The New College
SPANISH & ENGLISH Dictionary

THIRD EDITION

by
EDWIN B. WILLIAMS
Late Professor of Romance Languages
University of Pennsylvania

Editor-in-chief of the Third Edition:
ROGER J. STEINER
Emeritus Professor of Linguistics
University of Delaware

AMSCO SCHOOL PUBLICATIONS, INC.
315 Hudson Street / New York, N.Y. 10013

THE NEW COLLEGE SPANISH & ENGLISH DICTIONARY, THIRD EDITION

Cover design by Mel Haber
Cover photograph of Spain, Plaza de España, Seville by Image Bank
Composition by Maryland Composition Company, Inc.

When ordering this book, please specify:
either **R 760 P** or SPANISH DICTIONARY

Please visit our Website at:
www.amscopub.com

ISBN 978-1-56765-489-9
NYC Item 56765-489-8

Published by Amsco School Publications, Inc., by arrangement with the copyright owners.

Printed in the United States of America

10 08

CONTENTS

PREFACE TO THE FIRST EDITION

This book is based on primary spoken and written sources. It is designed for speakers of either language who wish to find words or the meanings of words in the foreign language. Its purpose is, therefore, fourfold. It gives to the English-speaking users (1) the Spanish words they need to express their thoughts in Spanish and (2) the English meanings of Spanish words they need to understand Spanish, and to the Spanish-speaking users (3) the English words they need to express their thoughts in English and (4) the Spanish meanings of English words they need to understand English.

To accomplish the purpose of (1) and (3), discriminations are provided in the source language except that, because of the special facility with which the subject of the verb can be shown in Spanish and because of the convenience of showing the object with personal **a,** discriminations in the form of subject and/or object are given in Spanish on the English-Spanish side as well as on the Spanish-English side. For the purpose of (2) and (4) discriminations are not needed and are not given because the users will always have the context of what they hear or read to guide them. However, some glosses whose purpose is not to show discrimination but rather to elaborate on the meaning of what may be judged to be an unfamiliar or obscure word or expression in the user's native language are provided in that language.

All words are treated in a fixed order according to the parts of speech and the functions of verbs; and meanings with subject, usage, and regional labels come after more general meanings.

In order to facilitate the finding of the meaning and use sought for, changes within a vocabulary entry in part of speech and function of verb, in irregular inflection, in the gender of Spanish nouns, and in the pronunciation of English words are marked with parallels instead of the usual semicolons.

Periods are omitted after labels and grammatical abbreviations and at the end of vocabulary entries.

The feminine form of a Spanish adjective used as a noun (or a Spanish feminine noun having identical spelling with the feminine form of an adjective) that falls alphabetically in a separate position from the adjective is treated in that position and is listed again as a cross reference under the adjective.

The gender of Spanish nouns is shown on both sides of the Dictionary except that the gender of masculine nouns ending in **-o,** feminine nouns ending in **-a, -dad, -tad, -tud, -ión,** and **-umbre,** masculine nouns modified by an adjective ending in **-o,** and feminine nouns modified by an adjective ending in **-a,** is not shown on the English-Spanish side.

Numbers referring to the conjugations of irregular Spanish verbs are placed before the abbreviations indicating the part of speech. The list at the end of the Spanish-English part of the Dictionary includes models of all verbs that show a combination of two types of irregularity, e.g., **esforzar, seguir, teñir.**

Proper nouns and abbreviations are listed in their alphabetical position in the main body of the Dictionary. Thus **España** and **español** do not have to be looked up in two different parts of the book. And all subentries are listed in strictly alphabetical order.

The centered period is used in vocabulary entries of irregularly inflected words to mark off the final syllable that has to be detached before the syllable showing the inflection is added, e.g., **lá•piz** *m* (*pl* **-pices**) and **falsi•fy** [ˈfɔlsɪ,faɪ] *v* (*pret & pp* **-fied**).

The pronunciation of all English simple words is shown in a new adaptation of the symbols of the International Phonetic Alphabet and in brackets. The pronunciation of English compound words is not shown provided the pronunciation of the components is shown where they appear as independent vocabulary entries.

Since vocabulary entries are not determined on the basis of etymology, homographs are included in a single entry. When the pronunciation of an English homograph changes, this is shown in the proper place after parallels.

Edwin B. Williams

PRÓLOGO A LA PRIMERA EDICIÓN

Hemos basado este libro en fuentes originales del lenguaje hablado y escrito. Está destinado a los hablantes de uno u otro idioma que buscan palabras o significados de palabras en el idioma extranjero. Tiene, por lo tanto, los cuatro siguientes propósitos: al usuario de habla inglesa le suministra (1) las palabras españolas que necesita para expresar su pensamiento en español y (2) los significados ingleses de las palabras españolas que necesita para comprender el español; y al usuario de habla española le suministra (3) las palabras inglesas que necesita para expresar su pensamiento en inglés y (4) los significados españoles de las palabras inglesas que necesita para comprender el inglés.

Para lograr los propósitos indicados bajo los números (1) y (3), se suministran diferenciaciones (es decir, distinciones entre dos o más significados de una palabra) en la lengua-fuente; pero, dada la facilidad con que el sujeto del verbo puede indicarse en español y dada la conveniencia de destacar el objeto del verbo con la preposición **a,** las diferenciaciones consistentes en el sujeto o el objeto, o ambos, se dan en español tanto en la parte de inglés-español como en la parte de español-inglés. Para los propósitos indicados bajo los números (2) y (4) no se necesitan diferenciaciones y no se dan, porque el usuario siempre tendrá como guía el contexto de lo que oye o lee. Con todo, algunas glosas que no tienen por objeto indicar diferenciaciones sino más bien dilucidar el sentido de lo que parece ser una palabra o expresión raras u obscuras en la lengua nativa del usuario, se indican en esta lengua.

Los vocablos se tratan consecutivamente de acuerdo con las partes de la oración y las funciones verbales; y los significados marcados con calificativos de tema, uso y país van después de los significados más generales.

Para facilitar la búsqueda del significado y el uso deseados, los cambios en la parte de la oración y función verbal, en la flexión, en el género de los nombres españoles y en la pronunciación de las palabras inglesas van señalados con doble raya vertical, en vez del punto y coma de costumbre.

Se han omitido los puntos después de los calificativos y abreviaturas gramaticales y al fin de los artículos.

La forma femenina de un adjetivo español usado como sustantivo (o de un sustantivo femenino que se escribe lo mismo que la forma femenina de un adjetivo), que cae alfabéticamente en lugar apartado del adjetivo, se trata en este lugar y se consigna otra vez bajo el adjetivo con una referencia a la palabra traducida anteriormente.

El género de los nombres españoles aparece en ambas partes del Diccionario; pero no aparece en la parte de inglés-español el género de los nombres masculinos que terminan en **-o,** los nombres femeninos que terminan en **-a, -dad, -tad, -tud, -ión, y -umbre,** los nombres masculinos modificados por un adjetivo que termina en **-o** ni los nombres femeninos modificados por un adjetivo que termina en **-a.**

Los números que se refieren a los modelos de conjugación de los verbos españoles van antes de las abreviaturas que indican la parte de la oración. La lista completa de los modelos de conjugación incluye muchos que muestran una combinación de dos irregularidades, p.ej., **esforzar, seguir, teñir.**

Los nombres propios y las abreviaturas se consignan en su propio lugar alfabético en el texto del Diccionario. No hay, pues, que buscar **España** y **español** en dos partes distintas del libro. Y todos los artículos secundarios van colocados en riguroso orden alfabético.

Se usa el punto divisorio en los artículos de palabras de flexión irregular para señalar la sílaba final que debe separarse antes de agregar la sílaba que denota la flexión, p.ej., **lá•piz** (*pl* **-pices**) y **falsi•fy** [ˈfɔlsɪ,faɪ] *v* (*pret & pp* **-fied**).

La pronunciación de todas las palabras inglesas simples se muestra por medio de una nueva adaptación de los símbolos del Alfabeto Fonético Internacional y entre corchetes. No se muestra la pronunciación de las palabras inglesas compuestas cuando la pronunciación de los componentes consta en los lugares donde aparecen como artículos independientes.

Como la constitución de los artículos no se ha determinado a base de su etimología, se incluyen bajo un mismo artículo todos los homógrafos de una palabra. Cuando varía la pronunciación de un homógrafo inglés, se indica en su propio lugar después de la doble raya vertical.

Edwin B. Williams

PRÓLOGO A LA TERCERA EDICIÓN

De este diccionario del difunto y mundialmente conocido lexicógrafo Edwin Bucher Williams se han vendido muchos millones de ejemplares, los cuales les han servido como fuente de información a estudiantes, viajeros, traductores, lingüistas y lectores del mundo entero. Siendo yo uno de los colegas del Dr. Williams y autor de varios diccionarios, he asumido la responsabilidad de poner al día este diccionario.

Uno de los propósitos importantes de esta revisión es incluir los vocablos nuevos que se usan en las siguientes áreas: tecnología, comunicación, medio ambiente, economía y las ciencias. Las palabras empleadas en informática, medicina y genética aparecen traducidas en esta edición. Por ejemplo, este diccionario contiene más de cuatrocientos vocablos usados en informática. Otro propósito de esta edición es dar a conocer un diccionario que contenga el vocabulario del nuevo milenio. Así pues aparecen palabras de uso común y actual con sus correspondientes significados nuevos.

La lista de vocablos sigue la cronología alfabética nueva en la que la *ch* y la *ll* no se consideran letras separadas. Es decir, la *ch* no sigue a la *c* ni la *ll* sigue a la *l,* sino que cada letra sigue el orden tradicional del alfabeto internacional.

Quisiera poner de manifesto mi agradecimiento a todos los que me han ayudado a revisar esta edición. En especial agradezco la ayuda del Dr. Alfred R. Wedel y la de la profesora Sara Jane Jack DiLaura Morris.

En esta ocasión también quisiera hacer notar la labor editorial de Walter D. Glanze que hizo posible la segunda edición del diccionario. Espero que el presente diccionario le pueda ayudar a encontrar la palabra o la expresión más apropiada para entender en el momento de leer, escribir, escuchar o hablar.

Roger J. Steiner

PREFACE TO THE THIRD EDITION

This Dictionary by the world-famous lexicographer, the late Edwin Bucher Williams, became a standard source of bilingual information for students, travelers, translators, linguists, and readers worldwide. As one of Dr. Williams' colleagues with several published dictionaries to my credit, I have undertaken the responsibility of bringing this work up to date.

One of the important objectives of this revision is the addition of new words and meanings from the fields of science, technology, communications, environment, and economics. New words having to do with computers, medicine, and genetics find their translations here. For example, this Dictionary contains over four hundred entries of computer terms. Another important objective has been the creation of a dictionary of the actual speech of the new millennium by the inclusion of translations of new words widely used as well as translations of new meanings of everyday words.

The Spanish word list now follows the new alphabetical order in which *ch* no longer follows *c* and *ll* no longer follows *l* but instead take regular places in alphabetical order.

Appreciation must be expressed to all who have helped the revisor's task and special thanks should be given to Dr. Alfred R. Wedel and Professor Sara Jane Jack DiLaura Morris.

Furthermore, Walter D. Glanze must be recognized for the significant contributions he made to the Dictionary in his editorship of the second edition. It is our hope that this Dictionary will help you find the word or expression that you need in reading and writing as well as in listening and speaking.

Roger J. Steiner

LABELS AND GRAMMATICAL ABBREVIATIONS

abbr abbreviation—abreviatura
(acronym) acrónimo—a word formed from the initial letters or syllables of a series of words—palabra formada de las letras o sílabas iniciales de una serie de palabras
adj adjective—adjetivo
adv adverb—adverbio
(aer) aeronautics—aeronáutica
(aerosp) aerospace—aeroespacial
(agr) agriculture—agricultura
(alg) algebra—álgebra
(anat) anatomy—anatomía
(archaic) arcaico
(archeol) archeology—arqueología
(archit) architecture—arquitectura
(Arg) Argentine—argentino
(arith) arithmetic—aritmética
art article—artículo
(arti) artillery—artillería
(astr) astronomy—astronomía
(aut) automobiles—automóviles
(bact) bacteriology—bacteriología
(baseball) beisbol
(bb) bookbinding—encuadernación
(Bib) Biblical—bíblico
(billiards) billar
(biochem) biochemistry—bioquímica
(biol) biology—biología
(Bol) Bolivian—boliviano
(bowling) bolos
(bot) botany—botánica
(box) boxing—boxeo
(Brit) British—británico
(CAm) Central American—centroamericano
(cards) naipes
(carp) carpentry—carpintería
(chem) chemistry—química
(chess) ajedrez
(Chile) Chilean—chileno
(Col) Colombian—colombiano
(coll) colloquial—familiar
(com) commercial—comercial
comp comparative—comparativo
(compu) computers—informática
cond conditional—condicional
conj conjunction—conjunción
contr contraction—contracción
(C-R) Costa Rican—costarriqueño
(Cuba) Cuban—cubano
(culin) cooking—cocina
def definite—definido
dem demonstrative—demostrativo
(dent) dentistry—odontología
(dial) dialectal—dialectal
(eccl) ecclesiastical—eclesiástico
(ecol) ecology—ecología
(econ) economics—economía
(Ecuad) Ecuadorian—ecuatoriano
(educ) education—educación
(elec) electricity—electricidad
(electron) electronics—electrónica
(El Salv) El Salvador
(ent) entomology—entomología
(Esp) Spanish—español
f feminine noun—nombre femenino
(fa) fine arts—bellas artes
fem feminine—femenino
(fencing) esgrima
(feud) feudalism—feudalismo
(fig) figurative—figurado
(formal) formal
fpl feminine noun plural—nombre femenino plural
fsg feminine noun singular—nombre femenino singular
fut future—futuro
(gen) genetics—genética
(geog) geography—geografía
(geol) geology—geología
(geom) geometry—geometría
ger gerund—gerundio
(gram) grammar—gramática
(Guat) Guatemalan—guatemalteco
(heral) heraldry—heráldica
(hist) history—historia
(Hond) Honduran—hondureño
(hort) horticulture—horticultura
(hum) humorous—jocoso
(hunt) hunting—caza
(ichth) ichthyology—ictiología
imperf imperfect—imperfecto
impers impersonal—impersonal
impv imperative—imperativo
ind indicative—indicativo
indecl indeclinable—indeclinable
indef indefinite—indefinido
inf infinitive—infinitivo
(ins) insurance—seguros
interj interjection—interjección
interr interrogative—interrogativo
intr intransitive verb—verbo intransitivo
invar invariable—invariable
(iron) ironical—irónico
(Lat) Latin—latín
(law) derecho
(letterword) a word in the form of an abbreviation which is pronounced by sounding the names of its letters in succession and which functions as a part of speech—palabra en forma de abreviatura la cual se pronuncia haciendo sonar el nombre de cada letra

consecutivamente y que funciona como parte del discurso
(log) logic—lógica
m masculine noun—nombre masculino
(mach) machinery—maquinaria
(mas) masonry—albañilería
masc masculine—masculino
(math) mathematics—matemática
(mech) mechanics—mecánica
(med) medicine—medicina
(metal) metallurgy—metalurgia
(meteor) meteorology—meteorología
(Mex) Mexican—mejicano
mf masculine or feminine noun according to sex—nombre masculino o nombre femenino según el sexo
(mil) military—militar
(min) mining—minería
(mineral) mineralogy—mineralogía
(mountaineering) alpinismo
(mov) moving pictures—cine
mpl masculine noun plural—nombre masculino plural
msg masculine noun singular—nombre masculino singular
(mus) music—música
(myth) mythology—mitología
m & f masculine and feminine noun without regard to sex—nombre masculino y femenino sin tener en cuenta el sexo
(naut) nautical—náutico
(nav) naval—naval militar
neut neuter—neutro
(obs) obsolete—desusado
(obstet) obstetrics—obstetricia
(opt) optics—óptica
(orn) ornithology—ornitología
(paint) painting—pintura
(Pan) Panamanian—panameño
(Para) Paraguayan—paraguayo
(pathol) pathology—patología
(pej) pejorative—peyorativo
pers personal—personal
(Peru) Peruvian—peruano
(pharm) pharmacy—farmacia
(philol) philology—filología
(philos) philosophy—filosofía
(phonet) phonetics—fonética
(phot) photography—fotografía
(phys) physics—física
(physiol) physiology—fisiología
pl plural—plural
(poet) poetical—poético
(pol) politics & government—política y gobierno
poss possessive—posesivo
pp past participle—participio pasado
(P-R) Puerto Rican—puertorriqueño
prep preposition—preposición
pres present—presente
pret preterit—pretérito
pron pronoun—pronombre
(psychoanalysis) sicoanálisis
(psychol) psychology—sicología
(rad) radio—radio
ref reflexive verb—verbo reflexivo
reflex reflexive—reflexivo
rel relative—relativo
(rhet) rhetoric—retórica
(rr) railway—ferrocarril
s substantive—substantivo
(SAm) South American—sudamericano
(scornful) despreciativo
(sculp) sculpture—escultura
(S-D) Santo Domingo—República Dominicana
(sew) sewing—costura
sg singular—singular
SIGN displayed notice—placa, letrero, anuncio, cartel
(slang) jerga
spl substantive plural—substantivo plural
(sport) deporte
ssg substantive singular—substantivo singular
subj subjunctive—subjuntivo
super superlative—superlativo
(surg) surgery—cirugía
(surv) surveying—agrimensura
Ⓣtrademark—marca registrada
(taur) bullfighting—tauromaquia
(telg) telegraphy—telegrafía
(telp) telephony—telefonía
(telv) television—televisión
(tennis) tenis
(theat) theater—teatro
(theol) theology—teología
tr transitive verb—verbo transitivo
(typ) printing—imprenta
(Urug) Uruguayan—uruguayo
(U.S.A.) EE.UU.
v verb—verbo
var variant—variante
v aux auxiliary verb—verbo auxiliar
(Ven) Venezuelan—venezolano
(vet) veterinary medicine—veterinaria
(vulg) vulgar—grosero
(W-I) West Indian—antillano
(zool) zoology—zoología

SPANISH PRONUNCIATION

The Spanish alphabet has twenty-six letters. Note that **ñ** is considered to be a separate single letter and is so treated in the alphabetization of Spanish words. While **rr** is considered to be a distinct sign for a particular sound, it is not included in the alphabet and, except in syllabification—notably for the division of words at the end of a line—is not treated as a separate letter, perhaps because words never begin with it.

LETTER	NAME	SOUND
a	a	Like **a** in English **father,** e.g., **casa, fácil.**
b	be	When initial or preceded by **m,** like **b** in English **book,** e.g., **boca, combate.** When standing between two vowels and when preceded by a vowel and followed by **l** or **r,** like **v** in English **voodoo** except that it is formed with both lips, e.g., **saber, hablar, sobre.** It is generally silent before **s** plus a consonant and often dropped in spelling, e.g., **oscuro** for **obscuro.**
c	ce	When followed by **e** or **i,** like **th** in English **think** in Castilian, and like **c** in English **cent** in American Spanish, e.g., **acento, cinco.** When followed by **a, o, u,** or a consonant, like **c** in English **come,** e.g., **cantar, como, cubo, acto, creer.**
ch	che	Like **ch** in English **much,** e.g., **escuchar.**
d	de	Generally, like **d** in **dog,** e.g., **diente, rendir.** When standing between two vowels, when preceded by a vowel and followed by **r,** and when final, like **th** in English **this,** e.g., **miedo, piedra, libertad.**
e	e	At the end of a syllable, like **a** in English **fate,** but without the glide the English sound sometimes has, e.g., **beso, menos.** When followed by a consonant in the same syllable, like **e** in English **met,** e.g., **perla, selva.**
f	efe	Like **f** in English **five,** e.g., **flor, efecto.**
g	ge	When followed by **e** or **i,** like **h** in English **home,** e.g., **gente, giro.** When followed by **a, o, u,** or a consonant, like **g** in English **go,** e.g., **gato, gota, agudo, grande.**
h	hache	Always silent, e.g., **hombre, alcohol.**
i	i	Like **i** in English **machine,** e.g., **camino, ida.** When preceded or followed by another vowel, it has the sound of English **y,** e.g., **tierra, reina.**
j	jota	Like **h** in English **home,** e.g., **jardín, junto.**
k	ka	Like English **k,** e.g., **kilociclo.**
l	ele	Like **l** in English **laugh,** e.g., **lado, ala.**
ll	elle	Somewhat like **lli in William** in Castilian and like **y** in English **yes** in American Spanish, e.g., **silla, llamar.**
m	eme	Like **m** in English **man,** e.g., **mesa, amar.**

n	ene	Generally, like **n** in English **name,** e.g., **andar, nube.** Before **v,** like **m** in English **man,** e.g., **invierno, enviar.** Before **c** [k] and **g** [g], like **n** in English **drink,** e.g., **finca, manga.**
ñ	eñe	Somewhat like **ni** in English **onion,** e.g., **año, enseñar.**
o	o	At the end of a syllable, like **o** in English **note,** but without the glide the English sound sometimes has, e.g., **boca, como.** When followed by a consonant in the same syllable, like **o** in English **organ,** e.g., **poste, norte.**
p	pe	Like **p** in English **pen,** e.g., **poco, aplicar.** It is often silent in **septiembre** and **séptimo.**
q	cu	Like **c** in English **come.** It is always followed by **ue** or **ui,** in which the **u** is silent, e.g., **querer, quitar.** The sound of English **qu** is represented in Spanish by **cu,** e.g., **frecuente.**
r	ere	Strongly trilled, when initial and when preceded by **l, n,** or **s,** e.g., **rico, alrededor, honra, israelí.** Pronounced with a single tap of the tongue in all other positions, e.g., **caro, grande, amar.**
rr	erre	Strongly trilled, e.g., **carro, tierra.**
s	ese	Generally, like **s** in English **say,** e.g., **servir, casa, este.** Before a voiced consonant (**b, d, g** [g], **l, r, m, n**), like **z** in English **zero,** e.g., **esbelto, desde, rasgar, eslabón, mismo, asmo.**
t	te	Like **t** in English **stamp,** e.g., **tiempo, matar.**
u	u	Like **u** in English **rude,** e.g., **mudo, puño.** It is silent in **que, gui, que,** and **qui,** but not in **güe** and **güi,** e.g., **guerra, guisa, querer, quitar,** but **agüero, lingüístico.** When preceded or followed by another vowel, it has the sound of English **w,** e.g., **fuego, deuda.**
v	ve or uve	Like Spanish **b** in all positions, e.g., **vengo, invierno, uva, huevo.**
x	equis	When followed by a consonant, like s in English **say,** e.g., **expresar, sexto.** Between two vowels, like **gs,** e.g., **examen, existencia, exótico**; and in some words, like **s** in **say,** e.g., **auxilio, exacto.** In **México** (for **Méjico**), like Spanish **j.**
y	ye or i griega	In the conjunction **y,** like **i** in English **machine.** When standing next to a vowel or between two vowels, like **y** in English **yes,** e.g., **yo, hoy, vaya.**
z	zeda or zeta	Like **th** in English **think** in Castilian, and like **c** in English **cent** in American Spanish, e.g., **zapato, zona.**

DIPHTHONG	SOUND
ai, ay	Like **i** in English **might,** e.g., **baile, hay**
au	Like **ou** in English **pound,** e.g., **causa**
ei, ey	Like **ey** in English **they,** e.g., **reina, ley**
eu	Like **ayw** in English **hayward,** e.g., **deuda**
oi, oy	Like **oy** in English **boy,** e.g., **estoy**

Spanish-English
Español-Inglés

A

A, a (a) *f* first letter of the Spanish alphabet
a *prep* at; for, to; on, upon; in, into; by; from; **a decir verdad** to tell the truth; **a la española** in the Spanish manner; **a lo que parece** as it seems; **a no ser por** if it weren't for; **a saberlo yo** if I had known it; **oler a** to smell of
abacería *f* grocery store
abace•ro -ra *mf* grocer
abad *m* abbot
abadejo *m* codfish; (orn) kinglet; (ent) Spanish fly
abadesa *f* abbess
abadía *f* abbacy; abbey
abajar *ref* to lower oneself
abaje•ño -ña *adj* (Mex) coastal, lowland || *mf* (Mex) lowlander
abaje•ro -ra *adj* (Arg) lower, under || *f* (Arg) bellyband, bellystrap; (Arg) saddlecloth
abaji•no -na *adj* (Col, Chile) northern || *mf* (Col, Chile) northerner
abajo *adv* down, underneath; downwards; downstairs; **abajo de** down; **más abajo** lower down; **río abajo** downstream || *interj* down with. . .!
abalanzar §60 *tr* to hurl || *ref* to rush; venture; (*un caballo*) rear
abalear *tr* (SAm) to shoot
abalizar §60 *tr* to mark with buoys || *ref* (naut) to take bearings
abalorio *m* glass bead
abaluartar *tr* to bulwark
abanar *tr* to fan
abanderado *m* colorbearer
abanderar *tr* (*un buque*) to register
abanderizar §60 *tr* to organize into bands || *ref* to band together; (Chile, Peru) to join up
abandona•do -da *adj* deserted; neglected; slovenly
abandonar *tr* to abandon, forsake || *intr* to give up || *ref* to abandon oneself; give up
abandonismo *m* defeatism
abandonista *adj & mf* defeatist
abandono *m* abandon, abandonment; neglect; forlornness; yielding
abanicar §73 *tr* to fan
abanico *m* fan; fanlight; sword; **abanico de chimenea** fire screen
abaniquear *tr* to fan
abaniqueo *m* fanning; gesticulations
abanto *adj* skittish (*bull*)
abaratamiento *m* cheapening
abaratar *tr* to cheapen; (*precios*) lower || *intr & ref* to get cheap
abarca *f* sandal
abarcar §73 *tr* to embrace; encompass; surround; corner, monopolize
abarloar *tr* (naut) to bring alongside || *ref* to snuggle up
abarquillar *tr & ref* to curl up
abarraganamiento *m* illicit cohabitation
abarrancar *ref* to get into a difficult situation
abarrota•do -da *adj* overcrowded
abarrotar *tr* to bar; bind, fasten; jam, pack, stuff; overstock || *ref* to become a glut on the market
abarrote *m* (naut) packing; **abarrotes** groceries; hardware
abarrotería *f* (Guat) grocery store; (CAm) hardware store
abarrote•ro -ra *mf* grocer
abastecer §22 *tr* to supply, provide
abastecimiento *m* supplying; supplies, provisions
abasto *m* supply; abundance; **dar abasto** to be sufficient
abatanar *tr* to full
abatí *m* (Arg, Para) corn; corn whiskey
abatible *adj* collapsible, folding
abati•do -da *adj* downcast; abject, contemptible || *f* abatis
abatimiento *m* discouragement; descent
abatir *tr* to lower; knock down; shoot down; take apart; humble; discourage || *intr* (aer) to drift; (naut) to have leeway || *ref* to be discouraged; be humbled; drop, fall; swoop down
abdicar §73 *tr & intr* to abdicate
abdomen *m* abdomen
abecé *m* **A B C**
abecedario *m* **A B Cs**
abedul *m* birch
abeja *f* bee; **abeja asesina** killer bee; **abeja maestra** or **abeja reina** queen bee; **abeja obrera** worker bee
abejar *m* apiary, beehive
abejarrón *m* bumblebee
abeje•ro -ra *mf* beekeeper
abejorro *m* bumblebee
aberración *f* aberration; deviation
abertura *f* aperture; opening; crack, slit; cove; openness, frankness
abeto *m* fir tree; hemlock; **abeto del Norte, abeto falso** spruce tree

abier•to -ta *adj* open; frank
abigarra•do -da *adj* motley, variegated
abigeo *m* horse thief, cattle thief
abijar *tr* (Col) to sic
abiselar *tr* to bevel
abisma•do -da *adj* absorbed, lost in thought; mysterious
abismar *tr* to cast down; humble; spoil, ruin ‖ *ref* to sink; cave in; be humbled; give in; lose oneself; be surprised
abismo *m* abyss, chasm
abjurar *tr* to abjure; renounce
ablandabre•vas *m* (*pl* **-vas**) or **ablandahi•gos** *m* (*pl* **-gos**) good-for-nothing
ablandar *tr* to soften; soften up; soothe; loosen ‖ *intr* (*el tiempo*) to moderate ‖ *ref* to soften; relent; (*el tiempo*) moderate
ablativo *m* ablative
abnegación *f* abnegation; self-denial
abnega•do -da *adj* self-denying
abnegar *ref* to deny oneself; sacrifice oneself
aboba•do -da *adj* stupid, stupid-looking
abobar *tr* to make stupid ‖ *ref* to grow stupid
aboca•do -da *adj* (*vino*) mild, smooth; vulnerable; **abocado a** verging on
abocar §73 *tr* to bite; pour; bring near ‖ *intr* to enter ‖ *ref* to approach; have an interview
abochornar *tr* to overheat; make blush, embarrass ‖ *ref* to blush; wilt
abocinar *tr* to give a flare to ‖ *intr* to fall on the face ‖ *ref* to flare
abofa•do -da *adj* (Cuba, Mex) swollen
abofetear *tr* to slap in the face
abogacía *f* law, legal profession
abogaderas *fpl* (CAm) specious arguments
abogado *m* lawyer; **abogado criminalista** criminal lawyer; **abogado defensor** defense lawyer; **abogado de secano** quack lawyer; **abogado firmón** lawyer who will sign anything; **abogado trampista** shyster
abogar §44 *intr* to plead; **abogar por** to advocate, back
abolengo *m* ancestry, descent; inheritance
abolición *f* abolition
abolir §1 *tr* to revoke, repeal, abolish
abolladura *f* dent; bump, bruise; embossing
abollar *tr* to bump, bruise; dent; stun; emboss ‖ *ref* to get bumped, get bruised; dent, be dented
abollonar *tr* to emboss
abolorio *m* ancestry
abombar *tr* to make convex; stun, confound ‖ *ref* to rot, decompose
abominable *adj* abominable, very bad
abominación *f* abomination
abominar *tr* to detest, abominate ‖ *intr* — **abominar de** to abominate
abona•do -da *adj* trustworthy; apt, likely ‖ *mf* subscriber; (*al gas, electricidad, etc.*) consumer; (*a una localidad en el teatro*) season-ticket holder; (*al ferrocarril*) commuter
abonanzar §60 *intr* (*el tiempo*) to clear up; (*el viento*) abate
abonar *tr* to vouch for; certify; improve; fertilize; **abonar en cuenta a** to credit to the account of ‖ *intr* (*el tiempo*) to clear up ‖ *ref* to subscribe
abono *m* subscription; credit; installment; voucher; fertilizer, manure
abordar *tr* to approach; accost; undertake, plan; (naut) to board; (naut) to run afoul of; (naut) to dock ‖ *intr* to run afoul; (naut) to put into port
aborigen *adj invar* aboriginal, native; **aborígenes** *mpl* aborigines, natives
aborrascar §73 *ref* to get stormy
aborrecer §22 *tr* to abhor, detest, hate; bore ‖ *ref* to get bored
aborrecible *adj* abhorrent, hateful
aborrega•do -da *adj* (*nubes*) fleecy; (*cielo*) mackerel
aborregar *ref* (SAm) to become stupid
abortar *tr & intr* to abort
abortista *adj* pro-choice ‖ *mf* doctor who carries out abortions; pro-choice advocate ‖ *f* woman who has had an abortion
aborto *m* abortion; miscarriage; **aborto espontáneo** miscarriage
abotagar §44 *ref* to become bloated, swell up
abotonador *m* buttonhook
abotonar *tr* to button ‖ *intr* to bud
abovedar *tr* to arch, vault
abozalar *tr* to muzzle
abra *f* cove; vale; fissure; (Mex) clearing
abrasa•dor -dora *adj* burning, hot
abrasar *tr* to set fire to, burn; parch; nip; squander; shame ‖ *intr* to burn ‖ *ref* to burn; become parched; (fig) to be burning up
abrasi•vo -va *adj & m* abrasive
abrazadera *f* clasp, clip, clamp; (typ) bracket
abrazar §60 *tr* to embrace, clasp; include; take in ‖ *ref* (*dos personas*) to embrace
abrazo *m* embrace, hug
abrebo•cas *m* (*pl* **-cas**) mouth prop, mouth gag
abrebote•llas *m* (*pl* **-llas**) bottle opener
abrecar•tas *m* (*pl* **-tas**) knife, letter opener
abreco•ches *m* (*pl* **-ches**) doorman
abrela•tas *m* (*pl* **-tas**) can opener
abreos•tras *m* (*pl* **-tras**) oyster knife
abrevadero *m* watering place, drinking trough
abrevar *tr* to water; wet, soak; irrigate; size ‖ *ref* to drink
abreviación *f* abridgment, abbreviation, shortening; hastening
abreviar *tr* to abridge; abbreviate; shorten; hasten ‖ *intr* to be quick; **abreviar con** to make short work of
abreviatura *f* abbreviation; **en abreviatura** in a hurry
abridero *m* (Mex, P-R) dive, joint
abridor *m* opener; grafting knife; **abridor de guantes** glove stretcher
abridura *f* (act of) opening
abrigadero *m* windbreak
abrigar §44 *tr* to shelter; protect; (*esperanzas, sospechas*) harbor ‖ *ref* to take shelter; wrap oneself up

abrigo *m* shelter; aid, support; cover, wrap; overcoat; (naut) harbor; **abrigo antiaéreo** air-raid shelter; **abrigo de entretiempo** topcoat, spring-and-fall coat; **al abrigo de** sheltered from, protected from; sheltered by, protected by; (*ropa*) **de mucho abrigo** heavy
abril *m* April
abrillantar *tr* to polish; glaze
abrir *m* opening; **en un abrir y cerrar de ojos** in the twinkling of an eye || **§83** *tr* to open; unlock, unfasten; (*el apetito*) whet; (*el bosque*) clear || *intr* to open || *ref* to open; **abrirse a** or **con** to unbosom oneself to
abrochador *m* buttonhook
abrochar *tr* to button, hook, fasten
abrogación *f* repeal; abrogation
abrogar *tr* to repeal; abrogate; annul
abrojo *m* thistle, thorn; **abrojos** reef, hidden rocks
abrótano *m* southernwood
abruma•do -da *adj* hazy; foggy
abruma•dor -dora *adj* crushing, oppressing; overwhelming
abrumar *tr* to crush, oppress; overwhelm; annoy || *ref* to become foggy
abrup•to -ta *adj* abrupt, steep; rough, rugged
absceso *m* abscess
absenta *f* absinthe
ábsida *f* or **ábside** *m* apse
absolución *f* absolution; acquittal
absoluta *f* dogmatic statement; (mil) discharge
absolutamente *adv* absolutely; by no means
absolu•to -ta *adj* absolute; arbitrary || *m* absolute; **en absoluto** absolutely not || *f* see **absoluta**
absolvederas *fpl* — **tener buenas absolvederas** to be an indulgent confessor
absolver §47 & §83 *tr* to absolve; to solve, to answer
absorbente *adj* absorbent; (*interesante*) absorbing
absorber *tr* to absorb; use up; attract
absorción *f* absorption
absor•to -ta *adj* absorbed; entranced
abste•mio -mia *adj* abstemious
abstener §71 *ref* to abstain
abstensionismo *m* nonparticipation
abstinente *adj* abstinent
abstracción *f* abstraction; absorption, deep thought; **hacer abstracción de** to leave out, disregard
abstrac•to -ta *adj* abstract
abstraer §75 *tr* to abstract || *intr* — **abstraer de** to do without, leave aside || *ref* to be abstracted or absorbed; **abstraerse de** to do without, leave aside
abstraí•do -da *adj* absorbed in thought; withdrawn
abstru•so -sa *adj* abstruse
absurdidad *f* absurdity
absur•do -da *adj* absurd || *m* absurdity
abuchear *tr & intr* to boo, hoot
abuela *f* grandmother; (coll) granny; **cuénteselo a su abuela** tell that to the marines
abuelita *f* (coll) granny
abuelito *m* (coll) granddaddy
abuelo *m* grandparent; grandfather; **abuelos** grandparents; ancestors
abulta•do -da *adj* bulky, massive
abultar *tr* to enlarge; exaggerate || *intr* to be bulky
abundamiento *m* abundance; **a mayor abundamiento** with greater reason
abundancia *f* abundance, plenty
abundante *adj* abundant
abundar *intr* to abound
abur *interj* good-bye!, so long!
aburguesa•do -da *adj* middle-class, bourgeois
aburguesamiento *m* conversion to middle-class ways; (*en un barrio*) gentrification
aburguesar *ref* to become middle-class, become bourgeois; (*en un barrio*) gentrify
aburri•do -da *adj* bored; tiresome, stodgy
aburrimiento *m* weariness, fatigue; dullness
aburrir *tr* to bore, tire || *ref* to become bored
abusar *intr* to go too far; **abusar de** to abuse; impose on; overindulge in
abusión *f* superstition
abusi•vo -va *adj* abusive
abuso *m* abuse; imposition; **abuso de confianza** breach of trust; **abuso de información privilegiada** (econ) insider trading; **abusos deshonestos** sexual abuse; **abuso (sexual) infantil** child abuse
abyec•to -ta *adj* abject
A.C. *abbr* **año de Cristo**
aC *adj* (letterword) (**antes de Cristo**) B.C. (before Christ)
acá *adv* here, around here; **acá y allá** here and there; **de ayer acá** since yesterday; **¿de cuándo acá?** since when?; **desde entonces acá** since then; **más acá** here closer; **muy acá** right here
acaba•do -da *adj* complete, perfect; wornout, exhausted || *m* finish
acabamiento *m* end; completion; death; decline
acabar *tr* to end, finish, complete || *intr* to end; die; **acabar con** to put an end to; end in; **acabar de** to finish; have just, e.g., **acaba de salir** he has just left; **acababa de salir** he had just left; **acabar por** to end in; end by; **no acabar de decidirse** to be unable to make up one's mind || *ref* to end; be exhausted; be all over; run out of, e.g., **se me acabó el café** I have run out of coffee
acabóse *m* limit, last straw
acacia *f* acacia; **acacia falsa** locust tree
academia *f* academy; **academia de choferes** driving school; **academia de corte y confección** dressmaking school; **academia de idiomas** school of languages; **academia militar** military academy
académi•co -ca *adj* academic || *mf* academician
acaecer §22 *intr* to happen, occur
acaecimiento *m* happening, occurrence

acalenturar *ref* to get a fever
acallar *tr* to quiet, silence; pacify
acalora•do -da *adj* heated; warm; fiery, excited
acaloramiento *m* ardor; passion
acalorar *tr* to heat, warm; incite, encourage; stir up || *ref* to become heated; warm up
acampada *f* camp
acamar *tr* (*las mieses la lluvia o el viento*) to beat down, blow over
acampamento *m* camp, encampment
acampana•do -da *adj* bell-shaped
acampar *tr, intr & ref* to encamp
acanalar *tr* to groove; flute; channel; corrugate
acantila•do -da *adj* rocky; steep, precipitous || *m* cliff, bluff
acantonamiento *m* cantonment
acantonar *tr* to canton, quarter || *ref* to be quartered; **acantonarse en** to limit one's activities to
acaparar *tr* to corner; monopolize; hoard
acaramela•do -da *adj* candied; smooth, honey-tongued
acarar *tr* to bring face to face
acarear *tr* to bring face to face; face, brave
acariciar *tr* to caress; (*una ilusión*) cherish
acarraladura *f* (Chile, Peru) run (*in stockings*)
acarreadi•zo -za *adj* transportable
acarrear *tr* to cart, transport, carry along; cause, occasion || *ref* to incur, bring upon oneself
acarreo *m* cartage, drayage; conveyance
acartonar *ref* to shrivel up, become wizened
acasera•do -da *adj* (Chile, Peru) homeloving; (*parroquiano*) (Chile, Peru) regular || *mf* (Chile, Peru) stay-at-home, homebody; (Chile, Peru) regular customer
acaso *m* chance, accident; **al acaso** at random || *adv* maybe, perhaps; **por si acaso** in case of need, just in case
acatamiento *m* homage; respect
acatar *tr* to respect, hold in awe; observe
acatarrar *tr* to chill, give a cold to; (Chile, Mex) to bother, annoy || *ref* to catch cold; get tipsy
acaudala•do -da *adj* rich, well-to-do
acaudalar *tr* to acquire, accumulate
acaudillar *tr* to lead, command; direct
acceder *intr* to accede; agree
accesible *adj* accessible
accesión *f* accession; acquiescence; access, entry
accésit *m* second prize, honorable mention
acceso *m* access, approach; attack, fit, spell; **acceso prohibido** no admittance
acceso•rio -ria *adj* accessory || *m* accessory, fixture, attachment; **accesorios** (theat) properties
accidenta•do -da *adj* agitated; restless; rough, uneven || *mf* victim, casualty
accidental *adj* accidental; acting, protempore, temporary
accidentar *tr* to injure, hurt || *ref* to faint
accidente *m* accident; (*del terreno*) roughness, unevenness; fainting spell; **accidente aéreo** plane crash; **accidente de circulación, accidente de tráfico** traffic accident; **accidente ferroviario** train crash
acción *f* action; gesture; (*parte del capital de una sociedad*) share; stock certificate; **acción crecedera** growth stock; **acción de gracias** thanksgiving; **acción liberada** stock dividend; **acción popular** (law) class action; **poner en acción** to set in motion
accionar *tr* to drive || *intr* to gesticulate
accionista *mf* shareholder, stockholder
acebo *m* holly tree
acebuche *m* wild olive
acechar *tr* to watch, to spy on
acecho *m* watching, spying; **al acecho** or **en acecho** on the watch, spying
acecinar *tr* to dry-cure, dry-salt; (*el salmón o el arenque*) kipper || *ref* to shrivel up
acedar *tr* to turn sour; embitter || *ref* to turn sour; wither
acediá *f* sourness; crabbedness; heartburn
ace•do -da *adj* sour, tart; crabbed
aceitar *tr* to oil; grease
aceite *m* oil; olive oil; **aceite combustible** fuel oil; **aceite de hígado de bacalao** cod-liver oil; **aceite de linaza** linseed oil; **aceite de parafina** mineral oil; **aceite de ricino** castor oil; **aceite mineral** coal oil; **aceite solar** suntan lotion
aceite•ro -ra *adj* oil || *mf* oiler; oil dealer || *f* oilcan; oil cup; **aceiteras** cruet stand
aceito•so -sa *adj* oily, greasy
aceituna *f* olive
aceituno *m* olive tree
aceleración *f* acceleration
acelerador *m* accelerator
acelerar *tr & ref* to accelerate; hasten, hurry
acelga *f* Swiss chard
acémila *f* beast of burden, pack animal; dolt; drudge
acendra•do -da *adj* refined; stainless, spotless
acendrar *tr* to refine; purify, make stainless
acento *m* accent; emphasis; **acento agudo** acute accent; **acento circunflejo** circumflex accent; **acento grave** grave accent; **acento de altura** pitch accent; **acento ortográfico** written accent, accent mark; **acento prosódico** stress accent, tonic accent
acentuar §21 *tr* to accent; accentuate, emphasize
aceña *f* water-driven flour mill
acepción *f* meaning
acepillar *tr* to plane; brush; smooth
aceptable *adj* acceptable
aceptación *f* acceptance; **aceptación de personas** discrimination; partiality
aceptar *tr* to accept
acequia *f* irrigation ditch; (Bol, Col, Peru) stream, rivulet
acera *f* sidewalk
acera•do -da *adj* steel, steely; (fig) cutting, biting, sharp
acerar *tr* to steel, harden; line with a sidewalk || *ref* to harden; steel oneself

acer•bo -ba *adj* sour, bitter; harsh
acerca *adv* — **acerca de** about, with regard to
acercamiento *m* approach, rapprochement
acercar §73 *tr* to bring near or nearer || *ref* to approach, come near or nearer
acería *f* steel mill
acerico *m* small cushion; pincushion
acero *m* steel; sword; courage, spirit; **acero inoxidable** stainless steel
acérri•mo -ma *adj* all-out; (*enemigo*) bitter
acerrojar *tr* to bolt
acerta•do -da *adj* fit, right; skillful, sure; well-aimed
acertante *mf* winner
acertar §2 *tr* to hit; hit upon; figure out correctly; find; do right || *intr* to be right; succeed; guess right; **acertar a** to happen to; succeed in; **acertar con** to come upon; find
acertijo *m* conundrum, riddle
acervo *m* heap; assets, estate; shoal; store, fund, hoard
acetato *m* acetate
acéti•co -ca *adj* acetic
acetificar §73 *tr & ref* to acetify
acetileno *m* acetylene
acetona *f* acetone
achacar §73 *tr* to impute, attribute
achaco•so -sa *adj* ailing, sickly
achaparra•do -da *adj* stocky; stubby; chubby
achaparrar *ref* to become stunted
achaque *m* sickliness, indisposition; excuse, pretext; matter, subject; weakness; (coll) monthlies
achatar *tr* to flatten || *ref* (Mex) to become frightened, afraid
achica•do -da *adj* childish; abashed, disconcerted
achicador *m* scoop
achicar §73 *tr* to make smaller; humble; bail, to bail out
achicoria *f* chicory
achicharrar *tr* to scorch; bedevil || *ref* to get scorched
achicharronar *tr* to squash
achín *m* (CAm) peddler; door-to-door salesman
achiquitar *ref* to lose heart, cower
achispa•do -da *adj* tipsy.
achispar *tr* to make tipsy || *ref* to get tipsy
achuchar *tr* to incite; crumple, crush; jostle || *ref* (Arg, Urug) to shiver, have a chill
acia•go -ga *adj* unlucky, ill-fated, evil
acial *m* (CAm, Ecuad) whip
acíbar *m* aloes; bitterness, sorrow
acicalar *tr* to polish, burnish; dress, dress up || *ref* to get all dressed up
acicate *m* long-pointed spur; incentive, stimulus
acicatear *tr* to spur, urge
acidez *f* acidity
acidificar §73 *tr & ref* to acidify
áci•do -da *adj* acid, tart, sour || *m* acid; **ácido deoxirribonucleico (A.D.N.)** deoxyribonucleic acid, DNA
acierto *m* lucky hit, good shot; good guess; tact, prudence; ability, skill; accuracy; success
aci•mut *m* (*pl* **-muts**) azimuth
aclamación *f* acclaim, applause
aclamar *tr & intr* to acclaim, to hail, to cheer
aclarar *tr* to brighten, clear; rinse; explain || *intr* to get bright; clear up; dawn
aclarato•rio -ria *adj* explanatory
aclimatar *tr & ref* to acclimate
acne *f* acne
acobardar *tr* to cow, intimidate || *ref* to be frightened
acocear *tr* to kick; trample upon, ill-treat
acocil *m* Mexican crayfish; **estar como un acocil** (Mex) to blush, be abashed
acoda•do -da *adj* elbow-shaped
acodar *tr* (*el brazo*) to lean; prop; (hort) to layer || *ref* to lean
acodillar *tr* to bend at an angle || *ref* to double up; to bend, to crumple
acogencia *f* (CAm) acceptance; reception
acoger §17 *tr* to receive, welcome; accept || *ref* to take refuge; resort
acogida *f* reception, welcome; meeting place, confluence; refuge, shelter; **dar acogida a** (com) to honor
acolada *f* accolade
acolchar *tr* to quilt, pad
acolchí *m* (Mex) red-winged blackbird
acólito *m* acolyte; altar boy
acollador *m* (naut) lanyard
acomedi•do -da *adj* obliging
acometer *tr* to attack; undertake; (*el sueño, la enfermedad, el deseo a una persona*) overcome
acometida *f* attack; (*p.ej., de una línea eléctrica*) house connection
acomodación *f* accommodation
acomodadi•zo -za *adj* accommodating, obliging
acomoda•do -da *adj* convenient, suitable; comfort-loving; well-to-do
acomoda•dor -dora *adj* accommodating, obliging || *mf* usher
acomodar *tr* to accommodate; usher; reconcile; suit; furnish, supply || *intr* to be suitable, be convenient || *ref* to comply; come to terms; hire out; make oneself comfortable
acomodo *m* arrangement, adjustment; lodgings; job, position; (Chile) neatness, tidiness
acompañador *m* companion; accompanist
acompañamiento *m* accompaniment; escort, retinue; (theat) extras, supernumeraries
acompañanta *f* female companion or escort; accompanist
acompañante *m* companion; accompanist
acompañar *tr* to accompany; escort; enclose; sympathize with
acompaño *m* (CAm) meeting; encounter
acompasa•do -da *adj* rhythmic; slow; easy-going; cautious
acompleja•do -da *adj* full of complexes
aconchar *tr* to push to safety; (naut) to beach,

run aground || *ref* to take shelter; (naut) to run aground; (Chile) to form a deposit
acondiciona•do -da *adj* conditioned; **bien acondicionado** well-disposed; in good condition; **mal acondicionado** ill-disposed; in bad condition
acondicionador *m* conditioner; **acondicionador de aire** air conditioner
acondicionamiento *m* conditioning; **acondicionamiento del aire** air conditioning
acondicionar *tr* to condition; put in condition; repair; season || *ref* to qualify; find a job
acongojar *tr* to grieve, afflict || *ref* to grieve
aconsejable *adj* advisable
aconsejar *tr* to advise, counsel, warn || *ref* to seek advice, get advice
acontecer §22 *intr* to happen, occur
acontecimiento *m* happening, event
acopiar *tr* to gather together
acopio *m* gathering; stock; abundance
acoplado *m* (Arg, Chile, Urug) trailer trolley car
acoplamiento *m* coupling; joint; connection; linkage; linkup (in space)
acoplar *tr* to couple; join; connect; hitch; reconcile || *ref* to be reconciled; mate; be intimate
acoquinar *tr* to intimidate
acoraza•do -da *adj* armored, armor-plated; contrary || *m* battleship
acorazar §60 *tr* to armor-plate
acorchar *tr* to line with cork; turn into cork || *ref* to get spongy; wither, shrivel; become corky or pithy; get numb
acorchetar *tr* to bracket
acordar §61 *tr* to agree upon; authorize; reconcile; make level or flush; remind of; tune || *intr* to agree; blend || *ref* to be agreed, come to an agreement; remember; **acordarse de** to remember
acorde *adj* agreed, in accord; in tune || *m* accord; (mus) chord
acordeón *m* accordion
acordonar *tr* to cord, lace; (*monedas*) knurl, mill; rope off
acornar §61 *tr* gore; butt
acornear *tr* to gore; butt
acorralar *tr* to corral, corner; intimidate
acortar *tr* to shorten; reduce; slow down; check, stop || *ref* to become shorter; hold back; be timid; slow down; shrink
acosar *tr* to harass; pester
acosijar *tr* (Mex) to pursue, press, track down
acostar §61 *tr* to lay down; put to bed; (naut) to bring alongside || *ref* to lie down; go to bed; (CAm, Mex) to give birth
acostumbra•do -da *adj* accustomed; customary, usual
acostumbrar *tr* to accustom || *intr* to be accustomed || *ref* to accustom oneself; become accustomed
acotación *f* boundary mark; marginal note; elevation mark
acotamiento *m* boundary mark; marginal note; elevation mark; stage direction
acotar *tr* to mark off, map; annotate; admit, accept; check; vouch for; select; mark elevations on
acotillo *m* sledge hammer
acre *adj* acrid; austere; biting, mordant || *m* (*medida de superficie: 0.405 hectáreas*) acre
acrecentamiento *m* increase, growth; promotion
acrecentar §2 *tr* to increase; promote || *ref* to increase; bud, blossom
acreditar *tr* to accredit; credit; get a reputation for || *ref* to get a reputation, prove oneself
acree•dor -dora *adj* accrediting; deserving || *mf* creditor; **acreedor hipotecario** mortgagee
acribar *tr* to sift; riddle
acribillar *tr* to riddle; harass, plague, pester
acríli•co -ca *adj & m* acrylic
acriminar *tr* to incriminate; exaggerate
acrimonio•so -sa *adj* acrid; acrimonious
acriollar *ref* to acquire Spanish-American ways
acrisolar *tr* to purify, refine; reveal, bring out
acrobacia *f* acrobatics
acróbata *mf* acrobat
acrobatismo *m* acrobatics
acrónimo *m* acronym
acrópo•lis *adj* (*pl* **-lis**) acropolis
acróstico *m* acrostic
acta *f* minutes; certificate; **acta notarial** affidavit; **actas** proceedings, transactions; **levantar acta** to write up the minutes
actitud *f* attitude; **en actitud de** getting ready to
activar *tr* to activate; hasten, expedite
actividad *f* activity
activista *mf* activist
acti•vo -va *adj* active || *m* (com) assets; (com) credit side
acto *m* act; ceremony, function; commencement; thesis; **acto carnal** sexual intercourse; **acto continuo** right afterward; **acto reflejo** reflex action; **acto seguido** right afterward; **acto seguido de** right after; **en acto de servicio** in the line of duty; **hacer acto de presencia** to honor with one's presence
actor *m* actor, player; agent; **primer actor** leading man
ac•triz *f* (*pl* **-trices**) actress; **primera actriz** leading lady
actuación *f* acting, performance; action; operation; behavior; **actuación en directo** live performance; **actuaciones** legal proceedings
actual *adj* present, present-day; up-to-date || *m* current month
actualidad *f* present time; timeliness; **actualidades** current events; newsreel; **actualidad escénica** theater news; **actualidad gráfica** news in pictures
actualización *f* updating; (compu) upgrade
actualizar §60 *tr* to bring up to date; (compu) to upgrade
actualmente *adv* at present, at the present time
actuante *mf* participant
actuar §21 *tr* to actuate || *intr* to act; perform

actua•rio -ria *mf* actuary
acuaplano *m* aquaplane
acuarela *f* water color
acuario *m* aquarium; **Acuario** *m* (astr) Aquarius
acuartelar *tr* to billet, quarter
acuáti•co -ca *adj* aquatic
acuatizaje *m* (aer) alighting on water; (*de nave espacial*) splashdown
acuatizar §60 *intr* (aer) to alight on water
acuchilla•do -da *adj* knife-shaped; schooled by experience; (*vestido*) slashed
acuchillar *tr* to stab; stab to death; slash
acucia *f* zeal, diligence; yearning
acuciar *tr* to goad, prod; harass; yearn for
acuclillar *ref* to squat, crouch
acudir *intr* to come up, respond; apply; hang around; come to the rescue; **acudir a las urnas** to vote
acueducto *m* aqueduct
acuerdo *m* accord; agreement; memory; **¡de acuerdo!** agreed!, all right!; **de acuerdo con** in accord with; **de común acuerdo** with one accord; **estar en su acuerdo** to be in one's right mind; **ponerse de acuerdo** to come to an agreement; **recobrar su acuerdo** to come to; **tomar un acuerdo** to make a decision; **volver en su acuerdo** to come to; to change one's mind
acuitar *tr & ref* to grieve
acullá *adv* yonder, over there
acumulador *m* storage battery
acumular *tr* to accumulate, gather; store up || *intr & ref* to accumulate, gather
acunar *tr* to rock; cradle
acuñación *f* coining, minting; wedging
acuñar *tr* to coin, mint; wedge; key, lock; (typ) to quoin
acuo•so -sa *adj* watery; juicy
acupuntura *f* acupuncture
acurrucar §73 *ref* to squat, crouch; huddle
acusación *f* accusation
acusa•do -da marked || *mf* accused
acusa•dor -dora *adj* accusing || *mf* prosecuting attorney
acusar *tr* to accuse; show; (*recibo de una carta*) acknowledge || *ref* to confess
acusati•vo -va *adj & m* accusative
acuse *m* acknowledgment
acústi•co -ca *adj* acoustic || *f* acoustics
adagio *m* adage
adalid *m* chief; guide, leader; champion
adama•do -da *adj* womanish; chic, stylish
adamar *ref* to become effeminate
adán *m* dirty, ragged fellow; lazy, careless fellow || **Adán** *m* Adam
adaptación *f* adaptation
adaptar *tr* to adapt
adarga *f* oval or heart-shaped leather shield
adarvar *tr* to bewilder, stun
A. de C. *abbr* **año de Cristo**
a. de C. *abbr* **antes de Cristo** before Christ
adecentar *tr* to clean up, tidy up || *ref* to put on a clean shirt, dress up
adecua•do -da *adj* fitting, suitable
adecuar *tr* to fit, adapt
adefesio *m* nonsense; outlandish outfit; queer-looking fellow
adehala *f* gratuity, extra
adehesar *tr* to convert into pasture
a. de J.C. *abbr* **antes de Jesucristo**
adelanta•do -da *adj* precocious; bold, forward; (*reloj*) fast; **por adelantado** in advance || *m* provincial governor
adelantamiento *m* anticipation; advancement, promotion, progress
adelantar *tr* to move forward; outstrip, get ahead of; advance; promote; improve || *intr* to advance; improve; be fast || *ref* to move forward; gain; **adelantarse a** preempt
adelante *adv* ahead; forward; **más adelante** farther on; later || *interj* go ahead!; come in!
adelanto *m* advance, progress, improvement; advancement; payment in advance
adelfa *f* oleander
adelgazar §60 *tr* to make thin; taper; purify; argue subtly about; weaken, lessen || *intr & ref* to get thin; taper
ademán *m* attitude; gesture; **ademanes** manners; **en ademán de** getting ready to; **hacer ademán de** to make a move to
además *adv* moreover, besides; **además de** in addition to, besides
adentellar *tr* to sink one's teeth into
adentrar *intr & ref* to go in; **adentrarse en el mar** to go farther out to sea
adentro *adv* inside; **mar adentro** out at sea; **ser muy de adentro** to be like a member of the family; **tierra adentro** inland || **adentros** *mpl* inmost being, inmost thoughts; **en** or **para sus adentros** to oneself, to himself, etc.
adep•to -ta *adj* initiated || *mf* follower
aderezar §60 *tr* to dress, adorn; cook; (*una tela*) starch; season; repair; lead; (*bebidas*) mix; (*vinos*) blend || *ref* to dress, get ready
aderezo *m* dressing; seasoning, condiment; starch; finery; equipment; set of jewelry
adestrar §2 *tr & ref* var of **adiestrar**
adeuda•do -da *adj* indebted, in debt
adeudar *tr* to owe; to be liable for; charge || *intr* to become related by marriage || *ref* to run into debt
adeudo *m* debt, indebtedness; customs duty; charge, debit
adherencia *f* adhesion; **tener adherencias** to have connections
adherente *adj* adherent || *m* adherent; **adherentes** accessories
adherir §68 *intr & ref* to adhere; stick
adhesión *f* adherence, adhesion
adhesi•vo -va *adj* adhesive
adicción *f* addiction
adición *f* addition; (*en un café o restaurante*) check
adicionar *tr* to add; add to
adictivo *adj* addictive

adic•to -ta *adj* addicted; devoted || *mf* addict; fan, supporter
adiestramiento *m* training; breaking in
adiestrar *tr* to train; teach; lead, guide || *ref* to train, practice
adietar *tr* to put on a diet
adinera•do -da *adj* wealthy, well-to-do
adiós *m* adieu, good-bye || *interj* adieu!, good-bye!
aditamento *m* addition; accessory
aditi•vo -va *adj & m* additive
adivinación *f* prophecy; guessing, divination; **adivinación del pensamiento** mind reading
adivina•dor -dora *mf* guesser; good guesser; **adivinador del pensamiento** mind reader
adivinaja *f* riddle, puzzle
adivinanza *f* riddle; guess
adivinar *tr* to prophesy; guess, divine; (*un enigma*) solve; (*el pensamiento ajeno*) read
adivi•no -na *mf* fortuneteller; guesser
adjetivo *m* adjective
adjudicar §73 *tr* to adjudge, award || *ref* to appropriate
adjuntar *tr* to join, connect; add; enclose
adjun•to -ta *adj* added, attached; enclosed || *mf* associate || *m* adjunct; adjective
adminículo *m* aid, auxiliary; gadget; meddler; **adminículos** emergency equipment
administración *f* administration; management; headquarters; **administración pública** civil service
administra•dor -dora *mf* administrator, manager; **administrador de correos** postmaster
administrar *tr* to administer, manage
admiración *f* admiration; wonder; exclamation mark
admira•dor -dora *mf* admirer
admirar *tr* to admire; surprise || *ref* to wonder; **admirarse de** to wonder at
admisible *adj* admissible
admisión *f* admission; (mach) intake
admitir *tr* to admit; allow; accept, recognize; agree to; (compu) support
A.D.N. *m* (letterword) (**ácido deoxirribonucleico**) DNA (deoxyribonucleic acid)
adobar *tr* to repair, restore; dress, prepare; cook, stew; (*carne, pescado*) pickle; (*pieles*) tan
adobe *m* adobe
adobera *f* (SAm) brick-shaped cheese; mold for brick-shaped cheese
adobo *m* repairing; dressing; cooking; pickling; tanning; pickled meat or fish
adocena•do -da common, ordinary
adoctrinar *tr* to indoctrinate, teach, instruct
adolecer §22 *intr* to fall sick; **adolecer de** to suffer from || *ref* — **adolecerse de** (archaic) to sympathize with, feel sorry for
adolescencia *f* adolescence
adolescente *adj & mf* adolescent
adonde *conj* where, whither
adónde *adv* where, whither
adopción *f* adoption
adoptar *tr* to adopt
adoptivo *adj* adopted; adoptive
adoquín *m* paving stone, paving block; (coll) blockhead
adoquina•do -da *adj* paved with cobblestones || *m* cobblestone paving
adorable *adj* adorable
adoración *f* adoration, worship; **Adoración de los Reyes** Epiphany
adora•dor -dora *mf* adorer, worshiper || *m* suitor
adorar *tr & intr* to adore, worship
adormecer §22 *tr* to put to sleep || *ref* to go to sleep; get sleepy
adormeci•do -da *adj* sleepy, drowsy; numb; calm
adormidera *f* opium poppy
adormilar *ref* to doze, drowse
adornar *tr* to adorn; (*un cuento*) embroider
adornista *mf* decorator
adorno *m* adornment, decoration; **adorno de escaparate** window dressing
adosar *tr* to lean; push close
adquirir §40 *tr* to acquire; **adquirir en propiedad** to buy, purchase
adquisición *f* acquisition
adrede *adv* on purpose
Adriáti•co -ca *adj & m* Adriatic
adscribir §83 *tr* to attribute; assign
adscripción *f* attribution; assignment
aduana *f* customhouse; **aduana seca** inland customhouse; **exento de aduana** duty-free; **sujeto de aduana** dutiable
aduane•ro -ra *adj* customhouse; customs || *m* customhouse officer, customs inspector
aduar *m* Arab settlement; Gypsy camp; Indian ranch
adueñar *ref* to take possession
adujar *tr* (naut) to coil || *ref* (naut) to curl up
adular *tr* to flatter, fawn on
adu•lón -lona *adj* fawning, groveling || *mf* fawner
adúltera *f* adulteress
adulterar *tr* to adulterate || *intr* to commit adultery || *ref* to become adulterated, to spoil
adulterio *m* adultery
adúlte•ro -ra *adj* adulterous || *m* adulterer || *f* see **adúltera**
adultez *f* adulthood
adul•to -ta *adj & mf* adult
adulzar §60 *tr* to sweeten; (*metales*) soften
adunar *tr* to join, bring together
adundar *ref* (CAm) to become stupid
adus•to -ta *adj* grim, stern, gloomy; scorching hot
advenedi•zo -za *adj* strange; foreign || *mf* stranger; foreigner; outsider; parvenu, upstart; nouveau riche
advenimiento *m* advent, coming; accession; **esperar el santo advenimiento** to wait in vain
advenir §79 *intr* to come, arrive; happen
adverbio *m* adverb
adversa•rio -ria *mf* adversary
adversidad *f* adversity

advertencia *f* observation; notice, remark; warning; preface
adverti•do -da *adj* capable, clever, wide-awake
advertir §68 *tr* to notice, observe; notify, warn; point out || *ref* to become aware
Adviento *m* (eccl) Advent
adyacente *adj* adjacent
aeración *f* aeration; ventilation; air conditioning
aére•o -a *adj* air, aerial; overhead, elevated; airy, light, fanciful
aerobismo *m* aerobics
aerodinámi•co -ca *adj* aerodynamic, streamlined || *f* aerodynamics
aeródromo *m* aerodrome, airdrome; **aeródromo de urgencia** emergency landing field
aeroembolismo *s* decompression sickness
aeroespacial *adj* aerospace
aerofluyente *adj* streamlined
aerofoto *f* aerial photograph
aerofumigación *f* crop-dusting
aeromedicina *f* aviation medicine
aeromodelismo *m* model-airplane building
aeromodelista *mf* model-airplane builder
aeromodelo *m* model airplane
aeromotor *m* windmill; airplane motor
aeromoza *f* air hostess, stewardess
aeronáuti•co -ca *adj* aeronautic || *f* aeronautics
aeronave *f* airship; **aeronave cohete** rocket ship
aeropista *f* landing strip
aeroplano *m* aeroplane
aeroposta *f* air mail
aeropostal *adj* air-mail
aeropropulsor *m* airplane engine; **aeropropulsor por reacción** jet engine
aeropuerto *m* airport
aeroscala *f* transit point
aerosol *m* aerosol
aeróstato or **aerostato** *m* dirigible, balloon
aeroste•ro -ra *adj* aviation || *m* flyer; airman
aerotaxi *m* air taxi
aeroterrestre *adj* air-ground
aerovía *f* airway
afable *adj* affable, friendly, agreeable
afama•do -da *adj* noted, famous
afamar *tr* to make famous || *ref* to become famous
afán *m* hard work; eagerness, zeal; task; worry
afanar *tr* to press, hurry || *intr* to strive, toil || *ref* to strive, toil; busy oneself
afano•so -sa *adj* hard, laborious; hardworking
afarolar *ref* to make a fuss, get excited
afear *tr* to deface, disfigure; blame
afeblecer §22 *intr* to grow feeble, get thin
afección *f* affection, fondness; (med) affection
afectación *f* affectation
afecta•do -da *adj* affected; **estar afectado de** (*p.ej., los riñones*) to have (*e.g., kidney*) trouble
afectar *tr* to affect; hurt, injure || *ref* to be moved, be stirred
afecti•vo -va *adj* emotional
afec•to -ta *adj* fond; kind; affected; **afecto a** fond of; (*un empleo, un servicio, etc.*) attached to; **afecto de** suffering from || *m* affection, fondness; emotion
afectuo•so -sa *adj* affectionate; kind
afeitado *m* shave; **afeitado a ras** close shave
afeitar *tr* to shave; adorn; || *ref* to shave; paint
afeite *m* cosmetics, rouge, makeup
afeminación *f* effeminacy
afemina•do -da *adj* effeminate
afeminar *tr* to effeminate || *ref* to become effeminate
aferra•do -da *adj* stubborn, obstinate
aferrar *tr* to seize; catch; hook; (naut) to moor; (naut) to furl || *ref* to interlock, hook together; cling; insist
Afganistán, el Afghanistan
afga•no -na *adj & mf* Afghan
AFI *m* (letterword) (**Alfabeto Fonético Internacional**) IPA (International Phonetic Alphabet)
afianzar §60 *tr* to guarantee, vouch for; bail; fasten; prop up; grasp; support || *ref* to hold fast, steady oneself
afición *f* fondness, liking, taste; ardor, zeal; fans, public
aficiona•do -da *adj* fond; amateur; **aficionado a** fond of || *mf* amateur; fan, follower
aficionar *tr* to win, win the attachment of || *ref* — **aficionarse a** *or* **de** to become fond of; become a follower of, become a fan of
afiebra•do -da *adj* feverish
afiebrar *ref* (SAm) to get a fever
afi•jo -ja *adj* affixed || *m* affix
afila•do -da *adj* sharp; tapering; pointed; peaked
afilador *m* grinder, sharpener; razor strop
afilalápi•ces *m* (*pl* **-ces**) pencil sharpener
afilar *tr* to grind, sharpen; (*una navaja de afeitar*) strop; (Arg & Urug) to flirt with || *ref* to sharpen, get sharp; taper, get thin
afiliar §77 & regular *tr* to affiliate, take in || *ref* — **afiliarse a** to join
afiligranar *tr* to filigree; adorn, embellish
afilón *m* knife sharpener; razor strop
afín *adj* near, bordering; like, similar; related || *mf* relative by marriage
afinador *m* tuner; tuning hammer, tuning key
afinar *tr* to purify, refine, perfect; trim; tune
afincar §73 *intr & ref* to buy up real estate
afinidad *f* affinity; **por afinidad** by marriage
afirmar *tr* to strengthen, secure, fasten; assert || *ref* to hold fast; steady oneself
afirmati•vo -va *adj & f* affirmative
aflicción *f* affliction; sorrow, grief
afligir §27 *tr* to afflict, grieve; (Mex) to beat, whip || *ref* to grieve
aflojar *tr* to slacken, let go; loosen || *intr* to slacken, slow up; abate, lessen || *ref* to come loose; slacken
aflora•do -da *adj* flour; fine, elegant
aflorar *tr* to sift || *intr* to crop out
afluencia *f* flowing; affluence, abundance; crowd, jam, rush; fluency; **horas de afluencia** rush hour

afluente *adj* flowing; abundant; fluent || *m* tributary
afluir §20 *intr* to flow; pour, flock
afmo. *abbr.* **afectísimo**
afofar *tr* to make fluffy, make spongy
afonizar §60 *tr & ref* to unvoice
aforar *tr* to gauge, measure; appraise
aforismo *m* aphorism
afortuna•do -da *adj* fortunate; happy
afrancesa•do -da *adj & mf* Francophile
afrecho *m* bran
afrenta *f* affront
afrentar *tr* to affront || *ref* to be ashamed
afrento•so -sa *adj* outrageous, disgraceful
Africa *f* Africa
africa•no -na *adj & mf* African
afroamerica•no -na *adj & mf* Afro-American, African-American
afrodisía•co -ca *adj & m* aphrodisiac
afrontamiento *m* confrontation
afrontar *tr* to bring face to face; defy || *ref* — **afrontarse con** to confront, meet face to face
afuera *adv* outside || *interj* clear the way!, look out! || **afueras** *fpl* outskirts, environs
afuetada *f* or **afuetadura** *f* (SAm) beating
agachadiza *f* snipe; **hacer la agachadiza** to duck
agachar *tr* to lower, bend down || *ref* to crouch, squat; cower; (SAm) to give in, yield
agalla *f* gallnut; (*de pez*) gill; (*de ave*) ear lobe; **agallas** courage, guts
ágape *m* banquet, love feast
agarradera *f* hold, grip; handle; **tener agarraderas** to have connections
agarrada *f* brawl, fight, scrap
agarra•do -da *adj* stingy, tight || *f* see **agarrada**
agarrar *tr* to grab, grasp; take hold of; get, obtain || *intr* to take hold; take root; stick || *ref* to grapple; have a good hold; worry; **agarrarse a** to take hold of, cling to
agarro *m* clench, clutch, grip
agarrochar *tr* to jab with a goad
agarrón *m* brawl, fight; grip, tug
agarrotar *tr* to garrote; bind, tie up || *ref* to become numb
agasajar *tr* to regale, lionize, make a fuss over
agasajo *m* kindness, attention; lionization; favor, gift; treat; party
agavillar *tr* to bind or tie in sheaves || *ref* to band together
agazapar *tr* to grab, to nab || *ref* to crouch; to hide
agencia *f* agency; bureau; office; branch; (Chile) pawn shop; **agencia de cobros de cuentas** collection agency; **agencia de viajes** travel agency; **agencia de noticias** news agency; **agencia funeraria** funeral parlor; **agencia inmobiliaria** real-estate agency; **agencia matrimonial** marriage bureau
agenciar *tr* to manage to bring about; promote || *ref* to manage
agenda *f* notebook
agente *mf* agent; policeman; **agente de bolsa, agente de cambio** stockbroker; **agente de policía** police officer; **agente de publicidad** press agent; **agente de viajes** travel agent; **agente inmobiliario** realtor, real-estate agent; **agente viajero** traveling sales person
agigantar *tr* to make huge || *ref* to become huge
ágil *adj* agile; flexible, light, supple
agilitar *tr & ref* to limber up
agita•do -da *adj* agitated, excited, exalted; (*mar*) rough
agitar *tr* to agitate; shake; wave; stir || *intr* to agitate || *ref* to be agitated; shake; wave; get excited; (*el mar*) get rough
aglomeración *f* agglomeration; crowd; built-up area
aglomerado *m* briquet, coal briquet
aglutinar *tr* to stick together || *ref* to cake
agnósti•co -ca *adj & mf* agnostic
agobiar *tr* to overburden; exhaust, oppress
agolpar *ref* to flock, throng
agonía *f* agony, throes of death; agony, anguish; yearning; craving
agonizar §60 *tr* (*al moribundo*) to assist, attend; harass || *intr* to be in the throes of death
agorar §3 *tr* to augur, foretell
agore•ro -ra *adj* fortune-telling; ill-omened; superstitious || *mf* fortune-teller
agostar *tr* to burn up, to parch || *ref* to dry up; (*la esperanza, la felicidad*) fade away
agostero *m* harvest helper
agosto *m* August; harvest; harvest time; **hacer su agosto** to make hay while the sun shines
agota•do -da *adj* exhausted; suffering burnout; sold out; out of print
agotar *tr* to exhaust, wear out, use up || *ref* to become exhausted, be used up; go out of print; run out
agracia•do -da *adj* charming, graceful; nice, pretty || *mf* winner
agradable *adj* agreeable; pleasant
agradar *tr* to please || *intr* to be pleasing || *ref* to be pleased
agradecer §22 *tr* to thank; **agradecerle a uno una cosa** to thank someone for something
agradeci•do -da *adj* thankful, grateful; rewarding
agradecimiento *m* thanks, gratitude
agrado *m* agreeableness, graciousness; pleasure, liking
agrandar *tr* to enlarge || *ref* to grow larger
agranelar *tr* (*cuero*) to grain, pebble
agrapar *tr* to clamp
agrariense *adj & mf* agrarian
agra•rio -ria *adj* agrarian
agravar *tr* to weigh down; aggravate; exaggerate; oppress || *ref* to get worse
agraviar *tr* to wrong, offend || *ref* to take offense
agravio *m* wrong, offense; (law) tort; **agravios de hecho** assault and battery
agravio•so -sa *adj* offensive, insulting
agraz *m* (*pl* **agraces**) sour grape; sour-grape juice; bitterness, displeasure; **en agraz** prematurely

agredir §1 *tr* to attack, assault
agregado *m* aggregate; concrete block; attaché; (Arg) tenant farmer
agregar §44 *tr* to add; attach; appoint || *ref* to join
agremiado *m* union member
agremiar *tr* to unionize
agresión *f* aggression; **agresión con lesiones** (law) assault and battery
agresi•vo -va *adj* aggressive
agre•sor -sora *adj* aggressive || *mf* aggressor
agreste *adj* country, rustic; wild, rough; uncouth
agriar §77 & regular *tr* to make sour; exasperate || *ref* to turn sour; become exasperated
agrícola *adj* agricultural || *mf* farmer
agricultura *f* agriculture; **agricultura biológica** organic farming
agridulce *adj* bittersweet; sweet-and-sour
agriera *f* (Chile) heartburn; **agrieras** (Col) cruet stand
agrietar *tr & ref* to crack
agrimensor *m* surveyor
agrimensura *f* surveying
agringar §44 *ref* to act like a gringo
a•grio -gria *adj* sour, acrid; uneven, rough; brittle || **agrios** *mpl* citrus fruit
agronomía *f* agronomy
agropecua•rio -ria *adj* land-and-cattle, farm
agrumar *tr & ref* to curd, clot
agrupar *tr & ref* to group, cluster
agrura *f* sourness; unpleasantness; **agruras** citrus fruit
agua *f* water; (*de un tejado*) slope; **agua abajo** downstream; **agua arriba** upstream; **agua bendita** holy water; **agua corriente** running water; **agua de colonia** cologne; **agua de marea** tidewater; **agua de Seltz** club soda; **agua gaseosa** carbonated water; **agua nieve** sleet; **agua oxigenada** hydrogen peroxide; **agua pesada** heavy water; **agua potable** drinking water; **aguas** mineral springs; (*de sedas; de piedras preciosas*) water, sparkle; **aguas mayores** equinoctial tide; feces; **aguas menores** ordinary tide; urination; **aguas negras, residuales** *or* **servidas** sewage; **aguas pluviales** rainwater; **cubrir aguas** to have under roof; **entre dos aguas** under water, under the surface of the water; (coll) undecided
aguacate *m* avocado, alligator pear; pear-shaped emerald
aguacero *m* shower
aguada *f* source of water; water color; watering station
aguade•ro -ra *adj* water || *m* watering place
agua•do -da *adj* watery; thin, watered; weak, washed out, limp; dull, insipid || *f* see **aguada**
agua•dor -dora *mf* water carrier || *m* paddle, bucket
aguafies•tas *mf* (*pl* **-tas**) kill-joy, wet blanket, crapehanger
aguafortista *mf* etcher
aguafuerte *f* etching; **grabar al aguafuerte** to etch
aguaitar *intr* to spy, watch || *tr* to watch, wait for
aguaje *m* watering place; tidal wave; strong current; (*de buque*) wake
aguamala *f* jellyfish
aguamanil *m* ewer, wash pitcher; washstand
aguama•nos *m* (*pl* **-nos**) water for washing hands; washstand
aguamarina *f* aquamarine
aguanie•ves *f* (*pl* **-ves**) wagtail
aguano•so -sa *adj* watery, soaked
aguantada *f* patience, forbearance
aguantar *tr* to hold up, sustain; bear, endure, tolerate; hold back, control || *intr* to last, hold out || *ref* to restrain oneself; keep quiet; **aguantarse las lágrimas** to swallow one's tears
aguante *m* patience, endurance; strength, vigor
aguar §10 *tr* to water; spoil, mar || *ref* to become watery; fill up with water; be spoiled
aguardar *tr* to await, wait for; grant time to || *intr* to wait; **aguardar a que** to wait until
aguardentera *f* liquor bottle, brandy flask
aguardentería *f* liquor store
aguardento•so -sa *adj* brandy; (*voz*) whiskey
aguardiente *m* brandy; spirituous liquor; **aguardiente de caña** rum; **aguardiente de manzana** applejack
aguardo *m* hunter's blind
aguarrás *m* turpentine, oil of turpentine
aguasar *ref* (Arg & Chile) to become countrified
aguazal *m* swamp, pool
agudeza *f* acuteness, acuity; sharpness; witticism; **agudeza visual** visual acuity
agu•do -da *adj* acute; sharp; keen; witty
agüero *m* augury; omen; forecast
aguerri•do -da *adj* inured, hardened
aguijada *f* goad, spur; prod
aguijar *tr* to goad, spur, prod || *intr* to hurry along
aguijón *m* goad, spur; sting; thorn; stimulus; **dar coces contra el aguijón** to kick against the pricks
aguijonear to goad, incite; sting
águila *f* eagle; **¿águila o sol?** (Mex) heads or tails?; **águila ratonera** buzzard; **ser un águila** to be wide-awake, be a wizard
aguile•ño -ña *adj* aquiline; sharp-featured
aguilón *m* (*de grúa*) boom, jib; (*del tejado*) gable
aguinaldo *m* Christmas gift, Epiphany gift; Christmas carol
aguja *f* needle; hatpin; steeple, spire; (*del reloj*) hand; (electron) stylus; **aguja de calceta, punto** *or* **tejer** knitting needle; **aguja de gancho** crochet needle; **aguja de hacer media** knitting needle; **aguja de zurcir** darning needle; **agujas** (rr) switch; **buscar una aguja en un pajar** to look for a needle in a haystack
agujerear *tr* to make a hole in, pierce, perforate
agujerito *m* pinhole

agujero *m* hole; pincushion; **agujero negro** black hole
agujeta *f* (*de la jeringa*) needle; shoestring; **agujetas** stitches, twinges
agusanar *ref* to get wormy; become wormeaten
aguzanie•ves *f* (*pl* **-ves**) wagtail
aguzar §60 *tr* to sharpen; incite, stir up; stare at; (*las orejas*) prick up
ah-chís *interj* kerchoo!
aherrojar *tr* to fetter, shackle; oppress
aherrumbrar *tr & ref* to rust
ahí *adv* there; **de ahí que** hence; **por ahí** that way
ahija•do -da *mf* godchild; protégé ‖ *m* godson ‖ *f* goddaughter
ahilar *ref* to faint from hunger; waste away; grow poorly; turn sour
ahincar §73 *tr* to urge, press; importune ‖ *ref* to hasten
ahinco *m* earnestness, zeal, eagerness
ahitar *tr* to cloy, surfeit, stuff
ahi•to -ta *adj* surfeited, stuffed; fed up, disgusted ‖ *m* surfeit; indigestion
ahoga•do -da *adj* drowned; smothered; sunk; close, unventilated; **mate ahogado** stalemate; **perecer ahogado** to drown; **verse ahogado** to be swamped
ahogar §44 *tr* to drown; suffocate, smother; (*cal*) slake; (*plantas*) soak; oppress; extinguish; stalemate ‖ *ref* to drown; suffocate; drown oneself
ahogo *m* shortness of breath; great sorrow; stringency
ahondar *tr* to make deeper; go deep into ‖ *intr* to go deep, go deeper
ahora *adv* now; presently; **ahora bien** now then, so then; **ahora mismo** right now; **por ahora** for the present
ahorcajar *ref* to sit astride
ahorcar §73 *tr* to hang ‖ *ref* to hang, be hanged; hang oneself
ahorra•do -da *adj* saving, thrifty
ahorrar *tr* to save; spare ‖ *ref* to save or spare oneself
ahorrati•vo -va *adj* saving, thrifty; stingy ‖ *f* economy
ahorro *m* economy; **ahorros** savings
ahuchar *tr* to hoard
ahuecar §73 *tr* to hollow, hollow out; loosen, fluff up; **ahuecar la voz** to speak in deep and solemn tones ‖ *ref* to be puffed up
ahula•do -da *adj* waterproof, impermeable ‖ *m* overshoe
ahumar *tr* to smoke ‖ *intr* to be smoky ‖ *ref* to get smoked up; look or taste smoky; get drunk
ahusar *tr & ref* to taper
ahuyentar *tr* to put to flight; scare away ‖ *ref* to flee, run away
aira•do -da *adj* angry; wild; depraved
airar §4 *tr* to anger ‖ *ref* to get angry
aire *m* air; **aire acondicionado** air-conditioning; **aire-aire** (mil) air-to-air; **aire-superficie, aire-tierra** (mil) air-to-ground; **al aire libre** in the open air; **darse aires** to put on airs
airear *tr* to air, aerate, ventilate ‖ *ref* to get aired; catch cold
airón *m* aigrette, panache; gray heron
airo•so -sa *adj* airy; drafty; graceful, light; resplendent; successful
aislación *f* insulation
aislacionista *adj & mf* isolationist
aislador *m* insulator
aislamiento *m* isolation; (elec) insulation; **aislamiento acústico** soundproofing
aislar §4 *tr* to isolate; detach, separate; (*un jurado*) to sequester; (elec) to insulate ‖ *ref* to live in seclusion
ajá *interj* oho!
ajar *m* garlic field ‖ *tr* to crumple, muss; (*marchitar*) wither; tamper with; abuse, ill-treat ‖ *ref* to get mussed; wither
ajedrea *f* (bot) savory
ajedrecista *mf* chess player
ajedrez *m* chess; chess set
ajenjo *m* (*Artemisia*) wormwood; (*licor*) absinthe; (*sinsabores y penas*) (fig) wormwood, bitterness; **ajenjo del campo** or **ajenjo mayor** (*Artemisia absinthium*) wormwood
aje•no -na *adj* another's; extraneous, foreign; different; contrary; free; insane; uninformed; **lo ajeno** what belongs to someone else
ajetrear *tr* to drive, harass ‖ *ref* to bustle about; fidget
ajetreo *m* bustle, fuss
ají *m* (*pl* **ajíes**) chili; chili sauce; **ponerse como un ají** (Chile) to turn red as a tomato
aji•mez *m* (*pl* **-meces**) mullioned window
ajo *m* garlic; garlic clove; garlic sauce
ajorca *f* bracelet, anklet
ajornalar *tr* to hire by the day ‖ *ref* to hire out by the day
ajuar *m* housefurnishings; trousseau
ajuiciar *tr* to bring to one's senses ‖ *ref* to come to one's senses
ajustable *adj* adjustable
ajusta•do -da *adj* just, right; tight, closefitting
ajustar *tr* to adapt, fit, adjust; fine-tune; hire; arrange; reconcile; fasten; settle ‖ *intr* to fit ‖ *ref* to fit; hire out; be hired; come to an agreement
ajuste *m* fit; fitting, adjustment; hiring; arrangement; reconciliation; settlement; agreement
ajusticiar *tr* to execute, put to death
ala *f* wing; (*del sombrero*) brim; (*de puerta, mesa, etc.*) leaf; (*de pez*) fin; (*de hélice*) blade; (football) end; **ahuecar el ala** (coll) to beat it, to cut and run; **ala delta** hang gliding; hang glider; **ala en flecha** (aer) sweptback wing, **alas** boldness, courage; **volar con sus propias alas** to stand on one's own feet
Alá *m* Allah
alabanza *f* praise
alabar *tr* to praise ‖ *ref* to boast
alabarda *f* halberd

alabardero *m* halberdier; hired applauder, claqueur
alabastro *m* alabaster
álabe *m* drooping branch; bucket, paddle; cog
alabear *tr & ref* to warp
alabeo *m* warp, deformation, warping
alacena *f* cupboard, wall closet; (naut) locker; (Mex) booth, stall
alacrán *m* scorpion
ala•do -da *adj* winged
alamar *m* frog (*button and loop on a garment*)
alambica•do -da *adj* precious, oversubtle, finespun; begrudged
alambicar §73 *tr* to distill; refine to excess
alambique *m* still, alembic; (*de laboratorio*) retort; **por alambique** sparingly
alambrada *f* chicken wire; wire mesh; (mil) barbed wire; (elec) wiring
alambrado *m* chicken wire; wire mesh; wire fence; (elec) wiring; (mil) wire entanglement
alambraje *m* (elec) wiring
alambrar *tr* to fence with wire; string with wire; wire
alambre *m* wire; **alambre cargado** live wire; **alambre de púas** barbed wire; **alambre sin aislar** bare wire
alambrera *f* wire screen; wire cover
alameda *f* poplar grove; mall, shaded walk
álamo *m* poplar; **álamo de Italia** Lombardy poplar; **álamo negro** black poplar; **álamo temblón** aspen
alampar *ref* to have a craving
alancear *tr* to lance, spear
alano *m* mastiff, great Dane
alarde *m* display, ostentation; (mil) review; **hacer alarde de** to make a show of; boast of
alardear *intr* to boast, brag, show off
alardo•so -sa *adj* showy, ostentatious
alargar §44 *tr* to extend, lengthen, stretch; hand; to increase; let out || *ref* to go away, withdraw; grow longer; be long-winded
alarido *m* howl, shout, yell, whoop
alarma *f* alarm; (aer) alert; **alarma aérea** air-raid warning; **alarma antirrobo** burglar alarm; **alarma de incendios** fire alarm; **alarma de ladrones** burglar alarm; **falsa alarma** false alarm
alarmar *tr* to alarm; alert || *ref* to become alarmed
alarmista *mf* alarmist
alastrar *tr* (*las orejas*) to throw back; (naut) to ballast || *ref* to lie flat, cower
ala•zán -zana *adj* sorrel, reddish-brown || *mf* sorrel horse
alba *f* dawn, daybreak
albacea *m* executor || *f* executrix
albahaca *f* basil
albahaquero *m* flowerpot
alba•nés -nesa *adj & mf* Albanian
albañal *m* sewer, drain
albañil *m* mason, bricklayer
albañilería *f* masonry
albarán *m* rent sign; bulletin; (com) check list
albarca *f* sandal
albarda *f* packsaddle
albardilla *f* (*tejadillo sobre los muros*) coping; shoulder pad
albaricoque *m* apricot
albaricoquero *m* apricot tree
alba•tros *m* (*pl* **-tros**) albatross
albayalde *m* white lead
albear *intr* to turn white; (Arg) to get up at dawn
albedrío *m* free will; fancy, caprice, pleasure; **libre albedrío** free will
albéitar *m* veterinarian
alberca *f* pond, pool; tank, reservoir; **en alberca** roofless
albérchigo *m* clingstone peach
albergar §44 *tr* to shelter, harbor; house || *intr & ref* to take shelter; take lodgings
albergue *m* shelter, refuge; lodging; den, lair
albero *m* dishcloth, dishrag; white earth
al•bo -ba *adj* (poet) white || *f* see **alba**
albóndiga *f* meat ball, fish ball
albor *m* whiteness; dawn
alborada *f* dawn; morning serenade; reveille
alborear *intr* to dawn
albor•noz *m* (*pl* **-noces**) terry cloth; burnoose; cardigan; beach robe
alborota•do -da *adj* hasty, rash; noisy; rough
alborota•dor -dora *mf* agitator, rioter
alborotapue•blos *mf* (*pl* **-blos**) (coll) rabble rouser
alborotar *tr* to agitate, arouse, stir up || *intr* to make a racket || *ref* to get excited; riot; (*la mar*) get rough
alboroto *m* agitation, disturbance; noise, riot; **alborotos** (CAm) candied popcorn; **armar un alboroto** to raise a racket
alborozar §60 *tr* to gladden, cheer, overjoy, elate
alborozo *m* joy, merriment, elation
albricias *fpl* reward for good news; reward given on the occasion of some happy event; **en albricias de** as a token of || *interj* good news!, congratulations!
albufera *f* saltwater lagoon
ál•bum *m* (*pl* **-bumes**) album; **álbum de recortes** scrapbook
albumen *m* albumen
albúmina *f* albumin
albuminar *tr* (phot) to emulsify
albur *m* risk, chance
alcachofa *f* artichoke
alcahue•te -ta *mf* bawd, procurer, go-between; screen, fence; schemer; gossip
alcahuetear *tr* to procure; harbor || *intr* to pander
alcaide *m* governor, warden, jailer
alcalde *m* mayor, chief burgess; **alcalde de monterilla** small-town mayor; **tener el padre alcalde** to have a friend at court
alcaldesa *f* mayoress; mayor's wife
álcali *m* alkali
alcali•no -na *adj* alkaline
alcallería *f* pottery
alcana *f* henna

alcance *m* reach, scope, extent; range; pursuit; capacity; late news; import; coverage; brains, intelligence; **al alcance de** within reach of, within range of; **alcance de la vista** eyesight, eyeshot; **alcance del oído** earshot; **dar alcance a** to catch up with
alcancía *f* child's bank; bin, hopper
alcanfor *m* camphor
alcantarilla *f* sewer; culvert
alcantarillar *tr* to sewer
alcanza•do -da *adj* needy, hard up
alcanzar §60 *tr* to reach; overtake, catch up to; grasp; obtain; understand; live through ‖ *intr* to succeed; (*un arma de fuego*) carry; manage; suffice
alcaparrosa *f* vitriol
alcaravea *f* caraway
alcatraz *m* gannet, pelican
alcázar *m* fortress; castle, royal palace; quarterdeck
alce *m* elk, moose
alcista *adj* bullish ‖ *mf* (fig) bull
alcoba *f* bedroom; **alcoba de respeto** master bedroom
alcohol *m* alcohol
alcohóli•co -ca *adj & mf* alcoholic
alconafta *f* gasohol
alcor *m* hill, elevation, eminence
alcornoque *m* cork oak; blockhead
alcorque *m* cork-soled shoe; trench for water around a tree
alcorza *f* sugar paste, sugar icing; **ser una alcorza** (Arg) to be highly emotional
alcurnia *f* ancestry, lineage
alcuza *f* olive-oil can
aldaba *f* knocker, door knocker; bolt, crossbar; latch; hitching ring; **aldaba dormida** deadlatch; **tener buenas aldabas** to have pull
aldabonazo *m* knock on the door
aldea *f* village, hamlet; **la aldea mundial** the global village
aldea•no -na *adj* village; rustic ‖ *mf* villager
aleación *f* alloy
alear *tr* to alloy ‖ *intr* to flap the wings; to flap one's arms; to convalesce
aleccionar *tr* to teach, instruct; to train, to coach
aleda•ño -ña *adj* bordering ‖ *m* border, boundary
alega•dor -dora *adj* quarrelsome; litigious
alegar §44 *tr* to allege; to declare, assert ‖ *intr* (Col, Hond) to quarrel
alegoría *f* allegory
alegóri•co -ca *adj* allegoric(al)
alegrar *tr* to cheer, gladden; (*un fuego*) to stir ‖ *ref* to be glad, to rejoice; to get tipsy
alegre *adj* glad; bright; cheerful, lighthearted; careless; fast, spicy; **alegre de cascos** scatterbrained
alegría *f* cheer, joy, gladness; brightness, gaiety
aleja•do -da *adj* distant, remote
alejandri•no -na *adj & mf* Alexandrine
alejar *tr & ref* to move aside, move away
alelar *tr* to make stupid ‖ *ref* to grow stupid
aleluya *m & f* hallelujah ‖ *m* Easter time ‖ *f* doggerel; daub; **aleluya navideña** Christmas card ‖ *interj* hallelujah!
ale•mán -mana *adj & mf* German
Alemania *f* Germany
alenta•do -da *adj* brave, spirited; proud, haughty; well, healthy ‖ *f* deep breath
alentar §2 *tr* to encourage, cheer up ‖ *intr* to breathe ‖ *ref* to take heart; get well, recover
alerce *m* larch
alergia *f* allergy
alérgico *adj* allergic
alero *m* eaves
alerón *m* aileron
alerta *adv* on the alert ‖ *interj* watch out!, look out! ‖ *m* (mil) alert; (mil) watchword; **alerta avanzada** early warning
alertar *tr* to alert
aler•to -ta *adj* alert, watchful, vigilant
alesaje *m* bore
alesna *f* awl
aleta *f* small wing; (*de pez*) fin; (*de hélice*) blade; (zool) aleta; **aletas** (*natación*) flippers
aletargar §44 *tr* to benumb; put to sleep ‖ *ref* to get drowsy, fall asleep
aletear *intr* to flap the wings; flap, flip, flutter
aleve *adj* treacherous, perfidious
alevosía *f* treachery, perfidy
alevo•so -sa *adj* treacherous, perfidious
alfabetizar §60 *tr* to alphabetize; teach reading and writing to
alfabeto *m* alphabet
alfaneque *m* buzzard
alfanje *m* cutlass
alfarería *f* pottery
alfarero *m* potter
alféizar *m* splay; embrasure
alfeñicar §73 *tr* to candy, ice ‖ *ref* to grow thin; be affected, finical
alfeñique *m* almond-flavored sugar paste; affectation, prudery; thin, delicate person; weakling
alfé•rez *m* (*pl* **-reces**) (mil) second lieutenant; (mil) subaltern (Brit); **alférez de fragata** (nav) ensign; **alférez de navío** (nav) lieutenant (j.g.)
alfil *m* bishop
alfiler *m* pin; **alfiler de corbata** stickpin, scarfpin; **alfiler de madera** clothespin; **alfiler de seguridad** safety pin; **alfileres** pin money
alfilerar *tr* to pin, pin up
alfiletero *m* pincase, needlecase
alfombra *f* carpet; rug
alfombrar *tr* to carpet
alforfón *m* buckwheat
alforja *f* shoulder bag; traveling supplies; **pasarse a la otra alforja** to go too far, take too much liberty
alforza *f* pleat, tuck
al•foz *m* (*pl* **-foces**) outskirts; dependence; mountain pass
alga *f* alga; **alga marina** seaweed; **algas** algae
algaida *f* brush, thicket; sandbank
algalia *f* civet; catheter

algarabía *f* Arabic; (coll) gibberish, jabber; (coll) hubbub, uproar
algarada *f* outcry; uproar
algarroba *f* carob bean
algarrobo *m* carob
algazara *f* Moorish battle cry; din, uproar
álgebra *f* algebra
algebrai•co -ca *adj* algebraic
álgi•do -da *adj* cold, icy, frigid
algo *pron indef* something; anything; **algo por el estilo** something of the sort || *adv* somewhat, a little, rather
algodón *m* cotton; **algodón de azúcar** cotton candy; **algodón pólvora** guncotton; **estar criado entre algodones** to be brought up in comfort
algodoncillo *m* milkweed
algodono•so -sa *adj* cottony
alguacil *m* bailiff; mounted police officer at the head of the processional entrance of the bullfighters
alguien *pron indef* somebody, someone
algún *adj indef* apocopated form of **alguno,** used only before masculine singular nouns and adjectives
algu•no -na *adj indef* some, any; not any; **alguna vez** sometimes; ever || *pron indef* someone; **algunos** some
alhaja *f* jewel, gem; **buena alhaja** a bad egg, a sly fellow
alhajera *f* or **alhajero** *m* jewelry box
alharaca *f* fuss, ado, ballyhoo; **hacer alharacas** to make a fuss
alharaquien•to -ta *adj* fussy, noisy
alhe•lí *m* (*pl* **-líes**) gillyflower (*Matthiola incana*); wallflower (*Cheiranthus*)
alheña *f* henna; blight, mildew
alheñar *tr* to henna; blight, mildew || *ref* (*el pelo*) to henna
alhucema *f* lavender
alhumajo *m* pine needles
alia•do -da *adj* allied || *mf* ally
aliaga *f* furze, gorse
alianza *f* alliance; wedding ring; (Bib) covenant
aliar §77 *tr* to ally || *ref* to ally, become allied; form an alliance
alias *adj & m* alias
alicaí•do -da *adj* failing, weak; crestfallen, discouraged
alicates *mpl* pliers
Alicia *f* Alice
aliciente *m* inducement, incentive
alienar *tr* to alienate; enrapture
aliento *m* breath, breathing; courage, spirit; **dar aliento a** to encourage; **de mucho aliento** arduous, difficult, endless; **nuevo aliento** second wind; **sin aliento** out of breath
alifafe *m* complaint, indisposition
aligerar *tr* to lighten; alleviate, ease; hasten; shorten
aligustre *m* privet
alijador *m* lighter; lighterman; sander
alijar *tr* to unload, lighten; sandpaper
aligeramiento *m* easing; alleviation; **aligeramiento de impuestos** tax relief
alimaña *f* varmint, small predacious animal
alimentante *mf* person obliged to provide child support
alimentar *tr* to feed, nourish; (*por la fuerza*) to force-feed; (*p.ej., esperanzas*) to cherish, foster || *ref* to feed, nourish oneself
alimenti•cio -cia *adj* alimentary, nourishing
alimento *m* food, nourishment; encouragement; **alimento chatarra** (Mex) junk food; **alimentos** foodstuffs; allowance; alimony
alindar *tr* to mark off; embellish, prettify || *intr* to border, be contiguous
alineación *f* (auto) alignment; (sport) line-up
alinea•do -da *adj* lined up, aligned; **no alineado** nonaligned, Third World
alineamiento *m* (archeol, compu, pol) alignment
alinear *tr & ref* to align, line up
aliñar *tr* to dress, season
aliño *m* dressing, seasoning
aliquebra•do -da *adj* crestfallen
alisar *tr* to smooth; polish, sleek; iron lightly
aliso *m* alder tree
alistamiento *m* (mil) enrollment
alistar *tr* to list; enlist, enroll; stripe || *ref* to enlist, enroll; get ready
aliteración *f* alliteration
aliviar *tr* to alleviate, relieve, soothe; remedy; lighten; hasten || *ref* to get better, recover
alivio *m* alleviation, relief; remedy
aljaba *f* quiver
aljama *f* mosque; synagogue; Moorish quarter; ghetto
aljamía *f* Spanish of Moors and Jews; Spanish written in Arabic characters
aljez *m* gypsum
aljibe *m* water tender, tank barge; oil tanker; cistern
aljófar *m* imperfect pearl; (fig) dewdrops
aljofifa *f* floor mop
aljofifar *tr* to mop
allá *adv* there, over there; back there; **allá en** over in; back in; **el más allá** the beyond; **más allá** farther on, farther away; **más allá de** beyond; **por allá** thereabouts; that way
allanamiento *m* raid; break-in; **allanamiento de morada** breaking and entering
allanar *tr* to level, smooth, flatten; (*una dificultad*) iron out, overcome, get around; (*una casa*) break into; to subdue || *intr* to level off || *ref* to tumble down; yield, submit; humble oneself
allega•do -da *adj* near, close; related; partisan || *mf* relative; partisan
allegar §44 *tr* to collect, gather; reap || *intr* to approach || *ref* to approach; be attached, be a follower, agree
allende *adv* beyond; **allende de** besides, in addition to || *prep* beyond
allí *adv* there; **allí dentro** in there; **por allí** that way; around there

alma *f* soul, heart, spirit; (*persona*) living soul; crux, heart; sweetheart; (*de carril*) web; (*de cañón*) bore; (*de escalera*) newel; **alma gemela** soulmate; **dar el alma, entregar el alma, rendir el alma** to give up the ghost
almacén *m* warehouse; store, shop; grocery store, grocery; general store; storehouse; (phot) magazine; **almacén de ramos generales** (SAm) general store; **grandes almacenes** department store
almacenaje *m* storage; **almacenaje de datos** (compu) data storage, memory
almacenamiento *m* storage; (compu) (data) storage
almacenar *tr* to store; store up, hoard; (*datos*) (compu) to store
almacenero *s* grocer
almacenista *mf* storekeeper || *m* warehouseman
almáciga *f* seedbed, tree nursery
almádana *f* spalling hammer
almagre *m* red ocher
almajara *f* (hort) hotbed
alma-máter *f* driving force; university
almanaque *m* almanac; calendar
almeja *f* clam
almena *f* merlon
almenaje *m* battlement
almendra *f* almond; (*de cualquier fruto drupáceo*) kernel; **almendra amarga** bitter almond; **almendra de Málaga** Jordan almond; **almendra tostada** burnt almond
almendrado *m* macaroon
almendro *m* almond tree
almiar *m* haystack, hayrick
almíbar *m* simple syrup; fruit juice; **estar hecho un almíbar** to be as sweet as pie
almibarar *tr* to preserve in syrup; (*sus palabras*) honey || *intr* to candy
almidón *m* starch; paste; **almidón de maíz** cornstarch
almidona•do -da *adj* starched; spruce, dapper; stiff, prim
almidonar *tr* to starch
alminar *m* minaret
almiranta *f* admiral's wife; flagship
almirante *m* admiral
almi•rez *m* (*pl* **-reces**) brass mortar
almizcle *m* musk
almizclera *f* muskrat
almizclero *m* musk deer
almohada *f* pillow; **consultar con la almohada** to sleep it over
almohadilla *f* cushion; pad; (Chile) pincushion
almohaza *f* currycomb
almohazar §60 *tr* to currycomb
almoneda *f* auction; clearance sale
almonedar *tr* to auction
almorranas *fpl* piles, hemorrhoids
almorta *f* grass pea
almorzada *f* double handful, heavy breakfast
almorzar §35 *tr* to lunch on || *intr* to lunch, have lunch
almuecín *m* or **almuédano** *m* muezzin
almuerzo *m* lunch
alna•do -da *mf* stepchild
aloca•do -da *adj* mad, wild, reckless || *mf* madcap
alocar §73 *tr* to drive crazy
alocución *f* address, speech
áloe *m* or **aloe** *m* aloe; aloes
aloja•do -da *mf* guest, lodger
alojar *tr* to lodge; quarter, billet || *intr & ref* to lodge; be quartered or billeted
alojo *m* accommodations, lodging
alondra *f* lark
aloquecer §22 *ref* to go crazy, lose one's mind
alosa *f* shad
alpaca *f* alpaca; alpaca wool; alpaca cloth; German silver
alpargata *f* hemp sandal, espadrille
alpende *m* tool shed; lean-to, penthouse
Alpes *mpl* Alps
alpestre *adj* alpine
alpinismo *m* mountain climbing
alpi•no -na *adj* alpine
alpiste *m* canary seed, birdseed; **quedarse alpiste** to be disappointed
alquería *f* farmhouse
alquibla *f* kiblah
alquiladi•zo -za *adj & mf* hireling
alquilar *tr* to rent, let, hire || *ref* to hire out; be for rent
alquiler *m* rent, rental, hire; **alquiler de coches** car-rental service; **alquiler sin chófer** drive-yourself service; **de alquiler** for rent, for hire
alquimia *f* alchemy
alquitarar *tr* to distill
alquitrán *m* tar; **alquitrán de hulla** coal tar
alquitranado *m* tarpaulin
alquitranar *tr* to tar
alrededor *adv* around; **alrededor de** around; about, approximately || **alrededores** *mpl* environs, surroundings, outskirts, vicinity
Alsacia *f* Alsace
alsacia•no -na *adj & mf* Alsatian
alta *f* discharge from hospital; (mil) certificate of induction into active service; **dar de alta** to discharge from the hospital; **darse de alta** to join, be admitted; (mil) to report for duty
altane•ro -ra *adj* towering; arrogant, haughty
altar *m* altar; **altar mayor** high altar; **conducir al altar** to lead to the altar
alta•voz *m* (*pl* **-voces**) loudspeaker
altea *f* (bot) marshmallow
alteración *f* alteration; disturbance; uneven pulse; altercation, quarrel
alterar *tr* to alter; disturb; agitate, upset; falsify; lessen || *ref* to alter; be disturbed; be agitated; lessen; (*el pulso*) flutter
altercación *f* or **altercado** *m* argument, wrangle, bickering
altercar §73 *intr* to argue, bicker, wrangle
alternar *tr & intr* to alternate; **alternar con** to go around with
alternati•vo -va *adj* alternating, alternative || *f*

choice, option; admission as a matador; **no tener alternativa** to have no choice
alter•no -na *adj* alternate
alteza *f* sublimity || **Alteza** *f* (*tratamiento*) Highness
altibajo *m* downward thrust; **altibajos** uneven ground; ups and downs
altillo *m* hillock; (*oficina en una tienda o taller*) balcony; (Arg, Ecuad) attic, garret
altimetría *f* altimetry
altiplanicie *f* tableland
altitud *f* altitude; height
altivez *f* or **altiveza** *f* arrogance, haughtiness, pride
alti•vo -va *adj* haughty, proud; high, lofty
al•to -ta *adj* high; upper; top; loud; (*horas*) late; **ponerse tan alto** to take offense, be hoity-toity || *m* height, altitude; story, floor; stop, halt; **de alto a bajo** from top to bottom; **hacer alto** to stop; **pasar por alto** to overlook, disregard || *f* see **alta** || **alto** *adv* high up; loud; aloud || **alto** *interj* halt!
altoparlante *m* loudspeaker
altozanero *m* (Col) public errand boy
altozano *m* hill, knoll; upper part of town; (CAm, Col, Ven) parvis
altruísta *adj* altruistic || *mf* altruist
altura *f* height, altitude; high seas; juncture, point, stage; (mus) pitch; (naut) latitude; **a baja altura** low-level; **a estas alturas** at this juncture; **a la altura de** (naut) off; **estar a la altura de** to be up to, be equal to; be abreast of; **por estas alturas** around here
alucinación *f* hallucination
alucinante *adj* hallucinogenic
alud *m* avalanche
aludi•do -da *adj* above-mentioned
aludir *intr* to allude
alumbra•do -da *adj* lighted; enlightened; tipsy || *m* lighting; lighting system; **alumbrado de fondo** backlighting; **alumbrado público** street lighting
alumbramiento *m* lighting; childbirth, accouchement
alumbrar *tr* to light, illuminate; (*a los ciegos*) give sight to; enlighten; (*aguas subterráneas*) discover and bring to the surface || *intr* to have a child || *ref* to get tipsy
alumbre *m* alum
aluminio *m* aluminum
alumnado *m* student body
alum•no -na *mf* (*niño criado como si fuera hijo*) foster child; (*discípulo*) pupil, student; **alumno mimado** teacher's pet
alunizaje *m* lunar landing
alunizar §60 *intr* to land on the moon
alusión *f* allusion
álveo *m* bed of a stream, river bed
alvéolo *m* alveolus; (*de diente*) socket; (*de rueda de agua*) bucket
alza *f* rise, advance, increase; **jugar al alza** to bull the market
alzacuello *m* dog collar (*worn by clerics*)
alzada *f* height (*e.g., of a horse*)
alza•do -da *adj* (SAm) insolent; rebellious; *m* lump sum, cash settlement; front elevation; (bb) quire, gathering
alzapaño *m* curtain holder; tieback
alzapié *m* snare, trap
alzaprima *f* crowbar, lever; (*de instrumento de arco*) (mus) bridge
alzaprimar *tr* to pry, pry up; arouse, stir up
alzapuer•tas *m* (*pl* **-tas**) (archaic) dumb player, supernumerary
alzar §60 *tr* to raise, lift, hoist; pick up; (*la hostia*) elevate; hide, lock up; (*naipes*) cut; (bb) to gather || *ref* to rise, get up; revolt; **alzarse con** to abscond with
alzaválvu•las *m* (*pl* **-las**) tappet
alzo *m* (CAm) theft
a.m. *adj* (letterword) (**ante meridiem**) A.M.
AM *f* (letterword) A.M. (amplitude modulation)
ama *f* housekeeper; housewife, lady of the house; landlady, proprietress; **ama de casa** housewife; **ama de cría** or **de leche** wet nurse; **ama de llaves** housekeeper; **ama seca** dry nurse
amable *adj* amiable, kind, obliging; (*digno de ser amado*) lovable
amachinar *ref* to cohabit; get intimate
ama•do -da *adj & mf* beloved
ama•dor -dora *adj* fond, loving || *mf* lover
amadrigar §44 *tr* to welcome, receive with open arms || *ref* to burrow; go into seclusion
amaestra•dor -dora *mf* animal trainer
amaestrar *tr* to teach, coach; (*a los animales*) train
amagar §44 *tr* to show signs of, threaten; feint || *intr* to look threatening
amago *m* threat, menace; sign, indication; feint
amainar *tr* to lessen; (naut) to lower, shorten || *intr* to subside, die down; lessen; yield || *ref* to lessen; yield
amalgama *f* amalgam
amalgamar *tr & ref* to amalgamate
amamantar *tr* to nurse, to suckle
amancebamiento *m* cohabitation, concubinage, liaison
amancebar *ref* to cohabit, live in concubinage
amancillar *tr* to stain, spot; sully, tarnish
amanecer *m* dawn, daybreak || *v* **§22** *intr* to dawn, begin to get light; begin to appear; get awake, start the day
amanecida *f* dawn, daybreak
amanera•do -da *adj* mannered, affected
amansar *tr* (*animal*) to tame; (*caballo*) break; soothe, appease
amante *adj* fond, loving || *mf* lover
amaño *m* skill, cleverness, dexterity; trick; **amaños** tools, implements
amapola *f* poppy
amar *tr* to love
amaraje *m* alighting on water
amarar *intr* to alight on water
amargar §44 *tr* to make bitter; embitter; (*una*

tertulia, una velada) spoil || *intr & ref* to become bitter; become embittered
amar•go -ga *adj* bitter; sour; distressing || **amargos** *mpl* bitters
amargura *f* bitterness; sorrow, grief
amarillear *intr* to turn yellow, show yellow
amarillecer §22 *intr* to become yellow
amarillen•to -ta *adj* yellowish
amarillez *f* yellowness
amari•llo -lla *adj & m* yellow
amarra *f* mooring cable; **amarras** support, protection, moorings; **soltar las amarras** (naut) to cast off
amarradero *m* mooring
amarrar *tr* to moor; lash, tie up; (*las cartas*) stack
amartelar *tr* to make love to; make jealous || *ref* to fall in love; become jealous
amartillar *tr* to hammer; (*un arma de fuego*) to cock
amasar *tr* to knead; mix; massage; (*dinero*) amass; concoct
amatista *f* amethyst
Amazonas *m* Amazon (river)
ambages *mpl* ambiguity, quibbling; **sin ambages** straight to the point
ámbar *m* amber
Amberes *f* Antwerp
ambición *f* ambition
ambicionar *tr* to strive for, be eager for
ambicio•so -sa *adj* ambitious; eager; **ambicioso de figurar** social climber
ambientador *m* air freshener
ambiental *adj* environmental
ambiente *m* atmosphere; **medio ambiente** environment; situation
ambi•gú *m* (*pl* **-gúes**) buffet supper; bar, refreshment bar
ambigüedad *f* ambiguity
ambi•guo -gua *adj* ambiguous; (*género*) (gram) common
ámbito *m* boundary, limit; compass, scope
ambladura *f* amble
amblar *intr* to amble
am•bos -bas *adj & pron indef* both; **ambos a dos** both, both together
ambrosía *f* ragweed
ambulancia *f* ambulance; **ambulancia de correos** mail car, railway post office
ambulante *adj* itinerant, traveling || *m* railway mail clerk
ambulato•rio -ria *adj* ambulatory || *m* welfare center, public clinic; ambulance
amedrentar *tr* to frighten, scare
amelona•do -da *adj* melon-shaped; mentally retarded; lovesick
amén *interj* amen! || *m* amen || *adv* — **amén de** aside from; in addition to
amenaza *f* threat, menace
amenazar §60 *tr* to threaten, menace
amenguar §10 *tr* to lessen, diminish; belittle; dishonor
amenidad *f* amenity
amenizar §60 *tr* to make pleasant, brighten, cheer
ame•no -na *adj* agreeable, pleasant
amento *m* catkin
América *f* America; **la América Central** Central America; **la América del Norte** North America; **la América del Sur** South America; **la América Latina** Latin America
americana *f* sack coat, jacket
americanizar §60 *tr* to Americanize
america•no -na *adj & mf* American; Spanish-American || *f* see **americana**
amerizar §60 *intr* to alight on water
ametralladora *f* machine gun
ametrallar *tr* to machine-gun
amiba *f* amoeba
amiga *f* (*amistosa*) friend; (*amancebada*) lover; **amiga del alma** bosom friend
amigable *adj* amicable, friendly
amigacho *m* chum, crony, pal
amígdala *f* tonsil
amigdalitis *f* tonsillitis; quinsy
ami•go -ga *adj* friendly; fond || *mf* (*amistoso*) friend; (*amancebado*) lover; **amigo del alma** bosom friend || *f* see **amiga**
amigote *m* chum, crony, pal
amilanar *tr* to terrify, intimidate
aminorar *tr* to lessen, diminish
amistad *f* friendship; liaison; **hacer las amistades** to make up; **romper las amistades** to fall out, become enemies
amistar *tr* to bring together || *ref* to become friends
amisto•so -sa *adj* friendly
amniocentesis *f* amniocentesis
amnistía *f* amnesty
amnistiar §77 *tr* to amnesty, grant amnesty to
amo *m* head of family; landlord, proprietor; boss; **ser el amo del cotarro** to rule the roost
amoblar §61 *tr* to furnish
amodorrar *ref* to get drowsy; fall asleep; grow numb
amohinar *tr* to annoy, irritate, vex
amojonar *tr* to mark off with landmarks
amoladera *f* grindstone, whetstone
amolar §61 *tr* to grind, sharpen; bore, annoy
amoldar *tr* to mold; model, pattern, fashion; adjust, adapt
amonestación *f* admonition; marriage banns
amonestar *tr* to admonish, warn; publish the banns of
amoniáco *m* ammonia
amontonar *tr* to heap, pile; accumulate; hoard || *ref* to collect, gather; crowd; get angry; (Mex) to gang up
amor *m* love; **al amor del agua** with the current; obligingly; **al amor de la lumbre** by the fire, in the warmth of the fire; **amor cortés** courtly love; **amores** love affair; **amor propio** amour-propre; conceit; **por amor de** for the sake of
amorata•do -da *adj* livid, black-and-blue
amordazar §60 *tr* to muzzle; gag

amorío *m* love-making; love affair
amoro•so -sa *adj* loving, affectionate, amorous
amortajar *tr* to shroud; (carp) to mortise
amortecer §22 *tr* to deaden, muffle || *ref* to die away, become faint
amortiguador *m* shock absorber; door check; (*de automóvil*) bumper; **amortiguador de luz** dimmer; **amortiguador de ruido** muffler
amortiguar §10 *tr* to deaden, muffle; soften, tone down; dim; damp; (*un golpe*) cushion; (*ondas electromagnéticas*) damp
amortizar §60 *tr* to amortize; (*una deuda*) pay off
amoscar §73 *ref* to get peeved; (Mex) to blush, be embarrassed
amotina•do -da *adj* mutinous, rebellious || *mf* mutineer, rebel, rioter
amotinar *tr* to stir up; incite to mutiny || *ref* to rise up, mutiny, rebel
amover §47 *tr* to discharge, dismiss
amovible *adj* removable, detachable; temp
amparar *tr* to shelter, protect || *ref* to seek shelter; protect oneself
amparo *m* shelter, protection, refuge; stall; aid, favor
amperio *m* ampere
amperio-hora *m* (*pl* **amperios-hora**) ampere-hour
ampliable *adj* (compu) expandable
ampliación *f* amplification; (phot) enlargement
ampliar §77 *tr* to amplify, enlarge, widen; (phot) to enlarge
amplificador *m* amplifier
amplificar §73 *tr* to amplify; expand, enlarge; magnify
am•plio -plia *adj* ample; spacious, roomy, wide-ranging; wide-angle
amplitud *f* amplitude; roominess; **amplitud de banda** (compu) bandwidth
ampo *m* dazzling white; snowflake
ampolla *f* blister; water blister; bubble; cruet; bulb, light bulb
ampollar *tr & ref* to blister
ampolleta *f* vial; sandglass, hourglass; bulb, light bulb; cruet
ampulosidad *f* bombast, pomposity
ampulo•so -sa *adj* bombastic, pompous
amputa•do -da *mf* amputee
amputar *tr* to amputate
amueblar *tr* to furnish
amujera•do -da *adj* effeminate
amuleto *m* amulet, charm
amurallar *tr* to wall, wall in
amurcar §73 *tr* to gore
amusgar §44 *tr* (*las orejas el toro, el caballo*) to throw back
anacardo *m* cashew; cashew nut
anacróni•co -ca *adj* anachronistic
anacronismo *m* anachronism
ánade *mf* duck; **ánade real** mallard
anadear *intr* to waddle
anadeo *m* waddle, waddling
anales *mpl* annals
analfabetismo *m* illiteracy
analfabe•to -ta *adj & mf* illiterate
analgési•co -ca *adj* analgesic || *m* painkiller, analgesic
análi•sis *m & f* (*pl* **-sis**) analysis; **análisis costo-beneficio** cost-benefit analysis; **análisis de sistemas** systems analysis; **análisis gramatical** parsing; **análisis ocupacional** job analysis
analista *mf* analyst; annalist
analíti•co -ca *adj* analytic(al)
analizador *m* analyst; **analizador de léxico** (compu) scanner
analizar §60 *tr* to analyze; **analizar gramaticalmente** to parse
analogía *f* analogy; similarity
analógico *adj* analogical; (electron) analog
análo•go -ga *adj* analogous; similar
ana•ná *m* (*pl* **-naes**) pineapple
ananás *m* pineapple
anaquel *m* shelf
anaranja•do -da *adj & m* (*color*) orange
anarquía *f* anarchy
anárqui•co -ca *adj* anarchic(al)
anarquista *mf* anarch, anarchist
anatema *m & f* anathema; curse
anatomía *f* anatomy
anatómi•co -ca *adj* anatomic(al) || *mf* anatomist
anatomista *mf* anatomist
anca *f* croup, haunch; buttock, rump; **a ancas** or **a las ancas** mounted behind another person; **anca de rana** frog's leg; **dar ancas vueltas** (Mex) to give odds
ancheta *f* (Arg) foolishness; ridiculous act
an•cho -cha *adj* wide, broad; full, ample; loose, loose-fitting || *m* width, breadth; **ancho de banda** (compu) bandwidth
anchoa *f* anchovy
anchura *f* width, breadth; fullness, ampleness; looseness; comfort, ease
anchuro•so -sa *adj* wide, broad; spacious, roomy
ancianidad *f* old age
ancia•no -na *adj* old, aged || *mf* senior citizen || *m* old man; (eccl) elder || *f* old woman
ancla *f* anchor; **echar anclas** to cast anchor; **levar anclas** to weigh anchor
anclar *intr* to anchor
anclote *m* kedge, kedge anchor
ancón *m* bay, cove
áncora *f* anchor
ancorar *intr* to anchor
andada *f* thin, hard-baked cracker; **andadas** (*de conejos y otros animales*) tracks; **volver a las andadas** to revert to one's old tricks
andaderas *fpl* gocart, walker
anda•do -da *adj* gone by, elapsed; frequented, trodden; worn, used; ordinary || *m* gait || *f* see **andada**
andadores *mpl* leading strings
andadura *f* pace, gait; amble; (Mex) mount
Andalucía *f* Andalusia
anda•luz -luza *adj & mf* Andalusian
andaluzada *f* tall story, exaggeration, fish story

andamiaje *m* scaffolding
andamio *m* scaffold; platform
andanada *f* (naut) broadside; (taur) covered upper section; (coll) scolding; (fig) fusillade
andante *adj* walking; errant, wandering
andanza *f* wandering, rambling; fate, fortune
andar *m* gait, pace, walk || **§5** *tr* (*p.ej., dos millas*) to go; (*un camino*) go down or up || *intr* to go, walk; run; travel; act, behave; (*p.ej., un reloj*) go, run, work; be, feel; go by, pass, elapse; go (*to bear up, to last*), e.g., **anduve diez horas sin comer** I went ten hours without eating || *ref* to go by, to pass, to elapse; to go away; **andarse sin** to go without
andarie•go -ga *adj* wandering, roving; swift, fleet
andas *fpl* litter; stretcher; bier
andén *m* railway platform; quay; footpath
Andes *mpl* Andes
andinismo *m* mountain climbing in the Andes
andi•no -na *adj* Andean
andraje•ro -ra *mf* ragpicker
andrajo *m* rag, tatter; ragamuffin, scalawag
andrajo•so -sa *adj* ragged, raggedy, in tatters
Andrés *m* Andrew
andropausia *f* male menopause
andurriales *mpl* byways, out-of-the-way place
anea *f* cattail, bulrush
aneblar §2 *tr* to cloud; becloud || *ref* to become clouded; get dark
anécdota *f* anecdote
anega•do -da *adj* flooded; waterlogged
anegar §44 *tr* to flood; drown || *ref* to become flooded; drown
ane•jo -ja *adj* annexed; accessory || *m* annex; dependency; supplement
anemia *f* anemia; **anemia drepanocítica** sickle-cell anemia
anémi•co -ca *adj* anaemic
anestesia *f* anaesthesia
anestesiar *tr* anaesthetize
anestési•co -ca *adj & m* anaesthetic
aneurisma *m & f* aneurysm
anexar *tr* to annex
ane•xo -xa *adj* annexed; accessory || *m* annex; dependency
anfi•bio -bia *adj* amphibious
anfiteatro *m* amphitheater
anfitrión *m* host
anfitriona *f* hostess
ánfora *f* voting urn, ballot box
anfractuo•so -sa *adj* winding, tortuous
angarillas *fpl* handbarrow; panniers; cruet stand
ángel *m* angel; **ángel custodio** or **de la guarda** guardian angel; **ángel patudo** wolf in sheep's clothing; **tener ángel** to have great charm
angelical or **angéli•co -ca** *adj* angelic(al)
angelito *m* dead child; (coll) moppet
angina *f* angina; **angina de pecho** angina pectoris || **anginas** *fpl* quinsy
angloparlante *adj* English-speaking || *mf* speaker of English
anglosa•jón -jona *adj & mf* Anglo-Saxon
angos•to -ta *adj* narrow
anguila *f* eel; **anguilas** (*para botar un barco al agua*) ways; **escurrirse como una anguila** to be as slippery as an eel
angular *adj* angular
ángulo *m* angle; corner; **de ángulo plano** (phot) fish-eye
angulo•so -sa *adj* (*facciones*) angular
angurria *f* (SAm) raging hunger; greed
angustia *f* anguish, distress, grief
angustia•do -da *adj* distressed, grieved
angustiar *tr* to distress, afflict, grieve
angustio•so -sa *adj* distressed, grieved; worrisome
anhelar *tr* to crave, want badly || *intr* to pant; yearn; **anhelar por** to long for
anhélito *m* hard breathing
anhelo *m* craving; yearning, longing
anhelo•so -sa *adj* eager, yearning; breathless, panting
anhi•dro -dra *adj* anhydrous
Aníbal *m* Hannibal
anidar *tr* to harbor, shelter || *intr & ref* to nestle, make a nest; live
anilina *f* aniline
anilla *f* curtain ring; (*en la gimnasia*) ring; hoop
anillo *m* ring; cigar band; **anillo de boda** wedding ring; **anillo de compromiso** or **de pedida** engagement ring; **anillo sigilar** signet ring
ánima *f* soul; (*de arma de fuego*) bore
animación *f* animation; liveliness; bustle, movement
anima•do -da *adj* animated, lively
animador *m* (*de un café-cantante*) master of ceremonies
animal *adj & m* animal
animar *tr* to enliven; encourage; strengthen; drive || *ref* to take heart, feel encouraged
ánimo *m* mind, spirit; courage, valor, energy; attention, thought
animosidad *f* animosity, ill will
animo•so -sa *adj* brave, courageous; spirited; ready, disposed
aniña•do -da *adj* babyish, childish
anión *m* anion
aniquilar *tr* to annihilate, destroy || *ref* to be annihilated; decline, waste away; be humbled
anís *m* anise; anise-flavored brandy
aniversa•rio -ria *adj & m* anniversary
ano *m* anus
anoche *adv* last night
anochecer *m* nightfall, dusk || *v* **§22** *intr* to grow dark; arrive or happen at nightfall; end the day; go to sleep || *ref* to get dark; get cloudy; slip away
anochecida *f* nightfall, dusk
anodi•no -na *adj* innocuous, ineffective, harmless
ánodo *m* anode
anomalía *f* anomaly
anóma•lo -la *adj* anomalous

anonadar *tr* to annihilate, destroy; overwhelm; humble
anonimato *m* anonymity; **conservar el anonimato** to remain anonymous
anóni•mo -ma *adj* anonymous || *m* anonymous letter; anonymous person; pseudonym
anorexia *f* anorexia
anormal *adj* abnormal
anotar *tr* to annotate; note, jot down; point out
anquilosa•do -da *adj* stiff-jointed; old-fashioned; (*músculos*) stiff
ánsar *m* goose; wild goose
ansia *f* anxiety, anguish; eagerness; **ansias** (Ven) nausea
ansiar §77 & regular *tr* to long for, yearn for || *intr* to be madly in love
ansiedad *f* anxiety, worry; pain
ansio•so -sa *adj* anxious; anguished; longing; covetous
ant. *abbr* **anticuado**
anta *f* elk
antagonismo *m* antagonism
antaño *adv* last year; of yore, long ago
antárti•co -ca *adj* antarctic
ante *prep* before, in the presence of; in front of; at, with || *m* elk; buff
antea•do -da *adj* buff; (Mex) damaged, shopworn
anteanoche *adv* the night before last
anteayer *adv* the day before yesterday
antebrazo *m* forearm
antecámara *f* antechamber, anteroom
antecedente *adj* antecedent || *m* antecedent; **antecedentes** antecedents
anteceder *tr* to precede, go before
antece•sor -sora *mf* predecessor; ancestor
antedatar *tr* to antedate
antedi•cho -cha *adj* aforesaid, abovementioned
antelación *f* previousness, anticipation
antemano — de antemano in advance, beforehand
antena *f* (ent) antenna; (rad) antenna, aerial; **antena de conejo** rabbit ears; **en antena** on the air; **antena interior incorporada** built-in antenna; **antena parabólica** satellite dish; **llevar a las antenas** to put on the air
antenombre *m* title, honorific
anteojera *f* spectacle case; blinker, blinder
anteojo *m* eyeglass; spyglass; **anteojos** eyeglasses, spectacles; binoculars; blinkers; **anteojos bifocales** bifocals; **anteojos de sol** sunglasses: **anteojos oscuros** dark glasses
antepasa•do -da *adj* before last || **antepasados** *mpl* ancestors
antepecho *m* railing, guardrail; parapet; window sill
antepenúltima *f* antepenult
anteponer §54 *tr* to place in front; prefer
anteportada *f* half title, bastard title
anteportal *m* porch, vestibule
antepuerta *f* portière
antepuerto *m* entrance to a mountain pass; (naut) outer harbor
anterior *adj* front; previous; earlier
antes *adv* before; sooner, soonest; rather; previously; **antes bien** rather; on the contrary; **antes de** before; **antes (de) que** before; **cuanto antes** as soon as possible
antesala *f* antechamber; (*p.ej., de médico*) waiting room; **hacer antesala** to dance attendance
antiaére•o -a *adj* antiaircraft
anti-aliasing *m* (compu) anti-aliasing
antiamerica•no -na *adj* un-American
antiartísti•co -ca *adj* inartistic
antibalas *adj invar* bulletproof
antibéli•co -ca *adj* antiwar
antibióti•co -ca *adj & m* antibiotic
anticartel *adj* antitrust
anticientífi•co -ca *adj* unscientific
anticipación *f* preparation, anticipation; **con anticipación** in advance
anticipa•do -da *adj* future; advance; **por anticipado** in advance
anticipar *tr* to anticipate, hasten; to move ahead || *ref* to happen early; **anticiparse a** to anticipate, to get ahead of
anticipo *m* anticipation; advance payment, down payment; retaining fee, retainer
anticoncepti•vo -va *adj & m* contraceptive
anticongelante *m* antifreeze
anticonstitucional *adj* unconstitutional
anticua•do -da *adj* antiquated; old-fashioned; obsolete, obsolescent
anticua•rio -ria *adj* antiquarian || *mf* antiquarian, antiquary; antique dealer
anticuerpo *m* antibody
antideporti•vo -va *adj* unsportsmanlike
antiderrapante or **antideslizante** *adj* nonskid
antideslumbrante *adj* antiglare
antidetonante *adj & m* antiknock
antídoto *m* antidote
antieconómi•co -ca *adj* uneconomic(al)
antier *adv* the day before yesterday
antiesclavista *adj* antislavery || *mf* abolitionist
anti•faz *m* (*pl* **-faces**) veil, mask
antífona *f* anthem
antigás *adj invar* gas (*e.g., mask, shelter*)
antigramatical *adj* ungrammatical
antigravedad *f* weightlessness
antigualla *f* antique; relic, antique; has-been
antiguar §10 *intr & ref* to attain seniority
antigüedad *f* antiquity; seniority; (*mueble u otro objeto de arte antiguos*) antique; **antigüedades** antiquities; antiques
anti•guo -gua *adj* old; ancient; antique; former || *mf* veteran; senior
antihigiéni•co -ca *adj* unsanitary
antílope *m* antelope
antilla•no -na *adj & mf* West Indian
Antillas *fpl* Antilles
antimateria *f* antimatter
antimonio *m* antimony
antiobre•ro -ra *adj* antilabor
antiparras *spl* spectacles
antipatía *f* dislike, antipathy
antipáti•co -ca *adj* disagreeable, uncongenial

antipatrióti•co -ca *adj* unpatriotic
antiproyectil *adj* antimissile
antirreflejo *adj invar* nonreflecting
antirresbaladi•zo -za *adj* nonskid
antirrobo *adj invar* theft-proof, burglar-proof
antisemíti•co -ca *adj* anti-Semitic
antisépti•co -ca *adj & m* antiseptic
antisono•ro -ra *adj* soundproof
antitanque *adj* antitank
antiterrorista *adj invar & mf* antiterrorist
antíte•sis *f* (*pl* **-sis**) antithesis
antitóxi•co -ca *adj* antitoxic
antitoxina *f* antitoxin
antojadi•zo -za *adj* capricious, whimsical
antojar *ref* to seem; fancy; seem likely; have a notion to + *inf*; take a fancy to + *inf*
antojo *m* caprice, fancy, whim; snap judgment; birthmark; **antojos** moles, warts; **a su antojo** as one pleases
antología *f* anthology
antónimo *m* antonym
Antonio *m* Anthony
antorcha *f* torch; **antorcha a soplete** blowtorch
antracita *f* anthracite
ántrax *m* anthrax
antro *m* cave, cavern; (fig) den
antropología *f* anthropology
antruejo *m* carnival
anual *adj* annual
anualidad *f* annuity; year's pay; annual occurrence
anuario *m* yearbook; directory; bulletin, catalogue; **anuario telefónico** telephone directory
anublar *tr* to cloud; dim, darken; blight, wither || *ref* to become cloudy; be withered; (*las esperanzas de uno*) fade away
anudar *tr* to tie, fasten, knot; unite; resume || *ref* to get knotted; be united; fade away, wilt fail
anuente *adj* consenting
anular *tr* to annul; nullify; remove, discharge || *ref* to be passed over
anunciar *tr* to announce; advertise || *intr* to advertise
anunciante *mf* advertiser
anuncio *m* announcement; advertisement
anverso *m* obverse
anzuelo *m* fishhook; **picar en el anzuelo** or **tragar el anzuelo** to swallow the bait, swallow the hook
añadi•do -da *adj* additional || *m* false hair, switch
añadidura *f* addition; extra weight, extra measure; **de añadidura** extra, in the bargain; **por añadidura** besides
añadir *tr* to add; increase
añafil *m* straight Moorish trumpet
añagaza *f* bird call; decoy, lure; trap, trick
añe•jo -ja *adj* aged; stale; musty, rancid
añicos *mpl* bits, pieces; **hacer añicos** to tear to pieces, break to pieces; **hacerse añicos** to wear oneself out
añil *m* indigo; bluing
añilar *tr* to dye with indigo; (*la ropa blanca*) to blue
año *m* year; **año bisiesto** leap year; **año económico** fiscal year; **año lectivo** school year; **año luz** (*pl* **años luz**) light-year; **años** birthday; **año sabático** sabbatical; **cumplir . . . años** to be . . . years old; **primer año** (educ) first grade
añoranza *f* longing, sorrow
añorar *tr* to long for, sorrow for; grieve over || *intr* to yearn; sorrow, grieve
año•so -sa *adj* aged, old
aojada *f* (Col) skylight; (Col) transom
aojar *tr* to cast the evil eye on, jinx
aojo *m* evil eye, jinx
aovar *intr* to lay eggs
ap. *abbr* **aparte, apóstol**
apabilar *tr* to trim
apabullar *tr* to mash, crush; squelch
apacentar §2 *tr & ref* to pasture, graze; feed
apachurrar *tr* to crush, squash, mash
apacible *adj* gentle, mild; calm
apaciguamiento *m* pacification, appeasement
apaciguar §10 *tr* to pacify, appease || *ref* to calm down
apadrinar *tr* to sponsor; act as godfather for; back, support; second
apagabron•cas *m* (*pl* **-cas**) bouncer
apagador *m* extinguisher; (*de piano*) damper
apagaincen•dios *m* (*pl* **-dios**) fire extinguisher
apagar §44 *tr* to extinguish, put out; (*la luz, la radio*) turn off; (*la cal*) slake; (*el sonido*) damp, muffle; (*el fuego del enemigo*) silence; (*la sed*) quench; (*el dolor*) deaden || *ref* to go out; subside, calm down, fade away
apagón *m* blackout; (compu) power failure; **apagón parcial** brown-out; **apagón escalonado, apagón programado** rolling blackout
apalabrar *tr* to bespeak; consider || *ref* to agree
apalabrear *intr* (SAm) to make an appointment
apalancamiento *m* (econ, phys) leverage
apalancar §73 *tr* to raise with a lever or crowbar
apalear *tr* to shovel; beat; pile up
apandar *tr* to steal
apantallar *tr* to dazzle, amaze; (elec) to shield, screen
apañar *tr* to grasp; pick up; steal; repair, mend; wrap up || *ref* to be handy
apañuscar §73 *tr* to crumple, rumple; steal; (CAm, Col, Ven) to jam, crowd
aparador *m* sideboard, buffet; showcase; workshop; (Mex) show window, store window
aparar *tr* to prepare; adorn; block; (*las manos, la falda, el pañuelo, la capa*) hold out
aparato *m* apparatus; ostentation, show; exaggeration; radio set; television set; telephone; airplane; camera; bandage, application; (theat) scenery, properties; **aparato auditivo** hearing aid; **aparato de relojería** clockwork; **aparato de video** video recorder; **aparatos sanitarios** bathroom fixtures; **ponerse al aparato** to go or to come to the phone

aparato•so -sa *adj* showy, pompous, ostentatious
aparcamiento *m* parking; parking space; **aparcamiento subterraneo** underground garage
aparcar §44 *tr & intr* to park
aparcería *f* partnership, sharecropping
aparce•ro -ra *mf* partner, sharecropper; (Arg) customer
aparear *tr* to pair, match; mate || *ref* to pair; mate
aparecer §22 *intr & ref* to appear; show up
aparecido *m* ghost, specter
aparejador *m* builder
aparejar *tr* to prepare; prime, size; harness
aparejo *m* preparation; harness; set, kit; priming, sizing; (mas) bond; **aparejos** tools, implements, equipment
aparentar *tr* to feign, pretend; look, look to be
aparente *adj* apparent, seeming; evident; right, proper
aparición *f* apparition
apariencia *f* appearance, aspect; sign, indication; **salvar las apariencias** to save face
aparqueamiento *m* parking
aparquear *tr & intr* to park
aparqueo *m* parking
aparragar §44 *ref* to crouch, squat; (CAm) to loll, sprawl
apartadero *m* siding, side track; turnout
aparta•do -da *adj* distant, remote; aloof; (*camino*) side, back; different || *m* side room; post-office box; vocabulary entry; section
apartamento *m* apartment, apartment house
apartar *tr* to take aside; separate; push away; shunt; (*el ganado*) sort || *ref* to separate; move away, keep away, stand aside; withdraw; get divorced; give up
aparte *adv* apart, aside; **aparte de** apart from || *prep* apart from || *m* (theat) aside
apartheid [a'partej] *m* apartheid
apasiona•do -da *adj* passionate; devoted, tender, loving; sore
apasionar *tr* to impassion, appeal deeply to; afflict || *ref* to become impassioned; be stirred up; fall madly in love
apatía *f* apathy
apáti•co -ca *adj* apathetic
apatusco *m* ornament, finery
apdo. *abbr* **apartado**
apeadero *m* horse block; flag stop, wayside station; platform; temporary quarters
apear *tr* to help dismount, help down; bring down; remove; overcome; prop up || *ref* to dismount, get off; back down; stop, put up
apechugar §44 *intr* to push with the chest; **apechugar con** to make the best of
apedazar §60 *tr* to mend, patch; cut or tear to pieces
apedrear *tr* to stone; stone to death; pit; speckle || *intr* to hail || *ref* to be damaged by hail; be pitted
apegar §44 *ref* to become attached, grow fond
apego *m* attachment, fondness
apelación *f* medical consultation; remedy, help; (law) appeal
apelante *adj* appellate
apelar *intr* to appeal, make an appeal; have recourse; refer
apelativo *m* (CAm) surname, family name
apeldar *tr* — **apelderlas** (coll) to flee, run away
apellidar *tr* to call, name; proclaim
apellido *m* name; surname, last name, family name; **apellido de soltera** maiden name
apelmazar §60 *tr* to squeeze, compress || *ref* to cake
apelotonar *tr* to form into a ball || *ref* to form a ball; curl up
apenar *tr & ref* to grieve
apenas *adv* hardly, scarcely; **apenas si** hardly, scarcely || *conj* no sooner, as soon as
apéndice *m* appendage; (anat) appendix
apendicitis *f* appendicitis
apercancar §73 *ref* (Chile) to get moldy, mildew
apercibir *tr* to prepare; provide; warn; perceive; collect || *ref* to get ready; be provided; **apercibirse de** to notice
apergaminar *ref* to dry up, become yellow and wrinkled
aperitivo *m* appetizer
aperla•do -da *adj* pearly
apero *m* tools, equipment, outfit; riding gear
aperrear *tr* to set the dogs on; harass, plague, pester
apersogar §44 *tr* to tether
apersona•do -da *adj* — **bien apersonado** presentable; **mal apersonado** unpresentable
apersonar *ref* to appear in person; have an interview
apertura *f* opening
apesadumbrar or **apesarar** *tr & ref* to grieve
apestar *tr* to infect with the plague; corrupt; sicken, nauseate; infest || *intr* to stink || *ref* to be infected with the plague
apesto•so -sa *adj* stinking, foul-smelling; pestilent; sickening
apetecer §22 *tr* to hunger for, thirst for, crave
apetecible *adj* desirable, tempting
apetencia *f* hunger, appetite, craving
apetito *m* appetite
apetito•so -sa *adj* tasty; tempting; gourmand
ápex *m* apex
apiadar *tr* to move to pity; take pity on || *ref* to have pity
ápice *m* apex; bit, whit; crux; **estar en los ápices de** to be up in
apilar *tr & ref* to pile, pile up
apimpollar *ref* to sprout, put forth shoots
apiñar *tr & ref* to crowd, jam
apio *m* celery
apisonadora *f* road roller
apisonar *tr* to tamp; roll
aplacar §73 *tr* to placate, appease, pacify; (*la sed*) to quench
aplanacalles *m* (SAm) idler; lazy person
aplanar *tr* to smooth, make even; to astonish;

aplanar las calles to loaf, bum around || *ref* to collapse; become discouraged
aplanchar *tr* to iron
aplanetizar §60 *intr* to land on another planet
aplastar *tr* to flatten, crush, smash; dumbfound
aplaudida *f* applause
aplaudir *tr & intr* to applaud
aplauso *m* applause; **aplausos** applause
aplazada *f* or **aplazamiento** *m* delay; procrastination
aplazar §60 *tr* to postpone; convene; summon
aplicación *f* appliance, application; diligence
aplica•do -da *adj* industrious, studious; applied
aplicar §73 *tr* to apply; attribute || *ref* to apply; apply oneself
aplomar *tr* to plumb; make straight or vertical || *intr* to be vertical || *ref* to collapse; (Chile) to be embarrassed; (Mex) to be slow, be backward
aplomo *m* aplomb, poise, self-possession; gravity
apoca•do -da *adj* diffident, timid, irresolute; humble, lowly
apocar §73 *tr* to cramp, contract; narrow; humble, belittle
apodar *tr* to nickname; make fun of
apodera•do -da *adj* empowered, authorized || *m* proxy; attorney
apoderamiento *m* authorization; power of attorney
apoderar *tr* to empower, authorize || *ref* — **apoderarse de** to seize, grasp; take possession of
apodo *m* nickname
apofanía *f* ablaut
apogeo *m* apogee; (fig) height, apogee
apolilla•do -da *adj* moth-eaten, mothy
apolilladura *f* moth hole
apolillar *tr* (*la polilla, p.ej., las ropas*) to eat || *ref* to become moth-eaten
apoliti•co -ca *adj* apolitical, nonpolitical
apología *f* eulogy
apoltronar *ref* to loaf around; loll, sprawl
apontizaje *m* deck-landing
apontizar §60 *intr* to deck-land
apoplejía *f* apoplexy
apopléti•co -ca *adj & mf* apoplectic
aporcar §73 *tr* (*las hortalizas*) to hill
aporrear *tr* to beat, club, cudgel; annoy || *ref* to drudge, slave
aportación *f* contribution, input; dowry
aportar *tr* to contribute; bring; lead; (*como dote*) bring || *intr* to show up; reach port
aporte *m* contribution
aposentar *tr* to put up, lodge || *ref* to take lodging
aposento *m* lodging; room; inn
apostadero *m* stand, post; naval station
apostar *tr* to post, station || **§61** *tr* to bet, wager || *intr* to bet; compete
apostilla *f* note, comment
apóstol *m* apostle
apóstrofe *m & f* apostrophe (*words addressed to absent person*)
apóstrofo *m* apostrophe (*written sign*)
apostura *f* neatness, spruceness; bearing, carriage
apoyabra•zos *m* (*pl* **-zos**) armrest
apoyali•bros *m* (*pl* **-bros**) book end
apoyar *tr* to support, hold up; lean, rest; abet, back || *intr & ref* to lean, rest, be supported
apoyatura *f* (mus) grace note
apoyo *m* support, prop; backing, approval
applet *m* (compu) applet
apreciable *adj* appreciable; estimable
apreciación *f* appraisal
apreciar *tr* to appreciate; appraise; esteem
aprecio *m* appreciation, esteem
aprehender *tr* to apprehend, catch; think, conceive
aprehensión *f* apprehension
aprehensi•vo -va *adj* apprehensive
aprehensor *m* captor
apremiar *tr* to press, urge; compel, force; hurry; harass; (*a un deudor*) dun || *intr* to be urgent
apremio *m* pressure; urgency; compulsion; oppression; surtax for late payment; (*demanda de pago*) dun
aprender *tr & intr* to learn; **aprender haciendo** to learn by doing
apren•diz -diza *mf* apprentice; **aprendiz de imprenta** printer's devil
aprendizaje *m* apprenticeship; **pagar el aprendizaje** to pay for one's inexperience
aprensar *tr* to press; oppress
aprensión *f* apprehension; misgiving, prejudice
aprensi•vo -va *adj* apprehensive
apresar *tr* to grasp, seize; capture
aprestador *m* primer
aprestar *tr* to prepare; (*tejidos*) process; prime; size || *ref* to get ready
apresto *m* preparation; equipment; priming; sizing
apresurar *tr & ref* to hurry, hasten
apretadera *f* strap, rope; **apretaderas** pressure
apreta•do -da *adj* compact, tight; close, intimate; dense, thick; difficult, dangerous; mean, stingy; **estar muy apretado** to be in a bad way
apretar §2 *tr* to tighten; squeeze; pinch; hug; harass, importune; afflict, beset; (*un botón*) press; (*los puños*) clench; (*los dientes*) grit; (*la mano*) shake || *intr* to pinch; insist; get worse; push hard, press forward; **apretar a correr** to start running; **apretar con** to close in on || *ref* to grieve, be distressed; crowd
apretón *m* pressure, squeeze; struggle; dash, run; **apretón de manos** handshake
apretura *f* crush, jam; tightness; fix, trouble; need, want
aprietarropa *m* clothespin
¡aprieta! *interj* (coll) baloney!
aprieto *m* crush, jam; fix
aprisa *adv* fast, quickly
aprisco *m* sheepfold
aprisionar *tr* to imprison; bind, tie; shackle

aprobación *f* approbation, approval; pass, passing grade
aproba•do -da *adj* excellent || *m* pass
aprobar §61 *tr & intr* to approve; pass
aprontar *tr* to hand over without delay; expedite
apropia•do -da *adj* appropriate, fitting, proper; **ser apropiado para** to be suited to
apropiar *tr* to hand over; fit, adapt || *ref* to appropriate; pre-empt
aprovechable *adj* available, usable
aprovecha•do -da *adj* thrifty; stingy; diligent; well-spent || *mf* opportunist
aprovechar *tr* to make good use of, take advantage of; (*una caída de agua*) harness || *intr* to be useful; progress, improve || *ref* — **aprovecharse de** to avail oneself of, take advantage of
aprovisionar *tr* to provision, supply, furnish
aproxima•do -da *adj* approximate, rough
aproximar *tr* to bring near; approximate || *ref* to come near; approximate
aptitud *f* aptitude; suitability
ap•to -ta *adj* apt; suitable
apuesta *f* bet, wager **apuesta colectiva** football pool; **apuesta inicial** (cards) ante
apues•to -ta *adj* neat, spruce, elegant || *f* see **apuesta**
apulgarar *ref* to become mildewed
apunta•dor -dora *adj* (compu) pointing || *mf* prompter, prompt
apuntalar *tr* to prop up, underpin
apuntar *tr* to point; point at; aim; aim at; take note of; sharpen; stitch, darn, patch; correct; prompt; stake, to put up; (theat) to prompt || *intr* to begin to appear; dawn || *ref* (*el vino*) to begin to turn sour; register; get tipsy
apunte *m* note; reminder; rough sketch; stake; rogue, rascal; (theat) cue
apuñalar *tr & intr* to stab
apuñear *tr* to punch
apura•do -da *adj* needy, hard up; difficult, dangerous; hurried, rushed
apurar *tr* to purify, refine; clear up, verify; finish; drain, use up, exhaust; hurry, press; annoy || *ref* to worry, grieve; exert oneself, strive
apuro *m* need, want; grief, sorrow; haste, urgency; **apuros** financial embarrassment
aquejar *tr* to grieve, afflict
aquel, aquella *adj dem* (*pl* **aquellos, aquellas**) that, that . . . yonder
aquél, aquélla *pron dem* (*pl* **aquéllos, aquéllas**) that; that one, that one yonder; the one; the former || *m* charm, appeal
aquelarre *m* witches' Sabbath
aquello *pron dem* that; that thing, that matter
aquende *adv* on this side || *prep* on this side of
aquerenciar *ref* to become fond or attached
aquí *adv* here; **aquí dentro** in here; **de aquí en adelante** from now on; **por aquí** this way
aquiescencia *f* acquiescence
aquietar *tr* to quiet, calm
aquilatar *tr* to assay; check; refine
Aquiles *m* Achilles
aquilón *m* north wind
ara *f* altar; altar slab; **en aras de** for the sake of
árabe *adj* Arab, Arabian; (archit) Moresque || *mf* Arab, Arabian || *m* (*idioma*) Arabic
Arabia, la Arabia
arábi•go -ga *adj* Arabian, Arabic || *m* (*idioma*) Arabic; **estar en arábigo** (coll) to be Greek
arabismo *m* (*estudio, voz, rasgo*) Arabism
aracanga *f* macaw
arado *m* plow
Aragón *m* Aragon
arago•nés -nesa *adj & mf* Aragonese
arancel *m* tariff
arancelar *tr* (CAm) to pay
arancela•rio -ria *adj* tariff, customs
arándano *m* whortleberry; blueberry; **arándano agrio** cranberry
arandela *f* bobèche; (mach) washer
araña *f* spider; chandelier
arañar *tr* to scratch; scrape; scrape together
arañazo *m* scratch
araño *m* scratching
aráquida *f* peanut
arar *tr* to plow
arbitraje *m* arbitration
arbitrar *tr & intr* to arbitrate; referee; umpire
arbitra•rio -ria *adj* arbitrary
arbitrio *m* free will; means, ways; **arbitrios** excise taxes
arbitrista *mf* wild-eyed dreamer
árbi•tro -tra *mf* arbiter; referee || *m* umpire
árbol *m* tree; axle, shaft; **árbol del caucho** rubber plant; **árbol de levas** camshaft; **árbol de mando** drive shaft; **árbol de Navidad** Christmas tree; **árbol motor** drive shaft
arbola•do -da *adj* wooded; (*mar*) high || *m* woodland
arboleda *f* grove; (*vivero con fines científicos*) arboretum
arbollón *m* sewer, drain
arbotante *m* flying buttress
arbusto *m* shrub
arca *f* chest, coffer; tank; ark; **arca de agua** water tower; **arca de la alianza** ark of the covenant; **arca de Noé** ark, Noah's ark
arcada *f* arcade; archway; stroke of bow; **arcadas** retching
arcai•co -ca *adj* archaic
arcaísmo *m* archaism
arcaizante *adj* archaic
arcángel *m* archangel
arca•no -na *adj & m* secret
arcar §73 *tr* to arch
arce *m* maple tree
archiduque *m* archduke
archienemigo *m* archenemy
archipiélago *m* archipelago; (coll) maze, entanglement || **Archipiélago** *m* Aegean Sea
archiva•dor -dora *mf* file clerk || *m* filing cabinet; letter file
archivar *tr* to file; file away; hide away
archivero *m* city clerk

archivo *m* archives; files; filing; (Col) office; (compu) file
arcilla *f* clay; **arcilla figulina** potter's clay
arco *m* arch; (*de cuna o mecedor*) rocker; (elec, geom) arc; (mus) bow; **arco iris** rainbow; **arco triunfal** triumphal arch; memorial arch
arcón *m* large chest; bin, bunker
ardentía *f* heartburn; (*en las olas de la mar*) phosphorescence
arder *tr* to burn || *intr* to burn; blaze; **estar que arde** to be coming to a head || *ref* to burn up
ardid *m* artifice, trick, wile, gimmick
ardi•do -da *adj* burnt-up; bold, intrepid; angry
ardiendo *adj invar* burning
ardiente *adj* ardent; fiery, passionate; burning, hot
ardilla *f* squirrel; **ardilla de tierra** gopher; **ardilla ladradora** prairie dog; **ardilla listada** chipmunk
ardillón *m* gopher
ardite *m* old Spanish coin of little value; **no me importa un ardite** (coll) I don't care a hang; **no valer un ardite** to be not worth a straw
ardor *m* ardor; eagerness, fervor, zeal; vehemence; courage, dash
ardoro•so -sa *adj* fiery, enthusiastic; balky, restive
ar•duo -dua *adj* arduous, difficult
área *f* area; small plot; **área de descansar** rest area; **área de servicio** service area; **área sensible** (compu) hotspot
arena *f* sand; grit; arena; **arena movediza** quicksand; **arenas** arena; (pathol) stones
arenal *m* sandy place; quicksand
arenga *f* harangue
arengar *tr & intr* to harangue
arenis•co -ca *adj* sandy, gritty; sand || *f* sandstone
areno•so -sa *adj* sandy
arenque *m* herring
areómetro *m* hydrometer
arepa *f* corn griddle cake
arete *m* eardrop, earring
arfada *f* (naut) pitching
arfar *intr* (naut) to pitch
argadijo *m* or **argadillo** *m* bobbin, reel; restless fellow
argado *m* prank, trick, artifice
argamasa *f* mortar
argamasar *tr* to mortar, plaster; (*los materiales de construcción*) mix
árgana *f* (mach) crane; **árganas** panniers
Argel *f* Algiers
Argelia *f* Algeria
argeli•no -na *adj & mf* Algerian
argentar *tr* to silver
argenti•no -na *adj & mf* Argentine, Argentinean || **la Argentina** Argentina, the Argentine
argolla *f* large iron ring; (*que se pone en la nariz a un animal*) ring; engagement ring
argonauta *m* Argonaut
argot *m* argot
argucia *f* subtlety; trick
argüir §6 *tr* to argue, argue for; prove; accuse || *ref* to argue, dispute
argumenta•dor -dora *adj* argumentative || *mf* arguer
argumentar *tr* to argue for; prove || *intr & ref* to argue, dispute
argumento *m* argument
aria *f* (mus) aria
aridez *f* aridity, dryness
ári•do -da *adj* arid; (*aburrido, falto de interés*) dry
Aries *m* (astr) Aries
ariete *m* battering ram; **ariete hidráulico** hydraulic ram
arimez *m* projection
a•rio -ria *adj & mf* Aryan || *f* see **aria**
aris•co -ca *adj* churlish, surly, evasive; (*caballo*) vicious
arista *f* edge; (*intersección de dos planos*) ridge; (*del grano de trigo*) beard; **arista de encuentro** (archit) groin
aristocracia *f* aristocracy
aristócrata *mf* aristocrat
aristocráti•co -ca *adj* aristocratic
Aristóteles *m* Aristotle
aristotéli•co -ca *adj & mf* Aristotelian
aritméti•co -ca *adj* arithmetical || *mf* arithmetician || *f* arithmetic
arlequín *m* harlequin
arma *f* arm, weapon; **alzarse en armas** to rise up, rebel; **arma blanca** steel blade; **arma corta** pistol; **arma de fuego** firearm; **jugar a las armas** to fence; **sobre las armas** under arms
armada *f* fleet, armada; navy
armadía *f* raft, float
armadijo *m* trap, snare
arma•do -da *adj* armed; (*hormigón*) reinforced || *f* see **armada**
arma•dor -dora *mf* assembler || *m* recruiter of fishermen and whalers
armadura *f* armor; framework; skeleton; (elec) armature; (*de imán*) keeper
armamentismo *m* military preparedness
armamentis•to -ta *adj* militarist, arms || *mf* arms dealer
armamento *m* armament
armar *tr* to arm; (*un arma*) load; (*una bayoneta*) fix; mount, assemble; build; equip; (*el hormigón*) reinforce; (*una nave*) fit out; (*caballero*) dub; start, stir up; **armarla** to start a row || *ref* to arm oneself; get ready; balk
armario *m* closet, wardrobe; **armario botiquín** medicine cabinet; **armario de luna** wardrobe with mirror; **armario frigorífico** refrigerator
armatoste *m* hulk
armazón *f* frame; assemblage; skeleton; carcass
armella *f* screw eye, eyebolt
arme•nio -nia *adj & mf* American || **Armenia** *f* Armenia
armería *f* arms shop; arms museum; arms
armero *m* gunsmith; (*para las armas*) rack
armiño *m* ermine

armisticio *m* armistice
armonía *f* harmony
armóni•co -ca *adj & m* harmonic || *f* harmonica; **armónica de boca** mouth organ
armonio•so -sa *adj* harmonious
armonizar §60 *tr & intr* to harmonize
arnés *m* armor, coat of mail; harness; **arneses** harness, trappings; outfit, equipment; accessories
aro *m* hoop; rim; **aro de émbolo** piston ring
aroma *m* aroma, fragrance
aromáti•co -ca *adj* aromatic
arpa *f* harp
arpar *tr* to claw, scratch; tear, rend
arpegio *m* arpeggio
arpeo *m* grappling iron
arpía *f* harpy; shrew, jade
arpillera *f* burlap, sackcloth
arpista *mf* harpist
arpón *m* harpoon
arponear *tr & intr* to harpoon
arqueada *f* (mus) bow
arquear *tr* to arch; (*la lana*) beat; (*una nave*) gauge; to audit || *intr* to retch || *ref* to bow
arqueología *f* archeology
arquería *f* arcade
arquero *m* archer, bowman; goalkeeper, goalie
arquitecto *m* architect
arquitectóni•co -ca *adj* architectural
arquitectura *f* architecture; **arquitectura abierta** (compu) open-architecture
arrabal *m* suburb; **arrabales** outskirts
arracada *f* earring with pendant
arracimar *ref* to cluster, bunch
arraiga•do -da *adj* deep-rooted, ingrained; property-owning, landed
arraigar §44 *tr* to establish, strengthen || *intr* to take root || *ref* to take root; become settled
arraigo *m* taking root; stability; property, real estate
arramblar *tr* to cover with sand or gravel; sweep away
arrancadero *m* starting point
arrancar §73 *tr* to root up, pull out, pull up; snatch, wrest; (*lágrimas*) draw forth || *intr* to start; set sail; leave; originate
arranque *m* pull; fit, impulse; jerk, sudden start; sally, outburst; (aut) start, starter; (compu) start-up; **arranque a mano** (aut) hand cranking; **arranque automático** (aut) self-starter
arrapiezo *m* rag, tatter; whippersnapper
arras *fpl* earnest money, pledge; dowry
arrasar *tr* to level; wreck, demolish; fill to the brim || *intr* to clear up || *ref* to clear up; fill up
arrastra•do -da *adj* mean, crooked || *mf* wretch, crook
arrastrar *tr* to drag, drag along; drag down; impel || *intr* to drag, trail; crawl, creep; **arrastrar y soltar** (compu) drag and drop || *ref* to drag, trail; crawl, creep; drag on; cringe
arrastre *m* drag; crawl; washout; influence; haulage; (*influencia política y social*) (Cuba, Mex) drag
arrayán *m* myrtle
arre *interj* gee!, get up!
arreador *m* muleteer; (SAm) whip
arrear *tr* to drive || *intr* to hurry || *ref* to lose all one's money
arrebata•do -da *adj* rash, reckless; (*color del rostro*) flushed, ruddy
arrebatar *tr* to snatch; carry away; attract; move, stir || *ref* to be carried away, be overcome
arrebatiña *f* scuffle, scramble; **andar a la arrebatiña** to scramble
arrebato *m* rage, fury; ecstasy, rapture
arrebol *m* (*de las nubes*) red; (*de las mejillas*) rosiness; (*afeite*) rouge; **arreboles** red clouds
arrebozar §60 *tr* to muffle || *ref* to muffle one's face
arrebujar *tr* to jumble together; wrap || *ref* to wrap oneself up
arreciar *intr & ref* to grow worse; become more violent; grow stronger
arrecife *m* stone-paved road; dike; reef; **arrecife de coral** coral reef
arredrar *tr* to drive back; frighten || *ref* to draw back; shrink; be frightened
arregazar §60 *tr* to tuck up
arreglar *tr* to adjust, regulate, settle; arrange; fix, repair || *ref* to adjust, settle; arrange; conform; **arreglárselas** to manage, make out
arreglo *m* adjustment, regulation; settlement; arrangement; order, rule; agreement; **con arreglo a** in accordance with
arregostar *ref* to take a liking
arregosto *m* liking, taste
arrellanar *ref* to loll, sprawl; like one's work
arremangar §44 *tr* (*las mangas*) to turn up; (*la ropa*) to tuck up || *ref* to turn up one's sleeves; tuck up one's dress; take a firm stand
arremeter *tr* to attack, assail; (*un caballo*) to spur || *intr* to attack; be offensive to look at; **arremeter contra** to light into, sail into
arremetida *f* attack; (*de un caballo*) sudden start; push; short, wild run
arremolinar *ref* to crowd, mill around; whirl
arrendajo *m* (orn) jay; mimic
arrendar §2 *tr* to rent; (*una caballería*) tie || *ref* to rent, be rented
arreo *m* adornment; (SAm) drove; **arreos** harness, trappings
arrepenti•do -da *adj* repentant || *mf* penitent
arrepentimiento *m* repentance
arrepentir §68 *ref* to repent, be repentant; **arrepentirse de** (*p.ej., un pecado*) to repent
arrequives *mpl* finery; attendant circumstances
arresta•do -da *adj* bold, daring
arrestar *tr* to arrest || *ref* to rush boldly
arresto *m* arrest; boldness, daring; **arresto domiciliario** house arrest; **arresto preventivo** preventive detention; **bajo arresto** under arrest, in custody
arrezagar §44 *tr* to tuck up

arriada *f* flood
arriar §77 *tr* to flood; (naut) to lower, strike; slacken || *ref* to be flooded
arriba *adv* up, upward; above; upstairs; uptown; on top; **arriba de** up; **de arriba abajo** from top to bottom; from beginning to end; superciliously; **más arriba** farther up; **río arriba** upstream || *interj* up with . . . !
arribada *f* arrival (*by sea*); **de arribada** (naut) emergency
arribar *intr* to put into port; arrive; to recover, make a comeback; (naut) to fall off to leeward
arribista *adj & mf* parvenu, upstart
arribo *m* arrival
arricete *m* shoal, bar
arriendo *m* rent, rental; lease
arriero *m* muleteer
arriesga•do -da *adj* dangerous, risky; bold, daring
arriesgar §44 *tr* to risk, jeopardize || *ref* to take a risk
arriesgo *m* (SAm) risk; hazard
arrimadillo *m* wainscot
arrimar *tr* to bring close, move up; (*un golpe*) give; abandon, neglect; give up; get rid of || *ref* to come close, move up; snuggle up; lean; depend
arrinconar *tr* to corner; put aside; abandon, neglect; get rid of || *ref* to live in seclusion
arrisca•do -da *adj* enterprising; brisk, spirited; craggy
arriscar §73 *tr* to risk || *ref* to take a risk; (*las reses*) plunge over a cliff
arrisco *m* risk
arritmia *f* arrhythmia
arrivista *adj & mf* parvenu, upstart
arrizar §60 *tr* to reef
arroba *f* Spanish weight of about 25 pounds
arrobar *tr* to entrance, enrapture || *ref* to be enraptured
arrobo *m* ecstasy, rapture
arroce•ro -ra *adj* rice || *mf* rice grower; rice merchant
arrocinar *tr* to bestialize || *ref* to become bestialized; fall madly in love
arrodajar *ref* (CAm) to squat down with one's legs crossed
arrodillar *ref* to kneel, kneel down
arrogancia *f* arrogance
arrogante *adj* arrogant
arrogar §44 *tr* to adopt || *ref* to arrogate to oneself
arrojadi•zo -za *adj* for throwing, projectile
arroja•do -da *adj* bold, fearless, rash
arrojalla•mas *m* (*pl* **-mas**) flame thrower
arrojar *tr* to throw, hurl; emit; bring forth; yield || *ref* to rush, rush forward
arrojo *m* boldness, fearlessness, rashness
arrollado *m* (elec) coil
arrolla•dor -dora *adj* sweeping, devastating
arrollamiento *m* winding
arrollar *tr* to roll; roll up; wind, coil; (*al enemigo*) rout; dumbfound; knock down, run over
arropar *tr* to wrap, wrap up || *ref* to bundle up
arrope *m* grape syrup; honey syrup
arropía *f* taffy
arrostrar *tr* to face; to like || *intr* — **arrostrar con** or **por** to face, resist || *ref* to rush into the fight
arroyada *f* gully; flood, freshet
arroyo *m* stream, brook; gutter; street; (*de lágrimas, sangre, etc.*) stream
arroz *m* rice; **arroz integral** brown rice; **arroz salvaje** wild rice
arrozal *m* ricefield
arrufar *tr* to sic, incite
arruga *f* wrinkle; crease, rumple
arrugar §44 *tr* to wrinkle; crease, rumple; (*la frente*) to knit; (Cuba, Mex) to bother, annoy || *ref* to wrinkle; crease, rumple; shrink, shrivel; (Cuba, Mex) to lose courage, lose heart
arruinar *tr* to ruin || *ref* to go to ruin
arrullar *tr* to sing to sleep, lull to sleep; to court, woo || *intr* to coo || *ref* to coo; (*las palomas*) to bill
arrullo *m* billing and cooing; lullaby
arrumaje *m* stowage; ballast
arrumar *tr* to stow || *ref* to become overcast
arrumbar *tr* to cast aside, neglect; silence; (*una costa*) determine the lay of || *intr* (naut) to take bearings || *ref* to get seasick; (naut) to take bearings
arsenal *m* arsenal, armory; dockyard, shipyard
arsénico *m* arsenic
art. *abbr* **artículo**
arte *m & f* art; trick; knack; fishing gear; **artes y oficios** arts and crafts; **bellas artes** fine arts; **no tener arte ni parte en** to have nothing to do with
artefacto *m* artifact; appliance, device, contrivance; **artefactos de alumbrado** lighting fixtures; **artefactos sanitarios** bathroom fixtures
artemisa *f* sagebrush
arteria *f* artery
artería *f* craftiness, cunning
arte•ro -ra *adj* crafty, cunning, sly
artesa *f* trough; Indian canoe
artesanía *f* craftsmanship
artesa•no -na *mf* artisan, craftsman || *f* craftswoman
artesón *m* kitchen tub; coffer, caisson (*in ceiling*)
árti•co -ca *adj* arctic
articulación *f* articulation; (*de huesos*) joint; **articulación universal** universal joint
articular *tr* to articulate
articulista *mf* feature writer
artículo *m* article; item; joint; (*en un diccionario*) entry; **artículo de fondo** leader, editorial; **artículos de consumo** consumers' goods; **artículos de deporte** sporting goods; **artículos de primera necesidad** basic commodities; **artículos para caballeros** men's furnishings
artífice *mf* artificer; craftsman
artificial *adj* artificial

artificio *m* artifice; workmanship; appliance, device; cunning; trick, ruse
artificio•so -sa *adj* ingenious, skillful; cunning, scheming, deceptive
artillería *f* artillery
artillero *m* artilleryman, gunner
artilugio *m* contraption, jigger, gimmick
artimaña *f* trap; trick, cunning
artista *mf* artist
artísti•co -ca *adj* artistic
artolas *fpl* mule chair, cacolet
artríti•co -ca *adj & mf* arthritic
artritis *f* arthritis
arúspice *m* diviner, soothsayer
arveja *f* vetch, tare; (Chile) pea
arzobispo *m* archbishop
arzón *m* saddletree; **arzón delantero** saddlebow; **arzón trasero** cantle
as *m* ace; **as de fútbol** football star; **as de la pantalla** movie star; **as del volante** speed king
asa *f* handle; juice; **en asas** with arms akimbo
asa•do -da *adj* roasted; **bien asado** well done; **poco asado** rare || *m* roast
asador *m* spit
asadura *f* entrails
asalaria•do -da *mf* wage earner
asaltar *tr* to assail, assault, storm; overtake, overcome
asalto *m* assault, attack; (box) round; (mil) storm; **tomar por asalto** to take by storm
asamblea *f* assembly
asar *tr* to roast || *ref* to be burning up
asbesto *m* asbestos
ascendencia *f* ancestry
ascendente *adj* ascending; up
ascender §51 *tr* to promote; upgrade || *intr* to ascend, go up; be promoted; **ascender a** to amount to
ascendiente *adj* ascending; up || *mf* ancestor || *m* ascendancy, upper hand
ascensión *f* ascension, ascent
ascenso *m* ascent; promotion, upgrade
ascensor *m* elevator; freight elevator
ascensorista *mf* elevator operator
asceta *mf* ascetic
ascéti•co -ca *adj* ascetic
asco *m* disgust, nausea, loathing; **dar asco** to turn the stomach; **estar hecho un asco** to be filthy; **hacer ascos de** to turn one's nose up at; **ser un asco** to be contemptible; be worthless
ascua *f* ember, live coal; **estar sobre ascuas** to be on needles and pins || **ascuas** *interj* ouch!
asea•do -da *adj* clean, neat, tidy
asear *tr & ref* to clean up, tidy up; make one's toilet
asechamiento *m* or **asechanza** *f* snare, trap
asechar *tr* to set a trap for
asediar *tr* to besiege; harass
asedio *m* siege
asegundar *tr* to repeat right away
asegurable *adj* insurable
aseguración *f* insurance policy
asegura•do -da *adj* insured || *mf* policyholder
asegura•dor -dora *mf* insurer, underwriter
asegurar *tr* to fasten, secure; assure; assert; seize; imprison; (*garantizar por un precio contra determinado accidente o pérdida*) insure || *ref* to make sure; take out insurance
asemejar *tr* to make like; compare; resemble || *ref* to be similar
asenso *m* assent; **dar asenso a** to believe
asentada *f* sitting; **de una asentada** at one sitting
asentaderas *fpl* (coll) buttocks
asentadillas — a asentadillas sidesaddle
asenta•do -da *adj* sedate; stable || *f* see **asentada**
asentador *m* strap, razor strop
asentar §2 *tr* to seat; place; establish; tamp down, level; hone, sharpen; note down; (*un golpe*) impart; (*en la mente de uno*) impress; affirm; suppose || *intr* to be becoming || *ref* to sit down; be established, establish oneself; settle
asentimiento *m* assent
asentir §68 *intr* to assent
aseo *m* cleanliness, neatness, tidiness; care; toilet
asépti•co -ca *adj* aseptic
aseptizar §60 *tr* to purify, make aseptic
asequible *adj* accessible, obtainable
aserción *f* assertion
aserradero *m* sawmill
aserra•dor -dora *mf* sawyer; (coll) fiddler || *f* power saw
aserraduras *fpl* sawdust
aserrar §2 *tr* to saw
aserrín *m* sawdust
aserruchar *tr* (SAm) to saw
aserto *m* assertion
asesinar *tr* to assassinate, murder
asesinato *m* assassination, murder
asesi•no -na *adj* murderous || *mf* assassin, murderer
asesorar *tr* to advise || *ref* to seek advice; get advice
asestar *tr* to aim; shoot; (*un golpe*) deal
aseveración *f* assertion, declaration
aseverar *tr* to assert, declare
asfaltar *tr* to asphalt, blacktop
asfalto *m* asphalt; blacktop
asfixia *f* asphyxiation
asfixiar *tr* to asphyxiate
así *adv* so, thus; **así . . . como** both . . . and; **así como** as soon as; as well as; **así que** as soon as; with the result that; **así y todo** even so, anyhow; **por decirlo así** so to speak; **y así sucesivamente** and so on
Asia *f* Asia; **el Asia Menor** Asia Minor
asiáti•co -ca *adj & mf* Asian, Asiatic
asidero *m* handle; occasion, pretext
asi•duo -dua *adj* assiduous; frequent, persistent
asiento *m* seat; site; (*de un edificio*) settling; (*de una botella, una silla, etc.*) bottom; sediment; list, roll; wisdom, maturity; **asiento abatible** reclining seat; **asiento de rejilla** cane seat;

asiento lanzable (aer) ejection seat; **asientos** buttocks; **planchar el asiento** to be a wallflower; **tome Ud. asiento** have a seat
asignación *f* assignment; salary; allowance
asignar *tr* to assign
asignatorio *m* heir, inheritor
asignatura *f* course, subject
asila•do -da *mf* inmate
asilar *tr* to shelter; place in an asylum; silo || *ref* to take refuge; be placed in an asylum
asilla *f* fastener; collarbone; **asillas** shoulder pole
asilo *m* asylum; shelter, refuge; (*para menesterosos*) home; **asilo de huérfanos** orphan asylum; **asilo de locos** insane asylum; **asilo de pobres** poorhouse
asimetría *f* asymmetry
asimétri•co -ca *adj* asymmetrical
asimilar *tr* to compare; take in || *intr* to be alike || *ref* to assimilate; **asimilarse a** to resemble
asimismo *adv* also, likewise
asir §7 *tr* to grasp, seize || *intr* to take root || *ref* to take hold; fight, grapple; **asirse a** or **de** to cling to
Asiria *f* Assyria
asi•rio -ria *adj & mf* Assyrian
asistencia *f* attendance; assistance; reward; audience, persons present; welfare, social work; (Mex) sitting room, parlor; **asistencias** allowance, support; **asistencia sanitaria** health care; **asistencia social** welfare
asistenta *f* charwoman, cleaning woman
asistente *adj* attendant; present || *mf* assistant, helper; bystander, spectator, person present; (mil) orderly; **asistente social** social worker, case worker
asistir *tr* to assist, help; attend; serve, wait on || *intr* to be present; **asistir a** to be present at, attend
asma *f* asthma
asna *f* she-ass, jenny ass; **asnas** rafters
asnal *adj* donkey; brutish
asno *m* ass, donkey, jackass
asociación *f* association; **asociación de estudiantes** student union
asocia•do -da *adj* associated; associate || *mf* associate, partner
asociar *tr* to associate; take as partner || *ref* to become associated; become a partner; become partners
asolamiento *m* razing, destruction
asolar *tr* to parch, burn || *ref* to become parched || **§61** *tr* to raze, destroy
asoleada *f* or **asoleadura** *f* (SAm) sunstroke
asolear *tr* to sun || *ref* to bask in the sun, sunbathe; get sunburned
asomar *tr* (*p.ej., la cabeza*) to show, stick out || *intr* to begin to show or appear; show || *ref* to show, appear; stick out; get tipsy
asombradi•zo -za *adj* timid, shy
asombrar *tr* to shade; (*un color*) darken; frighten; astonish, amaze || *ref* to be frightened; be astonished, amazed
asombro *m* fright; astonishment
asombro•so -sa *adj* astonishing, amazing
asomo *m* mark, token, sign; appearance; **ni por asomo** nothing of the kind, not by a long shot
asordar *tr* to deafen
aspa *f* X-shaped figure; reel; (*de molino de viento*) wheel, vane; propeller blade
aspar *tr* to reel; crucify; annoy, harass || *ref* to writhe; take great pains
aspaviento *m* fuss, excitement
aspecto *m* aspect
aspereza *f* harshness; roughness; bitterness, sourness; gruffness
asperjar *tr* to sprinkle; sprinkle with holy water
áspe•ro -ra *adj* harsh; rough; bitter; gruff
áspid *m* asp
aspirador *m* vacuum cleaner; **aspirador de gasolina** (aut) vacuum tank
aspirante *m* applicant, candidate; **aspirante a cabo** private first class; **aspirante de marina** midshipman
aspirar *tr* to suck in, draw in; inhale || *intr* to aspire; inhale, breathe in
aspirina *f* aspirin
asquear *tr* to loathe || *ref* to be nauseated
asquero•so -sa *adj* disgusting, loathsome; nauseating; squeamish
asta *f* spear; shaft; flagpole, staff, mast; antler; (*de toro*) horn; **a media asta** at halfmast; **dejar en las astas del toro** to leave high and dry
asta•do -da *adj* horned || *m* bull
ástato *m* astatine
aster *m* aster
asterisco *m* asterisk
astil *m* handle; shaft
astilla *f* chip, splinter, sliver
astillar *tr & ref* to chip, splinter
Astillejos *mpl* (astr) Castor and Pollux
astillero *m* dockyard, shipyard
astro *m* star, heavenly body; (fig) star, leading light
astrofísica *f* astrophysics
astrología *f* astrology
astronauta *m* astronaut
astronáuti•co -ca *adj* astronautic || *f* astronautics
astronave *f* spaceship; **astronave tripulada** manned spaceship
astronavegación *f* space travel
astronomía *f* astronomy
astronómi•co -ca *adj* astronomic(al)
astróno•mo -ma *mf* astronomer
astro•so -sa *adj* ill-fated; vile, contemptible; ragged, shabby
astucia *f* cunning, craftiness; trick
asturia•no -na *adj & mf* Asturian
astu•to -ta *adj* astute, cunning; tricky
asueto *m* day off; leisure
asumir *tr* to assume, take on
asunción *f* assumption
asunto *m* subject, matter; affair, business; theme; **asuntos internacionales** world affairs
asurar *tr* to burn; parch; harass, worry

asurcar §73 *tr* to furrow, plow
asustadi•zo -za *adj* scary, skittish; **lo asustadizo** (*de un animal*) shyness
asustar *tr* to scare, frighten
atabal *m* kettledrum; timbrel
ataca•do -da *adj* irresolute, undecided; mean, stingy
atacar §73 *tr* to attack; attach, fasten; pack, jam; (*un barreno*) tamp; corner, contradict || *intr* to attack
ata•do -da *adj* timid, shy; weak, irresolute; insignificant; cramped || *m* pack, bundle, roll
ataguía *f* cofferdam
atajar *tr* to stop, intercept, interrupt; to partition off || *intr* to take a short cut || *ref* to be abashed
atajo *m* short cut; (*en un escrito*) cut
atalaya *m* guard, lookout || *f* watchtower; elevation
atalayar *tr* to watch from a watchtower; spy on
atanquía *f* depilatory ointment
atañer §70 *tr* to concern
ataque *m* attack; **ataque aéreo** air raid; **ataque cardíaco** or **ataque al corazón** heart attack; **ataque por sorpresa** surprise attack
atar *tr* to tie, fasten
ataracea *f* marquetry, inlaid work
atarantar *tr* to stun, daze
atardecer *m* late afternoon || *v* **§22** *intr* to draw toward evening; happen in the late afternoon
atarea•do -da *adj* busy
atarear *tr* to give an assignment to; overload with work || *ref* to toil, work hard, keep busy
atarjea *f* sewer
atarugar §44 *tr* to peg, wedge; plug; stuff, fill; silence, shut up || *ref* to become confused
atasajar *tr* to slash, hack; (*carne*) jerk
atascadero *m* mudhole; (fig) pitfall
atascar §73 *tr* to stop, stop up, clog, obstruct || *ref* to get stuck; stuff oneself; clog, get clogged
atasco *m* sticking, clogging; obstruction
ataúd *m* casket, coffin
ataujía *f* damascene work
ataujiar §77 *tr* to damascene
ataviar §77 *tr* to dress, adorn, deck out
atávi•co -ca *adj* atavistic
atavío *m* dress, adornment; **atavíos** finery, frippery, chiffons
atediar *tr* to tire, bore
ateísmo *m* atheism
ateísta *mf* atheist
atelaje *m* harness
atemorizar §60 *tr* to frighten
atemperar *tr* to soften, moderate, temper; adjust, adapt
Atenas *f* Athens
atención *f* attention; **en atención a** in view of
atender §51 *tr* to attend to; heed, pay attention to; take care of; (*a los parroquianos*) wait on
atener §71 *ref* — **atenerse a** to abide by, rely on
ateniense *adj & mf* Athenian
atenta•do -da *adj* moderate, prudent; cautious || *m* attempt, assault; **atentado suicida** suicide bombing; **atentado terrorista** terroristic attack
atentamente *adv* attentively, thoughtfully, carefully; **atentamente** *or* **a usted atentamente** *or* **lo saluda atentamente** Sincerely yours
atentar *tr* to attempt, try to commit || *intr* — **atentar a** or **contra** (*p.ej., la vida de una persona*) to attempt || **§2** *ref* to grope
aten•to -ta *adj* attentive; courteous, polite || *f* favor (*letter*)
atenuar §21 *tr* to extenuate
ate•o -a *adj & mf* atheist
aterciopela•do -da *adj* velvety
ateri•do -da *adj* stiff, numb with cold
aterrada *f* landfall
aterrajar *tr* to thread, tap
aterraje *m* landing
aterrar *tr* to terrify || **§2** *tr* to destroy, demolish; cover with earth || *intr* to land || *ref* to stand inshore
aterrizaje *m* landing; **aterrizaje a ciegas** blind landing; **aterrizaje aplastado** or **en desplome** pancake landing; **aterrizaje forzoso** emergency landing; **aterrizaje sin choque** soft landing
aterrizar §60 *intr* to land
aterronar *tr* to make lumpy || *ref* to cake, lump
aterrorizar §60 *tr* to terrify
atesorar *tr* to treasure; hoard; (*virtudes, perfecciones*) possess
atesta•do -da *adj* stuffed, jammed; obstinate, stubborn || *m* certificate
atestar *tr* (law) to attest || **§2 & regular** *tr* to jam, pack, stuff, cram; stuff
atestiguar §10 *tr* to attest, testify, depose
atezar §60 *tr* to tan; blacken || *ref* to become tanned, become sunburned
atiborrar *tr* to stuff || *ref* to stuff, stuff oneself
ático *m* top-floor apartment; (*de lujo*) penthouse; (*desván*) garret, loft
atiesar *tr* to stiffen; tighten || *ref* to become stiff; become tight
atildar *tr* to mark with a tilde, dash, or accent mark; point out; find fault with; tidy up, trim, adorn
atina•do -da *adj* careful, keen, wise
atinar *tr* to find, come upon || *intr* to guess, guess right; be right; manage
atirantar *tr* (Mex) to make taut; brace || *ref* (Mex) to die, pass away
atisbadero *m* peephole
atisbar *tr* to watch, spy on
atisbo *m* glimpse, look, peek
atizar §60 *tr* to stir, poke; snuff; rouse; (*p.ej., un puntapié*) let go
Atlánti•co -ca *adj & m* Atlantic
at•las *m* (*pl* **-las**) atlas
atleta *mf* athlete
atleticismo *m* athletics
atléti•co -ca *adj* athletic || *f* athletics
atmósfera *f* atmosphere
atmosféri•co -ca *adj* atmospheric

atoar *tr* (naut) to tow
atocha *f* esparto
atocinar *tr* (*un cerdo*) to cut up; make into bacon; (coll) to murder || *ref* to get angry; fall madly in love
atolladero *m* mudhole; obstacle, difficulty
atollar *intr & ref* to get stuck, get stuck in the mud
atolondra•do -da *adj* confused; scatterbrained
atolondrar *tr* to confuse, bewilder
atómi•co -ca *adj* atomic
átomo *m* atom
atóni•to -ta *adj* astounded, aghast
atontar *tr* to stun; to confuse, bewilder
atorar *tr* to clog, obstruct || *intr & ref* to stick, get stuck; choke
atormentar *tr* to torment; torture
atornillar *tr* to screw, screw on
atortillar *tr* (SAm) to squash, flatten
atortolar *tr* to rattle, scare, intimidate
atosigar §44 *tr* to poison; harass || *ref* to be in a hurry
atrabanca•do -da *adj* overworked; (Mex) hasty, rash; (Ven) deep in debt
atrabancar §73 *tr & intr* to rush through
atrabilia•rio -ria *adj* irascible, grouchy
atracada *f* quarrel, row
atracador *m* hold-up man
atracar §73 *tr* to hold up; bring up; stuff; (naut) to bring alongside, dock || *intr* (naut) to come alongside, dock || *ref* to stuff; quarrel
atracción *f* attraction; amusement
atraco *m* holdup, robbery; mugging
atracón *m* stuffing, gluttony; fight; push, shove
atracti•vo -va *adj* attractive || *m* attraction; attractiveness
atraer §75 *tr* to attract
atragantar *tr* to choke down || *ref* to choke; **atragantarse con** to choke on
atraillar §4 *tr* to leash; master, subdue
atrampar *ref* to fall into a trap; be stopped up; stick; get stuck
atrancar §73 *tr* to bar; obstruct || *intr* to stride; read falteringly || *ref* to get stuck; (*una ventana*) stick; (Mex) to stick to one's opinion
atrapamos•cas *m* (*pl* **-cas**) flytrap; (bot) Venus's-flytrap
atrapar *tr* to trap, catch; get, land, net
atrás *adv* back, backward; behind; before; previously; **atrás de** back of, behind; **hacerse atrás** to back up, move back; **hacia atrás** backwards; the other way
atrasa•do -da *adj* late; (*reloj*) slow; needy; back; retarded; in arrears; **atrasado de medios** short of funds; **atrasado de noticias** behind the times
atrasar *tr* to slow down; retard; set back, turn back; delay; leave behind; postdate || *intr* to be slow || *ref* to be slow; lose time; lag, stay behind; be late; be in debt
atraso *m* delay, slowness; backwardness; lag; **atrasos** arrears, delinquency
atravesada *f* (SAm) crossing
atravesar §2 *tr* to cross, go across; pierce; pass through, go through; put crosswise; stake, wager || *ref* to butt in; fight, wrangle; get stuck
atrayente *adj* attractive
atreguar §10 *tr* to give a truce to; grant an extension to || *ref* to agree to a truce
atrever *ref* to dare; **atreverse con** or **contra** to be impudent toward
atrevi•do -da *adj* bold, daring; impudent
atrevimiento *m* boldness, daring; impudence
atribuir §20 *tr* to attribute, ascribe || *ref* to assume
atribular *tr & ref* to grieve
atributo *m* attribute
atril *m* lectern; music stand
atrincherar *tr* to entrench || *ref* to dig in
atrio *m* hall, vestibule; court, courtyard; parvis
atri•to -ta *adj* contrite
atrocidad *f* atrocity; enormity
atrofia *f* atrophy
atrofiar *tr & ref* to atrophy
atrojar *tr* (*granos*) to garner; (Mex) to befuddle
atrona•do -da *adj* reckless, thoughtless
atronar §61 *tr* to deafen; stun || *intr* to thunder; to blare
atropella•do -da *adj* brusk, violent; hasty; tumultuous
atropellar *tr* to trample; knock down; run over; disregard; do hurriedly || *intr & ref* to act hastily or recklessly
atropello *m* trampling; knocking down; running over; abuse, insult; outrage
a•troz *adj* (*pl* **-troces**) atrocious; huge, enormous
atto. *abbr* **atento**
atufar *tr* to anger, irritate || *ref* to get angry; (*el vino*) turn sour
atún *m* tuna
aturdi•do -da *adj* reckless, harebrained
aturdir *tr* to stun; perplex, bewilder
atusar *tr* to trim; smooth || *ref* to dress fancily; (*el bigote*) twist
audacia *f* audacity
au•daz *adj* (*pl* **-daces**) audacious
audición *f* audition; hearing; concert; listening
audiencia *f* audience, hearing; audience chamber; royal tribunal; provincial high court
audífono *m* hearing aid; earphone
audio *adj & m* audio
audiofrecuencia *f* audio frequency
audiómetro *m* audiometer
audiovisual *adj* audiovisual
auditor *m* judge advocate; **auditor de guerra** judge advocate (*in army*); **auditor de marina** judge advocate (*in navy*)
auditorio *m* (*concurso de oyentes*) audience; (*local*) auditorium
auge *m* height, acme; boom; vogue; **estar en auge** to be booming
augur *m* augur
augurar *tr* to augur; wish || *intr* to augur
augurio *m* augury; wish
augus•to -ta *adj* august

aula *f* classroom, lecture room; **aula magna** assembly hall
aulaga *f* gorse, furze
aullar **§8** *intr* to howl
aullido *m* howl, howling
aúllo *m* howl
aumentar *tr* to augment, increase, enlarge; promote; exaggerate || *intr & ref* to augment, increase
aumento *m* augmentation, increase, enlargement; promotion; (Guat, Mex) postscript, addition; **ir en aumento** to be on the increase
aun *adv* even; **aun cuando** although
aún *adv* still, yet
aunar **§8** *tr & ref* to join, unite; combine, mix
aunque *conj* although, though
aúpa *interj* up!; **de aúpa** swanky; **los de aúpa** (taur) the picadors
aupar **§8** *tr* to help up; extol
aura *f* gentle breeze; breath; popularity; turkey vulture
áure•o -a *adj* gold, golden
aureola *f* halo, aureole
auricular *m* earpiece, receiver; **auricular de casco** headpiece
auriga *m* (poet) coachman, charioteer
aurora *f* aurora, dawn; roseate hue
ausencia *f* absence
ausentar *tr* to send away || *ref* to absent oneself
ausente *adj* absent; absent-minded || *mf* absentee
auspiciar *tr* to sponsor, foster, back
auspicio *m* auspice; **bajo los auspicios de** under the auspices of
auste•ro -ra *adj* austere; harsh; honest; penitent
Australia *f* Australia
australia•no -na *adj & mf* Australian
Austria *f* Austria
austrí•co -ca *adj & mf* Austrian
austro *m* south wind
auténtica *f* certificate; certification
autenticar **§73** *tr* to authenticate; probate
auténti•co -ca *adj* authentic; real || *f* see **auténtica**
autillo *m* tawny owl
autístia•co -ca *adj* autistic
auto *m* edict; short Biblical play; miracle play; auto; **auto de prisión** commitment, warrant for arrest; **auto sacramental** play in honor of the Sacrament; **autos de choque** bumper cars
autoabastecimiento *m* self-sufficiency
autoadhesi•vo -va *adj* self-adhesive
autoamortizable *adj* self-liquidating
autobanco *m* drive-in bank
autobiografía *f* autobiography
autobombo *m* self-glorification
autobús *m* autobus, bus
autocamión *m* motor truck
autocasa *f* motor home; mobile home; trailer
autocine *m* (Chile, Cuba) drive-in theater
autocinema *f* (Mex) drive-in theater
autocráti•co -ca *adj* autocratic(al)
autócto•no -na *adj* native, indigenous
autocue *m* (*dispositivo visual*) teleprompter
autodefensa *f* self-defense
autodestrucción *f* self-destruction
autodeterminación *f* self-determination
autodidac•to -ta *adj* self-taught
autodisciplina *f* self-discipline
autodominio *m* self-control
autódromo *m* automobile race track
autoedición *f* desktop publishing
autoediti•vo -va *adj* desktop publishing
autoejecutable *adj* (compu) stand-alone
auto-escuela *f* driving school
autógena *f* welding
autogestión *f* self-administration; independence
autogobierno *m* self-government
autografiar **§77** *tr* to autograph
autógra•fo -fa *adj & m* autograph
autoguia•do -da *adj* self-guided, homing
autolimpiador or **autolimpiante** *adj invar* self-cleaning
automación *f* automation
autómata *m* automaton
automáti•co -ca *adj* automatic; (compu) hands-off
automatización *f* automation
automatizado *adj* automated
automóvil *m* automobile, car
automovilista *mf* motorist
autonomía *f* autonomy; cruising radius
autóno•mo -ma *adj* autonomous, independent; (compu) off-line
autopega•do -da *adj* self-sealing
autopiano *m* player piano
autopista *f* expressway, freeway, superhighway; **autopista de peaje** turnpike
autopsia *f* autopsy
au•tor -tora *mf* author; (*de un crimen*) perpetrator || *f* authoress
autoreactor *m* ramjet (engine)
autoridad *f* authority; pomp, display
autorita•rio -ria *adj & mf* authoritarian
autoriza•do -da *adj* authoritative
autorizar **§60** *tr* to authorize; legalize; exalt
autorretrato *m* self-portrait
autoservicio *m* self-service; self-service store or restaurant; supermarket
autostop *m* hitchhiking; **viajar en autostop** to hitchhike
autostopista *mf* hitchhiker
auto-teatro *m* drive-in movie theater
autovía *m* railway motor coach || *f* turnpike, automobile road
auxiliar *adj* auxiliary || *mf* auxiliary; aid, helper; substitute teacher || *v* **§77 & regular** *tr* to aid, help, assist; (*a un moribundo*) attend
auxilio *m* aid, help, assistance; **acudir en auxilio a** or **de** to come to the aid of; **auxilio en carretera** road service; **primeros auxilios** first aid
avahar *tr* to steam; breathe warmth on || *intr* to steam, give off vapor || *ref* to steam, give off vapor; warm one's hands with one's breath
aval *m* indorsement; countersignature

avalancha *f* avalanche
avalorar *tr* to estimate; encourage
avaluación *f* appraisal, valuation
avaluar §21 *tr* to appraise, estimate
avalúo *m* appraisal, valuation
avance *m* advance; advance payment; (com) balance; (com) estimate; (mov) preview; **avance rápido** (mach, mov) fast forward
avante *adv* (naut) fore
avanza•do -da *adj* advanced; **avanzado de edad** advanced in years || *f* outpost, advance guard
avanzar §60 *tr* to advance, extend; propose || *intr & ref* to advance; approach
avanzo *m* balance sheet; estimate
avaricia *f* avarice
avaricio•so -sa *adj* avaricious
avarien•to -ta *adj* avaricious || *mf* miser
ava•ro -ra *adj* miserly || *mf* miser
avasallar *tr* to subject, subjugate, enslave || *ref* to submit
ave *f* bird; fowl; **ave canora** songbird; **ave de corral** barnyard fowl; **ave de mal agüero** Jonah, jinx; **ave de paso** bird of passage; **ave de rapiña** bird of prey; **ave fría** lapwing; **ave zancuda** wading bird
avecinar *tr* to bring near || *ref* to approach; take up residence
avecindar *tr* to domicile || *ref* to become a resident
avejentar *tr & ref* to age prematurely
avejigar §44 *tr, intr & ref* to blister
avellana *f* hazelnut, filbert
avellanar *tr* to countersink || *ref* to shrivel, shrivel up
avellano *m* hazel, hazel tree
avemaría *f* Hail Mary, Ave Maria; **al avemaría** at sunset; **en un avemaría** in a jiffy; **saber como el avemaría** to have a thorough knowledge of
avena *f* oats
avenar *tr* to drain
avenate *m* gruel, oatmeal gruel
avenencia *f* agreement; deal, bargain
avenida *f* avenue; allée; flood, freshet; gathering, assemblage; **avenida ajardinada** parkway
aveni•do -da *adj* — **bien avenido** in agreement; **mal avenido** in disagreement || *f* see **avenida**
avenimiento *m* agreement; reconciliation
avenir §79 *tr* to reconcile, bring together || *ref* to be reconciled, agree; compromise; correspond
aventa•dor -dora *mf* winnower || *m* fan
aventaja•do -da *adj* excellent, outstanding; advantageous
aventajar *tr* to advance; put ahead; excel || *ref* to advance, win an advantage; excel
aventar §2 *tr* to fan; winnow; scatter to the winds; blow; drive away || *ref* to swell up; flee, run away
aventón *m* (Guat, Mex, Peru) push, shove; (*llevada gratuita*) (Mex) free ride; **pedir aventón** (Mex) to hitchhike
aventura *f* adventure; danger, risk
aventura•do -da *adj* hazardous, venturesome
aventurar *tr* to adventure, venture, hazard || *ref* to adventure, take a risk; venture, to risk
aventure•ro -ra *adj* adventuresome, adventurous || *m* adventurer, soldier of fortune || *f* adventuress
avergonzar §9 *tr* to shame; embarrass || *ref* to be ashamed; be embarrassed
avería *f* aviary; breakdown, failure; (com) damage; (naut) average
averiar §77 *tr* to damage || *ref* to suffer damage; break down
averiguable *adj* ascertainable
averiguar §10 *tr* to ascertain, find out
aversión *f* aversion, dislike; **cobrar aversión a** to take a dislike for
aves•truz *m* (*pl* **-truces**) ostrich
avezar §60 *tr* to accustom || *ref* to become accustomed
aviación *f* aviation
avia•dor -dora *mf* aviator, flyer || *m* aviator, airman; (mil) airman; **aviador postal** airmail pilot || *f* aviatrix, airwoman
aviar §77 *tr* to make ready, prepare; equip, provide; **estar, encontrarse** or **quedar aviado** to be in a mess, be in a jam || *ref* to hurry; (aer) to take off
avia•triz (*pl* **-trices**) aviatrix
avidez *f* avidity, greediness
ávi•do -da *adj* avid, greedy, eager
aviejar *tr & ref* to age prematurely
aviento *m* winnowing fork, pitchfork
avie•so -sa *adj* crooked, distorted; evil-minded, perverse
avilantar *ref* to be insolent
avilantez *f* insolence; meanness
avillana•do -da *adj* rustic, boorish
avillanar *tr* to debase, make boorish || *ref* to become boorish
avinagra•do -da *adj* vinegarish, sour, crabbed
avinagrar *tr* to sour || *ref* to become sour; turn into vinegar
avío *m* provision; arrangement; load; **¡al avío!** let's go!; **avíos** equipment, tools, outfit; **avíos de pescar** fishing tackle
avión *m* airplane; (orn) martin; **avión birreactor** twin-jet plane; **avión de caza** pursuit plane; **avión a chorro, avión de propulsión a chorro** *or* **a reacción** jet plane; **avión de travesía** airliner; **avión supersónico** supersonic aircraft; **en avión** by plane
avión-correo *m* mailplane
avioneta *f* small plane; **avioneta de alquiler** taxiplane
avisaco•ches *m* (*pl* **-ches**) car caller
avisa•do -da *adj* prudent, wise; **mal avisado** rash, thoughtless
avisa•dor -dora *adj* warning || *mf* informer; ad-

viser || *m* electric bell; **avisador de incendio** fire alarm
avisar *tr* to advise, inform; warn; report on
aviso *m* advice, information; warning; care, prudence; dispatch boat; advertisement; **aviso clasificado** classified ad; **aviso fúnebre** death notice; **sobre aviso** on the lookout
avispa *f* wasp
avispa•do -da *adj* brisk, wide-awaker; smart, streetwise; (SAm) startled, scared
avispar *tr* to spur; to stir up || *ref* to fret, worry
avispón *m* hornet
avistar *tr* to descry || *ref* to meet, have an interview
avitaminosis *f* vitamin deficiency
avituallar *tr* to supply, provision || *ref* to take in supplies
avivar *tr* to brighten, enlive, revive || *intr & ref* to brighten, revive
avizor *adj* watchful, alert || *m* watcher; **avizores** (slang) eyes
avizorar *tr* to watch, spy on || *ref* to hide and watch, spy
ax *interj* ouch!, ow!
axioma *m* axiom
axiomáti•co -ca *adj* axiomatic
ay *interj* ay!, alas! **¡ay de mí!** woe is me! || *m* sigh
aya *f* nurse, governess
ayer *adj & m* yesterday
ayo *m* tutor
ayuda *m* valet; **ayuda de cámera** valet de chambre || *f* help, aid; enema
ayudanta *f* assistant; **ayudanta de cocina** kitchenmaid
ayudante *m* aid, assistant; adjutant; **ayudante de campo** aide-de-camp; **ayudante de mecánico** (coll) grease monkey
ayudantía *f* (*universidad*) assistantship
ayudar *tr* to aid, help, assist
ayunar *intr* to fast
ayu•no -na *adj* fasting; uninformed; **en ayunas** or **en ayuno** fasting; before breakfast; uninformed; missing the point || *m* fast, fasting
ayuntamiento *m* town or city council; town or city hall; sexual intercourse
azabacha•do -da *adj* jet, jet-black
azabache *m* jet; **azabaches** jet trinkets
aza•cán -cana *adj* menial || *mf* drudge || *m* water carrier
azada *f* hoe
azadón *m* hoe; grub hoe; **azadón de peto** or **de pico** mattock
azadonar *tr* to hoe
azafata *f* flight attendant; hostess
azafate *m* wicker tray
azafrán *m* saffron
azafrana•do -da *adj* saffron
azafranar *tr* to saffron
azahar *m* orange or lemon blossom
azar *m* chance, hazard; accident, misfortune; fate, destiny; losing card; losing throw; (*persona o cosa que traen mala suerte*) Jonah
azarar *ref* to go awry; get rattled
azaro•so -sa *adj* hazardous, risky; unlucky
ázi•mo -ma *adj* unleavened
azófar *m* brass
azoga•do da *adj* fidgety, restless || *m* quicksilver foil; **temblar como un azogado** to shake like a leaf
azogar §44 *tr* (*un espejo*) to silver || *ref* to have mercury poisoning; shake, become agitated
azogue *m* quicksilver; market place; (coll) mirror
azonza•do -da *adj* stupid, dumb
azor *m* goshawk
azorar *tr* to abash; excite, stir up
Azores *fpl* Azores
azotar *tr* to whip, scourge; beat; flail; beat down upon
azote *m* whip; lash; (fig) scourge; **azotes y galeras** tiresome fare
azotea *f* flat roof, roof terrace
azteca *adj & mf* Aztec
azúcar *m* sugar; **azúcar de caña** cane sugar; **azúcar de remolacha** beet sugar
azucarar *tr* to sugar, sugarcoat; sugar over
azucare•ro -ra *adj* sugar || *m* sugar bowl
azucena *f* Madonna lily, white lily
azufrar *tr* to sulfur
azufre *m* sulfur; brimstone
azul *adj & m* blue; **azul marino** navy blue
azular *tr* to color blue, dye blue
azulear *intr* to turn blue
azulejar *tr* to tile, cover with tiles
azulejo *m* glazed colored tile (orn) roller; (orn) indigo bunting; (orn) bee eater
azulones *mpl* blue jeans
azuzar §60 *tr* to sic; tease, incite

B

B, b (be) *f* second letter of the Spanish alphabet
B. *abbr* **Beato, Bueno**
baba *f* drivel, spittle, slobber; (*de culebras, peces, etc.*) slime
babear *intr* to slobber; froth
babel *m & f* (coll) bedlam, confusion; **estar en babel** to be daydreaming
babero *m* bib
Babia *f* — **estar en Babia** to be daydreaming
babieca *adj* silly, simple || *mf* simpleton
Babilonia *f* (*imperio*) Babylonia; (*ciudad*) Babylon
babilóni•co -ca *adj* Babylonian
babilo•nio -nia *adj & mf* Babylonian || *f* see **Babilonia**
bable *m* Asturian dialect; patois

babor *m* (naut) port
babosa *f* slug
babosada *f* (CAm, Mex) stupidity; foolish act
babosear *tr* to slobber over || *intr* to slobber
babo•so -sa *adj* slobbery; (*con las damas*) (coll) mushy || *m* (CAm) scoundrel || *f* see **babosa**
babucha *f* slipper, mule
babuino *m* baboon
bacalao or **bacallao** *m* codfish
baceta *f* (cards) widow
bacha *f* (Mex) (cigarette) butt
bache *m* hole, rut; blip; **bache aéreo** air pocket
bachi•ller -llera *adj* garrulous || *mf* garrulous person || **bachiller** *mf* bachelor (*holder of a bachelor's degree*); graduate with the equivalent of a high school diploma
bachillerar *tr* to confer the bachelor's degree on || *ref* to receive the bachelor's degree
bachillerato *m* secondary education; equivalent of a high school diploma; bachelor's degree
bachillerear *intr* to babble, prattle
bachillería *f* babble, prattle; gossip
bacía *f* basin, vessel; shaving dish
bacilo *m* bacillus
bacín *m* chamber pot
Baco *m* Bacchus
bacteria *f* bacterium
bacteria•no -na *adj* bacterial
bacteriología *f* bacteriology
bacterióIo•go -ga *mf* bacteriologist
báculo *m* staff; crook; (fig) staff, comfort; **báculo pastoral** crozier
badajo *m* clapper (*of a bell*)
badana *f* (dressed) sheepskin; **zurrarle a uno la badana** to tan someone's hide
badén *m* gully, gutter; speed bump
badil *m* fire shovel
badulaque *m* nincompoop
bagaje *m* beast of burden; (mil) baggage; (fig) stock of knowledge
bagatela *f* trinket; triviality; (Chile, Peru) pinball
bagazo *m* waste pulp, bagasse
bagre *adj* (Bol, Col) showy, gaudy; (CAm) sly, slick; (SAm) coarse, ill-bred; (Mex) stupid || *m* catfish
bahareque *m* (CAm, Col, Ven) small hut
bahía *f* bay; (compu) bay
bahorrina *f* slop; riffraff
bailable *adj* for dancing || *m* ballet
bailadero *m* dance floor, dance hall
baila•dor -dora *mf* dancer
bailar *tr* (*p.ej., un vals*) to dance; (*un trompo*) spin || *intr* to dance; spin; wobble
baila•rín -rina *mf* dancer; **bailarín de zapateo americano** tap dancer || *f* ballerina; **bailarina ombliguista** belly dancer
baile *m* dance; ball; ballet; **baile de etiqueta** dress ball, formal dance; **baile de los globos** bubble dance; **baile de máscaras** masked ball, masquerade ball; **baile de San Vito** (pathol) Saint Vitus's dance; **baile de trajes** costume ball, fancy-dress ball
baja *f* (*de los precios*) fall, drop; (*en la guerra*) casualty; **baja por maternidad** maternity leave; **dar baja** to go down, decline; **dar de baja** to drop; (mil) to mark absent; **darse de baja** to drop out; **jugar a la baja** to bear the market
bajaca *f* (Ecuad) hair ribbon
bajada *f* descent; slope; downspout; (rad) lead-in wire; **bajada de aguas** gutter
bajagua *f* (Mex) cheap tobacco
bajamar *f* low tide
bajar *tr* to lower, take down; bring down; (*la escalera*) go down, descend; humble; (compu) to download || *intr* to come down, go down; get off || *ref* to bend down; get off; humble oneself
bajel *m* ship, vessel
bajeza *f* humbleness, lowliness; meanness, baseness
bajío *m* shoal, sandbank; pitfall; lowland
bajista *adj* bearish || *mf* (fig) bear
ba•jo -ja *adj* low, under, lower; short; mean, base; lowly, humble; (mus) bass; **baja Edad Media** late Middle Ages; **bajos fondos sociales** underworld || *m* shoal, sandbank; (mus) bass || *f* see **baja** || **bajo** *adv* down; low, in a low voice || **bajo** *prep* under
bajón *m* bassoon; (*en el caudal, la salud, etc.*) decline, loss
bajonista *mf* bassoon player
bajorrelieve *m* bas-relief
bala *f* bullet; bale; **bala de fogueo** or **salva** blank, blank round; **bala de goma** rubber bullet; **bala expansiva** dumdum bullet; **bala fría** spent bullet; **bala perdida** stray bullet; **ni a bala** (SAm) under no circumstances
balaca *f* boasting, show
balaceo *m* or **balacera** *f* (SAm) shooting; shootout
balada *f* ballad; (mus) ballade
bala•dí *adj* (*pl* **-díes**) trivial, paltry, cheap
baladro *m* scream, shout, outcry
baladronada *f* boast, boasting
baladronear *intr* to boast, brag
bálago *m* chaff
balance *m* balance, balance sheet; rocking, swinging; hesitation, doubt; (*de una nave*) rolling; **balance de comprobación** trial balance
balancear *tr* to balance || *intr & ref* to rock, swing; hesitate, waver; (*la nave*) roll
balancín *m* balance beam; singletree; rocker arm; seesaw
balandra *f* sloop
balandrán *m* cassock
balanza *f* scales; balance; comparison, judgment; **balanza comercial** balance of trade; **balanza de pagos** balance of payments
balar *intr* to bleat; (coll) to pine
balastar *tr* to ballast
balasto *m* ballast
balaustre *m* baluster, banister
balay *m* wicker basket

balazo *m* shot; bullet wound
balbucear *tr* to stammer || *intr* to stammer, stutter; to babble, to prattle
balbucir **§1** *tr & intr* var of **balbucear**
Balcanes, los the Balkans
balcarrotas *fpl* (SAm) sideburns; (Mex) locks falling over sides of face
balcón *m* balcony
baldar *tr* to cripple; incapacitate; inconvenience; trump
balde *m* bucket, pail; **de balde** free, gratis; over, in excess; **en balde** in vain
baldear *tr* to wash with pails of water; (*una excavación*) bail out
baldí•o -a *adj* uncultivated; idle, lazy; careless; useless, vain; unfounded || *m* untilled land
baldón *m* insult; blot, disgrace
baldonar *tr* to insult; stain, disgrace
baldosa *f* floor tile, paving tile; flagstone
baldra•gas *m* (*pl* **-gas**) jellyfish
balduque *s* red tape, wrapping tape
balear *tr* to shoot at, shoot, shoot to death
baleo *m* (SAm) shooting
balido *m* bleat, bleating
balísti•co -ca *adj* ballistic
baliza *f* buoy, beacon; danger signal
balizaje *m* (aer) airway lighting; (naut) buoys
balizar **§60** *tr* to mark with buoys; mark off
ballena *f* whale; whalebone; (*de corsé*) stay
ballesta *f* crossbow; spring, auto spring
ba•llet *m* (*pl* **-llets**) ballet
balnea•rio -ria *adj* bathing || *m* watering place, spa
balompié *m* soccer
balón *m* ball; bale; balloon; cylinder; **balón de fútbol** football
baloncesto *m* basketball
balonvolea *m* volleyball
balota *f* ballot
balotar *intr* to ballot
balsa *f* pool, puddle; raft; float; corkwood; **balsa salvavidas** life float
bálsamo *m* balsam, balm
balsear *tr* to cross by raft; ferry across
balsero *m* ferryman
bálti•co -ca *adj* Baltic
baluarte *m* bulwark, bastion
balumba *f* confusion; row
bambalinas *fpl* (theat) flies, borders
bambolear *intr* to sway, reel, wobble
bambolla *f* hulk; show, sham; show-off
bam•bú *m* (*pl* **-búes**) bamboo
banana *f* banana; (rad) plug
banane•ro -ra *adj* banana || *m* banana tree
banano *m* banana tree
banas *fpl* (Mex) banns
banasta *f* hamper, large basket
banca *f* bench; banking; stand, fruit stand; (*en el juego*) bank; **banca de hielo** iceberg; **hacer saltar la banca** to break the bank
banca•rio -ria *adj* banking, bank
bancarrota *f* bankruptcy; **hacer bancarrota** to go bankrupt
bancarrote•ro -ra *adj & mf* bankrupt
banco *m* bench; bank; (*de peces*) school; **banco de ahorros** savings bank; **banco de arena** sandbank; **banco de coral** coral reef; **banco de datos** (compu) data bank; memory; **banco de esperma** or **semen** sperm bank; **banco de hielo** iceberg; **banco de liquidación** clearing house; **banco de nieve** snowdrift; **banco de sangre** blood bank
banda *f* band; ribbon; faction, party; flock; border, edge; bank, shore; (*de la mesa de billar*) cushion; **banda ciudadana** citizens band, CB; **banda de frecuencias** wave band; **banda de rodamiento** (aut) tread; **banda de tambores** drum corps; **banda sonora** sound track; (aut) rumble strip; **irse a la banda** (naut) to list
bandada *f* flock, covey; (*de gente*) (coll) flock
bandaje *m* tire
bandazo *m* swerving; (naut) lurch
bandear *tr* to go through, pierce; to pursue; to make love to || *ref* to manage
bandeja *f* tray; dish, platter
bandera *f* flag, banner; **con banderas desplegadas** with flying colors; **la bandera de las barras y las estrellas** the Stars and Stripes (U.S.A.)
banderilla *f* (taur) banderilla; **poner una banderilla a** to taunt; hit for a loan
banderín *m* (mil) color corporal; recruiting post
banderola *f* streamer, pennant; transom
bandido *m* bandit
bando *m* proclamation; faction, side
bandolera *f* bandoleer; female bandit; **en bandolera** across the shoulders
bandolero *m* highwayman, brigand
bandurria *f* Spanish lute
banquero *m* banker
banqueta stool, footstool; (Guat, Mex) sidewalk
banquete *m* banquet
banquetear *tr, intr & ref* to banquet
banquisa *f* floe, iceberg
bañadera *f* bathtub
bañado *m* chamber pot; marshland
baña•dor -dora *adj* bathing || *mf* bather || *m* bathing suit, swimsuit; **bañador de hombre** (Esp) swimming trunks
bañar *tr* to bathe; dip; coat by dipping || *ref* to bathe
bañera *f* bathtub
bañero *m* (SAm) lifeguard
bañista *mf* bather; frequenter of a spa or seaside resort
baño *m* bath; bathing; bathroom, washroom, restroom; bathtub; **baño de asiento** sitz bath; **baño de ducha** shower bath; **baño de espuma** bubble bath; **baño de lodo** *or* **fango** mudbath; **baño (de) María** double boiler; **baños** bathing place; spa
banyi *m* bungee jumping
bao *m* (naut) beam
baptista *adj & mf* Baptist

baptisterio *m* baptistery
baque *m* thud, thump; bump, bruise
baquelita *f* bakelite
ba•quet *m* (*pl* **-quets**) bucket seat
baqueta *f* ramrod; drumstick; **correr baquetas** or **pasar por baquetas** to run the gauntlet
baquía *f* knowledge of the road, paths, rivers, etc., of a region; manual skill
baquia•no -na *adj* skillful, expert ‖ *mf* scout, pathfinder, guide
báqui•co -ca *adj* Bacchic
bar *m* bar; cocktail bar
barahunda *f* uproar, tumult
baraja *f* (*de naipes*) deck, pack; gang, mob; confusion, mix-up
barajadura *f* shuffling; dispute, quarrel
barajar *tr* (*naipes*) to shuffle; jumble, to mix ‖ *intr* to shuffle; fight, quarrel ‖ *ref* to get jumbled or mixed
baranda *f* railing; (*de la mesa de billar*) cushion
barandilla *f* balustrade, railing
barata *f* cheapness; barter; (Mex) bargain sale; (Chile, Peru) cockroach; (Col, Mex) junk store
baratero *m* shopkeeper
baratía *f* (SAm) cheapness
baratija *f* trinket
baratillo *m* second-hand goods; second-hand shop; bargain counter
baratío *m* (CAm) junk store
bara•to -ta *adj* cheap ‖ *m* bargain sale; **dar de barato** to admit for the sake of argument; **de barato** gratis, free ‖ *f* see **barata** ‖ **barato** *adv* cheap
báratro *m* (poet) hell
baratura *f* cheapness
baraúnda *f* uproar, tumult
barba *f* (*parte de la cara*) chin; (*pelo en ella*) beard; (*del papel*) deckle edge; (*de ave*) gill, wattle; **barba española** Spanish moss; **barbas** whiskers; **barbas de chivo** goatee; **hacer la barba a** to shave; to bore, annoy; (Mex) to fawn on; **llevar por la barba** to lead by the nose; **mentir por la barba** (coll) to tell fish stories ‖ *m* (theat) old man
barbacoa *f* barbecue; (Col) kitchen cupboard; (Peru) attic
barbada *f* lower jaw of horse; bridle curb ‖ **la Barbada** Barbados
barbar *intr* to grow a beard; strike root
barbaridad *f* barbarism; outrage; piece of folly; large amount; **¡qué barbaridad!** how awful!, what nonsense!
barbarie *f* barbarity, barbarism
barbarismo *m* illiteracy; outrage; (gram) barbarism
bárba•ro -ra *adj* barbaric; barbarous ‖ *mf* barbarian
barbear *tr* to reach with the chin; be as high as ‖ *intr* to reach the same height; **barbear con** to be as high as
barbechar *tr* to plow for seeding; fallow
barbecho *m* fallow; **firmar como en un barbecho** to sign with one's eyes closed
barbería *f* barber shop
barberil *adj* barber
barbe•ro -ra *mf* barber; (Mex) flatterer
barbilampi•ño -ña *adj* smooth-faced, beardless; beginning, green
barbilla *f* tip of chin; (*de pluma*) barb; (*de pez*) wattle
bar•bón -bona *adj* bearded ‖ *m* graybeard; solemn old fellow; billy goat
barboquejo *m* chin strap
barbotar *tr & intr* to mutter, mumble
barbuchas *adj* beardless
barbu•do -da *adj* bearded, long-bearded, heavy-bearded ‖ *m* shoot, sucker
barbullar *tr & intr* to blabber
barca *f* small boat; bark; **barca perforador** offshore (oil) rig
barchi•lón -lona *mf* (Ecuad, Peru) nurse, orderly; (Arg, Bol, Peru) quack
barcia *f* chaff
barco *m* boat, ship; **barco cisternas** or **barco tanque** tanker; **barco de carga** cargo boat; **barco náufrago** shipwreck
barda *f* thatch; bard, horse armor
bardana *f* burdock
bardar *tr* to thatch; (*caballo*) bard
bardo *m* bard
baremo *m* (*escala*) scale; rate table
bargueño *m* carved inlaid secretary
bario *m* barium
barjuleta *f* haversack
barloventear *intr* to wander around; turn to windward
barlovento *m* windward
barman *m* bartender
bar•niz *m* (*pl* **-nices**) varnish; (*de la loza, la porcelana, etc.*) glaze; gloss, polish; (*conocimientos superficiales*) smattering; (aer) dope; (fig) veneer
barnizar **§60** *tr* to varnish
barómetro *m* barometer; **barómetro aneroide** aneroid barometer
barón *m* baron
baronesa *f* baroness
barquero *m* boatman
barquilla *f* (naut) log; (naut) log chip; (aer) nacelle, car
barquillero *m* waffle iron; harbor boatman
barquillo *m* cone; waffle
barquín *m* bellows
barra *f* bar; (*de dinamita*) stick; (*en el tribunal*) bar, railing; (*para pesas*) barbell; **barra colectora** (elec) bus bar; **barra de controles** (compu) control strip; **barra de espaciado, barra espaciadora** space bar; **barra de herramientas** (compu) tool bar; **barra de labios** or **para los labios** lipstick; **barra de menús** (compu) menu bar; **barra imantada** bar magnet; **barras paralelas** (sport) parallel bars
barrabasada *f* fiendish prank, mean trick

barraca *f* cabin, hut; cottage; storage shed; bunkhouse
barracón *m* barracks, bunkhouse; fair booth
barragana *f* concubine
barranca *f* gorge, ravine, gully
barranco *m* gorge, ravine, gully; difficulty, obstruction; cliff, precipice
barrar *tr* to daub, smear
barrear *tr* to barricade; bar shut
barredera *f* street sweeper
barre•dor -dora *mf* sweeper; **barredora de alfombras** carpet sweeper; **barredora de nieve** snowplow
barredura *f* sweeping; **barreduras** sweepings
barremi•nas *m* (*pl* **-nas**) mine sweeper
barrena *f* auger, drill, gimlet; (*espiga para taladrar*) bit; (aer) spin; **barrena picada** (aer) tail spin; **entrar en barrena** (aer) to go into a spin
barrenar *tr* to drill; (*un buque*) to scuttle; blast; upset, frustrate; violate
barrende•ro -ra *mf* sweeper
barreno *m* large drill; drill hole; blast hole; pride, vanity; (Chile) mania, pet idea; **dar barreno a** (*un buque*) to scuttle
barreño *m* earthen dishpan
barrer *tr* to sweep, sweep away; graze ‖ *intr* to sweep; **barrer hacia dentro** to look out for oneself
barrera *f* barrier; barricade; (mil) barrage; crockery cupboard; tollgate; (rr) crossing gate; (taur) fence around inside of ring; (taur) first row of seats; **barrera de arrecifes** barrier reef; **barrera de paso a nivel** (rr) crossing gate; **barrera de sonido** or **barrera sónica** sound barrier
barriada *f* district, quarter
barrial *m* (SAm) mudhole; muddy ground
barrica *f* cask, barrel
barricada *f* barricade
barrido *m or* **barrida** *f* (*con una escoba*) sweep; (*en béisbol*) slide; (mov, telv) wipe
barriga *f* belly; (*de una vasija, una pared, etc.*) bulge
barri•gón -gona or **barrigu•do -da** *adj* big-bellied
barril *m* barrel, keg, cask
barrilero *m* cooper, barrel maker
barrio *m* ward, quarter; suburb; **barrio bajo** slums; **barrio chino** Chinatown; **barrio comercial** shopping district, business district; **barrio periférico** suburb; **el otro barrio** the other world; **estar vestido de barrio** to be dressed in house clothes
barro *m* mud; clay; earthenware; pimple; (coll) money; (Arg, Urug) blunder
barro•co -ca *adj & m* baroque
barro•so -sa *adj* muddy; pimply
barrote *m* heavy bar; bolt; cross brace
barruntar *tr* to guess; to sense
barrunto *m* guess, conjecture; sign, token, foreboding
bartola *f* belly; **a la bartola** lazily
bartolina *f* (CAm, W-I) jail, dungeon
bártulos *mpl* household tools; **liar los bártulos** to pack up one's belongings
barullo *m* confusion, tumult
basar *tr* to base; build ‖ *ref* — **basarse en** to base one's judgment on, rely on
basca *f* nausea, squeamishness; fit of temper, tantrum
basco•so -sa *adj* nauseated, squeamish
báscula *f* scales; platform scale
base *f* base; basis; **a base de** on the basis of; **base de datos** database; **base de lanzamiento** launch site; **base imponible** tax base; **de las bases** grass roots; **las bases** the grass roots
bási•co -ca *adj* basic; **lo básico** the basics
Basilea *f* Basle, Basel
basílica *f* basilica
basilisco *m* basilisk; **estar hecho un basilisco** to be in a rage
basquear *intr* to be nauseated
basquetbol *m* basketball
bastante *adj* enough ‖ *adv* enough; fairly, rather ‖ *m* enough
bastar *intr* to be enough, suffice; abound, be more than enough ‖ *ref* to be self-sufficient
bastardilla *f* italics
bastar•do -da *adj & mf* bastard
bastedad *f* coarseness; roughness; (CAm) abundance; excess
bastidor *m* frame; stretcher; (theat) wing; **entre bastidores** behind the scenes
bastilla *f* hem
bastillar *tr* to hem
bas•to -ta *adj* coarse, rough; uncouth ‖ *m* packsaddle; (cards) club; **bastos** (cards) suit with figures representing clubs and considered to be equivalent to the English suit called clubs; **el basto** the ace of clubs
bastón *m* stick, staff; cane, walking stick; baton; **bastón de esquiar** ski pole or stick
bastoncillo *m* small stick; (*de la retina*) rod; cotton swab
bastonear *tr* to cane, beat
basura *f* sweepings; rubbish, litter, refuse, garbage; horse manure
basural *m* (SAm) dump; trash pile
basurero *m* trash can; rubbish dump; rubbish collector
basurita *f* trifle
bata *f* smock; dressing gown, wrapper; **bata de baño** bathrobe
batacazo *m* thud, bump
bataclán *m* (Cuba) burlesque show
bataclana *f* (Cuba) showgirl, stripteaser
batahola *f* racket, hubbub
batalla *f* battle; (*de un vehículo*) wheel base; (*de la silla de montar*) seat; (paint) battle piece; **batalla campal** pitched battle; **librar batalla** to do battle
batallar *intr* to battle, fight; hesitate, waver
bata•llón -llona *adj* (*cuestión*) controversial, moot ‖ *m* battalion
batata *f* sweet potato; (Arg) timidity

bate *m* baseball bat
batea *f* tray; flat-bottomed boat; (rr) flatcar
bateador *m* batter
batear *tr & intr* to bat
batel *m* small boat
batelero *m* boatman
batería *f* battery; footlights; **batería de cocina** kitchen utensils
baterista *mf* drummer
batiboleo *m* (Cuba, Mex) noise; confusion
bati•do -da *adj* (*camino*) beaten; (*tejido*) moiré ‖ *m* batter; milk shake; (rad) beat ‖ *f* battue; combing, search
batidor *m* beater; scout, ranger; **batidor de huevos** egg beater; **batidor de oro** goldbeater
batidora *f* beater, mixer
batiente *m* jamb; (*hoja de puerta*) leaf, door; (*de piano*) damper; wash, place where surf breaks
batihoja *m* goldbeater; sheet-metal worker
batimiento *m* beating; (phys) beat
batín *m* smoking jacket
batintín *m* Chinese gong
batir *tr* to beat; batter, beat down; (*las alas*) flap; (*manos*) clap; (*las olas*) ply; **batir tiendas** (mil) to strike camp
batiscafo *m* bathyscaphe
bato *m* simpleton, rustic
batuque *m* (Arg) uproar, rumpus, jamboree; **armar un batuque** (Arg) to raise a rumpus
baturrillo *m* hodgepodge
batuta *f* (mus) baton; **llevar la batuta** to boss the show
baudio *m* (compu) baud
baúl *m* trunk; **baúl mundo** large trunk; **baúl ropero** wardrobe trunk
bauprés *m* bowsprit
bautismo *m* baptism; **bautismo de aire** first flight
bautista *adj* Baptist ‖ *mf* Baptist; baptizer; **el Bautista** John the Baptist
bautisterio *m* baptistery
bautizar §60 *tr* to baptize; (*el vino*) water
bautizo *m* baptism; christening party
báva•ro -ra *adj & mf* Bavarian
Baviera *f* Bavaria
baya *f* berry
bayeta *f* baize
ba•yo -ya *adj* bay ‖ *m* bay horse ‖ *f* see **baya**
bayoneta *f* bayonet
bayonetear *tr* to bayonet
bayunca *f* or **bayuna** *f* (CAm) bar; tavern
baza *f* trick; **meter baza en** to butt into
bazar *m* bazaar
ba•zo -za *adj* yellowish-brown ‖ *m* yellowish brown; spleen ‖ *f* see **baza**
bazofia *f* refuse, offal, garbage
bazuca *f* bazooka
bazucar §73 *tr* to stir, shake; tamper with
BC *f* (letterword) (**banda ciudadana**) CB (citizens' band)
be *m* baa
beata *f* lay sister
beatería *f* cant, hypocrisy
beatificar §73 *tr* to beatify
beatísi•mo -ma *adj* most holy
bea•to -ta *adj* blessed; pious, devout; bigoted, prudish ‖ *mf* beatified person; devout person; bigot; churchgoer ‖ *f* see **beata**
bebé *m* baby; doll
bebede•ro -ra *adj* (archaic) drinkable ‖ *m* watering place; (Col, Ecuad, Mex) watering trough
bebedi•zo -za *adj* drinkable ‖ *m* potion, philter
bebe•dor -dora *adj* drinking ‖ *mf* drinker; hard drinker
beber *m* drink, drinking ‖ *tr & intr* to drink; **beber de** or **en** to drink out of ‖ *ref* to drink, drink up; (*p.ej., un libro*) to drink in
bebestible *adj* drinkable ‖ *m* drink
bebezón *f* (Col) drunk, spree
bebible *adj* drinkable
bebi•do -da *adj* tipsy, unsteady ‖ *f* drink
bebistrajo *m* dose, mixture
beborrotear *intr* to tipple
beca *f* scholarship, fellowship; (*de los colegiales*) sash
becacín *m* snipe, whole snipe
becacina *f* snipe, great snipe
becada *f* woodcock
beca•rio -ria *mf* scholar, fellow
becerra *f* snapdragon
becerrillo *m* calfskin
bece•rro -rra *mf* yearling calf ‖ *m* calfskin ‖ *f* see **becerra**
becuadro *m* (mus) natural sign
bedel *m* beadle
befa *f* jeer, flout, scoff
befar *tr* to jeer at, to scoff at ‖ *intr* (*un caballo*) to move the lips
be•fo -fa *adj* blobber-lipped; knock-kneed ‖ *m* (*de animal*) lip ‖ *f* see **befa**
behaviorismo *m* behaviorism
beisbol or **béisbol** *m* baseball
beisbolero *m* or **beisbolista** *m* baseball player
bejuco *m* cane, liana
beldad *f* beauty
beldar §2 *tr* to winnow
belén *m* crèche; bedlam, confusion; madhouse; gossip ‖ **Belén** Bethlehem
bel•fo -fa *adj* (*labio*) blobber; blobber-lipped ‖ *m* (*de animal*) lip; blobber lip
belga *adj & mf* Belgian
Bélgica *f* Belgium
bélgi•co -ca *adj* Belgian ‖ *f* see **Bélgica**
belicista *mf* warmonger
béli•co -ca *adj* warlike
belico•so -sa *adj* bellicose
beligerante *adj & mf* belligerent
belitre *adj* low, mean ‖ *m* scoundrel
bella•co -ca *adj* cunning, sly; wicked ‖ *mf* scoundrel
bellaquear *intr* to cheat, be crooked; (SAm) to be stubborn; rear
bellaquería *f* cunning, slyness; wickedness
belleza *f* beauty; **belleza exótica** glamour girl

be•llo -lla *adj* beautiful, fair
bellota *f* acorn; carnation bud
bem•bo -ba *adj* thick-lipped; (Mex) simple, silly || *mf* (*persona*) thicklips
bemol *adj & m* (mus) flat; **tener bemoles** to be a tough job
bencedrina *f* benzedrine
bencina *f* benzine
bendecir §11 *tr* to bless; consecrate; **bendecir la mesa** to say grace
bendición *f* benediction, blessing; godsend; (*en la mesa*) grace; **bendiciones** wedding ceremony; **echar la bendicióna** to have nothing more to do with
bendi•to -ta *adj* blessed, saintly; simple, silly; happy; (*agua*) holy; **como el pan bendito** as easy as pie || *m* simple-minded soul
benedícite *m* grace; **rezar el benedícite** to say grace
benedicti•no -na *adj & mf* Benedictine || *m* benedictine
beneficencia *f* beneficience; charity, welfare; social service
beneficia•do -da *mf* person or charity receiving the proceeds of a benefit performance
beneficiar *tr* to benefit; (*la tierra*) cultivate; (*una mina*) work, exploit; (*minerales*) process, reduce; (*una región del país*) serve; season; slaughter || *ref* — **beneficiarse de** to take advantage of
beneficia•rio -ria *mf* beneficiary
beneficio *m* benefit; profit, gain, yield; (*de una mina*) exploitation; smelting, ore reduction; benefit performance; **a beneficio de** for the benefit of; on the strength of; **beneficios sociales** fringe benefits
beneficio•so -sa *adj* beneficial, profitable
benéfi•co -ca *adj* charitable, benevolent
beneméri•to -ta *adj & mf* worthy; **benemérito de la patria** national hero
beneplácito *m* approval, consent
benevolencia *f* benevolence
benévo•lo -la *adj* benevolent, kind-hearted
bengala *f* Bengal light; (aer) flare
benignidad *f* benignity, mildness, kindness; (*del tiempo*) mildness
benig•no -na *adj* benign, mild, kind; (*tiempo*) clement, mild
benjamín *m* baby (*the youngest child*)
beodez *f* drunkenness
beo•do -da *adj & mf* drunk
bequista *mf* (CAm, Cuba) scholarship holder; grant winner
berbi•quí *m* (*pl* **-quíes**) brace; **berbiquí y barrena** brace and bit
berenjena *f* eggplant
berenjenal *m* eggplant patch; (coll) predicament, jam, fix
bergante *m* scoundrel, rascal
bergantín *m* (naut) brig; **bergantín goleta** (naut) brigantine
berilio *m* beryllium
berkelio *m* berkelium
berli•nés -nesa *adj* Berlin || *mf* Berliner
bermejear *intr* to turn bright red; look bright red
berme•jo -ja *adj* vermilion, bright-red
berme•jón -jona *adj* red, reddish
bermellón *m* vermilion
Bermudas, las Bermuda
berrear *intr* to bellow, low; bawl, yowl
berrenchín *m* rage, tantrum
berrido *m* bellow; scream, yowl
berrín *m* touchy person, cross child
berrinche *m* tantrum, conniption
berro *m* water cress
berza *f* cabbage
berzal *m* cabbage patch
berzas *m* or **berzotas** *m* dunderhead, flop
besalamano *m* (obs) announcement, written in the third person and marked B.L.M. (*kisses your hand*)
besamanos *m* levee, reception at court; throwing kisses; kissing the hand
besar *tr* to kiss; to graze || *ref* to bump heads together
beso *m* kiss; **beso francés** French kiss; **beso sonado** noisy kiss
bestia *adj* stupid || *mf* dunce || *f* beast; **bestia de carga** beast of burden
bestial *adj* beastly; (coll) terrific
besucar §73 *tr & intr* to keep on kissing || *ref* (coll) to neck, smooch
besu•cón -cona *adj* kissing || *mf* kisser
besuquear *tr & intr* to keep on kissing || *ref* (coll) to neck, smooch
betabel *m* (Mex) beet
betún *m* bitumen, pitch; shoe polish
bezo *m* blubber lip; proud flesh
bezu•do -da *adj* thick-lipped
biberón *m* nursing bottle
Biblia *f* Bible
bíbli•co -ca *adj* Biblical
bibliófi•lo -la *mf* bibliophile
bibliografía *f* bibliography
bibliógra•fo -fa *mf* bibliographer
biblioteca *f* library; **biblioteca de consulta** reference library; **biblioteca de préstamo, biblioteca circulante** lending library
bibliotecario -ria *mf* librarian
bibliotecnia *f* bookmaking; library science
biblioteconomía *f* library science
BIC *f* (acronym) (**Brigada de Investigación Criminal**) (*equivalent to the*) FBI (**Federal Bureau of Investigation**)
bicameral *adj* bicameral
bicarbonato *m* bicarbonate
bicherío *m* (SAm) vermin
bichero *m* boat hook
bicho *m* bug, insect; vermin; animal; fighting bull; simpleton; brat; **bicho viviente** living soul; **mal bicho** scoundrel; ferocious bull
bici *f* (coll) bike
bicicleta *f* bicycle
bidireccional *adj* bidirectional
bidón *m* (*bote, lata*) can; (*tonel de metal*) drum

biela *f* connecting rod
bielda *f* winnowing rack; winnowing
bieldar *tr* to winnow
bieldo *m* winnowing pitch rake
bien *adv* well; readily; very; indeed; all right; **ahora bien** now then; **bien como** just as; **bien que** although; **más bien** rather; somewhat; **no bien** as soon as; scarcely || *s* welfare; property; darling; **bienes** wealth, riches, possessions; **bienes de equipo** capital goods; **bienes de fortuna** worldly possessions; **bienes dotales** dower; **bienes inmuebles** real estate; **bienes muebles** personal property; **bienes raíces** real estate; **bienes relictos** estate; **bienes semovientes** livestock; **bien público** commonweal; **en bien de** for the sake of
bienal *adj* biennial
bienama•do -da *adj* dearly beloved
bienandanza *f* happiness, prosperity
bienaventura•do -da *adj* happy, blissful; blessed; simple
bienaventuranza *f* happiness, bliss; blessedness
bienestar *m* well-being, welfare
bienhabla•do -da *adj* well-spoken
bienhada•do -da *adj* fortunate, lucky
bienhe•chor -chora *adj* beneficent || *m* benefactor || *f* benefactress
bienintenciona•do -da *adj* well-meaning
bienio *m* biennium
bienquerencia *f* affection, fondness
bienquistar *tr* to bring together, reconcile
bienvenida *f* safe arrival; welcome; **dar la bienvenida a** to welcome
bienveni•do -da *adj* welcome || *f* see **bienvenida**
bienvivir *intr* to live in comfort; live decently, properly
bife (Arg, Bol, Urug) steak
bif•tec *m* (*pl* **-tecs**) beefsteak
bifurcar §73 *ref* to branch, fork
bigamia *f* bigamy
bíga•mo -ma *adj* bigamous || *mf* bigamist
bigornia *f* two-horn anvil
bigote *m* mustache; **bigotes** (*del gato*) whiskers; **tener bigotes** to have a mind of one's own
bigudí *m* hair curler
bikini *m* bikini (swimsuit)
bilingüe *adj* bilingual
bilis *f* bile; **descargar la bilis** to vent one's spleen
billar *m* billiards; billiard table; billiard room; **billar romano** pinball
billete *m* ticket; note, bill; **billete de abono** season ticket; commutation ticket; **billete de banco** bank note; **billete de ida y vuelta** round-trip ticket; **billete kilométrico** mileage ticket; **billete sencillo, billete de ida** one-way ticket; **medio billete** half fare
billetero *m* billfold; ticket agent
billón *m* (U.S.A.) trillion; (Brit) billion
bilma *f* (med) compresa
bimotor *adj* twin-motor || *m* twin-motor plane
bina•rio -ria *adj & m* binary
biodegradable *adj* biodegradable
bioéti•co -ca *adj* bioethical || *f* bioethics
biofísi•co -ca *adj* biophysical || *f* biophysics
biogenética *f* genetic engineering
biografía *f* biography
biógra•fo -fa *mf* biographer
bioingeniería *f* bioengineering
biología *f* biology
biólo•go -ga *mf* biologist
biomba *m* folding screen
biomédi•co -ca *adj* biomedical
biometría *f* biometrics
biométri•co -ca *adj* biometric
biónico -ca *adj* bionic
bioplasma *f* bioplasm
biopsia *f* biopsy
bioquími•co -ca *adj* biochemical || *mf* biochemist || *f* biochemistry
bioscopía *f* bioscopy
biosfera, biósfera *f* biosphere
biotecnología *f* biotechnology
bioterrorismo *m* bioterrorism
bióxido *m* dioxide; **bióxido de carbona** carbon dioxide
bip *m* bip
bipartición *f* fission, splitting
bípe•do -da *adj & mf* biped; human
biplano *m* biplane
biplaza *m* (aer) two-seater
birimbao *m* jews'-harp
birlar *tr* to knock down, shoot down; outwit; **birlar algo a alguien** to snitch something from someone
birlocha *f* kite
Birmania *f* Burma
birma•no -na *adj & mf* Burmese
biro *m* or **birome** *f* (Arg) ballpoint pen
birreta *f* biretta, red biretta
birrete *m* mortarboard, academic cap
bis *adj* (*en direcciones*) A, 1/2, e.g., **24 bis** 24a; 24 1/2 || *adv* bis, repeat; twice || *interj* encore! || *m* encore
bisabue•lo -la *mf* great-grandparent || *m* great-grandfather || *f* great-grandmother
bisagra *f* hinge
bisar *tr* to repeat
bisbisar *tr* to mutter, mumble
bisecar §73 *tr* to bisect
bisel *m* bevel edge
biselar *tr* to bevel
bisexual *adj & mf* bisexual
bisies•to -ta *adj* leap
bismuto *m* bismuth
bisnie•to -ta *mf* great-grandchild || *m* great-grandson || *f* great-granddaughter
biso•jo -ja *adj* squint-eyed, cross-eyed
bisonte *m* bison; buffalo
biso•ño -ña *adj* green, inexperienced || *mf* greenhorn, rookie
bisté *m* or **bistec** *m* beefsteak
bisun•to -ta *adj* dirty, greasy
bisutería *f* costume jewelry
bit *m* (compu) bit
bitácora *f* binnacle

bitoque *m* bung; (CAm) sewer; (Mex) spigot
Bizancio Byzantium
bizanti•no -na *adj & mf* Byzantine
bizarría *f* gallantry, bravery; magnanimity
biza•rro -rra *adj* gallant, brave; magnanimous
bizcar §73 *tr* to wink || *intr* to squint
biz•co -ca *adj* squint-eyed, cross-eyed
bizcocho *m* biscuit; cake, sponge cake; hardtack; bisque
bizma *f* poultice
bizmar *tr* to poultice
biznie•to -ta *mf* var of **bisnieto**
bizquear *intr* to squint
bizquera *f* squint
blanca *f* steel blade; **sin blanca** penniless
blanca•zo -za *adj* whitish
blan•co -ca *adj* white; (*tez*) fair; (*fuerza*) water; (*arma*) steel; (*cobarde*) yellow; blank || *mf* (*persona*) white; coward || *m* (*color*) white; blank; target; aim, object; interval; white heat; blank form; **dar en el blanco** to hit the mark; **en blanco** (*hoja*) blank; **hacer blanco** to hit the mark; **quedarse en blanco** to not get the point; to be disappointed || *f* see **blanca**
blancor *m* whiteness
blancura *f* whiteness; purity
blancuz•co -ca *adj* whitish; dirty-white
blandear *tr* to persuade; brandish || *intr & ref* to yield, give in
blandengue *adj* soft, colorless
blandir §1 *tr, intr & ref* to brandish
blan•do -da *adj* bland, soft; indulgent; flabby; sensual; cowardly; (*ojos*) tender
blandón *m* wax candle; candlestick
blandura *f* blandness, softness; tolerance; flabbiness; sensuality; flattery; mild weather; cowardice
blanqueadura *f* whitening; bleaching; whitewash
blanquear *tr* to whiten, bleach; blanch; whitewash; tin; (*dinero*) to launder; (*objetos robados*) to fence || *intr* to turn white
blanqueci•no -na *adj* whitish
blanqui•llo -lla *adj* white, whitish || *m* (Guat, Mex) egg; (Chile, Peru) white peach
blasfemar *tr* to blaspheme, curse
blasfemia *f* blasphemy
blasfe•mo -ma *adj* blasphemous || *mf* blasphemer
blasón *m* (*ciencia de los escudos de armas; escudo de armas*) heraldry; (heral) charge; (fig) glory, honor
blasonar *tr* to emblazon; (fig) to emblazon, extol || *intr* to boast; **blasonar de** to boast of being
bledo *m* straw; **no me importa un bledo** or **no se me da un bledo de ello** that doesn't matter a rap to me
blindaje *m* armor; (elec) shield
blindar *tr* to armor, armor-plate; (elec) to shield
B.L.M. *abbr* **besalamano**
bloc *m* (*pl* **bloques**) pad
blof *m* bluff
blofear *intr* to bluff
blon•do -da *adj* blond, fair, flaxen, light; (Arg) curly || *f* blond lace
bloque *m* block; (*de papel*) pad; **bloque de hormigón** concrete block
bloquear *tr* to blockade; (*un coche, un tren*) brake; (*créditos*) freeze
bloqueo *m* blockade; block; (*de crédito*) freezing; **bloqueo vertical** (telv) vertical hold
b.l.p. *abbr* **besa los pies**
blujins *mpl* blue jeans
blusa *f* blouse, smock; (*de mujer*) shirtwaist; (Col) jacket
boardilla *f* dormer window; garret
boato *m* show, pomp
bobada *f* folly, piece of folly
bobalías *mf* simpleton, dunce
bobali•cón -cona *adj* simple, silly || *mf* simpleton, nitwit
bobear *intr* to talk nonsense; to dawdle, loiter around
bobería *f* folly, nonsense
bóbilis—de bóbilis free, for nothing; without effort
bobina *f* bobbin; (elec) coil; **bobina de chispas** spark coil; **bobina de encendido** ignition coil, spark coil; **bobina de sintonía** tuning coil
bobinar *tr* to wind
bo•bo -ba *adj* simple, foolish, stupid || *mf* simpleton, fool || *m* (archaic) clown, jester
boca *f* mouth; speech; taste, flavor; (*del estómago*) pit; **a boca de jarro** immoderately; at close range; **boca de agua** hydrant; **boca de dragón** (bot) snapdragon; **boca de expendio** sales outlet; **boca de incendios** fire hydrant; **boca del estómago** (coll) pit of the stomach; **boca de metro** subway entrance; **boca de riego** hydrant; **buscarle a uno la boca** to draw someone out; **decir con la boca chica** to offer as a mere formality; **no decir esta boca es mía** to not say a word
bocacalle *f* street entrance; intersection
boca•caz *m* (*pl* **-caces**) spillway
bocadillo *m* tape, ribbon; snack, bite; balloon (*in cartoons*); sandwich
bocadito *m* little bit; (Cuba) cigarillo (*cigaret wrapped in tobacco*)
bocado *m* bite, morsel; bit; **bocado de Adán** Adam's apple; **no tener para un bocado** to not have a cent
bocal *m* narrow-mouthed pitcher; (*de un puerto*) narrows
bocallave *f* keyhole
bocamanga *f* cuff, wristband
bocanada *f* (*de líquido*) swallow; (*de humo*) puff; (*de viento*) gust; boasting
bocartear *tr* to crush, stamp
bocaza *f* loudmouth; gossip
bocera *f* smear on lips
boceto *m* sketch, outline; wax model, clay model
bocha *f* bowling ball

bochar *tr* (Mex, Ven) to turn down; (Mex, Ven) insult
boche *m* small hole in ground for boys' game; (Ven) slight, snub
bochinche *m* uproar, tumult, row
bochorno *m* sultry weather; blush, embarrassment, shame
bochorno•so -sa *adj* sultry, stuffy, sweltering; embarrassing, shameful
bocina *f* horn, trumpet; auto horn; phonograph horn; ear trumpet
bocio *m* goiter
bocoy *m* large barrel
boda *f* marriage, wedding; **bodas de Camacho** banquet, lavish feast; **bodas de oro** golden anniversary
bodega *f* wine cellar; dock warehouse; granary; grocery store; (*de nave*) hold; cellar; (*hombre que bebe mucho*) tank
bodegón *m* hash house, beanery; saloon; still life
bodegue•ro -ra *mf* cellarer; grocer
bodijo *m* unequal match; simple wedding
bodoque *m* lump; dunce, dolt; (Mex) bump, lump
bodoquera *f* peashooter
bodrio *m* (slang) (theat) turkey; **un bodrio** (coll) garbage
bóer *mf* Boer
bofe *adj invar* (CAm) unpleasant, disgusting || *m* (coll) lung; (P-R) cinch, snap; **echar el bofe** or **los bofes** to drudge, to grind; **bofes** lights (*of sheep, etc.*)
bofetada *f* slap in the face
boga *mf* rower || *f* vogue, fashion; rowing
bogar §44 *intr* to row
bogavante *m* lobster
bohardilla *f* dormer window; garret
bohe•mio -mia *adj & mf* Bohemian
bohío *m* hut, shack
boicotear *tr* to boycott
boicoteo *m* boycott, boycotting
boina *f* beret
boj *m* boxwood
boja *f* southernwood
bojar *tr* to measure the perimeter of; (*el cuero*) scrape clean || *intr* to measure
bola *f* ball; marble; bowling; shoe polish; shoeshine; (cards) grand slam; lie, deceit; (Mex) brawl, riot; **bola de alcanfor** moth ball; **bola de cristal** crystal ball; **bola de nieve** snowball; **bola de partido** match point; **bola rompedora** wrecking ball; **bolas** Gaucho lasso tipped with balls; **dejar que ruede la bola** to let things take their course; **raspar la bola** (Chile) to clear out, beat it
bolada *f* (*de una bola*) throw; luck, opportunity; (Arg) billiard stroke; (Chile) dainty, tidbit; (Guat, Mex) lie, fib
bolado *m* (CAm) rumor
bolazo *m* hit with a ball; **de bolazo** (coll) hurriedly, right away; (Mex) at random
bolchevique *adj & mf* Bolshevik
bolchevismo *m* Bolshevism
boleada *f* (Arg) hunting with bolas; (Mex) shoeshine; (Peru) flunking
bolear *tr* to throw; (Arg) to catch with bolas; (*zapatos*) (Mex) to shine; (SAm) to kick out, flunk || *intr* to play for fun; lie; boast || *ref* (Arg, Urug) to rear and fall backwards; upset; blush
bole•ro -ra *mf* bolero dancer || *m* bolero (*dance; music; jacket*); (Mex) bootblack || *f* bowling alley; **bolera encespada** bowling green
boleta *f* pass, permit, admission ticket; (mil) billet; ballot
boletería *f* ticket office
boletín *m* bulletin; ticket; form; press release; **boletín de calificiones, boletín de notas** report card; **boletín informativo, boletín de noticias** news bulletin
boleto *m* ticket
boliche *m* bowling; bowling alley; (SAm) hash house
bólido *m* fireball, bolide
bolígrafo *m* ballpoint pen
bolilápiz *m* (Mex) ballpoint pen
bolillo *m* bobbin for making lace; frame for stiffening lace cuffs
Bolivia *f* Bolivia
bolivia•no -na *adj & mf* Bolivian
bollo *m* bun, roll; bump, lump; dent; (*en un vestido*) puff; (*en adorno de tapicería*) tuft; **bollo de crema** cream puff
bo•lo -la *adj* (CAm, Mex) drunk; *m* ninepin, tenpin; dunce, blockhead; (*de escalera*) newel; (cards) slam; **bolos** bowling, ninepins, tenpins; **jugar a los bolos** to bowl
Bolonia *f* Bologna
bolsa *f* purse, pocketbook; pouch; stock exchange, stock market; (*en el vestido*) bag, pucker; grant, award; **bolsa de agua caliente** hotwater bottle; **bolsa de aguas** amnion; **bolsa de aire** (aut) air bag; **bolsa de comercio** commodity exchange; **bolsa de dormir** sleeping bag; **bolsa de hielo** ice bag; **bolsa de la compra** shopping bag; **bolsa de trabajo** employment bureau; **bolsa isotérmica** Thermos bottle; **bolsa negra** black market; **hacer bolsa** (*un vestido*) to bag; **jugar a la bolsa** to play the market
bolsear *tr* to pick the pocket of; (Arg, Bol, Urug) to jilt; (Chile) to sponge on
bolsero *m* (SAm) sponger; (Mex) pickpocket
bolsicalculadora *f* pocket calculator
bolsillo *m* pocket; purse, pocketbook
bolsista *m* broker, stockbroker, (CAm, Mex) pickpocket
bolsita *f* small bag; **bolsita de té** teabag
bolso *m* purse, pocketbook; **bolso de mano** handbag
bomba *f* pump; bomb; fire engine; lamp globe; high hat; firecracker; soap bubble; bombshell; (compu) bomb; **a prueba de bombas** bombproof; **bomba atómica** atomic bomb; **bomba coche** car bomb; **bomba cohete** rocket bomb;

bomba corazón-pulmón heart-lung machine; **bomba de aire** air pump; **bomba de engrase** grease gun; **bomba de hidrógeno** hydrogen bomb; **bomba de incendios** fire engine; **bomba de profundidad** depth bomb; **bomba de sentina** bilge pump; **bomba estomacal** stomach pump; **bomba neutrónica** neutron bomb; **bomba rompedora** blockbuster; **bomba volante** buzz bomb; **caer como una bomba** to fall like a bombshell; to burst in unexpectedly
bombachas *fpl* loose-fitting baggy trousers
bombardear *tr & intr* to bomb; bombard; **bombardear en picado** to dive-bomb
bombardeo *m* bombing; bombarding; **bombardeo en picado** dive bombing; **bombardeo por saturación** carpet bombing
bombardero *m* bomber; bombardier
bomba-reloj *f* time bomb
bombazo *m* bomb explosion; bomb hit; bomb damage
bombear *tr* to bomb; ballyhoo, puff up; pump; (SAm) to reconnoiter; (Col) to fire, dismiss || *ref* to camber, bulge
bombero *m* fireman; pumpman
bombilla *f* bulb, light bulb; lamp chimney; tube for sucking up maté; **bombilla de flash** flashbulb
bombillo *m* trap, stench trap; (naut) pump; (CAm, Col, Ven) light bulb
bombista *m* lamp maker, (*el que da bombos*) booster
bombita *f* (SAm) light bulb
bom•bo -ba *adj* astounded, stunned; (W-I) lukewarm || *m* bass drum; ballyhoo; (naut) barge, lighter; **dar bombo a** to ballyhoo, puff up; **irse al bombo** (Arg) to fail || *f* see **bomba**
bombón *m* bonbon, candy; (coll) cutie
bombona *f* carboy
bombonera *f* candy box
bona•chón -chona *adj* goodnatured, kind, simple
bonancible *adj* (*tiempo*) fair; (*mar*) calm; (*viento*) moderate
bonanza *f* fair weather, calm seas; prosperity, boom; rich ore pocket
bona•zo -za *adj* kind-hearted
bondad *f* kindness; favor; **tener la bondad de** to have the kindness to
bondado•so -sa *adj* kind, generous
bonete *m* cap, hat; candy bowl
bonetería *f* hat shop; notion store
bongo *m* (SAm) barge; canoe
boniato *m* sweet potato
bonificar §73 *tr* to improve; give a discount on
boni•to -ta *adj* pretty, nice; pretty good
bono *m* bond; voucher, certificate; **bonos alimenticios** food stamps
boñiga *f* manure, cow dung
boom *m* (*mercado, bolsa*) boom
boqueada *f* gasp of death
boquear *tr* to pronounce, utter || *intr* to gasp
boquerel *m* nozzle
boquete *m* gap, breach, opening
boquiabier•to -ta *adj* open-mouthed
boquian•cho -cha *adj* wide-mouthed
boquiangos•to -ta *adj* narrow-mouthed
boquihundi•do -da *adj* hollow-mouthed
boquilla *f* (*de instrumento de viento*) mouthpiece; (*de pipa*) stem; (*de cigarro*) tip; (*de aparato de alumbrado*) burner; cigar holder, cigarette holder; (*de manguera*) nozzle; opening in irrigation canal; opening at bottom of trouser leg
boquirro•to -ta *adj* garrulous
boquiverde *adj* obscene, smutty
bórax *m* borax
borbollar or **borbollear** *intr* to bubble up
borbollón *m* bubbling; **a borbollones** impetuously
borborigmos *mpl* rumbling of the bowels
borbotar *intr* to bubble up, bubble over
borce•guí *m* (*pl* **-guíes**) high shoe
borda *f* hut; (naut) gunwale; **arrojar, echar** or **tirar por la borda** to throw overboard
bordada *f* (naut) tack; **dar bordadas** (naut) to tack; pace to and fro
bordado *m* embroidery
bordadura *f* embroidery
bordar *tr* to embroider
borde *m* border, edge; fringe; rim; **borde de la acera** curb; **borde del mar** seaside
bordear *tr* to border || *intr* to go on the edge; (naut) to tack
borde•lés -lesa *adj* of Bordeaux || *mf* native of Bordeaux; Bordelais; **bordeleses** inhabitants of Bordeaux
bordo *m* (naut) board; (naut) side; (naut) tack; (Guat, Mex) dam, dike; **a bordo** (naut) on board; **al bordo** (naut) alongside; **de alto bordo** seagoing; distinguished, important
bordón *m* (*de tambor*) snare; pilgrim's staff; pet word; burden, refrain
bordonear *intr* to grope along with a stick; to go around begging
borgoña *m* Burgundy (*wine*) || **la Borgoña** Burgundy
borgo•ñón -ñona *adj & mf* Burgundian
boricua or **borinque•ño -ña** *adj & mf* Puerto Rican
borla *f* tassel; powder puff; **tomar la borla** to take a higher degree, take the doctor's degree
borne *m* binding post; (*de la lanza*) tip
bornear *tr* to bend, twist; (*sillares pesados*) set in place || *intr* to swing at anchor || *ref* to warp
borra *f* fuzz, nap, lint
borrachera *f* drunkenness; spree, binge; great exaltation; (coll) piece of folly; **pegarse una borrachera** to go on a binge
borrachería *f* (Mex) bar, tavern
borrachín *m* drunkard
borra•cho -cha *adj* drunk; (*habitualmente*) drinking || *mf* drunkard
borrador *m* blotter, day book; rough draft; eraser
borradura *f* striking out, scratching out

borraj *m* borax
borrajear *tr & intr* to scribble; doodle
borrar *tr* to scratch out, cross out; erase, rub out; darken, obscure; blot, smear
borrasca *f* storm, tempest; upset, setback
borrasco•so -sa *adj* stormy
borregos *mpl* fleecy clouds
borrica *f* she-ass; stupid woman
borrico *m* ass, donkey; sawhorse; stupid fellow, ass
borricón *m* or **borricote** *m* drudge
borrón *m* blot; rough draft; blemish; (fig) blot, stain
borronear *tr* to scribble
borro•so -sa *adj* blurred, smudgy, fuzzy; muddy, thick
boruca *f* noise, clamor, uproar
borujo *m* lump, clump
boscaje *m* woodland; (paint) woodland scene
bosque *m* forest, woodland; **bosque ecuatorial** *or* **pluvial** rain forest; **bosque maderable** timberland
bosquejar *tr* to sketch, outline; make a rough model of
bosquejo *m* sketch, outline; rough model
bostezar §60 *intr* to yawn, gape
bostezo *m* yawn, yawning
bota *f* shoe, boot; leather wine bag; liquid measure (*125 gallons or 516 liters*); **bota de agua** gum boot, rubber boot; **bota de esquiar** or **de esquí** ski boot; **bota de montar** riding boot; **ponerse las botas** (coll) to hit the jack pot, come out on top
botador *m* boat pole; punch, nailset
botadura *f* launching
botafuego *m* hothead, firebrand
botalón *m* (naut) boom; **botalón de foque** (naut) jib boom
botáni•co -ca *adj* botanical || *mf* botanist || *f* botany
botanista *mf* botanist
botar *tr* to throw, hurl; throw away, throw out; (*un buque*) launch; (*el timón*) shift; fire, dismiss; squander || *intr* to jump; bounce || *ref* (*un caballo*) to buck
botarate *m* madcap, wild man; spendthrift
bote *m* boat, small boat; can, jar, pot; bounce; blow, thrust; (Mex) jug, jail; **bote de paso** ferryboat; **bote de porcelana** apothecary's jar; **bote de remos** rowboat; **bote de salvamento** or **bote salvavidas** lifeboat; **de bote en bote** crowded, jammed; **de bote y voleo** thoughtlessly
botella *f* bottle
botica *f* drug store; medicine
botica•rio -ria *mf* druggist, apothecary
botija *f* earthenware jug with short narrow neck; (CAm, Ven) hidden treasure; (SAm) belly; **decirle a uno botija verde** (Cuba) to let someone have it, tell someone off; **estar hecho una botija** (*un niño*) to be cross and scream; (*una persona*) be fat, be pudgy
botijo *m* earthenware jar with spout and handle
botín *m* booty, plunder, spoils; spat, legging; (Chile) sock
botina *f* shoe, high shoe
botiquín *m* medicine kit, first-aid kit; medicine chest; first-aid station; (Ven) saloon
bo•to -ta *adj* (*sin filo o punta*) blunt, dull; (fig) dull, slow || *m* leather bag || *f* see **bota**
botón *m* button; (*de mueble o puerta*) knob; (*de reloj de bolsillo*) stem; (bot) bud; (compu) button; (elec) push button, switch; **apretar el botón del inodoro** to flush the toilet; **botón de oro** buttercup; **botón de puerta** doorknob; **botones** *msg* bellboy, bellhop
bou *m* fishing with a dragnet between two boats
bóveda *f* dome, vault; crypt; (aut) cowl; **bóveda celeste** canopy of heaven; **bóveda de seguridad** bank vault
boxeador *m* boxer; (Mex) brass knuckles
boxear *intr* to box
boxeo *m* boxing
bóxer *m* brass knuckles
boxibalón *m* punching bag
boya *f* buoy; **boya salvavidas** life buoy
boyante *adj* buoyant; lucky, successful; (*que no cala lo que debe calar*) (naut) light
boyera *f* or **boyeriza** *f* ox stable
boyerizo *m* or **boyero** *m* ox driver
boy scout [bojesˈkaut] *m* boy scout
bozal *adj* simple, stupid || *m* muzzle; head-harness bells; headstall
bozo *m* down on upper lip; lips, mouth; headstall
B.p. *abbr* **Bendición papal**
Br. *abbr* **bachiller**
bracear *intr* to swing the arms; swim with overhead strokes; struggle
brace•ro -ra *adj* arm, hand; thrown with the hand || *m* man who offers his arm to a lady; day laborer; migrant worker; **de bracero** arm in arm
bra•co -ca *adj* pug-nosed
braga *f* diaper, clout; hoisting rope; **bragas** panties, step-ins; breeches; **calzarse las bragas** to wear the pants
bragadura *f* crotch
braga•zas *m* (*pl* **-zas**) easy mark, henpecked fellow
braguero *m* (*para hernias*) truss; (*entrepiernas*) crotch
bragueta *f* fly
bragui•llas *m* (*pl* **-llas**) brat
Braille *m* Braille, braille
brama *f* rut, mating, mating time
bramante *adj* bellowing, roaring || *m* packthread, twine
bramar *intr* to bellow, roar; (*el viento*) howl; rage, storm
bramido *m* bellow, roar; howling; raging
brasa *f* live coal, red-hot coal
brasero *m* brazier; (Col) bonfire; (Mex) hearth, fireplace
Brasil, el Brazil
brasile•ño -ña *adj & mf* Brazilian

bravata *f* bravado, bragging; **echar bravatas** to talk big
bravatear *intr* to brag, boast
bravear *intr* to talk big, four-flush
braveza *f* bravery; ferocity; (*de los elementos*) fury, violence
braví•o -a *adj* ferocious; wild, untamed, uncultivated; crude, unpolished; (*mar*) rough, wild; (*terreno*) rough, rugged
bra•vo -va *adj* (*valiente*) brave; fine, excellent; fierce, savage, wild; (*mar*) rough; magnificent; angry, mad; (*perro*) vicious; (*toro*) game; boasting; (*chili*) strong || *interj* bravo!, ole!, olé!
bravu•cón -cona *adj* four-flushing || *mf* four-flusher
bravura *f* bravery; fierceness; gameness; bravado, boasting
braza *f* fathom
brazada *f* stroke, pull (*with the arm*); **brazada de pecho** breast stroke
brazado *m* armful, armload
brazal *m* arm band; **brazal de luto** mourning band
brazalete *m* bracelet
brazo *m* arm; (*de animal*) foreleg; **a brazo partido** hand to hand (*i.e., without weapons*); **asidos del brazo** arm in arm; **brazo de gitano** jelly roll; **brazo de mar** inlet, sound; **brazo derecho** right-hand man; **brazo lector** pickup arm; **brazo político** political wing; **brazos** hands, workmen; backers; **hecho un brazo de mar** dressed to kill
brea *f* tar, wood tar; calking substance; packing canvas; **brea seca** rosin
brear *tr* to annoy, mistreat, beat; tar
brebaje *m* beverage, drink
brecha *f* opening; (*en un muro*) breach; breakthrough; **brecha generacional** generation gap
brécol *m* or **brécoles** *mpl* broccoli
brega *f* fight, struggle, quarrel; trickery; drudgery
bregar §44 *intr* to strive, struggle, toil
breña *f* or **breñal** *m* or **breñar** *m* rocky thicket
breque *m* brake
brequear *tr & intr* to brake
bresca *f* honeycomb
Bretaña *f* Brittany; **la Gran Bretaña** Great Britain
brete *m* fetters, shackles; tight squeeze, fix
bretones *mpl* Brussels sprouts
breva *f* early fig; cinch, snap
breval *m* early-fig tree
breve *adj* brief, short; **en breve** shortly, soon
brevedad *f* brevity, shortness; **a la mayor brevedad** as soon as possible
brevete *m* note, mark
brezal *m* heath, moor
brezo *m* heath, heather
briba *f* loafing; **andar a la briba** to loaf around
bri•bón -bona *adj* loafing, crooked || *mf* loafer, crook, scab, rascal
bribonada *f* loafing, crookedness
bribonear *intr* to loaf around, be crooked
brida *f* bridle
bridge [bridz] *m* (cards) bridge; **bridge contrato** contract bridge; **bridge subastado** auction bridge
brigada *f* brigade; gang, squad; warrant officer; **brigada antiexplosivos** bomb squad; **brigada de salvamentos** rescue team
brillante *adj* bright, brilliant, shining || *m* diamond, gem
brillantez *f* brilliance
brillantina *f* brilliantine; metal polish
brillar *intr* to shine; sparkle
brillazón *f* (Arg, Bol, Urug) pampa mirage
brillo *m* brightness, brilliance; sparkle; **sacar brillo a** to shine
brillo•so -sa *adj* (*que brilla por el mucho uso*) shiny; shining, brilliant
brin *m* canvas
brincar §73 *tr* to bounce up and down; skip, skip over || *intr* to jump, leap; be touchy, get angry easily
brinco *m* bounce; jump, leap; **en dos brincos** or **en un brinco** in an instant
brindador *m* toaster
brindar *tr* to invite; offer; **brindar a uno con una cosa** to offer someone something || *intr* — **brindar a** or **por** to drink to, toast || *ref* — **brindarse a** to offer to
brin•dis *m* (*pl* **-dis**) toast
brío *m* spirit, enterprise; elegance; **cortar los bríos a** to cut the wings of
brio•so -sa *adj* spirited, lively, enterprising; elegant
brisa *f* breeze; residue of pressed grapes
brisera *f* or **brisero** *m* glass lamp shade (*for candles*)
británi•co -ca *adj* British, Britannic
brita•no -na *adj* British || *mf* Briton, Britisher
brizna *f* chip, particle; (Ven) drizzle
brl. *abbr* **barril**
broca *f* reel, spindle; drill, bit
brocado *m* brocade
brocal *m* (*de pozo*) curbstone; (*de bota*) mouthpiece; (*de banqueta*) (Mex) curb
brocamantón *m* diamond brooch
brocha *f* brush; loaded dice; **de brocha gorda** house (*painter*); (coll) crude, heavy-handed
brochada *f* stroke with a brush; rough sketch
brochazo *m* stroke with a brush
broche *m* clasp, clip, fastener; (*conjunto de dos piezas*) hook and eye; (Chile) paper clip; **broche de oro** punch line; **broche de presión** snap, catch; **broches** (Ecuad) cuff buttons
brocheta *f* skewer
bróculi *m* broccoli
broma *f* joke, jest; fun; prank; shipworm; **bromas aparte** joking aside; **en broma** in fun, jokingly; **gastar una broma a** to play a joke on
bromear *intr & ref* to joke, jest; have a good time
bromhídri•co -ca *adj* hydrobromic

bromista *adj* joking || *mf* joker
bromo *m* bromine
bromuro *m* bromide
bronca *f* row, quarrel; rough joke, poor joke; tongue-lashing (coll); **armar una bronca** to start a row
bronce *m* bronze; **bronce de cañón** gun metal
broncea•do -da *adj* bronze; tanned, brown, sunburned || *m* bronzing; bronze finish; tan, sunburn
bronceador *m* suntan lotion
broncear *tr, intr & ref* to bronze; tan, sunburn
bron•co -ca *adj* coarse, rough; gruff, crude; (*voz*) harsh, hoarse || *f* see **bronca**
bronquitis *f* bronchitis
broquel *m* buckler, shield; (fig) shield
broqueta *f* skewer
brota *f* bud, shoot
brotadura *f* budding, sprouting; gushing; (*de la piel*) eruption, rash
brotar *tr* to bring forth, produce || *intr* to bud, sprout; gush; (*la piel*) break out
brote *m* bud, shoot; outbreak; (*de petróleo*) gush, spurt
broza *f* (*maleza*) underbrush; (*hojas, ramas, cortezas*) brushwood; (*desperdicio*) trash, rubbish; printer's brush
bruces — dar or **caer de bruces** to fall on one's face
bruja *f* witch, sorceress; barn owl; (*mujer fea*) hag; (*mujer de mala vida*) prostitute; (W-I) spook
brujear *tr* (*bestias salvajes*) (Ven) to hunt || *intr* to practice witchcraft
brujería *f* witchcraft, sorcery, magic
brujo *m* sorcerer, wizard
brújula *f* (*flechilla*) magnetic needle; (*instrumento*) compass; (*agujero para la puntería*) sight; **perder la brújula** to lose one's touch
brujulear *tr* (*las cartas*) to uncover gradually; suspect
brulote *m* fire ship; (Arg, Chile, Bol) vulgarity, insult
bruma *f* fog, mist
brumo•so -sa *adj* foggy, misty
bruñido *m* burnish, polish; burnishing
bruñir §12 *tr* to burnish, polish; put rouge on; (CAm) to annoy
brus•co -ca *adj* brusque, gruff; sudden; (*curva*) sharp
bruselas *fpl* tweezers || **Bruselas** Brussels
brusquedad *f* brusqueness, gruffness; suddenness; (*de una curva*) sharpness
brutal *adj* brutal; sudden; huge, terrific; stunning
brutalidad *f* brutality; stupidity; tremendous amount
bruteza *f* brutality; (archaic) roughness
bru•to -ta *adj* brute; rough, coarse; stupid; gross || *mf* (*persona*) brute; blockhead || *m* (*animal*) brute
bu *m* (*pl* **búes**) bugaboo; **hacer el bu a** to scare, frighten
buceador *m* or **buceadora** *f* diver
bucear *intr* to dive, be a diver; delve, search
buceo *m* diving
buche *m* (*de ave*) craw, crop, maw; (*de líquido*) mouthful; (*del vestido*) bag, pucker; (*para secretos*) bosom; belly; (Ecuad) high hat; (Guat, Mex) goiter; **sacar el buche a** to make (*someone*) open up
bucle *m* curl, lock
Buda *m* Buddha
budín *m* pudding
buen *adj* var of **bueno,** used before masculine singular nouns
buenamente *adj* with ease; gladly, willingly; conveniently
buenaventura *f* fortune, good luck; (*adivinación*) fortune; **decirle a uno la buenaventura** to tell someone his fortune
bue•no -na *adj* good; kind; (*sano*) well; (*tiempo*) good, fine; all right; **a buenas** willingly; **¡buena es ésa** (or **ésta**)! that's a good one; **¡buena suerte!** good luck!; **de buenas a primeras** all of a sudden; from the start; **¿de dónde bueno?** where have you been?, what's new?
buey *m* ox, bullock, steer
búfa•lo -la *mf* buffalo
bufanda *f* muffler, scarf
bufar *intr* to snort
bufete *m* writing desk; law office; (*de un abogado*) clients; law practice; refreshment; (Col) bedpan; **abrir bufete** to open a law office
buffer *m* (compu) buffer
bufido *m* snort
bu•fo -fa *adj* comic; (Ven) spongy || *mf* buffoon
bu•fón -fona *adj* clownish || *m* clown, buffoon; jester; peddler
bufonada *f* buffoonery; sarcasm
bufonería *f* buffoonery; peddling
bufones•co -ca *adj* clownish; coarse, crude
bugui-bugui *m* boogie-woogie
buharda *f* dormer; dormer window; garret
buhardilla *f* dormer window; garret
búho *m* eagle owl; shy fellow
buhonería *f* peddler's kit; peddler's wares
buhonero *m* peddler, hawker
buitre *m* vulture
buje *m* axle box, bushing
bujería *f* gewgaw, trinket
bujía *f* (auto) spark plug; (phys) candle power; (CAm) light bulb
bulbo *m* bulb
bulevar *m* boulevard
bulevardero *m* boulevardier, man about town
Bulgaria *f* Bulgaria
búlga•ro -ra *adj & mf* Bulgarian
bulimia *f* bulimia
bulín *m* (SAm) (coll) bachelor pad
bulla *f* noise; crowd; loud argument
bullaje *m* crush, mob (*of people*)
bullanga *f* racket, disturbance
bullebulle *mf* busybody, bustler

bulle•ro -ra *adj* noisy; inflammatory
bullicio *m* brawl, riot, uprising; (*rumor que hace mucha gente*) rumble
bullicio•so -sa *adj* brawling, riotous, riproaring (coll); rumbling || *mf* rioter
bullir §13 *tr* to move || *intr* to boil; abound; bustle, hustle; swarm; move, stir; be restless || *ref* to move, stir
bulto *m* bulk, volume; bust, statue; parcel, piece of baggage; bump, swelling; pillowcase; form, mass; **a bulto** broadly, by guess; **buscar el bulto a** to keep after; **de bulto** evident; **escurrir** or **huir el bulto** to duck
bundle *m* (compu) bundle
buniato *m* sweet potato
buñuelo *m* cruller, fritter, bun; botch, bungle
buque *m* ship, vessel; (*de una nave*) hull; (*de cualquier cosa*) capacity; (C-R) doorframe; **buque almirante** admiral; **buque cisterna** tanker; **buque de guerra** warship; **buque de vapor** steamer, steamship; **buque de vela** sailboat; **buque escucha** vedette; **buque escuela** training ship; **buque fanal** or **buque faro** lightship; **buque mercante** merchantman, merchant vessel; **buque portaminas** mine layer; **buque tanque** tanker; **buque velero** sailing vessel
burbuja *f* bubble
burbujear *intr* to bubble
burca *f* (*velo para tapar a una mujer de pies a cabeza*) burqa (*body veil that covers a woman from head to toe*)
burdégano *m* hinny
burdel *m* brothel, disorderly house
burdeos *adj invar* maroon, deep red || *m* claret; Bordeaux wine; maroon, deep red || **el Burdeos** Bordeaux
bur•do -da *adj* coarse, rough
burear *tr* (Col) to fool || *intr* to have fun
burga *f* hot springs
bur•gués -guesa *adj* middle-class, bourgeois; (*antiartístico*) bourgeois || *m* middle-class man || *f* middle-class woman
burguesía *f* middle class, bourgeoisie; **alta burguesía** upper middle class; **pequeña burguesía** lower middle class
burla *f* hoax, trick; joke; ridicule; **burlas aparte** joking aside; **de burlas** in fun, for fun
burladero *m* safety island, safety zone; (*en las plazas de toros*) covert; (*en los túneles*) safety niche; hiding place
burla•dor -dora *adj* joking; deceptive || *mf* wag, prankster, practical joker || *m* seducer, libertine
burlar *tr* to make fun of; deceive; disappoint; outwit, frustrate; (*a una mujer*) seduce || *intr* to scoff || *ref* to joke; **burlarse de** to make fun of
burlería *f* derision, mockery; deception, trick; scorn, derision; fish story
burles•co -ca *adj* funny, comic, burlesque
burlete *m* weather stripping
bur•lón -lona *adj* joking || *mf* joker || *m* mockingbird
bu•ró *m* (*pl* **-rós**) writing desk; (Mex) night table
burócrata *mf* jobholder, bureaucrat
burra *f* she-ass; stupid woman; drudge (*woman*)
burrajear *tr & intr* to scribble; doodle
burra•jo -ja *adj* (Mex) coarse, stupid || *m* dung (*used as fuel*)
bu•rro -rra *adj* stupid, asinine || *m* donkey, jackass; sawbuck, sawhorse; (Mex) stepladder; **burro cargado de letras** learned jackass; **burro de carga** drudge || *f* see **burra**
bus *m* (compu) bus; **bus de control** control bus; **bus de datas** data bus; **bus de direcciones** address bus
bursátil *adj* stock-market
busca *f* search; **en busca de** in search of
busca•dor -dora *mf* searcher; (compu) search engine; **buscador de oro** gold prospector *o* digger
buscani•guas *m* (*pl* **-guas**) (Col) snake
buscapié *m* (*para dar a entender algo*) hint; (*para averiguar algo*) feeler || **busca•piés** *m* (*pl* **-piés**) snake
buscaplei•tos *mf* (*pl* **-tos**) troublemaker
buscar §73 *tr* to seek, hunt, look for; (Mex) to provoke; **buscar tres pies al gato** to be looking for trouble || *ref* to take care of oneself; **buscársela** to manage to get along; to ask for it
buscareta *f* wren
buscarrui•dos *mf* (*pl* **-dos**) troublemaker
buscavi•das *mf* (*pl* **-das**) snoop, busybody; go-getter
bus•cón -cona *adj* searching; cheating || *mf* seeker; thief, cheat; (min) prospector || *f* loose woman
busi•lis *m* (*pl* **-lis**) trouble; **ahí está el busilis** that's the trouble; **dar en el busilis** to hit the nail on the head
búsqueda *f* search, hunt
busto *m* bust
butaca *f* armchair, easy chair; orchestra seat
butifarra *f* Catalonian sausage; loose sock, loose stocking; (Peru) ham and salad sandwich
bution•do -da *adj* lewd, lustful
buuah *interj* boo-hoo!
buz *m* (*pl* **buces**) kiss of gratitude and reverence; lip; **hacer el buz** (archaic) to bow and scrape
buzo *m* diver; (Arg) sweatshirt; (Chile, Peru) sweatsuit
buzón *m* plug, stopper, mailbox, letter box; (*agujero para echar las cartas*) slot, letter drop; **buzón de alcance** special-delivery box; late-collection slot

C

C, c (ce) *f* third letter of the Spanish alphabet
c. *abbr* **capítulo, compañía, corriente, cuenta**
c *abbr* **caja, cargo, contra, corriente**
cabal *adj* exact; full, complete, perfect; **no estar en sus cabales** to be not in one's right mind || *adv* exactly; completely || *interj* right!
cábala *f* intrigue; divination
cabalgada *f* raid on horseback; gathering of riders
cabalgador *m* rider, horseman
cabalgadura *f* mount, horse; beast of burden
cabalgar §44 *intr* to go horseback riding
cabalgata *f* cavalcade
caballa *f* mackerel
caballada *f* drove of horses; nonsense, stupidity
caballaje *m* stud service
caballazo *m* collision of two horses, trampling by a horse; (Chile, Peru) bitter attack
caballerango *m* (Mex) stableman
caballeres•co -ca *adj* chivalric, knightly; gentlemanly
caballerete *m* (coll) dude
caballería *f* mount, horse, mule; cavalry; chivalry, knighthood; **andarse en caballerías** to fall all over oneself in compliments; **caballería andante** knight-errantry; **caballería mayor** horse, mule; **cabellería menor** ass, donkey
caballeriza *f* stable; stable hands
caballerizo *m* groom, stableman
caballe•ro -ra *adj* riding, mounted; stubborn || *m* knight, nobleman; gentleman; mister; horseman, cavalier, rider; **armar caballero** to knight; **caballero andante** knight errant; **caballero de industria** crook, adventurer, sharper; **Caballero de la triste figura** Knight of the Rueful Countenance (*Don Quijote*); **Caballeros** *SIGN* (*servicio de caballeros*) Men (*men's room*); **ir caballero en** to ride
caballerosidad *f* chivalry, gentlemanliness
caballerote *m* boorish fellow, cad
caballete *m* (*bastidor para sostener un cuadro o pizarra*) easel; (*de tejado*) ridge, hip; (*lomo de tierra*) ridge; (*artificio usado como soporte*) trestle, sawbuck, horse; (*de la nariz*) bridge; chimney cap; (*del ave*) breastbone; little horse
caballista *m* horseman; mounted smuggler || *f* horsewoman
caballito *m* rocking horse, hobbyhorse; **caballito de batalla** warhorse (*hackneyed work or idea*); **caballito del diablo** dragonfly; **caballito de mar** sea horse; **caballitos** (Mex) merry-go-round
caballo *m* horse; (*en ajedrez*) knight; playing card (*figure on horseback equivalent to queen*); (slang) heroin; **a caballo** on horseback; **a caballo de** astride; **a caballo regalado no se le mira el diente** never look a gift horse in the mouth; **caballo blanco** (*persona que da dinero para una empresa dudosa*) angel; **caballo de batalla** (*de una controversia*) gist, main point; hobbyhorse; warhorse (*hackneyed work or idea*); **caballo de carreras** race horse; **caballo de fuerza** French horsepower, metric horsepower; **caballo de tiro** draft horse; **caballo de Troya** Trojan horse; **caballo de vapor** French horsepower, metric horsepower; **caballo de vapor inglés** horsepower; **caballo mecedor** rocking horse, hobbyhorse; **caballo padre** stallion; **caballo semental** stallion
caballu•no -na *adj* horse, horselike
cabaña *f* cabin, hut; drove, flock; livestock; pastoral scene; (Arg) cattlebreeding ranch
cabañuelas *fpl* (Arg, Bol) first summer rains; (Mex) winter rains
caba•ret *m* (*pl* **-rets**) cabaret
cabecear *tr* (*un libro*) to put a headband on; (*el vino*) head; (*una media*) put a new foot on || *intr* to nod; bob the head; (*en señal de negación*) shake the head; (*los caballos*) toss the head; (*la caja de un carruaje*) lurch; (*un buque*) pitch
cabeceo *m* (*de la cabeza*) nod, bob, shake; (*de la caja del carruaje*) lurching; (*del buque*) pitch, pitching
cabecera *f* (*de cama, mesa, etc.*) head; bedside; headboard; headwaters; (*de una casa, un campo*) end; (*del capítulo de un libro*) heading; (*de periódico*) headline; capital, county seat; bolster, pillow; (typ) headpiece, vignette; **cabecera de cartel** top billing; **cabecera de puente** (mil) bridgehead
cabecilla *mf* scalawag || *m* ringleader || *f* **cabecilla de alfiler** pinhead
cabellar *intr* to grow hair; to put on false hair || *ref* to put on false hair
cabellera *f* head of hair; foliage; (*del cometa*) coma; (bot) mistletoe
cabello *m* hair; **cabello de Venus** maiden-hair; **cabellos de ángel** cotton candy; **en cabello** with the hair down; **en cabellos** bareheaded; **traído por los cabellos** farfetched
cabellu•do -da *adj* hairy
caber §14 *intr* to fit, go; have enough room; be possible; happen, befall; **no cabe duda** there is no doubt; **no cabe más** that's the limit; **no caber de** to be bursting with; **no caber en sí** to be beside oneself; be puffed up with pride; **todo cabe en** anything can be expected of
cabestrar *tr* to put a halter on
cabestrillo *m* sling
cabestro *m* halter; **llevar** or **traer del cabestro** to lead by the halter; (fig) to lead by the nose
cabeza *f* head; chief city, capital; **cabeza de chorlito** scatterbrains; (Arg) forgetful person; **cabeza de grabación** recording head; **cabeza de lectura** playback head; **cabeza de motín** ringleader; **cabeza de playa** beachhead; **cabeza de puente** bridgehead; **cabeza de turco** butt, scapegoat; **cabeza lectora** playback head; **cabeza mayor** head of cattle; **cabeza menor** head of sheep, goats, etc.; **de cabeza**

headfirst; on end; on one's own; by heart; **ir cabeza abajo** to go downhill; **irse de la cabeza** to go out of one's mind; **mala cabeza** headstrong person; **por su cabeza** on one's own; **romperse la cabeza** to rack one's brains
cabezada *f* butt with the head; blow on the head; (*de buque*) pitch, pitching; (*de bota*) instep; (*de libro*) headband; **dar cabezadas** to nod; (*un buque*) to pitch
cabezal *m* pillow, cushion; bolster; (electron) head; **cabezal de impresión** (compu) printhead
cabezo *m* hillock; summit, peak; reef
cabe•zón -zona *adj* big-headed; stubborn; (*licor*) (Chile) strong || *m* (*en la ropa*) hole for the head; tax register
cabezonada *f* stubbornness
cabezu•do -da *adj* big-headed; headstrong; (*vino*) heady
cabezuela *f* little head; (*harina gruesa del trigo*) middling; cornflower
cabida *f* room, space, capacity; influence, pull; **tener cabida en** to be included in
cabildear *intr* to lobby
cabildeo *m* lobbying
cabildero *m* lobbyist
cabildo *m* chapter (*of a cathedral*); chapter meeting; town hall
cabina *f* cabin; bathhouse, dressing room; **cabina de control** control room; **cabina de peaje** toll booth; **cabina de prensa** press box; **cabina de proyección** projection room **cabina telefónica** *or* **de teléfonos** telephone booth
cabio *m* rafter; joist
cabizba•jo -ja *adj* crestfallen, downcast
cable *m* cable; rope, hawser; **cable coaxial** coaxial cable; **cable de remolque** towline; **cable de retén** guy wire; **cables de arranque** jumper cables
cablegrafiar §77 *tr & intr* to cable
cablegráfi•co -ca *adj* cable
cablegrama *m* cablegram
cabo *m* end, tip; (*punta de tierra que penetra en el mar*) cape; (*mango*) handle; small bundle; small piece; boss, foreman; cord, rope, cable; (mil) corporal; **al cabo** finally, at last; **al cabo de** at the end of; **atar cabos** (coll) to put two and two together; **Cabo de Buena Esperanza** Cape of Good Hope; **Cabo de Hornos** Cape Horn; **cabos** (*de caballo*) paws, nose, and mane; eyes, eyebrows, and hair; clothing; **cabo suelto** loose end; **estar al cabo de** to be well informed about; **llevar a cabo** to carry out, to accomplish
cabotaje *m* coasting trade
cabra *f* goat; nanny goat; (Chile) light two-wheel carriage; (Chile) sawbuck; (Col, Cuba, Ven) trick, gyp, loaded dice; **cabras** light clouds
cabrahigo wild fig
cabrería *f* goat stable; goat-milk dairy
cabre•ro -ra *mf* goatherd
cabrestante *m* capstan
cabrilla *f* sawbuck, sawhorse; (ichth) grouper; **cabrillas** skipping stones; (*olas blancas en el mar*) whitecaps
cabrillear *intr* (*el mar*) to be covered with whitecaps; shimmer
cabrio *m* rafter; joist
cabrí•o -a *adj* goat; goatish || *m* herd of goats
cabriola *f* caper; somersault; **dar cabriolas** to cut capers
cabriolear *intr* to caper, frisk, prance
cabritilla *f* kid, kidskin
cabrito *m* kid; **cabritos** (Chile) popcorn
cabrón *m* buck, billy goat; complaisant cuckold; (Chile) pimp
cabronada *f* shamelessness; shameless forbearance
cabru•no -na *adj* goat
caca *f* (vulg) excrement; trash
cacahuate *adj* (Mex) pocked || *m* peanut
cacahuete *m* peanut
cacahuete•ro -ra *mf* peanut vendor
cacalote *m* (Mex) raven; (CAm, Mex) candied popcorn; (Cuba) break, blunder
cacao *m* chocolate tree; cocoa, chocolate; **pedir cacao** to call quits; **tener mucho cacao** (Guat) to have a lot of pep
cacaraña *f* pit, pock
cacarear *tr* to crow over, boast of || *intr* (*la gallina*) to cackle; (*el gallo*) crow
cacareo *m* (*de la gallina*) cackling; (*del gallo*) crowing; (*de una persona*) (coll) crowing, boasting
cacatúa *f* cockatoo
cacea *f* trolling; **pescar a la cacea** to troll
cacear *tr* to stir with a dipper or ladle || *intr* to troll
cacería *f* hunting; hunting party; (*animales cobrados en la caza*) bag; hunting scene
cacerola *f* casserole, saucepan
cacha•co -ca *adj* (SAm) sporty || *m* (SAm) sport, dude
cachada *f* thrust or wound made with the horns
cachalote *m* sperm whale
cachar *tr* to break to pieces; (*la madera*) slit, split; to butt with the horns; (Arg, Ecuad, Urug) to make fun of; (Chile) to grasp, understand
cacharpari *m* (Arg, Bol, Peru) send-off party
cacharro *m* crock, earthen pot; piece of crockery; piece of junk; (*viejo coche*) jalopy; (CAm, W-I) jail; (Col) trinket
cachaza *f* sloth, phlegm; rum; first froth on cane juice when boiled
cachazu•do -da *adj* slothful, phlegmatic || *mf* sluggard
caché *m* (compu) cache
cachear *tr* to frisk, search (*a suspect*)
cacheo *m* frisking
cachetada *f* box on the ear
cachete *m* slap in the face; cheek, swollen cheek; dagger
cachetear *tr* to box on the ear
cachetero *m* dagger; dagger man
cachetina *f* brawl, fistfight

cachicuer•no -na *adj* horn-handled
cachillada *f* brood, litter
cachimba *f* (*para fumar*) pipe; (Arg, Urug) well, spring; (Chile) revolver
cachimbo *m* (*para fumar*) pipe; (Cuba) sugar mill; **chupar cachimbo** (Ven) to smoke a pipe; (*un niño*) (Ven) to suck its finger
cachiporra *f* billy, bludgeon
cachivache *m* good-for-nothing; **cachivaches** broken pottery; pots and pans; junk, trash
cacho *m* slice, piece; (*mercadería que no se vende*) (Chile) drug on the market
cachón *m* (*ola de agua*) breaker; splash of water; **cachones** surf
cachon•do -da *adj* (*perra*) in rut; sexy
cacho•rro -rra *mf* cub, whelp, pup || *m* little pistol
cachucha *f* rowboat; cap; Andalusian dance
cachuela *f* gizzard; fricassee of pork
cachu•pín -pina *mf* (CAm, Mex) Spanish settler in Latin America
cacique *m* Indian chief; bossy fellow; (*en asuntos políticos*) (coll) boss; (Chile) lazy lummox; **cacique veranero** Baltimore oriole, hangbird
caciquismo *m* bossism
cacle *m* (Mex) sandal
caco *m* thief, pickpocket; coward
cacto *m* cactus
cacumen *m* summit; acumen, keen insight
cada *adj* each; every; **cada vez más** more and more; **cada vez que** whenever
cadalso *m* stand, platform; (*para la ejecución de un reo*) scaffold
cadarzo *m* floss, floss silk
cadáver *m* corpse, cadaver; carcass
cadavéri•co -ca *adj* cadaverous
cadena *f* chain; (telv) network; **cadena antirrobo** bicycle lock; **cadena de montaje** assembly line; **cadena de montañas** mountain range; **cadena de presidiarios** chain gang; **cadena llanta** tire chain; **cadena perpetua** life imprisonment; **tirar de la cadena** to flush the toilet
cadencia *f* cadence, rhythm
cadencio•so -sa *adj* rhythmical
cadenero *m* (surv) lineman
cadera *f* hip
cadete *m* (mil) cadet; (Arg, Bol) apprentice (*without pay*), errand boy
cadillo *m* burdock
cadmio *m* cadmium
caducar §73 *intr* to be in one's dotage; be worn out; lapse, expire
caducidad *f* feebleness; expiration
caedi•zo -za *adj* tottery, ready to fall over || *m* lean-to
caer §15 *intr* to fall; droop; fall due; be, be found; fade; (*el sol, el día, el viento*) decline; happen; **caer a** to face, overlook; **caer bien** to fit; be becoming; make a hit; **caer de plano** to fall flat; **caer en** (*cierto día*) to come on, fall on, happen on; (*cierta página*) be found on; **caer en cama** to fall ill; **caer en favor** to be in favor; **caer en la cuenta** to catch on, get the point; **caer en que** to realize that; **caer mal** to fit badly; be unbecoming; fall flat; **no caigo** (coll) I don't get it || *ref* to fall, fall down; be, be found; **caerse de su peso, caerse de suyo** to be self-evident; **caerse muerto de** (*p.ej., alegría, miedo, risa*) to be overcome with
café *adj* tan, brown || *m* coffee; coffee tree; coffee house; café; (Arg) reprimand; (Mex) tantrum; **café cantante** night club; **café de la acera** sidewalk café; **café de maquinilla, café de recuelo** drip coffee; **café descafeinado** decaffeinated coffee; **café exprés** *or* **expreso** espresso; **café instantáneo, café soluble** instant coffee; **café solo, negro, tinto** or **puro** black coffee; **café teatro** dinner theater
cafetal *m* coffee plantation
cafetalero *m* (SAm) coffee planter; coffee dealer
cafetear *intr* to drink coffee
cafetera *f* coffee pot; (Arg) jalopy; **cafetera eléctrica** electric percolator
cafetería *f* cafeteria
cafete•ro -ra *adj* coffee || *mf* coffee dealer; coffee-bean picker || *f* see **cafetera**
cafeto *m* coffee tree
cafeína *f* caffeine
cagar §44 *tr* to spot, stain, spoil || *intr* to defecate || *ref* to defecate; be scared
cagatin•ta *m* or **cagatin•tas** *m* (*pl* **-tas**) office drudge, penpusher
ca•gón -gona *adj* cowardly || *mf* coward
caída *f* fall; spill, tumble; drop; failure; blunder, slip; (*de una cortina*) hang; **a la caída de la noche** at nightfall; **a la caída del sol** at sunset; **caída de agua** waterfall; (phys) **caída libre** free fall; **caída radiactiva** fallout; **caídas** coarse wool; witticisms
caí•do -da *adj* fallen; (*cuello*) turndown; (*párpado, hombro*) drooping; dejected, crestfallen; **caído en desuso** obsolete || **caídos** *mpl* interest due; **los caídos** (*en la guerra*) the fallen || *f* see **caída**
caimán *m* alligator; schemer
Caín *m* Cain; **pasar las de Caín** (coll) to have a frightful time
Cairo, El Cairo
caja *f* box; case, chest, coffer; (*de caudales*) safe, strongbox; (*para dinero contante*) cashbox; (*dinero contante*) cash; (*ataúd*) casket, coffin; (*de reloj de bolsillo*) case; (*donde se pagan las cuentas en los hoteles*) desk; cashier's desk; (*del aparato de radio o televisión*) cabinet; (*de coche*) body; (*tambor*) drum; (*de fusil*) stock; (*de ascensor, de escalera*) shaft, well; (mach) housing; (typ) case; **caja alta** upper case; **caja baja** lower case; **caja clara** snare drum; **caja de ahorros** savings bank; **caja de cambio de marchas** transmission-gear box; **caja de caudales** safe; **caja de cigüeñal** crankcase; **caja de colores** paintbox;

caja de dientes (Col) false teeth; **caja de diálogo** (compu) dialog box; **caja de embalaje** packing box or case; **caja de enchufe** (elec) outlet; **caja de engranajes** gear case; **caja de escalera** stairwell; **caja de fuego** firebox; **caja de fusibles** fuse box; **caja de ingletes** miter box; **caja de menores** petty cash; **caja de registro** manhole; **caja de reloj** watchcase; **caja de resonancia** (fig) sounding board (*for ideas*); **caja de seguridad** safe; safe-deposit box; **caja de sorpresa** jack-in-the-box; **caja de velocidades** transmission-gear box; **caja fuerte** safe, bank vault; **caja negra** black box, flight recorder; **caja postal de ahorros** postal savings bank; **caja registradora** cash register; **despedir** or **echar con cajas destempladas** to send packing, give the gate

caje•ro -ra *mf* boxmaker; (*en un banco*) cashier, teller; (*en un hotel*) desk clerk; **cajero automático** automated teller machine

cajeta *f* little box; tobacco box; **de cajeta** (CAm, Mex) fine

cajetilla *f* pack (*of cigarettes*)

cajetín *m* rubber stamp; (typ) box

cajista *mf* compositor

cajón *m* large box, bin; (*caja movible de un mueble*) drawer; (*que se cierra con llave*) locker; (*que sirve de tienda*) booth, stall; (Chile) long gully; (Mex) dry-goods store; (SAm) coffin; **cajón de municiones** (mil) caisson; **cajón de sastre** (coll) odds and ends; muddlehead; **cajón hidráulico** caisson; **ser de cajón** to be in vogue, be the thing

cal *f* lime; **cal apagada** slaked lime; **cal viva** quicklime; **de cal y canto** strong, tough

cala *f* calla lily; cove, inlet; (*de fruta*) sample slice; (*de buque*) hold; suppository

calabacear *tr* (*a un alumno*) to flunk; (*una mujer a un pretendiente*) to jilt

calabacera *f* calabash, pumpkin, squash

calabaza *f* calabash, gourd, pumpkin, squash; dolt; **dar calabaza** a (*un alumno*) to flunk; (*un pretendiente*) to jilt

calabo•bos *m* (*pl* **-bos**) steady drizzle

calabocero *m* jailer, warden

calabozo *m* dungeon; cell, prison cell

calada *f* soaking; (*del ave de rapiña*) swoop; scolding

calado *m* openwork, drawn work; fretwork; (*del agua*) depth; (naut) draught

calafatear *tr* to caulk

calafateo *m* caulking

calamar *m* squid

calambre *m* cramp

calamidad *f* calamity

calamita *f* magnetic needle

calamito•so -sa *adj* calamitous

cálamo *m* reed, stalk; (poet) pen; (poet) flute, reed

calamoca•no -na *adj* (*algo embriagado*) tipsy; (*chocho*) doddering

calaña *f* nature, kind; pattern; fan

calar *tr* to pierce; soak; wedge; cut open work in; (*un melón*) cut a plug in; (*la bayoneta*) fix; (*un puente levadizo*) lower; (*las redes de pesca*) lower in the water; (*un buque cierta profundidad*) draw; (*a una persona o las intenciones de una persona*) size up, see through; (Arg) to stare at ‖ *ref* to get soaked, get drenched; (*introducirse*) slip in; (*el ave de rapiña*) swoop down; miss fire; (*el sombrero*) pull down tight; (*las gafas*) stick on; **calarse hasta los huesos** to get soaked to the skin

cala•to -ta *adj* (Peru) naked; (Peru) penniless

calavera *m* daredevil; libertine ‖ *f* skull; (*imitación de la calavera*) death's-head; (Mex) tail light

calaverada *f* recklessness, daredeviltry; escapade

calaverear *tr* to spoil, make ugly ‖ *intr* to act recklessly; go on a spree

calcado *m* tracing

calcañal *m* or **calcañar** *m* heel

calcar §73 *tr* to trace; copy, imitate; tread on

calce *m* wedge; iron tire; iron tip; (*de un documento*) (CAm, Mex, P-R) bottom, foot

calceta *f* stocking; fetter, shackle; **hacer calceta** to knit

calcetería *f* hosiery; hosiery shop

calcete•ro -ra *mf* hosier; stocking mender

calcetín *m* sock

calchona *f* (Chile) goblin, bogey; (Chile) witch, old hag

calcificar §73 *tr & ref* to calcify

calcio *m* calcium

calco *m* tracing; copy, imitation

calcula•dor -dora *adj* calculating; (*egoísta, interesado*) (fig) calculating ‖ *mf* calculator ‖ *f* (mach) calculator; **calculadora de bolsillo** pocket calculator

calcular *tr & intr* to calculate; (*suponer*) (fig) calculate; **calcular aproximadamente** to guesstimate (coll)

cálculo *m* calculation; (math, pathol) calculus; **cálculo aproximado** guesstimate (coll); **cálculo biliar** gallstone; **calculo renal** kidney stone

calda *f* heating, warming; **caldas** hot springs

caldeamiento *m* heating

caldear *tr* to heat; weld ‖ *ref* to get hot; get overheated

caldeo *m* heating; welding

caldera *f* boiler; pot, kettle; (Arg) coffee pot, teapot

calderero *m* boilermaker

calderilla *f* holy-water vessel; copper coin; small change; mountain currant

caldero *m* kettle, pot; (*reloj de bolsillo*) (Arg) turnip

calderón *m* caldron; (*signo*) (mus) pause, hold

caldillo *m* light broth; sauce for fricassee; (Mex) meat bits in broth

caldo *m* broth; sauce, gravy, dressing; salad dressing; (Mex) syrup; (Mex) sugar-cane juice; **caldo de cultivo** breeding ground;

(biol) culture medium; **caldo de la reina** eggnog; **caldos** wet goods
calefacción *f* heating; **calefacción por agua caliente** hot-water heat; **calefacción por aire caliente** hot-air heat
calefactor *m* heater man; (electron) heater, heater element
calefón *m* (Arg) hot-water heater
calendar *tr* to date
calendario *m* calendar; **calendario islámico** Muslim calendar; **hacer calendarios** to meditate; to make wild predictions
calenta•dor -dora *adj* heating ‖ *m* heater, space heater; warming pan; (*reloj de bolsillo*) turnip; **calentador a gas** gas heater; **calentador de agua** water heater
calentamiento *m* heating, warming; **calentamiento global, calentamiento del planeta** global warming
calentar §2 *tr* to heat; warm; beat; (Chile) to bore, annoy; **calentar la silla** (*detenerse demasiado*) to warm a chair ‖ *ref* to heat up, run hot; warm oneself; warm up; (*estar en celo las bestias*) be in heat; (Chile, Ven) to become annoyed, get angry
calentón *m* warm-up; **darse un calentón** to stop and warm up
calentura *f* fever, temperature
calenturien•to -ta *adj* feverish; exalted; (Chile) consumptive
calenturón *m* high fever
calenturo•so -sa *adj* feverish
calera *f* limekiln; limestone quarry
calesa *f* chaise
caleta *f* cove, inlet
caletre *m* judgment, acumen
calibración *f* (compu) calibration
calibrado *m* calibration
calibrador *m* calipers; **calibrador de alambre** wire gauge
calibrar *tr* to calibrate; to gauge
calibre *m* caliber; gauge; bore, diameter
calicanto *m* rubble masonry
cali•có *m* (*pl* **-cós**) calico
calidad *f* quality; condition, term; rank, nobility; importance; **a calidad de que** provided that; **calidad de vida** quality of life; **en calidad de** in the capacity of
cáli•do -da *adj* warm, hot
calidoscopio *m* kaleidoscope
calientaca•mas *m* (*pl* **-mas**) bed warmer
calienta•piés *m* (*pl* **-piés**) foot warmer
caliente *adj* hot; fiery, vehement; (*en celo*) hot; **caliente de cascos** hotheaded; **en caliente** while hot; at once
califa *m* caliph
califato *m* caliphate
calificación *f* qualification; (*nota en un examen*) grade, mark; rating, standing
califica•do -da *adj* skilled; qualified
calificar §73 *tr* to qualify; certify; ennoble; (*un examen*) mark; (*en los registros electorales*) (Chile) to register ‖ *ref* (archaic) to prove one's noble birth; (*en los registros electorales*) (Chile) to register
calificati•vo -va *adj* qualifying ‖ *m* (*nota en la escuela*) grade, mark; (*en un diccionario*) label
California *f* California; **la Baja California** Lower California
caligrafía *f* penmanship
calina *f* haze
calino•so -sa *adj* hazy
Calíope *f* Calliope
calipso *m* calypso ‖ **Calipso** *f* Calypso
calistenia *f* calisthenics
calisténi•co -ca *adj* calisthenic
cá•liz *m* (*pl* **-lices**) chalice; **cáliz de dolor** cup of sorrow
cali•zo -za *adj* lime, limestone ‖ *f* limestone
callada *f* (naut) abatement, lull; **a las calladas** or **de callada** on the quiet; **dar la callada por respuesta** to give no answer
calla•do -da *adj* silent; mysterious, secret ‖ *f* see **callada**
callampa *f* (Chile) felt hat; (Chile) large ear; (Chile) mushroom
callana *f* (SAm) Indian baking bowl; (*reloj de bolsillo*) (Chile) turnip; (Chile) behind; (Chile, Peru) flowerpot
callao *m* pebble
callar *tr* to silence; not mention; (*un secreto*) keep; calm, quiet ‖ *intr & ref* to become silent, keep silent; keep quiet, keep still; **callarse la boca** (coll) to shut up, clam up
calle *f* street; **calle ciega** dead end; **calle de doble sentido** two-way street; **calle de sentido único, calle de dirección única** one-way street; **calle de travesía** cross street; **calle mayor** main street; **dejar en la calle** to deprive of one's livelihood
calleja *f* side street, alley; subterfuge, pretext
callejear *intr* to walk around the streets, to ramble around
calleje•ro -ra *adj* street; gadabout ‖ *m* street guide; list of addresses of newspaper subscribers
callejón *m* alley, lane; **callejón sin salida** blind alley; standoff
callejuela *f* side street, alley; subterfuge, pretext
callicida *m* corn cure
callo *m* callus; (*en el pie*) corn; **callos** tripe
callo•so -sa *adj* callous
calma *f* calm; calm weather; quiet, tranquility; slowness; (*cesación*) letup, suspension; **calma chicha** dead calm; **calmas ecuatoriales** doldrums; **en calma** in suspension; (*mercado*) steady; (*mar*) calm, smooth
calmante *adj* soothing; pain-relieving ‖ *m* sedative
calmar *tr* to calm, soothe ‖ *intr* to grow calm; abate ‖ *ref* to calm down
calmazo *m* dead calm
cal•mo -ma *adj* barren, treeless; fallow, uncultivated ‖ *f* see **calma**
calmo•so -sa *adj* calm; slow, lazy

calmu•do -da *adj* calm; (*viento*) (naut) light; (*tiempo*) (naut) mild
caló *m* gypsy slang, underworld slang
calofriar **§77** *ref* to become chilled
calofrío *m* chill
calor *m* heat; warmth; (fig) warmth, enthusiasm; **hace calor** it is hot, it is warm; **tener calor** (*una persona*) to be hot, be warm
caloríf e•ro -ra *adj* heat || *m* heater, furnace; heating system; foot warmer
calorífu•go -ga *adj* heatproof; fireproof
caloro•so -sa *adj* warm, hot; (fig) warm, enthusiastic, hearty
calotear *tr* (Arg) to gyp, cheat
calpul *m* (Guat) gathering, meeting; (Hond) Indian mound
caluma *f* (Peru) gorge in the Andes; (Peru) Indian hamlet
calumnia *f* calumny, slander
calumniar *tr* to slander
calumnio•so -sa *adj* slanderous
caluro•so -sa *adj* warm, hot; (fig) warm, enthusiastic, hearty, rousing
calva *f* bald spot; bare spot, clearing; (*en un tejido*) worn spot
calvario *m* (*sufrimiento moral*) cross; series of misfortunes; string of debts || **Calvario** *m* Calvary; Stations of the Cross
calvero *m* clearing; clay pit
calvez *f* or **calvicie** *f* baldness
cal•vo -va *adj* bald; barren, bare || *f* see **calva**
calza *f* wedge; stocking; **calzas** hose, breeches, tights; **en calzas prietas** in a tight fix
calzada *f* highway, causeway; (S-D) sidewalk
calzado *m* footwear shoes
calzador *m* shoehorn
calzar **§60** *tr* to shoe, put shoes on; provide with shoes; (*cierto tamaño de zapatos, guantes, etc.*) wear, take; (*un zapato a una persona*) fit; wedge; (*una rueda*) block, scotch; (*la para de una mesa*) block up; tip or trim with iron; (*plantas*) (hort) to hill || *intr* (Arg) to get the place sought; **calzar bien** to wear good footwear; **calzar mal** to wear poor footwear || *ref* to get; (*zapatos, guantes*) put on, wear; put one's shoes on; (*a una persona*) dominate, manage
calzo *m* wedge; chock, skid
calzón *m* trousers, pants; **calzones** trousers, breeches; (Mex) boxer shorts; **calzarse los calzones** to wear the pants
calzonarias *fpl* (Col) suspenders
calzona•zos *m* (*pl* **-zos**) jellyfish; henpecked husband
calzoncillos *mpl* underdrawers, boxer shorts
cama *f* bed; (*para las bestias*) bedding, litter; **cama camarote** bunk bed; **cama de agua** water bed; **cama de matrimonio, cama doble** double bed; **cama de tamaño grande** king-sized bed; **cama elástica** trampoline; **cama imperial** four-poster; **cama individual** single bed; **cama nido** trundle bed; **camas gemelas** twin beds; **cama turca** day bed; **guardar cama** to be sick in bed
camachuelo *m* (orn) bullfinch
camada *f* brood, litter; layer, stratum; (*de ladrones*) den
camafeo *m* cameo
camaleón *m* chameleon
cámara *f* chamber; hall; (*cuerpo legislador*) house, chamber; (*aparato fotográfico*) camera; (*tubo de goma del neumático*) inner tube; (*del arma de fuego*) chamber, breech; (*para cartuchos*) magazine; board, council; (*mueble donde se conservan los alimentos*) icebox; (*evacuación*) bowels; (aer) cockpit; **cámara agrícola** grange; **cámara ardiente** funeral chamber; **cámara cinematografica** movie camera; **cámara de combustión** (aut) combustion chamber; **cámara de comercio** chamber of commerce; **cámara de compensación** clearing house; **cámara de disco** disk camera; **cámara de fuelle** folding camera; **cámara de las máquinas** (naut) engine room; **Cámara de los Comunes** House of Commons; **Cámara de los Lores** House of Lords; **cámara de oxígeno** oxygen tent; **Cámara de Representantes** House of Representatives; **cámara frigorífica** cold-storage room; **cámara indiscreta** candid camera; **cámaras** loose bowels; camera crew; **cámara séptica** septic tank
camarada *m* comrade
camarera *f* waitress; chambermaid, maid; (*en los barcos*) stewardess; (*que sirve a una reina o princesa*) lady in waiting
camarero *m* waiter; valet; (*en un barco o avión*) steward
camarilla *f* clique, coterie, cabal; palace coterie
camarín *m* boudoir; (theat) dressing room
cámaro *m* var of **camarón**
camarógrafo *m* cameraman
camarón *m* shrimp, prawn; (CAm, Col) tip, gratuity; (Ven) nap; **ponerse como un camarón** to blush
camarote *m* stateroom, cabin
camasquin•ce *mf* (*pl* **-ce**) meddlesome person, kibitzer
cambalachar *tr & intr* var of **cambalachear**
cambalache *m* exchange, swap; (Arg) second-hand shop
cambalachear *tr* to swap, exchange, trade off || *intr* to swap, exchange
cambiadis•cos *m* (*pl* **-cos**) record changer
cambiante *adj* changing; fickle; iridescent || **cambiantes** *mpl* iridescence
cambiar *tr* to change; exchange, swap || *intr* to change; **cambiar de** (*p.ej., sombreros, ropa, trenes*) change; **cambiar de marcha** to shift gears || *ref* to change
cambiavía *m* switch; switchman
cambio *m* change; exchange, swap; rate of exchange; (aut) shift; (rr) switch; **cambio automático** automatic transmission; **cambio de domicilio** change of address; **cambio de**

marchas, **cambio de velocidades** gearshift; **cambio de tribunal** (law) change of venue; **cambio extranjero** foreign exchange; **en cambio** on the other hand
cambista *mf* moneychanger; banker || *m* (Arg) switchman
cambullón *m* (Mex, Col, Ven) barter, exchange; (Chile) subversion; (Peru) scheming, trickery
camcórder *m* camcorder, videocámara
camelar *tr* to flirt with; cajole, tease, sweet-talk
camellero *m* camel driver
camello *m* camel
camellón *m* drinking trough; flower bed
camelo *m* flirtation; joke; false rumor
came•ro -ra *adj* bed || *mf* maker of bedding || *m* (Col) highway
camilla *f* stretcher; couch; round table with heater underneath; (Mex) clothing store
camillero *m* stretcher-bearer
caminante *mf* walker; traveler on foot || *m* groom attending his master's horse
caminar *tr* (*cierta distancia*) to walk || *intr* to walk; go; travel, journey; behave
caminata *f* long walk, hike; outing, jaunt
camine•ro -ra *adj* road, highway
camino *m* road, way; (*viaje*) journey; (*tira larga que se pone en mesas o pisos*) (SAm) runner; **a medio camino (entre)** halfway (between); **camino de** on the way to; **camino de herradura** bridle path; **camino de hierro** railway; **camino de ruedas** wagon road; **Camino de Santiago** Way of St. James (*Milky Way*); **camino de sirga** towpath; **camino de tierra** dirt road; **camino real** highroad; **camino trillado** beaten path; **echar camino adelante** to strike out
camión *m* truck, motor truck; (Mex) bus; **camión articulado** semitrailer; **camión celular** patrol wagon; **camión cisterna** tanker; **camión de la basura** garbage truck; **camión de mudanzas** moving van; **camión de reparto** pickup truck; **camión remolcador** tow truck; **camión volquete** dump truck
camionaje *m* trucking
camione•ro -ra *adj* truck || *m* trucker, teamster
camioneta *f* light truck; station wagon
camionetilla *f* (Guat) station wagon
camión-grua *m* tow truck
camionista *m* trucker, teamster
camisa *f* (*de hombre*) shirt; (*de mujer*) chemise; (*de la culebra*) slough; (*de un libro*) jacket; (*para papeles*) folder; (*de una pieza mecánica*) jacket, casing; (*de un horno de fundición*) lining; **camisa de agua** water jacket; **camisa de dormir** nightshirt; **camisa de fuerza** straitjacket; **camisa parda** brownshirt; **cambiarse la camisa** to become a turncoat
camisería *f* haberdashery; shirt factory
camise•ro -ra *mf* haberdasher; shirt maker
camiseta *f* (*interior*) undershirt; (*de traje de baño*) top; **camiseta gruesa, camiseta de entrenamientos** sweatshirt; **camiseta-T** (*camiseta exterior en forma de T*) T-shirt; **camiseta tanque** (*camiseta con tirantes, camiseta de espaldas desnudas*) tank top, tank
camisola *f* stiff shirt
camisolín *m* dickey, shirt front
camón *m* bay window; **camón de vidrios** glass partition
camorra *f* quarrel, row; **armar camorra** to raise Cain, raise a row; **buscar camorra** to be looking for trouble
camorrista *adj* quarrelsome || *mf* quarrelsome person
camote *m* onion; (Mex) sweet potato; (Chile) lie, fib; (Chile, Peru) sweetheart; (Arg, Ecuad) blockhead; (Mex) churl; (El Salv) black-and-blue mark; **tomar un camote** to become infatuated
camotear *tr* (Arg) to filch, snitch; (Guat) to bother || *intr* (Mex) to wander around aimlessly
campal *adj* pitched (*battle*)
campamento *m* camp; encampment
campana *f* bell; (*para la protección de plantas*) bell glass, bell jar; (*de las guarniciones de alumbrado eléctrico*) canopy; **campana de buzo** diving bell; **por campana de vacante** (Mex) rarely, seldom
campanada *f* stroke of a bell, ring of a bell; scandal
campanario *m* belfry, steeple
campanear *tr* (*las campanas*) to ring || *intr* to ring the bells || *ref* to strut
campanero *m* bell ringer; bell founder
campanil *adj* bell || *m* belfry, bell tower
campanilla *f* hand bell; door bell; bubble; (anat) uvula; **de (muchas) campanillas** of great importance
campano *m* cowbell
campante *adj* proud, satisfied; outstanding
campanu•do -da *adj* bell-shaped; pompous, high-sounding
campaña *f* campaign; cruise; countryside
campañol *m* fieldmouse, vole
campar *intr* to camp; to excel, stand out
campear *intr* to go to pasture; (*las sementeras*) turn green; stand out, excel; reconnoiter; ride through the fields to check the cattle
campecha•no -na *adj* frank, good-natured, cheerful || *f* (Mex) mixed drink; (Ven) hammock
campeche *m* logwood
campeón *m* champion; **campeón de venta** best seller
campeona *f* championess
campeonato *m* championship
campe•ro -ra *adj* unsheltered, in the open
campesi•no -na *adj* country, rural, peasant || *mf* peasant, farmer || *m* countryman || *f* countrywoman
campestre *adj* country, rural
camping *m* camping; campsite, campground
campiña *f* countryside, open country
campo *m* (*terreno sembradío; sitio o foco de*

varias actividades) field; (*en oposición a la ciudad*) country; ground, background; (*campamento*) (mil) camp; **a campo traviesa** across country; **campo de batalla** battlefield; **campo de concentración** concentration camp; **campo de ensayos** proving ground; **campo de golf** golf course *o* links; **campo de juego** playground; **campo de pruebas** testing ground; **campo de refugiados** refugee camp; **campo de tiro** range, shooting range; **campo magnético** magnetic field; **campo santo** cemetery; **levantar el campo** (mil) to break camp; **quedar en el campo** to fall in battle
camposanto *m* cemetery
campus *m* campus
camuesa *f* pippin (*apple*)
camueso *m* pippin (*tree*)
camuflaje *m* camouflage
camuflar *tr* to camouflage
can *m* dog; (*de arma de fuego*) trigger
cana *f* gray hair; **echar una cana al aire** to cut loose, step out; **peinar canas** to be getting old
Canadá, el Canada
canadiense *adj & mf* Canadian
canal *m* (*cauce artificial*) canal; (*estrecho en el mar*) channel; (anat) duct, canal; (compu, electron, rad, telv) channel; **Canal de la Mancha** English Channel; **Canal de Panamá** Panama Canal; **Canal de Suez** Suez Canal; **canal alimenticio** alimentary canal; **canales de distribución** (compu) distribution channels || *f* channel; (*conducto del tejado*) gutter; (*estría*) flute, groove; pipe; (*de un libro*) fore edge
canalización *f* (*de agua o gas*) mains, pipes; ductwork; (elec) wiring; **canalización de consumo** (elec) house current
canalizar §60 to channel; pipe; (elec) to wire
canalizo *m* (naut) waterway, fairway
canalla *m* churl, scoundrel || *f* riffraff, canaille
canallada *f* dirty trick, meanness
canalón *m* rain-water spout; shovel hat; **canalones** ravioli
canana *f* cartridge belt
canapé *m* sofa, couch
Canarias *fpl* Canaries
cana•rio -ria *adj & mf* Canarian || *m* canary, canary bird || *fpl* see **Canarias**
canasta *f* basket, hamper; **meter una canasta** (*en baloncesto*) to shoot a basket
canastilla *f* basket; (*ropa para el niño que ha de nacer*) layette; (*equipo de novia*) (dial) trousseau
canastillo *m* basket-weave tray
canasto *m* hamper || **canastos** *interj* confound it!
cáncamo *m* eyebolt; **cáncamo de argolla** ringbolt
cancanear *intr* to loaf around; stammer
cancel *m* storm door; folding screen
cancela *f* door of ironwork
cancelar *tr* to cancel; (*una deuda*) pay off
cáncer *m* cancer; **Cáncer** (astr) Cancer; **cáncer pulmonar** lung cancer
cancerología *f* cancer research; oncology
cancero•so -sa *adj* cancerous
cancha *f* field, ground; race track; golf links; tennis court; cockpit; (Urug) path, way; **estar en su cancha** (Arg, Chile, Urug) to be in one's element; **tener cancha** (Arg) to have pull || *interj* gangway!
canche *adj* (Col) tasteless, poorly seasoned; (CAm) blond
cancilla *f* lattice gate
canciller *m* chancellor
cancillería *f* chancellery
canción *f* song; poem, lyric poem; **canción de amor** love song; **canción de cuna** cradlesong, lullaby; **canción típica** folk song; **volver a la misma canción** to sing the same old song
cancionero *m* songbook; anthology
cancionista *mf* popular singer
canco *m* (Chile) flowerpot; (Chile) earthen jug; (Chile) chamber pot; (Bol) buttock; **cancos** (Chile) woman's broad hips
cancón *m* bugaboo; **hacer un cancón a** (Mex) to try to bluff
cancro *m* (bot, vet) canker; (pathol) cancer
candado *m* padlock
candar *tr* to lock, padlock
candela *f* candle; candlestick; fire, light; **con la candela en la mano** at death's door
candelabro *m* candelabrum
candelecho *m* elevated hut for watching the vineyard
candelero *m* candlestick, candleholder; brass olive-oil lamp; fishing torch
candelilla *f* catkin; (Arg, Chile) will-o'-the-wisp; glowworm
candida•to -ta *mf* candidate
candidatura *f* candidacy; list of candidates; voting paper
candidez *f* whiteness; innocence
cándi•do -da white; simple, innocent
candil *m* open olive-oil lamp
candilejas *fpl* footlights
candon•go -ga *adj* fawning, slick; loafing, shirking || *mf* fawner, flatterer; loafer, shirker || *f* fawning; teasing
candonguear *tr* to kid, tease || *intr* to scheme to get out of work
candor *m* innocence, ingenuousness
caneca *f* glazed earthen bottle
cane•co -ca *adj* (Arg, Bol) tipsy || *f* see **caneca**
canela *f* cinnamon; (*cosa fina*) (coll) peach
canela•do -da *adj* cinnamon-colored
cane•lo -la *adj* cinnamon || *m* (*árbol*) cinnamon || *f* see **canela**
canelón *m* rain-water spout; large icicle; cinnamon candy
cane•sú *m* (*pl* **-súes**) (*prenda*) guimpe; (*pieza de una prenda*) yoke
cangilón *m* jug, jar, bucket; (*de draga*) bucket, scoop; rut, track
cangrejo *m* crab

cangrena *f* gangrene
cangrenar *ref* to have gangrene
canguro *m* kangaroo
caníbal *adj & mf* cannibal
canica *f* (*bolita*) marble; (*juego*) marbles
canicie *f* whiteness (*of hair*)
canícula *f* dog days || **Canícula** *f* Dog Star
caniculares *mpl* dog days
cani•jo -ja *adj* (coll) weak, sickly || *mf* (coll) weakling
canilla *f* shank (*of leg*); (*espita, grifo*) tap; bobbin, spool; (Mex) strength
cani•no -na *adj* canine || *m* canine, canine tooth || *f* excrement of dogs
canje *m* exchange
canjear *tr* to exchange
ca•no -na *adj* gray; gray-haired; hoary, old || *f* see **cana**
canoa *f* canoe; launch
canoe•ro -ra *mf* canoeist
canon *m* canon
canóni•co -ca *adj* canonical || *f* rules of canonical life
canóniga *f* nap before eating; drunk
canónigo *m* canon
canonizar §60 *tr* to canonize; approve
canonjía *f* sinecure
cano•ro -ra *adj* (*voz*) melodious; (*ave*) song, sweet-singing
cano•so -sa *adj* gray-haired
canotié *m* straw hat, skimmer
cansa•do -da *adj* tired, weary; exhausted, worn-out; tiresome
cansancio *m* tiredness, fatigue
cansar *tr* to tire, weary; bore || *intr* be tiresome || *ref* to tire, get tired
cantable *adj* tuneful, singable || *m* (*del libreto de una zarzuela*) lyric; (*de una zarzuela*) musical passage
canta•dor -dora *mf* singer of popular songs
cantaletear *tr* to say over and over again; make fun of
cantalupo *m* cantaloupe
cantante *adj* singing || *mf* singer
cantar *m* song, singing; chant; **Cantar de los Cantares** Song of Songs || *tr* to sing; chant; sing of; **cantarlas claras** to speak out || *intr* to sing; chant; creak, squeak; (coll) squeal; **cantar de plano** to make a full confession
cántara *f* jug, pitcher
cantárida *f* Spanish fly
canta•rín -rina *adj* (*voz*) melodious; fond of singing || *mf* singer || *m* professional singer
cántaro *m* jug, pitcher, jugful; ballot box; **llover a cántaros** to rain pitchforks
canta•triz *f* (*pl* **-trices**) singer
cantautor *m* song writer
cantera *f* quarry; talent, genius
cántico *m* canticle
cantidad *f* quantity; amount; sum; **cantidad de movimiento** (mech) momentum
cantiga *f* poem of the troubadours
cantilena *f* ballad, song; **salir con la misma cantilena** to sing the same old song
cantimplora *f* siphon; carafe, decanter; (*frasco para llevar bebida*) canteen, water bottle; (Col) powder flask; (Guat) mumps
cantina *f* cantine; lunchroom, station restaurant; cafeteria; barroom
cantinera *f* camp follower
cantinero *m* bartender
canto *m* song; singing; (*división del poema épico*) canto; (*de notas iguales y uniformes*) chant; (*extremidad*) edge; (*esquina*) corner; (*de cuchillo*) back; (*de pan*) crust; stone, pebble; **canto de corte** cutting edge; **canto del cisne** swan song
cantonera *f* corner reinforcement; corner table, corner shelf; streetwalker
cantonero *m* corner loafer
can•tor -tora *adj* singing; (*pájaro*) song || *mf* singer || *m* chanter; minstrel; poet, bard
canto•so -sa *adj* rocky, stony
canturrear *tr & intr* to hum
canturreo *m* hum, humming
canzonetista *mf* popular singer
caña *f* cane; reed; stalk, stem; (*del brazo o la pierna*) long bone; (*de bota o media*) leg; wineglass; **caña de azúcar** sugarcane; **caña de la dirección** steering column; **caña de pescar** fishing rod, fishpole
cañada *f* glen, ravine, gully; cattle path; brook
cañamazo *m* canvas, burlap; embroidered canvas
cañamiel *f* sugarcane
cañamo *m* hemp
cañamones *mpl* birdseed
cañaveral *m* canebrake; sugarcane plantation
cañería *f* pipe; pipe line; piping; **cañería maestra** gas main, water main
cañero *m* pipe fitter, plumber; sugarcane dealer; (SAm) cheat; (SAm) bluffer
cañista *m* pipe fitter, plumber
caño *m* pipe, tube; gutter, sewer; ditch; (*chorro*) spurt, jet; (*canal angosto*) channel; organ pipe; (*río pequeño*) (Col) stream
cañón *m* (*pieza de artillería*) cannon; (*valle estrecho*) canyon; (*de arma de fuego; de pluma*) barrel; (*pluma de ave*) quill; (*de escalera*) well; (*de columna; de ascensor*) shaft; organ pipe; (Col) trunk of tree; **cañón antiaéreo** antiaircraft gun; **cañón antitanque** antitank gun; **cañón de campaña** field gun; **cañón de chimenea** flue, chimney flue; **cañón obús** howitzer
cañonear *tr* to cannonade, to shell
cañutazo *m* gossip
caoba *f* mahogany
caos *m* chaos
caóti•co -ca *adj* chaotic
cap. *abbr* **capitán, capítulo**
capa *f* cloak, cape, mantle; (*de pintura*) coat; (*lo que cubre*) bed, layer, thickness; (*apariencia, pretexto*) (fig) cloak, mask; **capa del cielo** canopy of heaven; **capa de ozono** ozone

layer; **andar de capa caída** to be on the decline, be in a bad way; (*comedia*) **de capa y espada** cloak and sword; (*intriga, espionaje*) cloak-and-dagger; **so capa de** under the guise of

capacidad *f* capacity; **capacidad competitiva** competitiveness

capacitar *tr* to enable, qualify; to empower ‖ *ref* to become qualified

capacha *f* fruit basket; (SAm) jail

capacho *m* fruit basket; hamper; (*de albañil*) hod

capar *tr* to geld, castrate; curtail

caparazón *m* caparison; horse blanket; nose bag; (*de crustáceo*) shell

caparrosa *f* vitriol

capa•taz *m* (*pl* **-taces**) overseer, foreman, boss

ca•paz *adj* (*pl* **-paces**) (*grande*) capacious, spacious; (*que tiene cierta aptitud; diestro, instruído*) capable; **capaz de** capable of; with a capacity of; **capaz para** competent in; qualified for; with room for

capcio•so *adj* crafty, deceptive

capea *f* amateur free-for-all bullfight

capear *tr* (*al toro*) to challenge; (*el mal tiempo*) weather; deceive, take in ‖ *intr* (naut) to lay to; (Guat) to play hooky

capellán *m* chaplain

capeo *m* capework (*of bullfighter*)

caperucita *f* little pointed hood; **Caperucita Roja** Little Red Ridinghood

caperuza *f* pointed hood; chimney cap

capilla *f* (*parte de una iglesia con altar*) chapel; (*de los reos de muerte*) death house; (*pliego suelto*) proof sheet; cowl, hood, cape; **estar en capilla** to be in the death house; to be on pins and needles; **estar expuesto en capilla ardiente** to be on view, to lie in state

capiller *m* churchwarden, sexton

capillo *m* baby cap; baptismal cap; hood; cocoon; (*del cigarro*) filler

capirotazo *m* fillip

capirote *m* hood; doctor's cap and hood; cardboard or paper cone (*worn on head*); fillip

capitación *f* poll tax

capital *adj* capital; main, principal; paramount; (*enemigo*) mortal ‖ *m* (*dinero que produce renta*) capital; (*dinero que se presta para producir renta*) principal; **capital aventurado** venture capital; **capital de inversión** investment capital; **el gran capital** big business ‖ *f* capital

capitalismo *m* capitalism

capitalista *adj* capitalistic ‖ *mf* capitalist; shareholder, investor

capitalizar **§60** *tr* to capitalize; (*los intereses devengados*) compound

capitán *m* captain; leader, **capitán de bandera** flag captain; **capitán de corbeta** (nav) lieutenant commander; **capitán del puerto** harbor master; **capitán general** general (in the Army)

capitana *f* flagship

capitanear *tr* to captain; lead, command

capitanía *f* captaincy; (mil) company

capitel *m* (*de una iglesia*) spire; (*de una columna*) capital

capitolio *m* capitol

capitoste *m* big shot

capítula *f* chapter (*of Scriptures*)

capitular *tr* to accuse; agree on ‖ *intr* to capitulate

capitulear *intr* (Arg, Chile, Peru) to lobby

capituleo *m* (Arg, Chile, Peru) lobbying

capitulero *m* (Arg, Chile, Peru) political henchman, lobbyist

capítulo *m* chapter; chapter house; subject, matter; errand; main point; **ganar capítulo** (coll) to win one's point; **llamar a capítulo** to take to task, call to account; **perder capítulo** to lose one's point

ca•pó *m* (*pl* **-pós**) hood (*of auto*)

capolar *tr* to cut to pieces, chop up

ca•pón -pona *adj* castrated ‖ *m* eunuch; (*pollo*) capon; bundle of firewood; (*golpe*) fillip ‖ *f* shoulder strap

caponera *f* coop for fattening capons; place of welcome; (*cárcel*) coop, jail

caporal *m* chief, leader; foreman (*on cattle ranch*)

capota *f* bonnet; (aer) cowling; (aut) top

capotaje *m* (aer) nosing over

capotar *intr* to upset; (aer) to nose over

capote *m* cape, cloak; (coll) frown, scowl; (Chile, Mex) beating; **capote de monte** poncho; **de capote** (Mex) on the sly; **dar capote a** to flabbergast; (*un rezagado*) to leave hungry; **decir para su capote** to say to oneself; **echar un capote** to turn the conversation

capotear *tr* (*al toro*) to challenge; (*dificultades*) evade, duck; beguile, take in; (*una obra teatral*) cut, make cuts in

capricho *m* caprice, whim, fancy

capricho•so -sa *adj* capricious, whimsical; willful

caprichu•do -da *adj* capricious, whimsical

Capricornio *m* (astr) Capricorn

cápsula *f* capsule; (*de botella*) cap

capsular *tr* to cap

captación *f* capture; (*de las aguas de un río*) harnessing; (rad) tuning in, picking up

captar *tr* to catch; (*la confianza de una persona*) win; (*las aguas de un río*) harness; (*las ondas radiofónicas*) tune in, pick up; (*lo que uno dice*) get, grasp ‖ *ref* to attract, win

captura *f* capture, catch

capturar *tr* to capture, catch

capucha *f* cowl, hood; circumflex accent

capuchina *f* garden nasturtium, Indian cress; Capuchin nun; confection of egg yolks

capucho *m* cowl, hood

capuchón *m* lady's cloak and hood; (*de una plumafuente*) cap; (aut) valve cap

capullo *m* cocoon; coarse spun silk; bud; **capullo de rosa** rosebud

capuzar §60 *tr* to throw in headfirst; (*un buque*) overload at the bow
caqui *adj* khaki ‖ *m* khaki; Japanese persimmon
caquinos *mpl* (Mex) guffaw, outburst of laughter
cara *f* face; look, countenance; façade, front; (*de disco de fonógrafo*) side; **a cara descubierta** openly; **cara a** facing; **cara a cara** face-to-face; **cara al público** with an audience; **cara de acelga** sallow face; **cara de ajo** vinegar face; **cara de hereje** (*persona de feo aspecto*) fright, baboon; **cara de vinagre** vinegar face; **¿cara o cruz?** heads or tails?, **¿cara o ceca?** (Arg) heads or tails?, **¿cara o sello?** heads or tails?; **dar la cara** to take the consequences; **de cara** in the face; facing; **echar a cara o cruz** to flip a coin; **hacer cara a** to stand up to; **tener buena cara** to look well, to look good; **tener mala cara** to look ill, to look bad
cárabe *m* amber
carabina *f* carbine; chaperon
caracol *m* snail; snail shell; (*de pelo*) curl; (*trazado en espiral*) spiral; (*del oído*) cochlea
carácter *m* (*pl* **caracteres**) character; (*marca que se pone a las reses*) brand
característi•co -ca *adj* characteristic ‖ *m* (theat) old man ‖ *f* characteristic; (theat) old woman
caracteriza•do -da *adj* distinguished
caracterizar §60 *tr* to characterize; to confer a distinction on; (*un personaje en la escena*) to interpret ‖ *ref* to dress and make up for a role
caradu•ro -ra *adj* brazen; shameless ‖ *f* scoundrel
caramba *interj* confound it!; upon my word!
carámbano *m* icicle
carambola *f* carom; double shot; trick, cheating
carambolear *intr* to carom ‖ *ref* to get tipsy
caramelo *m* caramel; drop, lozenge
carantamaula *f* ugly false face; (*persona*) ugly mug
carantoña *f* ugly false face; **carantoñas** adulation, fawning
carátula *f* mask; (*profesión de actor*) stage, theater; title page; (*de reloj*) (Mex, Guat) face
caravana *f* caravan; (*casa rodante*) trailer, travel trailer; **caravana fija** mobile home, trailer home
caray *m* var of **carey**
carbohielo *m* dry ice
carbóli•co -ca *adj* carbolic
carbón *m* (*de leña*) charcoal; (*de piedra*) coal; (*electrodo de carbono de la lámpara de arco o la pila*) carbon; black crayon; (*honguillo parásito*) smut; **carbón de bujía** cannel coal, jet coal; **carbón tal como sale** run-of-mine coal
carboncillo *m* charcoal, charcoal pencil
carbonera *f* bunker, coal bunker; coalbin; (Col) coal mine
carbonería *f* coalyard
carbone•ro -ra *adj* coal, charcoal; coaling ‖ *mf* coaldealer; charcoal burner ‖ *f* see **carbonera**
carbonilla *f* fine coal; (*en los cilindros*) carbon
carbonizar §60 *tr* to char
carbono *m* carbon
carbunclo *m* (*piedra*) carbuncle; (pathol) carbuncle, anthrax symptom
carbunco *m* (pathol) carbuncle, anthrax symptom
carbúnculo *m* (*piedra*) carbuncle
carburador *m* carburetor
carburo *m* carbide
carcacha *f* (Mex) jalopy
carcaj *m* quiver
carcajada *f* outburst of laughter
carcasa *f* rocket; framework; carcass, casing; (compu) cover; (compu) housing
cárcel *f* jail, prison; (*para oprimir dos piezas de madera encoladas*) clamp
carcele•ro -ra *adj* jail ‖ *m* jailer, warden
carcinóge•no -na *adj* carcinogenic; cancer-causing ‖ *m* carcinogen
carcinoma *f* carcinoma
carcoma *f* woodworm, borer; anxiety, worry; spendthrift
carcomer *tr* to bore, gnaw away at; undermine, harass ‖ *ref* to become worm-eaten
cardán *m* universal joint
cardenal *m* cardinal; cardinal bird; black-and-blue mark
cardenillo *m* verdigris
cárde•no -na *adj* purple; dapple-gray; (*agua*) opaline
cardía•co -ca *adj* cardiac ‖ *mf* (*persona que padece del corazón*) cardiac ‖ *m* (*remedio*) cardiac
cardinal *adj* cardinal
cardo *m* thistle
cardume *m* school (*of fish*)
carear *tr* to bring face to face; compare ‖ *intr* — **carear a** to overlook ‖ *ref* to meet face to face
carecer §22 *intr* — **carecer de** to lack, need, be in want of
carecimiento *m* lack, need, want
carencia *f* lack, need, want
carencia•do -da *adj* deprived, disadvantaged, needy
carente *adj* — **carente de** lacking
careo *m* meeting; confrontation
care•ro -ra *adj* dear, expensive
carestía *f* scarcity, want, dearth; high prices; **carestía de la vida** high cost of living
careta *f* mask; **careta antigás** gas mask
carey *m* hawksbill turtle; tortoise shell
carga *f* load, loading; (*mercancías que se transportan*) freight, cargo; (*peso u obligación que pesan sobre una persona*) burden; (*de substancia explosiva, de electricidad, de soldados contra el enemigo*) charge; charge, responsibility, obligation; **carga de familia** dependent; **carga de la prueba** burden of proof; **carga de profundidad** depth charge; **carga de punta** (elec) peak load; **carga por eje** axle load; **carga útil** payload; **echar la carga a** to put the blame on; **volver a la carga** to keep at it

cargaderas *fpl* (Col) suspenders
cargadero *m* loading platform; freight station
carga•do -da *adj* loaded; (*cielo*) overcast, cloudy; (*atmósfera, tiempo*) close, sultry; (*alambre eléctrico*) hot, charged; (*café, té*) strong; (*rato, hora*) busy; **cargado de años** along in years; **cargado de espaldas** round-shouldered, stoop-shouldered
cargador *m* loader, stevedore; carrier, porter; (*de acumulador*) charger
cargamento *m* load; (naut) loading; (naut) cargo, shipment
cargante *adj* boring, annoying, tiresome
cargar §44 *tr* (*un peso, mercancías; un carro, un mulo, un barco; un horno; un arma de fuego; a una persona*) to load; (*a una persona con un peso u obligación*) burden; (*un acumulador; al enemigo*) charge; (*a una persona*) charge with; entrust with; annoy, bore, weary; **cargar en cuenta a** (*una persona*) to charge to the account of; **cargar** (*a una persona*) **de** to charge with; burden with || *intr* to load; (*el viento*) turn; crowd; incline, tip; (*el acento*) fall; eat too much, drink too much; **cargar con** to pick up; walk away with; (*un fusil*) shoulder; take on; **cargar sobre** to rest on; bother, pester; devolve on || *ref* (*el cielo*) to become overcast; (*el viento*) turn; become annoyed, be bored; **cargarse de** to have a lot of; (*lágrimas*) be bathed in
cargaréme *m* receipt, voucher
cargazón *f* loading; (*en el estómago, la cabeza, etc.*) heaviness; mass of heavy clouds; (Arg) clumsy job; (Chile) good crop; **cargazón alta** (coll) high office; high official
cargo *m* job, position; duty, responsibility; burden, weight; management; (*falta que se atribuye a uno; cantidad que uno debe y la acción de anotarla*) charge; **a cargo de** in charge of; **cargo de conciencia** sense of guilt; **girar a cargo de** to draw on; **hacerse cargo de** to take charge of; to realize, become aware of; to look into; **librar a cargo de** to draw on; **vestir el cargo** to look the part
cargosear *tr* (Arg, Chile) to pester
cargo•so -sa *adj* annoying, bothersome; onerous, costly
carguero *m* (naut) freighter; (Arg, Urug) beast of burden
cariaconteci•do -da *adj* downcast, woebegone
cariar §77 *tr & intr* to decay
cariátide *f* caryatid
caribe *adj* Caribbean || *m* savage, brute
caricatura *f* (*descripción o figura grotescas; retrato festivo*) caricature; (*retrato festivo*) cartoon
caricaturista *mf* caricaturist; cartoonist
caricaturizar §60 *tr* to caricature; cartoon
caricia *f* caress; endearment
caridad *f* charity; **la caridad bien ordenada empieza por uno mismo** charity begins at home
caries *f* decay, tooth decay; caries
carilla *f* (*de colmenero*) mask; (*de libro*) page
carille•no -na *adj* full-faced
carillón *m* carillon
carine•gro -gra *adj* swarthy
cariño *m* love, affection; loved one; (Chile) gift, present; **cariños** caresses, endearments; (Arg) greetings
cariño•so -sa *adj* loving, affectionate
caripare•jo -ja *adj* stone-faced, impassive
carirraí•do -da *adj* brazen-faced, shameless
carisma *f* charisma
carismáti•co -ca *adj* charismatic
carita *f* little face; **dar** or **hacer carita** (*una mujer coqueta*) (Mex) to smile back
caritati•vo -va *adj* charitable
cariz *m* (*de la atmósfera, el tiempo*) appearance, look; (*de un asunto*) look, outlook; (*de la cara de uno*) look; **mal cariz** angry look, scowl
carlinga *f* (aer) cockpit
Carlomagno *m* Charlemagne
Carlos *m* Charles
carlota *f* pudding; **carlota rusa** charlotte russe || **Carlota** *f* Charlotte
carmelita *f* (Hond) station wagon
carmen *m* song, poem; house and garden (*in Granada*)
carmesí (*pl* **-síes**) *adj & m* crimson
carnada *f* bait; (coll) bait, trap
carnal; *adj* carnal; (*hermano*) full; (*primo*) first
carnaval *m* carnival
carne *f* (*parte blanda del cuerpo humano y del animal*) flesh; (*la comestible del animal*) meat; **carne de cañón** cannon fodder; **carne de cerdo asada** roast pork; **carne de cordero** lamb; **carne de gallina** goose flesh; **carne de horca** gallows bird; **carne de res** beef; **carne de ternera** veal; **carne de vaca asada** roast of beef; **carne de venado** venison; **carne fiambre** cold meat; **carne molina, carne picada** ground beef; **carne salada de res** corned beef; **carne sin hueso** cinch, snap; **carne y sangre** flesh and blood; **cobrar carnes** to put on flesh; **echar carnes** (Mex) to swear, curse; **en carnes** naked; **en vivas carnes** stark-naked
carné *m or* **carnet** *m* notebook; membership card; (Arg) dance card; **carné de conducir, conductor, chófer** *or* **manejo** driver's license; **carné de identidad** identification card
carnear *tr* (Arg, Chile, Urug) to butcher, slaughter; (Arg, Urug) to stab; (Chile) to take in, swindle
carnero *m* sheep; (*carne de este animal*) mutton; (*osario*) charnel house; family vault; (*persona que no tiene voluntad propia*) (Arg, Chile) sheep; **cantar para el carnero** (Arg, Bol, Urug) to die; **no hay tales carneros** there's no truth to it
carnicería *f* butcher shop, meat market; (fig) carnage, massacre
carnice•ro -ra *adj* carnivorous; bloodthirsty || *mf* butcher

carnosidad *f* fleshiness, corpulence; (*excrecencia carnosa anormal*) proud flesh
carno•so -sa *adj* fleshy; meaty, fat
ca•ro -ra *adj* dear, expensive; dear, beloved; || *f* see **cara** || **caro** *adv* dear, dearly; at a high price
carpa *f* tent; beach tent; marquee; awning; stand, stall (*at a fair*); (*de un circo*) big top; (zool) carp; **carpa de oxígeno** oxygen tent; **carpa dorada** goldfish
carpanta *f* raging hunger
carpeta *f* (*cubierta para mesas*) table cover; (*par de cubiertas para documentos*) letter file, portfolio; (*factura*) invoice; (Col) accounting department; (compu) folder; (Peru) writing desk
carpintería *f* carpentry; carpenter shop; **carpintería de taller** millwork
carpintero *m* carpenter, woodpecker; **carpintero de carreta** wheelwright
carra•co -ca *adj* old, decrepit || *f* (*barco viejo*) tub, hulk; (*instrumento de madera para producir un ruido desapacible*) rattle; (*berbiquí*) ratchet drill || **la Carraca** Cádiz navy yard
carraspear *intr* to be hoarse
carraspera *f* hoarseness
carrera *f* (*paso del que corre*) run; (*lucha de velocidad*) race; (*sitio para correr*) race track; (*espacio recorrido corriendo*) course, stretch; (*curso de la vida, profesión*) career; (*calle*) avenue, boulevard; (*raya, crencha*) part (*in hair*); (*en las medias*) run; (*hilera*) row, line; (*viga*) rafter, girder; (*movimiento del émbolo del motor*) stroke; **a carrera abierta** at full speed; **carrera a pie** footrace; **carrera armamentista** or **de armamentos** arms race; **carrera ascendente** upstroke; **carrera de baquetas** gauntlet; **carrera de caballos** horse race; **carrera de campanario** steeplechase; **carrera de obstáculos** obstacle race; steeplechase; **carrera de relevos** relay race; **carrera descendente** downstroke; **carrera de trotones** harness race; **carrera de vallas** hurdle race; **carrera espacial** space race; **carreras** horse racing, turf; racing
carrerista *adj* horsy || *mf* racegoer; auto racer; bicycle racer || *m* outrider || *f* (slang) streetwalker
carreta *f* cart; **carreta de bueyes** oxcart
carrete *m* reel, spool; fishing reel; (elec) coil
carretear *tr* to cart, haul; (*un carro, una carreta*) drive; (aer) to taxi || *intr* (aer) to taxi
carretera *f* highway, road; **carretera cerrada** *SIGN* road closed; **carretera de circunvalación** beltway; **carretera de doble calzada** divided highway; **carretera de peaje** turnpike; **carretera de vía libre** expressway, limited-access highway; **carretera secundaria** back road
carretería *f* carts; wagon work; carting business; wagon shop
carrete•ro -ra *adj* wagon, carriage || *m* wheelwright; teamster; charioteer; **jurar como un carretero** to swear like a trooper || *f* see **carretera**
carretilla *f* wheelbarrow; baggage truck; (*para enseñar a los niños a andar*) gocart; (*buscapiés*) snake, serpent; (Arg, Chile, Urug) jaw; **carretilla de mano** handcart; **carretilla elevadora** forklift truck; **de carretilla** offhand
carretón *m* cart, wagon, dray; gocart; (rr) truck; covered wagon
carricoche *m* covered wagon
carricuba *f* street sprinkler
carril *m* (*barra de acero en el ferrocarril*) rail, track; (*huella*) track, rut; (*hecho por el arado*) furrow; lane, path; (Chile) train; (Chile, P-R) railroad; **carril de toma** third rail
carrilera *f* track, rut
carrilero *m* (Peru) railroader
carrillera *f* jaw; chin strap
carrillo *m* cheek, jowl; pulley; **comer a dos carrillos** to eat like a glutton; have two sources of income; play both sides
carrito *m* shopping cart
carrizo *m* ditch reed
carro *m* cart, wagon; car, auto; (mach) carriage; **carro alegórico** float; **carro blindado** armored car; **carro bomba** car bomb; **carro correo** mail car; **carro de asalto** tank; **carro de combate** combat car, tank; **carro de equipajes** baggage car; **carro de mudanza** moving van; **carro de riego** street sprinkler; **carro frigorífero** refrigerator car; **carro fúnebre** hearse; **Carro Mayor** Big Dipper; **Carro Menor** Little Dipper; **carro romano** chariot; **pare Ud. el carro** hold your horses
ca•rró *m* (*pl* **-rrós**) diamond
carrocería *f* (*de automóvil*) body
carrocha *f* eggs (*of insect*)
carromato *m* covered wagon
carro•ño -ña *adj & f* carrion
carro-patrulla *f* (SAm) patrol car; police car
carroza *f* coach, carriage; **carroza alegórica** float; **carroza fúnebre** hearse
carruaje *m* carriage
carta *f* (*comunicación escrita*) letter; (*constitución escrita de un país*) charter; (*naipe*) card, playing card; map; **carta aérea** airmail letter; **carta blanca** carte blanche; **carta bomba** letter bomb; **carta calumniosa** poison-pen letter; **carta certificada** registered letter; **carta de amor** love letter; **carta de marear** (naut) chart; **carta de naturaleza** naturalization papers; **carta de vuelo** flight plan; **carta general** form letter; **carta por avión** airmail letter; **carta verde** green card; **poner las cartas boca arriba** to put one's cards on the table
cartabón *m* carpenter's square
cartagi•nés -nesa *adj & mf* Carthaginian
Cartago *f* Carthage
cartapacio *m* notebook; schoolboy's satchel; writing book; (*papeles contenidos en una carpeta*) file, dossier
cartear *intr* to play low cards (*in order to see*

how the game stands) || *ref* to write to each other

cartel *m* show bill, poster, placard; cartel, trust; (*pasquín*) lampoon; (*de toreros*) bill, lineup; (*del torero*) fame, reputation; **cartel de teatro** bill, show bill; **dar cartel a** to headline; **se prohibe fijar carteles** post no bills; **tener cartel** to be the rage

cartela *f* card; bracket

cartelera *f* billboard; (*en los periódicos*) amusement page, theater section

cartelero *m* billposter

cartelón *m* show bill

carteo *m* finessing; exchange of letters

cárter *m* (mach) housing; **cárter de engranajes** gearcase; **cárter del cigüeñal** crankcase

cartera *f* portfolio; pocket flap; **cartera de bolsillo** billfold, wallet

cartería *f* sorting room

carterista *m* pickpocket, purse snatcher

cartero *m* letter carrier, postman

cartilagino•so -sa *adj* gristly

cartílago *m* gristle

cartilla *f* primer, speller, reader; notebook; (*de la caja de ahorros*) deposit book; **cartilla de racionamiento** ration book

cartivana *f* (bb) hinge, joint

cartón *m* cardboard, pasteboard; cardboard box; **cartón de yeso y fieltro** plasterboard; **cartón picado** stencil; **cartón tabla** wallboard

cartoné — en cartoné (bb) in boards, bound in boards

cartucho *m* cartridge

cartulina *f* fine cardboard

casa *f* (*edificio para habitar*) house; (*hogar, domicilio*) home; (*establecimiento comercial o industrial*) firm, concern; (*familia*) household; (*escaque*) square; **a casa** home, homeward; **casa club** clubhouse; **casa consistorial** town hall, city hall; **casa cuartel** police station; **casa cuna** children's home; **casa de azotea** penthouse; **casa de baños** bathhouse; **casa de campo** country house; **casa de caridad** poorhouse; **casa de citas** house of assignation; **casa de correos** post office; **casa de empeños** pawnshop; **casa de expósitos** foundling home; **casa de fieras** menagerie; **casa de huéspedes** boarding house; **casa de juego** gambling house; **casa del guarda** gatehouse; **casa de locos** madhouse; **casa de modas** dress shop; **casa de moneda** mint; **casa de muñecas** dollhouse; **casa de préstamos** pawnshop; **casa de salud** private hospital; nursing home; **casa de socorro** first-aid station; **casa de vecindad** or **de vecinos** apartment house, tenement house; **casa discográfica** record company; **casa editorial** publishing house; **casa matriz** main office; **casa modelo** model home, sample home; **casa publica** brothel; **casa real** royal palace; royal family; **casa refugio** hostel for battered women; **casa rodante** trailer home, house trailer, mobile home; **casas baratas** low-cost housing; **casa solar** or **solariega** ancestral mansion, manor house; **casa y comida** board and lodging; **¡convida la casa!** the drinks are on the house!; **en casa** home, at home; **ir a buscar casa** to go house hunting; **poner casa** to set up housekeeping

casabe *m* var of **cazabe**

casaca *f* dress coat; marriage contract; (Guat, Hond) lively whispered conversation; **volver la casaca** to become a turncoat

casade•ro -ra *adj* marriageable

casa•do -da *adj* married || *mf* married person; **(los) no casados** (coll) singles

casal *m* country place; (Arg) pair, couple

casamente•ro -ra *adj* matchmaking || *mf* matchmaker

casamiento *m* marriage; wedding

casapuerta *f* entrance hall, vestibule

casaquilla *f* jacket

casar *tr* to marry; marry off; match; harmonize; (law) to annul, repeal || *intr* to marry, get married || *ref* to marry, get married; **no casarse con nadie** to get tied up with nobody

casa-remolque *m* trailer home, travel trailer

casatienda *f* store and home combined

cascabel *m* sleigh bell, jingle bell; rattlesnake; **ponerle cascabel al gato** to bell the cat

cascabelear *intr* to jingle; to act tactlessly

cascabeleo *m* jingle

cascabele•ro -ra *adj* tactless, thoughtless || *mf* featherbrain || *m* baby's rattle

cascabillo *m* jingle bell; chaff, husk; cup of acorn

cascada *f* cascade, waterfall

cascajo *m* pebble; gravel, rubble; broken jar; piece of junk; **estar hecho un cascajo** to be old and worn-out, be a wreck

cascanue•ces *m* (*pl* **-ces**) nutcracker

cascar §73 *tr* to crack, break, split; beat, strike, hit || *ref* to crack, break, split

cáscara *f* hull, peel, rind, shell; bark, crust; **cáscara rueda** (Arg) ring-around-a-rosy; **ser de la cáscara amarga** to be wild and flighty; hold advanced views; (Mex) to be determined

cascarón *m* eggshell

cascarra•bias *mf* (*pl* **-bias**) crab, grouch

casco *m* (*pieza que sirve para proteger la cabeza del soldado, el bombero, el obrero, etc.*) helmet, hard hat; (*uña de las caballerías*) hoof; (*pedazo de vasija rota*) potsherd; (*capa de la cebolla*) coat, shell; (*del sombrero*) crown; (*cuerpo de la nave*) hull; (*de un barco inservible*) hulk; (*barril, pipa*) barrel, tank, cask, vat; (*pieza del teléfono*) headset, headpiece; bottle; (mach) shell, casing; (*gajo de la naranja*) (Arg, Col, Chile) slice; (Peru) chest, breast; **casco antiguo** old part of town; **casco de población** or **casco urbano** city limits; **romperse los cascos** to rack one's brain

casera *f* landlady; housekeeper

casería *f* country place; customers

caserío *m* country house; small settlement, hamlet

case•ro -ra *adj* homemade; homeloving; (*remedio*) household; house, home; (*sencillo*) homely || *mf* owner, proprietor; renter; caretaker; janitor; huckster; vendor || *m* landlord || *f* see **casera**

caseta *f* (*casa sin piso alto*) cottage; (*de una feria*) stall, booth; bathhouse

casete *m & f* cassette || *m* cassette player, cassette recorder || *var* **cassette**

casi *adv* almost, nearly; **casi nada** next to nothing; **casi nunca** hardly ever

casilla *f* hut, shack, shed; cabin, lodge; stall, booth; (*escaque*) square; (*compartimiento en un mueble*) pigeonhole; (*división del papel rayado*) column, square; (*taquilla*) ticket office; (*de locomotora o camión*) cab; (Bol, Chile, Peru, Urug) post-office box; (Ecuad) water closet; (Cuba) bird trap; **sacarle a uno de sus casillas** to jolt someone out of his old habits; drive someone crazy

casille•ro -ra *mf* (rr) crossing guard || *m* filing cabinet, set of pigeonholes

casimir *m* cashmere

casino *m* casino; club; clubhouse

caso *m* case; chance; event; **caso de conformidad** in case you agree; **caso que** in case; **de caso pensado** deliberately, on purpose; **en todo caso** at all events; **hacer al caso** to be to the purpose; **hacer caso de** to take into account, pay attention to; **hacer caso omiso de** to pass over in silence, not mention; **no venir al caso** to be beside the point; **poner por caso** to take as an example; **venir al caso** to be just the thing

casorio *m* hasty marriage, unwise marriage

caspa *f* dandruff, scurf

cáspita *interj* well well!, upon my word!

caspo•so -sa *adj* full of dandruff

casquete *m* (*cubierta que se ajusta al casco de la cabeza*) skullcap; skull, cranium; (*pieza de la armadura que cubre el casco de la cabeza*) helmet; (*pieza del teléfono*) headset; **casquete polar** polar icecap

casquillo *m* butt, cap, tip; bushing, sleeve; ferrule; horseshoe

casquiva•no -na *adj* scatterbrained

cassette *m & f* cassette; **en cassette** on cassette || *m* cassette player, cassette recorder || *var* **casete**

casta *f* caste; kind, quality; breed, race

castaña *f* chestnut; (*moño*) knot, chignon; demijohn; **castaña de cajú** cashew nut; **castaña de Indias** horse chestnut; **castaña de Pará** Brazil nut

castañeta *f* castanet; snapping of the fingers

castañetear *tr* (*los dedos*) to snap, click; (*p.ej., una seguidilla*) click off with the castanets || *intr* to click; (*los dientes*) chatter

casta•ño -ña *adj* chestnut, chestnut-colored; (*p.ej., pelo*) brown; (*p.ej., ojos*) hazel || *m* brown; chestnut tree; **castaño de Indias** horse chestnut || *f* see **castaña**

castañuela *f* castanet; **estar como unas castañuelas** to be bubbling over with joy

castella•no -na *adj & mf* Castilian || *m* Castilian, Spanish (*language*) || *f* chatelaine

casticidad *f* purity, correctness (*in language*)

casticismo *m* purism

castidad *f* chastity

castiga•dor -dora *mf* punisher || *m* seducer, Don Juan

castigar §44 *tr* to punish, chastise; (*la carne*) mortify; (*los gastos*) cut down, curtail; (*obras, escritos*) correct, emend; (*un tornillo*) (Mex) tighten

castigo *m* punishment, chastisement

Castilla *f* Castile; **Castilla la Nueva** New Castile; **Castilla la Vieja** Old Castile

castillete *m* (min) derrick; tower

castillo *m* castle; (*montura sobre un elefante*) howdah; **castillo en el aire** castle in Spain, castle in the air; **castillo de naipes** house of cards; **castillo de proa** forecastle

casti•zo -za *adj* chaste, pure, correct; pureblooded; real, regular

cas•to -ta *adj* chaste, pure || *f* see **casta**

castor *m* beaver

castrar *tr* to castrate; (*una planta*) prune, cut back; weaken

casual *adj* casual, accidental, chance

casualidad *f* accident, chance; chance event; **por casualidad** by chance

casuca or **casucha** *f* shack, shanty

casulla *f* chasuble

cata *f* tasting; taste, sample

catacal•dos *mf* (*pl* **-dos**) rolling stone; busybody

catacumba *f* catacomb

catafoto *m* (rear) reflector

cata•lán -lana *adj & mf* Catalan, Catalonian

catalejo *m* spyglass

catalizador *m* catalytic converter

catalogar §44 *tr* to catalogue; to categorize

catálogo *m* catalogue, catalog

Cataluña *f* Catalonia

cataplasma *f* poultice; **cataplasma de mostaza** mustard plaster

catapulta *f* catapult

catapultar *tr* to catapult

catar *tr* to taste, sample; check, examine; be on the lookout for

catarata *f* cataract, waterfall; (pathol) cataract

catarro *m* (*inflamación de las membranas mucosas*) catarrh; (*resfriado*) head cold

catástrofe *f* catastrophe

catavino *m* cup for tasting wine

catavi•nos *m* (*pl* **-nos**) winetaster; (*borracho*) rounder

catear *tr* to hunt, look for; (*a un alumno*) to flunk; to explore; (*una casa*) to search

catecismo *m* catechism

cátedra *f* chair, professorship; academic subject; teacher's desk; classroom; **poner cátedra** to hold forth

catedral *f* cathedral

catedrático *m* university professor
categoría *f* category; status, standing; class, kind; condition, quality; **de categoría** prominent
caterva *f* throng, crowd
catéter *m* catheter
cateterizar §60 *tr* to catheterize
cátodo *m* cathode
católi•co -ca *adj* catholic; Catholic; **no estar muy católico** to be under the weather || *mf* Catholic; **católico romano** Roman Catholic
catorce *adj & pron* fourteen || *m* fourteen; (*en las fechas*) fourteenth
catorcea•vo -va *adj & m* fourteenth
catorza•vo -va *adj & m* fourteenth
catre *m* (SAm) cot; pad (slang); **catre de tijera** folding cot
catrecillo *m* campstool, folding canvas chair
ca•trín -trina *adj* (CAm, Mex) sporty, swell || *mf* (CAm, Mex) sport, dude
caucasia•no -na or **caucási•co -ca** *adj & mf* Caucasian
Cáucaso *m* Caucasus
cauce *m* river bed; channel, ditch, trench
cauchal *m* rubber plantation
caucho *m* rubber; rubber plant; (Col) rubber raincoat; **caucho esponjoso** foam rubber; **cauchos** (*chanclos*) rubbers
caución *f* precaution; (law) bail, security
caucionar *tr* to guard against; (law) to give bail for
caudal *adj* of great volume || *m* (*de agua*) volume; abundance; wealth
caudalo•so -sa *adj* of great volume; abundant; rich, wealthy
caudillo *m* chief, leader; military leader; caudillo, head of state
causa *f* cause; (law) suit, trial; (Chile) bite, snack; (Peru) potato salad; **a** or **por causa de** on account of, because of
causa•dor -dora *adj* causing || *mf* (*persona*) cause
causante *mf* (*persona*) cause; (law) principal, constituent; (Mex) taxpayer
causar *tr* to cause
causear *tr* (Chile) to get the best of || *intr* (Chile) to have a bite
causeo *m* (Chile) bite, snack
cáusti•co -ca *adj* caustic
cautela *f* caution
cautelo•so -sa *adj* cautious, guarded
cauterizar §60 *tr* to cauterize
cautín *m* soldering iron
cautivar *tr* to take prisoner; attract, win over; (*encantar*) captivate
cautiverio *m* or **cautividad** *f* captivity
cauti•vo -va *adj & mf* captive
cau•to -ta *adj* cautious
cavar *tr* to dig, dig up || *intr* (*una herida*) to go deep; (*el caballo*) to paw; **cavar en** to study thoroughly, to delve into
caverna *f* cavern, cave
cavidad *f* cavity
cavilar *tr* to brood over || *intr* to worry, fret
cavilo•so -sa *adj* suspicious, mistrustful; (CAm) gossipy; (Col) touchy
cayado *m* (*de pastor*) crook; (*de obispo*) crozier
cayo *m* key, reef; **Cayo Hueso** Key West; **Cayos de la Florida** Florida Keys
caz *m* (*pl* **caces**) flume, millrace
caza *m* pursuit plane, fighter; **caza de reacción** jet fighter || *f* chase, hunt; hunting; (*animales que se cazan*) game; **a caza de** on the hunt for; **caza al hombre** manhunt; **caza al tesoro** treasure hunt; **caza de brujas** witch-hunt; **caza de grillos** fool's errand, wild-goose chase; **caza submarina** underwater fishing; **ir de caza** to go hunting || *m* fighter plane
cazaautógra•fos *mf* (*pl* **-fos**) autograph seeker
cazabe *m* cassava, manioc; cassava bread
caza•dor -dora *adj* hunting || *m* hunter; huntsman; **cazador de alforja** trapper; **cazador de cabezas** head-hunter; **cazador de dotes** fortune hunter; **cazador de ratones** mouser; **cazador furtivo** poacher || *f* huntress; hunting jacket; jacket
cazafortunas *f* (pej) gold digger
cazanoti•cias (*pl* **-cias**) *m* newshawk || *f* newshen
cazasubmarinos *m* sub(marine) chaser
cazar §60 *tr* to chase; hunt; catch; (*en un descuido o error*) catch up; (*un descuido o error*) catch; (*adquirir con maña*) wangle; (*con halagos o engaños*) take in || *intr* to hunt
cazarreactor *m* jet fighter
cazcalear *intr* to buzz around
cazo *m* dipper, ladle; glue pot; (*de cuchillo*) back
cazonete *m* (naut) toggle
cazuela *f* earthen casserole; stew; (archaic) gallery for women; (SAm) chicken stew
cazu•rro -rra *adj* sullen, surly
cazuz *m* ivy
CD *m* (letterword) (**compact-disc, disco compacto**) CD (compact disk)
C. de J. *abbr* **Compañía de Jesús**
cebada *f* barley
cebadera *f* nose bag
cebador *m* (mach) primer
cebar *tr* (*a un animal*) to fatten; (*un horno*) feed; (*un arma de fuego, una bomba, un carburador*) prime; (*una pasión, la esperanza*) nourish; (*atraer*) lure; (*un clavo, un tornillo*) make catch, make take hold; (*un anzuelo*) bait || *intr* (*un clavo, un tornillo*) to catch, take hold || *ref* (*una enfermedad, una epidemia*) to rage; **cebarse en** to be absorbed in; vent one's fury on
cebo *m* fattening; feed; bait; lure; (*carga de un arma de fuego*) primer; priming
cebolla *f* onion; bulb; (*del velón*) oil receptacle
cebra *f* zebra
ce•bú *m* (*pl* **-búes**) zebu
ceca *f* mint; **de Ceca en Meca** or **de la Ceca a la Meca** hither and thither, from pillar to post
cecear *intr* to lisp

ceceo *m* lisp, lisping; *pronouncing some words with [θ] instead of [s],* e.g., **cinco** [ˈθinko] *instead of* **cinco** [ˈsinko]
cecina *f* dried beef
cedazo *m* sieve
ceder *tr* to yield, cede, give up || *intr* to yield, give way, give in; slacken, relax; go down, decline
cedro *m* cedar; **cedro de Virginia** juniper, red cedar
cedrón *m* (bot) lemon verbena
cédula *f* (*de papel*) slip; form, blank; rent sign; certificate, document; **cédula de vecindad** or **cédula personal** identification papers
cedulón *m* proclamation, public notice; (*pasquín*) lampoon
céfiro *m* zephyr
cegar **§66** *tr* to blind; (*un agujero*) plug, stop up; (*una puerta, una ventana*) wall up || *intr* to go blind; be blinded || *ref* to be blinded
cega•to -ta *adj* dim-sighted, weak-eyed
ceguedad *f* blindness
ceguera *f* blindness; blackout
Ceilán Ceylon
ceila•nés -nesa *adj & mf* Ceylonese
ceja *f* (*pelo sobre la cuenca del ojo*) eyebrow; edge, rim; cloud cap; clearing for a road; **arquear las cejas** to raise one's eyebrows; **fruncir las cejas** to knit one's brow; **quemarse las cejas** to burn the midnight oil
cejar *intr* to back up; turn back; slacken
cejijun•to -ta or **ceju•do -da** *adj* beetle-browed; scowling
celada *f* ambush; trap, trick
celador *m* guard (*e.g., in a museum*); (elec) lineman; (Urug) policeman
celaje *m* cloud effect; skylight, transom; ghost
celar *tr* to see to; watch over, keep an eye on; hide; carve
celda *f* cell; **celda de castigo** solitary confinement
celdilla *f* cell; niche
celebración *f* celebration; applause; (*de una reunión*) holding
celebrante *m* (*sacerdote*) celebrant
celebrar *tr* to celebrate; (*una reunión*) hold; (*aprobar*) welcome; (*un matrimonio*) perform; (*misa*) say || *intr* (*decir misa*) to celebrate; be glad || *ref* to take place, be held; be celebrated
célebre *adj* celebrated, famous; funny, witty; pretty
celebridad *f* (*fama; persona*) celebrity
celeridad *f* speed, swiftness
celeste *adj* celestial; sky-blue
celestial *adj* celestial, heavenly; stupid, silly
celestina *f* procuress, bawd
celestinaje *m* procuring, pandering
celibato *m* celibacy; bachelor
célibe *adj* celibate, single, unmarried || *mf* celibate, single person || *m* bachelor || *f* unmarried woman
celinda *f* mock orange
cellisca *f* sleet, sleet storm
cellisquear *intr* to sleet
celo *m* zeal; envy; (*impulso reproductivo en las bestias*) heat, rut; **celos** jealousy
celofán *m* or **celofana** *f* cellophane
celosía *f* (*celotipia*) jealousy; (*enrejado de listoncillos*) lattice window, jalousie
celo•so -sa *adj* (*que tiene celo*) zealous; (*que tiene celos*) jealous; fearful, distrustful; (naut) unsteady
celotipia *f* jealousy
celta *adj* Celtic || *mf* Celt || *m* (*idioma*) Celtic
célti•co -ca *adj* Celtic
célula *f* cell; **célula fonorreceptora** playback head; **célula fotoeléctrica** photoelectric cell, electric eye; **célula fotovoltaica** *or* **solar** solar cell; **células madre** stem cells
celuloide *m* celluloid; **llevar al celuloide** to put on the screen
cementado *adj* cemented; case-hardened
cementerio *m* cemetery
cemento *m* cement; concrete; **cemento armado** reinforced concrete
cena *f* supper; dinner; **cena de gala** banquet; **cena de negocios** business dinner, power lunch || **la Cena** the Last Supper
cena•dor -dora *mf* diner-out || *m* arbor, bower, summerhouse
cenaduría *f* (Mex) supper club
cenagal *m* quagmire
cenago•so -sa *adj* muddy, miry
cenaoscu•ras *mf* (*pl* **-ras**) recluse; skinflint
cenar *tr* to have for supper, have for dinner || *intr* to have supper, have dinner
cencerrada *f* tin-pan serenade
cencerrear *intr* to keep jingling; rattle, jangle; play out of tune
cencerro *m* cowbell; **a cencerros tapados** cautiously
cendal *m* gauze, sendal
cenefa *f* edging, trimming, border
cenicero *m* ash tray
cenicien•to -ta *adj* ashen, ash-gray || **la Cenicienta** Cinderella
cenit *m* zenith
ceniza *f* ash; ashes; **cenizas** ashes; **huir de las cenizas y caer en las brasas** to jump from the frying pan into the fire
ceni•zo -za *adj* ashen, ash-gray || *f* see **ceniza**
cenojil *m* garter
cenote *m* (Mex) deep underground water reservoir
censo *m* census; **censo electoral** electoral roll *o* register; **levantar el censo** to take the census
censor *m* censor; **censor jurado de cuentas** certified public accountant
censura *f* censure; censoring; gossip; **censura de cuentas** auditing
censurar *tr* (*criticar, reprobar*) to censure; (*formar juicio de*) censor
centauro *m* centaur
centa•vo -va *adj* hundredth || *m* hundredth; cent

centella *f* flash of lightning; flash of light; spark; (*de ingenio, de ira*) (fig) spark, flash
centellar or **centellear** *intr* to flash, spark; glimmer, gleam, twinkle
centenar *m* hundred; **a centenares** by the hundreds
centena•rio -ria *adj* centennial || *mf* centenarian || *m* centennial
cente•no -na *adj* hundredth || *m* rye
centési•mo -ma *adj & m* hundredth
centígra•do -da *adj* centigrade
centímetro *m* centimeter
cénti•mo -ma *adj* hundredth || *m* hundredth; centime
centinela *mf* (*persona*) watch, guard || *m & f* (*soldado*) sentinel, sentry; **hacer de centinela** to stand sentinel
centípedo *m* centipede
centón patchwork quilt, crazy quilt
central *adj* central || *m* sugar mill, sugar refinery || *f* headquarters, main office; powerhouse; (telp) exchange, central; **central de correos** main post office; **central de teléfonos** telephone exchange; **central nuclear** nuclear power station; **central sindical** labor union
centralista *mf* telephone operator
centralita *f* switchboard
centralizar §60 *tr & ref* to centralize
centrar *tr* to center; hit the center || *ref* to concentrate; stress
céntri•co -ca *adj* center, central; (*próximo al centro de la ciudad*) downtown
centrifugadora *f* centrifuge; spin-dryer
centrifugar §44 *tr* to spin-dry, spin
centro *m* center; middle; business district, downtown; club; object, goal, purpose; **centro comercial** shopping mall; **centro de control** mission control; **centro de estudios** private school; **centro de mesa** centerpiece; **centro de operaciones** (mil, naut) control room; **centro docente** educational institution; **centro espacial** space center; **centro estudiantil en el campus** student center; **pegar centro** (CAm) to hit the bull's-eye
Centro América *f* Central America
centroamerica•no -na *adj & mf* Central American
cénts. *abbr* **céntimos**
ceñi•do -da *adj* tight, tight-fitting; lithe, svelte; thrifty
ceñidor *m* belt, girdle, sash
ceñir §72 *tr* to gird; girdle; fasten around the waist; fasten, tie; abridge, shorten; surround; (*la espada*) gird on; (mil) to besiege || *ref* (*reducirse en los gastos*) to tighten one's belt; (*a pocas palabras*) restrict oneself; adapt oneself; **ceñirse a** (*p.ej., un muro*) to hug, keep close to
ceño *m* frown; (*del cielo, las nubes, el mar*) threatening look; (*cerco, aro*) hoop, ring, band; **arrugar el ceño** to knit one's brow; **mirar con ceño** to frown at
ceño•so -sa or **ceñu•do -da** *adj* beetlebrowed; frowning, grim, gruff
cepa *f* (*de árbol*) stump; (*de la cola del animal*) stub; (*de la vid*) vinestalk; (*de una famila o linaje*) strain; **de buena cepa** of well-known quality
cepillar *tr* to plane; brush; smooth; (SAm) to flatter
cepillo *m* (*instrumento para alisar la madera*) plane; (*utensilio para limpieza*) brush; (*cepo para limosnas*) charity box, poor box; (CAm, Mex) flatterer; **cepillo de cabeza** hairbrush; **cepillo de dientes** toothbrush; **cepillo de ropa** clothesbrush; **cepillo de uñas** nail brush
cepo *m* (*de limosnas*) poor box; (*rama de árbol*) bough, branch; (*trampa*) snare, trap; (*del yunque*) stock; (*para devanar la seda*) reel; clamp, vise; (*para asegurar a un reo*) stocks, pillory; **¡cepos quedos!** quiet!, stop it!
cera *f* wax; **cera de abejas** beeswax; **cera de los oídos** earwax; **cera de lustrar** polishing wax; **cera de pisos** floor wax; **ceras** honeycomb; **ser como una cera** to be wax in one's hands
cerámi•co -ca *adj* ceramic
cerbatana *f* peashooter; ear trumpet; spokesperson, go-between
cerca *m* close-up; **tener buen cerca** to look good at close quarters || *f* fence, wall; **cerca viva** hedge || *adv* near; **cerca de** near, close to; about; to, at the court of; **de cerca** closely; at close range
cercado *m* fence, wall; walled-in garden or field
cercanía *f* nearness, proximity; **cercanías** neighborhood, vicinity
cerca•no -na *adj* close, near; adjoining, neighboring; (*que debe acontecer en breve*) early
cercar §73 *tr* to fence in, wall in; encircle, surround; crowd around; (mil) to besiege
cercenar *tr* to clip, trim; curtail; cut out
cerciorar *tr* to inform, assure || *ref* to find out; **cerciorarse de** to ascertain, find out about
cerco *m* (*aro, anillo*) hoop, ring; (*marco de puerta o ventana*) casing, frame; (*círculo que aparece alrededor del sol o la luna*) halo; (*reunión de personas*) circle, group; fence, wall; (mil) siege; **poner cerco a** (mil) to lay siege to
cerda *f* bristle, horsehair; (*hembra del cerdo*) sow
cerdear *intr* to be weak in the forelegs; (*las cuerdas de un instrumento*) rasp, grate; hold back, look for excuses
Cerdeña *f* Sardinia
cerdo *m* hog; (*persona sucia*) pig, swine; (*hombre sin cortesía*) cad, ill-bred fellow; **cerdo de muerte** pig to be slaughtered; **cerdo de vida** pig not old enough to be slaughtered; **cerdo marino** porpoise
cerdo•so -sa *adj* bristly
cereal *adj & m* cereal
cerebro *m* brain; (*seso, inteligencia*) brain, brains

ceremonia *f* ceremony; formality; **de ceremonia** formal; **hacer ceremonias** to stand on ceremony; **por ceremonia** as a matter of form
ceremonio•so -sa *adj* ceremonious, punctilious; (*que gusta de ceremonias*) formal
cereza *f* cherry
cerezo *m* cherry tree
cerilla *f* wax taper; wax match
cerillera *f* or **cerillero** *m* match box
cerneja *f* fetlock
cerner §51 *tr* to sift; (*el horizonte*) scan || *intr* to bud, blossom; drizzle || *ref* to waddle; (*el ave*) soar, hover; (*un mal*) threaten; **cernerse sobre** (*amenazar*) to hang over
cernícalo *m* (orn) sparrow hawk; ignoramus; jag, drunk
cernir §28 *tr* to sift
cero *m* zero; **empezar de cero** to start from scratch; **ser un cero a la izquierda** to not count, be a nobody
cerote *m* shoemaker's wax; fear
cerotear *tr* (*el hilo*) to wax || *intr* (Chile) to drip
cerra•do -da *adj* closed; enclosed; close; incomprehensible; (*cielo*) cloudy, overcast; (*barba*) thick; (*curva*) sharp; quiet, reserved, secretive; dense, stupid
cerradura *f* lock; closing, locking; **cerradura embutida** mortise lock; **cerradura horaria de bloqueo** time delay lock
cerrajería *f* locksmith business; hardware; hardware store
cerrajero *m* locksmith; hardware dealer; (*el que trabaja el hierro frío*) ironworker
cerrar §2 *tr* to close, shut; lock; bolt; (*el puño*) clench; enclose; (*la radio*) turn off; **cerrar con llave** to lock || *intr* to close, shut; (*la noche*) fall; **cerrar con** (*el enemigo*) to close in on; **cerrar en falso** (*una puerta, cerradura, etc.*) to not catch || *ref* to close, to shut; lock; **cerrarse en falso** to not heal right
cerrazón *f* gathering storm clouds; (Arg) heavy fog
cerre•ro -ra *adj* free, loose; untamed; haughty; (Mex) rough, unpolished; (*café*) (Ven) bitter
cerril *adj* rough, uneven; wild, untamed; boorish, rough
cerrillar *tr* to knurl, mill
cerro *m* hill, hillock; (*entre dos surcos*) ridge; (*espinazo*) backbone; (*del animal*) neck; **en cerro** bareback; **echar por los cerros de Úbeda** to talk nonsense; **por los cerros de Úbeda** off the beaten path
cerrojo *m* bolt; **cerrojo dormido** dead bolt
certamen *m* literary competition; contest, match
certe•ro -ra *adj* certain, sure, accurate; well-informed; (*tiro*) well-aimed; (*tirador*) good, crack
certeza *f* certainty
certidumbre *f* certainty; sureness
certificación *f* certification; certificate
certifica•do -da *adj* registered || *m* registered letter, registered package; certificate; **certificado de acciones** (econ) share certificate; **certificado de defunción** death certificate; **certificado de estudios** transcript
certificar §73 *tr* to certify; (*una carta*) register
certitud *f* certainty
cerval *adj* deer; (*miedo*) intense
cervato *m* fawn
cervecería *f* brewery; beer saloon
cervece•ro -ra *adj* beer || *mf* brewer
cerveza *f* beer; **cerveza a presión, cerveza de barril** draught beer; **cerveza de marzo** bock beer; **cerveza negra** brown ale; **cerveza rubia** lager
cer•viz *f* (*pl* **-vices**) cervix; nape of the neck; **bajar** or **doblar la cerviz** to humble oneself; **levantar la cerviz** to raise one's head, become proud; **ser de dura cerviz** to be ungovernable
cesación *f* cessation, suspension
cesante *adj* retired, out of office || *mf* pensioner
cesantía *f* retirement; dismissal (*of a public official*)
cesar *intr* to stop, cease
César *m* Caesar
cese *m* ceasing; notice of retirement; **cese de alarma** all-clear; **cese de fuego** ceasefire
césped *m* lawn, sward; sod, turf
cesta *f* basket; (*para jugar a la pelota*) wicker scoop; **cesta de costura** sewing basket; **cesta para compras** market basket
cesto *m* basket; washbasket; **cesto de la colada** clothesbasket, washbasket; **estar hecho un cesto** to be overcome with sleep; **ser un cesto** to be crude and ignorant
cetrería *f* falconry
cetrero *m* falconer
cetri•no -na *adj* (*tez*) sallow; jaundiced, melancholy
cetro *m* scepter; (*para aves*) perch, roost; (eccl) verge; **cetro de bufón** bauble; **cetro de locura** fool's scepter; **empuñar el cetro** to ascend the throne
cf. *abbr* **confesor**
cg. *abbr* **centigramo**
chabacanada or **chabacanería** *f* crudeness, coarseness, vulgarity
chabaca•no -na *adj* crude, coarse, vulgar || *m* (Mex) apricot tree
chabola *f* shack, shanty; (mil) foxhole
chacal *m* jackal
chacanear *tr* (Chile) to spur, goad on; (Chile) to annoy, bother
chacare•ro -ra *mf* (SAm) farm laborer, field worker; (Col) quack doctor; (Urug) gossip
chacarrachaca *f* row, racket
cháchara *f* chatter, idle talk; **chacharas** trinkets, junk
chacharear *intr* to chatter
chacolotear *intr* to clatter
chacota *f* laughter, racket; **hacer chacota de** to make fun of
chacotear *intr* to laugh and make a racket
chacra *f* farm house; small farm; sown field

chacua•co -ca *adj* ugly, crude, boorish || *m* (CAm) cigar butt; (CAm) cheap cigar
chafallar *tr* to botch
chafandín *m* conceited ass
chafar *tr* to rumple, muss; flatten; cut short; (Chile) to dismiss, send off
chafarrinar *tr* to blot, stain
chafarrinón *m* blot, stain; **echar un chafarrinón a** to insult, throw mud at
chaflán *m* chamfer
chaflanar *tr* to chamfer
chal *m* shawl
cha•lán -lana *adj* horse-dealing || *mf* horse dealer; horse trader || *m* broncobuster, horse-breaker || *f* scow, flatboat
chalanear *tr* (*un negocio*) to pull off shrewdly; (*un caballo*) break; (Arg) to take advantage of || *intr* to horse-trade
chalanería *f* horse-trading
chalanes•co -ca *adj* horse-trading
chaleco *m* vest, waistcoat; **al chaleco** (Mex) by force; (Mex) for nothing; **chaleco salvavidas** life jacket
chalecón *m* (Mex) crook
chalupa *f* small two-master; launch, lifeboat; (Mex) corncake
chama•co -ca *mf* (Mex) youngster, urchin
chamago•so -sa *adj* (Mex) dirty, filthy; (Mex) botched
chamarasca *f* brushwood; brush fire
chamarille•ro -ra *mf* junk dealer, secondhand dealer || *m* gambler
chamari•llón -llona *mf* poor card player
chamarra *f* sheepskin jacket
chamarreta *f* loose jacket; square poncho
chamba *f* fluke, scratch; (Mex) work
chambelán *m* chamberlain; (Mex) atomizer, spray
chambergo *m* (orn) bobolink; (Arg) soft hat
chambe•rí *adj* (*pl* **-ríes**) (Peru) showy, flashy
cham•bón -bona *adj* awkward, clumsy; lucky
chambonada *f* awkwardness, clumsiness; stroke of luck
chambonear *intr* to foozle
chambra *f* blouse; (Ven) din, uproar
chambrana *f* trim (*around a door*)
chamburgo *m* (Col) stagnant water, puddle
chamico *m* jimson weed; **dar chamico a** (SAm) to bewitch
chamorrar *tr* to shear
champán *m* sampan; (coll) champagne
champaña *m* champagne
champión *m* (Arg, Urug) sneaker
cham•pú *m* (*pl* **-púes**) shampoo
chamuchina *f* rabble; populace
chamuscar **§73** *tr* to singe, scorch; (Mex) to undersell
chamusco *m* singe, scorch
chamusquina *f* singeing; fight, row, quarrel; **oler a chamusquina** to look like a fight; smack of heresy
chancar **§73** *tr* to crush; beat, beat up; botch
chance *m* (SAm) opportunity, chance
chancear *intr & ref* to joke, jest
chance•ro -ra *adj* joking, jesting
chancha *f* cheat, lie; (Chile) slut; **hacer la chancha** (Bol, Col, Chile) to play hooky
chanche•ro -ra *mf* (Arg, Chile) pork butcher
chan•cho -cha *adj* dirty, filthy || *m* pig || *f* see **chancha**
chanchulle•ro -ra *mf* crook
chanchullo *m* (coll) racket, monkeybusiness
canciller *m* chancellor
chancla *f* old shoe; house slipper
chancleta *mf* good-for-nothing || *f* slipper; (Ven) accelerator
chanclo *m* overshoe, rubber
chandal *m* or **chándal** *m* jump suit, gym suit, sweatsuit
changador *m* (SAm) errand boy
changarro *m* (Mex) small shop
chan•go -ga *adj* (Chile) dull, stupid; (Mex) sly, crafty || *mf* (Mex) monkey || *m* (Arg) house boy
chan•guí *m* (*pl* **-guíes**) trick, deception
chantaje *m* blackmail
chantajista *mf* blackmailer
chantar *tr* to put on; (SAm) to throw hard; (Urug) to keep waiting || *ref* (*p.ej., el sombrero*) to clap on
chantre *m* cantor, precentor
chanza *f* joke, jest
chao *interj* (coll) good-by
chapa *f* sheet, plate; (*hoja fina de madera*) veneer; (*en las mejillas*) flush; (coll) good sense, judgment; (Chile) lock, bolt; **chapa de circulación** (aut) license plate; **chapas** flipping coins
chapa•do -da *adj* plated; veneered; **chapado a la antigua** old-fashioned
chapalear *intr* (*el agua; las manos y los pies en el agua*) to splash; (*la herradura floja*) clatter
chapar *tr* to cover or line with sheets of metal; veneer
chaparrear *intr* to pour
chapa•rro -rra *mf* (Mex) child, little one; (Mex) runt || *m* scrub oak
chaparrón *m* downpour
chapea•do -da *adj* lined with sheets of metal; veneered || *m* plywood; veneer
chapear *tr* to cover or line with sheets of metal; veneer
chapista *m* tinsmith, tinman
chapitel *m* (*remate de torre*) spire; (*capitel de columna*) capital
chapodar *tr* to trim, clear of branches; to curtail
chapotear *tr* to sponge, moisten || *intr* to splash, splatter
chapucear *tr & intr* to botch, bungle
chapuce•ro -ra *adj* crude, rough; clumsy, slipshod, bungling || *mf* bungler; amateur || *m* blacksmith; junk dealer
chapurrar *tr & intr* to jabber
chapurreo *m* jabber
cha•puz *m* (*pl* **-puces**) duck, ducking

chapuzar §60 *tr, intr & ref* to duck
chaqué *m* cutaway coat, morning coat
chaqueta *f* jacket; **chaqueta americana** (Esp) blazer; **chaqueta salvavidas** life jacket
chaquete *m* backgammon
chaquetilla *f* short jacket; (Ecuad) lady's vest
chaquetón *m* reefer, pea jacket
charamusca *f* brushwood, firewood; (Mex) candy twist
charanga *f* (mil) brass band
charangue•ro -ra *adj* crude, rough; bungling, clumsy || *mf* bungler
charca *f* pool
charco *m* puddle
charcutería *f* delicatessen
charla *f* talk, chat; talk, lecture; chatter, prattle; bull session
charla•dor -dora *adj* garrulous; gossipy || *mf* chatterbox; gossip
charlar *intr* to talk, chat; chatter, prattle
charla•tán -tana *adj* garrulous; gossipy || *mf* chatterbox; gossip; charlatan
charlatanería *f* garrulity, loquacity
charlatanismo *m* charlatanism; garrulity, loquacity
charnela *f* (*de puerta; de molusco*) hinge; (mach) knuckle
charol *m* varnish; patent leather; lacquered tray; **calzarse las de charol** (Arg, Urug) to hit the jackpot; **darse charol** to blow one's own horn
charola•do -da *adj* shiny
charolar *tr* to varnish, lacquer
charpa *f* pistol belt; (*cabestrillo*) sling
charquear *tr* (*carne de vaca*) to jerk; slash, cut to pieces
charqui *m* jerked beef
charrada *f* country dance; boorishness; tawdry ornamentation
charretera *f* epaulet; garter; (*del aguador*) shoulder pad; (mil) shoulder strap
charriada *f* (Mex) rodeo
cha•rro -rra *adj* coarse, ill-bred; flashy, loud, showy; Salamanca || *mf* peasant; Salamanca peasant || *m* broad-brimmed hat; Mexican cowboy
chasca *f* brushwood
chascar §73 *tr* (*la lengua*) to click; (*algún manjar*) crunch; (*engullir*) swallow || *intr* to crack, crackle
chascarrillo *m* funny story
chas•co -ca *adj* (Arg, Bol) crinkly, crinkly-haired || *m* joke, trick; disappointment; **dar un chasco a** to play a trick on; **llevar** or **llevarse (un) chasco** to be disappointed
chas•cón -cona *adj* (Bol, Chile) disheveled; (Bol, Chile) bushy-haired; (Bol, Chile) clumsy, unskilled
cha•sis *m* (*pl* **-sis**) chassis
chasquear *tr* (*un látigo*) to crack; play a trick on; disappoint || *intr* to crack || *ref* to be disappointed
chasqui *m* (SAm) messenger, courier
chasquido *m* crack; crackle
chata *f* barge, scow; flatcar; bedpan; (Mex) dear, darling
chatarra *f* iron slag; junk, scrap iron
chatarrería *f* junk yard
chatarre•ro -ra *mf* junk dealer, scrapiron dealer
cha•to -ta *adj* flat; flat-nosed, blunt; commonplace; disappointed || *m* wineglass || *f* see **chata**
chatre *adj* (Chile, Ecuad) all dressed up
chauvinismo *m* chauvinism
chauvinista *adj & mf* chauvinist
cha•val -vala *adj* (coll) young || *m* lad || *f* lass
chaveta *f* cotter pin; **perder la chaveta** to go out of one's head
chayote *m* chayote, vegetable pear; dunce, fool
chazar §60 *tr* (*la pelota*) to stop; (*el sitio donde paró la pelota*) to mark
che *interj* (SAm) say!, hey!
checar *tr* (Mex) to check
chechén *m* (Mex) poison ivy
chécheres *mpl* trinkets, junk
che•co -ca *adj & mf* Czech
chelín *m* shilling
cheque *m* check; **cheque de viajeros** traveler's check; **cheque en blanco** blank check; **cheque sin fondos** bad check
chequear *tr* (CAm, W-I) to check
chequeo *m* control; checkup
chequera *f* checkbook
chévere *adj invar* terrific, fabulous; **¡que chévere!** terrific!
chica *f* lass, little girl; girl; my dear; **chica de cita** call girl; **chica de la vida alegre** party girl
chicalote *m* Mexican poppy
chicha *f* corn liquor; **no ser ni chicha ni limonada** to be good for nothing
chícharo *m* pea; (Col) poor cigar; (Mex) apprentice
chicharra *f* harvest fly, cicada; chatterbox; (*timbre*) buzzer; **cantar la chicharra** (coll) to be hot and sultry
chicharrón *m* residue of hog's fat; burnt meat; sunburned person; wrinkled person
chiche *adj invar* nice, pretty
chichear *tr & intr* to hiss
chi•chón -chona *adj* (CAm) easy; (SAm) joking; (Guat) large-breasted || *m* lump, bump on the head
chicle *m* chewing gum; **chicle de globo** bubble gum
chiclear *intr* (Mex) to chew gum
chi•co -ca *adj* small, little; young || *mf* child, youngster || *m* lad, little boy; young fellow; old man; hand, turn || *f* see **chica**
chicolear *intr* to pay compliments, to flirt || *ref* (Arg, Peru) to enjoy oneself
chico•te -ta *mf* husky youngster || *m* cigar; cigar stub; whip
chicotear *tr* to beat up; kill
chicue•lo -la *adj* small, little || *m* little boy || *f* little girl
chifla *f* hissing, whistling; paring knife; **estar de chifla** (Mex) to be in a bad humor

chifla•do -da *adj* (coll) daffy, nutty || *mf* crackbrain, nut, crackpot
chifladura *f* daffiness, nuttiness; whim, wild idea
chiflar *tr* (*a un actor*) to hiss; (*vino o licor*) to gulp down; (*el cuero*) to pare || *intr* to whistle; (*las aves*) (Guat, Mex) to sing || *ref* to go crazy
chifle *m* whistle; (*para cazar aves*) bird call; powder flask
chiflido *m* whistle, hiss
chiflón *m* (SAm) cold blast of air; rapids; slide of loose stone
chiíte *or* **chiita** *adj & mf* Shiite
chilaba *f* jellaba
Chile *m* Chile
chile•no -na *adj & mf* Chilean
chilla *f* fox call, hare call; clapboard; (Chile) small fox; (Mex) top gallery
chillar *intr* to shriek; to squeak; to hiss, sizzle; (*los colores*) to scream || *ref* to take offense
chillido *m* shriek, scream
chi•llón -llona *adj* shrill, high-pitched; screaming; (*color*) loud
chilote *m* (CAm) ear of corn
chimenea *f* chimney, smokestack; fireplace, hearth; stovepipe hat; (naut) funnel
chimpancé *m* chimpanzee
china *f* Chinese woman; china, porcelain; pebble; nursemaid; (Col) spinning top || **China** *f* China
chinche *mf* bore, tiresome person || *m* (*clavito de cabeza chata*) thumbtack || *f* (*insecto*) bedbug; **caer** or **morir como chinches** to die like flies
chinchorre•ro -ra *adj* gossipy, mischievous
chincho•so -sa *adj* boring, tiresome
chinero *m* china closet
chines•co -ca *adj* Chinese || **chinescos** *mpl* (mus) bell tree
chingar §44 *tr* to tipple; (CAm) to bob, dock; (CAm, Mex) to bother, annoy || *ref* to tipple; fail
chin•go -ga *adj* (CAm) short; (CAm) dull, blunt; (CAm) naked
chinguirito *m* cheap rum; swig of liquor
chi•no -na *adj & mf* Chinese || *m* (*idioma*) Chinese; (Col) boy, newsboy; (Mex) curl || *f* see **china**
chip *m* (compu, electron) chip
chipichipi *m* drizzle, mist
Chipre *f* Cyprus
chiquero *m* pigsty; bull pen
chiquillada *f* childish prank
chiqui•to -ta *adj* small, little || *mf* little one || *m* (*de vino*) snifter; (Arg) moment, instant || *f* five cents; **no andarse con** or **en chiquitas** to talk right off the shoulder
chiquitura *f* trifle, small matter
chiribita *f* spark; daisy; **chiribitas** spots before the eyes
chiribitil *m* garret; cubbyhole
chirimbolos *mpl* utensils, vessels
chirimía *f* hornpipe
chiripa *f* (billiards) fluke, scratch; stroke of luck
chirivía *f* parsnip
chirle *adj* insipid, tasteless
chirlo *m* slash or scar on the face
chirlota *f* (Mex) meadow lark
chirona *f* (coll) jail, jug, slammer
chirriar §77 *intr* to creak, squeak; shriek; hiss, sizzle; sing or play out of tune || *ref* (Col) to go on a spree; (Col) to shiver
chirrido *m* creak, squeak; shriek; hiss, sizzle
chirrión *m* squeaky cart; (SAm) whip
chis *interj* sh-sh!; **¡chis, chis!** pst!
chischás *m* clash of swords
chisguete *m* swig of wine; squirt
chisme *m* piece of gossip; trinket; **chisme de vecindad** idle talker; **chismes** gossip; articles; **chismes de aseo** toilet articles
chismear *intr* to gossip
chismo•so -sa *adj* gossipy, catty || *mf* gossip
chispa *f* spark; (*pequeña cantidad*) drop; sizzle; lightning; (fig) sparkle, wit; (coll) drunk, spree; (Col) rumor; **coger una chispa** to go on a drunk; **chispa de entrehierro** (elec) jump spark; **chispas** sprinkle (*of rain*); **dar chispa** (Guat, Mex) to work, to click; **echar chispas** to blow up, hit the ceiling
chispar *tr* to throw (someone) out
chispeante *adj* sparkling
chispear *intr* to spark; sparkle; drizzle, sprinkle
chispero *m* (CAm) spark plug
chis•po -pa *adj* tipsy || *m* swallow, drink || *f* see **chispa**
chisporrotear *intr* to spark, sputter, sizzle
chispo•so -sa *adj* sputtering, sparking
chisquero *m* pocket lighter
chistar *intr* to speak, say something; **no chistar** to not say a word
chiste *m* joke; witticism; **caer en el chiste** to get the point; **chiste picante** *or* **verde** dirty joke; **dar en el chiste** to hit the nail on the head
chistera *f* fish basket; (coll) top hat
chisto•so -sa *adj* funny; witty || *mf* funny person; wit
chita *f* anklebone; quoits; **a la chita callando** quietly, secretly; **dar en la chita** to hit the nail on the head
chiticalla *mf* (*persona que no revela lo que sabe*) (coll) clam || *f* (coll) secret
chito *interj* hush!, sh-sh!
chivar *ref* to squeal, snitch
chivato *m* kid, young goat; (*soplón*) squealer, snitch; (Bol) apprentice, helper; (Chile) cheap rum
chi•vo -va *mf* kid || *m* billy goat; (Mex) day's wage; (Col, Ecuad, Ven) fit of rage; **chivo expiatorio** *or* **emisario** scapegoat || *f* nanny goat; **chivas** (coll) personal items, baggage
chocante *adj* shocking; coarse, crude; (Col) annoying; (Mex) disagreeable
chocar §73 *tr* to shock, annoy, irritate; surprise; (*vasos*) clink; please; **¡choque Ud. esos cinco!** give me five! (*high five*) || *intr* to shock; collide; clash, fight

chocarre•ro -ra *adj* coarse, crude || *mf* crude joker
chocha *f* woodcock
chochear *intr* to be in one's dotage; dote, be infatuated
chochera *f* dotage; (Arg, Peru) favorite
cho•chez *f* (*pl* **-checes**) dotage; doting act or remark
cho•cho -cha *adj* doting; doddering || *m* stick of cinnamon candy; **chochos** candy to quiet a child || *f* see **chocha**
choclo *m* wooden overshoe; (Mex) low shoe; (SAm) tender ear of corn, sweet corn
chocolate *m* chocolate
chófer *m* chauffeur
chofeta *f* fire pan (*for lighting cigars*)
cholla *f* (coll) noodle, head; (coll) ability, brains
cho•lo -la *adj* half-breed (*Indian and white*) || *mf* Indian; half-breed; (Chile) coward; (SAm) darling
chomba *f* (Chile) sweater; (Arg) polo shirt
chomite *m* (Mex) coarse wool; (Mex) woolen skirt
chompa *f* (Bol, Peru) sweater; (Col, Ecuad) jacket
chontal *m* uneducated person
chopo *m* black poplar; gun, rifle; **chopo de Italia** Lombardy poplar; **chopo del Canadá** or **de Virginia** cottonwood; **chopo lombardo** Lombardy poplar
choque *m* shock; collision, impact; clash, conflict, skirmish; (elec) choke, choke coil; **choque en cadena** (aut) pileup, mass collision
choricería *f* sausage shop
chorizo *m* smoked pork sausage
chorlito *m* plover, golden plover; scatter-brains
chorrea•do -da *adj* dirty; spotty
chorrear *intr* to gush, spurt, spout; drip, splatter; trickle
chorrera *f* spout, channel; cut, gulley; rapids; lace front, jabot; (Arg) string, stream
chorrillo *m* constant stream; **irse por el chorrillo** to follow the current; **tomar el chorrillo de** to get the habit of
chorro *m* jet, spurt; stream, flow; **a chorros** in abundance; **chorro de arena** sandblasting
chotaca•bras *m* (*pl* **-bras**) goatsucker
chotear *tr* to make fun of; (Guat) to keep an eye on
choteo *m* jeering, mocking
chovinista *adj & mf* chauvinist
choza *f* hut, cabin, lodge
chubasco *m* squall, shower; (fig) temporary setback; **chubasco de agua** rainstorm; **chubasco de nieve** blizzard
chubasco•so -sa *adj* stormy, threatening
chucha *f* female dog, bitch; drunk, jag; (Col) opossum; (Col) body odor
chuchaque *m* (Ecuad) hangover
chuchear *tr* (*caza menor*) to trap || *intr* to whisper
chuchería *f* knickknack, trinket; delicacy, tidbit
chu•cho -cha *adj* (CAm) mean, stingy; (*fruto*) (Col) watery; (Col) wrinkled || *m* (coll) dog || *f* see **chucha**
chucruta *f* sauerkraut
chue•co -ca *adj* (Mex) twisted, bent; (SAm) bow-legged; (Mex) crippled || *m* (Mex) dealing in stolen goods || *f* stump; hockey; hockey ball
chufa *f* groundnut
chufletear *intr* to joke, jest
chula *f* flashy dame (*in lower classes of Madrid*)
chulada *f* light-hearted remark; vulgarity
chul•co -ca *mf* (Bol) baby (*youngest child*)
chulear *tr* to tease; (Mex) to flirt with
chuleta *f* chop, cutlet; slap, smack; (*de los estudiantes*) (coll) crib, pony; **chuleta de cerdo** pork chop; **chuleta de ternera** veal chop; **chuletas** sideburns, side whiskers
chu•lo -la *adj* flashy, sporty; foxy, slick; (Guat, Mex) pretty, cute || *m* sporty fellow (*in lower classes of Madrid*); pimp, procurer; gigolo; butcher's helper; (taur) attendant on foot || *f* see **chula**
chumbera *f* prickly pear
chume•ro -ra *mf* (CAm) apprentice
chunches *mpl* (CAm) junk, stuff
chunga *f* jest, fun
chunguear *ref* to jest, joke
chupa *f* frock, coat; (Arg) drunk, jag; (Arg) tobacco pouch
chupa•do -da *adj* thin, skinny; drunk; (*falda*) tight || *f* suck; pull (*on a cigar*)
chupador *m* teething ring, pacifier
chupaflor *m* (Mex, Ven) hummingbird
chupalla *f* straw hat
chupamirto *m* (Mex) hummingbird
chupar *tr* to suck; (*la hacienda ajena*) milk, sap; absorb || *intr* to suck || *ref* to get thin, lose strength; (*los labios*) smack
chupatin•tas *mf* (*pl* **-tas**) (coll) office drudge
chupete *m* (*para un niño*) pacifier; lollipop; **de chupete** fine, splendid
chupetín *m* (SAm) lollipop
chu•pón -pona *mf* swindler || *m* (bot) sucker, shoot; (mach) plunger; baby bottle; pacifier
chupópte•ro -ra *mf* sponger
chuquisa *f* (Chile, Peru) prostitute
churrasco *m* barbecue; (SAm) steak
churrasquear *tr* to barbecue
churre *m* filth, dirt, grease
churrete *m* dirty spot (*on hands or face*)
churrigueres•co -ca *adj* churrigueresque; loud, flashy, tawdry
chu•rro -rra *adj* (*lana*) coarse; (*carnero*) coarse-wooled || *m* coarse-wooled sheep; fritter; botch
churrulle•ro -ra *adj* gossipy, loquacious || *mf* gossip, chatterbox
churrusco *m* burnt piece of bread
churumbela *f* hornpipe, flageolet; maté cup; (Col) worry, anxiety; (Col, Ecuad) pipe
churumo *m* (coll) substance (*money, brains, etc.*)

chus *interj* here! (*to call a dog*); **no decir chus ni mus** to not say boo
chus•co -ca *adj* droll, funny; (Peru) ill-mannered; (*perro*) (Peru) mongrel
chusma *f* galley slaves; mob, rabble
chuza *f* (Mex) strike (*in bowling*)
C.I. *m* (letterword) (**cociente intelectual** *or* **de inteligencia**) I.Q. (Intelligence Quotient)
CIA [ˈsia], [ˈθia] *f* (acronym) (**Agencia Central de Inteligencia**) CIA (Central Intelligence Agency)
cía. *abbr* **compañia**
cía *f* hipbone
cianamida *f* cyanamide
cianuro *m* cyanide
ciar **§77** *intr* to back up; back water; ease up
ciberespacio *m* (compu) cyberspace
cibernética *f* cybernetics
ciberneti•co -ca *adj* cybernetic
ciborio *m* ciborium
cicatear *intr* to be stingy
cicate•ro -ra *adj* stingy ‖ *mf* miser, niggard
cica•triz *f* (*pl* **-trices**) scar
cicatrizar **§60** *tr* to heal; (*una impresión dolorosa*) (Arg) to heal ‖ *ref* to heal; to scar
Cicerón *m* Cicero
ciclamor *m* Judas tree; **ciclamor del Canadá** redbud
cícli•co -ca *adj* cyclic(al)
ciclismo *m* bicycle racing
ciclista *mf* bicyclist; bicycle racer
ciclo *m* cycle; series (of lectures); (*en las escuelas*) (Arg, Urug) term
ciclón *m* cyclone
cicuta *f* hemlock
cidra *f* citron (*fruit*)
cidrada *f* citron (*candied rind*)
cidro *m* citron (*tree or shrub*)
cie•go -ga *adj* blind; blocked, stopped up; **más ciego que un topo** blind as a bat ‖ *mf* blind person ‖ *m* blind man ‖ *f* blind woman; **a ciegas** blindly; thoughtlessly; without looking
cielo *m* sky, heavens; (*clima, tiempo*) skies, climate, weather; (*de una cama*) canopy; (*mansión de los bienaventurados*) Heaven; **a cielo abierto** in the open air, outdoors; **a cielo descubierto** openly; **a cielo raso** in the open air, outdoors; in the country; **cielo de la boca** roof of the mouth; **cielo máximo** (aer) ceiling; **cielo raso** ceiling; **llovido del cielo** heaven-sent, manna from heaven
cielorraso *m* ceiling
ciem•piés *m* (*pl* **-piés**) centipede
cien *adj* hundred, a hundred, one hundred
ciénaga *f* swamp, marsh, mudhole
ciencia *f* science; knowledge; learning; **a ciencia cierta** with certainty; **Ciencia Cristiano** Christian Science; **ciencia-ficción** science fiction; **ciencias** (educ) science; **ciencias biológicas** life sciences; **ciencias naturales** natural science; **ciencias políticas** political science
ciencia-ficción *f* science fiction
cieno *m* mud, mire, silt
cieno•so -sa *adj* muddy, miry, silty
ciento *adj* & *m* hundred, a hundred, one hundred; **por ciento** percent
cierne *m* budding, blossoming; **en cierne** in blossom; only beginning
cierrarrenglón *m* marginal stop
cierre *m* closing; shutting; snap, clasp, fastener; latch, lock; (*de una tienda, de la Bolsa*) close; (*paro de trabajo*) shutdown; **cierre cremallera** zipper; **cierre de portada** metal shutter (*of store front*); **cierre de puerta** door check; **cierre hermético** weather stripping; **cierre relámpago** zipper
cierro *m* closing; shutting; (Chile) fence, wall; (Chile) envelope
ciertamente *adv* certainly, truly, surely
cier•to -ta *adj* certain; a certain; (*acertado, verdadero*) true; (*seguro*) sure; **por cierto** for sure ‖ **cierto** *adv* surely, certainly
cierva *f* hind
ciervo *m* deer, stag, hart
cierzo *m* cold north wind
cifra *f* number, figure; number, amount; (*número*) cipher; (*escritura secreta*) code; (*enlace de dos o más letras empleado en sellos*) device, monogram, emblem; abbreviation; amount, sum; **en cifra** in code; in brief; mysteriously; **un número de seis cifras** a six-figure number
cifrar *tr* to cipher, code; abridge; calculate; **cifrar la dicha en** to base one's happiness in; **cifrar la esperanza en** to place one's hope in ‖ *ref* to be abridged; **cifrarse en** to be based on
cifrario *m* (com) code
cigarra *f* harvest fly, locust, cicada
cigarrera *f* cigar case; cigar girl
cigarrería *f* cigar store, tobacco store
cigarre•ro -ra *mf* cigar maker; cigar dealer ‖ *f* see **cigarrera**
cigarrillo *m* cigarette; **cigarrillo con filtro** filter cigarette
cigarro *m* cigar; **cigarro de papel** cigarette; **cigarro puro** cigar
cigoñal *m* well sweep; (*del motor de explosión*) crankshaft
cigüeña *f* stork; crank, winch
cigüeñal *m* var of **cigoñal**
cilampa *f* (CAm) drizzle
cilicio *m* haircloth, hair shirt
cilindrada *f* piston displacement
cilindrar *tr* to roll
cilíndri•co -ca *adj* cylindrical
cilindro *m* cylinder; roll, roller; (Mex) barrel organ, hand organ
cima *f* (*de árbol*) top; (*de montaña*) top, summit; **dar cima a** to complete, to carry out; **por cima** (coll) at the very top
cimarra *f* — **hacer cimarra** (Arg, Chile) to play hooky
cima•rrón -rrona *adj* (*animal*) wild, untamed;

(*planta*) wild; (*esclavo*) fugitive; (*marinero*) lazy; (*maté*) (Arg, Urug) black, bitter
cimarronear *intr* (Arg, Urug) to drink black maté || *ref* (*el esclavo*) to flee, run away
címbalo *m* cymbal
cimbel *m* decoy pigeon, stool pigeon
cimborio or **cimborrio** *m* dome
cimbrar or **cimbrear** *tr* to brandish; swing, sway; bend; thrash, beat || *ref* to swing, sway; shake
cimbre•ño -ña *adj* flexible, pliant; lithe, willowy
cimentar §2 *tr* to found, establish; lay the foundations of
cime•ro -ra *adj* top, uppermost
cimiento *m* foundation, groundwork; basis, source
cimitarra *f* scimitar
cinabrio *m* cinnabar
cinanquia *f* quinsy
cinc *m* (*pl* **cinces**) zinc
cincel *m* chisel, graver
cincelar *tr* to chisel, engrave
cincha *f* cinch; **a revienta cinchas** at breakneck speed; reluctantly
cinchar *tr* to cinch; band, hoop
cincho *m* girdle, sash; iron hoop; iron tire
cinco *adj & pron* five; **las cinco** five o'clock || *m* five; (*en las fechas*) fifth; **¡choque Ud. esos cinco!** or **¡vengan esos cinco!** put it here!, shake!; **decirle a uno cuántas son cinco** to tell someone what's what
cincograbado *m* zinc etching
cincuenta *adj, pron & m* fifty
cincuenta•vo -va *adj & m* fiftieth
cine *m* movie; **cine de verano** open-air movie theater; **cine en colores** color movies; **cine hablado** talkie; **cine mudo** silent movie; **cine parlante** talkie; **cine sonoro** sound movie
cineasta *mf* motion-picture producer; movie fan || *m* movie actor || *f* movie actress
cinedrama *m* screenplay
cinelandia *f* (coll) movieland
cinema *m* var of **cine**
cinemateca *f* film library
cinematografiar §77 *tr & intr* to cinematograph, film
cinematógrafo *m* cinematograph; motion picture; motion-picture projector; motion-picture theater
cinematurgo *m* scriptwriter
cinescopio (telv) *m* kinescope
cineteatro *m* movie house
cinéti•co -ca *adj* kinetic || *f* kinetics
cínga•ro -ra *adj & mf* gypsy
cíni•co -ca *adj* cynical; impudent; slovenly, untidy || *mf* cynic || *m* Cynic
cinismo *m* cynicism; impudence
cinta *f* ribbon; sweatband; (*tira de papel, celuloide, etc.*) tape; film; measuring tape; (*borde de la acera*) curb; fillet, scroll; **cinta adhesiva** adhesive tape; **cinta aislante** electric tape, friction tape; **cinta de enmascarar** masking tape; **cinta de medir** tape measure; **cinta de teleimpresor** ticker tape; **cinta durex**[T] Scotch tape[T]; **cinta magnética** magnetic tape; **cinta perforada** punched tape; **cinta virgen** blank tape
cintillo *m* hatband; fancy hat cord; ring set with a gem; (*borde de la acera*) (P-R) curb; hair ribbon
cinto *m* belt, girdle; waist
cintura *f* (*parte estrecha del cuerpo humano sobre las caderas*) waist; waistline; (*de una chimenea*) throat; **meter en cintura** to bring to reason
cinturón *m* belt, sash; sword belt; **cinturón de asiento** seat belt; **cinturón de seguridad** safety belt; **cinturón retráctil** retractable safety belt; **cinturón salvavidas** safety belt
cíper *m* (Mex) zipper
cipo *m* milestone; signpost; memorial pillar
cipote *adj* (Col, Ven) stupid; (Guat) chubby || *mf* (Hond, El Salv, Ven) brat
ciprés *m* cypress
circo *m* circus
circón *m* zircon
circonio *m* zirconium
circuitería *f* (compu) circuitry
circuito *m* circuit; (*de carreteras, ferrocarriles, etc.*) network; race track; **corto circuito** (elec) short circuit; **circuito integrado** integrated circuit; **televisión en circuito cerrado** closed-circuit television
circulación *f* circulation; traffic; **circulación rodada** vehicular traffic
circular *adj* circular || *f* circular, circular letter; **circular noticiera** newsletter || *tr & intr* to circulate
círculo *m* circle; club; clubhouse
circuncidar *tr* to circumcise; clip, curtail
circundante *adj* surrounding
circundar *tr* to surround, go around
circunferencia *f* circumference
circunfle•jo -ja *adj* circumflex
circunlocución *f* or **circunloquio** *m* circumlocution
circunnavegación *f* circumnavigation
circunnavegar §44 *tr* to circumnavigate
circunscribir §83 *tr* to circumscribe || *ref* to hold oneself down; be held down
circunscripción *f* circumscription; district, subdivision
circunspec•to -ta *adj* circumspect
circunstancia *f* circumstance
circunstancia•do -da *adj* circumstantial, detailed
circunstancial *adj* circumstantial
circunstanciar *tr* to circumstantiate, to describe in detail
circunstante *adj* surrounding; present || *mf* bystander, onlooker
circunveci•no -na *adj* neighboring
circunvolar §61 *tr* to fly around
cirial *m* (eccl) processional candlestick
ciriga•llo -lla *mf* gadabout

cirílico -ca *adj* Cyrillic
cirio *m* wax candle
Ciro *m* Cyrus
ciruela *f* plum; **ciruela claudia** greengage; **ciruela pasa** prune
ciruelo *m* plum, plum tree; stupid fellow
cirugía *f* surgery; **cirugía cosmética, decorativa** or **estética** cosmetic surgery; **cirugía plástica** plastic surgery
ciruja•no -na *mf* surgeon
ciscar §73 *tr* to soil, dirty; (Cuba, Mex) to shame; annoy ‖ *ref* to soil one's clothes, have an accident
cisco *m* culm; row, disturbance
cisma *m* schism; discord, disagreement; (Arg) worry, concern; (Col) gossip; (Col) fastidiousness
cismáti•co -ca *adj* schismatic; dissident; (Col) gossipy; (Col) fastidious ‖ *mf* schismatic; dissident
cisne *m* swan; (Arg) powder puff
cisterna *f* cistern; reservoir; toilet tank
cita *f* date, appointment, engagement; (*mención, pasaje textual*) citation, quotation; **cita a ciegas** blind date; **cita previa** by appointment; **darse cita** to make a date
citación *f* citation, quotation; (*ante un juez*) citation, summons
citar *tr* to make a date with, have an appointment with; cite, quote; (*ante un juez*) cite, summon; (*al toro*) incite, provoke ‖ *ref* to make a date, have an appointment
cítara *f* (mus) zither
citología *f* cytology; smear test; Pap smear, Pap test
ciudad *f* city; city council; **ciudad dormitorio** bedroom community; **ciudad sanitaria** hospital complex; **ciudad universitaria** university campus; **la ciudad Condal** Barcelona; **la ciudad del Apóstol** Santiago de Compostela; **la ciudad del Betis** Seville; **la ciudad del Cabo** Capetown or Cape Town; **la ciudad de los Califas** Cordova; **la ciudad de los Reyes** Lima, Peru; **la ciudad de María Santísima** Seville; **la ciudad Imperial or Imperial ciudad** Toledo
ciudadanía *f* citizenship
ciudada•no -na *adj* city; citizen; civic ‖ *mf* citizen; urbanite
ciudadela *f* citadel; (Cuba) tenement house
cívi•co -ca *adj* civic; city; domestic; public-spirited
civil *adj* civil; civilian ‖ *mf* civilian ‖ *m* guard, policeman
civilidad *f* civility
civilista *adj* civil-law ‖ *mf* authority on civil law; (Chile) antimilitarist
civilización *f* civilization
civilizar §60 *tr* to civilize
civismo *m* good citizenship
cizalla *f* shears; metal shaving, metal clipping; **cizalla de guillotina** gate shears, guillotine shears; **cizallas** shears
cizallar *tr* to shear
cizaña *f* darnel; contamination, corruption; discord; **sembrar cizaña** to sow discord
clac *m* (*pl* **claques**) opera hat, claque, crush hat; (*sombrero de tres picos*) cocked hat
clamar *tr* to cry out for ‖ *intr* to cry out; **clamar contra** to cry out against; **clamar por** to cry out for
clamor *m* clamor, outcry; (*toque de difuntos*) knell, toll; fame
clamorear *tr* to clamor for ‖ *intr* to clamor; (*tocar a muerto*) toll
clamoreo *m* clamoring; tolling
clamoro•so -sa *adj* clamorous; loud, noisy
clan *m* clan
clandestinista *mf* (Guat) bootlegger
clandesti•no -na *adj* clandestine
claque *f* claque, hired clappers
clara *f* bald spot; (*de un trozo de tela*) thin spot; (*en el tiempo lluvioso*) break, let-up; **clara de huevo** eggwhite
claraboya *f* (*ventana en el techo*) skylight; (*en la parte alta de la pared*) transom; (*esp. en las iglesias la parte superior de la nave que tiene una serie de ventanas*) clerestory
clarear *tr* to brighten, light up ‖ *intr* (*empezar a amanecer*) to get light, dawn; (*el mal tiempo*) clear up ‖ *ref* (*una tela*) to show through; show one's hand
clarecer §22 *ref* to dawn
clarete *m* claret
claridad *f* clarity; clearness; brightness; fame, glory; blunt remark; **claridades** plain language
clarido•so -sa *adj* (CAm, Mex) blunt, rude, plain-spoken
clarificar §73 *tr* to clarify; brighten, light up; (*lo que estaba turbio*) clear
clarín *m* clarion; fine cambric; (Chile) sweet pea
clarinada *f* clarion call; uncalled-for remark
clarinete *m* clarinet
clarión *m* chalk
clarividencia *f* clairvoyance; clear-sightedness
clarividente *adj* clairvoyant, far-sighted; clear-sighted ‖ *mf* clairvoyant
cla•ro -ra *adj* clear; (*de color*) light; (*pelo*) thin, sparse; (*té*) weak; famous, illustrious; (*cerveza*) light; **a las claras** publicly, openly, frankly ‖ *m* gap; (*en el bosque*) glade, clearing; space, interval; (*ventana u otra abertura*) light; (*claraboya*) skylight; (*en las nubes*) break; **claro de luna** brief moonlight; **de claro en claro** evidently; from one end to the other; **pasar la noche de claro en claro** to not sleep all night; **poner** or **sacar en claro** to explain, clear up; (*un borrador*) to copy ‖ *f* see **clara** ‖ **claro** *adv* clearly ‖ **claro** *interj* sure!, sure thing!, of course!; **¡claro está!, ¡claro que sí!** sure!, of course!
claror *m* brightness; **claror de luna** moonlight, moonglow
claru•cho -cha *adj* watery, thin
clase *f* class; classroom; lecture; **clase alta** upper

class; **clase baja** lower class; **clase media** middle class; **clase obrera** working class; **clase particular** private lesson; **clases** non-commissioned officers, warrant officers; **clases pasivas** pensioners
clasicista *mf* classicist
clási•co -ca *adj* classical ‖ *mf* classicist ‖ *m* classic
clasificador *m* filing cabinet
clasificar §73 *tr* to classify; class; sort; file; to categorize ‖ *ref* to class
clasismo *m* segregation
clasista *mf* segregationist
claudicar §73 *intr* (*cojear*) to limp; (*obrar defectuosamente*) bungle; back down
claustral *adj* cloistral
claustro *m* cloister; (*junta de la universidad*) faculty
cláusula *f* (*de un contrato u otro documento*) clause; (gram) sentence
clausula•do -da *adj* (*estilo*) choppy ‖ *m* series of clauses
clausular *tr* to close, finish, conclude
clausura *f* confinement; seclusion; enclosure; adjournment
clausurar *tr* (*una asamblea, un tribunal, etc.*) to close, adjourn; (*un comercio por orden gubernativa*) suspend, close up
clava *f* club
clavadista *mf* (Mex) diver
clava•do -da *adj* studded with nails; exact, precise; (*reloj*) stopped; sharp, e.g., **a las siete clavadas** at seven o'clock sharp ‖ *m* dive ‖ *f* (*en ajedrez*) pin; (*canasta marcada metiendo el balón con fuerza desde arriba*) slam dunk, dunk; (Mex) dive
clavar *tr* to nail; (*un clavo*) drive; (*una daga, un punzón*) stick; (*una piedra preciosa*) set; (*los ojos, la atención*) fix; (*a un caballo al herrarlo*) prick; cheat ‖ *ref* to prick oneself; get cheated; (Mex) to dive; **clavárselas** (CAm) to get drunk
clave *m* harpsichord ‖ *f* (*de un enigma, código, etc.*) key; (*piedra con que se cierra el arco*) (archit) keystone; (mus) clef; **clave de fa** bass clef; **clave de sol** treble clef
clavel *m* carnation, pink; **clavel de ramillete** sweet william; **clavel reventón** double-flowered carnation
clavellina *f* carnation, pink
clavelón *m* marigold
clave•ro -ra *mf* keeper of the keys ‖ *m* clove tree ‖ *f* nail hole
claveta *f* peg, wooden peg
clavetear *tr* to stud; tip, put a tip on; wind up, settle
clavicordio *m* clavichord
clavícula *f* clavicle, collarbone
clavija *f* pin, peg, dowel; (elec) plug; (mus) peg; **apretarle a uno las clavijas** to put the screws on someone
clavillo *m* or **clavito** *m* brad, tack; (*que sujeta las hojas de unas tijeras*) pin, rivet; clove
clavo *m* nail; (*capullo seco de la flor del clavero*) clove; migraine; keen sorrow; (*artículo que no se vende*) (Arg, Bol, Chile) drug on the market; (Col) bad deal; (Hond, Mex) rich vein of ore; (Ven) heartburn; **clavo de alambre** wire nail; **clavo de especia** (*flor*) clove; **clavo de herrar** horseshoe nail; **dar en el clavo** to hit the nail on the head
clemátide *f* clematis
clemencia *f* clemency
clemente *adj* clement, merciful
cleptóma•no -na *mf* kleptomaniac
clerecía *f* clergy
clerical *adj* & *m* clerical
clericato *m* or **clericatura** *f* priesthood
clerigalla *f* (contemptuous) priests
clérigo *m* cleric, priest; **clérigo de misa y olla** priestlet
clerizonte *m* shabby-looking priest; fake priest
clero *m* clergy
clerófo•bo -ba *adj* priest-hating ‖ *mf* priest hater
clic *m* click; snap; (compu) clic
clicar *intr* (compu) to click
cliché *m* (*lugar común*) cliché
cliente *mf* (*parroquiano de una tienda*) customer; (*de un abogado*) client; (*de un médico*) patient; (*de un hotel*) guest
clientela *f* customers; clientele; patronage, protection; practice
clima *m* climate; country, region; **clima artificial** air conditioning
climatización *f* air conditioning
climatizar §60 *tr* to air-condition
clíni•co -ca *adj* clinical ‖ *mf* clinician ‖ *f* clinic; private hospital; **clínica dental** dental office; **clínica de reposo** nursing home, convalescent home
clip *m* paper clip
cliquear *m*—**doble cliquear** (compu) double click ‖ *intr* (compu) to click
cliqueteo *m* clicking
clisar *tr* (typ) to plate
clisé *m* (*plancha clisada*) cliché, plate; (phot) plate; (*lugar común*) cliché
clo *m* cluck; **decir clo** (Chile) to kick the bucket; **hacer clo clo** (*la gallina clueca*) to cluck
cloaca *f* sewer
clocar §81 *intr* to cluck
clon *m* clone
clonar *tr* to clone
clónico *adj* clonal ‖ *m* (compu) clone
cloquear *intr* to cluck
cloqueo *m* cluck, clucking
clorhídri•co -ca *adj* hydrochloric
cloro *m* chlorine
clorofila *f* chlorophyll
cloroformizar §60 *tr* to chloroform
cloroformo *m* chloroform
cloruro *m* chloride
clóset *m* (SAm) closet, cupboard, cabinet
club *m* (*pl* **clubs**) club; **club de admiradores** fan club; **club náutico** yacht club
clubista *mf* club member

clue•co -ca *adj* broody; decrepit
c.m.b., C.M.B. *abbr* **cuyas manos beso**
coa *f* (Mex) hoe; (Chile) thieves' jargon
coacción *f* coercion, compulsion
coaccionar *tr* to coerce, compel
coacervar *tr* to pile up
coactar *tr* to coerce, compel
coadunar *tr & ref* to mix together
coadyuvar *tr & intr* to help, aid, assist
coagular *tr & ref* (*la sangre*) to coagulate; (*la leche*) curdle
coágulo *m* clot
coalición *f* coalition
coalla *f* woodcock
coartada *f* alibi
coartar *tr* to limit, restrict
coba *f* hoax; flattery
cobalto *m* cobalt
cobarde *adj* cowardly; timid; (*vista*) dim, weak || *mf* coward
cobardear *intr* to act cowardly; be timid
cobardía *f* cowardice; timidity
cobayo *m* guinea pig
cobertera *f* lid; bawd, procuress
cobertizo *m* shed; (*tejado saledizo*) covered balcony, penthouse
cobertor *m* bedcover, bedspread; lid
cobertura *f* cover; covering; (*garantía metálica*) coverage
cobija *f* curved tile; top, lid; short mantilla; (W-I) guano roof; **cobijas** bedclothes
cobijar *tr* to cover; shelter, protect
cobijo *m* covering; shelter, protection; (*hospedaje sin manutención*) lodging
cobra *f* team of mares used in threshing; (hunt) retrieval
cobra•dor -dora *adj* (*perro*) retrieving || *mf* collector; trolley conductor
cobranza *f* collecting; (hunt) retrieval
cobrar *tr* (*lo perdido*) to recover; (*lo que otro le debe*) collect; (*un cheque*) cash; (*cierto precio*) charge; acquire, get; (*una cuerda*) pull in; (*pedir, reclamar*) dun; (hunt) to retrieve; **cobrar afición a** to take a liking for; **cobrar al número llamado** (telp) to reverse the charges; **cobrar ánimo** to take courage; **cobrar carnes** to put on flesh; **cobrar fuerzas** to gain strength || *intr* to get hit || *ref* to recover, come to
cobre *m* copper; copper or brass kitchen utensils; **batir el cobre** to hustle, work with a will; **cobres** (mus) brasses
cobre•ño -ña *adj* copper
cobrero *m* coppersmith
cobri•zo -za *adj* coppery
cobro *m* collection; recovery; **cobro contra entrega** collect on delivery; **en cobro** in a safe place
coca *f* coca; (*en una cuerda*) kink; (coll) head; (slang) coke (*cocaine*); **de coca** (Mex) free; (Mex) in vain
cocaína *f* cocaine
cocción *f* cooking, baking; (*de objetos cerámicos*) baking, burning
cocear *intr* to kick; (*resistir*) balk, rebel
cocer §16 *tr* to cook; boil; (*pan; ladrillos*) bake; digest || *intr* to cook; boil; ferment || *ref* to suffer a long time
cochambre *m* dirty, stinking thing, pigsty
cochambro•so -sa *adj* dirty, stinking
coche *m* carriage; coach; car; taxi; (*puerco*) hog; **caminar en el coche de San Francisco** to go or to ride on shank's mare; **coche bar** (rr) club car; **coche bomba** fire engine; (coll) car bomb; **coche celular** Black Maria, prison van; **coche con puerta trasera** hatchback; **coche de alquiler** cab, hack; **coche de carreras** racing car; **coche de correos** mail car; **coche de plaza** or **de punto** cab, hack; **coche de reparto** (delivery) van; **coche de serie** (aut) stock car; **coche fúnebre** hearse; **coche rural** station wagon
coche-cama *m* (*pl* **coches-camas**) sleeping car
cochecillo *m* baby carriage; **cochecillo para inválidos** wheelchair; **cochecillo para niños** baby carriage
coche-comedor *m* (*pl* **coches-comedores**) (rr) diner, dining car
coche-correo *m* (*pl* **coches-correo**) (rr) mail car
coche-fumador *m* (*pl* **coches-fumadores**) (rr) smoker, smoking car
coche-habitación *m* (*pl* **coches-habitación**) trailer
cochera *f* coach house; livery stable; carbarn; garage
cochería *f* (Arg, Chile) livery stable
coche•ro -ra *adj* easy to cook || *m* coachman, driver; **cochero de punto** cabby, hackman || *f* see **cochera**
cocherón *m* coach house; (*depósito de locomotoras*) roundhouse
coche-salón *m* (*pl* **coches-salón**) (rr) parlor car
cochevira *f* lard
cochina *f* sow; (*mujer sucia y desaliñada*) trollop
cochinada *f* piggishness, filthiness; dirty trick
cochinillo *m* sucking pig
cochi•no -na *adj* piggish, filthy; (*tacaño*) stingy; (Ven) cowardly || *mf* hog; (*persona muy sucia*) (coll) pig, dirty person || *f* see **cochina**
cochite hervite *adj, adv & m* helter-skelter
cochitril *m* pigsty; den, hovel
cochura *f* batch of dough
coci•do -da *adj* cooked || *m* Spanish stew
cociente *m* quotient; **cociente intelectual** intelligence quotient
cocina *f* (*pieza*) kitchen; (*arte*) cooking, cuisine; (*aparato*) stove; **cocina de presión** pressure cooker; **cocina económica** kitchen stove
cocinar *tr* to cook || *intr* to meddle
cocine•ro -ra *mf* cook
cocinilla *m* meddler || *f* kitchenette; chafing dish; **cocinilla sin fuego** fireless cooker
coco *m* coconut; (*moño*) topknot, chignon; (*duende*) bogeyman; (*gesto, mueca*) face, gri-

mace; (*sombrero hongo*) (Col, Ecuad) derby hat; **hacer cocos** to make a face; (*los enamorados*) to make eyes
cocodrilo *m* crocodile
cócora *adj* boring, tiresome || *mf* bore, pest
coco•so -sa *adj* worm-eaten
cocotero *m* cocoanut palm or tree
cóctel *m* cocktail; cocktail party; **cóctel de frutas** fruit salad
coctelera *f* cocktail shaker
cocuma *f* (Peru) roast corn on the cob
codadura *f* (hort) layer
codal *adj* elbow || *m* prop, shoring
codazo *m* poke, nudge; **dar codazo a** (Mex) to tip off
codear *tr* (SAm) to sponge on || *intr* to elbow, elbow one's way || *ref* to hobnob, rub elbows
codelincuencia *f* complicity
codelincuente *mf* accomplice
codera *f* elbow patch; elbow itch
códice *m* codex
codicia *f* covetousness, greed, cupidity
codiciar *tr* to covet
codicilo *m* codicil
codicio•so -sa *adj* covetous, greedy; (*laborioso*) hard-working
codificación *f* codification; coding, encoding; (compu) coding; **codificación con colores** color coding; **codificación de barras** bar coding
codificar §73 *tr* to codify
código *m* code; **código barrado, código de barras** bar code; **código binario** binary code; **código de edificación** building code; **código de la zona, código territorial** (telp) area code; **código genético** genetic code; **código morse** Morse code; **codigo penal** criminal code; **código postal** zip code; **código universal de producto** universal product code (UPC)
codillo *m* (*de animal*) knee; (*estribo*) stirrup; (*de un tubo*) elbow; (*de la rama cortada*) stump
codo *m* elbow; (Guat, Mex) miser, tightwad; **dar de codo a** to nudge; to spurn; **empinar el codo** to crook the elbow; **hablar por los codos** to talk too much
codor•niz *f* (*pl* **-nices**) quail
coeducación *f* coeducation
coeficiente *adj & m* coefficient
coetáne•o -a *adj & mf* contemporary, peer
coexistencia *f* coexistence
coexistir *intr* to coexist
cofa *f* (naut) top; **cofa de vigía** (naut) crow's-nest
cofrade *mf* member, fellow member || *m* brother || *f* sister
cofradía *f* brotherhood, sisterhood; association, fraternity
cofre *m* coffer, chest, trunk
cogedor *m* dustpan; coal shovel, ash shovel
coger §17 *tr* to catch, seize, take hold of: collect, gather, pick; overtake; surprise; hold || *intr* to be, be located; fit || *ref* to get caught; cling; get involved
cogida *f* collecting, gathering, picking; (taur) hook
cogollo *m* (*de la lechuga*) heart; (*de la berza*) head; (*de una planta*) shoot; (*del árbol*) top; (*lo mejor*) cream, pick
cogote *m* back of the neck
cogotera *f* havelock
cogotu•do -da *adj* thick-necked; (coll) proud, stiff-necked; (SAm) moneyed
cogulla *f* cowl, frock; **cogulla de fraile** (bot) monkshood
cohabitar *intr* to live together; (*el hombre y la mujer*) cohabit
cohechar *tr* to bribe; plow just before sowing || *intr* to take a bribe
cohecho *m* bribe
coherede•ro -ra *mf* coheir || *f* coheiress
coherente *adj* coherent
cohesión *f* cohesion
cohete *m* (*fuego artificial*) rocket, skyrocket; (*motor a reacción*) rocket; (coll) fidgety person; **cohete borracho** jumping jack; **cohete de señales** (aer) flare; **cohete espacial** space rocket; **cohete intermedio** or **cohete de alcance medio** intermediate-range missile; **cohete lanzador** booster rocket; **cohete sonda** space probe
cohetería *f* missilery
cohibente *adj* (elec) nonconducting
cohibi•do -da *adj* timid, self-conscious
cohibir *tr* to check, restrain, inhibit; (Mex) to oblige
cohombro *m* cucumber
cohonestar *tr* to gloss over, rationalize
coima *f* rake-off paid to operator of a gambling table; concubine; (SAm) bribe
coincidencia *f* coincidence
coincidir *intr* to coincide; happen at the same time; be at the same time (*at a given place*); agree
coito *m* coition, coitus
coja *f* lame woman; lewd woman
cojear *intr* to limp; (*una mesa, una silla*) wobble; (*adolecer de algún vicio*) slip, lapse, have a weakness
cojera *f* (*anormalidad del que cojea*) lameness; (*movimiento del que cojea*) limp
cojijo *m* bug, insect; peeve
cojijo•so -sa *adj* peevish
cojín *m* cushion; (*para arrodillarse*) hassock
cojincillo *m* pad
cojinete *m* cushion; sewing cushion; (mach) bearing; **cojinete de bolas** ball bearing; **cojinete de rodillos** roller bearing
co•jo -ja *adj* lame, crippled; (*mesa, silla*) wobbly; (*pierna*) game || *mf* lame person, cripple || *f* see **coja**
cojón *m* testicle
cok *m* var of **coque**
col. *abbr* **colonia, columna**
col *f* cabbage; **col de Bruselas** Brussels sprouts

cola *f* (*de animal, de ave, de cometa*) tail; (*de un vestido*) train, trail; (*de personas que esperan turno*) queue; (*extremidad posterior*) tail end, rear end; (*de una clase de alumnos*) bottom; (*pasta fuerte*) glue; **cola del pan** bread line; **cola de milano** or **de pato** dovetail; **cola de pescado** isinglass; **cola de retazo** size, sizing; **hacer cola** to queue, to stand in line
colaboración *f* collaboration; (*en un periódico, coloquio, etc.*) contribution
colaboracionista *mf* collaborationist
colabora•dor -dora *adj* collaborating || *mf* collaborator; contributor
colaborar *intr* to collaborate; (*en un periódico, coloquio, etc.*) contribute
colación *f* (*cotejo; refacción ligera*) light meal; (*de un grado de universidad*) conferring; parish land; **sacar a colación** to mention, bring up; **traer a colación** to bring up; adduce as proof; bring up irrelevantly
colacionar *tr* to collate; compare; (*un beneficio*) confer
colactánea *f* foster sister
colactáneo *m* foster brother
colada *f* washing powder; wash; (*garganta entre montañas*) gulch; cattle run; **todo saldrá en la colada** it will all come out in the wash; the day of reckoning will come
coladera *f* strainer; (Mex) sewer
coladero *m* strainer; cattle run; narrow pass
cola•do -da *mf* (coll) gatecrasher; (coll) line jumper
colador *m* strainer, colander
colapez *f* or **colapiscis** *f* isinglass
colapso *m* breakdown, collapse; **colapso nervioso** nervous breakdown
colar *tr* (*un grado universitario*) to confer || **§61** *tr* (*un líquido*) to strain; bleach in hot lye, buck; (*metales*) cast; (*una moneda falsa*) pass off; **colar el hueso por** (coll) to squeeze through || *intr* to run, ooze; squeeze through; come in, slip in; drink wine; **colar a fondo** to sink; **no colar** (*una cosa*) to not be believed || *ref* to seep, seep through; slip in, slip through; make a slip; lie; **colarse de gorra** to crash the gate
colateral *adj* collateral || *ref* (*pariente*) collateral || *m* (com) collateral
colcha *f* quilt, counterpane, bedspread; **colcha de retazos** crazy quilt, patchwork quilt
colchón *m* mattress; **colchón de aire** air mattress; **colchón de muelles** or **resortes** bedspring, box spring, spring mattress; **colchón de plumas** feather bed
colcrén *m* cold cream
coleada *f* wag (*of the tail*); (Mex, Ven) throwing the bull by twisting its tail
colear *tr* (taur) to grab by the tail; (*la res*) (Mex, Ven) to throw by twisting the tail; (Col, Ven) to nag, harass; (Guat) to trail after; (*reprobar en un examen*) (Chile) to flunk || *intr* to wag the tail; stay alive, keep going; (*los últimos vagones de un tren*) sway; (aer) to fishtail; **colear en** (*cierta edad*) (CAm, W-I) to border on, be close to; **todavía colea** it's not over yet
colección *f* collection
coleccionar *tr* to collect
coleccionista *mf* collector; **coleccionista de sellos** stamp collector
colecta *f* collection for charity; (eccl) collect
colectar *tr* to collect; (*obras antes sueltas*) collect in one volume
colecti•cio -cia *adj* new, untrained, green; (*tomo*) omnibus
colecti•vo -va *adj* collective
colector *m* collector; catch basin; (elec) commutator; (aut) manifold
colega *mf* colleague || *m* confrere
colegial *m* schoolboy; (Mex) greenhorn, beginner
colegiala *f* schoolgirl
colegiatura *f* scholarship; (Mex) tuition
colegio *m* school, academy; (*sociedad de hombres de una misma profesión*) college (*e.g., of cardinals, electors*); **colegio concertado** private school receiving a state subsidy; **colegio privado** private school; **colegio público** public school; **colegio universitario** university
colegir **§57** *tr* to gather, collect; conclude, infer
cólera *m* cholera || *f* anger, wrath; (*bilis*) bile; **montar en cólera** to fly into a rage
coléri•co -ca *adj* choleric, irascible
colesterol *m* cholesterol
coleta *f* pigtail; (*del torero*) cue, queue; (coll) postscript; **cortarse la coleta** to quit the bull ring; to quit, retire; **tener** or **traer coleta** to have serious consequences
coletero *m* wren
coleto *m* buff jacket; (coll) body, one's body, oneself; **decir para su coleto** (coll) to say to oneself; **echarse al coleto** to eat up, drink up; read from cover to cover
colgadero *m* hanger, hook; clothes rack
colgadizo *m* lean-to, penthouse; projection over a door, canopy
colga•do -da *adj* pending, unsettled; **dejar colgado** to disappoint, frustrate; **quedarse colgado** to be disappointed, frustrated
colgador *m* clothes hanger, coat hanger
colgajo *m* rag, tatter
colgante *adj* hanging, dangling; (*puente*) suspension || *m* drop, pendant; (archit) festoon; (P-R) watch fob
colgar **§63** *tr* to hang; impute, attribute; (*a un alumno*) flunk; (*a un reo*) hang || *intr* to hang, hang down, dangle; droop; (telp) to hang up; **colgar de** to hang from, hang on; depend on || *ref* (compu) to crash
coli•brí *m* (*pl* **-bríes**) humming bird
coliche *m* (coll) at-home, open house
cóli•co -ca *adj & m* colic || *f* upset stomach
coliflor *f* cauliflower
coligar **§44** *ref* to join forces, make common cause

colilla *f* butt, stump, stub
co•lín -lina *adj* (*caballo o yegua*) bobtailed || *m* bobwhite; **colín de Virginia** bobwhite || *f* see **colina**
colina *f* hill, knoll
colindante *adj* adjacent, contiguous
colindar *intr* to be adjacent
colino•so -sa *adj* hilly
colirio *m* eyewash, eye drops
coliseo *m* coliseum; **Coliseo** Colosseum
colisión *f* collision; bruise, bump
colista *mf* person standing in line
colitis *f* colitis
collada *f* mountain pass; (naut) steady blow
collado *m* hill, height
collar *m* necklace; dog collar, horse collar; (*aro de hierro asegurado al cuello del malhechor*) collar, band; (*plumas del cuello de ciertas aves*) frill, ring; (*cadena que rodea el cuello como insignia*) cord, chain; (mach) collar
collera *f* horse collar; chain gang; **colleras** (Arg, Chile) cuff links
co•llón -llona *adj* cowardly || *mf* coward
colma•do -da *adj* abundant, plentiful || *m* food store, grocery store; seafood restaurant
colmar *tr* to fill up; (*las esperanzas de uno*) fulfill; overwhelm; **colmar de** to shower with, overwhelm with
colmena *f* beehive
colmenar *m* apiary
colmene•ro -ra *mf* beekeeper
colmillo *m* eyetooth, canine tooth; (*del elefante*) tusk; **tener el colmillo retorcido** to cut one's eyeteeth
col•mo -ma *adj* brimful, overflowing || *m* overflow; thatch, thatch roof; (*de un sorbete*) topping; **eso es el colmo** (coll) that's the limit; **para colmo de** to top off
colocación *f* (*acción de poner una persona o cosa en un lugar*) location; (*disposición de una cosa respecto del lugar que ocupa*) placement, niche; (*inversión de dinero*) investment; (*empleo*) position, employment, job
colocar §73 *tr* to place, put; (*una trampa*) set || *ref* to get placed, find a job; (*venderse*) sell
colodra *f* milk bucket; drinking horn; (*bebedor de vino*) (coll) toper
colofón *m* colophon
colofonia *f* rosin
coloide *adj* & *m* colloid
colon *m* colon; (gram) main clause
Colón *m* Columbus
colonia *f* colony; cologne; silk ribbon; housing development; (W-I) sugar plantation; **colonia nudista** nudist colony || **Colonia** *f* Cologne; **la Colonia del Cabo** Cape Colony
colonial *adj* colonial; overseas || **coloniales** *mpl* imported foods
colonizar §60 *tr* & *intr* to colonize
colono *m* colonist, settler; tenant farmer; (W-I) owner of sugar plantation
coloquial *adj* colloquial
coloquialismo *m* colloquialism
coloquio *m* colloquy, talk, conference
color *m* color; (*substancia para pintar*) paint; (*para pintarse el rostro*) rouge; **colores** (*bandera*) colors; (*persona*) **de color** of color, colored; (*zapatos*) tan; **sacar los colores a** to make blush; **so color de** under color of, under pretext of; **verlo todo de color de rosa** to see everything through rose-colored glasses
colora•do -da *adj* red, reddish; (*libre, obsceno*) off-color; (*aparentemente justo y razonable*) specious; **ponerse colorado** to blush
colorado•te -ta *adj* ruddy, sanguine
colorante *adj* & *m* coloring
colorar *tr* to color; dye; stain
colorear *tr* to color; (fig) to color, excuse, palliate || *ref* (*la cereza, el tomate, etc.*) to redden, turn red
colorete *m* rouge; **ponerse colorete** to put on rouge
colorir §1 *tr* to color; (fig) to color, palliate || *intr* to take on color
colosal *adj* colossal
coloso *m* colossus
columbrar *tr* to discern, descry, glimpse; to guess
columna *f* column; **columna de dirección** steering column; **quinta columna** fifth column
columnata *f* colonnade
columnista *mf* columnist
columpiar *tr* to swing || *ref* to swing; to seesaw; (coll) to swing, swagger
columpio *m* swing; **columpio de tabla** seesaw
colusión *f* collusion
coma *m* (pathol) coma || *f* comma; **coma decimal** (*en inglés se emplea el punto en arimética para separar los números enteros de las fracciones decimales*) decimal point; **coma flotante** (compu) floating-point
comadre *f* mother or godmother (*with respect to each other*); gossip (*woman*); friend, neighbor (*woman*)
comadrear *intr* to gossip, go around gossiping
comadreja *f* weasel
comadrería *f* gossip, idle gossip
comadre•ro -ra *adj* gossipy || *mf* gossip
comadrón *m* accoucheur
comadrona *f* midwife
comandancia *f* command; commander's headquarters; (mil) majority
comandante *m* commander, commandant; (mil) major
comandar *tr* (mil, nav) to command
comando *m* (compu, mil) command; **comando encajado** (compu) embedded command; **comando suicida** suicide squad
comarca *f* district, region, country
comarcar §73 *tr* to plant in a line at regular intervals || *intr* to border, be contiguous
comato•so -sa *adj* comatose
comba *f* bend, curve; warp, bulge; skipping rope: **saltar a la comba** to jump rope, skip rope

combar *tr* to bend, curve || *ref* to bend, curve; warp, bulge; sag

combate *m* combat, fight; **combate aéreo** dogfight; **combate revancha** (box) return bout; **fuera de combate** hors de combat; (box) knockout; **(el) combate asimétrico** (*guerra entre dos fuerzas armadas desiguales en la que la técnica militar de una de esas fuerzas es superior a la otra*) asymmetrical warfare

combatiente *adj & m* combatant

combatir *tr* to combat, fight; beat, beat upon || *intr & ref* to combat, fight, struggle

combinación *f* combination; (*de trenes*) connection

combinar *tr & ref* to combine

com•bo -ba *adj* bent, curved, crooked; warped || *m* trunk or rock to stand wine casks on || *f* see **comba**

combustible *adj* combustible || *m* (*substancia que arde con facilidad*) combustible; (*substancia que sirve para calentar, cocinar, etc.*) fuel; **combustible alternativo** alternative fuel

combustión *f* combustion

comede•ro -ra *adj* eatable || *m* manger, feed trough; (Mex) haunt, hangout; **limpiarle a uno el comedero** to deprive someone of his bread and butter

comedia *f* drama, play; theater; comedy; (fig) farce; **comedia cómica** (*drama de desenlace festivo*) comedy; **comedia musical** (theat) musical; **hacer la comedia** to pretend, make believe

comedian•te -ta *mf* hypocrite || *m* actor, comedian || *f* actress, comedienne

comedi•do -da *adj* courteous, polite; moderate; obliging, accommodating

comedimiento *m* courtesy, politeness; moderation

comediógra•fo -fa *mf* playwright

comedir §50 *ref* to be courteous; restrain oneself, be moderate; be obliging; **comedirse a** to offer to, volunteer to

comedón *m* blackhead

come•dor -dora *adj* heavy-eating || *m* dining room; restaurant, eating place; dining-room suite; **comedor de beneficencia** soup kitchen

comején *m* termite

comendador *m* prelate, prior; knight commander; (*de una orden militar*) commander

comensal *mf* dependent, servant; table companion

comentar *tr* to comment on || *intr* to comment; to gossip

comentario *m* comment, commentary; **comentarios** talk, gossip

comentarista *mf* commentator

comento *m* comment, commentary; deceit, falsehood

comenzar §18 *tr & intr* to commence, begin, start

comer *m* eating, food || *tr* to eat; to feed on; to gnaw away; to consume; (*alguna renta*) to enjoy; to itch; (*una pieza en el juego de damas*) to take; **comer vivo** to have it in for; **sin comerlo ni beberlo** (coll) without having anything to do with it; **tener qué comer** to have enough to live on || *intr* to eat; to dine, to have dinner; to itch || *ref* to eat up; (*las uñas*) to bite; (*el dinero*) (coll) to consume, eat up; (*omitir*) to skip, skip over; **comerse unos a otros** to be at loggerheads

comerciable *adj* marketable; sociable

comercial *adj* commercial, business

comercializar §60 *tr* to market; commercialize

comerciante *mf* merchant, trader, dealer; **comerciante al por mayor** wholesaler; **comerciante al por menor** retailer

comerciar *intr* to trade, deal

comercio *m* commerce, trade, business; store, shop; business center; commerce, intercourse; **comercio de artículos de regalo** gift shop; **comercio exterior** foreign trade

comestible *adj* eatable || *m* food, foodstuff; **comestibles** groceries

cometa *m* comet || *f* kite

cometer *tr* (*un crimen, una falta*) to commit; (*un negocio a una persona*) commit, entrust; (*figuras retóricas*) employ

cometido *m* assignment, duty; commitment

comezón *f* itch

comicastro *m* ham, ham actor

comicios *mpl* polls; **acudir a los comicios** to go to the polls

cómi•co -ca *adj* comic, comical; dramatic || *mf* actor; comedian; **cómico de la legua** strolling player, barnstormer || *f* actress; comedienne

comida *f* (*alimento*) food; (*el que se toma a horas señaladas*) meal; (*el principal de cada día*) dinner; **comida basura** junk food; **comida corrida** (Mex) table d'hôte; **comida de negocios** business lunch; **comida para llevar** take-out

comidilla *f* hobby; **la comidilla del pueblo** the talk of the town

comienzo *m* beginning, start; **a comienzos de** around the beginning of

comilitona *f* spread, feast

comillas *fpl* quotation marks

comi•lón -lona *adj* heavy-eating || *mf* hearty eater || *f* hearty meal, spread

cominear *intr* (*el hombre*) to fuss around like a woman

comiquear *intr* to put on amateur plays

comiquillo *m* ham, ham actor

comiquísi•mo -ma *adj* hilarious

comisar *tr* to seize, confiscate

comisaría *f* police station

comisario *m* commissary; commissioner; **comisario de a bordo** purser

comisión *f* commission; service charge; committee; (*recado*) errand; **comisión mixta** joint committee; **comisión permanente** standing committee

comisiona•do -da *mf* commissioner || *m* committeeman

comisionar *tr* to commission
comiso *m* seizure, confiscation; confiscated goods
comisura *f* corner (*e.g., of lips*)
comité *m* committee; **comité asesor** think tank; **comité de redacción** editorial board; **comité planeador** steering committee
comitente *mf* constituent
comitiva *f* retinue, suite; procession
como *adv* as, like; so to speak, as it were || *conj* as; when; if; so that; as soon as; as long as; inasmuch as; **así como** as well as; **como no** unless; **como que** because, inas much as; **como quien dice** so to speak; **tan luego como** as soon as
cómo *adv* how; why; what; **¿a cómo es. . . ?** how much is. . . ?; **¿cómo no?** why not?
cómoda *f* bureau, commode, chest
comodidad *f* comfort; convenience; advantage, interest
comodín *m* joker, wild card; gadget, jigger; excuse, alibi; (compu) wild card
cómo•do -da *adj* handy, convenient; comfortable || *f* see **cómoda**
como•dón -dona *adj* comfort-loving, self-indulgent, easy-going
compact-disc [kompak 'ðis(k)] *m* compact disk; compact disk player
compac•to -ta *adj* compact
compadecer §22 *tr* to pity, feel sorry for || *ref* to harmonize; **compadecerse con** to harmonize with; **compadecerse de** to pity, feel sorry for
compadraje *m* clique, cabal
compadrar *intr* to become a godfather; become friends
compadre *m* father or godfather (*with respect to each other*); friend, companion
compadrear *intr* to be close friends; (Arg, Urug) to brag, show off
compadrería *f* close companionship
compadrito *m* (Arg) bully
compaginación *f* combination, organization; (compu, typ) page setup *o* makeup
compaginar *tr* to arrange, put in order || *ref* to fit, agree; blend
companage *m* snacks, cold cuts
compañerismo *m* companionship
compañe•ro -ra *mf* companion; partner, comrade; mate; **compañero de armas** comrade in arms; **compañero de cama** bedfellow; **compañero de candidatura** (pol) running mate; **compañero de cuarto** roommate; **compañero de juego** playmate; **compañero de viaje** fellow traveler || *f* (*esposa*) helpmeet
compañía *f* company; society; (theat) troupe; **compañía de desembarco** (nav) landing force; **compañía matriz** parent company; **hacerle compañía a una persona** to keep someone company
compañón *m* testicle; **compañón de perro** orchid
comparación *f* comparison
comparar *tr* to compare
comparati•vo -va *adj* comparative
comparecencia *f* (law) appearance
comparecer §22 *intr* (law) to appear
comparendo *m* (law) summons
comparsa *mf* (theat) supernumerary, extra, super || *f* supernumeraries, extras
compartimiento *m* distribution, division; compartment, cubicle; **compartimiento estanco** watertight compartment
compartir *tr* to distribute, divide; share
compás *m* (*brújula*) compass; (*instrumento para trazar curvas*) compass or compasses; rule, measure; (mus) time, measure; (mus) bar, measure; (mus) beat; **a compás** (mus) in time; **compás de calibres** calipers; **compás de división** dividers; **llevar el compás** (mus) to keep time
compasible *adj* compassionate; pitiful
compasión *f* compassion; **¡por compasión!** for pity's sake!
compasi•vo -va *adj* compassionate
compatri•cio -cia *mf* or **compatriota** *mf* fellow countryman, compatriot
compeler *tr* to compel
compendiar *tr* to condense, summarize
compendio *m* compendium; **en compendio** in a word
compendio•so -sa *adj* compendious
compensación *f* compensation; (com) clearing, clearance
compensar *tr* to compensate; compensate for || *intr* to compensate || *ref* to be compensated for
competencia *f* (*aptitud*) competence; (*rivalidad*) competition; dispute; area, field; **competencia de atletismo** track and field meet; **competencia desleal** unfair competition; **de la competencia de** in the domain of; **sin competencia** unmatched (*prices*)
competente *adj* competent; reliable
competer *intr* to be incumbent
competición *f* competition
competi•dor -dora *adj* competing || *mf* competitor
competir §50 *intr* to compete; **poder competir** to be competitive
compilación *f* compilation
compila•dor -dora *mf* compiler || *m* (compu) compiler
compilar *tr* to compile
compinche *mf* chum, crony, pal
complacencia *f* complacency
complacer §22 *tr* to please, humor || *ref* to be pleased, take pleasure
complaciente *adj* obliging; indulgent
comple•jo -ja *adj & m* complex; **complejo de inferioridad** inferiority complex; **complejo deportivo** (sport) field house; **complejo turístico** tourist resort
complementar *tr* to complement
complemento *m* complement; completion; perfection; accessory; **complemento directo** (gram) direct object

completar *tr* to complete; perfect
comple•to -ta *adj* complete; (*autobús, tranvía*) full
complexión *f* constitution
complexiona•do -da *adj* — **bien complexionado** strong, robust; **mal complexionado** weak, frail
comple•xo -xa *adj* complex
complica•do -da *adj* complicated, complex
complicar §73 *tr* to complicate; involve || *ref* to become complicated; become involved
cómplice *mf* accomplice, accessory
complicidad *f* complicity
com•plot *m* (*pl* **-plots**) plot, intrigue
compone•dor -dora *mf* composer, compositor; typesetter; arbitrator; repairer || *m* stick, composing stick; **amigable componedor** mediator, umpire
componenda *f* compromise, settlement, reconciliation
componente *adj* component, constituent || *m* component, constituent; member || *f* (mech) component
componer §54 *tr* to compose; compound; mend, repair; pacify, reconcile; arrange, put in order; restore, strengthen; (*huesos dislocados*) (Am) to set; (Col) to bewitch || *ref* to compose oneself; get dressed; make up, become friends again; (*pintarse el rostro*) make up; **componérselas** to make out, manage
comportable *adj* bearable, tolerable
comportamentismo *m* behaviorism
comportamiento *m* behavior, conduct
comportar *tr* to support; bring about, entail || *ref* to act, behave
comporte *m* behavior; carriage, bearing
composición *f* composition; agreement; (*circunspección*) composure, restraint; **composición de textos** typesetting; **hacer una composición de lugar** to lay one's plans carefully
compositi•vo -va *adj* (gram) combining
composi•tor -tora *mf* composer || *m* (Arg, Urug) horse trainer, trainer of fighting cocks
compostura *f* composition; agreement; (*circunspección*) composure, restraint; repair, repairing, mending; (*aseo*) neatness; adulteration; (Arg, Urug) training
compota *f* compote, preserves; **compota de frutas** stewed fruit; **compota de manzanas** applesauce
compotera *f* (*vasija*) compote
compra *f* purchase, buy; shopping; **compra al contado** cash purchase; **compra apalancada, compra con financiación a jena** leveraged buyout; **compra a plazos** installment buying; **hacer compras, ir de compras** to go shopping
compra•dor -dora *mf* purchaser, buyer; shopper
comprar *tr* to purchase, buy; (*sobornar*) buy off || *intr* to shop
compraventa *f* dealing, business, bargain, trading; resale
comprender *tr* (*entender*) to understand; (*entender; abrazar*) comprehend; (*contener, incluir*) comprise
comprensible *adj* comprehensible, understandable
comprensión *f* understanding, comprehension; inclusion
comprensi•vo -va *adj* understanding, sympathetic; comprehensive; **comprensivo de** inclusive of
compresa *f* (med) compress; **compresa higiénica** sanitary napkin
compresión *f* compression
comprimido *m* tablet
comprimir *tr* to compress; restrain, repress; flatten
comprobación *f* checking, verification; proof
comprobante *adj* proving || *m* certificate, voucher, warrant; proof; claim check
comprobar §61 *tr* to check, verify; prove
comprometer *tr* to compromise, endanger, jeopardize; force, oblige; (*un negocio a un tercero*) entrust || *ref* to promise; commit oneself; become engaged
comprometi•do -da *adj* awkward, embarrassing; engaged to be married
comprometimiento *m* commitment, promise; predicament, awkward situation; compromise
compromiso *m* commitment, promise; appointment, engagement; predicament, awkward situation; betrothal; (com) obligation
compuerta *f* hatch, half door; floodgate, sluice; **compuerta de dique** (naut) caisson
compues•to -ta *adj & m* composite, compound
compulsar *tr* to collate; make an authentic copy of
compungi•do -da *adj* remorseful
compungir §27 *tr* to make remorseful || *ref* to feel remorse
compurgar §44 *tr* (*el reo; la pena*) (Mex) to finish serving
computadora *f or* **computador** *m* computer; **computadora de a bordo** *or* **de viaje** onboard computer; **computadora de sobremesa** *or* **de mesa** *or* **escritorio** desktop computer; **computadora doméstica** home computer; **computadora patrón** server; **computadora personal** personal computer; **computadora portátil** laptop computer
computadorizar §60 *tr* to computerize
computar *tr & intr* to compute
computerizar §60 *or* **computarizar §60** *tr* to computerize
computista *mf* computer programmer
computo *m* computation, calculation
comulgante *mf* (eccl) communicant
comulgar §44 *tr* to administer communion to || *intr* to take communion
comulgatorio *m* communion rail, altar rail
común *adj* common || *m* community; water closet; toilet; **el común de las gentes** the general run of people; **por lo común** commonly
comunal *adj* common; community || *m* community

comune•ro -ra *adj* popular || *m* shareholder
comunicación *f* communication; connection
comunicado *m* communiqué; letter to the editor, official announcement
comunica•dor -dora *adj* communicating
comunicante *mf* communicant, informant
comunicar §73 *tr* to communicate; notify, inform; connect, put into communication || *intr* to communicate || *ref* to communicate; communicate with each other
comunicati•vo -va *adj* communicative
comunidad *f* community; **Comunidad Económica Europea** European Economic Community
comunión *f* communion; political party; sect
comunismo *m* communism
comunista *mf* communist
comunistizar §60 *tr* to convert to communism || *ref* to become communistic
comunizar §60 *tr* to communize
con *prep* with; to, toward; in spite of; **con que** and so; whereupon; **con tal (de) que** provided that; **con todo** however, nevertheless
conato *m* effort, endeavor; (*delito que no llegó a consumarse*) attempt
cónca•vo -va *adj* concave
concebible *adj* conceivable
concebir §50 *tr & intr* to conceive
conceder *tr* to concede, admit; grant
concejal *m* alderman, councilman; **concejales** city fathers
concejo *m* town council; town hall; council meeting; (*expósito*) foundling
concentrar *tr & ref* to concentrate
concéntri•co -ca *adj* concentric
concepción *f* conception
concepto *m* concept; opinion, judgment; (*dicho ingenioso*) conceit, witticism; point of view; **en concepto de** under the head of; **tener buen concepto de** or **tener en buen concepto** to have a high opinion of, to hold in high esteem
conceptuar §21 *tr* to deem, judge, regard
conceptuo•so -sa *adj* witty, epigrammatic
concerniente *adj* relative
concernir §28 *tr* to concern
concertar §2 *tr* to concert; mend, repair; (*un casamiento; la paz*) arrange; (*huesos dislocados*) set; (*poner de acuerdo*) reconcile; (*un pacto*) conclude; harmonize || *intr* to concert; agree || *ref* to come to terms, become reconciled; agree
concertino *m* concertmaster
concertista *mf* (mus) manager; (mus) performer, soloist
concesión *f* concession, admission; grant
concesionario *m* licensee; (*comerciante*) dealer
concesi•vo -va *adj* concessive
concha *f* (*de molusco o crustáceo*) shell; (*cada una de las dos partes del caparazón de los moluscos bivalvos*) half shell; (*en que se sirve el pescado*) scallop; (*carey*) tortoise shell; oyster; shellfish; horseshoe bay; (theat) prompter's box; **concha de peregrino** scallop shell; (zool) scallop; (*ostras*) **en su concha** on the half shell; **tener muchas conchas** to be sly, cunning
conchabanza *f* comfort; collusion, cabal
conchabar *tr* to join, unite; hire || *ref* to gang up; hire out
conchabero *m* (Col) pieceworker
conciencia *f* (*conocimiento que uno tiene de su propia existencia*) consciousness; (*sentimiento del bien y del mal*) conscience; (*conocimiento*) awareness; **cobrar conciencia de** to become aware of; **en conciencia** in all conscience
concienzu•do -da *adj* conscientious; thorough
concierto *m* concert, harmony; (*función de música*) concert; (*composición de música*) concerto
concilia•dor -dora *adj* conciliatory
conciliar *tr* to conciliate, reconcile || *ref* (*el respeto, la estima, etc.*) to conciliate, win
concilio *m* (eccl) council
conci•so -sa *adj* concise
concitar *tr* to stir up, incite, agitate
conciudada•no -na *mf* fellow citizen
concluir §20 *tr* to conclude; convince || *intr & ref* to conclude, end
conclusión *f* conclusion
concluyente *adj* conclusive, convincing
concomitar *tr* to accompany, go with
concordancia *f* concordance; (gram, mus) concord
concordar §61 *tr* to harmonize; reconcile; make agree || *intr* to agree
concordia *f* concord; **de concordia** by common consent
concre•to -ta *adj* concrete
concubina *f* concubine
concubio *m* (archaic) bedtime
concuñada *f* sister-in-law
concuñado *m* brother-in-law
concurrencia *f* (*acaecimiento de varios sucesos en un mismo tiempo*) concurrence; (*competencia comercial*) competition; (*ayuda*) assistance, crowd, gathering, attendance
concurrente *adj* concurrent; competing || *mf* competitor, contender, entrant
concurri•do -da *adj* crowded, full of people; well-attended
concurrir *intr* to concur; gather, meet, come together; compete, contend; coincide; **concurrir con** (*p.ej., dinero*) to contribute
concursante *mf* contender
concursar *tr* to declare insolvent || *intr* to contend, compete
concurso *m* contest, competition; (*de gente*) concourse, crowd, throng; backing, coöperation; show, exhibition; **concurso de acreedores** meeting of creditors; **concurso de belleza** beauty contest; **concurso de televisión** quiz program; **concurso hípico** horse show
concusión *f* concussion; extortion, shakedown
condado *m* county; earldom

conde *m* count, earl; gypsy chief
condecoración *f* decoration
condecorar *tr* to decorate
condena *f* sentence; penalty, jail term; **condena judicial** conviction
condenación *f* condemnation; (*la eterna*) damnation
condena•do -da *adj* condemned; damned; (Chile) shrewd, clever || *mf* sentenced person; **los condenados** the damned
condenar *tr* to condemn; convict; (*a la pena eterna*) damn; (*p.ej., una ventana*) shut off, block up; (*una habitación*) padlock || *ref* to condemn oneself, confess one's guilt; (*a la pena eterna*) be damned
condensar *tr* to condense || *ref* to condense, be condensed
condesa *f* countess
condescendencia *f* acquiescence, compliance
condescender §51 *intr* to acquiesce, comply; **condescender a** to accede to
condescendiente *adj* acquiescent, obliging
condición *f* condition, state; position, situation; standing; nature, character, temperament; **a condición (de) que** on condition that; **en buenas condiciones** in good condition, in good shape; **tener condición** to have a bad temper
condicional *adj* conditional
condimentar *tr* to season
condimento *m* condiment, seasoning
condiscípulo *m* fellow student
condolencia *f* condolence; **expresar las condolencias a** to extend one's sympathy to
condoler §47 *ref* to condole; **condolerse de** to sympathize with, feel sorry for, commiserate with
condominio *m* condominium
condón *m* condom
condonar *tr* to condone, overlook
cóndor *m* condor; (Chile, Ecuad) gold coin
conducción *f* conveyance, transportation; guiding, leading; (aut) drive, driving; **conducción a la derecha** right-hand drive; **conducción a la izquierda** left-hand drive; **conducción interior** closed car
conducente *adj* conducive
conducir §19 *tr* to conduct; manage, direct; guide, lead; convey, transport; drive; employ, hire || *intr* to lead; conduce || *ref* to conduct oneself, behave
conducta *f* conduct; management, direction; guidance; conveyance; conduct, behavior
conductismo *m* behaviorism
conducto *m* pipe; conduit; (anat) duct, canal; agency, intermediary, channel; **por conducto de** through
conduc•tor -tora *adj* conducting || *mf* driver, motorist; (*cobrador en un vehículo público*) conductor || *m & f* (elec & phys) conductor; **buen conductor, buena conductora** good conductor; **mal conductor, mala conductora** bad or poor conductor || *m* (rr) engineman, engine driver
conectar *tr* to connect
conecti•vo -va *adj* connective
conejera *f* burrow, warren; (coll) joint, dive
conejillo *m* young rabbit; **conejillo de Indias** guinea pig
conejo *m* rabbit; **conejo de Pascua** Easter bunny
conexión *f* connection; linkage; (rad, telv) linkup
conexionar *tr* to connect; put in touch || *ref* to connect; make contacts
confabulación *f* collusion, connivance
confabular *ref* to connive, scheme, plot
confección *f* making, preparation, confection; tailoring; ready-made suit; **confección a medida** suit made to order; **de confección** ready-made
confeccionar *tr* (*ropa*) to make; (*una receta*) make up, concoct
confeccionista *mf* ready-made clothier
confederación *f* confederacy; alliance; **Confederación Helvética** Federal Republic of Switzerland
confedera•do -da *adj & mf* confederate
confederar *tr & ref* to confederate
conferencia *f* (*reunión para tratar asuntos internacionales, etc.*) conference; (*plática para tratar de algún negocio*) interview; (*disertación en público o en la universidad*) lecture; **conferencia a cobro revertido** (telp) collect call; **conferencia de prensa** press conference; **conferencia (en la) cumbre** summit (conference); **conferencia persona a persona** (telp) person-to-person call; **conferencia interurbana** (telp) long-distance call
conferenciante *mf* conferee; lecturer
conferenciar *intr* to confer, hold an interview
conferencista *mf* (Arg) lecturer
conferir §68 *tr* to confer, award, bestow; discuss; compare || *intr* to confer
confesante *mf* confessor
confesar §2 *tr, intr & ref* to confess
confesión *f* confession; denomination, faith, religion
confe•so -sa *adj* confessed; (*judío*) converted || *mf* converted Jew || *m* lay brother
confesonario *m* confessional
confesor *m* confessor
confiable *adj* reliable, dependable
confia•do -da *adj* unsuspecting; haughty, self-confident
confianza *f* confidence; self-confidence, self-assurance; familiarity; secret deal; **de confianza** reliable
confianzu•do -da *adj* overconfident; overfamiliar
confiar §77 *tr* to confide, entrust; strengthen the confidence of || *intr & ref* to confide, trust; **confiar** or **confiarse de** or **en** to confide in, trust in; rely on
confidencia *f* confidence; secret; **de mayor confidencia** top secret

confidencial *adj* confidential
confiden•te -ta *adj* trustworthy, faithful || *mf* confident || *m* spy; informer; secret agent; love seat
configurar *tr* to shape, form
confín *m* confine, border, boundary; **los confines** the confines
confina•do -da *adj* exiled || *m* prisoner
confinamiento *m* confinement; abutment
confinar *tr* to exile; confine || *intr* to border
confirmar *tr* to confirm
confiscar §73 *tr* to confiscate
confita•do -da *adj* hopeful, confident; (*bañado de azúcar*) candied
confitar *tr* (*frutas*) to candy; (*en almíbar*) preserve; (*endulzar*) sweeten
confite *m* candy, bonbon, confection; **confites** confectionery
confitera *f* candy box; candy jar
confitería *f* confectionery; confectionery store
confite•ro -ra *mf* confectioner || *f* see **confitera**
confitura *f* preserves, confiture; **confituras** confectionery
conflagración *f* conflagration
conflagrar *tr* to set fire to
conflicti•vo -va *adj* conflicting; anguished
conflicto *m* conflict; (*apuro*) fix, jam
confluencia *f* confluence
confluir §20 *intr* to flow together; crowd, gather
conformador *m* hat block
conformar *tr* to shape; (*un sombrero*) to block || *intr & ref* to conform, comply, yield, agree
conforme *adj* in agreement || *adv* depending on circumstances; fine, O.K.; **conforme a** according to || *conj* as, in proportion as; as soon as || *m* approval
conformidad *f* conformance, conformity; resignation
confort *m* comfort
confortable *adj* comfortable; comforting
confortante *adj* comforting; tonic || *mf* comforter || *m* tonic
confr. *abbr* **confesor**
confricar §73 *tr* to rub
confrontar *tr* (*poner en presencia; cotejar*) to confront || *intr* to border; to agree || *ref* to get along, agree; **confrontarse con** (*hacer frente a*) to confront
confundir *tr* to confuse; (*turbar, dejar desarmado*) confound || *ref* to become confused; (*en la muchedumbre*) get lost
confusión *f* confusion
confutar *tr* to confute
congal *m* (Mex) brothel, whorehouse
congelador *m* freezer
congelar *tr* to congeal, freeze; (*créditos*) (fig) to freeze || *ref* to congeal, freeze
congenial *adj* congenial (*having the same nature*)
congeniar *intr* to be congenial, get along well
congéni•to -ta *adj* congenital
congestión *f* congestion
congestionar *tr* to congest || *ref* to congest, become congested
conglobar *tr* to lump together
congoja *f* anguish, grief
congojo•so -sa *adj* distressing; distressed
congosto *m* narrow mountain pass
congraciar *tr* to win over || *ref* to ingratiate oneself; **congraciarse con** to get into the good graces of
congratulación *f* congratulation
congratular *tr* to congratulate || *ref* to congratulate oneself, rejoice
congregación *f* congregation; **la Congregación de los fieles** the Roman Catholic Church
congregar §44 *tr* to bring together || *ref* to congregate, come together
congresal *m* (Arg, Chile) congressman
congresista *mf* delegate; member of congress || *m* congressman || *f* congresswoman
congreso *m* (*asamblea legislativa*) congress; (*reunión para deliberar sobre intereses comunes*) meeting, convention
congrio *m* conger eel
cóni•co -ca *adj* conical
conjetura *f* conjecture, guess
conjeturar *tr & intr* to conjecture, guess
conjugación *f* conjugation
conjugar §44 *tr* to conjugate; combine
conjunción *f* conjunction; combination
conjuntamente *adv* together
conjuntista *m* chorus man || *f* chorus girl
conjunti•vo -va *adj* conjunctive; subjunctive
conjun•to -ta *adj* joined, combined, united || *m* whole, entirety, ensemble; unit; group; (theat) chorus; **de conjunto** general; **en conjunto** as a whole; **en su conjunto** in its entirety
conjura or **conjuración** *f* conspiracy, plot
conjuramentar *tr* to swear in || *ref* to take an oath
conjurar *tr* to swear in; conjure, entreat; conjure away, exorcise || *intr* to conspire, plot || *ref* to conspire, join in a conspiracy
conjuro *m* (*invocación supersticiosa*) conjuration; adjuration, entreaty
conllevar *tr* (*los trabajos*) to share in bearing; (*a una persona*) tolerate, stand for; (*las adversidades*) suffer
conmemorar *tr* to commemorate, memorialize
conmigo *pron* with me, with myself
conmilitón *m* fellow soldier
conminar *tr* to threaten
conmoción *f* commotion; concussion, shock
conmove•dor -dora *adj* touching, moving, stirring, rousing
conmover §47 *tr* to touch, move, affect; stir, stir up; shake, upset || *ref* to be touched, be moved
conmutación *f* commutation
conmutador *m* (elec) change-over switch; (SAm) telephone exchange
conmutar *tr* to commute
connivencia *f* connivance; **estar en connivencia** to connive

cono *m* cone; **cono de proa** nose cone; **cono de viento** (aer) wind cone, wind sock
conoce•dor -dora *adj* knowledgeable || *mf* expert, connoisseur
conocer §22 *tr* to know; meet, get to know; tell, distinguish; (law) to try || *intr* to know; **conocer de** or **en** to know, have knowledge of || *ref* to know oneself; know each other; meet, meet each other
conoci•do -da *adj* known, well-known, familiar; distinguished, prominent || *mf* acquaintance
conocimiento *m* knowledge; understanding; acquaintance; consciousness; (com) bill of lading; **con conocimiento de causa** knowingly, with full knowledge; **conocimiento de embarque** (com) bill of lading; **conocimientos** knowledge; **hablar con pleno conocimiento de causa** to know what one is talking about; **perder el conocimiento** to lose consciousness; **por su real conocimiento** (Arg) for real money; **recobrar el conocimiento** to regain consciousness; **venir en conocimiento de** to come to know
conque *adv* and so || *m* condition, terms
conquista *f* conquest
conquista•dor -dora *adj* conquering || *m* conqueror; (*ladrón de corazones*) lady-killer
conquistar *tr* to conquer; (*ganar la voluntad de*) win over
consabi•do -da *adj* well-known; above-mentioned
consagrar *tr* to consecrate; devote; dedicate; (*una nueva palabra*) authorize || *ref* to devote oneself; make a name for oneself
consciente *adj* conscious
conscripción *f* conscription
conscripto *m* conscript, draftee
consecución *f* obtaining, getting
consecuencia *f* (*correspondencia lógica entre sus elementos*) consistency; (*acontecimiento que resulta necesariamente de otro*) consequence; **en consecuencia** accordingly; **guardar consecuencia** to remain consistent; **traer a consecuencia** to bring in
consecuente *adj* (*que tiene proporción consigo mismo*) consistent; (*que sigue en orden a otra cosa*) consecutive
consecuti•vo -va *adj* consecutive
conseguir §67 *tr* to get, obtain; **conseguir** + *inf* to succeed in + *ger*
conseja *f* story, fairy tale; cabal
conseje•ro -ra *adj* advisory || *mf* advisor, counselor; councilor
consejo *m* advice, counsel; board; council; **consejos** advice; **un consejo** a piece of advice; **consejo de administración** board of directors; **consejo de guerra** court-martial; **consejo de redacción** editorial board; **consejo escolar** school board
consenso *m* consensus
consenti•do -da *adj* spoiled, pampered; (*marido*) indulgent
consenti•dor -dora *adj* acquiescent; pampering || *mf* acquiescent person; (*de niños*) pamperer || *m* cuckold
consentimiento *m* consent
consentir §68 *tr* to allow; admit; pamper, spoil || *intr* to consent; come loose; **consentir** + *inf* to think that + *ind;* **consentir con** to be indulgent toward; **consentir en** to consent to || *ref* to begin to crack up; (Arg) to be proud
conserje *m* janitor, concierge, super
conserva *f* preserves; preserved food; pickles; (naut) convoy; **conservas alimenticias** canned goods; **llevar en su conserva** (naut) to convoy; **navegar en (la) conserva** (naut) to sail in a convoy
conservación *f* conservation; preservation; self-preservation; maintenance, upkeep
conserva•dor -dora *adj* preservative; (pol) conservative || *mf* conservative || *m* curator
conservar *tr* to conserve, keep, maintain; preserve || *ref* to take good care of oneself; keep
conservati•vo -va *adj* conservative, preservative
conservatorio *m* (*p.ej., de música*) conservatory; (Arg) private school; (Chile) hothouse, greenhouse
conservera *f* cannery; (Mex) preserve dish
conservería *f* canning
conserve•ro -ra *adj* canning || *mf* canner || *f* see **conservera**
considerable *adj* considerable; large, great, important
consideración *f* consideration; **ser de consideración** to be of importance, be of concern; **someter a consideración** to take under advisement
considera•do -da *adj* (*que guarda consideración a los demás*) considerate; (*digno de respeto*) respected, esteemed; (*que obra con reflexión*) cautious, prudent
considerando *conj* & *m* whereas
considerar *tr* to consider; treat with consideration
consigna *f* slogan; watchword; (mil) orders; (rr) checkroom; **consigna automática** locker
consignación *f* consignment
consignar *tr* to consign; assign; state in writing, set forth
consignatario *m* consignee
consigo *pron* with him, with her, with them, with you; with himself, with herself, with themselves, with yourself or yourselves
consiguiente *adj* consequential; **ir** or **proceder consiguiente** to act consistently || *m* consequence; **por consiguiente** consequently, therefore
consilia•rio -ria *mf* advisor, counselor
consistencia *f* consistence, consistency
consistente *adj* consistent
consistir *intr* to consist; **consistir en** (*estar compuesto de*) to consist of; (*residir en*) consist in
consistorio *m* consistory; town council; town hall

conso•cio -cia *mf* copartner; companion, fellow member
consola *f* console, console table; bracket; (compu) console
consolación *f* consolation
consolar §61 *tr* to console
consolidar *tr* to fund, refund; strengthen; repair
consommé *m* consommé
consonancia *f* consonance; rhyme
consonante *adj* consonantal; rhyming || *m* rhyme || *f* consonant
consonar §61 *intr* to be in harmony; rhyme
cónsone *adj* harmonious || *m* (mus) chord
consorcio *m* consortium; partnership; fellowship
consorte *mf* consort, mate, spouse; partner, companion; **consortes** (law) colitigants; (law) accomplices
conspi•cuo -cua *adj* outstanding, prominent
conspiración *f* conspiracy
conspirar *intr* to conspire
constancia *f* constancy; certainty, proof
constante *adj* constant; steady, regular; sure, certain || *f* constant
constar *intr* to be clear, be certain; be on record; have the right rhythm; **constar de** to consist of; **hacer constar** to state, make known; **y para que conste** in witness whereof
constatación *f* proof
constatar *tr* to prove, establish, show
constelación *f* constellation; climate, weather; epidemic
consternar *tr* to depress, dismay
constipación *f* or **constipado** *m* cold, cold in the head
constipar *tr* (*los poros*) to stop up || *ref* to catch cold
constitución *f* constitution
constituir §20 *tr* to constitute; establish, found; **constituir en** to force into || *ref* — **constituirse en** to set oneself up as
constituti•vo -va *adj & m* constituent
constituyente *adj* (*para dictar o reformar la constitución*) constituent
constreñir §72 *tr* to constrain, force, compel; constrict, compress
construcción *f* construction; building, structure; **construcción de buques** shipbuilding
construc•tor -tora *adj* construction || *mf* builder, constructor; **constructor de buques** shipbuilder
construir §20 *tr* to build, construct
consuegro *m* fellow father-in-law (*with respect to the father of one's son-in-law or daughter-in-law*), father-in-law of one's child
consuelda *f* comfrey; **consuelda real** field larkspur; **consuelda sarracena** goldenrod
consuelo *m* consolation; joy, delight; **sin consuelo** inconsolably; to excess
consueta *m* (theat) prompter
consuetudina•rio -ria *adj* customary, usual
cónsul *m* consul
consulado *m* consulate, consulship; (*casa u oficina*) consulate
consular *adj* consular
consulta *f* consultation; opinion; reference
consultación *f* consultation
consultar *tr* to consult; take up, discuss; advise || *intr* to consult, confer
consulti•vo -va *adj* advisory
consul•tor -tora *mf* consultant
consultorio *m* dispensary
consuma•do -da *adj* consummate || *m* consommé
consumar *tr* to consummate; fulfill, carry out
consumerismo *m* consumerism
consumición *f* consumption; drink (*in bar or restaurant*)
consumi•do -da *adj* thin, weak, emaciated; fretful
consumi•dor -dora *mf* consumer; customer (*in bar or restaurant*)
consumir *tr* to consume; exhaust; harass, wear down || *ref* to consume, waste away; long, yearn
consumo *m* consumption; drink (*in bar or restaurant*); customers; **consumos** octroi (*a tax*)
consunción *f* consumption; (pathol) consumption
consuno *adv* — **de consuno** together, in accord
consunti•vo -va *adj* consumptive; (*crédito*) consumer
contabilidad *f* accounting, bookkeeping
contabilista *mf* accountant, bookkeeper
contabilizadora *f* computer
contabilizar §60 *tr* to enter in the ledger
contable *adj* countable || *mf* accountant, bookkeeper
contactar *intr* to contact, be in contact
contacto *m* contact; **ponerse en contacto con** to get in touch with
conta•do -da *adj* scarce, rare; **al contado** cash, for cash; **contados** a few; **de contado** right away; **por de contado** of course
contador *m* counter; accountant; (*que mide el agua, gas, electricidad*) meter; (law) receiver; **contador de abonado** house meter; **contador de Geiger** Geiger counter; **contador kilométrico** speedometer; **contador público titulado** certified public accountant
contaduría *f* accountancy; accountant's office; box office for advanced sales
contagiar *tr* to infect; corrupt
contagio *m* contagion
contagio•so -sa *adj* contagious
contaminación *f* contamination; **contaminación ambiental** environmental pollution
contaminante *m* pollutant
contaminar *tr* to contaminate; (*un texto*) corrupt; (*la ley de Dios*) break
contante *adj* (*dinero*) ready
contar §61 *tr* to count; regard, consider; tell, relate; **contar . . . años** to be . . . years old; **dejarse contar diez** (box) to take the count; **tiene sus horas contadas** his days are num-

bered || *intr* to count; **a contar desde** beginning with; **contar con** to count on, rely on; reckon with; expect to
contemplación *f* contemplation; leniency, condescension
contemplar *tr* to contemplate; be lenient to || *intr* to contemplate
contemporáne•o -a *adj* contemporaneous, contemporary || *mf* contemporary
contemporizar §60 *intr* to temporize
contención *f* containment; contention, strife; (law) suit, litigation
contencio•so -sa *adj* contentious
contender §51 *intr* to contend
contendiente *mf* contender, contestant
contenedor *m* container
contener §71 *tr* to contain || *ref* to contain oneself
conteni•do -da *adj* moderate, restrained || *m* content, contents
contenta *f* gift or treat; indorsement; (mil) certificate of good conduct; (law) release
contentadi•zo -za *adj* easy to please
contentamiento *m* contentment
contentar *tr* to content; reconcile; (com) to indorse
conten•to -ta *adj* content, contented, glad || *m* content, contentment; **a contento** to one's satisfaction; **no caber de contento** (coll) to be beside oneself with joy || *f* see **contenta**
conteo *m* calculation, estimate, count
contera *f* tip, metal tip
contesta *f* answer; (Mex) chat
contestación *f* answer; argument, debate; **mala contestación** back talk
contestador automático *m* answering machine
contestar *tr* to answer || *intr* to answer; agree
contesto *m* (Mex) reply
contexto *m* interweaving; context
conticinio *m* dead of night
contienda *f* contest, dispute, fight
contigo *pron* with thee, with you
conti•guo -gua *adj* contiguous, adjoining
continencia *f* continence
continental *adj* continental
continente *adj* continent || *m* (*cosa que contiene en sí a otra*) container; (*aire del semblante, compostura del cuerpo*) mien, bearing; (*gran extensión de tierra rodeada por los océanos*) continent
contingencia *f* contingency
contingente *adj* contingent || *m* contingent; share, quota
continuar §21 *tr & intr* to continue; **continuará** to be continued
continuidad *f* continuity
conti•nuo -nua *adj* continuous, continual; (mach) endless || **continuo** *adv* continuously
contonear *ref* to strut, swagger
contoneo *m* strut, swagger
contorcer §74 *ref* to writhe
contorno *m* contour, outline; **contornos** environs, neighborhood
contorsión *f* contortion
contra *prep* against; toward, facing; **contra reembolso** collect on delivery || *m* (*concepto opuesto*) con || *f* trouble, inconvenience; (*al comprador*) (Cuba) gift, extra; (Chile) antidote; **llevar la contra a** to disagree with
contraalmirante *m* rear admiral
contraatacar §73 *tr & intr* to counterattack
contraataque *m* counterattack
contrabajo *m* contrabass, double bass
contrabajón *m* double bassoon
contrabalancear *tr* to counterbalance
contrabalanza *f* counterbalance
contrabandear *intr* to smuggle
contrabandista *adj* smuggling; contraband || *mf* smuggler, contrabandist
contrabando *m* smuggling, contraband; **meter de contrabando** to smuggle, smuggle in
contrabarrera *f* second row of seats (*in bull ring*)
contracalle *f* parallel side street
contracarril *m* (rr) guardrail
contracción *f* contraction; (*reducción del ritmo normal de los negocios*) recession; (*al estudio*) (Chile, Peru) concentration
contracepti•vo -va *adj & m* contraceptive
contrachapado *m* plywood
contracorriente *f* countercurrent, crosscurrent; (*entre aguas*) undertow
contracultura *f* counterculture
contradecir §24 (*impv sg* **-dice**) *tr* to contradict
contradicción *f* contradiction
contradic•tor -tora *adj* contradictory || *mf* contradicter
contradicto•rio -ria *adj* contradictory
contraer §75 *tr* to contract; (*deudas*) incur; (*el discurso o idea*) condense || *ref* to contract; shrink; (Chile, Peru) to concentrate, apply oneself
contraescalón *m* riser (*of stairway*)
contraespía *mf* counterspy
contraespionaje *m* counterespionage
contrafallar *tr & intr* to overtrump
contrafallo *m* overtrump
contrafigura *f* counterpart
contrafuero *m* infringement, violation
contrafuerte *m* abutment, buttress
contragolpe *m* counterstroke; kickback; (box) counter
contrahace•dor -dora *adj* counterfeiting; fake || *mf* counterfeiter; fake; impersonator
contrahacer §39 *tr* to counterfeit, copy, imitate; fake; impersonate; (*un libro*) pirate || *ref* to pretend to be
contra•haz *f* (*pl* **-haces**) wrong side
contrahe•cho -cha *adj* counterfeit, fake; deformed
contrahechura *f* counterfeit, fake
contrahuella *f* riser (*of stairway*)
contralor *m* comptroller
contralto *mf* contralto (*person*) || *m* contralto (*voice*)

contraluz *f* view against the light; **a contraluz** against the light
contramaestre *m* foreman; (naut) boatswain; **segundo contramaestre** boatswain's mate
contramandar *tr* to countermand
contramandato *m* countermand
contramano *adv* — **a contramano** in the wrong direction, the wrong way
contramarcha *f* countermarch; reverse
contramarchar *intr* to countermarch; to go in reverse
contraofensiva *f* counteroffensive
contraorden *f* cancellation
contraparte *f* counterpart
contrapasar *intr* to go over to the other side
contrapelo *adv* — **a contrapelo** against the hair, against the grain; the wrong way; **a contrapelo de** against, counter to
contrapesar *tr* to offset, counterbalance
contrapeso *m* counterweight; counterbalance; (*para completar el peso de carne, etc.*) makeweight
contraponer §54 *tr* to set opposite; oppose; compare
contraportada *f* (*del disco*) flip side
contraprestación *f* return favor
contraproducente *adj* self-defeating, unproductive
contraprueba *f* second proof
contrapuerta *f* storm door; vestibule door
contrapuntear *tr* to sing in counterpoint; taunt, be sarcastic to || *ref* to taunt each other
contrapunto *m* counterpoint
contrapunzón *m* nailset, punch
contrariar §77 *tr* to counteract, oppose; annoy, provoke
contrariedad *f* opposition; interference; annoyance, bother
contra•rio -ria *adj* opposite, contrary; harmful || *mf* enemy, opponent, rival || *m* opposite, contrary; **al contrario** on the contrary; **de lo contrario** otherwise
contrarreferencia *f* cross reference
Contrarreforma *f* Counter Reformation
contrarregistro *m* (*para comprobar si algún género ha pasado por la frontera*) double check; (*de una experiencia científica*) control
contrarréplica *f* (law) rejoinder
contrarrestar *tr* to resist, counteract; (*la pelota*) return
contrarrevolución *f* counterrevolution
contrasentido *m* misinterpretation; mistranslation; nonsense
contraseña *f* countersign; baggage check; (compu) password; **contraseña de salida** (mov, theat) check
contrastar *tr* to resist; (*las pesas y medidas*) check || *intr* to resist; contrast
contraste *m* resistance; contrast; assayer; assayer's office; (naut) sudden shift in the wind
contratar *tr* to contract for; hire, engage
contratiempo *m* misfortune, disappointment, setback
contratista *mf* contractor
contrato *m* contract; **contrato de alquiler** rental agreement, lease
contratreta *f* counterplot
contratuerca *f* lock nut, jam nut
contravalidación *f* (*documento*) validation
contravalidar *tr* to validate; confirm
contraveneno *m* counterpoison, antidote
contravenir §79 *intr* to act contrary; **contravenir a** to contravene, act counter to
contraventana *f* window shutter
contravidriera *f* storm sash
contrayente *mf* contracting party (*to a marriage*)
contribución *f* contribution; tax; **contribución de sangre** military service; **contribución industrial** excise tax; **contribución territorial** land tax
contribui•dor -dora *mf* contributor; taxpayer
contribuir §20 *tr & intr* to contribute
contribuyente *mf* contributor; taxpayer
contrición *f* contrition
contrincante *m* competitor, rival; fellow candidate
contristar *tr* to sadden
contri•to -ta *adj* contrite
control *m* control, check; checkpoint; **control antidoping** drug test; **control de la natalidad** or **de los nacimientos** birth control; **control remoto** remote control
controlador *m* controller; **controlador aéreo** air-traffic controller; (compu) driver
controlar *tr* to control, check
controversia *f* controversy
controvertible *adj* controversial, controvertible
controvertir §68 *tr* to controvert
contubernio *m* cohabitation; evil alliance
contumacia *f* contumacy; (law) contempt
contu•maz *adj* (*pl* **-maces**) contumacious; germ-bearing; (law) guilty of contempt of court
contumelia *f* contumely
contundente *adj* bruising; impressive, convincing
contundir *tr* to bruise
conturbar *tr* to trouble, worry, upset
contusión *f* contusion
contusionar *tr* (Chile) to bruise
convalecencia *f* convalescence
convalecer §22 *intr* to convalesce, recover
convaleciente *adj & mf* convalescent
convalidar *tr* to confirm
conveci•no -na *adj* neighboring || *mf* neighbor
convencer §78 *tr* to convince
convencimiento *m* conviction
convención *f* (*acuerdo; conformidad; asamblea*) convention; political convention
convencional *adj* conventional
convenible *adj* docile, compliant; (*precio*) fair, reasonable
conveniencia *f* (*comodidad*) convenience; (*acuerdo, convenio*) agreement; fitness, suitability; (*formas sociales*) propriety; domestic

employment; **conveniencias** income, property

conveniencie•ro -ra *adj* comfort-loving

conveniente *adj* (*cómodo*) convenient; fit, suitable; advantageous; proper

convenio *m* pact, covenant, treaty; **convenio comercial** trade agreement

convenir §79 *intr* to agree; (*concurrir, juntarse*) convene; be suitable, be becoming; be important, be necessary; **conviene a saber** to wit, namely || *ref* to agree, come to an agreement

conventillo *m* (SAm) tenement house

convento *m* convent, monastery; **convento de religiosas** convent

converger §17 or **convergir §27** *intr* to converge; concur

conversa *f* chat, conversation

conversación *f* conversation

conversacional *adj* conversational

conversar *intr* to converse; live, dwell

conversión *f* conversion

conver•so -sa *adj* converted || *mf* convert || *m* lay brother || *f* see **conversa**

conversor *m* converter

convertible *adj* convertible || *m* (aut) convertible

convertidor *m* (electron) converter

convertir §68 *tr* to convert; turn || *ref* to convert; be converted; **convertirse en** to turn into, become

conve•xo -xa *adj* convex

convic•to -ta *adj* convicted, found guilty

convida•do -da *mf* guest, wedding guest || *f* treat

convidar *tr* to invite; treat; move, incite; **convidarle a uno con alguna cosa** to treat someone to something || *ref* to offer one's services

convincente *adj* convincing

convite *m* invitation; treat, banquet, party; **convite a escote** Dutch treat

conviviente *mf* live-in partner || *f* common-law wife

convivir *intr* to live together

convocar §73 *tr* to convoke, call together; (*p.ej., una huelga*) call; acclaim

convoy *m* convoy; escort; cruet stand; (rr) train

convoyar *tr* to convoy

convulsionar *tr* to convulse

conyugal *adj* conjugal

cónyuge *mf* spouse, consort || **cónyuges** *mpl* couple, husband and wife

co•ñac *m* (*pl* **-ñacs** or **-ñaques**) cognac

cooperacion *f* cooperation

cooperar *intr* to cooperate

cooperati•vo -va *adj* cooperative

cooptar *tr* to coopt

coordena•do -da *adj* coordinate || *f* (math) coordinate

coordinante *adj* (gram) coordinating

coordinar *tr & intr* to coordinate

copa *f* goblet, wineglass; (*del sombrero*) crown; brazier; vase; drink; sundae; (*del dolor*) (fig) cup; (cards) "copa"; (sport) cup; **copa de helado, copa helado** ice cream sundae; **copas** card suit with figures representing goblets and often considered to be equivalent to the English suit called hearts

copar *tr* (*la puesta equivalente a todo el dinero de la banca*) to cover; (*todos los puestos en una elección*) sweep; (mil) to cut off and capture

copartícipe *mf* copartner, joint partner

copear *intr* to sell wine or liquor by the glass; (coll) to tipple

copero *m* cabinet for wineglasses

copete *m* (*cabello levantado sobre la frente*) pompadour; (*de plumas; de una montaña*) crest; (*de un caballo*) forelock; (*de lana, cabello, plumas, etc.*) tuft; (*de un mueble*) top, finial; (*de un sorbete*) topping; **de alto copete** aristocratic, important; **tener mucho copete** to be high-hat

copetu•do -da *adj* tufted; high, lofty; high-hat

copia *f* plenty, abundance; copy; **copia al carbón** carbon copy; **copia de respaldo, copia de seguridad** backup copy; **copia en limpio** fair copy; **copia fiel** true copy

copiador *m* or **copiadora** *f* copy(ing) machine; duplicator

copiante *mf* copier, copyist

copiar *tr* to copy, copy down; **copiar y pegar** (compu) copy-and-paste

copiloto *m* copilot; co-driver

co•pión -piona *mf* (coll) copycat

copio•so -sa *adj* copious, abundant

copista *mf* copier, copyist

copla *f* couplet; ballad, popular song; **coplas** verse, poetry; **coplas de ciego** doggerel

cople•ro -ra *mf* vendor of ballads; poetaster

coplista *mf* poetaster

copo *m* bundle of cotton, flax, hemp, etc. to be spun; **copo de algodón** cotton ball; **copo de nieve** snowflake; **copos de avena** oatmeal; **copos de maíz** cornflakes; **copos de jabón** soap flakes

copón *m* ciborium, pyx

copo•so -sa *adj* bushy; flaky, woolly

coprotagonista *mf* costar

copu•do -da *adj* bushy, thick

copular *ref* to copulate

coque *m* coke

coqueluche *f* whooping cough

coqueta *adj* coquettish || *f* coquette, flirt; (W-I) dressing table

coquetear *intr* to coquette, flirt; try to please everybody

coquetería *f* coquetry, flirting; affectation

coque•tón -tona *adj* coquettish, kittenish || *m* flirt, lady-killer

coracha *f* leather bag

coraje *m* anger; mettle, spirit

coraju•do -da *adj* ill-tempered; (Arg) brave, courageous

coral *adj* (mus) choral || *m* (mus) chorale (*zoófito; esqueleto calizo del zoófito; color*) coral; **corales** coral beads

corambre *f* hides, skins

Corán *m* Koran

coranvo•bis *m* (*pl* **-bis**) fat solemn look
coraza *f* armor; cuirass; (sport) guard
corazón *m* heart; (*centro de una cosa*) core; **corazones** (*palo de la baraja norteamericana*) hearts; **de corazón** heartily; **hacer de tripas corazón** to pluck up courage
corazonada *f* impulsiveness; hunch, presentiment; entrails
corbata *f* necktie, cravat; scarf; **corbata de mariposa, corbata de lazo** bow tie; **corbata de nudo corredizo** four-in-hand tie
corbatín *m* bow tie
corbeta *f* corvette
Córcega *f* Corsica
corcel *m* steed, charger
corcha *f* cork bark; cork bucket (*for cooling wine*)
corchea *f* (mus) quaver, eighth note
corche•ro -ra *adj* cork || *f* cork bucket (*for cooling wine*)
corcheta *f* eye (*of hook and eye*)
corchete *m* snap; hook and eye; hook (*of hook and eye*); (*signo*) bracket; **corchete de presión** snap fastener
corcho *m* cork; cork, cork stopper; cork wine cooler; cork box; cork mat; **corcho bornizo, corcho virgen** virgin cork
corcova *f* nump, nunch
corcova•do -da *adj* humpbacked, hunchbacked || *mf* humpback, hunchback
corcovar *tr* to bend
corcovear *intr* to buck; grumble; (Mex) to be afraid
cordada *f* (mountaineering) party of two or three men roped together
cordaje *m* cordage; (naut) rigging
cordal *adj* wisdom (*tooth*) || *m* (mus) tail-piece
cordel *m* cord, string; (distance of) five steps; cattle run; **a cordel** in a straight line
cordelejo *m* string; **dar cordelejo a** to make fun of; (Mex) to keep putting off
cordera *f* ewe lamb; (*mujer dócil y humilde*) (fig) lamb
cordería *f* cordage
corderillo *m* lambskin
corderi•no -na *adj* lamb || *f* lambskin
cordero *m* lamb; lambskin; (*hombre dócil y humilde*) (fig) lamb
corderuna *f* lambskin
cordial *adj* cordial; (*dedo*) middle || *m* cordial
cordialidad *f* cordiality
cordillera *f* chain of mountains
cordobana *f* — **andar a la cordobana** to go naked
cordón *m* lace; (*de cuerda o alambre*) strand; cordon; milled edge of coin; (*de monje*) rope belt; **cordón de apertura** rip cord; **cordón umbilical** umbilical cord; **cordón verde** (ecol) green belt
cordoncillo *m* rib, ridge; braid; (*de monedas*) milling
cordura *f* prudence, wisdom
Corea *f* Korea; **la Corea del Norte** North Korea; **la Corea del Sur** South Korea
corea•no -na *adj & mf* Korean
corear *tr* to compose for a chorus; accompany with a chorus; join in singing; agree obsequiously with
coreografía *f* choreography
coriáce•o -a *adj* leathery
corista *m* choir priest; (theat) chorus man || *f* chorus girl, chorine
cori•to -ta *adj* naked; bashful, timid
cormorán *m* cormorant
cor•nac *m* (*pl* **-nacs**) or **cornaca** *m* mahout
cornada *f* hook with horns; goring; (*en la esgrima*) upward thrust
cornadura *f* or **cornamenta** *f* (*del toro, la vaca, etc.*) horns; (*del ciervo*) antlers
cornamusa *f* bagpipe
córnea *f* cornea
cornear *tr* to butt; to gore
corneja *f* daw, crow
cornejo *m* dogwood
córne•o -a *adj* horn, horny || *f* see **córnea**
corneta *f* bugle; swineherd's horn; **corneta acústica** ear trumpet; **corneta de llaves** cornet, cornet-à-pistons; **corneta de monte** hunting-horn
cornisa *f* cornice
cornisamento *m* (archit) entablature
corno *m* horn; dogwood; **corno inglés** (mus) English horn
Cornualles Cornwall
cornucopia *f* cornucopia; sconce with mirror
cornu•do -da *adj* horned, antlered; cuckold || *m* cuckold
coro *m* chorus; choir; choir loft; glee club; **a coros** alternately; **de coro** by heart; **hacer coro a** to echo
corolario *m* corollary
corona *f* (*cerco de metal; moneda; dignidad real; parte visible de una muela*) crown; (*cerco de flores*) garland, wreath; (*aureola*) halo; (*de eclesiástico*) tonsure; (*la que corresponde a un título nobiliario*) coronet; **corona nupcial** bridal wreath
coronación *f* coronation
coronamento *m* or **coronamiento** *m* coronation; completion, termination; (archit) coping; (naut) taffrail
coronar *tr* to crown; complete, finish; top, surmount; (checkers) to crown
coronel *m* colonel
coronelía *f* colonelcy
coronilla *f* (*de la cabeza*) crown; **andar or bailar de coronilla** to be hard at it; **estar hasta la coronilla** to be fed up
corotos *mpl* belongings; utensils
corpiño *m* bodice, waist; (Arg) brassiere
corporación *f* corporation
corporal *adj* corporal, bodily
corpu•do -da *adj* corpulent
corpulen•to -ta *adj* corpulent
corpúsculo *m* corpuscle; particle

corral *m* corral, stockyard; barnyard; fishpond; open-air theater; **corral de madera** lumberyard; **corral de vacas** pigpen; **hacer corrales** to play hooky

correa *f* strap, thong; shoulder strap; (aer, mach) belt; **correa de(l) ventilador** fan belt; **correa de seguridad** (aer, aut) safety belt; **correa elástica** bungee

corrección *f* (*acción de corregir; reprensión*) correction; (*calidad de correcto*) correctness

correcti•vo -va *adj & m* corrective

correc•to -ta *adj* correct

correc•tor -tora *mf* corrector; **corrector de estilo** copy editor; **corrector de pruebas, corrector de manuscrito** proofreader

corredera *f* track, slide; slide valve; (*del trombón*) slide; (naut) log; (naut) log line; (*puerta*) **de corredera** sliding

corredi•zo -za *adj* slide; sliding; (*nudo*) slip

corre•dor -dora *adj* running ‖ *mf* runner ‖ *m* corridor; porch, gallery; (*el que interviene en compras y ventas de efectos comerciales, etc.*) broker; (mil) scout; **corredor de apuestas** bookmaker; **corredor de bolsa** stockbroker; **corredor de la muerte** death row (*in prison*); **corredor de propiedades** real-estate agent, realtor

corregidor *m* Spanish magistrate; chief magistrate of Spanish town

corregir §57 *tr* to correct; temper, moderate ‖ *intr* (W-I) to have a bowel movement ‖ *ref* to mend one's ways

correlación *f* correlation

correlacionar *tr & intr* to correlate

correlati•vo -va *adj & m* correlative

corre•lón -lona *adj* (SAm) fast, swift; (Col, Mex) cowardly

correncia *f* bashfulness; looseness of the bowels

correntí•o -a *adj* running; free, easy ‖ *f* looseness of the bowels

corren•tón -tona *adj* jolly, full of fun

corrento•so -sa *adj* swift, rapid

correo *m* mail; post office; mail train; postman; courier; **correo aéreo** air mail; **correo electrónico** E-mail; **correo urgente** special delivery; **echar al correo** to mail, to post

correo•so -sa *adj* leathery, tough

correr *tr* (*un caballo*) to run, race; (*un riesgo*) run; travel over; overrun; (*una cortina*) draw; (*un toro*) fight; chase, pursue; auction; confuse; throw out; (compu) run; **correrla** to run around all night ‖ *intr* to run; race; pass, elapse; circulate, be common talk; be current; **a todo correr** at full speed; **correr a** to sell for; **correr a cargo de** or **por cuenta de** to be the business of; **correr con** to be on good terms with; be in charge of; (*mes*) **que corre** current ‖ *ref* (*a derecha o a izquierda*) to turn; be confused; be embarrassed, be ashamed; slide, glide; (*una bujía, un color*) run; go too far

correría *f* short trip, excursion; foray, raid

correspondencia *f* correspondence; contact, communication; agreement, harmony; (*en el metro*) connection; (*en una carretera*) interchange

corresponder *intr* to correspond; (*dos habitaciones*) communicate; **corresponder a** (*un beneficio, el afecto de una persona*) to return, reciprocate; concern; be up to ‖ *ref* (*comunicarse por escrito*) to correspond; (*dos cosas*) correspond with each other; be in agreement; be attached to each other

correspondiente *adj* corresponding; correspondent; respective ‖ *mf* correspondent

corresponsal *mf* correspondent

corretaje *m* brokerage

corretear *tr* to harass, pursue; (CAm) to drive away; (Chile) to speed up ‖ *intr* to race around

correveidi•le *mf* (*pl* **-le**) gossip; go-between

corrida *f* run; bullfight; (*carrera de entrenamiento de un caballo*) trial run; **corrida de banco** run on the bank; **corrida de toros** bullfight

corri•do -da *adj* (*peso, medida*) in excess; (*letra*) cursive; continued, unbroken; abashed, ashamed; worldly-wise, sophisticated ‖ *m* overhang; street ballad ‖ *f* see **corrida**

corriente *adj* (*agua*) running; (*actual*) current; common, ordinary; regular; well-known; fluent ‖ *adv* all right, O.K. ‖ *m* current month; **al corriente** on time; informed, aware, posted ‖ *f* current, stream; (elec) current; **corriente alterna** alternating current; **corriente continua** direct current; **corriente de aire** draft; **Corriente del Golfo** Gulf Stream; **corriente principal** *or* **dominante** mainstream; **ir contra la corriente** to go against the tide

corrillo *m* circle, clique

corrimiento *m* running; sliding; watery discharge; embarrassment, shyness; landslide; rheumatism

corro *m* (*cerco de gente; espacio circular*) ring; (*juego de niñas*) ring-around-a-rosy; **corro de brujas** fairy ring; **hacer corro** to make room

corroborar *tr* to corroborate; strengthen

corroer §62 *tr & ref* to corrode

corromper *tr* to corrupt; spoil; rot; seduce; bribe; annoy ‖ *intr* to smell bad ‖ *ref* to become corrupted; spoil; rot

corrosión *f* corrosion

corrosi•vo -va *adj & m* corrosive

corrugar §44 *tr* to shrink; wrinkle

corrupción *f* corruption; seduction; bribery; stench

corruptela *f* corruption

corruptible *adj* corruptible; (*p.ej., frutas*) perishable

corrusco *m* crust of bread

corsa *f* (naut) day's run

corsario *m* corsair

corsé *m* corset

cor•so -sa *adj & mf* Corsican ‖ *m* (naut) privateering; (SAm) drive, promenade ‖ *f* see **corsa**

corta *f* clearing, cutting, felling
cortaalam•bres *m* (*pl* **-bres**) wire cutter
cortabol•sas *m* (*pl* **-sas**) pickpocket
cortabordes *m* (hort) edger
cortacésped *m* lawn mower
cortaciga•rros *m* (*pl* **-rros**) cigar cutter
cortacircui•tos *m* (*pl* **-tos**) (elec) fuse; circuit breaker
cortacorriente *m* (elec) change-over switch
cortada *f* cut, cutting
cortadillo *m* drinking cup
corta•do -da *adj* (*estilo*) choppy; (SAm) hard up || *f* see **cortada**
corta•dor -dora *adj* cutting || *mf* cutter || *m* butcher || *f* (culin) shredder; (mach) cutter; **cortadora de césped** lawnmower
cortafrío *m* cold chisel
cortafuego *s* fire wall, firebreak
cortahie•los *m* (*pl* **-los**) icebreaker
cortalápi•ces *m* (*pl* **-ces**) pencil sharpener
cortante *adj* cutting, sharp || *m* butcher; butcher knife
cortapape•les *m* (*pl* **-les**) paper cutter
cortapi•cos *m* (*pl* **-cos**) (ent) earwig; **cortapicos y callares** little children should be seen and not heard
cortaplu•mas *m* (*pl* **-mas**) penknife
cortapu•ros *m* (*pl* **-ros**) cigar cutter
cortar *tr* to cut; trim; chop; cut off; cut out, omit; cut short; cut up; carve; (*la corriente; la ignición*) cut off || *intr* to cut; (*el viento, el frío*) be cutting; **cortar de vestir** to cut cloth; gossip || *ref* to become speechless; (*la leche*) curdle, turn sour; (*la piel*) chap, crack
cortarrenglón *m* marginal stop
cortaú•ñas *m* (*pl* **-ñas**) nail clipper
cortavi•drios *m* (*pl* **-drios**) glass cutter
cortaviento *m* windshield
corte *m* cut; cutting; (*filo de un arma, cuchillo, etc.; borde de un libro*) edge; cross section; (*de un vestido*) cut, fit; piece of material; harvest; **corte de energía, corte de luz** (elec) blackout; **corte de pelo** haircut; **corte de pelo a cepillo** crew cut; **corte de pelo cuadrado** flattop; **corte de traje** suiting || *f* (*de un rey*) court; (*corral*) yard; stable, fold; (*tribunal de justicia*) court; **Cortes** Parliament; **darse cortes** (SAm) to put on airs; **hacer la corte a** to pay court to; **la Corte** the Capital (*Madrid*)
cortedad *f* shortness; smallness; lack; bashfulness
cortejar *tr* to escort, attend, court; court, woo
cortejo *m* courting; courtship; (*séquito*) cortege; gift, treat; (coll) beau
cortera *f* (Chile) streetwalker
cortero *m* (Chile) day laborer
cortés *adj* courteous, polite, courtly
cortesana *f* courtesan
cortesana•zo -za *adj* overpolite, obsequious
cortesanía *f* courtliness
cortesa•no -na *adj* courtly, courteous || *m* courtier || *f* see **cortesana**
cortesía *f* courtesy, politeness, courtliness; gift, favor; (*inclinación de la cabeza o el cuerpo en señal de respeto*) curtsy; (*de una carta*) conclusion; **hacer una cortesía** to make a bow; curtsy
corteza *f* bark; peel, rind, skin; (*de pan, de la tierra*) crust; coarseness; (*envoltura exterior de un órgano*) cortex; (*de un átomo*) shell; **corteza cerebral** cortex
cortijo *m* farm, farmhouse
cortil *m* barnyard
cortina *f* curtain; **correr la cortina** to pull the curtain aside; **cortina de ducha** shower curtain; **cortina de hierro** Iron Curtain; **cortina de humo** smoke screen
cortinal *m* fenced-in field
cortinilla *f* shade, window shade
cortisona *f* cortisone
cor•to -ta *adj* short; dull; bashful, shy; speechless; **a la corta o a la larga** sooner or later; **desde muy corta edad** from earliest childhood || *f* see **corta**
cortocircuitar *tr & ref* (elec) to short-circuit
cortocircuito *m* (elec) short circuit
cortometraje *m* (mov) short
corva *f* ham, back of knee; (vet) curb
corvejón *m* gambrel, hock; (orn) cormorant
cor•vo -va *adj* arched, bent, curved || *m* hook || *f* see **corva**
cor•zo -za *mf* roe deer
cosa *f* thing; **cosa de** a matter of; **cosa de cajón** a matter of course; **cosa de mieles** something fine; **cosa de nunca acabar** endless bore; **cosa de oír** something worth hearing; **cosa de risa** something to laugh at; **cosa de ver** something worth seeing; **cosa nunca vista** something unheard-of; **cosa que** so that; **cosa rara** strange to say; **como si tal cosa** as if nothing had happened; **en cosa de** in a matter of; **no . . . gran cosa** not much; **no haber tal cosa** to be not so; **otra cosa** something else; **¿qué cosa?** what's new?
cosa•co -ca *adj & mf* Cossack || *m* Cossack (*horseman*)
coscolina *f* (Mex) loose woman
cos•cón -cona *adj* sly, crafty
cosecha *f* crop, harvest; harvest time; **cosecha de vino** vintage; **de su cosecha** (coll) out of one's own head
cosechadora *f* (mech) cotton picker
cosechar *tr* to harvest, reap || *intr* to harvest
coseche•ro -ra *mf* harvester, reaper; vintner
cose-pape•les *m* (*pl* **-les**) stapler
coser *tr* to sew; join, unite closely; **coser a preguntas** to riddle with questions; **coser a puñaladas** to cut to pieces || *intr* to sew; **ser coser y cantar** to be a cinch || *ref* — **coserse con** or **contra** to be closely attached to
cosméti•co -ca *adj & m* cosmetic
cósmi•co -ca *adj* cosmic
cosmonauta *mf* cosmonaut
cosmonave *f* spacecraft
cosmonavegación *f* space travel
cosmopolita *adj & mf* cosmopolitan

cosmos *m* cosmos; (bot) cosmos
coso *m* enclosure; arena; **coso taurino** bullring
cosquillas *fpl* tickling, ticklishness; **buscarle a uno las cosquillas** to try to irritate a person; **no sufrir cosquillas** or **tener malas cosquillas** to be touchy
cosquillear *tr* to tickle; tease, taunt; stir up the curiosity of; scare || *intr* to tickle || *ref* to be curious; enjoy oneself
cosquilleo *m* tickling, tickling sensation
cosquillo•so -sa *adj* ticklish; (*que se ofende fácilmente*) touchy
costa *f* coast, shore; cost, price; **a toda costa** at all costs; **Costa Brava** Mediterranean coast in province of Gerona, Spain; **Costa Firme** Spanish Main; **costa marítima** seacoast; **costas** (law) costs
costado *m* side; (*del ejército*) flank; (Mex) station platform; **costados** ancestors, stock
costal *m* bag, sack; **costal de los pecados** human body (*full of sin*); **estar hecho un costal de huesos** to be nothing but skin and bones
costanera *f* slope; **costaneras** rafters
costane•ro -ra *adj* sloping; coastal || *f* see **costanera**
costanilla *f* short steep street
costar §61 *intr* to cost; **cueste lo que cueste** cost what it may
costarricense or **costarrique•ño -ña** *adj & mf* Costa Rican
coste *m* cost; **a coste y costas** at cost; **de bajo costo** (compu) low-cost
costear *tr* to pay for, defray the cost of; sail along the coast of || *intr* to sail along the coast || *ref* to pay; pay one's way
coste•ño -ña *adj* sloping; coastal
coste•ro -ra *adj* coastal
costilla *f* rib; wealth; **costillas** back, shoulders
costillu•do -da *adj* heavy-set, broadshouldered
costo *m* cost; **costo de la vida** cost of living; **costo, seguro y flete** cost, insurance, and freight; **de bajo costo** low-cost
costo•so -sa *adj* costly, expensive; grievous
costra *f* scab, scale; (*moco de una vela*) snuff
costro•so -sa *adj* scabby, scaly
costumbre *f* custom, habit; **de costumbre** usual; usually; **tener por costumbre** to be in the habit of
costumbrista *mf* critic of manners and customs
costura *f* sewing, needlework; dressmaking; (*unión de dos piezas cosidas*) seam; **alta costura** fashion designing, haute couture
costurar or **costurear** *tr* (CAm, Mex) to sew
costurera *f* seamstress, dressmaker
costurero *m* sewing table
cota *f* coat of arms; coat of mail
cotarrera *f* gossipy woman
cotarro *m* night shelter (*for beggars and tramps*); **alborotar el cotarro** to raise a row
cotejar *tr* to compare, collate
cotejo *m* comparison, collation
cotidia•no -na *adj* daily, everyday
cotilla *f* gossip, tattletale
cotín *m* (sport) backstroke
cotización *f* quotation; dues
cotizante *adj* dues-paying
cotizar §60 *tr* to quote; prorate || *intr* to collect dues; pay dues
coto *m* term, limit, boundary; game preserve; hamlet; price-fixing agreement; (pathol) goiter; **coto de caza** game preserve; **poner coto a** to put a stop to
cotón *m* printed cotton
cotona *f* work shirt
cotonía *f* dimity
cotorra *f* parrot; parakeet; magpie; chatterbox; (Mex) night shelter
cotorrear *intr* to gossip, gabble
cotufa *f* Jerusalem artichoke; delicacy, tidbit; **hacer cotufas** (Bol) to be fastidious; **pedir cotufas en el golfo** to ask for the moon
coturno *m* buskin
covacha *f* cave; cubbyhole; shanty; doghouse
covachuelista *m* clerk, government clerk
coxcojita *f* hopscotch; **a coxcojita** hippety-hop
coy *m* (naut) hammock
coyunda *f* strap for yoking oxen; sandal string; marriage; tyranny
coyuntura *f* joint, articulation; (*sazón, oportunidad*) juncture
coz *f* (*pl* **coces**) kick; big end; ebb; (coll) insult; **dar coces contra el aguijón** to kick against the pricks
c.p.b., C.P.B. *abbr* **cuyos pies beso**
cps. *abbr* **compañeros**
crabrón *m* hornet
crac *m* (*ruido seco*) crack; crash; **hacer crac** to crash, fail
crack *m* (*droga*) crack; (coll) star, champion
cráneo *m* cranium, skull
crápula *f* drunkenness, debauchery; riffraff
crapulo•so -sa *adj* drunken; vicious, evil
crascitar *intr* to crow, croak
cra•so -sa *adj* fat, greasy, thick; (*ignorancia*) crass, gross
cráter *m* crater
creación *f* creation
crea•dor -dora *adj* creative || *mf* creator
crear *tr* to create; appoint; found || *ref* to make for oneself, build up; trump up
creati•vo -va *adj* creative
crecede•ro -ra *adj* growth; large enough to allow for growth
crecepelo *m* hair restorer
crecer §22 *intr* to grow; increase; (*el río*) rise, swell; (*la luna*) wax || *ref* to grow; take on more authority; get bolder
creces *fpl* growth, increase; excess, extra; **con creces** amply, in abundance
crecida *f* freshet, flood
creciente *adj* growing, increasing, burgeoning || *f* —**creciente de la luna** waxing of the moon, crescent; **creciente del mar** high tide, flood tide
crecimiento *m* growth, increase; **crecimiento cero** zero growth

credenciales *fpl* credentials
crédito *m* credit; **crédito de vivienda, crédito hipotecario** mortgage; **crédito en cuenta corriente** overdraft protection
credo *m* creed; credo; **con el credo en la boca** with one's heart in one's mouth; **en un credo** in a trice
crédu•lo -la *adj* credulous
creederas *fpl* — **tener buenas creederas** to be gullible
creencia *f* belief; (*crédito que se presta a un hecho*) credence; (*secta*) creed
creer §43 *tr & intr* to believe; **¡ya lo creo!** I should say so! ‖ *ref* to believe; believe oneself to be
creíble *adj* believable, credible
creí•do -da *adj* credulous; gullible
crema *f* cream; cold cream; shoe polish; (gram) diaeresis; **crema bronceadora** suntan lotion; **crema de afeitar** shaving cream; **crema dental** or **crema dentífrica** toothpaste; **crema desvanecedora** *or* **evanescente** vanishing cream
cremación *f* cremation
cremallera *f* rack; zipper
cremato•rio -ria *adj & m* crematory
crémor *m* cream of tartar
cremo•so -sa *adj* creamy
crencha *f* part (*in hair*); hair on each side of part
crepitar *intr* to crackle, sizzle
crepuscular *adj* twilight
crepúsculo *m* twilight
cresa *f* maggot
crespar *tr & ref* to curl
cres•po -pa *adj* curly; curled; angry, irritated; stylish, conceited; (*estilo*) turgid ‖ *m* curl
crespón *m* crape; **crespón fúnebre** crape; mourning band
cresta *f* crest; **cresta de eco** (electron) blip; **cresta de gallo** cockscomb; (bot) cockscomb
creta *f* chalk ‖ **Creta** *f* Crete
cretense *adj & mf* Cretan
cretona *f* cretonne
creyente *adj* believing ‖ *mf* believer
creyón *m* crayon
cría *f* brood, litter; breeding; raising, rearing; nursing; **al cría** at stud
criada *f* female servant, maid; **criada de casa, criada de servir** housemaid
criadero *m* nursery, tree nursery; fish hatchery; oyster bed
criadilla *f* testicle; potato
cria•do -da *adj* — **bien criado** well-bred; **mal criado** ill-bred ‖ *mf* servant ‖ *f* see **criada**
cria•dor -dora *mf* breeder ‖ *f* wet nurse
criamiento *m* care, upkeep
crianza *f* raising, rearing; nursing; (*urbanidad*) breeding, manners; **buena crianza** good breeding; **mala crianza** bad breeding
criar §77 *tr* to raise, rear, bring up; breed; grow; nurse, nourish; fatten; create; foster
criatura *f* (*toda cosa creada; persona que debe su cargo o situación a otra*) creature; little child, little creature
criba *f* screen, sieve
cribar *tr* to screen, sieve
cribo *m* screen, sieve
cric *m* (*pl* **crics**) jack (*for lifting objects*)
crimen *m* crime; **crimen de lesa majestad** lese majesty; **crímenes de oficinistas** white-collar crime
criminal *adj & mf* criminal
criminar *tr* to accuse, incriminate
criminología *f* criminology
crimino•so -sa *adj & mf* criminal
crines *fpl* mane
crío *m* (coll) baby, infant
crio•llo -lla *adj & mf* Creole
cripta *f* crypt
criptografía *f* cryptography
crisálida *f* chrysalis
crisantemo *m* chrysanthemum
cri•sis *f* (*pl* **-sis**) crisis; (*pánico económico*) depression, slump; mature judgment; **crisis del servicio doméstico** servant problem; **crisis de llanto** crying fit; **crisis de vivienda** housing shortage; **crisis energética** energy crisis; **crisis ministerial** cabinet crisis; **crisis nerviosa** fit of nerves
crisma *f* (coll) head, bean
crisol *m* crucible
crispar *tr* to cause to twitch ‖ *ref* to twitch
crispatura *f* twitch, twitching
crispir *tr* to grain, to marble
cristal *m* crystal; glass; pane of glass; mirror, looking glass; **cristal cilindrado** plate glass; **cristal de reloj** watch crystal; **cristal de roca** rock crystal; **cristal hilado** glass wool, spun glass; **cristal laminado** laminated glass, safety glass; **cristal tallado** cut glass
cristalera *f* China closet; sideboard; glass door
cristalería *f* glassworks, glass store; glassware; glass cabinet
cristali•no -na *adj* crystalline ‖ *m* lens, crystalline lens
cristalizar §60 *tr & ref* to crystallize
cristianar *tr* to baptize, christen
cristiandad *f* Christendom
cristianismo *m* Christianity
cristianizar §60 *tr* to Christianize
cristia•no -na *adj & mf* Christian ‖ *m* soul, person; Spanish; watered wine
Cristo *m* Christ; crucifix; **donde Cristo dió las tres voces** in the middle of nowhere
Cristóbal *m* Christopher
criterio *m* criterion
crítica *f* (*jucio sobre una obra literaria, etc.; censura de la conducta de alguno*) criticism; (*arte de juzgar una obra literaria, etc.*) critique; gossip
criticar §73 *tr & intr* to criticize
críti•co -ca *adj* critical; (*criticón*) critical (*fault-finding*) ‖ *mf* critic ‖ *f* see **crítica**
criti•cón -cona *adj* critical, faultfinding ‖ *mf* critic, faultfinder

critiquizar §60 *tr* to overcriticize
crizneja *f* braid of hair
croar *intr* to croak
croata *adj & mf* Croatian
crocante *m* almond brittle, peanut brittle
croché *m* crochet
crochet *m* (box) hook
crocitar *intr* to crow, croak
croco *m* crocus
croma•do -da *adj* chrome || *m* chromium plating
cromar *tr* to chrome
cromo *m* chromium
cromosoma *m* chromosome
crónica *f* chronicle; news chronicle, feature story
cróni•co -ca *adj* chronic; longstanding; (*vicio*) inveterate || *f* see **crónica**
cronista *mf* chronicler; reporter, feature writer; **cronista de radio** newscaster
cronología *f* chronology
cronometra•dor -dora *mf* (sport) timekeeper
cronometraje *m* (sport) clocking, timing
cronómetro *m* chronometer; stop watch
croqueta *f* croquette
cro•quis *m* (*pl* **-quis**) sketch
croscitar *intr* to crow, croak
crótalo *m* rattlesnake; castanet
cruce *m* crossing; crossroads, intersection; exchange (*e.g., of letters*); (*avería*) (elec) crossed wires, short circuit; **cruce a nivel** grade crossing; **cruce en trébol** cloverleaf intersection
crucero *m* crossroads; railroad crossing; (archit) transept; (aer, naut) cruise, cruising; (nav) cruiser; **crucero a nivel** grade crossing
crucial *adj* crucial
crucificar §73 *tr* to crucify
crucifijo *m* crucifix
crucifixión *f* crucifixion
crucigrama *m* crossword puzzle
cruda *f* (Mex) hangover
crudeza *f* crudeness, rawness; (*del agua*) hardness; harshness, roughness; blustering; **crudezas** undigested food
cru•do -da *adj* crude, raw; (*agua*) hard; harsh, rough; (*tiempo*) raw; (*lienzo*) unbleached; **estar crudo** (P-R) to be rusty; (Mex) to have a hangover || *f* see **cruda**
cruel *adj* cruel
crueldad *f* cruelty; **crueldad mental** mental cruelty
cruen•to -ta *adj* bloody
crujía *f* corridor, hall; hospital ward; block of houses; (naut) midship gangway; **crujía de piezas** suite of rooms; **sufrir una crujía** (coll) to have a hard time of it
crujido *m* creak; crackle; clatter; chatter; rustle
crujir *intr* to creak; crackle; clatter; chatter; rustle; crunch
crup *m* croup
crustáce•o -a *adj* crustaceous || *m* crustacean
cruz *f* (*pl* **cruces**) cross; (*de una moneda*) tails; (typ) dagger; **Cruz del Sur** Southern Cross; **Cruz Roja** Red Cross; **¡cruz y raya!** (coll) that's enough!; **de la cruz a la fecha** from beginning to end; **en cruz** crisscross **ponga una cruz** make an X
cruza *f* (SAm) intersection; crossbreeding
cruzada *f* (*expedición contra los infieles; propaganda contra un vicio*) crusade; crossroads, intersection
cruza•do -da *adj* crossed; (*de raza mixta*) cross; double-breasted || *m* (*el que toma parte en una cruzada*) crusader; (*caballero de una orden militar*) knight; twill || *f* see **cruzada**
cruzar §60 *tr* to cross; (*la tela*) twill; (*cartas*) exchange; crossbreed; (naut) to cruise, cruise over || *intr* to cross; cruise || *ref* to cross each other, cross one another's path; (*alistarse para una cruzada*) take the cross; **cruzarse con** (*otro automóvil*) to pass; **cruzarse de brazos** (*estar ocioso*) to cross one's arms
cs. *abbr* **céntimos, cuartos**
cte. *abbr* **corriente**
c/u *abbr* **cada uno**
cuad. *abbr* **cuadrado**
cuaderna *f* (naut) frame
cuaderno *m* notebook; folder; **cuaderno de bitácora** (naut) logbook; **cuaderno de espiral** spiral-bound notebook; **cuaderno de exámenes** (educ) blue book; **cuaderno de hojas cambiables** or **sueltas** loose-leaf notebook
cuadra *f* hall, large room; stable; dormitory, ward; croup, rump; block
cuadra•do -da *adj* square; square-shouldered; perfect || *m* square; (*regla*) ruler; (*en las medias*) clock; **cuadrado de las bases** baseball diamond; **de cuadrado** perfectly; (*que se mira frente a frente*) full-faced
cuadragési•mo -ma *adj & m* fortieth
cuadrangular *adj* quadrangular || *m* home run
cuadrángu•lo -la *adj* quadrangular || *m* quadrangle
cuadrante *m* quadrant; (*de reloj*) face, dial; **cuadrante solar** sundial
cuadrar *tr* to square; please; (*al toro*) (taur) to square off, line up || *ref* to square; stand at attention; take on a serious air
cuadrilla *f* group, party; crew, gang
cuadrillazo *m* (SAm) surprise attack
cuadrillo *m* (*saeta*) bolt (*arrow*)
cuadrimotor *m* four-motor plane
cua•dro -dra *adj* square || *m* square; (*lienzo, pintura*) painting, picture; (*marco de pintura, ventana, etc.*) frame; (*de jardín*) patch, flower bed; (*grupo de animales*) stud; staff, personnel; (baseball) cuadro; (mil) cadre; (sport) team; (theat) scene; (coll) sight, mess; **a cuadros** checked; **cuadro de costumbres** sketch of manners and customs; **cuadro de diálogo** (compu) dialog box; **cuadro de distribución** switchboard; **cuadro de mando** instrument panel; (aut) dashboard; **cuadro indicador** score board; **cuadro vivo** tableau; **en cuadro** square, e.g., **ocho pulgadas en cuadro** eight inches square; topsy-turvy; **quedarse en cua-**

dro to be all alone in the world; (mil) to be skeletonized || *f* see **cuadra**
cuadrúpe•do -da *adj & m* quadruped
cuádruple *adj & m* quadruple
cuadruplicar §73 *tr & ref* to quadruple
cuajada *f* curd
cuajado *m* mincemeat
cuajar *tr* to curd, curdle, thicken, jelly; please, suit || *intr* to take hold, catch on, jell, take shape; (Mex) to chatter, prattle || *ref* to curd, curdle, thicken, jelly; sleep sound; become crowded
cuajo *m* curd; (Mex) chatter, prattle; (*en la escuela*) (Mex) recess
cual *adj rel & pron rel* such as; **el cual** which; who; **lo cual** which; **por lo cual** for which reason || *adv* as || *prep* like
cuál *adj interr & pron interr* which, what; which one
cualidad *f* quality, characteristic, trait
cualquier *adj indef* (*pl* **cualesquier**) apocopated form of **cualquiera,** used only before masculine nouns and adjectives
cualquiera (*pl* **cualesquiera**) *pron indef* anyone; **cualquiera que** whichever; whoever || *adj indef* any || *adj rel* whichever || *m* (*persona poco importante*) nobody
cuan *adv* as
cuán *adv* how, how much
cuando *conj* when; although; in case; since; **aun cuando** even if, even though; **cuando más** at most; **cuando menos** at least; **cuando mucho** at most; **cuando quiera** whenever; **de cuando en cuando** from time to time || *prep* (coll) at the time of
cuándo *adv* when; **cuándo . . . cuándo** sometimes . . . sometimes; **¿de cuándo acá?** since when?; how come?
cuantía *f* quantity; importance; **delito de mayor cuantía** felony; **delito de menor cuantía** misdemeanor; **de mayor cuantía** first-rate; **de menor cuantía** second-rate, of little importance
cuantiar §77 *tr* to estimate, appraise
cuánti•co -ca *adj* quantum
cuantio•so -sa *adj* large, substantial
cuan•to -ta *adj rel & pron rel* as much as, whatever, all that which; **cuantos** as many as, all those who, everybody who; **unos cuantos** some few || **cuanto** *adv* as soon as; as long as; **cuanto antes** as soon as possible; **cuanto más . . . tanto más** the more . . . the more; **cuanto más que** all the more because; **en cuanto** as soon as; while; insofar as; **en cuanto a** as to, as for, regarding; **por cuanto** inasmuch as; **por cuanto . . . por tanto** inasmuch as . . . therefore || **cuan•to** *m* (*pl* **-ta**) quantum
cuán•to -ta *adj interr & pron interr* how much; **cuántos** how many || **cuánto** *adv* how, how much; how long; how long ago; **cada cuánto** how often
cuáque•ro -ra *adj & mf* Quaker
cuarenta *adj, pron & m* forty
cuarenta•vo -va *adj & m* fortieth
cuarentena *f* forty; quarantine; forty days, forty months, forty years; **poner en cuarentena** to quarantine; withhold one's credence in
cuaresma *f* Lent
cuaresmal *adj* Lenten
cuarta *f* fourth, fourth part; (*de la mano*) span; (CAm, W-I) horse whip
cuartago *m* nag, pony
cuartear *tr* to divide in four parts; divide; (*la aguja*) (naut) to box; (CAm, W-I) to whip || *ref* to crack, split; (taur) to step aside, dodge
cuartel *m* quarter; (*de una ciudad*) section, ward; (*terreno*) lot; flower bed; (mil) barracks; (*buen trato*) (mil) quarter; (*armazón de tablas para cerrar la escotilla*) (naut) hatch; (coll) house, home; **cuartel de bomberos** engine house, firehouse; **cuarteles** (mil) quarters; **cuartel general** (mil) headquarters
cuartelada *f* mutiny, military uprising
cuartelazo *m* (mil) coup, putsch; (mil) take-over
cuarte•rón -rona *mf* quadroon || *m* quarter; (*de puerta*) panel; (*de ventana*) shutter
cuarteto *m* quartet
cuartilla *f* sheet of paper
cuar•to -ta *adj* fourth; quarter || *m* fourth; quarter; room, bedroom; quarter-hour; **cuarto creciente** (*de la luna*) first quarter; **cuarto de aseo** powder room; **cuarto de baño** bathroom; **cuarto de dormir** bedroom; **cuarto de estar** living room; **cuarto de final** (sport) quarterfinal; **cuarto de huéspedes** guest room; **cuarto delantero** (*de la res*) forequarter; **cuarto de los niños** nursery; **cuarto de luna** quarter; **cuarto menguante** (*de la luna*) last quarter; **cuarto obscuro** (phot) darkroom; **cuartos** money, cash; **cuarto trasero** (*p.ej., de vaca*) rump || *f see* **cuarta**
cuarzo *m* quartz
cuasar *or* **cuásar** *m* quasar
cuate *adj* (Mex) twin; (Mex) like || *mf* (Mex) twin; (Mex) pal
cuatrilli•zo -za *mf* quadruplet
cuatrinca *f* foursome
cuatro *adj & pron* four; (Mex) deceit, swindle; **las cuatro** four o'clock || *m* four; (*en las fechas*) fourth; (*de voces*) quartet; **más de cuatro** (coll) quite a number
cuatrocien•tos -tas *adj & pron* four hundred || **cuatrocientos** *m* four hundred
cuba *f* cask, barrel; tub, vat; (*persona de mucho vientre*) (coll) tub; (*persona que bebe mucho*) (coll) toper; **cuba de riego** street sprinkler
cuba•no -na *adj & mf* Cuban
cubertería *f* silverware, cutlery
cubeta *f* keg, cask; pail; bowl, toilet bowl; (*del termómetro*) cup; (chem, phot) tray; (Mex) high hat
cubicaje *m* piston displacement, cylinder capacity
cubicar *tr* (*elevar al cubo*) to cube; measure the volume of; have a piston displacement of
cúbi•co -ca *adj* cubic; (*raíz*) cube

cubículo *m* cubicle; **cubículo de estudio** carrel
cubierta *f* cover; envelope; roof; (*de un libro*) paper cover; (*de un neumático*) casing, shoe; (*del motor de un coche*) hood; (naut) deck; **bajo cubierta separada** under separate cover; **cubierta de aterrizaje** (nav) flight deck; **cubierta de cama** bedcover; **cubierta de mesa** table cover; **cubierta de paseo** (naut) promenade deck; **cubierta de vuelo** (nav) flight deck; **cubierta principal** (naut) main deck; **cubierta sin cámara** tubeless tire; **entre cubiertas** (naut) between decks
cubiertamente *adv* secretly
cubier•to -ta *adj* covered; (*cielo*) overcast || *m* cover, roof, shelter; (*servicio de mesa para una persona*) cover; knife, fork, and spoon; table d'hôte, prix fixe; **a cubierto de** under cover of; protected from; **bajo cubierto** under cover, indoors || *f* see **cubierta**
cubil *m* (*de fieras*) lair, den; (*de arroyo*) bed
cubilete *m* (*de cocinero*) copper mold; dicebox; mince pie; high hat; (SAm) scheming, wire-pulling
cubo *m* bucket; (*de rueda*) hub; (*de un candelero; de una llave de caja*) socket, nozzle; cube; (mach) barrel, drum; (math) cube; (Arg) finger bowl; **cubo de (la) basura** garbage can
cubreasiento *m* seat cover
cubrecama *f* counterpane, bedcover
cubrecorsé *m* corset cover
cubrefuego *m* curfew
cubrelibro *m* jacket
cubrenuca *f* havelock
cubrerrueda *f* mudguard
cubresexo *m* G-string
cubretablero *m* (aut) cowl
cubretetera *f* cozy, tea cozy
cubrir §83 *tr* to cover, cover over, cover up || *ref* to cover oneself; be covered; put one's hat on; (*el cielo*) become overcast; (*satisfacer una deuda*) cover
cucaña *f* greased pole to be climbed as a game; (coll) cinch
cucañe•ro -ra *mf* loafer, parasite
cucar §73 *tr* to wink; to make fun of; (*la caza*) to sight; to incite, stir up || *intr* (*el ganado*) to go off on a run (*when bitten by flies*)
cucaracha *f* roach, cockroach
cucarache•ro -ra *adj* (W-I) sly, tricky; (W-I) amorous, lecherous
cucarda *f* cockade
cuchara *f* spoon; (*cazo*) dipper, ladle; (*para áridos; para achicar el agua en los botes*) scoop; (*de albañil*) trowel; (Mex) pick-pocket; **cuchara de postre** dessertspoon; **cuchara de servir** tablespoon; **cuchara de sopa** soupspoon; **media cuchara** (Mex) mason's helper; ordinary fellow; fellow with heavy accent; **meter su cuchara** to butt in
cucharada *f* spoonful; ladleful; scoop
cucharear *tr* to spoon, ladle out
cucharetear *intr* to stir the pot, stir with a spoon; to meddle
cucharilla *f* teaspoon; (*de soldador*) ladle
cucharón *m* large spoon; soup ladle, dipper; scoop; **despacharse con el cucharón** to look out for number one
cucheta *f* couchette; bunk bed
cuchichear *intr* to whisper
cuchilla *f* knife; (*hoja de arma blanca de corte*) blade; (*de patín de hielo*) runner; (*cerro escarpado*) hogback; (*de interruptor*) (elec) blade; (poet) sword; **cuchilla de afeitar** razor blade; **cuchilla de carnicero** butcher knife, cleaver
cuchillada *f* slash, gash, hack; **cuchilladas** fight, quarrel; **dar cuchillada** (*un actor o un teatro*) to be the hit of the town
cuchillería *f* cutlery; cutler's shop
cuchillero *m* cutler
cuchillo *m* knife; (*en un vestido*) gore; (naut) triangular sail; **cuchillo de trinchar** carving knife; **cuchillo de vidriero** putty knife; **pasar a cuchillo** to put to the sword
cuchitril *m* hovel, den
cuchufleta *f* joke, fun, wisecrack
cuchufletear *intr* to joke, make fun, wisecrack
cuclillas — en cuclillas squatting, crouching
cuclillo *m* cuckoo; (coll) cuckold
cu•co -ca *adj* sly, tricky; cute || *mf* sly person || *m* bogeyman; cuckoo; **hacer cuco a** to poke fun at
cu•cú *m* (*pl* **-cúes**) cuckoo (*call*) || *interj* peekaboo!
cuculla *f* cowl, hood
cucurucho *m* paper cone, ice-cream cone; **hacer cucurucho a** (Chile) to deceive, take in
cuelga *f* fruit hung up for keeping; birthday present
cuelgaca•pas *m* (*pl* **-pas**) cloak hanger
cuelgue *m* (compu) crash
cuello *m* (*del cuerpo*) neck; (*de una prenda*) collar; shirt collar; **cuello almidonado** stiff collar; **cuello alto** turtleneck; **cuello de botella** (aut) bottleneck; **cuello de camisa** shirtband; **cuello de cisne** gooseneck; **cuello de pajarita** or **doblado** wing collar; **cuello de pico** V neck; **levantar el cuello** to get back on one's feet again
cuenca *f* wooden bowl; (*del ojo*) socket; basin, river basin; **cuenca de polvo** dust bowl
cuenco *m* earthen bowl; hollow
cuenta *f* count, calculation; account; (*factura*) bill; (*en un restaurante*) check; (*del rosario*) bead; **abonar en cuenta a** to credit to the account of; **a cuenta** or **a buena cuenta** on account; **adeudar en cuenta a** to charge to the account of; **a fin de cuentas** after all; **caer en la cuenta** to get the point; **cargar en cuenta a** to charge to the account of; **correr por cuenta de** to be the responsibility of, to be under the administration of; **cuenta a cero, cuenta atrás** countdown; **cuenta conjunta** joint account; **cuenta corriente** current account; **cuenta de ahorros** savings account; **cuenta de crédito** charge account; **cuenta de**

gastos expense account; **cuenta de la vieja** counting on one's fingers; **cuenta de protección** standing count; **cuenta regresiva** countdown; **cuentas del gran capitán** overdrawn account; **cuentas galanas** illusions; **darse cuenta de** to realize, become aware of; **de cuenta** of importance; **más de la cuenta** too long; too much; **pedir cuentas a** to bring to account; **por la cuenta** apparently; **por mi cuenta** to my way of thinking; **tomar por su cuenta** to take upon oneself; **vamos a cuentas** (coll) let's settle this

cuentacorrentista *mf* depositor

cuentago•tas *m* (*pl* **-tas**) dropper, medicine dropper

cuentakilóme•tros *m* (*pl* **-tros**) odometer

cuente•ro -ra *adj* (coll) gossipy || *mf* (coll) gossip

cuentista *adj* (coll) gossipy || *mf* story teller; short-story writer; (coll) gossip

cuento *m* story, tale; short story; prop, support; tip, point; (*cómputo*) count; (coll) gossip, evil talk; (coll) disagreement; **cuento chino** (coll) baloney, rubbish; **cuento de hadas** fairty tale; **cuento del tío** (SAm) gyp, swindle; **cuento de nunca acabar** (coll) endless affair; **cuento de penas** (coll) hard-luck story; **cuento de viejas** old wives' tale; **Cuentos de Calleja** collection of nursery stories; **dejarse de cuentos** (coll) to come to the point; **estar en el cuento** to be well-informed; **¡ puro cuento!** pure fiction!; **sin cuento** countless; **traer a cuento** to bring up; **venir a cuento** (coll) to be opportune; **vivir del cuento** to live by one's wits

cuerda *f* cord, rope; watch spring; winding a watch or clock; (*acción de ahorcar*) hanging; fishing line; (aer, anat, geom) chord; (mus) string; **acabarse la cuerda** to run down, e.g., **se acabó la cuerda** the watch ran down; **bajo cuerda** secretly, underhandedly; **cuerda de presos** chain gang; **cuerda de remolcar** tow rope; **cuerda de tripa** (mus) catgut; **cuerda floja** tightrope, high wire; **cuerdas** (mus) strings; **cuerdas vocales** vocal cords; **cuerda tirante** tight rope; **dar cuerda a** to give free rein to; (*un reloj*) to wind; **estar en su cuerda** to be in one's element; **sin cuerda** unwound, rundown

cuer•do -da *adj* wise, prudent; sane || *f* see **cuerda**

cuerna *f* antler; horns

cuerno *m* horn; (mus) horn; **cuerno de caza** hunting horn; **cuerno de la abundancia** horn of plenty; **cuerno inglés** (mus) English horn

cuero *m* (*pellejo de buey*) hide; (*después de curtido*) leather; wineskin; **cuero cabelludo** scalp; **cuero en verde** rawhide; **en cueros** stark-naked

cuerpear *intr* (Arg) to duck, dodge

cuerpo *m* body; (*parte del vestido hasta la cintura*) waist; (*talle, aspecto*) build; (*de escritos, leyes, etc.*) corpus; corps, staff; (mil) corps; **cuerpo a cuerpo** hand to hand; **cuerpo celeste** heavenly body; **cuerpo compuesto** (chem) compound; **cuerpo de aviación** air corps; **cuerpo de baile** corps de ballet; **cuerpo de bomberos** fire brigade, fire company; **cuerpo de ejército** army corps; **cuerpo del delito** corpus delicti; **Cuerpo de Paz** Peace Corps; **cuerpo de policía** police force; **cuerpo de redacción** editorial staff; **cuerpo diplomático** diplomatic corps; **cuerpo electoral** electorate; **cuerpo médico** medical corps; **cuerpo simple** (chem) element, simple substance; **dar con el cuerpo en tierra** (coll) to fall flat on the ground; **de cuerpo entero** full-length; **de medio cuerpo** half-length; **descubrir el cuerpo** to drop one's guard; **en cuerpo** or **en cuerpo de camisa** in shirt sleeves; **estar de cuerpo presente** to be on view, to lie in state; **hacer del cuerpo** (coll) to have a movement of the bowels

cueru•do -da *adj* thick-skinned; annoying, boring; bold, shameless

cuervo *m* raven; **cuervo marino** cormorant; **cuervo merendero** rook

cuesco *m* (*de la fruta*) stone; (*del molino de aceite*) millstone; windiness

cuesta *f* hill, slope, grade; charity drive; **cuesta abajo** downhill; **cuesta arriba** up-hill; **llevar a cuestas** to be burdened with

cuestión *f* question; dispute, quarrel; matter; **cuestión batallona** much-debated question; **cuestión palpitante** burning question; **en cuestión de** in a matter of

cuestionable *adj* questionable

cuestionar *tr* to question || *intr* (Arg) to argue

cuestionario *m* questionnaire

cuestua•rio -ria or **cuestuo•so -sa** *adj* profitable, lucrative

cuetear *ref* (Col) to blow up, explode; (Col) to die, kick the bucket; (Mex) to get drunk

cueva *f* cave; cellar; (*de ladrones, fieras, etc.*) den

cufi•fo -fa *adj* (Chile) tipsy

cugulla *f* cowl

cui•co -ca *adj* foreign, outside || *m* (Mex) cop, policeman

cuidado *m* care, concern, worry; **¡cuidado con . . .!** beware of . . .!, look out for!; **de cuidado** dangerously; **estar de cuidado** to be dangerously ill; **pierda Ud. cuidado** don't worry; **salir de su cuidado** (*una mujer*) to be delivered; **tener cuidado** to beware, be careful

cuidadora *f* (Mex) governess, chaperon

cuidado•so -sa *adj* careful, concerned, worried; watchful

cuidar *tr* to take care of, watch over || *intr* — **cuidar de** to take care of, care for; care to || *ref* to take care of oneself; **cuidarse de** to care about; be careful to

cuita *f* trouble, worry; longing, yearning

cuja *f* bedstead

culata *f* buttock, haunch; (*de la escopeta*) butt;

(*de imán*) keeper, yoke; **culata de cilindro** cylinder head
culatazo *m* kick, recoil
culebra *f* snake; (*del alambique*) coil; **culebra de anteojos** cobra; **culebra de cascabel** rattlesnake; **saber más que las culebras** to be crafty
culebrear *intr* to wriggle; wind, meander, zigzag
culebrón *m* foxy fellow; (Mex) poor farce
cule•co -ca *adj* self-satisfied; madly in love
cu•lí *m* (*pl* **-líes**) coolie
culina•rio -ria *adj* culinary
culipandear *intr & ref* (CAm, W-I) to welsh, be evasive
culminar *intr* to culminate
culo *m* seat, behind, backside; (*de animal*) buttocks; (*de un vaso*) bottom; **culo de mal asiento** fidgety person; **volver el culo** to run away
culote *m* base
culpa *f* blame, guilt, fault; **echar la culpa a** to put the blame on; **tener la culpa** to be wrong, be to blame
culpable *adj* blamable, guilty, culpable
culpa•do -da *adj* guilty || *mf* culprit
culpar *tr* to blame, censure, accuse || *ref* to take the blame
cultedad *f* fustian, affectation
culteranismo *m* euphuism, Gongorism
cultiparlar *intr* to speak in a euphuistic manner
cultismo *m* learned word; cultism, Gongorism
cultiva•dor -dora *mf* grower, planter || *m & f* (mach) cultivator
cultivar *tr* to cultivate; till
cultivo *m* cultivation; **cultivo de secano** dry farming
cul•to -ta *adj* cultivated, cultured; (*vocablo*) learned || *m* worship; cult; **culto a la personalidad** personality cult
cultura *f* culture, cultivation
culturar *tr* to cultivate, till
cumbre *adj* top, greatest || *f* summit; acme, pinnacle; **conferencia en la cumbre** summit meeting
cúmel *m* kümmel
cumiche *m* (CAm) baby (*youngest member of family*)
cumpa *m* (SAm) pal, buddy; comrade
cúmplase *m* approval, O.K.
cumplea-ños *m* (*pl* **-ños**) birthday
cumpli•do -da *adj* full; perfect; (*en muestras de urbanidad*) correct || *m* correctness; courtesy; present
cumplimentar *tr* to compliment; to pay a complimentary visit to; to carry out, execute; (*un cuestionario*) to fill out
cumplimente•ro -ra *adj* effusive, obsequious
cumplimiento *m* (*muestra de urbanidad*) compliment; (*conducta decorosa*) correctness; fulfillment; perfection; **por cumplimiento** as a matter of pure formality
cumplir *tr* to fulfill, perform, execute; **cumplir años** to have a birthday; **cumplir . . . años** to be . . . years old || *intr* to fall due; to expire; to keep one's promise; to finish one's service in the army; **cumplir con** to fulfill; to fulfill one's obligation to; **cumplir por** to act on behalf of; to pay the respects of || *ref* to be fulfilled, to come true; to fall due; **cúmplase** approved
cumquibus *m* wherewithal
cúmulo *m* heap, pile, lot
cuna *f* cradle
cundido *m* olive, vinegar, and salt for shepherds; olive oil, cheese, and honey to make children eat
cundir *intr* to spread; swell, puff up; increase
cunear *tr* to cradle, rock in a cradle || *intr* to rock, swing, sway
cune•co -ca *mf* (Ven) baby (*youngest member of family*)
cuneta *f* gutter, ditch
cuña *f* wedge; (typ) quoin; **ser buena cuña** to take up a lot of room
cuñada *f* sister-in-law
cuñado *m* brother-in-law
cuñete *m* keg
cuño *m* die; stamp; mark
cuota *f* quota, share; fee, dues; tuition fee
cupé *m* coupé
cupo *m* quota, share; (Mex) capacity
cupón *m* coupon; **cupón de racionamiento** ration coupon; **cupón federal** *or* **alimenticio** food stamp; **cupón obsequio** gift certificate
cúpula *f* cupola; dome; **cúpula de bulbo** onion dome
cuquillo *m* cuckoo
cura *m* curate; (coll) priest; **este cura** (*yo*) (coll) yours truly (*I*) || *f* cure; care, treatment; **cura de aguas** water cure; **cura de almas** care of souls; **cura de hambre** starvation diet; **cura de reposo** rest cure; **cura de urgencia** first aid; **no tener cura** to be hopeless, be incorrigible
curaca *m* (SAm) boss, chief || *f* (Bol, Peru) priest's housekeeper
curación *f* cure, treatment
curade•ro -ra *mf* caretaker || *m* (law) guardian
curande•ro -ra *mf* quack, healer
curar *tr* (*a un enfermo*) to treat; (*sanar*) cure, heal; (*curtir*) cure; (*la madera*) season; (*una herida*) dress || *intr* to cure; recover; **curar de** to take care of; recover from; mind, pay attention to || *ref* to cure; cure oneself; get well, recover, get drunk; **curarse de** to recover from, get over; **curarse en salud** to be forewarned
curati•vo -va *adj & f* curative
curda *f* jag, drunk
cureña *f* gun carriage
curia *f* (hist) curia; (*de rey*) court; (*conjunto de abogados*) bar
curiales•co -ca *adj* hairsplitting, legalistic
curiosear *tr* to pry into || *intr* to snoop; browse around

curiosidad *f* curiosity; (*objeto de arte raro y curioso*) curio; neatness, tidiness; care, carefulness
curio•so -sa *adj* curious; neat, tidy; careful || *mf* busybody || *m* (Ven) healer, medical man
currinche *m* cub reporter; hit playwright
cu•rro -rra *adj* flashy, sporty || *m* sport, dandy
curruca *f* (orn) whitethroat; **curruca de cabeza negra** blackcap, warbler
curruta•co -ca *adj* dudish, sporty; chubby || *m* dude, sport || *f* chic dame
cursa•do -da *adj* skilled, experienced; (*asignatura*) taken
cursante *mf* student
cursar *tr* (*una materia, estudios*) to take, study; (*conferencias*) attend; (*una carta*) forward; (*un paraje*) frequent, to haunt || *intr* to study; be current
cursear *intr* to have diarrhea
cursería *f* cheapness, flashiness, vulgarity; flashy lot of people
cursi *adj* cheap, flashy, vulgar, loud || *m* sporty guy || *f* flashy dame
cursien•to -ta *adj* diarrheic
cursilería *f* cheapness, flashiness, vulgarity; flashy lot of people
cursillo *m* refresher course; short course of lectures
cursi•vo -va *adj* cursive; italic || *f* cursive; italics
curso *m* course; academic year, school year; price, quotation, current rate; **curso académico** academic year; **curso acelerado** *or* **intensivo** intensive course; **curso legal** legal tender; **curso por correspondencia** correspondence course; **cursos** loose bowels; **dar curso a** to give way to; to forward
cursor *m* slide; sliding contact; (compu) cursor; **cursor de procesiones** marshal
curtiduría *f* tannery
curtiembre *f* tannery
curtir *tr* (*las pieles*) to tan; (*el cutis de una persona*) tan, sunburn; harden, inure; **estar curtido en** to be skilled in, be expert in || *ref* to become tanned, sunburned; become hardened; be weather-beaten
curva *f* curve; bend; **curva de nivel** contour line
curvadura *f* painful exhaustion
cur•vo -va *adj* curved, bent || *f* see **curva**
cusca *f* (Col) jag, drunk; (Mex) prostitute, slut
cuscús *or* **cus-cus** *m* (culin) couscous
cúspide *f* (*de montaña*) peak; (*de diente*) cusp; apex, tip, top
custodia *f* custody, care; (*de un preso*) guard; (eccl) monstrance
custodiar *tr* to guard, watch over
custodio *m* custodian; guard
cususa *f* (CAm) rum
cutá•neo -nea *adj* cutaneous
cu•tí *m* (*pl* **-tíes**) bedtick, ticking
cutícula *f* cuticle
cutio *m* work, labor
cu•tis *m* (*& f*) (*pl* **-tis**) skin, complexion; **cutis anserina** goose flesh
cu•yo -ya *adj rel* whose
c/v *abbr* **cuenta de venta**

D

D, d (de) *f* fourth letter of the Spanish alphabet
d. — d. de C., d. de J.C. *adj abbr* (**después de Cristo, después de Jesucristo**) A.D. (Anno Domini)
D. *abbr* **don**
D.ª *abbr* **doña**
daca give me, hand over; **andar al daca y toma** to be at cross purposes
dactilógra•fo -fa *mf* typist || *m* typewriter
dactilograma *m* fingerprint
dádiva *f* gift, present
dadivo•so -sa *adj* liberal, generous
da•do -da *adj* given; **dado que** provided, as long as || *m* die; **cargar los dados** to load the dice; **dados** dice; **el dado está tirado** the die is cast
daga *f* dagger
dalia *f* dahlia
daltonia•no -na *var de* **daltónico**
daltóni•co -ca *adj* color-blind || *mf* color-blind person
dama *f* lady, dame; maid-in-waiting; (*en el juego de damas*) king; (*en el ajedrez y los naipes*) queen; (theat) leading lady; concubine, mistress; **dama de honor** bridesmaid; **dama joven** (theat) young lead; **damas** checkers; **Damas** (*ladies' room*) *SIGN* Ladies; Women; **damas chinas** Chinese checkers; **primera dama** (pol) first lady, First Lady; **señalar dama** (*en el juego de damas*) to crown a man
damajuana *f* demijohn
damasquina•do -da *adj & m* damascene
damasquinar *tr* to damascene
damasqui•no -na *adj* damascene
damero *m* checkerboard
damisela *f* young lady; courtesan
damnación *f* damnation
damnificar §73 *tr* to damage, hurt
da•nés -nesa *adj* Danish || *mf* Dane || *m* (*idioma*) Danish; Danish pastry
dáni•co -ca *adj* Danish
Danubio *m* Danube
danza *f* dance; dancing; dance team; **danza de cintas** Maypole dance; **danza de figuras**

square dance; **meter en la danza** to drag in, involve
danza•dor -dora *mf* dancer
danzar §60 *tr* to dance || *intr* to dance; butt in
danza•rín -rina *mf* dancer; meddler, scatterbrain
dañable *adj* harmful; reprehensible
daña•do -da *adj* bad, wicked; spoiled
dañar *tr* to hurt, damage, injure; spoil || *ref* to be damaged; spoil
dañi•no -na *adj* harmful, destructive, noxious; wicked
daño *m* damage, harm; (Arg) witchcraft; **a daño de** on the responsibility of; **daños y perjuicios** (law) damages; **en daño de** to the detriment of; **hacer daño** to be harmful; **hacer daño a** to hurt; **hacerse daño** to hurt oneself; to get hurt
daño•so -sa *adj* harmful, injurious
dar §23 *tr* to give; cause; hit, strike; (*el reloj la hora*) strike; (*cartas*) deal; (*un paseo*) take; (*los buenos días*) wish; (*un film*) show; (*una capa de pintura*) put on, apply; **dar a conocer** to make known; **dar a luz** to bring out, publish; **dar cuerda a** (*un reloj*) to wind; **dar curso a** to circulate; **dar de beber a** to give something to drink to; **dar de comer a** to give something to eat to; **dar la razón a** to admit that (*someone*) is right; **dar prestado** to lend; **dar palmadas** to clap the hands; **dar por** to consider as; **dar que hablar** to cause talk; to stir up criticism; **dar que hacer** to cause annoyance or trouble; **dar que pensar** to give food for thought; to give rise to suspicion || *intr* to take place; to hit, strike; (*el reloj; dos, tres, etc. horas*) to strike; to tell, intimate; **dar a** to overlook; **dar con** to run into; **dar contra** to run against, strike against; **dar de sí** to stretch, to give; **dar en** to overlook; to hit; to run into; to fall into; to be bent on; (*un chiste*) to catch on to; **dar sobre** to overlook; **dar tras** to pursue hotly || *ref* to give oneself up; to give in, yield; to occur, be found; **darse a** to devote oneself to; **darse a conocer** to make a name for oneself, make oneself known; to get to know each other; **darse cuenta de** to realize, become aware of; **darse la mano** to shake hands; **dárselas de** to pose as; **darse por aludido** to take the hint; **darse por entendido** to show an understanding; to show appreciation; **darse por ofendido** to take offense; **darse por vencido** to give up, to acknowledge defeat
dardo *m* dart; cutting remark
dares y tomares *mpl* quarrels, disputes
dársena *f* basin, marina, inner harbor
darvinia•no -na *adj & mf* Darwinian, Darwinist
darvinismo *m* Darwinism
data *f* date; (*en una cuenta*) item; (journ) byline; **de larga data** of long standing; **estar de mala data** to be in a bad humor
datar *tr & intr* to date; **datar de** to date from
dátil *m* date
datilera *f* date, date palm
dati•vo -va *adj & m* dative
dato *m* datum; basis, foundation; information; **datos** (compu) data
David *m* David
dC *adj* (letterword) (**después de Cristo**) A.D. (Anno Domini)
de *prep* of; from; about; **acompañado de** accompanied by; **cubierto de** covered with; **de noche** in the nighttime; **de no llegar nosotros a la hora** if we do not arrive on time; **más de** more than; **tratar de** to try to
deán *m* (eccl) dean
deanato *m* or **deanazgo** *m* deanship
debajo *adv* below, underneath; **debajo de** below, under
debate *m* debate; altercation, argument
debatir *tr & intr* to debate; fight, argue || *ref* to struggle
debe *m* debit
debelar *tr* to conquer, vanquish
deber *m* duty; (*deuda*) debt; homework, school work; **últimos deberes** last rites || *tr* to owe || *v aux* to have to, ought to, must, should; **deber de** must, most likely || *ref* to be committed; **deberse a** to be due to
debidamente *adv* duly
debi•do -da *adj* due, owed; proper, right; **debido a** due to
débil *adj* weak
debilidad *f* weakness, debility; **debilidad por** fondness for
debilitar *tr & ref* to weaken
débito *m* debt, debit; responsibility
debutante *mf* debutant(e), beginner
debutar *intr* to make one's start, appear for the first time
década *f* decade
decadencia *f* decadence
decadente *adj & mf* decadent
decaer §15 *intr* to decay, decline, fail, weaken; (naut) to drift from the course
decampar *intr* (mil) to decamp
decanato *m* deanship
decano *m* dean
decanta•do -da *adj* puffed-up, overrated
decantar *tr* to decant
decapitar *tr* to decapitate
decelerar *tr, intr & ref* to decelerate
decena *f* ten; about ten; **por decenas** in tens
decencia *f* decency
decenio *m* decade
decentar §2 *tr* to cut the first slice of; begin to damage || *ref* to get bedsores
decente *adj* decent, proper; decent-looking
decepción *f* disappointment
decepcionar *tr* to disappoint
dechado *m* sample, model, example; (*labor de las niñas*) sampler
decidi•do -da *adj* decided, determined
decidir *tr* to decide; persuade || *intr & ref* to decide
deci•dor -dora *adj* facile, fluent, witty

decimal *adj & m* decimal
déci•mo -ma *adj & m* tenth
decimocta•vo -va *adj* eighteenth
decimocuar•to -ta *adj* fourteenth
decimono•no -na *adj* nineteenth
decimonove•no -na *adj* nineteenth
decimoquin•to -ta *adj* fifteenth
decimosépti•mo -ma *adj* seventeenth
decimosex•to -ta *adj* sixteenth
decimoterce•ro -ra *adj* thirteenth
decimoter•cio -cia *adj* thirteenth
decir *m* say-so; **al decir de** according to || **§24** *tr* to say; tell; (*disparates*) talk; **como si dijéramos** so to speak, in a manner of speaking; **decir entre sí** to say to oneself; **decirle a uno cuántas son cinco** to tell a person what's what; **decir para sí** to say to oneself; **decir por decir** to talk for talk's sake; **decir que no** to say no; **decir que sí** to say yes; **decírselo a una persona deletreado** to spell it out to a person; **es decir** that is to say; **mejor dicho** rather; **¡por algo te lo dije!** I told you so!; **por decirlo así** so to speak || *intr* to suit, fit; **¡diga!** (*al contestar el teléfono*) hello! || *ref* to be said; be called; **se dice** it is said, they say
decisión *f* decision
decisi•vo -va *adj* decisive
declamar *tr & intr* to declaim
declaración *f* declaration; (*en bridge*) bid; **declaración de aduana** customs declaration; **declaración de derechos** bill of rights. **Declaración de la Independencia** Declaration of Independence; **declaración de la renta, declaración del impuesto sobre la renta** income tax return; **declaración de no culpabilidad** verdict of not guilty; **declaración jurada** sworn statement, affidavit
declarante *mf* declarant, deponent; (*en el juego de bridge*) bidder
declarar *tr* to declare; (*en bridge*) bid; (law) to depose || *ref* to declare oneself; break out, take place
declarati•vo -va *adj* declarative
declinación *f* declination; fall, drop; decline; (gram) declension
declinar *tr & intr* to decline
declive *m* descent, declivity, slope
declividad *f* declivity
decodificador *m* (telv) decoder
decollaje *m* (aer) take-off
decollar *intr* (aer) to take off
decomisar *tr* to seize, confiscate
decomiso *m* seizure, confiscation
decoración *f* decoration; memorizing; (theat) set, scenery; **decoraciones** (theat) scenery; **decoración interior** interior decoration
decorado *m* decoration; (theat) décor, scenery; memorizing
decora•dor -dora *mf* decorator
decorar *tr* to decorate; memorize
decoro *m* decorum; honor, respect; decency, propriety
decoro•so -sa *adj* decorous; respectful; decent
decrecer **§22** *intr* to decrease, grow smaller, grow shorter
decrepitar *intr* to crackle
decrépi•to -ta *adj* decrepit
decretar *tr* to decree
decreto *m* decree
decurso *m* course; **en el decurso de** in the course of
dedada *f* touch, spot; **dar una dedada de miel a** to feed the hopes of
dedal *m* thimble
dedalera *f* foxglove
dedeo *m* (mus) finger dexterity
dedicación *f* dedication; (*aplicación*) diligence
dedicar **§73** *tr* to dedicate; devote; autograph || *ref* to devote oneself
dedicatoria *f* dedication
dedil *m* fingerstall
dedillo *m* little finger; **saber** or **tener al dedillo** to have at one's finger tips, have a thorough knowledge of
dedo *m* finger; toe; bit; **alzar el dedo** (*en señal de dar palabra*) to raise one's hand; **cogerse los dedos** to burn one's fingers; **dedo anular** ring finger; **dedo auricular** little finger; **dedo cordial, de en medio,** *or* **del corazón** middle finger; **dedo gordo** thumb; big toe; **dedo índice** index finger, forefinger; **dedo meñique** little finger; **dedo mostrador** forefinger; **dedo pulgar** thumb; big toe; **estar a dos dedos de** to be within an ace of; **irse de entre los dedos** (coll) to slip between the fingers; **tener en la punta de los dedos** to have at one's fingertips
deducción *f* deduction; drawing off
deducir **§19** *tr* (*concluir*) to deduce; (*rebajar*) deduct; (law) to allege
defecar **§73** *intr* to defecate
defección *f* defection
defeccionar *intr & ref* (Chile) to defect
defecti•vo -va *adj* defective
defecto *m* defect; shortage, lack; **en defecto de** for lack of
defectuo•so -sa *adj* defective; lacking
defender **§51** *tr* to defend; protect; delay, interfere with
defensa *f* defense; fender, guard; (*del toro*) horn; (*del elefante*) tusk; (*del automóvil*) bumper; **defensa marítima** (Arg) sea wall; **defensa personal, defensa propia** self-defense
defensi•vo -va *adj & f* defensive
defen•sor -sora *adj* defending || *mf* defender; (law) counsel for the defense
deferencia *f* deference
deferente *adj* deferential
deferir **§68** *tr* to delegate || *intr* to defer
deficiencia *f* deficiency
deficiente *adj* deficient
défi•cit *m* (*pl* **-cits**) deficit
deficita•rio -ria *adj* deficit
definición *f* definition; decision, verdict

defini•do -da *adj* definite; sharp, defined; **bien definido** clear-cut
definir *tr* to define; settle, determine
definiti•vo -va *adj* definitive; **en definitiva** after all, in short
deflación *f* deflation
deflector *m* baffle
deformación *f* deformation; (rad) distortion
deformar *tr* to deform; disfigure; distort
deforme *adj* deformed
deformidad *f* deformity; gross error
defraudar *tr* to defraud, cheat; (*las esperanzas de una persona*) defeat; (*la claridad del día*) cut off
defuera *adv* outside; **por defuera** on the outside
defunción *f* decease, demise
degeneración *f* (*acción y efecto de degenerar*) degeneration; (*estado de degenerado; depravación*) degeneracy
degenera•do -da *adj & mf* degenerate
degenerar *intr* to degenerate
deglutir *tr & intr* to swallow
degollar §3 *tr* to cut the throat of; kill, massacre; (*un vestido*) cut low in the neck; (*el actor una obra dramática*) butcher, murder; become obnoxious to
degradante *adj* degrading
degradar *tr* to degrade; (mil) to break
degüello *m* throat-cutting; massacre; (*de un arma*) neck; **tirar a degüello** to try to harm
degustar *tr* (*probar*) to taste; (*percibir con deleite el sabor de*) to savor
dehesa *f* pasture land, meadow; (taur) range
deidad *f* deity
deificar §73 *tr* to deify
dejación *f* abandonment; (CAm, Chile, Col) negligence
dejadez *f* laziness; negligence; slovenliness; low spirits
deja•do -da *adj* lazy; negligent; slovenly; dejected
dejamiento *m* laziness; negligence; indolence, languor, indifference
dejar *tr* to leave; abandon; let, allow, permit; **dejar caer** to drop, let fall; **dejar feo** to slight; **dejar fresco** to leave in the lurch; **dejar por** + *inf or* **que** + *inf* to leave (*something*) to be + *pp*, e.g., **hemos dejado dos manuscritos por corregir** *or* **que corregir** we left two manuscripts to be corrected || *intr* to stop; **dejar de** to stop, cease; fail to || *ref* to be slovenly, neglect oneself; (*una barba*) grow; **dejarse de** (*disparates*) to cut out; (*preguntas*) stop asking; (*dudas*) put aside; **dejarse ver** to show up; be evident
dejillo *m* (*gusto que deja alguna comida*) aftertaste; (*acento regional*) local accent
dejo *m* (*gusto que deja alguna comida*) aftertaste; hint, touch; abandonment; slovenliness, neglect; local accent; (*placer o disgusto que queda después de hecha una cosa*) (fig) aftertaste
delación *f* accusation, denunciation
delantal *m* apron
delante *adv* before, ahead, in front; **delante de** before, ahead of, in front of
delantera *f* front; front row; advantage, lead; cowcatcher; **coger** or **tomar la delantera a** to get ahead of; get a start on; **delanteras** overalls
delante•ro -ra *adj* front, foremost, first || *m* — **delantero centro** (*fútbol*) center forward || *f* see **delantera**
delatar *tr* to accuse, denounce
delega•do -da *mf* delegate; **delegado de curso** student representative
delegar §44 *tr* to delegate
deleitable *adj* delectable, enjoyable
deleitar *tr & ref* to delight
deleite *m* delight
deleito•so -sa *adj* delightful
deletrear *tr & intr* to spell; decipher
deletreo *m* spelling
deleznable *adj* (*poco durable*) perishable; (*que se rompe fácilmente*) crumbly, fragile; (*que se desliza con facilidad*) slippery
delfín *m* (*primogénito del rey de Francia*) dauphin; (*mamífero cetáceo*) dolphin
delgadez *f* thinness, leanness; delicateness, lightness; perspicacity
delga•do -da *adj* thin, lean; delicate, light; sharp, perspicacious; (*terreno*) poor, exhausted || *adv* — **hilar delgado** to hew close to the line, split hairs
delgadu•cho -cha *adj* skinny; slight
deliberar *tr & intr* to deliberate
delicadeza *f* delicacy, delicateness; scrupulousness
delica•do -da *adj* delicate; scrupulous
delicia *f* delight
delicio•so -sa *adj* delicious, delightful
delicti•vo -va *adj* punishable; criminal
delincuencia *f* guilt, criminality
delincuente *adj* guilty, criminal || *mf* criminal
delineante *mf* designer || *m* draughtsman
delinquir §25 *intr* to transgress, be guilty
deliquio *m* faint, swoon; weakening
delirante *adj* delirious
delirar *intr* to be delirious, rant, rave; talk nonsense
delirio *m* delirium; nonsense
delito *m* crime; **delito de incendio** arson; **delito de lesa majestad** lese majesty; **delito de mayor cuantía** (law) felony; **delito de menor cuantía** (law) misdemeanor; **delito de sangre** violent crime
deludir *tr* to delude
demacra•do -da *adj* emaciated, wasted, thin
demago•go -ga *mf* demagogue
demanda *f* demand, petition; charity box; lawsuit; undertaking; (*del Santo Grial*) quest; **demanda colectiva** (law) class action; **demanda maxima** (elec) peak load; **en demanda de** in search of; **tener demanda** to be in demand
demanda•do -da *mf* (law) defendant

demandante *mf* (law) complainant, plaintiff
demandar *tr* to ask for, request; (law) to sue || *intr* (law) to sue, bring suit
demarcar §73 *tr* to demarcate
demás *adj* **— el demás . . .** the other. . . , the rest of the . . . ; **estar demás** to be useless, to be in the way; **lo demás** the rest; **por lo demás** furthermore, besides || *pron* others; **los demás** the others, the rest || *adv* besides; **por demás** in vain; too, too much
demasía *f* excess, surplus; daring, boldness; evil, guilt, wrong; insolence; **en demasía** excessively, too much
demasia•do -da *adj & pron* too much; **demasia•dos -das** too many || **demasiado** *adv* too, too much, too hard
demasiar §77 *intr* to go too far
demediar *tr* to divide in half; use up half of; reach the middle of || *intr* to be divided in half
dementa•do -da *adj* insane; demented
demente *adj* insane || *mf* lunatic
democracia *f* democracy
demócrata *mf* democrat
democráti•co -ca *adj* democratic
demoler §47 *tr* to demolish
demolición *f* demolition
demonía•co -ca *adj* demoniacal
demonio *m* demon, devil; **estudiar con el demonio** to be full of devilishness
demora *f* delay
demorar *tr & ref* to delay
demostración *f* demonstration
demostra•dor -dora *mf* demonstrator || *m* hand (*of clock*)
demostrar §61 *tr* to demonstrate
demostrati•vo -va *adj* demonstrative
demudar *tr* to change, alter; disguise, cloak || *ref* to change countenance, color
denegación *f* denial, refusal
denegar §66 *tr* to deny, refuse
denegrecer §22 *tr* to blacken || *ref* to turn black
dengo•so -sa *adj* affected, finicky, overnice; (Col) strutting
dengue *m* affectation, finickiness, overniceness; (Col) strut, swagger
denguear *ref* (Col) to strut, swagger
denigrar *tr* to defame, revile; insult
denominación *f* denomination
denoda•do -da *adj* bold, daring
denostar §61 *tr* to abuse, insult, mistreat
denotar *tr* to denote
densidad *f* density; darkness, confusion
den•so -sa *adj* dense; dark, confused; crowded, thick, close
denta•do -da *adj* toothed; (*sello de correo*) perforated || *m* gear; teeth
dentadura *f* set of teeth; **dentadura artificial** or **postiza** denture, false teeth
dental *adj & f* dental
dentellada *f* bite; tooth mark
dentellar *intr* (*los dientes*) to chatter
dentellear *tr* to nibble, nibble at
dentera *f* envy; eagerness; **dar dentera** to set the teeth on edge; make the mouth water
dentición *f* teething
dentífri•co -ca *adj* (*pasta, polvos*) tooth || *m* dentifrice
dentista *mf* dentist
dentistería *f* dentistry
dentística *f* (Chile) dentistry
dentro *adv* inside, within; **dentro de** inside, within; **dentro de poco** shortly; **por dentro** on the inside
denuedo *m* bravery, courage, daring
denuesto *m* abuse, insult, mistreatment
denuncia *f* denunciation; report; proclamation
denunciar *tr* to denounce; report; (*la guerra*) proclaim
deparar *tr* to furnish, provide; offer, present
departamento *m* department; (rr) compartment; (*piso*) apartment; naval district (*in Spain*)
departir *intr* to chat, converse
depauperación *f* impoverishment; exhaustion, weakening
depauperar *tr* to impoverish; exhaust, weaken
dependencia *f* dependence, dependency; branch, branch office; relationship, friendship; accessory; personnel
depender *intr* to depend; **depender de** to depend on; be attached to, belong to
dependienta *f* female employee, clerk
dependiente *adj* dependent; branch || *mf* employee, clerk
deplorable *adj* deplorable
deplorar *tr* to deplore
deponer §54 *tr* to depose; set aside, remove; (*las armas*) lay down || *intr* to depose; (*evacuar el vientre*) have a movement; (CAm, Mex) to vomit
deportación *f* deportation
deporta•do -da *mf* deportee
deportar *tr* to deport
deporte *m* sport; outdoor recreation
deportista *mf* sport fan || *m* sportsman || *f* sportswoman
deporti•vo -va *adj* sport, sports
depositante *mf* depositor
depositar *tr* to deposit; (*la esperanza, la confianza*) put, place; (*el equipaje*) check; (*a una persona en seguro*) commit; store || *ref* to deposit, settle
deposita•rio -ria *mf* trustee; (*de un secreto*) repository || *m* public treasurer
depósito *m* deposit; depot, warehouse; storage; tank, reservoir; (*de libros en una biblioteca*) stack; (mil) depot; **depósito comercial** *or* **franco** bonded warehouse; **depósito de agua** reservoir; **depósito de cadáveres** morgue; **depósito de cereales** grain elevator; **depósito de equipajes** (rr) checkroom; **depósito de gasolina** (aut) gas tank; **depósito de locomotoras** roundhouse; **depósito de municiones** munition dump
depravación *f* depravity, depravation
deprava•do -da *adj* depraved

depravar *tr* to deprave || *ref* to become depraved
deprecar §73 *tr* to entreat, implore
depreciación *f* depreciation
depreciar *tr & ref* to depreciate
depresión *f* depression; drop, dip; (*en un muro*) recess
deprimir *tr* to depress; press down; push in; belittle; humiliate || *ref* to be depressed; (*la frente de una persona*) recede
depurar *tr* to purify, cleanse; purge
derecha *f* right hand; right-hand side; (pol) right; **a la derecha** on the right, to the right
derechamente *adv* rightly; straight, direct; properly; wisely
derechazo *m* blow with the right; (box) right
dereche•ro -ra *adj* right, just
derechista *adj* rightist || *mf* rightist, right-winger
dere•cho -cha *adj* right; right-hand; right-handed; straight; upright, standing; (CAm) lucky || *m* right; law; exemption, privilege; road, path; (*de tela, papel, tabla*) right side; **derecho a la vida** right-to-life; **derecho consuetudinario** common law; **derecho de asilo** right of asylum; **derecho de gentes** law of nations, international law; **derecho de matrícula** registration fee; **derecho de reproducción** copyright; **derecho de subscripción** (*a una nueva emisión de acciones*) (com) right; **derecho de tránsito** *or* **paso** right of way; **derecho internacional** international law; **derecho penal** criminal law; **derechos** dues, fees, taxes; (*de aduana*) duties; **derechos de almacenaje** storage, cost of storage; **derechos de autor** royalty; **derechos del hombre** rights of man; **derechos de patente** patent rights; **derechos de propiedad literaria** *or* **derechos reservados** copyright; **derechos humanos** human rights; **según derecho** by right, by rights || *f* see **derecha** || **derecho** *adv* straight, direct; rightly
deriva (aer, naut) drift; **ir a la deriva** (naut) to drift, be adrift
derivado *m* by-product
derivar *tr* to derive || *intr & ref* to derive, be derived; (aer, naut) to drift
dermatitis *f* dermatitis
derogar §44 *tr* to abolish, destroy, repeal
derrabar *tr* to dock, cut off the tail of
derrama•do -da *adj* extravagant, lavish
derramamiento *m* pouring, spilling; shedding; spreading; lavishing, wasting
derramar *tr* to pour, spill; (*sangre*) shed; spread, publish abroad; (*dinero*) lavish, waste || *ref* to run over, overflow; spread, scatter; (*una corriente, un río*) open, empty; (*la plumafuente*) leak
derrame *m* pouring, spilling; (*de sangre*) shed, shedding; spread, scattering; lavishing, wasting; overflow; leakage; slope; chamfering; (pathol) discharge, effusion
derrapada *f* or **derrapaje** *f* (aut) skidding
derredor *m* circumference; **al** *or* **en derredor** around, round about
der(r)elicto *m* (naut) derelict
derrelínquir §25 *tr* to abandon, forsake
derrenga•do -da *adj* crooked, out of shape; crippled, lame
derrengar §44 or **§66** *tr* to bend, make crooked; cripple
derreniego *m* curse
derreti•do -da *adj* madly in love; (*mantequilla*) drawn || *m* concrete
derretimiento *m* thawing, melting; intense love, passion
derretir §50 *tr* to thaw, melt; (*la mantequilla*) draw; (*la hacienda*) squander || *ref* to thaw, melt; fall madly in love; be quite susceptible; be worried, be impatient
derribar *tr* to destroy, tear down, knock down; wreck; (*un árbol*) fell; bring down, shoot down; overthrow; humiliate || *ref* to fall down, tumble down; throw oneself on the ground
derribo *m* demolition, wrecking; (*de un árbol*) felling; overthrow; (*de un avión enemigo*) bringing down; **derribos** debris, rubble
derrocadero *m* rocky precipice
derrocar §73 or **§81** *tr* to throw or hurl from a height; ruin, wreck, tear down; bring down, humble, overthrow
derrocha•dor -dora *mf* wastrel, squanderer
derrochar *tr* to waste, squander
derroche *m* wasting, squandering, extravagance
derrota *f* defeat, rout; road, route, way; (*de embarcación*) course
derrotadamente *adv* shabbily, poorly
derrotar *tr* to rout, put to flight; wear out; ruin || *ref* (naut) to drift from the course
derrotero *m* course, route; ship's course
derrotismo *m* defeatism
derrotista *adj & mf* defeatist
derrubiar *tr & ref* to wash away, wear away
derrubio *m* washout
derruir §20 *tr* to tear down, demolish
derrumbadero *m* crag, precipice; hazard, risky business
derrumbamiento *m* headlong plunge; cave-in, collapse; **derrumbamiento de tierra** landslide
derrumbar *tr* to throw headlong || *ref* to plunge headlong; collapse, cave in, crumble
derrumbe *m* precipice; landslide; cave-in
derviche *m* dervish
desabonar *ref* to drop one's subscription
desabono *m* cancellation of subscription; discredit, disparagement
desabor *m* insipidity, tastelessness
desabotonar *tr* to unbutton || *intr* to blossom, bloom
desabri•do -da *adj* insipid, tasteless; gruff, surly; (*tiempo*) unsettled
desabrigar §44 *tr* to uncover, bare || *ref* to bare oneself; undress
desabrir *tr* to give a bad taste to; displease, embitter
desabrochar *tr* to unclasp, unbutton, unfasten || *ref* to unbosom oneself

desacalorar *ref* to cool off
desacatamiento *m* incivility, disrespect
desacatar *tr* to treat disrespectfully
desacato *m* incivility, disrespect, contempt; (*para con las cosas sagradas*) profanation
desacelerar *tr & ref* to decelerate
desacerta•do -da *adj* mistaken, wrong
desacertar §2 *intr* to be mistaken, be wrong
desacierto *m* error, mistake, blunder
desacomoda•do -da *adj* inconvenient; out of work; in straightened circumstances
desacomodar *tr* to inconvenience; discharge, dismiss
desacomodi•do -da *adj* (SAm) rude; impolite
desacomodo *m* discharge, dismissal
desaconseja•do -da *adj* ill-advised
desaconsejar *tr* to dissuade
desacordar §61 *tr* to put out of tune ‖ *ref* to get out of tune; become forgetful
desacorde *adj* out of tune; incongruous
desacostumbra•do -da *adj* unusual
desacostumbrar *tr* to break a habit
desacreditar *tr* to discredit; disparage
desacuerdo *m* discord, disagreement; error, mistake; unconsciousness; forgetfulness
desadaptación *f* maladjustment
desadeudar *tr* to free of debt ‖ *ref* to get out of debt
desadormecer §22 *tr* to awaken; free of numbness ‖ *ref* to get awake; shake off the numbness
desadorna•do -da *adj* unadorned, plain; bare, uncovered
desadverti•do -da *adj* unnoticed; inattentive
desadvertimiento *m* inadvertence
desafección *f* dislike
desafec•to -ta *adj* adverse, hostile; opposed ‖ *m* dislike
desaferrar *tr* to unfasten, loosen; make (*a person*) change his mind; (*las áncoras*) weigh
desafiar §77 *tr* to challenge, defy, dare; rival, compete with
desafición *f* dislike
desaficionar *tr* to cause to dislike
desafilar *tr* to make dull ‖ *ref* to become dull
desafina•do -da *adj* flat, out of tune, off key
desafinar *intr* to go out of tune; to go off key ‖ *reflex* to go out of tune
desafío *m* challenge, dare; rivalry, competition
desafora•do -da *adj* colossal, huge; disorderly, outrageous
desafortuna•do -da *adj* unfortunate
desafuero *m* excess, outrage
desagracia•do -da *adj* ungraceful, graceless
desagradable *adj* disagreeable
desagradar *tr & intr* to displease ‖ *ref* to be displeased
desagradeci•do -da *adj* ungrateful
desagradecimiento *m* ungratefulness
desagrado *m* displeasure
desagraviar *tr* to make amends to, indemnify
desagravio *m* amends, indemnification
desagregación *f* disintegration
desagregar §44 *ref* to disintegrate
desaguadero *m* drain, outlet; (*ocasión de continuo gasto*) (fig) drain
desaguar §10 *tr* to drain, empty; squander, waste ‖ *intr* to flow, empty ‖ *ref* to drain, be drained
desagüe *m* drainage, sewerage; drain, outlet
desaguisa•do -da *adj* illegal ‖ *m* offense, outrage, wrong
desahijar *tr* (*las crías del ganado*) to wean ‖ *ref* (*las abejas*) to swarm
desahogadamente *adv* freely; comfortably, easily; impudently
desahoga•do -da *adj* brazen, forward; roomy; in comfortable circumstances
desahogar §44 *tr* to relieve, comfort; (*deseos, pasiones*) give free rein to ‖ *ref* to take it easy, get comfortable; unbosom oneself, open up one's heart; get out of debt; **desahogarse en** (*denuestos*) to burst forth in
desahogo *m* brazenness; ample room; comfort; outlet, relief; comfortable circumstances
desahuciar *tr* to deprive of hope; evict, oust, disposses ‖ *ref* to lose all hope
desahucio *m* eviction, ousting, dispossession
desaira•do -da *adj* unattractive, unprepossessing; unsuccessful
desairar *tr* to slight, snub, disregard
desaire *m* slight, snub, disregard; unattractiveness, lack of charm
desajustar *tr* to put out of order ‖ *ref* to get out of order; disagree
desajuste *m* (mech) maladjustment
desalabanza *f* belittling, disparagement
desalabar *tr* to belittle, disparage
desala•do -da *adj* eager, in a hurry
desalar *tr* to desalt; clip the wings of ‖ *ref* to hasten, rush; **desalarse por** to be eager to
desalentar §2 *tr* to put out of breath; discourage ‖ *ref* to become discouraged
desalforjar *ref* to loosen one's clothing
desaliento *m* discouragement
desalinización *f* desalinization
desaliña•do -da *adj* slovenly, untidy; careless, slipshod
desaliño *m* slovenliness, untidiness; carelessness, neglect
desalma•do -da *adj* cruel, inhuman
desalojar *tr* to oust, evict; (*al enemigo*) to dislodge; (*el camino*) to clear ‖ *intr* to leave, move away, move out
desalquila•do -da *adj* vacant, unrented
desalterar *tr* to calm, quiet
desalumbra•do -da *adj* dazzled, blinded; confused, unsure of oneself
desamable *adj* unlikeable, unlovable
desamar *tr* to dislike, hate, detest
desamarrar *tr* to untie, unfasten; (naut) to unmoor
desamistar *ref* to fall out, become estranged
desamor *m* dislike, coldness; hatred
desamorrar *tr* to make (*a person*) talk
desamparar *tr* to abandon, forsake; give up

desamparo *m* abandonment, desertion; helplessness
desamuebla•do -da *adj* unfurnished
desandar §5 *tr* to retrace, go back over
desandraja•do -da *adj* ragged, in tatters
desangrar *tr* to bleed; drain; (fig) to bleed, impoverish || *ref* to lose a lot of blood
desanimación *f* discouragement, downheartedness
desanima•do -da *adj* discouraged, downhearted; (*reunión*) lifeless, dull
desanimar *tr* to discourage, dishearten || *ref* to become discouraged
desánimo *m* discouragement
desanublar *tr & ref* to clear up, brighten up
desanudar *tr* to untie; disentangle
desapacible *adj* unpleasant, disagreeable
desapadrinar *tr* to disavow; disapprove
desaparecer §22 *intr & ref* to disappear
desapareci•do -da *adj* missing; extinct || **desaparecidos** *mpl* missing persons
desaparecimiento *m* disappearance
desaparejar *tr* to unharness, unhitch; (naut) to unrig
desaparición *f* disappearance; (Ven) death
desapasiona•do -da *adj* dispassionate, impartial
desapego *m* dislike, coolness, indifference
desapercibi•do -da *adj* unprepared; wanting; unnoticed
desapiada•do -da *adj* merciless, pitiless
desaplica•do -da *adj* idle, lazy
desapodera•do -da *adj* headlong, impetuous; violent, wild; excessive
desapoderar *tr* to dispossess; deprive of power || *ref* — **desapoderarse de** to lose possession of, give up possession of
desapolillar *tr* to free of moths || *ref* to expose oneself to the weather
desapreciar *tr* to depreciate
desaprecio *m* depreciation
desaprender *tr* to unlearn
desaprensión *f* composure, nonchalance
desapretar §2 *tr* to slacken, loosen; (typ) to unlock
desaprobación *f* disapproval
desaprobar §61 *tr & intr* to disapprove
desapropiar *tr* to divest || *ref* — **desapropiarse de** to divest oneself of
desaprovecha•do -da *adj* unproductive; indifferent, lackadaisical
desaprovechar *tr* to not take advantage of || *intr* to slip back
desarmable *adj* dismountable
desarmador *m* hammer (*of gun*); (Mex) screwdriver
desarmamiento *m* disarmament; arms reduction
desarmar *tr* to disarm; dismount, dismantle, take apart; (*la cólera*) temper, calm || *intr & ref* to disarm
desarme *m* disarmament; dismantling, dismounting
desarraigar §44 *tr* to uproot, dig up; expel, drive out
desarregla•do -da *adj* out of order; slovenly, disorderly; intemperate
desarrimo *m* lack of support; standoffishness
desarrollador *m* (compu) developer
desarrollar *tr & intr* to develop; unroll, unfold || *ref* to develop; unroll, unfold; take place
desarrollo *m* development; unrolling, unfolding; **ayuda al desarrollo** developmental aid
desarropar *tr & ref* to undress
desarrugar §44 *tr & ref* to unwrinkle
desarzonar *tr* to unsaddle, unhorse
desasea•do -da *adj* dirty, unclean, slovenly
desasentar §2 *tr* to remove; displease || *ref* to stand up
desaseo *m* dirtiness, uncleanliness, slovenliness
desasir §7 *tr* to let go, let go of || *ref* to come loose; let go; **desasirse de** to let go of; give up, get free of
desasosegar §66 *tr* to disquiet, worry, disturb
desasosiego *m* disquiet, worry
desastra•do -da *adj* disastrous; unfortunate, wretched; ragged, shabby
desastre *m* disaster; **ir al desastre** to go to rack and ruin
desastro•so -sa *adj* disastrous
desatacar §73 *tr* to unbuckle, untie
desatar *tr* to untie, undo, unfasten; solve, unravel || *ref* to come loose; free oneself; (*la tempestad*) break loose; forget oneself, go too far; **desatarse en** (*denuestos*) to burst forth in
desatascar §73 *tr* to pull out of the mud; (*un conducto obstruído*) unclog; (*a una persona de un apuro*) extricate
desataviar §77 *tr* to disarray, undress
desatavío *m* disarray, undress, slovenliness
desate *m* (*de palabras*) flood; **desate del vientre** loose bowels
desatención *f* inattention; discourtesy, disrespect
desatender §51 *tr* to slight, disregard, pay no attention to
desatenta•do -da *adj* wild, disorderly, extreme
desaten•to -ta *adj* inattentive; discourteous, disrespectful
desatina•do -da *adj* wild, disorderly; foolish, nonsensical || *mf* fool
desatinar *tr* to bewilder, confuse || *intr* to talk nonsense, act foolishly; lose one's bearings
desatino *m* folly, nonsense; awkwardness, loss of touch
desatolondrar *tr* to bring to || *ref* to come to one's senses
desatollar *tr* to pull out of the mud
desatornillador *m* screwdriver
desatornillar *tr* to unscrew
desatraillar §4 *tr* to unleash
desatrampar *tr* to unclog
desatrancar §73 *tr* to unbar, unbolt; unclog
desatufar *ref* to get out of the close air; cool off, quiet down

desautoriza•do -da *adj* unauthorized
desavenencia *f* disagreement, discord
desavenir §79 *tr* to cause disagreement among || *ref* to disagree; **desavenirse con** to differ with, disagree with
desaventura *f* misfortune
desaviar §77 *tr* to mislead, lead astray
desavisa•do -da *adj* unadvised; ill-advised; thoughtless, careless
desayuna•do -da *adj* — **estar desayunado** to have had breakfast
desayunar *intr* to breakfast || *ref* to breakfast; **desayunarse con** to have breakfast on; **desayunarse de** to get the first news of
desayuno *m* breakfast
desazón *f* insipidity, tastelessness; annoyance, displeasure; discomfort
desazonar *tr* to make tasteless; annoy, displease || *ref* to feel ill
desbancar §73 *tr* to win the bank from; cut out, to supplant
desbandada *f* — **a la desbandada** helterskelter, in confusion
desbandar *ref* to run away; disband; desert
desbarajustar *tr* to put out of order || *ref* to get out of order, break down
desbarata•do -da *adj* debauched, corrupt || *mf* libertine
desbaratar *tr* to destroy, spoil, ruin; squander, waste; (mil) to rout, throw into confusion || *intr* to talk nonsense || *ref* to be unbalanced
desbarrancadero *m* precipice
desbastar *tr* to smooth off; waste, weaken; (*a una persona inculta*) polish || *ref* to become polished
desbautizar §60 *ref* to lose one's temper
desbeber *intr* (coll) to urinate
desbloquear *tr* to relieve the blockade of; (*crédito*) to unfreeze
desboca•do -da *adj* (*pieza de artillería*) widemouthed; (*herramienta*) nicked; (*caballo*) runaway; (*persona*) foul-mouthed
desbocar §73 *tr* to break the mouth of, break the spout of || *intr* (*un río*) to empty; (*una calle*) run, open, end || *ref* (*un caballo*) to run away, break loose; curse, swear
desbordamiento *m* overflow
desbordar *tr* to overwhelm || *intr & ref* to overflow
desbozalar *tr* to unmuzzle
desbravar *tr* to tame, break in || *intr & ref* to abate, moderate; cool off, calm down
desbrozar §60 *tr* to clear of underbrush, clear of rubbish
desbulla *f* oyster shell
desbulla•dor -dora *mf* oyster opener || *m* oyster fork
desbullar *tr* (*la ostra*) to open
descabal *adj* incomplete, imperfect
descabalgar §44 *intr* to dismount, alight from a horse
descabella•do -da *adj* disheveled; rash, wild
descabellar *tr* to muss, dishevel
descabeza•do -da *adj* crazy, rash, wild
descabezar §60 *tr* to behead; (*un árbol*) top; (*una dificultad*) get the best off; **descabezar el sueño** to doze, snooze || *intr* to border || *ref* to rack one's brains
descabullir §13 *ref* to sneak out, slip away; refuse to face the facts
descachalandra•do -da *adj* untidy; tattered
descacharra•do -da *adj* (CAm) dirty, slovenly, ragged
descaecer §22 *intr* to decline, lose ground
descaecimiento *m* weakness; depression, despondency
descalabazar §60 *ref* to rack one's brain
descalabra•do -da *adj* banged on the head; **salir descalabrado** to come out the loser, be worsted
descalabrar *tr* to bang on the head; knock down || *ref* to bang one's head
descalabro *m* misfortune, setback, loss
descalcificar §73 *tr* to decalcify
descalificar §73 *tr* to disqualify
descalzar §60 *tr* (*las botas, los guantes*) to take off; (*a una persona*) take the shoes or stockings off; undermine || *ref* to take one's shoes or stockings off; take one's gloves off; (*las botas, los guantes*) take off; (*el caballo*) lose a shoe
descal•zo -za *adj* barefooted; seedy, down at the heel
descamar *ref* to scale, scale off
descaminadamente *adv* off the road, on the wrong track
descaminar *tr* to mislead, lead astray || *ref* to get lost; run off the road
descamino *m* going astray; leading astray; nonsense; contraband, smuggled goods
descamisa•do -da *adj* shirtless, ragged || *m* wretch, ragamuffin
descampa•do -da *adj* free, open || *m* open country
descansadero *m* resting place, stopping place
descansa•do -da *adj* rested, refreshed; calm, restful
descansar *tr* to rest, relieve; (*la cabeza, el brazo*) rest, lean || *intr* to rest; lean; not worry; (*yacer en el sepulcro*) rest; **descansar en** to trust in
descanso *m* rest, time out; peace, quiet; (*de la escalera*) landing; (theat) intermission; (Chile) toilet
descantillar *tr* to chip off; deduct
descañonar *tr* to pluck; shave against the grain; gyp
descapiruzar §60 *tr* (Col) to muss, rumple, crumple
descapotable *adj & m* (aut) convertible
descara•do -da *adj* barefaced, brazen, saucy, sassy
descarar *ref* to be impudent; **descararse a** to have the nerve to
descarga *f* unloading; (*de un arma de fuego*) discharge; (com) discount; (elec) discharge;

descarga de aduana customhouse clearance; **descarga eléctrica** electric shock
descargar §44 *tr* to unload; (*de una deuda u obligación*) free; (*un arma de fuego*) discharge; (*un golpe*) strike, deal; (compu) to download; (elec) to discharge || *intr* to unload; (*un río*) empty; (*una calle, paseo*) open; (*una nube en lluvia*) burst || *ref* to unburden oneself; resign; **descargarse con** *or* **en uno de algo** to unload something on someone; **descargarse de** to get rid of; resign from; (*una imputación, un cargo*) clear oneself of
descargo *m* unloading; (*de una obligación*) discharge; (*del cargo que se hace a uno*) release, acquittal; receipt
descargue *m* unloading
descariño *m* coolness, indifference
descarnadamente *adv* right off the shoulder, bluntly
descarnar *tr* to remove the flesh from; chip; wear away; detach from earthly matters || *ref* to lose flesh
descaro *m* brazenness, effrontery
descarriar §77 *tr* to mislead, lead astray || *ref* to go wrong, go astray
descarrilamiento *m* derailment
descarrilar *intr* to jump the track; wander from the point || *ref* to jump the track
descartable *adj* disposable
descartar *tr* to cast aside, reject; discard || *ref* to shirk, evade; **descartarse de** (*un compromiso*) to shirk, evade
descarte *m* casting aside, rejection; discarding; (*cartas desechadas*) discard; shirking, evasion
descasar *tr* to divorce; disturb, disarrange
descascar §73 *tr* to husk, shell, peel || *ref* to break to pieces; jabber, talk too much
descascarar *tr* to shell, peel || *ref* to shell off, peel off
descascarillar *tr & ref* to shell, peel
descasta•do -da *adj* ungrateful, ungrateful to one's family
descaudala•do -da *adj* ruined, penniless
descendencia *f* descent
descendente *adj* descendent, descending; (*tren*) down
descender §51 *tr* to bring down, lower; (*la escalera*) descend, go down || *intr* to descend, go down; flow, run; decline
descendiente *mf* descendant
descenso *m* descent; (*de temperatura*) drop; decline
descentralizar §60 *tr* to decentralize
desceñi•do -da *adj* loose-fitting, loose
descepar *tr* to pull up by the roots; extirpate, exterminate
descerebrar *tr* to brain
descerraja•do -da *adj* corrupt, evil, wicked
deschavetar *intr* to get rattled; go mad; flip one's lid
descifrador *m* decoder
desciframiento *m* deciphering, decoding; resolving
descifrar *tr* to decipher, decode, figure out
desclasificar §73 *tr* to disqualify
descocer §16 *tr* to digest
descocholla•do -da *adj* (Chile) ragged
descoco *m* impudence, insolence
descodificador *m* decoder
descolar *tr* to dock, crop; (*a un empleado*) (CAm) to discharge, fire; (Mex) to slight, snub
descolgar §63 *tr* to unhook; take down, lower; (*el auricular*) pick up || *ref* to come down, come off; to show up suddenly; **descolgarse con** to blurt out
descollante *adj* prominent, outstanding; chief, main
descollar §61 *intr* to tower, stand out; (fig) to excel, stand out
descolón *m* (Mex) slight, snub
descolorar *tr & ref* to discolor, fade
descolori•do -da *adj* faded, off color
descomedi•do -da *adj* immoderate, excessive; rude, discourteous
descomedir §50 *ref* to be rude, be discourteous
descomer *intr* to have a bowel movement
descómo•do -da *adj* inconvenient
descompasa•do -da *adj* extreme, excessive
descompletar *tr* to break (*a set or series*)
descomponer §54 *tr* to decompose; disturb, disorganize; put out of order; set at odds || *ref* to decompose; (*una persona, la salud de una persona*) fall to pieces; (*el tiempo*) change for the worse; (*el rostro*) become distorted; (*un aparato*) get out of order; to lose one's temper; **descomponerse con** to get angry with
descomposición *f* decomposition; disorder, disorganization; discord
descompostura *f* decomposition; disorder, untidiness; brazenness
descompresión *f* decompression
descompues•to -ta *adj* out of order, brazen, discourteous; irritated; drunk
descomulgar §44 *tr* to excommunicate
descomunal *adj* huge, colossal, enormous, extraordinary; (coll) humongous
desconcerta•do -da *adj* out of order; disconcerted, baffled, bewildered; slovenly; unbridled
desconcertar §2 *tr* to put out of order; disturb, upset; (*un hueso*) dislocate; disconcert, bewilder
desconchabar *tr* to dislocate || *ref* to become dislocated; disagree, fall out
desconchado *m* scaly part of wall; (*en la porcelana*) chip
desconchar *tr & ref* to chip, chip off; scale off
desconcierto *m* disrepair; disorder, mismanagement; confusion; discomfiture; disagreement; lack of restraint; loose bowels
desconectar *tr* to detach; disconnect
desconfia•do -da *adj* distrustful, suspicious
desconfianza *f* distrust

desconfiar §77 *intr* to lose confidence; **desconfiar de** to lose confidence in, to distrust
desconformar *intr* to dissent, disagree || *ref* to not go well together
descongelación *f* thaw, thawing out; defrosting; (econ) unfreezing
descongelador *m* defroster
descongelante *mf* deicer
descongelar *tr* to melt; defrost, unfreeze; (*salarios, precios*) to unfreeze; (*cuenta*) to unfreeze
descongestión *f* decongestion; freeing up
descongestionar *tr* to decongest; free up
desconocer §22 *tr* to not know; disavow, disown; not recognize; slight, ignore; not see || *ref* to be unknown; be quite changed, be unrecognizable
desconocidamente *adv* unknowingly
desconoci•do -da *adj* unknown; strange, unfamiliar; ungrateful || *mf* unknown, unknown person
desconsentir §68 *tr* to not consent to
desconsidera•do -da *adj* ill-considered; inconsiderate
desconsola•do -da *adj* disconsolate, downhearted; (*estómago*) weak
desconsuelo *m* disconsolateness, grief; upset stomach
descontaminación *f* decontamination; **descontaminación de radiactividad** radioactive decontamination
descontar §61 *tr* to discount; deduct; take for granted; **dar por descontado que** to take for granted that
descontentadi•zo -za *adj* hard to please
desconten•to -ta *adj & m* discontent
descontinuar §21 *tr* to discontinue
descontrola•do -da *adj* uncontrolled; deregulated
descontrolar *tr* (com) deregulate; decontrol
desconvenar *tr* to call off
desconvenir §79 *intr* to disagree; not go together, not match; not be suitable || *ref* to disagree
desconvidar *tr* to cancel an invitation to; (*lo prometido*) take back
descopar *tr* to top (*a tree*)
descorazonar *tr* to discourage
descorchar *tr* to remove the bark from; (*una botella*) uncork; break into
descornar §61 *tr* to dehorn || *ref* to rack one's brains
descorrer *tr* to run back over; (*una cortina, un cerrojo*) draw || *intr & ref* to flow, run off
descortés *adj* discourteous, impolite
descortesía *f* discourtesy, impoliteness
descortezar §60 *tr* to strip the bark from; take the crust off; polish || *ref* to become polished
descoser *tr* to unstitch, rip || *ref* to loose one's tongue; (coll) to break wind
descosi•do -da *adj* disorderly, wild; indiscreet; desultory || *m* wild man; rip, open seam
descote *m* low neck
descoyuntar *tr* to dislocate; bore, annoy || *ref* (*p.ej., el brazo*) to throw out of joint
descrédito *m* discredit
descreer §43 *tr* to disbelieve; discredit || *intr* to disbelieve
descreí•do -da *adj* disbelieving, unbelieving || *mf* disbeliever, unbeliever
descriar §77 *ref* to spoil; waste away
describir §83 *tr* to describe
descripción *f* description
descripti•vo -va *adj* descriptive
descto. *abbr* **descuento**
descuadrar *intr* to disagree; **descuadrar con** (Mex) to displease
descuajar *tr* to liquefy, dissolve; uproot; discourage || *ref* to liquefy; drudge
descuartizar §60 *tr* to tear to pieces; quarter
descubierta *f* open pie; inspection; reconnoitering; (naut) scanning the horizon; **a la descubierta** openly; in the open; reconnoitering
descubiertamente *adv* clearly, openly
descubier•to -ta *adj* bareheaded; (*campo*) bare, barren; (*expuesto a reconvenciones*) under fire || *m* deficiency, shortage; overdraft; exposition of the Holy Sacrament; **al descubierto** in the open; unprotected; (*sin tener disponibles las acciones que se venden*) short, e.g., **vender al descubierto** to sell short || *f* see **descubierta**
descubri•dor -dora *mf* discoverer || *m* (mil) scout
descubrimiento *m* discovery
descubrir §83 *tr* to discover; uncover, lay open, reveal; invent; (*p.ej., una estatua*) unveil || *ref* to take off one's hat, uncover; be discovered; open one's heart
descuello *m* excellence, superiority; great height; haughtiness
descuento *m* discount; deduction, rebate
descuerar *tr* (Chile) to skin, flay; (Chile) to discredit, flay
descuerno *m* slight, snub
descuida•do -da *adj* careless, negligent, slipshod; slovenly, dirty; off guard
descuidar *tr* to overlook, neglect; divert, distract, relieve || *ref* to be careless, not bother; be diverted
descuide•ro -ra *mf* sneak thief
descuido *m* carelessness, negligence, neglect; slip, mistake, blunder; oversight; **al descuido** with studied carelessness; **en un descuido** when least expected
descuita•do -da *adj* carefree
desde *prep* since, from; after; **desde ahora** from now on; **desde entonces** since then, ever since; **desde hace** for, e.g., **estoy aquí desde hace cinco días** I've been here for five days; **desde luego** at once; of course; **desde que** since
desdecir §24 (*impv sg* **-dice**) *intr* to slip back; be out of harmony || *ref* — **desdecirse de** to take back, retract

desdén *m* scorn, disdain; **al desdén** with studied neglect
desdenta•do -da *adj* toothless
desdeñar *tr* to scorn, disdain || *ref* to be disdainful; **desdeñarse de** to loathe, despise; not deign to
desdeño•so -sa *adj* scornful, disdainful
desdicha *f* misfortune; indigence
desdicha•do -da *adj* unfortunate, unlucky; poor, wretched; backward, timid
desdinerar *tr* to impoverish
desdoblar *tr & intr* to unfold, spread open; split, divide
desdorar *tr* to remove the gold or gilt from; tarnish, sully; disparage
desdoro *m* tarnish, blemish, blot; disparagement
deseable *adj* desirable
desear *tr* to desire, wish
desecar §73 *tr & ref* to dry; drain
desechable *adj* disposable
desechar *tr* to discard, throw out, cast aside; underrate; blame, censure; (*la llave de una puerta*) turn
desecho *m* remainder; offal, rubbish; castoff; scorn, contempt; short cut; **desecho de hierro** scrap iron; **desechos militares** army surplus
desegregación *f* desegregation
desellar *tr* to unseal
desembalaje *m* unpacking
desembalar *tr* to unpack
desembarazar §60 *tr* to free, clear, empty, open || *ref* to free oneself; be cleared, emptied; **desembarazarse de** to get rid of
desembarazo *m* naturalness, lack of restraint; delivery, childbirth; **con desembarazo** naturally, readily
desembaracadero *m* wharf, pier, landing
desembarcar §73 *tr* to unload, debark, disembark || *intr* to land, debark, disembark; (*de un carruaje*) get out, alight; (*la escalera al plano bajo*) end || *ref* to land, debark, disembark
desembarco *m* landing, debarkation, disembarkation; (*de la escalera*) landing
desembarque *m* unloading, debarkation, disembarkation
desembocadura *f* (*de una calle*) opening, outlet; (*de un río*) mouth
desembocar §73 *intr* (*una calle*) open, to end; (*un río*) flow, empty
desembolsar *tr* to disburse, pay out
desembolso *m* disbursement, payment
desembragar §44 *tr* (*el motor*) to disengage || *intr* to throw the clutch out
desembrague *m* disengagement, clutch release
desembravecer §22 *tr* to tame; calm, quiet, pacify
desembriagar §44 *tr & ref* to sober up
desembrollar *tr* to untangle, unravel
desemejante *adj* — **desemejante de** dissimilar from or to, unlike; **desemejantes** dissimilar, unlike
desemejar *tr* to change, disfigure || *intr* to be different, not look alike
desempacar §73 *tr* to unpack, unwrap || *ref* to cool off, calm down
desempalagar §44 *tr* to rid of nausea || *ref* to get rid of nausea
desempañar *tr* (*el vidrio*) to wipe the steam, smear, *o* ice from; take the diaper off
desempapelar *tr* to unwrap; (*una pared, una habitación*) scrape the wallpaper from
desempaquetar *tr* to unpack; unwrap
desempatar *tr* to break the tie between; (*los votos*) break the tie in
desempate *m* tiebreaker; (pol) run-off; (sport) shootout
desempedrar §2 *tr* to remove the paving stones from; (*un sitio empedrado*) pound; **ir desempedrando la calle** to dash down the street
desempeñar *tr* (*un papel*) to play (*a rôle*); (*un cargo*) fill, perform; (*a uno de un empeño*) disengage; (*un deber*) discharge; free of debt; take out of hock || *ref* to get out of a jam; get out of debt
desempeño *m* acting, performance; disengagement; (*de un deber*) discharge; payment of a debt; taking out of hock
desempernar *tr* to unbolt
desemplea•do -da *adj & mf* unemployed
desempleo *m* unemployment; **desempleo en masa** mass unemployment
desempolvar *tr* to dust; renew, take up again || *ref* to brush up
desempolvorar *tr* to dust, dust off
desenamorar *tr* to alienate; *ref* to grow apart; **desenamorarse de** to get fed up with
desencadenar *tr* to unchain, unleash || *ref* to break loose
desencajar *tr* to dislocate; disconnect || *ref* to get out of joint; (*el rostro*) be contorted
desencaminar *tr* to lead astray, mislead
desencantamiento *m* disenchantment, disillusion
desencantar *tr* to disenchant, disillusion
desencantarar *tr* (*nombres o números*) to draw; (*un nombre o nombres*) exclude from balloting
desencanto *m* disenchantment, disillusion
desencarecer §22 *tr* to lower the price of || *intr & ref* to come down in price
desencerrar §2 *tr* to release, set free; disclose, reveal
desenchufar *tr* to unplug, disconnect
desencoger §17 *tr* to unfold, spread out || *ref* to relax, shake off one's timidity
desencolar *tr* to unglue || *ref* to become unglued
desenconar *tr* to take the soreness out of; calm down
desencriptar *tr* (compu) decrypt
desendiosar *tr* to bring down a peg
desenfadaderas *fpl* — **tener buenas desenfadaderas** to be resourceful
desenfada•do -da *adj* free, easy, unconstrained
desenfado *m* ease, naturalness; relaxation, calmness
desenfoca•do -da *adj* out of focus

desenfrena•do -da *adj* unbridled, wanton, licentious
desenfrenar *tr* to unbridle || *ref* to yield to temptation; fly into a passion; (*la tempestad, el viento*) break loose
desenfreno *m* unruliness, wantonness, licentiousness
desenfundar *tr* to take out of its sheath, bag, pillowcase, etc.
desenganchar *tr* to unhook, uncouple, unfasten, disengage; to unhitch
desenganche *m* unhooking, disengaging; unhitching
desengañar *tr* to disabuse, undeceive; disillusion; disappoint
desengaño *m* disabusing; disillusionment; disappointment; plain fact, plain truth
desengrana•do -da *adj* out of gear
desengranar *tr* to unmesh; disengage, throw out of gear
desengraso *m* (Chile) dessert
desenlace *m* outcome, result; (*de un drama, novela, etc.*) dénouement
desenlazar §60 *tr* to untie; solve; (*el nudo de un drama*) unravel
desenmarañar *tr* to disentangle; (*una cosa obscura*) unravel
desenmascarar *tr* to unmask || *ref* to take one's mask off
desenojar *tr* to appease, free of anger || *ref* to calm down; be amused
desenredar *tr* to disentangle; clear up || *ref* to extricate oneself
desenredo *m* disentanglement; (*de un drama, novela, etc.*) dénouement
desenrollar *tr* to unroll, unwind, unreel
desensartar *tr* to unstring, unthread
desensillar *tr* to unsaddle (*a horse*)
desentablar *tr* to disrupt; break off (*a bargain, friendship, etc.*)
desentender §51 *ref* — **desentenderse de** to take no part in, not participate in; affect ignorance of, pretend to be unaware of
desenterrar §2 *tr* to dig up; disinter; (fig) to unearth, dig up; (fig) to recall to mind
desentona•do -da *adj* out of tune, flat
desentonar *tr* to humble, bring down a peg || *intr* to be out of tune; be out of harmony || *ref* to talk loud and disrespectfully
desentono *m* dissonance, false note; loud tone of voice
desentornillar *tr* to unscrew
desentrampar *ref* to get out of debt
desentrañar *tr* to disembowel; figure out, unravel || *ref* to give away all that one has
desentrena•do -da *adj* out of training
desentronizar §60 *tr* to dethrone; strip of influence
desentumecer §22 *tr* to relieve of numbness || *ref* to be relieved of numbness
desenvainar *tr* to unsheathe; (*las uñas el animal*) show, stretch out; bare, uncover
desenvoltura *f* naturalness, ease of manner, offhandedness; fluency; lewdness, boldness (*chiefly in women*)
desenvolver §47 & §83 *tr* to unfold, unroll, unwrap; unwind; unravel, clear up; develop || *ref* to unroll; unwind; develop, evolve; extricate oneself; be forward
desenvuel•to -ta *adj* free and easy, offhand; fluent; brazen, bold, lewd
deseo *m* desire, wish
deseo•so -sa *adj* desirous, anxious
desequilibra•do -da *adj* unbalanced
desequilibrar *tr* to unbalance || *ref* to become unbalanced
desequilibrio *m* disequilibrium, imbalance; derangement, mental instability
deserción *f* desertion
desertar *tr & intr* to desert
desertor *m* deserter
deservicio *m* disservice
desesperación *f* despair; **ser una desesperación** to be unbearable
desespera•do -da *adj* despairing, desperate || *mf* desperate person
desesperanza *f* hopelessness
desesperanza•do -da *adj* hopeless
desesperanzar §60 *tr* to discourage || *ref* to lose hope
desesperar *tr* to drive to despair; exasperate || *intr* to lose hope; be exasperated || *ref* to be desperate, lose all hope
desestancar §73 *tr* to open up, unclog; make free of duty; open the market to
desestimar *tr* to hold in low regard; refuse, reject
deséxito *m* failure
desfachata•do -da *adj* brazen, impudent
desfachatez *f* brazenness, impudence
desfalcar §73 *tr & intr* to embezzle
desfalco *m* embezzlement
desfallecer §22 *tr* to weaken || *intr* to grow weak; faint, faint away; lose courage
desfalleci•do -da *adj* weak; faint
desfallecimiento *m* weakness; fainting; discouragement
desfavorable *adj* unfavorable
desfavoreci•do -da *adj* disadvantaged, underprivileged; unflattering
desfigurar *tr* to disfigure; distort, misrepresent; disguise; change, alter || *ref* to look different
desfiladero *m* defile, pass
desfilar *intr* to defile, parade, file by
desfile *m* review, parade
desflorar *tr* to deflower; mention in passing
desfogar §44 *tr* (*un horno*) to vent; (*la cal*) slake; (*una pasión*) give free rein to || *intr* (*una tempestad*) to break into rain and wind || *ref* to give vent to one's anger
desfondar *tr* to stave in; (*una nave*) bilge; (agr) to trench-plow
desforestar *tr* to deforest
desgaire *m* slovenliness; disdain, scorn; **al desgaire** scornfully; carelessly, with affected carelessness

desgajar *tr* to tear off; split off || *ref* to come off, come loose; arise, originate; separate, break away
desgana *f* lack of appetite; indifference; boredom; **a desgana** unwillingly, reluctantly
desgarba•do -da *adj* ungainly, uncouth
desgarrar *tr* to tear, rend; (*la flema*) cough up || *ref* to tear oneself away
desgarro *m* tear, rent; brazenness, effrontery; boasting, bragging; (Chile, Col) phlegm, mucus
desgasta•do -da *adj* worn (out); eroded; (*llanta*) treadless; (*tela*) threadbare
desgastar *tr* to wear away, wear down; to weaken, spoil || *ref* to wear away; grow weak, decline
desgaste *m* wear, wearing away
desgoberna•do -da *adj* ungovernable, uncontrollable
desgobernar §2 *tr* to misgovern; (*un hueso*) dislocate || *intr* (naut) to steer poorly || *ref* to twist and turn in dancing
desgobierno *m* misgovernment; dislocation
desgonzar §60 *tr* to unhinge; disconnect
desgracia *f* misfortune; (*acontecimiento adverso*) mishap; (*pérdida de favor*) disfavor, disgrace; (*aspereza en el trato*) gruffness; (*falta de gracia*) lack of charm; **correr con desgracia** to have no luck; **por desgracia** unfortunately
desgracia•do -da *adj* unfortunate; unattractive, unpleasant; disagreeable || *mf* wretch, unfortunate
desgraciar *tr* to displease; spoil || *ref* to spoil; fail; fall out, disagree
desgranar *tr* (*el maíz*) to shell; (*un racimo*) to pick the grapes from || *ref* (*piezas ensartadas*) to come loose
desgravación *f* tax relief; **desgravación fiscal** tax exemption
desgreña•do -da *adj* disheveled, straggly
desgreñar *tr* to dishevel || *ref* to get disheveled; pull each other's hair
deshabita•do -da *adj* unoccupied
deshabituar §21 *tr* to break a habit
deshacer §39 *tr* to undo; untie; take apart; wear away, consume, destroy; melt; put to flight, rout; (*un tratado o negocio*) violate || *ref* to get out of order; vanish, disappear; **deshacerse de** to get rid of; **deshacerse en** (*cumplidos*) to lavish; (*lágrimas*) burst into; **deshacerse por** to strive hard to
desharrapa•do -da *adj* ragged, in rags
deshebillar *tr* to unbuckle
deshebrar *tr* to unravel, unthread
deshecha *f* sham, pretense; dismissal; **hacer la deshecha** to feign, pretend; (Mex) to pretend lack of interest
deshe•cho -cha *adj* tired, exhausted, worn out; shattered, devastated, ruined; (meteor) violent, strong
deshelar §2 *tr* to thaw, melt; defrost; (aer) to deice || *intr* to thaw, melt
deshereda•do -da *adj* disinherited; underprivileged
desheredar *tr* to disinherit || *ref* to be a disgrace to one's family
desherrar §2 *tr* to unchain, unshackle; (*a una caballería*) unshoe
desherrumbrar *tr* to remove the rust from
deshidratar *tr* to dehydrate
deshielo *m* thaw; defrosting; détente
deshilachar *ref* to fray
deshila•do -da *adj* in a file; **a la deshilada** in single file; secretly || *m* openwork, drawn work
deshilar *tr* to unweave; (*reducir a hilos*) shred || *ref* to fray; get thin
deshilvana•do -da *adj* disconnected, desultory
deshincar §73 *tr* to pull up, pull out
deshinchar *tr* to deflate; (*la cólera*) give vent to || *ref* (*un tumor*) to go down; (*una persona orgullosa*) become deflated
deshojar *tr* to strip of leaves; tear the pages out of || *ref* to lose the leaves
deshollejar *tr* (*la uva*) to peel, skin; (*las habichuelas*) shell
deshollina•dor -dora *mf* chimney sweep; curious observer || *m* long-handled brush or broom
deshonestidad *f* dishonesty
deshones•to -ta *adj* dishonest; improper, indecent
deshonor *m* dishonor; disgrace
deshonorar *tr* to dishonor; degrade; disfigure
deshonra *f* dishonor; disrespect; **tener a deshonra** to consider improper
deshonrabue•nos *mf* (*pl* **-nos**) slanderer; (coll) black sheep
deshonrar *tr* to disgrace; (*a una mujer*) seduce; insult
deshonro•so -sa *adj* disgraceful, improper, discreditable
deshora *f* wrong time; **a deshora** at the wrong time, inopportunely; suddenly, unexpectedly
deshuesar *tr* (*la carne de un animal*) to bone; (*la fruta*) stone, take the pits out of
deshumedecer §22 *tr* to dehumidify
desidia *f* laziness, indolence
desidio•so -sa *adj* lazy, indolent || *mf* lazy person
desier•to -ta *adj* desert; deserted || *m* desert; wilderness
designar *tr* to designate; (*un trabajo*) plan
designio *m* design, plan, scheme
desigual *adj* unequal; unlike; rough, uneven; difficult; inconstant
desigualar *tr* to make unequal || *ref* to become unequal; (*aventajarse*) get ahead
desigualdad *f* inequality; roughness, unevenness
desilusión *f* disillusionment; disappointment
desilusionar *tr* to disillusion; disappoint || *ref* to become disillusioned; be disappointed
desimanar or **desimantar** *tr* to demagnetize
desimpresionar *tr* to undeceive
desinclina•do -da *adj* disinclined
desinencia *f* (gram) termination, ending

desinfectante *adj & m* disinfectant
desinfectar or **desinficionar** *tr* to disinfect
desinflación *f* deflation
desinflamar *tr* to take the soreness out of
desinflar *tr* to deflate; let the air out of; (*a una persona*) deflate
desinhibición *f* loss of inhibitions
desinsectación *f* insect control
desinsectar *intr* to exterminate insects
desintegración *f* disintegration
desintegrar *tr & ref* to disintegrate
desinterés *m* disinterestedness
desinteresa•do -da *adj* (*imparcial*) disinterested; (*poco interesado*) uninterested
desinteresar *ref* to lose interest
desintonizar §60 *tr* (rad) to tune out; (rad) to put out of tune
desintoxicación *f* detoxification; sobering (up)
desintoxicar *tr* to detoxify; sober up
desistir *intr* to desist
desjarretar *tr* to hamstring; bleed to excess
desjuicia•do -da *adj* lacking judgment, senseless
desjuntar *tr* to disjoin, separate
deslabonar *tr* to unlink; disconnect || *ref* to come loose; withdraw
deslastrar *tr* to unballast
deslava•do -da *adj* faded, colorless; barefaced || *mf* barefaced person
deslavar *tr* to wash superficially; fade, take the life out of
desleal *adj* disloyal; unfair
deslealtad *f* disloyalty
deslechar *tr* (Col) to milk
desleír §58 *tr* to dissolve; dilute; (*los colores, la pintura*) thin; (*sus pensamientos*) express too diffusely || *ref* to dissolve; become diluted
deslengua•do -da *adj* foul-mouthed, shameless
desliar §77 *tr* to untie, undo; unravel || *ref* to come untied
desligar §44 *tr* to untie, unbind; disentangle; excuse || *ref* to come untied, come loose
deslindar *tr* to mark the boundaries of; distinguish; define, explain
des•liz *m* (*pl* **-lices**) sliding; (*superficie lisa*) slide; slip, blunder; peccadillo, indiscretion
deslizade•ro -ra *adj* slippery || *m* slippery place; launching way
deslizadi•zo -za *adj* slippery
deslizador *m* (aer) glider
deslizar §60 *tr* to slide; (*decir por descuido*) let slip || *intr* to slide; slip; glide || *ref* to slide; slip; glide; slip away, sneak away; (*un reparo*) slip out; (*caer en una flaqueza*) slide back, backslide
deslomador *adj* backbreaking
deslomar *tr* to break or strain the back of || *ref* to break or strain one's back; **no deslomarse** to not strain oneself
desluci•do -da *adj* quiet, lackluster; dull, undistinguished
deslucir §45 *tr* to tarnish; deprive of charm, deprive of distinction; discredit
deslumbramiento *m* dazzle, glare; bewilderment, confusion
deslumbrante *adj* dazzling, ravishing; bewildering, confusing
deslumbrar *tr* to dazzle, bewilder, confuse
deslustra•do -da *adj* dull, flat, dingy; (*vidrio*) ground, frosted
deslustrar *tr* to tarnish; dull, dim; (*el vidrio*) frost; discredit || *ref* to tarnish
deslustre *m* tarnishing; dulling, dimming; discredit; (*del vidrio*) frosting
deslustro•so -sa *adj* ugly, unbecoming
desmadejar *tr* to enervate, weaken
desmagnetizar §60 *tr* to demagnetize
desmán *m* excess, misconduct; misfortune, mishap
desmanchar *tr* (Chile) to clean of spots
desmanda•do -da *adj* disobedient, unruly
desmandar *tr* to cancel, countermand || *ref* to misbehave; go away, keep apart; get out of control
desmanear *tr* to unfetter, unshackle
desmantela•do -da *adj* dilapidated
desmantelar *tr* to dismantle; (naut) to unmast; (naut) to unrig
desmaña *f* awkwardness, clumsiness
desmaña•do -da *adj* awkward, clumsy
desmaquillar *tr & ref* to take makeup off
desmaya•do -da *adj* faint, languid, weak; unconscious; (*color*) dull
desmayar *tr* to depress, discourage || *intr* to lose heart, be discouraged; falter || *ref* to faint
desmayo *m* depression, discouragement; faint, fainting fit; weeping willow
desmedi•do -da *adj* excessive; boundless, limitless
desmedir §50 *ref* to go too far, be impudent
desmedra•do -da *adj* weak, run-down
desmedrar *tr* to impair || *intr & ref* to decline, deteriorate
desmejorar *tr* to impair, spoil || *intr & ref* to decline, go into a decline
desmelenar *tr* to muss, dishevel, rumple
desmembrar §2 *tr* to dismember
desmemoria *f* forgetfulness
desmemoria•do -da *adj* forgetful
desmemoriar *ref* to become forgetful
desmentida *f* contradiction; **dar una desmentida a** to give the lie to
desmentir §68 *tr* to belie, give the lie to; conceal || *intr* to be out of line || *ref* to contradict oneself
desmenudear *tr & intr* (Col) to sell at retail
desmenuzar §60 *tr* to crumble; chop up; examine in detail; criticize harshly || *ref* to crumb, crumble
desmerece•dor -dora *adj* unworthy
desmerecer §22 *tr* to be unworthy of || *intr* to decline in value; **desmerecer de** to compare unfavorably with
desmesura *f* excess, lack of restraint
desmesura•do -da *adj* excessive, disproportionate; insolent || *mf* insolent person

desmigajar *tr & ref* to crumble, break up
desmigar §44 *tr & ref* to crumble, crumb
desmilitarizar §60 *tr* to demilitarize; **zona desmilitarizada** demilitarized zone
desmirria•do -da *adj* exhausted, emaciated, run-down
desmochar *tr* (*un árbol*) to top; (*al toro*) dehorn; (*una obra artística*) cut
desmodular *tr* to demodulate
desmola•do -da *adj* toothless
desmontable *adj* demountable, removable
desmontar *tr* (*un terreno*) to level; (*un bosque*) clear; dismantle, dismount, take apart, knock down; (*las piezas de artillería del enemigo*) knock out; (*al jinete el caballo*) unhorse, to throw; (*un arma de fuego*) uncock ‖ *ref* to dismount, alight
desmoralizar §60 *tr* to demoralize
desmoronadi•zo -za *adj* crumbly
desmoronar *tr* to wear away ‖ *ref* to wear away; crumble, decline
desmotadera *f* burler; **desmotadera de algodón** cotton gin
desmotar *tr* (*la lana*) to burl; (*el algodón*) gin
desmovilizar §60 *tr* to demobilize
desmurador *m* mouser
desnatadora *f* cream separator
desnatar *tr* to skim; remove the slag from; take the choicest part of
desnaturalizar §60 *tr* to denaturalize; (*el alcohol*) denature; alter, pervert
desnivel *m* unevenness; difference of level
desnivelar *tr* to make uneven ‖ *ref* to become uneven
desnudar *tr* to undress; strip, lay bare; (*la espada*) draw ‖ *ref* to undress, get undressed; become evident; **desnudarse de** to get rid of
desnudez *f* nakedness, nudity; bareness
desnudista *mf* nudist
desnu•do -da *adj* naked, nude; bare; destitute, penniless ‖ *m* nudity; (fa) nude; **desnudo integral** full-frontal nude
desnutrición *f* undernourishment, malnutrition
desnutri•do -da *adj* undernourished
desobedecer *tr & intr* to disobey
desobediencia *f* disobedience
desobediente *adj* disobedient
desocupación *f* unemployment; idleness, leisure
desocupa•do -da *adj* unemployed; idle; free, unoccupied, vacant, empty ‖ *mf* unemployed person
desocupar *tr* to empty, vacate, clear out ‖ *intr* (*una mujer*) to be delivered ‖ *ref* to become empty, vacated; become unemployed, become idle
desodorante *adj & m* deodorant
desodorizar §60 *tr* to deodorize
desoír §48 *tr* to not hear, pretend not to hear
desolación *f* desolation
desola•do -da *adj* desolate, disconsolate
desolar §61 *tr* to desolate, lay waste ‖ *ref* to be desolate, be disconsolate
desoldar §61 *tr* to unsolder ‖ *ref* to come unsoldered
desolla•do -da *adj* brazen, impudent
desollar §61 *tr* to skin, flay; harm, hurt; **desollar vivo** (*hacer pagar mucho más de lo justo*) fleece, skin alive; (*murmurar acerbamente de*) (coll) to flay
desopilar *ref* to roar with laughter
desopinar *tr* to defame, discredit
desorbita•do -da *adj* popeyed; crazy
desorbitar *tr* to pop wide-open
desorden *m* disorder
desordena•do -da *adj* disorderly, unruly; straggly
desordenar *tr* to put out of order ‖ *ref* to get out of order; be unruly; go too far
desoreja•do -da *adj* infamous, degraded; (*que canta mal*) (Peru) off tune; (Cuba) shameless; (Cuba) spendthrift, prodigal; (Guat) stupid; (Chile) without handles
desorganizar §60 *tr* to disorganize
desorientación *f* disorientation; confusedness; going astray
desorientar *tr* to lead astray; confuse
desovar *intr* to spawn
desove *m* spawning; spawning season
desovillar *tr* to unravel, disentangle; encourage
desoxidar *tr* to deoxidize; clean of rust
despabiladeras *fpl* snuffers
despabila•do -da *adj* wide-awake
despabilar *tr* (*una candela*) to snuff, trim; (*la hacienda*) dissipate; (*una comida*) dispatch; (*robar*) snitch; (*matar*) dispatch ‖ *ref* to brighten up; wake up; leave, disappear
despachaderas *fpl* surly reply; resourcefulness
despacha•do -da *adj* brazen, impudent; quick, resourceful
despachante *m* (Arg) clerk; **despachante te de aduana** (Arg) customhouse broker
despachar *tr* to send, ship; dispatch, expedite; discharge, dismiss; decide, settle; sell; (*a los parroquianos*) wait on; (*la correspondencia*) attend to; hurry; (*matar*) dispatch, kill ‖ *intr* to hurry; make up one's mind; work, be employed ‖ *ref* to hurry; (*una mujer*) be delivered; speak out
despacho *m* shipping; dispatch, expedition; discharge, dismissal; (*tienda*) store, shop; (*aposento para el estudio*) study; (*aposento para los negocios*) office; (*comunicación por telégrafo o teléfono*) dispatch; (Chile) attic; **despacho de billetes** ticket office; **despacho de localidades** box office; **estar al despacho** to be pending; **tener buen despacho** to be expeditious
despachurrar *tr* to crush, smash, squash; (*dejar sin tener que replicar*) squelch; (*lo que uno trata de decir*) butcher, murder
despacio *adv* slow, slowly; at leisure; (Arg, Chile) in a low voice
despacio•so -sa *adj* slow, easy-going
despampanante *adj* stunning, terrific
despampanar *tr* (*las vides*) to prune, trim; astound ‖ *intr* to give vent to one's feelings ‖ *ref* to fall and hurt oneself

despancar §73 *tr* to husk (*corn*)
desparejar *tr* (*dos cosas que forman pareja*) to break, separate (*a pair*)
desparpajar *tr* to tear apart || *intr* to rant, rave || *ref* to rant, rave; (CAm, Mex, W-I) to wake up
desparramar *tr* to scatter, spread; (*el agua*) to spill; (*la hacienda*) squander || *ref* to scatter, spread; make merry
despartir *tr* to divide, part, separate; to reconcile
despatarrada *f* split (*in dancing*); **hacer la despatarrada** to stretch out on the floor pretending to be ill or injured
despatarrar *tr* to dumbfound || *ref* to open one's legs wide, fall down with legs outspread; lie motionless; be dumbfounded
despavori•do -da *adj* terrified
despea•do -da *adj* footsore
despear *ref* to get sore feet
despecha•do -da *adj* spiteful, enraged
despechar *tr* to spite, enrage; (*destetar*) to wean || *ref* to be enraged; despair, lose hope
despecho *m* spite; despair; weaning; **a despecho de** despite, in spite of; **por despecho** out of spite
despechugar §44 *tr* to carve the breast of || *ref* (coll) to go with bare breast, bare one's breast
despecti•vo -va *adj* contemptuous; (gram) pejorative
despedazar §60 *tr* to break to pieces; (*la honra de uno*) to ruin; (*el alma de una persona*) break || *ref* to break to pieces; **despedazarse de risa** to split one's sides laughing
despedida *f* farewell, leave-taking; (*de una carta*) close, conclusion; (*copla final*) envoi
despedir §50 *tr* to throw; emit, send forth; discharge, dismiss; (*al que sale de la casa*) see off; (*un mal pensamiento*) banish; **despedir en la puerta** to see to the door || *ref* to take leave, say good-by; give up one's job; **despedirse a la francesa** to take French leave; **despedirse de** to take leave of, say good-by to
despega•do -da *adj* gruff, surly
despegar §44 *tr* to loosen, unglue, unseal; open; separate, detach || *intr* (aer) to take off || *ref* to come off; **despegarse con** to be unbecoming to
despego *m* dislike, indifference
despegue *m* (aer) takeoff; **despegue vertical** vertical takeoff
despeina•do -da *adj* unkempt
despeja•do -da *adj* (*frente*) wide; (*día, cielo*) clear, cloudless; bright, sprightly; (*en el trato*) unconstrained
despejar *tr* to clarify, explain; free; (*una incógnita*) (math) to find || *ref* to brighten up, cheer up; (*el cielo, el tiempo; una situación dificultosa*) clear up; (*un borracho*) sober up
despejo *m* ease, naturalness; talent, intelligence, understanding
despellejar *tr* to skin, flay; slander, malign
despelotar *ref* to disrobe
despeluzar §60 *tr* to muss the hair of; make the hair of (*a person*) stand on end || *ref* (*el pelo*) to stand on end
despeluznante *adj* hair-raising, horrifying
despenalización *f* legalization
despenalizar §60 *tr* to legalize; condone
despenar *tr* to console; (coll) to kill; (Chile) to deprive of hope
despender *tr* to spend, squander; (*el tiempo*) to waste
despensa *f* pantry; food supplies; day's marketing; stewardship; (naut) storeroom
despensero *m* butler, steward; (naut) storekeeper
despeñadamente *adv* hastily; boldly
despeñade•ro -ra *adj* precipitous || *m* precipice; danger, risk
despeñadi•zo -za *adj* precipitous
despeñar *tr* to hurl, throw, push || *ref* to hurl oneself, jump; fall headlong; (*en vicios, pecados, pasiones*) plunge downward
despeño *m* plunge; headlong fall; ruin, failure, collapse; (coll) loose bowels
despepitar *tr* to seed, remove the seeds from || *ref* to rush around madly, go around screaming; **despepitarse por** to be mad about
desperdicia•do -da *adj* wasteful, prodigal || *mf* spendthrift, prodigal
desperdiciar *tr* to waste, squander; (*la ocasión de aprovechar una cosa*) miss, lose
desperdicio *m* waste, squandering; **desperdicios** waste; waste products; by-products; rubbish; **no tener desperdicio** to be excellent, be useful
desperdigar §44 *tr* to separate, scatter
desperecer §22 *ref* to long eagerly
desperezar §60 *ref* to stretch, stretch one's arms and legs
desperfecto *m* blemish, flaw, imperfection
desperna•do -da *adj* footsore, weary
desperta•dor -dora *mf* awakener || *m* alarm clock; warning
despertar §2 *tr* to awaken; arouse, stir || *intr & ref* to awaken, wake up
despestañar *tr* to pluck the eyelashes of || *ref* to look hard, strain one's eyes
despiada•do -da *adj* cruel, pitiless
despichar *tr* to squeeze dry; (Col, Chile) to crush, flatten || *intr* (coll) to croak, die
despidiente *m* stick placed between a hanging scaffold and wall; **despidiente de agua** flashing
despido *m* layoff; dismissal, discharge
despier•to -ta *adj* wide-awake, alert; **soñar despierto** to daydream
despilfarra•do -da *adj* wasteful; ragged || *mf* prodigal; raggedy person
despilfarrar *tr* to squander, waste || *ref* to spend recklessly
despilfarro *m* squandering, waste, extravagance; slovenliness
despintar *tr* to remove the paint from; disfigure,

distort, spoil; **no despintarle a uno los ojos** to not take one's eyes from a person || *intr* to decline, slip back; **despintar de** to be unworthy of || *ref* to fade, wash off; **no despintársele a uno** to not fade from one's memory

despiojar *tr* to delouse; (coll) to free from poverty

despique *m* revenge

despistar *tr* to outwit, throw off the track || *ref* to run off the track, run off the road

desplacer *m* displeasure || **§22** to displease

desplantar *tr* to uproot; throw out of plumb || *ref* to get out of plumb; lose one's upright posture

desplaya•do -da *adj* broad, open, wide || *m* (Arg) wide sandy beach

desplayar *tr* to widen, spread out || *ref* (*el mar*) to recede from the beach

desplaza•do -da *adj* displaced || *mf* displaced person

desplazar §60 *tr* (*cierto peso de agua*) to displace; move, transport || *ref* to move

desplegar §66 *tr* to unfold, spread; display; explain; (compu) to run; (mil) to deploy || *ref* to unfold, spread out; (mil) to deploy

despliegue *m* unfolding, spreading out; display; (mil) deployment

desplomar *tr* to throw out of plumb || *ref* to get out of plumb; collapse, tumble; fall down in a faint; (*un trono*) crumble; (aer) to pancake

desplome *m* leaning; collapse, tumbling; falling in a faint; downfall; (aer) pancaking

desplumar *tr* to pluck; (*dejar sin dinero*) fleece || *ref* to molt

despoblado *m* wilderness, deserted spot

despoblar §61 *tr* to depopulate; lay waste; clear, lay bare

despojamiento *m* (econ) divestment

despojar *tr* to strip, despoil, divest; dispossess || *ref* to undress; **despojarse de** to divest oneself of; (*ropa*) take off

despojo *m* dispoilment; dispossession; booty, plunder, spoils; prey, victim; **despojos** scraps, leavings; mortal remains; second-hand building materials

despolarizar §60 *tr* to depolarize

despolvar *tr* to dust

despolvorear *tr* to dust, dust off; scatter

desportillar *tr* to chip, nick || *ref* to chip, chip off

desposa•do -da *adj* handcuffed; newly married || *mf* newlywed

desposar *tr* to marry || *ref* to be betrothed, get engaged; get married

desposeer §43 *tr* to dispossess || *ref* — **desposeerse de** to divest oneself of

desposorios *mpl* betrothal, engagement; marriage, nuptials

despostar *tr* to cut up, carve; butcher

déspota *m* despot

despóti•co -ca *adj* despotic

despotismo *m* despotism

despotricar §73 *intr & ref* to rave, rant

despreciable *adj* contemptible, despicable

despreciar *tr* to scorn, despise; slight, snub; overlook, forgive; reject || *ref* — **despreciarse de** to not deign to

despreciati•vo -va *adj* contemptuous, scornful

desprecio *m* scorn, contempt; slight, snub

desprender *tr* to loosen, unfasten, detach; emit, give off; (chem) to liberate || *ref* to come loose, come off; issue, come forth; **desprenderse de** to give up, part with; be deduced from

desprendi•do -da *adj* generous, disinterested

desprendimiento *m* loosening, detachment; emission, liberation; generosity, disinterestedness; landslide; (chem) liberation

despreocupación *f* relaxation; impartiality; indifference

despreocupa•do -da *adj* relaxed, unconcerned; impartial; indifferent

despreocupante *adj* relaxing

despreocupar *ref* to relax; **despreocuparse de** to forget about, be unconcerned about

desprestigiar *tr* to disparage, run down || *ref* to lose caste, lose one's standing, lose face

desprestigio *m* disparagement; loss of standing, discredit

despreveni•do -da *adj* off one's guard; **coger a uno desprevenido** to catch someone unawares

desproporciona•do -da *adj* disproportionate

despropósito *m* absurdity, nonsense; malapropism

desproveer §43 & §83 *tr* to deprive

desprovis•to -ta *adj* destitute; **desprovisto de** lacking, devoid of

después *adv* after, afterwards; **después de** after; **después (de) que** after

despuli•do -da *adj* ground (*glass*)

despumar *tr* to skim

despuntar *tr* to dull, blunt; (*un cabo o punta*) (naut) to double, round || *intr* to begin to sprout; (*empezar a amanecer*) dawn; stand out || *ref* to get dull

desquiciar *tr* to unhinge; shake loose, upset; unsettle, perturb; overthrow, undermine

desquitar *tr* to recover, retrieve; compensate || *ref* to retrieve a loss; get revenge, get even

desquite *m* recovery, retrieval; retaliation, revenge; (sport) return match

desrazonable *adj* unreasonable

desrielar *intr* to jump the track

destaca•do -da *adj* outstanding, distinguished

destacamiento *m* (mil) detachment; (mil) detail

destacar §73 *tr* to highlight, point up; emphasize; make stand out; (mil) to detach; (mil) to detail || *intr* to stand out, be conspicuous || *ref* to stand out, project; (fig) to stand out

destajar *tr* to arrange for, establish the terms for; (*la baraja*) cut; carve up

destaje•ro -ra or destajista *mf* pieceworker, jobber; free lance

destajo *m* piecework; job, contract; **a destajo** by the piece, by the job; freelancing; **hablar a destajo** to talk too much

destapar *tr* to open, uncover, take the lid off; uncock, unplug; reveal || *ref* to get uncovered; throw off the covers; unbosom oneself
destaponar *tr* to uncock, unplug; (*una botella; las fosas nasales*) unstop
destartala•do -da *adj* tumble-down, ramshackle
destazar §60 *tr* to carve up
destechar *tr* to unroof
destejar *tr* to remove the tiles from; leave unprotected
destejer *tr* to unbraid, unknit, unweave; upset, disturb
destellar *tr & intr* to flash
destello *m* flash, beam, sparkle
destempla•do -da *adj* disagreeable, unpleasant; inharmonious, out of tune; indisposed; (*clima; pulso*) irregular
destemplanza *f* unpleasantness; discord; indisposition; (*del pulso*) irregularity; (*del tiempo*) inclemency; excess
destemple *m* dissonance; indisposition; disorder, disturbance
desteñir §72 *tr* to discolor || *intr & ref* to fade
desternillante *adj* sidesplitting
desternillar *ref* — **desternillarse de risa** to split one's sides with laughter
desterra•do -da *adj* exiled || *mf* exile
desterrar §2 *tr* to exile, banish; (fig) to banish
destetar *tr* to wean || *ref* — **destetarse con** to have known since childhood
destete *m* weaning
destiempo *m* — **a destiempo** untimely
destiento *m* surprise, shock
destierro *m* exile; backwoods
destilación *f* distillation
destiladera *f* still; scheme, stratagem
destilar *tr* to distill; filter; exude || *intr* to drip
destilatorio *m* distillery; (*alambique*) still
destilería *f* distillery
destinación *f* destination
destinar *tr* to destine; assign, designate
destinata•rio -ria *mf* addressee; consignee; (*de homenaje, aplausos*) recipient
destino *m* (*lugar a donde va una persona o una remesa*) destination; (*suerte, encadenamiento fatal de los sucesos*) fate, destiny; employment; place of employment; **con destino a** bound for
destituir §20 *tr* to deprive; dismiss, discharge
destorcer §74 *tr* to untwist, straighten || *ref* to become untwisted; (naut) to drift
destornilla•do -da *adj* rash, reckless, out of one's head
destornillador *m* screwdriver
destornillar *tr* to unscrew || *ref* to lose one's head, go berserk
destoser *ref* to cough (*artificially, to attract attention*)
destrabar *tr* to loosen, untie, detach
destraillar §4 *tr* unleash
destral *m* hatchet
destreza *f* skill, dexterity
destripacuen•tos *m* (*pl* **-tos**) (coll) butter-in
destripar *tr* to disembowel, gut; crush, mangle; spoil (*a story by telling its outcome*)
destriunfar *tr* to force to play trump
destrocar §81 *tr* to swap back again
destronar *tr* to dethrone; overthrow
destroncar §73 *tr* to chop down; chop off; ruin; exhaust, wear out
destrozar §60 *tr* to shatter, break to pieces; destroy; squander; (*al ejército enemigo*) wipe out
destrozo *m* havoc, destruction; rout, annihilation, defeat
destrucción *f* destruction
destructi•vo -va *adj* destructive
destructor *m* (nav) destroyer
destruir §20 *tr* to destroy || *ref* (alg) to cancel each other
desuellaca•ras *m* (*pl* **-ras**) sloppy barber; scoundrel
desuello *m* skinning, flaying; shamelessness; (*precio excesivo*) (coll) highway robbery
desuncir §36 *tr* to unyoke
desunir *tr* to disunite; take apart || *ref* to disunite; come apart
desusa•do -da *adj* obsolete, out of use; uncommon, unusual; **estar desusado** (*perder la práctica*) to be rusty
desuso *m* disuse; **caído en desuso** obsolete
desvaí•do -da *adj* lank, ungainly; (*color*) dull
desvainar *tr* to shell
desvali•do -da *adj* helpless, destitute
desvalijar *tr* (*una valija, baúl, etc.*) to rifle; rob, wipe out
desvalorar *tr* to devalue
desvalorizar §60 *tr* to devalue
desván *m* garret, loft
desvanecedor *m* (phot) mask
desvanecer §22 *tr* to dispel, dissipate; (*una conspiración*) break up; (*la sospecha*) banish; (phot) to mask || *ref* to disappear, vanish, evanesce; evaporate; faint, faint away, swoon; (rad) to fade
desvanecimiento *m* disappearance, evanescence; dissipation; pride, vanity; faintness, fainting spell; (phot) masking; (rad) fading, fadeout
desvaria•do -da *adj* delirious, raving
desvariar §77 *intr* to be delirious, rave, rant
desvarío *m* delirium, raving; absurdity, nonsense, extravagance; whim, caprice; inconstancy
desvela•do -da *adj* wakeful, sleepless; watchful, vigilant; anxious, worried
desvelar *tr* to keep awake, not let sleep || *ref* to keep awake, go without sleep; be watchful, be vigilant; **desvelarse por** to be anxious about, be worried about
desvelo *m* wakefulness, sleeplessness; watchfulness, vigilance; anxiety, worry, concern
desvenar *tr* to strip (*tobacco*)
desvencija•do -da *adj* rickety, ramshackle
desvencijar *tr* to break, tear apart || *ref* to go to rack and ruin

desvendar *tr* to unbandage, undress
desventaja *f* disadvantage
desventaja•do -da *adj* disadvantaged; deprived
desventajo•so -sa *adj* disadvantageous
desventura *f* misfortune
desventura•do -da *adj* unfortunate; faint-hearted; stingy
desvergonza•do -da *adj* shameless, impudent
desvergüenza *f* shamelessness, impudence
desvestir §50 *tr & ref* to undress
desviación *f* deviation, deflection; detour; (rad, telv) drift
desviacionismo *m* deviationism
desviacionista *mf* deviationist
desviadero *m* (rr) siding, turnout
desvia•do -da *adj* devious; (gone) astray; off track; lost
desviar §77 *tr* to deviate, deflect; turn aside; dissuade; parry, ward off; (rr) to switch || *ref* to deviate, deflect; turn aside; branch off; be dissuaded
desvío *m* deviation, deflection; coldness, indifference; detour; (rr) siding, sidetrack
desvirgar §44 *tr* to deflower, ravish
desvirtuar §21 *tr* to weaken, spoil, impair
desvivir *ref* — **desvivirse por** to be crazy about; **desvivirse por** + *inf* to be eager to + *inf*, to do one's best to + *inf*
desvolvedor *m* wrench
desvolver §47 & §83 *tr* to alter, change; (*la tierra*) turn up; (*una tuerca o tornillo*) loosen, unscrew
detall *m* — **al detall** at retail
detalladamente *adv* in detail
detallar *tr* to detail, tell in detail; retail, sell at retail
detalle *m* detail; retail; **ahí está el detalle** that's the point
detallista *mf* retailer; person fond of details
detección *f* detection
detectar *tr* to detect
detective *m* detective
detector *m* detector; **detector de incendios** smoke detector; **detector de mentiras** lie detector
detención *f* detention, detainment; delay; care, thoroughness; arrest; **detención domiciliaria** house arrest; **detención preventiva** preventive detention
detener §71 *tr* to detain; stop; arrest; keep, retain; (*el aliento*) hold || *ref* to stop; linger, tarry
detenidamente *adv* carefully, thoroughly
deteni•do -da *adj* careful, thorough; hesitant, timid; stingy, mean || *mf* person held in custody
detenimiento *m* var of **detención**
detergente *adj & m* detergent
deteriorar *tr & ref* to deteriorate
deterioro *m* deterioration
determinación *f* determination; decision
determina•do -da *adj* determined, resolute; (*artículo*) (gram) definite
determinar *tr* to determine; cause, bring about || *ref* to decide
detestar *tr* to detest; curse; **detestar** + *inf* to hate to + *inf*
detonar *intr* to detonate
detraer §75 *tr* to withdraw, take away, detract; defame, vilify
detrás *adv* behind; **detrás de** behind, back of; **por detrás** behind; behind one's back; **por detrás de** behind the back of
detrimento *m* harm, detriment
deuce *m* (sport) deuce
deuda *f* debt; indebtedness
deu•do -da *mf* relative || *m* kinship || *f* see **deuda**
deu•dor -dora *adj* indebted || *mf* debtor; **deudor hipotecario** mortgagor; **deudor moroso** delinquent (*in payment*)
devalar *intr* (naut) to drift from the course
devaluación *f* devaluation
devanar *tr* to wind, roll; (*un cuento*) to unfold || *ref* (CAm, Mex, W-I) to roll with laughter; (CAm, Mex, W-I) to writhe in pain
devanear *intr* to talk nonsense; loaf around
devaneo *m* nonsense; loafing; flirtation
devastación *f* devastation
devastar *tr* to devastate
develar *tr* to reveal; (*p.ej., una estatua*) unveil
devengar §44 *tr* (*salarios*) to earn; (*intereses*) draw, earn
devoción *f* devotion
devolución *f* return, restitution; **devolución de impuestos** tax refund
devolver §47 & §83 *tr* to return, give back, send back; pay back; (coll) to vomit || *ref* to return, come back
devorar *tr* to devour
devo•to -ta *adj* devout; devoted; devotional || *mf* devotee; devout person; **devoto del volante** car enthusiast || *m* object of worship
D.F. *abbr* **Distrito Federal**
d/f *abbr* **días fecha**
dho. *abbr* **dicho**
día *m* day; daytime; daylight; **al día** per day; up to date; **al otro día** on the following day; **buenos días** good morning; **dar los días a** to wish (*someone*) many happy returns of the day; **de día** in the daytime, in the daylight; **día de años** birthday; **día de ayuno** fast day; **día de carne** meat day; **día de entresemana** weekday; **día de inauguración** (fa) private view; **Día de la Hispanidad, Día de la Raza** Columbus Day; **Día de la Madre** Mother's Day; **Día del Juicio Final** judgment day; **Día de los Caídos** Memorial Day; **Día de los Difuntos, Día de los Muertos** All Souls' Day; **Día de los Inocentes** (*día de engañabobos*) April Fools' Day (December 28th or April first); **Día del Padre** Father's Day; **día de maniobras** (mil) field day; **Día de Ramos** Palm Sunday; **Día de Reyes** Epiphany; **Día de Todos los Santos** All Saints' Day; **día de trabajo, día laborable** workday, weekday; **Día del Trabajo** Labor Day; **día de vigilia**

fast day; **día festivo oficial** legal holiday; **día hábil** workday; **día inhábil, día libre** day off; holiday; **día lectivo** school day; **día puente, día sandwich** day off between two holidays; **el Día de Año Nuevo** New Year's Day; **el Día de la Bandera** Flag Day (June 14th); **el día menos pensado** when least expected; **el mejor día** some fine day; **en cuatro días** in a few days; **en pleno día** in broad daylight; **en su día** in due time; **ocho días** a week; **poner al día** to bring up to date; **quince días** two weeks, a fortnight; **tener sus días** to be up in years; **un día sí y otro no** every other day; **vivir al día** to live from hand to mouth

diabetes *f* diabetes

diabéti•co -ca *adj & mf* diabetic

diablillo *m* imp

diablo *m* devil; (Chile) ox-drawn log drag; **ahí será el diablo** (coll) there will be the devil to pay; **diablo cojuelo** tricky devil; **diablos azules** delirium tremens

diablura *f* devilment, deviltry, mischief

diabóli•co -ca *adj* devilish, diabolical

diaconisa *f* deaconess

diácono *m* deacon

diacríti•co -ca *adj* diacritical

diadema *f* diadem; (*adorno femenino*) tiara

diáfa•no -na *adj* diaphanous

diafragma *m* diaphragm

diagno•sis *f* (*pl* **-sis**) diagnosis

diagnosticar §73 *tr* to diagnose

diagonal *adj* diagonal || *f* diagonal, bias

diagrama *m* diagram

dialecto *m* dialect

dialogar *intr* to talk

diálogo *m* dialogue

diamante *m* diamond; **diamantes** (*palo de la baraja norteamericana*) diamonds

diametral or **diamétri•co -ca** *adj* diametrical

diámetro *m* diameter

diana *f* bull's-eye; dartboard; (mil) reveille; **hacer diana** to hit the bull's-eye

diantre *m* devil || *interj* the devil!, the deuce!

diapasón *m* tuning fork; pitch pipe; (*p. ej., del violín*) finger board; **bajar el diapasón** to lower one's voice, to change one's tune

diapositiva *f* slide, lantern slide

dia•rio -ria *adj* daily || *m* diary; daily, daily paper; **diario de navegación** logbook; **diario hablado** newscast

diarismo *m* journalism

diarrea *f* diarrhea

diástole *f* diastole

diatermia *f* diathermy

diatriba *f* diatribe, screed

dibujado *m* (compu) display

dibujante *mf* sketcher, illustrator || *m* draftsman; **dibujante de chistes** cartoonist

dibujar *tr* to draw, sketch, design; outline || *ref* to be outlined; appear, show

dibujo *m* drawing, sketch, design; outline; **dibujo al carbón** charcoal drawing; **dibujo animado** animated cartoon; **no meterse en dibujos** to attend to one's business

di•caz *adj* (*pl* **-caces**) sarcastic, witty

dicción *f* diction; word

diccionario *m* dictionary; **diccionario bilingüe** bilingual dictionary; **diccionario de autoridades** dictionary of authorities (*definitions based upon quotations*); **diccionario de ideas afines, diccionario ideológico** thesaurus; **diccionario de sinónimos** synonym dictionary *o* thesaurus; **diccionario de uso** usage dictionary; **diccionario enciclopédico** encyclopedic dictionary; **diccionario etimológico** etymological dictionary

díceres *mpl* sayings; rumor(s)

dicha *f* happiness; luck; **por dicha** by chance

dicharache•ro -ra *adj* obscene, vulgar

dicharacho *m* obscenity, vulgarity; wisecrack

di•cho -cha *adj* said; **dicho y hecho** no sooner said than done; **mejor dicho** rather; **tener por dicho** to consider settled || *m* saying; promise of marriage, one's word; witticism; insult; **dicho de las gentes** talk, hearsay, gossip || *f* see **dicha**

dicho•so -sa *adj* happy; lucky, fortunate; annoying, tiresome

diciembre *m* December

dicloruro *m* dichloride

dicotomía *f* dichotomy; (*entre médicos*) split fee

dictado *m* dictation; **escribir al dictado** to take dictation; (*lo que otro dicta*) to take down

dictador *m* dictator

dictadura *f* dictatorship

dictáfono *m* dictaphone

dictamen *m* dictum, judgment, opinion

dictar *tr* to dictate; (*una ley*) promulgate; inspire, suggest; (*una conferencia*) give, deliver (*a lecture*)

dicterio *m* taunt, insult

didácti•co -ca *adj* didactic

diecinueve *adj & pron* nineteen || *m* nineteen; (*en las fechas*) nineteenth

diecinuevea•vo -va *adj & m* nineteenth

dieciocha•vo -va *adj m* eighteenth

dieciocho *adj & pron* eighteen || *m* eighteen; (*en las fechas*) eighteenth

dieciséis *adj & pron* sixteen || *m* sixteen; (*en las fechas*) sixteenth

dieciseisa•vo -va *adj & m* sixteenth

diecisiete *adj & pron* seventeen || *m* seventeen; (*en las fechas*) seventeenth

diecisietea•vo -va *adj & m* seventeenth

Diego *m* James

diente *m* tooth; (*de elefante y otros animales*) tusk, fang; (*de peine, sierra, rastrillo*) tooth; (*de rueda dentada*) cog; clove (of garlic); **dar diente con diente** to shake all over; **decir entre dientes** to mutter, to mumble; **diente canino** eyetooth, canine tooth; **diente de leche** milk tooth, baby tooth; **diente de león** dandelion; **estar a diente** to be famished; **tener buen diente** to be a hearty eater; **traer**

entre dientes to have a grudge against; to talk about
diére•sis *f* (*pl* **-sis**) diaeresis; (*señal que indica la metafonía*) umlaut
diesel *m* diesel engine; diesel fuel *o* oil; (*coche*) diesel
dieseléctri•co -ca *adj* diesel-electric
dies•tro -tra *adj* right; handy, skillful; shrewd, sly; favorable; **a diestro y siniestro** wildly, right and left || *m* expert fencer; bullfighter on foot; matador; halter, bridle || *f* right hand; **juntar diestra con diestra** to join forces
dieta *f* diet; **dieta blanda** soft food diet; **dieta hídrica** *or* **líquida** liquid diet; **dietas** per diem; **estar a dieta** to diet, be on a diet
dietario *m* family budget
dietista *mf* dietitian
diez *adj & pron* ten; **las diez** ten o'clock || *m* ten; (*en las fechas*) tenth
diezmar *tr* (*causar gran mortandad en*) to decimate; (*pagar el diezmo de*) tithe
diezmo *m* tithe
difamación *f* defamation, vilification
difamar *tr* to defame, vilify
diferencia *f* difference; **a diferencia de** unlike; **partir la diferencia** to split the difference
diferenciar *tr* to differentiate || *intr* (*discordar*) to differ, dissent || *ref* (*distinguirse una cosa de otra*) to differ, be different
diferente *adj* different
diferir §68 *tr* to defer, postpone, put off || *intr* to differ, be different
difícil *adj* difficult, hard; hard to please
difícilmente *adv* with difficulty
dificultad *f* difficulty; (*reparo que se opone a una opinión*) objection
dificultar *tr* to make difficult; consider difficult || *intr* to raise objections || *ref* to become difficult
dificulto•so -sa *adj* difficult, troublesome; objecting; (coll) ugly, homely
difidencia *f* distrust
difidente *adj* distrustful
difteria *f* diphtheria
difundir *tr* to diffuse; spread, disseminate; divulge, publish; broadcast || *ref* to diffuse; spread
difun•to -ta *adj & mf* deceased; **difunto de taberna** dead-drunk || *m* corpse
difu•so -sa *adj* diffuse; extended; wordy
digerible *adj* digestible
digerir §68 *tr* to digest; **no digerir** to not bear, not stand || *intr* to digest
digestible *adj* digestible
digestión *f* digestion
digesti•vo -va *adj & m* digestive
digesto *m* (law) digest
digital *adj* digital || *f* (bot) foxglove; (pharm) digitalis
digitalizar §60 *tr* to digitize
dígito *m* digit
dignación *f* condescension
dignar *ref* to deign, condescend
dignatario *m* dignitary, official
dignidad *f* dignity; bishop, archbishop
dignificar §73 *tr* to dignify
dig•no -na *adj* worthy; fitting, suitable; (*grave, decoroso*) dignified
digresión *f* digression
dije *m* amulet, charm, trinket; (*persona de excelentes cualidades*) jewel; person all dressed up; handy person
dilacerar *tr* to tear to pieces; (*la honra, el orgullo*) damage
dilación *f* delay
dilapidación *f* waste; squandering
dilapidar *tr* to squander
dilatación *f* expansion; serenity
dilatar *tr* to dilate, expand; defer, postpone; (*p.ej., la fama*) spread || *ref* to dilate, expand; spread; be wordy; delay
dilección *f* true love
dilec•to -ta *adj* dearly beloved
dilema *m* dilemma
diletante *adj & mf* dilettante
diletantismo *m* dilettantism
diligencia *f* diligence; step, démarche; errand; dispatch, speed; stagecoach; **hacer una diligencia** to do an errand; to have a bowel movement
diligente *adj* diligent; quick, ready
dilucidación *f* explanation; enlightenment
dilucidar *tr* to elucidate, explain
dilución *f* dilution
diluí•do -da *adj* dilute
diluir §20 *tr* to dilute; thin || *ref* to dilute; melt; dissolve
diluviar *intr* to rain hard, pour
diluvio *m* deluge
dimanar *intr* to spring up; **dimanar de** to spring from, originate in
dimensión *f* dimension
dimes *mpl* — **andar en dimes y diretes con** to bicker with
disminución *f* diminution, decrease, relaxation
diminuti•vo -va *adj & m* (gram) diminutive
diminu•to -ta *adj* tiny, diminutive; defective
dimisión *f* resignation
dimisorias *fpl* — **dar dimisorias a** to discharge, fire
dimitir *tr* to resign, resign from || *intr* to resign
din *m* (coll) dough, money
Dinamarca *f* Denmark
dinamar•qués -quesa *adj* Danish || *mf* Dane || *m* Danish (*language*)
dinámi•co -ca *adj* dynamic
dinamita *f* dynamite
dinamitar *tr* to dynamite
dínamo *f* dynamo
dinasta *m* dynast
dinastía *f* dynasty
dindán *m* ding-dong
dinerada *f* or **dineral** *m* large sum of money
dinero *m* money; currency; wealth; **dinero contante, efectivo** cash; **dinero contante y sonante** ready cash, spot cash; **dinero de bol-**

sillo pocket money; **dinero negro** undeclared income; **dinero sucio** (coll) blood money; **dinero suelto** change
dinero•so -sa *adj* moneyed, wealthy
dintel *m* lintel, doorhead
dióce•si *f* or **dióce•sis** *f* (*pl* **-sis**) diocese
diodo *m* diode
dios *m* god; **Dios mediante** God willing; **¡por Dios!** goodness!, for heaven's sake; **¡válgame Dios!** bless me!; **¡vaya con Dios!** off with you!
diosa *f* goddess
diploma *m* diploma
diplomacia *f* diplomacy
diploma•do -da *adj & mf* graduate
diplomar *tr & ref* to graduate
diplomáti•co -ca *adj* diplomatic ‖ *mf* diplomat
diptongar §44 *tr & ref* to diphthongize
diptongo *m* diphthong
diputación *f* congress; commission
diputa•do -da *mf* deputy, representative
diputar *tr* to commission, delegate; designate
dique *m* dike, jetty; dry dock; check, stop; **dique seco** dry dock
dirección *f* direction; (*señas en una carta*) address; administration, management; directorship; (aut) steering; **de dirección única** one-way; **dirección a la derecha** right-hand drive; **dirección a la izquierda** left-hand drive; **La Dirección General de Salud Pública** the Surgeon General; **perder la dirección** to lose control of the car
directamente *adv* directly, straight; first-hand
directi•vo -va *adj* managing ‖ *mf* director, manager ‖ *f* management
direc•to -ta *adj* direct; straight
direc•tor -tora *adj* directing, guiding; managing, governing ‖ *mf* director, manager; editor in chief; (*de un periódico*) editor; (*de una escuela*) principal; (*de una orquesta*) conductor; **director de escena** stage manager; **director de funeraria** funeral director; **director gerente** managing director; **director invitado** guest conductor
directorio *m* directorship; directory
dirigente *mf* leader, head, executive
dirigible *adj & m* dirigible
dirigir §27 *tr* to direct; manage; (*un automóvil*) steer; (*una carta; la palabra*) address; (*una obra*) dedicate ‖ *ref* to go, betake oneself; turn; **dirigirse a** to address; apply to
dirimir *tr* to dissolve, annul; (*una dificultad*) solve; (*una controversia*) settle, mediate
discado *m* dialing; **discado automático** *or* **directo** direct dialing
discar §73 *tr & intr* to dial
disceptar *intr* to discuss, debate
discerniente *adj* discerning
discernir §28 *tr* to discern; distinguish
disciplina *f* discipline; **disiplinas** scourge, whip
disciplina•do -da *adj* disciplined; (*flores*) many-colored
disciplinar *tr* to discipline; teach; scourge, whip
disciplinazo *m* lash
discípu•lo -la *mf* disciple; pupil
disco *m* disk; (*del gramófono*) record, disk; (sport) discus; **disco compacto** compact disk; **disco de cola** (rr) taillight; **disco de goma** (*para un grifo*) washer (*for a spigot*); **disco de identificación** identification tag; **disco de larga duración** long-playing record; **disco de señales** (rr) semaphore; **disco duro** *or* **rígido** hard disk; hard drive; **disco flexible** *or* **floppy** floppy disk; **disco óptico** video disk; **disco selector** (telp) dial; **disco vertebral** spinal disk; **disco volador** flying saucer; **siempre el mismo disco** the same old song ‖ *f* (*discoteca*) disco
discóbolo *m* discus thrower
discófi•lo -la *mf* record lover, discophile
dísco•lo -la *adj* ungovernable, wayward
disconforme *adj* disagreeing
discontinuar §21 *tr* to discontinue
discordancia *f* discordance
discordar §61 *intr* to be out of tune; disagree
discorde *adj* discordant, disagreeing; (mus) discordant, out of tune
discordia *f* discord
discoteca *f* discothèque, disco; record cabinet; record library; record store
discreción *f* discretion; wit; witticism; **a discreción** at discretion; (mil) unconditionally
discrepancia *f* discrepancy; dissent
discrepar *intr* to differ, disagree
discretear *intr* to try to be clever, try to sparkle
discre•to -ta *adj* (*juicioso*) discreet; (*discontinuo*) discrete; witty
discrimen *m* risk, hazard; difference
discriminación *f* discrimination
discriminar *tr* to discriminate against ‖ *intr* to discriminate
discriminato•rio -ria *adj* discriminatory
disculpa *f* excuse, apology
disculpar *tr* to excuse; pardon, overlook; **discúlpeme, por favor** excuse me, please ‖ *ref* to apologize; **disculparse con** to apologize to; **disculparse de** to apologize for
discurrir *tr* to contrive, invent; guess, conjecture ‖ *intr* to ramble, roam; occur, take place; discourse; reason; pass, elapse
discursi•to -ta *adj* long-winded; (coll) windy; *mf* windbag; big talker
discursi•vo -va *adj* meditative
discurso *m* discourse, speech; (*paso del tiempo*) course; **discurso de sobremesa** after-dinner speech
discusión *f* discussion
discutible *adj* debatable
discutir *tr* to discuss ‖ *intr* to discuss; argue
disecar §73 *tr* to dissect; (*un animal muerto*) stuff; (*una planta*) mount
diseminar *tr* to disseminate; scatter ‖ *ref* to scatter
disensión *f* (*oposición*) dissent; (*contienda*) dissension
disentería *f* dysentery

disentir §68 *intr* to dissent
diseñar *tr* to draw, sketch; design, outline; style (*clothes*)
diseño *m* drawing, sketch; design, outline; style
disertar *intr* to discourse, discuss
diser•to -ta *adj* fluent, eloquent
disfavor *m* disfavor
disforme *adj* formless; monstrous, ugly
disforzar §35 *ref* (Peru) to be prudish, be finical
dis•fraz *m* (*pl* **-fraces**) disguise; (*traje de máscara*) costume, fancy dress
disfrazar §60 *tr* to disguise ‖ *ref* to disguise oneself; wear fancy dress, masquerade, dress in costume
disfrutar *tr* to enjoy, to use ‖ *intr* — **disfrutar de** to enjoy, use; **disfrutar con** to enjoy, take enjoyment in
disfrute *m* enjoyment, use
disfunción *f* dysfunction
disgregar §44 *tr & intr* to disintegrate, break up
disgusta•do -da *adj* tasteless, insipid; sad, sorrowful; disagreeable; (Mex) hard to please
disgustar *tr* to displease ‖ *ref* to be displeased; fall out, become estranged
disgusto *m* displeasure; annoyance, unpleasantness; grief, sorrow; difference, quarrel; **a disgusto** against one's will
disidencia *f* dissidence; (*de una doctrina*) dissent
disidente *adj* dissident ‖ *mf* dissident, dissenter
disidir *intr* to dissent
disíla•bo -ba *adj* dissyllabic ‖ *m* dissyllable
disímil *adj* dissimilar
disimilar *tr & ref* to dissimilate
disimula•do -da *adj* sly, underhanded; **a lo disimulado** or **a la disimulada** underhandedly; **hacerse la disimulada** to feign ignorance
disimular *tr* to dissemble, dissimulate, hide, conceal; overlook, pardon ‖ *intr* to dissemble, dissimulate
disimulo *m* dissembling, dissimulation; indulgence
disipación *f* dissipation
disipa•do -da *adj* dissipated; spendthrift ‖ *mf* debauchee; spendthrift
disipar *tr* to dissipate ‖ *ref* to be dissipated; disappear, evanesce
dislate *m* nonsense
dislocar §73 *tr* to dislocate ‖ *ref* to dislocate; be dislocated
disloque *m* tops, top notch
disminución *f* diminution; decrease; **disminución física** handicap, disability
disminuir §20 *tr, intr & ref* to diminish
disociar *tr* to dissociate
disolución *f* dissolution; disbandment; (*relajación de costumbres*) dissoluteness, dissipation
disolu•to -ta *adj* dissolute ‖ *mf* debauchee
disolver §47 & §83 *tr* to dissolve; disband; destroy, ruin ‖ *intr & ref* to dissolve
disonancia *f* dissonance
disonar §61 *intr* to be dissonant, lack harmony, disagree; cause surprise; sound bad
dispar *adj* unlike, different; (*que no hace juego*) odd
disparada *f* sudden flight; **a la disparada** like a shot, in mad haste; **de una disparada** (Arg) right away; **tomar la disparada** (Arg) to take to one's heels
disparadero *m* trigger
disparador *m* trigger; (*de reloj*) escapement; **poner en el disparador** to drive mad
disparar *tr* to throw, hurl; shoot, fire ‖ *intr* to rant, talk nonsense; **disparar sobre** to snipe at ‖ *ref* to dash away, rush away; (*un caballo*) run away; (*una escopeta*) to go off; be beside oneself
disparata•do -da *adj* absurd, nonsensical; frightful
disparatar *intr* to talk nonsense; act foolishly
disparate *m* folly, nonsense; blunder, mistake; outrage
dispare•jo -ja *adj* unequal, different, uneven, disparate; rough, broken
disparidad *f* disparity
disparo *m* shot, discharge; nonsense; (compu) shot; (mach) release, trip; **cambiar disparos** to exchange shots
dispendio *m* waste, extravagance
dispendio•so -sa *adj* expensive
dispensar *tr* to excuse, pardon; exempt; dispense; dispense with; **dispénseme, por favor** excuse me, please
dispensario *m* dispensary; **dispensario de alimentos** soup kitchen
dispepsia *f* dyspepsia
dispersar *tr & ref* to disperse
displicente *adj* disagreeable; cross, fretful, peevish
disponer §54 *tr* to dispose, arrange; direct, order ‖ *intr* to dispose; **disponer de** to dispose of, have at one's disposal ‖ *ref* to prepare, get ready; get ready to die, make one's will
disponible *adj* available, disposable
disposición *f* disposition, arrangement, layout; inclination; preparation; disposal; predisposition; state of health; elegance; **estar a la disposición de** to be at the disposal of, be at the service of; **disposición testamentaria** provision of a will
dispositivo *m* appliance, device; (mil) force, deployment; **dispositivo de acceso** (compu) access mechanism; **dispositivo de alimentación** (compu) hopper; **dispositivo de almacenamiento** (compu) storage device; **dispositivo de postcombustión** (aer) afterburner; **dispositivo periférico** (compu) peripheral device
dispues•to -ta *adj* ready, prepared; comely, graceful; clever, skillful; **bien dispuesto** well-disposed; well, in good health; **mal dispuesto** ill-disposed, unfavorable; ill, indisposed
disputa *f* dispute; fight, struggle; **sin disputa** beyond dispute

disputar *tr* to dispute, question; argue over; fight for ‖ *intr* to dispute; debate, argue; fight
disquería *f* record shop
disque•ro -ra *mf* record dealer
disquete *or* **disquette** [disˋkete] *m* diskette, floppy disk
distancia *f* distance; **a distancia** at a distance; **a larga distancia** long-distance; **tomar distancia** to stand aside, stand off
distante *adj* distant
distar *intr* to be distant, be far; be different
distender §51 *tr* to distend; (*p.ej., las piernas*) stretch ‖ *ref* to distend; relax; (*un reloj*) run down
distensión *f* distension; relaxation of tension
distinción *f* (*honor, prerrogativa*) distinction; (*diferencia*) distinctness; **a distinción de** unlike
distingui•do -da *adj* distinguished; refined, urbane, smooth
distinguir §29 *tr* to distinguish; give distinction to; make out
distinti•vo -va *adj* distinctive ‖ *m* badge, insignia; distinction; distinctive mark
distin•to -ta *adj* distinct; different; **distintos** various, several
distorsión *f* distortion
distorsionar *tr* to distort, twist, bend
distracción *f* distraction; entertainment, relaxation; (*licencia en las costumbres*) dissipation; (*substracción de fondos*) embezzlement
distraer §75 *tr* to distract; amuse, divert, entertain; seduce; embezzle
distraí•do -da *adj* absent-minded, distracted; licentious, dissolute; (Chile, Mex) untidy, careless
distribución *f* distribution; electric supply system; timing gears, valve gears
distribui•dor -dora *adj* distributing ‖ *mf* distributor ‖ *m* (aut) distributor; slide valve; **distribuidor automático** vending machine
distribuir §20 *tr* to distribute
distrito *m* district; (rr) section; **distrito electoral** precinct; **distrito postal** zone, postal zone
disturbar *tr* to disturb
disturbio *m* disturbance
disuadir *tr* to dissuade
disyunti•vo -va *adj* disjunctive ‖ *f* dilemma
disyuntor *m* circuit breaker
dita *f* bond, surety
diuca *m* (Arg, Chile) teacher's pet ‖ *f* (Arg, Chile) finch (*Fringilla diuca*)
diuréti•co -ca *adj & m* diuretic
diur•no -na *adj* day, daytime
diva *f* goddess; (mus) diva
divagación *f* digression; wandering
divagar §44 *intr* to digress; ramble, wander
diván *m* divan; **diván cama** day bed
divergir §27 *intr* to diverge
diversidad *f* diversity; abundance
diversificación *f* diversification
diversificar §73 *tr & ref* to diversify
diversión *f* diversion
diver•so -sa *adj* diverse, different; **diversos** several, various, divers
divertidísi•mo -ma *adj* hilarious
diverti•do -da *adj* amusing, funny; (Am) tipsy
divertimiento *m* diversion, amusement
divertir §68 *tr* to divert; amuse ‖ *ref* to enjoy oneself, have a good time
dividendo *m* dividend
dividir *tr* to divide ‖ *ref* to divide, be divided; separate
divieso *m* boil
divinidad *f* divinity; (*persona dotada de gran belleza*) beauty
divinizar §60 *tr* to deify; exalt, extol
divi•no -na *adj* divine
divisa *f* badge; emblem; motto; goal, ideal; currency, foreign exchange; (com) script
divisar *tr* to descry, espy
división *f* division; (*deportes*) class, category; league
divisor *m* (math) divisor; **máximo común divisor** greatest common divisor; **divisor de voltaje** (rad) voltage divider
divisoria *f* dividing line; (geog) divide
di•vo -va *adj* godlike, divine ‖ *m* god; (mus) opera star ‖ *f* see **diva**
divorciar *tr* to divorce ‖ *ref* to divorce, get divorced
divorcio *m* divorce; divergency (*in opinion*); (Col) jail for women
divulgación *f* divulging, disclosure; popularization
divulgar §44 *tr* to divulge, disclose; popularize
D.ⁿ *abbr* **don**
D.N.A. *m* (letterword) (**ácido deoxirribonucleico**) DNA (deoxyribonucleic acid)
dobladillar *tr* to hem
dobladillo *m* hem
dobla•do -da *adj* rough, uneven; stocky, thickset; double-dealing ‖ *m* (mov) dubbing
doblaje *m* (mov) dubbing
doblar *tr* to double; fold, crease; bend; (*una esquina*) turn, round; (*un promontorio*) double; (*una película, generalmente en otro idioma*) dub; (bridge) to double; (Mex) to shoot down ‖ *intr* to turn; (*tocar a muerto*) toll; (mov, theat) to double, stand in; (bridge) to double ‖ *ref* to double; fold, crease; bend; bow, stoop; give in, yield
doble *adj* double; heavy, thick; stocky, thickset; deceitful, two-faced; **doble agente** *mf* double agent; **doble barba** (coll) double chin; **doble clic** (compu) double click; **doble contabilidad** double-entry bookkeeping; **doble fondo** false bottom; **doble juego** double dealing; **doble nacionalidad** dual citizenship; **doble personalidad** split personality; **doble tracción** four-wheel drive ‖ *adv* double, doubly ‖ *mf* (mov, theat) double, stand-in ‖ *m* double; fold, crease; (*toque de difuntos*) toll, knell; (*suma que se paga por la prórroga de una*

operación a plazos en la bolsa) margin; **al doble** doubly
doblegar §44 *tr* to fold; bend; (*una espada*) brandish, flourish; sway, dominate || *ref* to fold; bend; give in, yield
doblete *adj* medium || *m* (*piedra falsa; cada una de dos palabras que poseen un mismo origen*) doublet; (bridge) doubleton
do•blez *m* (*pl* **-bleces**) fold, crease; (*del pantalón*) cuff; duplicity, double-dealing
doce *adj & pron* twelve; **las doce** twelve o'clock || *m* twelve; (*en las fechas*) twelfth
docea•vo -va *adj & m* twelfth
docena *f* dozen; **docena del fraile** baker's dozen
docencia *f* teaching; (Arg) teaching staff
docente *adj* educational, teaching
dócil *adj* docile; soft, ductile
doc•to -ta *adj* learned || *mf* scholar
doc•tor -tora *mf* doctor || *f* (coll) blue-stocking
doctorado *m* doctorate
doctoran•do -da *mf* candidate for the doctor's degree
doctorar *tr* to grant the doctor's degree to || *ref* to get the doctor's degree
doctrina *f* doctrine; teaching, instruction; learning; catechism; preaching the Gospel
doctrinar *tr* to teach, instruct
doctrino *m* orphan (*in orphanage*); **parecer un doctrino** to look scared
documentación *f* documentation; **documentación del buque** ship's papers
documental *adj* documentary || *m* (mov) documentary
documentar *tr* to document
documento *m* document; **documento de prueba** (law) exhibit
dogal *m* (*para atar las caballerías*) halter; (*para ahorcar a un reo*) noose, halter, hangman's rope; **estar con el dogal a la garganta** or **al cuello** to be in a tight spot
dogmáti•co -ca *adj* dogmatic
do•go -ga *mf* bulldog
dolamas *fpl* or **dolames** *mpl* hidden defects of a horse; complaints, aches and pains
dolar §61 *tr* to hew
dólar *m* dollar
dolencia *f* ailment, complaint
doler §47 *tr* to ache, pain; grieve, distress; **dolerle a uno el dinero** to hate to spend money || *intr* to ache, hurt, pain || *ref* to complain; feel sorry; repent
doliente *adj* sick, ill; aching, suffering; sad, sorrowful || *mf* sufferer, patient || *m* mourner
dolo *m* deceit, fraud, guile
dolor *m* ache, pain; grief, sorrow; regret, repentance; **dolor de cabeza** headache; **dolor de muelas** toothache; **dolor de oído** earache; **dolor de yegua** (CAm) lumbago; **dolores de crecimiento** growing pains; **estar con dolores** to be in labor
dolori•do -da *adj* sore, painful; grieving, disconsolate
doloro•so -sa *adj* painful; sorrowful, sad
dolo•so -sa *adj* deceitful, guileful
domador *m* horsebreaker; animal tamer
domar *tr* to tame, break; master
domeñar *tr* to master, subdue
domesticar §73 *tr* to domesticate; tame
domésti•co -ca *adj* domestic, household || *mf* domestic, servant
domiciliar *tr* to domicile, settle; (*una carta*) (Mex) to address || *ref* to be domiciled, take up one's residence
domicilio *m* domicile, home; dwelling, house; **domicilio social** home office, company office
dominación *f* domination; (mil) eminence, high ground
dominante *adj* dominant; (*mandón*) domineering || *f* (mus) dominant
dominar *tr* to dominate; check, restrain, subdue; (*una ciencia, un idioma*) master || *intr* to dominate; (*mandar imperiosamente*) domineer || *ref* to restrain oneself
dómine *m* schoolmaster, Latin teacher; pedant
domingo *m* Sunday; **Domingo de Ramos** Palm Sunday; **Domingo de Resurrección, Domingo de Pascua** Easter Sunday; **guardar el domingo** to keep the Sabbath
dominguillo *m* tumbler
dominica•no -na *adj & mf* Dominican
dominio *m* dominion; domain; (*de una ciencia, de un idioma*) mastery; (*del aire*) supremacy; **dominio público** public domain
domi•nó *m* (*pl* **-nós**) (*traje*) domino; (*juego*) dominoes; (*fichas*) set of dominoes
dom.º *abbr* **domingo**
domo *m* dome
dompedro *m* four-o'clock
don *m* gift, present; talent, natural gift; Don (*Spanish title used before masculine Christian names*); **don de acierto** knack for doing the right thing; **don de errar** knack for doing the wrong thing; **don de gentes** charm, social grace; **don de lenguas** linguistic facility; **don de mando** ability to lead, generalship
dona *f* gift, present; **donas** wedding presents from the bridegroom to the bride
donación *f* gift, bequest; endowment
donada *f* lay sister
donado *m* lay brother
dona•dor -dora *mf* donor
donaire *m* charm, grace; witticism; cleverness
donairo•so -sa *adj* charming, graceful; witty; clever
donar *tr* to donate, give
doncel *adj* mild, mellow || *m* (*joven noble aun no armado caballero*) bachelor; (*hombre virgen*) virgin
doncella *f* maiden, virgin; housemaid; lady's maid; maid of honor; (Col, Ven) felon, whitlow
doncellez *f* maidenhood, virginity
doncellona *f* or **doncellueca** *f* unmarried woman, maiden lady
donde *conj* where; wherever; in which; **donde no** otherwise; **por donde quiera** anywhere,

everywhere || *prep* at or to the house, office, or store of

dónde *adv* where; **a dónde** where, whither; **de dónde** from where, whence; **por dónde** which way; for what cause, for what reason

dondequiera *adv* anywhere; **dondequiera que** wherever

dondiego *or* **donjúan** *m* four-o'clock, marvel-of-Peru; **dondiego de día** morning-glory; **dondiego de noche** four-o'clock

donillero *m* sharper, smoothy

donjuán *m* womanizer, Casanova, Don Juan, ladies' man || see **dondiego**

donosidad *f* charm, grace, wit

dono•so -sa *adj* charming, graceful, witty

donostiarra *adj* San Sebastian || *mf* native or inhabitant of San Sebastian

donosura *f* charm, grace, wit

doña *f* Doña (*Spanish title used before feminine Christian names*)

doñear *intr* (coll) to hang around women

doquier or **doquiera** *conj* wherever; **por doquier** everywhere

dorada *f* (ichth) gilthead

doradillo *m* fine brass wire

dora•do -da *adj* golden; gilt || *m* gilt, gilding; **dorados** bronze trimmings (*on furniture*) || *f* see **dorada**

dorar *tr* to gold-plate; gild; (*tostar ligeramente*) brown; (*paliar*) sugar-coat || *ref* to turn golden; turn brown

dormi•lón -lona *adj* sleepy || *mf* sleepyhead || *f* reclining armchair; mimosa; (Mex) headrest; (Ven) sleeping gown; **dormilonas** pearl earrings

dormir §30 *tr* to put to sleep; (*p.ej., una borrachera*) sleep off || *intr* to sleep; spend the night || *ref* to sleep; fall asleep; (*entorpecerse, p.ej., el pie*) go to sleep

dormirlas *m* hide-and-seek

dormitar *intr* to doze, nap

dormitorio *m* bedroom; (*muebles propios de esta habitación*) bedroom suit; **dormitorio común** (*en un colegio, cuartel*) dormitory; **dormitorio principal** master bedroom

dorsal *m* (sport) number (*worn on shirt*)

dorso *m* back

dos *adj & pron* two; **las dos** two o'clock || *m* two; (*en las fechas*) second

dosal•bo -ba *adj* (*horse*) with two white feet

doscien•tos -tas *adj & pron* two hundred || **doscientos** *m* two hundred

dosel *m* canopy, dais

doselera *f* valance, drapery

dosificación *f* dosage

dosificar §73 *tr* (*un medicamento*) to dose, give in doses

do•sis *f* (*pl* **-sis**) dose

dos-pie•zas *m* (*pl* **-zas**) two-piece bathing suit

dotación *f* (*de una mujer; de una fundación*) endowment; (nav) complement; (aer) crew; (*de remeros*) (sport) crew; staff, personnel

dotar *tr* to give a dowry to; endow; (*un buque*) staff, man; (*una oficina*) staff; equip; fix the wages for

dote *m & f* dowry, marriage portion || *m* (*en el juego de naipes*) stack of chips || *f* endowment, talent, gift; **dotes de mando** leadership

dovela *f* voussoir

doza•vo -va *adj & m* twelfth

d/p *abbr* **días plazo**

dracma *f* (*moneda griega*) drachma; (*peso farmacéutico*) dram

draga *f* dredge; (*barco*) dredger

dragado *m* dredging

dragami•nas *m* (*pl* **-nas**) mine sweeper

dragar §44 *tr* to dredge

dragón *m* dragon; (*planta*) snapdragon; (*soldado*) dragoon

dragonear *intr* to flirt; boast; **dragonear de** to boast of being; pretend to be, pass oneself off as

drama *m* drama

dramáti•co -ca *adj* dramatic || *mf* (*autor*) dramatist; actor || *f* (*arte y género*) drama

dramatizar §60 *tr* to dramatize

dramaturgo *m* dramatist

dramón *m* (coll) soap opera

drásti•co -ca *adj* drastic

dren *m* drain

drenaje *m* drainage

drenar *tr* to drain

drepanocitosis *f* sickle-cell anemia

driblar *tr & intr* to dribble

dril *m* (*tejido*) drill, duck; **dril de algodón** denim

driza *f* (naut) halyard

dro. *abbr* **derecho**

droga *f* drug; annoyance, bother; deceit, trick; (Chile, Mex, Peru) bad debt; (Cuba) drug on the market; **drogas milagrosas** wonder drugs

drogadic•to -ta *adj* drug-addicted || *mf* drug addict

drogado *m* doping, drugging

drogar §44 *tr* to dope

droguería *f* drug store; drug business; (*comercio de substancias usadas en química, industria, medicina, bellas artes*) drysaltery (Brit)

drogue•ro -ra *mf* druggist; drysalter (Brit)

droguista *mf* druggist; (coll) crook, cheat; (Arg) toper, drunk

droláti•co -ca *adj* droll, snappy

dromedario *m* dromedary; big heavy animal; brute (*person*)

druida *m* druid

dúa *f* (min) gang of workmen

dual *adj & m* dual

dualidad *f* duality; (Chile) tie vote

ducado *m* duchy, dukedom; (*moneda antigua*) ducat; **gran ducado** grand duchy

ducha *f* (*chorro de agua en una cavidad del cuerpo*) douche; (*chorro de agua sobre el cuerpo entero*) shower bath; (*lista en los tejidos*) stripe; **ducha en alfileres** needle bath

duchar *tr* to douche; give a shower bath to || *ref* to douche; take a shower bath

du•cho -cha *adj* experienced, expert, skillful ‖ *f* see **ducha**
dúctil *adj* ductile; easy to handle
duda *f* doubt; **sin duda** doubtless, no doubt, without doubt
dudable *adj* doubtful
dudar *tr* to doubt; question ‖ *intr* to hesitate; **dudar de** to doubt
dudo•so -sa *adj* doubtful; dubious
duela *f* stave (*of barrel*)
duelista *m* duelist
duelo *m* (*combate entre dos*) duel; grief, sorrow; bereavement, mourning; (*los que asisten a los funerales*) mourners; **batirse en duelo** to duel, to fight a duel; **duelos** hardships; **sin duelo** in abundance
duende *m* elf, goblin, sprite, brownie; gold cloth, silver cloth; (coll) restless daemon; **tener duende** to be burning within
due•ño -ña *mf* owner, proprietor; **dueño de sí mismo** one's own master; **ser dueño de** to be master of; be at liberty to, be free to ‖ *m* master, landlord ‖ *f* mistress, landlady, housekeeper; duenna; matron; **dueña de casa** housewife
duermevela *f* doze, light sleep; (*sueño fatigoso e interrumpido*) fitful sleep
dula *f* common pasture land; land irrigated from common ditch
dulce *adj* sweet; (*agua*) fresh; (*metal*) soft, ductile; gentle, mild, pleasant; (*manjur*) tasteless, insipid ‖ *m* candy; piece of candy; preserves; **dulce de almíbar** preserved fruit; **dulce de leche** candy milk, soft caramel; **dulces** candy
dulcera *f* candy dish, preserve dish
dulcería *f* candy store, confectionery store
dulce•ro -ra *adj* sweet-toothed ‖ *mf* confectioner ‖ *f* see **dulcera**
dulcificar §73 *tr* to sweeten; appease, mollify ‖ *ref* to sweeten, turn sweet
dulcinea *f* sweetheart; ideal
dulzaina *f* flageolet
dulza•rrón -rrona *adj* cloying, sickening
dulzo•so -sa *adj* sweetish
dulzura *f* sweetness; pleasantness, kindliness; (*del clima*) mildness; endearment, sweet word
duna *f* dune
dun•do -da *adj* (CAm, Col) simple, stupid ‖ *mf* (CAm, Col) simpleton
dúo *m* duet, duo
duodéci•mo -ma *adj & m* twelfth
duodeno *m* duodenum
duplica•do -da *adj & m* duplicate; **por duplicado** in duplicate
duplicar §73 *tr* to duplicate; double; repeat
duplicata *f* duplicate
duplicidad *f* (*falsedad*) duplicity; (*calidad de doble*) doubleness
du•plo -pla *adj & m* double
duque *m* duke; **gran duque** grand duke
duquesa *f* duchess; **gran duquesa** grand duchess
dura *f* durability; **de dura** or **de mucha dura** (coll) strong, durable
durable *adj* durable, lasting
duración *f* duration, endurance; (*espacio de tiempo del uso de una cosa*) life
durade•ro -ra *adj* durable, lasting
durante *prep* during, for
durar *intr* to last; remain; (*la ropa*) last, wear, wear well
durazno *m* peach; peach tree
dureza *f* hardness; harshness, roughness; **dureza de corazón** hardheartedness; **dureza de oído** hardness of hearing; **dureza de vientre** constipation
durmiente *adj* sleeping; **la Bella Durmiente** Sleeping Beauty ‖ *mf* sleeper ‖ *m* girder, sleeper, stringer; tie, railroad tie; (Ven) steel bar
du•ro -ra *adj* hard; (*huevo*) hard-boiled; harsh, rough; cruel; stubborn, obstinate; stiff; unbearable; strong, tough; stingy; (*tiempo*) stormy; **duro de corazón** hard-hearted; **duro de oído** hard of hearing; **duro de película** movie hero; **estar muy duro con** to be hard on; **ser duro de pelar** to be hard to put across; be hard to deal with ‖ *m* dollar (*Spanish coin worth five pesetas*) ‖ *f* see **dura** ‖ **duro** *adv* hard
dux *m* (*pl* **dux**) doge
d/v *abbr* **días vista**

E

E, e (e) *f* fifth letter of the Spanish alphabet
e *conj* (used before words beginning with *i* or *hi* not followed by a vowel) and
ea *interj* hey!
ebanista *m* cabinetmaker, woodworker
ebanistería *f* cabinetmaking, woodwork; cabinetmaker's shop
ébano *m* ebony
ebriedad *f* drunkenness
e•brio -bria *adj* drunk; (*p.ej., de ira*) blind ‖ *mf* drunk
ebrio•so -sa *adj* drinking ‖ *mf* drinker
ebullición *f* boiling
echacan•tos *m* (*pl* **-tos**) good-for-nothing
echacuer•vos *m* (*pl* **-vos**) pimp, procurer; cheat
echada *f* cast, throw; man's length; (Arg, Mex) boast, hoax
echadero *m* place to stretch out

echadi•zo -za *adj* discarded, waste; spying || *mf* founding || *m* spy
echa•do -da *adj* stretched out; (C-R) lazy, indolent; **estar echado** (CAm, Mex, P-R) to have an easy job (or easy life) || *f* see **echada**
echar *tr* to throw, throw away, throw out; issue, emit; publish; discharge, dismiss; swallow; (*p.ej., agua*) pour; (*p.ej., un cigarrillo*) smoke; (*la baraja*) deal; (*una partida de cartas*) play; (*una llave*) turn; (*un discurso*) deliver; (*un drama*) put on; (*maldiciones*) utter; (*pelo, dientes, renuevos*) grow, put forth; (*impuestos*) impose, levy; (*la buenaventura*) tell; (*precio, distancia, edad, etc.*) ascribe, attribute; (*una mirada*) cast; (*sangre*) shed; (*la culpa*) lay; (*una mano*) lend; **echar abajo** to demolish, destroy; overthrow; **echar a pasear** to dismiss unceremoniously; **echar a perder** to spoil, ruin; **echar a pique** to sink; **echar de menos** to miss; **echarla de** to claim to be, boast of being; **echarlo todo a rodar** to upset everything; hit the ceiling; **echar pulsos** to arm wrestle || *intr* — **echar a** to begin to; burst out (*e.g., crying*); **echar a perder** to spoil, ruin; **echar de ver** to notice, happen to see; **echar por** (*un empleo, un oficio*) to go into, take up; (*la derecha, la izquierda*) turn toward; (*un camino*) go down || *ref* to throw oneself; lie down, stretch out; (*el viento*) fall; (*un abrigo*) throw on; (*una gallina*) set; **echarse a** to begin to; **echarse a morir** to give up in despair; **echarse a perder** to spoil, be ruined; **echarse atrás** to back out; **echarse de ver** to be easy to see; **echárselas de** to claim to be, boast of being; **echarse sobre** to rush at, fall upon
echazón *f* jettison, jetsam
echiquier *m* Exchequer
ecléctico -ca *adj & mf* eclectic
eclesiásti•co -ca *adj & m* ecclesiastic
eclipsar *tr* to eclipse; (fig) to outshine || *ref* to be in eclipse; (fig) to disappear
eclipse *m* eclipse
eclip•sis *f* (*pl* **-sis**) var of **elipsis**
eclisa *f* (rr) fishplate
eco *m* echo; (*del tambor*) rumbling; **hacer eco** to echo; attract attention; **tener eco** to be well received, catch on
ecografía *f* ultrasound scan
ecógrafo *m* ultrasound scanner
ecología *f* ecology
ecológi•co -ca *adj* ecologic(al)
ecologista *mf* or **ecólogo** *m* ecologist
economato *m* stewardship; commissary, company store, coöperative store
economía *f* economy; want, poverty; **economía de la oferta** supply-side economics; **economía política** economics; **economías** savings
económi•co -ca *adj* economic; (*que gasta poco; poco costoso*) economical; cheap; miserly, niggardly
economista *mf* economist
economizar §60 *tr* to economize, save; avoid || *intr* to economize, save; skimp
ecónomo *m* steward, trustee; supply priest
ecosistema *m* ecosystem
ecuación *f* equation
ecuador *m* equator || **el Ecuador** Ecuador
ecuatorial *adj* equatorial
ecuánime *adj* calm, composed; impartial
ecuanimidad *f* equanimity; impartiality
ecuatoria•no -na *adj & mf* Ecuadoran, Ecuadorian
ecuestre *adj* equestrian
ecuméni•co -ca *adj* ecumenic(al)
eczema *m & f* eczema
edad *f* age; **edad crítica** change of life; **edad de quintas** draft age; **edad escolar** school age; **Edad Media** Middle Ages; **edad viril** prime of life; **mayor edad** majority; **menor edad** minority; **tercera edad** retirement years
edecán *m* aide-de-camp
edema *f* edema
Edén *m* (Bib) Eden
edición *f* edition; publication; **edición electrónica, edición digital** electronic publishing; **edición limitada** *or* **numerada** limited edition; **edición príncipe** first edition; **la segunda edición de** the spit and image of
edicto *m* edict
edificación *f* construction, building; buildings; (*inspiración con el buen ejemplo*) edification, uplift
edificante *adj* edifying
edificar §73 *tr* to construct, build; (*dar buen ejemplo a*) edify, uplift
edificio *m* edifice, building
editar *tr* to publish
edi•tor -tora *adj* publishing || *mf* publisher; (*revisor*) editor *m*; (compu, mov) editor || *f* publishing house
editorial *adj* publishing; editorial || *m* editorial || *f* publishing house
editorialista *mf* editorial writer
editorializar §60 *intr* (Urug) to editorialize
edredón *m* eider down
Eduardo *m* Edward
educación *f* education; upbringing, civility, manners; **educación a distancia** distance learning, correspondence courses; **educación especial** special education; **educación física** physical education
educacional *adj* educational
educa•dor -dora *mf* educator
educan•do -da *mf* pupil, student
educar §73 *tr* to educate; (*los sentidos*) train; (*al niño o al adolescente*) rear, bring up
educati•vo -va *adj* educational
edulcorante *adj* sweetening || *m* sweetener
EE.UU. *abbr* **Estados Unidos**
efectismo *m* sensationalism
efectista *adj* sensational, theatrical || *mf* sensationalist
efectivamente *adv* actually, really; as a matter of fact

efecti•vo -va *adj* actual, real; (*empleo, cargo*) regular, permanent; (*vigente*) effective; **hacer efectivo** to carry out; (*un cheque*) to cash; **hacerse efectivo** to become effective || *m* cash; **efectivo en caja** cash on hand

efecto *m* effect; end, purpose; article; (*en el juego de billar*) English; **a ese efecto** for that purpose; **al efecto** for the purpose; **con efecto** or **en efecto** indeed, as a matter of fact; **efecto dominó** domino effect; **efecto invernadero** (ecol) greenhouse effect; **efectos sonoros** sound effects; **efecto útil** efficiency, output; **llevar a efecto** or **poner en efecto** to put into effect, carry out; **surtir efecto** to work, have the desired effect

efectuar §21 *tr* to carry out, effect, effectuate || *ref* to take place

efervescencia *f* effervescence

efervescente *adj* effervescent

eficacia *f* efficacy

efi•caz *adj* (*pl* **-caces**) efficacious, effectual; efficient

eficiencia *f* efficiency

eficiente *adj* efficient

efigie *f* effigy

efíme•ro -ra *adj* ephemeral

efugio *m* evasion, subterfuge

efusión *f* effusion; (*manifestación de afectos muy viva*) warmth, effusiveness; **efusión de sangre** bloodshed

efusi•vo -va *adj* effusive

égida *f* aegis

egip•cio -cia *adj & mf* Egyptian

Egipto *m* Egypt

eglantina *f* sweetbriar

eglefino *m* haddock

égloga *f* eclogue

egoísmo *m* egoism

egoísta *adj* egoistic || *mf* egoist

egolatría *f* self-worship, self-glorification

egotismo *m* egotism

egotista *adj* egotistic(al) || *mf* egotist

egre•gio -gia *adj* distinguished, eminent

egresar *intr* to graduate

egreso *m* departure; graduation

eje *m* (*pieza alrededor de la cual gira un cuerpo*) axle, shaft; (*línea que divide en dos mitades; línea recta alrededor de la cual se supone que gira un cuerpo*) axis; (fig) core, crux, linchpin; **eje de balancín** rocker, rockershaft; **eje de carretón** axletree; **eje de transmisión** drive shaft; **eje motor** drive shaft; **eje tándem** dual axle; dual rear

ejecución *f* execution

ejecutante *mf* performer

ejecutar *tr* to execute; perform; (compu) run

ejecutivamente *adv* expeditiously

ejecuti•vo -va *adj* urgent, pressing; insistent; executive || *m* executive

ejecu•tor -tora *adj* executive || *mf* executor; (compu) player; **ejecutor de la justicia** executioner; **ejecutor testamentario** executor (*of a will*) || *f* — **ejecutora testamentaria** executrix

ejemplar *adj* exemplary || *m* pattern, model; (*de una obra impresa*) copy; precedent; (*caso que sirve de escarmiento*) example; **ejemplar de cortesía** complimentary copy; **ejemplar muestra** sample copy; **sin ejemplar** unprecedented; as a special case

ejemplarizar §60 *tr* to set an example to; exemplify

ejemplificar §73 *tr* to exemplify

ejemplo *m* example, instance; **por ejemplo** for example, for instance; **sin ejemplo** unexampled

ejercer §78 *tr* (*la medicina*) to practice; (*la caridad*) show, exercise; (*una fuerza*) exert || *intr* to practice; **ejercer de** to practice as, work as

ejercicio *m* exercise; drill, practice; (*de un cargo u oficio*) tenure; (*uso constante*) exertion; (*año económico*) fiscal year; **hacer ejercicio** to take exercise; (mil) to drill

ejercitar *tr* to exercise; practice; drill, train || *ref* to exercise; practice

ejército *m* army; **ejército permanente** standing army; **los tres ejércitos** the three arms of the service

ejido *m* commons

ejote *m* (Mex) string bean, green bean

el, la (*pl* **los, las**) *art def* the; **el** is used before masculine nouns and also before feminine nouns beginning with accented *a* or *ha,* e.g., *el agua* || *pron dem* that, the one; **el que** who, which, that; he who, the one that

él *pron pers masc* he, it; him, it

elabora•do -da *adj* elaborate; finished

elaborar *tr* to elaborate; (*una teoría*) work out; (*el metal, la madera*) fashion, to work

elación *f* magnanimity, nobility; (*de estilo y lenguaje*) pomposity

elástica *f* knit undershirt; **elásticas** (Ven) suspenders

elasticidad *f* elasticity

elásti•co -ca *adj* elastic || *m* elastic; bedspring || *f* see **elástica**

eléboro *m* hellebore

elección *f* election; choice

electi•vo -va *adj* elective

elec•to -ta *adj* elect

electorado *m* electorate

electorero *m* henchman, heeler

electricidad *f* electricity

electricista *mf* electrician

eléctrico -ca *adj* electric(al)

electrificar §73 *tr* to electrify

electrizar §60 *tr* to electrify

electro *m* electromagnet

electrocardiograma *m* electrocardiogram

electrochoque *m* (med) electroshock

electroafeitadora *f* electric shaver

electrocutar *tr* to electrocute

electrodo *m* electrode

electrodomésti•co -ca *adj* electric-appliance || *m* electric appliance

electróge•no -na *adj* generating electricity ‖ *m* electric generator
electroimán *m* electromagnet
electrólisis *f* electrolysis
electrólito *m* electrolyte
electromagnéti•co -ca *adj* electromagnetic
electromo•tor -tora or **-triz** *adj* (*pl* **-tores -toras -trices**) electromotive
electrón *m* electron
electróni•co -ca *adj* electronic ‖ *f* electronics
electrostáti•co -ca *adj* electrostatic
electrotecnia *f* electrical engineering
electrotipar *tr* to electrotype
electrotipo *m* electrotype
elefante *m* elephant; **elefante blanco** (fig) (SAm) white elephant
elegancia *f* elegance; style, stylishness
elegante *adj* elegant; stylish ‖ *mf* fashion plate
eleganto•so -sa *adj* elegant
elegía *f* elegy
elegía•co -ca *adj* elegiac
elegible *adj* eligible
elegir §57 *tr* to elect; choose, select
elemental *adj* (*primordial; simple, no compuesto*) elemental; (*que se refiere a los principios de una ciencia o arte; de fácil comprensión*) elementary
elemento *m* element; (*de una pila o batería*) cell; **elemento de compuestos** (gram) combining form; **elemento en rastro** trace element; **estar en su elemento** to be in one's element
elenco *m* catalogue, list, table; (theat) cast
elepé *adj* (*disco*) long-playing; LP ‖ *m* long-playing record
elevación *f* elevation; **elevación a potencias** (math) involution
eleva•do -da *adj* elevated, high; lofty, sublime
elevador *m* elevator, **elevador de granos** grain elevator
elevar *tr* to elevate, lift; (math) to raise ‖ *ref* to ascend, rise; be exalted; become conceited
elfo *m* elf
elidir *tr* to eliminate; (*una vocal*) elide
eliminar *tr* to eliminate; strike out ‖ *ref* (Mex) to go away, leave
elipse *f* (geom) ellipse
elip•sis *f* (*pl* **-sis**) (gram) ellipsis
elípti•co -ca *adj* (geom & gram) elliptic(al)
elisión *f* elision
elitista *adj & mf* elitist
ella *pron pers fem* she, it; her, it; (coll) the trouble
ello *pron pers neut* it; (coll) the trouble; **ello es que** the fact is that ‖ *m* (psychoanalysis) id
elocución *f* public speaking, elocution
elocuencia *f* eloquence
elocuente *adj* eloquent
elogiable *adj* praiseworthy
elogiar *tr* to praise, eulogize
elogio *m* praise, eulogy
elogio•so -sa *adj* laudatory, glowing
elote *m* (Mex, Guat) ear of corn, sweet corn; **coger asando elotes** (CAm) to catch in the act; **pagar los elotes** (CAm) to be the goat
elucidar *tr* to elucidate
eludir *tr* to elude, evade, avoid, sidestep
elusi•vo -va *adj* evasive; elusive
E.M. *abbr* **Estado Mayor**
emancipar *tr* to emancipate
embadurnamiento *m* daub, daubing
embadurnar *tr* to daub
embaír §1 *tr* to deceive, take in, hoax
embajada *f* embassy; ambassadorship; (iron) fine proposition
embajador *m* ambassador; **embajadores** ambassador and wife
embajadora *f* ambassadress
embalaje *m* packing; package; (sport) sprint
embala•dor -dora *mf* packer
embalar *tr* to pack ‖ *intr* (sport) to sprint ‖ *ref* (*el motor*) to race; (sport) to sprint
embaldosado *m* tile paving
embaldosar *tr* to pave with tile
embalsamar *tr* to embalm; perfume
embalsar *tr* to dam, dam up
embalse *m* dam; damming; backwater
embanastar *tr* to put in a basket; pack, jam, overcrowd
embanquetar *tr* (Mex) to line with sidewalks
embarazada *adj fem* pregnant ‖ *f* pregnant woman
embarazar §60 *tr* (*estorbar*) to embarrass; obstruct; make pregnant ‖ *ref* to be embarrassed, be encumbered; become pregnant
embarazo *m* embarrassment; obstruction; awkwardness; pregnancy
embarazo•so -sa *adj* embarrassing, troublesome
embarbillar *tr* to rabbet
embarcación *f* boat, ship; embarkation (*of passengers*)
embarcadero *m* pier, wharf; (rr) platform; **embarcadero de ganado** (Arg) loading chute; **embarcadero flotante** landing stage
embarcador *m* shipper
embarcar §73 *tr* to ship ‖ *intr* to entrain ‖ *ref* to embark, ship; get involved
embarco *m* embarkation (*of passengers*)
embargar §44 *tr* to embargo; paralyze; (law) to seize, attach
embargo *m* embargo; indigestion; (law) seizure, attachment; **sin embargo** however, nevertheless
embarnizar §60 *tr* to varnish
embarque *m* shipment, embarkation (*of freight*)
embarrada *f* blunder
embarrancar §73 *tr, intr & ref* to run into a ditch; (*una nave*) run aground
embarrar *tr* to splash with mud; smear, stain; (CAm, Mex) to involve in a shady deal; **embarrarla** (Arg) to spoil the whole thing
embarrilar *tr* to barrel, put in barrels
embarullar *tr* to muddle, make a mess of; bungle, botch
embastar *tr* to baste, stitch
embate *m* blow, attack; (*del mar*) beating, dash-

ing; (*de viento*) gust; **embates de la fortuna** hard knocks
embauca•dor -dora *mf* trickster; impostor; con man
embaucar §73 *tr* to trick, bamboozle, swindle
embaula•do -da *adj* crowded, packed, jammed
embaular §8 *tr* to put in a trunk; jam, pack in
embayar *ref* (Ecuad) to fly into a rage
embazar §60 *tr* to dye brown; hinder, obstruct; astound, dumbfound || *ref* to get bored; be upset, get sick in the stomach
embebecer §22 *tr* to entertain, amuse, fascinate, enchant
embeber *tr* to absorb, soak up; soak; contain, include; embed; contract, shrink || *intr* to contract, shrink || *ref* to be enchanted, be enraptured; become absorbed or immersed; become well versed
embebi•do -da *adj* (*vocal*) elided; (*columna*) engaged
embelecar §73 *tr* to cheat, dupe, bamboozle
embeleco *m* cheating, fraud; bore; **embelecos** cuteness
embeleñar *tr* to dope, stupefy; enchant, bewitch
embelequería *f* (Col, Mex, W-I) fraud, swindle
embelesar *tr* to charm, enrapture, fascinate
embeleso *m* charm, fascination, delight
embellece•dor -dora *adj* embellishing, beautifying || *m* (aut) hubcap || *f* beautician
embellecer §22 *tr* to embellish, beautify
embellecimiento *m* embellishment, beautification
embermejecer §22 *tr* to dye red; make blush || *ref* to blush
emberrinchar *ref* to fly into a rage
embestida *f* attack, assault; (*detención intempestiva*) buttonholing
embesti•dor -dora *mf* beat, sponger
embestir §50 *tr* to attack, assail; to strike; buttonhole, waylay || *intr* to attack, charge, rush
embetunar *tr* to blacken; cover with tar
embicar §73 *tr* (Mex) to turn upside down, tilt || *intr* (Arg, Chile) to run aground
emblandecer §22 *tr* to soften; placate, mollify || *ref* to soften, yield
emblanquecer §22 *tr* to whiten; bleach || *ref* to turn white
emblema *m* emblem
emblemáti•co -ca *adj* emblematic(al)
embobar *tr* to amaze, fascinate || *ref* to stand gaping
embocadero *m* mouth, outlet
embocadura *f* nozzle; (*de río*) mouth; (*del freno; de instrumento de viento*) mouthpiece; (*de cigarrillo*) tip; (*del vino*) taste; stage entrance
embocar §73 *tr* to catch in the mouth; put in the mouth; take on, undertake; gulp down; try to put over || *intr & ref* to enter, pass
embolada *f* stroke
embolado *m* bull with wooden balls on horns; (theat) minor role; (coll) trick, hoax
embolar *tr* (*los cuernos del toro*) to put wooden balls on; (*el calzado*) to shine || *ref* (CAm, Mex) to get drunk
embolia *f* embolism
émbolo *m* (mach) piston; **émbolo buzo** (mach) plunger
embolsar *tr* to pocket, take in
embonar *tr* to fertilize; suit, be becoming to
emboquillar *tr* (*los cigarrillos*) to put tips on; (*una galería o túnel*) cut an entrance in; (*las junturas entre los ladrillos*) (Chile) to point, chink
emborrachar *tr* to intoxicate || *ref* to get drunk; (*los colores de una tela*) run
emborrar *tr* to stuff, pad, wad; gulp down
emborrascar §73 *tr* to stir up, irritate || *ref* to get stormy; (*un negocio*) fail; (*la veta de una mina*) (Arg, CAm, Mex) to peter out
emborronar *tr* to blot; scribble
emboscada *f* ambush, ambuscade
emboscado *m* draft dodger
emboscar §73 *tr* (*tropas para sorprender al enemigo*) to ambush || *ref* to ambush, lie in ambush; shirk, take an easy way out
embota•do -da *adj* blunt, dull; (Chile) blackpawed
embotadura *f* bluntness, dullness
embotar *tr* to blunt, dull; dull, weaken; (*el tabaco*) put in a jar
embotella•do -da *adj* (*discurso*) prepared || *m* bottling; (*del tráfico*) bottleneck
embotellamiento *m* bottling; traffic jam
embotellar *tr* to bottle; (*un negocio*) tie up; (nav) to bottle up
embotijar *tr* (*un suelo*) to underlay with jugs || *ref* to swell up with anger
embovedar *tr* to vault, vault over; put in a vault
emboza•do -da *adj* muffled up || *mf* person muffled up to eyes
embozar §60 *tr* to muffle up to the eyes; (*p.ej., a un perro*) muzzle; disguise || *ref* to muffle oneself up to the eyes
embozo *m* muffler, cloak held over the face; fold back (*of bed sheet*); cunning, dissimulation; **quitarse el embozo** to drop one's mask
embragar §44 *tr* (*el motor*) to engage || *intr* to throw the clutch in
embrague *m* clutch; engagement
embravecer §22 *tr* to enrage, make angry || *ref* to get angry; (*el mar*) get rough
embraveci•do -da *adj* angry; rough, wild
embrear *tr* to tar, cover with tar; calk with tar
embregar §44 *ref* to wrangle
embriagar §44 *tr* to intoxicate, make drunk; enrapture || *ref* to get drunk
embriaguez *f* drunkenness; rapture
embridar *tr* to bridle; check, restrain
embriología *f* embryology
embrión *m* embryo; **en embrión** in embryo
embriona•rio -ria *adj* embryonic: **en estado embrionario** at the embryonic stage
embroca *f* poultice
embrocar §73 *tr* to empty; (*el toro al torero*)

to catch between the horns || *ref* (C-R) to fall on one's face; (Mex) to put on over the head
embrollar *tr* to tangle, muddle, embroil
embrollo *m* entanglement, muddle, embroilment; deception, trick
embromar *tr* to joke with, play jokes on; bore, annoy || *ref* to be bored, be annoyed
embrujar *tr* to bewitch
embrutecer §22 *tr* to brutify, stupefy
embrutecimiento *m* brutalization; coarsening
embuchado *m* pork sausage; subterfuge; (*de la urna electoral*) stuffing (of ballot box)
embudar *tr* to put a funnel in; trick, trap
embudista *adj* tricky, scheming || *mf* schemer
embudo *m* funnel; trick; (mil) shell hole; **embudo de bomba** (mil) bomb crater
embullar *tr* to stir up, excite, key up || *ref* to become excited, keyed up
emburujar *tr* to jumble, pile up || *ref* to wrap oneself up
embuste *m* lie, falsehood, trick; **embustes** baubles, trinkets; (*del niño*) cuteness
embuste•ro -ra *adj* lying, false, tricky || *mf* liar, cheat
embuti•do -da *adj* inlaid, flush || *m* inlay, marquetry; pork sausage; lace insertion
embutir *tr* to stuff, pack tight; insert; inlay; set flush; (*una hoja de metal*) fashion, hammer into shape || *ref* to squeeze in; stuff oneself
emergencia *f* emergence; emergency; **de emergencia** standby
emerger §17 *intr* to emerge; (*un submarino*) surface
eméri•to -ta *adj* emeritus; **professor emérito, profesora emérita** professor emeritus *o* emeritus professor
emersión *f* emersion; (*de un submarino*) surfacing
eméti•co -ca *adj & m* emetic
emigración *f* emigration; migration
emigra•do -da *mf* émigré
emigrante *adj & mf* emigrant
emigrar *intr* to emigrate; migrate
eminencia *f* eminence
eminente *adj* eminent
emisa•rio -ria *mf* emissary || *m* outlet
emisión *f* (*acción de exhalar; acción de lanzar ondas luminosas, etc.*) emission; (*títulos creados de una vez*) (com) issue; (*acción de emitir títulos nuevos*) (com) issuance; (rad) broadcast; **emisión seriada** (rad) serial
emi•sor -sora *adj* emitting; broadcasting || *m* (rad) transmitter || *f* broadcasting station
emitir *tr* to emit, send forth; issue, give out; (*p.ej., opiniones*) utter, express; (com) to issue; (rad) to broadcast
emoción *f* emotion
emocional *adj* emotional
emocionante *adj* moving, touching; thrilling, exciting
emocionar *tr* to move, stir; thrill
emoti•vo -va *adj* emotional
empacadi•zo -za *adj* (Arg) touchy
empaca•do -da *adj* (Arg) gruff, grim
empacar §73 *tr* to pack, crate || *ref* to be stubborn; (*un animal*) balk, get balky
empacha•do -da *adj* backward, fumbling
empachar *tr* to hinder, embarrass; disguise; surfeit, upset the stomach of || *ref* blush, be embarrassed; be upset, have indigestion
empacho *m* hindrance; embarrassment, bashfulness; indigestion
empacho•so -sa *adj* sickening; shameful
empa•cón -cona *adj* stubborn; balky
empadronar *tr* to register, take the census of || *ref* to register, be registered in the census
empalagar §44 *tr* to cloy, pall, surfeit; bore, weary
empalago•so -sa *adj* cloying, sickening, mawkish; boring, annoying; fawning
empalar *tr* impale
empalizada *f* palisade, stockade, fence
empalizar §60 *tr* to fence in
empalmar *tr* to splice, connect, join, couple; combine || *intr* to connect, make connections; **empalmar con** to connect with; follow, succeed
empalme *m* splice, connection, joint, coupling; combination; (elec) joint; (rr) connection, junction
empanada *f* pie; fraud
empanadilla *f* pie
empana•do -da *adj* unlighted, unventilated || *f* see **empanada**
empanar *tr* to crumb, bread; (*las tierras*) sow with wheat
empantanar *tr* to flood; obstruct
empaña•do -da *adj* dim, misty; blurred, fogged; (*voz*) flat
empañar *tr* (*a las criaturas*) to swaddle; blur, fog, dim, dull; tarnish, sully || *ref* to blur, fog, dim, dull
empañetar *tr* to plaster
empapa•do -da *adj* soaked up, drenched, waterlogged
empapar *tr* to soak; soak up, absorb; drench || *ref* to soak; be soaked; to become imbued; be surfeited
empapelado *m* papering, paper hanging; wallpaper; paper lining
empapela•dor -dora *mf* paper hanger
empapelar *tr* to wrap in paper; paper, line with paper; wallpaper; bring a criminal charge against
empaque *m* packing; look, appearance, mien; stiffness, stuffiness; brazenness
empaquetadura *f* gasket
empaquetar *tr* to pack; jam, stuff || *ref* to pack; pack in; dress up
empareda•do -da *mf* recluse || *m* sandwich
emparedar *tr* to wall in, confine
emparejar *tr* to pair, match; smooth, make level; even, make even; (*una puerta*) close flush || *intr* to come up, come abreast; **emparejar con** to catch up with || *ref* to pair, match
emparentar §2 *intr* to become related by mar-

riage; **emparentar con** (*buena gente*) to marry into the family of; (*una familia rica*) marry into
emparrado *m* arbor, bower
emparrillar *tr* to grill
empasta•dor -dora *mf* bookbinder
empastadura *f* binding
empastar *tr* (*un diente*) to fill; (*un libro*) bind with stiff covers; convert into pasture land || *ref* (Chile) to be overgrown with weeds
empaste *m* (*de diente*) filling; stiff binding
empastelar *tr* (typ) to pie
empatar *tr* (*en la votación y los juegos*) to tie; join, connect; tie, fasten || *intr* to tie || *ref* to tie; **empatársela a una persona** to be a match for someone; **empatárselo a una persona** (Guat, Hond) to put it over on someone
empate *m* tie, draw; standoff; (Col) penholder; (Ven) waste of time
empatía *f* empathy
empavar *tr* (Ecuad) to annoy; (Peru) to kid, razz
empavesado *m* (naut) dressing, bunting
empavesar *tr* to bedeck with flags and bunting; (*un buque*) dress; (*un monumento*) veil || *ref* to become overcast
empavonar *tr* to blue; grease, spread grease over || *ref* (CAm) to dress up
empecina•do -da *adj* stubborn
empecinamiento *m* stubbornness; determination
empecinar *tr* to tar; dip in pitch || *ref* to be stubborn; persist
empederni•do -da *adj* hardened, inveterate; hard-hearted
empedra•do -da *adj* cloud-flecked; pockmarked; (*caballo*) dark-spotted || *m* stone paving
empedrar §2 *tr* to pave with stones; bespatter
empegado *m* tarpaulin
empegar §44 *tr* to coat with pitch, dip in pitch; (*el ganado lanar*) mark with pitch
empeine *m* instep; (*de la bota*) vamp; (*enfermedad cutánea*) tetter; (*región central del hipogastrio*) pubes
empella *f* vamp
empellar *tr* to push, shove
empellar §31 *tr* to push, shove
empellón *m* push, shove; **a empellones** pushing, roughly
empelotar *ref* to get all tangled up; get into a row; take all one's clothes off; (Mex, W-I) to fall madly in love
empenachar *tr* to adorn with plumes
empeña•do -da *adj* (*disputa*) bitter, heated; **no empeñado** noncommitted
empeñar *tr* (*dar en prenda*) to pawn; (*una lucha*) launch, begin; (*prendar, hipotecar*) pledge; (*la palabra*) pledge; force, compel || *ref* to commit oneself, bind oneself; go into debt; (*una lucha, una disputa*) begin, start; **empeñarse en** to engage in; persist in, insist on
empeñe•ro -ra *mf* (Mex) pawnbroker
empeño *m* pledge, engagement, commitment; (*prenda*) pawn; pawnshop; persistence, insistence; eagerness, perseverance; effort, endeavor; pledge, backer, patron; favor, protection; **con empeño** eagerly
empeño•so -sa *adj* eager, persistent
empeorar *tr* to impair, make worse || *intr & ref* to get worse, deteriorate
empequeñecer §22 *tr* (*hacer más pequeño*) to make smaller, dwarf; (*amenguar la importancia de*) belittle || *ref* to get smaller, dwarf
emperador *m* emperor; **los emperadores** the emperor and empress
empera•triz *f* (*pl* **-trices**) empress
emperchar *tr* to hang on a clothes rack
emperejilar *tr & ref* to dress up, spruce up
emperezar §60 *tr* to delay, put off || *intr & ref* to get lazy
empericar §73 *ref* (Col, Ecuad) to get drunk; (Mex) to blush
emperifollar *tr & ref* to dress up gaudily
empernar *tr* to bolt
empero *conj* but, however, yet
emperrar *ref* to get stubborn
empezar §18 *tr & intr* to begin
empicar §73 *ref* to become infatuated
empicotar *tr* to pillory
empiema *m* empyema
empina•do -da *adj* high, lofty; steep; stiff, stuck-up || *f* (aer) zoom, zooming; **irse a la empinada** (*un caballo*) to rear
empinar *tr* to raise, lift; tip over; (*el codo*) crook; (aer) to zoom || *intr* to be a toper || *ref* to stand on tiptoe; (*un caballo*) rear; tower, rise high; (aer) to zoom
empingorota•do -da *adj* influential; proud, haughty
empingorotar *tr* to put on top || *ref* to climb up, get up; be stuck-up
empíre•o -a *adj & m* empyrean
empíri•co -ca *adj* empiric(al) || *mf* empiricist
empizarrado *m* slate roof
empizarrar *tr* to roof with slate
emplastar *tr* to put a plaster on; put make-up on; (*un negocio*) tie up, obstruct || *ref* to put make-up on; smear oneself up
emplásti•co -ca *adj* sticky
emplasto *m* plaster, poultice
emplazamiento *m* emplacement, location; (law) summons
emplazar §60 *tr* to place, locate; summon, summons
emplea•do -da *mf* employee; (*de oficina, de tienda*) clerk; **empleado público** civil servant
emplear *tr* to employ; use; (*el dinero*) invest; **estarle a uno bien empleado** to serve someone right || *ref* to be employed; busy oneself; **empleárselo mal** to act up, misbehave
empleo *m* employ, employment; use; job, position, occupation
empleomanía *f* eagerness to hold public office
empleóma•no -na *mf* public officeholder, bureaucrat

emplomar *tr* to lead; line with lead; (*un techo*) cover with lead; put a lead seal on; (*un diente*) (Arg) to fill
emplumar *tr* to put a feather on; adorn with feathers; tar and feather; (Hond) to thrash; **emplumarlas** (Col) to beat it || *intr* to fledge, grow feathers
emplumecer §22 *intr* to fledge, grow feathers
empobrecer §22 *tr* to impoverish || *intr & ref* to become poor
empodrecer §22 *intr & ref* to rot
empolla•do -da *adj* primed for an examination
empollar *tr* (*huevos*) to brood, hatch; (*estudiar con mucha detención*) bone up on || *intr* to grind, be a grind; **empollar sobre** to bone up on || *ref* to hatch; bone up on
empo•llón -llona *mf* (coll) grind
empolva•do -da *adj* (Mex) rusty
empolvar *tr* to cover with dust; (*el rostro*) powder || *ref* to get dusty; (*el rostro*) powder; (Mex) to get rusty
emponcha•do -da *adj* (SAm) poncho-wearing; (SAm) crafty, hypocritical; (SAm) suspicious-looking
emponzoñar *tr* to poison; corrupt
emporcar §81 *tr* to soil, dirty
emporra•do -da *adj* (*drogas*) high
empotra•do -da *adj* built-in; recessed
empotrar *tr* to embed, recess, fasten in a wall || *intr & ref* to fit, interlock
emprende•dor -dora *adj* enterprising
emprender *tr* to undertake; **emprenderla con** to squabble with, have it out with; **emprenderla para** to set out for
empreñar *tr* to make pregnant || *ref* to become pregnant
empresa *f* enterprise, undertaking; company, concern, firm; device, motto; (*la parte patronal*) management; **empresa anunciadora** advertising agency; **empresa de servicios públicos** public utility; **empresa de tranvías** traction company; **empresa tiburón** raider; **pequeña empresa** small business
empresarial *adj* managerial
empresa•rio -ria *mf* contractor; business leader, industrialist; manager; promoter; theatrical manager; **empresario de circo** showman; **empresario de pompas fúnebres** undertaker; **empresario de publicidad** advertising man; **empresario de teatro** impresario, theater manager
emprestar *tr* to borrow
empréstito *m* loan, government loan
empujar *tr* to push, shove; replace || *intr* to push, shove
empujatierra *f* bulldozer
empuje *m* push; (*fuerza o presión ejercidas por una cosa sobre otra*) thrust; (*espíritu emprendedor*) enterprise, push
empujón *m* hard push, shove; **tratar a empujones** to push around
empuñadura *f* (*de la espada*) hilt; first words of a story; (*de bastón o paraguas*) handle
empuñar *tr* to seize, grasp, clutch; (*un empleo o puesto*) obtain; (*la mano*) (Chile) to clench; (Bol) to punch; **empuñar el bastón** (fig) to seize the reins
emular *tr & intr* to emulate; **emular con** to emulate, vie with
ému•lo -la *adj* emulous || *mf* rival
emulsión *f* emulsion
emulsionar *tr* to emulsify
en *prep* at; in; into; by; on; of, e.g., **pensar en** to think of
enaceitar *tr* to oil || *ref* to get oily, get rancid
enagua *f* petticoat; skirt; **enaguas** petticoat
enagüillas *fpl* kilt, short skirt
enajenación *f* alienation; estrangement; rapture; (*distracción*) absent-mindedness; **enajenación mental** mental derangement
enajenar *tr* (*la propiedad, el dominio; a un amigo*) to alienate, estrange; enrapture, transport || *ref* to be enraptured, be transported; **enajenarse de** to dispossess oneself of; (*un amigo*) become alienated from
enaltecer §22 *tr* to exalt, extol
enamoradi•zo -za *adj* susceptible
enamora•do -da *adj* lovesick; (*propenso a enamorarse*) susceptible || *mf* sweetheart || *m* lover, boyfriend
enamorar *tr* to make love to; enamor, captivate || *ref* to fall in love
enamoricar §73 *ref* to trifle in love
enangostar *tr & ref* to narrow
ena•no -na *adj* dwarfish || *mf* dwarf
enarbolar *tr* to hoist, hang out; (*una espada*) brandish || *ref* to get angry; (*el caballo*) rear
enarcar §73 *tr* to arch; (*los toneles*) hoop || *ref* to become confused, be bashful; (*el caballo*) (Mex) to rear
enardecer §22 *tr* to inflame, excite || *ref* to get excited; (*una parte del cuerpo*) become inflamed, get sore
enarenar *tr* to throw sand on || *ref* (naut) to run aground
enastar *tr* (*una herramienta*) to put a handle on; (*una bandera*) put a shaft on
encabalgamiento *m* gun carriage; trestlework; (*en el verso*) enjambment
encabalgar §44 *tr* to provide with horses || *intr* to lean, rest
encaballar *tr* to overlap; (typ) to pie
encabezamiento *m* heading; (*fórmula con que comienza un documento*) opening words; tax list; tax rate; **encabezamiento de factura** billhead
encabezar §60 *tr* (*un escrito*) to put a heading or title on; head; register; (*vinos*) fortify
encabritar *ref* (*un caballo*) to rear; (*un buque*) shoot up, pitch up; (*un avión*) nose up
encadenar *tr* to chain, put in chains; brace, buttress; bind, tie together; tie down
encajar *tr* to fit, fit in, make fit; insert, put in; (*un golpe*) give, let go; (*dinero*) put away; (*un chiste*) tell at the wrong time; to palm off; throw, hurl, **encajar una cosa a uno** to foist

something on someone, palm something off on someone || *intr* to fit; (*una puerta*) close right || *ref* to squeeze one's way; (*una prenda de vestir*) put on; butt in, intrude
encaje *m* (*tejido de mallas*) lace; (*labor de taracea*) inlay, mosaic; recess, groove; fitting, matching; insertion; insert; appearance, look
encaje•ro -ra *mf* lacemaker; lace dealer
encajonado *m* cofferdam
encajonar *tr* to box, crate, case; squeeze in || *ref* (*un río*) to narrow, narrow down; squeeze in, squeeze through
encalambrar *ref* to get cramps
encalar *tr* (*espolvorear con cal*) to lime, sprinkle with lime; (*blanquear con cal*) whitewash
encalladero *m* sand bank, shoal
encallar *intr* to run aground; fail, get stuck
encallecer §22 *intr* (*la piel*) to become callous || *ref* to become callous; (fig) to become callous, become hardened
encalma•do -da *adj* (*mercado de valores*) dull, quiet; (*mar, viento*) becalmed
encalvecer §22 *intr* to get bald
encamar *tr* to spread out on the ground || *ref* to take to bed; (*el grano*) droop, bend over
encaminar *tr* to direct, show the way to; (*sus esfuerzos, su atención*) direct || *ref* to set out
encanalar *tr* to channel, pipe
encandecer §22 *tr* to make white-hot
encandila•do -da *adj* (*sombrero*) cocked; stiff, erect
encandilar *tr* to daze, befuddle; (*un fuego*) to stir || *ref* (*los ojos*) to flash
encanecer §22 *intr & ref* to turn gray; get old; become moldy
encanta•do -da *adj* absent-minded, distracted; (*casa*) rambling
encanta•dor -dora *adj* charming, enchanting || *mf* charmer || *f* enchantress
encantamiento *m* charm, enchantment
encantar *tr* to charm, enchant, bewitch
encante *m* auction sale; auction house
encanto *m* charm, enchantment, spell
encantusar *tr* to coax, wheedle
encañada *f* gorge, ravine
encañar *tr* (*el agua*) to pipe; (*las tierras*) drain; (*las plantas*) prop up; wind on a spool
encañizada *f* reed fence; weir
encañonar *tr* to pipe; wind on a spool; (*un pliego*) (typ) to tip in
encaperuzar §60 *tr* to put a hood on || *ref* to put on one's hood
encapotar *tr* to cloak || *ref* to frown; cloud over, become overcast
encaprichar *ref* to insist on getting one's way; become infatuated
encaracolado *m* spiral ornament, spiral work
encara•do -da *adj* — **bien encarado** well-featured; **mal encarado** ill-featured
encaramar *tr* to raise up, lift up; praise, extol; elevate, exalt || *ref* to climb, get on top; rise, tower; blush
encarar *tr* to aim, point; (*una dificultad*) face || *intr & ref* to come face to face
encarcelar *tr* to incarcerate, imprison, jail; (*piezas de madera recién encoladas*) clamp; plaster in || *ref* to stay indoors
encarecer §22 *tr* (*el precio*) to raise; raise the price of; extol; urge; overrate || *intr & ref* to rise, rise in price
encarecidamente *adv* earnestly, insistently, eagerly
encarga•do -da *mf* agent, representative; **encargado de negocios** chargé d'affaires
encargamiento *m* duty; obligation; charge
encargar §44 *tr* (*mercancías*) to order; (*confiar*) entrust; urge, warn || *ref* to take charge, be in charge; **encargarse del servicio de comida** to cater; **encargarse el buffet de** to cater (*a banquet, party, dinner*)
encargo *m* assignment, job, charge; (*pedido*) order; warning; **como de encargo** or **ni de encargo** just the thing, as if made to order
encariñamiento *m* endearment
encariñar *tr* to awaken love in || *ref* — **encariñarse con** to become fond of, become attached to
encarnación *f* incarnation, embodiment
encarna•do -da *adj* red; Caucasian-skin-("flesh")-colored; (*de forma humana*) incarnate
encarnar *tr* to incarnate, embody; (*el anzuelo*) bait || *intr* to become incarnate; (*una herida*) heal over
encarnecer §22 *intr* to put on flesh
encarniza•do -da *adj* bloodshot; bloody, fierce, bitter, hard-fought
encarnizar §60 *tr* to anger, provoke || *ref* to get angry; become fierce; **encarnizarse con** or **en** to be merciless to
encaro *m* aim; stare; blunderbuss
encarrilar *tr* to put back on the rails; set right, put on the right track; guide, direct
encarruja•do -da *adj* wrinkled; (*pelo*) kinky; (*terreno*) (Mex) rough
encartar *tr* to enroll, register; outlaw; (*un naipe*) slip in || *ref* to be unable to discard
encarte *m* (typ) insert
encartonar *tr* to cover with cardboard; (*libros*) bind in boards
encasar *tr* (*un hueso dislocado*) to set (*a broken bone*)
encasillado *m* set of pigeonholes; (*lista de candidatos apoyados por el gobierno*) government slate; (SAm) checkerwork
encasillar *tr* to pigeonhole; sort out, classify; (*el gobierno a un candidato*) slate
encasquetar *tr* (*un sombrero*) to stick on the head; (*una idea*) drive in; force on
encasquillar *tr* to put a tip on; (*un caballo*) shoe || *ref* to stick, get stuck
encastilla•do -da *adj* haughty, proud
encastillar *tr* to fortify with castles; pile up || *ref* to stick, get stuck; take to the hills; stick to one's opinion

encastrar *tr* to engage, mesh
encastre *m* engaging, meshing; groove, socket; insert
encauchar *tr* to cover with rubber, line with rubber
encausar *tr* to prosecute, sue, bring to trial
encausticar §73 *tr* to wax
encáustico *m* floor wax, furniture polish
encauzar §60 *tr* (*una corriente*) to channel; guide, direct
encavar *ref* to hide, burrow
encebollado *m* beef stew with onions
encefalopatía *f* brain disease; (vet) **encefalopatía espongiforme bovina** mad cow disease
encelar *tr* to make jealous || *ref* to get jealous; be in rut
encella *f* cheese mold
encenagar §44 *ref* to get covered with mud; wallow in vice
encencerrar *tr* (*al ganado*) to put a bell on
encendajas *fpl* kindling, brush
encendedor *m* lighter; **encendedor de bolsillo** pocket lighter
encender §51 *tr* to light, kindle; ignite, fire to; (*la luz, la radio*) turn on; (*la lengua*) burn; stir up, excite || *ref* to catch fire, ignite; become excited; blush
encendi•do -da *adj* bright, high-colored; red, flushed; keen, enthusiastic || *m* ignition
encenizar §60 *tr* to cover with ashes || *ref* to get covered with ashes
encepar *tr* to put in the stocks || *intr & ref* to take deep root
encera•do -da *adj* wax, wax-colored; (*huevo*) boiled || *m* oilcloth; tarpaulin; (*pizarra*) blackboard
encerar *tr* to wax || *intr & ref* (*el grano*) to ripen, turn yellow
encerotar *tr* (*el hilo*) to wax
encerradero *m* sheepfold; (taur) bull pen
encerrar §2 *tr* to shut in; lock in, lock up; contain, include; encircle; imply || *ref* to lock oneself in; go into seclusion; **encerrarse con** to be closeted with
encerrona *f* dilemma; tight spot; (coll) fix
encespedar *tr* to sod
encestar *tr* to put in a basket; (coll) to sink (*a basketball*)
enchapado *m* veneer
enchapar *tr* to veneer
encharcar §73 *tr* to make a puddle of; (*el estómago*) upset || *ref* to turn into a puddle; wallow in vice
enchavetar *tr* to key
enchichar *ref* (SAm) to get drunk; (CAm) to get angry
enchilada *f* (Guat, Mex) corn cake with tomato sauce seasoned with chili
enchilado *m* (Cuba, Mex) shellfish stew with chili sauce
enchilo•so -sa *adj* (CAm, Mex) spicy, hot
enchinar *tr* to pave with pebbles; (Mex) to curl || *ref* (Mex) to get goose flesh
enchispar *tr* to make drunk || *ref* to get drunk
enchivar *ref* (Col, Ecuad, CAm) to fly into a rage
enchufar *tr* (*un tubo o caño*) to fit; (*dos tubos o caños*) connect, connect together; (*dos negocios*) merge; (elec) to connect, plug in || *intr* to fit || *ref* to merge
enchufe *m* fitting; (*de tubo o caño*) male end; (*de dos tubos*) joint; (elec) connector; (elec) plug; (elec) receptacle; sinecure, easy job; **tener enchufe** to have pull, have a drag
enchufismo *m* spoils system; wire pulling
enchufista *m* spoilsman
encía *f* gum
encíclica *f* encyclical
enciclopedia *f* encyclopedia
enciclopédi•co -ca *adj* encyclopedic
encierro *m* locking up, confinement; sit-in; inclusion; encirclement; lockup, prison; solitary confinement; retirement, retreat; (taur) bull pen
encima *adv* above, overhead, on top; at hand, here now; besides, in addition; **de encima** (Chile) in the bargain; **echarse encima** to take upon oneself; **encima de** on, upon; above, over; **por encima** hastily, superficially; **por encima de** above, over; in spite of; **quitarse de encima** to get rid of, shake off
encina *f* holm oak, evergreen oak
encinta *adj* pregnant; **dejar encinta** to make pregnant
encintado *m* curb
encintar *tr* to trim with ribbons; provide with curbs
enclaustrar *tr* to cloister; hide away
enclavar *tr* to nail; pierce, transfix; (*el pie del caballo*) prick; cheat
enclave *m* enclave
enclavijar *tr* to dowel; (*un instrumento*) to peg
enclenque *adj* sickly, feeble
enclíti•co -ca *adj & m* enclitic
enclocar §81 *intr & ref* to brood
encofrado *m* planking, timbering; (*para el hormigón*) form
encoger §17 *tr* to shrink, shrivel; discourage; draw in || *intr* to shrink, shrivel || *ref* to shrink, shrivel; be discouraged; be bashful; (*humillarse*) cringe; (*en la cama*) curl up; **encogerse de hombros** to shrug one's shoulders
encogi•do -da *adj* bashful, timid
encogimiento *m* shrinkage; crouch; bashfulness, timidity; **encogimiento de hombros** shrug
encojar *tr* to cripple, lame || *ref* to become lame; feign illness
encolar *tr* to glue; (*la superficie que ha de pintarse*) size; (*el vino*) clarify; (*p.ej., una pelota*) throw out of reach
encolerizar §60 *tr* to anger || *ref* to get angry
encomendar §2 *tr* to commend, entrust, commit; knight || *ref* to commend oneself; send regards
encomiar *tr* to praise, extol

encomienda *f* charge, commission; commendation, praise; favor, protection; knight's cross; royal land grant (*with Indian inhabitants*); parcel post; (Mex) fruit stand
encomio *m* encomium
enconamiento *m* soreness; rancor, ill will
enconar *tr* to make sore, inflame; aggravate, irritate || *ref* to get sore, become inflamed; (*una herida; el ánimo de uno*) rankle, fester
enconchar *ref* to draw back into one's shell, keep aloof
encono *m* rancor, ill will; (Col, Chile, Mex, W-I) soreness
encono•so -sa *adj* sore, sensitive; harmful; rancorous
encontra•do -da *adj* opposite, facing; contrary; hostile; **estar encontrados** to be at odds
encontrar *tr* to encounter, meet; (*hallar*) find || *intr* to meet; collide || *ref* to meet, meet each other; be, be situated; find oneself; **encontrarse con** to meet, run into
encontrón *m* bump, jolt, collision
encopeta•do -da *adj* aristocratic, of noble descent; conceited, boastful
encorajar *tr* to encourage || *ref* to fly into a rage
encorajinar *ref* to fly into a rage; (Chile) to break up, go to ruin
encorchar *tr* (*botellas*) to cork; (*abejas*) to hive
encordar §61 *tr* (*un violín, una raqueta*) to string; wrap, wind up with rope
encordelar *tr* to string; tie with strings
encornudar *tr* to cuckold, make a cuckold of || *intr* to grow horns
encorralar *tr* to corral
encortinar *tr* to curtain
encorvada *f* stoop, bending over; **hacer la encorvada** to malinger
encorvar *tr* to bend over || *ref* to stoop, bend over; be partial, be biased
encovar §61 *tr & ref* to hide away
encrespar *tr* to curl; (*el pelo*) make stand on end; (*plumas*) ruffle; (*las olas*) stir up; irritate, anger || *ref* to curl; bristle, stand on end; (*el mar, las olas*) get rough; get involved; bristle, get angry
encresta•do -da *adj* proud, haughty
encriptar *tr* (compu) to encrypt
encrucijada *f* crossroads, street intersection; ambush, snare, trap
encrudecer §22 *tr* to make raw; aggravate
encuadernación *f* bookbinding; (*taller*) bindery; **encuadernación a la holandesa** half binding
encuaderna•dor -dora *mf* bookbinder
encuadernar *tr* to bind; **sin encuadernar** unbound
encuadrar *tr* (*encerrar en un marco o cuadro*) to frame; (*incluir dentro de sí*) encompass; (*encajar*) insert, fit in; (Arg) to summarize
encuadre *m* film adaptation; (mov & telv) frame
encubar *tr* to put in a cask or vat; (min) to shore up
encubierta *f* fraud, deception
encubrimiento *m* concealment; (law) complicity
encubrir §83 *tr* to hide, conceal || *ref* to hide; disguise oneself
encuentro *m* encounter, meeting; clash, collision; (*hallazgo*) find; (sport) game, match; **encuentro fronterizo** border clash; **llevarse de encuentro** (CAm, Mex, W-I) to knock down, run over; (CAm, Mex, W-I) to drag down to ruin; **mal encuentro** foul play; **salir al encuentro a** to go to meet; get ahead of; take a stand against
encuerar *tr* to strip of clothes; fleece || *ref* to strip, get undressed
encuesta *f* inquiry; **encuesta demoscópica** opinion poll; survey
encuestador *m* pollster
encuitar *ref* to grieve
encumbra•do -da *adj* high, lofty; sublime; influential
encumbramiento *m* height, elevation; exaltation
encumbrar *tr* to raise, elevate; exalt || *ref* to rise; be exalted; be proud; be flowery, use flowery speech; (*subir una cosa a mucha altura*) tower
encunar *tr* to cradle; catch between the horns
encurtido *m* pickle
encurtir *tr* to pickle
ende *adv* — **por ende** therefore
endeble *adj* feeble, weak; worthless
endecha *f* dirge
endechadera *f* hired mourner
endemia *f* endemic
endémi•co -ca *adj* endemic
endemonia•do -da *adj* possessed of the devil; furious, wild; (coll) devilish
endenantes *adv* recently
endentar §2 *tr & intr* to mesh
endentecer §22 *intr* to teethe
enderezar §60 *tr* to stand up; straighten; direct; put in order; regulate || *intr* to go straight || *ref* to stand up, straighten up; head, make one's way; go straight; (aer) to flatten out, level off
endeuda•do -da *adj* indebted
endeudamiento *m* indebtedness
endeudar *ref* to run into debt; acknowledge one's indebtedness
endevota•do -da *adj* pious, devout; fond, devoted
endiabla•do -da *adj* devilish; deformed, ugly; mean, wicked; (Arg) difficult, complicated
endilgar §44 *tr* to send, direct; to spring, unload
endiosar *tr* to deify || *ref* to get stuck-up; get absorbed
endominga•do -da *adj* Sunday; all dressed up
endomingar §44 *ref* to get dressed in one's Sunday best
endosante *mf* endorser
endosar *tr* (*un documento de crédito*) to endorse; (*una cosa poco grata*) unload
endosata•rio -ria *mf* endorsee
endoso *m* endorsement

endriago *m* fabulous monster
endri•no -na *adj* sloe-colored || *m* (*arbusto*) sloe, blackthorn || *f* (*fruto*) sloe
endrogar §44 *ref* to run into debt; take drugs
endulzar §60 *tr* to sweeten; make bearable
endura•dor -dora *adj* saving, stingy
endurar *tr* to harden; delay, put off; (*tolerar*) endure; save, spare || *ref* to get hard
endurecer §22 *tr* to harden; (*robustecer, acostumbrar*) inure
endureci•do -da *adj* hard, strong; inured; hardhearted; tenacious, obstinate
enebrina *f* juniper berry
enebro *m* juniper
enecha•do -da *adj & mf* foundling
eneldo *m* dill
enema *f* enema
enemiga *f* enmity, hatred
enemi•go -ga *adj* enemy; hostile || *mf* enemy, foe; **el enemigo malo** the Evil One || *f* see **enemiga**
enemistad *f* enmity
enemistar *tr* to make an enemy of; make enemies of || *ref* to become enemies
energéti•co -ca *adj* energy; power
energía *f* energy; power; **energía atómica** atomic power (or energy); **energías alternas** alternate energy sources; **energía eólica** windpower; **energía hidráulica** waterpower; **energía nuclear** nuclear power, nuclear energy; **energía solar** solar energy
enérgi•co -ca *adj* energetic
energúme•no -na *adj* fiendish || *mf* crazy person, wild person
enero *m* January
enervar *tr* to enervate; weaken
enési•mo -ma *adj* nth, umpteenth
enfadadi•zo -za *adj* peevish, irritable
enfadar *tr* to annoy, bother; anger
enfado *m* annoyance, bother; anger
enfado•so -sa *adj* annoying, disagreeable
enfaldar *ref* to tuck up one's skirt
enfardar *tr* to bale, pack
énfa•sis *m* (*pl* **-sis**) emphasis; bombast, affected speech
enfatizar §60 *tr* to emphasize
enfáti•co -ca *adj* emphatic; affected
enfermar *tr* to make sick || *intr* to get sick
enfermedad *f* sickness, illness, disease; **enfermedad del legionario** Legionnaires disease; **enfermedad del sueño** sleeping sickness; **enfermedad de transmisión sexual** sexually transmitted disease; **enfermedad mental** mental illness; **enfermedad venérea** venereal disease
enfermera *f* nurse; **enfermera ambulante** visiting nurse
enfermería *f* infirmary
enfermero *m* male nurse
enfermi•zo -za *adj* sickly; (*clima*) unhealthy
enfer•mo -ma *adj* sick, ill; (*enfermizo*) sickly; **enfermo de amor** lovesick; **los enfermos mentales** the insane || *mf* patient
enfermo•so -sa *adj* sickly
enfiestar *ref* to have a good time
enfilar *tr* to line up; (*p.ej., perlas*) string; aim; go down, go up; (mil) to enfilade || *intr* to bear
enfisema *m* emphysema
enflaquecer §22 *tr* to make thin; weaken || *intr* to get thin; flag, slacken || *ref* to get thin, lose weight
enflauta•do -da *adj* pompous, inflated
enflautar *tr* to blow up, inflate; cheat
enfocar §73 *tr* to focus; (fig) to size up
enfoque *m* focus, focusing; (fig) approach (*to a problem*)
enfoscar §73 *tr* to trim with mortar; patch with mortar; darken, make dark || *ref* to become sullen, become grouchy; become absorbed in business; become overcast
enfrailar *tr* to make a friar or monk of || *ref* to become a friar or monk
enfranque *m* shank
enfrascar §73 *tr* to bottle || *ref* to become involved, intangled; be sunk in work; have a good time
enfrenar *tr* (*un caballo*) to bridle; (*un tren*) brake; check
enfrentamiento *m* (*policía, masas*) confrontation
enfrentar *tr* to put face to face; (*p.ej., al enemigo*) face || *intr* to be facing || *ref* to meet face to face; **enfrentarse con** to stand up to; cope with
enfrente *adv* opposite, in front; **enfrente de** opposite, in front of; opposed to
enfriadera *f* bottle cooler, ice pail
enfriar §77 *tr* to cool, chill; kill || *intr & ref* to cool off
enfundar *tr* to sheathe, put in a case; stuff; (*un tambor*) muffle
enfurecer §22 *tr* to infuriate, anger || *ref* to rage
enfurruñar *ref* to sulk
engalanar *tr* to adorn, deck out, dress
engalla•do -da *adj* straight, erect; haughty
engallador *m* checkrein
enganchar *tr* to hook; (*un caballo*) hitch; (*un coche de ferrocarril*) couple; recruit; inveigle || *intr* to get caught || *ref* to get caught; (mil) to enlist
enganche *m* hook; hooking; hitching; coupling; inveigling; recruiting; enlisting; (rr) coupler
engañabo•bos *mf* (*pl* **-bos**) bamboozler
engaña•dor -dora *adj* deceptive; (*simpático*) winsome
engañar *tr* to deceive, cheat, fool; (*el tiempo*) while away; (*el sueño, el hambre*) ward off; wheedle || *ref* to be mistaken
engañifa *f* deception, trick
engaño *m* deception, deceit, fraud; mistake; falsehood; **llamarse a engaño** to back out because of fraud
engaño•so -sa *adj* deceptive
engargantar *tr* (*un ave*) to stuff the throat of || *intr & ref* to mesh, engage

engarzar §60 *tr* to link, string, wire; curl; enchase; (Col) to hook
engastar *tr* to enchase, mount, set
engaste *m* enchasing, mounting, setting
engatusar *tr* to coax, wheedle; inveigle, sweet-talk
engendrar *tr* to beget, engender; (geom) to generate
engendro *m* foetus; botch, bungle; (*criatura informe*) runt, stunt; **mal engendro** (coll) young tough
engolfar *intr* to go far out in the ocean || *ref* to go far out in the ocean; become deeply involved; be lost in thought
engoma•do -da *adj* (Chile) all dressed up || *m* (CAm) hangover
engomar *tr* to gum || *ref* to have a hangover
engorda *f* fattening; animals being fattened
engordar *tr* to fatten || *intr* to get fat; (coll) to get fat, get rich
engorro *m* bother, nuisance, obstacle
engorro•so -sa *adj* annoying
engoznar *tr* to hinge, to hang on a hinge
engranaje *m* gear, gears, teeth; (fig) link, connection; **engranaje de distribución** (aut) timing gears; **engranaje de tornillo sin fin** worm gear
engranar *tr* to gear, mesh; throw into gear || *intr* to gear, mesh
engrandecer §22 *tr* to amplify, enlarge, magnify; exalt, extol; enhance
engrane *m* gear; mesh
engranerar *tr* (*el grano*) to store
engrapa•dor -dora *mf* stapler
engrapar *tr* to clamp, cramp
engrasador *m* grease cup; **engrasador de pistón** grease gun
engrasar *tr* to grease; smear with grease
engrase *m* greasing; grease
engravar *tr* to spread gravel over
engredar *tr* to chalk, to clay
engreí•do -da *adj* conceited, vain
engreimiento *m* conceit, vanity
engreír §58 *tr* to make conceited; spoil, pamper || *ref* to become conceited
engreña•do -da *adj* disheveled
engrescar §73 *tr* to incite to fight; incite to merriment || *ref* to pick a fight; join in the fun
engrifar *tr* to curl, crisp || *ref* to curl up; stand on end; (*un caballo*) rear
engrillar *tr* to shackle, fetter || *ref* (*las patatas*) to sprout
engringar §44 *ref* to act like a foreigner
engrosar §61 *tr* to broaden; enlarge || *intr* to get fat || *ref* to broaden; swell, get bigger
engrudar *tr* to paste
engrudo *m* paste
engualdrapar *tr* to caparison
enguapear *ref* (Mex) to get drunk
enguirnaldar *tr* to garland, wreathe; trim, bedeck
engullir §13 *tr* to gulp down
engurrio *m* sadness, melancholy
enhebrar *tr* (*una aguja*) to thread; (*perlas*) string; (*mentiras*) rattle off
enhestar §2 *tr* to stand upright, erect; hoist, lift up
enhies•to -ta *adj* upright, straight, erect
enhilar *tr* to thread; direct; line up; (*ideas*) marshal || *intr* to set out
enhorabuena *adv* safely, luckily; **enhorabuena que** thank heavens that || *f* congratulations; **dar la enhorabuena a** to congratulate
enhoramala *adv* unluckily, under an unlucky star; **nacer enhoramala** to be born under an unlucky star; **vete enhoramala** go to the devil
enhornar *tr* to put into the oven
enigma *m* enigma, riddle, puzzle
enigmáti•co -ca *adj* enigmatic(al)
enjabonar *tr* to soap, lather; (*adular*) (coll) to soft-soap; (*reprender*) (coll) to upbraid
enjaezar §60 *tr* to harness, put trappings on
enjalbegado *m* whitewashing
enjalbegar §44 *tr* to whitewash; (*el rostro*) paint || *ref* to paint the face
enjambrar *intr* (*las abejas*) to swarm; to multiply in great numbers
enjambre *m* swarm
enjaretado *m* grating, lattice work
enjarrar *ref* (C-R, Mex) to stand with arms akimbo
enjaular *tr* to cage; jail, lock up
enjergar §44 *tr* to launch, get started, start on a shoestring
enjoyar *tr* to adorn with jewels; set with precious stones; adorn
enjuagadien•tes *m* (*pl* **-tes**) mouthwash
enjuagar §44 *tr* to rinse, rinse out
enjuague *m* rinse; rinsing water; mouthwash; rinsing cup; (coll) plot
enjugador *m* drier; clotheshorse
enjugama•nos *m* (*pl* **-nos**) towel, hand towel
enjugaparabri•sas *m* (*pl* **-sas**) windshield wiper
enjugar §44 *tr* (*secar*) to dry; (*el sudor*) wipe, wipe off; (*lágrimas*) wipe away; (*deudas, un déficit*) wipe out || *ref* to lose weight
enjuiciamiento *m* procedure; prosecution, impeachment, suit; trial; judgment, sentence
enjuiciar *tr* to prosecute, sue, impeach; try; judge
enjundio•so -sa *adj* fatty, greasy; solid, substantial
enju•to -ta *adj* (*tiempo, clima; ojos*) dry; lean, skinny; quiet, stolid || **enjutos** *mpl* brushwood; (*para excitar la gana de beber*) tidbits
enlabiar *tr* to entice, take in; press one's lips against
enlace *m* connection, linking, link; relationship; betrothal, engagement; marriage; (compu) linkage; (mil, phonet) liaison; (rad, telv) linkup; (rr) connection, junction; **enlace sindical** (Esp) shop steward
enlaciar *tr, intr & ref* to wither, wilt, shrivel; rumple

enladrillado *m* brickwork; bricklaying; brick paving
enladrillar *tr* to pave with bricks
enlajado *m* (Ven) flagstone
enlajar *tr* (Ven) to pave with flagstones
enlardar *tr* to baste
enlatado *m* canning
enlatar *tr* to can; roof with tin, line with tin
enlazar §60 *tr* to connect, link; lace; (*un animal con el lazo*) lasso || *intr* (*p.ej., dos trenes*) to connect || *ref* to be connected, be linked; connect; get married; become related by marriage
enlechar *tr* to grout
enlistonado *m* lathing, lath
enlistonar *tr* to lath
enlodar *tr* to muddy, smear with mud; plaster with mud; seal with mud; (fig) to sling mud at
enloquecer §22 *tr* to drive crazy || *intr* to go crazy
enloquecimiento *m* insanity, madness
enlosado *m* flagstone paving
enlosar *tr* to pave with flagstone
enlozar §60 *tr* to enamel
enlozado *m* enamelware
enlucido *m* plaster, coat (*of plaster*)
enlucir §45 *tr* (*una pared*) to plaster; (*la plata*) polish
enlutar *tr* to put in mourning, hang with crape; darken, sadden || *ref* to dress in mourning
enmaderar *tr* to cover with boards; build the framework for
enmagrecer §22 *tr* to make thin || *intr & ref* to get thin
enmalecer §22 *tr* to spoil || *ref* to get full of weeds, be overgrown with weeds
enmarañar *tr* to entangle; confuse || *ref* to become entangled; become overcast, get cloudy
enmarcar §73 *tr* to frame
enmarchitar *tr & ref* to wither
enmaridar *intr & ref* to take a husband
enmarillecer §22 *ref* to turn yellow, turn pale
enmasar *tr* (*tropas*) to mass
enmascaramiento *m* (compu) masking
enmascarar *tr* to mask; camouflage || *ref* to put on a mask; masquerade
enmasillar *tr* to putty, caulk
enmendación *f* emendation
enmendar §2 *tr* (*corregir*) to emend; (*reformar*) amend; (*resarcir*) make amends for || *ref* to amend, mend one's ways, go straight
enmienda *f* (*corrección*) emendation; (*propuesta de variante*) amendment; (*satisfacción del daño hecho*) amends
enmohecer §22 *tr* to make moldy; rust; neglect || *ref* to get moldy; rust; (*la memoria*) get rusty; fade away
enmontar *ref* (CAm, Mex, Col, Ven) to become overgrown with brush
enmudecer §22 *tr* to hush, silence || *intr* to hush up, keep quiet; become dumb, lose one's voice
enmuescar §73 *tr* to notch; (carp) to mortise
ennegrecer §22 *tr* to blacken, dye black || *ref* to turn black; (*el porvenir*) be black
ennoblecer §22 *tr* to ennoble; glorify, enhance
ennoblecimiento *m* ennoblement; glory, splendor; (*grandeza de alma*) nobility
enodio *m* fawn, young deer
enojada *f* (Mex) fit of anger
enojadi•zo -za *adj* irritable, ill-tempered
enojar *tr* to anger; annoy, vex || *ref* to get angry; **enojarse con** *or* **contra** to get angry with (*a person*); **enojarse de** to get angry at (*a thing*)
enojo *m* anger; annoyance, bother
eno•jón -jona *adj* (Chile, Ecuad, Mex) irritable, ill-tempered
enojo•so -sa *adj* annoying, bothersome
enorgullecer §22 *tr* to fill with pride, make proud || *ref* to be proud; **enorgullecerse de** to pride oneself on
enorme *adj* enormous, huge
enotecnia *f* wine making; oenology
enquiciar *tr* (*una puerta, una ventana*) to hang; fasten, make firm
enrabiar *tr* to enrage || *intr* to have rabies || *ref* to become enraged
enramar *tr* (*ramos*) to intertwine; adorn with branches || *intr* to sprout branches || *ref* to hide in the branches
enranciar *tr* to make rancid || *ref* to get rancid
enrarecer §22 *tr* to rarefy; make scarce || *intr* to become scarce || *ref* to rarefy; become scarce
enrarecimiento *m* (*p.ej., del aire*) thinness; scarceness, scarcity
enrasar *tr* to make flush; grade, level || *intr* to be flush
enratonar *ref* to get sick from eating mice; (Ven) to have a hangover
enredadera *adj* (*planta*) climbing || *f* climbing plant, vine
enreda•dor -dora *mf* gossip, busybody
enredar *tr* to catch in a net; (*redes, una trampa*) set; tangle up; involve, entangle; (*una pelea*) start; intertwine, interweave; endanger, compromise || *intr* to romp around, be frisky || *ref* to get tangled up; get involved, become entangled; (coll) to have an affair
enredijo *m* entanglement
enredo *m* tangle; involvement, entanglement, complication; restlessness; friskiness; mischievous lie; (*de una novela, un drama*) plot; (*trato ilícito de hombre y mujer*) liaison
enre•dón -dona *adj* scheming || *mf* schemer
enredo•so -sa *adj* entangled, complicated, difficult
enrejado *m* grating, trellis, latticework; iron railing; grill; openwork embroidery
enrejar *tr* to grate, lattice; (*una ventana*) put a grate on; fence with an iron grating; (*ladrillos, tablas*) pile alternately crosswise; (Mex) to darn
enrielar *tr* to make into ingots; lay rails on; put on the tracks; put on the right track
Enrique *m* Harry; Henry

enriquecer §22 *tr* to enrich || *intr & ref* to get rich
enrisca•do -da *adj* craggy, full of cliffs
enrizar §60 *tr & ref* to curl
enrocar §73 *tr & intr* (chess) to castle
enrodrigar §44 *tr* to prop, prop up
enrojar *tr* to redden, make red; (*el horno*) to heat up || *ref* to redden, turn red
enrojecer §22 *tr* to make red; make red-hot; make blush || *intr* to blush || *ref* to turn red; get red-hot; flush; get sore, get inflamed
enromar *tr* to make dull, make blunt
enronquecer §22 *tr* to make hoarse || *intr & ref* to get hoarse
enronquecimiento *m* hoarseness
enroque *m* (chess) castling
enroscar §73 *tr* to coil, twist, screw in || *ref* to coil, twist
enrubiar *tr* to bleach, make blond || *ref* to turn blond
enrubio *m* bleaching; bleaching lotion
enrular *tr & ref* (Arg) to curl
ensacar §73 *tr* to bag, put in a bag
ensaimada *f* twisted coffee cake
ensalada *f* salad; hodgepodge; fiasco, flop; **ensalada de repollo** (cole) slaw
ensaladera *f* salad bowl
ensalmar *tr* (*un hueso*) to set; treat or heal by incantation
ensalmo *m* incantation, spell; **como por ensalmo** as if by magic
ensalzar §60 *tr* to exalt, elevate, extol
ensamblar *tr* to assemble, join, fit together; **ensamblar a cola de milano** *or* **a cola de pato** to dovetail
ensanchador *m* glove stretcher
ensanchar *tr* to widen, enlarge; (*una prenda ajustada*) ease, let out; (*el corazón*) unburden || *intr & ref* to be proud and haughty
ensanche *m* widening, extension; (*de una calle*) extension; suburban development; allowance (*for enlargement of garment*)
ensandecer §22 *intr* to go crazy
ensangrenta•do -da *adj* bloody, gory
ensangrentar §2 *tr* to bathe in blood; stain with blood || *ref* to rage, go wild; (*p.ej., las manos*) bloody, make bloody
ensañar *tr* to anger, enrage || *ref* to be cruel, be merciless; (*una enfermedad*) rage
ensartar *tr* (*una aguja*) to thread; (*cuentas*) string; stick; rattle off || *ref* to squeeze in
ensayar *tr* to try, try on, try out; (*un espectáculo*) rehearse; (*minerales*) assay; teach, train; test || *ref* to practice
ensaye *m* assay
ensayista *mf* essayist; (Chile) assayer
ensayo *m* trying, trial; testing, test; (*género literario*) essay; (*de minerales*) assay; exercise, practice; (theat) rehearsal; **ensayo de choque** (aut) crash test; **ensayo general** dress rehearsal
ensenada *f* inlet, cove
enseña *f* standard, ensign
enseña•do -da *adj* trained, informed; (*perro de caza*) trained
enseñanza *f* teaching; education, instruction; (*ejemplo que sirve de experiencia*) lesson; **enseñanza superior** higher education
enseñar *tr* to teach; train; show, point out || *intr* to teach
enseñorear *ref* to control oneself; **enseñorearse de** to take possession of
enseres *mpl* utensils, equipment, household goods, chattels
enseriar *ref* to become serious
ensilado *m* silage
ensilaje *m* silage
ensillar *tr* to saddle
ensimismamiento *m* absorption in thought, deep thought
ensimismar *ref* to become absorbed in thought; (Chile, Ecuad, Peru) to be proud, be boastful
ensoberbecer §22 to make proud || *ref* to become proud; (*el mar, las olas*) swell, get rough
ensoberbecimiento *m* haughtiness
ensombrecer §22 *tr* to darken || *ref* to get dark; become sad and gloomy
ensoña•dor -dora *adj* dreamy || *mf* dreamer
ensopar *tr* to dip, dunk; soak, drench
ensordece•dor -dora *adj* deafening
ensordecer §22 *tr* to deafen; (*una consonante sonora*) unvoice || *intr* to become deaf; play deaf, not answer || *ref* to unvoice
ensortijar *tr* to curl, make curly; (*la nariz de un animal*) ring, put a ring in || *ref* to curl
ensuciar *tr* to dirty, soil; stain, smear; defile, sully || *ref* to soil oneself; take bribes
ensueño *m* dream; daydream
entablado *m* flooring; wooden framework
entablar *tr* to board, board up; (*un hueso roto*) splint; (*una conversación*) start; (*p.ej., una batalla*) launch; (*un pleito*) bring; (*las piezas del ajedrez y de las damas*) set up || *ref* (*el viento*) to settle
entable *m* boarding; (*en los juegos de ajedrez y damas*) position of men; (Col) business, undertaking
entablillar *tr* (*un hueso roto*) to splint
enta•blón -blona *adj* (Peru) blustering, bragging || *mf* (Peru) bully
entalegar §44 *tr* to bag, put in a bag; (*dinero*) hoard
entalladura *f* carving, sculpture; engraving; slot, groove, mortise; cut, incision (*in a tree*)
entallar *tr* to carve, sculpture; engrave; notch; groove, mortise; (*un traje*) fit, tailor || *intr* to take shape; (*el vestido*) fit; go well, be fitting
entallecer §22 *intr & ref* to shoot, sprout
entapizar §60 *tr* to tapestry, hang with tapestry; cover with a fabric; overgrow, spread over
entarimado *m* parquet, inlaid floor, hardwood floor
entarimar *tr* to parquet, to put an inlaid floor on || *ref* to put on airs

entarugar §44 *tr* to pave with wooden blocks || *ref* (*el sombrero*) (Ven) to stick on
ente *m* being; (coll) guy, odd fellow
enteca•do -da or **ente•co -ca** *adj* sickly, frail
enteleri•do -da *adj* shaking with cold, shaking with fright; sickly, frail
entena *f* lateen yard
entena•do -da *mf* stepchild || *m* stepson || *f* stepdaughter
entendederas *fpl* (coll) brains; **tener malas entendederas** (coll) to have no brains
entende•dor -dora *adj* understanding, intelligent || *mf* understanding person; **al buen entendedor, pocas palabras** a word to the wise is sufficient
entender *m* understanding, opinion || **§51** *tr* to understand; intend, mean || *intr* **—entender de** to be a judge of; be experienced as; **entender de razón** to listen to reason; **entender en** to be familiar with, deal with || *ref* to be understood; be meant; have a secret understanding; **entenderse con** to get along with; concern; (*una mujer*) have an affair with
entendi•do -da *adj* expert, skilled; informed; **no darse por entendido** to take no notice, pretend not to understand; **los entendidos** informed sources; **un entendido en** a well-informed person in
entendimiento *m* understanding
entenebrecer §22 *tr* to darken; confuse || *ref* to get dark; become confused
entera•do -da *adj* informed, posted; (Chile) conceited; (Chile) intrusive, meddlesome || *mf* insider
enterar *tr* to inform, acquaint; to pay; (Arg, Chile) to complete || *intr* (Chile) to get better; (Chile) to drift along || *ref* to find out; to recover; **enterarse de** to find out about, become aware of
entereza *f* entirety, completeness; wholeness; perfection; fairness; constancy, fortitude; strictness
enteri•zo -za *adj* in one piece
enternece•dor -dora *adj* moving, touching
enternecer §22 *tr* to move, touch || *ref* to be moved to pity
enternecimiento *m* pity, compassion
ente•ro -ra *adj* entire, whole, complete; honest, upright; firm, energetic; sound, vigorous; (*tela*) strong, heavy || *m* (arith) integer; payment; (Chile) balance; **por entero** entirely, wholly, completely
enterradero *m* (Arg, Urug) hideout, safe house
enterrador *m* gravedigger
enterramiento *m* burial, interment; (*hoyo*) grave; (*monumento*) tomb
enterrar §2 *tr* to bury, inter; outlive, survive || *ref* to hide away
entesar §2 *tr* to stretch, make taut
entibar *tr* to prop up, shore up || *intr* to rest, lean
entibiar *tr* to cool off; temper, moderate || *ref* to cool off, cool down
entidad *f* entity; importance, consequence, moment; body, organization
entierramuer•tos *m* (*pl* **-tos**) gravedigger
entierro *m* burial, interment; (*hoyo*) grave; (*monumento*) tomb; funeral; funeral cortege; buried treasure
entintar *tr* to ink; ink in; stain with ink; dye
entoldar *tr* to cover with awnings; adorn with hangings || *ref* to get cloudy, become overcast; swell with pride
entomología *f* entomology
entonación *f* intonation; blowing of bellows
entona•do -da *adj* arrogant; haughty; harmonious, in tune
entonar *tr* to intone; sing in tune; (*el órgano*) blow; (*colores*) harmonize; tone, tone up; (*alabanzas*) sound || *intr* to sing in tune || *ref* to be puffed up with pride
entonces *adv* then || *m* **— por aquel entonces** at that time
entonelar *tr* to put in barrels, put in casks
entongar §44 *tr* (Mex, W-I) to pile up, pile in rows; (Col) to drive crazy
entono *m* intoning; arrogance, haughtiness
entontecer §22 *tr* to make foolish, make stupid || *intr & ref* to become foolish, become stupid
entorchado *m* bullion; **ganar los entorchados** to win one's stripes
entorna•do -da *adj* ajar, half-closed
entornar *tr* to half-close; (*los ojos*) squint; (*una puerta*) leave ajar; (*volcar*) upset || *ref* to upset
entornillar *tr* to twist, screw up
entorno *m* environment
entorpecer §22 *tr* to stupefy; obstruct, delay; benumb; (*una cerradura, una ventana*) make stick || *ref* to stick, get stuck
entortar §61 *tr* to bend, make crooked; knock out the eye of || *ref* to bend, get crooked
entrada *f* entrance, entry; admission; arrival; income, receipts; admission ticket; entrance hall; (*artículo*) entry; (*número de personas que asisten a un espectáculo*) house; (*producto de cada función*) gate; (*amistad en alguna casa*) entree; (*naipes que guarda un jugador*) hand; (*de una comida*) first course (*served after the soup or appetizer and before the main course*); (*visita breve*) short call; (Col) down payment; (Mex) attack, onslaught; (compu, elec) input; **dar entrada a** to admit; to give an opening to; (*un buque*) to give the right of entry to; **entrada de aire** air intake; **entrada de gama** (compu) entry level; **entrada de taquilla** gate; **entrada general** top gallery; **entrada libre** open to the public; **entrada llena** full house; **mucha entrada** good house, good turnout; **se prohibe la entrada** no admittance
entra•do -da *adj* (Chile) officious, self-assertive; **entrado en años** advanced in years || *f* see **entrada**
entra•dor -dora *adj* (*enamoradizo*) susceptible; (Mex) lively, energetic; (Chile) officious, self-assertive

entrama•do -da *adj* half-timbered || *m* timber framework

entram•bos -bas *adj & pron indef* both; **entrambos a dos** both

entrampar *tr* to ensnare, trap; trick, deceive; overload with debt || *ref* to get trapped; be tricked; run into debt

entrante *adj* entering; (*p.ej., tren*) inbound, incoming; (*próximo, que viene*) next || *mf* entrant; **entrantes y salientes** (coll) hangers-on

entraña *f* internal organ; (fig) heart, center; **entrañas** entrails; (fig) heart, feeling; (fig) disposition, temper

entrañable *adj* close, intimate

entrañar *tr* to put away deep, bury deep; involve; (*malos pensamientos*) harbor || *ref* to go deep into; be buried deep; be close, be intimate

entrapajar *tr* to wrap up, bandage

entrar *tr* to bring in; overrun, invade; influence || *intr* to enter, go in, come in; (*un río*) empty; (*el viento, la marea*) rise; attack; begin; **entrar a matar** (taur) to go in for the kill; **entrar en** to enter, enter into, go into; fit into; adopt, take up; **que entra** next

entre *prep* (*en medio de*) between; (*en el número de*) among; (*en el intervalo de*) in the course of; **entre manos** at hand; **entre mí** to myself; **entre que** while; **entre tanto** meanwhile; **entre Ud. y yo** between you and me

entreabier•to -ta *adj* half-open; (*puerta*) ajar

entreabrir §83 *tr* to half-open; leave ajar

entreacto *m* entr'acte

entreca•no -na *adj* graying, grayish

entrecarril *m* (Ven) gauge

entrecejo *m* space between the eyebrows; frown; **fruncir el entrecejo** to frown; **mirar con entrecejo** to frown at

entrechocar §73 *ref* to collide, clash

entrecoger §17 *tr* to catch, seize; press hard, hold down

entrecoro *m* chancel

entrecorta•do -da *adj* broken, intermittent

entrecortar *tr* to break in on, keep interrupting

entre•cruz *m* (*pl* **-cruces**) interweaving

entrecruzar §60 *tr & ref* to intercross; interweave, interlace; to interbreed; to crisscross

entrecubiertas *fpl* between-decks

entredicho *m* interdiction, prohibition; (law) injunction; (Bol) alarm bell; **poner en entredicho** to cast doubt upon

entredós *m* (*tira de encaje*) insertion; (typ) long primer

entrefilete *m* short feature, special item

entrefi•no -na *adj* medium

entrega *f* delivery; (*p.ej., de una plaza fuerte*) surrender; (*cuaderno de un libro que se vende suelto*) fascicle; (*de una revista*) issue, number; **por entregas** in instalments

entregar §44 *tr* to deliver; hand over, surrender; fit in, insert; **entregarla** to die || *ref* to give in, surrender; abandon oneself; to devote oneself; **entregarse de** to take possession of, take charge of

entrehierro *m* (elec) spark gap; (phys) air gap

entrelazar §60 *tr* to interlace, interweave

entremediar *tr* to put between

entremedias *adv* in between; in the meantime; **entremedias de** between; among

entremés *m* hors d'œuvre, side dish; short farce (*inserted in an auto or performed between two acts of a comedia*)

entremesear *tr* (*una conversación*) to enliven

entremeter *tr* to put in, insert || *ref* to meddle, intrude, butt in

entremeti•do -da *adj* meddling, meddlesome || *mf* meddler, intruder, busybody

entremezclar *tr & ref* to intermingle, intermix

entremorir §30 & §83 *intr* to flicker, die out

entrenador *m* (sport) coach, trainer, handler

entrenamiento *m* (sport) coaching, training

entrenar *tr & ref* (sport) to coach, train

entrepaño *m* (*de una puerta*) panel; (*espacio entre dos columnas, etc.*) pier; shelf

entreparecer §60 *ref* to show through

entrepiernas *fpl* crotch; patches in the crotch of trousers; (Chile) bathing trunks

entrepuentes *mpl* between-decks; (naut) steerage

entrerrenglón *m* interline; space between the lines

entrerrenglonar *tr* to write between the lines

entrerriel *m* gauge

entrerrisa *f* giggle

entrerrosca *f* (mach) nipple

entresacar §73 *tr* to pick, pick out, select; cull, sift; (*árboles; el pelo*) thin out

entresemana *adv* (SAm) weekdays; workdays

entresijo *m* secret; mystery; **tener muchos entresijos** to be mysterious, be hard to figure out

entresuelo *m* mezzanine, entresol

entretallar *tr* to carve, engrave; carve in bas-relief; do openwork in; intercept

entretanto *adv* meantime, meanwhile || *m* meanwhile; **en el entretanto** in the meantime

entretecho *m* (Arg, Chile, Urug) attic, garret

entretejer *tr* to interweave

entretela *f* interlining

entretelar *tr* to interline

entretención *f* amusement, entertainment

entretener §71 *tr* to amuse, entertain; (*el tiempo*) while away; maintain, keep up; put off, delay; (*el dolor*) allay; (*el hambre*) stave off (*by taking a bite before mealtime*); try to get one's mind off || *ref* to amuse oneself, be amused

entreteni•do -da *adj* amusing, entertaining; (rad) continuous, undamped || *f* kept woman; **dar la entretenida a** *or* **dar con la entretenida a** to stall off by constant talk

entretenimiento *m* amusement, entertainment; upkeep, maintenance

entretiempo *m* in-between season; **de entretiempo** spring-and-fall (*coat*)

entreventana *f* pier
entrever **§80** *tr* to glimpse, descry, catch a glimpse of; guess, suspect
entreverar *tr* to mix || *ref* (Arg) to get all mixed together; (*dos grupos de caballería*) (Arg) to clash in hand-to-hand combat
entrevía *f* gauge
entrevista *f* interview
entrevistar *ref* to have an interview
entristecer **§22** *tr* to sadden, make sad || *ref* to sadden, become sad
entrojar *tr* to store in a granary
entrometer *tr & ref var of* **entremeter**
entrometi•do -da *adj & mf var of* **entremetido**
entronar *tr* to enthrone
entroncamiento *m* connection, relationship; (*de caminos, ferrocarriles*) junction
entroncar **§73** *tr* to prove relationship between || *intr* to be related; (*dos caminos, ferrocarriles, etc.*) connect
entronerar *tr* (*una bola de billar*) to pocket
entronizar **§60** *tr* to enthrone; exalt; popularize || *ref* to be puffed up with pride
entronque *m* connection, relationship; (*de caminos, ferrocarriles*) junction
entruchar *tr* to decoy, trick
entru•chón -chona *adj* tricky || *mf* trickster
entuerto *m* wrong, harm, injustice
entumecer **§22** *tr* to make numb || *ref* (*un miembro*) to get numb, go to sleep; (*el mar*) swell, get rough
entupir *tr* to stop up, clog; pack tight || *ref* to get stopped up, get clogged
enturbiar *tr* to stir up, make muddy; confuse, upset
entusiasmar *tr* to enthuse, make enthusiastic || *ref* to enthuse, become enthusiastic
entusiasmo *m* enthusiasm; inspiration
entusiasta *adj* enthusiastic || *mf* enthusiast
entusiásti•co -ca *adj* enthusiastic
enumerar *tr* to enumerate
enunciar *tr* to enunciate, enounce
enunciati•vo -va *adj* (gram) declarative
enuresis *f*—**enuresis nocturna** bedwetting
envainar *tr* to sheathe
envalentonar *tr* to embolden, make bold || *ref* to pluck up, take courage
envanecer **§22** *tr* to make vain || *ref* to become vain, get conceited
envanecimiento *m* vanity, conceit
envaramiento *m* stiffness
envarar *tr* to make numb, to stiffen || *ref* to get stiff; get numb
envasa•dor -dora *mf* packer || *f* processing plant, packer
envasar *tr* (*p.ej., trigo*) to pack, sack; (*p.ej., vino*) bottle; (*p.ej., pescado*) can; (*una espada*) thrust, poke; (*mucho vino*) put away; **envasar al vacío** to vacuum-pack || *intr* to tipple
envase *m* container; bottle, jar; can; packing; bottling; canning; **envase de hojalata** tin can
envedijar *ref* to get tangled; come to blows
envejecer **§22** *tr* to age, make old || *intr & ref* to age, grow old; get out of date
envejeci•do -da *adj* old, aged; experienced, tried
envenenar *tr* to poison; (*llenar de amargura*) envenom, embitter; (*las palabras o conducta de una persona*) put an evil interpretation on || *ref* to take poison
enverdecer **§22** *intr* to turn green
envergadura *f* (*de las alas abiertas del ave*) spread; (*ancho de una vela*) breadth; (aer) span, wingspread; (fig) compass, spread, reach
envés *m* wrong side; (*del cuerpo humano*) back
enviado *m* envoy
enviar **§77** *tr* to send; (*mercancías*) ship; **enviar a buscar** to send for; **enviar a paseo** to send on his way, dismiss without ceremony; **enviar por** to send for
enviciar *tr* to corrupt, vitiate; (*mimar*) spoil || *intr* to have many leaves and little fruit || *ref* to become addicted; **enviciarse con** *or* **en** to addict oneself to, become addicted to
envidar *tr* to bid against, bet against || *intr* to bid, bet
envidia *f* envy; desire
envidiable *adj* enviable
envidiar *tr* to envy, begrudge; desire, want
envidio•so -sa *adj* envious; greedy, covetous || *mf* envious person
envilecer **§22** *tr* to debase, vilify, revile || *ref* to degrade oneself
envío *m* sending; (*de mercancías*) shipment; (*de dinero*) remittance; (*en una obra*) autograph, inscription
envirota•do -da *adj* stiff, stuck-up
envite *m* bet; bid, offer, invitation; push, shove; (*apuesta adicional a un lance o suerte*) side bet; **al primer envite** right off, at the start
enviudar *intr* (*una mujer*) to become a widow; (*un hombre*) become a widower
envoltorio *m* bundle; (*defecto en el paño*) knot
envoltura *f* cover, wrapper, envelope; swaddling clothes
envolver **§47 & §83** *tr* to wrap, wrap up; (*hilo, cinta*) wind, roll up; (*al niño*) swaddle; imply, mean; involve; envelop; (*dejar cortado y sin salida en la disputa*) floor; (mil) to encircle || *ref* to become involved; have an affair
enyerbar *tr* (Col, Chile, Mex) to bewitch || *ref* to be covered with grass; (Mex) to fall madly in love; (Mex) to take poison
enyesar *tr* to plaster; put in a plaster cast; (*la tierra, el vino*) gypsum
enyugar **§44** *tr* to yoke
enzima *f* enzyme
enzolvar *tr* (Mex) to clog, stop up
epazote *m* (CAm, Mex) Mexican tea
E.P.D. *abbr* **en paz descanse**
epénte•sis *f* (*pl* **-sis**) epenthesis
eperlano *m* smelt
épica *f* epic poetry
epice•no -na *adj* (gram) epicene, common
épi•co -ca *adj* epic || *m* epic poet || *f* see **épica**

epicúre•o -a *adj* epicurean || *mf* epicurean, epicure
epidemia *f* epidemic
epidémi•co -ca *adj* epidemic
epidemiología *f* epidemiology
epidermis *f* epidermis; **tener la epidermis fina** or **sensible** to be touchy
Epifanía *f* Epiphany, Twelfth Day
epígrafe *m* epigraph; inscription; headline, title; device, motto
epigrama *m* epigram
epilepsia *f* epilepsy
epilépti•co -ca *adj & mf* epileptic
epilogar §44 *tr* to sum up, summarize
episcopalista *adj & mf* Episcopalian
episodio *m* episode
epistemología *f* epistemology
epístola *f* epistle
epitafio *m* epitaph
epíteto *m* epithet
epitomar *tr* to epitomize
epítome *m* epitome
E.P.M. *abbr* **en propia mano**
época *f* epoch; **época de paz** peacetime; **hacer época** to be epochmaking
epopeya *f* epic, epic poem
equidad *f* equity; (*templanza habitual*) equableness; (*moderación en el precio*) reasonableness
equiláte•ro -ra *adj* equilateral
equilibra•do -da *adj* balanced, well-balanced; well-adjusted; (fig) sensible, even-tempered
equilibrar *tr* to balance, equilibrate; even up; (*el presupuesto*) balance || *ref* to balance, equilibrate
equilibrio *m* equilibrium, balance, equipoise; (*del presupuesto*) balancing; **equilibrio político** balance of power
equilibrista *mf* balancer; tightrope walker, high-wire artist
equinoccial *adj* equinoctial
equinoccio *m* equinox
equipaje *m* baggage; piece of baggage; equipment; (naut) crew; **equipaje de mano** hand baggage
equipar *tr* to equip
equiparar *tr* to compare
equi•pier *m* (*pl* **-piers**) teammate
equipo *m* equipment, outfit; crew, gang; (sport) team; **equipo de alta fidelidad** stereo system; hi-fi system; **equipo de música** *or* **sonido** sound system; **equipo de novia** trousseau; **equipo de urgencia** first-aid kit; **equipo local** *or* **de casa** home team; **equipo móvil** outside broadcasting unit; **equipo visitante, equipo de fuera** visiting team
equitación *f* horsemanship, riding
equitati•vo -va *adj* fair, equitable; (*tranquilo*) equable
equivalente *adj & m* equivalent
equivaler §76 *intr* to be equal, be equivalent
equivocación *f* mistake; mistakenness
equivoca•do -da *adj* mistaken, wrong
equivocar §73 *tr* (*una cosa por otra*) to mistake, mix || *ref* to be mistaken, make a mistake; be wrong; **equivocarse con** to be mistaken for; **equivocarse de** to be wrong in, take the wrong . . .
equívo•co -ca *adj* equivocal, ambiguous || *m* equivocation, ambiguity; pun
equivoquista *mf* equivocator; punster
era *f* era, age; threshing floor; vegetable patch, garden bed; **era espacial** space-age;
eral *m* two-year-old bull
erario *m* state treasury
erección *f* erection; foundation, establishment
eremita *m* hermit
ergástulo *m* dungeon, slave prison
ergio *m* erg
ergotismo *m* argumentativeness; (pathol) ergotism
ergotista *adj invar* argumentative; dogmatic; *mf* dogmatist; know-it-all
erguir §33 *tr* to raise; straighten up || *ref* to straighten up; swell with pride
erial *adj* unplowed, uncultivated || *m* unplowed land, uncultivated land
erigir §72 *tr* to erect, build; found, establish; (*a nueva condición*) elevate || *ref* **—erigirse en** to be elevated to; set oneself up as
eriza•do -da *adj* bristling, bristly, spiny
erizar §60 *tr* to make stand on end, cause to bristle || *ref* to stand on end, to bristle
erizo *m* (*mamífero*) hedgehog; (*zurrón espinoso de la castaña*) bur, thistle; (*púas de hierro que coronan lo alto de una muralla*) cheval-de-frise; (*persona de carácter áspero*) curmudgeon; **erizo de mar** (zool) sea urchin
ermita *f* hermitage
ermita•ño -ña *mf* hermit
erogación *f* (*de bienes o caudales*) distribution; expenditure; (Peru, Ven) gift, charity; (Mex) outlay
erogar §44 *tr* to distribute; (Ecuad) to contribute; (Mex) to cause
erosión *f* erosion
erosionar *tr & ref* to erode
erradicar §73 *tr* to eradicate
erra•do -da *adj* mistaken, wrong
errar §34 *tr* to miss || *intr* to err, be mistaken, be wrong; wander || *ref* to be mistaken, be wrong
errata *f* erratum; printer's error
erróne•o -a *adj* erroneous
error *m* error, mistake; **error de imprenta, error tipográfico** misprint, printer's error; **error de pluma** clerical error; **salvo error u omisión** barring error or omission
eructar *intr* to belch, burp; (coll) to brag
eructo *m* belch, belching, burp
erudición *f* erudition, learning
erudi•to -ta *adj* erudite, learned || *mf* scholar, savant; **erudito a la violeta** egghead, highbrow
erugino•so -sa *adj* rusty
erumpir *intr* (*un volcán*) to erupt

erupción *f* eruption
esbel•to -ta *adj* slender, lithe, willowy
esbirro *m* bailiff, constable; (*el que ejecuta órdenes injustas*) myrmidon, henchman
esbozar §60 *tr* to sketch, outline
esbozo *m* sketch, outline
escabechar *tr* to pickle; (*el pelo, la barba*) dye; (*reprobar en un examen*) flunk; stab to death || *ref* to dye one's hair; (*el pelo, la barba*) dye
escabeche *m* pickle; pickled fish; hair dye
escabel *m* stool; footstool; (*para medrar*) stepping stone
escabio•so -sa *adj* mangy
escabro•so -sa *adj* scabrous, risqué; scabrous, uneven, rough, harsh
escabuche *m* weeding hoe
escabullir §13 *ref* to slip away, sneak away; slip out, wiggle out; slip through
escafandra *f* diving suit; **escafandra espacial** space suit
escafandrista *mf* diver
escala *f* (*escalera de mano*) ladder, stepladder; (*línea graduada de instrumento*) scale; (*de buque*) call; (*de avión*) stop; (*puerto donde toca una embarcación*) port of call; (*serie de las notas musicales*) scale; **en escala de** on a scale of; **en grande escala** on a large scale; **escala de cuerda** *or* **de viento** rope ladder; **escala de grises** (compu) grayscale; **escala móvil** (*de salarios*) sliding scale; **escala real** royal flush; **escala telescópica** extension ladder; **hacer escala** (naut) to call
escalada *f* scaling, climbing; breaking in; escalation
escalador *m* climber; (*ladrón*) burglar, housebreaker
escalación *f* escalation
escalafón *m* roster, roll, register
escalar *tr* (*subir, trepar*) to scale; break in, burglarize; (*la compuerta de la acequia*) open || *intr* to climb; (naut) to call || *ref* to escalate
escalofriante *adj* horrifying; spine-chilling; (*cifra*) incredible
escalato•rres *m* (*pl* **-rres**) steeplejack, human fly
escalda•do -da *adj* cautious, scared, wary; (*mujer*) lewd, loose
escaldar *tr* to scald; make red hot || *ref* to get scalded; chafe
escalera *f* stairs, stairway; (*portátil*) ladder; (*de naipes*) sequence; (*en el póker*) straight; **de escalera abajo** from below stairs, from the servants; **escalera de caracol, escalera espiral** spiral staircase; **escalera de escape** fire escape; **escalera de husillo** winding stairway; **escalera de incendios** fire escape; **escalera de mano** ladder; **escalera de salvamento** fire escape; **escalera de tijera** *or* **escalera doble** ladder; **escalera excusada** *or* **falsa** private stairs; **escalera extensible** extension ladder; **escalera hurtada** secret stairway; **escalera mecánica, móvil** *or* **rodante** escalator, moving stairway; **escalera real** royal flush
escalerilla *f* low step; car step; (*en las medias*) runner; (*de naipes*) sequence; thumb index
escalfar *tr* (*huevos*) to poach; (*el pan*) bake brown
escalinata *f* stone steps, front steps
escalo *m* burglary, breaking in
escalofria•do -da *adj* chilly
escalofrío *m* chill
escalón *m* step, rung; (*grada de la escalera*) tread; (fig) step, echelon, grade; (*paso con que uno adelanta sus pretensiones*) (fig) stepping stone; (mil) echelon; (rad) stage
escalonamiento *m* ranking; gradation
escalonar *tr* to space out, spread out; (*las horas de trabajo*) stagger; (mil) to echelon
escalope *m* (*loncha delgada de carne*) scallop (*thin slice of meat*)
escalpar *tr* to scalp
escalpelo *m* scalpel
escama *f* scale; fear, suspicion
escamar *tr* (*los peces*) to scale; (coll) to frighten || *ref* to be frightened
escamondar *tr* to trim, prune
escamo•so -sa *adj* scaly
escamotea•dor -dora *mf* prestidigitator; swindler
escamotear *tr* to whisk out of sight, cause to vanish; (*una carta*) palm; swipe, snitch
escampada *f* clear spell, break in rain
escampar *tr* to clear out || *intr* to stop raining; ease up; **¡ya escampa!** there you go again! || *ref* — **escamparse del agua** to get in out of the rain
escampavía *f* (naut) cutter, revenue cutter
escamujar *tr* (*un árbol, esp. un olivo*) to prune; (*ramas*) clear out
escanciar *tr* (*vino*) to pour, serve, drink || *intr* to drink wine
escandalizar §60 *tr* to scandalize || *ref* to be scandalized; be outraged, be exasperated
escandallo *m* (naut) sounding lead; (*del contenido de varios envases*) testing, sampling; cost accounting
escándalo *m* scandal; **causar escándalo** to make a scene
escandalo•so -sa *adj* scandalous; noisy, riotous; loud, flashy
escandina•vo -va *adj* & *mf* Scandinavian
escandir *tr* (*versos*) to scan
escanear *tr* (compu) to scan
escáner *m* scanner; scan; **escáner de TAC** CAT scanner
escanógrafo *m* scanner
escanograma *m* scan
escansión *f* scansion; (telv) scanning
escaño *m* settle, bench with a back; (*en las Cortes*) seat; park bench; (Guat) nag
escañuelo *m* footstool
escapada *f* escape, flight; short trip, quick trip
escapar *tr* to free, save; (*un caballo*) drive hard || *intr* to escape; flee, run away; **escapar en**

una tabla to have a narrow escape || *ref* to escape; flee, run away; (*el gas, el agua*) leak; **escapársele a uno** to let slip; not notice
escaparate *m* show window, showcase; (*armario con cristales*) cabinet; wardrobe, clothes closet; **escaparete de tienda** shop window
escaparatista *mf* window dresser
escapatoria *f* escape, getaway; (*de atenciones, deberes, etc.*) (fig) escape; (*efugio, pretexto*) (coll) evasion, subterfuge
escape *m* escape; flight; (*de gas, agua*) leak; (*de reloj*) escapement; (aut) exhaust valve; (aut) exhaust, exhaust pipe; **a escape** at full speed, on the run; **escape de rejilla** (rad) grid leak; **escape libre** (aut) cutout
escápula *f* shoulder blade, scapula
escaque *m* square; **escaques** chess
escarabajear *tr* to bother, worry, harass || *intr* to swarm, crawl; scrawl, scribble
escarabajo *m* black beetle; (*imperfección en los tejidos*) flaw; (*persona pequeña*) runt
escaramuza *f* skirmish
escaramuzar §60 *intr* to skirmish; (sport) scrimmage
escarapela *f* (*divisa en forma de lazo*) cockade; dispute ending in hair pulling
escarapelar *intr & ref* to quarrel, wrangle
escarbadien•tes *m* (*pl* **-tes**) toothpick
escarbar *tr* (*el suelo*) to scratch, scratch up; scavenge; (*la lumbre*) poke; (*los dientes, los oídos*) pick; pry into
escarcha *f* frost, hoarfrost
escarchar *tr* (*confituras*) to frost, put frosting on; (*la tierra del alfarero*) dilute with water; spangle || *intr* — **escarcha** there is frost
escardar or **escardillar** *tr* to weed, weed out
escardillo *m* weeding hoe
escariar *tr* to ream
escarlata *adj* scarlet || *f* scarlet fever
escarlatina *f* scarlet fever
escarmentar §2 *tr* to make an example of || *intr* to learn one's lesson
escarmiento *m* example, lesson, warning; caution, wisdom; punishment
escarnecer §22 *tr* to scoff at, make fun of
escarnio *m* scoff, scoffing
escarola *f* endive
escarpa *f* scarp, escarpment; (Mex) sidewalk
escarpa•do -da *adj* steep; abrupt, craggy
escarpia *f* hooked spike
escarpín *m* pump
escasamente *adv* barely; hardly
escasear *tr* to give sparingly; cut down on, avoid; bevel || *intr* to be scarce
escase•ro -ra *adj* sparing; saving, frugal; stingy || *mf* skinflint
escasez *f* (*falta de una cosa*) scarcity; (*pobreza*) need, want; (*mezquindad*) stinginess
esca•so -sa *adj* (*poco abundante*) scarce; (*no cabal*) scant; (*muy económico*) parsimonious, frugal; (*tacaño*) stingy; (*oportunidad*) dim, slim, slight; **estar escaso de** to be short of
escatimar *tr & intr* to scrimp
escena *f* (*parte del teatro donde se representan las obras*) stage; (*subdivisión de un acto*) scene; incident, episode; **en escena** onstage; **poner en escena** to stage
escenario *m* stage; (*disposición de la representación*) setting; (*guión de cine*) scenario; (*antecedentes de una persona o cosa*) background
escenarista *mf* scenarist
escéni•co -ca *adj* scenic
escenificar §73 *tr* to adapt for the stage
escépti•co -ca *adj* sceptic(al) || *mf* sceptic
Escila *f* Scylla; **entre Escila y Caribdis** between Scylla and Charybdis
Escipión *m* Scipio
escisión *f* (biol) fission; (surg) excision
esclarecer §22 *tr* to light up, brighten; explain, elucidate; ennoble || *intr* to dawn
esclareci•do -da *adj* noble, illustrious
esclavitud *f* slavery
esclavización *f* enslavement
esclavizar §60 *tr* to enslave
escla•vo -va *adj & mf* slave
escla•vón -vona *adj & mf* Slav
esclerosis múltiple *f* multiple sclerosis
esclusa *f* lock; floodgate; **esclusa de aire** caisson
esclusero *m* lock tender
escoba *f* broom
escobada *f* sweep; sweeping
escobar *tr* to sweep with a broom
escobazar §60 *tr* to sprinkle with a wet broom
escobén *m* (naut) hawse
escobilla *f* brush, whisk; gold and silver sweepings; (elec) brush
escocer §16 *intr* to smart, sting || *ref* to hurt; chafe, become chafed
esco•cés -cesa *adj* Scotch, Scottish || *mf* Scot || *m* Scotchman; (*whisky; dialecto*) Scotch; **los escoceces** the Scotch, the Scottish
Escocia *f* Scotland; **la Nueva Escocia** Nova Scotia
escofina *f* rasp
escofinar *tr* to rasp
escoger §17 *tr* to choose, pick out
escogi•do -da *adj* choice, select
escolar *adj* school || *m* pupil
escolaridad *f* schooling, school attendance; curriculum
escolimo•so -sa *adj* impatient, gruff, restless
escollar *intr* (Arg) to run aground on a reef; (Arg, Chile) to fail
escollera *f* jetty, breakwater
escollo *m* (*peñasco a flor de agua*) reef, rock; (*peligro*) pitfall; (*obstáculo*) stumbling block
escolta *f* escort
escoltar *tr* to escort
escombrar *tr* to clear out
escombro *m* (*pez*) mackerel; **escombros** debris, rubble, rubbish
esconder *tr* to hide, conceal; harbor, contain || *ref* to hide; lurk
escondi•do -da *adj* hidden; **a escondidas** se-

cretly; **a escondidas de** without the knowledge of
escondite *m* hiding place; (*juego de muchachos*) hide-and-seek; **jugar al escondite** to play hide-and-seek
escondrijo *m* hiding place
escopeta *f* shotgun; **escopeta blanca** gentleman hunter; **escopeta de caza** fowling piece; **escopeta de dos cañones** double-barreled shotgun; **escopeta de viento** air rifle; **escopeta negra** professional hunter
escopetazo *m* gunshot; gunshot wound; bad news, blow; (SAm) sarcasm; insult
escoplear *tr* to chisel
escoplo *m* chisel
escorbuto *m* scurvy
escoria *f* dross, scoria, slag; (fig) dross, dregs
escorial *m* cinder bank, slag dump
escorpión *m* scorpion; **Escorpión** *m* (astr) Scorpio
escorzar §60 *tr* to foreshorten
escorzo *m* foreshortening
escota *f* (naut) sheet
escota•do -da *adj* low-neck || *m* low neck
escotadura *f* low neck, low cut in neck
escotar *tr* to cut to fit; draw water from, drain; cut low in the neck || *intr* to go Dutch
escote *m* low neck, cleavage; (*encajes en el cuello de una vestidura*) tucker; **ir a escote** *or* **pagar a escote** to go Dutch
escotilla *f* (naut) hatchway, scuttle
escotillón *m* hatch, trap door, scuttle; (theat) trap door
escozor *m* burning, smarting, stinging; grief, sorrow
escriba *m* scribe
escribanía *f* court clerkship; desk; writing materials
escribano *m* court clerk; lawyer's clerk
escribiente *mf* clerk, office clerk; **escribiente a máquina** typist
escribir §83 *tr & intr* to write || *ref* to enroll, enlist; write to each other; **no escribirse** to be impossible to describe
escriño *m* casket, jewel case; straw basket
escri•to -ta *adj* streaked || *m* writing; (law) brief, writ; **escrito largo y pesado** screed; **poner por escrito** to write down, put in writing
escri•tor -tora *mf* writer
escritorio *m* writing desk; office; (compu) desktop; **escritorio ministro** kneehole desk, office desk; **escritorio norteamericano** rolltop desk
escritura *f* writing; script, handwriting, longhand; (law) deed, indenture; (law) sworn statement; **escritura al tacto** touch typewriting || **Escritura** *f* Scripture; **Sagrada Escritura** Holy Scripture, Holy Writ
escriturar *tr* to notarize; (*p.ej., a un actor*) book || *ref* (taur) to sign up for a fight
escrnía. *abbr* **escribanía**
escrno. *abbr* **escribano**
escrófula *f* scrofula
escrúpulo *m* scruple
escrupulo•so -sa *adj* scrupulous; exact
escrutar *tr* to scrutinize; (*los votos*) count
escrutinio *m* scrutiny; counting of votes
escuadra *f* (*pequeño número de personas o de soldados*) squad; (*pieza de metal para asegurar las ensambladuras*) angle iron; (*de carpintero*) square; (*de dibujante*) triangle; (nav) squadron
escuadrar *tr* (carp) to square
escuadrilla *f* (aer) squadron
escuadrón *m* (mil) squadron
escualidez *f* squalor
escuáli•do -da *adj* squalid
escualor *m* squalor
escucha *mf* listener || *m* (mil) scout, vedette || *f* listening; (*en un convento*) chaperon; **escuchas telefónicas** wiretapping; **escucha telefónica** wiretap; **estar de escucha** (coll) to eavesdrop
escuchar *tr* to listen to; (*atender a*) heed; (*radiotransmisiones*) monitor || *intr* to listen || *ref* to like the sound of one's own voice
escudar *tr* to shield
escudero *m* esquire; nobleman; lady's page
escudete *m* escutcheon; (*refuerzo en la ropa*) gusset; (*planchuela delante de la cerradura*) escutcheon, escutcheon plate
escudilla *f* bowl
escudo *m* shield; buckler; (*delante de la cerradura*) escutcheon plate; **escudo de armas** coat of arms; **escudo térmico** (*de una cápsula espacial*) heat shield
escudriñar *tr* to scrutinize
escuela *f* school; **escuela de artes y oficios** trade school; **escuela de párvulos** kindergarten; **escuela de verano** summer school; **escuela dominical** Sunday school; **Escuela Naval Militar** Naval Academy; **escuela nocturna** night school; **escuela preparatoria** prep school; **escuela pública** public school; **hacer escuela** to be the leader of a school (*of thought*)
escuelante *mf* (Mex) schoolteacher || *m* (Mex) schoolboy || *f* (Mex) schoolgirl
escuerzo *m* toad
escue•to -ta *adj* free, unencumbered; bare, unadorned
escuintle *adj* (Mex) sickly || *m* (*perro*) (Mex) mutt; (Mex) brat
esculcar §73 *tr* to frisk
esculpir *tr & intr* to sculpture, carve; engrave
escultismo *m* outdoor activities
escultista *m* outdoorsman
escultor *m* sculptor
escultora *f* sculptress
escultura *f* sculpture
escultural *adj* sculptural; statuesque
escupidera *f* cuspidor; chamber pot
escupidura *f* spit; fever blister
escupir *tr & intr* to spit
escurrepla•tos *m* (*pl* **-tos**) dish rack
escurridero *m* drainpipe; drainboard; slippery spot

escurridi•zo -za *adj* slippery
escurri•do -da *adj* narrow-hipped; abashed, confused
escurridor *m* colander
escurriduras *fpl* dregs, lees
escurrir *tr* (*una vasija; un líquido; la vajilla*) to drain; to wring, wring out; **escurrir el bulto** to duck || *intr* to drip, ooze, trickle; slide, slip || *ref* to drip, ooze, trickle; slide, slip; slip away; (*un reparo*) slip out
esdrúju•lo -la *adj* accented on the antepenult || *m* word or verse accented on the antepenult
ese, esa *adj dem* (*pl* **esos, esas**) that (*near you*) || **ese** *f* sound hole (*of violin*); **hacer eses** to reel, stagger
ése, ésa *pron dem* (*pl* **ésos, ésas**) that (*near you*); **ésa** your city
esencia *f* essence; **esencia de pera** banana oil; **quinta esencia** quintessence
esencial *adj & m* essential; **lo esencial** the basics
esfera *f* sphere; (*del reloj*) dial
esféri•co -ca *adj* spherical || *m* football
esfero *m* or **esferográfica** *f* (Col) ballpoint pen
esfinge *f* sphinx; spiteful woman
esforza•do -da *adj* brave, vigorous, enterprising
esforzar §35 *tr* to strengthen, invigorate; encourage || *ref* to exert oneself; strive
esfuerzo *m* effort, exertion, endeavor; courage, vigor, spirit
esfumar *tr* to stump || *ref* to disappear, fade away
esgarrar *tr* (*la flema*) to try to cough up || *intr* to clear the throat
esgrima *f* fencing
esgrimidura *f* fencing
esgrimir *tr* to wield, brandish; (*un argumento*) swing || *intr* to fence
esgrimista *mf* (Arg, Chile, Peru) fencer; (Chile) swindler, panhandler
esguazar §60 *tr* to ford
esguazo *m* fording; ford
esguince *m* dodge, duck; (*gesto de disgusto*) frown; twist, sprain, wrench
eslabón *m* (*de cadena*) link; (*hierro acerado para sacar fuego de un pedernal; cilindro de acero para afilar cuchillos*) steel
eslabonar *tr* to link; link together, string together || *intr* to link
eslálom *m* slalom
esla•vo -va *adj* Slav, Slavic || *mf* Slav || *m* (*idioma*) Slavic
esla•vón -vona *adj & mf* Slav
eslogan *m* (*consigna usada en fórmulas publicitarias*) slogan
eslora *f* (naut) length
eslova•co -ca *adj & mf* Slovak
esmaltar *tr* to enamel; embellish
esmalte *m* enamel; **esmalte para las uñas** nail polish
esmera•do -da *adj* careful, painstaking
esmeralda *f* emerald
esmerar *tr* to polish, shine; examine, check || *ref* to take pains, do one's best
esmeril *m* emery
esmeriladora *f* emery wheel
esmerilar *tr* to grind or polish with emery
esmero *m* care, neatness
esmoladera *f* grindstone
esmoquin *m* tuxedo, dinner coat
esnifar *tr & intr* (*heroína*) to sniff
esnob *adj* snobbish || *mf* (*pl* **esnobs**) snob
esnobismo *m* snobbery, snobbishness
esnobista *adj* snobbish
eso *pron dem* that; **a eso de** about; **eso es** that's it; that is; **por eso** for that reason; therefore
esófago *m* esophagus
espabila•do -da *adj* intelligent; bright
espabilar *ref* to know the ropes; be well informed
espaciador *m* space bar
espacial *adj* space, spatial
espaciar §77 (Arg, Chile) & **regular** *tr* to space; spread, scatter || *ref* to expatiate; amuse oneself, relax
espacio *m* space; **espacio de chispa** spark gap; **espacio exterior** outer space; **espacio libre** (*entre dos cosas*) clearance; **espacio muerto** (*en el cilindro de un motor*) clearance; **espacio-tiempo** space-time; **por espacio de** in the space of
espacio•so -sa *adj* spacious, roomy; slow, deliberate
espada *m* swordsman; (taur) matador || *f* sword; (cards) spade; **entre la espada y la pared** between the devil and the deep blue sea; **espadas** (cards) suit with figures representing swords and considered to be equivalent to the English suit called spades
espadachín *m* swordsman; (*amigo de pendencias*) bully
espadaña *f* cattail, bulrush, reed mace; (*campanario*) bell gable
espadilla *f* (*remo que se usa como timón*) scull; (*aguja para sujetar el pelo*) bodkin; red insignia of Order of Santiago
espadín *m* rapier
espadón *m* (coll) brass hat
espagueti *m* spaghetti
espalar *tr* to shovel
espalda *f* back; **a espaldas de uno** behind one's back; **de espaldas a** with one's back to; **espalda mojada** (pej) wetback; **tener buenas espaldas** to have broad shoulders; **volver las espaldas a** to turn a cold shoulder to
espaldar *m* (*de silla*) back; (*enrejado para plantas*) trellis, espalier
espaldarazo *m* slap on the back; (*ceremonia para armar caballero*) accolade; **dar el espaldarazo a** to accept, approve
espalera *f* trellis, espalier
espanglés *m* (hum) Spanglish
espantada *f* (*de un animal*) sudden flight; (*desistimiento ocasionado por el miedo*) cold feet
espantadi•zo -za *adj* shy, skittish, scary
espantajo *m* scarecrow; (*persona fea*) fright
espantamos•cas *m* (*pl* **-cas**) (*para poner a los*

caballos) fly net; (*aparato para asustar y alejar las moscas*) fly chaser
espantapája•ros *m* (*pl* **-ros**) scarecrow
espantar *tr* to scare, frighten; scare away || *ref* to get scared; be surprised, marvel
espanto *m* fright, terror; (*amenaza*) threat; ghost
espantosidad *f* fright; frightfulness; awfulness
espanto•so -sa *adj* frightening, terrifying
España *f* Spain; **la Nueva España** New Spain (*Mexico in the early days*)
espa•ñol -ñola *adj* Spanish; **a la española** in the Spanish manner || *mf* Spaniard || *m* (*idioma*) Spanish; **los españoles** the Spanish || *f* Spanish woman
españolería *f* Spanishness; hispanophilia
españolada *f* Spanish mannerism; Spanish remark
españolizar §60 *tr* to make Spanish, Hispanicize; translate into Spanish || *ref* to become Spanish
esparadrapo *m* (pharm) adhesive tape
esparaván *m* spavin
esparavel *m* mortarboard
esparcimiento *m* spreading, scattering, dissemination; diversion, relaxation; frankness, openness
esparcir §36 *tr* to spread, scatter; divert, relax || *ref* to spread, scatter; disperse; take it easy, relax
espárrago *m* asparagus; (*perno*) stud bolt; awning pole
esparrancar §73 *ref* to spread one's legs wide apart
esparta•no -na *adj & mf* Spartan
esparto *m* esparto grass
espasmo *m* spasm
espasmódi•co -ca *adj* spasmodic
espásti•co -ca *adj* spastic
espato *m* spar; **espato flúor** fluor spar
espátula *f* spatula; putty knife
especia *f* spice
especia•do -da *adj* spicy
especial *adj* especial, special
especialidad *f* speciality; (*ramo a que se consagra una persona o negocio*) specialty
especialista *mf* specialist
especializar §60 *tr, intr & ref* to specialize
especiar *tr* to spice
especie *f* (*categoría de la clasificación biológica*) species; (*clase, género*) sort, kind; (*caso, asunto*) matter; (*chisme, cuento*) news, rumor; appearance, pretext, show; remark; **en especie** in kind; **soltar una especie** to try to draw someone out
especie•ro -ra *mf* spice dealer || *m* spice box
especificar §73 *tr* to specify; itemize
específi•co -ca *adj* specific || *m* specific; patent medicine
espécimen *m* (*pl* **especímenes**) specimen
especio•so -sa *adj* (*engañoso*) specious; nice, neat, perfect
especiota *f* hoax, wild idea
espectáculo *m* spectacle; **dar un espectáculo** to make a scene; **espectáculo de atracciones** side show
especta•dor -dora *mf* witness; spectator
espectral *adj* ghostly
espectro *m* specter, phantom, ghost; (phys) spectrum
especular *tr* to check, examine; contemplate || *intr* to speculate
espejear *intr* to sparkle
espejismo *m* mirage
espejo *m* mirror, looking glass; model; **espejo de cuerpo entero** full-length mirror, pier glass; **espejo de retrovisión** rear-view mirror; **espejo de vestir** full-length mirror, pier glass; **espejo retrovisor** rear-view mirror
espelunca *f* cave, cavern
espeluznante *adj* hair-raising; nightmarish
espera *f* wait, waiting; (*puesto para cazar*) blind, hunter's blind; composure, patience, respite; delay; (law) stay; **no tener espera** to be of the greatest urgency
esperanza *f* hope; **tener puesta su esperanza en** to pin one's faith on
esperanza•do -da *adj* hopeful (*having hope*)
esperanza•dor -dora *adj* hopeful (*giving hope*)
esperanzar §60 *tr* to give hope to
esperanzo•so -sa *adj* hopeful, full of hope
esperar *tr* (*aguardar*) to wait for, await; (*tener esperanza de conseguir*) expect, hope for; **ir a esperar** to go to meet || *intr* to wait; hope; **esperar** + *inf* to hope to + *inf;* **esperar a que** to wait until; **esperar desesperando** to hope against hope; **esperar en** to put one's hope in; **esperar que** to hope that; **esperar sentado** to have a good wait
esperinque *m* smelt
esperma *f* sperm
esperpento *m* monstrosity; freak; nonsense
espesar *m* depth, thickness (*of woods*) || *tr* to thicken; (*un tejido*) weave tighter || *ref* to thicken, get thick or thicker
espe•so -sa *adj* thick; dirty, greasy; **lo espeso** (culin) thickness
espesor *m* thickness; (*de un fluido, gas, masa*) density
espesura *f* thickness; (*matorral*) thicket; (*cabellera muy espesa*) shock of hair; dirtiness, greasiness
espetar *tr* to skewer; pierce, pierce through; **espetar algo a** to spring something on || *ref* to be solemn, be pompous; settle down
espetón *m* (*hurgón*) poker; (*asador*) skewer, spit; jab, poke
espía *mf* spy; squealer || *f* (naut) warping; (*cuerda*) (naut) warp
espiar §77 *tr* to spy on || *intr* to spy; (naut) to warp
espichar *tr* to prick; (*dinero*) (Chile) to cough up; (Chile, Peru) to tap || *intr* (coll) to die || *ref* (Mex, W-I) to get thin
espiche *m* (*arma o instrumento puntiagudo*) prick; (naut) peg, bung
espichón *m* stab, prick

espiga *f* (bot) ear, spike; peg, pin, tenon; (*clavo sin cabeza*) brad; (*badajo*) clapper; (*de una llave*) stem
espigar §44 *tr* to glean; tenon, dowel || *intr* (*los cereales*) to form ears || *ref* to grow tall, shoot up
espigón *m* sharp point, spur; (*mazorca*) ear of corn; (*cerro puntiagudo*) peak; breakwater
espina *f* thorn, spine; (*de los peces*) fishbone; doubt, uncertainty; sorrow; (anat) spine; **dar mala espina a** to worry; **espina de pescado** herringbone; **espina de pez** fishbone; **espina dorsal** spinal column; **estar en espinas** to be on pins and needles
espinaca *f* spinach; **espinacas** spinach
espinal *adj* spinal
espinapez *m* herringbone; thorny matter, difficulty
espinar *m* thorny spot; (fig) thorny matter || *tr* to prick; (*árboles*) protect with thornbushes; hurt, offend
espinazo *m* backbone; (*de un arco*) keystone
espinel *m* trawl, trawl line
espineta *f* spinet
espinilla *f* (*de la pierna*) shin, shinbone; (*granillo en la piel*) blackhead
espino *m* hawthorn; **espino artificial** barbed wire; **espino negro** blackthorn
espinochar *tr* (*el maíz*) to husk
espino•so -sa or **espinu•do -da** *adj* thorny; (*pez*) bony; (*difícil*) (fig) thorny, knotty
espiocha *f* pickaxe
espión *m* spy
espionaje *m* spying, espionage
espira *f* turn
espiración *f* breathing; exhalation
espiral *adj* spiral || *f* (*línea curva que da vueltas alrededor de un punto*) spiral; (*del reloj*) hairspring; (*de humo*) curl, wreath
espirar *tr* to breath; encourage || *intr* to breathe; exhale, expire; (*el viento*) (poet) to blow gently
espiritismo *m* spiritualism
espirito•so -sa *adj* spirited, lively; (*licor*) spirituous
espíritu *m* spirit; (*mente*) mind; (*aparecido, fantasma*) ghost, spirit; **espíritu de equipo,** team spirit; **Espíritu Santo** Holy Ghost, Holy Spirit; **dar, despedir, exhalar** *or* **rendir el espíritu** to give up the ghost
espiritual *adj* spiritual; sharp, witty
espiritualismo *m* spiritualism
espita *f* tap, cock; (coll) tippler
espitar *tr* to tap
esplendidez *f* splendor, magnificence
espléndi•do -da *adj* splendid, magnificent; generous, open-handed; (poet) brilliant, radiant
esplendor *m* splendor
esplendoro•so -sa *adj* resplendent
espliego *m* lavender
esplín *m* melancholy
espolada *f* prick with spur; **espolada de vino** shot of wine
espolear *tr* to spur, spur on
espoleta *f* fuse; (*hueso*) wishbone
espolón *m* (*del gallo, una montaña, un buque de guerra*) spur; dike, jetty, mole, cut-water; (*prominencia córnea de las caballerías*) fetlock; (*sabañón*) chilblain
espolvorear *tr* (*quitar el polvo de; esparcir el polvo sobre*) dust; (*el azúcar*) sprinkle
esponja *f* sponge; (*sablista*) sponge, sponger; **beber como una esponja** to drink like a fish; **tirar la esponja** to throw in (or up) the sponge
esponja•do -da *adj* proud, puffed-up; fresh, healthy
esponjar *tr* to puff up, make fluffy || *ref* to puff up, become fluffy; be puffed up, be conceited; look fresh and healthy
esponjo•so -sa *adj* spongy
esponsales *mpl* betrothal, engagement
espontanear *ref* to make a clean breast of it; open one's heart
espontáne•o -a *adj* spontaneous || *m* (taur) spectator who jumps into the ring to take on the bull
espora *f* spore
esporádi•co -ca *adj* sporadic
esposa *f* wife; **esposas** handcuffs, manacles
esposar *tr* to handcuff, manacle
espo•so -sa *mf* spouse || *m* husband || *f* see **esposa**
espuela *f* spur; **echar la espuela** (coll) to take a nightcap; **espuela de caballero** delphinium, rocket larkspur; **espuela de galán** nasturtium
espuelar *tr* (SAm) to spur, goad
espuerta *f* two-handled esparto basket
espulgar §44 *tr* to delouse; scrutinize
espuma *f* foam; (*en un vaso de cerveza; saliva parecida a la espuma*) froth; (*película de impurezas en la superficie de un líquido*) scum; **crecer como espuma** to grow like weeds; to have a meteoric rise; **espuma de afeitar** shaving foam; **espuma de caucho** foam rubber; **espuma de jabón** lather; **espuma de mar** meerschaum; **espuma seca** carpet shampoo
espumadera *f* skimmer
espumajear *intr* to froth at the mouth
espumajo•so -sa *adj* foamy, frothy
espumante *adj* foaming; (*vino*) sparkling
espumar *tr* to skim || *intr* to foam, froth; (*el jabón*) lather, (*el vino*) sparkle; increase rapidly
espumarajo *m* froth, frothing at the mouth
espumilla *f* voile; (CAm, Ecuad) meringue
espumo•so -sa *adj* foamy, frothy; (*cubierto de una película*) scummy; (*jabonoso*) lathery; (*vino*) sparkling
espu•rio -ria *adj* spurious
espurrear or **espurriar** *tr* to squirt with water from the mouth
esputar *tr & intr* to spit
esputo *m* spit, saliva
esq. *abbr* **esquina**
esqueje *m* cutting, slip
esquela *f* note; announcement; death notice; **esquela amorosa** billet-doux

esqueléti•co -ca *adj* skeleton; skeletal, thin, wasted
esqueleto *m* skeleton; (CAm, Mex) blank form; (Chile) sketch, outline
esquema *m* scheme, diagram
es•quí *m* (*pl* **-quís**) ski; skiing; **esquí acuático** water ski; water skiing; **esquí alpino** downhill skiing; **esquí de fondo** cross-country skiing; **esquí remolcado** skijoring
esquia•dor -dora *adj* ski ‖ *mf* skier
esquiar §77 *intr* to ski
esquiciar *tr* to sketch
esquicio *m* sketch
esquifar *tr* (naut) to fit out, staff, man
esquife *m* skiff
esquiismo *m* skiing
esquila *f* sheepshearing; hand bell
esquilar *tr* to shear, fleece
esquilimo•so -sa *adj* fastidious, squeamish
esquilmar *tr* to harvest; (*las plantas el jugo de la tierra*) drain, exhaust; (*una fuente de riqueza*) drain, squander, use up; carry away, steal
esquilmo *m* harvest, farm produce; (Mex) farm scrapings
esquilmo•so -sa *adj* fastidious
esquimal *adj & mf* Eskimo
esquina *f* corner; (SAm) corner store; **a la vuelta de la esquina** around the corner; **doblar la esquina** to turn the corner; **hacer esquina** (*un edificio*) to be on the corner; **las cuatro esquinas** puss in the corner
esquina•do -da *adj* sharp-cornered; difficult, unsociable
esquinar *tr* to be on the corner of; put in the corner; alienate ‖ *intr* — **esquinar con** to be on the corner of ‖ *ref* — **esquinarse con** to fall out with
esquinazo *m* corner; (Arg, Chile) serenade; **dar esquinazo a** to give the slip to, to shake off
esquinencia *f* quinsy
esquinera *f* corner piece (*of furniture*)
esquirla *f* splinter, sliver
esquirol *m* scab, strikebreaker
esquisto *m* schist
esquite *m* (CAm, Mex) popcorn
esquivar *tr* to avoid, evade, shun; dodge, sidestep ‖ *ref* to withdraw; dodge
esquivez *f* aloofness, gruffness
esqui•vo -va *adj* aloof, gruff
esquizofrenia *f* schizophrenia
estable *adj* stable, permanent; full-time ‖ *mf* regular guest, permanent guest
establecer §22 *tr* to establish, institute ‖ *ref* to settle, take up residence; start a business, open an office
establecimiento *m* establishment; place of business; decree, ordinance, statute
establo *m* stable
estaca *f* stake, picket, pale; cudgel, club; (*clavo largo*) spike; (hort) cutting
estacada *f* stockade, palisade; dueling ground; **dejar en la estacada** to leave in the lurch; **quedarse en la estacada** to succumb on the field of battle, fall in a duel; fail; lose out
estacar §73 *tr* to stake, stake off; tie to a stake ‖ *ref* to stand stiff
estación *f* (*cada una de las cuatro divisiones del año*) season; (*sitio en que paran los trenes; radioemisora*) station; (*lugar en que se hace alto en un paseo, etc.*) stop; **estación balnearia** bathing resort; **estación de cabeza** (rr) terminal; **estación de carga** freight station; **estación de empalme** junction; **estación de esquí** ski resort; **estación de gasolina** gas station, filling station; **estación seca** dry season; **estación de las lluvias** rainy season; **estación de paso** (rr) way station; **estación depuradora** sewage-disposal plant; **estación de radiodifusión** broadcasting station; **estación de seguimiento** tracking station; **estación de servicio** service station; **estación de trabajo** (compu) workstation; **estación difusora** or **emisora** broadcasting station; **estación espacial** space station; **estación ferroviaria** railroad station; **estación gasolinera** gas station, filling station; **estación meteorológica** weather station; **estación orbital** orbital space station; **estación telefónica** telephone exchange
estacional *adj* seasonal
estacionamiento *m* stationing; parking; parking lot; **estacionamiento vigilado** attended parking
estacionar *tr* to park; to place, station ‖ *intr* to park ‖ *ref* to be stationary, level off; to park; **prohibido estacionar, se prohibe estacionar** no parking
estaciona•rio -ria *adj* stationary
estada *f* stay, stop
estadía *f* (*ante un pintor*) sitting; stop, stay; (com) demurrage
estadio *m* stadium; phase, stage; (*longitud*) furlong; **estadio de béisbol** ballpark, baseball stadium; **estadio de fútbol** football stadium; soccer stadium
estadista *mf* (*perito en estadística*) statistician ‖ *m* statesman
estadística *f* statistics
estadísti•co -ca *adj* statistical ‖ *m* statistician ‖ *f* see **estadística**
estadi•zo -za *adj* (*aire*) heavy, stifling; (*agua*) stagnant
estado *m* state; state, condition, status; statement, report; **en estado de buena esperanza** or **en estado interesante** in the family way; **estado asistencial, benefactor,** *or* **de bienestar** welfare state; **estado civil** marital status; **estado de ánimo** state of mind; **estado de cuentas** (com) statement; **estado de derecho** democracy; **estado libre asociado** commonwealth; **estado llano** commoners, common people; **estado mayor** (mil) staff; **estado mayor conjunto** joint chiefs of staff; **estado mayor general** general staff; **Estados**

Unidos *msg* the United States; **estado tapón** buffer state; **estar en estado de guerra** to be under martial law; **los Estados Unidos de América** *mpl* the United States of America; **los Estados Unidos Mexicanos** the United States of Mexico; **tomar estado** to take a wife; to go into the church
estado-policía *m* (*pl* **estados-policías**) police state
estadounidense or **estadunidense** *adj* American, United States || *mf* American
estafa *f* swindle, trick, shakedown; (*estribo*) stirrup
estafa•dor -dora *mf* (coll) rip-off artist || *m* con artist
estafar *tr* to swindle, trick; overcharge
estafeta *f* post, courier; post office; diplomatic mail
estallar *intr* to burst; explode; (*un incendio, una revolución; la guerra*) break out; (*la ira*) break forth
estallido *m* report, crash, explosion; crack; (*p.ej., de la guerra*) outbreak; **dar un estallido** to crash, explode
estambre *m* (*hebras de lana e hilo formado de ellas*) worsted; (bot) stamen; **estambre de la vida** course or thread of life
estampa *f* stamp, print, engraving; press, printing; footstep, track; aspect, appearance; **dar a la estampa** to publish, bring out; **parecer la estampa de la herejía** to be a sight, be a mess; **la propia estampa de** the very image of
estampado *m* printing, stamping; printed fabric, cotton print
estampar *tr* to stamp, print, engrave; (*en el ánimo*) fix, engrave; (*p.ej., el pie*) leave a mark of; (bb) to tool; (*arrojar con fuerza*) (coll) to dash, slam
estampida *f* report, crash, explosion; stampede
estampido *m* report, crash, explosion; **estampido sónico** (aer) sonic boom
estampilla *f* (*sello con letrero para estampar*) stamp; (*sello con una firma en facsímile*) rubber stamp; (*sello de correos o fiscal*) stamp
estampillar *tr* to stamp; rubber-stamp
estanca•do -da *adj* stagnant; (fig) stagnant, dead
estancar §73 *tr* to stanch; stem, check; (*un negocio*) suspend, hold up; corner; monopolize || *ref* to become stagnant, become choked up
estancia *f* stay, sojourn; (*aposento*) living room; day in hospital; cost of day in hospital; (*estrofa*) stanza; (mil) bivouac; (Arg, Urug, Chile) cattle ranch; (Col) small country place; (Ven) truck farm
estanciero *m* rancher, cattle raiser
estan•co -ca *adj* stanch, watertight || *m* government monopoly; cigar store, government store (*for sale of tobacco, matches, postage stamps, etc.*); archives; (Ecuad) liquor store
estándar *m* standard; **estándar de vida** standard of living
estandardizar §60 or **estandarizar §60** *tr* to standardize
estandarte *m* banner, standard
estandartizar §60 *tr* to standardize
estanque *m* basin, reservoir; pond, pool
estanque•ro -ra *mf* storekeeper, tobacconist; (Ecuad) saloonkeeper || *m* reservoir tender
estanquillo *m* cigar store, government store (*for sale of tobacco, matches, postage stamps, etc.*); (Col, Ecuad) bar, saloon; (Mex) booth, stand
estante *adj* located, being; settled, permanent || *m* shelf; shelving; bookcase, open bookcase
estantería *f* shelves, shelving; book stack
estañar *tr* to tin; tin-plate; solder; (Ven) to hurt, injure; (Ven) to fire
estaño *m* tin
estaquilla *f* peg, dowel, pin; (*clavo pequeño sin cabeza*) brad; (*clavo largo*) spike
estaquillar *tr* to peg, dowel; nail
estar §37 *v aux* (*to form progressive form*) to be, e.g., **están aprendiendo el español** they are learning Spanish || *intr* to be; be in, be home; be ready; **¿a cuántos estamos?** what day of the month is it?; **¡está bien!** O.K.!, all right!; **estar a** to cost, sell at; **estar bien** to be well; **estar bien con** to be on good terms with; **estar de** to be (*on a temporary basis*); **estar de más** to be in the way; be unnecessary; be idle; **estar de viaje** to be on a trip; **estar mal** to be sick, be ill; **estar mal con** to be on bad terms with; **estar para** to be about to; **estar por** to be for, be in favor of; to be about to; to have a mind to; to remain to be + *pp;* **estar sobre sí** to be wary, be on one's guard || *ref* (*p.ej., en casa*) to stay; (*p.ej., quieto*) to keep quiet
estarcido *m* stencil
estarcir §36 *tr* to stencil
estatal *adj* state
estáti•co -ca *adj* static; dumbfounded, speechless
estatificar §73 *tr* to nationalize
estatizar §60 *tr* to nationalize
estatorreactor *m* ramjet (engine)
estatua *f* statue; **Estatua de la Libertad** Statue of Liberty; **quedarse hecho una estatua** to stand aghast
estatuir §20 *tr* to order, decree; establish, prove
estatura *f* stature
estatuta•rio -ria *adj* statutory
estatuto *m* statute
estay *m* (naut) stay; **estay mayor** (naut) mainstay
este, esta *adj dem* (*pl* **estos, estas**) this || *m* east; east wind
éste, ésta *pron dem* (*pl* **éstos, éstas**) this one, this one here; the latter; **ésta** this city
estela *f* (*de un buque*) wake; (*de cohete, humo, cuerpo celeste, etc.*) trail
estenógrafo *m* (Cuba) ballpoint pen
estenotipia *f* stenotypy; machine stenography
estepa *f* steppe

estera *f* mat; matting; **cargado de esteras** out of patience
esterar *tr* to cover with matting || *intr* to bundle up for the cold
estercolar *m* dunghill || **§61** *tr* to dung, to manure
estercolero *m* manure pile, dunghill; manure collector
estéreo *adj & m* stereo
estereofonía *f* stereophonic sound system, stereo
estereofóni•co -ca *adj* stereophonic, stereo
estereoscópi•co -ca *adj* stereoscopic, stereo
estereotipa•do -da *adj* stereotyped
estéril *adj* (*que no produce nada*) sterile; (*inútil, vano*) futile
esterilización *f* sterilization
esterilizar §60 *tr* to sterilize || *ref* to become sterile
esterlina *adj fem* (*libra*) sterling (*pound*)
esternón *m* breastbone
estero *m* tideland; estuary; (Arg) swamp, marsh; (Chile) stream; (Col, Ven) pool, puddle
esterto *m* death rattle; (*ruido en ciertas enfermedades, perceptible por la auscultación*) stertor, rale; **estertor agónico** death rattle
esteta *mf* aesthete || *f* beautician
estéti•co -ca *adj* aesthetic || *f* aesthetics
estetoscopio *m* stethoscope
estiaje *m* low water
estiba *f* (naut) stowage
estibador *m* stevedore, longshoreman
estibar *tr* to pack, stuff; (naut) to stow
estiércol *m* dung, manure
esti•gio -gia *adj* Stygian || **Estigia** *f* Styx
estigma *m* stigma
estigmatizar §60 *tr* to stigmatize
estilar *tr* (*una escritura*) to draw up in proper form; be given to || *intr & ref* to be in fashion
estilete *m* (*puñal*) stiletto
estilo *m* style; stylus (*for writing*); **por el estilo** like that, of the kind; **por el estilo de** like; **estilo de vida** way of life; lifestyle; **estilo directo** (gram) direct discourse; **estilo indirecto** (gram) indirect discourse; **estilo libre** freestyle; **estilo mariposa** butterfly (*swimming stroke*)
estilográfica *f* fountain pen
estima *f* esteem; (naut) dead reckoning
estimable *adj* estimable; considerable; appreciable, computable; esteemed
estimación *f* esteem, estimation; estimate, evaluation
estimar *tr* (*tener en buen concepto*) to esteem; (*apreciar, valuar*) estimate; think, believe; appreciate, thank; be fond of, like; **estimar en poco** to hold in low esteem
estimativa *f* judgment; instinct
estimulante *adj & m* stimulant
estimular *tr* to stimulate
estímulo *m* stimulus
estío *m* summer
estipendio *m* stipend; wages
estípti•co -ca *adj* styptic; constipated; mean, stingy
estipular *tr* to stipulate
estiradamente *adv* scarcely, hardly; violently
estira•do -da *adj* conceited, stuck-up; prim, neat; tight, closefisted
estirar *tr* to stretch; (*alambre, metal*) draw; (*planchar ligeramente*) iron lightly; (*un escrito, discurso, cargo, etc.*) (fig) to stretch out; (*el dinero*) (fig) to stretch || *ref* to stretch; put on airs
estirón *m* jerk, tug; **dar un estirón** to grow up in no time
estirpe *f* race, stock, lineage; (*linaje*) strain, pedigree
estitiquez *f* constipation
estival *adj* summer
esto *pron dem* that; **en esto** at this point; **por esto** for this reason
estocada *f* thrust, stab, lunge; (*herida*) stab, stab wound; (*cosa que ocasiona dolor*) blow
Estocolmo *f* Stockholm
estofa *f* brocade; quality, kind
estofado *m* stew
estoi•co -ca *adj & mf* stoic
estóli•do -da *adj* stupid, imbecile
estómago *m* stomach; **estómago de avestruz** iron digestion; **tener buen estómago** *or* **mucho estómago** to be thick-skinned; have an easy conscience
estopa *f* (*de lino o cáñamo*) tow; (*de calafatear*) (naut) oakum; **estopa de acero** steel wool; **estopa de algodón** cotton waste
estopilla *f* (*tela muy sutil*) lawn; (*tela ordinaria de algodón*) cheesecloth
estoque *m* rapier; sword lily, gladiola
estoquear *tr* to stab with a rapier
estor *m* blind, shade, window shade
estorbar *tr* to hinder, obstruct; inconvenience, bother, annoy || *intr* to be in the way
estorbo *m* hindrance, obstruction; inconvenience, bother, annoyance
estorbo•so -sa *adj* hindering; bothersome, annoying
estornino *m* starling; **estornino de los pastores** grackle, myna
estornudar *intr* to sneeze
estornudo *m* sneeze, sneezing
estrado *m* (*tarima del trono*) dais; lecture platform; (archaic) lady's drawing room; **estrados** courtrooms, law courts; **citar para estrados** to subpoena
estrafala•rio -ria *adj* odd, eccentric; sloppy, sloppily dressed || *mf* screwball
estragar §44 *tr* to spoil, damage, vitiate
estrago *m* damage, ruin, havoc
estrambote *m* tail (*of sonnet*)
estrambóti•co -ca *adj* odd, weird
estrangul *m* (mus) reed, mouthpiece
estrangular *tr & ref* to strangle, choke
estraperlear *intr* to deal in the black market
estraperlista *adj* black-market || *mf* black-market dealer

estraperlo *m* black market
estrapontín *m* folding seat, jump seat
estratagema *f* stratagem; craftiness
estratega *m* strategist
estrategia *f* strategy; **alta estrategia** grand strategy
estratégi•co -ca *adj* strategic(al) || *m* strategist
estratificar §73 *tr & ref* to stratify
estrato *m* stratum, layer
estratosfera *f* stratosphere
estraza *f* rag; brown paper
estrechar *tr* (*reducir a menor ancho*) narrow; (*apretar*) tighten; press, pursue; force, compel; hug, embrace; squeeze; **estrechar la mano a** to shake hands with || *ref* to narrow down; contract; hug, embrace; (*reducir los gastos*) retrench; **estrecharse en** to squeeze in; **estrecharse la mano** (*dos personas*) to shake hands
estrechez *f* narrowness; rightness; (*amistad íntima*) closeness, intimacy; austerity, strictness; poverty, want, need; trouble, jam; **estrechez de miras** narrow outlook, narrow-mindedness; **hallarse en gran estrechez** to be in dire straits
estre•cho -cha *adj* narrow; tight; close, intimate; austere, strict; stingy, tight; poor, needy; mean || *m* (*paso angosto en el mar*) strait; fix, predicament
estrechura *f* narrowness; tightness; closeness, intimacy; austerity, strictness; trouble, predicament
estregar §66 *tr* to rub hard; scour
estregón *m* hard rub
estrella *f* star; (typ) asterisk, star; (mov & theat) star; (*hado, destino*) (fig) star; **estrella de los Alpes** edelweiss; **estrella de mar** starfish; **estrella de rabo** comet; **estrella filante** or **fugaz** shooting star; **estrella fulgurante** (astr) flare star; **estrella polar** polestar, North Star; **estrella vespertina** evening star; **ver las estrellas** (fig) to see stars
estrella•do -da *adj* (*cielo*) starry; star-spangled; star-shaped; (*huevos*) fried
estrellamar *m* starfish
estrellar *adj* star || *tr* to star, spangle with stars; (*huevos*) fry; shatter, dash to pieces || *ref* to be spangled with stars; crash; **estrellarse con** to clash with
estrellato *m* stardom; big time
estrellón *m* large star; (*fuego artificial*) star; smash-up
estremecer §22 *tr* to shake; (*el aire*) rend; (fig) to shake, upset || *ref* to shake, tremble, shiver, shudder
estrena *f* (*regalo que se da en señal de agradecimiento*) handsel; first use
estrenar *tr* to use for the first time, wear for the first time; (*un drama*) perform for the first time; (*un cine*) show for the first time; try out for the first time || *ref* to make the day's first transaction; appear for the first time; (*un drama, un cine*) open, premiere
estrenista *mf* first-nighter
estreno *m* beginning, debut; première, first performance; first use
estre•nuo -nua *adj* strenuous, vigorous, enterprising
estreñimiento *m* constipation
estreñir §72 *tr* to constipate
estrépito *m* racket, crash; fuss, show
estrepito•so -sa *adj* loud, noisy, boisterous; notorious; shocking
estreptomicina *f* (pharm) streptomycin
estría *f* flute, groove
estriar §77 *tr* to flute, groove
estribar *intr* to lean, rest; be based, depend
estriberón *m* stepping stone
estribillo *m* (*de un poema*) burden, refrain; pet word, pet phrase
estribo *m* (*de coche*) step; (*de automóvil*) running board; (*apoyo para el pie*) footboard; (*para el pie del jinete*) stirrup; abutment, buttress; (fig) foundation, support; **perder los estribos** to fly off the handle; lose one's head
estribor *m* starboard
estricnina *f* strychnine
estricote *m* (Ven) riotous living; **al estricote** hither and thither
estric•to -ta *adj* strict, severe, rigorous; proper, punctual; (*sentido de una palabra*) narrow
estrictura *f* (pathol) stricture
estrige *f* barn owl; (*Athene noctua*) little owl
estro *m* poetic inspiration; (*de animal*) rut, heat
estrofa *f* strophe, stanza, verse
estroncio *m* strontium
estropajo *m* mop; dishcloth; **servir de estropajo** to be forced to do the dirty work; be treated with indifference
estropajo•so -sa *adj* raggedy, slovenly; (*carne*) tough, leathery; spluttering
estropear *tr* to spoil, ruin, damage; abuse, mistreat; cripple, maim || *ref* to spoil, go to ruin; fail
estropicio *m* breakage; havoc, ruin; fracas, rumpus
estructura *f* structure
estruendo *m* noise, crash, boom; confusion, uproar; pomp, show; fame
estruendo•so -sa *adj* noisy, booming
estrujar *tr* to squeeze; press, crush, mash; bruise; rumple; drain, exhaust
estuante *adj* hot, burning
estuario *m* estuary; tideland
estucar §73 *tr* to stucco
estuche *m* case, box; (*caja y utensilios que se guardan en ella*) kit; casket, jewel case; (*para tijeras*) sheath; **estuche de maquillaje** compact, vanity case; **ser un estuche** to be a handy fellow
estuco *m* stucco; **estuco de París** plaster of Paris
estudia•do -da *adj* affected, studied
estudiantado *m* student body
estudiante *mf* student; **estudiante de profesorado** student teacher
estudiantil *adj* student

estudiar *tr* to study; (*la lección a una persona*) to hear (*someone's lesson*) || *intr* to study; **estudiar para . . .** to study to become . . .
estudio *m* study; (*aposento*) studio; (mus) étude; **altos estudios** advanced studies
estudio•so -sa *adj* studious || *m* student, scholar
estufa *f* stove; steam cabinet, steam room; foot stove; (*invernáculo*) hothouse; (Col, Mex) kitchen stove
estul•to -ta *adj* stupid, silly, foolish
estupefac•to -ta *adj* stupefied, dumbfounded
estupen•do -da *adj* stupendous; famous, distinguished
estúpi•do -da *adj* stupid || *mf* dolt
estupor *m* stupor; surprise, amazement
estuprar *tr* to rape, violate
estupro *m* rape, violation
estuque *m* stucco
esturión *m* sturgeon
etapa *f* stage; **a etapas pequeñas** by easy stages
éter *m* ether
etére•o -a *adj* ethereal
eternidad *f* eternity
eternizar §60 *tr* to prolong endlessly || *ref* to be endless, be interminable
eter•no -na *adj* eternal
éti•co -ca *adj* ethical || *f* ethics
etileno *m* ethylene
etilo *m* ethyl
étimo *m* etymon
etimología *f* etymology; **etimología popular** folk etymology
etíope *adj & mf* Ethiopian
etiópi•co -ca *adj & m* Ethiopic
etiqueta *f* (*marbete*) tag, label; (*ceremonial que se debe observar*) etiquette; (*ceremonial en la manera de tratarse*) formality; **de etiqueta** formal, full-dress; **de etiqueta menor** semiformal; **estar de etiqueta** to have become cool toward each other
etiquetado, etiquetaje *m* labeling
etiquetar *tr* to tag, label
etiquete•ro -ra *adj* formal, ceremonious; full of compliments
etiquez *f* (pathol) consumption
étni•co -ca *adj* ethnic(al); (gram) gentilic
etnografía *f* ethnography
etnología *f* ethnology
E.U.A. *abbr* **Estados Unidos de América**
eucalipto *m* eucalyptus
Eucaristía *f* Eucharist
eufemismo *m* euphemism
eufemísti•co -ca *adj* euphemistic
eufonía *f* euphony
eufóni•co -ca *adj* euphonic, euphonious
euforia *f* euphoria; endurance, fortitude
eufuísmo *m* euphuism
eufuísti•co -ca *adj* euphuistic
eugenesia *f* eugenics
eunuco *m* eunuch
euritmia *f* regular pulse
euro *m* east wind; **Euro** Euro(dollar)
eurodólar *m* Eurodollar
Europa *f* Europe
europe•o -a *adj & mf* European
eutanasia *f* euthanasia, mercy killing
eutrapelia *f* moderation; lightheartedness; simple pastime
evacuación *f* evacuation; **evacuación de basuras** garbage disposal
evacuar §21 & regular *tr* to evacuate; (*un trámite*) transact; (*una visita*) pay; (*un encargo, un asunto*) do, carry out; **evacuar el vientre** to have a bowel movement || *intr* to evacuate; have a bowel movement
evadi•do -da *adj* escaped || *mf* escapee
evadir *tr* to avoid, evade, elude || *ref* to evade; escape, flee
evaluar §21 *tr* to evaluate; value
evangéli•co -ca *adj* evangelic(al)
evangelio *m* gospel, gospel truth || **Evangelio** *m* Gospel, Evangel
evangelista *m* Gospel singer or chanter; (Mex) public writer, penman || **Evangelista** *m* Evangelist
evaporar *tr & ref* to evaporate
evaporizar §60 *tr, intr & ref* to vaporize
evasión *f* (*efugio, evasiva*) evasion; (*fuga*) escape
evasi•vo -va *adj* evasive || *f* loophole, pretext, excuse
evento *m* chance, happening, contingency; (Col) sports event; **a todo evento** in any event
eventual *adj* contingent; (*emolumentos; gastos*) incidental
eventualidad *f* eventuality, contingency; uncertainty
evidencia *f* evidence, obviousness; (*prueba judicial*) evidence; **evidencia moral** moral certainty
evidenciar *tr* to show, make evident
evidente *adj* evident, obvious
evitable *adj* avoidable
evitación *f* avoidance; prevention
evitar *tr* to avoid, shun; (*p.ej., el polvo*) keep off; prevent; **evitar** + *inf* to avoid + *ger;* save from + *ger,* e.g., **la luz de la luna nos evitó tener que encender los faroles** the light of the moon saved us from having to light the lights
evo *m* (poet) age, aeon; (theol) eternity
evoca•dor -dora *adj* suggestive
evocar §73 *tr* to evoke; (*p.ej., los demonios*) invoke
evolución *f* evolution; change, development (*of one's point of view, plans, conduct, etc.*)
evolucionar *intr* to evolve; change, develop; (mil & nav) to maneuver
evolucionista *adj & mf* evolutionist; evolutionary
ex *adj* ex- (*former*), e.g., **el ex presidente** the ex-president
ex abrupto *adv* brashly || *m* brash remark
exacción *f* (*de impuestos, deudas, multas, etc.*) exaction, levy; (*cobro injusto*) extortion
exacerbar *tr* to exacerbate, aggravate

exactitud *f* exactness; punctuality
exac•to -ta *adj* exact; punctual, faithful || **exacto** *interj* right!
exactor *m* tax collector
exagerar *tr* to exaggerate
exalta•do -da *adj* exalted; extreme, hotheaded; wrought-up; radical
exaltar *tr* to exalt; extol || *ref* to be wrought-up, get excited
examen *m* examination; **examen de ingreso** entrance examination; **examen médico** medical examination; **sufrir un examen** to take an examination
examinar *tr* to examine; inspect || *ref* to take an examination; **examinarse de ingreso** to take entrance examinations
exangüe *adj* bloodless; weak, exhausted; dead
exánime *adj* (*sin vida*) lifeless; (*desmayado*) faint, in a faint, lifeless
exasperar *tr* to exasperate
Exc.ª *abbr* **Excelencia**
excandecer §22 *tr* to incense, enrage
excarcelación *f* release
excarcelar *tr* (*a un preso*) to release
excavadora *f* power shovel
excavar *tr* to excavate; loosen soil around
excedente *adj* excess; excessive; on leave || *m* excess, surplus; **excedente de ganancia** profit margin
exceder *tr* (*ser mayor que*) to exceed; (*aventajar*) excel || *ref* to go too far, go to extremes; **excederse a sí mismo** to outdo oneself
excelencia *f* excellence, excellency; **por excelencia** par excellence; **Su Excelencia** Your Excellency
excelente *adj* excellent
excel•so -sa *adj* lofty, sublime || **el Excelso** the Most High
excéntrica *f* eccentric
excentricidad *f* eccentricity
excéntri•co -ca *adj* eccentric; (*barrio*) outlying || *mf* eccentric || *f* see **excéntrica**
excepción *f* exception; **a excepción de** with the exception of
excepcional *adj* exceptional
excepto *prep* except
exceptuar §21 *tr* to except; (*eximir*) exempt
excerpta or **excerta** *adj* excerpt
excesi•vo -va *adj* excessive; excess
exceso *m* excess; **exceso de equipaje** excess baggage; **exceso de peso** excess weight; **exceso de velocidad** speeding
excitable *adj* excitable
excitación *f* excitement; excitation
excitante *adj & m* stimulant
excitar *tr* to excite, stir up, stimulate || *ref* to become excited
exclamación *f* exclamation
exclamar *tr & intr* to exclaim
exclaustrar *tr* (*a un religioso*) to secularize
excluir §20 *tr* to exclude
exclusión *f* exclusion; **con exclusión de** to the exclusion of; **exclusión de contribución** tax deduction
exclusiva *f* rejection, turndown; sole right, monopoly; (*anticipación de una noticia por un periódico*) news beat
exclusive *adv* exclusively || *prep* exclusive of, not counting
exclusivista *adj* exclusive, clannish || *mf* snob
exclusi•vo -va *adj* exclusive, sole; exclusive, select, elite || *f* see **exclusiva**
Exc.ᵐᵒ *abbr* **Excelentísimo**
ex combatiente *m* ex-serviceman
excomulgar §44 *tr* to excommunicate; ostracize, banish
excomunión *f* excommunication
ex comunista *mf* ex-communist
ex convicto *m* ex-convict, ex-con (slang)
excoriar *tr* to skin || *ref* to skin oneself; (*p.ej., el codo*) skin
excrementar *intr* to have a bowel movement
excremento *m* excrement
exculpar *tr* to exculpate, exonerate
excursión *f* excursion, outing
excursionista *mf* excursionist, tourist
excusa *f* excuse; **a excusa** secretly; **excusa es decir** it is unnecessary to say
excusabaraja *f* basket with lid
excusable *adj* excusable; avoidable
excusadamente *adv* unnecessarily
excusa•do -da *adj* exempt; unnecessary; private, set apart; (*puerta*) side || *m* toilet
excusa•lí *m* (*pl* **-líes**) small apron
excusar *tr* to excuse; exempt; avoid; prevent; make unnecessary; **excusar** + *inf* to not have to + *inf* || *ref* to excuse oneself; apologize; **excusarse de** + *inf* to decline to + *inf*
exención *f* exemption
exencionar *tr* to exempt
exentamente *adv* freely; frankly, simply
exentar *tr* to exempt
exen•to -ta *adj* exempt; open, unobstructed; free, disengaged
exequias *fpl* obsequies
exfolia•dor -dora *adj* tear-off
exhalación *f* exhalation; flash of lightning; shooting star; fume, vapor; **como una exhalación** like a flash of lightning
exhalar *tr* to exhale, emit; (*suspiros, quejas*) breathe forth; **exhalar el último suspiro** to breathe one's last || *ref* to exhale; (*con el ejercicio violento del cuerpo*) breathe hard; hurry; crave
exhausti•vo -va *adj* exhaustive
exhaus•to -ta *adj* exhausted; wasted away
exheredar *tr* to disinherit
exhibición *f* exhibition; exhibit; **exhibición repetida** (telv) rerun
exhibición-venta *f* sales exhibit
exhibir *tr* to exhibit; showcase; (Mex) to pay || *ref* to make oneself evident
exhilarante *adj* exhilarating; (*gas*) laughing
exhortar *tr* to exhort
exhumar *tr* to exhume

exigencia *f* exigency, requirement
exigente *adj* exigent, demanding
exigir §27 *tr* to exact, require, demand
exi•guo -gua *adj* meager, scanty
exila•do -da *adj & mf* exile
exi•mio -mia *adj* choice, select, superior; distinguished
eximir *tr* to exempt
existencia *f* existence; **en existencia** in stock; **existencias** (com) stock
existente *adj* existing, extant; in stock
existir *intr* to exist
exitazo *m* smash hit, knockout
exitista *adj* (Arg) me-too || *mf* (Arg) me-tooer
éxito *m* (*resultado feliz*) success; (*canción, cine, etc. que ha tenido mucho éxito*) hit; (*resultado de un negocio*) outcome, result; **éxito de librería** best seller; **éxito de taquilla** box-office hit, sellout; **éxito de venta** best seller; **éxito rotundo** smash hit
exito•so -sa *adj* (Arg) successful
ex li•bris *m* (*pl* **-bris**) bookplate
exobiología *f* exobiology
éxodo *m* exodus; **éxodo de técnicos** brain drain
exonerar *tr* to exonerate, relieve; discharge, dismiss; **exonerar el vientre** to have a bowel movement
exorar *tr* to beg, entreat
exorbitante *adj* exorbitant
exorcizar §60 *tr* to exorcise
exornar *tr* to adorn, embellish
exóti•co -ca *adj* exotic; striking, stunning, glamorous
expandir *tr & ref* (Arg, Chile) to expand, extend, spread
expansión *f* expansion; (*manifestación efusiva*) expansiveness; (*difusión de una opinión*) spread; rest, recreation
expansionar *ref* to expand; open one's heart; relax, take it easy
expansi•vo -va *adj* expansive
expatria•do -da *adj & mf* expatriate
expectación *f* expectancy; **expectación de vida** life expectancy
expectativa *f* expectation; **estar a la expectativa de** to be expecting, be on the lookout for
expectorar *tr & intr* to expectorate
expediar *tr* to expedite; handle without delay; rush, speed
expedición *f* (*excursión para realizar una empresa*) expedition; (*remesa*) shipment; (*de un certificado, títulos, etc.*) issuance; (*agilidad, facilidad*) expedition
expedi•dor -dora *mf* sender, shipper
expediente *m* expedient; makeshift, apology; (*agilidad, facilidad*) expedition; (*todos los papeles correspondientes a un asunto*) dossier; (law) action, proceedings; **expediente académico** (educ) record
expedienteo *m* red tape
expedir §50 *tr* to send, ship, remit; (*títulos*) issue; (*despachar, cursar*) expedite
expeditar *tr* to expedite
expediti•vo -va *adj* expeditious
expedi•to -ta *adj* ready; clear, open, unencumbered
expeler *tr* to expel, eject
expende•dor -dora *mf* dealer, retailer; ticket agent; **expendedor de moneda falsa** distributor of counterfeit money
expendeduría *f* cigar store (*for sale of state-monopolized articles*)
expender *tr* to spend; dispense; sell at retail; (*moneda falsa*) circulate
expendio *m* shop, store; retail; (Mex) cigar store
expensar *tr* (Chile, Guat, Mex) to pay the cost of
expensas *fpl* expenses
experiencia *f* (*enseñanza que se adquiere con la práctica o con el vivir; suceso en que uno ha participado, cosa que uno ha experimentado*) experience; (*ensayo, experimento*) experiment
experimenta•do -da *adj* experienced
experimentar *tr* to experience, undergo, feel; test, try, try out || *intr* to experiment
experimento *m* experiment; **experimento piloto** pilot test, pilot run
exper•to -ta *adj & m* expert
expiación *f* expiation, atonement; purification
expiar §77 *tr* to expiate, atone for; purify
expirar *intr* to expire
explanación *f* grading, leveling; explanation
explanada *f* esplanade
explanar *tr* to grade, level; explain
explayar *tr* to enlarge, extend || *ref* to spread out, extend; go for an outing; expatiate, talk at length; **explayarse con** to unbosom oneself to
explicación *f* explanation
explicar §73 *tr* to explain; (*exponer*) expound; (*exculpar*) explain away; (*una clase*) teach || *intr* to explain || *ref* to explain oneself; understand, make out
explicati•vo -va *adj* explanatory
explíci•to -ta *adj* explicit
exploración *f* exploration; (mil) scouting; (astr, compu, mil, telv) scan, scanning
explora•dor -dora *mf* explorer || *m* boy scout; (compu) scanner; (mil) scout
explorar *tr* to explore; (astr, compu, mil, telv) to scan; (mil) to scout
explosión *f* explosion; (*de gases en un motor*) combustion
explosi•vo -va *adj & m* explosive || *f* (phonet) explosive
explotación *f* operation, running; exploitation; **explotación abusiva** (geol) overexploitation (of resources)
explotar *tr* to operate, run; (*una mina*) work; exploit || *intr* to explode
exponente *m* exponent; (fig) interpreter, apologist
exponer §54 *tr* to expose; (*explicar*) expound; (*a un niño recién nacido*) abandon || *intr* to

display, show, exhibit; (eccl) to expose the Host || *ref* to expose oneself; be on view
exportación *f* exportation, export; (*mercaderías que se exportan*) exports
exporta•dor -dora *mf* exporter
exportar *tr & intr* to export
exposición *f* exposition; (*a un peligro; con relación a los puntos cardinales*) exposure; (phot) exposure; (rhet) exposition; **exposición canina** dog show; **exposición comercial** *or* **industrial** trade fair; **exposición universal** world's fair
exposición-venta *f* sales exhibit
exposímetro *m* light meter
expósi•to -ta *mf* foundling
exposi•tor -tora *mf* exhibitor
exprés *m* express train; (Mex) express company
expresa•do -da *adj* above-mentioned
expresamente *adv* express, expressly
expresar *tr* to express || *ref* to express oneself
ex presidia•rio -ria *mf* ex-convict
expresión *f* expression; (*acción de exprimir*) squeezing; (*zumo exprimido*) juice; **expresiones** regards
expresi•vo -va *adj* expressive; kind, affectionate
expre•so -sa *adj* express || *m* (*tren muy rápido; correo extraordinario*) express; express company; (*café exprés*) espresso
exprimidera *f* squeezer; **exprimidera de naranjas** orange squeezer
exprimi•do -da *adj* lean, skinny; stiff, stuck-up; affected, prim, prudish
exprimidor *m* wringer; squeezer; **exprimidor de ropa** clothes wringer
exprimir *tr* to squeeze, press; (*p.ej., la ropa blanca*) wring, wring out; (*extraer apretando*) express
ex profeso *adv* on purpose
expropiar *tr* to expropriate
expues•to -ta *adj* dangerous, hazardous
expugnar *tr* to take by storm
expulsanie•ves *m* (*pl* **-ves**) snowplow
expulsar *tr* to expel
expulsión *f* expulsion; (compu) ejection
expurgar §44 *tr* to expurgate
exquisi•to -ta *adj* exquisite
extasiar §77 & regular *ref* to go into ecstasy
éxta•sis *m* (*pl* **-sis**) ecstasy
extáti•co -ca *adj* ecstatic
extemporal *adj* unseasonable
extemporáne•o -a *adj* unseasonable; untimely, inopportune
extender §51 *tr* to extend, stretch out, spread out; spread; (*un documento*) draw up || *ref* to extend, stretch out; spread; **extenderse a** *or* **hasta** to amount to
extendidamente *adv* at length, in detail
extensión *f* extension; (*vasta superficie, p.ej., del océano*) expanse; (*alcance, importancia*) extent; extending; (*de un cable*) extension cord; (compu, telp) extension
extensi•vo -va *adj* extensive; **hacer extensivos a** to extend (*e.g., good wishes*) to
exten•so -sa *adj* extensive, extended, vast; **por extenso** at length, in detail
extenuar §21 *tr* to weaken, emaciate
exterior *adj* exterior, outer, outside; foreign || *m* exterior, outside; appearance, bearing; **al exterior** *or* **a lo exterior** on the outside; outwardly; **del exterior** from abroad; **en el exterior** on the outside; abroad; **en exteriores** (mov) on location
exterioridad *f* externals, outward appearance; **exterioridades** pomp, show
exteriorista *adj* outgoing, outgiving || *mf* extrovert
exteriorizar §60 *tr* to reveal || *ref* to unbosom one's heart
exterminar *tr* to exterminate
exterminio *m* extermination
exter•no -na *adj* external || *mf* day pupil
extinción *f* extinction; cancellation, elimination
extinguidor *m* extinguisher; (SAm) (*incendios*) fire extinguisher
extinguir §29 *tr* to extinguish, put out; wipe out, put an end to; fulfil, carry out; (*un plazo, un tiempo*) spend, serve || *ref* to be extinguished, go out; come to an end
extin•to -ta *adj* (*volcán*) extinct; deceased || *mf* deceased
extintor *m* fire extinguisher; **extintor de espuma** foam extinguisher; **extintor de granada** fire grenade
extirpar *tr* to extirpate, eradicate
extorno *m* premium adjustment (*based on change in policy*)
extorsión *f* extortion; harm, damage
extorsionar *tr* to harm, damage; extort
extra *adj* extra; **extra de** in addition to, besides || *mf* (theat) extra, super || *m* (*de un periódico*) extra; extra, bonus
extracción *f* extraction; (*en la lotería*) drawing numbers; **extracción de raíces** (math) evolution
extractar *tr* (*un escrito*) to abstract
extracto *m* (*de un escrito*) abstract, summary; (pharm) extract; **extracto de carne** beef extract; **extracto de tomate** tomato paste
extractor *m* extractor; remover; **extractor de aire** ventilator; **extractor de humos** smoke evacuator
extracurricular *adj* extracurricular
extradición *f* extradition
extraer §75 *tr* to extract; pull; (*la raíz*) (math) to extract
extrafuerte *adj* heavy-duty
extragalácti•co -ca *adj* extragalactic
extraíble *adj* (compu) removable
extralimitar *ref* to go too far
extramural *adj* extramural
extanjerismo *m* borrowing
extranje•ro -ra *adj* foreign, alien || *mf* foreigner, alien; **extranjero enemigo** enemy alien || *m* foreign country; **al extranjero** abroad; **del extranjero** from abroad; **en el extranjero** abroad

extrañar *tr* to banish, expatriate; surprise; find strange; miss || *ref* to be surprised; refuse

extrañeza *f* strangeness, peculiarity; (*desavenencia*) estrangement; wonder, surprise

extra•ño -na *adj* foreign; (*raro, singular*) strange; extraneous; **extraño a** unconnected with || *mf* foreigner

extraoficial *adj* unofficial

extraordina•rio -ria *adj* extraordinary; extra, special || *m* extra dish; special mail; (*de un periódico*) extra

extrapla•no -na *adj* extra-flat

extrapolar *tr & intr* to extrapolate

extrarradio *m* outer edge of town

extrasensorial *adj* extrasensory

extraterrestre *adj* extraterrestrial; otherworldly

extravagancia *f* (*singularidad, ridiculez*) extravagance, wildness, folly

extravagante *adj* (*singular, ridículo*) extravagant, wild, foolish; (*correspondencia en la casa de correos*) in transit

extravia•do -da *adj* lost, misplaced; astray, gone astray; (*lugar*) out-of-the-way

extraviar §77 *tr* to lead astray, mislead; mislay, misplace || *ref* to get lost, go astray; go wrong; get out of line

extravío *m* going astray; loss; misleading; misconduct; misplacement

extrema *f* (*escasez grande*) extremity; (*de la vida*) end, last moment

extremar *tr* to carry far, carry to the limit || *ref* to strive hard

extremaunción *f* extreme unction; last rites (*Roman Catholic*)

extreme•ño -ña *adj* frontier

extremidad *f* extremity; end, tip; **extremidades** (*pies y manos*) extremities; **la última extremidad** one's last moment

extremismo *m* extremism

extremista *mf* extremist

extre•mo -ma *adj* extreme; utmost; critical, desperate || *m* extremity; (*de la calle*) end; (*del dedo*) tip; (*punto último*) extreme; great care; (*de una conversación, una carta*) point; winter pasture; **al extremo de** to the point of; **de extremo a extremo** from one end to the other; **hacer extremos** to be demonstrative, gush || *f* see **extrema**

extremo•so -sa *adj* extreme, forthright; effusive, gushy, demonstrative

extrínse•co -ca *adj* extrinsic

extroversión *f* extroversion

extroverti•do -da *mf* extrovert

exuberante *adj* exuberant; luxuriant

exudar *tr & intr* to exude

exultante *adj* exultant

exultar *intr* to exult

exvoto *m* votive offering

eyacular *tr & intr* to ejaculate

F

F, f (efe) *f* sixth letter of the Spanish alphabet

f.a.b. *abbr* **franco a bordo**

fabada *f* pork-and-bean stew (*in Asturias*)

fábrica *f* factory, plant; building, masonry; (eccl) vestry

fabricación *f* manufacture; **fabricación en serie** mass production

fabricante *mf* manufacturer

fabricar §73 *tr* to manufacture; devise, invent; fabricate

fabril *adj* factory

fabriquero *m* manufacturer; charcoal burner; churchwarden

fábula *f* fable; (*p.ej., de un drama*) plot, story; rumor, gossip; (*mentira*) story, lie; (*objeto de murmuración*) talk of the town

fabulario *m* book of fables

fabulo•so -sa *adj* fabulous

facción *f* faction; feature; battle; **estar de facción** (mil) to be on duty; **facciones** features

facciona•rio -ria *adj* factional

faceta *f* facet

facetada *f* (Mex) flat joke

face•to -ta *adj* (Mex) affected; (Mex) finicky || *f* see **faceta**

facha *mf* (*adefesio*) sight || *f* look, appearance; **facha a facha** face to face

fachada *f* façade; (*de un libro*) title page; look, build, bearing; **hacer fachada con** to overlook, to look out on

facha•do -da *adj* — **bien fachado** good-looking || *f* see **fachada**

fachenda *m* boaster, show-off || *f* boasting

fachendear *intr* to boast, show off

fachendista or **fachen•dón -dona** or **fachendo•so -sa** *adj* boastful || *mf* boaster, show-off

fachinal *m* (Arg) marshland

facial *adj* facial

fácil *adj* easy; pliant, yielding; likely; loose, wanton

facilidad *f* facility, ease, easiness; **facilidades de pago** easy payments

facilitar *tr* to facilitate, expedite; furnish, supply

facili•tón -tona *adj* bumbling, brash || *mf* bumbler

facinero•so -sa *adj* wicked || *mf* villain

facistol *m* choir desk

facón *m* (Arg, Urug) gaucho knife

facsimilar *tr* to facsimile; copy

facsímile *m* facsimile

factible *adj* feasible

factor *m* factor; commission merchant; baggageman; freight agent

factoría *f* trading post; (Ecuad, Peru) foundry; (Mex) factory
factura *f* invoice, bill; workmanship; **factura simulada** pro forma invoice; **según factura** as per invoice
facturación *f* invoicing, billing (*del equipaje*) checking
facturar *tr* to invoice, bill; (*el equipaje*) check
facultad *f* faculty; (*de la universidad*) school, college; knowledge, skill; power; **facultad de altos estudios** graduate school
facultar *tr* to empower, authorize
facultati•vo -va *adj* faculty; optional ‖ *m* doctor, physician
facundia *f* eloquence, fluency
facun•do -da *adj* eloquent, fluent
fada *f* fairy, witch
faena *f* work; toil; chore, task, job; (taur) windup; (taur) stunt, trick; (mil) fatigue, fatigue duty; (Guat, Mex, W-I) extra work, overtime; (Ecuad) morning work in the field; (Chile) gang of farm hands
faenero *m* (Chile) farm hand
fagot *m* bassoon
faisán *m* pheasant
faja *f* sash, girdle; bandage; band, strip; newspaper wrapper; (*de carretera*) lane; (*de tierra*) strip; **faja central** *or* **divisoria** median strip; **faja interior** sweatband (*in hat*); **faja medical** supporter
fajar *tr* to wrap; bandage; swaddle; (*un periódico o revista*) put a wrapper on; beat, thrash; to attack ‖ *ref* to put on a sash
fajardo *m* meat pie
fajín *m* sash
fajina *f* bundle of sticks; fire wood; (mil) call to quarters
fajo *m* bundle; (*de papel moneda*) roll; swig; (Mex) blow; (Mex) leather belt; **fajos** swaddling clothes
falacia *f* deception; deceitfulness
falange *f* phalanx
falangia *f* daddy-longlegs
fa•laz *adj* (*pl* **-laces**) deceitful; deceptive
falba•lá *m* (*pl* **-aes**) gore; flounce, ruffle
falce *m* sickle; falchion
falda *f* skirt, dress; (*regazo*) lap; flap; fold; (*del sombrero*) brim; foothill; (*mujer*) skirt; **cosido a las faldas de** tied to the apron strings of; **falda de tubo** straight skirt; **falda pantalón** split skirt
falde•ro -ra *adj* skirt; (*perro*) lap; lady-loving ‖ *m* lap dog
faldillas *fpl* skirts, coattails
faldón *m* coattail; shirttail; saddle flap
falible *adj* fallible
fáli•co -ca *adj* phallic
falla *f* failure, breakdown; defect; (geol) fault; (Mex) baby's bonnet
fallar *tr* to trump; judge, pass judgment on ‖ *intr* to fail, miss; misfire; sag, weaken; break down; judge, pass judgment; (compu) to crash
falleba *f* espagnolette
fallecer **§22** *intr* to die; fail, expire
falleci•do -da *adj* deceased, late
falli•do -da *adj* unsuccessful; bankrupt; (*deuda*) uncollectible
fallir **§13** *intr* to fail; (Ven) to go bankrupt
fa•llo -lla *adj* (Chile) silly, simple; **estar fallo a** to be out of (*cards of a suit*) ‖ *m* short suit; decision; judgment; verdict; **fallo cardíaco** heart failure; **fallo fotográfico** photo finish; **fallo humano** human error; **tener fallo a** or **de** to be out of ‖ *f* see **falla**
falo *m* penis, phallus
falsada *f* swoop (*of bird of prey*)
falsa•rio -ria *adj* lying ‖ *mf* falsifier, crook; liar
falsear *tr* to falsify; counterfeit; forge; (*la verdad*) distort; (*una cerradura*) pick; bevel ‖ *intr* to sag, buckle; give, give way
falsedad *f* falsity; (*mentira*) falsehood
falsete *m* falsetto; plug, tap; door (*between rooms*)
falsetista *f* falsetto
falsía *f* falsity, treachery; unsteadiness
falsificación *f* falsification; fake; counterfeit; forgery
falsificar **§73** *tr* to falsify; fake; counterfeit; forge
falsilla *f* guide lines
fal•so -sa *adj* false; counterfeit; (*caballo*) vicious ‖ *m* patch; **coger en falso** (Mex) to catch in a lie; **envidar en falso** to bluff
falta *f* fault; lack, want; misdeed; absence; (*ausencia de la clase*) cut; (sport) fault; foul; **a falta de** for want of; **echar en falta** to miss; **falta de ortografía** misspelling **hacer falta** to be needed; be lacking; **hacerle falta a uno** to need, e.g., **le hacen falta a Juan estos libros** John needs these books; to miss, e.g., **Ud. me hace mucha falta** I miss you very much; **sin falta** without fail
faltar *intr* to be missing, be lacking, be wanting; fall short; run out; be absent; fail; die; lack, need, e.g., **me falta dinero** I lack money, I need money; **faltar a la clase** to cut class; **faltar a la verdad** to fail to tell the truth; **faltar a una cita** to fail to keep an appointment; **faltar. . . para** to be . . . to, e.g., **faltan cinco minutos para las dos** it is five minutes to two; **faltar poco para** to come near; **faltar por** to remain to be, e.g., **faltan por escribir dos cartas** two letters remain to be written
fal•to -ta *adj* short, lacking; (*peso o medida*) short; (Arg) dull, stupid; (Col) proud, vain; **falto de** short of ‖ *f* see **falta**
fal•tón -tona *adj* dilatory, remiss; (Arg) simple-minded
falto•so -sa *adj* addlebrained; (Col) quarrelsome; (CAm, Mex) disrespectful
faltriquera *f* pocket; handbag; **faltriquera de reloj** watch fob; **rascarse la faltriquera** to cough up
falúa *f* barge, tender
falucho *m* felucca
fama *f* fame; reputation; rumor; (Chile) bull's-

eye; **correr fama** to be rumored; **es fama** it is said, it is rumored
faméli•co -ca *adj* famished, starving
familia *f* family; **familia de acogida** foster family; host family; **familia extensa** extended family; **familia monoparental** single-parent family; **venir de familia** to run in the family
familiar *adj* familiar; family; (*sin ceremonia*) informal; (*lenguaje, estilo*) colloquial || *m* member of the family; member of the household; acquaintance; **familiar dependiente** dependent
familiaridad *f* familiarity
familiarizar §60 *tr* to familiarize || *ref* to become familiar; become too familiar; familiarize oneself
famo•so -sa *adj* famous; (*excelente*) famous; (*formidable*) some, e.g., **famoso sujeto** some guy
fámu•lo -la *mf* (coll) servant
fanal *m* beacon, lighthouse; lantern; bell glass, bell jar; lamp shade
fanáti•co -ca *adj* fanatic(al); addicted || *mf* fanatic; addict; (sport) fan; **fanático de la gimnasia** fitness buff; **fanático del trabajo** workaholic
fanatismo *m* fanaticism
fanega *f* 1.58 bu.; **fanega de tierra** 1.59 acres
fanfarria *f* fanfare; blustering
fanfa•rŕon -rrona *adj* blustering, bragging; flashy || *mf* blusterer, braggart, showoff
fanfarronada *f* bluster, bravado
fanfarronnear *intr* to bluster, brag
fanfarronería *f* blustering, bragging, sword rattling
fanfurriña *f* pet, peeve
fango *m* mud, mire; **llenar de fango** (fig) to sling mud at
fango•so -sa *adj* muddy; sticky, gooey
fanguero *m* (Cuba, Mex, P-R) mud, quagmire
fantasear *tr* to dream of || *intr* to fancy, to daydream; **fantasear de** to boast of being
fantasía *f* fantasy; fancy, conceit, vanity; imagery; **con fantasía** (Arg) hard; **de fantasía** fancy, imitation; **tocar por fantasía** (Ven) to play by ear
fantasio•so -sa *adj* vain, conceited
fantasma *m* phantom, ghost; stuffed shirt; (telv) ghost; **fantasma magnético** magnetic curves || *f* scarecrow, hobgoblin
fantas•món -mona *adj* (coll) conceited || *mf* conceited person || *m* stuffed shirt; (coll) scarecrow
fantásti•co -ca *adj* fantastic; fancy; conceited
fantoche *m* puppet, marionette; nincompoop
faquín *m* street porter, errand boy
fara•lá *m* (*pl* **-laes**) ruffle, flounce; frill
faramalla *mf* cheat, swindler || *f* jabber, claptrap; bluff, fake; (Chile) bragging
faramalle•ro -ra *or* **farama•llón -llona** *adj* scheming, swindling || *mf* schemer, swindler
farándula *f* (*baile*) farandole; gossip, scheming; theater people; (*de gente*) (Arg) crush, milling
farandulear *intr* to boast, to show off
Faraón *m* Pharaoh
faraute *m* herald, messenger; interpreter; (*actor*) prologue; busybody
fardel *m* bag, bundle; sloppy person
fardo *m* bundle, package
farero *m* lighthouse keeper
farfa•lá *m* (*pl* **-laes**) ruffle, flounce
farfullar *tr* to jabber; (*p.ej., una lección*) to sputter through; (*p.ej., una tarea*) stumble through || *intr* to sputter, jabber
faringe *f* pharynx
fariseo *m* (Bib) Pharisee; (pej) hypocrite, pharisee
farmacéuti•co -ca *adj* pharmaceutical || *mf* pharmacist, druggist
farmacia *f* pharmacy, drug store; **farmacia de guardia** drug store open all night
fármaco *m* drug, medicine
faro *m* lighthouse, beacon; floodlight; (aut) headlight; (fig) beacon; **faro antiniebla** fog light; **faro piloto** (aut) spotlight; **faros de carretera** (aut) bright lights; **faros de cruce** (aut) dimmers; **faros de población** or **de situación** (aut) parking lights
farol *m* lamp, light; lantern; street light; (rr) headlight; (coll) conceited fellow; (Bol) bay window; **farol de tope** (naut) headlight; **faroles de situación** navigation lights
farola *f* lighthouse; street lamp, lamppost
farolear *intr* to boast, brag
farole•ro -ra *adj* boasting || *mf* boaster || *m* lamplighter
farolillo *m* heartseed; Canterbury bell; **farolillo veneciano** Chinese lantern, Japanese lantern
farota *f* minx, vixen
farotear *intr* (Col) to romp around, make a racket
faro•tón -tona *adj* brazen, cheeky || *mf* cheeky person
farra *f* salmon trout; (SAm) revelry
fárrago *m* hodgepodge
farrago•so -sa *adj* involved, dense, wordy, cumbersome; (*respiración*) labored
farraquista *m* scatterbrain; muddlehead
farrear *intr* to celebrate; (coll) to goof off
farro *m* grits
farru•co -ca *adj* bold, fearless; ill-humored || *mf* Galician abroad, Asturian abroad
farru•to -ta *adj* (Arg, Bol, Chile) sickly
farsa *f* farce; humbug
farsante *adj & mf* fake, fraud, humbug
fas — por fas o por nefas rightly or wrongly, in any event
fascinante *adj* fascinating
fascinar *tr* to fascinate, bewitch; cast a spell on, cast the evil eye on
fascismo *m* fascism
fascista *adj & mf* fascist
fase *f* phase; **tercera fase** (aer) burnout
fastidiar *tr* to bore, annoy; cloy, sicken; disappoint || *ref* to get bored; suffer, be a victim
fastidio *m* boredom, annoyance; distaste, nausea

fastidio•so -sa *adj* boring, annoying; cloying, sickening; annoyed, displeased
fas•to -ta *adj* happy, blessed || *m* pomp, show
fastuo•so -sa *adj* vain, pompous; magnificent
fatal *adj* fatal; bad, evil; (law) unextendible
fatalidad *f* fatality; misfortune
fatalismo *m* fatalism
fatalista *mf* fatalist
fatalmente *adv* fatally; inevitably; unfortunately; badly, poorly
fatídi•co -ca *adj* ominous, fateful
fatiga *f* fatigue; hard breathing; **fatigas** hardship
fatigante *adj* tiresome; fatiguing
fatigar §44 *tr* to fatigue, tire, weary; annoy, bother || *ref* to get tired
fatigo•so -sa *adj* fatiguing, tiring; trying tedious; (*respiración*) labored
fa•tuo -tua *adj* fatuous; conceited || *mf* simpleton
fatwa *m* (*decreto promulgado por un clérigo musulmán*) fatwa (*religious and legal decree issued by a Muslim cleric*)
fauces *fpl* (anat) fauces; (fig) jaws, mouth
fauna *f* fauna
fauno *m* faun
faus•to -ta *adj* happy, fortunate || *m* pomp, magnificence
fausto•so -sa *adj* magnificent
fau•tor -tora *mf* abettor, accomplice
favor *m* favor; **a favor de** under cover of; by means of; in favor of; **hágame Ud. el favor de** do me the favor of; **por favor** please; excuse me; **vender favores** to peddle influence
favorable *adj* favorable
favorecer §22 *tr* to favor; flatter
favoritismo *m* favoritism
favori•to -ta *adj & mf* favorite
fax *m* fax
faxear *tr* to fax; **mandar** *or* **enviar por fax** to fax
fayanca *f* unstable posture
faz *f* (*pl* **faces**) face; aspect, look; (*de monedas o medallas*) obverse; **faces** cheeks; **faz a faz** face to face
F.C. *abbr* ferrocarril
fe *f* faith; testimony, witness; certificate; **¡a fe mía!** upon my faith!; **dar fe de** to certify; **en fe de lo cual** in witness whereof; **fe de erratas** list of errata; **hacer fe** to be valid; **la fe del carbonero** simple faith
fealdad *f* ugliness
Febe *f* Phoebe
feble *adj* weak, sickly; (*moneda, aleación*) lacking in weight or fineness
Febo *m* Phoebus
febrero *m* February
febril *adj* feverish
fecha *f* date; **con fecha de** under date of; **de larga fecha** of long standing; **fecha de caducidad** (pharm) expiration date; **fecha de consumo preferente** use-before date; **fecha límite** cutoff date, closing date; **fecha de vencimiento** (com) due date, maturity date; (pharm) expiration date; **hasta la fecha** to date
fechador *m* (Chile, Mex) canceler, postmark
fechar *tr* to date
fechoría *f* misdeed, villainy
fécula *f* starch
feculen•to -ta *adj* starchy; fecal
fecundación *f* fertilization; **fecundación cruzada** cross-fertilization; **fecundación in vitro** in vitro fertilization
fecundar *tr* to fecundate, to fertilize
fecun•do -da *adj* fecund, fertile
federación *f* federation
federal *adj & mf* federal
federar *tr & ref* to federate
feéri•co -ca *adj* fairy
fehaciente *adj* authentic
feldespato *m* feldspar
felicidad *f* felicity, happiness; luck
felicitar *tr* to felicitate, congratulate, wish happiness to
feli•grés -gresa *mf* parishioner, church member
feligresía *f* parish; congregation
Felipe *m* Philip
fe•liz *adj* (*pl* **-lices**) happy; lucky; (*oportuno*) felicitous
fe•lón -lona *adj* perfidious, treacherous || *mf* wicked person
felonía *f* perfidy, treachery
felpa *f* plush; drubbing; severe reprimand; toweling, terry cloth
felpu•do -da *adj* plushy, downy || *m* mat, door mat
femenil *adj* feminine, womanly
femeni•no -na *adj* feminine; (*sexo*) female || *m* feminine
fementi•do -da *adj* false, treacherous
feminismo *m* feminism
fenecer §22 *tr* to finish, close || *intr* to come to an end; die
fé•nix *m* (*pl* **-nix** or **-nices**) phoenix
fenobarbital *m* phenobarbital
fenomenal *adj* phenomenal
fenómeno *m* phenomenon; monster, freak
fe•o -a *adj* ugly || *m* slight; **hacer un feo a** to slight || **feo** *adv* (Arg, Col, Mex) bad, e.g., **oler feo** to smell bad
feo•te -ta *adj* ugly, hideous
feral *adj* cruel, bloody
fe•raz *adj* (*pl* **-races**) fertile
féretro *m* bier
feria *f* weekday; market; fair; day off; (Mex) small change; (Mex) con man; (CAm, Mex) extra, tip, gratuity; **revolver la feria** to upset the applecart
ferial *adj* week (*day*); market (*day*) || *m* market; fair
feriante *adj* fair-going || *mf* fairgoer
feriar *tr* to buy, sell; give, present; (Mex) to give change for
feri•no -na *adj* wild, savage; (*tos*) whooping (*cough*)
fermentación *f* ferment; fermentation
fermentar *tr & intr* to ferment
fermento *m* ferment

ferocidad *f* ferocity, fierceness
ferósti•co -ca *adj* irritable; hideous
fe•roz *adj* (*pl* **-roces**) ferocious, fierce
férre•o -a *adj* iron
ferrería *f* ironworks, foundry
ferretear *tr* to trim with iron; work in iron
ferretería *f* ironworks; hardware; hardware store
ferrete•ro -ra *mf* hardware dealer
ferrocarril *m* railroad, railway; **ferrocarril de cremallera** rack railway, mountain railroad, cog railway
ferrocarrile•ro -ra *adj* railroad, rail || *m* railroader
ferrotipo *m* tintype
ferrovia•rio -ria *adj* railroad, rail || *m* railroader
fértil *adj* fertile
fertilizar §60 *tr* to fertilize
férula *f* flexible splint; ferule; **estar bajo la férula de** to be under the thumb of
férvi•do -da *adj* fervid; (*fiebre; sed*) burning
ferviente *adj* fervent
fervor *m* fervor, zeal
fervoro•so -sa *adj* ardent, zealous
festejar *tr* to fete, honor, entertain; celebrate; court, woo; (Mex) to beat, thrash
festejo *m* feast, entertainment; celebration; courting, wooing; (Peru) revelry; **festejos** public festivities
festín *m* feast, banquet
festinar *tr* to hurry through; (CAm) to entertain
festival *m* festival, music festival
festividad *f* festivity; feast day, witticism
festi•vo -va *adj* festive, gay; witty; (*digno no de celebrarse*) solemn
festón *m* festoon
festonear *tr* to festoon
fetiche *m* fetish
féti•do -da *adj* fetid, foul
feto *m* fetus
feú•co -ca *or* **feú•cho -cha** *adj* hideous, repulsive
feudal *adj* feudal
feudalismo *m* feudalism
feudo *m* fief; **feudo franco** freehold
fiable *adj* trustworthy
fiado *m* — **al fiado** on credit; **en fiado** on bail
fia•dor -dora *mf* bail; **salir fiador por** to go bail for || *m* fastener; catch, pawl; (Chile, Ecuad) chin strap
fiambre *adj* cold, cold-served; (*noticias*) old, stale || *m* cold lunch, cold food; stale news; (Arg) dull party; **fiambres** cold cuts
fiambrera *f* dinner pail, lunch basket
fiambrería *f* delicatessen
fianza *f* guarantee, surety; bond; bail; **fianza carcelera** bail
fiar §77 *tr* to entrust, confide; guarantee; give credit to; sell on credit || *intr & ref* to trust
fiasco *m* fiasco
fibra *f* fiber; (fig) fiber, strength, vigor; **fibra de vidrio** fiberglass; **fibra óptica** optical fiber; **fibras del corazón** heartstrings
fibrosis *f* — **fibrosis cística** cystic fibrosis
fibro•so -sa *adj* fibrous
ficción *f* fiction
ficciona•rio -ria *adj* fictional
fice *m* (ichth) hake
ficha *f* chip; counter; domino; filing card; police record; (elec) plug; **ficha catalográfica** index card; **ficha médica** medical records; **ficha perforada** punch card; **ficha policial** police record; **llevar ficha** to have a police record; **ser una buena ficha** to be a sly fox
ficha•dor -dora *mf* file clerk
fichar *tr* to file; play, move; blacklist; (Cuba) to cheat || *intr* (Col) to die
fichero *m* card index, filing cabinet; (compu) file
ficti•cio -cia *adj* fictitious
fidedig•no -na *adj* reliable, trustworthy
fideicomisa•rio -ria *mf* trustee
fideicomiso *m* trusteeship
fidelería *f* (Arg, Ecuad, Peru) vermicelli factory, noodle factory
fidelidad *f* fidelity; punctiliousness; **alta fidelidad** (rad) high fidelity
fideo *m* skinny person; (Arg) joke; (Arg) confusion, disorder; (culin) noodle; **fideos** noodles, vermicelli, pasta
fiducia•rio -ria *adj & mf* fiduciary
fiebre *f* fever; **fiebre aftosa** (vet) foot-and-mouth disease; **fiebre del heno** hay fever; **fiebre paludica** jungle fever; **fiebra tifoidea** typhoid fever
fiel *adj* faithful; exact; punctilious; honest, trustworthy || *m* inspector of weights and measures; (*en las balanzas*) pointer; (*de las tijeras*) pin; **fiel de romana** inspector of weights in a slaughterhouse; **los fieles** the faithful
fielato *m* inspector's office; octroi
fieltro *m* felt; felt hat; felt rug
fiera *f* wild animal; (*persona*) fiend; (taur) bull; **ser una fiera para** to be a fiend for
fierabrás *m* spitfire, little terror
fierecilla *f* shrew
fiereza *f* fierceness; cruelty; deformity
fie•ro -ra *adj* fierce, wild; cruel; deformed, ugly; huge, tremendous; **echar** *or* **hacer fieros** to bluster || *f* see **fiera**
fierro *m* (SAm) branding iron
fierros *mpl* (Ecuad, Mex) tools
fiesta *f* feast, holy day; holiday; celebration, festivity; **estar de fiesta** (coll) to be in a holiday mood; **Fiesta de la Hispanidad** *or* **Fiesta de la Raza** Columbus Day; **Fiesta de Todos los Santos** All Saints' Day; **fiesta onomástica** saint's day, birthday; **fiestas** holiday, vacation; **hacer fiesta** to take off (*from work*); **hacer fiestas a** to act up to, to fawn on; **la fiesta brava** bullfighting; **no estar para fiestas** to be in no mood for joking; **para fin de fiestas** to top it off; **se acabó la fiesta** let's drop it

fieste•ro -ra *adj* merry, cheerful || *mf* merry-maker, party-goer
figón *m* cheap restaurant
figura *f* figure; face, countenance; (*naipe*) face card; (mus) note; (theat) character; **figura retórica** figure of speech; **hacer figura** to cut a figure
figuración *f* representation; (Arg) status, social standing
figura•do -da *adj* figurative
figurante *mf* extra, super
figurar *tr* to depict, trace, represent; feign || *intr* to figure, be in the limelight || *ref* to figure, imagine
figurati•vo -va *adj* figurative, representative
figurería *f* face, grimace
figurilla *mf* silly little runt || *f* figurine
figurín *m* dummy, model; fashion plate
figurina *f* figurine
figurita *mf* silly little runt
figurón *m* stuffed shirt; **figurón de proa** (naut) figurehead
fija *f* hinge; trowel; (*caballo*) (Peru) sure bet; **la fija** sure thing
fijacarte•les *m* (*pl* **-les**) billposter
fijación *f* fixing, fastening; fixation, obsession; posting; **fijación de precios** price fixing
fijado *m* (phot) fixing
fija•dor -dora *adj* fixing || *m* carpenter who installs doors and windows; fixing bath; sprayer; (mas) pointer; hair set, hair spray
fijamárge•nes *m* (*pl* **-nes**) margin stop
fijapeína•dos *m* (*pl* **-dos**) hair set, hair spray
fijar *tr* to fix; fasten; (*carteles*) post; (*una fecha; los cabellos; una imagen fotográfica; los precios; la atención; una hora, una cita*) fix; (*residencia*) establish; paste, glue || *ref* to settle; notice; **fijarse en** to notice; pay attention to; be intent on
fijeza *f* firmness, stability; steadfastness; **mirar con fijeza** to stare at
fi•jo -ja *adj* fixed; firm, solid, secure, fast; sure, determined; **de fijo** surely || *f* see **fija**
fil *m* — **estar en fil** or **en un fil** to be alike; **fil derecho** leapfrog
fila *f* row, line; file; (*linea que los soldados forman de frente*) rank; dislike, hatred; **cerrar las filas** (mil) to close ranks; **en fila** in single file; **en filas** (mil) in active service; **fila india** single file, Indian file; **llamar a filas** (mil) to call to the colors; **pasarse a las filas de** to go over to; **romper filas** (mil) to break ranks
filamento *m* filament
filantropía *f* philanthropy
filántrop•po -pa *mf* philanthropist
filar *tr* (naut) to pay out slowly
filarmónica *f* (Mex) accordion
filarmóni•co -ca *adj* philharmonic
filatelia *f* philately
filatelista *mf* philatelist, stamp collector
filatería *f* fast talking; wordiness
filate•ro -ra *adj* fast-talking; wordy || *mf* fast talker; great talker
file•no -na *adj* cute, tiny
filete *m* (*de carne o pescado*) filet or fillet; filet mignon; (*asador*) spit; edge, rim; narrow hem; (*de tornillo*) thread; snaffle bit; (archit, bb) fillet; (typ) rule, fancy rule
filetear *tr* to fillet; (*un tornillo*) thread; (bb) to tool
filiación *f* filiation; description, characteristics; (mil) regimental register
filial *adj* filial || *f* affiliate, branch
filiar §77 *tr* to register || *ref* to enroll
filibustero *m* filibuster, buccaneer
filigrana *f* filigree; (*en el papel*) watermark
filipi•no -na *adj* Filipine, Filipino || *mf* Filipino || **Filipinas** *fpl* Philippines
filiste•o -a *adj & mf* Philistine || *m* tall, fat fellow
film *m* (*pl* **-films or filmes**) film
filmadora *f* movie camera
filmar *tr* to film, shoot
filmi•co -ca *adj* movie, film
filo *m* edge; ridge; dividing line; (CAm, Mex) hunger; **al filo de** at, at about; **dar filo a** to sharpen; **filo del viento** direction of the wind; **pasar al filo de la espada** to put to the sword; **por filo** exactly
filobús *m* trolley bus, trackless trolley
filología philology
filólo•go -ga *mf* philologist
filón *m* seam, vein; (fig) gold mine
filo•so -sa *adj* sharp
filosofía *f* philosophy
filosófi•co -ca *adj* philosophic(al)
filóso•fo -fa *mf* philosopher
filote *m* (Col) corn silk; (Col) ear of green corn
filtración *f* filtering; leak; (fig) leak, loss
filtrado *m* filtrate
filtrar *tr* to filter || *intr* to leak; ooze || *ref* to filter; (*el dinero*) leak away, disappear
filtro *m* filter; (*brebaje para conciliar el amor*) philter, love potion
filu•do -da *adj* (SAm) sharp-edged
filván *m* featheredge
fimo *m* dung, manure
fin *m* end; aim, purpose, end; **a fin de** to, in order to; **a fin de que** in order that, so that; **a fines de** toward the end of, late in; **al fin** finally; **al fin del mundo** far, far away; **al fin y a la postre** *or* **al fin y al cabo** after all, in the end; **dar fin a** to put an end to; **fin de semana** weekend; **por fin** finally, in short; **sin fin** endless; endlessly; **un sin fin de** no end of
fina•do -da *adj* deceased, late || *mf* deceased
final *adj* final || *m* end; (mus) finale; **final espectacular** (theat) grand finale; **por final** finally || *f* (sport) finals; **final de partido** windup
finalidad *f* end, purpose
finalista *mf* finalist
finalizar §60 *tr* to end, terminate; (*una escritura*) (law) to execute; **finalizar la sesión** (compu) to log out *o* off || *intr* to end, terminate
financiación *f* financing

financiamiento *m* (SAm) financial backing
financiar *tr* to finance
financie•ro -ra *adj* financial || *mf* financier
finanzas *fpl* finances
finar *intr* to die || *ref* to yearn
finca *f* property, piece of real estate; farm, ranch; **buena finca** sly fellow
fincar §73 *tr* (P-R) to cultivate, farm || *intr* to buy up real estate; (Col) to reside, rest, be based || *ref* to buy up real estate
fincha•do -da *adj* vain, conceited
fi•nés -nesa *adj* Finnic; Finnish || *mf* Finn || *m* (*idioma uraliano*) Finnic; (*idioma de Finlandia*) Finnish
fineza *f* fineness; kindness, courtesy; token of affection, favor
fingi•do -da *adj* fake, sham; false, deceitful
fingir §27 *tr & intr* to feign, pretend, fake || *ref* to pretend to be
finiquitar *tr* (*una cuenta*) to settle, to close; finish, wind up
finiquito *m* settlement, closing; **dar finiquito a** to settle, close; finish, wind up
finíti•mo -ma *adj* bordering, neighboring
fini•to -ta *adj* finite
finlan•dés -desa *adj* Finnish || *mf* Finn, Finlander || *m* Finnish
Finlandia *f* Finland
fi•no -na *adj* fine; (*ligero, casi transparente*) sheer; (*esbelto*) thin, slender; (*paño, papel, etc.*) thin; (*agua*) pure; polite, courteous; shrewd, cunning
finta *f* feint
finura *f* fineness, excellence; politeness, courtesy
finústi•co -ca *adj* overobsequious
firma *f* signature; signing; firm; firm name; mail to be signed; **con mi firma** under my hand; **firma en blanco** blank check
firmamento *m* firmament
firmante *adj* signatory || *mf* signer, signatory
firmar *tr & intr* to sign
firme *adj* firm, steady; solid, hard; staunch, unswerving; **¡firme!, ¡firmes!** (mil) attention! || *adv* firmly, steadily || *m* roadbed; **de firme** hard, e.g., **llover de firme** to rain hard
firmeza *f* firmness; constancy, fortitude
firmón *m* shyster who signs anything
fiscal *adj* fiscal, tax, treasury || *mf* treasurer; district attorney; busybody; **Fiscal General del Estado** Attorney General
fiscalizar §60 *tr* to control, inspect; prosecute; pry into
fisco *m* state treasury, exchequer
fisga *f* fish spear; prying, snooping; banter, raillery
fisgar §44 *tr* to harpoon, fish with a spear; pry into || *intr* to pry, snoop; mock, jeer || *ref* to mock, jeer
fis•gón -gona *mf* (coll) mocker, jester; (coll) snooper, busybody
físi•co -ca *adj* physical; (Mex, W-I) finicky, prudish || *mf* physicist || *m* physique || *f* physics; **física de las partículas** particle physics; **física del estado sólido** solid state physics; **física molecular** molecular physics; **física cuántica** quantum physics; **física nuclear** nuclear physics
fisiculturismo *m* bodybuilding
fisil *adj* fissionable
fisiología *f* physiology
fisiológi•co -ca *adj* physiological
fisión *f* fission; **fisión nuclear** nuclear fission
fisionable *adj* fissionable
fisonomía *f* physiognomy
fistol *m* sly fellow; (Mex) necktie pin
fisura *f* (anat, min) fissure; **fisura del paladar** cleft palate
fla•co -ca *adj* thin, skinny; feeble, weak, frail; insecure, unstable || *m* weak spot
flacu•cho -cha *adj* skinny
flagrante *adj* occurring, actual; **en flagrante** in the act
flamante *adj* bright, flaming; brand-new, spick-and-span
flameante *adj* flamboyant
flamear *intr* to flame; flare up (*with anger*); flutter, wave
flamen•co -ca *adj* Flemish; buxom; Andalusian gypsy; flashy, snappy, gypsyish || *mf* Fleming || *m* (*idioma*) Flemish; Andalusian gypsy dance, song, or music; (orn) flamingo
fláme•o -a *adj* flamelike
flamíge•ro -ra *adj* (poet) flaming; (archit) flamboyant
flan *m* custard
flanco *m* side, flank; **coger por el flanco** to catch off guard
Flandes *f* Flanders
flanquear *tr* to flank
flaquear *intr* to weaken, flag; become faint; become discouraged
flaqueza *f* thinness, skinniness; weakness; instability
flash *m* (*destello; aparato*) (phot) flash; **flash electrónico** flashgun; **flash informativo** first brief news report, flash
flashback *m* (*retrospectiva*) flashback
flato *m* gas; gloominess, melancholy
flato•so -sa *adj* flatulent, windy; gloomy, melancholy
flauta *f* flute; **flauta dulce** recorder
flautín *m* piccolo
flautista *mf* flautist, flutist
flebitis *f* phlebitis
flecha *f* arrow; (aer) sweepback
flechar *tr* (*el arco*) to draw; (*a una persona*) wound with an arrow, kill with an arrow; infatuate
flechero *m* archer, bowman
fleco *m* fringe; ragged edge; **flecos** bangs
fleje *m* iron strap, iron hoop; spring
flema *f* phlegm
flemáti•co -ca *adj* phlegmatic(al); (coll) cool
flemón *m* gumboil
flequillo *m* bangs

Flesinga *f* Flushing
fletante *m* shipowner; (Arg, Chile, Ecuad) conveyancer
fletar *tr* (*una nave*) to charter; (*ganado*) load; (*bestias de carga, carros, etc.*) (Arg, Chile, Ecuad, Mex) to hire || *ref* (Arg) to sneak in, slip in; (Cuba, Mex) to beat it, clear out
flete *m* (naut) freight, cargo; (Arg, Bol, Col, Urug) race horse; **salir sin flete** (Col, Ven) to beat it
flexible *adj* flexible; supple; (*sombrero*) soft || *m* soft hat; (elec) flexible cord
flexo *m* gooseneck lamp
flinflanear *intr* to tinkle
flip *m* eggnog
flip-flop *m* (compu) toggle; **flip-flop de conmutación** (compu) toggle switch
flirt *m* or **flirtación** *f* flirting
flirtear *intr* to flirt
flojear *intr* to ease up, idle; flag, weaken
flojedad *f* slackness; looseness; limpness; laziness; weakness
flojel *m* fluff, nap; down, soft feathers
flo•jo -ja *adj* slack, loose; limp; languid; lazy; weak; (*precios*) sagging; (*viento*) light; lax, careless; (*café, té*) weak
flor *f* flower; (*de árbol frutal*) blossom; (*del cuero*) grain; (fig) compliment, bouquet; **a flor de** even with, flush with; **a flor de agua** at water level; **decir flores a** to flatter; to flirt with; **flor de la edad** bloom of youth; **flor de la vida** prime of life; **flor del campo** wild flower; **flor de lis** (*escudo de armas de Francia*) lily, fleur-de-lis; **flor de mano** paper flower, artificial flower; **flor de Pascua** poinsettia; **la flor de la canela** the tops; **la flor y nata de** the cream of
flora *f* flora
floral *adj* floral
florcita *f* little flower; **andar de florcita** (Arg, Bol, Chile, Urug) to stroll around with a flower in one's buttonhole, take it easy
florear *tr* to flower, decorate with flowers; (*los naipes*) stack; (*harina*) bolt || *intr* (*la punta de la espada*) to quiver; twang away on a guitar; throw bouquets
florecer §22 *intr* to flower, blossom, bloom; (*prosperar*) flourish || *ref* to become moldy
floreciente *adj* flowering, florescent; flourishing, burgeoning
florenti•no -na *adj & mf* Florentine
floreo *m* idle talk; bright remark; (*de la punta de la espada*) quivering; (*de la guitarra*) twanging; (mus) flourish; **andarse con floreos** to beat about the bush
florera *f* flower girl
florería *f* flower shop
flore•ro -ra *adj* flattering, jesting || *mf* flatterer, jester; florist || *m* (*vaso para flores*) vase; (*maceta con flores*) flowerpot; flower stand, jardiniere; (*cuadro, pintura*) flower piece || *f* see **florera**
florescencia *f* florescence, flowering
floresta *f* woods, woodland; grove; rural setting; anthology
florete *m* (*esgrima*) fencing; (*espadín*) foil
floretear *tr* to decorate with flowers || *intr* to fence
flori•do -da *adj* flowery, full of flowers; choice, select
florilegio *m* anthology
floripondio *m* (SAm) angel's-trumpet
florista *mf* florist
floristería *f* flower shop
florón *m* large flower; finial; rosette; (typ) tailpiece, vignette
flota *f* fleet; **flota petrolera** tanker fleet
flotación *f* buoyancy
flotador *m* float
flotaje *m* log driving
flotante *adj* floating; (*barba*) flowing || *m* (Col) braggart
flotar *intr* to float; (*una bandera*) wave
flote *m* floating; **a flote** afloat
fluctuar §21 *intr* to fluctuate; bob up and down; wave; waver; be in danger
fluente *adj* fluent, flowing; (*hemorroides*) bleeding
fluidez *f* fluidity
flui•do -da *adj* fluid; (*estilo, lenguaje*) fluent || *m* fluid
fluir §20 *intr* to flow
flujo *m* flow, flux; (*acceso de la marea*) floodtide; **flujo de caja** cash flow; **flujo de datos** (compu) data flow; **flujo de risa** fit of noisy laughter; **flujo de texto** (compu) textflow; **flujo de vientre** loose bowels; **flujo y reflujo** ebb and flow
flúor *m* fluorine
fluorescencia *f* fluorescence
fluorescente *adj* fluorescent
fluorhídri•co -ca *adj* hydrofluoric
fluorización *f* fluoridation
fluorizar §60 *tr* to fluoridate
fluoroscopio *m* fluoroscope
fluoruro *m* fluoride
flux *m* (*en el póker*) flush; suit of clothes; **estar en flux** to be penniless; **hacer flux** to blow in everything without settling accounts; **tener flux** to be lucky
fluxión *f* (*acumulación morbosa de humores*) congestion; (*enrojecimiento de la cara y el cuello*) flush; (*constipado de narices*) cold in the head; **fluxión de muelas** swollen cheek; **fluxión de pecho** pneumonia
FM *f* (letterword) (**frecuencia modulada**) FM (frequency modulation)
foca *f* seal
focal *adj* focal
foco *m* focus; (*de vicios*) center; (*de un absceso*) core; electric light; floodlight; **iluminar con foco** to floodlight
fodo•lí *adj* (*pl* **-líes**) meddlesome
fodon•go -ga *adj* (Mex) dirty, slovenly
fo•fo -fa *adj* soft, fluffy, spongy
fogaje *m* (*contribución*) hearth money; blush,

flush; (Arg) fire, blaze; (Arg, Mex) rash, eruption
fogata *f* blaze, bonfire
fogón *m* cooking stove; (*de máquina de vapor*) firebox
fogonazo *m* flash; explosive flash
fogonero *m* fireman, stoker
fogosidad *f* fire, spirit, dash
fogo•so -sa *adj* fiery, spirited
fol. *abbr* **folio**
folgo *m* foot muff
foliar *tr* to folio
folio *m* folio; **al primer folio** right off; **de a folio** enormous; **en folio** folio
folklore *m* folklore
follaje *m* foliage; gaudy ornament; (*palabrería*) fustian
follar *tr* to shape like a leaf || §61 *tr* to blow with bellows
folletín *m* newspaper serial (*printed at bottom of page*); pamphlet
folleto *m* brochure, pamphlet, tract
fo•llón -llona *adj* careless, indolent, lazy; arrogant, cowardly || *mf* lazy loafer, knave || *m* noiseless rocket
fomentar *tr* to foment; foster, encourage, promote; warm
fonda *f* inn, restaurant; cheap restaurant, hash house; (Chile) refreshment stand
fondeadero *m* anchorage; roadstead
fondea•do -da *adj* well-heeled
fondear *tr* (*un buque*) to search; scrutinize, examine closely || *intr* to cast anchor || *ref* to save up for a rainy day
fondillos *mpl* seat (*of trousers*)
fondista *mf* innkeeper
fondo *m* bottom; (*de un cuarto, una tienda*) back, rear; (*del mar, de una piscina, etc.*) floor; (*de un cilindro, barril, etc.*) head; background; (*de una casa*) depth; (*de un paño*) ground; (*caudal*) fund; (*lo esencial*) bottom; (compu) background; **a fondo** thoroughly; **bajos fondos sociales** underworld, scum of the earth; **colar a fondo** to sink; **dar fondo** to cast anchor; **doble fondo** false bottom; **echar a fondo** to sink; **en el fondo** at bottom; **estar en fondos** to have funds available; **fondo de amortización** sinking fund; **fondo de comercio** goodwill; **fondo de fideicomiso** trust fund; **fondo de inversión mobiliaria** mutual fund; **fondo de pensiones** pension fund; **fondo de reptiles** slush fund; **fondo fiduciario** trust fund; **fondos** (*caudales, dinero*) funds; **irse a fondo** to go to the bottom; (*un negocio*) to fail; **tener buen fondo** to be good-natured
fonducho *m* cheap eating house
fonéti•co -ca *adj* phonetic
foniatría *f* speech correction
fónica *f* phonics
fono *m* (Chile) earphone
fonoabsorbente *adj* sound-absorbent; sound-deadening
fonocaptor *m* pickup
fonógrafo *m* phonograph; record player
fonología *f* phonology
fontanería *f* plumbing; water-supply system
fontane•ro -ra *adj* fountain || *m* plumber, tinsmith
footing *m* walking; jogging; hiking
foque *m* (naut) jib; (coll) piccadilly collar
foraji•do -da *adj* fugitive || *mf* fugitive, outlaw, bandit
foráne•o -a *adj* foreign, strange; offshore
foraste•ro -ra *adj* outside, strange; foreign || *mf* outsider, stranger
forbante *m* freebooter
forcejar or **forcejear** *intr* to struggle, resist, contend
forceju•do -da *adj* strong, husky, robust
fór•ceps *m* (*pl* **-ceps**) forceps
forestal *adj* forest
forja *f* forge; forging; silversmith's forge; foundry, ironworks; mortar
forjar *tr* to forge; build with stone and mortar; roughcast; (*mentiras*) forge || *ref* to forge; hatch, think up
forma *f* form, shape; way; (*de un libro*) format; **buena forma física** physical fitness; **de forma que** so that, with the result that; **en buena forma física** fit, healthy; **tener buenas formas** to have a good figure; to be physically fit
formación *f* formation; **formación de palabras** word formation
formal *adj* formal, ceremonious; express, definite; reliable; sedate; serious
formalidad *f* formality; reliability; seriousness
formar *tr* to form; to shape, fashion; train, educate || *intr* to form; form a line, stand in line || *ref* to form; form a line, stand in line; take form, grow, develop
formatear *tr* to format
formateo *m* (compu) formatting
formato *m* format; **formato de fichero** (compu) file format
formidable *adj* formidable
formidolo•so -sa *adj* scared, frightened; frightful, horrible
fórmula *f* formula; prescription; **por fórmula** as a matter of form
formular *tr* to formulate
formulario *m* form, blank; **formulario de pedido** order blank
fornicación *f* fornication
fornicar *intr* to fornicate; to have sex
forni•do -da *adj* well-built, husky, sturdy, hefty
foro *m* forum; (*abogacía*) bar (*del escenario*) back, rear
forrado *m* lining; padding
forraje *m* forage, fodder
forrajear *tr & intr* to forage
forrar *tr* to line; (*un vestido*) face; (*un libro, un paraguas*) cover; (*un lienzo*) stretch || *ref* (Guat, Mex) to stuff oneself
forro *m* lining; cover, covering; (naut) sheath-

ing, planking; **forro de freno** brake lining; **ni por el forro** not by a long shot
fortalecer §22 *tr* to fortify, strengthen
fortaleza *f* fortitude; strength, vigor; fortress, stronghold
fortificación *f* fortification
fortificante *m* tonic
fortificar §73 *tr* to fortify
fortín *m* small fort; bunker
fortui•to -ta *adj* fortuitous
fortuna *f* fortune; **correr fortuna** (naut) to ride the storm; **de fortuna** makeshift; **por fortuna** fortunately; **probar fortuna** to try one's luck
fortunón *m* windfall
forza•do -da *adj* forced; (*p.ej., entrada*) forcible; (*sonrisa*) (fig) forced; (*trabajos*) hard ‖ *m* galley slave
forzar §35 *tr* to force
forzo•so -sa *adj* unavoidable; strong, husky; (*trabajos*) hard; (*aterrizaje; marcha*) forced ‖ *f* — **hacer la forzosa a** to put the squeeze on
forzu•do -da *adj* strong, husky, robust
fosa *f* grave; (*of lions*) (Bib) den; (auto) pit; **fosa común** pauper's grave; **fosa marina** marine basin; **fosa nasal** nostril; **fosa séptica** septic tank
fosar *tr* to dig a ditch around
fos•co -ca *adj* dark; cross, sullen; (*tiempo*) threatening
fosfato *m* phosphate
fosforera *f* matchbox
fosforescente *adj* phosphorescent
fósforo *m* (*cuerpo simple*) phosphorus; match; **fósforo de seguridad** safety match
fósil *adj & m* fossil
foso *m* hole, pit; (*que rodea un castillo o fortaleza*) moat; (theat & aut) pit
fotingo *m* jalopy, jitney
foto *f* photo, picture; **foto de carnet, foto de pasaporte** passport photo; **foto fija** still
fotocélula *f* photoelectric cell
fotocopia *f* photocopy, Xerox copy
fotocopiador *m* or **fotocopiadora** *f* photocopier, Xerox machine
fotocopiar *tr* to photocopy, xerox
fotodrama *m* photoplay
fotofija *m* photo-finish camera
fotoeléctri•co -ca *adj* photoelectric
fotogéni•co -ca *adj* photogenic
fotograbado *m* photoengraving
fotografía *f* (*arte*) photography; (*imagen, retrato*) photograph; photograph gallery; **fotografía aérea** aerial photograph(y)
fotografiar §77 *tr & intr* to photograph
fotográfi•co -ca *adj* photographic
fotógra•fo -fa *mf* photographer
fotomatón *m* photo booth
fotómetro *m* light meter
fotoperiodismo *m* photojournalism
fotopila *f* solar battery
fotostatar *tr & intr* to photostat
fotóstato *m* photostat
fototubo *m* phototube
fra. *abbr* **factura**
frac *m* (*pl* **-fraques**) full-dress coat, tails, swallow-tailed coat
fracasar *intr* to fail; break to pieces
fracaso *m* failure; breakdown, crash
fracción *f* fraction; **fracción de segundo** split second
fraccionar *tr* to divide up; break up
fracciona•rio -ria *adj* fractional
fractura *f* fracture; breaking open, breaking in
fracturar *tr* to fracture; break open, break in ‖ *ref* (*p.ej., un brazo*) to fracture
fragancia *f* fragrance; good reputation
fragante *adj* fragrant; **en fragante** (archaic) in the act
fragata *f* frigate; **fragata ligera** corvette
frágil *adj* fragile; (*quebradizo; que cae fácilmente en el pecado*) frail; (Mex) poor, needy
fragmento *m* fragment
fragor *m* crash, roar, thunder
fragoro•so -sa *adj* noisy, thundering
fragosidad *f* roughness, unevenness; (*de un bosque*) thickness, denseness; rough road
frago•so -sa *adj* rough, uneven; thick, dense; noisy, thundering
fragua *f* forge
fraguar §10 *tr* to forge; hatch, scheme; (*mentiras*) forge ‖ *intr* to forge; (*la cal, el cemento*) set
fraile *m* friar, monk; **fraile de misa y olla** friarling; **fraile rezador** praying mantis
frambesia *f* (pathol) yaws
frambuesa *f* raspberry
frambueso *m* raspberry bush
francachela *f* feast, spread; carousal, high time; (Arg) excessive familiarity
francalete *m* strap with buckle
fran•cés -cesa *adj* French; **despedirse a la francesa** to take French leave ‖ *m* Frenchman; (*idioma*) French ‖ *f* Frenchwoman
francesada *f* French remark; French invasion of Spain in 1808
francesilla *f* French roll; (bot) turban buttercup
Francia *f* France
Francisca *f* Frances
francisca•no -na *adj & mf* Franciscan
Francisco *m* Francis
francmasón *m* Freemason
francmasonería *f* Freemasonry
fran•co -ca *adj* generous, liberal; outspoken, candid, frank; (*camino*) free, open; (*suelo*) loamy; free, gratis; Frankish; **franco a bordo** free on board; **franco de porte** postpaid ‖ *mf* Frank ‖ *m* franc; (*idioma*) Frankish
francolín *m* black partridge
franco•te -ta *adj* frank, wholehearted
francotirador *m* sniper
franela *f* flannel
frangente *m* accident, mishap
frangir §27 *tr* to break up, break to pieces
frangollar *tr* to bungle, to botch

frangollo *m* porridge; mash for cattle; bungle, botch

franja *f* fringe; strip, band; (opt) fringe

franjar *tr* to fringe

franquear *tr* to exempt; cross, go over; grant; free, enfranchise; (*un camino*) open, clear; (*una carta*) frank, pay the postage for; **a franquear en destino** postage will be paid by addressee || *ref* to yield; **franquearse con** to open one's heart to

franqueo *m* freeing, liberation; postage; **franqueo concertado** postage permit

franqueza *f* generosity; candidness, frankness; freedom

franquía *f* (naut) sea room; **en franquía** (naut & fig) in the open

franquicia *f* franchise; exemption, tax exemption; **franquicia aduanera** duty-free allowance; **franquicia postal** franking privilege

franquista *mf* Francoist

frasca *f* leaves, twigs, brush; (Guat, Mex) high jinks

frasco *m* flask; (*p.ej., de aceitunas*) jar

frase *f* phrase; (*oración cabal*) sentence; idiom; **frase hecha** saying, proverb; cliché; **gastar frases** to talk all around the subject

frasear *tr* to phrase || *intr* to talk all around the subject

frasquera *f* bottle frame, liquor case

fratás *m* plastering trowel

fraternal *adj* brotherly, fraternal

fraternidad *f* fraternity, brotherhood

fraternizar §60 *intr* to fraternize

frater•no -na *adj* brotherly, fraternal

fraude *m* fraud; **fraude fiscal** tax evasion

fraudulen•to -ta *adj* fraudulent

fray *m* fra

frecuencia *f* frequency; **alta frecuencia** high frequency; **baja frecuencia** low frequency; **con frecuencia** frequently; **frecuencia de reloj** (compu) clock time

frecuentar *tr* (*ir con frecuencia a*) to frequent; keep up, repeat

frecuente *adj* frequent; (*usual*) common

fregadero *m* sink, kitchen sink

frega•do -da *adj* annoying, bothersome; cunning; (SAm) stubborn; (P-R) brazen || *m* scrubbing; mopping; mess

frega•dor -dora *mf* dishwasher

fregar §66 *tr* (*restregar*) to rub; (*restregar para limpiar*) scrub, scour; (*el pavimento*) mop; (*los platos*) wash; annoy, bother

fregasue•los *m* (*pl* **-los**) mop, floor mop

frega•triz *f* (*pl* **-trices**) *var of* **fregona**

fre•gón -gona *adj* annoying, bothersome; brazen || *f* (*criada que friega el pavimento*) scrub woman; (*criada que lava la vajilla*) dishwasher, scullery maid

freidora *f* deep fryer

freiduría *f* fried-fish shop

freír §58 & §83 *tr* to fry; bore to death || *intr* to fry; **dejarle a uno freír en su aceite** to let someone stew in his own juice || *ref* to fry; be bored to death; **freírsele a** to try to fool, scheme to deceive

fréjol *m* kidney bean

frenar *tr* to bridle, check, hold back; (*un automóvil, tren*) brake

frene•sí *m* (*pl* **-síes**) frenzy

frenéti•co -ca *adj* frantic; mad, furious; wild

frenillo *m* muzzle; **no tener frenillo en la lengua** to not mince one's words

freno *m* (*parte de la brida*) bit; (*aparato para parar el movimiento de los vehículos*) brake; (fig) brake, check, curb; **freno de contrapedal** coaster brake; **freno de disco** disk brake; **freno de mano** handbrake; **freno de tambor** drum brake; **frenos antibloque** antilock brakes **frenos asistidos** power brakes; **frenos de aire, frenos neumáticos** air brakes; **morder el freno** to champ the bit

frenología *f* phrenology

frentazo *m* (Mex) rebuff

frente *m & f* (*de un edificio*) front || *m* (mil) front, front line; **al frente de** at the head of, in charge of || *f* brow, forehead; face, front; head; **a frente** straight ahead; **arrugar la frente** to knit the brow; **de frente** straight ahead; abreast; **en frente de** in front of; against, opposed to; **frente a** in front of; compared with

freo *m* channel, strait

fresa *f* strawberry; (*de fresadora*) cutter

fresado *m* milling, millwork

fresadora *f* milling machine

fresal *m* strawberry patch

fresar *tr* to mill

fresca *f* fresh air; cool part of the day; blunt remark, piece of one's mind

fresca•chón -chona *adj* bouncing, buxom; (*viento*) brisk

fresca•les *mf* (*pl* **-les**) forward sort of person

frescamente *adv* recently; cheekily, brazenly

fres•co -ca *adj* (*acabado de hacer o suceder*) fresh; (*moderadamente frío*) cool; (*pintura*) fresh, wet; (*tela, vestido*) light; calm, unruffled; buxom, ruddy; cheeky, fresh, sassy; **estar fresco** to be in a fine pinch; **quedarse tan fresco** to show no offense, be indifferent or unconcerned || *m* coolness; fresh air; fresh bacon; (fa) fresco; cool drink; **al fresco** in the open air; in the night air; **hace fresco** it is cool; **tomar el fresco** to go out for some fresh air || *f* see **fresca**

frescor *m* freshness; cool, coolness

fresco•te -ta *adj* plump and rosy

frescura *f* freshness; cool, coolness; unconcern, offhand manner; sharp reply; cheek, impudence

fresno *m* ash tree; (*madera*) ash

fresquera *f* meat closet, food cabinet, icebox

fresquería *f* ice-cream parlor, soft-drink store

fresque•ro -ra *mf* fish dealer; (Peru) soft drink vendor || *f* see **fresquera**

freudismo *m* Freudianism

freza *f* dung; spawning; hole made by game

frialdad *f* coldness; carelessness, laxity; stupidity; (pathol) frigidity; (pathol) impotence; (fig) coolness, coldness
friáti•co -ca *adj* chilly; awkward, stupid; (*ropa*) cold
fricar **§73** *tr* to rub
fricasé *m* fricassee
fricción *f* rubbing; massage; (pharm) rubbing liniment; (phys) friction
friccionar *tr* to rub; massage
friega *f* rubbing, massage; annoyance, bother; flogging, whipping
frigidez *f* frigidity; coldness
frígi•do -da *adj* frigid; cold
frigorífero *m* freezing chamber
frigorífi•co -ca *adj* refrigerating; cold-storage || *m* (Esp) refrigerator; (SAm) packing house, cold-storage plant
frijol *m* bean, kidney bean; **frijol colorado** kidney bean; **frijol de media luna** Lima bean; **¡frijoles!** (W-I) absolutely no!
frijolear *tr* (Guat) to annoy, molest
frijolizar **§60** *tr* (Peru) to bewitch
frí•o -a *adj* cold; dull, weak, colorless; (fig) cold, cool || *m* cold; **fríos** chills and fever; **coger frío** to catch cold; **hace frío** it is cold; **tener frío** (*una persona*) to be cold; **tomar frío** to catch cold
friole•ro -ra *adj* chilly || *f* trifle, trinket; snack, bite
frisar *tr* to rub; to fit, fasten; (naut) to calk || *intr* to agree, get along; **frisar con** *or* **en** to border on
friso *m* dado, wainscot; (archit) frieze
fri•són -sona *adj & mf* Frisian
fritada *f* fry
fri•to -ta *adj* fried; bored to death || *m* fry; (Ven) daily bread; **fritos** fried food
fritura *f* frying; fried food
frívo•lo -la *adj* frivolous; trifling
fronda *f* leaf; (*de helecho*) frond; sling-shaped bandage; **frondas** frondage, foliage
frondo•so -sa *adj* leafy; woodsy
frontalera *f* yoke pad
frontera *f* frontier, border; front, façade
fronteri•zo -za *adj* frontier, border; facing, opposite
fronte•ro -ra *adj* frontier, border, facing, opposite; front || *f* see **frontera**
frontín *m* (Mex) flip, fillip
fron•tis *m* (*pl* **-tis**) front, façade
frontispicio *m* frontispiece; (coll) face
frontón *m* (*encima de puertas o ventanas*) gable, pediment; pelota court; pelota wall; handball court
frotamiento *m* rubbing; (phys) friction
frotar *tr* to rub; to chafe || *ref* to rub
fro•tis *m* (*pl* **-tis**) (bact) smear; Pap smear, Pap test
fructuo•so -sa *adj* fruitful
frugal *adj* (*en comer y beber*) temperate; (*no muy abundante*) frugal
fruición *f* enjoyment, satisfaction; (*del mal ajeno*) evil satisfaction
fruiti•vo -va *adj* enjoyable
frunce *m* shirr, shirring, gathering
frunci•do -da *adj* grim, gruff, stern; (Chile) temperate; (Chile) sad, gloomy || *m* shirr, shirring, gathering
fruncir **§36** *tr* to wrinkle, pucker, pleat; (*la frente*) knit; (*los labios*) curl, purse; (*la verdad*) twist, disguise; shirr, gather || *ref* to affect modesty, be shocked
fruslería *f* trifle, trinket; (coll) futility, triviality
frusle•ro -ra *adj* futile, trivial, trifling || *m* rolling pin
frustrar *tr* to frustrate, thwart, scotch, stymie
fruta *f* fruit; **fruta confitada** candied fruit; **fruta del tiempo** fruit in season; **fruta de sartén** fritter, pancake; **frutas** fruit; **frutas agrias** citrus fruit; **fruta seca** dried fruit
frutal *adj* fruit || *m* fruit tree
frutería *f* fruit store
frute•ro -ra *adj* fruit || *mf* fruit dealer || *m* fruit dish; tray of imitation fruit
frutilla *f* (*del rosario*) bead; Chilean strawberry; gumdrop
fruto *m* (bot & fig) fruit; **fruto de bendición** legitimate offspring; **fruto prohibido** forbidden fruit; **frutos** produce; **fruto seco** nut; **frutos secos** nuts and dried fruit; **sacar fruto de** to derive benefit from
fu *interj* faugh! fie!; (*del gato*) spit!; **ni fu ni fa** neither this nor that
fucilazo *m* heat lightning, sheet lightning
fuego *m* fire; (*para encender un cigarrillo*) light; (*de arma de fuego*) firing; lighthouse, beacon; hearth, home; rash, eruption; sore, fever blister; **abrir fuego** to open fire; **echar fuego** to blow up, hit the ceiling; **¡fuego!** fire!; **fuego cruzado** crossfire; **fuego fatuo** will-o'-the-wisp; **fuego graneado** *or* **nutrido** drumfire; **fuego real** live ammunition; **fuegos artificiales** fireworks; **hacer fuego** to fire, shoot; **marcar a fuego** to brand; **pegar fuego a** to set fire to, set on fire; **poner a fuego y sangre** to lay waste; **prenderse fuego** to catch on fire; **romper fuego** to open fire; stir up a row; **tocar a fuego** to sound the fire alarm
fuel *or* **fuel-oil** *m* fuel oil
fuelle *m* fold, pucker, wrinkle; (*instrumento para soplar*) bellows; (*cubierta de coche*) folding carriage top; wind clouds; (*persona soplona*) gossip, talebearer
fuente *f* fountain, spring; grass roots; public hydrant; font, baptismal font; platter, tray; (compu, typ) font; (fig) source; **beber en buenas fuentes** to have good sources of information; **fuente de gasolina** gasoline pump; **fuente de horno** ovenproof dish; **fuente de los deseos** wishing well; **fuente de sodas** soda fountain; **fuente para beber** drinking fountain; **fuentes termales** hot springs
fuer *m* — **a fuer de** as a, by way of
fuera *adv* out, outside; away, out of town; **desde**

fuera from the outside; **fuera de** outside of; away from; out of; aside from; in addition to; **fuera de borda** outboard; outboard motor; **fuera de juego** offside; **fuera de la ley** outlaw; **fuera de que** aside from the fact that; **fuera de serie** outstanding; **fuera de sí** beside oneself; **por fuera** on the outside
fuerabordo *m* outboard motor; outboard
fuere•ño -ña *mf* (Mex) hick, stranger
fuero *m* law, statute; code of laws; jurisdiction; exemption, privilege; **fuero interior** conscience, inmost heart; **fueros** pride, arrogance
fuerte *adj* strong; hard; loud; heavy; **hacerse fuerte** to stick to one's guns; (mil) to hole up, to dig in || *adv* hard; loud || *m* fort, fortress; forte, strong point
fuerza *f* force, strength, power; (*de un ejército*) main body; literal meaning; (phys) force; **a fuerza de** by dint of, by force of; **a la fuerza** forcibly, by force; **a viva fuerza** by main strength; **fuerza aérea** air force; **fuerza de agua** water power; **fuerza de sangre** animal power; **fuerza disuasoria** deterrent; **fuerza mayor** (law) force majeure, act of God; **fuerza motriz** motive power; **fuerza pública** police; **fuerza viva** kinetic energy; **hacer fuerza** to strain, struggle; to carry weight; **por fuerza** perforce, necessarily; **ser fuerza** + *inf* to be necessary to + *inf*
fuete *m* whip
fufar *intr* (*el gato*) to spit
fuga *f* flight; (*salida de un gas o líquido*) leak; ardor, vigor; (mus) fugue; **darse a la fuga** to take flight, run away; **fuga de capitales** capital flight; **fuga de cerebros** brain drain; **poner en fuga** to put to flight
fugar §44 *ref* to flee, escape, run away
fu•gaz *adj* (*pl* **-gaces**) fleeting, passing; (*estrella*) shooting
fugiti•vo -va *adj & mf* fugitive
fugui•llas *m* (*pl* **-llas**) (coll) hustler
fula•no -na *mf* so-and-so
fulcro *m* fulcrum
fulgor *m* brilliance, radiance
fulgurar *intr* to flash
fullería *f* trickery, cheating
fulle•ro -ra *adj* crooked, cheating; rough, shoddy || *mf* crook, cheat; **fullero de naipes** cardsharp
fulmicotón *m* guncotton
fulminar *tr* to strike with lightning; strike dead; (*censuras, amenazas, etc.*) thunder; (*balas o bombas*) hurl
fumada *f* puff, whiff
fumadero *m* smoking room; **fumadero de opio** opium den
fuma•dor -dora *adj* smoking || *mf* smoker
fumar *tr* to smoke || *intr* to smoke; **fumar en pipa** to smoke a pipe; **se prohibe fumar** no smoking || *ref* to squander; stay away from; (*la clase*) cut
fumarada *f* (*de humo*) puff; (*de tabaco*) pipeful
fumigación *f* fumigation; **fumigación aérea** crop dusting
fumigar §44 *tr* to fumigate
fumista *m* stove or heater repairman; stove or heater dealer
fumistería *f* stove or heater shop
fumo•so -sa *adj* smoky
funámbu•lo -la *mf* ropewalker, high-wire artist
función *f* function; duty, office, function; (*espectáculo teatral*) show, performance; **entrar en funciones** to take office, take up one's duties; **función benéfica** charitable performance; **función de aficionados** amateur performance; **función de aficionados** amateur performance; **función de títeres** puppet show; **función gramatical** part of speech; **función secundaria** side show
funcional *adj* functional
funcionariado *m* bureaucracy
funcionario *m* functionary, public official, civil servant
funcione•ro -ra *adj* officious, fussy
fund. *abbr* **fundador**
funda *f* case, sheath, envelope, slip; (*para una espada*) scabbard; (*para proteger los muebles*) slip cover; **funda de almohada** pillowcase; **funda de asientos** seat cover; **funda de gafas** spectacle case
fundación *f* foundation
fundadamente *adv* with good reason; on good authority
funda•dor -dora *adj* founding || *mf* founder
fundamental *adj* fundamental
fundamentar *tr* to lay the foundations of
fundamento *m* foundation; (*razón, motivo*) grounds, reason; basis; reliability, sense; (Col) skirt
fundar *tr* to found, base || *ref* — **fundarse en** to be based on; base one's opinion on
fundente *adj* molten || *m* flux
fundería *f* foundry
fundible *adj* fusible
fundición *f* (*acción de fundir*) founding; (*fábrica*) foundry; (*herrería*) forge; (*hierro colado*) cast iron; (typ) font
fundi•do -da *adj* melted; (*individuo*) ruined; (elec) shorted, blown out
fundidor *m* founder, foundryman
fundillo *m* (Cuba, Mex) behind, buttocks
fundir *tr* (*p.ej., metales*) to found; (*campanas, estatuas*) cast; (*derretir para purificar*) smelt; (*colores*) mix; (*un filamento eléctrico*) burn out; to melt down || *intr* to smelt || *ref* to melt; fuse; (*un filamento eléctrico*) burn out; fail, founder; (fig) to fuse, merge; (*accidentalmente*) to melt down (*core of a nuclear reactor*)
fúnebre *adj* (*marcha, procesión*) funeral; (*triste*) funereal
funeral *adj* funeral; (*triste, lúgubre*) funereal || *m* funeral; **funerales** funeral
funerala — **a la funerala** (mil) with arms inverted (*as a token of mourning*)

funera•rio -ria *adj* funeral || *m* mortician, funeral director || *f* (*empresa*) undertaking establishment; (*local*) funeral home, funeral parlor
funes•to -ta *adj* ill-fated; sad, sorrowful; (*p.ej., influencia*) baneful
fungir §27 *intr* (CAm, Mex) to act, function
fungo *m* (pathol) fungus
fungo•so -sa *adj* fungous
funicular *adj & m* funicular; cable car
fuñique *adj* awkward; dull, tiresome
furgón *m* wagon, truck; (rr) freight car, boxcar; (rr) caboose; **furgón de municiones** (mil) caisson
furgoneta *f* light truck, delivery truck
furia *f* fury
furibun•do -da *adj* furious, frenzied
furio•so -sa *adj* furious; (*muy grande*) terrific, tremendous
furor *m* rage, furor; **causar furor** to make a splash, cause a stir; **hacer furor** to be all the rage
furti•vo -va *adj* furtive; sneaky, poaching
furúnculo *m* boil
fusa *f* (mus) demisemiquaver
fus•co -ca *adj* dark
fusela•do -da *adj* streamlined
fuselaje *m* fuselage
fusible *adj* fusible || *m* (elec) fuse
fusil *m* gun, rifle
fusilar *tr* to shoot, execute; plagiarize
fusilazo *m* (*tiro de fusil*) gunshot, rifle shot; (*relámpago sin ruido*) heat lightning, sheet lightning
fusilería *f* rifle corps; rifles, guns; (*descarga*) fusillade
fusión *f* fusion; melting; merger, amalgamation; **fusión de empresas** (com) merger; **fusión nuclear** nuclear fusion
fusionar *tr & ref* to fuse, merge
fusta *f* brushwood, twigs; teamster's whip
fustán *m* fustian; cotton petticoat; (Ven) skirt
fuste *m* wood, timber; shaft, stem; (fig) importance, substance
fustigar §44 *tr* to whip, lash; rebuke harshly
fútbol *or* **futbol** (Mex) *m* football (U.S.A.); soccer, football (Brit), association football; **fútbol americano** football (U.S.A.)
fútil *adj* futile, trifling, inconsequential
futilidad *f* futility
futre *m* (SAm) dandy, dude
futurista *adj* futuristic, futurist; space-age
futu•ro -ra *adj* future || *m* future; (gram) future; fiancé; **futuros** (com) futures || *f* fiancée

G

G, g (ge) *f* seventh letter of the Spanish alphabet
G. *abbr* gracia
gaba•cho -cha *adj & mf* Pyrenean; (coll) Frenchy || *m* (coll) Frenchified Spanish (*language*)
gabán *m* overcoat
gabardina *f* gabardine; raincoat with belt
gabarra *f* barge, lighter
gabarro *m* (*en una piedra*) nodule; (*en un tejido*) flaw, defect; mistake
gabinete *m* cabinet; (*de médico, abogado, etc.*) office; studio, study; laboratory; (Col) glassed-in balcony; **de gabinete** armchair, theoretical; **gabinete de aseo** washroom; **gabinete de imagen** public relations office; **gabinete estratégico** think tank; **gabinete de lectura** reading room; **gabinete fantasma** *or* **en la sombra** shadow cabinet
gablete *m* gable
gacela *f* gazelle
gaceta *f* government journal; newspaper; **mentir más que la gaceta** to lie like a trooper
gacetilla *f* town talk, gossip column; short item
gacetillero *m* gossip columnist
gacetista *mf* newspaper reader; newsmonger
gacha *f* watery mass; (Col, Ven) earthenware bowl; **gachas** mush, pap; porridge, gruel; mud; **gachas de avena** oatmeal; **hacerse unas gachas** to be mushy
ga•cho -cha *adj* turned down; flopping; (*sombrero*) slouch; **a gachas** on all fours || *f* see **gacha**
gachumbo *m* (SAm) hard fruit shell
gachu•pín -pina *mf* (CAm, Mex) (pej) Spanish settler in Latin America
gacilla *f* (CAm) safety pin
gaéli•co -ca *adj* Gaelic || *mf* Gael || *m* Gaelic (*language*)
gafa *f* clamp; (*enganche de los anteojos*) temple; **gafas** glasses; **gafas bifocales** bifocals; **gafas de bucear** diving goggles; **gafas de cerca** *or* **de leer** reading glasses; **gafas de esquiar** skiing goggles; **gafas de sol** *or* **gafas para sol** sunglasses; **gafas graduadas** prescription glasses; **gafas oscuras** *or* **negras** dark glasses
gafe *m* jinx, hoodoo
ga•fo -fa *adj* claw-handed; foot-sore || *f* see **gafa**
gaguear *intr* to stutter
gaita *f* hornpipe; hurdy-gurdy; chore, hard task; neck; **gaita gallega** bagpipe
gaite•ro -ra *adj* flashy, gaudy || *m* piper, bagpipe player
gajes *mpl* wages, salary; **gajes del oficio** cares of office, occupational annoyances
gajo *m* broken branch; (*de un racimo de uvas*) small stem; (*división interior de ciertas fru-*

tas) slice; (*de horca*) tine, prong; (*ramal de montes*) spur; curl

gala *f* fine clothes; (*lo más selecto*) choice, cream; tip, fee; **de gala** full-dress; **hacer gala de** to glory in; **llevarse la gala** to win approval

galafate *m* slick thief

galai•co -ca *adj* Galician

galán *m* good-looking fellow; lover, heartthrob, ladies' man; (*el que sirve de escolta a una dama*) escort, cavalier; (theat) leading man; **galán joven** (theat) juvenile; **primer galán** (theat) leading man

galancete *m* (theat) juvenile

gala•no -na *adj* elegant, graceful; spruce, smartly dressed; rich, tasteful

galante *adj* (*con las damas*) gallant; (*con los caballeros*) flirtatious; (*mujer*) wanton, loose

galantear *tr* to court, woo, make love to; sue, entreat

galantería *f* gallantry; charm, elegance; generosity

galanura *f* charm, elegance

galápago *m* pond tortoise; (*del arado*) moldboard; light saddle; ingot

galardón *m* reward, recompense

galardonar *tr* to reward, recompense

galaxia *f* galaxy

galbana *f* laziness; shiftlessness

galbano•so -sa *adj* lazy; phlegmatic

gale•no -na *adj* gentle; mild || *m* (coll) physician, doctor

galeón *m* (naut) galleon

galeote *m* galley slave

galera *f* covered wagon; women's jail; (*de hospital*) ward; (naut & typ) galley

galerada *f* wagonload; (typ) galley; (typ) galley proof

galería *f* gallery; **galería comercial** shopping mall; **galería de arte** art gallery; **galería de personajes famosos** hall of fame; **galería de tiro** shooting gallery; **galerías** department store; **hablar para la galería** to play to the gallery

galerna *f* stormy wind from the northwest (*on the northern coast of Spain*)

Gales *f* Wales; **el país de Gales** Wales; **la Nueva Gales del Sur** New South Wales

ga•lés -lesa *adj* Welsh || *m* Welshman; Welsh (*language*) || *f* Welsh woman

galguear *intr* (CAm, Mex, Arg) to be hungry

gal•go -ga *adj* (Col) sweet-toothed || *m* greyhound || *f* greyhound bitch; rolling stone; mange, rash; (mech) gauge

Galia, la Gaul

gálibo *m* template, pattern; (rr) gabarit

galicismo *m* Gallicism

gáli•co -ca *adj* Gallic || *m* syphilis; syphilitic

galillo *m* uvula; gullet

galimatí•as *m* (*pl* **-as**) gibberish, mumbo jumbo, nonsense; confusion

galiparia *f* Frenchified Spanish

galladura *f* tread (*of egg*)

gallardete *m* streamer, pennant

gallardía *f* gallantry; elegance; nobility; generosity

gallar•do -da *adj* gallant; elegant; noble; generous; (*temporal*) fierce

gallear *intr* to stand out, excel; shout, yell, threaten

galle•go -ga *adj & mf* Galician

gallera *f* cockpit

galleta *f* hardtack, ship biscuit; cracker; little pitcher; slap; **galleta integral** graham cracker

gallina *adj* chicken-hearted || *mf* chicken-hearted person || *f* hen; **estar como gallina en corral ajeno** to be like a fish out of water; **gallina ciega** blindman's buff; **gallina de Guinea** guinea fowl; **gallina ponedora** laying hen

gallinería *f* poultry shop; cowardice

galline•ro -ra *mf* poultry dealer || *m* hencoop, henhouse; poultry basket; top gallery; babel, madhouse

gallipavo *m* turkey; sour note

gallito *m* (*el que figura sobre los demás*) somebody; **gallito del lugar** cock of the walk

gallo *m* cock, rooster; false note, sour note; boss; frog in the throat; (box) bantam-weight; (Col, C-R, Mex) strong man; **gallo de bosque** wood grouse; **gallo de pelea** gamecock; **tener mucho gallo** to be cocky

gallofa *f* vegetables; French roll; talk, gossip

gallofear *intr* to beg, bum, loaf around

gallofe•ro -ra *adj* begging, loafing || *mf* beggar, loafer

ga•lo -la *adj* Gaulish || *mf* Gaul || *m* Gaulish (*language*)

galocha *f* clog, wooden shoe

galón *m* braid, galloon; (*medida para líquidos: 4,55 litros*) gallon; (mil) chevron, stripe

galopar *intr* to gallop

galope *m* gallop; **a galope** at a gallop; in great haste; **a galope tendido** on the run

galopea•do -da *adj* hasty, sketchy || *m* beating, punching

galopear *intr* to gallop

galopillo *m* scullion, kitchen boy

galopín *m* ragamuffin; (*hombre taimado*) wise guy; (naut) cabin boy

galpón *m* (SAm) iron shed; (Col) tile works

galvanizar §60 *tr* to electroplate; galvanize

galvanoplastia *f* electroplating

gama *f* doe, female fallow deer; (mus & fig) gamut; **de gama baja** (compu) low-level; **gama de frecuencias** wave band; (compu) frequency range; **gama media** (compu) midrange

gamberrismo *m* gangsterism, rowdyism

gambe•rro -rra *adj & mf* libertine || *m* hoodlum, tough, rowdy

gambeta *f* crosscaper; caper, prance

gambito *m* gambit

gammaglobulina *f* gamma globulin

gamo *m* buck, male fallow deer

gamón *m* asphodel

gamonal *m* field of asphodel; boss

gamuza *f* chamois
gana *f* desire; will; **darle a uno la gana de** to feel like, e.g., **le da la gana de trabajar** he feels like working; **de buena gana** willingly; **de gana** in earnest; willingly; **de mala gana** unwillingly; **tener ganas de** to feel like, to have a mind to
ganadería *f* cattle, livestock; brand, stock; cattle raising; cattle ranch
ganade•ro -ra *adj* cattle, livestock || *mf* cattle breeder; cattle dealer || *m* cattleman
ganado *m* cattle, livestock; **ganado bovino** cattle; **ganado caballar** horses; **ganado cabrío** goats; **ganado lanar** sheep; **ganado mayor** large farm animals (*cows, bulls, horses, and mules*); **ganado menor** small farm animals (*sheep, goats, pigs*); **ganado menudo** young cattle; **ganado moreno** swine; **ganado ovejuno** sheep; **ganado porcino** swine; **ganado vacuno** cattle
gana•dor -dora *adj* winning; earning; hardworking || *mf* winner; earner; **ganador sorpresa** dark horse
ganancia *f* gain, profit; (Guat, Mex) extra, bonus; **ganancias y pérdidas** profit and loss
ganancial *adj* profit
gananció•so -sa *adj* gainful, profitable; earning || *mf* earner
ganapán *m* errand boy; boor
ganapierde *m & f* giveaway
ganar *tr* (*dinero trabajando*) to earn; (*la victoria luchando*) win; (*beneficios en los negocios*) gain; (*a una persona en una contienda*) beat, defeat; (*aventajar*) excel; (*la voluntad de una persona*) win over; (*alcanzar*) reach; **ganar algo a alguien** to win something from someone; **ganar de comer** to earn a living || *intr* to earn; (*mejorar*) improve || *ref* to win over; **ganarse la vida** to earn a livelihood
ganchero *m* log driver; (Chile) odd-jobber; (Ecuad) gentle mount
ganchillo *m* crochet needle; crochet, crochet work; **hacer ganchillo** to crochet
gancho *m* hook; shepherd's crook; coaxer; procurer, pimp; hairpin; (Col, Ecuad) lady's saddle; **gancho de botalones** (naut) gooseneck; **gancho de nodriza** (Col) safety pin; **echar el gancho a** to hook in, to land; **tener gancho** (*una mujer*) to have a way with men
gandaya *f* (coll) bumming, loafing
gandujar *tr* to pleat, shirr
gan•dul -dula *adj* loafing, idling || *mf* loafer, idler
gandulear *intr* to loaf, idle
ganfo•rro -rra *mf* scoundrel
ganga *f* bargain
ganglio *m* ganglion
gangocho *m* burlap
gango•so -sa *adj* snuffling, nasal
gangrena *f* gangrene
gangrenar *tr & ref* to gangrene
gángster *m* gunman, gangster
gangsteril *adj* gangster(like)
gangsterismo *m* gangsterism; mobsterism
ganguear *intr* to snuffle, talk through the nose
gangue•ro -ra *adj* bargain-hunting; self-seeking || *mf* bargain hunter
gano•so -sa *adj* desirous; (*caballo*) (Chile) spirited, fiery
gan•so -sa *mf* dope, dullard || *m* goose; gander; **ganso bravo** wild goose || *f* female goose
Gante Ghent
ganzúa *f* (*garfio*) picklock, lock pick; (*persona*) picklock; pumper (*of secrets*)
gañán *m* farm hand; rough, husky fellow
gañido *m* yelp; croak
gañir **§12** *intr* (*el perro*) to yelp; (*p.ej., el cuervo*) croak
garabatear *tr* to scribble || *intr* to hook; beat about the bush; scribble
garabato *m* hook; pothook; scribbling; weeding hoe; (*bozal*) muzzle; (*de una mujer*) winsomeness; **garabato de carnicero** meathook; **garabatos** wiggling of hands and fingers
garabato•so -sa *adj* full of scrawls; winsome
garage *m* or **garaje** *m* garage
garagista *m* garbage man
garambaina *f* gaudy trimming; **garambainas** simpering, smirking; (coll) scribble
garante *adj* responsible || *mf* guarantor, voucher
garantía *f* guarantee, guaranty; warranty; **garantía anticorrosión** antirust warranty
garantir **§1** *tr* to guarantee
garantizar **§60** *tr* to guarantee
garañón *m* stud jackass; stud camel; stallion
garapiña *f* icing, sugar-coating; iced pineapple drink
garapiñar *tr* to ice, sugar-coat; candy
garapiñera *f* ice-cream freezer
garbanzo *m* chickpea, garbanzo (bean); **garbanzo negro** (fig) black sheep
garbeo *m* walk; promenade
garbillar *tr* to sieve, screen riddle
garbillo *s* sieve, screen; riddled ore
garbo *m* jauntiness, grace, fine bearing; generosity
garbo•so -sa *adj* jaunty, graceful, spruce, sprightly; generous
gardu•ño -ña *mf* (archaic) sneak thief || *f* stone marten, beech marten
garete *m* — **al garete** (naut) adrift
garfa *f* claw
garfio *m* hook, gaff
gargajear *intr* to cough up phlegm, hawk
gargajo *m* phlegm
garganta *f* throat; (*de un río, una vasija, etc.*) neck, throat; (*del pie*) instep; (*entre montañas*) ravine, gorge; (*del arado*) sheath; (*de una polea*) groove; (archit) shaft; **tener buena garganta** to have a good voice
gargantear *intr* to warble
gargantilla *f* necklace
gárgara *f* gargling; **gárgaras** (*líquido*) gargle; **hacer gárgaras** to gargle
gargarear *intr* to gargle
gargarismo *m* gargling; (*líquido*) gargle

gargarizar §60 *intr* to gargle
gárgola *f* gargoyle
garguero *m* gullet; (*caña del pulmón*) windpipe
garita *f* sentry box; porter's lodge; (*de una fortificación*) watchtower; railroad-crossing box; privy (*with one seat*); **garita de centinela** sentry box; **garita de señales** (rr) signal tower
garito *m* gambling den
garlito *m* fish trap; trap, snare
garlopa *f* jack plane, trying plane
garnar *intr* to drizzle
garra *f* claw, talon; catch, hook; **caer en las garras de** to fall into the clutches of
garrafa *f* carafe, decanter; **garrafa corchera** demijohn
garrafal *adj* awful, terrible
garrafiñar *tr* to snatch
garrafón *m* carboy, demijohn
garramar *tr* to snitch
garranchuelo *m* crab grass
garrapata *f* cattle tick, sheep tick; (mil) disabled horse; (Chile) little runt; (Mex) slut
garrapatear *intr* to scrawl, scribble
garrapato *m* pothook, scrawl; **garrapatos** scrawl
garri•do -da *adj* handsome, elegant
garroba *f* carob bean
garrocha *f* goad; (sport) pole
garrotazo *m* blow with a club
garrote *m* club, cudgel; garrote (*method of execution; iron collar used for such execution*); (Mex) brake; **dar garrote a** to garrote
garrote•ro -ra *adj* (Chile) stingy || *m* (Mex) brakeman
garrotillo *m* croup
garrucha *f* pulley, sheave
gárru•lo -la *adj* chirping; (*hablador*) garrulous; (*arroyo*) babbling; (*viento*) rustling
garúa drizzle
garuar §21 *intr* to drizzle
garulla *f* mob, rabble
garza *f* heron; **garza real** gray heron
gar•zo -za *adj* blue || *f* see **garza**
garzón *m* boy, youth; suitor; woman chaser
gas *m* gas; **gas de alumbrado** illuminating gas; **gas envasado** bottled gas; **gas exhilarante** *or* **hilarante** laughing gas; **gas lacrimógeno** tear gas; **gas mostaza** mustard gas; **gas neurotóxico** *or* **nervioso** nerve gas
gasa *f* gauze, chiffon; (*tira de gasa negra con que se rodea el sombrero en señal de luto*) hatband
Gascuña *f* Gascony
gasear *tr* to gas
gaseo•so -sa *adj* gaseous || *f* soda water, carbonated water
gasificar §73 *tr* to gasify; exalt, elate || *ref* to gasify
gasista *m* gas fitter; (Chile) gasworker
gasoducto *m* gas pipe line
gasógeno *m* gas generator, gas producer; mixture of benzine and alcohol used for lighting and cleaning
gas-oil or **gasoil** *m* diesel fuel, diesel oil; (*coche*) diesel
gasolina *f* gasoline
gasolinera *f* motor boat; gas station, filling station
gasómetro *m* gasholder, gas tank
gastadero *m* waste
gasta•do -da *adj* worn-out; used up; spent; (*chiste*) crummy, corny
gasta•dor -dora *adj & mf* spendthrift || *m* convict; (mil) sapper, pioneer
gastadura *f* worn spot
gastar *tr* (*dinero, tiempo*) to spend; (*en cosas inútiles*) waste; (*echar a perder con el uso*) wear out; (*consumir*) use up; (*p.ej., una barba*) wear; (*un coche*) keep; **gastarlas** to act, behave || *intr* to spend || *ref* to wear; wear out; become used up; waste away
gasto *m* cost, expense; wear; **gastos de conservación** *or* **de entretenimiento** upkeep; **gastos de explotación** operating expenses; **gastos de flete** shipping and handling; **gastos de viaje** travel expenses; **gastos fijos** overhead; **gastos menudos** petty expenses; **hacer el gasto** to do most of the talking; to be the subject of conversation; **hacer frente a los gastos** to meet expenses; **meterse en gastos con** to go to the expense of
gasto•so -sa *adj* wasteful, extravagant
gástri•co -ca *adj* gastric
gastronomía *f* gastronomy
gastróno•mo -ma *mf* gourmet
gata *f* she-cat; low-hanging cloud; Madrid woman; (Mex) maid, servant girl; **a gatas** on all fours, on hands and knees
gatada *f* catty act
gatatumba *f* faked attention, fake emotion, faked pain
gatazo *m* gyp
gatea•do -da *adj* catlike; grained, striped || *m* crawling, climbing; scratching, clawing
gatear *tr* to scratch, claw; snitch || *intr* to crawl, climb
gatera *f* cathole; (naut) hawsehole
gatería *f* cats; gang of toughs; fake humility
gate•ro -ra *adj* full of cats || *mf* cat lover || *f* see **gatera**
gates•co -ca *adj* catlike, feline
gatillo *m* (*de arma de fuego*) trigger; little pickpocket
gato *m* cat; tomcat; (*instrumento para levantar pesos*) jack, lifting jack; sly fellow; sneak thief; native of Madrid; **gato montés** wildcat; **gato rodante** dolly; **vender gato por liebre** to gyp, cheat
gatopardo *m* cheetah
gauchada *f* (SAm) sly trick; (SAm) good turn
gauchaje *m* (SAm) gathering of Gauchos
gauches•co -ca *adj* Gaucho
gau•cho -cha *adj* (SAm) Gaucho; (Arg, Chile) sly, crafty || *m* (SAm) Gaucho; (SAm) good horseman || *m* (Arg) mannish woman; (Arg) loose woman

gaulteria *f* wintergreen
gaveta *f* drawer, till
gavia *f* ditch, drain; (*ave*) gull; (min) gang of basket passers; (naut) topsail
gavilán *m* sparrow hawk; (*de la pluma*) nib; (*en la escritura*) hair stroke; ingrowing nail
gavilla *f* sheaf, bundle; gang
gaviota *f* sea gull
gavota *f* gavotte
gay [gaɪ], [geɪ] *adj & mf* (*homosexual*) gay
gaya *f* colored stripe; (*ave*) magpie
gayar *tr* to trim with colored stripes
ga•yo -ya *adj* cheerful, bright, showy || *m* (orn) jay || *f* see **gaya**
gayola *f* cage; jail
gayomba *f* Spanish broom
gazapa *f* lie
gazapatón *m* blunder, slip
gazapera *f* rabbit warren; gang, gang of thugs; brawl, row
gazapo *m* young rabbit; sly fellow; slip, boner, blunder; (*de actor*) fluff
gazmiar *tr* (*oliendo*) to sniff; (*comiendo*) nibble || *ref* to complain
gazmoñada *f* or **gazmoñería** *f* prudishness, priggishness
gazmoñe•ro -ra or gazmo•ño -ña *adj* prudish, priggish, strait-laced, demure || *mf* prude, prig
gaznápiro *m* gawk, boob, bumpkin
gaznate *m* gullet; (Mex) fritter
gazpacho *m* gazpacho (*cold vegetable soup*); (Hond) leftovers
gazuza *f* hunger
Gedeón *m* Gideon
gehena *m* Gehenna
géiser *m* geyser
gel *m* gel
gelatina *f* gelatine
gema *f* gem; (bot) bud
geme•lo -la *adj & mf* twin; **gemelos** twins; binoculars; cuff links; **gemelos de campo** field glasses; **gemelos de teatro** opera glasses || **Gemelos** *mpl* (astr) Gemini
gemido *m* moan, groan; wail, whine; howl, roar
Géminis *m* (astr) Gemini
gemiquear *intr* (Chile) to whine
gemir §50 *intr* to moan, groan; wail, whine; howl, roar
gen *m* gene
genciana *f* gentian
gendarme *m* policeman
genealogía *f* genealogy
generación *f* generation
genera•dor -dora *adj* generating || *m* generator
general *adj* general; common, usual; **en general** *or* **por lo general** in general || *m* general; **capitán general de ejército** five-star general; **general de brigada** brigadier, brigadier general; **general de división** major general || **generales** *fpl* general information, personal data
generala *f* general's wife; call to arms
generalato *m* generalship
generalidad *f* generality; majority; **la generalidad de** the general run of
generalísimo *m* generalissimo
generalizar §60 *tr & intr* to generalize || *ref* to become generalized
generar *tr* to generate
genéri•co -ca *adj* generic; (*artículo*) indefinite; (*nombre*) common; showing gender
género *m* kind, sort; way, manner; cloth, material; (biol, log) genus; (gram) gender; **de género** genre; **género chico** one-act play, one-act operetta; **género de punto** knit goods, knitwear; **género humano** humankind, human race, mankind; **género ínfimo** light vaudeville; **género novelístico** fiction; **género picaresco** burlesque; **géneros** goods, merchandise, material; **géneros de pieza** yard goods; **géneros para vestidos** dress goods
genero•so -sa *adj* generous; highborn; noble, magnanimous; (*vino*) rich, full
géne•sis *f* (*pl* **-sis**) genesis || **el Génesis** (Bib) Genesis
genéti•co -ca *adj* genetic || *f* genetics
genetista *mf* geneticist
genial *adj* inspired, geniuslike; pleasant, agreeable; temperamental
geniazo *m* fiery temper
genio *m* (*índole, carácter*) temperament, disposition; (*don altísimo de invención; persona que lo posee; espíritu tutelar, deidad pagana*) genius; fire, spirit
genital *adj* genital || **genitales** *mpl* genitals
geniti•vo -va *adj* genitive
genitourina•rio -ria *adj* genitourinary
genocida *adj* genocidal || *mf* genocide
genocidio *m* genocide
genoma *m* (gen) genome
Génova *f* Genoa
geno•vés -vesa *adj & mf* Genoese
gente *f* people; (*parentela, familia*) folks; race, nation; troops; **gente baja** lower classes, rabble; **gente bien** nice people; **gente de bien** decent people; **gente de capa parda** country people; **gente de coleta** bullfighters; **gente de edad** senior citizens; **gente de la cuchilla** butchers; **genta de la vida airada** bullies; underworld; **gente del bronce** bright, lively people; **gente del rey** convicts; **gente de mal vivir** toughs, underworld; **gente de mar** seafaring people; **gente de paz** (*palabras con las cuales se contesta al que pregunta ¿quién?*) friend; **gente de pluma** (coll) clerks; **gente de su majestad** convicts; **gente de trato** tradespeople; **gente forzada** convicts; **gente menuda** small fry; common people; **la gente de a pie** the ordinary citizen
gentecilla *f* mob, rabble
gentil *adj* heathen, gentile; elegant, genteel; noble || *mf* heathen, pagan
gentileza *f* elegance, gentility, courtesy; gallantry; show, splendor; (*hidalguía*) nobility
gentilhombre *m* (*pl* **gentileshombres**) gentleman; messenger to the king; my good man;

gentilhombre de cámara gentleman in waiting
genti·li·cio -cia *adj* national; family; (gram) gentile
gentilidad *f* heathendom
gentío *m* crowd, mob
gentualla or **gentuza** *f* rabble, riffraff
genui·no -na *adj* genuine
geofísi·co -ca *adj* geophysical || *mf* geophysicist || *f* geophysics
geografía *f* geography
geográfi·co -ca *adj* geographic(al)
geógra·fo -fa *mf* geographer
geología *f* geology
geológi·co -ca *adj* geologic(al)
geólo·go -ga *mf* geologist
geómetra *mf* geometrician
geometría *f* geometry; **geometría del espacio** solid geometry
geométri·co -ca *adj* geometric(al)
geopolíti·co -ca *adj* geopolitical || *f* geopolitics
geranio *m* geranium
gerencia *f* management; manager's office
gerente *m* manager, director; **gerente de publicidad** advertising manager; **gerente de ventas** sales manager
geriatría *f* geriatry
geriatra *adj* geriatrical || *mf* geriatrician
geriátri·co -ca *adj* geriatrical
germanía *f* gypsy slang; criminal slang
germa·no -na *adj* (hist) Germanic || *mf* Germanic tribe member
germanófo·no -na *adj* German-speaking || *mf* German speaker
germen *m* germ; **germen plasma** germ plasm
germicida *adj* germicidal || *m* germicide
germinal *adj* germ; germinal
germinar *intr* to germinate
gerontología *f* gerontology
gerundio *m* gerund; present participle; bombastic writer or speaker
gestación *f* gestation
gestear *intr* to make faces
gesticular *intr* to make a face, to make faces; (*hacer ademanes*) to gesticulate
gestión *f* step, measure; management; action, proceeding, negotiation
gestionar *tr* to promote, pursue; manage; negotiate
gesto *m* face; wry face, grimace; look, appearance; (*movimiento, ademán*) gesture
ges·tor -tora *adj* managing || *m* manager; **gestor de extensiones** (compu) extension manager
gestu·do -da *adj* cross-looking
ghetto *m* ghetto
giba *f* hump; annoyance
giga *f* jig
giganta *f* giantess
gigante *adj* giant || *m* giant; (*en las procesiones*) giant figure
gigantes·co -ca *adj* gigantic
gigantez *f* giant size
gigantilla *f* large-headed masked figure; little fat woman
gigan·tón -tona *mf* huge giant || *m* giant figure
gigote *m* chopped-meat stew; **hacer gigote** to chop up
gilí *or* **gili** *adj* foolish, stupid
gimnasia *f* gymnastics; health club; **gimnasia respiratoria** breathing exercises; **gimnasia sueca** Swedish movements, setting-up exercises
gimnasio *m* gymnasium; secondary school, academy
gimnasta *mf* gymnast
gimnásti·co -ca *adj* gymnastic || *f* gymnastics
gimotear *intr* to whine
gimoteo *m* whining
ginebra *f* gin; (*de voces*) buzz, din; confusion, disorder || **Ginebra** *f* Geneva
ginebri·no -na *adj & mf* Genevan
ginecología *f* gynecology
ginecológi·co -ca *adj* gynecologic(al)
ginecólo·go -ga *mf* gynecologist
ginesta *f* Spanish broom
gira *f* outing, excursion; **gira relámpago** whistle-stop tour
gira·do -da *mf* drawee
gira·dor -dora *mf* drawer
giralda *f* weathercock (*in the form of person or animal*)
girándula *f* girandole
girar *tr* (*una visita*) to pay; (com) to draw || *intr* to turn; rotate, gyrate; trade; (com) to draw
girasol *m* sunflower
girato·rio -ria *adj* revolving || *f* revolving bookcase
gi·ro -ra *adj* (Guat) drunk; (Mex) cocky || *m* turn; rotation; revolution; course, trend, turn; turn of phrase; boast, threat; gash, slash; line of business; trade; (com) draft; **giro a la vista** sight draft; **giro en U** (CAm) U-turn; **giro postal** money order || *f* see **gira**
giroflé *m* clove
giroscopio *m* gyroscope
gis *m* (Col) slate pencil
gitana *f* gypsy woman, gypsy girl
gitanada *f* gypsy trick; fawning, flattery
gitanería *f* band of gypsies; gypsy life; fawning, flattery
gitanes·co -ca *adj* gypsyish
gita·no -na *adj* gypsy; flattering; sly, tricky || *mf* gypsy || *m* Gypsy (*language*) || *f* see **gitana**
glaciación *f* freezing
glacial *adj* glacial; (*zona*) frigid; (fig) cold, indifferent
glaciar *m* glacier
gladiador *m* gladiator
gladiolo *m* gladiolus
glamoro·so -sa *adj* glamorous; glitzy (coll)
glamour *m* glamor; glitz (coll)
glándula *f* gland; **glándula cerrada** ductless gland
glaucoma *m* glaucoma
glasé *m* glacé silk

glasea•do -da *adj* glossy, shiny
glicerina *f* glycerin
global *adj* total; global, world-wide
globo *m* globe; bubble; speech balloon (*in comics*); (*aparato que, lleno de un gas, se eleva en el aire*) balloon; (*bomba de lámpara*) globe, lamp shade; (baseball) flyball; **globo de aire** (aut) air bag; **globo de aire caliente** hot-air balloon; **globo del ojo** eyeball; **globos de ayuda** (compu) balloon help; **globo sonda** trial balloon; **lanzar un globo sonda** (fig) to send up a trial balloon
glóbulo *m* globule; (physiol) corpuscle; **glóbulo rojo** red corpuscle, red blood cell; **glóbulo blanco** white corpuscle, white blood cell
gloria *f* glory; **ganar la gloria** to go to glory; **oler a gloria** to smell heavenly; **saber a gloria** to taste heavenly
gloriar §77 *tr* to glorify || *intr* to recite the rosary || *ref* to glory
glorieta *f* arbor, bower, summerhouse; public square; traffic circle
glorificar §73 *tr* to glorify || *ref* to glory
glorio•so -sa *adj* glorious; boastful
glosa *f* gloss
glosa•dor -dora *adj* commenting || *mf* commentator
glosar *tr* to gloss; audit; (Col) to scold || *intr* to find fault
glosario *m* glossary
glosopeda *f* (vet) foot-and-mouth disease
glóti•co -ca *adj* glottal
glo•tón -tona *adj* gluttonous || *mf* glutton
glotonería *f* gluttony
glucosa *f* glucose
gluglú *m* (*del agua*) gurgle, glug; (*del pavo*) gobble; **hacer gluglú** to gurgle, to glug
gluglutear *intr* to gobble
gnomo *m* gnome
gob. *abbr* **gobierno**
gobernación *f* governing; government; department of the interior; (Arg) territory
goberna•dor -dora *adj* governing || *mf* governor || *f* governor's wife
gobernalle *m* rudder, helm
gobernante *adj* governing || *mf* ruler || *m* self-appointed head
gobernar §2 *tr* to govern; guide, direct; control, rule; (*un buque*) steer || *intr* to govern; steer
governo•so -sa *adj* orderly
gobierno *m* government; governor's office, governorship; management; control, rule; guidance; (*de un buque*) navigability; **de buen gobierno** (*buque*) navigable; **gobierno de monigotes** puppet government; **gobierno doméstico** housekeeping; **gobierno en funciones** caretaker government; **gobierno exilado** government in exile; **para su gobierno** for your guidance; **servir de gobierno** to serve as a guide
goce *m* enjoyment
go•do -da *adj* Gothic || *mf* Goth; Spanish noble; (Arg, Chile) Spaniard
gofio *m* roasted corn meal
gol *m* goal; **gol de campo** field goal
gola *f* gullet
goldre *m* quiver
goleta *f* schooner
golf *m* golf
golfán *m* white water lily
golfista *mf* golfer
gol•fo -fa *mf* ragamuffin || *m* gulf; open sea; **golfo de Méjico** Gulf of Mexico; **golfo de Vizcaya** Bay of Biscay
Gólgota, el (Bib) Golgotha
golilla *f* gorget, ruff; magistrate's collar; pipe flange; (*de los caños de barro*) collar, sleeve; (*del gallo*) erectile bristles
gollería *f* delicacy, dainty; **pedir gollerías** to ask for too much
gollete *m* throat, neck; (*de botella*) neck
golondrina *f* swallow; **empresa golondrina** fly-by-night outfit
golosina *f* delicacy, tidbit; eagerness, appetite; trifle
golosinear *intr* to go around eating candy
golo•so -sa *adj* sweet-toothed; (*glotón*) gluttonous; (*apetitoso*) tasty
golpe *m* blow, stroke, hit; bump, bruise; heartbeat; crowd, throng, flock; (*del bolsillo*) flap; (*pestillo*) bolt, latch; (*de licor*) shot; surprise, wonder; (*infortunio*) blow; witticism; (*atraco*) heist (slang); **dar golpe** to make a hit; **de golpe** all at once, suddenly; **de golpe y porrazo** slambang; **de un golpe** at one stroke; **golpe de ariete** water hammer; **golpe de calor** heatstroke; **golpe de estado** coup d'état; **golpe de fortuna** stroke of luck; **golpe de gracia** coup de grâce; **golpe de mano** surprise attack; **golpe de mar** surge; **golpe de ojo** glance; **golpe de suerte** stroke of luck; **golpe de teatro** dramatic turn of events; **golpe de timón** change of direction; **golpe de tos** fit of coughing; **golpe de vista** glance, look; view; **golpe en vago** miss, flop; **golpe mortal** deathblow; **no dar golpe** to not raise a hand, not do a stroke of work
golpear *tr* to strike, hit, beat; bump, bruise || *intr* to beat, strike; (*el reloj*) tick; (*el motor de combustión interna*) knock
golpete *m* door catch, window catch
golpetear *tr & intr* to beat; rattle
golpismo *m* government by coup d'état
goma *f* gum, rubber; (*tira de goma elástica*) rubber band; (*neumático*) tire; **goma arábiga** gum arabic; **goma de borrar** eraser, rubber; **goma de mascar** chewing gum; **goma de pegar** glue, gum; **goma dos** plastic explosive; **goma espumosa** foam rubber; **goma laca** shellac
gomecillo *m* blind man's guide
gomia *f* bugaboo; waster; glutton
gomo•so -sa *adj* gum; gummy || *m* dude, dandy
góndola *f* gondola
gondolero *m* gondolier
gongo *m* gong

gonorrea *f* gonorrhea
gordal *adj* large-size
gordia•no -na *adj* Gordian
gordi•flón -flona or **gordin•flón -flona** *adj* chubby, pudgy, fatty || *mf* fatty
gor•do -da *adj* fat, plump; fatty, greasy; coarse; big, large; whopping big; (*agua*) hard || *mf* (*apelativo cariñoso*) (coll) dear, honey; (pej) fatty || *m* fat man; fat, suet; (*premio mayor*) first prize, jackpot || *f* fat woman || **gordo** *adv* — **hablar gordo** to talk big
gordura *f* fatness, plumpness, stoutness, corpulence; fat, grease
gorgojo *m* grub, weevil; dwarf, runt; **gorgojo del algodón** boll weevil
gorgojo•so -sa *adj* grubby
gorgón *m* (Col) concrete
gorgonear *intr* (*el pavo*) to gobble
gorgoritear *intr* to trill
gorgorito *m* trill
gorgotear *intr* to burble, gurgle
gorgotero *m* peddler, hawker
gorigori *m* lugubrious funeral chant
gorila *f* gorilla; (coll) thug; (coll) bodyguard; (coll) bouncer
gorjear *intr* to warble, trill || *ref* (*el niño*) to gurgle
gorra *f* cap; bumming, sponging; **andar de gorra** to sponge; **colarse de gorra** (coll) to crash the gate; **gorra de visera** cap; **vivir de gorra** to live on other people
gorrada *f* tipping the hat
gorrear *intr* (Ecuad) to sponge, mooch
gorretada *f* tipping the hat
gorrión *m* sparrow; **gorrión triguero** bunting
gorrista *adj* sponging || *mf* sponger
gorro *m* cap, bonnet; baby's bonnet; **gorro de dormir** nightcap
go•rrón -rrona *adj* sponging || *mf* sponger || *m* pivot; journal, gudgeon
gota *f* drop; (pathol) gout; **gota a gota** little by little; (*aparato*) (med) drip; **gotas** (pharm) drops; **gotas nasales** nose drops; **gotas para los ojos** eye drops; **sudar la gota gorda** to work one's head off
gotear *intr* to drip, dribble; (*llover a gotas espaciadas*) sprinkle
gotera *f* drip, dripping; mark left by dripping; (*en el techo*) leak; (*adorno de una cama*) valance; **estar lleno de goteras** to be full of aches and pains; **es una gotera** it's a constant drain; **goteras** aches, pains; (Col) environs, outskirts
gotero *m* (med) drip; (pharm) dropper
góti•co -ca *adj* Gothic; noble, illustrious || *m* Gothic
gotita *f* droplet
goto•so -sa *adj* gouty || *mf* gout sufferer
gozar §60 *tr* (*poseer*) to enjoy || *intr* to enjoy oneself; **gozar de** (*poseer*) to enjoy || *ref* to enjoy oneself; rejoice
gozne *m* hinge
gozo *m* joy, enjoyment; **no caber en sí de gozo** to be beside oneself with joy; **saltar de gozo** to leap with joy
gozo•so -sa *adj* joyful; **gozoso con** *or* **de** joyful over
gozque *m* or **gozquejo** *m* little yapping dog
grabación *f* recording; **grabación digital** digital recording; **grabación en video** video recording, videocassette recording; **grabación magnética** magnetic recording; **grabación sobre cinta** tape recording
grabado *adj* engraved, etched || *m* engraving; print, cut, picture; (*de disco*) recording **grabado al aguafuerte** etching; **grabado en cobre** copperplate; **grabado en hueco** intaglio; **grabado en madera** wood engraving, woodcut; **grabado en relieve** embossing; **grabado fuera de texto** inset, insert
graba•dor -dora *adj* recording || *mf* engraver; (compu) keyboarder || *f* recorder; **grabadora de cinta** tape recorder
grabador-reproductor *m* cassette recorder
grabadura *f* engraving
grabar *tr* to engrave; (*un sonido, una canción, un disco, etc.*) record; **grabar en** *or* **sobre cinta** to tape-record; **grabar en video** to videotape, to video || *ref* to become engraved, to be engraved
gracejada *f* (CAm, Mex) cheap comedy, clownishness
gracejar *intr* to be engaging, witty; joke
gracejo *m* lightness, winsome manner, charm; (CAm, Mex) clown
gracia *f* witticism, witty remark, joke; grace; gracefulness; favor; pardon; (*de un chiste*) point; name; **caer en gracia a** to be pleasing to; **de gracia** gratis; **decir dos gracias a** to tell someone a thing or two; **en gracia a** because of; **gracia de Dios** daily bread; air and sunshine; **gracias** thanks; **¡gracias!** thanks!; **gracias a** thanks to; **¡gracias a Dios!** thank heavens!; **hacer gracia** to be pleasing; **hacer gracia de algo a uno** to exempt or free someone from something; **hacerle a uno gracia** to strike someone as funny; **¡linda gracia!** nonsense!; **tener gracia** to be funny, be surprising
graciable *adj* kind, gracious; easy to grant
grácil *adj* thin, small, slender
gracio•so -sa *adj* (*que tiene donaire, gracia*) graceful; (*afable, fino*) gracious; (*agudo, chistoso*) funny, witty; (*que se da de balde*) free, gratis || *mf* comic || *m* gracioso (*merry, comic character in Spanish comedy*)
grada *f* step, stair; row of seats; grandstand; altar step; (agr) harrow; (*plano inclinado sobre el cual se construyen los barcos*) slip; **gradas** stone steps; (Chile, Peru) atrium; **gradas al aire libre** bleachers
gradar *tr* (agr) to harrow
gradería *f* stone steps; row of seats; bleachers; **gradería cubierta** grandstand
gradiente *m* (phys) gradient || *f* slope, gradient
grado *m* step; grade; degree; (*título que se da*

en las universidades) degree; (*sección en las escuelas*) grade, form, class; (mil) rank; **de buen grado** willingly; **de grado en grado** by degrees; **de grado o por fuerza** willy-nilly; **de mal grado** unwillingly; **en sumo grado** to a great extent; **mal de mi grado** unwillingly, against my wishes

graduación *f* gradation; (educ) graduation; (educ) graduation ceremony; (mil) rank; (*de las bebidas espirituosas*) strength, alcoholic content

gradua•do -da *adj* graduated; (*gafas*) prescription; (educ) graduate || *mf* (educ) graduate

gradual *adj* gradual

graduan•do -da *mf* (*persona próxima a graduarse en la universidad*) graduate (*candidate for a degree*)

graduar §21 *tr* to graduate, grade; (*un grifo, una válvula, etc.*) regulate; appraise, estimate || *ref* to graduate

grafía *f* graph

gráfi•co -ca *adj* graphic(al); printing; illustrated; picture, camera || *m* diagram || *f* graph

grafito *m* graphite

grafospasmo *m* writer's cramp

gragea *f* colored candy; sugar-coated pill

grajear *intr* (*los cuervos*) to caw; (*los niños*) gurgle

grajien•to -ta *adj* foul-smelling

gra•jo -ja *mf* rook, crow; chatterbox || *m* body odor

gral. *abbr* **general**

gramática *f* grammar; **gramática parda** shrewdness, mother wit

gramatical *adj* grammatical

gramáti•co -ca *adj* grammatical || *mf* grammarian || *f* see **gramática**

gramil *m* marking gauge, gauge

gramo *m* gram

gran *adj* apocopated form of **grande,** used only before nouns of both genders in the singular; **gran angular** wide-angle lens; **gran maestro** grand master; **gran ópera** grand opera; **gran público** general public; **gran slam** *m* (*conquista de todas las competencias en un circuito profesional*) grand slam; **gran superficie** *f* large supermarket; **la Gran Depresión** the Great Depression

grana *f* seed; seeding; seeding time; red; **dar en grana** to go to seed

granada *f* pomegranate; (*proyectil explosivo*) grenade; **granada de mano** hand grenade; **granada de metralla** shrapnel; **granada extintora** fire extinguisher, fire grenade

granadero *m* grenadier

granadilla *f* passionflower

granadina *f* grenadine

grana•do -da *adj* choice, select; mature, expert || *m* pomegranate; **granado blanco** rose of Sharon || *f* see **granada**

granalla *f* filings

granangular *adj* wide-angle

granate *m adj invar & m* garnet; deep-red, maroon

Gran Bretaña, la Great Britain

grande *adj* big, large; great; **grandes almacenes** department store || *mf* eldest; grown-up || *m* grandee || *f* jackpot, big prize

grandeza *f* bigness, largeness; greatness; (*tamaño*) size; (*magnificencia*) grandeur; grandees; grandeeship

grandi•llón -llona *adj* oversize, overgrown

grandio•so -sa *adj* grandiose, grand

grandor *m* size

granea•do -da *adj* spattered; (*fuego*) heavy and continuous

granear *tr* to sow; (*la pólvora; una piedra litográfica*) grain; stipple

granel — a granel in bulk, loose; at random; lavishly

granelar *tr* (*el cuero*) to grain

granero *m* granary

granete *m* center punch

graníf u•go -ga *adj* hail-dispersing

granito *m* granite

granizada *f* hailstorm; (Arg, Chile) iced drink

granizar §60 *tr* (*p.ej., golpes*) to hail; sprinkle || *intr* to hail

granizo *m* hail

granja *f* farm, grange; dairy; country place

granjear *tr* to earn, gain; win, win over || *ref* to win, win over

granjería *f* husbandry; gain, profit

granje•ro -ra *mf* farmer; merchant, trader

grano *m* grain; (*baya*) berry; (*baya de la uva*) grape; (*tumorcillo en la piel*) pimple; (*peso*) grain; **grano de belleza** beauty spot; **grano de café** coffee bean; **granos** (*fruto de los cereales*) grain; **ir al grano** to come to the point

granuja *m* scoundrel; (*muchacho vagabundo*) waif || *f* loose grape; grapeseed

granujo *m* pimple

granular *adj* granular; pimply || *tr & ref* to granulate

gránulo *m* granule

grapa *f* clamp, clip, staple

grapadora *f* stapler

grasa *f* fat, grease; (*polvo*) pounce; (Mex) shoe polish; **grasa de ballena** blubber; **grasas** slag

grasien•to -ta *adj* greasy

grasilla *f* pounce

gra•so -sa *adj* fatty, greasy || *m* fattiness, greasiness || *f* see **grasa**

grasones *mpl* wheat porridge

graso•so -sa *adj* greasy; (pathol) fatty

grata *f* wire brush; (*carta*) favor

gratificar §73 *tr* to gratify; reward, recompense; tip, fee

gratín *m* **— al gratín** au gratin

gratis *adv* gratis

gratisda•to -ta *adj* free, gratis

gratitud *f* gratitude

gra•to -ta *adj* pleasing; free; (Bol, Chile) grateful || *f* see **grata**

gratuidad *f* cost exemption; exemption from fees
gratui•to -ta *adj* gratuitous; free, gratis
grava *f* gravel; crushed stone
gravamen *m* burden, obligation; encumbrance, lien; assessment
gravar *tr* to burden, encumber; assess || *ref* to get worse
grave *adj* grave, serious, solemn; hard, difficult; (*que pesa*) heavy; (*sonido*) grave, deep, low; (*música*) majestic, noble; (*negocio*) important; (*enfermedad*) serious; (*acento*) grave; paroxytone
gravedad *f* gravity; seriousness; **de gravedad** seriously; gravely; **gravedad nula** weightlessness, zero gravity
gravedo•so -sa *adj* heavy, pompous
gravidez *f* pregnancy
grávi•do -da *adj* pregnant
gravitación *f* gravitation
gravitar *intr* to gravitate; **gravitar sobre** to weigh down on
gravo•so -sa *adj* burdensome, onerous, costly; boring, tiresome
graznar *intr* to caw, croak; cackle; (*al cantar*) (fig) cackle
graznido *m* caw, croak; cackle; (*canto que disuena mucho*) (fig) cackle
Grecia *f* Greece
grecia•no -na *adj* Grecian
gre•co -ca *adj & mf* Greek
greda *f* clay, fuller's earth
grega•rio -ria *adj* (*que vive confundido con otros*) gregarious; slavish, servile
gregoria•no -na *adj* Gregorian
gremial *adj* guild; trade-union, union || *m* guildsman; union member
gremio *m* guild, corporation; trade union, union; association, society
greña *f* confusion, entanglement; (*de cabello*) shock, tangled mop; **andar a la greña** to get into a hot argument; (*dos mujeres*) to pull each other's hair
greñu•do -da *adj* bushy-headed, shock-headed
gres *m* sandstone; stoneware
gresca *f* tumult, uproar; row, quarrel
grey *f* (*de ganado menor*) flock; group, party; nation, people; (*de fieles*) flock, congregation
grie•go -ga *adj* Greek || *mf* Greek || *m* (*idioma*) Greek; **hablar en griego** to not make sense
grieta *f* crack, crevice, chink; (*en la piel*) chap
grieta•do -da *adj* crackled || *m* crackleware
grietar *ref* to crack, split; (*la piel*) become chapped
gri•fo -fa *adj* (*pelo*) kinky, tangled; (*letra*) script; (W-I) colored; (Mex) drunk; (Col) conceited || *mf* (W-I) person of color; (Mex) drunk || *m* faucet, spigot, tap, cock; (myth) griffin; (Peru) gas station, (Mex) marijuana || *f* (Mex) marijuana
gril *m* grill, grillroom
grilla *f* female cricket; (rad) grid; (Col) fight, quarrel; (SAm) annoyance, bother; **¡ésa es grilla!** (coll) you expect me to believe that!
grillar *intr* (*el grillo*) to chirp || *ref* (*las semillas, bulbos, etc.*) to sprout
grillete *m* fetter, shackle
grillo *m* (*insecto*) cricket; (*brote tierno*) sprout, shoot; **grillos** fetters, shackles
grima *f* fright, horror; **dar grima** to grate on the nerves
grin•go -ga *mf* (disparaging) foreigner; (*anglosajón*) gringo; (SAm) blond or fair-haired person || *m* gibberish; **hablar en gringo** to talk nonsense
griñón *m* (*toca de monja*) wimple; (*melocotón*) nectarine
gripe *f* grippe, flu
gris *adj* gray; dull, gloomy || *m* gray; **hacer gris** (*el tiempo*) to be sharp, be brisk
grisáce•o -a *adj* grayish
gri•sú *m* (*pl* **-súes**) firedamp
grita *f* shouting; hubbub, uproar; **dar grita a** to hoot at
gritar *intr* to shout, cry out
gritería *f* shouting, outcry, uproar
grito *m* cry, shout; scream, shriek; **el Grito de Independencia** (hist) the declaration of Independence in some Latin American countries; **el último grito** the latest thing, all the rage; **poner el grito en el cielo** to raise the roof, scream wildly
gro. *abbr* **género**
Groenlandia *f* Greenland
grosella *f* currant; **grosella silvestre** gooseberry
grosellero *m* currant bush; **grosellero silvestre** gooseberry bush
grosería *f* grossness, coarseness; churlishness, rudeness; stupidity; vulgarity
grose•ro -ra *adj* gross, coarse; churlish, rude; stupid; vulgar || *mf* churl, boor
grosor *m* thickness, bulk
grosura *f* fat, suet, tallow; meat diet; coarseness, vulgarity
grotes•co -ca *adj* grotesque
grúa *f* crane, derrick; **grúa de bote** (naut) davit; **grúa de auxilio** wrecking crane; **grúa de caballete** gantry crane
grúa-remolque *m* tow truck
grue•so -sa *adj* big, thick, bulky, heavy; coarse, ordinary; stout, fat; (*mar*) rough, heavy; **en grueso** in gross, in bulk || *f* (*doce docenas*) gross
grulla *f* (orn) crane
grumete *m* ship's boy, cabin boy
grumo *m* clot, curd; bunch, cluster
grumo•so -sa *adj* clotty, curdly
gruñido *m* (*de cerdo*) grunt; (*de perro cuando amenaza*) growl; (*de persona*) grumble; (*de puerta*) creak; grumble, scolding
gruñir §12 *intr* (*el cerdo*) to grunt; (*el perro*) growl; (*una persona*) grumble; (*una puerta*) creak
gru•ñón -ñona *adj* grumpy, grumbly || *mf* crosspatch

grupa *f* croup, rump
grupada *f* squall
grupal *adj* group
grupo *m* group; (mach & elec) unit; **grupo de interés** *or* **presión** pressure group; **grupo electrógeno** generator; **grupo sanguíneo** blood group
grupúsculo *m* splinter group
gruta *f* grotto
grutes•co -ca *adj & m* (fa) grotesque
Gruyère *m* Swiss cheese
gte. *abbr* **gerente**
guaca *f* (Bol, Peru) Indian tomb; hidden treasure
guacal *m* crate
guacama•yo -ya *adj* (P-R) flashy, sporty || *m* macaw
guachapear *tr* to splash with the feet; bungle, botch || *intr* to clank, clatter
guachinan•go -ga *adj* flattering, sly || *mf* (disparaging term used by Cubans) Mexican
gua•cho -cha *adj* (SAm) homeless, orphan; (SAm) odd, unmatched
guadal *m* bog, swamp; sand hill, dune
Guadalupe *f* Gaudeloupe
guadama•cí *m* (*pl* **-cíes**) embossed leather
guadaña *f* scythe
guadañadora *f* mowing machine
guadañar *tr* to cut with a scythe
guadarnés *m* harness room; harness man
guagua *f* trifle; (SAm) baby; (W-I) bus; (Col) paca
guagüita *f* (Cuba, P-R) station wagon
guajada *f* (Mex) nonsense, folly
guaje *adj* (Hond, Mex) foolish, stupid || *m* (Hond, Mex) calabash, gourd; (CAm) piece of junk
guaji•ro -ra *mf* (W-I) peasant, yokel
guajolote *m* turkey; (Mex) simpleton
gualda *f* (bot) weld, dyer's rocket
gual•do -da *adj* yellow || *f* see **gualda**
gualdrapa *f* housing, trappings; dirty rag hanging from clothes
gualdrapear *tr* to line up head to tail || *intr* (*las velas*) to flap
Gualterio *m* Walter
guanaco *m* (SAm) dope, simpleton; (SAm) tall lanky fellow; (zool) guanaco
guanajo *m* (W-I) boob, dunce
guano *m* palm tree; bird manure
guante *m* glove; **arrojar el guante** to throw down the gauntlet; **echar un guante** to pass the hat; **guantes** tip, fee; **guantes de boxeo** boxing gloves; **guantes de cirujano** surgical gloves; **recoger el guante** to take up the gauntlet; **salvo el guante** excuse my glove
guantelete *m* gauntlet
guantería *f* glove shop
guantón *m* box on the ear
guapear *intr* to bluster, swagger; dress to kill
guape•tón -tona *adj* handsome; flashy, sporty; bold, fearless || *m* bully, tough
guapeza *f* good looks; flashiness, sportiness; (coll) boldness, daring; bravado
gua•po -pa *adj* handsome, good-looking; flashy, sporty; bold, daring || *m* (*hombre pendenciero*) bully; gallant, ladies' man
guapura *f* good looks
guarache *m* (Mex) leather sandal; (Mex) tire patch
guarapo *m* sugar-cane juice; fermented juice of sugar cane
guarda *mf* guard, custodian; security guard; **guarda jurado o jurada** security guard || *m* (Arg) trolley-car conductor; **guarda de la aduana** customhouse officer; **guarda forestal** forest ranger || *f* guard, custody; (*de la ley*) observance; (*de la espada*) guard; (*de la cerradura*) ward; (bb) flyleaf
guardabarrera *mf* (rr) gatekeeper
guardaba•rros *m* (*pl* **-rros**) fender, mudguard, dashboard
guardabosque *m* gamekeeper; forest ranger
guardabrisa *m* windshield; (naut) glass candle shade
guardacantón *m* spur stone
guardacarril *m* (rr) railguard
guardacar•tas *m* (*pl* **-tas**) letter file
guardaco•ches *m* (*pl* **-ches**) car watcher
guardacos•tas *m* (*pl* **-tas**) revenue cutter, coast guard cutter; **guardacostas** *mpl* (*servicio*) coast guard
guarda•dor -dora *adj* guarding, protecting; mindful, observant; stingy || *m* guardian, keeper; observer
guardaespal•das *m* (*pl* **-das**) bodyguard
guardafango *m* fender, mudguard
guardafre•nos *m* (*pl* **-nos**) (rr) brakeman, flagman
guardafuego *m* fender, fireguard
guardagu•jas *m* (*pl* **-jas**) (rr) switchman
guardajo•yas *m* (*pl* **-yas**) jewel case
guardalado *m* railing, parapet
guardalmacén *m* warehouseman; (Cuba) country station master
guardamalleta *f* valance
guardameta *m* goalkeeper
guardamue•bles *m* (*pl* **-bles**) warehouse, furniture warehouse
guardanieve *m* snowshed
guardapelo *m* locket
guardapolvo *m* (*sobretodo ligero*) duster; (*resguardo para preservar del polvo*) cover, cloth; (*del reloj*) inner lid; (*sobre una puerta o ventana*) hood
guardapuerta *f* storm door
guardar *tr* to guard; watch over; protect; put away; show, observe; save, e.g., **¡Dios guarde a la Reina!** God save the Queen! || *intr* to keep, save; **¡guarda!** look out!, watch out! || *ref* to be on one's guard; **guardarse de** to look out for, watch out for, guard against
guardarraya *f* (CAm, W-I) boundary line, property line
guardarropa *mf* keeper of the wardrobe || *m* (*armario donde se guarda la ropa*) wardrobe; (*local destinado a la custodia de ropa en es-*

tablecimientos públicos) checkroom, cloakroom; check boy || *f* check girl, hat girl
guardarropía *f* (theat) wardrobe
guardasilla *f* chair rail
guardaventana *f* storm window
guardavía *m* (rr) trackwalker, lineman
guardavida *m* lifeguard
guardavien•tos *m* (*pl* **-tos**) (*abrigo contra los vientos*) windbreak; (*mitra de chimenea*) chimney pot
guardavivo *m* bead, corner bead
guardería *f* guard, guardship; **guardería infantil** day nursery
guardesa *f* woman guard
guardia *m* guard, guardsman; **guardia civil** rural policeman; **guardia marina** midshipman, middy; **guardia tumbado** (Esp) speed bump; **guardia urbano** policeman || *f* (*cuerpo de hombres armados; manera de defenderse en la esgrima*) guard; (naut) watch; **de guardia** on duty; on guard; **guardia civil** rural police; **guardia de asalto** shock troops; **guardia de corps** (mil) bodyguard; **guardia de cuartillo** (naut) dogwatch; **guardia suiza** Swiss Guards
guar•dián -diana *mf* guardian || *m* watchman
guardilla *f* attic; attic room
guardo•so -sa *adj* careful, neat, tidy; (*que ahorra mucho*) thrifty; (*mezquino*) stingy
guarecer §22 *tr* to take in, give shelter to; keep, preserve; (*a un enfermo*) treat || *ref* to take refuge, take shelter
guarida *f* den, lair; shelter; haunt, hangout, hideout
guarismo *m* cipher, figure
guarnecer §22 *tr* to trim, adorn; equip, provide; bind, edge; (*joyas*) set; stucco, plaster; (*frenos*) line; (*un cojinete*) bush; (*una plaza fuerte*) man, garrison; (culin) garnish
guarnición *f* trimming; equipping; binding, edging; (*de joyas*) setting; stuccoing, plastering; (*de la espada*) guard; (*de frenos*) lining; (*del émbolo*) packing; (*tropa que guarnece un lugar*) garrison; (culin) garnish; **guarniciones** fixtures, fittings; (*de la caballería*) harness
guarnicionar *tr* to garrison
guarnicionero *m* harness maker
guaro *m* (CAm) sugar-cane liquor
gua•rro -rra *mf* hog
guasa *f* heaviness, churlishness; joking, kidding
guasca *f* rawhide; whip; **dar guasca a** to whip, thrash
guasería *f* (SAm) coarseness, crudity; (Chile) timidity
gua•so -sa *adj* (SAm) coarse, crude, uncouth || *mf* (Chile) peasant || *f* see **guasa**
gua•són -sona *adj* heavy, churlish; funny, comical || *mf* dullard, churl; joker, kidder
guata *f* wadding, padding; (Arg, Chile, Peru) belly, paunch; (*de una pared*) (Chile) bulging, warping; (Ecuad) boon companion; **echar guata** (Chile) to prosper
guatemalte•co -ca *adj & mf* Guatemalan
guáter *m* toilet, water closet
guau *m* (*ladrido del perro*) bowwow; (bot) woodbine, Virginia creeper; **guau guau** (*perro*) bowwow || *interj* bowwow!
guay *interj* — **¡guay de mí!** (poet) woe is me!
guayaba *f* guava, guava apple
guayabo *m* guava tree; lie, trick; (Col) hangover
guayaco *m* lignum vitae
Guayana *f* Guyana
gubernamental *adj* governmental; (*defensor*) strong-government
gubernati•vo -va *adj* governmental
gubia *f* gouge
guedeja *f* shock of hair; lion's mane
guerra *f* war, warfare; billiards; **guerra a muerte** war to the death; **guerra bacteriana** *or* **bacteriológica** germ warfare, biological warfare; **guerra civil** civil war; **guerra comercial** trade war; **guerra de almohadas** (Arg, Chile) pillow fight; **guerra de desgaste** war of attrition; **guerra de guerrillas** guerrilla warfare; **guerra de las dos Rosas** War of the Roses; **guerra de los Cien Años** Hundred Years' War; **guerra del Transvaal** Boer War; **guerra de ondas** radio jamming; **guerra de nervios** war of nerves; **guerra de precios** price war; **Guerra de Secesión** American Civil War; **guerra de trincheras** trench warfare; **guerra de Troya** Trojan War; **Guerra Fría** cold war; **Guerra Mundial** World War; **guerra nuclear** nuclear war; **guerra química** chemical warfare; **guerra relámpago** blitzkrieg; **hacer la guerra** to wage war
guerrea•dor -dora *adj* warring || *mf* warrior
guerrear *intr* to war, wage war, fight; struggle, resist
guerre•ro -ra *adj* war, warlike; warring; mischievous || *mf* fighter || *m* warrior, soldier, fighting man || *f* tight-fitting military jacket
guerrilla *f* band of skirmishers; guerrilla band; guerrilla warfare
guerrillear *intr* to skirmish; wage guerrilla warfare
guerrillero *m* guerrilla
guía *mf* guide, leader; adviser || *m* (mil) guide || *f* guide; guidance; directory; (*del viajero*) guidebook; (*caballo*) leader; (*de la bicicleta*) handle bar; (*del bigote*) turned-up end; (*de la sierra*) fence; marker; shoot, sprout; (mach) guide; (rr) timetable; **guías** reins; **guía sonora** sound track; **guía telefónica** *or* **de teléfonos** telephone directory; **guía turística** tourist guide
guiadera *f* (mach) guide
guiar §77 *tr* to guide, lead; (*un automóvil*) steer, drive; pilot; (*una planta, una vid*) train || *intr* to shoot, sprout || *ref* — **guiarse por** to be guided by, go by
guija *f* pebble; grass pea
guijarro *m* cobble, cobblestone
guije•ño -ña *adj* pebbly; hard-hearted

guijo *m* gravel
guijo•so -sa *adj* gravelly; pebbly
güila *f* (Mex) prostitute
guillame *m* rabbet plane
Guillermo *m* William
guillotina *f* guillotine; paper cutter
guillotinar *tr* to guillotine
guimbalete *m* pump handle
guinche *m* or **güinche** *m* (mach) crane
guinda *f* sour cherry
guindal *m* sour cherry tree
guindaleza *f* (naut) hawser
guindar *tr* to hoist, raise; win; (*ahorcar*) hang, string up
guindilla *m* policeman, cop; Guinea pepper
guindo *m* sour cherry tree
guindola *f* (naut) boatswain's chair; (naut) life buoy
guinea *f* (*moneda*) guinea
guineo *m* small banana
guinga *f* gingham
guiña *f* (Col, Ven) bad luck
guiñada *f* wink; (naut) yaw
guiñapo *m* rag, tatter; ragamuffin
guiñar *tr* (*el ojo*) to wink || *intr* to wink; (naut) to yaw || *ref* to wink at each other
guiño *m* wink; **hacer guiños a** to make eyes at; **hacerse guiños a** to make faces at each other
guión *m* banner, standard; cross (*carried before prelate in procession*); (*signo ortográfico*) hyphen; (*signo ortográfico largo*) dash; (mil) guidon; (mov & theat) scenario; (rad & telv) script; (mus) repeat sign; **guión de montaje** (mov) cutter's script; **guión de rodaje** (mov) shooting script
guionista *mf* (mov) scenarist; (mov) scriptwriter; (mov) subtitle writer
guirigay *m* gibberish; confusion, hubbub
guirindola *f* frill, jabot
guirlache *m* almond brittle, peanut brittle
guirnalda *f* garland, wreath
guisa *f* way, manner, wise; **a guisa de** in the manner of, like
guisado *m* stew, meat stew
guisante *m* pea; **guisante de olor** sweet pea
guisar *tr* to cook; stew; arrange, prepare || *intr* to cook
guiso *m* dish
guisote *m* hash
guita *f* twine; (coll) dough, money
guitarra *f* guitar; **guitarra clásica** Spanish guitar
guitarrista *mf* guitarist
gui•tón -tona *mf* tramp, bum
gula *f* gluttony; gorging, guzzling
gulo•so -sa *adj* gluttonous; guzzling
gumía *f* Moorish poniard
gurrumi•no -na *adj* weak, puny || *m* henpecked husband
gusanear *intr* to swarm
gusanera *f* nest of worms; ruling passion
gusanien•to -ta *adj* wormy, grubby
gusanillo *m* small worm; twist stitch; (*de la barrena*) spur; (coll) itch (*to do something*); **matar el gusanillo** (coll) to satisfy a desire or one's curiosity; to have a snack; to take a shot of liquor before breakfast
gusano *m* worm; **gusano de luz** glowworm; **gusano de seda** silk worm; **gusano de tierra** earthworm
gusano•so -sa *adj* wormy, grubby
gusarapo *m* waterworm, vinegar worm
gustación *f* tasting; taste
gustar *tr* to taste; try, sample; please, be pleasing to; like, e.g., **me gustan estas peras** I like these pears || *intr* to like e.g., **como Ud. guste** as you like; **gustar de** to like; like to
gustillo *m* slight taste, touch
gusto *m* taste; flavor; liking; caprice, whim; pleasure; **a gusto** as you like it; **con mucho gusto** with pleasure, gladly; **encontrarse a gusto** *or* **estar a gusto** to like it (*e.g., in the country*); **tanto gusto** so glad to meet you
gusto•so -sa *adj* tasty; agreeable, pleasant; ready, willing, glad
gutapercha *f* gutta-percha
gutural *adj* guttural

H

H, h (hache) *f* eighth letter of the Spanish alphabet
haba *f* bean, broad bean; (*simiente del café y el cacao*) bean; **ser habas contadas** to be a sure thing
Habana, La Havana
haber *m* salary, wages; credit, credit side; **haberes** property, wealth || *v* **§38** *tr* to have; get, get hold of || *v aux* to have, e.g., **lo he visto a menudo** I have seen it often; **haber de** + *inf* to be to + *inf*, e.g., **ha de llegar a mediodía** he is to arrive at noon || *v impers* there to be, e.g., **ha habido tres personas allí** there were three people there; **haber que** + *inf* to be necessary to + *inf;* **no hay de qué** you're welcome, don't mention it || *ref* to behave oneself; **habérselas con** to deal with; to have it out with
habichuela *f* kidney bean; **habichuela verde** string bean, green bean
hábil *adj* skillful, capable; (*día*) work
habilidad *f* skill, ability, capability; (*lo que se ejecuta con gracia*) feat; (*enredo, embuste*) scheme, trick

habilido•so -sa *adj* skillful
habilitación *f* qualification; backing, financing; equipping, outfitting; **habilitaciones** fixtures
habilitar *tr* to qualify; back, finance; equip, fit out; (*en un examen*) pass
habitabilidad *f* habitability; (aut) interior (space)
habitable *adj* inhabitable
habitación *f* habitation; (*edificio donde se habita*) house, home, dwelling; (*aposento de la casa o el hotel*) room; (*donde vive una especie vegetal o animal*) habitat
habitante *mf* (*de una casa*) dweller, occupant; (*de una población*) inhabitant
habitar *tr* to inhabit, live in; (*una casa, un piso*) occupy ‖ *intr* to live
hábitat *m* habitat
hábito *m* garment, dress; habit, custom; **ahorcar los hábitos** to doff the cassock, to leave the priesthood; to change jobs; **el hábito no hace al monje** clothes don't make the man
habitua•do -da *mf* habitué
habitual *adj* habitual; regular, usual
habituar §21 *tr* to accustom ‖ *ref* to become accustomed
habitud *f* relationship, connection; custom, habit
habla *f* speech; **al habla** speaking
hablada *f* talk, talking
habla•dor -dora *adj* talkative; gossipy ‖ *mf* talker, chatterbox; gossip
habladuría *f* cut, sarcasm; **andar con habladurías** to go around gossiping; **habladurías** hearsay
hablante *adj* speaking ‖ *mf* speaker
hablar *tr* (*una lengua*) to speak, talk; (*disparates*) talk ‖ *intr* to speak, talk; **es hablar por demás** it's wasted talk; **estar hablando** (*una pintura, una estatua*) to be almost alive; **hablar claro** to talk straight from the shoulder; **hablar por señas** to talk in sign language
hablilla *f* story, piece of gossip
hablista *mf* speaker, good speaker
hacede•ro -ra *adj* feasible, practicable
hacenda•do -da *adj* landed, property-owning ‖ *mf* landholder, property owner; cattle rancher; plantation owner
hacendar §2 *tr* (*el dominio de bienes raíces*) to pass on ‖ *ref* to buy property in order to settle down
hacende•ro -ra *adj* thrifty
hacendista *m* economist, fiscal expert; man of independent means
hacendo•so -sa *adj* hard-working, thrifty
hacer §39 *tr* (*crear, producir, formar*) to make; (*ejecutar, llevar a cabo*) do; (*un baúl*) pack; (*un papel*) play; (*un mandato*) give; (*un drama*) act, perform; pretend to be; (*una pregunta*) ask; **hace** ago, e.g., **hace un mes** a month ago; **hacer** + *inf* to have + *inf*, e.g., **le hice tomar un libro en la biblioteca** I had him get a book at the library; to make + *inf*, e.g., **el médico me hizo guardar cama** the doctor made me stay in bed; to have + *pp*, e.g., **hará construir una casa** he will have a house built; **hacer . . . que** to be . . . since, e.g., **hace un año que yo estuve aquí** it is a year since I was here; to be for . . . , e.g., **hace un año que estoy aquí** I have been here for a year; for expressions like **hacer frío** to be cold, see the noun ‖ *intr* to act; **hacer a** to fit; **hacer al caso** (coll) to be to the purpose; **hacer como que** + *ind* to pretend to + *inf;* **hacer de** to act as, work as; **hacer por** to try to ‖ *ref* to become, get to be, grow; **hacerse a** to become accustomed to; **hacerse a un lado** to step aside; **hacerse con** to make off with; **hacerse chiquito** to sing small; **hacérsele a uno difícil** to strike one as difficult; **hacerse viejo** to grow old; kill time
hacha *f* axe; (*hacha pequeña*) hatchet; torch, firebrand; four-wick wax candle; **hacha de armas** battleaxe
hachazo *m* blow with an axe
hachear *tr & intr* to hew, hack, or chop with an axe
hachero *m* torchbearer; (*candelero*) torch stand; (*leñador*) woodcutter
hachich *m* or **hachís** *m* hashish
hacho *m* torch; (*sitio elevado cerca de la costa*) beacon, beacon hill
hacia *prep* toward; (*cierta hora o época*) about, near; **hacia abajo** downward; **hacia adelante** forward; **hacia arriba** upward; **hacia atrás** backward; the wrong way; **hacia dentro** inward; **hacia fuera** outward
hacienda *f* farmstead, landed estate, country property; property, possessions; ranch; (Arg) cattle, livestock; **hacienda pública** public finance, federal income; **haciendas** household chores
hacina *f* pile, heap; shock, stack
hacinar *tr* to pile, heap, stack
hada *f* fairy; (*mujer que encanta por su belleza, gracia, etc.*) charmer; **hada madrina** fairy godmother
hadar *tr* (*determinar el hado*) to predestine, foreordain; (*pronosticar*) to foretell; (*encantar*) to charm, cast a spell on
hado *m* fate, destiny
haiga *m* (slang) flashy auto; (slang) sport
halagar §44 *tr* (*lisonjear*) to flatter; (*demostrar cariño a*) cajole, fawn on; (*agradar*) gratify, please
halago *m* flattery; cajolery; gratification; **halagos** flattery, blandishments
halagüe•ño -ña *adj* flattering; fawning; gratifying, pleasing; bright, rosy, promising
halar *tr* (naut) to haul, pull
halcón *m* falcon
halconear *intr* (*la mujer*) to chase after men
halconería *f* falconry
halconero *m* falconer
halda *f* skirt; **poner haldas en cinta** to pull up one's skirts to run; roll up one's sleeves
halieto *m* fish hawk, osprey

hálito *m* breath; vapor; (poet) gentle breeze
halitosis *f* halitosis
hallar *tr* to find; (*averiguar*) find out, discover || *ref* to find oneself; to be; **hallarse bien con** to be satisfied with; **hallárselo todo hecho** to never have to turn a hand; **no hallarse** to feel uncomfortable, not like it
hallazgo *m* (*cosa hallada*) find; (*acción de hallar*) finding, discovery; (*premio al que ha hallado una cosa perdida*) reward, finder's reward, e.g., **diez dólares de hallazgo** ten dollars reward
hallulla *f* bread baked on embers or hot stones; (Chile) fine bread
halo *m* halo
haló *interj* (*teléfono*) hello!
halógeno *m* halogen
haltera *f* barbell
halterio *m* dumbbell
halterofilia *f* weightlifting
halterofilista *mf* weight lifter
haluro *m* halide
hamaca *f* hammock
hamamelina *f* witch hazel
hambre *f* hunger; (*escasez general de comestibles*) famine; **matar de hambre** to starve to death; **morir de hambre** to starve to death, die of starvation; **pasar hambre** to go hungry; **tener hambre** to be hungry
hambrear *tr & intr* to starve, famish
hambrien•to -ta *adj* hungry, starving
hambruna *f* (SAm) mad hunger; (Ecuad) starvation
hamburguesa *f* hamburger
hamo *m* fishhook
hampa *f* underworld life; denizens of the underworld
hampes•co -ca *adj* underworld
hampón *m* bully, tough
hangar *m* (aer) hangar
hara•gán -gana *adj* idling, loafing, lazy || *mf* idler, loafer
haraganear *intr* to idle, loaf, hang around
harapien•to -ta *adj* ragged, tattered
harapo *m* rag, tatter; **andar** *or* **estar hecho un harapo** (coll) to go around in rags
harapo•so -sa *adj* ragged, tattered
hardware [ˋxardwer] *m* (compu) hardware
harén *m* harem
harina *f* (*especialmente del trigo*) flour; (*de cualquier grano*) meal; **estar metido en harina** to be deeply absorbed; to be fat and heavy; **harina de avena** oatmeal; **harina de maíz** cornmeal; **harina integral** whole-wheat flour; **ser harina de otro costal** to be a horse of another color
harine•ro -ra *adj* flour || *m* flour dealer; flour bin
harino•so -sa *adj* floury, mealy
harnear *tr* (Col, Chile) to sift
harnero *m* sieve
ha•rón -rona *adj* lazy || *mf* lazy loafer
harpillera *f* burlap, sackcloth
hartar *tr* to stuff, cram; satisfy, satiate; tire, bore; overwhelm, deluge || *intr* to have one's fill || *ref* to stuff; be satiated; tire, be bored
hartazgo *m* or **hartazón** *m* fill, bellyful; **darse un hartazgo** to eat one's fill; **darse un hartazgo de** to have or to get one's fill of
har•to -ta *adj* full, fed up; very much; **harto de** full of, fed up with, sick of || **harto** *adv* enough; very, quite
hartura *f* fill, satiety; full satisfaction; abundance
hasta *adv* even || *prep* until, till; to, as far as; down to, up to; as much as; **hasta ahora** up till now; **hasta aquí** so far; **hasta después** so long, good-by; **hasta la vista** *or* **hasta luego** so long, good-by; **hasta mañana** see you tomorrow; **hasta más no poder** to the utmost; **hasta no más** to the utmost; **hasta que** until, till
hastial *m* gable end; (*hombrón rústico*) bumpkin
hastiar §77 *tr* to surfeit, sicken, cloy; (*fastidiar*) bother, annoy, bore
hastío *m* surfeit, loathing, disgust; bother, annoyance, boredom
hataca *f* large wooden ladle; (*cilindro para extender la masa*) rolling pin
hatajo *m* small herd, small flock; (*p.ej., de disparates*) lot, flock
hato *m* (*de ganado vacuno*) herd; (*de ovejas*) flock; (*de ropa*) pack, bundle; (*de gente*) clique, ring; (*de gente malvada*) gang; everyday outfit; (*de disparates*) flock, lot; cattle ranch; **liar el hato** to pack up, pack one's baggage; **revolver el hato** to stir up trouble
Hawai *m* Hawaii
hawaia•no -na *adj & mf* Hawaiian || *m* (*idioma*) Hawaiian
haya *f* beech tree; (*madera*) beech || **La Haya** The Hague
hayaca *f* (Ven) mince pie
hayo *m* (Col) coca; (Col) coca leaves (*mixed for chewing*)
hayuco *m* beechnut, mast
haz *m* (*pl* **haces**) bunch, bundle; (*de leña*) fagot; (*de mieses*) sheaf; (*de rayos*) beam, pencil; (*de soldados*) file || *f* (*pl* **haces**) face; (*de la tierra*) surface; (*de paño o tela*) right side; (*de un edificio*) façade, front; **a sobre haz** on the surface; **ser de dos haces** to be two-faced
hazaña *f* feat, exploit, deed
hazañería *f* fuss
hazañe•ro -ra *adj* fussy
hazaño•so -sa *adj* gallant, courageous
hazmerreír *m* laughingstock, butt
he *adv* behold, lo and behold; **he aquí** here is, here are; **he allí** there is, there are
hebilla *f* buckle
hebra *f* thread; fiber; (*en la madera*) grain; (*del discurso*) (fig) thread; **de una hebra** (Chile) all at once; **pegar la hebra** to strike up a conversation; to keep on talking

hebre•o -a *adj & mf* Hebrew || *m* (*idioma*) Hebrew
hebro•so -sa *adj* fibrous, stringy
hecatombe *f* hecatomb
hechicera *f* witch, sorceress; (*mujer que por su belleza cautiva*) enchantress
hechicería *f* witchcraft, sorcery, wizardry; (fig) fascination, charm
hechice•ro -ra *adj* bewitching, charming, enchanting; magic || *mf* sorcerer, magician; charmer, enchanter || *m* wizard, sorcerer || *f* see **hechicera**
hechizar §60 *tr* to bewitch, cast a spell on; (fig) to bewitch, charm, enchant || *intr* to practice sorcery; (fig) to be charming, enchant
hechi•zo -za *adj* fake, artificial; (*de quita y pon*) detachable; made, manufactured; (*producto*) local, home || *m* spell, charm; magic, sorcery; (fig) magic, sorcery, glamour; (fig) charmer; **hechizos** (*de una mujer*) charms
he•cho -cha *adj* accustomed; finished; turned into; (*traje*) ready-made; (*llegado a la edad adulta*) full-grown || *m* act, deed; fact; event; (*hazaña*) feat; **de hecho** in fact; **en hecho de verdad** as a matter of fact; **estar en el hecho de** to catch on to; **hecho consumado** fait accompli || **hecho** *interj* all right!, OK!
hechura *f* form, shape, cut, build; creation, creature; workmanship; (Chile) drink, treat; **hechuras** cost of making; **no tener hechura** to be impracticable
hectárea *f* hectare (*surface measurement: 2.47 acres*)
heder §51 *tr* to bore, annoy, tire || *intr* to stink, reek
hediondez *f* stench, stink
hedion•do -da *adj* stinking, smelly; annoying, boring; obscene, filthy, dirty || *m* bean trefoil; skunk
hedor *m* stench, stink
hégira *f* hegira
helada *f* freezing; (*escarcha*) frost; **helada blanca** hoarfrost
heladera *f* refrigerator; (Chile) ice-cream tray
heladería *f* ice-cream parlor
hela•do -da *adj* cold, icy; (*pasmado por el miedo, la sorpresa, etc.*) frozen; (*esquivo, indiferente*) cold, chilly; (*cubierto de azúcar*) (Ven) iced || *m* cold drink; (*sorbete*) ice cream; **helado al corte** brick ice cream; **helado de agua** water ice || *f* see **helada**
hela•dor -dora *adj* freezing || *f* ice-cream freezer
helar §2 *tr* to freeze; harden, congeal; dumbfound; discourage || *intr* to freeze || *ref* to freeze; harden, congeal, set; (*cubrirse de hielo*) to ice
helecho *m* fern
heléni•co -ca *adj* Hellenic
hele•no -na *adj* Hellenic || *mf* Hellene
helero *m* glacier
hélice *f* helix; (*de un buque*) screw, propeller; (*de un avión*) propeller
helicóptero *m* helicopter
helio *m* helium
heliotropo *m* heliotrope
helipuerto *m* heliport
hematíe *m* red cell
hembra *adj invar* (*animal, planta, herramienta*) female; weak, thin, delicate || *f* female; (*del corchete*) eye; (*tuerca*) nut; **hembra de terraja** (mach) die
hembraje *m* (SAm) females of a flock or herd
hembrilla *f* (mach) female part or piece; (*armella*) eyebolt
hemeroteca *f* periodical library
hemiciclo *m* (*semicírculo*) hemicycle; (*gradería semicircular*) amphitheater; (*espacio central del salón de sesiones de las Cortes*) floor
hemisferio *m* hemisphere
hemistiquio *m* hemistich
hemofilia *f* hemophilia
hemoglobina *f* hemoglobin
hemorragia *f* hemorrhage
hemorroides *fpl* hemorrhoids
hemóstato *m* hemostat
henal *m* hayloft
henar *m* hayfield
henchir §50 *tr* to fill; (*un colchón*) stuff; (*a una persona, p.ej., de favores*) heap, shower || *ref* to be filled; stuff, stuff oneself
hendedura *f* crack, split, cleft
hender §51 *tr* to crack, split, cleave; (*el aire, las ondas*) cleave; make one's way through || *ref* to crack, split
hendidura *f* crack, split, cleft
henil *m* hayloft, haymow
henna *f* henna
heno *m* hay
heñir §72 *tr* to knead; **hay mucho que heñir** there's still a lot of work to do
hepatitis *f* hepatitis
heraldía *f* heraldry
heráldi•co -ca *adj* heraldic || *f* heraldry
heraldo *m* herald
herbáce•o -a *adj* herbaceous
herbajar *tr & intr* to graze
herbaje *m* herbage
herba•rio -ria *adj* herbal || *m* (*libro*) herbal; (*colección*) herbarium
herbicida *m* weed killer
herbo•so -sa *adj* grassy
hercúle•o -a *adj* herculean
heredad *f* country estate
heredar *tr & intr* to inherit; **heredar a** to inherit from
herede•ro -ra *mf* heir, inheritor; owner of an estate; **heredero forzoso** heir apparent || *m* heir || *f* heiress
heredita•rio -ria *adj* hereditary
hereje *mf* heretic
herejía *f* heresy; insult, outrage; outrageous price
herencia *f* heritage, inheritance; (*transmisión de caracteres biológicos*) heredity; (*patrimonio de un difunto*) estate

heréti•co -ca *adj* heretic(al)
herida *f* injury, wound; insult, outrage; **renovar la herida** to open an old sore; **tocar en la herida** to sting to the quick
heri•do -da *adj* hurt, wounded; (*ofendido*) hurt || *mf* injured person, wounded person; **los heridos** the injured, the wounded || *f* see **herida**
herir §68 *tr* to injure, hurt, wound; (*ofender*) hurt; (*golpear*) strike; (*el sol sobre*) beat down upon; (*un instrumento de cuerda*) play; (*la cuerda de un instrumento*) pluck; touch, move
hermana *f* sister; **hermana de leche** foster sister; **hermana gemela** twin sister; **hermana política** sister-in-law; **media hermana** half sister
hermanar *tr* to match, mate; combine, join; harmonize || *ref* to match; become attached as brothers or sisters or brother and sister
hermanastra *f* stepsister; half sister
hermanastro *m* stepbrother; half brother
hermandad *f* brotherhood; sisterhood; close friendship; close relationship
hermanita *f* (coll) sis
herma•no -na *adj* (*p.ej., idioma*) sister || *mf* companion, mate || *m* brother; **el Gran Hermano** Big Brother; **hermano de leche** foster brother; **hermano de sangre** blood brother; **hermano gemelo** twin brother; **hermano político** brother-in-law; **hermanos** brother and sister; brothers and sisters; **hermanos siameses** Siamese twins; **medio hermano** half brother; **primo hermano** first cousin || *f* see **hermana**
herméti•co -ca *adj* hermetic(al); air-tight; impenetrable; tight-lipped
hermosear *tr* to beautify, embellish
hermo•so -sa *adj* beautiful; (*caballero*) handsome
hermosura *f* beauty; (*mujer hermosa*) belle, beauty
hernia *f* hernia; **hernia de disco** slipped disc
héroe *m* hero
heroi•co -ca *adj* heroic; (*remedio*) desperate
heroína *f* heroine; (pharm) heroin
heroinómano *m* heroin addict
heroísmo *m* heroism
herrada *f* wooden bucket
herrador *m* horseshoer
herradura *f* horseshoe; **mostrar las herraduras** (*un caballo*) to kick, be vicious; (coll) to show one's heels
herraje *m* hardware, ironwork
herramental *adj* tool || *m* toolbox, tool bag
herramienta *f* tool; set of tools; (coll) teeth; (coll) horns; **herramienta de autor** (compu) authoring tool; **herramienta de desarrollo** (compu) development tool
herrar §2 *tr* (*guarnecer con hierro*) to fit with hardware; (*un caballo*) to shoe; (*marcar con hierro candente*) to brand; (*un barril*) to hoop
herrería *f* forge, blacksmith shop; blacksmithing; ironworks; rumpus
herrero *m* blacksmith; **herrero de grueso** ironworker; **herrero de obra** steelworker
herrete *m* tip, metal tip
herretear *tr* to tip, put a metal tip on
herrín *m* rust
herón *m* (*tejo de hierro horadado*) quoit; (*arandela*) washer
herrumbre *f* rust; (*honguillo parásito*) rust, plant rot
herrumbro•so -sa *adj* rusty
herventar §2 *tr* to boil
hervidero *m* boiling; bubbling spring; (*en el pecho*) rattle; (*de gente*) swarm
hervidor *m* boiler, cooker
hervir §68 *intr* to boil; (*el mar; una persona encolerizada*) boil, seethe; swarm, teem
hervor *m* boil, boiling; (*de la juventud*) fire, restlessness; **alzar el hervor** to begin to boil
hervoro•so -sa *adj* ardent, fiery, impetuous
heterócli•to -ta *adj* irregular; unconventional
heterodinar *tr* to heterodyne
heterodi•no -na *adj* heterodyne
heterodo•xo -xa *adj* heterodox
heterogeneidad *f* heterogeneity
heterogéne•o -a *adj* heterogeneous
heterosexual *adj & mf* heterosexual
hexámetro *m* hexameter
hez *f* (*pl* **heces**) (fig) scum, dregs; **heces** lees, dregs; feces, excrement
hiato *m* hiatus
hibisco *m* hibiscus
hibridación *f* hybridization
hibridar *tr & intr* to hybridize
híbri•do -da *adj & m* hybrid
hidal•go -ga *adj* noble, illustrious || *m* nobleman || *f* noblewoman
hidalguez *f* or **hidalguía** *f* nobility
hidra *f* hydra
hidratante *adj* moisturing
hidratar *tr & ref* to hydrate; to moisturize
hidrato *m* hydrate
hidráuli•co -ca *adj* hydraulic || *f* hydraulics
hidroala *m* (*vehículo mixto de buque y avión*) hydrofoil
hidroaleta *f* (*miembro alar del hidroala*) hydrofoil
hidroavión *m* hydroplane
hidrocarburo *m* hydrocarbon
hidroeléctri•co -ca *adj* hydroelectric
hidrófi•lo -la *adj* (*algodón*) absorbent (*cotton*)
hidrofobia *f* hydrophobia
hidrófu•go -ga *adj* waterproof
hidrógeno *m* hydrogen
hidropesía *f* dropsy
hidróxido *m* hydroxide
hiedra *f* ivy
hiel *f* bile, gall; (fig) gall, bitterness, sorrow; **echar la hiel** to strain, overwork
hielo *m* ice; (fig) coldness, coolness; **hielo flotante** drift ice, ice pack; **hielo seco** dry ice; **romper el hielo** (*quebrantar la reserva*) to break the ice
hiena *f* hyena

hienda *f* dung
hierba *f* grass; (*especialmente la que tiene propiedades medicinales*) herb; **hierba de la plata** honesty; **hierba del asno** evening primrose; **hierba de París** truelove; **hierba gatera** catnip; **hierba pastel** woad; **hierbas** grass, pasture; herb poison; years of age (*said of animals*); **mala hierba** weed; wayward young fellow
hierbabuena *f* mint
hierro *m* iron; (*marca candente que se pone a los ganados*) brand; **hierro colado** cast iron; **hierro colado en barras** pig iron; **hierro de desecho** scrap iron; **hierro de marcar** branding iron; **hierro dulce** wrought iron; **hierro fundido** cast iron; **hierro galvanizado** galvanized iron; **hierro ondulado** corrugated iron; **hierros** irons, fetters; **llevar hierro a Vizcaya** to carry coals to Newcastle
higa *f* baby's fist-shaped amulet; scorn, contempt; **dar higa** to misfire; **no dar dos higas por** to not give a rap for
hígado *m* liver; **echar los hígados** to strain, to overwork; **hígados** guts, courage; **malos hígados** hatred, grudge; **ser un hígado** to be a nuisance
higiene *f* hygiene
higiéni•co -ca *adj* hygienic
higo *m* fig; **higo chumbo** prickly pear; **higo paso** dried fig; **no valer un higo** to be not worth a continental
higuera *f* fig tree; **higuera chumba** prickly pear
hija *f* daughter; **hija adoptiva** adopted daughter; **hija política** daughter-in-law
hijas•tro -tra *mf* stepchild ‖ *m* stepson ‖ *f* stepdaughter
hi•jo -ja *mf* child; (*de un animal*) young; **hijo de bendición** legitimate child; good child; **hijo de la cuna** foundling; **hijo del amor** love child; **hijo de leche** foster child; **hijo único** only child ‖ *m* son; **cada hijo de vecino** every man Jack, every mother's son; **hijo adoptivo** adopted son; **hijo del agua** good sailor; good swimmer; **hijo de su padre** chip off the old block; **hijo de sus propias obras** self-made man; **hijo político** son-in-law; **hijo pródigo** prodigal son; **hijos** children; descendants ‖ *f* see **hija**
hijodalgo *m* (*pl* **hijosdalgo**) nobleman
hijuela *f* little girl, little daughter; (*tira de tela*) gore; branch drain; side path
hijuelero *m* rural postman
hijuelo *m* shoot, sucker
hila *f* row, line; (*acción de hilar*) spinning; **a la hila** in single file; **hilas** (*hebras para curar heridas*) lint
hilacha *f* shred, fraying; **hilacha de acero** steel wool; **hilacha de algodón** cotton waste; **hilacha de vidrio** spun glass; **hilachas** lint; **mostrar la hilacha** (Arg) to show one's worst side
hilachen•to -ta *adj* tattered; in rags
hilachos *mpl* (Mex) rags, tatters
hilacho•so -sa *adj* frayed, raggedy
hilada *f* row, line; (mas) course
hilado *m* spinning; (*hilo*) yarn, thread
hila•dor -dora *adj* spinning ‖ *mf* spinner ‖ *f* spinning machine
hilandería *f* spinning; spinning mill
hilande•ro -ra *adj* spinning ‖ *m* spinning mill
hilar *tr & intr* to spin; **hilar delgado** to hew close to the line; **hilar largo** to drag on
hilarante *adj* laughable; (*gas*) laughing
hilaza *f* yarn, thread; lint; **descubrir la hilaza** to show one's true nature
hilera *f* row, line; fine thread, fine yarn; (*parhilera*) ridgepole; (mil) file
hilo *m* thread; (*hebras retorcidas*) yarn; (*alambre*) wire; (*de perlas*) string; (*de agua*) thin stream; (*de luz*) beam; linen, linen fabric; (*de un discurso, de la vida*) (fig) thread; **hilo bramante** twine; **hilo de Escocia** lisle; **hilo de la muerte** end of life; **hilo de masa** (aut) ground wire; **hilo de medianoche** midnight sharp; **hilo dental** dental floss; **hilo de sutura** suture; **hilo de tierra** (elec) ground wire; **irse al hilo** or **tras el hilo de la gente** to follow the crowd; **manejar los hilos** to pull strings; **perder el hilo de** to lose the thread of
hilván *m* basting, tacking; basting stitch; (Chile) basting thread; (Ven) hem; **hablar de hilván** to jabber along
hilvanar *tr* to baste, tack; sketch, outline; (*hacer con precipitación*) hurry; (Ven) to hem ‖ *intr* to baste, tack
himnario *m* hymnal, hymn book
himno *m* hymn; **himno nacional** national anthem
him *m* neigh, whinny
hincadura *f* driving, thrusting, sticking
hincapié *m* stamping the foot; emphasis; **hacer hincapié en** to lay great stress on, to emphasize
hincar **§73** *tr* to drive, thrust, stick, sink; (*la rodilla*) go down on, fall on ‖ *ref* to kneel, kneel down; **hincarse de rodillas** to go down on one's knees
hincha *mf* (sport) fan, rooter ‖ *f* grudge, ill will
hinchable *adj* inflatable; (*goma de mascar*) bubble gum
hincha•do -da *adj* swollen; swollen with pride; (*estilo, lenguaje*) pompous, high-flown ‖ *m* (*de un neumático*) inflation ‖ *f* (sport) fans, rooters
hinchar *tr* to swell; inflate; (*un neumático*) pump up; exaggerate, embroider ‖ *ref* to swell; swell up, become puffed up (*with pride*)
hinchazón *f* swelling; vanity, conceit; (*del estilo, lenguaje*) bombast
hinchismo *m* (sport) fans, rooters
hin•dú -dúa (*pl* **-dúes -dúas**) *adj & mf* Hindoo, Hindu
hiniesta *f* Spanish broom
hinojo *m* fennel; **de hinojos** on one's knees
hipar *intr* to hiccup; (*los perros cuando siguen

la caza) pant, snuffle; (*gimotear*) whimper; be worn out; **hipar por** to long for; long to
hiperacidez *f* hyperacidity
hiperactivo *adj* hyperactive
hiperenlace *m* (compu) hyperlink
hiperenlazado *adj* (compu) hyperlinked
hipertexto *m* (compu) hypertext
hipertextual *adj* (compu) hypertext
hipérbola *f* (geom) hyperbola
hipérbole *f* (rhet) hyperbole
hiperbóli•co -ca *adj* (geom & rhet) hyperbolic
hipermétrope *adj* (path) far-sighted
hipersensible *adj* (*alérgico*) hypersensitive
hipertensión *f* hypertension, high blood pressure
hípica *f* (horseback) riding; equestrianism
hípi•co -ca *adj* horse, equine
hipnosis *f* hypnosis
hipnóti•co -ca *adj* hypnotic || *mf* hypnotic || *m* (*medicamento que provoca el sueño*) hypnotic
hipnotismo *m* hypnotism
hipnotista *mf* hypnotist
hipnotizar §60 *tr* to hypnotize
hipo *m* hiccup; longing, desire; **tener hipo contra** to have a grudge against; **tener hipo por** to desire eagerly
hipocondría•co -ca *adj* & *mf* hypochondriac
hipocresía *f* hypocrisy
hipócrita *adj* hypocritical || *mf* hypocrite
hipodérmi•co -ca *adj* hypodermic
hipódromo *m* hippodrome, race track
hipopótamo *m* hippopotamus
hiposulfito *m* hyposulfite
hipoteca *f* mortgage; **¡buena hipoteca!** you may believe it, if you want to!
hipotecar §73 *tr* to mortgage
hipoteca•rio -ria *adj* mortgage
hipotenusa *f* hypotenuse
hipóte•sis *f* (*pl* **-sis**) hypothesis; **hipótesis de guía** working hypothesis
hipotéti•co -ca *adj* hypothetic(al)
hiriente *adj* cutting, stinging
hirsu•to -ta *adj* hairy, bristly; (fig) brusque, gruff
hirviente *adj* boiling
hisopear *tr* to sprinkle with holy water
hisopo *m* (bot) hyssop; aspergillum, sprinkler of holy water; paint brush, shaving brush
hispalense *adj* & *mf* Sevillian
hispáni•co -ca *adj* & *mf* Hispanic
hispanista *mf* Hispanist
hispa•no -na *adj* Spanish; Spanish American || *mf* Spaniard; Spanish American
hispanohablante or **hispanoparlante** *adj* Spanish-speaking || *mf* speaker of Spanish
híspi•do -da *adj* bristly, spiny
histéri•co -ca *adj* hysterical
histerismo *m* hysteria
histología *f* histology
historia *f* history; story, tale; **de historia** notorious, infamous; **dejarse de historias** to come to the point; **historia clínica** medical history; **historia de lagrimitas** (coll) sob story; **historias** gossip, meddling; **historia universal** world history; **pasar a la historia** to become a thing of the past; **picar en historia** to turn out to be serious
historia•do -da *adj* richly adorned; overadorned; (*cuadro, dibujo*) storied
historial *adj* historical || *m* record, dossier; track record; **historical clínico** case history; **historial personal** resumé
historiar §77 & regular *tr* to tell the history of; tell the story of; (*un suceso histórico*) (fa) to depict
históri•co -ca *adj* historic(al)
historieta *f* anecdote, brief story; **historieta gráfica** comic strip
histrión *m* actor; juggler, buffoon
histrióni•co -ca *adj* histrionic
hita *f* brad; landmark, milestone
hi•to -ta *adj* fixed, firm; (*casa, calle*) next; (*caballo*) black || *m* (*clavo fijado en la tierra*) peg, hob; (*juego*) quoits; (*blanco*) target; (*mojón*) landmark, milestone; **dar en el hito** to hit the nail on the head; **mirar de hito en hito** to eye up and down || *f* see **hita**
Hno. *abbr* Hermano
hoba•chón -chona *adj* lumpish
hocicar §73 *tr* to nuzzle, root; keep on kissing || *intr* to nuzzle, root; run into a snag; (*la proa*) (naut) to dip
hocico *m* snout; (*de una persona*) snout; sour face; **caer de hocicos** to fall on one's face; **meter el hocico en todo** to poke one's nose into everything; **poner hocico** to make a face
hogaño *adv* this year; at the present time
hogar *m* fireplace, hearth; furnace; home; family life; (*hoguera*) bonfire
hogare•ño -ña *adj* home-loving || *mf* homebody, stay-at-home
hogaza *f* large loaf of bread
hoguera *f* bonfire
hoja *f* (*de planta, libro, mesa, muelle, puerta plegadiza, etc.; pétalo de flor*) leaf; (*de planta acuática*) pad; (*de papel*) sheet; blank sheet; (*de cuchillo, sierra, espada, etc.*) blade; (*hojuela de metal*) foil; (*de persiana*) slat; (*del patín*) runner; **doblar la hoja** to change the subject; **hoja clínica** clinical chart; **hoja de afeitar** razor blade; **hoja de cálculo** spreadsheet; **hoja de embalaje** packing slip; **hoja de encuadernador** (bb) endpaper; **hoja de estaño** tin foil; **hoja de estudios** transcript; **hoja de guarda** (bb) flyleaf; **hoja del anunciante** tear sheet; **hoja de lata** tin, tin plate; **hoja de nenúfar** lily pad; **hoja de paga** pay roll; **hoja de parra** fig leaf; **hoja de pedidos** order blank; **hoja de rodaje** (mov) shooting record; **hoja de ruta** waybill; **hoja de servicios** service record; **hoja de trébol** cloverleaf (*intersection*); **hoja maestra** master blade (*of spring*); **hojas del autor** (typ) advance sheets; **hoja suelta** leaflet, handbill; (bb) flyleaf; **hoja volante** leaflet, handbill

hojalata *f* tin, tin plate
hojalatería *f* tinsmith's shop; tinwork
hojalatero *m* tinsmith, tinner
hojaldrado *adj* (culin) flaky
hojaldre *m & f* puff paste
hojarasca *f* dead leaves; trash, rubbish; bluff, vain show
hojear *tr* to leaf through ‖ *intr* to scale off; (*las hojas de los árboles*) flutter
hojita *f* leaflet; **hojita de afeitar** razor blade
hojo•so -sa *adj* leafy
hojuela *f* (*hoja de otra compuesta*) leaflet; (*fruta de sartén*) pancake; (*hoja muy delgada de metal*) foil; **hojuela de estaño** tin foil
hola *interj* hey!, hello!
Holanda *f* Holland
holan•dés -desa *adj* Dutch; **a la holandesa** (*bb*) half-bound ‖ *mf* Hollander ‖ *m* Dutchman; (*idioma*) Dutch ‖ *f* Dutch woman
holga•chón -chona *adj* lazy, idle ‖ *mf* loafer, idler
holgadero *m* hangout
holga•do -da *adj* idle, unoccupied; (*vestido*) loose, full, roomy; (*que vive con bienestar*) fairly well-off
holganza *f* idleness, leisure; pleasure, enjoyment
holgar §63 *intr* to idle, be idle; take it easy, rest up; not fit, be too loose; be unnecessary, be of no use; be glad ‖ *ref* to be glad; be amused
holga•zán -zana *adj* idle, lazy ‖ *mf* idler, loafer
holgazanear *intr* to idle, loaf, bum around
hol•gón -gona *adj* pleasure-loving ‖ *mf* loafer, lizard
holgorio *m* fun, merriment
holgura *f* looseness, fulness; enjoyment, merriment; comfort, easy circumstances; (mach) play
hollar §61 *tr* to tread on, to trample on
hollejo *m* hull, peel, skin
hollín *m* soot
hollinar *tr* (Chile) to cover with soot
hollinien•to -ta *adj* sooty
holocausto *m* holocaust
holografía *f* holography
holograma *m* hologram
hombracho *m* big husky fellow
hombrada *f* manly act
hombradía *f* manliness, courage
hombre *m* man; husband, man; my boy, old chap; **buen hombre** good-natured fellow; **¡hombre al agua!** or **¡hombre a la mar!** man overboard!; **hombre bueno** arbiter, referee; **hombre de bien** honorable man; **hombre de buenas prendas** man of parts; **hombre de ciencia** scientist; **hombre de confianza** right-hand man; **hombre de dinero** man of means; **hombre de estado** statesman; **hombre de la calle** man in the street; **hombre de las cavernas** caveman; **hombre de letras** man of letters; **hombre del tiempo** weatherman; **hombre de mundo** man of the world; **hombre de negocios** businessman; **hombre de paja** puppet, straw man, front man; **hombre de suposición** man of straw; **hombre hecho** grown man; **hombre lobo** werewolf; **hombre orquesta** one-man band; **hombre público** public figure; **hombre rana** frogman, diver ‖ *interj* man alive!, upon my word!
hombre-anuncio *m* sandwich-board man
hombrear *tr* (Arg) to carry on the shoulders; (Mex) to aid, back ‖ *intr* to try to be somebody; (*una mujer*) to be mannish; **hombrear con** to try to be equal
hombrecillo *m* little man; (*lúpulo*) hop
hombrera *f* (*del vestido*) shoulder; shoulder pad; epaulet
hombre-rana *m* (*pl* **hombres-ranas**) frogman
hombría *f* manliness; **hombría de bien** honor, probity
hombrillo *m* (*de la camisa*) yoke; shoulder piece
hombro *m* shoulder; **arrimar el hombro** to lend a hand, put one's shoulder to the wheel; **encoger los hombros** to let one's shoulders droop; **encogerse de hombros** to shrug one's shoulders; to crouch, to shrink with fear; to not answer; **mirar por encima del hombro** to look down upon; **salir en hombros** to be carried off on the shoulders of the crowd
hombru•no -na *adj* mannish
homenaje *m* homage; (feud) homage; (Chile) gift, favor; **homenaje de boca** lip service; **rendir homenaje a** to swear allegiance to
homeópata *mf* homeopath
homeopatía *f* homeopathy
homicida *adj* homicidal ‖ *mf* homicide
homicidio *m* homicide
homilía *f* homily
homogeneidad *f* homogeneity
homogeneizar §60 *tr* to homogenize
homogéne•o -a *adj* homogeneous
homologación *f* confirmation, ratification; (sport) validation
homologar §44 *tr* to confirm, ratify; (*un récord*) (sport) to validate
homólo•go -ga *adj* homologous ‖ *m* colleague
homóni•mo -ma *adj* homonymous; of the same name ‖ *mf* namesake ‖ *m* homonym
homosexual *adj & mf* homosexual; gay
homúnculo *m* guy, little runt
honda *f* sling
hondazo *m* blow with a sling
hondear *tr* (naut) to sound
hondillos *mpl* patches in the crotch of pants
hon•do -da *adj* deep; (*terreno*) low ‖ *m* bottom ‖ *f* see **honda** ‖ **hondo** *adv* deep
hondón *m* (*de la aguja*) eye; (*de un vaso*) bottom; lowland
hondonada *f* lowland, ravine
hondura *f* depth, profundity; **meterse en honduras** to go beyond one's depth
hondure•ño -ña *adj & mf* Honduran
honestidad *f* decency; chastity; modesty; honesty, probity; fairness, reasonableness

hones•to -ta *adj* decent; chaste, pure; modest; honest, upright; (*precio*) fair, reasonable
hongo *m* fungus, mushroom; (*sombrero*) bowler, derby
honor *m* honor; **en honor a la verdad** as a matter of fact, to tell the truth; **hacer honor a** to do honor to; (*la firma*) to honor
honorable *adj* honorable
honora•rio -ria *adj* honorary || *s* fee, honorarium
honorífi•co -ca *adj* honorific
honra *f* honor; **tener a mucha honra** to be proud of
honradez *f* honesty, integrity
honra•do -da *adj* honorable
honrar *tr* to honor || *ref* to feel honored
honrilla *f* — **por la negra honrilla** out of concern for what people will say
honro•so -sa *adj* honorable
hopo *m* tuft, shock (*of hair*); bushy tail; **seguir el hopo a** (coll) to keep right after
hora *f* hour; (*momento determinado para algo*) time; **a la hora** on time; **a la hora de ahora** right now; **a la hora en punto** on the hour; **a las pocas horas** within a few hours; **dar hora** to fix a time; **dar la hora** (*el reloj*) to strike; **de última hora** up-to-date; most up-to-date; (*noticias*) late; **en buen hora** *or* **en hora buena** safely, luckily; all right; **en mal hora** *or* **en hora mala** unluckily, in an evil hour; **fuera de horas** after hours; **hasta altas horas** until late into the night; **hora de acostarse** bedtime; **hora de aglomeración** rush hour; **hora de cierre** closing time; curfew; **hora de comer** mealtime; **hora deshorada** fatal hour; **hora de verano** daylight-saving time; **hora de la verdad** (taur) kill; **hora legal** *or* **oficial** standard time; **hora pico, hora punta** peak hour; rush hour; **horas de afluencia** rush hour; **horas extra** overtime; **horas de consulta** office hours (*of a doctor*); **horas de ocio** leisure hours; **horas de oficina** office hours; **horas de punta** rush hour; **horas de visita** visiting hours; **horas de vuelo** flying time; **horas extraordinarias de trabajo** overtime; **horas libres** free time, spare time
horadar *tr* to drill, bore, pierce
hora•rio -ria *adj* hour || *m* hour hand; clock; (*de ferrocarriles*) timetable; **horario escolar** roster
horca *f* (*para levantar la paja*) pitchfork; (*para ahorcar a un condenado*) gallows, gibbet; (*de ajos, cebollas, etc.*) string
horcajadas — a horcajadas astride, astraddle
horcajadillas — a horcajadillas astride, astraddle
horcajadura *f* crotch
horcajo *m* (*confluencia de los ríos*) fork; (*para mulas*) yoke
horchata *f* orgeat
horcón *m* pitchfork; forked prop (*for fruit trees*); upright, prop
horda *f* horde
horero *m* (*reloj*) hour hand
horizontal *adj* & *f* horizontal
horizonte *m* horizon
horma *f* form, mold; shoe tree; hat block; **hallar la horma de su zapato** to meet one's match
hormiga *f* ant; (*enfermedad que causa comezón*) itch
hormigón *m* concrete; **hormigón armado** reinforced concrete
hormigonera *f* concrete mixer
hormigo•so -sa *adj* antlike; full of ants; ant-eaten; (*picante*) itchy
hormiguear *intr* (*ponerse en movimiento gente o animales*) to swarm; (*experimentar una sensación de hormigas corriendo por el cuerpo*) crawl, creep; abound, teem
hormiguero *m* anthill; (*de gente*) swarm, mob
hormillón *m* hat block
hormón *m* or **hormona** *f* hormone
hornacina *f* niche
hornada *f* (*cantidad que se cuece de una vez en un horno*) batch, bake; (*conjunto de individuos de una misma promoción*) crop
hornazo *m* Easter cake filled with hard-boiled eggs; Easter gift to Lenten preacher
horne•ro -ra *mf* baker
hornilla *f* kitchen grate; pigeonhole
hornillo *m* kitchen stove; hot plate; (*de la pipa de fumar*) bowl
horno *m* oven, furnace; (*para cocer ladrillos*) kiln; **al horno** baked, roast(ed); **alto horno** blast furnace; **de horno** ovenproof; **horno de cal** limekiln; **horno de fundición** smelting furnace; **horno de ladrillero** brickkiln; **horno (de) microondas** microwave; **resistente al horno** ovenproof
horóscopo *m* horoscope; **sacar un horóscopo** to cast a horoscope
horqueta *f* pitchfork; fork, prop; (*ángulo agudo en un río*) (Arg) bend
horquilla *f* pitchfork; (*de bicicleta*) fork; (*de microteléfono*) cradle; (*alfiler para sujetar el pelo*) hairpin
horrar *tr* to save
hórreo *m* granary; (in Asturias and Galicia) crib or granary raised on pillars (*to protect grain from mice and dampness*)
horrible *adj* horrible
horripilante *adj* hair-raising, blood-curdling
horror *m* horror; **tener horror a** to have a horror of
horrorizar §60 *tr* to horrify
horroro•so -sa *adj* horrid; hideous, ugly; nightmarish
hortaliza *f* vegetable
hortela•no -na *adj* garden || *mf* gardener
hortera *m* clerk, helper || *f* wooden bowl
hortícola *adj* horticultural
horticul•tor -tora *mf* horticulturist
horticultura *f* horticulture; gardening, truck farming
hos•co -ca *adj* dark, dark-skinned; sullen, grim, gloomy
hospedaje *m* lodging
hospedar *tr* to lodge || *ref* to lodge, stop, put up
hospedería *f* hospice; inn, hostelry

hospede•ro -ra *mf* innkeeper
hospicio *m* hospice; poorhouse; orphan asylum
hospital *m* hospital; **estar hecho un hospital** (*una persona*) to be full of aches and pains; (*una casa*) to be turned into a hospital; **hospital de campaña** field hospital; **hospital de la sangre** poor relations; **hospital de primera sangre** (mil) field hospital; **hospital robado** bare house
hospitala•rio -ria *adj* hospitable
hospitalidad *f* hospitality; (*estancia del enfermo en el hospital*) hospitalization
hospitalizar §60 *tr* to hospitalize
hosquedad *f* darkness; sullenness, grimness, gloominess
hostelería *f* restaurant and hotel business
hostería *f* inn, hostelry
hostia *f* sacrificial victim; wafer; (eccl) wafer, Host
hostigar §44 *tr* to scourge; harass; to pester; cloy, surfeit
hostigo•so -sa *adj* cloying, sickening
hostil *adj* hostile
hostilidad *f* hostility
hostilizar §60 *tr* to antagonize; (*al enemigo*) harry, harass
hotel *m* (*establecimiento donde se da comida y alojamiento por dinero*) hotel; (*casa particular lujosa*) mansion
hotele•ro -ra *adj* hotel || *mf* hotelkeeper
hoy *adv & s* today; **de hoy a mañana** any time now; **de hoy en adelante** from now on; **hoy día** nowadays
hoya *f* hole, pit, ditch; (*sepultura*) grave; valley; (*almáciga*) seedbed; river basin
hoyanca *f* potter's field
hoyo *m* hole; grave; pockmark; **el decimoctavo hoyo** (golf) the eighteenth hole; **un hoyo en uno** (golf) a hole in one
hoyo•so -sa *adj* full of holes
hoyuelo *m* dimple; (*juego de muchachos*) pitching pennies
hoz *f* (*pl* **hoces**) sickle; narrow pass, defile; **de hoz y de coz** headlong, recklessly
hozar §60 *tr & intr* to nuzzle, root
hta. *abbr* **hasta**
huacal *m* var of **guacal**
huachinango *m* (Mex) red snapper
hucha *f* workingman's chest; (*alcancía*) toy bank; (*dinero ahorrado*) savings, nest egg
huchear *intr* to cry, shout
hue•co -ca *adj* hollow; (*mullido*) soft, fluffy, spongy; (*voz*) deep, resounding; vain, conceited; (*estilo, lenguaje*) affected, pompous || *m* hollow; interval; (*en un muro, una hilera de coches, etc.*) opening; (*empleo sin proveer*) opening; **hueco de la axila** armpit; **hueco de escalera** stair well
huélfago *m* (vet) heaves
huelga *f* (*ocio*) rest, leisure, idleness; recreation; pleasant spot; (*cesación del trabajo en señal de protesta*) strike; (mach) play; **huelga de brazos caídos** sit-down strike; **huelga de celo** (Esp) work-to-rule strike; **huelga de hambre** hunger strike; **huelga general** general strike; **huelga patronal** lockout; **huelga por solidaridad** sympathy strike; **huelga salvaje** (Esp) wildcat strike; **huelga sentada** sit-down strike; **ir a la huelga** or **ponerse en huelga** to go on strike
huelguista *mf* striker
huella *f* track, footprint; trace, mark; rut; (*acción de hollar*) tread, treading; (*peldaño en que se asienta el pie*) tread; **huella dactilar** or **digital** fingerprint; **huella de sonido** sound track; **huella genética** genetic fingerprint; **seguir las huellas de** to follow in the footsteps of
huérfa•no -na *adj* orphan; orphaned; alone, deserted || *mf* orphan; (Chile, Peru) foundling
hue•ro -ra *adj* rotten; (fig) empty, hollow; (Guat, Mex) blond; **salir huero** (coll) to flop, turn out bad || *mf* (Guat, Mex) blond
huerta *f* truck farm; extensive gardens and orchards; irrigated region
huerte•ro -ra *mf* (Arg, Peru) gardener
huerto *m* (*de árboles frutales*) orchard; (*de verduras*) kitchen garden
huesa *f* grave
huesear *intr* to beg (alms)
huesillo *m* (Chile, Peru) sun-dried peach
hueso *m* bone; (*de ciertas frutas*) stone, pit; drudgery; **a otro perro con ese hueso** tell that to the marines; **calarse hasta los huesos** to get soaked to the skin; **hueso de la alegría** crazy bone, funny bone; **hueso de la suerte** wishbone; **hueso duro de roer** a hard nut to crack; **la sin hueso** the tongue; **no dejarle a uno un hueso sano** to beat someone up; to pick someone to pieces; **no poder con sus huesos** to be all in; **soltar la sin hueso** to talk too much; to pour forth insults; **tener los huesos molidos** to be all fagged out
hueso•so -sa *adj* bony
hués•ped -peda *mf* (*persona alojada en casa ajena*) guest; (*persona que hospeda a otra en su casa*) host; (*mesonero*) innkeeper, host; (*persona alojada en un hotel*) guest, client; (biol) host
hueste *f* followers; (*ejército*) army, host
huesu•do -da *adj* bony, big-boned
hueva *f* roe, fish roe
hueve•ro -ra *mf* egg dealer || *f* eggcup; oviduct
huevo *m* egg; **huevo a la plancha** fried egg; **huevo al plato** shirred egg; **huevo del té** tea ball; **huevo de Pascua** Easter egg; **huevo de zurcir** darning egg or gourd; **huevo duro** hard-boiled egg; **huevo escalfado** poached egg; **huevo estrellado** or **frito** fried egg; **huevo pasado por agua** soft-boiled egg; **huevos revueltos** scrambled eggs
huída *f* flight; (*de un líquido*) leak; (*ensanche en un agujero*) flare, splay; (*de caballo*) shying
huidi•zo -za *adj* fugitive; evasive
huincha *f* (SAm) tape; (SAm) tape measure; **huincha adhesiva** Scotch[T] tape; **huincha aisladora** friction tape

huipil *m* (Mex) colorful poncho worn by Indian women
huir §20 *tr* to flee, avoid, shun; (*el cuerpo*) duck || *intr* to flee; (*el tiempo*) fly; (*de la memoria*) to slip || *ref* to flee
hule *m* (*tela impermeable*) oilcloth; rubber; (taur) blood, goring
hulear *intr* (CAm) to gather rubber
hulla *f* coal; **hulla azul** tide power; wind power; **hulla blanca** white power; water power
hullera *f* colliery, coal mine
humanidad *f* humanity; fatness
humanista *adj & mf* humanist
humanita•rio -ria *adj & mf* humanitarian
huma•no -na *adj* (*perteneciente al hombre*) human; (*compasivo, misericordioso; civilizador*) humane
humanoide *adj & mf* humanoid
humareda *f* cloud of smoke
humeante *adj* smoking, smoky; steamy, reeking
humear *tr* (SAm) to fumigate || *intr* to smoke; steam, reek; put on airs; (*reliquias de un alboroto, enemistad, etc.*) last, persist
humectador *m* humidifier
humectante *adj* moisturizing
humectar *tr* to moisturize
humedad *f* humidity, dampness, moisture
humedecer §22 *tr* to humidify, dampen, moisten, wet
húme•do -da *adj* humid, damp, moist
humero *m* smokestack, chimney
húmero *m* humerus
humidificador *m* air humidifier
humildad *f* humility
humilde *adj* humble
humilladero *m* calvary, road shrine; prie-dieu
humillante *adj* humiliating
humillar *tr* (*abatir el orgullo de*) to humble; (*avergonzar*) humiliate; (*la cabeza*) bow; (*el cuerpo, las rodillas*) bend || *ref* to humble oneself; cringe, grovel
humo *m* smoke; steam, fume; **a humo de pajas** lightly, thoughtlessly; **bajar los humos a** (coll) to humble, take down a peg; **echar más humo que una chimenea** to smoke like a chimney; **humos** airs, conceit; hearths, homes; **irse todo en humo** to go up in smoke; **tragar el humo** to inhale; **vender humos** to peddle influence
humor *m* humor; **de mal humor** out of humor; **estar de humor para** to be in the humor for; **seguir el humor a** to humor
humorismo *m* humor, humorousness
humorista *mf* humorist; cartoonist; comic
humorísti•co -ca *adj* humorous
humo•so -sa *adj* smoky
hundible *adj* sinkable
hundir *tr* to sink; plunge; (*abrumar*) overwhelm; confound, confute; destroy, ruin || *ref* to sink; collapse; settle, cave in; come to ruin; disappear, vanish
húnga•ro -ra *adj & mf* Hungarian || *m* (*idioma*) Hungarian
Hungría *f* Hungary
hupe *m* punk
huracán *m* hurricane
hurañía *f* shyness, unsociability
hura•ño -ña *adj* shy, unsociable
hurgar §44 *tr* to poke; (fig) to stir up, incite; **peor es hurgallo** (i.e., **hurgarlo**) better keep hands off || *intr* to poke; scavenge || *ref* (*la nariz*) to pick
hurgón *m* poker; thrust, stab
hurgonazo *m* (*con hurgón*) poke; jab, stab, thrust
hurgonear *tr* to poke; to jab, to stab at
hurgonero *m* poker
hu•rón -rona *adj* shy, diffident || *mf* prier, snooper; shy person, diffident person || *m* ferret
huronear *tr* to ferret, hunt with a ferret; to ferret out
huronera *f* ferret hole; lair, hiding place
hurra *interj* hurrah!, hurray!
hurtadillas — a hurtadillas by stealth, on the sly; **a hurtadillas de** unbeknown to
hurtar *tr* to steal; (*en pesos y medidas*) cheat; (*el suelo*) wear away; plagiarize; **hurtar el cuerpo** to dodge, duck || *ref* to withdraw, hide
hurto *m* thieving; theft; **a hurto** stealthily, on the sly; **coger con el hurto en las manos** to catch with the goods; **hurto mayor** grand larceny
husma *f* snooping; **andar a la husma** to go around snooping
husmear *tr* to scent, smell out; pry into || *intr* (*la carne*) to smell bad, become gamy
husmo *m* gaminess, high odor; **estar al husmo** to wait for a chance
huso *m* (*para hilar*) spindle; (*para devanar*) bobbin; (*cilindro del torno*) drum; **huso horario** time zone; **ser más derecho que un huso** to be as straight as a ramrod
huta *f* hunter's blind
huy *interj* ouch!
huyente *adj* (*frente*) receding; (*ojeada*) shifty

I

I, i (i) *f* ninth letter of the Spanish alphabet
ib. *abbr* **ibídem**
ibéri•co -ca *adj* Iberian
ibe•ro -ra *adj & mf* Iberian
íbice *m* ibex
ice•berg *m* (*pl* **-bergs**) iceberg

iconoclasia *f or* **iconoclasmo** *m* iconoclasm
iconoclasta *mf* iconoclast
iconoscopio *m* (telv) iconoscope
ictericia *f* jaundice
ictericia•do -da *adj* jaundiced
ictiología *f* ichthyology
ida *f* going; departure; rashness; sally; trail; **de ida y vuelta** round-trip; **idas y venidas** comings and goings
idea *f* idea; **mudar de idea** to change one's mind
ideal *adj & m* ideal
idealista *adj & mf* idealist
idealizar §60 *tr* to idealize
idear *tr* to think up, devise
idemista *adj* yessing ‖ *mf* yesser; yes-man
idénti•co -ca *adj* identic(al); (*muy parecido*) very similar
identidad *f* identity, sameness
identificación *f* identification; **identificación genética** genetic fingerprinting
identifica•dor -dora *adj* identifying ‖ *m*—**identificador** *m* **de llamada** (telp) caller ID
identificar §73 *tr* to identify
ideología *f* ideology
idíli•co -ca *adj* idyllic
idilio *m* idyll
idioma *m* language; (*modo particular de hablar*) idiom, speech
idiomáti•co -ca *adj* idiomatic; language, linguistic
idiosincrasia *f* idiosyncrasy
idiota *adj* idiotic ‖ *mf* idiot
idiotez *f* idiocy
idiotismo *m* ignorance; (*idiotez*) idiocy; (gram) idiom
i•do -da *adj* wild, scatterbrained; drunk ‖ **los idos** the dead ‖ *f* see **ida**
idolatrar *tr* to idolize
idolatría *f* idolatry; (*amor excesivo a una persona*) idolization
ídolo *m* idol
idoneidad *f* fitness, suitability
idóne•o -a fit, suitable
idus *mpl* ides
iglesia *f* church; **entrar en la iglesia** to go into the church; **llevar a la iglesia** to lead to the altar
iglesie•ro -ra *adj* (Arg) church-going ‖ *mf* (Arg) church goer
igna•ro -ra *adj* ignorant
ignición *f* combustion; (aut) ignition
ignominio•so -sa *adj* ignominious
ignorancia *f* ignorance
ignorante *adj* ignorant ‖ *mf* ignoramus
ignorar *tr* to not know, be ignorant of
igno•to -ta *adj* unknown
igual *adj* equal; (*liso, llano*) smooth, even, level; (*no variable*) firm, constant, equable; indifferent; **me es igual** it makes no difference to me ‖ *mf* equal, peer ‖ *m* equal; equal sign; **al igual de** like, after the fashion of; **al igual que** as; while, whereas; **en igual de** instead of; **sin igual** without equal, peerless
iguala *f* equalization; agreement; (*fee*) retainer
igualización *f* equalization; agreement
igualar *tr* to equal; (*alisar, allanar*) smooth, even, level; make equal, match; deem equal ‖ *intr & ref* to be equal
igualdad *f* equality; smoothness, evenness; **igualdad de ánimo** equanimity; **igualdad de oportunidades** equal opportunity
igualmente *adv* likewise; **igualmente que** the same as
ijada *f* (*de animal*) flank; (*del cuerpo humano*) loin; (*dolor en estas partes*) stitch; **tener su ijada** to have its weak side or point
ijadear *intr* to pant
ijar *m* flank; loin
ilegal *adj* illegal
ilegible *adj* illegible
ilegíti•mo -ma *adj* illegitimate
ile•so -sa *adj* unscathed, unharmed
iletra•do -da *adj* unlettered, uncultured
ilíci•to -ta *adj* illicit, unlawful
ilimita•do -da *adj* limitless
ilitera•to -ta *adj* illiterate
ilógi•co -ca *adj* illogical
ilote *m* ear of corn
iludir *tr* to elude, evade
iluminación *f* illumination
iluminador *m* lighting engineer
iluminar *tr* to illuminate, light, light up ‖ *ref* to light up, brighten
ilusión *f* illusion; (*esperanza infundada*) delusion; enthusiasm, zeal; dream; **forjarse** *or* **hacerse ilusiones** to kid oneself, indulge in wishful thinking
ilusionar *tr* to delude ‖ *ref* to have illusions, indulge in wishful thinking; be enraptured, be beguiled
ilusionista *mf* prestidigitator, magician
ilusi•vo -va *adj* illusive
ilu•so -sa *adj* deluded, misguided; (*propenso a ilusionarse*) visionary
iluso•rio -ria *adj* illusory
ilustración *f* illustration; enlightenment; illustrated magazine
ilustra•do -da *adj* illustrated; learned, informed; enlightened
ilustrar *tr* (*adornar con grabados alusivos al texto*) to illustrate; make illustrious, make famous; explain, elucidate; enlighten ‖ *ref* to become famous; be enlightened
ilustre *adj* illustrious
imagen *f* image; picture; **en imagen** on camera
imaginación *f* imagination
imaginar *tr, intr & ref* to imagine
imagina•rio -ria *adj* imaginary
imaginati•vo -va *adj* imaginative ‖ *f* imagination; understanding
imaginería *f* fancy colored embroidery; carving or painting of religious images
imán *m* magnet; (fig) lodestone; **imán de herradura** horseshoe magnet; **imán inductor** (elec) field magnet
imanar or **imantar** *tr* to magnetize

imbatible *adj* unbeatable
imbécil *adj & mf* imbecile
imbecilidad *f* imbecility
imberbe *adj* beardless
imbíbi•to -ta *adj* including; included
imbornal *m* drain hole
imborrable *adj* indelible; unforgettable
imbuir §20 *tr* to imbue
imitación *adj invar* imitation ‖ *f* imitation; **a imitación de** in imitation of; **de imitación** imitation, fake
imita•do -da *adj* imitated; mock, sham; imitation
imitar *tr* to imitate
impaciencia *f* impatience
impacientar *tr* to make impatient ‖ *ref* to get impatient
impaciente *adj* impatient
impacto *m* impact, hit; (*señal que deja el proyectil*) mark; **impacto directo** direct hit
impa•go -ga *adj* unpaid, outstanding ‖ *m* nonpayment
impar *adj* odd, uneven; (*que no tiene igual*) unmatched ‖ *m* odd number
imparcial *adj* impartial; (*que no entra en ningún partido*) nonpartisan
impartir *tr* to distribute, impart; (*lecciones*) to give
impasse [im 'pas] *m* impasse; (*in bridge*) finesse
impasible *adj* impassible, impassive
impávi•do -da *adj* dauntless, fearless, intrepid
impecable *adj* impeccable
impedancia *f* impedance
impedi•do -da *adj* disabled, crippled
impedimento *m* impediment, obstacle, hindrance
impedir §50 *tr* to hinder, prevent
impeler *tr* to impel; spur, incite
impenetrable *adj* impenetrable
impenitente *adj & mf* impenitent
impensable *adj* unthinkable
impensa•do -da *adj* unexpected
imperar *intr* to rule, reign, command
imperati•vo -va *adj & m* imperative
imperceptible *adj* imperceptible
imperdible *m* safety pin
imperdonable *adj* unpardonable, unforgivable
imperecede•ro -ra *adj* imperishable, undying
imperfección *f* imperfection
imperfec•to -ta *adj & m* imperfect
imperial *adj* imperial ‖ *f* imperial, roof (*of a coach or bus*)
imperialista *adj & mf* imperialist
impericia *f* unskillfulness, inexpertness
imperio *m* empire; dominion, sway
imperio•so -sa *adj* (*que manda con imperio*) imperious; (*indispensable*) imperative
imperi•to -ta *adj* unskilled, inexpert
impermeable *adj* impermeable; waterproof ‖ *m* raincoat
impersonal *adj* impersonal
impertérri•to -ta *adj* dauntless, intrepid
impertinencia *f* impertinence; irrelevance; fussiness
impertinente *adj* impertinent; (*que no viene al caso*) irrelevant; (*nimiamente susceptible*) fussy ‖ **impertinentes** *mpl* lorgnette
impetrar *tr* to beg (for); obtain by entreaty
ímpetu *m* impetus; force; haste
impetuo•so -sa *adj* impetuous
impiedad *f* (*falta de religión*) impiety; (*falta de compasión*) pitilessness
impí•o -a *adj* (*irreligioso*) impious; (*falto de compasión*) pitiless
impla *f* wimple
implacable *adj* relentless
implantar *tr* to implant; introduce
implementos *mpl* implements; tools
implicar §73 *tr* (*envolver*) to implicate; (*incluir en esencia*) imply ‖ *intr* to stand in the way
implíci•to -ta *adj* implicit, implied
implorar *tr* to implore
implume *adj* featherless
imponente *adj* imposing ‖ *mf* depositor, investor
imponer §54 *tr* (*la voluntad de uno, silencio, tributos*) to impose; (*dinero a rédito*) invest; (*dinero en depósito*) deposit; instruct; impute falsely ‖ *intr* to dominate, command respect ‖ *ref* (*responsabilidades*) to assume; command attention, command respect; **imponerse a** to dominate, command the respect of; **imponerse de** to learn, to find out
imponible *adj* taxable
impopular *adj* unpopular
impopularidad *f* unpopularity
importación *f* importation; import; imports
importa•dor -dora *mf* importer
importancia *f* importance; (*extensión, tamaño*) size; **ser de la importancia de** to be the concern of
importante *adj* important; large
importar *tr* (*introducir en un país*) to import; amount to; involve, imply; concern ‖ *intr* to import; be important; matter
importe *m* amount
importunar *tr* to importune
importu•no -na *adj* (*molesto*) importunate; (*fuera de sazón*) inopportune
imposibilita•do -da *adj* paralyzed, disabled
imposibilitar *tr* to make impossible ‖ *ref* to become paralyzed, become disabled
imposible *adj* impossible
imposición *f* (*de la voluntad de uno*) imposition; burden, demand; imposture; (*de dinero*) deposit; (typ) make-up; **imposición de contribuciones** taxation; **imposición de manos** laying on of hands
impos•tor -tora *mf* impostor; slanderer
impostura *f* imposture
impotable *adj* undrinkable
impotencia *f* impotence
impotente *adj* impotent
impracticable *adj* impracticable, impassable; impractical
impreci•so -sa *adj* imprecise; vague

impregnar *tr* to impregnate, saturate
impremedita•do -da *adj* unpremeditated
imprenta *f* printing; printing shop; (*lo que se publica impreso*) printed matter; (*máquina para imprimir o prensar; conjunto de periódicos o periodistas*) press
imprentar *tr* (*la ropa*) (Chile) to press, iron; (Ecuad) to mark
imprescindible *adj* indispensable, essential
impresentable *adj* unpresentable
impresión *f* (*efecto producido en el ánimo; señal que una cosa deja en otra por presión*) impression; (*acción de imprimir*) printing; (*los ejemplares de una edición*) edition, issue; hard copy; (phot) print; **impresión dactilar** or **digital** fingerprint; **impresión subordinada** (compu) background printing
impresionable *adj* impressionable
impresionante *adj* impressive
impresionar *tr* to impress; (*un disco fonográfico*) record; (phot) to expose || *intr* to make an impression || *ref* to be impressed
impreso *m* printed paper or book; **impreso derivado** (compu) printout; **impreso de solicitud** application form; **impresos** printed matter
impre•sor -sora *mf* printer || *f* (compu) printer; **impresora de chorro de tinta** (compu) ink-jet printer; **impresora de margarita** daisy-wheel printer; **impresora láser** *or* **de láser** laser printer; **impresora matricial** dot-matrix printer
imprevisible *adj* unforeseeable
imprevisión *f* improvidence, lack of foresight
imprevi•sor -sora *adj* improvident
imprevis•to -ta *adj* unforeseen, unexpected || **imprevistos** *mpl* emergencies, unforeseen expenses
imprimar *tr* to prime
imprimir *tr* (*respeto, miedo; movimiento*) to impart || **§83** *tr* to stamp, imprint, impress; (*un disco fonográfico*) press; (typ) to print
improbable *adj* improbable
improbar §61 *tr* to disapprove
improbidad *f* dishonesty; hardness, arduousness
ímpro•bo -ba *adj* dishonest; (*trabajo*) arduous
improcedente *adj* wrong; unfit, untimely
improducti•vo -va *adj* unproductive; unemployed
impronunciable *adj* unpronounceable
improperar *tr* to insult, revile
improperio *m* insult, affront
impropi•cio -cia *adj* unpropitious
impro•pio -pia *adj* improper; (*ajeno*) foreign
impróspe•ro -ra *adj* unsuccessful
impróvi•do -da *adj* unprepared
improvisación *f* improvisation; meteoric rise; (mus) impromptu
improvisadamente *adv* suddenly, unexpectedly; extempore
improvisar *tr & intr* to improvise
improvi•so -sa *adj* unforeseen, unexpected
imprudencia *f* imprudence; **imprudencia temeraria** criminal negligence
imprudente *adj* imprudent
impudicia *f* immodesty
impúdi•co -ca *adj* immodest
impues•to -ta *adj* informed || *m* tax; **impuesto al valor añadido** *or* **agregado, impuesto sobre el valor añadido** *or* **agregado** value-added tax; **impuesto de consumo, impuesto interno** excise tax; **impuesto de lujo** luxury tax; **impuesto de retención** *or* **retenido** withholding tax; **impuesto sobre donaciones** gift tax; **impuesto sobre la plusvalía** capital gains tax; **impuesto sobre la renta** (*de las personas físicas*), **impuesto sobre los ingresos** income tax; **impuesto sobre las utilidades excedentes** *or* **las ganancias excesivas** excess profits tax; **impuesto sobre las ventas** sales tax; **impuesto sucesorios, impuesto sobre sucesiones, impuesto a la herencia** inheritance tax; **impuesto único** flat tax
impugnar *tr* to impugn, contest, impeach
impulsar *tr* to impel; drive
impulsión *f* impulse, drive
impulsi•vo -va *adj* impulsive
impulso *m* impulse
impune *adj* unpunished
impunidad *f* impunity
impureza *f* impurity
impu•ro -ra *adj* impure; unclean
imputar *tr* to impute; credit on account
inabordable *adj* unapproachable
inacabable *adj* endless, interminable
inaccesible *adj* inaccessible
inacción *f* inaction
inacentua•do -da *adj* unaccented
inactividad *f* inactivity
inacti•vo -va *adj* inactive
inadaptación *f* maladjustment
inadecua•do -da *adj* inadequate; unsuited
inadvertencia *f* inadvertence, oversight
inadverti•do -da *adj* inadvertent, unwitting; careless, thoughtless; unseen, unnoticed
inagotable *adj* inexhaustible
inaguantable *adj* unbearable
inalámbri•co -ca *adj* wireless
inalcanzable *adj* unattainable
inamisto•so -sa *adj* unfriendly
inamovible *adj* irremovable; undetachable; (*incorporado*) built-in
inamovilidad *f* irremovability; tenure, permanent tenure
inane *adj* inane
inanición *f* starvation
inanima•do -da *adj* inanimate, lifeless
inapelable *adj* unappealable; unavoidable
inapetencia *f* loss of appetite
inapreciable *adj* inappreciable; imperceptible
inarmóni•co -ca *adj* unharmonious
inarrugable *adj* wrinkle-free, permanent-press
inarticula•do -da *adj* inarticulate
inartísti•do -ca *adj* inartistic
inasequible *adj* unattainable; unobtainable

inastillable *adj* nonshatterable, shatter-proof
inatacable *adj* unattackable; **inatacable por** resistant to
inaudi•to -ta *adj* unheard-of; outrageous
inauguración *f* inauguration; (*de una estatua*) unveiling
inaugural *adj* inaugural
inaugurar *tr* to inaugurate; (*p.ej., una estatua*) unveil
inaveriguable *adj* unascertainable
inca *mf* Inca
incai•co -ca *adj* Inca, Incan
incalificable *adj* unqualifiable; (*infame, atroz*) unspeakable
incambiable *adj* unchangeable
incandescente *adj* incandescent
incansable *adj* untiring, indefatigable
incapacitar *tr* to incapacitate; (law) to declare incompetent
inca•paz *adj* (*pl* **-paces**) incapable, unable; not large enough; stupid; (law) incompetent; frightful, unbearable
incasable *adj* unmarriageable; opposed to marriage; (*por su fealdad*) unable to find a husband
incautar *ref* — **incautarse de** to hold until claimed; (law) to seize, attach
incau•to -ta *adj* unwary, heedless
incendajas *fpl* kindling
incendiar *tr* to set on fire || *ref* to catch fire
incendia•rio -ria *adj* incendiary || *mf* incendiary, firebug, arsonist
incendio *m* fire; (fig) fire, passion
incensar §2 *tr* to incense, burn incense before; (fig) to flatter
incensario *m* censer, incense burner
incenti•vo -va *adj & m* incentive
inceremonio•so -sa *adj* unceremonious
incertidumbre *f* uncertainty, incertitude
incesante *adj* unceasing
incesto *m* incest
incestuo•so -sa *adj* incestuous
incidencia *f* incidence; **por incidencia** by chance
incidente *adj* incident; incidental || *m* incident
incidir *tr* to make an incision in || *intr* — **incidir en culpa** to fall into guilt; **incidir en** *or* **sobre** to strike, impinge on
incienso *m* incense; (*olíbano*) frankincense
incier•to -ta *adj* uncertain
incineración *f* incineration; (*de cadáveres*) cremation
incinerar *tr* to incinerate; (*cadáveres*) cremate
incipiente *adj* incipient
incisión *f* incision; (*mordacidad en el lenguaje*) incisiveness, sarcasm
incisi•vo -va *adj* incisive; biting, sarcastic
inci•so -sa *adj* (*estilo del escritor*) choppy || *m* comma; clause; sentence
incitar *tr* to incite
incivil *adj* rude, impolite
inciviliza•do -da *adj* uncivilized
inclemencia *f* inclemency; **a la inclemencia** in the open, without shelter
inclemente *adj* inclement
inclinación *f* inclination; bent, leaning, propensity; nod, bow
inclinar *tr, intr & ref* to incline; bend, bow
ínclí•to -ta *adj* illustrious, renowned
incluir §20 *tr* to include; (*en una carta*) inclose
inclusa *f* foundling home
incluse•ro -ra *mf* foundling
inclusión *f* inclusion; friendship
inclusive *adv* inclusive, inclusively || *prep* including
inclusi•vo -va *adj* inclusive
inclu•so -sa *adj* inclosed || *f* see **inclusa** || **incluso** *adv* inclusively; (*hasta, aun*) even || **incluso** *prep* including
incobrable *adj* uncollectible; irrecoverable
incógni•to -ta *adj* (*no conocido*) unknown; (*que no se da a conocer*) incognito || *mf* (*persona*) incognito || *m* (*condición de no ser conocido*) incognito; **de incógnito** (*sin ser conocido*) incognito || *f* (math & fig) unknown quantity
incoherente *adj* incoherent
íncola *m* inhabitant
incolo•ro -ra *adj* colorless
incólume *adj* unharmed, safe
incombustible *adj* incombustible, fireproof; cold, indifferent
incomerciable *adj* unmarketable
incomible *adj* uneatable, inedible
incomodar *tr* to inconvenience, disturb
incomodidad *f* inconvenience; annoyance, discomfort
incómo•do -da *adj* inconvenient; annoying, uncomfortable || *m* inconvenience; discomfort
incomparable *adj* incomparable
incompartible *adj* unsharable
incompasi•vo -va *adj* pitiless, unsympathetic
incompatible *adj* incompatible; (*acontecimientos, citas, horas de clase, etc.*) conflicting; (compu, electron, med, pharm) incompatible
incompetente *adj* incompetent
incompetible *adj* unmatchable
incomple•to -ta *adj* incomplete
incomponible *adj* unmendable, beyond repair
incomprable *adj* unpurchasable
incomprensible *adj* incomprehensible
incomprensión *f* incomprehension
incomunicación *f* isolation, solitary confinement
incomunica•do -da *adj* incommunicado; in solitary confinement
inconcebible *adj* inconceivable, unthinkable
inconclu•so -sa *adj* unfinished
inconcluyente *adj* inconclusive
inconcu•so -sa *adj* undeniable
incondicional *adj* unconditional
incone•xo -xa *adj* unconnected; (*inaplicable*) irrelevant
inconfidente *adj* distrustful
inconformidad *f* nonconformity; disagreement

inconformista *mf* nonconformist
inconfundible *adj* unmistakable
incon•gruo -grua *adj* incongruous
inconocible *adj* unknowable
inconquistable *adj* unconquerable; (*que no se deja vencer con ruegos y dádivas*) unbending, unyielding
inconsciencia *f* unconsciousness; unawareness
inconsciente *adj* unconscious; unaware; **lo inconsciente** the unconscious
inconsecuencia *f* (*falta de consecuencia o correspondencia en dichos y hechos*) inconsistency
inconsecuente *adj* inconsistent; (*que no se deduce de otra cosa*) inconsequential
inconsidera•do -da *adj* inconsiderate
inconsiguiente *adj* inconsequential, illogical
inconsistencia *f* (*falta de cohesión*) inconsistency
inconsistente *adj* inconsistent
inconsolable *adj* inconsolable
inconstante *adj* inconstant
inconstitucional *adj* unconstitutional
inconsútil *adj* seamless
incontable *adj* countless, innumerable
incontenible *adj* irrepressible
incontestable *adj* incontestable
incontinente *adj* incontinent || *adv* at once, instantly
incontrastable *adj* invincible; inconvincible; (*argumento*) unanswerable
incontrovertible *adj* incontrovertible
inconveniencia *f* inconvenience; unsuitability; impoliteness; impropriety
inconveniente *adj* inconvenient; unsuitable; impolite; improper || *m* drawback; disadvantage; objection
incordio *m* bore, nuisance
incorporación *f* incorporation, embodiment
incorpora•do -da *adj* (*el que estaba echado*) sitting up; (*montado en la construcción*) built-in
incorporar *tr* to incorporate, embody || *ref* to incorporate; (*el que estaba echado*) sit up; **incorporarse a** to join
incorrec•to -ta *adj* incorrect
incrédu•lo -la *adj* incredulous || *mf* disbeliever, doubter
increíble *adj* incredible
incremento *m* increment, increase
increpar *tr* to chide, rebuke
incriminar *tr* to incriminate; (*un delito, falta, defecto*) exaggerate the gravity of
incruen•to -ta *adj* bloodless
incrustar *tr* to incrust, ingrain; (*embutir por adorno*) inlay
incubadora *f* incubator
incubar *tr & intr* to incubate || *ref* (fig) to be brewing
incuestionable *adj* unquestionable
inculcar §73 *tr* to inculcate || *ref* to become obstinate
inculpable *adj* blameless, guiltless
inculpar *tr* to accuse, blame
incultivable *adj* untillable
incul•to -ta *adj* uncultivated, untilled; uncultured; (*estilo*) coarse, sloppy
incumbencia *f* responsibility, obligation
incumbir *intr* — **incumbir a** to be incumbent on, to be incumbent upon
incumplimiento *m* nonfulfillment
incunable *m* incunabulum
incurable *adj & mf* incurable
incuria *f* carelessness, negligence
incurio•so -sa *adj* careless, negligent
incurrir *intr* — **incurrir en** to incur
incursión *f* incursion, inroad, raid
indagación *f* investigation, research
indagatorio *m* deposition of the accused
indagar §44 *tr* to investigate
indebidamente *adv* unduly
indebi•do -da *adj* undue; wrong
indecencia *f* indecency
indecente *adj* indecent
indecible *adj* unspeakable, unutterable
indeci•so -sa *adj* undecided, indecisive; (*contorno, forma*) vague, obscure
indeclinable *adj* unavoidable; (gram) indeclinable
indecoro•so -sa *adj* improper
indefectible *adj* unfailing
indefendible *adj* indefensible
indefen•so -sa *adj* defenseless, undefended
indefinible *adj* indefinable
indefini•do -da *adj* indefinite; limitless; vague
indeleble *adj* indelible
indelibera•do -da *adj* unpremeditated
indelica•do -da *adj* indelicate
indemne *adj* unharmed, undamaged
indemnidad *f* (*seguridad contra un daño*) indemnity
indemnización *f* (*compensación*) indemnity, indemnification; **indemnización por despido** severance pay
indemnizar §60 *tr* to indemnify
independencia *f* independence
independiente *adj & mf* independent
independizar §60 *tr* to free, emancipate || *ref* to become independent
indescriptible *adj* indescribable
indeseable *adj & mf* undesirable
indesea•do -da *adj* unwanted
indesmallable *adj* runproof
indestructible *adj* indestructible
indetermina•do -da *adj* indeterminate; (gram) indefinite
indevo•to -ta *adj* impious; not fond, not devoted
indexar *tr* (econ) to index
india *f* wealth, riches; **Indias Occidentales** West Indies; **la India** India
indiana *f* printed calico
india•no -na *adj & mf* Spanish American; East Indian; West Indian || *m* man back from America with great wealth; **indiano de hilo negro** (coll) skinflint || *f* see **indiana**

indicación *f* indication; **por indicación de** at the direction of
indica•do -da *adj* appropriate, advisable; **muy indicado** just the thing, just the person
indica•dor -dora *adj* indicating, pointing || *m* indicator; gauge; (*de tránsito*) traffic signal; (compu) flag; **indicator de velocidad** speedometer
indicar §73 *tr* to indicate
indicati•vo -va *adj & m* indicative
índice *m* index; index finger; **el Índice** (eccl) the Index; **índice con pestañas, índice en el corte** thumb index; **índice de audiencia** (telv) ratings; **índice del costo de (la) vida** cost-of-living index; **índice de materias, índice temático** table of contents; **índice de mortalidad** death rate; **índice de natalidad** birth rate; **índice de precios al consumo** *or* **al consumidor** consumer price index
indiciar *tr* to betoken, indicate; surmise, suspect; (econ) to index
indicio *m* sign, token, indication; **indicios vehementes** circumstantial evidence
indiferente *adj* indifferent; (*que no importa*) immaterial
indígena *adj* indigenous || *mf* native
indigente *adj* indigent
indigestar *ref* to be indigestible; be disliked, be unbearable
indigestible *adj* indigestible
indigestión *f* indigestion
indignación *f* indignation
indigna•do -da *adj* indignant
indignar *tr* to anger, provoke || *ref* to become indignant
indignidad *f* (*falta de mérito*) unworthiness; (*acción reprobable*) indignity
indig•no -na *adj* unworthy
índigo *m* indigo
in•dio -dia *adj & mf* Indian || *f* see **india**
indirec•to -ta *adj* indirect || *f* hint, innuendo; **indirecta del padre Cobos** broad hint
indiscernible *adj* indiscernible
indiscre•to -ta *adj* indiscreet
indiscrimina•do -da *adj* indiscriminate; nondiscriminating
indisculpable *adj* inexcusable
indiscutible *adj* undeniable
indisoluble *adj* indissoluble
indispensable *adj* unpardonable; indispensable
indisponer §54 *tr* (*alterar la salud de*) to indispose, upset; disturb, upset; **indisponer a uno con** to set someone against, prejudice someone against || *ref* to become indisposed; **indisponerse con** to fall out with
indisponible *adj* unavailable
indispues•to -ta *adj* indisposed
indistintamente *adv* indistinctly; indiscriminately, without distinction
indistin•to -ta *adj* indistinct
individual *adj* individual; (*habitación en un hotel; partido de tenis*) single
individualidad *f* individuality
indivi•duo -dua *adj* individual; indivisible || *mf* (*persona indeterminada*) (coll) individual || *m* (*cada persona*) individual; (*miembro de una corporación*) member, fellow
indócil *adj* unteachable; headstrong, unruly
indocumenta•do -da *adj* unidentified; unqualified || *mf* nobody (*person of no account*); person without identity papers
indochi•no -na *adj & mf* Indo-Chinese || **la Indochina** Indochina
indoeurope•o -a *adj & m* Indo-European
índole *f* kind, class; nature, disposition, temper
indolente *adj* stolid, impassive; (*perezoso*) indolent
indolo•ro -ra *adj* painless
indoma•do -da *adj* untamed
indone•sio -sia *adj & mf* Indonesian || **la Indonesia** Indonesia
inducción *f* induction
inducido *m* (*de dínamo o motor*) (elec) armature
inducir §19 *tr* to induce
inductor *m* (*de dínamo o motor*) (elec) field
indudable *adj* doubtless
indulgente *adj* indulgent
indultar *tr* to pardon; free, exempt
indulto *m* pardon; exemption
indumentaria *f* clothing, dress; historical study of clothing
indumento *m* clothing, dress
industria *f* industry; **de industria** on purpose; **industria artesanal** *or* **casera** cottage industry; **industria en crecimiento** *or* **en expansión** growth industry
industrial *adj* industrial || *m* industrialist
industrializar §60 *tr* to industrialize
industriar *tr* to teach, instruct, train || *ref* to get along, manage
industrio•so -sa *adj* industrious
inédi•to -ta *adj* unpublished; new, novel, unknown
inefable *adj* ineffable
ineficacia *f* inefficacy
inefi•caz *adj* (*pl* **-caces**) ineffectual, ineffective; inefficient; incompetent
ineficiente *adj* inefficient; incompetent
inelegible *adj* ineligible
ineluctable *adj* inevitable, inescapable
ineludible *adj* inescapable
inenarrable *adj* indescribable
inencogible *adj* unshrinkable
inencontrable *adj* unobtainable
inequidad *f* inequity
inequívo•co -ca *adj* unmistakable
inercia *f* inertia
inerme *adj* unarmed
inerte *adj* inert; slow, sluggish
inescrupulo•so -sa *adj* unscrupulous
inescrutable or **inescudriñable** *adj* inscrutable
inespera•do -da *adj* unexpected, unforeseen; unhoped for
inestable *adj* unstable
inevitable *adj* unavoidable, inevitable
inexactitud *f* inaccuracy, inexactness

inexac•to -ta *adj* inaccurate, inexact
inexcusable *adj* inexcusable, unpardonable; unavoidable; indispensable
inexistencia *f* nonexistence
inexorable *adj* inexorable
inexperiencia *f* inexperience
inexplicable *adj* inexplicable, unexplainable
inexplica•do -da *adj* unexplained, unaccounted for
inexplora•do -da *adj* unexplored; (*mar*) uncharted
inexpresable *adj* inexpressible
inexpues•to -ta *adj* (phot) unexposed
inexpugnable *adj* impregnable; firm, unshakable
inextinguible *adj* undying; perpetual, lasting; (*sed*) unquenchable; (*risa*) uncontrollable
inextirpable *adj* ineradicable
infalible *adj* infallible
infamación *f* defamation
infamar *tr* to defame, discredit
infame *adj* infamous; vile, frightful, despicable || *mf* scoundrel
infamia *f* infamy
infancia *f* infancy
infan•do -da *adj* odious, unmentionable
infanta *f* female child; infanta (*any daughter of a king of Spain; wife of an infante*)
infante *m* male child; infante (*any son of a king of Spain who is not heir to the throne*); (mil) infantryman; **infante de coro** choirboy
infantería *f* infantry; **infantería de marina** marines, marine corps
infantil *adj* children's, childlike, childhood or child (*before the noun*), e.g., **la población infantil** the child population; (pej) childish, infantile
infarto *m* (heart) infarct, heart attack
infatigable *adj* indefatigable
infatuar §21 *tr* to make vain || *ref* to become vain
infaus•to -ta *adj* fatal, unlucky
infección *f* infection
infeccionar *tr* to infect
infeccio•so -sa *adj* infectious
infectar *tr* to infect
infec•to -ta *adj* foul, corrupt; infected; fetid
infecun•do -da *adj* sterile, barren
infe•liz (*pl* **-lices**) *adj* unhappy; simple, goodhearted || *m* wretch, poor soul
inferior *adj* inferior; lower; **inferior a** inferior to; lower than; less than; smaller than || *m* inferior
inferioridad *f* inferiority
inferir §68 *tr* to infer; lead to, entail; (*una herida*) inflict; (*una ofensa*) cause, offer
infernáculo *m* hopscotch
infernal *adj* infernal
infernar §2 *tr* to damn; irritate, annoy
infernillo *m* chafing dish
infestar *tr* to infest || *ref* to become infested
inficionar *tr* to infect || *ref* to become infected
infidelidad *f* infidelity; (*conjunto de infieles*) unbelievers
infidente *adj* faithless, disloyal
infiel *adj* (*falto de fidelidad*) unfaithful; (*no exacto*) inaccurate, inexact; (*no cristiano*) infidel || *mf* infidel
infierno *m* hell; **en el quinto infierno** *or* **en los quintos infiernos** far, far away; out in the boondocks
infijo *m* (gram) infix
infiltrar *tr & ref* to infiltrate
ínfi•mo -ma *adj* lowest; humblest, most abject; meanest, vilest
infinidad *f* infinity
infiniti•vo -va *adj & m* infinitive
infini•to -ta *adj* infinite || *m* infinite; (math) infinity || **infinito** *adv* greatly, very much
infirme *adj* infirm
inflación *f* inflation; (*vanidad*) conceit
inflaciona•rio -ria *adj* inflationary
inflado *m* inflation (*of a tire*)
inflamable *adj* inflammable, flammable
inflamación *f* ignition, inflammation; ardor, enthusiasm; (pathol) inflammation
inflamar *tr* to set on fire; inflame || *ref* to catch fire; become inflamed
inflar *tr* to inflate; exaggerate; puff up with pride || *ref* to inflate; be puffed up with pride
inflexible *adj* inflexible; unyielding, unbending
inflexión *f* inflection; **inflexión vocálica** (*metafonía*) umlaut
inflexionar *tr* to umlaut
infligir §27 *tr* to inflict
influencia *f* influence
influenciar *tr* to influence
influenza *f* influenza
influir §20 *intr* to have influence; have great weight; **influir en** *or* **sobre** to influence
influjo *m* influence; rising tide
influyente *adj* influential
información *f* information; (law) judicial inquiry, investigation; **informaciones** testimonial
informal *adj* (*que no se ajusta a las reglas debidas*) informal; unreliable
informar *tr & intr* to inform || *ref* to inquire, find out
informática *f* computer science, computers
informáti•co -ca *adj* computer || *mf* computer specialist, computer programmer
informati•vo -va *adj* informational; (*sección de un periódico*) news || *m* (telv) news, news program
informatizar §60 *tr* to computerize || *ref* to become computerized
informe *adj* shapeless, formless; misshapen || *m* piece of information; report; **informes** information; **informes confidenciales** inside information
infortuna•do -da *adj* unfortunate, unlucky
infortunio *m* misfortune; (*acaecimiento desgraciado*) mishap
infracción *f* infraction, infringement

infraconsumo *m* underconsumption
infrac•to -ta *adj* unperturbable
infraestructura *f* substructure; groundwork; (rr) roadbed
inframundo *m* underworld
infrarro•jo -ja *adj & m* infrared
infrascri•to -ta *adj* undersigned; hereinafter mentioned
infrecuente *adj* infrequent
infringir §27 *tr* to infringe, break, violate
infructuo•so -sa *adj* fruitless, unfruitful
ínfulas *fpl* conceit, airs; **darse ínfulas** to put on airs
infunda•do -da *adj* unfounded, groundless, baseless
infundio *m* lie, fib
infundir *tr* to infuse, instill
infusión *f* infusion; (*acción de echar agua sobre el que se bautiza*) sprinkling; **estar en infusión para** to be all set for
ingeniar *tr* to think up ‖ *ref* to manage; **ingeniarse a** *or* **para** to manage to; **ingeniarse para ir viviendo** to manage to get along
ingeniería *f* engineering; **ingeniería genética** genetic engineering
ingenie•ro -ra *mf* engineer; **ingeniero de caminos, canales y puertos** government civil engineer; **ingeniero químico** chemical engineer
ingenio *m* talent, creative faculty; talented person; cleverness, skill, wit; (*artificio mecánico*) apparatus, device; (*del encuadernador*) paper cutter; engine of war; **afilar** *or* **aguzar el ingenio** to sharpen one's wits; **ingenio de azúcar** sugar refinery
ingeniosidad *f* ingenuity; wittiness
ingenio•so -sa *adj* (*dotado de ingenio; hecho con ingenio*) ingenious; (*agudo, sutil*) witty
ingéni•to -ta *adj* innate, inborn
ingente *adj* huge, enormous
ingenuidad *f* ingenuousness
inge•nuo -nua *adj* ingenuous
ingerir §68 *tr & ref* var of **injerir**
ingestión *f* (food) consumption; ingestion
Inglaterra *f* England
ingle *f* groin
in•glés -glesa *adj* English; **a la inglesa** in the English manner ‖ *m* Englishman; (*idioma*) English; **el inglés medio** Middle English; **los ingleses** the English ‖ *f* Englishwoman
ingramatical *adj* ungrammatical
ingratitud *f* ingratitude, ungratefulness
ingra•to -ta *adj* (*desagradecido*) ungrateful; (*desagradecido; desagradable, áspero; improductivo*) thankless ‖ *mf* ingrate
ingravidez *f* lightness, tenuousness; (*gravedad nula*) weightlessness
ingrávi•do -da *adj* light, tenuous; weightless
ingrediente *m* ingredient
ingresa•do -da *mf* new student
ingresar *tr* to deposit ‖ *intr* to enter, become a member; (*beneficios*) come in ‖ *ref* (Mex) to enlist
ingreso *m* entrance; admission; **ingresos** income, revenue; **ingresos brutos** gross income; **ingresos netos** net income; **ingresos por trabajo personal, ingresos en concepto de salario** earned income
íngri•mo -ma *adj* solitary, alone
inhábil *adj* unable; unskillful; unfit, unqualified; ineligible; **en horas inhábiles** outside office hours
inhabilidad *f* inability; unskillfulness; unfitness; unsuitability; ineligibility
inhabilitar *tr* to disable, to disqualify, to incapacitate
inhabita•do -da *adj* uninhabited
inhabitua•do -da *adj* unaccustomed
inhalar *tr* to inhale
inherente *adj* inherent
inhibir *tr* to inhibit
inhospitala•rio -ria *adj* inhospitable
inhóspi•to -ta *adj* inhospitable
inhumanidad *f* inhumanity
inhuma•no -na *adj* inhuman, inhumane; (Chile) filthy
iniciación *f* initiation
inicial *adj & f* initial
iniciar *tr* to initiate; **iniciar la sesión** (compu) to log in *o* to log on ‖ *ref* to be initiated
iniciativa *f* initiative
ini•cuo -cua *adj* wicked, iniquitous
inigualable *adj* incomparable
iniguala•do -da *adj* unequaled
inimaginable *adj* unimaginable, unthinkable
ininteligente *adj* unintelligent
ininteligible *adj* unintelligible
ininterrumpi•do -da *adj* uninterrupted
iniquidad *f* iniquity
injerencia *f* interference, meddling
injerir §68 *tr* to insert, introduce; (*alimentos*) take in; (hort) to graft ‖ *ref* to interfere, meddle, intrude
injertar *tr* (hort & surg) to graft
injerto *m* (hort & surg) graft; transplant
injuria *f* offense, insult; abuse, wrong; damage, harm
injuriar *tr* to offend, insult; abuse, wrong; harm, damage
injurio•so -sa *adj* offensive, insulting; abusive; harmful; (*lenguaje*) profane
injusticia *f* injustice
injustifica•do -da *adj* unjustified
injus•to -ta *adj* unjust
inmacula•do -da *adj* immaculate
inmanejable *adj* unmanageable; unhandy
inmarcesible *adj* unfading
inmaterial *adj* immaterial
inmaturo -ra *adj* immature
inmediación *f* immediacy; proximity, nearness; **inmediaciones** neighborhood, outskirts, vicinity
inmediatamente *adv* immediately; **inmediatamente que** as soon as
inmedia•to -ta *adj* immediate; close, adjoining, next; next above; next below; (*pago*) prompt;

venir a las inmediatas to get into the thick of the fight
inmejorable *adj* superb, unsurpassable
inmemorial *adj* immemorial
inmen•so -sa *adj* immense
inmensurable *adj* immeasurable
inmereci•do -da *adj* undeserved
inmergir §27 *tr* to immerse
inmersión *f* immersion
inmigración *f* immigration
inmigrante *mf* immigrant
inmigrar *intr* to immigrate
inminente *adj* imminent
inmiscuir §20 & regular *tr* to mix ‖ *ref* to meddle, interfere
inmobilia•rio -ria *adj* real-estate
inmoble *adj* motionless; firm, constant
inmodera•do -da *adj* immoderate
inmodes•to -ta *adj* immodest
inmódi•co -ca *adj* excessive
inmoral *adj* immoral
inmortal *adj* immortal, deathless ‖ *mf* immortal
inmortalizar §60 *tr* to immortalize
inmotiva•do -da *adj* groundless; unmotivated
inmovilizar §60 *tr* to immobilize; (*un caudal*) tie up
inmueble *m* property, piece of real estate; **inmuebles** real estate
inmun•do -da *adj* dirty, filthy
inmune *adj* immune
inmunidad *f* immunity
inmunizar §60 *tr* to immunize
inmunodeficiencia *f* immunodeficiency
inmutar *tr* to change, alter; disturb, upset ‖ *ref* to change, alter; change countenance; **sin inmutarse** without batting an eye
inna•to -ta *adj* innate, inborn; natural
innatural *adj* unnatural
innavegable *adj* (*río*) unnavigable; (*embarcación*) unseaworthy
innecesa•rio -ria *adj* unnecessary
innegable *adj* undeniable
innoble *adj* ignoble
innocuidad *f* harmlessness
inno•cuo -cua *adj* harmless
innovación *f* innovation
innovar *tr* to innovate
innumerable *adj* innumerable
inocencia *f* innocence
inocentada *f* simpleness; blunder; (Ecuad) April Fools' joke
inocente *adj & mf* innocent; **coger por inocente** to make an April fool of
inocen•tón -tona *adj* simple, gullible ‖ *mf* gull, dupe
inoculación *f* inoculation
inocular *tr* to inoculate; contaminate, pervert
inodo•ro -ra *adj* odorless ‖ *m* deodorizer; (*excusado que funciona con agua corriente*) toilet
inofensi•vo -va *adj* inoffensive
inolvidable *adj* unforgettable
inope *adj* impecunious
inopia *f* indigence
inoportu•no -na *adj* inopportune, untimely
inorgáni•co -ca *adj* inorganic
inortodo•xo -xa *adj* unorthodox
inoxidable *adj* (*acero*) stainless; inoxidizable
inquietante *adj* disquieting, upsetting
inquietar *tr* to disquiet, worry; stir up, excite
inquie•to -ta *adj* anxious, worried
inquietud *f* disquiet, worry, concern
inquili•no -na *mf* tenant, renter
inquina *f* aversion, dislike, ill will
inquirir §40 *tr* to inquire, inquire into
inquisición *f* inquiry; inquisition
insabible *adj* unknowable
insaciable *adj* insatiable
insalubre *adj* unhealthy
insania *f* insanity
insa•no -na *adj* insane; imprudent
insatisfacción *f* dissatisfaction
insatisfe•cho -cha *adj* unsatisfied
inscribir §83 *tr* to inscribe; (educ) to enroll; (law) to record ‖ *ref* to enroll, register
inscripción *f* inscription; enrollment, registration
insecticida *adj & m* insecticide
insecto *m* insect
insegu•ro -ra *adj* insecure, unsafe; uncertain
inseminación *f* insemination; **inseminación artificial** artificial insemination
insensa•to -ta *adj* foolish, stupid
insensible *adj* callous, hard-hearted, unfeeling, insensitive; imperceptible
inseparable *adj* inseparable; undetachable ‖ *mf* inseparable ‖ *m* lovebird
insepul•to -ta *adj* unburied
inserción *f* insertion
inserir §68 *tr* to insert; (*injertar*) graft, engraft
insertar *tr* to insert
inservible *adj* useless
insidia *f* snare, ambush; plotting
insidiar *tr* to ambush, waylay; trap, trick
insidio•so -sa *adj* insidious
insigne *adj* noted, famous, renowned
insignia *f* badge, decoration, insignia; banner, standard
insignificante *adj* insignificant
insince•ro -ra *adj* insincere
insinuación *f* insinuation, hint
insinuante *adj* engaging, slick, crafty; suggestive
insinuar §21 *tr* to insinuate; suggest, hint at ‖ *ref* to creep in, slip in; ingratiate oneself; flow, run; **insinuarse en** to work one's way in
insípi•do -da *adj* insipid, vapid
insistir *intr* to insist
ínsi•to -ta *adj* inbred, innate
insociable *adj* unsociable
insolación *f* (pathol) sunstroke
insolencia *f* insolence
insolentar *tr* to make insolent ‖ *ref* to become insolent
insolente *adj* insolent
insóli•to -ta *adj* unusual
insoluble *adj* insoluble

insolvencia *f* insolvency
insomne *adj* sleepless
insomnio *m* insomnia
insondable *adj* fathomless; inscrutable
insonorización *f* soundproofing
insonoriza•do -da *adj* soundproof
insonorizar §60 *tr* to soundproof
insono•ro -ra *adj* soundproof
insospecha•do -da *adj* unsuspected
insostenible *adj* untenable
inspección *f* inspection; inspectorship; **inspección técnica de vehículos (I.T.V.)** car inspection
inspeccionar *tr* to inspect
inspec•tor -tora *mf* inspector
inspiración *f* inspiration; inhalation
inspirante *adj* inspiring
inspirar *tr & intr* to inspire; (*atraer a los pulmones*) inhale, breathe in || *ref* to be inspired
instalación *f* plant, factory; outfit, equipment; arrangements, fittings; installment; **instalación sanitaria** plumbing
instalador *m* (compu) installer
instalar *tr* to install || *ref* to settle
instantáne•o -a *adj* instantaneous || *f* snapshot
instante *m* instant, moment; **al instante** right away, immediately; **en un instante** in a flash; **por instantes** uninterruptedly; any time
instantemente *adv* insistently, urgently
instar *tr* to press, urge || *intr* to be pressing, be urgent
instaurar *tr* to restore; reestablish
instigar §44 *tr* to instigate
instilar *tr* to instill
instinti•vo -va *adj* instinctive
instinto *m* instinct
institución *f* institution; **instituciones** (*de un Estado*) constitution; (*de una ciencia, arte, etc.*) principles
instituir §20 *tr* to institute, found
instituto *m* institute; (*de una orden religiosa*) rule, constitution; **instituto de segunda enseñanza** *or* **de enseñanza media** high school
institu•triz *f* (*pl* **-trices**) governess
instrucción *f* instruction; education, training
instructi•vo -va *adj* instructive
instruc•tor -tora *mf* teacher, instructor || *m* (mil) drillmaster || *f* instructress
instruí•do -da *adj* well-educated; well-posted
instruir §20 *tr* to instruct; (*un proceso o expediente*) draw up
instrumentar *tr* to instrument
instrumentista *mf* instrumentalist
instrumento *m* instrument; (*persona que se emplea para alcanzar un resultado*) tool; **instrumento de cuerda** (mus) stringed instrument; **instrumento de viento** (mus) wind instrument
insubordina•do -da *adj* insubordinate
insubstituíble *adj* irreplaceable
insudar *intr* to drudge
insuficiente *adj* insufficient
insufrible *adj* insufferable
ínsula *f* island; one-horse town
insular *adj* insular || *mf* islander
insulina *f* insulin
insulsez *f* tastelessness; dullness, heaviness
insul•so -sa *adj* tasteless; dull, heavy
insultada *f* insult
insultar *tr* to insult || *ref* to faint, swoon
insulto *m* insult; fainting spell
insume *adj* expensive
insumergible *adj* unsinkable
insuperable *adj* insurmountable
insurgente *adj & mf* insurgent
insurrección *f* insurrection
intachable *adj* blameless, irreproachable
intac•to -ta *adj* intact, untouched
integración *f* integration
integrado *adj* integrated; (compu) integrated
integrante *mf* (sport) member (*of a team, the Hall of Fame, etc.*)
integrar *tr* to integrate
integridad *f* integrity; virginity
ínte•gro -gra *adj* integral, whole; honest
intelecto *m* intellect
intelectual *adj & mf* intellectual
intelectualidad *f* intellectuality; (*conjunto de los intelectuales de un país o región*) intelligentsia
inteligencia *f* intelligence; **estar en inteligencia con** to be in collusion with; **inteligencia artificial** artificial intelligence
inteligente *adj* intelligent; trained, skilled
inteligible *adj* intelligible
intemperancia *f* intemperance
intemperante *adj* intemperate
intemperie *f* inclement weather; **a la intemperie** in the open, unsheltered
intempesti•vo -va *adj* unseasonable, inopportune, untimely
intención *f* intention; (*cautelosa advertencia*) caution; (*instinto dañino de un animal*) viciousness; **con intención** deliberately, knowingly; **de intención** on purpose
intendencia *f* intendance; (SAm) mayoralty
intendente *m* intendant; quartermaster general; (SAm) mayor
intensar *tr & ref* to intensify
intensidad *f* intensity
intensificar §73 *tr & ref* to intensify
intensión *f* intensity
intensi•vo -va *adj* intensive
inten•so -sa *adj* intense
intentar *tr* to try, to attempt; intend; try out
intento *m* intent, purpose; **de intento** on purpose
intentona *f* rash attempt (*to rob, escape, etc.*)
interacción *f* interaction
interacti•vo -va *adj* interactive
interamerica•no -na *adj* inter-American
intercalar *tr* to intercalate, insert
intercambiar *tr & ref* to interchange, swap
intercambio *m* interchange, exchange
interceder *intr* to intercede
interceptar *tr* to intercept

intercep•tor -tora *mf* interceptor || *m* trap; separator; (aer) interceptor
interdecir §24 *tr* to interdict, forbid
interés *m* interest; **intereses creados** vested interests; **poner a interés** to put out at interest
interesa•do -da *adj* interested || *mf* interested party
interesante *adj* interesting
interesar *tr* to interest; involve || *intr* to be interesting || *ref* — **interesarse en** *or* **por** to be interested in, take an interest in
interescolar *adj* interscholastic, intercollegiate
interfase *f* interface
interfaz *f* (compu) interface
interfec•to -ta *adj* murdered || *mf* victim of murder
interferencia *f* (compu, phys, rad, sport, telv) interference
interferir §68 *tr* to interfere with || *intr* to interfere
interferón *m* (pharm) interferon
interfono *m* intercom
ínterin *adv* meanwhile || *conj* while, as long as || *m* (*pl* **intérines**) temporary incumbency
interinar *tr* to fill temporarily, fill in an acting capacity
interi•no -na *adj* temporary, acting, interim
interior *adj* interior, inner, inside; home, domestic || *m* interior, inside; mind, soul; **interiores** entrails, insides
interioridad *f* inside; **interioridades** inside story, private matters
interiorista *mf* interior decorator
interjección *f* interjection
interlinear *tr* to interline; (typ) to space, lead
interlocu•tor -tora *mf* speaker, party; interviewer
intermedia•rio -ria *adj* & *mf* intermediary || *m* (com) middleman
interme•dio -dia *adj* intermediate || *m* interval, interim; (mus) intermezzo; (theat) intermission, entr'acte
intermitente *adj* intermittent; blinking, flashing || *m* (aut) direction or turning light, blinker
internacional *adj* international
internacionalizar §60 *tr* to internationalize
interna•do -da *mf* (mil) internee || *m* boarding school
internamiento *m* internment; commitment (*to an institution*)
internar *tr* to send inland; intern; hospitalize; commit (*to an institution*) || *intr* to move inland || *ref* to move inland; take refuge, hide; insinuate oneself; **internarse en** to go deeply into
internauta *mf* (compu) Internet user
internáutico *adj* (compu) internet
internet *f* (compu) Internet
internista *mf* internist
inter•no -na *adj* internal; inside || *mf* boarding-school student; **interno de hospital** intern
interpelar *tr* to seek the protection or aid of; interrogate; interpellate
interpolar *tr* to interpolate; interpose; interrupt briefly
interponer §54 *tr* to interpose; appoint as mediator || *ref* to intervene, intercede
interprender *tr* to take by surprise
interpresa *f* surprise action; surprise seizure
interpretación *f* interpretation
interpretar *tr* to interpret
intérprete *mf* interpreter
interracial *adj* interracial
interrogación *f* interrogation; question mark
interrogar §44 *tr* & *intr* to question, interrogate
interrumpir *tr* to interrupt
interruptor *m* (elec) switch; **interruptor automático** (elec) circuit breaker; **interruptor del encendido** (aut) ignition switch; **interruptor de resorte** (elec) snap switch
intersección *f* (geom) intersection
intersticio *m* interstice; interval
interurba•no -na *adj* long-distance; (*tren*) intercity
intervalo *m* interval
intervención *f* intervention; inspection; (*de cuentas*) audit, auditing; (surg) operation; **intervención de los precios** price control; **intervención quirúrgica** (med) operation; **no intervención** nonintervention
intervenir §79 *tr* to take up, work on; inspect, supervise; (*cuentas*) audit; (*un teléfono*) tap; (surg) operate on || *intr* to mediate, intervene, intercede; participate; happen
interventor *m* election supervisor; (com) auditor
inter•viev *m* (*pl* **-vievs**) interview
intervievar *tr* to interview
intesta•do -da *adj* & *mf* intestate
intesti•no -na *adj* internal; domestic || *m* intestine; **intestino delgado** small intestine; **intestino grueso** large intestine
intimación *f* announcement, notification
intimar *tr* to announce || *intr* & *ref* to become well-acquainted, to become intimate
intimidad *f* intimacy, closeness; (*parte íntima o personal*) privacy
intimidar *tr* to intimidate
ínti•mo -ma *adj* intimate; (*más interno*) innermost
intitular *tr* to entitle || *ref* to use a title; be called
intocable *mf* untouchable
intolerante *adj* & *mf* intolerant
into•so -sa *adj* unshorn; ignorant; (*libro o revista*) uncut || *mf* ignoramus
intoxicación *f* intoxication; poisoning; **intoxicación alimenticia** food poisoning
intoxicar §73 *tr* to poison, intoxicate
intracruzamiento *m* inbreeding
intranáutico *adj* intranet
intranquilidad *f* uneasiness, worry
intranquilizar §60 *tr* to make uneasy, worry
intranqui•lo -la *adj* uneasy, worried
intransigente *adj* & *mf* intransigent, die-hard
intransiti•vo -va *adj* intransitive
intrascendente *adj* unimportant; nonessential

intratable *adj* unmanageable; impassable; unsociable
intravenosa *adj* intravenous
intrepidez *f* intrepidity
intrépi•do -da *adj* intrepid
intriga *f* intrigue
intrigar §44 *tr* (*excitar la curiosidad de*) to intrigue || *intr* to intrigue || *ref* to be intrigued
intrinca•do -da *adj* intricate
intrincar §73 *tr* to complicate; confuse, bewilder
intríngu•lis *m* (*pl* **-lis**) hidden motive, mystery
intrínse•co -ca *adj* intrinsic(al)
introducción *f* introduction
introducir §19 *tr* to introduce; insert, put in || *ref* to gain access; meddle, interfere, intrude
introito *m* (*de un escrito o una oración*) introduction; (*de un poema dramático*) prologue; (eccl) introit
intromisión *f* interference
introspecti•vo -va *adj* introspective
introverti•do -da *mf* introvert
intru•so -sa *adj* intrusive || *mf* intruder, interloper
intuición *f* intuition
intuir §20 *tr* to guess, sense
intuito *m* view, glance, look; **por intuito de** in view of
inundación *f* flood, inundation
inundar *tr* to flood, inundate
inurba•no -na *adj* discourteous, unmannerly
inusita•do -da *adj* (*no ordinario*) unusual; obsolete, out of use
inusual *adj* unusual
inútil *adj* useless
invadir *tr* to invade
invalidar *tr* to invalidate
invalidez *f* invalidity
inváli•do -da *adj* invalid, null and void; (med) disabled, handicapped || *mf* invalid
invariable *adj* invariable
invasión *f* invasion
inva•sor -sora *mf* invader
invectiva *f* invective
invectivar *tr* to inveigh against
invencible *adj* invincible
invención *f* invention; finding, discovery; deception
invendible *adj* unsalable
inventar *tr* to invent
inventariar §77 & regular *tr* to inventory
inventario *m* inventory; muster roll
inventi•vo -va *adj* inventive || *f* inventiveness
invento *m* invention
inven•tor -tora *adj* inventive || *mf* inventor
inverecun•do -da *adj* shameless, brazen
inverisímil *adj* improbable, unlikely
invernáculo *m* greenhouse, hothouse, conservatory
invernada *f* wintertime; (SAm) pasture land; (Ven) torrential rain
invernadero *m* greenhouse, hothouse; winter resort; winter pasture
invernal *adj* winter || *m* cattle shed (*in winter-pasture land*)
invernar §2 *intr* to winter; be winter
inverni•zo -za *adj* winter; wintery
inverosímil *adj* improbable, unlikely
inversión *f* inversion; (*de dinero*) investment; (gram) inverted order
inversionista *adj* investment || *mf* investor
inver•so -sa *adj* inverse, opposite; **a** *or* **por la inversa** on the contrary
inversor *m* investor
invertebra•do -da *adj & m* invertebrate
inverti•do -da *adj* inverted
invertir §68 *tr* to invert; (*dinero*) invest; (*tiempo*) spend; reverse
investidura *f* investment, investiture; station, standing
investigación *f* investigation, research; **investigación mercológica** market research; **investigación y desarrollo** research and development
investiga•dor -dora *adj* investigative; **labor investigadora** research (work) || *mf* investigator; researcher; **investigador de campo** fieldworker
investigar §44 *tr* to investigate || *intr* to research
investir §50 *tr* — **investir con** or **de** (*poner en posesión de*) to invest with
invetera•do -da *adj* inveterate, confirmed
invic•to -ta *adj* unconquered
invidencia *f* blindness
invidente *adj* blind || *mf* blind person
invierno *m* winter; rainy season
inviolabilidad *f* inviolability; undamageability
invisible *adj* invisible || *m* (Mex) hair net; **en un invisible** in an instant
invitación *f* invitation
invita•do -da *mf* guest; **invitado de honor** guest of honor
invitar *tr* to invite
invocar §73 *tr* to invoke
involunta•rio -ria *adj* involuntary
invulnerable *adj* invulnerable
inyección *f* injection; **inyección secundaria** booster shot
inyectable *adj* injectable || *m* ampule, phial
inyecta•do -da *adj* bloodshot, inflamed
inyectar *tr* to inject || *ref* to become congested; become inflamed
ionizar §60 *tr* to ionize || *ref* to be ionized
ionosfera *f* ionosphere
ir §41 *intr* to go; be becoming, fit, suit; be at stake; **ir a** + *inf* to be going to + *inf* (*to express futurity*); **ir a buscar** to go get, go for; **ir a parar en** to end up in; **ir con cuidado** to be careful; **ir con miedo** to be afraid; **ir con tiento** to watch one's step; **ir de caza** to go hunting; **ir de pesca** to go fishing; **lo que va de** so far (as); **¡qué va!** of course not!; **¡vaya!** the deuce!; what a. . . ! || *ref* to go away; leak; wear away; get old; break to pieces
ira *f* anger, wrath, ire

iracun•do -da *adj* angry, wrathful, irate
Irak, el Iraq
Irán, el Iran
ira•nés -nesa or ira•nio -nia *adj & mf* Iranian
ira•qués -quesa or **iraquiano -na** *adj & mf* Iraqi
iris *m* (*pl* **iris**) (*del ojo*) iris; rainbow
Irlanda *f* Ireland; **Irlanda del Norte** Northern Ireland
irlan•dés -desa *adj* Irish ‖ *m* Irishman; (*idioma*) Irish; **los irlandeses** the Irish ‖ *f* Irishwoman
ironía *f* irony
iróni•co -ca *adj* ironic(al)
ironizar §60 *tr* to ridicule
irracional *adj* irrational
irradiar *tr* to radiate, irradiate; (*difundir*) broadcast; (med) to irradiate ‖ *intr* to radiate
irrazonable *adj* unreasonable
irreal *adj* unreal
irrealidad *f* unreality
irrebatible *adj* irrefutable
irreconocible *adj* unrecognizable
irrecuperable *adj* irretrievable
irrecusable *adj* unimpeachable
irredimible *adj* irredeemable
irreemplazable *adj* irreplaceable
irreflexión *f* rashness, thoughtlessness
irreflexi•vo -va *adj* rash, thoughtless
irregular *adj* irregular ‖ *m* (mil) irregular
irregularidad *f* irregularity; embezzlement
irrelevante *adj* irrelevant
irreligio•so -sa *adj* irreligious
irrellenable *adj* nonrefillable
irremediable *adj* irremediable
irremisible *adj* unpardonable
irreparable *adj* irreparable
irreprimible *adj* irrepressible
irreprochable *adj* irreproachable
irresistible *adj* irresistible
irresoluble *adj* unworkable, unsolvable
irrespetuo•so -sa *adj* disrespectful
irresponsable *adj* irresponsible
irresuel•to -ta *adj* hesitant, wavering
irreverente *adj* irreverent
irreversible *adj* irreversible
irrevocable *adj* irrevocable
irrigación *f* irrigation
irrigar §44 *tr* to irrigate
irrisible *adj* laughable, absurd
irrisión *f* derision, ridicule; laughingstock
irriso•rio -ria *adj* derisory, laughable, ridiculous
irritante *adj & m* irritant
irritar *tr* to irritate ‖ *ref* to become exasperated
irrompible *adj* unbreakable
irrumpir *intr* to burst in; **irrumpir en** to burst into
irrupción *f* sudden attack; invasion
Isabel *f* Elizabeth
isi•dro -dra *mf* hick, jake, yokel
isla *f* island; (*manzana de casas*) block; **isla de peatones** or **isla de seguridad** safety zone (for pedestrians); **islas Baleares** Balearic Islands; **Islas Británicas** British Isles; **Islas Canarias** Canary Islands; **Islas de Barlovento** Windward Islands; **Islas de Sotavento** Leeward Islands; **Islas Filipinas** Philippine Islands; **Islas Malvinas** Falkland Islands; **Islas Vírgenes** Virgin Islands
Islam, el Islam
islámi•co -ca *adj* Islamic
islamismo *m* Islamism
islan•dés -desa *adj* Icelandic ‖ *mf* Icelander ‖ *m* (*idioma*) Icelandic
Islandia *f* Iceland
isle•ño -ña *adj* island ‖ *mf* islander; (Cuba) Canarian
isleta *f* traffic island
islote *m* isle
ismo *m* (pej) ism
isométri•co -ca *adj* isometric
isométrica *f* isometrics
isósce•les *adj* (*pl* **-les**) isosceles
isótopo *m* isotope
Israel *m* Israel
israe•lí (*pl* **-líes**) *adj & mf* Israeli
israelita *adj & mf* Israelite
istmo *m* isthmus
Italia *f* Italy
italia•no -na *adj & mf* Italian
itáli•co -ca *adj* Italic; (typ) italic ‖ *f* (typ) italics
itinera•rio -ria *adj & m* itinerary
izar §60 *tr* (naut) to hoist, haul up
izquierda *f* left hand; left-hand side; (pol) left; **a la izquierda** left, on the left, to the left
izquierdear *intr* to go wild, go astray, go awry
izquierdista *adj* leftist ‖ *mf* leftist, leftwinger
izquierdizante *adj* leftish
izquier•do -da *adj* left; left-hand; left-handed; crooked; **levantarse del izquierdo** to get out of bed on the wrong side ‖ *f* see **izquierda**

J

J, j (jota) *f* tenth letter of the Spanish alphabet
jabalcón *m* strut, brace
jaba•lí *m* (*pl* **-líes**) wild boar
jabalina *f* javelin; wild sow
jabardillo *m* (*de insectos*) noisy swarm; noisy throng
jabeque *m* (naut) xebec; gash in the face
jabón *m* soap; cake of soap; **dar jabón a** to softsoap; **dar un jabón a** (coll) to upbraid, to reprimand; **jabón de afeitar** shaving soap; **jabón de Castilla** Castile soap; **jabón de tocador** or **de olor** toilet soap; **jabón de sastre**

soapstone, French chalk, tailor's chalk; **jabón en escamas** soap flakes; **jabón en polvo** soap powder; **jabón neutro** mild soap

jabonado *m* soaping; (*ropa lavada o por lavar*) wash

jabonadura *f* soaping; **dar una jabonadura a** to lambaste, upbraid; **jabonaduras** soapy water; soapsuds

jabonar *var* of **en jabonar**

jaboncillo *m* small bar of soap; **jaboncillo de sastre** soapstone, French chalk, tailor's chalk

jabone•ro -ra *adj* soap; (*toro*) yellowish, dirty-white || *mf* soapmaker; soap dealer || *f* soap dish

jabonete *m* cake of toilet soap

jabono•so -sa *adj* soapy, lathery

jaca *f* pony, jennet

jacal *m* (Guat, Mex, Ven) hut, shack

jácara *f* merry ballad; cheerful song and dance; night revelers; story, argument; fake, hoax, lie; annoyance, bother

jacarear *intr* to go serenading, go singing in the street; be disagreeable

jáca•ro -ra *adj & m* braggart || *f* see **jácara**

jacinto *m* hyacinth

jaco *m* nag, jade; gray parrot

Jacobo *m* (*reyes de Inglaterra*) James

jactancia *f* boasting, bragging

jactancio•so -sa *adj* boastful, bragging

jactar *ref* to boast, brag; **jactarse de** to boast of

jade *m* jade

jadeante *adj* panting

jadear *intr* to pant

jadeo *m* panting

ja•ez *m* (*pl* **-eces**) harness, piece of harness; ilk, stripe, kind; **jaeces** trappings

jaguar *m* jaguar

jagüel *m* (Arg) reservoir

jaharrar *tr* to plaster

Jaime *m* James

jalar *tr* to pull; flirt with || *intr* to get out, beat it || *ref* to get drunk

jalbegar §44 *tr* to whitewash; (*el rostro*) to paint || *ref* to paint the face

jalbegue *m* whitewash; whitewashing; paint, make-up

jalda•do -da *adj* bright-yellow

jalea *f* jelly; **hacerse una jalea** to be madly in love

jalear *tr* (*a los que bailan y cantan*) to animate with clapping and shouting; (*a los perros*) to incite, urge on; (Chile) to tease, pester || *intr* to dance the jaleo || *ref* to have a noisy time; swing and sway

jaleo *m* cheering, shouting; jamboree; jaleo (*vivacious Spanish solo dance*)

jalis•co -ca *adj* (Guat, Mex) drunk || *m* (Mex) straw hat

jalma *f* small packsaddle

jalón *m* surveying rod, range pole; (Guat, Mex) swig of liquor; (CAm) beau; **jalón de mira** leveling rod

jalonar *tr* to stake out, mark out

jalonear *tr* (Mex) to pull, jerk

jalonero *m* (surv) rodman

jamaica *m* Jamaica rum || *f* (Mex) charity fair

jamaica•no -na or jamaiqui•no -na *adj & mf* Jamaican

jamar *tr* to eat

jamás *adv* never; ever

jamba *f* jamb

jambaje *m* doorframe, window frame

jamelgo *m* jade, nag

jamete *m* samite

jamón *m* ham

jamona *adj* (coll) buxom, full-figured; (Esp, coll) stunning, attractive || *f* buxom middle-aged woman

jamugas *fpl* mule chair

jánda•lo -la *adj & mf* Andalusian

Jantipa *f* or **Jantipe** *f* Xanthippe

Japón, el Japan

japo•nés -nesa *adj & mf* Japanese || *m* (*idioma*) Japanese

jaque *m* (*lance del ajedrez*) check; bully; **dar jaque a** to check; **dar jaque mate a** to checkmate; **en jaque** in check; **estar muy jaque** to be full of pep; **jaque mate** checkmate; **tener en jaque** to hold a threat over the head of || *interj* check!

jaquear *tr* to check; (*al enemigo*) harass

jaqueca *f* sick headache, migraine; **dar una jaqueca a** to bore to death

jaqueco•so -sa *adj* boring, tiresome

jaquemar *m* jack (*figure that strikes a clock bell*)

jarabe *m* syrup; sweet drink; **jarabe de pico** lip service, idle promise

jarana *f* merrymaking; rumpus; carousal, spree; trick, deceit; jest, joke; small guitar; **ir de jarana** to go on a spree

jaranear *tr* (CAm, Col) to swindle, cheat || *intr* to go on a spree; raise a rumpus; joke

jarane•ro -ra *adj* merrymaking; cheerful, merry || *mf* merrymaker, reveler

jarano *m* sombrero

jarcia *f* fishing tackle; jumble, mess; **jarcias** tackle, rigging; **jarcia trozada** junk (*old cable*)

jardín *m* garden, flower garden; (baseball) field, outfield; (naut) privy, latrine; **jardín botánico de árboles** arboretum; **jardín central** (baseball) center field; **jardín de la infancia** kindergarten; **jardín derecho** (baseball) right field; **jardines colgantes** hanging gardens; **jardín izquierdo** (baseball) left field

jardinera *f* jardiniere, flower stand; basket carriage; summer trolley car, open trolley car; window box

jardinería *f* gardening

jardine•ro -ra *mf* gardener; **jardinero adornista** landscape gardener || *m* (baseball) fielder, outfielder || *f* see **jardinera**

jardinista *mf* landscape gardener

jarea *f* (Mex) hunger

jarear *intr* (Bol) to stop for a rest || *ref* (Mex) to flee, run away; (Mex) to swing, sway; (Mex) to die of starvation
jareta *f* (sew) casing
jari•fo -fa *adj* showy, spruce, natty
jaro•cho -cha *adj* brusk, bluff || *m* insulting fellow; Veracruz peasant
jarope *m* syrup; nasty potion
jarra *f* jug, jar, water pitcher; **de jarras** or **en jarras** with arms akimbo
jarrete *m* hock, gambrel
jarretera *f* garter
jarro *m* pitcher; **echar un jarro de agua (fría) a** to pour cold water on
jarrón *m* (*vaso para adornar chimeneas, consolas, etc.*) vase; (*sobre un pedestal*) urn
jaspe *m* jasper
jaspea•do -da *adj* marbled, speckled || *m* marbling, speckling
jaspear *tr* to marble, speckle
jateo *m* foxhound
ja•to -ta *mf* calf
Jauja *f* utopia, promised land, bed of roses; **¿Estamos aquí o en Jauja?** Where do you think you are, at a vacation resort?; **¡esto es Jauja!** this is the life!
jaula *m* cage; (*embalaje de listones de madera*) crate; (Mex) open freight car; (Cuba, P-R) police wagon
jauría *f* pack (*of hounds*)
java•nés -nesa *adj & mf* Javanese || *m* (*idioma*) Javanese
jazmín *m* jasmine; **jasmín de la India** gardenia
jazz *m* jazz
J.C. *abbr* **Jesucristo**
jeans [(d)ʒins] *mpl* jeans
jebe *m* alum; (SAm) rubber
jedive *m* khedive
jefa *f* female head or leader; **jefa de bomberos** fire chief; **jefa de ruta** hostess (*on a bus*)
jefatura *f* headship, leadership; (*de policía*) headquarters
jefe *m* chief, boss, head, leader; (*de una tribu*) chieftain; **jefe de bomberos** fire chief; **jefe de cocina** chef; **jefe do coro** choirmaster; **jefe de equipajes** (rr) baggage master; **jefe de estación** stationmaster; **jefe del estado** chief of state; **jefe del gobierno** chief executive; **jefe de redacción** editor in chief; **jefe de ruta** guide; **jefe de taller** supervisor, foreman; **jefe de tren** (rr) conductor; **jefe de tribu** chieftain; **jefe de ventas** sales manager; **quedar jefe** (Chile) to gamble away everything
jején *m* gnat, sandfly
jenabe *m* or **jenable** *m* mustard
jengibre *m* ginger
Jenofonte *m* Xenophon
jeque *m* sheik
jerarca *m* hierarch, head
jerarquía *f* hierarchy; **de jerarquía** important
jeremiada *f* jeremiad
jeremiquear *intr* to moan; pour out one's troubles
jerez *m* sherry
jerga *f* slang; jargon; mumbo jumbo, gobbledegook; coarse cloth; straw mattress; **jerga periodística** (pej) journalese
jergón *m* straw mattress; ill-fitting clothes; (*persona torpe y estúpida*) lummox
Jericó Jericho
jerife *m* shereef
jerigonza *f* jargon; mumbo jumbo, gobbledegook; vulgar language; thieves or gypsies language, secret language; piece of folly
jeringa *f* syringe; (*para inyectar materias blandas en una máquina*) gun; annoyance, plague; **jeringa de engrase** or **grasa** grease gun
jeringar §44 *tr* to syringe; inject; give an enema to; plague
jeringazo *m* injection, shot; squirt
jeringuilla *f* (*jeringa pequeña*) syringe; (bot) mock orange
Jerjes *m* Xerxes
jeroglífi•co -ca *adj & m* hieroglyphic
Jerónimo *m* Jerome
jer•sey *m* (*pl* **-seis**) jersey, sweater
Jerusalén Jerusalem
Jesucristo *m* Jesus Christ
jesuíta *adj & m* Jesuit
jesuíti•co -ca *adj* Jesuitic(al)
Jesús *m* Jesus; (*imagen del niño Jesús*) bambino; **en un decir Jesús** in an instant; **¡Jesús, María y José!** my gracious!
jeta *f* hog's snout, pig face; (*rostro de una persona*) phiz, mug; **estar con tanta jeta** to make a long face; **poner jeta** to pucker one's lips
jet lag *m* (*cansancio causado por el desfase horario*) jet lag
jetu•do -da *adj* thick-lipped; grim, gruff
Jhs. *abbr* **Jesús**
jíba•ro -ra *mf* (W-I) white peasant
jibia *f* cuttlefish
jícara *f* chocolate cup; (CAm, Mex, W-I) calabash cup
jícaro *m* calabash (tree)
jifia *f* swordfish
jilguero *m* linnet, goldfinch
jilote *m* (Mex) green ear of corn
jineta *f* (zool) genet
jinete *m* rider, horseman
jinetear *tr* (*caballos cerriles*) to break in || *intr* to show off one's horsemanship
jinglar *intr* to swing, to rock
jingle [(d)ʒingel] *m* (*anuncio rimado y cantado*) (rad, telv) jingle
jingoísmo *m* jingoism
jingoísta *adj & mf* jingo
jipa•to -ta *adj* pale, wan; insipid, tasteless; (Guat) drunk
jipijapa *m* Panama hat || *f* jipijapa; strip of jipijapa straw
jira *f* strip of cloth; outing, picnic; trip, tour; swing, political trip
jirón *m* rag, tatter, shred; (*de una falda*) facing;

pennant; bit, drop, shred; **hacer jirones** to tear to shreds
jitomate *m* (Mex) tomato
joco•so -sa *adj* jocose, jocular
jocotal *m* (CAm, Mex) Spanish plum (*tree*)
jocote *m* (CAm, Mex) Spanish plum (*fruit*)
jocoyote *m* (Mex) baby (*youngest child*)
jofaina *f* washbowl, basin
jogging *m* jogging; **hacer jogging** (*correr despacio*) to jog
jojoto *m* (Ven) sweet corn
jolgorio *m* fun, merriment
jonrón *m* (baseball) home run; **jonrón con casa llena** grand slam
Jordán *m* Jordan (*river*); **ir al Jordán** to be born again
Jordania *f* Jordan (*country*)
jorda•no -na *adj & mf* Jordanian
jorguín *m* sorcerer, wizard
jorguina *f* sorceress, witch
jorguinería *f* sorcery, witchcraft
jornada *f* journey, trip, stage; day's journey; (*horas del trabajo diario del obrero*) workday; (*tiempo que dura la vida de un hombre*) lifetime; battle; (*muerte*) passing; summer residence of diplomat or diplomatic corps; event, occasion; undertaking; (mil) expedition; (*de un drama*) (archaic) act; **a grandes** *or* **largas jornadas** by forced marches; **al fin de la jornada** in the end; **caminar por sus jornadas** to proceed with circumspection; **hacer mala jornada** to get nowhere; **jornada ordinaria** full time; **jornada reducida** reduced working hours
jornal *m* day's work; day's pay; **a jornal** by the day; **jornal mínimo** minimum wage
jornalero *m* day laborer
joroba *f* hump; annoyance, bother
joroba•do -da *adj* humpbacked, hunchbacked; annoyed, bothered || *mf* humpback, hunchback
jorobar *tr* to annoy, pester
jorongo *m* (Mex) poncho; (Mex) woolen blanket
José *m* Joseph
jota *f* (*letra del alfabeto*) J; jota (*Spanish folk dance and music*); jot, iota, tittle; vegetable soup; **sin faltar una jota** with not a whit left out
joven *adj* young; **ser joven de esperanzas** to have a bright future || *mf* youth, young person; **de joven** as a youth, as a young man, as a young woman
jovial *adj* jovial
joya *f* jewel; (*brocamantón*) diamond brooch; (*agasajo*) gift, present; (*persona o cosa de mucha valía*) (fig) jewel, gem; **joya de familia** heirloom; **joyas** jewelry; trousseau; **joyas de fantasía** costume jewelry; **joyas de la corona** crown jewels
joyante *adj* glossy
joyelero *m* jewel case, casket
joyería *f* (*conjunto de joyas*) jewelry; jewelry shop; jewelry trade
joye•ro -ra *mf* jeweler || *m* jewel case, casket
joystick [(d)ʒojstik] *m* (electron, compu) joystick
Juan *m* John; **Buen Juan** sap, easy mark; **Juan Español** the Spanish people, the typical Spaniard; **San Juan Bautista** John the Baptist
Juana *f* Jane, Jean, Joan; **Juana de Arco** Joan of Arc, Jeanne d'Arc; **juanas** glove stretcher
juanete *m* bunion; high cheekbone
Juanito *m* Jack
jubilación *f* retirement; (*renta de la persona jubilada*) pension, retirement annuity
jubila•do -da *adj* retired || *mf* retired person, pensioner
jubilar *tr* to retire, pension; throw out || *intr* to rejoice; retire, be pensioned || *ref* to rejoice; retire, be pensioned; (Col) to decline, go to pieces; (CAm, Ven) to play hooky; (Cuba, Mex) to become a past master
jubileo *m* much coming and going, great doings; (eccl) jubilee; **por jubileo** once in a long time
júbilo *m* jubilation
jubilo•so -sa *adj* jubilant, joyful
jubón *m* jerkin
judaísmo *m* Judaism
judeo-cristia•no -na *adj* Judeo-Christian
judería *f* (*raza judaica*) Jewry; (*barrio de los judíos*) ghetto
judía *f* kidney bean, string bean; **judía de careta** black-eyed bean; **judía de la peladilla** lima bean; **judía verde** (Esp) green bean
judicatura *f* judicature; (*cargo de juez*) judgeship
judicial *adj* judicial, judiciary
judí•o -a *adj* Jewish || *mf* Jew || *f* see **judía**
juego *m* (*acción de jugar*) play, playing; (*ejercicio recreativo en el cual se gana o se pierde*) game; (*vicio de jugar*) gambling; (*lugar donde se ejecutan ciertos juegos*): (bowling) alley; (tennis) court; (baseball) field; (*tantos necesarios para ganar la partida*) game; (*colección de cosas*) kit; (*de muebles*) suit, suite; (*de café*) service; (*de vajilla, libros, sillas*) set; (*de luces, colores, aguas*) play; (mach) play; (*p.ej., de diplomacia*) (fig) game; **a juego** to match, e.g., **una silla a juego** a chair to match; **conocer el juego de** to see through, to have the number of; **en juego** at hand; **hacer juego** to match; **hacer juego con** to match, to go with; **juego de adivinanzas** guessing game; **juego de alcoba** bedroom suit; **juego de azar** game of chance; **juego de bolas** (mach) ball bearing; **juego de campanas** chimes; **juego de comedor** dining-room suit; **juego de envite** gambling game, game played for money; **juego de escritorio** desk set; **juego de la cuna** cat's cradle; **juego de la pulga** tiddlywinks; **juego de las pajitas** jackstraws; **juego del corro** ring-around-a-rosy; **juego de llaves** set of keys; **juego del salto** leapfrog; **juego del tres en raya** tick-tack-toe played with movable counters or pebbles; **juego de manos** legerdemain,

sleight of hand; roughhousing; **juego de niños** (*cosa muy fácil*) child's play; **juego de palabras** play on words, pun; **juego de pelota** ball game; pelota; **juego de piernas** footwork; **juego de por ver** (Chile) game played for fun; **juego de prendas** game of forfeits, forfeits; **juego de suerte** game of chance; **juego de tejo** shuffleboard; **juego de timbres** glockenspiel; **juego de vocablos** or **voces** play on words, pun; **juego limpio** fair play; **juego público** gambling house; **juegos de sociedad** parlor games; **juegos malabares** juggling; flimflam; **juego sucio** foul play; **no ser cosa de juego** to be no laughing matter; **por juego** in fun, for fun; **verle a uno el juego** to be on to someone

juerga *f* carousal, spree; **juerga de borrachera** drinking bout, binge; **ir de juerga** (coll) to go on a spree

juerguista *mf* carouser, reveler

jue•ves *m* (*pl* **-ves**) Thursday; **Jueves Santo** Maundy Thursday

juez *m* (*pl* **jueces**) judge; **juez de alzadas** appellate judge; **juez de guardia** coroner; **juez de instrucción** examining magistrate; **juez de paz** justice of the peace; **juez de salida** (sport) starter; **juez de silla** umpire; **juez de tiempo** (sport) timekeeper

jugada *f* (*lance*) play, throw, stroke, move; **mala jugada** dirty trick

juga•dor -dora *mf* player; gambler; **jugador de manos** prestidigitator; **jugador de ventaja** sharper

jugar §42 *tr* (*p.ej., un naipe, una partida de juego*) to play; (*una espada*) wield; (*arriesgar*) stake, risk; (*las manos, los dedos*) move; **jugarle a uno las bebidas** to match someone for the drinks ‖ *intr* to play; to gamble; (*hacer juego dos cosas*) match; (*intervenir*) figure, participate; **jugar a** (*p.ej., los naipes, el tenis*) to play; **jugar con** (*un contrario*) to play; (*una persona; los sentimientos de una persona*) toy with; match; **jugar en** to have a hand in ‖ *ref* (*p.ej., la vida*) to risk; to be at stake; **jugarse el todo por el todo** to stake all, shoot the works

jugarreta *f* bad play, poor play; mean trick, dirty trick

juglar *m* minstrel, jongleur; (*bufón*) (archaic) juggler

juglaría *f* minstrelsy

jugo *m* (*p.ej., de la naranja*) juice; (*de la carne*) gravy; (*líquido orgánico*) juice; (fig) gist, essence, substance; **en su jugo** (culin) au jus; **jugo de muñeca** elbow grease

jugo•so -sa *adj* juicy; substantial, important

juguete *m* toy, plaything; (*burla*) joke, jest; (theat) skit; **de juguete** toy, e.g., **soldado de juguete** toy soldier; **juguete de movimiento** mechanical toy; **por juguete** for fun, in fun

juguetear *intr* to frolic, romp, sport

juguete•ro -ra *adj* toy ‖ *mf* toy dealer ‖ *m* whatnot, étagère

juguete-sorpresa *m* (*pl* **juguetes-sorpresa**) jack-in-the-box

jugue•tón -tona *adj* playful, frisky

juicio *m* judgment, opinion; (*prudencia*) sense; (law) trial, prosecution; **estar en su cabal juicio** to be in one's right mind; **estar fuera de juicio** to be out of one's mind; **juicio de Dios** (hist) ordeal; **pedir en juicio** (law) to sue

juicio•so -sa *adj* judicious, wise

julepe *m* julep; scolding; scare, fright

julepear *tr* to scold; whip; (SAm) to scare, frighten; (Mex) to weary, tire out

julio *m* July

julo *m* lead cow, lead mule

jumen•to -ta *mf* ass, donkey

juncal *adj* willowy, rushy; (fig) willowy, lissome

juncia *f* sedge; **vender juncia** to boast, brag

junco *m* (*embarcación china*) junk; (bot) rush, bulrush; **junco de Indias** (bot) rattan; **junco de laguna** (bot) rush, bulrush

junco•so -sa *adj* rushy, full of rushes

jungla *f* jungle

junio *m* June

junípero *m* juniper

junquera *f* rush, bulrush

junquillo *m* jonquil

junta *f* meeting, conference; board, council; junction, union; joint, seam; (*empaquetadura*) gasket; (*arandela*) washer; **junta de comercio** board of trade; **junta de charnela** (mach) knuckle; **junta de sanidad** board of health; **junta directiva** board of directors; **juntas** (mas) pointing; **junta universal** (mach) universal joint

juntamente *adv* together; at the same time

juntar *tr* to join, unite; gather, gather together; (*una puerta*) half-close ‖ *ref* to gather together; go along; copulate

jun•to -ta *adj* joined, united; **jun•tos -tas** together ‖ *f* see **junta** ‖ **junto** *adv* together; at the same time; **junto a** near, close to; **junto con** along with, together with; **todo junto** at the same time, all at once

juntura *f* junction; (*p.ej., de una cañería; de un hueso*) joint; connection, coupling

Júpiter *m* (astr, myth) Jupiter

jura *f* oath

jura•do -da *adj* (*enemigo*) sworn ‖ *m* (*conjunto de ciudadanos encargados de determinar la culpabilidad del acusado; conjunto de examinadores de un certamen*) jury; (*cada uno de los expresados individuos*) juror; juryman

juramentar *tr* to swear in ‖ *ref* to take an oath, be sworn in

juramento *m* oath; (*voto, reniego*) curse, swearword; **prestar juramento a** to swear to; **tomar juramento a** to swear in

jurar *tr* to swear; (*la verdad de una cosa*) swear to; swear allegiance to ‖ *intr* (*pronunciar un juramento*) to swear, take an oath; (*echar votos o reniegos*) swear, curse; **jurar** + *inf* to swear to + *inf* ‖ *ref* to swear; **jurársela** or

jurárselas a uno to have it in for someone, swear to get even with someone
jure•ro -ra *mf* (SAm) false witness
jurídi•co -ca *adj* juridical
jurisconsulto *m* (*el que escribe sobre el derecho*) jurist; (*jurisperito*) legal expert
jurisdicción *f* jurisdiction
jurisperito *m* jurist, legal expert
jurisprudencia *f* jurisprudence; case law
jurista *mf* jurist
juro *m* right of perpetual ownership; **de juro** inevitably, for sure
justa *f* joust, tournament
justamente *adv* just, just at that time; justly; (*ajustadamente*) tightly
justar *intr* to joust, to tilt
justicia *f* justice; (*castigo de muerte*) execution; **de justicia** justly, deservedly; **hacer justicia a** to do justice to; **ir por justicia** to go to court, to bring suit
justicie•ro -ra *adj* just, fair; stern, righteous
justificable *adj* justifiable
justifica•do -da *adj* (*hecho*) just, right; (*persona*) just, upright
justificante *m* voucher, proof
justificar §73 *tr* to justify; (typ) to justify
justillo *m* jerkin, waist
justipreciar *tr* to estimate, appraise
jus•to -ta *adj* just; right, exact; (*apretado*) tight || *mf* just person || *f* see **justa** || **justo** *adv* just; right, in tune; tight; (*con estrechez*) in straitened circumstances
ju•to -ta *mf* Jute
juvenil *adj* juvenile, youthful
juventud *f* youth; young people
juzgado *m* court of law; courtroom; court of one judge
juzgar §44 *tr & intr* to judge; **a juzgar por** judging by; **juzgar de** to judge, pass judgment on

K

K, k (ka) *f* eleventh letter of the Spanish alphabet
karate *m* or **karaté** *m* karate
karateka *m o f* karate player
kermesse *f var* of **quermés**
keroseno *m* kerosene, coal oil
kg. *abbr* **kilogramo**
kilate *m var* of **quilate**
kilo *m* kilo, kilogram
kilociclo *m* kilocycle
kilogramo *m* kilogram
kilometraje *m* kilometrage, distance in kilometers
kilométri•co -ca *adj* kilometric; (coll) interminable, long-drawn-out
kilómetro *m* kilometer (*.621 miles*)
kilovatio *m* kilowatt
kilovatio-hora *m* (*pl* **kilovatios-hora**) kilowatt-hour
kimono *m var* of **quimono**
kinescopio *m* (telv) kinescope
kiosco *m var* of **quiosco**
kirieleisón *m* dirge; **cantar el kirieleisón** to beg mercy
kit *m* kit
km. *abbr* **kilómetro**
knock-out [ˈnokau(t)] *m* (box) knockout
K.O. *abbr* knock-out
kph. *abbr* **kilómetros por hora**
kv. *abbr* **kilovatio**
kv-h *abbr* **kilovatio-hora**

L

L, l (ele) twelfth letter of the Spanish alphabet
la *art def fem* of **el** || *pron pers fem* her, it; you || *pron dem* that, the one; **la que** who, which, that; she who, the one that
laberinto *m* labyrinth, maze
labia *f* fluency, smoothness; **con mucha labia** smooth-spoken
labial *adj & f* labial
labio *m* lip; (fig) edge, lip; **chuparse los labios** to smack one's lips; **labio leporino** harelip; **leer en los labios** to lip read
labiolectura *f* lip reading
labio•so -sa *adj* fluent, smooth
labor *f* labor, work; (*cultivo de los campos*) farming, tilling; (*obra de coser, bordar, etc.*) needlework, fancywork, embroidery; **hacer labor** to match; **labor blanca** linen work, linen embroidery; **labor de ganchillo** crocheting
laborable *adj* workable; arable, tillable; (*día*) work
laborante *m* journeyman; political henchman
laborar *tr* to work || *intr* to scheme
laboratorio *m* laboratory; **laboratorio de idiomas** language laboratory; **laboratorio espacial** space laboratory; Skylab

laborio•so -sa *adj* (*trabajador*) laborious, industrious; (*trabajoso*) laborious, arduous
laborismo *m* British Labour Party
laborista *adj* Labour || *mf* Labourite
laborterapia *f* work therapy
labra *f* carving
labrada *f* fallow ground (*to be sown the following year*)
labrade•ro -ra *adj* arable, tillable
labra•do -da *adj* wrought, fashioned; carved; figured, embroidered || *m* carving; **labrado de madera** wood carving || *f* see **labrada**
labra•dor -dora *adj* work; farm || *mf* farmer; (*campesino*) peasant || *m* plowman; **el Labrador** Labrador
labrantí•o -a *adj* farm || *m* farmland
labranza *f* farming; farm, farmland
labrar *tr* to work, fashion; (*la piedra, la madera*) carve; (*arar*) plow; (*construir o mandar construir*) build; till, cultivate; cause, bring about || *intr* to make a lasting impression
labrie•go -ga *mf* peasant
laca *f* lacquer; shellac; **laca de uñas** nail polish; **lacas** lacquer ware
lacayo *m* lackey, footman
lacear *tr* to tie with a bow; adorn with bows; (*la caza*) drive within shot; (*la caza menor*) trap, snare
lacería *f* poverty, want; trouble, bother; leprosy
lacerio•so -sa *adj* poor, needy
lacero *m* lassoer; poacher; dogcatcher
la•cio -cia *adj* faded, withered; languid; (*cabello*) lank, straight
lacóni•co -ca *adj* laconic
lacra *f* fault, defect; (*señal dejada por una enfermedad*) mark, remains; sore; scab, scar
lacrimóge•no -na *adj* tear, tear-producing
lacrimo•so -sa *adj* lachrymose, tearful
lactar *tr* to suckle
lácte•o -a *adj* milky
lacustre *adj* lake
ladear *tr* to tip, tilt; bend, lean; (*un avión*) bank || *intr* to tip, tilt; bend, lean; turn away, turn off; (*la aguja de brújula*) deviate || *ref* to tip, tilt; bend, lean; be equal, be even; (Chile) to fall in love; **ladearse a** (*un dictamen, un partido*) to lean to or toward
ladeo *m* tipping, tilting; bending, leaning; inclination, bent
lade•ro -ra *adj* side, lateral || *f* hillside
ladilla *f* crab louse; **pegarse como ladilla** to stick like a leech
ladi•no -na *adj* crafty, sly, cunning; polyglot
lado *m* side; direction; (*del hilo telefónico*) end; **al lado** nearby; **dejar a un lado** to leave aside; **de lado** square, e.g., **diez centímetros de lado** ten centimeters square; **de otro lado** on the other hand; **de un lado** on the one hand; **echar a un lado** to cast aside; to finish up; **hacer lado** to make room; **hacerse a un lado** to step aside; **lados** backers, advisers; **mirar de lado** *or* **de medio lado** to look askance at; to sneak a look at; **ponerse al lado de** to take sides with; **por el lado de** in the direction of; **tirar por su lado** to pull for oneself
ladrar *tr* (*p.ej., injurias*) to bark || *intr* to bark
ladrido *m* bark, barking; slander, blame
ladrillador *m* bricklayer
ladrillal *m* brickyard
ladrillo *m* brick; (*azulejo*) tile; (*p.ej., de chocolate*) cake; **ladrillo de fuego** *or* **ladrillo refractario** firebrick
la•drón -drona *adj* thievish, thieving || *mf* thief || *m* sluice gate; **ladrón de corazones** heartbreaker, lady-killer
ladronera *f* den of thieves; thievery; (*alcancía*) child's bank
ladronerío *m* (Arg) gang of thieves; (Arg) wave of thieving
ladronzue•lo -la *mf* petty thief
lagaña *f* var of **legaña**
lagar *m* wine press; olive press; (*establecimiento*) winery
lagarta *f* female lizard; sly woman; (ent) gypsy moth
lagartija *f* green lizard; wall lizard
lagarto *m* lizard; sly fellow; (Mex) fop, dandy; **lagarto de Indias** alligator
lago *m* lake
lagotear *tr & intr* to flatter, wheedle
lágrima *f* tear; (*de cualquier licor*) drop; **beberse las lágrimas** to hold back one's tears; **deshacerse en lágrimas** to weep one's eyes out; **lágrimas de cocodrilo** crocodile tears; **llorar a lágrima viva** to shed bitter tears
lagrimear *intr* to weep easily, be tearful; (*los ojos*) fill
lagrimo•so -sa *adj* tearful; (*ojos*) watery
laguna *f* (*lago pequeño*) lagoon; (*hueco, omisión*) lacuna, gap
laical *adj* lay
laicismo *m* secularism
lai•co -ca *adj* lay, secular || *mf* layperson; **laicos** laity || *m* layman
laja *f* slab, flagstone
lama *f* mud, ooze, slim; pond scum
lambrija *f* earthworm; skinny person
lamedero *m* salt lick
lame•dor -dora *adj* licking || *mf* licker || *m* syrup; **dar lamedor** to lose at first in order to take in one's opponent
lamedura *f* lick, licking
lamentable *adj* lamentable
lamentación *f* lamentation
lamentar *tr, intr & ref* to lament, mourn
lamento *m* lament
lamento•so -sa *adj* lamentable; plaintive
lamer *tr* to lick; lap, lap against; (*las llamas un tejado*) to lick || *ref* (*p.ej., los dedos*) to lick
lame•rón -rona *adj* (coll) sweet-toothed
lametada *f* lap, lick
lámina *f* sheet, plate, strip; (*plancha grabada*) engraving; (*pintura en cobre*) copper plate; (*figura estampada*) cut, picture, illustration
laminador *m* rolling mill
laminar *tr* to laminate; (*el hierro, el acero*) roll

lampadario *m* floor lamp
lámpara *f* lamp, light; (*mancha en la ropa*) grease spot, oil spot; (rad) vacuum tube; **atizar la lámpara** to fill up the glasses again; **lámpara de alcohol** spirit lamp; **lámpara de arco** arc lamp, arc light; **lámpara de bolsillo** flashlight; **lámpara de carretera** (aut) bright light; **lámpara de cruce** (aut) dimmer; **lámpara de flash** flashbulb; **lámpara de pie** floor lamp; **lámpara de sobremesa** table lamp; **lámpara de socorro** trouble light; **lámpara de soldar** blowtorch; **lámpara de techo** ceiling light; (aut) dome light; **lámpara inundante** floodlight; **lámpara testigo** pilot light
lamparilla *f* rushlight; aspen; nightlight
lampi•ño -ña *adj* beardless; hairless
lampista *mf* lamplighter ‖ *m* tinsmith, plumber, glazier, electrician
lana *f* wool; (CAm) common person; (CAm) swindler; **lana de acero** steel wool; **lana de ceiba** kapoc; **lana de escorias** mineral wool, rock wool; **lana de vidrio** fiberglass
lance *m* cast, throw; (*en la red*) catch, haul; (*accidente en el juego*) play, move, stroke; (*ocasión crítica*) chance, pass, juncture; incident, event; (*riña*) row, quarrel; (taur) capework; **de lance** cheap; secondhand; **echar buen lance** to have a break; **lance de honor** affair of honor, duel; **tener pocos lances** to be dull and uninteresting
lancero *m* lancer, spearman, pikeman
lanceta *f* (surg) lancet; (Mex, SAm) sting
lancha *f* barge, lighter; flagstone, slab; (naut) longboat; (nav) launch; (Ecuad) mist, fog; (Ecuad) frost; **lancha automóvil** launch, motor launch; **lancha de auxilio** lifeboat (*stationed on shore*); **lancha de carreras** speedboat; **lancha de desembarco** (nav) landing craft; **lancha salvavidas** lifeboat (*on shipboard*)
lanchar *intr* (Ecuad) to get foggy; (Ecuad) to freeze
lancinante *adj* piercing
lan•dó *m* (*pl* **-dós**) landau
landre *f* swollen gland; hidden pocket
lanería *f* wool shop; **lanerías** woolens, woolen goods
langosta *f* (*insecto*) locust; (*crustáceo*) lobster, spiny lobster
langostera *f* lobster pot
langostín *m* or **langostino** *m* prawn (*Peneus*)
langostón *m* green grasshopper
languidecer §22 *intr* to languish
languidez *f* languor
lángui•do -da *adj* languid, languorous
lano•so -sa *adj* woolly
lanu•do da *adj* woolly; (Ecuad, Ven) coarse, illbred
lanza *f* lance, pike; (*de la manguera*) nozzle; (*palo de coche*) wagon pole
lanzabom•bas *m* (*pl* **-bas**) (aer) bomb release; (mil) trench mortar
lanzacohe•tes *m* (*pl* **-tes**) rocket launcher
lanzadera *f* shuttle; (compu) launcher; **parecer una lanzadera** to buzz around
lanza•do -da *adj* sloping; (*salida de una carrera*) (sport) running (*start*)
lanza•dor -dora *mf* thrower; **lanzador de lodo** (fig) mudslinger ‖ *m* launcher; (aer) jettison gear; (baseball) pitcher
lanzaespu•mas *m* (*pl* **-mas**) foam extinguisher
lanzagranadas *m* grenade launcher
lanzalla•mas *m* (*pl* **-mas**) flame thrower
lanzamiento *m* throw, hurl, fling, launch; (*de un buque*) launching; (*de un cohete*) shot, launch; (*p.ej., de víveres*) (aer) airdrop; (*de bombas*) (aer) release; (*de paracaidistas*) (aer) jump; (law) dispossession; (naut) steeve; **lanzamiento de bala** (sport) shot put
lanzami•nas *m* (*pl* **-nas**) (nav) mine layer
lanzamisiles *m* missile launcher
lanzapla•tos *m* (*pl* **-tos**) trap
lanzar §60 *tr* to throw, hurl, fling; (*un proyecto, un cohete, maldiciones, una ofensiva, un producto nuevo, un buque*) launch; (*una mirada*) cast; vomit, throw up; (*flores, hojas una planta*) put forth; (*una advertencia*) toss, toss out; (aer) to airdrop; (*bombas*) (aer) to release; (law) to dispossess ‖ *ref* to launch, launch forth; throw oneself; dash, rush; (aer) to jump; (sport) to sprint
lanzatorpe•dos *m* (*pl* **-dos**) (nav) torpedo tube
laña *f* clamp; rivet
lañar *tr* to clamp; (*objetos de porcelana*) rivet
lapicero *m* pencil holder; mechanical pencil; ballpoint pen; **lapicero fuente** fountain pen
lápida *f* tablet, stone; **lápida supulcral** gravestone
lapidar *tr* to stone to death
lá•piz *m* (*pl* **-pices**) (*grafito*) black lead; (*barrita que sirve para escribir*) pencil, lead pencil; **lápiz de bolilla** (Para) ballpoint pen; **lápiz de labios** lipstick; **lápiz de pizarra** slate pencil; **lápiz de pasta** (Chile) ballpoint pen; **lápiz de plomo** graphite; **lápiz estíptico** styptic pencil; **lápiz labial** lipstick; **lápiz luminoso, fotosensible** *or* **óptico** (compu) light pen
lapizar §60 *tr* to mark or line with a pencil
la•pón -pona *adj* Lapp ‖ *mf* Lapp, Laplander ‖ *m* (*idioma*) Lapp
Laponia *f* Lapland
lapso *m* lapse
laquear *tr* to lacquer
lardo•so -sa *adj* greasy, fatty
larga *f* long billiard cue; **dar largas a** to postpone, put off
largamente *adv* at length, extensively; in comfort; generously; long, for a long time
largar §44 *tr* to let go, release; ease, slack; utter; (*un golpe*) deal, strike, give; (naut) to unfurl; (Col) to give ‖ *ref* to move away; get away, sneak away, beat it; take to sea; (*el ancla*) to come loose
lar•go -ga *adj* long; abundant; liberal, generous; quick, ready; shrewd, cunning; (naut) loose, slack; **a la larga** in the long run, in the end;

a lo largo lengthwise; at great length; far away; **a lo largo de** along; along with; throughout; in the course of; (*el mar*) far out in; **a lo más largo** at most; **hacerse a lo largo** to get out in the open sea; **largo de lengua** loose-tongued; **largo de uñas** light-fingered; **pasar de largo** to pass without stopping; take a quick look; miss; **ponerse de largo** to come out, make one's debut; **vestir de largo** to wear long clothes || *m* length || *f* see **larga** || **largo** *adv* at length, at great length; abundantly || **largo** *interj* get out of here!

largometraje *m* full-featured film, full-length movie

largor *m* length

larguero *m* (*palo, madero*) stringer; (*almohada larga*) bolster; (aer) longeron

largueza *f* length; liberality, generosity

larguiru•cho -cha *adj* gangling, lanky

largura *f* length

lárice *m* larch tree

laringe *f* larynx

larínge•o -a *adj* laryngeal

laringitis *f* laryngitis

laringoscopio *m* laryngoscope

larva *f* larva; mask; (*duende*) hobgoblin

lasca *f* advantage, benefit

lascar §73 *tr* (naut) to pay out, slacken; (Mex) to scratch, bruise; (*un objeto de porcelana*) (Mex) to chip

lascivia *f* lasciviousness

lasci•vo -va *adj* lascivious; playful

láser *m* laser

la•so -sa *adj* tired, exhausted; weak, wan

lástima *f* pity; (*quejido*) complaint; **contar lástimas** to tell a hard-luck story; **dar lástima** to be pitiful; **es lástima (que)** it is a pity (that); **estar hecho una lástima** to be a sorry sight; **hacer lástima** to be pitiful; **llorar lástimas** to put on a show of tears; **poner lástima** to be pitiful; **¡qué lástima!** what a pity!, what a shame!; **¡qué lástima de saliva!** what a waste of breath!

lastimar *tr* to hurt, injure; hurt, offend; bruise || *ref* to hurt oneself; bruise oneself; complain

lastime•ro -ra *adj* hurtful, injurious; pitiful, sad, doleful

lastimo•so -sa *adj* pitiful

lastra *f* slab, flagstone

lastrar *tr* (aer & naut) to ballast

lastre *m* (aer & naut) ballast; (fig) wisdom, maturity; (coll) food; (rr) (Chile) ballast

lat. *abrr* **latín, latitud**

lata *f* (*hojalata*) tin, tin plate; (*envase*) tin, tin can; (*madero sin pulir*) log; (*tabla delgada*) lath; annoyance, bore; **dar la lata a** (coll) to pester; **es una lata** that's terribly boring; **estar en la lata** (Col) to be penniless; **¡que lata!** what a nuisance! what a curse!

latebra *f* hiding place

latebro•so -sa *adj* furtive, secretive

latente *adj* latent

lateral *adj* lateral

latido *m* (*del perro*) yelp; (*del corazón*) beat, throb; (*dolor*) pang, twinge

latifundio *m* large neglected landed estate

latigazo *m* lash; crack of whip; (*reprensión áspera*) lashing; whiplash

látigo *m* whip, horsewhip; cinch strap

latiguear *tr* to lash, whip || *intr* crack a whip

latiguillo *m* small whip; (*del actor u orador*) claptrap

latín *m* Latin; **latín de cocina** dog Latin; **latín rústico** or **vulgar** Vulgar Latin; **saber latín** or **mucho latín** to be very shrewd

latinajo *m* dog Latin; Latin word or phrase (*slipped into the vernacular*)

latinar or **latinear** *intr* to use Latin

lati•no -na *adj* Latin; (naut) lateen || *mf* Latin

Latinoamérica *f* Latin America

latinoamerica•no -na *adj* Latin-American || *mf* Latin American

latir *tr* (Ven) to annoy, bore, molest || *intr* (*el perro*) to bark, yelp; (*el corazón*) beat, throb; **me late que** (Mex) I have a hunch that

latitud *f* latitude

la•to -ta *adj* broad || *f* see **lata**

latón *m* brass; (Cuba) garbage pail

lato•so -sa *adj* annoying, boring || *mf* bore

latrocinio *m* thievery; thievishness

laucha *f* (Arg, Chile) mouse

laúd *m* (mus) lute; (zool) leatherback turtle

laudable *adj* laudable

láudano *m* laudanum

laudato•rio -ria *adj* laudatory

laudo *m* (law) finding, decision

láurea *f* laurel wreath

laurea•do -da *adj & mf* laureate

laurean•do -da *mf* graduate, candidate for a degree

laurear *tr* to trim or adorn with laurel; crown with laurel; decorate, honor, reward

laurel *m* laurel; (*de la victoria*) laurels; **dormirse sobre sus laureles** to rest or sleep on one's laurels

láure•o -a *adj* laurel || *f* see **láurea**

lauréola *f* crown of laurel, laurel wreath; (*aureola*) halo

lava *f* lava; (min) washing

lavable *adj* washable

lavabo *m* washstand; washroom, lavatory; (*retrete, servicios*) toilet; **lavabos** *SIGN* rest rooms

lavaca•ras *mf* (*pl* **-ras**) fawner, flatterer, bootlicker

lavaco•ches *m* (*pl* **-ches**) car washer

lavada *f* wash(ing)

lavade•dos *m* (*pl* **-dos**) finger bowl

lavadero *m* laundry; (*tabla de lavar*) washboard; (*a orillas de un río*) washing place; (Guat, Mex, SAm) placer

lava•do -da *adj* brazen, fresh, impudent || *m* wash, washing; **lavado a seco** dry cleaning; **lavado cerebral** or **de cerebro** brainwashing; **lavado químico** dry cleaning

lava•dor -dora *mf* washer || *m* (phot) washer ||

f washing machine; **lavadora de platos** *or* **de vajilla** dishwasher
lavadura *f* washing; (*agua sucia; rozadura de una cuerda*) washings
lavafru•tas *m* (*pl* **-tas**) fruit washing bowl, finger bowl
lavaluneta *s* windshield washer
lavama•nos *m* (*pl* **-nos**) (*pila con caño y llave*) washstand; (*jofaina*) washbowl
lavanda *f* lavender
lavandera *f* laundress, laundrywoman, washerwoman; (orn) sandpiper
lavandero *m* launderer, laundryman
lavándula *f* lavender
lavao•jos *m* (*pl* **-jos**) eyecup
lavaparabri•sas *m* (*pl* **-sas**) windshield washer
lavapla•tos (*pl* **-tos**) *mf* (*persona*) dishwasher || *m* (*aparato*) dishwasher; (Chile) kitchen sink
lavar *tr & ref* to wash; **lavarle el cerebro a** to brainwash
lavativa *f* enema; annoyance, bore
lavatorio *m* washing; washstand; toilet; washroom; (*ceremonia de lavar los pies*) maundy; (med) wash, lotion
lavavajillas *m* dishwasher
lavazas *fpl* dirty water, wash water
laxante *adj & m* laxative
laxar *tr* to ease, slack; (*el vientre*) loosen
la•xo -xa *adj* lax, slack; (fig) lax, loose
laya *f* spade; kind, quality
layar *tr* to spade, dig with a spade
lazada *f* bowknot
lazar §60 *tr* to lasso
lazarillo *m* blind man's guide
lazari•no -na *adj* leprous || *mf* leper
lázaro *m* raggedy beggar; **estar hecho un lázaro** to be full of sores
lazo *m* bow, knot, tie; lasso, lariat; snare, trap; bond, tie; **armar lazo a** to set a trap for; **caer en el lazo** to fall into the trap; **lazo de amor** truelove knot; **lazo de unión** (fig) tie, bond
Ldo. *abbr* **Licenciado**
le *pron pers* to him, to her, to it; to you; him; you
leal *adj* loyal, faithful; reliable, trustworthy || *m* loyalist
lealtad *f* loyalty; reliability, trustworthiness
le•brel -brela *mf* whippet, small greyhound
lebrillo *m* earthen washtub
lebrón *m* large hare; coward; (Mex) slicker
lección *f* lesson; (*interpretación de un pasaje*) reading; **dar la lección** to recite one's lesson; **echar** *or* **señalar lección** to assign the lesson; **tomar una lección a** to hear the lesson of
leccionista *mf* private tutor
lechada *f* grout; whitewash; (*para hacer papel*) pulp; (CAm, Mex, W-I) whitewash
lechar *tr* to milk; (CAm, Mex, W-I) to whitewash
leche *f* milk; (coll) sperm; **estar con la leche en los labios** to lack experience, to be young and inexperienced; **leche condensada** condensed milk; **leche de magnesia** milk of magnesia; **leche de manteca** buttermilk; **leche desnatada** skim milk; **leche en polvo** milk powder; **leche entera** whole milk; **leche hidratante** moisturing lotion; **tener mala leche** to have a terribly bad temper
lechecillas *fpl* sweetbread
lechera *f* milkmaid, dairymaid; (*vasija para guardar la leche*) milk can; (*vasija para servir la leche*) milk pitcher
lechería *f* dairy, creamery
leche•ro -ra *adj* (*que da leche*) milch; (*perteneciente a la leche*) milk; (*cicatero*) (coll) stingy || *m* milkman, dairyman; (coll) lucky dog || *f* see **lechera**
lecho *m* bed; (*especie de sofá*) couch; (*cauce de río*) bed; layer, stratum; **abandonar el lecho** to get up (*from illness*); **lecho de plumas** (fig) feather bed
le•chón -chona *adj* filthy, sloppy || *mf* suckling pig; (*persona sucia, desaseada*) pig || *m* pig || *f* sow
lecho•so -sa *adj* milky || *m* papaya (*tree*) || *f* papaya (*fruit*)
lechuga *f* lettuce; head of lettuce; (*fuelle formado en la tela*) frill; **lechuga repollada** iceberg lettuce; **lechuga romana** romaine lettuce
lechugui•no -na *adj* stylish, sporty || *m* dandy || *f* stylish young lady
lechuza *f* barn owl, screech owl; owllike woman
lechu•zo -za *adj* owlish; (*muleto*) yearling || *m* bill collector; summons server; owllike fellow || *f* see **lechuza**
lecti•vo -va *adj* school (*e.g., day*)
lec•tor -tora *adj* reading || *mf* reader; foreign-language teacher; (*empleado que anota el consumo registrado por el contador de agua, gas o electricidad*) meter reader; **lector mental** mind reader || *m*—**lector CD-ROM** CD-ROM drive; **lector digital** digital scanner; **lector óptico** optical scanner
lectura *f* reading; broad culture; public lecture; college subject; (*interpretación de un pasaje*) reading; (electron) playback; (typ) pica; **lectura de la mente** mind reading; **lectura óptica** optical scanner
leer §43 *tr* to read || *intr* to read; lecture; **leer en** to read (*someone's thoughts*) || *ref* to read, e.g., **este libro se lee con facilidad** this book reads easily
leg. *abbr* **legal, legislatura**
lega *f* lay sister
legación *f* legation
legado *m* (*don que se hace por testamento*) legacy; (*enviado diplomático*) legate
legajo *m* file, docket, dossier
legal *adj* legal; faithful, prompt, right
legalidad *f* legality; faithfulness, promptness
legalizar §60 *tr* to legalize; authenticate
légamo *m* slime, ooze
legamo•so -sa *adj.* slimy, oozy
legaña *f* gum (*on edge of eyelids*)
legaño•so -sa *adj* gummy

legar §44 *tr* to bequeath, will
legata•rio -ria *mf* legatee
legenda•rio -ria *adj* legendary
legible *adj* legible
legión *f* legion
legionario *m* legionnaire
legislación *f* legislation; laws
legisla•dor -dora *adj* legislating || *mf* legislator
legislar *intr* to legislate
legislati•vo -va *adj* legislative
legislatura *f* (session of a) legislature
legista *m* law professor; law student
legitimar *tr* to legitimate; legitimize
legitimidad *f* legitimacy
legíti•mo -ma *adj* legitimate
le•go -ga *adj* lay; uninformed || *m* layman; lay brother || *f* see **lega**
legua *f* league; **a leguas** far, far away
leguleyo *m* pettifogger
legumbre *f* (*hortaliza*) vegetable; (bot) legume; (Chile) vegetable stew
leíble *adj* legible, readable
leída *f* reading
leí•do -da *adj* well-read; **leído y escribido** (coll) posing as learned || *f* see **leída**
lejanía *f* distance, remoteness
leja•no -na *adj* distant, remote; (*pariente*) distant
lejía *f* lye; bleach; wash water; severe rebuke
lejiadora *f* washing machine
lejos *adv* far; **a lo lejos** in the distance; **de lejos** or **desde lejos** from a distance || *m* glimpse; look from afar; **tener buen lejos** to look good at a distance
le•lo -la *adj* stupid, inane
lema *m* motto, slogan; theme; headword
len *adj* soft, flossy
lena *f* spirit, vigor; breathing
lencería *f* linen goods, dry goods; linen closet; dry-goods store
lence•ro -ra *mf* linen dealer, dry-goods dealer
lendrera *f* fine-toothed comb
lendro•so -sa *adj* nitty, lousy
lene *adj* (*suave al tacto*) soft; (*ligero*) light; kind, agreeable
lengua *f* (anat) tongue; (*idioma*) language, tongue; (*de tierra, de fuego, de zapato; badajo de campana; lengua de un animal usada como alimento*) tongue; **buscar la lengua a** to pick a fight with; **dar la lengua** to chew the rag; **hacerse lenguas de** to rave about; **írsele a** (*uno*) **la lengua** to blab; **lengua madre** or **matriz** mother tongue (*language from which another is derived*); **lengua materna** mother tongue (*language acquired by reason of nationality*); **morderse la lengua** to hold one's tongue; **tener en la lengua** to have on the tip of one's tongue; **tener la lengua gorda** to talk thick; to be drunk; **tener mala lengua** to be blasphemous; to have an evil tongue; **tener mucha lengua** to be a great talker; **tirar de la lengua a** to draw out; **tomar en lenguas** to gossip about; **tomar lengua** or **lenguas** to pick up news
lenguado *m* sole
lenguaje *m* language; **lenguaje de bajo nivel** (compu) low-level language; **lenguaje de programación** computer language; **lenguaje ensamblador** (compu) assembly language; **lenguaje gestual** *or* **de gestos** sign language
lengua•raz (*pl* **-races**) *adj* foul-mouthed, scurrilous; polyglot || *mf* linguist
len•guaz *adj* (*pl* **-guaces**) garrulous
lengüeta *f* (*de la balanza*) pointer, needle; (*del zapato*) tongue; (anat) epiglottis; (carp) tongue; (*de un instrumento de viento*) (mus) reed; (Chile) paper cutter; (Mex) petticoat fringe; (SAm) chatterbox
lengüetada *f* licking, lapping
lengüetear *intr* to stick the tongue out; flicker, flutter; jabber, rant; lick
lengüilar•go -ga *adj* foul-mouthed, scurrilous
lengüisu•cio -cia *adj* (Mex, P-R) foul-mouthed, scurrilous
lenidad *f* lenience
lenocinio *m* pandering, procuring
lente *m & f* lens; **lente de aumento** magnifying glass; **lente de contacto** *or* **lente invisible** contact lens; **lentes** *mpl* nose glasses; **lentes bifocales** bifocals; **lentes de aumento, de fórmula** *or* **ópticos** prescription glasses; **lentes de nariz** *or* **de pinzas** pince-nez; **lentes de sol** sunglasses; **lentes negros** *or* **oscuros** dark glasses; **lente telefotográfica** tele(photo)lens
lenteja *f* lentil; (*del reloj*) bob, pendulum bob
lentejuela *f* sequin, spangle
lentillas *fpl* contact lenses
lentitud *f* slowness
len•to -ta *adj* slow; sticky; (*fuego*) low
leña *f* firewood, kindling wood; **cargar de leña** to give a drubbing to; **llevar leña al monte** to carry coals to Newcastle
leña•dor -dora *mf* woodcutter || *m* woodsman
leñame *m* lumber, timber; stock of firewood
leñero *m* wood merchant; wood purchaser; (*sitio donde se guarda la leña*) woodshed
leño *m* (*madera*) wood; (*tronco de árbol, limpio de ramas*) log; sap, blockhead; (poet) ship, vessel; **dormir como un leño** to sleep like a log
leño•so -sa *adj* woody
Leo *m* (astr) Leo
león *m* lion
leona *f* lioness
leona•do -da *adj* tawny, fulvous
leonera *f* lion cage, den of lions; dive, gambling joint; junk room, lumber room
leonero *m* lion keeper; keeper of a gambling joint
leontina *f* watch chain
leopardo *m* leopard
leopoldina *f* watch fob; (mil) Spanish shako
leotardo *m* leotard
lépa•ro -ra *adj* (CAm, Mex) indecent, improper

lepe *m* (Ven) flip in the ear; **saber más que Lepe** to be wide-awake
leperada *f* (CAm, Mex) coarseness, vulgarity
lepisma *f* (ent) silver fish, fish moth
lepori•no -na *adj* hare, harelike
lepra *f* leprosy
leprosería *f* leper house
lepro•so -sa *adj* leprous ‖ *mf* leper
lerdera *f* (CAm) laziness, apathy; (CAm) slowness
ler•do -da *adj* slow, dull; coarse, crude
lesbiana *f* lesbian
lesbianismo *m* lesbianism
lesbia•no -na *adj* lesbian
lésbi•co -ca *adj* lesbian
lesión *f* harm, hurt; (pathol) lesion
lesionar *tr* to harm, hurt, injure
lesi•vo -va *adj* harmful, injurious
lesna *f* awl
le•so -sa *adj* hurt, harmed, injured; wounded; offended; perverted; (SAm) simple, foolish
leste *m* (naut) east
letal *adj* lethal, deadly
letame *m* manure
letanía *f* litany; (*enumeración seguida*) litany
letárgi•co -ca *adj* lethargic
letargo *m* lethargy
letargo•so -sa *adj* lethargic
le•tón -tona *adj* Lettish ‖ *mf* Lett ‖ *m* (*idioma*) Lettish, Lett
Letonia *f* Latvia
letra *f* (*del alfabeto*) letter; (*modo de escribir propio de una persona*) hand, handwriting; (*de una canción*) words, lyric; (com) draft; (typ) type; (*sentido material*) (fig) letter; **a la letra** (*al pie de la letra*) to the letter; **a letra vista** (com) at sight; **bellas letras** belles lettres; **cuatro letras** *or* **dos letras** (*esquela, cartita*) a line; **en letras de molde** in print; **escribir en letra de molde** to print; **las letras y las armas** the pen and the sword; **letra a la vista** (com) sight draft; **letra bastardilla, cursiva** *or* **itálica** italic script, italics; **letra de cambio** (com) bill of exchange; **letra de imprenta** (typ) type; **letra de mano** handwriting; **letra de molde** printed letter; **letra mayúscula** uppercase letter, capital letter; **letra menuda** fine print; (fig) cunning; **letra minúscula** lowercase letter; **letra muerta** dead letter; **letra negrilla** (typ) boldface; **letra pequeña** small print; **letra redonda** *or* **redondilla** (typ) roman; **letras** (*literatura*) letters; (coll) a few words, a line; **primeras letras** elementary education, three R's
letra•do -da *adj* learned, lettered; pedantic ‖ *m* lawyer
letrero *m* sign, notice; (*p.ej., en una botella*) label; **letrero luminoso** neon sign
letrina *f* privy, latrine; (*cloaca*) sewer; (*cosa sucia*) (fig) cesspool
letrista *mf* lyricist, writer of lyrics (*for songs*); calligrapher, engrosser
leucemia *f* leukemia
leucorrea *f* leucorrhea
leudar *tr* to leaven, ferment with yeast ‖ *ref* (*la masa con la levadura*) to rise
leu•do -da *adj* leavened, fermented
leva *f* weighing anchor; (mach) cam; (mil) levy; (CAm, Col) trick; (CAm, Col) swindle
levada *f* (*de la espada, el florete, etc.*) flourish; (*de los astros*) rise; (*del émbolo*) stroke
levadi•zo -za *adj* (*puente*) lift
levadura *f* leaven; leavening; yeast; (*tabla*) board; **levadura comprimida** yeast cake; **levadura de cerveza** brewer's yeast; **levadura en polvo** baking powder
levantaco•ches *m* (*pl* **-ches**) auto jack
levantada *f* rising, getting up (*from bed or from sickbed*)
levantamiento *m* rise, elevation; insurrection, revolt, uprising; **levantamiento del cadáver** inquest; **levantamiento del censo** census taking; **levantamiento de planos** surveying
levantar *tr* to raise, lift, elevate; agitate, rouse, stir up; (*una sesión*) adjourn; (*la mesa*) clear; (*la voz*) raise; (*el campo*) break; (*gente para el ejército; un sitio; fondos*) raise; (*el ancla*) weigh; straighten up; build, construct, erect; establish, found; **levantar casa** to break up housekeeping; **levantar planos** to make a survey ‖ *ref* to rise; (*de la cama*) get up; (*de una silla*) stand up; straighten up; (*sublevarse*) rise up, rebel
levantaválvu•las *m* (*pl* **-las**) valve lifter
levantaventana *m* sash lift
levante *m* east; (*viento*) levanter; (CAm, P-R) slander, libel ‖ **Levante** *m* (*países de la parte oriental del Mediterráneo*) Levant; northeastern Mediterranean shores of Spain, especially around Valencia, Alicante, and Murcia
levanti•no -na *adj* Levantine; of the northeastern Mediterranean shores of Spain ‖ *mf* Levantine; native or inhabitant of the northeastern Mediterranean shores of Spain
levar *tr* (*el ancla*) to weigh ‖ *ref* to set sail
leve *adj* (*de poco peso*) light; slight, trivial, trifling
levedad *f* lightness; trivialness
leviatán *m* (Bib & fig) leviathan
levita *m* deacon ‖ *f* coat, frock coat
levitón *m* heavy frock coat
léxi•co -ca *adj* lexical ‖ *m* lexicon; (*caudal de voces de un autor*) vocabulary; (*conjunto de vocablos de una lengua o dialecto*) wordstock
lexicografía *f* lexicography
lexicográfi•co -ca *adj* lexicographic(al)
lexicógra•fo -fa *mf* lexicographer
lexicología *f* lexicology
lexicón *m* lexicon
ley *f* law; loyalty, devotion; norm, standard; (*de un metal*) fineness; **a ley de caballero** on the word of a gentleman; **de buena ley** sterling, genuine; **ley de la oferta y la demanda** law of supply and demand; **ley de la selva** law of the jungle; **ley del menor esfuerzo** line of least resistance; **ley marcial** martial law;

tener or **tomar ley a** to become devoted to; **venir contra una ley** to break a law
leyenda *f* legend; caption
leyente *adj* reading || *mf* reader
lezna *f* awl
lía *f* plaited esparto rope; **lías** lees, dregs
lianza *f* (Chile) account, credit (*in a store*)
liar **§77** *tr* to tie, bind; tie up, wrap up; (*un cigarillo*) roll; embroil, involve; **liarlas** to beat it; kick the bucket || *ref* to join together, be associated; have a liaison; become embroiled, become involved; **liárselos** to roll one's own (*i.e., cigarettes*)
liba•nés -nesa *adj & mf* Lebanese
Libano, el Lebanon
libar *tr* to suck; taste, sip || *intr* to pour out a libation; imbibe
libelo *m* lampoon, libel; (law) petition
libélula *f* dragonfly
liberación *f* liberation; (*cancelación de la carga que grava un inmueble*) redemption; (*de una cuenta*) settlement, closing; quittance
liberal *adj* liberal; (*expedito*) quick, ready; (pol) liberal; (*de amplias miras*) (Arg) liberal-minded || *mf* (pol) liberal
liberalidad *f* liberality
liberar *tr* to free
libertad *f* liberty, freedom; **libertad bajo fianza** *or* **palabra, libertad provisional** bail; **libertad condicional** parole; **libertad de cátedra** academic freedom; **libertad de cultos** freedom of worship; **libertad de empresa** free enterprise; **libertad de enseñanza** academic freedom; **libertad de imprenta** freedom of the press; **libertad de los mares** freedom of the seas; **libertad de palabra** freedom of speech, free speech; **libertad de reunión** freedom of assembly; **libertad vigilada** probation; **plena libertad** free hand; **tomarse la libertad de** to take the liberty to
liberta•do -da *adj* bold, daring; free, brash, unrestrained
liberta•dor -dora *mf* liberator
libertar *tr* to liberate, set free; (*de un peligro, la muerte, etc.*) save
liberta•rio -ria *adj* anarchistic
libertinaje *m* licentiousness, profligacy; impiety, ungodliness
liberti•no -na *adj & mf* libertine
liber•to -ta *mf* (law) probationer || *m* freedman || *f* freedwoman
libídine *f* lewdness, lust; (*impulso a las actividades sexuales*) libido
libidino•so -sa *adj* libidinous
libido *f* libido
libra *f* pound; **Libra** *f* (astr) Libra; **libra esterlina** pound sterling
libraco *m* or **libracho** *m* trashy book
libra•do -da *mf* (com) drawee
libra•dor -dora *mf* (com) drawer
libranza *f* (com) draft; **libranza postal** money order
librar *tr* to free; save, spare; (*la esperanza*) place; (*batalla*) give, join; (com) to draw || *intr* to be delivered, give birth; (*una religiosa*) receive a visitor in the locutory; (com) to draw; **librar bien** to come off well, succeed; **librar mal** to come off badly, fail || *ref* to free oneself; escape
libre *adj* free; free, brash, outspoken; free, unmarried; free, loose, licentious; innocent, guiltless; **libre albedrío** (philos) free will; **libre comercio** free trade; **libre de culpa** (*seguro, divorcio*) no-fault; **libre de porte** postage prepaid; **libre empresa** *or* **mercado** free market
librea *f* livery
librecambio *m* free trade
librecambista *mf* freetrader
librepensa•dor -dora *adj* freethinking || *mf* freethinker
librería *f* bookstore, bookshop; book business; (*mueble*) bookshelf; **librería de viejo** second-hand bookshop
libreril *adj* book
librero *m* bookseller; (*encuadernador*) bookbinder; (Cuba, Mex) bookshelf
libres•co -ca *adj* bookish
libreta *f* notebook; **libreta de banco** bankbook
libreto *m* (mus) libretto
librillo *m* earthen washtub; (*de papel de fumar, de sellos, etc.*) book
libro *m* book; **ahorcar los libros** to become a dropout; **a libro abierto** at sight; **hacer libro nuevo** to turn over a new leaf; **libro a la rústica** paperbound book; **libro de bolsillo** pocketbook, paperback; **libro de caballerías** romance of chivalry; **libro de cocina** cookbook; **libro de cheques** checkbook; **libro de chistes** joke book; **libro de lance** second-hand book; **libro de mayor venta** best seller; **libro de memoria** memo book; **libro de recuerdos** scrapbook; **libro de registro** guest book; **libro de tapa dura** hardback; **libro de teléfonos** telephone book; **libro de texto** textbook; **libro de visitas** visitors' book; **libro diario** day book; **libro en imágenes** picture book; **libro en rústica** paperbound book, paperback; **libro mayor** (com) ledger; **libro talonario** checkbook, stub book
libro-registro *m* (com) book
licencia *f* license; leave of absence; (mil) furlough; **licencia absoluta** (mil) discharge; **licencia de armas** gun permit; **licencia de caza** hunting permit; **licencia de conducción, de conducir** *or* **de manejar** driver's license; **licencia de pesca** fishing permit; **licencia por enfermedad** sick leave; **licencia por maternidad** maternity leave
licencia•do -da *adj* pedantic || *mf* licenciate || *m* lawyer; (mil) discharged soldier; university student (*wearing the long student gown*)
licenciar *tr* to license; allow, permit; confer the degree of licenciate or master on; (mil) to discharge || *ref* to receive the degree of licenciate

or master; become dissolute; (mil) to be discharged

licenciatura *f* licenciate, master's degree; graduation with a licenciate or master's degree; work leading to a licenciate or master's degree

licencio•so -sa *adj* licentious

liceo *m* (*sociedad literaria, establecimiento de enseñanza popular*) lyceum; (*instituto de segunda enseñanza*) (Chile) lycée; (Mex) primary school

licitación *f* bidding

licita•dor -dora *mf* bidder

licitar *tr* to bid on; (Arg) to buy at auction, to sell at auction || *intr* to bid

líci•to -ta *adj* fair, just; licit, legal

licor *m* (*bebida espiritosa; cuerpo líquido*) liquor; (*bebida espiritosa preparada por mezcla de azúcar y substancias aromáticas*) liqueur

licorera *f* cellaret

licorista *mf* distiller; liquor dealer

licoro•so -sa *adj* spirituous, alcoholic; (*vino*) rich, generous

licuar §21 & regular *tr* to liquefy

lid *f* fight, combat; dispute, argument; **en buena lid** by fair means

líder *adj* leading || *m* leader

liderar *tr & intr* to lead, be the leader

lidia *f* fight; bullfight

lidiadera *f* (Ecuad) quarreling, bickering

lidia•dor -dora *mf* fighter || *ref* bullfighter

lidiar *tr* (*un toro*) to fight || *intr* to fight; **lidiar con** to fight with; have to put up with

liebre *f* hare; (*hombre cobarde*) coward

liendre *f* nit

lien•to -ta *adj* damp, dank

lienza *f* strip of cloth

lienzo *m* linen (cloth); linen handkerchief; (*de edificio o pared*) face, front; (*pintura sobre lienzo*) canvas

liga *f* (*cinta elástica para asegurar las medias*) garter; (*aleación*) alloy; (*materia pegajosa para cazar pájaros*) birdlime; (*confederación, alianza*) league; (*muérdago*) mistletoe; band; **liga de goma** rubber band

ligado *m* (mus & typ) ligature

ligadura *f* tie, bond; (mus) ligature, glide; (surg) ligature

ligamento *m* ligament; **ligamento de la corva** (anat) hamstring

ligar §44 *tr* to tie, bind; join, combine; alloy; (*bebidas*) mix; (surg) to ligate || *ref* to league together; be committed; be bound or attached (*e.g., in friendship*)

ligereza *f* lightness; speed, rapidity; fickleness, inconstancy; tactlessness

lige•ro -ra *adj* light; (*té*) weak; (*tejido*) light, thin; quick; slight; **a la ligera** lightly; quickly; unceremoniously; **de ligero** thoughtlessly, rashly; **ligero de cascos** light-headed, scatterbrained; **ligero de lengua** loose-tongued; **ligero de pies** lightfooted; **ligero de ropa** scantily clad || **ligero** *adv* fast, rapidly

lignito *m* lignite

ligustro *m* privet

lija *f* (*pez*) dogfish; (*papel que sirve para pulir*) sandpaper; **darse lija** (W-I) to boast, brag, pat oneself on the back

lijar *tr* to sand, sandpaper

lila *adj* silly, simple || *m* lilac (*color*) || *f* lilac (*plant and flower*)

li•lac *f* (*pl* **-laques**) lilac

liliputiense *adj & mf* Lilliputian

lima *f* (*herramienta*) file; sweet lime; sweetlime tree; (*del tejado*) hip; hip rafter; correcting, polishing; **lima de uñas** nail file; **lima hoya** valley (*of roof*)

limadura *f* filing; (*partecillas*) filings

limalla *f* filings

limar *tr* to file; file down; polish, touch up; smooth, smooth over; (*cercenar*) curtail

limaza *f* (*babosa*) slug; (Ven) large file

limazo *m* slime, sliminess

limbo *m* (*borde*) edge; (theol) limbo; **estar en el limbo** to be quite distraught

limen *m* (physiol, psychol & fig) threshold

limenso *m* (Chile) honeydew melon

lime•ño -ña *adj & mf* Limean

limero *m* sweet-lime tree

limita•do -da *adj* limited; dull-witted

limitador *m* — **limitador de corriente** clock meter; slot meter

limitar *tr* to limit; cut down, reduce || *intr* — **limitar con** to border on

límite *m* limit; boundary, border

limítrofe *adj* bordering

limo *m* slime, mud

limón *m* lemon; lemon tree; (*de un coche o carro*) shaft

limonada *f* lemonade

limoncillo *m* citronella

limonera *f* shaft

limonero *m* lemon tree

limosna *f* alms

limosnear *intr* to beg

limosne•ro -ra *adj* almsgiving, charitable || *mf* almsgiver; beggar || *m* alms box

limo•so -sa *adj* slimy, muddy

limpia *f* cleaning

limpiaba•rros *m* (*pl* **-rros**) scraper, foot scraper

limpiabo•tas *m* (*pl* **-tas**) shoeshiner, bootblack; (fig) flatterer

limpiacrista•les *m* (*pl* **-les**) windshield washer

limpiachimene•as *m* (*pl* **-as**) chimney sweep

limpiadien•tes *m* (*pl* **-tes**) toothpick

limpia•dor -dora *adj* cleaning || *mf* cleaner

limpiadura *f* cleaning; **limpiaduras** cleanings, dirt

limpiama•nos *m* (*pl* **-nos**) (Guat, Hond) towel

limpiamente *adv* in a clean manner; with ease, skillfully; simply, sincerely; unselfishly

limpiameta•les *m* (*pl* **-les**) metal polish

limpianieve *m* snowplow

limpiaparabri•sas *m* (*pl* **-sas**) windshield wiper

limpia•piés *m* (*pl* **-piés**) (Mex) door mat

limpiapi•pas *m* (*pl* **-pas**) pipe cleaner

limpiaplu•mas *m* (*pl* **-mas**) penwiper
limpiar *tr* to clean; (*purificar*) cleanse; (*de culpas*) exonerate; (*un árbol*) clean out, prune; (*zapatos*) shine; (*hurtar*) snitch; (*a una persona en el juego*) clean out; (*dinero en el juego*) clean up; (mil) to mop up; **limpiarle a uno de** to clean someone out of ‖ *ref* to clean, clean oneself
limpiaú•ñas *m* (*pl* **-ñas**) nail cleaner, orange stick
limpiaví•as *m* (*pl* **-as**) track cleaner
limpieza *f* (*acción de limpiar*) cleaning; (*calidad de limpio*) cleanness; (*hábito del aseo*) cleanliness; neatness, tidiness; honesty; chastity; ease, skill; (*observancia de las reglas en los juegos*) fair play; **limpieza de bolsa** emptiness of the pocketbook; **limpieza de la casa** house cleaning; **limpieza en seco** dry cleaning
lim•pio -pia *adj* clean; (*que tiene el hábito del aseo*) cleanly; neat, tidy; honest; chaste; clear, free; **dejar limpio** to clean out; **en limpio** (com) net; **estar limpio** to have no (criminal) record; be clean; **limpio de polvo y paja** free, for nothing; net, after deducting expenses; **poner en limpio** to make a clear or fair copy of; **quedar limpio** to be cleaned out; **sacar en limpio** to make a clear or clean copy of; deduce, understand ‖ *f* see **limpia** ‖ **limpio** *adv* fair; cleanly; **jugar limpio** to play fair
limpión *m* (*limpiadura ligera*) lick; (coll) cleaner; (Col) scolding; (Col, Ven) dustcloth; (Ecuad) dishcloth
limusina *f* limousine
lín. *abbr* **línea**
lina *f* (Chile) coarse wool
linaje *m* lineage; class, description; **linaje humano** mankind
linaju•do -da *adj* highborn ‖ *mf* highborn person
linaza *f* flaxseed, linseed
lince *adj* keen, shrewd, discerning; (*ojos*) keen ‖ *m* lynx; (fig) keen person
lincear *tr* to see into
linchamiento *m* lynching
linchar *tr* to lynch
lindante *adj* bordering, adjoining
lindar *intr* to border, be contiguous; **lindar con** to border on
linde *m & f* limit, boundary
linde•ro -ra *adj* bordering, adjoining ‖ *m* edge; boundary stone, landmark ‖ *f* limit, boundary; (bot) spicebush
lindeza *f* prettiness, niceness; elegance; witticism, funny remark; flirting; **lindezas** insults
lin•do -da *adj* pretty, nice; fine, perfect; **de lo lindo** a lot, a great deal; wonderfully ‖ *m* dude, sissy
lindura *f* prettiness, niceness
línea *f* line; (*contorno de una figura, un vestido*) lines; figure, waistline; **conservar la línea** to keep one's figure; **en línea** (compu) on line; **leer entre líneas** to read between the lines; **línea aérea** airline; **línea central** mainstream; **línea de agua** water line; **línea de batalla** line of battle; **línea de empalme** (rr) branch line; **línea de flotación** water line; **línea de fuego** firing line; **línea de fuerza** (elec) power line; (phys) line of force; **línea del partido** party line; **línea de mira** line of sight; **línea de montaje** assembly line; **línea de pleamar** high-water mark; **línea de puntos** dotted line; **línea de tiro** (mil) line of fire; **línea férrea** railway; **línea internacional de cambio de fecha** international date line; **línea suplementaria** (mus) added line, ledger line
lineal *adj* linear
lineamentos *mpl* lineaments
linfa *f* lymph; (poet) water
linfáti•co -ca *adj* lymphatic
lingote *m* ingot, slug; (naut) ballast bar
lingual *adj & f* lingual
lingüísta *mf* linguist
lingüísti•co -ca *adj* linguistic ‖ *f* linguistics
linimento *m* liniment
lino *m* flax; (*tela*) linen; (poet) sail
linóleo *m* linoleum
linón *m* lawn
linotipia *f* linotype
linotípi•co -ca *adj* linotype
linotipista *mf* linotype operator
linotipo *m* linotype
linterna *f* lantern; flashlight
lío *m* bundle; (*de papeles*) batch; (coll) muddle, mess; (coll) affair, fling, liaison; **armar un lío** to raise a row; **hacerse un lío** to get into a jam
liofilización *f* freeze-drying
liofilizar §60 *tr* to freeze-dry
lionesa — a la lionesa (culin) lyonnaise
liorna *f* hubbub, uproar ‖ **Liorna** *f* Leghorn
lio•so -sa *adj* trouble-making; knotty, troublesome
liq.ⁿ *abbr* **liquidación**
líq.º *abbr* **líquido**
liquen *m* lichen
liquidación *f* (*de una cuenta*) sale, closeout; **liquidación total** sellout
liquidar *tr* to liquefy; (com) to liquidate ‖ *intr* (com) to liquidate ‖ *ref* to liquefy
liquidez *f* liquidity
líqui•do -da *adj & m* liquid; (com) net ‖ *f* (phonet) liquid
lira *f* (mus) lyre; (*numen de un poeta*) inspiration; poems, poetry
lírica *f* lyric poetry
líri•co -ca *adj* lyric(al); (*músico, operístico*) lyric; fantastic, utopian ‖ *m* lyric poet; (Arg, Ven) visionary ‖ *f* see **lírica**
lirio *m* (bot) iris; **lirio blanco** (*azucena*) Madonna lily; **lirio de agua** (bot) calla, calla lily; **lirio de los valles** (bot) lily of the valley
lirismo *m* lyricism; spellbinding; fancy, illusion
lirón *m* (bot) water plantain; (zool) dormouse; (coll) sleepyhead
lis *m* (bot) lily ‖ *f* (bot) iris; (heral) fleur-de-lis
Lisboa *f* Lisbon

lisia•do -da *adj* hurt, injured; crippled; (*muy deseoso*) eager || *mf* cripple
lisiar *tr* to hurt, injure; cripple || *ref* to become crippled
lisimaquia *f* loosestrife
li•so -sa *adj* even, smooth; (*vestido*) plain, unadorned; (*franco, sincero*) simple, plain-dealing; brash, insolent; **liso y llano** simple, easy
lisonja *f* flattery
lisonjear *tr* to flatter; please || *intr* to flatter
lisonje•ro -ra *adj* flattering; pleasing || *mf* flatterer
lista *f* list; (*tira*) strip; (*en un tejido*) colored stripe; (*recuento en alta voz de las personas que deben estar en un lugar*) roll call; **lista de bajas** casualty list; **lista de comidas** bill of fare; **lista de correos** general delivery; **lista de dotación** (naut) muster roll; **lista de la compra** shopping list; **lista de espera** waiting list; **lista de frecuencia** frequency list; **lista de invitados** guest list; **lista de pagos** pay roll; **lista de revista** (mil) muster roll; **lista negra** blacklist; **pasar lista** to call the roll
listar *tr* to list
listero *m* roll keeper, timekeeper
listín *m* telephone directory; (S-D) newspaper
lista•do -da *adj* striped || *m* list; (compu) hard copy, printout; **listado electoral** electoral roll
lis•to -ta *adj* ready; quick, prompt; alert, wide-awake; **estar listo** to be ready; to be finished; **listo de manos** light-fingered; **pasarse de listo** to be shrewd, be clever || *f* see **lista**
listón *m* (*cinta*) ribbon, tape; (*pedazo de tabla angosta*) lath, strip of wood
listonado *m* lath, lathing
lisura *f* evenness, smoothness; plainness; candor; brashness, insolence
lit. *abbr* **literalmente**
lite *f* lawsuit
litera *f* (*vehículo llevado por hombres o por animales*) litter; (*cama fija en los camarotes*) berth, bunk bed; **litera alta** upper berth; **litera baja** lower berth
literal *adj* literal
litera•rio -ria *adj* literary
litera•to -ta *adj* literary || *mf* literary person; **literatos** literati
literatura *f* literature; **literatura de escape** *or* **de evasión** escape literature; **literatura infantil** children's books
litigación *s* litigation
litigante *adj & mf* litigant
litigar §44 *tr & intr* to litigate
litigio *m* litigation, lawsuit; dispute
litigio•so -sa *adj* litigious
litina *s* (chem) lithia
litio *m* (chem) lithium
litisexpensas *fpl* (law) costs
litografía *f* (*arte de grabar en piedra para la reproducción en estampa*) lithography; (*estampa*) lithograph
litografiar §77 *tr* to lithograph
litógra•fo -fa *mf* lithographer
litoral *adj* coastal, littoral || *m* coast, shore
litro *m* liter
liturgia *f* liturgy
litúrgi•co -ca *adj* liturgic(al)
liviandad *f* lightness; inconstancy, fickleness; lewdness
livia•no -na *adj* light, lightweight; inconstant, fickle; lewd || *m* leading donkey; **livianos** lights, lungs
lívi•do -da *adj* livid
liza *f* combat, fight; (*campo para lidiar*) lists; **entrar en liza** to enter the lists
llaga *f* sore, ulcer; sorrow, grief; (*entre dos ladrillos*) (mas) seam, joint; (fig) ulcer
llagar §44 *tr* to make sore; hurt
llama *f* flame, blaze; marsh, swamp; (zool) llama; (fig) fire, passion; **llama piloto** pilot light; **saltar de las llamas y caer en las brasas** to jump out of the frying pan into the fire
llamada *f* call; (*movimiento con que se llama la atención de uno*) sign, signal; knock, ring; reference, reference mark; (mil) call, call to arms; (Mex) cowardice; **batir** *or* **tocar a llamada** (mil) to sound the call to arms; **llamada a filas** (mil) call to the colors; **llamada a quintas** draft call; **llamada interurbana** long distance call; **llamada por cobrar** collect call; **llamada telefónica** telephone call; **llamada urbana** local call
llamadera *f* goad
llama•do -da *adj* so-called || *f* see **llamada**
llama•dor -dora *mf* caller || *m* messenger; door knocker; push button
llamamiento *m* call; calling, vocation
llamar *tr* to call; (*dar nombre a*) name, call; summon; invoke, call upon; (*la atención*) attract || *intr* to call; (*golpear en la puerta*) knock; (*hacer sonar la campanilla*) ring; (*el viento*) (naut) to veer || *ref* to be called, be named; **se llama Juan** his name is John
llamarada *f* blaze, flare-up; (*encendimiento repentino del rostro*) flush; (fig) flare-up, outburst
llamarón *m* flare-up
llamati•vo -va *adj* showy, loud, flashy, gaudy; (*manjar*) thirst-raising
llamazar *m* swamp, marsh
llame *m* (Chile) bird net, bird trap
llamear *intr* to blaze, flame, flash
lla•món -mona *adj* (Mex) cowardly
llampo *m* (Chile) ore
llana *f* trowel, float; plain; **dar de llana** to smooth with the trowel
llanada *f* plain
llanero *m* ranger, plainsman
llaneza *f* plainness, simplicity; familiarity; sincerity
lla•no -na *adj* even, level, smooth; (*parecido a un plano geométrico*) plane; (*sencillo*) plain, simple; clear, evident; (*palabras*) frank; accented on the next to last syllable || *m* plain; (*de la escalera*) landing || *f* see **llana**
llanque *m* (Peru) rawhide sandal

llanta *f* (*cerco exterior de la rueda*) tire (*of iron or rubber*); (*borde exterior de la rueda*) rim; (*pieza de hierro más ancha que gruesa*) iron flat; **llanta de goma** rubber tire; **llanta de invierno** snow tire; **llanta de oruga** (*de un tractor de oruga*) track

llanto *m* weeping, crying; **en llanto** in tears

llanura *f* evenness, level, smoothness; (*terreno extenso y llano*) plain

llapan•go -ga *adj* (Ecuad) barefooted

llares *m* pothanger

llave *adj* key ‖ *f* (*pieza para abrir y cerrar las cerraduras*) key; (*herramienta*) wrench; (*grifo*) faucet, spigot, cock; (*de arma de fuego*) cock; (elec) switch; (*de un instrumento de viento*) (mus) key; (*de un enigma, secreto, traducción, cifra; lugar estratégico más propicio*) key; **bajo llave** under lock and key; **echar la llave a** to lock; **llave de caja** socket wrench; **llave de caño** pipe wrench; **llave de contacto** *or* **de encendido** ignition key; **llave de cubo** socket wrench; **llave de chispa** flintlock; **llave de estufa** damper; **llave de mandíbulas dentadas** alligator wrench; **llave de paso** stopcock; passkey; **llave de purga** drain cock; **llave de tubo** box wrench; **llave espacial** space key; **llave inglesa** monkey wrench; **llave maestra** master key, skeleton key; **llave para tubos** pipe wrench

llave•ro -ra *mf* keeper of the keys; (*carcelero*) turnkey ‖ *m* key ring

llavín *m* latchkey

llegada *f* arrival

llegar §44 *tr* to bring up, bring close ‖ *intr* to arrive; happen; **llegar a** to arrive at; reach; amount to; be equal to; **llegar a** + *inf* to come to + *inf;* succeed in + *ger;* **llegar a ser** to become ‖ *ref* to come close

llena *f* flood

llenado *m* filling

llena•dor -dora *adj* (*alimento*) (Chile) filling

llenar *tr* to fill; (*un formulario*) fill out; (*ciertas condiciones*) fulfill; satisfy; (*colmar*) overwhelm ‖ *intr* (*la luna*) to be full ‖ *ref* to fill, fill up; stuff oneself; **llenarse a rebosar** to be filled to overflowing

llene *m* filling; full tank

lle•no -na *adj* full; **lleno a rebosar** full to overflowing; **lleno de goteras** full of aches and pains ‖ *m* fill, plenty; fulness, full enjoyment; completeness; full moon; (*en el teatro*) full house ‖ *f* see **llena**

lleva or **llevada** *f* carrying, conveying; ride; **lleva gratuita** free ride

llevade•ro -ra *adj* bearable, tolerable

llevar *tr* (*transportar*) to carry; (*traer consigo*) take; (*conducir*) lead; carry away, take away; (*cuentas, libros; la anotación en los naipes*) keep; (*la correspondencia con una persona*) carry on; (*un drama a la pantalla*) put on; (*buena o mala vida*) lead; (*aguantar*) bear, stand for; (*castigo*) suffer; get, obtain; win; (*cierto precio*) charge; (*traje, vestido*) wear; (*armas*) bear; (*cierto tiempo*) have been, e.g., **llevo ocho días en cama** I have been in bed for a week; (*ropa*) **a todo llevar** for all kinds of wear; **llevar** (*cierto tiempo*) **a** (*uno*) to be older than (*someone*) by (*a certain age*); (*cierta distancia*) **a** (*uno*) to be ahead of (*someone*) by (*a certain distance*); (*cierto peso*) **a** (*uno*) to be heavier than (*someone*) by (*a certain weight*); **llevar a las antenas** to put on the air; **llevarla hecha** to have it all figured out; **llevar puesto** to wear, to have on; **llevar** + *pp* to have + *pp,* e.g., **lleva conseguidas muchas victorias** he has won many victories ‖ *ref* to carry away; take, take away; carry off; win; get along; **llevarse algo a alguien** to take something away from someone

lloradue•los *mf* (*pl* **-los**) crybaby, sniveler

lloralásti•mas *mf* (*pl* **-mas**) poverty-crying skinflint

llorar *tr* to weep over; mourn, lament ‖ *intr* to weep, cry; (*los ojos*) water, run

llorera *f* crying; sobbing

lloriquear *intr* to whine, to whimper

lloriqueo *m* whining, whimpering

lloro *m* weeping, crying; tears

llo•rón -rona *adj* weeping, crying ‖ *mf* weeper, crybaby ‖ *m* weeping willow; pendulous plume ‖ *f* hired mourner

lloro•so -sa *adj* weepy; sad, tearful

llovedi•zo -za *adj* (*agua*) rain; (*techo*) leaky

llover §47 *tr* (*enviar como lluvia*) to rain ‖ *intr* to rain; **como llovido** unexpectedly; **llueva o no** rain or shine; **llueve** it is raining ‖ *ref* (*el techo*) to leak

llovido *m* stowaway

llovizna *f* drizzle

lloviznar *intr* to drizzle

llovizno•so -sa *adj* moist, damp (*from drizzle*); drizzly

lluvia *f* rain; rain water; (*copia, muchedumbre*) (fig) shower, downpour; **lluvia ácida** acid rain; **lluvia de estrellas** meteor shower; **lluvia radiactiva** *or* **nuclear** fallout, radioactive fallout

lluvio•so -sa *adj* rainy

lo *art def neut* (used with *masc sg* form of adj) the, e.g., **lo bueno** the good; what is, e.g., **lo útil** what is useful; **lo mío** what is mine; (used with *adv* or inflected *adj*) the + noun, e.g., **lo aprisa que habla** the speed with which he speaks; **lo tacaños que son** the stinginess of them; how, e.g., **Ud., no sabe lo felices que son** you do not know how happy they are; **lo más** as . . . as, e.g., **lo más temprano posible** as early as possible ‖ *pron pers masc* him, it; you; (with **estar, ser, parecer,** and the like, it stands for an adjective or noun understood and is either not translated or is translated by "so"), e.g., **Ud. está preparado pero ella no lo está** you are ready but she is not ‖ *pron dem* that; **de lo que** + *verb* than + *verb,* e.g., **ese libro ha costado más dinero de lo que**

vale that book cost more money than it is worth; **lo de** the matter of, the question of, e.g., **lo de sus deudas** the matter of your debts; **lo de que** the fact that, the statement that; **lo de siempre** the same old story; **lo que** what, that which; **todo lo que** all (that), e.g., **me dió todo lo que tenía** he gave me all he had

loa *f* praise; (*del teatro antiguo*) prologue; short dramatic poem

loable *adj* laudable, praiseworthy

loar *tr* to praise

loba *f* she-wolf; ridge

lobagante *m* lobster (*Homarus*)

lobanillo *m* wen, cyst

lobato *m* wolf cub

lobizón *or* **lobisón** (SAm) werewolf

lo•bo -ba *adj* & *mf* (Mex) half-breed || *m* wolf; **coger** or **pillar un lobo** (coll) to go on a jag; **desollar** or **dormir un lobo** to sleep off a drunk; **lobo acuático** *or* **de río** otter; **lobo cervario** lynx; **lobo de mar** (ichth) sea wolf; (coll) old salt, sea dog; **lobo marino** seal; **lobo solitario** (fig) lone wolf || *f* see **loba**

lóbre•go -ga *adj* dark, dismal; gloomy

lobreguez *f* darkness; gloominess

lobu•no -na *adj* wolf, wolfish

locación *f* lease

local *adj* local || *m* quarters, place

localidad *f* (*lugar, sitio*) location, locanty; (*plaza en un tren*) accommodations; (theat) seat

localización *f* localization; location; **localización de averías** trouble shooting

localizar §60 *tr* (*limitar a un punto determinado*) to localize; (*determinar el lugar de*) locate

loc. cit. *abbr* **loco citado** (Lat) (**en el lugar citado**) l.c. (in the place cited)

locería *f* pottery

loción *f* wash; (pharm) lotion; **loción facial** after-shave lotion, loción para después de afeitarse

lo•co -ca *adj* crazy, insane, mad; terrific, wonderful; **estar loco por** to be crazy about, to be mad about; **loco de amor** madly in love; **loco de atar** raving mad; **loco perenne** insane, demented; full of fun; **loco rematado** stark-mad; **volver loco** to drive crazy || *mf* crazy person, lunatic || *m* (*bufón*) fool

locomotora *f* engine, locomotive; **locomotora de maniobras** shifting engine

locro *m* (SAm) meat and vegetable stew

lo•cuaz *adj* (*pl* **-cuaces**) loquacious

locución *f* expression, locution; idiomatic phrase, idiom

locuela *f* speech, way of speaking

locue•lo -la *adj* wild, frisky || *f* see **locuela**

locura *f* insanity, madness; folly, madness

locu•tor -tora *mf* announcer, commentator

locutorio *m* (*en un convento de monjas*) parlor, locutory; telephone booth

lodazal *m* mudhole

lodo *m* mud, mire; (*substancia que sirve para cerrar junturas, tapar grietas, etc.*) (chem) lute

lodo•so -sa *adj* muddy

logaritmo *m* logarithm

logia *f* (*p.ej., de francmasones*) lodge; (archit) loggia

logicial *m* (compu) software

lógi•co -ca *adj* logical || *mf* logician || *f* logic

logísti•co -ca *adj* logistic(al) || *f* logistics

logo *m* logo

logopedía *f* speech correction

logotipo *m* logo

logrado -da *adj* successful

lograr *tr* to get, obtain; achieve, attain; **lograr** + *inf* to succeed in + *ger* || *ref* to be successful

logrear *intr* to be a moneylender; profiteer

logre•ro -ra *adj* moneylending; profiteering || *mf* moneylender; profiteer; (Chile) sponger

logro *m* attainment, success; gain, profit; usury; **dar** or **prestar a logro** to lend at usurious rates

loma *f* low hill, elevation

lombriguera *f* wormhole in the ground; (bot) tansy

lom•briz *f* (*pl* **-brices**) worm, earthworm; (pathol) worm; (*persona muy alta y delgada*) beanpole; **lombriz de tierra** earthworm; **lombriz solitaria** tapeworm

lomera *f* (*de la guarnición*) backstrap; (*del tejado*) ridgepole; (bb) backing

lominhies•to -ta *adj* high-backed; conceited

lomo *m* (*de animal, libro, cuchillo*) back; (*tierra que levanta el arado*) ridge; (*carne de lomo del animal*) loin; (*pliegue del tejido*) crease; (bb) spine; **loma de burro** (SAm) speed bump; **lomos** ribs

lona *f* canvas; sailcloth; (Mex) burlap

loncha *f* slab, flagstone; slice, strip

lonchería *f* snack bar

londinense *adj* London || *mf* Londoner

Londres *m* London; **el Gran Londres** Greater London

longáni•mo -ma *adj* long-suffering

longaniza *f* pork sausage

longevidad *f* longevity

longe•vo -va *adj* long-lived

longitud *f* length; (astr & geog) longitud; **longitud de onda** wave length

lonja *f* exchange, market; marketplace; commodity exchange; grocery store; wool warehouse; (*de carne*) slice; (*de cuero*) strip; (*a la entrada de un edificio*) elevated parvis; (Arg) rawhide; (Esp) fish market

lonjeta *f* bower, summerhouse

lonjista *mf* grocer

lontananza *f* (*de una pintura*) background; **en lontananza** in the distance, on the horizon

loor *m* praise

loquear *intr* to talk nonsense, play the fool; carry on, have a high time

loquera *f* insanity

loquería *f* (Chile) madhouse
loque•ro -ra *mf* guard in a mental hospital ‖ *m* (Arg) confusion, pandemonium; (Arg) madhouse
loques•co -ca *adj* crazy; funny, jolly
lorán *m* (naut) loran
lord *m* (*pl* **lores**) lord
lo•ro -ra *adj* dark-brown ‖ *m* parrot; cherry laurel; (Chile) spy; (Chile) glass bedpan; (Chile) third degree
losa *f* slab, flagstone; tomb
losange *m* lozenge; (baseball) diamond
lote *m* lot, share, portion; lottery prize; (compu) batch; (Cuba, Mex) remnant; (Arg) dunce, simpleton; (Col) swallow, swig; (*de terreno*) (Cuba, Mex) lot
lotear *tr* (Chile) to divide up, divide into lots
lotería *f* lottery; (*juego casero*) lotto; (*cosa insegura, riesgo*) gamble
lote•ro -ra *mf* vendor of lottery tickets
lotizar §60 *tr* (Peru) to divide into lots
loto *m* lotus
loza *f* (*barro cocido y barnizado*) porcelain; crockery, earthenware; **loza fina** china, chinaware
lozanear *intr* to be luxuriant; be full of life ‖ *ref* (*deleitarse*) to luxuriate
lozanía *f* luxuriance, verdure; exuberance, vigor; pride, haughtiness
loza•no -na *adj* luxuriant, verdant; exuberant, vigorous; proud, haughty
lubricante *adj & m* lubricant
lubricar §73 *tr* to lubricate
lúbri•co -ca *adj* (*resbaladizo; lascivo*) lubricious (slippery; lewd)
lubrificar §73 to lubricate
lucera *f* skylight
lucerna *f* large chandelier; (*abertura, tronera*) loophole
lucero *m* bright star; (*planeta*) Venus; (*ventanillo en un muro*) light; **lucero del alba** *or* **de la mañana** morning star; **lucero de la tarde** evening star; **luceros** (poet) eyes
lucha *f* fight; (*disputa*) quarrel; (*actividad forzada*) struggle; (*combate cuerpo a cuerpo*) wrestling; **lucha antipolución** antipollution movement (or campaign); **lucha de la cuerda** (sport) tug of war; **lucha libre** freestyle wrestling; **lucha por la vida** struggle for existence
lucha•dor -dora *mf* fighter, wrestler
luchar *intr* (*combatir*) to fight; (*disputar*) quarrel; (*esforzarse*) struggle; (*pelear cuerpo a cuerpo*) wrestle
luci•do -da *adj* generous, magnificent; brilliant, successful; sumptuous; (Arg) striking, dashing
lúci•do -da *adj* lucid
luciente *adj* bright, shining
luciérnaga *f* glowworm, firefly
lucifer *m* overbearing fellow ‖ **Lucifer** *m* Lucifer
lucífe•ro -ra *adj* (poet) bright, dazzling ‖ *m* morning star; (Col) match
lucimiento *m* brilliance, luster; show, dash; success; **quedar** or **salir con lucimiento** to come off with flying colors
lu•cio -cia *adj* shiny ‖ *m* salt pool; (*pez*) pike, luce
lucir §45 *tr* to light, light up; show, display; (*p.ej., un traje nuevo*) sport; help; plaster ‖ *intr* to shine ‖ *ref* to dress up; come off with great success; (*sobresalir, distinguirse*) shine; flop, e.g., **lucido me quedé** I was a flop
lucrar *tr* to get, obtain ‖ *intr & ref* to profit, make money
lucrati•vo -va *adj* lucrative
lucro *m* gain, profit; **lucros y daños** profit and loss
lucro•so -sa *adj* lucrative
luctuo•so -sa *adj* sad, mournful, gloomy
ludibrio *m* derision, mockery, scorn
ludir *tr, intr & ref* to rub, rub together
luego *adv* next, then; therefore; soon; once in a while; **desde luego** right away; of course; **hasta luego** good-bye, so long; **luego como** as soon as; **luego de** after, right after; **luego que** as soon as
luen•go -ga *adj* long
lúes *f* pestilence; **lúes canina** distemper; **lúes venérea** syphilis
lugano *m* (orn) siskin
lugar *m* place; site, spot; job, position; (*espacio*) room, space; (*asiento*) seat; village, hamlet; (geom) locus; **dar lugar** to make room; **dar lugar a** to give cause for; give rise to; **en lugar de** instead of, in place of; **hacer lugar** to make room; **lugar común** (*expresión trivial*) commonplace; (*retrete*) toilet, water closet; **lugar de cita** tryst; **lugar de cría** (zool) breeding ground; **lugares estrechos** close quarters; **lugar geométrico** locus; **lugar religioso** place of burial
lugarejo *m* hamlet
lugare•ño -ña *adj* village ‖ *mf* villager
lugarteniente *m* lieutenant
luge *m* sled
lúgubre *adj* dismal, gloomy, lugubrious
luir §20 *tr* (naut) to gall, wear; (Chile) to muss, rumple; (*vasijas de barro*) (Chile) to polish ‖ *ref* (Chile) to rub, wear away
Luis *m* Louis
luisa *f* (bot) lemon verbena; **Luisa** Louise
lujo *m* luxury; **de lujo** de luxe; **gastar mucho lujo** to live in high style; **lujo de** abundance of, excess of
lujo•so -sa *adj* luxurious
lujuria *f* lust, lechery
lujuriante *adj* (*lozano*) luxuriant, lush; (*libidinoso*) lustful
lujuriar *intr* to lust, be lustful; (*los animales*) copulate
lujurio•so -sa *adj* lustful, lecherous ‖ *mf* lecher
lu•lo -la *adj* (Chile) lank, slender ‖ *m* (Chile) bundle
lu•lú *m* (*pl* **-lúes**) spitz dog

lumbago *m* lumbago
lumbre *f* light; fire; (*para encender el cigarrillo*) light; (*hueco en un muro por donde entra la luz*) light; brightness, brilliance; knowledge, learning; **echar lumbre** to blow one's top; **lumbre del agua** surface of the water; **lumbres** tinderbox; **ni por lumbre** not for love or money; **ser la lumbre de los ojos de** to be the light of the eyes of
lumbrera *f* light, source of light; light, lamp; (*abertura por donde entran el aire y la luz*) louver; skylight; dormer window; air duct, ventilating shaft; (*persona insigne*) light, luminary; (mach) port; **lumbreras** eyes
luminar *m* luminary
luminiscente *adj* luminescent
lumino•so -sa *adj* luminous; (*idea*) bright
luminotecnia *f* lighting engineering
lun. *abbr* **lunes**
luna *f* moon; moonlight; (*tabla de cristal*) plate glass; (*espejo*) mirror; (*de los anteojos*) lens, glass; whim; **estar de buena luna** to be in a good mood; **estar de mala luna** to be in a bad mood; **luna de miel** honeymoon; **luna llena** full moon; **luna menguante** waning moon; **luna nueva** new moon; **media luna** half moon; (*figura de cuarto de luna creciente o menguante*) crescent; **quedarse a la luna de Valencia** to be disappointed
lunar *adj* lunar || *m* (*mancha de la piel*) mole; (*punto en un diseño de puntos*) polka dot; (fig) stain, blot, stigma; **lunar postizo** beauty spot
lunáti•co -ca *adj & mf* lunatic
lu•nes *m* (*pl* **-nes**) Monday; **hacer San Lunes** to knock off on Monday
luneta *f* (*de los anteojos*) lens, glass; orchestra seat; (aut) rear window
lunfardo *m* (Arg) thief; underworld slang
lupa *m* magnifying glass
lupanar *m* brothel, bawdyhouse
lupia *mf* (Hond) quack, healer || *f* wen, cyst; **lupias** (Col) small amount of money, small change
lúpulo *m* (*vid*) hop; (*flores desecadas de la vid*) hops
luquete *m* slice of orange or lemon used to flavor wine; (Chile) bald spot; (*en la ropa*) (Chile) spot, hole
lu•rio -ria *adj* (Mex) mad, crazy
lusitanismo *m* Lusitanism
lusita•no -na *adj & mf* Lusitanian, Portuguese
lustrabo•tas *m* (*pl* **-tas**) shoeshiner
lustrar *tr* to shine, polish || *intr* to wander, roam
lustre *m* shine, polish; luster, gloss; (*fama, gloria*) (fig) luster
lustrina *f* (Chile) shoe polish
lustro *m* five years; chandelier
lustro•so -sa *adj* shining, bright, lustrous
lutera•no -na *adj & mf* Lutheran
luto *m* (*señal exterior de duelo*) mourning; (*duelo, aflicción*) sorrow, bereavement; **estar de luto** to be in mourning; **ir de luto** to wear black; **lutos** crape; **luto riguroso** deep mourning
lutocar *m* (Chile) trash cart
luz *f* (*pl* **luces**) light; window, light; electricity; (*dinero*) money; cash; **a primera luz** at dawn; **a toda luz** *or* **a todas luces** everywhere; by all means; **dar a luz** to have a child; to give birth to; to bring out; to publish; **entre dos luces** at twilight; halfseas over; **luces de carretera, luces largas, luces altas** (aut) bright lights; **luces de ciudad** parking lights; **luces de cruce** (aut) dimmers; **luces de placa** license plate lights; **luz de balizaje** (aer) marker light; **luz de cortesía** *or* **estribo** courtesy light; **luz de matrícula** license-plate light; **luz de parada** stop light; **luz estroboscópica** strobe (light); **luz interior** (aut) courtesy light; **luz trasera** taillight; **sacar a luz** to bring to light; **salir a luz** to come to light; come out, be published; take place; **ver la luz** to see the light, see the light of day
Luzbel *m* Lucifer

M

M, m (eme) *f* thirteenth letter of the Spanish alphabet
m. *abbr* **mañana, masculino, meridiano, metro, minuto, muerto**
maca *f* flaw, blemish; bruise (*on fruit*); spot, stain; hammock
maca•co -ca *adj* ugly, misshapen || *m* — **macaco de la India** rhesus
macadamizar §60 *tr* to macadamize
macadán *m* macadam
macana *f* cudgel, club; drug on the market; nonsense; (Arg) botch; (Arg) lie, trick
macanear *intr* to fib, lay it on; (Col, Ven) to manage (well)
macanu•do -da *adj* terrific, swell, grand; (Col, Ecuad) strong, husky
macarrón *m* macaroon; **macarrones** macaroni
macear *tr* to mace, hammer || *intr* to pester, bore
macelo *m* slaughterhouse
macero *m* macebearer
maceta *f* stone hammer; flowerpot; flower vase; (*de herramienta*) handle; (*de cantero*) hammer; (Mex) head
macfarlán *m* inverness cape

macha *f* (Bol) drunkenness; (Arg) joke; (Bol) mannish woman
machaca *mf* pest, bore || *f* crusher
machacar §73 *tr* to crush, mash, pound || *intr* to pester, bore
macha•cón -cona *adj* boring, tiresome, importunate || *mf* bore
machada *f* flock of billy goats; stupidity
machado *m* hatchet
machamartillo — a machamartillo solidly, firmly, lastingly
machaque•ro -ra *adj* tiresome, boring || *mf* bore
machar *tr* to crush, grind, pound || *ref* (Bol, Ecuad) to get drunk
machete *m* machete, cane knife
machi *mf* (Chile) quack, healer
machihembrar *tr* (*ensamblar a ranura y lengüeta*) to feather; (*ensamblar a caja y espiga*) mortise
machina *f* derrick, crane; pile driver; (P-R) merry-go-round
machismo *m* machismo; male chauvinism
machista *m* male chauvinist
macho *adj invar* (*animal, planta, herramienta*) male; strong, robust; dull, stupid || *m* sledge hammer; abutment, pillar; male; he-mule; dullard; (*del corchete*) hook; (mach) male piece; (coll) he-man; (C-R) blond foreigner; **macho cabrío** he-goat, billy goat; **macho de aterrajar** or **macho de terraja** (mach) tap, screw tap
machona *f* (Arg, Bol, Ecuad, Guat) mannish woman
macho•rro -rra *adj* barren, sterile || *f* barren woman; (Mex) mannish woman
machucar §73 *tr* to beat, pound, bruise
machu•cho -cha *adj* sedate, judicious; elderly
macilen•to -ta *adj* pale, wan, gaunt
macillo *m* hammer (*of piano*)
macis *m* mace (*spice*)
macizar §60 *tr* to fill in, fill up
maci•zo -za *adj* solid; massive || *m* solid; flower bed; bulk, mass; massif; wall space
macrobióti•co -ca *adj* macrobiotic
macroeconómi•co -ca *adj* macroeconomic || *f* macroeconomics
macrofotografía *f* macrophotography
macu•co -ca *adj* (Chile) sly, cunning; (Arg, Chile, Ven) important, notable; (Ecuad) old, worthless; (Arg, Chile, Peru) strong, husky || *m* (Arg, Bol, Col) overgrown boy
mácula *f* spot; stain; blemish; trick, deception
madamita *m* (coll) sissy
madeja *f* hank, skein; tangle of hair; (*hombre flojo*) jellyfish; **madeja sin cuenda** hopeless tangle
madera *m* Madeira wine || *f* wood; piece of wood; knack, flair; makings; **madera aserradiza** lumber; **madera contrachapada** plywood; **madera de sierra** lumber; **madera laminada** plywood; **madera número 1** (*golf*) driver; **tener madera de** to have what it takes to, to be suited for
maderada *f* raft, float
maderaje *m* or **maderamen** *m* woodwork
maderería *f* lumberyard
madere•ro -ra *adj* lumber || *m* lumberman; carpenter; log driver
madero *m* log, beam; ship, vessel; blockhead
madrasta *f* stepmother; bother
madraza *f* doting mother
madre *adj* mother || *f* mother; matron; womb; main sewer; river bed; dregs; sediment; (Mex) (coll) prostitute; **madre adoptiva** foster mother; **madre alquilada, de alquiler** *or* **suplente** surrogate mother; **madre biológica** biological mother; **madre de leche** wet nurse; **madre patria** mother country, old country; **madre política** mother-in-law; stepmother; **madre soltera** single *o* unmarried mother; **sacar de madre** to annoy, to upset
madreperla *f* (*molusco*) pearl oyster; (*nácar*) mother-of-pearl
madreselva *f* honeysuckle
madriga•do -da *adj* twice-married; (*toro*) that has sired; worldly-wise
madriguera *f* burrow, lair, den; warren
madrile•ño -ña *adj* Madrid || *mf* native or inhabitant of Madrid
madrina *f* godmother; patroness, protectress; prop, shore, brace; joke; leading mare; **madrina de guerra** war mother; **primera madrina de boda** matron of honor
madrugada *f* early morning, dawn; early rising
madruga•dor -dora *adj* early-rising || *mf* early riser
madrugar §44 *intr* to get up early; be out in front
madurar *tr* to ripen; mature; think out || *intr* to ripen; mature
madurez *f* ripeness; maturity
madu•ro -ra *adj* ripe; mature
maestra *f* teacher; elementary girls' school; **maestra de escuela** schoolmistress
maestranza *f* arsenal, armory; navy yard; order of equestrian knights
maestría *f* mastery; mastership
maes•tro -tra *adj* master; masterly; chief, main; (*perro*) trained || *m* master; teacher; (*en la música y la pintura*) maestro; **maestro de capilla** choirmaster; **maestro de ceremonias** master of ceremonies; **maestro de equitación** riding master; **maestro de escuela** elementary schoolteacher; **maestro de esgrima** fencing master; **maestro de obras** master builder || *f* see **maestra**
Magallanes *m* Magellan
magancear *intr* (Col, Chile) to loaf around
magan•to -ta *adj* dull, spiritless
magia *f* magic
magiar *adj & mf* Magyar; Hungarian
mági•co -ca *adj* magic || *mf* magician, wizard || *f* magic
magín *m* fancy, imagination
magisterio *m* teaching; teachers
magistrado *m* magistrate

magistral *adj* masterly
magnáni•mo -ma *adj* magnanimous
magnesio *m* magnesium; (phot) flashlight
magnéti•co -ca *adj* magnetic
magnetismo *m* magnetism
magnetizar §60 *tr* magnetize
magneto *m & f* magneto
magnetofón *m* or **magnetófono** *m* tape recorder
magnetoscopia *f* video recorder
magnificar §73 *tr* to magnify; exalt
magnífi•co -ca *adj* magnificent
magnitud *f* magnitude
mag•no -na *adj* great, e.g., **Alejandro Magno** Alexander the Great
mago *m* magician; soothsayer; (fig) wizard, expert; **Magos de Oriente** Wise Men of the East
ma•gro -gra *adj* lean, thin || *m* loin of pork || *f* slice of ham
maguar §10 *ref* (Ven, W-I) to be disappointed
magüeta *f* heifer
magüeto *m* young bull
maguey *m* century plant
magullar *tr* to bruise || *ref* to get bruised
magullón *m* bruise; contusion
Mahoma *m* Muhammad
mahones *mpl* (P-R, S-D) blue jeans
mahonesa *f* mayonnaise
maído *m* meow
maitines *mpl* matins
maíz *m* maize, Indian corn; **comer maíz** to accept bribes; **maíz en la mazorca** corn on the cob; **maíz terno** sweet corn
maizal *m* cornfield
maja *f* flashy dame
majada *f* sheepfold; dung, manure
majaderear *tr* to bother, annoy
majadería *f* nonsensical remark; bother, nuisance
majade•ro -ra *adj* pestiferous, stupid || *mf* bore, dunce || *m* pestle
majar *tr* to crush, mash, grind, pound; annoy, bother
majestad *f* majesty
majestuo•so -sa *adj* majestic
ma•jo -ja *adj* sporty; handsome, dashing; pretty, nice; all dressed up || *mf* sport || *m* bully || *f* see **maja**
mal *adj* apocopated form of **malo**, used only before nouns in masculine singular || *adv* badly, poorly; wrong; hardly, scarcely; **mal de** short of; **mal que le pese** in spite of him || *m* evil; damage, harm; wrong; sickness; misfortune; **mal de altura, mal de (las) alturas, mal de (las) montañas** altitude or mountain sickness; **mal de Alzheimer** Alzheimer's disease; **mal de la tierra** homesickness; **mal de mar** seasickness; **mal de Parkinson** Parkinson's disease; **mal de piedra** (pathol) stone; **mal de rayos** radiation sickness; **mal de vuelo** airsickness; **por mal de mis pecados** to my sorrow; **tener a mal** to object to; **¡mal haya . . . !** curses on . . . !
mala *f* mail; mailbag; mailboat
malabarista *mf* juggler; sneak thief
malacate *m* whim; (*hoisting machine*) (Mex, Hond) spindle
malaconseja•do -da *adj* ill-advised
malacrianza *f* var of **malcriadez**
malagradeci•do -da *adj* ungrateful
malandante *adj* unlucky, unfortunate
malandanza *f* bad luck, misfortune
malan•drín -drina *adj* evil, wicked || *mf* scoundrel, rascal
malaria *f* malaria
malaventura *f* misfortune
mala•yo -ya *adj & mf* Malay
mala•zo -za *adj* perverse; evil; wicked
malbaratar *tr* to undersell; squander
malcasa•do -da *adj* mismated; undutiful
malcasar *tr* to mismate || *intr & ref* to be mismated
malcaso *m* treachery
malconten•to -ta *adj & mf* malcontent
malcriadez *f* rudeness; bad manners
malcria•do -da *adj* ill-bred
malcriar §77 *tr* to spoil, pamper
maldad *f* evil, wickedness
maldecir §11 *tr* to curse || *intr* to curse, damn; **maldecir de** to slander, vilify
maldición *f* malediction, curse; oath, curse
maldispues•to -ta *adj* ill, indisposed; unwilling, ill-disposed
maldi•to -ta *adj* damned, accursed; wicked; (Mex) coarse, crude, indecent; **no saber maldita la cosa de** to not know a single thing about || **el Maldito** the Evil One || *f* (coll) tongue; **soltar la maldita** to talk too much
maleante *adj* wicked, evil || *mf* crook, hoodlum, rowdy
malear *tr* to spoil; corrupt || *ref* to spoil, get spoiled; be corrupted
malecón *m* levee, dike, mole, jetty
maledicencia *f* calumny, slander
maleficiar *tr* to damage, harm; to curse, bewitch, cast a spell on
maleficio *m* curse, spell; witchcraft
maléfi•co -ca *adj* evil; harmful
malentender §51 *tr* to misunderstand
malentendido *m* misunderstanding, misapprehension
malestar *m* malaise, indisposition
maleta *m* bungler; ham bullfighter || *f* valise; **hacer la maleta** to pack up
maletín *m* satchel, bag; briefcase
malevolencia *f* malice, malevolence
malévo•lo -la *adj* malevolent
maleza *f* thicket, underbrush; weeds
malfuncionamiento *m* malfunction
malgasta•do -da *adj* ill-spent
malgastar *tr* to waste, squander
malgenio•so -sa *adj* ill-tempered, irritable
malhabla•do -da *adj* foul-mouthed
malhada•do -da *adj* ill-starred
malhe•cho -cha *adj* deformed || *m* misdeed
malhe•chor -chora *mf* malefactor || *f* malefactress

malherir §68 *tr* to injure badly
malhumora•do -da *adj* ill-humored
malicia *f* (*maldad*) evil; (*bellaquería, malevolencia*) malice; insidiousness, trickiness; suspicion
malicio•so -sa *adj* evil; malicious; insidious, tricky
malignar *tr* to corrupt, vitiate; spoil
malignidad *f* malignity
malig•no -na *adj* (*malévolo; pernicioso*) malign; (*malicioso; perjudicial*) malignant; (pathol) malignant
malintenciona•do -da *adj* ill-disposed, evil-minded
malla *f* mesh, meshing; (*de la armadura*) mail; (*traje*) tights; bathing suit, swimsuit
mallete *m* mallet
Mallorca *f* Majorca
mallor•quín -quina *adj & mf* Majorcan
malmaridada *f* faithless wife
malmeter *tr* to lead astray, misguide; alienate, estrange
ma•lo -la *adj* bad, poor, evil; (*travieso*) naughty, mischievous; (*enfermo*) sick, ill; (*que no es como debiera ser*) wrong; (*inflamado, dolorido*) sore; **a la mala** (Cuba, P-R) by force; (Mex) insincere; (Mex) mean; **estar de malas** to be out of luck; **lo malo es que** the trouble is that; **mala hierba** weed; **mala leche** (coll) foul or nasty mood; **mala pasada** dirty trick; **mala pata** (coll) bad luck; **malas artes** cunning; **malas lenguas** (coll) malicious tongues; **malo con** *or* **para con** mean to; **malos tratos** ill-treatment; **por malas o por buenas** willingly or unwillingly; **ser malo de engañar** to be hard to trick || **el Malo** the Evil One || *f* see **mala**
malogra•do -da *adj* late, ill-fated
malograr *tr* to miss || *ref* to fail; come to an untimely end
malogro *m* failure, disappointment
maloliente *adj* malodorous, foul-smelling
malón *m* mean trick; (SAm) Indian incursion; (Chile) surprise party
malpara•do -da *adj* hurt; **salir malparado (de)** to fail (in), come out worsted (in)
malparar *tr* to mistreat
malparir *intr* to miscarry, have a miscarriage
malparto *m* miscarriage
malquerencia *f* dislike
malquerer §55 *tr* to dislike
malquistar *tr* to alienate, estrange || *ref* to become alienated
malquis•to -ta *adj* disliked, unpopular
malrotar *tr* to squander
malsa•no -na *adj* unhealthy
malsín *m* mischief-maker
malsonante *adj* obnoxious, odious
malsufri•do -da *adj* impatient
malta *m* malt || *f* asphalt, tar; dark beer; (Chile) premium beer
maltraer §75 *tr* to abuse, ill-treat; call down, scold
maltratar *tr* to abuse, ill-treat, maltreat; damage, spoil
maltre•cho -cha *adj* battered, damaged
malu•co -ca *or* **malu•cho -cha** *adj* sickish, upset
malva *f* mallow; **malva arbórea** hollyhock, rose mallow; **ser como una malva** to be meek and mild
malva•do -da *adj* evil, wicked || *mf* evildoer
malvarrosa *f* hollyhock, rose mallow
malvavisco *m* marsh mallow
malvender *tr* to sell at a loss
malversación *f* graft, embezzlement, misappropriation
malversar *tr & intr* to graft, embezzle
malvezar §60 *tr* to give bad habits to || *ref* to acquire bad habits
Malvinas, las the Falkland Islands
mama *f* (anat) mama, breast; (zool) mamma, mammary gland; (coll) mamma, mama
ma•má *f* (*pl* **-más**), ma, mama, momma, mamma
mamada *f* suck; sucking; cinch; advantageous deal; easy profit
mama•lón -lona *adj* (Ven, W-I) loafing || *mf* (Cuba) sponger
mamama *f* (Hond) granny
mamamama *f* (Peru) granny
mamar *tr* to suck; learn as a child; swallow; wangle; **mamola** he was taken in || *intr* to suck || *ref* to swallow; (*obtener sin mérito*) wangle; (SAm) to get drunk; **mamarse a uno** to get the best of someone; take someone in; (Col, Chile, Peru) to do away with someone
mamarracho *m* mess, sight; (*hombre ridículo*) milksop
mamelón *m* knoll, mound
mami *f* (coll) mommy
mamífe•ro -ra *adj* mammalian || *m* mammal, mammalian
mamita *f* (coll) mommy
mamografía *f* mammogram; mammography
mamola *f* chuck (*under the chin*); **hacer la mamola a** to chuck under the chin; take in, make a fool of
ma•món -mona *adj* sucking; fond of sucking; (Col) boring || *mf* suckling; (*persona crédula*) (coll) sucker || *m* shoot, sucker, (Guat, Hond) club; (Mex) soft cake || *f* chuck (*under chin*)
mamonear *tr* (Guat, Hond) to beat, cudgel; (S-D) to put off, delay; (*el tiempo*) (S-D) to waste
mamotreto *m* memo book; batch of papers; hulk, bulk
mampara *f* screen; folding screen; (Peru) glass door
mamparo *m* bulkhead
mampostería *f* rubble, rubblework; masonry, stone masonry
ma•mut *m* (*pl* **-muts**) mammoth
manada *f* (*de ganado vacuno*) herd, drove; (*de ganado lanar*) flock; (*de lobos*) pack; (*de gente*) gang, troop; (*de hierba, trigo, etc.*) handful

manade•ro -ra *adj* flowing || *m* spring, source; shepherd
manantial *adj* flowing, running || *m* spring, source; (fig) source
manar *tr* to run with || *intr* to pour forth, run; abound
manaza *f* big hand
mancar §73 *tr* to maim, cripple || *intr* (*el viento*) (naut) to abate, subside
manca•rrón -rrona *adj* (*caballería*) skinny, worn-out; (Chile) tired out, exhausted || *m* old nag; (Chile, Peru) dam, dike
manceba *f* mistress, concubine
mancebía *f* bawdyhouse, brothel; wild oats; youth
mance•bo -ba *adj* youthful || *m* youngster; youth, young man; (*en una farmacia, barbería, etc.*) helper || *f* see **manceba**
mancerina *f* saucer with hook to hold chocolate cup
mancha *f* spot, stain; (*de vegetación*) patch; speckle; (fig) stain, blot; **mancha de petróleo** oil slick; **mancha solar** sunspot
manchar *tr* to spot, stain; speckle; splatter; (fig) to stain, disgrace || *intr* to spot; **¡mancha!** wet paint!
mancilla *f* spot, blemish
mancillar *tr* to spot, blemish
man•co -ca *adj* armless, one-armed; one-handed; defective, faulty || *mf* cripple || *m* (Chile) old nag
mancomún — de mancomún jointly, in common
mancomunar *tr* to unite, combine; (*fuerzas, caudales, etc.*) pool || *ref* to unite, combine
mancomunidad *f* association, union; (*asociación de provincias*) commonwealth
mancornar §61 *tr* (*un novillo*) to throw and hold on the ground; (*una res vacuna*) tie a horn and front leg of; (*dos reses*) tie together by the horns; (coll) to join, bring together
mancornas or **mancuernas** *fpl* (Mex) cuff links
mancuernillas *fpl* (Guat, Hond) cuff links
manda *f* gift, offer; bequest, legacy
mandade•ro -ra *mf* messenger || *m* errand boy
mandado *m* order, command; errand; **hacer un mandado** to run an errand
manda•más *m* (*pl* **-mases**) (slang) big shot; (*jefe político*) (slang) boss
mandamiento *m* order, command; (Bib) commandment; (law) writ; **los cinco mandamientos** the five fingers of the hand
mandar *tr* to order, command; (*legar*) bequeath; (*enviar*) send; **mandar a distancia** to operate by remote control; **mandar** + *inf* to have + *inf*, e.g., **la mandé leer en voz alta** I had her read aloud || *intr* to be in command, be the boss; **mandar llamar** to send for; **mandar por** to send for; **mande Ud.** I beg your pardon || *ref* (*un enfermo*) to manage to get around; (*dos piezas*) be communicating; **mandarse con** (*otra pieza*) to communicate with; be rude to
mandarina *f* tangerine
mandatario *m* agent, proxy; chief executive
mandato *m* mandate; term (*of office*)
mandíbula *f* jaw, jawbone; **reír a mandíbula batiente** to roar with laughter
mandil *m* apron
mando *m* command; control, drive; **alto mando** (mil) high command; **mando a distancia** remote control; **mando a punta de dedo** fingertip control; **mando de las válvulas** timing gears; **mando por botón** push-button control; **tener el mando y el palo** to be the boss, rule the roost
mandolina *f* mandolin
man•dón -dona *adj* bossy || *mf* domineering person || *m* (*en las minas*) boss, foreman; (*en las carreras de caballos*) (Chile) starter
mandrágora *f* mandrake
mandril *m* (mach) chuck
mandrilar *tr* to bore
manea *f* hobble
manear *tr* to hobble
manecilla *f* (*de reloj*) hand; clasp, book clasp; (bot) tendril; (typ) fist, index
manejable *adj* manageable
manejar *tr* to manage; handle, wield; (*un automóvil*) drive || *ref* to behave; get around, move about
manejo *m* management; handling; intrigue, scheming; horsemanship; driving; **manejo a distancia** remote control; **manejo doméstico** housekeeping
manera *f* manner, way; **a la manera de** in the manner of; like; **de manera que** so that; **de ninguna manera** nohow, by no means; **en gran manera** to a great extent; extremely; **sobre manera** exceedingly
manga *f* (*parte del vestido*) sleeve; (*tubo de caucho*) hose; waterspout; (bridge) game; **en mangas de camisa** in shirt-sleeves; **ir de manga** to be in cahoots; **manga de agua** waterspout; cloudburst; **manga de camisa** shirt-sleeve; **manga de incendio** fire hose; **manga de riego** watering hose; **manga de ventilación** ventilation shaft; **manga de viento** whirlwind, windsock; **manga marina** waterspout; **mangas** extras, profits
mangana *f* lasso
manganear *tr* to lasso; (Peru) to annoy, bother
manganeso *m* manganese
mango *m* handle; **mango de escoba** broomstick; (aer) stick, control stick
mangonear *tr* to plunder || *intr* to loaf around; meddle; dabble
mangosta *f* mongoose
mangote *m* sleeve protector
manguera *f* hose; (*tubo de ventilación*) funnel
mangueta *f* fountain syringe; door jamb
manguitero *m* furrier
manguito *m* muff; sleeve guard; coffee cake; (mach) sleeve
ma•ní *m* (*pl* **-níes** or **-nises**) peanut
manía *f* mania; craze, whim; grudge; **manía**

persecutoria *or* **de persecución** persecution complex; **tener manía a** to dislike

maniabier•to -ta *adj* open-handed

manía•co -ca *adj* maniac(al) || *mf* maniac

maníaco-depresi•vo -va *adj* manic-depressive

maniatar *tr* to tie the hands of

maniáti•co -ca *adj* stubborn; queer, eccentric; (*entusiasta*) crazy || *mf* crank, eccentric

manicero *m* peanut vendor

manicomio *m* madhouse, insane asylum

manicor•to -ta *adj* closefisted, tight

manicu•ro -ra *mf* manicure, manicurist || *f* manicure, manicuring

mani•do -da *adj* shabby, worn; hackneyed; (culin) high || *f* haunt, hangout

manifestación *f* manifestation; (*reunión pública para dar a conocer un sentimiento u opinión*) demonstration

manifestante *mf* demonstrator

manifestar §2 *tr* to manifest; (*el Santísimo Sacramento*) expose || *intr* to demonstrate || *ref* to become manifest

manifies•to -ta *adj* manifest || *m* manifesto; (eccl) exposition of the Host; (naut) manifest

manigua *f* (Mex, W-I) thicket, jungle; **irse a la manigua** (W-I) to revolt

manija *f* handle; clamp; crank

manilar•go -ga *adj* ready-fisted; generous

manilla *f* bracelet; handcuff, manacle

manillar *m* handle bar

maniobra *f* handling; lever; maneuver; (naut) gear, tackle

maniobrar *intr* to work with the hands; maneuver; (rr) to shift

maniota *f* hobble

manipulación *f* manipulation; operation, use; (*de alimentos*) handling

manipula•dor -dora *mf* manipulator || *m* (telg) key

manipular *tr* to manipulate

mani•quí *m* (*pl* **-quíes**) manikin, mannequin; (*para exponer prendas de ropa*) dress form; (*de pintores y escultores*) lay figure; (fig) puppet; **ir hecho un maniquí** to be a fashion plate || *f* (*mujer joven que luce los trajes de última moda*) mannequin, model

manirro•to -ta *adj* lavish, prodigal

manivací•o -a *adj* empty-handed

manivela *f* crank; **manivela de arranque** starting crank

manjar *m* dish, food, tidbit, delicacy; lift, recreation

mano *m* first to play, e.g., **soy mano** I'm first || *f* hand; (*de cuadrúpedo*) forefoot; (*de pintura*) coat; (*de papel*) quire; (*saetilla de reloj u otro instrumento*) hand; (*lance en un juego*) round, hand; (*del elefante*) trunk; pestle, masher; **a la mano** at hand, on hand; within reach; understandable; **a mano airada** violently; **asidos de la mano** hand in hand; **bajo mano** underhandedly; **caer en manos de** to fall into the hands of; **¡dame esa mano!** put it here!; **dar la mano** to lend a hand; **darse las manos** to join hands; to shake hands; **de las manos** hand in hand; **de primera mano** at first hand; firsthand; **de segunda mano** secondhand; **echar mano de** to resort to; **echar una mano** to lend a hand; to play a game; **en buena mano está** after you, you drink first; **escribir a la mano** to take dictation; **escribir a manos de** to write in care of; **estrecharse la mano** to shake hands; **ganarle a uno por la mano** to steal a march on someone; **lavarse las manos de** to wash one's hands of; **llegar a las manos** to come to blows; **malas manos** awkwardness; **mano de gato** cat's-paw; master hand, master touch; **mano de obra** labor; workmanship; **mano derecha** right-hand man; **mano de santo** sure cure; **¡manos a la obra!** let's get to work!; **manos libres** outside work; **manos limpias** extras, perquisites; clean hands; **manos puercas** graft; **probar la mano** to try one's hand; **tener mano con** to have a pull with; **tener mano izquierda** to be on one's toes; **untar la mano a** to grease the palm of; **venir a las manos** to come to blows; **vivir de la mano a la boca** to live from hand to mouth

manojo *m* bunch, bundle, handful; **a manojos** in abundance

manopla *f* gauntlet; postilion's whip; (Chile) knuckles, brass knuckles

manosear *tr* to finger, paw; muss, rumple; fiddle with; pet || *ref* to spoon, neck

manotada *f* slap

manotear *tr* to slap, smack; (Arg, Mex) to steal, snitch; || *intr* to gesticulate

manquedad *f* lack of one or both hands or arms; disability; deficiency

mansalva — a mansalva without risk; without warning; **a mansalva de** safe from

mansarda *f* mansard, mansard roof

mansedumbre *f* gentleness, mildness, meekness; tameness

mansión *f* stay, sojourn; abode, dwelling; **hacer mansión** to stop, stay

man•so -sa *adj* gentle, mild, meek; tame || *m* bellwether; farm

manta *f* blanket; heavy shawl; (coll) beating, thrashing; (Chile, Ecuad) poncho; (Col, Mex, Ven) coarse cotton cloth; **a manta de Dios** copiously; **dar una manta a** to toss in a blanket; **manta de coche** lap robe; **manta de viaje** steamer rug; **tirar de la manta** to let the cat out of the bag

mantear *tr* to toss in a blanket; abuse, mistreat

manteca *f* (*grasa de los animales, esp. la del cerdo*) lard; butter; pomade; (*dinero*) (slang) dough; **como manteca** smooth as butter; **manteca de maní** (SAm) peanut butter; **manteca de puerco** lard; **manteca de vaca** butter

mantecado *m* custard ice cream, French ice cream

mantecón *m* mollycoddle, milksop

mantel *m* tablecloth; altar cloth

mantelería *f* table linen

mantelillo *m* embroidered centerpiece
mantelito *m* lunch cloth
mantener §71 *tr* to maintain; keep; keep up; sustain, defend || *ref* to keep, remain, continue
mantenida *f* kept woman
mantenido *m* (*hombre que vive a expensas de su mujer*) (Guat, Mex, W-I) gigolo; (Guat, Mex, W-I) sponger
mantenimiento *m* maintenance; food, support, living
manteo *m* mantle, cloak
mantequera *f* churn, butter churn; butter dish
mantequería *f* creamery; delicatessen
mantequilla *f* butter; **mantequilla azucarada** hard sauce; **mantequilla de maní** peanut butter; **mantequilla derretida** drawn butter
mantilla *f* mantilla (*silk or lace head scarf*); **mantillas** swaddling clothes
mantillo *m* humus, mold
manto *m* mantle, cloak; (*de chimenea*) mantel; (*ropa talar de algunos religiosos, catedráticos, alumnos*) robe, gown; (fig) cloak
mantón *m* shawl, kerchief
mantra *f* (*lema, consigna, eslogan, máxima*) mantra
manuable *adj* handy
manual *adj* (*que se hace con las manos*) hand; (*fácil de manejar*) handy; easy; easy to understand; easy-going; manual; (compu) hands-on || *m* manual, handbook; notebook
manubrio *m* handle; crank, winch
manuela *f* open hack (*in Madrid*)
manufactura *f* (*fábrica*) factory; (*obra fabricada*) manufacture
manufacturar *tr* to manufacture
manuscribir §83 *tr* to write by hand
manuscri•to -ta *adj* manuscript, handwritten || *m* manuscript
manutención *f* maintenance; care, upkeep; shelter, protection
manutener §71 *tr* (law) to maintain, support
manzana *f* apple; (*conjunto aislado de varias casas contiguas*) block, city block; (*remate en un mueble*) knob, finial; **manzana de Adán** (Chile) Adam's apple
manzanar *m* apple orchard
manzanilla *f* camomile; (*aceituna pequeña; vino blanco*) manzanilla (*small olive; white wine*); (*remate en un mueble*) knob, finial
manzano *m* apple tree
maña *f* skill, dexterity; cunning, craftiness; bad habit, vice; (*de lino, cáñamo, etc.*) bunch; sister; **darse maña** to manage, contrive; **hacer maña** (Col) to fool around
mañana *adv* tomorrow; **¡hasta mañana!** see you tomorrow!; **pasado mañana** the day after tomorrow || *m* tomorrow; (*tiempo venidero*) morrow || *f* morning; **de la mañana, de mañana** in the morning; **muy de mañana** very early in the morning; **por la mañana** in the morning; **tomar la mañana** to get up early; have a shot of liquor before breakfast
mañanear *intr* to be in the habit of getting up early
mañane•ro -ra *adj* morning; early-rising
mañanica *f* early morning, break of day
mañanita *f* woman's bed jacket
mañear *tr* to manage craftily || *intr* to act with cunning
mañerear *intr* (Arg) to dawdle, dilly-dally
mañería *f* sterility
mañe•ro -ra *adj* clever, shrewd; simple, easy; skittish
ma•ño -ña *mf* (coll) Aragonese || *m* brother || *f* see **maña**
maño•so -sa *adj* skillful, clever; crafty, tricky; vicious
mañuela *f* craftiness, trickiness
mañue•las *mf* (*pl* **-las**) tricky person
mapa *m* map; **mapa de bits** (compu) bitmap; **mapa de imágenes, mapa de vínculos** image map; **mapa itenerario** road map || *f* — **llevarse la mapa** to take the prize
mapache *m* coon, raccoon
mapamundi *m* map of the world; (coll) buttocks, behind
mapurite *m* (CAm) skunk
maque *m* lacquer
maquear *tr* to lacquer; (Mex) to varnish
maqueta *f* (*en tamaño reducido*) maquette; (*en tamaño natural*) mock-up; (*de un libro*) dummy
maquetación *f* layout, page makeup
maquetar *tr* to do the layout of; (compu) lay out
maquiavéli•co -ca *adj* Machiavellian
maquillador *m* (theat) make-up man
maquillaje *m* (theat) make-up
maquillar *tr & ref* to make up
máquina *f* machine; (*motor*) engine; locomotive; plan, project; (fig) machinery; (coll) heap, pile, lot; (Cuba) auto; (Chile) ganging up; **escribir a máquina** to typewrite; **máquina de afeitar** safety razor; **máquina de apostar** gambling machine; **máquina de calcular** calculator; **máquina de componer** typesetter; **máquina de coser** sewing machine; **máquina de escribir** typewriter; **máquina de frutas** slot machine; **máquina de lavar** washing machine; **máquina de sumar** adding machine; **máquina de volar** flying machine; **máquina de votar, máquina registradora de votos** voting machine; **máquina expendedora** *or* **vendedora** vending machine; **máquina fotográfica** camera; **máquina sacaperras** slot machine; **máquina tragamonedas, traganíqueles, tragaperras** *or* **sacacuartos** slot machine
maquinación *f* machination, scheming
máquina-herramienta *f* (*pl* **máquinas-herramientas**) machine tool
maquinal *adj* mechanical
maquinar *tr* to plot, scheme
maquinaria *f* machinery; applied mechanics
maquinilla *f* windlass, winch; clippers; **maqui-**

nilla cortapelos clippers, hair clippers; **maquinilla de afeitar** safety razor; **maquinilla de rizar** curling iron

maquinista *mf* (*persona que fabrica máquinas*) machinist; (*persona que dirige una máquina o locomotora*) engineer; **segundo maquinista** (naut) machinist

mar *m & f* sea; tide, flood; **alta mar** high seas; **a mares** abundantly, copiously; **arrojarse a la mar** to plunge, take great risks; **baja mar** low tide; **correr los mares** to follow the sea; **hablar de la mar** to talk wildly, talk on and on; **hacerse a la mar** to put to sea; **la mar de** (fig) oceans of, large numbers of; **mar alta** rough sea; **mar ancha** high seas; **mar bonanza** calm sea; **mar Caribe** Caribbean Sea, Caribbean; **mar de fondo** swell; **mar de las Antillas** Caribbean Sea; **mar de las Indias** Indian Ocean; **mar de nubes** cloud bank; **mar gruesa** rough or heavy sea; **mar Latino** Mediterranean Sea; **mar llena** high tide; **mar patrimonial** territorial waters; **mar territorial** *or* **jurisdiccional** territorial waters; **meter la mar en un pozo** to attempt the impossible; **meterse mar adentro** (fig) to go beyond one's depth

maraña *f* undergrowth, thicket; silk waste; (*de hilo, pelo, etc.*) tangle; trick, scheme; puzzle

marañón *m* cashew

maraño•so -sa *adj* scheming ‖ *mf* schemer

maravilla *f* wonder, marvel; (bot) marigold, calendula; **a las maravillas** or **a las mil maravillas** magnificently; **a maravilla** wonderfully well; **por maravilla** rarely, occasionally

maravillar *tr* to astonish ‖ *ref* to wonder, marvel; **maravillarse con** or **de** to marvel at, wonder at

maravillo•so -sa *adj* wonderful, marvelous

marbete *m* label, tag; baggage check; edge, border; **marbete engomado** sticker

marca *f* mark; (*tipo de producto*) make, brand; (*de tamaño*) standard; score; record; height-measuring device; **de marca** outstanding; **marca de agua** watermark; **marca de fábrica** trademark; **marca de reconocimiento** (naut) landmark, seamark; **marca de taquilla** box-office record; **marca registrada** registered trademark

marca•do -da *adj* marked, pronounced

marcador *m* scoreboard; bookmark; felt-tipped pen highlighter

marcaje *m* (sport) scoring; (sport) interfering; (telp) dialing

marcapaso *m* or **marcapasos** *m* (heart) pacemaker

marcar §73 *tr* to mark; brand; embroider; (*p.ej., un pañuelo*) initial; (*la hora un reloj*) show; (*un tanto*) make, score; (*el número telefónico*) dial ‖ *ref* (*un buque*) to take bearings

marcear *tr* to shear ‖ *ref* to be Marchlike

marcha *f* march; (*funcionamiento*) running, operation; (*p.ej., de los astros*) course, path; (*desenvolvimiento de un asunto*) course, march, progress; (*grado de velocidad*) rate of speed; (*de los engranajes*) (aut) speed; **cambiar de marcha** to shift gears; **en marcha** on the march; underway; in motion; **marcha atrás** reverse; **marcha del hambre** hunger march; **marcha directa** high gear; **marcha forzada** (mil) forced march

marchamo *m* customhouse mark; (Arg, Bol) tax on slaughtered cattle

marchante *adj* commercial ‖ *m* dealer, merchant; customer

marchapié *m* running board

marchar *intr* to march; run, work, go; leave, go away; come along, proceed; **marchar en vacío** to idle ‖ *ref* to leave, go away

marchitar *tr* to wilt, wither ‖ *ref* to wilt, wither languish

marchi•to -ta *adj* withered, faded; (fig) languid

marcial *adj* martial; gallant, noble

marcia•no -na *adj & mf* Martian

marco *m* frame; framework; (*de pesas y medidas*) standard

marea *f* tide; tideland; gentle sea breeze; dew; drizzle; **marea alta** high tide; **marea baja** low tide; **marea creciente** or **entrante** flood tide; **marea menguante** ebb tide; **marea muerta** neap tide; **marea negra** oil slick; **marea viva** spring tide; **rendir la marea** to stem the tide

marea•do -da *adj* nauseated, sick, lightheaded; seasick

mareaje *m* navigation, seamanship; (*de un buque*) course

marear *tr* to sail; annoy, pester ‖ *intr* to be annoying ‖ *ref* to get sick, get giddy; get seasick; be damaged at sea; fade

marejada *f* heavy sea; (*de desorden*) stirring, undercurrent; **marejada de fondo** ground swell

maremagno *m* or **maremágnum** *m* big mess

mareo *m* nausea, dizziness, sickness; seasickness; annoyance

marfil *m* ivory

marfile•ño -ña *adj* ivory

mar•fuz -fuza *adj* (*pl* **-fuces -fuzas**) cast aside, rejected; deceptive

marga *f* marl

margar §44 *tr* to marl

margarita *f* pearl; (bot) daisy; **margarita de los prados** English daisy; (compu) daisy wheel; **Margarita** Margaret

margen *m & f* margin; border, edge; marginal note; bank, riverbank; **al margen de** aloof from; outside of; independent of; aside from; **dar margen para** to give occasion for; **dejar al margen** to leave out, sideline; **quedar al margen** to be left out of

marginal *adj* marginal

marginar *tr* to ostracize, sideline, push to one side ‖ *intr* to cut oneself off

María *f* Mary

mariache *m* Mexican band and singers

marica *adj* (pej) queer; wimpish || *m* (pej) gay; wimp, sissy || *f* magpie
mari•cón -cona *adj* (pej) queer; wimpish || *m* (pej) gay; wimp
maridable *adj* marital
maridaje *m* married life; (fig) union
maridar *tr* to combine, unit || *intr* to get married; to live as man and wife
marido *m* husband
mariguana *f* marihuana
mariguanza *f* (Chile) hocus-pocus; (Chile) pirouette; **mariguanzas** (Chile) clowning; (Chile) powwowing
marimacho *m* mannish woman
marimandona *f* queen bee, bossy woman
marimarica *m* sissy
marimorena *f* fight, row
marina *f* navy; (*conjunto de buques*) marine, fleet; (*cuadro o pintura*) seascape; shore, seaside; sailing, navigation; **marina de guerra** navy; **marina mercante** merchant marine
marinar *tr* to marinate, salt; (*un buque*) staff, man || *intr* to be a sailor
marine [ma'rin(e)] *m* (*soldado de infantería de marina*) marine
marinera *f* sailor blouse; (*blusa de niño*) middy, middy blouse
marinería *f* sailoring; sailors
marine•ro -ra *adj* sea, marine; seaworthy; seafaring || *m* mariner, seaman, sailor; **marinero de agua dulce** (*el que ha navegado poco*) landlubber (*person unacquainted with the sea*); **marinero matalote** (*hombre de mar, rudo y torpe*) landlubber (*awkward and unskilled seaman*) || *f* see **marinera**
marines•co -ca *adj* sailor; sailorly
mari•no -na *adj* marine, sea || *m* mariner, seaman, sailor || *f* see **marina**
marioneta *f* marionette, puppet
mariposa *f* butterfly; butterfly valve; wing nut; rushlight; (Col) blindman's buff; **mariposa nocturna** moth
mariposear *intr* to flit about; be fickle
mariposón *m* (Cuba, Guat, Mex) fickle flirt
mariquita *mf* (pej) gay; wimp, sissy || *f* (ent) ladybird
marisabidilla *f* bluestocking
mariscal *m* blacksmith; (mil) marshal; **mariscal de campo** (mil) field marshal
marisco *m* shellfish; **mariscos** seafood
marisma *f* swamp, marsh, salt marsh
marisquería *f* seafood store, seafood restaurant
maríti•mo -ma *adj* maritime; marine, sea
maritor•nes *f* (*pl* **-nes**) mannish maidservant, wench
marmita *f* pot, boiler, kettle
marmitón *m* kitchen scullion
mármol *m* marble
marmóre•o -a *adj* marble
marmosete *m* vignette
marmota *f* marmot; sleepyhead; worsted cap; **marmota de Alemania** hamster; **marmota de América** ground hog, woodchuck
maroma *f* hemp rope, esparto rope; acrobatic stunt
maromear *intr* to perform acrobatic stunts, walk the tight rope; wobble, sway from side to side (*e.g., in politics*); hesitate
marome•ro -ra *mf* acrobat, tightrope walker; weaseler; opportunist
marqués *m* marquis; **los marqueses** the marquis and marchioness
marquesa *f* marchioness, marquise; (*sobre la puerta de un hotel*) marquee
marquesina *f* cover over field tent; (*sobre la puerta de un hotel*) marquee; locomotive cab
marquetería *f* cabinetwork, woodwork; (*taracea*) marquetry
marra•jo -ja *adj* sly, tricky; (*toro*) vicious
marrana *f* sow; slattern, slut
marranada *f* piggishness, filth
marranalla *f* rabble, riffraff
marra•no -na *adj* base, vile; dirty, sloppy || *mf* hog || *m* male hog, boar; filthy person, hog; cad, cur || *f* see **marrana**
marrar *intr* to miss, fail; go astray
marras *adv* long ago; **hacer marras que** (Bol, Ecuad) to be a long time since
marro *m* game resembling quoits and played with a stone; (*juego de muchachos*) tag; (*ladeo*) dodge, duck; slip, miss
marrón *adj invar* brown; tan (*shoes*); **marrón oscuro** dark brown || *m* brown; candied chestnut; stone (*used as a sort of quoit*)
marro•quí (*pl* **-quíes**) *adj & mf* Moroccan || *m* morocco, morocco leather
marro•quín -quina *adj & mf* var of **marroquí**
marrubio *m* horehound
marrue•co -ca *adj & mf* Moroccan
Marruecos *m* Morocco
marrulle•ro -ra *adj* cajoling, wheedling || *mf* cajoler, wheedler
Marsella *f* Marseille
marsopa *f* or **marsopla** *f* porpoise
mart. *abbr* **martes**
marta *f* pine marten; **marta cebellina** sable, Siberian sable; **marta del Canadá** fisher
Marte *m* (astr, myth) Mars
mar•tes *m* (*pl* **-tes**) Tuesday; **martes de carnaval** *or* **carnestolendas** Shrove Tuesday
martillar *tr* to hammer; pester, worry || *intr* to hammer
martillazo *m* blow with a hammer
martillear *tr & intr* var of **martillar**
martillero *m* (Chile) auctioneer
martillo *m* hammer; auction house; (*persona*) scourge; (mus) tuning hammer; (*de arma de fuego*) cock
martín *m* — **martín pescador** (*pl* **martín pescadores**) kingfisher
martinete *m* drop hammer; pile driver; (*del piano*) hammer
martinico *m* ghost, goblin
mártir *mf* martyr
martirio *m* martyrdom
márts. *abbr* **mártires**

marullo *m* surge, swell
marxista *adj & mf* Marxist or Marxian
marzo *m* March
mas *conj* but
más *adv* more; most; **a lo más** at most, at the most; **a más de** besides, in addition to; **como el que más** as the next one, as well as anybody; **cuando más** at the most; **de más** extra; too much, too many; **estar de más** to be in the way; be unnecessary; be superfluous; **los más de** most of, the majority of; **más bien** rather; **más de** + *número* more than; **más de lo que** + *verbo* more than; **más que** more than; better than; **no . . . más** no longer; **no . . . más nada** nothing more; **no . . . más que** only || *prep* plus || *m* more; (*signo de adición*) plus
masa *f* mass; (*pasta que se forma con agua y harina*) dough; (*masa aplastada*) mash; nature, disposition; (Chile, Ecuad) puff paste; (*p.ej., de un automóvil*) (elec) ground; **las masas** the masses
masada *f* farm
masadero *m* farmer
masaje *m* massage; **masaje facial** facial
masajear *tr* to massage
masajista *m* masseur || *f* masseuse
masar *tr* to knead; massage
mascar §73 *tr* to chew; mumble, mutter || *ref* (*un cabo*) (naut) to gall
máscara *mf* (*persona*) mask, mummer || *f* mask; (*traje, disfraz*) masquerade; **máscara antigás** gas mask; **máscara facial** face pack
mascarada *f* masquerade
mascarilla *f* half mask; false face; death mask
mascarón *m* false face; (*persona fea*) fright; (archit) mask; **mascarón de proa** (naut) figurehead
mascota *f* mascot
mascujar *tr & intr* to chew with difficulty; mumble
masculi•no -na *adj* masculine; (*sexo*) male; (*traje*) men's || *m* masculine
mascullar *tr & intr* to mumble, mutter; to chew with difficulty
masera *f* kneading trough
masilla *f* putty
masita *f* (mil) money withheld for clothing; (Arg, Bol) cake
masón *m* Mason
masonería *f* Masonry
masoquis•to -ta *adj* masochistic || *mf* masochist
mastelero *m* (naut) topmast
masticar §73 *tr* to chew, masticate; meditate on; mumble
mástil *m* (*de una embarcación*) mast; (*de un violín o guitarra*) neck; stalk; (*de pluma*) shaft, stem; upright
mas•tín -tina *mf* mastiff; **mastín danés** Great Dane
mastodonte *m* mastodon
mastuerzo *m* (bot) cress; dolt
masturbación *f* masturbation
masturbar *tr & ref* to masturbate
mat. *abbr* **matématica**
mata *f* bush, shrub; blade, sprig; brush, underbrush; **mata de pelo** crop of hair, head of hair; **mata parda** chaparro (*oak*); **saltar de la mata** to come out of hiding
mataca•bras *m* (*pl* **-bras**) cold blast from the north
matacán *m* dog poison
matacande•las *m* (*pl* **-las**) candle snuffer
matadero *m* abattoir, slaughterhouse; drudgery
mata•dor -dora *mf* killer || *m* matador; **matador de mujeres** lady-killer
matadura *f* sore, gall
matafue•gos *m* (*pl* **-gos**) fire extinguisher; (*oficial*) fireman
matalo•bos *m* (*pl* **-bos**) wolf's-bane
mata•lón -lona *mf* skinny old nag
matalotaje *m* (naut) ship stores; mess, hodgepodge
matamale•zas *m* (*pl* **-zas**) weed killer
matamari•dos *f* (*pl* **-dos**) many times a widow
matamo•ros *m* (*pl* **-ros**) bully
matamos•cas *m* (*pl* **-cas**) fly swatter; flypaper
matanza *f* slaughter, massacre; butchering; pork products; (CAm) butcher shop; (Ven) slaughterhouse
matape•rros *m* (*pl* **-rros**) harum-scarum, street urchin
matar *tr* to kill; butcher; (*el fuego, la luz*) put out; (*la cal*) slack; (*el metal*) mat; (*un color*) tone down; (*un naipe*) spot; play a card higher than; (*a un caballo*) gall; bore to death; (*el tiempo, el hambre, etc.*) (fig) to kill || *intr* to kill || *ref* to kill oneself; drudge, overwork; be disappointed; **matarse con** to quarrel with; **matarse por** to struggle for; struggle to
matarratas *m* rat poison; (*aguardiente de mala calidad*) rotgut
matarro•tos *m* (*pl* **-tos**) (Chile) pawnshop
matasa•nos *m* (*pl* **-nos**) quack doctor
matasellar *tr* to cancel, postmark
matase•llos *m* (*pl* **-llos**) postmark
matasie•te *m* (*pl* **-te**) bully, swashbuckler
matatí•as *m* (*pl* **-as**) moneylender, pawnbroker
matazar•zas *m* (*pl* **-zas**) weed killer
mate *adj* dull, flat || *m* checkmate; (SAm) maté; (SAm) maté gourd; **dar mate a** to checkmate; make fun of; **dar mate ahogado a** to stalemate; **mate ahogado** stalemate
matear *tr* to plant at regular intervals; make dull; (Chile) to checkmate || *ref* (*el trigo*) to sprout; (*un perro de caza*) hunt through the bushes
matemáti•co -ca *adj* mathematical || *mf* mathematician || *f* mathematics; **matemáticas** mathematics
materia *f* matter; material, stuff; **materia clasificada** classified information; **materia colorante** dyestuff; **materia de guerra** matériel; **materia prima** *or* **primera materia** raw material
material *adj* material; (*grosero*) crude || *m* mate-

rial; (*conjunto de objetos necesario para un servicio*) matériel; (typ) matter, copy; **material de guerra** matériel; **material fijo** (rr) permanent way; **material móvil** or **rodante** (rr) rolling stock
materialismo *m* materialism
materialista *mf* materialist; (Mex) truck driver
materializar §60 *tr* (*beneficios*) to realize
maternal *adj* maternal, mother; (*afectos, cuidados, etc.*) motherly
maternidad *f* maternity; motherhood
mater•no -na *adj* maternal, mother
matinal *adj* morning
matinée *f* matinée; dressing gown, wrapper
ma•tiz *m* (*pl* **-tices**) shade, hue, nuance
matizar §60 *tr* (*diversos colores*) to blend; (*un color, un sonido*) shade; (*en cuanto al color*) match
matón *m* bully, browbeater
matorral *m* thicket, underbrush
matraca *f* rattle, noisemaker; taunting, bantering; bore, pest; **dar matraca a** to taunt, to tease
matraquear *intr* to make a racket; to taunt, tease
ma•traz *m* (*pl* **-traces**) flask
matre•ro -ra *adj* cunning, shrewd || *m* (SAm) cheat, swindler
matriarca *f* matriarch
matricida *adj* matricidal || *mf* matricide
matricidio *m* matricide
matrícula *f* register, roster, roll; license; registry; (educ) enrollment
matricular *tr & ref* to matriculate, enroll
matrimonialmente *adv* as husband and wife
matrimoniar *intr* to marry, get married
matrimonio *m* marriage, matrimony; (*marido y mujer*) married couple; **matrimonio consensual** common-law marriage
ma•triz *adj* (*pl* **-trices**) main, first, mother || *f* matrix; (*de libro talonario*) stub; screw nut; first draft; **matriz activa** (compu) active-matrix; **matriz de puntos** dot matrix
matrona *f* matron; matronly lady
matronal *adj* matronly
matun•go -ga *adj* skinny, full of sores || *m* old nag
maturran•go -ga *adj* (SAm) poor, clumsy || *m* (SAm) stranger; (SAm) old nag || *f* trickery
Matusalén *m* Methuselah; **vivir más años que Matusalén** to be as old as Methuselah
matute *m* smuggling; smuggled goods; gambling den
matutear *intr* to smuggle
matute•ro -ra *mf* smuggler
matutinal or **matuti•no -na** *adj* morning
maula *mf* lazy loafer; poor pay; tricky person, cheat || *f* junk, trash; remnant; trickery
maulería *f* remnant shop; trickiness
maullar §8 *intr* to meow
maullido *m* or **maúllo** *m* meow
mausoleo *m* mausoleum
máxima *f* maxim; principle
máxime *adv* chiefly, mainly, especially
máxi•mo -ma *adj* maximum; top; superlative || *m* maximum || *f* see **máxima**
may. *abbr* **mayúscula**
maya *f* May queen; English daisy
mayal *m* flail
mayear *intr* to be Maylike
mayestáti•co -ca *adj* royal
mayido *m* meow
mayo *m* May; Maypole
mayonesa *f* mayonnaise
mayor *adj* greater; larger; older, elder; greatest; largest; oldest, eldest; major; elderly; (*calle*) main; (*altar; misa*) high; **hacerse mayor de edad** to come of age; **ser mayor de edad** to be of age || *m* chief, head, superior; **al por mayor** wholesale; **mayor de edad** (*persona de edad legal*) major; **mayores** elders; ancestors, forefathers; **mayor general** staff officer
mayoral *m* boss, foreman; head shepherd; stagecoach driver; (Arg) streetcar conductor
mayorazgo *m* primogeniture; entailed estate descending by primogeniture; first-born son
mayordoma *f* stewardess, housekeeper
mayordomo *m* steward, butler, majordomo
mayoreo *m* wholesale
mayoría *f* (*mayor edad; el mayor número, la mayor parte*) majority; superiority; **alcanzar su mayoría de edad** to come of age; **mayoría cómoda** solid majority; **mayoría de edad** majority
mayoridad *f* majority
mayorista *adj* (Arg, Chile) wholesale || *mf* (Arg, Chile) wholesaler
mayorita•rio -ria *adj* majority
mayormente *adv* chiefly, mainly, mostly
mayúscu•lo -la *adj* (*letra*) capital; egregious; tremendous || *f* capital, capital letter
maza *f* mace; heavy drumstick; bore, pedant; **la maza y la mona** constant companions; **maza de gimnasia** Indian club
mazacote *m* barilla; concrete, cement; botched job; tough, doughy food; (coll) bore
mazar §60 *tr* to churn
mazmorra *f* dungeon
mazo *m* mallet, maul; bunch; (*de la campana*) clapper; (*hombre fastidioso*) bore, pest
mazonería *f* stone masonry; (*obra de relieve*) relief; gold or silver embroidery
mazorca *f* ear of corn; cocoa bean; (*husada*) spindleful; (*de un balustre*) spindle; **comer maíz de** *or* **en la mazorca** to eat corn on the cob
mazorral *adj* coarse, crude
m/c *abbr* **mi cargo, mi cuenta, moneda corriente**
m/cta *abbr* **mi cuenta**
m/cte *abbr* **moneda corriente**
me (used as object of verb) *pron pers* me, to me || *pron reflex* myself; to myself
meada *f* urination, water; urine stain
meadero *m* urinal
meados *mpl* urine

meaja *f* crumb; **meaja de huevo** tread
meandro *m* meander; wandering speech, wandering writing
mear *tr* to urinate on || *intr & ref* to urinate
Meca, La Mecca
¡mecachis! *interj* wow!, geez!
mecáni•co -ca *adj* mechanical; low, mean || *m* (*obrero perito en el arreglo de las máquinas*) mechanic; (*obrero que fabrica y compone máquinas*) machinist; workman, repairman; driver, chauffeur; **mecánicos** (CAm, Cuba, S-D) blue jeans || *f* mechanics; (*aparato que da movimiento a un artefacto*) machinery, works; meanness; **mecánicas** household chores
mecánico-dentista *m* dental technician
mecanismo *m* mechanism, machinery
mecanizar §60 *tr* to mechanize; motorize
mecanógrafa *f* typist
mecanografía *f* typewriting; **mecanografía al tacto** touch typewriting
mecanografiar §77 *tr & intr* to typewrite
mecanógra•fo -fa *mf* typist, typewriter
mecapale•ro -ra *m* (Mex) messenger, porter
mece•dor -dora *adj* swinging, rocking || *m* stirrer; (*columpio*) swing || *f* rocker, rocking chair; glider
mecer §46 *tr* (*un líquido*) to stir; (*la cuna*) rock || *ref* to rock, swing
mecha *f* (*de vela o bujía*) wick; (*tubo de pólvera*) fuse; lock of hair; (*para mechar carne*) slice of bacon; bundle of thread; (Col, Ecuad, Ven) joke
mechar *tr* (*la carne*) to lard, interlard
mechera *f* shoplifter
mechero *m* (*p.ej., de cigarrillos*) lighter, pocket lighter; (*de aparato de alumbrado*) burner; (*de candelero*) socket; shoplifter; **mechero encendedor** pilot, pilot light
mechón *m* cowlick; (Guat) torch
medalla *f* medal; medallion
medallón *m* medallion; (*joya en que se colocan retratos, etc.*) locket
médano *m* dune, sandbank
media *f* stocking; (math) mean; **media corta** (Arg) sock; **media media** (Arg, Ecuad, Ven) sock; **y media** half past, e.g., **las dos y media** half past two
mediación *f* mediation
media•do -da *adj* half over; half-full; **a mediados de** about the middle of; **mediada la tarde** in the middle of the afternoon
media•dor -dora *mf* mediator
mediana *f* long billiard cue
medianería *f* party wall; party fence
mediane•ro -ra *adj* middle; mediating || *mf* mediator; partner; owner of a row house
medianía *f* average; (*persona que carece de dotes relevantes*) mediocrity
media•no -na *adj* middling, medium; average, fair; mediocre || *f* see **mediana**
medianoche *f* midnight; small meat pie
mediante *adj* interceding || *prep* by means of, by virtue of
mediar *intr* to be half over; be in the middle; intercede, mediate; elapse; take place
mediatinta *f* half-tone
medible *adj* measurable
medical *adj* medical
medicamento *m* medicine
medicamento•so -sa *adj* medicinal
medicastro *m* quack
medicina *f* medicine; **medicina alternativa** alternative medicine; **medicina forense** *or* **legal** forensic medicine; **medicina general** general medicine
medicinar *tr* to treat || *ref* to take medicine
medición *f* measurement; metering
médi•co -ca *adj* medical || *mf* doctor, physician; **médico de cabecera** family physician; **médico de urgencia** emergency doctor; **médico forense** forensic scientist; (law) medical examiner; **médico general** general practitioner
medida *f* measurement; measure; caution, moderation; **a medida de** in proportion to; according to; **a medida que** in proportion as; **en la medida que** to the extent that; **hecho a la medida** custom-made; **medida para áridos** dry measure; **medida para líquidos** liquid measure; **medidas prontas de seguridad** (Urug) emergency security measures; **tomarle a uno las medidas** to take someone's measure, size up someone
medidamente *adv* with moderation
medidor *m* measurer; (Mex, SAm) meter
medie•ro -ra *mf* hosier; partner
medieval *adj* medieval
medievalista *mf* medievalist
medievo *m* Middle Ages
me•dio -dia *adj* middle; medium; medieval; half; a half, e.g., **media libra** a half pound; half a, e.g., **media naranja** half an orange; average, mean; mid, in the middle of, e.g., **a media tarde** in mid afternoon, in the middle of the afternoon; **a medias** half; half-and-half; **ir a medias (con)** to go halves (with), go fifty-fifty (with) || *m* middle; medium, environment; step, measure; means; (*en el espiritismo*) medium; (baseball) shortstop; (arith) half; (*del ruedo*) (taur) center; **a medio** half; **en medio de** in the middle of; in the midst of; **justo medio** happy medium, golden mean; **medio ambiente** environment; situation; **medio centro** (*deporte*) center half; **medios audiovisuales** audiovisual aids; **medios de comunicación** mass media; **por medio de** by means of; **quitarse de en medio** to get out of the way || *f* see **media** || **medio** *adv* half
mediocre *adj* mediocre
mediocridad *f* mediocrity
mediodía *m* noon, midday; south; **en pleno mediodía** at high noon; **hacer mediodía** to stop for the noon meal
mediquillo *m* quack

medir §50 *tr* to measure || *intr* to measure || *ref* to act with moderation
meditabun•do -da *adj* meditative
meditar *tr* to meditate; plan, contemplate || *intr* to meditate
mediterráne•o -a *adj* inland || **Mediterráne•o -ne•a** *adj & m* Mediterranean
mé•dium *m* (*pl* **-dium** or **diums**) medium
medra *f* growth, prosperity
medrana *f* fear
medrar *intr* to thrive, prosper, improve
medro *m* growth, prosperity; **medros** progress
medro•so -sa *adj* fearful, scared; frightful, terrible
médula *f* or **medula** *f* marrow, medulla; (bot) pith; (fig) pith, gist, essence; **médula espinal** spinal cord; **médula ósea** bone marrow
medular *adj* pithy
medusa *f* jellyfish
mefistoféli•co -ca *adj* Mephistophelian
megaciclo *m* megacycle
megáfono *m* megaphone
megahercio *or* **megaherzio** *m* megahertz
me•go -ga *adj* meek, gentle, mild
megohmio *m* megohm
Méj. *abbr* **Méjico**
mejica•no -na *adj & mf* Mexican
Méjico *m* Mexico; Mexico City; **Nuevo Méjico** New Mexico
meji•do -da *adj* beaten with sugar and milk
mejilla *f* cheek
mejor *adj* better; best; (*licitador*) highest; **a lo mejor** unexpectedly; perhaps, maybe; **el mejor día** some fine day || *adv* better; best; **mejor dicho** rather
mejora *f* growth, improvement; higher bid; alteration
mejoramiento *m* improvement
mejorana *f* sweet marjoram
mejorar *tr* to improve; (*los licitadores el precio de una cosa*) raise; **mejorando lo presente** present company excepted || *intr & ref* to improve, get better, recover; make progress; (*el tiempo*) to clear up; **¡que se mejore!** get well!
mejoría *f* improvement; (*en una enfermedad*) betterment, recovery
mejunje *m* brew, potion, mixture
mela•do -da *adj* honey-colored || *m* thick cane syrup
melancolía *f* (*tristeza vaga*) melancholy; (*depresión moral*) melancholia
melancóli•co -ca *adj* melancholy
melaza *f* molasses
melchor *m* German silver
melcocha *f* taffy, molasses candy
melena *f* hair falling over the eyes; long hair, loose hair; (*del león*) mane; (*del caballo*) forelock; **andar a la melena** to pull each other's hair; to get into a fight; **estar en melena** (coll) to have one's hair down
melenu•do -da *adj* (coll) long-haired, hippie type || *mf* long-hair, hippie
melga *f* ridge made by plow; (Col, Chile) plot of ground to be sown; (Hond) small piece of work to be finished
melindre *m* honey fritter; narrow ribbon; prudery, finickiness
melindrear *intr* to be prudish, be finicky
melindro•so -sa *adj* prudish, finicky
mella *f* dent, nick, notch; gap, hollow; harm, injury; **hacer mella a** to have an effect on; **hacer mella en** to harm
mellar *tr* to dent, nick, notch; harm
melli•zo -za *adj & mf* twin
melocotón *m* peach tree; peach
melocotonero *m* peach tree
melodía *f* melody
melodio•so -sa *adj* melodious
melodramáti•co -ca *adj* melodramatic
melóma•no -na *mf* music lover, long-hair
melón *m* melon; (*Cucumis melo*) muskmelon; blockhead; bald head; **melón de agua** watermelon
melo•so -sa *adj* sweet, honeyed; gentle, mild, mellow
membrana *f* membrane; (*del teléfono, micrófono*) diaphragm
membrete *m* note, memo; letterhead; heading; written invitation
membrillero *m* quince tree
membrillo *m* quince; quince tree
membru•do -da *adj* brawny, burly
memeches — a memeches (CAm) on horseback
memela *f* (CAm, Mex) cornmeal pancake
me•mo -ma *adj* foolish, simple || *mf* fool, simpleton
memorán•dum *m* (*pl* **-dum**) memorandum book, notebook; (*sección en los periódicos*) professional services; (*papel con membrete*) letterhead
memorar *tr & ref* to remember
memoria *f* memory; (*exposición de ciertos hechos*) memoir; account, record; (*ordenador*) data storage, memory; **de memoria** by heart; **encomendar a la memoria** to commit to memory; **hablar de memoria** (coll) to say the first thing that comes to one's mind; **hacer memoria de** to bring up; **memoria de acceso aleatorio, memoria ROM** (compu) read-only memory; **memoria de acceso aleatorio** *or* **directo, memoria RAM** (compu) random access memory; **memorias** memoirs
memorial *m* memorandum book; memorial, petition; (law) brief
memorizar §60 *tr* to memorize
mena *f* ore
menaje *m* household furniture; school supplies
mención *f* mention
mencionar *tr* to mention
men•daz *adj* (*pl* **-daces**) mendacious || *mf* liar
mendicante *adj & mf* mendicant
mendigante *adj* begging, mendicant || *mf* beggar, mendicant

mendigar §44 *tr* to beg for || *intr* to beg, go begging
mendi•go -ga *mf* beggar
mendiguez *f* begging
mendo•so -sa *adj* false, wrong
mendrugo *m* crumb, crust
menear *tr* to stir, shake; wiggle; (*la cola*) wag; (*un negocio*) manage; **peor es meneallo** (i.e., **menearlo**) better keep hands off, let sleeping dogs lie || *ref* to shake; wiggle; wag; hustle, bestir oneself
meneo *m* stirring, shaking; wagging; hustling; drubbing, thrashing
menester *m* need; want, lack; job, occupation; **haber menester** to be necessary, to be need for; **menesteres** bodily needs; property; implements, tools; **ser menester** to be necessary
menestero•so -sa *adj* needy || *mf* needy person
menestra *f* vegetable stew
menes•tral -trala *mf* mechanic
meng. *abbr* **menguante**
mengua *f* want, lack; poverty; decline; decrease, diminution; **en mengua de** to the discredit of
mengua•do -da *adj* timid, cowardly; simple, silly; mean, stingy; wretched, miserable; poor, needy; fatal
menguante *adj* decreasing; declining; waning || *f* decrease; decline; low water; ebb tide; **menguante de la luna** wane, waning of the moon
menguar §10 *tr* to diminish, lessen; discredit || *intr* to diminish, lessen; decline; decrease; (*la luna*) wane; (*la marea*) fall
mengue *m* (coll) devil
menina *f* young lady-in-waiting
menino *m* noble page of the royal family
menopausia *f* menopause
menor *adj* less, lesser; smaller; younger; least; smallest; youngest; slightest; minor || *m* minor; **al por menor** retail; **menor de edad** minor; **por menor** retail; in detail, minutely || *f* minor premise
Menorca *f* Minorca
menoría *f* inferiority, subordination; (*tiempo de menor edad*) minority
menorista *adj* (Arg, Chile) retail || *mf* (Arg, Chile) retailer
menor•quín -quina *adj & mf* Minorcan
menos *adv* less; fewer; least; fewest; **al menos** at least; **a lo menos** at least; **a menos que** unless; **echar de menos** to miss; **¡menos mal!** lucky break!; **menos mal que** it is a good thing that; **no poder menos de** + *inf* to not be able to help + *ger;* **por lo menos** at least; **tener en menos** to think little of; **venir a menos** to decline; become poor || *prep* less, minus; (*al decir la hora*) of, to, e.g., **las tres menos diez** ten minutes of (or to) three || *m* less; (*signo de resta o sustracción*) minus, minus sign
menoscabar *tr* to lessen, diminish, reduce; damage; discredit
menoscabo *m* lessening, reduction; damage; discredit; **con menoscabo de** to the detriment of
menoscuenta *f* part payment
menospreciable *adj* despicable, contemptible
menospreciar *tr* to underestimate, underrate; scorn, despise
menosprecio *m* underestimation; scorn
mensaje *m* message; **mensaje al operador** (compu) voice menu, prompt
mensajería *f* public conveyance; **mensajerías** transportation company; shipping line
mensaje•ro -ra *mf* messenger || *m* harbinger
men•so -sa *adj* (Mex) foolish, stupid
menstruar §21 *intr* to menstruate
menstruo *m* menses
mensual *adj* monthly
mensualidad *f* monthly pay, monthly installment
ménsula *f* bracket; elbow rest
mensurar *tr* to measure
menta *f* mint; **menta piperita** peppermint; **menta romana** or **verde** spearmint
menta•do -da *adj* famous, renowned
mentar §2 *tr* to mention
mente *f* mind
mentecatería or **mentecatez** *f* simpleness, folly
menteca•to -ta *adj* simple, foolish || *mf* simpleton, fool
mentidero *m* hangout; gossip column
mentir §68 *tr* to disappoint || *intr* to lie; be misleading; (*un color*) clash; **¡miento!** my mistake!
mentira *f* lie; error, mistake; **mentira inocente** *or* **oficiosa** *or* **piadosa** white lie; **parece mentira** it's hard to believe
mentirilla *f* fib, white lie; **de mentirillas** for fun
mentirón *m* whopper
mentiro•so -sa *adj* lying; false, deceptive; full of errors || *mf* liar
men•tís *m* (*pl* **-tís**) insulting contradiction; **dar un mentís a** to give the lie to
mentón *m* chin
me•nú *m* (*pl* **-nús**) menu; **menú desplegable** (compu) pull-down menu; **menú pegajoso** (compu) sticky menu
menudamente *adv* in detail; at retail
menudear *tr* to make frequently; tell in detail; (Col) to sell at retail || *intr* to happen frequently, be frequent; go into detail; (Arg) to grow, increase
menudencia *f* smallness; trifle; meticulousness; **menudencias** pork products; (Col, Mex) giblets
menudeo *m* constant repetition; detailed accounting; **al menudeo** at retail
menudillos *mpl* giblets
menu•do -da *adj* small, slight, minute; futile, worthless; meticulous; common, vulgar; petty || *m* innards (*of fowl and other animals*); rice coal; (Mex) soup made with tripe; **al menudo** at retail; **a menudo** often; **menudos** small change; **por menudo** in detail; at retail

meñique *adj* little, tiny; (*dedo*) little || *m* little finger

meollo *m* marrow; pith; (*seso*) brain; brains, intelligence; gist, marrow, essence

me•ón -ona *adj* (*niño*) piddling; (*niebla*) dripping

mequetrefe *m* whippersnapper

mercachifle *m* peddler; small dealer

mercadear *intr* to deal, trade

merca•der -dera *mf* merchant; **mercader de grueso** wholesale merchant

mercadería *f* merchandise, commodity; **mercaderías** goods, merchandise

mercado *m* market; **lanzar al mercado** to put on the market; **mercado alcista** bull market; **mercado bajista** *or* **en baja** bear market; **Mercado Común** Common Market; **mercado de capitales** capital market; **mercado de dinero, mercado monetario** money market; **mercado de divisas** foreign exchange market; **mercado de futuros** futures market; **mercado de materias primas** commodities market; **mercado de pulgas** flea market; **mercado de valores** stock market; **mercado negro** black market

mercaduría *f* commodity

mercancía *f* trade, commerce; merchandise; piece of merchandise; **mercancías** goods, merchandise || **mercancías** *msg* (*pl* **-as**) freight train

mercante *adj* & *m* merchant

mercantil *adj* mercantile

mercar §73 *tr* to buy || *intr* to trade

merced *f* pay, wages; favor, grace; **a merced de** at the mercy of; **merced a** thanks to; **merced de agua** distribution of irrigating water; **vuestra merced** your grace

mercena•rio -ria *adj* mercenary || *m* mercenary; day laborer, hireling

mercería *f* haberdashery, notions store; dry-goods store; hardware store

mercología *f* marketing

mercurio *m* mercury || **Mercurio** (astr, myth) Mercury

merecer §22 *tr* to deserve, merit; (*lo que se desea*) attain; (*alabanza*) win; (*cierta suma*) be worth; **merecer la pena** to be worthwhile || *intr* to be deserving; **merecer bien de** to deserve the gratitude of

mereci•do -da *adj* deserved || *m* just deserts; **llevar su merecido** to get what's coming to one

mereciente *adj* deserving

merecimiento *m* desert, merit

merendar §2 *tr* to lunch on, have for lunch; keep an eye on, peep at || *intr* to lunch || *ref* to manage to get; (*en el juego*) (Chile) to clean out

merendero *m* lunchroom; picnic grounds

merendona *f* fine spread

merengar §44 *tr* to whip (*cream*)

merengue *m* meringue

mere•triz *f* (*pl* **-trices**) harlot

meridiana *f* lounge, couch; afternoon nap; meridian line; **a la meridiana** at noon

meridia•no -na *adj* meridian; bright, dazzling || *m* meridian || *f* see **meridiana**

meridional *adj* southern || *mf* southerner

merienda *f* lunch, snack; hunchback

meri•no -na *adj* merino; (*cabello*) thick and curly || *mf* merino || *m* merino shepherd; merino wool

mérito *m* merit, desert; value, worth; **hacer mérito de** to make mention of; **hacer méritos** to try to please, put one's best foot forward

merito•rio -ria *adj* meritorious || *m* volunteer worker; unpaid learner, apprentice

merluza *f* (*pez*) hake; drunk, spree

merma *f* decrease, reduction; leakage, shrinkage

mermar *tr* to decrease, reduce || *intr* to decrease, shrink, dwindle

mermelada *f* marmalade

me•ro -ra *adj* mere, pure; (Col, Ven) alone || *m* grouper, jewfish || **mero** *adv* (CAm) almost, soon

merodea•dor -dora *adj* marauding || *m* marauder

merodear *intr* to maraud

mes *m* month; monthly pay; menses; **caer en el mes del obispo** to come at the right time

mesa *f* table; (*mostrador*) counter; (*escritorio*) desk; (*de arma blanca o herramienta*) flat side; (*de escalera*) landing; (*comida*) fare, food; (*conjunto de dirigentes*) board; **alzar la mesa** to clear the table; **hacer mesa limpia** to clean up (*in gambling*), **levantar la mesa** to clear the table; **mesa auxiliar** side table; **mesa de batalla** sorting table; **mesa de billar** billiard table, pool table; **mesa de centro, mesa ratona, mesa de café** coffee table; **mesa de extensión** extension table; **mesa de juego** gambling table; **mesa de milanos** scanty fare; **mesa de noche, mesa de luz** (SAm) bedside table; **mesa de trucos** pool table; **mesa nido** nest of tables; **mesa perezosa** drop table; **poner la mesa** to set or lay the table; **tener a mesa y mantel** to feed, support; **tener mesa** to keep open house

mesana *f* (naut) mizzen

mesar *tr* (*los cabellos*) to tear, pull out || *ref* — **mesarse los cabellos** to pull out one's hair; pull out each other's hair

mescolanza *f* jumble, hodgepodge, medley

meseguería *f* harvest watch

mesera *f* waitress

mesero *m* journeyman on monthly pay; waiter

meseta *f* plateau, tableland; (*de escalera*) landing

Mesías *m* Messiah

mesilla *f* mantel, mantelpiece; (*de escalera*) landing; window sill

mesita *f* stand, small table; **mesita portateléfono** telephone table

mesnada *f* armed retinue; band, company

mesón *m* inn, tavern; (Chile) bar; (Chile) counter
mesone•ro -ra *adj* inn, tavern || *mf* innkeeper, tavern keeper
mester *m* (archaic) craft, trade; (archaic) literary genre; **mester de clerecía** clerical verse of the Middle Ages; **mester de juglaría** popular minstrelsy of the Middle Ages
mesti•zo -za *adj & mf* half-breed; (*perro*) mongrel
mesura *f* dignity, gravity; calm, restraint; courtesy, civility
mesura•do -da *adj* dignified, sedate; calm, restrained; polite; moderate, temperate
mesurar *tr* to temper, moderate || *ref* to act with restraint
meta *f* goal
metafonía *f* umlaut
metáfora *f* metaphor
metafóri•co -ca *adj* metaphorical
metal *m* metal; money; (*de la voz*) timbre; condition, quality; (mus) brass; **el vil metal** filthy lucre; **metal blanco** nickel silver; **metal de imprenta** type metal
metale•ro -ra *adj* (Bol, Chile, Peru) metal || *m* (Bol, Chile, Peru) metalworker
metáli•co -ca *adj* metallic || *m* metalworker; cash, coin
metalistería *f* metalwork
metalizar §60 *tr* to make metallic; put a metal coating on; turn into cash || *ref* to become mercenary
metaloide *m* nonmetal
metalurgia *f* metallurgy
metamorfo•sis *f* (*pl* **-sis**) metamorphosis
metano *m* methane
metástasis *f* metastasis
metate *m* (CAm, Mex) flat stone on which corn is ground
metáte•sis *f* (*pl* **-sis**) metathesis
mete•dor -dora *mf* smuggler
metedura *f* disgrace, shame; **metedura de pata** (coll) blunder, boo-boo
meteduría *f* smuggling
metemuer•tos *m* (*pl* **-tos**) stagehand; busybody, meddler
meteo *f* weather bureau, weather report
meteóri•co -ca *adj* meteoric
meteoro *m* or **metéoro** *m* meteor; atmospheric phenomenon
meteorología *f* meteorology
meter *tr* to put, place; insert; (*un ruido*) make; (*miedo*) cause; (*mentiras*) tell; (*chismes, enredos*) start; (*dinero en el juego*) stake; to smuggle; (*un golpe*) strike || *ref* to project; meddle, butt in; **meterse a** to set oneself up as; take it upon oneself to; **meterse con** to pick a quarrel with; **meterse en** to get into; to plunge into; empty into
meticulo•so -sa *adj* meticulous; shy, timid
meti•do -da *adj* close, tight; rich, abundant; meddlesome; **muy metido con** on close terms with; **muy metido en** deeply involved in || *m* push; punch; strong lye; loose leaf; (*tela*) seam
metódi•co -ca *adj* methodic(al)
metodista *adj & mf* Methodist
método *m* method
metraje *m* distance or length in meters; (*cine*) **de corto metraje** short; (*cine*) **de largo metraje** full-length
metralla *f* scrap iron; grapeshot; shrapnel
métri•co -ca *adj* metric(al) || *f* prosody
metro *m* meter; ruler; tape measure; subway; **metro plegadizo** folding rule
metrónomo *m* metronome
metrópoli *f* metropolis; mother country
metropolita•no -na *adj* metropolitan || *m* subway; (eccl) metropolitan
Méx. *abbr* **México**
mexcal *m* agave liquor
mexica•no -na *adj & mf* Mexican
México *m* Mexico; Mexico City; **Nuevo México** New Mexico
mezcal *m* var of **mexcal**
mezcla *f* mixture; (*argamasa*) mortar; (*tejido*) tweed
mezclar *tr* to mix; blend || *ref* to mix; (*introducirse uno entre otros*) mingle; intermarry; meddle
mezclilla *f* light tweed
mezcolanza *f* jumble, hodgepodge, medley
mezquinar *tr* to be stingy with || *intr* to be stingy
mezquindad *f* meanness, stinginess; need, poverty; smallness, tininess; wretchedness
mezqui•no -na *adj* mean, stingy; needy, poor; small, tiny; wretched
mezquita *f* mosque
mi *adj poss* my
mí (*used as object of a preposition*) *pron pers* me || *pron reflex* myself
miar §77 *intr* to meow
miau *m* meow
mica *f* mica; (Guat) flirt; **ponerse una mica** (CAm) to go on a jag
mi•cho -cha *mf* pussy cat
mico *m* long-tailed monkey; libertine; hoodlum; **dar mico** to not keep a date
microbio *m* microbe, germ
microbiología *f* microbiology
microbiólo•go -ga *mf* microbiologist
microbús *m* (Chile) jitney
microchip [ˌmikroˈtsip] *m* (*pl* **-chips**) microchip
microcirugía *f* microsurgery
microeconómi•co -ca *adj* microeconomic || *f* microeconomics
microfaradio *m* microfarad
microficha *f* microcard
micro•film *m* (*pl* **-films** or **-filmes**) microfilm
microfilmar *tr* to microfilm
micrófono *m* microphone
microinformáti•co -ca *adj* microcomputer || *f* microcomputing
microlentilla *f* contact lens
microonda *f* microwave
microondas *m* microwave oven, microwave

microordenador *m* microcomputer

micropelícula *f* microfilm

microprocesador *m* chip, microprocessor

microscópi•co -ca *adj* microscopic

microscopio *m* microscope

microsurco *adj invar* microgroove ‖ *m* microgroove

microteléfono *m* handset, French telephone

miedo *m* fear, dread; **miedo cerval** great fear; **por miedo de** for fear of; **por miedo (de) que** for fear that; **tener miedo (a)** to be afraid (of); **tener miedo de** to be in fear of, be afraid of; be afraid to

miedo•so -sa *adj* fearful, afraid

miel *f* honey; (*jarabe saturado*) molasses; **dejar con la miel en los labios** to spoil the fun for; **hacerse de miel** to be peaches and cream

mielga *f* lucerne

miembro *m* member; (*extremidad del hombre y los animales*) member, limb

mientes *fpl* mind, thought; wish, desire; **caer en las mientes** *or* **en mientes** to come to mind; **parar** *or* **poner mientes en** to reflect on; **venírsele a uno a las mientes** to come to one's mind

mientras *conj* while; whereas; **mientras que** while; whereas; **mientras tanto** meanwhile

miérco•les *m* (*pl* **-les**) Wednesday; **miércoles de ceniza** Ash Wednesday

mies *f* cereal, grain; harvest time; **mieses** grain fields

miga *f* (*porción pequeña*) bit; (*parte más blanda del pan*) crumb; (fig) substance; **hacer buenas migas con** to get along well with; **migas** fried crumbs

migaja *f* bit, piece; (*de inteligencia*) smattering; **migajas** crumbs; leavings

migajón *m* crumb; substance

migar §44 *tr* (*el pan*) to crumb; (*p. ej., la leche*) put crumbs in

migraña *f* migraine

migrato•rio -ria *adj* migratory

miguelear *tr* (CAm) to make love to

miguele•ño -ña *adj* (Hond) impolite, discourteous

mijo *m* millet

mil *adj & m* thousand, a thousand, one thousand; **a las mil quinientas** at an unearthly hour

milagre•ro -ra *adj* superstitious; miracle-working

milagro *m* (*hecho sobrenatural*) miracle; (*cosa rara*) wonder; votive offering; **colgar el milagro a** to put the blame on; **vivir de milagro** to have a hard time getting along; have had a narrow escape

milagrón *m* fuss, excitement

milagro•so -sa *adj* miraculous; marvelous, wonderful

milano *m* burr, down; (orn) kite

mil•deu *m* (*pl* **-deues**) mildew

milena•rio -ria *adj* millennial ‖ *m* millennium

milenio *m* millennium

milenrama *f* yarrow

milési•mo -ma *adj & m* thousandth

miliamperio *m* milliampere

milicia *f* militia; soldiery; warfare; military service

milicia•no -na *adj* military ‖ *m* militiaman

miligramo *m* milligram

milímetro *m* millimeter

militante *adj* militant

militar *adj* military; army ‖ *m* soldier, military man ‖ *intr* to fight, go to war; struggle; serve in the army; (*surtir efecto*) militate

militarismo *m* militarism

militarista *adj & mf* militarist

militarizar §60 *tr* to militarize

mílite *m* soldier

milla *f* mile

millar *m* thousand

millarada *f* about a thousand; **echar millaradas** to boast about one's wealth

millo *m* millet

millón *m* million

millona•rio -ria *adj* of a million or more inhabitants ‖ *mf* millionaire

milpa *f* (CAm, Mex) cornfield

mimar *tr* to fondle, pet; pamper, indulge, spoil

mimbre *m & f* (bot) osier; wicker, withe

mimbrear *intr & ref* to sway

mimbre•ño -ña *adj* willowy

mimbrera *f* (bot) osier, osier willow

mimbro•so -sa *adj* osier; (*hecho de mimbre*) wicker

mimeografiar §77 *tr* to mimeograph

mimeógrafo *m* mimeograph

mímica *f* mimicry; sign language

mimo *m* (*entre los griegos y romanos*) mime; fondling, petting; pampering

mimo•so -sa *adj* delicate, tender, finicky, fussy

mina *f* mine; (*de lápiz*) lead; (fig) mine, gold mine, storehouse; underground passage; (SAm) moll; **explotar una mina** to work a mine; **mina de carbón** *or* **mina hullera** coal mine; **voló la mina** the truth is out

minado *m* mine work; (nav) mining

mina•dor -dora *adj* (nav) mine-laying ‖ *m* (mil) miner; (nav) mine layer

minar *tr* to mine; undermine; consume; plug away at ‖ *intr* to mine

minarete *m* minaret

mineraje *m* mining; **mineraje a tajo abierto** strip mining

mineral *adj & m* mineral

mineralogía *f* mineralogy

minería *f* mining; mine operators

mine•ro -ra *adj* mining ‖ *m* miner; mine operator; (fig) source, origin

mingitorio *m* street urinal

min•gón -gona *adj* (Ven) spoiled, pampered

miniar *tr* to paint in miniature; (*un manuscrito*) illuminate

miniatura *f* miniature

miniaturización *f* miniaturization

minifalda *f* miniskirt

míni•mo -ma *adj* minimum; tiny, small, minute; least, smallest || *m* minimum || *f* tiny bit
mini•no -na *mf* kitty, pussy
miniordenador *m* minicomputer
ministerial *adj* ministerial
ministerio *m* ministry, cabinet, department; **formar ministerio** to form a government; **ministerio de Hacienda** Treasury Department (U.S.A.); Treasury (Brit); **ministerio de la Gobernación** Department of the Interior (U.S.A.); Home Office (Brit); **ministerio del Ejército** Department of the Army (U.S.A.); War Office (Brit); **ministerio de Marina** Department of the Navy (U.S.A.); Board of Admiralty (Brit); **Ministerio de Relaciones Exteriores** *or* **de Asuntos Exteriores** State Department; Foreign Ministry; **ministerio radiofónico** (eccl) radio ministry; **ministerio televisivo** (eccl) television ministry
ministrar *tr* to administer; furnish
ministro *m* minister; bailiff, constable; **ministro de asuntos exteriores** foreign minister; **ministro de Gobernación** Home Secretary (Brit); **ministro de Hacienda** Secretary of the Treasury (U.S.A.); Chancellor of the Exchequer (Brit); **ministro de Justicia** Attorney General (U.S.A.); **primer ministro** prime minister, premier
minorar *tr* to diminish, reduce; weaken
minorati•vo -va *adj & m* laxative
minoría *f* minority
minoridad *f* minority
minorista *m* retailer
minorita•rio -ria *adj* minority
minucia *f* trifle; **minucias** minutiae
minucio•so -sa *adj* minute, meticulous
minué *m* or **minuete** *m* minuet
minúscu•lo -la *adj* (*letra*) small; small, tiny || *f* small letter
minusvalía *f* disability, physical handicap, mental handicap; (econ) drop in value
minusváli•do -da *adj* physically or mentally handicapped, disabled || *mf* disabled person, physically or mentally handicapped person
minuta *f* first draft, rough draft; memorandum; menu, bill of fare; roll, list
minutero *m* minute hand
minu•to -ta *adj* minute || *m* minute || *f* see **minuta**
mí•o -a *adj poss* mine; of mine, e.g., **un amigo mío** a friend of mine || *pron poss* mine
miope *adj* near-sighted || *mf* near-sighted person
miopía *f* near-sightedness
mira *f* (*de arma de fuego, telescopio, etc.*) sight; aim, object, purpose; target; watchtower; **estar a la mira** to be on the lookout; **poner la mira en** to have designs on
mirada *f* glance, look; **apuñalar con la mirada** to look daggers at; **mirada de soslayo** side glance
miradero *m* (*lugar desde donde se mira*) lookout; (*persona o cosa que es objeto de la atención pública*) cynosure
mira•do -da *adj* cautious, circumspect; **bien mirado** highly regarded || *f* see **mirada**
mirador *m* belvedere; bay window, oriel
miramiento *m* considerateness, courtesy, regard; look; **sin miramientos** without consideration
miranda *f* eminence, vantage point
mirar *tr* to look at, watch; consider, contemplate; **mirar bien** to look with favor on; **mirar por encima** to glance at || *intr* to look, glance; **¡mira!** look out!; **mirar a** to look at, glance at; face, overlook; aim at; aim to; **mirar por** to look after || *ref* to look at oneself; look at oneself; look at each other; **mirarse en ello** to watch one's step; **mirarse en una persona** to be all wrapped up in a person
mirasol *m* sunflower
miríada *f* myriad
mirilla *f* peephole; (*para dirigir visuales*) target; (phot) finder
miriñaque *m* hoop skirt, crinoline; bauble, trinket; (Arg) cowcatcher
mirística *f* nutmeg tree
mirlar *ref* to try to look important
mirlo *m* blackbird; solemn look; **mirlo blanco** rare bird; **soltar el mirlo** to start to jabber
mirmidón *m* tiny fellow, nincompoop
mi•rón -rona *adj* onlooking; nosy || *mf* onlooker; (*de una partida de juego*) kibitzer; busybody
mirra *f* myrrh
mirto *m* myrtle
misa *f* mass; **cantar misa** to say mass; **como en misa** in dead silence; **misa campal** *or* **de campaña** open-air mass; **misa cantada** sung mass; **misa de difuntos** Requiem mass; **misa de prima** early mass; **misa mayor** *or* **solemne** High Mass; **misa rezada** Low Mass
misal *m* missal
misantropía *f* misanthropy
misántropo *m* misanthrope
misar *intr* to say mass; to hear mass
misario *m* acolyte
misceláne•o -a *adj* miscellaneous || *f* miscellany
miserable *adj* miserable, wretched; mean, stingy; despicable, vile || *mf* cur, cad; wretch; miser
miseran•do -da *adj* pitiful
miserear *intr* to be stingy
miseria *f* misery, wretchedness; poverty; stinginess; trifle, pittance; **comerse de miseria** to live in great poverty
misericordia *f* compassion, mercy, pity
misericordio•so -sa *adj* merciful
míse•ro -ra *adj* miserable, wretched || *mf* wretch
mísil *or* **misil** *m* missile; **mísil antibalístico** antiballistic missile; **mísil crucero** cruise missile; **mísil dirigible** guided missile
misión *f* mission; ration for harvesters; **ir a misiones** to go away as a missionary
misional *adj* missionary
misionario *m* missionary; envoy, messenger
misione•ro -ra *adj & mf* missionary
misi•vo -va *adj & f* missive

mismísi•mo -ma *adj* very same, self-same
mis•mo -ma *adj & pron indef* same; own, very; -self, e.g., **ella misma** herself; myself, e.g., **yo mismo** I myself; yourself, himself, herself, itself; **así mismo** likewise, also; **casi lo mismo** much the same; **lo mismo** just the same; **lo mismo me da** it's all the same to me; **mismo . . . que** same . . . as, **por lo mismo** for that very reason || **mismo** *adv* right, e.g., **ahora mismo** right now; **aquí mismo** right here
mistela *f* flavored brandy; needled must, spiked must
misterio *m* mystery; **hablar de misterio** to talk mysteriously
misterio•so -sa *adj* mysterious
misticismo *m* mysticism
místi•co -ca *adj* mystic(al) || *mf* mystic
mistificación *f* hoax, mystification
mistificar §73 *tr* to hoax, mystify
mistifori *m* hodgepodge
misturera *f* (Peru) flower girl
mita *f* mite, cheese mite; (SAm) Indian slave labor; (*turno en el trabajo*) (Arg, Chile) shift, turn
mitad *f* half; middle; **a (la) mitad de** halfway through; **cara mitad** better half; **en la mitad de** in the middle of; **la mitad de** half the; **mitad y mitad** half-and-half; **por la mitad** in half, in the middle
míti•co -ca *adj* mythical
mitigar §44 *tr* to mitigate, appease, allay
mitin *m* (*pl* **mitins** or **mítines**) meeting, rally
mito *m* myth
mitología *f* mythology
mitológi•co -ca *adj* mythological
mitón *m* mitten
mitra *f* chimney pot; (eccl) miter
mixtificación *f* hoax, mystification
mixtificar §73 *tr* to hoax, mystify
mixtifori *m* hodgepodge
mixtión *f* mixture
mix•to -ta *adj* mixed || *m* compound number; sulphur match; explosive compound
mixtura *f* mixture
mixturar *tr* to mix
mixturera *f* (Peru) flower girl
miz *interj* here, pussy!, here, kitty!
mízcalo *m* edible milk mushroom
m/l *abbr* **mi letra**
m/n *abbr* **moneda nacional**
mobilia•rio -ria *adj* personal (*property*) || *m* furniture, suite of furniture
moblaje *m* furniture, suite of furniture
moblar §61 *tr* to furnish
moca *m* Mocha coffee || *f* (Ecuad) mudhole; (Mex) wineglass
mocador *m* handkerchief
mocar §73 *tr* to blow the nose of || *ref* to blow one's nose
mocarro *m* snot
mocasín *m* moccasin
mocear *intr* to act young; sow one's wild oats
mocedad *f* youth; wild oats
mocerío *m* young people
mocero *adj masc* woman-crazy
mocetón *m* strapping young fellow
mocetona *f* buxom young woman
mochar *tr* to butt; chop off; (Arg) to rob; (Col) to fire
mochil *m* errand boy for farmers in the field
mochila *f* knapsack, haversack; backpack; tool bag; (mil) ration
mochín *m* (slang) executioner
mo•cho -cha *adj* blunt, stub, flat; (*árbol*) topped; stub-horned; mutilated; (Mex) reactionary || *m* butt end
mochuelo *m* (orn) little owl; (*de una o más palabras*) omission; **cargar con el mochuelo** *or* **tocarle a** (*uno*) **el mochuelo** to get the worst of a deal
mocil *adj* youthful
moción *f* motion, movement; (*en junta deliberante*) motion; **hacer** or **presentar una moción** to make a motion
mocionante *mf* mover
mocionar *tr & intr* to move
mocito -ta *adj* young || *mf* youngster
moco *m* (*humor segregado por una membrana mucosa*) mucus; (*mocarro*) snot; (*extremo del pabilo de una vela*) snuff; **a moco de candil** by candle light; **llorar a moco tendido** to cry like a baby; **moco de pavo** crest of a turkey; trifle; (bot) cockscomb
moco•so -sa *adj* snotty, snively; rude, illbred; flip, saucy; mean, worthless || *mf* brat
moda *f* fashion, mode, style; **a la moda de** after the fashion of, in the style of; **alta moda** haute couture; **de moda** in fashion; **fuera de moda** out of fashion; **pasar de moda** to go out of fashion
modales *mpl* manners
modalidad *f* manner, way, nature, kind
modelado *m* modeling; (compu, fa) modeling
modelar *tr* to model; to form, shape; to mold || *ref* to model; **modelarse sobre** to pattern oneself after
modelismo *m* model making
modelización *f* (econ) modeling
modelo *adj invar* model, e.g., **ciudad modelo** model city || *mf* model, mannequin, fashion model || *m* model, pattern; form, blank; equal, peer; (compu) style; **modelo estrella** (aut) crest-line model
modem *m* (compu) modem
modera•do -da *adj* moderate
moderador *m* regulator; (*para retardar el efecto de los neutrones*) moderator
moderar *tr* to moderate, control, restrain || *ref* to moderate, control oneself, restrain oneself
modernizar §60 *tr* to modernize
moder•no -na *adj* modern
modestia *f* modesty
modes•to -ta *adj* modest
modicidad *f* moderateness, reasonableness
módi•co -ca *adj* moderate, reasonable

modificante *adj* modifying || *m* (gram) modifier
modificar §73 *tr* to modify
modismo *m* idiom
modista *f* dressmaker; **modista de sombreros** milliner
modistería *f* dressmaking; ladies' dress shop
modistilla *f* dressmaker's helper; unskilled dressmaker
modisto *m* ladies' tailor
modo *m* manner, mode, way; (gram) mood, mode; **al** *or* **a modo de** like, on the order of; **de buen modo** politely; **de ese modo** at that rate; **de tal modo que** with the result that; **de modo que** so that; and so; **de ningún modo** by no means, nohow; **de todos modos** anyhow, at any rate; **en cierto modo** after a fashion; **modo de empleo** usage; instructions for use; **modo de ser** nature, disposition; **modo subordinado** (compu) background mode; **por modo de** as, by way of; **sobre modo** extremely; **uno a modo de** a sort of, a kind of
modorra *f* drowsiness, heaviness
modorrar *tr* to make drowsy || *ref* to get drowsy, fall asleep; (*la fruta*) get squashy
modo•rro -rra *adj* drowsy, heavy; dull, stupid; (*fruta*) squashy || *f* see **modorra**
modo•so -sa *adj* quiet, well-behaved
modrego *m* boor, awkward fellow
modulación *f* modulation; **modulación de altura** *or* **de amplitud** amplitude modulation; **modulación de frecuencia** frequency modulation
modular *tr & intr* to modulate
módulo *m* module; **módulo lunar** lunar lander, lunar module
modulo•so -sa *adj* harmonious
mofa *f* jeering, scoffing, mockery
mofeta *f* skunk; (*gas pernicioso que se desprende de las minas*) blackdamp, firedamp
moflete *m* fat cheek, jowl
mofletu•do -da *adj* fat-cheeked
mo•gol -gola *adj & mf* Mongol, Mongolian
mogollón *m* — **comer a mogollón** (coll) to sponge
mo•gón -gona *adj* one-horned, broken-horned
mogote *m* knoll, hillock; stack of sheaves; budding antler
mohatra *f* fake sale; cheating
mohien•to -ta *adj* moldy, musty; (*hierro*) rusty
mohín *m* face, grimace
mohina *f* annoyance, displeasure
mohi•no -na *adj* sad, melancholy, moody; (*caballo, buey, vaca*) black, black-nosed || *mf* hinny || *m* blue magpie || *f* see **mohina**
moho *m* mold, must; (*del hierro*) rust; laziness; **no dejar criar moho** to keep in constant use, to use up quickly
moho•so -sa *adj* moldy, rusty; (*hierro*) rusty; (*chiste*) stale
Moisés *m* Moses
moja•do -da *adj* wet; (*p.ej., por la lluvia*) drenched, soaked; (*húmedo*) moist; (phonet) liquid || *m* (Mex) (pej) wetback
mojar *tr* to wet; (*la lluvia a una persona*) drench, soak; (*humedecer*) dampen, moisten; (*ensopar*) dunk; stab || *intr* — **mojar en** to get mixed up in || *ref* to get wet; get drenched, get soaked
mojarrilla *mf* jolly person
moje *m* or **mojete** *m* sauce, gravy
mojicón *m* muffin, bun; slap in the face
mojiganga *f* masquerade, mummery; clowning
mojigatería or **mojigatez** *f* hypocrisy; prudery, sanctimoniousness
mojiga•to -ta *adj* hypocritical; prudish, sanctimonious, strait-laced || *mf* hypocrite; prude, sanctimonious person
mojinete *m* (*de un muro*) coping; (*de un tejado*) ridge; (Arg) gable; (Chile) gable end
mojón *m* boundary stone, landmark; (*montón sin orden*) pile, heap; (*guía en desplobado*) road mark; (*porción de excremento humano*) turd
moldar *tr* to mold; put molding on
molde *m* mold; pattern; cast, stamp, matrix; (*persona*) model, ideal; (*letra*) **de molde** printed; **venir de molde** to be just right
moldear *tr* to mold; (*vaciar*) cast; put molding on
moldura *f* molding
moldurar *tr* to put molding on
mole *adj* soft || *m* (Mex) stew seasoned with chili sauce || *f* bulk, mass
molécula *f* molecule
molende•ro -ra *mf* miller, grinder || *m* chocolate grinder; (CAm) grinding table
moler §47 *tr* (*granos*) to grind, mill; annoy, harass, weary; tire out, fatigue; chew; **moler a palos** to beat up
molesquina *f* moleskin
molestar *tr* to disturb, molest; bother, annoy; tire, weary || *ref* to bother; be annoyed; **molestarse en** to take the trouble to
molestia *f* disturbance, discomfort; annoyance, bother, nuisance
moles•to -ta *adj* bothersome, troublesome; boring, tedious; bored, tired
molesto•so -sa *adj* bothersome
moleteado *m* knurl
moletear *tr* to knurl
molibdeno *m* molybdenum
molicie *f* softness; effeminacy; voluptuous living
moli•do -da *adj* ground; exhausted, worn out
molienda *f* grinding, milling; (*cantidad que se muele de una vez*) grist; (*molino*) mill; bore, annoyance; fatigue, weariness
molimiento *m* grinding; weariness
moline•ro -ra *adj* mill || *m* miller || *f* miller's wife
molinete *m* little mill; ventilating fan; (*juguete de papel*) windmill; (*movimiento que se hace con el bastón*) twirl; (*con la espada*) flourish; (naut) windlass; (*rueda de cohetes*) (Mex) pinwheel

molinillo *m* hand mill; **molinillo de café** coffee grinder

molino *m* mill; **luchar con los molinos de viento** to tilt at windmills; **molino de agua, molino hidráulico** waterwheel; **molino de papel** paper mill; **molino de sangre** animal-driven mill; **molino de viento** windmill; **molino harinero** gristmill, flour mill

mollar *adj* soft, tender; mushy, squashy; (*carne*) lean; profitable; gullible, easily taken in

mollear *intr* to give, yield; bend

molleja *f* gizzard; **criar molleja** to get lazy; **mollejas** sweetbread

mollejón *m* grindstone; big fat loafer; good-natured fellow

mollera *f* crown (*of the head*); brains, sense; **cerrado de mollera** stupid; **duro de mollera** stubborn

mollete *m* muffin

molli•no -na *adj* drizzly || *f* drizzle

mollizna *f* drizzle

moloc *m* (Ecuad) mashed potatoes

molondrón *m* lazy bum; (Ven) large inheritance, much money

molusco *m* mollusk

momentáne•o -a *adj* momentary

momento *m* moment; **a cada momento** constantly, all the time; **al momento** at once; **de un momento a otro** at any moment; **momento de torsión** (mech, phys) torque

momería *f* clowning

mome•ro -ra *adj* clowning || *mf* clown

momia *f* mummy

momificar §73 *tr* to mummify

mo•mio -mia *adj* lean, skinny || *m* extra; (*ganga*) bargain; sinecure || *f* see **momia**

momo *m* face, grimace; (coll) caress

mona *f* female monkey; Barbary ape; ape, copycat; drunkenness; (*persona*) drunk; (taur) guard for right leg; **dormir la mona** to sleep off a drunk; **pillar una mona** to go on a jag; **pintar la mona** to put on airs

monacal *adj* monachal

monacato *m* monkhood

monacillo *m* altar boy, acolyte

monada *f* monkeyshine; (*gesto*) face, grimace, monkey face; darling; cuteness; flattery; folly, childishness

monaguillo *m* altar boy, acolyte

monaquismo *m* monasticism

monarca *m* monarch

monarquía *f* monarchy

monárqui•co -ca *adj* monarchic(al) || *mf* monarchist

monasterio *m* monastery

monásti•co -ca *adj* monastic

monda *f* pruning, trimming; parings, peelings; beating, whipping

mondadien•tes *m* (*pl* **-tes**) toothpick

mondadura *f* pruning, trimming, **mondaduras** peelings

mondar *tr* to clean; prune, trim; peel, pare, hull, husk; (*quitar con engaño los bienes a*) fleece; beat, whip

mon•do -da *adj* clean; pure; **mondo y lirondo** pure, unadulterated || *f* see **monda**

mondonga *f* kitchen wench

mondongo *m* intestines, insides; (*del hombre*) guts

monear *intr* to act like a monkey; boast || *ref* (Hond) to plug away; (Hond) to punch each other

moneda *f* coin; money; **la Moneda** the government of Chile; **moneda corriente** currency; common knowledge; **moneda de curso legal, moneda legal** legal tender; **moneda falsa** counterfeit; **moneda menuda** change; **moneda metálica** *or* **sonante** specie; **moneda suelta** change; **pagar en la misma moneda** to pay back in one's own coin

monedar *tr* to coin, mint

monedero *m* moneybag; **monedero falso** counterfeiter

monería *f* monkeyshine; cuteness; childishness

mones•co -ca *adj* apish

moneta•rio -ria *adj* monetary

mon•gol -gola *adj & mf* Mongol, Mongolian

monigote *m* lay brother; rag figure, stuffed form; botched painting, botched statue; sap, boob

monipodio *m* collusion, deal, plot

monís *m* trinket; **monises** money, dough

mónita *f* cunning, smoothness, slickness

monitor *m* monitor

monja *f* nun; **monjas** lingering sparks in burning paper

monje *m* monk

monjía *f* monkhood

monjil *adj* nunnish || *m* nun's dress

mono -na *adj* cute, nice; blond; (*cabello*) red || *m* monkey, ape; (*traje de faena*) overalls, dungarees; whippersnapper, squirt; (*drogas*) withdrawal symptom; (coll) clown; (taur) attendant of picador; (Chile) pyramid of fruit or vegetables; **estar de monos** to be on the outs; **mono de Gibraltar** Barbary ape || *f* see **mona**

monóculo *m* monocle

monogamia *f* monogamy

monografía *f* monograph

monograma *m* monogram

monolíti•co -ca *adj* monolithic

monologar §44 *intr* to soliloquize

monólogo *m* monologue

monomanía *f* monomania

monomio *m* monomial

mono•no -na *adj* cute, sweet

monopatín *m* scooter; skateboard

monoplano *m* monoplane

monopolio *m* monopoly

monopolizar §60 *tr* to monopolize

monorriel *m* monorail

monosabio *m* (taur) attendant of picador

monosílabo *m* monosyllable

monoteísta *adj* monotheistic || *mf* monotheist

monotipia *f* or **monotipo** *m* monotype
monotonía *f* monotony
monóto•no -na *adj* monotonous
monóxido *m* monoxide
monseñor *m* monseigneur; (eccl) monsignor
monserga *f* gibberish
monstruo *m* monster
monstruosidad *f* monstrosity
monstruo•so -sa *adj* monstrous
monta *f* sum, total; **de poca monta** of little account
montacar•gas *m* (*pl* **-gas**) hoist, freight elevator
montadero *m* horse block
montadura *f* mounting; (*de una caballería de silla*) harness; (*engaste*) setting, mount
montaje *m* montage; setting up; (mach) assembly; (rad) hookup
montanero *m* forest ranger
montante *m* post, upright; (*suma*) amount; (*hueco cuadrilongo sobre una puerta*) transom; (*ventana en forma de abanico*) fanlight; (*espadón*) broadsword ‖ *f* flood tide
montaña *f* mountain; mountain country; **la Montaña** the Province of Santander, Spain; **montaña de hielo** iceberg; **montaña rusa** roller coaster
monta•ñés -ñesa *adj* mountain ‖ *mf* mountaineer, highlander
montaño•so -sa *adj* mountainous
montapla•tos *m* (*pl* **-tos**) dumbwaiter
montar *tr* to mount, get on; (*un caballo, una bicicleta, los hombros de una persona*) ride; (*un servicio*) set up, establish; (*un fusil*) cock; (*una piedra preciosa*) set, mount; (*el caballo a la yegua*) cover; (*un reloj*) wind; (elec) to hook up; (mach) to assemble, to mount; (*la guardia*) (mil) to mount; (*un cabo*) (naut) to round; (*un buque*) (naut) to command; (*importar*) amount to ‖ *intr* to mount; get on top; weigh, be important; **montar en cólera** to fly into a rage; **tanto monta** it's all the same ‖ *ref* to mount; get on top
monta•raz *adj* (*pl* **-races**) backwoods; wild, untamed ‖ *m* forester, warden
monte *m* mountain, mount; woods, woodland; obstruction, interference; backwoods, wilds; bank, kitty; dirty head of hair; **andar al monte** to take to the woods; **monte alto** forest; **monte bajo** thicket, brushwood; **monte de piedad** pawnshop; **monte pío** pension fund for widows and orphans; mutual benefit society; **monte tallar** tree farm
montear *tr* to hunt, track down; make a working drawing of; arch, vault
montecillo *m* mound, hillock
montepío *m* pension fund for widows and orphans; mutual benefit society
montera *f* cloth cap; glass roof; wife of hunter; bullfighter's black bicorne; (Hond) drunk, jag
montería *f* hunting, big-game hunting; hunting party; (Bol, Ecuad) canoe to shoot the rapids; (Mex) lumberman's camp
monterilla *f* (naut) moonsail
montero *m* hunter, huntsman; (Mex) sawmill
montés or **montesi•no -na** *adj* wild (*e.g., goat*)
montículo *m* mound, hillock
montilla *f* montilla (*a pale dry sherry*)
monto *m* sum, total
montón *m* pile, heap; (*de gente*) crowd; lot, great deal, great many; **a, de,** or **en montón** taken together; **a montones** in abundance; **ser del montón** to be quite ordinary
montonera *f* heap, pile; band of mounted rebels
montonero *m* guerrilla
montu•no -na *adj* wooded; wild, untamed, rustic
montuo•so -sa *adj* wooded, woody; rugged, hilly
montura *f* (*cabalgadura*) mount; (*de una cabalgadura*) harness; seat, saddle; (*de una piedra preciosa, de un instrumento astronómico*) mounting; (*de gafas*) frame
monumento *m* monument
monzón *m* monsoon
moña *f* doll; mannequin; ribbon, hair ribbon; drunk, jag
moño *m* topknot; crest, top; (Col) caprice, whim; (*de caballo*) (Chile) forelock; **moños** frippery
moquear *intr* to snivel
moqueo *m* snivel, sniveling
moquero *m* handkerchief
moquete *m* punch in the nose
moquillo *m* runny nose; (vet) distemper
moquita *f* mucus, snivel
mor *m* — **por mor de** for love of; because of
mora *f* black mulberry; blackberry, brambleberry; white mulberry
morada *f* dwelling; stay, sojourn
mora•do -da *adj* purple, mulberry ‖ *f* see **morada**
moral *adj* moral ‖ *m* black mulberry tree ‖ *f* (*ciencia de la conducta; conducta*) morals; (*espíritu, confianza*) morale; (*p.ej., de una fábula*) moral
moraleja *f* moral
moralidad *f* morality; (*de una fábula*) moral
moraliza•dor -dora *adj* moralistic, moralizing
morar *intr* to live, dwell
moratoria *f* moratorium
mórbi•do -da *adj* (*perteneciente a la enfermedad*) morbid; soft, delicate, mellow
morbo *m* sickness, illness; **morbo gálico** syphilis; **morbo regio** jaundice
morbo•so -sa *adj* morbid, diseased
morcilla *f* blood pudding, black pudding; (*añadidura que mete un actor en su papel*) gag
mor•daz *adj* (*pl* **-daces**) mordant, mordacious, sharp, caustic
mordaza *f* (*pañuelo o instrumento que se pone en la boca para impedir el hablar*) gag; (*aparato que sirve para apretar*) clamp, jaw; pipe vise; **poner la mordaza a** to gag
mordedura *f* bite
morder **§47** *tr* to bite; nibble at; wear away; gossip about, ridicule; (Mex, Ven, W-I) to

cheat; **morder el polvo** to bite the dust || *intr* to bite; take hold
mordicar **§73** *tr & intr* to bite, sting
mordida *f* bite; (Mex) bribe; (*para eludir una multa*) (Mex) payoff
mordiente *m* mordant
mordiscar **§73** *tr* to nibble at || *intr* to nibble, gnaw away; champ
mordisco *m* nibble, bite; champ
more•no -na *adj* brown, dark-brown; dark, dark-complexioned; (*de la raza negra*) black; mulato || *mf* black person; mulato || *m* brunet || *f* brunette; loaf of brown bread; rick of new-mown hay
morería *f* Moorish quarter; Moorish land
moretón *m* black-and-blue mark
morfina *f* morphine
morfinomanía *f* morphine habit, drug habit
morfinóma•no -na *adj* addicted to morphine, addicted to drugs || *mf* morphine addict, drug addict
morfología *f* morphology
moribun•do -da *adj* moribund, dying || *mf* dying person
morillo *m* andiron, firedog
morir **§30 & §83** *intr* to die; (*el fuego, la luz, etc.*) die away; **morir ahogado** to drown; **morir de risa** to die laughing; **morir de viejo** to die of old age; **morir helado** to freeze to death; **morir quemado** to burn to death; **morir vestido** to die a violent death || *ref* to die; be dying; die away, die out; (*una pierna, un brazo*) go to sleep; **morirse por** to be crazy about; be dying to
moris•co -ca *adj* Morisco, Moorish || *mf* Moor converted to Christianity (*after the Reconquest*); (*descendiente de mulato y española o de mulata y español*) (Mex) Morisco
mo•ro -ra *adj* Moorish; (*vino*) unwatered || *mf* Moor; **hay moros en la costa** there's trouble brewing; **moro de paz** man of peace || *f* see **mora**
moro•cho -cha *adj* strong, robust; (SAm) dark
morón *m* mound, knoll; moron
moron•do -da *adj* bare, stripped
moronga *f* (CAm, Mex) sausage
moro•so -sa *adj* slow, tardy; (*retrasado en el pago de deudas*) delinquent
morra *f* (*de la cabeza*) top, crown; (*de gato*) purr; **andar a la morra** to come to blows
morrada *f* slap, punch; (*golpe dado con la cabeza*) butt
morral *m* nose bag; (*saco de cazador*) game bag; (*de soldado, viandante, etc.*) knapsack; boor, lout
morralla *f* small fish; (*gente de escaso valor*) rabble, trash; (*mezcla de cosas inútiles*) junk, trash; (Mex) change, small change
morriña *f* blues, melancholy; **morriña de la tierra** homesickness
morriño•so -sa *adj* sickly; (coll) blue, melancholy
morrión *m* helmet; (mil) bearskin
morro *m* (*cosa redonda*) knob; (*monte redondo*) knoll; (*guijarro*) pebble; (*saliente que forman los labios*) snout; **beber a morro** (slang) to drink out of the bottle; **estar de morro** *or* **de morros** to be on the outs; **poner morro** to make a snout; **por el morro** just like that, simply so
morrocotu•do -da *adj* strong, thick, heavy; (*asunto, negocio*) weighty; big, enormous; (Col) rich, wealthy; (Chile) graceless, monotonous
morsa *f* walrus
mortaja *f* shroud, winding sheet; cigarette paper; (carp) mortise
mortal *adj* mortal; deadly; mortally ill; deathly pale; sure, conclusive || *m* mortal
mortalidad *f* mortality; death rate
mortandad *f* massacre, mortality, butchery
morteci•no -na *adj* dead; dying; failing, weak; **hacer la mortecina** to play dead, to play possum
mortero *m* (*recipiente que sirve para machacar; argamasa*) mortar; (*en los molinos de aceite*) nether stone; (arti) mortar
mortífe•ro -ra *adj* deadly
mortificar **§73** *tr* to vex, annoy, bother; mortify || *ref* (Mex) to be mortified, be embarrassed
mortual *m* (CAm, Mex) inheritance
mortuo•rio -ria *adj* mortuary, funeral; (*casa*) of the deceased || *m* (archaic) funeral
morucco *m* ram
moru•no -na *adj* Moorish
mosai•co -ca *adj* Mosaic || *m* tile, paving tile; mosaic; **mosaico de madera** marquetry
mosca *f* fly; (*barba*) imperial; cash, dough; disappointment; bore, nuisance; **aflojar la mosca** to shell out, to fork out; **mosca borriquera** horsefly; **mosca de las frutas** fruit fly; **mosca del vinagre** fruit fly; **mosca muerta** hypocrite; **moscas** sparks; **moscas volantes** spots before the eyes; **papar moscas** to gape, gawk
moscareta *f* (orn) flycatcher
moscona *f* hussy, brazen woman
Moscú Moscow
mosquear *tr* (*moscas*) to shoo; beat, whip; answer sharply || *intr* (Mex) to sneak a ride || *ref* to shake off annoyances; take offense
mosquero *m* flytrap; fly swatter
mosquete *m* musket
mosquetear *intr* (Arg, Bol) to snoop
mosquete•ro -ra *adj* idle || *mf* (Arg, Bol) bystander, snooper || *m* musketeer || *f* wallflower
mosquetón *m* snap hook
mosquitera *f* or **mosquitero** *m* mosquito net; fly net
mosquito *m* (*Culex pungens*) mosquito; (*insecto parecido al anterior*) gnat; (coll) tippler
mostacera *f* mustard jar
mostacho *m* mustache; spot on the face
mostachón *m* macaroon
mostaza *f* mustard; (*semilla; munición*) mus-

tard seed; **subírsele a** (*uno*) **la mostaza a las narices** to fly into a rage
mosto *m* must; **mosto de cerveza** wort
mostrador *m* (*en las tiendas*) counter; (*en las tabernas*) bar; (*de reloj*) dial
mostrar §61 *tr* to show ‖ *ref* to show; show oneself to be
mostrear *tr* to spot, splash
mostren•co -ca *adj* ownerless, unclaimed; (*que no tiene casa ni hogar*) homeless; (*animal*) stray; slow, dull; fat, heavy ‖ *mf* dolt, dullard
mota *f* mote, speck; (*en el paño*) burl, knot; hill, rise; defect, fault; (Mex, W-I) powder puff
mote *m* device, emblem, riddle; (*apodo*) nickname; (Chile) mistake; (SAm) stewed corn
motear *tr* to speck, speckle; dapple, mottle ‖ *intr* (Peru) to eat stewed corn
motejar *tr* to call names; scoff at, make fun of; **motejar de** to brand as
motín *m* mutiny, riot
motinista *m* (Peru) rioter
motivar *tr* to explain, account for; rationalize
moti•vo -va *adj* motive ‖ *m* motive, reason; (mus) motif; **con motivo de** because of; on the occasion of; **de su motivo propio** on his own accord; **motivo conductor** (mus) leitmotif; **motivos** grounds, reasons; (Chile) finickiness, prudery
moto *m* guidepost, landmark ‖ *f* motorcycle; **moto de motocross** trail bike
motobomba *f* fire truck, fire engine
motocarro *m* three-wheel delivery truck
motocicleta *f* motorcycle
motociclista *mf* motorcyclist
motocine *m* drive-in theater
motogrúa *f* truck crane
motoli•to -ta *adj* simple, stupid; **vivir de motolito** to be a sponger, live on other people ‖ *f* (orn) wagtail; (Ven) decent woman
motón *m* (naut) block, pulley
motonáuti•co -ca *adj* motorboat ‖ *f* motorboating
motonaustismo *m* (sport) motorboating
motonave *f* motor launch; motor ship
motoneta *f* motor scooter; moped; light three-wheel delivery truck
mo•tor -tora *adj* motor, motive ‖ *m* motor, engine; **motor a chorro** jet engine; **motor de arranque** (aut) starter, starting motor; **motor de búsqueda** (compu) search engine; **motor de cuatro tiempos** four-cycle engine; **motor de dos tiempos** two-cycle engine; **motor de explosión** internal-combustion engine; **motor de inyección** fuel-injection engine; **motor de reacción** jet engine; **motor fuera borda** outboard motor; **motor térmico** heat engine ‖ *f* small motor boat
motorista *mf* motorist; motorcyclist; motorcycle racer ‖ *m* motorcycle policeman; motorman
motorización *f* motorization
motorizar §60 *tr* to motorize
motosegadora *f* power mower
motovelero *m* (naut) motor sailer
motriz *adj fem* (*fuerza*) motive
movedi•zo -za *adj* shaky, unsteady; fickle, inconstant; (*arena*) quick, shifting
mover §47 *tr* to move; (*la cola el perro*) wag; (*discordia*) stir up ‖ *intr* to move; abort, miscarry; bud, sprout ‖ *ref* to move; be moved
movible *adj* movable; fickle, inconstant, changeable
móvil *adj* movable, mobile; fickle, changeable; moving ‖ *m* moving body; cause, motive
movilidad *f* mobility; **movilidad ascendente** upward mobility
movilización *f* mobilization; demonstrations, action
movilizar §60 *tr* to mobilize
movimiento *m* movement, motion; **movimiento continuo** *or* **perpetuo** perpetual motion; **movimientos oculares rápidos** rapid eye movement; **movimiento feminista** women's liberation (movement)
moza *f* girl, lass; mistress, concubine; maid, kitchen maid; (*en algunos juegos de naipes*) last hand; wash bat; **buena moza** or **real moza** good-looking woman; **moza de fortuna** or **del partido** prostitute; **moza de taberna** barmaid
mozalbete *m* lad, young fellow
mozárabe *adj* Mozarabic ‖ *mf* Mozarab
mo•zo -za *adj* young, youthful; single, unmarried ‖ *m* youth, lad; (*camarero*) waiter; (*criado*) servant; porter; (*cuelgacapas*) cloak hanger; **buen mozo** *or* **real mozo** handsome fellow; **mozo de caballerías** hostler, stable boy; **mozo de café** waiter; **mozo de cámara** (naut) cabin boy; **mozo de ciego** blind man's guide; **mozo de cordel** street porter, public errand boy; **mozo de cuadra** stable boy; **mozo de cuerda** public errand boy; **mozo de espuelas** groom who walks in front of master's horse; **mozo de esquina** street porter, public errand boy; **mozo de estación** station porter; **mozo de estoques** (taur) sword handler; **mozo de hotel** porter, bellhop; **mozo de paja y cebada** hostler (*at an inn*); **mozo de restaurante** waiter ‖ *f* see **moza**
mozue•lo -la *mf* youngster ‖ *m* lad, young fellow ‖ *f* lass, young woman
m/p *abbr* **mi pagaré**
m/r *abbr* **mi remesa**
Mro. *abbr* **Maestro**
M.S. *abbr* **manuscrito**
mtd. *abbr* **mitad**
mu *m* moo ‖ *f* bye-bye; **ir a la mu** to go bye-bye
muaré *adj invar & m* moiré
muca•mo -ma *mf* (Arg, Urug) house servant ‖ *f* (Arg, Chile, Urug) servant girl
muceta *f* (*de los doctores en los actos universitarios*) hood; (eccl) mozzetta
muchacha *f* girl; young woman; servant girl
muchachada *f* youthful prank
muchachez *f* boyishness, girlishness

mucha•cho -cha *adj* young, youthful || *mf* youth, young person; servant || *m* boy || *f* see **muchacha**
muchedumbre *f* crowd, multitude, flock
mu•cho -cha *adj* much, a lot of, a great deal of; (*tiempo*) a long || *pron* much, a lot, a great deal || **mu•chos -chas** *adj & pron* many || **mucho** *adv* much; (*más de lo regular*) hard; often; a long time; **con mucho** by far; **ni con mucho** or **ni mucho menos** not by a long shot; **por mucho que** however much; **sentir mucho** to be very sorry; **tener mucho de** to take after
muco•so -sa *adj* mucous || *f* mucous membrane
múcura *f* (Bol, Col, Ven, W-I) water pitcher; (Col) thickhead
muda *f* change; change of voice; change of clothes; (*cambio de plumas o de piel*) molt, molting; molting season; **estar de muda** to be changing one's voice; **estar en muda** (coll) to keep too quiet; **hacer la muda** to molt; **muda de ropa** change of clothing
mudable *adj* fickle, inconstant
mudada *f* change of clothing; move, change of residence
mudadi•zo -za *adj* fickle, inconstant
mudanza *f* change; (*cambio de domicilio*) moving; fickleness, inconstancy; (*en el baile*) figure
mudar *tr* to change || *intr* to change; **mudar de** to change || *ref* to change; change clothing; move; move away; have a bowel movement; **mudarse de** to change
mudez *f* muteness, dumbness; continued silence
mu•do -da *adj* dumb, mute; (phonet) voiceless, surd || *mf* mute || *f* see **muda**
mueblaje *m* furniture, suite of furniture
mueble *adj* movable || *m* piece of furniture; (*p.ej., de un aparato de radio*) cabinet; **muebles** furniture
mueblería *f* furniture shop
mueblista *mf* furniture dealer
mueca *f* face, grimace
muela *f* grindstone; knoll, mound; back tooth, grinder; **muela cordal** wisdom tooth; **muela de esmeril** emery wheel; **muela del juicio** wisdom tooth; **muela de molino** millstone
muellaje *m* dockage, wharfage
muelle *adj* soft; voluptuous || *m* (*pieza elástica de metal*) spring; (*obra en la orilla del mar o de un río*) dock, wharf, pier; (rr) freight platform; **muelle real** mainspring
muérdago *m* mistletoe
muérgano *m* (Col, Ven) piece of junk, drug on the market; (Col, Ecuad, Ven) boor, nobody
muermo *m* (vet) glanders
muerte *f* death; **cada muerte de obispo** once in a blue moon; **dar la muerte a** to put to death; **de mala muerte** crummy, not much of a; **estar a la muerte** to be at death's door; **muerte cerebral** brain death; **muerte chiquita** nervous shudder; **muerte de cuna** cot death, sudden infant death syndrome; **muerte súbita** (*en fútbol*) sudden death; (*en tenis*) sudden death
muer•to -ta *adj* dead; (*apagado, marchito*) flat, dull; (*cal, yeso*) slaked; **muerto de** dying of; **muerto por** crazy about || *mf* corpse, dead person || *m* (*en los naipes*) dummy; **hacerse el muerto** to play possum; play deaf; **tocar a muerto** to toll
muesca *f* nick, notch; (carp) mortise
muestra *f* (*porción de un producto que sirve para conocer su calidad*) sample; model, specimen; (*rótulo sobre una tienda u hotel*) sign; show, exhibition, indication; (*esfera de reloj*) dial, face; (*parada del perro para levantar la caza*) set; (*ademán, porte*) bearing; **dar muestras de** to show signs of
mugido *m* moo, low; bellow, roar
mugir §27 *intr* (*la res vacuna*) to moo, low; (*con ira*) bellow; (*el viento, el mar*) roar
mugre *f* dirt, filth, grime
mugrien•to -ta *adj* dirty, filthy, grimy
muguete *m* lily of the valley
mujer *f* woman; (*esposa*) wife; **mujer de gobierno** housekeeper; **mujer de la limpieza** cleaning woman; **mujer de negocios** businesswoman; **mujer de su casa** good manager; **mujer fatal** vamp, femme fatale; **mujer golpeada** *or* **maltratada** battered woman, battered wife; **mujer policía** policewoman; **mujer taxista** woman taxi driver; **ser mujer** to be a grown woman
mujeren•go -ga *adj* (Arg, Urug, CAm) effeminate
mujerie•go -ga *adj* feminine, womanly; effeminate, womanish; fond of women; **a mujeriegas** sidesaddle || *m* flock of women; womanizer
mujeril *adj* womanly; womanish
mújol *m* mullet, striped mullet
mula *f* mule, she-mule; junk, trash; (Arg) ingrate, traitor; (Arg) hoax; (C-R) jag, drunk; (Guat, Hond) anger, rage; (Mex) drug on the market; (Ven) flask; **devolver la mula** (CAm) to pay back in one's own coin; **echar la mula a** (Mex) to rake over the coals; **en mula de San Francisco** on shank's mare
mulada *f* drove of mules
muladar *m* dungheap, dunghill; dump, trash heap; filth
mula•to -ta *adj & mf* mulatto
muleta *f* (*palo para apoyarse al andar*) crutch; muleta (*cloth attached to a stick, used by the matador*); support, prop; snack
muletilla *f* cross-handle cane; pet word, pet phrase; (taur) muleta
mulli•do -da *adj* soft, fluffy || *m* stuffing (*for cushions, pillows, etc.*) || *f* bedding, litter (*for animals*)
mullir §13 *tr* to soften, fluff up; (*la cama*) beat up, shake up; (*la tierra*) loosen around a stalk || *ref* to get fluffy
mulo *m* mule
multa *f* fine

multar *tr* to fine
multicopista *m* copying machine
multilateral *adj* multilateral
multiláte•ro -ra *adj* multilateral
multimedia *f* (compu) multimedia
multinacionales *mpl* multinational corporations
multiplataforma *f* (compu) multiplatform
múltiple *adj* multiple, manifold || *m* manifold; **múltiple (de) admisión** intake manifold; **múltiple (de) escape** exhaust manifold; **múltiple (de) uso** multipurpose
multiplicar §73 *tr, intr & ref* to multiply
multiplicidad *f* multiplicity
múlti•plo -pla *adj* multiple, manifold || *m* (math) multiple
multipropiedad *f* time share
multitarea *f* (compu) multitasking
multitud *f* multitude
multiusuario *adj invar* multiuser
munda•no -na *adj* mundane, worldly; (*mujer*) loose
mundial *adj* worldwide, world
mundillo *m* arched clotheshorse; cushion for making lace; warming pan; guelder-rose, cranberry tree; world (*of artists, scholars, etc.*)
mundo *m* world; **así va el mundo** so it goes; **desde que el mundo es mundo** since the world began; **echar al mundo** to bring into the world; to bring forth; **el mundo del espectáculo** show business, entertainment business; **el otro mundo** the other world; **gran mundo** high society; **medio mundo** (*mucha gente*) half the world; **nada del otro mundo** nothing special, no great thing; **tener mucho mundo** to know one's way around; **todo el mundo** everybody; **ver mundo** to see the world, to travel
mundonuevo *m* peep show
munición *f* munition, ammunition; **de munición** (mil) government issue; (coll) done hurriedly
municionar *tr* to supply with munition
municipal *adj* municipal || *m* policeman
munícipe *m* citizen
municipio *m* municipality; town council
munidad *f* susceptibility to infection
munífi•co -ca *adj* munificent
muñeca *f* (*figurilla infantil con que juegan las niñas*) doll; (*parte del cuerpo humano en donde se articula la mano con el brazo*) wrist; manikin, dress form; (*mujer linda; mozuela frívola*) doll; (*como apelativo*) (coll) honey, darling; (coll), pull, influence; **muñeca de trapo** rag doll, rag baby; **muñeca parlante** talking doll
muñeco *m* doll (*representing a male child or animal*); dummy, manikin; (*como apelativo*) (coll) honey, darling; (*joven afeminado*) (pej) namby-pamby, sissy; (fig) puppet; (coll) lad, little fellow; **muñeco de nieve** snowman
muñequera *f* strap for wrist watch, wristband
muñequilla *f* (mach) chuck; (Arg, Chile) young ear of corn
muñidor *m* heeler, henchman
muñir §12 *tr* to convoke, summon; (pol) to fix, rig
muñón *m* (*p.ej., de un brazo cortado*) stump; (mach) journal, gudgeon; **muñón de cola** dock
mural *adj* mural
muralla *f* wall, rampart
murar *tr* to surround with a wall
murciélago *m* bat
murga *f* tin-pan band; trouble, bother; torment
muriente *adj* dying, faint
murmujear *tr & intr* to mumble
murmullar *intr* to murmur
murmullo *m* murmur; whisper; (*de aguas corrientes*) ripple; (*del viento*) rustle
murmurar *tr* to murmur, mutter; murmur at || *intr* to murmur, mutter; whisper; (*las aguas corrientes*) ripple, purl; (*el viento*) rustle; gossip
muro *m* wall; **muro del sonido** sound barrier
murria *f* (coll) blues, dejection
musa *f* muse; **las Musas** the Muses; **soplarle a uno la musa** to be inspired to write poetry; be lucky at games of chance
musaraña *f* shrew, shrewmouse; bug, worm; **mirar a las musarañas** to stare vacantly
músculo *m* muscle
musculo•so -sa *adj* muscular
muselina *f* muslin
museo *m* museum; **museo de cera** waxworks
muserola *f* noseband
mus•go -ga *adj* dark-brown || *m* moss
musgo•so -sa *adj* mossy, moss-covered
música *f* music; (*músicos que tocan juntos*) band; noise, racket; **con la música a otra parte** don't bother me, get out; **música ambiental** background music; piped *o* canned music; **música celestial** nonsense; **música de cámara** chamber music; **música de fondo** background music; **poner en música** to set to music
musical *adj* musical
musicalidad *f* musicianship
music-hall *s* vaudeville theater, burlesque show
músi•co -ca *adj* musical || *mf* musician; composer; **músico callejero** street musician; **músico mayor** bandmaster || *f* see **música**
musicología *f* musicology
musicólo•go -ga *mf* musicologist
musiquero *m* music cabinet
musitar *tr & intr* to mutter, mumble
muslo *m* thigh; (*de ave cocida*) leg, drumstick
mustiar *ref* to wither
mus•tio -tia *adj* sad, gloomy; (*marchito*) withered; (Mex) hypocritical; (Mex) standoffish
musul•mán -mana *adj & mf* Muslim
mutación *f* mutation; unsettled weather, change of weather; (biol) mutation, sport; (theat) change of scene
mutila•do -da *adj* crippled || *mf* cripple
mutilar *tr* to mutilate; cripple
múti•lo -la *adj* mutilated; crippled

mutis *m* silence; (theat) exit; **hacer mutis** to keep quiet; (theat) to exit
mutua *f* mutual savings bank, benefit society; **mutua de seguros** mutual insurance company
mutual *adj* mutual
mutualidad *f* mutuality; mutual benefit; mutual benefit association
mutualista *mf* member of a mutual benefit association
mu•tuo -tua *adj* mutual, reciprocal
muy *adv* very; very much; too, e.g., **es muy tarde para dar un paseo tan largo** it is too late to take such a long walk; **muy de noche** late at night; **Muy señor mío** Dear Sir

N

N, n (ene) *f* fourteenth letter of the Spanish alphabet
n/ *abbr* **nuestro**
N. *abbr* **Norte**
nabo *m* turnip; (naut) mast
Nabucodonosor *m* Nebuchadnezzar
nácar *m* mother-of-pearl
nacara•do -da *adj* mother-of-pearl
nacatamal *m* (CAm, Mex) meat-filled tamale
nacela *f* nacelle
nacencia *f* birth; growth, tumor
nacer §22 *intr* to be born; bud, take rise, originate, appear; dawn || *ref* bud, shoot, sprout; (*abrirse la ropa por las costuras*) split
naci•do -da *adj* born; natural, innate; apt, proper, fit; **nacida** née or nee || *m* human being; growth, boil
naciente *adj* incipient; resurgent; (*sol*) rising || *m* east
nacimiento *m* birth; origin, beginning, fountainhead; descent, lineage; (*de agua*) spring, fountainhead; crèche
nación *f* nation
nacional *adj* national; domestic || *mf* national || *m* militiaman
nacionalidad *f* nationality
nacionalismo *m* nationalism
nacionalista *adj & mf* nationalist
nacionalizar §60 *tr* to nationalize || *ref* to be naturalized; become a citizen
nacista *adj & mf* Nazi
naco *m* (Arg, Bol, Urug) black rolled leaf of chewing tobacco; (Arg) fear, scare; (Col) stewed corn; (Col) mashed potatoes
nada *pron indef* nothing, not . . . anything; **de nada** don't mention it, you're welcome || *adv* not at all
nadaderas *fpl* water wings
nada•dor -dora *adj* swimming, floating || *mf* swimmer || *m* (Chile) fishnet float
nadar *intr* to swim; float; fit loosely or too loosely; **nadar en** (*riqueza*) to be rolling in; (*suspiros*) be full of; (*sangre*) be bathed in
nadear *tr* to destroy, wipe out
nadería *f* trifle
nadie *pron indef* nobody, not . . . anybody; **nadie más** nobody else; **nadie más que** nobody but || *m* nobody; **un don nadie** a nonentity
nado — a nado swimming, floating; **echarse a nado** to dive in; **pasar a nado** to swim across
NAFTA [ˈnafta] *m* (acronym) (**Tratado de Librecambio de Norteamérica**) NAFTA (North Atlantic Free Trade Agreement)
nafta *f* naphtha
nagual *m* (Guat, Hond) (*dícese de un animal*) inseparable companion; (Mex) sorcerer, wizard; (Mex) lie
nagualear *intr* (Mex) to lie; (Mex) to be out looking for trouble all night
naguas *fpl* petticoat
naipe *m* playing card; deck of cards; **naipe de figura** face card; **tener buen naipe** to be lucky
naire *m* mahout
nalga *f* buttock; **nalgas** buttocks, rump, behind (coll), bottom (coll)
nalgada *f* shoulder, ham; blow on or with the buttocks
nana *f* grandma; lullaby, cradlesong; (CAm, Mex, W-I) child's nurse; (Arg, Chile, Urug) child's complaint
napa *f* leather; (*de agua*) aquifer; (*de gas*) layer; fake fleece
napoleóni•co -ca *adj* Napoleonic
napolita•no -na *adj & mf* Neapolitan
naranja *f* orange; **media naranja** (coll) sidekick, better half; **naranja amarga** *or* **cajel** sour orange; **¡naranjas!** nonsense! || *m* (*color*) orange
naranjada *f* orangeade; orange juice; orange marmalade
naranjal *m* orange grove
naranjo *m* orange tree; boob, simpleton
narciso *m* narcissus; fop, dandy; **narciso trompón** daffodil || **Narciso** *m* Narcissus
narcóti•co -ca *adj & m* narcotic
narcotizar §60 *tr* to dope, drug
narcotraficante *mf* drug dealer
narguile *m* hookah
narigada *f* (SAm) pinch of snuff
nari•gón -gona *adj* big-nosed || *m* big nose
narigu•do -da *adj* big-nosed; nose-shaped
nariguera *f* nose ring

na•riz *f* (*pl* **-rices**) nose; nostril; sense of smell; (*del vino*) bouquet; **nariz de pico de loro** hooknose; **sonarse las narices** to blow one's nose; **tabicarse las narices** to hold one's nose; **tener agarrado por las narices** to lead by the nose
narración *f* narration
narra•dor -dora *adj* narrating ‖ *mf* narrator
narrar *tr* to narrate
narrati•vo -va *adj* narrative ‖ *f* (*relato; habilidad en narrar*) narrative
narria *f* sled, sledge, drag
nasal *adj & f* nasal
nasalizar §60 *tr* to nasalize
nata *f* cream; whipped cream; élite, choice; skim, scum
natación *f* swimming
natal *adj* natal; native ‖ *m* birth; birthday
natali•cio -cia *adj* birth ‖ *m* birthday
natalidad *f* birth rate
naterón *m* cottage cheese
natillas *fpl* custard
natividad *f* birth; Christmas; (*día; festividad; pintura*) Nativity
nati•vo -va *adj* native; natural; natural-born; innate
na•to -ta *adj* born, e.g., **criminal nato** born criminal ‖ *f* see **nata**
natural *adj* natural; native; (mus) natural ‖ *mf* native ‖ *m* temper, disposition, nature; **al natural** au naturel; rough, unfinished; live; **del natural** from life, from nature
naturaleza *f* nature; disposition, temperament; nationality; **naturaleza muerta** still life
naturalidad *f* naturalness; nationality
naturalismo *m* naturalism
naturalista *mf* naturalist
naturalización *f* naturalization
naturalizar §60 *tr* to naturalize; acclimatize ‖ *ref* to become naturalized; go native
naturalmente *adv* naturally; easily, readily
naturismo *m* nudism; natural lifestyle
naturista *adj* natural; nudist ‖ *mf* nudist
naufragar §44 *intr* to be shipwrecked; fail
naufragio *m* shipwreck; failure, ruin
náufra•go -ga *adj* shipwrecked ‖ *mf* shipwrecked person ‖ *m* shark
náusea *f* nausea; **dar náuseas a** to nauseate; sicken, disgust; **tener náuseas** to be nauseated, be sick at one's stomach
nauseabun•do -da *adj* nauseating, nauseous, loathsome, sickening
nauta *m* mariner, sailor
náuti•co -ca *adj* nautical ‖ *f* sailing, navigation
nava *f* hollow plain between mountains
navaja *f* folding knife; razor; penknife; tusk of wild boar; razor clam; evil tongue; **navaja automática, de botón** *or* **de resorte** (Mex) switchblade; **navaja barbera** straight razor
navajada *f* or **navajazo** *m* slash, gash
navajero *m* razor case; razor cloth
naval *adj* naval; nautical; **naval militar** naval
nava•rro -rra *adj & mf* Navarrese ‖ **Navarra** *f* Navarre
navazo *m* garden in sandy marshland
nave *f* ship, vessel; (*de un taller, fábrica, tienda, iglesia, etc.*) aisle; commercial ground floor; hall, shed, bay, building; **nave central** *or* **principal** (archit) nave; **nave lateral** (archit) aisle
navegable *adj* navigable
navegación *f* navigation; sailing; sea voyage; **navegación astronómica** celestial navigation; **navegación a vela** sailing; **navegación espacial** space travel
navega•dor -dora or navegante *adj* navigating ‖ *mf* navigator ‖ *m* (compu) navigator
navegante *mf* navigator
navegar §44 *tr* to sail ‖ *intr* to navigate, sail; move around; (Mex) to suffer, bear
navel *f* (*pl* **-vels**) navel orange
Navidad *f* Christmas; Christmas time; **¡Felices Navidades!** Merry Christmas!; **contar** *or* **tener muchas Navidades** to be pretty old
navidal *m* Christmas card
navide•ño -ña *adj* Christmas
navie•ro -ra *adj* ship, shipping ‖ *m* shipowner; outfitter
navío *m* ship, vessel; **navío de guerra** warship
náyade *f* naiad
nazare•no -na *adj & mf* Nazarene ‖ *m* penitent in Passion Week procession ‖ **nazarenas** *fpl* (SAm) large gaucho spurs
nazi *adj & mf* Nazi
N.B. *abbr* **nota bene** (Lat) (**nótese bien** note well)
nébeda *f* catnip
neblina *f* fog, mist
neblino•so -sa *adj* foggy, misty
nebulo•so -sa *adj* nebulous, cloudy, misty, hazy, vague; gloomy, sullen ‖ *f* nebula
necedad *f* foolishness, stupidity, nonsense
necesa•rio -ria *adj* necessary ‖ *f* water closet, privy
neceser *m* toilet case; sewing kit; **neceser de belleza** vanity case; **neceser de costura** workbasket
necesidad *f* necessity; need, want; starvation; **de necesidad** from weakness; of necessity; **necesidad mayor** bowel movement; **necesidad menor** urination
necesita•do -da *adj* necessitous, poor, needy; **estar necesitado de** to be in need of ‖ *mf* needy person
necesitar *tr* to necessitate; need; **necesitar** + *inf* to have to, need to + *inf* ‖ *intr* to be in need; **necesitar de** to be in need of, need ‖ *ref* to be needed, be necessary
ne•cio -cia *adj* foolish, stupid; imprudent; stubborn; touchy ‖ *mf* fool
necrología *f* necrology; obituary
necromancia *f* necromancy
néctar *m* nectar
neerlan•dés -desa *adj* Netherlandish, Dutch ‖ *mf* Netherlander ‖ *m* Dutchman; (*idioma*) Netherlandish or Dutch ‖ *f* Dutchwoman
nefalista *mf* teetotaler
nefan•do -da *adj* base, infamous

nefas•to -ta *adj* ominous, fatal, tragic
negable *adj* deniable
negación *f* negation; denial; refusal
nega•do -da *adj* unfit, incompetent; dull, indifferent
negar §66 *tr* to deny; refuse; prohibit; disown; conceal || *intr* to deny || *ref* to avoid; refuse; deny oneself to callers; **negarse a** to refuse; **negarse a** + *inf* to refuse to + *inf*
negati•vo -va *adj* negative || *f* negative; denial; refusal
negligencia *f* negligence
negligente *adj* negligent
negociable *adj* negotiable
negociación *f* negotiation; deal, matter
negociado *m* department, bureau; affair, business; (SAm) illegal dealing; (Chile) store
negociante *m* dealer, trader
negociar *tr* to negotiate || *intr* to negotiate; deal, trade
negocio *m* business; affair, deal, transaction; profit; (SAm) store
negocio•so -sa *adj* businesslike
negrear *intr* to turn black; look black
negre•ro -ra *adj* slave-trading; (fig) slave-driving || *mf* slave trader; (fig) slave driver
negrilla *f* (typ) boldface
ne•gro -gra *adj* black, dark; Black *o* black (*person*); gloomy; fatal, wicked; (coll) broke || *mf* Black *o* black (*person*); dear, darling || *m* black; **negro de humo** lampblack
negror *m* or **negrura** *f* blackness
negruz•co -ca *adj* blackish
néme•sis *f* (*pl* **-sis**) (*justo castigo; castigador*) nemesis || **Némesis** Nemesis
nemoro•so -sa *adj* (poet) woody, sylvan
ne•ne -na *mf* baby; dear, darling || *m* rascal, villain
nenúfar *m* white water lily
neo- *prefix* new
neocelan•dés -desa *adj* New Zealand || *mf* New Zealander
neoesco•cés -cesa *adj & mf* Nova Scotian
neófi•to -ta *mf* neophyte
neologismo *m* neologism
neomejica•no -na *adj & mf* New Mexican
neomicina *f* neomycin
neón *m* neon
neoyorki•no -na *adj* New York || *mf* New Yorker
Nepal, el Nepal
nepa•lés -lesa *adj & mf* Nepalese
nepente *m* nepenthe
neptunio *m* neptunium
Neptuno *m* (astr, myth) Neptune
Nerón *m* Nero
nervio *m* nerve; (*del ala del insecto*) rib; strength, vigor
nerviosidad *f* nervousness
nervio•so -sa *adj* nervous; energetic, vigorous, sinewy; (*célula; centro; tónico*) nerve; (*sistema; enfermedad; postración, colapso*) nervous
nervosidad *f* nervosity; ductility, flexibility; (*de un argumento*) force, cogency
nervo•so -sa *adj* var of **nervioso**
nervu•do -da *adj* vigorous, sinewy
nervura *f* backbone (*of book*)
nesga *f* gore
nesgar §44 *tr* to gore
ne•to -ta *adj* net
neumáti•co -ca *adj* pneumatic; air || *m* tire; **neumático desinflado** flat tire
neumonía *f* pneumonia
neuralgia *f* neuralgia
neurología *f* neurology
neurona *f* neuron
neuro•sis *f* (*pl* **-sis**) neurosis; **neurosis de guerra** shell shock
neuróti•co -ca *adj & mf* neurotic
neutral *adj & mf* neutral
neutralidad *f* neutrality
neutralismo *m* neutralism
neutralista *adj & mf* neutralist
neutralizar §60 *tr* to neutralize
neu•tro -tra *adj* neuter; (*que no es de un color ni de otro*) neutral; (bot, chem, elec, phonet, zool) neutral; (*verbo*) intransitive
neutrón *m* neutron
neva•do -da *adj* snow-covered; snow-white || *f* snowfall
nevar §2 *tr* to make snow-white || *intr* to snow
nevasca *f* snowfall; snowstorm, blizzard
nevazón *f* (SAm) snowfall
nevera *f* icebox, refrigerator; icehouse; (P-R) jail
nevería *f* ice-cream parlor
neve•ro -ra *mf* ice-cream dealer || *m* place of perpetual snow; perpetual snow || *f* see **nevera**
nevisca *f* snow flurry
neviscar §73 *intr* to snow lightly
nevo *m* mole; **nevo materno** birth mark
nevo•so -sa *adj* snowy
ni *conj* neither, nor; **ni . . . ni** neither . . . nor; **ni . . . siquiera** not even
niacina *f* niacin
nicaragüense or **nicaragüe•ño -ña** *adj & mf* Nicaraguan
nicho *m* niche
Nicolás *m* Nicholas
nicotina *f* nicotine
nidada *f* (*huevos en el nido*) nestful of eggs; (*pajarillos en el nido*) nest, brood, hatch
nidal *m* (*donde la gallina pone sus huevos*) nest; nest egg; haunt; source; basis, foundation
nido *m* nest; haunt; home; source; (*de ladrones*) nest, den
niebla *f* fog, mist, haze; mildew; fog, confusion; **hay niebla** it is foggy; **niebla artificial** smoke screen; **niebla tóxica** smog
nie•to -ta *mf* grandchild || *m* grandson; **nietos** grandchildren || *f* granddaughter
nieve *f* snow; water ice
nigromancia *f* necromancy
nihilismo *m* nihilism
nihilista *mf* nihilist
Nilo *m* Nile; **Nilo Azul** Blue Nile
nilón *m* nylon
nimbo *m* nimbus; halo

nimiedad *f* excess; fussiness, fastidiousness; timidity
ni•mio -mia *adj* excessive; fussy, fastidious; tiny
ninfa *f* nymph; **ninfa marina** mermaid
ninfea *f* white water lily
ningún *adj indef* apocopated form of **ninguno,** used only before masculine singular nouns and adjectives
ningu•no -na *adj indef* no, not any ‖ *pron indef* none, not any; neither, neither one; **ninguno de los dos** neither one ‖ **ninguno** *pron indef* nobody, no one
niña *f* child, girl; (*del ojo*) pupil; **niña del ojo** apple of one's eye; **niña exploradora** girl scout; **niña mimada** favorite, pet; spoiled girl; **niña probeta** test-tube baby (girl)
niñada *f* childishness
niñera *f* nursemaid
niñería *f* childishness; trifle
niñero -ra *adj* fond of children ‖ *f* see **niñera**
niñez *f* childhood; childishness; (fig) infancy
ni•ño -ña *adj* childlike, childish; young, inexperienced ‖ *mf* child; (*persona joven e inexperta*) babe; **desde niño** from childhood; **niño expósito** foundling; **niño travieso** imp ‖ *m* child, boy; **niño bonito** playboy; **niño de coro** choirboy; **niño de la bola** child Jesus; lucky fellow; **niño explorador** boy scout; **niño gótico** playboy; **niño mimado** favorite, pet; spoiled boy; **niño probeta** test-tube baby (boy) ‖ *f* see **niña**
ni•pón -pona *adj & mf* Nipponese
níquel *m* nickel
niquelar *tr* to nickel-plate
nirvana, el nirvana
níspero *m* medlar (*tree and fruit*)
níspola *f* medlar (*fruit*)
nitidez *f* brightness, clearness; sharpness
níti•do -da *adj* bright, clear; sharp
nitrato *m* nitrate
nítri•co -ca *adj* nitric
nitro *m* niter; **nitro de Chile** saltpeter
nitrógeno *m* nitrogen
nitroglicerina *f* nitroglycerine
nitro•so -sa *adj* nitrous
nitruro *m* nitride
nivel *m* level; **a bajo nivel** low-level; **en dos niveles** split-level; **nivel de burbuja** spirit level; **nivel de vida** standard of living; **nivel freático** water table; **nivel sonoro** noise level
nivelar *tr* to level; even, make even, grade; survey
NN *abbr* **ningún nombre** *initials on the grave of an unidentified person*
no *adv* not; no; **¿cómo no?** why not?; of course, certainly; **creer que no** to think not, believe not; **¿no?** is it not so?; **no bien** no sooner; **no más que** not more than; only; **no sea que** lest; **no . . . sino** only; **ya no** no longer
nobabia *f* (aer) dope
noble *adj* noble ‖ *m* noble, nobleman
nobleza *f* nobility
noche *f* night, nighttime; darkness; **buenas noches** good evening; good night; **de la noche a la mañana** overnight; unexpectedly, suddenly; **de noche** at night, in the nighttime; **esta noche** tonight; **hacer noche en** to spend the night in; **hacerse de noche** to grow dark; **muy de noche** late at night; **por la noche** at night, in the nighttime; **Noche Buena** Christmas Eve; **noche de estreno** (theat) first night; **Noche de Uvas** New Year's Eve; **Noche Vieja** New Year's Eve; watch night
Nochebuena *f* Christmas Eve
nochebueno *f* Christmas cake; Yule log
nochero *m* sleepwalker
noción *f* notion, idea; rudiment
nocividad *f* harmfulness
noci•vo -va *adj* noxious, harmful
noctur•no -na *adj* nocturnal; lonely, sad, melancholy; night, nighttime
nodo *m* (astr, med, phys) node
No-Do *m* (acronym) (**Noticiario y Documentales**) newsreel; newsreel theater
nodriza *f* wet nurse; vacuum tank
Noé *m* Noah
nogal *m* walnut tree; **nogal de la brujería** witch hazel
nómada or **nómade** *adj & mf* nomad
nomádi•co -ca *adj* nomadic
nomás *adv* just, only
nombradía *f* fame, renown, reputation
nombra•do -da *adj* famous
nombramiento *m* naming; appointment
nombrar *tr* to name; appoint
nombre *m* name; fame, reputation; nickname; watchword; noun; **del mismo nombre** (elec) like; **de nombres contrarios** (elec) unlike; **nombre artístico** stage name; pen name; **nombre comercial** trade name; **nombre de lugar** place name; **nombre de pila** first name; **nombre de soltera** maiden name; **nombre propio** proper name; **nombre sustantivo** noun; **nombre supuesto** alias
nomeolvi•des *f* (*pl* **-des**) forget-me-not
nómina *f* list, roll; payroll
nominal *adj* nominal; noun
nominar *tr* to name; appoint
nominati•vo -va *adj & m* nominative
non *adj* odd, uneven ‖ *m* odd number
nonada *f* trifle, nothing
no•no -na *adj & m* ninth
nopal *m* prickly pear
norcorea•no -na *adj & mf* North Korean
nordestada *f* or **nordeste** *m* (*viento*) northeaster (*wind*)
noria *f* chain pump; (*pozo*) draw well; Ferris wheel; treadmill, drudgery
norma *f* norm, standard; rule, regulation; method; (carp) square
normal *adj* normal; standard; perpendicular
Normandía *f* Normandy
norman•do -da *adj & mf* Norman ‖ *m* Norseman
norte *m* north; north wind; (*guía*) (fig) polestar, lodestar
Norteamérica *f* North America; America, the United States
norteamerica•no -na *adj & mf* North American; (*estadunidense*) American

norte•ño -ña *adj* northern
norue•go -ga *adj & mf* Norwegian || **Noruega** *f* Norway
nos (used as object of verb) *pron pers* us; to us || *pron reflex* ourselves, to ourselves; each other, to each other
noso•tros -tras *pron pers* we; us; ourselves
nostalgia *f* nostalgia
nota *f* note; (*en la escuela*) mark, grade; (*en el restaurante*) check; (mus) note; **nota a pie de página** footnote; **nota de adorno** grace note; **nota de prensa** press release; **notas necrológicas** obituaries; **nota tónica** keynote
notables *mpl* notables; prominent persons; (coll) VIPs
notación *f* notation; **notación en clave** coding
notar *tr* to note; dictate; annotate; criticize; discredit || *reflex*—**nótese bien** note well, note bene
notario *m* notary, notary public
noticia *f* news; notice, information; notion, rudiment; knowledge; **noticias de actualidad** news of the day; **noticias de última hora** late news; **noticia de último momento** (rad, telv) flash; **una noticia** a piece of news, a news item
noticiar *tr* to notify; give notice of
noticia•rio -ria *adj* news || *m* up-to-the-minute news; newsreel; newscast; **noticiario gráfico** picture page; **noticiario teatral** theater page
noticie•ro -ra *adj* news || *m* newsman, reporter; late news
noticio•so -sa *adj* informed; learned; well-informed; newsy || *m* news item
notificar §73 *tr* to notify; report on
no•to -ta *adj* known, well-known || *m* south wind || *f* see **nota**
notoriedad *f* general knowledge; fame
noto•rio -ria *adj* manifest, well-known
nov. *abbr* **noviembre**
novatada *f* hazing; beginner's blunder
nova•to -ta *adj* beginning || *mf* beginner; freshman
novecien•tos -tas *adj & pron* nine hundred || **novecientos** *m* nine hundred
novedad *f* newness, novelty; news; fashion; happening; change; failing health; **sin novedad** as usual; safe; well; without anything happening
novel *adj* new, inexperienced, beginning || *m* beginner
novela *f* novel; story, lie; (telv) soap opera; **novela de vaqueros** novel of western life; **novela policíaca** *or* **policial** detective story; **novela por entregas** serial
novele•ro -ra *adj* fond of novelty; fond of fiction; gossipy; fickle
noveles•co -ca *adj* novelistic, fictional; romantic, fantastic
novelista *mf* novelist
novelísti•co -ca *adj* fictional || *f* fiction
novelizar §60 *tr* to fictionalize
nove•no -na *adj & m* ninth
noventa *adj, pron & m* ninety
noventa•vo -va *adj & m* ninetieth
novia *f* fiancée; bride; (*enamorada*) girlfriend; **novia de guerra** war bride
noviazgo *m* engagement, courtship
novi•cio -cia *adj & mf* novice
noviembre *m* November
novilla *f* heifer
novillada *f* drove of young bulls; (taur) fight with young bulls by aspiring bullfighters
novillero *m* herdsman of young cattle; (taur) aspiring fighter, untrained fighter; truant
novillo *m* young bull; (coll) cuckold; (Mex, P-R) fiancé; **hacer novillos** to play truant
novilunio *m* new moon
novio *m* suitor; fiancé; bridegroom; (*enamorado*) boyfriend; **novios** engaged couple; bride and groom, newlyweds
novocaína *f* novocaine
nro. *abbr* **nuestro**
N.S. *abbr* **Nuestro Señor**
ntro. *abbr* **nuestro**
nubada *f* local shower; abundance
nubarrón *m* storm cloud
nube *f* cloud; **andar** (*los precios*) **por las nubes** to be sky-high; **bajar de las nubes** to come back to or down to earth; **poner en** *or* **sobre las nubes** to praise to the skies
nube-hongo *f* mushroom cloud
nubla•do -da *adj* cloudy; bleary (*eyes*) || *m* storm cloud; impending danger; abundance; **aguantar el nublado** to suffer resignedly
nublar *tr* to cloud, cloud over || *ref* to become cloudy
nu•blo -bla *adj* cloudy || *m* storm cloud
nublo•so -sa *adj* cloudy; adverse, unfortunate
nubosidad *f* clouding, clouds
nubo•so -sa *adj* cloudy
nuca *f* nape
nuclear *adj* nuclear
núcleo *m* nucleus; core; (*de nuez*) kernel; (*de la fruta*) stone; (*de un electroimán*) core
nudillo *m* knuckle; stocking stitch; plug (*in wall*)
nudismo *m* nudism
nudista *adj & mf* nudist
nudo *m* knot; bond, tie, union; crux; tangle, plot; difficulty; (*en el drama*) crisis; center, juncture; (bot) node; (naut) knot; **cortar el nudo gordiano** to cut the Gordian knot; **hacérsele a** (*uno*) **un nudo en la garganta** to get a lump in one's throat; **nudo corredizo** granny knot
nudo•so -sa *adj* knotted, knotty
nuera *f* daughter-in-law
nues•tro -tra *adj poss* our || *pron poss* ours
nueva *f* news; piece of news; **nuevas** *fpl* news
Nueva York *m & f* New York; **el Gran Nueva York** Greater New York
Nueva Zelandia New Zealand
nueve *adj & pron* nine; **las nueve** nine o'clock || *m* nine; (*en las fechas*) ninth
nue•vo -va *adj* new; **de nuevo** again, anew; **nuevo flamante** brand-new; **¿qué hay de**

nuevo? what's new? || *mf* novice; freshman || *f* see **nueva**
nuevomejica•no -na *adj & mf* New Mexican
Nuevo Méjico *m* New Mexico
nuez *f* (*pl* **nueces**) nut; walnut; Adam's apple; **nuez dura** (*árbol*) hickory; hickory nut; **nuez moscada** nutmeg
nulidad *f* nullity; incapacity; nobody
nu•lo -la *adj* null, void, worthless
núm. *abbr* **número**
numen *m* deity; inspiration
numeral *adj* numeral
numerar *tr* to number; count; numerate
numerario *m* cash, coin, specie
numéri•co -ca *adj* numerical
número *m* number; (*de un periódico*) copy, issue; (*de zapatos*) size; lottery ticket; **cargar** or **cobrar al número llamado** (telp) to reverse the charges; **de número** (*dícese de los individuos de una sociedad*) regular; **medio número** half size; **mirar por el número uno** to look out for number one; **número de identificación personal** Personal Identification Number (PIN); **número de matrícula** license number; **número de serie** series number; **número de teléfono** telephone number; **número equivocado** (telp) wrong number; **número impar** odd number; **número par** even number; **número romano** Roman numeral
numero•so -sa *adj* numerous
nunca *adv* never; **no . . . nunca** not . . . ever, never; **nunca jamás** nevermore
nupcial *adj* nuptial
nupcialidad *f* marriage rate
nupcias *fpl* nuptials, marriage; **casarse en segundas nupcias** to marry the second time
nutria *f* otter
nutrición *f* nutrition
nutri•do -da *adj* great, intense, robust, vigorous, steady; full, abounding, rich, heavy; (*carácter, letra*) thick; (*cañoneo*) heavy, sustained
nutrimento *m* or **nutrimiento** *m* nourishment, nutriment
nutrir *tr* to nourish, feed; supply, stock; support, back up; fill to overflowing
nu•triz *f* (*pl* **-trices**) wet nurse

Ñ

Ñ, ñ (eñe) *f* fifteenth letter of the Spanish alphabet
ñadi *m* (Chile) broad, shallow swamp
ñajú *m* okra, gumbo
ñam ñam *interj* (coll) yum yum!
ñámbar *m* Jamaica rosewood
ñame *m* yam; (W-I) blockhead, dunce
ñan•dú *m* (*pl* **-dúes**) nandu, American ostrich
ña•ño -ña *adj* close, intimate; spoiled, overindulged || *m* elder brother || *f* elder sister; nursemaid; dear
ñapa *f* something thrown in, lagniappe; **de ñapa** in the bargain
ñaque *m* junk, pile of junk
ña•to -ta *adj* pug-nosed; (Arg) ugly, deformed
ñeque *adj* (Am) strong, vigorous; (*dícese de los ojos*) drooping || *m* slap, blow; pep
ñiqueñaque *m* (coll) trash
ñisca *f* bit, fragment; excrement
ñoclo *m* macaroon
ñolombre *m* old peasant; **¡viene ñolombre!** here comes the bogeyman
ñon•go -ga *adj* slow, lazy; foolish, stupid; tricky; suspicious
ñoñería *f* or **ñoñez** *f* timidity; inanity; dotage
ño•ño -ña *adj* timid; inane; doting

O

O, o (o) sixteenth letter of the Spanish alphabet
o *conj* or; **o . . . o** either . . . or
oa•sis *m* (*pl* **-sis**) oasis
ob. *abbr* **obispo**
obduración *f* obduracy
obedecer §22 *tr* (with personal **a**) to obey || *intr* to obey; **obedecer a** to yield to, be due to, be in keeping with, arise from
obediencia *f* obedience
obediente *adj* obedient
obelisco *m* obelisk; (typ) dagger
obertura *f* (mus) overture
obesidad *f* obesity
obe•so -sa *adj* obese
obispo *m* bishop
óbito *m* decease, demise
obituario *m* obituary
objeción *f* objection
objetable *adj* objectionable (*open to objection*)
objetar *tr* to object; (*dudas*) raise; (*una razón contraria*) set up, offer, present; object to
objeti•vo -va *adj & m* objective; **objetivo de ojo de pez** fish-eye lens
objeto *m* object; subject matter; **objetos de co-**

tillón favors; **objeto volante no identificado, objeto volador no identificado (ovni)** unidentified flying object (UFO)
oblea *f* wafer; pill, tablet; **hecho una oblea** nothing but skin and bones
obli•cuo -cua *adj* oblique
obligación *f* obligation, duty; bond, debenture; **obligaciones** family responsibilities
obligacionista *mf* bondholder
obliga•do -da *adj* obliged, grateful; required, customary; submissive; (mus) obbligato || *m* (mus) obbligato
obligar §44 *tr* to obligate; oblige
obliterar *tr* to cancel
oblon•go -ga *adj* oblong
oboe *m* oboe; oboist
oboísta *mf* oboist
óbolo *m* mite
obra *f* work; **obra de** a matter of; **obra de consulta** reference work; **obra maestra** masterpiece; **obra pía** charity; useful effort; **obra prima** shoemaking; **obras** construction, repairs, alterations; **obra segunda** shoe repairing; **poner por obra** to undertake, set to work on
obra•dor -dora *mf* worker || *m* workman; shop, workshop || *f* workingwoman
obraje *m* manufacture; processing
obrajero *m* foreman; (Arg) lumberman; (Bol) artisan
obrar *tr* to build; perform; work || *intr* to work; act, operate, proceed; have a movement of the bowels; **obra en mi poder** I have at hand, I have in my possession
obrera *f* workingwoman
obrerismo *m* labor; labor movement
obre•ro -ra *adj* working; labor || *m* workman; **los obreros** labor || *f* see **obrera**
obrero-patronal *adj* labor management
obscenidad *f* obscenity
obsce•no -na *adj* obscene
obscurecer §22 *tr* to darken; dim; discredit; cloud, confuse || *intr* to grow dark || *ref* to cloud over; become dimmed; fade away
obscuridad *f* obscurity; darkness
obscu•ro -ra *adj* obscure; dark; gloomy; uncertain, dangerous; **a obscuras** in the dark || *m* dark; (paint) shading
obsequia•do -da *mf* recipient; guest of honor
obsequiar *tr* to fawn over, flatter; present, give; court, woo
obsequio *m* flattery; gift; attention, courtesy; **en obsequio de** in honor of; **obsequio del autor** (*un libro*) compliments of the author
obsequio•so -sa *adj* obsequious; obliging, courteous
observación *f* observation
observa•dor -dora *adj* observant || *mf* observer
observancia *f* observance; deference, respectfulness
observar *tr* to observe
observatorio *m* observatory
obsesión *f* obsession
obsesionar *tr* to obsess
obsole•to -ta *adj* obsolete
obstaculizar §60 *tr* to prevent; obstruct, stymie
obstáculo *m* obstacle
obstante *adj* standing in the way; **no obstante** however, nevertheless; in spite of
obstar *intr* to stand in the way; **obstar a** *or* **para** to hinder, check, oppose
obstetricia *f* obstetrics
obstétri•co -ca *adj* obstetrical || *mf* obstetrician
obstinación *f* obstinacy
obstina•do -da *adj* obstinate
obstinar *ref* to be obstinate
obstrucción *f* obstruction
obstruccionar *tr* to hinder, obstruct
obstruir §20 *tr* to obstruct; block; stop up
obtención *f* obtaining
obtener §71 *tr* to obtain; keep
obtenible *adj* obtainable
obturación *f* plugging up, sealing off
obturador *m* stopper, plug; (aut) choke; (aut) throttle; (phot) shutter; **obturador de guillotina** drop shutter
obtu•so -sa *adj* obtuse
obús *m* howitzer; shell; (*de válvula de neumático*) plunger
obvención *f* extra, bonus, incidental
obvencional *adj* incidental
obviar §77 & regular *tr* to obviate, prevent || *intr* to stand in the way
ob•vio -via *adj* obvious; unnecessary
oca *f* goose
ocasión *f* occasion; opportunity, chance; bargain; danger, risk; **aprovechar la ocasión** to improve the occasion; **aprovechar la ocasión de** to avail oneself of the opportunity to; **asir la ocasión por la melena** to take time by the forelock; **de ocasión** secondhand
ocasiona•do -da *adj* dangerous, risky; exposed, subject, liable; annoying
ocasionar *tr* to occasion, cause; stir up; endanger
ocasional *adj* occasional; causal; causing; (*causa*) responsible; accidental
ocaso *m* west; (*de un cuerpo celeste*) setting; sunset; decline; end, death
occidental *adj* western; occidental
occidente *m* occident
oceáni•co -ca *adj* oceanic
océano *m* ocean; **Océano Atlántico** Atlantic Ocean; **Océano Índico** Indian Ocean; **Océano Pacífico** Pacific Ocean
oceanografía *f* oceanography
oceanógra•fo -fa *mf* oceanographer
ocha•vo -va *adj* eighth; octagonal || *m* eighth; octagon
ochenta *adj, pron & m* eighty
ochenta•vo -va *adj & m* eightieth
ocho *adj & pron* eight; **las ocho** eight o'clock || *m* eight; (*en las fechas*) eighth
ochocien•tos -tas *adj & pron* eight hundred || **ochocientos** *m* eight hundred
ocio *m* idleness, leisure; distraction, pastime; spare time
ocio•so -sa *adj* idle; useless, needless

oclusión *f* occlusion
oclusi•vo -va *adj & f* occlusive
ocote *m* (Mex) torch pine
octava *f* octave
octavilla *f* handbill; eight-syllable verse
octavín *m* piccolo
octa•vo -va *adj* eighth ‖ *mf* octoroon ‖ *m* eighth ‖ *f* see **octava**
oct.[e] *abbr* **octubre**
octogési•mo -ma *adj & m* eightieth
octubre *m* October
ocular *adj* ocular, eye ‖ *m* eyepiece, eyeglass, ocular
oculista *mf* oculist; fawner, flatterer
ocultar *tr & ref* to hide
ocul•to -ta *adj* hidden, concealed; (*misterioso, sobrenatural*) occult
ocupación *f* occupation; occupancy; employment
ocupa•do -da *adj* busy; occupied; **ocupada** pregnant
ocupante *adj* occupying ‖ *mf* occupant ‖ **ocupantes** *mpl* occupying forces
ocupar *tr* to occupy; busy, keep busy; employ; bother, annoy; attract the attention of ‖ *ref* to be occupied; be busy; be preoccupied; bother
ocurrencia *f* occurrence; witticism; bright idea
ocurrente *adj* witty
ocurrir *intr* to occur, happen; come; (*venir a la mente*) occur
oda *f* ode
odiar *tr* to hate
odio *m* hate, hatred
odio-amor *m* love-hate
odio•so -sa *adj* odious, hateful
Odisea *f* Odyssey
odómetro *m* (aut) odometer
odontología *f* odontology, dentistry
odontólo•go -ga *mf* odontologist, dentist
odre *m* goatskin wine bag; (coll) toper
OEA *f* (letterword) (**Organización de Estados Americanos**) OAS (Organization of American States)
oeste *m* west; west wind
ofender *tr & intr* to offend ‖ *ref* to take offense
ofensa *f* offense
ofensi•vo -va *adj & f* offensive
ofen•sor -sora *adj* offending ‖ *mf* offender
oferta *f* offer; gift, present; **oferta pública de adquisición (OPA)** takeover bid; **oferta y demanda** supply and demand
oficial *adj* official ‖ *m* official, officer; skilled workman; clerk, office worker; journeyman; commissioned officer; **oficial de derrota** navigator
oficiar *tr* to announce officially in writing; (*la misa*) celebrate; officiate at ‖ *intr* to officiate; **oficiar de** to act as
oficina *f* office; shop; pharmacist's laboratory; **oficina de objetos perdidos** lost-and-found department
oficines•co -ca *adj* office, clerical; bureaucratic
oficinista *mf* clerk, office worker
oficio *m* office, occupation; function, role; craft, trade; memo, official note; (eccl) office, service; **de oficio** officially; professionally; **hacer oficios de** to function as; **tomar por oficio** to take to, keep at
oficio•so -sa *adj* diligent; obliging; officious, meddlesome; profitable; unofficial
ofimática *f* (compu) business applications
ofrecer *tr & intr* to offer; (*una recepción*) give ‖ *ref* to offer; offer oneself; happen
ofrecimiento *m* offer, offering; **ofrecimiento de presentación** introductory offer
ofrenda *f* offering; gift
ofrendar *tr* to make offerings of; contribute
oftalmología *f* ophthalmology
oftalmólo•go -ga *mf* ophthalmologist
ofuscación *f* obfuscation; (mental) derangement
ofuscar **§73** *tr* to obfuscate; dazzle
ogro *m* ogre
Oh *interj* O!, Oh!
ohmio *m* ohm
oíble *adj* audible
oída *f* hearing; **de** or **por oídas** by hearsay
oído *m* hearing; ear; **al oído** by listening; confidentially; **decir al oído** to whisper; **hacer** *or* **tener oídos de mercader** to turn a deaf ear; **ser todo oídos** to be all ears
oír **§48** *tr* to hear; listen to; (*una conferencia*) attend; **oír** + *inf* to hear + *inf,* e.g., **oí entrar a mi hermano** I heard my brother come in; hear + *ger,* e.g., **oí cantar a la muchacha** I heard the girl singing; hear + *pp,* e.g., **oí tocar la campana** I heard the bell rung; **oír decir que** to hear that; **oír hablar de** to hear about ‖ *intr* to hear; listen; **¡oíga!** say!, listen!; the idea!, the very idea!
ojada *f* (Col) skylight
ojal *m* buttonhole; eyelet; grommet
ojalá *interj* God grant . . . !, would to God . . . !, I hope so!; **¡ojalá que** would that . . . !, I hope that . . . !
ojeada *f* glimpse, glance; **buena ojeada** eyeful
ojear *tr* to eye, stare at; cast the evil eye on; (*la caza*) start, rouse; frighten, startle
ojera *f* eyecup, eyeglass; **ojeras** (*bajo los párpados inferiores*) rings, circles
ojeriza *f* grudge, ill will
ojero•so -sa *adj* with rings or circles under the eyes
ojete *m* eyelet, eyehole
ojienju•to -ta *adj* dry-eyed, tearless
ojituer•to -ta *adj* cross-eyed
ojiva *f* ogive, pointed arch
ojo *m* eye; (*de la escalera*) opening, well; (*del puente*) bay, span; (*de agua*) spring; **a ojos vistas** visibly, openly; **costar un ojo de la cara** to cost a mint, cost a fortune; **dar los ojos de la cara por** to give one's eyeteeth for; **hasta los ojos** up to one's ears; **mirar con ojos de carnero degollado** to make sheep's eyes at; **no pegar el ojo** to not sleep a wink; **ojo de buey** (archit, meteor, naut) bull's-eye; (bot) oxeye; (naut) porthole; **ojo de la cerradura** keyhole; **ojo de pez** (phot) fish eye; **ojo mágico** peephole; **ojo morado, moro** (Mex), **a la funerala** (Esp), **en com-**

pota (SAm) *or* **en tinta** (Chile) black eye; **ponerle un ojo morado a alguien** to give someone a black eye; **poner los ojos en blanco** to roll one's eyes; **saltar a los ojos** to be self-evident; **valer un ojo de la cara** to be worth a mint || *interj* beware!; look out!; attention!; **¡mucho ojo!** be careful!, watch out!; **¡ojo con . . . !** look out for . . . !; **¡ojo, mancha!** fresh paint!
ojota *f* (SAm) sandal; (SAm) tanned llama hide
okey *interj* O.K., all right
ola *f* wave; (*de gente apiñada*) surge
ole *m* or **olé** *m* bravo || *interj* bravo!
oleada *f* big wave; (*de gente apiñada*) surge, swell
oleaje *m* surge, rush of waves
óleo *m* oil; holy oil; oil painting; **los santos óleos** extreme unction
oleoducto *m* pipe line
oler §49 *tr* to smell; pry into; sniff out || *intr* to smell, smell fragrant, smell bad; **no oler bien** to look suspicious; **oler a** to smell of, smell like; smack of
olfatear *tr* to smell, scent, sniff; (*p.ej., un buen negocio*) scent, sniff out
olfato *m* smell, sense of smell; scent; keen insight
olíbano *m* frankincense
oliente *adj* smelling, odorous
oligarquía *f* oligarchy
Olimpíada *or* **Olimpiada** *f* Olympiad
olímpi•co -ca *adj* Olympian; Olympic; haughty
oliscar §73 *tr* to smell, scent, sniff; investigate || *intr* to smell bad
oliva *f* olive; olive tree; barn owl; olive branch, peace
olivar *m* olive grove
olivillo *m* mock privet
olivo *m* olive tree; **tomar el olivo** (taur) to duck behind the barrier; beat it
olla *f* pot, kettle; stew; eddy, whirlpool; **olla a** *or* **de presión** pressure cooker; **olla común** *or* **popular** soup kitchen; **olla freidora** deep fryer
ollería *f* potter's shop
ollero *m* potter
olmeda *f* or **olmedo** *m* elm grove
olmo *m* elm tree
olor *m* odor; promise, hope; trace, suspicion; **olores** (Chile, Mex) spice, condiment
oloro•so -sa *adj* odorous, fragrant
olote *m* (CAm & Mex) cob, corncob
OLP *f* (letterword) (**Organización para la Liberación de Palestina**) PLO (Palestine Liberation Organization)
olvidadi•zo -za *adj* forgetful; ungrateful
olvida•do -da *adj* forgetful; ungrateful
olvidar *tr & intr* to forget; **olvidar** + *inf* to forget to + *inf* || *ref* to forget oneself; **olvidarse de** to forget; **olvidarse de** + *inf* to forget to + *inf;* **olvidársele a uno** to forget, e.g., **se me olvidó mi pasaporte** I forgot my passport; **olvidársele a uno** + *inf* to forget to + *inf,* e.g., **se me olvidó cerrar la ventana** I forgot to close the window
olvido *m* forgetfulness; oblivion
ombligo *m* navel; (*centro, punto medio*) (fig) navel
omino•so -sa *adj* ominous
omisión *f* omission; oversight, neglect
omi•so -sa *adj* neglectful, remiss
omitir *tr* to omit; overlook, neglect
ómni•bus *adj* (*tren*) accommodation || *m* (*pl* **-bus**) bus, omnibus; (Esp) slow train; **ómnibus de dos pisos** double-decker
omnímo•do -da *adj* all-inclusive
omnipotente *adj* omnipotent
omnisciente or **omnis•cio -cia** *adj* omniscient
omnívo•ro -ra *adj* omnivorous
omóplato *m* shoulder blade
once *adj & pron* eleven; **las once** eleven o'clock || *m* eleven; (*en las fechas*) eleventh
oncea•vo -va *adj & m* eleventh
once•no -na *adj & mf* eleventh
oncología *f* oncology
onda *f* wave; flicker; (*en el pelo*) wave; **estar en la misma onda** to be on the same wavelength; **onda corta** short wave; **onda larga** long wave; **onda portadora** (rad) carrier wave; **ondas entretenidas** (rad) continuous waves
ondear *tr* (*en el pelo*) to wave || *intr* to wave; ripple; flow; flicker; be wavy || *ref* to wave, sway, swing
ondo•so -sa *adj* wavy
ondulación *f* undulation; wave; wave motion
ondula•do -da *adj* wavy, ripply; rolling; corrugated || *m* (*en el pelo*) wave
ondular *tr* (*el pelo*) to wave || *intr* to undulate; (*una bandera*) wave, flutter; (*las ondas del mar*) billow; (*una culebra*) wriggle
onero•so -sa *adj* onerous, burdensome
ónice *m* or **ónique** *m* or **ónix** *m* onyx
onomásti•co -ca *adj* of proper names || *m* name day || *f* study of proper names
onomatopéyi•co -ca *adj* onomatopoeic
ONU [ˋonu] *f* (acronym) (**Organización de las Naciones Unidas**) UN (United Nations)
onza *f* (*28,35 gramos*) ounce; (zool) snow leopard
onza•vo -va *adj & m* eleventh
OPA [ˋopa] *f* (acronym) (**Oferta Pública de Adquisición**) takeover bid
opa•co -ca *adj* opaque; sad, gloomy
ópalo *m* opal
opción *f* option, choice; **de opción multiple** multiple-choice; **opción de compra** call option; **opción de enajenación** *or* **de venta** put option; **opción de futuro** futures option; **opción nula** *or* **opción cero** zero option
ópera *f* opera; **ópera bufa** comic opera; **ópera semiseria** light opera; **ópera seria** grand opera
operación *f* operation; transaction; **operación de vigilancia** stakeout (slang)
opera•dor -dora *mf* operator; cameraman; pro-

jectionist; (compu, electron) operator; **operador de consola** (compu) keyboarder

operar *tr* to operate on || *intr* to operate; work || *ref* to occur, come about; be operated on

opera•rio -ria *mf* worker || *m* workman || *f* working woman

opereta *f* operetta

operista *mf* opera singer

operísti•co -ca *adj* operatic

opia•to -ta *adj m & f* opiate

opinable *adj* moot

opinar *intr* to opine; think; pass judgment

opinión *f* opinion, view; reputation, public image

opio *m* opium

opípa•ro -ra *adj* sumptuous, lavish

oponer §54 *tr* to oppose; (*resistencia*) to offer, put up || *ref* to oppose each other; face each other; **oponerse a** to oppose, be opposed to; be against, resist; compete for

oporto *m* port, port wine

oportunidad *f* opportunity; opportuneness; **oportunidades** *fpl* witticisms

oportunista *adj* opportunistic || *mf* opportunist

oportu•no -na *adj* opportune, timely; proper; witty

oposición *f* opposition; competitive examination

oposi•tor -tora *adj* rivaling, competing || *mf* opponent; competitor

opresión *f* oppression

opresi•vo -va *adj* oppressive

opre•sor -sora *adj* oppressive || *mf* oppressor

oprimir *tr* to oppress; squeeze, press

oprobiar *tr* to defame, revile

oprobio *m* opprobrium

oprobio•so -sa *adj* opprobrious

optar *tr* to choose; assume || *intr* — **optar entre** to choose between; **optar por** to choose to

ópti•co -ca *adj* optical || *mf* optician || *f* optics

óptimamente *adv* to perfection

óptimismo *m* optimism

optimista *adj* optimistic || *mf* optimist

ópti•mo -ma *adj* fine, excellent

optometrista *mf* optometrist

opues•to -ta *adj* opposite, contrary

opugnar *tr* to attack; lay siege to; contradict

opulen•to -ta *adj* opulent

opúsculo *m* short work, opuscule

oquedad *f* hollow; hollowness

ora *conj* — **ora . . . ora** now . . . now, now . . . then

oración *f* oration, speech; prayer; sentence; **oración dominical** Lord's Prayer; **ponerse en oración** to get down on one's knees

oráculo *m* oracle

ora•dor -dora *mf* orator, speaker; **orador de plazuela** soapbox orator; **orador de sobremesa** after-dinner speaker; **orador invitado** guest speaker

oraje *m* rough weather, storm

oral *adj* oral

orangután *m* orangutan

orar *intr* to pray; make a speech

orato•rio -ria *adj* oratorical || *m* oratorio; (*capilla privada*) oratory || *f* (*arte de la elocuencia*) oratory

orbe *m* orb; world

órbita *f* orbit

orca *f* killer whale

Órcadas *fpl* Orkney Islands

órdago — **de órdago** (coll) swell, real

orden *m & f* order; **hasta nueva orden** until further notice; **orden** *f* **de allanamiento** search warrant; **orden** *m* **de colocación** word order; **orden de pago** money order; **orden judicial** court order; **orden sacerdotal** *or* **sagrada** ordination

ordenación *f* order, arrangement; ordination

ordena•do -da *adj* tidy, orderly, organized

ordenador *m* computer; **ordenador de a bordo** *or* **de viaje** on-board computer; **ordenador de sobremesa** *or* **de mesa** *or* **de escritorio** desktop computer; **ordenador doméstico** home computer; **ordenador patrón** server; **ordenador personal** personal computer; **ordenador portátil** laptop computer

ordenancista *adj* strict, severe || *mf* taskmaster, disciplinarian, martinet

ordenanza *m* errand boy; (mil) orderly || *f* ordinance; order, system; command; **ser de ordenanza** to be the rule

ordenar *tr* to order; put in order; ordain || *ref* to be ordained, take orders

ordeñadero *m* milk pail

ordeñar *tr* to milk

ordeño *m* milking

ordinal *adj* orderly; ordinal || *m* ordinal

ordinariez *f* coarseness, crudeness

ordina•rio -ria *adj* ordinary || *m* daily household expenses; delivery man

orear *tr* to air || *ref* to be aired; dry in the air; take an airing

orégano *m* pot or wild marjoram, winter sweet

oreja *f* ear; (*del zapato*) flap; (*de martillo*) claw; lug, flange, **aguzar las orejas** to prick up one's ears; **con las orejas caídas** crestfallen; **con las orejas tan largas** all ears; **descubrir** *or* **enseñar las orejas** to give oneself away

oreja•no -na *adj* (*res*) unbranded; (*animal*) skittish; shy; cautious

orejera *f* earflap, earmuff

orejeta *f* lug

ore•jón -jona *adj* coarse, uncouth; (Mex) skinny || *m* strip of dried peach; pull on the ear; (*de la hoja de un libro*) dog-ear

oreju•do -da *adj* big-eared

oreo *m* breeze

orfanato *m* orphanage

orfandad *f* orphanage, orphanhood

orfebre *m* goldsmith; silversmith

orfelinato *m* (SAm) orphanage

Orfeo *m* Orpheus

orfeón *m* glee club, choral society

organ•dí *m* (*pl* **-díes**) organdy

orgáni•co -ca *adj* organic

organillero -ra *mf* organ-grinder
organillo *m* barrel organ, hand organ, hurdy-gurdy
organismo *m* organism; organization
organista *mf* organist
organización *f* organization; **Organización de las Naciones Unidas (ONU)** United Nations (UN); **Organización de los Estados Americanos (OEA)** Organization of American States (OAS); **Organización del Tratado del Sudeste Asiático (O.T.A.S.E.)** Southwest Asia Treaty Organization (SEATO); **Organización para el Tratado del Atlántico Norte (O.T.A.N.)** North Atlantic Treaty Organization (NATO)
organizar §60 *tr* to organize
órgano *m* organ; (*de una máquina*) part; (*medio, conducto*) organ; (mus) organ
orgasmo *m* orgasm
orgía *f* orgy
orgiásti•co -ca *adj* orgiastic
orgullo *m* haughtiness; pride
orgullo•so -sa *adj* haughty; proud
oriental *adj* eastern; oriental
orientación *f* orientation; **orientación profesional** vocational guidance; **orientación sexual** sexual orientation
orienta•dor -dora *adj* orienting, guiding || *mf* guidance counselor
orientar *tr* to orient; guide, direct; (*una vela*) trim || *ref* to orient oneself; find one's bearings
oriente *m* east; source, origin; east wind; youth || **Oriente** *m* Orient; **el Cercano Oriente** the Near East; **el Extremo Oriente** the Far East; **el Lejano Oriente** the Far East; **el Oriente Medio** the Middle East; **el Próximo Oriente** the Near East; **gran oriente** (*logia masónica central*) grand lodge
orificar §73 *tr* to fill with gold
orífice *m* goldsmith
orificio *m* orifice, aperture, hole
origen *m* origin; source
original *adj* original; strange, odd, quaint || *m* original; character; **de buen original** on good authority; **original de imprenta** copy
originar *tr & ref* to originate, start
orilla *f* border, edge; margin; bank, shore; sidewalk; breeze; **orillas** (Arg, Mex) outskirts; **salir a la orilla** to manage to get through
orillar *tr* to put a border or edge on; trim || *intr* to come up to the shore
orillo *m* selvage, list
orín *m* rust; **orines** urine; **tomarse de orines** to get rusty
orina *f* urine
orinal *m* chamber pot
orinar *tr* to pass, urinate || *intr & ref* to urinate
oriun•do -da *adj & mf* native; **ser oriundo de** to come from, hail from
orla *f* border, edge; trimming, fringe
orlar *tr* to border, put an edge on; trim, trim with a fringe
orn. *abbr* **orden**
ornamentar *tr* to ornament, adorn
ornamento *m* ornament, adornment
ornar *tr* to adorn
ornato *m* adornment, show
oro *m* gold; (cards) "oro"; **de oro y azul** all dressed up; **oro batido** gold leaf; **oro de ley** standard gold; **oros** (cards) suit with figures representing gold coins and often considered to be equivalent to the English suit called diamonds; **poner de oro y azul** to rake over the coals; **ponerle colores al oro** to gild the lily
oron•do -da *adj* big-bellied; hollow, spongy, puffed up; pompous, self-satisfied
oropel *m* tinsel; glitz; **gastar mucho oropel** to put up a big front
oropéndola *f* golden oriole
orozuz *m* licorice
orquesta *f* orchestra; **orquesta típica** regional orchestra
orquestar *tr* to orchestrate
órquide *f* or **orquídea** *f* orchid
ortiga *f* nettle; **ser como unas ortigas** to be a grouch
orto *m* rise (*of sun or star*)
ortodoncia *f* orthodontics; **aparato de ortodoncia** orthodontic appliance, braces
ortodo•xo -xa *adj* orthodox
ortografía *f* orthography; spelling
ortografiar §77 *tr & intr* to spell
oruga *f* caterpillar
orujo *m* bagasse of grapes or olives
orzuelo *m* sty
os *pron pers & reflex* (used as object of verb and corresponding to **vos** and **vosotros**) you, to you; yourself, to yourself; yourselves, to yourselves; each other, to each other
osa *f* she-bear; **Osa Mayor** Great Bear; **Osa Menor** Little Bear
osadía *f* boldness, daring
osa•do -da *adj* bold, daring
osamenta *f* skeleton; bones
osar *intr* to dare
osario *m* ossuary, charnel house
oscilar *intr* to oscillate; fluctuate; waver, hesitate
ósculo *m* kiss
oscurecer §22 *tr, intr & ref* var of **obscurecer**
oscuridad *f* var of **obscuridad**
oscu•ro -ra *adj & m* var of **obscuro**
osera *f* bear's den
osificar §73 *tr & ref* to ossify
osito *m* — **osito de felpa, osita de peluche** teddy bear
oso *m* bear; **hacer el oso** to make a fool of oneself; to make love in the open; **oso blanco** polar bear; **oso hormiguero** ant bear; anteater; **oso lavador** raccoon; **oso pardo** brown bear
ostensorio *m* (eccl) monstrance
ostentar *tr* to show; make a show of || *ref* to show off; boast
ostentati•vo -va *adj* ostentatious
ostento *m* portent, prodigy

ostento•so -sa *adj* magnificent, showy
osteópata *mf* osteopath
osteopatía *f* osteopathy
ostión *m* large oyster
ostra *f* oyster; **ostras en su concha** oyster cocktail, oysters on the half shell
ostracismo *m* ostracism
ostral *m* oyster bed, oyster farm
ostrería *f* oysterhouse
ostre•ro -ra *adj* oyster || *m* oysterman; oyster bed, oyster farm
osu•do -da *adj* bony
osu•no -na *adj* bearish, bearlike
OTAN, O.T.A.N., la [ˋotan] *f* (acronym) (**Organización del Tratado del Atlántico Norte**) NATO (North Atlantic Treaty Organization)
OTASE, O.T.A.S.E., la [oˋtase] *f* (acronym) (**Organización del Tratado del Sudeste Asiático**) SEATO (South-East Asia Treaty Organization)
otate *m* Mexican giant grass (*Guadua amplexifolia*); otate stick
otero *m* hillock, knoll
otomán *m* ottoman
otoma•no -na *adj & mf* Ottoman || *f* ottoman
otoñal *adj* autumnal
otoño *m* autumn, fall
otorgar §44 *tr* to agree to; grant, confer; (law) to execute
o•tro -tra *adj indef* other, another || *pron indef* other one, another one; **como dijo el otro** as someone said
ovación *f* ovation
ovacionar *tr* to give an ovation to
oval *adj* oval
óvalo *m* oval
ovante *adj* victorious, triumphant
ovario *m* ovary
oveja *f* ewe, female sheep; **oveja negra** (fig) black sheep; **oveja perdida** (fig) lost sheep
oveje•ro -ra *adj* sheep || *mf* sheep raiser
oveju•no -na *adj* sheep, of sheep
ove•ro -ra *adj* blossom-colored; egg-colored
overol *m* overalls, dungarees
ovillar *tr* to wind up; sum up || *intr* to form into a ball || *ref* to curl up into a ball
ovillo *m* ball of yarn; ball, heap; tangled ball; **hacerse un ovillo** to cower, recoil; (*hablando*) get all tangled up
ovni, OVNI *m* (acronym) (**objeto volante no identificado**) UFO (Unidentified Flying Object)
óvulo *m* ovule; ovum
oxear *tr & intr* to shoo
oxiacanta *f* hawthorn
oxidación *f* oxidation
oxidar *tr* to oxidize || *ref* to oxidize; get rusty
óxido *m* oxide; **óxido de carbono** carbon monoxide; **óxido de mercurio** mercuric oxide
oxígeno *m* oxygen
oxíto•no -na *adj* oxytone
oxte *interj* get out!, beat it!, **sin decir oxte ni moxte** without opening one's mouth
oyente *mf* hearer; (*a la radio*) listener; (*en la escuela*) auditor
ozono *m* ozone
ozonosfera *f* ozonosphere

P

P, p (pe) *f* seventeenth letter of the Spanish alphabet
P. *abbr* **Padre, Papa, Pregunta**
pabellón *m* pavilion, building; bell tent; flag, banner; (*de fusiles*) stack; canopy; summerhouse; (*de instrumento de viento*) bell; **pabellón auricular** outer ear
pabilo or **pábilo** *m* wick
Pablo *m* Paul
pábulo *m* food; support, encouragement, fuel
pacana *f* pecan
paca•to -ta *adj* mild, gentle
pacer §22 *tr* to pasture, graze; gnaw, eat away || *intr* to pasture, graze
pacha•cho -cha *adj* (Chile) short-legged; (Chile) lax, lazy; (Chile) chubby
pa•chón -chona *adj* (CAm) shaggy, hairy, wooly || *m* (*perro*) pointer; (*hombre flemático*) sluggard
pachorra *f* sluggishness, indolence
pachotada *f* silliness
paciencia *f* patience
paciente *adj & mf* patient
pacienzu•do -da *adj* long-suffering
pacifica•dor -dora *adj* peace || *mf* peacemaker
pacificar §73 *tr* to pacify || *intr* to sue for peace || *ref* to calm down
pacífi•co -ca *adj* pacific; **el (océano) Pacífico** the Pacific (Ocean)
pacifismo *m* pacifism
pacifista *adj & mf* pacifist
pa•co -ca *adj* (Chile) bay, reddish || *m* paco, alpaca; Moorish sniper; sniper || **Paco** *m* Frank
pacotilla *f* trash, junk; (Chile) rabble, mob; **hacer su pacotilla** to make a cleanup; **ser de pacotilla** to be shoddy, be poorly made
pacotille•ro -ra *mf* (Chile, Ven) peddler
pactar *tr* to agree upon || *intr* to come to an agreement
pacto *m* pact, covenant, agreement, deal; **pacto de caballeros** gentlemen's agreement; **pacto de no agresión** nonaggression pact

padecer §22 *tr* to suffer; be victim of || *intr* to suffer
padrastro *m* stepfather; hangnail
padre *adj* huge; (Peru) terrific || *m* father; stallion, sire; **padres** parents; ancestors; **padres de la patria** founding fathers; **tener el padre alcalde** to have pull
padrenuestro *m* Lord's Prayer
padrina *f* godmother
padrinazgo *m* godfathership; sponsorship, patronage
padrino *m* godfather; sponsor; (*en un desafío*) second; **padrino de boda** best man; **padrinos** godparents
padrón *m* poll, census; pattern, model; memorial column; indulgent father; stallion; (Col) stock bull
padrote *m* stock animal; (Mex) pimp, procurer
paella *f* (culin) paella
paf *interj* bang!
pág. *abbr* **página**
paga *f* pay, payment; wages; fine; **como paga y señal** on account; as down payment
paga-alquiler *f* rent, rent money
pagadero -ra *adj* payable
paga•do -da *adj* pleased, cheerful; **estamos pagados** we are quits; **pagado de sí mismo** self-satisfied, conceited
paga•dor -dora *adj* paying || *mf* payer || *m* paymaster
paganismo *m* paganism
paga•no -na *adj & mf* pagan; (pej) heathen || *m* (Esp) (coll) easy mark
pagar §44 *tr* to pay; pay for; (*una bondad, una visita*) return || *intr* to pay; **sin pagar** without paying, scot-free || *ref* to become fond; be flattered; boast; be satisfied
pagaré *m* promissory note, I.O.U.
página *f* page
paginar *tr* to page
pago *m* payment; (*de viñas u olivares*) district, region; **pago contra reembolso** collect on delivery
pagote *m* scapegoat
paila *f* large pan
pairar *intr* (naut) to lie to
país *m* country, land; landscape; **el país de Gales** Wales; **el país de México** Mexico; **los Países Bajos** (*Bélgica, Holanda y Luxemburgo*) the Low Countries; (*Holanda*) The Netherlands; **países no alineados** Third World countries
paisaje *m* landscape; **paisaje lunar** moonscape
paisajista *mf* landscape painter
paisa•no -na *adj* of the same country || *mf* peasant; civilian; (Mex) Spaniard || *m* fellow countryman; **de paisano** in civies
paja *f* straw; chaff; trash, rubbish; **no dormirse en las pajas** to not let the grass grow under one's feet; **no levantar paja del suelo** to not lift a hand, not do a stroke of work
pájara *f* paper kite; paper rooster; bird; crafty female
pajarera *f* aviary; large bird cage
pajarería *f* flock of birds; bird store; pet shop
pajare•ro -ra *adj* bright, cheerful; bright-colored, gaudy || *m* bird dealer; bird fancier || *f* see **pajarera**
pajarita *f* paper kite; bow tie; wing collar, piccadilly
pájaro *m* bird; crafty fellow; expert; **pájaro bobo** penguin; motmot; **pájaro carpintero** woodpecker; **pájaro de cuenta** big shot; **pájaro mosca** hummingbird
pajarota *f* or **pajarotada** *f* hoax, canard
paje *m* page; valet; dressing table; (naut) cabin boy
pajilla *f* cornhusk cigarette; **pajilla de madera** excelsior
paji•zo -za *adj* straw; straw-colored; straw-thatched
pajuela *f* short straw; sulfur match or fuse; toothpick; (Bol) match
Pakistán, el var of **Paquistán**
pakista•ní (*pl* **-níes**) *adj & mf var of* **paquistaní**
pala *f* shovel; (*de remo, de la azada, etc.*) blade; (*del panadero*) peel; scoop; racket; (*del calzado*) upper; (*de excavadora*) bucket; shoulder strap; (coll) cunning, craftiness
palabra *f* word; speech; (*de una canción*) words; (*derecho para hablar en asambleas*) floor; **palabra de moda** buzz word; **palabras mayores** words, angry words; **remojar la palabra** to wet one's whistle; **usar de la palabra** to speak, make a speech
palabre•ro -ra *adj* wordy, windy || *mf* windbag
palabrota *f* (coll) vulgarity, obscenity, cussword, swearword
palabru•do -da *adj* talkative; chattering
palacie•go -ga *adj* palace, court || *m* courtier
palacio *m* palace; mansion; **palacio municipal** city hall
palada *f* shovelful; (*de remo*) stroke
paladar *m* palate; taste; gourmet
paladear *tr* to taste, relish
paladín *m* champion, hero
palafrén *m* palfrey
palanca *f* lever; pole; crowbar; influence; influential person; **palanca de cambios** gearshift; **palanca de mando** (aer) joystick; **palanca de mayúsculas** shift key
palancada *f* leverage
palangana *f* washbowl, basin
palanganear *intr* to brag, give oneself airs
palanganero *m* washstand
palangre *m* trawl, trawl line
palanqueta *f* jimmy; **palanquetas** (Arg) dumbbell
palatal *adj & f* palatal
palco *m* (theat) box
palear *tr* to beat, pound; shovel
palenque *m* paling, palisade; (SAm) hitching post; (C-R) Indian ranch; (Chile) pandemonium
paleta *f* palette; small shovel; trowel; (*de una rueda*) paddle; blade, bucket, vane; shoulder

blade; (*dulce con un palito que sirve de mango*) lollipop; **paleta flotante** (compu) floating palette
paletilla *f* shoulder blade
paleto *m* fallow deer; rustic, yokel
palia *f* altar cloth; (eccl) pall
paliacate *m* (Mex) bandanna
paliar §77 & regular *tr* to palliate
palidecer §22 *intr* to pale, to turn pale
palidez *f* paleness, pallor
páli•do -da *adj* pale, pallid
palillo *m* toothpick; drumstick; bobbin; **palillos** chopsticks; castanets; rudiments; trifles
palinodia *f* backdown; **cantar la palinodia** to eat crow, eat humble pie
palique *m* chit-chat, small talk
paliquear *intr* to chat, to gossip
palito *m* small stick; **palito de pescado** (culin) fish stick
paliza *f* beating, thrashing
palizada *f* fenced-in enclosure; stockade; embankment
pallador *m* (SAm) Gaucho minstrel
palma *f* (*de la mano*) palm; (*árbol y hoja*) palm; **batir palmas** to clap, to applaud; **llevarse la palma** to carry off the palm
palmada *f* slap; hand, applause, clapping; **dar palmadas** to clap hands
palma•rio -ria *adj* clear, evident
palmatoria *f* candlestick, candleholder
palmera *f* date palm
palmito *m* palmetto; woman's face; slender figure
palmo *m* span, palm; **dejar con un palmo de narices** (coll) to disappoint
palmotear *tr* to pat; clap, applaud || *intr* to clap, applaud
palo *m* stick; pole; staff; handle; tree; (*golpe*) whack; (*madera*) wood; (*grupo de naipes de la baraja*) suit; (naut) mast; **dar palos de ciego** to lay about, swing wildly; **de tal palo tal astilla** like father like son; **palo de escoba** broomstick; **palo de mesana** (naut) mizzenmast; **palo en alto** (fig) big stick; **palo mayor** (naut) mainmast; **servir del palo** to follow suit
paloma *f* pigeon, dove; prostitute; (fig) dove, meek person; **paloma mensajera** carrier pigeon; **palomas** whitecaps
palomar *m* pigeon house, dovecot
palomilla *f* doveling; small butterfly; white horse; (*del caballo*) back; pillow block, journal bearing; (CAm, Mex) rabble, scum; **palomillas** whitecaps
palomita *f* doveling; (baseball) fly; **palomitas** popcorn
palpable *adj* palpable
palpar *tr* to touch, feel; grope through || *intr* to grope
palpitante *adj* throbbing; thrilling; (*cuestión*) burning
palpitar *intr* to palpitate, throb; (*un afecto*) flash, break forth
pálpito *m* (SAm) hunch
palta *f* (SAm) alligator pear, avocado (*fruit*)
palto *m* (SAm) alligator pear, avocado (*tree*)
palúdi•co -ca *adj* marshy; malarial
paludismo *m* malaria
palur•do -da *adj* rustic, boorish || *mf* rustic, boor
pampa *f* pampa; **La Pampa** the Pampas
pámpana *f* vine leaf
pámpano *m* tendril; vine leaf
pan *m* bread; loaf; loaf of bread; wheat; food; livelihood; pie dough; (*de jabón, cera, etc.*) cake; gold foil or leaf; silver foil or leaf; **como el pan bendito** as easy as pie; **de pan llevar** arable, tillable; **llamar al pan pan y al vino vino** to call a spade a spade; **pan de carne** meat loaf; **pan de los ángeles** communion wafer; **panes** grain, breadstuff; **pan integral** whole-wheat bread; **pan moreno** *or* **negro** brown bread; **venderse como pan bendito** to sell like hot cakes || **Pan** *m* Pan
pana *f* corduroy; (aut) breakdown
panacea *f* panacea
panadería *f* bakery; baking business
panade•ro -ra *mf* baker; (Chile) flatterer
panadizo *m* felon; sickly person
panal *m* honeycomb
pana•má *m* (*pl* **-maes**) Panama hat
paname•ño -ña *adj & mf* Panamanian
panamerica•no -na *adj* Pan-American
pancarta *f* placard, poster
pancho *m* paunch, belly; (SAm) hot dog
pancista *adj* weaseling || *mf* weaseler
páncre•as *m* (*pl* **-as**) pancreas
pandear *intr & ref* to warp, bulge, buckle, sag, bend
pandeo *m* warp, deformation, warping
pandereta *f* tambourine
pandilla *f* party, faction; gang, band; picnic, excursion
pan•do -da *adj* bulging; slow-moving; slow, deliberate
pandorga *f* kite; fat, lazy woman
panecillo *m* roll, crescent
panel *m* panel; departures board; **panel de control** (compu) control panel
panfleto *m* pamphlet
paniaguado *m* servant, minion; protégé, favorite
páni•co -ca *adj* panic, panicky || *m* panic
panizo *m* Italian millet; (Chile) gangue; (Chile) abundance
panocha *f* ear of grain; ear of corn; pancake made of corn and cheese; (Mex) panocha (*brown sugar*)
panoja *f* ear of grain; ear of corn
panorama *m* panorama
pano•so -sa *adj* mealy
panqué *m* or **panqueque** *m* pancake
pantalán *m* pier, wooden pier
pantalla *f* lamp shade; fire screen; motion-picture screen; television screen; (*persona que encubre a otra*) blind; (*cine, arte del cine*) screen; fan; visual display unit; **llevar a la**

pantalla to put on the screen; **pantalla acústica** loudspeaker; baffle; **pantalla ancha** wide screen; **pantalla de plata** silver screen; **pantalla divida** (compu, mov, telv) split screen; **pequeña pantalla** television screen; **servir de pantalla a** to be a blind for

pantalón *m* trousers; **calzarse los pantalones** to wear the pants; **pantalones** trousers, pants; **pantalones azules** (CAm) blue jeans; **pantalones de mezclilla** (C-R, Mex) blue jeans; **pantalones con peto, pantalon de peto** jeans, dungarees, overalls

pantano *m* bog, marsh, swamp; dam, reservoir; trouble, obstacle

pantano•so -sa *adj* marshy, swampy; muddy; knotty, difficult

panteísmo *m* pantheism

panteón *m* pantheon, mausoleum; cemetery

pantera *f* panther

pantomima *f* pantomime

pantoque *m* (naut) bilge

pantorrilla *f* calf (*of leg*)

pants *mpl* (Mex) sweatsuit, tracksuit

pantufla *f* or **pantuflo** *m* house slipper

panty *m* panty hose

panza *f* paunch, belly

panzu•do -da *adj* paunchy, big-bellied

pañal *m* diaper; shirttail; **pañales** swaddling clothes; infancy; early stages

pañe•ro -ra *adj* dry-goods, cloth || *mf* dry-goods dealer, clothier

paño *m* cloth; rag; (*de agujas*) paper; (*ancho de la tela*) breadth; (*mancha en el rostro*) spot; (*en p.ej., un espejo*) blur; sailcloth, canvas; **al paño** off-stage; **conocer el paño** to know one's business, to know the ropes; **paño de adorno** doily; **paño de cocina** washrag, dishcloth; **paño de lágrimas** helping hand, stand-by; **paño de mesa** tablecloth; **paño de tumba** crape; **paño higiénico** sanitary napkin; **paño mortuorio** pall; **paños menores** underclothing; **paños tibios** appeasement attempts

pañuelo *m* handkerchief; shawl; **pañuelo de hierbas** bandanna

papa *m* pope || *f* potato; fake, hoax; food, grub; snap, cinch; **ni papa** nothing; **papa dulce** sweet potato; **papas a la francesa** (Col, Mex) French fries, fries; **papas chip** (Urug) potato chips; **papas fritas** French fries, fries; potato chips

pa•pá *m* (*pl* **-pás**) papa, daddy

papada *f* double chin; (*de animal*) dewlap; (Guat) stupidity

papado *m* papacy

papagayo *m* parrot

papalina *f* sunbonnet; drunk

papana•tas *m* (*pl* **-tas**) simpleton, gawk

Papanicolau *m* Pap smear, Pap test

paparrucha *f* hoax; trifle; **paparruchas** baloney, tripe

papel *m* paper; piece of paper; role, part; character, figure; **desempeñar** *or* **hacer un papel** to play a role; **papel alquitranado** tar paper; **papel cebolla** onionskin; **papel crepé** crepe paper; **papel de empapelar** wallpaper; **papel de esmeril** emery paper; **papel de estaño** tin foil; **papel de estraza** brown wrapping paper; **papel de excusado** toilet paper; **papel de fumar** cigarette paper; **papel de lija** sandpaper; **papel de oficio** foolscap; **papel (de) periódico** *or* **prensa** newsprint; **papel de seda** tissue paper; **papel de segundón** (fig) second fiddle; **papel de tornasol** litmus paper; **papel filtrante** filter paper; **papel higiénico** toilet paper; **papel moneda** paper money; **papel pintado** wallpaper; **papel secante** blotting paper; **papel viejo** waste paper; **papel volante** handbill, printed leaflet

papelada *f* farce; ridiculous act

papeleo *m* paperwork; red tape

papelera *f* paper case; writing desk; wastebasket; paper factory; (compu) trash can

papelería *f* stationery store; mess of papers, litter

papelerío *m* paper work

papele•ro -ra *adj* paper; boastful, showy || *mf* stationer; paper manufacturer; (Mex) paperboy || *f* see **papelera**

papeleta *f* slip of paper; card, file card; ticket; **papeleta de empeño** pawn ticket

papelista *m* paper maker, paper manufacturer; stationer; paper hanger

pape•lón -lona *adj* bluffing, four-flushing || *mf* bluffer, four-flusher || *m* thin cardboard

papelonear *intr* to bluff, to four-flush

papelote *m* worthless piece of paper; paper kite

papel-prensa *m* newsprint

papera *f* goiter; mumps

papila *f* — **papila gustativa** taste bud

papilla *f* pap; guile, deceit; baby food; puree

papiro *m* papyrus

papirote *m* fillip, flick; nincompoop

paq. *abbr* **paquete**

paquear *tr* to snipe at || *intr* to snipe

paque•te -ta *adj* self-important, pompous; (Arg) chic, dolled-up || *m* package, parcel, bundle, bale; sport, dandy; **darse paquete** (Guat, Mex) to put on airs; **en paquete aparte** under separate cover, in a separate package; **paquete de autor** (compu) authoring package; **paquetes postales** parcel post

Paquistán, el Pakistan

paquista•ní (*pl* **-níes**) or **paquistano -na** *adj & mf* Pakistani

Paquita *f* Fanny

par *adj* like, similar, equal; (math) even || *mf* peer, equal || *m* pair, couple; (elec, mech) couple; (math) even number; **a pares** in twos; **de par en par** wide-open; completely; overtly; **par de torsión** (mech, phys) torque; **¿pares o nones?** odd or even?; **sin par** without equal, peerless || *f* par; **a la par** equally; jointly; at the same time; at part; neck and neck, even up; **bajo la par** below par, under par; **sobre la par** above par

para *prep* to, for; towards; compared to; (*antes de*) by; **para** + *inf* in order to + *inf;* **para con** towards; **para que** in order that, so that
parabién *m* congratulation
parábola *f* parable
parabri•sa *m* or **parabri•sas** *m* (*pl* **-sas**) windshield
paracaí•das *m* (*pl* **-das**) parachute; **lanzar en paracaídas** to airdrop; **lanzarse en paracaídas** to parachute; **salvarse en paracaídas** to parachute to safety
paracaidismo *m* parachute jumping; (sport) sky diving
paracaidista *mf* parachutist; (coll) gatecrasher || *m* paratrooper
parachis•pas *m* (*pl* **-pas**) spark arrester
paracho•ques *m* (*pl* **-ques**) bumper
parachutar *intr* to parachute
paracorto *m* (Col, Ven) shortstop
parada *f* stop; end; stay; shutdown; (*en el juego*) stake; dam; (*para el ganado*) stall; stud farm; (*en la esgrima*) parry; (*tiro de caballerías de reemplazo*) relay; (mil) parade, dress parade, review; **parada de taxi** taxi stand; **parada opcional** flag stop **paradas cortas** (baseball) (Mex) shortstop
paradero *m* end; whereabouts; stopping place; wayside station
para•do -da *adj* slow, spiritless, witless; idle, unemployed; closed; proud, stiff; **quedar bien parado** to be lucky; **quedar mal parado** to be unlucky || *f* see **parada**
paradoja *f* paradox
paradóji•co -ca *adj* paradoxical
parador *m* inn, wayside inn; motel; **parador de carretera** drive-in restaurant; **parador en corto** (baseball) (Mex) shortstop
parafina *f* paraffin
paragol•pes *m* (*pl* **-pes**) buffer, bumper
para•guas *m* (*pl* **-guas**) umbrella
Paraguay, el Paraguay
paraguaya•no -na or **paragua•yo -ya** *adj & mf* Paraguayan
paragüero *m* umbrella man; umbrella stand
paraíso *m* paradise
paraje *m* place, spot; state, condition
paralela *f* parallel, parallel line; **paralelas** parallel bars
paralelizar §60 *tr* to parallel, compare
parale•lo -la *adj* parallel || *m* (geog) parallel || *f* see **paralela**
paráli•sis *f* (*pl* **-sis**) paralysis; **parálisis agitante** *or* **temblorosa** Parkinson's disease; **parálisis cerebral** cerebral palsy
paralíti•co -ca *adj & mf* paralytic
paralizar §60 *tr* to paralyze || *ref* to become paralyzed
parámetro *m* parameter; established boundary
páramo *m* high barren plain; bleak windy spot; (Bol, Col, Ecuad) cold drizzle
paranie•ves *m* (*pl* **-ves**) snow fence
paraninfo *m* assembly hall, auditorium
paranoi•co -ca *adj & mf* paranoiac
parapeto *m* parapet
parapléji•co -ca *adj & mf* paraplegic
parar *tr* to stop; check; change; prepare; put up, stake; parry; order; get, acquire; (*la atención*) fix; (*la caza*) point; (typ) to set || *intr* to stop; (*en un hotel*) put up; **parar en** to become; run to, run as far as || *ref* to stop; stop work; stand; turn, become; (*el perro de muestra*) point; (*el pelo*) stand on end; **pararse en** to pay attention to
pararra•yo *m* or **pararra•yos** *m* (*pl* **-yos**) (*barra metálica que sirve para preservar los edificios del rayo*) lightning rod; (*dispositivo que sirve para preservar una instalación eléctrica de la electricidad atmosférica o de las chispas que produce*) lightning arrester
parasíti•co -ca *adj* parasitic
parási•to -ta *adj* parasitic; (elec) stray || *m* parasite; **parásitos atmosféricos** atmospherics, static
parasol *m* parasol
parato•pes *m* (*pl* **-pes**) bumper
Parcas *fpl* Fates
parcela *f* particle; plot of ground; subdivision; (compu) site
parcelación *f* (*parcela*) subdivision
parcelar *tr* to parcel, divide into lots
parchar *tr* to mend, patch
parche *m* plaster, sticking plaster; patch; eyepatch; drum; drumhead; daub, botch, splotch; **parche poroso** porous plaster
parcial *adj* partial; partisan || *mf* partisan
parcialidad *f* partiality
par•co -ca *adj* frugal, sparing; moderate
parcómetro *m* parking meter
pardal *m* linnet; sly fellow
pardiez *interj* by Jove!
pardillo *m* linnet
par•do -da *adj* brown, drab; dark; cloudy; (*voz*) dull, flat; (*cerveza*) dark; mulatto || *mf* mulatto || *m* brown, drab; leopard
pardus•co -ca *adj* dark-brown, drabbish
parea•do -da *adj* rhymed || *m* couplet
parear *tr* to pair; match || *ref* to pair off
parecer *m* opinion; look, mien, countenance || *v* **§22** *intr* to appear; show up; look, seem; **me parece que. . . .** I think that. . . . || *ref* to look alike, resemble each other; **parecerse a** to look like
pareci•do -da *adj* like, similar; **bien parecido** good-looking; **parecido a** like, e.g., **esta casa es parecida a la otra** this house is like the other one; **parecidos** alike, e.g., **estas casas son parecidas** these houses are alike || *m* similarity, resemblance, likeness; **tener un gran parecido** to be a good likeness
pared *f* wall; **dejar pegado a la pared** to nonplus; **paredes** house
pareja *f* pair, couple; dancing partner; **correr parejas** *or* **a las parejas** to be abreast, arrive together; go together, match, be equal; **correr parejas con** to keep up with, keep abreast of; **parejas** (*de naipes*) pair

pareje•ro -ra *adj* even, equal; servile, fawning; forward, overfamiliar || *m* race horse
pare•jo -ja *adj* equal, like; even, smooth; **parejos** neck and neck, even up || *m* (CAm) dancing partner || *f* see **pareja**
parentela *f* kinsfolk, relations
parentesco *m* relationship; bond, tie
parénte•sis *m* (*pl* **-sis**) parenthesis; break, interval
parhilera *f* ridgepole
paria *mf* pariah, outcast
paridad *f* par, parity; comparison; equality; exchange rate
parien•te -ta *adj* related || *mf* relative; (coll) spouse
parihuela *f* handbarrow; (*camilla*) stretcher
parir *tr* to bear, give birth to, bring forth || *intr* to give birth; come forth, come to light; talk well
París *m* Paris
parisiense *adj & mf* Parisian
parking *m* parking (space); parking lot
parlamentar *intr* to talk, chat; parley
parlamento *m* parliament; parley; speech; (theat) speech
parlan•chín -china *adj* jabbering || *mf* chatterbox
parlante *m* loudspeaker
parlar *intr* to speak with facility; chatter, talk too much; (*el loro*) talk
parle•ro -ra *adj* loquacious, garrulous; gossipy; (*ave*) singing, song; (*ojos*) expressive; (*arroyo, fuente*) babbling
parlotear *intr* to prattle, jabber, chin
parloteo *m* jabber, prattle
paro *m* shutdown, work stoppage; strike; lockout; titmouse; (*de dados*) (SAm) throw; **paro cardíaco** heart failure; **paro forzoso** layoff
parodia *f* parody, travesty
parodiar *tr* to parody, travesty, burlesque
parón *m* stop; delay; **parón cíclico** rolling blackout
paroxíto•no -na *adj & m* paroxytone
parpadear *intr* to blink, wink; flicker
parpadeo *m* blinking, winking; flicker
párpado *m* eyelid
parque *m* park; parking; parking lot; **parque de atracciones** amusement park; **parque eólico** wind farm;
parqué *m* floor, inlaid floor
parqueadero *m* (Col) parking lot
parquear *tr* to park
parquímetro *m* parking meter
parra *f* grapevine; earthen jug
párrafo *m* paragraph; chat
parral *m* grape arbor
parranda *f* spree, party; (Col) large number; **andar de parranda** to go out on a spree, go out to celebrate
parricida *mf* patricide, parricide
parricidio *m* patricide, parricide
parrilla *f* grill, gridiron, broiler; grate, grating; grillroom, grill; **asar a la parrilla** to broil; grill
parrillada *f* barbecue
párroco *m* parish priest
parroquia *f* parish; parish church; customers, clientele
parroquial *adj* parochial
parroquia•no -na *mf* parishioner; customer
parte *m* dispatch, communiqué, report; (SAm) ticket, fine; **parte de defunción** death certificate; **parte meteorológico** weather report || *f* part; share; party; side; direction; (*papel de un actor*) role; (law) party; **de un mes a esta parte** for about a month past; **en ninguna otra parte** nowhere else; **en ninguna parte** nowhere; **ir a la parte** to go shares; **la mayor parte** most, the majority; **parte del león** lion's share; **parte de por medio** (theat) bit part, walk-on; **partes** parts, gifts, talent; faction; parts, genitals; **por otra parte** in another direction; elsewhere; on the other hand; **por todas partes** everywhere; **salva sea la parte** excuse me for not mentioning where
partea•guas *m* (*pl* **-guas**) divide, ridge
partear *tr* to deliver
parte•luz *m* (*pl* **-luces**) mullion, sash bar
partenogénesis *f* parthenogenesis
Partenón *m* Parthenon
partera *f* midwife
partición *f* partition, division
participación *f* participation
participar *tr* to notify, inform; give notice of || *intr* to participate; partake
participio *m* participle
partícula *f* particle
particular *adj* particular; peculiar; private, personal || *m* particular; matter, subject; individual; **particular a particular** (telp) person-to-person
particulizar §60 *tr* to itemize || *ref* to stand out; specialize
partida *f* departure; entry, item; certificate; party, group, band; band of guerrillas; game; (*de cartas*) hand; (*de tenis*) set; lot, shipment; behavior; **mala partida** mean trick; **partida de campo** picnic; **partida doble** (com) double entry; **partida sencilla** (com) single entry
partida•rio -ria or **partidista** *adj & mf* partisan, sympathizer
parti•do -da *adj* generous, open-handed || *m* (pol) party; decision; profit; advantage; step, measure; deal, agreement; protection, support; (*casamiento que elegir*) match; district, county; (sport) team; (sport) game, match; **partido de béisbol** ball game; **partido de desempate** play-off; **partido de homenaje** benefit game *o* match; **tomar partido** to take a stand, take sides || *f* see **partida**
partir *tr* to divide; distribute; share; split, split open; break, crack; upset, disconcert || *intr* to start, depart, leave, set out; **a partir de** beginning with || *ref* to become divided; crack, split
partisa•no -na *mf* (mil) partisan

partitura *f* (mus) score
parto *m* childbirth, confinement; newborn child; offspring; **estar de parto** to be in labor, be confined; **parto del ingenio** brain child
parva *f* light breakfast (*on fast days*); heap of unthreshed grain; heap, pile
parvulario *m* nursery school; kindergarten
parvulista *mf* kindergarten teacher
párvu•lo -la *adj* small, tiny; simple, innocent; humble || *mf* child, tot; (*niño*) kindergartner
pasa *f* raisin; (*del pelo de los negros*) kink; **pasa de Corinto** currant
pasada *f* passage; passing; **de pasada** in passing, hastily; **mala pasada** mean trick
pasade•ro -ra *adj* passable || *f* stepping stone; walkway, catwalk
pasadizo *m* passage, corridor, hallway, alley; catwalk
pasa•do -da *adj* past; gone by; overripe, spoiled; overdone; stale; burned out; antiquated; faded || *m* past; **pasados** ancestors || *f* see **pasada**
pasa•dor -dora *mf* smuggler || *m* door bolt; bolt, pin; hatpin; brooch; stickpin; safety pin; strainer
pasaje *m* passage; fare; fares; passengers; **cobrar el pasaje** to collect fares
pasaje•ro -ra *adj* passing, fleeting; (*camino, calle*) common, traveled || *mf* passenger; hotel guest; **pasajero colgado** straphanger; **pasajero no presentado** no-show
pasamano *m* lace trimming; (*baranda*) handrail; (naut) gangway
pasamonta•ña *m* or **pasamonta•ñas** *m* (*pl* **-ñas**) ski mask, storm hood
pasaporte *m* passport
pasapuré *m* potato masher
pasar *m* livelihood || *tr* to pass; cross; take across; send, transfer, transmit; (*contrabando*) slip in; spend; swallow; excel; overlook, stand for; undergo, suffer; (*un libro*) go through; (*una película*) show; dry in the sun; tutor; study with or under; **pasarlo** to get along; live; (*dícese de la salud*) be; **pasar por alto** to disregard; omit, leave out, skip || *intr* to pass; go; pass away; pass over; happen; last; spread; get along; yield; come in, e.g., **pase Ud.** come in; **pasar de** to go beyond, exceed; to go above; be more than; **pasar por** to pass by, down, through, over, etc.; pass as, pass for; stop or call at; **pasar sin** to do without || *ref* to pass; go; excel; pass over; get along; pass away; take an examination; leak; go too far; become overripe, become overcooked; rot; melt; burn out; (*una llave, un tornillo*) not fit, be loose; forget; **pasarse por** to stop or call at; **pasarse sin** to do without
pasarela *f* footbridge; catwalk, gangplank
pasatiempo *m* pastime
Pascua *f* (*fiesta cristiana*) Easter; (*fiesta judía*) Passover; (*Navidad*) Christmas; (*Epifanía*) Epiphany; (*Pentecostés*) Pentecost; **dar las pascuas a** to wish (*someone*) a Happy New Year; **de Pascuas a Ramos** once in a blue moon; **estar como unas pascuas** (coll) to be bubbling over with joy; **¡Felices Pascuas!** Merry Christmas!; **Pascuas Florida** *or* **de Resurrección** Easter; **pascuas** Christmas to Epiphany; **santas pascuas** (coll) that's that
pase *m* (*en fútbol, baloncesto, rugby; permiso; billete gratuito; movimiento de las manos del mesmerista or del torero*) pass; (*en la esgrima*) feint; **pase de cortesía** complimentary ticket
paseante *adj* strolling || *mf* stroller
pasear *tr* to walk; promenade, show off || *intr* to take a walk; go for a ride || *ref* to take a walk; go for a ride; wander, ramble; take it easy
paseíllo *m* processional entrance of bullfighters
paseo *m* walk, stroll, promenade; ride; drive; avenue; **dar un paseo** to take a walk; take a ride; **enviar a paseo** to send on his way, dismiss without ceremony; **paseo de caballos** bridle path; **paseo de la cuadrilla** processional entrance of the bullfighters
pasillo *m* short step; passage, corridor; (theat) short piece, sketch
pasión *f* passion
pasi•vo -va *adj* passive; (*pensión*) retirement || *m* liabilities; debit side
pasmar *tr* to chill; frostbite; stun, benumb; dumbfound, astound || *ref* to chill; become frostbitten; be astounded; get lockjaw; (*los colores*) become dull or flat
pasmo *m* cold; lockjaw, tetanus; astonishment; wonder, prodigy
pasmo•so -sa *adj* astounding; awesome
paso *m* step; pace; (*de la escalera*) step; gait; walk; passing; passage; step, measure, démarche; pass, permit; strait; footstep, footprint; incident, happening; (*de hélice, tornillo*) pitch; (elec) pitch; (rad) stage; (theat) short piece, sketch, skit; **al paso** in passing, on the way; **al paso que** at the rate that; (*a la vez que, mientras*) while, whereas; **ceder el paso** to make way; to keep clear; **de paso** in passing; at the same time; **paso a nivel** grade crossing; **paso de ganado** cattle crossing; **paso de ganso** goose step; **paso de gatos** (Mex) catwalk; **paso de peatones** crosswalk; **paso elevado** overpass; **paso fronterizo** border crossing; **paso subterráneo** underpass
paspa *f* (SAm) crack in the lips
pasquín *m* lampoon
pasquinar *tr* to lampoon
pasta *f* pasta; paste; pastry; mash; cardboard; board binding; (*de un diente*) filling; (*dinero*) (coll) dough; **pasta dentrífica, dental** *or* **de dientes** toothpaste; **pasta de papel** wood pulp; **pasta de té** (Esp) cookie; **pasta española** marbled leather binding, tree calf; **pastas** noodles, macaroni, spaghetti, etc.; **pasta seca** cookie
pastar *tr & intr* to graze
pastel *m* pie; pastry roll; pastel; settlement, pacification; cheat, trick; (typ) pi; (typ) smear;

(coll) plot, deal; **descubrir el pastel** to blab a secret; **pastel de cumpleaños** birthday cake; **pastel de picadillo de fruta** mince pie
pastelería *f* pastry; pastry shop
pastele•ro -ra *mf* pastry cook
pastelillo *m* tart, cake; (*de mantequilla*) pat
pasterizar §60 *tr* to pasteurize
pastilla *f* tablet, lozenge, drop; (*pequeña masa pastosa*) dab; (*de jabón, chocolate, etc.*) cake
pastinaca *f* parsnip
pasto *m* pasture; grass; food, nourishment; **a pasto** to excess; in abundance; **a todo pasto** freely, without restriction; **de pasto** ordinary, everyday
pastor *m* shepherd; pastor
pastora *f* shepherdess
pastoral *adj & f* pastoral
pastorear *tr* (*a las ovejas o los fieles*) to shepherd; lie in ambush for; spoil, pamper; (Arg, Urug) to court
pasto•so -sa *adj* pasty, doughy; (*voz*) mellow; (Arg, Chile) grassy
pastura *f* pasture; fodder
pasu•do -da *adj* kinky
pata *f* paw, foot, leg; (*de un mueble*) leg; female duck; **a cuatro patas** on all fours; **estirar la pata** to kick the bucket; **meter la pata** to butt in, to put one's foot in it; **pata de cabra** crowbar; **pata de gallo** crow's-foot; blunder; piece of nonsense; **pata de palo** peg leg, wooden leg; **pata galana** game leg; lame person; **patas arriba** on one's back, upside down; topsy-turvy; **patas de rana** (SAm) flippers
patada *f* kick; stamp, stamping; step; footstep, track; **en dos patadas** in a jiffy; **patada corta** onside kick; **patada de inicio** kickoff; **patada fija** place kick; **patada voladora** dropkick
patalear *intr* to kick; stamp the feet
pataleta *f* fit; feigned fit or convulsion; (dial) tantrum
patán *m* churl, boor, lout; peasant, yokel
pataplún *interj* kerplunk!, crash!, wham!
patata *f* potato; **patatas fritas** (Esp) French fries, fries; potato chips
patear *tr* to kick; trample on || *intr* to stamp one's foot; bustle around; kick
patentar *tr* to patent
patente *adj* patent, clear, evident || *f* grant, privilege, warrant; patent; **de patente** (Chile) excellent, first-class; **patente de circulación** owner's license; **patente de invención** patent; **patente de sanidad** bill of health
paternal *adj* paternal, fatherly
paternidad *f* paternity, fatherhood; **paternidad literaria** authorship
pater•no -na *adj* paternal
pateta *m* (coll) the devil; cripple
patéti•co -ca *adj* pathetic
patetismo *m* pathos
patibula•rio -ria *adj* hair-raising
patíbulo *m* scaffold
patiesteva•do -da *adj* bowlegged
patilla *f* small paw or foot; pocket flap; watermelon; (compu) pinhole; (naut) compass; **patillas** sideburns, side whiskers
patín *m* small patio; skate; skid, slide, runner; (*ave marina*) petrel; **patín de cuchilla** *or* **de hielo** ice skate; **patín de ruedas** roller skate
patinada *f* (SAm) (aut) skidding
patinadero *m* skating rink
patina•dor -dora *mf* skater
patinaje *m* skating; skidding; **patinaje artístico** figure skating; **patinaje de fantasía** fancy skating; **patinaje de figura** figure skating; **patinaje de velocidad** speed skating
patinar *intr* to skate; skid; slip
patinazo *m* skid; slip; slip, blunder
patinete *m* scooter; (SAm) skateboard
patio *m* patio, court, yard; campus; (rr) yard, switchyard; (theat) (Esp) orchestra; **patio de operaciones** (com) floor (*or an exchange*); **patio de recreo** playground
patituer•to -ta *adj* crooked-legged; crooked, lopsided
patizam•bo -ba *adj* knock-kneed
pa•to -ta *adj* (SAm) (coll) broke || *mf* duck; **pagar el pato** to be the goat; **pato de flojel** eider duck; **pato real** mallard || *m* drake; (Esp) (coll) clodhopper
patochada *f* blunder, stupidity
patojo *m* (CAm) street urchin
patología *f* pathology
patológi•co -ca *adj* pathological
patota *f* (Arg, Urug) teenage gang
patraña *f* fake, humbug, hoax
patria *f* country; mother country, fatherland, native land; birthplace; (*p.ej., de las artes*) home; **patria chica** native region, hometown; **patria potestad** parental authority
patriarca *m* patriarch
Patricia *f* Patricia
patri•cio -cia *adj & mf* patrician || *m* **Patricio** Patrick
patrimonio *m* patrimony
pa•trio -tria *adj* native, home; paternal || *f* see **patria**
patriota *mf* patriot
patrióti•co -ca *adj* patriotic
patriotismo *m* patriotism
patrocinar *tr* to sponsor, patronize
patrocinio *m* sponsorship
pa•trón -trona *mf* employer, boss; owner; sponsor, protector; host; patron; patron saint; (*de un barco*) skipper || *m* landlord; master; foreman; pattern, standard; **patrón oro** gold standard; **patrón picado** stencil || *f* landlady; hostess; patroness
patronal *adj* management, employers
patronato *m* employers' association; foundation; board of trustees; patronage
patronear *tr* to skipper
patro•no -na *mf* employer, boss; sponsor, protector; patron || *m* landlord; boss, foreman; lord of the manor; **los patronos** the management || *f* landlady; hostess; patroness
patrulla *f* patrol; gang, band

patrullar *tr & intr* to patrol
paulati•no -na *adj* slow, gradual
pausa *f* pause; slowness, delay; (mus) rest
pausa•do -da *adj* slow, calm, deliberate ‖ **pausado** *adv* slowly, calmly
pausar *tr & intr* to slow down
pauta *f* ruler; guide lines; guideline, rule, guide, standard, model
pava *f* turkey hen; **pelar la pava** to make love at a window
pavesa *f* ember, cinder, spark
pavimentar *tr* to pave
pavimento *m* pavement
pa•vo -va *adj* (coll) silly, stupid ‖ *mf* turkey ‖ *m* turkey; turkey cock; **comer pavo** to be a wallflower; **pavo real** peacock ‖ *f* see **pava**
pavón *m* bluing; peacock
pavonar *tr* to blue
pavonear *intr & ref* to strut, swagger; grandstand
pavor *m* fear, terror, dread
pavoro•so -sa *adj* frightful, dreadful
payador *m* (SAm) gaucho minstrel
payasada *f* clownishness, clownish remark
payaso *m* clown; laughingstock
paz *f* (*pl* **paces**) peace; peacefulness; **dejar en paz** to leave alone, stop pestering; **estar en paz** to be even; to be quits; **hacer las paces con** to make peace with, to come to terms with; **salir en paz** to break even
pazgua•to -ta *adj* simple, doltish ‖ *mf* simpleton, dolt
pazpuerca *f* slut, slattern
P.D. *abbr* **posdata**
peaje *m* toll
peatón *m* pedestrian; rural postman
pebete *m* punk, joss stick; fuse; (*cosa hedionda*) (coll) stinker
peca *f* freckle
pecado *m* sin
peca•dor -dora *adj* sinning, sinful ‖ *mf* sinner
pecamino•so -sa *adj* sinful
pecar §73 *intr* to sin; **pecar de** to be too, e.g., **pecar de confiado** to be too trusting
pecera *f* fish globe, fish bowl
pechada *f* bump or push with the chest; tossing an animal (*with a bump of horse's chest*); bumping contest between two horsemen
pechar *tr* to pay as a tax; fulfill; take on; drive one's horse against; bump with the chest; strike for a loan ‖ *ref* (*dos jinetes*) to vie in a bumping contest
pechera *f* shirt front, shirt bosom; chest protector; (*del delantal*) bib; breast strap; (coll) bosom; **pechera postiza** dickey
pecho *m* chest; breast, bosom; heart, courage; **dar el pecho** to nurse, suckle; face it out; **de dos pechos** double-breasted; **de un solo pecho** single-breasted; **echar el pecho al agua** to put one's shoulder to the wheel; (coll) to speak out; **en pechos de camisa** in shirt sleeves; **tomar a pecho** to take to heart; **¡pecho al agua!** take heart!, put your shoulder to the wheel!
pechuga *f* (*del ave*) breast; slope, hill; brass, cheek; treachery, perfidy; (coll) bosom, breast
pechu•gón -gona *adj* big-chested; brazen ‖ *mf* sponger ‖ *m* slap or blow on the chest; fall on the chest
pecino•so -sa *adj* slimy
pecio *m* flotsam
pecíolo *or* **peciolo** *m* leafstalk
pécora *f* head of sheep; **buena pécora** *or* **mala pécora** schemer, scheming woman
peco•so -sa *adj* freckly, freckle-faced
peculado *m* embezzlement, peculation
peculiar *adj* peculiar
pecunia•rio -ria *adj* pecuniary
pedagogía *f* pedagogy
pedal *mf* pedal, treadle
pedalear *intr* to pedal
pedante *adj* pedantic ‖ *mf* pedant
pedantería *f* pedantry
pedantes•co -ca *adj* pedantic
pedantismo *m* pedantry
pedazo *m* piece; **hacer pedazos** to break to pieces; **hacerse pedazos** (coll) to fall to pieces; to strain, to wear oneself out; **pedazo de alcornoque, de animal** *or* **de bruto** dolt, imbecile, good-for-nothing; **pedazo del alma, de las entrañas** *or* **del corazón** (*niño*) darling, apple of one's eye; **pedazo de pan** (*pequeña cantidad*) crumb; (*precio bajo*) song
pederastia *f* pederasty
pedernal *m* flint; flintiness; flint-hearted person
pedestal *m* pedestal
pedestre *adj* pedestrian, prosaic, ordinary, dull
pedestrismo *m* walking; foot racing; cross-country racing
pediatra *mf* pediatrician
pediatría *f* pediatrics
pedicu•ro -ra *mf* podiatrist ‖ *f* pedicure
pedido *m* request; (*encargo de mercancías*) order
pedigüe•ño -ña *adj* insistent, demanding, bothersome
pedir §50 *tr* to ask, ask for; request; demand, require; need; ask for the hand of; (*mercancías*) order; (gram) to govern; **pedir prestado a** to borrow from ‖ *intr* to ask; beg; bring suit; **a pedir de boca** opportunely; as desired
pedorre•ro -ra *adj* flatulent ‖ *f* flatulence; (orn) tody; **pedorreras** tights
pedrada *f* stoning; hit or blow with a stone; hint, taunt
pedregal *m* rocky ground; pile of rocks
pedrego•so -sa *adj* stony, rocky; suffering from gallstones ‖ *mf* sufferer from gallstones
pedrejón *m* boulder
pedrera *f* quarry, stone quarry
pedrería *f* precious stones, jewelry
pedrusco *m* boulder
pedúnculo *m* stem, stalk
peer §43 *intr & ref* to break wind

pega *f* sticking; pitch varnish; drubbing; (*en un examen*) catch question; trick, joke; (W-I) work, jobs; **de pega** (coll) fake

pegadi•zo -za *adj* sticky; catching, contagious; sponging; fake, imitation

pegajo•so -sa *adj* sticky; contagious; tempting; soft, gentle; mushy

pegamento *m* glue, adhesive

pegapega *f* glue

pegar §44 *tr* to stick, paste; fasten, attach, tie; (*carteles*) post; (*fuego*) set; (*una enfermedad*) transmit; (*un botón*) sew on; (*un grito*) let out; (*un salto*) take; (*un golpe, una bofetada*) let go; beat; **no pegar el ojo** to not sleep a wink || *intr* to stick, catch; take root, take hold; cling; join; fit, match; be fitting; pass, be accepted; beat; knock || *ref* to stick, catch; take root, take hold; hang on, stick around; (*una enfermedad*) be catching; **pegársela a uno** to make a fool of someone

pegatina *f* sticker (or tag)

pegotear *intr* to hang around, sponge

peina•do -da *adj* groomed; effeminate || *m* hairdo, coiffure; (*manera de componer el pelo*) hairstyle; (*policía, soldados*) search; **peinado al agua** finger wave

peina•dor -dora *mf* hairdresser || *m* wrapper, dressing gown; dressing table

peinar *tr* to comb; (*policía, soldados*) search; **peinar a la moda** to style || *ref* to comb oneself, comb one's hair

peine *m* comb; sly fellow

peineta *f* back comb

p. ej. *abbr* **por ejemplo** for example

pelada *f* pelt, sheepskin

peladero *m* wasteland

peladilla *f* sugar almond; small pebble

peladillo *m* clingstone peach

pela•do -da *adj* bare; bald; barren; penniless; (*decena, centena, etc.*) even || *m* raggedy fellow; (W-I) haircut || *f* see **pelada**

pelafus•tán -tana *mf* derelict, good-for-nothing

pelaga•tos *m* (*pl* **-tos**) wretch, ragamuffin

pelaje *m* coat, fur; (*especie, calidad*) sort, stripe

pelapapas *m or* **pelapatatas** *m* potato peeler

pelar *tr* (*pelo*) to cut; (*pelo, plumas*) pluck, pull out; peel, skin, husk, hull, shell; (*los dientes*) show; (*en el juego*) clean out; beat, thrash || *ref* to peel off; lose one's hair; get a haircut; clear out, make a getaway; **pelárselas por** to crave; crave to

pelazón *f* poverty; misery

peldaño *m* step

pelea *f* fight; quarrel, dustup; struggle; **pelea de gallos** cockfight

pelear *intr* to fight; quarrel; struggle || *ref* to fight, fight each other

pele•ón -ona *adj* pugnacious, quarrelsome; (*vino*) cheap, ordinary || *mf* quarrelsome person || *m* cheap wine || *f* row, scuffle, fracas

peletería *f* furriery; fur shop; (Cuba) shoe store

pelete•ro -ra *mf* furrier; (Cuba) shoe dealer

peliagu•do -da *adj* furry, long-haired; arduous, ticklish

película *f* film; motion picture; **película de dibujos** animated cartoon; **película del Oeste** western; **película de terror** *or* **miedo, película horripilante** horror movie; **película de video** video film; **película muda** silent movie

pelicule•ro -ra *adj* moving-picture || *mf* scenario writer || *m* movie actor || *f* movie actress

peligrar *intr* to be in danger

peligro *m* danger, peril, risk; **peligro de muerte** *SIGN* danger; **peligro para la seguridad** security risk; **ponerse en peligro de paz** to be alerted for war

peligro•so -sa *adj* dangerous

pelillo *m* trifle; **echar pelillos a la mar** to bury the hatchet; **no pararse en pelillos** to not bother about trifles, pay no attention to small matters; **no tener pelillos en la lengua** to speak right out

pelirro•jo -ja *adj* red-haired, redheaded || *mf* redhead

pellejo *m* skin; pelt, rawhide; peel, rind; wineskin; (*la vida de uno*) (coll) hide, skin; (coll) sot, drunkard; **dar, dejar** *or* **perder el pellejo** to die

pellizcar §73 to pinch; nip; take a pinch of || *ref* to long, pine

pellizco *m* pinch; nip; bit, pinch

pelo *m* hair; (*en las frutas y el cuerpo humano*) down; (*del paño*) nap; (*de la madera*) grain; (*de un animal*) coat; (*en las piedras preciosas*) flaw; (*del caballo*) color; (*en el billar*) kiss; (*del reloj*) hairspring; hair trigger; fiber, filament; raw silk; **al pelo** with the hair, with the nap; perfectly, to the point; **con todos sus pelos y señales** chapter and verse; **en pelo** bareback; **escapar por un pelo** to escape by a hair-breadth, have a narrow escape; **no tener pelos en la lengua** to be outspoken, not mince words; **ponerle a uno los pelos de punta** to make one's hair stand on end; **tomar el pelo a** to make fun of, make a fool of; **venir a pelo** to come in handy

pe•lón -lona *adj* bald, hairless; dull, stupid; penniless

Pélope *m* Pelops

peloponense *adj & mf* Peloponnesian

Peloponeso *m* Peloponnesus

pelo•so -sa *adj* hairy

pelota *f* ball; ball game; handball; **en pelota** stripped; stark-naked; **pelota acuática** water polo; **pelota de fútbol** (*balón*) football; **pelota fuera del cuadro** (baseball) foul ball; **pelota rodada** (baseball) grounder; **pelota vasca** pelota, jai alai

pelotari *mf* pelota player

pelotear *intr* to knock a ball around; wrangle, argue

pelotera *f* row, brawl

pelotón *m* large ball; gang, crowd; platoon; **pelotón de fusilamiento** firing squad; **pelotón de los torpes** awkward squad

peltre *m* pewter
peluca *f* wig
peluche *m* plush, pile
pelu•do -da *adj* hairy, furry; bushy
peluquear *tr* (Col, Ven) to cut the hair of || *intr* (Col, Ven) to get a haircut
peluquería *f* hairdresser's, barbershop
peluque•ro -ra *mf* hairdresser; barber; wigmaker
peluquín *m* hairpiece; toupee
pelusa *f* down; lint, fuzz; nap; jealousy, envy
pena *f* punishment; penalty; pain, hardship, toil; sorrow, grief; effort, trouble; **a duras penas** hardly, with great difficulty; **de pena** of a broken heart; **pena capital, pena de muerte** capital punishment; **pena corporal** corporal punishment; **pena pecuniaria** fine; **pena privativa de libertad** imprisonment; **¡qué pena!** what a pity!; **so pena de** on pain of, under penalty of; **valer la pena** to be worthwhile (to)
penacho *m* crest; tuft, plume; arrogance; (bot) tassel
pena•do -da *adj* afflicted, grieved; difficult || *mf* convict
penalidad *f* trouble, hardship; (law) penalty
penalizar §60 *tr* to punish; penalize
penar *tr* to penalize; punish || *intr* to suffer; linger; **penar por** to pine for, long for || *ref* to grieve
penca *f* pulpy leaf; cowhide; **coger una penca** to get a jag on
penco *m* nag, jade; boor
pendejo *m* pubes; pubic hair; (coll) coward
pendencia *f* dispute, quarrel, fight; pending litigation
pendencie•ro -ra *adj* quarrelsome || *mf* wrangler
pender *intr* to hang, dangle; depend; be pending
pendiente *adj* pendent, hanging, dangling; pending; under way; expecting; **estar pendiente de** (*las palabras de una persona*) to hang on; depend on; be in the process of || *m* earring, pendant; watch chain || *f* slope, grade; dip, pitch
péndola *f* feather; pendulum; clock; pen, quill; queen post
pendolón *m* king post
pendón *m* banner, standard, pennon
péndulo *m* pendulum; clock
pene *m* penis
penetrar *tr* to penetrate; pierce; grasp, fathom || *intr* to penetrate || *ref* to grasp, fathom; realize; become convinced
penicilina *f* penicillin
península *f* peninsula
peninsular *adj & mf* peninsular; (*ibero*) Peninsular
penique *m* penny
penitencia *f* penitence; penance; **hacer penitencia** to do penance; eat sparingly; take potluck
penitente *adj & mf* penitent
penol *m* (naut) yardarm
peno•so -sa *adj* arduous, difficult; suffering; conceited; shy
pensa•dor -dora *adj* thinking || *mf* thinker
pensamiento *m* thought; (*planta y flor*) pansy
pensar §2 *tr* to think; think over; (*un naipe, un número, etc.*) think of; intend to; **pensar de** to think of, e.g., **¿qué piensa Ud. de este libro?** what do you think of this book? || *intr* to think; **pensar en** (*dirigir sus pensamientos a*) to think of (*to turn one's thoughts to*)
pensati•vo -va *adj* pensive, thoughtful
pensión *f* pension; annuity; allowance; boardinghouse; (*para ampliar estudios*) fellowship; **pensión alimenticia** alimony; **pension completa** board and lodging; **pensión de invalidez** disability benefit; **pensión de jubilación** retirement pension; **pensión vitalicia** annuity
pensionar *tr* to pension
pensionista *mf* pensioner; boarder, guest; boarding-school pupil; **medio pensionista** day boarder
pentagrama *m* staff, musical staff
Pentecostés, el Pentecost
penúlti•mo -ma *adj* penultimate; next to last || *f* penult
penumbra *f* penumbra; semidarkness, half-light
penuria *f* shortage
peña *f* rock, boulder; cliff; club, group, circle
peñasco *m* pinnacle; crag
peñasco•so -sa *adj* rocky, craggy
peñón *m* rock, spire; **peñón de Gibraltar** rock of Gibraltar
peón *m* laborer; pedestrian; foot soldier; farm hand; (*en el ajedrez*) pawn; (*en las damas*) man; top, peg top; spindle, axle; (taur) attendant; **peón de albañil** *or* **de mano** construction worker; **peón caminero** road worker
peor *adj & adv* worse; worst
pepa *f* (*de la manzana*) (Col) seed; (*del durazno*) (Arg) stone; (*canica*) (Arg) marble; (Col) lie, cheat, trick
pepe *mf* founding || *m* bib; **Pepe** *m* Joe
pepinillo *m* gherkin
pepino *m* cucumber; **me importa un pepino** I couldn't care less
pepita *f* seed, pip; nugget; (vet) pip
peque *m* tot
pequén *m* (Chile) burrowing owl
peque•ñez *f* (*pl* **-ñeces**) smallness; infancy; trifle
peque•ño -ña *adj* little, small; young; low, humble
pequeño-burgués *adj* petit bourgeois
Pequín *m* Peking
pequi•nés -nesa *adj & mf* Pekinese
pera *f* pear; goatee; cinch, sinecure; pear-shaped bulb; pear-shaped switch
peral *m* pear tree
perca *f* (ichth) perch
percance *m* mischance, misfortune; **percances** perquisites

percatar *ref* **—percatarse de** to be aware of; beware of, guard against
percebe *m* barnacle; fool, sap
percepción *f* perception; collection
percha *f* perch, pole, roost; clothes tree; coat hanger; coat hook; barber pole
perchero *m* rack, clothes rack, clothes hanger
percibir *tr* to perceive; collect
percudir *tr* to tarnish, dull; spread through
percutor *m* firing pin
perde•dor -dora *adj* losing || *mf* loser
perder §51 *tr* to lose; waste, squander; (*un tren, una ocasión*) miss; (*una asignatura*) flunk; ruin; spoil || *intr* to lose; fade || *ref* to get lost; miscarry; sink; become ruined; spoil; go to the dogs
perdición *f* perdition; loss; outrage; ruination
pérdida *f* loss; waste; ruination; **no tener pérdida** to be easy to find; **pérdida de reclamable** tax loss
perdi•do -da *adj* (*bala*) stray, wild; (*manga*) wide, loose; fruitless; (*horas*) off, spare, idle; distracted; inveterate; madly in love || *m* profligate, rake
perdido•so -sa *adj* unlucky; easily lost
perdigón *m* young partridge; profligate; heavy loser; (*alumno*) failure; **perdigones** (*granos de plomo*) shot; **perdigón zorrero** buckshot
per•diz *f* (*pl* **-dices**) partridge
perdón *m* pardon, forgiveness; **con perdón** by your leave; **perdóneme** *or* **perdón** pardon me, excuse me
perdonable *adj* pardonable
perdonar *tr* to pardon, forgive, excuse; **no perdonar** to not miss, not omit
perdula•rio -ria *adj* careless, sloppy; incorrigible, vicious || *mf* good-for-nothing, profligate
perdurable *adj* long-lasting; everlasting
perdurar *intr* to last, last a long time, survive
perecede•ro -ra *adj* perishable; mortal || *m* extreme want
perecer §22 *intr* to perish; suffer; be in great want || *ref* to pine; **perecerse por** to be dying for; (*una mujer*) be mad about
peregrinación *f* peregrination; pilgrimage
peregri•no -na *adj* wandering, traveling; foreign; rare, strange; beautiful; mortal; (*ave*) migratory || *mf* pilgrim
perejil *m* parsley; (coll) frippery
perenne *adj* perennial
pereza *f* laziness; slowness
perezo•so -sa *adj* lazy; slow, dull, heavy || *mf* lazybones; sleepyhead || *m* (zool) sloth
perfección *f* perfection
perfeccionar *tr* to perfect, improve
perfec•to -ta *adj & m* perfect
perfidia *f* perfidy
pérfi•do -da *adj* perfidious
perfil *m* profile; side view; cross section; thin stroke; outline, sketch; **perfil aerodinámico** streamlining; **perfiles** finishing touches; courtesies
perfila•do -da *adj* (*cara*) long and thin; (*nariz*) well-formed; (*facciones*) delicate; streamlined
perfilar *tr* to profile, outline; perfect, polish, finish || *ref* to be outlined; show one's profile, stand sidewise; stand out; dress up
perforación *f* perforation; drilling; puncture; keypunching
perfora•dor -dora *adj* perforating; drilling || *f* pneumatic drill, rock drill
perforar *tr* to perforate; drill, bore; puncture; (*una tarjeta*) punch
perforista *mf* keypuncher
perfumar *tr* to perfume
perfume *m* perfume
pergamino *m* parchment
pergenio *m* rascal
pericia *f* skill, expertness
periclitar *intr* to be in jeopardy, be shaky
perico *m* (*pelo postizo*) periwig; (*cocaine*) (slang) snow, coke; (slang) chamber pot; (CAm) compliment (Col, Ecuad) drunk; (Mex) big talker; (orn) parakeet; **perico entre ellas** ladies' man; **perico ligero** (zool) sloth
periferia *f* periphery; surroundings
periféri•co -ca *adj* outlying; (anat, compu, med) peripheral
perifollos *mpl* finery, frippery, chiffons
perilla *f* pear-shaped ornament; goatee; knob, doorknob; (*del arzón*) pommel; (*de la oreja*) lobe; **de perilla** apropos, to the point
periodísti•co -ca *adj* newspaper, journalistic
periódi•co -ca *adj* periodic || *m* newspaper; periodical; **periódico sensacionalista** tabloid
periodismo *m* journalism
periodista *mf* journalist || *m* newspaperman || *f* newspaperwoman
período *m* period; compound sentence; (phys) cycle; **período lectivo** (*en la escuela*) term
peripues•to -ta *adj* dudish, all spruced up, sporty
periquete *m* jiffy; **en un periquete** in a jiffy
periquito *m* parakeet; lovebird; **periquito de Australia** budgerigar
periscopio *m* periscope
peri•to -ta *adj* skilled, skillful; expert || *m* expert
perjudicar §73 *tr* to damage, impair, hurt, prejudice
perjudicial *adj* harmful, injurious, detrimental, prejudicial
perjuicio *m* harm, injury, damage, prejudice; **en perjuicio de** to the detriment of
perjurar *intr* to commit perjury; swear, be profane || *ref* to commit perjury; perjure oneself
perjurio *m* perjury
perla *f* pearl; **de perlas** perfectly
perlesía *f* palsy
permanecer §22 *intr* to stay, remain
permanencia *f* permanence; stay, sojourn
permanente *adj* permanent || *f* permanent wave
permisi•vo -va *adj* permissive
permiso *m* permission; permit; time off; (*en el monedaje*) tolerance; leave; **con permiso** excuse me; **permiso de circulación** (aut) own-

er's license, registration; **permiso de conducir** *or* **de conducción** driver's license; **permiso para perro** dog license

permitir *tr* to permit, allow; **¿me permite, por favor?** excuse me ‖ *ref* to be permitted; **no se permite fumar** no smoking

permutar *tr* to interchange; barter; to permute

pernear *intr* to kick; hustle; fuss, fret

pernera *f* trouser leg

pernicio•so -sa *adj* pernicious

pernil *m* trouser leg; (*anca y muslo*) ham

perno *m* bolt; **perno con anillo** ringbolt; **perno roscado** screw bolt

pernoctar *intr* to spend the night

pero *conj* but, yet ‖ *m* but; fault, defect; **poner pero a** to find fault with

perogrullada *f* platitude, inanity

peroración *f* peroration; harangue

peróxido *m* peroxide; **peróxido de hidrógeno** hydrogen peroxide

perpendicular *adj* & *f* perpendicular

perpetrar *tr* to perpetrate

perpetuar §21 *tr* to perpetuate

perpe•tuo -tua *adj* perpetual; life

perplejidad *f* perplexity; worry, anxiety

perple•jo -ja *adj* perplexed; worried, anxious; baffling, perplexing

perra *f* bitch; tantrum; drunkenness

perrada *f* pack of dogs; dirty trick

perrera *f* kennel, doghouse; tantrum; toil, drudgery

perro *m* dog; **el perro del hortelano** the dog in the manger; **perro caliente** (slang) hot dog; **perro callejero** stray dog; **perro cobrador** retriever; **perro de aguas** spaniel; **perro de lanas** poodle; **perro de muestra** pointer; **perro de presa** bulldog; **perro faldero** lap dog; **perro lebrel** hound; **perro marino** dogfish, shark; **perro raposero** foxhound; **perro salchicha** dachshund; **perro viejo** (coll) wise old owl

perro-lazarillo *m* (*pl* **perros-lazarillos**) Seeing Eye dog

persa *adj* & *mf* Persian

persecución *f* persecution; pursuit; annoyance, harassment

perseguir §67 *tr* to persecute; pursue; annoy, harass

perseverar *intr* to persevere

persiana *f* slatted shutter; flowered silk; louver; **persiana del radiador** (aut) louver; **persiana veneciana** Venetian blind

persistir *intr* to persist

persona *f* person; personage; **persona de la tercera edad** senior citizen; **persona desplazada** displaced person; **persona física** *or* **natural** individual; **personas** people; **por persona** per capita

personaje *m* personage; (theat) character; person of importance

personal *adj* personal ‖ *m* personnel, staff, force; **personal docente** teaching staff

personalidad *f* personality

personificar §73 *tr* to personify

perspectiva *f* perspective; outlook, prospect; appearance

perspi•caz *adj* (*pl* **-caces**) perspicacious, discerning; keen-sighted

persuadir *tr* to persuade

persuasión *f* persuasion

pertenecer §22 *intr* to belong; pertain ‖ *ref* to be independent, be free

perteneciente *adj* pertaining

pértiga *f* pole, rod, staff

perti•naz *adj* (*pl* **-naces**) pertinacious; (*dolor de cabeza*) persistent

pertinente *adj* pertinent, relevant

pertrechos *mpl* supplies, provisions, equipment; tools; **pertrechos de guerra** ordnance

perturbar *tr* to perturb; disturb; upset, disconcert; confuse, interrupt

Perú, el Peru

perua•no -na *adj* & *mf* Peruvian

perulí *m* lollipop

perversidad *f* perversity

perversión *f* perversion

perver•so -sa *adj* perverse; wicked, depraved ‖ *mf* profligate

perverti•do -da *mf* pervert

pervertir §68 *tr* to pervert ‖ *ref* to become perverted; go to the bad

pesa *f* weight; (CAm, Col, Ven) butcher shop

pesacar•tas *m* (*pl* **-tas**) letter scales

pesadez *f* heaviness; slowness; tiresomeness; harshness; (phys) gravity

pesadilla *f* nightmare

pesa•do -da *adj* heavy; slow; tiresome; stodgy; harsh; boring

pesadumbre *f* sorrow, grief; trouble; weight, heaviness

pesaje *m* weighing; (sport) weigh-in

pésame *m* condolence; **dar el pésame a** to extend one's sympathy to

pesantez *f* (phys) gravity

pesar *m* sorrow, regret; **a pesar de** in spite of ‖ *tr* to weigh; make sorry ‖ *intr* to weigh; be heavy; cause regret, cause sorrow

pesaro•so -sa *adj* sorrowful, regretful

pesca *f* fishing; catch; **ir de pesca** to go fishing; **pesca de arrastre** trawling; **pesca de bajura** off-shore fishing; **pesca de gran altura** deep-sea fishing

pescadería *f* fish market; fish store; fish stand

pescade•ro -ra *mf* fish dealer, fishmonger

pescado *m* fish (*that has been caught*)

pesca•dor -dora *adj* fishing ‖ *m* fisherman ‖ *f* fisherwoman, fishwife

pescante *m* coach box; (*de una grúa*) jib; (aut) front seat; (naut) davit; (theat) trap door

pescar §73 *tr* to fish; fish for; fish out; (*peces*) catch; (coll) to manage to get ‖ *intr* to fish

pescozón *m* slap on the neck or head

pescuezo *m* neck

pesebre *m* crib, rack, manger; crèche

pesero *m* (CAm, Col, Ven) butcher; (Mex) shared taxi

pesimismo *m* pessimism
pesimista *adj* pessimistic || *mf* pessimist
pési•mo -ma *adj* very bad, abominable
peso *m* weight; scale, balance; burden, load; judgment, good sense; (*unidad monetaria*) peso; **caerse de su peso** to be self-evident; **llevar el peso de la batalla** to bear the brunt of the battle; **peso atómico** atomic weight; **peso gallo** bantamweight; **peso ligero** lightweight; **peso medio** *or* **mediano** middleweight; **peso molecular** molecular weight; **peso mosca** flyweight; **peso pesado** heavyweight; **peso pluma** featherweight; **peso semipesado** light heavyweight; **peso welter, peso semimediano** welterweight
pespuntar *tr & intr* to backstitch
pespunte *m* backstitch
pesquera *f* fishery; fishing grounds; (*presa para detener los peces*) weir
pesquería *f* fishing; fishery
pesque•ro -ra *adj* fishing || *m* fishing boat || *f* see **pesquera**
pesquis *m* acumen, keenness
pesquisa *m* (Arg) detective || *f* inquiry, investigation
pesquisar *tr* to investigate, inquire into
pestaña *f* eyelash; flange; fringe, edging; index tab; (compu) tab
pestañear *intr* to wink, blink; **sin pestañear** without batting an eye
peste *f* pest, plague; epidemic; stink, stench; abundance; (Col, Peru) head cold; (Chile) smallpox; **pestes** insults
pesticida *m* pesticide
pestífe•ro -ra *adj* pestiferous; stinking
pestilencia *f* pestilence
pestillo *m* bolt; doorlatch
petaca *f* cigar case; cigarette case; tobacco pouch; leather-covered hamper
pétalo *m* petal
petardear *tr* to swindle || *intr* (aut) to backfire
petardeo *m* swindling; (aut) backfire
petardo *m* petard; bomb; swindle, cheat
petate *m* sleeping bag; bedding; luggage; cheat; poor soul; **liar el petate** to pack up and get out; to kick the bucket
petición *f* petition; request; plea; (law) claim, bill; **a petición de** at the request of; **petición de mano** formal betrothal
petimetre *m* dude, sport, dandy
petirrojo *m* redbreast, robin
Petrarca *m* Petrarch
petrificar §73 *tr & ref* to petrify
petróleo *m* petroleum; **petróleo combustible** fuel oil
petrole•ro -ra *adj* oil, petroleum || *mf* oil dealer || *m* oil tanker
petroquími•co -ca *adj* petrochemical
petulancia *f* flippancy, pertness
petulante *adj* flippant, pert
pez *m* (*pl* **peces**) fish; reward, just desert; **como un pez en el agua** snug as a bug in a rug; **peces de colores** goldfish; **pez de plata** (ent) silverfish; **pez gordo** (coll) big shot, bigwig; **salga pez o salga rana** blindly, hit or miss || *f* pitch, tar
pezón *m* stem; nipple, teat
pezonera *f* linchpin
pezuña *f* hoof
piado•so -sa *adj* merciful; pitiful; pious
piafar *intr* (*el caballo*) to paw, to stamp
piano *m* piano; **piano de cola** grand piano; **piano de media cola** baby grand; **piano mecánico** player piano; **piano vertical** upright piano
piar §77 *intr* to peep, chirp
pica *f* pike; pikeman; picador's goad; (Col) pique, resentment; **picas** (*palo de la baraja norteamericana*) spades
picada *f* peck; bite; (Bol) knock at the door; (Arg, Bol, Urug) narrow ford; (SAm) path, trail
picadillo *m* (*carne, verduras, ajos, etc., reducidos a pequeños trozos*) hash; (*carne picada*) mincemeat
pica•do -da *adj* perforated; pitted; (*tabaco*) cut; (*hielo*) cracked; (*mar*) choppy; piqued || *m* mincemeat; (aer) dive, nosedive; **picado con motor** (aer) power dive || *f* see **picada**
picador *m* horsebreaker; (*torero de a caballo*) picador (*mounted bullfighter*); chopping block; meat grinder
picadura *f* bite, prick, sting; nick; puncture; cut tobacco; (*en un diente*) cavity
picaflor *m* hummingbird
picahie•los *m* (*pl* **-los**) ice pick
picamade•ros *m* (*pl* **-ros**) green woodpecker
picante *adj* biting, pricking, stinging; piquant, juicy, racy; (SAm) highly seasoned || *m* mordancy; piquancy
pícap *m* (Bol, Chile, Col) *var of* **pick-up**
picapedrero *m* stonecutter
picaplei•tos *m* (*pl* **-tos**) troublemaker; shyster, pettifogger
picaporte *m* latch; latchkey; door knocker
picar §73 *tr* to prick, pierce, puncture; sting; bite; burn; peck; nibble; pit, pock; mince, chop up, cut up; stick, poke; spur; goad; perforate; (*hielo*) crack; harass, pursue; tame; pique, annoy || *intr* to itch; (*el sol*) burn; nibble; have a smattering; be catching; (*los negocios*) pick up; (aer) to dive; (*caer en el lazo*) (coll) to bite; **picar en** to nibble at; dabble in; **picar muy alto** aim high, expect too much || *ref* to rot; (*la ropa*) be moth-eaten; (*el vino*) turn sour; (*un diente*) be decayed; (*el mar*) get rough; be offended; get drunk; (*drogas*) get a fix, shoot up; **picarse de** to boast of being
picardía *f* roguishness, knavery; crudeness, coarseness; mischief
picares•co -ca *adj* roguish, rascally; picaresque; rough, coarse, crude; witty, humorous
píca•ro -ra *adj* roguish; scheming, tricky; low, vile; mischievous || *mf* rogue; schemer
picaza *f* magpie

picazón *f* itch, itching; annoyance
pícea *f* spruce tree
pichel *m* pewter tankard
pichón -chona *mf* darling || *m* young pigeon; **pichón de barro** clay pigeon
pick-up *m* pickup; phonograph
pico *m* beak, bill; (*de jarra*) spout, nozzle; (*del yunque*) beak; (*del pañuelo*) corner; nib, tip; (*de la pluma de escribir*) point; peak; (*herramienta*) pick; (*de dinero*) pile, lot; talkativeness; (elec) peak; (naut) bow, prow; **callar el pico** to shut up; **darse el pico** (*las palomas*) to bill; **pico de oro** silver-tongue; **tener mucho pico** to talk too much; **y pico** odd, e.g., **trescientos y pico** three hundred odd; a little after, e.g., **a las tres y pico** a little after three o'clock
picor *m* (*del paladar*) smarting; itch, itching, burning
pico•so -sa *adj* pockmarked
picota *f* pillory; peak, point, spire
picotazo *m* peck
picotear *tr* to peck || *intr* (*el caballo*) to toss the head; chatter, jabber, gab; (*las mujeres*) wrangle
pie *m* foot; footing; foothold; base, stand; caption; (*de copa*) stem; (*de la cama*) footboard; cause, origin, reason; (*de la página*) foot, bottom; (theat) cue; (Chile) down payment; **a cuatro pies** on all fours; **al pie de fábrica** at the factory; **al pie de la letra** literally; **al pie de la obra** (com) delivered; **a pie** on foot, walking; **buscar cinco** (*or* **tres**) **pies al gato** to be looking for trouble; **de pie** standing; up and about; firm, steady; firmly, steadily; **en pie de guerra** on a war footing; **ir a pie** to go on foot, to walk; **morir al pie del cañón** to die in the harness, to die with one's boots on; **nacer de pie** *or* **de pies** to be born with a silver spoon in one's mouth; **pie de atleta** athlete's foot; **pie de cabra** crowbar; **pie de fotografía** caption; **pie de imprenta** imprint, printer's mark; **pie derecho** upright, stanchion; **pie equino** clubfoot; **pie marino** sea legs; **pie plano** flatfoot; **pie quebrado** (*de verso*) short line; **vestirse por los pies** to be a man
piedad *f* (*devoción a las cosas santas*) piety; (*misericordia*) pity, mercy
piedra *f* stone; rock; (*pedernal*) flint; heavy hailstone; (pathol) stone; **piedra angular** cornerstone; (fig) cornerstone, keystone; **piedra arenisca** sandstone; **piedra azul** (chem) bluestone; **piedra berroqueña** granite; **piedra caliza** *or* **de cal** limestone; **piedra de albardilla** copestone; **piedra de amolar** grindstone; **piedra de chispa** flint; **piedra de pipas** meerschaum; **piedra imán** loadstone; **piedra miliar** *or* **miliaria** milestone; **piedra movediza** rolling stone; **piedra pómez** pumice, pumice stone; **piedra rojiza** brownstone
piel *f* skin; hide, pelt; fur; leather; (*de las frutas*) peel, skin; **piel de cabra** goatskin; **piel de foca** sealskin; **piel de gallina** goose flesh; **piel de naranja** orange peel; **piel sintética** synthetic leather
pienso *m* feed, feeding; **ni por pienso** by no means, don't think of it
pierna *f* leg; post, upright; **dormir a pierna suelta** *or* **tendida** to sleep like a log; **estirar la pierna** to lie down on the job; kick the bucket; **estirar** *or* **extender las piernas** to stretch one's legs, go for a walk; **ser buena pierna** (Arg, Urug) to be a good-natured fellow
pieza *f* (*órgano de una máquina o artefacto; obra dramática; composición suelta de música; cañón; figura que sirve para jugar a las damas, al ajedrez, etc.; moneda*) piece; (*objeto; mueble; porción de tela*) piece or article; (*habitación, cuarto*) room; **buena pieza** hussy; sly fox; **pieza de autos** (law) item entered in evidence; **pieza de convicción** piece of evidence; **pieza de recambio** *or* **de repuesto** spare part; **quedarse en una pieza** *or* **hecho una pieza** to be dumbfounded, stand motionless
pífano *m* fife; fifer
pifia *f* (billiards) miscue; (coll) miscue, slip
pifiar *intr* to miscue
pigmentar *tr & ref* to pigment
pigmento *m* pigment
pigme•o -a *adj & mf* pygmy
pijama *f* pajamas
pila *f* basin; trough; sink; font; pile, heap; (elec) battery, cell; (elec & phys) pile; **pila de linterna** flashlight battery; **pila para pájaros** bird bath
pilar *m* (*de una fuente*) basin, bowl; pillar; stone post, milestone; (*persona*) (fig) pillar || *tr* (*el grano*) to crush, pound
Pilatos *m* Pilate
píldora *f* pill; bad news; **píldora para dormir** sleeping pill
pileta *f* sink; basin, bowl; font; swimming pool
pillar *tr* to pillage, plunder; catch
pi•llo -lla *adj* roguish, rascally; sly, crafty || *m* rogue, rascal; crafty fellow
pilluelo *m* scamp, little scamp
pilón *m* pylon; drinking trough; loaf of sugar; counterpoise; drop hammer; (Mex, Ven) tip, gratuity; **de pilón** in addition, on top of it
pilotar *tr* to pilot
pilote *m* pile
piloto *m* pilot; first mate; (Chile) hail fellow well met; **piloto automático** (aer) automatic pilot; **piloto de pruebas** test pilot
pimentero *m* pepper, black pepper; pepperbox
pimentón *m* cayenne pepper, red pepper; (*condimento preparado moliendo pimientos encarnados secos*) paprika
pimienta *f* pepper, black pepper; allspice, pimento; allspice tree
pimiento *m* (*planta*) pepper, black pepper; Guinea pepper
pimpante *adj* smart, spruce

pimpollo *m* sucker, shoot, sprout; rosebud; (*árbol nuevo*) sapling; handsome youth
PIN *m* (acronym) (*número de identificación personal*) PIN (personal identification number); **pin** (*broche*) pin; little bit; (compu) pin
pina *f* fellow
pinacoteca *f* picture gallery
pináculo *m* pinnacle
pincel *m* brush; painter; painting; (*de luz*) pencil, beam
pincelada *f* brush stroke; touch, finish, flourish
pincelar *tr* to paint; picture; (med) to pencil
pincha *f* kitchenmaid
pinchar *tr* to prick, jab, pierce, puncture; stir up, prod, provoke || *intr* to have a puncture; **no pinchar ni cortar** to have no say || *ref* (*drogas*) to get a fix, shoot up
pinchazo *m* prick, jab, puncture; provocation; **a prueba de pinchazos** puncture-proof
pinche *m* scullion, kitchen boy; helper
pincho *m* thorn, prick; snack; spike
pincia•no -na *adj* Valladolid || *mf* native or inhabitant of Valladolid
pingajo *m* rag, tatter
pingo *m* rag, tatter, ragamuffin; horse; **andar** *or* **ir de pingo** (*una mujer*) to gad about
pingüe *adj* oily, greasy, fat; abundant, rich; fertile; profitable
pingüino *m* penguin
pinito *m* first step, little step; **hacer pinitos** to begin to walk; (fig) to take the first steps
pino *m* pine tree; first step; **hacer pinos** to begin to walk; (fig) to take the first steps
pinocha *f* pine needle
pinta *m* scoundrel || *f* spot, mark, sign; dot; pint
pintacilgo *m* goldfinch
pintada *f* Guinea hen
pinta•do -da *adj* spotted, mottled; tipsy; accented; **el más pintado** the aptest one; the shrewdest one; the best one; **venir como pintado** to be just the thing || *m* (*acto de pintar*) painting || *f* see **pintada**
pintar *tr* to paint; (*una letra, un acento, etc.*) draw; picture, depict; put an accent mark on; **pintarla** to put it on, put on airs || *intr* to paint; begin to turn red, begin to ripen; show, turn out || *ref* to paint, put on make-up; begin to turn red, begin to ripen
pintarrajear *tr* to daub, smear
pin•to -ta *adj* speckled, spotted || *f* see **pinta**
pin•tor -tora *mf* painter; **pintor de brocha gorda** painter, house painter; dauber
pintores•co -ca *adj* picturesque
pintura *f* (*color preparado para pintar*) paint; (*arte; obra pintada*) painting; **hacer pinturas** to prance; **no poder ver ni en pintura** to not be able to stand the sight of
pinture•ro -ra *adj* showy, conceited || *mf* show-off
pinza *f* clothespin; (*de langosta, cangrejo, etc.*) claw; **pinzas** pliers; pincers; tweezers; forceps
pinzón *m* pump handle; (orn) finch
piña *f* fir cone, pine cone; knob; plug; cluster, knot; pineapple
piñonear *intr* (*un arma de fuego*) to click; reach the age of puberty; (coll) to be an old goat
piñoneo *m* click (*of a firearm*)
pí•o -a *adj* pious; merciful, compassionate; (*caballo*) pied, dappled || *m* peeping, chirping
piocha *f* jeweled head adornment; artificial flower made of feathers; pick
piojo *m* louse
piojo•so -sa *adj* lousy; mean, stingy
piola *f* string, cord
pione•ro -ra *adj* & *mf* pioneer
pipa *f* (*para fumar tabaco*) pipe; (*medida para vinos*) butt; wine cask; (*simiente*) pip; (mus) pipe, reed; (coll) handgun; **pipa de espuma de mar** meerschaum pipe; **pipa de riego** watering cart; **pipa de tierra** clay pipe
pipí *m* (coll) pee, urine; **hacer pipí** to pee, urinate
pipiolo *m* (CAm, Mex) child
pique *m* pique, resentment; eagerness; (*insecto*) chigger; (*naipe*) spade; **a pique** steep; **a pique de** in danger of; on the verge of; **echar a pique** to sink; ruin; **irse a pique** to sink; go to ruin, be ruined; **piques** (*palo de la baraja norteamericana*) spades
piquera *f* bung, bunghole; (Mex) dive, joint
piquete *m* sharp jab; small hole; stake, picket; (*de soldados, de huelguistas*) picket; **piquete de ejecución** firing squad; **piquete de salvas** firing squad
pira *f* pyre
piragua *f* pirogue; (sport) single shell
piragüismo *m* canoeing
piragüista *m* (sport) crewman
pirámide *f* pyramid
pirata *mf* pirate; **pirata aéreo** hijacker; **pirata informático** (comp) hacker
piratear *intr* to pirate, be a pirate
piratería *f* piracy; **piratería aérea** hijacking, skyjacking, air piracy; **piratería informática** (compu) hacking
pirca *f* (SAm) dry stone wall
pirco *m* (Chile) succotash
pirine•o -a *adj* Pyrenean || **Pirineos** *mpl* Pyrenees
pirita *f* pyrites
piróofficial•go -ga *adj* fire-eating || *mf* fire-eater
piropear *tr* to flatter, flirt with
piropo *m* garnet, carbuncle; flattery, compliment, flirtatious remark
piróscafo *m* steamship
pirotecnia *f* pyrotechnics
pirotécni•co -ca *adj* pyrotechnical || *m* powder maker, fireworks manufacturer
pirueta *f* pirouette; somersault; caper
piruetear *intr* to pirouette
pisada *f* tread; footstep; footprint; trampling
pisapape•les *m* (*pl* **-les**) paperweight
pisar *tr* to trample, tread on, step on; tamp, pack down; (*p.ej., uvas*) tread; cover part of; ram; (*una tecla*) strike; (mus) to pluck; (coll) to abuse, tread all over; **pisar algo a alguien** to

snitch something from someone || *intr* to be right above; step || *ref* (Arg) to guess wrong, come out wrong
pisaverde *m* fop, dandy
piscina *f* swimming pool; fishpond; **piscina de hidromasaje** whirlpool
Piscis *m* (astr) Pisces
pisco *m* Peruvian brandy
pisicorre *f* (W-I) station wagon
piso *m* tread; floor; flooring; (*de una carretera*) surface; flat, apartment; (aut) floorboard; **buscar piso** to be looking for a place to live; **piso alto** top floor; **piso bajo** street floor, ground floor; **piso franco** safe house; **piso piloto** (Esp) model apartment; **piso principal** main floor, second floor; **primer piso** second floor
pisón *m* ram, tamper
pisotear *tr* to trample, tread on, tread under foot; abuse, tread all over
pisotón *m* stamp, tread
pista *f* track; trace, trail; clew; race track; (*de bolera*) alley; (*de cabaret*) floor; (aer) runway; (compu, sport) track; **pista de aterrizaje** landing strip; **pista de esqui** ski run; **pista de patinar** *or* **patinaje** skating rink
pisto *m* (*para los enfermos*) chicken broth; vegetable cutlet; jumbled speech or writing; mess; (CAm, Mex) money
pistola *f* pistol; sprayer; rock drill; **pistola de arzón** horse pistol; **pistola engrasadora** *or* **de engrase** grease gun; **pistola de fogueo** starting pistol
pistolera *f* holster
pistolerismo *m* gangsterism
pistolero *m* gangster, gunman
pistón *m* piston
pistonear *intr* to knock
pistoneo *m* knock
pistonu•do -da *adj* stunning, swank
pita *f* century plant; hiss, hissing; glass marble; string, thread
pitar *tr* to pay, pay off; (*a un torero*) whistle disapproval of || *intr* to blow a whistle, whistle; blow the horn, honk, beep; talk nonsense; **no pitar** to not be popular; **salir pitando** to run away, dash away
pitazo *m* blast, toot, honk; (SAm) whistle
pitear *intr* to whistle
pitido *m* whistle, whistling; beep, honk
pitillera *f* cigarette maker; cigarette case
pitillo *m* cigarette
pito *m* whistle; horn; fife; fifer; cigarette; jackstone; (*insecto*) tick; woodpecker; (coll) continental, straw, tinker's damn
pitón *m* lump, sprig; tenderling; (*del cuerno*) tip; nozzle, spout; python
pitonisa *f* witch, siren; pythoness
pitorro *m* spout, nozzle
pitu•so -sa *adj* tiny, cute || *mf* tot
piular *intr* to peep, chirp
pivotar *intr* to pivot
pivote *m* pivot; **pivote de dirección** (aut) kingpin
pixel *m* (compu) pixel
píxide *f* pyx
pizarra *f* slate; blackboard
pizarrero *m* roofer, slater
pizarrín *m* slate pencil
pizca *f* mite, whit, jot
placa *f* plaque, tablet; badge; plate; slab, sheet; scab; dog tag; (anat, elec, electron, phot, zool) plate; (compu) board; **placa base** circuit board; **placa de circuitos impresos** printed circuit board; **placa de energía solar** solar cell; **placa de hielo** black ice; **placa de identidad** (mil) identity tag, dog tag; **placa de matrícula** license plate; **placa de silicio** silicon chip; **placa giratoria** (*de ferrocarril; de gramófono*) turntable; **placa hija** (compu) daughterboard; **placa lógica** (compu) logic board; **placa madre** (comp) motherboard
placaminero *m* persimmon
placebo *m* placebo
pláceme *m* congratulation
placente•ro -ra *adj* pleasant, agreeable
placer *m* pleasure; sandbank, reef; **a placer** at one's convenience || *v* **§52** *tr* to please
place•ro -ra *adj* public || *mf* market vendor; loafer, town gossip
pláci•do -da *adj* placid; pleasing
plaga *f* plague; pest; scourge; abundance; sore; clime, region
plagar §44 *tr* to plague, infest; (*de minas*) sow
plagiar *tr* to plagiarize
plagio *m* plagiarism; abduction, kidnaping
plan *m* plan; level, height; **plan de estudios** *or* **plan escolar** curriculum
plana *f* plain, flat country; trowel; cooper's plane; page
plancha *f* plate, sheet; iron, flatiron; gangplank; (coll) blunder; (Chile) false teeth; **a la plancha** grilled; (*huevo*) fried; **plancha de blindaje** armor plate; **plancha de vapor** steam iron; **plancha de vela** *or* **de windsurf** sailboard, windsurfer
planchado *m* ironing; pressing
planchar *tr* (*la ropa interior blanca*) to iron; (*un traje de hombre*) to press || *intr* to be a wallflower
planchear *tr* to plate
planear *tr* to plan, outline; (*una tabla*) plane || *intr* to hover; (aer) to volplane, glide
planeta *m* planet
planicie *f* plain
planificación *f* planning; **planificación familiar** family planning; **planificación urbana** town planning
planificar §73 *tr* to plan
planilla *f* list, roll, schedule; (*de candidatos para un puesto público*) (Mex) panel; (Mex) ballot; (Mex) commutation ticket
pla•no -na *adj* plane; level, smooth, even; flat || *m* plan; map; (*superficie*) plane; (aer) plane; **de plano** clearly, plainly, flatly; flat; **levantar**

un plano to make a survey; **plano acotado** contour map; **plano corto** close-up; **plano general** pan shot; **plano inclinado** inclined plane; **plano largo** long shot; **plano picado** aerial view; **primer plano** foreground || *f* see **plana**

planta *f* (*del pie*) sole; foot; plan; project; floor plan; (*del personal de una oficina*) roster; plant, factory; (bot) plant; (sport) stance; **de planta** from the ground up; **echar plantas** to swagger, bully; **planta baja** ground floor, first floor; **planta del sortilegio** (bot) witch hazel; **tener buena planta** to make a fine appearance

plantar *tr* to plant; establish, found; (*un golpe*) plant; jilt; (*en la calle, en la cárcel*) throw || *ref* to take a stand; gang together; (*un animal*) balk; land, arrive

plantear *tr* to plan, outline; establish, execute, carry out; state, set up, expound, pose

plantel *m* nursery garden; educational establishment; staff, team; (sport) lineup

plantificar **§73** *tr* to plan, outline; (*un golpe*) plant; (*en la calle, la cárcel*) throw || *ref* to land, arrive

plantilla *f* plantlet, young plant; insole; reinforced sole; model, pattern, template; (*de empleados*) staff; (*del personal de una oficina*) roster; plan, design; (*bizcocho*) ladyfinger

plantío *m* planting; garden patch; tree nursery

plantón *m* (*que ha de ser transplantado*) shoot; graft; guard, watchman; waiting, standing around

plañide•ro -ra *adj* mournful, plaintive || *f* hired mourner

plañir **§12** *tr* to lament, grieve over || *intr* to lament, grieve, bewail

plaqueta *f* small slab: (biol) platelet

plasma *m* plasma

plasmar *tr* to mold, shape

plasta *f* paste, soft mass; flattened object; poor job, bungle

plástica *f* (*arte de plasmar*) plastic; plastic arts

plásti•co -ca *adj* plastic; pliable; vivid, expressive || *m* (*substancia*) plastic || *f* see **plástica**

plastifica•do -da *adj* laminated

plata *f* silver; (*moneda o monedas*) silver; wealth; money; **en plata** briefly, to the point; plainly; **plata de ley** sterling silver

plataforma *f* platform; platform car; (*del ferrocarril*) roadbed; (*programa político*) platform; (*de lanzamiento de cohete*) pad; **plataforma giratoria** (rr) turntable; **plataforma petrolífera** oil rig

platal *m* piles of money, fortune

platanal *m* or **platanar** *m* banana plantation

plátano *m* banana; plantain; banana tree; plane tree; plantain tree; **plátano de occidente** buttonwood tree; **plátano de sombra** sycamore

platea *f* (theat) orchestra, parquet

platea•do -da *adj* silvered; silver-plated; (coll) well-to-do

platear *tr* to silver, coat or plate with silver

platero *m* silversmith; jeweler

plática *f* talk, chat; talk, informal lecture; sermon

platicar **§73** *tr* to talk over, discuss || *intr* to talk, chat; discuss; preach

platija *f* (ichth) flounder

platillo *m* plate; saucer; (*de la balanza*) pan; (mus) cymbal; **platillo volador** *or* **volante** flying saucer

platina *f* slide; platen; tape deck

platino *m* platinum

plato *m* dish; plate; (*de una comida*) course; daily fare; **plato fuerte** main course; **plato giratorio** (*del gramófono*) turntable; **plato llano** *or* **liso** dinner plate

pla•tó *m* (*pl* **-tós**) (mov) set

Platón *m* Plato

platóni•co -ca *adj* platonic

platu•do -da *adj* rich

plausible *adj* praiseworthy; acceptable

playa *f* beach, shore, strand; **playa infantil** sand pile

playera *f* fishwoman; beach shoe; **playeras** (Esp) sneakers

plaza *f* plaza, square; market place; town, city; fortified town; space, room; yard; office, employment; character, reputation; seat; **sentar plaza** to enlist; **plaza de armas** parade ground; public square; **plaza de gallos** cockpit; **plaza de toros** bullring; **plaza mayor** main square

plazo *m* term; time; time limit; date of payment; instalment; **a plazo** on credit, on time; **en plazos** in installments

pleamar *f* high tide, high water

plebe *f* common people

plebiscito *m* plebiscite, referendum

plebe•yo -ya *adj & mf* plebeian

plegadi•zo -za *adj* folding; pliable

plegar **§66** *tr* to fold; crease; pleat || *ref* to yield, give in

plegaria *f* prayer; noon call to prayer

pleito *m* litigation, lawsuit; dispute, quarrel; fight; **pleito de acreedores** bankruptcy proceedings; **pleito homenaje** (feud) homage; **pleito viciado** mistrial

plenilunio *m* full moon

plenitud *f* fullness, abundance

ple•no -na *adj* full; **en plena marcha** in full swing; **en pleno rostro** right in the face

pletina *f* platen; tape deck

pleuresia *f* pleurisy

pliego *m* (*de papel*) sheet; folder, cover, envelope; bid, specification; sealed letter; printer's proof

pliegue *m* fold, crease, pleat; **pliegue de tabla** box pleat

plisar *tr* to pleat

plomada *f* carpenter's lead pencil; plummet; plumb bob; sinker, sinkers; scourge tipped with lead balls

plomar *tr* to seal with lead

plomazo *m* (Guat, Mex, W-I) gunshot

plomería *f* lead roofing; leadwork, plumbing
plomero *m* leadworker; plumber
plomi•zo -za *adj* lead, leaden
plomo *m* lead; (*pedazo de plomo; bala*) lead; (elec) fuse; (coll) bore; **a plomo** plumb, perpendicularly; straight down; just right
pluma *f* feather; quill; plume; pen; faucet; (CAm) hoax; (Chile) crane, derrick; **pluma esferográfica** ballpoint pen; **pluma estilográfica** *or* **pluma fuente** fountain pen
plumaje *m* plumage
plúmbe•o -a *adj* lead
plumero *m* (*caja o vaso para las plumas*) penholder; feather duster
plumífe•ro -ra *adj* (*escritor*) hack, second-rate; (poet) feathered || *m* padded or quilted jacket, ski jacket; hack writer; newshound
plumilla *f* small feather; (*de la pluma fuente*) point, tip; (Ven) ballpoint pen
plumón *m* down; feather bed; (Mex) felt-tipped pen
plumo•so -sa *adj* downy, feathery
plural *adj & m* plural
pluriempleo *m* moonlighting
plus *m* extra, bonus
plusmarca *f* (sport) record
plusmarquista *mf* (sport) record holder
plusvalía *f* appreciation (*in value*); capital gain
Pluto *m* (myth) Pluto
Plutón *m* (astr) Pluto
plutonio *m* plutonium
población *f* population; village, town, city
poblada *f* (SAm) riot, mob
pobla•do -da *adj* thick, bushy || *m* town, community || *f* see **poblada**
poblar §61 *tr* to people, populate; found, settle, colonize; (*un estanque, una colmena*) stock; (*con árboles*) plant || *intr* to settle, colonize; multiply, be prolific || *ref* to become full, covered, or crowded
pobre *adj* poor || *mf* pauper; beggar
pobreza *f* poverty, want; poorness
po•cho -ca *adj* faded, discolored; overripe; rotten; (Chile) chubby
pocilga *f* pigpen
poción *f* potion, dose
po•co -ca *adj & pron* (*comp & super* **menos**) little; few, e.g., **poca gente** few people; **pocos** few; **unos pocos** a few || **poco** *adv* little; **a poco** shortly afterwards; **a poco de** shortly after; **dentro de poco** shortly; **por poco** almost, nearly; **tener en poco** to hold in low esteem, think little of; **un poco (de)** a little
podar *tr* to prune, to trim
podenco *m* hound
poder *m* power; power of attorney, proxy; **el cuarto poder** the fourth estate; **obra en mi poder** I have at hand, I have in my possession; **poder adquisitivo** purchasing power || *v* **§53** *intr* to be possible; be able, have power or strength; **a más no poder** as hard as possible; **no poder con** to not be able to stand, not be able to manage; **no poder más** to be exhausted, be all in; **no poder menos de** to not be able to keep from, not be able to help || *v aux* to be able to, may, can, might, could; **no poder ver** to not be able to stand
poderhabiente *mf* attorney, proxy
poderío *m* power, might; wealth, riches; sway, dominion
podero•so -sa *adj* powerful, mighty; wealthy, rich
podio *m* podium
podre *f* pus
podredumbre *f* corruption, putrefaction; pus; deep grief
poema *m* poem
poesía *f* poetry; poem; **bella poesía** (fig) fairy tale
poeta *m* poet
poéti•co -ca *adj* poetic(al) || *f* poetics
poetisa *f* poetess
pola•co -ca *adj* Polish || *mf* Pole || *m* (*idioma*) Polish
polaina *f* legging
polar *adj* pole; polar || *f* polestar
polarizar §60 *tr* to polarize
polea *f* pulley
poleame *m* (naut) tackle
polen *m* pollen
polerón *m* (Chile) sweatshirt
policía *m* policeman || *f* police; policing; politeness; cleanliness; neatness; **policía acostado** (Col) speed bump; **policía urbana** street cleaning
policía•co -ca or policial *adj* police; (*novela*) detective
policial *adj* police; crime, detective
poliéster *m* polyester
polifacéti•co -ca *adj* many-sided
políga•mo -ma *adj* polygamous || *mf* polygamist
poliglo•to -ta *adj* polyglot || *mf* polyglot, linguist
polígono *m* polygon
polígrafo *m* prolific writer; copying machine; ballpoint pen; lie detector
polilla *f* moth
polinizar §60 *tr* to pollinate
polinomio *m* polynomial
polio *f* (path) polio
pólipo *m* polyp
polisón *m* bustle
polista *mf* poloist, polo player
politeísta *adj* polytheistic || *mf* polytheist
política *f* politics; policy; manners, politeness, courtesy; **política de café** parlor politics; **política del buen vecino** Good Neighbor Policy
políti•co -ca *adj* political; politic, tactful; polite, courteous; -in-law; e.g., **padre político** father-in-law || *mf* politician || *f* see **política**
polivalente *adj* manifold; (chem, bact) polyvalent
póliza *f* policy, contract; draft, check; customhouse permit; **póliza de seguros** insurance policy
polizón *m* bum, tramp; stowaway
polizonte *m* cop, policeman

polla *f* pullet; (*puesta*) stake, kitty; (*apuesta*) football pool; (coll) penis
pollera *f* poultry woman; chicken coop; poultry yard; go-cart; (Arg, Chile) skirt
pollero *m* poulterer; poultry yard
polli•no -na *mf* donkey, ass
polli•to -ta *mf* chick; (*persona joven*) chick, chicken
pollo *m* chicken; (*persona joven*) chicken
polo *m* pole; popsicle; (*juego*) polo; **polo de agua** water polo; **polo de atracción popular** drawing card; **polo de desarrollo** growth area
pololear *tr* to bother, annoy; (Chile) to flirt with
polo•lo -la *adj* (Chile) youngster ‖ *m* (Chile) flirt; side job
Polonia *f* Poland
pol•trón -trona *adj* idle, lazy, comfort-loving ‖ *f* easy chair
polución *f* (*del ambiente*) pollution
polvareda *f* cloud of dust; rumpus
polvera *f* compact, powder case
polvo *m* dust; powder; pinch of snuff; **morder el polvo** to bite the dust; **polvo dentífrico** tooth powder; **polvo eres y en polvo te convertirás** ashes to ashes, dust to dust; **polvos** dust; powder; **polvos compactos** face powder; **polvo de hornear** baking powder; **polvos de la madre Celestina** (coll) hocus-pocus; **polvos de talco** talcum powder
pólvora *f* powder, gunpowder; fireworks; (*persona avispada*) live wire; **correr como pólvora en reguero** to spread like wildfire; **pólvora de algodón** guncotton
polvorear *tr* to dust, sprinkle with dust or powder
polvorien•to -ta *adj* dusty; powdery
polvorín *m* powder magazine; powder flask; powder keg (fig); (ent) tick; (Chile) spitfire
polvoro•so -sa *adj* dusty; **poner pies en polvorosa** to take to one's heels
pomada *f* pomade
pómez *f* pumice stone
pomo *m* (*de la guarnición de la espada*) pommel; (*bola aromática*) pomander; (*frasco para perfume*) flacon; **pomo de puerta** doorknob
pompa *f* pomp; soap bubble; swell, bulge; (*de la ropa*) billowing, ballooning; (*de las alas del pavo real*) spread; (naut) pump; **pompa fúnebre** funeral
pompis *m* behind, butt, rear end
pompo•so -sa *adj* pompous; high-flown, highfalutin
pómulo *m* cheekbone
ponche *m* (*bebida*) punch; **ponche de huevo** eggnog
ponchera *f* punch bowl
pon•cho -cha *adj* lazy, careless, easygoing; (Col) chubby ‖ *m* poncho; greatcoat
ponderar *tr* to weigh; ponder, ponder over; exaggerate; praise to the skies; balance; weight
ponencia *f* paper, report
poner §54 *tr* to put, place, lay, set; arrange, dispose; (*una observación*) put in; (*una pieza dramática*) put on; (*la mesa*) set; assume, suppose; (*una ley, un impuesto*) impose; wager, stake; (*huevos*) lay; (*por escrito*) set down, put down; (*tiempo*) take; (*p.ej., miedo*) cause; make, turn; (*la luz, la radio*) turn on; (*marcha directa*) (aut) to go in; **poner a prueba** to test out; **poner en acción** to set in motion; **poner en limpio** to make a clean copy of; **poner por encima** to prefer, put ahead ‖ *ref* to put or place oneself; become, get, turn; (*el sol, los astros*) set; (*sombrero, saco, etc.*) put on; dress, dress up; get spotted; get, reach, arrive; **ponerse a** to set out to, begin to; **ponerse tan alto** to take offense, become hoity-toity
poniente *m* west; west wind
ponqué *m* poundcake
pontífice *m* pontiff
pontón *m* pontoon; pontoon bridge; (*buque viejo*) hulk
ponzoña *f* poison
ponzoño•so -sa *adj* poisonous
popa *f* poop, stern
popote *m* (Mex) straw for brooms; (*para tomar refrescos*) (Mex) straw
populache•ro -ra *adj* popular; cheap, vulgar; rabble-rousing ‖ *mf* rabble-rouser
populacho *m* populace, mob, rabble
popular *adj* popular
popularizar §60 *tr* to popularize
populo•so -sa *adj* populous
popu•rrí *m* (*pl* **-rríes**) medley
poquedad *f* paucity, scantiness; scarcity; timidity; trifle
poqui•to -ta *adj* very little; timid, shy, backward
por *prep* by; through, over; via, by way of; in, e.g., **por la mañana** in the morning; for; because of; for the sake of; on account of; in exchange for; in order to; as; about, e.g., **por Navidad** about Christmastime; out of, e.g., **por ignorancia** out of ignorance; times, e.g., **tres por cuatro** four times three; **estar por** to be on the point of, be ready to; be still to be, e.g., **la carta está por escribir** the letter is still to be written; **ir por** to go for, to go after; to follow; **por ciento** per cent; **por ejemplo** for example; **por entre** among, between; **por que** because; in order that; **por qué** why; **por** + *adj* or *adv* + **que** however
porcelana *f* porcelain, chinaware; (*usado por los plateros*) enamel; (Mex) washbowl
porcentaje *m* percentage
porche *m* porch, portico
porción *f* portion
pordiosear *intr* to beg, go begging
pordiose•ro -ra *mf* beggar
porfía *f* persistence, stubbornness, obstinacy; **a porfía** in emulation; insistently
porfia•do -da *adj* persistent, stubborn, obstinate; opinionated
porfiar §77 *intr* to persist; argue stubbornly
pórfido *m* porphyry

pormenor *m* detail, particular
pormenorizar §60 *tr* to detail, tell in detail; to itemize
porno *adj* (coll) porn
pornografía *f* pornography
poro *m* pore
poro•so -sa *adj* porous
poroto *m* (SAm) bean, string bean; (Chile) little runt
porque *conj* because; in order that
porqué *m* reason why; quantity, share; wherewithal, money
porquería *f* dirt, filth; trifle; crudity; (*alimento dañoso a la salud*) junk
porra *f* club, bludgeon; bore, nuisance; boasting; (*pelos enredados*) (Arg, Bol) knot, tangle; (Mex) claque
porrazo *m* clubbing; blow, bump, thump
porro *m* (*marijuana*) joint
porta *f* porthole
portaavio•nes *m* (*pl* **-nes**) aircraft carrier, flattop
portacandado *m* hasp
portada *f* front, façade; portal; title page; (*de una revista*) cover; **falsa portada** half title
portadis•cos *m* (*pl* **-cos**) turntable
porta•dor -dora *adj* (*onda*) (rad, telv) carrier || *mf* bearer; carrier || *m* waiter's tray
portaequipaje *m* (aut) trunk
portaequipa•jes *m* (*pl* **-jes**) baggage rack
portaestandarte *mf* standard-bearer, color guard
portaguan•tes *m* (*pl* **-tes**) (aut) glove compartment
portal *m* vestibule, entrance hall; porch, portico; arcade; city gate; (*de un túnel*) portal *m;* crèche
portalámpa•ras *m* (*pl* **-ras**) (elec) socket
portalón *m* gate, portal; (*en el costado del buque*) gangway
portamira *m* (surv) rodman
portamone•das *m* (*pl* **-das**) pocketbook
portanue•vas *mf* (*pl* **-vas**) newsmonger
portañuela *f* (*de los pantalones*) fly; (Col, Mex) carriage door
portapape•les *m* (*pl* **-les**) brief case; (compu) clipboard
portaplu•mas *m* (*pl* **-mas**) penholder
portar *tr* to carry, bear; (hunt) to retrieve || *ref* to behave, conduct oneself
portase•nos *m* (*pl* **-nos**) brassiere
portátil *adj* portable
portatinte•ro *m* inkstand
portavian•das *m* (*pl* **-das**) dinner pail
porta•voz *m* (*pl* **-voces**) megaphone; mouthpiece, spokesperson
portazgo *m* toll, road toll
portazo *m* bang, slam
porte *m* portage; carrying charge, freight; postage; behavior, conduct; dress, bearing; size, capacity; (Chile) birthday present; **porte concertado** mailing permit; **porte pagado** postage prepaid, freight prepaid
portear *tr* to carry, transport || *intr* to slam || *ref* (*las aves*) to migrate
portento *m* prodigy, wonder
portento•so -sa *adj* portentous, extraordinary
porte•ño -ña *adj* Buenos Aires; Valparaiso; pertaining to any large South American city with a port || *mf* native or inhabitant of Buenos Aires, Valparaiso or any large South American city with a port
porte•ro -ra *mf* doorkeeper; gatekeeper; (sport) goalkeeper || *m* porter, janitor, super; doorman; **portero electrónico** automatic door opener
portezuela *f* small door; (*de un coche o automóvil*) door; pocket flap
pórtico *m* portico, porch; little gate
portilla *f* porthole; private cart road, private cattle pass
portillo *m* gap, opening; nick, notch; (*puerta chica en otra mayor*) wicket; gate; narrow pass; side entrance
portorrique•ño -ña *adj & mf* Puerto Rican
portua•rio -ria *adj* port, harbor, dock || *m* dock hand, dock worker
Portugal *m* Portugal
portu•gués -guesa *adj & mf* Portuguese
porvenir *m* future
pos — en pos de after, behind; in pursuit of
posa *f* knell, toll
posada *f* inn, wayside inn; lodging; boardinghouse; home, dwelling; camp; **posadas** (Mex) pre-Christmas celebration
posade•ro -ra *mf* innkeeper; **posaderas** buttocks
posafuentes *m* table mat
posar *tr* to put down || *intr* to put up, lodge; alight, perch; pose || *ref* to alight, perch; settle; rest
posavasos *m* coaster
posbéli•co -ca *adj* postwar
posdata *f* postscript
pose *f* pose; (phot) exposure
poseer §43 *tr* to own, possess, hold; have a mastery of || *ref* to control oneself
posesión *f* possession; **tomar posesión** (*un cargo*) to take up
posesionar *tr* to give possession to || *ref* to take possession
posesor *m* owner
poseta *f* (Ven) toilet, washroom
posfecha *f* postdate
posguerra *f* postwar period, postwar years
posible *adj* possible; **hacer todo lo posible** to do one's best || **posibles** *mpl* means, income, property
posición *f* position; standing; (aer, naut) fix
positi•vo -va *adj* positive || *f* (phot) print, positive
poso *m* sediment, dregs; grounds; rest, quiet; **poso del café** coffee grounds
posponer §54 *tr* to subordinate; think less of
posta *f* (*de caballos*) relay; posthouse; stage;

stake, wager; slice; **a posta** on purpose; **por la posta** posthaste; **postas** buckshot

postal *adj* postal ‖ *f* post card; **postal ilustrada** picture post card

poste *m* post, pillar, pole; **poste de alumbrado** or **de farol** lamppost; **poste de telégrafo** telegraph pole; (*persona muy alta y delgada*) beanpole; **poste indicador** road sign

póster *m* poster; **póster central** centerfold

postergar §44 *tr* to delay, postpone; pass over

posteridad *f* posterity; posthumous fame

posterior *adj* back, rear; later, subsequent

postgrado *m* postgraduate course

postgradua•do -da *adj* postgraduate ‖ *mf* graduate student

postigo *m* (*puerta chica en otra mayor*) wicket; (*puertecilla en una ventana*) peep window; (*puerta excusada*) postern; shutter

postilla *f* (med) scab

posti•zo -za *adj* false, artificial; (*cuello*) detachable ‖ *m* switch, false hair, rat

postóni•co -ca *adj* posttonic

postor *m* bidder; **el mejor postor** the highest bidder

postración *f* prostration

postrar *tr* to prostrate; weaken, exhaust ‖ *ref* to collapse, be prostrated; prostrate oneself

postre *adj* last, final; **a la postre** at last; afterwards ‖ *m* dessert; **postres** dessert

postulación *f* postulation; nomination

postulante *mf* applicant, candidate

póstu•mo -ma *adj* posthumous

postura *f* posture; attitude, stand; stake, wager; agreement, pact; egg, eggs; (*de huevos*) laying; **postura del sol** sunset

potabilizar §60 *tr* to make drinkable

potable *adj* drinkable

potaje *m* pottage, vegetable stew; broth; dried vegetables; jumble; (*bebida*) mixture; scheme

potasa *f* potash

potasio *m* potassium

pote *m* pot, jug; flowerpot; **a pote** in abundance

potencia *f* potency; power; **potencia de choque** striking power

potenciación *f* (math) involution

potencial *adj & m* potential

potenciar *tr* (*las aguas de un río; el entusiasmo de una persona*) to harness; (*elevar a una potencia*) (math) to raise

potentado *m* potentate

potente *adj* powerful; big, huge

potestad *f* power

potista *mf* toper, soak

potosí *m* great wealth, gold mine

potra *f* filly; hernia, rupture

potranca *f* young mare

potro *m* colt; pest, annoyance

pozal *m* bucket, pail

pozo *m* well; pit; whirlpool; (min) shaft; (naut) hold; (Chile, Col) pool, puddle; (Ecuad) spring, fountain; **pozo artesiano** artesian well; **pozo de ciencia** fountain of knowledge; **pozo de lanzamiento** launching silo; **pozo de lobo** (mil) foxhole; **pozo de ventilación** ventilation shaft; **pozo negro, séptico** *or* **ciego** septic tank, cesspool

P.P. *abbr* **porte pagado, por poder**

p.p.^{do} *abbr* **próximo pasado**

práctica *f* practice; method; skill; **prácticas** studies, training

prácticamente *adv* through practice, by experience

practicante *adj* practicing ‖ *mf* practitioner; nurse; medical intern; student teacher; churchgoer

practicar §73 *tr* to practice; bring about; (*un agujero*) make, cut

prácti•co -ca *adj* practical; skillful, practiced; practicing ‖ *m* medical practitioner; (naut) pilot ‖ *f* see **práctica**

pradera *f* meadowland; prairie

prado *m* meadow, pasture; promenade

Praga *f* Prague

pral. *abbr* **principal**

pralte. *abbr* **principalmente**

prángana — estar en la prángana (Mex, W-I) to be broke; (P-R) to be naked

preámbulo *m* preamble; evasion; **no andarse en preámbulos** to come to the point

prebéli•co -ca *adj* prewar

prebenda *f* sinecure, easy job; perk, privilege; (eccl) prebend

preca•rio -ria *adj* precarious

precaución *f* precaution

precaver *tr* to stave off, head off ‖ *intr & ref* to be on one's guard; **precaverse contra or de** to guard against

precavido -da *adj* cautious

precedente *adj* preceding ‖ *m* precedent

preceder *tr & intr* to precede

precepto *m* precept; order, injunction; **los preceptos** the Ten Commandments

preces *fpl* devotions; supplications

precia•do -da *adj* esteemed, valued; precious, valuable; boastful, proud

preciar *tr* to appraise, estimate ‖ *ref* to boast

precintar *tr* to bind, strap; seal

precio *m* price; value, worth; esteem, credit; **a precio de quemazón** at a giveaway price; **precio al por mayor** wholesale price; **precio al por menor** retail price; **precio cerrado** fixed price; **precios de cierre** closing prices; **precio tope** ceiling price

preciosidad *f* preciousness; beauty, gem, jewel

precio•so -sa *adj* precious; valuable; witty; beautiful

preciosura *f* beauty; pretty woman

precipicio *m* precipice; destruction

precipitación *f* precipitation; **precipitación acuosa** rainfall; **precipitación radiactiva** fallout

precipitar *tr* to precipitate; rush, hurl, throw headlong ‖ *ref* to rush, throw oneself headlong

precipito•so -sa *adj* precipitous, rash, reckless; risky, dangerous

precisar *tr* to state precisely, specify; fix; need;

oblige, force; determine || *intr* to be necessary; be important; be urgent; **precisar de** to need
precisión *f* precision; necessity, obligation; (Chile) haste; **precisiones** data
preci•so -sa *adj* necessary; precise; (Ven) haughty
precita•do -da *adj* above-mentioned
precla•ro -ra *adj* illustrious, famous
preconizar §60 *tr* to proclaim, commend publicly
pre•coz *adj* (*pl* **-coces**) precocious; early (*detection*)
predato•rio -ria *adj* predatory
predecir §24 *tr* to predict, foretell
prédica *f* Protestant sermon; harangue
predicar §73 *tr* to preach; praise to the skies; scold, preach to
predicción *f* prediction; **predicción del tiempo** weather forecasting
predilec•to -ta *adj* favorite, preferred
predio *m* property, estate
predisponer §54 *tr* to predispose
predominante *adj* predominant
preeminente *adj* preeminent
preencogi•do -da *adj* preshrunk
preescolar *adj & m* preschool
preestreno *m* (mov) preview
prefabricar §73 *tr* to prefabricate
prefacio *m* preface
preferencia *f* preference; right of way; (*en un estadio, los mejores localidades*) skybox; **de preferencia** preferably, **tener preferencia** to have the right of way
preferente *adj* preferable; favored; (*acciones*) preferred
preferible *adj* preferable
preferir §68 *tr* to prefer
prefigurar *tr* to foreshadow
prefijar *tr* to prefix; prearrange
prefijo *m* prefix; (telecommunications) code
pregón *m* proclamation, public announcement (*by town crier*)
pregonar *tr* to proclaim, announce publicly; hawk; reveal; outlaw; praise openly
pregonero *m* auctioneer; town crier; barker
preguerra *f* prewar period
pregunta *f* question; **hacer una pregunta** to ask a question
preguntar *tr* to ask; to question || *intr* to ask, inquire; **preguntar por** to ask after or for || *ref* to ask oneself; wonder
pregun•tón -tona *adj* inquisitive || *mf* inquisitive person
prejudicio *m* or **prejuicio** *m* prejudgment; prejudice
prelado *m* prelate
preliminar *adj & m* preliminary; **preliminares** (*de un libro*) front matter
preludio *m* prelude
prematu•ro -ra *adj* premature || *mf* premature baby
premedita•do -da *adj* premeditated
premia•do -da *adj* winning || *mf* prizewinner
premiar *tr* to reward; give an award to
premio *m* reward, prize; premium; **a premio** at a premium; **primer premio** blue ribbon, first prize; **premio de consolación** consolation prize; **premio de enganche** (mil) bounty; **premio gordo** first prize; jackpot
premio•so -sa *adj* tight, close; bothersome; strict, rigid; slow, dull
premisa *f* premise; mark, token, clue
premura *f* pressure, haste, urgency
premuro•so -sa *adj* pressing, urgent
prenda *f* pledge; security; pawn; jewel, household article; garment, article of clothing; gift, talent; darling, loved one; **en prenda** in pawn; **en prenda de** as a pledge of; **prenda perdida** forfeit; **prendas** (*juego*) forfeits; **prendas interiores** underwear
prendar *tr* to pawn; pledge; charm, captivate || *ref* — **prendarse de** to take a liking for, fall in love with
prendedero *m* or **prendedor** *m* fillet, brooch; stickpin
prender *tr* to seize, grasp; catch; imprison; dress up; pin; fasten || *intr* to catch; catch fire; take root; turn out well || *ref* to dress up; be fastened; catch hold
prendería *f* second-hand shop
prende•ro -ra *mf* second-hand dealer
prenombra•do -da *adj* above-mentioned; foregoing
prensa *f* press; printing press; vise; press, newspapers; press, frame; **entrar en prensa** to go to press; **meter en prensa** to put the squeeze on; **prensa amarilla** yellow press; **prensa taladradora** drill press
prensado *m* pressing; (*lustre de los tejidos prensados*) sheen
prensador *m* (CAm) paper clip
prensar *tr* to press; squeeze
preña•do -da *adj* pregnant; sagging, bulging; full, charged
preñez *f* pregnancy; fullness; impending danger; inherent confusion
preocupación *f* (*posesión anticipada; cuidado, desvelo*) preoccupation; (*posesión anticipada*) preoccupancy; bias, prejudice
preocupar *tr* to preoccupy, worry || *ref* to become preoccupied, be worried
preparación *f* preparation
prepara•do -da *adj* ready, prepared || *m* (pharm) preparation
preparar *tr* to prepare || *ref* to prepare, get ready
preparati•vo -va *adj* preparatory || *m* preparation, readiness
preponderante *adj* preponderant
preposición *f* preposition
prepóste•ro -ra *adj* reversed, upset, out of order, inopportune
prepucio *m* foreskin, prepuce
prerrogativa *f* prerogative
presa *f* capture, seizure; catch, prey; booty, spoils; dam; trench, ditch, flume; bit, morsel; fang, tusk, claw; fishweir; (sport) hold; **hacer**

presa to seize; **ser presa de** to be a victim of; be prey to
presagiar *tr* to presage, forebode
presagio *m* presage, omen, token
présbita or **présbite** *adj* far-sighted || *mf* far-sighted person
presbiteria•no -na *adj & mf* Presbyterian
prescindir *intr* — **prescindir de** to leave aside, leave out, disregard; do without, dispense with; avoid
prescribir §83 *tr & intr* to prescribe
presencia *f* presence; show, display; **presencia de ánimo** presence of mind
presenciar *tr* to witness, be present at
presentación *f* presentation; format; (*de una persona en el trato de otra u otras*) introduction; (*de un nuevo automóvil, libro, etc.*) appearance
presenta•dor -dora *mf* (telv) moderator, anchor
presentar *tr* to present; introduce || *ref* to present oneself; appear, show up; introduce oneself
presente *adj* present; **hacer presente** to notify of, remind of; **tener presente** to bear or keep in mind || *interj* here!, present! || *m* present, gift; person present
presentimiento *m* presentiment, premonition
presentir §68 *tr* to have a presentiment of
preservar *tr* to preserve, protect
preservati•vo -va *adj & m* preventive; preservative; condom
presidencia *f* presidency; chairmanship
presidenta *f* president; chair, chairperson, chairwoman
presidente *mf* president; chairman; presiding judge; chair, chairperson || *m* chairman
presidiario *m* convict
presidio *m* garrison; fortress; citadel; penitentiary; imprisonment; hard labor; aid, help
presidir *tr* to preside over; dominate || *intr* to preside
presilla *f* loop, fastener; clip; paper clip; shoulder strap
presión *f* pressure; (*cerveza*) **a presión** on draught; **presión de inflado** tire pressure
presionar *tr* to press; put pressure on || *intr* to press; **presionar sobre** to put pressure on
pre•so -sa *adj* seized; imprisoned || *mf* prisoner; convict; **preso preventivo** pretrial prisoner || *f* see **presa**
prestación *f* provision; (compu) feature; **prestaciones** benefits; **prestaciones económicas** financial assistance; **prestaciones por desempleo** unemployment compensation; **prestaciones sociales** welfare
presta•do -da *adj* lent, loaned; **dar prestado** to lend; **pedir** or **tomar prestado** to borrow
prestamista *mf* moneylender; pawnbroker
préstamo *m* loan; **préstamo lingüístico** loan word, borrowing; **préstamo puente** bridge loan
prestar *tr* to lend, loan; (*oído; ayuda; noticias*) give; (*atención*) pay; (*un favor*) do; (*un servicio*) render; (*juramento*) take; (*silencio*) keep; (*paciencia*) show || *intr* (*un paño, la ropa*) give, yield; be useful || *ref* to lend oneself, lend itself
prestata•rio -ria *mf* borrower
presteza *f* speed, promptness, readiness
prestidigitación *f* sleight of hand
prestidigita•dor -dora *adj* captivating || *mf* magician; faker, impostor
prestigio *m* prestige; good standing; spell; illusion
prestigio•so -sa *adj* captivating, spellbinding; famous, renowned; illusory
pres•to -ta *adj* quick, prompt, ready; nimble; (compu, telp) prompt || **presto** *adv* right away
presumi•do -da *adj* conceited, vain || *mf* would-be; showoff
presumir *tr* to presume || *intr* to boast, be conceited
presunción *f* presumption; conceit
presuntuo•so -sa *adj* conceited, vain
presuponer §54 *tr* to presuppose; budget
presupuestar *tr* to budget; (*el coste de una obra*) estimate
presupuesto *m* budget; reason, motive; supposition; estimate
presuro•so -sa *adj* speedy, quick, hasty; zealous, persistent
pretencio•so -sa *adj* pretentious, showy; conceited, vain
pretender *tr* to claim, pretend to; try for, try to do; be a suitor for || *intr* to insist; **pretender** + *inf* to try to + *inf*
pretendiente *mf* pretender, claimant; office seeker || *m* suitor
pretensión *f* pretension; claim; pretense; presumption; effort, pursuit
pretéri•to -ta *adj & m* past
pretil *m* parapet, railing; walk along a parapet
pretina *f* girdle, belt; waistband
pretóni•co -ca *adj* pretonic
prevalecer §22 *intr* to prevail; take root; thrive
prevaler §76 *ref* — **prevalerse de** to avail oneself of, take advantage of
prevaricar §73 *intr* to collude, connive; play false; transgress; rave, be delirious
prevención *f* preparation; prevention; foresight; warning; prejudice; stock, supply; jail, lockup; guardhouse; **a** *or* **de prevención** spare, emergency
preveni•do -da *adj* prepared, ready; foresighted, forewarned; stocked, full
prevenir §79 *tr* to prepare, make ready; forestall, prevent, anticipate; overcome; warn; prejudice || *intr* (*una tempestad*) to come up || *ref* to get ready; come to mind
prever §80 *tr* to foresee
pre•vio -via *adj* previous; preliminary; after, with previous, subject to, e.g., **previo acuerdo** subject to agreement; **cita previa** by appointment
previsión *f* prevision, foresight; foresightedness; forecast; **previsión del tiempo** weather forecasting

previ•sor -sora *adj* far-sighted
previsualización *f* (compu) preview
prevoste *mf* (U.S.A.) (*responsable del profesorado universitario*) provost
prie•to -ta *adj* dark, blackish; stingy, mean; tight, compact; dark-complexioned || *mf* (W-I) darling
prima *f* early morning; bonus, bounty; (ins) premium; (mil) first quarter of the night; (*cuerda*) (mus) treble
pri•mal -mala *adj & mf* yearling
prima•rio -ria *adj* primary || *m* (elec) primary
primavera *f* spring, springtime; cowslip, primrose; robin
primer *adj* apocopated form of **primero,** used only before masculine singular nouns and adjectives
prime•ro -ra *adj* first; former; early; primary; prime; (*materia*) raw || *m* first; **a primeros de** around the beginning of || **primero** *adv* first
primicia *f* first fruits
primige•nio -nia *adj* original, primitive
primiti•vo -va *adj* primitive
pri•mo -ma *adj* first; prime, excellent; skillful; (*materia*) raw || *mf* cousin; sucker, dupe; **primo carnal** *or* **primo hermano** first cousin, cousin-german || *f* see **prima** || **primo** *adv* in the first place
primogéni•to -ta *adj & mf* first-born
primor *m* care, skill, elegance; beauty
primoro•so -sa *adj* careful, skillful, elegant; fine, exquisite
princesa *f* princess; **princesa viuda** dowager princess
principal *adj* principal, main, chief; first, foremost; essential, important; famous, illustrious; (*piso*) second || *m* principal, head, chief
príncipe *m* prince; **portarse como un príncipe** to live like a prince; **príncipe consorte** prince consort; **príncipe de Asturias** heir apparent of the King of Spain; **príncipe de Gales** prince of Wales; **príncipe heredero** crown prince; **príncipes** prince and princess
principiante *adj* beginning || *mf* beginner, apprentice, novice, amateur
principiar *tr, intr & ref* to begin
principio *m* start, beginning; principle; origin, source; (culin) entree; **a principios de** around the beginning of; **en un principio** at the beginning; **principio de admiración** inverted exclamation point; **principio de interrogación** inverted question mark
pringar §44 *tr* to dip or soak in grease or fat; spot or stain with grease; make bleed; slander, run down; splash || *intr* to meddle; (CAm, Mex) to drizzle || *ref* to peculate
pringo•so -sa *adj* greasy, fatty
prioridad *f* priority; **de máxima prioridad** of the highest priority
prisa *f* hurry, haste; urgency; crush, crowd; **darse prisa** to hurry, make haste; **estar de prisa** or **tener prisa** to be in a hurry
prisión *f* seizure, capture; imprisonment; prison; **prisión celular** cell house; **prisiones** shackles, fetters
prisione•ro -ra *mf* prisoner; (*cautivo de una pasión o afecto*) captive; **prisionero de guerra** prisoner of war, POW || *m* setscrew; studbolt
prisma *m* prism
prismáticos *mpl* binoculars
priva•do -da *adj* private || *m* (*de un alto personaje*) favorite || *f* cesspool
privar *tr* to deprive; forbid, prohibit || *intr* to be in vogue; prevail; be in favor || *ref* to deprive oneself; **privarse de** to give up
privilegiar *tr* to grant a privilege to
privilegio *m* privilege
pro *m & f* profit, advantage; **¡buena pro!** good appetite!; **de pro** of note, of worth; **el pro y el contra** the pros and the cons; **en pro de** on behalf of
proa *f* (aer) nose; (naut) prow
probable *adj* probable, likely
probador *m* fitting room; **probador beta** (compu) beta tester
probar §61 *tr* to prove; test; try; (*clothing*) try on; try out; sample; fit; suit; (*vino*) touch || *intr* to taste; **probar de** to take a taste of || *ref* to try on
probidad *f* probity, integrity, honesty
problema *m* problem
pro•caz *adj* (*pl* **-caces**) impudent, insolent, bold
procedencia *f* origin, source; point of departure
procedente *adj* coming, originating; proper
proceder *m* conduct, behavior || *intr* to proceed; originate; behave; be proper
procedimiento *m* procedure; proceeding; process
procelo•so -sa *adj* tempestuous, stormy
prócer *adj* high, lofty || *m* hero, leader
procesado *adj* (compu) enhanced
procesador *m* processor; **procesador de alimentos** food processor; **procesador de textos** *or* **palabras** word processor
procesamiento *m* (law) prosecution; (com) turnaround; (compu) processing; **procesamiento de datos** data processing; **procesamiento de textos** or **palabras** word processing: **procesamiento por lotes** batch processing
procesar *tr* to sue, prosecute; indict; try; (compu) to process, data-process; to enhance
procesión *f* procession; origin, emergence
proceso *m* process; progress; suit, lawsuit; **proceso verbal** minutes
proclama *f* proclamation; marriage banns
proclamar *tr* to proclaim; acclaim
proclíti•co -ca *adj & m* proclitic
procurador *m* attorney, solicitor; proxy
procurar *tr* to strive for; manage as attorney; yield, produce; try to
prodigar §44 *tr* to lavish; squander; waste || *ref* to be a show-off
prodigio *m* prodigy

prodigio•so -sa *adj* prodigious, marvelous; fine, excellent
pródigo -ga *adj* prodigal; lavish || *mf* prodigal
producción *f* production; crop, yield, produce; **producción en masa** *or* **en serie** mass production
producir §19 *tr* to produce; yield, bear; cause, bring about || *ref* to explain oneself; come about; take place
producto *m* product; produce; proceeds
proeza *f* prowess; feat, stunt
prof. *abbr* **profeta**
profanar *tr* to profane
profa•no -na *adj* profane; indecent, immodest; worldly; lay || *mf* profane; worldly person; layman
profecía *f* prophecy || **las Profecías** (Bib) the Prophets
proferir §68 *tr* to utter
profesar *tr & intr* to profess
profesión *f* profession; **profesión de fe** confession of faith
profe•sor -sora *mf* teacher, professor; **profe•sor -sora adjunto** assistant professor, associate professor; **profe•sor -sora suplente** substitute teacher
profesorado *m* faculty, teaching staff; teaching profession
profeta *m* prophet
profetisa *f* prophetess
profetizar §60 *tr* to prophesy
profilácti•co -ca *adj & m* prophylactic; preventive || *m* condom || *f* hygiene
prófu•go -ga *adj & mf* fugitive || *m* slacker, draft dodger
profundidad *f* profundity; depth
profundizar §60 *tr* to deepen; fathom, get to the bottom of
profun•do -da *adj* profound; deep
profu•so -sa *adj* profuse, abundant
progenie *f* descent, lineage, progency
progno•sis *f* (*pl* **-sis**) prognosis; (*del tiempo*) forecast
programa *m* program; **programa continuo** (mov) continuous showing; **programa concurso** (telv) game show; **programa de estudios** curriculum; **programa (para ordenador)** program(me), software
programación *f* (compu) program(m)ing; (telv) scheduling
programador *m* or **programadora** *f* (compu) program(m)er
programar *tr* to program; (compu) program(me)
progresar *intr* to progress
progresista *adj & mf* (pol) progressive
progreso *m* progress; **hacer progresos** to make progress
prohibido *adj* forbidden; prohibited; *SIGNs:* **prohibido el paso** *or* **la entrada** no admission, no admittance, no entry; **prohibido estacionar** no parking; **prohibido fijar carteles** post no bills; **prohibido fumar** no smoking
prohibir *tr* to prohibit, forbid || *ref* to be forbidden or prohibited; **se prohibe fijar carteles** post no bills; **se prohibe fumar** no smoking; **se prohibe la entrada** no admission, no admittance, no entry
prohijar *tr* to adopt
prohombre *m* (*en los gremios de los artesanos*) master; leader, head; (coll) big shot
prójimo *m* fellow man, fellow creature, neighbor; fellow
pról. *abbr* **prólogo**
prole *f* kids, offspring; brood (pej)
proletariado *m* proletariat
proleta•rio -ria *adj & m* proletarian
proliferar *intr* to proliferate
prolífi•co -ca *adj* prolific
proli•jo -ja *adj* tedious, too long; fussy, fastidious; long-winded; tiresome
prologar §44 *tr* to preface, write a preface for
prólogo *m* prologue; preface
prolongar §44 *tr* to prolong, extend; (geom) to produce
promediar *tr* to divide into two equal parts; average || *intr* to mediate; be half over
promedio *m* average, mean; middle
promesa *f* promise
promete•dor -dora *adj* promising
prometer *tr & intr* to promise || *ref* to become engaged
prometi•do -da *adj* engaged, betrothed || *m* promise; fiancé || *f* fiancée
prominente *adj* prominent
promiso•rio -ria *adj* promissory
promoción *f* promotion; advancement; (*conjunto de individuos que obtienen un grado en un mismo año*) class, year, crop
promontorio *m* promontory, headland; unwieldy thing
promo•tor -tora *adj* (com) development || *mf* promoter, developer; instigator; **promotora inmobiliaria** development company; **promotor comercial** *or* **de ventas** sales representative; **promotor inmobiliario** property developer
promover §47 *tr* to promote; advance, further
promulgar §44 *tr* to promulgate
pronombre *m* pronoun
pronosticar §73 *tr* to prognosticate, foretell
pronóstico *m* prognostic, forecast; almanac; (med) prognosis
pron•to -ta *adj* quick, speedy; prompt; ready || *m* jerk; sudden impulse, fit of anger || **pronto** *adv* right away, soon; early; promptly; **lo más pronto posible** as soon as possible; **tan pronto como** as soon as
pronunciación *f* pronunciation; (law) pronouncement
pronuncia•do -da *adj* marked; (*curva*) sharp; (*pendiente*) steep; bulky
pronunciamiento *m* insurrection, uprising;

(*golpe de estado militar*) pronunciamento; (law) decree

pronunciar *tr* to pronounce; utter; (*un discurso*) make, deliver; decide on || *ref* to rebel; declare oneself

pro-opción *f* pro-choice

propaganda *f* propaganda; advertising

propagar §44 *tr* to propagate; spread; broadcast

propalar *tr* to divulge, spread

proparoxíto•no -na *adj & m* proparoxytone

propasar *ref* to go too far, take undue liberty

propender *intr* to tend, incline, be inclined

propensión *f* propensity; predisposition

propen•so -sa *adj* inclined, disposed, prone

propiciar *tr* to propitiate; support, favor, sponsor

propi•cio -cia *adj* propitious, favorable

propiedad *f* property; ownership; naturalness, likeness; **es propiedad** copyrighted; **propiedad horizontal** condominium; **propiedad industrial** patent rights; **propiedad inmobiliaria** real estate; **propiedad intelectual** *or* **literaria** copyright

propieta•rio -ria *mf* owner; **propietario de una vivienda** home owner || *m* proprietor || *f* proprietress

propina *f* tip, fee, gratuity

propinar *tr* (*algo a beber*) to offer; (*medicamentos*) prescribe or administer; (*palos, golpes, etc.*) give || *ref* (*una bebida*) to treat oneself to

propin•cuo -cua *adj* near, close at hand

pro•pio -pia *adj* proper, suitable; peculiar, characteristic; natural; same; himself, herself, etc.; own || *m* messenger; native; **propios** public lands

proponer §54 *tr* to propose; propound; (*a una persona para un empleo*) name, present || *ref* to plan; propose

proporción *f* proportion; opportunity

proporciona•do -da *adj* proportionate; fit, suitable

proporcionar *tr* to furnish, provide, supply, give; proportion; adapt, adjust

proposición *f* proposition, proposal; **proposición dominante** main clause

propósito *m* aim, purpose, intention, objective; subject matter; **a propósito** by the way; apropos, fitting; in place; **a propósito de** apropos of; **de propósito** on purpose; **fuera de propósito** irrelevant, beside the point

propuesta *f* proposal, proposition

propulsar *tr* to propel, drive

propulsión *f* propulsion; **propulsión a chorro** jet propulsion; **propulsión a cohete** rocket propulsion

pror. *abbr* **procurador**

prorratear *tr* to prorate

prórroga *f* extension, renewal

prorrogar §44 *tr* to defer, postpone, extend

prorrumpir *intr* to spurt, shoot forth; break forth, burst out

prosa *f* prose; chatter, idle talk

prosai•co -ca *adj* prose; prosaic, dull

proscribir §83 *tr* to outlaw, proscribe

proscrip•to -ta *mf* exile, outlaw

prosecución *f* continuation, prosecution; pursuit

proseguir §67 *tr* to continue, carry on || *intr* to continue

prosélito *m* proselyte

prosista *mf* prose writer; chatterbox

prosódi•co -ca *adj* (*acento*) stress

prospectar *tr & intr* to prospect

prosperar *tr* to make prosper || *intr* to prosper, thrive

prosperidad prosperity

próspe•ro -ra *adj* prosperous, thriving, successful

próstata *f* (anat) prostate (gland)

prosternar *ref* to prostrate oneself

prostituir §20 *tr* to prostitute || *ref* to prostitute oneself; become a prostitute

prostituta *f* prostitute

prosu•do -da *adj* (Chile, Ecuad, Peru) pompous, solemn

protagonista *mf* protagonist

protagonizar §60 *tr* to play the leading rôle of

protección *f* protection; **protección aduanera** protective tariff; **protección a la infancia** child welfare; **protección de datos, protección de la información** data protection

proteger §17 *tr* to protect

protegida *f* protégée

protegido *m* protégé

proteína *f* protein

proter•vo -va *adj* perverse

protesta *f* protest; pledge, promise

protestante *adj & mf* Protestant

protestar *tr* to protest, asseverate; (*la fe*) profess || *intr* to protest; **protestar de** (*aseverar con ahinco*) to protest (*to state positively*); **protestar contra** (*negar la validez de*) to protest (*to deny forcibly*)

protocolo *m* protocol

protoplasma *m* protoplasm

prototipo *m* prototype

protozoario *m* or **protozoo** *m* protozoön

provecho *m* advantage, benefit; profit, gain; advance, progress; **¡buen provecho!** good luck!; good appetite!; **de provecho** useful; **provechos** perquisites

provecho•so -sa *adj* advantageous, beneficial; profitable; useful

provec•to -ta *adj* old, ripe

proveedor -dora *mf* supplier, provider, purveyor; steward; (compu) provider

proveer §43 & §83 *tr* to provide, furnish; supply; resolve, settle || *intr* to provide; **proveer a** to provide for, cater to || *ref* to supply oneself; have a bowel movement

provenir §79 *intr* to come, arise

Provenza, la Provence

provenzal *adj & mf* Provençal

proverbio *m* proverb

providencia *f* providence, foresight; step, measure

providencial *adj* providential
provincia *f* province
provisión *f* provision; supply, stock; **provisiones de boca** foodstuffs
proviso•rio -ria *adj* provisory, provisional
provocar §73 *tr* to provoke; promote, bring about; incite, tempt, move ‖ *intr* to provoke; vomit
provocati•vo -va *adj* suggestive
proxeneta *mf* go-between
proximidad *f* proximity, closeness; **proximidades** neighborhood
próxi•mo -ma *adj* next; near; neighboring, close; early; **próximo pasado** last
proyección *f* projection; influence
proyectar *tr* to project; cast; design ‖ *ref* to project, stick out; (*una sombra*) be projected, fall
proyectil *m* projectile; **proyectil buscador del blanco** homing missile; **proyectil dirigido** or **teleguiado** guided missile
proyecto *m* project; **proyecto de ley** bill
proyector *m* projector, searchlight; projection machine
prudencia *f* prudence
prudente *adj* prudent
prueba *f* proof; trial, test, shakedown; examination; (*de un traje*) fitting; (*de un alimento o una bebida*) sample, sampling; evidence; acrobatics; sleight of hand; (sport) event; **a prueba** on approval, on trial; **a prueba de** proof against, -proof, e.g., **a prueba de escaladores** burglarproof; **a prueba de incendio** fireproof; **prueba de acidez** (chem) litmus test; **prueba de alcohol** alcohol-level test; **prueba de fuego** acid test; **prueba de nivel** placement test; **pruebas de planas** page proof; **pruebas de primeras** first proof (*for proofreader*); **pruebas de segundas** galley proof (*for author*); **prueba sobre el terreno** field test
pruebista *mf* acrobat
prurito *m* itching; eagerness, itch
psicoanálisis *m* psychoanalysis
psicoanalizar §60 *tr* to psychoanalyze
psicodéli•co -ca *adj* psychedelic
psicología *f* psychology
psicológi•co -ca *adj* psychologic(al)
psicólo•go -ga *mf* psychologist
psicópata *mf* psychopath
psico•sis *f* (*pl* **-sis**) psychosis
psicoterapia *f* psychotherapy; **psicoterapia de grupo** group therapy
psicóti•co -ca *adj & mf* psychotic
psique *f* cheval glass ‖ **Psique** *f* Psyche
psiquiatra *mf* psychiatrist
psiquiatría *f* psychiatry
psíqui•co -ca *adj* psychic
P.S.M. *abbr* **por su mandato**
pte. *abbr* **parte, presente**
púa *f* point; prick, barb; tine, prong; (*del fonógrafo*) needle, stylus; (*del peine*) tooth; thorn; (*del puerco espín*) spine, quill; sting; graft; plectrum; tricky person
pubertad *f* puberty
pubia•no -na *adj* pubic
publicación *f* publication
publicar §73 *tr* to publish; publicize
publicidad *f* publicity; advertising; **publicidad de lanzamiento** advance publicity
publicita•rio -ria *adj* publicity; advertising
públi•co -ca *adj & m* public
pucha *f* (W-I) small bouquet; (Mex) crescent roll
púcher *m* (*drogas*) pusher
puchero *m* pot, kettle; stew; daily bread; pouting; **hacer pucheros** to pout, screw up one's face
pucho *m* fag end, remnant; (*de cigarro*) stump; trifle, trinket; (*el hijo menor*) baby
puden•do -da *adj* ugly, shameful; obscene; (*partes*) private
pudiente *adj* powerful; well-off, well-to-do
pudín *m* pudding
pudor *m* modesty, shyness; chastity
pudoro•so -sa *adj* modest, shy; chaste
pudrición *f* rot, rotting
pudrir §83 *tr* to rot; worry ‖ *intr* to be dead and buried ‖ *ref* to rot; be worried; (*en la cárcel*) languish
pueblo *m* people; common people; town, village; **pueblo fantasma** ghost town
puente *m* bridge; (dent, mus) bridge; (aut) axle, rear axle; **hacer puente** to take the intervening day off; **puente aéreo** airlift; air shuttle; **puente colgante** suspension bridge; **puente de engrase** grease lift; **puente levadizo** drawbridge, lift bridge; **puente peatonal** footbridge
puer•co -ca *adj* piggish, hoggish; dirty, filthy; slovenly; coarse, mean; lewd ‖ *m* hog; **puerco espín** *or* **espino** porcupine; **puerco salvaje** wild boar ‖ *f* sow; slattern, slut
puericia *f* childhood
puericultura *f* child rearing, infant care
pueril *adj* puerile, childish
puerilidad *f* puerility, childishness
puerro *m* leek; (*mariguana, hachich*) joint
puerta *f* door, doorway; gate, gateway; **a puerta cerrada** or **a puertas cerradas** behind closed doors; **de puerta a puerta** door-to-door; **puerta de (la) calle** street door; **puerta de vaivén** swinging door; **puerta giratoria** revolving door
puerto *m* harbor, port; haven; mountain pass; **puerto aéreo** airport; **puerto artificial** man-made harbor; **puerto de arribada** port of call; **puerto de mar** seaport; **puerto franco** free port; **puerto deportivo** marina; **puerto marítimo** dock, port; **puerto seco** frontier customhouse; **puerto serie** (compu) serial port
puertorrique•ño -ña *adj & mf* Puerto Rican
pues *adv* then, well; yes, certainly; why; anyhow; **pues bien** well then; **pues que** since ‖

conj for, since, because, inasmuch as || *interj* well!, then!

puesta *f* setting; laying; putting; (*dinero apostado*) stake; **a puesta del sol** *or* **a puestas del sol** at sunset; **puesta a punto** adjustment; carrying out, completion; **puesta a tierra** (elec) grounding; **puesta de largo** coming out, social debut

pues•to -ta *adj* dressed; **puesto que** since, inasmuch as || *m* place; booth, stand; office; station; barracks; (*para cazadores*) blind; **puesto a punto** (aut) tune-up; **puesto de socorro** first-aid station || *f* see **puesta**

púgil *m* pugilist

pugilato *m* boxing; fist fight

pugilismo *m* pugilism

pugna *f* fight, battle; struggle, conflict; **en pugna** at issue; **en pugna con** at odds with

pugnar *intr* to fight, struggle; strive, persist

pug•naz *adj* (*pl* **-naces**) pugnacious

pujante *adj* powerful, mighty, vigorous

pujar *tr* (*un proyecto*) to push; (*un precio*) raise, bid up || *intr* to struggle, strain; falter; (*por decir una cosa*) grope; snivel; **pujar para adentro** (CAm, W-I) to keep silent, say nothing

pul•cro -cra *adj* neat, tidy, trim; circumspect

pulga *f* flea; **de malas pulgas** peppery, hot-tempered; **hacer de una pulga un camello** or **un elefante** to make a mountain out of a molehill; **no aguantar pulgas** to stand for no nonsense

pulgada *f* inch

pulgar *m* thumb

Pulgarcito *s* Tom Thumb

puli•do -da *adj* pretty; neat; polished; clean, spotless

pulimentar *tr* to polish

pulimento *m* polish

pulir *tr* to polish; finish; give a polish to

pulla *f* dig, cutting remark; filthy remark; witticism

pulmón *m* lung; **pulmón de acero** or **de hierro** iron lung

pulmonía *f* pneumonia

pulóver *m* sweater, pullover

pulpa *f* pulp

púlpito *m* pulpit

pulpo *m* octopus

pulque *m* (Mex) agave brandy

pulsación *f* pulsation, throb, beat; strike, striking; (*del pianista, el mecanógrafo*) touch

pulsar *tr* (*un botón*) to push; (*un piano, arpa, guitarra*) play; (*una tecla*) strike, press; (*una cuerda*) pluck; feel or take the pulse of; sound out, examine || *intr* to pulsate, throb, beat

pulsear *intr* to hand-wrestle

pulsera *f* bracelet; wristlet, watch strap; **pulsera de pedida** engagement bracelet

pulso *m* pulse; steadiness, steady hand; tact, care, caution; bracelet; wrist watch; **a pulso** with hand and wrist; by main strength; (*dibujo*) freehand; **sacar a pulso** to carry out against odds; **tomar el pulso a** to take the pulse of

pulular *intr* to swarm; bud, sprout

pulverizar §60 *tr* to pulverize; atomize; spray

pum *interj* bang!

puma *m* cougar

puna *f* (SAm) bleak tableland in the Andes; (SAm) mountain sickness

pundonor *m* point of honor; face

pundonoro•so sa *adj* punctilious, scrupulous; haughty, dignified

pungir §27 *tr* to prick; sting

punk *adj* punk || *mf & m* punk

punta *f* (*extremo agudo*) point; tip, end; (*del cigarro*) butt; nail; point, cape, headland; (*del toro*) horn; (*del asta del ciervo*) tine, prong; style, graver; touch, tinge, trace; (*del vino*) souring; (elec) point; **de punta** on end; on tiptoe; state-of-the-art; **de punta en blanco** in full armor; in full regalia; **estar de punta (con)** to be at odds (with); **punta de combate** (*del torpedo*) warhead; **punta de lanza** spearhead; **punta de París** wire nail; **sacar punta a** to put a point on, to sharpen; **tener en la punta de la lengua** to have on the tip of one's tongue

puntabola *f* (Bol) ballpoint pen

puntada *f* hint; (sew) stitch; (*dolor agudo*) stitch, sharp pain

puntal *m* prop, support; stay, stanchion; backing, support; bite, snack; (naut) depth of hold

puntapié *m* kick; **echar a puntapiés** to kick out

puntear *tr* to dot, mark with dots; (*guitarra*) pluck; stipple; stitch || *intr* (naut) to tack

puntera *f* toe, toe patch; leather tip; (coll) kick

puntería *f* aim, aiming; marksmanship

puntero *m* pointer; (*del reloj*) hand; stonecutter's chisel; punch; leading animal

puntiagu•do -da *adj* sharp-pointed

puntilla *f* brad; narrow lace edging; (*de la pluma fuente*) point; (carp) tracing point; dagger; **de puntillas** on tiptoe; **puntilla francesa** finishing nail

puntillero *m* bullfighter who delivers coup de grace with dagger

puntillo•so -sa *adj* punctilious

punto *m* (*señal de dimensiones poco perceptibles*) point, dot; stitch, loop; mesh; (*rotura en un tejido de punto*) break; jot; cabstand, hackstand; (*en inglés se emplea la coma en aritmética para agrupar las cifras de un entero*) comma (*used to group the digits of an integer*); (gram) period; (math, typ, sport, fig) point; **a buen punto** opportunely; **al punto** at once; **a punto de** on the point of; **a punto fijo** for certain; **de punto** knitted; **dos puntos** (gram) colon; **en punto** sharp, on the dot; **poner a punto** to fine-tune; **poner punto final a** to wind up, to bring to an end; **punto de admiración** exclamation mark or point; **punto de aguja** knitting; **punto de Hungría** herringbone; **punto de media** knitwork; **punto de mira** aim; center of attraction; **punto de ruptura** breaking point; **punto de vista** point of view; **¡punto en boca!** mum's

the word!; **punto interrogante** question mark; **punto muerto** dead center; (aut) neuter; **puntos suspensivos** suspension points; **puntos y rayas** dots and dashes; **punto y coma** *msg* semicolon
puntuación *f* punctuation; mark, grade; scoring
puntual *adj* punctual; certain, sure; exact, accurate
puntualizar §60 *tr* to fix in the memory; give a detailed account of; finish; draw up
puntuar §21 *tr & intr* to punctuate; score
puntura *f* puncture, prick
punzada *f* prick; shooting pain; (*del remordimiento*) pang
punzante *adj* sharp, pricking; barbed, biting, caustic
punzar §60 *tr* to prick, puncture, punch; to sting; to grieve || *intr* to sting
punzón *m* punch; pick; burin, graver; budding horn, tenderling; **punzón de marcar** center punch
puñada *f* punch
puñado *m* handful, bunch
puñal *m* dagger, poniard
puñalada *f* stab; blow, sudden sorrow; **puñalada de misericordia** coup de grâce; **puñalada trapera** stab in the back
puñetazo *m* punch; bang with the fist
puño *m* fist; cuff; wristband; grasp; fistful, handful; hilt; (*p.ej., del paraguas*) handle; (*del bastón*) head; punch; **como un puño** whopping big; tiny, microscopic; close-fisted; **de su propio puño** *or* **de su puño y letra** in his own hand, in his own writing; **puño de hierro** brass knuckles
pupa *f* pimple; fever blister
pupila *f* (*del ojo*) pupil
pupi•lo -la *mf* boarder; orphan, ward; pupil || *f* see **pupila**
pupitre *m* writing desk
puquio *m* (SAm) spring or pool of fresh, clear water
puré *m* purée; **puré de patatas** mashed potatoes; **puré de tomates** stewed tomatoes
purera *f* cigar case
pureza *f* purity
purga *f* purge; purgative; drain valve
purgante *adj & m* purgative
purgar §44 *tr* to purge; physic; drain; purify, refine; expiate; (*pasiones*) control, check; (*sospechas*) clear away || *ref* to take a physic; unburden oneself
puridad *f* purity
purificar §73 *tr* to purify
purita•no -na *adj & mf* puritan; Puritan
pu•ro -ra *adj* pure; sheer; (*cielo*) clear; out-and-out, outright; **de puro** completely, totally; because of being || *m* cigar
púrpura *f* purple
purpura•do -da *adj* purple || *m* (eccl) cardinal
purpúre•o -a *adj* purple
pusilánime *adj* pusillanimous, lily-livered
pústula *f* pustule
puta *f* whore
putañear or **putear** *intr* to whore around
putati•vo -va *adj* supposed; (law) putative
putrefac•to -ta *adj* rotten, putrid
pútri•do -da *adj* putrid, rotten
puya *f* steel point; (*del gallo*) spur

Q

Q, q (cu) *f* eighteenth letter of the Spanish alphabet
q.b.s.m. *abbr* **que besa su mano**
q.e.p.d. *abbr* **que en paz descanse**
q.e.s.m. *abbr* **que estrecha su mano**
quántum *m* (*pl* **quanta**) quantum
quásar *m* quasar
que *pron rel* that, which; who, whom; **el que** he who; which, the one which; who, the one who || *adv* than || *conj* that; for, because; let, e.g., **que entre** let him come in; **a que** I'll bet that
qué *adj & pron interr* what, which; **¿qué tal?** how?; hello, how's everything? || *interj* what!; what a!; how!
quebrada *f* gorge, ravine, gap; brook; failure, bankruptcy
quebradi•zo -za *adj* brittle, fragile; frail
quebra•do -da *adj* weakened; bankrupt; ruptured; rough; winding || *m* (math) fraction || *f* see **quebrada**
quebrantable *adj* breakable
quebrantar *tr* to break; break open; break out of; grind, crush; soften, mollify; (*un contrato; la ley; un hábito; un testamento; el corazón de una persona*) break || *ref* to break; become broken
quebranto *m* break, breaking; heavy loss; great sorrow; discouragement
quebrar §2 *tr* to break; bend, twist; crush; overcome; temper, soften || *intr* to break; fail; weaken, give in || *ref* to break; weaken; become ruptured
queda *f* curfew
quedar *intr* to remain; stay; be left; be left over; stop, leave off; turn out; be; be found, be located; **quedar en** to agree on; agree to; **quedar por** + *inf* or **sin** + *inf* to remain to be + *pp* || *ref* to remain; stay; stop; be; be left; put up; **quedarse con** to keep, to take; **quedarse tan fresco** to show no offense

que•do -da *adj* quiet, still; gentle || *f* see **queda** || **quedo** *adv* softly, in a low voice; gropingly
quehacer *m* work, task, chore
queja *f* complaint, lament; whine, moan
quejar *ref* to complain, lament; whine, moan
quejido *m* complaint, whine, moan
quejumbre *f* complaining, whine, moan
quejumbro•so -sa *adj* complaining; whining, whiny
quema *f* fire; burning; **a quema ropa** pointblank; **de quema** distilled; **hacer quema** (Arg, Bol) to hit the mark
quemada *f* burnt brush; (Mex) fire
quemadero *m* incinerator; (*poste destinado para quemar a los condenados a la pena de fuego*) stake
quema•do -da *adj* burned; burnt out; angry || *m* burnt brush; **oler a quemado** to smell of fire; **saber a quemado** to taste burned || *f* see **quemada**
quema•dor -dora *adj* burning; incendiary || *m* burner
quemadura *f* burn; (agr) smut
quemar *tr* to burn; scald; set on fire; scorch; frostbite; sell too cheap; (CAm, Mex) to betray, inform against || *intr* to burn, be hot || *ref* to burn; be burning up; fret; (*estar cercano a lo que se busca*) be warm, be hot; **quemarse las cejas** to burn the midnight oil
quemarropa — a quemarropa point-blank
quemazón *f* burn; burning; intense heat; (*de un fusible*) blowout; itch; cutting remark; pique, anger; (hum) bargain sale; (Arg, Bol, Chile) mirage on the pampas
que•pis *m* (*pl* **-pis**) kepi
queque *m* cake
querella *f* complaint; dispute, quarrel; lawsuit
querellar *ref* to complain; whine; sue
querencia *f* liking, affection; attraction; love of home; (*de animales*) haunt; favorite spot
querencio•so -sa *adj* homing; (*sitio*) favorite
querer *m* love, affection; liking, fondness || *v* §55 *tr* to wish, want, desire; like; love; **como quiera** anyhow; anyway; **como quiera que** whereas; inasmuch as; no matter how; **cuando quiera** any time; **donde quiera** anywhere; **querer bien** to love; **sin querer** unwillingly; unintentionally || *v aux* to wish to, want to, desire to; will; be about to, be trying to, e.g., **quiere llover** it is trying to rain; **querer decir** to mean; **querer más** to prefer to, would rather
queri•do -da *adj* dear || *mf* lover; paramour; dearie || *f* mistress
quermés *f* or **quermese** *f* bazaar; village or country fair
queroseno *m* var of **keroseno**
querubín *m* cherub
quesadilla *f* cheesecake; sweet pastry
quese•ro -ra *adj* cheesy || *mf* cheesemonger; cheesemaker || *f* cheese board; cheese mold; cheese dish
queso *m* cheese; **medio queso** tailor's ironing board; **queso crema** cream cheese; **queso de cerdo** headcheese; **queso de nata** cream cheese; **queso de soja** bean curd, tofu; **queso fundido** processed cheese; **queso helado** brick ice cream; **queso para extender** *or* **para untar** cheese spread
quevedos *mpl* nose glasses
quiá *interj* oh, no!
quicio *m* pivot hole (*of hinge*); **fuera de quicio** out of order; **sacar de quicio** to put out of order; unhinge
quiebra *f* crack; damage, loss; bankruptcy
quien *pron rel* who, whom; he who, she who; someone who, anyone who
quién *pron interr* who, whom
quienquiera *pron indef* anyone, anybody; **quienquiera que** whoever; **a quienquiera que** whomever
quie•to -ta *adj* quiet, calm; virtuous
quietud *f* quiet, calm, stillness
quijada *f* jaw, jawbone
quijotes•co -ca *adj* quixotic
quilate *m* carat
quilla *f* keel; (*de ave*) breastbone; **dar de quilla** (naut) to keel over
quilo *m* kilogram; **sudar el quilo** to slave, be a drudge
quimera *f* chimera; dispute, quarrel
química *f* chemistry
quími•co -ca *adj* chemical || *mf* chemist || *f* see **química**
quimicultura *f* tank farming
quimioterapia *f* chemotherapy
quimono *m* kimono
quina *f* cinchona, Peruvian bark
quincalla *f* hardware
quincallería *f* hardware store; hardware business; hardware factory
quincalle•ro -ra *mf* hardware merchant
quince *adj & pron* fifteen || *m* fifteen; (*en las fechas*) fifteenth
quincea•vo -va *adj & m* fifteenth
quince•no -na *adj & m* fifteenth || *f* fortnight, two weeks; two weeks' pay
quincuagési•mo -ma *adj & m* fiftieth
quiniela *f* pelota game of five; soccer lottery; daily double; (Arg, Urug) numbers game
quinien•tos -tas *adj & pron* five hundred || **quinientos** *m* five hundred
quinina *f* quinine
quinqué *m* student lamp, oil lamp
quinquenal *adj* five-year
quinta *f* villa, country house; draft, induction; **ir a quintas** to be drafted; **redimirse de las quintas** to be exempted from the draft
quintacolumnista *mf* fifth columnist
quintal *m* quintal, hundredweight
quintar *tr* to draft
quinteto *m* quintet
quintilla *f* five-line stanza of eight syllables and two rhymes; any five-line stanza with two rhymes
quintilli•zo -za *mf* quint, quintuplet

Quintín — armar la de San Quintín to raise a rumpus, raise a row
quin•to -ta *adj* fifth || *m* fifth; lot; pasture; draftee || *f* see **quinta**
quinza•vo -va *adj & m* fifteenth
quiosco *m* kiosk, summerhouse; stand; **quiosco de música** bandstand; **quiosco de necesidad** comfort station; **quiosco de periódicos** newsstand
quiquiri•quí *m* (*pl* **-quíes**) cock-a-doodle-doo; cock of the walk
quirófano *m* operating room
quiromancia *f* or **quiromancía** *f* palmistry
quiropodista *mf* chiropodist
quiroprácti•co -ca *adj* chiropractic || *mf* chiropractor
quirúrgi•co -ca *adj* surgical
quirurgo *m* surgeon
quiscal *m* grackle
quisicosa *f* puzzler
quisqui•do -da *adj* (Arg) constipated
quisquilla *f* trifle, triviality; **pararse en quisquillas** to bicker, make a fuss over trifles; **quisquillas** hairsplitting, quibbling
quisquillo•so -sa *adj* trifling; touchy; fastidious; hairsplitting
quiste *m* cyst
quis•to -ta *adj* — **bien quisto** well-liked, welcome; **mal quisto** disliked, unwelcome
quitaesmalte *m* nail-polish remover
quitaman•chas *mf* (*pl* **-chas**) (*persona*) clothes cleaner, spot remover || *m* (*substancia*) clothes cleaner, spot remover
quitamo•tas *mf* (*pl* **-tas**) bootlicker, apple polisher
quitanie•ve *m* or **quitanie•ves** *m* (*pl* **-ves**) snowplow
quitapie•dras *m* (*pl* **-dras**) cowcatcher
quitapintura *m* paint remover
quitapón *m* pompon for draft mules; **de quitapón** detachable, removable
quitar *tr* to remove; take away; (*la mesa*) clear; (*esfuerzo, trabajo*) save; (*tiempo*) take; free; parry; **quitar algo a algo** to take something off something, remove something from something; **quitar algo a uno** to remove something from someone; take something away from someone || *intr* — **de quita y pon** detachable, removable || *ref* (*el sombrero, una prenda de vestir*) to take off; (*el sombrero en señal de cortesía*) tip; (*una mancha*) come out, come off; (*un vicio*) give up; withdraw
quitasol *m* parasol, sunshade
quite *m* removal; hindrance; dodge; (*en la esgrima*) parry; (taur) passes made with the cape to draw the bull away from the man in danger
quizá or **quizás** *adv* maybe, perhaps
quó•rum *m* (*pl* **-rum**) quorum

R

R, r (ere) *f* nineteenth letter of the Spanish alphabet
R. *abbr* **respuesta, Reverencia, Reverendo**
rabada *f* hind quarter, rump
rabadilla *f* base of the spine
rábano *m* radish; **rábano picante** or **rusticano** horseradish; **tomar el rábano por las hojas** to be on the wrong track
ra•bí *m* (*pl* **-bíes**) rabbi
rabia *f* anger, rage; (*hidrofobia*) rabies; **tener rabia a** to have a grudge against
rabiar *intr* to rage, rave; get mad; go mad, have rabies; **que rabia** like the deuce; **rabiar por** to be dying for; be dying to
rabieta *f* tantrum
rabillo *m* leafstalk; flower stalk; (*en los cereales*) mildew spot; (*del ojo*) corner
rabio•so -sa *adj* mad, rabid
rabo *m* tail; (*del ojo*) corner; (fig) tail, train; **rabo verde** (CAm) old rake
ra•bón -bona *adj* bobtail; (Chile) bare, naked; (Mex) mean, wretched || *f* camp follower; **hacer rabona** to play hooky
rabotada *f* swish of the tail; coarse remark
rabu•do -da *adj* long-tailed
racha *f* split, crack; chip; squall, gust of wind; streak of luck
racial *adj* racial
racimar *ref* to cluster, gather together
racimo *m* bunch; cluster; (*de perlas*) string
raciocinio *m* reasoning
ración *f* ration; allowance; **ración de hambre** starvation wages
racional *adj* rational
racionamiento *m* rationing
racionar *tr* to ration
racismo *m* racism
racista *adj & mf* racist
rada *f* (naut) road, roadstead
radar *m* radar
radiación *f* radiation
radiacti•vo -va *adj* radioactive
radia•dor -dora *adj* radiating || *m* radiator
radiante *adj* radiant; (*alegre, sonriente*) radiant
radiar *tr* to radiate; radio; broadcast; cross out, erase || *intr* to radiate
radicación *f* taking root; (math) evolution
radical *adj & m* radical
radicar **§73** *intr* to take root; be located || *ref* to take root; settle; (*un negocio*) be based

radio *m* edge, outskirts; (*de una rueda*) spoke, rung; (*de acción*) radius; (chem) radium; (math) radius || *m & f* radio; **radio a** *or* **de transistores** transistor radio
radioacti•vo -va *adj* radioactive
radioaficiona•do -da *mf* ham operator, radio ham
radiodespertador *m & f* clock radio
radiodifundir *tr & intr* to broadcast
radiodifusión *f* broadcasting
radioemisora *f* radio station, transmitter
radioescucha *mf* radio listener; radio monitor
radiofrecuencia *f* radio frequency
radiografía *f* X ray (*photograph*); **hacer una radiografía de** to X-ray
radiografiar §77 *tr* to X-ray; radio
radiográfi•co -ca *adj* X-ray
radiograma *m* radio message, radiogram
radiola *f* record player
radiología *f* radiology
radiólo•go -ga *mf* radiologist
radioperturbación *f* jamming
radioteléfono *m* radio(tele)phone
radioterapia *f* radiotherapy
radioyente *mf* radio listener
raer §56 *tr* to scrape, scrape off; smooth, level; wipe || *ref* to become frayed, wear away
ráfaga *f* gust, puff; gust of wind; flash of light; (*de ametralladora*) burst; **ráfaga violenta** (aer) wind shear
raí•do -da *adj* threadbare; barefaced
ra•íz *f* (*pl* **-íces**) root; grass roots; **a raíz de** close to the root of; even with; right after, hard upon; **de raíz** by the root; completely; **echar raíces** to take root
raja *f* crack, split; splinter, chip; slice
raja•do -da *adj* (coll) cowardly, wimpish || *mf* (coll) coward, wimp
rajar *tr* to crack, split; splinter, chip; slice || *intr* to boast; chatter || *ref* to crack, split; splinter, chip; (Mex, CAm, W-I) to back down, break one's promise
rajatabla — a rajatabla desperately, ruthlessly
ralea *f* kind, quality; breed, ilk
ralear *intr* to thin out; be true to form
ralentí *m* slow motion; (auto) idling
rallador *m* grater
rallar *tr* to grate; grate on, annoy
rallo *m* grater; scraper; rasp; (*de la regadera*) spout, nozzle; unglazed porous jug (*for cooling water by evaporation*)
ra•lo -la *adj* sparse, thin
RAM [rram] *f* (acronym) (**memoria de acceso aleatorio** *or* **directo**) (compu) RAM (random access memory)
rama *f* branch, bough; **andarse por las ramas** to beat about the bush; **en rama** raw; unbound, in sheets; in the grain
Ramadán *m* Ramadan
ramaje *m* branches, foliage
ramal *m* (*de una cuerda*) strand; halter; branch; (rr) branch line
ramalazo *m* lash; (*señal en el cutis por un golpe o enfermedad*) spot, pock; sharp pain; blow, sudden sorrow
rambla *f* dry ravine; avenue, boulevard
ramera *f* whore, harlot
ramificar §73 *tr & ref* to ramify
ramillete *m* bouquet; centerpiece, epergne; (bot) cluster
ramo *m* branch, limb; bouquet, cluster; (*de géneros, negocios, etc.*) line; (*p.ej., de una ciencia*) branch; (*de una enfermedad*) touch, slight attack
ramojo *m* brushwood, dead wood
ramonear *intr* to trim twigs; browse
rampa *f* ramp; cramp; (aer) apron; (Bol) litter, stretcher; **rampa de lanzamiento** launching pad
ram•plón -plona *adj* (*zapato*) heavy, coarse; common, vulgar
ramplonería *f* coarseness, vulgarity
rana *f* frog; **no ser rana** to be a past master; **rana toro** bullfrog
ranchar *ref* (Col, Ven) to balk
ranchear *tr* to sack, pillage || *intr & ref* to build huts, form a settlement
ranchera *f* (Ven) station wagon
ranchero *m* messman; rancher, ranchman
rancho *m* mess, food, meal; meeting, gathering; camp; thatched hut; ranch; (naut) stock of provisions; (Arg) straw hat; **hacer rancho** to make room; **hacer rancho aparte** to be a lone wolf, go one's own way
ran•cio -cia *adj* rank, rancid, stale; (*vino*) old; old, ancient; old, old-fashioned
randa *m* pickpocket || *f* lace trimming
rango *m* rank; class, nature; pomp, splendor; (*elevada condición social*) status, standing
ranura *f* groove; slot; (compu) slot
rapagón *m* stripling
rapar *tr* to shave; crop; scrape; snatch, filch || *ref* to shave; (*una vida regalada*) lead
ra•paz (*pl* **-paces**) *adj* thievish; rapacious; (zool) predatory || *m* young boy, lad
rapaza *f* young woman, lass
rapé *m* snuff
rápi•do -da *adj* rapid || *m* (rr) express; **rápidos** (*de un río*) rapids
raposa *f* fox; female fox; (*persona*) (coll) fox
raposo *m* male fox; foxy fellow; slipshod fellow
raptar *tr* to abduct; kidnap
rapto *m* abduction; kidnaping; rapture; faint, swoon
rap•tor -tora *mf* kidnapper
raque *m* beachcombing; **andar al raque** to go beachcombing
raquear *intr* to beachcomb
raquero *m* priate; beachcomber
raqueta *f* racket; battledore; badminton; snowshoe; **raqueta y volante** battledore and shuttlecock
raquíti•co -ca *adj* (*que padece raquitis*) rickety; flimsy, weak, miserable
raquitis *f* rickets
raramente *adv* rarely, seldom; oddly

rareza *f* rareness; rarity; oddness, strangeness; peculiarity
ra•ro -ra *adj* rare; odd, strange; thin, sparse
ras *m* evenness; **a ras** close, even, flush; **a ras de** even with, flush with; **ras con ras** flush, at the same level; grazing
rasar *tr* to graze, skim || *ref* to clear up
rascacie•los *m* (*pl* **-los**) skyscraper
rascamoño *m* fancy hairpin; (bot) zinnia
rascar §73 *tr* to scrape; scuff; scratch; scrape clean || *ref* (*una cicatriz, un grano*) to pick; get drunk
rasete *m* satinet
rasga•do -da *adj* (*boca; ventana*) wide-open; (*ojos*) large; outspoken; (Col) generous || *m* tear, rip, rent
rasgar §44 *tr* to tear, rip || *ref* to become torn
rasgo *m* (*de una pluma de escribir*) flourish, stroke; trait, characteristic; feat, deed; flash of wit, bright remark; **a grandes rasgos** in bold strokes; **rasgos** (*de la cara*) features
rasguear *tr* to thrum on || *intr* to make a flourish
rasgón *m* tear, rip, rent
rasguñar *tr* to scratch; sketch, outline
rasguño *m* scratch; sketch, outline
ra•so -sa *adj* smooth, flat, level, even; common, plain; clear, cloudless; (coll) brazen, shameless || *m* flat country; satin; **al raso** in the open
raspa *f* stalk, stem; (*de mazorca de maíz*) beard; (*de pez*) spine, backbone; shell, rind; (CAm, Mex) dirty trick, nasty joke
raspadura *f* scraping; erasure; pan sugar
raspar *tr* to scrape, scrape off; scratch, scratch out; graze; (*el vino*) bite; take, steal; (W-I) to dismiss, fire; (W-I) to scold || *intr* (Ven) to go away; (Ven) to die
raspear *tr* (SAm) to scold || *intr* (*una pluma*) to scratch
rastra *f* rake; harrow; drag; track, trail; (*p.ej., de cebollas*) string; (naut) drag; **pescar a la rastra** to trawl
rastracuero *m* show-off; upstart; sharper, adventurer
rastreador *m* dredge; (nav) mine sweeper
rastreo *m* investigation, research; (*por pescadores*) trawling; (aerosp) tracking; **rastreo policial** (*de una zona*) sweep, thorough search
rastrear *tr* to trail, track, trace; drag; dredge; check into || *intr* to rake; skim the ground, fly low
rastre•ro -ra *adj* dragging, trailing; creeping; low-flying; groveling, cringing; low, vile
rastrillar *tr* to rake; (*cáñamo, lino*) hatchel, comb; (Arg, Col) to shoot, to fire; (*un fósforo*) (Arg, Col) to strike (*a match*)
rastrillo *m* rake; hackle, hatchel, flax comb; (*de cerradura o llave*) ward; grating, iron grate; (rr) cowcatcher
rastro *m* rake; harrow; track, trail; scent; trace, vestige; slaughterhouse; wholesale meat market; rag fair; **rastro de condensación** (aer) contrail
rastrojo *m* stubble
rasura *f* shaving; scraping
rasurar *tr & ref* to shave
rata *adj* (coll) stingy, tightfisted || *mf* (coll) miser, tightwad || *f* rat; female rat; **rata de alcantarilla** sewer rat; **rata del trigo** hamster
ratear *tr* to apportion; snitch
ratería *f* baseness, meanness, vileness; petty thievery; petty theft
rate•ro -ra *adj* thievish; trailing, dragging; base, vile || *mf* sneak thief, pickpocket
raticida *f* rat poison
ratificar §73 *tr* to ratify
rato *m* time, while, little while; **a ratos** from time to time; **a ratos perdidos** in spare time, in one's leisure hours; **buen rato** pleasant time; large amount; **pasar el rato** to waste one's time; **un rato** awhile
ratón *m* mouse; (Ven) hangover; (compu) mouse; **cazar ratones** to mouse; **ratón de biblioteca** bookworm
ratonera *f* (*trampa*) mousetrap; (*agujero*) mousehole; nest of mice; hut, shop
raudal *m* stream, torrent; abundance
rau•do -da *adj* rapid, swift, impetuous
raya *f* stripe; (*línea fina; pez*) ray; (*en la imprenta, la escritura y la telegrafía*) dash; (*de los pantalones*) crease; (*en los cabellos*) part; boundary line, limit; (*para impedir la comunicación del incendio en los campos*) firebreak; (*del espectro*) (phys) line; (Mex) pay, wages; **a rayas** striped; **hacerse la raya** to part one's hair; **pasar de la raya** to go too far; **tener a raya** to keep within bounds
raya•no -na *adj* bordering; borderline
rayar *tr* (*papel*) to rule, line; stripe; scratch, score, mark; cross out; underscore || *intr* to border; stand out; (*el alba, el día, la luz, el sol*) begin, arise, come forth; **rayar en** to verge on, border on || *ref* (Col) to get rich
rayo *m* (*de luz*) ray; (*de rueda*) spoke; lightning, flash of lightning, stroke of lightning, thunderbolt; (*persona*) (fig) live wire; **como un rayo** quick as a flash; **de rayos X** X-ray; **echar rayos** to blow up, hit the ceiling; **rayo láser** laser beam; **rayo mortífero** death ray; **rayos X** X-rays
rayón *m* rayon
raza *f* race; breed, stock; crack, slit; quality; ray of light (*coming through a crack*)
razón *f* reason; right, justice; account, story; (*cantidad o grado medidos por otra cosa tomada como unidad*) rate; for information, e.g., *SIGN* **Se alquila. Razón: portería** For rent. Get information from the super, e.g., *SIGN* **Se vende auto. Razón: este establecimiento** Auto for sale. Inquire within; (math) ratio; **a razón de** at the rate of; **con razón o sin ella** right or wrong; **hacer la razón** to return a toast; join at table; **meterse en razón** to listen to reason; **no tener razón** to be wrong; **razón social** firm name, trade name; **tener razón** to be right; be in the right

razonable *adj* reasonable
razonar *tr* to reason, reason out; itemize || *intr* to reason
reabrir §83 *tr & ref* to reopen
reacción *f* reaction; feedback (pol) right wing; **reacción en cadena** chain reaction
reaccionar *intr* to react
reacciona•rio -ria *adj & mf* reactionary
rea•cio -cia *adj* stubborn, obstinate
reactivo *m* reagent
reactor *m* jet engine; jet plane; (chem, phys) reactor: **reactor de agua en ebullición** boiling-water reactor: **reactor de gas** gas-cooled reactor; **reactor nuclear** nuclear reactor; **reactor reproductor** breeder reactor
real *adj* real; royal; fine, splendid || *m* army camp; fairground; real (*old Spanish coin; Spanish money of a value equal to a quarter of a peseta*)
realce *m* embossment, raised work; enhancement, luster; emphasis; **bordar a realce** to embroider in relief; (fig) to embroider, to exaggerate
realeza *f* royalty
realidad *f* reality; truth; **hecho realidad** come true, e.g., **un sueño hecho realidad** a dream come true; **realidad virtual** virtual reality
realimentación *f* (electron, rad) feedback
realismo *m* realism
realista *mf* (*persona que tiende a ver las cosas como son*) realist; (*partidario de la monarquía*) royalist
realización *f* realization, fulfillment; achievement; sale; **realización de beneficios** profit taking
realizar §60 *tr* to fulfill; carry out; turn into cash || *ref* to become fulfilled; be carried out
realquilar *tr* to sublet
realzar §60 *tr* to raise, elevate; emboss; enhance, set off; emphasize
reanimar *tr* to revive, restore; cheer, encourage || *ref* to revive, recover one's spirits
reanudar *tr* to renew, resume
reaparecer §22 *intr* to reappear
reasentamiento *s* resettlement
reata *f* rope to keep animals in single file; single file; **de reata** in single file; in blind submission; next, following
rebaba *f* burr, fin
rebaja *f* rebate; diminution
rebajar *tr* to lower; diminish, reduce; rebate; (*precios*) mark down; (*a una persona*) deflate; (carp) to rabbet || *ref* to stoop; humble oneself
rebajo *m* rabbet, groove; offset, recess
rebalsar *tr* to dam || *ref* to become dammed up; be checked; pile up, accumulate
rebanada *f* slice
rebanar *tr* to slice; cut through
rebañadera *f* grapnel
rebaño *m* flock
rebarbati•vo -va *adj* crabbed, surly
rebasar *tr* to exceed; overflow; sail past
rebatiña *f* grabbing, scramble; **andar a la rebatiña** to scramble
rebatir *tr* to repel, drive back; check; resist; strengthen; rebut, refute; deduct, rebate; beat hard
rebato *m* alarm, call to arms; alarm, excitement; (mil) surprise attack
rebeca *f* cardigan
rebelar *ref* to revolt, rebel; resist; break away
rebelde *adj* rebellious; stubborn || *mf* rebel
rebeldía *f* rebelliousness; defiance, stubbornness
rebelión *f* rebellion, revolt
rebe•lón -lona *adj* balky, restive
rebobinar *tr* to rewind; unwind
reborde *m* flange, rim, collar
rebosar *tr* to cause overflow || *intr* to overflow, run over; be in abundance; **rebosar de** *or* **en** to overflow with, burst with; be rich in; have an abundance of || *ref* to overflow, run over
rebotar *tr* to bend back; repel; annoy, worry || *intr* to bounce; bounce back, rebound, ricochet || *ref* to become annoyed, become worried
rebote *m* bounce; rebound, ricochet
rebozar §60 *tr* (*la cara*) to muffle up; cover with batter || *ref* to muffle up, muffle oneself up
rebozo *m* muffling; muffler; shawl; **de rebozo** secretly; **sin rebozo** frankly, openly
rebullicio *m* hubbub, loud uproar
rebullir §13 *intr* to stir, begin to move; give signs of life || *ref* to stir, begin to move
rebulta•do -da *adj* bulky, massive
rebusca *f* seeking, searching; gleaning; leavings, refuse
rebusca•do -da *adj* affected, unnatural, recherché
rebuscar §73 *tr* to seek after; search into; to glean
rebuznar *intr* to bray; talk nonsense
rebuzno *m* braying; nonsense
recade•ro -ra *mf* messenger || *m* errand boy
recado *m* errand; message; gift, present; daily marketing; compliments, regards; safety, security; equipment, outfit; **mandar recado** to send word; **recado de escribir** writing materials
recaer §15 *intr* to fall again; fall back; relapse; backslide; **recaer en** to fall to; **recaer sobre** to fall upon, devolve upon
recaída *f* relapse; backsliding
recalar *tr* to soak, saturate || *intr* to sight land
recalcar §73 *tr* to press, squeeze; cram, pack, stuff; (*sus palabras*) stress || *intr* (naut) to list, heel; **recalcar en** to lay stress on || *ref* to harp on the same string; sprawl; (*p.ej., la muñeca*) sprain
recalentar §2 *tr* to overheat; (*la comida*) to warm over
recalmón *m* (naut) lull
recamado *m* embroidery
recamar *tr* to embroider

recámara *f* dressing room; (*de un arma de fuego*) breech, chamber; reserve, caution; (Mex) bedroom

recamarera *f* (Mex) chambermaid

recambio *m* spare part; (*parte, rueda, etc.*) **de recambio** spare

recapacitar *tr* to run over in one's mind || *intr* to refresh one's memory; reflect

recargable *adj* rechargeable

recargar §44 *tr* to reload; overload; recharge; overcharge; overadorn; (*una cuota de impuesto*) increase; (elec) to recharge || *ref* to become more feverish

recargo *m* new burden; extra charge; new charge; (*que paga el contribuyente moroso*) penalty; (pathol) rise in temperature; **recargo de tarifa** extra fare

recata•do -da *adj* cautious, circumspect; modest; shy

recatar *tr* to hide, conceal || *ref* to hide; be afraid to take a stand

recato *m* caution, reserve; modesty

recauchutaje *m* recapping, retreading

recauchutar *tr* to recap, retread

recaudar *tr* (*impuestos, tributos*) to gather, collect; guard, watch over

recaudo *m* tax collecting; care, precaution; bail, surety; **a buen recaudo** under guard, in safety

recelar *tr* to fear, distrust || *intr & ref* to fear, be afraid

recelo *m* fear, distrust

recelo•so -sa *adj* fearful, distrustful

recensión *f* review, book review

recepción *f* reception; reception desk

recepcionista *m* room clerk || *f* receptionist

receptáculo *m* receptacle; shelter, refuge

receptador *m* (coll) fence, holder of stolen goods

receptar *tr* to receive, welcome; (*delincuentes*) hide, conceal; (*cosas robadas*) receive

recepti•vo -va *adj* receptive; susceptible

receptor *m* receiver; (med) recipient; **receptor de cabeza** headpiece; **receptor telefónico** receiver

recesión *f* (econ) recession

receta *f* recipe; (pharm) prescription

recetar *tr* (*un medicamento*) to prescribe; request

rechazar §60 *tr* to refuse, reject; repel, drive back

rechazo *m* rejection; rebound, recoil

rechifla *f* catcall

rechiflar *tr & intr* to catcall, hiss || *ref* to make fun

rechinar *intr* to creak, grate, squeak; act with bad grace; (Mex) to rage

rechistar *intr* to stir, say a word; **sin rechistar** without protest

rechon•cho -cha *adj* chubby, tubby, plump

rechupete — de rechupete fine, wonderful

recibí *m* receipt; received payment

recibida *f* reception; admission

recibi•dor -dora *mf* receiver; receiving teller; ticket collector || *m* reception room

recibimiento *m* reception; welcome; reception room; (*visita en que una persona recibe a sus amistades*) at home

recibir *tr* to receive; (*visitas*) entertain || *intr* to receive; entertain || *ref* to be received, be admitted; **recibirse de** to be admitted to practice as; be graduated as

recibo *m* reception; receipt; hall; parlor; at home; **acusar recibo de** to acknowledge receipt of; **estar de recibo** to be at home; **ser de recibo** to be acceptable

reciclable *adj* recyclable

reciclado *m* or **reciclaje** *m* recycling

reciclar *tr* to recycle

recién *adv* (used before past participles) recently, just, newly, e.g., **recién llegado** newly arrived; just now, recently

reciente *adv* recently

recinto *m* area, enclosure, place

re•cio -cia *adj* strong; thick, coarse, heavy; harsh; hard, bitter, arduous; (*tiempo*) severe; swift, impetuous || **recio** *adv* strongly; swiftly; hard; loud

reciprocidad *f* reciprocity

recípro•co -ca *adj* reciprocal

recital *m* (*de música o poesía*) recital

recitar *tr* to recite; (*un discurso*) deliver

reclamación *f* claim, demand; objection; protest, complaint

reclamar *tr* to claim, demand; (*un ave*) decoy, lure || *intr* to cry out, protest, complain

réclame *or* **reclame** *m & f* advertisement

reclamo *m* bird call; decoy bird; (*para aves*) lure; allurement, attraction; advertisement; blurb, puff; reference; (typ) catchword; (SAm) complaint

reclinar *tr* (*p.ej., la cabeza*) to lean, bend || *ref* to recline

reclinatorio *m* prie-dieu; couch, lounge

recluir §20 *tr* to seclude, shut in; imprison || *ref* to go into seclusion

reclusión *f* seclusion; imprisonment

reclu•so -sa *adj* secluded; imprisoned || *mf* prisoner; inmate

recluta *m* recruit || *f* recruiting; (*del ganado disperso*) (Arg) roundup

reclutar *tr* to recruit; (Arg) to round up

recobrar *tr* to recover || *ref* to recover; come to

recobro *m* recovery; (*de un motor*) pickup

recodar *intr* to lean; bend, twist, turn, wind

recodo *m* bend, twist, turn

recoger §17 *tr* to pick up; gather, collect; harvest; shorten, draw in; keep; welcome; lock up || *ref* to take shelter, take refuge; withdraw; (*echarse en la cama*) retire; go home; cut down expenses

recogida *f* collection; withdrawal; suspension; **recogida de basuras** garbage collection

recogimiento *m* gathering, collecting; harvesting; seclusion, retreat; concentration; self-communion

recolectar *tr* to gather, gather in; (*el algodón*) pick
recombina•do -da *adj* (*genética*) recombinant
recomendable *adj* commendable
recomendar §2 *tr* to recommend; commend
recompensa *f* recompense, reward
recompensar *tr* to recompense, reward
recompostura *f* repair
recomprar *tr* to buy back, repurchase
reconcentrar *tr* to bring together; (*un sentimiento o afecto*) conceal, disguise || *ref* to come together; be absorbed in thought
reconciliar *tr* to reconcile || *ref* to become reconciled
recóndi•to -ta *adj* hidden, concealed
reconfortar *tr* to comfort, cheer
reconocer §22 *tr* to recognize; admit, acknowledge; examine; (mil) to reconnoiter || *intr* (mil) to reconnoiter || *ref* to be clear
reconoci•do -da *adj* grateful
reconocimiento *m* recognition; admission, acknowledgment; gratitude; reconnaissance; **reconocimiento médico** medical examination
reconquista *f* reconquest
reconsiderar *tr* to reconsider
reconstruir §20 *tr* to reconstruct, rebuild, recast; (*a crime*) to reenact
recontar §61 *tr* (*volver a contar; narrar*) to recount (*to count again; narrate*)
reconvenir §79 *tr* to expostulate with, to remonstrate with
reconversión *f* reconversion
recopila•dor -dora *mf* compiler
recopilar *tr* to compile
record *or* **récord** *m* (*pl* **records**) (sport) record; **batir un record** to break a record; **establecer un récord** to make a record
recordar §61 *tr* to remember; remind || *intr* to remember; get awake; come to; **si mal no recuerdo** if I remember correctly
recordati•vo -va *adj* reminding, reminiscent || *m* reminder
recordatorio *m* reminder; memento
record•man (*pl* **-men**) record holder
recorrer *tr* to go over, go through; look over, look through; (*un libro*) run through; overhaul
recorrido *m* trip, run, route; (*del émbolo*) stroke; repair
recortado *m* cutout
recortar *tr* to trim, cut off; (*figuras en una tela, en un papel*) cut out; outline || *ref* to stand out
recorte *m* cutting; (*de un periódico*) clipping; dodge, duck; **recortes** cuttings, trimmings
recostar §61 *tr* to lean || *ref* to lean, lean back, sit back
recova *f* poultry business; poultry stand; (Arg) portico; (SAm) food market
recoveco *m* bend, turn, twist; subterfuge, trick
recreación *f* recreation
recrear *tr* to amuse; reenact || *ref* to take pleasure in
recreo *m* recreation; place of amusement
recrudecer §22 *intr & ref* to flare up, get worse
rectángu•lo -la *adj* right-angled || *m* rectangle
rectificar §73 *tr* to rectify; (*un cilindro de motor*) rebore
rec•to -ta *adj* straight; (*ángulo*) right; right, just, righteous || *m* rectum
rec•tor -tora *adj* governing, managing || *mf* principal, superior || *m* rector; (*de una universidad*) rector, president
recua *f* drove; (*de personas o cosas*) string, line
recuadro *m* panel, square; (*sección de un impreso encerrada dentro de un marco*) box; (compu) frame; window
recubrir §83 *tr* to cover, cap, coat
recuento *m* count; recount; inventory; **recuento de personas** head count
recuerdo *m* memory, remembrance; keepsake, souvenir
recuero *m* muleteer
recular *intr* to back up; (*un arma de fuego*) recoil; back down
reculón *m* backing; **a reculones** backing away, recoiling
recuperación *f* recovery; rehabilitation
recuperar *tr & ref* to recuperate, recover; (compu) to restore
recurrir *intr* to resort, have recourse; revert
recurso *m* recourse; resource; resort; appeal, petition
recusar *tr* to refuse, reject; (law) to challenge
red *f* net; netting; network, system; baggage netting; (compu) network; (fig) net, snare, trap; **a red barredera** with a clean sweep; **red barredera** dragnet
redacción *f* writing; editing; wording; editorial staff; newspaper office, city room
redactar *tr* to write up; edit
redac•tor -tora *mf* writer; editor, newspaper editor; **redactor en jefe** editor in chief; **redactor publicitario** copy writer
redada *f* (*de peces*) catch, netful; (*p.ej., de criminales*) haul, roundup
redecilla *f* hair net
rededor *m* surroundings; **al rededor (de)** around
redención *f* redemption; help, recourse
reden•tor -tora *mf* redeemer
redibujado *m* (compu) display
redi•cho -cha *adj* overprecise
redición *f* constant repetition
redil *m* sheepfold
redimir *tr* to redeem; ransom; buy back
rediscado *m* redial
redistribuir §20 *tr* to redistribute, reshuffle
rédito *m* income, revenue, yield
redituar §21 *tr* to yield, produce
redobla•do -da *adj* stocky, heavy-built; heavy, strong; (mil) double-quick
redoblar *tr* to double; clinch; repeat || *intr* (*un tambor*) to roll
redoble *m* doubling; clinching; repeating; roll of a drum
redoma *f* phial, flask

redoma•do -da *adj* sly, crafty
redonda *f* district, neighborhood; (mus) semibreve; **a la redonda** around, roundabout; **en redondas** (typ) in roman type
redondea•do -da *adj* round, rounded
redondear *tr* to round, make round; round off; round out || *ref* to be well-off; be out of debt
redondel *m* circle; round cloak; (*espacio destinado a la lidia*) (taur) ring
redondilla *f* eight-syllable quatrain with rhyme abba
redon•do -da *adj* round; straightforward; (*terreno*) pasture; honest; stupid || *m* ring, circle; cash || *f* see **redonda**
redopelo *m* row, scuffle; **al redopelo** against the grain, the wrong way; roughly, violently
reducir §19 *tr & ref* to reduce; **reducirse a** to come to, amount to; be obliged to
reducto *m* (fort) redoubt
redundante *adj* redundant
redundar *intr* to redound; overflow; **redundar en** to redound to
reduplicación *f* doubling
reelección *f* reelection
rellamada *f* redial
reembarcar §73 *tr, intr & ref* to reship, reembark
reembarco *m* reshipment (*of persons*), reembarkation
reembarque *m* reshipment (*of goods*)
reembolsar *tr* to reimburse; refund || *ref* to collect a debt, be reimbursed
reembolso *m* reimbursement; refund; **contra reembolso** collect on delivery; cash on delivery
reemplazar §60 *tr* to replace
reemplazo *m* replacement; (mil) replacements; (*hombre que sirve en lugar de otro*) (mil) replacement
reencuadernar *tr* (bb) to rebind
reencuentro *m* collision; (*de tropas*) clash
reenganchar *tr & ref* to reenlist
reentrada *f* reentry
reestrenar *tr* (theat) to revive
reestreno *m* (theat) revival
reexamen *m* or **reexaminación** *f* reexamination
reexpedición *f* forwarding, reshipment
reexpedir §50 *tr* to forward, reship
refacción *f* refreshment; allowance; repair, repairs; extra, bonus; spare part
refaccionar *tr* to finance; (SAm) to repair, renovate
refajo *m* underskirt, slip
referencia *f* reference; account, report
referendo *m* referendum
referi•do -da *adj* above-mentioned
referir §68 *tr* to refer; tell, report || *ref* to refer
refinamiento *m* refinement
refinar *tr* to refine; polish, perfect
refinería *f* refinery
reflector *s* reflector; spotlight; searchlight; floodlight; reflecting telescope; **iluminar con reflector** to floodlight
reflejar *tr* to reflect; reflect on; show, reveal || *intr* to reflect
reflejo *m* glare; reflection; reflex; **reflejo condicionado** conditioned reflex; **reflejo patelar** *or* **rotuliano** knee jerk
reflexión *f* reflection
reflexionar *tr* to reflect on or upon || *intr* to reflect
reflugo *m* ebb
refocilar *tr* to cheer; strengthen || *intr* (Arg, Urug) to lighten || *ref* to be cheered; take it easy
reforma *f* reform; reformation; alteration, renovation || **la Reforma** the Reformation
reformación *f* reformation
reformar *tr* to reform; mend, repair; alter, renovate; revise; reorganize || *ref* to reform; hold oneself in check
reforzar §35 *tr* to reinforce; strengthen; encourage
refracción *f* refraction
refracta•rio -ria *adj* rebellious, unruly, stubborn; ovenproof
refrán *m* proverb, saying
refregar §66 *tr* to rub; upbraid
refrenar *tr* to curb, rein; check, restrain
refrendar *tr* to countersign; authenticate; visé; repeat
refrescar §73 *tr* to refresh; cool, refrigerate || *intr & ref* to refresh; refresh oneself; cool off; go out for fresh air; (*el viento*) (naut) to blow up
refresco *m* refreshment; cold drink, soft drink
refriega *f* fray, scuffle, scrimmage
refrigerador *m* refrigerator; ice bucket
refrigerio *m* coolness; relief; pick-me-up, light lunch
refuerzo *m* reinforcement
refugia•do -da *mf* refugee
refugiar *tr* to shelter || *ref* to take refuge
refugio *m* refuge; hospice; shelter; haunt; (*para peatones en medio de la calle*) safety zone; **refugio antiaéreo** air-raid shelter; **refugio antinuclear** fallout shelter; **refugio fiscal** tax shelter
refundición *f* recast; revision; (*de una pieza dramática*) adaptation
refundir *tr* to recast; revise; (*una pieza dramática*) adapt || *intr* to redound
refunfuñar *intr* to grumble, growl
refutar *tr* to refute
regadera *f* watering can; street sprinkler
regadí•o -a *or* **regadi•zo -za** *adj* irrigable || *m* irrigated land
regala *f* gunwale
regala•do -da *adj* dainty, delicate; pleasing, pleasant; (*vida*) of ease
regalar *tr* to give; regale, entertain; treat; caress, fondle; indulge
regalía *f* privilege, perquisite; bonus; royalty; (Arg, Chile) muff
regaliz *m* licorice
regalo *m* gift, present; treat; joy, pleasure; **re-**

galo de boda *or* casamiento wedding present; **regalos de fiesta** favors
rega•lón -lona *adj* comfort-loving, pampered; (*vida*) soft, easy
regañar *tr* to scold || *intr* to growl, snarl; grumble; quarrel; scold
regaño *m* scolding; growl, snarl; grumble
regar §66 *tr* to water, sprinkle; irrigate; spread, sprinkle, strew
regate *m* dodge, duck; (fig) dodge, subterfuge
regatear *tr* to haggle over; sell at retail; avoid, shun || *intr* to haggle, bargain; duck, dodge; (naut) to race
regazo *m* lap
regeneración *f* feedback; (biol) regeneration
regenerar *tr & ref* to regenerate
regente *m* director, manager; registered pharmacist; (typ) foreman
regicida *mf* regicide
regicidio *m* regicide
regi•dor -dora *adj* ruling, governing || *m* alderman, councilman
régimen *m* (*pl* **regímenes**) regime; diet; rate; management; (gram) government; **régimen de hambre** starvation diet; **régimen de justicia** rule of law; **régimen de vida** lifestyle
regimental *adj* regimental
regimentar §2 *tr* to regiment
regimiento *m* regiment; rule, government; city council
re•gio -gia *adj* regal, royal; magnificent
región *f* region
regionalismo *f* regionalism
regir §57 *tr* to rule, govern; control, manage; guide, steer; (gram) to govern || *intr* to prevail, be in force
registra•dor -dora *adj* registering; recording || *m* registrar, recorder; inspector; **registrador de vuelo** flight recorder || *f* cash register
registrar *tr* to register; record; examine, inspect; search, frisk (*a suspect*); || *ref* to register; be recorded; take place
registro *m* registration, registry; recording; examination, inspection, shakedown; electoral roll; entry, record; bookmark; manhole; (*de chimenea*) damper; (*de reloj*) regulator; (*de órgano*) (mus) stop; (*de piano*) (mus) pedal
regla *f* rule, regulation; (*para trazar líneas*) ruler; measure, moderation; order; menstruation; **regla de cálculo** slide rule; **reglas** monthlies, menses; **regla T** T-square
reglamenta•rio -ria *adj* prescribed, statutory
reglamento *m* rules, regulations
reglar *tr* to regulate; (*papel*) rule || *ref* to guide oneself, be guided
regleta *f* (typ) lead
regletear *tr* (typ) to lead, space
regocijar *tr* to cheer, delight || *ref* to rejoice
regocijo *m* cheer, delight, rejoicing
regoldar §3 *intr* to belch
regolfar *intr & ref* to surge back, flow back, back up
regorde•te -ta *adj* dumpy, plump
regresar *intr* to return
regreso *m* return; **estar de regreso** to be back
regüeldo *m* belch, belching
reguero *m* drip, trickle; (*señal que deja una cosa que se va vertiendo*) track; irrigating ditch; **ser un reguero de pólvora** to spread like wildfire
regulador *m* regulator; (*de locomotora*) throttle; (mach) governor
regular *adj* regular; fair, moderate, medium; **por lo regular** as a rule || *tr* to regulate; put in order; throttle
rehabilitación *f* rehabilitation; renovation
rehacer §39 *tr* to remake, make over, do over; mend, repair, renovate || *ref* to recover, rally
rehén *m* hostage; **llevarse en rehenes** to carry off as a hostage; **toma de rehenes** hostage taking
rehilandera *f* pinwheel
rehilar *intr* to quiver; whiz by
rehilete *m* shuttlecock; (*que se lanza por diversión*) dart; dig, cutting remark; (taur) banderilla
rehuir §20 *tr* to avoid, shun; shrink from; refuse; dislike || *intr & ref* to flee
rehusar *tr* to refuse, turn down
reimpresión *f* reprint
reimprimir §83 *tr* to reprint
reina *f* queen; **reina claudia** greengage; **reina de belleza** beauty queen; **reina de las fiestas** carnival queen; **reina de los prados** meadowsweet; **reina madre** queen mother; **reina Margarita** aster, China aster; **reina viuda** queen dowager
reinado *m* reign
reinar *intr* to reign; prevail
reincidir *intr* to backslide; repeat an offense
reingreso *m* reentry
reiniciar *tr* (compu) to restart
reino *m* kingdom; **Reino Unido** United Kingdom
reinstalar *tr* to reinstate, reinstall
reintegrar *tr* to refund, pay back
reintegro *m* refund, payment
reír §58 *tr* to laugh at || *intr & ref* to laugh; **reír de** *or* **reírse de** to laugh at
reja *f* grate, grating, grille; plowshare, colter; **entre rejas** behind bars
rejilla *f* screen; grating; lattice, latticework; cane, cane upholstery; foot brasier; fire grate; (electron) grid; (*de acumulador*) (elec) grid; (rr) baggage rack
rejón *m* spear; dagger; (taur) lance
rejonear *tr* (*el jinete al toro*) (taur) to jab with a lance made to break off in the bull's neck
rejuntado *m* (mas) pointing
rejuvenecimiento *m* rejuvenation
relación *f* relation; account, list; (*en un drama*) speech; **relación de ciego** blind man's ballad; **relaciones** betrothal, engagement; **relaciones públicas** public relations; **relaciones raciales** race relations
relacionar *tr* to relate || *ref* to be related

relai *m* or **relais** *m* (elec) relay
relajación *f* or **relajamiento** *m* relaxation; slackening; laxity; rupture, hernia
relajar *tr* to relax; slacken; debauch || *intr* to relax || *ref* to relax, become relaxed; become debauched; be ruptured
relamer *ref* to lick one's lips; gloat; to relish; boast; slick oneself up
relami•do -da *adj* prim, overnice
relámpago *m* flash of lightning; flash of wit; **como un relámpago** in a flash
relampaguear *intr* to lighten; flash
relatar *tr* to relate, report
relati•vo -va *adj* relative
relato *m* story; statement, report
relé *m* (elec) relay; **relé de televisión** television relay system
releer §43 *tr* to reread
relegar §44 *tr* to relegate; banish, exile; shelve, lay aside
relente *m* night dew, light drizzle
relevador *m* (elec) relay
relevancia *f* relevance; significance
relevante *adj* outstanding
relevar *tr* to emboss; make stand out; relieve; release; absolve; replace || *intr* to stand out in relief
relevo *m* (elec) relay; (mil) relief; **relevos** (sport) relay race
relicario *m* shrine; (*medallón*) locket
relieve *m* relief; merit, distinction; **en relieve** in relief; **poner de relieve** to point out; to make stand out; **relieves** scraps, leftovers
religión *f* religion
religio•so -sa *adj* religious
relinchar *intr* to neigh
relincho *m* neigh, neighing; cry of joy
reliquia *f* relic; trace, vestige; **reliquia de familia** heirloom
rellano *m* (*en la pendiente de un terreno*) level stretch; (*de escalera*) landing
rellenar *tr* to refill; fill up; stuff; pad; fill out; cram, stuff || *ref* to fill up; cram, stuff oneself
relle•no -na *adj* full, packed; stuffed || *m* refill; filling, stuffing; padding, wadding; (*en un escrito*) filler
reloj [reˋlo], [reˋlox] *m* watch; clock; meter; **como un reloj** like clockwork; **conocer el reloj** to know how to tell time; **reloj automático** (culin, electron) timer; **reloj de arena** sandglass, hourglass; **reloj de bolsillo** pocket watch; **reloj de caja** grandfather's clock; **reloj de carillón** chime clock; **reloj de cuarzo** quartz watch; **reloj de cuclillo** cuckoo clock; **reloj de ocho días cuerda** eight-day clock; **reloj de pie** grandfather's clock, tall-case clock; **reloj de pulsera** wristwatch; **reloj de sol** sundial; **reloj despertador** alarm clock; **reloj digital** *or* **numérico** *m* digital clock, digital watch; **reloj registrador** time clock
relojera *f* watch case; watch pocket
relojería *f* watchmaking, clockmaking; watchmaker's shop
reloje•ro -ra *mf* watchmaker, clockmaker || *f* see **relojera**
reluciente *adj* shining, brilliant, flashing
relucir §45 *intr* to shine
relumbrar *intr* to shine, dazzle, glare
relumbre *m* beam, sparkle; flash; dazzle, glare
relumbrón *m* flash, glare; tinsel; **de relumbrón** showy, tawdry
REM [rem] *m* (acronym) (**movimientos oculares rápidos**) REM (rapid eye movement)
remachar *tr* (*un clavo ya clavado*) to clinch; (*un roblón*) rivet; stress, emphasize || *ref* (Col) to maintain strict silence
remache *m* clinching; riveting; rivet
remanso *m* dead water, backwater
remar *intr* to row; toil, struggle
remata•do -da *adj* hopeless; **loco rematado** raving mad
rematador *m* auctioneer
rematar *tr* to finish, put an end to; finish off, kill off; (*en una subasta*) knock down || *intr* to end || *ref* to come to ruin
remate *m* end; crest, top, finial; closing; highest bid; (*en una subasta*) sale; **de remate** hopelessly
rembolsar *tr* to reimburse; repay; redeem
rembolso *m* reimbursement; **contra rembolso** C.O.D. (cash on delivery)
remecer §46 *tr & ref* to shake, swing, rock
remedar *tr* to copy, imitate; ape, mimic; mock
remediar *tr* to remedy; help; prevent; (*del peligro*) free, save
remediava•gos *m* (*pl* **-gos**) short cut
remedio *m* remedy; help; recourse; **no hay remedio** *or* **no hay más remedio** it can't be helped; **no tener remedio** to be unavoidable
remedión *m* (theat) substitute performance
remedo *m* copy, imitation; poor imitation
remendar §2 *tr* to patch, mend, repair; darn; emend, correct; touch up
remen•dón -dona *mf* mender, repairer; shoe mender; tailor (*who does mending*)
reme•ro -ra *mf* rower || *m* oarsman
remesa *f* remittance; shipment
remesar *tr* to remit; ship
remezón *m* hard shake; tremor
remiendo *m* patch; mending, repair; retouching; emendation, correction; job printing, job work; **a remiendos** piecemeal
remilga•do -da *adj* prim and finicky; affected, smirking
remilgar §44 *intr* to be prim and finicky; smirk
remilgo *m* primness, affectation
remira•do -da *adj* circumspect, discreet
remisión *f* remission; reference
remitente *mf* sender, shipper
remitido *m* (*noticia de un particular a un periódico*) personal; letter to the editor
remitir *tr* to remit; forward, send, ship; refer; defer, postpone; pardon, forgive || *intr* to

remit, let up; refer || *ref* to remit, let up; defer, yield
remo *m* oar; leg, arm, wing; toil, labor; (sport) rowing; **aguantar los remos** to lie or rest on one's oars
remoción *f* discharge, dismissal; removal
remodelación *f* remodeling
remodelar *tr* to remodel
remojar *tr* to soak, steep, dip; celebrate with a drink; **remojar la palabra** to wet one's whistle
remojo *m* soaking, steeping; **poner en remojo** to put off until later; to let soak
remolacha *f* beet; **remolacha azucarera** sugar beet
remolcador *m* tug, tugboat; towboat; tow car
remolcar §73 *tr* to tow; take in tow
remoler §47 *tr* to grind up; bore
remolinear *tr, intr & ref* to eddy, whirl about
remolino *m* eddy, whirlpool; swirl, whirl; disturbance, commotion; throng, crowd; cowlick
remo•lón -lona *adj* lazy, indolent || *mf* shirker, quitter
remolonear *intr* to refuse to budge
remolque *m* tow; towing; trailer; **a remolque** in tow
remontar *tr* to mend, repair; frighten away; elevate, raise up; (*p.ej., un río*) go up || *intr* (*en el tiempo*) go back || *ref* to rise, rise up; soar; (*en el tiempo*) go back
remontuar *m* stem-winder
remoquete *m* punch; nickname; sarcasm; flirting
rémora *f* hindrance, obstacle
remordimiento *m* remorse
remo•to -ta *adj* remote; unlikely; **estar remoto** to be rusty
remover §47 *tr* to remove; shake; stir; disturb, upset; dismiss, discharge || *ref* to move away
removible *adj* removable
remozar §60 *tr* to rejuvenate || *ref* to become rejuvenated
rempujar *tr* to push, jostle
rempujón *m* push, jostle
remuda *f* change, replacement; change of clothes
remudar *tr* to change, replace; move around
remuneración *f* remuneration; **remuneración por rendimiento** piece wage
renacer §22 *intr* to be reborn, be born again; recover
renacimiento *m* rebirth; renaissance
renacuajo *m* tadpole; (coll) shrimp, little squirt
Renania *f* Rhineland
ren•co -ca *adj* lame
rencor *m* rancor; **guardar rencor** to bear malice
rendición *f* surrender; submission; fatigue, exhaustion; yield
rendi•do -da *adj* tired, worn-out; submissive
rendija *f* crack, split, slit
rendimiento *m* submission; exhaustion; yield; output; (*de una persona*) performance; (aut, compu) performance; (mech) efficiency
rendir §50 *tr* to conquer; subdue; surrender; exhaust, wear out; return, give back; yield, produce; (*gracias, obsequios, homenaje*) render || *intr* to yield || *ref* to surrender; yield, give in; be exhausted, be worn out
renegar §66 *tr* to deny vigorously; abhor, detest || *intr* to curse; be insulting; **renegar de** to deny; curse; abhor, detest
renegociación *f* renegotiation
Renfe, la acronym for **la Red Nacional de los Ferrocarriles Españoles** the Spanish National Railroad System
renglón *m* line; **a renglón sequido** right below; **leer entre renglones** to read between the lines
reniego *m* curse
reno *m* reindeer
renombra•do -da *adj* renowned, famous
renombre *m* renown, fame
renovar §61 *tr* to renew; renovate; transform, restore; remodel
renquear *intr* to limp
renta *f* income; private income; annuity; public debt; rent; **renta de aduanas** customs duties; **renta gravable** *or* **imponible** taxable income; **renta nacional** gross national product; **renta vitalicia** life annuity
rentabilizar §60 *tr* to achieve a return on
rentable *adj* profitable
rentar *tr* to produce, yield
rentista *mf* bondholder; financier; person of independent means
renuente *adj* reluctant, unwilling
renuevo *m* sprout, shoot; renewal
renuncia *f* renunciation; resignation; (law) waiver, quit-claim, relinquishment
renunciar *tr* to renounce; resign, relinquish || *intr* to renounce; (*no servir al palo que se juega*) renege; **renunciar a** to give up, renounce, waive
renuncio *m* slip, mistake; (*en juegos de naipes*) renege; lie
reñi•do -da *adj* on bad terms; bitter, hard-fought
reñir §72 *tr* (*regañar*) to scold; (*una batalla, un desafío*) fight || *intr* to fight; be at odds, fall out
re•o -a *adj* guilty, criminal || **reo** *mf* offender, criminal; (law) defendant
reojo — de reojo askance, out of the corner of one's eye; hostilely
reorganizar §60 *tr & ref* to reorganize
reorientación *f* reorientation
reóstato *m* rheostat
repanchigar or **repantigar §44** *ref* to sprawl, loll
reparar *tr* to repair, mend; make amends for; notice, observe; (*un golpe*) parry || *intr* to stop; **reparar en** to notice, pay attention to || *ref* to stop; refrain
reparo *m* repairing, repairs; notice, observation; doubt, objection; shelter; bashfulness
repa•rón -rona *adj* faultfinding || *mf* fault-finder
repartida *f* distribution; issuing
repartir *tr* to distribute; (*naipes*) deal

reparto *m* distribution; (*de naipes*) deal; (theat) cast; **reparto de acciones gratis** stock dividend
repasar *tr* to repass; retrace; review; revise; (*la ropa*) mend
repasata *f* scolding, reprimand
repaso *m* revision; (*de una lección*) review; mending; reprimand
repatriar §77 *tr* to repatriate; send home || *intr & ref* to be repatriated; go or come home
repeler *tr* to repel, repulse
repente *m* start, sudden movement; **de repente** suddenly
repenti•no -na *adj* sudden, unexpected
repentista *mf* (mus) improviser; (mus) sight reader
repentizar §60 *intr* to improvise; (mus) to sight-read, perform at sight
repercutir *intr* to rebound; reecho, reverberate
repertorio *m* repertory
repetición *f* repetition; (mus) repeat; **repetición de la jugada** (sport) instant replay
repetir §50 *tr & intr* to repeat
repicar §73 *tr* to mince, chop up; ring, sound; sting again || *intr* peal, ring out, resound || *ref* to boast, be conceited
repique *m* chopping, mincing; peal, ringing; squabble, quarrel
repiqueteo *m* pealing, ringing; beating, rapping
repisa *f* shelf, ledge; bracket; **repisa de chimenea** mantelpiece; **repisa de ventana** window sill
replantear *tr* to lay out again; reaffirm, reimplement
replegar §66 *tr* to fold over and over || *ref* to fold, fold up; (mil) to fall back
reple•to -ta *adj* replete, full, loaded; fat, chubby
réplica *f* answer, retort; replica; (geol) aftershock
replicar §73 *tr* to argue against || *intr* to answer back, retort
repli•cón -cona *adj* saucy, flip
repliegue *m* fold, crease; (mil) falling back
repoblación *f* resettlement; (agr) restocking
repollitos *mpl* — **repollitos de Bruseles** Brussels sprouts
repollo *m* cabbage; (*p.ej., de lechuga, col*) head
reponer §54 *tr* to replace, put back; restore; (*una pieza dramática*) revive; **repuso** he replied || *ref* to recover; calm down
reportaje *m* reporting; news coverage; report
reportar *tr* to check, restrain; get, obtain; bring, carry; report || *ref* to restrain or control oneself
reporte *m* report, news report; gossip
repórter *m* reporter
reporte•ro -ra *mf* reporter
reposa cabezas *f* (aut) headrest
reposar *intr & ref* to rest, repose; take a nap; (*en la sepultura*) lie, be at rest; (*poso, sedimento*) settle
reposición *f* replacement; (*de la salud*) recovery; (theat) revival
reposo *m* rest, repose
repostar *tr, intr & ref* to stock up; refuel
repostería *f* pastry shop, confectionery; pantry
reposte•ro -ra *mf* pastry cook, confectioner
repregunta *f* (law) cross-examination
repreguntar *tr* (law) to cross-examine
reprender *tr* to reprehend, scold
represa *f* dam; damming; repression, check; (*de un buque*) recapture
represalia *f* reprisal; retaliation
represar *tr* to dam; repress, check; (*de un buque*) to recapture
representación *f* representation; dignity, standing; performance; **en representación de** representing; **representación exclusiva** sole dealership
representante *adj* representing || *mf* representative; actor, player; (com) agent, representative; **representante sindical** shop steward
representar *tr* to represent; show, express; state, declare; act, perform, play, reenact; (*determinada edad*) appear to be || *ref* to imagine
representati•vo -va *adj* representative
reprimenda *f* reprimand
reprimir *tr* to repress
reprobación *f* reproof; flunk, failure
reprobar §61 *tr* to reprove; flunk, fail
reprochar *tr* to reproach
reproche *m* reproach
reproducción *f* reproduction; breeding
reproducir §19 *tr & ref* to reproduce; breed; repeat
reproduc•tor -tora *adj* breeding; reproductive || *mf* breeding animal || *m* — **reproductor de casetes** cassette player; **reproductor de discos compactos** compact disk player; **reproductor de video** videorecorder || *f var* of **reproductor** *m*
repro•pio -pia *adj* balky
reptar *intr* to crawl; to cringe
reptil *m* reptile
república *f* republic
republica•no -na *adj & mf* republican || *m* patriot
repudiar *tr* to repudiate, disown, disavow
repues•to -ta *adj* secluded; spare, extra || *m* stock, supply; serving table; pantry; **de repuesto** spare, extra
repugnante *adj* repugnant, disgusting
repugnar *tr* to conflict with; contradict; object to, avoid; revolt, be repugnant to || *intr* to be repugnant
repujar *tr* to emboss
repulgar §44 *tr* to hem, border
repulgo *m* hem, border
repuli•do -da *adj* highly polished; all dolled up
repulsar *tr* to reject, refuse
repulsi•vo -va *adj* repulsive
repuntar *tr* (*animales dispersos*) (Arg, Chile, Urug) to round up || *intr* to begin to appear; (naut) to begin to rise; (naut) to begin to ebb || *ref* to begin to turn sour; fall out
repuso see **reponer**
reputación *f* reputation, repute
reputar *tr* to repute; esteem

requebra•dor -dora *adj* flirtatious || *mf* flirt
requebrar §2 *tr* to break into smaller pieces; flatter, flirt with
requemar *tr* to burn again; parch; overcook; inflame; bite, sting || *ref* to become tanned or sunburned; smolder, burn within
requerir §68 *tr* to notify; summon; request; urge; check, examine; require; seek, look for; reach for; court, make love to
requesón *m* cottage cheese
requiebro *m* fine crushing; flattery, flattering remarks, flirtation
requisi•to -ta *adj* requisite || *m* requisite, requirement; accomplishment; **requisito previo** prerequisite
res *f* head of cattle; beast; **reses** cattle; **res muerta** carcass
resabio *m* unpleasant aftertaste; bad habit, vice
resabio•so -sa *adj* sly, crafty; (*caballo*) vicious
resaca *f* surge, surf; undertow; (com) redraft; (slang) hangover
resalir §65 *intr* to jut out, project
resaltar *tr* to emphasize || *intr* to bounce, rebound; jut out, project; stand out
resanar *tr* to retouch, patch, repair
resarcir §36 *tr* to indemnify, make amends to; (*un daño, un agravio*) repay; (*una pérdida*) make good; to mend, repair || *ref* — **resarcirse de** to make up for
resbaladi•zo -za *adj* slippery; skiddy; risky; (*memoria*) shaky
resbalar *intr* to slide; skid; slip || *ref* to slide; slip; (fig) to slip, to misstep
rescatar *tr* to ransom, redeem; rescue; (*el tiempo perdido*) make up for; relieve; atone for; (Mex) to resell
rescate *m* ransom, redemption; rescue; salvage; ransom money; **rescate financiero** bailout
rescindir *tr* to rescind
rescoldera *f* heartburn
rescoldo *m* embers; smoldering; doubt, scruple; **arder en rescoldo** to smolder
resenti•do -da *adj* resentful
resentimiento *m* resentment; sorrow, disappointment
resentir §68 *ref* to be resentful; **resentirse de** to feel the bad effects of; resent; suffer from
reseña *f* outline; book review; newspaper account; summary, report; (mil) review
reseñador *m* reviewer; critic
reseñar *tr* to outline; (*un libro*) review; (mil) to review
reserva *f* reserve; reservation; **con** *or* **bajo la mayor reserva** in strictest confidence; **de reserva** standby; **reserva de caza** game preserve; **reservas** (*dudas*) reservations
reservar *tr* to reserve; put aside; postpone; exempt; keep secret || *ref* to save oneself, bide one's time; beware, be distrustful
resfriado *m* cold, head cold
resfriar §77 *tr* to cool, chill || *intr* to turn cold || *ref* to catch cold; cool off, grow cold
resguardar *tr* to defend; protect, shield || *ref* to take shelter; protect oneself
resguardo *m* defense; protection; check, voucher, collateral; (naut) wide berth, sea room
residencia *f* residence; impeachment; **residencia de ancianos** nursing home; home for the aged; **residencia de estudiantes, residencia universitaria** college dormitory
residenciar *tr* to call to account; impeach
residente *adj* resident, live-in || *mf* (med) intern, resident; (pol) resident
residir *intr* to reside
residuo *m* residue, remains; remainder; **residuos peligrosos** hazardous waste; **residuos nucleares** *or* **radioactivos** nuclear *o* radioactive waste
resignación *f* resignation
resignar *tr* to resign || *ref* to resign, become resigned; **resignarse con** (*p.ej., su suerte*) to be resigned to
resina *f* resin
resistencia *f* resistance; strength; **resistencia de rejilla** (electron) grid leak
resistente *adj* resistant; strong; (hort) hardy; **resistente al rayado** scratch-resistant
resistir *tr* to bear, stand; (*la tentación*) resist || *intr* to resist; hold out; **resistir a** (*la violencia; la risa*) resist; refuse to || *ref* to resist; struggle; **resistirse a** to refuse to
resma *f* ream
resobrina *f* grandniece, greatniece
resobrino *m* grandnephew, greatnephew
resollar §61 *intr* to breathe; breathe hard, pant; stop for a rest
resolución *f* resolution; **en resolución** in brief, in a word
resolver §47 & §83 *tr* to resolve; solve; decide on; dissolve || *ref* to resolve; make up one's mind
resonar §61 *intr* to resound, echo
resoplar *intr* to puff; snort
resoplido *m* puffing; snort
resorte *m* spring; springiness; means; province, scope; rubber band; **resorte espiral** coil spring; **tocar resortes** to pull wires, pull strings
respailar *intr* — **ir respailando** to scurry along
respaldar *m* back; || *tr* to back; indorse || *ref* to lean back; sprawl
respaldo *m* back; backing; indorsement
respectar *tr* (with personal **a**) to concern; **por lo que respecta a . . .** as far as . . . is concerned
respecti•vo -va *adj* respective
respecto *m* respect, reference, relation; **al respecto** in the matter; **respecto a** or **de** with respect to, in or with regard to
respetable *adj* respectable
respetar *tr* to respect
respeto *m* respect; consideration; **campar por sus respetos** to be inconsiderate, go one's (his, her, etc.) own way; **de respeto** spare, extra

respetuo•so -sa *adj* respectful; awesome, impressive; humble, obedient
respigón *m* hangnail
respingar §44 *intr* to balk, shy; (*elevarse el borde, p.ej., de la falda*) curl up; give in unwillingly
respin•gón -gona *adj* (*nariz*) snubby, upturned; surly, churlish
respiración *f* respiration; **respiración artificial** artificial respiration; **contener la respiración** to hold one's breath
respirar *tr* to breathe || *intr* to breathe; breathe freely; breathe a sigh of relief; catch one's breath, stop for a rest; **no respirar** to not breathe a word; **sin respirar** without respite, without letup
respiro *m* breathing; respite, breather, breathing spell; (*para el pago de una deuda*) extension of time
resplandecer §22 *intr* to shine; flash, glitter
resplandeciente *adj* brilliant; resplendent
resplandor *m* brilliance, radiance; resplendence; glare
responder *tr* to answer || *intr* to answer, respond; correspond; answer back; **responder de** (*una cosa*) to answer for; **responder por** (*una persona*) to answer for
respon•dón -dona *adj* (coll) saucy
responsable *adj* responsible; **responsable de** responsible for
responsabilizar *tr* to put in charge; hold responsible || *ref* to assume responsibility
respuesta *f* answer, response
resquebrajar *tr & ref* to crack, split
resquemar *tr & intr* to bite, sting || *ref* to be parched; (*resentirse sin manifestarlo*) smolder
resquemo *m* bite, sting
resquicio *m* crack, chink; chance, opportunity
restablecer §22 *tr* to reestablish, restore || *ref* to recover
restañar *tr* to retin; (*sangre*) stanch, stop the flow of
restar *tr* to deduct; reduce; take away; (*una pelota*) return; subtract || *intr* to remain, be left
restaurante *m* restaurant; **restaurante automático** automat; **restaurante autoservicio** cafeteria
restaurar *tr* to restore; to recover
restitución *f* restitution, return
restituir §20 *tr* to return, give back; restore || *ref* to return, come back
resto *m* rest, remainder, residue; (*en juegos de naipes*) stakes; (*de una pelota*) return; **a resto abierto** without limit; **echar el resto** to stake all, shoot the works; **restos** remains, mortal remains; **restos de serie** remnants
restregar §66 *tr* to rub hard; scrub hard
restringir §27 *tr* to restrict; constrict, to contract
resucitar *tr & intr* to resuscitate; resurrect; revive
resuello *m* breathing; hard breathing, panting
resuel•to -ta *adj* resolute, resolved, determined; prompt, quick
resulta *f* result; outcome; vacancy; **de resultas de** as a result of
resultado *m* result
resultar *intr* to result; prove to be, turn out to be; be, become
resumen *m* summary, résumé; recap (coll); **en resumen** in brief, in a word
resumir *tr* to summarize, sum up; recap (coll) || *ref* to be reduced, be transformed
resurrección *f* resurrection
retachar *tr* (Mex) to ricochet
retacho *m* (Mex) ricochet
retaguardia *f* rearguard
retal *m* piece, remnant
retama *f* Spanish broom; **retama de escoba** furze
retar *tr* to challenge, dare; blame, find fault with
retardación *f* retardation
retardar *tr* to retard, slow down
retardo *m* retard, delay
retazo *m* piece, remnant; scrap, fragment
retén *m* store, stock, reserve; catch, pawl; (mil) reserve
retener §71 *tr* to retain, keep, withhold; detain, arrest; (*el pago de un haber*) stop
retentiva *f* memory; recall
reticente *adj* deceptive, misleading; noncommital
retina *f* retina
retintín *m* jingle, tinkling; (*en el oído*) ringing; tone of reproach, sarcasm, mockery
retiñir §12 *intr* to jingle, tinkle (*los oídos*) ring
retirada *f* retirement, withdrawal; place of refuge; (mil) retreat, retirement; (*toque*) (mil) retreat; **batirse en retirada** to beat a retreat
retirar *tr* to retire, withdraw; take away; pull back || *ref* to retire, withdraw; (mil) to retire
reto *m* challenge, dare; threat
retocar §73 *tr* to retouch; touch up; (*un disco de fonógrafo*) play back
retoño *m* sprout, shoot, sucker
retorcer §74 *tr* to twist; twist together; (*las manos*) wring; (fig) to twist, misconstrue || *ref* to twist; writhe
retóri•co -ca *adj* rhetorical || *f* rhetoric
retornar *tr* to return, give back; back, back up || *intr & ref* to return, go back
retorno *m* return; barter, exchange; reward, requital; **retorno terrestre** (elec) ground
retorta *f* (chem) retort
retozar §60 *intr* to frolic, gambol, romp
retozo *m* frolic, gambol, romping; **retozo de la risa** giggle, titter
reto•zón -zona *adj* frolicsome, frisky
retracción *f* retraction; (pathol) atrophy
retractar *tr & ref* to retract
retráctil *adj* retractable
retraer §75 *tr* to bring again, bring back; dissuade || *ref* to withdraw, retire; take refuge
retraí•do -da *adj* solitary; reserved, shy
retransmisión *f* rebroadcasting
retransmitir *tr* to rebroadcast

retrasa•do -da *adj* (mentally) retarded
retrasar *tr* to delay, retard; put off; (*un reloj*) set or turn back || *intr* to be too slow; (*en los estudios*) be or fall behind || *ref* to delay, be late, be slow, be behind time; (*un reloj*) go or be slow
retraso *m* delay; **tener retraso** to be late
retratar *tr* to portray; photograph; imitate || *ref* to sit for a portrait; have one's picture taken
retrato *m* portrait; photograph; copy, imitation; description; **el vivo retrato de** the living image of
retrepar *ref* to lean back, lean back in the chair
retreta *f* (mil) retreat, tattoo; outdoor band concert
retrete *m* toilet, lavatory, bathroom
retribuir §20 *tr* to repay, pay back
retroacti•vo -va *adj* retroactive
retroalimentación *f* (psychol) feedback
retroceder *intr* to retrogress; back away; back down, back out
retroceso *m* retrogression, throwback; (*de un arma de fuego*) recoil; (*de una enfermedad*) flare-up; (mach, mov) rewind(ing)
retrocohete *m* retrorocket
retrodisparo *m* retrofiring
retropropulsión *f* (aer) jet propulsion
retrospecti•vo -va *adj* retrospective || *f* (mov) flashback
retrovirus *m* retrovirus
retrovisor *m* rear-view mirror
retrucar §73 *intr* to answer, reply; (billiards) kiss
retruco *m* (billiards) kiss
retruécano *m* pun
retumbar *intr* to resound, rumble, boom
retumbo *m* resounding, rumble, echo
reumáti•co -ca *adj & mf* rheumatic
reumatismo *m* rheumatism
reubicación *f* relocation
reubicar §73 *tr* to relocate, resettle
reunificación *f* reunification
reunión *f* reunion, gathering, meeting; assemblage; **reunión de atletismo** field day
reunir §59 *tr* to join, unite; assemble, gather together, bring together; reunite; (*dinero*) raise || *ref* to unite; assemble, gather together, come together, meet; reunite
reválida *f* final examination (*for a higher degree*)
revalorar *tr* to revaluate
revalorizar §60 *tr* to revaluate
revejecer §22 *intr & ref* to grow old before one's time
revelación *f* revelation
revelado *m* (phot) development
revela•dor -dora *adj* revealing, telltale || *m* (phot) developer
revelar *tr* to reveal; (phot) to develop
revender *tr* to resell; retail
reventa *f* resale
reventar §2 *tr* to smash, crush; burst, blow out, explode; ruin; annoy, bore; (*a una persona*) work to death; (*a un caballo*) run to death || *intr* to burst, blow out, explode; (*las olas*) break; (*morir*) croak; (*de ira*) blow up, hit the ceiling; **reventar por** to be dying to || *ref* to burst, blow out, explode; be worked to death; (*un caballo*) be run to death
reventón *m* burst; (aut) blowout
rever §80 *tr* to revise, review; (*un caso legal*) retry
reverberar *intr* to reverberate
reverbero *m* reflector; street lamp; chafing dish
reverencia *f* reverence; bow, curtsy
reverenciar *tr* to revere, reverence || *intr* to bow, curtsy
reveren•do -da *adj & m* reverend
reversible *adj* reversible
reverso *m* back; wrong side; reverse
revertir §68 *intr* to revert
revés *m* back, reverse; wrong side; backhand; (*desgracia, contratiempo*) reverse, setback; **al revés** wrong side out; inside out; upside down; backwards
revestir §50 *tr* to put on, don; cover, coat, face, line, surface; assume, take on; disguise; (*un cuento*) adorn; invest || *ref* to put on vestments; be haughty; gird oneself
revirar *tr* to turn, twist; turn over
revisada *f* examination; revision
revisar *tr* to revise, review, check; audit; (med) to examine
revisión *f* revision, review, check; **revisión médica** (Esp) checkup, medical examination
revisionismo *m* revisionism
revisionista *adj & mf* revisionist
revisor *m* inspector, examiner; (rr) conductor, ticket collector
revista *f* review; magazine; journal, review; (mil) review; (theat) review, revue; (law) new trial
revistar *tr* (mil) to review
revivir *tr & intr* to revive
revocable *adj* reversible
revocar §73 *tr* to revoke; dissuade; drive back, drive away; plaster, stucco
revocatoria *f* (SAm) recall; repeal; cancellation
revolar §61 *intr & ref* to flutter, flutter around
revolcar §81 *tr* to knock down; (*a un adversario*) floor; (*a un alumno en un examen*) flunk, fail || *ref* to wallow, roll around; be stubborn
revolotear *tr* to fling up || *intr* to flutter, flutter around, flit
revoltijo *m* or **revoltillo** *m* mess, jumble; stew
revolto•so -sa *adj* rebellious, riotous; (*niño*) unruly, mischievous; complicated; winding || *mf* troublemaker, rioter
revolución *f* (mech, hist, pol) revolution; **revolución de palacio** coup d'état
revoluciona•rio -ria *adj & mf* revolutionary
revolver §47 & §83 *tr* to shake; stir; turn around; turn upside down; wrap up; mess up; disturb; (*sus pasos*) retrace; alienate, estrange || *intr* to retrace one's steps || *ref* to retrace

one's steps; turn around; toss and turn; (*un astro en su órbita*) revolve; (*el mar*) get rough
revólver *m* revolver
revuelco *m* upset, tumble; wallowing
revuelo *m* whirl, flying around; stir, commotion
revuel•to -ta *adj* restless; in a mess; (meteor) rough; unsettled || *f* revolution, revolt, uprising; disturbance; turning point; fight, row
rey *m* king; swineherd; **los Reyes Católicos** Ferdinand and Isabella; **los Reyes Magos** the Three Wise Men; **ni rey ni roque** nobody; **rey de zarza** wren; **reyes** king and queen; **Reyes** Epiphany
reyerta *f* quarrel, wrangle
reyezuelo *m* (orn) kinglet; **reyezuelo moñudo** goldcrest
rezaga•do -da *mf* straggler, laggard
rezagar **§44** *tr* to outstrip, leave behind; postpone || *ref* to fall behind
rezago *m* unused or surplus material
rezar **§60** *tr* (*una oración*) to pray; (*una oración; la misa*) say; (coll) to say, to read; (*anunciar*) (coll) to call for || *intr* to pray; grumble; (coll) to say, to read; **rezar con** to concern
rezo *m* prayer; devotions
rezón *m* grapnel
rezongar **§44** *tr* (CAm) to scold || *intr* to grumble, growl
rezonificar **§73** *tr* to rezone
rezumar *intr* to ooze, seep || *ref* to ooze, seep; to leak; (*una especie*) leak out
ría *f* estuary, fiord
riachuelo *m* rivulet, streamlet
riada *f* flood, freshet
ribazo *m* slope, embarkment
ribera *f* bank, shore; riverside, riverbank
ribere•ño -ña *adj* riverside
ribero *m* levee, dike
ribete *m* edge, trimming, border; (*a un cuento*) embellishment
ribetear *tr* to edge, trim, border, bind
Ricardo *m* Richard
ri•co -ca *adj* rich; dear, darling
ridiculez *f* absurdity
ridiculizar **§60** *tr* to ridicule
ridícu•lo -la *adj* ridiculous; touchy || *m* ridiculous situation; **poner en ridículo** to ridicule, expose to ridicule
riego *m* irrigation; watering
riel *m* ingot; curtain rod; rail
rielar *intr* to shimmer, gleam; (poet) to twinkle
rienda *f* rein; **a rienda suelta** swiftly, violently; with free rein
riente *adj* laughing; bright, cheerful
riesgo *m* risk, danger; **correr riesgo** to run or take a risk; **de alto riesgo** high-risk
riesgo•so -sa *adj* risky; dangerous
rifa *f* raffle; fight, quarrel
rifar *tr* to raffle, raffle off || *intr* to raffle; fight, quarrel
rifle *m* rifle
rigidez *f* stiffness, rigidity; inflexibility; **rigidez cadavérica** rigor mortis
rígi•do -da *adj* rigid, stiff; strict, severe
rigor *m* rigor; **de rigor** usual, a must, de rigueur; **rigor mortis** rigor mortis
riguro•so -sa *adj* rigorous; severe
rima *f* rhyme; **rimas** poems, poetry
rimar *tr & ref* to rhyme
rimbombante *adj* resounding; flashy
rímel *m* mascara
rimero *m* heap, pile
Rin *m* Rhine
rincón *m* corner; nook; piece of land; (coll) home; (box) corner
rinconera *f* corner piece of furniture; corner table; corner cupboard
ringla *f,* **ringle** *m* or **ringlera** *f* row, tier
ringorrango *m* curlicue; frill, frippery
rinoceronte *m* rhinoceros
riña *f* fight, scuffle; **riñas callejeras** street fight
riñón *m* kidney; (fig) heart, center, interior; **tener bien cubierto el riñón** to be well-heeled
río *m* river; **pescar en río revuelto** to fish in troubled waters
riostra *f* brace, stay; guy wire
riostrar *tr* to brace, stay
ripia *f* shingle
ripio *m* debris; rubble; (*palabras inútiles empleadas para completar el verso*) padding; **no perder ripio** to not miss a trick
riqueza *f* riches, wealth; richness; **riquezas del subsuelo** mineral resources
risa *f* laugh, laughter
risco *m* cliff, crag; honey fritter
risible *adj* laughable
risotada *f* guffaw, horse laugh
ristra *f* string of onions, string of garlic; (coll) string, row, file
ristre *m* lance rest
risue•ño -ña *adj* smiling
rítmi•co -ca *adj* rhythmic(al)
ritmo *m* rhythm; **a gran ritmo** at great speed
rito *m* rite
rival *mf* rival
rivalidad *f* rivalry; enmity
rivalizar **§60** *intr* to vie, compete; **rivalizar con** to rival
riza•do -da *adj* curly; ripply || *m* curl, curling; rippling
rizador *m* curling iron, hair curler
rizar **§60** *tr & ref* to curl; (*la superficie del agua*) ripple
ri•zo -za *adj* curly || *m* curl, ringlet; ripple; (aer) loop; **rizar el rizo** (aer) to loop the loop
ro *interj* — **¡ro ro!** hushaby!, bye-bye!
roba•dor -dora *mf* robber, thief
róbalo or **robalo** *m* (*Labrax lupus*) bass; (*Centropomus undecimalis*) snook
robar *tr* to rob, steal; (*un naipe o ficha de dominó*) draw || *intr & ref* to steal
Roberto *m* Robert
robinete *m* faucet, spigot, cock
roblar *tr* to clinch, rivet

roble *m* oak; (*Quercus robur*) British oak tree; husky fellow
roblón *m* rivet
robo *m* robbery, theft; (*naipe tomado del monte*) draw; **robo a mano armada** armed robbery; **robo con escalamiento** burglary
ro•bot *m* (*pl* **-bots**) robot; **robot de cocina** processor
robótica *f* robotics
robotización *f* use of robots; robotization
robus•to -ta *adj* robust
roca *f* rock; **roca de fonda, roca firme** bedrock
rocalla *f* pebbles; stone chips; large glass bead
rocallo•so -sa *adj* stony, pebbly
roce *m* rubbing; close contact; sideswipe
rociada *f* sprinkling; dew; (*de balas, piedras, etc.*) shower; (*de invectivas*) volley
rociadera *f* sprinkling can
rociar §77 *tr* to sprinkle; spray; bedew; scatter || *intr* to drizzle; **rocía** there is dew
rocín *m* hack, nag; work horse, draft horse; riding horse; rough guy
rocío *m* dew; drizzle; sprinkling
rock and roll *or* **rocanrol** *m* rock and roll, rock-'n'-roll
rocke•ro -ra *mf* rock singer
roco•so -sa *adj* rocky
rodada *f* rut, track
roda•do -da *adj* (*fácil, flúido*) rounded, fluent; (*tránsito*) vehicular || *f* see **rodada**
rodadura *f* rolling; rut; (*de neumático*) tread
rodaja *f* disk, caster; round slice
rodaje *m* wheels; (*de una película cinematográfica*) shooting, filming; **en rodaje** (aut) being run in; (mov) being filmed
rodamiento *m* bearing; (*de un neumático*) tread; **rodamientos** running gear
Ródano *m* Rhone
rodante *adj* rolling; on wheels; (Chile) wandering
rodapié *m* baseboard, washboard
rodar §61 *tr* to roll; (*una película cinematográfica*) shoot, film, take; screen, project; drag along; (*una llave*) turn; (*la escalera*) roll down; (*un nuevo coche*) run in; (*válvulas de un motor*) grind || *intr* to roll, roll along; roll down; rotate, revolve; tumble; roam, wander about; (*por medio de ruedas*) run; prowl
Rodas *f* Rhodes
rodear *tr* to surround; round up || *intr* to go around; go by a roundabout way; beat about the bush || *ref* to turn, twist, toss about
rodela *f* buckler, target; padded ring
rodeo *m* detour, roundabout way; dodge, duck; rodeo, roundup; **andar con rodeos** to beat about the bush; **dar un rodeo** to go a roundabout way
rodilla *f* knee; floor rag, mop; padded ring; **de rodillas** kneeling, on one's knees
rodillera *f* kneepad; baggy knee; (*de prenda de vestir*) knee; (*del órgano*) (mus) knee swell
rodillo *m* roller; rolling pin; road roller; inking roller; (*de la máquina de escribir*) platen
rodrigar §44 *tr* to prop, prop up, stake
rodrigón *m* prop, stake
roer §62 *tr* to gnaw, gnaw away at; (*un hueso*) pick; wear down
rogar §63 *tr & intr* to beg; pray; **hacerse de rogar** to like to be coaxed
Rogelio *m* Roger
roger *interj* (*¡comprendido!*) roger!
roí•do -da *adj* miserly, stingy
ro•jo -ja *adj* red; ruddy; red-haired; Red || *mf* (*comunista*) Red || *m* red; **al rojo** to a red heat; **rojo oscuro** deep red, maroon
rola *or* **roletazo** *m* (sport) ground ball
rollar *tr* to roll, roll up
rolli•zo -za *adj* round, cylindrical; plump, stocky || *m* round log
rollo *m* roll, coil; roller, rolling pin; round log; yoke pad; role; (*de tela*) bolt
ROM [rrom] *f* (acronym) (**memoria de acceso aleatorio**); (compu) ROM (read-only memory)
romadizo *m* cold in the head
romance *adj* (*neolatino*) Romance || *m* Romance language; Spanish language; romance of chivalry; octosyllabic verse with alternate lines in assonance; narrative poem in octosyllabic verse; ballad; **romance heroico** hendecasyllabic verse with alternate lines in assonance
romancero *m* collection of Old Spanish romances
romancillo *m* verse of less than eight syllables with alternate lines in assonance
románi•co -ca *adj* (*neolatino*) Romance, Romanic; (*arquitectura*) Romanesque || *m* Romanesque
roma•no -na *adj & mf* Roman
romanticismo *m* romanticism
románti•co -ca *adj* romantic
romanza *f* (mus) romance, romanza
romería *f* pilgrimage; crowd, gathering
rome•ro -ra *mf* pilgrim || *m* rosemary
ro•mo -ma *adj* blunt, dull; flat-nosed
rompeáto•mos *m* (*pl* **-mos**) atom smasher
rompecabe•zas *m* (*pl* **-zas**) riddle, puzzle, brain teaser; (*figura que ha sido cortada en trozos menudos y que hay que recomponer*) jigsaw puzzle
rompehie•los *m* (*pl* **-los**) iceboat, icebreaker
rompehuel•gas *m* (*pl* **-gas**) strikebreaker
rompeo•las *m* (*pl* **-las**) mole, breakwater
romper §83 *tr* to break; break through; break up; tear || *intr* to break; (*las flores*) break open, burst open; break down; **romper a** to start to, burst out
rompiente *m* reef, shoal; (*oleaje que choca contra las rocas*) breaker
rompope *m* alcoholic eggnog
ron *m* rum; **ron de laurel** *or* **de malagueta** bay rum
ronca *f* (*época del celo*) rut; cry of buck in rutting season; bullying

roncar §73 *intr* to snore; (*el viento, el mar*) roar; cry in rutting season; bully
ronce•ro -ra *adj* slow, poky; grouchy
roncha *f* weal, welt; black-and-blue mark
ronchar *tr* to crunch
ron•co -ca *adj* hoarse; harsh || *f* see **ronca**
ronda *f* (*de un policía; de visitas; de cigarros o bebidas*) round; (*juego del corro*) (Chile) ring-around-a-rosy; **ronda negociadora** round of negotiations
rondar *tr* to go around; fly around; patrol; hang around; court || *intr* to patrol by night; gad about at nighttime; go serenading; prowl; (mil) to make the rounds
ronpope *m* alcoholic eggnog
ronquedad *f* hoarseness; harshness
ronquera *f* hoarseness
ronquido *m* snore; rasping sound
ronronear *intr* to purr
ronroneo *m* purr, purring
ronzal *m* halter
ronzar §60 *tr* to crunch, munch
roña *f* scab, mange; sticky dirt; pine bark; stinginess; spite, ill will; (Col) malingering; **jugar a roña** (Peru) to play for fun
roño•so -sa *adj* scabby, mangy; dirty, filthy; stingy; spiteful
ropa *f* clothing, clothes; dry goods; **a quema ropa** point-blank; **ropa blanca** linen; **ropa de cama** bed linen; bedclothes; **ropa de mesa** tablecloths; **ropa dominguera** Sunday best; **ropa hecha** ready-made clothes; **ropa interior** *or* **íntima** underwear; **ropa sucia** laundry
ropaje *m* clothes, clothing, apparel; gown, robe; drapery
ropaveje•ro -ra *mf* old-clothes dealer
rope•ro -ra *mf* ready-made clothier; wardrobe keeper || *m* wardrobe, clothes closet
roque *m* rook, castle
roque•ño -ña *adj* rocky; hard, flinty
rorro *m* baby; (Mex) doll
rosa *f* rose; **rosa de los vientos** or **rosa náutica** (naut) compass card; **rosas** popcorn; **verlo todo de color de rosa** to see everything through rose-colored glasses
rosa•do -da *adj* rose-colored, rosy; pink; flushed || *f* frost
rosaleda or **rosalera** *f* rose garden
rosario *m* rosary; (*de sucesos*) string; chain pump
ros•bif *m* (*pl* **-bifs**) roast beef
rosca *f* coil, spiral; (*de una espiral*) turn; twisted roll; (*de un tornillo*) thread; (Chile) padded ring
roscar §73 *tr* to thread
roseta *f* sprinkling spout or nozzle; red spot on cheek; **rosetas** popcorn
rosetón *m* rose window
rosita *f* little rose; (Chile) earring; **rositas** popcorn
rosquilla *f* coffeecake, doughnut, cruller
rostro *m* face; snout; beak; flea market; **de rostro entero** (*retrato*) full-faced
rostropáli•do -da *mf* (Esp) paleface
rota *f* rout, defeat; (naut) route, course
rotación *f* rotation; (econ) turnover
rotisería *f* fast-food restaurant; delicatessen
rótula *f* lozenge; kneecap; knuckle
rotulador *m* felt pen, highlighter
rotular *tr* to label, title, letter
rótulo *m* label, title; poster, show bill
rotun•do -da *adj* round; rotund, sonorous, full; peremptory
rotura *f* break, breaking; breach, opening; tear, tearing
roturación *f* (agr) reclamation
roya *f* (agr) blight, rust
rozamiento *m* rubbing; friction; (*desavenencia*) (fig) friction
rozar §60 *tr* to graze; scrape, sideswipe; border on; grub, stub; (*las tierras*) clear; (*la hierba*) nibble; (*leña menuda*) cut and gather || *intr* to graze by || *ref* to be on close terms, rub elbows, hobnob; falter, stammer; be alike
roznar *tr* to crunch || *intr* to bray
roznido *m* crunch, crunching noise; bray, braying
Rte. *abbr* **Remite**
rubéola *or* **rubeola** *f* German measles, rubella
ru•bí *m* (*pl* **-bíes**) ruby; (*de un reloj*) ruby, jewel
rubia *f* blonde; station wagon; peseta; **rubia oxigenada** peroxide blonde; **rubia platino** platinum blonde
rubia•les *mf* (*pl* **-les**) goldilocks
ru•bio -bia *adj* blond, fair; golden || *m* blond || *f* see **rubia**
rublo *m* ruble
rubor *m* bright red; blush, flush; bashfulness
ruborizar §60 *tr* to make blush || *ref* to blush
rúbrica *f* title, heading; (*rasgo después de la firma de uno*) flourish
rubricación *f* listing; itemization
ru•bro -bra *adj* red || *m* title, heading; (Chile) (com) entry
rudimento *m* rudiment
ru•do -da *adj* coarse, rough; rude, crude, dull, stupid; hard, severe
rueca *f* distaff; spinning wheel
rueda *f* wheel; caster, roller; (*de gente*) ring, circle; round slice; pinwheel; (*de la cola del pavo*) spread; sunfish; **hacer la rueda** (*el pavo*) to spread its tail; **hacer la rueda a** to play up to; **rueda de andar** treadmill; **rueda de cadena** sprocket, sprocket wheel; **rueda de escape** escapement wheel; **rueda de fuego** pinwheel; **rueda de identificación, rueda de sospechosos** lineup; **rueda dentada** gearwheel; **rueda de paletas** paddle wheel; **rueda de prensa** press conference; **rueda de recambio** spare wheel; **rueda de tornillo sin fin** worm wheel; **rueda motriz** drive wheel
ruedo *m* turn, rotation; round mat; selvage; hemline; (taur) ring; **a todo ruedo** at all events
ruego *m* request, entreaty; prayer
ru•fián -fiana *mf* bawd, go-between || *m* cur, cad
ru•fo -fa *adj* sandy, sandy-haired; curly-haired

rugido *m* roar; (*de las tripas*) rumble
rugir **§27** *intr* to roar; rumble
rugo•so -sa *adj* rugged, wrinkled
ruibarbo *m* rhubarb
ruido *m* noise; rumor; row, rumpus; **ruido blanco** white noise; **ruido de fondo** background noise; **ruido de sables** saber rattling
ruido•so -sa *adj* noisy; loud; sensational
ruin *adj* base, mean, vile; stingy; (*animal*) vicious
ruina *f* ruin
ruindad *f* baseness, meanness, vileness; stinginess; viciousness
ruino•so -sa *adj* tottery, run-down
ruiseñor *m* nightingale
ruleta *f* roulette; (CAm, Arg) tape measure
ruletero *m* (Mex) cruising taxi driver (*in search of fares*)
rulo *m* roll; rolling pin; (hair) curler
ruma•no -na *adj* & *mf* Rumanian
rumbo *m* bearing, course, direction; pomp, show; generosity; (CAm) noisy celebration; **(con) rumbo a** in the direction of, bound for; **hacer** *or* **poner rumbo a** to set a course for, to head for; **por aquellos rumbos** in those parts
rumbo•so -sa *adj* pompous, magnificent; generous
rumiar *tr* & *intr* to ruminate
rumor *m* rumor; (*de voces*) murmur, buzz; rumble; **rumores** hearsay
rumorear *tr* to rumor, circulate by a rumor || *intr* to murmur, buzz, rumble || *ref* to be rumored; **se rumorea que** it is rumored that
rumoro•so -sa *adj* noisy, loud, rumbling
runfla *f* or **runflada** *f* string, row; (*en los naipes*) sequence
ruptor *m* (elec) contact breaker
ruptura *f* rupture, break; crack, split; (*cesación de relaciones*) rupture
Rusia *f* Russia
ru•so -sa *adj* & *mf* Russian
rúst. *abbr* **rústica**
rústi•co -ca *adj* rustic; coarse, crude, clumsy; (*latín*) Vulgar; **en rústica** paper-bound || *m* rustic, peasant
ruta *f* route; **ruta aérea** air lane; **ruta ecológica** nature trail
rutilante *adj* shining, sparkling
rutina *f* routine
rutina•rio -ria *adj* routine, monotonous

S

S, s (ese) *f* twentieth letter of the Spanish alphabet
S. *abbr* **San, Santo, sobresaliente, sur**
sábado *m* Saturday; (eccl) the Sabbath
sábalo *m* shad
sabana *f* savanna, pampa; **ponerse en la sabana** (Ven) to get rich overnight; **sábana ajustable, de cuatro picos** *or* **de cajón** (Mex) fitted sheet
sábana *f* sheet; altar cloth
sabandija *f* insect, bug, worm; (*persona*) vermin; **sabandijas** (*animales o personas*) vermin
sabanilla *f* kerchief; altar cloth
sabañón *m* chilblain
sabáti•co -ca *adj* sabbatical
sabe•dor -dora *adj* aware, informed
sabelotodo *m* (*pl* **sabelotodo**) know-it-all, wise guy
saber *m* knowledge, learning || *v* **§64** *tr* & *intr* to know; to find out; to taste; **a saber** namely, to wit; **me sabe mal** I'm sorry, I regret; **no saber dónde meterse** to not know which way to turn; **que yo sepa** as far as I know; **saber a** to taste of; smack of; **saber a poco** to be just a taste, taste like more; **saber de** to be aware of; hear from || *ref* to know; be or become known
sabidi•llo -lla *adj* & *mf* know-it-all
sabi•do -da *adj* well-known; (coll) learned, well-informed; **de sabido** certainly, surely
sabiduría *f* wisdom; knowledge, learning
sabiendas — a sabiendas knowingly, consciously; **a sabiendas de que** knowing that, aware that
sabihon•do -da *adj* & *mf* know-it-all
sa•bio -bia *adj* wise; learned; (*animal*) trained || *mf* wise person, scholar, scientist || *m* wise man, sage
sablazo *m* stroke with a saber, wound made by a saber; sponging; **dar un sablazo a** to hit for a loan
sable *m* saber, cutlass; (coll) sponging
sablear *tr* to hit for a loan, sponge on || *intr* to go around sponging
sablista *mf* sponger
sabor *m* taste, flavor
saborcillo *m* slight taste, touch
saborear *tr* to flavor; taste; savor; entice; || *ref* to smack one's lips; **saborearse de** to taste; to savor
sabotaje *m* sabotage
sabotear *tr* & *intr* to sabotage
sabro•so -sa *adj* tasty, savory, delicious
sabueso *m* bloodhound; sleuth
saburro•so -sa *adj* (*boca*) foul; (*lengua*) coated
sacaboca•do *m* or **sacaboca•dos** *m* (*pl* **-dos**) ticket punch; sure thing

sacabotas *m* (*pl* **-tas**) bootjack
sacacor•chos *m* (*pl* **-chos**) corkscrew
sacaman•chas *mf* (*pl* **-chas**) clothes cleaner, spot remover; dry cleaner; dyer
sacamue•las *m* (*pl* **-las**) tooth puller; quack, cheat
sacamuer•tos *m* (*pl* **-tos**) stagehand
sacapintura *m* paint remover
sacapun•tas *m* (*pl* **-tas**) pencil sharpener
sacar §73 *tr* (*un clavo, una espada, agua, una conclusión*) to draw; pull out; pull up; take out; extract, remove; show; bring out, publish; find out, solve; (*un secreto*) elicit, draw out; copy; (*una fotografía*) take; except, exclude; get, obtain; produce, invent, imitate; (*un premio*) win; (*una pelota*) serve; (*el pecho*) stick out; **sacar a bailar** to drag in; **sacar al perro con correa** to walk the dog with a leash; **sacar a relucir** to bring up unexpectedly; **sacar en claro** or **en limpio** to recopy clearly; deduce, clear up ‖ *ref* (Mex) to make off
sacarina *f* saccharin
sacasi•llas *m* (*pl* **-llas**) stagehand
sacerdocio *m* priesthood
sacerdote *m* priest
saciar *tr* to satiate
saco *m* bag, sack; coat, jacket; sack, plunder, pillage; (*de mentiras*) pack; **saco de arena** (box) punching bag; (mil) sandbag; **saco de dormir** sleeping bag; **saco de noche** overnight bag; **saco terreno** sandbag
sacramento *m* sacrament
sacrificar §73 *tr* to sacrifice; slaughter ‖ *intr* to sacrifice ‖ *ref* to sacrifice; sacrifice oneself
sacrificio *m* sacrifice; **sacrificio del altar** Sacrifice of the Mass
sacrilegio *m* sacrilege
sacríle•go -ga *adj* sacrilegious
sacristán *m* sacristan; sexton; **sacristán de amén** yes man
sacristía *f* sacristy, vestry
sa•cro -cra *adj* sacred
sacudida *f* shake, jar, jolt, jerk, bump; (elec) shock
sacudi•do -da *adj* intractable; determined ‖ *f* see **sacudida**
sacudir *tr* to shake; beat; jar, jolt; rock; shake off ‖ *ref* to shake, to shake oneself; rock; **sacudirse bien** to wangle one's way out
sádi•co -ca *adj* sadistic ‖ *mf* sadist
saeta *f* arrow, dart; (*del reloj*) hand; magnetic needle
saetilla *f* small arrow; (*del reloj*) hand; magnetic needle; (bot) arrowhead
saetín *m* flume, millrace
sa•gaz *adj* (*pl* **-gaces**) sagacious; keen-scented
Sagitario *m* (astr) Sagittarius
sagra•do -da *adj* sacred ‖ *m* asylum, haven, sanctuary; **acogerse a sagrado** to take sanctuary
sagrario *m* sanctuary, shrine; ciborium
sahariana *f* tight-fitting military jacket
sahornar *ref* to skin oneself
sahumar *tr* to perfume with smoke or incense; (Chile) to gold-plate, silver-plate
sainete *m* one-act farce; flavor, relish, spice, zest; sauce, seasoning; tidbit
sa•jón -jona *adj & mf* Saxon
sal *f* salt; grace, charm; wit; (CAm) misfortune; **sal de sosa** washing soda; **sales aromáticas** smelling salts; **sal gema** rock salt
sala *f* hall; drawing room, living room, sitting room; **sala de alumbramiento** (med) delivery room; **sala de batalla** sorting room; **sala de calderas** boiler room; **sala de control** (rad, telv) control room; **sala de enfermos** infirmary; **sala de espera** waiting room; **sala de estar** living room, sitting room; **sala de fiestas** night club; **sala de juntas** boardroom; **sala de cine** motion picture theater; **sala de máquinas** engine room; **sala de partos** (med) delivery room; **sala de redacción** newsroom; **sala de urgencias, sala de guardia** (med) emergency room; **sala recreativa con videojuegos** video arcade
saladillo *m* salted peanut
Salamina *f* Salamis
salar *tr* to salt; spoil, ruin; bring bad luck to
salario *m* wages, pay; **salario de hambre** starvation wages
salchicha *f* sausage; **salchicha ahumada** baloney, bologna; **salchicha de Frankfurt** *or* **salchicha de Viena** (Arg. Col) *or* **salchicha alemana** (Ven) frankfurter
salchiche•ro -ra *mf* pork butcher
salchichonería *f* (Mex) delicatessen
salcochar *tr* to boil in salt water
salcocho *m* food boiled in salt water
saldar *tr* to settle, liquidate; sell out
saldo *m* settlement; balance; remnant; bargain; **saldo de mercancías** job lot; **saldo deudor** debit balance
salero *m* saltshaker, saltcellar; salt lick; grace, charm, wit
salero•so -sa *adj* charming, winsome, lively; salty, witty
salgar §44 *tr* (*el ganado*) to salt
salida *f* start; departure; exit; outcome, result; subterfuge; pretext; outlay, expenditure; projection; outlying fields; (compu, elec) output; (sport) start; (mil) sally, sortie; (coll) witticism, sally; **salida de artistas** stage door; **salida de baño** bathrobe; **salida de incendios** fire exit; **salida del sol** sunrise; **salida de teatro** evening wrap; **salida de teatros** aftertheater party; **salida de tono** irrelevancy, impropriety; **salida en falso, salida nula** (sport) false start; **salida impresa** (compu) printout, hard copy; **salida lanzada** (sport) running start; **tener salida** to sell well; to be popular with the boys
sali•do -da *adj* bulging, prominent, projecting; (coll) in heat; horny, hot ‖ *mf* (Ven) (coll) busybody
saliente *adj* projecting; (*p.ej., tren*) outbound;

(*sol*) rising ‖ *m* east ‖ *f* projection; (*de la carretera*) shoulder

salir §65 *intr* to go out, come out; leave, go away, depart; sail; run out, come to an end; appear, show up; (*una mancha*) come out, come off; (*p.ej., el sol*) rise; shoot, spring, come up; project, stick out; make the first move; result, turn out; be elected; **salga lo que saliere** come what may; **salir a** to amount to; open into; resemble, look like; **salir al encuentro a** to go to meet; take a stand against; get ahead of; **salir bien en un examen** to pass an examination; **salir con bien** to be successful; **salir de** to depart from; cease being; get rid of; (*p.ej., su juicio, sentido*) lose; **salir disparado** to start like a shot; **salir pitando** to start off on a mad run; blow up, hit the ceiling; **salir reprobado** (*en un examen*) to fail ‖ *ref* to slip out, escape; slip off, run off; leak; boil over; **salirse con la suya** to have one's own way; carry one's point

salitre *m* saltpeter

saliva *f* saliva; **gastar saliva** to rattle along; to waste one's breath

salmo *m* psalm

salmón *m* salmon

salmuera *f* brine, pickle; salty food or drink

salobre *adj* brackish, saltish

salón *m* living room, parlor, sitting room; salon, drawing room; (*de un buque*) saloon; meeting room; reception room; **salón de actos** auditorium; **salón de baile** ballroom; **salón de belleza** beauty parlor; **salón de juegos, salón recreativo** amusement arcade; **Salón de la Fama** Hall of Fame; **salón del automóvil** automobile show; **salón de refrescos** ice-cream parlor; **salón de tertulia** *or* **salón social** lounge

saloncillo *m* (*p.ej., de un teatro*) rest room

salpicadero *m* control panel; (aut) dashboard

salpicar §73 *tr* to splash, splatter; sprinkle

salpimentar §2 *tr* to salt and pepper, season with salt and pepper; (fig) to sweeten

salpullido *m* rash, eruption

salpullir §13 *tr* to cause a rash on; splotch ‖ *ref* to break out

salsa *f* sauce, dressing, gravy; **salsa de ají** chili sauce; **salsa de tomate** catsup, ketchup; **salsa inglesa** Worcestershire sauce

salsamentaría *f* (Col) delicatessen

salsera *f* gravy dish; small saucer (*to mix paints*)

saltaban•co *m* or **saltaban•cos** *m* (*pl* **-cos**) quack, mountebank; prestidigitator; nuisance

saltamon•tes *m* (*pl* **-tes**) grasshopper

saltar *tr* to jump, jump over; skip, skip over ‖ *intr* to jump, leap, hop, skip; bounce; shoot up, spurt; come loose, come off; crack, break, burst; chip; project, stick out; **saltar a la vista** *or* **los ojos** to be self-evident; **saltar por** to jump over, jump out of ‖ *ref* to skip; come off

saltatum•bas *m* (*pl* **-bas**) burying parson

salteador *m* highwayman, holdup man

saltear *tr* to attack, hold up, waylay; take by surprise

saltimbanco *m* var of **saltabanco**

salto *m* jump, leap, bound; skip; dive; fall, waterfall; leapfrog; **salto con pértiga** *or* **garrocha** pole vault; **salto de altura** high jump; **salto de ángel** swan dive; **salto de anuncios comerciales** (electron) commercial scan; **salto de cama** morning wrap, dressing gown; **salto de carpa** jackknife; **salto de esquí** ski jump; **salto de longitud** long jump; **salto de viento** (naut) sudden shift in the wind; **salto en el tiempo** time warp; **salto mortal** somersault; **salto ornamental** fancy dive

sal•tón -tona *adj* (*eyes*) bulging; (SAm) wary

salubre *adj* healthful, salubrious

salud *f* health; welfare; salvation; greeting; **gastar, vender** *or* **verter salud** to radiate health ‖ *interj* greetings!; **¡salud y pesetas!** health and wealth!

saludar *tr* to greet, salute, hail, bow to; give regards to ‖ *intr* to salute; bow

saludo *m* greeting, salute, bow; salutation; **saludo final** conclusion

salutación *f* salutation, greeting, bow

salva *f* greeting, welcome; salvo; oath; tray; (*de aplausos; de una batería de artillería*) round

salvado *m* bran

salva•dor -dora *mf* savior, saver, rescuer ‖ **el Salvador** the Saviour; (*país de la América Central*) El Salvador

salvadore•ño -ña *adj & mf* Salvadoran

salvaguardar *tr* to safeguard

salvaguardia *m* bodyguard, escort ‖ *f* safeguard, safe-conduct; protection, shelter

salvajada *f* atrocity

salvaje *adj* wild, uncultivated; savage; stupid ‖ *mf* savage; dolt

salvaji•no -na *adj* wild; (*de la carne de los animales monteses*) gamy ‖ *f* wild animal; wild animals

salvamante•les *m* (*pl* **-les**) coaster

salvamento *m* salvation; lifesaving; rescue; salvage; place of safety

salvar *tr* to save, rescue; to salvage; (*una dificultad*) avoid, overcome; (*un obstáculo*) clear, get around; (*una distancia*) cover, get over; rise above; jump over; make an exception of; **salvar apariencias** to save face ‖ *ref* to save oneself, escape danger; be saved; **sálvese el que pueda** every man for himself

salvavi•das *m* (*pl* **-das**) life preserver; lifeboat; (*empleado de una estación de salvamento*) lifeguard

salvedad *f* reservation, exception

salvia *f* (bot) sage

sal•vo -va *adj* safe; omitted; **a salvo** safe, out of danger; **a salvo de** safe from ‖ **salvo** *prep* save, except for; **salvo error u omisión (s.e.u.o)** barring error or omission; **salvo que** unless ‖ *f* see **salva**

salvoconducto *m* safe-conduct

sámara *f* (bot) key, key fruit

san *adj* apocopated and unstressed form of **santo**
sanaloto•do *m* (*pl* **-do**) cure-all
sanar *tr* to cure, heal ‖ *intr* to heal; recover
sanción *f* (*aprobación*) sanction; (*castigo, pena*) penalty
sancionar *tr* (*aprobar*) to sanction; (*imponer pena a*) penalize
sancochar *tr* to parboil
sandalia *f* sandal
sándalo *m* (yellow) sandalwood
san•dez *f* (*pl* **-deces**) folly, nonsense; piece of folly
sandía *f* watermelon
san•dio -dia *adj* foolish, nonsensical
sándwich [ˈsaŋgwitʃ] *m or* **sándwiche** [ˈsaŋgwitʃe] *m* sandwich; roll; (Esp) toasted sandwich
saneamiento *m* sanitation, drainage; guarantee
sanear *tr* to guarantee; indemnify; make sanitary, drain, dry up
sangrar *tr* to bleed; drain; tap; (typ) to indent; (coll) to rob ‖ *intr* to bleed; **estar sangrando** to be new or recent; be plain or obvious ‖ *ref* to have oneself bled; (*los colores*) run
sangre *f* blood; **a sangre** by horsepower; **a sangre fría** in cold blood; **pura sangre** *m* thoroughbred; **sangre torera** bullfighting in the blood
sangría *f* bleeding; outlet, draining; ditch, trench; (*bebida*) sangria; tap; tapping; (typ) indentation
sangrien•to -ta *adj* bloody; bleeding; cruel, sanguinary
sangrigor•do -da *adj* unpleasant
sangrilige•ro -ra *adj* nice, pleasant
sangripesa•do -da *adj* unpleasant
sangüesa *f* raspberry
sangüeso *m* raspberry bush
sanguijuela *f* leech
sanguina•rio -ria *adj* sanguinary, bloodthirsty
sanidad *f* healthiness; healthfulness; health; sanitation; **sanidad pública** health department
sanita•rio -ria *adj* sanitary; health, public health ‖ *mf* health worker ‖ *m* (Col, Mex, Ven) toilet, lavatory; **sanitarios** bathroom fixtures
sa•no -na *adj* hale, healthy; healthful; sound; sane; earnest, sincere; safe, sure; whole, untouched, unharmed; **sano y salvo** safe and sound, surely
santiague•ro -ra *adj* Santiago de Cuba ‖ *mf* native or inhabitant of Santiago de Cuba
santia•gués -guesa *adj* Santiago de Compostela ‖ *mf* native or inhabitant of Santiago de Compostela
santiagui•no -na *adj* Santiago de Chile ‖ *mf* native or inhabitant of Santiago de Chile
santiamén *m* jiffy; **en un santiamén** in the twinkling of an eye
santidad *f* holiness, sanctity, saintliness; **su Santidad** his Holiness
santificar §73 *tr* to sanctify, hallow, consecrate; (*las fiestas*) keep; excuse, justify
santiguar §10 *tr* to bless, make the sign of the cross over; punish, slap, abuse ‖ *ref* to cross oneself, make the sign of the cross
san•to -ta *adj* holy, saintly, blessed; (*día*) livelong; artless, simple; **santo y bueno** well and good ‖ *mf* saint ‖ *m* name day; image of a saint; **a santo de** because of; **desnudar a un santo para vestir a otro** to rob Peter to pay Paul; **írsele a uno el santo al cielo** to forget what one was up to; **santo y seña** password, watchword
Santo Domingo Hispaniola
santuario *m* sanctuary, shrine; (Col) buried treasure; (Col, Ven) Indian idol
santu•rrón -rrona *adj* sanctimonious ‖ *mf* sanctimonious person
saña *f* fury, rage; cruelty
sañu•do -da *adj* furious, enraged; cruel
sapiente *adj* wise, intelligent
sapo *m* toad; (coll) stuffed shirt; (Chile) little runt
saque *m* (*en el tenis*) serve, service; server; service line; (Col) distillery; **tener buen saque** to be a heavy eater and drinker
saquear *tr* to sack, plunder, pillage, loot
Sara *f* Sarah
sarampión *m* measles
sarao *m* soirée, evening party
sarape *m* (Guat, Mex) bright-colored woolen poncho
sarcasmo *m* sarcasm
sarcásti•co -ca *adj* sarcastic
sardina *f* sardine; **como sardinas en banasta** *or* **en lata** packed in like sardines
sar•do -da *adj & mf* Sardinian
sarga *f* serge
sargento *m* sergeant
sarmiento *m* vine shoot, running stem
sarna *f* scabies, itch; (vet) mange
sarno•so -sa *adj* itchy, mangy
sarrace•no -na *adj & mf* Saracen
sarracina *f* scuffle, free fight; bloody brawl
sarro *m* crust; (*p.ej., en la lengua*) fur; (*en los dientes*) tartar, plaque
sarta *f* string; line, fine, series
sartén *f* frying pan; **saltar de la sartén y dar en las brasas** to jump from the frying pan into the fire
sastre *m* tailor
satélite *m* satellite; **satélite de comunicaciones** communications satellite; **satélite espía** spy satellite
satelizar §60 *tr* to put into orbit; (pol) to make a satellite of ‖ *ref* to go into orbit
satén *m* sateen
satíri•co -ca *adj* satiric(al) ‖ *mf* satirist
satirizar §60 *tr & intr* to satirize
satisfacción *f* satisfaction
satisfacer §39 *tr & intr* to satisfy ‖ *ref* to satisfy oneself, be satisfied, take satisfaction
satisfacto•rio -ria *adj* satisfactory

saturar *tr* to saturate; satiate
Saturno *m* (astr, myth) Saturn
sauce *m* willow tree; **sauce de Babilonia** *or* **sauce llorón** weeping willow
saúco *m* elder, elderberry
savia *f* sap
saxofón *m* or **saxófono** *m* saxophone
saya *f* skirt; petticoat
sayo *m* smock frock, tunic; garment
sazón *f* ripeness; season; time, occasion; taste, seasoning; **a la sazón** at that time; **en sazón** in season, ripe; on time, opportunely
sazonar *tr* to ripen; season ‖ *ref* to ripen, mature
s/c *abbr* **su cuenta**
S.E. *abbr* **Su Excelencia**
se *pron reflex* himself, to himself; herself, to herself; itself, to itself; themselves, to themselves; yourself, to yourself; yourselves, to yourselves; oneself, to oneself; each other, to each other ‖ *pron pers* (used before the pronouns **lo, la, le,** etc.) to him, to her, to it, to them, to you
sebo *m* tallow; fat, suet
seca *f* drought; dry season
secador *m* drier, hair drier
secadora *f* clothes drier
secafir•mas *m* (*pl* **-mas**) blotter
secano *m* dry land, unwatered land
secansa *f* sequence
secante *m* blotting paper
secar §73 *tr* to dry, wipe dry; annoy, bore ‖ *ref* to dry, get dry; dry oneself; wither; be dry, be thirsty; (*un pozo*) run dry
secarropa *f* clothes dryer; **secarropa de travesaños** clotheshorse
sección *f* section; cross section; **sección de fondo** editorial section
secesión *f* secession
se•co -ca *adj* dry; dried up, withered; lank, lean; harsh, sharp; (*bebida*) straight, indifferent; plain, unadorned ‖ *f* see **seca**
secreta•rio -ria *adj* confidential, trusted ‖ *mf* secretary
secreter *m* secretary (*writing desk*)
secre•to -ta *adj* secret ‖ *m* secret; secrecy; hiding place, secret drawer; (*mecanismo oculto para abrir una cerradura*) key; **el secreto bancario** client confidentiality; **en el secreto de las cosas** on the inside; **secreto a voces** open secret
secta *f* sect
secta•rio -ria *adj & mf* sectarian
sector *m* sector; group; area; **sector de distribución** house current, power line; **sector en expansión** (econ) growth area
se•cuaz *adj* (*pl* **-cuaces**) partisan ‖ *mf* partisan, follower
secuela *f* sequel, result; (*consecuencia indirecta*) fallout
secuencia *f* sequence
secuestrar *tr* to kidnap; (*un avión*) to hijack; (law) to sequester
secular *adj* secular
secundar *tr* to second, back
secunda•rio -ria *adj* secondary ‖ *m* (elec) secondary
sed *f* thirst; drought; **tener sed** to be thirsty
seda *f* silk; **como una seda** smooth as silk; easy as pie; sweet-natured; **seda encerada** *or* **dental** dental floss
sedal *m* fish line; (*sutura*) suture
sedán *m* sedan; **sedán de reparto** delivery truck
sede *f* (*p.ej., del gobierno*) seat; (eccl) see; **Santa Sede** Holy See; **sede social** headquarters, head office
sedenta•rio -ria *adj* sedentary
sede•ño -ña *adj* silk, silken
sedición *f* sedition
sedicio•so -sa *adj* seditious
sedien•to -ta *adj* thirsty; (*terreno*) dry; anxious, eager
sedimento *m* sediment
sedo•so -sa *adj* silky
seducción *f* seduction; charm, captivation
seducir §19 *tr* to seduce; tempt, lead astray; charm, captivate
seducti•vo -va *adj* seductive; tempting; charming, captivating
seduc•tor -tora *adj* seductive; tempting; charming ‖ *mf* seducer; tempter; charmer
sefar•dí (*pl* **-díes**) *adj* Sephardic ‖ *mf* Sephardi
sega•dor -dora *adj* harvesting ‖ *m* harvestman ‖ *f* harvester; mowing machine; **segadora de césped** lawn mower; **segadora trilladora** combine
segar §66 *tr* to reap, harvest, mow; mow down ‖ *intr* to reap, harvest, mow
segazón *f* harvest; harvest time
seglar *adj* secular, lay ‖ *m* layman ‖ *f* laywoman
segmento *m* segment; **segmento de émbolo** piston ring
segregación *f* segregation
segregacionismo *m* policy of segregation
segregacionista *adj & mf* segregationist
segregar §44 *tr* to segregate
seguida *f* series, succession; **de seguida** without interruption, continuously; at once; in a row; **en seguida** at once, immediately
seguidilla *f* Spanish stanza made up of a quatrain and a tercet; **seguidillas** seguidilla (*Spanish dance and music*)
segui•do -da *adj* continued, successive; straight, direct; running, in a row; **todo seguido** straight ahead ‖ *f* see **seguida**
segui•dor -dora *mf* follower
seguimiento *m* chase, hunt, pursuit; continuation; (*de vehículos espaciales*) tracking
seguir §67 *tr* to follow; pursue; continue; dog, hound ‖ *intr* to go on, continue; still be, be now; keep + *ger* ‖ *ref* to follow, ensue; issue, spring
según *prep* according to, as per; **según que** according as ‖ *conj* as, according as
segunda *f* double meaning; (aut & mus) second
segundero *m* second hand; **segundero central** sweep-second, center-second

segun•do -da *adj* second || *m* second; deputy, second in command; **ser sin segundo** to be second to none || *f* see **segunda**
segur *f* axe; sickle
segurador *s* security, bondsman
seguramente *adv* probably, surely, almost certainly
seguridad *f* security; safety; surety; certainty; assurance; confidence; **seguridad ciudadana** public safety; **seguridades** reassurance; **seguridad social** social security
segu•ro -ra *adj* sure, certain; secure, safe; reliable; constant; steady, unfailing || *m* assurance, certainty; safety; confidence; insurance; **a buen seguro** surely, truly; **seguro contra accidentes** accident insurance; **seguro de desempleo** *or* **desocupación** unemployment insurance; **seguro de enfermedad** health insurance; **seguro de incendios** fire insurance; **seguro de vida** life insurance; **sobre seguro** without risk || **seguro** *adv* surely || *interj* sure thing!
seis *adj & pron* six; **las seis** six o'clock || *m* six; (*en las fechas*) sixth
seiscien•tos -tas *adj & pron* six hundred || **seiscientos** *m* six hundred
selección *f* selection
seleccionar *tr* to select, choose
selecti•vo -va *adj* selective
selec•to -ta *adj* select, choice
sellar *tr* to seal; stamp; close; finish up
sello *m* seal; stamp; signet; wafer; **sello aéreo** air-mail stamp; **sello de correo** postage stamp; **sello de urgencia** special-delivery stamp; **sello fiscal** revenue stamp
selva *f* forest, woods; jungle; **selva tropical** rain forest
selváti•co -ca *adj* woodsy; rustic, wild; forest
semáforo *m* semaphore; traffic light
semana *f* week; week's pay; **semana inglesa** five-day work week
semanal *adj* weekly
semanalmente *adv* weekly
semana•rio -ria *adj & m* weekly
semánti•co -ca *adj* semantic || *f* semantics
semblante *m* face, mien, countenance; appearance, expression, look
semblanza *f* biographical sketch, portrait
sembrado *m* sown ground, grain field
sembrar **§2** *tr* to seed, sow; scatter, spread; sprinkle
semejante *adj* like, similar; such; **semejante a** like; **semejantes** alike, e.g., **estas sillas son semejantes** these chairs are alike || *m* resemblance, likeness; fellow, fellow man
semejanza *f* similarity, resemblance; simile; **a semejanza de** like
semejar *tr* to resemble, be like || *intr & ref* to be alike; **semejar a** *or* **semejarse a** to resemble, be like
semen *m* semen
semental *adj* (*animal*) stud, breeding || *m* sire; stallion; stock bull; virile man
semestral *adj* semester
semestre *m* semester
semibola *f* little slam
semibreve *f* (mus) whole note
semiconductor *m* semiconductor
semiconsciente *adj* semiconscious
semicul•to -ta *adj* semilearned
semidifun•to -ta *adj* half-dead
semidormi•do -da *adj* half-asleep
semifinal *adj & f* (sport) semifinal
semilla *f* seed; **semilla de césped** grass seed
semillero *m* seedbed
seminario *m* seminary; seminar; nursery
semi-remolque *m* semitrailer
semita *mf* Semite || *m* (*idioma*) Semitic
semíti•co -ca *adj* Semitic
semivi•vo -va *adj* half-alive
semovientes *mpl* stock, livestock
sempiter•no -na *adj* everlasting
Sena *m* Seine
senado *m* senate
senador *m* senator
senaduría *f* senatorship
sencillez *f* simplicity, plainness, candor; **sencillez de manejo** (compu) ease of use
senci•llo -lla *adj* simple, plain, candid; single || *m* change, loose change; (*disco*) single; (Esp, Mex) one-way ticket
senda *f* path, footpath
sendero *m* path, footpath, byway
sen•dos -das *adj pl* one each, one to each, e.g., **les dio sendos libros** he gave one book to each of them, he gave each of them a book
senectud *f* age, old age
senil *adj* senile
senilidad *f* senility
senilismo *m* (pathol) senility
seno *m* bosom, breast; lap; heart; womb; bay, gulf; cavity, hollow, recess; asylum, refuge
sensación *f* sensation
sensatez *f* good sense
sensa•to -ta *adj* sensible
sensibilizar **§60** *tr* to sensitize
sensible *adj* appreciable, perceptible, noticeable, sensible; considerable; sensitive; deplorable, regrettable
sensiblería *f* mawkishness
sensible•ro -ra *adj* mawkish
sensiti•vo -va *adj* (*de los sentidos*) sense, sensitive; sentient; stimulating
senso•rio -ria *adj* sensory
sensual *adj* sensual, sensuous
sentada *f* sitting; (*ocupación del lugar*) sit-in; **de una sentada** at one sitting
senta•do -da *adj* seated; settled; stable, permanent; sedate; **dar por sentado** to take for granted || *f* see **sentada**
sentar **§2** *tr* to seat; settle; fit, suit; agree with || *ref* to sit, sit down; settle, settle down
sentencia *f* maxim; (law) sentence

sentenciar *tr* to sentence; (*una cuestión*) to decide; (*p.ej., un libro a la hoguera*) to consign
senti•do -da *adj* felt; deep-felt; sensitive; eloquent; **darse por sentido** to take offense || *m* sense, meaning; direction; consciousness; **sentido común** common sense
sentimiento *m* sentiment; feeling; sorrow, regret
sentir *m* feeling; opinion; judgment || **§68** *tr* to feel; hear; be or feel sorry for; sense || *intr* to feel; be sorry, feel sorry || *ref* to feel; feel oneself to be; be resentful; crack, be cracked; **sentirse de** to feel; have a pain in; resent
seña *f* sign, mark, token; password, watchword; **por las señas** to all appearances; **por más señas** *or* **para más señas** to be more specific; **seña de tráfico** traffic sign; **señas** address; description; details; **hablar por señas** to talk in sign language; **señas particulares** distinguishing marks; **señas personales** physical description
señal *f* sign, mark, token; landmark; bookmark; trace, vestige; scar; signal; traffic light; representation; reminder; pledge; brand; down payment; **señal de humo** smoke signal; **Señal de la Cruz** (eccl) Sign of the Cross; **señal de ocupado** (telp) busy signal; **señal de tramo** (rr) block signal; **señal de vídeo** video signal; **señal digital** fingerprint; **señal para marcar** (telp) dial tone
señala *f* (Chile) earmark (*on livestock*)
señala•do -da *adj* noted, distinguished
señalar *tr* to mark; show, indicate; point at, point out; signal; brand; determine, fix; appoint; sign and seal; scar; threaten || *ref* to distinguish oneself, excel
señalizar §60 *tr* to signal
señor *m* sir, mister; lord, master, owner; **muy señor mío** Dear Sir; **señores** Mr. and Mrs.; ladies and gentlemen
señora *f* madam, missus; mistress, owner; wife; **muy señora mía** Dear Madam; **Nuestra Señora** our Lady; **señora de compañía** chaperon; **Señoras** (*women's room*) *SIGN* Women, Ladies; powder room
señorear *tr* to dominate, rule; master, control; seize, take control of; tower over; excel || *intr* to strut, swagger || *ref* to strut, swagger; control oneself; **señorearse de** to seize, take control of
señoría *f* lordship; ladyship; rule, sway
señoril *adj* lordly; haughty; majestic
señorío *m* dominion, sway, rule; mastery; arrogance, lordliness, majesty; gentry, nobility
señorita *f* young lady; miss
señorito *m* master; young gentleman; playboy
señuelo *m* decoy, lure; bait; enticement
separación *f* separation; **separación de poderes** (pol) separation of powers
separa•do -da *adj* separate; separated; apart; **por separado** separately; under separate cover
separar *tr* to separate; dismiss, discharge || *ref* to separate; resign
separata *f* reprint, offprint
sept.^{e} *abbr* **septiembre**
septeto *m* septet
sépti•co -ca *adj* septic
septiembre *m* September
sépti•mo -ma *adj & m* seventh
sepulcro *m* sepulcher, tomb, grave; **santo sepulcro** Holy Sepulcher
sepultar *tr* to bury; hide away
sepultura *f* burial; grave; **estar con un pie en la sepultura** to have one foot in the grave
sepulturero *m* gravedigger
sequedad *f* dryness, drought; gruffness, surliness
sequía *f* drought
séquito *m* retinue, suite; following, popularity
ser *m* being; essence; life || *v* **§69** *v aux* (to form passive voice) to be, e.g., **el discurso fue aplaudido por todos** the speech was applauded by everybody || *intr* to be; **a no ser por** if it were not for; **a no ser que** unless; **érase que se era** once upon a time there was; **es decir** that is to say; **sea lo que fuere** be that as it may; **ser de** to belong to; become of; be, e.g., **el reloj es de oro** the watch is gold; **ser de ver** to be worth seeing; **soy yo** it is me, it is I
serafín *m* seraph; great beauty (*person*)
serena *f* night love song; night dew, night air
serenar *tr* to calm; pacify; cool; settle
serenata *f* serenade
serenidad *f* serenity; **serenidad del espíritu** peace of mind
sere•no -na *adj* serene, calm; clear, cloudless || *m* night watchman; night dew, night air || *f* see **serena**
serial *adj* serial || *m* (telv) serial; **serial lacrimógeno** soap opera; **serial radiado** (rad) serial
serie *f* series; **de serie** serial; stock, e.g., **coche de serie** stock car; **en serie** mass; **fuera de serie** custom-built, special; outsize
seriedad *f* seriousness; reliability; sternness, severity; solemnity
serigrafía *f* silk screen
se•rio -ria *adj* serious; reliable; stern; solemn
sermón *m* sermon
sermonear *tr & intr* (coll) to sermonize, lecture
seropositi•vo -va *adj* HIV positive; seropositive
serpear or **serpentear** *intr* to wind, meander; wriggle, squirm
serpentín *m* coil
serpiente *f* serpent, snake; **serpiente de cascabel** rattlesnake
serranía *f* range of mountains, mountainous country
serra•no -na *adj* highland, mountain || *mf* highlander, mountaineer
serrar §2 *tr* to saw
serrería *f* sawmill
serrín *m* sawdust
serrucho *m* handsaw
Servia *f* Serbia
servicial *adj* accommodating, obliging

servicio *m* service; service charge; (tennis) service, serve; toilet, washroom, restroom; **en acto de servicio** in the line of duty; **fuera de servicio** out of service; inoperative; (coll) down; **libre servicio** self-service; **servicio de grúa** (aut) towing service; **servicio de mensajes** answering service; **servicio postventa** customer service; **servicio telegráfico y telefónico** wire service; **servicios** toilet, washroom, restroom; **servicio secreto** Secret Service

servi•dor -dora *mf* servant; humble servant; (compu, tennis) server; **servidor de chat** (compu) chat server; **servidor remoto** (compu) remote server; **servidor de Ud.** your servant, at your service || *m* waiter; suitor || *f* waitress

servidumbre *f* servitude; servants, help; compulsion; (law) easement; **servidumbre de la gleba** serfdom; **servidumbre de paso** (law) right of way; **servidumbre de vía** (rr) right of way

servil *adj* servile

servilleta *f* napkin

servilletero *m* napkin ring

ser•vio -via *adj & mf* Serbian || *f* see **Servia**

servir §50 *tr* to serve; help, wait on; (*un pedido*) fill; (tennis) serve; **para servir a Ud.** at your service || *intr* to serve; (*en los naipes*) follow suit; **servir de** to serve as; be used as; **servir para** to be good for, be used for || *ref* to help oneself, serve oneself; have the kindness to, deign to; **servirse de** to use, make use of; **sírvase** please

serv.º *abbr* **servicio**

servocroata *adj & mf* Serbo-Croatian

servodirección *f* (aut) power steering

servoembrague *m* (aut) automatic clutch

servofreno *m* power brake

sésamo *m* sesame; **sésamo ábrete** open sesame

sesenta *adj, pron & m* sixty

sesenta•vo -va *adj & m* sixtieth

sesgar §44 *tr* (*el paño*) to cut on the bias; bevel, slant, slope, skew

ses•go -ga *adj* beveled, slanting, sloped; oblique; stern; calm || *m* bevel; bias; slant, slope, skew; turn; compromise; **al sesgo** obliquely; on the bias

sesión *f* session; sitting; meeting; (*cada representación de un drama o película*) show; **sesión continua** (mov) continuous showing; **sesión de espiritistas** séance, spiritualistic séance; **sesión de gimnasia** workout

sesionar *intr* to be in session

seso *m* brain; brains, intelligence; **calentarse** *or* **devanarse los sesos** to rack one's brain

sestear *intr* to take a siesta; (*el ganado*) rest in the shade

sesu•do -da *adj* brainy; (Chile) stubborn

seta *f* bristle; toadstool

setecien•tos -tas *adj & m* seven hundred || **setecientos** *m* seven hundred

setenta *adj, pron & m* seventy

setenta•vo -va *adj & m* seventieth

seto *m* fence; **seto vivo** hedge, quickset

seudónimo *m* pseudonym, pen name

s.e.u.o. *abbr* **salvo error u omisión**

seve•ro -ra *adj* severe; stern; strict

sevicia *f* ferocity, cruelty

sexo *m* sex; **el bello sexo** the fair sex; **el sexo feo** the sterner sex

sextante *m* sextant

sex•to -ta *adj & m* sixth

sexual *adj* sexual, sex

shareware *m* (compu) shareware

shií *mf* Shiite; **los shiíes** the Shia

si *conj* if; whether; I wonder if; **por si acaso** just in case; **si acaso** if by chance; **si no** otherwise

sí *adv* yes; indeed; (gives emphasis to verb and is often equivalent to English auxiliary verb) **él sí habla español** he does speak Spanish || *pron reflex* himself, herself, itself, themselves; yourself, yourselves; oneself; each other || *m* (*pl* **-síes**) yes; **dar el sí** to say yes

sia•més -mesa *adj & mf* Siamese

siberia•no -na *adj & mf* Siberian

sibila *f* sibyl

sicalipsis *f* spiciness, suggestiveness

sicalípti•co -ca *adj* spicy, suggestive, sexy

Sicilia *f* Sicily

sicilia•no -na *adj & mf* Sicilian

sico. . . var of **psico. . .**

sicofanta *m* or **sicofante** *m* informer, spy; slanderer

sico•sis *f* (*pl* **-sis**) psychosis; (*afección de la piel*) sycosis

SIDA, el sida *m* (*acronym*) (**síndrome de inmunodeficiencia adquirida**) AIDS (acquired immunodeficiency syndrome)

sideral or **sidére•o -a** *adj* sidereal

siderurgia *f* iron and steel industry

sidra *f* cider; **sidra achampañada** hard cider

siega *f* reaping, mowing; harvest; crop

siembra *f* sowing; seeding; seedtime; sown field

siempre *adv* always; **de siempre** usual; **para siempre** or **por siempre** forever; **por siempre jamás** forever and ever; **siempre que** whenever; provided

siempreviva *f* everlasting flower

sien *f* temple (*of head*)

sierpe *f* serpent, snake

sierra *f* saw; sierra, mountain range; **sierra circular** buzz saw; **sierra continua** band saw; **sierra de armero** hacksaw; **sierra de bastidor** bucksaw; **sierra de cadena** chain saw; **sierra de hilar** ripsaw; **sierra de través** crosscut saw; **sierra de vaivén** jig saw; **sierra sin fin** band saw

sier•vo -va *mf* slave; servant; **siervo de la gleba** serf

sieso *m* anus

siesta *f* siesta; hot time of day; **echarse una siesta** to take a siesta; **siesta del carnero** nap before lunch

siete *adj & pron* seven; **las siete** seven o'clock

|| *m* seven; (*en las fechas*) seventh; (coll) V-shaped tear or rip
sífilis *f* syphilis
sifón *m* siphon; siphon bottle; (*tubo doblemente acodado*) trap
sig.[e] *abbr* **siguiente**
sigilar *tr* to seal, stamp; conceal, keep silent
sigilo *m* seal; concealment, reserve; stealth; **sigilo profesional** client confidentiality; **sigilo sacramental** inviolable secrecy of the confessional
sigilo•so -sa *adj* tight-lipped; reserved
sigla *f* initial; abbreviation, symbol
siglo *m* (*cien años*) century; (*comercio de los hombres*) world; (*largo tiempo*) age; **siglo de la ilustración** *or* **de las luces** Age of Enlightenment
signar *tr* to mark; sign; make the sign of the cross over
signatura *f* library number; (mus & typ) signature
significación *f* significance
significado *m* meaning
significar §73 *tr* to signify, mean; point out, make known || *intr* to be important
significati•vo -va *adj* significant; meaningful
signo *m* sign; mark; sign of the cross; fate, destiny; **signo de igual** equal sign; **signo de admiración** exclamation mark; **signo de interrogación** *or* **pregunta** question mark; **signo de más** plus sign; **signo de menos** minus sign; **signo de puntuación** punctuation mark; **signo externo** status symbol
siguiente *adj* following; next
sij *adj & mf* Sikh
sílaba *f* syllable; **última sílaba** ultima
silbar *tr* (*p.ej., una canción*) to whistle; (*un silbato*) blow; (*a un actor*) hiss || *intr* to whistle; (*ir zumbando por el aire*) whiz, whiz by
silbato *m* whistle
silbido *m* whistle, whistling, hiss; (rad) howling, squealing; **silbido de oídos** ringing in the ears
silbo *m* whistle, hiss
silenciador *m* silencer; (aut) muffler
silencio *m* silence; (*toque que manda que cada cual se acueste*) (mil) taps; (mus) rest
silencio•so -sa *adj* silent, noiseless; quiet, still || *m* (aut) muffler
sílfide *f* sylph
silla *f* chair; **silla alta** high chair; **silla de balanza** rocking chair; **silla de cubierta** deck chair; **silla de junco** rush-bottomed chair; **silla de manos** sedan chair; **silla de montar** saddle, riding saddle; **silla de ruedas** wheel chair; **silla de tijera** folding chair; **silla eléctrica** (*castigo*) electric chair; **silla giratoria** swivel chair; **silla hamaca** (Arg) rocking chair; **silla plegadiza** folding chair; **silla poltrona** armchair, easy chair; **sillas apilables** chairs that can be stacked or nested
sillar *m* ashlar
silleta *f* bedpan; chair, seat
sillico *m* chamber pot, commode
sillín *m* saddle (*of bicycle*)
sillón *m* armchair, easy chair; **sillón de orejas** wing chair
silo *m* silo; cave, dark place
silogismo *m* syllogism
silueta *f* silhouette
silueteado *s* (compu) outlining
silva *f* (*materias escritas sin orden*) miscellany; verse of iambic hendecasyllables intermingled with seven-syllable lines
silvestre *adj* wild; rustic, uncultivated
silvicul•tor -tora *mf* forester || *m* woodman, woodsman
silvicultura *f* forestry
sima *f* chasm, abyss
simbióti•co -ca *adj* symbiotic
simbóli•co -ca *adj* symbolic(al)
simbolizar §60 *tr* to symbolize
símbolo *m* symbol; **Símbolo de la fe** or **de los Apóstoles** Apostles' Creed
simetría *f* symmetry
simétri•co -ca *adj* symmetric(al)
simiente *f* seed, sperm
símil *adj* like, similar || *m* similarity; (rhet) simile
similar *adj* similar
similigrabado *m* (typ) half-tone
similor *m* ormolu, similor; **de similor** fake, sham
simio *m* monkey
simpatía *f* affection, attachment, liking; friendliness; congeniality; **simpatías** (pol) sympathies; **tomar simpatía a** to take a liking for
simpáti•co -ca *adj* agreeable, pleasant, likeable, congenial, nice, delightful
simpatizante *mf* sympathizer
simpatizar §60 *intr* to be congenial, get on well together; **simpatizar con** to get on well with
simple *adj* simple; single || *mf* simpleton || *m* (*planta medicinal*) simple
simpleza *f* simpleness; stupidity
simplificar §73 *tr* to simplify
simulacro *m* phantom, vision; idol, image; semblance, show; pretense; sham battle; **simulacro de ataque aéreo** air-raid drill; **simulacro de combate** sham battle; (mil) war game; **simulacro de incendio** fire drill
simula•do -da *adj* fake; (com) pro forma
simulador *m* (compu) simulator
simular *tr* to simulate, feign, fake || *intr* to malinger; pretend
simultanear *tr* to do simultaneously || *intr* to work simultaneously
simultáne•o -a *adj* simultaneous
sin *prep* without; **sin embargo** nevertheless, however; **sin que** + *subj* without + *ger*
sinagoga *f* synagogue
sinapismo *m* mustard plaster; bore, nuisance
sincerar *tr* to vindicate, justify
sinceridad *f* sincerity
since•ro -ra *adj* sincere
síncopa *f* (phonet) syncope
sincopa•do -da *adj* syncopated
síncope *m* fainting spell

sincróni•co -ca *adj* synchronous
sincronización *f* synchronization, sync, synch
sincronizar §60 *tr & intr* to synchronize; **estar sincronizado con** to be synchronized with, to be in sync with
sindicar §73 *tr & ref* to syndicate
sindicato *m* syndicate; labor union
síndico *m* trustee; (*en una quiebra*) receiver
sin•diós (*pl* **-diós**) *adj* godless || *mf* atheist
síndrome *m* syndrome; **síndrome de abstinencia** withdrawal symptoms; **síndrome de choque tóxico** toxic-shock syndrome; **síndrome de inmunodeficiencia adquirida (SIDA)** acquired immunodeficiency syndrome (AIDS)
sinecura *f* sinecure
sinfín *m* endless amount, number
sinfonía *f* symphony
sinfóni•co -ca *adj* symphonic
singladura *f* (naut) day's run
singular *adj* singular; special; single || *m* singular; **en singular** in particular
singularizar §60 *tr* to distinguish, single out || *ref* to distinguish oneself, stand out
sinhueso *f* (coll) tongue
sinies•tro -tra *adj* evil, perverse; calamitous, disastrous || *m* calamity, disaster || *f* left hand, left-hand side
sinnúmero *m* great amount, great number
sino *conj* but, except; **no . . . sino** only; **no . . . sino que** only; **no sólo . . . sino que** not only . . . but also || *m* fate, destiny
sinóni•mo -ma *adj* synonymous || *m* synonym
sinop•sis *f* (*pl* **-sis**) synopsis
sinrazón *f* wrong, injustice
sinsabor *m* displeasure; anxiety, trouble, worry
sinsonte *m* mockingbird
sinsostenismo *m* (coll) braless fashion
sintaxis *f* syntax
sínte•sis *f* (*pl* **-sis**) synthesis
sintéti•co -ca *adj* synthetic(al)
sintetizar §60 *tr* to synthesize
síntoma *m* symptom; sign; **síntoma de abstinencia** withdrawal symptom
sintonía *f* (rad, telv) tuning; (rad, telv) theme song; **en sintonía con** in tune with; **de mayor sintonía** high viewer rating; **para una mejor sintonía** for better reception
sintonizar §60 *tr* (*el aparato receptor*) to tune; (*la estación emisora*) tune in
sinuo•so -sa *adj* sinuous, winding; wavy; evasive
sinvergüenza *adj* brazen, shameless || *mf* scoundrel, rascal
sionismo *m* Zionism
siquí. . . var of **psiquí. . .**
siquiera *adv* even; at least || *conj* although, even though
sirena *f* siren; mermaid; **sirena de la playa** bathing beauty; **sirena de niebla** foghorn
sirga *f* towrope, towline
sirgar §44 *tr* to tow
Siria *f* Syria
si•rio -ria *adj & mf* Syrian || **Sirio** *m* (astr) Sirius || *f* see **Siria**
sirvienta *f* maid, servant girl
sirviente *m* servant; waiter
sisa *f* petty theft; (*para fijar los panes de oro*) sizing
sisal *m* sisal, sisal hemp
sisar *tr* to filch, snitch; (*lo que se ha de dorar*) size
sisear *tr* to hiss || *intr* to hiss; sizzle
siseo *m* hiss, hissing; sizzle, sizzling
sismógrafo *m* seismograph
sismología *f* seismology
sistema *m* system; **el Sistema** the Establishment, established order
sistematizar §60 *tr* to systematize
sístole *f* systole
sitial *m* place of honor
sitiar *tr* to surround, hem in; siege, besiege
sitin *m* (Mex) sit-in
sitio *m* place, spot, room; location, site; country place; seat; cattle ranch; taxi stand; (mil) siege
si•to -ta *adj* situated, located
situación *f* situation, position; **pedir situación** (aer) to ask for bearings
situar §21 *tr* to situate, locate, place; (*dinero*) place, invest; (*un pedido*) place || *ref* to take a position; settle; take place; (aer) to get one's bearings
s.l. *abbr* **sin lugar**
S.M. *abbr* **Su Majestad**
smog *m* smog
smo•king *m* (*pl* **-kings**) tuxedo, dinner coat
so *prep* under, e.g., **so pena de** under penalty of || *interj* whoa!; you. . . !, e.g., **¡so animal!** you beast!
sobaco *m* armpit
sobajar *tr* to crush, to rumple; to humiliate
sobaquera *f* (*en el vestido*) armhole; (*para resguardar del sudor la parte del vestido correspondiente al sobaco*) shield
sobaquina *f* underarm odor, body odor
sobar *tr* to knead; massage; beat, slap; paw, pet, feel; annoy, be fresh to; flatter; (*un hueso dislocado*) (CAm) to set; (*la cabalgadura*) (Arg) to tire out; (Col) to flay, skin; (P-R) to bribe
soberanía *f* sovereignty
sobera•no -na *adj* sovereign; superb || *mf* sovereign || *m* (*moneda*) sovereign
sober•bio -bia *adj* proud, haughty; arrogant; magnificent, superb || *f* pride, haughtiness; arrogance; magnificence
so•bón -bona *adj* malingering; fresh, mushy, spoony
soborna•do -da *adj* twisted; out of shape
sobornar *tr* to bribe
soborno *m* bribery; (SAm) extra load; **de soborno** (Bol) in addition; **soborno de testigo** (law) subornation of perjury
sobra *f* extra, surplus; **sobras** leftovers, leavings; trash
sobradillo *m* penthouse
sobra•do -da *adj* excessive, superfluous; bold,

daring; rich, wealthy || *m* attic, garret || **sobrado** *adv* too
sobrante *adj* remaining, leftover, surplus || *m* leftover, surplus
sobrar *tr* to exceed, surpass || *intr* to be more than enough; be in the way; be left, remain
sobre *prep* on, upon; over; above; about; near; after; in addition to; out of, e.g., **en nueve casos sobre diez** in nine out of ten cases || *m* envelope; **sobre de ventanilla** window envelope
sobrealimentar *tr* to overfeed; supercharge
sobrecama *f* bedspread
sobrecarga *f* overload, extra load; overcharge; surcharge
sobrecargar §44 *tr* to overload, overburden; overcharge; surcharge; (aer) to pressurize
sobrecargo *m* (naut) supercargo; purser || *f* flight attendant, stewardess
sobrecejo *m* frown
sobreceño *m* frown
sobrecoger §17 *tr* to surprise, catch; scare, terrify || *ref* to be surprised; be scared; **sobrecogerse de** to be seized with
sobrecubierta *f* extra cover; (*de un libro*) jacket, dust jacket
sobredi•cho -cha *adj* above-mentioned
sobredosis *f* overdose
sobreestimar *tr* to overestimate
sobreexcitar *tr* to overexcite || *ref* to become overexcited
sobreexponer §54 *tr* to overexpose
sobreexposición *f* overexposure
sobregirar *tr & intr* to overdraw
sobregiro *m* overdraft
sobreherido *adj* slightly wounded
sobrehombre *m* superman
sobrehuma•no -na *adj* superhuman
sobrellevar *tr* to bear, carry; (*la carga de otra persona*) ease; (*los trabajos o molestias de la vida*) share; (*molestias*) suffer with patience
sobremanera *adv* exceedingly, beyond measure
sobremesa *f* tablecloth, table cover; (compu) desktop; **de sobremesa** desk, e.g., **reloj de sobremesa** desk clock; after-dinner, e.g., **discurso de sobremesa** after-dinner speech
sobremodo *adv* var of **sobremanera**
sobrenadar *intr* to float
sobrenatural *adj* supernatural
sobrenombrar *tr* to surname; nickname
sobrenombre *m* surname; nickname
sobrentender §51 *tr* to understand || *ref* to be understood, be implied
sobrepasar *tr* to excel, surpass, outdo; exceed; overtake || *ref* to outdo each other; go too far
sobrepeine *adv* slightly, briefly || *m* hair trimming
sobrepe•lliz *f* (*pl* **-llices**) surplice
sobreponer §54 *tr* to superpose, put on top; superimpose || *ref* to control oneself; triumph over adversity; **sobreponerse a** to overcome
sobreprecio *m* extra charge, surcharge
sobreproducción *f* overproduction
sobrepujar *tr* to excel, surpass
sobresaliente *adj* projecting; conspicuous, outstanding; (*en un examen*) distinguished || *mf* substitute; understudy
sobresalir §65 *intr* to project, jut out; stand out, excel
sobresaltar *tr* to assail, rush upon; startle, frighten || *intr* to stand out clearly || *ref* to be startled, be frightened; start, wince
sobresalto *m* fright, scare; start, shock, wince; **de sobresalto** suddenly, unexpectedly
sobrescribir §83 *tr* to address
sobrescrito *m* address
sobrestante *m* boss, foreman
sobresueldo *m* extra wages, extra pay
sobretiro *m* offprint
sobretodo *adv* especially || *m* overcoat, topcoat
sobrevenir §79 *intr* to happen, take place; supervene, set in; **sobrevenir a** to overtake
sobrevidriera *f* window screen; window grill; storm window
sobrevivencia *f* (Ecuad) survival
sobreviviente *adj* surviving || *mf* survivor
sobrevivir *intr* to survive; **sobrevivir a** to survive, outlive
sobrevolar §61 *tr* to overfly
sobriedad *f* sobriety, moderation
sobrina *f* niece
sobrino *m* nephew
so•brio -bria *adj* sober, moderate, temperate
socaire *m* (naut) lee; **al socaire de** (naut) under the lee of; (coll) under the shelter of; **estar al socaire** to shirk
socapa *f* subterfuge; **a socapa** clandestinely
socarrén *m* eaves
socarrar *tr* to singe, scorch
soca•rrón -rrona *adj* crafty, cunning, sly; sneering; roguish
socavar *tr* to undermine, dig under
socavón *m* cave-in; cave; (min) gallery
sociable *adj* sociable
social *adj* social; company, e.g., **edificio social** company building
socialismo *m* socialism
socialista *mf* socialist
sociedad *f* society; company, firm; **buena sociedad** (*mundo elegante*) society; **sociedad anónima** stock company; **sociedad de control** holding company; **sociedad de ahorro y préstamos, sociedad de crédito hipotecario** savings and loan institution; **Sociedad de las Naciones** League of Nations; **sociedad distribuidora** (wholesale) distributor; **sociedad financiera** finance company; **sociedad inmobiliaria** (Esp) development company
so•cio -cia *mf* partner; companion; member; **socio accionista** shareholder; **socio capitalista** silent partner; **socio de número** full member; **socio vitalicio** life member || *m* fellow; (scornful) guy
sociología *f* sociology
socorrer *tr* to aid, help, succor

socorri•do -da *adj* ready; handy, useful; hackneyed, trite, worn; well stocked
socorrismo *m* first aid
socorro *m* aid, help, succor
socoyote *m* (Mex) baby, youngest son
socráti•co -ca *adj* Socratic
soda *f* soda; soda water
sodio *m* sodium
so•ez *adj* (*pl* **-eces**) base, mean, vile
so•fá *m* (*pl* **-fás**) sofa; **sofá cama** sofa bed
soflama *f* glow, flicker; blush; deceit, cheating
soflamar *tr* to flimflam; make blush || *ref* to become scorched
sofocante *adj* suffocating, sweltering; stifling
sofocar §73 *tr* to choke, suffocate, stifle, smother; quench, extinguish; make blush; bother, harass || *ref* to choke, suffocate; blush; get excited; get out of breath
sofoco *m* blush, embarrassment
sofrenar *tr* (*un caballo*) to check suddenly; (*una pasión*) control; chide, reprimand
software [ˈsofwer] *m* (compu) software
soga *m* sly fellow || *f* rope, cord; **dar soga a** to make fun of; **hacer soga** to lag behind
soja *f* soy, soy bean
sojuzgar §44 *tr* to subjugate, subdue
sol *m* sun; sunlight; sunny side; **de sol a sol** from sunrise to sunset; **hacer sol** to be sunny; **soles** (poet) eyes; **tomar el sol** to sunbathe, sun oneself
solamente *adv* only
solana *f* sunny spot; sun porch
solanera *f* sunburn; sunny spot
solano *m* east wind; (bot) nightshade
solapa *f* lapel; pretext, pretense; flap
solapa•do -da *adj* overlapping; cunning, underhanded, sneaky
solapar *tr* to put lapels on; overlap; conceal, cover up || *intr* to overlap
solapo *m* lapel; flap; chuck under chin
solar *adj* solar; ancestral || *m* ground, plot; backyard; manor house, ancestral mansion; noble lineage; (Cuba) tenement || *v* **§61** *tr* to pave, floor; (*zapatos*) sole
solarie•go -ga *adj* ancestral; manorial
solario *m* sun porch
so•laz *m* (*pl* **-laces**) solace, consolation; recreation; **a solaz** with pleasure
soldada *f* wages, pay
soldadera *f* (Mex) camp follower
soldadesca *f* soldiery; undisciplined troops
soldado *m* soldier; **soldado de a pie** foot soldier; **soldado de juguete** toy soldier; **soldado de marina** marine; **soldado de plomo** tin soldier; **soldado de primera** private first class; **soldado raso** buck private; **soldados** soldiers; troops
soldadura *f* solder; soldering; weld; welding; **soldadura al arco** arc welding; **soldadura autógena** welding; **soldadura a tope** butt welding; **soldadura por puntos** spot welding
soldar §61 *tr* to solder; (*sin materia extraña*) weld || *ref* (*los huesos*) to knit
solear *tr* to sun || *ref* to sun, sun oneself
soledad *f* solitude, loneliness; longing, grieving; lonely spot
soledo•so -sa *adj* solitary, lonely; longing, grieving
solemne *adj* solemn; (*error, mentira, etc.*) downright
solenoide *m* solenoid
soler §47 *intr* to be accustomed to
solera *f* crossbeam; lumber, timber; mother liquor, mother of the wine; blend of sherry; old vintage sherry; tradition, standing; (Chile) curb; (Mex) brick, tile, stone; **de solera** *or* **de rancia solera** of the good old school, of the good old times
soletilla *f* (Esp) ladyfinger
solevantar *tr* to raise up; rouse, stir up, incite || *ref* to rise up; revolt
solevar *tr* to raise up; incite to rebellion || *ref* to rise up; revolt
solicitante *mf* petitioner; applicant
solicitar *tr* to solicit, ask for; apply for; woo, court; drive, pull; (*la atención*) attract; (phys) to attract
solíci•to -ta *adj* solicitous; careful, diligent; obliging; fond, affectionate
solicitud *f* solicitude; petition, request; application
solidar *tr* to harden; establish, prove
solida•rio -ria *adj* jointly liable; jointly binding; **solidario con** *or* **de** integral with
solidarizar §60 *ref* to declare one's solidarity (with); identify (with)
solidez *f* solidity; strength, soundness; constancy
sóli•do -da *adj* solid; strong, sound || *m* solid
soliloquio *m* soliloquy
solista *adj* (*p.ej., instrumento*) (mus) solo || *mf* (mus) soloist
solita•rio -ria *adj* solitary; lonely || *mf* hermit, recluse, solitary || **en solitario** alone, solo || *m* (*juego y diamante*) solitaire || *f* tapeworm
sóli•to -ta *adj* accustomed, customary
soliviantar *tr* to rouse, stir up, incite
soliviar *tr* to lift, lift up
sollastre *m* scullion
sollozar §60 *intr* to sob
sollozo *m* sob
so•lo -la *adj* only, sole; alone; lonely; (*p.ej., whisky*) straight, neat (coll); (*café*) black; **a mis solas** alone, all by myself; **a solas** alone, unaided || *pron* only one || *m* (mus) solo
sólo *adv* only, solely; **sólo para adultos** X-rated
solomillo *m* sirloin
solomo *m* sirloin; loin of pork
solsticio *m* solstice
soltador *m* release; **soltador del margen** margin release
soltar §61 *tr* to untie, unfasten, loosen; let go; let go of; (*una observación*) drop, let slip; (*el agua*) turn on || *ref* to get loose or free; come loose, come off; loosen up; burst out; thaw out, let oneself go

solte•ro -ra *adj* single, unmarried || *m* bachelor || *f* unmarried woman
solterona *f* older unmarried woman
soltura *f* looseness; agility, ease, freedom; fluency; dissoluteness; release
solución *f* solution
solucionar *tr* to solve, resolve
solventar *tr* (*lo que uno debe*) to settle, pay up; (*una dificultad*) solve
solvente *adj* solvent; (*fuente*) believable; reliable || *m* solvent
sombra *f* (*falta de luz brillante*) shade; (*imagen obscura que proyecta un cuerpo opaco*) shadow; shady side; darkness; parasol; ignorance; ghost, spirit; grace, charm, wit; favor, protection; luck; **a la sombra** in the shade; in jail; **a sombra de tejado** stealthily, sneakingly; **ni por sombra** by no means; without any notice; **no ser su sombra** to be but a shadow of one's former self; **sombra (de ojos)** eye shadow; **tener buena sombra** to be likeable; to bring good luck
sombrear *tr* to shade; (*un dibujo*) hatch
sombrerera *f* bandbox, hatbox
sombrerería *f* hat store, hat factory; millinery shop
sombrere•ro -ra *mf* hatter, hat maker || *f* see **sombrerera**
sombrero *m* hat; **sombrero de copa** high hat, top hat; **sombrero de muelles** opera hat; **sombrero de paja** straw hat; **sombrero de pelo** high hat; **sombrero de tres picos** three-cornered hat; **sombrero gacho** slouch hat; **sombrero hongo** derby; **sombrero jarano** sombrero
sombrilla *f* parasol, sunshade; **sombrilla de playa** beach umbrella; **sombrilla protectora** (mil) umbrella
sombrí•o -a *adj* shady; somber; gloomy
sombro•so -sa *adj* shadowy, full of shadows; shady
some•ro -ra *adj* brief, summary; slight; superficial, shallow
someter *tr* to subdue, subject; (*razones, reflexiones; un negocio*) submit || *ref* to yield, submit, surrender
someti•do -da *adj* humble, submissive
sometimiento *m* subjection
somier *m* bedspring, spring mattress
somnolencia *f* sleepiness, drowsiness
somorgujar *tr* to plunge, submerge || *intr* to dive, || *ref* to plunge
son *m* sound; news, rumor; pretext, motive; manner, mode; **en son de** in the manner of, by way of; as
sona•do -da *adj* talked-about; famous, noted
sonaja *f* jingle
sonajero *m* rattle, child's rattle
sonámbu•lo -la *mf* sleepwalker, somnambulist
sonar §61 *tr* to sound, ring; (*un instrumento de viento, un silbato*) blow; (*un instrumento de viento*) play || *intr* to sound, ring; (*un reloj*) strike; seem; sound familiar; **sonar a** to sound like, have the appearance of || *ref* to be rumored; (*las narices*) blow
sonda *f* sounding; plummet, lead; drill; (med) catheter; (surg) probe, sound; **sonda espacial** space probe
sondar or **sondear** *tr & intr* to sound, probe; to sound out; to sink a borehole (in)
sondeo *m* poll, survey; test drilling; (aerosp, meteor) exploration; (naut) sounding
sonetizar §60 *intr* to sonneteer
soneto *m* sonnet
sóni•co -ca *adj* sonic
sonido *m* sound; report, rumor; **sonido absoluto** absolute pitch; **sonido silencioso** ultrasound
sonoridad *f* sonority
sonorizar §60 *intr* (*una película cinematográfica*) to record sound effects on; (*una consonante sorda*) voice || *ref* to voice
sono•ro -ra *adj* sound; clear, loud, resounding
sonreír §58 *intr & ref* to smile
sonriente *adj* smiling
sonrisa *f* smile
sonrojar or **sonrojear** *tr* to make one blush || *ref* to blush
sonrojo *m* blush; word that causes blushing
sonrosar or **sonrosear** *tr* to rose-color; make blush || *ref* to become rose-colored; blush
sonsacar §73 *tr* to pilfer; entice away; elicit, draw out
son•so -sa *adj* stupid
sonsonete *m* rhythmical tapping; sing-song
soña•dor -dora *adj* dreamy || *mf* dreamer
soñar §61 *tr* to dream; **ni soñarlo** not even in a dream, by no means || *intr* to dream; **soñar con** to dream of; **soñar despierto** to daydream
soñolien•to -ta *adj* sleepy, dozy, drowsy, somnolent; lazy
sopa *f* (*pan u otra cosa empapada en un líquido*) sop; soup; **hecho una sopa** soaked to the skin, sopping wet; **sopa de pastas** noodle soup
sopapo *m* chuck under the chin; blow, slap
sopetear *tr* to dip, dunk; abuse
sopetón *m* slap, box; **de sopetón** suddenly
sopista *mf* beggar
soplar *tr* to blow; blow away; blow up, inflate; snitch, swipe; inspire; prompt; tip off; (*la dama a un rival*) cut out; squeal on, snitch || *intr* to blow; squeal || *ref* to be puffed up, be conceited; swill, gulp, gobble
soplete *m* blowpipe
soplillo *m* blower, fan; chiffon, silk gauze; light sponge cake
soplo *m* blowing, blast; breath; gust of wind; instant, moment; (*informe dado en secreto*) tip; squealing; squealer
so•plón -plona *adj* tattletale || *mf* tattletale, squealer, snitch
sopor *m* sleepiness, drowsiness; stupor
soporífico *m* soporific; nightcap
soportal *m* porch, portico, arcade
soportar *tr* to support, hold up, bear; endure, suffer; (compu) support

soporte *m* support, bearing, rest, standard; base, stand; (compu) support
soprano *mf* (*persona*) soprano ‖ *m* (*voz*) soprano
sor *f* (used before names of nuns) Sister
sorber *tr* to sip; absorb, soak up
sorbete *m* sherbet, water ice
sorbetera *f* ice-cream freezer; high hat
sorbo *m* sip; gulp
sordera or **sordez** *f* deafness
sórdi•do -da *adj* sordid
sordina *f* silencer; (mus) mute; (mus) damper; **a la sordina** silently, on the quiet
sor•do -da *adj* deaf; silent, mute; muffled, dull; (*dolor, ruido*) dull ‖ *mf* deaf person; **hacerse el sordo** to pretend to be deaf; turn a deaf ear
sordomu•do -da *adj* deaf and dumb ‖ *mf* deaf-mute
sorgo *m* sorghum, broomcorn
sorna *f* sluggishness; cunning; sarcasm
sorochar *ref* to blush; (SAm) to become mountain-sick
soroche *m* flush, blush; (SAm) mountain sickness; (Bol, Chile) silver-bearing galena
sorprendente *adj* surprising
sorprender *tr* to surprise; catch; (*un secreto*) discover ‖ *ref* to be surprised
sorpresa *f* surprise; surprise package
sorpresi•vo -va *adj* surprising
sortear *tr* to draw or cast lots for; raffle; choose by lot; dodge; duck through ‖ *intr* to draw or cast lots
sorteo *m* drawing, casting of lots; raffle; choosing by lot; dodging; (taur) workout, performance
sortija *f* ring; curl; hoop; **sortija de sello** signet ring
sortilegio *m* sorcery, witchery
sortíle•go -ga *mf* fortuneteller ‖ *m* sorcerer ‖ *f* sorceress
sosa *f* soda
sosega•do -da *adj* calm, quiet, peaceful
sosegar §66 *tr* to calm, quiet, allay ‖ *intr* to become calm, rest ‖ *ref* to calm down, quiet down
sosiega *f* nightcap
sosiego *m* calm, quiet, serenity
sosla•yo -ya *adj* slanting, oblique; **al soslayo** or **de soslayo** slantingly; askance
so•so -sa *adj* insipid; tasteless; dull, inane ‖ *f* see **sosa**
sospecha *f* suspicion
sospechar *tr* to suspect
sospecho•so -sa *adj* suspicious; suspect ‖ *m* suspect
sostén *m* support; (*de un buque*) steadiness; brassiere
sostener §71 *tr* to support, hold up; sustain; maintain; bear, stand ‖ *ref* to remain
sosteni•do -da *adj* & *m* (mus) sharp
sota *m* (Chile) boss, foreman ‖ *f* (*en los naipes*) jack; jade, hussy
sotana *f* soutane, cassock
sótano *m* basement, cellar
sotavento *m* (naut) leeward
soterrar §2 *tr* to bury; hide away
soto *m* grove; brush, thicket, copse
so•viet *m* (*pl* **-viets**) soviet
soviéti•co -ca *adj* soviet, sovietic
sovoz — a sovoz sotto voce, in a low tone
soya *f* soybean
Sr. *abbr* **Señor**
Sra. *abbr* **Señora**
Srta. *abbr* **Señorita**
S.S.S. *abbr* **su seguro servidor**
ss.ss. *abbr* **seguros servidores**
statu quo *or* **status quo** *m* status quo
stock *m* stock; inventory; **tener en stock** to carry; have in stock
streaker [(e)ˋstriker] *mf* (*persona que corre desnuda en un lugar público*) streaker
strip-tease [(e)sˋtriptis] *s* striptease
striptise•ro -ra [*(e)sˋtripti ˋsero(a)*] *mf* stripper, striptease artist
su *adj poss* his, her, its, their, your, one's
suave *adj* suave, smooth, soft; gentle, mild, meek
suavizador *m* razor strop
suavizar §60 *tr* to smooth, ease, sweeten, soften, mollify; (*una navaja de afeitar*) strop
subalter•no -na *adj* & *mf* subaltern, subordinate
subasta *f* auction, auction sale; **sacar a pública subasta** to sell at auction
subasta•dor -dora *mf* auctioneer
subastar *tr* to auction, sell at auction
subcampe•ón -ona *mf* (sport) runner-up
subcentral *f* (elec) substation
subconsciencia *f* subconscious, subconsciousness
subconsciente *adj* subconscious
subdesarrolla•do -da *adj* underdeveloped
súbdi•to -ta *adj* & *mf* subject
subentender §51 *tr* to understand ‖ *ref* to be understood, be implied
subestimar *tr* to underestimate
subfusil *m* submachine gun
subi•do -da *adj* high, fine, superior; strong, intense; (*color*) bright; high, high-priced ‖ *f* rise; ascent; (*p.ej., al trono*) accession
subir *tr* to raise; lift; carry up; (*p.ej., una escalera*) go up; (mus) to raise the pitch of ‖ *intr* to go up, come up; rise; get worse; spread; **subir a** to climb; climb on; get in or into; get on, mount ‖ *ref* to rise
súbi•to -ta *adj* sudden, unexpected; hurried; hasty, impetuous ‖ **súbito** *adv* suddenly
subjeti•vo -va *adj* subjective
subjunti•vo -va *adj* & *m* subjunctive
sublevación *f* uprising, revolt
sublevado *m* rebel, insurrectionist
sublevar *tr* to incite to rebellion ‖ *ref* to revolt
submarinista *mf* (sport) scuba diver; skin diver ‖ *m* (nav) submariner
submari•no -na *adj* underwater, submarine ‖ *m* submarine
subnormal *adj* (mentally) retarded

suboficial *m* sergeant major; noncommissioned officer
subordina•do -da *adj & mf* subordinate
subordinar *tr* to subordinate
subproducto *m* by-product
subrayar *tr* to underline; emphasize
subrepti•cio -cia *adj* surreptitious
subsanar *tr* to excuse, overlook; correct, repair
subscribir §83 *tr* to subscribe; subscribe to, endorse; subscribe to or for; sign; sign up || *ref* to subscribe
subseguir §67 *intr & ref* to follow next
subsidiar *tr* to subsidize
subsidiarias *fpl* feeder industries
subsidiario *m* subsidiary
subsidio *m* subsidy; aid, help
subsiguiente *adj* subsequent
subsistencia *f* subsistence, sustenance
subsistir *intr* to subsist
subsóni•co -ca *adj* subsonic
substancia *f* substance
substanciar *tr* to abstract, abridge
substanti•vo -va *adj & m* substantive
substitución *f* replacement; (chem, law, math) substitution
substitui•dor -dora *adj & mf* substitute
substituir §20 *tr* to replace; substitute for, take the place of || *intr* to take someone's place || *ref* to be replaced; relieve each other
substituti•vo -va *adj & m* substitute
substitu•to -ta *mf* substitute; surrogate
substraer §75 *tr* to remove; deduct; rob, steal; subtract || *ref* to withdraw; **substraerse a** to evade, avoid, slip away from
subte *m* (Arg, Urug) subway
subteniente *m* second lieutenant
subterráne•o -a *adj* subterranean, underground || *m* subterranean; (Arg) subway
subtitular *tr* to subtitle
subtítulo *m* subtitle, subheading
suburbio *m* suburb; outlying slum
subvención *f* subvention, subsidy
subvencionar *tr* to subvention, subsidize
subvenir §79 *intr* to provide; **subvenir a** to provide for; (*gastos*) defray
subvertir §68 *tr* to subvert
subyugar §44 *tr* to subjugate, subdue
sucedáne•o -a *adj & m* substitute; surrogate
suceder *tr* to succeed, follow || *intr* to happen; **suceder a** (*p.ej., el trono*) to succeed to || *ref* to follow one another
sucesi•vo -va *adj* successive; **en lo sucesivo** in the future
suceso *m* event, happening; issue, outcome; **sucesos de actualidad** current events
suciedad *f* dirt, filth; dirtiness, filthiness
su•cio -cia *adj* dirty, filthy; base, low; tainted; blurred; (sport) foul || **sucio** *adv* (sport) foully, unfairly
sucumbir *intr* to succumb
sucursal *f* branch, branch office
sudadera *f* sweatshirt; (Col) sweatsuit
suda•do -da *adj* sweaty
Sudamérica *f* South America
sudamerica•no -na *adj & mf* South American
sudar *tr* to sweat; cough up || *intr* to sweat; (*trabajar mucho*) sweat
sudario *m* shroud, winding sheet
sudcorea•no -na *adj & mf* South Korean
sudor *m* sweat; (fig) sweat, toil; **chorrear de sudor** to swelter
sudoro•so -sa *adj* sweaty
Suecia *f* Sweden
sue•co -ca *adj* Swedish || *mf* Swede || *m* (*idioma*) Swedish
suegra *f* mother-in-law
suegro *m* father-in-law
suela *f* sole; sole leather; (*fish*) sole
sueldacostilla *f* grape hyacinth
sueldo *m* salary, pay, wage; **a sueldo** salaried; (*gángster*) on a contract, hired (to kill)
suelo *m* ground, soil, land; floor, flooring; pavement; (*p.ej., de una botella*) bottom; (aut) floorboard; **no pisar en el suelo** to walk on air; **suelo franco** loam; **suelo natal** *or* **patrio** home country
suel•to -ta *adj* loose; free; easy; swift, agile, nimble; fluent; bold, daring; (*ejemplar*) single; (*verso*) blank; odd, separate; spare; bulk; **suelto de lengua** loose-tongued || *m* small change; news item
sueñecillo *m* nap; **descabezar un sueñecillo** to take a nap
sueño *m* sleep; dream; (*cosa de gran belleza*) (fig) dream; **conciliar el sueño** to manage to go to sleep; **ni por sueños** by no means; **no dormir sueño** to not sleep a wink; **tener sueño** to be sleepy; **último sueño** (*muerte*) last sleep; **sueño hecho realidad** dream come true; **sueños dorados** daydreams
suero *m* serum
suerte *f* fortune, luck; piece of luck; chance; fate, lot; kind, sort; way, manner; feat, trick; (taur) play, suerte; (Peru) lottery ticket; **de esta suerte** in this way; **de suerte que** so that, with the result that; **la suerte está echada** the die is cast; **suerte de capa** (taur) capework
suerte•ro -ra *adj* fortunate, lucky || *m* (coll) lucky dog
sué•ter *m* (*pl* **-ters**) sweater
suficiente *adj* sufficient; adequate; fit, competent
sufijo *m* suffix
sufragar §44 *tr* to help, support, favor; defray || *intr* (SAm) to vote
sufragio *m* help, succor; benefit; (*voto*) suffrage
sufragismo *m* woman suffrage
sufragista *mf* woman-suffragist || *f* suffragette
sufri•do -da *adj* long-suffering; (*color*) serviceable; (*marido*) complaisant
sufrir *tr* to suffer; undergo, experience; support, hold up; tolerate; (*un examen*) take || *intr* to suffer
sugerencia *f* suggestion
sugerir §68 *tr* to suggest
sugestión suggestion

sugestionar *tr* to influence by suggestion
sugesti•vo -va *adj* suggestive; stimulating, striking, conspicuous
suicida *adj* suicidal || *mf* suicide victim
suicidar *ref* to commit suicide
suicidio *m* suicide; **suicidio terrorista** suicide bombing
Suiza *f* Switzerland
sui•zo -za *adj & mf* Swiss || *f* see **Suiza**
sujeción *f* subjection; surrender; fastening; fastener
sujetador *m* bra(ssiere)
sujetahilo *m* (elec) binding post
sujetapape•les *m* (*pl* **-les**) paper clip
sujetar *tr* to subject; subdue; fasten, tighten || *ref* to subject oneself, submit; stick, adhere
suje•to -ta *adj* subject, liable; able, capable || *m* subject; fellow, individual; **buen sujeto** good egg
sulfato *m* sulfate
sulfito *m* sulfite
sulfúri•co -ca *adj* sulfuric
sulfuro *m* sulfide; **sulfuro de hidrógeno** hydrogen sulfide
sulfuro•so -sa *adj* sulfurous
sultán *m* sultan; (*galanteador*) sheik
suma *f* sum, addition; summary; sum and substance; **en suma** in short, in a word
sumadora *f* adding machine
sumamente *adv* extremely, exceedingly
sumar *tr* to add; sum up; amount to || *intr* to add; amount; **suma y sigue** add and carry || *ref* to add up; adhere
suma•rio -ria *adj & m* summary
sumergir §27 *tr* to submerge || *ref* to submerge; (*un submarino*) dive
sumersión *f* submersion; (*de un submarino*) dive
sumidad *f* top, apex, summit
sumidero *m* drain, sewer; sink
suministrar *tr* to provide, supply
suministro *m* provision, supply; **suministros** supplies
sumir *tr* to sink; press down; overwhelm || *ref* to sink; (*p.ej., los carrillos, el pecho*) be sunken; shrink, shrivel; cower; (*p.ej., el sombrero*) pull down
sumisión *f* submission (*sometimiento*) subjection
sumi•so -sa *adj* submissive
su•mo -ma *adj* high, great, extreme; supreme; **a lo sumo** at most, at the most || *f* see **suma**
suncho *m* hoop
suní *adj & mf* Sunni
sunita *adj & mf* Sunni
suntuo•so -sa *adj* sumptuous
supeditar *tr* to hold down, oppress
superar *tr* to surpass, excel; conquer
superávit *m* (com) surplus
supercarburante *m* high-test fuel
supercheria *f* fraud, deceit
superficial *adj* superficial; surface
superficie *f* surface; exterior, outside; area; **gran superficie** large supermarket; **superficie de sustentación** (aer) airfoil
super•fluo -flua *adj* superfluous
superhombre *m* superman
superintendente *mf* superintendent, supervisor; **superintendente de patio** (rr) yardmaster
superior *adj* superior; upper; higher; **superior a** superior to; higher than; more than; larger than || *m* superior
superiora *f* mother superior
superiordad *f* superiority; authorities
superlati•vo -va *adj & m* superlative
supermercado *m* supermarket
super•no -na *adj* highest, supreme
superpetrolero *m* supertanker
superpoblar §61 *tr* to overpopulate
superponer §54 *tr* to superpose
superproduction *f* overproduction
supersóni•co -ca *adj* supersonic || *f* supersonics
superstición *f* superstition
supersticio•so -sa *adj* superstitious
supertanquero *m* (SAm) supertanker
superventas *adj* best-selling || *m & f* best-seller
supervisar *tr* to supervise
supervivencia *f* survival; (law) survivorship
súpi•to -ta *adj* sudden; impatient; (Col) dumbfounded
suplantar *tr* to supplant by treachery; (*un documento*) to alter fraudulently
suplefal•tas *mf* (*pl* **-tas**) substitute, fill-in
suplemento *m* supplement; excess fare; **suplemento dominical** (*periódico*) Sunday supplement
suplente *adj* substitute || *mf* covering doctor; understudy; (educ) sub, substitute (teacher); (sport) sub, substitute
súplica *f* entreaty, supplication; request
suplicante *adj & mf* suppliant
suplicar §73 *tr & intr* to entreat, implore; (law) to petition
suplicio *m* torture; punishment, execution; anguish
suplir *tr* to supplement, make up for; replace, take the place of; (*un defecto de otra persona*) cover up; (gram) to understand
suponer §54 *tr* to suppose; presuppose, imply; entail || *intr* to have weight, have authority
suposición *f* supposition; distinction; falsehood, imposture
supositorio *m* suppository
supradi•cho -cha *adj* above-mentioned
supre•mo -ma *adj* supreme
supresión *f* suppression, elimination, omission; cancellation; deletion
suprimir *tr* to suppress, eliminate, do away with; cancel; delete
supues•to -ta *adj* supposed, assumed, hypothetical; **supuesto que** since, inasmuch as || *m* assumption, hypothesis; **dar por supuesto** to take for granted; **por supuesto** of course, naturally, surely || *interj* sure thing!
supurar *intr* suppurate, discharge pus
sur *m* south; south wind

Suramérica *f* South America
surcar §73 *tr* to furrow; plough; cut through; streak through
surco *m* furrow; wrinkle, rut, cut; (*del disco gramofónico*) groove; **echarse en el surco** to lie down on the job
surcorea•no -na *adj & mf* South Korean
sure•ño -ña *adj* southern || *mf* southerner
surestada *f* (Arg) southeaster
surf *m* surfing
surfing *m* surfing
surfista *mf* windsurfer, surfer
surgir §27 *intr* to spout, spurt; come forth, spring up; arise, appear
suripanta *f* (hum) chorus girl; (scornful) slut, jade
surmenage *m* breakdown, burnout, exhaustion
surrealismo *m* surrealism
surti•do -da *adj* assorted || *m* assortment; supply, stock
surtidor *m* jet, spout, fountain; **surtidor de gasolina** gasoline pump
surtir *tr* to furnish, provide, supply || *intr* to spout, spurt, shoot up
susceptible *adj* susceptible; touchy
suscitar *tr* to stir up, provoke; (*dudas, una cuestión*) to raise
susodi•cho -cha *adj* above-mentioned
suspender *tr* to hang; suspend; astonish; postpone; fail, flunk || *ref* to be suspended
suspensión *f* suspension; astonishment; withdrawal, discontinuation; **suspensión de fuegos** cease fire; **suspensión de pagos** bankruptcy protection; **suspensión hidráulica** hydraulic suspension
suspen•so -sa *adj* suspended, hanging; baffled, bewildered; (theat) closed || *m* flunk, condition
suspensores *mpl* suspenders
suspensorio *m* jockstrap, supporter
suspi•caz *adj* (*pl* **-caces**) suspicious, distrustful
suspirar *intr* to sigh
suspiro *m* sigh; ladyfinger; (mus) quarter rest
sustentación *f* support, prop; (aer) lift
sustentar *tr* to sustain, support, feed; maintain; (*una tesis*) defend
sustento *m* sustenance, support, food; maintenance
susto *m* scare, fright
susurrar *tr* to whisper || *intr* to whisper; murmur, rustle, purl, hum; be bruited about || *ref* to be bruited about
susurro *m* whisper; murmur, rustle, purling, hum
susu•rrón -rrona *adj* whispering || *mf* whisperer
sutil *adj* subtle; keen, observant; thin, delicate
sutura *f* suture
suturar *tr* to suture, stitch
su•yo -ya *adj poss* of his, of hers, of yours, of theirs, e.g., **un amigo suyo** a friend of his; *pron poss* his, hers, yours, theirs, its, one's; **hacer de las suyas** to be up to one's old tricks; **salirse con la suya** to have one's way; to carry one's point

T

T, t (te) *f* twenty-first letter of the Spanish alphabet
t. *abbr* **tarde**
taba *f* anklebone; (*del carnero*) knucklebone; (*juego*) knucklebones
tabacale•ro -ra *adj* tobacco || *mf* tobacco grower || *f* cigarette factory
tabaco *m* tobacco; cigar; snuff; (Cuba, CAm, Mex) punch; **tabaco en rama** leaf tobacco; **tabaco sin humo** smokeless tobacco
tabalada *f* bump, thump, heavy fall; slap
tabalear *tr* to rock, sway || *intr* to drum with the fingers
tabanazo *m* slap; slap in the face
tabanco *m* stand, stall, booth
tábano *m* horsefly, gadfly
tabanque *m* treadle wheel
tabaola *f* noise, hubbub
tabaquera *f* snuffbox; (*de la pipa de fumar*) bowl; (Arg, Chile) tobacco pouch
tabaquería *f* tobacco shop, cigar store
tabaque•ro -ra *adj* tobacco || *mf* tobacconist; cigar maker || *m* (Bol) pocket handkerchief || *f* see **tabaquera**
tabardete *m* or **tabardillo** *m* sunstroke; harum-scarum
tabarra *f* bore, tiresome talk
taberna *f* tavern, saloon, barroom, pub
tabernáculo *m* tabernacle
tabernera *f* barmaid
tabernero *m* tavern keeper; bartender
tabica *f* (*para cubrir un hueco*) board; (*del frente de un escalón*) riser
tabicar §73 *tr* to close up, shut up; wall up
tabilla *f* tablet; splint; bulletin board; **tabilla con sujetapapeles** clipboard
tabique *m* thin wall; partition wall, partition
tabla *f* (*de madera*) board; (*de metal*) sheet; (*de piedra*) slab; (*de tierra*) strip; (*cuadro pintado en una tabla*) panel; (*lista, catálogo; índice de materias*) table; **escapar** or **salvarse en una tabla** to have a narrow escape; **tabla de armonía** (mus) sounding board; **tabla de lavar** washboard; **tabla de planchar** ironing board; **tabla de salvación** lifesaver, helping hand; **tabla de windsurf** windsurfer; **tablas** draw, tie; (*escenario del teatro*) stage; (*de la plaza de toros*) barrier; **tener tablas** to have stage presence

tablado *m* flooring; scaffold; (*escenario del teatro*) stage
tablear *tr* to cut into boards; divide into plots or patches; level, grade
tablero *m* boarding; timber; table top; gambling table; cutting board; checkerboard, chessboard; counter; blackboard; **poner al tablero** to risk; **tablero de instrumentos** (aer) control panel; (aut) dashboard
tableta *f* small board; (*taco de papel; comprimido, pastilla*) tablet
tabletear *intr* to rattle
tablista *mf* windsurfer
tabloide *adj & m* (*de formato reducido*) tabloid
tablón *m* plank; beam; **tablón de mensajes** (compu) message board
tabloncillo *m* (taur) seat in last row
ta•bú *m* (*pl* **-búes**) taboo
tabuco *m* hovel
tabulador *m* tabulator
tabular *tr* to tabulate
taburete *m* stool
tac *m* tick
TAC *f* (acronym) (**tomografía axial computacional**) CAT (computerized axial tomography)
tacada *f* stroke (*of a billiard cue*)
taca•ño -ña *adj* stingy
tacha *f* defect, fault, flaw
tachar *tr* to erase; strike out; blame, find fault with
tacho *m* tin sheet; (Arg) garbage can; (Arg) watch; (Arg, Chile) boiler; (Cuba) sugar pan
tachón *m* scratch, erasure; ornamental tack or nail; trimming
tachonar *tr* to adorn with ornamental tacks; trim with ribbon; spangle, stud
tachuela *f* tack; hobnail; (Chile, Mex) runt, half pint; (SAm) drinking cup
táci•to -ta *adj* tacit; silent
tacitur•no -na *adj* taciturn; melancholy
taco *m* bung, plug; wad, wadding; billiard cue; pad, tablet; drumstick; snack, bite; drink; oath, curse, swearword; heel; muddle, mess; (Mex) rolled-up tortilla with fillings, taco
tacón *m* heel
taconear *tr* (Chile) to fill, stuff || *intr* to click the heels; strut
taconeo *m* click, clicking (*of heels*)
tácti•co -ca *adj* tactical || *m* tactician || *f* tactics
tacto *m* (sense of) touch; (*del dactilógrafo, el pianista, el instrumento*) touch; skill; tact
Tadeo *m* Thaddeus
tafetán *m* taffeta; **tafetanes** flags, colors; finery; **tafetán inglés** court plaster
tafilete *m* morocco leather; sweatband
tagarote *m* sparrow hawk; scrivener; lout; gentleman sponger
tagua *f* (Chile) mud hen; (*arbusto*) (SAm) ivory palm; (*fruto*) (SAm) ivory nut
taguara *f* (Ven) hash house, cheap restaurant
taha•lí *m* (*pl* **-líes**) baldric
tahona *f* horse-driven flour mill; bakery
ta•hur -hura *adj* gambling; cheating || *mf* gambler; cheat; cardsharp
tailan•dés -desa *adj & mf* Thai
Tailandia *f* Thailand
taima•do -da *adj* sly, crafty; (Arg, Ecuad) lazy; (Chile) gruff, sullen
Taiwán *m* Taiwan
tajada *f* cut; slice, sliver; hoarseness; drunk
tajadero *m* chopping block
tajalá•piz *m* (*pl* **-pices**) pencil sharpener
tajamar *m* cutwater; dike, dam
tajar *tr* to cut; slice; (*un lápiz*) sharpen
tajo *m* cut; cutting edge; chopping block; execution block; steep cliff || **Tajo** *m* Tagus
tal *adj indef* such; such a || *pron indef* so-and-so; such a thing; someone || *adv* so; in such a way; **con tal (de) que** provided (that); **¿qué tal?** how?; hello!, how's everything?
talabarte *m* sword belt
talabartero *m* saddler, harness maker
talache *m* or **talacho** *m* (Mex) mattock
taladrar *tr* to bore, drill, pierce, perforate; (*un billete*) punch; (*un problema*) get to the bottom of
taladro *m* drill; auger; drill hole; drill press
tálamo *m* bridal bed
talán *m* ding-dong
talante *m* countenance, mien; desire, will, pleasure; way, manner
talar *adj* (*traje, vestidura*) long || *tr* (*árboles*) to fell; destroy, lay waste
talco *m* tinsel; talc; **talco en polvo** talcum powder
talega *f* bag, sack; **talegas** money, wealth
talego *m* big bag, sack; slob; **tener talego** to have money tucked away
taleguilla *f* small bag; bullfighter's breeches
talento *m* talent
talento•so -sa *adj* talented
talismán *m* talisman
talla *f* cut; carving; height, stature; size; ransom; reward; (*diamante*) cut, polish; (Arg) chatting, prattle; (CAm) fraud, lie; (Col) beating, thrashing; **talla dulce** intaglio; **talla especial** half-size
tallar *tr* to carve; (*una piedra preciosa*) cut; (*naipes*) deal; appraise; engrave; grind; size up; (Col) beat, thrash || *intr* (Arg) to chat, converse; (Chile) to make love
tallarín *m* noodle
talle *m* shape, figure, stature; waist; fit; appearance, outline; (*de prendas*) waistline
taller *m* shop, workshop; factory, mill; atelier, studio; laboratory; **taller agremiado** closed shop; **taller carrocero** (aut) body shop; **taller franco** open shop; **taller penitenciario** workhouse
tallo *m* stem, stalk; shoot, sprout; (Col) cabbage
talón *m* heel; (aut) lug, flange; check, voucher, coupon; (*de un cheque*) stub; **talón conformado** certified check; **talón de Aquiles** Achilles' heel; **talón sin fondos** bad check

talona•rio -ria *adj* stub || *m* stub book, checkbook
talonear *intr* to dash along
talud *m* slope
tamal *m* (CAm, Mex) tamale; (Chile) bundle; (coll) intrigue
tamañi•to -ta *adj* so small; very small; confused, disconcerted
tama•ño -ña *adj* so big; such a big; very big, very large; so small; **abrir tamaños ojos** to open one's eyes wide || *m* size; **tamaño bolsillo** pocket-size; **tamaño carné** passport-size; **tamaño natural** life-size
tambaleante *adj* staggering
tambalear *intr & ref* to stagger, reel, totter
también *adv* also, too
tambo *m* (Arg, Chile) brothel; (SAm) roadside inn; (Arg, Urug) dairy
tambor *m* drum; (*persona que toca el tambor*) drummer; sieve, screen; eardrum, coffee roaster; **a tambor batiente** with drums beating; in triumph; **tambor mayor** drum major
tamborilear *tr* to praise to the skies || *intr* to drum
Támesis *m* Thames
ta•miz *m* (*pl* **-mices**) sieve; sifter
tamizar §60 *tr* to sift, sieve
tamo *m* fuzz, fluff
tampoco *adv* neither, not either; **ni yo tampoco** nor I either, neither do I
tampón *m* stamp pad
tan *adv* so; **tan . . . como** or **cuan** as . . . as; **tan siquiera** at least; **un tan** + *adj* such a + *adj* || *m* boom (*of a drum*)
tanatología *f* thanatology
tanda *f* turn; shift, relay; task; coat, layer; game, match; flock, lot, pack; show; habit, bad habit
tangente *adj & f* tangent; **escaparse, irse** *or* **salir por la tangente** to evade the issue
Tánger *f* Tangier
tanguista *f* hostess (*in a night club*)
ta•no -na *adj & mf* (Arg) Neapolitan, Italian
tanque *m* tank; (dial) dipper, drinking cup; **tanque de almacenamiento** storage tank; **tanque de gasolina** (aut) gas tank
tantán *m* tom-tom; clanging; boom
tantear *tr* to compare; size up; probe, test, feel out; sketch, outline; keep the score of || *intr* to keep score; to grope; **¡tantee Ud!** just imagine!, fancy that!
tanteo *m* comparison; careful consideration; test, probe, trial; trial and error; score
tan•to -ta *adj & pron indef* so much; as much; **tanto . . . como** as much . . . as; both . . . and; **tan•tos -tas** so many; as many; **tantos . . . como** as many . . . as; **y tantos** odd, or more, e.g., **veinte y tantos** twenty odd, twenty or more || *m* copy; counter, chip; point; portion, part; **apuntar los tantos** to keep score; **entre tanto** in the meantime; **estar al tanto de** to be aware of, to be or keep informed about; **poner al tanto de** to make aware of, to keep informed of; **por lo tanto** or **por tanto** therefore || **tanto** *adv* so much; so hard; so often; so long; as much
tañer §70 *tr* (*un instrumento músico*) to play; (*una campana*) to ring || *intr* to drum with the fingers
tañido *m* sound, tone; twang; ring, tang
tapa *f* lid, cover, top, cap; (*de un cilindro, un barril*) head; (*de una compuerta*) gate; (*de un libro*) board cover; shirt front; (aut) valve cap; **levantarse** *or* **saltarse la tapa de los sesos** to blow one's brains out; **tapa de rosca** screw top; **tapas** appetizer, free lunch
tapabalazo *m* fly (*of trousers*)
tapabarro *m* (Chile) mudguard
tapaboca *f* slap in the mouth; muffler; squelch, squelcher
tapacu•bo *m* or **tapacu•bos** *m* (*pl* **-bos**) (aut) hubcap
tapadera *f* lid, cover, cap
tapagote•ras *m* (*pl* **-ras**) (Arg) roofing cement; (Col) roofer
tapaguje•ros *m* (*pl* **-ros**) (coll) bungling mason; substitute, replacement
tapar *tr* to cover; cover up, hide; plug, stop, stop up; conceal; obstruct; wrap up; (*un diente*) (Chile) to fill
tapara *f* (Ven) gourd; **vaciarse como una tapara** (Ven) to spill all one knows
taparrabo *m* loincloth; bathing trunks
tapera *f* (SAm) ruins; (SAm) shack
tapete *m* rug; runner; table scarf; **estar sobre el tapete** to be on the carpet, be under discussion; **tapete verde** card table, gambling table
tapia *f* mud wall, adobe wall
tapiar *tr* to wall up, wall in; close up
tapicería *f* tapestries; upholstery; tapestry shop; upholstery shop
tapicero *m* tapestry maker; upholsterer; carpet maker; carpet layer
ta•piz *m* (*pl* **-pices**) tapestry
tapizar §60 *tr* to tapestry; upholster; carpet; cover
tapón *m* stopper, cork; cap; bottle cap; bung, plug; (elec) fuse; (surg) tampon; **tapón de algodón** (surg) swab; **tapón de cubo** (aut) hubcap; **tapón de desagüe** drain plug; **tapón de rosca** screw top; **tapón de tráfico** traffic jam; **tapón de vaciado** (aut) drain plug; **tapón para el oído** earplug
taponar *tr* to plug, stop up; (surg) to tampon
taponazo *m* pop
taque *m* click; knock, rap
taqué *m* (aut) tappet
taquigrafía *f* shorthand, stenography
taquigrafiar §77 *tr* to take down in shorthand || *intr* to take shorthand
taquígra•fo -fa *mf* stenographer
taquilla *f* ticket rack; ticket window; ticket office; box office; gate, take; file; (C-R) inn, tavern
taquille•ro -ra *adj* box-office || *mf* ticket agent
taquimeca *mf* shorthand-typist
taquimecanógra•fo -fa *mf* shorthand-typist

tarabilla *f* millclapper; catch; turnbuckle; (*de la hebilla de la correa*) tongue; chatterbox; jabber; **soltar la tarabilla** to talk a blue streak
tarabita *f* (*clavillo de la hebilla*) tongue; (SAm) rope of rope bridge
taracea *f* marquetry, inlaid work
tarambana *adj & mf* (coll) crackpot
tararear *tr & intr* to hum
tarasca *f* dragon (*in Corpus Christi procession*); (*mujer fea*) hag
tarascada *f* bite; tart reply
tardanza *f* slowness, delay, tardiness
tardar *intr* to be long, be slow; be late; **a más tardar** at the latest; **tardar en** + *inf* to be late in + *ger* || *ref* to be long, be slow; be late
tarde *adv* late; too late; **hacerse tarde** to grow late; **tarde o temprano** sooner or later || *f* afternoon; evening; **de la tarde a la mañana** overnight; suddenly, in no time; unexpectedly
tardecer **§22** *intr* to grow dark, grow late
tardí•o -a *adj* late, delayed; dilatory, tardy; slow
tar•do -da *adj* slow; late; slow, dull, dense
tar•dón -dona *mf* poke, slow poke
tarea *f* task, job; care, worry
tarifa *f* tariff; price list; rate; fare; (telp) toll; **tarifa recargada** extra fare
tarima *f* platform; stand, stool; low bench; (*entablado para dormir*) bunk
tarjeta *f* card; (compu) card; **tarjeta de buen deseo** *or* **de felicitación** greeting card; **tarjeta de cobro automático** debit card; **tarjeta de crédito** credit card; **tarjeta de embarque** boarding pass; **tarjeta de visita** calling card, visiting card; **tarjeta inteligente** smart card; **tarjeta navideña** Christmas card; **tarjeta perforada** punch card; **tarjeta postal** post card; **tarjeta telefónica** phonecard; **tarjeta verde** green card
tarjetero *m* card case; card index
tarquín *m* mire, slime, mud
tarro *m* jar; milk pail; horn; (SAm) top hat
tarta *f* tart, cake; pan
tartajear *intr* to stutter
tartalear *intr* to stagger, sway; be speechless
tartamudear *intr* to stutter, stammer
tartamudeo *m* stuttering, stammering
tartamu•do -da *mf* stutterer, stammerer
tartán *m* Scotch plaid
tarugo *m* wooden plug; wooden paving block; (Guat, Mex) dolt, blockhead
tasa *f* appraisal; measure, standard; rate; ceiling price; **tasa de cambio** exchange rate; **tasa de interés** interest rate; **tasa de mortalidad** mortality rate; **tasa de natalidad** birthrate
tasación *f* appraisal; regulation
tasajo *m* jerked beef
tasar *tr* to appraise; regulate; hold down, keep within bounds; grudge
tasca *f* dive, joint; tavern; (Peru) surf, breakers
tata *m* daddy || *f* nursemaid; little sister
tate *m* hashish; hashish user
tato *m* little brother
tatuaje *m* tattoo, tattooing
tatuar **§21** *tr & ref* to tattoo
tauri•no -na *adj* bullfighting
Tauro *m* (astr) Taurus
taurófi•lo -la *mf* bullfight fan
tauromaquia *f* bullfighting
taxear *intr* (aer) to taxi
taxi *m* taxi, taxicab || *f* taxi dancer
taxista *mf* taxi driver
taza *f* cup; (*de la fuente*) basin; (*del inodoro*) bowl; **taza de café** coffee cup; **taza para té** teacup
te *pron pers & reflex* thee, to thee; you, to you; thyself, to thyself; yourself, to yourself
té *m* tea; **té bailable** tea dance
tea *f* torch, firebrand
teatral *adj* theatrical
teatre•ro -ra *mf* theatergoer
teatro *m* theater; **dar teatro a** to ballyhoo; **teatro de estreno** first-run house; **teatro de guiñol, marionetas** *or* **títeres** puppet theater; **teatro de la ópera** opera house; **teatro de repetorio** stock company
teatrólo•go -ga *mf* theater critic || *m* actor || *f* actress
Tebas *f* Thebes
tebe•o -a *adj & mf* Theban || *m* comic book, funny paper
teca *f* teak
techado *m* roof; **bajo techado** indoors
techar *tr* to roof
techo *m* ceiling; roof; (*sombrero*) hat; **techo corredizo** sunroof; **techo de paja** thatched roof
techumbre *f* ceiling; roof
teckel [ˈtekel] *s* dachshund
tecla *f* (*de piano, máquina de escribir, etc.*) key; touchy subject; **dar en la tecla** to get the knack of it; **tecla de cambio** shift key; **tecla de destello** (telp) flash button; **tecla de escape** margin release; **tecla de espacios** space bar; **tecla de retroceso** backspacer; **tecla de silencio** mute button
teclado *m* keyboard; (compu) keypad; **teclado manual** (mus) manual; **teclado numérico** (compu, electron, telv) numeric keypad
teclear *tr* to feel out; (compu) to keyboard || *intr* to run over the keys; drum, thrum; (Chile) to be at death's door; (*un jugador*) (Chile) to be losing one's last cent
tecleo *m* fingering; touch; (*de la máquina de escribir*) click
técni•co -ca *adj* technical || *m* technician; expert; **técnico en informática** computer engineer || *f* technique; technics
tecnología *f* technology; **de alta tecnología** high-tech
tecolote *m* eagle owl (*of Central America*); (Mex) night policeman
tedio *m* ennui, boredom
tedio•so -sa *adj* tedious, boresome
teja *f* roofing tile; shovel hat; yew tree; linden

tree; **a toca teja** (coll) in cash; **teja de madera** shingle
tejadillo *m* cover, top; (*de coche*) roof
tejado *m* tile roof; roof; **tejado de vidrio** (fig) glass house
tejama•ní *m* (*pl* **-níes**) shake (*long shingle*)
teja•no -na *adj & mf* Texan
tejar *m* tile works || *tr* to tile, roof with tiles
teja•roz *m* (*pl* **-roces**) eaves
teje•dor -dora *adj* weaving; scheming || *mf* weaver; schemer
tejer *tr & intr* to weave
tejido *m* weave, texture; web; fabric, textile; tissue; (biol & fig) tissue; **tejido adhesivo** friction tape; **tejido conjuntivo** (anat) connective tissue; **tejido de saco** (Mex) burlap; **tejido de punto** knitted fabric, jersey
tejo *m* disk; quoit; yew tree
tejón *m* badger
tela *f* cloth, fabric; (*de cebolla*) skin; (*del insecto*) web; film; (bb) cloth; (paint) canvas; (*dinero*) (slang) dough; **poner en tela de juicio** to question, doubt; **tela de alambre** wire screen; **tela de araña** spider web, cobweb; **tela de toalla** terry cloth; **tela emplástica** court plaster; **tela metálica** chicken wire; wire screen
telar *m* loom; frame; embroidery frame; (bb) sewing press
telaraña *f* spiderweb; cobweb; **telaraña mundial** (compu) World-Wide Web
telebanco *m* ATM machine
telecomedia serial *f* sitcom
telecomunicaciones *fpl* telecommunications
teleconferencia *f* conference call
telecontrol *m* remote control
telediario *m* daytime television news
teledifundir *tr & intr* to telecast
teledifusión *f* telecasting; telecast
teledirigi•do -da *adj* remote-controlled
telefax *m* fax, telefax
teleférico *m* cable car, cable railway
telefilm *m or* **telefilme** *m* made-for-television movie
telefonar *tr & intr* to telephone
telefonazo *m* telephone call
telefonear *tr & intr* to telephone
telefonema *m* telephone message
telefonista *mf* telephone operator
teléfono *m* telephone; **teléfono automático** dial telephone; **teléfono celular** cellphone, cellular telephone; **teléfono inalámbrico** *or* **sin hilos** cordless telephone; **teléfono interno** extension phone; **teléfono portátil** *or* **móvil** mobile phone; **teléfono público** pay phone; **teléfono rojo** hotline
teleg. *abbr* **telégrafo, telegrama**
telegrafiar §77 *tr & intr* to telegraph
telegrafista *mf* telegrapher
telégrafo *m* telegraph; **telégrafo de banderas** wigwagging; **telégrafo de máquinas** (naut) engine-room telegraph; **telégrafo sin hilos** wireless telegraph
telegrama *m* telegram
teleimpresor *m* teletype, teleprinter
Telémaco *m* Telemachus
telemando *m* remote control
telemetrar *tr* to telemeter
telemetría *f* telemetry
telémetro *m* telemeter; (mil) range finder
telen•do -da *adj* sprightly, lively
teleobjectivo *m* telephoto (lens)
telepatía *f* telepathy, mental telepathy
telerreceptor *m* television set
telescopar *tr & ref* to telescope
telescopio *m* telescope
telesilla *f* chair lift
telespecta•dor -dora *mf* viewer, televiewer; **telespectadores** television audience
telesquí *m* ski lift, ski tow
teleta *f* blotter, blotting paper
teletipo *m* teletype
teletubo *m* (telv) picture tube
televidente *mf* viewer, televiewer
televisar *tr* to televise
televisión *f* television; **televisión en circuito cerrado** closed-circuit television; **televisión en colores** color television; **televisión por cable** cable television
televi•sor -sora *adj* televising; television || *m* television set || *f* television transmitter
telón *m* drop curtain; **telón de acero** (fig) Iron Curtain; **telón de boca** (theat) front curtain; **telón de fondo** or **foro** (theat) backdrop
tema *m* theme, subject; exercise; (gram) stem; (mus) theme || *f* fixed idea; persistence; grudge; **a tema** in emulation
temario *m* agenda
temblar §2 *intr* to tremble, shake, quiver, shiver; **estar temblando** to teeter
tem•blón -blona *adj* shaking, tremulous || *m* aspen tree
temblor *m* tremor, shaking, trembling; **temblor de tierra** earthquake
tembloro•so -sa *adj* trembling, shaking, tremulous
tem•bo -ba *adj* (Col) silly, stupid
temer *tr & intr* to fear
temera•rio -ria *adj* rash, reckless, foolhardy
temeridad *f* rashness, recklessness, foolhardiness, temerity
temero•so -sa *adj* frightful, dread; timid; fearful
temible *adj* dreadful, terrible, fearful
temor *m* fear, dread
témpano *m* small drum; drumhead; (*de barril*) head; (*de tocino*) flitch; (*de hielo*) iceberg, floe; (archit) tympan; (mus) kettledrum
temperamental *adj* temperamental
temperamento *m* temperament; conciliation, compromise; weather
temperar *tr* to temper, soften, moderate, calm; tune || *intr* to go to a warmer climate
temperatura *f* temperature; weather; **temperatura ambiente** room temperature
temperie *f* weather, state of the weather
tempestad *f* storm, tempest; **tempestad de**

arena sandstorm; **tempestades de risas** gales of laughter
tempesti•vo -va *adj* opportune, timely
tempestuo•so -sa *adj* stormy, tempestuous
templa•do -da *adj* temperate; moderate; lukewarm, medium; brave, courageous; drunk, tipsy; (SAm) in love; (CAm, Mex) clever
templanza *f* temperence; mildness
templar *tr* to temper; soften; ease, dilute; (*colores*) blend; (*velas*) trim || *intr* (*el tiempo*) to warm up || *ref* to temper; moderate; fall in love; die
temple *m* weather, state of the weather; temper, disposition; humor; average; dash, boldness; (*del acero, el vidrio, etc.*) temper
templo *m* temple
témpora *f* Ember days
temporada *f* season; period; (*p.ej., de buen tiempo*) spell; **de temporada** temporarily; vacationing; **temporada baja** off season
temporal *adj* temporal; temporary || *m* weather; storm, tempest; spell of rainy weather
temporáne•o -a or **tempora•rio -ria** *adj* temporary
temporizar §60 *intr* to temporize; putter around
temprane•ro -ra *adj* early
tempra•no -na *adj* early || **temprano** *adv* early
tenacidad *f* tenacity; persistence
tenacillas *fpl* sugar tongs; hair curler; tweezers; snuffers
te•naz *adj* (*pl* **-naces**) tenacious; persistent
tenazas *fpl* pincers, pliers; tongs
tenazón — a or **de tenazón** without taking aim; offhand
tenazuelas *fpl* tweezers
tendedera *f* clothesline; litter
tendedero *m* drier, frame for drying clothes; drying ground
tendencia *f* tendency
tender §51 *tr* to spread; stretch out; extend; reach out; offer, tender; (*la ropa*) hang out; (*con una capa de cal o yeso*) coat; (*un puente*) throw, build; (*una trampa*) set; (*conductores eléctricos, vías de ferrocarril, cañerías*) lay; (*la cama*) make; (*un cadáver*) lay out || *intr* to tend || *ref* to stretch out; throw one's cards on the table; run at full gallop
ténder *m* (naut, rr) tender
tenderete *m* stand, booth
tende•ro -ra *mf* shopkeeper, storekeeper; grocer || *m* tentmaker
tendido *m* (*p.ej., de un cable*) laying; (*de una cortina de humo*) spreading; (*de alambres*) hanging, stretching; wires; (*trecho de ferrocarril*) stretch; (*ropa que tiende la lavandera*) wash; (*de cal o yeso*) coat; (*del tejado*) slope; (*de panes*) batch; (taur) uncovered stand; (Col) bedclothes
tendón *m* tendon; **tendón de Aquiles** Achilles' heel; **tendón del corvejón** (*del caballo*) hamstring
tenducho *m* (pej) miserable old store
tenebro•so -sa *adj* dark, gloomy; (*negocio*) dark, shady; (*estilo*) obscure
tenedor *m* holder, bearer; fork, table fork; **tenedor de acciones** stockholder; **tenedor de bonos** bondholder; **tenedor de libros** bookkeeper
teneduría *f* bookkeeping
tenencia *f* tenure, tenancy; (mil & nav) lieutenancy
tener §71 *tr* to have; hold; keep; own, possess; consider; (*recibir*) get; esteem; stop; **no tenerlas todas consigo** to be alarmed, dismayed; **no tener nada que ver con** to have nothing to do with; **no tener sobre qué caerse muerto** to not have a cent to one's name; **tener que** to have to; for expressions like **tener hambre** to be hungry, see the noun || *ref* to stop; catch oneself, keep from falling; consider oneself; fit, go
tenería *f* tannery
tenida *f* meeting, session; reception
teniente *adj* holding, owning; unripe; mean, miserly; hard of hearing || *m* lieutenant; **teniente coronel** lieutenant colonel; **teniente de navío** (nav) lieutenant
tenis *m* tennis
tenista *mf* tennis player || *mpl* sneakers
tenor *m* tenor, character, import, drift; (mus) tenor; **a tenor de** in accordance with
tenorio *m* lady-killer
tensión *f* tension, stress; (elec) tension, voltage; (mech) stress; **tensión arterial** or **sanguínea** blood pressure
ten•so -sa *adj* tense, tight, taut
tentación *f* temptation
tentáculo *m* tentacle, feeler
tenta•dor -dora *adj* tempting || *m* tempter
tentar §2 *tr* to touch; (*el camino*) feel; try, attempt; examine; try out, test; tempt; probe
tentati•vo -va *adj* tentative || *f* attempt; trial, feeler
tentempié *m* snack, bite; (*juguete*) tumbler
tenue *adj* tenuous; light, soft; faint, subdued; (*estilo*) simple
teñir §72 *tr* to dye; stain; tinge, shade, color
teocracia *f* theocracy
teología *f* theology; **no meterse en teologías** to keep out of deep water; **teología liberacionista** liberation theology
teorema *m* theorem
teoría *f* theory; **teoría ondulatoria** wave theory
tepe *m* turf, sod
tequila *m* (Mex) tequila (*distilled liquor*)
terapeuta *mf* therapist
terapéuti•co -ca *adj* therapeutic(al) || *f* therapeutics
terapia *f* therapy; **terapia vocacional** occupational therapy
tercena *f* government tobacco warehouse; (Ecuad) butcher shop
tercer *adj* this apocopated form of **tercero** is used before masculine singular nouns and adjectives

tercermundista *adj* Third World
terce•ro -ra *adj* third; **Tercer Mundo** Third World; nonaligned nations ‖ *mf* third; mediator; go-between ‖ *m* procurer, bawd; referee, umpire
terceto *m* tercet; trio
terciar *tr* to place diagonally; divide into three parts; (*p.ej., la capa, el fusil*) to swing over one's shoulder; (*licor*) water ‖ *intr* to intercede, mediate ‖ *ref* to happen; be opportune
tercia•rio -ria *adj* tertiary
ter•cio -cia *adj* third ‖ *m* third; (mil) corps; **hacer buen tercio a** to do a good turn
terciopelo *m* velvet
ter•co -ca *adj* stubborn; hard, resistant
Teresa *f* Theresa
tergiversar *tr* to slant, twist, distort
terliz *m* ticking
termal *adj* thermal; steam
termas *fpl* hot baths
térmi•co -ca *adj* temperature; steam; steam-generated
terminación *f* termination
terminal *adj* terminal ‖ *m* (elec) terminal; **terminal de trabajo** workstation
terminante *adj* final, definitive, peremptory
terminar *tr* to end, terminate; finish ‖ *intr* to end, terminate; **terminar de operar** (compu) to log out *o* off
término *m* end, limit; boundary; bearing, manner; term; **medio término** subterfuge, evasion; compromise; **primer término** foreground; (mov) close-up; **segundo término** middle distance; **término medio** average; **último término** background
termistor *m* (elec) thermistor
termita *f or* **térmite** *m* termite
termoaislante *adj* heat-insulated
termodinámi•co -ca *adj* thermodynamic ‖ *f* thermodynamics
termómetro *m* thermometer; **termómetro clínico** clinical thermometer
termonuclear *adj* thermonuclear
termopar *m* (elec) thermocouple
Termópilas, las Thermopylae
ter•mos *m* (*pl* **-mos**) thermos bottle; hot-water heater; **termos de acumulación** (elec) off-peak heater
termosifón *m* hot-water boiler
termostato *m* thermostat
terna *f* trio
terne•jo -ja *adj* (Ecuad, Peru) peppy, energetic
ternera *f* calf; (*carne*) veal
terneza *f* tenderness; fondness; love; **ternezas** flirting, flirtation
ternilla *f* gristle
terno *m* suit of clothes; oath, curse; trio; piece of luck; (Col) cup and saucer; (W-I) set of jewelry
ternura *f* tenderness; fondness, love
terquedad *f* stubbornness; hardness, resistance
terraja *f* diestock
terral *adj* (*viento*) land ‖ *m* land breeze
Terranova *m* (*perro*) Newfoundland (*dog*) ‖ *f* (*isla y provincia*) Newfoundland (*island and province*)
terraplén *m* fill; embankment; terrace, platform; earthwork, rampart
terrateniente *mf* landholder, landowner
terraza *f* terrace; veranda; flat roof; (*de jardín*) border; edge; sidewalk cafe; glazed jar with two handles
terremoto *m* earthquake
terrenal *adj* earthly, mundane, worldly
terre•no -na *adj* terrestrial; mundane, worldly ‖ *m* land, ground, terrain; lot, plot; (sport) field; (fig) field, sphere; **sobre el terreno** on the spot; with data in hand; **terreno echadizo** refuse dump
terre•ro -ra *adj* earthly; of earth; humble ‖ *m* pile, heap; mark, target; terrace; public square; (min) dump
terrestre *adj* terrestrial; ground, land
terrible *adj* terrible; gruff, surly, ill-tempered
territorio *m* territory
terromontero *m* hill, butte
terrón *m* clod; lump, cake; (*de tierra*) divot
terror *m* terror
terrorismo *m* terrorism, frightfulness
terrorista *adj & mf* terrorist; **terrorista suicida** suicide bomber
terro•so -sa *adj* earthly, dirty
terruño *m* piece of ground; soil; country, native soil
ter•so -sa *adj* smooth, glossy, polished; smooth, limpid, flowing
tertulia *f* party, social gathering; literary gathering; game room; (compu) newsgroup; **estar de tertulia** to sit around and talk
tertulia•no -na *mf* party-goer; regular member
Tesalia, la Thessaly
te•sis *f* (*pl* **-sis**) thesis
te•so -sa *adj* taut, tight, tense ‖ *m* top of hill; (*en superficie lisa*) rough spot
tesón *m* grit, pluck, tenacity
tesone•ro -ra *adj* obstinate, stubborn, tenacious
tesorería *f* treasury
tesore•ro -ra *mf* treasurer
tesoro *m* treasure; treasury; treasure house; thesaurus
Tespis *m* Thespis
testa *f* head; front; head, brains; **testa coronada** crowned head
testaferro *m* dummy, figurehead, straw man
testamento *m* testament, will; **Antiguo Testamento** Old Testament; **Nuevo Testamento** New Testament; **Viejo Testamento** Old Testament
testar *tr* (Ecuad) to cross out ‖ *intr* to make a will
testaru•do -da *adj* stubborn, pig-headed
testear *tr* (compu) to test out
testera *f* front; (*de animal*) forehead; (*de coche*) back seat
testículo *m* testicle
testificar §73 *tr & intr* to testify

testigo *mf* witness; **testigo de cargo** witness for the prosecution; **testigo de descargo** witness for the defense; **testigo de Jehová** Jehovah's Witness; **testigo de vista, testigo ocular,** or **testigo presencial** eyewitness || *m* (*evidencia*) witness; (*en un experimento*) control; **testigo falso** straw man

testimoniar *tr* to attest, testify to, bear witness to

testimonio *m* testimony; affidavit; false witness; **testimonio de oídas** hearsay evidence

tes•tuz *m* (*pl* **-tuces**) (*p.ej., de caballo*) face; nape

teta *f* teat; breast; tit (slang)

tetera *f* teapot; teakettle

tetilla *f* nipple

tétri•co -ca *adj* dark gloomy; sad, sullen, gloomy

textil *adj & m* textile

texto *m* text; **fuera de texto** tipped-in

textura *f* texture

tez *f* complexion

ti *pron pers* thee; you

tía *f* aunt; old lady, old woman; bawd; **no hay tu tía** there's no chance; **tía abuela** great-aunt, grandaunt; **tía segunda** cousin once removed

tiara *f* tiara

tibante *adj* (Col) haughty, proud

tibia *f* shinbone; pipe, flute

ti•bio -bia *adj* tepid, lukewarm; (SAm) angry || *f* see **tibia**

tibor *m* large porcelain vase; chamber pot

tiburón *m* shark

tic *m* (pathol) tic

Ticiano, El Titian

tictac *m* tick-tock

tiempo *m* time; weather; (gram) tense; (*de un motor de combustión interna*) cycle; (*de una sinfonía*) (mus) movement; (mus) tempo; **darse buen tiempo** to have a good time; **de cuatro tiempos** (mach) four-cycle; **de dos tiempos** (mach) two-cycle; **de un tiempo a esta parte** for some time now; **el Tiempo** Father Time; **fuera de tiempo** untimely, at the wrong time; **hacer buen tiempo** to be clear; **mucho tiempo** a long time; **tiempo compartido** time-sharing; time-share; **tiempo complementario** (sport) overtime; **tiempo de devolución** *or* **respuesto** (compu) turnaround time; **tiempo de exposición** (phot) shutter speed; **tiempo libre** spare time; **tiempo muerto** (sport) time out; **tiempo real** (compu) real time; **tiempos de paz** peacetime; **tiempo suplementario** (com) overtime; **tomarse tiempo** to bide one's time

tienda *f* store, shop; tent; **ir de tiendas** to go shopping; **tienda de campaña** army tent; camping tent; **tienda de comestibles** *or* **alimentación** grocery store, grocery; **tienda de modas** ladies dress shop; **tienda de objetos de regalo** gift shop; **tienda de raya** (Mex) company store

tienta *f* cleverness; probe; (taur) testing the mettle of a young bull; **andar a tientas** to grope in the dark; feel one's way

tiento *m* touch; blind man's stick; ropewalker's pole; steady hand; care, caution; mahlstick; blow, hit; swig; **andarse con tiento** to watch one's step; **perder el tiento** to lose one's touch

tier•no -na *adj* tender; loving; tearful; soft

tierra *f* earth; ground; land; dirt; (elec) ground; **dar en tierra con** to upset, overthrow, ruin; **echar tierra a** to hush up; **en tierra, mar y aire** on land, on sea, and in the air; **irse a tierra** to topple, to collapse; **la tierra de nadie** (mil) no-man's-land; **tierra adentro** inland; **tierra de pan llevar** wheat land, cereal-growing land; **tierra firme** mainland; land, terra firma; **Tierra Firme** Spanish Main; **Tierra Santa** Holy Land; **tierras de labranza** farmland; **tierra y escombros** landfill; **tomar tierra** to land; to fine one's way around; **venir** or **venirse a tierra** to topple, to collapse; **ver tierras** to see the world, to go traveling

tierral *m* cloud of dust

tie•so -sa *adj* stiff; tight, taut, tense; stubborn; bold, enterprising; strong, well; stiff, stuck-up; **tenérselas tiesas a** *or* **con** to stand up to || **tieso** *adv* hard

ties•to -ta *adj* stiff; tight, taut, tense; stubborn || *m* flowerpot; (*pedazo roto*) postherd || **tiesto** *adv* hard

tiesura *f* stiffness

ti•fo -fa *adj* full, satiated || *m* typhus; **tifo de América** yellow fever; **tifo de Oriente** bubonic plague

tifón *m* waterspout; typhoon

tigra *f* tigress; (female) jaguar

tigre *m* tiger; (male) jaguar

tijera *f* scissors, shears; sawbuck; **buena tijera** good cutter; good eater; gossip; **tijeras** scissors, shears

tijeretear *tr* to snip, clip, cut; meddle with || *intr* to gossip

tila *f* linden tree; linden-blossom tea

tildar *tr* to put a tilde or dash over; erase, strike out; **tildar de** to brand as

tilde *m & f* tilde; accent mark; superior dash; blemish, flaw; censure || *f* jot, tittle

tiliche *m* (CAm, Mex) trinket

tiliche•ro -ra *mf* (CAm) peddler

tilín *m* ting-a-ling

tilo *m* linden tree; linden-blossom tea

tilo•so -sa *adj* (CAm) dirty, filthy

timar *tr* to snitch; swindle || *ref* to make eyes at each other

timba *f* game of chance; gambling den; (CAm, Mex) belly

timbal *m* kettledrum; (*pastel relleno*) casserole

timbrar *tr* to stamp

timbre *m* stamp, seal; tax stamp; stamp tax; deed of glory; (phonet & phys) timbre; **timbre de agua** watermark; **timbre fiscal** reve-

nue stamp; **timbre nasal** twang; **timbres** glockenspiel
timidez *f* shyness; timidity
tími•do -da *adj* timid, bashful
timo *m* theft, swindle, shakedown; lie; catch phrase
timón *m* (*del arado*) beam; rudder; (fig) helm; **timón de dirección** (aer) vertical rudder; **timón de profundidad** (aer) elevator
timonel *m* helmsman, steersman
timonera *f* (naut) pilot house, wheelhouse
timora•to -ta *adj* God-fearing; chicken-hearted
tímpano *m* eardrum; kettledrum
tina *f* large earthen jar; wooden vat; bathtub
tinaja *f* large earthen jar
tincazo *m* (Arg, Ecuad) fillip
tinglado *m* shed; intrigue, trick; (zool) leatherback
tinieblas *fpl* darkness
tino *m* feel (*for things*); good aim; knack; insight, wisdom; **coger el tino** to get the knack of it
tinta *f* ink; tint, hue; dyeing; **de buena tinta** on good authority; **tinta china** India ink; **tinta simpática** invisible ink
tinte *m* dye; dyeing; dyer's shop; (fig) coloring, false appearance
tinterillo *m* clerk, lawyer's clerk; pettifogger
tintero *m* inkstand, inkwell
tintín *m* clink; jingle
tintinear *intr* to clink; jingle
tin•to -ta *adj* red || *m* red table wine || *f* see **tinta**
tintorería *f* dyeing; dyeing establishment; dry-cleaning establishment
tintore•ro -ra *mf* dyer; dry cleaner
tintura *f* dye; dyeing; rouge; tincture; (fig) smattering; **tintura de tornasol** litmus, litmus solution; **tintura de yodo** iodine
tiña *f* ringworm; stinginess; **tiña podal** athlete's foot
tiño•so -sa *adj* scabby, mangy; stingy
tío *m* uncle; old man; guy, fellow; **el Tío Sam** (coll) Uncle Sam; **el Tío Tom** (pej) Uncle Tom; **tío abuelo** great-uncle, granduncle; **tíos** uncle and aunt; **tío segundo** cousin once removed
tiovivo *m* merry-go-round, carrousel
tipiadora *f* (*máquina*) typewriter; (*mujer*) typist
tipiar *tr & intr* to type, typewrite
tipicista *adj* regional, local
típi•co -ca *adj* typical; regional; quaint
tipismo *m* quaintness
tipista *mf* typist, typewriter
tiple *mf* soprano (*person*); treble-guitar player || *m* soprano (*voice*); treble guitar
tipo *m* type; (*de descuento, de interés, de cambio*) rate; shape, figure, build; fellow, guy, specimen; (compu) style; **tener buen tipo** to have a good figure; **tipo de cambio** exchange rate; **tipo de ensayo** *or* **prueba** eye-chart type; **tipo de impuesto** tax rate; **tipo de interés** interest rate; **tipo de letra** typeface; **tipo menudo** small print
tipografía *f* typography
típula *f* (ent) daddy-longlegs
tira *m* (Arg, Chile, Col) detective || *f* strip; **hecho tiras** (Chile) in rags; **tira emplástica** (Arg) court plaster; **tira proyectable** film strip; **tiras cómicas** comics, funnies; **tira y afloja** hard bargaining
tirabala *f* popgun
tirabuzón *m* corkscrew; corkscrew curl
tirada *f* throw; distance, stretch; time, period; printing; edition, issue; shooting party, hunting party; tirade; **de** *or* **en una tirada** at one stroke; **tirada aparte** reprint
tira•do -da *adj* dirt-cheap; (*letra*) cursive || *f* see **tirada**
tira•dor -dora *mf* shot, good shot || *m* knob; doorknob; pull chain; **tirador certero** sharpshooter; **tirador emboscado** sniper
tirafondo *m* wood screw
tiraje *m* draft; printing, edition
tiramira *f* long, narrow mountain range; (*de personas o cosas*) string; distance, stretch
tiranía *f* tyranny
tiráni•co -ca *adj* tyrannic(al)
tira•no -na *adj* tyrannous || *mf* tyrant
tirante *adj* tense, taut, tight; (fig) tense, strained || *m* (*de los arreos de una caballería*) trace; (*de una prenda*) shoulder strap; **tirantes** suspenders; shoulder straps
tirantez *f* tenseness, tautness, tightness; strain
tirar *tr* to throw, cast, fling; throw away; shoot, fire; (*alambre*) draw, pull, stretch; (*una línea*) draw; (*una coz, un pellizco*) give; print; attract; tear down, knock down; (phot) to print || *intr* to pull; last; appeal, have an appeal; (*una chimenea*) draw; (*a la derecha, a la izquierda*) bear, turn; **ir tirando** to get along; **tirar a** to shoot at; (*la espada*) handle; shade into; tend to; aspire to; **tirar de** to pull, pull on; (*una espada*) draw; attract; boast of being; **tira y afloja** give and take; hot and cold || *ref* to rush, throw oneself; give oneself over; lie down; serve time (in prison)
tirilla *f* neckband; **tirilla de bota** bootstrap; **tirilla de camisa** collarband
tiritar *intr* to shiver
tiro *m* throw; shot; charge, load; (*estampido*) report; rifle range; (*p.ej., de chimenea*) draft; (*de caballos*) team; (*de escalera*) flight; (*de las guarniciones*) trace; (*de un paño*) length; pull cord, pull chain; reach; hurt, damage; trick; theft; (min) shaft; (sport) drive, shot; (*alusión desfavorable*) shot; (fig) shot, marksman; **a tiro de fusil** within gunshot; **a tiro de piedra** within a stone's throw; **matar a tiros** to shoot to death; **ni a tiros** not for love nor money; **poner el tiro muy alto** to hitch one's wagon to a star; **tiro al blanco** target practice; **tiro al plato** trapshooting; **tiro al vuelo** trapshooting; **tiro con arco** archery; **tiro de la pesa** (sport) shot put

tirón *m* tyro, novice; jerk; tug, pull; **de un tirón** all at once; at a stretch
tirotear *tr* to snipe at, blaze away at || *ref* to fire at each other; bicker
tirria *f* dislike, grudge; **tener tirria a** to have it in for
tisana *f* tea, infusion
tísi•co -ca *adj* tubercular || *mf* tubercular person, tubercular
tisis *f* consumption, tuberculosis
titáni•co -ca *adj* colossal, titanic
titanio *m* titanium
tít. *abbr* **título**
títere *m* marionette, puppet; fixed idea; whipper-snapper, nincompoop; (*testaferro*) puppet, straw man, figurehead; **no dejar títere con cabeza** or **cara** to upset the applecart; **títeres** puppet show
titilar *tr* to titillate || *intr* to flutter, quiver; twinkle
titubear *intr* to stagger, totter; stammer, stutter; waver, hesitate
titular *m* bearer, holder; incumbent; headline || *f* capital letter || *tr* to title, entitle || *intr* to receive a title || *ref* to be called; call oneself
titulillo *m* running head
título *m* title; titled person; regulation; bond; certificate; diploma, degree, qualifications; headline; **a título de** as a, by way of, on the score of; **título de propiedad** title deed; **títulos** credentials
tiza *f* chalk
tiznar *tr* to soil with soot; spot, stain; to defame || *ref* to become soiled; get spotted or stained; (Arg, Chile, CAm) to get drunk
tizne *m & f* soot || *m* firebrand
tiznón *m* smudge, spot of soot
tizón *m* brand, firebrand; wheat smut; brand, dishonor
tizonear *intr* to stir up the fire
tlapalería *f* (Mex) paint store
toalla *f* towel; **toalla higiénica** sanitary napkin; **toalla refrescante** towelette; **toalla rusa** Turkish towel; **toalla sin fin** roller towel
toallero *m* towel rack
toar *tr* (naut) to tow
tobar *tr* (Col) to tow
tobera *f* (aerosp) nozzle
tobillera *f* anklet; (sport) ankle support; (coll) subdeb; (coll) flapper
tobillo *m* ankle
tobo *m* (Ven) bucket
tobogán *m* toboggan; chute, slide
toca *f* toque; headdress
tocadis•cos *m* (*pl* **-cos**) record player; **tocadiscos automático** record changer
toca•do -da *adj* (*echado a perder; medio loco*) touched; **tocado de la cabeza** touched in the head || *m* hairdo, coiffure; headdress
toca•dor -dora *mf* performer; player || *m* boudoir; dressing table; dressing case, toilet case
tocante *adj* touching; **tocante a** concerning, with reference to
tocar §73 *tr* to touch; touch on; feel; ring; toll; strike; come to know, suffer, feel; (*el cabello*) do; (*un tambor*) beat; (mus) to play; (paint) to touch up || *intr* to touch; **tocar a** to knock at; pertain to, concern; fall to the lot of; be the turn of; (*el fin*) approach; **tocar en** (*un puerto*) to touch at; (*tierra*) touch; touch on; approach, border on || *ref* to put one's hat on, cover one's head; touch each other; be related; make one's toilet; become mentally unbalanced; (*el sombrero*) tip; **tocárselas** to beat it
toca•yo -ya *mf* namesake
tochimbo *m* (Peru) smelting furnace
to•cho -cha *adj* rough, coarse, crude
tocino *m* bacon; salt pork
tocón *m* stump
tocuyo *m* (SAm) coarse cotton cloth
todavía *adv* still, yet; **todavía no** not yet
to•do -da *adj* all, whole, every; any || *m* whole; everything; **con todo** still, however; **del todo** wholly, entirely; **jugar el todo por el todo** to stake everything, shoot the works; **sobre todo** above all, especially; **todo el que** everybody who; **todo lo que** all that; **todos** all, everybody; **todos cuantos** all those who
todopodero•so -sa *adj* all-powerful, almighty
todoterreno *m* off-road four-wheel drive vehicle; (fam) jack-of-all-trades
tofu *m* tofu
toga *f* (academic) gown; (*disfraz*) toga
toldilla *f* poop, poop deck
toldería *f* (SAm) Indian camp, Indian village
toldo *m* awning; pride, haughtiness; (SAm) Indian hut
tole *m* hubbub, uproar; **tole tole** gossip, talk; **tomar el tole** to run away
tolerancia *f* tolerance; **por tolerancia** on sufferance
tolerar *tr* to tolerate
tolete *m* club, cudgel; raft; (Cuba) dunce
toletole *m* (Col) persistence, obstinacy; (Ven) merry life of a wanderer
tolla *f* quagmire; (Cuba) watering trough
tolon•dro -dra *adj* scatterbrained || *mf* scatterbrain || *m* bump, lump
tolva *f* hopper; chute
tolvanera *f* dust storm
tom. *abbr* **tomo**
toma *f* taking; seizure, capture; tap; intake; inlet; (elec) tap, outlet; (compu, elec) plug; (elec) terminal; (*de rapé*) pinch; **toma de datos** (compu) data capture; **toma de poder** take-over; **toma de posesión** installation, induction; inauguration; **toma de tierra** (aer) landing; (rad) ground connection; **toma directa** high gear
toma-corrien•te *m* or **toma-corrien•tes** *m* (*pl* **-tes**) (elec) current collector; (elec) tap, outlet; (elec) plug
tomadero *m* handle; intake, inlet
toma•dor -dora *mf* (com) drawee; thief; drinker, toper

tomar *tr* to take; get; seize; take on; (*un resfriado*) catch; (*p.ej., el desayuno*) have, eat; (*el café, un trago*) take, drink; **tomar a bien** to take in the right spirit; **tomar a mal** to take offense at; **tomarla con** to pick a quarrel with; have a grudge against; **tomar prestado** to borrow; **tomar sobre sí** to take upon oneself || *intr* to take, turn || *ref* to take; (*p.ej., el desayuno*) have, eat; (*el café*) take, drink; get rusty
tomate *m* tomato; (*en medias, calcetines, etc.*) tear, run
tomavis•tas *m* (*pl* **-tas**) movie camera; cameraman
tómbola *f* raffle, charity raffle
tomillo *m* thyme
tomo *m* volume; bulk, importance, consequence; **de tomo y lomo** of consequence; bulky and heavy
ton. *abbr* **tonelada**
ton *m* — **sin ton ni son** without rhyme or reason
tonada *f* air, melody, song; singsong; (Cuba) hoax; (*pronunciación particular*) (Arg, Chile) accent
tonel *m* cask, barrel
tonelada *f* (*unidad de peso; unidad de volumen; unidad de desplazamiento*) ton; (*medida de capacidad para el vino*) tun
tonelaje *m* tonnage
tonele•ro -ra *mf* barrelmaker, cooper
tonga *f* coat, layer; (Arg, Col) task; (Col) sleep; (Cuba) heap, pile
tongo *m* (coll) fix; **hubo tongo** it was fixed, it was rigged
tongonear *ref* to strut, swagger
tóni•co -ca *adj & m* tonic || *f* (mus) keynote
tonillo *m* singsong; (*pronunciación particular*) accent
tono *m* tone; tune; (mus) pitch; (mus) key; (*de un instrumento de bronce*) (mus) slide; **dar el tono** to set the standard; **darse tono** to put on airs; **de buen tono** stylish, elegant; **estar a tono** to be in style; **poner a tono** (*un motor de automóvil*) to tune up; **tono de marcar, tono de discado** dial tone; **tono mayor** (mus) major key; **tono menor** (mus) minor key
tonsila *f* tonsil
tonsilitis *f* tonsilitis
tonsurar *tr* to shear, clip
tontear *intr* to talk nonsense, act foolishly
tontería *f* foolishness, nonsense
ton•to -ta *adj* foolish, stupid, silly; **a tontas y a locas** wildly, recklessly; in disorder, haphazardly || *mf* fool, dolt; **tonto de capirote** blatant fool, utter fool
tonu•do -da *adj* (Arg) magnificent, showy, conceited
topacio *m* topaz
topar *tr* to butt; bump; run into, encounter || *intr* to butt; succeed; lie, be found; **topar con** *or* **en** to run into, encounter
tope *adj* (*precio*) top; (*fecha*) last || *m* butt; bumper; bump, collision; rub, difficulty; limit; scuffle; masthead; (Mex) speed bump; **al tope** *or* **a tope** end to end; flush; **estar hasta el tope** *or* **los topes** to be loaded to the gunwales; be fed up; **tope de puerta** doorstop
topera *f* molehill
topetada *f* butt
topetar *tr* to butt || *intr* to butt; **topetar con** to bump, bump into; to run across
topetón *m* butt; bump, collision, fender-bender
tópi•co -ca *adj* local || *m* topic; (med) external application
topinera *f* molehill; **beber como una topinera** to drink like a fish
topo *m* mole; blunderer; stumbler, awkward person
topografía *f* topography
toque *m* touch; (*de una campana*) tolling; (*del tambor*) beat; sound; knock; stroke; check, test; (*punto esencial*) gist; (paint) touch; (coll) blow; **dar un toque a** to put to the test; feel out, sound out; **toque a muerto** knell, toll; **toque de diana** reveille; **toque de queda** curfew; **toque de retreta** (mil) tattoo; **toque de tambor** drumbeat
torada *f* drove of bulls
tó•rax *m* (*pl* **-rax**) thorax
torbellino *m* whirlwind; (*persona bulliciosa*) harum-scarum
torcecuello *m* (orn) wryneck
torcedura *f* twist; sprain; dislocation
torcer **§74** *tr* to twist; bend; turn; sprain; (*la cara*) screw up; (*el tobillo*) wrench; turn; (*interpretar mal*) distort, misconstrue || *intr* to turn || *ref* to twist; bend; sprain, dislocate; turn sour; go crooked; fail
torci•do -da *adj* twisted; crooked; bent; skew; (*ojos*) cross; (*persona o conducta*) crooked; (Guat) unlucky || *f* wick, lampwick; curlpaper
tor•do -da *adj* dapple-gray || *mf* dapple-gray horse || *m* thrush; starling
torear *tr* (*toros*) to fight; banter, tease, string along || *intr* to fight bulls, be a bullfighter
toreo *m* bullfighting; (taur) performance
tore•ro -ra *adj* bullfighting || *mf* bullfighter
toril *m* (taur) bull pen
tormenta *f* storm; adversity, misfortune
tormento *m* torment, torture; anguish
tormento•so -sa *adj* stormy; (*barco*) stormridden
tormo *m* (*terrón*) divot
torna *f* return; dam; tap; **se han vuelto las tornas** the luck has changed; **volver las tornas** to give tit for tat
tornar *tr* to return, give back; turn, make || *intr* to return; turn; **tornar a** + *inf* verb + again, e.g., **tornó a abrir la puerta** he opened the door again || *ref* to turn, become
tornasol *m* sunflower; litmus; iridescence
tornasola•do -da *adj* changeable, iridescent
tornavía *m* (rr) turntable
torna•voz *m* (*pl* **-voces**) sounding board; **hacer tornavoz** to cup one's hands to one's mouth
tornear *tr* to turn, turn up || *intr* to go around; tourney; muse, meditate

torneo *m* tourney; match, tournament; **torneo radiofónico** quiz program

tornillo *m* (*cilindro que entra en la tuerca*) screw; (*clavo con resalto helicoidal*) bolt; (*instrumento con dos mandíbulas*) vise; (mil) desertion; (CAm, Ven) screw tree; **apretar los tornillos a** to put the screws on; **tener flojos los tornillos** to have a screw loose; **tornillo de mariposa** *or* **de orejas** thumbscrew; **tornillo de presión** setscrew; **tornillo para metales** machine screw

torniquete *m* (*para contener hemorragias*) tourniquet; (*torno para cerrar un paso*) turnstile; **dar torniquete a** to twist the meaning of

torno *m* turn, revolution; (*máquina simple que consiste en un cilindro que gira sobre su eje*) winch, windlass; (*de alfarero*) potter's wheel; (*instrumento con dos mandíbulas*) vise; (*máquina herramienta que sirve para labrar metal o madera*) lathe; (*de coche*) brake; (*de un río*) bend, turn; revolving server; **en torno a** *or* **de** around; **torno de alfarero** potter's wheel; **torno de banco** bench vise; **torno de hilar** spinning wheel

toro *m* bull; **asir al toro por las astas** to take the bull by the horns; **los toros** bullfighting; **toro corrido** smart fellow; **toros** bullfight

torón *m* strand

toronja *f* grapefruit

toronjo *m* grapefruit (*tree*)

torpe *adj* slow, heavy; clumsy, awkward; stupid; lewd; crude, ugly; heavy-handed

torpedear *tr* to torpedo

torpedero *m* (baseball) shortstop

torpedo *m* torpedo; touring car

torpeza *f* torpidity, slowness; clumsiness, awkwardness; stupidity; lewdness; turpitude; crudeness, ugliness

torrar *tr* to toast

torre *f* tower; watchtower; (*en el ajedrez*) castle, rook; **torre de apartamentos** high-rise; **torre de control** control tower; **torre del homenaje** donjon, keep; **torre de lanzamiento** launching tower; **torre de marfil** (fig) ivory tower; **torre de perforación** oil rig, drilling rig; **torre de vigía** (naut) crow's nest; **torre de vigilancia** fire tower; **torre maestra** donjon, keep; **torre reloj** clock tower; **torres gemelas** twin towers

torreja *f* (dial, Am) French toast

torrentada *f* flash flood

torrente *m* torrent

torreón *m* (archit) turret

torreta *f* (nav) turret

tórri•do -da *adj* torrid

torrija *f* French toast

torta *f* cake; (typ) font; slap; **ser tortas y pan pintado** to be a cinch; **torta a la plancha** hot cake, griddle cake

torticolis *m* or **tortícolis** *m* wryneck, stiff neck

tortilla *f* omelet; (CAm, Mex) tortilla (*cornmeal cake*); **tortilla a la española** potato omelet; **tortilla a la francesa** plain omelet; **tortilla de tomate** Spanish omelet

tórtola *f* turtledove

tortolito *m* (coll) lover, lovebird

tórtolo *m* (coll) lovebird

tortuga *f* tortoise, turtle; **tortuga boba** loggerhead; **tortuga de agua dulce** terrapin

tortuo•so -sa *adj* winding; (fig) devious

tortura *f* torture

torturar *tr* to torture

tor•vo -va *adj* grim, stern

tos *f* cough; **tos ferina** *or* **convulsa** whooping cough

tosca•no -na *adj* Tuscan ‖ **la Toscana** Tuscany

tos•co -ca *adj* coarse, rough; uncouth

toser *intr* to cough

tósigo *m* poison; sorrow

tosiguero *m* poison ivy

tosquedad *f* coarseness, roughness; uncouthness

tostada *f* piece of toast; toast; **dar** *or* **pegar la tostada** *or* **una tostada a** to cheat, trick; **tostadas** toast

tosta•do -da *adj* brown; tan, sunburned ‖ *m* toasting; roasting ‖ *f* see **tostada**

tostador *m* toaster, roaster

tostar §61 *tr & ref* to toast; roast; tan, burn

tostón *m* roasted chickpea; toast dipped in olive oil; roast pig; scorched food

total *adj & m* total ‖ *adv* in a word

totalidad *f* totality; entirety; **en su totalidad** in its entirety

totalitario *adj* totalitarian

totémi•co -ca *adj* —**pilar totémico** totem pole

tóxi•co -ca *adj & m* toxic

toxicomanía *f* drug addiction

toxicóma•no -na *adj* drug-addicted ‖ *mf* drug addict

tozu•do -da *adj* stubborn

tpo. *abbr* **tiempo**

traba *f* bond, tie; clasp, lock; hobble, clog; obstacle, hindrance

traba•do -da *adj* tied, fastened; joined, connected; robust, sinewy; (*sílaba*) checked; tongue-tied; (*ojos*) (Col) cross

trabaja•do -da *adj* overworked, worn-out; strained, forced, labored; busy; elaborate, carefully thought-out

trabaja•dor -dora *adj* working; industrious, hard-working ‖ *mf* worker, toiler; **trabajador autónomo, independiente** *or* **por su cuenta propia** self-employed worker; **trabajador no cualificado** unskilled worker ‖ *m* workman, workingman ‖ *f* workingwoman

trabajar *tr* to work; till, bother, disturb; (*a una persona*) work, drive ‖ *intr* to work; strain; warp; **trabajar en** or **por** to strive to ‖ *ref* to strive, exert oneself

trabajo *m* work; workmanship; trouble; (*en contraposición de capital*) labor; **costar trabajo** + *inf* to be hard to + *inf;* **trabajo a destajo** piecework; **trabajo a domicilio** homework; **trabajo a jornal** timework; **tra-**

bajo de campo field work; **trabajo de esclavos** slave labor; **trabajo de menores** child labor; **trabajo de oficina** clerical work; **trabajo de taller** shopwork; **trabajo en tiempo compartido** time-sharing; **trabajo preliminar, trabajo de base** groundwork; **trabajos** hardships, tribulations; **trabajos forzados** or **forzosos** hard labor, penal labor

trabajoadicto *m* (coll) workaholic

trabajo•so -sa *adj* arduous, laborious; (*maganto*) wan, languid; (*falto de espontaneidad*) labored; unpleasant, annoying

trabalen•guas *m* (*pl* **-guas**) tongue twister, jawbreaker

trabar *tr* to join, unite; catch, seize; fasten; fetter; lock; begin; (*una batalla*) join; (*una conversación, amistad*) strike up || *intr* to take hold || *ref* to become entangled; jam; to foul; **trabársele a uno la lengua** to become tongue-tied

trabe *f* beam

trabilla *f* gaiter strap; belt loop; end stitch

trabuco *m* blunderbuss; popgun

trac *m* stage fright

tracale•ro -ra *adj* (CAm, Mex, W-I) cheating, tricky || *mf* (CAm, Mex, W-I) cheat, trickster

tracción *f* traction; **doble tracción** four-wheel drive; **tracción delantera** front-wheel drive; **tracción total, integral** *or* **a las cuatro ruedas** four-wheel drive; **tracción trasera** rear-wheel drive

tractor *m* tractor; **tractor de oruga** caterpillar tractor

tradición *f* tradition

tradicionista *mf* folklorist

traducción *f* translation; **traducción automática** *or* **mecánica** machine translation; **traducción directa** decoding (*translation from a language in which the translators are less skilled than they are in the language into which they are translating*); **traducción inversa** encoding (*translation into a language in which the translators are less skilled than they are in the language from which they are translating*); **traducción simultánea** simultaneous translation

traducir §19 *tr* to translate; to convey (*e.g., one's sentiments*) || *ref* — **traducirse en** to result in, to lead to

traduc•tor -tora *mf* translator

traer §75 *tr* to bring; bring on; draw, pull; make, keep; wear; have, carry; **traer a mal traer** to abuse, mistreat || *intr* — **traer y llevar** to gossip || *ref* to dress; behave; **traérselas** to get worse and worse, cause a lot of trouble

tráfago *m* traffic, trade; toil, drudgery

trafa•gón -gona *adj* hustling, lively; slick, tricky || *mf* hustler, live wire

traficante *mf* dealer, merchant

traficar §73 *intr* to deal, trade, traffic; travel about

tráfico *m* trade; traffic

tragaderas *fpl* gullibility; tolerance; **tener buenas tragaderas** to be too gullible

tragalda•bas *mf* (*pl* **-bas**) glutton; easy mark

tragale•guas *mf* (*pl* **-guas**) (coll) great walker

traga•luz *m* (*pl* **-luces**) skylight, bull's-eye; cellar window

tragamone•das *m* (*pl* **-das**) or **tragape•rras** *m* (*pl* **-rras**) slot machine

tragar §44 *tr* to swallow; swallow up; gulp down; (*a duras penas*) to force down; (*creer fácilmente*) swallow; overlook; **no poder tragar** to not be able to stomach || *intr & ref* to swallow

tragasable *m* sword swallower

tragavenado *f* (SAm) anaconda

tragaviro•tes *m* (*pl* **-tes**) stuffed shirt

tragedia *f* tragedy

trági•co -ca *adj* tragic(al) || *m* tragedian

trago *m* swallow; swig; misfortune; **a tragos** slowly

tra•gón -gona *adj* gluttonous || *mf* glutton

traición *f* treachery, betrayal; (*delito contra la patria*) treason; treacherous act; **alta traición** high treason; **a traición** treacherously; **hacer traición a** to betray

traicionar *tr* to betray

traicione•ro -ra *adj* treacherous; treasonable || *mf* traitor

traída *f* conveyance, transfer; (Guat) sweetheart; **traída de aguas** water supply

traí•do -da *adj* worn, threadbare || *f* see **traída**

trai•dor -dora *adj* treacherous; treasonable || *mf* traitor; betrayer || *m* villain || *f* traitoress

traílla *f* leash; road scraper

traje *m* suit; clothes; dress; gown; **cortar un traje a** to gossip about; **traje a la medida** suit made to order; **traje de baño** bathing suit, swimsuit; swimming trunks; **traje de calle** street clothes; **traje de ceremonia** *or* **de etiqueta** dress suit; full dress; evening clothes; **traje de faena** (mil) fatigue clothes; **traje de luces** bullfighter's costume; **traje de malla** tights; **traje de montar** riding habit; **traje de neoprene** *or* **neopreno** wet suit; **traje de novia** wedding dress; **traje de paisano** civilian clothes; **traje hecho** ready-made suit; **traje largo** *or* **de gala** evening dress; **traje sastre** lady's tailor-made suit; **traje serio** formal dress; **vestir su primer traje largo** to come out, make one's debut

trajear *tr* to dress, clothe

trajín *m* carrying, transfer, conveyance; going and coming; bustle, commotion

trajinar *tr* to carry, convey; (Arg, Chile) to poke into; (Arg, Chile) to deceive; (Pan) to annoy || *intr* to bustle around

tralla *f* lash, whiplash, whipcord

trallazo *m* whiplash

trama *f* weft, woof; plot, scheme, machination; (*de un drama o novela*) plot

tramar *tr* to weave; plot, scheme; (*un enredo*) hatch (*a plot*)

trambucar §73 *intr* (Col, Ven) to be shipwrecked; (Col, Ven) to go out of one's mind

tramitación *f* transaction, negotiation; procedure, steps; **tramitación automática de datos** data processing

tramitar *tr* to transact, negotiate

trámite *m* step, procedure; proceeding; transaction

tramo *m* tract; stretch; (*de una escalera*) flight; (*de un puente*) span; (*de un canal entre dos esclusas*) level

tramontana *f* north; north wind; pride, haughtiness

tramoya *f* stage machinery; scheme

tramoyista *adj* scheming, tricky || *mf* schemer, impostor || *m* stagehand

trampa *f* trap; trap door; gimmick; (*de un mostrador*) flap; (*de los pantalones*) fly; **armar una trampa a** to lay a trap for; **trampa explosiva** (mil) booby trap

trampear *tr* to trick, swindle || *intr* to cheat; manage to get along

trampilla *f* peephole in the floor; (*de los pantalones*) fly; (*de un secreter*) top, lid; (*de una mesa*) leaf, hinged leaf

trampolín *m* diving board; springboard; ski jump

trampo•so -sa *adj* tricky, crooked || *mf* cheat, swindler

tranca *f* beam, pole; crossbar; (Arg, Chile) drunk, spree; (P-R) dollar; **a trancas y barrancas** through fire and water

trancar §73 *tr* to bar || *intr* to stride along

trance *m* crisis; peril; trance; **a todo trance** at any cost; **último trance** (*de la vida*) last stage, end

tranco *m* long stride; threshold

tranquera *f* palisade, fence

tranquilamente *adv* calmly, peacefully

tranquilidad *f* tranquillity, peace

tranquilizante *adj* reassuring, soothing, calming; (med) tranquilizing || *m* tranquilizer

tranquilizar §60 *tr, intr & ref* to tranquilize, calm down

tranquilla *f* feeler

tranquillo *m* knack

tranqui•lo -la *adj* tranquil, calm

transacción *f* settlement, compromise; transaction

transaéreo *m* airliner

transar *tr* to settle || *intr* to yield, give in, compromise

transatlánti•co -ca *adj & m* transatlantic

transbordador *m* ferry; **transbordador espacial** space shuttle

transbordar *tr* to transship; transfer || *intr* to transfer, change trains

transbordo *m* transshipment; transfer

transcribir §83 *tr* to transcribe

transcripción *f* transcription

transcurrir *intr* to pass, elapse

transcurso *m* course (*of time*)

transepto *m* transept

transeúnte *adj* transient || *mf* transient; passer-by

transexual *adj & mf* transsexual

transferencia *f* transfer

transferir §68 *tr* to transfer; postpone

transformador *m* transformer

transformar *tr* to transform || *ref* to transform, be transformed

transformista *mf* quick-change artist

tránsfuga *mf* turncoat; fugitive

transfusión *f* transfusion; **transfusión de sangre** transfusion, blood transfusion

transgredir §1 *tr* to transgress

transgresión *f* transgression

transi•do -da *adj* overcome, paralyzed; mean, cheap, stingy

transigencia *f* compromise; compromising

transigente *adj* compromising

transigir §27 *tr* (law) to settle out of court || *intr* to compromise, give in, give way; **transigir con** to put up with, tolerate

transistor *m* transistor

transistorizar §60 *tr* transistorize

transitable *adj* passable, practicable

transitar *intr* to go, walk; to travel

transiti•vo -va *adj* transitive

tránsito *m* transit; traffic; stop; passage; transfer

transito•rio -ria *adj* transitory

translúci•do -da *adj* translucent

transmisión *f* transmission; transfer; broadcast; broadcasting; (aut, biol, med) transmission; **transmisión automática** automatic transmission; **transmisión de datos** (compu) data transmission; **transmisión del pensamiento** thought transference

transmisor *m* transmitter; **transmisor de órdenes** (naut) engine-room telegraph

transmitir *tr & intr* to transmit

transmudar *tr* to transfer; persuade, convince

transmutar *tr, intr & ref* to transmute

transparecer §22 *intr* to show through

transparencia *f* transparency; slide

transparentar *ref* to show through

transparente *adj* transparent || *m* curtain, window curtain; **transparente de resorte** window blind or shade

transpirar *intr* to transpire; (*dejarse conocer una cosa secreta*) transpire; perspire, sweat

transplantar *tr* to transplant

transponer §54 *tr* to transpose; disappear behind || *ref* (*ocultarse detrás del horizonte*) to set; get sleepy

transportar *tr* to transport; (mus) to transpose

transporte *m* transport; transportation; (aer & naut) transport; **transporte colectivo** *or* **público** public transportation; **transporte de tropas** troop carrier

transportista *mf* transport worker

tranvía *m* trolley, trolley car, streetcar; **tranvía de sangre** horsecar

tranzar §60 *tr* to cut off, rip off; plait, braid

trapacear *tr* to chear, swindle
trapacería *f* cheating, swindling
trapace•ro -ra *adj* cheating, swindling ‖ *mf* cheat, swindler
trapajo *m* rag, tatter
trápala *adj* chattering; cheating ‖ *mf* chatterbox; cheat ‖ *m* loquacity ‖ *f* noise, uproar; (*del trote de un caballo*) clatter; cheating
trapear *tr* to mop
trapecio *m* (geom) trapezoid; (sport) trapeze
trapecista *mf* trapeze performer
trape•ro -ra *mf* ragpicker; junk dealer
trapiche *m* sugar mill; olive press; ore crusher
trapicheo *m* (coll) crooked deal, monkey business
trapien•to -ta *adj* raggedy, in rags
trapío *m* flipness, pertness; (*del toro de lidia*) spirit
trapisonda *f* brawl, row; scheming
trapisondista *mf* schemer
trapo *m* rag; (naut) canvas, sails; bullfighter's bright-colored cape; (*de la muleta*) cloth; **a todo trapo** full sail; **poner como un trapo** to rake over the coals; **sacar los trapos a la colada, a relucir** *or* **al sol** to wash one's dirty linen in public; **soltar el trapo** to burst out crying, to burst out laughing; **trapo de cocina** dishtowel; **trapo del polvo** *or* **de sacudir** dust cloth; **trapos** rags, duds; **trapos de cristianar** Sunday best
trapo•so -sa *adj* raggedy, in rags
tráquea *f* trachea, windpipe
traquea•do -da *adj* (*sendero*) (Arg) beaten
traquear *tr* to shake, rattle; fool with ‖ *intr* to crackle; rattle, chatter
traqueo *m* shake, rattle, chatter
traquetear *tr & intr* to rattle, jerk
tras *prep* after; behind; **tras de** behind; in addition to
trasatlánti•co -ca *adj & m var of* **transatlántico**
trasbordador *m var of* **transbordador**
trasbordar *tr & intr var of* **trasbordar**
trasbordo *m var of* **transbordo**
trascendencia *f* penetration, keenness; importance
trascendente *adj* penetrating; important
trascender §51 *tr* to go into, dig up ‖ *intr* to smell; come to be known, leak out
trascendi•do -da *adj* keen, perspicacious
trascocina *f* scullery
trascorral *m* backyard; backside
trascribir §83 *tr var of* **transcribir**
trascripción *f var of* **transcripción**
trascuarto *m* back room
trascurrir *intr var of* **transcurrir**
trascurso *m var of* **transcurso**
trasegar §66 *tr* to upset, turn topsy-turvy; decant, draw off
trase•ro -ra *adj* back, rear ‖ *m* buttock, rump
trasferir §68 *tr var of* **transferir**
trasformador *m var of* **transformador**
trasformar *tr & intr var of* **transformar**
trásfuga *mf var of* **tránsfuga**
trasfusión *f var of* **transfusión**
trasgo *m* goblin, hobgoblin; imp
trashojar *tr* to leaf through
trashumante *adj* nomadic, migrating
trasiego *m* upset, disorder; decantation
traslación *f* (astr) movement, passage; (math) translation
trasladar *tr* to transfer; postpone; copy, transcribe; transmit; move; (eccl, math) translate ‖ *intr* to go; move
traslado *m* transfer; copy, transcript; moving; (eccl) translation; **traslado de jurisdicción** (law) change of venue
traslapar *tr, intr & ref* to overlap
traslapo *m* lap, overlap
traslúci•do -da *adj var of* **translúcido**
traslucir §45 *tr* to guess ‖ *intr* to leak out ‖ *ref* to be translucent; leak out
traslumbrar *tr* to dazzle ‖ *ref* to be dazzled; vanish
trasluz *m* diffused light; glint, gleam; **al trasluz** against the light
trasmisión *f var of* **transmisión**
trasmisor *m var of* **transmisor**
trasmitir *tr & intr var of* **transmitir**
trasmóvil *m* (Col) mobile unit, radio pickup
trasmudar *tr var of* **transmudar**
trasmundo *m* afterlife, future life
trasmutar *tr, intr & ref var of* **transmutar**
trasnocha•do -da *adj* stale; haggard, rundown; hackneyed ‖ *f* last night; sleepless night; (mil) night attack
trasnocha•dor -dora *mf* night owl
trasnochar *tr* (*un problema*) to sleep over ‖ *intr* to spend the night; spend a sleepless night; stay up late
trasoír §48 *tr* to hear wrong
traspapelar *tr* to mislay ‖ *ref* to become mislaid
trasparecer §22 *intr var of* **transparecer**
trasparencia *f var of* **transparencia**
trasparente *adj & m var of* **transparente**
traspasar *tr* to cross, cross over; send; transfer; move; pierce, transfix; pain, grieve ‖ *ref* to go too far
traspié *m* slip, stumble; trip
traspirar *intr var of* **transpirar**
trasplantar *tr var of* **transplantar**
trasponer §54 *tr & ref var of* **transponer**
trasportar *tr var of* **transportar**
trasporte *m var of* **transporte**
trasportista *mf var of* **transportista**
traspunte *m* (theat) callboy
traspuntín *m* flap seat, folding seat, jump seat
trasquilar *tr* to crop, lop; (*las ovejas*) shear; curtail
trastazo *m* whack, blow
traste *m* fret; **dar al traste con** to throw away, ruin, spoil
trastera *f* attic, junk room
trastienda *f* back room
trasto *m* piece of furniture; piece of junk; good-for-nothing; **trastos** tools, implements, utensils; arms, weapons; junk; muleta and sword

trastornar *tr* to upset; overturn; disturb; perplex; daze, make dizzy; persuade
trastorno *m* upset; disturbance
trastrocar §81 *tr* to turn around, reverse, change
trasudor *m* cold sweat
trasueño *m* blurred dream, vague recollection
trasuntar *tr* to copy; abstract, sum up
trasunto *m* copy; record; likeness
trasvasar *tr* to decant; to transfer; (compu) to download
trasverter §51 *intr* to run over, overflow
trasvolar §61 *tr* to fly over
trata *f* traffic, trade, slave trade; **trata de blancas** white slavery; **trata de esclavos** slave trade
tratado *m* (*escrito, libro*) treatise; (*convenio entre gobiernos*) treaty; agreement
tratamiento *m* treatment; title; handling; **apear el tratamiento** to leave off the title
tratante *mf* dealer, trader
tratar *tr* to handle; deal with; treat; **tratar a uno de** to address someone as; charge someone with being || *intr* to deal; treat; try; **tratar de** to deal with; treat of; come in contact with; try to || *ref* to deal; behave; (*bien o mal*) live; **tratarse de** to deal with; be a question of
trate•ro -ra *mf* (Chile) pieceworker
trato *m* treatment; deal, agreement; manner; business; title; friendly relations; **tener buen trato** to be very nice, be very pleasant; **trato colectivo** collective bargaining; **trato doble** double-dealing; **¡trato hecho!** it's a deal!
traumatismo *m* traumatism; **traumatismo cervical** whiplash injury
traumatología *f* orthopedics; orthopedic department
través *m* bend, bias, turn; reverse, misfortune; (naut) beam; **al** *or* **a través de** through, across; **dar al través con** to do away with; **mirar de través** to squint; look at out of the corner of one's eye
travesaño *m* crosspiece; (*de cama*) bolster; (*p.ej., de una sila*) rung
travesear *intr* to romp, carry on; sparkle, be witty; lead a wild life
travesía *f* crossing, voyage; crossroad; distance, passage; cross wind; (Arg, Bol) wasteland; (Chile) west wind
travesti•do -da *adj & mf* transvestite
travestismo *m* transvestism
travesura *f* prank, antic, caper; mischief; sparkle, wit; slick trick
traviesa *f* crossing, voyage; rafter; side bet; (rr) tie
travie•so -sa *adj* cross; keen, shrewd; restless, fidgety; naughty, mischievous; debauched
trayecto *m* journey, passage, course; stretch, run
trayectoria *f* trajectory; path
traza *f* plan, design; scheme; means; appearance; mark, trace; footprint; streak, trait; **tener trazas de** to show signs of; look like
trazar §60 *tr* to plan, design; outline; trace; (*una línea*) draw; lay out, plot
trazo *m* line, stroke; trace; outline
trebejo *m* implement; chessman
trébol *m* clover; (*naipe*) club; **tréboles** (*palo de la baraja norteamericana*) clubs
trece *adj & pron* thirteen || *m* thirteen; (*en las fechas*) thirteenth; **estarse, mantenerse** *or* **seguir en sus trece** to stand firm
trecea•vo -va *adj & m* thirteenth
trecho *m* stretch; while; **a trechos** at intervals
tregua *f* truce; respite, letup
treinta *adj & pron* thirty || *m* thirty; (*en las fechas*) thirtieth
treinta•vo -va *adj & m* thirtieth
tremar *intr* to tremble, shake
tremen•do -da *adj* frightful, terrible, tremendous; (*muy grande*) tremendous
trementina *f* turpentine
tremer *intr* to tremble, shake
tremolar *tr & intr* to wave
tren *m* (*de coches o vagones; de ondas*) train; outfit, equipment; following, retinue; show, pomp; (*de la vida*) way; **tren aerodinámico de lujo** (rr) streamliner; **tren ascendente** (rr) up train; **tren correo** (rr) mail train; **tren de aterrizaje** (aer) landing gear; **tren de laminadores** rolling mill; **tren de lavado** car wash; **tren de mercancías** *or* **cargo** freight train; **tren de mudadas** moving company; **tren descendente** (rr) down train; **tren de viajeros** passenger train; **tren de vida** way of life, lifestyle; **tren ómnibus** (rr) local train; **tren rápido** (rr) flyer
treno *m* dirge
trenza *f* braid, plait; tress; (*p.ej., de ajos*) string; **en trenzas** with her hair down
trenzar §60 *tr* to braid, plait || *intr* to caper; prance
trepa•dor -dora *adj* climbing || *mf* climber || *f* (bot) climber
trepar *tr* to climb; drill, bore || *intr* to climb; **trepar por** to climb up || *ref* to lean back
trepidar *intr* to shake, vibrate; (Chile) to hesitate, waver
tres *adj & pron* three; **las tres** three o'clock || *m* three; (*en las fechas*) third
trescien•tos -tas *adj & pron* three hundred || **trescientos** *m* three hundred
tresillo *m* ombre; three-piece living-room suite; (mus) triplet
tresnal *m* (agr) shock
treta *f* trick, scheme; (*del esgrimidor*) feint
treza•vo -va *adj & m* thirteenth
triángulo *m* triangle
triar §77 *tr* to sort
tribu *f* tribe
tribuna *f* tribune, rostrum, platform; grandstand; (*en la iglesia*) gallery; **tribuna de la prensa** press box; **tribuna del órgano** (mus) organ loft; **tribuna de los acusados** (law) dock
tribunal *m* tribunal, court; **el Tribunal Supremo** the Supreme Court; **tribunal de apelación** appellate court; **tribunal militar**

court martial; military court; **tribunal tutelar de menores** juvenile court
tributar *tr* (*contribuciones, impuestos, etc.*) to pay; (*admiración, gratitud, etc.*) render
tributario-ria *adj* tributary; tax; **ser tributario de** to be indebted to || *m* tributary
tributo *m* tribute; tax
tricornio *m* tricorn, three-cornered hat
trifocal *adj* trifocal
trifulca *f* wrangle, squabble
trigési•mo -ma *adj & m* thirtieth
trigo *m* wheat; (slang) dough, money; **trigo entero** whole wheat; **trigo sarraceno** buckwheat
trigonometría *f* trigonometry
trigue•ño -ña *adj* swarthy, olive-skinned
trilla *f* threshing
trilla•do -da *adj* (*sendero*) beaten; trite, commonplace
trilladora *f* threshing machine
trillar *tr* to thresh; mistreat; frequent
trilli•zo -za *mf* triplet
trillón *m* British trillion; quintillion (*in U.S.A.*)
trilogía *f* trilogy
trimestral *adj* quarterly
trimestre *m* quarter
trinado *m* trill, warble
trinar *intr* to trill, warble, quaver; get angry
trinca *f* trinity
trincar §73 *tr* to bind, lash, tie fast; crush; (slang) to kill || *intr* to take a drink
trinchar *tr* to carve, slice
trinchera *f* cut; trench; trench coat
trineo *m* sleigh, sled
Trinidad *f* Trinity
trino *m* trill
trinquete *m* pawl, ratchet; (naut) foresail
trin•quis *m* (*pl* **-quis**) drink, swig
trío *m* sorting; trio; (mus) trio
tripa *f* gut, intestine; belly; (*del cigarro*) filler; **hacer de tripas corazón** to pluck up courage
triple *adj & m* triple
triplica•do -da *adj & m* triplicate; **por triplicado** in triplicate
triplicar §73 *tr* to triplicate || *intr* to treble
trípode *m* tripod
tríptico *m* triptych
tripu•do -da *adj* big-bellied, potbellied
tripulación *f* crew
tripulante *m* crew member
tripular *tr* to man; fit out, equip
trique *m* crack, swish; **a cada trique** at every turn; **triques** (Mex) tools, implements
triquiñuela *f* chicanery, subterfuge
triquitraque *m* clatter; firecracker
tris *m* crackle; shave, inch; trice
trisar *tr* (Chile) to crack, chip || *intr* to chirp
triscar §73 *tr* to mix; (*una sierra*) set || *intr* to stamp the feet; romp, frisk around; (Col) to gossip
trismo *m* lockjaw
triste *adj* sad; dismal, gloomy; (*despreciable, ridículo*) sorry
tristeza *f* sadness; gloominess
tris•tón -tona *adj* wistful, melancholy
tritón *m* eft, newt, triton; (*hombre experto en la natación*) merman
trituradora *f* crushing machine; shredder
triturar *tr* to grind, crush; abuse; shred (*documents*)
triunfal *adj* triumphal
triunfante *adj* triumphant
triunfar *intr* to triumph; trump; **triunfar de** to triumph over; trump
triunfo *m* triumph; trump; **sin triunfo** no trump
trivial *adj* trivial; trite, commonplace; (*sendero*) beaten
trivialidad *f* triviality; triteness
triza *f* shred; **hacer trizas** to tear to pieces
trizar §60 *tr* to tear to pieces
trocar §81 *tr* to exchange, swap; barter; confuse, twist, distort || *intr* to swap || *ref* to change; change seats
trocha *f* trail, narrow path; gauge
trofeo *m* trophy; victory
troj *f* or **troje** *f* granary; olive bin
trole *m* trolley pole
trolebús *m* trolley bus, trackless trolley
tromba *f* (*de polvo, agua, etc.*) whirl, column; whirlwind; **en tromba** en masse; **tromba marina** waterspout; **tromba terrestre** tornado
trombón *m* trombone; **trombón de varas** slide trombone
trombosis *f* thrombosis
trompa *f* (*del elefante*) trunk; waterspout; top; nozzle; (anat) duct, tube; (mus) horn; (Col, Chile) cowcatcher; **trompa de armonía** French horn; **trompa de caza** hunting horn; **trompa de Eustaquio** Eustachian tube; **trompa de Falopio** Fallopian tube
trompada *f* bump, collision; punch
trompar *intr* to spin a top
trompeta *f* trumpet; bugle, clarion; good-for-nothing; drunkenness
trompetear *intr* to trumpet, sound the trumpet
trompetilla *f* ear trumpet; Bronx cheer
trompicar §44 *tr* to trip, make stumble || *intr* to stumble
trompicón *m* stumble
trompiza *f* fist fight
trompo *m* (*juguete*) top; (*en el ajedrez*) man; (*buque malo y pesado*) tub
tronada *f* thunderstorm
tronar §61 *tr* (Mex) to shoot || *intr* to thunder; fail, collapse; **por lo que pueda tronar** just in case
troncar §44 *tr* to cut off the head of; (*un escrito*) cut, shorten
troncha *f* slice; cinch
tronchar *tr* to smash, split; chop off
tronco *m* (*del cuerpo, del árbol, de una familia, del ferrocarril*) trunk; (*leño*) log; (*de caballerías*) team; sap, fathead; **estar hecho un tronco** to be knocked out; be sound asleep

tronera *m* madcap, roisterer || *f* embrasure, loophole; louver; (*de la mesa de billar*) pocket
tronido *m* thunderclap
trono *m* throne
tronquista *m* driver, teamster
tronzar §60 *tr* to shatter, break to pieces; pleat; wear out
tropa *f* troop; herd, drove; **en tropa** straggling, without formation; **la tropa** the troops; **tropas de asalto** shock troops, storm troops
tropecien•tos -tas *adj* (coll) hundreds of, umpteen
tropel *m* crowd, throng; rush, hurry; jumble; **de** *or* **en tropel** in a mad rush
tropelía *f* mad rush; outrage
tropero *m* (Arg) cowboy
tropezar §18 *tr* to strike || *intr* to stumble; slip, blunder; **tropezar con** *or* **en** to stumble over, trip over; run into; come upon
trope•zón -zona *adj* stumbling || *m* stumble; stumbling block; **a tropezones** by fits and starts; falteringly; **dar un tropezón** to stumble, trip
tropical *adj* tropic(al)
trópico *m* tropic
tropiezo *m* stumble; stumbling block; slip, blunder, fault; obstacle; quarrel
tropilla *f* (Arg, Urug) drove of horses following a leading mare
troposfera *f* troposphere
troquel *m* die
trotaconven•tos *f* (*pl* **-tos**) procuress, bawd
trotamun•dos *m* (*pl* **-dos**) globetrotter
trotar *intr* to trot; to hustle
trote *m* trot; chore; **al trote** right away; **para todo trote** for everyday wear; **trote de perro** jog trot
trotona *f* chaperone
troupe *f* troupe
trovador *m* troubadour
trovadores•co -ca *adj* troubadour
trovero *m* trouvère
Troya *f* Troy; **ahí fué Troya** it's a shambles; **¡arda Troya!** come what may!
troya•no -na *adj & mf* Trojan
troza *f* log
trozar §60 *tr* to break to pieces; (*un tronco*) cut into logs
trozo *m* piece, fragment; block; excerpt, selection
trucha *f* trout
truco *m* contrivance, device; trick, gimmick; pocketing of ball; **truco de naipes** card trick; **trucos** pool
truculen•to -ta *adj* truculent
trueno *m* thunder, thunderclap; shot, report; rake, roué; **trueno gordo** finale (*of fireworks*); big scandal; **truenos** (Ven) heavy shoes
trueque *m* barter; exchange, swap; trade-in; **a trueque de** in exchange for; **trueques** (Col) change
trufa *f* truffle; fib, lie
tru•hán -hana *adj* crooked; clownish || *mf* crook; clown
trujal *m* wine press; oil press
trulla *f* noise, bustle; crowd; trowel
truncar §73 *tr* to cut off the head of; (*palabras o frases*) cut, slash; cut off, interrupt
trusas *fpl* trunk hose; trunks
tu *adj poss* thy, your
tú *pron pers* thou, you
tubérculo *m* (*rizoma engrosado, p.ej., de la patata*) tuber; (*protuberancia*) tubercle
tuberculosis *f* tuberculosis
tubería *f* tubing; piping
tubo *m* tube; pipe; **tubo de desagüe** drainpipe; **tubo de ensayo** test tube; **tubo de escape** exhaust pipe; **tubo de humo** flue; **tubo de imagen** picture tube; **tubo de vacío** vacuum tube; **tubo digestivo** alimentary canal; **tubo sonoro** chime
tuerca *f* nut; **tuerca de aletas, tuerca mariposa** wing nut
tuer•to -ta *adj* crooked, bent; one-eyed; **a tuertas** upside down; crosswise; **a tuertas o a derechas** rightly or wrongly; thoughtlessly || *mf* one-eyed person || *m* wrong, harm, injustice; **tuertos** afterpains
tuétano *m* marrow; pith; **hasta los tuétanos** through and through; head over heels
tufi•llas *mf* (*pl* **-llas**) touchy person
tufillo *m* whiff, smell
tufo *m* fume, vapor; sidelock; foul odor, foul breath; **tufos** airs, conceit
tugurio *m* shepherd's hut; hovel
tuición *f* protection, custody
tulipán *m* tulip
tullecer §22 *tr* to abuse, mistreat || *intr* to be crippled
tulli•do -da *adj* paralyzed, crippled || *mf* paralytic, cripple
tullir §13 *tr* to cripple, paralyze; abuse, mistreat || *ref* to become crippled or paralyzed
tumba *f* grave, tomb; tombstone; arched top; felling of trees
tumbacuarti•llos *mf* (*pl* **-llos**) old soak
tumbar *tr* to knock down; catch, trick; stun || *intr* to tumble; capsize || *ref* to lie down
tumbo *m* fall, tumble; boom, rumble; crisis; rise and fall of sea; rough surf
tumbona *f* hammock
tumor *m* tumor
túmulo *m* catafalque
tumulto *m* tumult
tuna *f* loafing, bumming; (bot) prickly pear
tunante *adj* bumming, loafing; crooked, tricky || *mf* bum, loafer; crook
tundidora *f* lawn mower
tuneci•no -na *adj & mf* Tunisian
túnel *m* tunnel; **túnel de lavado** car wash
tunes *mpl* (Col) little steps, first steps
Túnez (*ciudad*) Tunis; (*país*) Tunisia
tungsteno *m* tungsten
túnica *f* tunic

tu•no -na *adj* crooked, tricky ‖ *mf* crook ‖ *f* see **tuna**
tupé *m* toupee; nerve, cheek, brass
tupi•do -da *adj* thick, dense, compact; dull, stupid; clogged up
tupir *tr* to pack tight ‖ *ref* to stuff, stuff oneself
turba *f* crowd, mob; peat
turbamulta *f* job, rabble
turbar *tr* to disturb, trouble; stir up ‖ *ref* to be confused
turbiedad *f* muddiness; confusion
turbina *f* turbine
tur•bio -bia *adj* turbid, muddy, cloudy; confused; obscure
turbión *m* squall, thunderstorm; (*p.ej., de balas*) (fig) hail
turbocompresor *m* turbocharger
turbohélice *m* turboprop
turbopropulsor *m* turboprop (*engine*)
turborreactor *m* turbojet (*engine*)
turbosupercargador *m* turbosupercharger
turbulen•to -ta *adj* turbulent
tur•co -ca *adj* Turkish ‖ *mf* Turk ‖ *m* (*idioma*) Turkish ‖ *f* (coll) binge; boozing; **coger una turca** to get drunk
turfista *adj* horsy ‖ *m* turfman
turismo *m* touring; touring car
turista *mf* tourist
turísti•co -ca *adj* tourist; touring
turnar *intr* to alternate, take turns
tur•nio -nia *adj* (*ojos*) cross; cross-eyed; (*que mira con ceño*) cross-looking
turno *m* turn, shift; **aguardar turno** to wait one's turn; **por turno** in turn; **turno de tarde** swing shift; **turno diurno** day shift
turón *m* polecat
turquesa *s* turquoise
Turquía *s* Turkey
turrón *m* nougat; plum
tusa *f* corncob; corn silk; (Chile) mane; (Col) pockmark; (CAm, W-I) trollop
tusar *tr* to shear, clip, cut
tutear *tr* to thou, address familiarly ‖ *ref* to thou each other, address each other familiarly
tutela *f* guardianship; protection
tutelar *adj* guardian; protecting ‖ *tr* to protect, shelter, guide
tu•tor -tora *or* **-triz** *mf* (*pl* **-trices**) guardian; tutor
tu•yo -ya *adj poss* of thee ‖ *pron poss* thine, yours
tuza *f* gopher

U

U, u (u) *f* twenty-second letter of the Spanish alphabet
u *conj* (used before words beginning with *o* or *ho*) or
U. *abbr* **usted**
ubicación *f* (compu) location
ubicar §73 *tr* to locate, place ‖ *intr* & *ref* to be situated
ubi•cuo -cua *adj* ubiquitous
ubre *f* udder
Ucrania *f* Ukraine
ucrania•no -na *adj* & *mf* Ukrainian
ucra•nio -nia *adj* & *mf* Ukrainian ‖ *f* see **Ucrania**
Ud. *abbr* **usted**
Uds. *abbr* **ustedes**
uf *interj* oof!; whew!; eugh!, yuck!
ufanar *ref* —**ufanarse con** or **de** to boast of, be proud of
ufanía *f* pride, conceit; cheer, satisfaction; ease, smoothness
ufa•no -na *adj* proud, conceited; cheerful, satisfied; easy, smooth
uh *interj* boo!; huh!; oh!, aw!
ujier *m* doorman, usher
úlcera *f* ulcer, fester, sore; (*en la boca*) canker; **úlcera de decúbito** bedsore
ulcerar *tr* & *ref* to ulcerate, fester
ulterior *adj* ulterior; subsequent
ulteriormente *adv* subsequently, later
últimamente *adv* finally; lately, recently
ultimar *tr* to finish, end, conclude, wind up; kill, finish off
ultimátum *m* (*pl* **-tums**) ultimatum; definite decision
últi•mo -ma *adj* last, latest; final; excellent, superior; (*precio*) lowest, final; most remote; (*piso*) top; (*hora*) late; **a la última** in the latest fashion; **a última hora** at the eleventh hour; **a últimos de** toward the end of, in the latter part of; **de última hora** last-minute; **en las últimas** at death's door; **estar a la última** to be up to date, be well-informed; **la Última Cena** the Last Supper; **por último** at last, finally; **última voluntad** last wishes; **últimos sacramentos** last rites; **último suplicio** capital punishment
ultraatmosféri•co -ca *adj* outer (*space*)
ultracongelación *f* deep freezing
ultracongelador *m* deep freezer
ultraeleva•do -da *adj* (rad) ultrahigh
ultrajar *tr* to outrage, offend
ultraje *m* outrage, offense
ultrajo•so -sa *adj* outrageous, offensive
ultramar *m* country overseas
ultramari•no -na *adj* overseas ‖ **ultramarinos** *mpl* groceries, delicatessen
ultranza — a ultranza *adj* out-and-out, fanati-

cal || *adv* tooth and nail, to the death, at all costs
ultrarro•jo -ja *adj & m* infrared
ultrasecre•to -ta *adj* top secret
ultrasonido *m* ultrasound
ultratumba *adv* beyond the grave
ultraviola•do -da *or* **ultravioleta** *adj & m* ultraviolet
ululación *f* howl; whoop; (*del buho*) hoot; (*del disco del fonógrafo*) wow
ulular *intr* to howl; whoop; (*el buho*) hoot
ululato *m* howl; (*del buho*) hoot
umbilical *adj* umbilical
umbral *m* threshold, doorsill; (*madero que sostiene el muro encima de un vano*) lintel; (physiol, psychol & fig) threshold; **atravesar** *or* **pisar los umbrales** to cross the threshold; **estar en los umbrales de** to be on the threshold of
umbralada *f* (Col) threshold
umbrí•o -a *adj* shady || *f* shady side
umbro•so -sa *adj* shady
un, una (the apocopated form **un** is used before masculine singular nouns and adjectives and before feminine singular nouns beginning with stressed *a* or *ha*) *art indef* (*pl* **unos, unas**) a || *adj* one
unánime *adj* unanimous
unanimidad *f* unanimity
unción *f* unction
uncir §36 *tr* (*bueyes*) to yoke, hitch
undéci•mo -ma *adj & m* eleventh
undo•so -sa *adj* wavy
ungir §27 *tr* to smear with ointment or with oil; anoint
ungüento *m* unguent, ointment, salve
únicamente *adv* only, solely
úni•co -ca *adj* only, sole; (*sin otro de su especie*) unique; one, e.g., **precio único** one price; **eres hijo único** you're an only child
unicornio *m* unicorn
unidad *f* (*concepto de una sola cosa o persona; cantidad que se toma como medida común de todas las demás de su clase; el número entero más pequeño*) unit; (*indivisión; armonía de conjunto; el número uno*) unity; **unidad de disco, unidad de disquette** (compu) disk drive; **unidad de proceso** (compu) processor
uni•do -da *adj* united; smooth, even; close-knit
unifamiliar *adj* (*casa*) one-family
unificar §73 *tr* to unify
uniformar *tr* to make uniform; provide with a uniform
uniforme *adj* uniform || *m* uniform; **uniforme de gala** (mil) full dress
uniformidad *f* uniformity
unilateral *adj* unilateral
unión *f* union; double ring
unir *tr & ref* to unite
unisex [ˈunisɛks] *adj* unisex
unisonancia *f* (mus) unison; (*de un orador*) monotony
unísono — al unísono in unison; unanimously; **al unísono de** in unison with
unita•rio -ria *adj* unit
universal *adj* universal; all-purpose; (*teclado de máquina de escribir*) standard
universidad *f* university
universita•rio -ria *adj* university || *mf* university student, college student || *m* university professor
universo *m* universe
u•no -na *adj* one; **unos** *or* **unas** some, a few, about || *pron* one, someone; **a una** of one accord; **la una** one o'clock; **somos uno** we are one; **uno a otro, unos a otros** each other, one another; **uno que otro** one or more, a few; **u•nos -nas** some; pair of, e.g., **unas gafas** a pair of glasses; **unas tijeras** a pair of scissors; **unos cuantos** some; **uno y otro** both || *pron indef* one, e.g., **uno no sabe qué hacer aquí** one does not know what to do here || *m* (*unidad y signo que la representa*) one
untar *tr* to smear, grease; anoint; bribe || *ref* to get smeared; grease oneself; embezzle
unto *m* grease; (*gordura del cuerpo del animal*) fat; (Chile) shoe polish; **unto de Méjico** or **de rana** bribe money
untuo•so -sa *adj* unctuous, greasy, sticky
uña *f* nail, fingernail, toenail; (*pezuña*) hoof; (*del ancla*) fluke, bill; (mach) claw, gripper; **enseñar** *or* **mostrar las uñas** to show one's teeth; **ser largo de uñas** to have long fingers; **ser uña y carne** to be hand in glove; **tener en la uña** to have on the tip of one's fingers
uñada *f* scratch, nail scratch; (*impulso dado con la uña*) flip
uñero *m* ingrowing nail; (*inflamación del dedo en la raíz de la uña*) whitlow
ural *adj* Ural || **Urales** *mpl* Urals
uranio *m* uranium
urbanidad *f* urbanity
urbanismo *m* city planning
urbanista *mf* city planner
urbanísti•co -ca *adj* city-planning || *f* city planning, urban development
urbanizar §60 *tr* (*convertir en poblado*) to urbanize; refine; polish
urba•no -na *adj* urban, city; (*atento, cortés*) urbane || *m* policeman
urbe *f* metropolis
urdema•las *mf* (*pl* **-las**) schemer
urdimbre *f* warp; scheme, scheming; **estar en la urdimbre** (Chile) to be thin, be emaciated
urdir *tr* (*los hilos*) to warp; (*una conspiración*) hatch
urente *adj* burning, smarting
uretra *f* urethra
urgencia *f* urgency; **de urgencia** special delivery
urgente *adj* urgent; (*correo*) special delivery
urgir §27 *intr* to be urgent
urina•rio -ria *adj* urinary || *m* urinal
urna *f* glass case; ballot box; (*para guardar las*

cenizas de los cadáveres) urn; **acudir** or **ir a las urnas** to go to the polls
urología *f* urology
urraca *f* magpie; **ser una urraca** (coll) to be a pack rat
urticaria *f* hives
Uruguay , el Uruguay
urugua•yo -ya *adj & mf* Uruguayan
usa•do -da *adj* (*empleado; gastado por el uso; acostumbrado*) used; skilled, experienced; (*vocablo*) **poco usado** rare
usanza *f* use, usage, custom
usar *tr* to use, make use of; (*un cargo, un oficio*) follow || *intr* **—usar** + *inf* to be accustomed to + *inf;* **usar de** to use, have recourse to; **usar de la palabra** to speak, make a speech || *ref* to be the custom
usina *f* factory, plant; powerhouse; (*estación de tranvía*) (Arg) carbarn
uso *m* use; custom, usage; wear, wear and tear; habit, practice; **al uso** according to custom; **en buen uso** in good condition; **hacer uso de la palabra** to speak, make a speech
usted *pron pers* you
usual *adj* (*de uso común*) usual; (*que se usa con facilidad*) usable; sociable
usualmente *adv* usually
usua•rio -ria *mf* user
usufructo *m* use, enjoyment
usufructuar §21 *tr* to enjoy the use of
usura *f* usury; profit; **pagar con usura** to pay back a thousandfold
usurero *m* loan shark; profiteer
usurpar *tr* to usurp
utensilio *m* utensil
útero *m* uterus, womb
útil *adj* useful || **útiles** *mpl* utensils, tools, equipment
utilería *f* (Arg) properties, stage equipment
utilero *m* (Arg) property man
utilidad *f* utility, usefulness; profit, earnings; (compu) utility
utilita•rio -ra *adj* utilitarian
utilizable *adj* usable
utilizar §60 *tr* to utilize, use || *ref* **— utilizarse con, de** or **en** to make use of; **utilizarse para** to be good for
utopía *f* utopia
utopista *adj & mf* utopian
UU. *abbr* **ustedes**
uva *f* grape; wart on eyelid; (*baya*) berry; **estar hecho una uva** to have a load on; **uva crespa** gooseberry; **uva de Corinto** currant; **uva de raposa** nightshade; **uva espín** or **espina** gooseberry; **uva pasa** raisin; **uvas verdes** (*de la fábula de Esopo*) sour grapes
uve *f* (*letra del alfabeto*) **V**
uy *interj* ooh!; oh!; ah!, oh!; ow!, ouch!; (Ven) hey!, look out!

V

V, v (ve *or* uve) *f* twenty-third letter of the Spanish alphabet
V. *abbr* **usted, vease, venerable**
V.A. *abbr* **Vuestra Alteza**
vaca *f* cow; (*cuero*) cowhide; (*carne de vaca o de buey*) beef; gambling pool; **hacer vaca** (Peru) to play truant; **vaca de la boda** (coll) goat, laughingstock; friend in need; **vaca de leche** milch cow; **vaca de San Antón** (ent) ladybird; **vaca sagrada** sacred cow
vacación *f* (*cargo que está sin proveer*) vacancy; **de vacaciones** on vacation; **vacaciones** vacation; **vacaciones retribuídas** vacation with pay
vacancia *f* vacancy
vacante *adj* vacant || *f* vacancy
vacar §73 *intr* (*un empleo, un cargo*) to be vacant, be unfilled; take off, take a vacation; **vacar a** to attend to; **vacar de** to lack, be devoid of
vacia•do -da *adj* hollow-ground || *m* cast, casting; plaster cast
vaciante *f* ebb tide
vaciar §77 & regular *tr* to empty, drain; to clear out; cast, mold; (*formar un hueco en*) hollow out; sharpen on a grindstone; copy, transcribe; explain in detail || *intr* to empty; flow; (*el agua en el río*) fall, go down || *ref* to blab
vacilación *f* vacillation; flickering; hesitancy, hesitation
vacilada *f* (Mex) spree, high time; (Mex) drunk
vacilante *adj* vacillating; (*luz*) flickering; (*irresoluto*) hesitant
vacilar *intr* to vacillate; (*la luz*) flicker; shake, wobble; (*estar irresoluto*) hesitate, waver
vací•o -a *adj* empty; (*hueco*) hollow; idle; useless, unsuccessful; (*vaca*) barren; presumptuous || *m* emptiness; (*laguna, abertura; vacante*) vacancy; (*espacio que no contiene ninguna materia*) void; (*espacio de que se ha extraído el aire*) vacuum; (*ijada*) side, flank; **de vacío** light, unloaded; **hacer el vacío a** to isolate
vacuidad *f* vacuity, emptiness
vacuna *f* (*enfermedad de las vacas*) cowpox; (*virus cuya inoculación preserva de una enfermedad determinada*) vaccine
vacunación *f* vaccination
vacunar *tr* to vaccinate
vacu•no -na *adj* bovine; cowhide || *f* see vacuna

va•cuo -cua *adj* vacant || *m* cavity, hollow
vadear *tr* (*un río*) to ford; wade through; overcome; sound out || *ref* to behave; manage
vado *m* ford; expedient, resource; **al vado o a la puente** one way or another; **no hallar vado** to see no way out; **tentar el vado** to feel one's way
vagabundear *intr* to wander, roam; loaf around
vagabun•do -da *adj* vagabond || *mf* vagabond, tramp; wanderer
vagancia *f* loafing, vagrancy
vagar *m* leisure; **con vagar** slowly; **estar de vagar** to have nothing to do || **§44** *intr* to wander, roam; be idle; have plenty of leisure; (*una cosa*) lie around; (*p.ej., una sonrisa por los labios*) play
vagido *m* cry of a newborn baby
vagina *f* vagina
vagneria•no -na *adj & mf* Wagnerian
va•go -ga *adj* wandering, roaming; idle, loafing; lax, loose; hesitating, wavering; (*indefinido, indeciso*) vague; (*mirada*) blank || *m* vagabond; idler, loafer; **en vago** shakily; in vain; in the air; **poner en vago** to tilt
vagón *m* car, railroad car; **vagón cama** sleeping car; **vagón carbonero** coal car; **vagón cerrado** boxcar; **vagón cisterna** tank car; **vagón comedor** (Esp) dining car; **vagón de carga** freight car; **vagón de cola** caboose; **vagón de ganado** stock car; **vagón de mercancías** freight car; **vagón de plataforma** flatcar; **vagón frigorífico** refrigerator car; **vagón mirador** observation car; **vagón restaurante** dining car; **vagón salón** chair car; **vagón tolva** hopper-bottom car; **vagón volquete** dump car
vagoneta *f* tip car; station wagon
vaguear *intr* to wander around
vaguedad *f* vagueness; vague remark
vaguido *m* faintness, fainting spell
vaharada *f* breath, exhalation
vahear *intr* to emit odors, give forth an aroma
vahido *f* faintness, fainting spell
vaho *m* odor, aroma, vapor, fume
vaina *f* sheath; scabbard; knife case; (*de ciertas semillas*) pod, husk; annoyance, bother; (Col) luck, stroke of luck
vainica *f* hemstitch
vainilla *f* vanilla
vainita *f* (Ven) string bean
vaivén *m* swing, seesaw, backward and forward motion; unsteadiness, inconstancy; risk, chance
vajilla *f* dishes, set of dishes; **lavar la vajilla** to wash the dishes; **vajilla de oro** gold plate; **vajilla de plata** silver plate, silverware; **vajilla de porcelana** chinaware
vale *m* promissory note; voucher; farewell; (Ven) chum, pal; **vale respuesta** reply coupon
valede•ro -ra *adj* valid, effective
vale•dor -dora *mf* defender, protector; (Mex) friend, companion
valedura *f* (Mex) favor, protection
valencia *f* (chem) valence
valentía *f* bravery, valor; feat, exploit; dash, boldness; boast; **pisar con valentía** to strut, swagger
valen•tón -tona *adj* arrogant, boastful || *mf* braggart, boaster || *f* bragging
valer *m* worth, merit, value || **§76** *tr* to defend, protect; favor, patronize; avail; yield; be worth, be valued at; be equal to; suit; **valer la pena** to be worthwhile (to); **valerle a uno** + *inf* to help someone to + *inf,* to get someone to + *inf;* **valer lo que pesa** to be worth its (his, her, etc.) weight in gold; **valga lo que valiere** come what may; **¡válgame Dios!** bless my soul!, so help me God! || *intr* to have worth; be worthy; be valuable; be valid; prevail; hold, count; have influence; **hacer valer** (*sus derechos*) to assert; make felt; make good; turn to account; **más vale** it is better (to); **¡vale!** O.K.!, all right!; **valer para** to be useful for; **valer por** to be equal to || *ref* to help oneself; defend oneself; **valerse de** to make use of, avail oneself of
valero•so -sa *adj* valorous, brave; strong, active, effective
va•let *m* (*pl* **-lets**) (cards) jack
valía *f* value, worth; favor, influence; **mayor valía** or **plus valía** appreciation, increased value; unearned increment
validación *f* validation
validar *tr* to validate
validez *f* validity; strength, vigor
vali•do -da *adj* highly esteemed, influential || *m* court favorite; prime minister
váli•do -da *adj* valid; strong, robust
valiente *adj* valiant; strong, robust; fine, excellent; (*grande y excesivo*) terrific || *m* brave fellow; bully
valija *f* satchel, brief case; mailbag, mailpouch; mail; **valija diplomática** diplomatic pouch
valimiento *m* favor, protection; favor at court, favoritism
valio•so -sa *adj* valuable; influential; wealthy
valla *f* fence, railing; barricade; hindrance, obstacle; (sport) hurdle; (W-I) cockpit; **valla paranieves** snow fence
vallado *m* barricade, stockade
valle *m* valley; river bed; valley dwellings; **valle de lágrimas** vale of tears
va•lón -lona *adj & mf* Walloon
valor *m* value, worth; valor, courage; meaning, import; efficacy; equivalence; (*rédito*) income, return; effrontery; (*persona, cosa o cualidad dignas de ser poseídas*) (fig) asset; **¿cómo va ese valor?** how are you?; **valor aparente** *or* **facial** face value; **valor de rescate** (ins) surrender value; **valores** securities; **valor nominal** par value; face value
valoración *f* valuation, appraisal
valorar or **valorear** *tr* (*poner precio a*) to value, appraise; enhance the value of
valorizar **§60** *tr* to value; enhance the value of; sell off (*for quick realization*)

vals *m* waltz
valsar *intr* to waltz
valuación *f* valuation, appraisal
valuar §21 *tr* to estimate
válvula *f* valve; **válvula corrediza** slide valve; **válvula de admisión** intake valve; **válvula de escape** exhaust valve; **válvula de escape libre** cutout; **válvula de seguridad** safety valve; **válvula en cabeza** valve in the head, overhead valve
vampiresa *f* vampire
vampíri•co -ca *adj* vampire; ghoulish
vampiro *m* vampire; (*persona que se deleita con cosas horribles*) ghoul
vanadio *m* vanadium
vanagloriar §77 & regular *ref* to boast
vanaglorio•so -sa *adj* vainglorious, conceited, boastful
vanamente *adv* vainly
vandalismo *m* vandalism
vánda•lo -la *adj & mf* Vandal; (fig) vandal
vanguardia *f* (mil & fig) vanguard, van; **a la vanguardia** in the vanguard; **de vanguardia** state-of-the-art
vanguardismo *m* avant-garde
vanguardista *adj* avant-garde || *mf* avant-gardist
vanidad *f* vanity; (*fausto*) pomp, show; **ajar la vanidad de** to take down a peg; **hacer vanidad de** to boast of
vanido•so -sa *adj* vain, conceited
va•no -na *adj* vain; hollow, empty; **en vano** in vain || *m* opening in a wall
vapor *m* steam; (*el visible: exhalación, vaho, niebla, etc.*) vapor; steamer, steamboat; **al vapor** at full speed; **vapores** gas (*belched*); blues; **vapor volandero** tramp steamer
vaporar *tr & ref* to evaporate
vaporizador *m* atomizer, sprayer
vaporizar §60 *tr* to vaporize; spray || *ref* to vaporize
vaporo•so -sa *adj* vaporous
vapular or **vapulear** *tr* whip, flog
vaquería *f* drove of cattle; dairy; (Mex) party
vaqueri•zo -za *adj* cattle || *f* winter stable for cattle
vaque•ro -ra *adj* cattle; denim || *mf* cattle tender; (Peru) truant || *m* cow hand; cowboy; **vaqueros** blue jeans, dungarees, jeans
vaqueta *f* leather; (P-R) strop; **zurrarle a uno la vaqueta** to tan someone's hide
vaquillona *f* (Arg, Chile) heifer
vara *f* pole, rod, staff; (*de carruaje*) shaft; (*bastón de mando*) wand; measuring stick; (taur) thrust with goad; **tener vara alta** to have the upper hand; **vara alcándara** shaft; **vara alta** upper hand; **vara buscadora** divining rod (*ostensibly to discover water or metals*); **vara de adivinar** divining rod; **vara de oro** goldenrod; **vara de pescar** fishing rod; **vara de San José** goldenrod
vara-alta *m* boss
varada *f* beaching; running aground
varadero *m* repair dock, dry dock
varapalo *m* long pole; setback, disappointment, reverse
varar *tr* (*una embarcación*) to beach || *intr* to run aground; (*un negocio*) come to a standstill
varear *tr* (*los frutos de los árboles*) to beat down, knock down; beat, strike; (taur) to goad; (*los caballos de carreras*) (SAm) to exercise, train || *ref* to lose weight, get thin
varec *m* (bot) wrack
varenga *f* (naut) floor, floor timber
vareta *f* twig, stick; lime twig for catching birds; colored stripe; cutting remark; hint; **irse de vareta** to have diarrhea
variable *adj & f* variable
variación *f* variation; **variación magnética** magnetic deviation
varia•do -da *adj* varied; variegated
variante *adj & f* variant
variar §77 to vary, change || *intr* to vary, change; be different; **variar de** *or* **en opinión** to change one's mind
varice *f* or **várice** *f* varicose veins
varicela *f* chicken pox
varico•so -sa *adj* varicose
variedad *f* variety; **variedades** variety show, vaudeville
varilla *f* rod, stem, twig; (*bastón de mando*) wand; (*de paraguas, abanico, etc.*) rib; (*del corsé*) stay; (*de rueda*) wire spoke; jawbone; (Mex) peddler's wares; **varilla de nivel** dipstick; **varilla de virtudes** wand, magician's wand
varillaje *m* ribs, ribbing; (*de máquina de escribir*) type bars
varille•ro -ra *adj* (*caballo*) (Ven) race || *m* (Mex) peddler
va•rio -ria *adj* (*de diversos colores; que tiene variedad*) various, varied; fickle, inconstant; **varios** various; several
varón *adj* male, e.g., **hijo varón** male child || *m* man, male; grown man, adult male; man of standing; **santo varón** plain artless fellow
varonía *f* male issue
varonil *adj* manly, virile; courageous
Varsovia *f* Warsaw
vasa•llo -lla *adj & mf* vassal
vas•co -ca *adj & mf* Basque (*of Spain and France*) || *m* Basque (*language*)
vas•cón -cona *adj & mf* Basque (*of old Spain*)
vasconga•do -da *adj & mf* Basque (*of Spain*) || *m* Basque (*language*) || **las Vascongadas** the Basque Provinces
vascuence *adj & m* Basque (*language*) || *m* gibberish
vaselina *f* Vaseline^T, petroleum jelly
vasera *f* kitchen shelf; bottle rack, tumbler rack
vasija *f* container, vessel
vaso *m* tumbler, glass; vase, flower jar; (anat) duct, vessel; **vaso de engrase** (mach) grease cup; **vaso de noche** pot, chamber pot; **vaso graduado** measuring glass; **vaso sanguíneo** blood vessel
vástago *m* shoot, sapling; scion, offspring; rod,

stem; **vástago de émbolo** piston rod; **vástago de válvula** valve stem
vastedad *f* vastness
vas•to -ta *adj* vast
vate *m* bard, seer, poet
váter *m* toilet, water closet
vataije *m* wattage
vaticinar *tr* to prophesy, predict
vaticinio *m* prophecy, prediction
vatídi•co -ca *adj* prophetical || *mf* prophet
vatímetro *m* wattmeter
vatio *m* watt
vatio-hora *m* (*pl* **vatios-hora**) watt-hour
vaya *f* jest, jeer
Vd. *abbr* (obs) **usted** || **see Ud.**
Vds. *abbr* (obs) **ustedes** || **see Uds.**
V.E. *abbr* **Vuestra Excelencia**
vece•ro -ra *adj* alternating; yielding in alternate years || *mf* person waiting his turn
vecinamente *adv* nearby
vecindad *f* neighborhood, vicinity; residency; residents; **hacer mala vecindad** to be a bad neighbor
vecindario *m* neighborhood, community; people, population
veci•no -na *adj* neighboring; like, similar || *mf* neighbor; resident, citizen
veda *f* prohibition; (*de la caza y la pesca*) closed season
vedado *m* game preserve
vedar *tr* to forbid, prohibit; hinder, stop; veto
vedija *f* fleece, tuft of wool; mat of hair; matted hair
vee•dor -dora *adj* curious, spying || *mf* busybody || *m* supervisor, overseer, inspector
vega *f* fertile plain; (Cuba) tobacco plantation
vegetación *f* vegetation; **vegetaciones adenoideas** adenoids
vegetal *adj & m* vegetable
vegetaria•no -na *adj & mf* vegetarian
vego•so -sa *adj* (Chile) damp, wet
vehemencia *f* vehemence
vehemente *adj* vehement
vehículo *m* vehicle; **vehículo espacial** space vehicle
veinta•vo -va *adj & m* twentieth
veinte *adj & pron* twenty; **a las veinte** late, untimely || *m* twenty; (*en las fechas*) twentieth
veintena *f* score, twenty
veintiún *adj* this apocopated form of **veintiuno** is used before masculine singular nouns and adjectives
veintiu•no -na *adj & pron* twenty-one || *m* twenty-one; (*en las fechas*) twenty-first || *f* (*juego de naipes*) twenty-one
vejación *f* vexation, annoyance
vejamen *m* vexation, annoyance; bantering, taunting
vejar *tr* to vex, annoy; taunt
vejestorio *m* old dodo
vejete *m* little old fellow
vejez *f* old age; oldness; dotage; platitude, old story; **a la vejez, viruelas** can one ignore the passing years?
vejiga *f* (*órgano que recibe la orina de los riñones*) bladder; (*ampolla*) blister; (*saco hecho de piel, goma, etc.*) bag, pouch, bladder; **vejiga de la bilis** *or* **de la hiel** gall bladder
vela *f* wakefulness; pilgrimage; evening; work in the evening; sail; sailboat; awning; (*cilindro con una torcida que sirve para alumbrar*) candle; vigil (*before Eucharist*); (Mex) scolding; **a toda vela** full sail; **a vela** under sail; **a vela llena** under full sail; **en vela** awake; **estar a dos velas** (coll) to be broke; **hacerse a la vela** to set sail; **vela latina** lateen sail; **vela mayor** mainsail; **vela romana** Roman candle
velada *f* evening party, soirée; vigil, watch
vela•do -da *adj* veiled, hidden; (phot) light-struck || *f* see **velada**
velador *m* pedestal table, gueridon; wooden candlestick; watchman; (SAm) night table; (Mex) lamp globe
velaje *m* or **velamen** *m* (naut) canvas, sails
velar *adj & f* velar || *tr* to watch over; guard; (*la guardia*) keep; hold a wake over; (*cubrir con un velo*) veil; (phot) to fog; (fig) to veil, hide, conceal || *intr* to stay awake; stay awake working; keep vigil; (*el viento*) keep up all night; (*un escollo, un peñasco*) stick up out of the water; **velar por** *or* **sobre** to watch over || *ref* (phot) to fog, be light-struck
velatorio *m* wake; viewing
veleidad *f* whim, caprice; fickleness, flightiness
veleido•so -sa *adj* whimsical, capricious; fickle, flighty
vele•ro -ra *adj* swift-sailing || *m* sailboat
veleta *mf* (*persona inconstante*) weathercock || *f* vane, weathervane, weathercock; (*de un molino*) rudder vane; (*de la caña de pescar*) bob; streamer, pennant; **veleta de manga** (aer) air sleeve, air sock
velís *m* (Mex) valise
velita *f* little candle
vello *m* down, fuzz; body hair
vellocino *m* fleece; **vellocino de oro** Golden Fleece
vellón *m* fleece; unsheared sheepskin; lock of wool; copper coin; copper-silver alloy
vello•so -sa *adj* downy, hairy, fuzzy
velludillo *m* velveteen
vellu•do -da *adj* shaggy, hairy, fuzzy || *m* (*felpa*) plush; (*terciopelo*) velvet
velo *m* veil; taking the veil; confusion, perplexity; (*disfraz*) veil; (*de lágrimas*) mist; (phot) fog; **correr el velo** to pull aside the curtain, to dispel the mystery; **tomar el velo** to take the veil; **velo del paladar** soft palate; **velo que cubre el cuerpo** body veil
velocidad *f* (*rapidez*) speed, velocity; (mech) velocity; **en gran velocidad** (rr) by express; **en pequeña velocidad** (rr) by freight; **primera velocidad** (aut) low gear; **segunda velocidad** (aut) second; **tercera velocidad**

(aut) high gear; **velocidad con respecto al suelo** (aer) ground speed; **velocidad de crucero** cruising speed; **velocidad de giro** (compu) spin rate; **velocidad de obturación** shutter speed; **velocidad media de transferencia** (compu) baud rate; **velocidad permitida** speed limit
velocímetro *m* speedometer
velón *m* brass olive-oil lamp
velorio *m* evening party or bee; wake; wake for a dead child; dull party; come-on
ve•loz *adj* (*pl* **-loces**) swift, speedy; agile, quick
vena *f* vein; (*en piedras*) grain; (fig) poetical inspiration; **estar en vena** to be all set, be inspired; sparkle with wit; **vena de loco** fickle disposition
venablo *m* dart, javelin; **echar venablos** to burst forth in anger
venado *m* deer, stag; **pintar el venado** (Mex) to play hooky
venáti•co -ca *adj* fickle, unsteady; daffy, nutty
vence•dor -dora *adj* conquering, victorious || *mf* conqueror, victor
vencejo *m* band, string; (orn) European swift, black martin
vencer §78 *tr* to vanquish, conquer; excel, outdo; overcome, surmount || *intr* to conquer, be victorious; (*un plazo*) be up; (*un contrato*) expire; (*una letra*) mature, fall due || *ref* to control oneself; (*un camino*) bend, turn; (Chile) to wear out, become useless
vencetósigo *m* milkweed, tame poison
venci•do -da *adj* conquered; (com) due, mature, payable
vencimiento *m* (*acción de vencer*) victory; (*hecho de ser vencido*) defeat; (com) expiration, maturity
venda *f* (*para ligar un miembro herido*) bandage; (*para tapar los ojos*) blindfold
vendaje *m* bandage, dressing; **vendaje enyesado** plaster cast
vendar *tr* (*un miembro, una herida*) to bandage; (*los ojos*) blindfold; (*cegar*) (fig) to blind; (*engañar*) (fig) to hoodwink
vendaval *m* strong southeasterly wind from the sea; strong wind, gale
vendedera *f* saleswoman, saleslady
vende•dor -dora *adj* selling || *mf* salesclerk, sales representative; (law) vendor || *m* salesman || *f* saleswoman
vendehu•mos *mf* (*pl* **-mos**) influence peddler
vendeja *f* public sale
vender *tr* to sell; betray, sell out; **vender salud** to be the picture of health || *intr* to sell; **¡vendo, vendo, vendí!** going, going, gone! || *ref* to sell oneself; sell, be for sale; betray oneself, give oneself away; **venderse caro** to be hard to see; be quite a stranger; **venderse en** (*p.ej., cien pesetas*) to sell for; **venderse por** to pass oneself off as
ven•dí *m* (*pl* **-díes**) certificate of sale
vendible *adj* salable, marketable
vendimia *f* vintage; (fig) big profit
vendimia•dor -dora *mf* vintager
vendimiar *tr* (*la uva*) to gather, harvest; (*las viñas*) gather the grapes of; make off with; kill
venduta *f* public sale; (W-I) greengrocery
Venecia *f* (*ciudad*) Venice; (*provincia*) Venetia
venecia•no -na *adj & mf* Venetian
veneno *m* poison, venom
veneno•so -sa *adj* poisonous, venomous
venera *f* scallop shell; (*manantial de agua*) spring; **empeñar la venera** to go all out, spare no expense
venerable *adj* venerable
venerar *tr* to venerate, revere; worship
venére•o -a *adj* venereal || *m* venereal disease
venero *m* (*de agua*) spring; (*filón de mineral*) lode, vein; (fig) source
venezola•no -na *adj & mf* Venezuelan
Venezuela *f* Venezuela
venga *interj*—**¡venga, date prisa!** (coll) come on, hurry up!
venga•dor -dora *adj* avenging || *mf* avenger
venganza *f* vengeance, revenge
vengar §44 *tr* to avenge || *ref* to take revenge; **vengarse de** to take revenge on
vengati•vo -va *adj* vengeful, vindictive
venia *f* forgiveness, pardon; leave, permission; bow, greeting
venida *f* coming; return; flood, freshet
venide•ro -ra *adj* coming, future || **venideros** *mpl* successors, posterity
venir §79 *intr* to come; **que viene** coming, next; **venga lo que viniere** come what may; **venir** + *ger* to be + *ger;* **venir a** + *inf* to come to + *inf;* to amount to + *ger;* to happen to + *inf;* to finally + *inf,* e.g., **después de una larga enfermedad, vino a morir** after a long illness he finally died; **venir a ser** to turn out to be || *ref* to ferment; **venirse abajo** to collapse
veno•so -sa *adj* venous
venta *f* sale; roadside inn; (Chile) refreshment stand; (S-D) grocery store; **de venta** *or* **en venta** on sale, for sale; **ser una venta** to be an expensive place; **venta al contado** cash sale; **venta al descubierto** short sale; **venta al por mayor** wholesale; **venta al por menor** retail; **venta a plazos** installment plan; **venta de garaje** garage sale; **venta por catálogo** *or* **correo** mail order
ventaja *f* advantage; (*en juegos o apuestas*) odds; extra pay; head start
ventajo•so -sa *adj* advantageous
ventalla *f* valve
ventana *f* window; (*de la nariz*) nostril; (compu) window; **echar la casa por la ventana** to go to a lot of expense; **ventana batiente** casement; **ventana de guillotina** sash window; **ventana desplegable** (compu) pop-up window; **ventana salediza** bay window
ventanal *m* church window; picture window
ventanear *intr* to be at the window all the time

ventanilla *f* (*de coche, de banco, de sobre*) window; ticket window; (*de la nariz*) nostril
ventanillo *m* (*postigo de puerta o ventana*) wicket; (*mirilla*) peephole
ventar **§2** *tr* to sniff; to snoop into || *intr* to snoop, pry around
ventarrón *m* gale, windstorm
ventear *tr* to sniff; dry in the wind; snoop into || *intr* to snoop, pry around || *impers* — **ventea** it is windy || *ref* (*henderse*) to split; break wind; spend a lot of time in the open
vente•ro -ra *mf* innkeeper
ventilador *m* ventilator; fan; (naut) funnel; **ventilador aspirador** exhaust fan; **ventilador de aspas, ventilador hélice** ceiling fan
ventilar *tr* to ventilate; (fig) to air, ventilate
ventisca *f* drift, snowdrift; (*borrasca*) blizzard
ventiscar **§73** *intr* to snow and blow; (*la nieve*) drift
ventisquero *m* snowdrift; blizzard; snowcapped mountain; glacier
ventolera *f* blast of wind; (*molinete*) pinwheel; vanity, pride; wild idea; (Mex) wind
ventosa *f* vent, air hole; **pegar una ventosa a** to swindle
ventosear *intr* to break wind
vento•so -sa *adj* windy || *f* see **ventosa**
ventregada *f* brood, litter; outpouring, abundance
ventrículo *m* ventricle
ventrílo•cuo -cua *mf* ventriloquist
ventriloquia *f* or **ventriloquismo** *m* ventriloquism
ventura *f* happiness; luck, chance; danger, risk; **a la ventura** at random; at a risk; **por ventura** perhaps, perchance; **probar ventura** to try one's luck
venture•ro -ra *adj* adventurous; fortunate, lucky || *mf* adventurer
ventu•ro -ra *adj* future, coming || *f* see **ventura**
venturón *m* stroke of luck
venturo•so -sa *adj* fortunate, lucky
Venus *m* (astr) Venus || *f* (myth) Venus; (*mujer de belleza*) Venus
venus•to -ta *adj* beautiful, graceful
ver *m* (*vista*) sight; (*apariencia*) appearance; opinion; **a mi ver** in my opinion || **§80** *tr* to see; look at; (law) to hear, try; **no poder ver** to not be able to bear; **no tener nada que ver con** to have nothing to do with; **ver** + *inf* to see + *inf,* e.g., **vi entrar a mi hermano** I saw my brother come in; to see + *ger,* e.g., **ví bailar a la muchacha** I saw the girl dancing; to see + *pp.* e.g., **ví ahorcar al criminal** I saw the criminal hanged; **ver venir a uno** to see what someone is up to || *intr* to see; **a más ver** so long; **a ver** let's see; **hasta más ver** good-bye, so long; **ver de** to try to; **ver y creer** seeing is believing || *ref* to be seen; be obvious; see oneself; see each other; meet; (*encontrarse*) be, find oneself; **verse con** to see, have a talk with; **ya se ve** of course, certainly
vera *f* edge, border; **a la vera de** near, beside; **de veras** in truth; **jugar de veras** to play for keeps; **veras** truth, reality; earnestness
veracidad *f* veracity, truthfulness
veranda *f* verandah; bay window, closed porch
veraneante *mf* summer vacationist, summer resident
veranear *intr* to summer
veranie•go -ga *adj* summer; unimportant, insignificant
veranillo *m* Indian summer; **veranillo de San Martín** Indian summer
ve•raz *adj* (*pl* **-races**) veracious, truthful
verbena *f* fair, country fair, night festival; (bot) verbena
verbigracia *adv* for example
verbo *m* verb || **Verbo** *m* (theol) Word
verbo•so -sa *adj* verbose, wordy
verdacho *m* green earth
verdad *f* truth; **a la verdad** in truth, as a matter of fact; **de verdad** really; **la verdad desnuda** the plain truth; **¿no es verdad?** *or* **¿verdad?** isn't that so? *La traducción al inglés de esta pregunta depende generalmente de la aseveración que la precede. Si la aseveración es afirmativa, la pregunta es negativa, p.ej.,* **Ud. vivió aquí. ¿No es verdad?** You lived here. Did you not?; *Si la aseveración es negativa, la pregunta es afirmativa, p.ej.,* **Ud. no vivió aquí. ¿No es verdad?** You did not live here? Did you? *Si el sujeto de la aseveración es un nombre sustantivo, va representado en la pregunta con un pronombre personal, p.ej.,* **Juan no estuvo aquí anoche. ¿No es verdad?** John was not here last evening. Was he?; **ser verdad** to be true; **verdad trillada** truism
verdade•ro -ra *adj* true; real; (*que dice siempre la verdad*) truthful
verde *adj* green; young, youthful; (*viuda*) merry; (*cuento*) shady, off-color; **están verdes** they're hard to reach || *m* green; foliage, verdure
verdear *intr* to turn green, look green
verdecer **§22** *intr* to turn green, grow green again
verdecillo *m* (orn) greenfinch
verdemar *m* sea green
verdete *m* verdigris
verdín *m* fresh green; (*capa verde en aguas estancadas*) mold, pond scum; (*cardenillo*) verdigris
verdise•co -ca *adj* half-dry
verdor *m* verdure; youth
verdo•so -sa *adj* greenish
verdugado *m* hoop skirt
verdugo *m* shoot, sucker; (*estoque*) rapier; (*azote*) scourge; (*roncha*) welt; executioner, hangman; torment; butcher bird, shrike
verdugón *m* wale, weal
verdulería *f* greengrocery
verdule•ro -ra *mf* greengrocer || *f* fishwife
verdura *f* greenness; vegetable; (*color verde de*

las plantas) verdure; (*obscenidad*) smuttiness; **verduras** vegetables, greens
verecundia *f* bashfulness, shyness
verecun•do -da *adj* bashful, shy
vereda *f* path, lane; sidewalk
veredicto *m* verdict
verga *f* (anat) penis; (naut) yard
vergel *m* flower and fruit garden
vergonzo•so -sa *adj* (*que causa vergüenza*) shameful; (*que tiene vergüenza*) ashamed; (*que se avergüenza con facilidad*) bashful, shy; (*que causa humillación*) embarrassing; shabby, wretched || *mf* bashful person || *m* armadillo
vergüenza *f* (*arrepentimiento*) shame; (*oprobio*) shamefulness, disgrace; (*pudor, timidez*) bashfulness, shyness; (*desconcierto, humillación*) embarrassment; (*pundonor*) dignity, face; public punishment; **¡qué vergüenza!** shame on you!; **tener vergüenza** to be ashamed; **vergüenzas** privates, genitals
vericueto *m* rough, rocky ground
verídi•co -ca *adj* truthful
verificación *f* verification; checking, testing, inspection; **verificación a la ventura** spot check
verifica•dor -dora *adj* verifying || *m* meter inspector; checker, inspector; **verificador ortográfico** (compu) spell checker
verificar §73 *tr* to verify, check; (*llevar a cabo*) carry out; (*los contadores de agua, gas y electricidad*) inspect || *ref* to prove true; take place
verja *f* iron gate, iron fence, grating
ver•mú *m* (*pl* **-mús**) vermouth; matinée
vernácu•lo -la *adj* vernacular
verónica *f* (bot) veronica; (taur) veronica (*graceful pass in which the bullfighter waits for the bull with open cape*)
veroniquear *intr* (taur) to perform veronicas
verosímil *adj* likely, probable
verraco *m* male hog, boar
verraquear *intr* to grunt, grumble; cry hard
verruga *f* wart; bore, nuisance
verrugo *m* miser
versal *adj & f* capital
versalilla or **versalita** *f* small capital
Versalles Versailles
versar *intr* — **versar acerca de** *or* **sobre** to deal with, treat of || *ref* — **versarse en** to be or become versed in
versátil *adj* fickle; versatile; (*arma*) multipurpose
versículo *m* verse (*in the Bible*)
versificación *f* versification
versificar §73 *tr & intr* to versify
versión *f* version; translation
verso *m* verse; (typ) verso; **versos pareados** rhymed couplet
vertebra•do -da *adj & m* vertebrate
vertedero *m* dump; weir, spillway
verter §51 *tr* (*un líquido, un polvo*) to pour; (*un recipiente*) empty; (*lágrimas; luz; sangre*) shed; (*descargar*) dump; translate || *intr* to flow || *ref* to run, empty
vertical *adj & f* vertical
vértice *m* vertex
vertido *m* spilling, spillage; dumping
vertiente *m & f* (*declive*) slope; (*colina por donde corre el agua*) shed || *f* (Arg, Col, Chile) spring, fountain
vertigino•so -sa *adj* dizzy; fast, sudden
vértigo *m* vertigo, dizziness; fit of insanity
vesícula *f* vesicle; **vesícula biliar** gall bladder
veso *m* polecat
Véspero *m* Vesper
vesperti•no -na *adj* evening || *m* evening sermon
vestíbulo *m* vestibule; (theat) foyer, lobby
vestido *m* clothing, dress; (*de mujer*) gown, dress; (*de hombre*) suit; costume; **vestido de baño** (Col) swimsuit; **vestido de ceremonia** dress suit; **vestido de etiqueta** evening clothes; **vestido de etiqueta de mujer** *or* **vestido de noche** evening gown; **vestido de novia** wedding dress; **vestido de gala** (mil) full dress; **vestido de serio** evening clothes; **vestido de tarde-noche** cocktail dress
vestidura *f* clothing; (*del sacerdote*) vestment
vestigio *m* vestige, trace; track, footprint
vestir §50 *tr* to dress, clothe; adorn; cover up; disguise; (*tal o cual vestido*) wear; put on; **vestir el cargo** to look the part || *intr* to dress; (*una prenda o la materia*) be dressy; **vestir de** (*p.ej., blanco*) to dress in; **vestir de etiqueta** to dress in evening clothes; **vestir de paisano** to dress in civilian clothes || *ref* to dress, get dressed; dress oneself; (*de una enfermedad*) be up, be about; **vestirse de** (*nubes, flores, hierba, etc.*) to be covered with; (*importancia, humildad, etc.*) assume
vestuario *m* (*las prendas de uno*) wardrobe; dressing room; bathhouse; checkroom, cloakroom; (mil) uniform; (sport) locker room; (theat) dressing room
Vesubio, el Vesuvius
veta *f* vein; streak, stripe; **descubrir la veta de** to be on to
vetar *tr* to veto
vetea•do -da *adj* veined, striped || *m* graining || *f* (Ecuad) whipping
vetear *tr* to grain, stripe; (Eucad) to whip, flog
veteranía *f* experience, know-how
vetera•no -na *adj & mf* veteran
veterina•rio -ria *adj* veterinary || *mf* veterinarian || *f* veterinary medicine
vetus•to -ta *adj* old, ancient
vez *f* (*pl* **veces**) time; (*tiempo de hacer una cosa por turno*) turn; **a la vez** at the same time; **a la vez que** while; **alguna vez** sometimes; ever; **a su vez** in turn; on his part; **a veces** at times, sometimes; **cada vez** every time; **cada vez más** more and more; **cuántas veces** how often; **de una vez** at one time; once and for all; **de vez en cuando** once in a while; **dos veces** twice; **en vez de** instead of; **esperar**

vez to wait one's turn; **hacer las veces de** to take the place of; **las más veces** most of the time; **muchas veces** often; **otra vez** again; **raras veces** *or* **rara vez** seldom, rarely; **repetidas veces** over and over again; **tal vez** perhaps; **tomar la vez a** to get ahead of; **una que otra vez** once in a while; **una vez** once

veza *f* vetch, spring vetch

v.g. or **v.gr.** *abbr* **verbigracia**

vía *f* road, route, way; (*par de rieles y el suelo en que se asientan*) (rr) track; (*el mismo carril*) (rr) rail, track; (anat) passage, tract; (fig) way; **por la vía de** via; **por vía aérea** by air; **por vía bucal** by mouth; **vía aérea** airway; **vía ancha** (rr) broad gauge; **vía de acceso** on ramp, entrance; **vía de agua** waterway; (naut) leak; **vía de salida** off ramp, exit; **vía estrecha** (rr) narrow gauge; **vía férrea** railway; **vía fluvial** waterway; **Vía Láctea** Milky Way; **vía muerta** (rr) siding; **vía normal** (rr) standard gauge; **vía principal** mainstream; **vía pública** thoroughfare; **vías de hecho** (law) assault and battery ‖ *prep* via

viable *adj* feasible

viaducto *m* viaduct

viajante *adj* traveling ‖ *mf* traveler; traveling sales representative, traveling salesman

viajar *tr* to sell on the road; (*ciertas comarcas*) cover as salesman ‖ *intr* to travel, journey

viaje *m* trip, journey; travel book; water supply; (*drogas*) trip; **¡buen viaje!** bon voyage!; **viaje de bodas** honeymoon; **viaje de estudios** field trip; **viaje de ida y vuelta** *or* **viaje redondo** round trip; **viaje de negocios** business trip; **viaje de placer** pleasure trip; **viaje de pruebas** shakedown cruise, trial cruise; **viaje organizado** package tour

viaje•ro -ra *adj* traveling ‖ *mf* traveler; passenger

vial *adj* road, highway ‖ *m* tree-lined road

vianda *f* food, viand; meal

viandante *mf* traveler; itinerant

víbora *f* viper

vibración *f* vibration

vibrar *tr* to vibrate; (*la voz; la r*) roll; (*una lanza*) hurl ‖ *intr* to vibrate ‖ *ref* to be thrilled

vicaría *f* vicarage

vicario *m* vicar

vicealmirante *m* vice-admiral

vicepresiden•te -ta *mf* vice-president

viceversa *adv* vice versa

viciar *tr* to vitiate; (*una proposición*) to slant ‖ *ref* to become vitiated; give oneself up to vice; become addicted; (*una tabla*) warp

vicio *m* vice; pampering, spoiling; luxuriance, overgrowth; fault, defect; (law) flaw, error; **hablar de vicio** to talk all the time, talk too much; **quejarse de vicio** to be a chronic complainer

vicio•so -sa *adj* vicious; faulty, defective; strong, robust; luxuriant, overgrown; dissolute; (*niño*) spoiled

víctima *f* victim, **víctima propiciatoria** scapegoat

victimar *tr* to kill, murder

victoria *f* victory

victorio•so -sa *adj* victorious

vid *f* vine, grapevine

vida *f* life; living, livelihood; **darse buena vida** to live high; live in comfort; **de por vida** for life; **en mi vida** never; **escapar con vida** to have a narrow escape; **ganar** or **ganarse la vida** to earn one's livelihood, make a living; **hacer por la vida** to get a bite to eat; **mudar de vida** to mend one's ways; **¡por vida mía!** upon my soul!; **vida airada** licentious living; **vida amorosa** love life; **vida ancha** loose living; **vida de familia** *or* **de hogar** home life; **vida mía** my darling

vidalita *f* (Arg, Chile, Urug) mournful love song

vidente *mf* clairvoyant ‖ *m* prophet, see ‖ *f* seeress

video *or* **vídeo** (Esp) *m* video; videocassette; videotape; videocassette recorder; **en video** on video

videocámara *f* video camera, camcorder

videocasete *or* **videocassette** *m* videocassette

videocinta *f* videotape

videoclip *m* video clip

videoclub *m* video club

videoconferencia *f* videoconference

video disco *m* videodisk

videófono *m* videophone

videograbación *f* videotape recording, videotaping, videocassette recording

videograbador *m or* **videograbadora** *f* videocassette recorder, videotape recorder

videograbar *tr* to video, to videotape

videograma *m* videotape recording

videojuego *m* video game

videopiratería *f* video piracy

videoproyector *m* video projector

videoseñal *f* video signal, picture signal

videoteca *f* video library

videoterminal *m* (compu) terminal, visual display unit (VDU)

videotexto *m* videotext

videotocadiscos *m* videodisk player

vidria•do -da *adj* glazed; brittle ‖ *m* glaze, glazing; glazed pottery; dishes

vidriar §77 & regular *tr* to glaze ‖ *ref* (*los ojos*) to become glassy

vidriera *f* glass window, glass door; shop-window, store window; **vidriera de colores** *or* **vidriera pintada** stained-glass window

vidriería *f* glassworks; glass store

vidriero *m* glass blower, glassworker; glazier; glass dealer

vidrio *m* glass; piece of glass; windowpane; **pagar los vidrios rotos** to take the blame, to be the goat; **vidrio cilindrado** plate glass; **vidrio de aumento** magnifying glass; **vidrio de color** stained glass; **vidrio deslustrado** ground glass; **vidrio tallado** cut glass

vidrio•so -sa *adj* glassy, vitreous; (*quebradizo*) brittle; (*resbaladizo*) slippery; (*que se resiente fácilmente*) touchy; (*mirada, ojos*) (fig) glassy

vieira *f* (*molusco*) scallop; (*concha*) scallop shell

vie•jo -ja *adj* old || *m* old man; **viejo verde** old goat, old rake || *f* old woman

vie•nés -nesa *adj & mf* Viennese || *f* (Chile) frankfurter

viento *m* wind; course, direction; (*cuerda que mantiene una cosa derecha*) guy; (*gases intestinales*) wind; **ceñir el viento** (naut) to sail close to the wind; **viento de cola** (aer) tail wind; **viento en popa** (naut) tail wind; **vientos alisios** trade winds

vientre *m* belly; (*parte de la ondulación entre dos nodos*) (phys) loop; **evacuar** *or* **exonerar el vientre** to have a bowel movement; **vientre flojo** loose bowels

vier•nes *m* (*pl* **-nes**) Friday; **Viernes Santo** Good Friday

viertea•guas *m* (*pl* **-guas**) *m* flashing

vietna•més -mesa *adj & mf* Vietnamese

viga *f* beam, girder, rafter; **estar contando las vigas** to gaze blankly at the ceiling; **viga de celosía** lattice girder

vigencia *f* force, operation; (*de una póliza de seguro*) life; **en vigencia** in force, in effect

vigente *adj* effective, in force

vigési•mo -ma *adj & m* twentieth

vigía *m* lookout, watch; **vigía de incendios** firewarden || *f* watch; watchtower; (naut) rock, reef

vigiar §77 *tr* to watch over

vigilancia *f* vigilance, watchfulness; **bajo vigilancia médica** under the care of a physician

vigilante *adj* vigilant, watchful || *m* guard, watchman; **vigilante nocturno** night watchman

vigilar *tr* to watch over; look out for || *intr* to watch, keep guard

vigilia *f* vigil; wakefulness; night work, night study; (*víspera*) eve; (mil) guard, watch; **comer de vigilia** to fast, abstain from meat

vigor *m* vigor; **en vigor** in force; into effect

vigoriza•dor -dora *adj* invigorating || *m* tonic; **vigorizador del cabello** hair tonic

vigorizante *adj* invigorating

vigorizar §60 *tr* to invigorate; encourage

vigoro•so -sa *adj* vigorous

vigueta *f* small beam, small girder

VIH *m* (letterword) (*Virus de Inmunodeficiencia-Humana*) HIV (Human Immunodeficiency Virus)

vihuela *f* Spanish lute

vil *adj* vile, base, mean || *mf* scoundrel

vilano *m* bur, down

vileza *f* vileness, baseness

vilipendiar *tr* to scorn, despise

vilipendio•so -sa *adj* contemptible

villa *f* town; (*casa de recreo en el campo*) villa; **la Villa** the city (*Madrid*)

villancico *m* carol, Christmas carol

villanes•co -ca *adj* boorish, crude, rustic

villanía *f* humbleness, humble birth; vileness, meanness; foul remark

villa•no -na *adj* base, vile; rude, impolite || *mf* peasant; knave, scoundrel

villorrio *m* small country town

vilo — en vilo in the air; (fig) up in the air

vilorta *f* reed hoop; (*arandela*) washer

vinagre *m* vinegar; (*persona de genio áspero*) grouch

vinagrera *f* (bot) sorrel; (SAm) heartburn; **vinagreras** cruet stand

vinagreta *f* French dressing, vinaigrette sauce

vinagro•so -sa *adj* vinegary

vinariego *m* vineyardist

vinatería *f* wine business; wine shop

vinate•ro -ra *adj* wine || *m* wine dealer, vintner

vincha *f* sweatband; hairband

vincular *tr* to bind, tie, unite; continue, perpetuate; (*esperanzas*) found, base; (law) entail || *ref* (compu) link

vínculo *m* bond, tie; (law) entail; **vínculos** (compu) links

vindicar §73 *tr* (*vengar*) to avenge; (*exculpar*) vindicate

vindicta *f* revenge

vinicul•tor -tora *mf* winegrower

vinicultura *f* winegrowing

vinilo *m* vinyl

vino *m* wine; sherry reception, wine party; **tener mal vino** to be a quarrelsome drunk; **vino cubierto** dark-red wine; **vino de Jerez** sherry; **vino del terruño** local wine; **vino de mesa** table wine; **vino de Oporto** port wine; **vino de pasto** table wine; **vino de postre** after-dinner wine; **vino de segunda** second-run wine; **vino de solera** solera sherry; **vino espumante** *or* **espumoso** sparkling wine; **vino tinto** red table wine

vinolen•to -ta *adj* too fond of wine

viña *f* vineyard; **ser una viña** to be a mine; **tener una viña** to have a sinecure

viña•dor -dora *mf* vineyardist, vinedresser || *m* guard of a vineyard

viñedo *m* vineyard

viñeta *f* vignette, headpiece

viola *f* (mus) viola

violación *f* rape; (*de una ley*) violation; (*de un acuerdo*) breaking

viola•dor -dora *mf* violator; rapist

viola•do -da *adj & m* violet (*color*)

violar *m* bed of violets || *tr* to violate; ravish, rape; profane, desecrate; tamper with; (*una ley; un acuerdo*) break

violencia *f* violence

violentar *tr* to do violence to; (*p.ej., una casa*) break into || *ref* to force oneself

violen•to -ta *adj* violent

violeta *m* (*color; colorante*) violet || *f* (bot) violet

violín *m* violin; (billiards) bridge, cue rest; **embolsar el violín** (Arg, Ven) to cower, to slink away
violinista *mf* violinist
violón *m* (mus) bass viol; **tocar el violón** to talk nonsense
violoncelista *mf* cellist, violoncellist
violoncelo *m* (mus) cello, violoncello
violonchelista *mf* cellist, violoncellist
violonchelo *m* (mus) cello, violoncello
VIP *mf* (letterword) (**notable** *m*) VIP (Very Important Person); **VIPS** VIPs
vira *f* welt; (*saetilla*) dart
virada *f* turn, change of direction; (naut) tack
virago *f* mannish woman
viraje *m* turn, swerve; (phot) toning
virar *tr* (naut) to wind; (naut) to tack, veer; (phot) to tone || *intr* to turn, swerve; (naut) to tack, veer
virgen *adj* virgin || *f* virgin, maiden; **la Virgen y el niño** (fa) the Madonna and child
virginidad *f* virginity
Virgo *m* (astr) Virgo
vírgula *f* rod; thin line, light dash
virgulilla *f* fine line; diacritic mark
virilidad *f* virility
virin•go -ga *adj* (Col) naked
virolen•to -ta *adj* pock-marked; having smallpox
virología *f* virology
virote *m* (*saeta*) bolt; sporty young fellow; (coll) stuffed shirt
virrey *m* viceroy
virtual *adj* virtual
virtud *f* virtue
virtuosismo *m* virtuosity
virtuo•so -sa *adj* virtuous || *m* virtuoso
viruela *f* smallpox; pock mark; **viruelas locas** chicken pox
virulencia *f* virulence
virulen•to -ta *adj* violent, rabid; (med) virulent
vi•rus *m* (*pl* **-rus**) virus; **Virus de Inmunodeficiencia Humana** Human Immunodeficiency Virus; **virus del Sida (VIH)** AID's virus (HIV); **virus informáticos** computer virus
viruta *f* shaving
virutilla *f* thin shaving; **virutillas de acero** steel wool
visado *m* visa
visaje *m* face, grimace
visar *tr* to visa; to O.K.; (arti & surv) to sight
vísceras *fpl* viscera
visco *m* birdlime
viscosa *f* viscose
viscosilla *f* rayon thread
visco•so -sa *adj* viscous || *f* see **viscosa**
visera *f* (*del yelmo, de las gorras, del parabrisas del automóvil, etc.*) visor; (*pequeña pantalla que se pone en la frente para resguardar la vista*) eyeshade; (W-I) blinder, blinker
visible *adj* visible; (*manifiesto*) evident; (*que llama la atención*) conspicuous
visigo•do -da *adj* Visigothic || *mf* Visigoth
visillo *m* window curtain, window shade
visión *f* vision; view; (*persona fea y ridícula*) sight, scarecrow; **ver visiones** to be seeing things; **visión de túnel** (opt) tunnel vision; **visión negra** (*del aviador*) blackout
visionar *tr* to contemplate, look at
visiona•rio -ria *adj & mf* visionary
visir *m* vizier; **gran visir** grand vizier
visita *f* visit; visitor, caller, guest; inspection; **ir de visitas** to go calling; **pagar la visita a** to return the call of; **tener visita** to have callers; **visita de cumplido** *or* **de cortesía** courtesy call; **visita guiada** guided tour; **visita de médico** (fig) brief visit
visita•dor -dora *mf* frequent caller || *m* inspector || *f* (Hond, Ven) enema
visitante *adj* visiting || *mf* visitor, guest
visitar *tr* to visit; inspect
visite•ro -ra *adj* visiting; (*médico*) fond of making calls || *mf* visitor
vislumbrar *tr* to descry, glimpse; surmise, suspect || *ref* (*verse confusamente por la distancia*) glimmer; (*aparecer en la distancia*) loom
vislumbre *f* glimpse, glimmer; **vislumbres** inkling, notion
viso *m* sheen, gleam; (*de ciertas telas*) luster; streak, strain; appearance, thin veneer; elevation, height; colored material worn under transparent outer garment; **a dos visos** with a double purpose; **de viso** conspicuous; **hacer visos** to be iridescent
visón *m* mink
visor *m* (aer) bombsight; (phot) finder
víspera *f* eve, day before; **en vísperas de** on the eve of; **víspera de año nuevo** New Year's Eve; **víspera de Navidad** Christmas Eve; **vísperas** (eccl) vespers, evensong
vista *mf* custom-house inspector || *f* (*sentido del ver*) vision, sight; (*paisaje que se ve desde un punto; estampa que representa un lugar*) view; (*panorama, perspectiva*) vista; comparison; purpose, design; (*ojeada*) glance, look; interview; eye; eyes; (law) hearing, trial; **a la vista** (com) at sight; **a vista de** in view of; compared with; **con vistas a** with a view to; **de vista** by sight; **doble vista** second sight; **hacer la vista gorda ante** to shut one's eyes to; **hasta la vista** good-bye, so long; **medir con la vista** to size up; **saltar a la vista** to be self-evident; **tener a la vista** to keep one's eyes on; (*p.ej., una carta*) to have at hand; **torcer la vista** to squint; **vista a ojo de pájaro** bird's-eye view; **vistas** (*aberturas de un edificio*) lights, openings; view, outlook; visible parts, parts that show
vistazo *m* look, glance
vistillas *fpl* eminence, height; **irse a las vistillas** to try to get a look at one's opponent's cards
vis•to -ta *adj* evident, obvious; in view of; **bien visto** looked upon with approval; **mal visto**

looked upon with disapproval; **no visto** *or* **nunca visto** unheard-of; **por lo visto** apparently, judging from the facts; **visto bueno** approved, O.K.; **visto que** whereas, inasmuch as || *m* whereas || *f* see **vista**
visto•so -sa *adj* showy, flashy, loud
visual *adj* visual || *f* line of sight
visualizador *m* (compu) visual display unit; viewer
visualizar §60 *tr* (compu) to display; to view
vital *adj* vital
vitali•cio -cia *adj* life, lifetime || *m* life-insurance policy; life annuity
vitalidad *f* vitality
vitalizar §60 *tr* to vitalize
vitamina *f* vitamin
vitan•do -da *adj* hateful, odious; being shunned
vitela *f* vellum
viticul•tor -tora *mf* grape grower, vineyardist
viticultura *f* grape growing
vitola *f* cigar size; mien, appearance; (Cuba) cigar band
vítor *interj* hurray! || *m* panegyric tablet; triumphal pageant
vitorear *tr* to cheer, acclaim
vitral *m* stained-glass window
vítre•o -a *adj* vitreous, glassy
vitrina *f* showcase, glass cabinet; shopwindow; **mirar vitrinas** to windowshop
vitriólì•co -ca *adj* (chem) vitriolic
vitro *m*—**in vitro** (*fertilización*) in vitro
vitrola *f* record player
vituallas *fpl* victuals
vituperable *adj* vituperable
vituperar *tr* to vituperate
viuda *f* widow; **viuda de marido vivo** *or* **viuda de paja** grass widow
viudedad *f* widowhood; dower; widow's pension
viudez *f* (*estado de viuda*) widowhood; (*estado de viudo*) widowerhood
viu•do -da *adj* left a widow; left a widower || *m* widower || *f* see **viuda**
viva *interj* viva!, long live!, hurrah! || *m* viva
vivacidad *f* longevity; vivacity, liveliness; brightness, brilliance
vivande•ro -ra *mf* (mil) sutler, camp follower
vivaque *m* bivouac; guardhouse; police headquarters; **estar al vivaque** to bivouac
vivaquear *intr* to bivouac
vivar *m* warren, burrow; aquarium || *tr* to cheer, acclaim
vivara•cho -cha *adj* vivacious, lively
vi•vaz *adj* (*pl* **-vaces**) long-lived; vivacious, lively; keen, perceptive; (bot) perennial
víveres *mpl* food, provisions, victuals
vivero *m* tree nursery; fishpond; (*origen de cosas perjudiciales*) (fig) hotbed
viveza *f* agility, briskness; ardor, vehemence; sharpness, keenness; perception; brightness, brilliance; witticism; (*de los ojos*) sparkle; (*acción o palabra poco consideradas*) thoughtlessness
vivide•ro -ra *adj* livable
víví•do -da *adj* quick, perceptive; lively
vivienda *f* dwelling; life, way of life; **vivienda unifamiliar** one-family house
viviente *adj* living, alive
vivificar §73 *tr* to vivify, enliven
vivir *m* life, living || *tr* (*una experiencia o ventura*) to live; (*toda la vida; la vejez*) live out; (*habitar*) live in || *intr* to live; **¿quién vive?** (mil) who goes there?; **vivir de** (*p.ej., carne*) to live on; **vivir para ver** to live and learn; **vivir y dejar vivir** to live and let live
vivisección *f* vivisection
vi•vo -va *adj* living, alive, live; (*lleno de vida; intenso*) live; (*sutil, agudo*) sharp, keen; (*dolor*) acute; (*carne*) raw; active, effective; (*luz*) bright, intense; (*pronto y ágil*) quick; (*idioma*) living, modern; **de viva voz** viva voce, by word of mouth; **herir en lo vivo** to cut or to sting to the quick || *mf* living person; **los vivos y los muertos** the quick and the dead || *m* edging, border; (vet) mange
Vizcaya *f* Biscay; **llevar hierro a Vizcaya** to carry coals to Newcastle
vizconde *m* viscount
vizcondesa *f* viscountess
V.M. *abbr* **Vuestra Majestad**
V.°B.° *abbr* **visto bueno**
vocablista *mf* punster
vocablo *m* word; **jugar del vocablo** to pun; **vocablo cabeza de artículo** headword
vocabulario *m* vocabulary
vocación *f* vocation, calling
vocal *adj* vocal || *mf* director || *f* vowel
vocalista *mf* singer, vocalist
vocativo *m* vocative
voceador *m* town crier; barker (*e.g., at a fair*); (Col, Ecuad) paper boy
vocear *tr* to cry, shout; cheer, acclaim; call, page; boast about publicly || *intr* to shout
vocería *f* shouting, outcry; spokesmanship
vocerío *m* shouting, outcry
vocero *m* spokesman, mouthpiece
vociferar *tr* (*injurias*) to shout; boast loudly about || *intr* to vociferate, shout
vocingle•ro -ra *adj* loudmouthed; loud, talkative
vo•dú *m* (*pl* **-dúes**) voodoo
voduísta *adj & mf* voodoo
vol. *abbr* **volumen, voluntad**
volada *f* short flight; (*del jugador de billar*) (Arg) stroke; (Col, Ecuad) trick; (*noticia inventada*) (Mex) hoax
voladi•zo -za *adj* projecting || *m* projection
vola•do -da *adj* (typ) superior || *f* see **volada**
vola•dor -dora *adj* flying; hanging, dangling; swift, fast || *m* rocket; flying fish
voladura *f* blast, explosion
volandas — **en volandas** in the air; fast

volante *adj* flying; unsettled || *m* shuttlecock; battledore and shuttlecock; (*rueda que regula el movimiento de una máquina*) flywheel; (*rueda de mano para la dirección del automóvil*) steering wheel; (*pieza del reloj movida por la espiral*) balance wheel; flunkey, lackey; (*criado que iba a pie delante del coche o caballo*) outrunner; (*de papel*) slip, leaflet; (sew) flounce, ruffle; **un buen volante** a good driver
volan•tín -tina *adj* unsettled || *m* fish line; kite
volantista *m* driver, man at the wheel
volan•tón -tona *mf* fledgling || *f* (Ven) loose woman
volapié *m* (taur) running sword thrust; a **volapié** half running, half flying; half walking, half swimming
volar §61 *tr* (*llevar en un aparato de aviación*) to fly; blow up, explode; irritate; (*una letra, tipo o signo*) (typ) to raise || *intr* to fly; fly away; disappear; jut out, project; (*una especie*) spread rapidly; (*p.ej., una torre*) rise in the air; **volar sin motor** (aer) to glide || *ref* to fly away; fly off the handle
volatería *f* fowling with decoys; **de volatería** offhand
volátil *adj* volatile
volatilizar *tr & ref* to volatilize
volatín *m* ropewalker, acrobat, tumbler
volatine•ro -ra *mf* ropewalker, acrobat, tumbler
volcán *m* volcano
volcar §81 *tr* to upset, overturn, dump; tip, tilt; (*a una persona un olor fuerte*) to make dizzy; change the mind of; irritate, tease || *intr* to upset || *ref* to turn upside down
volear *tr* (tennis) to volley
vóleibol *or* **voleibol** *m* volleyball
voleo *m* (tennis) volley; reeling punch; **del primer voleo** *or* **de un voleo** with a smash, all at once; **sembrar a voleo** to sow, broadcast
volframio *m* wolfram, tungsten
volibol *m* (Col, Mex, Ven) volleyball
volquete *m* dumpcart, dump truck
voltai•co -ca *adj* voltaic
voltaje *m* voltage
volta•rio -ria *adj* fickle, inconstant; (Chile) willful; (Chile) sporty
voltea•do -da *mf* (Col) turncoat, deserter
voltear *tr* to upset, turn over; turn around; move, transform || *intr* to roll over, tumble
volteo *m* upset, overturning; tumbling; (P-R) scolding
voltereta *f* tumble; turning up card to determine trump; **voltereta lateral** cartwheel
voltímetro *m* voltmeter
voltio *m* volt
volti•zo -za *adj* curled, twisted; fickle
voluble *adj* easily turned; fickle, inconstant
volumen *m* volume; **volumen sonoro** volume; (geom) volume
volumino•so -sa *adj* voluminous
voluntad *f* will; (*amor, cariño*) fondness, love; **a voluntad** at will; **buena voluntad** willingness; **de buena voluntad** willingly; **de mala voluntad** unwillingly; **de su propia voluntad** of one's own volition; **última voluntad** last wishes; **última voluntad y testamento** last will and testament; **voluntad de hierro** iron will
voluntariedad *f* willfulness
volunta•rio -ria *adj* (*que se hace por espontánea voluntad*) voluntary; (*que tiene voluntad obstinada*) willful; (*que se presta voluntariamente a hacer algo*) volunteer || *mf* volunteer
voluntario•so -sa *adj* willful
voluptuo•so -sa *adj* (*que inspira complacencia en los placeres sensuales*) voluptuous; (*dado a los placeres sensuales*) voluptuary || *mf* voluptuary
voluta *f* (archit) scroll, volute; (*p.ej., de humo*) ring
volvedor *m* screwdriver; (Col) extra, something thrown in; **volvedor de machos** tap wrench
volver §47 & §83 *tr* to turn; turn upside down; turn inside out; return, send back, give back; (*una puerta*) push to, pull to; translate; vomit || *intr* to turn; return, come back; **volver a** + *inf* verb + again, e.g., **volvió a abrir la puerta** he opened the door again; **volver a marcar** *or* **discar** (telp) to redial; **volver en sí** to come to; **volver por** to defend, stand up for || *ref* to become; turn around; return, come back; change one's mind; turn, turn sour; **volverse atrás** to back out; **volverse contra** to turn on
vomitar *tr* to vomit, throw up; (*fuego los cañones*) belch forth; (*maldiciones*) utter; (*un secreto*) let out; (*lo que uno retiene indebidamente*) cough up || *intr* to vomit, throw up; come across, disgorge
vómito *m* vomit, vomiting; **provocar a vómito** to nauseate; **vómitos del embarazo** morning sickness
voracidad *f* voracity
vorágine *f* whirlpool, vortex
vo•raz *adj* (*pl* **-races**) voracious
vormela *f* polecat
vórtice *m* vortex
vos *pron pers* (subject of verb and object of preposition; takes plural form of verb but is singular in meaning; used in addressing the Deity, the Virgin, etc., and distinguished persons; in Spanish America is much used instead of **tú**) you
voso•tros -tras *pron pers* (plural of **tú**) you
votación *f* vote, voting; **votación de desempate** runoff election
votante *adj* voting || *mf* voter
votar *tr* to vote for; (*sí, no*) vote; (*p.ej., un cirio a la Virgen*) vow || *intr* to vote; vow; swear, curse
voti•vo -va *adj* votive
voto *m* (*sufragio; derecho de votar; persona que da su voto*) vote; (*promesa solemne*) vow; (*exvoto*) votive offering; (*blasfemia*) oath, curse; wish, desire; **echar votos** to swear, to

curse; **regular los votos** to tally the votes; **voto de amén** vote of a yes man; yes man; **voto de calidad** casting vote; **voto informativo** straw vote; **voto por correspondencia** *or* **correo** absentee ballot; **votos** good wishes; **¡voto va!** come now!

voz *f* (*pl* **voces**) voice; (*vocablo*) word; **aclarar la voz** to clear one's throat; **a una voz** with one voice; **a voces** shouting; **a voz en cuello** or **en grito** at the top of one's voice; **correr la voz que** to be rumored that; **dar voces** to shout, cry out; **de viva voz** viva voce, by word of mouth; **en alta voz** aloud, in a loud voice; **en voz baja** in a low voice; **llevar la voz cantante** to have the say, be the boss; **voces** outcry

voz-guía *f* (*diccionario*) entry word

vro. *abbr* **vuestro**

V.S. *abbr* **Vueseñoría, Vuestra Señoría**

vuelco *m* upset, overturn; (compu) dump; **dar un vuelco** to turn over, overturn, alter drastically

vuelo *m* flight; flying; (*de una falda*) flare, fullness; projection; lace cuff trimming; **al vuelo** at once; on the wing; scattered at random; (chess) en passant; **alzar el vuelo** to take flight; to dash away; **echar a vuelo las campanas** to ring a full peal; **tirar al vuelo** to shoot on the wing; **tocar a vuelo las campanas** to ring a full peal; **vuelo a ciegas** (aer) blind flying; **vuelo a vela** glide, gliding, soaring; **vuelo de distancia** (aer) long-distance flight; **vuelo de enlace** connecting flight; **vuelo de ensayo** *or* **de prueba** (aer) test flight; **vuelo espacial tripulado** manned space flight; **vuelo libre** hang gliding; **vuelo planeado** (aer) volplane; **vuelo rasante** (aer) hedgehopping; **vuelo regular** scheduled flight; **vuelo sin escala** (aer) nonstop flight; **vuelo sin motor** (aer) glide, gliding, soaring

vuelta *f* turn; (*regreso; devolución*) return; (*dinero sobrante de un pago*) change; (*de un camino*) bend, turn; (*del pantalón*) cuff; cuff trimming; (*paseo corto*) stroll; (*revés*) other side; (*paliza*) beating, whipping; (*en un cabo*) loop; (*en la media*) clock; (*mudanza*) change; **a la vuelta** on returning; please turn the page; **a la vuelta de** at the end of; at the turn of; (*la esquina*) around; **a vuelta de** about; **a vuelta de correo** by return mail; **dar cien vueltas a** to run rings around, be way ahead of; **dar la vuelta de campana** to turn somersault; **darse una vuelta a la redonda** to tend to one's own business; **dar una vuelta** to take a stroll, take a walk; take a look; change one's ways; **dar vuelta** to turn around; (*el vino*) turn sour; **dar vuelta a** to reverse, turn around; **estar de vuelta** to be back; **media vuelta** about-face; **quedarse con la vuelta** to keep the change; **vuelta al ruedo** (taur) lap of honor; **vuelta de campana** somersault; **vuelta de carro** (Mex) cartwheel; **vuelta de honor** (sport) lap of honor; **vuelta del mundo** trip around the world; **vuelta de manos** handspring; **vuelta en redondo** complete turn; **vuelta en U** (CAm) U-turn

vuelto *m* change

vues•tro -tra (corresponds to **vos** and **vosotros**) *adj poss* your || *pron poss* yours

vulcanizar §60 *tr* to vulcanize

vulgacho *m* populace, mob

vulgar *adj* vulgar, popular, common, vernacular

vulgarismo *m* popular expression; (philol) popular word, popular form

vulgarizar §60 *tr* to popularize; translate into the vernacular || *ref* to associate with the people

Vulgata *f* Vulgate

vulgo *adv* commonly || *m* common people; (*personas que en una materia sólo conocen la parte superficial*) laity || *adv* commonly known as

vulnerable *adj* vulnerable

vulnerar *tr* to hurt, injure; (*la reputación de una persona*) damage; (*una ley, un precepto*) break

vulpeja *f* she-fox, vixen

V.V. or **VV** *abbr* **ustedes**

X

X, x (equis) *f* twenty-fourth letter of the Spanish alphabet

xenia *f* xenia

xenofobia *f* xenophobia

xenófo•bo -ba *mf* xenophobe

xenón *m* xenon

xerocopia *f* Xerox copy, Xerox[T]

xerocopiar §77 *tr* to xerox, to make a Xerox (copy) of || *intr* to make Xerox copies

xerografía *f* xerography; Xerox copy, Xerox[T] *m*

xerografiar §77 *tr* to xerox, to make a Xerox copy of || *intr* to make Xerox copies

Xerox[T] *m* Xerox[T]

xilema *f* xylem

xilofono *m* (mus) xylophone

xilografía *f* (*arte*) xylography; (*grabado*) xylograph

xpiano *abbr* **cristiano**

Xpo *abbr* **Cristo**

xptiano *abbr* **cristiano**

Xpto *abbr* **Cristo**

xunde *m* (Mex) reed basket, palm basket

Y

Y, y (ye) *f* twenty-fifth letter of the Spanish alphabet
y *conj* and
ya *adv* already; right away; now; **no ya** not only; **ya no** no longer; **ya que** since, inasmuch as
yac *m* (*bandera de proa*) (naut) jack; (*bóvido del Tibet*) yak
yacer §82 *intr* to lie
yacija *f* bed, couch; (*sepultura*) grave
yacimiento *m* bed, field, deposit; **yacimiento de petróleo** oil field
yámbi•co -ca *adj* iambic
yambo *m* iamb, iambus
yanqui *adj & mf* Yankee
yapa *f* bonus, extra, allowance; **de yapa** in the bargain, extra
yarda *f* (*0.91 metro*) yard
yate *m* yacht
yedra *f* ivy
yegua *f* mare; (CAm) cigar butt
yeguada *f* stud
yelmo *m* helmet
yema *f* (*de huevo*) yolk; candied yolk; (*del invierno*) dead; (*renuevo*) bud; (fig) cream; **dar en la yema** to put one's finger on the spot; **yema del dedo** finger tip; **yema mejida** eggnog
yente — yentes y vinientes *mpl* habitués, frequenters
yerba *f* var of **hierba**
yer•mo -ma *adj* deserted, uninhabited; (*suelo*) unsown; (*mujer*) not pregnant || *m* desert, wilderness
yerno *m* son-in-law
yerro *m* error, mistake; **yerro de cuenta** miscalculation; **yerro de imprenta** printer's error
yer•to -ta *adj* stiff, rigid
yesca *f* punk, tinder; (*cosa que excita una pasión*) fuel; **echar una yesca** to strike a light
yeso *m* gypsum; plaster cast
yo *pron pers* I; **soy yo** it's me, it is I; present, here
yodhídri•co -ca *adj* hydriodic
yodo *m* iodine
yoduro *m* iodide
yoga *f* yoga
yogui *m* yogi
yogurt *m* yogurt
yola *f* shell (*boat*)
yonquí *m* (*drogas*) junkie drug addict
yugo *m* yoke; **sacudir el yugo** to throw off the yoke
Yugoeslavia *f* Yugoslavia
yugoesla•vo -va *adj & mf* Yugoslav
yugular *adj & f* jugular || *tr* to cut off, nip in the bud
yunque *m* anvil; drudge, work horse
yunta *f* yoke, team
yupi *mf* yuppie, yuppy || *interj* yippee!, whoopee!, hooray!
yute *m* jute
yuxtaponer §54 *tr* to juxtapose
yuyo *m* (Arg, Chile) weed; **yuyos** (Col, Ecuad, Peru) greens

Z

Z, z (zeda or zeta) *f* twenty-sixth letter of the Spanish alphabet
zabordar *intr* (naut) to run aground
zabullir §13 *tr* (*p.ej., a un perro*) to duck, give a ducking to; throw, hurl || *ref* (*meterse debajo del agua con ímpetu*) to dive; (*esconderse rápidamente*) duck
zacapela *f* or **zacapella** *f* row, rumpus
zacate *m* (CAm, Mex) hay, fodder; **zacate de empaque** excelsior
zacateca *m* (Cuba) undertaker, gravedigger
zacatín *m* old-clothes market
zacear *tr* (*al perro*) to chase away || *intr* to lisp
zafaduría *f* (Arg) brazenness, effrontery
zafar *tr* to adorn, bedeck; loosen, untie; clear, free; (*un buque*) lighten || *ref* to slip away; slip off, come off; **zafarse de** to get out of
zafarrancho *m* (naut) clearing the decks; (coll) havoc, ravage; (coll) scuffle, row; **zafarrancho de combate** (naut) clearing the deck for action
za•fio -fia *adj* rough, uncouth, boorish
zafiro *m* sapphire
za•fo -fa *adj* unhurt, intact; (naut) free, clear || **zafo** *prep* (Col) except
zafra *f* olive-oil can; drip jar; sugar crop; sugar making; sugar-making season; (min) rubbish, muck
zaga *f* rear; load carried in the rear; (mil) rear guard; **a la zaga, a zaga** *or* **en zaga** behind, in the rear; **no ir en zaga a** to not be behind, be as good as
zagal *m* young fellow; strapping young fellow; shepherd boy; footboy
zagala *f* lass, maiden; young shepherdess
zaguán *m* vestibule, hall, entry
zague•ro -ra *adj* back, rear || *m* (sport) back, backstop
zaherir §68 *tr* to upbraid, reproach; scold shamefully
zahones *mpl* chaps, hunting breeches
zaho•rí *m* (*pl* **-ríes**) keen observer; seer, clairvoyant

zahurda *f* pigpen
zai•no -na *adj* treacherous, false; (*caballo*) vicious; (*caballo*) dark-chestnut; **mirar a lo zaino** *or* **de zaino** to look askance at
za•lá *f* (*pl* **-laes**) Muslim prayer; **hacer la zalá a** to fawn on
zalagarda *f* ambush; skirmish; (*trampa para cazar animales*) trap; trick; row, rumpus; mock fight
zalamería *f* flattery, cajolery
zalame•ro -ra *adj* flattering, fawning ‖ *mf* flatterer, fawner
zalea *f* unsheared sheepskin
zalear *tr* to drag around, shake; (*al perro*) chase away
zalema *f* salaam
zamacuco *m* blockhead; sullen fellow; drunkenness
zamacueca *f* cueca (*Chilean courtship dance*)
zamarra *f* undressed sheepskin; sheepskin jacket
zam•bo -ba *adj* knock-kneed
zambra *f* merrymaking, celebration; Moorish boat
zambucar §73 *tr* to slip away, hide away
zambullida *f* dive, plunge; (fencing) thrust to the breast
zambulli•dor -dora *adj* diving, plunging ‖ *mf* diver, plunger ‖ *m* (orn) diver, loon
zambullir §13 *tr* (*p.ej., a un perro*) to duck, give a ducking to; throw, hurl ‖ *ref* (*meterse debajo del agua con ímpetu*) to dive; (*esconderse rápidamente*) duck
zampa *f* pile, bearing pile
zampacuarti•llos *mf* (*pl* **-llos**) toper, soak
zampalimos•nas *mf* (*pl* **-nas**) bum, ordinary bum
zampar *tr* to slip away, hide away; gobble down ‖ *ref* to slip away, hide away
zampator•tas *mf* (*pl* **-tas**) glutton; boor
zampear *tr* (*el terreno*) to strengthen with piles and rubble
zampoña *f* shepherd's pipe, rustic flute; nonsense, folly
zampuzar §60 *tr* to duck, give a ducking to; slip away, hide away
zanahoria *f* carrot
zanca *f* long leg; (*de la escalera*) horse
zancada *f* long stride; **en dos zancadas** in a flash, in a jiffy
zancadilla *f* booby trap; **echar la zancadilla a** to stick out one's foot and trip
zancajo *m* heel; **no llegar a los zancajos a** to not come up to, not be equal to
zancajo•so -sa *adj* duck-toed; down-at-the-heel
zancarrón *m* dirty old fellow
zanco *m* stilt; **en zancos** from a vantage point
zancu•do -da *adj* long-legged; (orn) wading ‖ *m* mosquito ‖ *f* wading bird
zanfonía *f* hurdy-gurdy
zangala *f* buckram
zangamanga *f* trick
zanganada *f* impertinence, impudence
zanganear *intr* to loaf around
zángano *m* (ent) drone; (fig) drone, loafer; (CAm) scoundrel
zangarrear *intr* to thrum a guitar
zangolotear *tr* to jiggle ‖ *intr* to fuss around ‖ *ref* to jiggle, flop around, rattle
zangoloteo *m* jiggle, jiggling, rattle; fuss, bother
zanguanga *f* malingering; flattery; **hacer la zanguanga** to malinger
zanguan•go -ga *adj* slow, lazy ‖ *mf* loafer ‖ *f* see **zanguanga**
zanja *f* ditch, trench; (SAm) gully; **abrir las zanjas** to lay the foundations
zanquear *intr* to waddle; to rush around
zanquilar•go -ga *adj* leggy, long-legged
zanquituer•to -ta *adj* bandy-legged
zapa *f* spade; sharkskin, (mil) sap
zapapico *m* mattock, pickax
zapar *tr* (mil) to sap, mine, excavate
zaparrastrar *intr* — **ir zaparrastrando** to go along trailing one's clothes on the ground
zapateado *m* clog dance, tap dance
zapatear *tr* to hit with the shoe; tap with the feet; abuse, ill-treat ‖ *intr* to tap-dance; (*las velas*) flap ‖ *ref* — **zapatearse con** to hold out against
zapateo *m* tapping; stamping; **zapateo americano** tap dance
zapatería *f* shoemaking; shoemaker's shop; (*tienda*) shoe store
zapate•ro -ra *adj* poorly cooked ‖ *mf* shoemaker; shoe dealer; **quedarse zapatero** to not take a trick; **¡zapatero, a tus zapatos!** stick to your last!; **zapatero de viejo** *or* **zapatero remendón** cobbler, shoemaker
zapatilla *f* slipper; (*escarpín*) pump; (*del grifo*) washer; (*del florete*) leather tip or button; cloven hoof; **zapatillas** sneakers
zapato *m* shoe, low shoe; **andar con zapatos de fieltro** to gumshoe; **como tres en un zapato** hard up; like sardines; **zapato de cordón** lace-up shoe; **zapato de goma, zapato de hule** (Mex) sneaker, tennis shoe, gym shoe; **zapato de salón** pump; **zapato de tacón alto** high-heeled shoe; **zapato inglés** low shoe
zapatón *m* (Guat, SAm) overshoe
zapear *tr* (*al gato*) to scare away, chase away
zaque *m* wineskin; tippler, drunk
zaquiza•mí *m* (*pl* **-míes**) attic, garret; hovel, pigpen
zar *m* czar
zarabanda *f* (mus) saraband; noise, confusion, uproar; (Mex) beating, thrashing
zaragata *f* scuffle, row; **zaragatas** (W-I) flattery
zaranda *f* sieve, screen; colander; (Ven) horn; (Ven) top
zarandajas *fpl* odds and ends, trinkets
zarandar *tr* to sift, screen; winnow, pick out, select; jiggle ‖ *ref* to jiggle; swagger, strut
zaraza *f* chintz, printed cotton
zarcillo *m* eardrop; (bot) tendril
zarigüeya *f* opossum
zarina *f* czarina

zarpa *f* claw, paw; (naut) weighing anchor
zarpar *tr* (*el ancla*) (naut) to weigh (*anchor*) || *intr* (naut) to weigh anchor, set sail
zarpo•so -sa *adj* mud-splashed
zarracatería *f* cajolery, insincere flattery
zarracatín *m* sharp trader
zarramplín *m* botcher, bungler
zarrien•to -ta *adj* mud-splashed
zarza *f* blackberry, bramble (*bush*)
zarzamora *f* blackberry (*fruit*)
zarzaparrilla *f* sarsaparilla
zarzo *m* hurdle, wattle
zarzo•so -sa *adj* brambly
zarzuela *f* small bramble; (theat) zarzuela (*Spanish musical comedy*); **zarzuela grande** three-act zarzuela
zas *interj* bang!; zap!; **¡zas, zas!** bing, bang!
zascandilear *intr* to meddle, scheme
zepelín *m* zeppelin
Zeus *m* Zeus
zigzag *m* zigzag
zigzaguear *intr* to zigzag
zinc *m* (*pl* **zinces**) zinc
zipizape *m* scuffle, row, rumpus
ziszás *m* zigzag
zoca *f* public square
zócalo *m* (archit) socle; (*de una pared*) dado; (compu) slot; (rad) socket; (Mex) public square, center square
zoca•to -ta *adj* (*fruto*) corky, pithy; left; left-handed || *mf* left-handed person
zoclo *m* clog, wooden shoe
zo•co -ca *adj* left; left-handed || *mf* left-handed person || *m* clog, wooden shoe; Moroccan market place; (archit) socle; **andar de zocos en colodros** to jump from the frying pan into the fire || *f* see **zoca**
zodíaco *or* **zodiaco** *m* zodiac
zofra *f* Moorish carpet, Moorish rug
zollipar *intr* to sob
zollipo *m* sob
zolo•cho -cha *adj* stupid, simple || *mf* simpleton
zona *m* (pathol) shingles || *f* zone; (*banda, faja*) belt, girdle; **zona a batir** target area; **zona catastrófica** disaster area; **zona de escaramuza** line of scrimmage; **zona de estacionamiento** (mil) staging area; **zona desmilitarizada** demilitarized zone; **zona industrial** industrial park; **zona siniestrada** disaster area; **zona urbana deprimida** inner-core, inner-city
zonificar §73 *tr* to zone
zon•zo -za *adj* tasteless, insipid; dull, inane || *mf* dolt, dimwit
zoófito *m* zoophyte
zoología *f* zoology
zoológi•co -ca *adj* zoologic(al) || *s* zoo
zoólo•go -ga *mf* zoologist
zoom [sum], [θum] *m* zoom lens, zoom
zopen•co -ca *adj* dull, stupid || *mf* dullard, blockhead
zopilote *m* (Mex, CAm) turkey buzzard, turkey vulture
zo•po -pa *adj* crippled; awkward, gauche || *mf* cripple
zoquete *m* (*de madera*) block, chunk, end; (*de pan*) bit, crust; chump, lout
zoquetu•do -da *adj* coarse, crude
zorra *f* fox; female fox; cunning person; prostitute; drunkenness; dray, truck; **pillar una zorra** to get drunk
zorrera *f* (*cueva de zorros*) foxhole; smoke-filled room; worry, confusion
zorrería *f* foxiness, craftiness
zorre•ro -ra *adj* sly, foxy; slow, heavy, tardy || *f* see **zorrera**
zorrillo *m* skunk
zorro *m* male fox; (*piel*) fox; (*hombre taimado*) fox; **estar hecho un zorro** to be overwhelmed with sleep; be dull and sullen; **zorros** duster
zorral *m* (orn) fieldfare; sly fellow; (Chile) simpleton
zozobra *f* capsizing, sinking; anxiety
zozobrar *tr* (*un buque*) to sink; (*un negocio*) wreck || *intr* to capsize, sink; (*la embarcación en la tempestad*) wallow; (*un negocio*) be in great danger; be greatly worried || *ref* to capsize, sink
zueco *m* clog, wooden shoe, sabot
zulacar §73 *tr* to waterproof
zulaque *m* waterproofing
zullar *ref* to have a bowel movement; break wind
zullen•co -ca *adj* windy, flatulent
zulú *adj & mf* (*pl* **-lús** o **-lúes**) Zulu
zumaque *m* sumach; wine
zumaya *f* (*autillo*) tawny owl; (*chotacabras*) goatsucker
zumba *f* bell worn by leading mule; (Mex) drunkenness; **hacer zumba a** to make fun of; **sin zumba** (Mex) in a rush, in a hurry
zumbador *m* buzzer; (Mex) pauraque; (Mex, CAm, W-I) hummingbird
zumbar *tr* to make fun of; (*un golpe, una bofetada*) let have || *intr* to buzz; zoom; (*los oídos*) ring; **zumbar a** (*frisar con*) to be close to, border on || *ref* (Cuba) to go too far, forget oneself; (P-R) to rush ahead; **zumbarse de** to make fun of
zumbido *m* buzz; zoom; blow, smack; **zumbido de ocupación** (telp) busy signal; **zumbido de oídos** ringing in the ears
zum•bón -bona *adj* waggish, playful || *mf* wag, jester
zumien•to -ta *adj* juicy
zumo *m* juice; advantage, profit; **zumo de cepas** or **de parras** fruit of the vine
zumo•so -sa *adj* juicy
zunchar *tr* to band, hoop
zuncho *m* band, hoop
zupia *f* (*del vino*) dregs; slop, wine full of dregs; (fig) junk, trash
zurcido *m* darning; darn; invisible mending
zurcir §36 *tr* to darn; (*una mentira*) hatch, concoct; (*unas mentiras*) weave (*a tissue of lies*)
zurdazo *m* (box) left, blow with the left

zur•do -da *adj* left; left-handed; **a zurdas** with the left hand; the wrong way || *mf* left-handed person

zurear *intr* to coo

zuro *m* stripped corncob

zurra *f* dressing, currying; scuffle, quarrel; drubbing, thrashing; (*trabajo o estudio continuados*) grind

zurrapa *f* thread, filament; trash, rubbish; **con zurrapas** in a sloppy manner

zurrar *tr* (*el cuero*) to dress, curry; get the best of; (*censurar con dureza*) dress down; (*castigar con azotes*) drub, thrash || *ref* (*hacer sus necesidades involuntariamente*); to soil oneself; be scared to death; (Arg) to break wind noiselessly

zurriagar §44 *tr* to whip, horsewhip

zurriago *m* whip, lash

zurribanda *f* rain of blows; rumpus, scuffle

zurrir *intr* to buzz, grate

zurrón *m* shepherd's leather bag; leather bag; (*cáscara*) husk

zurrona *f* loose, evil woman

zurullo *m* soft roll; turd

zurupeto *m* unregistered broker; shyster notary

zuta•no -na *mf* so-and-so

Spanish Irregular Verbs

All simple tenses are shown in these tables if they contain one irregular form or more, except the conditional (which can always be derived from the stem of the future indicative) and the imperfect and future subjunctive (which can always be derived from the third plural preterit indicative minus the last syllable **-ron**).

The numbers are those that accompany the respective verbs and verbs of identical patterns where they are listed in their alphabetical places in this Dictionary. The letters (a) to (h) identify the tenses as follows:

(a) gerund
(b) past participle
(c) imperative
(d) present indicative
(e) present subjunctive
(f) imperfect indicative
(g) future indicative
(h) preterit indicative

§1 **abolir:** defective verb used only in forms whose endings contain the vowel **i**

§2 **acertar**
(c) **acierta,** acertad
(d) **acierto, aciertas, acierta,** acertamos, acertáis, **aciertan**
(e) **acierte, aciertes, acierte,** acertemos, acertéis, **acierten**

§3 **agorar:** like **§61** but with diaeresis on the **u** of **ue**
(c) **agüera,** agorad
(d) **agüero, agüeras, agüera,** agoramos, agoráis, **agüeran**
(e) **agüere, agüeres, agüere,** agoremos, agoréis, **agüeren**

§4 **airar**
(c) **aíra,** airad
(d) **aíro, aíras, aíra,** airamos, airáis, **aíran**
(e) **aíre, aíres, aíre,** airemos, airéis, **aíren**

§5 **andar**
(h) **anduve, anduviste, anduvo, anduvimos, anduvisteis, anduvieron**

§6 **argüir:** like **§20** but with diaeresis on **u** in forms with accented **i** in the ending
(a) **arguyendo**
(b) **argüído**
(c) **arguye,** argüid
(d) **arguyo, arguyes, arguye,** argüimos, argüís, **arguyen**
(e) **arguya, arguyas, arguya, arguyamos, arguyáis, arguyan**
(h) argüí, argüiste, **arguyó,** argüimos, argüisteis, **arguyeron**

§7 **asir**
(d) **asgo,** ases, ase, asimos, asís, asen
(e) **asga, asgas, asga, asgamos, asgáis, asgan**

§8 **aunar**
(c) **aúna,** aunad
(d) **aúno, aúnas, aúna,** aunamos, aunáis, **aúnan**
(e) **aúne, aúnes, aúne,** aunemos, aunéis, **aúnen**

§9 **avergonzar:** combination of **§3** and **§60**
(c) **avergüenza,** avergonzad
(d) **avergüenzo, avergüenzas, avergüenza,** avergonzamos, avergonzáis, **avergüenzan**
(e) **avergüence, avergüences, avergüence, avergoncemos, avergoncéis, avergüencen**
(h) **avergoncé,** avergonzaste, avergonzó, avergonzamos, avergonzasteis, avergonzaron

§10 **averiguar**
(e) **averigüe, averigües, averigüe, averigüemos, averigüéis, averigüen**
(h) **averigüé,** averiguaste, averiguó, averiguamos, averiguasteis, averiguaron

§11 **bendecir**
(a) **bendiciendo**
(c) **bendice,** bendecid
(d) **bendigo, bendices, bendice,** bendecimos, bendecís, **bendicen**
(e) **bendiga, bendigas, bendiga, bendigamos, bendigáis, bendigan**
(h) **bendije, bendijiste, bendijo, bendijimos, bendijisteis, bendijeron**

§12 **bruñir**
(a) **bruñendo**
(h) bruñí, bruñiste, **bruñó,** bruñimos, bruñisteis, **bruñeron**

§13 **bullir**
(a) **bullendo**
(h) bullí, bulliste, **bulló,** bullimos, bullisteis, **bulleron**

§14 **caber**
(d) **quepo,** cabes, cabe, cabemos, cabéis, caben
(e) **quepa, quepas, quepa, quepamos, quepáis, quepan**
(g) **cabré, cabrás, cabrá, cabremos, cabréis, cabrán**
(h) **cupe, cupiste, cupo, cupimos, cupisteis, cupieron**

§15 **caer**
(a) **cayendo**
(b) **caído**
(d) **caigo,** caes, cae, caemos, caéis, caen
(e) **caiga, caigas, caiga, caigamos, caigáis, caigan**
(h) caí, **caíste, cayó, caímos, caísteis, cayeron**

§16 **cocer:** combination of **§47** and **§78**
(c) **cuece,** coced
(d) **cuezo, cueces, cuece,** cocemos, cocéis, **cuecen**
(e) **cueza, cuezas, cueza, cozamos, cozáis, cuezan**

§17 **coger**
(d) **cojo,** coges, coge, cogemos, cogéis, cogen
(e) **coja, cojas, coja, cojamos, cojáis, cojan**

§18 **comenzar:** combination of §2 and **§60**
(c) **comienza,** comenzad
(d) **comienzo, comienzas, comienza,** comenzamos, comenzáis, **comienzan**
(e) **comience, comiences, comience, comencemos, comencéis, comiencen**
(h) **comencé,** comenzaste, comenzó, comenzamos, comenzasteis, comenzaron

§19 **conducir**
(d) **conduzco,** conduces, conduce, conducimos, conducís, conducen
(e) **conduzca, conduzcas, conduzca, conduzcamos, conduzcáis, conduzcan**
(h) **conduje, condujiste, condujo, condujimos, condujisteis, condujeron**

§20 **construir**
(a) **construyendo**
(b) **construído**
(c) **construye,** construid
(d) **construyo, construyes, construye,** construimos, construís, **construyen**
(e) **construya, construyas, construya, construyamos, construyáis, construyan**
(h) construí, construiste, **construyó,** construimos, construisteis, **construyeron**

§21 **continuar**
(c) **continúa,** continuad
(d) **continúo, continúas, continúa,** continuamos, continuáis, **continúan**
(e) **continúe, continúes, continúe,** continuemos, continuéis, **continúen**

§22 **crecer**
(d) **crezco,** creces, crece, crecemos, crecéis, crecen
(e) **crezca, crezcas, crezca, crezcamos, crezcáis, crezcan**

§23 **dar**
(d) **doy,** das, da, damos, dais, dan
(e) **dé,** des, **dé,** demos, deis, den
(h) **di, diste, dio, dimos, disteis, dieron**

§24 **decir**
(a) **diciendo**
(b) **dicho**
(c) **di,** decid
(d) **digo, dices, dice,** decimos, decís, **dicen**
(e) **diga, digas, diga, digamos, digáis, digan**
(g) **diré, dirás, dirá, diremos, diréis, dirán**
(h) **dije, dijiste, dijo, dijimos, dijisteis, dijeron**

§25 delinquir
(d) **delinco,** delinques, delinque, delinquimos, delinquís, delinquen
(e) **delinca, delincas, delinca, delincamos, delincáis, delincan**

§26 desosar: like **§61** but with **h** before **ue**
(c) **deshuesa,** desosad
(d) **deshueso, deshuesas, deshuesa,** desosamos, desosáis, **deshuesan**
(e) **deshuese, deshueses, deshuese,** desosemos, desoséis, **deshuesen**

§27 dirigir
(d) **dirijo,** diriges, dirige, dirigimos, dirigís, dirigen
(e) **dirija, dirijas, dirija, dirijamos, dirijáis, dirijan**

§28 discernir
(c) **discierne,** discernid
(d) **discierno, disciernes, discierne,** discernimos, discernís, **disciernen**
(e) **discierna, disciernas, discierna,** discernamos, discernáis, **disciernan**

§29 distinguir
(d) **distingo,** distingues, distingue, distinguimos, distinguís, distinguen
(e) **distinga, distingas, distinga, distingamos, distingáis, distingan**

§30 dormir
(a) **durmiendo**
(c) **duerme,** dormid
(d) **duermo, duermes, duerme,** dormimos, dormís, **duermen**
(e) **duerma, duermas, duerma, durmamos, durmáis, duerman**
(h) dormí, dormiste, **durmió,** dormimos, dormisteis, **durmieron**

§31 empeller
(a) **empellendo**
(h) empellí, empelliste, **empelló,** empellimos, empellisteis, **empelleron**

§32 enraizar: combination of **§4** and **§60**
(c) **enraíza,** enraizad
(d) **enraízo, enraízas, enraíza,** enraizamos, enraizáis, **enraízan**
(e) **enraíce, enraíces, enraíce, enraicemos, enraicéis, enraícen**
(h) **enraicé,** enraizaste, enraizó, enraizamos, enraizasteis, enraizaron

§33 erguir: combination of **§29** and **§50** or **§68**
(a) **irguiendo**
(c) **irgue** or **yergue,** erguid
(d) **irgo, irgues, irgue,** / **yergo, yergues, yergue,** } erguimos, erguís, { **irguen** / **yerguen**
(e) **irga, irgas, irga,** / **yerga, yergas, yerga,** } **irgamos, irgáis,** { **irgan** / **yergan**
(h) erguí, erguiste, **irguió,** erguimos, erguisteis, **irguieron**

§34 errar: like **§2** but with initial **ye** for **ie**
(c) **yerra,** errad
(d) **yerro, yerras, yerra,** erramos, erráis, **yerran**
(e) **yerre, yerres, yerre,** erremos, erréis, **yerren**

§35 esforzar: combination of **§60** and **§61**
(c) **esfuerza,** esforzad
(d) **esfuerzo, esfuerzas, esfuerza,** esforzamos, esforzáis, **esfuerzan**
(e) **esfuerce, esfuerces, esfuerce, esforcemos, esforcéis, esfuercen**
(h) **esforcé,** esforzaste, esforzó, esforzamos, esforzasteis, esforzaron

§36 esparcir
(d) **esparzo,** esparces, esparce, esparcimos, esparcís, esparcen
(e) **esparza, esparzas, esparza, esparzamos, esparzáis, esparzan**

§37 estar
(c) **está,** estad
(d) **estoy, estás, está,** estamos, estáis, **están**
(c) **esté, estés, esté,** estemos, estéis, **estén**
(h) **estuve, estuviste, estuvo, estuvimos, estuvisteis, estuvieron**

§38 haber
(c) **he,** habed
(d) **he, has, ha, hemos,** habéis, **han** (*v impers*) **hay**
(e) **haya, hayas, haya, hayamos, hayáis, hayan**
(g) **habré, habrás, habrá, habremos, habréis, habrán**
(h) **hube, hubiste, hubo, hubimos, hubisteis, hubieron**

§39 hacer
(b) **hecho**
(c) **haz,** haced
(d) **hago,** haces, hace, hacemos, hacéis, hacen
(e) **haga, hagas, haga, hagamos, hagáis, hagan**
(g) **haré, harás, hará, haremos, haréis, harán**
(h) **hice, hiciste, hizo, hicimos, hicisteis, hicieron**

§40 inquirir
(c) **inquiere,** inquirid
(d) **inquiero, inquieres, inquiere,** inquirimos, inquirís, **inquieren**
(e) **inquiera, inquieras, inquiera,** inquiramos, inquiráis, **inquieran**

§41 ir
(a) **yendo**
(c) **ve, vamos,** id
(d) **voy, vas, va, vamos, vais, van**
(e) **vaya, vayas, vaya, vayamos, vayáis, vayan**
(f) **iba, ibas, iba, íbamos, ibais, iban**
(h) **fui, fuiste, fue, fuimos, fuisteis, fueron**

§42 jugar: like **§63** but with radical **u**
(c) **juega,** jugad
(d) **juego, juegas, juega,** jugamos, jugáis, **juegan**
(e) **juegue, juegues, juegue, juguemos, juguéis, jueguen**
(h) **jugué,** jugaste, jugó, jugamos, jugasteis, jugaron

§43 leer
(a) **leyendo**
(b) **leído**
(h) leí, **leíste, leyó, leímos, leísteis, leyeron**

§44 ligar
(e) **ligue, ligues, ligue, liguemos, liguéis, liguen**
(h) **ligué,** ligaste, ligó, ligamos, ligasteis, ligaron

§45 lucir
(d) **luzco,** luces, luce, lucimos, lucís, lucen
(e) **luzca, luzcas, luzca, luzcamos, luzcáis, luzcan**

§46 mecer
(d) **mezo,** meces, mece, mecemos, mecéis, mecen
(e) **meza, mezas, meza, mezamos, mezáis, mezan**

§47 mover
(c) **mueve,** moved
(d) **muevo, mueves, mueve,** movemos, movéis, **mueven**
(e) **mueva, muevas, mueva,** movamos, mováis, **muevan**

§48 oír
(a) **oyendo**
(b) **oído**
(c) **oye, oíd**
(d) **oigo, oyes, oye, oímos,** oís, **oyen**
(e) **oiga, oigas, oiga, oigamos, oigáis, oigan**
(h) oí, **oíste, oyó, oímos, oísteis, oyeron**

§49 oler: like **§47** but with **h** before **ue**
(c) **huele,** oled
(d) **huelo, hueles, huele,** olemos, oléis, **huelen**
(e) **huela, huelas, huela,** olamos, oláis, **huelan**

§50 **pedir**
(a) **pidiendo**
(c) **pide,** pedid
(d) **pido, pides, pide,** pedimos, pedís, **piden**
(e) **pida, pidas, pida, pidamos, pidáis, pidan**
(h) pedí, pediste, **pidió,** pedimos, pedisteis, **pidieron**

§51 **perder**
(c) **pierde,** perded
(d) **pierdo, pierdes, pierde,** perdemos, perdéis, **pierden**
(e) **pierda, pierdas, pierda,** perdamos, perdáis, **pierdan**

§52 **placer**
(d) **plazco,** places, place, placemos, placéis, placen
(e) **plazca, plazcas, plazca, plazcamos, plazcáis, plazcan**
(h) plací, placiste, plació (or **plugo**), placimos, placisteis, placieron

§53 **poder**
(a) **pudiendo**
(c) (**puede,** poded)
(d) **puedo, puedes, puede,** podemos, podéis, **pueden**
(e) **pueda, puedas, pueda,** podamos, podáis, **puedan**
(g) **podré, podrás, podrá, podremos, podréis, podrán**
(h) **pude, pudiste, pudo, pudimos, pudisteis, pudieron**

§54 **poner**
(b) **puesto**
(c) **pon,** poned
(d) **pongo,** pones, pone, ponemos, ponéis, ponen
(e) **ponga, pongas, ponga, pongamos, pongáis, pongan**
(g) **pondré, pondrás, pondrá, pondremos, pondréis, pondrán**
(h) **puse, pusiste, puso, pusimos, pusisteis, pusieron**

§55 **querer**
(c) **quiere,** quered
(d) **quiero, quieres, quiere,** queremos, queréis, **quieren**
(e) **quiera, quieras, quiera,** queramos, queráis, **quieran**
(g) **querré, querrás, querrá, querremos, querréis, querrán**
(h) **quise, quisiste, quiso, quisimos, quisisteis, quisieron**

§56 **raer**
(a) **rayendo**
(b) **raído**
(d) **raigo** (or **rayo**), raes, rae, raemos, raéis, raen
(e) **raiga** (or **raya**), **raigas, raiga, raigamos, raigáis, raigan**
(h) raí, **raíste, rayó, raímos, raísteis, rayeron**

§57 **regir:** combination of **§27** and **§50**
(a) **rigiendo**
(c) **rige,** regid
(d) **rijo, riges, rige,** regimos, regís, **rigen**
(e) **rija, rijas, rija, rijamos, rijáis, rijan**
(h) regí, registe, **rigió,** regimos, registeis, **rigieron**

§58 **reír**
(a) **riendo**
(b) **reído**
(c) **ríe, reíd**
(d) **río, ríes, ríe, reímos,** reís, **ríen**
(e) **ría, rías, ría, riamos, riáis, rían**
(h) reí, **reíste, rió, reímos, reísteis, rieron**

§59 **reunir**
(c) **reúne,** reunid
(d) **reúno, reúnes, reúne,** reunimos, reunís, **reúnen**
(e) **reúna, reúnas, reúna,** reunamos, reunáis, **reúnan**

§60 **rezar**
(e) **rece, reces, rece, recemos, recéis, recen**
(h) **recé,** rezaste, rezó, rezamos, rezasteis, rezaron

§61 **rodar**
(c) **rueda,** rodad
(d) **ruedo, ruedas, rueda,** rodamos, rodáis, **ruedan**
(e) **ruede, ruedes, ruede,** rodemos, rodéis, **rueden**

§62 **roer**
(a) **royendo**
(b) **roído**
(d) roo (**roigo,** or **royo**), roes, roe, roemos, roéis, roen
(e) roa (**roiga,** or **roya**), roas, roa, roamos, roáis, roan
(h) roí, **roíste, royó, roímos, roísteis, royeron**

§63 **rogar:** combination of **§44** and **§61**
(c) **ruega,** rogad
(d) **ruego, ruegas, ruega,** rogamos, rogáis, **ruegan**
(e) **ruegue, ruegues, ruegue, roguemos, roguéis, rueguen**
(h) **rogué,** rogaste, rogó, rogamos, rogasteis, rogaron

§64 **saber**
(d) **sé,** sabes, sabe, sabemos, sabéis, saben
(e) **sepa, sepas, sepa, sepamos, sepáis, sepan**
(g) **sabré, sabrás, sabrá, sabremos, sabréis, sabrán**
(h) **supe, supiste, supo, supimos, supisteis, supieron**

§65 **salir**
(c) **sal,** salid
(d) **salgo,** sales, sale, salimos, salís, salen
(e) **salga, salgas, salga, salgamos, salgáis, salgan**
(g) **saldré, saldrás, saldrá, saldremos, saldréis, saldrán**

§66 **segar:** combination of **§2** and **§44**
(c) **siega,** segad
(d) **siego, siegas, siega,** segamos, segáis, **siegan**
(e) **siegue, siegues, siegue, seguemos, seguéis, sieguen**
(h) **segué,** segaste, sego, segamos, segasteis, segaron

§67 **seguir:** combination of **§29** and **§50**
(a) **siguiendo**
(c) **sigue,** seguid
(d) **sigo, sigues, sigue,** seguimos, seguís, **siguen**
(e) **siga, sigas, siga, sigamos, sigáis, sigan**
(h) seguí, seguiste, **siguió,** seguimos, seguisteis, **siguieron**

§68 **sentir**
(a) **sintiendo**
(c) **siente,** sentid
(d) **siento, sientes, siente,** sentimos, sentís, **sienten**
(e) **sienta, sientas, sienta, sintamos, sintáis, sientan**
(h) sentí, sentiste, **sintió,** sentimos, sentisteis, **sintieron**

§69 **ser**
(c) **sé,** sed
(d) **soy, eres, es, somos, sois, son**
(e) **sea, seas, sea, seamos, seáis, sean**
(f) **era, eras, era, éramos, erais, eran**
(h) **fui, fuiste, fue, fuimos, fuisteis, fueron**

§70 **tañer**
(a) **tañendo**
(h) tañí, tañiste, **tañó,** tañimos, tañisteis, **tañeron**

§71 **tener**
(c) **ten,** tened
(d) **tengo, tienes, tiene,** tenemos, tenéis, **tienen**

(e) **tenga, tengas, tenga, tengamos, tengáis, tengan**
(g) **tendré, tendrás, tendrá, tendremos, tendréis, tendrán**
(h) **tuve, tuviste, tuvo, tuvimos, tuvisteis, tuvieron**

§72 **teñir:** combination of **§12** and **§50**
(a) **tiñendo**
(c) **tiñe,** teñid
(d) **tiño, tiñes, tiñe,** teñimos, teñis, **tiñen**
(e) **tiña, tiñas, tiña, tiñamos, tiñais, tiñan**
(h) teñí, teñiste, **tiño,** teñimos, teñisteis, **tiñeron**

§73 **tocar**
(e) **toque, toques, toque, toquemos, toquéis, toquen**
(h) **toqué,** tocaste, tocó, tocamos, tocasteis, tocaron

§74 **torcer:** combination of **§47** and **§78**
(c) **tuerce,** torced
(d) **tuerzo, tuerces, tuerce,** torcemos, torcéis, **tuercen**
(e) **tuerza, tuerzas, tuerza, torzamos, torzáis, tuerzan**

§75 **traer**
(a) **trayendo**
(b) **traído**
(d) **traigo,** traes, trae, traemos, traéis, traen
(e) **traiga, traigas, traiga, traigamos, traigáis, traigan**
(h) **traje, trajiste, trajo, trajimos, trajisteis, trajeron**

§76 **valer**
(d) **valgo,** vales, vale, valemos, valéis, valen
(e) **valga, valgas, valga, valgamos, valgáis, valgan**
(g) **valdré, valdrás, valdrá, valdremos, valdréis, valdrán**

§77 **variar**
(c) **varía,** variad
(d) **varío, varías, varía,** variamos, variáis, **varían**
(e) **varíe, varíes, varíe,** variemos, variéis, **varíen**

§78 **vencer**
(d) **venzo,** vences, vence, vencemos, vencéis, vencen
(e) **venza, venzas, venza, venzamos, venzáis, venzan**

§79 **venir**
(a) **viniendo**
(c) **ven,** venid
(d) **vengo, vienes, viene,** venimos, venís, **vienen**
(e) **venza, venzas, venza, venzamos, venzáis, venzan**
(g) **vendré, vendrás, vendrá, vendremos, vendréis, vendrán**
(h) **vine, viniste, vino, vinimos, vinisteis, vinieron**

§80 **ver**
(b) **visto**
(d) **veo,** ves, ve, vemos, veis, ven
(e) **vea, veas, vea, veamos, veáis, vean**
(f) **veía, veías, veía, veíamos, veíais, veían**

§81 **volcar:** combination of **§61** and **§73**
(c) **vuelca,** volcad
(d) **vuelco, vuelcas, vuelca,** volcamos, volcáis, **vuelcan**
(e) **vuelque, vuelques, vuelque, volquemos, volquéis, vuelquen**
(h) **volqué,** volcaste, volcó, volcamos, volcasteis, volcaron

§82 **yacer**
(c) **yaz** (or yace), yaced
(d) **yazco (yazgo,** or **yago),** yaces, yace, yacemos, yacéis, yacen
(e) **yazca (yazga,** or **yaga), yazcas, yazca, yazcamos, yazcáis, yazcan**

§83 The following verbs, some of which are included in the foregoing table, and their compounds have irregular past participles, as shown in the following table:

abrir ——— **abierto**
cubrir ——— **cubierto**
decir ——— **dicho**
escribir ——— **escrito**
freir ——— **frito**
hacer ——— **hecho**
imprimir ——— **impreso**
morir ——— **muerto**
poner ——— **puesto**
proveer ——— **provisto**
pudrir ——— **podrido**
romper ——— **roto**
solver ——— **suelto**
ver ——— **visto**
volver ——— **vuelto**

English-Spanish
Inglés-Español

A

A, a [e] primera letra del alfabeto inglés
a [e] *art indef* un
AA [ˈeˈe] *s* (letterword) (**Alcoholics Anonymous**) Alcohólicos Anónimos
aback [əˈbæk] *adv* atrás; **to be taken aback** quedar desconcertado; **to take aback** desconcertar
abaft [əˈbæft] *adv* a popa, en popa ‖ *prep* detrás de
abandon [əˈbændən] *s* abandono ‖ *tr* abandonar
abandonment [əˈbændənmənt] *s* abandono, abandonamiento; desembarazo
abase [əˈbes] *tr* degradar, humillar
abash [əˈbæʃ] *tr* avergonzar
abate [əˈbet] *tr* disminuir, reducir; deducir ‖ *intr* disminuir, moderarse
aba•tis [ˈæbətɪs] *s* (*pl* **-tis**) abatida
abattoir [ˈæbəˌtwar] *s* matadero
abba•cy [ˈæbəsi] *s* (*pl* **-cies**) abadía
abbess [ˈæbɪs] *s* abadesa
abbey [ˈæbi] *s* abadía
abbot [ˈæbət] *s* abad *m*
abbreviate [əˈbrivɪˌet] *tr* abreviar
abbreviation [əˌbrivɪˈeʃən] *s* (*shortening*) abreviación; (*shortened form*) abreviatura
A B C [ˌeˌbiˈsi] *s* abecé *m;* **A B C's** abecedario
abdicate [ˈæbdɪˌket] *tr & intr* abdicar
abdomen [ˈæbdəmən] o [æbˈdomən] *s* abdomen *m*
abduct [æbˈdʌkt] *tr* raptar, secuestrar
abduction [æbˈdʌkʃən] *s* rapto; secuestro
abed [əˈbɛd] *adv* en cama, acostado
aberration [ˌæbɛˈreʃən] *s* aberración; (*mind*) extravío
abet [əˈbɛt] *v* (*pret & pp* **abetted;** *ger* **abetting**) *tr* incitar (*a una persona, esp. al mal*); fomentar (*el crimen*)
abeyance [əˈbe•əns] *s* suspensión; **in abeyance** en suspenso
ab•hor [æbˈhɔr] *v* (*pret & pp* **-horred;** *get* **-horring**) *tr* aborrecer, detestar
abhorrence [əbˈhɔrəns] *s* aversión; aborrecimiento
abhorrent [æbˈhɔrənt] *adj* aborrecible, detestable
abide [əˈbaɪd] *v* (*pret & pp* **abode** o **abided**) *tr* esperar; tolerar ‖ *intr* permanecer; **to abide by** cumplir con; atenerse a
abili•ty [əˈbɪlɪti] *s* (*pl* **-ties**) habilidad, capacidad; talento
abject [æbˈdʒɛkt] *adj* abyecto, servil
abjure [æbˈdʒur] *tr* abjurar
ablative [ˈæblətɪv] *s* ablativo
ablaut [ˈæblaʊt] *s* apofonía
ablaze [əˈblez] *adj* brillante; ardiente; encolerizado ‖ *adv* en llamas, ardiendo
able [ˈebəl] *adj* hábil, capaz; **to be able to** poder
able-bodied [ˈebəlˈbɑdid] *adj* sano; fornido; experto
abloom [əˈblum] *adj* floreciente ‖ *adv* en flor
abnormal [æbˈnɔrməl] *adj* anormal
aboard [əˈbord] *adv* a bordo; al bordo; **all aboard!** ¡señores viajeros al tren!; **to go aboard** ir a bordo; **to take aboard** embarcar ‖ *prep* a bordo de; (*a train*) en
abode [əˈbod] *s* domicilio, residencia
abolish [əˈbɑlɪʃ] *tr* eliminar, suprimir, abolir
abolition [ˌæbəˈlɪʃən] *s* abolición
A-bomb [ˈeˌbɑm] *s* bomba atómica
abominable [əˈbɑmɪnəbəl] *adj* abominable
abomination [əˌbɑmɪˈneʃən] *s* abominación
aborigines[ˌæbəˈrɪdʒɪˌniz] *spl* aborígenes ***mf***
abort [əˈbɔrt] *tr & intr* abortar
abortion [əˈbɔrʃən] *s* aborto
abortionist [əˈbɔrʃənɪst] *s* abortista ***mf***
abound [əˈbaʊnd] *intr* abundar
about [əˈbaʊt] *adv* casi; aquí; **to be about to** estar a punto de, estar para ‖ *prep* acerca de; con respecto a; cerca de; hacia, a eso de; **to be about** tratar de
about-face [əˈbaʊtˈfes] *s* (*reversal of policy*) cambio de opinión; (mil) media vuelta ‖ intr cambiar de opinión; (mil) dar media vuelta
above [əˈbʌv] *adj* antedicho ‖ *adv* arriba, encima ‖ *prep* sobre, encima de, más alto que; superior a; **above all** sobre todo
above-mentioned [əˈbʌvˈmɛnʃənd] *adj* sobredicho, antedicho, susodicho, prenombrado
abrasive [əˈbresɪv] o [əˈbreziv] *adj & s* abrasivo
abreast [əˈbrɛst] *adj & adv* de frente; **to be abreast of** correr parejas con; estar al corriente de
abridge [əˈbrɪdʒ] *tr* abreviar; disminuir; condensar, resumir
abroad [əˈbrɔd] *adv* al extranjero; en el extranjero; fuera de casa
abrupt [əˈbrʌpt] *adj* brusco; repentino; áspero; abrupto, escarpado
abscess [ˈæbsɛs] *s* absceso
abscond [æbˈskɑnd] *intr* irse a hurtadillas; **to abscond with** alzarse con
absence [ˈæbsəns] *s* ausencia

absent [ˈæbsənt] *adj* ausente ‖ [æbˈsɛnt] *tr*—**to absent oneself** ausentarse
absentee [ˌæbsənˈti] *s* ausente *mf*
absentee ballot *s* voto por correspondencia *or* correo
absent-minded [ˈæbsəntˈmaɪndɪd] *adj* distraído, absorto
absinthe [ˈæbsɪnθ] *s* (*plant*) absintio, ajenjo; (*drink*) absenta, ajenjo
absolute [ˈæbsəˌlut] *adj & s* absoluto
absolutely [ˈæbsəˌlutli] *adv* absolutamente ‖ [ˌæbsəˈlutli] *adv* (coll) positivamente
absolute pitch *s* (mus) sonido absoluto; (*ability*) oído absoluto
absolution [ˈæbsəˈluʃən] *s* absolución
absolve [æbˈsɑlv] *tr* absolver
absorb [æbˈsɔrb] *tr* absorber; **to be** o **become absorbed** ensimismarse
absorbent [æbˈsɔrbənt] *adj* absorbente; (*cotton*) hidrófilo
absorbing [æbˈsɔrbɪŋ] *adj* absorbente
absorption [æbˈsɔrpʃən] *s* abstracción; embebecimiento; absorción
abstain [æbˈsten] *intr* abstenerse
abstemious [æbˈstimɪ•əs] *adj* abstemio, sobrio
abstinent [ˈæbstɪnənt] *adj* abstinente
abstract [ˈæbstrækt] *adj* abstracto ‖ *s* resumen *m*, sumario, extracto ‖ *tr* resumir, compendiar, extractar ‖ [æbˈstrækt] *tr* abstraer; quitar
abstruse [æbˈstrus] *adj* abstruso
absurd [æbˈsʌrd] o [æbˈzʌrd] *adj* absurdo
absurdi•ty [æbˈsʌrdɪti] o [æbˈzʌrdɪti] *s* (*pl* **-ties**) absurdidad, absurdo
abundance [əˈbʌndəns] *s* abundancia, copia; (CAm) bastedad
abundant [əˈbʌndənt] *adj* abundante
abuse [əˈbjus] *s* maltrato; injuria, insulto; (*bad practice; injustice*) abuso ‖ [əˈbjuz] *tr* maltratar; injuriar, insultar; (*to misapply, take unfair advantage of*) abusar de
abusive [əˈbjusiv] *adj* injurioso, insultante; abusivo
abut [əˈbʌt] *v* (*pret & pp* **abutted;** *ger* **abutting**) *intr*—**to abut on** confinar con, terminar en
abutment [əˈbʌtmənt] *s* confinamiento; estribo, contrafuerte *m*
abyss [əˈbɪs] *s* abismo
AC, A.C. [ˈeˈsi] *s* (letterword) (**alternating current**) corriente alterna
academic [ˌækəˈdɛmɪk] *adj* académico
academic costume *s* toga, traje *m* de catedrático
academic freedom *s* libertad de cátedra, libertad de enseñanza
academician [əˌkædəˈmɪʃən] *s* académico
academic subjects *spl* materias no profesionales, materias escolares
academic year *s* año escolar
acade•my [əˈkædəmi] *s* (*pl* **-mies**) academia
accede [ækˈsid] *intr* acceder; **to accede to** acceder a, condescender a; (*e.g., the throne*) ascender a, subir a
accelerate [ækˈsɛləˌret] *tr* acelerar ‖ *intr* acelerarse
accelerator [ækˈsɛləˌretər] *s* acelerador *m*
accent [ˈæksɛnt] *s* acento ‖ [ˈæksɛnt] o [ækˈsɛnt] *tr* acentuar
accent mark *s* acento ortográfico
accentuate [ækˈsɛntʃʊˌet] *tr* acentuar
accept [ækˈsɛpt] *tr* aceptar
acceptable [ækˈsɛptəbəl] *adj* aceptable
acceptance [ækˈsɛptəns] *s* aceptación
access [ˈæksɛs] *s* acceso
accessible [ækˈsɛsɪbəl] *adj* accesible
accession [ækˈsɛʃən] *s* accesión; (*to a dignity*) ascenso; (*of books in a library*) adquisición
access mechanism *s* (compu) dispositivo de acceso
accesso•ry [ækˈsɛsəri] *adj* accesorio ‖ *s* (*pl* **-ries**) accesorio; (*to a crime*) cómplice *mf*
accident [ˈæksɪdənt] *s* accidente *m;* **by accident** por casualidad
accidental [ˌæksɪˈdɛntəl] *adj* accidental
acclaim [əˈklem] *s* aclamación ‖ *tr & intr* aclamar
acclimate [ˈæklɪˌmet] *tr* aclimatar ‖ *intr* aclimatarse
accolade [ˌækəˈled] *s* acolada; elogio, premio
accommodate [əˈkɑməˌdet] *tr* acomodar; alojar
accommodating [əˈkɑməˌdetɪŋ] *adj* acomodadizo, servicial
accommodation [əˌkɑməˈdeʃən] *s* acomodación; **accommodations** facilidades, comodidades; (*in a train*) localidad; (*in a hotel*) alojamiento
accompaniment [əˈkʌmpənɪmənt] *s* acompañamiento
accompanist [əˈkʌmpənɪst] *s* acompañante *m*
accompa•ny [əˈkʌmpəni] *v* (*pret & pp* **-nied**) *tr* acompañar
accomplice [əˈkɑmplɪs] *s* cómplice *mf*, codelincuente *mf*
accomplish [əˈkɑmplɪʃ] *tr* realizar, llevar a cabo
accomplished [əˈkɑmplɪʃt] *adj* realizado; culto, talentoso; (*fact*) consumado
accomplishment [əˈkɑmplɪʃmənt] *s* realización; **accomplishments** prendas, talentos
accord [əˈkɔrd] *s* acuerdo; **in accord with** de acuerdo con: **of one's own accord** de buen grado, voluntariamente; **with one accord** de común acuerdo ‖ *tr* conceder, otorgar ‖ *intr* concordar, avenirse
accordance [əˈkɔrdəns] *s* conformidad; **in accordance with** de acuerdo con
according [əˈkɔrdɪŋ] *adj* — **according as** según que; **according to** según
accordingly [əˈkɔrdɪŋli] *adv* en conformidad; por consiguiente
accordion [əˈkɔrdɪ•ən] *s* acordeón *m;* filarmónica (Mex)
accost [əˈkɔst] o [əˈkɑst] *tr* abordar, acercarse a
account [əˈkaʊnt] *s* informe *m,* relato; cuenta; estado de cuenta; importancia; **by all ac-**

counts según el decir general; **of no account** de poca importancia; **on account** como paga y señal; **on account of** a causa de; **to bring to account** pedir cuentas a; **to buy on account** comprar a plazos; **to turn to account** sacar provecho de, hacer valer || *intr*—**to account for** explicar; responder de
accountable [ə'kaʊntəbəl] *adj* responsable; explicable
accountant [ə'kaʊntənt] *s* contador *m*, contable *m*
accounting [ə'kaʊntɪŋ] *s* arreglo de cuentas; contabilidad
accouterments [ə'kutərmənts] *spl* equipo
accredit [ə'krɛdɪt] *tr* acreditar
accrue [ə'kru] *intr* acumularse; resultar
acct. *abbr* **account**
accumulate [ə'kjumjə,let] *tr* acumular || *intr* acumularse
accuracy ['ækjərəsi] *s* exactitud, precisión
accurate ['ækjərɪt] *adj* exacto
accusation [,ækjə'zeʃən] *s* acusación
accusative [ə'kjuzətɪv] *adj & s* acusativo
accuse [ə'kjuz] *tr* acusar
accustom [ə'kʌstəm] *tr* acostumbrar
ace [es] *s* as *m;* **to be within an ace of** estar a dos dedos de
acetate ['æsɪ,tet] *s* acetato
acetic acid [ə'sitɪk] *s* ácido acético
aceti•fy [ə'sɛtɪ,faɪ] *v* (*pret & pp* **-fied**) *tr* acetificar || *intr* acetificarse
acetone ['æsɪ,ton] *s* acetona
acetylene [ə'sɛtɪ,lin] *s* acetileno
acetylene torch *s* soplete oxiacetilénico
ache [ek] *s* achaque *m,* dolor *m* || *int* doler
achieve [ə'tʃiv] *tr* llevar a cabo; alcanzar, ganar, lograr
achievement [ə'tʃivmənt] *s* realización; (*feat*) hazaña
Achilles' heel [ə'kɪliz] *s* talón *m* de Aquiles
Achilles tendon *s* tendón *m* de Aquiles
acid ['æsɪd] *adj* ácido; agrio, mordaz || *s* ácido
acidi•fy [ə'sɪdɪ,faɪ] *v* (*pret & pp* **-fied**) *tr* acidificar || *intr* acidificarse
acidi•ty [ə'sɪdɪti] *s* (*pl* **-ties**) acidez *f*
acid rain *s* lluvia ácida
acid test *s* prueba decisiva, prueba de fuego
acknowledge [æk'nɑlɪdʒ] *tr* reconocer; acusar (*recibo de una carta*); agradecer (*p.ej., un favor*)
acknowledgment [æk'nɑlɪdʒmənt] *s* reconocimiento; (*of receipt of a letter*) acuse *m;* (*of a favor*) agradecimiento
acme ['ækmi] *s* auge *m,* colmo
acne ['ækni] *s* acné *m & f,* acne *f*
acolyte ['ækə,laɪt] *s* acólito
acorn ['ekɔrn] o ['ekərn] *s* bellota
acoustic [ə'kustɪk] *adj* acústico || **acoustics** *ssg* acústica
acquaint [ə'kwent] *tr* informar, poner al corriente; **to be acquainted** conocerse; **to be acquainted with** conocer; estar al corriente de
acquaintance [ə'kwentəns] *s* conocimiento; (*person*) conocido
acquiesce [,ækwɪ'ɛs] *intr* consentir, condescender, asentir
acquiescence [,ækwɪ'ɛsəns] *s* consentimiento, condescendencia, aquiescencia
acquire [ə'kwaɪr] *tr* adquirir
acquired im•mune'-de•fi'cien•cy syndrome (AIDS) *s* síndrome *m* de inmunodeficiencia adquirida (SIDA)
acquisition [,ækwɪ'zɪʃən] *s* adquisición
acquit [ə'kwɪt] *v* (*pret & pp* **acquitted;** *ger* **acquitting**) *tr* absolver, exculpar; **to acquit oneself** conducirse, portarse
acquittal [ə'kwɪtəl] *s* absolución, exculpación
acre ['ekər] *s* acre *m* (*medida de superficie: 0.405 hectáreas*)
acrid ['ækrɪd] *adj* acre, acrimonioso
acrobat ['ækrə,bæt] *s* acróbata *mf*
acrobatic [,ækrə'bætɪk] *adj* acrobático || **acrobatics** *ssg* (*profession*) acrobatismo; *spl* (*stunts*) acrobacia
acronym ['ækrənɪm] *s* acrónimo
acropolis [ə'krɑpəlɪs] *s* acrópolis *f*
across [ə'krɔs] o [ə'krɑs] *prep* al través de; al otro lado de; **to come across** encontrarse con; **to go across** atravesar
across'-the-board' *adj* comprensivo, general
acrostic [ə'krɔstɪk] o [ə'krɑstɪk] *s* acróstico
acrylic [ə'krɪlɪk] *adj & s* acrílico
act [ækt] *s* acto; (law) decreto; **in the act** en flagrante || *tr* representar; desempeñar (*un papel*); **to act the fool** hacer el bufón; **to act the part of** hacer o desempeñar el papel de || *intr* actuar; funcionar, obrar; conducirse; **to act as if** hacer como que; **to act for** representar; **to act up** travesear; **to act up to** hacer fiestas a
acting ['æktɪŋ] *adj* interino || *s* actuación
action ['ækʃən] *s* acción; **to take action** tomar medidas
activate ['æktɪ,vet] *tr* activar
active ['æktɪv] *adj* activo
ac'tive-ma'trix *s* (compu) matriz activa
activi•ty [æk'tɪvɪti] *s* (*pl* **-ties**) actividad
act of God *s* fuerza mayor
actor ['æktər] *s* actor *m*
actress ['æktrɪs] *s* actriz *f*
actual ['æktʃʊ•əl] *adj* real, efectivo
actually ['æktʃʊ•əli] *adv* en realidad
actuar•y ['æktʃʊ,ɛri] *s* (*pl* **-ies**) actuario (de seguros)
actuate ['æktʃʊ,et] *tr* actuar; estimular, mover
acuity [ə'kju•ɪti] *s* agudeza
acumen [ə'kjumən] *s* cacumen *m,* perspicacia
acupuncture ['ækjə,pʌŋktʃər] *s* acupuntura
acute [ə'kjut] *adj* agudo
acute accent *s* acento agudo
A.D. ['e'di] *adj* (letterword) (**Anno Domini**) dC, d. de C., d. de J.C. (después de Cristo, después de Jesucristo)
ad [æd] *s* (coll) anuncio
adage ['ædɪdʒ] *s* adagio, refrán *m*

Adam [ˈædəm] *s* Adán *m*
adamant [ˈædəmənt] *adj* firme, inexorable
Adam's apple *s* nuez *f* (de la garganta)
adapt [əˈdæpt] *tr* adaptar; refundir (*un drama*)
adaptation [ˌædæpˈteʃən] *s* adaptación; (*of a play*) refundición
add [æd] *tr* agregar, añadir; sumar ‖ *intr* sumar; **to add up to** subir a; (coll) querer decir
added line *s* (mus) línea suplementaria
adder [ˈædər] *s* víbora; serpiente *f*
addict [ˈædɪkt] *s* adicto; (*to sports, music, hobby*) fanático
addicted [əˈdɪktəd] *adj* — **to be addicted** ser adicto; (*to sports, music, hobby*) ser fanático; **to be addicted to drugs** ser drogadicto; **to become addicted to** enviciarse con o en
addiction [əˈdɪkʃən] *s* adicción; (*to sports, music, hobby*) afición
addictive [əˈdɪktɪv] *adj* adictivo (*que forma hábito*)
adding machine *s* sumadora
addition [əˈdɪʃən] *s* adición; **in addition** de pilón; **in addition to** además de
additive [ˈædɪtɪv] *adj & s* aditivo
address [əˈdrɛs] o [ˈædrɛs] *s* dirección; consignación ‖ [əˈdrɛs] *s* alocución, discurso; **to deliver an address** hacer uso de la palabra ‖ *tr* dirigirse a; dirigir (*p.ej., una alocución, una carta*); consignar
address bus *s* (compu) bus *m*, bus de direcciones
addressee [ˌædrɛˈsi] *s* destinatario; (com) consignatario
adduce [əˈdjus] o [əˈdus] *tr* aducir
adenoids [ˈædəˌnɔɪdz] *spl* vegetaciones adenoides
adept [əˈdɛpt] *adj & s* experto, perito
adequate [ˈædɪkwɪt] *adj* suficiente
adhere [ædˈhɪr] *intr* adherir, adherirse; conformarse
adherence [ædˈhɪrəns] *s* adhesión
adherent [ædˈhɪrənt] *adj & s* adherente *m*
adhesion [ædˈhiʒən] *s* (*sticking*) adherencia; (*support, loyalty*) adhesión; (pathol) adherencia; (phys) adherencia o adhesión
adhesive [ædˈhisɪv] *adj* adhesivo
adhesive tape *s* cinta adhesiva; (pharm) esparadrapo
adieu [əˈdju] o [əˈdu] *interj* ¡adiós! ‖ *s* (*pl* **adieus** o **adieux**) adiós *m;* **to bid adieu to** desperdirse de
adjacent [əˈdʒesənt] *adj* adyacente
adjective [ˈædʒɪktɪv] *adj & s* adjetivo
adjoin [əˈdʒɔɪn] *tr* lindar con ‖ *intr* colindar
adjoining [əˈdʒɔɪnɪŋ] *adj* colindante, contiguo
adjourn [əˈdʒʌrn] *tr* prorrogar, suspender ‖ *intr* prorrogarse, suspenderse; (coll) ir
adjournment [əˈdʒʌrnmənt] *s* prorrogación, suspensión
adjust [əˈdʒʌst] *tr* ajustar, arreglar; corregir, verificar; (ins) liquidar
adjustable [əˈdʒʌstəbəl] *adj* ajustable, arreglable
adjustment [əˈdʒʌstmənt] *s* ajuste *m*, arreglo; (ins) liquidación de la avería
adjutant [ˈædʒətənt] *s* ayudante *m*
ad•lib [ˌædˈlɪb] *v* (*pret & pp* **-libbed;** *ger* **-libbing**) *tr & intr* improvisar
administer [ædˈmɪnɪstər] *tr* administrar; **to administer an oath** tomar juramento ‖ *intr* — **to administer to** cuidar de
administrator [ædˈmɪnɪsˌtretər] *s* administrador *m*
admiral [ˈædmɪrəl] *s* almirante *m;* buque *m* almirante
admiral•ty [ˈædmɪrəlti] *s* (*pl* **-ties**) almirantazgo
admire [ædˈmaɪr] *tr* admirar
admirer [ædˈmaɪrər] *s* admirador *m;* enamorado
admissible [ædˈmɪsɪbəl] *adj* admisible
admission [ædˈmɪʃən] *s* admisión; (*in a school*) ingreso; (*reception*) recibida; precio de entrada; **no admission** se prohibe la entrada; *SIGN* prohibido el paso; *SIGN* prohibido la entrada; **to gain admission** lograr entrar
ad•mit [ædˈmɪt] *v* (*pret & pp* **-mitted;** *ger* **-mitting**) *tr* admitir ‖ *intr* dar entrada; **to admit of** admitir, permitir
admittance [ædˈmɪtəns] *s* admisión; derecho de entrar; **no admittance** acceso prohibido, se prohibe la entrada; *SIGN* prohibido el paso; *SIGN* prohibida la entrada
admonish [ædˈmɑnɪʃ] *tr* amonestar
ado [əˈdu] *s* bulla, excitación
adobe [əˈdobi] *s* adobe *m;* casa de adobe
adolescence [ˌædəˈlɛsəns] *s* adolescencia
adolescent [ˌædəˈlɛsənt] *adj & s* adolescente *mf*
adopt [əˈdɑpt] *tr* adoptar
adopted [əˈdɑptəd] *adj* adoptado; (*child; country*) adoptivo
adoption [əˈdɑpʃən] *s* adopción
adoptive [əˈdɑptɪv] *adj* adoptivo
adorable [əˈdorəbəl] *adj* adorable
adore [əˈdor] *tr* adorar
adorn [əˈdɔrn] *tr* adornar
adornment [əˈdɔrnmənt] *s* adorno
adrenal gland [ædˈrinəl] *s* glándula suprarrenal
Adriatic [ˌedrɪˈætɪk] *adj & s* Adriático
adrift [əˈdrɪft] *adj & adv* al garete, a la deriva
adroit [əˈdrɔɪt] *adj* diestro
adult [əˈdʌlt] o [ˈædʌlt] *adj & s* adulto
adulterate [əˈdʌltəˌret] *tr* adulterar
adulterer [əˈdʌltərər] *s* adúltero
adulteress [əˈdʌltərɪs] *s* adúltera
adulter•y [əˈdʌltəri] *s* (*pl* **-ies**) adulterio
adulthood [əˈdʌltˌhʊd] *s* adultez *f*
advance [ædˈvæns] *adj* adelantado; anticipado ‖ *s* adelanto, avance *m;* aumento, subida; **advances** propuestas; requerimiento amoroso; propuesta indecente; préstamo; **in advance** de antemano, por anticipado ‖ *tr* adelantar ‖ *intr* adelantar; adelantarse
advanced [ædˈvænst] *adj* avanzado; **advanced in years** avanzado de edad, entrado en años

advanced standing *s* traspaso de matrículas, traspaso de crédito académico
advanced studies *spl* altos estudios
advancement [æd'vænsmənt] *s* adelanto, avance *m;* subida; promoción
advance publicity *s* publicadad de lanzamiento
advantage [æd'væntɪdʒ] *s* ventaja; lasca; **to take advantage of** aprovecharse de; abusar de, engañar
advantageous [,ædvən'tedʒəs] *adj* ventajoso
advent ['ædvɛnt] *s* advenimiento || **Advent** *s* (eccl) Adviento
adventure [æd'vɛntʃər] *s* aventura || *tr* aventurar || *intr* aventurarse
adventurer [æd'vɛntʃərər] *s* aventurero
adventuresome [æd'vɛntʃərsəm] *adj* aventurero
adventurous [æd'vɛntʃərəs] *adj* aventurero
adverb ['ædvʌrb] *s* adverbio
adversar•y ['ædvər,sɛri] *s* (*pl* **-ies**) adversario
adversi•ty [æd'vʌrsɪti] *s* (*pl* **-ties**) adversidad
advertise ['ædvər,taiz] *tr & intr* anunciar
advertisement [,ædvər'taɪzmənt] o [æd'vʌrtɪzmənt] *s* anuncio
advertiser ['ædvər,taɪzər] *s* anunciante *mf*
advertising ['ædvər,taɪzɪŋ] *s* propaganda, publicidad, anuncios; reclame *m & f*
advertising agency *s* empresa anunciadora
advertising campaign *s* campaña de publicidad
advice [æd'vaɪs] *s* consejo; aviso, noticia; **a piece of advice** un consejo
advisable [æd'vaɪzəbəl] *adj* aconsejable
advise [æd'vaɪz] *tr* aconsejar, asesorar; advertir, avisar
advisement [æd'vaɪzmənt] *s* consideración; **to take under advisement** someter a consideración
advisory [æd'vaɪʒəri] *adj* consultivo
advocate ['ædvə,ket] *s* defensor *m;* (law) abogado || *tr* abogar por
Aegean Sea [ɪ'dʒi•ən] *s* Archipiélago; (*of the ancients*) mar Egeo
aegis ['idʒɪs] *s* égida; **under the aegis of** bajo los auspicios de
aerate ['ɛret] o ['e•ə,ret] *tr* airear
aerial ['ɛrɪ•əl] *adj* aéreo || *s* antena
aerialist ['ɛrɪ•əlɪst] *s* (*on trapeze*) trapecista *mf;* (*on tightrope*) equilibrista *mf*
aerial photograph *s* aerofoto *f,* fotografía aérea
aerial photography *s* fotografía aérea
aerial view *s* plano picado
aerobics [ə'robɪks] *s* aerobismo
aerodrome ['ɛrə,drom] *s* aeródomo
aerodynamic [,ɛrodaɪ'næmɪk] *adj* aerodinámico || **aerodynamics** *ssg* aerodinámica
aeronaut ['ɛrə,nɔt] *s* aeronauta *mf*
aeronautic [,ɛrə'nɔtɪk] *adj* aeronáutico || **aeronautics** *ssg* aeronáutica
aerosol ['ɛrə,sol] *s* aerosol *m*
aerospace ['ɛro,spes] *adj* aeroespacial
aesthete ['ɛsθit] *s* esteta *mf*
aesthetic [ɛs'θɛtɪk] *adj* estético || **aesthetics** *ssg* estética
afar [ə'far] *adv* lejos
affable ['æfəbəl] *adj* afable
affair [ə'fɛr] *s* asunto, negocio; lance *m;* (*fling, liaison*) (coll) amorío, lío; encuentro, combate *m;* **affairs** negocios
affect [ə'fɛkt] *tr* influir en; impresionar, enternecer; (*to assume; to pretend*) afectar; aficionarse a
affectation [,æfɛk'teʃən] *s* afectación
affected [ə'fɛktɪd] *adj* afectado
affection [ə'fɛkʃən] *s* afecto, cariño, afección; (pathol) afección
affectionate [ə'fɛkʃənɪt] *adj* afectuoso, cariñoso
affidavit [,æfɪ'devɪt] *s* declaración jurada, acta notarial
affiliate [ə'fɪlɪ,et] *adj* afiliado || *s* afiliado; filial *f* || *tr* afiliar || *intr* afiliarse
affini•ty [ə'fɪnɪti] *s* (*pl* **-ties**) afinidad
affirm [ə'fʌrm] *tr & intr* afirmar
affirmative [ə'fʌrmətɪv] *adj* afirmativo || *s* afirmativa
affirmative action *s* discriminación positiva, acción afirmativa (*determinada a favorecer a ciertos grupos*)
affix ['æfɪks] *s* añadidura; (gram) afijo || [ə'fɪks] *tr* añadir; atribuir (*p.ej., culpa*); poner (*una firma, sello, etc.*)
afflict [əflɪkt] *tr* afligir; **to be afflicted with** sufrir de, adolecer de
affliction [ə'flɪkʃən] *s* aflicción, desgracia; achaque *m*
affluence ['æflu•əns] *s* (*abundance*) afluencia; (*wealth*) opulencia
afford [ə'fɔrd] *tr* proporcionar; **to be able to afford (to)** poder darse el lujo de, poder permitirse
affray [ə'fre] *s* pendencia, riña
affront [ə'frʌnt] *s* afrenta || *tr* afrentar
Afghan ['æfgæn] *adj & s* afgano
Afghanistan [æf'gænɪ,stæn] *s* el Afganistán
afire [ə'faɪr] *adj & adv* ardiendo
aflame [ə'flem] *adj & adv* en llamas
afloat [ə'flot] *adj & adv* a flote; a bordo; inundado; sin rumbo; (*rumor*) en circulación
afoot [ə'fʊt] *adj & adv* a pie; en marcha
afoul [ə'faʊl] *adj & adv* enredado; en colisión; **to run afoul of** enredarse con
afraid [ə'fred] *adj* asustado; **to be afraid** tener miedo
Africa ['æfrɪkə] *s* Africa
African ['æfrɪkən] *adj & s* africano
African-American ['æfrɪkənə'mɛrikən] *adj & s* afroamericano
Afro-American ['æfro•ə'mɛrɪkən] *adj & s* afroamericano
aft [æft] *adj & adv* en popa
after ['æftər] *adj* siguiente || *adv* después || *prep* después de; según; **after all** al fin y al cabo || *conj* después de que
af'terburn'er *s* (aer) dispositivo de postcombustión

af′ter-din′ner speaker *s* orador *m* de sobremesa
after-dinner speech *s* discurso de sobremesa
af′ter•hours′ *adv* después del trabajo
af′ter•life′ *s* vida venidera; resto de la vida
aftermath [ˈæftər,mæθ] *s* segunda siega; consecuencias, consecuencias desastrosas
af′ter•noon′ *s* tarde *f*
af′ter•shave′ lotion *s* loción facial
aftershock [ˈæftərˈʃɑk] *s* réplica
af′ter•taste′ *s* dejo, gustillo, resabio
af′ter•thought′ *s* idea tardía, expediente tardío
afterward [ˈæftəwərd] *adv* después, luego
af′ter•while′ *adv* dentro de poco
again [əˈgɛn] *adv* otra vez, de nuevo; además; **to** + *inf* + **again** volver a + *inf,* p.ej., **he will come again** volverá a venir
against [əˈgɛnst] *prep* contra; cerca de; en contraste con; por; para
agape [əˈgep] *adj* abierto de par en par ‖ *adv* con la boca abierta
age [edʒ] *s* edad; (*old age*) vejez *f;* (*one hundred years; a long time*) siglo; edad mental; **of age** mayor de edad; **to come of age** alcanzar su mayoría de edad, llegar a mayor edad; **under age** menor de edad ‖ *tr* envejecer ‖ *intr* envejecer, envejecerse
aged [edʒd] *adj* de la edad de ‖ [ˈedʒɪd] *adj* anciano, viejo
ageless [ˈedʒlɪs] *adj* eternamente joven
agen•cy [ˈedʒənsi] *s* (*pl* **-cies**) agencia; mediación
agenda [əˈdʒɛndə] *s* agenda, temario
agent [ˈədʒənt] *s* agente *m*
agglomeration [ə,glɑməˈreʃən] *s* aglomeración
aggrandizement [əˈgrændɪzmənt] *s* engrandecimiento
aggravate [ˈægrə,vet] *tr* agravar; (coll) exasperar, irritar
aggregate [ˈægrɪ,get] *adj & s* agregado ‖ *tr* agregar, juntar; ascender a
aggression [əˈgrɛʃən] *s* agresión
aggressive [əˈgrɛsɪv] *adj* agresivo
aggressor [əˈgrɛsər] *s* agresor *m*
aghast [əˈgæst] *adj* horrorizado
agile [ˈædʒɪl] *adj* ágil
agitate [ˈædʒɪ,tet] *tr & intr* agitar
aglow [əˈglo] *adj & adv* fulgurante
agnostic [ægˈnɑstɪk] *adj & s* agnóstico
ago [əˈgo] *adv* hace, p.ej., **two days ago** hace dos días
ago•ny [ˈægəni] *s* (*pl* **-nies**) angustia, congoja; (*anguish; death struggle*) agonía
agrarian [əˈgrɛrɪ•ən] *adj* agrario ‖ *s* agrariense *mf*
agree [əˈgri] *intr* estar de acuerdo, ponerse de acuerdo; sentar bien; (gram) concordar
agreeable [əˈgri•əbəl] *adj* (*to one's liking*) agradable; (*willing to consent*) acorde, conforme
agreement [əˈgrimənt] *s* acuerdo, convenio, pacto; concordancia; **in agreement** de acuerdo
agriculture [ˈægrɪ,kʌltʃər] *s* agricultura
agronomy [əˈgrɑnəmi] *s* agronomía
aground [əˈgraʊnd] *adv* encallado, varado; **to run aground** encallar, varar
ague [ˈegju] *s* escalofrío; fiebre *f* intermitente
ahead [əˈhɛd] *adj & adv* delante, al frente; **ahead of** antes de; delante de; al frente de; **to get ahead (of)** adelantarse (a)
ahoy [əˈhɔɪ] *interj* — **ship ahoy!** ¡ah del barco!
aid [ed] *s* ayuda, auxilio; (mil) ayudante *m* ‖ *tr* ayudar, auxiliar; **to aid and abet** auxiliar e incitar, ser cómplice de ‖ *intr* ayudar
aide [ed] *s* ayudante *m;* (mil) edecán *m*
aide-de-camp [ˈeddəˈkæmp] *s* (*pl* **aides-de-camp**) ayudante *m* de campo, edecán *m*
AIDS [edz] *s* (*acronym*) (**acquired immunodeficiency syndrome**) el sida, SIDA (síndrome de inmunodeficiencia adquirida)
ail [el] *tr* inquietar; **what ails you?** ¿qué tiene Ud.? ‖ *intr* sufrir, estar enfermo
aileron [ˈelə,rɑn] *s* alerón *m*
ailing [ˈelɪŋ] *adj* enfermo, achacoso
ailment [ˈelmənt] *s* enfermedad, achaque *m*
aim [em] *s* puntería; intento; punto de mira ‖ *tr* apuntar, encarar; dirigir (*p.ej., una observación*) ‖ *intr* apuntar
air [ɛr] *s* aire *m;* **by air** por vía aérea; **in the open air** al aire libre; **on the air** en antena, en la radio; **to let the air out of** desinflar; **to put on airs** darse aires; **to put on the air** llevar a las antenas; **to walk on air** no pisar en el suelo ‖ *tr* airear, ventilar; radiodifundir; (fig) ventilar
air′-a•tom′ic *adj* aeroatómico
air bag *s* (aut) globo de aire, bolsa de aire
air′borne′ *adj* aerotransportado
air brakes *spl* frenos de aire comprimido, frenos neumáticos
air′-condi′tion *tr* climatizar
air-conditioned [ˈɛrkənˈdɪʃənd] *adj* climatizado, refrigerado
air conditioner *s* acondicionador *m* de aire
air conditioning *s* acondicionamiento del aire, clima *m* artificial, climatización
air corps *s* cuerpo de aviación
air′craft′ *ssg* máquina de volar; *spl* máquinas de volar
aircraft carrier *s* portaaviones *m*
air′drop′ *s* suministro por paracaídas ‖ *tr* lanzar enparacaídas
air field *s* campo de aviación
air′foil′ *s* superficie *f* de sustentación
air force *s* fuerza aérea, ejército del aire
air freshener *s* ambientador *m*
air gap *s* (phys) entrehierro
air′-ground′ *adj* aeroterrestre
air humidifier *s* humidificador *m*
air intake *s* entrada de aire
air lane *s* ruta aérea
air′lift′ *s* puente aéreo ‖ *tr* aerotransportar
air′line′ *s* línea aérea
airliner *s* transaéreo, avión *m* de travesía
airmail *s* correo aéreo, aeroposta
air′mail′ letter *s* carta aérea, carta por avión

airmail stamp *s* sello aéreo
air mattress *s* colchón *m* de aire
air′plane′ *s* avión *m,* aparato
airplane carrier *s* portaaviones *m*
air pocket *s* bache aéreo
air pollution *s* contaminación atmosférica
air′port′ *s* aeropuerto
air pump *s* bomba de aire
air raid *s* ataque aéreo
air′-raid′ drill *s* simulacro de ataque aéreo
air-raid shelter *s* abrigo antiaéreo
air-raid warning *s* alarma aérea
air rifle *s* escopeta de viento, escopeta de aire comprimido
air′ship′ *s* aeronave *f*
air show *s* demostración de acrobacia aérea
air shuttle *s* puente aéreo
air′sick′ *adj* mareado en el aire
air′sick′ness *s* mal *m* de vuelo
air sleeve o **sock** *s* veleta de manga
air′strip′ *s* pista de aterrizaje
air taxi *s* aerotaxi *m*
air′tight′ *adj* herméticamente cerrado, estanco al aire
air-to-air [ˈɛrtəˈɛr] *adj* (mil) aire-aire
air-to-ground [ˈɛrtəˈgraund] *adj* (mil) aire-superficie, aire-tierra
air′-traff′ic controller *s* controlador aéreo
air′waves′ *spl* ondas de radio
air′way′ *s* aerovía, vía aérea
airway lighting *s* balizaje *m*
air•y [ˈɛri] *adj* (*comp* **-ier;** *super* **-iest**) airoso; aireado; alegre; impertinente; (coll) afectado
aisle [aɪl] *s* (*in theater, movie, etc.*) pasillo; (*in a store, factory, etc.*) nave *f;* (archit) nave *f* lateral; (*any of the long passageways of a church*) (archit) nave *f*
ajar [əˈdʒɑr] *adj* entreabierto, entornado
akimbo [əˈkɪmbo] *adj & adv* — **with arms akimbo** en jarras
akin [əˈkɪn] *adj* emparentado; semejante
alabaster [ˈæləˌbæstər] *s* alabastro
alarm [əˈlɑrm] *s* alarma ‖ *tr* alarmar
alarm clock *s* reloj *m* despertador
alarmist [əˈlɑrmɪst] *s* alarmista *mf*
alas [əˈlæs] o [əˈlɑs] *interj* ¡ay!, ¡ay de mí!
Alaska [əˈlæskə] *s* Alaska
Albanian [ælˈbenɪ•ən] *adj & s* albanés *m*
albatross [ˈælbəˌtrɔs] o [ˈælbəˌtrɑs] *s* albatros *m*
album [ˈælbəm] *s* álbum *m*
albumen [ælˈbjumən] *s* (*albumin*) albúmina; (bot) albumen *m;* (*egg white*) clara (de huevo)
alchemy [ˈælkɪmi] *s* alquimia
alcohol [ˈælkəˌhɔl] o [ˈælkəˌhɑl] *s* alcohol *m*
alcoholic [ˌælkəˈhɔlɪk] o [ˌælkəˈhɑlɪk] *adj & s* alcohólico
al′co•hol-lev′el test *s* prueba de alcohol
alcove [ˈælkov] *s* gabinete *m,* rincón *m;* (*in bedroom*) trasalcoba; (*in garden*) cenador *m*
alder [ˈɔldər] *s* aliso
alder•man [ˈɔldərmən] *s* (*pl* **-men** [mən]) concejal *m*
ale [el] *s* ale *f* (*cerveza inglesa, obscura, espesa y amarga*)
alembic [əˈlɛmbɪk] *s* alambique *m*
alert [əˈlʌrt] *adj* listo, vivo; vigilante ‖ *s* (aer) alarma; (mil) alerta *m;* **to be on the alert** estar sobre aviso, estar alerta ‖ *tr* alertar
Aleutian Islands [əˈluʃən] *spl* islas Aleutas, islas Aleutianas
Alexandrine [ˌælɪgˈzændrɪn] *adj & s* alejandrino
algae [ˈældʒi] *spl* algas
algebra [ˈældʒɪbrə] *s* álgebra
algebraic [ˌældʒɪˈbre•ɪk] *adj* algebraico
Algeria [ælˈdʒɪrɪ•ə] *s* Argelia
Algerian [ælˈdʒɪrɪ•ən] *adj & s* argelino
Algiers [ælˈdʒɪrz] *s* Argel *f*
alias [ˈelɪ•əs] *adv* alias ‖ *s* alias *m,* nombre supuesto
ali•bi [ˈælɪˌbaɪ] *s* (*pl* **-bis**) coartada; (coll) excusa
Alice [ˈælɪs] *s* Alicia
alien [ˈelɪ•ən] *adj & s* extranjero
alienate [ˈeljəˌnet] o [ˈelɪ•əˌnet] *tr* enajenar, alienar; desenamorar
alight [əˈlaɪt] *v* (*pret & pp* **alighted** o **alit** [əˈlɪt]) *intr* bajar, apearse; posarse (*un ave*)
align [əˈlaɪn] *tr* alinear ‖ *intr* alinearse
alignment [əˈlaɪnmənt] *s* (auto) alineación; (archeol, compu, pol) alineamiento
alike [əˈlaɪk] *adj* semejantes; **to look alike** parecerse ‖ *adv* igualmente
alimentary canal [ˌælɪˈmɛntəri] *s* canal alimenticio, tubo digestivo
alimony [ˈælɪˌmoni] *s* pensión alimenticia
alive [əˈlaɪv] *adj* vivo, viviente; animado; **alive to** despierto para, sensible a; **alive with** hormigueante en
alka•li [ˈælkəˌlaɪ] *s* (*pl* **-lis** o **-lies**) álcali *m*
alkaline [ˈælkəˌlaɪn] *adj* alcalino
all [ɔl] *adj indef* todo, todos; todo el, todos los ‖ *pron indef* todo; todos, todo el mundo; **after all** sin embargo; **all of** todo el, todos los; **all that** todo lo que, todos los que; **for all I know** que yo sepa; a lo mejor; **not at all** nada; no hay de qué ‖ *adv* enteramente; **all along** desde el principio; a lo largo de; **all at once** de golpe; **all too** excesivamente
Allah [ˈælə] *s* Alá *m*
all-American [ˈɔləˈmɛrɪkən] *adj* típicamente americano; (sport) de clase internacional
all-around [ˈɔləˈraund] *adj* amplio; (*versatile*) completo
allay [əˈle] *tr* aliviar, calmar
all-clear [ˈɔlˈklɪr] *s* cese *m* de alarma
allege [əˈlɛdʒ] *tr* alegar
alleged [əˈlɛdʒd] *adj* alegado, supuesto
allegiance [əˈlidʒəns] *s* fidelidad, lealtad; homenaje *m;* **to swear allegiance to** jurar fidelidad a; rendir homenaje a
allegoric(al) [ˌælɪˈgɑrɪk(əl)] o [ˌælɪˈgɔrɪk(əl)] *adj* alegórico
allego•ry [ˈælɪˌgori] *s* (*pl* **-ries**) alegoría
allergic [əˈlʌrdʒɪk] *adj* alérgico

aller•gy [ˈælərdʒi] *s* (*pl* **-gies**) alergia
alleviate [əˈlivɪ,et] *tr* aliviar
alleviation [ə,livɪˈeʃən] *s* aligeramiento
alley [ˈæli] *s* callejuela; paseo arbolado, paseo de jardín; (bowling) pista; (tennis) espacio lateral
All Fools' Day *s var* de **April Fools' Day**
Allhallows [,ɔlˈhæloz] *s* día *m* de todos los santos
alliance [əˈlaɪ•əns] *s* alianza
alligator [ˈælɪ,getər] *s* caimán *m*
alligator pear *s* aguacate *m*
alligator wrench *s* llave *f* de mandíbulas dentadas
alliteration [ə,lɪtəˈreʃən] *s* aliteración
all-knowing [ˈɔlˈno•ɪŋ] *adj* omnisciente
allocate [ˈælə,ket] *tr* asignar, distribuir
allot [əˈlɑt] *v* (*pret & pp* **allotted;** *ger* **allotting**) *tr* asignar, distribuir
all'-out' *adj* total, supremo; acérrimo
allow [əˈlaʊ] *tr* dejar, permitir; admitir; conceder ‖ *intr* **— to allow for** tener en cuenta; **to allow of** permitir; admitir
allowance [əˈlau•əns] *s* permiso; concesión; ración; descuento, rebaja; tolerancia; **to make allowance for** tener en cuenta
alloy [ˈælɔɪ] o [əˈlɔɪ] *s* aleación, liga ‖ [əˈlɔɪ] *tr* alear, ligar
all'-pow'er•ful *adj* todopoderoso
all'-pur'pose *adj* universal, para todo uso
all right *adj* bueno ‖ *adv* bien ‖ *interj* ¡bueno!, ¡de acuerdo!; **all right?** ¿okey?, ¿vale?
All Saints' Day *s* Día *m* de Todos los Santos
All Souls' Day *s* Día *m* de los Difuntos
allspice [ˈɔl,spaɪs] *s* pimienta inglesa
all'-star' game *s* (sport) juego de estrellas
allude [əˈlud] *intr* aludir
allure [əˈlʊr] *s* tentación, encanto, fascinación ‖ *tr* tentar, encantar
alluring [əˈlʊrɪŋ] *adj* tentador, encantador, fascinante
allusion [əˈluʒən] *s* alusión
all'-weath'er *adj* para todo tiempo
al•ly [ˈælaɪ] o [əˈlaɪ] *s* (*pl* **-lies**) aliado ‖ [əˈlaɪ] *v* (*pret & pp* **-lied**) *tr* aliar ‖ *intr* aliarse
almanac [ˈɔlmə,næk] *s* almanaque *m*
almighty [ɔlˈmaɪti] *adj* todopoderoso
almond [ˈɑmənd] o [ˈæmənd] *s* almendra
almond brittle *s* crocante *m*
almond tree *s* almendro
almost [ˈɔlmost] o [ɔlˈmost] *adv* casi
alms [amz] *s* limosna
aloe [ˈælo] *s* áloe *m*
aloft [əˈlɔft] o [əˈlɑft] *adv* arriba; (aer) en vuelo; (naut) en la arboladura
alone [əˈlon] *adj* solo; **let alone** sin mencionar; y mucho menos; **to let alone** no molestar; no mezclarse en ‖ *adv* solamente
along [əˈlɔŋ] o [əˈlɑŋ] *adv* conmigo, consigo, etc.; **all along** desde el principio; **along with** junto con ‖ *prep* a lo largo de
along'side' *adv* a lo largo; (naut) al costado; **to bring alongside** acostar ‖ *prep* a lo largo de; (naut) al costado de
aloof [əˈluf] *adj* apartado; reservado ‖ *adv* lejos, a distancia
aloud [əˈlaʊd] *adv* alto, en voz alta
alphabet [ˈælfə,bɛt] *s* alfabeto
alpine [ˈælpaɪn] *adj* alpestre, alpino
Alps [ælps] *spl* Alpes *mpl*
already [ɔlˈrɛdi] *adv* ya
alright *var* de **all right**
Alsace [ælˈses] o [ˈælsæs] *s* Alsacia
Alsatian [ælˈseʃən] *adj & s* alsaciano
also [ˈɔlso] *adv* también
alt. *abbr* **alternate, altitude**
altar [ˈɔltər] *s* altar *m;* **to lead to the altar** conducir al altar
altar boy *s* acólito, monaguillo
altar cloth *s* sabanilla, palia
al'tar•piece' *s* retablo
altar rail *s* comulgatorio
alter [ˈɔltər] *tr* alterar ‖ *intr* alterarse
alteration [,ɔltəˈreʃən] *s* alteración; (*in a building*) reforma; (*in clothing*) arreglo
alternate [ˈɔltərnɪt] o [ˈæltərnɪt] *adj* alterno ‖ [ˈɔltər,net] o [ˈæltər,net] *tr & intr* alternar
alternating current *s* corriente alterna o alternativa
alternative [ɔlˈtʌrnətɪv] *adj* alternativo ‖ *s* alternativa
alternative fuel *s* combustible alternativo
alternative medicine *s* medicina alternativa
although [ɔlˈðo] *conj* aunque
altimetry [ælˈtɪmɪtri] *s* altimetría
altitude [ˈæltɪ,tjud] *s* altitud, altura
altitude sickness *s* mal *m* de alturas o de montañas
al•to [ˈælto] *s* (*pl* **-tos**) contralto
altogether [,ɔltəˈgɛðər] *adv* enteramente; en conjunto
altruist [ˈæltrʊ•ɪst] *s* altruísta *mf*
altruistic [,æltrʊˈɪstɪk] *adj* altruísta
alum [ˈæləm] *s* alumbre *m*
aluminum [əˈlumɪnəm] *s* aluminio
alum•na [əˈlʌmnə] *s* (*pl* **-nae** [ni]) graduada
alum•nus [əˈlʌmnəs] *s* (*pl* **-ni** [naɪ]) graduado
alveo•lus [ælˈvi•ələs] *s* (*pl* **-li** [,laɪ]) alvéolo
always [ˈɔlwɪz] o [ˈɔlwez] *adv* siempre
Alzheimer's disease [ˈɑlts,haɪmərz] *s* enfermedad *f* de Alzheimer, mal *m* de Alzheimer
A.M. o **AM** [ˈeˈɛm] *adj* (letterword) (**ante meridiem**) a.m., de la mañana ‖ *s* (letterword) (**amplitude modulation**) AM *f*
Am. *abbr* **America, American**
amalgam [əˈmælgəm] *s* amalgama *f*
amalgamate [əˈmælgə,met] *tr* amalgamar ‖ *intr* amalgamarse
amass [əˈmæs] *tr* amontonar; amasar (*dinero*)
amateur [ˈæmətʃər] *adj & s* aficionado; (*beginner*) chapucero, principiante *mf;* (sport) amateur
amaze [əˈmez] *tr* asombrar, maravillar
amazing [əˈmezɪŋ] *adj* asombroso, maravilloso
Amazon [ˈæmə,zɑn] *s* (*river*) Amazonas *m*

ambassador [æm'bæsədər] *s* embajador *m*
ambassadress [æm'bæsədrɪs] *s* embajadora
amber ['æmbər] *adj* ambarino || *s* ámbar *m*
ambigui•ty [,æmbɪ'gju•ɪti] *s* (*pl* **-ties**) ambigüedad
ambiguous [æm'bɪgju•əs] *adj* ambiguo
ambition [æm'bɪʃən] *s* ambición
ambitious [æm'bɪʃəs] *adj* ambicioso
amble ['æmbəl] *s* ambladura || *intr* amblar
ambulance ['æmbjələns] *s* ambulancia
ambush ['æmbʊʃ] *s* emboscada; **to lie in ambush** estar emboscado || *tr* (*to station in ambush*) emboscar; (*to lie in wait for and attack*) insidiar || *intr* emboscarse
ame•ba [ə'mibə] *s* (*pl* **-bas** o **-bae** [bi]) amiba
amelioration [ə,miljə'reʃən] *s* mejoramiento
amen ['e'mɛn] o ['a'mɛn] *interj* ¡amén! || *s* amén *m*
amenable [ə'minəbəl] o [ə'mɛnəbəl] *adj* dócil; responsable
amend [ə'mɛnd] *tr* enmendar || *intr* enmendarse || **amends** *spl* enmienda; **to make amends for** enmendar
amendment [ə'mɛndmənt] *s* enmienda
ameni•ty [ə'minɪti] o [ə'mɛnɪti] *s* (*pl* **-ties**) amenidad
America [ə'mɛrɪkə] *s* América
American [ə'mɛrɪkən] *adj & s* americano; norteamericano, estadounidense
Americanize [ə'mɛrɪkə,naɪz] *tr* americanizar
amethyst ['æmɪθɪst] *s* amatista
amiable ['emɪ•əbəl] *adj* amable, bonachón
amicable ['æmɪkəbəl] *adj* amigable
amid [ə'mɪd] *prep* en medio de
amidship [ə'mɪdʃip] *adv* en medio del navío
amiss [ə'mɪs] *adj* inoportuno; malo || *adv* inoportunamente; mal; **to take amiss** llevar a mal, tomar en mala parte
ami•ty ['æmɪti] *s* (*pl* **-ties**) amistad
ammeter ['æm,mitər] *s* anmetro, amperímetro
ammonia [ə'monɪ•ə] *s* (*gas*) amoníaco; (*liquid*) agua amoníacal
ammunition [,æmjə'nɪʃən] *s* munición
amnes•ty ['æmnɪsti] *s* (*pl* **-ties**) amnistía || *v* (*pret & pp* **-tied**) *tr* amnistiar
amniocentesis [,æmnɪ•osen'tisɪs] *s* amniocentesis *f*
amnion ['æmnɪ•ɑn] *s* bolsa de aguas
amoeba [ə'mibə] *s var* de **ameba**
among [ə'mʌŋ] *prep* entre, en medio de, en el número de
amorous ['æmərəs] *adj* amoroso; erótico, sensual, voluptuoso
amortize ['æmər,taɪz] *tr* amortizar
amount [ə'maʊnt] *s* cantidad, importe *m* || *intr* — **to amount to** ascender a; significar
amp. *abbr* **ampere, amperage**
ampere ['æmpɪr] *s* amperio
am'pere-hour' *s* amperio-hora *m*
amphibious [æm'fɪbɪ•əs] *adj* anfibio
amphitheater ['æmfɪ,θɪ•ətər] *s* anfiteatro
ample ['æmpəl] amplio; bastante, suficiente; abundante
amplifier ['æmplɪ,faɪ•ər] *s* amplificador *m*
ampli•fy ['æmplɪ,faɪ] *v* (*pret & pp* **-fied**) *tr* amplificar || *intr* espaciarse
amplitude [æ||mplɪ,tjud] *s* amplitud
amplitude modulation *s* modulación de amplitud
ampule ['æmpjul] *s* inyectable *m*
amputate ['æmpjə,tet] *tr* amputar
amputee ['æmpju'ti] *s* amputado
amuck [ə'mʌk] *adv* frenéticamente; **to run amuck** atacar a ciegas
amulet ['æmjəlɪt] *s* amuleto
amuse [ə'mjuz] *tr* divertir, entretener
amusement [ə'mjuzmənt] *s* diversión, entretenimiento; pasatiempo, recreación; (*in a park or circus*) atracción
amusement arcade *s* salón *m* de juegos, salón recreativo
amusement park *s* parque *m* de atracciones
amusing [ə'mjuzɪŋ] *adj* divertido, gracioso
an [æn] o [ən] *art indef* (antes de sonido vocal) un
anachronism [ə'nækrə,nɪzəm] *s* anacronismo
anachronistic [ə,nækrə'nɪstɪk] *adj* anacrónico
anaemia [ə'nimɪ•ə] *s* anemia
anaemic [ə'nimɪk] *adj* anémico
anaesthesia [,ænɪs'θiʒə] *s* anestesia
anaesthetic [,ænɪs'θɛtik] *adj & s* anestésico
anaesthetize [æ'nɛsθɪ,taɪz] *tr* anestesiar
analog ['ænəlog] *adj* (electron) analógico
analogous [ə'næləgəs] *adj* analogo
analo•gy [ə'nælədʒi] *s* (*pl* **-gies**) analogía
analyse ['ænə,laɪz] *tr* analizar
analy•sis [ə'nælɪsɪs] *s* (*pl* **-ses** [,siz]) análisis *m & f*
analyst ['ænəlɪst] *s* analista *mf*
analytic(al) [,ænə'lɪtɪk(əl)] *adj* analítico
analyze ['ænə,laɪz] *tr* analizar
anarchist ['ænərkɪst] *s* anarquista *mf*
anarchy ['ænərki] *s* anarquía
anathema [ə'næθɪmə] *s* anatema *m & f*
anatomic(al) [,ænə'tɑmɪk(əl)] *adj* anatómico
anato•my [ə'nætəmi] *s* (*pl* **-mies**) anatomía
ancestor ['ænsɛstər] *s* antecesor *m,* antepasado
ances•try ['ænsɛstri] *s* (*pl* **-tries**) abolengo, alcurnia
anchor ['æŋkər] *s* ancla, áncora; (telv) presentador; (fig) áncora; **to cast anchor** echar anclas; **to weigh anchor** levar anclas || *tr* sujetar con el ancla || *intr* anclar, ancorar
ancho•vy ['æntʃovi] *s* (*pl* **-vies**) anchoa
ancient ['enʃənt] *adj* antiguo
and [ænd] o [ənd] *conj* y; **and so forth** y así sucesivamente
Andean [æn'di•ən] *adj & s* andino
Andes ['ændiz] *spl* Andes *mpl*
andirons ['ænd,aɪ•ərnz] *spl* morillos
Andrew ['ændru] *s* Andrés *m*
anecdote ['ænɪk,dot] *s* anécdota
anemia [ə'nimɪ•ə] *s* anemia
anemic [ə'nimɪk] *adj* anémico
aneroid barometer ['ænə,rɔɪd] *s* barómetro aneroide

anesthesia [ˌænɪsˈθiʒə] *s* anestesia
anesthetic [ˌænɪsˈθɛtɪk] *adj & s* anestésico
anesthetize [æˈnɛsθɪˌtaɪz] *tr* anestesiar
aneurysm [ˈænjəˌrɪzəm] *s* aneurisma *m*
anew [əˈnju] o [əˈnu] *adv* de nuevo, nuevamente
angel [ˈendʒəl] *s* ángel *m;* (*financial backer*) caballo blanco
angelic(al) [ænˈdʒɛlɪk(əl)] *adj* angélico, angelical
anger [ˈæŋgər] *s* cólera, ira ‖ *tr* encolerizar, airar
angina pectoris [æñˈdʒainə ˈpɛktərɪs] *s* angina de pecho
angle [ˈæŋgəl] *s* ángulo; punto de vista ‖ *intr* pescar con caña; intrigar
angle iron *s* angulo de hierro, hierro angular
angler [ˈæŋglər] *s* pescador *m* de caña; intrigante *mf*
Anglo-Saxon [ˌæŋgloˈsæksən] *adj & s* anglosajón *m*
an•gry [ˈæŋgri] *adj* (*comp* **-grier;** *super* **-griest**) encolerizado, airado; (pathol) inflamado, irritado; **to become angry at** enojarse de; **to become angry with** enojarse con o contra
anguish [ˈæŋgwɪʃ] *s* angustia, congoja
angular [ˈæŋgjələr] *adj* angular; (*features*) anguloso
anhydrous [ænˈhaɪdrəs] *adj* anhidro
aniline dyes [ˈænɪlɪn] o [ˈænɪˌlaɪn] *s* colores *mpl* de anilina
animal [ˈænɪməl] *adj & s* animal *m*
animal spirits *spl* ardor *m,* vigor *m,* vivacidad
animated cartoon [ˈænɪˌmetɪd] *s* película de dibujos, dibujo animado
animation [ˌænɪˈmeʃən] *s* animación
animosi•ty [ˌænɪˈmɑsɪti] *s* (*pl* **-ties**) animosidad
anion [ˈænˌaɪ•ən] *s* anión *m*
anise [ˈænɪs] *s* anís *m*
aniseed [ˈænɪˌsid] *s* grano de anís
anisette [ˌænɪˈzɛt] *s* anisete *m*
ankle [ˈæŋkəl] *s* tobillo
an'kle•bone' *s* hueso del tobillo
ankle support *s* tobillera
anklet [ˈæŋklɪt] *s* ajorca; (*sock*) tobillera
annals [ˈænəlz] *spl* anales *mpl*
anneal [əˈnil] *tr* recocer
annex [ˈænɛks] *s* anexo; (*of a building*) pabellón *m* ‖ [əˈnɛks] *tr* anexar
annihilate [əˈnaɪ•ɪˌlet] *tr* aniquilar
anniversa•ry [ˌænɪˈvʌrsəri] *adj* aniversario ‖ *s* (*pl* **-ries**) aniversario
annotate [ˈænəˌtet] *tr* anotar
announce [əˈnaʊns] *tr* anunciar
announcement [əˈnaʊnsmənt] *s* anuncio
announcer [əˈnaʊnsər] *s* anunciador *m;* (rad) locutor *m*
annoy [əˈnɔɪ] *tr* fastidiar, molestar; majaderear; pololear; (Cuba, Mex) ciscar
annoyance [əˈnɔɪ•əns] *s* fastidio, molestia
annoying [əˈnɔɪ•ɪŋ] *adj* fastidioso, molesto
annual [ˈænjʊ•əl] *adj* anual ‖ *s* publicación anual; planta anual
annui•ty [əˈnju•ɪti] o [əˈnu•ɪti] *s* (*pl* **-ties**) anualidad; renta vitalicia, pensión vitalicia
an•nul [əˈnʌl] *v* (*pret & pp* **-nulled;** *ger* **-nulling**) *tr* anular, invalidar
anode [ˈænod] *s* ánodo
anoint [əˈnɔɪnt] *tr* ungir, untar
anomalous [əˈnɑmələs] *adj* anómalo
anoma•ly [əˈnɑməli] *s* (*pl* **-lies**) anomalía
anon. *abbr* **anonymous**
anonymity [ˌænəˈnɪmɪti] *s* anonimato
anonymous [əˈnɑnɪməs] *adj* anónimo; **to remain anonymous** conservar el anonimato
another [əˈnʌðər] *adj & pron indef* otro
answer [ˈænsər] *s* contestación, respuesta; solución ‖ *tr* contestar, responder; resolver (*un problema o un enigma*) ‖ *intr* contestar, responder; **to answer for** responder de (*una cosa*); responder por (*una persona*)
answering machine *s* contestador automático
answering service *s* servicio de mensajes
ant [ænt] *s* hormiga
antagonism [ænˈtægəˌnɪzəm] *s* antagonismo
antagonize [ænˈtægəˌnaɪz] *tr* oponerse a; enemistar, enajenar
antarctic [æntˈɑrktɪk] *adj* antártico ‖ **the Antarctic** las Tierras Antárticas
ante [ˈæntɪ] *s* (cards) apuesta inicial ‖ *intr* poner el dinero de la apuesta inicial
antecedent [ˌæntɪˈsidənt] *adj* antecedente ‖ *s* antecedente *m;* **antecedents** antecedentes *mpl;* antepasados
antechamber [ˈæntɪˌtʃembər] *s* antecámara
antedate [ˈæntɪˌdet] *tr* antedatar; preceder
antelope [ˈæntɪˌlop] *s* antílope *m*
anten•na [ænˈtɛnə] *s* (*pl* **-nae** [ni]) (ent) antena ‖ *s* (*pl* **-nas**) (rad) antena
antepenult [ˌæntɪˈpinʌlt] *s* antepenúltima
anteroom [ˈæntɪˌrum] *s* antecámara
anthem [ˈænθəm] *s* himno; antífona
ant'hill' *s* hormiguero
antholo•gy [ænˈθɑlədʒi] *s* (*pl* **-gies**) antología
Anthony [ˈænθənɪ] *s* Antonio
anthracite [ˈænθrəˌsaɪt] *s* antracita
anthrax [ˈænθræks] *s* ántrax *m;* (*symptom*) carbunco, carbunculo
anthropology [ˌænθrəˈpɑlədʒi] *s* antropología
antiaircraft [ˌæntɪˈɛrˌkræft] *adj* antiaéreo
anti-aliasing [ˈæntaɪˈeli•əsɪŋ] *s* (compu) antialiasing *m*
antiballistic missile [ˈæntɪbəˈlɪstɪk] *s* mísil antibalístico
antibiotic [ˌæntɪbaɪˈɑtɪk] *adj & s* antibiótico
antibod•y [ˈæntɪˌbadi] *s* (*pl* **-ies**) anticuerpo
anticipate [ænˈtɪsɪˌpet] *tr* esperar, prever; anticipar; (*to get ahead of*) anticiparse a; impedir; prometerse (*p.ej., un placer*); temerse (*algo desagradable*)
antics [ˈæntɪks] *spl* cabriolas, gracias, travesuras
antidote [ˈæntɪˌdot] *s* antídoto
antifreeze [ˌæntɪˈfriz] *s* anticongelante *m*
antiglare [ˌæntɪˈglɛr] *adj* antideslumbrante
antiknock [ˌæntɪˈnɑk] *adj & s* antidetonante *m*
antilabor [ˌæntɪˈlebər] *adj* antiobrero
Antilles [ænˈtɪliz] *spl* Antillas

antilock brakes [ˋæntɪˋlɑk] *spl* frenos antibloque
antimatter [ˋæntɪˌmætər] *s* antimateria
antimissile [ˌæntɪˋmɪsɪl] *adj* antiproyectil
antimony [ˋæntɪˌmoni] *s* antimonio
antipas•to [ˌɑntɪˋpɑsto] *s* (*pl* **-tos**) aperitivo, entremés *m*
antipa•thy [ænˋtɪpəθi] *s* (*pl* **-thies**) antipatía
antipollution movement [ˌæntɪpəˋluʃən] *s* lucha antipolución
antiquar•y [ˋæntɪˌkwɛri] *s* (*pl* **-ies**) anticuario
antiquated [ˋæntɪˌkwetɪd] *adj* anticuado
antique [ænˋtik] *adj* antiguo ‖ *s* antigüedad
antique dealer *s* anticuario
antique store *s* tienda de antigüedades
antiqui•ty [ænˋtɪkwɪti] *s* (*pl* **-ties**) antigüedad
anti-Semitic [ˌæntɪsɪˋmɪtɪk] *adj* antisemítico
antiseptic [ˌæntɪˋsɛptɪk] *adj* & *s* antiséptico
antislavery [ˌæntɪˋslevəri] *adj* antiesclavista
antitank [ˌæntɪˋtæŋk] *adj* antitanque
antiterrorist [ˌæntɪˋtɛrərɪst] *adj* & *s* antiterrorista *mf*
antithe•sis [ænˋtɪθɪsɪs] *s* (*pl* **-ses** [ˌsiz]) antítesis *f*
antitoxin [ˌæntɪˋtɑksɪn] *s* antitoxina
antitrust [ˌæntɪˋtrʌst] *adj* anticartel
antiwar [ˌæntɪˋwɔr] *adj* antibélico
antler [ˋæntlər] *s* cuerna
antonym [ˋæntənɪm] *s* antónimo
Antwerp [ˋæntwərp] *s* Amberes *f*
anus [ˋenəs] *s* ano
anvil [ˋænvɪl] *s* yunque *m*
anxie•ty [æŋˋzaɪ•əti] *s* (*pl* **-ties**) ansiedad, inquietud; ansia, anhelo
anxious [ˋæŋkʃəs] *adj* ansioso, inquieto; anhelante; **to be anxious to** tener ganas de
any [ˋɛni] *adj indef* algún, cualquier; todo; **any place** dondequiera; **any time** cuando quiera; alguna vez ‖ *pron indef* alguno, cualquiera ‖ *adv* algo
an′y•bod′y *pron indef* alguno, alguien, cualquiera, quienquiera; todo el mundo; **not anybody** nadie
an′y•how′ *adv* de cualquier modo; de todos modos; sin embargo
an′y•one′ *pron indef* alguno, alguien, cualquiera
an′y•thing′ *pron indef* algo, alguna cosa; cualquier cosa; todo cuanto; **anything at all** cualquier cosa que sea; **anything else** cualquier otra cosa; **anything else?** ¿algo más?; **not anything** nada
an′y•way′ *adv* de cualquier modo; de todos modos; sin embargo
an′y•where′ *adv* dondequiera; adondequiera; **not anywhere** en ninguna parte
apace [əˋpes] *adv* aprisa
apart [əˋpɑrt] *adv* aparte; en pedazos; **to fall apart** caerse a pedazos; desunirse; ir al desastre; **to live apart** vivir separados; vivir aislado; **to stand apart** mantenerse apartado; **to take apart** descomponer, desarmar, desmontar; **to tell apart** distinguir
apartheid [əˋpɑrtet] *s* apartheid *m*
apartment [əˋpɑrtmənt] *s* apartamento
apartment house *s* casa de pisos
apathetic [ˌæpəˋθɛtɪk] *adj* apático
apa•thy [ˋæpəθi] *s* (*pl* **-ties**) apatía; lerdera
ape [ep] *s* mono ‖ *tr* imitar, remedar
aperture [ˋæpərtʃər] *s* abertura, orificio
apex [ˋepɛks] *s* (*pl* **apexes** o **apices** [ˋæpɪˌsiz]) ápex *m*, ápice *m*
aphorism [ˋæfəˌrɪzəm] *s* aforismo
aphrodisiac [ˌæfrəˋdɪzɪˌæk] *adj* & *s* afrodisíaco
apiar•y [ˋepɪˌɛri] *s* (*pl* **-ies**) abejar *m*, colmenar *m*
apiece [əˋpis] *adv* cada uno; por persona
apish [ˋepɪʃ] *adj* monesco; tonto
aplomb [əˋplɑm] *s* aplomo, sangre fría
apogee [ˋæpəˌdʒi] *s* apogeo
Apologetic [əˌpɑləˋdʒɛtɪk] *adj* lleno de excusas
apologist [əˋpɑlədʒɪst] *s* defensor *m;* exponente *m*
apologize [əˋpɑləˌdʒaɪz] *intr* excusarse, disculparse; **to apologize for** disculparse de; **to apologize to** disculparse con
apology [əˋpɑlədʒi] *s* (*pl* **-gies** excusa; (*makeshift*) expediente *m*
apoplectic [ˌæpəˋplɛktɪk] *adj* & *s* apoplético
apoplexy [ˋæpəˌplɛksi] *s* apoplejía
apostle [əˋpɑsəl] *s* apóstol *m*
apostrophe [əˋpɑstrəfi] *s* (*written sign*) apóstrofo; (*words addressed to absent person*) apóstrofe *m* & *f*
appall [əˋpɔl] *tr* espantar, pasmar
appalling [əˋpɔlɪŋ] *adj* aterrador, espantoso, pasmoso
appara•tus [ˌæpəˋretəs] o [ˌæpəˋrætəs] *s* (*pl* **-tus** o **-tuses**) aparato
apparel [əˋpærəl] *s* indumentaria, vestido, ropaje *m*
apparent [əˋpærənt] *adj* aparente
apparition [ˌæpəˋrɪʃən] *s* aparición
appeal [əˋpil] *s* súplica, instancia, solicitud; atracción, interés *m;* (law) apelación ‖ *intr* ser atrarente; **to appeal to** (*to make an entreaty to*) suplicar; (*to be attractive to*) atraer, interesar; (law) apelar a
appear [əˋpɪr] *intr* (*to come into sight; to be in sight; to be published*) aparecer; (*to come into sight; to be in sight; to look; to seem*) parecer; (*to come before the public*) presentarse; (*to come before a court*) comparecer
appearance [əˋpɪrəns] *s* (*act of appearing*) aparición; (*outward look*) apariencia, aspecto; (law) comparecencia
appease [əˋpiz] *tr* apaciguar
appeasement [əˋpizmənt] *s* apaciguamiento
appellate [əˋpɛlɪt] *adj* apelante
appellate court *s* tribunal *m* de apelación
appellate judge *s* juez *m* de alzadas
appendage [əˋpɛndɪdʒ] *s* apéndice *m*
appendicitis [əˌpɛndɪˋsaɪtɪs] *s* apendicitis *f*
appen•dix [əˋpɛndɪks] *s* (*pl* **-dixes** o **-dices** [dɪˌsiz]) apéndice *m*
appertain [ˌæpərˋten] *intr* relacionarse

appetite [ˈæpɪ,taɪt] *s* apetito
appetizer [ˈæpɪ,taɪzər] *s* aperitivo
appetizing [ˈæpɪ,taɪzɪŋ] *adj* apetitoso
applaud [əˈplɔd] *tr & intr* aplaudir
applause [əˈplɔz] *s* aplauso, aplausos
apple [ˈæpəl] *s* manzana
ap′ple•jack′ *s* aguardiente *m* de manzana
apple of the eye *s* niña del ojo
apple pie *s* pastel *m* de manzana
apple polisher *s* (slang) quitamotas *mf*
ap′ple•sauce′ *s* compota de manzanas; (slang) música celestial
applet [ˈæplɛt] *s* (compu) applet *m*
apple tree *s* manzano
appliance [əˈplaɪ•əns] *s* artificio, dispositivo, aparato; aplicación
applicant [ˈæplɪkənt] *s* aspirante *mf*, pretendiente *mf*, solicitante *mf*
application [,æplɪˈkeʃən] *s* aplicación; (*for admission, funds, a job*) solicitud; (compu) aplicación
ap•ply [əˈplaɪ] *v* (*pret & pp* **-plied**) *tr* aplicar ‖ *intr* aplicarse; dirigirse; **to apply for** pedir, solicítar
appoint [əˈpɔɪnt] *tr* designar, nombrar; señalar; amueblar
appointment [əˈpɔɪntmənt] *s* designación, nombramiento; empleo, puesto; cita; **appointments** instalación, accesorios, adornos; **by appointment** cita previa
apportion [əˈporʃən] *tr* prorratear
appraisal [əˈprezəl] *s* tasación, valoración, apreciación
appraise [əˈprez] *tr* tasar, valorar, apreciar
appreciable [əˈpriʃi•əbəl] *adj* apreciable; sensible
appreciate [əˈpriʃi,et] *tr* apreciar; aprobar; comprender; estar agradecido por ‖ *intr* subir de valor
appreciation [ə,priʃiˈeʃən] *s* aprecio; agradecimiento; plusvalía, aumento de valor
appreciative [əˈpriʃi,etɪv] *adj* apreciador; agradecido
apprehend [,æprɪˈhɛnd] *tr* aprehender, prender; comprender; temer
apprehension [,æprɪˈhɛnʃən] *s* aprehensión; (*fear, worry*) aprensión; comprensión
apprehensive [,æprɪˈhɛnsɪv] *adj* (*fearful, worried*) aprehensivo, aprensivo
apprentice [əˈprɛntɪs] *s* aprendiz *m*, meritorio; chumero, chumera (CAm) ‖ *tr* poner de aprendiz
apprenticeship [əˈprɛntɪs,ʃɪp] *s* aprendizaje *m*
apprise o **apprize** [əˈpraɪz] *tr* informar; apreciar, tasar
approach [əˈprotʃ] *s* acercamiento; vía de entrada; proposición; (*to a problem*) enfoque *m* ‖ *tr* abordar, acercarse a; (*to bring closer*) acercar ‖ *intr* acercarse, aproximarse
approbation [,æprəˈbeʃən] *s* aprobación
appropriate [əˈpropri•ɪt] *adj* apropiado, a propósito ‖ [əˈpropri,et] *tr* apropiarse; asignar, destinar (*el parlamento determinada suma a un determinado fin*)
approval [əˈpruvəl] *s* aprobación; **on approval** a prueba
approve [əˈpruv] *tr & intr* aprobar
approximate [əˈprɑksɪmɪt] *adj* aproximado ‖ [əˈprɑksɪ,met] *tr* aproximar ‖ *intr* aproximarse
apricot [ˈeprɪ,kɑt] o [ˈæprɪ,kɑt] *s* albaricoque *m*
apricot tree *s* albaricoquero
April [ˈeprɪl] *s* abril *m*
April fool *s* — **to make an April fool of** coger por inocente
April Fools' Day *s* Día *m* de los Inocentes, el primer día de abril
apron [ˈeprən] *s* delantal *m;* (*of a workman*) mandil *m;* **tied to the apron strings of** cosido a las faldas de
apropos [,æprəˈpo] *adj* oportuno ‖ *adv* a propósito; **apropos of** a propósito de
apse [æps] *s* ábside *m*
apt [æpt] *adj* apto; a propósito; dispuesto, inclinado
aptitude [ˈæptɪ,tjud] *s* aptitud
aquamarine [,ækwəməˈrin] *s* aguamarina
aquaplane [ˈækwə,plen] *s* acuaplano ‖ *intr* correr en acuaplano
aquari•um [əˈkwɛrɪ•əm] *s* (*pl* **-ums** o **-a** [ə]) acuario
Aquarius [əˈkwɛrɪ•əs] *s* (astr) Acuario
aquatic [əˈkwætɪk] o [əˈkwɑtɪk] *adj* acuático ‖ **aquatics** *spl* deportes acuáticos
aqueduct [ˈækwə,dʌkt] *s* acueducto
aquiline nose [ˈækwɪ,laɪn] *s* nariz aguileña
Arab [ˈærəb] *adj* árabe ‖ *s* árabe *mf;* caballo árabe
Arabia [əˈrebɪ•ə] *s* la Arabia
Arabian [əˈrebɪ•ən] *adj* árabe; arábigo ‖ *s* árabe *mf*
Arabic [ˈærəbɪk] *adj* arábigo ‖ *s* árabe *m*, arábigo
arbiter [ˈɑrbɪtər] *s* árbitro
arbitrary [ˈɑrbɪ,trɛri] *adj* arbitrario
arbitrate [ˈɑrbɪ,tret] *tr & intr* arbitrar
arbitration [,ɑrbɪˈtreʃən] *s* arbitraje *m*
arbor [ˈɑrbər] *s* emparrado, glorieta
arbore•tum [,ɑrbəˈritəm] *s* (*pl* **-tums** o **-ta** [tə]) jardín botánico de árboles, arboleda (*vivero con fines científicos*)
arbutus [ɑrˈbjutəs] *s* madroño
arc [ɑrk] *s* arco
arcade [ɑrˈked] *s* arcada, galería
arch. *abbr* **archaic, archaism, archipelago, architect**
arch [ɑrtʃ] *adj* astuto; travieso; principal ‖ *s* arco ‖ *tr* arquear, enarcar; atravesar
archaeology [,ɑrkɪˈɑlədʒi] *s* arqueología
archaic [ɑrˈke•ɪk] *adj* arcaico
archaism [ˈɑrke,ɪzəm] *s* arcaísmo
archangel [ˈɑrk,endʒəl] *s* arcángel *m*
archbishop [ˈɑrtʃˈbɪʃəp] *s* arzobispo
archduke [ˈɑrtʃˈdjuk] *s* archiduque *m*

archene•my [ˈartʃ,ɛnɪmi] *s* (*pl* **-mies**) archienemigo
archeology [,arkɪˈalədʒi] *s* arqueología
archer [ˈartʃər] *s* arquero, flechero
archery [ˈartʃəri] *s* tiro de flechas *or* con arco
archipela•go [,arkɪˈpɛləgo] *s* (*pl* **-gos** o **-goes**) archipiélago
architect [ˈarkɪ,tɛkt] *s* arquitecto
architectural [,arkɪˈtɛktʃərəl] *adj* arquitectónico, arquitectural
architecture [ˈarkɪ,tɛktʃər] *s* arquitectura
archives [ˈarkaɪvz] *spl* archivo
arch′way′ *s* arcada
arc lamp *s* lámpara de arco
arctic [ˈarktɪk] *adj* ártico ‖ **the Arctic** las Tierras Articas
arc welding *s* soldadura de arco
ardent [ˈardənt] *adj* ardiente
ardor [ˈardər] *s* ardor *m*
arduous [ˈardjʊ•əs] *adj* arduo, difícil; enérgico; (*steep*) escarpado
area [ˈɛrɪ•ə] *s* área, superficie *f;* comarca, región; zona; patio
area code *s* (telp) código de la zona, prefijo local, código territorial
ar′ea•way′ *s* entrada baja de un sótano
aren't *contr* **are not**
Argentina [,ardʒənˈtinə] *s* la Argentina
Argentine [ˈardʒən,tin] o [ˈardʒən,taɪn] *adj & s* argentino ‖ **the Argentine** la Argentina
Argentinean [,ardʒənˈtɪnɪ•ən] *adj & s* argentino
argot [ˈargət] *s* argot *m*
argue [ˈargju] *tr* argüir; **to argue into** persuadir a + *inf;* **to argue out of** disuadir de + *inf* ‖ *intr* argüir
argument [ˈargjəmənt] *s* argumento; disputa
argumentative [,argjəˈmɛntətɪv] *adj* argumentador; ergotista *masc*
aria [ˈarɪ•ə] o [ˈɛrɪ•ə] *s* (mus) aria
arid [ˈærɪd] *adj* árido
aridity [əˈrɪdɪti] *s* aridez *f*
Aries [ˈɛriz] *s* (astr) Aries *m*
aright [əˈraɪt] *adv* acertadamente; **to set aright** rectificar
arise [əˈraɪz] *v* (*pret* **arose** [əˈroz]; *pp* **arisen** [əˈrɪzən]) *intr* levantarse; subir; aparecer; **to arise from** provenir de
aristocra•cy [,ærɪsˈtakrəsi] *s* (*pl* **-cies**) aristocracia
aristocrat [əˈrɪstə,kræt] *s* aristócrata *mf*
aristocratic [ə,rɪstəˈkrætɪk] *adj* aristocrático
Aristotelian [,ærɪstəˈtilɪ•ən] *adj & s* aristotélico
Aristotle [ˈærɪs,tatəl] *s* Aristóteles *m*
arithmetic [əˈrɪθmətɪk] *s* aritmética
arithmetical [,ærɪθˈmɛtɪkəl] *adj* aritmético
arithmetician [ə,rɪθməˈtɪʃən] *s* aritmético
ark [ark] *o* **Noah's Ark** *s* arca de Noe
ark of the covenant *s* arca de la alianza
arm [arm] *s* brazo; (*weapon*) arma; **arm in arm** de bracero, asidos del brazo; **in arms** de pecho, de teta; **the three arms of the service** los tres ejércitos; **to arm wrestle** echar pulsos; **to be up in arms** estar en armas; **to keep at arm's length** mantener a distancia; mantenerse a distancia; **to lay down one's arms** rendir las armas; **to rise up in arms** alzarse en armas; **under arms** sobre las armas ‖ *tr* armar ‖ *intr* armarse
armament [ˈarməmənt] *s* armamento
armature [ˈarmə,tʃər] *s* armadura; (*of a dynamo or motor*) (elec) inducido
arm′chair′ *adj* de gabinete ‖ *s* butaca, sillón *m,* silla de brazos
armed robbery *s* robo a mano armada
Armenian [arˈminɪ•ən] *adj & s* armenio
armful [ˈarm,fʊl] *s* brazado
arm′hole′ *s* (*in clothing*) sisa
armistice [ˈarmɪstɪs] *s* armisticio
armor [ˈarmər] *s* armadura; coraza, blindaje *m* ‖ *tr* acorazar, blindar
armored car *s* carro blindado
armorial bearings [arˈmorɪ•əl] *spl* blasón *m,* escudo de armas
armor plate *s* plancha de blindaje
ar′mor-plate′ *tr* acorazar, blindar
armor•y [ˈarməri] *s* (*pl* **-ies**) arsenal *m;* (*arms factory*) armería
arm′pit′ *s* sobaco, axila
arm′rest′ *s* apoyabrazos *m*
arms race *s* carrera armanentista
ar•my [ˈarmi] *adj* militar, castrense ‖ *s* (*pl* **-mies**) ejército
army corps *s* cuerpo de ejército
army surplus *s* desechos militares
aroma [əˈromə] *s* aroma *m,* fragancia
aromatic [,ærəˈmætɪk] *adj* aromático
around [əˈraʊnd] *adv* alrededor, a la redonda; en la dirección opuesta ‖ *prep* alrededor de, en torno a o de; cerca de; (*the corner*) a la vuelta de
arouse [əˈraʊz] *tr* despertar; excitar, incitar
arpeg•gio [arˈpɛdʒo] *s* (*pl* **-gios**) arpegio
arraign [əˈren] *tr* acusar; presentar al tribunal
arraignment [əˈrenmənt] *s* comparecencia ante el juez
arrange [əˈrendʒ] *tr* arreglar, disponer; (mus) adaptar, refundir
array [əˈre] *s* orden *m;* orden *m* de batalla; adorno, atavío ‖ *tr* poner en orden; poner en orden de batalla; adornar, ataviar
arrears [əˈrɪrz] *spl* atrasos; **in arrears** atrasado en pagos
arrest [əˈrɛst] *s* arresto, prisión; detención; **under arrest** bajo arresto ‖ *tr* arrestar; detener; atraer (*la atención*)
arresting [əˈrɛstɪŋ] *adj* impresionante
arrhythmia [əˈrɪθmi•ə] *s* arritmia
arrival [əˈraɪvəl] *s* llegada; (*person*) llegado
arrive [əˈraɪv] *intr* llegar; tener éxito
arrogance [ˈærəgəns] *s* arrogancia
arrogant [ˈærəgənt] *adj* arrogante
arrogate [ˈærə,get] *tr* — **to arrogate to oneself** arrogarse
arrow [ˈæro] *s* flecha
ar′row-head′ *s* punta de flecha; (bot) saetilla
arsenal [ˈarsənəl] *s* arsenal *m*

arsenic [ˈɑrsɪnɪk] *s* arsénico
arson [ˈɑrsən] *s* incendio premeditado
arsonist [ˈɑrsənɪst] s incendiario
art [ɑrt] *s* arte *m & f*
arter•y [ˈɑrtəri] *s* (*pl* **-ies**) arteria
artesian well [ɑrˈtiʒən] *s* pozo artesiano
artful [ˈɑrtfəl] *adj* astuto, mañoso; diestro, ingenioso
art gallery *s* galería de arte
arthritic [ɑrˈθrɪtɪk] *adj & s* artrítico
arthritis [ɑrˈθraɪtɪs] *s* artritis *f*
artichoke [ˈɑrtɪ,tʃok] *s* alcachofa
article [ˈɑrtɪkəl] *s* artículo; **an article of clothing** una prenda de vestir
articulate [ɑrˈtɪkjəlɪt] *adj* claro, distinto; capaz de hablar ‖ [ɑrˈtɪkjə,let] *tr* articular
artifact [ˈɑrtɪ,fækt] *s* artefacto
artifice [ˈɑrtɪfɪs] *s* artificio
artificial [,ɑrtɪˈfɪʃəl] *adj* artificial
artificial insemination *s* inseminación artificial
artificial intelligence *s* inteligencia artificial
artificial respiration *s* respiración artificial
artillery [ɑrˈtɪləri] *s* artillería
artillery•man [ɑrˈtɪlərimən] *s* (*pl* **-men** [mən]) artillero
artisan [ˈɑrtɪzən] *s* artesano
artist [ˈɑrtɪst] *s* artista *mf*
artistic [ɑrˈtɪstɪk] *adj* artístico
artistry [ˈɑrtɪstri] *s* habilidad artística
artless [ˈɑrtlɪs] *adj* sencillo, natural; ingenuo, inocente; (*crude, clumsy*) chabacano
arts and crafts *spl* artes y oficios
art•y [ˈɑrti] *adj* (*comp* **-ier;** *super* **-iest**) (coll) ostentosamente artístico
Aryan [ˈɛrɪ•ən] o [ˈɑrjən] *adj & s* ario
as [æz] o [əz] *pron rel* que; **the same as** el mismo que ‖ *adv* tan; **as . . . as** tan . . . como; **as for** en cuanto a; **as long as** mientras que; ya que; **as many as** tantos como; **as much as** tanto como; **as regards** en cuanto a; **as soon as** tan pronto como; **as soon as possible** cuanto antes, los más pronto posible; **as though** como si; **as to** en cuanto a; **as well** también; **as yet** hasta ahora ‖ *conj* como; que; ya que; a medida que; **as it seems** por lo visto, según parece ‖ *prep* por, como; **as a rule** por regla general
asbestos [æsˈbɛstəs] *s* asbesto, amianto
ascend [əˈsɛnd] *tr* subir a (*p.ej., el trono*) ‖ *intr* ascender
ascendancy [əˈsɛndənsi] *s* ascendiente *m*
ascension [əˈsɛnʃən] *s* ascensión
Ascension Day *s* fiesta de la Ascensión
ascent [əˈsɛnt] *s* ascensión, subida; ascenso, promoción
ascertain [,æsərˈten] *tr* averiguar
ascertainable [,æsərˈtenəbəl] *adj* averiguable
ascetic [əˈsɛtɪk] *adj* ascético ‖ *s* asceta *mf*
ascorbic acid [əˈskɔrbɪk] *s* ácido ascórbico
ascribe [əˈskraɪb] *tr* atribuir
aseptic [əˈsɛptɪk] o [eˈsɛptɪk] *adj* aséptico
ash [æʃ] *s* ceniza; (*tree; wood*) fresno; **ashes** ceniza, cenizas; (*mortal remains*) cenizas; **ashes to ashes, dust to dust** polvo eres y en polvo te convertirás
ashamed [əˈʃemd] *adj* avergonzado; **to be ashamed** tener vergüenza
ashlar [ˈæʃlər] *s* sillar *m*
ashore [əˈʃor] *adv* en tierra, a tierra
ash tray *s* cenicero
Ash Wednesday *s* miércoles *m* de ceniza
Asia [ˈeʒə] o [ˈeʃə] *s* Asia
Asia Minor *s* el Asia Menor
Asian [ˈeʒən] o [ˈeʃən] o **Asiatic** [,eʒɪˈætɪk] o [,eʃiˈætɪk] *adj & s* asiático
aside [əˈsaɪd] *adv* aparte; **aside from** además de; **to step aside** hacerse a un lado ‖ *s* (theat) aparte *m*
asinine [ˈæsɪ,naɪn] *adj* tonto, necio
ask [æsk] o [ɑsk] *tr* (*to request*) pedir; (*to inquire of*) preguntar; hacer (*una pregunta*); invitar; **to ask in** invitar a entrar ‖ *intr*—**to ask about, after,** o **for;** preguntar por; **to ask for** pedir
askance [əˈskæns] *adv* al sesgo, de soslayo; con desdén, sospechosamente
asleep [əˈslip] *adj* dormido; **to fall asleep** dormirse
asp [æsp] *s* áspid *m*
asparagus [əˈspærəgəs] *s* espárrago
aspect [ˈæspɛkt] *s* aspecto
aspen [ˈæspən] *s* tiemblo, álamo temblón
aspersion [əˈspʌrʒən] o [əˈspʌrʃən] *s* calumnia, difamación
asphalt [ˈæsfɔlt] *s* asfalto ‖ *tr* asfaltar
asphyxiate [æsˈfɪksɪ,et] *tr* asfixiar
aspirant [əˈspaɪrənt] o [ˈæspɪrənt] *s* pretendiente *mf,* candidato
aspire [əˈspaɪr] *intr* aspirar
aspirin [ˈæspɪrɪn] *s* aspirina
ass [æs] *s* asno; (coll) imbécil *m*
assail [əˈsel] *tr* asaltar, acometer
assassin [eˈsæsɪn] *s* asesino
assassinate [əˈsæsɪ,net] *tr* asesinar
assassination [ə,sæsɪˈneʃən] *s* asesinato
assault [əˈsɔlt] *s* asalto ‖ *tr* asaltar
assault and battery *s* vías de hecho, agresión con lesiones
assay [əˈse] o [ˈæse] *s* ensaye *m;* muestra de ensaye ‖ [əˈse] *tr* ensayar; apreciar
assemble [əˈsɛmbəl] *tr* reunir; (mach) armar, montar ‖ *intr* reunirse
assem•bly [əˈsɛmbli] *s* (*pl* **-blies**) asamblea; reunión; (mach) armadura, montaje *m*
assembly hall *s* aula magna, paraninfo; salón *m* de sesiones
assembly language *s* (compu) lenguaje *m* ensamblador
assembly line *s* línea de montaje, cadena de montaje
assembly plant *s* fábrica de montaje
assembly room *s* sala de reunión; (mach) taller *m* de montaje
assent [əˈsɛnt] *s* asentimiento, asenso ‖ *intr* asentir
assert [əˈsʌrt] *tr* afirmar, aseverar, declarar; **to**

assert oneself imponerse, hacer valer sus derechos
assertion [əˈsʌrʃən] *s* aserción, aseveración
assess [əˈsɛs] *tr* amillarar, gravar; fijar (*daños y perjuicios*); apreciar, estimar
assessment [əˈsɛsmənt] *s* amillaramiento, gravamen *m;* fijación; apreciación, estimación
asset [ˈæsɛt] *s* posesión, ventaja; (*person, thing, or quality worth having*) (fig) valor *m;* **assets** (com) activo
assiduous [əˈsɪdjʊ•əs] *adj* asiduo
assign [əˈsaɪn] *tr* asignar
assignment [əˈsaɪnmənt] *s* asignación, cometido; lección
assimilate [əˈsɪmɪ,let] *tr* asimilarse (*los alimentos, el conocimiento*) ‖ *intr* asimilarse
assist [əˈsɪst] *tr* ayudar, asistir, auxiliar
assistant [əˈsɪstənt] *adj & s* auxiliar *mf,* ayudante *mf*
assistant professor *s* profesor adjunto
assistantship [əˈsɪstənt,ʃip] *s* ayudantía
assn. *abbr* **association**
associate [əˈsoʃi•ɪt] *adj* asociado ‖ *s* asociado, socio ‖ [əˈsoʃi,et] *tr* asociar ‖ *intr* asociarse
associate professor *s* profesor asociado
association [ə,soʃiˈeʃən] *s* asociación
assort [əˈsɔrt] *tr* clasificar, ordenar
assortment [əˈsɔrtmənt] *s* surtido; clase *f,* grupo
asst. *abbr* **assistant**
assume [əˈsum] o [əˈsjum] *tr* asumir (*p.ej., responsabilidades*); arrogarse; suponer, dar por sentado
assumption [əˈsʌmpʃən] *s* asunción; suposición
assurance [əˈʃʊrəns] *s* aseguramiento; seguridad, confianza; (com) seguro
assure [əˈʃʊr] *tr* asegurar; (com) asegurar
astatine [ˈæstə,tin] *s* ástato
aster [ˈæstər] *s* (bot) aster *m;* (*China aster*) reina Margarita
asterisk [ˈæstə,rɪsk] *s* asterisco, estrella
astern [əˈstʌrn] *adv* por la popa
asthma [ˈæzmə] o [ˈæsmə] *s* asma *f*
astonish [əˈstɑnɪʃ] *tr* asombrar
astonishing [əˈstɑnɪʃɪŋ] *adj* asombroso
astound [əˈstaʊnd] *tr* pasmar
astounding [əˈstaʊndɪŋ] *adj* pasmoso
astraddle [əˈstrædəl] *adv* a horcajadas
astray [əˈstre] *adv* por mal camino; **to go astray** extraviarse; **gone astray** desviado; **to lead astray** extraviar
astride [əˈstraɪd] *adv* a horcajadas ‖ *prep* a horcajadas de
astrology [əˈstrɑlədʒi] *s* astrología
astronaut [ˈæstrə,nɔt] *s* astronauta *m*
astronautic [,æstrəˈnɔtɪk] *adj* astronáutico ‖ **astronautics** *s* astronáutica
astronavigation [,æstro,nævɪˈgeʃən] *s* astronavigación
astronomer [əˈstrɑnəmər] *s* astrónomo
astronomic(al) [,æstrəˈnɑmɪk(əl)] *adj* astronómico
astronomy [əˈstrɑnəmi] *s* astronomía
astrophysics [,æstroˈfɪzɪks] *s* astrofísica
astute [əˈstjut] *adj* astuto, sagaz
asunder [əˈsʌndər] *adv* a pedazos, en dos
asylum [əˈsaɪləm] *s* asilo
asymmetrical [ˈesɪˈmɛtrɪkəl] *adj* asimétrico
asymmetrical warfare *s* (*warfare between two enemies of very different size and capabilities*) (el) combate asimétrico (*guerra entre dos fuerzas armadas desiguales en la que la técnica militar de una de esas fuerzas es superior a la otra*)
asymmetry [əˈsɪmɪtri] *s* asimetria
at (@) [æt] *prep* (comp) la arroba
at [æt] o [ət] *prep* en, p.ej., **I saw her at the library** la ví en la biblioteca; a, p.ej., **at five o'clock** a las cinco; de, p.ej., **to be surprised at** estar sorprendido de; **to laugh at** reírse de; en casa de, p.ej., **at John's** en casa de Juan
atavistic [,ætəˈvɪstɪk] *adj* atávico
atheism [ˈeθi,ɪzəm] *s* ateísmo
atheist [ˈeθi•ɪst] *s* ateísta *mf,* ateo
Athenian [əˈθinɪ•ən] *adj & s* ateniense *mf*
Athens [ˈæθɪnz] *s* Atenas *f*
athlete [ˈæθlit] *s* atleta *mf*
athlete's foot *s* pie *m* de atleta, tiña podal
athletic [æθˈlɛtɪk] *adj* atlético ‖ **athletics** *s* atletismo
athletic supporter *s* suspensorio(s)
Atlantic [ætˈlæntɪk] *adj & s* Atlántico
Atlantic Ocean *s* Océano Atlántico
atlas [ˈætləs] *s* atlas *m*
ATM [ˈeˈtiˈɛm] *s* (letterword) (**automated teller machine**) cajero automático, telebanco
atmosphere [ˈætməs,fɪr] *s* atmósfera
atmospheric [,ætməsˈfɛrɪk] *adj* atmosférico ‖ **atmospherics** *spl* parásitos atmosféricos
atom [ˈætəm] *s* átomo
atom bomb *s* bomba atómica
atomic [əˈtɑmɪk] *adj* atómico
atomic bomb *s* bomba atómica
atomic weight *s* peso atómico
atomize [ˈætə,maɪz] *tr* atomizar
atomizer [ˈætə,maɪzər] *s* pulverizador *m,* vaporizador *m*
atom smasher *s* rompeátomos *m*
atone [əˈton] *intr* dar reparación; **to atone for** dar reparación por, expiar
atonement [əˈtonmənt] *s* reparación, expiación
atop [əˈtɑp] *adv* encima ‖ *prep* encima de
atrocious [əˈtroʃəs] *adj* atroz; (coll) abominable, muy malo
atroci•ty [əˈtrɑsɪti] *s* (*pl* **-ties**) atrocidad
atro•phy [ˈætrəfi] *s* (pathol) atrofia, retracción ‖ *v* (*pret & pp* **-phied**) *tr* atrofiar ‖ *intr* atrofiarse
attach [əˈtætʃ] *tr* atar, ligar; atribuir (*p.ej., importancia*); (law) embargar; **to be attached to** aficionarse a; (*to be officially associated with*) depender de
attaché [,ætəˈʃe] *s* agregado
attachment [əˈtætʃmənt] *s* atadura, enlace *m;* atribución; apego, cariño; accesorio; (law) embargo

attack [əˈtæk] *s* ataque *m* ‖ *tr & intr* atacar
attain [əˈten] *tr* alcanzar, lograr
attainment [əˈtenmənt] *s* consecución, logro; **attainments** dotes *fpl,* prendas
attempt [əˈtɛmpt] *s* tentativa; (*assault*) atentado, conato ‖ *tr* procurar, intentar; (*e.g., the life of a person*) atentar a o contra
attend [əˈtɛnd] *tr* atender, asistir; asistir a (*p.ej., la escuela*); auxiliar (*a un moribundo*) ‖ *intr* atender; **to attend to** atender a
attendance [əˈtɛndəns] *s* asistencia, concurrencia.
attendant [əˈtɛndənt] *adj & s* asistente *mf;* concomitante *m*
attended parking *s* estacionamiento vigilado
attention [əˈtɛnʃən] *s* atencion; **attention!** ¡atención!; (mil) ¡firme!, ¡firmes!; **to attract attention** llamar la atención; **to call attention to** hacer presente; **to come to attention** (mil) ponerse en posición de firme(s); **to pay attention to** hacer caso de
attentive [əˈtɛntɪv] *adj* atento
attenuate [əˈtɛnjʊ,et] *tr* adelgazar; debilitar ‖ *intr* debilitarse; desaparecer
attest [əˈtɛst] *tr* atestiguar; juramentar ‖ *intr* dar fe; **to attest to** dar fe de
attic [ˈætɪk] *s* buharda, guardilla, desván *m*
attire [əˈtaɪr] *s* atavío, traje *m* ‖ *tr* ataviar, vestir
attitude [ˈætɪ,tjud] o [ˈætɪ,tud] *s* actitud, ademán *m*
attorney [əˈtʌrni] *s* abogado; procurador *m*
Attorney General *s* Fiscal *mf* General del Estado
attract [əˈtrækt] *tr* atraer; llamar (*la atención*)
attraction [əˈtrækʃən] *s* atracción; (*personal charm*) atractivo
attractive [əˈtræktɪv] *adj* atractivo; (*agreeable, interesting*) atrayente
attribute [ˈætrɪ,bjut] *s* atributo ‖ [əˈtrɪbjʊt] *tr* atribuir
auburn [ˈɔbərn] *adj & s* castaño rojizo
auction [ˈɔkʃən] *s* almoneda, remate *m,* subasta ‖ *tr* rematar, subastar
auction bridge *s* bridge *m* subastado
auctioneer [,ɔkʃənˈɪr] *s* subastador *m,* rematador *m* ‖ *tr & intr* rematar, subastar
auction house *s* martillo
audacious [ɔˈdeʃəs] *adj* audaz
audaci•ty [ɔˈdæsɪti] *s* (*pl* **-ties**) audacia
audience [ˈɔdɪ•əns] *s* (*hearing; formal interview*) audiencia; público, auditorio
audio [ˈɔdɪ,o] *adj & s* audio
audio frequency *s* audiofrecuencia
audiometer [,ɔdɪˈɑmɪtər] *s* audiómetro
audiovisual [,ɔdɪ•oˈvɪʒu•əl] *adj* audiovisual
audiovisual aids *spl* medios audiovisuales
audit [ˈɔdɪt] *s* intervención ‖ *tr* intervenir
audition [ɔˈdɪʃən] *s* audición ‖ *tr* dar audición a
auditor [ˈɔdɪtər] *s* oyente *mf;* (com) interventor *m*
auditorium [,ɔdɪˈtorɪ•əm] *s* auditorio, anfiteatro, paraninfo
auger [ˈɔgər] *s* barrena
augment [ɔgˈmɛnt] *tr & intr* aumentar
augur [ˈɔgər] *s* augur *m* ‖ *tr & intr* augurar; **to augur well** ser de buen agüero
augu•ry [ˈɔgəri] *s* (*pl* **-ries**) augurio
august [ɔˈgʌst] *adj* augusto ‖ **August** [ˈɔgəst] *s* agosto
aunt [ænt] o [ɑnt] *s* tía
aurora [eˈrorə] *s* aurora
auspice [ˈɔspɪs] *s* auspicio; **under the auspices of** bajo los auspicios de
auspicious [ɔsˈpɪʃəs] *adj* favorable, propicio
austere [ɔsˈtɪr] *adj* austero
Australia [ɔˈstreljə] *s* Australia
Australian [ɔˈstreljən] *adj & s* australiano
Austria [ˈɔstrɪ•ə] *s* Austria
Austrian [ˈɔstrɪ•ən] *adj & s* austríaco
authentic [ɔˈθɛntɪk] *adj* auténtico
authenticate [ɔˈθɛntɪ,ket] *tr* autenticar
author [ˈɔθər] *s* autor *m,* escritor *m*
authoress [ˈɔθərɪs] *s* autora, escritora
authoring package *s* (compu) paquete *m* de autor
authoring tool *s* (compu) herramienta de autor
authoritarian [ɔ,θɔrɪˈtɛrɪ•ən] *adj & s* autoritario
authoritative [ɔˈθɔrɪ,tetɪv] *adj* autorizado; (*dictatorial*) autoritario
authori•ty [ɔˈθɔrɪti] *s* (*pl* **-ties**) autoridad; **on good authority** de buena tinta, de fuente fidedigna
authorize [ˈɔθə,raɪz] *tr* autorizar
authorship [ˈɔθər,ʃip] *s* paternidad literaria
autistic [ɔˈtɪstɪk] *s* autístico
au•to [ˈɔto] *s* (*pl* **-tos**) (coll) auto, coche *m*
autobiogra•phy [,ɔtobaɪˈɑgrəfi] *s* (*pl* **-phies**) autobiografía
autobus [ˈɔto,bʌs] *s* autobús *m*
autocratic(al) [,ɔtəˈkrætɪk(əl)] *adj* autocrático
autograph [ˈɔtə,græf] *adj & s* autógrafo ‖ *tr* autografiar
autograph hunter *s* cazaautógrafos *m*
automat [ˈɔtə,mæt] *s* restaurante automático
automated [ˈɔtəmetəd] *adj* automatizado
automated teller machine (ATM) *s* cajero automático
automatic [,ɔtəˈmætɪk] *adj* automático
automatic clutch *s* embrague *m* automático
automatic pilot *s* (aer) piloto automático
automatic redial *s* (telp) rellamada automática, rediscado automático
automatic transmission *s* cambio automático, transmisión automática
automation [,ɔtəˈmeʃən] *s* automación, automatización
automa•ton [ɔˈtɑmə,tɑn] *s* (*pl* **-tons** o **-ta** [tə]) autómata
automobile [,ɔtəmoˈbil] u [,ɔtəˈmobil] *s* automóvil *m*
automobile show *s* salón *m* del automóvil
autonomous [ɔˈtɑnəməs] *adj* autónomo
autonomy [ɔˈtɑnəmi] *s* autonomía
autop•sy [ˈɔtɑpsi] *s* (*pl* **-sies**) autopsia

autumn [ˈɔtəm] *s* otoño
autumnal [ɔˈtʌmnəl] *adj* otoñal
auxilia•ry [ɔgˈzɪljəri] *adj* auxiliar || *s* (*pl* **-ries**) auxiliar *mf;* **auxiliaries** tropas auxiliares
av. *abbr* **avenue, average, avoirdupois**
avail [əˈvel] *s* provecho, utilidad || *tr* beneficiar; **to avail oneself of** aprovecharse de, valerse de || *intr* aprovechar
available [əˈveləbəl] *adj* disponible; **to make available to** poner a la disposición de
avalanche [ˈævə,læntʃ] *s* alud *m,* avalancha
avant-garde [ə,vɑntˈgɑrd] *adj* vanguardista || *s* vanguardismo
avarice [ˈævərɪs] *s* avaricia
avaricious [,ævəˈrɪʃəs] *adj* avaricioso, avariento
Ave. *abbr* **Avenue**
avenge [əˈvɛndʒ] *tr* vengar; **to avenge oneself on** vengarse en
avenue [ˈævə,njʊ] o [ˈævə,nu] *s* avenida
aver [əˈvʌr] *v* (*pret & pp* **averred;** *ger* **averring**) *tr* afirmar, declarar
average [ˈævərɪdʒ] *adj* común, mediano, ordinario || *s* promedio, término medio; (naut) avería || *tr* calcular el término medio de; prorratear; ser de un promedio de
averse [əˈvʌrs] *adj* renuente, contrario
aversion [əˈvʌrʒen] *s* aversión, antipatía; cosa aborrecida
avert [əˈvʌrt] *tr* apartar, desviar; impedir
aviar•y [ˈevɪ,ɛri] *s* (*pl* **-ies**) avería, pajarera
aviation [,evɪˈeʃən] *s* aviación
aviator [ˈevɪ,etər] *s* aviador *m*
avid [ˈævɪd] *adj* ávido
avidity [əˈvɪdɪti] *s* avidez *f*
avocado [,ævəˈkɑdo] *s* aguacate *m*
avocation [,ævəˈkeʃən] *s* distracción, diversión
avoid [əˈvɔid] *tr* evitar
avoidable [əˈvɔɪdəbəl] *adj* evitable
avoidance [əˈvɔɪdəns] *s* evitación
avow [əˈvaʊ] *tr* admitir, confesar
avowal [əˈvaʊ•əl] *s* admisión, confesión
await [əˈwet] *tr* aguardar, esperar
awake [əˈwek] *adj* despierto || *v* (*pret & pp* **awoke** [əˈwok] o **awaked**) *tr & intr* despertar
awaken [əˈwekən] *tr & intr* despertar
awakening [əˈwekənɪŋ] *s* despertamiento; desilusión
award [əˈwɔrd] *s* premio; condecoración; adjudicación || *tr* conceder; adjudicar
aware [əˈwɛr] *adj* enterado; **to become aware of** enterarse de, darse cuenta de
awareness [əˈwɛrnɪs] *s* conciencia
away [əˈwe] *adj* ausente; distante || *adv* lejos; a lo lejos; **away from** lejos de; **to do away with** deshacerse de; **to get away** escapar; **to go away** irse; **to make away with** robar, hurtar; **to run away** fugarse; **to send away** enviar; despedir; **to take away** llevarse; quitar
awe [ɔ] *s* temor *m* reverencial || *tr* infundir temor reverencial a
awesome [ˈɔsəm] *adj* imponente
awestruck [ˈɔ,strʌk] *adj* espantado
awful [ˈɔfəl] *adj* atroz, horrible; impresionante; (coll) muy malo, muy feo, enorme
awfully [ˈɔfəli] *adv* atrozmente, horriblemente; (coll) muy, excesivamente
awfulness [ˈɔfəlnɪs] *s* espantosidad (SAm)
awhile [əˈhwaɪl] *adv* un rato, algún tiempo
awkward [ˈɔkwərd] *adj* desmañado, torpe, lerdo; embarazoso, delicado
awl [ɔl] *s* alesna, lezna
awning [ˈɔnɪŋ] *s* toldo
AWOL [ˈewɔl] *adj* (letterword) (**absent without leave**) ausente sin permiso
ax [æks] *s* hacha
axiom [ˈæksɪ•əm] *s* axioma *m*
axiomatic [,æksɪ•əˈmætɪk] *adj* axiomático
axis [ˈæksɪs] *s* (*pl* **axes** [ˈæksiz]) *s* eje *m*
axle [ˈæksəl] *s* eje *m,* árbol *m*
axle load *s* carga por eje
ax'le•tree' *s* eje *m* de carretón
ay [aɪ] *adv & s* sí || [e] *adv* siempre; **for ay** por siempre || [e] *interj* ¡ay!
aye [aɪ] *adv & s* sí || [e] *adv* siempre; **for aye** por siempre
azimuth [ˈæzɪmɔθ] *s* acimut *m,* azimut *m*
Azores [əˈzorz] o [ˈezorz] *spl* Azores *fpl*
Aztec [ˈæztɛk] *adj & s* azteca *mf*
azure [ˈæʒər] o [ˈeʒər] *adj & s* azul *m*

B

B, b [bi] segunda letra del alfabeto inglés
b. *abbr* **bass, bay, born, brother**
baa [bɑ] *s* be *m,* balido || *intr* balar
babble [ˈbæbəl] *s* barboteo; charla; (*of a brook*) murmullo || *tr* barbotar; decir indiscretamente || *intr* barbotar; murmurar (*un arroyo*)
babe [beb] *s* rorro, criatura, (*innocent, gullible person*) niño; (slang) chica, chica hermosa
baboon [bæˈbun] *s* babuíno
ba•by [ˈbebi] *s* (*pl* **-bies**) rorro, criatura, bebé *m;* (*the youngest child*) benjamín *m* || *v* (*pret & pp* **-bied**) *tr* mimar; tratar como niño
baby boomers *spl generación nacida durante los veinte años inmediatamente después de la segunda guerra mundial*
baby carriage *s* cochecillo para niños
baby grand *s* piano de media cola
babyhood [ˈbebi,hʊd] *s* primera infancia, niñez
babyish [ˈbebi•ɪʃ] *adj* aniñado, infantil
ba'by-sit' *intr* hacer de niñera
baby-sitter *s* niñera tomada por horas
baby teeth *spl* dientes *mpl* de leche
baccalaureate [,bækəˈlɔrɪ•ɪt] *s* bachillerato
bachelor [ˈbætʃələr] *s* (*unmarried man*) sol-

tero; (*holder of bachelor's degree*) bachiller *mf;* (*apprentice knight*) doncel *m*
bachelorhood [ˈbætʃələr,hʊd] *s* celibato, soltería (*del hombre*)
bacil•lus [bəˈsɪləs] *s* (*pl* **-li** [laɪ]) bacilo
back [bæk] *adj* trasero, posterior; atrasado || *adv* atrás, detrás; de vuelta; (*ago*) hace; **back of** detrás de; **to go back to** remontarse a; **to send back** devolver || *s* espalda; dorso; (*of a coin*) reverso; (*of a chair*) espaldar *m,* respaldo; (*of an animal, of a book*) lomo; (*of a hall, a room*) fondo; (*of a writing, a book*) final *m;* **behind one's back** a espaldas de uno; **on one's back** postrado, en cama; a cuestas || *tr* mover hacia atrás; apoyar, respaldar || *intr* moverse hacia atrás; **to back down** u **out** volverse atrás, echarse atrás; **to back up** retroceder; regolfar (*el agua*)
back'ache' *s* dolor *m* de espalda
back'bone' *s* espinazo; (*of a book*) nervura; (*strength of character*) firmeza, resistencia
back'break'ing *adj* deslomador
back'down' *s* palinodia, retractación
back'drop' *s* telón *m* de fondo o de foro
backer [ˈbækər] *s* sostenedor *m,* defensor *m;* (*of a business venture*) impulsador *m*
back'fire' *s* (aut) petardeo || *intr* (aut) petardear; (coll) fracasar, fallar
backgammon [ˈbæk,gæmən] *s* chaquete *m*
back'ground' *s* fondo; antecedentes *mpl;* conocimientos, educación; (*of a painting*) lontananza; (compu) fondo
background mode *s* (compu) modo subordinado
background music *s* música de fondo, música ambiental
background noise *s* ruido de fondo
background printing *s* (compu) impresión subordinada
backing [ˈbækɪŋ] *s* apoyo, sostén *m;* garantía, respaldo; financiamiento; (bb) lomera
back'lash' *s* (mach) contragolpe *m;* (mach) juego; (fig) reacción violenta
back'light'ing *s* alumbrado de fondo
back'log' *s* (com) reserva de pedidos pendientes; (*e.g., of work*) acumulación
back number *s* número atrasado; (coll) persona anticuada
back'pack' *s* mochila
back pay *s* sueldo retrasado
back'rest' *s* respaldo
back road *s* carretera secundaria
back seat *s* puesto secundario; **to take a back seat** perder influencia
back'side' *s* espalda; trasero
back'slide' *v* (*pret & pp* **-slid** [,slɪd]) *intr* reincidir
backspacer [ˈbæk,spesər] *s* tecla de retroceso
back'stage' *adv* detrás del telón; entre bastidores
back'stairs' *adj* indirecto, secreto
back stairs *spl* escalera trasera; (fig) medios indirectos
back'stitch' *s* pespunte *m* || *tr & intr* pespuntar
back'stop' *s* reja o red *f* para detener la pelota
back'swept' wing *s* (aer) ala en flecha
back talk *s* respuesta insolente
back'-to-back' *adj* consecutivo
back'up copy *s* copia de respaldo, copia de seguridad
backward [ˈbækwərd] *adj* atrasado, tardío; tímido || *adv* de atrás; de espaldas; al revés; cada vez peor; para atrás, hacia atrás
back'wa'ter *s* remanso; (fig) atraso, yermo
back'woods' *spl* monte *m,* región alejada de los centros de población
back yard *s* patio trasero, corral trasero
bacon [ˈbekən] *s* tocino
bacteria [bækˈtɪrɪ•ə] *pl de* **bacterium**
bacterial [bækˈtɪrɪ•əl] *adj* bacteriano
bacteriologist [bæk,tɪrɪˈɑlədʒɪst] *s* bacteriólogo
bacteriology [bæk,tɪrɪˈɑlədʒi] *s* bacteriología
bacteri•um [bækˈtɪrɪ•əm] *s* (*pl* **-a** [ə]) bacteria
bad [bæd] *adj* (*comp* **worse** [wʌrs]; *super* **worst** [wʌrst]) malo; (*money*) falso; (*debt*) incobrable; (slang) bueno; **from bad to worse** de mal en peor; **to be in bad** (coll) caer en desgracia; **to be too bad** ser lástima; **to go to the bad** (coll) ir por mal camino; (coll) arruinarse; **to look bad** tener mala cara
bad breath *s* mal aliento
bad check *s* cheque *m* o talón *m* sin fondos
badge [bædʒ] *s* divisa, insignia
badger [ˈbædʒər] *s* tejón *m*
bad luck *s* mala suerte, mala pata (coll)
badly [ˈbædli] *adv* mal; con urgencia; gravemente
badly off *adj* malparado; muy enfermo
badminton [ˈbædmɪntən] *s* juego del volante
baffle [ˈbæfəl] *s* deflector *m;* (rad) pantalla acústica || *tr* confundir; burlar, frustrar
baffling [ˈbæflɪŋ] *adj* perplejo, desconcertador
bag [bæg] *s* saco; saquito de mano; (*in clothing*) bolsa; (*purse*) bolso; (*take of game*) caza; **to be in the bag** (slang) ser cosa segura || *v* (*pret & pp* **bagged;** *ger* **bagging**) *tr* ensacar; coger, cazar || *intr* hacer bolsa (*un vestido*)
bagel [ˈbegəl] *s* panecillo en forma de rosca
baggage [ˈbægɪdʒ] *s* equipaje *m;* (mil) bagaje *m*
baggage car *s* furgón *m* de equipajes
baggage check *s* contraseña de equipajes
baggage rack *s* red *f* de equipajes
baggage room *s* sala de equipajes
bag•gy [ˈbægi] *adj* (*comp* **-gier;** *super* **-giest**) holgado; (*pants*) bombacho, ancho
bag'pipe' *s* gaita, cornamusa
bag'pi'per *s* gaitero
bail [bel] *s* caución, fianza; libertad bajo fianza o palabra, libertad provisional; **to go bail for** salir fiador por || *tr* caucionar, afianzar; achicar (*la embarcación; el agua*); **to bail out** salir fiador por; achicar || *intr* achicar; **to bail out** lanzarse en paracaídas
bailiff [ˈbelɪf] *s* algualcil *m,* corchete *m*

bailiwick [ˈbelɪwɪk] *s* alguacilazgo; **to be in the bailiwick of** ser de la pertenencia de
bail′out′ *s* rescate financiero
bait [bet] *s* carnada, cebo; señuelo; **to swallow the bait** tragar el anzuelo ‖ *tr* cebar, encarnar (*el anzuelo*); tentar, seducir; (*to pester*) hostigar
baize [bez] *s* bayeta (*para mesas de juego*)
bake [bek] *tr* cocer al horno; cocer (*loza, gres, etc.*)
baker [ˈbekər] *s* panadero, hornero
baker's dozen *s* docena del fraile
baker•y [ˈbekəri] *s* (*pl* **-ies**) panadería
baking powder [ˈbekɪŋ] *s* levadura en polvo, polvo de hornear
baking soda *s* bicarbonato de sosa
bal. *abbr* **balance**
balance [ˈbæləns] *s* (*instrument for weighing*) balanza; (*state of equilibrium*) equilibrio; (*amount left over*) resto; (*amount still owed*) saldo; (*statement of debits and credits*) balance *m;* **to lose one's balance** perder el equilibrio; **to strike a balance** hacer o pasar balance ‖ *tr* balancear; equilibrar; equilibrar, nivelar (*el presupuesto*) ‖ *intr* equilibrarse; (*to waver*) balancear
balanced [ˈbælənst] *adj* equilibrado
balance of payments *s* balanza de pagos
balance of power *s* equilibrio político
balance of trade *s* balanza comercial
balance sheet *s* balance *m,* avanzo
balco•ny [ˈbælkəni] *s* (*pl* **-nies**) balcón *m;* (*in a theater*) galería, paraíso
bald [bɔld] *adj* calvo; franco, directo
bald eagle *s* águila de cabeza blanca (*ave heráldica de EE.UU.*)
baldness [ˈbɔldnɪs] *s* calvicie *f*
baldric [ˈbɔldrɪk] *s* tahalí *m*
bale [bel] *s* bala ‖ *tr* embalar
Balearic [ˌbælɪˈærɪk] *adj* balear
Balearic Islands *spl* islas Baleares
baleful [ˈbelfəl] *adj* funesto, maligno
balk [bɔk] *tr* burlar, frustrar ‖ *intr* emperrarse, resistirse
Balkan [ˈbɔlkən] *adj* balcánico ‖ **the Balkans** los Balcanes
balk•y [ˈbɔki] *adj* (*comp* **-ier;** *super* **-iest**) rebelón, repropio
ball [bɔl] *s* bola, pelota; esfera, globo; (*of wool, yarn*) ovillo; (*of finger*) yema; (*projectile*) bala; (*dance*) baile *m*
ballad [ˈbæləd] *s* balada
ballade [bəˈlɑd] *s* (mus) balada
ballast [ˈbæləst] *s* (aer, naut) lastre *m;* (rr) balasto ‖ *tr* lastrar; balastar
ball bearing *s* cojinete *m* de bolas
ballerina [ˌbæləˈrinə] *s* bailarina
ballet [ˈbæle] *s* ballet *m,* baile *m*
ball game *s* partido de béisbol
ballistic [bəˈlɪstɪk] *adj* balístico
balloon [bəˈlun] *s* globo; (aer) globo, aeróstato; (*in cartoons*) bocadillo
balloon help *s* (compu) globos *mpl* de ayuda
ballot [ˈbælət] *s* balota; sufragio ‖ *intr* balotar
ballot box *s* urna electoral
ball′park *s* estadio de béisbol
ball′play′er *s* pelotero; beisbolero
ball′ point′ pen *s* bolígrafo, pluma estilográfica; biro (Arg); birome *f* (Arg, Urug); puntabola, punto bola (Bol); lapicero (CAm, Col); lápiz *m* de pasta (Chile); esferográfica, esfero (Col); estenógrafo (Cuba); lápiz *m* de bolilla (Peru); plumilla (Ven)
ball′room′ *s* salón *m* de baile
ballyhoo [ˈbælɪˌhu] *s* alharaca, bombo ‖ *tr* dar teatro a, dar bombo a
balm [bɑm] *s* bálsamo
balm•y [ˈbɑmi] *adj* (*comp* **-ier;** *super* **-iest**) bonancible, suave
baloney [bəˈloni] *s* (coll) salchicha ahumada; (slang) tonterías ‖ *interj* (coll) ¡aprieta!
balsam [ˈbɔlsəm] *s* bálsamo
Baltic [ˈbɔltɪk] *adj* báltico
Baltimore oriole [ˈbɔltɪˌmor] *s* cacique veranero
baluster [ˈbæləstər] *s* balaustre *m*
bamboo [bæmˈbu] *s* bambú *m*
bamboozle [bæmˈbuzəl] *tr* (coll) embaucar, engañar
bamboozler [bæmˈbuzlər] *s* (coll) embaucador *m,* engañabobos *mf*
ban [bæn] *s* prohibición; excomunión, entredicho; (*of marriage*) amonestación ‖ *v* (*pret & pp* **banned;** *ger* **banning**) *tr* prohibir; excomulgar
banana [bəˈnænə] *s* banana, plátano; (*tree*) banano, bananero, plátano
banana oil *s* esencia de pera
band [bænd] *s* banda; (*of people*) cuadrilla; (*of a hat*) cintillo; (*of a cigar*) anillo; liga de goma; (mus) banda, música, charanga ‖ *intr* abanderizarse
bandage [ˈbændɪdʒ] *s* venda ‖ *tr* vendar
bandanna [bænˈdænə] *s* pañuelo de hierbas
band′box′ *s* sombrerera
bandit [ˈbændɪt] *s* bandido
band saw *s* sierra continua, sierra sin fin
band′stand′ *s* quiosco de música
band′width *s* (compu) ancho de banda; (electron) amplitud de banda
baneful [ˈbenfəl] *adj* nocivo, venenoso; (*e.g., influence*) funesto
bang [bæŋ] *adv* de golpe ‖ *interj* ¡pum! ‖ *s* golpazo; (*of a door*) portazo; **bangs** flequillo ‖ *tr* golpear con ruido; cerrar (*p.ej., una puerta*) de golpe ‖ *intr* hacer estrépito
banish [ˈbænɪʃ] *tr* desterrar; despedir (*p.ej., miedo*)
banishment [ˈbænɪʃmənt] *s* destierro
banister [ˈbænɪstər] *s* balaustre *m*
bank [bæŋk] *s* banco; (*in certain games*) banca; (*small container for coins*) alcancía; (*of a river*) ribera, orilla; (*of earth, snow, clouds*) montón *m* ‖ *tr* depositar o guardar (*dinero*) en un banco; amontonar; cubrir (*un fuego*)

con cenizas || *intr* depositar dinero; **to bank on** (coll) contar con
bank account *s* cuenta de banco
bank'book' *s* libreta de banco
banker ['bæŋkər] *s* banquero
banking ['bæŋkɪŋ] *adj* bancario || *s* banca
bank note *s* billete *m* de banco
bank roll *s* lío de papel moneda
bankrupt ['bæŋkrʌpt] *adj & s* bancarrotero; **to go bankrupt** hacer bancarrota || *tr* hacer quebrar; arruinar
bankrupt•cy ['bæŋkrʌptsi] *s* (*pl* **-cies**) bancarrota
bankruptcy protection *s* suspensión de pagos
bank vault *s* bóveda de seguridad
banner ['bænər] *s* bandera, estandarte *m*
banner headline *s* gran titular *m*
banquet ['bæŋkwɪt] *s* banquete *m,* cena de gala || *tr & intr* banquetear
bantamweight ['bæntəm,wet] *s* (box) peso gallo
banter ['bæntər] *s* burla, chanza || *intr* burlar, chancear
baptism ['bæptɪzəm] *s* bautismo, bautizo; (fig) bautismo
Baptist ['bæptɪst] *adj & s* baptista *mf,* bautista *mf*
baptister•y ['bæptɪstəri] *s* (*pl* **-ies**) baptisterio, bautisterio
baptize ['bæptaɪz] *tr* bautizar
bar. *abbr* **barometer, barrel, barrister**
bar [bɑr] *s* barra; (*of door or window*) tranca; (*of jail*) reja; barrera; (*legal profession*) abogacía; (*members of legal profession*) curia; (*of public opinion*) tribunal *m;* (mus) barra; (*unit between two bars*) (mus) compás *m;* **behind bars** entre rejas || *prep* salvo; **bar none** sin excepción || *v* (*pret & pp* **barred;** *ger* **barring**) *tr* barrear, atrancar; impedir; prohibir; excluir
bar association *s* colegio de abogados
barb [bɑrb] *s* púa, lengüeta; (*of a pen*) barbilla
Barbados [bɑr'bedoz] *s* la Barbada
barbarian [bɑr'bɛrɪ•ən] *s* bárbaro
barbaric [bɑr'bærɪk] *adj* bárbaro
barbarism ['bɑrbə,rɪzəm] *s* barbaridad *f;* (gram) barbarismo
barbari•ty [bɑr'bærɪti] *s* (*pl* **-ties**) barbarie *f*
barbarous ['bɑrbərəs] *adj* bárbaro
Barbary ape ['bɑrbəri] *s* mono de Gibraltar
barbecue ['bɑrbɪ,kju] *s* (*grill*) barbacoa, parrilla; (*food*) parrillada; (*social gathering*) barbacoa, parrillada
barbed [bɑrbd] *adj* armado de púas; mordaz, punzante
barbed wire *s* alambre *m* de espino, alambre de púas
bar'bell' *s* barra con pesas, haltera
barber ['bɑrbər] *adj* barberil || *s* barbero peluquero
barber pole *s* percha de barbero
bar'ber•shop' *s* barbería, peluquería
bar code *s* código de barras, código barrado
bar coding *s* codificación de barras
bard [bɑrd] *s* bardo; (*horse armor*) barda || *tr* bardar
bare [bɛr] *adj* desnudo; (*head*) descubierto; (*unfurnished*) desamueblado; (*wire*) sin aislar; mero, sencillo, puro || *tr* desnudar; descubrir
bare'back' *adj & adv* en pelo, sin silla
barefaced ['bɛr,fest] *adj* desvergonzado
bare'foot' *adj* descalzo || *adv* con los pies desnudos
bareheaded ['bɛr,hɛdɪd] *adj* descubierto || *adv* con la cabeza descubierta
barelegged ['bɛr,lɛgɪd] o ['bɛr,lɛgd] *adj* con las piernas desnudas
barely ['bɛrli] *adv* aspenas; escasamente
bargain ['bɑrgɪn] *s* (*deal*) convenio, trato; (*cheap purchase*) ganga, ocasión; **in the bargain** de añadidura || *tr* — **to bargain away** vender regalado || *intr* negociar; (*to haggle*) regatear
bargain counter *s* baratillo
bargain sale *s* venta de saldos
barge [bɑrdʒ] *s* gabarra, lanchón *m;* bongo (SAm) || *intr* moverse pesadamente; **to barge in** entrar sin pedir permiso, entrar sin llamar a la puerta
barium ['bɛrɪ•əm] *s* bario
bark [bɑrk] *s* (*of tree*) corteza; (*of dog*) ladrido; (*boat*) barca || *tr* ladrar (*p.ej., injurias*) || *intr* ladrar
barker ['bɑrkər] *s* voceador *m,* pregonero
barley water *s* hordiate *m*
bar magnet *s* barra imantada
barn [bɑrn] *s* granero, troje *m;* caballeriza, establo; cochera
barnacle ['bɑrnəkəl] *s* cirrópodo
barn owl *s* lechuza, oliva
barn'yard' *s* corral *m*
barnyard fowl *spl* aves *fpl* de corral
barometer [bə'rɑmɪtər] *s* barómetro
baron ['bærən] *s* barón *m*
baroness ['bærənɪs] *s* baronesa
baroque [bə'rok] *adj & s* barroco
barracks ['bærəks] *spl* cuartel *m*
barrage [bə'rɑʒ] *s* (*dam*) presa; (mil) barrera de fuego
barrel ['bærəl] *s* barril *m,* tonel *m;* (*of a gun, pen, etc.*) cañón *m*
barrel organ *s* organillo
barren ['bærən] *adj* árido, estéril
barricade [,bærɪ'ked] *s* barricada, barrera || *tr* barrear
barrier ['bærɪ•ər] *s* barrera
barrier reef *s* barrera de arrecifes
barrister ['bærɪstər] *s* (Brit) abogado
bar'room' *s* bar *m,* cantina
bar'tend'er *s* cantinero, tabernero, barman *m*
barter ['bɑrtər] *s* trueque *m* || *tr* trocar
base [bes] *adj* bajo, humilde; infame, vil; (*metal*) bajo de ley || *s* base *f;* (*of electric light*

or vacuum tube; of projectile) culote *m;* (mus) bajo || *tr* basar
base′ball′ *s* béisbol *m;* pelota de béisbol
baseball player *s* beisbolero, beisbolista *m*
base′board′ *s* rodapié *m*
Basel [ˈbɑzəl] *s* Basilea
baseless [ˈbeslɪs] *adj* infundado
basement [ˈbesmənt] *s* sótano
bashful [ˈbæʃfəl] *adj* encogido, tímido
basic [ˈbesɪk] *adj* básico || **basics** *spl*—**the basics** lo básico, lo esencial; **we must get back to basics** tenemos que replantearnos todo desde cero
basilica [bəˈsɪlɪkə] *s* basílica
basil [ˈbæzəl] *s* albahaca
basin [ˈbesɪn] *s* jofaina, palangana; (*of a fountain*) tazón *m;* (*of a river*) cuenca; (*of a harbor*) dársena
ba•sis [ˈbesɪs] *s* (*pl* **-ses** [siz]) base *f;* **on the basis of** a base de
bask [bæsk] o [bɑsk] *intr* asolearse, calentarse
basket [ˈbæskɪt] *s* cesta; (*large basket*) cesto; (*with two handles*) canasta; (*with lid*) excusabaraja; (*in basketball*) canasta, cesto; **to shoot a basket** meter una canasta, tirar al cesto
bas′ket•ball′ *s* baloncesto, basquetbol *m*
basket case *s* (coll) caso perdido
Basle [bɑl] *s* Basilea
Basque [bæsk] *adj & s* (*of Spain*) vascongado; (*of Spain and France*) vasco; (*of old Spain*) vascón *m*
bas-relief [ˌbɑrɪˈlif] *s* bajo relieve
bass [bes] *adj & s* (mus) bajo || [bæs] (ichth) róbalo; (ichth) micróptero
bass clef *s* clave *f* de fa
bass drum *s* bombo
bass horn *s* tuba
bas•so [ˈbæso] *s* (*pl* **-sos** o **-si** [si]) (mus) bajo
bassoon [bəˈsun] *s* bajón *m*
bass viol [ˈvaɪ•əl] *s* violón *m,* contrabajo
bastard [ˈbæstərd] *adj & s* bastardo
bastard title *s* anteportada
baste [best] *tr* (*to sew slightly*) hilvanar; (*to moisten with drippings while roasting*) enlardar; (*to thrash*) azotar; (*to scold*) regañar
bastion [ˈbæstʃən] *s* baluarte *m,* bastión *m*
bat. *abbr* **battalion, battery**
bat [bæt] *s* palo; (coll) golpe *m;* (zool) murciélago || *v* (*pret & pp* **batted;** *ger* **batting**) *tr* golpear; batear (*una pelota*); **without batting an eye** sin inmutarse, sin pestañear || *intr* golpear
batch [bætʃ] *s* (*of bread*) hornada; (*of papers*) lío, pila; (*group*) grupo, tanda; (compu) lote *m,* batch *m,* todo de golpe
batch processing *s* (compu) procesamiento por lotes
bath [bæθ] *s* baño
bathe [beð] *tr* bañar || *intr* bañarse; **to go bathing** ir a bañarse
bather [ˈbeðər] *s* bañista *mf*
bath′house′ *s* casa de baños; caseta de baños
bathing beauty *s* sirena de la playa
bathing suit *s* traje *m* de baño, bañador *m*
bathing trunks *spl* taparrabo
bath′robe′ *s* albornoz *m,* bata de baño; bata, peinador *m*
bath′room′ *s* baño, cuarto de baño
bathroom fixtures *spl* (aparatos) sanitarios
bath′tub′ *s* bañera, baño
bathyscaphe [ˈbæθəˌskæf] *s* batiscafo
baton [bæˈtɑn] *s* bastón *m;* (mus) batuta
battalion [bəˈtæljən] *s* batallón *m*
batter [ˈbætər] *s* pasta, batido; (*baseball*) bateador *m* || *tr* magullar, estropear
battered woman *or* **wife** *s* mujer golpeada o maltratada
battering ram *s* ariete *m*
batter•y [ˈbætəri] *s* (*pl* **-ies**) batería; (*primary*) (elec) pila; (*secondary*) (elec) acumulador *m;* (law) violencia
battle [ˈbætəl] *s* batalla; **to do battle** librar batalla || *tr* batallar
battle array *s* orden *m* de batalla
battle cry *s* grito de combate
battledore [ˈbætəlˌdor] *s* raqueta; **battledore and shuttlecock** raqueta y volante
bat′tlefield′ *s* campo de batalla
battle front *s* frente *m* de combate
battlement [ˈbætəlmənt] *s* almenaje *m*
battle piece *s* (paint) batalla
bat′tle•ship′ *s* acorazado
bauble [ˈbɔbəl] *s* chuchería; cetro de bufón
baud [bɔd] *s* (compu) baudio
baud rate *s* (compu) velocidad media de transferencia
Bavaria [bəˈvɛrɪ•ə] *s* Baviera
Bavarian [bəˈvɛrɪ•ən] *adj & mf* bávaro
bawd [bɔd] *s* (archaic) alcahuete *m,* alcahueta
bawd•y [ˈbɔdi] *adj* (*comp* **-ier;** *super* **-iest**) indecente, obsceno
bawl [bɔl] *s* voces *fpl,* gritos || *tr* — **to bawl out** (slang) regañar || *intr* vocear, gritar; llorar ruidosamente
bay [be] *adj* bayo || *s* bahía; aullido, ladrido; caballo bayo; (bot) laurel *m;* (compu) bahía; **to keep at bay** tener a raya || *intr* aullar, ladrar
Bay of Biscay *s* golfo de Vizcaya
bayonet [ˈbe•ənɪt] *s* bayoneta || *tr* herir o matar con bayoneta
bay rum *s* ron *m* de laurel, ron de malagueta
bay window *s* ventana salediza, mirador *m*
bazooka [bəˈzukə] *s* bazuca
B.C. [ˈbiˈsi] *adj* (letterword) (**before Christ**) aC, a. de C., a. de J.C. (antes de Cristo, antes de Jesucristo)
be [bi] *v* (*pres* **am** [æm], **is** [ɪz] **are** [ɑr]; *pret* **was** [wɑz] o [wʌz], **were** [wʌr]; *pp* **been** [bɪn]) *intr* estar; ser; tener, p.ej., **to be cold** tener frío; **to be wrong** no tener razón; tener la culpa; **here is** o **here are** aquí tiene Ud.; **there is** o **there are** hay || *v aux* estar, p.ej., **he is studying** está estudiando; ser, p.ej., **she was hit by a car** fue atropellada por un coche; deber, p.ej., **what am I to do?** ¿qué debo

hacer? ‖ *v impers* ser, p.ej., **it is necessary to get up early** es necesario levantarse temprano; haber, p.ej., **it is sunny** hay sol; hacer, p.ej., **it is cold** hace frío

beach [bitʃ] *s* playa

beach'comb' *intr* raquear; **to go beachcombing** andar al raque

beach'comb'er *s* raquero; vago de playa

beach'front' property *s* terreno frente a la playa

beach'head' *s* cabeza de playa

beach robe *s* albornoz *m*

beach shoe *s* playera

beach tent *s* carpa

beach umbrella *s* sombrilla de playa

beach wagon *s* rubia, coche *m* rural

beacon [ˈbikən] *s* señal luminosa; (*lighthouse*) faro; (*hill overlooking sea*) hacho; radiofaro; (*guide*) faro ‖ *tr* iluminar, guiar ‖ *intr* brillar

bead [bid] *s* cuenta; (*of glass*) abalorio; (*of sweat*) gota; (*moulding on corner of wall*) guardavivo; **to say** o **tell one's beads** rezar el rosario

beagle [ˈbigəl] *s* sabueso

beak [bik] *s* pico; cabo, promontorio

beam [bim] *s* (*of wood*) viga; (*of light, heat, etc.*) rayo; (naut) bao; (*direction perpendicular to the keel*) (naut) través *m;* (*of hope*) (fig) rayo; **on the beam** siguiendo el haz del radiofaro; (coll) siguiendo el buen camino ‖ *tr* emitir (*luz, ondas*) ‖ *intr* brillar; sonreír alegremente

bean [bin] *s* frijol *m;* haba (*Vicia faba*); alubia, judía (*Phaseolus vulgaris*); (*of coffee, cocoa*) haba; (slang) cabeza

bean curd *s* tofu *m,* queso de soja

bean'pole' *s* rodrigón *m* para frijoles; (*tall, skinny person*) (coll) poste *m* de telégrafo

bear [bɛr] *s* oso; (*in stock market*) bajista *mf* ‖ *v* (*pret* **bore** [bor]; *pp* **borne** [born]) *tr* cargar; traer; llevar (*armas*); apoyar; aguantar; sentir, experimentar; producir, rendir (*frutos; interés*); (*to give birth to*) parir; tener (*amor, odio*); **to bear out** confirmar ‖ *intr* dirigirse, volver; **to bear on** referirse a; **to bear up** no perder la esperanza; **to bear with** ser indulgente para con

beard [bɪrd] *s* barba; (*of wheat*) arista

beardless [ˈbɪrdlɪs] *adj* imberbe

bearer [ˈbɛrər] *s* portador *m*

bearing [ˈbɛrɪŋ] *s* porte *m,* presencia; referencia, relación; (mach) cojinete *m;* **bearings** orientación; **to lose one's bearings** desorientarse

bearish [ˈbɛrɪʃ] *adj* bajista

bear market *s* (com) mercado bajista o en baja

bear'skin' *s* piel *f* de oso; (*military cap*) morrión *m*

beast [bist] *s* bestia

beast•ly [ˈbistli] *adj* (*comp* **-lier;** *super* **-liest**) bestial; (coll) muy malo ‖ *adv* (coll) muy mal

beast of burden *s* bestia de carga, acémila

beat [bit] *s* golpe *m;* (*of heart*) latido; (*of rhythm*) compás *m;* marca del compás; (mus) tiempo; (phys) batimiento; (rad) batido; (*of a policeman*) ronda; (*sponger*) (slang) embestidor *m* ‖ *v* (*pret* **beat;** *pp* **beat** o **beaten**) *tr* azotar, pegar; batir; sacudir (*una alfombra*); aventajar; llevar (*el compás*); tocar (*un tambor*); (*a una persona en una contienda*) ganar; **to beat it** (slang) largarse; **to beat up** batir (*p.ej., huevos*); (slang) aporrear ‖ *intr* batir; latir (*el corazón*); **to beat against** azotar

beaten [ˈbitən] *adj* batido; (*vanquished*) vencido, batido; (*tired*) cansado, abatido

beaten path *s* camino trillado

beater [ˈbitər] *s* batidor *m;* (*mixer*) batidora

beati•fy [bɪˈætɪˌfaɪ] *v* (*pret & pp* **-fied**) *tr* beatificar

beating [ˈbitɪŋ] *s* golpeo; (*of wings*) aleteo; (*with a whip*) paliza; (*defeat*) derrota

beat'-up' *adj* (coll) (*delapidated*) destartalado; (*ragged*) andrajoso

beau [bo] *s* (*pl* **beaus** o **beaux** [boz]) galán *m,* cortejo; novio; elegante *m*

beautician [bjuˈtɪʃən] *s* embellecedora, esteta *mf,* esteticista *mf*

beautiful [ˈbjutɪfəl] *adj* bello, hermoso

beauti•fy [ˈbjutɪˌfaɪ] *v* (*pret & pp* **-fied**) *tr* hermosear, embellecer

beau•ty [ˈbjuti] *s* (*pl* **-ties**) beldad *f,* belleza; (*person*) preciosura

beauty contest *s* concurso de belleza

beauty parlor *s* salón *m* de belleza

beauty queen *s* reina de belleza

beauty sleep *s* primer sueño (*antes de medianoche*)

beauty spot *s* lunar postizo; sitio pintoresco

beaver [ˈbivər] *s* castor *m;* piel *f* de castor

becalm [bɪˈkɑm] *tr* calmar, serenar

because [bɪˈkɔz] *conj* porque; **because of** por, por causa de

beck [bɛk] *s* seña (*con la cabeza o la mano*); **at the beck and call of** a la disposición de

beckon [ˈbɛkən] *s* seña (*con la cabeza o la mano*) ‖ *tr* llamar por señas; atraer, tentar ‖ *intr* hacer señas

be•come [bɪˈkʌm] *v* (*pret* **-came;** *pp* **-come**) *tr* convenir, sentar bien ‖ *intr* hacerse; llegar a ser; ponerse, volverse; convertirse en; **to become of** ser de, p.ej., **what will become of the soldier?** ¿qué será del soldado? hacerse, p.ej., **what became of his pencil?** ¿qué se hizo su lápiz?

becoming [bɪˈkʌmɪŋ] *adj* conveniente, decente; que sienta bien

bed [bɛd] *s* cama; (*of a river*) cauce *m;* (*of flower garden*) macizo; **to go to bed** acostarse; **to take to bed** encamarse

bed and board *s* pensión completa, casa y comida

bed'bug' *s* chinche *f*

bed'cham'ber *s* alcoba, cuarto de dormir

bed'clothes' *spl* ropa de cama

bed'cov'er *s* cubrecama, cobertor *m*

bedding [ˈbɛdɪŋ] *s* ropa de cama; (*for animals*) cama

bedev•il [bɪˋdɛvəl] *v* (*pret & pp* **-iled** o **-illed;** *ger* **-iling** o **-illing**) *tr* atormentar, confundir
bed′fast′ *adj* postrado en cama
bed′fel′low *s* compañero o compañera de cama; (fig) (*associate*) socio, socia
bedlam [ˋbɛdləm] *s* confusión, desorden *m,* tumulto
bed linen *s* ropa de cama
bed′pan′ *s* silleta
bed′post′ *s* pilar *m* de cama
bedridden [ˋbɛd,rɪdən] *adj* postrado en cama
bed′rock′ *s* (*principle*) fundamento; (min) roca de fondo, roca firme
bed′room′ *s* alcoba, cuarto de dormir
bedroom community *s* ciudad *f* dormitorio
bed′side′ *s* cabecera
bedside table *s* mesa de noche, mesa de luz (SAm)
bed′sore′ *s* úlcera de decúbito; **to get bedsores** decentarse
bed′spread′ *s* sobrecama, cobertor *m*
bed′spring′ *s* colchón *m* de muelles, somier *m*
bed′stead′ *s* cuja
bed′time′ *s* hora de acostarse
bed warmer *s* calientacamas *m*
bed′wetting *s* enuresis nocturna
bee [bi] *s* abeja
beech [bitʃ] *s* haya
beech′nut′ *s* hayuco
beef [bif] *s* carne *f* de vaca; ganado vacuno de engorde; (coll) fuerza muscular; (slang) queja ‖ *tr* — **to beef up** (coll) reforzar ‖ *intr* (slang) quejarse; (slang) soplar
beef cattle *s* ganado vacuno de engorde
beef extract *s* extracto de carne
beef′steak′ *s* biftec *m*
bee′hive′ *s* colmena
bee′line′ *s* — **to make a beeline for** ir en línea recta hacia, ir derecho a
beep [bip] (coll) pitido ‖ *tr & intr* (coll) pitar
beer [bɪr] *s* cerveza; **dark beer** cerveza parda, cerveza negra; **light beer** cerveza clara
beer belly *s* (coll) panza (*de bebedor de cerveza*)
beeswax [ˋbɪz,wæks] *s* cera de abejas ‖ *tr* encerar
beet [bit] *s* remolacha
beetle [ˋbitəl] *s* escarabajo
beetle-browed [ˋbitəl,braʊd] *adj* cejijunto; (*sullen*) ceñudo
beet sugar *s* azúcar *m* de remolacha
be•fall [bɪˋfɔl] *v* (*pret* **-fell** [ˋfɛl]; *pp* **-fallen** [ˋfɔlən]) *tr* acontecer a ‖ *intr* acontecer
befitting [bɪˋfɪtɪŋ] *adj* conveniente; decoroso
before [bɪˋfor] *adv* antes; delante, enfrente ‖ *prep* (*in time*) antes de; (*in place*) delante de; (*in the presence of*) ante ‖ *conj* antes (de) que
before′hand′ *adv* de antemano, con anticipación
befriend [bɪˋfrɛnd] *tr* ofrecer amistad a, amparar, proteger
befuddle [bɪˋfʌdəl] *tr* aturdir, confundir
beg [bɛg] *v* (*pret & pp* **begged;** *ger* **begging**) *tr* pedir, rogar, solicitar; mendigar; huesar ‖ *intr* mendigar; **to beg off** excusarse
be•get [bɪˋgɛt] *v* (*pret* **-got** [ˋgɑt]; *pp* **-gotten** o **-got;** *ger* **-getting**) *tr* engendrar
beggar [ˋbɛgər] *s* mendigo; pobre *mf;* pícaro, bribón *m;* sujeto, tipo
be•gin [bɪˋgɪn] *v* (*pret* **-gan** [ˋgæn]; *pp* **-gun** [ˋgʌn]; *ger* **-ginning**) *tr & intr* comenzar, empezar; **beginning with** a partir de
beginner [bɪˋgɪnər] *s* principiante *mf;* iniciador *m*
beginner's luck *s* suerte *f* de principiante
beginning [bɪˋgɪnɪŋ] *s* comienzo, principio
begrudge [bɪˋgrʌdʒ] *tr* dar de mala gana; envidiar
beguile [bɪˋgaɪl] *tr* engañar; divertir, entretener; engañar (*el tiempo*)
behalf [bɪˋhæf] — **on behalf of** en nombre de; a favor de
behave [bɪˋhev] *intr* conducirse, comportarse; portarse bien; funcionar
behavior [bɪˋhevjər] *s* conducta, comportamiento; funcionamiento
behaviorism [bɪˋhevjə,rɪzəm] *s* behaviorismo, conductismo
behead [bɪˋhɛd] *tr* decapitar, descabezar
behind [bɪˋhaɪnd] *adv* detrás; hacia atrás; con retraso; **to stay behind** quedarse atrás ‖ *prep* detrás de; **behind the back of** a espaldas de; **behind the times** astrasado de noticias; **behind time** tarde ‖ *s* (slang) trasero, pompis *m*
behold [bɪˋhold] *v* (*pret & pp* **-held** [ˋhɛld]) *tr* contemplar ‖ *interj* ¡he aquí!
beholden [bɪˋholdən] *adj*—**to be beholden to someone for something** estar en deuda con alguien por algo
behoove [bɪˋhuv] *tr* convenir, tocar
being [ˋbi•ɪŋ] *adj* existente; **for the time being** por ahora, por el momento ‖ *s* ser, ente *m*
belch [bɛltʃ] *s* eructo, regüeldo ‖ *tr* vomitar (*p.ej., llamas, injurias*) ‖ *intr* eructar, regoldar
beleaguer [bɪˋligər] *tr* sitiar, cercar
bel•fry [ˋbɛlfri] *s* (*pl* **-fries**) campanario
Belgian [ˋbɛldʒən] *adj & s* belga *mf*
Belgium [ˋbɛldʒəm] *s* Bélgica
be•lie [bɪˋlaɪ] *v* (*pret & pp* **-lied** [ˋlaɪd]; *ger* **-lying** [ˋlaɪ•ɪŋ]) *tr* desmentir
belief [bɪˋlif] *s* creencia
believable [bɪˋlivəbəl] *adj* creíble; (*source*) solvente
believe [bɪˋliv] *tr & intr* creer
believer [bɪˋlivər] *s* creyente *mf*
belittle [bɪˋlɪtəl] *tr* empequeñecer, despreciar
bell [bɛl] *s* campana; (*electric bell*) timbre *m,* campanilla; (*ring of bell*) campanada ‖ *intr* bramar, berrear
bell′boy′ *s* botones *m*
belle [bɛl] *s* beldad *f,* belleza
belles-lettres [,bɛlˋlɛtrə] *spl* bellas letras
bell gable *s* espadaña
bell glass *s* fanal *m*
bell′hop′ *s* botones *m*
bellicose [ˋbɛlɪ,kos] *adj* belicoso

belligerent [bə'lɪdʒərənt] *adj & s* beligerante *mf*
bellow ['bɛlo] *s* bramido; **bellows** fuelle *m,* barquín *m* ‖ *tr* gritar ‖ *intr* bramar
bell ringer *s* campanero
bellwether ['bɛl,wɛðər] *s* manso
bel•ly ['bɛli] *s* (*pl* **-lies**) barriga, vientre *m;* estómago ‖ *v* (*pret & pp* **-lied**) *intr* hacer barriga; hacer bolso (*las velas*)
bel'ly•ache' *s* (slang) dolor *m* de barriga ‖ *intr* (slang) quejarse
belly button *s* (coll) ombligo
belly dance *s* (coll) danza del vientre
bellyful ['bɛlɪ,fʊl] *s* (slang) panzada
bel'ly-land' *intr* (aer) aterrizar de panza
belong [bɪ'lɔŋ] *intr* pertenecer; deber estar
belongings [bɪ'lɔŋɪŋz] *spl* pertenencias, efectos; corotos
beloved [bɪʌvɪd] o [bɪ'lʌvd] *adj & s* querido, amado
below [bɪ'lo] *adv* abajo; (*in a text*) más abajo; bajo cero, p.ej., **ten below** diez grados bajo cero ‖ *prep* debajo de; inferior a
belt [bɛlt] *s* cinturón *m;* (aer, mach) correa; (geog) faja, zona; **to tighten one's belt** ceñirse
belt'way *s* carretera de circunvalación
bemoan [bɪ'mon] *tr* deplorar, lamentar
bench [bɛntʃ] *s* banco; (law) tribunal *m*
bend [bɛnd] *s* curva; (*in a road, river, etc.*) recodo, vuelta ‖ *v* (*pret & pp* **bent** [bɛnt]) *tr* encorvar; doblar (*un tubo; la rodilla*); inclinar (*la cabeza*); dirigir (*sus esfuerzos*) ‖ *intr* encorvarse; doblarse; inclinarse
beneath [bɪ'niθ] *adv* abajo ‖ *prep* debajo de; inferior a
benediction [,bɛnɪ'dɪkʃən] *s* bendición *f*
benefaction [,bɛnɪ'fækʃən] *s* beneficio
benefactor ['bɛnɪ,fæktər] o [,bɛnɪ'fæktər] *s* bienhechor *m*
benefactress ['bɛnɪ,fæktrɪs] o [,bɛnɪ'fæktrɪs] *s* bienhechora
beneficence [bɪ'nɛfɪsəns] *s* beneficencia
beneficent [bɪ'nɛfɪsənt] *adj* bienhechor
beneficial [,bɛnɪ'fɪʃəl] *adj* beneficioso
beneficiar•y [,bɛnɪ'fɪʃɪ,ɛri] *s* (*pl* **-ies**) beneficiario
benefit ['bɛnɪfɪt] *s* beneficio; lasca; **benefits** prestaciones; **for the benefit of** a beneficio de ‖ *tr* beneficiar
benefit game *s* partido de homenaje
benefit match *s* partido de homenaje
benefit performance *s* beneficio
benefit society *s* mutua
benevolence [bɪ'nɛvələns] *s* benevolencia
benevolent [bɪ'nɛvələnt] *adj* benévolo; (*e.g., institution*) benéfico
benign [bɪ'naɪn] *adj* benigno
benigni•ty [bɪ'nɪgnɪti] *s* (*pl* **-ties**) benignidad
bent [bɛnt] *adj* encorvado, doblado, torcido; **bent on** resuelto a, empeñado en; **bent over** cargado de espaldas ‖ *s* encorvadura; inclinación *f,* propensión *f*
benzedrine ['bɛnzə,drin] *s* bencedrina
benzine [bɛn'zin] *s* bencina
bequeath [bɪ'kwið] o [bɪ'kwiθ] *tr* legar
bequest [bɪ'kwɛst] *s* manda, legado
berate [bɪ'ret] *tr* regañar, reñir
be•reave [bɪ'riv] *v* (*pret & pp* **-reaved** o **-reft** ['rɛft]) *tr* despojar, privar; desconsolar
bereavement [bɪ'rivmənt] *s* despojo, privación *f;* desconsuelo
berkelium [bər'kilɪ•əm] *s* berkelio
Berliner [bər'lɪnər] *s* berlinés *m*
berm [bʌrm] *s* arcén *m,* berma *f*
Bermuda [bər'mjudə] *s* las Bermudas
ber•ry ['bɛri] *s* (*pl* **-ries**) baya; (*of coffee plant*) grano, haba
berserk ['bʌrsʌrk] *adj* frenético ‖ *adv* frenéticamente
berth [bʌrθ] *s* (*bed*) litera; (*room*) camarote *m;* (*for a ship*) amarradero; (coll) empleo, puesto
beryllium [bə'rɪlɪ•əm] *s* berilio
be•seech [bɪ'sitʃ] *v* (*pret & pp* **-sought** ['sɔt] o **-seeched**) *tr* suplicar
be•set [bɪ'sɛt] *v* (*pret & pp* **-set;** *ger* **-setting**) *tr* acometer, acosar; cercar, sitiar
beside [bɪ'saɪd] *adv* además, también ‖ *prep* cerca de, junto a; en comparación de; excepto; **beside oneself** fuera de sí; **beside the point** incongruente
besiege [bɪ'sidʒ] *tr* asediar, sitiar
besmirch [bɪ'smʌrtʃ] *tr* ensuciar, manchar
best [bɛst] *adj super* mejor; óptimo ‖ *adv super* mejor; **had best** debería ‖ *s* (lo) mejor; (lo) más; **at best** a lo más; **to do one's best** hacer lo mejor posible; **to get the best of** aventajar, sobresalir; **to make the best of** sacar el mejor partido de
best man *s* padrino de boda
bestow [bɪ'sto] *tr* otorgar, conferir; dedicar
best-seller *s* superventas *m;* (*book*) bestseller *m,* éxito de librería; (*product*) éxito de venta, campeón *m* de venta
bet [bɛt] *s* apuesta ‖ *v* (*pret & pp* **bet** o **betted;** *ger* **betting**) *tr & intr* apostar; **I bet!** ¡a que sí!; apuesto a que; **to bet on** apostar por; **you bet** (slang) ya lo creo
beta tester ['betə] *s* (compu) probador *m* beta
Bethlehem ['bɛθlɪ,hɛm] *s* Belén *m*
betray [bɪ'tre] *tr* traicionar; descubrir, revelar
betrayal [bɪ'tre•əl] *s* traición; descubrimiento, revelación
betroth [bɪ'troð] o [bɪ'trɔθ] *tr* prometer en matrimonio; **to become betrothed** desposarse
betrothal [bɪ'troðəl] o [bɪ'trɔθəl] *s* desposorios, esponsales *mpl*
betrothed [bɪ'troðd] o [bɪ'trɔθt] *s* prometido, novio
better ['bɛtər] *adj comp* mejor; **it is better to** más vale; **to grow better** mejorarse; **to make better** mejorar ‖ *adv comp* mejor; más; **had better** debería; **to like better** preferir ‖ *s* superior; ventaja; **to get the better of** llevar la ventaja a ‖ *tr* aventajar; mejorar; **to better oneself** mejorar su posición

betterment [ˋbɛtərmənt] *s* mejoramiento; (*in an illness*) mejoría
between [bɪˋtwin] *adv* en medio, entremedias ‖ *prep* entre; **between you and me** entre Ud. y yo; acá para los dos
be•tween′-decks′ *s* entrecubiertas, entrepuentes *mpl*
between decks *adv* entrecubiertas
bev•el [ˋbɛvəl] *adj* biselado ‖ *s* (*instrument*) cartabón *m;* (*sloping part*) bisel *m* ‖ *v* (*pret & pp* **-eled** o **-elled;** *ger* **-eling** o **-elling**) *tr* biselar
beverage [ˋbɛvərɪdʒ] *s* bebida
bev•y [ˋbɛvi] *s* (*pl* **-ies**) (*of birds*) bandada; (*of girls*) grupo
bewail [bɪˋwel] *tr & intr* lamentar
beware [bɪˋwɛr] *tr* guardarse de ‖ *intr* tener cuidado; **beware of . . .!** ¡ojo con . . .!, ¡cuidado con . . .!; **to beware of** guardarse de
bewilder [bɪˋwɪldər] *tr* aturdir, dejar perplejo, desatinar
bewilderment [bɪˋwɪldərmənt] *s* aturdimiento, perplejidad
beyond [bɪˋjɑnd] *adv* más allá, más lejos ‖ *prep* más allá de; además de; no capaz de; **beyond a doubt** fuera de duda; **beyond the reach of** fuera del alcance de ‖ *s* — **the great beyond** el más allá, el otro mundo
bias [ˋbaɪ•əs] *s* sesgo, diagonal *f;* prejuicio; (electron) polarización de rejilla ‖ *tr* predisponer, prevenir
Bib. *abbr* **Bible, Biblical**
bib [bɪb] *s* babero; pepe *m;* (*of apron*) pechera
Bible [ˋbaɪbəl] *s* Biblia
Biblical [ˋbɪblɪkəl] *adj* bíblico
bibliographer [,bɪblɪˋɑgrəfər] *s* bibliógrafo
bibliogra•phy [,bɪblɪˋɑgrəfi] *s* (*pl* **-phies**) bibliografía
bibliophile [ˋbɪblɪ•ə,faɪl] *s* bibliófilo
bicameral [baɪˋkæmərəl] *adj* bicameral
bicarbonate [baɪˋkɑrbə,net] *s* bicarbonato
bicker [ˋbɪkər] *s* discusión ociosa ‖ *intr* discutir ociosamente
bicycle [ˋbaɪsɪkəl] *s* bicicleta ‖ *intr* ir en bicicleta
bicycle lock *s* cadena antirrobo
bicyclist [ˋbaɪ,sɪklɪst] *s* ciclista *mf*
bid [bɪd] *s* oferta, postura; (*in bridge*) declaración ‖ *v* (*pret* **bade** [bæd] o **bid;** *ger* **bidden** [ˋbɪdən]) *tr & intr* ofrecer, pujar, licitar; (*in bridge*) declarar
bidder [ˋbɪdər] *s* postor *m;* (*in bridge*) declarante *mf;* **the highest bidder** el mejor postor
bidding [ˋbɪdɪŋ] *s* mandato, orden *f;* postura; (*in bridge*) declaración
bide [baɪd] *tr* — **to bide one's time** esperar la hora propicia
bidirectional [ˋbaɪdɪˋrɛkʃənəl] *adj* bidireccional
biennial [baɪˋɛnɪ•əl] *adj* bienal
bier [bɪr] *s* féretro, andas
bifocal [baɪˋfokəl] *adj* bifocal ‖ **bifocals** *spl* anteojos, gafas o lentes *mpl & fpl* bifocales
big [bɪg] *adj* (*comp* **bigger;** *super* **biggest**) grande; (*considerable*) importante; (*grown-up*) adulto; **big with child** preñada ‖ *adv* (coll) con jactancia; **to talk big** (coll) hablar gordo
bigamist [ˋbɪgəmɪst] *s* bígamo
bigamous [ˋbɪgəməs] *adj* bígamo
bigamy [ˋbɪgəmi] *s* bigamia
big-bellied [ˋbɪg,bɛlɪd] *adj* panzudo
big brother *s* hermano mayor; **Big Brother** el Hermano Mayor
big business *s* el gran capital
big cheese *s* (slang) pez gordo
Big Dipper *s* Carro Mayor, Osa Mayor
big game *s* caza mayor
big-hearted [ˋbɪg,hɑrtɪd] *adj* magnánimo, generoso, de gran corazón
bigot [ˋbɪgət] *s* intolerante *mf,* fanático
bigoted [ˋbɪgətɪd] *adj* intolerante, fanático
bigot•ry [ˋbɪgətri] *s* (*pl* **-ries**) intolerancia, fanatismo
big shot *s* (coll) pájaro de cuenta, señorón *m,* capitoste *m*
big stick *s* palo en alto
big ticket *adj* (coll) caro, costoso
big time *s* (coll) estrellato
big toe *s* dedo gordo o grande (*del pie*)
big top *s* carpa de circo
big wheel *s* (coll) pez gordo
big′wig *s* (coll) pez gordo
bike [baɪk] *s* (coll) bici *f;* moto *f* ‖ *intr* (coll) ir en bici; ir en moto
biker [ˋbaɪkər] *s* (coll) ciclista *mf;* motociclista *mf*
bikini [bɪˋkini] *s* bikini *m*
bile [baɪl] *s* bilis *f*
bilge [bɪldʒ] *s* pantoque *m* ‖ *tr* desfondar
bilge pump *s* bomba de sentina
bilge water *s* agua de pantoque
bilge ways *spl* anguilas
bilingual [baɪˋlɪŋgwəl] *adj* bilingüe
bilingual dictionary *s* diccionario bilingüe
bilious [ˋbɪljəs] *adj* bilioso
bilk [bɪlk] *tr* estafar, trampear
bill [bɪl] *s* (*statement of charges for goods or service*) cuenta, factura; (*paper money*) billete *m;* (*poster*) cartel *m,* aviso; cartel de teatro; (*draft of law*) proyecto de ley; (*handbill*) hoja suelta; (*of bird*) pico; (com) giro, letra de cambio ‖ **Bill** apodo de Guillermo ‖ *tr* facturar; cargar en cuenta a; anunciar por carteles ‖ *intr* darse el pico (*las palomas*); acariciarse (*los enamorados*); **to bill and coo** acariciarse y arrullarse
bill′board′ *s* cartelera
billet [ˋbɪlɪt] *s* (mil) boleta; (mil) alojamiento ‖ *tr* (mil) alojar
billet-doux [ˋbɪleˋdu] *s* (*pl* **billets-doux** [ˋbɪleˋduz]) esquela amorosa
bill′fold′ *s* cartera de bolsillo, billetero
billiards [ˋbɪljərdz] *s* billar *m*
billiard table *s* mesa de billar, mesa de trucos
billion [ˋbɪljən] *s* (U.S.A.) mil millones; (Brit) billón *m*
bill of exchange *s* letra de cambio
bill of fare *s* lista de comidas, menú *m*

bill of lading [ˈledɪŋ] *s* conocimiento de embarque
bill of rights *s* declaración de derechos
bill of sale *s* escritura de venta
billow [ˈbɪlo] *s* oleada, ondulación ‖ *intr* ondular, hincharse
bill′post′er *s* fijacarteles *m,* fijador *m* de carteles
bil•ly [ˈbɪli] *s* (*pl* **-lies**) cachiporra
billy club *s* (coll) porra, cachiporra
billy goat *s* macho cabrío
bin [bɪn] *s* arcón *m,* hucha
binary [ˈbaɪnəri] [ˈbaɪnari] *adj & s* binario
binary code *s* código binario
bind [baɪnd] *v* (*pret & pp* **bound** [baʊnd]) *tr* ligar, atar; juntar, unir; (*with a garland*) enguirlandar; ribetear (*la orilla del vestido*); agavillar (*las mieses*); vendar (*una herida*); encuadernar (*un libro*); estreñir (*el vientre*)
binder•y [ˈbaɪndəri] *s* (*pl* **-ies**) taller *m* de encuadernación
binding [ˈbaɪndɪŋ] *s* atadura; (*of a book*) encuadernación
binge [bɪndʒ] *s* (slang) borrachera; turca; **to go on a binge** (slang) pegarse una mona, coger una turca
binnacle [ˈbɪnəkəl] *s* bitácora
binoculars [bɪˈnɑkjələrz] o [baɪˈnɑkjələrz] *spl* gemelos, prismáticos
biochemical [ˌbaɪ•əˈkɛmɪkəl] *adj* bioquímico
biochemist [ˌbaɪ•əˈkɛmɪst] *s* bioquímico
biochemistry [ˌbaɪ•əˈkɛmɪstri] *s* bioquímica
biodegradable [ˌbaɪ•ədɪˈgredədəl] *adj* biodegradable
bioethical [ˌbaɪ•oˈɛθɪkəl] *adj* bioético
bioethics [ˌbaɪ•oˈɛθɪks] *s* bioética
bioengineering [ˌbaɪ•oˈɛndʒəˈnɪrɪŋ] *s* bioingeniería
biog. *abbr* **biographical, biography**
biographer [baɪˈɑgrəfər] *s* biógrafo
biographic(al) [ˌbaɪ•əˈgræfɪk(əl)] *adj* biográfico
biogra•phy [baɪˈɑgrəfi] *s* (*pl* **-phies**) biografía
biological clock [ˈbaɪəˈlɑdʒɪkəl] *s* reloj *m* biológico *or* interno
biological father *s* padre biológico
biological mother *s* madre biológica
biological warfare *s* guerra biológica o bacteriológica
biologist [baɪˈɑlədʒɪst] *s* biólogo
biology [baɪˈɑlədʒi] *s* biología
biomedical [ˌbaɪ•oˈmɛdɪkəl] *adj* biomédico
biometric(al) [ˈbaɪ•oˈmɛtrɪk(əl)] *adj* biométrico ‖ **biometrics** [ˈbaɪ•oˈmɛtrɪks] *s* biometría
bionic [ˌbaɪˈɑnɪk] *adj* biónico
biophysical [ˌbaɪ•əˈfɪzɪkəl] *adj* biofísico
biophysics [ˌbaɪ•əˈfɪzɪks] *s* biofísica
bioplasm [ˈbaɪ•əˌplæzəm] *s* bioplasma
biopsy [ˈbaɪ•ɑpsi] *s* biopsia
bioscopy [baɪˈɑskəpɪ] *s* bioscopía
biosphere [ˈbaɪ•osfɪr] *s* biosfera, biósfera
biotechnology [ˈbaɪ•otɛkˈnɑlədʒi] *s* biotecnología
bioterrorism [baɪˌoˈtɛrərɪzəm] *s* bioterrorismo
bip [bɪp] *s* bip
biped [ˈbaɪpɛd] *adj & s* bípedo
birch [bʌrtʃ] *s* abedul *m* ‖ *tr* azotar, varear
bird [bʌrd] *s* ave *f,* pájaro
bird bath *s* pila para pájaros
bird cage *s* jaula
bird call *s* reclamo
bird′lime′ *s* liga
bird of passage *s* ave *f* de paso
bird of prey *s* ave *f* de rapiña
bird′seed′ *s* alpiste *m,* cañamones *mpl*
bird's′-eye′ view *s* vista a ojo de pájaro
bird shot *s* perdigones *mpl*
birth [bʌrθ] *s* nacimiento; (*childbirth*) parto; origen *m*
birth certificate *s* partida de nacimiento
birth control *s* limitación de la natalidad, control de la natalidad, control de los nacimientos
birth′day′ *s* cumpleaños *m,* natal *m,* día *m* de años; (*of any event*) aniversario; **to have a birthday** cumplir años
birthday cake *s* pastel *m* de cumpleaños
birthday present *s* regalo de cumpleaños
birth′mark′ *s* antojo, nevo materno
birth′place′ *s* suelo natal, patria, lugar *m* de nacimiento
birth rate *s* índice *m or* tasa de natalidad
birth′right′ *s* derechos de nacimiento; primogenitura
Biscay [ˈbɪske] *s* Vizcaya
biscuit [ˈbɪskɪt] *s* panecillo redondo; bizcocho
bisect [baɪˈsɛkt] *tr* bisecar ‖ *intr* empalmar (*dos caminos*)
bisexual [ˈbaɪˈsɛkʃʊ•əl] *adj & s* bisexual *mf*
bishop [ˈbɪʃəp] *s* obispo; (*in chess*) alfil *m*
bismuth [ˈbɪzməθ] *s* bismuto
bison [ˈbaɪsən] *s* bisonte *m*
bit [bɪt] *s* poquito, pedacito; (*of food*) bocado; (*of time*) ratito; (*part of bridle*) bocado, freno; (*for drilling*) barrena; (compu) bit *m;* **a good bit** una buena cantidad
bitch [bɪtʃ] *s* (*dog*) perra; (*fox*) zorra; (*wolf*) loba; (vulg) mujer *f* de mal genio
bite [baɪt] *s* mordedura; (*of bird or insect*) picadura; (*burning sensation on tongue*) resquemo; (*of food*) bocado; (*snack*) (coll) tentempié *m,* refrigerio ‖ *v* (*pret* **bit** [bɪt]; *pp* **bit** o **bitten** [ˈbɪtən]) *tr* morder; picar (*los peces, los insectos*); resquemar (*la lengua los alimentos*); comerse (*las uñas*) ‖ *intr* morder; picar; resquemar; (*to be caught by a trick*) (slang) picar
biting [ˈbaɪtɪŋ] *adj* penetrante; mordaz, picante
bit′map *s* (compu) mapa *m* de bits
bitter [ˈbɪtər] *adj* amargo; (*e.g., struggle*) encarnizado; **to the bitter end** hasta el extremo; hasta la muerte
bitter almond *s* almendra amarga
bitterness [ˈbɪtərnɪs] *s* amargura
bitumen [bɪˈtjumən] *s* betún *m*
bivou•ac [ˈbɪvʊˌæk] *s* vivaque *m* ‖ *v* (*pret & pp* **-acked; *ger* -acking**) *intr* vivaquear
bizarre [bɪˈzɑr] *adj* original, raro

bk. *abbr* **bank, block, book**
blab [blæb] o **blabber** [ˈblæbər] *tr & intr* (coll) barbullar; **to blab a secret** descubrir el pastel
black [blæk] *adj* negro; **Black** or **black** (*person*) negro ‖ *s* negro; luto; **Black** or **black** (*person*) negro; **to wear black** ir de luto
black′-and-blue′ *adj* encardenalado, amoratado
black′-and-white′ *adj* en blanco y negro
black′ber′ry *s* (*pl* **-ries**) (*bush*) zarza; (*fruit*) zarzamora
black′bird′ *s* mirlo
black′board′ *s* encerado, pizarra
black box *s* registrador *m* de vuelo, caja negra
black coffee *s* café negro, solo, tinto *or* puro
black′damp′ *s* mofeta
blacken [ˈblækən] *tr* ennegrecer; (*to defame*) desacreditar, denigrar
black eye *s* ojo morado; **to give someone a black eye** ponerle un ojo morado a alguien
blackguard [ˈblægɑrd] *s* bribón *m,* canalla *m* ‖ *tr* injuriar, vilipendiar
black′head′ *s* espinilla, comedón *m*
black hole *s* (astr) agujero negro
black ice *s* placa de hielo
blackish [ˈblækɪʃ] *adj* negruzco
black′jack′ *s* (*club*) cachiporra; (*flag*) bandera negra (*de pirata*) ‖ *tr* aporrear
black′list *s* lista negra ‖ *tr* poner en la lista negra
black′mail′ *s* chantaje *m* ‖ *tr* amenazar con chantaje
blackmailer [ˈblæk,melər] *s* chantajista *mf*
black market *s* estraperlo, mercado negro
blackness [ˈblæknɪs] *s* negror *m,* negrura
black′out′ *s* (*of a community*) apagón *m,* corte *m* de luz, corte de energía; (*in theater*) apagamiento de luces; (*of aviators*) visión negra; (pathol) pérdida de la memoria
black sheep *s* (fig) oveja negra
black′smith′ *s* (*man who works with iron*) herrero; (*man who shoes horses*) herrador *m*
black′thorn′ *s* espino negro, endrino
black tie corbata de smoking; smoking *m*
black′top *s* asfalto ‖ *tr* asfaltar
bladder [ˈblædər] *s* vejiga
blade [bled] *s* (*of a knife, sword*) hoja; (*of a propeller*) aleta; (*of a fan*) paleta; (*of an oar*) pala; (*of an electric switch*) cuchilla; (*sword*) espada; tallo de hierba; (coll) gallardo joven
blame [blem] *s* culpa ‖ *tr* culpar
blameless [ˈblemlɪs] *adj* inculpable, irreprochable
blanch [blæntʃ] *tr* blanquear ‖ *intr* palidecer
bland [blænd] *adj* apacible; suave; (*character; weather*) blando
blandish [ˈblændɪʃ] *tr* engatusar, lisonjear
blank [blæŋk] *adj* en blanco; blanco, vacío; (*stare, look*) vago; (*bullet*) bala de fogueo, bala de salva ‖ *s* blanco; papel blanco; formulario
blank check *s* firma en blanco; (fig) carta blanca; cheque *m* en blanco
blanket [ˈblæŋkɪt] *adj* general, comprensivo ‖ *s* manta, frazada; (fig) capa, manto ‖ *tr* cubrir con manta; cubrir, obscurecer
blank tape *s* cinta virgen
blare [blɛr] *intr* atronar
blasé [blɑˈze] *adj* hastiado
blaspheme [blæsˈfim] *tr* blasfemar contra ‖ *intr* blasfemar
blasphemous [ˈblæsfɪməs] *adj* blasfemo
blasphe•my [ˈblæsfɪmi] *s* (*pl* **-mies**) blasfemia
blast [blæst] *s* (*of wind*) ráfaga; (*of air, sand, water*) chorro; (*of bellows*) soplo; (*of a horn*) toque *m;* carga de pólvora; voladura, explosión; **full blast** en plena marcha ‖ *tr* (*to blow up*) volar; arruinar; infamar, maldecir
blast furnace *s* alto horno
blast′off′ *s* lanzamiento de cohete
blatant [ˈbletənt] *adj* descarado, patente; ruidóso; vocinglero; intruso; chillón, cursi
blaze [blez] *s* llamarada; (*fire*) incendio; (*bonfire*) hoguera; luz *f* brillante ‖ *tr* encender, inflamar; **to blaze a trail** abrir una senda ‖ *intr* encenderse; resplandecer
blazer [ˈblezər] *s* chaqueta americana (Esp)
bldg. *abbr* **building**
bleach [blitʃ] *s* blanqueo ‖ *tr* blanquear; colar (*la ropa*)
bleachers [ˈblitʃərz] *spl* gradas al aire libre, gradería
bleak [blik] *adj* desierto, yermo, frío, triste
blear•y [ˈblɪri] *adj* (*comp* **-ier;** *super* **-iest**) (*eyes*) nublado; (*view*) borroso
bleat [blit] *s* balido ‖ *intr* balar
bleed [blid] *v* (*pret & pep* **bled** [blɛd]) *tr & intr* sangrar
bleep [blip] *s* sonido agudo ‖ *intr* emitir un sonido agudo
blemish [ˈblɛmɪʃ] *s* mancha ‖ *tr* manchar
blend [blɛnd] *s* mezcla; armonía ‖ *v* (*pret & pp* **blended** o **blent** [blɛnt]) *tr* mezclar; armonizar; fusionar ‖ *intr* mezclarse; armonizar; fusionarse
bless [blɛs] *tr* bendecir; **to be blessed with** estar dotado de
blessed [ˈblɛsɪd] *adj* bendito, santo
blessedness [ˈblɛsɪdnɪs] *s* bienaventuranza
blessing [ˈblɛsɪŋ] *s* bendición
blight [blaɪt] *s* niebla, roya; ruina ‖ *tr* anublar; arruinar
blimp [blɪmp] *s* dirigible pequeño
blind [blaɪnd] *adj* ciego ‖ *s* (*window shade*) estor *m,* transparente *m* de resorte; (*Venetian blind*) persiana; pretexto, subterfugio ‖ *tr* cegar; (*to dazzle*) deslumbrar; (*to deceive*) cegar, vendar
blind alley *s* callejón *m* sin salida
blind date *s* cita a ciegas
blinder [ˈblaɪndər] *s* anteojera
blind flying *s* (aer) vuelo a ciegas
blind′fold′ *adj* vendado de ojos ‖ *s* venda ‖ *tr* vendar los ojos a
blind landing *s* aterrizaje *m* a ciegas
blind man *s* ciego
blind′man's′ buff *s* gallina ciega

blindness [ˈblaɪndnɪs] *s* ceguedad
blind′side *tr* coger desprevenido, atacar de improviso
blink [blɪŋk] *s* guiñada, parpadeo ‖ *tr* guiñar (*el ojo*) ‖ *intr* guiñar, parpadear, pestañear; oscilar (*la luz*)
blinkers [ˈblɪŋkərz] *spl* (*blinders*) anteojeras; (aut) intermitentes *mpl*
blinking [ˈblɪŋkɪŋ] *adj* intermitente
blip [blɪp] *s* bache *m;* (*sound*) bip *m;* (electron) cresta de eco, señal luminosa
bliss [blɪs] *s* bienaventuranza, felicidad
blissful [ˈblɪsfəl] *adj* bienaventurado, feliz
blister [ˈblɪstər] *s* ampolla, vejiga ‖ *tr* ampollar ‖ *intr* ampollarse
blithe [blaɪð] *adj* alegre, animado
blitzkrieg [ˈblɪts,krig] *s* guerra relámpago
blizzard [ˈblɪzərd] *s* ventisca, chubasco de nieve
bloat [blot] *tr* hinchar ‖ *intr* hincharse, abotagarse
block [blɑk] *s* bloque *m;* (*of hatter*) horma; (*of houses*) manzana; (*for chopping meat*) tajo; estorbo, obstáculo ‖ *tr* cerrar, obstruir; conformar (*un sombrero*)
blockade [blɑˈked] *s* bloqueo ‖ *tr* bloquear
blockade runner *s* forzador *m* de bloqueo
block and tackle *s* aparejo de poleas
block′bust′er *s* (coll) bomba rompedora
block′head′ *s* tonto, zoquete *m*
block signal *s* (rr) señal *f* de tramo
blond [blɑnd] *adj* rubio, blondo ‖ *s* rubio (*hombre rubio*)
blonde [blɑnd] *s* rubia (*mujer rubia*)
blood [blʌd] *s* sangre *f;* **in cold blood** a sangre fría
blood bank *s* banco de sangre
blood brother *s* hermano de sangre
bloodcurdling [ˈblʌd,kʌrdlɪŋ] *adj* horripilante
blood group *s* grupo sanguíneo
blood′hound′ *s* sabueso
blood money *s* (coll) dinero sucio
blood poisoning *s* envenenamiento de la sangre
blood pressure *s* presión arterial
blood pudding *s* morcilla
blood relation *s* pariente consanguíneo
blood′shed′ *s* efusión de sangre
blood′shot′ *adj* inyectado en sangre, rojo
blood′stream′ *s* corriente *f* sanguínea
blood test *s* análisis *m* de sangre
blood′thirst′y *adj* sanguinario
blood transfusion *s* transfusión de sangre
blood vessel *s* vaso sanguíneo
blood•y [ˈblʌdi] *adj* (*comp* **-ier;** *super* **-iest**) sangriento ‖ *v* (*pret & pp* **-ied**) *tr* ensangrentar
bloom [blum] *s* florecimiento; flor *f* ‖ *intr* florecer
blossom [ˈblɑsəm] *s* brote *m,* flor *f;* **in blossom** en cierne ‖ *intr* cerner, florecer
blot [blɑt] *s* borrón *m* ‖ *v* (*pret & pp* **blotted;** *ger* **blotting**) *tr* (*to smear*) borrar; secar con papel secante; **to blot out** borrar ‖ *intr* borrarse; echar borrones (*una pluma*)
blotch [blɑtʃ] *s* manchón *m;* (*in the skin*) erupción
blotter [ˈblɑtər] *s* teleta, secafirmas *m*
blouse [blaʊs] *s* blusa
blow [blo] *s* (*hit, stroke*) golpe; (*blast of air*) soplo, soplido; (*blast of wind*) ventarrón *m;* (*of horn*) toque *m,* trompetazo; (*sudden sorrow*) estocada, ramalazo; (*boaster*) (slang) fanfarrón *m;* **to come to blows** venir a las manos ‖ *v* (*pret* **blew** [blu]; *pp* **blown**) ‖ *tr* soplar; sonar, tocar (*un instrumento de viento*); silbar (*un silbato*); sonarse (*las narices*); quemar (*un fusible*); (slang) malgastar (*dinero*); **to blow out** apagar soplando; quemar (*un fusible*); **to blow up** (*with air*) inflar; (*e.g., with dynamite*) volar, hacer saltar; ampliar (*una foto*) ‖ *intr* soplar; (*to pant*) jadear, resoplar; fundirse (*un fusible*); (slang) fanfarronear; **to blow out** apagarse con el aire; quemarse, fundirse (*un fusible*); reventar (*un neumático*); **to blow up** volarse; (*to fail*) fracasar; (*with anger*) (slang) estallar, reventar
blow′gun *s* cerbatana
blow′out′ *s* (aut) reventón *m;* (*of a fuse*) quemazón *f;* (slang) tertulia concurrida, festín *m*
blow′pipe′ *s* (*torch*) soplete *m;* (*peashooter*) cerbatana
blow′torch′ *s* antorcha a soplete, lámpara de soldar
blubber [ˈblʌbər] *s* grasa de ballena; lloro ruidoso ‖ *intr* llorar ruidosamente
bludgeon [ˈblʌdʒən] *s* cachiporra ‖ *tr* aporrear; intimidar
blue [blu] *adj* azul; abatido, triste ‖ *s* azul *m;* **the blues** la murria, la morriña ‖ *tr* azular; añilar (*la ropa blanca*) ‖ *intr* azularse
blue′ber′ry *s* (*pl* **-ries**) arándano
blue book *s* (educ) cuaderno de exámenes
blue chip *s* valor *m* de primera fila
blue′jay′ *s* cianocita
blue jeans *spl* blujins *mpl,* vaqueros; pantalones de mezclilla (C-R, Mex); mecánicos (CAm, Cuba, S-D); pantalones azules (CAm); azulones (El Salv); mahones (P-R, S-D)
blue moon *s* cosa muy rara; **once in a blue moon** cada muerte de obispo, de Pascuas a Ramos
blue′-pen′cil *tr* marcar o corregir con lápiz azul
blue′print′ *s* plano, proyecto; (phot) cianotipo; (fig) programa *m* ‖ *tr* copiar a la cianotipia
blue ribbon *adj* selecto, de élite; máximo ‖ *s* primer premio
blue′stock′ing *s* (coll) marisabidilla
blue streak *s* (coll) rayo; **to talk a blue streak** (coll) soltar la tarabilla
bluff [blʌf] *adj* escarpado ‖ *s* risco, peñasco escarpado; (*deception*) farol *m,* blof *m;* **to call someone's bluff** cogerle la palabra a uno ‖ *intr* farolear, papelonear
blunder [ˈblʌndər] *s* disparate *m,* desatino, metedura de pata (coll) ‖ *intr* disparatar, desatinar
blunt [blʌnt] *adj* despuntado, embotado; brusco, franco, directo ‖ *tr* despuntar, embotar

bluntness [ˈblʌntnɪs] *s* embotadura; brusquedad, franqueza
blur [blʌr] *s* borrón *m,* mancha || *v* (*pret & pp* **blurred;** *ger* **blurring**) *tr* empañar; obscurecer (*la vista*) || *intr* empañarse
blurb [blʌrb] *s* anuncio efusivo
blurt [blʌrt] *tr* — **to blurt out** soltar abrupta e impulsivamente
blush [blʌʃ] *s* rubor *m,* sonrojo || *intr* ruborizarse, sonrojarse
bluster [ˈblʌstər] *s* tumulto, gritos; jactancia || *intr* soplar con furia (*el viento*); bravear, fanfarronear
blustery [ˈblʌstəri] *adj* tempestuoso; (*wind*) violento; (*swaggering*) fanfarrón
blvd. *abbr* **boulevard**
boar [bor] *s* (*male swine*) verraco; (*wild hog*) jabalí *m*
board [bord] *s* tabla; (*to post announcements*) tablero; (*table with meal*) mesa; (*daily meals*) pensión; (*organized group*) junta, consejo; (compu) placa; (naut) bordo; **in boards** (bb) en cartoné; **on board** en el tren; (naut) a bordo || *tr* entablar; subir a (*un tren*); embarcarse en (*un buque*) || *intr* hospedarse; estar de pupilo
board and lodging *s* mesa y habitación, pensión completa
boarder [ˈbordər] *s* pensionista *mf,* pupilo
boarding house *s* pensión, casa de huéspedes
boarding pass *s* tarjeta de embarque
boarding school *s* escuela de internos
board of directors *s* consejo de administración, junta directiva
board of health *s* junta de sanidad
board of trade *s* junta de comercio
board of trustees *s* consejo de administración
board′room′ *s* (com) sala de juntas
board′walk′ *s* paseo entablado a la orilla del mar
boast [bost] *s* jactancia, baladronada || *intr* jactarse, baladronear, bravatear
boastful [ˈbostfəl] *adj* jactancioso
boat [bot] *s* barco, buque *m,* nave *f;* (*small boat*) bote *m;* **to be in the same boat** correr el mismo riesgo
boat hook *s* bichero
boat′house′ *s* casilla para botes
boating [ˈbotɪŋ] *s* paseo en barco
boat•man [ˈbotmən] *s* (*pl* **-men** [mən]) barquero, lanchero
boat race *s* regata
boatswain *s* [ˈbosən] *s* contramaestre *m*
boatswain's chair *s* guindola
bob [bɑb] *s* (*of pendulum of clock*) lenteja; (*of plumb line*) plomo; (*of a fishing line*) corcho; (*of a horse*) cola cortada; (*of a girl*) pelo cortado corto; (*jerky motion*) sacudida || *v* (*pret & pp* **bobbed;** *ger* **bobbing**) *tr* cortar corto || *intr* agitarse, menearse; **to bob up and down** subir y bajar con sacudidas cortas
bobbin [ˈbɑbɪn] *s* broca, canilla, bobina
bobby pin [ˈbɑbi] *s* horquillita para el pelo
bob′by•socks′ *spl* (coll) tobilleras (*de jovencita*)
bobbysoxer [ˈbɑbɪˌsɑksər] *s* (coll) tobillera
bobolink [ˈbɑbəˌlɪŋk] *s* chambergo
bob′sled′ *s* doble trineo articulado
bob′tail′ *s* animal *m* rabón; cola corta; cola cortada
bob′white′ *s* colín *m* de Virginia
bock beer [bɑk] *s* cerveza de marzo
bode [bod] *tr & intr* anunciar, presagiar; **to bode ill** ser un mal presagio; **to bode well** ser un buen presagio
bodice [ˈbɑdɪs] *s* jubón *m,* corpiño
bodily [ˈbɑdɪli] *adj* corporal, corpóreo || *adv* en persona; en conjunto
bod•y [ˈbɑdi] *s* (*pl* **-ies**) cuerpo; (*of a carriage or auto*) caja, carrocería
body building *s* fisiculturismo
bod′y•guard′ *s* (mil) guardia de corps; guardaespaldas *m*
body odor *s* sobaquina
body shop *s* taller *m* carrocero
body veil *s* velo que cubre el cuerpo
Boer [bor] o [bʊr] *s* bóer *mf*
Boer War *s* guerra del Transvaal
bog [bɑg] *s* pantano || *v* (*pret & pp* **bogged;** *ger* **bogging**) *intr* — **to bog down** atascarse, hundirse
bo′gey•man′ *s* (*pl* **-men** [ˌmɛn]) duende *m,* espantajo
bogus [ˈbogəs] *adj* (coll) fingido, falso
Bohemian [boˈhimɪ•ən] *adj & s* bohemio
boil [bɔɪl] *s* hervor *m,* ebullición; (pathol) divieso, furúnculo || *tr* hacer hervir, herventar || *intr* hervir, bullir; **to boil over** salirse (*un líquido*) al hervir
boiler [ˈbɔɪlər] *s* caldera; (*for cooking*) marmita, olla
boiler room *s* sala de calderas
boiling [ˈbɔɪlɪŋ] *adj* hirviente, hirviendo || *s* hervor *m,* ebullición
boiling point *s* punto de ebullición
boil′ing-wa′ter reactor *s* reactor *m* de agua en ebullición
boisterous [ˈbɔɪstərəs] *adj* bullicioso, ruidoso, estrepitoso
bold [bold] *adj* audaz, arrojado, osado; descarado, impudente; temerario
bold′face′ *s* (typ) negrilla, negrita
boldness [ˈboldnɪs] *s* audacia, arrojo, osadía; descaro, impudencia; temeridad
Bolivia [boˈlɪvɪ•ə] *s* Bolivia
Bolivian [boˈlɪvɪ•ən] *adj & s* boliviano
boll weevil [bol] *s* gorgojo del algodón
Bologna [bəˈlonjə] *s* Bolonia
bologna [bəˈlonə] *s* salchicha ahumada
boloney *var de* **baloney**
Bolshevik [ˈbɑlʃəvɪk] o [ˈbolʃəvɪk] *adj & s* bolchevique *mf*
Bolshevism [ˈbɑlʃəˌvɪzəm] o [ˈbolʃəˌvɪzəm] *s* bolchevismo
bolster [ˈbolstər] *s* (*of bed*) larguero, travesaño; refuerzo, soporte *m* || *tr* apoyar, sostener; animar, alentar
bolt [bolt] *s* perno; (*to fasten a door*) cerrojo,

pasador *m;* (*arrow*) cuadrillo; (*of lightning*) rayo; (*of cloth or paper*) rollo || *tr* empernar; acerrojar; deglutir de una vez; cribar, tamizar; disidir de (*un partido político*) || *intr* salir de repente; disidir; desbocarse (*un caballo*)
bolter [ˈboltər] *s* disidente *mf;* (*sieve*) criba, tamiz *m*
bolt from the blue *s* rayo en cielo sin nubes; suceso inesperado
bomb [bɑm] *s* bomba; (compu) bomba || *tr* bombear, bombardear
bombard [bɑmˈbɑrd] *tr* bombardear; (*e.g., with questions*) asediar
bombardment [bɑmˈbɑrdmənt] *s* bombardeo
bombast [ˈbɑmbæst] *s* ampulosidad
bombastic [bɑmˈbæstɪk] *adj* ampuloso
bomb crater *s* (mil) embudo de bomba
bomber [ˈbɑmər] *s* bombardero; (*political assassin*) terrorista *mf*
bomb'proof' *adj* a prueba de bombas
bomb release *s* lanzabombas *m*
bomb'shell' *s* bomba; **to fall like a bombshell** caer como una bomba
bomb shelter *s* refugio antiaéreo
bomb'sight' *s* mira de bombardeo, visor *m*
bomb squad *s* brigada antiexplosivos
bona fide [ˈbonə,faɪdə] *adj & adv* de buena fe
bonbon [ˈbɑn,bɑn] *s* bombón *m,* confite *m*
bond [bɑnd] *s* (*tie, union*) enlace *m,* vínculo, lazo de unión; (*interest-bearing certificate*) bono, obligación; (*surety*) fianza; (mas) aparejo; **bonds** cadenas, grillos; **in bond** en depósito bajo fianza
bondage [ˈbɑndɪdʒ] *s* cautiverio, servidumbre
bonded warehouse *s* depósito comercial
bond'hold'er *s* obligacionista *mf,* tenedor *m* de bonos
bonds•man [ˈbɑndzmən] *s* (*pl* **-men** [mən]) fiador *m*
bone [bon] *s* hueso; (*of fish*) espina; **bones** esqueleto; (*mortal remains*) huesos; castañuelas; (*dice*) (coll) dados; **to have a bone to pick with** tener una queja con; **to make no bones about** no andarse con rodeos en || *tr* desosar; quitar la espina a; emballenar (*un corsé*) || *intr* — **to bone up on** (coll) empollar, estudiar con ahinco
bone'-dry' *adj* completamente seco
bone'head' *s* (coll) estúpido
boneless [ˈbonlɪs] *adj* mollar, desosado; (*fish*) sin espinas
bone marrow *s* médula ósea
boner [ˈbonər] *s* (coll) patochada, plancha, gazapo
bonfire [ˈbɑn,faɪr] *s* hoguera, fogata
bonnet [ˈbɑnɪt] *s* gorra; (*sunbonnet*) papalina; (*of auto*) cubierta, capó *m*
bonus [ˈbonəs] *s* prima, plus *m;* dividendo extraordinario
bon•y [ˈboni] *adj* (*comp* **-ier;** *super* **-iest**) osudo; descarnado; (*fish*) espinoso
boo [bu] *s* rechifla; **not to say boo** no decir ni chus ni mus || *tr & intr* abuchear, rechiflar || *interj* ¡uh!
boo-boo [ˈbubu] *s* (slang) metedura de pata
boo•by [ˈbubi] *s* (*pl* **-bies**) (coll) bobalicón *m,* zopenco; el peor jugador
booby prize *s* premio al peor jugador
booby trap *s* (*mine*) trampa explosiva; (*trick*) zancadilla
boo-hoo [ˈbuˈhu] *interj* ¡buuah!
booing [ˈbuɪŋ] *s* abucheo
book [bʊk] *s* libro; (*bankbook*) libreta; (*book containing records of business transactions*) libro-registro; (*of cigaret paper, stamps, etc.*) librillo; **to keep books** llevar libros || *tr* reservar (*un pasaje*); escriturar (*a un actor*)
bookbinder [ˈbʊk,baɪndər] *s* encuadernador *m*
book'bind'er•y *s* (*pl* **-ies**) encuadernación (*taller*)
book'bind'ing *s* encuadernación (*acción, arte*)
book'case' *s* armario para libros, estante *m* para libros
book end *s* apoyalibros *m*
bookie [ˈbʊki] *s* (coll) corredor *m* de apuestas
booking [ˈbʊkɪŋ] *s* (*of passage*) reservación; (*of an actor*) escritura
booking clerk *s* taquillero (*que despacha pasajes o localidades*)
bookish [ˈbʊkɪʃ] *adj* libresco
book'keep'er *s* tenedor *m* de libros
book'keep'ing *s* teneduría de libros, contabilidad
book'mak'er *s* corredor *m* de apuestas
book'mark' *s* registro, señal *f,* marcador *m*
book'plate' *s* ex libris *m*
book review *s* reseña
book'sell'er *s* librero
book'shelf' *s* (*pl* **-shelves** [,ʃɛlvz] estante *m* para libros
book'stand' *s* (*rack*) atril *m;* mostrador *m* para libros; puesto de venta para libros
book'store' *s* librería
book'worm' *s* polilla que roe los libros; (fig) ratón *m* de biblioteca
boom [bum] *s* (*sudden prosperity*) auge *m,* boom *m;* (*noise*) estampido, trueno; (*of a crane*) aguilón *m;* (naut) botalón *m* || *intr* hacer estampido, tronar; estar en auge, retumbar
boomerang [ˈbumə,ræŋ] *s* bumerán *m*
boomers [ˈbumərz] *abbr* **baby boomers**
boom town *s* pueblo en bonanza
boon [bun] *s* bendición, dicha
boon companion *s* buen compañero
boon'docks' *spl* (coll) selva; **out in the boondocks** en los quintos infiernos
boondoggle [ˈbun,dɑgəl] *s* trabajo pagado innecesario
boor [bʊr] *s* patán *m,* rústico
boorish [ˈbʊrɪʃ] *adj* rústico, zafio
boost [bust] *s* empujón *m* hacia arriba; (*in price*) alza; alabanza; ayuda || *tr* empujar hacia arriba; alzar (*el precio*); alabar; ayudar
booster [ˈbustər] *s* cohete *m* lanzador; primera

etapa de un cohete lanzador; (*enthusiastic backer*) bombista *mf*
booster shot *s* inyección secundaria
boot [but] *s* bota; **to boot** de añadidura, además; **to die with one's boots on** morir al pie del cañón ‖ *tr* dar un puntapié a; **to boot out** (slang) poner en la calle; **to boot (up)** (comp) (*load*) cargar, hacer el cebado de; (comp) (*start*) prender
boot'black' *s* limpiabotas *m*
boot camp *s* (mil) campamento de entrenamiento de reclutas
booth [buθ] *s* casilla, quiosco; (*to telephone, to vote, etc.*) cabina; (*at a fair or market*) puesto
boot'jack' *s* sacabotas *m*
boot'leg' *adj* contrabandista; de contrabando ‖ *s* contrabando de licores ‖ *v* (*pret & pp* **-legged;** *ger* **-legging**) *tr* pasar de contrabando ‖ *intr* contrabandear en bebidas alcohólicas
bootlegger [ˈbutˌlɛgər] *s* destilador *m* clandestino, contrabandista *m*
boot'leg'ging *s* contrabando en bebidas alcohólicas
bootlicker [ˈbutˌlɪkər] *s* (slang) quitamotas *mf*, lavacaras *mf*
boot'strap' *s* tirilla de bota; **by one's bootstraps** por sí mismo, sin ayuda ajena
boo•ty [ˈbuti] *s* (*pl* **-ties**) botín *m*, presa
booze [buz] *s* (coll) bebida alcohólica ‖ *intr* borrachear
borax [ˈboræks] *s* bórax *m*
Bordeaux [bɔrˈdo] *s* Burdeos
border [ˈbɔrdər] *adj* frontero, fronterizo ‖ *s* borde *m*, margen *m & f;* frontera; **borders** bambalinas ‖ *tr* bordear; deslindar ‖ *intr* confinar
border clash *s* encuentro fronterizo
border crossing *s* paso fronterizo
bor'der•line' *adj* incierto, indefinido ‖ *s* frontera
bore [bor] *s* (*drill hole*) barreno; (*size of hole*) calibre *m;* (*of firearm*) alma, ánima; (*of cylinder*) alesaje *m;* (*wearisome person*) latoso, machaca *mf;* fastidio ‖ *tr* aburrir, fastidiar; barrenar, hacer (*un agujero*)
boredom [ˈbordəm] *s* aburrimiento, fastidio
boring [ˈborɪŋ] *adj* aburrido, pesado; **that's terribly boring** es una lata
born [bɔrn] *adj* nacido; (*natural, by birth*) nato, innato; **to be born** nacer
borough [ˈbʌro] *s* (*town*) villa; distrito electoral de municipio
borrow [ˈbɑro] o [ˈbɔro] *tr* pedir o tomar prestado; apropiarse (*p.ej., una idea*); incorporar (*un elemento lingüístico extranjero*); **to borrow trouble** tomarse una molestia sin motivo alguno
borrower [ˈbɑro•ər] o [ˈbɔro•ər] *s* prestatario
borrowing [ˈbɑro•ɪŋ] o [bɔro•ɪŋ] *s* préstamo; préstamo lingüístico, extranjerismo
bosom [ˈbʊzəm] *s* seno; (*of shirt*) pechera; corazón *m*, pecho
bosom friend *s* amigo de la mayor confianza
Bosporus [ˈbɑspərəs] *s* Bósforo
boss [bɔs] o [bɑs] *s* (coll) amo, capataz *m*, mandamás *m*, jefe *m;* (*in politics*) (coll) cacique *m;* protuberancia ‖ *tr* (coll) mandar, dominar
boss•y [ˈbɔsi] *adj* (*comp* **-ier;** *super* **-iest**) mandón
botanical [bəˈtænɪkəl] *adj* botánico
botanist [ˈbɑtənɪst] *s* botánico
botany [ˈbɑtəni] *s* botánica
botch [bɑtʃ] *s* remiendo chapucero ‖ *tr* remendar chapuceramente
both [boθ] *adj & pron* ambos ‖ *adv* igualmente ‖ *conj* a la vez; **both . . . and** tanto . . . como, así . . . como
bother [ˈbɑðər] *s* molestia, fastidio ‖ *tr* molestar, fastidiar ‖ *intr* molestarse, fastidiarse
bothersome [ˈbɑðərsəm] *adj* incómodo, molesto, fastidioso
bottle [ˈbɑtəl] *s* botella, frasco ‖ *tr* embotellar; **to bottle up** (nav) embotellar
bottled gas *s* gas envasado
bot'tle•neck' *s* gollete *m;* (*in traffic*) embotellado; (fig) cuello de botella
bottle opener [ˈopənər] *s* abrebotellas *m*
bottom [ˈbɑtəm] *adj* (*price*) (el) más bajo; (*e.g., dollar*) último ‖ *s* fondo; (*of a chair*) asiento; (*of jar*) culo; (coll) trasero; **at bottom** en el fondo; **to bottom out** tocar fondo; **to go to the bottom** irse a pique
bottomless [ˈbɑtəmlɪs] *adj* sin fondo, insondable
bottom line *s* (econ) balance *m;* **the bottom line** (fig) lo esencial, lo primordial
boudoir [buˈdwɑr] *s* tocador *m*
bough [bau] *s* rama
bouillon [ˈbʊljɑn] *s* caldo
boulder [ˈboldər] *s* pedrejón *m*
boulevard [ˈbʊləˌvɑrd] *s* bulevar *m*
bounce [baʊns] *s* rebote *m* ‖ *tr* hacer botar; (slang) despedir ‖ *intr* botar, rebotar; saltar; **to bounce along** dar saltos al andar
bouncer [ˈbaʊnsər] *s* (coll) gorila *m*, apagabroncas *m*
bouncing [ˈbaʊnsɪŋ] *adj* frescachón, vigoroso; (*baby*) gordinflón
bound [baʊnd] *adj* atado, ligado; (*book*) encuadernado; dispuesto, propenso; puesto en aprendizaje; **bound for** con destino a, con rumbo a; **bound in boards** (bb) encartonado, en cartoné; **bound up in** entregado a, muy adicto a; absorto en ‖ *s* salto; (*of a ball*) bote *m;* límite *m*, confín *m;* **bounds** región, comarca; **out of bounds** fuera de los límites; **within bounds** a raya
bounda•ry [ˈbaʊndəri] *s* (*pl* **-ries**) límite *m*, frontera; (*established*) parámetro
boundary mark *s* (*annotation*) acotamiento
boundary stone *s* mojón *m*
bounder [ˈbaʊndər] *s* persona vulgar y malcriada
boundless [ˈbaʊndlɪs] *adj* ilimitado, inmenso
bountiful [ˈbaʊntɪfəl] *adj* generoso, liberal; abundante

boun•ty [ˈbaʊnti] *s* (*pl* **-ties**) generosidad, liberalidad; don *m,* favor *m;* galardón *m,* premio; (*bonus*) prima; (mil) premio de enganche
bouquet [buˈke] *s* ramillete *m;* (*aroma of a wine*) nariz *f*
bourgeois [ˈbʊrʒwɑ] *adj & s* burgués *m*
bourgeoisie [ˌbʊrʒwɑˈzi] *s* burguesía
bout [baʊt] *s* encuentro; rato; (*of an illness*) ataque *m*
bow [baʊ] *s* inclinación, reverencia; (*of a ship*) proa ‖ *tr* inclinar (*la cabeza*) ‖ *intr* inclinarse; **to bow and scrape** hacer reverencias obsequiosas; **to bow to** saludar, inclinarse delante ‖ [bo] *s* (*for shooting an arrow*) arco; lazo, nudo; (mus) arco; (*stroke of bow*) (mus) arqueada ‖ *tr* (mus) tocar con arco ‖ *intr* arquearse
bowdlerize [ˈbaʊdləˌraɪz] *tr* expurgar
bowel [ˈbaʊ•əl] *s* intestino; **bowels** intestinos; (*inner part*) entrañas
bowel movement *s* evacuación del vientre; **to have a bowel movement** evacuar el vientre
bower [ˈbaʊ•ər] *s* emparrado, glorieta
bower•y [ˈbaʊ•əri] *adj* frondoso, sombreado ‖ *s* (*pl* **-ies**) finca, granja
bowknot [ˈboˌnɑt] *s* lazada
bowl [bol] *s* (*for soup or broth*) escudilla, cuenco; (*for washing hands*) jofaina, palangana; (*of toilet*) cubeta, taza; (*of fountain*) tazón *m;* (*of spoon*) paleta; (*of pipe*) hornillo; (*hollow place*) concavidad, cuenco ‖ *tr* — **to bowl over** tumbar ‖ *intr* jugar a los bolos; **to bowl along** rodar
bowlegged [ˈboˌlɛgd] o [ˈboˌlɛgɪd] *adj* patiestevado
bowler [ˈbolər] *s* jugador *m* de bolos; (Brit) sombrero hongo
bowling [ˈbolɪŋ] *s* juego de bolos, boliche *m*
bowling alley *s* bolera, boliche *m*
bowling green *s* bolera encespada
bowshot [ˈboˌʃɑt] *s* tiro de flecha
bowsprit [ˈbaʊsprit] o [ˈbosprɪt] *s* bauprés *m*
bow tie [bo] *s* corbata de mariposa, pajarita
bowwow [ˈbaʊˌwaʊ] *interj* ¡guau! ‖ *s* guau guau *m*
box [bɑks] *s* caja; (*slap*) bofetada; (*plant*) boj *m;* (*in newspaper*) recuadro; (theat) palco ‖ *tr* encajonar; (*to slap*) abofetear; (naut) cuartear (*la aguja*) ‖ *intr* boxear
boxˈcarˈ *s* vagón *m* de carga cerrado
boxer [ˈbɑksər] *s* embalador *m;* (sport) boxeador *m*
boxers [ˈbɑksərz] o **boxer shorts** *spl* calzoncillos *mpl,* calzones *mpl* (Mex), interiores *mpl* (Col, Ven)
boxing [ˈbɑksɪŋ] *s* embalaje *m;* (sport) boxeo
boxing gloves *spl* guantes *mpl* de boxeo
box office *s* taquilla, despacho de localidades; boletería
boxˈ-ofˈfice hit *s* éxito de taquilla
box-office record *s* marca de taquilla
box pleat *s* pliegue *m* de tabla
box seat *s* asiento de palco
box spring *s* colchón *m* de resortes
boxˈwoodˈ *s* boj *m*
box wrench *s* llave *f* de tubo
boy [bɔɪ] *s* muchacho; (*servant*) mozo; (coll) compadre *m*
boycott [ˈbɔɪkɑt] *s* boicoteo ‖ *tr* boicotear
boyˈfriendˈ *s* (*sweetheart*) novio, enamorado; (*friend*) amigo, compañero
boyhood [ˈbɔɪhʊd] *s* muchachez *f;* muchachería
boyish [ˈbɔɪ•ɪʃ] *adj* amuchachado, muchachil
boy scout *s* niño explorador
bra [brɑ] *s* (coll) portasenos *m,* sostén *m,* sujetador *m*
brace [bres] *s* riostra; berbiquí *m;* **braces** (Brit) tirantes *mpl;* (*on teeth*) aparato de ortodoncia ‖ *tr* arriostrar; asegurar, vigorizar; **to brace oneself** (coll) cobrar ánimo ‖ *intr* — **to brace up** (coll) cobrar ánimo
brace and bit *s* berbiquí y barrena
bracelet [ˈbreslɪt] *s* brazalete *m,* pulsera
bracer [ˈbresər] *s* (coll) trago de licor
bracing [ˈbresɪŋ] *adj* fortificante, tónico
bracket [ˈbrækɪt] *s* puntal *m,* soporte *m;* ménsula, repisa; (*mark used in printing*) corchete *m;* clase *f,* categoría ‖ *tr* acorchetar; agrupar
brackish [ˈbrækɪʃ] *adj* salobre
brad [bræd] *s* clavito, estaquilla
brag [bræg] *s* jactancia ‖ *v* (*pret & pp* **bragged;** *ger* **bragging**) *intr* jactarse, bravatear, palanganear
braggart [ˈbrægərt] *s* fanfarrón *m*
braid [bred] *s* (*flat strip of cotton, silk, etc.*) cinta, galón *m;* (*something braided*) trenza ‖ *tr* encintar, galonear; trenzar
Braille, braille [brel] *s* Braille *m*
brain [bren] *s* cerebro; **brains** cerebro, inteligencia; **to rack one's brains** devanarse los sesos ‖ *tr* descerebrar
brainchild *s* parto del ingenio
brainˈ-deadˈ *adj* clínicamente muerto
brain death *s* muerte *f* cerebral
brain drain *s* (coll) éxodo de técnicos, fuga de cerebros
brainless [ˈbrenlɪs] *adj* tonto, sin seso
brain power *s* capacidad mental
brainˈstormˈ *s* acceso de locura; confusión mental; buena idea, hallazgo
brain teaser *s* rompecabezas *m*
brain trust *s* grupo de peritos
brainˈwashˈ *tr* lavarle el cerebro a
brainˈwashˈing *s* lavado de cerebro
brain wave *s* onda encefálica; (coll) buena idea, hallazgo
brainˈworkˈ *s* trabajo intelectual
brain•y [ˈbreni] *adj* (*comp* **-ier;** *super* **-iest**) (coll) inteligente, sesudo
braise [brez] *tr* soasar y cocer (*la carne*) a fuego lento en vasija bien tapada
brake [brek] *s* freno; breque *m;* (*for dressing flax*) agramadera; (*thicket*) matorral *m;* (*fern*) helecho común ‖ *tr* frenar; brequear; agramar (*el lino o el cañamo*)

brake band *s* cinta de freno
brake drum *s* tambor *m* de freno
brake lining *s* forro o cinta de freno
brake•man [ˋbrekmən] *s* (*pl* **-men** [mən]) guardafrenos *m*
brake shoe *s* zapata de freno
bramble [ˋbræmbəl] *s* frambueso, zarza
bram•bly [ˋbræmbli] *adj* (*comp* **-blier;** *super* **-bliest**) zarzoso
bran [bræn] *s* afrecho, salvado
branch [bræntʃ] *s* (*of tree*) rama; (*smaller branch; branch cut from tree; of a science, etc.*) ramo; (*of vine*) sarmiento; (*of road, railroad*) ramal *m;* (*of candlestick, river, etc.*) brazo; (*of a store, bank*) sucursal *f* ‖ *intr* ramificarse; **to branch out** extender sus actividades
branch line *s* ramal *m,* línea de empalme
branch office *s* sucursal *f*
brand [brænd] *s* (*kind, make*) marca; (*trademark*) marca de fábrica; (*branding iron*) hierro de marcar; (*mark stamped with hot iron*) hierro; (*dishonor*) tizón *m* ‖ *tr* poner marca de fábrica en; herrar con hierro candente; tiznar (*la reputación de una persona*); **to brand as** tildar de
brandied [ˋbrændid] *adj* macerado en aguardiente
branding iron *s* hierro de marcar; fierro
brandish [ˋbrændɪʃ] *tr* blandear
brand′-new′ *adj* nuevecito, flamante
bran•dy [ˋbrændi] *s* (*pl* **-dies**) aguardiente *m*
brash [bræʃ] *adj* atrevido, impetuoso; descarado, respondón ‖ *s* acceso, ataque *m*
brass [bræs] *s* latón *m;* (*in army and navy*) (slang) los mandamases; (coll) descaro; **brasses** (mus) cobres *mpl*
brass band *s* banda, charanga
brass hat *s* (slang) espadón *m,* mandamás *m*
brassiere [brəˋzɪr] *s* portasenos *m,* sostén *m,* sujetador *m*
brass knuckles *spl* llave inglesa, bóxer *m*
brass tack *s* clavito dorado de tapicería; **to get down to brass tacks** (coll) entrar en materia
brass winds *spl* (mus) cobres *mpl,* instrumentos músicos de metal
brass•y [ˋbræsi] *adj* (*comp* **-ier;** *super* **-iest**) hecho de latón; metálico; descarado
brat [bræt] *s* rapaz *m,* mocoso, braguillas *m*
brava•do [brəˋvɑdo] *s* (*pl* **-does** o **-dos**) bravata
brave [brev] *adj* bravo, valiente ‖ *s* valiente *m;* guerrero indio norteamericano ‖ *tr* hacer frente a, arrostrar; desafiar, retar
bravery [ˋbrevəri] *s* bravura, valor *m*
bra•vo [ˋbrɑvo] *interj* ¡bravo! ‖ *s* (*pl* **-vos**) bravo
brawl [brɔl] *s* pendencia, reyerta; alboroto ‖ *intr* armar pendencia; alborotar
brawler [ˋbrɔlər] *s* pendenciero; alborotador *m*
brawn [brɔn] *s* fuerza musculosa
brawn•y [ˋbrɔni] *adj* (*comp* **-ier;** *super* **-iest**) fornido, musculoso
bray [bre] *s* rebuzno ‖ *intr* rebuznar
braze [brez] *s* soldadura de latón ‖ *tr* soldar con latón; cubrir de latón; adornar con latón
brazen [ˋbrezən] *adj* de latón; descarado ‖ *tr* — **to brazen through** llevar a cabo descaradamente
brazier [ˋbreʒər] *s* brasero
Brazil [brəˋzɪl] *s* el Brasil
Brazilian [brəˋzɪljən] *adj* & *s* brasileño
Brazil nut *s* castaña de Pará, coquito del Brasil
breach [britʃ] *s* (*opening*) abertura; (*in a wall*) brecha; abuso, violación ‖ *tr* abrir brecha en
breach of faith *s* falta de fidelidad
breach of peace *s* perturbación del orden público
breach of promise *s* incumplimiento de la palabra de matrimonio o de un acuerdo
breach of trust *s* abuso de confianza
bread [brɛd] *s* pan *m* ‖ *tr* empanar
bread and butter *s* pan *m* con mantequilla; (coll) pan de cada día
bread crumbs *spl* pan rallado
breaded [ˋbrɛdɪd] *adj* empanado
bread line *s* cola del pan
breadth [brɛdθ] *s* anchura; alcance *m,* extensión; (*e.g., of judgment*) amplitud *f*
bread′win′ner *s* sostén *m* de la familia
break [brek] *s* rompimiento; interrupción; intervalo, pausa; (*split*) hendidura, grieta; (*in prices*) baja; (*in clouds*) claro; (*from jail*) evasión, huída; (*among friends*) ruptura; (*luck, good or bad*) (slang) suerte *f;* (slang) disparate *m;* **to give someone a break** abrirle a uno la puerta ‖ *v* (*pret* **broke** [brok]; *pp* **broken**) *tr* romper, quebrar; cambiar (*un billete*); comunicar (*una mala noticia*); suspender (*relaciones*); faltar a (*la palabra*); batir (*un récord*); cortar (*un circuito*); quebrantar (*un testamento; un hábito*); romper, violar (*una ley*); violar (*un acuerdo*); levantar (*el campo*); (mil) degradar; **to break in** forzar (*una puerta*); **to break open** abrir por la fuerza ‖ *intr* romperse, quebrarse; reventar; aclarar (*el tiempo*); bajar (*los precios*); quebrantarse (*la salud*); **to break down** perder la salud; prorrumpir en llanto; **to break even** salir sin ganar ni perder; **to break in** entrar por fuerza; irrumpir en; **to break loose** desprenderse; escaparse; desbocarse (*un caballo*); desencadenarse (*una tempestad*); **to break out** estallar, declararse; (*in laughter, weeping*) romper; (*on the skin*) brotar granos; **to break through** abrirse paso; abrir paso por entre; **to break up** desmenuzarse; levantarse (*una reunión*); **to break with** romper con
breakable [ˋbrekəbəl] *adj* rompible
breakage [ˋbrekɪdʒ] *s* estropicio; indemnización por objetos rotos
break′down′ *s* mal éxito; avería, pana; (*in health*) colapso, surmenage *m;* (*in negotiations*) ruptura; análisis *m*
breaker [ˋbrekər] *s* cachón *m,* rompiente *m*
breakfast [ˋbrɛkfəst] *s* desayuno ‖ *intr* desayunar

breakfast food *s* cereal *m* para el desayuno
break'-in *s* allanamiento, entrada forzada
breaking and entering *s* allanamiento de morada
breaking point *s* punto de ruptura
break'neck' *adj* vertiginoso; **at breakneck speed** a mata caballo, a velocidad suicida
break of day *s* alba, amanecer *m*
break'through' *s* (mil) brecha, ruptura; (fig) descubrimiento sensacional
break'up' *s* disolución, dispersión; desplome *m;* (*in health*) postración
break'wa'ter *s* rompeolas *m,* escollera
breast [brɛst] *s* pecho, seno; (*of fowl*) pechuga; (*of garment*) pechera; **to make a clean breast of it** confesarlo todo
breast'bone' *s* esternón *m;* (*of fowl*) quilla
breast drill *s* berbiquí *m* de pecho
breast'pin' *s* alfiler *m* de pecho
breaststroke *s* brazada de pecho
breath [brɛθ] *s* aliento, respiración; **out of breath** sin aliento; **short of breath** corto de resuello; **to gasp for breath** respirar anhelosamente; **to hold one's breath** contener la respiración; **under one's breath** por lo bajo, en voz baja
breathe [brið] *tr* respirar; **to breathe one's last** dar el último suspiro ‖ *intr* respirar; **to breathe freely** cobrar aliento; **to breathe in** aspirar; **to breathe out** espirar
breathing exercises *spl* gimnasia respiratoria
breathing spell *s* respiro, rato de descanso
breathless [ˈbrɛθlɪs] *adj* falto de aliento, jadeante; intenso, vivo; sin aliento
breath'tak'ing *adj* conmovedor, imponente
breech [britʃ] *s* culata, recámara; **breeches** [ˈbrɪtʃiz] calzones *mpl;* (coll) pantalones *mpl;* **to wear the breeches** (coll) calzarse los pantalones
breed [brid] *s* casta, raza; clase *f,* especie *f* ‖ *v* (*pret & pp* **bred** [brɛd] *tr* criar, reproducir ‖ *intr* criar; criarse, reproducirse
breeder [ˈbridər] *s* (*of animals*) criador *m;* (*animal*) reproductor *m*
breeder reactor *s* (phys) reactor *m* reproductor
breeding animal *s* reproductor *m,* reproductora *f*
breeding [ˈbridɪŋ] *s* cría; crianza, modales *mpl;* **bad breeding** mala crianza; **good breeding** buena crianza
breeding ground *s* (zool) lugar de cría; (fig) semillero; (*liquid*) caldo de cultivo
breeze [briz] *s* brisa
breez•y [ˈbrizi] *adj* (*comp* **-ier;** *super* **-iest**) airoso; animado, vivo; (coll) desenvuelto, vivaracho
brethren [ˈbrɛðrɪn] *spl* hermanos o hermanas de una hermandad
brevi•ty [ˈbrɛvɪti] *s* (*pl* **-ties**) brevedad
brew [bru] *s* calderada de cerveza; mezcla ‖ *tr* fabricar (*cerveza*); preparar (*té*); (fig) tramar, urdir ‖ *intr* amenazar (*una tormenta*)
brewer [ˈbru•ər] *s* cervecero
brewer's yeast *s* levadura de cerveza
brewer•y [ˈbru•əri] *s* (*pl* **-ies**) cervecería, fábrica de cerveza
bribe [braɪb] *s* soborno, mordida (Mex); **to take bribes** comer maíz ‖ *tr* sobornar
briber•y [ˈbraɪbəri] *s* (*pl* **-ies**) soborno
bric-a-brac [ˈbrɪkə,bræk] *s* chucherías, curiosidades *fpl*
brick [brɪk] *s* ladrillo; (coll) buen sujeto ‖ *tr* enladrillar
brick'bat' *s* pedazo de ladrillo; (coll) palabra hiriente
brickkiln [ˈbrɪk,kɪln] *s* horno de ladrillero
bricklayer [ˈbrɪk,le•ər] *s* ladrillador *m*
brick'yard' *s* ladrillal *m*
bridal [ˈbraɪdəl] *adj* nupcial; de novia
bridal wreath *s* corona nupcial
bride [braɪd] *s* desposada, novia
bride'groom' *s* desposado, novio
bridesmaid [ˈbraɪdz,med] *s* madrina de boda
bridge [bridʒ] *s* puente *m;* (*of nose*) caballete *m;* (*card game*) bridge *m;* (dent) puente ‖ *tr* tender un puente sobre; salvar (*un obstáculo*); colmar, llenar (*un vacío*)
bridge'head' *s* (mil) cabeza de puente
bridge loan *s* préstamo puente
bridle [ˈbraɪdəl] *s* brida ‖ *tr* embridar ‖ *intr* engallarse, erguirse
bridle path *s* camino de herradura
brief [brif] *adj* breve, corto, conciso ‖ *s* resumen *m;* (law) escrito; **in brief** en resumen ‖ *tr* resumir; dar consejos anticipados a; dar informes a
brief case *s* cartera, maletín *m,* portafolio
briefing [ˈbrifɪŋ] *s* órdenes *fpl,* instrucciones; (*of the press*) informe *m,* sesión informativa
brier [ˈbraɪ•ər] *s* zarza; brezo blanco
brig [brɪg] *s* (naut) bergantín *m;* prisión en buque de guerra
brigade [brɪˈged] *s* brigada
brigadier [,brɪgəˈdɪr] *s* general *m* de brigada
brigand [ˈbrɪgənd] *s* bandolero
brigantine [ˈbrɪgən,tin] *s* (naut) bergantín *m* goleta
bright [braɪt] *adj* brillante; (*e.g., day*) claro; (*color*) subido; listo, inteligente, despierto; (*idea, thought*) luminoso; (*disposition*) alegre, vivo
brighten [ˈbraɪtən] *tr* abrillantar; alegrar, avivar ‖ *intr* avivarse; alegrarse; despejarse (*el cielo*)
bright lights *spl* luces *fpl* brillantes; (aut) luces de carretera, luces largas, luces altas
brilliance [ˈbrɪljəns] o **brilliancy** [ˈbrɪljənsi] *s* brillantez *f,* brillo
brilliant [ˈbrɪljənt] *adj* brillante
brillantine [ˈbrɪljəntin] *s* brillantina
brim [brɪm] *s* borde *m;* (*of hat*) ala
brim'stone' *s* azufre *m*
brine [braɪn] *s* salmuera, agua salobre
bring [brɪŋ] *v* (*pret & pp* **brought** [brɔt]) *tr* traer; llevar; **to bring about** efectuar; **to bring back** devolver; **to bring down** abatir; **to bring forth** sacar a luz; **to bring in** traer

a colación; servir (*una comida*); introducir, presentar; **to bring into play** poner en juego; **to bring on** causar, producir; **to bring out** sacar; presentar al público; **to bring suit** poner pleito; **to bring to** sacar de un desmayo; **to bring together** reunir; confrontar; reconciliar; **to bring to pass** efectuar, llevar a cabo; **to bring up** arrimar (*p.ej., una silla*); educar, criar; traer a colación; **to bring upon oneself** atraerse (*un infortunio*)

bringing-up [ˈbrɪŋɪŋˈʌp] *s* educación, crianza

brink [brɪŋk] *s* borde *m,* margen *m;* **on the brink of** al borde de

brink'man•ship *s* política del borde del abismo

brisk [brɪsk] *adj* animado, vivo, vivaz

bristle [ˈbrɪsəl] *s* cerda ‖ *intr* erizarse, encresparse; (*to be visibly annoyed*) encresparse

bris•tly [ˈbrɪsli] *adj* (*comp* **-tlier;** *super* **-tliest**) cerdoso, erizado

Britannic [brɪˈtænɪk] *adj* británico

britches *var* de **breeches**

British [ˈbrɪtɪʃ] *adj* británico ‖ **the British** los britanos

Britisher [ˈbrɪtɪʃər] *s* britano

British Isles *sp* Islas Británicas

Briton [ˈbrɪtən] *s* britano

Brittany [ˈbrɪtəni] *s* Bretaña

brittle [ˈbrɪtəl] *adj* quebradizo, frágil

broach [brotʃ] *s* (*skewer*) asador *m,* espetón *m;* (*ornamental pin*) broche *m,* prendedero ‖ *tr* sacar a colación

broad [brɔd] *adj* ancho; liberal, tolerante; (*day, noon, etc.*) pleno

broad'cast' *s* radiodifusión, transmisión; audición, programa radiotelefónico ‖ *v* (*pret & pp* **-cast**) *tr* difundir, esparcir ‖ (*pret & pp* **-cast** o **-casted**) *tr* radiodifundir, radiar, emitir

broadcasting station *s* emisora, estación de radiodifusión

broad'cloth' *s* paño fino

broaden [ˈbrɔdən] *tr* ensanchar ‖ *intr* ensancharse

broad'loom' *adj* tejido en telar ancho y en color sólido

broad-minded [ˈbrɔdˈmaɪndɪd] *adj* tolerante, de amplias miras

broad-shouldered [ˈbrɔdˈʃoldərd] *adj* ancho de espaldas

broad'side' *s* (naut) costado; (naut) andanada; (coll) torrente *m* de injurias

broad'sword' *s* espada ancha

Broad'way' *s* distrito de salas de teatro de Nueva York

brocade [broˈked] *s* brocado

broccoli [ˈbrɑkəli] *s* brécol *m,* brécoles *mpl*

brochure [broˈʃʊr] *s* folleto

brogue [brog] *s* acento irlandés

broil [brɔɪl] *tr* asar a la parrilla ‖ *intr* asarse

broiler [ˈbrɔɪlər] *s* parrilla; pollo para asar a la parrilla

broke [brok] *adj*—**to be broke** (coll) estar pelado, estar a dos velas, estar planchado (Chile); **to go for broke** (coll) jugarse el todo por el todo

broken [ˈbrokən] *adj* roto, quebrado; agotado; amansado; (*accent*) chapurrado; suelto

bro'ken-down' *adj* abatido; descompuesto; destartalado

broken-hearted [ˈbrokənˈhartɪd] *adj* abrumado por el dolor

broker [ˈbrokər] *s* corredor *m*

brokerage [ˈbrokərɪdʒ] *s* corretaje *m*

bromide [ˈbromaɪd] *s* bromuro; (slang) trivialidad

bromine [ˈbromin] *s* bromo

bronchitis [brɑŋˈkaɪtɪs] *s* bronquitis *f*

bron•co [ˈbrɑŋko] *s* (*pl* **-cos**) potro cerril

bron'co•bust'er *s* domador *m* de potros; vaquero

bronze [brɑnz] *adj* bronceado ‖ *s* bronce *m* ‖ *tr* broncear ‖ *intr* broncearse

brooch [brotʃ] o [brutʃ] *s* alfiler *m* de pecho, prendedero, pasador *m*

brood [brud] *s* cría; nidada; casta, raza; (*offspring*) (pej) prole *f* ‖ *tr* empollar ‖ *intr* enclocar; **to brood on** meditar con preocupación

brook [brʊk] *s* arroyo ‖ *tr* — **to brook no** no tolerar, no aguantar

broom [brum] o [brʊm] *s* escoba; (bot) hiniesta

broom'corn' *s* sorgo

broom'stick' *s* palo de escoba

bros. *abbr* **brothers**

broth [brɔθ] o [brɑθ] *s* caldo, potaje *m*

brothel [ˈbrɑθəl] o [ˈbrɑðəl] *s* burdel *m;* (Mex) congal *m*

brother [ˈbrʌðər] *s* hermano

brotherhood [ˈbrʌðər,hʊd] *s* (*relationship*) fraternidad; (*association*) hermandad; (eccl) cofradía

broth'er-in-law' *s* (*pl* **brothers-in-law**) cuñado, hermano político; (*husband of one's wife's or husband's sister*) concuñado

brotherly [ˈbrʌðərli] *adj* fraternal

brow [braʊ] *s* (*forehead*) frente *f;* (*eyebrow*) ceja; **to knit one's brow** fruncir las cejas

brow'beat' *v* (*pret* **-beat;** *pp* **beaten**) *tr* intimidar con mirada ceñuda

brown [braʊn] *adj* (*eyes; dress; shoe; paint*) marrón, café; (*hair*) castaño; (*skin; egg*) moreno; (*suntanned*) bronceado, tostado por el sol ‖ *s* marrón *m,* castaño, moreno ‖ *tr* poner moreno; tostar, quemar, broncear; (culin) dorar

brown ale *s* cerveza negra

brown bear *s* oso pardo

brown bread *s* pan moreno *or* integral

brown'fields' *spl* terrenos *mpl* contaminados por residuos peligrosos

brownie [ˈbra ni] *s* (*sprite*) duende *m;* (*cake*) bizcocho de chocolate y nueces; **Brownie** (*girl scout*) niña exploradora

brownish [ˈbraʊnɪʃ] *adj* que tira a moreno

brown'-out' *s* apagón *m* parcial

brown rice *s* arroz *m* integral

brown'shirt' *s* camisa marrón

brown'stone *s* piedra rojiza
brown study *s* absorción, pensamiento profundo, ensimismamlento
brown sugar *s* azúcar terciado
brown wrapping paper *s* papel *m* de estraza
browse [braʊz] *intr* (*to nibble at twigs*) ramonear; (*to graze*) pacer; hojear un libro ociosamente; **to browse about** o **around** curiosear
bruise [bruz] *s* contusión, magulladura, magullón *m* || *tr* contundir, magullar || *intr* contundirse, magullarse
brunet [bru'nɛt] *adj* moreno || *s* moreno (*hombre moreno*)
brunette [bru'nɛt] *s* morena (*mujer morena*)
brunt [brʌnt] *s* fuerza, choque *m,* empuje *m;* (*e.g., of a battle*) peso, (lo) más reñido
brush [brʌʃ] *s* brocha, cepillo, escobilla; (*stroke*) brochada; (*light touch*) roce *m;* (*brief encounter*) encuentro, escaramuza; (*growth of bushes*) maleza; (elec) escobilla || *tr* acepillar; (*to graze*) rozar; **to brush aside** echar a un lado || *intr* pasar ligeramente; **to brush up on** repasar
brush'-off' *s* (coll) despedida brusca; **to give the brush-off to** (coll) darle calabazas a
brush'wood' *s* broza, ramojo
brusque [brʌsk] *adj* brusco, rudo
brusqueness ['brʌsknɪs] *s* brusquedad
Brussels ['brʌsəlz] *s* Bruselas
Brussels sprouts *spl* bretones *mpl,* col *f* de Bruselas, repollitos de Bruselas
brutal ['brutəl] *adj* brutal, bestial
brutali•ty [bru'tælɪti] *s* (*pl* **-ties**) brutalidad, crueldad
brutalization [,brutələ'zeʃən] *s* embrutecimiento
brute [brut] *adj* bruto; (*force*) inconsciente, ciego || *s* bruto
brutish ['brutɪʃ] *adj* abrutado, estúpido
bu. *abbr* **bushel**
bubble ['bʌbəl] *s* burbuja; ampolla; ilusión, quimera || *intr* burbujear; **to bubble over** desbordar, rebosar
bubble bath *s* baño de espuma
bubble gum *s* chicle *m* de globo
buck [bʌk] *s* (*goat*) cabrón *m;* (*deer*) gamo; (*rabbit*) conejo; (*of a horse*) corveta, encorvada; (*youth*) pisaverde *m;* (slang) dólar *m;* **to pass the buck** (coll) echar la carga a otro || *tr* hacer frente a, resistir a; (*to butt*) acornear, topetar; colar (*la ropa*); **to buck up** (coll) alentar, animar || *intr* botarse, encorvarse; **to buck against** embestir contra
bucket ['bʌkɪt] *s* balde *m,* cubo; (*of a well*) pozal *m;* **to kick the bucket** (slang) estirar la pata, liar el petate
bucket seat *s* baquet *m*
buckle ['bʌkəl] *s* hebilla; (*bend, bulge*) alabeo, pandeo || *tr* abrochar con hebilla || *intr* (*to bend, bulge*) alabearse, pandear; **to buckle down to** (coll) dedicarse con empeño a
buck private *s* (slang) soldado raso
buckram ['bʌkrəm] *s* zangala; (bb) bocací *m,* bucarán *m*
buck'saw' *s* sierra de bastidor
buck'shot' *s* postas
buck'tooth' *s* (*pl* **-teeth**) diente *m* saliente
buck'wheat' *s* alforfón *m,* trigo sarraceno
bud [bʌd] *s* botón *m,* brote *m;* **to nip in the bud** cortar de raíz || *v* (*pret & pp* **budded;** *ger* **budding**) *intr* abotonar, brotar
Buddha ['budə] *s* Buda *m*
bud•dy ['bʌdi] *s* (*pl* **-dies**) (coll) camarada *m,* cumpa *m* (coll) muchachito
budge [bʌdʒ] *tr* mover || *intr* moverse
budget ['bʌdʒɪt] *s* presupuesto || *tr* presuponer, presupuestar
budgetary ['bʌdʒɪ,tɛri] *adj* presupuestario
buff [bʌf] *adj* de ante || *s* (*leather*) ante *m;* color *m* de ante; chaqueta de ante; rueda pulidora; (coll) piel desnuda; (*fan, enthusiast*) aficionado || *tr* dar color de ante a; pulimentar
buffa•lo ['bʌfə,lo] *s* (*pl* **-loes** o **-los**) búfalo || *tr* (slang) intimidar
buffer ['bʌfər] *s* amortiguador *m* de choques; tope *m,* paragolpes *m;* pulidor *m;* (compu) buffer *m*
buffer state *s* estado tapón
buffet [bʊ'fe] *s* (*piece of furniture*) aparador *m;* restaurante *m* de estación || ['bʌfɪt] *tr* abofetear, golpear, pegar
buffet car *s* coche *m* bar
buffet lunch *s* servicio de bufet
buffet supper *s* ambigú *m,* bufet *m*
buffoon [bə'fun] *s* bufón *m,* payaso
buffooner•y [bə'funəri] *s* (*pl* **-ies**) bufonada, chocarrería
bug [bʌg] *s* insecto, bicho, sabandija; microbio; (*bedbug*) (Brit) chinche *f;* (coll) defecto; (coll) micrófono escondido; (slang) entusiasta *mf* || *v* (*pret & pp* **bugged;** *ger* **bugging**) *tr* (*spy*) esconder un micrófono en; (*bother*) fastidiar
bug'bear' *s* espantajo; aversión
bug•gy ['bʌgi] *adj* (*comp* **-gier;** *super* **-giest**) infestado de bichos; (slang) loco || *s* (*pl* **-gies**) calesa
bugle ['bjugəl] *s* corneta
bugle call *s* toque *m* de corneta
bugler ['bjuglər] *s* corneta *m*
build [bɪld] *s* forma, hechura, figura; (*of human being*) talle *m* || *v* (*pret & pp* **built** [bɪlt]) *tr* construir, edificar; componer; establecer, fundar; crearse (*p.ej., una clientela*)
builder ['bɪldər] *s* constructor *m;* aparejador *m,* maestro de obras
building ['bɪldɪŋ] *s* construcción; edificio; (*one of several in a group*) pabellón *m*
building and loan association *s* sociedad *f* de crédito para la construcción
building code *s* código de edificación
building lot *s* solar *m*
building site *s* terreno para construir
building trades *spl* oficios de edificación

build′-up′ *s* acumulación, formación; (coll) propaganda anticipada
built′in′ *adj* integrante, incorporado, empotrado
built′-up′ *adj* armado, montado; (*land*) aglomerado
bulb [bʌlb] *s* (*of plant*) bulbo; (*of thermometer*) bola, cubeta; (*of syringe*) pera; (*of electric light*) ampolla, bombilla
Bulgaria [bʌlˈgɛrɪ•ə] *s* Bulgaria
Bulgarian [bʌlˈgɛrɪ•ən] *adj & s* búlgaro
bulge [bʌldʒ] *s* protuberancia, bulto, bombeo; **to get the bulge on** (coll) llevar la ventaja a ‖ *intr* hacer bulto, bombearse
bulging [ˈbʌldʒɪŋ] *adj* salido; (*pockets*) repleto; (*eyes*) saltón
bulimia [bjuˈlimi•ə] *s* bulimia
bulk [bʌlk] *s* bulto, volumen *m;* (*main mass*) grueso; **in bulk** a granel ‖ *intr* abultar, hacer bulto; tener importancia
bulk′head′ *s* mamparo; tabique hermético
bulk•y [ˈbʌlki] *adj* (*comp* **-ier;** *super* **-iest**) abultado, voluminoso, grueso
bull [bʊl] *s* toro; (*in stockmarket*) alcista *m;* (*papal document*) bula; (*absurdity*) disparate *m;* **to take the bull by the horns** asir al toro por las astas ‖ *tr* — **to bull the market** jugar al alza
bull′dog′ *s* dogo, perro de presa
bulldoze [ˈbʊl,doz] *tr* coaccionar, intimidar con amenazas
bulldozer [ˈbʊl,dozər] *s* explanadora de empuje, empujatierra
bullet [ˈbʊlɪt] *s* bala
bulletin [ˈbʊlətɪn] *s* boletín *m;* comunicado; (*of a school*) anuario
bulletin board *s* tablilla
bul′let•proof′ *adj* a prueba de balas, blindado, antibalas
bull′fight′ *s* corrida de toros
bull′fight′er *s* torero
bull′fight′ing *adj* torero ‖ *s* toreo, los toros
bull′finch′ *s* (orn) camachuelo
bull′frog′ *s* rana toro
bull-headed [ˈbʊl,hɛdɪd] *adj* obstinado, terco
bull′horn′ *s* megáfono
bullion [ˈbʊljən] *s* oro en barras, plata en barras; (*twisted fringe*) entorchado
bullish [ˈbʊlɪʃ] *adj* obstinado; (*market*) en alza; (*speculator*) alcista; optimista
bullock [ˈbʊlək] *s* buey *m*
bull market *s* (com) mercado alcista
bull′pen′ *s* (taur) toril *m;* (*jail*) (coll) prevención, calabozo; (baseball) (*place*) zona de calentamiento; (*pitchers*) lanzadores *mpl* de reserva
bull′ring′ *s* plaza de toros, coso taurino
bull session *s* (coll) charla
bull's-eye [ˈbʊlz,aɪ] *s* (*of a target*) diana; (archit, meteor, naut) ojo de buey; **to hit the bull's-eye** hacer diana
bul•ly [ˈbʊli] *adj* (coll) excelente, magnífico ‖ *s* (*pl* **-lies**) matón *m,* valentón *m* ‖ *v* (*pret & pp* **-lied**) *tr* intimidar, maltratar
bulrush [ˈbʊl,rʌʃ] *s* junco; junco de laguna; (*Typha*) anea, espadaña; (Bib) papiro
bulwark [ˈbʊlwərk] *s* baluarte *m* ‖ *tr* abaluartar; defender, proteger
bum [bʌm] *s* (slang) holgazán *m;* (slang) vagabundo; (slang) mendigo ‖ *v* (*pret & pp* **bummed;** *ger* **bumming**) *tr* (slang) mendigar ‖ *intr* holgazanear; (slang) vagabundear; (slang) mendigar
bumblebee [ˈbʌmbəl,bi] *s* abejorro
bump [bʌmp] *s* (*collision*) topetón *m;* (*shake*) sacudida; (*on falling*) batacazo; (*of plane in rough air*) rebote *m;* (*swelling*) hinchazón *f,* chichón *m;* protuberancia ‖ *tr* dar contra, topar; (*to bruise*) abollar ‖ *intr* chocar; dar sacudidas; **to bump into** tropezar con; encontrarse con
bumper [ˈbʌmpər] *adj* (coll) abundante, grande ‖ *s* tope *m,* paratopes *m;* (aut) amortiguador *m,* parachoques *m;* vaso lleno
bumper cars *spl* autos de choque
bumpkin [ˈbʌmpkɪn] *s* patán *m,* palurdo
bumptious [ˈbʌmpʃəs] *adj* engreído, presuntuoso
bump•y [ˈbʌmpi] *adj* (*comp* **-ier;** *super* **-iest**) (*ground*) desigual, áspero; (*air*) agitado
bun [bʌn] *s* buñuelo, bollo; (*of hair*) castaña
bunch [bʌntʃ] *s* manojo, puñado; (*of grapes, bananas, etc.*) racimo; (*of flowers*) ramillete *m;* (*of people*) grupo ‖ *tr* agrupar, juntar ‖ *intr* agruparse; arracimarse
bundle [ˈbʌndəl] *s* atado, bulto, lío, paquete *m;* (*of papers*) legajo; (*of wood*) haz *m;* (compu) bundle *m* ‖ *tr* atar, liar, empaquetar, envolver; **to bundle off** despedir precipitadamente; **to bundle up** arropar ‖ *intr* — **to bundle up** arroparse
bung [bʌŋ] *s* bitoque *m,* tapón *m*
bungalow [ˈbʌŋgə,lo] *s* bungalow *m,* casa de una sola planta
bungee [ˈbʌndʒi] *s* correa elástica
bungee jumping *s* banyi *m*
bung′hole′ *s* piquera, boca de tonel
bungle [ˈbʌŋgəl] *s* chapucería ‖ *tr & intr* chapucear
bungler [ˈbʌŋglər] *s* chapucero
bungling [ˈbvŋglɪŋ] *adj* chapucero ‖ *s* chapucería
bunion [ˈbʌnjən] *s* juanete *m*
bunk [bʌŋk] *s* tarima; (slang) palabrería vana, música celestial
bunk bed *s* litera, cucheta, cama camarote
bunker [ˈbʌŋkər] *s* carbonera; (mil) fortín *m,* búnker *m*
bunk′house′ *s* barraca, barracón *m*
bun•ny [ˈbʌni] *s* (*pl* **-nies**) conejito
bunting [ˈbʌntɪŋ] *s* banderas colgadas como adorno; (*of a ship*) empavesado; (orn) gorrión triguero
buoy [bɔɪ] o [ˈbu•i] *s* boya; boya salvavidas, guindola ‖ *tr* — **to buoy up** mantener a flote; animar, alentar

buoyancy [ˈbɔɪ•ənsi] o [ˈbujənsi] *s* flotación; alegría, animación
buoyant [ˈbɔɪ•ənt] o [ˈbujənt] *adj* boyante; alegre, animado
bur [bʌr] *s* erizo, vilano
burble [ˈbʌrbəl] *s* burbujeo ‖ *intr* burbujear
burden [ˈbʌrdən] *s* carga; (*of a speech*) tema *m;* (*of a poem*) estribillo ‖ *tr* cargar; agobiar, gravar
burden of proof *s* peso de la prueba
burdensome [ˈbʌrdənsəm] *adj* gravoso, oneroso
burdock [ˈbʌrdak] *s* bardana, cadillo
bureau [ˈbjʊro] *s* cómoda; despacho, oficina; departamento, negociado
bureaucra•cy [bjʊˈrɑkrəsi] *s* (*pl* **-cies**) burocracia; funcionariado
bureaucrat [ˈbjʊrə,kræt] *s* burócrata *mf*
bureaucratic [,bjʊrəˈkrætɪk] *adj* burocrático
burgeoning [ˈbʌrdʒənɪn] *adj* creciente, floreciente
burger [ˈbʌrgər] *s* (coll) hamburguesa
burgess [ˈbʌrdʒɪs] *s* burgués *m,* ciudadano; alcalde *m* de un pueblo o villa
burglar [ˈbʌrglər] *s* escalador *m*
burglar alarm *s* alarma de ladrones, alarma antirrobo
bur′glar•proof′ *adj* a prueba de escaladores; antirrobo
burglar•y [ˈbʌrgləri] *s* (*pl* **-ies**) robo con escalamiento
Burgundian [bərˈgʌndɪ•ən] *adj & s* borgoñón *m*
Burgundy [ˈbʌrgəndi] *s* la Borgoña; (*wine*) borgoña *m*
burial [ˈbɛrɪ•əl] *s* entierro
burial ground *s* cementerio
burlap [ˈbʌrlæp] *s* arpillera
burlesque [bərˈlɛsk] *adj* burlesco, festivo ‖ *s* parodia ‖ *tr* parodiar
burlesque show *s* espectáculo de bailes y cantos groseros, music-hall *m;* bataclán *m* (SAm)
bur•ly [ˈbʌrli] *adj* (*comp* **-lier;** *super* **-liest**) fornido, corpulento, membrudo
Burma [ˈbʌrmə] *s* Birmania
Bur•mese [bərˈmiz] *adj* birmano ‖ *s* (*pl* **-mese**) birmano
burn [bʌrn] *s* quemadura, quemazón *f* ‖ *v* (*pret & pp* **burned** o **burnt** [bʌrnt]) *tr* quemar ‖ *intr* quemar, quemarse; estar encendido (*p.ej., un faro*); **to burn out** quemarse (*un fusible*); fundirse (*una bombilla*); **to burn within** requemarse
burner [ˈbʌrnər] *s* (*of furnace*) quemador *m;* (*of gas fixture or lamp*) mechero
burning [ˈbʌrnɪŋ] *adj* ardiente ‖ *s* quema, incendio
burning question *s* cuestión palpitante
burnish [ˈbʌrnɪʃ] *s* bruñido ‖ *tr* bruñir ‖ *intr* bruñirse
burnoose [bərˈnus] *s* albornoz *m*
burn′out′ *s* (coll) agotamiento, surmenage *m;* (aer) tercera fase
burnt almond [bʌrnt] *s* almendra tostada
burp [bʌrp] *s* eructo ‖ *tr* (*a baby*) hacer eructar ‖ *intr* eructar
burqa [ˈbʌrkɑ] *s* (*body veil that covers a woman from head to toe*) burca (*velo para tapar a una mujer de pies a cabeza*)
burr [bʌr] *s* (*of plant*) erizo; (*of cut in metal*) rebaba
burrow [ˈbʌro] *s* madriguera, conejera ‖ *tr* hacer madrigueras en; socavar ‖ *intr* amadrigarse; esconderse
bursar [ˈbʌrsər] *s* tesorero universitario
burst [bʌrst] *s* explosión, reventón *m,* estallido; (*of machine gun*) ráfaga; salida brusca ‖ *v* (*pret & pp* **burst**) *tr* reventar ‖ *intr* reventar, reventarse; partirse (*el corazón*); **to burst into** irrumpir en (*un cuarto*); desatarse en (*amenazas*); prorrumpir en (*lágrimas*); **to burst out crying** deshacerse en lágrimas; **to burst with laughter** reventar de risa
bur•y [ˈbɛri] *v* (*pret & pp* **-ied**) *tr* enterrar; **to be buried in thought** estar absorto en meditación; **to bury the hatchet** hacer la paz, echar pelillos a la mar
burying ground *s* cementerio
bus. *abbr* **business**
bus [bʌs] *s* (*pl* **busses** o **buses**) autobús *m;* (compu) bus *m* ‖ *tr* llevar en un autobús
bus boy *s* ayudante *m* de camarero
bus•by [ˈbʌzbi] *s* (*pl* **-bies**) morrión *m* de húsar, colbac *m*
bush [bʊʃ] *s* arbusto; (*scrubby growth*) matorral *m,* monte *m;* **to beat about the bush** andar con rodeos
bushel [ˈbʊʃəl] *s* medida para áridos (*35,24 litros en E.U.A. y 36,38 litros en Inglaterra*)
bushing [ˈbʊʃɪŋ] *s* buje *m,* forro
bush•y [ˈbʊʃi] *adj* (*comp* **-ier;** *super* **-iest**) arbustivo; peludo, lanudo; espeso
business [ˈbɪznɪs] *adj* comercial, de negocios ‖ *s* negocio, comercio; (*company, concern*) empresa; (*job, employment*) empleo, oficio; (*matter*) asunto, cuestión; (*duty*) obligación; (*right*) derecho; **on business** por negocios; **to have no business to** no tener derecho a; **to make it one's business to** proponerse; **to mean business** (coll) obrar en serio, hablar en serio; **to mind one's own business** no meterse en lo que no le importa a uno; **to send about one's business** mandar a paseo
business applications *spl* (compu) ofimática
business dinner *s* cena de negocios
business district *s* barrio comercial
businesslike [ˈbɪznɪs,laɪk] *adj* práctico, sistemático, serio
business lunch *s* comida de negocios
business•man [ˈbɪznɪs,mæn] *s* (*pl* **-men** [,mɛn]) comerciante *m,* hombre *m* de negocios
business suit *s* traje *m* de calle
business trip *s* viaje *m* de negocios
bus′iness wom′an *s* mujer *f* de negocios
busing [ˈbʌsɪŋ] *s* (educ) *transporte diario de*

escolares en autobús fuera de su zona para favorecer la integración racial

bus•man [ˈbʌsmən] *s* (*pl* **-men** [mən]) conductor *m* de autobús

bust [bʌst] *s* busto; (*of woman*) pecho; (slang) fracaso, borrachera || *tr* (slang) reventar, romper; (slang) arruinar; (slang) golpear, pegar || *intr* (slang) reventar, fracasar

buster [ˈbʌstər] *s* (coll) muchachito

bustle [ˈbʌsəl] *s* (*of woman's dress*) polisón *m;* (*activity*) alboroto, bullicio || *intr* ajetrearse, menearse

bus•y [ˈbɪzi] *adj* (*comp* **-ier;** *super* **-iest**) ocupado; (*e.g., street*) concurrido; (*medling*) intruso, entremetido || *v* (*pret & pp* **-ied**) *tr* ocupar; **to busy oneself with** ocuparse de

busybod•y [ˈbɪzɪ,bɑdi] *s* (*pl* **-ies**) entremetido, fisgón *m*

busy signal *s* (telp) señal *f* de ocupado

but [bʌt] *adv* sólo, solamente, no . . . más que; **but for** a no ser por; **but little** muy poco || *prep* excepto, salvo; **all but** casi || *conj* pero; sino, p.ej., **nobody came but John** no vino sino Juan

butcher [ˈbʊtʃər] *s* carnicero; pesero (CAm, Col, Ven) || *tr* matar (*reses para el consumo*); dar muerte a; (*to bungle*) chapucear

butcher knife *s* cuchilla de carnicero

butcher shop *s* carnicería; pesa (CAm, Col, Ven)

butcher•y [ˈbʌtʃəri] *s* (*pl* **-ies**) (*wanton slaughter*) matanza, carnicería

butler [ˈbʌtlər] *s* despensero, mayordomo

butt [bʌt] *s* (*of gun*) culata; (*of cigaret*) colilla, punta; (*of horned animal*) cabezada, topetada, topetón *m;* (*target*) blanco; hazmerreír *m;* (*large cask*) pipa; (*rear end*) pompis *m* || *tr* topar, topetar; acornear || *intr* dar cabezadas; **to butt against** confinar con; **to butt in** (slang) entremeterse

butter [ˈbʌtər] *s* mantequilla || *tr* untar con mantequilla; **to butter up** (coll) adular, lisonjear

but′ter•cup′ *s* botón *m* de oro

butter dish *s* mantequillera

but′ter•fly′ *s* (*pl* **-flies**) mariposa; (*swimming stroke*) estilo mariposa

butter knife *s* cuchillo mantequillero

but′ter•milk′ *s* leche *f* de manteca

but′ter•scotch′ *s* bombón *m* escocés, bombón hecho con azúcar terciado y mantequilla

buttocks [ˈbʌtəks] *spl* nalgas; fundillo (Cuba, Mex)

button [ˈbʌtən] *s* botón *m;* (*switch*) botón; (compu) botón || *tr* abotonar, abrocharse

but′ton•hole′ *s* ojal *m* || *tr* detener con conversación

but′ton•hook *s* abotonador *m*

but′ton•wood′ tree *s* plátano de occidente

buttress [ˈbʌtrɪs] *s* contrafuerte *m;* (fig) apoyo, sostén *m* || *tr* estribar; (fig) apoyar, sostener

butt weld *s* soldadura a tope

buxom [ˈbʌksəm] *adj* rolliza, frescachona

buy [baɪ] *s* (coll) compra; (*bargain*) (coll) ganga || *v* (*pret & pp* **bought** [bɔt]) *tr* comprar; **to buy back** recomprar; **to buy off** comprar, sobornar; **to buy out** comprar la parte de (*un socio*); **to buy up** acaparar

buyer [ˈbaɪ•ər] *s* comprador *m*

buzz [bʌz] *s* zumbido || *intr* zumbar; **to buzz about** ajetrearse, cazcalear

buzzard [ˈbʌzərd] *s* águila ratonera

buzzer [ˈbʌzər] *s* zumbador *m,* chicharra

buzz saw *s* sierra circular

buzz word *s* palabra de moda

by [baɪ] *adv* cerca; a un lado; **by and by** luego || *prep* por; cerca de, al lado de; (*not later than*) para; **by far** con mucho; **by the way** de paso; a propósito

by-and-by [ˈbaɪ•əndˈbaɪ] *s* porvenir *m*

bye-bye [ˈbaɪˈbaɪ] *s* mu *f;* **to go bye-bye** ir a la mu || *interj* (coll) ¡adiosito!; (*to a child*) ¡ro ro!

bygone [ˈbaɪ,gɔn] o [ˈbaɪ,gɑn] *adj* pasado || *s* pasado; **let bygones be bygones** olvidemos lo pasado

bylaw [ˈbaɪ,lɔ] *s* reglamento, estatuto

by′line′ *s* (journ) data

bypass [ˈbaɪ,pæs] *s* desviación; tubo de paso || *tr* desviar; eludir

by′-prod′uct *s* subproducto, derivado

bystander [ˈbaɪ,stændər] *s* asistente *mf,* circunstante *mf*

byway [ˈbaɪ,we] *s* camino apartado

byword [ˈbaɪ,wʌrd] *s* objeto de oprobio; refrán *m,* muletilla; apodo

Byzantine [ˈbɪzən,tin] o [bɪˈzæntin] *adj & s* bizantino || **byzantine** *adj* complejo

Byzantium [bɪˈzænʃi•əm] o [bɪˈzæntɪ•əm] *s* Bizancio

C

C, c [si] tercera letra del alfabeto inglés

c. *abbr* **cent, center, centimeter**

C. *abbr* **centigrade, Congress, Court**

cab [kæb] *s* coche *m* de plaza o de punto; taxi *m;* (*of a truck*) casilla

cabaret [,kæbəˈre] *s* cabaret *m*

cabbage [ˈkæbɪdʒ] *s* col *f,* berza

cab driver *s* cochero de plaza; taxista *mf*

cabin [ˈkæbɪn] *s* (*hut, cottage*) cabaña; (aer) cabina; (naut) camarote *m*

cabin boy *s* mozo de cámara
cabinet [ˈkæbɪnɪt] *s* (*piece of furniture for displaying objects*) escaparate *m,* vitrina; (*for a radio*) caja, mueble *m;* (*closet*) armario, clóset *m;* (*private room; ministry of a government*) gabinete *m*
cab′inet•ma′ker *s* ebanista *m*
cab′inet•ma′king *s* ebanistería
cable [ˈkebəl] *adj* cablegráfico ‖ *s* cable *m;* cablegrama *m* ‖ *tr & intr* cablegrafiar
cable address *s* dirección cablegráfica
cable car *s* tranvía *m* de tracción por cable; funicular *m;* teleférico
cablegram [ˈkebəl,græm] *s* cablegrama *m*
cable television *s* televisión por cable
caboose [kəˈbus] *s* (rr) furgón de cola
cab′stand′ *s* punto de coches, punto de taxis
cache [kæʃ] *s* escondrijo; víveres escondidos; (compu) caché *m* ‖ *tr* depositar en un escondrijo; ocultar
cachet [kæˈʃe] *s* sello
cackle [ˈkækəl] *s* (*of a hen*) cacareo; (*idle talk*) charla ‖ *intr* cacarear; charlar
cac•tus [ˈkæktəs] *s* (*pl* **-tuses** o **-ti** [taɪ]) cacto
cad [kæd] *s* sinvergüenza *mf;* **to behave like a cad** tener mala leche
cadaver [kəˈdævər] *s* cadáver *m*
cadaverous [kəˈdævərəs] *adj* cadavérico
caddie [ˈkædi] *s* caddie *m* (*muchacho que lleva los utensilios en el juego de golf*) ‖ *intr* servir de caddie
cadence [ˈkedəns] *s* cadencia
cadet [kəˈdɛt] *s* hermano menor, hijo menor; (*student at military school*) cadete *m*
cadmium [ˈkædmɪ•əm] *s* cadmio
cadre [ˈkædri] *s* (mil) cuadro
Caesar [ˈsizər] *s* César *m*
café [kæˈfe] *s* bar *m,* cabaret *m;* restaurante *m*
café society *s* gente *f* del mundo elegante que frecuenta los cabarets de moda
cafeteria [,kæfəˈtɪrɪ•ə] *s* cafetería, restaurante autoservicio; (*in a station, school, or hospital*) cantina
caffeine [kæˈfin] *s* cafeína
cage [kedʒ] *s* jaula ‖ *tr* enjaular
cageling [ˈkedʒlɪŋ] *s* pájaro enjaulado
ca•gey [ˈkedʒi] *adj* (*comp* **-gier;** *super* **-giest**) (coll) astuto
cahoots [kəˈhuts] *s* — **to be in cahoots** (slang) confabularse (*dos o más personas*); **to go cahoots** (slang) entrar por partes iguales
Cain [ken] *s* Caín *m;* **to raise Cain** (slang) armar camorra
Cairo [ˈkaɪro] *s* El Cairo
caisson [ˈkesən] *s* cajón *m* hidráulico; (mil) cajón de municiones; (mil) furgón *m* de municiones; (naut) compuerta de dique
cajole [kəˈdʒol] *tr* adular, lisonjear, halagar
cajoler•y [kəˈdʒoləri] *s* (*pl* **-ies**) adulación, lisonja, halago
cake [kek] *s* pastel *m,* bollo, queque *m;* (*small cake*) pastelillo; (*sponge cake*) bizcocho; (*of fish*) fritada; (*of earth*) terrón *m;* (*of soap*) pan *m,* pastilla; (*of ice*) témpano; **to take the cake** (coll) ser el colmo ‖ *intr* apelmazarse, aterronarse
calabash [ˈkælə,bæʃ] *s* calabacera; jícaro; (*fruit*) calabaza
calamitous [kəˈlæmɪtəs] *adj* calamitoso
calami•ty [kəˈlæmɪti] *s* (*pl* **-ties**) calamidad
calci•fy [ˈkælsɪ,faɪ] *v* (*pret & pp* **-fied**) calcificar ‖ *intr* calcificarse
calcium [ˈkælsɪ•əm] *s* calcio
calculate [ˈkælkjə,let] *tr* calcular; (*to reckon*) (coll) calcular ‖ *intr* calcular; **to calculate on** contar con
calculating [ˈkælkjə,letɪŋ] *adj* de calcular; astuto, intrigante
calculator [ˈkælkjəletər] *s* (*person*) calculador *m;* (mach) calculadora
calcu•lus [ˈkælkjələs] *s* (*pl* **-luses** o **-li** [,laɪ]) (math, pathol) cálculo
caldron [ˈkɔldrən] *s* calderón *m*
calendar [ˈkæləndər] *s* calendario, almanaque *m*
calf [kæf] o [kɑf] *s* (*pl* **calves** [kævz] o [kɑvz]) ternero; (*of the leg*) pantorrilla
calf′skin′ *s* becerro, becerrillo
caliber [ˈkælɪbər] *s* calibre *m*
calibrate [ˈkælɪ,bret] *tr* calibrar
calibration [ˈkæləˈbreʃən] *s* calibrado; (compu) calibración
cali•co [ˈkælɪ,ko] *s* (*pl* **-coes** o **-cos**) calico *m,* indiana
California [,kælɪˈfɔrnɪ•ə] *s* California
calipers [ˈkælɪpərz] *spl* calibrador *m,* compás *m* de calibres
caliph [ˈkelɪf] o [ˈkælɪf] *s* califa *m*
caliphate [ˈkælɪ,fet] *s* califato
calisthenic [,kælɪsˈθɛnɪk] *adj* calisténico ‖ **calisthenics** *spl* calistenia
calk [kɔk] *tr var* de **caulk**
call [kɔl] *s* llamada; visita; (*of a boat or airplane*) escala; vocación; **within call** al alcance de la voz ‖ *tr* llamar; convocar (*p.ej., una huelga*); **to call back** mandar volver; **to call down** (coll) reprender, regañar; **to call in** hacer entrar; (*from circulation*) retirar; **to call off** aplazar, suspender; desconvocar; **to call out** llamar (*a uno*) que salga; **to call together** convocar, reunir; **to call up** llamar por teléfono; evocar, recordar ‖ *intr* llamar, gritar; hacer una visita; (naut) hacer escala; **to call on** acudir a; visitar; **to call out** gritar; **to go calling** ir de visitas
calla lily [ˈkælə] *s* cala, lirio de agua
call bell *s* timbre *m* de llamada
call′boy′ *s* (*in a hotel*) botones *m;* (theat) traspunte *m*
caller [ˈkɔlər] *s* visitante *mf;* (telp) persona que llama
caller ID *s* (telp) identificador *m* de llamada
call girl *s* chica de cita
calling [ˈkɔlɪŋ] *s* profesión, vocación
calling card *s* tarjeta de visita

calliope [kəˈlaɪ•əpi] o [ˈkælɪ•op] *s* (mus) órgano de vapor ‖ **Calliope** [kəˈlaɪ•əpi] *s* Calíope *f*
call number *s* número de teléfono; (*of a book*) número de clasificación
call option *s* (com) opción de compra
callous [ˈkæləs] *adj* calloso; (fig) duro, insensible
call to arms *s* — **to sound the call to arms** (mil) batir o tocar a llamada
call to the colors *s* (mil) llamada a filas
callus [ˈkæləs] *s* callo
calm [kɑm] *adj* tranquilo, quieto; (*sea*) bonancible ‖ *s* tranquilidad, calma ‖ *tr* tranquilizar, calmar ‖ *intr* — **to calm down** tranquilizarse, calmarse; abonanzar, calmar (*el viento, el tiempo*)
calmness [ˈkɑmnɪs] *s* tranquilidad, calma
calorie [ˈkæləri] *s* caloría
calum•ny [ˈkæləmni] *s* (*pl* **-nies**) calumnia
calva•ry [ˈkælvəri] *s* (*pl* **-ries**) (*at the entrance to a town*) humilladero ‖ **Calvary** *s* Calvario
calyp•so [kəˈlɪpso] *s* (*pl* **-sos**) calipso ‖ **Calypso** *s* Calipso *f*
cam [kæm] *s* leva
cambric [ˈkembrɪk] *s* batista
camcorder [ˈkæmˈkɔrdər] *s* videocámara, camcórder *m*
camel [ˈkæməl] *s* camello
came•o [ˈkæmɪ•o] *s* (*pl* **-os**) camafeo
camera [ˈkæmərə] *s* cámara (fotográfica), máquina fotográfica; **on camera** en imagen
camera crew *s* camarógrafos, cámaras *mf*
camera•man [ˈkæmərə,mæn] *s* (*pl* **-men** [,mɛn]) camarógrafo, tomavistas *m*
camomile [ˈkæmə,maɪl] *s* manzanilla
camouflage [ˈkæmə,flɑʒ] *s* camuflaje *m* ‖ *tr* camuflar
camp [kæmp] *s* campamento ‖ *intr* acampar
campaign [kæmˈpen] *s* campaña ‖ *intr* hacer campaña
campˈfireˈ *s* hoguera de campamento
campground *s* camping *m*
camphor [ˈkæmfər] *s* alcanfor *m*
campˈstoolˈ *s* silla de tijera, catrecillo
campus [ˈkæmpəs] *s* campus *m,* recinto (*de la universidad*)
camˈshaftˈ *s* árbol *m* de levas
can [kæn] *s* bote *m,* envase *m,* lata ‖ *v* (*pret & pp* **canned;** *ger* **canning**) *tr* envasar, enlatar ‖ *v* (*pret & cond* **could**) *v aux* **he can come tomorrow** puede venir mañana; **can you swim?** ¿sabe Ud. nadar?
Canada [ˈkænədə] *s* el Canadá
Canadian [kəˈnedɪ•ən] *adj & s* canadiense
canal [kəˈnæl] *s* canal *m*
canard [kəˈnɑrd] *s* rumor falso, bulo
canar•y [kəˈnɛri] *s* (*pl* **-ies**) canario ‖ **Canaries** *spl* Canarias
can•cel [ˈkænsəl] *v* (*pret & pp* **-celed** o **-celled;** *ger* **-celing** o **-celling**) *tr* cancelar, eliminar, suprimir; matasellar, obliterar (*sellos de correo*)
canceler [ˈkænsələr] *s* matasellos *m*
cancellation [,kænsəˈleʃən] *s* cancelación, eliminación, supresión; revocatoria; (*of stamps*) obliteración
cancer [ˈkænsər] *s* cáncer *m;* **Cancer** *s* (astr) Cáncer *m*
cancerous [ˈkænsərəs] *adj* canceroso
candela•brum [,kændəˈlebrəm] *s* (*pl* **-bra** [brə] o **-brums**) candelabro
candid [ˈkændɪd] *adj* franco, sincero; imparcial
candida•cy [ˈkændɪdəsi] *s* (*pl* **-cies**) candidatura
candidate [ˈkændɪ,det] *s* candidato; (*for a degree*) graduando
candid camera *s* cámara indiscreta
candied fruit *s* fruta confitada
candle [ˈkændəl] *s* bujía, candela, vela
canˈdle•holdˈer *s* candelero, palmatoria
canˈdle•lightˈ *s* luz *f* de vela; crepúsculo
candlepower *s* bujía
canˈdle•stickˈ *s* candelero, palmatoria
candor [ˈkændər] *s* franqueza, sinceridad; imparcialidad
can•dy [ˈkændi] *s* (*pl* **-dies**) bombón *m,* confite *m,* dulce *m;* dulces *mpl* ‖ *v* (*pret & pp* **-died**) *tr* almibarar, confitar, garapiñar ‖ *intr* almibararse
candy box *s* bombonera, confitera
candy store *s* confitería, dulcería
cane [ken] *s* (*plant; stem*) caña; (*walking stick*) bastón *m;* (*for chair seats*) junco, mimbre *m,* rejilla
cane seat *s* asiento de rejilla
cane sugar *s* azúcar *m* de caña
canine [ˈkenaɪn] *adj* canino ‖ *s* (*tooth*) canino; perro
canker [ˈkænkər] *s* úlcera (en la boca); (bot, vet) cancro
canned goods *spl* conservas alimenticias
canned music *s* (coll) música ambiental
canner•y [ˈkænəri] *s* (*pl* **-ies**) conservera, fábrica de conservas
cannibal [ˈkænɪbəl] *adj & s* caníbal *mf*
canning [ˈkænɪŋ] *adj* conservero ‖ *s* conservería
cannon [ˈkænən] *s* cañón *m;* cañones
cannonade [,kænəˈned] *s* cañoneo ‖ *tr* cañonear
cannon ball *s* bala de cañón
cannon fodder *s* carne *f* de cañón
can•ny [ˈkæni] *adj* (*comp* **-nier;** *super* **-niest**) cauteloso, cuerdo; astuto
canoe [kəˈnu] *s* canoa; bongo (SAm)
canoeing [kəˈnu•ɪŋ] *s* piraguismo
canoeist [kəˈnu•ɪst] *s* canoero
canon [ˈkænən] *s* canon *m;* (*priest*) canónigo
canonical [kəˈnɑnɪkəl] *adj* canónico; aceptado, auténtico, establecido ‖ **canonicals** *spl* vestiduras sacerdotales
canonize [ˈkænə,naɪz] *tr* canonizar
canon law *s* cánones *mpl,* derecho canónico
canon•ry [ˈkænənri] *s* (*pl* **-ries**) canonjía
can opener [ˈopənər] *s* abrelatas *m*
cano•py [ˈkænəpi] *s* (*pl* **-pies**) dosel *m,* pabellón *m;* (*over an entrance*) marquesina; (*for electrical fixtures*) campana
canopy of heaven *s* bóveda celeste

can't *contr* **can not** *o* **cannot**
cant [kænt] *s* hipocresía; jerga, jerigonza
cantaloupe [ˈkæntəˌlop] *s* cantalupo
cantankerous [kænˈtæŋkərəs] *adj* de mal genio, pendenciero
canteen [kænˈtin] *s* (*shop*) cantina; (*water flask*) cantimplora; (mil) centro de recreo
canter [ˈkæntər] *s* medio galope ‖ *intr* ir a medio galope
canticle [ˈkæntɪkəl] *s* cántico
cantilever [ˈkæntɪˌlivər] *adj* voladizo ‖ *s* viga voladiza
cantle [ˈkæntəl] *s* arzón trasero
cantonment [kænˈtɑnmənt] *s* acantonamiento
cantor [ˈkæntər] *s* chantre *m;* (*in a synagogue*) cantor *m* principal
canvas [ˈkænvəs] *s* cañamazo, lona; (naut) vela, lona; (*painting*) lienzo; **under canvas** (mil) en tiendas; (naut) con las velas izadas
canvass [ˈkænvəs] *s* pesquisa, escrutinio; (*of votes*) solicitación ‖ *tr* escrutar, solicitar; discutir detenidamente
canyon [ˈkænjən] *s* cañón *m*
cap. *abbr* **capital, capitalize**
cap [kæp] *s* gorra, gorra de visera; (*of academic costume*) birrete *m;* (*of bottle*) cápsula; (*e.g., of a fountain pen*) capuchón *m* ‖ *v* (*pret & pp* **capped;** *ger* **capping**) *tr* cubrir con gorra; capsular (*una botella*); **to cap the climax** ser el colmo
capabili•ty [ˌkepəˈbɪlɪti] *s* (*pl* **-ties**) habilidad, capacidad
capable [ˈkepəbəl] *adj* hábil, capaz
capacious [kəˈpeʃəs] *adj* espacioso, capaz
capaci•ty [kəˈpæsɪti] *s* (*pl* **-ties**) (*room, space; ability, aptitude*) capacidad; (*status, function*) calidad; **in the capacity of** en calidad de
cap and gown *s* birrete y toga
caparison [kəˈpærɪsən] *s* caparazón *m* ‖ *tr* engualdrapar
cape [kep] *s* cabo, promontorio; (*garment*) capa, esclavina
Cape Colony *s* la Colonia del Cabo
Cape Horn *s* el Cabo de Hornos
Cape of Good Hope *s* Cabo de Buena Esperanza
caper [ˈkepər] *s* (*frolic*) cabriola; (*prank*) travesura; **to cut capers** dar cabriolas; hacer travesuras ‖ *intr* cabriolear; retozar
Capeˈtownˈ *o* **Cape Town** *s* El Cabo, la Ciudad del Cabo
capeˈworkˈ *s* (taur) suerte *f* de capa, lance *m*
capital [ˈkæpɪtəl] *adj* capital ‖ *s* (*money*) capital *m;* (*city*) capital *f;* (*top of a column*) capitel *m;* **to make capital out of** sacar beneficio de
capital flight *s* fuga de capitales
capital gain *s* plusvalía *f*
capital gains tax *s* impuesto sobre la plusvalía
capital goods *spl* bienes *mpl* de equipo
capitalism [ˈkæpɪtəˌlɪzəm] *s* capitalismo
capitalist [ˈkæpɪtəˌlɪst] *adj & s* capitalista *mf*
capitalize [ˈkæpɪtəˌlaɪz] *tr* escribir con mayúscula; capitalizar ‖ *intr* — **to capitalize on** aprovecharse de
capital letter *s* letra mayúscula
capital market *s* mercado de capitales
capital punishment *s* pena capital, pena de muerte, último suplicio
capitol [ˈkæpɪtəl] *s* capitolio
capitulate [kəˈpɪtʃəˌlet] *intr* capitular
capon [ˈkepɑn] *s* capón *m*
caprice [kəˈpris] *s* capricho, antojo; veleidad
capricious [kəˈprɪʃəs] *adj* caprichoso, antojadizo
Capricorn [ˈkæprɪˌkɔrn] *s* (astr) Capricornio
capsize [ˈkæpsaɪz] *tr* volcar ‖ *intr* volcar; tumbar, zozobrar (*un barco*)
capstan [ˈkæpstən] *s* cabrestante *m*
capˈstoneˈ *s* coronamiento
capsule [ˈkæpsəl] *s* cápsula
Capt. *abbr* **Captain**
captain [ˈkæptən] *s* capitán *m* ‖ *tr* capitanear
captain•cy [ˈkæptənsi] *s* (*pl* **-cies**) capitanía
caption [ˈkæpʃən] *s* título; (*in a movie*) subtítulo; (*under a picture*) leyenda, pie *m*
captivate [ˈkæptɪˌvet] *tr* cautivar, encantar
captive [ˈkæptɪv] *adj & s* cautivo
captivi•ty [kæpˈtɪvɪti] *s* (*pl* **-ties**) cautividad, cautiverio
captor [ˈkæptər] *s* aprenhensor *m*
capture [ˈkæptʃər] *s* apresamiento, captura; (*of a stronghold*) toma ‖ *tr* apresar, capturar; tomar (*una plaza*); captar (*p.ej., la atención de una persona*)
car [kɑr] *s* coche *m,* automóvil *m;* (*of an elevator*) caja, carro; (*of a balloon*) barquilla; (rr) vagón *m,* coche
carafe [kəˈræf] *s* garrafa
caramel [ˈkærəməl] *o* [ˈkɑrməl] *s* (*burnt sugar*) caramelo; bombón *m* de caramelo
carat [ˈkærət] *s* quilate *m*
caravan [ˈkærəˌvæn] *s* caravana
caraway [ˈkærəˌwe] *s* alcaravea
carˈbarnˈ *s* cochera de tranvías
carbide [ˈkɑrbaɪd] *s* carburo
carbine [ˈkɑrbaɪn] *s* carabina
carbolic acid [kɑrˈbɑlɪk] *s* ácido carbólico
car bomb *s* coche bomba, carro bomba
carbon [ˈkɑrbən] *s* (*chemical element*) carbono; (*pole of arc light or battery*) carbón *m;* papel *m* carbón; (*in auto cylinders*) carbonilla
carbon copy *s* copia al carbón; (fig) réplica
carbon dioxide *s* bióxido de carbono, anhídrido carbónico
carbon monoxide *s* óxido de carbono, monóxido de carbono
carbon paper *s* papel *m* carbón
carˈboyˈ *s* bombona, garrafón *m*
carbuncle [ˈkɑrbʌŋkəl] *s* (*stone*) carbunclo, carbúnculo; (*biol*) furúnculo, divieso; (*symptom of anthrax*) carbunco, carbunclo
carburetor [ˈkɑrbəˌretər] *s* carburador *m*
car caller *s* avisacoches *m*
carcass [ˈkɑrkəs] *s* cadáver de animal; (*for*

meat) res muerta; (*framework*) armazón *m & f,* carcasa
carcinogen [kɑrˈsɪnəjən] *s* carcinógeno
carcinoma [ˌkɑrsəˈnomə] *s* carcinoma
card [kɑrd] s tarjeta; (*for playing games*) naipe *m,* carta; (*for filing*) ficha; (*person*) (coll) sujeto, tipo; (compu) tarjeta
card'board' *s* cartón *m*
cardboard binding *s* encuadernación en pasta
card case *s* tarjetero
card catalogue *s* catálogo de fichas
cardiac [ˈkɑrdɪˌæk] *adj* cardíaco ‖ *s* (*medicine; sufferer*) cardíaco
cardigan [ˈkɑrdɪgən] *s* albornoz *m,* rebeca
cardinal [ˈkɑrdɪnəl] *adj* cardinal; purpurado ‖ *s* (*prelate; bird*) cardenal *m;* número cardinal
card index *s* fichero, tarjetero
card party *s* tertulia de baraja
card'sharp' *s* fullero, tahur *m*
card trick *s* truco de naipes
care [kɛr] *s* (*worry*) inquietud, ansiedad; (*watchful attention*) esmero; (*charge*) cargo, custodia; **care of** suplicada en casa de; **to take care of oneself** cuidarse ‖ *intr* inquietarse, preocuparse; **to care for** cuidar (de) *or* (á); (*love*) amar, querer; **to care to** tener ganas de; **I couldn't care less** me importe un pepino
careen [kəˈrin] *intr* inclinarse; mecerse precipitadamente
career [kəˈrɪr] *adj* de carrera ‖ *s* carrera
care'free' *adj* despreocupado, libre de cuidados
careful [ˈkɛrfəl] *adj* (*acting with care*) cuidadoso; (*done with care*) esmerado; **to be careful to** cuidarse de
careless [ˈkɛrlɪs] *adj* descuidado, negligente
carelessness [ˈkɛrlɪsnɪs] *s* descuido, negligencia
caress [kəˈrɛs] *s* caricia ‖ *tr* acariciar ‖ *intr* acariciarse
caretaker [ˈkɛrˌtekər] *s* curador *m,* guardián *m,* custodio
caretaker government *s* gobierno en funciones
care'worn' *adj* fatigado, rendido, agobiado
car'fare' *s* pasaje *m* de tranvía o autobús
car•go [ˈkɑrgo] *s* (*pl* **-goes** o **-gos**) carga, cargamento
Caribbean [ˌkærɪˈbi•ən] o [kəˈrɪbɪ•ən] *adj* caribe ‖ *s* mar *m* Caribe
caricature [ˈkærɪkətʃər] *s* caricatura ‖ *tr* caricaturizar
carillon [ˈkærɪˌlɑn] o [kəˈrɪljən] *s* carillón *m*
car'load' *s* furgonada, vagonada
carnage [ˈkɑrnɪdʒ] *s* carnicería, matanza
carnation [kɑrˈneʃən] *adj* encarnado ‖ *s* clavel *m,* clavel reventón
carnival [ˈkɑrnɪvəl] *adj* carnavalesco ‖ *s* (*period before Lent*) carnaval *m;* verbena, espectáculo de atracciones
carnival queen *s* reina de las fiestas
car•ol [ˈkærəl] *s* canción alegre, villancico ‖ *v* (*pret & pp* **-oled** o **-olled;** *ger* **-oling** o **-olling**); *tr* celebrar con villancicos ‖ *intr* cantar con alegría
carom [ˈkærəm] *s* carambola ‖ *intr* carambolear
carousal [kəˈraʊzəl] *s* juerga, borrachera, jarana
carouse [kəˈraʊz] *intr* emborracharse, jaranear
carp [kɑrp] *s* (*pez*) carpa ‖ *intr* quejarse
carpenter [ˈkɑrpəntər] *s* carpintero
carpentry [ˈkɑrpəntri] *s* carpintería
carpet [ˈkɑrpɪt] *s* alfombra; **to be on the carpet** estar sobre el tapete ‖ *tr* alfombrar
carpet bombing *s* bombardeo por saturación
carpet shampoo *s* espuma seca
carpet sweeper *s* barredora de alfombras
carrel [ˈkærəl] *s* cubículo de estudio
car'-rent'al service *s* alquiler *m* de coches
carriage [ˈkærɪdʒ] *s* carruaje *m;* (*cost of carrying*) porte *m,* transporte *m;* (*bearing*) porte *m,* continente *m;* (mach) carro
carrier [ˈkærɪ•ər] *s* portador *m,* transportador *m;* portador de gérmenes; empresa de transportes; (*mailman*) cartero; vendedor *m* de periódicos; portaaviones *m;* (rad) onda portadora
carrier pigeon *s* paloma mensajera
carrier wave *s* (rad) onda portadora
carrion [ˈkærɪ•ən] *adj* carroño; inmundo ‖ *s* carroña; inmundicia
carrot [ˈkærət] *s* zanahoria
carrousel [ˌkærəˈzɛl] *s* caballitos, tiovivo
car•ry [ˈkæri] *v* (*pret & pp* **-ried**) *tr* llevar, portar, traer; transportar; sostener (*una carga*); **to carry away** llevarse; encantar, entusiasmar; **to carry into effect** llevar a cabo; **to carry one's point** salirse con la suya; **to carry out** llevar a cabo; **to carry the day** quedar victorioso, ganar la palma; **to carry weight** ser de peso ‖ *intr* tener alcance; **to carry on** continuar, perseverar; (coll) travesear; (coll) comportarse de un modo escandaloso; (coll) hacer locuras
cart [kɑrt] *s* carreta, carro ‖ *tr* carretear
carte blanche [ˈkɑrtˈblɑnʃ] *s* carta blanca
cartel [kɑrˈtɛl] *s* cartel *m*
cart horse *s* caballo de tiro
cartilage [ˈkɑrtɪlɪdʒ] *s* cartílago
cartoon [kɑrˈtun] *s* caricatura; (*comic strip*) tira cómica; (*film*) película de dibujos ‖ *tr* caricaturizar
cartoonist [kɑrˈtunɪst] *s* caricaturista *mf;* humorista *mf,* dibujante *mf* de chistes
cartridge [ˈkɑrtrɪdʒ] *s* cartucho
cartridge belt *s* canana
cart'wheel *s* (*gymnastics*) voltereta lateral, rueda carreta (Mex), vuelta de carro (Mex)
carve [kɑrv] *tr* trinchar (*carne*); esculpir, tallar
carving knife [ˈkɑrvɪŋ] *s* cuchillo de trinchar
car wash *s* tren *m or* túnel *m* de lavado
car washer *s* lavacoches *m*
caryatid [ˌkærɪˈætɪd] *s* cariátide *f*
cascade [kæsˈked] *s* cascada
case [kes] *s* (*instance; form of a word*) caso; (*box*) caja; (*small container*) estuche *m;* (*for cigarettes*) pitillera; (*sheath*) vaina, funda; (gram) caso; (law) causa, pleito; **in case** caso que; **in no case** de ninguna manera ‖ *tr* encajo-

nar, enfundar; **to case the joint** (slang) reconocer el terreno
case′-hardened *adj* (metal) cementado, endurecido
case history *s* historial clínico; evolución de un caso social
case law *s* jurisprudencia
case load *s* número de casos
casement [ˈkesmənt] *s* ventana batiente; bastidor *m* (*de la ventana*)
case worker *s* asistente *mf* social
cash [kæʃ] *s* dinero contante; pago al contado; **cash on delivery** contra reembolso, pago contra entrega; **to pay cash** pagar al contado ‖ *tr* cobrar (*un cheque el portador*); abonar, pagar (*un cheque el banco*) ‖ *intr* — **to cash in on** (coll) sacar provecho de
cash and carry *s* pago al contado con transporte a cargo del comprador
cash′box′ *s* caja
cashew [ˈkæʃu] *s* anacardo, marañón *m*
cashew nut *s* anacardo, nuez *f* de marañón
cash flow *s* flujo de caja, cash-flow *m*
cashier [kæˈʃɪr] *s* cajero ‖ *tr* destruir; (*in the army*) degradar
cashier's check *s* cheque *m* de caja
cashier's desk *s* caja
cashmere [ˈkæʃmɪr] *s* casimir *m*, cachemir *m*
cash on hand *s* efectivo en caja
cash payment *s* pago al contado
cash purchase *s* compra al contado
cash register *s* caja registradora
cash sale *s* venta al contado
casing [ˈkesɪŋ] *s* caja, cubierta, envoltura; (*of door or window*) marco, cerco; (*of tire*) cubierta; (sew) jareta
cask [kæsk] o [kɑsk] *s* casco, pipa, tonel *m*
casket [ˈkæskɪt] *s* (*box for valuables*) cajita, joyero; (*coffin*) caja, ataúd *m*
cassava [kəˈsɑvə] *s* cazabe *m*, casabe *m*
casserole [ˈkæsə,rol] *s* cacerola; (*dish cooked in a casserole*) timbal *m*
cassette [kæˈsɛt] *s* (*audio*) cassette *m & f*, casete *m & f*; (*video*) videocassette *m*, cinta de video, vídeo (Esp), videocinta (Esp); (phot) chasis *m*; **on cassette** en cassette; en videocassette
cassette deck *s* platina, pletina
cassette player *s* pasacintas *m*, reproductor *m* de casetes, casete (Esp), pasacassettes *m* (Arg), tocacassettes (Chile)
cassette recorder *s* grabadora, grabador *m* (de cassettes), casete *m* (Esp)
cassock [ˈkæsək] *s* balandrán *m*, sotana
cast [kæst] *s* echada, tiro; forma, molde *m*; aire *m*, semblante *m*; matiz *m*, tinte *m*; (*of actors*) reparto ‖ *v* (*pret & pp* **cast**) *tr* echar, tirar; volver (*los ojos*); proyectar (*una sombra*); colar, fundir (*metales*); depositar (*votos*); echar (*suertes*); (theat) repartir (*papeles*); **to cast aside** desechar; **to cast loose** soltar; **to cast out** arrojar, echar fuera; despedir, desterrar ‖ *intr* echar los dados; arrojar el sedal o el anzuelo; **to cast about** revolver proyectos; **to cast off** (naut) soltar las amarras
castanet [,kæstəˈnɛt] *s* castañuela, castañeta
cast′a•way′ *adj & s* proscrito, réprobo; náufrago
caste [kæst] *s* casta; **to lose caste** desprestigiarse
caster [ˈkæstər] *s* ruedecilla de mueble; (*cruet stand*) angarillas, vinagreras; frasco
Castile [kæsˈtil] *s* Castilla
Castilian [kæsˈtɪljən] *adj & s* castellano
casting [ˈkæstɪŋ] *s* fundición, pieza fundida; (theat) reparto
casting vote *s* voto de calidad
cast iron *s* hierro colado, hierro fundido
cast′-i′ron *adj* de hierro colado; fuerte, endurecido; duro, inflexible
castle [ˈkæsəl] *s* castillo; (chess) roque *m*, torre *f* ‖ *tr & intr* (chess) enrocar
castles in Spain o **castles in the air** *spl* castillos en el aire
cast′off′ *adj* abandonado, desechado; (*clothing*) de desecho ‖ *s* desecho
castor oil [ˈkæstər] *s* aceite *m* de ricino
castrate [ˈkæstret] *tr* capar, castrar
casual [ˈkæʒu•əl] *adj* casual, fortuito; descuidado, indiferente
casual•ty [ˈkæʒu•əlti] *s* (*pl* **-ties**) desgracia, accidente *m*; accidentado, víctima; (*in war*) baja
casualty list *s* lista de bajas
CAT [kæt] *s* (acronym) (**computerized axial tomography**) TAC *f* (tomografía axial computacional)
cat. *abbr* **catalog, catalogue, catechism**
cat [kæt] *s* gato; mujer maligna; **to bell the cat** ponerle cascabel al gato; **to let the cat out of the bag** revelar el secreto
catacomb [ˈkætə,kom] *s* catacumba
Catalan [ˈkætə,læn] *adj & s* catalán *m*
catalog, catalogue [ˈkætə,lɔg] o [ˈkætə,lɑg] *s* catálogo ‖ *tr* catalogar
Catalonia [,kætəˈlonɪ•ə] *s* Cataluña
Catalonian [,kætəˈlonɪ•ən] *adj & s* catalán *m*
catalytic converter [ˈkætəˈlɪtɪk] *s* catalizador *m*
catapult [ˈkætə,pʌlt] *s* catapulta ‖ *tr* catapultar
cataract [ˈkætə,rækt] *s* catarata; (pathol) catarata
catarrh [kəˈtɑr] *s* catarro
catastrophe [kəˈtæstrəfi] *s* catástrofe *f*
cat′call′ *s* rechifla ‖ *tr & intr* rechiflar
catch [kætʃ] *s* (*of a ball*) cogida; (*of fish*) pesca; (*of a lock*) cerradera, pestillo; (*booty*) botín *m*, presa; (*fastener*) broche *m*; (*good match*) buen partido ‖ *v* (*pret & pp* **caught** [kɔt]) *tr* asir, coger, atrapar; llegar a oír; coger (*un resfriado*); (*to come upon suddenly*) sorprender; comprender; capturar (*al delincuente*); **to catch fire** encenderse; **to catch hold of** agarrar, coger; apoderarse de; **to catch it** (coll) merecerse un regaño; **to catch oneself** contenerse; recobrar el equilibrio; **to catch sight of** alcanzar a ver; **to catch up** arrebatar; coger al vuelo; (*in a mistake*) cazar ‖ *intr* pegarse (*una enfermedad*); enredarse; encenderse; **to catch at** agarrarse a, tratar de asir; **to catch on**

prender en (*p.ej., un gancho*); comprender, coger el tino; **to catch up** salir del atraso; (*in one's debts*) ponerse al día; **to catch up with** emparejar con

catcher [ˈkætʃər] *s* (baseball) receptor, parador *m*

catching [ˈkætʃɪŋ] *adj* pegajoso, contagioso; atrayente, cautivador

catch question *s* pega

catchup [ˈkætʃəp] *s* salsa de tomate condimentada

catch′word′ *s* lema *m,* palabra de efecto; (*actor's cue*) pie *m;* (typ) reclamo

catch•y [ˈkætʃi] *adj* (*comp* **-ier;** *super* **-iest**) (*tune*) animado, vivo; (*title of a book*) impresionante, llamativo; (*question*) intrincado; (*breathing*) espasmódico

catechism [ˈkætɪˌkɪzəm] *s* catecismo

categorize [ˈkætəgəraɪz] *tr* catalogar, clasificar

catego•ry [ˈkætɪˌgori] *s* (*pl* **-ries**) categoria (*sports*) division

cater [ˈketər] *tr* (*banquet, wedding, party*) encargarse el buffet de ‖ *intr* encargarse del servicio de comida; **to cater to** proveer a

cater-cornered [ˈkætərˌkɔrnərd] *adj* diagonal ‖ *adv* diagonalmente

caterer [ˈketərər] *s* abastecedor *m,* proveedor *m* de alimentos (*esp. para fiestas caseras*)

caterpillar [ˈkætərˌpɪlər] *s* oruga

caterpillar tractor *s* tractor *m* de oruga

cat′fish′ *s* bagre *m*

cat′gut′ *s* (mus) cuerda de tripa; (surg) catgut *m*

Cath. *abbr* **Catholic**

cathartic [kəˈθɑrtɪk] *adj & s* catártico

cathedral [kəˈθidrəl] *s* catedral *f*

catheter [ˈkæθɪtər] *s* catéter *m,* sonda

catheterize [ˈkæθɪtəˌraɪz] *tr* cateterizar

cathode [ˈkæθod] *s* cátodo

catholic [ˈkæθəlɪk] *adj* católico ‖ **Catholic** *adj & s* católico

catkin [ˈkætkɪn] *s* candelilla, amento

cat nap *s* sueñecito

catnip [ˈkætnɪp] *s* hierba gatera, nébeda

cat-o'-nine-tails [ˌkætəˈnaɪnˌtelz] *s* azote *m* con nueve ramales

CAT scan *s* imagen dada por el escáner TAC

CAT scanner *s* escáner *m* de TAC

cat's cradle *s* juego de la cuna

cat's-paw o **catspaw** [ˈkætsˌpɔ] *s* mano *f* de gato, instrumento

catsup [ˈkætsəp] o [kɛtʃəp] *s* salsa de tomate condimentada

cat′tail′ *s* anea, espadaña; amento

cattle [ˈkætəl] *s* ganado vacuno o bovino

cattle crossing *s* paso de ganado

cattle•man [ˈkætəlmən] *s* (*pl* **-men** [mən]) *s* ganadero

cattle raising *s* ganadería

cattle ranch *s* hacienda de ganado

cat•ty [ˈkæti] *adj* (*comp* **-tier;** *super* **-tiest**) (*like a cat*) felino, gatuno; (*spiteful*) malicioso; (*gossipy*) chismoso

cat′walk′ *s* pasadero, pasarela, paso de gatos (Mex)

Caucasian [kɔˈkeʒən] *adj & s* caucasiano, caucásico

Caucasus [ˈkɔkəsəs] *s* Cáucaso

caucus [ˈkɔkəs] *s* junta de políticos

cauliflower [ˈkɔlɪˌflaʊ•ər] *s* coliflor *f*

caulk [kɔk] *tr* enmasillar; (naut) calafatear

caulking [ˈkɔkɪŋ] *s* enmasillado; (naut) calafateo

cause [kɔz] *s* causa; (*person*) causante *mf* ‖ *tr* causar

cause′way′ *s* (*highway*) calzada; calzada elevada

caustic [ˈkɔstɪk] *adj* cáustico

cauterize [ˈkɔtəˌraɪz] *tr* cauterizar

caution [ˈkɔʃən] *s* (*carefulness*) cautela; (*warning*) advertencia, amonestación ‖ *tr* advertir, amonestar

cautious [ˈkɔʃəs] *adj* cauteloso, cauto

cavalcade [ˌkævəlˈked] o [ˈkævəlˌked] *s* cabalgata

cavalier [ˌkævəˈlɪr] *adj* (*haughty*) altivo, desdeñoso; (*offhand*) alegre, desenvuelto, inceremonioso ‖ *s* (*horseman*) caballero; (*lady's escort*) galán *m*

caval•ry [ˈkævəlri] *s* (*pl* **-ries**) caballería

cavalry•man [ˈkævəlrimən] *s* (*pl* **-men** [mən]) soldado de caballería

cave [kev] *s* cueva, caverna ‖ *intr* — **to cave in** hundirse; (*to give in, yield*) (coll) ceder, rendirse

cave′-in′ *s* hundimiento, derrumbe *m,* socavón *m*

caveman *s* hombre grosero, hombre *m* de las cavernas

cavern [ˈkævərn] *s* caverna

cav•il [ˈkævɪl] *v* (*pret & pp* **-iled** o **-illed;** *ger* **-iling** o **-illing**) *intr* buscar quisquillas

cavi•ty [ˈkævɪti] *s* (*pl* **-ties**) cavidad; (*in a tooth*) picadura

cavort [kəˈgɔrt] *intr* (coll) cabriolar

caw [kɔ] *s* graznido ‖ *intr* graznar

CB [ˈsiˈbi] *s* (letterword) (**citizens' band**) BC *f* (banda ciudadana)

cc. *abbr* **cubic centimeter**

CD [ˈsiˈdi] *s* (letterword) (**compact disk**) CD *m* (compact-disc, disco compacto)

CD-ROM drive [ˈsiˈdiˈrom] *s* lector *m* CD-ROM

cease [sis] *tr* parar, suspender ‖ *intr* cesar; cesar de, dejar de + *inf*

cease′fire′ *s* cese *m* de fuego ‖ *intr* suspender hostilidades

ceaseless [ˈsislɪs] *adj* incesante, continuo

cedar [ˈsidər] *s* cedro

cede [sid] *tr* ceder, traspasar

ceiling [ˈsilɪŋ] *s* techo, cielo raso; (aer) techo, cielo máximo

ceiling fan *s* ventilador *m* de aspas, ventilador hélice

ceiling price *s* precio tope

celebrant [ˈsɛlɪbrənt] *s* celebrante *m*

celebrate [ˋsɛlɪˌbret] *tr* celebrar ‖ *intr* (*to say mass*) celebrar; divertirse, festejarse; far-rear
celebrated [ˋsɛlɪˌbretɪd] *adj* célebre, renombrado
celebration [ˌsɛlɪˋbreʃən] *s* celebración; diversión, festividad
celebri•ty [sɪˋlɛbrɪti] *s* (*pl* **-ties**) (*fame; famous person*) celebridad
celery [ˋsɛləri] *s* apio
celestial [sɪˋlɛstʃəl] *adj* celeste, celestial
celestial navigation *s* navegación astronómica
celiba•cy [ˋsɛlɪbəsi] *s* (*pl* **-cies**) celibato
celibate [ˋsɛlɪbɪt] *adj* & *s* célibe *mf*
cell [sɛl] *s* (*of convent or jail*) celda; (*of honeycomb*) celdilla; (*of electric battery*) elemento; (*of plant or animal; of photoelectric device; of political group*) célula; (compu) celda
cellar [ˋsɛlər] *s* sótano; (*for wine*) bodega
cellaret [ˌsɛləˋrɛt] *s* licorera
cell house *s* prisión celular
cellist o **'cellist** [ˋtʃɛlɪst] *s* violoncelista *mf*
cel•lo o **'cel•lo** [ˋtʃɛlo] *s* (*pl* **-los**) violoncelo
cellophane [ˋsɛləˌfen] *s* celofán *m*
cellphone [ˋsɛlfon] *s* teléfono celular
cellular telephone [ˋsɛljələr] *s* teléfono celular
celluloid [ˋsɛljəˌlɔɪd] *s* celuloide *m*
Celt [sɛlt] o [kɛlt] *s* celta *mf*
Celtic [ˋsɛltɪk] o [ˋkɛltɪk] *adj* céltico ‖ *s* (*language*) celta *m*
cement [sɪˋmɛnt] *s* cemento ‖ *tr* revestir con cemento; (*la amistad*) consolidar
cemeter•y [ˋsɛmɪˌtɛri] *s* (*pl* **-ies**) cementerio
censer [ˋsɛnsər] *s* incensario
censor [ˋsɛnsər] *s* censor *m* ‖ *tr* censurar
censure [ˋsɛnʃər] *s* censura ‖ *tr* censurar
census [ˋsɛnsəs] *s* censo; **to take the census** levantar el censo
cent. *abbr* **centigrade, central, century**
cent [sɛnt] *s* centavo
centaur [ˋsɛntɔr] *s* centauro
centennial [sɛnˋtɛnɪ•əl] *adj* & *s* centenario
center [ˋsɛntər] *adj* centrista ‖ *s* centro ‖ *tr* centrar
cen'ter fold *s* póster *m* central
center half *s* (*ball games*) medio centro
cen'ter•piece' *s* centro de mesa; (fig) eje *m*, foco
center punch *s* granete *m*, punzón *m* de marcar
centigrade [ˋsɛntɪˌgred] *adj* centígrado
centimeter [ˋsɛntɪˌmitər] *s* centímetro
centipede [ˋsɛntɪˌpid] *s* ciempiés *m*
central [ˋsɛntrəl] *adj* central ‖ *s* (telp) central *f*, central de teléfonos; (*operator*) telefonista *mf*
Central America *s* Centro América, la América Central
Central American *adj* & *mf* centroamericano
Central Intelligence Agency (CIA) *s* agencia central de inteligencia
centralize [ˋsɛntrəˌlaɪz] *tr* centralizar ‖ *intr* centralizarse
centrifuge [ˋsɛntrəfjudʒ] *s* centrifugadora
centu•ry [ˋsɛntʃəri] *s* (*pl* **-ries**) siglo
century plant *s* pita, maguey *m*
ceramic [sɪˋræmɪk] *adj* cerámico
cereal [ˋsɪrɪ•əl] *adj* & *s* cereal *m*
cerebral palsy [ˋsɛrəbrəl] *s* parálisis *f* cerebral
ceremonious [ˌsɛrɪˋmonɪ•əs] *adj* ceremonioso, etiquetero
ceremo•ny [ˋsɛrɪˌmoni] *s* (*pl* **-nies**) ceremonia; **to stand on ceremony** hacer ceremonias, ser etiquetero
certain [ˋsʌrtən] *adj* cierto; **a certain** cierto; **for certain** por cierto
certainly [ˋsɛrtənli] *adj* ciertamente; (*gladly*) con mucho gusto
certain•ty [ˋsʌrtənti] *s* (*pl* **-ties**) certeza; **with certainty** a ciencia cierta
certificate [sərˋtɪfɪkɪt] *s* certificación, certificado; (*of birth, death, etc.*) partida, fe *f;* (*document representing financial assets*) título ‖ [sərˋtɪfɪˌket] *tr* certificar
certified check *s* talón conformado
certified public accountant [ˋsʌrtɪˌfaɪd] *s* contador público, censor jurado de cuentas
certi•fy [ˋsʌrtɪˌfaɪ] *v* (*pret* & *pp* **-fied**) *tr* certificar
cervix [ˋsʌrvɪks] *s* (*pl* **cervices** [sərˋvaɪsiz]) cerviz *f*
cessation [sɛˋseʃən] *s* cesación
cessation of hostilities *s* suspensión de hostilidades
cesspool [ˋsɛsˌpul] *s* pozo negro; (fig) sitio inmundo
Ceylon [sɪˋlɑn] *s* Ceilán
Ceylo•nese [ˌsiləˋniz] *adj* ceilanés ‖ *s* (*pl* **-nese**) ceilanés *m*
cf. *abbr* **confer,** i.e., **compare**
C.F.I., c.f.i. *abbr* **cost, freight, and insurance**
cg. *abbr* **centigram**
ch. *abbr* **chapter, church**
chafe [tʃef] *s* fricción, roce *m;* desgaste *m;* irritación ‖ *tr* (*to rub*) frotar; (*to rub and make sore*) escocer, (*to wear*) desgastar; irritar ‖ *intr* escocerse; desgastarse; irritarse
chaff [tʃæf] *s* barcia; paja menuda; broza, desperdicio
chafing dish [ˋtʃefɪŋ] *s* cocinilla, infernillo
chagrin [ʃəˋgrɪn] *s* desazón *f*, disgusto ‖ *tr* desazonar, disgustar
chain [tʃen] *s* cadena ‖ *tr* encadenar
chain gang *s* cadena de presidiarios, collera, cuerda de presos
chain reaction *s* reacción en cadena
chain saw *s* sierra de cadena
chain'smoke' *intr* fumar un pitillo tras otro
chair [tʃɛr] *s* silla; (*de catedrático*) cátedra; presidencia; (*e.g., of a university department*) presidente *m*, presidenta; **to take the chair** presidir la reunión; abrir la sesión ‖ *tr* presidir (*una reunión*)
chair lift *s* telesilla
chair•man [ˋtʃɛrmən] *s* (*pl* **-men** [mən]) presidente *mf*
chairmanship [ˋtʃɛrmənˌʃɪp] *s* presidencia
chair'per'son *s* presidente *m*, presidenta
chair rail *s* guardasilla
chalice [ˋtʃælɪs] *s* cáliz *m*

chalk [tʃɔk] *s* (*soft white limestone*) creta; (*piece used for writing*) tiza ‖ *tr* marcar o escribir con tiza; **to chalk up** apuntar; marcar (*un tanto*)
challenge [ˈtʃælɪndʒ] *s* desafío; (law) recusación ‖ *tr* desafiar; (law) recusar
chamber [ˈtʃembər] *s* cámara; (*of a gun*) recámara; dormitorio; **chambers** oficina de juez
chamberlain [ˈtʃembərlɪn] *s* chambelán *m*
chamˊber•maid *s* camarera
chamber music *s* música de cámara
chamber of commerce *s* cámara de comercio
chamber pot *s* orinal *m*
chameleon [kəˈmilɪ•ən] *s* camaleón *m*
chamfer [ˈtʃæmfər] *s* chaflán *m* ‖ *tr* chaflanar
cham•ois [ˈʃæmi] *s* (*pl* **-ois**) gamuza
champ [tʃæmp] *s* mordisco; (slang) campeón *m* ‖ *tr & intr* mordiscar; (*el freno*) morder
champagne [ʃæmˈpen] *s* champaña *m*
champion [ˈtʃæmpɪ•ən] *s* campeón *m* ‖ *tr* defender
championess [ˈtʃæmpɪ•ənɪs] *s* campeona
championship [ˈtʃæmpɪ•ən,ʃip] *s* campeonato
chance [tʃæns] o [tʃɑns] *adj* casual, imprevisto ‖ *s* oportunidad, ocasión; casualidad, suerte *f;* probabilidad; peligro, riesgo; chance *m* (SAm); **by chance** por casualidad; **to not stand a chance** no tener probabilidad de éxito; **to take a chance** probar fortuna; comprar un billete de lotería; **to take chances** probar fortuna; **to wait for a chance** esperar la oportunidad ‖ *intr* acontecer; **to chance on** o **upon** tropezar con; **to chance to** acertar a
chancel [ˈtʃænsəl] o [ˈtʃɑnsəl] *s* entrecoro
chanceller•y [ˈtʃænsələri] o [ˈtʃɑnsələrɪ] *s* (*pl* **-ies**) cancillería
chancellor [ˈtʃænsələr] *s* canciller *m*
chandelier [,ʃændəˈlɪr] *s* araña de luces
change [tʃendʒ] *s* cambio, mudanza; suelto, moneda suelta; (*surplus money returned with a purchase*) vuelta; (*of clothing*) muda; **for a change** por variedad; **to keep the change** quedarse con la vuelta; ‖ *tr* cambiar, mudar; cambiar de, mudar de; reemplazar; **to change clothes** cambiar de ropa; **to change gears** cambiar de velocidades; **to change hands** cambiar de dueño; **to change money** cambiar moneda; **to change one's mind** cambiar de parecer; **to change trains** cambiar de tren, transbordar ‖ *intr* cambiar, mudar; corregirse
changeable [ˈtʃendʒəbəl] *adj* cambiable; inconstante, cambiante, mudable
change of clothing *s* muda de ropa
change of heart *s* arrepentimiento, conversión
change of life *s* cesación natural de las reglas
change of voice *s* muda (*de voz*)
chan•nel [ˈtʃænəl] *s* (*body of water joining two others*) canal *m;* (*bed of river*) álveo, cauce *m;* (*means of communication*) vía; (*passage*) conducto; (*groove*) ranura, surco; (compu, electron, rad, telv) canal *m;* **the Channel** el Canal de la Mancha ‖ *v* (*pret & pp* **-neled** o **-nelled;** *ger* **-neling** o **-nelling**) *tr* acanalar; canalizar (*esfuerzos, dinero, etc.*)
chant [tʃænt] *s* (*song*) canción; (*song sung in a monotone*) canto ‖ *tr & intr* cantar
chanter [ˈtʃæntər] *s* cantor *m;* (*priest*) chantre *m*
chanticleer [ˈtʃæntɪ,klɪr] *s* el gallo
chaos [ˈke•ɑs] *s* caos *m*
chaotic [keˈɑtɪk] *adj* caótico
chap. *abbr* **chaplain, chapter**
chap [tʃæp] *s* (*jaw*) mandíbula; (*cheek*) mejilla; (*crack in the skin*) grieta; chico, tipo; **chaps** zahones *mpl* ‖ *v* (*pret & pp* **chapped;** *ger* **chapping**) *tr* agrietar, rajar ‖ *intr* agrietarse, rajarse
chapel [ˈtʃæpəl] *s* capilla
chaperon o **chaperone** [ˈʃæpə,ron] *s* carabina, señora de compañía ‖ *tr* acompañar (*una señora a una o más señoritas*)
chaplain [ˈtʃæplɪn] *s* capellán *m*
chaplet [ˈtʃæplɪt] *s* (*wreath for head*) guirnalda; rosario
chapter [ˈtʃæptər] *s* capítulo; (*of the Scriptures*) capítula; (*of a cathedral*) cabildo
chapter and verse *adv* con todos sus pelos y señales
char [tʃɑr] *v* (*pret & pp* **charred;** *ger* **charring**) *tr* carbonizar; (*to scorch*) socarrar
character [ˈkærɪktər] *s* carácter *m;* (*conspicuous person; person in a play or novel*) personaje *m;* (*part or role in a play*) papel *m;* (*fellow*) (coll) tipo, sujeto
character assassination *s* asesinato de carácter
characteristic [,kærɪktəˈrɪstɪk] *adj* característico ‖ *s* característica
characterize [ˈkærɪktə,raɪz] *tr* caracterizar
charˊcoalˊ *s* carbón *m* de leña; (*for sketching*) carboncillo; (*sketch*) dibujo al carbón
charcoal burner *s* (*person*) carbonero; horno para hacer carbón de leña
charge [tʃɑrdʒ] *s* (*of an explosive, of electricity, of soldiers against the enemy; responsibility*) carga; (*accusation; amount owed; recording of amount owed*) cargo; encargamiento; (heral) blasón *m;* (*attack*) embestida; **in charge of** a cargo de; **to put in charge** responsabilizar; **to reverse the charges** (telp) cargar al número llamado; **to take charge of** hacerse cargo de ‖ *tr* cargar; cobrar (*cierto precio*); (*to order*) encargar, mandar; cargar (*un acumulador; al enemigo*); **to charge to the account of someone** cargarle a uno en cuenta; **to charge with** cargar de ‖ *intr* embestir
charge account *s* cuenta de crédito
chargé d'affaires [ʃɑrˈʒe dəˈfɛr] *s* (*pl* **chargés d'affaires**) encargado de negocios
charger [ˈtʃɑrdʒər] *s* caballo de guerra; (*of a battery*) cargador *m*
chariot [ˈtʃærɪ•ət] *s* carro romano
charioteer [,tʃærɪ•əˈtɪr] *s* carretero, auriga *m*
charisma [kəˈrɪzmə] *s* carisma
charismatic [,kɑrɪzˈmætɪk] *adj* carismático

charitable [ˈtʃærɪtəbəl] *adj* caritativo
chari•ty [ˈtʃærɪti] *s* (*pl* **-ties**) caridad; asociación de beneficencia, obra pía; **charity begins at home** la caridad bien ordenada empieza por uno mismo
charity performance *s* función benéfica
charlatan [ˈʃɑrlətən] *s* charlatán *m*
charlatanism [ˈʃɑrlətən,ɪzəm] *s* charlatanismo
Charlemagne [ˈʃɑrlə,men] *s* Carlomagno
Charles [tʃɑrlz] *s* Carlos *m*
charm [tʃɑrm] *s* encanto, hechizo; (*trinket*) amuleto, dije *m* || *tr* encantar, hechizar
charming [ˈtʃɑrmɪŋ] *adj* encantador
charnel [ˈtʃɑrnəl] *adj* cadavérico, horrible || *s* carnero, osario
chart [tʃɑrt] *s* mapa geográfico; (naut) carta de marear; cuadro, diagrama *m* || *tr* bosquejar; **to chart a course** trazar una ruta
charter [ˈtʃɑrtər] *s* carta (de privilegio) || *tr* alquilar (*un autobús*); fletar (*un barco*)
charter member *s* socio fundador
char•woman [ˈtʃɑr,wʊmən] *s* (*pl* **-women** [,wɪmɪn]) alquilona, asistenta
chase [tʃes] *s* caza, persecución || *tr* cazar, perseguir; **to chase away** ahuyentar
chasm [ˈkæzəm] *s* abismo
chas•sis [ˈtʃæsi] *s* (*pl* **-sis** [siz]) chasis *m*
chaste [tʃest] *adj* casto; (*style*) castizo
chasten [ˈtʃesən] *tr* castigar, corregir
chastise [tʃæsˈtaɪz] *tr* castigar
chastity [ˈtʃæstɪti] *s* castidad
chasuble [ˈtʃæzjəbəl] *s* casulla
chat [tʃæt] *s* charla, plática || *v* (*pret & pp* **chatted;** *ger* **chatting**) *intr* charlar, platicar; (comp) chatear
chat room *s* (compu) charla de chat
chat server *s* (compu) servidor *m* de chat
chatelaine [ˈʃætə,len] *s* castellana
chattel [ˈtʃætəl] *s* bienes *mpl* muebles; **chattels** enseres *mpl*
chatter [ˈtʃætər] *s* (*talk*) cháchara; (*rattling*) traqueo; (*of teeth*) castañeteo; (*of birds*) chirrido || *intr* chacharear; traquear; castañetear, dentellar (*los dientes*)
chat'ter•box' *s* charlador *m,* tarabilla
chattering [ˈtʃætərɪŋ] *adj* palabrudo
chauffeur [ˈʃofər] o [ʃoˈfʌr] *s* chófer *m*
chauvinism [ˈʃovɪnɪzəm] *s* chauvinismo
chauvinist [ˈʃovɪnɪst] *adj & s* chovinista *mf;* (*sexist*) machista *mf*
cheap [tʃip] *adj* barato; (*charging low prices*) no carero, baratero; (*flashy*) cursi; baladí; **to feel cheap** sentirse avergonzado || *adv* barato
cheapen [ˈtʃipən] *tr* abaratar
cheapness [ˈtʃipnɪs] *s* baratura; baratía; (*flashiness*) cursilería
cheat [tʃit] *s* trampa, fraude *m;* (*person*) trampista *mf,* defraudador *m* || *tr* trampear, defraudar
check [tʃɛk] *s* (*of bank*) cheque *m;* (*for baggage*) talón *m,* contraseña; (*in a restaurant*) cuenta; (*in theater or movie*) contraseña, billete *m* de salida; (*restraint*) freno; (*to hold a door*) amortiguador *m;* (*in chess*) jaque *m;* inspección; comprobación, verificación; (*cloth*) paño a cuadros; **in check** en jaque; **to hold in check** contener, refrenar || *interj* ¡jaque! || *tr* parar súbitamente; contener, refrenar; amortiguar; facturar (*equipajes*); inspeccionar; comprobar, verificar; marcar, señalar; chequear; (*in chess*) jaquear, dar jaque a; **to check up** comprobar, verificar || *intr* pararse súbitamente; corresponder punto por punto; **to check in** (*at a hotel*) llegar e inscribirse; **to check out** pagar la cuenta y despedirse; (slang) morir
check'book' *s* talonario (de cheques), chequera
checker [ˈtʃɛkər] *s* inspector *m;* cuadro; dibujo a cuadros; (*in game of checkers*) ficha, pieza; **checkers** damas, juego de damas || *tr* marcar con cuadros; diversificar, variar
check'er•board' *s* damero, tablero
check girl *s* moza de guardarropa
checking account *s* cuenta corriente
check'mate' *s* mate *m,* jaque *m* mate || *tr* dar mate a, dar jaque mate a; (fig) derrotar completamente
check'out' *s* (*from a hotel*) salida; hora de salida; (*in a self-service retail store*) revisión y pago, caja
checkout counter *s* mostrador *m* de revisión
check'point' *s* punto de inspección, control *m*
check'rein' *s* engallador *m*
check'room' *s* guardarropa *m;* (rr) consigna, depósito de equipajes
check'up' *s* verificación rigurosa; chequeo; (*of an automobile*) revisión; (med) reconocimiento general, revisión médica (Esp)
cheek [tʃik] *s* mejilla, carrillo; (coll) descaro, frescura
cheek'bone' *s* pómulo
cheek by jowl *adv* cara a cara, en estrecha intimidad
cheek•y [ˈtʃiki] *adj* (*comp* **-ier;** *super* **-iest**) (coll) descarado, fresco
cheer [tʃir] *s* alegría, regocijo; (*shout*) viva *m,* aplauso; **what cheer?** ¿qué tal? || *tr* alegrar, animar; aplaudir, vitorear; dar la bienvenida a, con vivas y aplausos || *intr* alegrarse, animarse; **cheer up!** ¡ánimo!
cheerful [ˈtʃirfəl] *adj* alegre
cheerio [ˈtʃirɪ,o] *interj* (coll) ¡hola! ¡qué tal!; (coll) ¡adiós! ¡hasta la vista!
cheerless [ˈtʃirlɪs] *adj* sombrío, triste
cheese [tʃiz] *s* queso
cheese'bur,ger *s* hamburguesa con queso
cheese'cloth' *s* estopilla
cheese spread *s* queso para extender
cheetah [ˈtʃitə] *s* gatopardo; leopardo indio
chef [ʃɛf] *s* primer cocinero, jefe *m* de cocina
chem. *abbr* **chemical, chemist, chemistry**
chemical [ˈkɛmɪkəl] *adj* químico || *s* producto químico, substancia química
chemical engineer *s* ingeniero químico
chemical warfare *s* guerra química
chemise [ʃəˈmiz] *s* camisa (de mujer)

chemist [ˈkɛmɪst] *s* químico
chemistry [ˈkɛmɪstri] *s* química
chemotherapy [ˌkimoˈθɛrəpi] *s* quimioterapia
cherish [ˈtʃɛrɪʃ] *tr* acariciar; (*a hope*) abrigar, acariciar
cher•ry [ˈtʃɛri] *s* (*pl* **-ries**) (*fruit; color*) cereza; (*tree*) cerezo
cher•ub [ˈtʃɛrəb] *s* (*pl* **-ubim** [əbɪm]) querubín *m* ‖ *s* (*pl* **-ubs**) niño angelical
chess [tʃɛs] *s* ajedrez *m*
chess'board' *s* tablero de ajedrez
chess•man [ˈtʃɛsˌmæn] *s* (*pl* **-men** [ˌmɛn]) pieza de ajedrez, trebejo
chess player *s* ajedrecista *mf*
chess set *s* ajedrez *m*
chest [tʃɛst] *s* (*part of body*) pecho; (*receptacle*) cajón *m*, cofre *m;* (*piece of furniture*) cómoda
chestnut [ˈtʃɛsnət] *s* (*tree, wood, color*) castaño; (*fruit*) castaña
chest of drawers *s* cómoda
cheval glass [ʃəˈvæl] *s* psique *f*
chevalier [ˌʃɛvəˈlɪr] *s* caballero
chevron [ˈʃɛvrən] *s* galón *m* en forma de V invertida
chew [tʃʊ] *s* mascadura ‖ *tr* mascar; **to chew gum** chiclear; **to chew the rag** (slang) dar la lengua ‖ *intr* mascar
chewing gum *s* goma de mascar, chicle *m*
chg. *abbr* **charge**
chic [ʃik] *adj & s* chic *m*
chicaner•y [ʃɪˈkenəri] *s* (*pl* **-ies**) triquiñuela
chick [tʃɪk] *s* pollito; (slang) polla
chicken [ˈtʃikən] *s* pollo; (*young person*) pollo; (*young girl*) polla
chicken coop *s* pollera
chickenhearted [ˈtʃikənˌhɑrtɪd, varicela] *adj* gallina
chicken pox *s* viruelas locas, varicela
chicken wire *s* alambrada, tela metálica
chick'pea' *s* garbanzo
chico•ry [ˈtʃikəri] *s* (*pl* **-ries**) achicoria
chide [tʃaɪd] *v* (*pret* **chided** o **chid** [tʃɪd]; *pp* **chided, chid** o **chidden** [ˈtʃɪdən]) *tr* reprender, regañar
chief [tʃif] *adj* principal ‖ *s* jefe *m;* (*of American Indians*) cacique *m*
chief executive *s* jefe *m* del gobierno
chief justice *s* presidente *m* de sala; presidente del tribunal supremo
chiefly [ˈtʃifli] *adv* principalmente, mayormente
chief of staff *s* jefe *m* del estado mayor
chief of state *s* jefe *m* del estado
chieftain [ˈtʃiftən] *s* (*of a clan or tribe*) jefe *m;* adalid *m,* caudillo
chiffon [ʃɪˈfɑn] *s* gasa, soplillo; **chiffons** atavíos, perifollos
chiffonier [ˌʃifəˈnɪr] *s* cómoda alta
chignon [ˈʃinjɑn] *s* castaña, moño
chilblain [ˈtʃilˌblen] *s* sabañón *m*
child [tʃaɪld] *adj* (*before a noun: child, children's*) infantil ‖ *s* (*pl* **children** [ˈtʃildrən]) *s* (*infant, youngster*) niño; pipiolo (CAm, Mex); (*one's offspring*) hijo; descendiente *mf;* **with child** encinta, embarazada
child abuse *s* maltrato infantil; (*sexual*) abusos sexual infantil, abusos deshonestos
child'birth' *s* alumbramiento, parto
childhood [ˈtʃaɪldhʊd] *s* niñez *f,* puericia; **from childhood** desde niño
childish [ˈtʃaɪldɪʃ] *adj* aniñado, pueril, infantil
childishness [ˈtʃaɪldɪʃnɪs] *s* puerilidad
child labor *s* trabajo de menores
childless [ˈtʃaɪldlɪs] *adj* sin hijos
child'like' *adj* aniñado
child'-rear'ing *s* puericultura
children's books *s* literatura infantil
children's home *s* casa cuna
child's play *s* juego de niños
child welfare *s* protección a la infancia
Chile [ˈtʃili] *s* Chile *m*
Chilean [ˈtʃilɪ•ən] *adj & s* chileno
chili sauce [ˈtʃili] *s* ají *m,* salsa de ají
chill [tʃil] *adj* frío ‖ *s* frío desapacible; (*sensation of cold*) escalofrío; (*lack of cordiality*) frialdad ‖ *tr* enfriar ‖ *intr* calofriarse
chill•y [ˈtʃili] *adj* (*comp* **-ier;** *super* **-iest**) (*causing shivering*) frío; (*sensitive to cold*) escalofriado, friolero; (*indifferent*) (fig) frío
chime [tʃaɪm] *s* campaneo, repique *m;* tubo sonoro; **chimes** juego de campanas ‖ *tr & intr* campanear, repicar
chime clock *s* reloj *m* de carillón
chimera [kaɪˈmɪrə] o [kɪˈmɪrə] *s* quimera
chimney [ˈtʃimni] *s* chimenea; (*for a lamp*) tubo
chimney cap *s* caperuza
chimney flue *s* cañón *m* de chimenea
chimney pot *s* mitra, guardavientos *m*
chimney sweep *s* limpiachimeneas *m,* deshollinador *m*
chimpanzee [tʃimˈpænzi] o [ˌtʃimpænˈzi] *s* chimpancé *m*
chin [tʃin] *s* barba, mentón *m;* **to keep one's chin up** (coll) no desanimarse ‖ *v* (*pret & pp* **chinned;** *ger* **chinning**) *intr* (coll) charlar
china [ˈtʃaɪnə] *s* china, porcelana ‖ **China** *s* China
china closet *s* chinero
Chinatown [ˈtʃaɪnətaʊn] *s* barrio chino
chi'na•ware' *s* porcelana, vajilla de porcelana
Chi•nese [tʃaɪˈniz] *adj* chino ‖ *s* (*pl* **-nese** chino
Chinese checkers *s* damas chinas
Chinese gong *s* batintín *m*
Chinese lantern *s* farolillo veneciano
Chinese puzzle *s* problema embrollado
chink [tʃɪŋk] *s* grieta, hendidura; sonido metálico
chin strap *s* barboquejo, carrillera
chintz [tʃints] *s* zaraza
chip [tʃip] *s* astilla, brizna; (*in china*) desconchado; (*in poker*) ficha; (compu, electron) chip *m;* **chip off the old block** hijo de su padre *or* madre ‖ *v* (*pret & pp* **chipped;** *ger* **chipping**) *tr* astillar (*la madera*); desconchar (*la porcelana*); **to chip in** contribuir con su cuota ‖ *intr* astillarse; desconcharse

chipmunk [ˈtʃɪp,mʌŋk] *s* ardilla listada
chipper [ˈtʃɪpər] *adj* (coll) alegre, jovial, vivo
chiropodist [kaɪˈrɑpədɪst] o [kɪˈrɑpədɪst] *s* quiropodista *mf*
chiropractor [ˈkaɪrə,præktər] *s* quiropráctico
chirp [tʃʌrp] *s* chirrido, gorjeo ‖ *intr* chirriar, gorjear; hablar alegremente
chis•el [ˈtʃɪzəl] *s* (*for wood*) escoplo, formón *m;* (*for stone and metal*) cincel *m* ‖ *v* (*pret & pp* **-eled** o **-elled;** *ger* **-eling** o **-elling**) *tr* escoplear; cincelar; (slang) estafar
chit-chat [ˈtʃɪt,tʃæt] *s* charla, palique *m;* hablilla, chismes *mpl*
chivalric [ˈʃɪvəlrɪk] o [ʃɪˈvælrɪk] *adj* caballeresco
chivalrous [ˈʃɪvəlrəs] *adj* caballeroso
chivalry [ˈʃɪvəlri] *s* (*knighthood*) caballería; (*gallantry, gentlemanliness*) caballerosidad
chloride [ˈkloraɪd] *s* cloruro
chlorine [ˈklorin] *s* cloro
chloroform [ˈklorə,fɔrm] *s* cloroformo ‖ *tr* cloroformizar
chlorophyll [ˈklorəfɪl] *s* clorofila
chock-full [ˈtʃɑkˈfʊl] *adj* de bote en bote, colmado
chocolate [ˈtʃɑkəlɪt] *s* chocolate *m*
choice [tʃɔɪs] *adj* escogido, selecto, superior ‖ *s* elección, selección; lo más escogido; **to have no choice** no tener alternativa
choir [kwaɪr] *s* coro
choir′boy′ *s* niño de coro, infante *m* de coro
choir desk *s* facistol *m*
choir loft *s* coro
choir′mas′ter *s* jefe *m* de coro, maestro de capilla
choke [tʃok] *s* estrangulación; (*of carburetor*) cierre *m,* obturador *m;* (elec) choque *m* ‖ *tr* ahogar, sofocar, estrangular; obstruir, tapar; (aut) obturar; **to choke down** atragantar ‖ *intr* sofocarse; atragantarse; **to choke on** atragantarse con
cholera [ˈkɑlərə] *s* cólera *m*
choleric [ˈkɑlərɪk] *adj* colérico
cholesterol [kəˈlɛstə,rol] *s* colesterol *m*
choose [tʃuz] *v* (*pret* **chose** [tʃoz]; *pp* **chosen** [ˈtʃozən]) *tr* escoger, elegir ‖ *intr* — **to choose between** optar entre; **to choose to** optar por
chop [tʃɑp] *s* golpe *m* cortante; (*of meat*) chuleta; **chops** boca, labios ‖ *v* (*pret & pp* **chopped;** *ger* **chopping**) *tr* cortar, tajar; picar (*la carne*); **to chop off** tronchar; **to chop up** desmenuzar
chopper [ˈtʃɑpər] *s* (*person*) tajador *m;* (*tool*) hacha; (*of butcher*) cortante *m;* (slang) helicóptero
chopping block *s* tajo
chop•py [ˈtʃɑpi] *adj* (*comp* **-pier;** *super* **-piest**) (*sea*) agitado, picado; (*wind*) variable; (*style*) cortado, inciso
chop shop *s* (coll) *lugar oculto por desmontar autos robados*
chop′sticks′ *spl* palillos
choral [ˈkorəl] *adj* coral
chorale [koˈrɑl] *s* coral *m*
choral society *s* orfeón *m*
chord [kɔrd] *s* (*harmonious combination of tones*) (mus) acorde *m;* (aer, anat, geom) cuerda
chore [tʃor] *s* tarea, quehacer *m*
choreography [,korɪˈɑgrəfi] *s* coreografía
chorine [koˈrin] *s* (slang) corista, suripanta
chorus [ˈkorəs] *s* coro; (*refrain of a song*) estribillo
chorus girl *s* corista, conjuntista
chowder [ˈtʃaʊdər] *s* estofado de almejas o pescado o papas o legumbres
Chr. *abbr* **Christian**
Christ [kraɪst] *s* Cristo
christen [ˈkrɪsən] *tr* bautizar
Christendom [ˈkrɪsəndəm] *s* cristiandad
christening [ˈkrɪsənɪŋ] *s* bautismo, bautizo
Christian [ˈkrɪstʃən] *adj & s* cristiano
Christianity [,krɪstʃɪˈænɪti] *s* cristianismo
Christianize [ˈkrɪstʃə,naɪz] *tr* cristianizar
Christian name *s* nombre *m* de pila
Christian Science *s* (eccl) Ciencia Cristiana
Christmas [ˈkrɪsməs] *adj* navideño ‖ *s* Navidad, Pascua de Navidad, Pascua
Christmas card *s* tarjeta navideña
Christmas carol *s* villancico
Christmas Eve *s* Nochebuena
Christmas gift *s* aguinaldo, regalo de Navidad
Christmas tree *s* árbol *m* de Navidad
Christopher [ˈkrɪstəfər] *s* Cristóbal *m*
chrome [krom] *adj* cromado ‖ *s* cromo ‖ *tr* cromar
chromium [ˈkromɪ•əm] *s* cromo
chro•mo [ˈkromo] *s* (*pl* **-mos**) (*colored picture*) cromo; (*piece of junk*) (slang) trasto
chromosome [ˈkromə,som] *s* cromosoma *m*
chron. *abbr* **chronological, chronology**
chronic [ˈkrɑnɪk] *adj* crónico
chronicle [ˈkrɑnɪkəl] *s* crónica ‖ *tr* narrar en una crónica; narrar, contar
chronicler [ˈkrɑnɪklər] *s* cronista *mf*
chronolo•gy [krəˈnɑlədʒi] *s* (*pl* **-gies**) cronología
chronometer [krəˈnɑmɪtər] *s* cronómetro
chrysanthemum [krɪˈsænθɪməm] *s* crisantemo
chub•by [ˈtʃʌbi] *adj* (*comp* **-bier;** *super* **-biest**) rechoncho, regordete
chuck [tʃʌk] *s* (*throw*) echada, tirada; (*under the chin*) mamola; (*of a lathe*) mandril *m* ‖ *tr* arrojar; **to chuck under the chin** hacer la mamola a
chuckle [ˈtʃʌkəl] *s* risa ahogada ‖ *intr* reírse con risa ahogada
chug [tʃʌg] *s* ruido explosivo sordo; (*of a locomotive*) resoplido ‖ *v* (*pret & pp* **chugged;** *ger* **chugging**) *intr* hacer ruidos explosivos sordos, moverse con ruidos explosivos sordos
chum [tʃʌm] *s* (coll) compinche *mf;* compañero de cuarto ‖ *v* (*pret & pp* **chummed;** *ger* **chumming**) *intr* (coll) ser compinche, ser compinches; (coll) compartir un cuarto

chum•my[ˈtʃʌmi] *adj* (*comp* **-mier;** *super* **-miest**) muy amigable, íntimo
chump [tʃʌmp] *s* tarugo, zoquete *m;* (coll) estúpido, tonto
chunk [tʃʌnk] *s* trozo, pedazo grueso
church [tʃʌrt] *s* iglesia
churchgoer [ˈtʃʌrtʃ,go•ər] *s* practicante *mf,* devoto
church member *s* feligrés *m*
Church of England *s* Iglesia Anglicana
church'yard' *s* patio de iglesia; cementerio
churl [tʃʌrl] *s* palurdo, patán *m*
churlish [ˈtʃʌrlɪʃ] *adj* palurdo, insolente
churn [tʃʌrn] *s* mantequera || *tr* mazar (*leche*); hacer (*mantequilla*) en una mantequera; agitar, revolver || *intr* revolverse
chute [ʃut] *s* cascada, salto de agua; rápidos; conducto inclinado; (*e.g., into a swimming pool*) tobogán *m;* (*e.g., for grain*) tolva; paracaídas *m*
CIA [ˈsiˈaɪˈe] *s* (letterword) (**Central Intelligence Agency**) CIA *f* (Agencia Central de Inteligencia)
cibori•um [sɪˈborɪ•əm] *s* (*pl* **-a** [ə]) (*canopy*) ciborio, baldaquín *m;* (*cup*) copón *m*
cicada [səˈkedə] *s* chicharra, cigarra
Cicero [ˈsɪsə,ro] *s* Cicerón *m*
cider [ˈsaɪdər] *s* sidra
C.I.F., c.i.f. *abbr* **cost, insurance, and freight**
cigar [sɪˈgɑr] *s* cigarro, puro
cigar band *s* anillo de cigarro
cigar case *s* cigarrera, petaca
cigar cutter *s* cortacigarros *m*
cigaret o **cigarette** [,sɪgəˈrɛt] *s* cigarrillo, pitillo
cigarette case *s* pitillera
cigarette holder *s* boquilla
cigarette lighter *s* mechero, encendedor *m* de bolsillo
cigarette paper *s* papel *m* de fumar
cigar holder *s* boquilla
cigar store *s* estanco, tabaquería
cinch [sɪntʃ] *s* (*of saddle*) cincha; (*sure grip*) (coll) agarro; (*something easy*) (slang) breva || *tr* cinchar; (coll) agarrar
cinder [ˈsɪndər] *s* ceniza; (*coal burning without flame*) pavesa
cinder bank *s* escorial *m*
Cinderella [,sɪndəˈrɛlə] *s* la Cenicienta
cinder track *s* pista de cenizas
cinema [ˈsɪnəmə] *s* cine *m*
cinnabar [ˈsɪnə,bɑr] *s* cinabrio
cinnamon [ˈsɪnəmən] *s* canela
cipher [ˈsaɪfər] *s* cifra; cero; (*nonentity*) cero a la izquierda; (*key to a cipher*) clave *f* || *tr* cifrar; calcular
circle [ˈsʌrkəl] *s* círculo || *tr* circundar; dar la vuelta a; girar alrededor de
circuit [ˈsʌrkɪt] *s* circuito; **circuit board** *s* placa base
circuit breaker *s* disyuntor *m,* cortacircuitos
circuitous [sərˈkju•ɪtəs] *adj* indirecto, tortuoso
circuitry [ˈsʌrkɪtrɪ] *s* sistema *m* de circuitos; (compu) circuitería
circular [ˈsʌrkjələr] *adj* tortuoso; circular || *s* circular *f,* carta circular
circularize [ˈsʌrkjələ,raɪz] *tr* anunciar por circular; enviar circulares a
circulate [ˈsʌrkjə,let] *tr & intr* circular
circumcise [ˈsʌrkəm,saɪz] *tr* circuncidar
circumference [sərˈkʌmfərəns] *s* circunferencia
circumflex [ˈsʌrkəm,flɛks] *adj* circunflejo
circumflex accent *s* acento circunflejo
circumlocution [,sʌrkəmloˈkjuʃən] *s* circunlocución, circunloquio
circumnavigate [,sʌrkəmˈnævɪ,get] *tr* circunnavegar
circumnavigation [,sʌrkəm,nævɪˈgeʃən] *s* circunnavegación
circumscribe [,sʌrkəmˈskraɪb] *tr* circunscribir
circumspect [ˈsʌrkəm,spɛkt] *adj* circunspecto
circumstance [ˈsʌrkəm,stæns] *s* circunstancia; ceremonia, ostentación; **in easy circumstances** acomodado; **under no circumstances** de ninguna manera, ni a bala
circumstantial [,sʌrkəmˈstænʃəl] *adj* (*derived from circumstances*) circunstancial; (*detailed*) circunstanciado
circumstantial evidence *s* (law) indicios vehementes
circumstantiate [,sʌrkəmˈstænʃi,et] *tr* apoyar con pruebas y detalles; (*to describe in detail*) circunstanciar
circumvent [,sʌrkəmˈvɛnt] *tr* (*to catch by a trick*) entrampar, embaucar; (*to outwit*) burlar; (*to keep away from, get around*) evitar
circus [ˈsʌrkəs] *s* circo
cistern [ˈsɪstərn] *s* cisterna, aljibe *m*
citadel [ˈsɪtədəl] *s* ciudadela
citation [saɪˈteʃən] *s* (*of a text*) cita; (*before a court of law*) citación; (*for gallantry*) mención
cite [saɪt] *tr* (*to quote; to summon*) citar; (*for gallantry*) mencionar
citizen [ˈsɪtɪzən] *s* ciudadano, (*civilian*) paisano
citizen•ry [ˈsɪtɪzənri] *s* (*pl* **-ries**) conjunto de ciudadanos
citizens band *s* banda ciudadana
citizenship [ˈsɪtɪzən,ʃɪp] *s* ciudadanía
citron[ˈsɪtrən] *s* (*fruit*) cidra; (*tree*) **cidro;** (*candied rind*) cidrada
citronella [,sɪtəˈnɛlə] *s* limoncillo (*Andropogon nardus*); aceite *m* de limoncillo
citrus fruit [ˈsɪtrəs] *s* agrios, frutas cítricas
cit•y [ˈsɪti] *s* (*pl* **-ies**) ciudad
city clerk *s* archivero
city council *s* ayuntamiento
city editor *s* redactor de periódico encargado de noticias locales
city fathers *spl* concejales *mpl*
city hall *s* casa consistorial, ayuntamiento
city plan *s* plano de la ciudad
city planner *s* urbanista *mf*
city planning *s* urbanismo
city room *s* redacción
cit'y-state' *s* ciudad-estado *f*

civic [ˈsɪvɪk] *adj* cívico || **civics** *s* estudio de los deberes y derechos del ciudadano
civic-mindedness [ˈmaɪndɪdnɪs] *s* civismo
civies [ˈsɪvɪz] *spl* (coll) traje *m* de paisano; **in civies** (coll) de paisano, de civil
civil [ˈsɪvɪl] *adj* civil; cortés
civilian [sɪˈvɪljən] *adj* civil || *s* civil *mf,* paisano; **civilians** civiles, civilidad
civilian clothes *spl* traje *m* de paisano
civili•ty [sɪˈvɪlɪti] *s* (*pl* **-ties** cortesía, educación
civilization [ˌsɪvɪlɪˈzeʃən] *s* civilización
civilize [ˈsɪvɪˌlaɪz] *tr* civilizar
civil servant *s* funcionario del estado
civil service *s* administración pública
civil war *s* guerra civil; **Civil War** (U.S.A.) Guerra de Secesión
civvies *var de* **civies**
claim [klem] *s* demanda, pretensión, reclamación || *tr* demandar, pretender, reclamar; afirmar, declarar; **to claim to** + *inf* pretender + *inf*
claim check *s* comprobante *m*
clairvoyance [klɛrˈvɔɪ•əns] *s* clarividencia
clairvoyant [klɛrˈvɔɪ•ənt] *adj* & *s* clarividente *mf*
clam [klæm] *s* almeja; (*tight-lipped person*) (coll) chiticalla *m* || *intr* — **to clam up** (coll) callarse la boca
clamber [ˈklæmər] *intr* — **to clamber up** subir gateando
clamor [ˈklæmər] *s* clamor *m,* clamoreo || *intr* clamorear
clamorous [ˈklæmərəs] *adj* clamoroso
clamp [klæmp] *s* abrazadera, grapa; (*vise-like device*) mordaza || *tr* agrapar, afianzar con abrazadera; sujetar en una mordaza || *intr* — **to clamp down on** (coll) apretar los tornillos a
clan [klæn] *s* clan *m*
clandestine [klænˈdɛstɪn] *adj* clandestino
clang [klæŋ] *s* tantán *m,* sonido metálico resonante || *tr* hacer sonar fuertemente || *intr* sonar fuertemente
clank [klæŋk] *s* sonido metálico seco || *tr* hacer sonar secamente || *intr* sonar secamente
clannish [ˈklænɪʃ] *adj* exclusivista
clap [klæp] *s* golpe seco; (*of the hands*) palmada; (*of thunder*) estampido || *v* (*pret & pp* **clapped;** *ger* **clapping**) *tr* batir (*palmas*); palmotear, aplaudir; **to clap shut** cerrar de golpe || *intr* palmotear, dar palmadas
clap of thunder *s* estampido de trueno
clapper [ˈklæpər] *s* palmoteador *m;* (*of a bell*) badajo; (*to cause grain to slide*) tarabilla
clap'trap' *s* faramalla; (*of an actor*) latiguillo
claque [klæk] *s* (*paid clappers*) claque *f;* (*crush hat*) clac *m*
claret [ˈklærɪt] *s* clarete *m*
clari•fy [ˈklærɪˌfaɪ] *v* (*pret & pp* **-fied**) *tr* clarificar; encolar (*el vino*)
clarinet [ˈklærɪˈnet] *s* clarinete *m*
clarion [ˈklærɪ•ən] *adj* claro, brillante || *s* clarín *m*
clarity [ˈklærɪti] *s* claridad
clash [klæʃ] *s* choque *m,* encontrón *m;* estruendo, ruido || *intr* chocar, entrechocarse
clasp [klæsp] *s* (*fastener*) abrazadera, cierre *m;* (*for, e.g., a necktie*) broche *m;* (*buckle*) hebilla; (*embrace*) abrazo; (*grip*) agarro || *tr* abrochar; abrazar; agarrar, apretar (*la mano*); apretarse (*la mano*)
class [klæs] *s* clase *f;* ó (slang) elegancia, buen tono; (*sports*) división || *tr* clasificar || *intr* clasificarse
class action *s* (law) acción popular, demanda colectiva
class consciousness *s* sentimiento de clase
classic [ˈklæsɪk] *adj* & *s* clásico; **the classics** las obras clásicas
classical [ˈklæsɪkəl] *adj* clásico
classical scholar *s* erudito en las lenguas clásicas
classicist [ˈklæsɪsɪst] *s* clasicista *mf*
classified [ˈklæsɪˌfaɪd] *adj* clasificado; clasificado como secreto
classified ads *spl* anuncios clasificados en secciones, avisos clasificados
classi•fy [ˈklæsɪˌfaɪ] *v* (*pret & pp* **-fied**) *tr* clasificar
class'mate' *s* compañero de clase
class'room' *s* aula, sala de clase
class struggle *s* lucha de clases
class•y [ˈklæsi] *adj* (*comp* **-ier;** *super* **-iest**) (slang) elegante
clatter [ˈklætər] *s* estruendo confuso; algazara, gresca; (*of hoofs*) trápala || *intr* caer o moverse con estruendo confuso; hablar rápida y ruidosamente; **to clatter down the stairs** bajar la escalera ruidosamente
clause [klɔz] *s* (*article in a legal document*) cláusula; (gram) oración dependiente
clavichord [ˈklævɪˌkɔrd] *s* clavicordio
clavicle [ˈklævɪkəl] *s* clavícula
clavier [ˈklævɪ•ər] o [kləˈvɪr] *s* teclado || [kləˈvɪr] *s* instrumento musical con teclado
claw [klɔ] *s* garra, uña; (*of lobster, crab, etc.*) pinza; (*of hammer, wrench, etc.*) oreja; (coll) dedos, mano *f* || *tr* (*to clutch*) agarrar; (*to scratch*) arañar; (*to tear*) desgarrar
clay [kle] *adj* arcilloso || *s* arcilla
clay pigeon *s* pichón *m* de barro
clay pipe *s* pipa de tierra
clean [klin] *adj* limpio; distinto, neto, nítido; completo || *adv* completamente; **to come clean** (slang) confesarlo todo || *tr* limpiar; (*to tidy up*) asear; **to be cleaned out** (*of money*) (slang) quedar limpio; **to clean out** limpiar; (slang) dejar limpio || *intr* limpiarse; asearse; **to clean up** limpiarse; (coll) llevárselo todo; (*in gambling*) (slang) hacer mesa limpia; **to clean up after someone** limpiar lo que alguno ha ensuciado
clean bill of health *s* patente limpia de sanidad
cleaner [ˈklinər] *s* limpiador *m;* (*dry cleaner*) tintorero; (*preparation*) quitamanchas *m;* **to send to the cleaners** (slang) dejar limpio

cleaning [ˈklinɪŋ] *s* limpieza
cleaning fluid *s* quitamanchas *m*
cleaning woman *s* mujer *f* de la limpieza
cleanliness [ˈklɛnlɪnɪs] *s* limpieza
clean·ly [ˈklɛnli] *adj* (*comp* **-lier;** *super* **-liest**) limpio (*que tiene el hábito del aseo*)
cleanse [klɛnz] *tr* limpiar, lavar, depurar
clean-shaven [ˈklinˈʃevən] *adj* lisamente afeitado
clean′up′ *s* limpieza general; (*profit*) gran ganancia
clear [klɪr] *adj* claro; (*cloudless*) despejado; (*of debts, etc.*) libre ‖ *adv* claro, claramente; **clear through** de parte a parte ‖ *tr* despejar (*un bosque*); clarificar (*lo que estaba turbio*); (*to make less dark*) aclarar; saltar por encima de; (*to prove the innocence of*) absolver; sacar (*una ganancia neta*); abonar, acreditar; liquidar (*una cuenta*); (*in the customhouse*) despachar; salvar (*un obstáculo*); levantar (*la mesa*); desmontar (*un terreno*); **to clear out** vaciar, desocupar; **to clear the way** abrir camino; **to clear up** esclarecer, aclarar ‖ *intr* clarificarse; aclararse; **to clear away** irse, desaparecer; **to clear up** abonanzarse (*el tiempo*); despejarse (*el cielo, el tiempo*)
clearance [ˈklɪrəns] *s* aclaración; abono, acreditación; espacio libre; (*in a cylinder*) espacio muerto; (com) compensación
clearance sale *s* venta de liquidación
clear′-cut′ *adj* claro, bien definido
clearing [ˈklɪrɪŋ] *s* (*in a woods*) claro; (com) compensación
clearing house *s* cámara de compensación
clear-sighted [ˈklɪrˈsaɪtɪd] *adj* clarividente, perspicaz
cleat [klit] *s* abrazadera, listón *m*
cleavage [ˈklivɪdʒ] *s* división, hendidura; (*bosom*) escote *m;* (fig) desunión
cleave [kliv] *v* (*pret & pp* **cleft** [klɛft] o **cleaved**) *tr* rajar, partir; hender (*las aguas un buque, los aires una flecha*) ‖ *intr* adherirse, pegarse; apegarse, ser fiel
cleaver [ˈklivər] *s* cortante *m,* cuchilla de carnicero
clef [klɛf] *s* (mus) clave *f*
cleft palate [klɛft] *s* fisura del paladar
clematis [ˈklɛmətɪs] *s* clemátide *f*
clemen·cy [ˈklɛmənsi] *s* (*pl* **-cies** clemencia; (*of the weather*) benignidad
clement [ˈklɛmənt] *adj* clemente; (*weather*) benigno
clench [klɛntʃ] *s* agarro ‖ *tr* agarrar; apretar, cerrar (*el puño, los dientes*)
cler·gy [ˈklɛrdʒi] *s* (*pl* **-gies**) clerecía, clero
clergy·man [ˈklɛrdʒimən] *s* (*pl* **-men** [mən]) clérigo, pastor *m*
cleric [ˈklɛrɪk] *s* clérigo
clerical [ˈklɛrɪkəl] *adj* (*of clergy*) clerical; (*of office work*) oficinesco ‖ *s* clérigo, eclesiático; (*supporter of power of clergy*) clerical *m;* **clericals** (coll) hábitos clericales
clerk [klʌrk] *s* (*in a store*) dependiente *mf;* (*in an office*) oficinista *mf;* (*in a city hall*) archivero; (*in a church*) lego, seglar *m;* (*in law office, in court*) escribano
clever [ˈklɛvər] *adj* hábil, diestro, mañoso; inteligente
cleverness [ˈklɛvərnɪs] *s* habilidad, destreza, maña; inteligencia
clew [klu] *s* indicio, pista
cliché [kliˈʃe] *s* (*printing plate*) clisé *m;* (*trite expression*) cliché *m*
click [klɪk] *s* golpecito; (*of typewriter*) tecleo; (*of firearm*) piñoneo; (*of heels*) taconeo; (*of tongue*) claqueo, chasquido; (compu) clic *m* ‖ *tr* hacer sonar con un golpecito seco; chascar (*la lengua*); **to click the heels** taconear; cuadrarse (*un soldado*) ‖ *intr* sonar con un golpecito seco; piñonear (*el gatillo de un arma de fuego*); claquear (*la lengua*); (compu) clicar, cliquear, hacer clic
client [ˈklaɪ•ənt] *s* cliente *mf;* cliente de abogado
clientele [ˌklaɪ•ənˈtɛl] *s* clientela
cliff [klɪf] *s* acantilado, escarpa, risco
climate [ˈklaɪmɪt] *s* clima *m*
climax [ˈklaɪmæks] *s* colmo; orgasmo; **to cap the climax** ser el colmo
climb [klaɪm] *s* subida, trepa ‖ *tr & intr* escalar, subir, trepar
climber [ˈklaɪmər] *s* trepador *m;* ambicioso de figurar; (bot) enredadera, trepadora
clinch [klɪntʃ] *s* agarro, abrazo; (*of a nail*) remache *m* ‖ *tr* afianzar, sujetar; agarrar, abrazar; apretar (*el puño*); remachar (*un clavo ya clavado*); resolver decisivamente
cling [klɪŋ] *v* (*pret & pp* **clung** [klʌŋ]) *intr* adherirse, pegarse; **to cling to** agarrarse a, asirse de
cling′stone′ peach *s* albérchigo, peladillo
clinic [ˈklɪnɪk] *s* clínica
clinical [ˈklɪnɪkəl] *adj* clínico
clinical chart *s* hoja clínica
clinician [klɪˈnɪʃən] *s* clínico
clink [kliŋk] *s* tintín *m* ‖ *tr* hacer tintinear; chocar (*vasos, copas*) ‖ *intr* tintinear
clinker [ˈklɪŋkər] *s* escoria de hulla
clip [klɪp] *s* tijereteo, esquileo; grapa, pinza; (*to fasten papers*) sujetapapeles *m,* presilla de alambre; **at a good clip** a buen paso ‖ *v* (*pret & pp* **clipped;** *ger* **clipping**) *tr* tijeretear, esquilar; (*to fasten with a clip*) afianzar, sujetar; recortar (*p.ej., un cupón*); (*to overcharge*) estafar ‖ *intr* moverse con rapidez
clip′board′ *s* tablilla con sujetapapeles; (compu) portapapeles *m*
clipper [ˈklɪpər] *s* tijera, cizalla; **clippers** maquinilla cortapelos; tijeras podadoras
clipping [ˈklɪpɪŋ] *s* tijereteo, esquileo; (*from a newspaper*) recorte *m*
clique [klik] *s* pandilla, corrillo ‖ *intr* — **to clique together** apandillarse
cliquish [ˈklikɪʃ] *adj* exclusivista
clk. *abbr* **clerk, clock**

cloak [klok] *s* capote *m; (disguise, excuse)* capa || *tr* encapotar; disimular, encubrir
cloak-and-dagger [ˈklokənˈdægər] *adj* de capa y espada (*dícese de duelos, espionaje, etc.*)
cloak-and-sword [ˈklokənˈsord] *adj* de capa y espada (*dícese, p.ej., de las costumbres caballerescas*)
cloak hanger *s* cuelgacapas *m*
cloak'room' *s* guardarropa *m;* (Brit) excusado
clock [klɑk] *s* reloj *m* (de pared o de mesa); (*in a stocking*) cuadrado || *tr* registrar; (sport) cronometrar
clock'mak'er *s* relojero
clock radio *s* radiodespertador *m & f*
clock time *s* (compu) frecuencia de reloj
clock tower *s* torre *f* reloj
clock'wise' *adj & adv* en el sentido de las agujas del reloj
clock'work' *s* mecanismo de relojería; **like clockwork** como un reloj
clod [klɑd] *s* terrón *m*
clod'hop'per *s* (coll) patán *m,* pato (Esp); **clodhoppers** zapatos fuertes de trabajo
clog [klɑg] *s* estorbo, obstáculo; (*wooden shoe*) zueco; (*dance*) zapateado; (*hobble on animal*) traba || *v* (*pret & pp* **clogged;** *ger* **clogging**) *tr* atascar || *intr* atascarse; bailar el zapateado
clog dance *s* zapateado
cloister [ˈklɔɪstər] *s* claustro || *tr* enclaustrar
cloistral [ˈklɔɪstrəl] *adj* claustral
clonal [ˈklonəl] *adj* clónico
clone [klon] *s* clon *m;* (compu) clónico || *tr* clonar
close [klos] *adj* cercano, próximo; casi igual; (*translation*) fiel, exacto; (*fabric*) compacto; (*weather, atmosphere*) pesado, sofocante; (*stingy*) tacaño; (*battle, race, election*) reñido; (*friend*) íntimo; (*shut in, enclosed*) cerrado; (*narrow*) estrecho || *adv* cerca; **close to** cerca de || [kloz] *s* fin *m,* terminación; (*of business, of stock market*) cierre *m;* **at the close of day** a la caída de la tarde; **to bring to a close** poner término a; **to come to a close** tocar a su fin || *tr* cerrar; (*to cover*) tapar; (*to finish*) concluir; saldar (*una cuenta*); cerrar (*un trato*); **to close in** cerrar, encerrar; **to close ranks** cerrar las filas || *intr* cerrar, cerrarse; **to close in on** cerrar con (*el enemigo*)
close call [klos] *s* (coll) escape *m* por un pelo
closed *adj* cerrado
closed car [klozd] *s* coche cerrado, conducción interior
closed chapter *s* asunto concluído
closed circuit *s* circuito cerrado; **closed-circuit television** televisión en circuito cerrado
closed season *s* veda
closed shop *s* taller agremiado
closefisted [ˈklosˈfɪstɪd] *adj* cicatero, tacaño, manicorto
close-fitting [ˈklosˈfɪtɪŋ] *adj* ajustado, ceñido al cuerpo
close-knit [ˈklosnɪt] *adj* unido
close-lipped [ˈklosˈlɪpt] *adj* callado, reservado
closely [ˈklosli] *adv* de cerca; estrechamente; fielmente; atentamente
closeness [ˈklosnəs] *s* proximidad; (*intimacy*) intimidad
closeout [ˈklozaʊt] *s* liquidación
close quarters [klos] *spl* lugar muy estrecho, lugares estrechos
close shave [klos] *s* afeitado a ras; (coll) escape *m* por un pelo
closet [ˈklɑzɪt] *adj* (*gay; racist*) encubierto, de clóset || *s* (*wall*) alacena, closet *m;* (*wardrobe*) armario; (*small private room*) aposento, gabinete *m;* (*for keeping clothing*) guardarropa *m;* (*toilet*) retrete *m* || *tr* — **to be closeted with** encerrarse con
close-up [ˈklos,ʌp] *s* fotografía de cerca, plano corto; (mov) vista cerca
closing [ˈklozɪŋ] *s* cerradura, cierre *m*
closing date *s* fecha límite
closing prices *spl* precios de cierre
closing time *s* hora de cierre
clot [klɑt] *s* grumo, coágulo || *v* (*pret & pp* **clotted;** *ger* **clotting**) *intr* engrumecerse, coagularse
cloth [klɔθ] o [klɑθ] *s* paño, tela; ropa clerical; (*canvas, sails*) lona, trapo, vela; (*for binding books*) tela; **the cloth** la clerecía
clothe [kloð] *v* (*pret & pp* **clothed** o **clad** [klæd]) *tr* trajear, vestir; cubrir; (*e.g., with authority*) investir
clothes [kloz] o [kloθz] *spl* ropa, vestidos
clothes'bas'ket *s* cesto de la ropa, cesto de la colada
clothes'brush' *s* cepillo de ropa
clothes closet *s* ropero
clothes dryer *s* secadora de ropa, secarropa
clothes hanger *s* colgador *m,* perchero
clothes'horse' *s* enjugador *m,* secarropa de travesaños
clothes'line' *s* cordel *m* para tender la ropa, tendedera
clothes'pin' *s* pinza, alfiler *m* de madera
clothes tree *s* percha
clothier [ˈklot͡ʃjər] *s* (*person who sells ready-made clothes*) ropero; (*dealer in cloth*) pañero
clothing [ˈkloðɪŋ] *s* ropa, vestidos, ropaje *m*
cloud [klaʊd] *s* nube *f* || *tr* anublar || *intr* — **to cloud over** anublarse
cloud bank *s* mar *m* de nubes
cloud'burst' *s* aguacero, chaparrón *m*
cloud-capped [ˈklaʊd,kæpt] *adj* coronado de nubes
cloudless [ˈklaʊdlɪs] *adj* despejado, sin nubes
cloud of dust *s* polvareda, nube *f* de polvo
cloud•y [ˈklaʊdi] *adj* (*comp* **-ier;** *super* **-iest**) nuboso, nublado; (*muddy, turbid*) turbio; confuso, obscuro; melancólico, sombrío
clove [klov] *s* (*flower*) clavo de especia; (*spice*) clavo; (*of garlic*) diente *m*

clover [ˈklovər] *s* trébol *m;* **to be in clover** vivir en el lujo
clo′ver·leaf′ *s* (*pl* **-leaves** [ˌlivz]) *s* (*highway access*) cruce *m* en trébol; (bot) hoja de trébol
clove tree *s* clavero
clown [klaʊn] *s* bufón *m,* payaso; (*rustic*) patán *m* ‖ *intr* hacer el payaso
clownish [ˈklaʊnɪʃ] *adj* bufonesco; rústico
cloy [klɔɪ] *tr* hastiar, empalagar
club [klʌb] *s* porra, clava; club *m,* casino; (cards) trébol *m* (*baraja francesa*); **clubs** (cards) tréboles; un palo negro de naipes representandos tréboles estilizados; equivalente al palo de bastos; **ace of clubs** el basto ‖ *v* (*pret & pp* **clubbed;** *ger* **clubbing**) *tr* aporrear ‖ *intr* — **to club together** unirse; formar club
club car *s* coche *m* club, coche bar
club′foot′ *s* pie *m* deforme *or* equino
club′house′ *s* casa club; (*in a stadium*) club *m* de tribuna
club member *s* clubista *mf*
club soda *s* agua de Seltz
cluck [klʌk] *s* cloqueo, clo clo ‖ *intr* cloquear, hacer clo clo
clue [klu] *s* indicio, pista
clump [klʌmp] *s* (*of earth*) terrón *m;* (*of trees or shrubs*) grupo; pisada fuerte ‖ *intr* — **to clump along** andar pesadamente
clum·sy [ˈklʌmzi] *adj* (*comp* **-sier;** *super* **-siest**) (*worker*) chapucero, desmañado, torpe; (*work*) chapucero, tosco, grosero
cluster [ˈklʌstər] *s* grupo; (*of grapes or other things growing or joined together*) racimo ‖ *intr* arracimarse; **to cluster around** reunirse en torno a; **to cluster together** agruparse
clutch [klʌtʃ] *s* (*grasp, grip*) agarro, apretón *m* fuerte; (aut) embrague *m;* (aut) pedal *m* de embrague; **to fall into the clutches of** caer en las garras de; **to throw the clutch in** embragar; **to throw the clutch out** desembragar ‖ *tr* agarrar, empuñar
clutter [ˈklʌtər] *tr* — **to clutter up** cubrir o llenar desordenadamente
cm. *abbr* **centimeter**
c/o *abbr* **in care of,** e.g., **John Delgado, c/o Mary Ramírez** Juan Delgado, en casa de María Ramírez *or:* María Ramírez, para entregar a Juan Delgado
Co. *abbr* **Company, County**
coach [kotʃ] *s* coche *m,* diligencia; (*tutor*) profesor *m* particular; (aut) coche cerrado; (rr) coche de viajeros, coche ordinario *m;* (sport) entrenador *m,* director técnico ‖ *tr* aleccionar; preparar; (sport) entrenar ‖ *intr* entrenarse
coach house *s* cochera
coaching [ˈkotʃɪŋ] *s* lecciones *fpl* particulares; (sport) entrenamiento
coach·man [ˈkotʃmən] *s* (*pl* **-men** [mən]) *s* cochero
coagulate [koˈægjəˌlet] *tr* coagular ‖ *intr* coagularse
coal [kol] *s* carbón *m,* hulla ‖ *tr* proveer de carbón ‖ *intr* proveerse de carbón
coal′bin′ *s* carbonera
coal bunker *s* carbonera
coal car *s* vagón carbonero
coal′deal′er *s* carbonero
coaling [ˈkolɪŋ] *adj* carbonero ‖ *s* toma de carbón
coalition [ˌko·əˈlɪʃən] *s* unión; (*alliance between states or factions*) coalición
coal mine *s* mina de carbón
coal oil *s* aceite *m* mineral
coal scuttle *s* cubo para carbón
coal tar *s* alquitrán *m* de hulla
coal′yard′ *s* carbonería
coarse [kors] *adj* (*of inferior quality*) basto, burdo; (*composed of large particles*) grueso; (*crude in manners*) grosero, rudo, vulgar
coarseness [ˈkorsnɪs] *s* bastedad
coast [kost] *s* costa; **the coast is clear** ya no hay peligro ‖ *tr* costear ‖ *intr* deslizarse cuesta abajo; **to coast along** avanzar sin esfuerzo
coastal [ˈkostəl] *adj* costero
coaster [ˈkostər] *s* salvamanteles *m,* posavasos *m*
coaster brake *s* freno de contrapedal
coast guard *s* guardacostas *mpl;* guardia *m* de los guardacostas
coast guard cutter *s* escampavía de los guardacostas
coasting trade *s* cabotaje *m*
coast′land′ *s* litoral *m*
coast′line′ *s* línea de la costa
coast′wise′ *adj* costanero ‖ *adv* a lo largo de la costa
coat [kot] *s* (*jacket*) americana, saco; (*topcoat*) abrigo, sobretodo; (*of an animal*) lana, pelo; (*of paint*) capa, mano *f* ‖ *tr* cubrir, revestir; dar una capa de pintura a
coated [ˈkotɪd] *adj* revestido; (*tongue*) saburoso
coat hanger *s* colgador *m*
coating [ˈkotɪŋ] *s* revestimiento; (*of paint*) capa; (*of plaster*) enlucido
coat of arms *s* escudo de armas
coat′room′ *s* guardarropa *m*
coat′tail′ *s* faldón *m*
coax [koks] *tr* engatusar
coaxial cable [koˈæksɪ·əl] *s* cable *m* coaxial
cob [kɑb] *s* zuro; **to eat corn on the cob** comer maíz en la mazorca
cobalt [ˈkobɔlt] *s* cobalto
cobbler [ˈkɑblər] *s* remendón *m,* zapatero de viejo
cob′ble·stone′ *s* guijarro
cob′web′ *s* telaraña
coca [ˈkokə] *s* coca
cocaine [koˈken] *s* cocaína
cock [kɑk] *s* (*rooster*) gallo; (*faucet, valve*) espita, grifo; (*of firearm*) martillo; (*weathervane*) veleta; caudillo, jefe *m* ‖ *tr* amartillar (*un arma de fuego*); ladear (*la cabeza*); enderezar, levantar
cockade [kɑˈked] *s* cucarda, escarapela

cock-a-doodle-doo [ˈkakə,dudəlˈdu] *s* quiquiriquí *m*
cock-and-bull story [ˈkakəndˈbʊl] *s* cuento absurdo, cuento increíble
cocked hat [kakt] *s* sombrero de candil, sombrero de tres picos; **to knock into a cocked hat** (slang) apabullar
cockeyed [ˈkak,aɪd] *adj* bisojo, bizco; (coll) encorvado, torcido; (slang) disparatado, extravagante
cock'fight' *s* pelea de gallos
cockney [ˈkakni] *s* londinense *mf* de la clase pobre que habla un dialecto característico; dialecto de la clase pobre de Londres
cock of the walk *s* quiquiriquí *m,* gallito del lugar
cock'pit' *s* gallera; (aer) carlinga
cock'roach' *s* cucaracha
cockscomb [ˈkaks,kom] *s* cresta de gallo; gorro de bufón; (bot) cresta de gallo, moco de pavo
cock'sure' *adj* muy seguro de sí mismo
cock'tail' *s* coctel *m;* (*of fruit, oysters, etc.*) aperitivo
cocktail party *s* coctel *m*
cocktail shaker [ˈʃekər] *s* coctelera
cock•y [ˈkaki] *adj* (*comp* **-ier;** *super* **-iest**) (coll) arrogante, hinchado; **to be cocky** (coll) tener mucho gallo
cocoa [ˈkoko] *s* cacao; (*drink*) chocolate *m*
coconut [ˈkokə,nʌt] *s* coco
coconut palm o **tree** *s* cocotero
cocoon [kəˈkun] *s* capullo
C.O.D., c.o.d. [ˈsiˈoˈdi] (letterword) (**collect on delivery**) *adv* contra reembolso ‖ *s* entrega contra reembolso
cod [kad] *s* abadejo, bacalao
coddle [ˈkadəl] *tr* consentir, mimar
code [kod] *s* (*of laws; of manners; of signals*) código; (*of telegraphy*) alfabeto; (*secret system of writing*) cifra, clave *f;* (com) cifrario; (compu) código; (telecommunications) código, prefijo; **in code** en cifra ‖ *tr* (*to put in code*) cifrar; (compu) codificar
code word *s* clave telegráfica
codex [ˈkodɛks] *s* (*pl* **codices** [ˈkodɪ,siz] o [ˈkadɪ,siz]) *s* códice *m*
cod'fish' *s* abadejo, bacalao
codger [ˈkadʒər] *s* — **old codger** (coll) anciano, tío
codicil [ˈkadɪsɪl] *s* codicilo; apéndice *m*
codi•fy [ˈkadɪ,faɪ] o [ˈkodɪ,faɪ] *v* (*pret & pp* **-fied**) *tr* codificar
coding [ˈkodɪŋ] *s* (compu) codificación; (mus) cifrado, notación en clave
cod'-liv'er oil *s* aceite *m* de hígado de bacalao
co-driver [ˈkoˈdraɪvər] *s* copiloto *mf*
coed o **co-ed** [ˈko,ɛd] *s* alumna de una escuela coeducativa
coeducation [,ko,ɛdʒəˈkeʃən] *s* coeducación
coefficient [,ko•ɪˈfɪʃənt] *adj & s* coeficiente *m*
coerce [koˈʌrs] *tr* forzar, coactar
coercion [koˈʌrʃən] *s* compulsión, coacción
coeval [koˈivəl] *adj & s* coetáneo
coexist [,ko•ɪgˈzɪst] *intr* coexistir
coexistence [,ko•ɪgˈzɪstəns] *s* coexistencia
coffee [ˈkɔfi] o [ˈkafi] *s* café *m;* (*plant*) cafeto; **black coffee** café solo; **to drink coffee** cafetear
coffee bean *s* grano de café
cof'fee•cake' *s* rosquilla (que se come con el café), bizcocho con fruta seca
coffee cup *s* taza de café
coffee dealer *s* cafetalero
coffee grinder *s* molinillo de café
coffee grounds *spl* poso del café
coffee mill *s* molinillo de café
coffee plantation *s* cafetal *m*
coffee planter *s* cafetalero
coffee pot *s* cafetera
coffee table *s* mesa de centro, mesa ratona, mesa de café (al lado de un sofá)
coffee tree *s* cafeto
coffer [ˈkɔfər] o [ˈkafər] *s* arca, cofre *m;* **coffers** tesoro, fondos
cof'fer•dam' *s* ataguía, encajonado
coffin [ˈkɔfɪn] o [ˈkafɪn] *s* ataúd *m*
cog [kag] *s* diente *m* (*de rueda dentada*); rueda dentada; **to slip a cog** equivocarse
cogency [ˈkodʒənsi] *s* fuerza (*de un argumento*)
cogent [ˈkodʒənt] *adj* fuerte, convincente
cogitate [ˈkadʒɪ,tet] *tr & intr* cogitar, meditar
cognac [ˈkanjæk] *s* coñac *m*
cognizance [ˈkagnɪzəns] o [ˈkanɪzəns] *s* conocimiento; **to take cognizance of** enterarse de
cognizant [ˈkagnizənt] o [ˈkanɪzənt] *adj* sabedor, enterado
cog railway *s s* ferrocarril *m* de cremallera
cog'wheel' *s* rueda dentada
cohabit [koˈhæbɪt] *intr* cohabitar
coheir [koˈɛr] *s* coheredero
cohere [koˈhɪr] *intr* adherirse, pegarse; conformarse, corresponder
coherent [koˈhɪrənt] *adj* coherente
cohesion [koˈhiʒən] *s* cohesión
coiffeur [kwaˈfʌr] *s* peluquero
coiffure [kwaˈfjʊr] *s* peinado, tocado
coil [kɔɪl] *s* (*something wound in a spiral*) rollo; (*single turn of spiral*) vuelta; (*of a still*) serpentín *m;* (*of hair*) rizo; (*of a spring*) espiral *f;* (elec) carrete *m* ‖ *tr* arrollar, enrollar; (naut) adujar ‖ *intr* arrollarse, enrollarse; (*like a snake*) serpentear
coil spring *s* resorte *m* espiral
coin [kɔɪn] *s* moneda; (*wedge*) cuña; **to pay back in one's own coin** pagar en la misma moneda; **to toss a coin** echar a cara o cruz ‖ *tr* acuñar; forja, inventar (*palabras o frases*)
coincide [,ko•ɪnˈsaɪd] *intr* coincidir
coincidence [koˈɪnsɪdəns] *s* coincidencia
coition [koˈɪʃən] o **coitus** [ˈko•ɪtəs] *s* coito
coke [kok] *s* coque *m,* cok *m,* coke *m;* (slang) coca *or* perico (*cocaína*)
Coke[1] *s* Coca-Cola
col. *abbr* **colored, colony, column**

colander [ˈkʌləndər] o [ˈkɑləndər] *s* colador *m,* escurridor *m*
cold [kold] *adj* frío; **to be cold** (*said of a person's body*) tener frío; (*said of the weather*) hacer frío || *s* frío; (*indisposition*) resfriado; **to catch cold** resfriarse, coger un resfriado
cold blood *s* — **in cold blood** a sangre fría
cold chisel *s* cortafrío
cold comfort *s* poca consolación
cold cream *s* colcrén *m*
cold cuts *spl* fiambres *mpl*
cold feet *spl* (coll) desánimo, miedo
cold'heart'ed *adj* duro, insensible
cold meat *s* carne *f* fiambre
coldness [ˈkoldnɪs] *s* frialdad
cold shoulder *s* — **to turn a cold shoulder on** (coll) tratar con suma frialdad
cold snap *s* corto rato de frío agudo
cold storage *s* conservación en cámara frigorífica
Cold War *s* Guerra Fría
coleslaw [ˈkol,slɔ] *s* ensalada de col
colic [ˈkɑlɪk] *adj & s* cólico
coliseum [,kɑlɪˈsi•əm] *s* coliseo
colitis [kəˈlaɪtɪs] *s* colitis *f*
coll. *abbr* **colleague, collection, college, colloquial**
collaborate [kəˈlæbə,ret] *intr* colaborar
collaborationist [kə,læbəˈreʃənɪst] *s* colaboracionista *mf*
collaborator [kəˈlæbə,retər] *s* colaborador *m*
collapse [kəˈlæps] *s* desplome *m;* (*in business*) fracaso; (pathol) colapso || *intr* desplomarse; fracasar; postrarse, sufrir colapso
collapsible [kəˈlæpsɪbəl] *adj* abatible, plegable, desmontable
collar [ˈkɑlər] *s* cuello; (*of dog, horse*) collar *m;* (mach) collar
col'lar•band' *s* tirilla de camisa
col'lar•bone' *s* clavícula
collate [kəˈlet] o [ˈkɑlet] *tr* colacionar, cotejar
collateral [kəˈlætərəl] *adj* colateral || *s* (*relative*) colateral *mf;* (com) colateral *m*
collateral damage *s* (mil) daños *mpl* incidentales; (mil) bajas *fpl* entre la población civil
collateral mail *s* correo contaminado por las esporas del ántrax
collation [kəˈleʃən] *s* (*act of comparing; light meal*) colación
colleague [ˈkɑlig] *s* colega *mf*
collect [ˈkɑlɛkt] *s* (eccl) colecta || [kəˈlɛkt] *tr* acumular, reunir; colectar, recaudar (*impuestos*); coleccionar (*sellos de correo, antigüallas*); recolectar (*cosechas*); cobrar (*pasajes*); recoger (*billetes; el correo*); **to collect oneself** reponerse || *intr* acumularse
collect call *s* llamada por cobrar, conferencia a cobro revertido
collected [kəˈlɛktɪd] *adj* sosegado, dueño de sí mismo
collection [kəˈlɛkʃən] *s* colección; (*of taxes*) recaudación; (*of mail*) recogida
collection agency *s* agencia de cobros de cuentas
collective [kəˈlɛktɪv] *adj* colectivo
collect on delivery *adv* contra reembolso || *s* entrega contra reembolso
collector [kəˈlɛktər] *s* (*of stamps, antiques*) coleccionista *mf;* (*of taxes*) recaudador *m;* (*of tickets*) cobrador *m*
college [ˈkɑlɪdʒ] *s* universidad, colegio universitario; (*division of university*) facultad; (*of cardinals, electors, etc.*) colegio
college dormitory *s* residencia de estudiantes, residencia universitaria
collide [kəˈlaɪd] *intr* chocar; **to collide with** chocar con
collie [ˈkɑli] *s* perro pastoril escocés
collier [ˈkɑljər] *s* barco carbonero; minero de carbón
collier•y [ˈkɑljəri] *s* (*pl* **-ies**) mina de carbón
collision [kəˈlɪʒən] *s* colisión
colloid [ˈkɑlɔɪd] *adj & s* coloide *m*
colloquial [kəˈlokwɪ•əl] *adj* coloquial, familiar
colloquialism [kəˈlokwɪ•ə,lɪzəm] *s* coloquialismo
collo•quy [ˈkɑləkwi] *s* (*pl* **-quies**) coloquio
collusion [kəˈluʒən] *s* colusión, confabulación; **to be in collusion with** estar en inteligencia con
cologne [kəˈlon] *s* agua de colonia, colonia || **Cologne** *s* Colonia
colon [ˈkolən] *s* (anat) colon *m;* (gram) dos puntos
colonel [ˈkʌrnəl] *s* coronel *m*
colonel•cy [ˈkʌrnəlsi] *s* (*pl* **-cies**) coronelía
colonial [kəˈlonɪ•əl] *adj* colonial || *s* colono
colonize [ˈkɑlə,naɪz] *tr & intr* colonizar
colonnade [,kɑləˈned] *s* columnata
colo•ny [ˈkɑləni] *s* (*pl* **-nies**) colonia
colophon [ˈkɑlə,fɑn] *s* colofón *m*
color [ˈkʌlər] *s* color; **the colors** los colores, la bandera; **to call to the colors** llamar a filas; **to give** o **to lend color to** dar visos de probabilidad a; **under color of** so color de, bajo pretexto de; **with flying colors** con banderas desplegadas || *tr* colorar, colorear; (*to excuse, palliate*) colorear; (*to dye*) teñir || *intr* sonrojarse, ponerse colorado, demudarse
col'or-blind' *adj* daltoniano, daltónico
color coding *s* codificación con colores
colored [ˈkʌlərd] *adj* de color; (*specious*) colorado
colorful [ˈkʌlərfəl] *adj* colorido; pintoresco
color guard *s* (mil) portaestandarte *mf*
coloring [ˈkʌlərɪŋ] *adj & s* colorante *m*
colorless [ˈkʌlərlɪs] *adj* incoloro; (fig) insulso
color photography *s* fotografía en colores
color salute *s* (mil) saludo con la bandera
color sergeant *s* sargento abanderado
color screen *s* (phot) pantalla de color
color television *s* televisión en colores
colossal [kəˈlɑsəl] *adj* colosal

Colosseum [ˈkaləˈsi•əm] *s* Coliseo
colossus [kəˈlasəs] *s* coloso
colt [kolt] *s* potro
Columbus [kəˈlʌmbəs] *s* Colón *m*
Columbus Day *s* Día de la Raza, Día o Fiesta de la Hispanidad
column [ˈkaləm] *s* columna
columnist [ˈkaləmɪst] *s* columnista *mf*
com. *abbr* **comedy, commerce, common**
Com. *abbr* **Commander, Commissioner, Committee**
coma [ˈkomə] *s* (pathol) coma *m*
comb [kom] *s* peine *m;* (*currycomb*) almohaza; (*of rooster*) cresta; cresta de ola ‖ *tr* peinar; explorar con minuciosidad
com•bat [ˈkambæt] *s* combate *m* ‖ [ˈkambæt] o [kəmˈbæt] *v* (*pret & pp* **-bated** o **-batted;** *ger* **-bating** o **-batting**) *tr & intr* combatir
combatant [ˈkambətənt] *adj & s* combatiente *m*
combat duty *s* servicio de frente
combination [ˌkambɪˈneʃən] *s* combinación
combine [ˈkambaɪn] *s* monopolio; segadora trilladora; (coll) combinación ‖ [kəmˈbaɪn] *tr* combinar ‖ *intr* combinarse
combining form *s* (gram) elemento de compuestos
combustible [kəmˈbʌstɪbəl] *adj* combustible; (fig) ardiente, impetuoso ‖ *s* combustible *m*
combustion [kəmˈbʌstʃən] *s* combustión
combustion chamber *s* cámara de combustión
come [kʌm] *v* (*pret* **came** [kem]; *pp* **come**) *intr* venir; **come on!** ¡venga!; **to come about** suceder; **to come across** encontrarse con; **to come after** venir detrás de; venir después de; venir por, venir en busca de; **to come again** volver; **to come apart** desunirse, desprenderse; **to come around** restablecerse; volver en sí; rendirse; ponerse de acuerdo; cambiar de dirección; **to come at** alcanzar; **to come back** volver; rehabilitarse; **to come before** anteponerse; **to come between** interponerse; desunir, separar; **to come by** conseguir; **to come down** bajar; (*in social position, etc.*) descender; (*from one person to another*) ser transmitido; **to come downstairs** bajar (*de un piso a otro*); **to come down with** enfermarse de; **to come for** venir por, venir en busca de; **to come forth** salir; aparecer; **to come forward** avanzar; presentarse; **to come from** venir de; provenir de; **to come in** entrar; entrar en; empezar; ponerse en uso; **to come in for** conseguir, recibir; **to come into one's own** ser reconocido; **to come off** desprenderse; acontecer; **to come out** salir; salir a luz; ponerse de largo (*una joven*); divulgarse (*una noticia*); **to come out for** anunciar su apoyo de; **to come out with** descolgarse con; **to come over** dejarse persuadir; pasar, p.ej., **what's come over him?** ¿qué le ha pasado?; **to come through** salir bien, tener éxito; ganar; **to come to** volver en sí; **to come together** juntarse, reunirse; **to come true** hacerse realidad; **to come up** subir; presentarse; **to come upstairs** subir (*de un piso a otro*); **to come up to** acercarse a; subir a; estar a la altura de; **to come up with** proponer
come'back' *s* rehabilitación; (slang) respuesta aguda; **to stage a comeback** rehabilitarse
comedian [kəˈmidɪ•ən] *s* cómico, comediante *m;* autor *m* de comedias
comedienne [kəˌmidɪˈɛn] *s* cómica, comedianta
come'down' *s* humillación, revés *m*
come•dy [ˈkamədi] *s* (*pl* **-dies**) comedia cómica; (*comicalness*) comicidad
come•ly [ˈkʌmli] *adj* (*comp* **-lier;** *super* **-liest**) (*attractive*) donairoso, gracioso; (*decorous*) conveniente, decente
comet [ˈkamɪt] *s* cometa *m*
comfort [ˈkʌmfərt] *s* comodidad, confort *m;* (*encouragement, consolation*) confortación; (*person*) confortador *m;* (*bed cover*) colcha, cobertor *m* ‖ *tr* confortar
comfortable [ˈkʌmfərtəbəl] *adj* cómodo, confortable; (*fairly well off*) holgado; (*salary*) (coll) suficiente
comforter [ˈkʌmfərtər] *s* confortador *m,* consolador *m;* colcha, cobertor *m;* bufanda de lana
comforting [ˈkʌmfərtɪŋ] *adj* confortante
comfrey [ˈkʌmfri] *s* consuelda
comic [ˈkamɪk] *adj* cómico ‖ *s* cómico; periódico cómico; **comics** tiras cómicas
comical [ˈkamɪkəl] *adj* cómico
comic book *s* tebeo
comic opera *s* ópera cómica, ópera bufa
comic strip *s* tira cómica
coming [ˈkʌmɪŋ] *adj* que viene, venidero; prometedor ‖ *s* venida
coming out *s* (*of stocks, bonds, etc.*) emisión; (*of a young girl*) puesta de largo, entrada en sociedad
comma [ˈkamə] *s* coma; (*in Spanish the period is used to group the digits of an integer*) punto (*empleado en aritmética para agrupar las cifras de un entero*)
command [kəˈmænd] *s* (*commanding*) dominio, mando; (*order, direction*) mandato, orden *f;* (*e.g., of a foreign language*) dominio; (compu, mil) comando; **to be in command of** estar al mando de; **to take command** tomar el mando ‖ *tr* mandar, ordenar; dominar (*un idioma extranjero*); merecer (*p.ej., respeto*); (mil) comandar ‖ *intr* mandar
commandant [ˌkamənˈdænt] o [ˌkamənˈdant] *s* comandante *m*
commandeer [ˌkamənˈdɪr] *tr* reclutar forzosamente; expropiar; (coll) apoderarse de
commander [kəˈmændər] *s* comandante *m;* (*of a military order*) comendador *m*
commandment [ˌkəˈmændmənt] *s* (Bib) mandamiento
commando [kəˈmændo] *s* (mil) comando
commemorate [kəˈmɛməˌret] *tr* conmemorar
commence [kəˈmɛns] *tr & intr* comenzar, empezar

commencement [kə'mɛnsmənt] *s* comienzo, principio; día *m* de graduación; ceremonia de graduación
commend [kə'mɛnd] *tr* (*to entrust*) encargar, encomendar; (*to recommend*) recomendar; (*to praise*) alabar, elogiar
commendable [kə'mɛndəbəl] *adj* recomendable
commendation [,kamən'deʃən] *s* encargo, encomienda; recomendación; alabanza, elogio
comment ['kamɛnt] *s* comentario, comento || *intr* comentar; **to comment on** comentar
commentar•y ['kamən,tɛri] *s* (*pl* **-ies**) comentario
commentator ['kamən,tetər] *s* comentarista *mf*
commerce ['kamərs] *s* comercio
commercial [kə'mʌrʃəl] *adj* comercial || *s* anuncio publicitario radiofónico o televisivo; (rad & telv) programa publicitario
commercial scan *s* (electron) salto de anuncios comerciales
commiserate [kə'mɪzə,ret] *intr* — **to commiserate with** condolerse de
commiseration [kə,mɪzə'reʃən] *s* conmiseración
commissar [,kamɪ'sar] *s* comisario (*en Rusia*)
commissar•y ['kamɪ,sɛri] *s* (*pl* **-ies**) (*deputy*) comisario; (*store*) economato
commission [kə'mɪʃən] *s* comisión; (mil) nombramiento; **to put in commission** poner en uso; poner (*un buque*) en servicio activo; **to put out of commission** inutilizar, descomponer; retirar (*un buque*) del servicio activo || *tr* comisionar; poner en uso; poner (*un buque*) en servicio activo; (mil) nombrar
commissioned officer *s* oficial *m*
commissioner [kə'mɪʃənər] *s* comisario; (*person authorized by a commission*) comisionado
com•mit [kə'mɪt] *v* (*pret & pp* **-mitted;** *ger* **-mitting**) *tr* cometer (*un crimen, una falta; un negocio a una persona*); (*to hand over*) confiar, entregar; dar, empeñar (*la palabra*); (*to bind, pledge*) comprometer; internar (*a un demente*); (*to memory*) encomendar; **to commit oneself** comprometerse, empeñarse; **to commit to writing** poner por escrito
commitment [kə'mɪtmənt] *s* responsibilidad; (*pledge*) compromiso; (*institutionalization*) internamiento; (*court order*) auto de prisión
committee [kə'mɪti] *s* comité *m,* comisión
commode [kə'mod] *s* (*chest of drawers*) cómoda; (*washstand*) lavabo; (*chamber pot*) sillico
commodious [kə'modɪ•əs] *adj* espacioso, holgado
commodities market *s* mercado de materias primas
commodi•ty [kə'madɪti] *s* (*pl* **-ties**) artículo de consumo, mercancía
commodity exchange *s* bolsa mercantil, bolsa de comercio
common ['kamən] *adj* común || *s* campo común, ejido; **commons** estado llano; (*of a school*) refectorio; **the Commons** (Brit) los Comunes
common carrier *s* empresa de transportes públicos
commoner ['kamənər] *s* plebeyo; (Brit) miembro de la Cámara de los Comunes
common law *s* derecho consuetudinario
com'mon-law' marriage *s* matrimonio consensual
common-law wife *s* conviviente *f*
Common Market *s* Mercado Común
com'mon•place' *adj* común, trivial, ordinario || *s* lugar *m* común, trivialidad
common sense *s* sentido común
com'mon-sense' *adj* cuerdo, razonable
common stock *s* acción ordinaria; acciones ordinarias
commonweal ['kamən,wil] *s* bien público
com'mon•wealth' *s* estado, nación; república; (*state of U.S.A.*) estado; (*self-governing associated country*) estado libre asociado; (*association of states*) mancomunidad
commotion [kə'moʃən] *s* conmoción
commune [kə'mjun] *intr* conversar; (eccl) comulgar
communicant [kə'mjunɪkənt] *s* comunicante *mf;* (eccl) comulgante *mf*
communicate [kə'mjunɪ,ket] *tr* comunicar || *intr* comunicarse
communicating [kə'mjunɪ,ketɪŋ] *adj* comunicador
communication [kə,mjunə'keʃən] *s* comunicación
communications satellite *s* satélite *m* de comunicaciones
communicative [kə'mjunɪ,ketɪv] *adj* comunicativo
communion [kə'mjunjən] *s* comunión; **to take communion** comulgar
communion rail *s* comulgatorio
communion wafer *s* (eccl) pan *m* de los ángeles
communiqué [kə,mjunɪ'ke] o [kə'mjunɪ,ke] *s* comunicado, parte *m*
communism ['kamjə,nɪzəm] *s* comunismo
communist ['kamjənɪst] *s* comunista *mf*
communi•ty [kə'mjunɪti] *s* (*pl* **-ties**) vecindario; (*group of people living together*) comunidad
communize ['kamjə,naɪz] *tr* comunizar
commutation ticket [,kamjə'teʃən] *s* billete *m* de abono
commutator ['kamjə,tetər] *s* (elec) colector *m*
commute [kə'mjut] *tr* conmutar || *intr* viajar con billete de abono
commuter [kə'mjutər] *s* abonado al ferrocarril
comp. *abbr* **compare, comparative, composer, composition, compound**
compact [kəm'pækt] *adj* compacto; breve, preciso || ['kampækt] *s* convenio, pacto; estuche *m* de afeites
compact disk *s* disco compacto, compact-disc *m*
compact disk player *s* compact-disc *m,* reproductor *m* de discos compactos

companion [kəm'pænjən] *s* compañero
companionable [kəm'pænjənəbəl] *adj* afable, sociable, simpático
companionship [kəm'pænjən,ʃɪp] *s* compañerismo
companionway [kəm'pænjən,we] *s* (naut) escalera de cámara
compa•ny ['kʌmpəni] *s* (*pl* **-nies**) compañía; visita, visitas, invitado, invitados; (naut) tripulación; **to be good company** ser compañero alegre; **to keep company** ir juntos (*un hombre y una mujer*); **to keep someone company** hacerle compañía a una persona; **to part company** separarse; enemistarse
company building *s* edificio social
company office *s* domicilio social
comparative [kəm'pærətɪv] *adj & s* comparativo
compare [kəm'pɛr] *s* — **beyond compare** sin comparación, sin par ‖ *tr* comparar
comparison [kəm'pærɪsən] *s* comparación
compartment [kəm'pɑrtmənt] *s* compartimiento; (rr) departamento
compass ['kʌmpəs] *s* brújula, compás *m;* ámbito, recinto; alcance *m,* extensión; **compass** o **compasses** (*for drawing circles*) compás *m*
compass card *s* (naut) rosa náutica, rosa de los vientos
compassion [kəm'pæʃən] *s* compasión
compassionate [kəm'pæʃənɪt] *adj* compasivo
com•pel [kəm'pɛl] *v* (*pret & pp* **-pelled;** *ger* **-pelling**) *tr* forzar, obligar, compeler; imponer (*respeto, silencio*)
compendious [kəm'pɛndɪ•əs] *adj* compendioso
compendi•um [kəm'pɛndɪ•əm] *s* (*pl* **-ums** o **-a** [ə]) compendio
compensate ['kɑmpən,set] *tr & intr* compensar; **to compensate for** compensar
compensation [,kɑmpən'seʃən] *s* compensación
compete [kəm'pit] *intr* competir
competence ['kɑmpɪtəns] o **competency** ['kɑmpɪtənsi] *s* (*aptitude; legal capacity*) competencia; (*sufficient means to live comfortably*) buen pasar *m*
competent ['kɑmpɪtənt] *adj* competente
competition [,kɑmpɪ'tɪʃən] *s* (*rivalry*) competencia; (*in a match, examination, etc.*) certamen *m,* concurso; (*in business*) concurrencia
competitive [kəm'pɛtɪtɪv] *adj* — **to be competitive** poder competir
competitive examination *s* oposición
competitiveness [kəm'pɛtɪtɪvnɪs] *s* capacidad competiva
competitive prices *spl* precios de competencia
competitor [kəm'pɛtɪtər] *s* competidor *m*
compilation [,kɑmpɪ'leʃən] *s* compilación, recopilación
compile [kəm'paɪl] *tr* compilar, recopilar
compiler [kəm'paɪlər] *s* (*of a dictionary*) compilador *m;* (*of a compilation*) recopilador *m;* (compu) compilador
complacence [kəm'plesəns] o **complacency** [kəm'plesənsi] *s* (*quiet satisfaction*) complacencia; satisfacción de sí mismo
complacent [kəm'plesənt] *adj* (*willing to please*) complaciente; satisfecho de sí mismo
complain [kəm'plen] *intr* quejarse
complainant [kəm'plenənt] *s* (law) demandante *mf*
complaint [kəm'plent] *s* queja; reclamo; (*grievance*) agravio; (*illness*) enfermedad, mal *m;* (law) demanda, querella
complaisance [kəm'plezəns] o ['kɑmplɪ,zæns] *s* amabilidad, cortesía
complaisant [kəm'plezənt] o ['kɑmplɪ,zænt] *adj* amable, cortés
complement ['kɑmplɪmənt] *s* complemento; (nav) dotación ‖ *tr* complementar
complete [kəm'plit] *adj* completo ‖ *tr* completar, terminar, realizar
completion [kəm'pliʃən] *s* terminación, realización
complex [kəm'plɛks] o ['kɑmplɛks] *adj* (*not simple*) complexo; (*composite*) complejo; (*intricate*) complicado ‖ ['kɑmplɛks] *s* complejo; (psychol) complejo; (coll) obsesión
complexion [kəm'plɛkʃən] *s* (*constitution*) complexión; (*texture of skin, esp. of face*) tez *f;* aspecto general, índole *f*
compliance [kəm'plaɪ•əns] *s* condescendencia; sumisión, rendimiento; **in compliance with** de acuerdo con, en conformidad con
complicate ['kɑmplɪ,ket] *tr* complicar
complicated ['kɑmplɪ,ketɪd] *adj* complicado
complication ['kɑmplɪ,keʃən] *s* complicación
complici•ty [kəm'plɪsɪti] *s* (*pl* **-ties**) complicidad, codelincuencia
compliment ['kɑmplɪmənt] *s* (*show of courtesy*) cumplimiento; (*praise*) alabanza, halago; perico (CAm); **compliments** saludos, recuerdos; **compliments of the author** (*complimentary copy*) cortesía del autor, obsequio del autor ‖ ['kɑmplɪ,mɛnt] *tr* cumplimentar; alabar, halagar
complimentary copy [,kɑmplɪ'mɛntəri] *s* ejemplar *m* de cortesía, pase de favor
complimentary ticket *s* billete *m* de regalo, pase *m* de cortesía
com•ply [kəm'plaɪ] *v* (*pret & pp* **-plied**) *intr* conformarse; **to comply with** conformarse con, obrar de acuerdo con
component [kəm'ponənt] *adj* componente ‖ *m* componente *m*
compose [kəm'poz] *tr* componer; **to be composed of** estar compuesto de
composed [kəm'pozd] *adj* sosegado, tranquilo
composer [kəm'pozer] *s* (mus) compositor *m,* músico
composing stick *s* componedor *m*
composite [kəm'pɑzɪt] *adj & s* compuesto
composition [,kɑmpə'zɪʃən] *s* composición
compositor [kəm'pɑzɪtər] *s* cajista *mf,* componedor *m*
composure [kəm'poʒər] *s* serenidad, sosiego

compote [ˈkampot] *s* (*stewed fruit*) compota; (*dish*) compotera

compound [ˈkampaʊnd] *adj* compuesto || *s* compuesto; (gram) vocablo compuesto || [kamˈpaʊnd] *tr* componer, combinar; (*interest*) capitalizar

comprehend [ˌkamprɪˈhɛnd] *tr* comprender

comprehensible [ˌkamprɪˈhɛnsɪbəl] *adj* comprensible

comprehension [ˌkamprɪˈhɛnʃən] *s* comprensión

comprehensive [ˌkamprɪˈhɛnsɪv] *adj* comprensivo, inclusivo, completo

compress [ˈkamprɛs] *s* (med) compresa, bilma || [kəmˈprɛs] *tr* comprimir

compression [kəmˈprɛʃən] *s* compresión

comprise o **comprize** [kəmˈpraɪz] *tr* abarcar, comprender, incluir

compromise [ˈkamprəˌmaɪz] *s* (*adjustment*) componenda, transigencia, transacción; (*endangering*) comprometimiento || *tr* (*by mutual concessions*) componer, transigir; (*to endanger*) comprometer, exponer || *intr* transigir, avenirse

comptroller [kənˈtrolər] *s* contralor *m*, interventor *m*

compulsory [kəmˈpʌlsəri] *adj* obligatorio

computable [kəmˈpjutəbəl] *adj* calculable

computation [ˌkampjuˈteʃən] *s* cálculo, cómputo

compute [kəmˈpjut] *tr & intr* computar, calcular

computer [kəmˈpjutər] *adj* informático || *s* ordenador *m*, computador *m;* (*person*) computador *m*, calculador *m;* **computers** informática; **on computer** computarizado; **to work in computers** trabajar en informática

computer chip *s* chip

computer dating *s* citas computerizadas

computer engineer *s* técnico en informática

computerize [kəmˈpjutəraɪz] *tr* computarizar, informatizar; (*a business office*) instalar ordenadores en

computer language *s* lenguaje *m* de programación

computer programmer *s* programador *m*, computista *mf*

computer programming *s* programación

computer science *s* informática

computer specialist *s* informático

computer virus *s* virus *m* informático

comrade [ˈkamræd] o [ˈkamrɪd] *s* camarada *m;* cumpa *m* (SAm) *mf*, compañero; compa *m* (SAm)

comrade in arms *s* compañero de armas

con. *abbr* **conclusion, consolidated, contra**

con [kan] *s* (*opposite opinion*) contra *m;* (*slang*) engaño || *v* (*pret & pp* **conned;** *ger* **conning**) *tr* leer con atención, aprender de memoria; (*slang*) engañar

concave [ˈkankev] o [kanˈkev] *adj* cóncavo

conceal [kənˈsil] *tr* encubrir, ocultar

concealment [kənˈsilmənt] *s* encubrimiento, ocultación; (*place*) escondite *m*

concede [kənˈsid] *tr* conceder

conceit [kənˈsit] *s* (*vanity*) orgullo, engreimiento; (*witty expression*) concepto, dicho ingenioso

conceited [kənˈsitɪd] *adj* orgulloso, engreído

conceivable [kənˈsivəbəl] *adj* concebible

conceive [kənˈsiv] *tr & intr* concebir

concentrate [ˈkansənˌtret] *tr* concentrar || *intr* concentrarse; **to concentrate on** o **upon** reconcentrarse en

concentration camp *s* campo de concentración

concentric [kənˈsɛntrɪk] *adj* concéntrico

concept [ˈkansɛpt] *s* concepto

conception [kənˈsɛpʃən] *s* concepción

concern [kənˈsʌrn] *s* (*business establishment*) empresa, casa comercial, razón *f* social; (*worry*) inquietud, preocupación; (*relation, reference*) concernencia; (*matter*) asunto, negocio || *tr* atañer, concernir; interesar; **as concerns** respecto de; **to whom it may concern** a quien pueda interesar, a quien corresponda

concerning [kənˈsʌrnɪŋ] *prep* respecto de, tocante a

concert [ˈkansərt] *s* concierto || [kənˈsʌrt] *tr & intr* concertar

conˈcert•masˈter *s* concertino

concer•to [kənˈtʃɛrto] *s* (*pl* **-tos** o **-ti** [ti]) concierto

concession [kənˈsɛʃən] *s* concesión

concessive [kənˈsɛsɪv] *adj* concesivo

concierge [ˌkansɪˈʌrʒ] *s* conserje *m*

conciliate [kənˈsɪlɪˌet] *tr* conciliar; conciliarse (*el respeto, la estima*)

conciliatory [kənˈsɪlɪ•əˌtori] *adj* conciliador

concise [kənˈsaɪs] *adj* conciso

conclude [kənˈklud] *tr & intr* concluir

concluding [kənˈkludɪŋ] *adj* final

conclusion [kənˈkluʒən] *s* conclusión; (*of a letter*) despedida

conclusive [kənˈklusɪv] *adj* concluyente

concoct [kənˈkakt] *tr* confeccionar; (*a story*) forjar, inventar

concomitant [kənˈkamɪtənt] *adj & s* concomitante *m*

concord [ˈkaŋkərd] *s* concordia; (gram, mus) concordancia

concordance [kənˈkərdəns] *s* concordancia

concourse [ˈkaŋkors] *s* (*of people*) concurso; (*of streams*) confluencia; bulevar *m*, gran via; (*of railroad station*) gran salón *m*

concrete [ˈkankrit] o [kanˈkrit] *adj* concreto; de hormigón || *s* hormigón *m*

concrete block *s* bloque *m* de hormigón

concrete mixer *s* hormigonera, mezcladora de hormigón

concubine [ˈkaŋkjəˌbaɪn] *s* concubina

con•cur [kənˈkʌr] *v* (*pret & pp* **-curred;** *ger* **-curring**) *intr* concurrir

concurrence [kənˈkʌrəns] *s* (*happening together*) concurrencia; (*agreement*) acuerdo

concussion [kənˈkʌʃən] *s* concusión

condemn [kən'dɛm] *tr* condenar
condemnation [,kandɛm'neʃən] *s* condenación
condense [kən'dɛns] *tr* condensar || *intr* condensarse
condensed milk *s* leche condensada
condescend [,kandɪ'sɛnd] *intr* dignarse
condescending [,kandɪ'sɛndɪŋ] *adj* condescendiente con inferiores
condescension [,kandɪ'sɛnʃən] *s* dignación, aire *m* protector
condiment ['kandɪmənt] *s* condimento
condition [kən'dɪʃən] *s* condición; **on condition that** a condición (de) que || *tr* acondicionar
conditional [kən'dɪʃənəl] *adj* condicional
conditioned reflex [kən'dɪʃənd] *s* reflejo acondicionado
condo *abbr* **condominium**
condole [kən'dol] *intr* condolerse
condolence [kən'doləns] *s* condolencia
condom ['kandəm] *s* preservativo, condón *m*
condominium [,kandə'mɪni•əm] *s* condominio, propiedad horizontal
condone [kən'don] *tr* condonar; (*legally*) despenalizar
condor ['kandər] *s* cóndor *m*
conduce [kən'djus] *intr* conducir
conducive [kən'djusɪv] *adj* conducente, contribuyente
conduct ['kandʌkt] *s* conducta || [kən'dʌkt] *tr* conducir; **to conduct oneself** conducirse, comportarse
conductor [kən'dʌktər] *s* conductor *m,* guía *mf;* (elec & phys) conductor *m,* conductora *f;* (rr) revisor *m;* (*on trolley or bus*) cobrador *m*
conduit ['kandɪt] o ['kandʊ•ɪt] *s* canal *f* para alambres o cables
cone [kon] *s* cono; (*of pastry*) barquillo; (*of paper*) cucurucho
confedera•cy [kən'fɛdərəsi] *s* (*pl* **-cies**) confederación; (*for unlawful purpose*) conjuración
confederate [kən'fɛdərɪt] *s* confederado; cómplice *mf* || [kən'fɛdə,ret] *tr* confederar || *intr* confederarse
con•fer [kən'fʌr] *v* (*pret & pp* **-ferred;** *ger* **-ferring**) *tr* conferir || *intr* conferenciar, consultar
conference ['kanfərəns] *s* conferencia, coloquio
conference call *s* teleconferencia
confess [kən'fɛs] *tr* confesar || *intr* confesar, confesarse
confession [kən'fɛʃən] *s* confesión
confessional [kən'fɛʃənəl] *s* confesonario
confession of faith *s* profesión de fe
confessor [kən'fɛsər] *s* confesante *mf;* (*priest*) confesor *m*
confide [kən'faɪd] *tr* confiar || *intr* confiar, confiarse; **to confide in** confiarse en
confidence ['kanfɪdəns] *s* confianza; (*secret*) confidencia; **in strictest confidence** bajo la mayor reserva
confident ['kanfɪdənt] *adj* seguro || *s* confidente *m,* confidenta
confidential [,kanfɪ'dɛnʃəl] *adj* confidencial
confine ['kanfaɪn] *s* confín *m;* **the confines** los confines || [kən'faɪn] *tr* (*to keep within limits*) limitar, restringir; (*to keep shut in*) encerrar; **to be confined** estar de parto; **to be confined to bed** tener que guardar cama
confinement [kən'faɪnmənt] *s* limitación; encierro; parto, sobreparto
confirm [kən'fʌrm] *tr* confirmar
confirmed [kən'fʌrmd] *adj* confirmado; empedernido, inveterado
confiscate ['kanfɪs,ket] *tr* confiscar
conflagration [,kanflə'greʃən] *s* conflagración
conflict ['kanflɪkt] *s* conflicto; (*of interests, class hours, etc.*) incompatibilidad || [kən'flɪkt] *intr* chocar, desavenirse
conflicting [kən'flɪktɪŋ] *adj* contradictorio; (*events, appointments, class hours, etc.*) incompatible, conflictivo
confluence ['kanflʊ•əns] *s* confluencia
conform [kən'fɔrm] *intr* conformar, conformarse
conformance [kən'fɔrməns] *s* conformidad
conformi•ty [kən'fɔrmɪti] *s* (*pl* **-ties**) conformidad
confound [kan'faʊnd] *tr* confundir || ['kan'faʊnd] *tr* maldecir; **confound it!** ¡maldito sea!
confounded [kan'faundɪd] *adj* confundido; aborrecible; maldito
confrere ['kanfrɛr] *s* colega *m*
confront [kən'frʌnt] *tr* (*to face boldly*) confrontarse con, hacer frente a; (*to meet face to face*) encontrar cara a cara; (*to bring face to face; to compare*) confrontar
confrontation [,kanfrʌn'teʃən] *s* enfrentamiento
confuse [kən'fjuz] *tr* confundir
confusedness [kən'fjuzɪdnɪs] *s* desorientación
confusion [kən'fjuʒən] *s* confusión
confute [kən'fjut] *tr* confutar
congeal [kən'dʒil] *tr* congelar || *intr* congelarse
congenial [kən'dʒinjəl] *adj* simpático; agradable; compatible; (*having the same nature*) congenial
congenital [kən'dʒɛnɪtəl] *adj* congénito
conger eel ['kaŋgər] *s* congrio
congest [kən'dʒɛst] *tr* congestionar || *intr* congestionarse
congestion [kən'dʒɛstʃən] *s* congestión
congratulate [kən'grætʃə,let] *tr* congratular, felicitar
congratulation [kən,grætʃə'leʃən] *s* congratulación, felicitación
congregate ['kaŋgrɪ,get] *intr* congregarse
congregation [,kaŋgrɪ'geʃən] *s* congregación; feligresía, fieles *mf* (*de una iglesia*)
congress ['kaŋgrɪs] *s* congreso
congress•man ['kaŋgrɪsmən] *s* (*pl* **-men** [mən]) congresista *m*
conical ['kanɪkəl] *adj* cónico

conj. *abbr* **conjugation, conjunction**
conjecture [kən'dʒɛktʃər] *s* conjetura ‖ *tr & intr* conjeturar
conjugal ['kandʒəgəl] *adj* conyugal
conjugate ['kandʒə,get] *tr* conjugar
conjugation [,kandʒə'geʃən] *s* conjugación
conjunction [kən'dʒʌŋkʃən] *s* conjunción
conjuration [,kandʒə'reʃən] *s* (*superstitious invocation*) conjuro; (*magic spell*) hechizo
conjure [kən'dʒʊr] *tr* (*to appeal to solemnly*) conjurar ‖ ['kʌndʒər] o ['kandʒər] *tr* (*to exorcise, drive away*) conjurar; **to conjure away** conjurar; **to conjure up** evocar; crear, suscitar (*dificultades*)
con man [kan] *s* (coll) embaucador *m*, embaucadora, estafador *m*
connect [kə'nɛkt] *tr* conectar; asociar, relacionar ‖ *intr* enlazarse; asociarse, relacionarse; empalmar, enlazar (*dos trenes*)
connecting flight *s* vuelo de enlace
connecting rod *s* biela
connection [kə'nɛkʃən] *s* conexión; (*relative*) pariente *mf;* (*of trains*) combinación, enlace *m,* empalme *m;* (*in subway*) correspondencia; **in connection with** con respecto a; juntamente con
connective tissue [kə'nɛktɪv] *s* (anat) tejido conjunctivo
conning tower ['kanɪŋ] *s* torreta de mando
conniption [kə'nɪpʃən] *s* pataleta, berrinche *m*
connive [kə'naɪv] *intr* confabularse, estar en connivencia
conquer ['kaŋkər] *tr* vencer; (*by force of arms*) conquistar ‖ *intr* triunfar
conqueror ['kaŋkərər] *s* conquistador *m,* vencedor *m*
conquest ['kaŋkwɛst] *s* conquista
conscience ['kanʃəns] *s* conciencia; **in all conscience** en conciencia
conscientious [,kanʃɪ'ɛnʃəs] *adj* concienzudo
conscientious objector [ab'dʒɛktər] *s* objetante *m* de conciencia
conscious ['kanʃəs] *adj* (*aware of one's own existence*) consciente; (*deliberate*) intencional; (*self-conscious*) encogido, tímido; **to become conscious** volver en sí
consciousness ['kanʃəsnɪs] *s* conciencia, conocimiento
consciousness raising *s* concienciación
conscript ['kanskrɪpt] *s* conscripto, quinto ‖ [kən'skrɪpt] *tr* reclutar
conscription [kən'skrɪpʃən] *s* conscripción, quinta
consecrate ['kansɪ,kret] *tr* consagrar
consecutive [kən'sɛkjətɪv] *adj* (*successive*) consecutivo; (*continuous*) consecuente
consensus [kən'sɛnsəs] *s* consenso; **the consensus of opinion** la opinión general
consent [kən'sɛnt] *s* consentimiento; **by common consent** de común acuerdo ‖ *intr* consentir; **to consent to** consentir en
consequence ['kansɪ,kwɛns] *s* consecuencia; aires *mpl* de importancia
consequential [,kansɪ'kwɛnʃəl] *adj* consiguiente; importante; altivo, pomposo
consequently ['kansɪ,kwɛntli] *adv* por consiguiente
conservation [,kansər'veʃən] *s* conservación
conservatism [kən'sʌrvə,tɪzəm] *s* conservadurismo
conservative [kən'sʌrvətɪv] *adj* (*preservative*) conservativo; (*disposed to maintain existing views and institutions*) conservador; cauteloso, moderado ‖ *s* preservativo; conservador *m*
conservato•ry [kən'sʌrvə,tori] *s* (*pl* **-ries**) (*school of music*) conservatorio; (*greenhouse*) invernadero
consider [kən'sɪdər] *tr* considerar
considerable [kən'sɪdərəbəl] *adj* considerable
considerate [kən'sɪdərɪt] *adj* considerado
consideration [kən,sɪdə'reʃən] *s* consideración; **for a consideration** por un precio; **in consideration of** en consideración de; en cambio de; **on no consideration** bajo ningún concepto; **out of consideration for** por respeto a; **without due consideration** sin reflexión
considering [kən'sɪdərɪŋ] *adv* (coll) teniendo en cuenta las circunstancias ‖ *prep* en vista de, en razón de ‖ *conj* en vista de que
consign [kən'saɪn] *tr* consignar
consignee [,kansaɪ'ni] *s* consignatario
consignment [kən'saɪnmənt] *s* consignación
consist [kən'sɪst] *intr* — **to consist in** consistir en; **to consist of** consistir en, constar de
consisten•cy [kən'sɪstənsi] *s* (*pl* **-cies**) (*firmness, amount of firmness*) consistencia; (*logical connection*) consecuencia
consistent [kən'sɪstənt] *adj* (*holding firmly together*) consistente; (*agreeing with itself or oneself*) consecuente; **consistent with** (*in accord with*) compatible con
consisto•ry [kən'sɪstəri] *s* (*pl* **-ries**) consistorio
consolation [,kansə'leʃən] *s* consolación, consuelo
consolation prize *s* premio de consolación
console ['kansol] *s* consola; mesa de consola; (compu) consola ‖ [kən'sol] *tr* consolar
consommé [,kansə'me] *s* consumado, consommé *m*
consonant ['kansənənt] *adj & s* consonante *f*
consort ['kansɔrt] *s* consorte *mf;* embarcación que acompaña a otra ‖ [kən'sɔrt] *tr* asociar ‖ *intr* asociarse; armonizar, concordar
consorti•um [kən'sɔrʃɪ•əm] *s* (*pl* **-a** [ə]) consorcio
conspicuous [kən'spɪkjʊ•əs] *adj* manifiesto, claro, evidente; llamativo, vistoso, sugestivo; conspicuo, notable
conspira•cy [kən'spɪrəsi] *s* (*pl* **-cies**) conspiración, conjuración
conspire [kən'spaɪr] *intr* conspirar, conjurar
constable ['kanstəbəl] o ['kʌnstəbəl] *s* policía *m,* guardia *m,* alguacil *m*
constancy ['kanstənsi] *s* constancia; fidelidad

constant [ˈkɑnstənt] *adj* constante; incesante; fiel || *s* constante *f*
constellation [ˌkɑnstəˈleʃən] *s* constelación
constipate [ˈkɑnstɪˌpet] *tr* estreñir
constipation [ˌkɑnstɪˈpeʃən] *s* estreñimiento, estitiquez *f*
constituen•cy [kənˈstɪtʃʊ•ənsi] *s* (*pl* **-cies**) votantes *mpl;* clientela; comitentes *mpl;* distrito electoral
constituent [kənˈstɪtʃʊ•ənt] *adj* constitutivo, componente; (*having power to create or revise a constitution*) constituyente || *s* constitutivo, componente *m;* (*person who appoints another to act for him*) comitente *m*
constitute [ˈkɑnstɪˌtjut] *tr* constituir
constitution [ˌkɑnstɪˈtjuʃən] *s* constitución
constrain [kənˈstren] *tr* constreñir; detener, encerrar; restringir
construct [kənˈstrʌkt] *tr* construir
construction [kənˈstrʌkʃən] *s* construcción; interpretación
construction worker *s* peón *m* de albañil o de mano
construe [kənˈstru] *tr* interpretar; deducir, inferir; traducir; (*to combine syntactically*) construir; (*to explain the syntax of*) analizar
consul [ˈkɑnsəl] *s* cónsul *m*
consular [ˈkɑnsələr] *adj* consular
consulate [ˈkɑnsəlɪt] *s* consulado
consulship [ˈkɑnsəlˌʃip] *s* consulado
consult [kənˈsʌlt] *tr & intr* consultar
consultant [kənˈsʌltənt] *s* consultor *m*
consultation [ˌkɑnsəlˈteʃən] *s* (*consulting*) consulta; (*meeting*) consulta, consultación
consume [kənˈsum] o [kənˈsjum] *tr* consumir; (*to absorb the interest of*) preocupar; || *intr* consumirse
consumer [kənˈsumər] *s* consumidor *m;* (*of gas, electricity, etc.*) abonado
consumer credit *s* crédito consuntivo
consumer goods *spl* bienes *mpl* de consumo
consumerism [kənˈsuməˌrɪzəm] *s* consumerismo
consumer price index *s* índice *m* de precios al consumidor
consummate [kənˈsʌmɪt] *adj* consumado || [ˈkɑnsəˌmet] *tr* consumar
consumption [kənˈsʌmpʃən] *s* consunción, consumo; (pathol) consunción, tisis *f*
consumptive [kənˈsʌmptɪv] *adj* consuntivo; (path) tísico || *s* tísico
cont. *abbr* **contents, continental, continued**
contact [ˈkɑntækt] *s* contacto; (elec) contacto; (elec) toma de corriente || *tr* (coll) ponerse en contacto con || *intr* contactar
contact breaker *s* (elec) ruptor *m*
contact lens *s* lente *m* de contacto, lente invisible, lentilla, microlentilla
contagion [kənˈtedʒən] *s* contagio
contagious [kənˈtedʒəs] *adj* contagioso
contain [kənˈten] *tr* contener; **to contain oneself** contenerse, refrenarse
container [kənˈtenər] *s* continente *m,* recipiente *m,* vaso, caja, envase *m,* contenedor *m*
containment [kənˈtenmənt] *s* contención, refrenamiento
contaminate [kənˈtæmɪˌnet] *tr* contaminar
contamination [kənˌtæmɪˈneʃən] *s* contaminación
contd. *abbr* **continued**
contemplate [ˈkɑntəmˌplet] *tr & intr* contemplar; pensar, proyectar
contemplation [ˌkɑntəmˈpleʃən] *s* contemplación; intención, propósito
contemporaneous [kənˌtɛmpəˈrenɪ•əs] *adj* contemporáneo
contemporar•y [kənˈtɛmpəˌrɛri] *adj* contemporáneo, coetáneo || *s* (*pl* **-ies**) contemporáneo, coetáneo
contempt [kənˈtɛmpt] *s* desprecio; (law) contumacia
contemptible [kənˈtɛmptɪbəl] *adj* despreciable
contemptuous [kənˈtɛmptʃʊ•əs] *adj* despreciativo, desdeñoso
contend [kənˈtɛnd] *tr* sostener, mantener || *intr* contender
contender [kənˈtɛndər] *s* contendiente *mf,* concurrente *mf*
content [kənˈtɛnt] *adj & s* contento || [ˈkɑntɛnt] *s* contenido; **contents** contenido || [kənˈtɛnt] *tr* contentar
contented [kənˈtɛntɪd] *adj* contento, satisfecho
contentedness [kənˈtɛndɪdnɪs] *s* contentamiento, satisfacción
contention [kənˈtɛnʃən] *s* (*strife; dispute*) contención; (*point argued for*) argumento
contentious [kənˈtɛnʃəs] *adj* contencioso
contentment [kənˈtɛntmənt] *s* contentamiento, contento
contest [ˈkɑntɛst] *s* (*struggle, fight*) contienda; (*competition*) competencia, concurso || [kənˈtɛst] *tr* disputar; tratar de conseguir || *intr* contender
contestant [kənˈtɛstənt] *s* contendiente *mf*
context [ˈkɑntɛkst] *s* contexto
contiguous [kənˈtɪgjʊ•əs] *adj* contiguo
continence [ˈkɑntɪnəns] *s* continencia
continent [ˈkɑntɪnənt] *adj & s* continente *m;* **the Continent** la Europa continental
continental [ˌkɑntɪˈnɛntəl] *adj* continental || **Continental** *s* habitante *mf* del continente europeo
contingen•cy [kənˈtɪndʒənsi] *s* (*pl* **-cies**) contingencia
contingent [kənˈtɪndʒənt] *adj & s* contingente *m*
continual [kənˈtɪnjʊ•əl] *adj* continuo
continue [kənˈtɪnjʊ] *tr & intr* continuar; **to be continued** continuará
continui•ty [ˌkɑntɪˈnju•ɪti] o [ˌkɑntɪˈnu•ɪti] *s* (*pl* **-ties**) continuidad; (mov, rad, telv) guión *m;* (rad, telv) comentarios o anuncios entre las partes de un programa
continuous [kənˈtɪnjʊ•əs] *adj* continuo
continuous showing *s* (mov) sesión continua

continuous waves *spl* (rad) ondas entretenidas
contortion [kən'tɔrʃən] *s* contorsión
contour ['kantʊr] *s* contorno
contour line *s* curva de nivel
contour map *s* plano acotado
contraband ['kantrə,bænd] *adj* contrabandista || *s* contrabando
contrabass ['kantrə,bes] *s* contrabajo
contraceptive [,kantrə'sɛptɪv] *adj & s* anticonceptivo, contraceptivo; (*condom*) preservatívo, condón *m*
contract ['kantrækt] *s* contrato; **on a contract** (*to kill*) a sueldo || ['kantrækt] o [kən'trækt] *tr* contraer (*p.ej., matrimonio* || *intr* (*to shrink*) contraerse; (*to enter into an agreement*) comprometerse; **to contract for** contratar
contract bridge *s* bridge *m* contrato
contraction [kən'trækʃən] *s* contracción
contractor [kən'træktər] *s* contratista *mf*
contradict [,kantrə'dɪkt] *tr* contradecir
contradiction [,kantrə'dɪkʃən] *s* contradicción
contradictory [,kantrə'dɪktəri] *adj* (*involving contradiction*) contradictorio; (*inclined to contradict*) contradictor
contrail ['kan,trel] *s* (aer) estela de vapor, rastro de condensación
contral•to [kən'trælto] *s* (*pl* **-tos**) (*person*) contralto *mf;* (*voice*) contralto *m*
contraption [kən'træpʃən] *s* (coll) artilugio, dispositivo
contra•ry ['kantrɛri] *adv* contrariamente || *adj* contrario || [kən'trɛri] *adj* obstinado, terco || ['kantrɛri] *s* (*pl* **-ries**) contrario; **on the contrary** al contrario
contrast ['kantræst] *s* contraste *m* || [kən'træst] *tr* comparar; poner en contraste || *intr* contrastar
contravene [,kantrə'vin] *tr* contradecir; contravenir a (*una ley*)
contribute [kən'trɪbjut] *tr* contribuir || *intr* contribuir; (*to a newspaper, conference, etc.*) colaborar
contribution [,kantrɪ'bjuʃən] *s* contribución; (*to a newspaper, conference, etc.*) colaboración
contributor [kən'trɪbjutər] *s* contribuidor *m,* contribuyente *mf;* colaborador *m*
contrite [kən'traɪt] *adj* contrito
contrition [kən'trɪʃən] *s* contrición
contrivance [kən'traɪvəns] *s* aparato, dispositivio; idea, plan *m,* designio
contrive [kən'traɪv] *tr* (*to devise*) idear, inventar; (*to scheme up*) maquinar, tramar; (*to bring about*) efectuar; **to contrive to** + *inf* ingeniarse a + *inf* || *intr* maquinar
con•trol [kən'trol] *s* gobierno, mando; chequeo; (*of a scientific experiment*) contrarregistro, control *m;* **controls** mandos; **to get under control** conseguir dominar (*un incendio*) || *v* (*pret & pp* **-trolled;** *ger* **-trolling**) *tr* gobernar, mandar; comprobar, controlar; **to control oneself** dominarse
control bus *s* (compu) bus *m* de control
controlling interest *s* (el) mayor porcentaje de acciones
control panel *s* (aer) tablero de instrumentos; (compu) panel *m* de control
control room *s* (mil, naut) centro de operaciones; (rad, telv) sala de control
control stick *s* (aer) mango de escoba, palanca de mando
control strip *s* (compu) barra de controles
control tower *s* torre *f* de control
controversial [,kantrə'vʌrʃəl] *adj* controvertible, disputable; disputador
controver•sy ['kantrə,vʌrsi] *s* (*pl* **-sies**) controversia, polémica
controvert ['kantrə,vʌrt] o [,kantrə'vʌrt] *tr* (*to argue against*) contradecir; (*to argue about*) controvertir
contumacious [,kantju'meʃəs] *adj* contumaz
contuma•cy ['kantjʊməsi] *s* (*pl* **-cies**) contumacia
contume•ly ['kantjʊmɪli] *s* (*pl* **-lies**) contumelia
contusion [kən'tjuʒən] *s* contusión; magullón *m*
conundrum [kə'nʌndrəm] *s* acertijo, adivinanza; problema complicado
convalesce [,kanvə'lɛs] *intr* convalecer
convalescence [,kanvə'lɛsəns] *s* convalecencia
convalescent [,kanvə'lɛsənt] *adj & s* convaleciente *mf*
convalescent home *s* clínica de reposo
convene [kən'vin] *tr* convocar || *intr* convenir, reunirse
convenience [kən'vinjəns] *s* comodidad, conveniencia; **at your earliest convenience** a la primera oportunidad que Ud. tenga
convenient [kən'vinjənt] *adj* cómodo, conveniente; próximo
convent ['kanvɛnt] *s* convento; convento de religiosas
convention [kən'vɛnʃən] *s* (*agreement*) convención, conveniencia; (*accepted usage*) costumbre *f,* conveniencia social, convención; (*meeting*) congreso, convención
conventional [kən'vɛnʃənəl] *adj* convencional
conventionali•ty [kən,vɛnʃə'nælɪti] *s* (*pl* **-ties**) precedente *m* convencional
converge [kən'vʌrʒ] *intr* convergir
conversant [kən'vʌrsənt] *adj* familiarizado, versado
conversation [,kanvər'seʃən] *s* conversación
conversational [,kanvər'seʃənəl] *adj* conversacional
converse ['kanvʌrs] *adj & s* contrario || [kən'vʌrs] *intr* conversar
conversion [kən'vʌrʒən] *s* conversión; (*unlawful appropriation*) malversación
convert ['kanvʌrt] *s* convertido, converso || [kən'vʌrt] *tr* convertir || *intr* convertirse
converter [kən'vʌrtər] *s* (electron) convertidor *m;* (compu) conversor *m*
convertible [kən'vʌrtɪbəl] *adj* convertible || *s* (aut) convertible *m,* descapotable *m*
convex ['kanvɛks] o [kan'vɛks] *adj* convexo
convey [kən've] *tr* llevar, transportar; comuni-

car, participar (*informes*); transferir, traspasar (*bienes de una persona a otra*)
conveyance [kən've•əns] *s* transporte *m;* comunicación, participación; vehículo; (*transfer of property*) traspaso; escritura de traspaso
convict ['kɑnvɪkt] *s* reo convicto, presidiario ‖ [kən'vɪkt] *tr* probar la culpabilidad de; declarar convicto (*a un acusado*)
conviction [kən'vɪkʃən] *s* convencimiento; condena, fallo de culpabilidad
convince [kən'vɪns] *tr* convencer
convincing [kən'vɪnsɪŋ] *adj* convincente
convivial [kən'vɪvɪ•əl] *adj* jovial
convocation [,kɑnvə'keʃən] *s* asamblea
convoke [kən'vok] *tr* convocar
convoy ['kɑnvɔɪ] *s* convoy *m,* conserva ‖ *tr* convoyar
convulse [kən'vʌls] *tr* convulsionar; agitar; **to convulse with laughter** mover a risas convulsivas
coo [ku] *intr* arrullar
cook [kʊk] *s* cocinero ‖ *tr* cocer, cocinar, guisar; **to cook up** (coll) falsificar; (coll) maquinar, tramar ‖ *intr* cocer, cocinar
cook'book' *s* libro de cocina
cookie ['kʊki] *s* var de **cooky**
cooking ['kʊkɪŋ] *s* cocina, arte *m* de cocinar
cook'stove' *s* cocina económica
cook•y ['kʊki] *s* (*pl* **-ies**) pasta seca, pastelito dulce, pasta de té (Esp)
cool [kul] *adj* fresco; frío, indiferente ‖ *s* fresco ‖ *tr* refrescar; moderar ‖ *intr* refrescarse; moderarse; **to cool off** refrescarse; serenarse
cooler ['kulər] *s* heladera, refrigerador *m;* refrigerante *m;* cárcel *f*
cool'-head'ed *adj* sereno, tranquilo, juicioso
coolie ['kuli] *s* culí *m*
coolish ['kulɪʃ] *adj* fresquito
coolness ['kulnɪs] *s* fresco, frescura; (fig) frialdad
coon [kun] *s* mapache *m,* oso lavandero
coop [kup] *s* gallinero; (*for fattening capons*) caponera; jaula, redil *m;* (*jail*) (slang) caponera; **to fly the coop** (slang) escabullirse ‖ *tr* encerrar en un gallinero; enjaular; **to coop up** emparedar
coop. *abbr* **cooperative**
cooper ['kupər] *s* barrilero, tonelero
cooperate [ko'ɑpə,ret] *intr* cooperar
cooperation [ko,ɑpə'reʃən] *s* cooperación
cooperative [ko'ɑpə,retɪv] *adj* cooperativo
coopt [ko'ɑpt] *tr* cooptar
coordinate [ko'ɔrdɪnɪt] *adj* coordenado; (gram) coordinante ‖ *s* (math) coordenada ‖ [ko'ɔrdɪ,net] *tr & intr* coordinar
cootie ['kuti] *s* (slang) piojo
cop [kɑp] *s* (slang) polizonte *m* ‖ *v* (*pret & pp* **copped;** *ger* **copping**) *tr* (slang) hurtar
copartner [ko'pɑrtnər] *s* consocio, copartícipe *mf*
cope [kop] *intr* — **to cope with** hacer frente a, enfrentarse con
cope'stone' *s* piedra de albardilla
copier ['kɑpɪ•ər] *s* (*person who copies*) copiante *mf,* copista *mf,* imitador *m;* (*apparatus*) copiador *m,* copiadora
copilot ['ko,paɪlət] *s* copiloto
coping ['kopɪŋ] *s* albardilla
copious ['kopɪ•əs] *adj* copioso
copper ['kɑpər] *adj* cobreño; (*in color*) cobrizo ‖ *s* cobre *m;* (*coin*) calderilla, vellón *m;* (slang) polizonte *m*
cop'per•head' *s* víbora de cabeza de cobre
cop'perplate' *s* grabado en cobre
cop'per•smith' *s* cobrero
coppery ['kɑpəri] *adj* cobreño; (*in color*) cobrizo
coppice ['kɑpɪs] o **copse** [kɑps] *s* soto, monte bajo
copulate ['kɑpjə,let] *intr* copularse
cop•y ['kɑpi] *s* (*pl* **-ies**) copia; (*of a book*) ejemplar *m;* (*of a magazine*) número; (*document to be reproduced in print*) original *m,* manuscrito ‖ *v* (*pret & pp* **-ied**) *tr* copiar
cop'y-and-paste' *intr* (compu) copiar y pegar
cop'y•book' *s* cuaderno de escritura
cop'y•cat' *s* (coll) copión *m,* copiona; (*before a substantive*) de imitación
copy editor *s* corrector *m* de estilo, editor *m*
copy reader *s* corrector *m* de manuscrito, corrector de pruebas
cop'y•right' *s* (derechos de) propiedad literaria *or* intelectual; derechos de reproducción ‖ *tr* registrar en el registro de la propiedad literaria
copy writer *s* escritor publicitario
co•quet [ko'kɛt] *v* (*pret & pp* **-quetted;** *ger* **-quetting**) *intr* coquetear; burlarse
coquet•ry ['kokətri] o [ko'kɛtri] *s* (*pl* **-ries**) coquetería; burla
coquette [ko'kɛt] *s* coqueta
coquettish [ko'kɛtɪʃ] *adj* coqueta
cor. *abbr* **corner, coroner, correction, corresponding**
coral ['kɑrəl] o ['kɔrəl] *adj* coralino ‖ *s* coral *m*
coral reef *s* arrecife *m* de coral
cord [kɔrd] *s* cordón *m;* piola ‖ *tr* acordonar
cordial ['kɔrdʒəl] *adj* cordial ‖ *s* licor tónico; (*medicine*) cordial *m*
cordiali•ty [kɔr'dʒælɪti] *s* (*pl* **-ties**) cordialidad
cordless telephone |'kɔrdləs| *s* teléfono inalámbrico, teléfono sin hilos
corduroy ['kɔrdə,rɔɪ] *s* pana; **corduroys** pantalones *mpl* de pana
core [kor] *s* corazón *m;* (*of an electromagnet*) núcleo
corespondent [,korɪs'pɑndənt] *s* cómplice *mf* del demandado en juicio de divorcio
cork [kɔrk] *s* corcho; corcho, tapón *m* de corcho; tapón (*de cualquier materia*) ‖ *tr* encorchar, tapar con corcho
corking ['kɔrkɪŋ] *adj* (slang) brutal, extraordinario
cork oak *s* alcornoque *m*
cork'screw' *s* sacacorchos *m,* tirabuzón *m*
cormorant ['kɔrmərənt] *s* cormorán *m,* cuervo marino

corn [kɔrn] *s* (*in U.S.A.*) maíz *m;* (*in England*) trigo; (*in Scotland*) avena; grano (*de maíz, trigo*); (*on the foot*) callo; (coll) aguardiente *m;* (slang) trivialidad
corn bread *s* pan *m* de maíz
corn′cake′ *s* tortilla de maíz
corn′cob′ *s* mazorca de maíz, carozo
corncob pipe *s* pipa de fumar hecha de una mazorca de maíz
corn′crib′ *s* granero para maíz
corn cure *adj* callicida *m*
cornea [ˈkɔrnɪ•ə] *s* córnea
corned beef *s* carne salada de res
corner [ˈkɔrnər] *s* ángulo; (*esp. where two streets meet*) esquina; (*inside angle formed by two or more surfaces; secluded place; region, quarter*) rincón *m;* (*of eye*) comisura, rabillo; (*of lips*) comisura; (*awkward position*) apuro, aprieto; monopolio; **around the corner** a la vuelta de la esquina; **to turn the corner** doblar la esquina; pasar el punto más peligroso ‖ *tr* arrinconar; monopolizar
corner cupboard *s* rinconera
corner room *s* habitación de esquina
cor′ner•stone′ *s* piedra angular; (*of a new building*) primera piedra
cornet [kɔrˈnɛt] *s* corneta
corn exchange *s* bolsa de granos
corn′field′ *s* (*in U.S.A.*) maizal *m;* (*in England*) trigal *m;* (*in Scotland*) avenal *m*
corn′flakes *spl* hojuelas de maíz
corn flour *s* harina de maíz
corn′flow′er *s* cabezuela
corn′husk′ *s* perfolla
cornice [ˈkɔrnɪs] *s* cornisa
Cornish [ˈkɔrnɪʃ] *adj & s* córnico
corn liquor *s* chicha
corn meal *s* harina de maíz
corn on the cob *s* maíz *m* en la mazorca
corn plaster *s* emplasto para los callos
corn silk *s* cabellos, barbas del maíz
corn′stalk′ *s* tallo de maíz
corn′starch′ *s* almidón *m* de maíz
cornucopia [,kɔrnəˈkopɪ•ə] *s* cornucopia
Cornwall [ˈkɔrn,wɔl] *s* Cornualles
corn•y [ˈkɔrni] *adj* (*comp* **-ier;** *super* **-iest**) de maíz; (coll) gastado, trivial, pesado
corollar•y [ˈkɑrə,lɛri] o [ˈkɔrə,lɛri] *s* (*pl* **-ies**) corolario
coronation [,kɑrəˈneʃən] o [,kɔrəˈneʃən] *s* coronación
coroner [ˈkɑrənər] o [ˈkɔrənər] *s* juez *m* de guardia
coroner's inquest *s* pesquisa dirigida por el juez de guardia
coronet [ˈkɑrə,nɛt] o [ˈkɔrə,nɛt] *s* (*worn by members of nobility*) corona; (*ornamental band of jewels worn on head*) diadema *f*
Corp. *abbr* **Corporation**
corporal [ˈkɔrpərəl] *adj* corporal ‖ *s* (mil) cabo
corporal punishment *s* pena corporal
corporation [,kɔrpəˈreʃən] *s* (*provincial, municipal, or service entity*) corporación; sociedad anónima por acciones
corps [kor] *s* (*pl* **corps** [korz]) cuerpo; (mil) cuerpo
corps de ballet [kɔr də bæˈlɛ] *s* cuerpo de baile
corpse [kɔrps] *s* cadáver *m*
corpulent [ˈkɔrpjələnt] *adj* corpulento
corpuscle [ˈkɔrpəsəl] *s* corpúsculo, partícula; (physiol) glóbulo
corpus delicti [ˈkɔrpəsdɪˈlɪktaɪ] *s* (law) cuerpo del delito
cor•ral [kəˈræl] *s* corral *m* ‖ *v* (*pret & pp* **-ralled;** *ger* **-ralling**) *tr* acorralar
correct [kəˈrɛkt] *adj* correcto; (*proper*) cumplido ‖ *tr* corregir
correction [kəˈrɛkʃən] *s* corrección
corrective [kəˈrɛktɪv] *adj & s* correctivo
correctness [kəˈrɛktnɪs] *s* corrección; cumplimiento, cumplido
correlate [ˈkɔrə,let] *tr* correlacionar ‖ *intr* correlacionarse
correlation [,kɔrəˈleʃən] *s* correlación
correlative [kəˈrɛlətɪv] *adj & s* correlativo
correspond [,kɑrɪˈspɑnd] o [,kɔrɪˈspɑnd] *intr* corresponder; (*to communicate by writing*) corresponderse
correspondence [,kɑrɪˈspɑndəns] o [,kɔrɪˈspɑndəns] *s* correspondencia
correspondence course *s* curso por correspondencia
correspondence school *s* escuela por correspondencia
correspondent [,kɑrɪˈspɑndənt] o [,kɔrɪˈspɑndənt] *adj* correspondiente ‖ *s* correspondiente *mf;* (*for a newspaper*) corresponsal *mf*
corresponding [,kɑrɪˈspɑndɪŋ] o [,kɔrɪˈspɑndɪŋ] *adj* correspondiente
corridor [ˈkɑrɪdər] o [ˈkɔrɪdər] *s* corredor *m,* pasillo
corroborate [kəˈrɑbə,ret] *tr* corroborar
corrode [kəˈrod] *tr* corroer ‖ *intr* corroerse
corrosion [kəˈroʒən] *s* corrosión
corrosive [kəˈrosɪv] *adj & s* corrosivo
corrugated [ˈkɑrə,getɪd] o [ˈkɔrə,getɪd] *adj* acanalado, ondulado
corrupt [kəˈrʌpt] *adj* corrompido ‖ *tr* corromper ‖ *intr* corromperse
corruption [kəˈrʌpʃən] *s* corrupción
corsage [kɔrˈsɑʒ] *s* (*bodice*) corpiño, jubón *m;* (*bouquet*) ramillete *m* que se lleva en el pecho o la cintura
corsair [ˈkɔr,sɛr] *s* corsario
corset [ˈkɔrsɪt] *s* corsé *m*
corset cover *s* cubrecorsé *m*
Corsica [ˈkɔrsɪkə] *s* Córcega
Corsican [ˈkɔrsɪkən] *adj & s* corso
cortege [kɔrˈteʒ] *s* procesión; (*retinue*) cortejo, séquito
cor•tex [ˈkɔr,tɛks] *s* (*pl* **-tices** [tɪ,siz]) corteza; corteza cerebral
cortisone [ˈkɔrtɪ,son] *s* cortisona
corvette [kɔrˈvɛt] *s* corbeta
cosmetic [kɑzˈmɛtɪk] *adj & s* cosmético

cosmetic surgery *s* cirugía plástica
cosmic [ˈkazmɪk] *adj* cosmico
cosmonaut [ˈkazmə,nɔt] *s* cosmonauta *mf*
cosmopolitan [,kazməˈpalɪtən] *adj & s* cosmopolita *mf*
cosmos [ˈkazməs] *s* cosmos *m;* (bot) cosmos
Cossack [ˈka,sæk] *adj & s* cosaco
cost [kɔst] o [kast] *s* coste *m,* costo; **at cost** a coste y costas; **at all costs** a toda costa; **costs** (law) costas ‖ *v* (*pret & pp* **cost**) *intr* costar; **cost what it may** cueste lo que cueste
cost accounting *s* escandallo
co-star [ˈkoˈstar] *s* coprotagonista *mf*
Costa Rican [ˈkastə ˈrikən] o [ˈkɔste ˈrikən] *adj & s* costarricense *mf,* costarriqueño
cost′-ben′e•fit analysis *s* análisis costebeneficio
cost exemption *s* gratuidad
cost, insurance, and freight costo, seguro y flete
cost•ly [ˈkɔstli] o [ˈkastli] *adj* (*comp* **-lier;** *super* **-liest**) costoso, dispendioso; (*lavish*) pródigo; (*magnificent*) suntuoso
cost′-of-liv′ing index *s* índice *m* del costo de la vida
costume [ˈkastjum] *s* traje *m;* (*garb worn on stage, at balls, etc.*) disfraz *m,* traje de época
costume ball *s* baile *m* de trajes
costume jewelry *s* joyas de fantasía, bisutería
cot [kat] *s* catre *m*
cot death *s* muerte *f* de cuna
coterie [ˈkotəri] *s* círculo, grupo; (*clique*) corrillo
cottage [ˈkatɪdʒ] *s* cabaña; casita de campo
cottage cheese *s* naterón *m,* requesón *m*
cottage industry *s* industria artesanal
cotter pin [ˈkatər] *s* chaveta
cotton [ˈkatən] *s* algodón *m* ‖ *intr* — **to cotton up to** (coll) aficionarse a
cotton ball *s* copo de algodón
cotton candy algodón de azúcar
cotton field *s* algodonal *m*
cotton gin *s* desmotadera de algodón
cotton picker [ˈpɪkər] *s* recogedor *m* de algodón; (mech) cosechadora de algodón
cot′ton•seed′ *s* semilla de algodón
cottonseed oil *s* aceite *m* de algodón
cotton waste *s* hilacha de algodón, estopa de algodón
cot′ton•wood′ *s* chopo del Canadá, chopo de Virginia
cottony [ˈkatəni] *adj* algodonoso
couch [kaʊtʃ] *s* canapé *m,* diván *m* ‖ *tr* expresar
cougar [ˈkugər] *s* puma *m*
cough [kɔf] o [kaf] *s* tos *f* ‖ *tr* — **to cough up** arrojar por la boca; (slang) sudar, entregar ‖ *intr* toser; (*artificially, to attract attention*) destoserse
cough drop *s* pastilla para la tos
cough syrup *s* jarabe *m* para la tos
could [kʊd] *v aux* pude, podía; podría
couldn't *contr* **could not**
council [ˈkaʊnsəl] *s* (*deliberative or legislative assembly*) consejo; (*of a municipality*) concejo; (eccl) concilio
council•man [ˈkaʊnsəlmən] *s* (*pl* **-men** [mən]) concejal *m*
councilor [ˈkaʊnsələr] *s* consejero
coun•sel [ˈkaʊnsəl] *s* consejo; (*advisor*) consejero; (*consultant*) consultor *m;* (*lawyer*) abogado consultor; **to keep one's own counsel** no revelar sus intenciones ‖ *v* (*pret & pp* **-seled** o **-selled;** *ger* **-seling** o **-selling**) *tr* aconsejar ‖ *intr* aconsejarse
counselor [ˈkaʊnsələr] *s* consejero, orientador *m;* abogado
count [kaʊnt] *s* (*act of counting*) cuenta, recuento; (*result of counting*) suma, total *m;* (*nobleman*) conde *m;* (*charge*) (law) cargo; **to take the count** (box) dejarse contar diez ‖ *tr* contar; **to count off** separar contando; **to count out** no incluir; (sport) declarar vencido ‖ *intr* contar; (*to be worth consideration*) valer; **to count for** valer; **to count on** contar con
countable [ˈkaʊntəbəl] *adj* contable
count′-down′ *s* cuenta a cero, cuenta atrás
countenance [ˈkaʊntɪnəns] *s* cara, rostro, semblante *m;* (*composure*) compostura, serenidad; **to keep one's countenance** contenerse; **to lose countenance** conturbarse; **to put out of countenance** avergonzar, confundir ‖ *tr* aprobar, apoyar, favorecer
counter [ˈkaʊntər] *adj* contrario ‖ *adv* en el sentido opuesto; **counter to** a contrapelo de ‖ *s* contador *m;* (*piece of wood or metal for keeping score*) ficha; (*board in shop over which business is transacted*) mostrador *m;* (box) contragolpe *m* ‖ *tr* oponerse a; contradecir ‖ *intr* (box) dar un contragolpe; **to counter with** replicar con
coun′ter•act′ *tr* contrarrestar, contrariar
coun′ter•attack′ *s* contraataque *m* ‖ **coun′ter•attack′** *tr & intr* contraatacar
coun′ter•bal′ance *s* contrabalanza, contrapeso ‖ **coun′ter•bal′ance** *tr* contrabalancear, contrapesar
coun′ter•clock′wise′ *adj & adv* en el sentido contrario al de las agujas del reloj
coun′ter•cul′ture *s* contracultura
coun′ter•es′pionage *s* contraespionaje *m*
counterfeit [ˈkaʊntərfɪt] *adj* contrahecho, falsificado ‖ *s* contrahechura, falsificación; moneda falsa ‖ *tr* contrahacer, falsificar
counterfeiter [ˈkaʊntər,fɪtər] *s* contrahacedor *m,* falsificador *m;* monedero falso
counterfeit money *s* moneda falsa
countermand [ˈkaʊntər,mænd] o [ˈkaʊntər,mand] *s* contramandato ‖ *tr* contramandar; hacer volver
coun′ter•march′ *s* contramarcha ‖ *intr* contramarchar
coun′ter•offen′sive *s* contraofensiva
coun′ter•pane′ *s* cubrecama
coun′ter•part′ *s* contraparte *f;* copia, duplicado
coun′ter•plot′ *s* contratreta ‖ *v* (*pret & pp* **-plot-**

ted; *ger* **-plotting)** *tr* complotar contra (*la treta de otro u otros*)
coun′ter•point′ *s* contrapunto
Counter Reformation *s* Contrarreforma
coun′ter•rev′olu′tion *s* contrarevolución
coun′ter•sign′ *s* contraseña ‖ *tr* refrendar
coun′ter•sink′ *v* (*pret & pp* **-sunk**) *tr* avellanar
coun′ter•spy′ *s* (*pl* **-spies**) contraespía *mf*
coun′ter•stroke′ *s* contragolpe *m*
coun′ter•weight′ *s* contrapeso
countess [ˈkaʊntɪs] *s* condesa
countless [ˈkaʊntlɪs] *adj* incontable, innumerable
countrified [ˈkʌntrɪ,faɪd] *adj* campesino, rústico
coun•try [ˈkʌntri] *s* (*pl* **-tries**) (*territory of a nation*) país *m;* (*land of one's birth*) patria; (*not the city*) campo
country club *s* club *m* campestre
country cousin *s* isidro
country estate *s* heredad, hacienda de campo
country gentleman *s* propietario acomodado de finca rural
country house *s* casa de campo, quinta
country life *s* vida rural
country•man [ˈkʌntrimən] *s* (*pl* **-men** [mən]) compatriota *m;* campesino
country people *s* gente *f* del campo, gente de capa parda
coun′try•side′ *s* campiña
coun′try•wide′ *adj* nacional
country•woman [ˈkʌntrɪ,wʊmən] *s* (*pl* **-women** [,wɪmɪn]) compatriota *f;* campesina
coun•ty [ˈkaʊnti] *s* (*pl* **-ties**) (*small political unit*) partido; (*domain of a count*) condado
county seat *s* cabeza de partido
coup [ku] *s* golpe *m*
coup de grâce [ku də ˈgrɑs] *s* puñalada de misericordia, golpe *m* de gracia
coup d'état [ku deˈtɑ] *s* golpe *m* de estado, revolución de palacio
coupé [kuˈpe] *s* cupé *m*
couple [ˈkʌpəl] *s* par *m;* (*man and wife*) matrimonio; (*two people dancing together*) pareja; (elec, mech) par *m;* (*two more or less*) (coll) par *m* ‖ *tr* acoplar, juntar, unir ‖ *intr* juntarse, unirse
coupler [ˈkʌplər] *s* (rr) enganche *m*
couplet [ˈkʌplɪt] *s* copla, pareado
coupon [kuˈpɑn] o [kjuˈpɑn] *s* (*of a bond*) cupón *m;* (*piece detached from larger piece*) talón *m*
courage [ˈkʌrɪdʒ] *s* valor *m,* ánimo; firmeza, resolución; **to have the courage of one's convictions** ajustarse abiertamente con su conciencia; **to pluck up courage** hacer de tripas corazón
courageous [kəˈredʒəs] *adj* valiente, animoso
courier [ˈkʌrɪ•ər] o [ˈkʊrɪ•ər] *s* estafeta, mensajero; guía *m*
course [kors] *s* (*onward movement*) curso; (*of a ship*) derrota, rumbo; (*of time*) transcurso; (*of events*) marcha; (*in school*) asignatura, curso; (*of a meal*) plato; campo de golf; (mas) hilada; **in the course of** en el decurso de; **of course** por supuesto, naturalmente; **to set a course for** hacer *or* poner rumbo a
court [kort] *s* (*of justice*) tribunal *m;* (*of a king*) corte *f;* (*open space enclosed by a building*) atrio, patio; (*for tennis*) cancha, pista; **to pay court to** hacer la corte a ‖ *tr* cortejar; buscar, solicitar
courteous [ˈkʌrtɪ•əs] *adj* cortés
courtesan [ˈkʌrtɪzən] o [ˈkortɪzən] *s* cortesana
courte•sy [ˈkʌrtɪsi] *s* (*pl* **-sies**) cortesía
courtesy call *s* visita de cumplido o de cortesía
courtesy light *s* (aut) luz *f* interior, luz de cortesía
court′house′ *s* palacio de justicia
courtier [ˈkortɪ•ər] *s* cortesano, palaciego
court jester *s* bufón *m*
court•ly [ˈkortli] *adj* (*comp* **-lier;** *super* **-liest**) cortés, cortesano; (*pertaining to the court*) cortesano
courtly love *s* amor *m* cortés
court′-mar′tial *s* (*pl* **courts-martial**) consejo de guerra, tribunal *m* militar ‖ *v* (*pret & pp* **-tialed** o **-tialled;** *ger* **-tialing** o **-tialling**) *tr* someter a consejo de guerra
court′room′ *s* sala de justicia, tribunal *m*
courtship [ˈkortʃɪp] *s* cortejo, galanteo; noviazgo
court′yard′ *s* atrio, patio
couscous [ˈkuskus] *s* (culin) cuscús, cus-cus
cousin [ˈkʌzɪn] *s* primo, prima; (*once removed*) tío segundo, tía segunda
cove [kov] *s* cala, ensenada
covenant [ˈkʌvənənt] *s* convenio, pacto; contrato; (Bib) alianza ‖ *tr & intr* pactar
cover [ˈkʌvər] *s* cubierta; (*of a magazine*) portada; (*place for one person at table*) cubierto; (*for a bed*) cobertor *m;* (compu) carcasa; **to take cover** ocultarse; **under cover** bajo cubierto, bajo techado; oculto; disfrazado; **under cover of** (*e.g., the night*) a cubierto de; so capa de; **under separate cover** bajo cubierta separada, por separado ‖ *tr* cubrir; (*to line, to coat*) recubrir, revestir; recorrer (*cierta distancia*); cubrirse (*la cabeza*); tapar (*una olla*) ‖ *intr* cubrirse
coverage [ˈkʌvərɪdʒ] *s* (*amount or space covered*) alcance *m;* (*of news*) reportaje *m;* (*funds to meet liabilities*) cobertura
coveralls [ˈkʌvər,ɔlz] *s* mono
cover charge *s* precio del cubierto
covered [ˈkʌvərd] *adj* cubierto; (*wire*) forrado; (*bridge*) cubierto
covered wagon *s* carromato
cover girl *s* (coll) muchacha hermosa en la portada de una revista
covering [ˈkʌvərɪŋ] *s* cubierta, envoltura
covert [ˈkʌvərt] *adj* disimulado, secreto
cov′er•up′ *s* efugio, subterfugio
covet [ˈkʌvɪt] *tr* codiciar
covetous [ˈkʌvɪtəs] *adj* codicioso
covetousness [ˈkʌvɪtəsnɪs] *s* codicia

covey [ˈkʌvi] *s* (*brood*) nidada; (*in flight*) bandada; corro, grupo
cow [kaʊ] *s* vaca ‖ *tr* acobardar, intimidar
coward [ˈkaʊ•ərd] *s* cobarde *mf;* rajado (coll)
cowardice [ˈkaʊ•ərdɪs] *s* cobardía; llamada (Mex)
cowardly [ˈkaʊ•ərdli] *adj* cobarde; rajado (coll); correlón (Col, Mex); llamón (Mex) ‖ *adv* cobardemente
cow'bell' *s* cencerro
cow'boy' *s* vaquero; gaucho (Arg)
cowcatcher [ˈkaʊ,kætʃər] *s* quitapiedras *m,* rastrillo; trompa (Col, Chile)
cower [ˈkaʊ•ər] *intr* agacharse
cow'herd' *s* vaquero, pastor *m* de ganado vacuno
cow'hide' *s* cuero; (*whip*) zurriago ‖ *tr* zurriagar
cowl [kaʊl] *s* capucha, cogulla; (aer) cubierta del motor; (aut) cubretablero, bóveda
cow'lick' *s* mechón *m,* remolino (*pelos que se levantan sobre la frente*)
cowpox [ˈkaʊ,pɑks] *s* vacuna
coxcomb [ˈkɑks,kom] *s* petimetre *m,* mequetrefe *m*
coxswain [ˈkɑksən] o [ˈkɑk,swen] *s* timonel *m;* contramaestre *m*
coy [kɔɪ] *adj* recatado, modesto; coquetón
co•zy [ˈkozi] *adj* (*comp* **-zier;** *super* **-ziest**) cómodo ‖ *s* (*pl* **-zies**) cubretetera
C.P.A. *abbr* **certified public accountant**
cr. *abbr* **credit, creditor**
crab [kræb] *s* cangrejo; (*grouch*) cascarrabias *mf*
crab apple *s* manzana silvestre
crabbed [ˈkræbɪd] *adj* avinagrado, ceñudo
crab grass *s* garranchuelo
crab louse *s* ladilla
crack [kræk] *adj* (coll) de primera clase; (*shot*) (coll) certero ‖ *s* grieta, hendidura; (*noise*) crujido, estallido; (*drug*) crack *m;* (coll) instante *m,* momento; (*joke*) (slang) chiste *m;* **at the crack of dawn** al romper el alba ‖ *tr* agrietar, hender; chasquear (*un látigo*); abrir (*una caja fuerte*) por la fuerza; cascar (*nueces*); descifrar (*un código*); (slang) decir (*un chiste*); (slang) descubrir (*un secreto*); **to crack a smile** (slang) sonreír; **to crack up** (coll) alabar, elogiar ‖ *intr* agrietarse; crujir; cascarse (*la voz de una persona*); enloquecerse; ceder, someterse; **to crack up** fracasar; perder la salud; estrellarse (*un avión*)
cracked [krækt] *adj* agrietado; (*ice*) picado; (coll) mentecato, loco
cracker [ˈkrækər] *s* galleta
crack'head *s* (slang) adicto al crack
crack'le•ware' *s* grietado
crack'pot' *adj & s* (coll) chiflado, excéntrico
crack'up' *s* fracaso; colisión; derrota; (aer) aterrizaje violento; (coll) colapso
cradle [ˈkredəl] *s* cuna; (*of handset*) horquilla ‖ *tr* acunar
cra'dle•song' *s* canción de cuna, arrullo
craft [kræft] o [krɑft] *s* arte *m,* arte manual; astucia, maña; nave *f* ‖ *spl* naves
craftiness [ˈkræftɪnɪs] *s* astucia
crafts•man [ˈkræftsmən] *s* (*pl* **-men** [mən]) artesano; artista *m*
craftsmanship [ˈkræftsmən,ʃɪp] *s* artesanía
craft•y [ˈkræfti] o [ˈkrɑfti] *adj* (*comp* **-ier;** *super* **-iest**) astuto, mañoso
crag [kræg] *s* peñasco, despeñadero
cram [kræm] *v* (*pret & pp* **crammed;** *ger* **cramming**) *tr* atascar, atracar, embutir; (coll) aprender apresuradamente ‖ *intr* atracarse; (*to study hard*) (coll) empollar
cramp [kræmp] *s* (*metal bar*) grapa, laña; (*clamp*) abrazadera; (*painful contraction of muscle*) calambre *m;* **cramps** retortijón *m* de tripas ‖ *tr* engrapar, lañar; apretar; dar calambre a
cranber•ry [ˈkræn,bɛri] *s* (*pl* **-ries**) arándano rojo y agrio
crane [kren] *s* (*bird*) grulla; (*derrick*) grúa, guinche *m,* güinche *m* ‖ *tr* estirar (*el cuello*) ‖ *intr* estirar el cuello
crani•um [ˈkrenɪ•əm] *s* (*pl* **-a** [ə]) cráneo
crank [kræŋk] *s* manivela, manubrio; (coll) estrafalario ‖ *tr* hacer girar (*el motor*) con la manivela
crank'case' *s* caja de cigüeñal, cárter *m* del cigüeñal
crank'shaft' *s* cigüeñal *m*
crank•y [ˈkræŋki] *adj* (*comp* **-ier;** *super* **-iest**) malhumorado; (*queer*) estrafalario
cran•ny [ˈkræni] *s* (*pl* **-nies**) hendidura, grieta, rendija
crape [krep] *s* crespón *m;* crespón fúnebre, crespón negro
crape'hang'er *s* (slang) aguafiestas *mf*
craps [kræps] *s* juego de dados; **to shoot craps** jugar a los dados
crash [kræʃ] *s* caída, desplome *m;* colisión, choque *m;* estallido, estrépito; fracaso; crac financiero; lienzo grueso; (aer) aterrizaje violento; (compu) cuelgue *m* ‖ *interj* ¡pataplún! ‖ *tr* romper con estrépito, estrellar; **to crash a party** (slang) asistir a una fiesta sin invitación; **to crash the gate** (slang) colarse de gorra ‖ *intr* caer, desplomarse; romperse con estrépito, estallar; (*in business*) quebrar; aterrizar violentamente, estrellarse (*un avión*); (compu) colgarse, fallar; **to crash into** chocar con ‖ *interj* ¡pataplun!
crash dive *s* sumersión instantánea (*de submarino*)
crash landing *s* aterrizaje violento
crash program *s* programa intensivo
crash test *s* (aut) ensayo de choque
crass [kræs] *adj* espeso, tosco; (*ignorance, mistake*) craso
crate [kret] *s* (*box made of slats*) jaula; (*basket*) banasta, cuévano ‖ *tr* embalar en jaula, embalar con listones
crater [ˈkretər] *s* cráter *m*
cravat [krəˈvæt] *s* corbata

crave [krev] *tr* anhelar, ansiar; pedir (*indulgencia*) || *intr* — **to crave for** anhelar, ansiar; pedir con insistencia
craven [ˈkrevən] *adj & s* cobarde *mf*
craving [ˈkrevɪŋ] *s* anhelo, ansia, deseo ardiente
craw [krɔ] *s* buche *m*
crawl [krɔl] *s* arrastre *m;* gateado || *intr* reptar, arrastarse, gatear; (*to have a feeling of insects on skin*) hormiguear; **to crawl along** andar paso a paso; **to crawl up** trepar
crayon [ˈkre•ən] *s* creyón *m*
craze [krez] *s* boga, moda; locura, manía || *tr* enloquecer
cra•zy [ˈkrezi] *adj* (*comp* **-zier;** *super* **-ziest**) loco; (*rickety*) desvencijado; achacoso, débil; **crazy as a bedbug** (slang) loco de atar; **to be crazy about** (coll) estar loco por; **to drive crazy** volver loco
crazy bone *s* hueso de la alegría
crazy quilt *s* centón *m,* colcha de retazos
creak [krik] *s* crujido, rechinamiento || *intr* crujir, rechinar
creak•y [ˈkriki] *adj* (*comp* **-ier;** *super* **-iest**) crujidero, rechinador
cream [krim] *s* crema; (*e.g., of society*) crema, nata y flor || *tr* desnatar (*la leche*)
cream cheese *s* queso crema, queso de nata
creamer•y [ˈkriməri] *s* (*pl* **-ies**) mantequería, quesería, lechería
cream puff *s* bollo de crema
cream separator *s* desnatadora
cream•y [ˈkrimi] *adj* (*comp* **-ier;** *super* **-iest**) cremoso
crease [kris] *s* arruga, pliegue *m;* (*in trousers*) raya || *tr* arrugar, plegar
create [kriˈet] *tr* crear
creation [kriˈeʃən] *s* creación
creative [kriˈetɪv] *adj* creativo
creator [kriˈetər] *s* creador *m*
creature [ˈkritʃər] *s* criatura; (*being, strange being*) ente *m;* animal *m*
credence [ˈkridəns] *s* creencia; **to give credence to** dar fe a
credentials [krɪˈdɛnʃəlz] *spl* credenciales *fpl*
credible [ˈkrɛdɪbəl] *adj* creíble
credit [ˈkrɛdɪt] *s* crédito; **to take credit for** atribuirse el mérito de || *tr* acreditar; **to credit a person with** atribuirle a una persona el mérito de
creditable [ˈkrɛdɪtəbəl] *adj* honorable, estimable
credit card *s* tarjeta de crédito
creditor [ˈkrɛdɪtər] *s* acreedor *m*
cre•do [ˈkrido] o [ˈkredo] *s* (*pl* **-dos**) credo
credulous [ˈkrɛdʒələs] *adj* crédulo; creído
creed [krid] *s* credo
creek [krik] *s* arroyo, riachuelo
creep [krip] *v* (*pret & pp* **crept** [krɛpt]) *intr* arrastrarse; (*on all fours*) gatear; (*to climb*) trepar; (*with a sensation of insects*) hormiguear; **to creep up on** acercarse insensiblemente a
creeper [ˈkripər] *s* planta rastrera, planta trepadora
creeping [ˈkripɪŋ] *adj* lento, progresivo; (*plant*) rastrero || *s* arrastramiento
cremate [ˈkrimet] *tr* incinerar
cremation [krɪˈmeʃən] *s* cremación, incineración
Creole [ˈkri•ol] *adj & s* criollo
crepe paper *s* papel *m* crepé
crescent [ˈkrɛsənt] *s* (*moon in first or last quarter*) creciente *f* de la luna; (*shape of moon in either of these phases*) media luna; panecillo (*en forma de media luna*)
cress [krɛs] *s* mastuerzo
crest [krɛst] *s* cresta
crestfallen [ˈkrɛst,fɔlən] *adj* cabizbajo
Cretan [ˈkritən] *adj & s* cretense *mf*
Crete [krit] *s* Creta
cretonne [krɪˈtɑn] *s* cretona
crevice [ˈkrɛvɪs] *s* grieta
crew [kru] *s* equipo; (*of a ship*) dotación, tripulación; (*group, esp. of armed men*) banda, cuadrilla
crew cut *s* corte *m* de pelo a cepillo
crib [krɪb] *s* pesebre *m;* camita de niño; (coll) plagio; (*student's pony*) (coll) chuleta || *v* (*pret & pp* **cribbed;** *ger* **cribbing**) *tr & intr* (coll) hurtar
cricket [ˈkrɪkɪt] *s* (ent) grillo; (sport) cricquet *m;* (coll) juego limpio
crier [ˈkraɪ•ər] *s* pregonero
crime [kraɪm] *s* crimen *m,* delito
criminal [ˈkrɪmɪnəl] *adj & s* criminal *mf;* delictivo
criminal code *s* código penal
criminal law *s* derecho penal
criminal negligence *s* imprudencia temeraria
criminology [,krɪməˈnɑlədʒi] *s* criminología
crimp [krɪmp] *s* rizado, rizo; **to put a crimp in** (coll) estorbar, impedir || *tr* rizar
crimple [ˈkrɪmpəl] *tr* arrugar, rizar || *intr* arrugarse, rizarse
crimson [ˈkrɪmzən] *adj & s* carmesí *m* || *intr* enrojecerse
cringe [krɪndʒ] *intr* arrastrarse, reptar, encogerse
crinkle [ˈkrɪŋkəl] *s* arruga, pliegue *m;* (*in the water*) rizo u onda || *tr* arrugar, plegar || *intr* arrugarse
cripple [ˈkrɪpəl] *s* zopo, lisiado || *tr* lisiar, estropear; dañar, perjudicar
cri•sis [ˈkraɪsɪs] *s* (*pl* **-ses**) [siz]) crisis *f*
crisp [krɪsp] *adj* frágil, quebradizo; (*air, weather*) refrescante; decisivo
crisscross [ˈkrɪskrɔs] *adj* entrecruzado || *adv* en cruz || *tr* entrecruzar || *intr* entrecruzarse
criteri•on [kraɪˈtɪrɪ•ən] *s* (*pl* **-a** [ə]) u **-ons**) criterio
critic [ˈkrɪtɪk] *s* crítico; (*reviewer*) reseñador; (*faultfinder*) criticón *m*
critical [ˈkrɪtɪkəl] *adj* crítico; (*faultfinding*) criticón
criticism [ˈkrɪtɪ,sɪzəm] *s* crítica

criticize [ˈkrɪtɪ,saɪz] *tr & intr* criticar
critique [krɪˈtik] *s* (*art of criticism*) crítica; ensayo crítico
croak [krok] *s* (*of raven*) graznido; canto de ranas || *intr* graznar (*el cuervo*); croar (*la rana*); (*morir*) (slang) reventar
Croat [ˈkro•æt] *s* (*native or inhabitant*) croata *mf;* (*language*) croata *m*
Croatian [kroˈeʃən] *adj & mf* croata *mf*
cro•chet [kroˈʃe] *s* croché *m* || *v* (*pret & pp* **-cheted** [ˈʃed]; *ger* **-cheting** [ˈʃe•ɪŋ]) *tr* trabajar con aguja de gancho || *intr* hacer croché
crocheting [kroˈʃə•ɪŋ] *s* labor *f* de ganchillo
crochet needle *s* aguja de gancho
crock [krɑk] *s* cacharro, vasija de barro cocido
crockery [ˈkrɑkəri] *s* loza
crocodile [ˈkrɑkə,daɪl] *s* cocodrilo
crocodile tears *spl* lágrimas de cocodrilo
crocus [ˈkrokəs] *s* azafrán *m,* croco
crone [kron] *s* vieja acartonada, vieja arrugada
cro•ny [ˈkroni] *s* (*pl* **-nies**) compinche *mf*
crook [krʊk] *s* gancho, garfio; curva; (*of shepherd*) cayado; (coll) fullero, ladrón *m;* chalecón *m* (Mex) || *tr* encorvar; (slang) empinar (*el codo*) || *intr* encorvarse
crooked [ˈkrʊkɪd] *adj* encorvado, torcido; (*person or his conduct*) torcido; **to go crooked** (coll) torcerse
croon [krun] *intr* cantar con voz suave, cantar con melancolía exagerada
crooner [ˈkrunər] *s* cantor de voz suave, cantor melancólico
crop [krɑp] *s* cosecha; (*head of hair*) cabellera; cabello corto; (*of a bird*) buche *m;* (*whip*) látigo; (*of appointments, promotions, heroes, etc.*) hornada || *v* (*pret & pp* **cropped;** *ger* **cropping**) *tr* desmochar (*un árbol*); desorejar (*a un animal*); esquilar, trasquilar || *intr* — **to crop out** o **up** aflorar; asomar, dejarse ver, manifestarse inesperadamente
crop dusting *s* aerofumigación, fumigación aérea
croquet [kroˈke] *s* crocquet *m*
croquette [kroˈkɛt] *s* croqueta
crosier [ˈkroʒər] *s* báculo pastoral, cayado
cross [krɔs] *adj* transversal, travieso; (*breed*) cruzado; malhumorado, enfadado || *s* cruz *f;* (*of races; of two roads*) cruce *m;* **to take the cross** (*to join a crusade*) cruzarse || *tr* cruzar; (*to oppose*) contrariar, frustrar; **to cross off** *or* **out** tachar; **to cross oneself** hacerse la señal de la cruz; **to cross one's mind** ocurrírsele a uno; **to cross one's t's** poner travesaño a las tes, poner el palo a las tes || *intr* cruzar; cruzarse; **to cross over** atravesar de un lado a otro
cross'bones' *spl* huesos cruzados (*símbolo de la muerte*)
cross'bow' *s* ballesta
cross'breed' *v* (*pret & pp* **-bred** [,brɛd]) *tr* cruzar (*animales o plantas*)
cross'coun'try *adj* a campo traviesa; a través del país
cross-country skiing *s* esquí *m* de fondo
cross'cur'rent contracorriente *f;* (fig) tendencia encontrada
crosscut saw [ˈkrɔscʌt] *s* sierra de través
cross'-exam'i•na'tion *s* interrogatorio riguroso; (law) repregunta
cross'ex•am'ine *tr* interrogar rigurosamente; (law) repreguntar
cross-eyed [ˈkrɑs,aɪd] *adj* bisojo, bizco, ojituerto
cross-fertilization [ˈkrɔsˈfʌrtələˈzeʃən] *s* fecundación cruzada
cross'fire *s* fuego cruzado
crossing [ˈkrɑsɪŋ] *s* (*of lines, streets, etc.*) cruce *m;* (*of the ocean*) travesía; (*of a river*) vado; (rr) crucero, paso a nivel
crossing gate *s* barrera, barrera de paso a nivel
crossing point *s* punto de cruce
cross'patch' *s* (coll) gruñón *m*
cross'piece' *s* travesaño
cross'-pol'lina'tion [ˈpɑləˈneʃən] *s* polinización cruzada
cross reference *s* contrarreferencia, remisión
cross'road' *s* vía transversal; **crossroads** encrucijada, cruce *m;* **at the crossroads** en el momento crítico
cross section *s* corte *m* transversal; (fig) sección representativa
cross street *s* calle traviesa, calle de travesía
cross'walk' *s* paso de peatones
cross'word' puzzle *s* crucigrama *m*
crotch [krɑtʃ] *s* (*forked piece*) horcajadura, bifurcación; (*between legs*) entrepierna, bragadura, horcajadura
crotchety [ˈkrɑtʃiti] *adj* caprichoso, estrambótico, de mal genio
crouch [kraʊtʃ] *s* posición agachada || *intr* agacharse, acuclillarse
croup [krup] *s* garrotillo, **crup** *m;* (*of horse*) anca, grupa
croupier [ˈkrupɪ•ər] *s* crupié *m*
crouton [ˈkrutɑn] *s* corteza de pan
crow [kro] *s* corneja, grajo, chova; (*cry of the cock*) quiquiriquí *m;* (*crowbar*) alzaprima; **as the crow flies** a vuelo de pájaro; **to eat crow** (coll) cantar la palinodia; **to have a crow to pick with** (coll) tener que habérselas con || *intr* cantar (*el gallo*); jactarse; **to crow over** jactarse de
crow'bar' *s* alzaprima, pie *m or* pata de cabra
crowd [kraʊd] *s* gentío, multitud; (*flock of people*) caterva, tropel *m;* (*mob, common people*) populacho, vulgo; (*clique, set*) corrillo, grupo || *tr* apiñar, apretar, atestar; (*to push*) empujar || *intr* apiñarse, apretarse, atestarse; (*to mill around*) arremolinarse
crowded [ˈkraʊdɪd] *adj* atestado, concurrido
crown [kraʊn] *s* corona; (*of hat*) copa || *tr* coronar; (checkers) coronar; (slang) golpear en la cabeza
crowned head *s* testa coronada
crown jewels *spl* joyas de la corona
crown prince *s* príncipe heredero

crown princess *s* princesa heredera
crow's'-foot' *s* (*pl* **-feet'**) pata de gallo
crow's'-nest' *s* (naut) cofa de vigía, torre *f* de vigía
crucial [ˈkruʃəl] *adj* crucial; difícil, penoso
crucible [ˈkrusɪbəl] *s* crisol *m*
crucifix [ˈkrusɪfɪks] *s* crucifijo
crucifixion [ˌkrusɪˈfɪkʃən] *s* crucifixión
cruci•fy [ˈkrusɪˌfaɪ] *v* (*pret & pp* **-fied**) *tr* crucificar
crude [krud] *adj* (*raw, unrefined*) crudo; (*lacking culture*) grosero, tosco; (*unfinished*) basto, sin labrar
crudi•ty [ˈkrudɪti] *s* (*pl* **-ties**) crudeza; grosería, tosquedad; bastedad
cruel [ˈkru•əl] *adj* cruel
cruel•ty [ˈkru•əlti] *s* (*pl* **-ties**) crueldad
cruet [ˈkru•ɪt] *s* ampolleta
cruet stand *s* angarillas, vinagreras
cruise [kruz] *s* viaje *m* por mar; (aer, naut) crucero || *tr* (naut) cruzar || *intr* cruzar; (coll) andar de un lado a otro
cruise missile *s* misil *m* crucero
cruiser [ˈkruzər] *s* (nav) crucero
cruising [ˈkruzɪŋ] *adj* de crucero || *s* (aer, naut) crucero
cruising radius *s* autonomía
cruising speed *s* velocidad de crucero
cruller [ˈkrʌlər] *s* buñuelo
crumb [krʌm] *s* migaja; (*soft part of bread*) miga; (*given to a beggar*) mendrugo || *tr* desmigar (*el pan*); (culin) empanar, cubrir con pan rallado; limpiar (*la mesa*) de migajas || *intr* desmigarse, desmenuzarse
crumble [ˈkrʌmbəl] *tr* desmenuzar || *intr* desmenuzarse; (*to fall to pieces gradually*) desmoronarse
crum•my [ˈkrʌmi] *adj* (*comp* **-mier;** *super* **-miest**) (slang) desaseado, sucio; (slang) de mal gusto, de mala muerte
crumple [ˈkrʌmpəl] *tr* arrugar, ajar, chafar || *intr* arrugarse, ajarse
crunch [krʌntʃ] *tr* ronchar, ronzar || *intr* crujir
crusade [kruˈsed] *s* cruzada || *intr* hacer una cruzada
crusader [kruˈsedər] *s* cruzado
crush [krʌʃ] *s* aplastamiento; (*of people*) aglomeración, bullaje *m;* **to have a crush on** (slang) estar perdido por || *tr* aplastar, machacar, magullar; (*to grind*) moler; bocartear (*el mineral*); (*to oppress, grieve*) abrumar
crush hat *s* clac *m*
crust [krʌst] *s* corteza; corteza de pan; (*scab*) costra
crustacean [krʌsˈteʃən] *s* crustáceo
crustaceous [krʌsˈteʃəs] *adj* crustáceo
crust•y [ˈkrʌsti] *adj* (*comp* **-ier;** *super* **-iest**) (*scabby*) costroso; áspero, grosero, rudo
crutch [krʌtʃ] *s* muleta
crux [krʌks] *s* punto capital; enigma *m*
cry [kraɪ] *s* (*pl* **cries**) grito; (*weeping*) lloro, llorera; (*of peddler*) pregón *m;* (*of wolf*) aullido; (*of bull*) bramido; **in full cry** en plena persecución; **to have a good cry** desahogarse en lágrimas abundantes || *v* (*pret & pp* **cried**) *tr* decir a gritos; (*to announce publicly*) pregonar; **to cry one's eyes** o **heart out** llorar amargamente; **to cry out** decir a gritos; pregonar || *intr* gritar; (*to weep*) llorar; aullar (*el lobo*); bramar (*el toro*); **to cry for** clamar por; **to cry for joy** llorar de alegría; **to cry out** clamar; **to cry out against** clamar contra; **to cry out for** clamar, clamar por
cry'ba'by *s* (*pl* **-bies**) llorón *m,* llorona, lloraduelos *mf*
crypt [krɪpt] *s* cripta
cryptic(al) [ˈkrɪptɪk(əl)] *adj* enigmático, misterioso
cryptography [krɪpˈtagrəfi] *s* criptografía
crystal [ˈkrɪstəl] *s* cristal *m*
crystal ball *s* bola de cristal
crystalline [ˈkrɪstəlɪn] o [ˈkrɪstəˌlaɪn] *adj* cristalino
crystallize [ˈkrɪstəˌlaɪz] *tr* cristalizar || *intr* cristalizarse
C.S. *abbr* **Christian Science, Civil Service**
ct. *abbr* **cent**
cu. *abbr* **cubic**
cub [kʌb] *s* cachorro
Cuban [ˈkjubən] *adj & s* cubano
cubbyhole [ˈkʌbɪˌhol] *s* chiribitil *m*
cube [kjub] *adj* (*root*) cúbico || *s* cubo; (*of ice*) cubito || *tr* cubicar
cubic [ˈkjubɪk] *adj* cúbico
cubicle [ˈkjubɪkəl] *s* (*room*) cubículo; (*space*) compartimiento
cub reporter *s* (coll) reportero novato
cuckold [ˈkʌkəld] *adj & s* cornudo || *tr* encornudar
cuckoo [ˈkʊkʊ] *adj* (slang) mentecato, loco || *s* cuclillo, cuco; (*call of cuckoo*) cucú *m*
cuckoo clock *s* reloj *m* de cuclillo
cucumber [ˈkjukəmbər] *s* pepino
cud [kʌd] *s* bolo alimenticio; **to chew the cud** rumiar
cuddle [ˈkʌdəl] *s* abrazo cariñoso || *tr* abrazar con cariño || *intr* estar abrazados, arrimarse cariñosamente
cudg•el [ˈkʌdʒəl] *s* garrote *m,* porra; **to take up the cudgels for** salir a la defensa de || *v* (*pret & pp* **-eled** o **-elled;** *ger* **-eling** o **-elling**) *tr* apalear, aporrear
cue [kju] *s* señal *f,* indicación; (*hint*) indirecta; (*role*) papel *m;* (*rod used in billiards*) taco; (*of hair*) coleta; (*of people in line*) cola; (theat) apunte *m*
cuff [kʌf] *s* (*of shirt*) puño; (*of trousers*) doblez *f,* vuelta; (*blow*) bofetada || *tr* abofetear
cuff links *spl* gemelos
cuirass [kwɪˈræs] *s* coraza
cuisine [kwɪˈzin] *s* cocina (*arte culinario*)
culinary [ˈkjulɪˌnɛri] *adj* culinario
cull [kʌl] *tr* (*to choose, pick*) entresacar, escoger; (*to gather, pluck*) coger, recoger
culm [kʌlm] *s* (*coal dust*) cisco; (*stalk of grasses*) caña, tallo

culminate [ˈkʌlmɪ,net] *intr* culminar; **to culminate in** conducir a, terminar en
culpable [ˈkʌlpəbəl] *adj* culpable
culprit [ˈkʌlprɪt] *s* acusado; reo
cult [kʌlt] *s* culto; secta
cultivate [ˈkʌltɪ,vet] *tr* cultivar
cultivated [ˈkʌltɪ,vetɪd] *adj* culto, cultivado
cultivation [,kʌltɪˈveʃən] *s* (*of the land, the arts, one's memory, etc.*) cultivo; (*refinement*) cultura
cultivator [ˈkʌltɪ,vetər] *s* (mach) cultivador *m,* cultivadora
culture [ˈkʌltʃər] *s* cultura
cultured [ˈkʌltʃərd] *adj* culto
culture medium *s* (biol) caldo de cultivo
culvert [ˈkʌlvərt] *s* alcantarilla
cumbersome [ˈkʌmbərsəm] *adj* incómodo, molesto; (*clumsy*) pesado, inmanejable
cunning [ˈkʌnɪŋ] *adj* (*sly*) astuto; (*clever*) hábil; (*attractive*) gracioso, mono ‖ *s* astucia; habilidad, destreza
cup [kʌp] *s* taza; (*of thermometer*) cubeta; (mach) vaso de engrase; (sport) copa; (*of sorrow*) (fig) copa; **in one's cups** borracho ‖ *v* (*pret & pp* **cupped;** *ger* **cupping**) *tr* ahuecar dando forma de taza o copa a; poner ventosa a
cupboard [ˈkʌbərd] *s* alacena, aparador *m,* armario, clóset *m*
cupidity [kjʊˈpɪdɪti] *s* codicia
cupola [ˈkjupələ] *s* cúpula
cur [kʌr] *s* perro mestizo, perro de mala raza; (*despicable fellow*) canalla *m*
curate [ˈkjʊrɪt] *s* cura *m*
curative [ˈkjʊrətɪv] *adj* curativo ‖ *s* curativa
curator [kjʊˈretər] *s* conservador *m*
curb [kʌrb] *s* (*of sidewalk*) encintado; (*of well*) brocal *m;* (*of bit*) barbada; (*market*) bolsín *m;* (*check, restraint*) freno; (vet) corva ‖ *tr* contener, refrenar
curb′stone′ *s* piedra de encintado; brocal *m* de pozo
curd [kʌrd] *s* cuajada ‖ *tr* cuajar ‖ *intr* cuajarse
curdle [ˈkʌrdəl] *tr* cuajar; **to curdle the blood** horrorizar ‖ *intr* cuajar
cure [kjʊr] *s* cura, curación ‖ *tr* curar ‖ *intr* curar; curarse
cure′-all′ *s* sanalotodo
curfew [ˈkʌrfju] *s* queda, cubrefuego; toque *m* de queda; hora de cierre
curi•o [ˈkjʊrɪ,o] *s* (*pl* **-os**) curiosidad
curiosi•ty [,kjʊrɪˈɑsɪti] *s* (*pl* **-ties**) curiosidad
curious [ˈkjʊrɪ•əs] *adj* curioso
curl [kʌrl] *s* bucle *m,* rizo; (*spiral-shaped curl*) tirabuzón *m;* (*of smoke*) espiral *f;* (*curling*) rizado ‖ *tr* encrespar, ensortijar, rizar; (*to coil, to roll up*) arrollar; fruncir (*los labios*) ‖ *intr* encresparse, ensortijarse, rizarse; arrollarse; **to curl up** arrollarse; (*in bed*) encogerse; (*to break up, collapse*) (coll) desplomarse
curler [ˈkʌrlər] *s* (*hair*) rulo, bigudí *m*
curlicue [ˈkʌrlɪ,kju] *s* ringorrango
curling iron *s* rizador *m,* maquinilla de rizar
curl′pa′per *s* torcida, papelito para rizar el pelo
curl•y [ˈkʌrli] *adj* (*comp* **-ier;** *super* **-iest**) crespo, rizo
curmudgeon [kərˈmʌdʒən] *s* cicatero, tacaño, erizo
currant [ˈkʌrənt] *s* pasa de Corinto; (*Ribes alpinum*) calderilla
curren•cy [ˈkʌrənsi] *s* (*pl* **-cies**) moneda corriente, dinero en circulación; uso corriente
current [ˈkʌrənt] *adj* corriente ‖ *s* corriente *f;* (elec) corriente *f*
current events *spl* actualidades, sucesos de actualidad
curricu•lum [kəˈrɪkjələm] *s* (*pl* **-lums** o **-la** [lə]) plan *m* de estudios
cur•ry [ˈkʌri] *s* (*pl* **-ries**) cari *m* ‖ *v* (*pret & pp* **-ried**) *tr* curtir (*las pieles*); almohazar (*el caballo*); **to curry favor** procurar complacer
cur′ry•comb′ *s* almohaza ‖ *tr* almohazar
curse [kʌrs] *s* maldición; (*profane oath*) reniego, voto; (*evil, misfortune*) calamidad ‖ *tr* maldecir ‖ *intr* jurar, echar votos; echar carnes (Mex)
cursed [ˈkʌrsɪd] o [kʌrst] *adj* maldito; aborrecible
cursive [ˈkʌrsɪv] *adj* cursivo ‖ *s* cursiva
cursor [ˈkʌrsər] *s* (compu) cursor *m*
cursory [ˈkʌrsəri] *adj* apresurado, rápido, superficial, de paso
curt [kʌrt] *adj* áspero, brusco; corto, conciso
curtail [kərˈtel] *tr* acortar, abreviar, cercenar
curtain [ˈkʌrtən] *s* cortina; (theat) telón *m;* **to draw the curtain** correr la cortina; **to drop the curtain** (theat) bajar el telón ‖ *tr* encortinar; separar con cortina; cubrir, ocultar
curtain call *s* llamada a la escena para recibir aplausos
curtain raiser [ˈrezər] *s* (theat) pieza preliminar
curtain ring *s* anilla
curtain rod *s* riel *m*
curt•sy [ˈkʌrtsi] *s* (*pl* **-sies**) cortesía, reverencia ‖ *v* (*pret & pp* **-sied**) *intr* hacer una cortesía
curve [kʌrv] *s* curva ‖ *tr* encorvar ‖ *intr* encorvarse; volver, virar
curved [kʌrvd] *adj* curvo, encorvado; (*crooked*) combo
cushion [ˈkʊʃən] *s* cojín *m,* almohada; (*of billiard table*) baranda ‖ *tr* amortiguar
cusp [kʌsp] *s* cúspide *f*
cuspidor [ˈkʌspɪ,dɔr] *s* escupidera
cuss *var de* **curse**
cuss′word [kʌs] *s* (coll) palabrota
custard [ˈkʌstərd] *s* flan *m,* natillas
custodian [kəsˈtodɪ•ən] *s* custodio; (*of a house or building*) casero
custo•dy [ˈkʌstədi] *s* (*pl* **-dies**) custodia; **in custody** en prisión; **to take into custody** prender
custom [ˈkʌstəm] *s* costumbre; (*customers*) parroquia, clientela; **customs** aduana; derechos de aduana
customary [ˈkʌstə,mɛri] *adj* acostumbrado, de costumbre

cus′tom-built′ *adj* hecho por encargo, fuera de serie
customer [ˈkʌstəmər] *s* parroquiano, cliente *mf;* (*of a café or restaurant*) consumidor *m;* (coll) individuo, sujeto, tipo
customer service *s* servicio postventa
cus′tom•house′ *adj* aduanero ‖ *s* aduana
cus′tom-made′ *adj* hecho a la medida
customs clearance *s* despacho de aduana
customs declaration *s* declaración de aduana
customs duties *mpl* renta de aduanas
customs officer *s* aduanero
custom tailor *s* sastre *m* a la medida
custom work *s* trabajo hecho a la medida
cut [kʌt] *s* corte *m;* (*piece cut off*) tajada; (*wound*) cuchillada; (*for a canal, highway, etc.*) desmonte *m;* (*shortest way*) atajo; (*in prices, wages, etc.*) reducción; (*of a garment*) corte *m,* hechura; (*in winnings, earnings, etc.*) parte *f;* (*diamond*) talla; (typ) estampa, grabado; (tennis) golpe *m* cortante; (*absence from school*) (coll) falta de asistencia; (*snub*) (coll) desaire *m;* (coll) palabra hiriente ‖ *v* (*pret & pp* **cut;** *ger* **cutting**) *tr* cortar; practicar (*un agujero*); reducir (*gastos*); capar, castrar; desleír, diluir; (coll) ausentarse de, faltar a (*la clase*); (coll) desairar; (coll) herir; **to cut down** cortar; derribar cortando; castigar (*gastos*); **to cut off** cortar; desheredar; amputar (*una pierna*); (elec) cortar (*la corriente, la ignición*); cerrar (*el carburador*); **to cut open** abrir cortando; **to cut out** cortar; sacar cortando; labrar; suprimir, omitir; (*to take the place of*) desbancar; soplar (*la dama a un rival*); (slang) dejarse de (*disparates*); **to cut short** terminar de repente; interrumpir, chafar; **to cut teeth** endentecer; **to cut up** desmenuzar, despedazar; criticar severamente; (coll) afligir ‖ *intr* cortar; cortarse; salir (*los dientes*); (coll) fumarse la clase; **to cut and run** (coll) largarse, ahuecar el ala, tomarse los vientos (SAm); **to cut in** entrar de repente; interrumpir; (*in a dance*) cortar o separar la pareja; **to cut under** vender a menor precio que; **to cut up** (slang) travesear, hacer travesuras; (slang) jaranear
cut-and-dried [ˈkʌtənˈdraɪd] *adj* dispuesto de antemano; monótono, poco interesante
cutaneous [kjʊˈtenɪ•əs] *adj* cutáneo
cutaneous anthrax *s* el ántrax que penetra en el cuerpo por la piel
cutaway coat [ˈkʌtə,we] *s* chaqué *m*
cut′back′ *s* reducción; discontinuación, incumplimiento; (mov) retorno a una época anterior
cute [kjut] *adj* (coll) mono, monono; (coll) astuto, listo
cut glass *s* cristal tallado
cuticle [ˈkjutɪkəl] *s* cutícula
cutie [ˈkjuti] *s* (coll) bombón *m,* monina
cutlass [ˈkʌtləs] *s* alfanje *m*
cutler [ˈkʌtlər] *s* cuchillero
cutlery [ˈkʌtləri] *s* cuchillería; (*knives, forks, and spoons*) cubierto
cutlet [ˈkʌtlɪt] *s* chuleta; croqueta
cutoff date [ˈkʌtɔf] *s* fecha límite
cut′out′ *s* (*design to be cut out*) recortado; (aut) escape *m* libre, válvula de escape libre
cut′-rate′ *adj* de precio reducido
cutter [ˈkʌtər] *s* cortador *m;* (*machine*) cortadora; (naut) escampavía
cut′throat′ *adj* asesino; implacable ‖ *s* asesino
cutting [ˈkʌtɪŋ] *adj* cortante; hiriente, mordaz ‖ *s* corte *m;* (*from a newspaper*) (Brit) recorte *m;* (hort) esqueje *m*
cutting edge *s* canto de corte
cuttlefish [ˈkʌtəl,fɪʃ] *s* jibia
cut′wa′ter *s* espolón *m,* tajamar *m*
cwt. *abbr* **hundredweight**
cyanamide [saɪˈænə,maɪd] *s* cianamida; cianamida de calcio
cyanide [ˈsaɪ•ə,naɪd] *s* cianuro
cybernetic [,saɪbərˈnɛtɪk] *adj* cibernético ‖ **cybernetics** [,saɪbərˈnɛtɪks] *s* cibernética
cyberspace [ˈsaɪbərˈspes] *s* (compu) ciberespacio
cycle [ˈsaɪkəl] *s* ciclo; bicicleta; (*of an internal-combustion engine*) tiempo; (phys) periódo ‖ *intr* montar en bicicleta
cyclic(al) [ˈsaɪklɪk(əl)] o [ˈsɪklɪk(əl)] *adj* cíclico
cyclone [ˈsaɪklon] *s* ciclón *m*
cyl. *abbr* **cylinder, cylindrical**
cylinder [ˈsɪlɪndər] *s* cilindro, balón *m*
cylinder block *s* bloque *m* de cilindros
cylinder bore *s* alesaje *m*
cylinder head *s* (*of steam engine*) tapa del cilindro; (*of gas engine*) culata del cilindro
cylindric(al) [sɪˈlɪndrɪk(əl)] *adj* cilíndrico
cymbal [ˈsɪmbəl] *s* címbalo, platillo
cynic [ˈsɪnɪk] *adj & s* cínico
cynical [ˈsɪnɪkəl] *adj* cínico
cynicism [ˈsɪnɪ,sɪzəm] *s* cinismo
cynosure [ˈsaɪnə,ʃʊr] o [ˈsɪnə,ʃʊr] *s* blanco de las miradas; guía, norte *m*
cypress [ˈsaɪprəs] *s* ciprés *m*
Cyprus [ˈsaɪprəs] *s* Chipre *f*
Cyrillic [sɪˈrɪlɪk] *adj* cirílico
Cyrus [ˈsaɪrəs] *s* Ciro
cyst [sɪst] *s* quiste *m*
cystic fibrosis [ˈsɪstɪkfaɪˈbrosəs] *s* (pathol) fibrosis cística
cytology [saɪˈtɑlədʒɪ] *s* citología
czar [zɑr] *s* zar *m;* (fig) autócrata *m*
czarina [zɑˈrinə] *s* zarina
Czech [tʃɛk] *adj & s* checo

D

D, d [di] cuarta letra del alfabeto inglés
d. *abbr* **date, day, dead, degree, delete, diameter, died, dollar, denarius (penny)**
D. *abbr* **December, Democrat, Duchess, Duke, Dutch**
D.A. *abbr* **District Attorney**
dab [dæb] *s* toque ligero; masa pastosa || *v* (*pret & pp* **dabbed;** *ger* **dabbing**) *tr* tocar ligeramente, frotar suavemente
dabble [ˈdæbəl] *tr* salpicar || *intr* chapotear; **to dabble in** meterse en; jugar a (*la Bolsa*); especular en (*granos*)
dachshund [ˈdɑksʊnt] *s* teckel mf, perro salchicha
dad [dæd] *s* (coll) papi *m*
dad•dy [ˈdædi] *s* (*pl* **-dies**) (coll) papi *m*
daffodil [ˈdæfədɪl] *s* narciso trompón
daff•y [ˈdæfi] *adj* (*comp* **-ier;** *super* **-iest**) (coll) chiflado
dagger [ˈdægər] *s* daga, puñal *m;* (typ) cruz *f,* obelisco; **to look daggers at** apuñalar con la mirada
dahlia [ˈdæljə] *s* dalia
dai•ly [ˈdeli] *adj* cotidiano, diario || *adv* diariamente || *s* (*pl* **-lies**) diario
dain•ty [ˈdenti] *adj* (*comp* **-tier;** *super* **-tiest**) delicado || *s* (*pl* **-ties**) golosina
dair•y [ˈdɛri] *s* (*pl* **-ies**) lechería, vaquería
dais [ˈde•ɪs] *s* estrado
dai•sy [ˈdezi] *s* (*pl* **-sies**) margarita
daisy wheel *s* (compu) margarita
dais'y-wheel printer *s* (compu) impresora de margarita
dal•ly [ˈdæli] *v* (*pret & pp* **-lied**) *intr* juguetear, retozar; tardar, malgastar el tiempo
dam [dæm] *s* represa, embalse *m;* (*female quadruped*) madre *f;* (dent) dique *m* || *v* (*pret & pp* **dammed;** *ger* **damming**) *tr* represar, embalsar; cerrar, tapar, obstruir
damage [ˈdæmɪdʒ] *s* daño, perjuicio; (*to one's reputation*) desdoro; (com) avería; **damages** daños y perjuicios || *tr* dañar, perjudicar; averiar
damascene [ˈdæmə,sin] o [,dæməˈsin] *adj* damasquino || *s* ataujía, damasquinado || *tr* ataujiar, damasquinar
dame [dem] *s* dama, señora; (coll) mujer *f*
damn [dæm] *s* terno; **I don't give a damn** (slang) maldito lo que me importa; **that's not worth a damn** (slang) eso no vale un pito || *interj* ¡caray! || *tr* condenar (a pena eterna); condenar; maldecir || *intr* maldecir, echar ternos
damnation [dæmˈneʃən] *s* damnación; (theol) condenación
damned [dæmd] *adj* condenado (a pena eterna); abominable, detestable || **the damned** los condenados (a pena eterna)
damp [dæmp] *adj* húmedo, mojado || *s* humedad; (*firedamp*) grisú *m* || *tr* humedecer, mojar; (*to deaden, muffle*) amortecer, amortiguar; (*to discourage*) abatir, desalentar; (elec) amortiguar (*ondas electromagnéticas*)
dampen [ˈdæmpən] *tr* humedecer, mojar; amortecer, amortiguar; abatir, desalentar
damper [ˈdæmpər] *s* (*of chimney*) registro; (*of piano*) apagador *m,* sordina
damsel [ˈdæmzəl] *s* señorita, damisela
dance [dæns] *s* baile *m,* danza || *tr & intr* bailar, danzar
dance band *s* orquesta de jazz
dance floor *s* pista de baile
dance hall *s* salón *m* de baile
dancer [ˈdænsər] *s* bailador *m,* danzador *m;* (*professional*) bailarín *m*
dancing partner *s* pareja (de baile)
dandelion [ˈdændɪ,laɪ•ən] *s* diente *m* de león
dandruff [ˈdændrəf] *s* caspa
dan•dy [ˈdændi] *adj* (*comp* **-dier;** *super* **-diest**) (coll) excelente, magnífico || *s* (*pl* **-dies**) currutaco, petimetre *m;* lagarto (Mex)
Dane [den] *s* danés *m,* dinamarqués *m*
danger [ˈdendʒər] *s* peligro
dangerous [ˈdendʒərəs] *adj* peligroso; riesgoso
dangle [ˈdæŋgəl] *tr & intr* colgar flojamente, colgar en el aire
Danish [ˈdenɪʃ] *adj & s* danés *m,* dinamarqués *m*
Danish (pastry) *s* danés *m*
dank [dæŋk] *adj* malsano y húmedo
Danube [ˈdænjʊb] *s* Danubio
dapper [ˈdæpər] *adj* aseado, apuesto
dapple [ˈdæpəl] *adj* habado, rodado || *tr* motear
dare [dɛr] *s* desafío, reto || *tr* retar; **to dare to** (*to challenge to*) desafiar a || *intr* osar, atreverse; **I dare say** talvez; **to dare to** (*to have the courage to*) atreverse a
dare'dev'il *s* calavera *m,* temerario
daring [ˈdɛrɪŋ] *adj* atrevido, osado || *s* atrevimiento, osadía
dark [dɑrk] *adj* obscuro; (*in complexion*) moreno; secreto, oculto; (*gloomy*) lóbrego; (*beer*) pardo || *s* obscuridad, tinieblas; noche *f;* **in the dark** a obscuras
Dark Ages the *spl* la Edad de las Tinieblas, la Alta Edad Media; (fig) la prehistoria, las tinieblas
dark-complexioned [ˈdarkkəmˈplɛkʃənd] *adj* moreno
darken [ˈdɑrkən] *tr* obscurecer; entristecer; cegar || *intr* obscurecerse
dark glasses *spl* gafas o lentes oscuras *or* negras
dark horse *s* ganador sorpresa; candidato nombrado inesperadamente
darkly [ˈdɑrkli] *adv* obscuramente; secretamente, misteriosamente
dark meat *s* carne *f* del ave que no es la pechuga
darkness [ˈdɑrknɪs] *s* obscuridad
dark'room' *s* (phot) cuarto obscuro
darling [ˈdɑrlɪŋ] *adj & s* querido, amado; predilecto; (*as address*) chata (Mex)

darn [dɑrn] *adj* (coll) maldito ‖ *adv* muy, sumamente ‖ *interj* ¡caray! ‖ *tr & intr* zurcir; (coll) maldecir
darnel [ˋdɑrnəl] *s* cizaña
darning [ˋdɑrnɪŋ] *s* zurcido
darning needle *s* aguja de zurcir
dart [dɑrt] *s* dardo; (*small missile used in a game*) rehilete *m* ‖ *intr* lanzarse, precipitarse; volar como dardo
dart′board *s* diana
Darwinian [dɑrˋwɪni•ən] *adj* darviniano
Darwinism [ˋdɑrwəˌnɪzəm] *s* darvinismo
dash [dæʃ] *s* arranque *m;* (*splash*) rociada; carrera corta; (*spirit*) brío; pequeña cantidad; (*in printing, writing, telegraphy*) raya ‖ *tr* lanzar; estrellar, romper; frustar (*las esperanzas de uno*); rociar, salpicar; **to dash off** escribir de prisa; **to dash to pieces** hacer añicos ‖ *intr* estrellarse (*las olas del mar*); lanzarse, precipitarse; **to dash by** pasar corriendo; **to dash in** entrar como un rayo
dash′board′ *s* tablero de instrumentos; cuadro de mando; (aut) guardabarros *m,* salpicadero
dashing [ˋdæʃɪŋ] *adj* brioso; ostentoso, vistoso ‖ *s* (*of waves*) embate *m*
dastard [ˋdæstərd] *adj & s* vil *mf,* miserable *mf,* cobarde *mf*
data [ˋdetə] *spl* datos, información ‖ *s* (compu) datos
data bank *s* banco de datos, almacenamiento
database [ˋdetəbes] *s* base *f* de datos
data bus *s* (compu) bus *m* de datos
data capture *s* (compu) toma de datos
data flow *s* (compu) flujo de datos
da′ta-proc′ess *tr & intr* procesar
data processing *s* procesamiento de datos, proceso de datos; tramitación automática de datos
data protection *s* protección de datos, protección de la información
data storage *s* memoria, almacenamiento
data transmission *s* (compu) transmisión de datos
date [det] *s* (*time*) fecha, data; (*palm*) datilera; (*fruit*) dátil *m;* (*appointment*) (coll) cita; **out of date** anticuado, fuera de moda; **to date** hasta la fecha; **under date of** con fecha de ‖ *tr* fechar, datar; (coll) tener cita con ‖ *intr* —**to date from** datar de
date line *s* línea de cambio de fecha
date palm *s* palmera (datilera)
dative [ˋdetɪv] *adj & s* dativo
datum [ˋdetəm] o [ˋdætəm] *s* (*pl* **data** [ˋdetə] o [ˋdætə]) dato
daub [dɔb] *s* embadurnamiento ‖ *tr* embadurnar
daughter [ˋdɔtər] *s* hija
daughter′board *s* (compu) placa hija
daughter-in-law [ˋdɔtərɪnˌlɔ] *s* (*pl* **daughters-in-law**) nuera, hija política
daunt [dɔnt] *tr* asustar, espantar; desanimar, acobardar
dauntless [ˋdɔntlɪs] *adj* atrevido, intrépido, impávido
dauphin [ˋdɔfɪn] *s* delfín *m*
davenport [ˋdævənˌport] *s* gran sofá *m* (*a veces convertible en cama*)
David [ˋdevɪd] *s* David *m*
davit [ˋdævɪt] *s* (naut) pescante *m,* grúa de bote
daw [dɔ] *s* corneja
dawdle [ˋdɔdəl] *intr* malgastar el tiempo, haronear
dawn [dɔn] *s* amanecer *m,* alba ‖ *intr* amanecer; despuntar (*el día, la mañana*); empezar a mostrarse; **to dawn on** empezar a hacerse patente a
day [de] *adj* diurno ‖ *s* día *m;* (*of travel, work, worry, etc.*) jornada; (*from noon to noon*) (naut) singladura; **any day now** de un día para otro; **by day** de día; **day off** día inhábil, día libre; **per day** al día; **the day after** el día siguiente; **the day after tomorrow** pasado mañana; **the day before** la víspera; la víspera de; **the day before yesterday** anteayer; **to call it a day** (coll) dejar de trabajar; **to win the day** ganar la jornada
daybed *s* diván *m* cama
day′break′ *s* amanecer *m*
day care *s* servicio de guardería infantil
day′care center *s* guardería infantil
day coach *s* (rr) coche *m* de viajeros
day′dream′ *s* ensueño ‖ *intr* soñar despierto
day laborer *s* jornalero
day′light′ *s* luz *f* del día; amanecer *m;* **in broad daylight** en pleno día; **to see daylight** comprender; ver el fin de una tarea difícil
day′light′-sav′ing time *s* hora de verano
day nursery *s* guardería infantil
day off *s* asueto
day of reckoning *s* día *m* de ajustar cuentas
day shift *s* turno diurno
day′time′ *adj* diurno ‖ día *m*
daze [dez] *s* aturdimiento; **in a daze** aturdido ‖ *tr* aturdir
dazzle [ˋdæzəl] *s* deslumbramiento ‖ *tr* deslumbrar
dazzling [ˋdæzlɪŋ] *adj* deslumbrante
DC, D.C. [ˋdiˋsi] *s* (letterword) (**direct current**) corriente continua
deacon [ˋdikən] *s* diácono
deaconess [ˋdikənɪs] *s* diaconisa
dead [dɛd] *adj* muerto; (coll) cansado ‖ *adv* (coll) completamente, muy ‖ *s* — **in the dead of night** en plena noche; **the dead** los muertos; **the dead of winter** lo más frío del invierno
dead beat *s* (slang) gorrón *m;* (slang) holgazán *m*
dead bolt *s* cerrojo dormido
dead calm *s* calma chicha, calmazo
dead center *s* punto muerto
dead′drunk′ *adj* difunto de taberna
deaden [ˋdɛdən] *tr* amortiguar, amortecer
dead end *s* callejón *m* sin salida, calle ciega
dead′latch′ *s* aldaba dormida
dead′-let′ter office *s* departamento de cartas no reclamadas

dead'line' *s* línea vedada; fin *m* del plazo
dead'lock' *s* cerradura dormida; desacuerdo insuperable ‖ *tr* estancar
dead•ly [ˋdɛdli] *adj* (*comp* **-lier;** *super* **-liest**) mortal; (*sin*) capital; abrumador
dead'pan *adj* sin expresión, de póquer ‖ *adv* de manera inexpresiva ‖ *s* semblante *m* sin expresión
dead reckoning *s* (naut) estima
dead ringer [ˋrɪŋər] *s* segunda edición
dead'wood' *s* leña seca; cosa inútil, gente *f* inútil
deaf [dɛf] *adj* sordo; **to turn a deaf ear** hacerse el sordo, hacer oídos de mercader
deaf and dumb *adj* sordomudo
deafen [ˋdɛfən] *tr* asordar, ensordecer
deafening [ˋdɛfənɪŋ] *adj* ensordecedor
deaf'-mute' *s* sordomudo
deafness [ˋdɛfnɪs] *s* sordera
deal [dil] *s* negocio, trato, pacto; (*of cards*) mano *f;* turno de dar; (*share*) parte *f,* porción; (coll) convenio secreto; **a good deal (of)** o **a great deal (of)** mucho; **to make a great deal of** hacer fiestas a ‖ *v* (*pret & pp* **dealt** [dɛlt]) *tr* asestar (*un golpe*); repartir (*la baraja*) ‖ *intr* negociar, comerciar; intervenir; (*in card games*) ser mano; **to deal with** entender en; tratar de; tratar con
dealer [ˋdilər] *s* comerciante *mf,* concesionario; (*of cards*) repartidor *m*
dean [din] *s* decano; (eccl) deán *m*
deanship [ˋdinʃɪp] *s* decanato; (eccl) deanato, deanazgo
dear [dɪr] *adj* (*beloved*) caro, querido; (*expensive*) caro; (*charging high prices*) carero; **dear me!** ¡Dios mío! ‖ *s* querido
dearie [ˋdɪri] *s* (coll) queridito
dearth [dʌrθ] *s* carestía
death [dɛθ] *s* muerte *f;* **to bleed to death** morir desangrado; **to bore to death** matar de aburrimiento; **to burn to death** morir quemado; **to choke to death** morir atragantado; **to die a violent death** morir vestido; **to freeze to death** morir helado; **to put to death** dar la muerte a; **to shoot to death** matar a tiros; **to stab to death** escabechar; **to starve to death** morir de hambre; (*kill*) matar de hambre
death'bed' *s* lecho de muerte
death'blow' *s* golpe *m* mortal
death certificate *s* fe *f* de óbito, partida o parte *m* de defunción, certificado de defunción
deathless [ˋdɛθlɪs] *adj* inmortal, eterno
deathly [ˋdɛθli] *adj* mortal, de muerte ‖ *adv* mortalmente; excesivamente
death notice *s* aviso fúnebre
death penalty *s* pena de muerte
death rate *s* índice *m* de mortalidad
death rattle *s* estertor agónico
death ray *s* rayo mortífero
death row *s* corredor *m* de la muerte, pabellón *m* de los condenados a muerte
death warrant *s* sentencia de muerte; fin *m* de toda esperanza
death'watch' *s* vela de un difunto; guardia de un reo de muerte
debacle [deˋbɑkəl] *s* desastre *m,* ruina, derrota; (*in a river*) deshielo
de•bar [dɪˋbɑr] *v* (*pret & pp* **-barred;** *ger* **-barring**) *tr* excluir; prohibir
debark [dɪˋbɑrk] *tr & intr* desembarcar
debarkation [ˌdibɑrˋkeʃən] *s* (*of passengers*) desembarco; (*of freight*) desembarque *m*
debase [dɪˋbes] *tr* degradar; falsificar
debatable [dɪˋbetəbəl] *adj* disputable
debate [dɪˋbet] *s* debate *m* ‖ *tr* debatir ‖ *intr* debatir; deliberar
debauchee [ˌdɛbɔˋʃi] o [ˌdɛbɔˋtʃi] *s* libertino, disoluto
debaucher•y [dɪˋbɔtʃəri] *s* (*pl* **-ies**) libertinaje *m,* crápula
debenture [dɪˋbɛntʃər] *s* (*bond*) obligación; (*voucher*) vale *m*
debilitate [dɪˋbɪlɪˌtet] *tr* debilitar
debili•ty [dɪˋbɪlɪti] *s* (*pl* **-ties**) debilidad
debit [ˋdɛbɪt] *s* debe *m;* (*entry on debit side*) cargo ‖ *tr* adeudar, cargar
debit balance *s* saldo deudor
debit card *s* tarjeta de cobro automático
debonair [ˌdɛbəˋnɛr] *adj* elegante y desenvuelto; cortés, afable
debris [deˋbri] *s* despojos, ruinas
debt [dɛt] *s* deuda; **to run into debt** endeudarse, entramparse
debtor [ˋdɛtər] *s* deudor *m*
debut [deˋbju] o [ˋdebju] *s* estreno, debut *m,* **to make one's debut** estrenarse, debutar; ponerse de largo, entrar en sociedad (*una joven*)
debutante [ˌdɛbjʊˋtɑnt] o [ˋdɛbjəˌtænt] *s* joven *f* que se pone de largo; debutante *f*
dec. *abbr* **deceased**
decade [ˋdɛked] *s* década, decenio
decadence [dɪˋkedəns] *s* decadencia
decadent [dɪˋkedənt] *adj & s* decadente *mf*
decaf [ˋdikæf] *s* café descafeinado
decaffeinated [ˋdiˋkæfənetəd] *adj* (*coffee*) descafeinado; (*soft drink*) sin cafeína
decant [dɪˋkænt] *tr* (*wine*) decantar; (chem) trasvasar
decanter [dɪˋkæntər] *s* garrata
decapitate [dɪˋkæpɪˌtet] *tr* decapitar
decay [dɪˋke] *s* (*decline*) decaimiento, descaecimiento; (*rotting*) podredumbre; (*of teeth*) caries *f* ‖ *tr* pudrir ‖ *intr* pudrirse; decaer; cariarse (*los dientes*)
decease [dɪˋsis] *s* fallecimiento ‖ *intr* fallecer
deceased [dɪˋsist] *adj & s* difunto
deceit [dɪˋsit] *s* engaño, fraude *m*
deceitful [dɪˋsitfəl] *adj* engañoso, fraudulento
deceive [dɪˋsiv] *tr & intr* engañar
decelerate [dɪˋsɛləˌret] *tr* desacelerar ‖ *intr* desacelerarse
December [dɪˋsɛmbər] *s* diciembre *m*
decen•cy [ˋdisənsi] *s* (*pl* **-cies**) decencia; (*propriety*) buena educación
decent [ˋdisənt] *adj* decente, decoroso; (*kind*) amable

decentralize [dɪˈsɛntrəˌlaɪz] *tr* descentralizar
deception [dɪˈsɛpʃən] *s* engaño
deceptive [dɪˈsɛptɪv] *adj* engañoso
decide [dɪˈsaɪd] *tr & intr* decidir
decimal [ˈdɛsɪməl] *adj & s* decimal *m*
decimal point *s* punto decimal; (*in Spanish the comma is used to separate the decimal fraction from the integer*) coma decimal
decimate [ˈdɛsɪˌmet] *tr* diezmar
decipher [dɪˈsaɪfər] *tr* descifrar
deciphering [dɪˈsaɪfərɪŋ] *s* desciframiento
decision [dɪˈsɪʒən] *s* decisión
decisive [dɪˈsaɪsɪv] *adj* decisivo; determinado, resuelto
deck [dɛk] *s* (*of cards*) baraja; (*of ship*) cubierta; (*sun deck*) terraza; **between decks** (naut) entre cubiertas ‖ *tr* — **to deck out** adornar, engalanar
deck chair *s* silla de cubierta
deck hand *s* marinero de cubierta
deckle-edged [ˈdɛkəlˈɛdʒd] *adj* de barba
declaim [dɪˈklem] *tr & intr* declamar
declaration [ˌdɛkləˈreʃən] *s* declaración; **Declaration of Independence** Declaración de Independencia
declarative [dɪˈklærətɪv] *adj* declarativo; (gram) enunciativo
declare [dɪˈklɛr] *tr & intr* declarar
declension [dɪˈklɛnʃən] *s* declinación
declination [ˌdɛklɪˈneʃən] *s* declinación
decline [dɪˈklaɪn] *s* bajada, declinación; (*in prices*) baja; (*in health, wealth, etc.*) bajón *m;* (*of sun*) ocaso ‖ *tr & intr* declinar; rehusar
declivi•ty [dɪˈklɪvɪti] *s* (*pl* **-ties**) declividad, declive *m*
decode [diˈkod] *tr* descodificar; (*messages*) descifrar; (*to translate*) traducir (*por traducción directa*)
decoder [diˈkodər] *s* (*person*) descifrador *m;* (compu, mil, telv) descodificador *m*
decoding [diˈkodɪŋ] *s* desciframiento; (*translation*) traducción directa; (compu) descodificación
décolleté [ˌdekɑlˈte] *adj* escotado
decompose [ˌdikəmˈpoz] *tr* descomponer ‖ *intr* descomponerse
decomposition [ˌdikɑmpəˈzɪʃən] *s* descomposición
decompression [ˌdikəmˈprɛʃən] *s* descompresión
decompression sickness *s* aeroembolismo
decongest [ˌdikənˈdʒɛst] *tr* descongestionar
decongestion [ˌdikənˈdʒɛstʃən] *s* descongestión
decontamination [ˌdikəmˌtæmɪˈneʃən] *s* descontaminación; **radioactive decontamination** descontaminación de radiactividad
decon•trol [ˌdikənˈtrol] *v* (*pret & pp* **-trolled;** *ger* **-trolling**) descontrolar
décor [deˈkɔr] *s* decoración; (theat) decorado
decorate [ˈdɛkəˌret] *tr* decorar; (*with medal, badge*) condecorar
decoration [ˌdɛkəˈreʃən] *s* decoración; (*medal, badge*) condecoración
decorator [ˈdɛkəˌretər] *s* decorador *m;* (*of interiors*) adornista *mf*
decorous [ˈdɛkərəs] o [dɪˈkorəs] *adj* decoroso
decorum [dɪˈkorəm] *s* decoro
decoy [dɪˈkɔɪ] o [ˈdikɔɪ] *s* añagaza, señuelo; (*person*) entruchón *m* ‖ [dɪˈkɔɪ] *tr* atraer con señuelo; entruchar
decoy pigeon *s* cimbel *m*
decrease [ˈdikris] *s* disminución ‖ [dɪˈkris] *tr* disminuir ‖ *intr* disminuir, disminuirse
decree [dɪˈkri] *s* decreto ‖ *tr* decretar
decrepit [dɪˈkrɛpɪt] *adj* decrépito
de•cry [dɪˈkraɪ] *v* (*pret & pp* **-cried**) *tr* censurar, denigrar
decrypt [diˈkrɪpt] *tr* (compu) desencriptar
dedicate [ˈdɛdɪˌket] *tr* dedicar
dedication [ˌdɛdɪˈkeʃən] *s* dedicación; (*inscription in a book*) dedicatoria
deduce [dɪˈdjus] *tr* deducir (*inferir, concluir; derivar*)
deduct [dɪˈdʌkt] *tr* deducir (*rebajar, substraer*)
deduction [dɪˈdʌkʃən] *s* deducción
deed [did] *s* acto, hecho; (*feat, exploit*) hazaña; (law) escritura ‖ *tr* traspasar por escritura
deem [dim] *tr & intr* creer, juzgar
deep [dip] *adj* profundo; (*sound*) grave; (*color*) subido; de hondo, p.ej., **two meters deep** dos metros de hondo; **deep in debt** cargado de deudas; **deep in thought** absorto en la meditación ‖ *adv* hondo; **deep into the night** muy entrada la noche
deepen [ˈdipən] *tr* profundizar ‖ *intr* profundizarse
deep freeze *s* congelador *m,* freezer *f*
deep freezer *s* ultracongelador *m*
deep freezing *s* ultracongelación, congelación
deep fryer *s* freidora, olla freidora
deep kiss *s* beso profundo
deep-laid [ˈdipˌled] *adj* concebido con astucia
deep mourning *s* luto riguroso
deep-rooted [ˈdipˌrutɪd] *adj* profundamente arraigado
deep′-sea′ fishing *s* pesca de gran altura
deep-seated [ˈdipˌsitɪd] *adj* profundamente arraigado
deer [dɪr] *s* ciervo, venado
deer′skin′ *s* piel *f* de ciervo
def. *abbr* **defendant, deferred, definite**
deface [dɪˈfes] *tr* desfigurar
de facto [diˈfækto] *adv* de hecho
defamation [ˌdɛfəˈmeʃən] o [ˌdifəˈmeʃən] *s* difamación
defame [dɪˈfem] *tr* difamar
default [dɪˈfɔlt] *s* falta, incumplimiento; **by default** (sport) por no presentarse; **in default of** por falta de ‖ *tr* dejar de cumplir; no pagar ‖ *intr* faltar; (sport) perder por no presentarse
defeat [dɪˈfit] *s* derrota ‖ *tr* derrotar, vencer
defeatism [dɪˈfitɪzəm] *s* derrotismo
defeatist [dɪˈfitɪst] *adj & s* derrotista *mf*
defecate [ˈdɛfɪˌket] *intr* defecar
defect [dɪˈfɛkt] o [ˈdifɛkt] *s* defecto, imperfección ‖ [dɪˈfɛkt] *intr* desertar

defection [dɪˈfɛkʃən] *s* defección; (*lack, failure*) falta
defective [dɪˈfɛktɪv] *adj* defectivo, defectuoso
defend [dɪˈfɛnd] *tr* defender
defendant [dɪˈfɛndənt] *s* (law) demandado, acusado
defender [dɪˈfɛndər] *s* defensor *m*
defense [dɪˈfɛns] *s* defensa
defense lawyer *s* abogado defensor
defenseless [dɪˈfɛnslɪs] *adj* indefenso
defensive [dɪˈfɛnsɪv] *adj* defensivo ‖ *s* defensiva
de•fer [dɪˈfʌr] *v* (*pret & pp* **-ferred;** *ger* **-ferring**) *tr* aplazar, diferir ‖ *intr* deferir
deference [ˈdɛfərəns] *s* deferencia
deferential [ˌdɛfəˈrɛnʃəl] *adj* deferente
deferment [dɪˈfʌrmənt] *s* aplazamiento, dilación
defiance [dɪˈfaɪ•əns] *s* oposición; desafío, provocación; **in defiance of** sin mirar a, a despecho de
defiant [dɪˈfaɪ•ənt] *adj* provocante, hostil
deficien•cy [dɪˈfɪʃənsi] *s* (*pl* **-cies**) carencia, deficiencia; (com) descubierto
deficient [dɪˈfɪʃənt] *adj* deficiente, defectuoso
deficit [ˈdɛfɪsɪt] *adj* deficitario ‖ *s* déficit *m*
defile [dɪˈfaɪl] o [ˈdifaɪl] *s* desfiladero ‖ [dɪˈfaɪl] *tr* corromper, manchar ‖ *intr* desfilar
define [dɪˈfaɪn] *tr* definir
definite [ˈdɛfɪnɪt] *adj* definido
definition [ˌdɛfɪˈnɪʃən] *s* definición
definitive [dɪˈfɪnɪtɪv] *adj* definitivo
deflate [dɪˈflet] *tr* desinflar
deflation [dɪˈfleʃən] *s* desinflación; (*of prices*) deflación
deflect [dɪˈflɛkt] *tr* desviar ‖ *intr* desviarse
deflower [diˈflaʊ•ər] *tr* desflorar
deforest [diˈfɑrɛst] o [diˈfɔrɛst] *tr* desforestar, despoblar
deform [dɪˈfɔrm] *tr* deformar
deformed [dɪˈfɔrmd] *adj* deforme
deformi•ty [dɪˈfɔrmɪti] *s* (*pl* **-ties**) deformidad
defraud [dɪˈfrɔd] *tr* defraudar
defray [diˈfre] *tr* sufragar, subvenir a
defrost [diˈfrɔst] *tr* descongelar, deshelar; (*a windshield*) desempañar
defroster [diˈfrɔstər] *s* descongelador *m*
deft [dɛft] *adj* diestro, hábil
defunct [dɪˈfʌŋkt] *adj* difunto
de•fy [dɪˈfaɪ] *v* (*pret & pp* **-fied**) *tr* desafiar, provocar
deg. *abbr* **degree**
degeneracy [dɪˈdʒɛnərəsi] *s* degeneración
degenerate [dɪˈdʒɛnərɪt] *adj & s* degenerado ‖ [dɪˈdʒɛnəˌret] *intr* degenerar
degrade [dɪˈgred] *tr* degradar
degrading [dɪˈgredɪŋ] *adj* degradante
degree [dɪˈgri] *s* grado; **by degrees** de grado en grado; **to take a degree** graduarse, recibir un grado o título
dehumidifier [ˌdihjuˈmɪdɪˌfaɪ•ər] *s* deshumedecedor *m*
dehydrate [diˈhaɪdret] *tr* deshidratar
deice [diˈaɪs] *tr* deshelar
deicer [diˈaɪsər] *s* descongelante *m*
dei•fy [ˈdi•ɪˌfaɪ] *v* (*pret & pp* **-fied**) *tr* deificar
deign [den] *intr* dignarse
dei•ty [ˈdi•ɪti] *s* (*pl* **-ties**) deidad; **the Deity** Dios *m*
dejected [dɪˈdʒɛktɪd] *adj* abatido
dejection [dɪˈdʒɛkʃən] *s* abatimiento
del. *abbr* **delegate, delete**
delay [dɪˈle] *s* retraso, tardanza; parón ‖ *tr* retrasar ‖ *intr* demorarse
delectable [dɪˈlɛktəbəl] *adj* deleitable
delegate [ˈdɛlɪgɪt] *s* diputado, delegado; (*to a convention*) congresista *mf* ‖ [ˈdɛlɪˌget] *tr* delegar
delete [dɪˈlit] *tr* borrar, suprimir
deletion [dɪˈliʃən] *s* supresión
deliberate [dɪˈlɪbərɪt] *adj* pensado, reflexionado; (*slow in deciding*) cauto, circunspecto; (*slow in moving*) espacioso, lento ‖ [dɪˈlɪbəˌret] *tr & intr* deliberar
delica•cy [ˈdɛlɪkəsi] *s* (*pl* **-cies**) delicadeza; (*choice food*) golosina
delicatessen [ˌdɛlɪkəˈtɛsən] *s* fiambrería, charcutería, salsamentaría (Col), salchichonería (Mex)
delicious [dɪˈlɪʃəs] *adj* delicioso, sabroso
delight [dɪˈlaɪt] *s* deleite *m,* delicia ‖ *tr* deleitar ‖ *intr* deleitarse
delightful [dɪˈlaɪtfəl] *adj* deleitoso, ameno, exquisito
delinquen•cy [dɪˈlɪŋkwənsi] *s* (*pl* **-cies**) culpa; (*in payment of debt*) morosidad; (*debt in arrears*) atrasos
delinquent [dɪˈlɪŋkwənt] *adj* culpado; (*in payment*) moroso, atrasado; no pagado ‖ *s* culpado; deudor moroso
delirious [dɪˈlɪrɪ•əs] *adj* delirante
deliri•um [dɪˈlɪrɪ•əm] *s* (*pl* **-ums** o **-a** [ə]) delirio
deliver [dɪˈlɪvər] *tr* entregar; asestar (*un golpe*); pronunciar, recitar (*un discurso*); transmitir, rendir (*energía*); partear (*a la mujer que está de parto*)
deliver•y [dɪˈlɪvəri] *s* (*pl* **-ies**) entrega; (*of mail*) distribución, reparto; (*of a speech*) declamación; (*childbirth*) alumbramiento, parto
delivery•man [dɪˈlɪvərimən] *s* (*pl* **-men** [mən]) mozo de reparto
delivery room *s* sala de alumbramiento, sala de partos
delivery service *s* servicio a domicilio
delivery truck *s* sedán *m* de reparto
dell [dɛl] *s* vallecito
delouse [diˈlaʊs] *tr* despiojar
delphinium [dɛlˈfɪnɪ•əm] *s* (*Delphinium ajacis*) espuela de caballero; (*Delphinium consolida*) consuelda real
delude [dɪˈlud] *tr* deludir, engañar
deluge [ˈdɛljudʒ] *s* diluvio ‖ *tr* inundar
delusion [dɪˈluʃən] *s* engaño, decepción
de luxe [dɪˈlʌks] *adj & adv s* de lujo
delve [dɛlv] *intr* cavar; **to delve into** cavar en
demagnetize [diˈmægnɪˌtaɪz] *tr* desimantar
demagogue [ˈdɛməˌgɑg] *s* demagogo

demand [dɪ`mænd] o [dɪ`mɑnd] *s* demanda; **to be in demand** tener demanda ‖ *tr* demandar perentoriamente
demanding [dɪ`mændɪŋ] *adj* exigente
demarcate [dɪ`mɑrket] o [`dimɑr,ket] *tr* demarcar
démarche [de`marʃ] *s* diligencia, gestión, paso
demeanor [dɪ`minər] *s* conducta, porte *m*
demented [dɪ`mɛntɪd] *adj* demente, dementado
demigod [`dɛmɪ,gɑd] *s* semidiós *m*
demijohn [`dɛmɪ,dʒɑn] *s* damajuana
demilitarize [di`mɪlɪtə,raɪz] *tr* desmilitarizar
demilitarized zone *s* zona desmilitarizada
demimonde [`dɛmɪ,mɑnd] *s* mujeres de vida alegre
demise [dɪ`maɪz] *s* fallecimiento
demisemiquaver [,dɛmɪ`sɛmɪ,kwevər] *s* (mus) fusa
demitasse [`dɛmɪ,tæs] o [`dɛmɪ,tɑs] *s* taza pequeña
demobilize [di`mobɪ,laɪz] *tr* desmovilizar
democra•cy [dɪ`mɑrkrəsi] *s* (*pl* **-cies**) democracia; estado de derecho
democrat [`dɛmə,kræt] *s* demócrata *mf*
democratic [,dɛmə`krætɪk] *adj* democrático
demodulate [di`mɑdjə,let] *tr* desmodular
demolish [dɪ`mɑlɪʃ] *tr* demoler
demolition [,dɛmə`lɪʃən] o [,dimə`lɪʃən] *s* demolición
demon [`dimən] *s* demonio
demoniacal [,dimə`naɪ•əkəl] *adj* demoníaco
demonstrate [`dɛmən,stret] *tr* demostrar ‖ *intr* demostrar; (*to show feelings in public gatherings*) manifestar
demonstration [,dɛmən`streʃən] *s* demostración; (*public show of feeling*) manifestación, movilización
demonstrative [dɪ`mɑnstrətɪv] *adj* demostrativo; (*giving open exhibition of emotion*) extremoso
demonstrator [`dɛmən,stretər] *s* demostrador *m;* manifestante *mf*
demoralize [dɪ`mɔrə,laɪz] *tr* desmoralizar
demote [dɪ`mot] *tr* degradar
demotion [dɪ`moʃən] *s* degradación
de•mur [dɪ`mʌr] *v* (*pret & pp* **-murred;** *ger* **-murring**) *intr* poner reparos
demure [dɪ`mjʊr] *adj* modesto, recatado; grave, serio
demurrage [dɪ`mʌrɪdʒ] *s* (com) estadía
den [dɛn] *s* (*of animals, thieves*) madriguera; (*dirty little room*) cuchitril *m;* lugar *m* de retiro; cuarto de estudio; (*of lions*) (Bib) fosa
denaturalize [di`nætjərə,laɪz] *tr* desnaturalizar
denatured alcohol [di`netʃərd] *s* alcohol desnaturalizado
denial [dɪ`naɪ•əl] *s* denegación; negación, desmentida
denim [`dɛnɪm] *s* dril *m* de algodón
denizen [`dɛnɪzən] *s* habitante *mf,* vecino
Denmark [`dɛnmɑrk] *s* Dinamarca
denomination [dɪ,nɑmɪ`neʃən] *s* denominación; categoría, clase *f;* secta, confesión, comunión
denote [dɪ`not] *tr* denotar
dénouement [denu`mɑ̃] *s* desenlance *m*
denounce [dɪ`naʊns] *tr* denunciar
dense [dɛns] *adj* denso; estúpido
densi•ty [`dɛnsɪti] *s* (*pl* **-ties**) densidad
dent [dɛnt] *s* abolladura, mella ‖ *tr* abollar, mellar ‖ *intr* abollarse, mellarse
dental [`dɛntəl] *adj & s* dental *f*
dental floss *s* hilo dental, seda encerada
dental office *s* clínica dental
dental technician *s* mecánico-dentista *m*
dentrifrice [`dɛntɪfrɪs] *s* dentífrico
dentist [`dɛntɪst] *s* dentista *mf*
dentistry [`dɛntɪstri] *s* odontología
denture [`dɛntʃər] *s* dentadura artificial
denunciation [dɪ,nʌnsɪ`eʃən] o [dɪ,nʌnʃɪ`eʃən] *s* denuncia
de•ny [dɪ`naɪ] *v* (*pret & pp* **-nied**) *tr* (*to declare not to be true*) negar; (*to refuse*) denegar; **to deny oneself to callers** negarse ‖ *intr* negar; denegar
deodorant [di`odərənt] *adj & s* desodorante *m*
deodorize [di`odə,raɪz] *tr* desodorizar
deoxidize [di`ɑksɪ,daɪz] *tr* desoxidar
deoxyribonucleic acid (DNA) [dɪ`ɑksɪ`rɪbə`nukle•ɪk] *s* ácido deoxirribonucleico (A.D.N., D.N.A.)
dep. *abbr* **department, departs, deputy**
depart [dɪ`pɑrt] *intr* partir, salir, irse; desviarse
department [dɪ`pɑrtmənt] *s* departamento; sección *f;* (*of government*) ministerio
department store *s* grandes almacenes *mpl*
departure [dɪ`pɑrtʃər] *s* partida, salida; desviación
depend [dɪ`pɛnd] *intr* depender; **to depend on** depender de
dependable [dɪ`pɛndəbəl] *adj* confiable, fidedigno
dependence [dɪ`pɛndəns] *s* dependencia
dependen•cy [dɪ`pɛndənsi] *s* (*pl* **-cies**) dependencia; (*country, territory*) posesión
dependent [dɪ`pɛndənt] *adj* dependiente ‖ *s* carga de familia, familiar *m* dependiente
depict [dɪ`pɪkt] *tr* describir, representar, pintar
deplete [dɪ`plit] *tr* agotar, depauperar
deplorable [dɪ`plorəbəl] *adj* deplorable
deplore [dɪ`plor] *tr* deplorar
deploy [dɪ`plɔɪ] *tr* (mil) desplegar ‖ *intr* (mil) desplegarse
deployment [dɪ`plɔɪmənt] *s* (mil) despliegue *m*
depolarize [di`polə,raɪz] *tr* despolarizar
depopulate [di`pɑpjə,let] *tr* despoblar
deport [dɪ`port] *tr* deportar; **to deport oneself** conducirse, portarse
deportation [,dipor`teʃən] *s* deportación
deportee [,dipor`ti] *s* deportado
deportment [dɪ`portmənt] *s* conducta, comportamiento
depose [dɪ`poz] *tr & intr* deponer
deposit [dɪ`pɑzɪt] *s* depósito; (*down payment*)

señal *f,* pago anticipado; (min) yacimiento ‖ *tr* depositar ‖ *intr* depositarse
depositor [dɪˈpɑzɪtər] *s* cuentacorrentista *mf,* imponente *mf*
depot [ˈdipo] o [ˈdɛpo] *s* almacén *m,* depósito; (mil) depósito; (rr) estación
depraved [dɪˈprevd] *adj* depravado
depravi•ty [dɪˈprævɪti] *s* (*pl* **-ties**) depravación
deprecate [ˈdɛprɪˌket] *tr* desaprobar
depreciate [dɪˈpriʃiˌet] *tr* (*to lower value or price of*) depreciar; (*to disparage*) desapreciar ‖ *intr* depreciarse
depreciation [dɪˌpriʃiˈeʃən] *s* (*drop in value*) depreciación; (*disparagement*) desaprecio
depress [dɪˈprɛs] *tr* deprimir; desanimar, desalentar; bajar (*los precios*)
depression [dɪˈprɛʃən] *s* depresión; desaliento; (*slump*) crisis *f*
deprive [dɪˈpraɪv] *tr* privar
deprived [dɪˈpraɪvd] *adj* desventajado
dept. *abbr* **department**
depth [dɛpθ] *s* profundidad; (*of a house, of a room*) fondo; **in the depth of night** en mitad de la noche; **in the depth of winter** en pleno invierno; **to go beyond one's depth** meterse en agua demasiado profunda; (fig) meterse en honduras
depth charge *s* carga de profundidad
depth of hold *s* (naut) puntal *m*
deputize [ˈdɛpjəˌtaɪz] *tr* nombrar como segundo
depu•ty [ˈdɛpjəti] *s* (*pl* **-ties**) diputado, segundo; (pol) diputado
derail [dɪˈrel] *tr* hacer descarrilar ‖ *intr* descarrilar
derailment [dɪˈrelmənt] *s* descarrilamiento
derange [dɪˈrendʒ] *tr* desarreglar, descomponer; trastornar el juicio a
derangement [dɪˈrendʒmənt] *s* desarreglo, descompostura; locura; obfuscación
der•by [ˈdʌrbi] *s* (*pl* **-bies**) sombrero hongo
deregulate [diˈrɛgjəˌlet] *tr* descontrolar
derelict [ˈdɛrɪlɪkt] *adj* abandonado; negligente ‖ *s* pelafustán *m;* (naut) derrelicto
deride [dɪˈraɪd] *tr* burlarse de, ridiculizar
derision [dɪˈrɪʒən] *s* burla, irrisión
derisory [dəˈraɪsəri] *adj* irrisorio
derive [dɪˈraɪv] *tr & intr* derivar
dermatitis [ˌdʌrməˈtaɪtɪs] *s* dermatitis *f*
derogatory [dɪˈrɑgəˌtori] *adj* despreciativo
derrick [ˈdɛrɪk] *s* grúa; (min) castillete *m*
dervish [ˈdʌrvɪʃ] *s* derviche *m*
desalinization [dɪˌselɪnɪˈzeʃən] *s* desalinización
desalt [diˈsɔlt] *tr* desalar
descend [dɪˈsɛnd] *tr* bajar, descender (*la escalera*) ‖ *intr* bajar, descender; **to descend on** caer sobre, invadir
descendant [dɪˈsɛndənt] *adj* descendente ‖ *s* descendiente *mf*
descendent [dɪˈsɛndənt] *adj* descendente
descent [dɪˈsɛnt] *s* (*passing from higher to lower state*) descenso; (*extraction; lineage*) descendencia; cuesta, bajada; invasión
describe [dɪˈskraɪb] *tr* describir
description [dɪˈskrɪpʃən] *s* descripción
descriptive [dɪˈskrɪptɪv] *adj* descriptivo
desecrate [ˈdɛsɪˌkret] *tr* profanar
desegregate [ˈdiˈsɛgrɪget] *tr & intr* eliminar la segregación racial (de *or* en)
desegregation [diˌsɛgrɪˈgeʃən] *s* desegregación
desert [ˈdɛzərt] *adj & s* desierto, yermo ‖ [dɪˈzʌrt] *s* mérito; **he received his just deserts** llevó su merecido ‖ *tr* desertar de ‖ *intr* desertar
deserter [dɪˈzʌrtər] *s* desertor *m*
desertion [dɪˈzʌrʃən] *s* deserción; abandono de cónyuge
deserve [dɪˈzʌrv] *tr & intr* merecer
deservedly [dɪˈzʌrvɪdli] *adv* merecidamente
design [dɪˈzaɪn] *s* diseño; (*combination of details; art of designing*) dibujo; (*plan, scheme*) designio; **to have designs on** poner la mira en ‖ *tr* deseñar, dibjuar; idear, proyectar ‖ *intr* diseñar, dibujar
designate [ˈdɛzɪgˌnet] *tr* designar
designing [dɪˈzaɪnɪŋ] *adj* intrigante, maquinador
desirable [dɪˈzaɪrəbəl] *adj* deseable
desire [dɪˈzaɪr] *s* deseo ‖ *tr* desear
desirous [dɪˈzaɪrəs] *adj* deseoso
desist [dɪˈzɪst] *intr* desistir
desk [dɛsk] *s* bufete *m,* escritorio; (*lectern*) atril *m;* (*clerk's counter in a hotel*) caja
desk clerk *s* cajero, recepcionista *m*
desk pad *s* bloc *m* de notas
desk set *s* juego de escritorio
desk'top *s* (compu) escritorio, sobremesa
desk'top computer *s* ordenador *m* de sobremesa o de mesa, computadora de sobremesa o de mesa; ordenador *or* computadora de escritorio
desk'top publishing *s* autoedición
desolate [ˈdɛsəlɪt] *adj* (*hopeless*) desolado; despoblado, yermo, desierto; solitario; (*dismal*) lúgubre ‖ [ˈdɛsəˌlet] *tr* desconsolar; (*to lay waste*) desolar, devastar; despoblar
desolation [ˌdɛsəˈleʃən] *s* (*devastation; great affliction*) desolación; (*dreariness*) lobreguez *f*
despair [dɪˈspɛr] *s* desesperación ‖ *intr* desesperar, desesperarse
despairing [dɪˈspɛrɪŋ] *adj* desesperado
despera•do [ˌdɛspəˈredo] o [ˌdɛspəˈrɑdo] *s* (*pl* **-does** o **-dos**) criminal dispuesto a todo
desperate [ˈdɛspərɪt] *adj* dispuesto a todo; (*bitter, excessive*) encarnizado; (*hopeless*) desesperado; (*remedy*) heroico
despicable [ˈdɛspɪkəbəl] *adj* despreciable, ruin, infame
despise [dɪˈspaɪz] *tr* despreciar, desdeñar
despite [dɪˈspaɪt] *prep* a despecho de
desponden•cy [dɪˈspɑndənsi] *s* (*pl* **cies**) abatimiento, desaliento
despondent [dɪˈspɑndənt] *adj* abatido, desalentado
despot [ˈdɛspɑt] *s* déspota *m*
despotic [dɛsˈpɑtɪk] *adj* despótico
despotism [ˈdɛspəˌtɪzəm] *s* despotismo

dessert [dɪˈzʌrt] *s* postre *m*
dessert′spoon *s* cuchara de postre
destination [ˌdɛstɪˈneʃən] *s* (*end of a journey or shipment*) destino; (*purpose*) destinación
destine [ˈdɛstɪn] *tr* destinar
desti•ny [ˈdɛstɪni] *s* (*pl* **-nies**) destino
destitute [ˈdɛstɪˌtjut] *adj* (*being in complete poverty*) indigente; (*lacking, deprived*) desprovisto
destitution [ˌdɛstɪˈtjuʃən] *s* indigencia
destroy [dɪˈstrɔi] *tr* destruir
destroyer [dɪˈstrɔɪ•ər] *s* (nav) destructor *m*
destruction [dɪˈstrʌkʃən] *s* destrucción
destructive [dɪˈstrʌktɪv] *adj* destructivo
desultory [ˈdɛsəlˌtori] *adj* deshilvanado, descosido
detach [dɪˈtætʃ] *tr* desprender, separar; (mil) destacar
detachable [dɪˈtætʃəbəl] *adj* desprendible, separable; (*collar*) postizo
detached [dɪˈtætʃt] *adj* separado, suelto; imparcial, desinteresado
detached retina *s* desprendimiento de retina
detachment [dɪˈtætʃmənt] *s* desprendimiento, separación; imparcialidad, desinterés *m;* (mil) destacamento
detail [dɪˈtel] o [ˈditel] *s* detalle *m,* pormenor *m;* (mil) destacamento; **details** señas *fpl* ‖ [dɪˈtel] *tr* detallar; (mil) destacar
detain [dɪˈten] *tr* detener; tener preso
detect [dɪˈtɛkt] *tr* detectar
detection [dɪˈtɛkʃən] *s* detección
detective [dɪˈtɛktɪv] *adj* policial ‖ *s* detective *m*
detective story *s* novela policíaca o policial
detector [dɪˈtɛktər] *s* detector *m*
detention [dɪˈtɛnʃən] *s* detención
de•ter [dɪˈtʌr] *v* (*pret & pp* **-terred;** *ger* **-terring**) *tr* impedir, refrenar
detergent [dɪˈtəʌrdʒənt] *adj & s* detergente *m*
deteriorate [dɪˈtɪrɪ•əˈret] *tr* deteriorar ‖ *intr* deteriorarse
determination [dɪˌtʌrməˈneʃən] *s* resolución; empecinamiento
determine [dɪˈtʌrmɪn] *tr* determinar
deterrent [dɪˈtʌrənt] *s* impedimento, refrenamiento, fuerza disuasoria
detest [dɪˈtɛst] *tr* detestar, aborrecer
dethrone [dɪˈθron] *tr* destronar
detonate [ˈdɛtəˌnet] o [ˈditəˌnet] *tr* hacer estallar ‖ *intr* detonar
detour [ˈditʊr] o [dɪˈtʊr] *s* desvío; rodeo, vuelta; manera indirecta ‖ *tr* desviar (*el tráfico*) ‖ *intr* desviarse
detoxification [diˌtɑksəfəˈkeʃən] *s* desintoxicación
detoxi•fy [diˈtɑksəˌfaɪ] *v* (*pret & pp* **-fied**) *tr* desintoxicar
detract [dɪˈtrækt] *tr* detraer ‖ *intr* **— to detract from** disminuir, rebajar
detriment [ˈdɛtrɪmənt] *s* perjuicio, detrimento; **to the detriment of** en perjuicio de
detrimental [ˌdɛtrɪˈmɛntəl] *adj* perjudicial
deuce [djus] o [dus] *s* (*in cards*) dos *m;* (*in tennis*) deuce *m;* **the deuce!** ¡demonio!
devaluation [diˌvæljʊˈeʃən] *s* desvalorización, devaluación
devastate [ˈdɛvəsˌtet] *tr* devastar
devastation [ˌdɛvəsˈteʃən] *s* devastación
develop [dɪˈvɛləp] *tr* desarrollar, desenvolver; (phot) revelar; explotar (*una mina*) ‖ *intr* desarrollarse, desenvolverse; evolucionar, manifestarse
developer [dɪˈvɛləpər] *s* fomentador *m;* (compu) desarrollador *m;* (phot) revelador *m*
development [dɪˈvɛləpmənt] *s* desarrollo, desenvolvimiento; (phot) revelado; (*of a mine*) explotación; acontecimiento nuevo
developmental aid [dɪˌvɛləpˈmɛntəl] *s* ayuda al desarrollo
development company *s* sociedad *or* promotora inmobiliaria (Esp), empresa promotora
development tool *s* (compu) herramienta de desarrollo
deviate [ˈdivɪˌet] *tr* desviar ‖ *intr* desviarse
deviation [ˌdivɪˈeʃən] *s* desviación
deviationism [ˌdivɪˈeʃəˌnɪzəm] *s* desviacionismo
deviationist [ˌdivɪˈeʃənɪst] *s* desviacionista *mf*
device [dɪˈvaɪs] *s* dispositivo, aparato; (*trick*) ardid *m,* treta; (*motto*) lema *m,* divisa; (compu) dispositivo; **to leave someone to his own devices** dejarle a uno que haga lo que se le antoje
dev•il [ˈdɛvəl] *s* diablo; **between the devil and the deep blue sea** entre la espada y la pared; **to raise the devil** (slang) armar un alboroto ‖ *v* (*pret & pp* **iled** o **-illed;** *ger* **-iling** o **illing**) *tr* condimentar con picantes; (coll) acosar, molestar
devilish [ˈdɛvəlɪʃ] *adj* diabólico
devilment [ˈdɛvəlmənt] *s* (*mischief*) diablura; (*evil*) maldad
devil•try [ˈdɛvəltri] *s* (*pl* **-tries**) maldad, crueldad; (*mischief*) diablura
devious [ˈdɪvɪ•əs] *adj* (*straying*) desviado, extraviado; (*roundabout; shifty*) tortuoso
devise [dɪˈvaɪz] *tr* idear, inventar; (law) legar
devoid [dɪˈvɔɪd] *adj* desprovisto
devote [dɪˈvot] *tr* dedicar
devoted [dɪˈvotɪd] *adj* (*zealous, ardent*) devoto; dedicado
devotee [ˌdɛvəˈti] *s* devoto
devotion [dɪˈvoʃən] *s* devoción; (*to study, work, etc.*) dedicación; **devotions** oraciones, preces *fpl*
devour [dɪˈvaʊr] *tr* devorar
devout [dɪˈvaʊt] *adj* devoto; cordial, sincero
dew [dju] o [du] *s* rocío
dew′drop′ *s* gota de rocío
dew′lap′ *s* papada
dew•y [ˈdju•i] o [ˈdu•i] *adj* rociado
dexterity [dɛksˈtɛrɪti] *s* destreza
D.F. *abbr* **Defender of the Faith**
diabetes [ˌdaɪ•əˈbitɪs] *s* diabetes *f*
diabetic [ˌdaɪ•əˈbɛtɪk] *adj & s* diabético

diabolic(al) [ˌdaɪ•əˈbɑlɪk(əl)] *adj* diabólico
diacritical [ˌdaɪ•əˈkrɪtɪkəl] *adj* diacrítico
diadem [ˈdaɪ•əˌdɛm] *s* diadema *f*
diaere•sis [daɪˈɛrɪsɪs] *s* (*pl* **-ses** [ˌsiz]) diéresis *f*
diagnose [ˌdaɪ•əgˈnos] *tr* diagnosticar
diagno•sis [ˌdaɪ•əgˈnosɪs] *s* (*pl* **-ses** [siz]) diagnosis *f*, diagnóstico
diagonal [daɪˈægənəl] *adj* & *s* diagonal *f*
diagram [ˈdaɪ•əˌgræm] *s* diagrama *m*
dial. *abbr* **dialect**
dial [ˈdaɪ•əl] *s* (*of radio*) cuadrante *m;* (*of watch*) cuadrante *m*, esfera, muestra; (*of telephone*) disco selector ‖ *tr* sintonizar (*el radiorreceptor*); marcar (*el número telefónico*); llamar (*a una persona*) por teléfono automático ‖ *intr* (telp) marcar
dialect [ˈdaɪ•əˌlɛkt] *s* dialecto
dialing [ˈdaɪ•əlɪŋ] *s* (telp) marcaje *m*, discado; (*of a lock*) marcador *m*
dialog box *s* (compu) caja de diálogo, cuadro de diálogo
dialogue [ˈdaɪ•əˌlɔg] *s* diálogo
dial telephone *s* teléfono automático
dial tone *s* (telp) señal *f* para marcar, tono de marcar, tono de discado
diam. *abbr* **diameter**
diameter [daɪˈæmɪtər] *s* diámetro
diametric(al) [ˌdaɪ•əˈmɛtrɪk(əl)] *adj* diamétrico
diamond [ˈdaɪmənd] *s* diamante *m;* (*figure of a rhombus*) losange *m;* (*playing card*) carró *m*, diamante *m;* (baseball) diamante *m*, cuadro; (*field*) campo de béisbol; (cards) diamante *m* (*baraja francesa*); **diamonds** (cards) un palo rojo de naipes representandos losanges; equivalente al palo de oros
diaper [ˈdaɪpər] *s* pañal *m*
diaphanous [daɪˈæfənəs] *adj* diáfano
diaphragm [ˈdaɪ•əˌfræm] *s* diafragma *m*
diarrhea [ˌdaɪ•əˈri•ə] *s* diarrea; **to have diarrhea** cursear
dia•ry [ˈdaɪ•əri] *s* (*pl* **-ries**) diario
diastole [daɪˈæstəli] *s* diástole *f*
diathermy [ˈdaɪ•əˌθʌrmi] *s* diatermia
diatribe [ˈdaɪ•ətraɪb] *s* diatriba
dice [daɪs] *spl* dados; (*small cubes*) cubitos; **to load the dice** cargar los dados ‖ *tr* cortar en cubos
dice′box′ *s* cubilete *m*
dichloride [daɪˈkloraɪd] *s* dicloruro
dichoto•my [daɪˈkɑtəmi] *s* (*pl* **-mies**) dicotomía
dickey [ˈdɪki] *s* camisolín *m*, pechera postiza
dict. *abbr* **dictionary**
dictaphone [ˈdɪktəˌfon] *s* dictáfono
dictate [ˈdɪktet] *s* mandato ‖ [ˈdɪktet] o [dɪkˈtet] *tr* dictar; mandar
dictation [dɪkˈteʃən] *s* dictado; (*orders; giving orders*) mandato; **to take dictation** escribir al dictado
dictator [ˈdɪktetər] o [dɪkˈtetər] *s* dictador *m*
dictatorship [dɪkˈtetərʃɪp] *s* dictadura
diction [ˈdɪkʃən] *s* dicción
dictionar•y [ˈdɪkʃənˌɛri] *s* (*pl* **-ies**) diccionario
dic•tum [ˈdɪktəm] *s* (*pl* **-ta** [tə]) dictamen *m;* aforismo, sentencia
didactic(al) [daɪˈdæktɪk(əl)] o [dɪ-ˈdæktɪk(əl)] *adj* didáctico
didn't *contr* **did not**
die [daɪ] *s* (*pl* **-dice** [daɪs]) dado; **the die is cast** la suerte está echada ‖ *s* (*pl* **dies**) (*for stamping coins, medals, etc.*) troquel *m;* (*for cutting threads*) hembra de terraja ‖ *v* (*pret* & *pp* **died;** *ger* **dying**) *intr* morir; **to be dying** estar agonizando; **to die laughing** morir de risa
die′hard′ *adj* & *s* intransigente *mf*
diesel [ˈdizəl] *s* coche *m or* camión *m* diesel, diesel *m*, gas-oil *m*
die′sel-elec′tric *adj* dieseleléctrico
diesel engine *s* diesel *m*
diesel fuel *s* gas-oil *m*, diesel *m*
diesel oil *s* gas-oil *m*, diesel *m*
die′stock′ *s* terraja
diet [ˈdaɪ•ət] *s* dieta, régimen alimenticio ‖ *intr* estar a dieta
dietitian [ˌdaɪ•əˈtɪʃən] *s* dietista *mf*
diff. *abbr* **difference, different**
differ [ˈdɪfər] *intr* (*to be different*) diferir, diferenciarse; (*to dissent*) diferenciar; **to differ with** desavenirse con
difference [ˈdɪfərəns] *s* diferencia; **to make no difference** no importar; **to split the difference** partir la diferencia
different [ˈdɪfərənt] *adj* diferente
differentiate [ˌdɪfəˈrɛnʃiˌet] *tr* diferenciar ‖ *intr* diferenciarse
difficult [ˈdɪfɪˌkʌlt] *adj* difícil
difficul•ty [ˈdɪfɪˌkʌlti] *s* (*pl* **-ties**) dificultad
diffident [ˈdɪfɪdənt] *adj* apocado, tímido
diffuse [dɪˈfjus] *adj* difuso ‖ [dɪˈfjuz] *tr* difundir ‖ *intr* difundirse
dig [dɪg] *s* (*poke*) empuje *m;* (*jibe*) pulla, palabra hiriente ‖ *v* (*pret* & *pp* **dug** [dʌg] o **digged;** *ger* **digging**) *tr* cavar, excavar; **to dig up** desenterrar ‖ *intr* cavar, excavar; **to dig in** (coll) poner manos a la obra; (mil) antrincherarse; **to dig under** socavar
digest [ˈdaɪdʒɛst] *s* compendio, resumen *m;* (law) digesto ‖ [dɪˈdʒɛst] o [daɪˈdʒɛst] *tr* & *intr* digerir
digestible [dɪˈdʒɛstɪbəl] o [daɪˈdʒɛstɪbəl] *adj* digerible, digestible
digestion [dɪˈdʒɛstʃən] o [daɪˈdʒɛstʃən] *s* digestión
digestive [dɪˈdʒɛstɪv] o [daɪˈdʒɛstɪv] *adj* & *s* digestivo
digit [ˈdɪdʒɪt] *s* (anat) dedo; (math) dígito, cifra
digital [ˈdɪdʒətəl] *adj* digital
digital clock *s* reloj numérico *or* digital
digitalis [ˌdɪdʒəˈtæləs] *s* (pharm) digital *f*
digital recording *s* grabación digital
digital scanner *s* lector *m* digital
digital telephone *s* teléfono digital
digital watch *s* reloj numérico *or* digital
digitize [ˈdɪdʒətaɪz] *tr* digitalizar

dignified [ˈdɪgnɪ,faɪd] *adj* digno, grave, decoroso
digni•fy [ˈdɪgnɪ,faɪ] *v* (*pret & pp* **-fied**) *tr* dignificar; engrandecer el mérito de
dignitar•y [ˈdɪgnɪ,tɛri] *s* (*pl* **-ies**) dignatario
digni•ty [ˈdɪgnɪti] *s* (*pl* **-ties**) dignidad; **to stand upon one's dignity** ponerse tan alto
digress [dɪˈgrɛs] o [daɪˈgrɛs] *intr* divagar
digression [dɪˈgrɛʃən] o [daɪˈgrɛʃən] *s* digresión, divagación
dike [daɪk] *s* dique *m;* (*bank of earth thrown up in digging*) montón *m;* (*causeway*) arrecife *m,* malecón *m*
dilapidated [dɪˈlæpɪ,detɪd] *adj* destartalado, desvencijado
dilate [daɪˈlet] *tr* dilatar ‖ *intr* dilatarse
dilatory [ˈdɪlə,tori] *adj* tardío
dilemma [dɪˈlɛmə] *s* dilema *m,* disyuntiva; encerrona
dilettan•te [,dɪləˈtænti] *adj* diletante ‖ *s* (*pl* **-tes** o **-ti** [ti]) diletante *mf*
diligence [ˈdɪlɪdʒəns] *s* diligencia; dedicación
diligent [ˈdɪlɪdʒənt] *adj* diligente
dill [dɪl] *s* eneldo
dillydal•ly [ˈdɪlɪ,dæli] *v* (*pret & pp* **-lied**) *intr* malgastar el tiempo, haraganear
dilute [dɪˈlut] o [daɪˈlut] *adj* diluído ‖ [dɪˈlut] *tr* diluir ‖ *intr* diluirse
dilution [dɪˈluʃən] *s* dilución
dim. *abbr* **diminutive**
dim [dɪm] *adj* (*comp* **dimmer;** *super* **dimmest**) débil, indistinto, confuso; obscuro, poco claro; (*chance*) escaso; (*not clearly understanding*) torpe, lerdo; **to take a dim view of** mirar escépticamente ‖ *v* (*pret & pp* **dimmed;** *ger* **dimming**) *tr* amortiguar (*la luz*); poner (*un faro*) a media luz; disminuir ‖ *intr* obscurecerse
dime [daɪm] *s* moneda de diez centavos
dimension [dɪˈmɛnʃən] *s* dimensión
diminish [dɪˈmɪnɪʃ] *tr* disminuir ‖ *intr* disminuir, disminuirse
diminution [,dɪməˈnuʃən] *s* disminución
diminutive [dɪˈmɪnjətɪv] *adj* (*tiny*) diminuto; (gram) diminutivo ‖ *s* diminutivo
dimi•ty [ˈdɪmɪti] *s* (*pl* **-ties**) cotonía
dimly [ˈdɪmli] *adv* indistintamente
dimmer [ˈdɪmər] *s* amortiguador *m* de luz; (aut) lámpara de cruce, luz *f* de cruce
dimple [ˈdɪmpəl] *s* hoyuelo
dimwit [ˈdɪm,wɪt] *s* (slang) mentecato, bobo
dim•witted [ˈdɪm,wɪtɪd] *adj* (slang) mentecato, bobo
din [dɪn] *s* estruendo, ruido ensordecedor ‖ *v* (*pret & pp* **dinned;** *ger* **dinning**) *tr* ensordecer con mucho ruido; repetir insistentemente; impresionar con repetición ruidosa ‖ *intr* sonar estrepitosamente
dine [daɪn] *tr* dar de comer a; obsequiar con una cena o comida ‖ *intr* cenar, comer; **to dine out** cenar fuera de casa
diner [ˈdaɪnər] *s* invitado a una cena, convidado a una comida; coche-comedor *m*
ding-dong [ˈdɪŋ,dɔŋ] *s* dindán *m*
din•gy [ˈdɪndʒi] *adj* (*comp* **-gier;** *super* **-giest**) deslustrado, sucio
dining car *s* coche-comedor *m,* vagón *m* restaurante, vagón comedor (Esp)
dining room *s* comedor *m*
din′ing-room′ suite *s* juego de comedor
dinner [ˈdɪnər] *s* cena, comida; (*formal meal*) banquete *m*
dinner coat o **jacket** *s* smoking *m*
dinner pail *s* fiambrera, portaviandas *m*
dinner plate *s* plato llano o liso
dinner set *s* vajilla
dinner theater *s* café teatro
dinner time *s* hora de la cena o comida
dint [dɪnt] *s* abolladura; **by dint of** a fuerza de ‖ *tr* abollar
diocese [ˈdaɪ•əˈsis] o [ˈdaɪ•əsis] *s* diócesi *f* o diócesis *f*
diode [ˈdaɪ•od] *s* diodo
dioxide [daɪˈɑksaɪd] *s* dióxido
dip [dɪ] *s* zambullida, inmersión; baño corto; (*in a road*) depresión; (*of magnetic needle*) inclinación ‖ *v* (*pret & pp* **dipped;** *ger* **dipping**) *tr* sumergir; sacar con cuchara; (*bread*) sopetear; **to dip the colors** saludar con la bandera ‖ *intr* sumergirse; inclinarse hacia abajo; desaparecer súbitamente; **to dip into** hojear (*un libro*); meterse en (*un comercio*); **to dip into one's purse** gastar dinero
diphtheria [dɪfˈθɪrɪ•ə] *s* difteria
diphthong [ˈdɪfθɔŋ] *s* diptongo
diphthongize [ˈdɪfθɔŋ,gaɪz] *tr* diptongar ‖ *intr* diptongarse
diploma [dɪˈplomə] *s* diploma *m*
diploma•cy [dɪˈploməsi] *s* (*pl* **-cies**) diplomacia
diplomat [ˈdɪplə,mæt] *s* diplomático
diplomatic [,dɪpləˈmætɪk] *adj* diplomático
diplomatic corps *s* cuerpo diplomático
diplomatic pouch *s* valija diplomática
dipper [ˈdɪpər] *s* cazo, cucharón *m*
dip′stick′ *s* varilla de nivel
dire [daɪr] *adj* horrendo, espantoso
direct [dɪˈrɛkt] o [daɪˈrɛkt] *adj* directo; franco, sincero ‖ *tr* dirigir; mandar, ordenar
direct current *s* corriente continua
direct dialing *s* discado automático, discado directo
direct discourse *s* (gram) estilo directo
direct hit *s* blanco directo, impacto directo
direction [dɪˈrɛkʃən] o [daɪˈrɛkʃən] *s* dirección; instrucción; **directions** (*for use*) modo de empleo
direction light *s* (aut) intermitente *m*
direct object *s* (gram) complemento directo
director [dɪˈrɛktər] o [daɪˈrɛktər] *s* director *m,* administrador *m;* (*member of a governing body*) vocal *m*
directorship [dɪˈrɛktərʃɪp] o [daɪˈrɛktərʃɪp] *s* dirección, directorio
directo•ry [dɪˈrɛktəri] o [daɪˈrɛktəri] *s* (*pl* **-ries**) (*list of names and addresses; board of direc-*

tors) directorio; anuario telefónico, guía telefónica; (compu) directorio
dirge [dʌrdʒ] *s* endecha, canto fúnebre, treno; (eccl) misa de réquiem
dirigible [ˈdɪrɪdʒɪbəl] *adj & s* dirigible *m*
dirt [dʌrt] *s* (*soil*) tierra, suelo; (*dust*) polvo; (*mud*) barro, lodo; excremento; (*accumulation of dirt*) suciedad; (*moral filth*) suciedad, porquería, obscenidad; (*gossip*) chismes *mpl*
dirtˈcheapˈ *adj* tirado, muy barato
dirt road *s* camino de tierra
dirt•y [ˈdʌrti] *adj* (*comp* **-ier;** *super* **-iest**) puerco, sucio; berroso, enlodado; polvoriento; (*obscene*) hediondo; bajo, vil ‖ *v* (*pret & pp* **-tied**) *tr* ensuciar
dirty linen *s* ropa sucia; **to air one's dirty linen in public** sacar los trapos sucios a relucir
dirty trick *s* (coll) perrada, mala partida, mala pasada
disabili•ty [ˌdɪsəˈbɪlɪti] *s* (*pl* **-ties**) incapacidad, inhabilidad, minusvalía; disminución (*física*)
disability benefit *s* pensión de invalidez
disable [dɪsˈebəl] *tr* incapacitar, inhabilitar, lisiar; (law) descalificar
disabled *adj* minusválido, descapacitado; (mil, naut) inutilizado
disabled veteran *s* lisiado de guerra
disabuse [ˌdɪsəˈbjuz] *tr* desengañar
disadvantage [ˌdɪsədˈvæntɪdʒ] *s* desventaja ‖ *tr* perjudicar
disadvantaged [ˌdɪsədˈvæntɪdʒd] *adj & s* desfavorecido, carenciado
disadvantageous [dɪsˌædvənˈtedʒəs] *adj* desventajoso
disagree [ˌdɪsəˈgri] *intr* desavenirse, desconvenirse; (*to quarrel*) altercar, contender; **to disagree with** no estar de acuerdo con; no sentar bien
disagreeable [ˌdɪsəˈgri•əbəl] *adj* desagradable
disagreement [ˌdɪsəˈgrimənt] *s* desavenencia, desacuerdo; disensión; inconformidad
disappear [ˌdɪsəˈpɪr] *intr* desaparecer, desaparecerse
disappearance [ˌdɪsəˈpɪrəns] *s* desaparecimiento, desaparición
disappoint [ˌdɪsəˈpɔɪnt] *tr* decepcionar, desilusionar, chasquear; **to be disappointed** chasquearse, llevarse chasco
disappointment [ˌdɪsəˈpɔɪntmənt] *s* decepción, desilusión, chasco
disapproval [ˌdɪsəˈpruvəl] *s* desaprobación
disapprove [ˌdɪsəˈpruv] *tr & intr* desaprobar
disarm [dɪsˈɑrm] *tr* desarmar ‖ *intr* desarmar, desarmarse
disarmament [dɪsˈɑrməmənt] *s* desarme *m,* desarmamiento
disarming [dɪsˈɑrmɪŋ] *adj* congraciador, simpático, encantadoro
disarray [ˌdɪsəˈre] *s* desorden *m;* (*in apparel*) desatavío ‖ *tr* desordenar; desataviar
disaster [dɪˈzæstər] desastre *m,* siniestro
disaster area *s* zona siniestrada o catastrófica
disastrous [dɪˈzæstrəs] *adj* desastroso, desastrado
disavow [ˌdɪsəˈvaʊ] *tr* desconocer, negar, repudiar
disband [dɪsˈbænd] *tr* disolver (*una asamblea*); licenciar (*tropas*) ‖ *intr* desbandarse
dis•bar [dɪsˈbɑr] *v* (*pret & pp* **-barred;** *ger* **-barring**) *tr* (law) expulsar del foro
disbelief [ˈdɪsbɪˈlif] *s* incredulidad
disbelieve [ˈdɪsbɪˈlig] *tr & intr* descreer
disburse [dɪsˈbʌrs] *tr* desembolsar
disbursement [dɪsˈbʌrsmənt] *s* desembolso
disc. *abbr* **discount, discoverer**
disc [dɪsk] *s* disco
discard [dɪsˈkɑrd] *s* descarte *m;* **to put into the discard** desechar ‖ *tr* descartar; desechar
discern [dɪˈzʌrn] o [dɪˈsʌrn] *tr* discernir, percibir
discerning [dɪˈzʌrnɪŋ] o [dɪˈsʌrnɪŋ] *adj* discerniente, perspicaz
discharge [dɪsˈtʃɑrdʒ] *s* (*of a gun, of a battery*) descarga; (*of a prisoner*) liberación; (*of a duty*) desempeño; (*of a debt, of an obligation*) descargo; (*from a job*) despedida, remoción; (mil) certificado de licencia; (pathol) derrame *m* ‖ *tr* descargar; desempeñar (*un deber*); libertar (*a un preso*); despedir, remover (*a un empleado*); (*from the hospital*) dar de alta; (mil) licenciar ‖ *intr* descargar (*un tubo, río, etc.*); descargarse (*un arma de fuego*)
disciple [dɪˈsaɪpəl] *s* discípulo
disciplinarian [ˌdɪsɪplɪˈnɛrɪ•ən] *s* ordenancista *mf*
discipline [ˈdɪsɪplɪn] *s* disciplina; castigo ‖ *tr* disciplinar; castigar
disclaim [dɪsˈklem] *tr* desconocer, negar
disclose [dɪsˈkloz] *tr* divulgar, revelar; descubrir
disclosure [dɪsˈkloʒər] *s* divulgación, revelación; descubrimiento
disco [ˈdɪsko] *abbr* **discotheque**
discolor [dɪsˈkʌlər] *tr* descolorar ‖ *intr* descolorarse
discomfiture [dɪsˈkʌmfɪtʃər] *s* desconcierto; frustración
discomfort [dɪsˈkʌmfərt] *s* incomodidad ‖ *tr* incomodar
disconcert [ˌdɪskənˈsʌrt] *tr* desconcertar, confundir
disconnect [ˌdɪskəˈnɛkt] *tr* desunir, separar; desconectar
disconsolate [dɪsˈkɑnsəlɪt] *adj* desconsolado, desolado
discontent [ˌdɪskənˈtɛnt] *adj & s* descontento ‖ *tr* descontentar
discontented [ˌdɪskənˈtɛntɪd] *adj* descontento
discontinue [ˌdɪskənˈtɪnjʊ] *tr* descontinuar
discord [ˈdɪskɔrd] *s* desacuerdo, discordia; discordancia
discordance [dɪsˈkɔrdəns] *s* discordancia
discotheque [ˌdɪskoˈtɛk] *s* discoteca
discount [ˈdɪskaʊnt] *s* descuento ‖ [ˈdɪskaʊnt] o [dɪsˈkaʊnt] *tr* descontar; descontar por exagerado

discount rate *s* tipo de descuento, tasa de descuento; tipo de redescuento
discourage [dɪsˈkʌrɪdʒ] *tr* desalentar, desanimar; desaprobar; disuadir
discouragement [dɪsˈkʌrɪdʒmənt] *s* desaliento; desaprobación; disuasión
discourse [ˈdɪskors] o [dɪsˈkors] *s* discurso ‖ [dɪsˈkors] *intr* discurrir
discourteous [dɪsˈkʌrtɪ•əs] *adj* descortés
discourte•sy [dɪsˈkʌrtəsi] *s* (*pl* **-sies**) descortesía
discover [dɪsˈkʌvər] *tr* descubrir
discover•y [dɪsˈkʌvəri] *s* (*pl* **-ies**) descubrimiento
discredit [dɪsˈkrɛdɪt] *s* descrédito ‖ *tr* desacreditar
discreditable [dɪsˈkrɛdɪtəbəl] *adj* deshonroso
discreet [dɪsˈkrit] *adj* discreto
discrepan•cy [dɪsˈkrɛpənsi] *s* (*pl* **-cies**) discrepancia
discrete [dɪsˈkrit] *adj* discreto
discretion [dɪsˈkrɛʃən] *s* discreción; **at discretion** a discreción
discriminate [dɪsˈkrɪmɪˌnet] *intr* discriminar; **to discriminate against** discriminar
discrimination [dɪsˌkrɪmɪˈneʃən] *s* discriminación
discriminatory [dɪsˈkrɪmɪnəˌtori] *adj* discriminatorio
discus [ˈdɪskəs] *s* (sport) disco
discuss [dɪsˈkʌs] *tr & intr* discutir
discussion [dɪsˈkʌʃən] *s* discusión
discus thrower [ˈθro•ər] *s* discóbolo
disdain [dɪsˈden] *s* desdén *m* ‖ *tr* desdeñar
disdainful [dɪsˈdenfəl] *adj* desdeñoso
disease [dɪˈziz] *s* enfermedad
diseased [dɪˈzizd] *adj* morboso
disembark [ˌdɪsɛmˈbɑrk] *tr & intr* desembarcar
disembarkation [dɪsˌɛmbɑrˈkeʃən] *s* (*of passengers*) desembarco; (*of freight*) desembarque *m*
disembowel [ˌdɪsɛmˈbaʊ•əl] *tr* desentrañar
disenchant [ˌdɪsɛnˈtʃænt] *tr* desencantar
disenchantment [ˌdɪsɛnˈtʃæntmənt] *s* desencanto
disengage [ˌdɪsɛnˈgedʒ] *tr* (*from a pledge*) desempeñar; (*to disconnect*) desenganchar; desembragar (*el motor*)
disengagement [ˌdɪsɛnˈgedʒmənt] *s* desempeño; desenganche *m;* desembrague *m*
disentangle [ˌdɪsɛnˈtæŋgəl] *tr* desenredar
disentanglement [ˌdɪsɛnˈtæŋgəlmənt] *s* desenredo
disestablish [ˌdɪsɛsˈtæblɪʃ] *tr* separar (*la Iglesia*) del Estado
disfavor [dɪsˈfevər] *s* disfavor *m*
disfigure [dɪsˈfɪgjər] *tr* desfigurar
disfranchise [dɪsˈfræntʃaɪz] *tr* privar de los derechos de ciudadanía
disgorge [dɪsˈgɔrdʒ] *tr & intr* vomitar
disgrace [dɪsˈgres] *s* deshonra, vergüenza; disfavor *m;* metedura ‖ *tr* deshonrar, avergonzar; despedir con ignominia
disgraceful [dɪsˈgresfəl] *adj* deshonroso, vergonzoso
disgruntle [dɪs•grʌntəl] *tr* disgustar, enfadar
disguise [dɪsˈgaɪz] *s* disfraz *m* ‖ *tr* disfrazar
disgust [dɪsˈgʌst] *s* asco, repugnancia ‖ *tr* dar asco a, repugnar
disgusting [dɪsˈgʌstɪŋ] *adj* asqueroso, repugnante; bofe (CAm)
dish [dɪʃ] *s* (*any container used at table*) vasija; (*shallow, circular dish; its contents*) plato; **to wash the dishes** lavar la vajilla, fregar los platos; (telv) antena parabólica ‖ *tr* servir en un plato; (slang) arruinar
dish antenna *s* antena parabólica
dish′cloth′ *s* albero; (*for washing*) trapo
dishearten [dɪsˈhɑrtən] *tr* descorazonar, desalentar, desanimar
dishev•el [dɪˈʃɛvəl] *v* (*pret & pp* **-eled** o **-elled;** *ger* **-eling** o **-elling**) desgreñar, desmelenar
dishonest [dɪsˈɑnɪst] *adj* deshonesto, no honrado, ímprobo
dishones•ty [dɪsˈɑnɪsti] *s* (*pl* **-ties**) deshonestidad, falta de honradez, improbidad
dishonor [dɪsˈɑnər] *s* deshonra, deshonor *m* ‖ *tr* deshonrar, deshonorar; (com) no aceptar, no pagar
dishonorable [dɪsˈɑnərəbəl] *adj* ignominioso, deshonroso
dish′pan′ *s* paila de lavar la vajilla
dish rack *s* escurreplatos *m*
dish′rag′ *s* albero; (*for washing*) trapo
dish′tow′el *s* paño para secar platos, trapo de cocina
dish′wash′er *s* (*person*) fregona; (*machine*) lavaplatos *m,* lavavajillas *m*
dish′wa′ter *s* agua de lavar platos, agua sucia
disillusion [ˌdɪsɪˈluʒən] *s* desilusión ‖ *tr* desilusionar
disillusionment [ˌdɪsɪˈluʒənmənt] *s* desilusión
disinclination [dɪsˌɪnklɪˈneʃən] *s* aversión, desafición
disinclined [ˌdɪsɪnˈklaɪnd] *adj* desinclinado
disinfect [ˌdɪsɪnˈfɛkt] *tr* desinfectar, desinficionar
disinfectant [ˌdɪsɪnˈfɛktant] *adj & s* desinfectante *m*
disingenuous [ˌdɪsɪnˈdʒɛnjʊ•əs] *adj* insincero, poco ingenuo
disinherit [ˌdɪsɪnˈhɛrɪt] *tr* desheredar
disintegrate [dɪsˈɪntɪˌgret] *tr* desagregar, desintegrar ‖ *intr* desagregarse, desintegrarse
disintegration [dɪsˌɪntɪˈgreʃən] *s* desagregación, desintegración
disin•ter [ˌdɪsɪnˈtʌr] *v* (*pret & pp* **-terred;** *ger* **-terring**) *tr* desenterrar
disinterested [dɪsˈɪntəˌrɛstɪd] o [dɪsˈɪntrɪstɪd] *adj* desinteresado
disinterestedness [dɪsˈɪntəˌrɛstɪdɪnɛs] o [dɪsˈɪntrɪstɪdnɪs] *s* desinterés *m*
disjunctive [dɪsˈdʒʌŋktɪv] *adj* disyuntivo
disk [dɪsk] *s* disco
disk brake *s* freno de disco
disk camera *s* cámara de disco

disk drive *s* (compu) unidad de disco, unidad de disquete, disquetera
diskette [dɪsˈkɛt] *s* disquete *m*
disk jockey *s* (rad) locutor *m* de un programa de discos
dislike [dɪsˈlaɪk] *s* aversión, antipatía; **to take a dislike for** cobrar aversión a || *tr* desamar
dislocate [ˈdɪslo,ket] *tr* dislocar, dislocarse (*un hueso*)
dislodge [dɪsˈlɑdʒ] *tr* desalojar
disloyal [dɪsˈlɔɪ•əl] *adj* desleal
disloyal•ty [dɪsˈlɔɪ•əlti] *s* (*pl* **-ties**) deslealtad
dismal [ˈdɪzməl] *adj* lúgubre, tenebroso; terrible, espantoso
dismantle [dɪsˈmæntəl] *tr* desarmar, desmontar
dismay [dɪsˈme] *s* consternación || *tr* consternar
dismember [dɪsˈmɛmbər] *tr* desmembrar
dismiss [dɪsˈmɪs] *tr* despedir, destituir; desechar; alejar del pensamiento, echar en olvido
dismissal [dɪsˈmɪsəl] *s* despedida, destitución
dismount [dɪsˈmaʊnt] *tr* desmontar || *intr* desmontarse
disobedience [,dɪsəˈbidɪ•əns] *s* desobediencia
disobedient [,dɪsəˈbidɪ•ənt] *adj* desobediente
disobey [,dɪsəˈbe] *tr & intr* desobedecer
disorder [dɪsˈɔrdər] *s* desorden *m* || *tr* desordenar
disorderly [dɪsˈɔrdərli] *adj* desordenado; alborotador, revoltoso
disorderly conduct *s* conducta contra el orden público
disorderly house *s* (*brothel*) burdel *m,* lupanar *m*
disorganize [dɪsˈɔrgə,naɪz] *tr* desorganizar
disorientation [dɪs,ɔrienˈteʃən] *s* desorientación
disown [dɪsˈon] *tr* desconocer, repudiar
disparage [dɪsˈpærɪdʒ] *tr* desacreditar, desdorar
disparagement [dɪsˈpærɪdʒmənt] *s* descrédito, desdoro
disparate [ˈdɪspərɪt] *adj* disparejo
dispari•ty [dɪsˈpærɪti] *s* (*pl* **-ties**) disparidad
dispassionate [dɪsˈpæʃənɪt] *adj* desapasionado
dispatch [dɪsˈpætʃ] *s* despacho || *tr* despachar; (coll) despabilar (*una comida*)
dis•pel [dɪsˈpɛl] *v* (*pret & pp* **-pelled;** *ger* **-pelling**) *tr* desvanecer, disipar
dispensa•ry [dɪsˈpɛnsəri] *s* (*pl* **-ries**) dispensario
dispense [dɪsˈpɛns] *tr* dispensar (*medicamentos*); administrar (*justicia*); expender (*p.ej., gasolina*); (*to exempt*) eximir || *intr* — **to dispense with** deshacerse de; pasar sin, prescindir de
disperse [dɪsˈpʌrs] *tr* dispersar || *intr* dispersarse
displace [dɪsˈples] *tr* remover, trasladar; despedir, deponer; reemplazar; desplazar (*un volumen de agua*)
displaced person *s* persona desplazada
display [dɪsˈple] *s* despliegue *m;* exhibición, exposición; ostentación; (compu) dibujado, redibujado; (compu, electron) visualizador *m* || *tr* (*to unfold; to reveal*) desplegar; (*to exhibit, show*) exhibir, exponer; (*to show ostentatiously*) ostentar; (compu) visualizar
display cabinet *s* vitrina, escaparate *m*
display window *s* escaparate *m* de tienda
displease [dɪsˈpliz] *tr* desagradar, disgustar, desplacer
displeasing [dɪsˈplizɪŋ] *adj* desagradable
displeasure [dɪsˈplɛʒər] *s* desagrado, disgusto, desplacer *m*
disposable [dɪsˈpozəbəl] *adj* (available for any use) disponible; (*made to be thrown away after serving its purpose*) desechable, descartable
disposal [dɪsˈpozəl] *s* disposición; donación, liquidación, venta; **at the disposal of** a la disposición de; **to have at one's disposal** disponer de
dispose [dɪsˈpoz] *tr* disponer; inducir, mover || *intr* disponer; **to dispose of** disponer de; deshacerse de; dar, vender; acabar con
disposition [,dɪspəˈzɪʃən] *s* disposición; índole *f,* genio, natural *m;* ajuste *m,* arreglo; venta
dispossess [,dɪspəˈzɛs] *tr* desposeer; (*to evict, oust*) desahuciar
disproof [dɪsˈpruf] *s* confutación, refutación
disproportionate [,dɪsprəˈporʃənɪt] *adj* desproporcionado
disprove [dɪsˈpruv] *tr* confutar, refutar
dispute [dɪsˈpjut] *s* disputa; **beyond dispute** sin disputa; **in dispute** disputado || *tr & intr* disputar
disquali•fy [dɪsˈkwɑlɪ,faɪ] *v* (*pret & pp* **-fied**) *tr* descalificar, desclasificar, inhabilitar; **disqualified** descalificado, inhabilitado
disquiet [dɪsˈkwaɪ•ət] *s* desasosiego, inquietud || *tr* desasosegar, inquietar
disregard [,dɪsrɪˈgɑrd] *s* desatención, desaire *m* || *tr* desatender, desairar, pasar por alto
disrepair [,dɪsrɪˈpɛr] *s* desconcierto, descompostura
disreputable [dɪsˈrɛpjətəbəl] *adj* desacreditado, de mala fama; raído, usado, desaliñado
disrepute [,dɪsrɪˈpjut] *s* descrédito, mala fama; **to bring into disrepute** desacreditar, dar mala fama a
disrespect [,dɪsrɪˈspɛkt] *s* desacato || *tr* desacatar
disrespectful [,dɪsrɪˈspɛktfəl] *adj* irrespetuoso
disrobe [dɪsˈrob] *tr* desnudar || *intr* desnudarse, despelotarse
disrupt [dɪsˈrʌpt] *tr* romper; (*to throw into disorder*) desbaratar
dissatisfaction [,dɪssætɪsˈfækʃən] *s* desagrado, descontento, insatisfacción
dissatisfied [dɪsˈsætɪs,faɪd] *adj* descontento
dissatis•fy [dɪsˈsætɪs,faɪ] *v* (*pret & pp* **-fied**) *tr* descontentar
dissect [dɪˈsɛkt] *tr* disecar
dissemble [dɪˈsɛmbəl] *tr* disimular || *intr* disimular; obrar hipócritamente
disseminate [dɪˈsɛmɪ,net] *tr* diseminar, difundir
dissension [dɪˈsɛnʃən] *s* disensión
dissent [dɪˈsɛnt] *s* disensión; (*nonconformity*)

disidencia || *intr* disentir; (*from doctrine or authority*) disidir
dissenter [dɪˋsɛntər] *s* disidente *mf*
disservice [dɪˋsʌrvɪs] *s* deservicio
dissidence [ˋdɪsɪdəns] *s* disidencia
dissident [ˋdɪsɪdənt] *adj & s* disidente *mf*
dissimilar [dɪˋsɪmɪlər] *adj* disímil, desemejante
dissimilate [dɪˋsɪmɪ,let] *tr* disimilar || *intr* disimilarse
dissimulate [dɪˋsɪmjə,let] *tr & intr* disimular
dissipate [ˋdɪsɪ,pet] *tr* disipar || *intr* disiparse; entregarse a la disipación
dissipated [ˋdɪsɪ,petɪd] *adj* disipado, disoluto
dissipation [,dɪsɪˋpeʃən] *s* disipación
dissociate [dɪˋsoʃi,et] *tr* disociar
dissolute [ˋdɪsə,lut] *adj* disoluto
dissolution [,dɪsəˋluʃən] *s* disolución
dissolve [dɪˋzɑlv] *tr* disolver || *intr* (*to have the power of dissolving*) disolver; (*to pass into a liquid*) disolverse
dissonance [ˋdɪsənəns] *s* disonancia
dissuade [dɪˋswed] *tr* disuadir
dissyllabic [,dɪsɪˋlæbɪk] *adj* disílabo, disilábico
dissyllable [dɪˋsɪləbəl] *s* disílabo
dist. *abbr* **distance, distinguish, district**
distaff [ˋdɪstæf] o [ˋdɪstɑf] *s* rueca
distaff side *s* rama femenina de la familia
distance [ˋdɪstəns] *s* distancia; **at a distance** a distancia; **in the distance** a lo lejos; **to keep at a distance** no permitir familiaridades; **to keep one's distance** mantenerse a distancia
distance learning *s* educación a distancia
distant [ˋdɪstənt] *adj* distante; (*relative*) lejano; (*not familiar*) frío, indiferente
distaste [dɪsˋtest] *s* aversión, repugnancia
distasteful [dɪsˋtestfəl] *adj* desagradable, repugnante
distemper [dɪsˋtɛmpər] *s* enfermedad; (*of dogs*) moquillo
distend [dɪsˋtɛnd] *tr* ensanchar, distender || *intr* ensancharse, distender
distension [dɪsˋtɛnʃən] *s* ensanche *m,* distensión
distill [dɪsˋtɪl] *tr* destilar
distillation [,dɪstɪˋleʃən] *s* destilación
distiller•y [dɪsˋtɪləri] *s* (*pl* **-ies**) destilería, destilatorio
distinct [dɪsˋtɪŋkt] *adj* distinto; cierto, indudable; (*not blurred*) nítido, bien definido
distinction [dɪsˋtɪŋkʃən] *s* distinción; (*distinguishing characteristic*) distintivo
distinctive [dɪsˋtɪŋktɪv] *adj* distintivo
distinguish [dɪsˋtɪŋgwɪʃ] *tr* distinguir
distinguished [dɪsˋtɪŋgwɪʃt] *adj* distinguido
distort [dɪsˋtɔrt] *tr* deformar, torcer; distorsionar; (*the truth*) falsear
distortion [dɪsˋtɔrʃən] *s* deformación, torcimiento; (*of the truth*) falseamiento; (rad) deformación, distorsión
distract [dɪsˋtrækt] *tr* distraer
distraction [dɪsˋtrækʃən] *s* distracción
distraught [dɪsˋtrɔt] *adj* trastornado, perplejo, aturdido
distress [dɪsˋtrɛs] *s* pena, aflicción, angustia; infortunio, peligro || *tr* apenar, afligir, angustiar
distressing [dɪsˋtrɛsɪŋ] *adj* penoso, angustioso
distress signal *s* señal *f* de socorro
distribute [dɪsˋtrɪbjut] *tr* distribuir, repartir
distribution [,dɪstrɪˋbjuʃən] *s* distribución, repartimiento, repartida
distribution channels *spl* (compu) canales *mpl* de distribución
distributor [dɪsˋtrɪbjətər] *s* distribuidor *m;* (aut) distribuidor
district [ˋdɪstrɪkt] *s* comarca, región; (*of a city*) barrio; (*administrative division*) distrito || *tr* dividir en distritos
district attorney *s* fiscal *mf*
distrust [dɪsˋtrʌst] *s* desconfianza || *tr* desconfiar de
distrustful [dɪsˋtrʌstfəl] *adj* desconfiado
disturb [dɪsˋtʌrb] *tr* disturbar, incomodar, molestar; desordenar, revolver; inquietar, dejar perplejo; perturbar (*el orden público*)
disturbance [dɪsˋtʌrbəns] *s* disturbio, molestia; desorden *m,* revuelta; inquietud; tumulto, trastorno
disuse [dɪsˋjus] *s* desuso
ditch [dɪtʃ] *s* zanja || *tr* zanjar; echar en una zanja; (slang) deshacerse de || *intr* amarar forzosamente
ditch reed *s* carrizo
dither [ˋdɪðər] *s* agitación, temblor; **to be in a dither** (coll) estar muy agitado
dit•to [ˋdɪto] *s* (*pl* **-tos**) lo mismo; (*symbol*) íd.; copia, duplicado || *tr* copiar, duplicar
ditto mark *s* la sigla "(*es decir:* íd.)
dit•ty [ˋdɪti] *s* (*pl* **-ties**) cancioneta
diuretic [,daɪəˋrɛtɪk] *adj & s* diurético
div. *abbr* **dividend, division**
diva [ˋdivɑ] *s* (mus) diva
divan [ˋdaɪvæn] o [dɪˋvæn] *s* diván *m*
dive [daɪv] *s* zambullida; (*of a submarine*) sumersión; (aer) picado; (coll) leonera, tasca || *v* (*pret & pp* **dived** o **dove** [dov]) *intr* zambullirse; (*to work as a diver*) bucear; sumergirse (*un submarino*); (aer) picar
dive′-bomb′ *tr & intr* bombardear en picado
dive bombing *s* bombardeo en picado
diver [ˋdaɪvər] *s* zambullidor *m;* buceador; (*person who works under water*) escafandrista *mf,* buzo; (orn) zambullidor *m*
diverge [dɪˋvʌrdʒ] o [daɪˋvʌrdʒ] *intr* divergir
divers [ˋdaɪvərz] *adj* diversos, varios
diverse [dɪˋvʌrs] o [daɪˋvʌrs] *adj* (*different*) diverso; (*of various kinds*) variado
diversification [dɪ′vʌrsɪfɪˋkeʃən] o [daɪ,vʌrsɪfɪˋkeʃən] *s* diversificación
diversi•fy [dɪˋvʌrsɪ,faɪ] o [daɪˋvʌrsɪ,faɪ] *v* (*pret & pp* **-fied**) *tr* diversificar || *intr* diversificarse
diversion [dɪˋvʌrʒən] o [daɪˋvʌrʒən] *s* diversión
diversi•ty [dɪˋvʌrsɪti] o [daɪˋvʌrsɪti] *s* (*pl* **-ties**) diversidad
divert [dɪˋvʌrt] o [daɪˋvʌrt] *tr* apartar, divertir;

(*to entertain*) divertir, entretener; (mil) divertir
diverting [dɪˈvʌrtɪŋ] o [daɪˈvʌrtɪŋ] *adj* divertido
divest [dɪˈvɛst] o [daɪˈvɛst] *tr* desnudar; despojar, desposeer; **to divest oneself of** desposeerse de
divestment [dɪˈvɛstmənt] *s* (econ) despojamiento
divide [dɪˈvaɪd] *s* (geog) divisoria ‖ *tr* dividir ‖ *intr* dividirse
divided highway *s* carretera de doble calzada
dividend [ˈdɪvɪ,dɛnd] *s* dividendo
dividers [dɪˈvaɪdərz] *spl* compás *m* de división
divination [,dɪvɪˈneʃən] *s* adivinación
divine [dɪˈvaɪn] *adj* divino ‖ *s* sacerdote *m,* clérigo ‖ *tr* adivinar
diving [ˈdaɪvɪŋ] *s* zambullida; buceo
diving bell *s* campana de buzo
diving board *s* trampolín *m*
diving goggles *spl* gafas de bucear
diving suit *s* escafandra
divining rod [dɪˈvaɪnɪŋ] *s* vara de adivinar; (*ostensibly to discover water or metals*) vara buscadora
divini•ty [dɪˈvɪnɪti] *s* (*pl* **-ties**) divinidad; teología; **the Divinity** Dios *m*
division [dɪˈvɪʒən] *s* división
divisor [dɪˈvaɪzər] *s* (math) divisor *m*
divorce [diˈvors] *s* divorcio; **to get a divorce** divorciarse ‖ *tr* divorciar (*los cónyuges*); divorciarse de (*la mujer o el marido*) ‖ *intr* divorciarse
divorcee [dɪvorˈsi] *s* persona divorciada; mujer divorciada
divot [ˈdɪvət] *s* tormo, terrón *m* (*de tierra*)
divulge [dɪˈvʌldʒ] *tr* divulgar, revelar
dixie [ˈdɪksi] *s* (*jazz*) dixie *m;* **Dixie** *los estados del sur en EE.UU.*
dizziness [ˈdɪzɪnɪs] *s* vértigo; confusión, perplejidad
diz•zy [ˈdɪzi] *adj* (*comp* **-zier;** *super* **-ziest**) (*suffering or causing dizziness*) vertiginoso; confuso, perplejo; aturdido, incauto; (coll) tonto
DNA [ˈdiˈɛnˈe] *s* (letterword) (**deoxyribonucleic acid**) A.D.N. *m,* D.N.A. *m* (ácido deoxirribonucleico)
do. *abbr* **ditto**
do [du] *v* (*tercera persona* **does** [dʌz]; *pret* **did** [dɪd]; *pp* **done** [dʌn]) *tr* hacer; resolver (*un problema*); recorrer (*cierta distancia*); cumplir con (*un deber*); aprender (*una lección*); componer (*la cama*); tocar (*el cabello*); rendir (*homenaje*); **to do one's best** hacer todo lo posible; **to do over** volver a hacer; repetir; renovar; **to do right by** tratar bien; **to do someone out of something** (coll) defraudar algo a alguien; **to do to death** despachar, matar; **to do up** empaquetar; poner en orden; almidonar y planchar (*una camisa*) ‖ *intr* actuar, obrar; conducirse; servir, ser suficiente; estar, hallarse; **how do you do?** ¿cómo está Ud.?; **that will do** eso sirve, eso es bastante; no digas más; **to have done** haber terminado; **to have done with** no tener más que ver con; **to have nothing to do with** no tener nada que ver con; **to have to do with** tratar de; **to do away with** suprimir; matar; **to do for** servir para; **to do well** salir bien; **to do without** pasar sin ‖ *v aux* úsase 1) en oraciones interrogativas: **Do you speak Spanish?** ¿Habla Ud. español?; 2) en oraciones negativas; **I do not speak Spanish** No hablo español; 3) para substituir a otro verbo en oraciones elípticas; **Did you go to church this morning? Yes, I did** ¿Fué Ud. a la iglesia esta mañana? Sí, fuí; 4) para dar más energía a la oración; **I do believe what you told me** Yo sí creo lo que me dijo Ud.; 5) en inversiones después de ciertos adverbios; **Seldom does he come to see me** él rara vez viene a verme; 6) en tono suplicante con el imperativo; **Do come in** pase Ud., por favor
docent [ˈdosənt] *s* conferenciante *mf;* (*person*) guía *mf*
docile [ˈdɑsɪl] *adj* dócil
dock [dɑk] *s* (*wharf*) muelle *m;* (*waterway between two piers*) dársena; (*area including piers and waterways*) puerto de mar; muñón *m* de cola; (law) tribuna de los acusados ‖ *tr* (naut) atracar en el muelle; derrabar, descolar (*a un animal*); reducir o suprimir (*el salario*) ‖ *intr* (naut) atracar
dockage [ˈdɑkɪdʒ] *s* entrada en un puerto; (*charges*) muellaje *m*
docket [ˈdɑkɪt] *s* actas, orden *m* del día; lista de causas pendientes; **on the docket** (coll) pendiente, entre manos
dock hand *s* portuario
dock'yard' *s* arsenal *m,* astillero
doctor [ˈdɑktər] *s* doctor *m;* (*physician*) médico ‖ *tr* medicinar; (coll) componer, reparar ‖ *intr* (coll) ejercer la medicina; (coll) tomar medicinas
doctorate [ˈdɑktərɪt] *s* doctorado
doctrine [ˈdɑktrɪn] *s* doctrina
document [ˈdɑkjəmənt] *s* documento ‖ [ˈdɑkjə,mɛnt] *tr* documentar
documenta•ry [,dɑkjəˈmɛntəri] *adj* documental ‖ *s* (*pl* **-ries**) documental *m*
documentation [,dɑkəmɛnˈteʃən] *s* documentación
doddering [ˈdɑdərɪŋ] *adj* chocho, temblón
dodge [dɑdʒ] *s* esguince *m,* regate *m;* (fig) regate ‖ *tr* evitar (*un golpe*); (fig) evitar mañosamente ‖ *intr* regatear, hurtar el cuerpo; **to dodge around the corner** voltear la esquina
do•do [ˈdodo] *s* (*pl* **-dos** o **-does**) (coll) inocente *m* de ideas anticuadas
doe [do] *s* cierva, gama, coneja
doeskin [ˈdo,skɪn] *s* ante *m,* piel *f* de ante; tejido fino de lana
doesn't *contr* **does not**
doff [dɑf] o [dɔf] *tr* quitarse (*el sombrero, la ropa*)
dog [dɔg] o [dɑg] *s* perro; **dog in the manger**

perro del hortelano; **to go to the dogs** darse al abandono; **lucky dog** (coll) lechero, suertero; **to put on the dog** (coll) darse ínfulas || *v* (*pret & pp* **dogged;** *ger* **dogging**) *tr* acosar, perseguir
dog'catch'er *s* lacero
dog collar *s* collar *m* de perro; (*clerical collar*) alzacuello
dog days *spl* canícula, caniculares *mpl*
doge [dodʒ] dux *m*
dog'-eared *adj* (*book*) sobado y con las esquinas dobladas
dog'fight *s* pelea de perros; (aer) combate aéreo
dogged ['dɔgɪd] *adj* tenaz, terco
doggerel ['dɔgərəl] *s* coplas de ciego
dog•gy ['dɔgi] *adj* (*comp* **-gier;** *super* **-giest**) emperejilado || *s* (*pl -gies*) perrito
doggy bag *s bolsita para llevarse las sobras a casa*
dog'house' *s* perrera
dog in the manger *s* el perro del hortelano
dog Latin *s* latinajo, latín *m* de cocina
dog license *s* permiso para perro
dogmatic [dɑg'mætɪk] *adj* dogmático; ergotista
dog racing *s* carreras de galgos
dog's-ear ['dɔgzəɪr] *s* orejón *m*
dog show *s* exposición canina
dog's life *s* vida miserable
Dog Star *s* Canícula
dog tag *s* placa; (*for soldiers*) placa de identificación *or* de identidad
dog'-tired' *adj* cansadísimo
dog'tooth' *s* (*pl* **-teeth**) [,tiθ] colmillo
dog track *s* galgódromo
dog'watch' *s* (naut) guardia de cuartillo
dog'wood' *s* cornejo
doi•ly ['dɔɪli] *s* (*pl* **-lies**) pañito de adorno
doings ['du•ɪŋz] *spl* acciones, obras, actividad
doldrums ['dɑldrəmz] *spl* (naut) calmas ecuatoriales; desanimación, inactividad
dole [dol] *s* limosna; subsidio a los desocupados || *tr* — **to dole out** distribuir en pequeñas porciones
doleful ['dolfəl] *adj* triste, lúgubre
doll [dɑl] *s* muñeca || *intr* — **to doll up** (slang) emperejilarse
dollar ['dɑlər] *s* dólar *m*
dollar mark *s* signo del dólar
doll'house *s* casa de muñecas
dol•ly ['dɑli] *s* (*pl* **-lies**) muñequita; (*low, wheeled frame for moving heavy loads*) gato rodante
dolphin ['dɑlfɪn] *s* delfín *m*
dolt [dolt] *s* bobalicón *m*
doltish ['doltɪʃ] *adj* bobalicón
dom. *abbr* **domestic, dominion**
domain [do'men] *s* dominio, heredad, propiedad; (*of learning*) campo
dome [dom] *s* cúpula, domo
dome light *s* (aut) lámpara de techo
domestic [də'mɛstɪk] *adj & s* doméstico
domesticate [də'mɛstɪ,ket] *tr* domesticar
domestic partner *s* conviviente *mf*
domicile ['dɑmɪsɪl] o ['dɑmɪ,saɪl] *s* domicilio || *tr* domiciliar
dominance ['dɑmɪnəns] *s* dominación
dominant ['dɑmɪnənt] *adj & s* dominante *f*
dominate ['dɑmɪ,net] *tr & intr* dominar
domination [,dɑmɪ'neʃən] *s* dominación
domineer [,dɑmɪ'nɪr] *intr* dominar
domineering [,dɑmɪ'nɪrɪŋ] *adj* dominante, mandón
Dominican [də'mɪnɪkən] *adj & s* dominicano
dominion [də'mɪnjən] *s* dominio
domi•no ['dɑmɪ,no] *s* (*pl* **-noes** o **-nos**) (*costume*) dominó *m;* (*half mask*) antifaz *m;* persona que lleva dominó; ficha (*del juego de dominó*); **domino effect** efecto de dominó; **dominoes** *ssg* dominó (*juego*); **domino theory** teoría del efecto domino de domino
don [dɑn] *s* caballero, señor *m,* personaje *m* de alta categoría; (coll) preceptor *m,* socio de uno de los colegios de las Universidades de Oxford y Cambridge || *v* (*pret & pp* **donned;** *ger* **donning**) *tr* ponerse (*el sombrero, la ropa*)
donate ['donet] *tr* dar, donar
donation [do'neʃən] *s* donación
done [dʌn] *adj* hecho, terminado; cansado, rendido; bien asado
done for *adj* (coll) cansado, rendido, agotado; (coll) arruinado, destruído; (coll) fuera de combate; (coll) muerto
donjon ['dʌndʒən] *s* torre *f* del homenaje
donkey ['dɑŋki] *s* asno, burro
donnish ['dɑnɪʃ] *adj* magistral, pedantesco
donor ['donər] *s* donador *m*
don't *contr* **do not**
doodle ['dudəl] *tr & intr* borrajear
doom [dum] *s* ruina, perdición, muerte *f;* condena, juicio; juicio final; hado, destino || *tr* condenar; sentenciar a muerte; predestinar a la ruina, a la muerte
doomsday ['dumz,de] *s* día *m* del juicio final; día del juicio
door [dor] *s* puerta; (*of a carriage or automobile*) portezuela; (*one part of a double door*) hoja, batiente *m;* **behind closed doors** a puertas cerradas; **to see to the door** acompañar a la puerta
door'bell' *s* campanilla de puerta, timbre *m* de puerta
door check *s* amortiguador *m,* cierre *m* de puerta
door'frame' *s* bastidor *m* de puerta, marco de puerta
door'head' *s* dintel *m*
door'jamb' *s* jamba de puerta
door'knob' *s* botón *m* de puerta, pomo de puerta
door knocker *s* aldaba
door latch *s* pestillo
door•man ['dormən] *s* (*pl* **-men** [mən]) portero; (*one who helps people in and out of cars*) abrecoches *m*
door'mat' *s* felpudo de puerta
door'nail' *s* clavo de adorno para puertas; **dead as a doornail** (coll) muerto sin duda alguna
door'post' *s* jamba de puerta

door scraper *s* limpiabarros *m*
door′sill′ *s* umbral *m*
door′step′ *s* escalón *m* delante de la puerta; escalera exterior
door′stop′ *s* tope *m* de puerta
door′-to-door′ *adj & adv* de puerta a puerta
door′way′ *s* puerta, portal *m*
dope [dop] *s* grasa lubricante; (aer) barniz *m,* nobabia; (slang) bobo, tonto; (slang) informes *mpl;* (slang) narcótico ‖ *tr* (slang) narcotizar, drogar; **to dope out** (slang) descifrar
dope fiend *s* (slang) toxicómano
dope sheet *s* (slang) hoja confidencial sobre los caballos de carreras
dormant [ˈdɔrmənt] *adj* durmiente, latente
dormer window [ˈdɔrmər] *s* buharda, buhardilla
dormito•ry [ˈdɔrmɪ,tori] *s* (*pl* **-ries**) dormitorio común; (*in a university*) residencia de estudiantes, colegio mayor (Esp)
dor•mouse [ˈdɔr,maʊs] *s* (*pl* **-mice** [,maɪs]) lirón *m*
dosage [ˈdosɪdʒ] *s* dosificación
dose [dos] *s* dosis *f;* (coll) mal trago ‖ *tr* medicinar; dosificar (*un medicamento*)
dossier [ˈdɑsɪ,e] *s* expediente *m*
dot [dɑt] *s* punto; **on the dot** (coll) en punto ‖ *v* (*pret & pp* **dotted;** *ger* **dotting**) *tr* (*to make with dots*) puntear; poner punto a; **to dot one's i's** poner los puntos sobre las íes
dotage [ˈdotɪdʒ] *s* chochera, chochez *f;* **to be in one's dotage** chochear
dotard [ˈdotərd] *s* viejo chocho
dot-com [ˈdɑtˈkɑm] *s* (compu) .com (*puntocom*) ‖ *adv* por la internet
dote [dot] *intr* chochear; **to dote on** estar chocho por
doting [ˈdotɪŋ] *adj* chocho
dot matrix [ˈmetrɪks] *s* matriz *f* de puntos
dot′-matrix printer *s* impresora matricial
dots and dashes *spl* (telg) puntos y rayas
dotted line [ˈdɑtɪd] *s* línea de puntos; **to sign on the dotted line** firmar un acuerdo
double [ˈdʌbəl] *adj* doble ‖ *adv* doble; dos juntos ‖ *s* doble *m,* duplo; (mov, theat) doble *mf;* **doubles** (tennis juego de dobles ‖ *tr* doblar; ser el doble de; (bridge) doblar ‖ *intr* doblarse; (mov, theat, bridge) doblar; **to double up** doblarse en dos; ocupar una misma habitación, dormir en una misma cama (*dos personas*)
double agent *s* doble agente *mf*
double-barreled [ˈdʌbəlˈbærəld] *adj* de dos cañones; (fig) para dos fines
double bass [bes] *s* contrabajo
double bassoon *s* contrabajón *m*
double bed *s* cama de matrimonio
double boiler *s* baño (de) María
double-breasted [ˈdʌbəlˈbrɛstɪd] *adj* cruzado, de dos pechos
double chin *s* papada, doble barba
double click *s* (compu) doble cliquear *m,* doble clic *m*
dou′ble-cross′ *tr* traicionar (*a un cómplice*)
double date *s* cita de dos parejas
doub′le-deal′er *s* embustero, impostor *m*
double dealing *s* doble juego
double-edged [ˈdʌbəlˈɛdʒd] *adj* de dos filos
double entry *s* (com) partida doble
doub′le-en′try bookkeeping *s* doble contabilidad
double feature *s* (mov) programa *m* doble, programa de dos películas de largo metraje
doubleheader [ˈdʌbəlˈhɛdər] *s* tren *m* con dos locomotoras; (baseball) dos partidos jugados sucesivamente
double-jointed [ˈdʌbəlˈdʒɔɪntɪd] *adj* de articulaciones dobles
dou′ble-park′ *tr & intr* aparcar en doble fila
dou′ble-quick′ *adj & adv* a paso ligero ‖ *s* paso ligero ‖ *intr* marchar a paso ligero
doublet [ˈdʌblɪt] *s* (*close-fitting jacket*) jubón *m;* (*counterfeit stone; each of two words having the same origin*) doblete *m*
double talk *s* (coll) galimatías *m;* (coll) habla ambigua para engañar
double time *s* pago doble por horas extraordinarias de trabajo; (mil) paso redoblado
doubleton [ˈdʌbəltən] *s* doblete *m*
double track *s* doble vía
doubling [ˈdʌbliŋ] *s* reduplicación
doubt [daʊt] *s* duda; **beyond doubt** sin duda; **if in doubt** en caso de duda; **no doubt** sin duda ‖ *tr* dudar, dudar de ‖ *intr* dudar
doubter [ˈdaʊtər] *s* incrédulo
doubtful [ˈdaʊtfəl] *adj* dudoso
doubtless [ˈdaʊtlɪs] *adj* indudable ‖ *adv* sin duda; probablemente
douche [duʃ] *s* ducha; (*instrument*) jeringa ‖ *tr* duchar ‖ *intr* ducharse
dough [do] *s* masa, pasta; (*money*) (slang) pasta
dough′boy′ *s* (coll) soldado norteamericano de infantería
dough′nut′ *s* rosquilla, buñuelo
dough•ty [ˈdaʊti] *adj* (*comp* **-tier;** *super* **-tiest**) (hum) fuerte, valiente
dough•y [ˈdo•i] *adj* (*comp* **-ier;** *super* **-iest**) pastoso
dour [daʊr] o [dʊr] *adj* triste, melancólico, austero
douse [daʊs] *tr* empapar, mojar, salpicar; (slang) apagar (*la luz*)
dove [dʌv] *s* paloma
dovecote [ˈdʌv,kot] *s* palomar *m*
dove′tail′ *s* cola de milano, cola de pato ‖ *tr* ensamblar a cola de milano, ensamblar a cola de pato; (*to make fit*) encajar ‖ *intr* (*to fit*) encajar; concordar, corresponder
dowager [ˈdaʊ•ədʒər] *s* viuda con título o bienes que proceden del marido, p.ej., **dowager duchess** duquesa viuda; (coll) matrona, señora anciana respetable
dow•dy [ˈdaʊdi] *adj* (*comp* **-dier;** *super* **-diest**) desaliñado
dow•el [ˈdaʊ•əl] *s* clavija ‖ *v* (*pret & pp* **-eled** o **-elled;** *ger* **-eling** o **-elling**) *tr* enclavijar

dower [ˈdaʊ•ər] *s* (*widow's portion*) viudedad; (*marriage portion*) dote *m & f;* (*natural gift*) prenda ‖ *tr* señalar viudedad a; dotar

down [daʊn] *adj* descendente; abatido, triste; enfermo, malo; acostado, echado; (*money, payment*) anticipado; (*storage battery*) agotado; (mach) (coll) fuera de servicio ‖ *adv* abajo; hacia abajo; en tierra; al sur; por escrito; al contado; **down and out** arruinado; sin blanca; **down from** desde; **down on one's knees** de rodillas: **down to** hasta; **down under** entre los antípodas; **down with . . . !** ¡abajo . . . !; **to get down to work** aplicarse resueltamente al trabajo; **to go down** bajar; **to lie down** acostarse; **to sit down** sentarse ‖ *prep* bajando; **down the river** río abajo; **down the street** calle abajo ‖ *s* (*of fruit and human body*) vello; (*of birds*) plumón *m;* descenso, revés *m* de fortuna; (*sand hill*) duna ‖ *tr* derribar; (coll) tragar

down'cast' *adj* cariacontecido

down'fall' *s* caída, ruina; chaparrón *m;* nevazo

down'grade' *adj* (coll) pendiente, en declive ‖ *adv* (coll) cuesta abajo ‖ *s* bajada, declive *m;* **to be on the downgrade** decaer, declinar ‖ *tr* disminuir la categoría de

downhearted [ˈdaʊn,hɑrtɪd] *adj* abatido, desanimado

down'hill' *adj* pendiente ‖ *adv* cuesta abajo; **to go downhill** ir cabeza abajo

downhill skiing *s* esquí *m* alpino

down'link *s* (aerosp) transmisión de datos del satélite a la tierra

down'load *tr* (compu) trasvasar, descargar, bajar

down'pour' *s* aguacero, chaparrón *m*

down'right' *adj* absoluto, categórico; franco; claro ‖ *adv* absolutamente

down'stairs' *adj* de abajo ‖ *adv* abajo ‖ *s* piso inferior, pisos inferiores; (*the help*) la servidumbre

down'stream' *adv* aguas abajo, río abajo

down'stroke' *s* carrera descendente

down'town' *adj* céntrico ‖ *adv* al centro de la ciudad, en el centro de la ciudad ‖ *s* barrios céntricos, calles céntricas

down train *s* tren *m* descendente

down'trend' *s* tendencia a la baja

downtrodden [ˈdaʊn,trɑdən] *adj* pisoteado, oprimido

downward [ˈdaʊnwərd] *adj* descendente ‖ *adv* hacia abajo; hacia una época posterior

down•y [ˈdaʊni] *adj* (*comp* **-ier;** *super* **-iest**) plumoso, felpudo, velloso; suave, blando

dow•ry [ˈdaʊri] *s* (*pl* **-ries**) dote *m & f*

doz. *abbr* **dozen**

doze [doz] *s* duermevela, sueño ligero ‖ *intr* dormitar

dozen [ˈdʌzən] *s* docena

dozy [ˈdozi] *adj* soñoliento

D.P. *abbr* **displaced person**

dpt. *abbr* **department**

dr. *abbr* **debtor, drawer, dram**

Dr. *abbr* **debtor, Doctor**

drab [dræb] *adj* (*comp* **drabber;** *super* **drabbest**) gris amarillento; monótono ‖ *s* gris amarillento; ramera; mujer desaliñada

drach•ma [ˈdrækmə] *s* (*pl* **-mas** o **-mae** [mi]) dracma

draft [dræft] *s* corriente *f* de aire; (*pulling; current of air in a chimney*) tiro; (*sketch, outline*) bosquejo; (*first form of a writing*) borrador *m;* (*drink*) bebida, trago; (com) giro, letra de cambio, libranza; aire inspirado; (naut) calado; (mil) conscripción, quinta; **drafts** damas, juego de damas; **on draft** a presión; **to be exempted from the draft** redimirse de las quintas ‖ *tr* dibujar; bosquejar; hacer un borrador de; redactar (*un documento*); (mil) quintar; **to be drafted** (mil) ir a quintas

draft age *s* edad *f* de quintas

draft beer *s* cerveza a presión

draft board *s* (mil) junta de reclutamiento

draft call *s* llamada a quintas

draft dodger [ˈdɑdʒər] *s* emboscado

draftee [,dræfˈti] *s* conscripto, quinto

draft horse *s* caballo de tiro

drafting room *s* sala de dibujo

drafts•man [ˈdræftsmən] *s* (*pl* **-men** [mən]) dibujante *m;* (*man who draws up documents*) redactor *m;* (*in checkers*) peón *m*

draft treaty *s* proyecto de convenio

draft•y [ˈdræfti] *adj* (*comp* **-ier;** *super* **-iest**) airoso, con corrientes de aire

drag [dræg] *s* (*sledge for conveying heavy bodies*) narria; (*on a cigarette*) chupada; fumada; (naut) rastra; (aer) resistencia al avance; (fig) estorbo, impedimento; **to have a drag** (slang) tener buenas aldabas, tener enchufe ‖ *v* (*pret & pp* **dragged;** *ger* **dragging**) *tr* arrastrar; (naut) rastrear ‖ *intr* arrastrarse por el suelo; avanzar muy lentamente; decaer (*el interés*); **to drag on** ser interminable, prolongarse interminablemente

drag and drop *intr* (comp) arrastrar y soltar

drag'net' *s* red barredera

dragon [ˈdrægən] *s* dragón *m*

drag'on-fly' *s* (*pl* **-flies**) caballito del diablo, libélula

dragoon [drəˈgun] *s* (*soldier*) dragón *m* ‖ *tr* tiranizar; forzar, constreñir

drain [dren] *s* dren *m,* desaguadero, desagüe *m;* (surg) dren *m;* (*source of continual expense*) (fig) desaguadero ‖ *tr* drenar, desaguar; avenar (*terrenos húmedos*); escurrir (*una vasija; un líquido*) ‖ *intr* desaguarse; escurrirse

drainage [ˈdrenɪdʒ] *s* drenaje *m,* desagüe *m*

drain'board' *s* escurridero

drain cock *s* llave *f* de purga

drain'pipe' *s* tubo de desagüe, escurridero

drain plug *s* tapón *m* de desagüe; (aut) tapón de vaciado

drake [drek] *s* pato

dram [dræm] *s* dracma; trago de aguardiente

drama [ˈdrɑmə] o [ˈdræmə] *s* drama *m;* (*art and genre*) dramática

dramatic [drəˈmætɪk] *adj* dramático ‖ **dramatics** *ssg* representación de aficionados; *spl* obras representadas por aficionados
dramatist [ˈdræmətɪst] *s* dramático
dramatize [ˈdræməˌtaɪz] *tr* dramatizar
dram'shop' *s* bar *m,* taberna
drape [drep] *s* cortina, colgadura; (*hang of a curtain, skirt, etc.*) caída ‖ *tr* cubrir con colgaduras; adornar con colgaduras; disponer los pliegues de (*una colgadura, una prenda de vestir*)
draper•y [ˈdrepəri] *s* (*pl* **-ies**) colgaduras, ropaje *m*
drastic [ˈdræstɪk] *adj* drástico
draught [dræft] *s & tr* var de **draft**
draught beer *s* cerveza a presión
draw [drɔ] *s* (*in a game or other contest*) empate *m;* (*in chess or checkers*) tablas; (*in a lottery*) sorteo; (*card drawn from the bank*) robo; (*of a drawbridge*) compuerta; (*of a chimney*) tiro ‖ *v* (*pret* **drew** [dru]; *pp* **drawn** [drɔn]) *tr* tirar (*una línea; alambre*); (*to attract*) tirar; (*to pull*) tirar de; derretir (*la mantequilla*); sacar (*un clavo, una espada, agua, una conclusión*); atraerse (*aplausos*); atraer (*a la gente*); aspirar (*el aire*); llamar (*la atención*); dar (*un suspiro*); correr (*una cortina*); cobrar (*un salario*); sacarse (*un premio*); empatar (*una partida*); robar (*fichas, naipes*); levantar (*un puente levadizo*); calar (*un buque cierta profundidad*); hacer (*una comparación*); consumir (*amperios*); (*to sketch in lines*) dibujar; (*to sketch in words*) redactar; (com) girar, librar; (com) devengar (*interés*); **to draw forth** hacer salir; **to draw off** sacar, extraer; trasegar (*un líquido*); **to draw on** ocasionar, provocar; ponerse (*p.ej., los zapatos*); (com) girar a cargo de; **to draw oneself up** enderezarse con dignidad; **to draw out** (*to persuade to talk*) sonsacar, tirar de la lengua a; **to draw up** redactar (*un documento*); (mil) ordenar para el combate ‖ *intr* tirar, tirar bien (*una chimenea*); empatar; echar suertes; atraer mucha gente; dibujar; **to draw aside** apartarse; **to draw back** retroceder, retirarse; **to draw near** acercarse; acercarse a; **to draw to a close** estar para terminar; **to draw together** juntarse, unirse
draw'back' *s* desventaja, inconveniente *m*
draw'bridge' *s* puente levadizo
drawee [ˌdrɔˈi] *s* girado, librado
drawer [ˈdrɔ•ər] *s* dibujante *mf;* (com) girador *m,* librador *m* ‖ [drɔr] *s* cajón *m,* gaveta; **drawers** calzoncillos
drawing [ˈdrɔ•ɪŋ] *s* dibujo; (*in a lottery*) sorteo
drawing board *s* tablero de dibujo
drawing card *s* polo de atracción popular
drawing room *s* sala, salón *m*
draw'knife' *s* (*pl* **-knives** [ˌnaɪvz]) cuchilla de dos mangos
drawl [drɔl] *s* habla lenta y prolongada ‖ *tr* decir lenta y prolongadamente ‖ *intr* hablar lenta y prolongadamente
drawn butter [drɔn] *s* mantequilla derretida
drawn work *s* calado, deshilado
dray [dre] *s* carro fuerte, camión *m;* (*sledge*) narria
drayage [ˈdre•ɪdʒ] *s* acarreo
dread [drɛd] *adj* espantoso, terrible ‖ *s* pavor *m,* terror *m* ‖ *tr & intr* temer
dreadful [ˈdrɛdfəl] *adj* espantoso, terrible; (coll) feo, desagradable
dread'naught' *s* (nav) gran buque acorazado
dream [drim] *s* sueño, ensueño; (*thing of great beauty*) sueño; (*fancy, illusion*) ensueño; **dream come true** sueño hecho realidad ‖ *v* (*pret & pp* **dreamed** o **dreamt** [drɛmt]) *tr* soñar; **to dream up** (coll) imaginar, inventar; ‖ *intr* soñar; **to dream of** soñar con
dreamer [ˈdrimər] *s* soñador *m*
dream'land' *s* reino del ensueño
dream'world' *s* tierra de la fantasía
dream•y [ˈdrimi] *adj* (*comp* **-ier;** *super* **-iest**) soñador; visionario; vago
drear•y [ˈdrɪri] *adj* (*comp* **-ier;** *super* **-iest**) sombrío, triste; monótono, pesado
dredge [drɛdʒ] *s* draga ‖ *tr* dragar, rastrear; (culin) enharinar, rebozar; **to dredge up** (*scandal*) desenterrar
dredger [ˈdrɛdʒər] *s* draga (*barco*)
dredging [ˈdrɛdʒɪŋ] *s* dragado
dregs [drɛgz] *spl* heces *fpl;* (*of society*) hez *f*
drench [drɛntʃ] *tr* mojar, empapar
dress [drɛs] *s* ropa, vestidos; vestido de mujer; (*skirt*) falda; traje *m* de etiqueta; (*of a bird*) plumaje *m* ‖ *tr* vestir; (*to provide with clothing*) trajear; peinar (*el pelo*); curar (*una herida*); zurrar (*el cuero*); empavesar (*un barco*); adornar, ataviar; aderezar, aliñar (*los manjares*); **to dress down** (coll) reprender; **to get dressed** vestirse ‖ *intr* (*to put one's clothing on*) vestirse; (*to wear clothes*) vestir; (mil) alinearse; **to dress up** vestirse de etiqueta; ponerse de veinticinco alfileres; disfrazarse
dress ball *s* baile *m* de etiqueta
dress coat *s* frac *m*
dresser [ˈdrɛsər] *s* tocador *m;* cómoda con espejo; (*sideboard*) aparador *m;* **to be a good dresser** vestir con elegancia
dress form *s* maniquí *m*
dress goods *spl* géneros para vestidos
dressing [ˈdrɛsɪŋ] *s* adorno; (*for food*) aliño, salsa; (*stuffing for fowl*) relleno; (*fertilizer*) abono; (*for a wound*) vendaje *m*
dress'ing-down' *s* (coll) repasata, regaño
dressing gown *s* bata, peinador *m*
dressing room *s* cuarto de vestir; (theat) camarín *m*
dressing station *s* (mil) puesto de socorro
dressing table *s* tocador *m;* peinador *m*
dress'mak'er *s* costurera, modista
dress'mak'ing *s* costura, modistería
dressmaking school *s* academia de corte y confección
dress rehearsal *s* ensayo general

dress shirt *s* camisa de pechera almidonada, camisa de pechera de encaje
dress shop *s* casa de modas
dress suit *s* traje *m* de etiqueta
dress tie *s* corbata de smoking, corbata de frac
dress·y [ˈdrɛsi] *adj* (*comp* **-ier;** *super* **-iest**) (coll) elegante; (*showy*) acicalado, vistoso, peripuesto
dribble [ˈdrɪbəl] *s* goteo; (coll) llovizna ‖ *tr* (sport) driblar ‖ *intr* gotear; (*at the mouth*) babear; (sport) driblar
driblet [ˈdrɪblɪt] *s* gotita; pedacito
dried beef [draɪd] *s* cecina
dried fig *s* higo paso
dried fruit *s* fruta seca
dried peach *s* orejón *m*
drier [ˈdraɪ·ər] *s* enjugador *m;* (*for hair*) secador *m;* (*for clothes*) secadora; (*rack for drying clothes*) tendedero (de ropa)
drift [drɪft] *s* movimiento; (*of sand, snow*) montón *m;* (*movement of snow*) ventisca; tendencia, dirección; intención, sentido; (aer, naut) deriva; (rad, telv) desviación ‖ *intr* flotar a la deriva; amontonarse (*la nieve*); ventiscar; (aer, naut) derivar, ir a la deriva; (fig) vivir sin rumbo
drift ice *s* hielo flotante
driftʹwoodʹ *s* madera flotante; madera llevada por el agua; madera arrojada a la playa por el agua; (*people*) vagos
drill [drɪl] *s* taladro; instrucción; (*fabric*) dril *m;* (mil) ejercicio ‖ *tr* taladrar; instruir; (mil) enseñar el ejercicio a ‖ *intr* adiestrarse; (mil) hacer el ejercicio
drilling rig *s* torre *f* de perforación
drillʹmasʹter *s* amaestrador *m;* (mil) instructor *m*
drill press *s* prensa taladradora
drink [drɪŋk] *s* bebida; **the drinks are on the house!** ¡convida la casa! ‖ *v* (*pret* **drank** [dræŋk]; *pp* **drunk** [drʌŋk]) *tr* beber; beberse (*su sueldo*); **to drink down** beber de una vez; **to drink in** beber (*las palabras de una persona*); beberse (*un libro*); aspirar (*el aire*) ‖ *intr* beber; **to drink out of** beber de o en; **to drink to the health of** beber a o por la salud de
drinkable [ˈdrɪŋkəbəl] *adj* bebedizo, potable
drinker [ˈdrɪŋkər] *s* bebedor *m*
drinking [ˈdrɪŋkɪŋ] *s* (el) beber
drinking cup *s* taza para beber
drinking fountain *s* fuente *f* para beber
drinking song *s* canción báquica, canción de taberna
drinking spree *s* bebezón *m;* bimba (Mex)
drinking trough *s* abrevadero
drinking water *s* agua para beber, agua potable
drip [drɪp] *s* goteo; gotas; (med) gota a gota, gotero ‖ *v* (*pret & pp* **dripped;** *ger* **dripping**) *intr* caer gota a gota, gotear
drip coffee *s* café *m* de maquinilla, café de recuelo
dripʹ-dryʹ *adj* de lava y pon
drip pan *s* colector *m* de aceite
drive [draɪv] *s* paseo en coche; calzada; fuerza, vigor *m;* urgencia; campaña vigorosa; venta a bajo precio; (aut) tracción (*delantera o trasera*); (mach) transmissión, mando ‖ *v* (*pret* **drove** [drov]; *pp* **driven** [ˈdrɪvən]) *tr* conducir, guiar, manejar (*un automóvil*); clavar, hincar (*un clavo*); arrear (*a las bestias*); (*in a carriage or auto*) llevar (*a una persona*); empujar, impeler; estimular; forzar, compeler; obligar a trabajar mucho; (sport) golpear con gran fuerza; **to drive away** ahuyentar; **to drive away** ahuyentar; **to drive back** rechazar; **to drive mad** volver loco ‖ *intr* ir en coche; **to drive at** aspirar a; querer decir; **to drive hard** trabajar mucho; **to drive in** entrar en coche; entrar en (*un sitio*) en coche; **to drive on the right** circular por la derecha; **to drive out** salir en coche; **to drive up** llegar en coche
drive-in restaurant [ˈdraɪv,ɪn] *s* parador *m* de carretera
drive-in theater *s* auto-teatro, motocine *m;* autocine *m* (Chile, Cuba); autocínema *f* (Mex)
driv·el [ˈdrɪvəl] *s* (*slobber*) baba; (*nonsense*) bobería ‖ *v* (*pret* **-eled** o **-elled;** *ger* **eling** o **-elling**) *intr* babear; (*to talk nonsense*) bobear
driver [ˈdraɪvər] *s* conductor *m;* (*of a carriage*) cochero; (*of a locomotive*) maquinista *m;* (*of pack animals*) arriero; (*golf club*) madera número 1; (compu) controlador *m;* driver *m*
driver's license *s* licencia de conducción, de conducir *or* de manejar, permiso de conducir o de conducción, carné de conducir, conductor, chófer *or* manejo
drive shaft *s* árbol *m* de mando, eje *m* motor
driveʹwayʹ *s* calzada; camino de entrada para coches
drive wheel *s* rueda motriz
driveʹ-your·selfʹ service *s* alquiler *m* sin chófer
driving range *s* *campo de golf diseñado para practicar tiros de salida*
driving school *s* auto-escuela, academia de choferes
drizzle [ˈdrɪzəl] *s* llovizna ‖ *intr* lloviznar, garnar
droll [drol] *adj* chusco, gracioso
dromedar·y [ˈdrɑmə,dɛri] *s* (*pl* **-ies**) dromedario
drone [dron] *s* zángano; (*buzz, hum*) zumbido; (*of bagpipe*) bordón *m,* roncón *m;* avión radiodirigido ‖ *tr* decir monótonamente ‖ *intr* hablar monótonamente; (*to live in idleness*) zanganear; (*to buzz, hum*) zumbar
drool [drul] *s* (*slobber*) baba; (slang) bobería ‖ *intr* babear; (slang) bobear
droop [drup] *s* inclinación ‖ *intr* caer, colgar; inclinarse; marchitarse; abatirse; encamarse (*el grano*)
drooping [ˈdrupɪŋ] *adj* (*eyelid, shoulder*) caído
drop [drɑp] *s* gota; (*slope*) pendiente *f;* (*earring*) pendiente *m;* (*in temperature*) descenso; (*of supplies from an airplane*) lan-

zamiento; (*trap door*) escotillón *m;* (*gallows*) horca; (*lozenge*) pastilla; (*small amount*) chispa; (*slit for letters*) buzón *m;* (*curtain*) telón *m;* **a drop in the bucket** una gota en el mar; **drops** (pharm) gotas || *v* (*pret & pp* **dropped;** *ger* **dropping**) *tr* dejar caer; echar (*una carta*) al buzón; bajar (*una cortina*); soltar (*una indirecta*); escribir (*una esquela*); omitir, suprimir; abandonar, dejar; echar (*el ancla*); borrar de la lista (*a un alumno*); lanzar (*bombas o suministros de un avión*) || *intr* caer; bajar; cesar, terminar; **to drop dead** caer muerto; **to drop in** entrar al pasar, visitar de paso; **to drop off** desaparecer; quedarse dormido; morir de repente; **to drop out** desaparecer; retirarse; darse de baja

drop curtain *s* telón *m*

drop hammer *s* martinete *m*

drop in value *s* minusvalía

drop'kick' *s* (sport) patada voladora

drop'-leaf' table *s* mesa de hoja plegadiza

droplet [ˋdrɑplɛt] *s* gotita

drop'light' *s* lámpara colgante

drop'out' *s* fracasado, desertor *m* escolar; **to become a dropout** ahorcar los libros

dropper [ˋdrɑpər] *s* cuentagotas *m,* gotero

drop shutter *s* obturador *m* de guillotina

dropsical [ˋdrɑpsɪkəl] *adj* hidropico

dropsy [ˋdrɑpsi] *s* hidropesía

drop table *s* mesa perezosa

dross [drɔs] o [drɑs] *s* (*of metals*) escoria; (fig) escoria, hez *f*

drought [draʊt] *s* (*long period of dry weather*) sequía; (*dryness*) sequedad

drove [drov] *s* manada, rebaño, hato; gentío, multitud

drover [ˋdrovər] *s* ganadero

drown [draʊn] *tr* ahogar; (*inundate*) anegar || *intr* ahogarse; anegarse

drowse [draʊz] *intr* adormecerse, amodorrarse

drow•sy [ˋdraʊzi] *adj* (*comp* **-sier;** *super* **-siest**) soñoliento, modorro

drub [drʌb] *v* (*pret & pp* **drubbed;** *ger* **drubbing**) *tr* apalear, pegar, tundir; derrotar completamente

drudge [drʌdʒ] *s* yunque *m,* esclavo del trabajo || *intr* afanarse

drudger•y [ˋdrʌdʒəri] *s* (*pl* **-ies**) trabajo penoso

drug [drʌg] *s* droga, medicamento; narcótico; **drug on the market** macana, artículo invendible || *v* (*pret & pp* **drugged;** *ger* **drugging**) *tr* narcotizar; mezclar con drogas

drug addict *s* toxicómano, drogadicto; (coll) yonquí *m*

drug'-ad•dict'ed *adj* drogadicto

drug addiction *s* toxicomania

drug dealer *s* narcotraficante *mf*

druggist [ˋdrʌgɪst] *s* boticario, farmacéutico

drug habit *s* vicio de los narcóticos

drug store *s* farmacia, botica, droguería

drug test *s* control *m* antidoping

drug traffic *s* contrabando de narcóticos

druid [ˋdru•ɪd] *s* druida *m*

drum [drʌm] *s* (*cylinder; instrument of percussion*) tambor *m;* (*container for oil, gasoline, etc.*) bidón *m* || *v* (*pret & pp* **drummed;** *ger* **drumming**) *tr* reunir a toque de tambor; **to drum up trade** fomentar ventas || *intr* tocar el tambor; (*with the fingers*) teclear

drum'beat' *s* toque *m* de tambor

drum brake *s* freno de tambor

drum corps *s* banda de tambores

drum'fire' *s* fuego graneado, fuego nutrido

drum'head' *s* parche *m* de tambor

drum major *s* tambor *m* mayor

drummer [ˋdrʌmər] *s* tambor *m,* baterista *mf,* tamborilero; agente viajero

drum'stick' *s* baqueta, palillo; (coll) muslo (*de ave cocida*)

drunk [drʌŋk] *adj* borracho; bolo (CAm, Mex); **to get drunk** emborracharse; coger una turca; embolarse (CAm, Mex) enchicharse (SAm) || *s* (coll) borracho; (*spree*) (coll) borrachera

drunkard [ˋdrʌŋkərd] *s* borrachín *m*

drunken [ˋdrʌŋkən] *adj* borracho

drunk driver *s* conductor *m* en estado de embriaguez

drunken driving *s* — **to be arrested for drunken driving** ser arrestado por conducir en estado de embriaguez

drunkenness [ˋdrʌŋkənnɪs] *s* embriaguez *f;* bimba (Mex)

dry [draɪ] *adj* (*comp* **drier;** *super* **driest**) seco; (*thirsty*) sediento; (*dull, boring*) árido || *s* (*pl* **drys**) (*prohibitionist*) (coll) seco || *v* (*pret & pp* **dried**) *tr* secar; (*to wipe dry*) enjugar || *intr* secarse; **to dry up** secarse completamente; (slang) callar, dejar de hablar

dry cell *s* pila seca

dry'-clean' *tr* lavar en seco, limpiar en seco

dry cleaner *s* tintorero

dry cleaning *s* lavado a seco, limpieza en seco

dry'-clean'ing establishment *s* tintorería

dry dock *s* dique seco, varadero

dryer [ˋdraɪ•ər] *s* var de **drier**

dry'eyed' —*adj* ojienjuto

dry farming *s* cultivo de secano

dry goods *spl* mercancías de tejidos y de confección

dry ice *s* carbohielo, hielo seco

dry measure *s* medida para áridos

dryness [ˋdraɪnɪs] *s* sequedad; (*e.g., of a speaker*) aridez *f*

dry nurse *s* ama seca

dry season *s* estación de la seca

dry wash *s* ropa lavada y secada pero no planchada

d.s. *abbr* **days after sight, daylight saving**

D.S.T. *abbr* **Daylight Saving Time**

dual [ˋdju•ə] o [ˋdu•əl] *adj & s* dual *m*

dual axle *s* eje tandem

dual citizenship *s* doble nacionalidad

duali•ty [djuˋælɪti] *s* (*pl* **-ties**) dualidad

dub [dʌb] *s* (slang) jugador *m* torpe || *v* (*pret & pp* **dubbed;** *ger* **dubbing**) *tr* apellidar; armar caballero; (mov) doblar

dubbing [ˈdʌbɪŋ] *s* doblado, doblaje *m*
dubious [ˈdubɪ•əs] *adj* dudoso
ducat [ˈdʌkət] *s* ducado
duchess [ˈdʌtʃɪs] *s* duquesa
duch•y [ˈdʌtʃi] *s* (*pl* **-ies**) ducado
duck [dʌk] *s* pato; (*female*) pata; agachada rápida; (*in the water*) zambullida; **ducks** (coll) pantalones *mpl* de dril ‖ *tr* bajar rápidamente (*la cabeza*); (*in water*) chapuzar; (coll) esquivar, evitar (*un golpe*) ‖ *intr* chapuzar; **to duck out** (coll) escabullirse
duck′-toed′ *adj* zancajoso
duct [dʌkt] *s* conducto, canal *m*
ductile [ˈdʌktɪl] *adj* dúctil
ductless gland [ˈdʌktlɪs] *s* glándula cerrada
duct′work′ *s* canalización
dud [dʌd] *s* (slang) bomba que no estalla; (slang) fracaso; **duds** (coll) trapos, prendas de vestir
dude [dud] *s* caballerete *m*
due [dju] o [du] *adj* debido; aguardado, esperado; pagadero; **due to** debido a; **to fall due** vencer; **when is the train due?** ¿a qué hora debe llegar el tren? ‖ *adv* directamente, derecho ‖ *s* deuda; **dues** derechos; (*of a member*) cuota; **to get one's due** llevar su merecido; **to give the devil his due** ser justo hasta con el diablo
due date *s* fecha de vencimiento
duel [ˈdju•əl] o [ˈdu•əl] *s* duelo; **to fight a duel** batirse en duelo ‖ *v* (*pret & pp* **dueled** o **duelled;** *ger* **dueling** o **duelling**) *intr* batirse en duelo
duelist o **duellist** [ˈdju•əlɪst] o [ˈduəlɪst] *s* duelista *m*
dues-paying [ˈdjuz,pe•ɪŋ] o [ˈduz,peɪŋ] *adj* cotizante
duet [djuˈɛt] o [duˈɛt] *s* dúo
duke [djuk] *s* duque *m*
dukedom [ˈdjukdəm] *s* ducado
dull [dʌl] *adj* (*not sharp*) embotado, romo; (*color*) apagado; (*sound; pain*) sordo; (*stupid*) lerdo, torpe; (*business*) inactivo, muerto; (*boring*) aburrido, tedioso; (*flat*) deslucido, deslustrado ‖ *tr* embotar, enromar; deslucir, deslustrar; enfriar (*el entusiasmo*) ‖ *intr* embotarse, enromarse; deslucirse, deslustrarse
dullard [ˈdʌlərd] *s* estúpido
duly [ˈdjuli] o [ˈduli] *adv* debidamente
dumb [dʌm] *adj* (*lacking the power to speak*) mudo; (coll) estúpido, torpe
dumb′bell′ *s* halterio; (slang) estúpido, tonto
dumb creature *s* animal *m,* bruto
dumb show *s* pantomima
dumb′wait′er *s* montaplatos *m*
dumdum bullet [ˈdʌmdʌm] *s* bala expansiva
dumfound [,dʌmˈfaʊnd] *tr* pasmar, dejar sin habla
dum•my [ˈdʌmi] *adj* falso, fingido, simulado ‖ *s* (*pl* **-mies**) (*dress form*) maniquí *m;* cabeza para pelucas; (*in card games*) muerto; cartas del muerto; (*figurehead, straw man*) testaferro; (*skeleton copy of a book*) maqueta; imitación, copia; (slang) estúpido
dump [dʌmp] *s* basurero, vertedero; montón *m* de basuras; (compu) vuelco; (mil) deposito de municiones; (min) terrero; **to be down in the dumps** (coll) tener murria ‖ *tr* descargar, verter; vaciar de golpe; vender en grandes cantidades y a precios inferiores a los corrientes
dumping [ˈdʌmpɪŋ] *s* descarga, vertido; venta en grandes cantidades y a precios inferiores a los corrientes
dumpling [ˈdʌmplɪŋ] *s* bola de pasta rellena de fruta o carne
dump truck *s* camión *m* volquete
dump•y [ˈdʌmpi] *adj* (*comp* **-ier;** *super* **-iest**) regordete, rollizo
dun [dʌn] *adj* bruno, pardo, castaño ‖ *s* acreedor importuno; (*demand for payment*) apremio ‖ *v* (*pret & pp* **dunner;** *ger* **dunning**) *tr* importunar para el pago, apremiar (*a un deudor*)
dunce [dʌns] *s* zopenco, bodoque *m*
dunce cap *s* capirote *m* que se le pone al alumno torpe
dune [djun] o [dun] *s* duna, médano
dung [dʌŋ] *s* estiércol *m* ‖ *tr* estercolar
dungarees [,dʌŋgəˈriz] *spl* (*jeans*) jeans *mpl,* vaqueros, pantalones *mpl* de peto; (*workmen's*) overal *m,* mono (Esp)
dungeon [ˈdʌndʒən] *s* calabozo, mazmorra; (*fortified tower of medieval castle*) torre *f* del homenaje
dung′hill′ *s* estercolar *m;* lugar inmundo
dunk [dʌŋk] *s* (basketball) clavada (*canasta marcada metiendo el balón con fuerza desde arriba*) ‖ *tr* sopetear, ensopar; (basketball) clavar
duo [ˈdju•o] o [ˈdu•o] *s* dúo
duode•num [,du•əˈdinəm] *s* (*pl* **-na** [nə]) duodeno
dupe [djup] o [dup] *s* víctima, primo, inocentón *m* ‖ *tr* embaucar, engañar
duplex house [ˈduplɛks] *s* casa para dos familias
duplicate [ˈduplɪkɪt] *adj & s* duplicado; **in duplicate** por duplicado ‖ [ˈduplɪ,ket] *tr* duplicar
duplici•ty [djuˈplɪsɪti] *s* (*pl* **-ties**) duplicidad
durable [ˈdjʊrəbəl] o [ˈdʊrəbəl] *adj* durable, duradero
durable goods *spl* artículos duraderos
duration [djʊˈreʃən] o [dʊˈreʃən] *s* duración
during [ˈdjʊrɪŋ] *prep* durante
dusk [dʌsk] *s* crepúsculo
dust [dʌst] *s* polvo; **to bite the dust** morder el polvo ‖ *tr* (*to free of dust*) desempolvar; (*to sprinkle with dust*) polvorear; **to dust off** desempolvar
dust bowl *s* cuenca de polvo
dust′cloth′ *s* trapo del polvo *or* de sacudir
dust cloud *s* nube *f* de polvo, polvareda
duster [ˈdʌstər] *s* paño, plumero; (*light overgarment*) guardapolvo
dust jacket *s* sobrecubierta
dust′pan′ *s* pala para recoger la basura
dust rag *s* trapo para quitar el polvo

dust storm *s* tolvanera
dust'up *s* pelea
dust•y ['dʌsti] *adj* (*comp* **-ier;** *super* **-iest**) polvoriento; (*grayish*) grisáceo
Dutch [dʌtʃ] *adj* holandés; (slang) alemán || *s* (*language*) holandés *m;* (*language*) (slang) alemán *m;* **in Dutch** (coll) en la desgracia; (slang) en un apuro; **the Dutch** los holandeses; (slang) los alemanes; **to go Dutch** (coll) pagar a escote
Dutch•man ['dʌtʃmən] *s* (*pl* **-men** [mən]) holandés *m;* (slang) alemán *m*
Dutch treat *s* (coll) convite *m* a escote
dutiable ['djutɪ•əbəl] *adj* sujeto a derechos de aduana
dutiful ['djutɪfəl] *adj* obediente, sumiso, solícito
du•ty ['djuti] *s* (*pl* **-ties**) deber *m;* (*task*) faena, quehacer *m;* (*tax*) derechos de aduana; **in the line of duty** en acto de servicio; **off duty** libre; **on duty** de servicio, de guardia; **to do one's duty** cumplir con su deber; **to take up one's duties** entrar en funciones
du'ty-free' *adj* libre de derechos, franquicia aduanera
DVD ['di'vi'di] *s* (letterword) (**digital versatile disc**) DVD *m* (videodisco versátil y digital)
dwarf [dwɔrf] *adj & s* enano || *tr* achicar, empequeñecer || *intr* achicarse, empequeñecerse
dwarfish ['dwɔrfɪʃ] *adj* enano, diminuto
dwell [dwɛl] *v* (*pret & pp* **dwelled** o **dwelt** [dwɛlt]) *intr* vivir, morar; **to dwell on** o **upon** hacer hincapié en
dwelling ['dwɛlɪŋ] *s* morada, vivienda
dwindle ['dwɪndəl] *intr* disminuir; decaer, consumirse
dwt. *abbr* **pennyweight**
dye [daɪ] *s* tinte *m,* tintura, color *m* || *v* (*pret & pp* **dyed;** *ger* **dyeing**) *tr* teñir
dyed-in-the-wool ['daɪdɪnðə,wul] *adj* intransigente
dyeing ['daɪ•ɪŋ] *s* tinte *m,* tintura
dyer ['daɪ•ər] *s* tintorero
dye'stuff' *s* materia, colorante
dying ['daɪ•ɪŋ] *adj* moribundo
dynamic [daɪ'næmɪk] o [dɪ'næmɪk] *adj* dinamico
dynamite ['daɪnə,maɪt] *s* dinamita || *tr* dinamitar
dyna•mo ['daɪnə,mo] *s* (*pl* **-mos**) dínamo *f*
dynast ['daɪnæst] *s* dinasta *m*
dynas•ty ['daɪnəsti] *s* (*pl* **-ties**) dinastía
dysentery ['dɪsən,tɛri] *s* disentería
dysfunction [dɪs'fʌŋʃən] *s* disfunción
dyspepsia [dɪs'pɛpsɪ•ə] o [dɪs'pɛpʃə] *s* dispepsia
dz. *abbr* **dozen**

E

E, e [i] quinta letra del alfabeto inglés
ea. *abbr* **each**
each [itʃ] *adj indef* cada || *pron indef* cada uno; **each other** nos, se; uno a otro, unos a otros || *adv* cada uno; por persona
eager ['igər] *adj* (*enthusiastic*) ardiente, celoso; **eager for** muy deseoso de; **eager to** + *inf* muy deseoso de + *inf*
eagerness ['igərnɪs] *s* ardor *m,* celo; deseo ardiente, empeño
eagle ['igəl] *s* águila
eagle owl *s* buho
ear [ɪr] *s* (*organ and sense of hearing*) oído; (*external part*) oreja; (*of corn*) mazorca; (*of wheat*) espiga; **all ears** con las orejas tan largas; **to be all ears** ser todo oídos, abrir tanto oído; **box on the ear** guantón *m;* **to prick up one's ears** aguzar las orejas; **to turn a deaf ear** hacer o tener oídos de mercader
ear'ache' *s* dolor *m* de oído
ear'drop' *s* arete *m*
ear'drum' *s* tímpano
ear'flap' *s* orejera
earl [ʌrl] *s* conde *m*
earldom ['ʌrldəm] *s* condado
ear•ly ['ʌrli] (*comp* **-lier;** *super* **-liest**) *adj* (*occurring before customary time*) temprano; (*prompt in detecting*) precoz; (*first in a series*) primero; (*far back in time*) primero, remoto, antiguo; (*occurring in near future*) cercano, próximo || *adv* temprano; al principio; en los primeros tiempos; **as early as** (*a certain time of day*) ya a; (*a certain time or date*) ya en; **as early as possible** lo más pronto posible; **early in** (*e.g., the month of December*) ya en; **early in the morning** muy de mañana; **early in the year** a principios del año; **to rise early** madrugar
early bird *s* (coll) madrugador *m*
early mass *s* misa de prima
early riser *s* madrugador *m*
ear'ly-warn'ing *adj* de alerta avanzada
ear'mark' *s* señal *f,* distintivo || *tr* destinar, poner aparte (*para un fin determinado*)
ear'muff' *s* orejera
earn [ʌrn] *tr* ganar, ganarse; (*to get as one's due*) merecerse; (com) devengar (*intereses*) || *intr* ganar; rendir
earned income *s* ingresos en concepto de salario, ingresos por trabajo personal
earnest ['ʌrnɪst] *adj* serio, grave; **in earnest** en serio, de buena fe || *s* arras
earnest money *s* arras
earnings ['ʌrnɪŋz] *s* ganancia; salario, ingresos

ear of corn *s* ilote *m;* chilote (CAm); **green ear of corn** jilote (Mex)
ear′phone′ *s* audífono
ear′piece′ *s* auricular *m*
ear′plug *s* tapón *m* para el oído
ear′ring′ *s* arete *m,* pendiente *m*
ear′shot′ *s* alcance *m* del oído; **within earshot** al alcance del oído
ear′split′ting′ *adj* ensordecedor
earth [ʌrθ] *s* tierra; **to come back to** o **down to earth** bajar de las nubes
earthen [ˋʌrθən] *adj* de tierra; de barro
ear′then•ware′ *s* loza, vasijas de barro
earthly [ˋʌrθli] *adj* terrenal; concebible, posible; **to be of no earthly use** no servir para nada
earth′quake′ *s* terremoto, temblor *m* de tierra
earth′work′ *s* terraplén *m*
earth′worm′ *s* lombriz *f* de tierra
earth•y [ˋʌrθi] *adj* (*comp* **-ier;** *super* **-iest**) terroso; (*worldly*) mundanal; (*unrefined*) grosero; franco, sincero
ear′wax′ *s* cera de los oídos
ease [iz] *s* facilidad; (*readiness, naturalness*) desenvoltura, soltura; (*comfort, well-being*) comodidad, bienestar *m;* **ease of use** (compu) sencillez *f* de manejo; **with ease** con facilidad ‖ *tr* facilitar; aligerar (*un peso*); (*to let up on*) aflojar, soltar; aliviar, mitigar ‖ *intr* aliviarse, mitigarse, disminuir; moderar la marcha
easel [ˋizəl] *s* caballete *m*
easement [ˋizmənt] *s* alivio; (law) servidumbre
easily [ˋizɪli] *adv* fácilmente; suavemente; sin duda; probablemente
easiness [ˋizɪnɪs] *s* facilidad; desenvoltura, soltura; (*e.g., of motion of a machine*) suavidad; indiferencia
east [ist] *adj* oriental, del este ‖ *adv* al este, hacia el este ‖ *s* este *m*
Easter [ˋistər] *s* (eccl) Pascua, Pascua Florida *or* de Resurrección
Easter bunny *s* conejo de Pascua
Easter egg *s* huevo de Pascua (*huevo duro decorado*)
Easter Monday *s* lunes *m* de Pascua de Resurrección
Easter vacation *s* vacaciones de Semana Santa
eastern [ˋistərn] *adj* oriental
East′er•tide′ *s* aleluya *m,* tiempo de Pascua
eastward [ˋistwərd] *adv* hacia el este
east wind *s* solano
eas•y [ˋizi] *adj* (*comp* **-ier;** *super* **-iest**) fácil; (*conducive to ease*) cómodo; (*not tight*) holgado; (*amenable*) manejable; (*not forced or hurried*) lento, pausado, moderado; **to have an easy job** (o **life**) estar echado (CAm, Mex, P-R) ‖ *adv* (coll) fácilmente; (coll) despacio; **to take it easy** (coll) descansar, holgar; (coll) ir despacio
easy chair *s* poltrona, silla poltrona
eas′y•go′ing *adj* despacioso, comodón
easy mark *s* (coll) víctima, inocentón *m*
easy money *s* dinero ganado sin pena; (com) dinero abundante
easy payments *spl* facilidades de pago
eat [it] *v* (*pret* **ate** [et]; *pp* **eaten** [ˋitən]) *tr* comer; **to eat away** corroer; **to eat up** comerse ‖ *intr* comer
eatable [ˋitəbəl] *adj* comestible ‖ **eatables** *spl* comestibles *mpl*
eaves [ivz] *spl* alero, socarrén *m,* tejaroz *m*
eaves′drop′ *v* (*pret & pp* **-dropped;** *ger* **-dropping**) *intr* escuchar a escondidas, estar de escucha
ebb [ɛb] *s* reflujo; decadencia ‖ *intr* bajar (*la marea*); decaer
ebb and flow *s* flujo y reflujo
ebb tide *s* marea menguante
ebon•y [ˋɛbəni] *s* (*pl* **-ies**) ébano; color *m* de ébano; (*skin; hair*) negro como el ébano
ebullient[ɪˋbʌljənt] *adj* hirviente; entusiasta
eccentric [ɛkˋsɛntrɪk] *adj* excéntrico ‖ *m* (*odd person*) excéntrico; (*device*) excéntrica
eccentrici•ty [ˌɛksɛnˋtrɪsɪti] *s* (*pl* **-ties**) excentricidad
ecclesiastic [ɪˌkliziˋæstɪk] *adj & s* eclesiástico
echelon [ˋɛʃəˌlɑn] *s* escalón *m;* (mil) escalón ‖ *tr* (mil) escalonar
ech•o [ˋɛko] *s* (*pl* **-oes**) eco ‖ *tr* repetir (*un sonido*); imitar ‖ *intr* hacer eco
éclair [eˋklɛr] *s* bollo de crema
eclectic [ɛkˋlɛktɪk] *adj & s* ecléctico
eclipse [ɪˋklɪps] *s* eclipse *m* ‖ *tr* eclipsar
eclogue [ˋɛklɔg] o [ˋɛklɑg] *s* égloga
ecologic(al) [ˌikəˋlɑdʒɪk(əl)] *adj* ecológico
ecologist [iˋkɑlədʒɪst] *s* ecologista *mf,* ecólogo
ecology [iˋkɑlədʒi] *s* ecología
economic [ˌikəˋnɑmɪk] *adj* económico (*perteneciente a la economía*)
economical [ˌikəˋnɑmɪkəl] *adj* económico (*ahorrador; poco costoso*)
economics [ˌikəˋnɑmɪks] *s* economía política
economist [ɪˋkɑnəmɪst] *s* economista *mf*
economize [ɪˋkɑnəˌmaɪz] *tr & intr* economizar
econo•my [ɪˋkɑnəmi] *s* (*pl* **-mies**) economía
ecosystem [ˋikoˌsɪstəm] *s* ecosistema *m*
ecsta•sy [ˋɛkstəsi] *s* (*pl* **-sies**) éxtasis *m*
ecstatic [ˋɛkˋstætɪk] *adj* extático
Ecuador [ˋɛkwəˌdɔr] *s* el Ecuador
Ecuadoran [ˌɛkwəˋdorən] o **Ecuadorian** [ˌɛkwhəˋdorɪ•ən] *adj & s* ecuatoriano
ecumenic(al) [ˌɛkjəˋmɛnɪk(əl)] *adj* ecuménico
eczema [ˋɛksɪmə] o [ɛgˋzimə] *s* eczema *m & f,* eccema *m & f*
ed. *abbr* **edited, edition, editor**
ed•dy [ˋɛdi] *s* (*pl* **-dies**) remolino ‖ *v* (*pret & pp* **-died**) *tr & intr* remolinear
edelweiss [ˋedəlˌvaɪs] *s* estrella de los Alpes
edema [ɪˋdimə] *s* edema
Eden [ˋidən] *s* (Bib) Edén *m;* **Garden of Eden** Jardín *m* del Edén
edge [ɛdʒ] *s* (*of a knife, sword, etc.*) filo, corte *m;* (*of a cup, glass, piece of paper, piece of cloth, an abyss, etc.*) borde *m;* (*of a piece of cloth; of a body of water*) orilla; (*of a table*)

canto; (*of a book*) corte *m;* (*of clothing*) ribete *m;* (slang) ventaja; **on edge** de canto; (fig) nervioso; **to have the edge on** (coll) llevar ventaja a; **to set the teeth on edge** dar dentera ‖ *tr* afilar, aguzar; bordear; ribetear (*un vestido*) ‖ *intr* avanzar de lado; **to edge in** lograr entrar

edger [ˈɛdʒər] *s* (hort) cortabordes *m*

edgeways [ˈɛdʒ,wez] *adv* de filo, de canto; **to not let a person get a word in edgeways** no dejarle a una persona decir ni una palabra

edging [ˈɛdʒɪŋ] *s* borde *m;* (*trimming*) orla, ribete *m*

edgy [ˈɛdʒi] *adj* agudo, angular; nervioso, irritable

edible [ˈɛdɪbəl] *adj & s* comestible *m*

edict [ˈidɪkt] *s* edicto

edification [,ɛdɪfɪˈkeʃən] *s* edificación

edifice [ˈɛdɪfɪs] *s* edificio

edi•fy [ˈɛdɪ,faɪ] *v* (*pret & pp* **-fied**) *tr* edificar

edifying [ˈɛdɪ,faɪ•ɪŋ] *adj* edificante

edit. *abbr* **edited, edition, editor**

edit [ˈɛdɪt] *tr* preparar para la publicación; dirigir, redactar (*un periódico*)

edition [ɪˈdɪʃən] *s* edición

editor [ˈɛdɪtər] *s* (*of a newspaper or magazine*) director *m,* redactor *m;* (*of a manuscript*) revisor *m;* (*of an editorial*) cronista *mf;* (compu, mov) editor *m*

editorial [,ɛdɪˈtorɪ•əl] *adj* editorial ‖ *s* editorial *m,* artículo de fondo

editorial board *s* comité *m* de redacción, consejo de redacción

editorial staff *s* redacción, cuerpo de redacción

editor in chief *s* jefe *m* de redacción, director *m,* redactor *m* en jefe

educate [ˈɛdʒʊ,ket] *tr* educar, instruir

education [,ɛdʒʊˈkeʃən] *s* educación, instrucción

educational [,ɛdʒʊˈkeʃənəl] *adj* educativo, educacional

educational institution *s* centro docente

educator [ˈɛdʒʊ,ketər] *s* educador *m*

Edward [ˈɛdwərd] *s* Eduardo

eel [il] *s* anguila; **to be as slippery as an eel** escurrirse como una anguila

ee•rie o **ee•ry** [ˈɪri] *adj* (*comp* **-rier;** *super* **-riest**) espectral, misterioso

efface [ɪˈfes] *tr* destruir; borrar; **to efface oneself** retirarse, no dejarse ver

effect [ɪˈfɛkt] *s* efecto; **in effect** vigente; en efecto, en realidad; **to feel the effects of** resentirse de; **to go into effect** o **to take effect** hacerse vigente, entrar en vigor; **to put into effect** poner en vigor ‖ *tr* efectuar

effective [ɪˈfɛktɪv] *adj* eficaz; (*actually in effect*) efectivo; (*striking*) impresionante; **to become effective** hacerse efectivo, entrar en vigencia

effectual [ɪˈfɛktʃʊ•əl] *adj* eficaz

effectuate [ɪˈfɛktʃʊ,et] *tr* efectuar

effeminacy [ɪˈfɛmɪnəsi] *s* afeminación

effeminate [ɪˈfɛmɪnɪt] *adj* afeminado

effervesce [,ɛfərˈvɛs] *intr* estar en efervescencia

effervescence [,ɛfərˈvɛsəns] *s* efervescencia

effervescent [,ɛfərˈvɛsənt] *adj* efervescente

effete [ɪˈfɪt] *adj* estéril, infructuoso; afectado; decadente

efficacious [,ɛfɪˈkeʃəs] *adj* eficaz

effica•cy [ˈɛfɪkəsi] *s* (*pl* **-cies**) eficacia

efficien•cy [ɪˈfɪʃənsi] *s* (*pl* **-cies**) eficiencia; (mech) rendimiento, efecto útil

efficient [ɪˈfɪʃənt] *adj* eficiente, eficaz; (*person*) competente; (mech) de buen rendimiento

effi•gy [ˈɛfɪdʒi] *s* (*pl* **-gies**) efigie *f*

effort [ˈɛfɔrt] *s* esfuerzo, empeño

effronter•y [ɪˈfrʌntəri] *s* (*pl* **-ies**) desfachatez *f,* descaro

effusion [ɪˈfjuʒən] *s* efusión

effusive [ɪˈfjusɪv] *adj* efusivo, expansivo

e.g., *abbr* **exempli gratia** (Lat) (**for example**) p.ej., vg., e.g. (por ejemplo)

egg [ɛg] *s* huevo; (slang) buen sujeto ‖ *tr* **to egg on** incitar, instigar

egg beat′er *s* batidor *m* de huevos

egg′cup′ *s* huevera

egg′head′ *s* intelectual *mf,* erudito

eggnog [ˈɛg,nɑg] *s* caldo de la reina, yema mejida, ponche *m* de huevo, flip *m,* ronpope *m*

egg′plant′ *s* berenjena

egg′shell′ *s* cascarón *m,* cáscara de huevo

egg white *s* clara de huevo

egoism [ˈɛgo,ɪzəm] o [ˈigo,ɪzəm] *s* egoísmo

egoist [ˈɛgo•ɪst] o [ˈigo•ɪst] *s* egoísta *mf*

egotism [ˈɛgo,tɪzəm] o [ˈigɑ,tɪzəm] *s* egotismo

egotist [ˈɛgotɪst] o [ˈigotɪst] *s* egotista *mf*

egregious [ɪˈgridʒəs] *adj* enorme, escandaloso, atroz, flagrante, mayúsculo

egress [ˈgrɛs] *s* salida

Egypt [ˈedʒɪpt] *s* Egipto

Egyptian [ɪˈdʒɪpʃən] *adj & s* egipcio

eider [ˈaɪdər] *s* pato de flojel

eid′erdown′ *s* edredón *m*

eight [et] *adj & pron* ocho ‖ *s* ocho; **eight o'clock** las ocho

eighteen [ˈetˈtin] *adj, pron & s* dieciocho, diez y ocho

eighteenth [ˈetˈtinθ] *adj & s* (*in a series*) decimoctavo; (*part*) dieciochavo ‖ *s* (*in dates*) dieciocho, diez y ocho

eighth [etθ] *adj & s* octavo, ochavo ‖ *s* (*in dates*) ocho

eight hundred *adj & pron* ochocientos ‖ *s* ochocientos *m*

eightieth [ˈetɪ•ɪθ] *adj & s* (*in a series*) octogésimo; (*part*) ochentavo

eigh•ty [ˈeti] *adj & pron* ochenta ‖ *s* (*pl* **-ties**) ochenta *m*

either [ˈiðər] o [ˈaɪðər] *adj* uno u otro, cada . . . (de los dos), cualquier . . . de los dos; ambos ‖ *pron* uno u otro, cualquiera de los dos ‖ *adv* — **not either** tampoco, no . . . tampoco ‖ *conj* — **either . . . or** o . . . o

ejaculate [ɪˈdʒækjə,let] *tr & intr* exclamar; (physiol) eyacular

eject [ɪˈdʒɛkt] *tr* arrojar, expulsar, echar; (*to evict*) desahuciar
ejection [ɪˈdʒɛkʃən] *s* expulsión; (*of a tenant*) desahucio; (compu) expulsión
ejection seat *s* (aer) asiento lanzable
eke [ik] *tr* — **to eke out** ganarse (*la vida*) con dificultad
elaborate [ɪˈlæbərɪt] *adj* (*done with great care*) elaborado; (*detailed, ornate*) primoroso, recargado ‖ [ɪˈlæbə,ret] *tr* elaborar ‖ *intr* — **to elaborate on** o **upon** explicar con más detalles
elapse [ɪˈlæps] *intr* pasar, transcurrir
elastic [ɪˈlæstɪk] *adj* & *s* elástico
elasticity [,ilæsˈtɪsɪti] *s* elasticidad
elated [ɪˈletɪd] *adj* alborozado, regocijado
elation [ɪˈleʃən] *s* alborozo, regocijo
elbow [ˈɛlbo] *s* codo; (*in a river*) recodo; (*of a chair*) brazo; **at one's elbow** a la mano; **out at the elbows** andrajoso, enseñando los codos; **to crook the elbow** empinar el codo; **to rub elbows** codearse, rozarse; **up to the elbows** hasta los codos ‖ *tr* — **to elbow one's way** abrirse paso a codazos ‖ *intr* codear
elbow grease *s* mucho trabajo, fuerza, energía física
elbow patch *s* codera
elbow rest *s* ménsula
el'bow•room' *s* espacio suficiente; libertad de acción
elder [ˈɛldər] *adj* mayor, más antiguo ‖ *s* mayor, señor *m* mayor; (eccl) anciano, patriarca *m;* (eccl) miembro del consejo
el'der•ber'ry *s* (*pl* **-ries**) saúco; baya del saúco
elderly [ˈɛldərli] *adj* viejo, anciano
elder statesman *s* veterano de la política
eldest [ˈɛldɪst] *adj* (el) mayor, (el) más antiguo
elec. *abbr* **electrical, electricity**
elect [ɪˈlɛkt] *adj* (*chosen*) escogido; (*selected but not yet installed*) electo ‖ *s* elegido; **the elect** los elegidos ‖ *tr* elegir
election [ɪˈlɛkʃən] *s* elección
electioneer [ɪ,lɛkʃəˈnɪr] *intr* solicitar votos
elective [ɪˈlɛktɪv] *adj* electivo ‖ *s* asignatura electiva
electoral roll [ɪˈlɛktərəl] *s* registro, listado electoral, censo (Esp)
electorate [ɪˈlɛktərɪt] *s* electorado, cuerpo electoral
electric(al) [ɪˈlɛktrɪk(əl)] *adj* eléctrico
electric appliance *s* electrodoméstico
electric chair *s* silla eléctrica
electric eye *s* célula fotoeléctrica
electrician [,ɛlɛkˈtrɪʃən] *s* electricista *mf*
electricity [,ɛlɛkˈtrɪsɪti] *s* electricidad
electric shaver *s* electroafeitadora
electric shock *s* descarga eléctrica
electric tape *s* cinta aislante
electri•fy [ɪˈlɛktrɪ,faɪ] *v* (*pret* & *pp* **-fied**) *tr* (*to provide with electric power*) electrificar; (*to communicate electricity to; to thrill*) electrizar
electrocardiogram [ɪ,lɛktroˈkɑrdɪ,əgræm] *s* electrocardiograma *m*
electrocute [ɪˈlɛktrə,kjut] *tr* electrocutar
electrode [ɪˈlɛktrod] *s* electrodo
electrolysis [,ɛlɛkˈtrɑlɪsɪs] *s* electrólisis *f*
electrolyte [ɪˈlɛktrə,laɪt] *s* electrólito
electromagnet [ɪ,lɛktrəˈmægnɪt] *s* electro, electroimán *m*
electromagnetic [ɪ,lɛktrəmægˈnɛtɪk] *adj* electromagnético
electromotive [ɪ,lɛktrəˈmotɪv] *adj* electromotor
electron [ɪˈlɛktrɑn] *s* electrón *m*
electronic [,ɛlɛkˈtrɑnɪk] *adj* electrónico; **electronic publishing** edición electrónica, edición digital ‖ **electronics** *s* electrónica
electroplating [ɪˈlɛktrə,pletɪŋ] *s* galvanoplastia
electroshock [ɪˈlɛktrə,ʃɑk] *s* (med) electrochoque *m*
electrostatic [ɪ,lɛktrəˈstætɪk] *adj* electrostático
electrotype [ɪˈlɛktrə,taɪp] *s* electrotipo ‖ *tr* electrotipar
eleemosynary [,ɛlɪˈmɑsɪ,nɛri] *adj* limosnero
elegance [ˈɛlɪgəns] *s* elegancia
elegant [ˈɛlɪgənt] *adj* elegante, elegantoso
elegiac [,ɛlɪˈdʒaɪ•æk] o [ɪˈlidʒɪ,æk] *adj* elegíaco
ele•gy [ˈɛlɪdʒi] *s* (*pl* **-gies**) elegía
element [ˈɛlɪmənt] *s* elemento; (chem) cuerpo simple; **to be in one's element** estar en su elemento
elementary [,ɛlɪˈmɛntəri] *adj* elemental
elephant [ˈɛlɪfənt] *s* elefante *m*
elevate [ˈɛlɪ,vet] *tr* elevar
elevated [ˈɛlɪ,vetɪd] *adj* elevado ‖ *s* (coll) ferrocarril aéreo o elevado
elevation [,ɛlɪˈveʃən] *s* elevación
elevator [ˈɛlɪ,vetər] *s* ascensor *m;* elevador *m* (Am); (*for freight*) montacargas *m;* (*for hoisting grain*) elevador de granos; (*warehouse for storing grain*) depósito de cereales; (aer) timón *m* de profundidad
eleven [ɪˈlɛvən] *adj* & *pron* once ‖ *s* once *m;* **eleven o'clock** las once
eleventh [ɪˈlɛvənθ] *adj* & *s* (*in a series*) undécimo, onceno; (*part*) onzavo ‖ *s* (*in dates*) once *m*
eleventh hour *s* último momento
elf [ɛlf] *s* (*pl* **elves** [elvz]) elfo, trasgo; enano
elicit [ɪˈlɪsɪt] *tr* sacar, sonsacar
elide [ɪˈlaɪd] *tr* elidir
eligible [ˈɛlɪdʒɪbəl] *adj* elegible; deseable, aceptable
eliminate [ɪˈlɪmɪ,net] *tr* eliminar
elision [ɪˈlɪʒən] *s* elisión
elite [eˈlit] *adj* selecto ‖ *s* — **the elite** la élite
elitist [eˈlitɪst] *adj* & *s* elitista *mf*
Elizabeth [əˈlɪzəbɛθ] *s* Isabel *f*
elk [ɛlk] *s* alce *m*
ellipse [ɪˈlɪps] *s* (geom) elipse *f*
ellip•sis [ɪˈlɪpsɪs] *s* (*pl* **-ses** [siz]) (gram) elipsis *f*
elliptic(al) [ɪˈlɪptɪk(əl)] *adj* (geom & gram) elíptico

elm tree [ɛlm] *s* olmo
elope [ɪˈlop] *intr* fugarse con un amante
elopement [ɪˈlopmənt] *s* fuga con un amante
eloquence [ˈɛləkwəns] *s* elocuencia
eloquent [ˈɛləkwənt] *adj* elocuente
else [ɛls] *adj* — **nobody else** ningún otro, nadie más; **nothing else** nada más; **somebody else** algún otro, otra persona; **something else** otra cosa; **what else** qué más, qué otra cosa; **who else** quién más; **whose else** de qué otra persona ‖ *adv* de otro modo; **how else** de qué otro modo; **or else** si no, o bien; **when else** en qué otro tiempo; a qué otra hora; **where else** en qué otra parte
else'where' *adv* en otra parte, a otra parte
elucidate [ɪˈlusɪˌdet] *tr* elucidar
elude [ɪˈlud] *tr* eludir
elusive [ɪˈlusɪv] *adj* fugaz, efímero; evasivo; elusivo; (*baffling*) deslumbrador
emaciated [ɪˈmeʃiˌetɪd] *adj* enflaquecido, macilento
E-mail [ˈimæl] *s* correo electrónico, E-mail *m*
emancipate [ɪˈmænsɪˌpet] *tr* emancipar
embalm [ɛmˈbɑm] *tr* embalsamar
embankment [ɛmˈbæŋkmənt] *s* terraplén *m*
embar•go [ɛmˈbɑrgo] *s* (*pl* **-goes**) embargo ‖ *tr* embargar
embark [ɛmˈbɑrk] *intr* embarcarse
embarkation [ˌɛmbɑrˈkeʃən] *s* (*of passengers*) embarco; (*of freight*) embarque *m*
embarrass [ɛmˈbærəs] *tr* (*to make feel self-conscious*) avergonzar; (*to put obstacles in the way of*) embarazar; (*to leave without money*) poner en apuros de dinero
embarrassing [ɛmˈbærəsɪŋ] *adj* desconcertante, vergonzoso; embarazoso
embarrassment [ɛmˈbærəsmənt] *s* desconcierto, vergüenza; (*interference; perplexity*) embarazo; (*financial difficulties*) apuros
embas•sy [ˈɛmbəsi] *s* (*pl* **-sies**) embajada
em•bed [ɛmˈbɛd] *v* (*pret & pp* **-bedded;** *ger* **-bedding**) *tr* empotrar, encajar
embedded command *s* (compu) comando encajado
embellish [ɛmˈbɛliʃ] *tr* embellecer
embellishment [ɛmˈbɛlɪʃmənt] *s* embellecimiento
ember [ˈɛmbər] *s* ascua, pavesa; **embers** rescoldo
Ember days *spl* témpora
embezzle [ɛmˈbɛzəl] *tr & intr* desfalcar, malversar
embezzlement [ɛmˈbɛzəlmənt] *s* desfalco, malversación
embezzler [ɛmˈbɛzlər] *s* malversador *m*
embitter [ɛmˈbɪtər] *tr* blasonar; (fig) blasonar
emblem [ˈɛmbləm] *s* emblema *m*
emblematic(al) [ˌɛmbləˈmætɪk(əl)] *adj* emblemático
embodiment [ɛmˈbɑdɪmənt] *s* incorporación; personificación, encarnación
embod•y [ɛmˈbɑdi] *v* (*pret & pp* **-ied**) *tr* incorporar; personificar, encarnar
embolden [ɛmˈboldən] *tr* envalentonar
embolism [ˈɛmbəˌlɪzəm] *s* embolia
emboss [ɛmˈbɔs] o [ɛmˈbɑs] *tr* (*to raise in relief*) realzar; abollonar (*metal*); repujar (*cuero*)
embossing *s* grabado en relieve
embrace [ɛmˈbres] *s* abrazo ‖ *tr* abrazar ‖ *intr* abrazarse
embrasure [ɛmˈbreʒər] *s* alféizar *m*
embroider [ɛmˈbrɔɪdər] *tr* bordar, recamar
embroider•y [ɛmˈbrɔɪdəri] *s* (*pl* **-ies**) bordado, recamado
embroil [ɛmˈbrɔɪl] *tr* embrollar; (*to involve in contention*) envolver
embroilment [ɛmˈbrɔɪlmənt] *s* embrollo; (*in contention*) envolvimiento
embry•o [ˈɛmbrɪˌo] *s* (*pl* **-os**) embrión *m;* **in embryo** en embrión
embryology [ˌɛmbrɪˈɑlədʒi] *s* embriología
embryonic [ˌɛmbrɪˈɑnɪk] *adj* embrionario; **at the embryonic stage** en estado embrionario
embryonic cloning *s* reproducción embrionaria asexual
embryonic stem cell research *s* investigaciones en células madre de embriones
emend [ɪˈmɛnd] *tr* enmendar
emendation [ˌimɛnˈdeʃən] *s* enmienda
emerald [ˈɛmərəld] *s* esmeralda
emerge [ɪˈmʌrdʒ] *intr* emerger
emergence [ɪˈmʌrdʒəns] *s* emergencia (*acción de emerger*)
emergen•cy [ɪˈmʌrdʒənsi] *s* (*pl* **-cies**) emergencia (*caso urgente*)
emergency exit *s* salida de auxilio
emergency landing *s* aterrizaje forzoso
emergency landing field *s* aeródromo de urgencia
emergency physician *s* médico de urgencia
emergency room *s* (med) sala de urgencias, sala de guardia
emergency security measures *spl* (Urug) medidas prontas de seguridad
emeritus [ɪˈmɛrɪtəs] *adj* emérito; **professor emeritus** *o* **emeritus professor** profesor emérito, profesora emérita
emersion [ɪˈmʌrʒən] o [ɪˈmʌrʃən] *s* emersión
emery [ˈɛməri] *s* esmeril *m*
emery cloth *s* tela de esmeril
emery wheel *s* esmeriladora, rueda de esmeril, muela de esmeril
emetic [ɪˈmɛtɪk] *adj & s* emético
emigrant [ˈɛmɪgrənt] *adj & s* emigrante *mf*
emigrate [ˈɛmɪˌgret] *intr* emigrar
émigré [emiˈgre] o [ˈɛmɪˌgre] *s* emigrado
eminence [ˈɛmɪnəns] *s* eminencia
eminent [ˈɛmɪnənt] *adj* eminente
emissar•y [ˈɛmɪˌsɛri] *s* (*pl* **-ies**) emisario
emission [ɪˈmɪʃən] *s* emisión
emit [ɪˈmɪt] *v* (*pret & pp* **emitted;** *ger* **emitting**) *tr* emitir
emotion [ɪˈmoʃən] *s* emoción
emotional [ɪˈmoʃənəl] *adj* emocional, emotivo
emperor [ˈɛmpərər] *s* emperador *m*

empathy [ˈɛmpəθi] *s* empatía
empha•sis [ˈɛmfəsɪs] *s* (*pl* **-ses** [ˌsiz]) énfasis *m,* hincapié *m,* importancia, acento
emphasize [ˈɛmfəˌsaɪz] *tr* acentuar, hacer hincapié en, enfatizar; (*to highlight*) poner de relieve, hacer resaltar
emphatic [ɛmˈfætɪk] *adj* enfático
emphysema [ˌɛmfɪˈsimə] *s* enfisema *m*
empire [ˈɛmpaɪr] *s* imperio
empiric(al) [ɛmˈpɪrɪk(əl)] *adj* empírico
empiricist [ɛmˈpɪrɪsɪst] *s* empírico
emplacement [ɛmˈplesmənt] *s* emplazamiento
employ [ɛmˈplɔɪ] *s* empleo ‖ *tr* emplear
employee [ɛmˈplɔɪ•i] o [ˌɛmplɔɪˈi] *s* empleado
employer [ɛmˈplɔɪ•ər] *s* patrono
employment [ɛmˈplɔɪmənt] *s* empleo, colocación
employment agency *s* agencia de colocaciones
empower [ɛmˈpaʊ•ər] *tr* autorizar, facultar; habilitar, permitir
empress [ˈɛmprɪs] *s* emperatriz *f*
emptiness [ˈɛmptɪnɪs] *s* vaciedad, vacuidad
emp•ty [ˈɛmpti] *adj* (*comp* **-tier;** *super* **-tiest**) vacío; (coll) hambriento ‖ *v* (*pret & pp* **-tied**) *tr & intr* vaciar
empty-handed [ˈɛmptiˈhændɪd] *adj* manivacío
empty-headed [ˈɛmptiˈhɛdɪd] *adj* tonto, ignorante
empye•ma [ˌɛmpɪˈimə] *s* (*pl* **-mata** [mətə]) empiema *m*
empyrean [ˌɛmpɪˈri•ən] *adj & s* empíreo
emulate [ˈɛmjəˌlet] *tr & intr* emular
emulator [ˈɛmjəˌletər] *s* émulo
emulous [ˈɛmjələs] *adj* émulo
emulsi•fy [ɪˈmʌlsɪˌfaɪ] *v* (*pret & pp* **-fied**) *tr* emulsionar
emulsion [ɪˈmʌlʃən] *s* emulsión
enable [ɛnˈebəl] *tr* habilitar, facilitar
enact [ɛnˈækt] *tr* decretar, promulgar; hacer el papel de
enactment [ɛnˈæktmənt] *s* ley *f;* (*of a law*) promulgación; (*of a play*) representación
enam•el [ɛnˈæməl] *s* esmalte *m* ‖ *v* (*pret & pp* **-eled** o **-elled;** *ger* **-eling** o **-elling**) *tr* esmaltar
enam′el•ware′ *s* utensilios de cocina de hierro esmaltado
enamor [ɛnˈæmər] *tr* enamorar
encamp [ɛnˈkæmp] *tr* acampar ‖ *intr* acampar, acamparse
encampment [ɛnˈkæmpmənt] *s* acampamiento
enchant [ɛnˈtʃænt] *tr* encantar
enchanting [ɛnˈtʃæntɪŋ] *adj* encantador
enchantment [ɛnˈtʃæntmənt] *s* encanto
enchantress [ɛnˈtʃæntrɪs] *s* encantadora
enchase [ɛnˈtʃes] *tr* engastar
encircle [ɛnˈsʌrkəl] *tr* encerrar, rodear; (mil) envolver
enclitic [ɛnˈklɪtɪk] *adj & s* enclítico
enclose [ɛnˈkloz] *tr* encerrar; (*in a letter*) remitir adjunto, adjuntar, incluir
enclosed [ɛnˈklozd] *adj* cerrado; (*in a letter*) adjunto; **please find enclosed . . .** se adjunta, se acompaña . . .
enclosure [ɛnˈkloʒər] *s* recinto; cosa inclusa, carta inclusa, documento anexo
encode [ɛnˈkod] *tr* codificar; (*messages*) cifrar; (*to translate*) traducir (*por traducción inversa*) ‖ *intr* cifrar mensajes
encoder [ɛnˈkodər] *s* (compu) codificador *m*
encoding [ɛnˈkodɪŋ] *s* codificación; (*translation*) traducción inversa; (compu) codificación
encomi•um [ɛnˈkomɪ•əm] *s* (*pl* **-ums** o **-a** [ə]) encomio
encompass [ɛnˈkʌmpəs] *tr* encuadrar, abarcar
encore [ˈɑnkor] *s* bis *m* ‖ *interj* ¡otra (vez)!, ¡que se repita! ‖ *tr* pedir la repetición de (*p.ej., de una pieza o canción*); pedir la repetición a (*un actor*)
encounter [ɛnˈkaʊntər] *s* encuentro ‖ *tr* encontrar, encontrarse con ‖ *intr* batirse, combatirse
encourage [ɛnˈkʌrɪdʒ] *tr* animar, alentar; (*to foster*) fomentar
encouragement [ɛnˈkʌrɪdʒmənt] *s* ánimo, aliento; fomento
encroach [ɛnˈkrotʃ] *intr* — **to encroach on** o **upon** pasar los límites de; abusar de; invadir, entremeterse en
encrypt [ɛnˈkrɪpt] *tr* (compu) encriptar
encumber [ɛnˈkʌmbər] *tr* embarazar, estorbar, impedir; (*to load with debts, etc.*) gravar
encumbrance [ɛnˈkʌmbrəns] *s* embarazo; estorbo; gravamen *m*
encyclical [ɛnˈsɪklɪkəl] o [ɛnˈsaɪklɪkəl] *s* encíclica
encyclopedia [ɛnˌsaɪkləˈpidɪ•ə] *s* enciclopedia
encyclopedic [ɛnˌsaɪkləˈpidɪk] *adj* enciclopédico
encyclopedic dictionary *s* diccionario enciclopédico
end [ɛnd] *s* (*in time*) fin *m;* (*in space*) extremo, remate *m;* (*e.g., of the month*) fines *mpl;* (*small piece*) cabo, pieza, fragmento; (*purpose*) intento, objeto, fin, mira; **at the end of** al cabo de; a fines de; **in the end** al fin; **no end of** (coll) un sin fin de; **to make both ends meet** pasar con lo que se tiene; **to no end** sin efecto; **to stand on end** poner de punta; ponerse de punta; erizarse, encresparse (*el pelo*); **to the end that** a fin de que ‖ *tr* acabar, terminar ‖ *intr* acabar, terminar; desembocar (*p.ej., una calle*); **to end up** acabar, morir; **to end up as** acabar siendo, parar en (*p.ej., ladrón*)
endanger [ɛnˈdendʒər] *tr* poner en peligro
endear [ɛnˈdɪr] *tr* hacer querer; **to endear oneself to** hacerse querer por
endearment [ɛnˈdɪrmənt] *s* encariñamento
endeavor [ɛnˈdɛvər] *s* esfuerzo, empeño ‖ *intr* esforzarse, empeñarse
endemic [ɛnˈdɛmɪk] *adj* endémico ‖ *s* endemia
ending [ˈɛndɪŋ] *s* fin *m,* terminación; (gram) desinencia, terminación
endive [ˈɛndaɪv] *s* escarola
endless [ˈɛndlɪs] *adj* interminable; (*chain, screw, etc.*) sin fin

end'most' *adj* último, extremo
endorse [ɛn'dɔrs] *tr* endosar; (fig) apoyar, aprobar
endorsee [,ɛndɔr'si] *s* endosatario
endorsement [ɛn'dɔrsmənt] *s* endoso; (fig) apoyo, aprobación
endorser [ɛn'dɔrsər] *s* endosante *mf*
endow [ɛn'daʊ] *tr* dotar
endowment [ɛn'daʊmənt] *adj* dotal ‖ *s* (*of an institution*) dotación; (*gift, talent*) dote *f,* prenda
end paper *s* hoja de encuadernador
endurance [ɛn'djʊrəns] o [ɛn'dʊrəns] *s* aguante *m,* paciencia; (*ability to hold out*) resistencia, fortaleza; (*lasting time*) duración
endure [ɛn'djʊr] o [ɛn'dʊr] *tr* aguantar, tolerar, sufrir ‖ *intr* durar; sufrir con paciencia
enduring [ɛn'djʊrɪŋ] o [ɛn'dʊrɪŋ] *adj* duradero, permanente, resistente
enema ['ɛnəmə] *s* enema, ayuda; (*liquid and apparatus*) lavativa
ene•my ['ɛnəmi] *adj* enemigo ‖ *s* (*pl* **-mies**) enemigo
enemy alien *s* extranjero enemigo
energetic [,ɛnər'dʒɛtɪk] *adj* enérgico, vigoroso
ener•gy ['ɛnərdʒi] *s* (*pl* **-gies**) energía; **alternative energy sources** energías alternativas
energy crisis *s* crisis energética
en'ergy-sav'ing *adj* de ahorro energético
enervate ['ɛnər,vet] *tr* enervar
enfeeble [ɛn'fibəl] *tr* debilitar
enfold [ɛnfold] *tr* arrollar, envolver
enforce [ɛn'fors] *tr* hacer cumplir, poner en vigor; obtener por fuerza; (*e.g., obedience*) imponer; (*an argument*) hacer valer
enforcement [ɛn'forsmənt] *s* compulsión; (*e.g., of a law*) ejecución
enfranchise [ɛn'fræntʃaɪz] *tr* franquear, libertar; conceder el derecho de sufragio a
eng. *abbr* **engineer, engraving**
engage [ɛn'gedʒ] *tr* ocupar, emplear; alquilar, reservar; atraer (*p.ej., la atención de una persona*); engranar con; trabar batalla con; **to be engaged, to be engaged to be married** estar prometido, estar comprometido para casarse; **to engage someone in conversation** entablar conversación con una persona ‖ *intr* empeñarse, comprometerse; empotrar, encajar; engranar; **to engage in** ocuparse en
engaged [ɛn'gedʒd] *adj* comprometido, prometido; (*column*) embebido, entregado
engagement [ɛn'gedʒmənt] *s* ajuste *m,* contrato, empeño; esponsales *mpl,* palabra de casamiento; (*duration of betrothal*) noviazgo; (*appointment*) cita; (mil) acción, batalla
engagement ring *s* anillo de compromiso, anillo de pedida
engaging [ɛn'gedʒɪŋ] *adj* agraciado, simpático
engender [ɛn'dʒɛndər] *tr* engendrar
engine ['ɛndʒɪn] *s* máquina; (*of automobile*) motor *m;* (rr) máquina, locomotora
engine driver *s* maquinista *m*
engineer [,ɛndʒə'nɪr] *s* ingeniero; (*engine driver*) maquinista *m* ‖ *tr* dirigir o construir como ingeniero; llevar a cabo con acierto
engineering [,ɛndʒə'nɪrɪŋ] *s* ingeniería
engine house *s* cuartel *m* de bomberos
engine•man ['ɛndʒɪnmən] *s* (*pl* **-mən** [mən]) maquinista *m,* conductor *m* de locomotora
engine room *s* sala de máquinas; (naut) cámara de las máquinas
en'gine-room' telegraph *s* (naut) transmisor *m* de órdenes, telégrafo de máquinas
England ['ɪŋglənd] *s* Inglaterra
English ['ɪŋglɪʃ] *adj* inglés ‖ *s* inglés *m;* (*in billiards*) efecto; **the English** los ingleses
English Channel *s* Canal *m* de la Mancha
English daisy *s* margarita de los prados
English horn *s* (mus) corno inglés, cuerno inglés
English•man ['ɪŋglɪʃmən] *s* (*pl* **-men** [mən]) inglés *m*
Eng'lish-speak'ing *adj* de habla inglesa, angloparlante
Eng'lish•wom'an *s* (*pl* **-wom'en**) inglesa
engraft [ɛn'græft] *tr* (hort & surg) injertar; (fig) implantar
engrave [ɛn'grev] *tr* grabar; (*in the memory*) grabar
engraver [ɛn'grevər] *s* grabador *m*
engraving [ɛn'grevɪŋ] *s* grabado
engross [ɛn'gros] *tr* absorber; poner en limpio; copiar caligáficamente
engrossing [ɛn'grosɪŋ] *adj* acaparador, absorbente
engulf [ɛn'gʌlf] *tr* hundir, inundar
enhance [ɛn'hæns] *tr* realzar; aumentar; mejorar; (compu) procesar
enhanced [ɛn'hænst] *adj* mejorado; (compu) procesado
enhancement [ɛn'hænsmənt] *s* realce *m;* aumento; mejora
enigma [ɪ'nɪgmə] *s* enigma *m*
enigmatic(al) [,ɪnɪg'mætɪk(əl)] *adj* enigmático
enjambment [ɛn'dʒæmmənt] o [ɛn'dʒæmbmənt] *s* encabalgamiento
enjoin [ɛn'dʒɔɪn] *tr* encargar, ordenar
enjoy [ɛn'dʒɔɪ] *tr* gozar; **to enjoy** + *ger* gozarse en + *inf;* **to enjoy oneself** divertirse
enjoyable [ɛn'dʒɔɪ•əbəl] *adj* agradable, deleitable
enjoyment [ɛn'dʒɔɪmənt] *s* (*pleasure*) placer *m;* (*pleasurable use*) goce *m*
enkindle [ɛn'kɪndəl] *tr* encender
enlarge [ɛn'lɑrdʒ] *tr* agrandar, aumentar; (phot) ampliar ‖ *intr* agrandarse, aumentar; (*to talk at length*) explayarse; exagerar; **to enlarge on** o **upon** tratar con más extensión; exagerar
enlargement [ɛn'lɑrdʒmənt] *s* agrandamiento, aumento; (phot) ampliación
enlighten [ɛn'laɪtən] *tr* ilustrar, instruir
enlightenment [ɛn'laɪtənmənt] *s* ilustración, instrucción; dilucidación
enlist [ɛn'lɪst] *tr* alistar; ganar (*a una persona; el favor, los servicios de una persona*) ‖ *intr*

alistarse; **to enlist in** (*a cause*) poner empeño en
enliven [ɛn`laɪvən] *tr* avivar, animar
enmesh [ɛn`mɛʃ] *tr* enredar
enmi•ty [`ɛnmɪti] *s* (*pl* **-ties**) enemistad
ennoble [ɛn`nobəl] *tr* ennoblecer
ennui [`ɑnwi] *s* aburrimiento, tedio
enormous [ɪ`nɔrməs] *adj* enorme
enough [ɪ`nʌf] *adj, adv & s* bastante *m* ‖ *interj* ¡basta!, ¡no más!
enounce [ɪ`naʊns] *tr* enunciar; pronunciar
en passant [,ɑn pæ`sɑnt] *adv* (chess) al vuelo
enrage [ɛn`redʒ] *tr* enrabiar, encolerizar
enrapture [ɛn`ræptʃər] *tr* embelesar, transportar, arrebatar
enrich [ɛn`rɪtʃ] *tr* enriquecer
enroll [ɛn`rol] *tr* inscribir; (educ) matricular; (mil) alistar ‖ *intr* inscribirse; matricularse; alistarse
enrollment [ɛn`rolmənt] *s* inscripción; (educ) matrícula; (mil) alistamiento; número de socios; (educ) número de estudiantes
en route [ɑn `rut] *adv* en camino; **en route to** camino de, rumbo a
ensconce [ɛn`skɑns] *tr* esconder, abrigar; **to ensconce oneself** instalarse cómodamente
ensemble [ɑn`sɑmbəl] *s* conjunto; grupo de músicos que tocan o cantan juntos; traje armonioso
ensign [`ɛnsaɪn] *s* (*standard*) enseña, bandera; (*badge*) divisa, insignia ‖ [`ɛnsən] o [`ɛnsaɪn] *s* (nav) alférez *m* de fragata
enslave [ɛn`slev] *tr* esclavizar
enslavement [ɛn`slevmənt] *s* esclavización
ensnare [ɛn`snɛr] *tr* entrampar
ensue [ɛn`su] *intr* seguirse; resultar
ensuing [ɛn`su•ɪŋ] *adj* siguiente; resultante
ensure [ɛn`ʃʊr] *tr* asegurar, garantizar
entail [ɛn`tel] *s* (law) vínculo ‖ *tr* acarrear, ocasionar; (law) vincular
entangle [ɛn`tæŋgəl] *tr* enmarañar, enredar
entanglement [en`tæŋgəlmənt] *s* enmarañamiento, enredo
enter [`ɛntər] *tr* entrar en (*una habitación*); entrar por (*una puerta*); (*in the customhouse*) declarar; (*to make a record of*) registrar, asentar; matricular (*a un alumno*); matricularse en; hacer miembro a; hacerse miembro de; (*to undertake*) emprender; asentar (*un pedido*); **to enter one's head** metérsele a uno en la cabeza ‖ *intr* entrar; (theat) entrar en escena, salir; **to enter into** entrar en; celebrar (*p.ej., un contrato*); **to enter on** o **upon** emprender
enterprise [`ɛntər,praɪz] *s* (*undertaking*) empresa; (*spirit, push*) empuje *m*
enterprising [`ɛntər,praɪzɪŋ] *adj* emprendedor
entertain [,ɛntər`ten] *tr* entretener, divertir; (*to show hospitality to*) recibir; considerar, abrigar (*esperanzas, ideas, etc.*) ‖ *intr* recibir
entertainer [,ɛntər`tenər] *s* (*host*) anfitrión *m;* (*in public*) actor *m,* bailador *m,* músico, vocalista *mf* (*esp. en un café cantante*)
entertaining [,ɛntər`tenɪŋ] *adj* entretenido
entertainment [,ɛntər`tenmənt] *s* entretenimiento, diversión; atracción, espectáculo; buen recibimiento; (*of hopes, ideas, etc.*) consideración, abrigo
entertainment business *s* el mundo del espectáculo
enthrall [ɛn`θrɔl] *tr* cautivar, encantar; esclavizar, sojuzgar
enthrone [ɛn`θron] *tr* entronizar
enthuse [ɛn`θuz] o [ɛn`θjuz] *tr* (coll) entusiasmar ‖ *intr* (coll) entusiasmarse
enthusiasm [ɛn`θuzɪ,æzəm] *s* entusiasmo
enthusiast [ɛn`θuzi,æst] *s* entusiasta *mf;* devoto
enthusiastic [ɛn,θuzɪ`æstɪk] *adj* entusiástico
entice [ɛn`taɪs] *tr* atraer, tentar; inducir al mal, extraviar
enticement [ɛn`taɪsmənt] *s* atracción, tentación; extravío
entire [ɛn`taɪr] *adj* entero
entirely [ɛn`taɪrli] *adv* enteramente; (*exclusively*) solamente
entire•ty [ɛtaɪrti] *s* (*pl* **-ties**) entereza; conjunto, totalidad
entitle [ɛn`taɪtəl] *tr* dar derecho a; (*to give a name to; to honor with a title*) intitular
enti•ty [`ɛntɪti] *s* (*pl* **-ties**) entidad
entomb [ɛn`tum] *tr* sepultar
entombment [ɛn`tummənt] *s* sepultura
entomology [,ɛntə`mɑlədʒi] *s* entomología
entourage [,ɑntu`rɑʒ] *s* cortejo, séquito
entrails [`ɛntrelz] *spl* entrañas
entrain [ɛn`tren] *tr* despachar en el tren ‖ *intr* embarcar, salir en el tren
entrance [`ɛntrəns] *s* entrada, ingreso; (theat) entrada en escena ‖ [ɛn`træns] *tr* arrebatar, encantar
entrance examination *s* examen *m* de ingreso; **to take entrance examinations** examinarse de ingreso
entrancing [ɛn`trænsɪŋ] *adj* arrebatador, encantador
entrant [`ɛntrənt] *s* entrante *mf;* (sport) concurrente *mf*
en•trap [ɛn`træp] *v* (*pret & pp* **-trapped;** *ger* **-trapping**) *tr* entrampar
entreat [ɛn`trit] *tr* rogar, suplicar
entreat•y [ɛn`triti] *s* (*pl* **-ies**) ruego, súplica
entree [`ɑntre] *s* entrada, ingreso; (culin) entrada, principio
entrench [ɛn`trɛntʃ] *tr* atrincherar ‖ *intr* — **to entrench on** o **upon** infringir, violar
entrust [ɛn`trʌst] *tr* confiar
en•try [`ɛntri] *s* (*pl* **-tries**) entrada; (*item*) partida, entrada; (*in a dictionary*) artículo; (sport) concurrente *mf;* **no entry** se prohibe la entrada; *SIGN* prohibido el paso; *SIGN* prohibida la entrada
entry level *s* (compu) entrada de gama
entry word *s* entrada (*del artículo*)
entwine [ɛn`twaɪn] *tr* entretejer, entrelazar
enumerate [ɪ`numə,ret] *tr* enumerar
enunciate [ɪ`nʌnsɪ,et] o [ɪ`nʌnʃɪ,et] *tr* enunciar; pronunciar

envelop [ɛn`vɛləp] *tr* envolver
envelope [`ɛnvə,lop] o [`ɑnvə,lop] *s* (*for a letter*) sobre *m;* (*wrapper*) envoltura
envenom [ɛn`vɛnəm] *tr* envenenar
enviable [`ɛnvɪ•əbəl] *adj* envidiable
envious [`ɛnvɪ•əs] *adj* envidioso
environment [ɛn`vaɪrənmənt] *s* medio ambiente; entorno; (*surroundings*) inmediaciones
environmental [ɛn,vaɪrən`mɛntəl] *adj* ambiental
environmental pollution *s* contaminación ambiental
environs [ɛn`vaɪrəns] *spl* inmediaciones, alrededores *mpl*
envisage [ɛn`vɪzɪdʒ] *tr* (*to look in the face of*) encarar; considerar, representarse
envoi [`ɛnvɔɪ] *s* despedida (*copla al fin de una composición poética*)
envoy [`ɛnvɔɪ] *s* (*diplomatic agent*) enviado; (*short concluding stanza*) despedida
en•vy [`ɛnvi] *s* (*pl* **-vies**) envidia || *v* (*pret & pp* **-vied**) *tr* envidiar
enzyme [`ɛnzaɪm] *s* enzima *f*
epaulet o **epaulette** [`ɛpə,lɛt] *s* charretera
epenthe•sis [ɛ'pɛnθɪsɪs] *s* (*pl* **-ses** [,siz]) epéntesis *f*
epergne [ɪ`pʌrn] o [e`pɛrn] *s* ramillete *m,* centro de mesa
ephemeral [ɪ`fɛmərəl] *adj* efímero
epic [`ɛpɪk] *adj* épico || *s* epopeya
epicure [`ɛpɪ,kjʊr] *s* epicúreo
epicurean [,ɛpɪkjʊ`ri•ən] *adj & s* epicúreo
epidemic [,ɛpɪ`dɛmɪk] *adj* epidémico || *s* epidemia
epidemiology [,ɛpɪ,dimɪ`ɑlədʒi] *s* epidemiología
epidermis [,ɛpɪ`dʌrmɪs] *s* epidermis *f*
epigram [`ɛpɪ,græm] *s* epigrama *m*
epilepsy [`ɛpɪ,lɛpsi] *s* epilepsia
epileptic [,ɛpɪ`lɛptɪk] *adj & s* epiléptico
Epiphany [ɪ`pɪfəni] *s* Epifanía, Día *m* de Reyes
Episcopalian [ɪ,pɪskə`pelɪ•ən] *adj & s* episcopalista *mf*
episode [`ɛpɪ,sod] *s* episodio
epistemology [ɪ,pɪstɪ`mɑlədʒi] *s* epistemología
epistle [ɪ`pɪsəl] *s* epístola
epitaph [`ɛpɪ,tæf] *s* epitafio
epithet [`ɛpɪ,θɛt] *s* epíteto
epitome [ɪ`pɪtəmi] *s* epítome *m;* (fig) esencia, personificación
epitomize [ɪ`pɪtə,maɪz] *tr* epitomar; (fig) encarnar, personificar
epoch [`ɛpək] o [`ipɑk] *s* época
epochal [`ɛpəkəl] *adj* memorable, trascendental
ep'och-mak'ing *adj* que hace época
equable [`ɛkwəbəl] o [`ikwəbəl] *adj* constante, uniforme; sereno
equal [`ikwəl] *adj* igual; **equal to** a la altura de || *s* igual *mf* || *v* (*pret & pp* **equaled** o **equalled;** *ger* **equaling** o **equalling**) *tr* (*to be equal to*) igualarse a o con; (*to make equal*) igualar
equali•ty [ɪ`kwɑlɪti] *s* (*pl* **-ties**) igualdad, paridad
equalize [`ikwə,laɪz] *tr* igualar; (*to make uniform*) equilibrar
equally [`ikwəli] *adv* igualmente
equal opportunity *s* igualdad de oportunidades
equal sign *s* signo de igualdad
equanimity [,ikwə`nɪmɪti] *s* ecuanimidad, igualdad de ánimo
equate [i`kwet] *tr* poner en ecuación; considerar equivalente(s)
equation [i`kweʃən] *s* ecuación
equator [i`kwetər] *s* ecuador *m;* **to cross the equator** cruzar el ecuador
equatorial [`ɛkwə`tɔri•əl] *adj* ecuatorial
equer•ry [`ɛkwəri] o [ɪ`kwɛri] *s* (*pl* **-ries**) caballerizo
equestrian [ɪ`kwɛstrɪ•ən] *adj* ecuestre || *m* jinete *m,* caballista *m*
equestrian sport *s* hípica
equilateral [,ikwɪ`lætərəl] *adj* equilátero
equilibrium [,ikwɪ`lɪbrɪ•əm] *s* equilibrio
equinoctial [,ikwɪ`nɑkʃəl] *adj* equinoccial
equinox [`ikwɪ,nɑks] *s* equinoccio
equip [ɪ`kwɪp] *v* (*pret & pp* **equipped;** *ger* **equipping**) *tr* equipar
equipment [ɪ`kwɪpmənt] *s* equipo, avíos, pertrechos; aptitud, capacidad
equipoise [`ikwɪ,pɔɪz] o [`ɛkwɪ,pɔɪz] *s* equilibrio; contrapeso || *tr* equilibrar; equipesar
equitable [`ɛkwɪtəbəl] *adj* equitativo
equi•ty [`ɛkwɪti] *s* (*pl* **-ties**) (*fairness*) equidad; valor líquido
equivalent [ɪ`kwɪvələnt] *adj & s* equivalente *m*
equivocal [ɪ`kwɪvəkəl] *adj* equívoco
equivocate [ɪ`kwɪvə,ket] *intr* usar de equívocos para engañar, mentir
equivocation [ɪ,kwɪvə`keʃən] *s* equívoco
ER *abbr* **emergency room**
era [`ɪrə] o [`irə] *s* era
eradicate [ɪ`rædɪ,ket] *tr* erradicar
erase [ɪ`res] *tr* borrar
eraser [ɪ`resər] *s* goma de borrar; (*for blackboard*) cepillo
erasure [ɪ`reʃər] o [ɪ`reʒər] *s* borradura, tachón *m*
ere [ɛr] *prep* antes de || *conj* antes de que; más bien que
erect [ɪ`rɛkt] *adj* derecho, enhiesto, erguido; (*hair*) erizado || *tr* (*to set in upright position*) erguir, enhestar; erigir (*un edificio*); armar, montar (*una máquina*)
erection [ɪ`rɛkʃən] *s* erección
erg [ʌrg] *s* ergio
ermine [`ʌrmɪn] *s* armiño; (fig) toga, judicatura
erode [ɪ`rod] *tr* erosionar || *intr* erosionarse
erosion [ɪ`roʒən] *s* erosión
err [ʌr] *intr* errar, equivocarse, marrar; pecar, marrar
errand [`ɛrənd] *s* mandado, recado, comisión; **to run an errand** hacer un mandado
errand boy *s* recadero, mandadero

erratic [ɪˋrætɪk] *adj* irregular, inconstante, variable; excéntrico
erra•tum [ɪˋretəm] o [ɪˋrɑtəm] *s* (*pl* **-ta** [tə]) errata
erroneous [ɪˋronɪ•əs] *adj* erróneo
error [ˋɛrər] *s* error *m;* **human error** fallo humano
erudite [ˋɛrʊ,daɪt] *adj* erudito
erudition [,ɛrʊˋdɪʃən] *s* erudición
erupt [ɪˋrʌpt] *intr* hacer erupción (*la piel, los dientes de un niño*); erumpir (*un volcán*)
eruption [ɪˋrʌpʃən] *s* erupción
escalate [ˋɛskə,let] *intr* escalarse
escalation [,ɛskə,ˋleʃən] *s* escalada, escalación
escalator [ˋɛskə,letər] *s* escalera mecánica, móvil o rodante
escallop [ˋɛsˋkæləp] *s* concha de peregrino; (*on edge of cloth*) festón *m* ‖ *tr* hornear a la crema y con migajas de pan; cocer (*p.ej., ostras*) en su concha; festonear
escapade [,ɛskəˋped] *s* calaverada, aventura atolondrada; (*flight*) escapada
escape [ɛsˋkep] *s* (*getaway*) escape *m,* escapatoria; (*from responsibilities, duties, etc.*) escapatoria ‖ *tr* evitar, eludir; **to escape someone** escapársele a uno; olvidársele a uno ‖ *intr* escapar, escaparse; **to escape from** escaparse a (*una persona*); escaparse de (*la cárcel*)
escapee [,ɛskəˋpi] *s* evadido
escapement [ɛsˋkepmənt] *s* escape *m*
escarpment [ɛsˋkɑrpmənt] *s* escarpa
eschew [ɛsˋtʃu] *tr* evitar, rehuir
escort [ˋɛskɔrt] *s* escolta; (*man or boy who accompanies a woman or girl in public*) acompañante *m,* caballero, galán *m* ‖ [ɛsˋkɔrt] *tr* escoltar
escutcheon [ɛsˋkʌtʃən] *s* escudo de armas; (*plate in front of lock on door*) escudo, escudete *m*
Eski•mo [ˋɛskɪ,mo] *adj* esquimal ‖ *s* (*pl* **-mos** o **-mo**) esquimal *mf*
esopha•gus [iˋsɑfəgəs] *s* (*pl* **-gi** [,dʒaɪ]) esófago
esp. *abbr* **especially**
espalier [ɛsˋpæljər] *s* espaldar *m,* espalera
especial [ɛsˋpɛʃəl] *adj* especial
espionage [ˋɛspɪ•ənɪdʒ] o [,ɛspɪ•əˋnɑʒ] *s* espionaje *m*
esplanade [,ɛspləˋned] *s* explanada
espousal [ɛsˋpaʊzəl] *s* desposorios; (*of a cause*) adhesión
espouse [ɛsˋpaʊz] *tr* casarse con; (*to advocate, adopt*) abogar por, adherirse a
espresso [ɛsˋprɛso] *s* expreso, café *m* exprés
Esq. *abbr* **Esquire** (*después del apellido*)
esquire [ɛsˋkwaɪr] o [ˋɛskwaɪr] *s* escudero ‖ **Esquire** *s* antiguo título de cortesía que se usa en vez de **Mr.**
essay [ˋɛse] *s* ensayo
essayist [ˋɛse•ɪst] *s* ensayista *mf*
essence [ˋɛsəns] *s* esencia
essential [ɛˋsɛnʃəl] *adj & s* esencial *m*
est. *abbr* **established, estate, estimated**
establish [ɛsˋtæblɪʃ] *tr* establecer
establishment [ɛsˋtæblɪʃmənt] *s* establecimiento; **the Establishment** (*established order*) el Sistema, la clase dirigente
estate [ɛsˋtet] *s* estado; situación social; (*landed property*) finca, hacienda, heredad; (*a person's possessions*) bienes *mpl,* propiedad; (*left by a decedent*) herencia, bienes relictos
esteem [ɛsˋtim] *s* estima ‖ *tr* estimar
esthete [ˋɛsθit] *s* esteta *mf*
esthetic [ɛsˋθɛtɪk] *adj* estético ‖ **esthetics** *ssg* estética
estimable [ˋɛstɪməbəl] *adj* estimable
estimate [ˋɛstɪmɪt] *s* (*calculation of value, judgment of worth*) estimación; (*statement of cost of work to be done*) presupuesto ‖ [ˋɛstɪ,met] *tr* (*to judge, deem*) estimar; presupuestar (*el coste de una obra*)
estimation [,ɛstɪˋmeʃən] *s* estimación
estrangement [ɛsˋtrendʒmənt] *s* extrañeza
estuar•y [ˋɛstʃʊ,ɛri] *s* (*pl* **-ies**) estero
etc. *abbr* (**et cetera**) etc. (*etcétera*)
et cetera [ɛtˋsɛtərə] *adv* etcétera
etch [ɛtʃ] *tr & intr* grabar al agua fuerte
etcher [ˋɛtʃər] *s* aguafortista *mf*
etching [ˋɛtʃɪŋ] *s* aguafuerte *f*
eternal [ɪˋtʌrnəl] *adj* eterno
eterni•ty [ɪˋtʌrnɪti] *s* (*pl* **-ties**) eternidad
ether [ˋiθər] *s* éter *m*
ethereal [ɪˋθɪrɪ•əl] *adj* etéreo
ethical [ˋɛθɪkəl] *adj* ético
ethics [ˋɛθɪks] *ssg* ética
Ethiopian [,iθɪˋopɪ•ən] *adj & s* etíope *mf*
Ethiopic [,iθɪˋopɪk] *adj & s* etiópico
ethnic(al) [ˋɛθnɪk(əl)] *adj* étnico
ethnography [ɛθˋnɑgrəfi] *s* etnografía
ethnology [ɛθˋnɑlədʒi] *s* etnología
ethyl [ˋɛθɪl] *s* etilo
ethylene [ˋɛθɪ,lin] *s* etileno
etiquette [ˋɛtɪ,kɛt] *s* etiqueta
et seq. *abbr* **et sequens, et sequentes, et sequentia** (*and the following*)
étude [eˋtjud] *s* (mus) estudio
etymological dictionary [,ɛtəməˋlɑdʒɪkəl] *s* diccionario etimológico
etymology [,ɛtɪˋmɑlədʒi] *s* etimología
ety•mon [ˋɛtɪ,mɑn] *s* (*pl* **-mons** o **-ma** [mə]) étimo
eucalyp•tus [,jukəˋlɪptəs] *s* (*pl* **-tuses** o **-ti** [taɪ]) eucalipto
Eucharist [ˋjukərɪst] *s* Eucaristía
euchre [ˋjukər] *s* juego de naipes ‖ *tr* (coll) ser más listo que
eugenics [jʊˋdʒɛnɪks] *s* eugenesia
eulogistic [,juləˋdʒɪstɪk] *adj* elogiador
eulogize [ˋjulə,dʒaɪz] *tr* elogiar
eulo•gy [ˋjulədʒi] *s* (*pl* **-gies**) elogio
eunuch [ˋjunək] *s* eunuco
euphemism [ˋjufɪ,mɪzəm] *s* eufemismo
euphemistic [,jufɪˋmɪstɪk] *adj* eufemístico
euphonic [juˋfɑnɪk] *adj* eufónico
eupho•ny [ˋjufəni] *s* (*pl* **-nies**) eufonía
euphoria [juˋforɪ•ə] *s* euforia

euphuism [ˈjufju,ɪzəm] *s* eufuísmo
euphuistic [,jufjuˈɪstɪk] *adj* eufuístico
Euro *abbr* **Eurodollar**
Eurodollar [ˈjʊro,dɑlər] *s* eurodólar *m*
Europe [ˈjʊrəp] *s* Europa
European [,jʊrəˈpi•ən] *adj & s* europeo
European Economic Community *s* Comunidad Económica Europea
euthanasia [,juθəˈneʒə] *s* eutanasia
evacuate [ɪˈvækjʊ,et] *tr & intr* evacuar
evacuation [ɪ,vækjʊˈeʃən] *s* evacuación
evade [ɪˈved] *tr* evadir || *intr* evadirse
evaluate [ɪˈvæljʊ,et] *tr* evaluar
Evangel [ɪˈvændʒəl] *s* Evangelio
evangelic(al) [,ivænˈdʒɛlɪk(əl)] o [,ɛvənˈdʒɛlɪk(əl)] *adj* evangélico
Evangelist [ɪˈvændʒəlɪst] *s* Evangelista *m*
evaporate [ɪˈvæpə,ret] *tr* evaporar || *intr* evaporarse
evasion [ɪˈveʒən] *s* evasión, evasiva
evasive [ɪˈvesɪv] *adj* evasivo; elusivo
eve [iv] *s* víspera; **on the eve of** en vísperas de
even [ˈivən] *adj* (*smooth*) parejo, llano, liso; (*number*) par; constante, uniforme, invariable; (*temperament*) apacible, sereno; exacto, igual; **even up** a la par, parejos; **even with** al nivel de; **to be even** estar en paz; no deber nada a nadie; **to get even** desquitarse || *adv* aun, hasta; sin embargo; también; exactamente, igualmente; **even as** así como; **even if** aunque, aun cuando; **even so** aun así; **even though** aunque, aun cuando; **even when** aun cuando; **not even** ni . . . siquiera; **to break even** salir sin ganar ni perder; (*in gambling*) salir en paz || *tr* allanar, igualar; **to even up** equilibrar
evening [ˈivnɪŋ] *adj* vespertino || *s* tarde *f*
evening clothes *spl* traje *m* de etiqueta
evening dress *s* traje largo o de gala
evening gown *s* vestido de noche (*de mujer*)
evening primrose *s* hierba del asno
evening star *s* estrella vespertina, lucero de la tarde
evening wrap *s* salida de teatro
e′ven•song′ *s* canción de la tarde; (eccl) vísperas
event [ɪˈvɛnt] *s* acontecimiento, suceso; (*outcome*) resultado; (*public function*) acto; (sport) prueba; **at all events** o **in any event** en todo caso; **in the event that** en caso que
e′ven-tem′pered *adj* equilibrado
eventful [ɪˈvɛntfəl] *adj* lleno de acontecimientos; importante, memorable
eventual [ɪˈvɛntʃʊ•əl] *adj* final
eventuali•ty [ɪˈvɛntʃʊˈælɪti] *s* (*pl*-**ties**) eventualidad
eventually [ɪˈvɛntʃʊ•əli] *adv* finalmente, con el tiempo
eventuate [ɪˈvɛntʃʊ,et] *intr* concluir, resultar
ever [ˈɛvər] *adv* (*at all times*) siempre; (*at any time*) jamás, nunca, alguna vez; **as ever** como siempre; **as much as ever** tanto como antes; **ever since** (*since that time*) desde entonces; después de que; **ever so** muy; **ever so much** muchísimo; **hardly ever** o **scarcely ever** casi nunca; **not . . . ever** no . . . nunca
ev′er•glade′ *s* tierra pantanosa cubierta de hierbas altas
ev′er•green′ *adj* siempre verde || *s* planta siempre verde; **evergreens** ramas colgadas como adorno
ev′er•last′ing *adj* sempiterno; (*lasting indefinitely*) duradero; (*wearisome*) aburrido, cansado || *s* eternidad; (bot) siempreviva
ev′er•more′ *adv* eternamente; **for evermore** para siempre jamás
every [ˈɛvri] *adj* todos los; (*each*) cada, todo; (*being each in a series*) cada, p.ej., **every three days** cada tres días; **every bit** (coll) todo, p.ej., **every bit a man** todo un hombre; **every now and then** de vez en cuando; **every once in a while** una que otra vez; **every other day** cada dos días, un día sí y otro no; **every which way** (coll) por todas partes; (coll) en desarreglo
ev′ery•bod′y *pron indef* todo el mundo
ev′ery•day′ *adj* de todos los días; cotidiano, diario; común, ordinario
every man Jack o **every mother's son** *s* cada hijo de vecino
ev′ery•one′ o **every one** *pron indef* cada uno, todos, todo el mundo
ev′ery•thing′ *pron indef* todo
ev′ery•where′ *adv* en o por todas partes; a todas partes
evict [ɪˈvɪkt] *tr* desahuciar
eviction [ɪˈvɪkʃən] *s* desahucio
evidence [ˈɛvɪdəns] *s* evidencia; (law) prueba
evident [ˈɛvɪdənt] *adj* evidente
evil [ˈɛivəl] *adj* malo, malvado, malazo, maléfico || *s* mal *m*, maldad
e′vil•do′er *s* malhechor *m*, malvado
e′vil•do′ing *s* malhecho, maldad
evil eye *s* mal *m* de ojo
evil-minded [ˈivəlˈmaɪndɪd] *adj* mal pensado, malintencionado
Evil One, the el enemigo malo
evince [ɪˈvɪns] *tr* manifestar, mostrar
evoke [ɪˈvok] *tr* evocar
evolution [,ɛvəˈluʃən] *s* evolución; (math) extracción de raíces, radicación
evolutionary [,ɛvəˈluʃə,nɛri] o **evolutionist** [,ɛgəˈluʃənɪst] *s* evolucionista *mf*
evolve [ɪˈvɑlv] *tr* desarrollar; desprender (*olores, gases, calor*) || *intr* evolucionar
ewe [ju] *s* oveja
ewer [ˈju•ər] *s* aguamanil *m*
ex. *abbr* **examination, example, except, exchange, executive**
ex [ɛks] *prep* sin incluir, sin participación en || *s* (*pl* **exes**) la letra X; (coll) ex marido, ex mujer
ex- *adj* (*former*) ex, e.g., **the ex-president** el ex presidente
exact [ɛgˈzækt] *adj* exacto || *tr* exigir
exacting [ɛgˈzæktɪŋ] *adj* exigente
exaction [ɛgˈzækʃən] *s* exacción

exactly [ɛg'zæktli] *adv* exactamente; (*sharp, on the dot*) en punto
exactness [ɛg,zæktnɪs] *s* exactitud
exaggerate [ɛg'zædʒə,ret] *tr* exagerar
exalt [ɛg'zɔlt] *tr* exaltar, ensalzar
exam [ɛg'zæm] *s* (coll) examen *m*
examination [ɛg,zæmɪ'neʃən] *s* examen *m;* (med) reconocimiento médico, examen médico; **to take an examination** sufrir un examen, examinarse
examine [ɛg'zæmɪn] *tr* examinar; (med) reconocer, examinar, revisar
example [ɛg'zæmpəl] o [ɛg'zɑmpəl] *s* ejemplo; (*case serving as a warning to others*) ejemplar *m;* (*of mathematics*) problema *m;* **for example** por ejemplo
exasperate [ɛg'zæspə,ret] *tr* exasperar
excavate ['ɛkskə,vet] *tr* excavar
exceed [ɛk'sid] *tr* exceder; sobrepasar (*p.ej., el límite de velocidad*)
exceedingly [ɛk'sidɪŋli] *adv* sumamente, sobremanera
ex•cel [ɛk'sɛl] *v* (*pret & pp* **-celled;** *ger* **-celling**) *tr* aventajar ‖ *intr* sobresalir
excellence ['ɛksələns] *s* excelencia
excellen•cy ['ɛksələnsi] *s* (*pl* **-cies**) excelencia; **Your Excellency** Su Excelencia
excelsior [ɛk'sɛlsɪ•ər] *s* pajilla de madera, virutas de madera
except [ɛk'sɛpt] *prep* excepto; **except for** sin; **except that** a menos que ‖ *tr* exceptuar
exception [ɛk'sɛpʃən] *s* excepción; **to take exception** poner reparos, objetar; ofenderse; **with the exception of** a excepción de
exceptional [ɛk'sɛpʃənəl] *adj* excepcional
excerpt ['ɛksʌrpt] *s* excerta, selección ‖ [ɛk'sʌrpt] *tr* escoger
excess ['ɛksɛs] o [ɛk'sɛs] *adj* excedente, sobrante ‖ [ɛk'sɛs] *s* (*amount or degree by which one thing exceeds another*) exceso, excedente *m;* (*excessive amount; immoderate indulgence, unlawful conduct*) exceso; **in excess of** más que, superior a
excess baggage *s* exceso de equipaje
excess fare *s* suplemento
excessive [ɛk'sɛsɪv] *adj* excesivo
ex'cess-prof'its tax *s* impuesto sobre beneficios extraordinarios, impuesto sobre ganancias excesivas, impuesto sobre las utilidades excedentes
excess weight *s* exceso de peso
exchange [ɛks'tʃendʒ] *s* (*of greetings, compliments, blows, etc.*) cambio; (*of prisoners, merchandise, newspapers, credentials, etc.*) canje *m;* periódico de canje; (*place for buying and selling*) bolsa, lonja; estación telefónica, central *f* de teléfonos; **in exchange for** en cambio de, a trueque de ‖ *tr* cambiar; canjear (*prisioneros, mercancías, etc.*); darse, hacerse (*cortesías*); **to exchange greetings** saludarse; **to exchange shots** cambiar disparos
exchange rate *s* tipo de cambio, tasa de cambio, paridad
exchequer [ɛks'tʃɛkər] o ['ɛkstʃɛkər] *s* tesorería; fondos nacionales
excise tax [ɛk'saɪz] o ['ɛksaɪz] *m* impuesto interno, impuesto de consumo
excitable [ɛk'saɪtəbəl] *adj* excitable
excite [ɛk'saɪt] *tr* excitar
excitement [ɛk'saɪtmənt] *s* excitación
exciting [ɛk'saɪtɪŋ] *adj* emocionante, conmovedor; (*stimulating*) excitante
exclaim [ɛks'klem] *tr & intr* exclamar
exclamation [,ɛksklə'meʃən] *s* exclamación
exclamation mark o **point** *s* punto de admiración
exclude [ɛks'klud] *tr* excluir
exclusion [ɛks'kluʒən] *s* exclusión; **to the exclusion of** con exclusión de
exclusive [ɛks'klusɪv] *adj* exclusivo; (*clannish*) exclusivista; (*expensive*) (coll) carero; (*fashionable*) (coll) muy de moda; **exclusive of** con exclusión de
excommunicate [,ɛkskə'mjunɪ,ket] *tr* excomulgar
excommunication [,ɛkskə,mjunɪ'keʃən] *s* excomunión
ex'-com'munist *s* ex comunista *mf*
ex'-con' *s* (slang) ex convicto
ex'-con'vict *s* ex presidiario
excoriate [ɛks'korɪ,et] *tr* (fig) desollar, vituperar
excrement ['ɛkskrəmənt] *s* excremento
excruciating [ɛks'kruʃɪ,etɪŋ] *adj* atroz, agudísimo, vivísimo
exculpate ['ɛkskʌl,pet] o [ɛks'kʌlpet] *tr* exculpar
excursion [ɛks'kʌrʒən] *s* excursión, gira
excursionist [ɛks'kʌrʒənɪst] *s* excursionista *mf*
excusable [ɛks'kjusəbəl] *adj* excusable
excuse [ɛks'kjus] *s* excusa ‖ [ɛks'kjuz] *tr* excusar, disculpar; dispensar, perdonar; **excuse me, please** por favor; (con) permiso; ¿me permite, por favor?, dispénseme, por favor; discúlpeme, por favor; (*apologizing*) perdón, perdóneme; **excuse me!** ¡perdón!, ¡perdone!, ¡perdone Ud.!
execute ['ɛksɪ'kjut] *tr* ejecutar; (law) celebrar, finalizar (*una escritura*)
execution [,ɛksɪ'kjuʃən] *s* ejecución
executioner [,ɛksɪ'kjuʃənər] *s* ejecutor *m* de la justicia, verdugo
executive [ɛg'zɛkjətɪv] *adj* ejecutivo ‖ *m* poder ejecutivo; (*of a school, business, etc.*) dirigente *mf*
Executive Mansion *s* (U.S.A.) palacio presidencial
executor [ɛg'zɛkjətər] *s* albacea *m,* ejecutor testamentario
executrix [ɛg'zɛkjətrɪks] *s* albacea *f,* ejecutora testamentaria
exemplary [ɛg'zɛmpləri] o ['ɛgzəm,plɛri] *adj* ejemplar
exempli•fy [ɛg'zɛmplɪ,faɪ] *v* (*pret & pp* **-fied**) *tr* ejemplificar

exempt [ɛg'zɛmpt] *adj* exento ‖ *tr* eximir, exentar
exemption [ɛg'zɛmpʃən] *s* exención
exercise ['ɛksər,saɪz] *s* ejercicio; ceremonia; **to take exercise** hacer ejercicio ‖ *tr* ejercer (*p.ej., caridad, influencia*); ejercitar (*un arte, profesión, etc.; adiestrar con el ejercicio*); inquietar, preocupar; poner (*cuidado*) ‖ *ref* ejercitarse
exert [ɛg'zʌrt] *tr* ejercer (*una fuerza*); **to exert oneself** esforzarse
exertion [ɛg'zʌrʃən] *s* esfuerzo, empeño; (*active use*) ejercicio
exhalation [,ɛks•hə'leʃən] *s* (*of gas, vapors, etc.*) exhalación; (*of air from lungs*) espiración
exhale [ɛks'hel] o [ɛg'zel] *tr* exhalar (*gases, vapores*); espirar (*el aire aspirado*) ‖ *intr* exhalarse; espirar
exhaust [ɛg'zɔst] *s* escape *m;* tubo de escape ‖ *tr* (*to wear out, fatigue; to use up*) agotar; hacer el vacío en; apurar (*todos los medios*)
exhaust fan *s* ventilador *m* aspirador
exhaustion [ɛg'zɔstʃən] *s* agotamiento
exhaustive [ɛg'zɔstɪv] *adj* exhaustivo; comprensivo
exhaust manifold *s* múltiple *m* de escape
exhaust pipe *s* tubo de escape
exhaust valve *s* válvula de escape
exhibit [ɛg'zɪbit] *s* exhibición; (law) documento de prueba ‖ *tr* exhibir
exhibition [,ɛksɪ'bɪʃən] *s* exhibición
exhibitor [ɛg'zɪbɪtər] *s* expositor *m*
exhilarating [ɛg'zɪlə,retɪŋ] *adj* alegrador, regocijador, alborozador
exhort [ɛg'zɔrt] *tr* exhortar
exhume [ɛks'hjum] *tr* exhumar
exigen•cy ['ɛksɪdʒənsi] *s* (*pl* **-cies**) exigencia
exigent ['ɛksɪdʒənt] *adj* exigente
exile ['ɛgzaɪl] o ['ɛksaɪl] *s* destierro; (*person*) desterrado ‖ *tr* desterrar
exist [ɛg'zɪst] *intr* existir
existence [ɛg'zɪstəns] *s* existencia
existing [ɛg'zɪstɪŋ] *adj* existente
exit ['ɛgzɪt] o ['ɛksɪt] *s* salida ‖ *intr* salir
exobiology [,ɛksobaɪ'ɑlədʒi] *s* exobiología
exodus ['ɛksədəs] *s* éxodo
exonerate [ɛg'zɑnə,ret] *tr* (*to free from blame*) exculpar; (*to free from an obligation*) exonerar
exorbitant [ɛg'zɔrbɪtənt] *adj* exorbitante
exorcise ['ɛksɔr,saɪz] *tr* exorcizar
exotic [ɛg'zɑtɪk] *adj* exótico
exp. *abbr* **expenses, expired, export, express**
expand [ɛks,pænd] *tr* dilatar (*un gas, el metal*); (*to enlarge, develop*) ampliar, ensanchar; (*to unfold, stretch out*) desplegar, extender; (math) desarrollar (*una ecuación*) ‖ *intr* dilatarse; ampliarse, ensancharse; desplegarse, extenderse
expandable [ɛks'pændəbəl] *adj* (compu) ampliable
expanse [ɛks'pæns] *s* extensión
expansion [ɛks'pænʃən] *s* expansión
expansive [ɛks'pænsɪv] *adj* expansivo
expatiate [ɛks'peʃɪ,et] *intr* espaciarse, explayarse
expatriate [ɛks'petrɪ•ɪt] *adj* & *s* expatriado
expect [ɛks'pɛkt] *tr* esperar; (coll) creer, suponer
expectan•cy [ɛks'pɛktənsi] *s* (*pl* **-cies**) expectación
expectant mother [ɛks'pɛktənt] *s* futura madre
expectation [,ɛks'pɛkteʃən] *s* expectativa
expectorate [ɛks'pɛktə,ret] *tr* & *intr* expectorar
expedien•cy [ɛks'pidɪ•ənsi] *s* (*pl* **-cies**) conveniencia, oportunidad; ventaja personal
expedient [ɛks'pidɪ•ənt] *adj* conveniente, oportuno; egoísta, ventajoso; (*acting with self-interest*) ventajista ‖ *s* expediente *m*
expedite ['ɛkspɪ,daɪt] *tr* apresurar, despachar; expediar; dar curso a (*un documento*)
expedition [,ɛkspɪ'dɪʃən] *s* expedición
expeditious [,ɛkspɪ'dɪʃəs] *adj* expeditivo
expeditiously [,ɛkspɪ'dɪʃəsli] *adv* ejecutivamente
ex•pel [ɛks'pɛl] *v* (*pret & pp* **-pelled;** *ger* **-pelling**) *tr* expeler, expulsar
expend [ɛks'pɛnd] *tr* gastar, consumir
expendable [ɛks'pɛndəbəl] *adj* gastable; (*to be thrown away after use*) desechable; (*soldier*) sacrificable
expenditure [ɛks'pɛndɪtʃər] *s* gasto, consumo
expense [ɛks'pɛns] *s* gasto; **expenses** gastos, expensas; **to go to the expense of** meterse en gastos con; **to meet expenses** hacer frente a los gastos
expense account *s* cuenta de gastos
expensive [ɛks'pɛnsɪv] *adj* caro, costoso, dispendioso; (*charging high prices*) carero
experience [ɛks'pɪrɪ•əns] *s* experiencia ‖ *tr* experimentar
experienced [ɛksɪ'ənst] *adj* experimentado
experiment [ɛks'perɪmənt] *s* experiencia, experimento ‖ [ɛks'pɛrɪ,mɛnt] *intr* experimentar
expert ['ɛkspərt] *adj* & *s* experto
expiate ['ɛkspɪ,et] *tr* expiar
expiation [,ɛkspɪ'eʃən] *s* expiación
expiration date *s* (pharm) fecha de caducidad o vencimiento
expire [ɛks'paɪr] *tr* expeler (*el aire de los pulmones*) ‖ *intr* expirar (*expeler el aire de los pulmones; acabarse, p.ej., un plazo; fallecer*)
explain [ɛks'plen] *tr* explicar; **to explain away** descartar con explicaciones; (*to make excuse for*) explicar ‖ *intr* explicar, explicarse
explanation [,ɛksplə'neʃən] *s* explicación; dilucidación
explanatory [ɛks'plænə,tori] *adj* explicativo
explicit [ɛks'plɪsɪt] *adj* explícito
explode [ɛks'plod] *tr* volar, hacer saltar; desacreditar (*una teoría*) ‖ *intr* explotar, estallar, reventar
exploit ['ɛksplɔɪt] *s* hazaña, proeza ‖ [ɛks'plɔɪt] *tr* explotar
exploitation [,ɛksplɔɪ'teʃən] *s* explotación

exploration [,ɛksplə'reʃən] *s* exploración; (aerosp, meteor) sondeo
explore [ɛks'plor] *tr* explorar
explorer [ɛks'plorər] *s* explorador *m*
explosion [ɛks'ploʒən] *s* explosión; (*of a theory*) refutación
explosive [ɛks'plosɪv] *adj* explosivo ‖ *s* explosivo; (phonet) explosiva
exponent [ɛks'ponənt] *s* exponente *m*, expositor *m;* (math) exponente *m*
export ['ɛksport] *adj* de exportación ‖ *s* exportación; **exports** (*articles exported*) exportación ‖ [ɛks'port] o ['ɛksport] *tr & intr* exportar
exportation [,ɛkspor'teʃən] *s* exportación
exporter [ɛksportər] *s* exportador *m*
expose [ɛks'poz] *tr* exponer; (*to unmask*) desenmascarar; (*the Host*) manifestar, exponer; (phot) impresionar
exposé [,ɛkspo'ze] *s* desenmascaramiento
exposition [,ɛkspə'zɪʃən] *s* exposición; (rhet) exposición
expostulate [ɛks'pɑstʃə,let] *intr* protestar; **to expostulate with** reconvenir
exposure [ɛks'poʒər] *s* (*to a danger; position with respect to points of compass*) exposición; (*unmasking*) desenmascaramiento; (phot) exposición
expound [ɛks'paʊnd] *tr* exponer
express [ɛks'prɛs] *adj* expreso ‖ *adv* (*for a special purpose*) expresamente; por expreso ‖ *s* expreso; **by express** (rr) en gran velocidad ‖ *tr* expresar; (*to squeeze out*) exprimir; enviar por expreso; **to express oneself** expresarse
express company *s* compañía de transportes rápidos
expression [ɛks'prɛʃən] *s* expresión
expressive [ɛks'prɛsɪv] *adj* expresivo
expressly [ɛks'prɛsli] *adv* expresamente
express•man [ɛks'prɛsmən] *s* (*pl* **-men** [mən]) (U.S.A.) empleado del servicio de transportes rápidos
express train *s* tren expreso
express'way' *s* carretera de vía libre, autopista rápida
expropriate [ɛks'proprɪ,et] *tr* expropiar
expulsion [ɛks'pʌlʃən] *s* expulsión
expunge [ɛks'pʌndʒ] *tr* borrar, cancelar, arrasar
expurgate ['ɛkspər,get] *tr* expurgar
exquisite ['ɛkskwɪzɪt] o [ɛks'kwɪzɪt] *adj* exquisito; agudo, vivo; sensible
ex-service•man [,ɛks'sʌrvɪs,mæn] *s* (*pl* **-men** [,mɛn]) ex militar *m*, ex combatiente *m*
extant ['ɛkstənt] o [ɛks'tænt] *adj* existente
extemporaneous [ɛks,tɛmpə'renɪ•əs] *adj* sin preparación; (*made for the occasion*) provisional
extempore [ɛks'tɛmpəri] *adj* improvisado ‖ *adv* improvisadamente
extemporize [ɛks'tɛmpə,raɪz] *tr & intr* improvisar
extend [ɛks'tɛnd] *tr* extender; dar, ofrecer; hacer extensivos (*p.ej., vivos deseos*); prorrogar (*un plazo*) ‖ *intr* extenderse
extended [ɛks'tɛndɪd] *adj* extenso; prolongado
extended family *s* familia extensa
extension [ɛks'tɛnʃən] *s* extensión; prolongación (compu, telp) extensión
extension cord *s* extensión, alargador *m*
extension ladder *s* escalera extensible
extension manager *s* (compu) gestor *m* de extensiones
extension phone *s* teléfono interno
extension table *s* mesa de extensión
extensive [ɛks'tɛnsɪv] *adj* (*having great extent*) extenso; (*characterized by extension*) extensivo
extent [ɛks'tɛnt] *s* extensión; **to a certain extent** hasta cierto punto; **to a great extent** en sumo grado; **to the full extent** en toda su extensión
extenuate [ɛks'tɛnjʊ,et] *tr* (*to make seem less serious*) atenuar; (*to underrate*) menospreciar, no dar importancia a
exterior [ɛks'tɪrɪ•ər] *adj & s* exterior *m*
exterminate [ɛks'tʌrmɪ,net] *tr* exterminar; (*insects*) desinsectar
external [ɛks'tʌrnəl] *adj* externo ‖ **externals** *spl* exterioridad
extinct [ɛks'tɪŋkt] *adj* desaparecido; (*volcano*) extinto
extinguish [ɛks'tɪŋgwɪʃ] *tr* extinguir
extinguisher [ɛks'tɪŋgwɪʃər] *s* extinguidor *m*, extintor *m*
extirpate ['ɛkstər,pet] o [ɛks'tʌrpet] *tr* extirpar
ex•tol [ɛks'tol] o [ɛks'tɑl] *v* (*pret & pp* **-tolled;** *ger* **-tolling**) *tr* ensalzar
extort [ɛks'tɔrt] *tr* obtener por amenazas, fuerza o engaño
extortion [ɛks'tɔrʃən] *s* extorción
extra ['ɛkstrə] *adj* extra; (*spare*) de repuesto ‖ *adv* extraordinariamente ‖ *s* (*of a newspaper*) extra *m;* pieza de repuesto; (*something additional*) extra *m;* (theat) extra *mf*, figurante *mf*, comparsa *mf*
extract ['ɛkstrækt] *s* selección; (pharm) extracto ‖ [ɛks'trækt] *tr* (*to pull out, remove*) extraer; seleccionar (*pasajes de un libro*); (math) extraer
extraction [ɛks'trækʃən] *s* extracción
extracurricular [,ɛkstrəkə'rɪkjələr] *adj* extracurricular
extradition [,ɛkstrə'dɪʃən] *s* extradición
extra fare *s* recargo de tarifa, tarifa recargada
ex'tra-flat' *adj* extraplano
extragalactic [,ɛkstrəgə'læktɪk] *adj* extragaláctico
extramural [,ɛkstrə'mjʊrəl] *adj* extramural
extraneous [ɛks'trenɪ•əs] *adj* ajeno, extraño
extraordinary [,ɛkstrə'ɔrdɪ,nɛri] o [ɛks'trɔrdɪ,nɛri] *adj* extraordinario
extrapolate [ɛks'træpə,let] *tr & intr* extrapolar
extrasensory [,ɛkstrə'sɛnsəri] *adj* extrasensorio

extraterrestrial [,ɛkstrətə'rɛstrɪ•əl] *adj* extraterrestre
extravagance [ɛks'trævəgəns] *s* derroche *m,* prodigalidad, gasto excesivo; (*wildness, folly*) extravagancia
extravagant [ɛks'trævəgənt] *adj* derrochador, pródigo, gastador; (*wild, foolish*) extravagante
extreme [ɛks'trim] *adj & s* extremo; **in the extreme** en sumo grado; **to go to extremes** excederse, propasarse
extremely [ɛks'trimli] *adv* extremadamente, sumamente
extreme unction *s* extremaunción
extremism [ɛks'trimɪzəm] *s* extremismo
extremi•ty [ɛks'trɛmɪti] *s* (*pl* **-ties**) extremidad; (*great want*) extrema necesidad; **extremities** medidas extremas; (*hands and feet*) extremidades
extricate ['ɛsktrɪ,ket] *tr* desembarazar, desenredar
extrinsic [ɛks'trɪnsɪk] *adj* extrínseco
extroversion [,ɛkstrə'vʌrʒən] *s* extroversión
extrovert ['ɛkstrə,vʌrt] *s* extrovertido
extrude [ɛks'trud] *intr* resaltar, sobresalir
exuberant [ɛg'zubərənt] *adj* exuberante
exude [ɛg'zud] o [ɛk'sud] *tr & intr* exudar
exult [ɛg'zʌlt] *intr* exultar, gloriarse
exultant [ɛg'zʌltənt] *adj* exultante
eye [aɪ] *s* ojo; (*of hook and eye*) hembra, corcheta; **to catch one's eye** llamar la atención a uno; **to feast one's eyes on** deleitar la vista en; **to lay eyes on** alcanzar a ver; **to make eyes at** hacer guiños a; **to roll one's eyes** poner los ojos en blanco; **to see eye to eye** estar completamente de acuerdo; **to shut one's eyes to** hacer la vista gorda ante; **without batting an eye** sin pestañear, sin inmutarse ‖ *v* (*pret & pp* **eyed;** *ger* **eying** o **eyeing**) *tr* ojear; **to eye up and down** mirar de hito en hito
eye'ball' *s* globo del ojo
eye'bolt' *s* armella, cáncamo
eye'brow' *s* ceja; **to raise one's eyebrows** arquear las cejas
eye'cup' *s* ojera, lavaojos *m*
eye'drops' *spl* gotas para los ojos, colirio
eyeful ['aɪfʊl] *s* (coll) buena ojeada
eye'glass' *s* (*of optical instrument*) ocular *m;* (*eyecup*) ojera, lavaojos *m;* **eyeglasses** gafas, anteojos
eye'lash' *s* pestaña
eyelet ['aɪlɪt] *s* ojete *m,* ojal *m;* (*hole to look through*) mirilla
eye'lid' *s* párpado
eye of the morning *s* sol *m*
eye opener ['opənər] *s* noticia asombrosa o inesperada; (coll) trago de licor
eye'patch *s* parche *m*
eye'piece' *s* ocular *m*
eye'shade' *s* visera
eye shadow *s* crema para los párpados; sombra (de ojos)
eye'shot' *s* alcance *m* de la vista
eye'sight' *s* vista; (*range*) alcance *m* de la vista
eye socket *s* cuenca del ojo
eye'sore' *s* cosa que ofende la vista
eye'strain' *s* vista fatigada
eye'-test' chart *s* escala tipográfica oftalmométrica, tipo de ensayo, tipo de prueba
eye'tooth' *s* (*pl* **teeth'**) colmillo, diente canino; **to cut one's eyeteeth** (coll) tener el colmillo retorcido; **to give one's eyeteeth for** (coll) dar los ojos de la cara por
eye'wash' *s* colirio; (coll) cuento chino, tontería, halago para engañar
eye'wit'ness *s* testigo ocular, testigo presencial
ey•rie o **ey•ry** ['ɛri] *s* (*pl* **-ries**) nido de águilas, nido de aves de rapiña; (fig) altura, morada elevada

F

F, f [ɛf] sexta letra del alfabeto inglés
f. *abbr* **feminine, folio**
F. *abbr* **Fahrenheit, Friday**
fable ['febəl] *s* fábula
fabric ['fæbrɪk] *s* tejido; textura; (*structure*) fábrica
fabricate ['fæbrɪ, ket] *tr* fabricar
fabrication [,fæbrɪ'keʃən] *s* fabricación; mentira
fabulous ['fæbjələs] *adj* fabuloso
façade [fə'sɑd] *s* fachada
face [fes] *s* cara, rostro; (*of cloth*) haz *f;* (*of earth*) faz *f;* (*grimace*) mueca; (*of watch*) esfera, muestra; (*impudence*) descaro; **face-to-face** cara a cara; **in the face of** en presencia de; **to keep a straight face** contener la risa; **to lose face** desprestigiarse; **to save face** salvar las apariencias; **to show one's face** dejarse ver ‖ *tr* volver la cara hacia; arrostrar; revestir (*un muro*); forrar (*un vestido*); **facing** cara a ‖ *intr* — **to face about** volver la mirada; dar media vuelta; cambiar de opinión; **to face on** dar a o sobre; **to face up to** encararse con
face card *s* figura, naipe *m* de figura
face lifting *s* cirugía estética
face pack *s* máscara facial
face powder *s* polvos de tocador, polvos compacto
facet ['fæsɪt] *s* faceta
face value *s* valor *m* nominal; (fig) valor aparente o facial

facial [ˈfeʃəl] *adj* facial || *s* masaje *m* facial
facilitate [fəˈsɪlɪˌtet] *tr* facilitar
facili•ty [fəˈsɪlɪti] *s* (*pl* **-ties**) facilidad
facing [ˈfesɪŋ] *s* revestimiento, paramento
facsimile [fækˈsɪmɪli] *s* facsímile *m* || *tr* facsimilar
fact [fækt] *s* hecho; **in fact** en realidad; **the fact is that** ello es que
faction [ˈfækʃən] *s* facción; discordia
factional [ˈfækʃənəl] *adj* faccionario
factionalism [ˈfækʃənəˌlɪzəm] *s* parcialidad, partidismo
factor [ˈfæktər] *s* factor *m* || *tr* descomponer en factores
facto•ry [ˈfæktəri] *s* (*pl* **-ries**) fábrica
factual [ˈfæktʃʊ•əl] *adj* verdadero, objetivo
facul•ty [ˈfækəlti] *s* (*pl* **-ties**) facultad; (*division of university*) facultad; (*teaching staff*) cuerpo docente, profesorado
fad [fæd] *s* afición pasajera, moda pasajera
fade [fed] *tr* desteñir || *intr* desteñir, desteñirse; apagarse (*un sonido*); (rad) desvanecerse
fade'out' *s* desaparición gradual; (rad) desvanecimiento
fag [fæg] *s* (pej) maricón *m* || *tr*—**to fag out** cansar
faggot [ˈfægət] *s* haz *m* de leña; (pej) maricón *m*
fail [fel] *s*—**without fail** sin falta || *tr* faltar a; reprobar, suspender (*a un alumno*); salir mal en (*un examen*) || *intr* malograrse, fracasar; salir mal (*un alumno*); fallar (*un motor*); (com) quebrar, hacer bancarrota; **to fail to** dejar de
failure [ˈfeljər] *s* malogro, fracaso, mal éxito; (*student*) perdigón *m;* (com) quiebra
faint [fent] *adj* débil; **to feel faint** sentirse desfallecido || *s* desmayo || *intr* desmayarse
faint-hearted [ˈfentˈhɑrtɪd] *adj* cobarde, tímido, apocado
fair [fɛr] *adj* justo, imparcial; regular, ordinario; favorable, propicio; (*hair*) rubio; (*complexion*) blanco; (*sky*) despejado; (*weather*) bueno, bonancible || *adv* imparcialmente; **to play fair** jugar limpio || *s* (*exhibition*) feria; (*carnival*) quermese *m,* verbena
fair copy *s* copia en limpio
fair'ground' *s* real *m,* campo de una feria
fairly [ˈfɛrli] *adv* justamente; bastante
fair-minded [ˈfɛrˈmaɪndɪd] *adj* justo, imparcial
fairness [ˈfɛrnɪs] *s* justicia, imparcialidad; (*of weather*) serenidad; (*of complexion*) blancura
fair play *s* juego limpio, limpieza
fair'-sized' *adj* bastante grande
fair'-trade agreement *s* convenio comercial (*sobre los precios mínimos*)
fair'weath'er *adj*—**a fair-weather friend** amigo del buen viento
fair•y [ˈfɛri] *adj* feérico || *s* (*pl* **-ies**) hada
fairy godmother *s* hada madrina
fair'y•land' *s* tierra de las hadas
fairy ring *s* corro de brujas
fairy tale *s* cuento de hadas; (fig) bella poesía
faith [feθ] *s* fe *f;* **to break faith with** faltar a la palabra dada a; **to keep faith with** cumplir la palabra dada a; **to pin one's faith on** tener puesta su esperanza en; **upon my faith!** ¡a fe mía!
faithful [ˈfeθfəl] *adj* fiel, leal || **the faithful** los fieles
faithless [ˈfeθlɪs] *adj* infiel, desleal
fake [fek] *adj* (coll) falso, fingido || *s* impostura, patraña; (*person*) farsante *mf* || *tr & intr* falsificar, fingir
faker [ˈfekər] *s* (coll) impostor *m,* patrañero; (*peddler*) (coll) buhonero
falcon [ˈfɔkən] o [ˈfɔlkən] *s* halcón *m*
Falkland Islands, the [ˈfɔklənd] *s* las Malvinas
fall [fɔl] *adj* otoñal || *s* caída; (*of water*) catarata, salto de agua; (*of prices*) baja; (*autumn*) otoño; **falls** catarata, caída de agua || *v* (*pret* **fell** [fɛl]; *pp* **fallen** [ˈfɔlən]) *intr* caer, caerse; **to fall apart** caerse a pedazos; **to fall back** (mil) replegarse; **to fall behind** quedarse atrás; **to fall down** caerse; **to fall due** vencer (*una letra*); **to fall flat** caer tendido; no tener éxito; **to fall for** (slang) ser engañado por; (slang) enamorarse de; **to fall in** desplomarse (*un techo*); ponerse de acuerdo; **to fall in with** trabar amistades con; ponerse de acuerdo con; **to fall off** caer de; disminuir; **to fall out** desavenirse; **to fall out of** caerse de; **to fall out with** esquinarse con; **to fall over** caerse; (coll) adular, halagar; **to fall through** fracasar, malograrse; **to fall to** recaer (*la herencia, la elección*) en; **to fall under** estar comprendido en
fallacious [fəˈleʃəs] *adj* erróneo, engañoso
falla•cy [ˈfæləsi] *s* (*pl* **-cies**) error *m,* equivocación
fall guy *s* (slang) cabeza de turco
fallible [ˈfælɪbəl] *adj* falible
falling star *s* estrella fugaz
Fallopian tube [fəˈlopi•ən] *s* trompa de Falopio
fall'out' *s* caída radiactiva, precipitación radiactiva; (*side effect*) secuela
fallout shelter *s* refugio antinuclear
fallow [ˈfælo] *adj* barbechado; **to lie fallow** estar en barbecho (*tierra labrantía*); (fig) quedar sin emplear, quedar sin ejecutar (*una cosa provechosa*) || *s* barbecho || *tr* barbechar
false [fɔls] *adj* falso; (*hair, teeth, etc.*) postizo || *adv* falsamente; **to play false** traicionar
false alarm *s* falsa alarma
false bottom *s* doble fondo
false colors *spl* pretextos falsos
false friend *s* (*deceptive cognate*) falso amigo
false-hearted [ˈfɔlsˈhɑrtɪd] *adj* pérfido
falsehood [ˈfɔls•hʊd] *s* falsedad
false pretenses *spl* falsas apariencias
false start *s* (sport) salida en falso, salida nula
false teeth *s* dentadura postiza, caja de dientes (Col), plancha (Chile)
falset•to [fɔlˈsɛto] *s* (*pl* **-tos**) (*voice*) falsete *m;* (*person*) falsetista *m*
falsi•fy [ˈfɔlsɪˌfaɪ] *v* (*pret & pp* **-fied**) *tr* falsifi-

car; (*to disprove*) refutar || *intr* falsificar; mentir
falsi•ty [ˈfɔlsɪti] *s* (*pl* **-ties**) falsedad
falter [ˈfɔltər] *s* vacilación; (*in speech*) balbuceo || *intr* vacilar; balbucear
fame [fem] *s* fama
famed [femd] *adj* afamado
familiar [fəˈmɪljər] *adj* familiar; conocido; común; **familiar with** familiarizado con
familiari•ty [fəˌmɪlɪˈærɪti] *s* (*pl* **-ties**) familiaridad; conocimiento
familiarize [fəˈmɪljəˌraɪz] *tr* familiarizar
fami•ly [ˈfæmɪli] *adj* familiar; **in the family way** (coll) en estado de buena esperanza; **to run in the family** venir de familia || *s* (*pl* **-lies**) familia
family man *s* hombre casero
family name *s* apellido
family physician *s* médico de cabecera
family planning *s* planificación familiar
family tree *s* árbol genealógico
famish [ˈfæmɪʃ] *tr & intr* hambrear
famished [ˈfæmɪʃt] *adj* famélico
famous [ˈfeməs] *adj* famoso; (*notable, excellent*) (coll) famoso
fan [fæn] *s* abanico; ventilador *m;* (coll) hincha *mf,* aficionado || *v* (*pret & pp* **fanned;** *ger* **fanning**) *tr* abanicar; (*to winnow*) aventar; ahuyentar con abanico; avivar (*el fuego*); excitar (*las pasiones*); (slang) azotar || *intr* abanicarse; **to fan out** salir (*un camino*) en todas direcciones
fanatic [fəˈnætɪk] *adj & s* fanático
fanatical [fəˈnætɪkəl] *adj* fanático
fanaticism [fəˈnætɪˌsɪzəm] *s* fanatismo
fan belt *s* correa de(l) ventilador
fancied [ˈfænsid] *adj* imaginario
fancier [ˈfænsɪ•ər] *s* aficionado; visionario; (*of animals*) criador aficionado
fanciful [ˈfænsɪfəl] *adj* fantástico, extravagante; imaginativo
fan club *s* club *m* de admiradores
fan•cy [ˈfænsi] *adj* (*comp* **-cier;** *super* **-ciest**) de fantasía, de imitación; fino, de lujo, precioso; ornamental; primoroso; fantástico, extravagante || *s* (*pl* **-cies**) fantasía; afición, gusto; **to take a fancy to** aficionarse a, prendarse de || *v* (*pret & pp* **-cied**) *tr* imaginar
fancy dress *s* traje *m* de fantasía, disfraz *m*
fan′cy•work′ *s* (sew) labor *f* (ornamental)
fanfare [ˈfænfɛr] *s* fanfarria
fang [fæŋ] *s* colmillo; (*of reptile*) diente *m*
fan′light′ *s* montante *m* (*en forma de abanico*)
fanny [ˈfænɪ] *s* (slang) trasero
fantastic(al) [fænˈtæstɪk(əl)] *adj* fantástico
fanta•sy [ˈfæntəsi] *s* (*pl* **-sies**) fantasía
far [fɑr] *adj* lejano; **on the far side of** del otro lado de || *adv* lejos; **as far as** hasta; en cuanto; **as far as I am concerned** por lo que a mí me toca; **as far as I know** que yo sepa; **by far** con mucho; **far and near** por todas partes; **far away** muy lejos; **far be it from me** no lo permita Dios; **far better** mucho mejor; **far different** muy diferente; **far from** lejos de; **far from it** ni con mucho; **far into** hasta muy adentro de; hasta muy tarde de; **far more** mucho más; **far off** a gran distancia; **how far** cuán lejos; **how far is it?** ¿cuánto hay de aquí?; **in so far as** en cuanto; **thus far** hasta ahora; **thus far this year** en lo que va del año; **to go far towards** contribuir mucho a
faraway [ˈfɑrəˌwe] *adj* lejano, distante; abstraído, preocupado
farce [fɑrs] *s* farsa; (*ridiculous act*) papelada
farcical [ˈfɑrsɪkəl] *adj* ridículo
fare [fɛr] *s* pasaje *m;* pasajero; alimento; comida; **to collect fares** cobrar el pasaje || *intr* pasarlo, p.ej., **how did you fare?** ¿cómo lo pasó Ud.?
Far East *s* Extremo Oriente, Lejano Oriente
fare′well′ *s* despedida; **to bid farewell to** o **to take farewell of** despedirse de || *interj* ¡adiós!
far•fetched [ˈfarˈfɛtʃt] *adj* traído por los pelos
far-flung [ˈfɑrˈflʌŋ] *adj* de gran alcance, vasto; (*distant*) remoto, lejano
farm [fɑrm] *adj* agrícola; agropecuario || *s* granja; terreno agrícola || *tr* cultivar, labrar (*la tierra*) || *intr* cultivar la tierra y criar animales
farmer [ˈfɑrmər] *s* granjero; agricultor *m*
farm′hand *s* peón *m,* mozo de granja
farm′house′ *s* alquería, cortijo
farming [ˈfɑrmɪŋ] *s* agricultura, labranza
farm′land *s* tierras de labranza
farm′yard′ *s* corral *m* de granja
far′-off′ *adj* lejano, distante
far-reaching [ˈfɑrˈritʃɪŋ] *adj* de mucho alcance
far-sighted [ˈfɑrˈsaɪtɪd] *adj* previsor, clarividente; (path) présbita, hipermétrope
farther [ˈfɑrðər] *adj* más lejano; adicional || *adv* más lejos, más allá; además, también; **farther on** más adelante
farthest [ˈfɑrðɪst] *adj* (el) más lejano; último || *adv* más lejos; más
farthing [ˈfɑrðɪŋ] *s* (Brit) cuarto de penique
Far West *s* (U.S.A.) Lejano Oeste
fascinate [ˈfæsɪˌnet] *tr* fascinar
fascinating [ˈfæsɪˌnetɪŋ] *adj* fascinante, cautivador
fascism [ˈfæʃizəm] *s* fascismo
fascist [ˈfæʃist] *adj & s* fascista *mf*
fashion [ˈfæʃən] *s* moda, boga; estilo, manera; alta sociedad; **after a fashion** en cierto modo; **in fashion** de moda; **out of fashion** fuera de moda; **to go out of fashion** pasar de moda || *tr* labrar, forjar
fashion designing *s* alta costura
fashion plate *s* figurín *m;* (*person*) (coll) figurín *m,* elegante *mf;* **to be a fashion plate** (coll) ir hecho un maniquí
fashion show *s* desfile *m* de modas
fast [fæst] *adj* rápido, veloz; (*clock*) adelantado; fijado; disipado; (*friend*) fiel || *adv* aprisa, rápidamente; firmemente; (*asleep*) profundamente; **to hold fast** mantenerse firme; **to live fast** vivir de una manera disipada || *s*

ayuno; **to break one's fast** romper el ayuno || *intr* ayunar
fast day *s* día *m* de ayuno
fasten [ˈfæsən] *tr* fijar; atar; abrochar; cerrar con llave; (*one's belt*) ajustarse; (*blame*) aplicar || *intr* fijarse
fastener [ˈfæsənər] *s* asilla; (*snap, clasp*) cierre *m;* (*for papers*) sujetapapeles *m*
fast′-food′ *adj* de comida rápida
fast forward *s* (mach, mov) avance rápido
fastidious [fæsˈtɪdɪ•əs] *adj* quisquilloso, descontentadizo
fasting [ˈfæstɪŋ] *s* ayuno
fat [fæt] *adj* (*comp* **fatter;** *super* **fattest**) gordo; poderoso; opulento; (*profitable*) pingüe; (*spark*) caliente; **to get fat** engordar || *s* grasa; (*suet*) gordo, sebo
fatal [ˈfetəl] *adj* fatal
fatalism [ˈfetə,lɪzəm] *s* fatalismo
fatalist [ˈfetəlɪst] *s* fatalista *mf*
fatali•ty [fəˈtælɪti] *s* (*pl* **-ties**) fatalidad; (*in accidents, war, etc.*) muerte *f*
fate [fet] *s* sino, hado; **the Fates** las Parcas || *tr* condenar, predestinar
fated [ˈfetɪd] *adj* hadado, predestinado
fateful [ˈfetfəl] *adj* fatídico; fatal
fat′head′ *s* (coll) tronco, estúpido
father [ˈfɑðər] *s* padre *m,* papá; (*an elderly man*) (coll) tío || *tr* servir de padre a; engendrar; inventar
fatherhood [ˈfɑðər,hʊd] *s* paternidad
fa′ther-in-law′ *s* (*pl* **fathers-in-law**) suegro
fa′ther•land′ *s* patria
fatherless [ˈfɑðərlɪs] *adj* huérfano de padre, sin padre
fatherly [ˈfɑðərli] *adj* paternal
Father's Day *s* Día *m* del Padre
Father Time *s* el Tiempo
fathom [ˈfæðəm] *s* braza || *tr* sondear; profundizar
fathomless [ˈfæðəmlɪs] *adj* insondable
fatigue [fəˈtig] *s* fatiga; (mil) faena || *tr* fatigar, cansar
fatigue clothes *spl* (mil) traje *m* de faena
fatigue duty *s* faena
fatten [ˈfætən] *tr & intr* engordar
fat•ty [ˈfæti] *adj* (*comp* **-tier;** *super* **-tiest**) graso; (pathol) grasoso; (*chubby*) (coll) gordiflón || *s* (*pl* **-ties**) (pej) gordiflón *m*
fatuous [ˈfætʃʊ•əs] *adj* fatuo; irreal, ilusivo
fatwa [ˈfætwɑ] *s* (*religious and legal decree issued by a Muslim cleric*) fatwa *m* (*decreto promulgado por un clérigo musulmán*)
faucet [ˈfɔsɪt] *s* grifo
fault [fɔlt] *s* (*misdeed, blame*) culpa; (*defect*) vicio, falta; (geol) falla; (sport) falta; **it's your fault** Ud. tiene la culpa; **to a fault** excesivamente; **to find fault with** culpar, echar la culpa a; hallar defecto en
fault′find′ing *adj* criticón, reparón || *s* manía de criticar
faultless [ˈfɔltlɪs] *adj* perfecto, impecable
fault•y [ˈfɔlti] *adj* (*comp* **-ier;** *super* **-iest**) defectuoso, imperfecto
faun[fɔn] *s* fauno
fauna [ˈfɔnə] *s* fauna
favor [ˈfevər] *s* favor *m;* (*letter*) atenta, grata; **do me the favor to** hágame Ud. el favor de; **by your favor** con permiso de Ud.; **favors** regalos de fiesta, objetos de cotillón; **to be in favor with** disfrutar del favor de; **to be out of favor** caer en desgracia || *tr* favorecer; (coll) parecerse a
favorable [ˈfevərəbəl] *adj* favorable
favorite [ˈfevərɪt] *adj & s* favorito
favoritism [ˈfevərɪ,tɪzəm] *s* favoritismo
fawn [fɔn] *s* cervato || *intr*—**to fawn on** adular servilmente; hacer fiestas a
fax [fæks] *s* (*machine; message*) fax *m* || *tr* faxear, mandar por fax, enviar por fax
faze [fez] *tr* (coll) molestar, desanimar
FBI [,ɛf,biˈaɪ] *s* (letterword) (**Federal Bureau of Investigation**) FBI; Negociado Federal de Investigaciones (*equivalente a la*) BIC (**Brigada de Investigación Criminal**)
fear [fɪr] *s* miedo; **for fear of** por miedo de, por temor de; **for fear that** por miedo (de) que; **no fear** no hay peligro; **to be in fear of** tener miedo de || *tr & intr* temer
fearful [ˈfɪrfəl] *adj* medroso; (coll) enorme, muy malo
fearless [ˈfɪrlɪs] *adj* arrojado, intrépido
feasible [ˈfɪsɪbəl] *adj* factible, viable
feast [fist] *s* fiesta; (*sumptuous meal*) festín *m,* banquete *m* || *tr & intr* banquetear; **to feast on** regalarse con
feat [fit] *s* hazaña, proeza
feather [ˈfɛðər] *s* pluma; (*plume; arrogance*) penacho; clase *f,* género; **in fine feather** de buen humor; en buena salud || *tr* emplumar; (carp) machihembrar; **to feather one's nest** hacer todo para enriquecerse
feather bed *s* colchón *m* de plumas; (*comfortable situation*) lecho de plumas
feath′er•bed′ding *s* empleo de más obreros de lo necesario (*exigido por los sindicatos*)
feath′er•brain′ *s* cascabelero
feath′er•edge′ *s* (*of board*) bisel *m;* (*of sharpened tool*) filván *m*
feath′er•weight′ *s* (sport) peso pluma
feathery [ˈfɛðəri] *adj* plumoso
feature [ˈfitʃər] *s* facción; característica, rasgo distintivo; película principal; artículo principal; (compu) prestación; **features** facciones || *tr* delinear; ofrecer como cosa principal; (coll) destacar, hacer resaltar
feature writer *s* articulista *mf*
February [ˈfɛbru,ɛri] *s* febrero
feces [ˈfisiz] *spl* heces *fpl,* excremento
feckless [ˈfɛklɪs] *adj* irresponsable; ineficaz, sin valor; inútil, fútil
federal [ˈfɛdərəl] *adj & s* federal *mf*
Federal Republic of Switzerland *s* Confederación Helvética

federate [ˈfɛdə,ret] *adj* federado ‖ *tr* federar ‖ *intr* federarse
federation [,fɛdəˈreʃən] *s* federación
fedora [fɪˈdorə] *s* sombrero de fieltro suave con ala vuelta
fed up [fɛd] *adj* harto; **to get fed up with** desenamorarse de
fee [fi] *s* honorarios; (*for admission, tuition, etc.*) cuota, precio; (*tip*) propina ‖ *tr* pagar; dar propina a
feeble [ˈfibəl] *adj* débil; caedizo
feeble-minded [ˈfibəlˈmaɪndɪd] *adj* imbécil; irresoluto, vacilante
feed [fid] *s* alimento, comida; (mach) dispositivo de alimentación ‖ *v* (*pret & pp* **fed** [fɛd]) *tr* alimentar; (*e.g., a dog*) dar de comer a ‖ *intr* alimentarse
feed′back′ *s* regeneración; (psychol) retroalimentación; comentarios *fpl,* reacción; informaciones *fpl;* comentario privado y confidencial; (electron, rad) realimentación
feed bag *s* cebadera, morral *m*
feeder industries *spl* subsidiarias *fpl*
feed pump *s* bomba de alimentación
feed trough *s* comedero
feed wire *s* (elec) conductor *m* de alimentación
feel [fil] *s* sensación; (*sense of what is right*) tino ‖ *v* (*pret & pp* **felt** [fɛlt]) *tr* sentir; (*e.g., with the hands*) palpar, tentar; tomar (*el pulso*); tantear (*el camino*) ‖ *intr* (*sick, tired, etc.*) sentirse; palpar; **to feel bad** sentirse mal; condolerse; **to feel cheap** avergonzarse; **to feel comfortable** sentirse a gusto; **to feel for** buscar tentando; condolerse de; **to feel like** tener ganas de; **to feel safe** sentirse a salvo; **to feel sorry** sentir; arrepentirse; **to feel sorry for** compadecer; arrepentirse de
feeler [ˈfilər] *s* (*something said to draw someone out*) buscapié *m,* tranquilla; **feelers** (*of insect*) anténulas, palpos; (*of mollusk*) tentáculos
feeling [ˈfilɪŋ] *s* (*with senses*) sensación; (*impression, emotion*) sentimiento; presentimiento; parecer *m*
feign [fen] *tr* aparentar, fingir ‖ *intr* fingir; **to feign to be** fingirse
feint [fent] *s* (*threat*) finta; (*of fencer*) pase *m,* treta ‖ *intr* hacer una finta
feldspar [ˈfɛld,spɑr] *s* feldespato
felicitate [fəˈlɪsɪ,tet] *tr* felicitar
felicitous [fəˈlɪsɪtəs] *adj* (*opportune*) feliz; elocuente
fell [fɛl] *adj* cruel, feroz, mortal ‖ *tr* talar (*árboles*)
fellow [ˈfɛlo] *s* (coll) mozo, tipo, sujeto; (coll) pretendiente *m;* prójimo; (*of a society*) socio, miembro; (*holder of fellowship*) pensionista *mf*
fellow being *s* prójimo
fellow citizen *s* conciudadano
fellow countryman *s* compatriota *mf*
fellow man *s* prójimo
fellow member *s* consocio
fellowship [ˈfɛlo,ʃɪp] *s* compañerismo; (*for study*) pensión
fellow traveler *s* compañero de viaje
felon [ˈfɛlən] *s* delincuente *mf* de mayor cuantía; (pathol) panadizo
felo•ny [ˈfɛləni] *s* (pl **-nies**) delito de mayor cuantía; **to compound a felony** aceptar dinero para no procesar
felt [fɛlt] *s* fieltro
felt′-tipped′ pen *s* rotulador *m,* marcador *m;* plumón *m* (Mex)
female [ˈfimel] *adj* (*sex*) femenino; (*animal, plant, piece of a device*) hembra ‖ *s* hembra
feminine [ˈfɛmɪnɪn] *adj & s* femenino
feminism [ˈfɛmɪ,nɪzəm] *s* feminismo
fen [fɛn] *s* pantano
fence [fɛns] *s* cerca, cercado; (*for stolen goods*) alcahuete *m;* receptador; (*of a saw*) guía; **on the fence** (coll) indeciso ‖ *tr* cercar; (*stolen goods*) blanquear ‖ *intr* esgrimir
fencing [ˈfɛnsɪŋ] *s* (*art*) esgrima; (*act*) esgrimidura
fend [fɛnd] *tr*—**to fend off** apartar, resguardarse de ‖ *intr*—**to fend for oneself** (coll) tirar por su lado
fender [ˈfɛndər] *s* (*mudguard*) guardafango, guardabarros *m;* (*of locomotive*) quitapiedras *m;* (*of trolley car*) salvavidas *m;* (*of fireplace*) guardafuego
fen′der•ben′der *s* (coll) topetón *m*
fennel [ˈfɛnəl] *s* hinojo
ferment [ˈfʌrmɛnt] *s* fermento; fermentación ‖ [fərˈmɛnt] *tr & intr* fermentar
fern [fʌrn] *s* helecho
ferocious [fəˈroʃəs] *adj* feroz
feroci•ty [fəˈrɑsɪti] *s* (*pl* **-ties**) ferocidad
ferret [ˈfɛrɪt] *s* hurón *m* ‖ *tr*—**to ferret out** huronear ‖ *intr* huronear
Ferris wheel [ˈfɛrɪs] *s* rueda de feria, noria
fer•ry [ˈfɛri] *s* (*pl* **-ries**) bote *m* de paso, ferryboat *m* ‖ *v* (*pret & pp* **-ried**) *tr* pasar (*viajeros, mercancías*) a través del río ‖ *intr* cruzar el río en barco
fer′ry•boat′ *s* bote *m* de paso, ferry-boat *m*
fertile [ˈfʌrtɪl] *adj* fértil
fertilize [ˈfʌrtɪ,laɪz] *tr* abonar, fertilizar; (*to impregnate*) fecundar
fervid [ˈfʌrvɪd] *adj* férvido, vehemente
fervor [ˈfʌrvər] *s* fervor *m*
fervent [ˈfʌrvənt] *adj* ferviente, fervoroso
fester [ˈfɛstər] *s* úlcera ‖ *tr* enconar ‖ *intr* enconarse (*una herida; el ánimo de uno*)
festival [ˈfɛstɪvəl] *adj* festivo ‖ *s* fiesta; (*of music*) festival *m*
festive [ˈfɛstɪv] *adj* festivo
festivi•ty [fɛsˈtɪvɪti] *s* (*pl* **-ties**) festividad
festoon [fɛsˈtun] *s* festón *m* ‖ *tr* festonear
fetch [fetʃ] *tr* ir por, hacer venir, traer; venderse a, venderse por
fetching [ˈfɛtʃɪŋ] *adj* (coll) encantador, atractivo
fete [fet] *s* fiesta ‖ *tr* festejar
fetid [ˈfɛtɪd] o [ˈfitɪd] *adj* fétido

fetish [ˈfitɪʃ] o [ˈfɛtɪʃ] *s* fetiche *m*
fetlock [ˈfɛtlɑk] *s* espolón *m;* (*tuft of hair*) cerneja
fetter [ˈfɛtər] *s* grillete *m,* grillo || *tr* engrillar; impedir
fettle [ˈfɛtəl] *s* estado, condición; **in fine fettle** en buena condición
fetus [ˈfitəs] *s* feto
feud [fjud] *s* odio hereditario, enemistad de larga duración
feudal [ˈfjudəl] *adj* feudal
feudalism [ˈfjudəˌlɪzəm] *s* feudalismo
fever [ˈfivər] *s* fiebre *f,* calentura
fever blister *s* escupidura, fuegos en los labios
feverish [ˈfivəriʃ] *adj* febril, calenturiento
few [fju] *adj & pron* pocos, no muchos; **a few** unos pocos, unos cuantos; **quite a few** muchos
fiancé [ˌfi•ɑnˈse] *s* novio, prometido; novillo (Mex, P-R)
fiancée [ˌfi•ɑnˈse] *s* novia, prometida
fias•co [fɪˈæsko] *s* (*pl* **-cos** o **-coes**) fiasco
fiat [ˈfi•æt] *s* orden *m,* decreto
fib [fɪb] *s* mentirilla || *v* (*pret & pp* **fibbed;** *ger* **fibbing**) *intr* decir mentirillas, macanear
fiber [ˈfaɪbər] *s* fibra; carácter *m,* índole *f*
fi'berglass' *s* fibra de vidrio, lana de vidrio
fibrous [ˈfaɪbrəs] *adj* fibroso
fickle [ˈfɪkəl] *adj* inconstante, veleidoso
fiction [ˈfɪkʃən] *s* (*invention*) ficción; (*branch of literature*) novelística; **pure fiction!** ¡puro cuento!
fictional [ˈfɪkʃənəl] *adj* novelesco
fictionalize [ˈfɪkʃənəˌlaɪz] *tr* novelizar
fictitious [ˈfɪkˈtɪʃəs] *adj* ficticio
fiddle [ˈfɪdəl] *s* violín *m* || *tr* tocar (*un aire*) con el violín; **to fiddle away** (coll) malgastar || *intr* tocar el violín; **to fiddle with** manosear
fiddler [ˈfɪdlər] *s* (coll) violinista *mf*
fiddling [ˈfɪdlɪŋ] *adj* (coll) despreciable, insignificante
fideli•ty [fɪˈdɛlɪti] *s* (*pl* **-ties**) fidelidad
fidget [ˈfɪdʒɪt] *intr* agitarse, menearse; **to fidget with** manosear
fidgety [ˈfɪdʒɪti] *adj* inquieto, nervioso
fiduciar•y [fɪˈdjuʃiˌɛri] *adj* fiduciario || *s* (*pl* **-ies**) fiduciario
fie [faɪ] *interj* (archaic or hum) ¡qué vergüenza!
fief [fif] *s* feudo
field [fild] *adj* (mil) de campaña || *s* campo; (*sown with grain*) sembrado; (baseball) jardín *m;* (elec) campo magnético; (*of motor or dynamo*) (elec) inductor *m;* (compu) campo
field day *s* (mil) día de maniobras; (sport) reunión de atletismo; **to have a field day** darse gusto
fielder [ˈfildər] *s* (baseball) jardinero
field glasses *spl* gemelos de campo
field goal *s* (sport) gol *m* de campo
field hockey *s* hockey *m* sobre hierba
field hospital *s* hospital *m* de campaña
field house *s* (sport) complejo deportivo
field magnet *s* imán *m* inductor
field marshal *s* (mil) mariscal *m* de campo
field'mouse *s* campañol *m*
field'piece' *s* cañón *m* de campaña
field test *s* prueba sobre el terreno
field trip *s* viaje *m* de estudio
field'work' *s* trabajo de campo
field'work'er *s* investigador *m* de campo
fiend [find] *s* diablo; (*person*) fiera; **to be a fiend for** ser una fiera para
fiendish [ˈfindɪʃ] *adj* diabólico
fierce [firs] *adj* feroz, fiero; (*wind*) furioso; (coll) muy malo
fierceness [ˈfɪrsnɪs] *s* ferocidad, fiereza; furia
fier•y [ˈfaɪri] *adj* (*comp* **-ier;** *super* **-iest**) ardiente, caliente; brioso
fife [faɪf] *s* pífano
fifteen [ˈfɪfˈtin] *adj, pron & s* quince *m*
fifteenth [ˈfɪfˈtinθ] *adj & s* (*in a series*) decimoquinto; (*part*) quinzavo || *s* (*in dates*) quince *m*
fifth [fɪfθ] *adj & s* quinto || *s* (*in dates*) cinco
fifth column *s* quinta columna
fiftieth [ˈfɪftɪ•ɪθ] *adj & s* (*in a series*) quincuagésimo; (*part*) cincuentavo
fif•ty [ˈfɪfti] *adj & pron* cincuenta || *s* (*pl* **-ties**) cincuenta *m*
fif'ty-fif'ty *adv*—**to go fifty-fifty** (coll) ir a medias
fig. *abbr* **figure, figuratively**
fig [fɪg] *s* higo, breva; (*tree*) higuera; (*merest trifle*) bledo
fight [faɪt] *s* lucha, pelea, revuelta; animo, brío; **to pick a fight with** meterse con, buscar la lengua a || *tr* luchar con; dar (*batalla*); lidiar (*al toro*) || *intr* luchar, pelear; **to fight shy of** tratar de evitar
fighter [ˈfaɪtər] *s* luchador *m,* peleador *m;* (*warrior*) combatiente *m;* (*game person*) porfiador *m;* (aer) avión *m* de combate, caza *m*
fig leaf *s* hoja de higuera; (*on statues*) hoja de parra
figment [ˈfɪgmənt] *s* ficción, invención
figurative [ˈfɪgjərətɪv] *adj* figurado; (*representing by a likeness*) figurativo
figure [ˈfɪgjər] *s* figura; (*bodily form*) talle *m;* precio; número, cifra; **a six-figure number** un número de seis cifras; **to be good at figures** ser listo en aritmética; **to cut a figure** hacer figura; **to have a good figure** tener buen tipo; **to keep one's figure** conservar la línea || *tr* adornar con figuras; figurarse, imaginar; suponer, calcular; **to figure out** descifrar || *intr* figurar; **to figure on** contar con
fig'ure•head' *s* (naut) figurón *m* de proa, mascarón *m* de proa; (*straw man*) testaferro
figure of speech *s* figura retórica
figure skating *s* patinaje artístico
figurine [ˌfɪgjəˈrin] *s* figurilla, figurina
filament [ˈfɪləmənt] *s* filamento
filbert [ˈfɪlbərt] *s* avellana
filch [fɪltʃ] *tr* birlar, ratear
file [faɪl] *s* fila, hilera; (*tool*) lima; (*collection of papers*) archivo; (*cabinet*) archivador *m,*

fichero; (compu) archivo, fichero || *tr* poner en fila; limar; archivar, clasificar; anotar || *intr* desfilar; **to file for** solicitar
file case *s* fichero
file clerk *s* fichador *m*
file format *s* (compu) formato de fichero
filet [fɪˈle] o [ˈfɪle] *s* filete *m* || *tr* cortar en filetes
filet mignon [miˈnon] *s* filete *m*, solomillo (Esp), lomo (SAm)
filial [ˈfɪlɪ•əl] o [ˈfɪljəl] *adj* filial
filiation [ˌfɪlɪˈeʃən] *s* filiación
filibuster [ˈfɪlɪˌbʌstər] *s* obstrucción (*de la aprobación de una ley*); obstruccionista *mf;* (*buccaneer*) filibustero || *tr* obstruir (*la aprobación de una ley*)
filigree [ˈfɪlɪˌgri] *adj* afiligranado || *s* filigrana || *tr* afiligranar
filing [ˈfaɪlɪŋ] *s* (*of documents*) clasificación; limadura; **filings** limadura, limalla
filing cabinet *s* archivador *m*, clasificador *m*
filing card *s* ficha
Filipi•no [ˌfɪlɪˈpino] *adj* filipino || *s* (*pl* **-nos**) filipino
fill [fɪl] *s* (*sufficiency*) hartazgo; (*place filled with earth*) terraplén *m;* **to have** o **get one's fill of** darse un hartazgo de || *tr* llenar; rellenar; despachar (*un pedido*); tapar (*un agujero*); empastar (*un diente*); inflar (*un neumático*); llenar, ocupar (*un puesto*); colmar (*lagunas*); **to fill out** llenar (*un formulario*) || *intr* llenarse; rellenarse; **to fill in** hacer de suplente; **to fill up** ahogarse de emoción
filler [ˈfɪlər] *s* relleno; (*of cigar*) tripa; *sizing* aparejo; (*in a writing*) relleno
fillet [ˈfɪlɪt] *s* cinta, tira; (*for hair*) prendedero; (archit, bb) filete *m* || *tr* filetear || [ˈfɪle] o [ˈfɪlɪt] *s* (*of meat or fish*) filete *m* || *tr* cortar en filetes
filling [ˈfɪlɪŋ] *s* (*of a tooth*) empaste *m;* (*e.g., of a turkey*) relleno; (*of cigar*) tripa
filling station *s* estación gasolinera
fillip [ˈfɪlɪp] *s* aguijón *m*, estímulo; (*with finger*) capirotazo
fil•ly [ˈfɪli] *s* (*pl* **-lies**) potra; (coll) muchacha retozona
film [fɪlm] *s* película; (mov) película, film *m;* (phot) película || *tr* filmar
film library *s* cinemateca
film star *s* estrella de la pantalla
filmstrip *s* tira proyectable
film•y [ˈfɪlmi] *adj* (*comp* **-ier;** *super* **-iest**) delgadísimo, diáfano, sutil
filter [ˈfɪltər] *s* filtro || *tr* filtrar || *intr* filtrarse
filtering [ˈfɪltərɪŋ] *s* filtración
filter paper *s* papel *m* filtrante
filter tip *s* embocadura de filtro
filth [fɪlθ] *s* suciedad, porquería
filth•y [ˈfɪlθi] *adj* (*comp* **-ier;** *super* **-iest**) sucio, puerco
filthy lucre [ˈlukər] *s* (coll) el vil metal (*dinero, raíz de muchos males*)
filtrate [ˈfɪltret] *s* filtrado || *tr* filtrar || *intr* filtrarse
fin. *abbr* **finance**
fin [fɪn] *s* aleta
final [ˈfaɪnəl] *adj* final; (*last in a series*) último; decisivo, terminante || *s* examen *m* final; **finals** (sport) final *f*
finale [fɪˈnɑli] *s* (mus) final *m*
finalist [ˈfaɪnəlɪst] *s* finalista *mf*
finally [ˈfaɪnəli] *adv* finalmente, por último
finance [ˈfaɪnæns] *s* financiación; **finances** finanzas || *tr* financiar
financial assistance *s* prestaciones económicas
finance company *s* sociedad financiera
financial [faɪˈnænʃəl] *adj* financiero
financier [ˌfaɪnənˈsɪr] *s* financiero
financing [ˈfaɪnænsɪŋ] *s* financiación, financiamiento
finch [fɪntʃ] *s* pinzón *m*
find [faɪnd] *s* hallazgo || *v* (*pret & pp* **found** [faʊnd]) *tr* hallar, encontrar; **to find out** averiguar, darse cuenta de || *intr* (*law*) pronunciar fallo; **to find out about** informarse de
finder [ˈfaɪndər] *s* (*of camera*) visor *m;* (*of microscope*) portaobjeto cuadriculado
finding [ˈfaɪndɪŋ] *s* descubrimiento; (law) laudo, fallo
fine [faɪn] *adj* fino; (*weather*) bueno; divertido || *adv* (coll) muy bien; **to feel fine** (coll) sentirse muy bien de salud || *s* multa, pena pecuniaria || *tr* multar
fine arts *spl* bellas artes
fineness *s* fineza; (*of metal*) ley *f*
fine print *s* letra menuda, tipo menudo
finer•y [ˈfaɪnəri] *s* (*pl* **-ies**) adorno, galas, atavíos
fine-spun [ˈfaɪnˌspʌn] *adj* estirado en hilo finísimo; (fig) alambicado
finesse [fɪˈnɛs] *s* sutileza; (*in bridge*) impasse *m* || *tr* hacer el impasse con || *intr* hacer un impasse
fine-toothed comb [ˈfaɪnˌtuθt] *s* lendrera, peine *m* de púas finas; **to go over with a fine-toothed comb** escudriñar minuciosamente
fine′-tune′ *tr* poner a punto, ajustar
finger [ˈfɪŋgər] *s* dedo; **to burn one's fingers** cogerse los dedos; **to put one's finger on the spot** poner el dedo en la llaga; **to slip between the fingers** irse de entre los dedos; **to snap one's fingers at** tratar con desprecio; **to twist around one's little finger** manejar a su gusto || *tr* manosear; (slang) acechar, espiar; (slang) identificar
fingerboard *s* (*of guitar*) diapasón *m;* (*of piano*) teclado
finger bowl *s* lavadedos *m*, lavafrutas *m*
finger dexterity *s* (mus) dedeo
fingering [ˈfɪŋgərɪŋ] *s* manoseo; (mus) digitación
fin′ger•nail′ *s* uña
fingernail polish *s* esmalte *m* para las uñas
fin′ger•print′ *s* huella digital, dactilograma *m* || *tr* tomar las huellas digitales de
finger tip *s* punta del dedo; **to have at one's**

finger tips tener en la punta de los dedos, saber al dedillo
finial [ˈfɪnɪ•əl] *s* florón *m*
finical [ˈfɪnɪkəl] o **finicky** [ˈfɪnɪki] *adj* delicado, melindroso
finish [ˈfɪnɪʃ] *s* acabado; fin *m,* conclusión ‖ *tr* acabar; **to be finished** estar listo ‖ *intr* acabar; **to finish** + *ger* acabar de + *inf;* **to finish by** + *ger* acabar por + *inf*
finishing nail *s* puntilla francesa
finishing school *s* escuela particular de educación social para señoritas
finishing touch *s* toque *m* final, última mano
finite [ˈfaɪnaɪt] *adj* finito
finite verb *s* forma verbal flexional
Finland [ˈfɪnlənd] *s* Finlandia
Finlander [ˈfɪnləndər] *s* finlandés *m*
Finn [fɪn] *s* (*member of a Finnish-speaking group of people*) finés *m;* (*native or inhabitant of Finland*) finlandés *m*
Finnish [ˈfɪnɪʃ] *adj* finlandés ‖ *s* (*language*) finlandés *m*
fir [fʌr] *s* abeto
fire [faɪr] *s* fuego; (*destructive burning*) incendio; **through fire and water** a trancos y barrancos; **to be on fire** estar ardiendo; **to be under enemy fire** estar expuesto al fuego del enemigo; **to catch fire** encenderse; **to hang fire** estar en suspensión; **to open fire** abrir fuego, romper el fuego; **to set on fire, to set fire to** pegar fuego a; **under fire** bajo el fuego del enemigo; acusado, inculpado ‖ *interj* (mil) ¡fuego! ‖ *tr* encender; calentar (*el horno*); cocer (*ladrillos*); disparar (*un arma de fuego*); pegar (*un tiro*); excitar (*la imaginación*); (coll) despedir (*a un empleado*) ‖ *intr* encenderse; **to fire on** hacer fuego sobre; **to fire up** cargar el horno; calentar el horno
fire alarm *s* alarma de incendios, avisador *m* de incendios; **to sound the fire alarm** tocar a fuego
fire′arm′ *s* arma de fuego
fire′ball′ *s* bola de fuego; (*lightning*) rayo en bola
fire′bird′ *s* cacique veranero
fire′boat′ *s* buque *m* con mangueras para incendios
fire′box′ *s* caja de fuego, fogón *m*
fire′brand′ *s* tizón *m;* (*hothead*) botafuego
fire′break′ *s* raya, cortafuego
fire′brick′ *s* ladrillo refractario
fire brigade *s* cuerpo de bomberos
fire′bug′ *s* (coll) incendiario
fire chief *s* jefe *m* de bomberos; jefa de bomberos
fire company *s* cuerpo de bomberos; compañía de seguros
fire′crack′er *s* triquitraque *m*
fire′damp′ *s* grisú *m,* mofeta
fire department *s* servicio de bomberos
fire′dog′ *s* morillo
fire drill *s* simulacro de incendio
fire engine *s* coche *m* bomba, bomba de incendios, motobomba
fire escape *s* escalera de salvamento
fire exit *s* salida de incendios
fire extinguisher *s* extintor *m,* apagafuegos *m,* extinguidor *m*
fire′fly′ *s* (*pl* **-flies**) luciérnaga
fire′guard′ *s* guardafuego
fire hose *s* manguera para incendios
fire′house′ *s* cuartel *m* de bomberos, estación de incendios
fire insurance *s* seguro contra incendios
fire irons *spl* badil *m* y tenazas
fireless cooker [ˈfaɪrlɪs] *s* cocinilla sin fuego
fire•man [ˈfaɪrmən] *s* (*pl* **-men** [mən]) (*man who stokes fires*) fogonero; (*man who extinguishes fires*) bombero
fire′place′ *s* chimenea, chimenea francesa
fire plug *s* boca de agua
fire power *s* (mil) potencia de fuego
fire′proof′ *adj* incombustible; a prueba de incendio ‖ *tr* hacer incombustible
fire sale *s* venta de mercancías averiadas en un incendio
fire screen *s* pantalla de chimenea
fire ship *s* brulote *m*
fire shovel *s* badil *m*
fire′side′ *s* hogar *m*
fire tower *s* torre *f* de vigilancia
fire′trap′ *s* edificio sin medios adecuados de escape en caso de incendio
fire wall *s* cortafuego
fire′ward′en *s* vigía *m* de incendios
fire′wa′ter *s* aguardiente *m*
fire′wood′ *s* leña
fire′works′ *spl* fuegos artificiales
firing [ˈfaɪrɪŋ] *s* encendimiento; (*of bricks*) cocción; (*of a gun*) disparo; (*of soldiers*) tiroteo; (*of an internal-combustion engine*) encendido; (*of an employee*) (coll) despedida
firing line *s* línea de fuego, frente *m* de batalla
firing order *s* (aut) orden *m* del encendido
firing pin *s* percutor *m*
firing squad *s* (*for saluting at a burial*) piquete *m* de salvas; (*for executing*) pelotón *m* de fusilamiento, piquete *m* de ejecución
firm [fʌrm] *adj* firme ‖ *s* empresa, casa comercial
firmament [ˈfʌrməmənt] *s* firmamento
firm name *s* razón *f* social
firmness [ˈfʌrmnɪs] *s* firmeza
first [fʌrst] *adj* primero ‖ *adv* primero; **first of all** ante todo ‖ *s* primero; (aut) primera (velocidad); (mus) voz *f* principal; **at first** al principio; en primer lugar; **from the first** desde el principio
first aid *s* cura de urgencia, primeros auxilios
first′-aid′ kit *s* botiquín *m,* equipo de urgencia
first-aid station *s* puesto de socorro, puesto de primera intención
first′-born′ *adj & s* primogénito
first′-class′ *adj* de primera, de primera clase ‖ *adv* en primera clase

first cousin *s* primo hermano
first draft *s* borrador *m*
first edition *s* edición príncipe
first finger *s* dedo índice, dedo mostrador
first floor *s* piso bajo, planta baja
first fruits *spl* primicia
first grade *s* (educ) primer año
first′-hand′ *adj* de primera mano ‖ *adv* directamente
First Lady *s* (*president's wife*) Primera Dama
first lieutenant *s* teniente
firstly [ˈfʌrstli] *adv* en primer lugar
first mate *s* (naut) piloto
first name *s* nombre *m* de pila
first night *s* (theat) noche *f* de estreno
first′-night′er *s* (theat) estrenista *mf*
first officer *s* (naut) piloto
first prize *s* primer premio, premio gordo
first quarter *s* cuarto creciente (*de la luna*)
first′-rate′ *adj* de primer orden; (coll) excelente ‖ *adv* (coll) muy bien
first′-run′ house *s* teatro de estreno
fiscal [ˈfɪskəl] *adj* (*pertaining to public treasury*) fiscal; económico ‖ *s* (*public prosecutor*) fiscal *m*
fiscal year *s* año económico, ejercicio
fish [fɪʃ] *s* pez *m;* (*that has been caught, that is ready to eat*) pescado; **to be like a fish out of water** estar como gallina en corral ajeno; **to be neither fish nor fowl** no ser carne ni pescado; **to drink like a fish** beber como una topinera, beber como una esponja ‖ *tr* pescar ‖ *intr* pescar; **to fish for compliments** buscar alabanzas; **to go fishing** ir de pesca; **to take fishing** llevar de pesca
fish′bone′ *s* espina de pez
fish bowl *s* pecera
fisher [ˈfɪʃər] *s* pescador *m;* embarcación de pesca; (zool) marta del Canadá
fisher•man [ˈfɪʃərmən] *s* (*pl* **-men** [mən]) pescador *m;* pescadora; barco pesquero
fisher•y [ˈfɪʃəri] *s* (*pl* **-ies**) (*activity*) pesca; (*business*) pesquería; (*grounds*) pesquera
fish′-eye′ *adj* (phot) de ángulo plano
fish-eye lens *s* objectivo de ojo de pez
fish glue *s* cola de pescado
fish hawk *s* halieto
fish′hook′ *s* anzuelo
fishing [ˈfɪʃɪŋ] *adj* pesquero ‖ *s* pesca
fishing ground *s* pesquería, pesquera
fishing permit *s* licencia de pesca
fishing reel *s* carrete *m*
fishing rod *s* caña de pescar
fishing tackle *s* aparejo de pescar, avíos de pescar
fishing torch *s* candelero
fish line *s* sedal *m*
fish market *s* pescadería, lonja (Esp)
fish′plate′ (rr) eclisa
fish′pole *s* caña de pescar
fish′pool′ *s* piscina
fish spear *s* fisga
fish stick *s* (culin) palito de pescado
fish story *s* (coll) andaluzada, patraña; **to tell fish stories** (coll) mentir por la barba
fish′tail′ *s* (aer) coleadura ‖ *intr* (aer) colear
fish′wife′ *s* (*pl* **-wives** [ˌwaɪvz]) pescadera; (*foul-mouthed woman*) verdulera
fish′worm′ *s* lombriz *f* de tierra (*cebo para pescar*)
fish•y [ˈfɪʃi] *adj* (*comp* **-ier;** *super* **-iest**) que huele o sabe a pescado; (coll) dudoso, inverosímil
fission [ˈfɪʃən] *s* (biol) escisión, biopartición; (phys) fisión
fissionable [ˈfɪʃənəbəl] *adj* fisionable; físil
fissure [ˈfɪʃər] *s* hendidura, grieta; (anat, min) fisura
fist [fɪst] *s* puño; (typ) manecilla; **to shake one's fist at** amenazar con el puño
fist fight *s* pelea con los puños
fisticuff [ˈfɪstɪˌkʌf] *s* puñetazo; **fisticuffs** pelea a puñetazos
fit [fɪt] *adj* (*comp* **-fitter;** *super* **-fittest**) apropiado, conveniente; apto; sano; en buena forma física; **fit to be tied** (coll) impaciente, encolerizado; **fit to eat** bueno de comer; **to feel fit** gozar de buena salud; **to see fit** juzgar conveniente ‖ *s* ajuste *m,* talle *m;* (*of one piece with another*) encaje *m;* (*of coughing*) acceso, ataque *m;* (*of anger*) arranque *m,* chivo; **by fits and starts** intermitentemente ‖ *v* (*pret & pp* **-fitted;** *ger* **fitting**) *tr* ajustar, entallar; cuadrar, sentar; encajar; cuadrar con (*p.ej., las señas de una persona*); equipar, preparar; servir para; estar de acuerdo con (*p.ej., los hechos*); **to fit out** o **up** pertrechar ‖ *intr* ajustar; encajar; sentar; **to fit in** caber en; encajar en
fitful [ˈfɪtfəl] *adj* caprichoso; intermitente, vacilante
fitness [ˈfɪtnɪs] *s* conveniencia; aptitud; tempestividad; (*physical fitness*) buena forma física
fitness buff *s* fanático de la gimnasia
fitness center *s* gimnasio destinado a los ejercicios físicos
fitted sheet [ˈfɪtəd] *s* sábana ajustable o de cuatro picos
fitter [ˈfɪtər] *s* ajustador *m;* (*of machinery*) montador *m;* (*of clothing*) probador *m*
fitting [ˈfɪtɪŋ] *adj* apropiado, conveniente, justo ‖ *s* ajuste *m;* encaje *m;* (*of a garment*) prueba; tubo de ajuste; **fittings** accesorios, avíos; (*iron trimmings*) herraje *m*
fitting room *s* probador *m*
five [faɪv] *adj & pron* cinco ‖ *s* cinco; **five o'clock** las cinco
five hundred *adj & pron* quinientos ‖ *s* quinientos *m*
five′-year′plan *s* plan *m* quinquenal
fix [fiks] *s* (*solution*) arreglo; (*predicament*) (coll) aprieto, apuro; (*secret prearrangement*) (coll) tongo, arreglo; (slang) dosis *f;* (aer, naut) posición; **in a tight fix** (coll) en calzas prietas; **to be in a fix** (coll) hallarse en un aprieto; **to get a fix** (*drugs*) picarse, pincharse ‖ *tr* arreglar, componer, reparar; fijar (*una*

fecha; los cabellos; una imagen fotográfica; los precios; la atención; una hora, una cita); calar (*la bayoneta*); (coll) desquitarse con; (pol) muñir || *intr* fijarse; **to fix on** decidir, escoger
fixed [fɪkst] *adj* fijo
fixed price *s* precio cerrado
fixing [ˈfɪksɪŋ] *adj* fijador || *s* (*fastening*) fijación; (phot) fijado
fixing bath *s* fijador *m*
fixture [ˈfɪkstʃər] *s* accesorio, artefacto; (*of a lamp*) guarnición; **fixtures** (*e.g., of a store*) instalaciones
fizz [fɪz] *s* ruido sibilante; bebida gaseosa; (Brit) champaña || *intr* hacer un ruido sibilante
fizzle [ˈfɪzəl] *s* (coll) fracaso || *intr* chisporrotear débilmente; (coll) fracasar
flabbergast [ˈflæbər,gæst] *tr* (coll) dejar sin habla, dejar estupefacto
flab•by [ˈflæbi] *adj* (*comp* **-bier;** *super* **-biest**) flojo, lacio
flack [flæk] *s* agente *mf* de publicidad, encargado de prensa; publicidad || véase **flak**
flag [flæg] *s* bandera; (compu) indicador *m* || *v* (*pret & pp* **flagged;** *ger* **flagging**) *tr* hacer señal a (*una persona*) con una bandera; hacer señal de parada a (*un tren*) || *intr* aflojar, flaquear
flag captain *s* (nav) capitán *m* de bandera
Flag Day *s* el Día de la Bandera (*14 de junio*)
flageolet [,flædʒəˈlɛt] *s* chirimía, dulzaina
flagger [ˈflægər] *s* persona con bandera que regula el tráfico
flag•man [ˈflægmən] *s* (*pl* **-men** [mən]) (rr) guardafrenos *m;* (rr) guardavía *m*
flag of truce *s* bandera de parlamento
flag′pole′ *s* asta de bandera; (surv) jalón *m*
flagrant [ˈflegrənt] *adj* enorme, escandaloso
flag′ship′ *s* (nav) capitana
flag′staff′ *s* asta de bandera
flag′stone′ *s* losa
flag stop *s* parada opcional; (rr) apeadero
flail [flel] *s* mayal *m* || *tr* golpear con mayal; golpear, azotar
flair [flɛr] *s* instinto, perspicacia
flak [flæk] *s* fuego antiaéreo; (fig) críticas
flake [flek] *s* (*thin piece*) hojuela; (*of snow*) copo || *intr* desprenderse en hojuelas; caer en copos pequeños
flak•y [ˈfleki] *adj* (*comp* **-ier;** *super* **-iest**) escamoso, laminoso; (*piecrust*) hojaldrado; (*eccentric*) (slang) raro, loco
flamboyant [flæmˈbɔɪ•ənt] *adj* flameante; llamativo; rimbombante; (archit) flameante, flamígero
flame [flem] *s* llama || *tr* (*to sterilize with a flame*) llamear || *intr* flamear
flamethrower [ˈθro•ər] *s* lanzallamas *m*
flaming [ˈflemɪŋ] *adj* llameante; flamante, resplandeciente; apasionado
flamin•go [fləˈmɪŋgo] *s* (*pl* **-gos** o **-goes**) flamenco
flammable [ˈflæməbəl] *adj* inflamable
Flanders [ˈflændərz] *s* Flandes *f*
flange [flændʒ] *s* pestaña
flank [flæŋk] *s* flanco; *tr* flanquear
flannel [ˈflænəl] *s* franela
flap [flæp] *s* (*fold in clothing; of a hat*) falda; (*of a pocket*) cartera; (*of a table*) hoja plegadiza; (*of shoe*) oreja; (*of an envelope*) tapa; (*of wings*) aletazo; (*of the counter in a store*) trampa; (coll) jaleo, lío || *v* (*pret & pp* **flapped;** *ger* **flapping**) *tr* golpear con ruido seco; batir, sacudir (*las alas*) || *intr* aletear; flamear con ruido
flare [flɛr] *s* llamarada, destello; cohete *m* de señales; (aer) bengala; (*outward curvature*) abocinamiento; (*of a dress*) vuelo || *tr* abocinar || *intr* arder con gran llamarada, destellar; (*to spread outward*) abocinarse; **to flare up** inflamarse; recrudecer (*una enfermedad*); encolerizarse
flare star *s* (astr) estrella fulgurante
flare′-up′ *s* llamarada; (*of an illness*) retroceso; (coll) llamarada, arrebato de cólera
flash [flæʃ] *s* (*of light*) destello; (*insight*) rasgo, relámpago; (*explosion; flash from gun*) fogonazo; (*of lightning*) relámpago, rayo; (phot) flash *m;* (rad, telv) noticia de último momento, flash informativo; **in a flash** en un instante; **quick as a flash** como un rayo, como un relámpago || *tr* quemar (*pólvora*); enviar (*un mensaje*) como un rayo || *intr* destellar, centellear; relampaguear (*los ojos*); **to flash by** pasar como un rayo
flash′back′ *s* (mov) escena retrospectiva, flashback *m*
flashbulb *s* (phot) lámpara de flash, bombilla de flash
flash button *s* (telp) tecla de destello
flasher [ˈflæʃər] *s* emisor *m* de destellos; (slang) exhibicionista *m*
flash flood *s* torrentada, avenida repentina
flashgun *s* flash electrónico
flashing [ˈflæʃɪŋ] *adj* intermitente || *s* (*in construction*) tapajuntas *m*
flash′light′ *s* linterna eléctrica, lámpara eléctrica de bolsillo; (*of a lighthouse*) luz *f* intermitente, fanal *m* de destellos; (*for taking photographs*) flash *m,* relámpago
flashlight battery *s* pila de linterna
flashlight bulb *s* bombilla de linterna
flash sign *s* anuncio intermitente
flash•y [ˈflæʃi] *adj* (*comp* **-ier;** *super* **-iest**) chillón, llamativo
flask [flæsk] *s* frasco; frasco de bolsillo; (*for laboratory use*) matraz *m,* redoma
flat [flæt] *adj* (*comp* **flatter;** *super* **flattest**) plano; (*nose; boat*) chato; (*surface*) mate, deslustrado; (*beer*) muerto; (*tire*) desinflado; (*e.g., denial*) terminante; (mus) bemol || *adv*—**to fall flat** caer de plano; (fig) no surtir efecto, no tener éxito || *s* banco, bajío; (Brit) apartamento, piso (Esp); (mus) bemol *m;* (*tire*) neumático desinflado, pinchazo
flat′boat′ *s* chalana

flat′car′ *s* vagón *m* de plataforma
flat′foot′ *s* pie plano
flat-footed [ˈflæt,futɪd] *adj* de pies planos; (coll) inflexible
flat′head′ *s* (*of a bolt*) cabeza chata; clavo, tornillo o perno de cabeza chata; (coll) tonto, mentecato
flat′i′ron *s* plancha
flat tax *s* impuesto único
flatten [ˈflætən] *tr* allanar, aplanar; chafar, aplastar; achatar ‖ *intr* allanarse, aplanarse; aplastarse; achatarse; **to flatten out** ponerse horizontal, enderezarse
flatter [ˈflætər] *tr* lisonjear; cepillar (*to make more attractive than is*) favorecer ‖ *intr* lisonjear
flatterer [ˈflætərər] *s* lisonjero; (coll) limpiabotas *m*
flattering [ˈflætərɪŋ] *adj* lisonjero
flatter•y [ˈflætəri] *s* (*pl* **-ies**) lisonja
flat tire *s* neumático desinflado, pinchazo
flat′top′ *s* (*haircut*) corte *m* de pelo cuadrado; (naut) portaaviones *m*
flatulence [ˈflætʃələns] *s* flatulencia
flat′ware′ *s* vajilla de plata; vajilla de porcelana
flaunt [flɔnt] *tr* ostentar hacer gala de
flautist [ˈflɔtɪst] *s* flautista *mf*
flavor [ˈflevər] *s* sabor *m,* gusto; condimento, sazón *f;* (*of ice cream*) clase *f* ‖ *tr* saborear; condimentar, sazonar; aromatizar, perfumar
flavoring [ˈflevərɪŋ] *s* condimento, sainete *m*
flaw [flɔ] *s* defecto, imperfección; (*crack*) grieta; (law) vicio
flawless [ˈflɔlɪs] *adj* perfecto, entero
flax [flæks] *s* lino
flaxen [ˈflæksən] *adj* blondo, rubio
flax′seed′ *s* linaza
flay [fle] *tr* desollar
flea [fli] *s* pulga
flea′bite′ *s* picadura de pulga; molestia insignificante
flea market *s* mercado de pulgas, rostro (Esp)
fleck [flɛk] *s* pinta, punto; partícula, pizca ‖ *tr* puntear
fledgling [ˈflɛdʒlɪŋ] *s* pajarito, volantón *m;* (fig) novato, novel *m*
flee [fli] *v* (*pret & pp* **fled** [flɛd]) *tr & intr* huir
fleece [flis] *s* (*coat of wool*) lana; (*wool shorn at one time; tuft of wool or hair*) vellón *m* ‖ *tr* esquilar; (*to strip of money*) desplumar
fleec•y [ˈflisi] *adj* (*comp* **-ier;** *super* **-iest**) lanudo; (*clouds*) aborregado
fleet [flit] *adj* veloz ‖ *s* armada; (*of merchant vessels, airplanes, automobiles*) flota
fleeting [ˈflitɪŋ] *adj* fugaz, efímero
Fleming [ˈflɛmɪŋ] *s* flamenco
Flemish [ˈflɛmɪʃ] *adj & s* flamenco
flesh [flɛʃ] *s* carne *f;* **in the flesh** en persona
flesh and blood *s* carne y sangre
fleshiness [ˈflɛʃinɪs] *s* carnosidad
fleshless [ˈflɛʃlɪs] *adj* descarnado
flesh wound *s* herida superficial
flesh•y [ˈflɛʃi] *adj* (*comp* **-ier;** *super* **-iest**) carnoso
flex [flɛks] *tr* doblar ‖ *intr* doblarse
flexible [ˈflɛksɪbəl] *adj* flexible
flexible cord *s* (elec) flexible *m*
flick [flɪk] *s* (*with finger*) papirote *m;* (*with whip*) latigazo; ruido seco ‖ *tr* golpear rápida y ligeramente
flicker [ˈflɪkər] *s* llama trémula; (*of eyelids*) parpadeo; (*of emotion*) temblor momentáneo ‖ *intr* flamear con llama trémula; aletear
flier [ˈflaɪ•ər] *s* aviador *m;* tren rápido; (coll) negocio arriesgado; (coll) hoja volante
flight [flaɪt] *s* fuga, huída; (*of an airplane*) vuelo; (*of birds*) bandada; (*of stairs*) tramo; (*of fancy*) arranque *m;* **to put to flight** poner en fuga; **to take flight** darse a la fuga
flight attendant *s* sobrecargo, sobrecarga
flight deck *s* (nav) cubierta de vuelo
flight plan *s* carta de vuelo
flight recorder *s* registrador *m* de vuelo, caja negra
flight•y [ˈflaɪti] *adj* (*comp* **-ier;** *super* **-iest**) veleidoso; casquivano
flim•flam [ˈflɪm,flæm] *s* (coll) engaño, trampa; (coll) tontería ‖ *v* (*pret & pp* **-flammed;** *ger* **-flamming**) *tr* (coll) engañar, trampear
flim•sy [ˈflɪmzi] *adj* (*comp* **-sier;** *super* **-siest**) débil, endeble, flojo
flinch [flɪntʃ] *intr* encogerse de miedo
fling [flɪŋ] *s* echada, tiro; baile escocés muy vivo; **to go on a fling** echar una cana al aire; **to have a fling at** ensayar, probar; **to have one's fling** correrla, mocear ‖ *v* (*pret & pp* **flung** [flʌŋ]) *tr* arrojar; (*e.g., on the floor, out the window, in jail*) echar; **to fling open** abrir de golpe; **to fling shut** cerrar de golpe
flint [flɪnt] *s* pedernal *m*
flint′lock′ *s* llave *f* de chispa; (*gun*) trabuco de chispa
flint•y [ˈflɪnti] *adj* (*comp* **-ier;** *super* **-iest**) pedernalino; (fig) empedernido
flip [flɪp] *adj* (*comp* **flipper;** *super* **flippest**) (coll) petulante ‖ *s* capirotazo ‖ *v* (*pret & pp* **flipped;** *ger* **flipping**) *tr* echar de un capirotazo, mover de un tirón; **to flip a coin** echar a cara o cruz; **to flip one's lid** (coll) deschavetar; **to flip shut** cerrar de golpe (*p. ej., un abanico*)
flippancy [ˈflɪpənsi] *s* petulancia
flippant [ˈflɪpənt] *adj* petulante
flipper [ˈflɪpər] *s* (*swimming aid*) aleta; (*in pinball machine*) flipper *m;* (zool) aleta; **flippers** patas de rana (Esp)
flip side *s* contraportada (*del disco*)
flirt [flʌrt] *s* (*woman*) coqueta; (*man*) galanteador *m* ‖ *intr* coquetear (*una mujer*); galantear (*un hombre*); **to flirt with** flirtear con; pololear (Chile); acariciar (*una idea*); jugar con (*la muerte*)
flit [flɪt] *v* (*pret & pp* **flitted;** *ger* **flitting**) *intr* revolotear, volar; pasar rápidamente
flitch [flɪtʃ] *s* hoja de tocino

float [flot] *s* (*raft*) balsa; (*of fishing line*) flotador *m;* (*of mason*) llana; carroza alegórica, carro alegórico ‖ *tr* poner a flote; lanzar (*una empresa*); emitir (*acciones, bonos, etc.*) ‖ *intr* flotar
floating [ˈflotɪŋ] *adj* flotante
floating palette *s* (compu) paleta flotante
floatʹing-pointʹ *s* (compu) coma flotante
flock [flɑk] *s* (*of birds*) bandada; (*of sheep*) grey *f,* rebaño, manada; (*of people*) muchedumbre; (*e.g., of nonsense*) hatajo; (*of faithful*) grey *f,* rebaño ‖ *intr* congregarse, reunirse; llegar en tropel
floe [flo] *s* banquisa, témpano
flog [flɑg] *v* (*pret & pp* **flogged;** *ger* **flogging**) *tr* azotar, fustigar
flood [flʌd] *s* inundación; (*caused by heavy rain*) diluvio; (*sudden rise of river*) crecida; (*of tide*) pleamar *f;* (*of words, etc.*) diluvio, torrente *m* ‖ *tr* inundar; (*to overwhelm*) abrumar ‖ *intr* desbordar, rebosar; entrar a raudales
floodʹgateʹ *s* (*of a dam*) compuerta; (*of a canal*) esclusa
floodʹlightʹ *s* foco, reflector *m* ‖ *tr* iluminar con foco *or* reflector
flood tide *s* pleamar *f,* marea montante
floor [flor] *s* (*inside bottom surface of room*) piso, suelo; (*story of a building*) piso, alto; (*of the sea, a swimming pool, etc.*) fondo; (*of an assembly hall*) hemiciclo; (naut) varenga; **to ask for the floor** pedir la palabra; **to have the floor** tener la palabra; **to take the floor** tomar la palabra ‖ *tr* entarimar; derribar, echar al suelo; (coll) confundir, envolver, revolcar (*al adversario en controversia*); (coll) vencer
floorʹboard *s* (auto) suelo, piso
floor lamp *s* lámpara de pie
floor mop *s* fregasuelos *m,* estropajo
floor plan *s* planta
floor show *s* espectáculo de cabaret
floor timber *s* (naut) varenga
floorʹwalkʹer *s* jefe *m* de sección
floor wax *s* cera de pisos
flop [flɑp] *s* fracaso, caída; (*person*) berzas *m,* berzotas *m;* **to take a flop** caerse ‖ *v* (*pret & pp* **flopped;** *ger* **flopping**) *intr* agitarse; caerse; venirse abajo; fracasar; **to flop over** volcarse; cambiar de partido
floppy disk [ˈflɑpi] *s* disco flexible, disco floppy, disquete *m,* disquette *m*
flora [ˈflorə] *s* flora
floral [ˈflorə] *s* flora
Florentine [ˈflɔrən,tin] *adj & s* florentino
florescence [floˈrɛsəns] *s* florescencia
florid [ˈflɔrɪd] *adj* (*complexion*) encarnado; (*showy, ornate*) florido
Florida Keys [ˈflɔrɪdə] *s* Cayos de la Florida
florist [ˈflorɪst] *s* florero, florista *mf*
floss [flɑs] *s* cadarzo; (*of corn*) cabellos
floss silk *s* seda floja sin torcer
floss•y [ˈflɑsi] *adj* (*comp* **-ier;** *super* **-iest**) ligero, velloso; (slang) cursi, vistoso
flotsam [ˈflɑtsəm] *s* pecio
flotsam and jetsam *s* pecios, despojos; (*trifles*) baratijas; gente *f* trashumante, gente perdida
flounce [flaʊns] *s* faralá *m,* volante *m* ‖ *tr* adornar con faralaes o volantes ‖ *intr* moverse airadamente
flounder [ˈflaʊndər] *s* platija ‖ *intr* forcejear, obrar torpemente, andar tropezando
flour [flaʊr] *adj* harinero ‖ *s* harina
flourish [ˈflʌrɪʃ] *s* (*with the sword*) molinete *m;* (*with the pen*) plumada, rasgo; (*as part of signature*) rúbrica; (mus) floreo ‖ *tr* blandir (*la espada*) ‖ *intr* florecer, prosperar
flourishing [ˈflʌrɪʃɪŋ] *adj* floreciente, próspero
flour mill *s* molino de harina
floury [ˈflaʊri] *adj* harinoso
flout [flaʊt] *tr* mofarse de, burlarse de ‖ *intr* mofarse, burlarse
flow [flo] *s* flujo ‖ *intr* fluir; subir (*la marea*); ondear (*el pelo en el aire*); **to flow into** desaguar en, desembocar en; **to flow over** rebosar; **to flow with** nadar en, abundar en
flower [ˈflaʊ•ər] *s* flor *f* ‖ *tr* florear ‖ *intr* florecer
flower bed *s* macizo, parterre *m*
flower garden *s* jardín *m*
flower girl *s* florera; (*at a wedding*) damita de honor
flower piece *s* ramillete *m;* (*painting*) florero
flowʹer•potʹ *s* tiesto, maceta
flower shop *s* floristería
flower show *s* exposición de flores
flower stand *s* florero
flowery [ˈflaʊ•əri] *adj* florido, cubierto de flores
flu [flu] *s* (coll) gripe *f,* influenza
fluctuate [ˈflʌktʃʊ,et] *intr* fluctuar
flue [flu] *s* cañón *m* de chimenea; tubo de humo
fluency [ˈflu•ənsi] *s* afluencia, facundia
fluent [ˈflu•ənt] *adj* (*flowing*) fluente; afluente, facundo, flúido
fluently [ˈflu•əntli] *adv* corrientemente
fluff [flʌf] *s* pelusa, tamo; vello, pelusilla; (*of an actor*) gazapo ‖ *tr* esponjar, mullir ‖ *intr* esponjarse
fluff•y [ˈflʌfi] *adj* (*comp* **-ier;** *super* **-iest**) fofo, esponjoso, mullido; velloso
fluid [ˈflu•ɪd] *adj & s* flúido
fluidity [fluˈɪdɪti] *s* fluidez *f*
fluke [fluk] *s* (*of anchor*) uña; (*in billiards*) chiripa
flume [flum] *s* caz *m,* saetín *m*
flunk [flʌŋk] *s* (coll) reprobación ‖ *tr* (coll) reprobar, dar calabazas a; perder (*un examen o asignatura*) ‖ *intr* (coll) fracasar, salir mal; **to flunk out** (coll) tener que abandonar los estudios por no poder aprobar
flunk•y [ˈflʌŋki] *s* (*pl* **-ies**) lacayo; adulador *m*
fluor [ˈflu•ɔr] *s* fluorita
fluorescence [,flu•əˈrɛsəns] *s* fluorescencia
fluorescent [,flu•əˈrɛsənt] *adj* fluorescente
fluoridate [ˈflu•ərɪ,det] *tr* fluorizar
fluoridation [ˈflu•ərɪˈdeʃən] *s* fluorización
fluoride [ˈflu•ə,raɪd] *s* fluoruro
fluorine [ˈflu•ə,rin] *s* flúor *m*
fluorite [ˈflu•ə,raɪt] *s* fluorita

fluoroscope [ˈflu•ərəˌskop] *s* fluoroscopio
flur•ry [ˈflʌri] *s* (*pl* **-ries**) agitación; (*of wind*) racha, ráfaga; (*of rain*) chaparrón *m;* (*of snow*) nevisca || *v* (*pret & pp* **-ried**) *tr* agitar
flush [flʌʃ] *adj* rasante, nivelado; (*set in, in order to be flush*) embutido; abundante; robusto, vigoroso; próspero, bien provisto; coloradote; (*in printing*) justificado; **flush with** a ras de || *adv* ras con ras, al mismo nivel || *s* (*of water*) flujo repentino; (*in the cheeks*) rubor *m;* sonrojo; (*in the springtime*) floración repentina; (*of joy*) acceso; (*of youth*) vigor *m;* chorro del inodoro; (*in poker*) flux *m* || *tr* (*to cause to blush*) abochornar; (*to flush out*) limpiar con un chorro de agua; hacer saltar (*una liebre*); **to flush the toilet** tirar de la cadena, apretar el botón del inodoro || *intr* abochornarse, estar encendido (*el rostro*); (*to gush*) brotar
flush outlet *s* (elec) caja de enchufe embutida
flush switch *s* (elec) llave embutida
flush tank *s* depósito de limpia
flush toilet *s* inodoro con chorro de agua
fluster [ˈflʌstər] *s* confusión, aturdimiento || *tr* confundir, aturdir
flute [flut] *s* (*of a column*) estría; (mus) flauta || *tr* estriar, acanalar
flutist [ˈflutɪst] *s* flautista *mf*
flutter [ˈflʌtər] *s* aleteo, revoloteo; confusión, turbación || *intr* aletear, revolotear; flamear, ondear; agitarse; alterarse (*el pulso*); palpitar (*el corazón*)
flux [flʌks] *s* (*flow; flowing of tide*) flujo; (*for fusing metals*) flujo, fundente *m*
fly [flaɪ] *s* (*pl* **flies**) mosca; (*of trousers*) portañuela, bragueta; (*for fishing*) mosca artificial; **flies** (theat) bambalinas; **to die like flies** morir como chinches || *v* (*pret* **flew** [flu]; *pp* **flown** [flon]) *tr* hacer volar (*una cometa*); dirigir (*un avión*); (*to carry in an airship*) volar; atravesar en avión; desplegar, llevar (*una bandera*) || *intr* volar; huir; ondear (*una bandera*); **to fly off** salir volando; desprenderse; **to fly open** abrirse de repente; **to fly over** trasvolar; **to fly shut** cerrarse de repente
fly ball *s* (baseball) palomita, globo
fly′blow′ *s* cresa
fly′-by-night′ *adj* indigno de confianza
fly′catch′er *s* moscareta, papamoscas *m*
fly chaser *s* espantamoscas *m*
flyer [ˈflaɪ•ər] *s* var de **flier**
fly′-fish′ *tr & intr* pescar con moscas artificiales
flying [ˈflaɪ•ɪŋ] *adj* volante; rápido, veloz || *s* aviación
flying boat *s* hidroavión *m*
flying buttress *s* arbotante *m*
flying colors *spl* gran éxito
flying field *s* campo de aviación
flying saucer *s* platillo volante, disco volador
flying sickness *s* mal *m* de altura
flying start *s* salida lanzada; **to get off to a flying start** empezar con muy buen pie
flying time *s* horas de vuelo
fly in the ointment *s* mosca muerta que malea el perfume
fly′leaf′ *s* (*pl* **-leaves′**) guarda, hoja de guarda
fly net *s* (*for a bed*) mosquitero; (*for a horse*) espantamoscas *m*
fly′pa′per *s* papel *m* matamoscas
fly′speck′ *s* mancha de mosca
fly′swatter [ˈswɑtər] *s* matamoscas *m*
fly′trap′ *s* atrapamoscas *m*
fly′weight′ *s* peso mosca
fly′wheel′ *s* volante *m*
FM [ˈɛfˈɛm] *s* (letterword) (**frequency modulation**) FM *f* (modulación de frecuencia)
foal [fol] *s* potro || *intr* parir (*la yegua*)
foam [fom] *s* espuma || *intr* espumar
foam extinguisher *s* lanzaespumas *m,* extintor *m* de espuma
foam rubber *s* caucho esponjoso, espuma de caucho
foam•y [ˈfomi] *adj* (*comp* **-ier;** *super* **-iest**) espumoso, espumajoso
fob [fɑb] *s* faltriquera de reloj; (*chain*) leopoldina; (*ornament*) dije *m*
F.O.B. *abbr* **free on board**
focal [ˈfokəl] *adj* focal
fo•cus [ˈfokəs] *s* (*pl* **-cuses** o **-ci** [saɪ]) foco; **in focus** enfocado; **out of focus** desenfocado || *v* (*pret & pp* **-cused** o **-cussed;** *ger* **-cusing** o **-cussing**) *tr* enfocar; fijar (*la atención*) || *intr* enfocarse
fodder [ˈfɑdər] *s* forraje *m*
foe [fo] *s* enemigo
fog [fɑg] o [fɔg] *s* niebla; (phot) velo || *v* (*pret & pp* **fogged;** *ger* **fogging**) *tr* envolver en niebla; (*to blur*) empañar; (phot) velar || *intr* empañarse; (phot) velarse
fog bank *s* banco de nieblas
fog bell *s* campana de nieblas
fog′bound′ *adj* atascado en la niebla, envuelto en la niebla
fog•gy [ˈfɑgi] o [ˈfɔgi] *adj* (*comp* **-gier;** *super* **-giest**) neblinoso, brumoso; confuso; (phot) velado; **it is foggy** hay neblina
fog′horn′ *s* sirena de niebla
fog light *s* faro antiniebla
foible [ˈfɔɪbəl] *s* flaqueza, lado flaco
foil [fɔɪl] *s* (*thin sheet of metal*) hojuela, laminilla; (*of mirror*) azogado, plateado; contraste *m,* realce *m;* (*sword*) florete *m* || *tr* frustrar; azogar, platear (*un espejo*)
foist [fɔɪst] *tr* — **to foist something on someone** encajar una cosa a uno
fol. *abbr* **folio, following**
fold [fold] *s* pliegue *m,* doblez *m;* arruga; (*for sheep*) aprisco, redil *m;* (*of the faithful*) rebaño || *tr* plegar, doblar; cruzar (*los brazos*); **to fold up** doblar (*p.ej., un mapa*) || *intr* plegarse, doblarse
folder [ˈfoldər] *s* (*covers for holding papers*) carpeta; (*pamphlet*) folleto; (compu) carpeta
folderol [ˈfɑldəˌrɑl] *s* tontería, necedad; bagatela

folding [ˈfoldɪŋ] *adj* plegadizo, plegable; plegador
folding camera *s* cámara de fuelle
folding chair *s* silla de tijera, silla plegadiza; (*of canvas*) catrecillo
folding cot *s* catre *m* de tijera
folding door *s* puerta plegadiza
folding rule *s* metro plegadizo
foliage [ˈfolɪ•ɪdʒ] *s* follaje *m*
foli•o [ˈfolɪ•o] *adj* en folio || *s* (*pl* **-os**) (*sheet*) folio; infolio, libro en folio || *tr* foliar
folk [fok] *adj* popular, tradicional, del pueblo || *s* (*pl* **folk** o **folks**) gente *f;* **folks** (coll) gente (*familia*)
folk etymology *s* etimología popular
folk'lore' *s* folklore *m*
folk music *s* música folklórica
folk song *s* canción típica, canción tradicional
folk•sy [ˈfoksi] *adj* (*comp* **-sier;** *super* **-siest**) (coll) sociable, tratable; (*like common people*) (coll) plebeyo
folk'way' *s* costumbre tradicional
follicle [ˈfɑlɪkəl] *s* folículo
follow [ˈfɑlo] *tr* seguir; sequir el hilo de; interesarse en (*las noticias del día*) || *intr* seguir; resultar; **as follows** como sigue; **it follows** síguese
follower [ˈfɑlo•ər] *s* seguidor *m;* secuaz *mf,* partidario; imitador *m;* discípulo
following [ˈfɑlo•ɪŋ] *adj* siguiente || *s* séquito; partidarios
fol'low-up' *adj* consecutivo; recordativo || *s* carta recordativa, circular recordativa
fol•ly [ˈfɑli] *s* (*pl* **-lies**) desatino, locura; empresa temeraria; **follies** revista teatral
foment [foˈment] *tr* fomentar
fond [fɑnd] *adj* afectuoso, cariñoso; **to become fond of** encariñarse con, aficionarse a o de
fondle [ˈfɑndəl] *tr* acariciar, mimar
fondness [ˈfɑndnɪs] *s* afición, cariño
font [fɑnt] *s* (*source; source of water*) fuente *f;* (*for holy water*) pila; (*of type*) fundición, fuente *f;* (compu) fuente
food [fud] *adj* alimenticio || *s* comida, alimento; **food for thought** cosa en qué pensar
food poisoning *s* intoxicación alimenticia
food processor *s* procesador *m* de alimentos, robot *m* de cocina
food stamps *spl* cupones alimenticios o federales; bonos-alimenticios
food'stuffs' *spl* comestibles *mpl,* víveres *mpl*
fool [ful] *s* tonto, necio; (*jester*) bufón *m;* (*person imposed on*) inocente *mf,* víctima; **to make a fool of** poner en ridículo; **to play the fool** hacer el tonto || *tr* embaucar, engañar; **to fool away** malgastar (*tiempo, dinero*) || *intr* tontear; **to fool around** (coll) malgastar el tiempo; **to fool with** (coll) ajar, manosear
fooler•y [ˈfuləri] *s* (*pl* **-ies**) locura, tontería, babosada
fool'har'dy *adj* (*comp* **-dier;** *super* **-diest**) temerario
fooling [ˈfulɪŋ] *s* broma; engaño; **no fooling** hablando en serio
foolish [ˈfulɪʃ] *adj* tonto; ridículo; gilí
fool'proof' *adj* (coll) a prueba de mal trato; (coll) infalible
fools'cap' *s* gorro de bufón; papel *m* de oficio
fool's errand *s* caza de grillos
fool's scepter *s* cetro de locura
foot [fut] *s* (*pl* **feet** [fit]) pie *m;* (*unit of measurement: 30.48 centimeters*) pie; **to drag one's feet** ir a paso de caracol; **to have one foot in the grave** estar con un pie en la sepultura; **to put one's best foot forward** (coll) hacer méritos; **to put one's foot in it** (coll) meter la pata; (coll) tirarse una plancha; **to stand on one's own feet** volar con sus propias alas; **to tread under foot** hollar || *tr* pagar (*la cuenta*); **to foot it** andar a pie; bailar
footage [ˈfutɪdʒ] *s* distancia o largura en pies
foot'-and-mouth' disease' *s* (vet) fiebre aftosa, glosopeda
foot'ball' *s* fútbol, futbol americano (Mex); (*ball*) balón *m,* pelota de fútbol
football player *s* futbolista *mf*
football pool *s* apuesta colectiva, polla
football stadium *s* estadio de fútbol
foot'board' *s* (*support for foot*) estribo; (*of bed*) pie *m*
foot'bridge' *s* pasarela, puente *m* para peatones, puente peatonal
foot'fall' *s* paso
foot'hill' *s* colina al pie de una montaña
foot'hold' *s* arraigo, pie *m;* **to gain a foothold** ganar pie
footing [ˈfutɪŋ] *s* pie *m,* p.ej., **he lost his footing** perdió el pie; **on a friendly footing** en relaciones amistosas; **on an equal footing** en pie de igualdad; **on a war footing** en pie de guerra
foot'lights' *spl* candilejas, batería; (fig) tablas, escena
foot'loose' *adj* libre, no comprometido
foot•man [ˈfutmən] *s* (*pl* **-men** [mən]) lacayo, criado de librea
foot'note' *s* nota al pie de la página
foot'path' *s* senda para peatones
foot'print' *s* huella
foot race *s* carrera a pie
foot'rest' *s* apoyapié *m,* descansapié *m*
foot rule *s* regla de un pie
foot soldier *s* soldado de a pie
foot'sore' *adj* despeado
foot'step' *s* paso; **to follow in the footsteps of** seguir los pasos de
foot'stone' *s* lápida al pie de una sepultura
foot'stool' *s* escabel *m,* escañuelo
foot warmer *s* calientapiés *m*
foot'wear' *s* calzado
foot'work' *s* juego de piernas
foot'worn' *adj* (*road*) trillado; (*person*) despeado
foozle [ˈfuzəl] *s* chambonada; (coll) chambón

m, torpe *m* || *tr* chafallar; errar (*un golpe*) de manera torpe || *intr* chambonear
fop [fɑp] *s* currutaco, petimetre *m;* lagarto (Mex)
for [fər] *prep* para; por; como, p.ej., **he uses his living room for an office** usa la sala como oficina; de, p.ej., **time for bed** hora de acostarse; desde hace, p.ej., **he has been here for a week** está aquí desde hace una semana; en honor de; a pesar de; **for example** por ejemplo || *conj* pues, porque
for. *abbr* **foreign**
forage [ˈfɔrɪdʒ] *adj* forrajero || *s* forraje *m* || *tr & intr* forrajear; saquear
foray [ˈfɑre] o [ˈfɔre] *s* correría; saqueo || *intr* hacer correrías
for•bear [fɔrˈbɛr] *v* (*pret* **-bore** [ˈbor]; *pp* **-borne** [ˈborn]) *tr* abstenerse de || *intr* contenerse
forbearance [fɔrˈbɛrəns] *s* abstención; paciencia
for•bid [fɔrˈbɪd] *v* (*pret* **-bade** [ˈbæd] o **-bad** [ˈbæd]; *pp* **-bidden** [ˈbɪdən]; *ger* **-bidding**) *tr* prohibir
forbidden fruit *s* fruto prohibido
forbidding [fɔrˈbɪdɪŋ] *adj* repugnante, repulsivo
force [fors] *s* fuerza; (*staff of workers*) personal *m;* (*of soldiers, police, etc.*) cuerpo; (phys) fuerza; **by force** a la mala (Cuba, P-R); **by force of** a fuerza de; **by main force** con todas sus fuerzas; **in force** vigente, en vigor; en gran número; **to join forces** juntar diestra con diestra || *tr* forzar; obligar; **to force back** hacer retroceder; **to force down** obligar a aterrizar; tragar (*a duras penas*); **to force open** abrir por fuerza; **to force through** llevar a cabo por fuerza
forced [forst] *adj* forzado
forced air *s* aire *m* a presión
forced landing *s* aterrizaje forzado o forzoso
forced march *s* marcha forzada
force′-feed′ *tr* alimentar por la fuerza
forceful [ˈforsfəl] *adj* enérgico, eficaz
for•ceps [ˈfɔrsəps] *s* (*pl* **-ceps** o **-cipes** [sɪ,piz]) (dent, surg) pinzas; (obstet) fórceps *m*
force pump *s* bomba impelente
forcible [ˈforsɪbəl] *adj* eficaz, convincente; forzado
ford [ford] *s* vado || *tr* vadear
fore [for] *adj* anterior; (naut) de proa || *adv* antes, anteriormente; delante; (naut) avante || *interj* ¡ojo!, ¡cuidado! || *s* delantera; **to the fore** destacado; a mano; vivo
fore and aft *adv* de popa a proa
fore′arm′ *s* antebrazo || **fore•arm′** *tr* armar de antemano; prevenir
fore′bear′ *s* antepasado
forebode [forˈbod] *tr* (*to portend*) presagiar; (*to have a presentiment of*) presentir, prever
foreboding [forˈbodɪŋ] *s* presagio; presentimiento
fore′cast′ *s* pronóstico || *v* (*pret & pp* **-cast** o **-casted**) *tr* pronosticar
forecastle [ˈfoksəl], [ˈfor,kæsəl], o [ˈfor,kɑsəl] *s* castillo de proa
fore•close′ *tr* excluir; extinguir el derecho de redimir (*una hipoteca*); privar del derecho de redimir una hipoteca
fore•doom′ *tr* condenar de antemano, predestinar al fracaso
fore edge *s* canal *f*
fore′fa′ther *s* antepasado
fore′fin′ger *s* dedo índice, dedo mostrador
fore′front′ *s* puesto delantero; sitio de actividad más intensa; **in the forefront** a vanguardia
fore•go′ *v* (*pret* **-went′**; *pp* **-gone′**) *tr & intr* preceder
foregoing [ˈfor,go•ɪŋ] o [forˈgo•ɪŋ] *adj* anterior, precedente, prenombrado
fore′gone′ conclusion *s* resultado inevitable; decisión adoptada de antemano
fore′ground′ *s* primer plano, primer término
forehanded [ˈfor,hændɪd] *adj* (*thrifty*) ahorrado; hecho de antemano
forehead [ˈfɑrɪd] o [ˈfɔrɪd] *s* frente *f*
foreign [ˈfɑrɪn] *adj* extranjero, exterior; **foreign to** (*not belonging to or connected with*) ajeno a
foreign affairs *spl* asuntos exteriores
for′eign-born′ *adj* nacido en el extranjero
foreigner [ˈfɑrɪnər] *s* extranjero
foreign exchange *s* cambio extranjero; (*currency*) divisa
foreign exchange market *s* mercado de divisas
foreign minister *s* ministro de asuntos exteriores
foreign ministry *s* ministerio de relaciones exteriores
foreign office *s* ministerio de asuntos exteriores
foreign service *s* servicio diplomático y consular; servicio militar extranjero
foreign trade *s* comercio extranjero
fore′leg′ *s* brazo, pata delantera
fore′lock′ *s* mechón *m* de pelo sobre la frente; (*of a horse*) copete *m;* **to take time by the forelock** asir la ocasión por la melena
fore•man [ˈformən] *s* (*pl* **-men** [mən]) capataz *m,* mayoral *m,* sobrestante *m;* (*in a machine shop*) contramaestre *m,* jefe *m* de taller; (law) presidente *m* del jurado
foremast [ˈformәst], [ˈfor,mæst], o [ˈfor,mɑst] *s* palo de trinquete
foremost [ˈfor,most] *adj* primero, principal, más eminente
fore′noon′ *adj* matinal || *s* mañana
fore′part′ *s* parte delantera; primera parte
fore′paw′ *s* pata delantera
fore′quar′ter *s* cuarto delantero
forensic medicine [fəˈrɛnsɪk] *s* medicina forense, medicina legal
fore′run′ner *s* precursor *m;* predecesor *m;* antepasado; anuncio, presagio
fore•sail [ˈforsəl] o [ˈfor,sel] *s* trinquete *m*
fore•see′ *v* (*pret* **-saw′**; *pp* **-seen′**) *tr* prever

foreseeable [for'si•əbəl] *adj* previsible
fore•shad'ow *tr* presagiar, prefigurar
fore•short'en *tr* escorzar
fore•short'ening *s* escorzo
fore'sight' *s* previsión, presciencia
fore'sight'ed *adj* previsor, presciente
fore'skin' *s* prepucio
forest ['fɑrɪst] o 'fɔrɪst] *adj* forestal || *s* bosque *m,* selva
fore•stall' *tr* impedir, prevenir; anticipar; acaparar
forester ['fɔrəstər] *s* silvicultor *m;* guarda *mf* forestal
forest ranger ['rendʒər] *s* guarda *m* forestal, montanero
forestry ['fɑrɪstri] o ['fɔrɪstri] *s* silvicultura, ciencia forestal
fore'taste' *s* goce anticipado, conocimiento anticipado
fore•tell' *v* (*pret & pp* **-told'**) *tr* predecir; presagiar
fore'thought' *s* premeditación; providencia, previsión
forever [fɔr'ɛvər] *adv* por siempre; siempre
fore•warn' *tr* prevenir, poner sobre aviso
fore'wom'an *s* (law) presidente *f* de jurado
fore'word' *s* advertencia, prefacio
forfeit ['fɔrfɪt] *adj* perdido || *s* multa, pena; prenda perdida; **forfeits** (*game*) prendas || *tr* perder el derecho a
forfeiture ['fɔrfɪtʃər] *s* multa, pena; prenda perdida
forgather [fɔr'gæðər] *intr* reunirse; encontrarse; **to forgather with** asociarse con
forge [fordʒ] *s* fragua; (*blacksmith shop*) herrería || *tr* fraguar, forjar; falsificar (*la firma de otra persona*); fraguar, forjar (*mentiras*) || *intr* fraguar, forjar; **to forge ahead** avanzar despacio y con esfuerzo
forger•y ['fordʒəri] *s* (*pl* **-ies**) falsificación
for•get [fɔr'gɛt] *v* (*pret* **-got** [gɑt]; *pp* **-got** o **-gotten;** *ger* **-getting**) *tr* olvidar, olvidarse de, olvidársele a uno, p.ej., **he forgot his overcoat** se le olvidó su abrigo; **forget it!** ¡no se preocupe!; **to forget oneself** no pensar en sí mismo; ser distraído; propasarse
forgetful [fɔr'gɛtfəl] *adj* olvidado, olvidadizo; descuidado
forgetfulness [fɔr'gɛtfəlnɪs] *s* olvido; descuido
for•get'-me-not' *s* nomeolvides *m*
forgivable [fɔr'gɪvəbəl] *adj* perdonable
for•give [fɔr'gɪv] *v* (*pret* **-gave'**; *pp* **-giv'en**) *tr* perdonar
forgiveness [fɔr'gɪvnɪs] *s* perdón *m;* misericordia
forgiving [fɔr'gɪvɪŋ] *adj* perdonador, misericordioso, clemente
for•go [fɔr'go] *v* (*pret* **-went'**; *pp* **-gone'**) *tr* privarse de
fork [fɔrk] *s* horca; (*of a gardener; of bicycle*) horquilla; (*of two rivers*) horcajo; (*of railroad*) ramal *m;* (*of a tree*) horqueta; (*for eating*) tenedor *m* || *tr* ahorquillar; cargar con horquilla; (*in chess*) amenazar (*dos piezas*); **to fork out** (slang) entregar, sudar || *intr* bifurcarse
forked [fɔrkt] *adj* ahorquillado
forked lightning *s* relámpago en zigzag
fork'lift' truck *s* carretilla elevadora de horquilla
forlorn [fɔr'lɔrn] *adj* desamparado; desesperado; miserable
forlorn hope *s* empresa desesperada
form [fɔrm] *s* forma; (*paper to be filled out*) formulario; (*construction to give shape to cement*) encofrado; (*type in a frame*) molde *m* || *tr* formar || *intr* formarse
formal ['fɔrməl] *adj* formal, ceremonioso; etiquetero
formal attire *s* vestido de etiqueta
formal call *s* visita de cumplido
formali•ty [fɔr'mælɪti] *s* (*pl* **-ties**) (*standard procedure*) formalidad; ceremonia, etiqueta
formal party *s* reunión de etiqueta
formal speech *s* discurso de aparato
format ['fɔrmæt] *s* formato, presentación; (compu, typ) formato || *tr* formatear
formatting ['fɔrmætiŋ] *s* (compu) formateo
formation [fɔr'meʃən] *s* formación
former ['fɔrmər] *adj* (*preceding*) anterior; (*long past*) antiguo; primero (*de dos*); **the former** aquél
formerly ['fɔrmərli] *adv* antes, en tiempos pasados
form'-fit'ting *adj* ceñido al cuerpo
formidable ['fɔrmɪdəbəl] *adj* formidable
formless ['fɔrmlɪs] *adj* informe
form letter *s* carta general
formu•la ['fɔrmjələ] *s* (*pl* **-las** o **-lae** [,li] fórmula
formulate ['fɔrmjə,let] *tr* formular
fornicate ['fɔrnə,ket] *intr* fornicar
fornication [,fɔrnə'keʃən] *s* fornicación
for•sake [fɔr'sek] *v* (*pret* **-sook** ['sʊk]; *pp* **-saken** ['sekən]) *tr* abandonar, desamparar; dejar
fort [fort] *s* fuerte *m,* fortaleza
forte [fort] *s* (*strong point*) fuerte *m,* caballo de batalla || ['forte] *adj* (mus) fuerte
forth [forθ] *adv* adelante; **and so forth** y así sucesivamente; **from this day forth** de hoy en adelante; **to go forth** salir
forth'com'ing *adj* próximo, venidero
forth'right' *adj* directo, franco, sincero || *adv* derecho; sinceramente, francamente; en seguida
forth'with' *adv* inmediatamente
fortieth ['fɔrtɪ•ɪθ] *adj & s* (*in a series*) cuadragésimo; (*part*) cuarentavo
fortification [,fɔrtɪfɪ'keʃən] *s* fortificación
forti•fy ['fɔrtɪ,faɪ] *v* (*pret & pp* **-fied**) *tr* fortificar; encabezar (*vinos*)
fortitude ['fɔrtɪ,tjud] *s* fortaleza, firmeza
fortnight ['fɔrtnaɪt] *s* quincena, dos semanas
fortress ['fɔrtrɪs] *s* fortaleza
fortuitous [fɔr'tju•ɪtəs] *adj* fortuito

fortunate [ˋfɔrt∫ənɪt] *adj* afortunado
fortune [ˋfɔrtjən] *s* fortuna; (*money*) platal *m;* **to make a fortune** enriquecerse; **to tell someone his fortune** decircle a uno la buenaventura
fortune hunter *s* cazador *m* de dotes
for′tune•tel′ler *s* adivino, agorero
for•ty [ˋfɔrti] *adj & pron* cuarenta ‖ *s* (*pl* **-ties**) cuarenta *m*
fo•rum [ˋforəm] *s* (*pl* **-rums** o **-ra** [rə]) foro; (*e.g., of public opinion*) tribunal *m*
forward [ˋfɔrwərd] *adj* delantero; precoz; atrevido, impertinente ‖ *adv* hacia adelante; **to bring forward** pasar a cuenta nueva; **to come forward** adelantarse; **to look forward to** esperar con placer anticipado ‖ *tr* cursar, hacer seguir, reexpedir; fomentar, patrocinar
fossil [ˋfɑsɪ] *adj & s* fósil *m*
foster [ˋfɑstər] o [ˋfɔstər] *adj* adoptivo, de leche, de crianza ‖ *tr* fomentar
foster brother *s* hermano de leche
foster family *s* familia de acogida
foster home *s* hogar *m* de adopción
foster mother *s* madre adoptiva; (*nurse*) ama de leche
foster sister *s* hermana de leche
foul [faʊl] *adj* sucio, puerco; (*air*) viciado; (*wind*) contrario; (*weather*) malo; obsceno; pérfido; (*breath*) fétido; (baseball) fuera del cuadro; (sport) falta, faul *m,* foul *m*
foul ball *s* (baseball) pelota fuera del cuadro
foul-mouthed [ˋfaʊlˋmaʊðd] o [ˋfaʊlˋmaʊθt] *adj* deslenguado
foul play *s* mal encuentro; (sport) juego sucio
foul′spo′ken *adj* malhablado
found [faʊnd] *tr* fundar; (*to melt, to cast*) fundir
foundation [faʊnˋde∫ən] *s* fundación; (*endowment*) dotación; (*basis*) fundamento; (*masonry support*) cimiento
founder [ˋfaʊndər] *s* fundador *m;* (*of metals*) fundidor *m* ‖ *intr* despearse (*un caballo*); hundirse, irse a pique (*un buque*); (*to fail*) fracasar
Founding Fathers, the *spl* los padres de la patria; (U.S.A.) los fundadores de la nación americana
foundling [ˋfaʊndlɪŋ] *s* niño expósito; pepe *mf*
foundling hospital *s* casa de expósitos
found•ry [ˋfaʊndri] *s* (*pl* **-ries**) fundición
foundry•man [ˋfaʊndrɪmən] *s* (*pl* **-men** [mən]) fundidor *m*
fount [faʊnt] *s* fuente *f*
fountain [ˋfaʊntən] *s* fuente *f,* manantial *m*
foun′tain•head′ *s* nacimiento; (fig) fuente *f*
fountain pen *s* pluma estilográfica, pluma fuente
fountain syringe *s* mangueta
four [for] *adj & pron* cuatro ‖ *s* cuatro; **four o'clock** las cuatro; **on all fours** a gatas
four′-cy′cle *adj* (mach) de cuatro tiempos
four′-cyl′inder *adj* (mach) de cuatro cilindros
four′-flush′ *intr* (coll) bravear, papelonear
fourflusher [ˋfor,flʌ∫ər] *s* bravucón *m*
four-footed [ˋforˋfʊtɪd] *adj* cuadrúpedo
four hundred *adj & pron* cuatrocientos ‖ *s* cuatrocientos *m;* **the four hundred** la alta sociedad
four′-in-hand′ *s* corbata de nudo corredizo; coche tirado por cuatro caballos
four′-lane′ *adj* cuadriviario
four′-leaf′ *adj* cuadrifoliado
four-legged [ˋforˋlɛgɪd] o [ˋforˋlɛgd] *adj* de cuatro patas; (*schooner*) de cuatro mástiles
four′-let′ter word *s* palabra impúdica de cuatro letras, palabrota
four′-mo′tor plane *s* cuadrimotor *m*
four′-o'clock′ *s* dondiego
four′post′er *s* cama imperial
four′score′ *adj* cuatro veintenas de
foursome [ˋforsəm] *s* cuatrinca; cuatro jugadores; juego de cuatro
fourteen [ˋforˋtin] *adj, pron & s* catorce *m*
fourteenth [ˋforˋtinθ] *adj & s* (*in a series*) decimocuarto; (*part*) catorzavo ‖ *s* (*in dates*) catorce *m*
fourth [forθ] *adj & s* cuarto ‖ *s* (*in dates*) cuatro
fourth estate *s* cuarto poder
four′-way′ *adj* de cuatro direcciones; (elec) de cuatro terminales
four-wheel drive *s* tracción total, integral o a las cuatro ruedas, doble tracción, todoterreno
fowl [faʊl] *s* ave *f;* aves; gallina; gallo; carne *f* de ave
fowling piece *s* escopeta de caza
fox [fɑks] *s* zorra; (*fur*) zorro; (*cunning person*) (fig) zorro ‖ *tr* (coll) engañar con astucia
fox′glove′ *s* dedalera
fox′hole′ *s* zorrera; (mil) pozo de lobo
fox′hound′ *s* perro raposero, perro zorrero
fox hunt *s* caza de zorras
fox terrier *s* fox-terrier *m* (*casta de perro de talla pequeña*)
fox trot *s* trote corto (*de caballo*); fox-trot *m* (*baile de compás cuaternario*)
fox•y [ˋfɑksi] *adj* (*comp* **-ier;** *super* **-iest**) (coll) hermosa y erótica; zorrero, astuto, taimado
foyer [ˋfɔɪ•ər] *s* (*of a private house*) vestíbulo; (theat) salón *m* de entrada, vestíbulo
fr. *abbr* **fragment, franc, from**
Fr. *abbr* **Father, French, Friday**
Fra [frɑ] *s* (*Brother*) fray *m*
fracas [ˋfrekəs] *s* alboroto, riña
fraction [ˋfræk∫ən] *s* fracción; porción muy pequeña
fractional [ˋfræk∫ənəl] *adj* fraccionario; insignificante
fractious [ˋfræk∫əs] *adj* reacio, rebelón; quisquilloso, regañón
fracture [ˋfrækt∫ər] *s* fractura ‖ *tr* fracturar; (*e.g., an arm*) fracturarse; *intr* fracturarse
fragile [ˋfrædʒɪl] *adj* frágil
fragment [ˋfrægmənt] *s* fragmento
fragrance [ˋfregrəns] *s* fragancia
fragrant [ˋfregrənt] *adj* fragante
frail [frel] *adj* (*not robust*) débil; (*easily broken; morally weak*) frágil ‖ *s* cesto de junco

frail•ty [ˈfrelti] *s* (*pl* **-ties**) debilidad; (*moral weakness*) fragilidad
frame [frem] *s* (*of a picture, mirror*) marco, (*of glasses*) montura, armadura; (*structure*) armazón *f,* esqueleto; (*for embroidering*) bastidor *m;* (*of government*) sistema *m;* (compu) recuadro; (mov, telv) encuadre *m;* (naut) cuaderna ‖ *tr* (*to put in a frame*) enmarcar; formar, forjar; construir; redactar, formular; (slang) incriminar (*a un inocente*)
frame house *s* casa de madera
frame of mind *s* manera de pensar
frame′-up′ *s* (slang) treta, trama para incriminar a un inocente
frame′work′ *s* armazón *f,* esqueleto, entramado
franc [fræŋk] *s* franco
France [fræns] o [frɑns] *s* Francia
Frances [ˈfrænsɛs] *s* Francisca
franchise [ˈfræntʃaɪz] *s* franquicia, privilegio; (*right to vote*) sufragio
Francis [ˈfrænsɪs] *s* Francisco
Franciscan [frænˈsɪskən] *adj & s* franciscano
frank [fræŋk] *adj* franco, sincero ‖ *s* carta franca, envío franco; franquicia postal; sello de franquicia ‖ *tr* franquear ‖ **Frank** *s* (*member of a Frankish tribe*) franco; (*masculine name*) Paco
frankfurter [ˈfræŋkfərtər] *s* salchicha (de Frankfurt), salchicha de Viena (Arg, Col), vienesa (Chile), frankfurter *m* (Urug), salchicha alemana (Ven)
frankincense [ˈfræŋkɪn,sɛns] *s* olíbano
Frankish [ˈfræŋkɪʃ] *adj & s* franco
frankness [ˈfræŋknɪs] *s* franqueza, abertura, sinceridad
frantic [ˈfræntɪk] *adj* frenético
frappé [fræˈpe] *adj* helado ‖ *s* refresco helado de zumo de frutas
frat [fræt] *s* (slang) club *m* de estudiantes
fraternal [frəˈtʌrnəl] *adj* fraternal
fraterni•ty [frəˈtʌrnɪti] *s* (*pl* **-ties**) (*brotherliness*) fraternidad; cofradía; asociación secreta; (U.S.A.) club *m* de estudiantes
fraternize [ˈfrætər,naɪz] *intr* fraternizar
fraud [frɔd] *s* fraude *m;* embelequería (Col, Mex, W-I); (*person*) (coll) impostor *m*
fraudulent [ˈfrɔdjələnt] *adj* fraudulento
fraught [frɔt] *adj*—**fraught with** cargado de, lleno de
fray [fre] *s* combate *m,* riña, batalla ‖ *intr* deshilacharse, raerse
freak [frik] *s* (*sudden fancy*) capricho, antojo; (*person, animal*) fenómeno, esperpento
freakish [ˈfrikɪʃ] *adj* caprichoso, antojadizo; raro, fantástico
freckle [ˈfrɛkəl] *s* peca
freckle-faced [ˈfrɛkəl,fest] *adj* pecoso
freckly [ˈfrɛkli] *adj* pecoso
free [fri] *adj* (*comp* **freer** [ˈfri•ər]; *super* **freest** [ˈfri•ɪst]) libre; gratis, franco; liberal, generoso; **to be free with** dar abundantemente; **to set free** libertar ‖ *adv* libremente; en libertad; de balde, gratis ‖ *v* (*pret & pp* **freed** [frid]; *ger* **freeing** [ˈfri•ɪŋ]) *tr* libertar, poner en libertad; soltar; exentar, eximir
free and easy *adj* despreocupado
freebooter [ˈfri,butər] *s* forbante *m,* filibustero, pirata *m*
free′born′ *adj* nacido libre; propio de un pueblo libre
freedom [ˈfridəm] *s* libertad
freedom of speech *s* libertad de palabra
freedom of the press *s* libertad de imprenta
freedom of the seas *s* libertad de los mares
freedom of worship *s* libertad de cultos
free enterprise *s* libertad de empresa
free fall *s* (phys) caída libre
free fight *s* sarracina, riña tumultuaria
free′-for-all′ *s* concurso abierto a todo el mundo; sarracina, riña tumultuaria
free hand *s* plena libertad, carta blanca
free′hand′ drawing *s* dibujo a pulso
freehanded [ˈfri,hændɪd] *adj* dadivoso, generoso
free′hold′ *s* (law) feudo franco
freelance *s* soldado mercenario; periodista *mf* sin empleo fijo; (*writer not on regular salary*) destajista *mf*
free lunch *s* tapas, enjutos
free•man [ˈfrimən] *s* (*pl* **-men** [mən]) hombre *m* libre; ciudadano
free market *s* libre empresa *or* mercado
Free′ma′son *s* francmasón *m*
Free′ma′sonry *s* francmasonería
free of charge *adj* gratis, de balde
free on board *adj* franco a bordo
free port *s* puerto franco
free ride *s* llevada gratuita
free service *s* servicio post-venta
free′-spo′ken *adj* franco, sin reserva
free′stone′ *adj & s* abridero
free′style *s* (sport) estilo libre
freestyle wrestling *s* lucha libre
free′think′er *s* librepensador *m*
free thought *s* librepensamiento
free time *s* horas libres
free trade *s* librecambio *or* libre comercio
free′trad′er *s* librecambista *mf*
free′way′ *s* autopista
free will *s* libre albedrío
freeze [friz] *s* helada ‖ *v* (*pret* **froze** [froz]; *pp* **frozen**) *tr* helar; congelar (*créditos, fondos, etc.*) ‖ *intr* helarse; congelarse; helársele a uno la sangre (*p.ej., de miedo*)
freeze′-dry′ *v* (*pret & pp* **-dried**) *tr* liofilizar
freeze drying *s* liofilización
freezer [ˈfrizər] *s* heladora, sorbetera
freezing [ˈfrizɪŋ] *s* glaciación
freight [fret] *s* carga; (naut) flete *m;* **by freight** como carga; (rr) en pequeña velocidad ‖ *tr* enviar por carga
freight car *s* vagón *m* de carga, vagón de mercancías
freighter [ˈfretər] *s* buque *m* de carga, carguero
freight platform *s* (rr) muelle *m*
freight station *s* (rr) estación de carga

freight train *s* mercancías *msg,* tren *m* de mercancías
freight yard *s* (rr) patio de carga
French [frɛntʃ] *adj & s* francés *m;* **the French** los franceses
French chalk *s* jaboncillo de sastre
French doors *spl* puertas vidrieras dobles
French dressing *s* salsa francesa, vinagreta
French fries *spl* papas fritas, patatas fritas (Esp), papas a la francesa (Col, Mex)
French horn *s* (mus) trompa de armonía
French horsepower *s* caballo de fuerza, caballo de vapor
French kiss *s* beso profundo (*en la boca con la lengua*)
French leave *s* despedida a la francesa; **to take French leave** despedirse a la francesa
French•man [ˈfrɛntʃmən] *s* (*pl* **-men** [mən]) francés *m*
French telephone *s* microteléfono
French toast *s* torrija
French window *s* puerta ventana
French'wom'an *s* (*pl* **-wom'en**) francesa
frenzied [ˈfrɛnzid] *adj* frenético
fren•zy [ˈfrɛnzi] (*pl* **-zies**) frenesí *m*
frequen•cy [ˈfrikwənsi] *s* (*pl* **-cies**) frecuencia
frequency list *s* lista de frecuencia
frequency modulation *s* modulación de frecuencia
frequency range *s* (compu) gama de frecuencias
frequent [ˈfrikwənt] *adj* frecuente ‖ [frɪˈkwɛnt] o [ˈfrikwənt] *tr* frecuentar
frequently [ˈfrikwəntli] *adv* con frecuencia, frecuentemente
fres•co [ˈfrɛsko] *s* (*pl* **-coes** o **-cos**) fresco ‖ *tr* pintar al fresco
fresh [freʃ] *adj* fresco; (*water*) dulce; (*wind*) fresquito; novicio, inexperto; (*cheeky*) (slang) fresco; (*toward women*) (slang) atrevido; **fresh paint!** ¡ojo mancha! ‖ *adv* recientemente, recién; **fresh in** (coll) recién llegado, acabado de llegar; **fresh out** (coll) recién agotado
freshen [ˈfrɛʃən] *tr* refrescar ‖ *intr* refrescarse
freshet [ˈfrɛʃit] *s* avenida, crecida
fresh•man [ˈfrɛʃmən] *s* (*pl* **-men** [mən]) novato; estudiante *mf* de primer año
freshness [ˈfrɛʃnɪs] *s* frescura; (*cheek*) (slang) frescura
fresh' wa'ter *adj* de agua dulce; no acostumbrado a navegar; de poca monta
fret [frɛt] *s* (*interlaced design*) calado; (mus) ceja, traste *m;* queja ‖ *v* (*pret & pp* **fretted;** *ger* **fretting**) *tr* adornar con calados ‖ *intr* irritarse, quejarse, agitarse
fretful [ˈfrɛtfəl] *adj* irritable, enojadizo, displicente
fret'work' *s* calado
Freudianism [ˈfrɔɪdɪ•ə,nɪzəm] *s* freudismo
friar [ˈfraɪ•ər] *s* fraile *m*
fricassee [,frikəˈsi] *s* fricasé *m*
friction [ˈfrikʃən] *s* fricción, rozamiento; (fig) desavenencia, rozamiento
friction tape *s* cinta aislante
Friday [ˈfraɪdi] *s* viernes *m*
fried [fraɪd] *adj* frito
fried egg *s* huevo a la plancha, huevo frito o estrellado
fried food *s* fritura, fritos
friend [frɛnd] *s* amigo; (*in answer to "Who is there?"*) gente *f* de paz; **to be friends with** ser amigo de; **to make friends** trabar amistades; **to make friends with** hacerse amigo de
friend•ly [ˈfrɛndli] *adj* (*comp* **-lier;** *super* **-liest**) amigo, amistoso, amigable
friendly fire *s* (mil) fuego amigo
friendship [ˈfrɛndʃip] *s* amistad
fries [fraɪz] *spl* (*French fries*) (coll) papas fritas
frieze [friz] *s* (archit) friso
frigate [ˈfrɪgɪt] *s* fragata
fright [fraɪt] *s* susto, espanto; (*grotesque or ridiculous person*) (coll) espantajo; **to take fright at** asustarse de
frighten [ˈfraɪtən] *tr* asustar, espantar; **to frighten away** espantar, ahuyentar ‖ *intr* asustarse
frightful [ˈfraɪtfəl] *adj* espantoso, horroroso; (coll) feúcho, repugnante; (coll) enorme, tremendo
frightfulness [ˈfraɪtfəlnɪs] *s* espanto, horror *m;* terrorismo; espantosidad (SAm)
frigid [ˈfrɪdʒɪd] *adj* frío; (fig) frío; (*zone*) glacial
frigidity [frɪˈdʒɪdɪti] *s* frialdad; (pathol) frialdad; (fig) frialdad, frigidez *f*
frill [fril] *s* lechuga; (*of birds and other animals*) collarín *m;* (*frippery*) (coll) ringorrango; (*in dress, speech etc.*) (coll) afectación
fringe [frɪndʒ] *s* franja, orla; (opt) franja ‖ *tr* franjar, orlar
fringe benefits *spl* beneficios accesorios; beneficios sociales
fripper•y [ˈfrɪpəri] *s* (*pl* **-ies**) (*flashiness*) cursilería; (*flashy clothes*) perejil *m,* perifollos
frisk [frɪsk] *tr* (*a person for concealed weapons*) cachear, registrar
frisk•y [ˈfrɪski] *adj* (*comp* **-ier;** *super* **-iest**) juguetón, retozón; (*horse*) fogoso
fritter [ˈfrɪtər] *s* fruta de sartén; fragmento ‖ *tr*—**to fritter away** desperdiciar, malgastar poco a poco
frivolous [ˈfrɪvələs] *adj* frívolo
frizz [frɪz] *s* (*pl* **frizzes**) rizo, pelo rizado apretadamente ‖ *v* (*pret & pp* **frizzed;** *ger* **frizzing**) *tr* rizar, rizar apretadamente
frizzle [ˈfrɪzəl] *s* rizo apretado; chirrido, siseo ‖ *tr* rizar apretadamente; asar o freír en parrilla ‖ *intr* chirriar, sisear
friz•zly [ˈfrɪzli] *adj* (*comp* **-zlier;** *super* **-zliest**) muy ensortijado
fro [fro] *adv*—**to and fro** de acá para allá; **to go to and fro** ir y venir
frock [frɑk] *s* vestido; bata, blusa; (*of priest*) vestido talar
frock coat *s* levita
frog [frɑg] o [frɔg] *s* rana; (*button and loop on a garment*) alamar *m;* (*in throat*) ronquera, gallo

frog′man′ *s* (*pl* **-men′**) hombre rana *m*
frol•ic [ˈfrɑlɪk] *s* juego alegre, travesura; fiesta, holgorio ‖ *v* (*pret & pp* **-icked;** *ger* **-icking**) *intr* juguetear, travesear, jarancar
frolicsome [ˈfrɑlɪksəm] *adj* juguetón, travieso
from [frʌm], [frɑm] o [frəm] *prep* de; desde; de parte de; según; a, p.ej., **to take something away from someone** quitarle algo a alguien
front [frʌnt] *adj* delantero; anterior ‖ *s* frente *m & f;* (*of a shirt*) pechera; (*of a book*) principio; apariencia falsa (*p.ej., de riqueza*); ademán estudiado; (mil) frente *m;* **in front of** delante de, frente a, en frente de; **to put on a front** (coll) gastar mucho oropel; **to put up a bold front** (coll) hacer de tripas corazón ‖ *tr* (*to face*) dar a; (*to confront*) afrontar, arrostrar; (*to supply with a front*) poner frente o fachada a ‖ *intr*—**to front on** dar a; **to front towards** mirar hacia
frontage [ˈfrʌntɪdʒ] *s* fachada, frontera; terreno frontero
front desk *s* (*in a hotel*) recepción
front door *s* puerta de entrada
frontier [frʌnˈtɪr] *adj* fronterizo ‖ *s* frontera
frontiers•man [frʌnˈtɪrzmən] *s* (*pl* **-men** [mən]) hombre *m* de la frontera, explorador *m*
frontispiece [ˈfrʌntɪsˌpis] *s* (*of book*) portada; (archit) frontispicio
front man *s* testaferro, hombre *m* de paja
front matter *s* preliminares *mpl* (*de un libro*)
front page *s* primera plana
front porch *s* soportal *m*
front room *s* cuarto que da a la calle
front row *s* primera fila
front seat *s* asiento delantero
front steps *spl* escalones *mpl* de acceso a la puerta de entrada
front view *s* vista de frente
front′-wheel′ drive *s* tracción delantera
frost [frɔst] o [frɑst] *s* (*freezing*) helada; (*frozen dew*) escarcha; (slang) fracaso ‖ *tr* cubrir de escarcha; escarchar (*confituras*); helar (*el frío las plantas*); deslustrar (*el vidrio*)
frost′bit′ten *adj* dañado por la helada; quemado por la helada o la escarcha
frosted glass *s* vidrio deslustrado
frosting [ˈfrɔstɪŋ] o [frɑstɪŋ] *s* garapiña; (*of glass*) deslustre *m*
frost•y [ˈfrɔsti] o [ˈfrɑsti] *adj* (*comp* **-ier;** *super* **-iest**) cubierto de escarcha; escarchado; frío, poco amistoso; canoso, gris
froth [frɔθ] o [frɑθ] *s* espuma; frivolidad, vanidad ‖ *intr* espumar, echar espuma; (*at the mouth*) espumajear
froth•y [ˈfrɔθi] o [ˈfrɑθi] *adj* (*comp* **-ier;** *super* **-iest**) espumoso; frívolo, vano
froward [ˈfrowərd] *adj* díscolo, indócil
frown [fraʊn] *s* ceño, entrecejo ‖ *intr* fruncir el entrecejo; **to frown at** o **on** mirar con ceño, desaprobar
frows•y o **frowz•y** [ˈfraʊzi] *adj* (*comp* **-ier;** *super* **-iest**) desaseado, desaliñado; maloliente; mal peinado
frozen foods [ˈfrozən] *spl* viandas congeladas
frugal [ˈfrugəl] *adj* (*moderate in the use of things*) parco; (*not very abundant*) frugal
fruit [frut] *adj* (*tree*) frutal; (*boat, dish*) frutero ‖ *s* (*such as apple, pear, strawberry*) fruta; frutas, p.ej., **I like fruit** me gustan las frutas; (*part containing seed*) fruto; (*effect, result*) (fig) fruto
fruit′cake′ *s* torta de frutas
fruit cup *s* compota de frutas picadas
fruit fly *s* mosca del vinagre; mosca de las frutas
fruitful [ˈfrutfəl] *adj* fructuoso
fruition [fruˈɪʃən] *s* buen resultado, cumplimiento; **to come to fruition** lograrse cumplidamente
fruit jar *s* tarro para frutas
fruit juice *s* jugo de frutas
fruitless [ˈfrutlɪs] *adj* infructuoso
fruit of the vine *s* zumo de cepas o de parras
fruit salad *s* ensalada de frutas, macedonia de frutas, cóctel *m* de frutas
fruit stand *s* puesto de frutas
fruit store *s* frutería
frumpish [ˈfrʌmpɪʃ] *adj* basto, desgarbado, desaliñado
frustrate [ˈfrʌstret] *tr* frustrar
fry [fraɪ] *s* (*pl* **fries**) fritada ‖ *v* (*pret & pp* **fried**) *tr & intr* freír
frying pan [ˈfraɪ•ɪŋ] *s* sartén *f;* **to jump from the frying pan into the fire** saltar de la sartén y dar en las brasas
ft. *abbr* **foot, feet**
fudge [fʌdʒ] *s* dulce *m* de chocolate
fuel [ˈfju•əl] *s* combustible *m;* (fig) pábulo; **alternative fuel** combustible alternativo ‖ *v* (*pret & pp* **fueled** o **fuelled;** *ger* **fueling** o **fuelling**) *tr* aprovisionar de combustible ‖ *intr* aprovisionarse de combustible
fuel cell *s* cámara de combustible, célula electrógena
fuel′-injec′tion engine *s* motor *m* de inyección
fuel oil *s* aceite *m* combustible, aceite fuel, fuel *m,* fuel-oil *m*
fuel tank *s* depósito de combustible
fugitive [ˈfjudʒɪtɪv] *adj & s* fugitivo
fugue [fjug] *s* (mus) fuga
ful•crum [ˈfʌlkrəm] *s* (*pl* **-crums** o **-cra** [krə]) fulcro
fulfill [fʊlˈfɪl] *tr* (*to carry out*) cumplir, realizar; cumplir con (*una obligación*); llenar (*una condición*)
fulfillment [fʊlˈfɪlmənt] *s* cumplimiento, realización
full [fʊl] *adj* lleno; (*dress, garment*) amplio, holgado; (*formal dress*) de etiqueta; (*voice*) sonoro, fuerte; (*of food*) harto; **full of aches and pains** lleno de goteras; **full of fun** muy divertido, muy chistoso; **full of play** muy juguetón; **full to overflowing** lleno a rebosar ‖ *adv* completamente; **full many (a)** muchísimos; **full well** muy bien, perfectamente ‖ *s* colmo; **in full** por completo; sin abreviar; **to the full** completamente ‖ *tr* abatanar

full-blooded [ˈfʊlˈblʌdɪd] *adj* vigoroso; completo, pletórico; de raza
full-blown [ˈfʊlˈblon] *adj* (*flower, blossom*) abierto; desarrollado, maduro
full-bodied [ˈfʊlˈbɑdid] *adj* fuerte, espeso, consistente; aromático
full dress *s* traje *m* de etiqueta; (mil) uniforme *m* de gala
full′-dress′ coat *s* frac *m*
full-faced [ˈfʊlˈfest] *adj* carilleno; (*view*) de cuadrado; (*portrait*) de rostro entero
full′-fig′ured *adj* robusto, corpulento, jamona
full-fledged [ˈfʊlˈflɛdʒd] *adj* hecho y derecho, nada menos que
full-grown [ˈfʊlˈgron] *adj* crecido, completamente desarrollado
full house *s* lleno, entrada llena; (poker) fulján *m*
full′-length′ mirror *s* espejo de cuerpo entero, espejo de vestir
full-length movie *s* largometraje *m*, cinta de largo metraje
full load *s* plena carga; (aer) peso total
full member *s* socio de número
full moon *s* luna llena, plenilunio
full name *s* nombre *m* y apellidos
full′-page′ *adj* a página entera
full powers *spl* plenos poderes, amplias facultades
full sail *adv* a todo trapo
full′-scale′ *adj* de tamaño natural; total, completo; pleno
full-sized [ˈfʊlˈsaɪzd] *adj* de tamaño natural
full speed *adv* a toda velocidad
full stop *s* parada completa; (gram) punto
full swing *s* plena actividad
full tilt *adv* a toda velocidad
full′-time′ *adj* a tiempo completo
full′-view′ *adj* de vista completa
full volume *s* (rad) máximo de volumen
fully [ˈfuli] o [ˈfulli] *adv* completamente; cabalmente; por lo menos
fulsome [ˈfʊlsəm] *adj* bajo, craso, de mal gusto
fumble [ˈfʌmbəl] *tr* no coger (*la pelota*), dejar caer (*la pelota*) desmañadamente; manosear desmañadamente ‖ *intr* revolver papeles; titubear; andar a tientas; (*in one's pockets*) buscar con las manos
fume [fjum] *s* humo, vapor *m*, gas *m*, vaho ‖ *tr* (*to treat with fumes*) ahumar ‖ *intr* (*to give off fumes*) humear; (*to show anger*) echar pestes; **to fume at** echar pestes contra
fumigate [ˈfjumɪ,get] *tr* fumigar
fumigation [,fjumɪˈgeʃən] *s* fumigación
fun [fʌn] *s* divertimiento; broma, chacota; **to be fun** ser divertido; **to have fun** divertirse; **to make fun of** reírse de, burlarse de
function [ˈfʌŋkʃən] *s* función ‖ *intr* funcionar
functional [ˈfʌŋkʃənəl] *adj* funcional
functionar•y [ˈfʌŋkʃə,nɛri] *s* (*pl* **-ies**) funcionario
fund [fʌnd] *s* fondo; **funds** fondos ‖ *tr* consolidar (*una deuda*)
fundamental [,fʌndəˈmɛntəl] *adj* fundamental ‖ *s* fundamento
fundamentalism [,fʊndəˈmɛntəlɪzem] *s* fundamentalismo, integrismo; (eccl) *creencia basada en la interpretación literal de los escritos sagrados*
fundamentalist [,fʊndəˈmɛntəlɪst] *s* fundamentalista *mf*, integrista *mf;* (eccl) *persona que cree en la interpretación literal de los escritos sagrados*
funeral [ˈfjunərəl] *adj* funeral; (*march, procession*) fúnebre; (*expense*) funerario ‖ *s* funeral *m*, funerales *mpl*, pompa fúnebre (*de cuerpo presente*); **it's not my funeral** (slang) no corre a mi cuidado
funeral director *s* empresario de pompas fúnebres
funeral home o **parlor** *s* funeraria, agencia funeraria
funeral service *s* oficio de difuntos, misa de cuerpo presente
funereal [fjuˈnɪrɪ•əl] *adj* fúnebre
fungous [ˈfʌŋgəs] *adj* fungoso
fungus [ˈfʌŋgəs] *s* (*pl* **funguses** o **fungi** [ˈfʌndʒaɪ]) hongo; (pathol) fungo
funicular [fjuˈnɪkjələr] *adj & s* funicular *m*
funk [fʌŋk] *s* (coll) miedo, cobardía; cobarde *mf;* **in a funk** asustado
fun•nel [ˈfʌnəl] *s* embudo; (*smokestack*) chimenea; (*tube for ventilation*) manguera, ventilador *m* ‖ *v* (*pret & pp* **-neled** o **-nelled;** *ger* **-neling** o **-nelling**) *tr* verter por medio de un embudo
funnies [ˈfʌniz] *spl* páginas cómicas, tiras cómicas, tebeo
fun•ny [ˈfʌni] *adj* (*comp* **-nier;** *super* **-niest**) cómico; divertido, chistoso; (coll) extraño, raro; **to strike someone as funny** hacerle a uno gracia
funny bone *s* hueso de la alegría
funny paper *s* páginas cómicas
fur [fʌr] *s* piel *f;* abrigo de pieles; (*on the tongue*) sarro
furbelow [ˈfʌrbə,lo] *s* (*ruffle*) faralá *m;* (*frippery*) ringorrango
furbish [ˈfʌrbɪʃ] *tr* acicalar, limpiar; **to furbish up** renovar
furious [ˈfjʊrɪ•əs] *adj* furioso
furl [fʌrl] *tr* enrollar; (naut) aferrar
fur-lined [ˈfʌr,laɪnd] *adj* forrado con pieles
furlong [ˈfʌrlɔŋ] o [ˈfʌrlɑŋ] *s* estadio
furlough [ˈfʌrlo] *s* licencia ‖ *tr* dar licencia a
furnace [ˈfʌrnɪs] *s* horno; (*to heat a house*) calorífero
furnish [ˈfʌrnɪʃ] *tr* amueblar; proporcionar, suministrar
furnishings [ˈfʌrnɪʃɪŋz] *spl* muebles *mpl;* (*things to wear*) artículos
furniture [ˈfʌrnɪtʃər] *s* muebles *mpl*, mobiliario; (naut) aparejo; **a piece of furniture** un mueble
furniture dealer *s* mueblista *mf*
furniture store *s* mueblería

furrier [ˈfʌrɪ•ər] *s* peletero
furrier•y [ˈfʌrɪ•əri] *s* (*pl* **-ies**) peletería
furrow [ˈfʌro] *s* surco ‖ *tr* surcar
further [ˈfʌrðər] *adj* adicional; nuevo; más lejano ‖ *adv* además; más lejos ‖ *tr* adelantar, promover, fomentar
furtherance [ˈfʌrðərəns] *s* adelantamiento, promoción, fomento
furthermore [ˈfʌrðər,mor] *adv* además
furthest [ˈfʌrðɪst] *adj* (el) más lejano ‖ *adv* más lejos
furtive [ˈfʌrtɪv] *adj* furtivo
fu•ry [ˈfjUri] *s* (*pl* **-ries**) furia
furze [fʌrz] *s* aulaga; retama de escoba
fuse [fjuz] *s* (*tube or wick filled with explosive material*) mecha; (*device for detonating an explosive charge*) espoleta; (elec) fusible *m,* cortacircuitos *m,* tapón *m;* **to burn out a fuse** quemar un fusible ‖ *tr* fundir; (*to unite*) fusionar ‖ *intr* fundirse; fusionarse
fuse box *s* caja de fusibles
fuselage [ˈfjuzəlɪdʒ] *s* fuselaje *m*
fusible [ˈfjuzɪbəl] *adj* fundible, fusible
fusillade [,fjuzɪˈled] *s* fusilería; (*e.g., of questions*) andanada ‖ *tr* atacar o matar con una descarga de fusilería, fusilar
fusion [ˈfjuʒən] *s* fusión
fuss [fʌs] *s* alharaca, hazañería; (coll) disputa por ligero motivo; **to make a fuss** hacer alharacas; **to make a fuss over** hacer fiestas a; disputar sobre ‖ *tr* atolondrar, inquietar, confundir ‖ *intr* hacer alharacas, inquietarse por bagatelas
fuss•y [ˈfʌsi] *adj* (*comp* **-ier;** *super* **-iest**)] alharaquiento, alborotado; descontentadizo, quisquilloso, melindroso; funcionero, hazañero; muy adornado
fustian [ˈfʌstʃən] *s* (*coarse cloth*) fustán *m;* (*sort of velveteen*) pana; (*bombast*) cultedad, follaje *m*
fust•y [ˈfʌsti] *adj* (*comp* **-ier;** *super* **-iest**) mohoso, rancio; que huele a cerrado; pasado de moda
futile [ˈfjutɪl] *adj* (*unproductive*) estéril; (*unimportant*) fútil
futili•ty [fjuˈtɪlɪti] *s* (*pl* **-ties**) esterilidad; futilidad
future [ˈfjutʃər] *adj* futuro ‖ *s* futuro, porvenir *m;* (gram) futuro; **futures (option)** (com) futuros, opción de futuro; **in the future** en el futuro; **in the near future** en un futuro próximo
futuristic [ˈfjutʃəˈrɪstɪk] *s* futurista
futures market *s* mercado de futuros
fuzz [fʌz] *s* (*as on a peach*) pelusa, vello; (*in pockets and corners*) borra, tamo; **the fuzz** (pej) la policía
fuzz•y [ˈfʌzi] *adj* (*comp* **-ier;** *super* **-iest**) cubierto de pelusa, velloso; polvoriento; (*indistinct*) borroso

G

G, g [dʒi] *s* séptima letra del alfabeto inglés
G. *abbr* **German, Gulf**
g. *abbr* **gender, genitive, gram**
gab [gæb] *s* (coll) cotorreo ‖ (*pret & pp* **gabbed;** *ger* **gabbing**) *intr* (coll) cotorrear
gabardine [ˈgæbər,din] *s* gabardina
gabble [ˈgæbəl] *s* cotorreo, parloteo ‖ *intr* cotorrear, parlotear
gable [ˈgebəl] *s* (*of roof*) aguilón *m;* (*over a door or window*) gablete *m,* frontón *m*
gable end *s* hastial *m*
gable roof *s* tejado de dos aguas
gad [gæd] *v* (*pret & pp* **gadded;** *ger* **gadding**) *intr* callejear, andar de acá para allá; **to gad about** pindonguear (*una mujer*)
gad'a•bout' *adj* callejero ‖ *s* cirigallo; (*woman*) pindonga
gad'fly' *s* (*pl* **-flies**) tábano
gadget [ˈgædʒɪt] *s* adminículo, chisme *m,* artilugio
Gael [gel] *s* gaélico
Gaelic [ˈgelɪk] *adj & s* gaélico
gaff [gæf] *s* garfio, arpón *m;* **to stand the gaff** (slang) tener aguante
gag [gæg] *s* mordaza; (*interpolation by an actor*) morcilla; (*joke*)) chiste *m,* payasada ‖ *v* (*pret & pp* **gagged;** *ger* **gagging**) *tr* amordazar; dar bascas a ‖ *intr* sentir bascas, arquear
gage [gedʒ] *s* (*pledge*) prenda; (*challenge*) desafío
gaie•ty [ˈge•ɪti] *s* (*pl* **-ties**) alegría, algazara, diversión; (*of colors*) viveza
gaily [ˈgeli] *adv* alegremente
gain [gen] *s* ganancia; (*increase*) aumento ‖ *tr* ganar; (*to reach*) alcanzar ‖ *intr* ganar terreno; mejorar (*un enfermo*); adelantarse (*un reloj*); **to gain on** ir alcanzando
gainful [ˈgenfəl] *adj* ganancioso, provechoso
gain'say' *v* (*pret & pp* **-said** [ˈsed] o [ˈsɛd]) *tr* negar; contradecir; prohibir
gait [get] *s* paso, manera de andar
gaiter [ˈgetər] *s* polaina corta
gal. *abbr* **gallon**
gala [ˈgelə] *adj* de gala ‖ *s* fiesta
galax•y [ˈgæləksi] *s* (*pl* **-ies**) galaxia
gale [gel] *s* ventarrón *m;* **gales of laughter** tempestades de risas; **to weather the gale** correr el temporal; (fig) ir tirando
Galician [gəˈlɪʃən] *adj & s* gallego
gall [gɔl] *s* bilis *f,* hiel *f;* vejiga de la bilis; (*some-*

thing bitter) (fig) hiel *f;* rencor *m,* odio; (*gallnut*) agalla; (*audacity*) (coll) descaro || *tr* lastimar rozando; irritar || *intr* raerse; (naut) mascarse (*un cabo*)
gallant [ˋgælənt] o [geˋlænt] *adj* (*attentive to women*) galante; (*pertaining to love*) amoroso || [ˋgælənt] *adj* (*stately, grand*) gallardo; (*spirited, daring*) hazañoso; (*showy, gay*) vistoso, festivo || *s* hombre *m* valiente; (*man attentive to women*) galán *m*
gallant•ry [ˋgæləntri] *s* (*pl* **-ries**) galantería; gallardía
gall bladder *s* vejiga de la bilis, vesícula biliar
gall duct *s* conducto biliar
galleon [ˋgælɪ•ən] *s* (naut) galeón *m*
galler•y [ˋgæləri] *s* (*pl* **-ies**) galería; (*in church, theater, etc.*) tribuna; (*cheapest seats in theater*) gallinero; **to play to the gallery** (coll) hablar para la galería
galley [ˋgæli] *s* (naut & typ) galera; (naut) cocina
galley proof *s* (typ) galerada, pruebas de segundas
galley slave *s* galeote *m;* (*drudge*) esclavo del trabajo
Gallic [ˋgælɪk] *adj* gálico
galling [ˋgɔlɪŋ] *adj* irritante, ofensivo
gallivant [ˋgælɪ,vænt] *intr* andar a placer
gall′nut′ *s* agalla
gallon [ˋgælən] *s* galón *m* (*medida: 3.79 litros*)
galloon [gə′lun] *s* galón *m* (*cinta*)
gallop [ˋgæləp] *s* galope *m;* **at a gallop** a galope || *tr* hacer galopar || *intr* galopar; **to gallop through** (fig) hacer muy aprisa
gal•lows [′gæloz] *s* (*pl* **-lows** o **-lowses**) horca
gallows bird *s* (coll) carne *f* de horca
gall′stone′ *s* cálculo biliar
galore [gəˋlor] *adv* en abundancia
galosh [gəˋlɑʃ] *s* chanclo alto
galvanize [ˋgælvə,naɪz] *tr* galvanizar
galvanized iron *s* hierro galvanizado
gambit [′gæmbɪt] *s* gambito
gamble [ˋgæmbəl] *s* (coll) empresa arriesgada || *tr* aventurar en el juego; **to gamble away** perder en el juego || *intr* jugar; (*in the stock market*) especular, aventurarse
gambler [ˋgæmblər] *s* jugador *m;* especulador *m*
gambling [ˋgæmblɪŋ] *s* juego
gambling den *s* garito
gambling house *s* casa de juego, juego público
gambling table *s* mesa de juego
gam•bol [ˋgæmbəl] *s* cabriola, retozo, salto || *v* (*pret & pp* **-boled** o **-bolled;** *gen* **-boling** o **-bolling**) *intr* cabriolar, retozar, saltar
gambrel [ˋgæmbrəl] *s* corvejón *m*
gambrel roof *s* techo a la holandesa
game [gem] *adj* bravo, peleón; dispuesto, resuelto; (*leg*) cojo; de caza || *s* (*form of play*) juego; (*single contest*) partida; (*score*) tantos; (*in bridge*) manga; (*any sport*) deporte *m;* (*animal or bird hunted for sport or food*) caza; (*any pursuit*) actividad; (*pursuit of diplomacy*) juego; **the game is up** estamos frescos **to make game of** burlarse de; **to play the game** jugar limpio
game bag *s* morral *m*
game bird *s* ave *f* de caza
game′cock′ *s* gallo de pelea
game′keep′er *s* guardabosque *m*
game of chance *s* juego de azar
game preserve *s* vedado, coto de caza
game show *s* (telv) programa concurso
game warden *s* guardabosque *m*
gamma globulin [ˋgæmə] *s* gammaglobulina *f*
gamut [ˋgæmət] *s* (mus & fig) gama
gam•y [ˋgemi] *adj* (*comp* **-ier;** *super* **-iest**) (*having flavor of uncooked game*) salvajino; bravo, peleón
gander [ˋgændər] *s* ganso
gang [gæŋ] *adj* múltiple || *s* (*of workmen*) brigada, cuadrilla; (*of thugs*) pandilla || *intr* — **to gang up** acuadrillarse; **to gang up against** u **on** atacar juntos; conspirar contra
gangling [ˋgæŋglɪŋ] *adj* larguirucho
gangli•on [ˋgæŋglɪ•ən] *s* (*pl* **-ons** o **-a** [ə]) ganglio
gang′plank′ *s* plancha pasarela
gangrene [ˋgæŋgrin] *s* gangrena || *tr* gangrenar || *intr* gangrenarse
gangster [ˋgæŋstər] *adj* gangsteril || *s* gángster *m,* pistolero
gangsterism [ˋgæŋstə,r zəm] *s* gangsterismo; acciones de los gangsters
gang′way′ *s* (*passageway*) pasillo; (*gangplank*) plancha, pasarela; (*in ship's side*) portalón *m* || *interj* ¡abran paso!, ¡paso libre!
gantlet [ˋgɔntlɪt] *s* (rr) vía traslapada
gan•try [ˋgæntri] *s* (*pl* **-tries**) caballete *m,* poíno; (rr) puente *m* transversal de señales
gantry crane *s* grúa de caballete
gap [gæp] *s* (*break, open space*) laguna; (*in a wall*) boquete *m;* (*between mountains*) garganta, quebrada; (*between two points of view*) sima
gape [gep] o [gæp] *s* abertura, brecha; (*yawn*) bostezo; mirada de asombro; **the gapes** ganas de bostezar || *int.* estar abierto de par en par; bostezar; embobarse; **to gape at** mirar embobado; **to stand gaping** embobarse
garage [gəˋrɑz] *s* garage *m*
garage sale *s* venta de garaje, feria americana (Mex), ventuta (Col)
garb [gɑrb] *s* vestidura || *tr* vestir
garbage [ˋgɑrbɪdʒ] *s* basuras, desperdicios, bazofia
garbage can *s* cubo para bazofia, latón *m* de la basura, cubo de la basura
garbage collection *s* recogida de basuras
garbage disposal *s* evacuación de basuras
garbage heap *s* basural *m* (CAm)
garbage truck *s* camión *m* de la basura
garble [ˋgɑrbəl] *tr* mutilar (*un texto*)
garden [ˋgɑrdən] *s* (*of vegetables*) huerto; (*of flowers*) jardín *m*

gardener [ˈgɑrdənər] *s* (*of vegetables*) hortelano; (*of flowers*) jardinero
gardenia [gɑrˈdinɪ•ə] *s* gardenia, jazmín *m* de la India
gardening [ˈgɑrdənɪŋ] *s* horticultura; jardinería
garden party *s* recepción al aire libre, garden-party *m*
gargle [ˈgɑrgəl] *s* gargarismo ‖ *intr* gargarizar
gargoyle [ˈgɑrgɔɪl] *s* gárgola
garish [ˈgɛrɪʃ] *adj* charro, chillón, cursi
garland [ˈgɑrlənd] *s* guirnalda
garlic [ˈgɑrlɪk] *s* ajo
garment [ˈgɑrmənt] *s* prenda de vestir
garner [ˈgɑrnər] *tr* (*to gather, collect*) acopiar; adquirir; (*cereales*) entrojar
garnet [ˈgɑrnɪt] *adj & s* granate *m*
garnish [ˈgɑrnɪʃ] *s* adorno; (culin) aderezo, condimento de adorno ‖ *tr* adornar; (culin) aderezar; (law) embargar
garret [ˈgærɪt] *s* buhardilla, desván *m*
garrison [ˈgærɪsən] *s* plaza fuerte; (*troops*) guarnición ‖ *tr* guarnecer, guarnicionar (*una plaza fuerte*); guarnecer una plaza fuerte de (*tropas*)
garrote [gəˈrɑt] o [gəˈrot] *s* estrangulación para robar; (*method of execution; iron collar used for such execution*) garrote *m* ‖ *tr* estrangular; estrangular para robar; agarrotar, dar garrote a
garrulous [ˈgærələs] *adj* gárrulo, locuaz
garter [ˈgɑrtər] *s* liga, jarretera
garth [gɑrθ] *s* patio de claustro
gas [gæs] *s* gas *m;* gasolina; (coll) palabrería ‖ *v* (*pret & pp* **gassed;** *ger* **gassing**) *tr* abastecer de gas; (*to attack, asphyxiate, or poison with gas*) gasear; abastecer de gasolina ‖ *intr* despedir gas; (slang) charlar
gas′bag′ *s* (aer) cámara de gas; (slang) charlatán *m*
gas burner *s* mechero de gas
gas′-cooled reac′tor *s* reactor *m* de gas
Gascony [ˈgæskəni] *s* Gascuña
gas engine *s* motor *m* a gas
gaseous [ˈgæsɪ•əs] *adj* gaseoso
gas fitter *s* gasista *m*
gas generator *s* gasógeno
gash [gæʃ] *s* cuchillada, chirlo ‖ *tr* acuchillar
gas heat *s* calefacción por gas
gas′hold′er *s* gasómetro
gasi•fy [ˈgæsɪ,faɪ] *v* (*pret & pp* **-fied**) *tr* gasificar ‖ *intr* gasificarse
gas jet *s* mechero de gas; llama de gas
gasket [ˈgæskɪt] *s* empaquetadura
gas′light′ *s* luz *f* de gas
gas main *s* cañería de gas
gas mask *s* careta *or* máscara antigás
gas meter *s* contador *m* de gas
gasohol [ˈgæsə,hɔl] *s* alconafta
gasoline [ˈgæsə,lin] o [,gæsəˈlin] *s* gasolina
gasoline pump *s* poste *m* distribuidor *m* de gasolina, surtidor *m* de gasolina
gasp [gæsp] *s* respiración entrecortada; (*of death*) boqueada ‖ *tr* decir con voz entrecortada ‖ *intr* boquear
gas producer *s* gasógeno
gas range *s* cocina a gas
gas station *s* estación gasolinera
gas stove *s* cocina a gas
gas tank *s* (aut) depósito de gasolina, tanque *m* de gasolina
gastric [ˈgæstrɪk] *adj* gástrico
gastronomy [gæsˈtrɑnəmi] *s* gastronomía
gas′works′ *s* fábrica de gas
gate [get] *s* puerta; (*in fence or wall; of bird cage*) portillo; (*of sluice or lock*) compuerta; (*number of people paying admission; amount they pay*) entrada, taquilla; (rr) barrera; (fig) entrada, camino; **to crash the gate** (coll) colarse de gorra
gate′crash′er *s* (coll) colado, paracaidista *mf*
gate′house *s* casa del guarda
gate′keep′er *s* portero; (rr) guardabarrera *mf*
gate′post′ *s* poste *m* de una puerta de cercado
gate′way′ *s* entrada, paso, camino
gather [ˈgæðər] *tr* recoger, reunir; recolectar (*la cosecha*); coger (*leña, flores, etc.*); cubrirse de (*polvo*); recoger (*una persona sus pensamientos*); (bb) alzar; (sew) fruncir; (*to deduce*) (fig) calcular, deducir; **to gather oneself together** componerse ‖ *intr* reunirse; amontonarse; saltar (*lágrimas*)
gathering [ˈgæðərɪŋ] *s* reunión; recolección; (bb) alzado; (sew) frunce *m*
gaud•y [ˈgɔdi] *adj* (*comp* **-ier;** *super* **-iest**) cursi, chillón, llamativo
gauge [gedʒ] *s* medida, norma; calibre *m;* (*of liquid in a container*) nivel *m;* (*of carpenter*) gramil *m;* (*of gasoline*) medidor *m;* (mec) galga; (rr) ancho de vía, entrevía ‖ *tr* medir; calibrar; graduar; aforar (*la cantidad de agua de una coriente*); arquear (*una nave*)
gauge glass *s* tubo indicador, vidrio de nivel
Gaul [gɔl] *s* la Galia; (*native*) galo
Gaulish [ˈgɔlɪʃ] *adj & s* galo
gaunt [gɔnt] o [gɑnt] *adj* desvaído, macilento; hosco, tétrico
gauntlet [ˈgɔntlɪt] o [ˈgɑntlɪt] *s* guantelete *m;* guante con puño abocinado; carrera de baquetas; (rr) vía traslapada; **to run the gauntlet** correr baquetas, pasar por baquetas; **to take up the gauntlet** recoger el guante; **to throw down the gauntlet** arrojar el guante
gauze [gɔz] *s* gasa, cendal *m*
gavel [ˈgævəl] *s* mazo, martillo
gavotte [gəˈvɑt] *s* gavota
gawk [gɔk] *s* (coll) palurdo, papanatas *m* ‖ *intr* (coll) mirar de modo impertinente; papar moscas, mirar embobado
gawk•y [ˈgɔki] *adj* (*comp* **-ier;** *super* **-iest**) desgarbado, torpe, bobo
gay [ge] *adj* (*homosexual*) gay; (*cheerful*) (obs) alegre, festivo; (*brilliant*) (obs) vistoso; (obs) amigo de los placeres ‖ *s* gay *mf*
gaye•ty [ˈge•ɪti] *s* var de **gaiety**
gaze [gez] *s* mirada fija ‖ *intr* mirar fijamente

gazelle [gə'zɛl] *s* gacela
gazette [gə'zɛt] *s* periódico; anuncio oficial
gazetteer [,gæzə'tɪr] *s* diccionario geográfico
gazpacho [gəz'pɑtʃo] *s* (*cold vegetable soup*) gazpacho
gear [gɪr] *s* pertrechos, utensilios; (*of transmission, steering, etc.*) mecanismo, aparato; rueda dentada; (*two or more toothed wheels meshed together*) engranaje *m;* **out of gear** desengranado; (fig) descompuesto; **to throw into gear** engranar; **to throw out of gear** desengranar; (fig) descomponer || *tr & intr* engranar
gear'box' *s* caja de engranajes; (aut) caja de velocidades
gear case *s* caja de engranajes
gear'shift' *s* cambio de marchas, cambio de velocidades, palanca de cambios
gear'wheel' *s* rueda dentada
gee [dʒi] *interj* ¡caramba!; **gee up!** (*get up! said to a horse*) ¡arre!; **geez!** ¡mecachis!
Gehenna [gɪ'hɛnə] *s* gehena *m*
Geiger counter ['gaɪgər] *s* contador *m* de Geiger
gel [dʒɛl] *s* gel *m* || *v* (*pret & pp* **gelled;** *ger* **gelling**) *intr* cuajarse en forma de gel
gelatine ['dʒɛlətɪn] *s* gelatina
geld [gɛld] *v* (*pret & pp* **gelded** o **gelt** [gɛlt]) *tr* castrar
gem [dʒɛm] *s* gema, piedra preciosa; (fig) joya, preciosidad
Gemini ['dʒɛmɪ,naɪ] *s* (*constellation*) Géminis *m* o Gemelos; (*sign of zodiac*) Géminis *m*
gen. *abbr* **gender, general, genitive, genus**
gender ['dʒɛndər] *s* (gram) género; (coll) sexo
gene [dʒin] *s* gen *m,* gene *m*
genealo•gy [,dʒɛnɪ'ælədʒi] *s* (*pl* **-gies**) genealogía
general ['dʒɛnərəl] *adj & s* general *m;* **general of the army** capitán general de ejército; **in general** en general o por lo general
general delivery *s* lista de correos
generalissi•mo [,dʒɛnərə'lɪsɪmo] *s* (*pl* **-mos**) generalísimo
generali•ty [,dʒɛnə'rælɪti] *s* (*pl* **-ties**) generalidad
generalize ['dʒɛnərə'laɪz] *tr & intr* generalizar
generally ['dʒɛnərəli] *adv* por lo general
general medicine *s* medicina general
general practitioner *s* médico general
gen'eral-pur'pose *adj* de uso general, para todo uso
generalship ['dʒɛnərəl,ʃɪp] *s* generalato; don *m* de mando
general staff *s* estado mayor
general store *s* almacén *m*
general strike *s* huelga general
generate ['dʒɛnə,ret] *tr* (*to beget*) engendrar; generar (*electricidad*); (geom) engendrar
generating station *s* central *f*
generation ['dʒɛnə'reʃən] *s* generación
generation gap *s* brecha generacional
generator ['dʒɛnə,retər] *s* generador *m*
generic [dʒɪ'nɛrɪk] *adj* genérico
generous ['dʒɛnərəs] *adj* generoso; abundante, grande
gene•sis ['dʒɛnɪsɪs] *s* (*pl* **-ses** [,siz]) génesis *f* || **Genesis** *s* (Bib) el Génesis
gene splicing *s* empalme genético
genetic [dʒɪ'nɛtɪk] *adj* genético
genetic code *s* código genético
genetic engineering *s* ingeniería genética, biogenética
genetic fingerprinting *s* identificación genética, huella genética
geneticist [dʒə'nɛtəsɪst] *s* genetista *mf,* especialista *mf* en genètica
genetics [dʒɪ'nɛtɪks] *s* genética
Geneva [dʒɪ'nivə] *s* Ginebra
Genevan [dʒɪ'nivən] *adj & s* ginebrino
genial ['dʒinɪ•əl] *adj* afable, complaciente
genie ['dʒini] *s* genio
genital ['dʒɛnɪtəl] *adj* genital || **genitals** *spl* genitales *mpl,* órganos genitales
genitive ['dʒɛnɪtɪv] *adj & s* genitivo
genitourinary [,dʒɛnəto'jʊrɪ,nɛrɪ] *adj* genitourinario
genius ['dʒinjəs] o ['dʒinɪ•əs] *s* (*pl* **geniuses**) (*great inventive gift; person possessing it*) genio || *s* (*pl* **genii** ['dʒinɪ,aɪ]) (*guardian spirit; pagan deity*) genio
Genoa ['dʒɛno•ə] *s* Génova
genocidal [,dʒɛnə'saɪdəl] *adj* genocida
genocide ['dʒɛnə'saɪd] *s* (*act*) genocidio; (*person*) genocida *mf*
Geno•ese [,dʒɛno'iz] *adj* genovés || *s* (*pl* **-ese**) genovés *m*
genome ['dʒinom] *s* (gen) genoma *m*
genre ['ʒɑnrə] *adj* de género
gent. o **Gent.** *abbr* **gentleman, gentlemen**
genteel [dʒɛn'til] *adj* gentil, elegante; cortés, urbano
gentian ['dʒɛnʃən] *s* genciana
gentile ['dʒɛntɪl] o ['dʒɛntaɪl] *adj* gentilicio; (gram) gentilicio || ['dʒɛntaɪl] *adj & s* no judío; cristiano; (*pagan*) gentil *mf*
gentili•ty [dʒɛn'tɪlɪti] *s* (*pl* **-ties**) gentileza
gentle ['dʒɛntəl] *adj* apacible, benévolo; dulce, manso, suave; cortés, fino; (*e.g., tap on the shoulder*) ligero
gen'tle•folk' *s* gente bien nacida
gentle•man ['dʒɛntəlmən] *s* (*pl* **-men** [mən]) *s* caballero; (*attendant to a person of high rank*) gentilhombre *m*
gentlemanly ['dʒɛntəlmənli] *adj* caballeroso
Gentlemen *s* (*men's room*) *SIGN* Caballeros
gentlemen's agreement *s* pacto de caballeros (*acuerdo verbal*)
gentle sex *s* bello sexo, sexo débil
gentrification ['dʒɛntrəfə'keʃən] *s* aburguesamiento
gentrify ['dʒɛntrəfaɪ] *v* (*pret & pp* **-fied**) *intr* aburguesarse
gentry ['dʒɛntri] *s* gente bien nacida
genuflect ['dʒɛnjəflɛkt] *intr* hacer una genuflexión
genuine ['dʒɛnjʊ•ɪn] *adj* genuino; sincero, franco

genus [ˈdʒinəs] *s* (*pl* **genera** [ˈdʒɛnərə] o **genuses**) (biol, log) género
geog. *abbr* **geography**
geographer [dʒɪˈɑgrəfər] *s* geógrafo
geographic(al) [ˌdʒi•əˈgræfɪk(əl)] *adj* geográfico
geogra•phy [dʒɪˈɑgrəfi] *s* (*pl* **-phies**) geografía
geol. *abbr* **geology**
geologic(al) [ˌdʒi•əˈlɑdʒɪk(əl)] *adj* geológico
geologist [dʒɪˈɑlədʒɪst] *s* geólogo
geology [dʒɪˈɑlədʒi] *s* (*pl* **-gies**) geología
geom. *abbr* **geometry**
geometric(al) [ˌdʒi•əˈmɛtrɪk(əl)] *adj* geométrico
geometrician [dʒɪˌɑmɪˈtrɪʃən] *s* geómetra *mf*
geome•try [dʒɪˈɑmɪtri] *s* (*pl* **-tries**) geometría
geophysics [ˌdʒi•əˈfɪzɪks] *s* geofísica
geopolitics [ˌdʒi•əˈpɑlɪtɪks] *s* geopolítica
George [dʒɔrdʒ] *s* Jorge *m*
geranium [dʒɪˈrenɪ•əm] *s* geranio
geriatrical [ˌdʒɛrɪˈætrɪkəl] *adj* geriátrico
geriatrician [ˌdʒɛrɪ•əˈtrɪʃən] *s* geriatra *mf*
geriatrics [ˌdʒɛrɪˈætrɪks] *s* geriatría
germ [dʒʌrm] *s* (biol, bot) germen *m;* (med) microbio, germen; (*beginning*) germen
German [ˈdʒʌrmən] *adj & s* alemán *m*
germane [dʒərˈmen] *adj* pertinente, relacionado
Germanic [dʒʌrˈmænɪk] adj germánico; (hist) germano
German measles *s* rubéola, rubeola
German silver *s* melchor *m,* alpaca
German speaker *s* germanófono
Ger'man-speak'ing *adj* germanófono
Germany [ˈdʒʌrməni] *s* Alemania
germ carrier *s* portador *m* de gérmenes
germ cell *s* célula germen
germicidal [ˌdʒʌrmɪˈsaɪdəl] *adj* germicida
germicide [ˈdʒʌrmɪˌsaɪd] *s* germicida *m*
germinate [ˈdʒʌrmɪˌnet] *intr* germinar
germ plasm *s* germen *m* plasma
germ theory *s* teoría germinal
germ warfare *s* guerra bacteriana, guerra bacteriológica
gerontology [ˌdʒɛrɑnˈtɑlədʒi] *s* gerontología
gerund [ˈdʒɛrənd] *s* gerundio
gerundive [dʒɪˈrʌndɪv] *s* gerundio adjetivo
gestation [dʒɛsˈteʃən] *s* gestación
gesticulate [dʒɛsˈtɪkjəˌlet] *intr* accionar, manotear
gesticulation [dʒɛsˌtɪkjəˈleʃən] *s* ademán *m,* manoteo
gesture [ˈdʒɛstʃər] *s* ademán *m,* gesto; demostración, muestra ‖ *intr* hacer ademanes, hacer gestos
get [gɛt] *v* (*pret* **got** [gɑt]; *pp* **got** o **gotten** [ˈgɑtən]; *ger* **getting**) *tr* conseguir, obtener; recibir; ir por, buscar; tomar (*p.ej., un billete*); alcanzar; encontrar, hallar; hacer (*p.ej., la comida*); resolver (*un problema*); aprender de memoria; captar (*una estación emisora*); **to get across** hacer aceptar; hacer comprender; **to get back** recobrar; **to get down** descolgar; (*to swallow*) tragar; **to get off** quitar (*p.ej., una mancha*); **to get someone to** + *inf* lograr que alguien + *subj;* **to get** + *pp* hacer + *inf;* **to have got** (coll) tener; **to have got to** + *inf* (coll) tener que + *inf* ‖ *intr* (*to become*) hacerse, ponerse, volverse; (*to arrive*) llegar; **get up!** (*to an animal*) ¡arre!; **to get about** estar levantado (*un convaleciente*); **to get along** seguir andando; irse; ir tirando; tener éxito; llevarse bien; **to get along in years** ponerse viejo; **to get along with** congeniar con; **to get angry** enfadarse; **to get around** divulgarse; salir mucho, ir a todas partes; eludir; manejar (*a una persona*); **to get away** conseguir marcharse; evadirse; **to get away with** llevarse, escaparse con; (coll) hacer impunemente; **to get back** volver, regresar; **to get back at** (coll) desquitarse con; **to get behind** quedarse atrás; apoyar, abogar por; **to get by** lograr pasar; (*to manage to shift*) (coll) arreglárselas; **to get going** ponerse en marcha; **to get in** entrar; volver a casa; llegar (*un tren*); **to get in with** llegar a ser amigo de; **to get married** casarse; **to get off** apearse; marcharse; **to get old** envejecer; **to get on** subir; llevarse bien; **to get out** salir, marcharse, divulgarse; **to get out of** bajar de (*un coche*); librarse de; perder (*la paciencia*); **to get out of the way** quitarse de en medio; **to get run over** ser atropellado; **to get through** pasar por entre; terminar; **to get to be** llegar a ser; **to get under way** ponerse en camino; **to get up** levantarse; **to not get over it** (coll) no volver de su asombro
get'a•way' *s* escapatoria, escape *m;* (*of an automobile*) arranque *m*
get'-to•geth'er *s* reunión, tertulia
get'-up' *s* (coll) disposición, presentación; (coll) atavío, traje *m*
gewgaw [ˈgjugɔ] *adj* cursi, charro, chillón ‖ *s* fruslería, chuchería; adorno, charro
geyser [ˈgaɪzər] *s* géiser *m* ‖ [ˈgizər] *s* (Brit) calentador *m* de agua
ghast•ly [ˈgæstli] o [ˈgɑstli] *adj* (*comp* **-lier;** *super* **-liest**) cadavérico, espectral; espantoso, horrible
Ghent [gɛnt] *s* Gante
gherkin [ˈgʌrkɪn] *s* pepinillo
ghet•to [ˈgɛto] *s* (*pl* **-tos**) ghetto
ghost [gost] *s* espectro, fantasma *m;* (telv) fantasma *m;* **not a ghost of a** ni sombra de; **to give up the ghost** entregar el alma, rendir el alma
ghost•ly [ˈgostli] *adj* (*comp* **-lier;** *super* **-liest**) espectral
ghost story *s* cuento de fantasmas
ghost town *s* pueblo fantasma
ghostwriter *s* colaborador anónimo, escritor anónimo de obras firmadas por otra persona
ghoul [gul] *s* demonio que se alimenta de cadáveres; ladrón *m* de tumbas; (*person who revels in horrible things*) vampiro
ghoulish [ˈgulɪʃ] *adj* vampírico, horrible
G.H.Q. *abbr* **General Headquarters**

GI [ˋdʒiˋaɪ] *adj* (coll) reglamentario ‖ *s* (*pl* **GI's**) (coll) soldado estadounidense
giant [ˋdʒaɪ•ənt] *adj & s* gigante *m*
giantess [ˋdʒaɪ•əntɪs] *s* giganta
gibberish [ˋdʒɪbərɪʃ] o [ˋgɪbərɪʃ] *s* guirigay *m*
gibbet [ˋdʒɪbɪt] *s* horca ‖ *tr* ahorcar; poner a la vergüenza
gibe [dʒaɪb] *s* remoque *m,* mofa ‖ *intr* mofarse; **to gibe at** mofarse de
giblets [ˋdʒɪblɪts] *spl* menudillos
giddiness [ˋgɪdɪnɪs] *s* vértigo, vahido; falta de juicio
gid•dy [ˋgɪdi] *adj* (*comp* **-dier;** *super* **-diest**) vertiginoso; mareado; casquivano, ligero de cascos
Gideon [ˋgɪdɪ•ən] *s* (Bib) Gedeón *m*
gift [gɪft] *s* regalo; (*natural ability*) don *m,* dote *f,* prenda
gift certificate *s* cupón obsequio
gifted [ˋgɪftɪd] *adj* talentoso; muy inteligente
gift horse *s* **—never look a gift horse in the mouth** a caballo regalado no se le mira el diente
gift of gab *s* (coll) facundia, labia
gift shop *s* comercio de objetos de regalo, tienda de regalos
gift tax *s* impuesto sobre donaciones
gift'wrap' *v* (*pret & pp* **-wrapped;** *ger* **-wrapping**) *tr* envolver en paquete regalo
gigantic [dʒaɪˋgæntɪk] *adj* gigantesco
giggle [ˋgɪgəl] *s* risita, risa ahogada, retozo de la risa ‖ *intr* reírse bobamente
gigo•lo [ˋdʒɪgə,lo] *s* (*pl* **-los**) acompañante *m* profesional de mujeres; (*man supported by a woman*) mantenido
gild [gɪld] *v* (*pret & pp* **gilded** o **gilt** [gɪlt]) *tr* dorar
gilding [ˋgɪldɪŋ] *s* dorado
gill [gɪl] *s* (*of fish*) agalla; (*of cock*) barba ‖ [dʒɪl] *s* cuarta parte de una pinta
gillyflower [ˋdʒɪlɪ,flaʊ•ər] *s* alhelí *m*
gilt [gɪlt] *adj & s* dorado
gilt-edged [ˋgɪlt,ɛdʒd] *adj* de toda confianza, de lo mejor que hay
gilt'head' *s* dorada
gimcrack [ˋdʒɪm ,kræk] *adj* de oropel ‖ *s* chuchería
gimlet [ˋgɪmlɪt] *s* barrena de mano
gimmick [ˋgɪmɪk] *s* truco, ardid *m;* (*misleading catch*) trampa; (*gadget*) artilugio
gin [dʒɪn] *s* (*alcoholic liquor*) ginebra; desmotadera de algodón; trampa; (*fish trap*) garlito; torno de izar ‖ *v* (*pret & pp* **ginned;** *ger* **ginning**) *tr* desmotar
gin fizz *s* ginebra con gaseosa
ginger [ˋdʒɪndʒər] *s* jenjibre *m;* (coll) energía, viveza
ginger ale *s* cerveza de jengibre gaseosa
gin'ger•bread' *s* pan *m* de jengibre; adorno charro
gingerly [ˋdʒɪndʒərli] *adj* cauteloso, cuidadoso ‖ *adv* cautelosamente
gin'ger•snap' *s* galletita de jengibre
gingham [ˋgɪŋəm] *s* guinga
giraffe [dʒɪˋræf] *s* jirafa
girandole [ˋdʒɪrən,dol] *s* girándula
gird [gʌrd] *v* (*pret & pp* **girt** [gʌrt] o **girded**) *tr* ceñir; (*to equip*) dotar; (*to prepare*) aprestar; (*to surround, hem in*) rodear, encerrar
girder [ˋgʌrdər] *s* viga, trabe *f*
girdle [ˋgʌrdəl] *s* faja; corsé pequeño ‖ *tr* ceñir; circundar, rodear
girl [gʌrl] *s* muchacha, niña, chica; (*daughter*) hija, niña; (*servant*) moza
girlfriend *s* (*sweetheart*) novia, enamorada; (*friend*) amiga, compañera
girlhood [ˋgʌrlhʊd] *s* muchachez *f;* juventud femenina
girlish [gʌrlɪʃ] *adj* de muchacha; juvenil
girl scout *s* niña exploradora
girth [gʌrθ] *s* (*band*) cincha; (*waistband*) pretina; circunferencia
gist [dʒɪst] *s* esencia
give [gɪv] *s* elasticidad ‖ *v* (*pret* **gave** [gev]; *pp* **given** [ˋgɪvən] *tr* dar; ocasionar (*molestia, trabajo, etc.*); representar (*una obra dramática*); (*lessons*) impartir; pronunciar (*un discurso*); **to give away** dar de balde; revelar; llevar (*a la novia*); (coll) traicionar; **to give back** devolver; **to give forth** despedir (*p.ej., olores*); **to give oneself up** entregarse; **to give up** abandonar, dejar (*un empleo*); renunciar ‖ *intr* dar; dar de sí; romperse (*p.ej., una cuerda*); **to give in** ceder, rendirse; **to give out** agotarse; no poder más; **to give up** darse por vencido
give'-and-take' *s* concesiones mutuas; conversación sazonada de burlas
give'a•way' *s* (coll) revelación involuntaria; (coll) traición; (*e.g., in checkers*) (coll) ganapierde *m & f*
given [ˋgɪvən] *adj* dado; (math) conocido; **given that** dado que, suponiendo que
given name *s* nombre *m* de pila
giver [ˋgɪvər] *s* dador *m,* donador *m*
gizzard [ˋgɪzərd] *s* molleja
glacial [ˋgleʃəl] *adj* glacial
glacier [ˋgleʃər] *s* glaciar *m,* helero
glad [glæd] *adj* (*comp* **gladder;** *super* **gladdest**) alegre, contento; **to be glad (to)** alegrarse (de)
gladden [ˋglædən] *tr* alegrar
glade [gled] *s* claro, claro herboso (*en un bosque*)
glad hand *s* (coll) acogida efusiva
gladiator [ˋglædɪ,etər] *s* gladiador m
gladiolus [ˋglædiˋoləs] *s* gladiolo
gladly [ˋglædli] *adv* alegremente; de buena gana, con mucho gusto
gladness [ˋglædnɪs] *s* alegría, regocijo
glad rags *spl* (slang) trapitos de cristianar; (slang) vestido de etiqueta
glamorous [ˋglæmərəs] *adj* fascinador, elegante, glamoroso, sofisticado
glamour [ˋglæmər] *s* fascinación, elegancia, hechizo, glamour *m*
glamour girl *s* belleza exótica

glance [glæns] *s* ojeada, vistazo, golpe *m* de vista; **at a glance** de un vistazo; **at first glance** a primera vista ‖ *intr* lanzar una mirada; **to glance at** lanzar una mirada a; examinar de paso; **to glance off** desviarse de soslayo; desviarse de, al chocar; **to glance over** mirar por encima
gland [glænd] *s* glándula
glanders [ˈglændərz] *spl* muermo
glandulous [ˈglændʒələs] *adj* glanduloso
glare [glɛr] *s* fulgor *m* deslumbrante, luz intensa; mirada feroz, mirada de indignación ‖ *intr* relumbrar; lanzar miradas feroces; **to glare at** echar una mirada feroz a
glaring [ˈglɛrɪŋ] *adj* deslumbrante, relumbrante; (*look*) feroz, penetrante; manifiesto, que salta a la vista
glass [glæs] *s* vidrio, cristal *m;* (*tumbler*) vaso, copa; (*mirror*) espejo; (*glassware*) vajilla de cristal; **glasses** anteojos, gafas
glassblower [ˈblo•ər] *s* soplador *m* de vidrio, vidriero
glass case *s* vitrina
glass cutter *s* cortavidrios *m*
glass door *s* puerta vidriera
glassful [ˈglæsfʊl] *s* vaso
glassine [glæˈsin] *s* papel *m* cristal
glass′ware′ *s* cristalía, vajilla de vidrio
glass wool *s* cristal hilado
glass′works′ *s* cristalería vidriería
glass′work′er *s* vidriero
glass•y [ˈglæsi] *adj* (*comp* **-ier;** *super* **-iest**) vidiroso
glaucoma [glɔˈkomə] *s* glaucoma *m*
glaze [glez] *s* vidriado, esmalte *m;* (*of ice*) capa resbaladiza ‖ *tr* vidriar, esmaltar; garapiñar (*golosinas*)
glazier [ˈgleʒər] *s* vidriero
gleam [glim] *s* destello, rayo de luz; luz *f* tenue; (*of hope*) rayo ‖ *intr* destellar; brillar con luz tenue
glean [glin] *tr* espigar; (*to gather bit by bit, e.g., out of books*) espigar
glee [gli] *s* alegría, regocijo
glee club *s* orfeón *m,* coro *m*
glib [glɪb] *adj* (*comp* **glibber;** *super* **glibbest**) locuaz; (*tongue*) suelto; fácil e insincero
glide [glaɪd] *s* deslizamiento; (aer) vuelo sin motor, planeo, vuelo a vela; (mus) ligadura ‖ *intr* deslizarse; (aer) volar sin motor, planear; **to glide along** pasar suavemente
glider [ˈglaɪdər] *s* (aer) planeador *m,* deslizador *m;* (*seat*) mecedora
glimmer [ˈglɪmər] *s* luz *f* tenue; (*faint perception*) vislumbre *f* ‖ *intr* brillar con luz tenue; (*to appear faintly*) vislumbrarse
glimmering [ˈglɪmərɪŋ] *adj* tenue, trémulo ‖ *s* luz *f* tenue; vislumbre *f*
glimpse [glɪmps] *s* vislumbre *f;* **to catch a glimpse of** entrever, vislumbrar ‖ *tr* vislumbrar
glint [glɪnt] *s* destello, rayo ‖ *intr* destellar
glisten [ˈglɪsən] *s* centelleo ‖ *intr* centellear
glitter [ˈglɪtər] *s* resplandor *m,* brillo ‖ *intr* resplandecer, brillar
glitz [glɪts] *s* (coll) oropel *m,* glamour *m*
glitzy [ˈglɪtsi] *adj* (coll) glamoroso, deslumbrante
gloaming [ˈglomɪŋ] *s* crepúsculo vespertino
gloat [glot] *intr* relamerse; **to gloat over** mirar con satisfacción maligna
global [ˈglobəl] *adj* global
global village, the *s* la aldea mundial
global warming *s* calentamiento global, calentamiento del planeta
globe [glob] *s* globo
globetrotter [ˈglob,trɑtər] *s* trotamundos *m*
globule [ˈglɑbjʊl] *s* glóbulo
glockenspiel [ˈglɑkən,spil] *s* juego de timbres, órgano de campanas
gloom [glum] *s* lobreguez *f* tinieblas, obscuridad; abatimiento, tristeza; aspecto abatido
gloom•y [ˈglumi] *adj* (*comp* **-ier;** *super* **-iest**) (*dark; sad*) lóbrego; pesimista
glori•fy [ˈglorɪ,faɪ] *v* (*pret & pp* **-fied**) *tr* glorificar; (*to enhance*) realzar
glorious [ˈglorɪ•əs] *adj* glorioso; espléndido, magnífico; (coll) alegre
glo•ry [ˈglori] *s* (*pl* **-ries**) gloria; **to go to glory** ganar la gloria; (slang) fracasar ‖ *v* (*pret & pp* **-ried**) *intr* gloriarse
gloss [glɑs] *s* brillo, lustre *m;* (*note, commentary*) glosa; glosario ‖ *tr* (*to annotate*) glosar; lustrar, satinar; **to gloss over** disculpar, paliar
glossa•ry [ˈglɑsəri] *s* (*pl* **-ries**) glosario
gloss•y [ˈglɑsi] *adj* (*comp* **-ier;** *super* **-iest**) brillante, lustroso; (*silk*) joyante
glottal [ˈglɑtəl] *adj* glótico
glove [glʌv] *s* guante *m*
glove compartment *s* portaguantes *m*
glove stretcher *s* ensanchador *m,* juanas *fpl*
glow [glo] *s* (*light of incandescence*) resplandor *m;* (*e.g., of sunset*) brillo, esplendor *m;* sensación de calor; color *m* en las mejillas ‖ *intr* brillar sin llama; estar encendido (*el rostro, el cielo*); estar muy animado
glower [ˈglaʊ•ər] *s* ceño, mirada ceñuda ‖ *intr* mirar con ceño
glowing [ˈglo•ɪŋ] *adj* ardiente, encendido; radiante; entusiasta, elogioso
glow′worm′ *s* gusano de luz, luciérnaga
glucose [ˈglukos] *s* glucosa
glue [glu] *s* cola, goma de pegar, pegamento ‖ *tr* encolar; pegar fuertemente
gluey [ˈglu•i] *adj* (*comp* **gluier;** *super* **gluiest**) pegajoso; (*smeared with glue*) encolado
glug [glʌg] *s* gluglú *m* ‖ *v* (*pret & pp* **glugged;** *ger* **glugging**) *intr* hacer gluglú (*el agua*)
glum [glʌm] *adj* (*comp* **glummer;** *super* **glummest**) hosco
glut [glʌt] *s* abundancia, gran acopio; exceso; **to be a glut on the market** abarrotarse ‖ *v* (*pret & pp* **glutted;** *ger* **glutting**) *tr* hartar, saciar; inundar (*el mercado*); obstruir
glutton [ˈglʌtən] *adj & s* glotón *m*
gluttonous [ˈglʌtənəs] *adj* glotón

glutton•y [ˈglʌtəni] *s* (*pl* **-ies**) glotonería, gula
glycerine [ˈglɪsərɪn] *s* glicerina
G-man [ˈdʒi,mæn] *s* (*pl* **-men** [,mɛn]) (coll) agente *m* de la policía federal
G.M.T. *abbr* **Greenwich mean time**
gnarl [nɑrl] *s* nudo ‖ *tr* torcer ‖ *intr* gruñir
gnarled [nɑrld] *adj* nudoso, retorcido
gnash [næʃ] *tr* hacer rechinar (*los dientes*) ‖ *intr* hacer rechinar los dientes
gnat [næt] *s* jején *m*
gnaw [nɔ] *tr* roer; practicar (*un agujero*) royendo
gnome [nom] *s* gnomo
go [go] *s* (*pl* **goes**) ida; (coll) energía, ímpetu *m;* (coll) boga; (coll) ensayo; (*for traffic*) paso libre; **it's a go** (coll) es un trato hecho; **it's all the go** (coll) hace furor; **it's no go** (coll) es imposible; **on the go** (coll) en continuo movimiento; **to make a go of** (coll) lograr éxito en ‖ *v* (*pret* **went** [wɛnt]; *pp* **gone** [gɔn] o [gɑn]) *tr* (coll) soportar, tolerar; **to go it alone** obrar sin ayuda ‖ *intr* ir; (*to work, operate*) funcionar, marchar; andar (*p.ej., desnudo*); volverse (*p.ej., loco*); **going, going, gone!** ¡vendo, vendo, vendí!; **so it goes** así va el mundo; **to be going to** + *inf* ir a + *inf;* **to be gone** haber ido; haberse agotado; haber dejado de ser; **to go against** ir en contra de; **to go ahead** seguir adelante; **to go away** irse, marcharse; **to go back** volver; **to go by** pasar por; guiarse por; atenerse a; **to go down** bajar; hundirse (*un buque*); **to go fishing** ir de pesca; **to go for** ir por; **to go get** ir por, ir a buscar; **to go house hunting** ir a buscar casa; **to go hunting** ir de caza; **to go in** entrar; entrar en; (*to fit in*) caber en; **to go in for** dedicarse a, interesarse por; **to go into** entrar en; investigar; (aut) poner (*p.ej., primera*); **to go in with** asociarse con; **to go off** irse, marcharse; llevarse a cabo; estallar (*p.ej., una bomba*); dispararse (*un fusil*); **to go on** seguir adelante; ir tirando; **to go on** + *ger* seguir + *ger;* **to go on with** continuar; **to go out** salir; pasar de moda; apagarse (*un fuego, una luz*); declararse en huelga; (*for entertainment, etc.*) salir; **to go over** tener éxito; releer; examinar, revisar; pasar por encima de; **to go over to** pasarse a las filas de; **to go through** pasar por; llegar al fin de; agotar (*una fortuna*); **to go with** ir con, acompañar; salir con (*una muchacha*); hacer juego con; **to go without** andarse sin, pasarse sin
goad [god] *s* aguijada, aguijón *m* ‖ *tr* aguijonear; (SAm) espuelar
go'-a•head' *adj* (coll) emprendedor ‖ *s* (coll) señal *f* para seguir adelante, luz *f* verde
goal [gol] *s* meta; (*in football*) gol *m*
goal'keep'er *s* guardameta *m,* portero
goal line *s* raya de la meta
goal post *s* poste *m* de la meta
goat [got] *s* cabra; (*male goat*) macho cabrío; (coll) víctima inocente; **to be the goat** (slang) pagar el pato; **to get the goat of** (slang) tomar el pelo a; **to ride the goat** (coll) ser iniciado en una sociedad secreta
goatee (goˈti] *s* perilla, barbas de chivo
goat'herd' *s* cabrero
goat'skin' *s* piel *f* de cabra
goat'suck'er *s* chotacabras *m*
gob [gɑb] *s* (coll) masa informe y pequeña; (coll) marinero de guerra
gobble [ˈgɑbəl] *s* gluglú *m* ‖ *tr* engullir; **to gobble up** engullirse ávidamente; (coll) asir de repente, apoderarse ávidamente de ‖ *intr* engullir; gluglutear, gorgonear (*el pavo*)
gobbledegook [ˈgɑbəldɪ,gʊk] *s* (pej) jerga, jerigonza, galimatías *m*
go'-be•tween' *s* (*intermediary*) medianero; (*in promoting marriages*) casamentero; (*in shady love affairs*) alcahuete *m,* alcahueta
goblet [ˈgɑblɪt] *s* copa
goblin [ˈgɑblɪn] *s* duende *m,* trasgo
go'-by' *s* (coll) desaire *m;* **to give someone the go-by** (coll) negarse al trato de alguien
go'cart' *s* andaderas; cochecito para niños; carruaje ligero
God [gɑd] *s* dios *m;* **God forbid** no lo quiera Dios; **God grant** permita Dios; **God willing** Dios mediante
God'child' *s* (*pl* **chil'dren**) ahijado, ahijada
god'daugh'ter *s* ahijada
goddess [ˈgɑdɪs] *s* diosa
god'fa'ther *s* padrino; (fig) padrino (*un señor de cierta edad que da su ayuda y su apoyo*)
God'-fear'ing *adj* timorato; devoto, pío
God'for•sak'en *adj* dejado de la mano de Dios; (coll) desolado, desierto
God'head' *s* divinidad ‖ **Godhead** *s* Dios *m*
godless [ˈgɑdlɪs] *adj* infiel, impío; desalmado, malvado
god•ly [ˈgɑdli] *adj* (*comp* **-lier;** *super* **-liest**) devoto, pío
god'moth'er *s* madrina
god'send' *s* cosa llovida del cielo, bendición
god'son' *s* ahijado
God'speed' *s* bienandanza, buena suerte, buen viaje *m*
go'-get'ter *s* (slang) buscavidas *mf,* persona emprendedora
goggle [ˈgɑgəl] *intr* volver los ojos; abrir los ojos desmesuradamente
goggle-eyed [ˈgɑgəl,aɪd] *adj* de ojos saltones
goggles [ˈgɑgəlz] *spl* anteojos de camino, gafas contra el polvo
going [ˈgo•ɪŋ] *adj* en marcha, funcionando; **going on** casi, p.ej., **it is going on nine o'clock** son casi las nueve ‖ *s* ida, partida
going concern *s* empresa que marcha
goings on *spl* actividades; bulla, jarana
goiter [ˈgɔɪtər] *s* bocio, coto
gold [gold] *adj* áureo, de oro; dorado ‖ *s* oro
gold'beat'er *s* batidor *m* de oro, batihoja *m*
goldbeater's skin *s* venza
gold brick *s* — **to sell a gold brick** (coll) vender gato por liebre
gold'crest' *s* reyezuelo moñudo

gold digger [ˈdɪgər] *s* (min) buscador de oro; (*woman*) (pej) cazafortunas *f*
golden [ˈgoldən] *adj* áureo, de oro; (*gilt*) dorado; (*hair*) rubio; excelente, favorable, floreciente
golden age *s* edad de oro, siglo de oro
golden anniversary *s* bodas de oro
golden calf *s* becerro de oro
golden mean *s* justo medio
golden plover *s* chorlito
gold′en•rod′ *s* vara de oro, vara de San José
golden rule *s* regla de la caridad cristiana
golden wedding *s* bodas de oro
gold-filled [ˈgold,fɪld] *adj* empastado en oro
gold′finch′ *s* jilguero, pintacilgo
gold′fish′ *s* carpa dorada, pez *m* de color; peces *mpl* de colores
goldilocks [ˈgoldɪ ,lɑks] *s* rubiales *mf*
gold leaf *s* pan *m* de oro
gold mine *s* mina de oro; **to strike a gold mine** (fig) encontrar una mina
gold plate *s* vajilla de oro
gold′-plate′ *tr* dorar
gold′smith′ *s* orfebre *m*
gold standard *s* patrón *m* oro
golf [gɑlf] *s* golf *m* ‖ *intr* jugar al golf
golf club *s* palo de golf; asociación de jugadores de golf
golf course *s* campo de golf, cancha (de golf)
golfer [ˈgɑlfər] *s* golfista *mf*
golf links *spl* campo de golf, cancha (de golf)
Golgotha [ˈgɑlgəθə] *s* el Gólgota
gondola [ˈgɑndələ] *s* góndola
gondolier [,gɑndəˈlɪr] *s* gondolero
gone [gɔn] o [gɑn] *adj* agotado; arruinado; desaparecido; muerto; **gone on** (coll) enamorado de
gong [gɔŋ] o [gɑŋ] *s* batintín *m*
gonorrhea [,gɑnəˈri•ə] *s* gonorrea
goo [gu] *s* (slang) substancia pegajosa
good [gʊd] *adj* (*comp* **better;** *super* **best**) bueno; **good and . . .** (coll) muy, p.ej., **good and cheap** muy barato; **good for** bueno para; capaz de hacer; capaz de pagar; capaz de vivir (*cierto tiempo*); **to be good at** tener talento para; **to be no good** (coll) no servir para nada; (coll) ser un perdido; **to make good** tener éxito; cumplir (*sus promesas*); pagar (*una deuda*); responder de (*los daños*) ‖ *s* bien *m,* provecho, utilidad; **for good** para siempre; **for good and all** de una vez para siempre; **goods** efectos; géneros, mercancías; **the good** lo bueno; los buenos; **to catch with the goods** (slang) coger en flagrante; **to deliver the goods** (slang) cumplir lo prometido; **to do good** hacer el bien; dar salud o fuerzas a; **to the good** de sobra, en el haber; **what is the good of . . . ?** ¿para qué sirve . . . ?
good afternoon *s* buenas tardes
good′by′ o **good′bye′** *s* adiós *m* ‖ *interj* ¡adiós!
good day *s* buenos días
good evening *s* buenas noches, buenas tardes
good fellow *s* (coll) buen chico, buen sujeto
good′-for-noth′ing *adj* inútil, sin valor ‖ *s* pelafustán *m* perdido
Good Friday *s* Viernes Santo
good graces *spl* favor *m,* estimación
good-hearted [ˈgʊdˈhɑrtɪd] *adj* de buen corazón
good-humored [ˈgʊdˈjumərd] *adj* de buen humor; afable
good-looking [ˈgʊdˈlʊkɪŋ] *adj* guapo, bien parecido
good looks *spl* hermosura, guapeza
good luck *interj* ¡buena suerte!
good•ly [ˈgʊdli] *adj* (*comp* **-lier;** *super* **-liest**) considerable; bien parecido, hermoso; bueno, excelente
good morning *s* buenos días
good-natured [ˈgʊdˈnetʃərd] *adj* bonachón, afable
Good Neighbor Policy *s* política del buen vecino
goodness [ˈgʊdnɪs] *s* bondad; **for goodness' sake!** ¡por Dios!; **goodness knows!** ¡quién sabe! ‖ *interj* ¡válgame Dios!
good night *s* buenas noches
good sense *s* buen sentido, sensatez *f*
good-sized [ˈgʊdˈsaɪzd] *adj* bastante grande, de buen tamaño
good speed *s* adiós *m* y buena suerte
good-tempered [ˈgʊdˈtɛmpərd] *adj* de natural apacible
good time *s* rato agradable; **to have a good time** divertirse; **to make good time** ir a buen paso; llegar en poco tiempo
good turn *s* favor *m,* servicio
good way *s* buen trecho
goodwill *s* buena voluntad; (com) buen nombre *m,* clientela, fondo de comercio
good•y [ˈgʊdi] *adj* (coll) beatuco, santurrón ‖ *s* (*pl* **-ies**) (coll) golosina ‖ *interj* (coll) ¡qué bien!, ¡qué alegría!
gooey [ˈgu•i] *adj* (*comp* **gooier;** *super* **gooiest**) (slang) pegajoso, fangoso
goof [guf] *s* (slang) tonto ‖ *tr & intr* (slang) chapucear ‖ *intr* — **to goof off** farrear
goof•y [ˈgufɪ] *adj* (*comp* **-ier;** *super* **-iest**) (slang) tonto, mentecato
goon [gun] *s* (*roughneck*) (coll) gamberro, canalla *m;* (coll) terrorista *m* de alquiler; (slang) estúpido
goose [gus] *s* (*pl* **geese** [gis] ánsar *m,* ganso, oca; **to cook one's goose** malbaratarle a uno los planes; **to kill the goose that lays the golden eggs** matar la gallina de los huevos de oro ‖ *s* (*pl* **gooses**) plancha de sastre
goose′ber′ry *s* (*pl* **-ries**) (*plant*) grosellero silvestre; (*fruit*) grosella silvestre
goose egg *s* huevo de oca; (slang) cero
goose flesh *s* carne *f* de gallina
goose′neck′ *s* cuello de cisne; (naut) gancho de botalones
goose pimples *spl* carne *f* de gallina
goose step *s* (mil) paso de ganso

G.O.P. ['dʒi'o'pi] *s* (letterword) (**Grand Old Party**) (U.S.A.) Partido Republicano
gopher ['gofər] *s* ardilla de tierra, ardillón *m;* (*Geomys*) tuza
Gordian knot ['gɔrdɪ•ən] *s* nudo gordiano; **to cut the Gordian knot** cortar el nudo gordiano
gore [gor] *s* sangre derramada, sangre cuajada; (*insert in a piece of cloth*) cuchillo, nesga ‖ *tr* (*to pierce with a horn*) acornar; poner cuchillo o nesga a; nesgar
gorge [gɔrdʒ] *s* garganta, desfiladero; (*in a river*) atasco de hielo ‖ *tr* atiborrar ‖ *intr* atiborrarse
gorgeous ['gɔrdʒəs] *adj* primoroso, brillante, magnífico, suntuoso
gorilla [gə'rɪlə] *s* gorila
gorse [gɔrs] *s* aulaga
gor•y ['gori] *adj* (*comp* **-ier;** *super* **-iest**) ensangrentado, sangriento
gosh [gɑʃ] *interj* ¡caramba!
goshawk ['gɑs,hɔk] *s* azor *m*
gospel ['gɑspəl] *s* evangelio ‖ **Gospel** *s* Evangelio
gospel truth *s* evangelio, pura verdad
gossamer ['gɑsəmər] *s* telaraña flotante; gasa sutilísima; tela impermeable muy delgada; impermeable *m* de tela muy delgada
gossip ['gɑsɪp] *s* chismes *m;* (*person*) chismoso, bocaza; **piece of gossip** chisme *m* ‖ *intr* chismear
gossip column *s* mentidero
gossip columnist *s* gacetillero, cronista *mf* social
gossipy ['gɑsɪpɪ] *adj* chismoso
Goth [gɑθ] *s* godo; (fig) bárbaro
Gothic ['gɑθɪk] *adj* & *s* gótico
gouge [gaʊdʒ] *s* gubia; (*cut made with a gouge*) muesca; (coll) estafa ‖ *tr* excavar con gubia; (coll) estafar
goulash ['gulɑʃ] *s* puchero húngaro
gourd [gord] o [gʊrd] *s* calabaza
gourmand ['gʊrmənd] *s* gastrónomo; glotón *m,* goloso
gourmet ['gʊrme] *s* gastrónomo delicado
gout [gaʊt] *s* gota
gov. *abbr* **governor, government**
govern ['gʌvərn] *tr* gobernar; (gram) regir ‖ *intr* gobernar
governess ['gʌvərnɪs] *s* aya, institutriz *f*
government ['gʌvərnmənt] *s* gobierno; (gram) régimen *m*
governmental [,gʌvərn'mɛntəl] *adj* gubernamental, gubernativo
government in exile *s* gobierno exilado
governor ['gʌvərnər] *s* gobernador *m;* (*of a jail, castle, etc.*) alcaide *m;* (mach) regulador *m*
governorship ['gʌvərnər,ʃɪp] *s* gobierno
govt. *abbr* **government**
gown [gaʊn] *s* (*of a woman*) vestido; (*of a professor, judge, etc.*) toga; (*of a priest*) traje *m* talar; (*dressing gown*) bata, peinador *m;* (nightgown) camisa de dormir
G.P.O. *abbr* **General Post Office, Government Printing Office**
gr. *abbr* **gram, grams, grain, grains, gross**
grab [græb] *s* asimiento, presa; (coll) robo ‖ *v* (*pret & pp* **grabbed;** *ger* **grabbing**) *tr* asir, agarrar; arrebatar ‖ *intr* — **to grab at** tratar de asir
grace [gres] *s* (*charm; favor; pardon*) gracia; (*prayer at table*) benedícite *m;* (*extension of time*) demora; **to be in the good graces of** gozar del favor de; **to say grace** rezar el benedícite; **with good grace** de buen talante ‖ *tr* adornar, engalanar; favorecer
graceful ['gresfəl] *adj* agraciado, gracioso
grace note *s* apoyatura, nota de adorno
gracious ['greʃəs] *adj* graciable, gracioso; misericordioso ‖ *interj* ¡válgame Dios!
grackle ['grækəl] *s* (*myna*) estornino de los pastores; (*purple grackle*) quiscal *m*
grad. *abbr* **graduate**
gradation [gre'deʃən] *s* (*gradual change*) paso gradual; (*arrangement in grades*) graduación; (*step in a series*) paso, grado
grade [gred] *s* grado; (*slope*) pendiente *f;* (*mark for work in class*) calificación, nota; **to make the grade** lograr subir la cuesta; vencer los obstáculos ‖ *tr* graduar, calificar; dar nota a (*un alumno*); explanar, nivelar
grade crossing *s* (rr) paso a nivel, cruce *m* a nivel
grade school *s* escuela elemental
gradient ['gredɪ•ənt] *adj* pendiente ‖ *s* pendiente *f;* (phys) gradiente *m*
gradual ['grædʒʊ•əl] *adj* paulatino
gradually [grædʒʊ•əli] *adv* paulatinamente, gradualmente, poco a poco
graduate ['grædʒʊ•ɪt] *adj* graduado ‖ *s* graduado; (*candidate for a degree*) graduando; (*for measuring*) vasija graduada ‖ ['grædʒʊ,et] *tr* graduar ‖ *intr* graduarse
graduate school *s* facultad de altos estudios
graduate student *s* estudiante graduado, postgraduado
graduate work *s* altos estudios
graduation [,grædʒʊ'eʃən] *s* graduación; ceremonia de graduación
graft [græft] *s* (hort & surg) injerto; (coll) soborno político, ganancia ilegal ‖ *tr & intr* (hort & surg) injertar; (coll) malversar
graham bread ['gre•əm] *s* pan *m* integral
graham cracker *s* galleta integral
graham flour *s* harina de trigo sin cerner
grain [gren] *s* (*small seed; tiny particle of sand, etc.; small unit of weight*) grano; (*cereal seeds*) granos; (*in stone*) vena; (*in wood*) fibra; **against the grain** a contrapelo ‖ *tr* granear (*la pólvora; una piedra litográfica*); crispir, vetear (*la madera*); granular (*una piel*)
grain elevator *s* elevador *m* de granos; (*tall building where grain is stored*) depósito de cereales
grain'field' *s* sembrado

graining [ˈgrenɪŋ] *s* veteado
gram [græm] *s* gramo
grammar [ˈgræmər] *s* gramática
grammarian [grəˈmɛrɪ•ən] *s* gramático
grammar school *s* escuela pública elemental
grammatical [grəˈmætɪkəl] *adj* gramático
grana•ry [ˈgrænəri] *s* (*pl* **-ries**) granero
grand [grænd] *adj* espléndido, grandioso; importante, principal
grand'aunt' *s* tía abuela
grand'child' *s* (*pl* **-chil'dren**) nieto, nieta
grand'dad *s* abuelo
grand'dad'dy *s* (coll) abuelito; **the granddaddy of** (*first example*) el padre de
grand'daugh'ter *s* nieta
grand duchess *s* gran duquesa
grand duchy *s* gran ducado
grand duke *s* gran duque *m*
grandee [grænˈdi] *s* grande *m* de España
grandeur [ˈgrændʒər] o [ˈgrændʒʊr] *s* grandeza, magnificencia
grand'fa'ther *s* abuelo; (*forefather*) antepasado
grandfather's clock *s* reloj *m* de caja, reloj de pie
grand finale *s* (theat) final *m* espectacular
grandiose [ˈgrændɪ,os] *adj* grandioso; hinchado, pomposo
grand jury *s* jurado de acusación
grand larceny *s* hurto mayor
grand lodge *s* gran oriente *m*
grandma [ˈgrænd ,mɑ], [ˈgræm ,mɑ], o [ˈgræmə] *s* (coll) abuela, abuelita
grand master *s* gran maestro
grand'moth'er *s* abuela
grand'neph'ew *s* resobrino
grand'niece *s* resobrina
grand opera *s* ópera seria, gran ópera
grandpa [ˈgrænd,pɑ], [ˈgræn,pɑ], o [ˈgræmpə] *s* (coll) abuelo, abuelito
grand'par'ent *s* abuelo, abuela
grand piano *s* piano de cola
grand slam *s* (*in baseball*) jonrón *m* con casa llena; (*in bridge, golf, tennis*) gran slam *m;* (cards) bola
grand'son' *s* nieto
grand'stand' *s* gradería cubierta, tribuna || *intr* pavonearse
grand strategy *s* alta estrategia
grand total *s* gran total *m,* suma de totales
grand'un'cle *s* tío abuelo
grand vizier *s* gran visir *m*
grange [grendʒ] *s* (*farm with barns, etc.*) granja; (*organization of farmers*) cámara agrícola
granite [ˈgrænɪt] *s* granito, piedra berroqueña
granny [ˈgræni] *s* (coll) abuelita; (*old woman*) (coll) abuela
granny knot *s* nudo corredizo
grant [grænt] o [grɑnt] *s* concesión; donación, subvención; traspaso de propiedad || *tr* conceder; dar (*permiso, perdón*); transferir (*bienes inmuebles*); **to take for granted** dar por sentado; tratar con indiferencia
grantee [grænˈti] o [grɑnˈti] *s* cesionario
grant'-in-aid' *s* (*pl* **grants-in-aid**) subvención concedida por el gobierno para obras de utilidad pública; pensión para estimular conocimientos científicos, literarios, artísticos
grantor [grænˈtɔr] or [grɑnˈtɔr] *s* cesionista *mf,* otorgante *mf*
grant winner *s* bequista *mf* (CAm, Cuba)
granular [ˈgrænjələr] *adj* granular
granulate [ˈgrænjə,let] *tr* granular || *intr* granularse
granule [ˈgrænjʊl] *s* gránulo
grape [grep] *s* (*fruit*) uva; (*vine*) vid *f*
grape arbor *s* parral *m*
grape'fruit' *s* (*fruit*) toronja; (*tree*) toronjo
grape hyacinth *s* sueldacostilla
grape juice *s* zumo de uva
grape'shot' *s* metralla
grape'vine' *s* vid *f,* parra; **by the grapevine** por vías secretas, por vías misteriosas
graph [græf] *s* (*diagram*) gráfica; (gram) grafía
graphic(al) [ˈgræfɪk(əl)] *adj* gráfico
graphite [ˈgræfaɪt] *s* grafito
graph paper *s* papel cuadriculado
grapnel [ˈgræpnəl] *s* rebañadera; (*anchor*) rezón *m*
grapple [ˈgræpəl] *s* asimiento, presa; lucha cuerpo a cuerpo || *tr* asir, agarrar || *intr* agarrarse; luchar a brazo partido; **to grapple with** luchar a brazo partido con; tratar de resolver
grappling iron *s* arpeo
grasp [græsp] *s* asimiento; (*power, reach*) poder *m,* alcance *m;* (fig) comprensión; **to have a good grasp of** saber a fondo; **within the grasp of** al alcance de || *tr* (*with hand*) empuñar; (*to get control of*) apoderarse de; (fig) comprender || *intr* — **to grasp at** tratar de asir; aceptar con avidez
grasping [ˈgræspɪŋ] *adj* avaro, codicioso
grass [ˈgræs] *s* hierba; (*pasture land*) pasto; (*lawn*) césped *m;* **to go to grass** ir a pacer; disfrutar de una temporada de descanso; gastarse, arruinarse; morir; **to not let the grass grow under one's feet** no dormirse en las pajas
grass court *s* cancha de césped
grass'hop'per *s* saltamontes *m*
grass pea *s* almorta, guija
grass'-roots' *adj* de la gente común, de las bases || *spl* raíz *f,* fuente *f;* (pol) nivel *m* local; **the grass roots** las bases
grass seed *s* semilla de césped
grass widow *s* viuda de paja, viuda de marido vivo
grass•y [ˈgræsi] *adj* (*comp* **-ier;** *super* **-iest**) herboso
grate [gret] *s* (*at a window*) reja; (*for cooking*) parrilla || *tr* (*to put a grate on*) enrejar; rallar (*p.ej., queso*) || *intr* crujir, rechinar; **to grate on** (fig) rallar
grateful [ˈgretfəl] *adj* agradecido; (*pleasing*) agradable
grater [ˈgretər] *s* rallador *m*

grati•fy [ˋgrætɪ,faɪ] *v* (*pret & pp* **-fied**) *tr* complacer, gratificar
gratifying [ˋgrætɪ,faɪ•ɪŋ] *adj* grato, satisfactorio
grating [ˋgretɪŋ] *adj* áspero, irritante; (*sound*) chirriante || *s* enrejado, rejilla
gratis [ˋgretɪs] o [ˋgrætɪs] *adj* gracioso, gratuito || *adv* gratis, de balde
gratitude [ˋgrætɪ,tjud] *s* gratitud, reconocimiento
gratuitous [grəˋtju•ɪtəs] o [grəˋtu•ɪtəs] *adj* gratuito
gratui•ty [grəˋtju•ɪti] *s* (*pl* **-ties**) propina; feria (CAm, Mex)
grave [grev] *adj* (*serious, dangerous; important*) grave; solemne; (*sound; accent*) grave || *s* sepulcro, sepultura; **to have one foot in the grave** estar con un pie en la sepultura
grave accent *s* acento grave
gravedigger [ˋgrev ,dɪgər] *s* enterrador *m,* sepulturero, entierramuertos *m*
gravel [ˋgrævəl] *s* grava, cascajo
graven image [ˋgrevən] *s* ídolo
grave′stone′ *s* lápida sepulcral
grave′yard′ *s* camposanto
gravitate [ˋgrævɪ,tet] *intr* gravitar; ser atraído
gravitation [,grævɪˋteʃən] *s* gravitación
gravi•ty [ˋgrævɪti] *s* (*pl* **-ties**) gravedad
gravure [grəˋvjʊr] *s* fotograbado
gra•vy [ˋgrevi] *s* (*pl* **-vies**) (*juice from cooking meat*) jugo; (*sauce made with this juice*) salsa; (slang) ganga, breva
gravy dish *s* salsera
gray [gre] *adj* gris; (*gray-haired*) cano, canoso || *s* gris *m;* traje *m* gris || *intr* encanecer
gray′beard′ *s* anciano, viejo
gray-haired [ˋgre,hɛrd] *adj* canoso
gray′hound′ *s* galgo
grayish [ˋgre•ɪʃ] *adj* grisáceo; (*person; hair*) entrecano
gray matter *s* substancia gris; (*intelligence*) (coll) materia gris
gray′scale *s* (compu) escala de grises
graze [grez] *tr* (*to touch lightly*) rozar; (*to scratch lightly in passing*) raspar; pacer (*la hierba*); apacentar (*el ganado*); (*to lead to the pasture*) pastar || *intr* pacer, pastar
grease [gris] *s* grasa || [gris] o [griz] *tr* engrasar; (slang) sobornar
grease cup [gris] *s* vaso de engrase
grease gun [gris] *s* engrasador *m* de pistón, jeringa de engrase, bomba de engrase, pistola engrasadora o de engrase
grease lift [gris] *s* puente *m* de engrase
grease monkey *s* (coll) ayudante *mf* de mecánico
grease paint [gris] *s* maquillaje *m*
grease pit [gris] *s* fosa de engrase
grease spot [gris] *s* lámpara, mancha de grasa
greas•y [ˋgrisi] o [ˋgrizi] *adj* (*comp* **-ier;** *super* **-iest**) grasiento, pringoso
great [gret] *adj* grande; (coll) excelente || **the great** los grandes
great′-aunt′ *s* tía abuela
Great Bear *s* Osa Mayor
Great Britain [ˋbrɪtən] *s* la Gran Bretaña
great′coat′ *s* gabán *m* de mucho abrigo
Great Dane *s* mastín *m* danés
Great Depression, the *s* la Gran Depresión
Greater London *s* el Gran Londres
Greater New York *s* el Gran Nueva York
great′-grand′child′ *s* (*pl* **-chil′dren**) bisnieto, bisnieta
great′-grand′daugh′ter *s* bisnieta
great′-grand′fa′ther *s* bisabuelo
great′-grand′moth′er *s* bisabuela
great′-grand′par′ent *s* bisabuelo, bisabuela
great′-grand′son′ *s* bisnieto
greatly [ˋgretli] *adj* grandemente
great′-neph′ew *s* resobrino
greatness [ˋgretnɪs] *s* grandeza
great′-niece′ *s* resobrina
great′-un′cle *s* tío abuelo
Grecian [ˋgriʃən] *adj & s* griego
Greece [gris] *s* Grecia
greed [grid] *s* codicia, avaricia; (*in eating and drinking*) glotonería
greed•y [ˋgridi] *adj* (*comp* **-ier;** *super* **-iest**) codicioso, avaro; glotón
Greek [grik] *adj & s* griego
green [grin] *adj* verde; inexperto || *s* verde *m;* (*lawn*) césped *m;* **greens** verduras
green′back′ *s* (U.S.A.) billete *m* de banco (*de dorso verde*)
green bean *s* habichuela verde, judía verde (Esp), ejote *m* verde (Mex)
green belt *s* (ecol) cordón *m* verde
green card *s* (pol) carta verde, tarjeta verde
green corn *s* maíz tierno
green earth *s* verdacho
greener•y [ˋgrinəri] *s* (*pl* **-ies**) (*foliage*) verdura; (*hothouse*) invernáculo
green-eyed [ˋgrin,aɪd] *adj* de ojos verdes; celoso
green′gage′ *s* ciruela claudia, reina claudia
green grasshopper *s* langostón *m*
green′horn′ *s* novato; (*dupe*) primo, inocentón *m;* papanatas *m,* isidro; colegial *mf* (Mex)
green′house′ *s* invernáculo, invernadero; **the greenhouse effect** (ecol) el efecto invernadero
greenish [ˋgrinɪʃ] *adj* verdoso
Greenland [ˋgrinlənd] *s* Groenlandia
greenness [ˋgrinnɪs] *s* verdura, verdor *m;* falta de experiencia
green′room′ *s* saloncillo; chismería de teatro
green thumb *s* pulgares *mpl* verdes (*don de criar plantas*)
green vegetables *spl* verduras
Greenwich Mean Time [ˋgrɛnɪtʃ], [ˋgrɪnɪdʒ] *s* hora de Greenwich
greet [grit] *tr* saludar; acoger, recibir; presentarse a (*los ojos u los oídos de uno*)
greeting [ˋgritɪŋ] *s* saludo; acogida, recibimiento || **greetings** *interj* ¡salud!
greeting card *s* tarjeta de buen deseo
gregarious [grɪˋgɛrɪ•əs] *adj* (*living in the midst*

of others) gregario; (*fond of the company of others*) sociable
Gregorian [grɪˈgorɪ•ən] *adj* gregoriano
grenade [grɪˈned] *s* granada; (*to put out fires*) granada extintora
grenade launcher *s* lanzagranadas *m*
grenadier [ˌgrɛnəˈdɪr] *s* granadero
grenadine [ˌgrɛnəˈdin] *s* granadina
grey [gre] *adj, s & intr* var de **gray**
grid [grɪd] *s* parrilla, rejilla; (*electron*) rejilla; (*of a storage battery*) (elec) rejilla
griddle [ˈgrɪdəl] *s* plancha
grid′dle•cake′ *s var* de **pancake**
grid′i′ron *s* parrilla; campo de fútbol
grid leak *s* (electron) resistencia de rejilla, escape *m* de rejilla
grief [grif] *s* aflicción, pesar *m;* (coll) desgracia, disgusto; **to come to grief** fracasar, arruinarse
grievance [ˈgrivəns] *s* agravio, injusticia; despecho, disgusto; motivo de queja
grieve [griv] *tr* afligir, penar ‖ *intr* afligirse, apenarse; **to grieve over** añorar
grievous [ˈgrivəs] *adj* doloroso, penoso; atroz, cruel; (*deplorable*) lastimoso
griffin [ˈgrɪfɪn] *s* (myth) grifo
grill [grɪl] *s* parrilla; (*restaurant*) gril *m,* parrilla ‖ *tr* (culin) asar a la parilla, emparrillar; someter (*a un acusado*) a un interrogatorio muy apremiante
grille [grɪl] *s* reja, verja; (*of an automobile*) parrilla, rejilla
grill′room′ *s* parrilla, gril *m*
grim [grɪm] *adj* (*comp* **grimmer;** *super* **grimmest**) (*fierce*) cruel, feroz; (*repellent*) horrible, siniestro; (*unyielding*) formidable, implacable; (*stern-looking*) ceñudo
grimace [ˈgrɪməs] o [grɪˈmes] *s* mueca, gesto ‖ *intr* hacer muecas, gestear
grime [graɪm] *s* mugre *f;* (*soot*) tizne *m & f*
grim•y [ˈgraɪmi] *adj* (*comp* **-ier;** *super* **-iest**) mugriento; tiznado
grin [grɪn] *s* sonrisa bonachona; mueca (*mostrando los dientes*) ‖ *v* (*pret & pp* **grinned;** *ger* **grinning**) *intr* sonreírse bonachonamente; hacer una mueca (*mostrando los dientes*)
grind [graɪnd] *s* molienda; (*long hard work or study*) (coll) zurra; (*student*) (coll) empollón *m* ‖ *v* (*pret & pp* **ground** [graʊnd]) *tr* moler; (*to sharpen*) afilar, amolar; tallar (*lentes*); pulverizar; picar (*carne*); rodar (*las válvulas de un motor*); dar vueltas a (*un manubrio*) ‖ *intr* hacer molienda; molerse; rechinar; (coll) echar los bofes
grinder [ˈgraɪndər] *s* (*to sharpen tools*) muela, esmoladera; (*to grind coffee, pepper, etc.*) molinillo; (*back tooth*) muela
grind′stone′ *s* esmoladera, piedra de amolar; **to keep one's nose to the grindstone** trabajar con ahinco
grin•go [ˈgrɪŋgo] *s* (*pl* **-gos**) (pej) gringo
grip [grɪp] *s* (*grasp*) asimiento; (*with hand*) apretón *m;* (*handle*) asidero; saco de mano; **to come to grips (with)** luchar cuerpo a cuerpo (con); arrostrarse (con) ‖ *v* (*pret & pp* **gripped;** *ger* **gripping**) *tr* asir, agarrar; tener asido; absorber (*la atención*); absorber la atención a (*una persona*)
gripe [graɪp] *s* (coll) queja; **gripes** retortijón *m* de tripas ‖ *intr* (coll) quejarse, refunfuñar
grippe [grɪp] *s* gripe *f*
gripping [ˈgrɪpɪŋ] *adj* conmovedor, impresionante
gris•ly [ˈgrɪzli] *adj* (*comp* **-lier;** *super* **-liest**) espantoso, espeluznante
grist [grɪst] *s* (*batch of grain for one grinding*) molienda; (*grain that has been ground*) harina; (coll) acopio, acervo; **to be grist to one's mill** (coll) serle a uno de mucho provecho
gristle [ˈgrɪsəl] *adj* (*comp* **-tlier;** *super* **-tliest**) cartilaginoso, ternilloso
grist′mill′ *s* molino harinero
grit [grɪt] *s* arena, guijo fino; (fig) ánimo, valentía; **grits** farro, sémola ‖ *v* (*pret & pp* **gritted;** *ger* **gritting**) *tr* hacer rechinar (*los dientes*); cerrar fuertemente (*los dientes*)
grit•ty [ˈgrɪti] *adj* (*comp* **-tier;** *super* **-tiest**) arenoso; (fig) valiente, resuelto
griz•zly [ˈgrɪzli] *adj* (*comp* **-zlier;** *super* **-zliest**) grisáceo; canoso ‖ *s* (*pl* **-zlies**) oso gris
grizzly bear *s* oso gris
groan [gron] *s* gemido, quejido ‖ *intr* gemir, quejarse; estar muy cargado, crujir por exceso de peso
grocer [ˈgrosər] *s* tendero, abacero, almacenero
grocer•y [ˈgrosəri] *s* (*pl* **-ies**) tienda de comestibles, almacén *m,* abacería; **groceries** comestibles *mpl*
grocery store *s* tienda de comestibles, almacén *m,* albacería
grog [grɑg] *s* grog *m*
grog•gy [ˈgrɑgi] *adj* (*comp* **-gier;** *super* **-giest**) (coll) inseguro, vacilante; (*shaky, e.g., from a blow*) (coll) atontado; (coll) borracho
groin [grɔɪn] *s* (anat) ingle *f;* (archit) arista de encuentro
groom [grum] *s* (*bridegroom*) novio; mozo de caballos ‖ *tr* asear, acicalar; almohazar (*caballos*); enseñar (*a un político*) para presentarse como candidato
grooms•man [ˈgrumzmən] *s* (*pl* **-men** [mən]) padrino de boda
groove [gruv] *s* ranura; (*of a pulley*) garganta; (*of a phonograph record*) surco; (*mark left by a wheel*) rodada; (coll) rutina, hábito arraigado ‖ *tr* ranurar, acanalar
grope [grop] *intr* andar a tientas; (*for words*) pujar; **to grope for** buscar a tientas, buscar tentando; **to grope through** palpar (*p.ej., la obscuridad*)
gropingly [ˈgropɪŋli] *adv* a tientas
grosbeak [ˈgrosˌbik] *s* pico duro
gross [gros] *adj* (*dense, thick*) denso, espeso; (*coarse; vulgar*) grosero; (*fat, burly*) grueso; (*with no deductions*) bruto ‖ *s* conjunto, totalidad; (*twelve dozen*) gruesa; **in gross** en grueso ‖ *tr* obtener un ingreso bruto de

gross income *s* ingreso bruto
grossly [ˈgrosli] *adv* aproximadamente
gross national product *s* renta nacional
grotesque [groˈtɛsk] adj (*ridiculous, extravagant*) grotesco; (fa) grutesco || *s* (fa) grutesco
grot•to [ˈgrɑto] *s* (*pl* **-toes** o **-tos**) gruta
grouch [graʊtʃ] *s* (coll) mal humor *m;* (*person*) (coll) cascarrabias *mf,* vinagre *m* || *intr* (coll) refunfuñar
grouch•y [ˈgraʊtʃi] *adj* (*comp* **-ier;** *super* **-iest**) (coll) gruñón, malhumorado
ground [graʊnd] *adj* molido || *s* (*earth, soil, land*) tierra; (*piece of land*) terreno; (*basis, foundation*) causa, fundamento; motivo, razón *f;* (elec) tierra; (*body of automobile corresponding to ground*) (elec) masa; (elec) borne *m* de tierra; **ground for complaint** motivo de queja; **grounds** terreno; jardines *mpl;* causa, fundamento; (*of coffee*) posos; **on the ground of** con motivo de; **to break ground** empezar la excavación; **to fall to the ground** fracasar, abandonarse; **to gain ground** ganar terreno; **to give ground** ceder terreno; **to lose ground** perder terreno; **to stand one's ground** mantenerse firme; **to yield ground** ceder terreno || *tr* establecer, fundar; (elec) poner a tierra; **grounded** (coll) (*kept at home for disciplinary reasons*) castigado, e.g., **I can't go to the party because I'm grounded** no puedo ir a la fiesta porque estoy castigado; **to be grounded** estar sin volar (*un avión*); **to be well grounded** ser muy versado || *intr* (naut) encallar, varar
ground ball *s* (sport) roletazo, rola
ground beef *s* carne molina, carne picada
ground connection *s* (rad) toma de tierra
ground crew *s* (aer) personal *m* de tierra
grounder [ˈgraʊndər] *s* (baseball) pelota rodada
ground floor *s* piso bajo
ground glass *s* vidrio deslustrado
ground hog *s* marmota de América
ground lead [lid] *s* (elec) conductor *m* a tierra
groundless [ˈgraʊndlɪs] *adj* infundado; inmotivado
ground plan *s* primer proyecto; (*of a building*) planta
ground speed *s* (aer) velocidad con respecto al suelo
ground swell *s* marejada de fondo
ground troops *spl* (mil) tropas terrestres
ground wire *s* (rad) alambre *m* de tierra; (aut) hilo de masa
groundˈworkˈ *s* (*preparation*) trabajo preliminar, trabajo de base; (archit) infraestructura
ground zero (*terroristic*) punto de explosión; (mil) punto de detonación de una bomba atómica; **Ground Zero** *lugar de la destrucción del Centro del Comercio Mundial de Nueva York*
group [grup] *adj* grupal; colectivo || *s* grupo || *tr* agrupar || *intr* agruparse
group therapy *s* psicoterapia de grupo
grouse [graʊs] *s* perdiz blanca, bonasa americana, gallo de bosque; (slang) refunfuño || *intr* (slang) refunfuñar
grout [graʊt] *s* lechada || *tr* enlechar
grove [grov] *s* arboleda, bosquecillo
grov•el [ˈgrʌvəl] o [ˈgrɑvəl] *v* (*pret & pp* **-eled** o **-elled;** *ger* **-eling** o **-elling)** *intr* arrastrarse servilmente; rebajarse servilmente; deleitarse en vilezas
grow [gro] *v* (*pret* **grew** [gru]; *pp* **grown** [gron] *tr* cultivar (*plantas*); criar (*animales*); dejarse (*la barba*) || *intr* crecer; cultivarse; criarse; brotar, nacer; (*to become*) hacerse, ponerse, volverse; **to grow angry** enfadarse; **to grow old** envejecerse; **to grow out of** tener su origen en; perder (*p.ej., la costumbre*); **to grow together** adherirse el uno al otro; **to grow up** crecer, desarrollar
grower [ˈgro•ər] *s* cultivador *m*
growing child [ˈgro•ɪŋ] *s* muchacho de creces
growing pains *spl* dolores *mpl* de crecimiento
growl [graʊl] *s* gruñido; refunfuño || *intr* gruñir (*el perro*); refunfuñar
grownˈupˈ *adj* adulto; juicioso || *s* (*pl* **grown-ups**) adulto; **grown-ups** personas mayores
growth [groθ] *s* crecimiento; desarrollo; aumento; (*of trees, grass, etc.*) cobertura; (pathol) tumor *m*
growth area *s* polo de desarrollo; (econ) sector *m* en expansión
growth fund *s* fondo común de inversión orientado al crecimiento
growth industry *m* industria en crecimiento o en expansión
growth stock *s* acción crecedera
grub [grʌb] *s* (*drudge*) esclavo del trabajo; (*larva*) gorgojo; (coll) comida, alimento || *v* (*pret & pp* **grubbed;** *ger* **grubbing**) *tr* arrancar (*tocones*); desmalezar (*un terreno*) || *intr* cavar; trabajar como esclavo
grub•by [ˈgrʌbi] *adj* (*comp* **-bier;** *super* **-biest**) gorgojoso; sucio, roñoso
grudge [grʌdʒ] *s* rencor *m,* inquina; **to have a grudge against** guardar rencor a, tener inquina a || *tr* dar de mala gana; envidiar
grudgingly [ˈgrʌdʒɪŋli] *adv* de mala gana
gru•el [ˈgru•əl] *s* avenate *m,* gachas *f* || *v* (*pret & pp* **-eled** o **-elled;** *ger* **-elling** o **-elling**) *tr* agotar, castigar cruelmente
gruesome [ˈgrusəm] *adj* espantoso, horripilante
gruff [grʌf] *adj* áspero, brusco, rudo; (*voice, tone*) ronco
grumble [ˈgrʌmbəl] *s* gruñido, refunfuño; ruido sordo y prolongado || *intr* gruñir, refunfuñar; retumbar
grump•y [ˈgrʌmpi] *adj* (*comp* **-ier;** *super* **-iest**) gruñón, malhumorado
grunt [grʌnt] *s* gruñido || *intr* gruñir
grunt work *s* (slang) trabajo de baja categoría
G-string [ˈdʒiˌstrɪŋ] *s* (*loincloth*) taparrabo; (*worn by women entertainers*) cubresexo
gt. *abbr* **great; gutta** (Lat) **drop**
g.u. *abbr* **genitourinary**
Guadeloupe [ˌgwɑdəˈlup] *s* Guadalupe *f*

guarantee [,gaerən'ti] *s* garantía; (*guarantor*) garante *mf;* persona de quien otra sale fiadora || *tr* garantizar
guarantor ['gærən,tɔr] *s* garante *mf*
guaran•ty ['gærənti] *s* (*pl* **-ties**) garantía || *v* (*pret & pp* **-tied**) *tr* garantizar
guard [gɑrd] *s* (*act of guarding; part of handle of sword*) guarda; (*person who guards or takes care of something*) guarda *mf;* (*group of armed men; posture in fencing*) guardia; (*member of group of armed men*) guardia *m;* (*in front of trolley car*) salvavidas *m;* (sport) coraza; (rr) guardabarrera *mf;* (rr) guardafrenos *m;* **off guard** desprevenido; **on guard** alerta, prevenido; de centinela; **to mount guard** montar la guardia; **under guard** a buen recaudo || *tr* guardar || *intr* estar de centinela; **to guard against** guardarse de, precaverse contra o de
guard'house' *s* cuartel *m* de la guardia; prisión militar
guardian ['gɑrdɪ•ən] *adj* tutelar || *s* guardián *m;* (law) curador *m,* tutor *m*
guardian angel *s* ángel *m* custodio, ángel de la guarda
guardianship ['gɑrdɪ•ən,ʃɪp] *s* amparo, protección; (law) curaduría, tutela
guard'rail' *s* baranda; (naut) barandilla; (rr) contracarril *m*
guard'room' *s* cuarto de guardia; cárcel *f* militar
guards•man ['gɑrdzmən] *s* (*pl* **-men** [mən]) guardia *m,* soldado de guardia
Guatemalan [,gwɑtɪ'mɑlən] *adj & s* guatemalteco
guerrilla [gə'rɪlə] *s* guerrillero; montonero
guerrilla warfare *s* guerra de guerrillas
guess [gɛs] *s* conjetura suposición; adivinación || *tr & intr* conjeturar, suponer; (*to judge correctly*) acertar, adivinar; (coll) creer, suponer; **I guess so** (coll) creo que sí, me parece que sí
guessing game *s* juego de adivinanzas
guesstimate ['gɛstəmət] *s* (coll) cálculo aproximado || *tr* (coll) calcular aproximadamente
guess'work' *s* conjetura; **by guesswork** por conjeturas
guest [gɛst] *s* invitado, invitada; (*lodger*) huésped *mf,* alojado, alojada; (*caller*) visitante *mf,* visita; (*of a hotel*) huésped, cliente *m,* clienta; (*of a boarding house*) pensionista *mf;* (*at a wedding*) convidado, convidada
guest book *s* libro de registro
guest conductor *s* director invitado
guest list *s* lista de invitados
guest of honor *s* invitado de honor
guest room *s* cuarto de huéspedes
guest speaker *s* orador invitado
guffaw [gə'fɔ] *s* risotada, carcajada || *intr* risotear, reír a carcajadas
guidance ['gaɪdəns] *s* guía, gobierno, dirección; **for your guidance** para su gobierno
guidance counselor *s* orientador, consejero
guide [gaɪd] *s* (*person*) guía *mf;* (*book*) guía; (*guidance*) guía; dirección; poste *m* indicador; (mach) guía, guiadera; (mil) guía *m* || *tr* guiar
guide'board' *s* señal *f* de carretera
guide'book' *s* guia *m,* guía del viajero
guided missile ['gaɪdɪd] *s* proyectil dirigido o teleguiado; misil *m* dirigible
guide dog *s* perro-lazarillo
guided tour *s* visita guiada
guide'line' *s* cuerda de guía; norma, pauta, directorio
guide'post' *s* poste *m* indicador
guidon ['gaɪdən] *s* (mil) guión *m;* (mil) portaguión *m*
guild [gɪld] *s* (*medieval association of craftsmen*) gremio; asociación benéfica
guild'hall' *s* casa consistorial
guile [gaɪl] *s* astucia, dolo, maña
guileful ['gaɪlfəl] *adj* astuto, doloso, mañoso
guileless ['gaɪllɪs] *adj* cándido, inocente, sencillo
guillotine ['gɪlə,tin] *s* guillotina || [,gɪlə'tin] *tr* guillotinar
guilt [gɪlt] *s* culpa
guiltless ['gɪltlɪs] *adj* inocente, libre de culpa
guilt•y ['gɪlti] *adj* (*comp* **-ier;** *super* **-iest**) culpable; (*charged with guilt*) culpado; (*found guilty*) reo
guimpe [gɪmp] o [gæmp] *s* canesú *m*
guinea ['gɪni] *s* (*monetary unit*) guinea; gallina de Guinea
guinea fowl *s* pintada, gallina de Guinea
guinea hen *s* pintada, gallina de Guinea (*hembra*)
guinea pig *s* conejillo de Indias; (fig) cobayo
guise [gaɪz] *s* traje *m;* aspecto, semejanza; **under the guise of** so capa de
guitar [gɪ'tɑr] *s* guitarra
guitarist [gɪ'tɑrɪst] *s* guitarrista *mf*
gulch [gʌltʃ] *s* barranco, quebrada
gulf [gʌlf] *s* golfo
Gulf of Mexico *s* golfo de Méjico
Gulf Stream *s* Corriente *f* del Golfo
gull [gʌl] *s* gaviota; (coll) bobo || *tr* estafar, engañar
gullet ['gʌlɪt] *s* gaznate *m,* garguero; esófago
gullible ['gʌlɪbəl] *adj* crédulo; creído; **to be too gullible** tener buenas tragaderas
gul•ly ['gʌli] *s* (*pl* **-lies**) barranca, arroyada; (*channel made by ain water*) badén *m*
gulp [gʌlp] *s* trago || *tr* — **to gulp down** engullir; reprimir (*p.ej., sollozos*) || *intr* respirar entrecortadamente
gum [gʌm] *s* goma; chanclo de goma; (*firm flesh around base of teeth*) encía; (*mucous on edge of eyelid*) legaña || *v* (*pret & pp* **gummed;** *ger* **gumming**) *tr* engomar || *intr* exudar goma
gum arabic *s* goma arábiga
gum'boil' *s* flemón *m*
gum boot *s* bota de agua
gum'drop' *s* frutilla

gum•my [ˋgʌmi] *adj* (*comp* **-mier;** *super* **-miest**) gomoso; (*eyelid*) legañoso
gumption [ˋgʌmpʃən] *s* ánimo, iniciativa, empuje *m,* fuerza; juicio, seso
gum′shoe′ *s* chanclo de goma; (coll) detective *m* ‖ *v* (*pret & pp* **-shoed;** *ger* **-shoeing**) *intr* (slang) andar con zapatos de fieltro
gun [gʌn] *s* escopeta, fusil *m;* cañón *m;* (*for injections*) jeringa; (coll) revólver *m;* **to stick to one's guns** mantenerse en sus trece ‖ *v* (*pret & pp* **gunned;** *ger* **gunning**) *tr* hacer fuego sobre; (slang) acelerar rápidamente (*un motor, un avión*) ‖ *intr* andar a caza; disparar; **to gun for** ir en busca de; buscar para matar
gun′boat′ *s* cañonero
gun carriage *s* cureña, encabalgamiento
gun′cot′ton *s* fulmicotón *m,* algodón *m* pólvora, pólvora de algodón
gun′fire′ *s* fuego (*de armas de fuego*); cañoneo
gun•man [ˋgʌnmən] *s* (*pl* **-men** [mən]) bandido armado, pistolero; gángster *m*
gun metal *s* bronce *m* de cañón; metal pavonado
gunnel [ˋgʌnəl] *s* (naut) borda, regala
gunner [ˋgʌnər] *s* artillero; cazador *m*
gunnery [ˋgʌnəri] *s* artillería
gunny sack [ˋgʌni] *s* saco de yute
gun permit *s* licencia de armas
gun′pow′der *s* pólvora
gun′run′ner *s* contrabandista *m* de armas de fuego
gun′run′ning *s* contrabando de armas de fuego
gun′shot′ *s* escopetazo, tiro de fusil; alcance *m* de un fusil; **within gunshot** a tiro de fusil
gunshot wound *s* escopetazo
gun′smith′ *s* armero
gun′stock′ *s* caja de fusil
gun-toting [ˋgʌnˋtotɪŋ] *adj* armado
gunwale [ˋgʌnəl] *s* (naut) borda, regala
gup•py [ˋgʌpi] *s* (*pl* **-pies**) lebistes *m*
gurgle [ˋgʌrgəl] *s* gorgoteo, gluglú *m;* (*of a child*) gorjeo ‖ *intr* gorgotear, hacer gluglú; gorjearse (*el niño*)
gush [gʌʃ] *s* borbollón *m,* chorro ‖ *intr* surgir, salir a borbollones; (coll) hacer extremos, ser extremoso
gusher [ˋgʌʃər] *s* pozo de chorro de petróleo; (coll) personal extremosa
gushing [ˋgʌʃɪŋ] *adj* surgente; (coll) extremoso ‖ *s* borbollón *m,* chorro; (coll) efusión, extremos
gush•y [ˋgʌʃi] *adj* (*comp* **-ier;** *super* **-iest**) (coll) efusivo, extremoso
gusset [ˋgʌsɪt] *s* escudete *m*
gust [gʌst] *s* (*of wind*) ráfaga; (*of rain*) aguacero; (*of smoke*) bocanada; (*of noise*) explosión; (*of anger or enthusiasm*) arrebato
gusto [ˋgʌsto] *s* deleite *m,* entusiasmo; **with gusto** con sumo placer
gust•y [ˋgʌsti] *adj* (*comp* **-ier;** *super* **-iest**) tempestuoso, borrascoso
gut [gʌt] *s* tripa; cuerda de tripa; **guts** tripas; (slang) agallas ‖ *v* (*pret & pp* **gutted;** *ger* **gutting**) *tr* destripar; destruir lo interior de
gutta-percha [ˋgʌtəˋpʌrtʃə] *s* gutapercha
gutter [ˋgʌtər] *s* (*on side of road*) cuneta; (*in street*) arroyo; (*of roof*) canal *f;* (*ditch formed by rain water*) badén *m;* barrios bajos
gut′ter-snipe′ *s* pilluelo, hijo de la miseria; gamberro
guttural [ˋgʌtərəl] *adj* gutural ‖ *s* sonido gutural
guy [gaɪ] *s* viento, cable *m* de retén; (coll) tipo, tío, sujeto
Guyana [gaɪˋænə] *s* Guayana
guy wire *s* cable *m* de retén
guzzle [ˋgʌzəl] *tr & intr* beber con exceso
guzzler [ˋgʌzlər] *s* borrachín *m*
gym [dʒɪm] *s* (coll) gimnasio
gymnasi•um [dʒɪmˋnezɪ•əm] *s* (*pl* **-ums** o **-a** [ə]) gimnasio
gymnast [ˋdʒɪmnæst] *s* gimnasta *mf*
gymnastic [dʒɪmˋnæstɪk] *adj* gimnástico ‖ **gymnastics** *spl* gimnasia, gimnástica
gym shoe *s* zapato de goma
gym suit *s* chandal *m,* chándal *m*
gynecologic(al) [ˌgaɪnəkoˋlɑdʒɪk(əl)] o [ˌdʒaɪnəkoˋlɑdʒɪk(əl)] *adj* ginecológico
gynecologist [ˌgaɪnəˋkɑlədʒɪst] o [ˌdʒaɪnəˋkɑlədʒɪst] *s* ginecólogo
gynecology [ˌgaɪnəˋkɑlədʒi] o [ˌdʒaɪnəˋkɑlədʒi] *s* ginecología
gyp [dʒɪp] *s* (slang) estafa, timo; (*person*) (slang) estafador *m,* timador *m* ‖ *v* (*pret & pp* **gypped;** *ger* **gypping**) *tr* (slang) estafar, timar
gypsum [ˋdʒɪpsəm] *s* yeso, aljez *m*
gyp•sy [ˋdʒɪpsi] *adj* gitano ‖ *s* (*pl* **-sies**) gitano ‖ **Gypsy** *s* gitano (*idioma*)
gypsy moth *s* lagarta
gyrate [ˋdʒaɪret] *intr* girar
gyroscope [ˋdʒaɪrəˌskop] *s* giroscopio

H

H, h [etʃ] octava letra del alfabeto inglés
haberdasher•y [ˋhæbərˌdæʃəri] *s* (*pl* **-ies**) tienda de artículos para hombres; artículos para hombres
habit [ˋhæbɪt] *s* costumbre *f,* hábito; (*costume*) traje *m;* **to be in the habit of** acostumbrar
habitat [ˋhæbɪˌtæt] *s* hábitat *m*
habitation [ˌhæbɪˋteʃən] *s* habitación
habit-forming [ˋhæbɪt ˌfɔrmɪŋ] *adj* enviciador
habitual [həˋbɪtʃʊ•əl] *adj* habitual
habitué [həˌbɪtʃʊˋe] *s* habituado
hack [hæk] *s* (*cut*) corte *m;* (*notch*) mella;

(*cough*) tos seca; coche *m* de alquiler; caballo de alquiler; caballo de silla; (*old nag*) rocín *m;* escritor *m* a sueldo || *tr* cortar, machetear
hacker [ˈhækər] *s* (*online vandal*) pirata *mf* informáti•co -ca
hacking [ˈhækɪŋ] *s* (*online vandalism*) piratería informática
hack•man [ˈhækmən] *s* (*pl* **-men** [mən]) cochero de punto
hackney [ˈhækni] *s* caballo de silla; coche *m* de alquiler; esclavo del trabajo
hackneyed [ˈhæknid] *adj* trillado, gastado
hack'saw' *s* sierra de armero, sierra de cortar metales
haddock [ˈhædək] *s* eglefino
hadn't *contr* **had not**
haft [hæft] o [hɑft] *s* mango, puño
hag [hæg] *s* (*ugly old woman*) tarasca; (*witch*) bruja
haggard [ˈhægərd] *adj* ojeroso, macilento
haggle [ˈhægəl] *intr* regatear
Hague,The [heg] La Haya
ha-ha [hɑˈhɑ] *interj* ¡ja,ja!
hail [hel] *s* (*frozen rain*) granizo; (*greeting*) saludo; **within hail** al alcance de la voz || *interj* ¡salud!, ¡salve! || *tr* saludar; dar vivas a, acoger con vivas; aclamar; granizar (*p.ej., golpes*) || *intr* granizar; **to hail from** venir de, ser oriundo de
Hail Mary *s* avemaría
hail'stone' *s* piedra de granizo
hail'storm' *s* granizada
hair [hɛr] *s* pelo, cabellos; **to a hair** con la mayor exactitud; **to cut the hair of** peluquear; **to get in one's hair** (slang) enojarle a uno; **to have one's hair down** estar en melena; **to let one's hair down** (slang) hablar con mucha desenvoltura; **to make one's hair stand on end** ponerle a uno los pelos de punta; **to not turn a hair** no inmutarse; **to split hairs** pararse en quisquillas
hair'breadth' *s* (el) grueso de un pelo, casi nada; **to escape by a hairbreadth** escapar por un pelo
hair'brush' *s* cepillo de cabeza
hair'cloth' *s* tela de crin; (*worn as a penance*) cilicio
hair curler [ˈkʌrlər] *s* rizador *m,* tenacillas, bigudí *m,* rulo
hair'cut' *s* corte *m* de pelo; **to get a haircut** cortarse el pelo, peluquear
hair'do' *s* (*pl* **-dos**) peinado, tocado
hair'dress'er *s* peinador *m,* peluquero
hair dryer *s* secador *m*
hair dye *s* tinte *m* para el pelo
hairless [ˈhɛrlɪs] *adj* pelón
hair net *s* redecilla
hair piece *s* peluquín *m*
hair'pin' *s* horquilla
hair-raising [ˈhɛr,rezɪŋ] *adj* (coll) espeluznante, horripilante
hair restorer [rɪˈstorər] *s* crecepelo
hair ribbon *s* cinta para el cabello
hair set *s* fijapeinados *m*
hair shirt *s* cilicio
hairsplitting [ˈhɛr,splɪtɪŋ] *adj* quisquilloso || *s* quisquillas
hair spray *s* laca
hair'spring' *s* espiral *f*
hair'style' *s* peinado
hair tonic *s* vigorizador *m* del cabello
hair•y [ˈhɛri] *adj* (*comp* **-ier;** *super* **-iest**) peludo, cabelludo
hake [hek] *s* merluza; (genus: *Urophycis*) fice *m*
halberd [ˈhælbərd] *s* alabarda
halberdier [,hælbərˈdɪr] *s* alabardero
halcyon days [ˈhælsɪ•ən] *s* días tranquilos, época de paz
hale [hel] *adj* sano, robusto; **hale and hearty** sano y fuerte || *tr* llevar a la fuerza
half [hæf] *adj* medio; **a half** o **half a** medio; **half the** la mitad de || *adv* medio, p.ej., **half asleep** medio dormido; a medio, p.ej., **half finished** a medio acabar; a medias, p.ej., **half owner** dueño a medias; **half past** y media, p.ej., **half past three** las tres y media; **half . . . half** medio . . . medio || *s* (*pl* **halves** [hævz]) mitad; (arith) medio; **in half** por la mitad; **to go halves ir** a medias
half'-and-half' *adj* mitad y mitad; indeterminado || *adv* a medias, en partes iguales || *s* mezcla de leche y crema; mezcla de dos cervezas inglesas
half'back' *s* (football) medio
half-baked [ˈhæf,bekt] *adj* a medio cocer; incompleto; poco juicioso, inexperto
half binding *s* (bb) encuadernación a la holandesa, media pasta
half'-blood' *s* mestizo; medio hermano
half boot *s* bota de media caña
half'-bound' *adj* (bb) a la holandesa
half'-breed' *s* mestizo
half brother *s* medio hermano, hermanastro
half-cocked [ˈhæfˈkakt] *adv* (coll) con precipitación; **to go off half-cocked** obrar precipitadamente y antes del momento propio
half fare *s* medio billete
half'-full' *adj* mediado
half-hearted [ˈhæf,hartɪd] *adj* indiferente, frío
half holiday *s* mañana o tarde *f* de asueto
half hose *spl* calcetines *mpl*
half'-hour *s* media hora; **on the half-hour** a la media en punto, cada media hora
half leather *s* (bb) encuadernación a la holandesa, media pasta
half'-length' *adj* de medio cuerpo
half'-mast' *s* — **at half mast** a media asta
half moon *s* media luna
half mourning *s* medio luto
half note *s* (mus) nota blanca
half pay *s* media paga; medio sueldo
halfpen•ny [ˈhepəni] o [ˈhepni] *s* (*pl* **-nies**) medio penique
half pint *s* media pinta
half'-seas' over *adj* — **to be half-seas over**

(slang) estar entre dos velas, estar entre dos luces
half shell *s* (*either half of a bivalve*) concha; (*oysters*) **on the half shell** en su concha
half sister *s* media hermana, hermanastra
half′-size′ *adj* de mitad de tamaño, de talla especial; reducido a la mitad ‖ *s* medio número; talla especial
half sole *s* media suela
half′-sole′ *tr* poner media suela a
half′-staff′ *s* — **at half-staff** a media asta
half through *prep* a la mitad de
half-timbered [ˈhæf,tɪmbərd] *adj* entramado
half title *s* anteportada, falsa portada
half′tone′ *s* (phot & paint) mediatinta; (typ) similigrabado
half′-track′ *s* media oruga, semitractor *m*
half′-truth′ *s* verdad a medias
half′way′ *adj* a medio camino; incompleto, hecho a medias ‖ *adv* a medio camino; **halfway through** a la mitad de; **to meet halfway** partir el camino con; partir la diferencia con; hacer concesiones mutuas (*dos personas*)
half′way house′ *s* (*for limited detention*) centro de reinserción social
half-witted [ˈhæf ,wɪtɪd] *adj* imbécil; necio, tonto
halibut [ˈhælɪbət] *s* halibut *m*
halide [ˈhælaɪd] o [ˈhelaɪd] *s* (chem) haluro
halitosis [,hælɪˈtosɪs] *s* halitosis *f*, aliento fétido
hall [hɔl] (*passageway*) corredor *m;* (*entranceway*) vestíbulo, zaguán *m;* (*large meeting room*) sala, salón *m;* (*assembly room of a university*) paraninfo; (*building, e.g., of a university*) edificio
halleluiah o **hallelujah** [,hælɪˈlujə] *s* aleluya *m & f* ‖ *interj* ¡aleluya!
hall′mark′ *s* marca de constraste; (*distinguishing feature*) (fig) sello
hal•lo [həˈlo] *s* (*pl* **-los**) grito ‖ *interj* ¡hola!; (*to incite dogs in hunting*) ¡sus! ‖ *intr* gritar
hall of fame *s* galería de personajes famosos; **Hall of Fame** Salón *m* de la Fama
hallow [ˈhælo] *tr* santificar
hallowed [ˈhælod] *adj* santo, sagrado
Halloween o **Hallowe′en** [,hæloˈin] *s* víspera de Todos los Santos
hallucination [hə,lusɪˈnefən] *s* alucinación
hallucinogenic [hə,lusɪnoˈdʒɛnɪk] *adj* alucinante
hall′way′ *s* corredor *m;* vestíbulo, zaguán *m*
ha•lo [ˈhelo] *s* (*pl* **-los** o **-loes**) halo
halogen [ˈhælədʒən] *s* halógeno
halt [hɔlt] *adj* cojo, renco ‖ *s* alto, parada; **to call a halt** mandar hacer alto; **to come to a halt** pararse, detenerse, interrumpirse ‖ *tr* parar, detener ‖ *intr* hacer alto ‖ *interj* ¡alto!
halter [ˈhɔltər] *s* (*for leading or fastening horse*) cabestro, ronzal *m*, dogal *m;* (*noose*) dogal *m*, cuerda de ahorcar; muerte *f* en la horca
halting [ˈhɔltɪŋ] *adj* cojo, renco; vacilante
halve [hæv] *tr* partir en dos, partir por la mitad
halyard [ˈhæljərd] *s* (naut) driza
ham [hæm] *s* (*part of leg behind knee*) corva; (*thigh and buttock*) pernil *m;* (*cured meat from hog's hind leg*) jamón *m;* (slang) comicastro; (slang) aficionado (*a la radio*); **hams** nalgas
ham and eggs *spl* huevos con jamón
hamburger [ˈhæm,bʌrgər] *s* hamburguesa
hamlet [ˈhæmlɪt] *s* aldehuela, caserío
hammer [ˈhæmər] *s* martillo; (*of piano*) macillo, martinete *m;* **to go under the hammer** venderse en pública subasta ‖ *tr* martillar; **to hammer out** formar a martillazos; sacar en limpio a fuerza de mucho esfuerzo ‖ *intr* martillar; **to hammer away** trabajar asiduamente
hammock [ˈhæmək] *s* hamaca
ham operator *s* (*radio ham*) radioaficionado
hamper [ˈhæmpər] *s* canasto, cesto grande con tapa ‖ *tr* estorbar, impedir
hamster [ˈhæmstər] *s* marmota de Alemania, rata del trigo
ham•string [ˈhæm,strɪŋ] *s* (anat) ligamento de la corva; (*of horse*) tendón *m* del corvejón ‖ *v* (*pret & pp* **-strung**) *tr* desjarretar; (fig) estropear, incapacitar
hand [hænd] *adj* (*done or operated with the hands*) manual ‖ *s* mano *f;* (*workman*) obrero, peón *m;* (*way of writing*) escritura, puño y letra; (signature) firma; (*clapping of hands*) salva de aplausos; (*of clock or watch*) mano *f;* manecilla; (*all the cards in one's hand*) juego; (*a round of play*) mano *f;* (*player*) jugador *m;* (*source, origin*) fuente *f;* (*skill*) destreza; **all hands** (naut) toda la tripulación; (coll) todas; **at first hand** de primera mano; directamente, de buena tinta; **at hand** disponible; **hand in glove** uña y carne; **hand in hand** asidos de la mano; juntos; **hands-on** (compu) manual; **hands up!** ¡arriba las manos! **hand to hand** cuerpo a cuerpo; **in hand** entre manos; **in his own hand** de su propio puño; **on hand** entre manos; disponible; **on hands and knees** (*crawling*) a gatas; (*beseeching*) de rodillas; **on the one hand** por una parte; **on the other hand** por otra parte; **out of hand** luego, en seguida; desmandado; **to be at hand** obrar en mi (nuestro) poder (*una carta*); **to change hands** mudar de manos; **to clap hands** batir palmas; **to eat out of one's hand** aceptar dócilmente la autoridad de uno; **to fall into the hands of** caer en manos de; **to have a hand in** tomar parte en; **to have one's hands full** estar ocupadísimo; **to hold hands** tomarse de las manos; **to hold up one's hands** (*as a sign of surrender*) alzar las manos; **to join hands** darse las manos; casarse; **to keep one's hands off** no tocar, no meterse en; **to lend a hand** echar una mano; **to live from hand to mouth** vivir al día, vivir de la mano a la boca; **to not lift a hand** no levantar paja del suelo; **to play into the hands of** hacer el caldo gordo a; **to raise one's hand** (*in taking an oath*) alzar el dedo; **to shake hands** estre-

charse la mano; **to show one's hand** descubrir su juego; **to take in hand** hacerse cargo de; tratar, estudiar (*una cuestión*); **to throw up one's hands** darse por vencido; **to try one's hand** probar la mano; **to turn one's hand to** dedicarse a, ocuparse en; **to wash one's hands of** lavarse las manos de; **under my hand** con mi firma, bajo mi firma, de mi puño y letra; **under the hand and seal of** firmado y sellado por || *tr* dar, entregar; **to hand in** entregar; **to hand on** transmitir; **to hand out** repartir

hand'bag' *s* saco de noche; bolso de señora

hand baggage *s* equipaje *m* de mano

hand'ball' *s* pelota; juego de pelota a mano

hand'bill' *s* hoja volante

hand'book' manual *m;* guía de turistas; registro para apuestas

hand'brake' *s* freno de mano

hand'breadth' *s* palmo menor

hand'car' *s* (rr) carrito de mano

hand'cart' *s* carretilla de mano

hand control *s* mando a mano

hand'cuff' *s* manilla; **handcuffs** manillas, esposas || *tr* poner esposas a

handful [ˈhændˌful] *s* puñado, manojo

hand glass *s* espejo de mano; lupa

hand grenade *s* granada de mano

hand gun *s* (coll) pipa

hand'-held' calculator *s* calculador a mano

handi-cap [ˈhændɪˌkæp] *s* desventaja, obstáculo; (sport) handicap *m;* (med) disminución, minusvalía || *v* (*pret & pp* **-capped;** *ger* **-capping**) *tr* poner trabas a; (sport) handicapar

handicraft [ˈhændɪˌkræft] *s* destreza manual; arte mecánica

handiwork [ˈhændɪˌwʌrk] *s* hechura, trabajo; obra manual

handkerchief [ˈhæŋkərtʃif] *s* pañuelo

handle [ˈhændəl] *s* (*of a basket, crock, pitcher*) asa; (*of a shovel, rake, etc.*) mango; (*of an umbrella, sword*) puño; (*of a door, drawer*) tirador *m;* (*of a hand organ*) manubrio; (*of a water pump*) guimbalete *m;* (*opportunity, pretext*) asidero; **to fly off the handle** (slang) salirse de sus casillas || *tr* manosear, manipular; dirigir, manejar, gobernar; comerciar en || *intr* manejarse

handle bar *s* manillar *m,* guía

handler [ˈhændlər] *s* (sport) entrenador *m*

handling [ˈhændlɪŋ] *s* manejo; tratamiento; (*touching*) manipulación; (compu) gestión; **shipping and handling** gastos de flete

hand'made' *adj* hecho a mano

hand'maid' o **hand'maid'en** *s* criada, sirvienta

hand'-me-down' *s* (coll) prenda de vestir de segunda mano

hand organ *s* organillo

hand'out' *s* comida que se da de limosna; comunicado de prensa

hand-picked [ˈhænd ˌpɪkt] *adj* escogido a mano; escogido escrupulosamente; escogido con motivos ocultos

hand'rail' *s* barandilla, pasamano

hand'saw' *s* serrucho, sierra de mano

hand'set' *s* microteléfono

hand'shake' *s* apretón *m* de manos

hands'-off' *adj* teórico; (compu) automático; (pol) de no intervención

handsome [ˈhænsəm] *adj* hermoso, elegante, guapo; considerable

hands'-on' *adj* práctico; (compu) manual

hand'spring' *s* voltereta sobre las manos, vuelta de manos

hand'-to-hand' *adj* cuerpo a cuerpo

hand'-to-mouth' *adj* inseguro, precario; impróvido

hand'work' *s* trabajo a mano

hand'-wres'tle *intr* pulsear

hand'-writ'ing *s* escritura; (*writing by hand which characterizes a particular person*) letra

hand'writ'ten *adj* manuscrito, escrito a mano

hand•y [ˈhændi] *adj* (*comp* **-ier;** *super* **-iest**) (*easy to handle*) manuable; (*within easy reach*) próximo, a la mano; (*skillful*) diestro, hábil; **to come in handy** venir a pelo

handy man *s* dije *m,* factótum *m*

hang [hæŋ] *s* (*of a dress, curtain, etc.*) caída; (*skill; insight*) tino; **I don't care a hang** (coll) no me importa un bledo; **to get the hang of it** (coll) coger el tino || *v* (*pret & pp* **hung** [hʌŋ]) *tr* colgar; tender (*la ropa mojada*); pegar (*el papel pintado*); fijar (*un cartel, un letrero*); enquiciar (*una puerta, una ventana*); bajar (*la cabeza*); **hang it!** (coll) ¡caramba!; **to hang up** colgar (*el sombrero*); impedir los progresos de || *intr* colgar, pender; estar agarrado; vacilar; **to hang around** esperar sin hacer nada; haraganear; rondar; **to hang on** colgar de; depender de; estar pendiente de (*las palabras de una persona*); estar sin acabar de morir; agarrarse; **to hang out** asomarse; (slang) recogerse, alojarse; **to hang over** (*to threaten*) cernerse sobre; **to hang together** mantenerse unidos; **to hang up** (telp) colgar || *v* (*pret* **hanged** o **hung**) *tr* ahorcar || *intr* ahorcarse

hangar [ˈhæŋər] o [ˈhæŋgɑr] *s* cobertizo; (aer) hangar *m*

hang'bird' *s* pájaro de nido colgante; (*Baltimore oriole*) cacique veranero

hanger [ˈhæŋər] *s* colgador, *m,* suspensión; (*hook*) colgadero

hang'er•on' *s* (*pl* **hangers-on**) secuaz *mf;* parásito; (*sponger*) pegote *m*

hang glider *s* ala delta

hang gliding *s* ala delta, vuelo libre

hanging [ˈhæŋɪŋ] *adj* colgante, pendiente || *s* ahorcadura, muerte *f* en la horca; **hangings** colgaduras

hanging gardens *spl* jardines *mpl* colgantes

hang•man [ˈhæŋmən] *s* (*pl* **-men** [mən]) verdugo

hang'nail' *s* padrastro, respigón *m*

hang'out' *s* sitio muy frequentado, punto de reunión, mentidero
hang'o'ver *s* resaca, cruda (CAm, Mex), guayabo (Col), ratón *m* (Ven); (*survival*) vestigio, reliquia
hang'up *s* (coll) complejo, problema *m*, trauma *m*
hank [hæŋk] *s* madeja ‖ **Hank** apodo de Enrique *m*
hanker [ˈhæŋkər] *intr* sentir anhelo
Hannibal [hænɪbəl] *s* Aníbal *m*
haphazard [ˌhæpˈhæzərd] *adj* casual, fortuito, impensado ‖ *adv* al acaso, a la ventura
hapless [ˈhæplɪs] *adj* desgraciado, desventurado
happen [ˈhæpən] *intr* acontecer, suceder; (*to turn out*) resultar; (*to be the case by chance*) dar la casualidad; **to happen in** entrar por casualidad; **to happen on** encontrarse con; **to happen to** hacerse de; **to happen to** + *inf* por casualidad + *ind*, p.ej., **I happened to see her at the theater** por casualidad la vi en el teatro
happening [ˈhæpənɪŋ] *s* acontecimiento, suceso
happily [ˈhæpɪli] *adv* felizmente
happiness [ˈhæpɪnɪs] *s* felicidad
hap•py [ˈhæpi] *adj* (*comp* **-pier;** *super* **-piest**) feliz; (*pleased*) contento; **to be happy to** alegrarse de, tener gusto en
hap'py-go-luck'y *adj* irresponsable, impróvido ‖ *adv* a la buenaventura
happy hour *s* el consumo de bebidas alcohólicas en un bar (*durante la rebaja en los precios de las consumiciones*)
happy medium *s* justo medio
Happy New Year *interj* ¡Feliz Año Nuevo!
harangue [həˈræŋ] *s* arenga ‖ *tr & intr* arengar
harass [ˈhærəs] o [həˈræs] *tr* acosar, hostigar; molestar, vejar
harbinger [ˈhɑrbɪndʒər] *s* precursor *m;* anuncio, presagio ‖ *tr* anunciar, presagiar
harbor [ˈhɑrbər] *adj* portuario ‖ *s* puerto ‖ *tr* albergar; alcahuetar, encubrir (*delincuentes u objetos robados*); guardar (*sentimientos de odio*)
harbor master *s* capitán *m* de puerto
hard [hɑrd] *adj* duro; (*difficult*) difícil; (*water*) crudo, duro; (*solder*) fuerte; (*work*) asiduo; (*drinker*) empedernido; espiritoso, fuertemente alcohólico; **to be hard on** (*to treat severely*) ser muy duro con; (*to wear out fast*) gastar, echar a perder ‖ *adv* duro; fuerte; mucho; **hard upon** a raíz de; **to drink hard** beber de firme; **to rain hard** llover de firme
hard and fast *adj* inflexible, riguroso ‖ *adv* firmemente
hard'back *s* libro de tapa dura
hard'ball *s* béisbol *m;* **to play hardball** (coll) ser implacable
hard bargaining *s* tira y afloja
hard-bitten [ˈhɑrdˈbɪtən] *adj* terco, tenaz, inflexible
hard-boiled [ˈhɑrdˈbɔɪld] *adj* (*egg*) duro, muy cocido; duro, inflexible
hard candy *s* caramelos
hard cash *s* dinero contante y sonante
hard cider *s* sidra muy fermentada
hard coal *s* antracita
hard copy *s* impresión *f*, salida impresa; (compu) listado
hard core *adj* incondicional, a ultranza
hard disk *s* (compu) disco duro, disco rígido
hard drive *s* (compu) disco duro, disco rígido
hard-earned [ˈhɑrdˈʌrnd] *adj* ganado a pulso
harden [ˈhɑrdən] *tr* endurecer ‖ *intr* endurecerse
hardening [ˈhɑrdənɪŋ] *s* endurecimiento
hard facts *spl* realidades
hard-fought [ˈhɑrdˈfɔt] *adj* reñido
hard-hat *adj* de obreros; (pej) reaccionario; **hard-hat area** zona de casco obligatorio
hard-headed [ˈhɑrdˈhɛdɪd] *adj* astuto, sagaz; terco, tozudo
hard-hearted [ˈhɑrdˈhɑrtɪd] *adj* duro de corazón
hardihood [ˈhɑrdɪˌhʊd] *s* audacia, resolución; descaro, insolencia
hardiness [ˈhɑrdɪnɪs] *s* fuerza, robustez; audacia, resolución
hard labor *s* trabajos forzados
hard luck *s* mala suerte
hard'-luck' story *s* (coll) cuento de penas; **to tell a hard-luck story** (coll) contar lástimas
hardly [ˈhɑrdli] *adv* apenas; escasamente; casi no; (*with great difficulty*) a duras penas; (*grievously*) penosamente; **hardly ever** casi nunca
hardness [ˈhɑrdnɪs] *s* dureza; (*of water*) crudeza
hard of hearing *adj* duro de oído, teniente
hard-pressed [ˈhɑrdˈprɛst] *adj* acosado; (*for money*) apurado, alcanzado
hard rubber *s* vulcanita
hard sauce *s* mantequilla azucarada
hard'-shell' clam *s* almeja redonda
hard'-shell' crab *s* cangrejo de cáscara dura
hardship [ˈhɑrdʃɪp] *s* penalidad, infortunio, apuro
hard'tack' *s* galleta, sequete *m*
hard times *spl* período de miseria, apuros
hard to please *adj* difícil de contentar
hard up *adj* (coll) apurado, alcanzado
hard'ware' *s* ferretería, quincalla; (*metal trimmings*) herraje *m;* (compu) hardware *m*, equipo, maquinaria, soporte *m* físico
hardware•man [ˈhɑrdˌwɛrmən] *s* (*pl* **-men** [mən]) ferretero, quincallero
hardware store *s* ferretería, quincallería
hard-won [ˈhɑrdˌwʌn] *adj* ganado a pulso
hard'wood' *s* madera dura; árbol *m* de madera dura
hardwood floor *s* entarimado
har•dy [ˈhɑrdi] *adj* (*comp* **-dier;** *super* **-diest**) fuerte, robusto; audaz, resuelto; (*rash*) temerario; (hort) resistente
hare [hɛr] *s* liebre *f*

harebrained [ˈhɛr,brend] *adj* atolondrado
hare'lip *s* labio leporino
harelipped [ˈhɛr ,lɪpt] *adj* labiohendido
harem [ˈhɛrəm] *s* harén *m*
hark [hɑrk] *intr* escuchar; **to hark back** volver (*la jauría*) sobre la pista; **to hark back to** volver a, recordar
harken [ˈhɑrkən] *intr* escuchar, atender
harlequin [ˈhɑrləkwɪn] *s* arlequín *m*
harlot [ˈhɑrlət] *s* meretriz *f*
harm [hɑrm] *s* daño, perjuicio ‖ *tr* dañar, perjudicar, hacer daño a
harmful [ˈhɑrmfəl] *adj* dañoso, perjudicial; maléfico; (*e.g., pests*) dañino
harmfulness [ˈhɑrmfəlnɪs] *s* nocividad
harmless [ˈhɑrmlɪs] *adj* innocuo, inofensivo
harmlessness [ˈhɑrmlɪsnɪs] *s* innocuidad
harmonic [hɑrˈmɑnɪk] *adj & s* armónico
harmonica [hɑrˈmɑnɪkə] *s* armónica
harmonious [hɑrˈmonɪ•əs] *adj* armonioso
harmonize [ˈhɑrmə,naɪz] *tr & intr* armonizar
harmo•ny [ˈhɑrməni] *s* (pl **-nies**) armonía
harness [ˈhɑrnɪs] *s* arreos, guarniciones; **to get back in the harness** volver a la rutina; **to die in the harness** morir al pie del cañón ‖ *tr* enjaezar, poner las guarniciones a; enganchar; captar (*las aguas de un río*)
harness maker *s* guarnicionero
harness race *s* carrera con sulky, carrera de trotones
harp [hɑrp] *s* arpa ‖ *intr* — **to harp on** repetir porfiadamente
harpist [ˈhɑrpɪst] *s* arpista *mf*
harpoon [hɑrˈpun] *s* arpón *m* ‖ *tr & intr* arponear
harpsichord [ˈhɑrpsɪ ,kɔrd] *s* clave *m*
har•py [ˈhɑrpi] *s* (*pl* **-pies**) arpía
harrow [ˈhæro] *s* (agr) grada ‖ *tr* (agr) gradar; atormentar
harrowing [ˈhæro•ɪŋ] *adj* horripilante, espantoso
har•ry [ˈhæri] *v* (*pret & pp* **-ried**) *tr* acosar, hostilizar, hostigar; atormentar, molestar ‖ **Harry** Enrique *m*
harsh [hɑrʃ] *adj* (*to touch, taste, eyes, hearing*) áspero; duro, cruel
harshness [ˈhɑrʃnɪs] *s* aspereza; dureza, crueldad
hart [hɑrt] *s* ciervo
harum-scarum [ˈhɛrəmˈskɛrəm] *adj* atolondrado ‖ *adv* atolondradamente ‖ *s* mataperros *m*
harvest [ˈhɑrvɪst] *s* cosecha; corte *m* ‖ *tr & intr* cosechar
harvester [ˈhɑrvɪstər] *s* cosechero; (*helper*) agostero; (*machine*) segadora
harvest home *s* entrada de los frutos; fiesta de segadores; canción de segadores
harvest moon *s* luna de la cosecha
has-been [ˈhæzˈbɪn] *s* (coll) antigualla
hash [hæʃ] *s* picadillo ‖ *tr* picar
hash house *s* fonda, taguara (Ven)
hashish [ˈhæʃiʃ] *s* hachich *m;* (coll) tate *m*
hashish user *s* (coll) tate *m*
hasn't *contr* **has not**
hasp [hæsp] o [hɑsp] *s* portacandado; (*of book covers*) broche *m*
hassle [ˈhæsəl] *s* (coll) riña, disputa
hassock [ˈhæsək] *s* cojín *m* (*para arrodillarse*)
haste [hest] *s* prisa; **in haste** de prisa; **to make haste** darse prisa
hasten [ˈhesən] *tr* apresurar; apretar (*el paso*) ‖ *intr* apresurarse
hast•y [ˈhesti] *adj* (*comp* **-ier;** *super* **-iest**) apresurado, inconsiderado, impulsivo, colérico
hat [hæt] *s* sombrero; **to keep under one's hat** (coll) callar, no divulgar; **to throw one's hat in the ring** (coll) decidirse a bajar a la arena
hat'band' *s* cintillo; (*worn to show mourning*) gasa
hat block *s* horma, conformador *m*
hat'box' *s* sombrerera
hatch [hætʃ] *s* (*brood*) cría, nidada; (*trap door*) escotillón *m;* (*lower half of door*) media puerta; (*opening in ship's deck*) escotilla; (*lid for opening in ship's deck*) cuartel *m* ‖ *tr* empollar (*huevos*); sombrear (*un dibujo*); maquinar, tramar ‖ *intr* empollarse; salir del huevo
hatch'back *s* coche *m* con puerta trasera
hat'-check' girl *s* guardarropa
hatchet [ˈhætʃit] *s* destral *m,* hacha pequeña; **to bury the hatchet** envainar la espada
hatch'way' *s* (*trap door*) escotillón *m;* (*opening in ship's deck*) escotilla
hate [het] *s* odio, aborrecimiento ‖ *tr & intr* odiar, aborrecer, detestar
hateful [ˈhetfəl] *adj* odioso, aborrecible
hat'pin' *s* aguja de sombrero, pasador *m*
hat'rack' *s* percha
hatred [ˈhetrɪd] *s* odio, aborrecimiento
hat shop *s* bonetería
hatter [ˈhætər] *s* sombrerero
haughtiness [ˈhɔtɪnɪs] *s* altanería, altivez *f*
haugh•ty [ˈhɔti] *adj* (*comp* **-tier;** *super* **-tiest**) altanero, altivo
haul [hɔl] *s* (*pull, tug*) tirón *m;* (*amount caught*) redada; (*distance transported*) trayecto, recorrido; (*roundup, e.g., of thieves*) redada ‖ *tr* acarrear, transportar; (naut) halar
haunch [hɔntʃ] o [hɑntʃ] *s* (*hip*) cadera; (*hind quarter of an animal*) anca; (*leg of animal used for food*) pierna
haunt [hɔnt] o [hɑnt] *s* guarida, nidal *m,* querencia ‖ *tr* andar por, vagar por; frecuentar; inquietar, molestar; perseguir (*las memorias a una persona*)
haunted house *s* casa de fantasmas
haute couture [ot kuˈtyr] *s* alta moda
Havana [həˈvænə] *s* La Habana
have [hæv] *v* (*pret & pp* **had** [hæd]) *tr* tener; (*to get, to take*) tomar; **to have and to hold** (úsase sólo en el infinitivo) para ser poseído en propiedad; **to have got** (coll) tener, poseer; **to have got to** + *inf* (coll) tener que + *inf;* **to have it in for** (coll) tener tirria a; **to have it out with** (coll) habérselas con, emprenderla

con; **to have on** llevar puesto; **to have** (*something*) **to do with** tener que ver con; **to have what it takes to** tener madera de; **to have** + *inf* hacer, mandar + *inf,* p.ej., **I had him go out that door** le hice salir por esa puerta; **to have** + *pp* hacer, mandar + *inf,* p.ej., **I had my watch repaired** hice componer mi reloj ‖ *intr* — **to have at** atacar, embestir; **to have to** + *inf* tener que + *inf;* **to have to do with** (*to be concerned with*) tratar de; (*to have connections with*) tener relaciones con ‖ *v aux* haber, p.ej., **he has studied his lesson** ha estudiado su lección

havelock [ˈhævlɑk] *s* cogotera

haven [ˈhevən] *s* puerto; abrigo, asilo, buen puerto

have-not [ˈhæv,nɑt] *s* — **the haves and the have-nots** (coll) los ricos y los desposeídos

haven't *contr* **have not**

haversack [ˈhævər,sæk] *s* barjuleta; (*of soldier*) mochila

havoc [ˈhævək] *s* estrago, estragos; **to play havoc with** hacer grandes estragos en

haw [hɔ] *s* (*of hawthorn*) baya, simiente *f;* (*in speech*) vacilación ‖ *interj* ¡a la izquierda! ‖ *tr & intr* volver a la izquierda

haw'-haw' *s* carcajada

Hawaii o **Hawai'i** [həˈwaɪ•i] *s* Hawai *m*

Hawaiian o **Hawai'ian** [həˈwaɪ•ən] *adj & s* hawaiano

hawk [hɔk] *s* halcón *m,* gavilán *m,* cernícalo; (*mortarboard*) esparavel *m;* (*sharper*) (coll) fullero ‖ *tr* pregonar; **to hawk up** arrojar tosiendo ‖ *intr* carraspear, gargajear

hawker [ˈhɔkər] *s* buhonero

hawksbill turtle [ˈhɔks,bil] *s* carey *m*

hawse [hɔz] *s* (naut) muz *m;* (*hole*) (naut) escobén *m;* (naut) longitud de cadenas

hawse'hole' *s* (naut) escobén *m*

hawser [ˈhɔzər] *s* (naut) guindaleza

haw'thorn' *s* espino, oxiacanta

hay [he] *s* heno; **to hit the hay** (slang) acostarse; **to make hay while the sun shines** hacer su agosto

hay fever *s* fiebre *f* del heno

hay'field' *s* henar *m*

hay'fork' *s* horca; (*machine*) elevador *m* de heno

hay'loft' *s* henil *m,* henal *m*

hay'mak'er *s* (box) golpe *m* que pone fuera de combate

haymow [ˈhe,maʊ] *s* henil *m;* acopio de heno

hay'rack' *s* pesebre *m*

hayrick [ˈhe,rɪk] *s* almiar *m*

hay ride *s* paseo de placer en carro de heno

hay'seed' *s* simiente *f* de heno; (coll) patán *m,* campesino

hay'stack' *s* almiar *m*

hay'wire' *adj* (coll) decompuesto; **to go haywire** (*person*) volverse loco; (*machine*) descomponerse; (*plans*) desbaratarse

hazard [ˈhæzərd] *s* peligro, riesgo; (*chance*) acaso, azar *m;* (golf) obstáculo; **at all hazards** por grande que sea el riesgo ‖ *tr* arriesgar; aventurar (*una opinión*)

hazardous [ˈhæzərdəs] *adj* peligroso, arriesgado

hazardous waste *s* residuos *mpl* peligrosos

hazardous waste site *s* terreno contaminado por residuos peligrosos

haze [hez] *s* calina, bruma; (fig) confusión, vaguedad ‖ *tr* dar novatada a

hazel [ˈhezəl] *adj* castaño claro ‖ *s* avellano

ha'zel•nut *s* avellana

hazing [ˈhezɪŋ] *s* novatada

ha•zy [ˈhezi] *adj* (*comp* **-zier;** *super* **-ziest**) calinoso, brumoso; confuso, vago

H-bomb [ˈetʃ,bɑm] *s* bomba de hidrógeno

hdqrs. *abbr* **headquarters**

he [hi] *pron pers* (*pl* **they**) él ‖ *s* (*pl* **hes**) macho, varón *m*

head [hɛd] *s* cabeza; (*of a bed*) cabecera; (*caption*) encabezamiento; (*of a boil*) centro; (*on a glass of beer*) espuma; (*of a drum*) parche *m;* (*of a cane*) puño; (*of a barrel, cylinder, etc.*) fondo, tapa; (*of cylinder of automobile engine*) culata; crisis *f,* punto decisivo; (electron) cabezal *m;* **at the head of** al frente de; **from head to foot** de pies a cabeza; **head over heels** en un salto mortal; hasta los tuétanos; precipitadamente; **heads** (*of a coin*) cara; **heads or tails?** ¿cara o cruz?, ¿águila o sol? (Mex), ¿cara o sello? (SAm), ¿cara o seca? (Arg); **over one's head** fuera del alcance de uno; (*going to a higher authority*) por encima de uno; **to be out of one's head** (coll) delirar; **to come into one's head** pasarle a uno por la cabeza; **to go to one's head** subírsele a uno a la cabeza; **to keep one's head;** no perder la cabeza; **to head for** hacer o poner rumbo a; **to keep one's head above water** no dejarse vencer; **to put heads together** consultarse entre sí; **to not make head or tail of** no ver pies ni cabeza a ‖ *tr* acaudillar, dirigir, mandar; estar a la cabeza de (*p.ej., la clase*); venir primero en (*una lista*) ‖ *intr* — **to head towards** dirigirse hacia

head'ache' *s* dolor *m* de cabeza

head'band' *s* banda, cinta para la cabeza; (*of a book*) cabezada

head'board' *s* cabecera de cama

head'cheese' *s* queso de cerdo

head cold *s* resfriado

head count *s* recuento de personas

head'dress' *s* (*style of hair*) tocado; prenda para la cabeza

header [ˈhɛdər] *s* (compu) cabecera; **to take a header** (coll) caerse de cabeza

head'first' *adv* de cabeza; precipitadamente

head'gear' *s* sombrero; (*for protection*) casco

head'hunt'er *s* cazador *m* de cabezas

heading [ˈhɛdɪŋ] *s* encabezamiento; (*of a letter*) membrete *m;* (*of a chapter of a book*) cabecera

headland [ˈhɛdlənd] *s* promontorio

headless [ˈhɛdlɪs] *adj* sin cabeza; sin jefe; estúpido
head′light′ *s* (aut) faro; (naut) farol *m* de tope; (rr) farol *m*
head′line′ *s* (*of newspaper*) cabecera; (*of a page of a book*) titulillo, título de página ‖ *tr* poner cabecera a; (slang) destacar, dar cartel a (*un actor*)
head′lin′er *s* (slang) atracción principal
head′long′ *adj* de cabeza; precipitado ‖ *adv* de cabeza; precipitadamente
head•man [ˈhɛd,mæn] *s* (*pl* **-men** [,mɛn]) caudillo, jefe *m*
head′mas′ter *s* director *m* de un colegio
head′most′ *adj* delantero, primero
head office *s* oficina central, sede *f* social
head of hair *s* cabellera
head′-on′ *adj & adv* de frente; **head-on collision** colisión de frente
head′phone′ *s* auricular *m* de casco, receptor *m* de cabeza
head′piece′ *s* (*any covering for head*) casco, yelmo, morrión *m;* (*brains, judgment*) cabeza, juicio; cabecera de cama; (*headset*) auricular *m* de casco, receptor *m* de cabeza; (typ) cabecera, viñeta
head′quar′ters *s* centro de dirección, sede *f* social; (*of police*) jefatura; (mil) cuartel *m* general
head′rest′ *s* apoyo para la cabeza; (aut) reposa cabezas
head′set′ *s* auricular *m* de casco, receptor *m* de cabeza
head′ship′ *s* jefatura, dirección
head start *s* ventaja; (*program*) *programa de enseñanza preescolar para niños carenciados*
head′stone′ *s* (*cornerstone*) piedra angular; (*on a grave*) lápida sepulcral
head′stream′ *s* afluente *m* principal
head′strong′ *adj* cabezudo, terco
head′wait′er *s* jefe *m* de camareros, encargado de comedor
head′wa′ters *spl* cabecera
head′way′ *s* avance *m,* progreso; espacio libre; **to make headway** avanzar, progresar
head′wear′ *s* prendas de cabeza
head wind *s* viento de frente, viento por la proa
head′word *s* vocablo cabeza de artículo, lema *m*
head′work′ *s* trabajo intelectual
head•y [ˈhɛdi] *adj* (*comp* **-ier;** *super* **-iest**) excitante, emocionante; impetuoso, violento; (*intoxicating*) cabezudo; (*clever*) sesudo
heal [hil] *tr* curar, sanar; cicatrizar; remediar (*un daño*) ‖ *intr* curar, sanar; cicatrizarse; remediarse
healer [ˈhilər] *s* sanador *m*
health [hɛlθ] *s* salud *f;* **to be in good health** estar bien de salud; **to be in poor health** estar mal de salud; **to drink to the health of** beber a la salud de; **to radiate health** verter salud; **to your health!** ¡a su salud!
health care *s* asistencia sanitaria
health club *m* gimnasio
healthful [ˈhɛlθfəl] *adj* saludable; sano
health insurance *s* seguro de enfermedad
health•y [ˈhɛlθi] *adj* (*comp* **-ier;** *super* **-iest**) sano; saludable
heap [hip] *s* montón *m* ‖ *tr* amontonar, apilar; (*to supply with, e.g., favors*) colmar; (*to bestow in great quantity*) dar generosamente ‖ *intr* amontonarse, apilarse
hear [hɪr] *v* (*pret & pp* **heard** [hʌrd]) *tr* oír; **to hear it said** oírlo decir ‖ *intr* oír; **hear! hear!** ¡bravo!; **to hear about;** oír hablar de; **to hear from** tener noticias de; **to hear of** oír hablar de; **to hear tell of** oír hablar de; **to hear that** oír decir que
hearer [ˈhɪrər] *s* oyente *mf*
hearing [ˈhɪrɪŋ] *s* (*sense*) oído; (*act*) oída; audiencia; **in the hearing of** en presencia de; **within hearing** al alcance del oído
hearing aid *s* aparato auditivo, audífono
hear′say′ *s* rumores *mpl,* habladurías *fpl;* **by hearsay** de o por oídas; **hearsay evidence** testimonio de oídas
hearse [hʌrs] *s* coche *m* fúnebre, carroza fúnebre
heart [hɑrt] *s* corazón *m;* (*e.g., of lettuce*) cogollo; (cards) corazón (*baraja francesa*); **after one's heart** enteramente del gusto de uno; **by heart** de memoria; **heart and soul** de todo corazón; **hearts** (cards) un palo rojo de naipes representandos corazones estilizados y equivalente al palo de copas; **to break the heart of** partir el corazón de; **to die of a broken heart** morir de pena; **to eat one's heart out** sufrir en silencio; **to get to the heart of** llegar al fondo de; **to have one's heart in one's work;** trabajar con entusiasmo; **to have one's heart in the right place** tener buenas intenciones; **to lose heart** descorazonarse; **to open one's heart to** descubrirse con; **to take heart** cobrar aliento; **to take to heart** tomar a pecho; **to wear one's heart on one's sleeve** llevar el corazón en la mano; **with all one's heart** con toda el alma de uno; **with one's heart in one's mouth** con el credo en la boca
heart′ache′ *s* angustia, congoja
heart attack *s* ataque *m* al corazón, ataque cardíaco
heart′beat′ *s* latido del corazón
heart′break′ *s* angustia, dolor *m* abrumador
heart′break′er *s* ladrón *m* de corazones
heartbroken [ˈhɑrt,brokən] *adj* transido de dolor, muerto de pena
heart′burn′ *s* acedía, resculdera; (*jealousy*) celos
heart disease *s* enfermedad del corazón
hearten [ˈhɑrtən] *tr* alentar, animar
heart failure *s* debilidad coronaria, fallo cardíaco; (*death*) paro del corazón; (*faintness*) desfallecimiento, desmayo
heartfelt[ˈhɑrt,fɛlt] *adj* cordial, sentido, sincero
hearth [hɑrθ] *s* hogar *m*

hearth′stone′ *s* solera del hogar; (*home*) hogar *m*
heartily [ˈhɑrtɪli] *adv* cordialmente; con buen apetito; de buena gana; bien, mucho
heartless [ˈhɑrtlɪs] *adj* cruel, inhumano
heart′-lung′ machine *s* bomba corazón-pulmón
heart pacemaker *s* marcapaso, marcapasos *m*
heart rate *s* ritmo cardíaco
heart-rending [ˈhɑrt,rɛndɪŋ] *adj* angustioso, que parte el corazón
heart′seed′ *s* farolillo
heart′sick′ *adj* afligido, desconsolado
heart′strings′ *spl* fibras del corazón, entretelas
heart′-to-heart′ *adj* franco, sincero
heart trouble *s* — **to have heart trouble** enfermar del corazón
heart′wood′ *s* madera de corazón
heart•y [ˈhɑrti] *adj* (*comp* **-ier;** *super* **-iest**) cordial, sincero; sano, fuerte; (*meal*) abundante; (*laugh*) bueno; (*eater*) grande
heat [hit] *adj* térmico ‖ *s* calor *m;* (*warming of a room, house, etc.*) calefacción; (*rut of animals*) celo; (*in horse racing*) carrera de prueba; (fig) ardor *m,* ímpetu *m;* **in heat** en celo ‖ *tr* calentar; calefaccionar (*p.ej., una casa*); (fig) acalorar, excitar ‖ *intr* calentarse; (fig) acalorarse, excitarse
heated [ˈhitɪd] *adj* acalorado
heater [ˈhitər] *s* calentador *m;* (*for central heating*) calorífero; (electron) calefactor *m*
heath [hiθ] *s* (*shrub*) brezo; (*tract of land*) brezal *m*
hea•then [ˈhiðən] *adj* gentil, pagano; irreligioso ‖ *s* (*pl* **-then** o **-thens**) gentil *mf,* pagano
heathendom [ˈhiðəndəm] *s* gentilidad
heather [ˈhɛðər] *s* brezo
heating [ˈhitɪŋ] *adj* calentador ‖ *s* calefacción
heat′-in′su•lat•ed *adj* termoaislante
heat lightning *s* fucilazo, relámpago de calor
heat shield *s* blindaje térmico, escudo térmico
heat′stroke′ *s* insolación; golpe *m* de calor
heat wave *s* (phys) onda calorífica; (coll) ola de calor
heave [hiv] *s* esfuerzo para levantar; esfuerzo para levantarse; **heaves** (vet) huélfago ‖ *v* (*pret & pp* **heaved** o **hov** [hov]) *tr* alzar, levantar; arrojar, lanzar; exhalar (*un suspiro*) ‖ *intr* levantarse y bajar alternativamente; palpitar (*el pecho*); elevarse; hacer esfuerzos por vomitar
heaven [ˈhɛvən] *s* cielo; **for heaven's sake!** o **good heavens!** ¡válgame Dios!; **heavens** (*firmament*) cielo ‖ **Heaven** *s* cielo (*mansión de los bienaventurados*)
heavenly [ˈhɛvənli] *adj* (*body*) celeste; (*life, home*) celestial; (fig) celestial
heavenly body *s* astro, cuerpo celeste
heav•y [ˈhɛvi] *adj* (*comp* **-ier;** *super* **-iest**) (*of great weight*) pesado; (*liquid*) espeso, denso; (*cloth, paper, sea, line*) grueso; (*traffic*) denso; (*crop, harvest*) abundante, copioso; (*expense*) fuerte; (*rain*) recio; (*features*) basto; (*eyes*) agravado; (*gunfire*) fragoroso; (*heart*) abatido, triste; (*drinker*) grande; (*stock market*) postrado; (*clothing*) de mucho abrigo ‖ *adv* pesadamente; **to hang heavy;** pasar (*el tiempo*) con gran lentitud
heav′y•du′ty *adj* extrafuerte
heav′y han′ded *adj* torpe, inepto
heavy-hearted [ˈhɛviˈhɑrtɪd] *adj* afligido, acongojado
heav′y•set′ *adj* costilludo, espaldudo
heav′y•wa′ter *s* agua pesada
heav′y•weight′ *s* (box) peso pesado
Hebrew [ˈhibru] *adj & s* hebreo
hecatomb [ˈhɛkə,tom] *s* hecatombe *f*
heck [hɛk] *interj* (coll) ¡caray!; **what the heck** ¡qué diablos!
heckle [ˈhɛkəl] *tr* interrumpir (*a un orador*) con preguntas impertinentes
hectare [ˈhɛk,tɛr] *s* (*surface measurement: 2.5 acres*) hectárea
hectic [ˈhɛktɪk] *adj* (coll) agitado, turbulento
he'd *contr* **he had; he would**
hedge [hedʒ] *s* cercado, vallado; (*of bushes*) seto vivo; apuesta compensatoria; (*in stock market*) operación compensatoria ‖ *tr* cercar con vallado; cercar con seto vivo; **to hedge in** encerrar, rodear ‖ *intr* no querer comprometerse; hacer apuestas compensatorias; hacer operaciones compensatorias
hedge′hog′ *s* erizo; (*porcupine*) puerco espín *m*
hedge′hop′ *v* (*pret & pp* **-hopped;** *ger* **-hopping**) *intr* (aer) volar rasando el suelo
hedgehopping [ˈhɛdʒ,hɑpɪŋ] *s* (aer) vuelo rasante
hedge′row′ *s* cercado de arbustos, seto vivo
heed [hid] *s* atención, cuidado; **to take heed** ir con cuidado ‖ *tr* atender a, hacer caso de ‖ *intr* atender, hacer caso
heedless [ˈhidlɪs] *adj* desatento, descuidado
heehaw [ˈhi,hɔ] *s* (*of donkey*) rebuzno; risotada ‖ *intr* rebuznar; reír groseramente
heel [hil] *s* (*of foot*) calcañar *m,* talón *m;* (*of stocking or shoe*) talón *m;* (*raised part of shoe below heel*) tacón *m;* (slang) sinvergüenza *mf;* **down at the heel** desaliñado, mal vestido; **to cool one's heels** (coll) hacer antesala; **to kick up one's heels** (slang) mostrarse alegre; **to show a clean pair of heels** o **to take to one's heels** poner pies en polvorosa
heft•y [ˈhɛfti] *adj* (*comp* **-ier;** *super* **-iest**) (*heavy*) pesado; (*strong*) fuerte, fornido
hegemo•ny [hɪˈdʒɛməni] o [ˈhedʒɪ-,moni] *s* (*pl* **-nies**) hegemonía
heg., hej., o **h.** *abbr* (*honorific applied to someone who has made a pilgrimage to Mecca*) **hegira**
hegira [hɪˈdʒəɪrə] o [ˈhɛdʒɪrə] *s* fuga, huída; (eccl) hégira
heifer [ˈhɛfər] *s* novilla, vaquilla
height [hɑɪt] *s* altura; (*e.g., of folly*) colmo
heighten [ˈhaɪtən] *tr* hacer más alto; (*to increase the amount of*) aumentar; (*to set off, bring out*) realzar ‖ *intr* aumentarse
heinous [ˈhenəs] *adj* atroz, nefando

heir [ɛr] *s* heredero
heir apparent *s* (*pl* **heirs apparent**) heredero forzoso
heirdom [ˈɛrdəm] *s* herencia
heiress [ˈɛrɪs] *s* heredera
heirloom [ˈɛr,lum] *s* joya de familia, reliquia de familia
heist [haɪst] *s* (slang) golpe *m,* atraco
helicopter [ˈhɛlɪ,kɑptər] *s* helicóptero
heliotrope [ˈhilɪ•ə,trop] *s* heliotropo
heliport [ˈhɛlɪ,port] *s* helipuerto
helium [ˈhilɪ•əm] *s* helio
helix [ˈhilɪks] *s* (*pl* **helixes** o **helices** [ˈ*hɛlɪ,siz*]) hélice *f*
he'll (contr) **he will**
hell [hɛl] *s* infierno
hell-bent [ˈhɛlˈbɛnt] *adj* (slang) muy resuelto; **hell-bent on** (slang) empeñado en
hell'cat' *s* (*bad-tempered woman*) arpía, mujer perversa; (*witch*) bruja
hellebore [ˈhɛlɪ,bor] *s* eléboro
Hellene [ˈhɛlin] *s* heleno
Hellenic [hɛˈlɛnik] *adj* helénico
hell'fire' *s* fuego del infierno
hellish [ˈhɛlɪʃ] *adj* infernal
hel•lo [hɛˈlo] *s* saludo ‖ *interj* ¡qué tal!; (*on telephone*) ¡hola!, ¡aló! (Col), ¡dígame! (Mex), ¡buenó! (Mex)
helm [hɛlm] *s* barra del timón; rueda del timón; (fig) timón *m* ‖ *tr* dirigir, gobernar
helmet [ˈhɛlmɪt] *s* casco; (*of ancient armor*) yelmo
helms•man [ˈhɛlmzmən] *s* (*pl* **-men** [mən]) timonel *m*
help [hɛlp] *s* ayuda, socorro; (*of food*) ración; (*relief*) remedio, p.ej., **there's no help for it** no hay remedio; criados; empleados; obreros; **to come to the help of** acudir en socorro de ‖ *interj* ¡socorro! ‖ *tr* ayudar, socorrer; aliviar, mitigar; (*to wait on*) servir; **it can't be helped** no hay remedio; **so help me God!** ¡así Dios me salve!; **to help down** ayudar a bajar; **to help a person with his coat** ayudarle a una persona a ponerse el abrigo; **to help oneself** valerse por sí mismo; servirse; **to help up** ayudar a subir; ayudar a levantarse; **to not be able to help** + *ger* no poder menos de + *inf,* p.ej., **he can't help laughing** no puede menos de reír ‖ *intr* ayudar
helper [ˈhelpər] *s* ayudante *mf;* (*in a drug store, barbershop, etc.*) mancebo
helpful [ˈhɛlpfəl] *adj* útil, provechoso; servicial
helping [[ˈhɛlpɪŋ] *s* ración (*de alimento*)
helpless [ˈhɛlplɪs] *adj* (*weak*) débil; (*powerless*) impotente; (*penniless*) desvalido; (*confused*) perplejo; (*situation*) irremediable
help'mate' *s* compañero; (*wife*) compañera
helter-skelter [ˈhɛltərˈskɛltər] *adj, adv & s* cochite hervite *m*
hem [hɛm] *s* tos fingida; (*of a garment*) bastilla, dobladillo ‖ *interj* ¡ejem! ‖ *v* (*pret & pp* **hemmed;** *ger* **hemming**) *tr* bastillar, dobladillar; **to hem in** encerrar, rodear ‖ *intr* destoserse; vacilar; **to hem and haw** vacilar al hablar; ser evasivo
hemisphere [ˈhɛmɪ,sfɪr] *s* hemisferio
hemistich [ˈhɛmɪ,stɪk] *s* hemistiquio
hem'line' *s* ruedo de la falda, borde *m* de la falda
hem'lock' *s* (*Tsuga canadensis*) abeto del Canadá; (*herb and poison*) cicuta
hemoglobin [,hɛməˈglobɪn] o [,himəˈglobɪn] *s* hemoglobina
hemophilia [,hɛməˈfɪlɪ•ə] o [,himəˈfɪlɪ•ə] *s* hemofilia
hemorrhage [ˈhɛmərɪdʒ] *s* hemorragia
hemorrhoids [ˈhɛmə,rɔɪdz] *spl* hemorroides *fpl*
hemostat [ˈhɛmə,stæt] o [ˈhimə,stæt] *s* hemóstato
hemp [hɛmp] *s* cáñamo
hemstitch [ˈhɛm,stɪtʃ] *s* vainica ‖ *tr* hacer vainica en ‖ *intr* hacer vainica
hen [hɛn] *s* gallina
hence [hɛns] *adv* de aquí; desde ahora; por lo tanto, por consiguiente; de aquí a, p.ej., **three weeks hence** de aquí a tres semanas
hence'forth' *adv* de aquí en adelante
hench•man [ˈhɛntʃmən] *s* (*pl* **-men** [mən]) secuaz *m,* servidor *m;* muñidor *m*
hen'coop' *s* gallinero
hen'house' *s* gallinero
henna [ˈhɛnə] *s* alcana, alheña; (*dye*) henna *f* ‖ *tr* alheñarse (*el pelo*)
hen'peck' *tr* dominar (*la mujer al marido*)
henpecked husband *s* calzonazos *m,* gurrumino
Henry [ˈhɛnrɪ] *s* Enrique *m*
hep [hɛp] *adj* (slang) enterado; **to be hep to** (slang) estar al corriente de
hepatitis [ˈhɛpəˈtaɪtəs] *s* hepatitis *f*
her [hʌr] *adj poss* su; el . . . de ella ‖ *pron pers* la; ella; **to her** le; a ella
herald [ˈhɛrəld] *s* heraldo; anunciador *m* ‖ *tr* anunciar; ser precursor de
heraldic [hɛˈrældɪk] *adj* heráldico
herald•ry [ˈhɛrəldri] *s* (*pl* **-ries**) (*office or duty of herald*) heraldía; (*science of armorial bearings*) blasón *m,* heráldica; (*heraldic device; coat of arms*) blasón; pompa heráldica
herb [ʌrb] o [hʌrb] *s* hierba; hierba aromática; hierba medicinal
herbaceous [hʌrˈbeʃəs] *adj* herbáceo
herbage [ˈʌrbɪdʒ] o [ˈhʌrbɪdʒ] *s* herbaje *m*
herbal [ˈʌrbəl] o [ˈhʌrbəl] *adj & s* herbario
herbalist [ˈhʌrbəlɪst] o [ˈʌrbəlɪst] *s* herbolario
herbari•um [hʌrˈbɛrɪ•əm] *s* (*pl* **-ums** o **-a** [ə]) herbario
herb doctor *s* herbolario
herculean [hʌrˈkulɪ•ən] *adj* (*hard to perform*) penoso, laborioso; (*strong, big*) hercúleo
herd [hʌrd] *s* manada, rebaño, hato; (*of people*) chusma, multitud ‖ *tr* reunir en manada; reunir ‖ *intr* reunirse en manada; reunirse, ir juntos
herds•man [ˈhʌrdzmən] *s* (*pl* **-men** [mən]) manadero; (*of sheep*) pastor *m;* (*of cattle*) vaquero
here [hɪr] *adj* presente ‖ *adv* aquí; **here and**

there acá y allá; **here is** o **here are** aquí tiene Ud.; **that's neither here nor there** eso no viene al caso || *s* — **the here and the hereafter** esta vida y la futura || *interj* ¡presente!
hereabouts [ˈhɪrə,baʊts] *adv* por aquí, cerca de aquí
here•af'ter *adv* de aquí en adelante; en lo sucesivo; en la vida futura || **the hereafter** la otra vida, el más allá
here•by' *adv* por esto; por la presente
hereditary [hɪˈrɛdɪ,tɛri] *adj* hereditario
heredi•ty [hɪˈrɛdɪti] *s* (*pl* **-ties**) herencia
here•in' *adv* aquí dentro; en este asunto
here•of' *adv* de esto
here•on' *adv* en esto, sobre esto
here's *contr* **here is**
here•sy [ˈhɛrəsi] *s* (*pl* **-sies**) herejía
heretic [ˈhɛrətɪk] *adj* herético || *s* hereje *mf*
heretical [hɪˈrɛtɪkəl] *adj* herético
heretofore [,hɪtrʊˈfor] *adv* antes, hasta ahora
here'u•pon' *adv* en esto, sobre esto; en seguida
here•with' *adv* adjunto, con la presente; de este modo
heritage [ˈhɛrɪtɪdʒ] *s* herencia
hermetic(al) [hʌrˈmɛtɪk(əl)] *adj* hermético
hermit [ˈhʌrmɪt] *s* eremita *m*, ermitaño
hermitage [ˈhʌrmɪtɪdʒ] *s* ermita
herni•a [ˈhʌrnɪ•ə] *s* (*pl* **-as** o **-ae** [,i]) hernia
he•ro [ˈhɪro] *s* (*pl* **-roes**) héroe *m*
heroic [hɪˈro•ɪk] *adj* heroico || **heroics** *spl* verso heroico; lenguaje rimbombante
heroin [ˈhɛro•ɪn] *s* heroína (*polvo cristalino*); (slang) caballo
heroin addict *s* heroinómano
heroine [ˈhɛro•ɪn] *s* heroína (*mujer*)
heroism [ˈhɛro,ɪzəm] *s* heroísmo
heron [ˈhɛrən] *s* garza; (*Ardea cinerea*) airón *m*, garza real
herring [ˈhɛrɪŋ] *s* arenque *m*
her'ring•bone *s* (*in fabrics*) espina de pescado; (*in hardwood floors*) espinapez *m*, punto de Hungría
hers [hʌrz] *pron poss* el suyo, el de ella; suyo
herself [hʌrˈsɛlf] *pron pers* ella misma; sí, sí misma; se, p.ej., **she enjoyed herself** se divirtió; **with herself** consigo
he's *contr* **he is; he has**
hesitan•cy [ˈhɛzɪtənsi] *s* (*pl* **-cies**) vacilación
hesitant [ˈhɛzɪtənt] *adj* vacilante
hesitate [ˈhɛzɪ,tet] *intr* vacilar, titubear; (*to stutter*) titubear
hesitation [,hɛzɪˈteʃən] *s* vacilación
heterodox [ˈhɛtərə,dɑks] *adj* heterodoxo
heterodyne [ˈhɛtərə,daɪn] *adj* heterodino || *tr* heterodinar
heterogenei•ty [,hɛtərədʒɪˈni•ɪti] *s* (*pl* **-ties**) heterogeneidad
heterogeneous [,hɛtərəˈdʒinɪ•əs] *adj* heterogéneo
heterosexual [ˈhɛtəroˈsɛkʃʊəl] *adj & s* heterosexual *mf*
hew [hju] *v* (*pret* **hewed;** *pp* **hewed** o **hewn**) *tr* cortar, tajar; (*with an ax*) hachear; labrar (*madera*); picar (*piedra*); **to hew down** derribar a hachazos || *intr* — **to hew close to the line** (coll) hilar delgado
hex [hɛks] *s* (coll) bruja; (coll) hechizo || *tr* (coll) embrujar
hexameter [hɛksˈæmɪtər] *s* hexámetro
hey [he] *interj* ¡oye!, ¡oiga!
hey'day' *s* época de mayor prosperidad
hi [haɪ] *interj* (coll) ¡hola!, ¡oyé!
hia•tus [haɪˈetəs] *s* (*pl* **-tuses** o **-tus**) (*gap*) abertura, laguna; (*in a text; in verse*) hiato
hibernate [ˈhaɪbər,net] *intr* invernar; estar inactivo
hibiscus [hɪˈbɪskəs] o [haɪˈbɪskəs] *s* hibisco
hiccough o **hiccup** [ˈhɪkəp] *s* hipo || *intr* hipar
hick [hɪk] *adj & s* (coll) campesino, palurdo
hicko•ry [ˈhɪkəri] *s* (*pl* **-ries**) nuez encarcelada, nuez dura (*árbol*)
hickory nut *s* nuez encarcelada, nuez dura (*fruto*)
hidden [ˈhɪdən] *adj* escondido, oculto; obscuro
hide [haɪd] *s* cuero, piel *f;* **hides** corambre *f;* **neither hide nor hair** ni un vestigio; **to tan someone's hide** (coll) zurrarle a uno la badana || *v* (*pret* **hid** [hɪd]; *pp* **hid** o **hidden** [ˈhɪdən]) *tr* esconder, ocultar || *intr* esconderse, ocultarse; **to hide out** (coll) recatarse
hide'-and-seek' *s* escondite *m;* **to play hide-and-seek** jugar al escondite
hide'bound' *adj* fanático, obstinado, dogmático
hideous [ˈhɪdɪ•əs] *adj* (*very ugly*) feote; (*heinous*) atroz, nefando; (*distressingly large*) brutal, enorme
hide'-out' *s* (coll) guarida, refugio, escondrijo
hiding [ˈhaɪdɪŋ] *s* ocultación; (*place of concealment*) escondite *m*, escondrijo; **in hiding** escondido, oculto; (*in ambush*) emboscado
hiding place *s* escondite *m*, escondrijo
hie [haɪ] *v* (*pret & pp* **hied;** *ger* **hieing** o **hying**) *tr* — **hie thee home** apresúrate a volver a casa || *intr* apresurarse, ir volando
hierar•chy [ˈhaɪ•ə,rɑrki] *s* (*pl* **-chies**) jerarquía
hieroglyphic [,haɪ•ərəˈglɪfɪk] *adj & s* jeroglífico
hi-fi [ˈhaɪˈfaɪ] *adj* de alta fidelidad || *s* alta fidelidad
hi-fi fan *s* aficionado a la alta fidelidad
hi-fi set *s* equipo de alta fidelidad
hi-fi stereo sound *s* sonido estereofónico de alta fidelidad
higgledy-piggledy [ˈhɪgəldiˈpɪgəldi] *adj* confuso, revuelto || *adv* confusamente, revueltamente
high [haɪ] *adj* alto; (*river*) crecido; (*sound*) agudo; (*wind*) fuerte; (coll) borracho; (*intoxicated*) embriagado; (*drugs*) emporrado; (culin) manido; **high and dry** abandonado, desamparado; **high and mighty** (coll) muy arrogante || *adv* en sumo grado; a gran precio; **to aim high** poner el tiro muy alto; **to come high** venderse caro || *s* (aut) marcha directa; **on high** en el cielo
high altar *s* altar *m* mayor
high'ball' *s* highball *m*

high blood pressure *s* hipertensión arterial
high'born' *adj* linajudo, de ilustre cuna
high'boy' *s* cómoda alta con patas altas
high'brow' *adj & s* (coll) intelectual *mf*
high chair *s* silla alta
high command *s* alto mando
high cost of living *s* carestía de la vida
higher education *s* enseñanza superior
high'-end *s* (compu) gama alta
higher-up [ˌhaɪ•ərˈʌp] *s* (coll) superior jerárquico
high explosive *s* explosivo rompedor
highfalutin [ˌhaɪfəˈlutən] *adj* (coll) pomposo, presuntuoso
high fidelity *s* alta fidelidad
high'-fre'quency *adj* de alta frecuencia
high gear *s* marcha directa, toma directa
high'-grade' *adj* de calidad superior
high-handed [ˈhaɪˈhændɪd] *adj* arbitrario
high hat *s* sombrero de copa
high'-hat' *adj* (coll) copetudo, esnob; **to be high-hat** tener mucho copete ‖ **high'-hat'** *v* (*pret & pp* **-hatted;** *ger* **-hatting**) *tr* desairar
high-heeled shoe [ˈhaɪˌhild] *s* zapato de tacón alto
high horse *s* ademán *m* arrogante
high'jack' *tr* var de **hijack**
high jinks [dʒɪŋks] *spl* (slang) jarana, payasada
high jump *s* salto de altura
highland [ˈhaɪlənd] *s* región montañosa; **highlands** montañas, tierras altas
high life *s* alta sociedad, gran mundo
high'light' *s* elemento sobresaliente ‖ *tr* destacar
highlighter [ˈhaɪlaɪtər] *s* (*pen*) rotulador *m,* marcador *m*
highly [ˈhaɪli] *adv* altamente; en sumo grado; a gran precio; con aplauso general; **to speak highly of** decir mil bienes de
High Mass *s* misa cantada, misa mayor
high-minded [ˈhaɪˈmaɪndɪd] *adj* noble, magnánimo
highness [ˈhaɪnɪs] *s* altura ‖ **Highness** *s* Alteza
high noon *s* pleno mediodía
high-pitched [ˈhaɪˈpɪtʃt] *adj* agudo; tenso, impresionable
high-powered [ˈhaɪˈpaʊ•ərd] *adj* de alta potencia
high'-pres'sure *adj* de alta presión; (fig) emprendedor, enérgico ‖ *tr* (coll) apremiar
high-priced [ˈhaɪˈpraɪst] *adj* de precio elevado
high priest *s* sumo sacerdote
high'-rise *adj* de muchos pisos, de una torre ‖ *s* edificio de muchos pisos; torre *f* de apartamentos
high'-risk *adj* de alto riesgo
high'road' *s* camino real
high school *s* escuela de segunda enseñanza
high sea *s* mar gruesa; **high seas** alta mar
high society *s* alta sociedad, gran mundo
high'-speed' *adj* de alta velocidad
high-spirited [ˈhaɪˈspɪrɪtɪd] *adj* animoso; vivaz; (*horse*) fogoso
high spirits *spl* alegría, buen humor *m,* animación
high-strung [ˈhaɪˈstrʌŋ] *adj* tenso, impresionable
high-tech [ˈhaɪˈtɛk] *adj* de alta tecnología
high'-test' fuel *s* supercarburante *m*
high tide *s* pleamar *f,* marea alta; (fig) punto culminante
high time *s* hora, p.ej., **it is high time for you to go** ya es hora de que Ud. se marche; (slang) jarana, parranda
high treason *s* alta traición
high water *s* aguas altas; pleamar *f,* marea alta
high'wa'ter mark *s* línea de pleamar; (*highest point*) cénit *m,* apogeo
high'way' *s* carretera
highway•man [ˈhaɪˌwemən] *s* (*pl* **-men** [mən]) salteador *m* de caminos
high'way' robbery *s* (*unfair price*) robo a mano armada
high wire *s* cuerda floja
high'wire' artist *s* equilibrista *mf,* funámbulo
hijack [ˈhaɪˌdʒæk] *tr* (coll) robar (*a un contrabandista de licores*); (coll) robar (*el licor a un contrabandista*)
hijacker [ˈhaɪˌdʒækər] *s* pirata aéreo
hijacking [ˈhaɪˌdʒækɪŋ] *s* piratería aérea
hike [haɪk] *s* caminata, marcha; (*increase, rise*) aumento ‖ *tr* elevar de un tirón; aumentar ‖ *intr* dar una caminata
hiker [ˈhaɪkər] *s* caminador *m,* aficionado a las caminatas
hilarious [hɪˈlɛrɪ•əs] o [haɪˈlɛrɪ•əs] *adj* jubiloso, regocijado, animadísimo; (*comic*) comiquísimo, divertidísimo
hill [hɪl] *s* colina, collado ‖ *tr* aporcar (*las hortalizas*)
hillbil•ly [ˈhɪlˌbɪli] *s* (*pl* **-lies**) (coll) rústico montañés (*del sur de los EE.UU.*)
hillock [ˈhɪlək] *s* altozano, montecillo
hill'side' *s* ladera
hill'top' *s* cumbre *f,* cima
hill•y [ˈhɪli] *adj* (*comp* **-ier;** *super* **-iest**) colinoso; (*steep*) empinado
hilt [hɪlt] *s* empuñadura, puño; **up to the hilt** completamente
him [hɪm] *pron pers* le, lo; él; **to him** le; a él
himself [hɪmˈsɛlf] *pron pers* él mismo; sí, sí mismo; se, p.ej., **he enjoyed himself** se divirtió; **with himself** consigo
hind [haɪnd] *adj* posterior, trasero ‖ *s* cierva
hinder [ˈhɪndər] *tr* estorbar, impedir; obstruccionar
hindmost [ˈhaɪndˌmost] *adj* postrero, último
Hindoo [ˈhɪndu] *adj & s* hindú *m*
hind'quar'ter *s* cuarto trasero
hindrance [ˈhɪndrəns] *s* estorbo, impedimento, obstáculo
hind'sight' *s* (*of a firearm*) mira posterior; percepción tardía, sabiduría tardía
Hindu [ˈhɪndu] *adj & s* hindú *m*
hinge [hɪndʒ] *s* (*of a door*) charnela, gozne *m,* bisagra; (*of a mollusk*) charnela; (bb) car-

tivana; punto capital || *tr* engoznar || *intr* — **to hinge on** depender de

hin•ny [ˈhɪni] *s* (*pl* **-nies**) burdégano, mohino

hint [hɪnt] *s* indirecta, insinuación; **to take the hint** darse por aludido || *tr & intr* insinuar; indicar; **to hint at** aludir indirectamente a

hinterland [ˈhɪntər,lænd] *s* región interior

hip [hɪp] *s* cadera; (*of a roof*) caballete *m,* lima; **to shoot from the hip** (coll) no tener pelos en la lengua || *interj*—**hip, hip, hurrah!** ¡hurra!, ¡viva!

hip'bone' *s* cía, hueso de la cadera

hipped [hɪpt] *adj* (*livestock*) renco; (*roof*) a cuatro aguas; **hipped on** (coll) obsesionado por

hippety-hop [ˈhɪpɪtɪˈhɑp] *adv* (coll) a coxcojita

hip•po [ˈhɪpo] *s* (*pl* **-pos**) (coll) hipopótamo

hippodrome [ˈhɪpə,drom] *s* hipódromo

hippopota•mus [,hipəˈpɑtəməs] *s* (*pl* **-muses** o **-mi** [,maɪ]) hipopótamo

hippy o **hippie** [ˈhɪpi] *s* (*pl* **-pies**) hippy *mf,* melenudo

hip roof *s* tejado a cuatro aguas

hire [haɪr] *s* alquiler *m;* precio; salario; **for hire** de alquiler || *tr* alquilar (*p.ej., un coche*); ajustar (*p.ej., a un criado*) || *intr* —**to hire out** ajustarse

hired girl *s* (coll) criada

hired man *s* (coll) mozo de campo

hireling [ˈhaɪrlɪŋ] *adj & s* alquiladizo

his [hɪz] *adj poss* su; el . . . de él || *pron poss* el suyo, el de él; suyo

Hispanic [hɪsˈpanɪk] *adj & s* hispánico

Hispaniola [,hɪspənˈjolə] *s* Santo Domingo

hispanist [ˈhɪspənɪst] *s* hispanista *mf*

hispanophilia [hɪs,pænoˈfɪli•ə] *s* españolería

hiss [hɪs] *s* siseo, silbido || *tr* sisear, silbar (*p.ej., una escena, a un actor por malo*) || *intr* sisear, silbar

histology [hɪsˈtɑlədʒi] *s* histología

historian [hɪsˈtorɪ•ən] *s* historiador *m*

historic(al) [hɪsˈtɔrɪk(əl)] *adj* histórico

histo•ry [ˈhɪstəri] *s* (*pl* **-ries**) historia

histrionic [,hɪstrɪˈɑnɪk] *adj* histriónico; teatral || **histrionics** *s* actitud teatral, modales *mpl* teatrales

hit [hɪt] *s* golpe *m;* (*of a bullet*) impacto; (*blow that hits its mark*) tiro certero; (*sarcastic remark*) cansura acerba; (baseball) batazo; (coll) éxito; **to make a hit** (coll) dar golpe; **to make a hit with** caer en la gracia de (*una persona*) || *v* (*pret & pp* **hit;** *ger* **hitting**) *tr* golpear, pegar; dar con, dar contra, chocar con; dar en (*p.ej., el blanco*); censurar acerbamente; (*to run over in a car*) atropellar; afectar mucho (*un acontecimiento a una persona*); **to hit it off with** congeniar con || *intr* chocar; **to hit against** dar contra; **to hit on** (*an idea*) dar con (*lo que se busca*); (*to make sexual advances to*) (coll) tratar deligarse con

hit'-and-run' *adj* que atropella y se da a la huída

hitch [hɪtʃ] *s* (*jerk*) tirón *m;* dificultad; obstáculo; **without a hitch** a pedir de boca, sin tropiezo || *tr* (*to tie*) atar, sujetar; enganchar (*un caballo*); uncir (*bueyes*); (slang) casar

hitch'hike' *intr* (coll) hacer autostop, viajar en autostop

hitch'hik'er *s* autostopista *mf*

hitching post *s* poste *m* para atar a las cabalgaduras

hither [ˈhɪðər] *adv* acá, hacia acá; **hither and thither** acá y allá

hith'er•to' *adv* hasta ahora, hasta aquí

hit'-or-miss' *adj* descuidado, casual

hit record *s* (coll) disco de mucho éxito

hit'-run' *adj* que atropella y se da a la huída

HIV [ˈeɪtʃˈaɪˈvi] *s* (letterword) (**Human Immunodeficiency Virus**) VIH *m* (Virus de Inmunodeficiencia Humana)

HIV positive *adj* seropositivo; **to be HIV positive** ser portador del virus del SIDA

hive [haɪv] *s* (*box for bees*) colmena; (*swarm*) enjambre *m;* **hives** (pathol) urticaria || *tr* encorchar (*abejas*)

hoard [hord] *s* (*of money, provisions, etc.*) cúmulo; tesoro escondido || *tr* acumular secretamente; atesorar (*dinero*) || *intr* guardar víveres, atesorar dinero

hoarding [ˈhordɪŋ] *s* acumulación secreta; atesoramiento

hoar'frost' *s* helada blanca, escarcha

hoarse [hors] *adj* ronco

hoarseness [ˈhorsnɪs] *s* ronquedad; (*from a cold*) ronquera

hoar•y [ˈhori] *adj* (*comp* **-ier;** *super* **-iest**) cano, canoso; (*old*) vetusto

hoax [hoks] *s* pajarota, mistificación || *tr* mistificar

hobble [ˈhɑbəl] *s* (*limp*) cojera; (*rope used to tie legs of animal*) manea, traba || *tr* dejar cojo; manear, trabar; dificultar || *intr* cojear; tambalear

hobble skirt *s* falda de medio paso

hob•by [ˈhɑbi] *s* (*pl* **-bies**) comidilla, afición favorita, trabajo preferido; **to ride a hobby** entregarse demasiado al tema favorito

hob'by•horse' *s* (*stick with horse's head*) caballito; (*rocking horse*) caballo mecedor

hob'gob'lin *s* duende *m,* trasgo; (*bogy*) bu *m,* coco

hob'nail' *s* tachuela || *tr* clavetear con tachuelas; (fig) atropellar

hob•nob [ˈhɑb,nɑb] *v* (*pret & pp* **-nobbed;** *ger* **-nobbing**) *intr* codearse, rozarse; beber juntos

ho•bo [ˈhobo] *s* (*pl* **-bos** o **-boes**) vagabundo

Hobson's choice [ˈhɑbsənz] *s* alternativa entre la cosa ofrecida o ninguna

hock [hɑk] *s* jarrete *m,* corvejón *m* || *tr* (*to hamstring*) desjarretar; (coll) empeñar

hockey [ˈhɑki] *s* hockey *m,* chueca

hock'shop' *s* (slang) casa de empeños, monte *m* de piedad

hocus-pocus [ˈhokəsˈpokəs] *s* (*meaningless formula*) abracadabra *m;* burla, engaño; juego de manos

hod [hɑd] *s* capacho, cuezo; cubo para carbón

hodgepodge [ˈhɑdʒ,pɑdʒ] *s* baturrillo
hoe [ho] *s* azada, azadón *m* || *tr & intr* azadonar
hog [hɑg] o [hɔg] *s* cerdo, puerco || *v* (*pret & pp* **hogged;** *ger* **hogging**) *tr* (slang) tragarse lo mejor de
hoggish [ˈhɑgɪʃ] o [ˈhɔgɪʃ] *adj* comilón; glotón; egoísta
hogs'head' *s* pipa de 63 galones o más; medida de capacidad de 63 galones
hog'wash' *s* bazofia; (fig) disparates *mpl,* tonterías
hoist [hɔɪst] *s* (*apparatus for lifting*) montacargas *m,* torno izador, grúa; empujón *m* hacia arriba || *tr* alzar, levantar; enarbolar (*p.ej., una bandera*); (naut) izar
hoity-toity [ˈhɔɪtiˈtɔɪti] *adj* frívolo, veleidoso; arrogante, altanero; **to be hoity-toity** ponerse tan alto
hokum [ˈhokəm] *s* (coll) música celestial, tonterías
hold [hold] *s* (*grip*) agarro; (*handle*) asa, mango; autoridad, dominio; (*in wrestling*) presa; (aer) cabina de carga; (*electron*) sostén *m;* (mus) calderón *m;* (naut) bodega; (telv) control *m* de imagen; **to be on hold** (telp) estar esperando; **to take hold of** agarrar, coger; apoderarse de || *v* (*pret & pp* **held** [hɛld]) *tr* tener, retener; (*to hold up, support*) apoyar, sostener; (*e.g., with a pin*) sujetar; contener, tener cabida para; ocupar (*un cargo, puesto, etc.*); celebrar (*una reunión*); sostener (*una opinión*); (mus) sostener (*una nota*); **hold the line, please** no cuelgue, por favor; **to hold back** detener; retener; contener; **to hold in** refrenar; **to hold one's own** mantenerse firme, no perder terreno; **to hold over** aplazar, diferir; **to hold up** apoyar, sostener; (*to rob*) (coll) atracar || *intr* ser valedero, seguir vigente; pegarse; **hold on!** ¡un momento!; **to hold back** refrenarse; **to hold forth** poner cátedra; **to hold off** esperar; mantenerse a distancia; **to hold on** agarrarse bien; **to hold on to** asirse de; **to hold out** no cejar; ir tirando; **to hold out for** insistir en
hold button *s* botón *m* de sostén
holder [ˈholdər] *s* tenedor *m,* posesor *m;* (*for a cigar or cigaret*) boquilla; (*to hold, e.g., a hot plate*) cojinillo; (*e.g., of a passport*) titular *m;* asa, mango
holding [ˈholdɪŋ] *s* tenencia, posesión; **holdings** valores habidos
holding company *s* sociedad de control, compañía tenedora, holding *m*
hold'out *s* persona que mantiene su negativa
hold'o'ver *s* remanente *m;* (mov, theat) continuación en cartel
hold'up' *s* (*stop, delay*) detención; atraco, asalto; precio excesivo
hole [hol] *s* agujero; (*in cheese, bread, etc.*) ojo; (*in a road*) bache *m;* (*den of animals; den of vice*) guarida; (*dirty, disorderly dwelling*) cochitril *m;* **eighteenth hole** (golf) decimoctavo hoyo; **hole in one** (golf) hoyo en uno; **in the hole** adeudado, perdidoso; **to burn a hole in one's pocket** írsele a uno (*el dinero*) de entre las manos; **to pick holes in** (coll) poner reparos a || *intr* — **to hole up** encovarse; buscar un rincón cómodo
holiday [ˈhɑlɪ,de] *s* día festivo; vacación
holiness [ˈholɪnɪs] *s* santidad; **his Holiness** su Santidad
Holland [ˈhɑlənd] *s* Holanda
Hollander [ˈhɑləndər] *s* holandés *m*
hollow [ˈhɑlo] *adj* hueco; (*voice*) ahuecado, sepulcral; (*eyes, cheeks*) hundido; falso, engañoso || *adv* — **to beat all hollow** (coll) derrotar completamente || *s* hueco, cavidad; (*small valley*) vallecito || *tr* ahuecar, excavar
hol•ly [ˈhɑli] *s* (*pl* **-lies**) acebo
hol'ly•hock' *s* malva arbórea
Hol'ly•wood' *s* distrito de estudios cinematográficos; (fig) el mundo del espectáculo
holm oak [hom] *s* encina
holocaust [ˈhɑlə,kɔst] *s* holocausto
hologram [ˈhɑləgræm] *s* holograma *m*
holography [hoˈlɑgrəfɪ] *s* holografía
holster [ˈholstər] *s* pistolera
ho•ly [ˈholi] *adj* (*comp* **-lier;** *super* **-liest**) santo; (*e.g., writing*) sagrado; (*e.g., water*) bendito
Holy Ghost *s* Espíritu Santo
holy orders *spl* órdenes sagradas; **to take holy orders** recibir las órdenes sagradas, ordenarse
Holy Scripture *s* Sagrada Escritura
Holy See *s* Santa Sede
Holy Sepulcher *s* santo sepulcro
Holy Spirit *s* Espíritu Santo
holy water *s* agua bendita
Holy Writ *s* Sagrada Escritura
homage [ˈhɑmɪdʒ] o [ˈɑmɪdʒ] *s* homenaje *m;* (feud) homenaje, pleito homenaje
home [hom] *adj* casero, doméstico; nacional || *s* casa, domicilio, hogar *m;* (*native heath*) patria chica; (*of the arts, etc.*) patria; (*for the sick, poor, etc.*) asilo; (sport) meta; **at home** en casa; en su propio país; (*ready to receive callers*) de recibo; (*at ease, comfortable*) a gusto; (sport) en campo propio; **away from home** fuera de casa; **make yourself at home** está Ud. en su casa || *adv* en casa; a casa; **to see home** acompañar a casa; **to strike home** dar en lovivo || *intr* volver a casa; (aer) autodirigirse; **to home in on** acércarse a, centrarse en
home'bod'y *s* (*pl* **-ies**) hogareño
homebred [ˈhom,brɛd] *adj* doméstico; sencillo, inculto, tosco
home'brew' *s* cerveza o vino caseros
homecoming [ˈhom,kʌmɪŋ] *s* regreso al hogar
home computer *s* ordenador doméstico, computadora doméstica
home country *s* suelo natal
home delivery *s* distribución a domicilio
home front *s* frente doméstico
home'land' *s* tierra natal, patria
homeless [ˈhomlɪs] *adj* sin casa, sin hogar
home life *s* vida de familia

home-loving [ˈhom,lʌvɪŋ] *adj* casero, hogareño
home•ly [ˈhomli] *adj* (*comp* **-lier;** *super* **-liest**) (*not attractive or good-looking*) feo; (*plain, not elegant*) sencillo, llano
homemade [ˈhomˈmed] *adj* casero, hecho en casa
homemaker [ˈhom,mekər] *s* ama de casa
home office *s* domicilio social, oficina central ‖ **Home Office** *s* (Brit) ministerio de la Gobernación
homeopath [ˈhomɪ•ə,pæθ] o [ˈhɑmɪ•ə,pæθ] *s* homeópata *mf*
homeopathy [,homɪˈɑpəθi] o [,hɑmɪˈɑpəθi] *s* homeopatía
home owner *s* propietario de una vivienda
home plate *s* (baseball) puesto meta
home port *s* puerto de origen
homer *var* de **home run**
home rule *s* autonomía, gobierno autónomo
home run *s* (baseball) jonrón *m,* cuadrangular *m*
home′sick′ *adj* nostálgico; **to be homesick (for)** sentir nostalgia (de)
home′sick′ness *s* nostalgia, mal *m* de la tierra
homespun [ˈhom,spʌn] *adj* hilado en casa; sencillo, llano
home′stead′ *s* casa y terrenos, heredad
home stretch *s* esfuerzo final, último trecho
home team *s* equipo local o de casa
home town *s* ciudad natal
homeward [ˈhomwərd] *adj* de regreso ‖ *adv* hacia casa; hacia su país
home′work′ *s* trabajo a domicilio; (*of a student*) deber *m,* trabajo escolar
homey [ˈhomi] *adj* (*comp* **homier;** *super* **homiest**) (coll) íntimo, cómodo
homicidal [,hɑmɪˈsaɪdəl] *adj* homicida
homicide [ˈhɑmɪ,saɪd] *s* (*act*) homicidio; (*person*) homicida *mf*
homi•ly [ˈhɑmɪli] *s* (*pl* **-lies**) homilía
homing [ˈhomɪŋ] *adj* (*animal*) querencioso; (*weapon*) buscador del blanco
homing pigeon *s* paloma mensajera
hominy [ˈhɑmɪni] *s* maíz molido
homogenei•ty [,hɑmədʒɪˈni•ɪti] *s* (*pl* **-ties**) homogeneidad
homogeneous [,hɑməˈdʒinɪ•əs] *adj* homogéneo
homogenize [həˈmɑdʒə,naɪz] *tr* homogeneizar
homonym [ˈhɑmənɪm] *s* homónimo
homonymous [həˈmɑnɪməs] *adj* homónimo
homosexual [,hɑməˈsɛkʃʊ•əl] *adj & s* homosexual *mf*
Honduran [hɑnˈdʊrən] *adj & s* hondureño
hone [hon] *s* piedra de afilar ‖ *tr* afilar, amolar, asentar
honest [ˈɑnɪst] *adj* honrado, probo, recto; (*money*) bien adquirido; sincero; genuino
honesty [ˈɑnɪsti] *s* honradez *f,* probidad, rectitud; (bot) hierba de la plata
hon•ey [ˈhʌni] *adj* meloso, dulce; (coll) querido ‖ *s* miel *f;* (coll) vida mía; **it's a honey** (slang) es una preciosidad ‖ *v* (*pret & pp* **-eyed** o **-ied**) *tr* enmelar, endulzar con miel; adular, lisonjear
hon′ey•bee′ *s* abeja doméstica, abeja de miel
hon′ey•comb′ *s* panal *m* ‖ *tr* (*to riddle*) acribillar; llenar, penetrar
hon′ey•dew′ melon *s* melón muy dulce, blanco y terso
honeyed [ˈhʌnid] *adj* dulce, enmelado; melodioso; adulador
honey locust *s* acacia de tres espinas
hon′ey•moon′ *s* luna de miel; viaje *m* de bodas ‖ *intr* pasar la luna de miel
honeysuckle [ˈhʌni,sʌkəl] *s* madreselva
honk [hɑŋk] *s* (*of wild goose*) graznido; (*of automobile horn*) bocinazo ‖ *tr* tocar (*la bocina*) ‖ *intr* graznar (*el ganso silvestre*); tocar la bocina
honkytonk [ˈhɑŋki,tɑŋk] *s* (slang) sala de fiestas de mala muerte
honor [ˈɑnər] *s* (*distinction; award for distinction; integrity*) honor *m;* (*good reputation; chastity*) honor, honra ‖ *tr* honrar; hacer honor a (*su firma*); aceptar y pagar (*una letra*)
honorable [ˈɑnərəbəl] *adj* (*behaving with honor; performed with honor*) honrado; (*bringing honor; associated with honor*) honroso; (*worthy, of honor*) honorable
honorary [ˈɑnə,rɛri] *adj* honorario
honorific [,ɑnəˈrɪfɪk] *adj* honorífico ‖ *s* antenombre *m*
honor system *s* acatamiento voluntario del reglamento
hood [hʊd] *s* capilla; (*one with a point*) caperuza; (*one which covers the face*) capirote *m;* (*worn with academic gown*) muceta, capirote *m;* (*of a chimney*) sombrerete *m;* (aut) capó *m,* cubierta; (slang) gamberro ‖ *tr* encapirotar; ocultar
hoodlum [ˈhudləm] *s* (coll) gamberro, maleante *m*
hoodoo [ˈhudu] *s* (*body of primitive rites*) vudú *m;* (coll) mala suerte ‖ *tr* traer mala suerte a
hood′wink′ *tr* burlar, engañar, vendar
hooey [ˈhu•i] *s* (slang) música celestial
hoof [huf] o [hʊf] *s* casco, pezuña; **on the hoof** (*cattle*) vivo, en pie ‖ *tr & intr* (coll) caminar; **to hoof it** (coll) caminar, ir a pie; (coll) bailar
hoof′-and-mouth′ disease *s* (vet) fiebre aftosa, glosopeda
hoof′beat′ *s* pisada, ruido de la pisada (*de animal ungulado*)
hook [hʊk] *s* gancho; (*for fishing*) anzuelo; (*to join two things*) enganche *m;* (*bend, curve*) ángulo, recodo; (box) crochet *m,* golpe *m* de gancho; (*of hook and eye*) corchete *m,* macho; **by hook or by crook** por fas o por nefas; **to swallow the hook;** tragar el anzuelo ‖ *tr* enganchar; (*to bend*) encorvar, doblar; coger, pescar (*un pez*); (*to wound with the horns*) acornar ‖ *intr* engancharse; encorvarse, doblarse
hookah [ˈhʊkə] *s* narguile *m*

hook and eye *s* broche *m,* corchete *m* (*macho y hembra*)
hook and ladder *s* carro de escaleras de incendio
hooked rug *s* tapete *m* de crochet
hook'nose' *s* nariz *f* de pico de loro
hook'up' *s* montaje *m*
hook'worm' *s* anquilostoma *m*
hooky [ˈhʊki] *s* — **to play hooky** hacer novillos
hooligan [ˈhulɪgən] *s* gamberro
hooliganism [ˈhulɪgən,ɪzəm] *s* gamberrismo
hoop [hup] o [hʊp] *s* aro ‖ *tr* herrar, enarcar, enzunchar
hoop skirt *s* miriñaque *m*
hoot [hut] *s* resoplido, ululato; grito ‖ *tr* reprobar a gritos; echar a gritos (*p.ej., a un cómico*) ‖ *intr* resoplar, ulular; **to hoot at** dar grita a
hoot owl *s* autillo, cárabo
hop [hɑp] *s* saltito; (coll) vuelo en avión; (coll) sarao; (coll) baile *m;* lúpulo, hombrecillo; **hops** (*dried flowers of hop vine*) lúpulo ‖ *v* (*pret & pp* **hopped;** *ger* **hopping**) *tr* cruzar de un salto; (coll) atravesar (*p.ej., el mar*) en avión; (coll) subir a (*un tren, taxi, etc.*) ‖ *intr* saltar, brincar; (*on one foot*) saltar a la pata coja
hope [hop] *s* esperanza ‖ *tr & intr* esperar; **to hope for** esperar
hope chest *s* ajuar *m* de novia
hopeful [ˈhopfəl] *adj* (*feeling hope*) esperanzado; (*giving hope*) esperanzador
hopefully [ˈhopfəli] *adv* (*expectantly*) expectante, esperanzadamente; (*it is to be hoped*) se espera es de esperarse, si Dios quiere
hopeless [ˈhoplɪs] *adj* desesperanzado, (*situation*) desesperado
hopper [ˈhɑpər] *s* (*funnel-shaped container*) tolva; (*of blast furnace*) tragante *m;* (compu) dispositivo de alimentación
hopper car *s* (rr) vagón *m* tolva
hop'scotch' *s* infernáculo
horde [hord] *s* horda
horehound [ˈhor,haʊnd] *s* marrubio; extracto de marrubio
horizon [həˈraɪzən] *s* horizonte *m*
horizontal [,hɑrɪˈzɑntəl] o [,hɔrɪˈzɑntəl] *adj & s* horizontal *f*
hormone [ˈhɔrmon] *s* hormón *m* u hormona
horn [hɔrn] *s* (*bony projection on head of certain animals*) cuerno; (*of bull*) asta, cuerno; (*of moon, anvil, etc.*) cuerno; (*of automobile*) bocina; (mus) cuerno; (*French horn*) (mus) trompa de armonía; **to blow one's own horn** cantar sus propias alabanzas; **to pull in one's horns** contenerse, volverse atrás ‖ *intr* — **to horn in** (slang) entrometerse (en)
hornet [ˈhɔrnɪt] *s* crabrón *m,* avispón *m*
hornet's nest *s* panal *m* del avispón; **to stir up a hornet's nest** (coll) armar camorra, armar cisco
horn of plenty *s* cuerno de la abundancia
horn'pipe' *s* chirimía
horn-rimmed glasses [ˈhɔrnˈrɪmd] *spl* anteojos de concha
horn•y [ˈhɔrni] *adj* (*comp* **-ier;** *super* **-iest**) córneo; (*callous*) calloso; (*having hornlike projections*) cornudo; (slang) caliente, cachondo (Esp)
horoscope [ˈhɑrə,skop] o [ˈhɔrə,skop] *s* horóscopo; **to cast a horoscope** sacar un horóscopo
horrible [ˈhɑrɪbəl] o [ˈhɔrɪbəl] *adj* horrible; (coll) muy desagradable
horrid [ˈhɑrɪd] o [ˈhɔrɪd] *adj* horroroso; (coll) muy desagradable
horri•fy [ˈhɑrɪ,faɪ] o [ˈhɔrɪ,faɪ] *v* (*pret & pp* **-fied**) *tr* horrorizar
horror [ˈhɑrər] o [ˈhɔrər] *s* horror *m;* **to have a horror of** tener horror a
horror movie *s* película de terror, película horripilante
hors d'oeuvre [ɔrˈdʌrv] *s* (*pl* **hors d'oeuvres** [ɔrˈdʌrvz]) *s* entremés *m*
horse [hɔrs] *s* caballo; (*of carpenter*) caballete *m;* **hold your horses** (coll) pare Ud. el carro; **to back the wrong horse** (coll) jugar a la carta mala; **to be a horse of another color** (coll) ser harina de otro costal
horse'back' *s* — **on horseback** a caballo ‖ *adv* — **to ride horseback** montar a caballo
horseback riding *s* hípica
horse blanket *s* manta para caballo
horse'break'er *s* domador *m* de caballos
horse'car' *s* tranvía *m* de sangre; (*for transporting horses*) remolque *m,* trailer *m*
horse chestnut *s* (*tree*) castaño de Indias; (*nut*) castaña de Indias
horse collar *s* collera
horse dealer *s* chalán *m*
horse doctor *s* veterinario
horse'fly' *s* (*pl* **-flies**) mosca borriquera, tábano
horse'hair' *s* crines *fpl* de caballo; (*fabric*) tela de crin
horse'hide' *s* cuero de caballo
horse laugh *s* risotada
horse•man [ˈhɔrsmən] *s* (*pl* **-men** [mən]) jinete *m,* caballista *m*
horsemanship [ˈhɔrsmən,ʃɪp] *s* equitación, manejo
horse meat *s* carne *f* de caballo
horse opera *s* (U.S.A.) melodrama *m* del Oeste
horse pistol *s* pistola de arzón
horse'play' *s* chanza pesada, payasada
horse'pow'er *s* caballo de vapor inglés
horse race *s* carrera de caballos
horse'rad'ish *s* (*plant*) rábano picante o rusticano; (*condiment*) mostaza de los alemanes
horse sense *s* (coll) sentido común
horse'shoe' *s* herradura
horseshoe magnet *s* imán *m* de herradura
horseshoe nail *s* clavo de herrar
horse show *s* concurso hípico
horse'tail' *s* cola de caballo
horse thief *s* abigeo, cuatrero
horse'-trade' *intr* chalanear
horse trading *s* chalanería

horse'-trad'ing *adj* chalanesco
horse'whip' *s* látigo || *v* (*pret & pp* **-whipped;** *ger* **-whipping**) *tr* dar latigazos a
horse•woman [ˈhɔrs,wʊmən] *s* (*pl* **-women** [,wɪmɪn]) amazona, caballista *f*
hors•y [ˈhɔrsi] *adj* (*comp* **-ier;** *super* **-iest**) caballar, hípico; (*interested in horses and horse racing*) carrerista, turfista; (coll) desmañado
horticultural [,hɔrtɪˈkʌltʃərəl] *adj* hortícola
horticulture [ˈhɔrtɪ,kʌltʃər] *s* horticultura
horticulturist [,hɔrtɪˈkʌltʃərɪst] *s* horticultor *m*
hose [hoz] *s* (*stocking*) media; (*sock*) calcetín *m;* (*flexible tube*) manguera || **hose** *spl* calzas
hosier [ˈhoʒər] *s* mediero, calcetero
hosiery [ˈhoʒəri] *s* calcetas; calcetería
hospice [ˈhɑspɪs] *s* hospicio
hospitable [ˈhɑspɪtəbəl] o [hɑsˈpɪtəbəl] *adj* hospitalario
hospital [ˈhɑspɪtəl] *s* hospital *m*
hospital complex *s* ciudad sanitaria
hospitali•ty [,hɑspɪˈtælɪti] *s* (*pl* **-ties**) hospitalidad
hospitalize [ˈhɑspɪtə,laɪz] *tr* hospitalizar
host [host] *s* anfitrión *m,* anfitriona, huésped *m,* huéspeda; (*innkeeper*) mesonero, posadero; (*army*) hueste *m;* (*great number*) multitud, muchedumbre; (*fed on by a parasite*) huésped *m;* (compu) ordenador que controla las comunicaciones en una red que administra una base de datos; (rad, telv, theat) presentador *m,* animador *m* || **Host** *s* (eccl) hostia || *tr* (*a meal, function*) organizar; (rad, telv, theat) presentar
hostage [ˈhɑstɪdʒ] *s* rehén *m;* **to be held a hostage** quedar en rehenes
hostel•ry [ˈhɑstəlri] *s* (*pl* **-ries**) parador *m,* hostería
hostess [ˈhostɪs] *s* anfitriona; dueña, patrona; (*in a night club*) tanguista; azafata; (*e.g., on a bus*) jefa de ruta
hostile [ˈhɑstɪl] *adj* hostil
hostili•ty [hɑsˈtɪlɪti] *s* (*pl* **-ties**) hostilidad
hostler [ˈhɑslər] o [ˈɑslər] *s* mozo de cuadra, mozo de paja y cebada
hot [hɑt] *adj* (*comp* **hotter;** *super* **hottest**) (*water, air, coffee, etc.*) caliente; (*climate, country; taste*) cálido; (*fiery, excitable*) caluroso; (*pursuit*) enérgico; (*in rut*) caliente; (coll) muy radiactivo; **to be hot** (*said of a person*) tener calor; (*said of the weather*) hacer calor; **to make it hot for** (coll) hostilizar
hot air *s* (slang) palabrería, música celestial
hot'-air' balloon *s* globo de aire caliente
hot'-air' furnace *s* calorífero de aire
hot and cold running water *s* circulación de agua fría y caliente
hot baths *spl* caldas, termas
hot'bed' *s* (hort) almajara; (*e.g., of vice*) sementera, semillero
hot-blooded [ˈhɑtˈblʌdɪd] *adj* apasionado; temerario, irreflexivo
hot cake *s* torta a la plancha; **to sell like hot cakes** (coll) venderse como pan bendito
hot dog *s* perro caliente, pancho (SAm) || *interj* (slang) ¡caray!
hotel [hoˈtɛl] *adj* hotelero || *s* hotel *m*
ho•tel'-keep'er *s* hotelero
hotel room *s* habitación de hotel
hot'head' *s* botafuego
hot-headed [ˈhɑtˈhɛdɪd] *adj* caliente de cascos
hot'house' *s* estufa, invernáculo
hot'line' *s* teléfono rojo
hot plate *s* hornillo, calientaplatos *m*
hot'spot' *s* (compu) área sensible
hot springs *spl* fuentes *fpl* termales
hot-tempered [ˈhɑtˈtɛmpərd] *adj* irascible
hot water *s* — **to be in hot water** (coll) estar en calzas prietas
hot-water bottle *s* bolsa de agua caliente
hot-water heater *s* calentador *m* de acumulación
hot-water heating *s* calefacción por agua caliente
hot-water tank *s* depósito de agua caliente
hound [haʊnd] *s* podenco, perro de caza, perro lebrel; **to follow the hounds** o **to ride the hounds** cazar a caballo con jauría || *tr* acosar, hostigar
hour [aʊr] *s* hora; **by the hour** por horas; **in an evil hour** en hora mala; **on the hour** a la hora en punto cada hora; **to keep late hours** acostarse tarde; **to work long hours** trabajar muchas horas cada día
hour'glass' *s* reloj *m* de arena
hour hand *s* horario, horero
hourly [ˈaʊrli] *adj* de cada hora; por hora || *adv* cada hora; muy a menudo
house [haʊs] *s* (*pl* **houses** [ˈhaʊzɪz]) casa; (*legislative body*) cámara; teatro; (*size of audience*) entrada, p.ej., **a good house** mucha entrada; **to keep house** tener casa puesta; hacer los que haceres domésticos; **to put one's house in order** arreglar sus asuntos || [haʊz] *tr* domiciliar, alojar, hospedar
house arrest *s* arresto domiciliario
house'boat' *s* barco vivienda
house'break'er *s* escalador *m*
housebreaking [ˈhaʊs,brekɪŋ] *s* escalo, allanamiento de morada
housebroken [ˈhaʊs,brokən] *adj* (*perro o gato*) enseñado (*a hábitos de limpieza*)
housecleaning *s* limpieza de la casa
house coat *s* bata
house'fly' *s* (*pl* **-flies**) mosca domestica
houseful [ˈhaʊs,fʊl] *s* casa llena
house'hold' *adj* casero, doméstico || *s* casa, familia
house'hold'er *s* dueño de la casa; jefe *m* de familia
house'-hunt' *intr* — **to go house-hunting** ir a buscar casa
house'keep'er *s* ama de llaves, mujer *f* de gobierno
house'keep'ing *s* manejo doméstico, gobierno

doméstico; **to set up housekeeping** poner casa
housekeeping apartment *s* apartamento con cocina
house′maid′ *s* criada de casa
house meter *s* contador *m* de abonado
house′moth′er *s* mujer encargada de una residencia de estudiantes
house of cards *s* castillo de naipes
house of ill fame *s* lupanar *m,* casa de prostitución
house painter *s* pintor *m* de brocha gorda
house physician *s* médico residente
house′top′ *s* tejado; **to shout from the housetops** pregonar a los cuatro vientos
house trailer *s* casa rodante, caravana
housewarming [ˈhaʊs,wɔrmɪŋ] *s* fiesta para celebrar el estreno de una casa; **to have a housewarming** estrenar la casa
house′wife′ *s* (*pl* **-wives**) ama de casa, madre *f* de familia
house′work′ *s* quehaceres domésticos
housing [ˈhaʊzɪŋ] *s* (*of a horse*) gualdrapa; (aut) cárter *m;* (mach) caja, bastidor *m;* (compu) carcasa
housing shortage *s* crisis *f* de viviendas
hovel [ˈhʌvəl] *s* casucha, choza; (*shed for cattle, tools, etc.*) cobertizo
hover [ˈhʌvər] *intr* cernerse (*un ave*); (*to hesitate; to be in danger*) fluctuar; asomar (*p.ej., una sonrisa en los labios de uno*)
how [haʊ] *adv* cómo; (*at what price*) a cómo; **how do you do?** (formal) ¿cómo está usted?; **how early** cuándo, a qué hora; **how else** de qué otra manera; **how far** hasta dónde; cuánto, p.ej., **how far is it to the airport?** ¿cuánto hay de aquí al aeropuerto?; **how long** cuánto tiempo; **how many** cuántos; **how much** cuánto; lo mucho que; **how often** cuántas veces; **how old are you?** ¿cuántas años tiene Ud.?; **how soon** cuándo, a qué hora; **how** + *adj qué* + *adj,* p.ej., **how beautiful she is!** ¡qué hermosa es!; lo + *adj,* p.ej., **you know how intelligent he is** Ud. sabe lo inteligente que es; **to know how to** + *inf* saber + *inf*
howdah [ˈhaʊdə] *s* castillo
how•ev′er *adv* no obstante, sin embargo; por muy . . . que, por mucho . . . que
howitzer [ˈhaʊ•ɪtsər] *s* cañón *m* obús
howl [haʊl] *s* aullido; chillido; risa muy aguda; (*of wind*) bramido ‖ *tr* decir a gritos; **to howl down** imponerse a gritos a (*una persona*) ‖ *intr* aullar; chillar; reír a más no poder; bramar (*el viento*)
howler [ˈhaʊlər] *s* aullador *m;* (coll) plancha, desacierto
hoyden [ˈhɔɪdən] *s* muchacha traviesa, tunantuela
H.P. *abbr* **horsepower**
hr. *abbr* **hour**
hub [hʌb] *s* cubo; (fig) centro, eje *m*
hubbub [ˈhʌbəb] *s* gritería, alboroto
hub′cap′ *s* tapacubo, embellecedor *m*
huck′ster [ˈhʌkstər] *s* (*peddler*) buhonero; vendedor *m* ambulante de hortalizas; vil traficante *m,* sujeto ruin
huddle [ˈhʌdəl] *s* (coll) reunión secreta; **to go into a huddle** (coll) conferenciar en secreto ‖ *intr* acurrucarse, arrimarse
hue [hju] *s* matiz *m;* gritería; **hue and cry** vocería de indignación
huff [hʌf] *s* arrebato de cólera; **in a huff** encolerizado, ofendido
hug [hʌg] *s* abrazo ‖ *v* (*pret & pp* **hugged;** *ger* **hugging**) *tr* abrazar; apretar con los brazos; ahogar entre los brazos; navegar muy cerca de (*la costa*); ceñirse a (*p.ej., un muro*) ‖ *intr* abrazarse
huge [hjudʒ] *adj* enorme, descomunal
huh [hʌ] *interj* ¡eh!
hulk [hʌlk] *s* (*body of an old ship*) casco; (*clumsy old ship*) carcamán *m,* carraca; (*old ship tied up at a wharf and used as a warehouse, prison, etc.*) pontón *m;* (*shell of an old building, piece of furniture, machine, etc.; heavy, unwieldy person*) armatoste *m*
hulking [ˈhʌlkɪŋ] *adj* grueso, pesado
hull [hʌl] *s* (*of ship or hydroplane*) casco; (*of a dirigible*) armazón *f;* (*of certain vegetables*) hollejo, vaina ‖ *tr* deshollejar, desvainar; mondar, pelar
hullabaloo [ˈhʌləbə,lu] o [,hʌləbəˈlu] *s* alboroto, gritería, tumulto
hum [hʌm] *s* canturreo, tarareo; (*of a bee, machine, etc.*) zumbido ‖ *interj* ¡ejem! ‖ *v* (*pret & pp* **hummed;** *ger* **humming**) *tr canturrear, tararear* ‖ *intr* canturrear, tararear; (*to buzz*) zumbar; (coll) estar muy activo
human [ˈhjumən] *adj* humano (*perteneciente al hombre*) ‖ *s* ser humano
human being *s* ser humano
humane [hjuˈmen] *adj* humano (*compasivo*)
Human Immunodeficiency Virus *s* Virus *m* de Inmunodeficiencia Humana; **HIV** VIH
humanist [ˈhjumənɪst] *adj & s* humanista *mf*
humanitarian [hju,mænɪˈtɛrɪ•ən] *adj & s* humanitario
humani•ty [hjuˈmænɪti] *s* (*pl* **-ties**) humanidad
hu′man•kind′ *s* género humano
human nature *s* naturaleza humana
humanoid [ˈhjumə,nɔɪd] *adj & s* humanoide *mf*
humble [ˈhʌmbəl] *adj* humilde ‖ *tr* humillar
humble pie *s* — **to eat humble pie** cantar la palinodia
hum′bug′ *s* patraña; (*person*) patrañero ‖ *v* (*pret & pp* **-bugged;** *ger* **-bugging**) *tr* embaucar, engaitar
hum′drum′ *adj* monótono, tedioso
humer•us [ˈhjumərəs] *s* (*pl* **-i** [,aɪ]) húmero
humid [ˈhjumɪd] *adj* húmedo
humidifier [hjuˈmɪdɪ,faɪ•ər] *s* humectador *m*
humidi•fy [hjuˈmɪdɪ,faɪ] *v* (*pret & pp* **-fied**) *tr* humedecer
humidity [hjuˈmɪdɪti] *s* humedad
humiliate [hjuˈmɪlɪ,et] *tr* humillar

humiliating [hju'mılı,etıŋ] *adj* humillante
humili•ty [hju'mılıti] *s* (*pl* **-ties**) humildad
hummingbird ['hʌmıŋ,bʌrd] *s* colibrí *m,* pájaro mosca
humongous [hju'mʌŋəs] *adj* (coll) descomunal
humor ['hjumər] o ['jumər] *s* humor *m;* **out of humor** de mal humor; **to be in the humor for** estar de humor para ‖ *tr* seguir el humor a; manejar con delicadeza
humorist ['hjumərıst] *s* humorista *mf*
humorous ['hjumərəs] *adj* humorístico
hump [hʌmp] *s* corcova, joroba; (*in the ground*) montecillo
hump'back' *s* corcova, joroba; (*person*) corcovado, jorobado
humus ['hjuməs] *s* mantillo
hunch [hʌntʃ] *s* corcova, joroba; (*premonition*) (coll) corazonada ‖ *tr* encorvar ‖ *intr* encorvarse
hunch'back' *s* corcova, joroba; (*person*) corcovado, jorobado
hundred ['hʌndrəd] *adj* cien ‖ *s* ciento, cien; **a hundred** u **one hundred** ciento; cien; **by the hundreds** a centenares
hundredth ['hʌndredθ] *adj & s* centésimo
hun'dred•weight' *s* quintal *m*
Hundred Years' War *s* guerra de los Cien Años
Hungarian [hʌŋ'gɛrı•ən] *adj & s* húngaro
Hungary ['hʌŋgəri] *s* Hungría
hunger ['hʌŋgər] *s* hambre *f* ‖ *intr* hambrear; **to hunger for** tener hambre de
hunger march *s* marcha del hambre
hunger strike *s* huelga de hambre
hun•gry ['hʌŋgri] *adj* (*comp* **-grier;** *super* **-griest**) hambriento; **to be hungry** tener hambre; galguear (Arg, CAm, Mex); **to go hungry** pasar hambre
hunk [hʌŋk] *s* (coll) buen pedazo, pedazo grande
hunt [hʌnt] *s* (*act of hunting*) caza; (*hunting party*) cacería; (*a search*) busca; **on the hunt for** a caza de ‖ *tr* cazar; (*to seek, look for*) buscar ‖ *intr* cazar; buscar; **to go hunting** ir de caza; **to hunt for** buscar; **to take hunting** llevar de caza
hunter ['hʌntər] *s* cazador *m;* perro de caza
hunting ['hʌntiŋ] *adj* de caza ‖ *s* (*act*) caza; (*art*) cacería, montería
hunting dog *s* perro de caza
hunting ground *s* cazadero
hunting horn *s* cuerno *or* trompa de caza
hunting jacket *s* cazadora
hunting lodge *s* casa de montería
hunting permit *s* licencia de caza
hunting season *s* época de caza
huntress ['hʌntrıs] *s* cazadora
hunts•man ['hʌntsmən] *s* (*pl* **-men** [mən]) cazador *m,* montero
hurdle ['hʌrdəl] *s* (*hedge over which horses must jump*) zarzo; (*wooden frame over which runners and horses must jump*) valla; (fig) obstáculo; **hurdles** carrera de vallas ‖ *tr* saltar por encima de
hurdle race *s* carrera de vallas
hurdy-gur•dy ['hʌrdi'gʌrdi] *s* (*pl* **-dies**) organillo
hurl [hʌrl] *s* lanzamiento ‖ *tr* lanzar
hurrah [hʊ'rɑ] o **hurray** [hʊ're] *s* viva *m* ‖ *interj* ¡viva!, ¡hurra!; **hurrah for . . .** ¡viva!. . . ‖ *tr* aplaudir, vitorear ‖ *intr* dar vivas
hurricane ['hʌrı,ken] *s* huracán *m*
hurried ['hʌrid] *adj* apresurado; hecho de prisa
hur•ry ['hʌri] *s* (*pl* **-ries**) prisa; **to be in a hurry** tener prisa, estar de prisa ‖ *v* (*pret & pp* **-ried**) *tr* apresurar, dar prisa a ‖ *intr* apresurarse, darse prisa; **to hurry after** correr en pos de; **to hurry away** marcharse de prisa; **to hurry back** volver de prisa; **to hurry up** darse prisa
hurt [hʌrt] *adj* (*injured*) lastimado, herido; (*offended*) resentido, herido ‖ *s* (*harm*) daño; (*injury*) herida; (*pain*) dolor *m* ‖ *v* (*pret & pp* **hurt**) *tr* (*to harm*) dañar, perjudicar; (*to injure*) lastimar, herir; (*to offend*) ofender, herir; (*to pain*) doler ‖ *intr* doler
hurtle ['hʌrtəl] *intr* lanzarse con violencia, pasar con gran estruendo
husband ['hʌzbənd] *s* marido, esposo ‖ *tr* manejar con economía
husband•man ['hʌzbəndmən] *s* (*pl* **-men** [mən]) agricultor *m,* granjero
husbandry ['hʌzbəndri] *s* agricultura, labranza; buena dirección, buen gobierno (*de la hacienda de uno*)
hush [hʌʃ] *s* silencio ‖ *interj* ¡chito! ‖ *tr* callar; **to hush up** echar tierra a (*un escándalo*) ‖ *intr* callarse
hushaby ['hʌʃə,baı] *interj* ¡ro ro!
hush'-hush' *adj* muy secreto
hush money *s* precio del silencio
husk [hʌsk] *s* cáscara, hollejo, vaina; (*of corn*) perfolla ‖ *tr* descascarar, deshollejar, desvainar; espinochar (*el maíz*)
husk•y ['hʌski] *adj* (*comp* **-ier;** *super* **-iest**) fortachón, fornido; (*voice*) ronco
hus•sy ['hʌzi] o ['hʌsi] *s* (*pl* **-sies**) buena pieza, moza descarada; mujer desvergonzada
hustle ['hʌsəl] *s* (coll) energía, vigor *m* ‖ *tr* apresurar; echar a empellones ‖ *intr* apresurarse; (coll) menearse, trabajar con gran ahinco
hustler ['hʌslər] *s* trafagón *m,* buscavidas *mf*
hut [hʌt] *s* casucha, choza
hyacinth ['haı•əsınθ] *s* jacinto
hybrid ['haıbrıd] *adj & s* híbrido
hybridization [,haıbrıdı'zeʃən] *s* hibridación
hybridize ['haıbrı,daız] *tr & intr* hibridar
hy•dra ['haıdrə] *s* (*pl* **-dras** o **-drae** [dri]) hidra
hydrant ['haıdrənt] *s* boca de agua, boca de riego; (*water faucet*) grifo
hydrate ['haıdret] *s* hidrato ‖ *tr* hidratar ‖ *intr* hidratarse
hydraulic [haı'drɔlık] *adj* hidráulico ‖ **hydraulics** *s* hidráulica
hydraulic ram *s* ariete hidráulico
hydraulic suspension *s* suspensión hidraúlica
hydriodic [,haıdrı'ɑdık] *adj* yodhídrico
hydrobromic [,haıdrə'bromık] *adj* bromhídrico

hydrocarbon [ˌhaɪdrəˈkɑrbən] *s* hidrocarburo
hydrochloric [ˌhaɪdrəˈklorɪk] *adj* clorhídrico
hydroelectric [ˌhaɪdro•ɪˈlɛtrɪk] *adj* hidroeléctrico
hydrofluoric [ˌhaɪdrəfluˈɔrɪk] *adj* fluorhídrico
hydrofoil [ˈhaɪdrəˌfɔɪl] *s* superficie hidrodinámica; (*wing designed to lift vessel*) hidroaleta; (*vessel*) hidroala *m*
hydrogen [ˈhaɪdrədʒən] *s* hidrógeno
hydrogen bomb *s* bomba de hidrógeno
hydrogen peroxide *s* peróxido de hidrógeno
hydrogen sulfide *s* sulfuro de hidrógeno
hydrometer [haɪˈdrɑmɪtər] *s* areómetro
hydrophobia [ˌhaɪdrəˈfobɪ•ə] *s* hidrofobia
hydroplane [ˈhaɪdrəˌplen] *s* hidroavión *m*
hydroxide [haɪˈdrɑksaɪd] *s* hidróxido
hyena [haɪˈinə] *s* hiena
hygiene [ˈhaɪdʒin] *s* higiene *f*
hygienic [ˌhaɪdʒɪˈɛnɪk] *adj* higiénico
hymn [hɪm] *s* himno
hymnal [ˈhɪmnəl] *s* himnario
hyper [ˈhaɪpər] *var* de **hyperactive**
hyperacidity [ˌhaɪpərəˈsɪdɪti] *s* hiperacidez *f*
hy′per•ac′tive *adj* hiperactivo
hyperbola [haɪˈpʌrbələ] *s* (geom) hipérbola
hyperbole [haɪˈpʌrbəli] *s* (rhet) hipérbole *f*
hyperbolic [ˌhaɪpərˈbɑlɪk] *adj* (geom & rhet) hiperbólico
hy′per•link *s* (compu) hiperenlace *m*
hy′per•linked′ *adj* (compu) hiperenlazado
hypersensitive [ˌhaɪpərˈsɛnsɪtɪv] *adj* extremadamente sensible; (*allergic*) hipersensible
hypertension [ˌhaɪpərˈtɛnʃən] *s* hipertensión
hy′per•text *adj* (compu) hipertextual || *s* (compu) hipertexto
hyphen [ˈhaɪfən] *s* guión *m*
hyphenate [ˈhaɪfəˌnet] *tr* unir con guión; escribir con guión
hypno•sis [hɪpˈnosɪs] *s* (*pl* **-ses** [siz]) hipnosis *f*
hypnotic [hɪpˈnɑtɪk] *adj* hipnótico || *s* (*person; sedative*) hipnótico
hypnotism [ˈhɪpnəˌtizəm] *s* hipnotismo
hypnotist [ˈhɪpnətɪst] *s* hipnotista *mf*
hypnotize [ˈhɪpnəˌtaɪz] *tr* hipnotizar
hypochondriac [ˌhaɪpəˈkɑndrɪˌæk] *s* hipocondríaco
hypocri•sy [hɪˈpɑkrəsi] *s* (*pl* **-sies**) hipocresía
hypocrite [ˈhɪpəkrɪt] *s* hipócrita *mf*
hypocritical [ˌhɪpəˈkrɪtɪkəl] *adj* hipócrita
hypodermic [ˌhaɪpəˈdʌrmɪk] *adj* hipodérmico
hyposulfite [ˌhaɪpəˈsʌlfaɪt] *m* hiposulfito
hypotenuse [haɪˈpɑtɪˌnus] *s* hipotenusa
hypothe•sis [haɪˈpɑθɪsɪs] *s* (*pl* **-ses** [ˌsiz] hipótesis *f*
hypothetic(al) [ˌhaɪpəˈθɛtɪk(əl)] *adj* hipotético
hyssop [ˈhɪsəp] *s* (bot) hisopo
hysteria [hɪsˈtɪrɪ•ə] *s* histerismo, histeria
hysteric [hɪsˈtɛrɪk] *adj* histérico || **hysterics** *s* paroxismo histérico
hysterical [hɪsˈtɛrɪkəl] *adj* histérico

I

I, i [aɪ] novena letre del alfabeto inglés
I [aɪ] *pron pers* (*pl* **we** [wi]) yo; **it is I** soy yo
iambic [aɪˈæmbɪk] *adj* yámbico
iam•bus [aɪˈæmbəs] *s* (*pl* **-bi** [baɪ]) yambo
ib. *abbr* **ibidem**
Iberian [aɪbˈɪrɪ•ən] *adj* ibérico || *s* ibero
ibex [ˈaɪbɛks] *s* (*pl* **ibexes** o **ibices** [ˈɪbɪˌsiz]) íbice *m*, cabra montés
ibid. *abbr* **ibidem**
ice [aɪs] *s* hielo; **to break the ice** (*to overcome reserve*) romper el hielo; **to cut no ice** (coll) no importar nada; **to skate on thin ice** (coll) buscar el peligro || *tr* helar; enfriar con hielo; (*to cover with icing*) garapiñar || *intr* helarse
ice age *s* época glacial
ice bag *s* bolsa para hielo
iceberg [ˈaɪsˌbʌrg] *s* banquisa, iceberg *m*
iceberg lettuce *s* lechuga repollada
ice′boat′ *s* cortahielos *m*, rompehielos *m;* trineo con vela para deslizarse sobre el hielo
ice′bound′ *adj* rodeado de hielo; de tenido por el hielo
ice′box′ *s* nevera, fresquera
ice′break′er *s* cortahielos *m*, rompehielos *m*
ice′cap′ *s* bolsa para hielo; manto de hielo
ice cream *s* helado
ice′-cream′ cone *s* cucurucho de helado, barquillo de helado
ice-cream freezer *s* heladora, garapiñera
ice-cream parlor *s* salón *m* de refrescos, tienda de helados
ice-cream soda *s* agua gaseosa con helado
ice cream sundae *s* copa de helado, copa helado con frutas, jarabes o nueces
ice cube *s* cubito de hielo
ice hockey *s* hockey *m* sobre patines
Iceland [ˈaɪslənd] *s* Islandia
Icelander [ˈaɪsˌlændər] *s* islandés *m*
Icelandic [aɪsˈlændɪk] *adj* islandés || *s* islandés *m* (*idioma*)
ice•man [ˈaɪsˌmæn] *s* (*pl* **-men** [ˌmɛn]) vendedor *m* de hielo, repartidor *m* de hielo
ice pack *s* hielo flotante; bolsa de hielo
ice pail *s* enfriadera
ice pick *s* picahielos *m*
ice skate *s* patín *m* de cuchilla, patín de hielo
ice skating *s* patinaje *m* sobre hielo
ice tray *s* bandejita de hielo

ice water *s* agua helada
ichthyology [ˌɪkθɪˋɑlədʒi] *s* ictiología
icicle [ˋaɪsɪkəl] *s* carámbano
icing [ˋaɪsɪŋ] *s* garapiña, capa de azúcar; (aer) formación de hielo
iconoclasm [aɪˋkɑnəˌklæzəm] *s* iconoclasia, iconoclasmo
iconoclast [aɪˋkɑnəˌklæst] *s* iconoclasta *mf*
icy [ˋaɪsi] *adj* (*comp* **icier;** *super* **iciest**) cubierto de hielo; (*slippery*) resbaladizo; (fig) frío
id. *abbr* **idem**
id [ɪd] *s* (psychoanalysis) ello
I.D. *abbr* **identity card**
I'd *contr* **I would**
idea [aɪˋdi•ə] *s* idea
ideal [aɪˋdi•əl] *adj & s* ideal *m*
idealist [aɪˋdi•əlɪst] *adj & s* idealista *mf*
idealize [aɪˋdi•əˌlaɪz] *tr* idealizar
identic(al) [aɪˋdɛntɪk(əl)] *adj* idéntico
identification [aɪˌdɛntɪfɪˋkeʃən] *s* identificación
identification tag *s* disco de identificación
identify [aɪˋdɛntɪˌfaɪ] *v* (*pret & pp* **-fied**) *tr* identificar ‖ *intr* — **to identify with** solidarizar con
identi•ty [aɪˋdɛntɪti] *s* (*pl* **-ties**) identidad
identity card *s* carta de identificación
identity tag *s* placa de identidad
ideolo•gy [ˌaɪdɪˋɑlədʒi] o [ˌɪdɪˋɑlədʒi] *s* (*pl* **-gies**) ideología
ides [aɪdz] *spl* idus *mpl*
idio•cy [ˋɪdɪ•əsi] *s* (*pl* **-cies**) idiotez *f*
idiom [ˋɪdɪ•əm] *s* (*expression that is contrary to the usual patterns of the language*) modismo; (*style of language*) idioma *m,* lenguaje *m;* (*style of an author*) estilo; (*character of a language*) índole *f*
idiomatic [ˌɪdɪ•əˋmætɪk] *adj* idiomático
idiosyncra•sy [ˌɪdɪ•əˋsɪnkrəsi] *s* (*pl* **-sies**) idiosincrasia
idiot [ˋɪdɪ•ət] *s* idiota *mf*
idiotic [ˌɪdɪ•ˋɑtɪk] *adj* idiota
idle [ˋaɪdəl] *adj* desocupado, ocioso; **at idle moments** a ratos perdidos; **to run idle** marchar en ralentí ‖ *tr* — **to idle away** gastar ociosamente (*el tiempo*) ‖ *intr* estar ocioso, holgar; marchar (*un motor*) en ralentí
idleness [ˋaɪdəlnɪs] *s* desocupación, ociosidad
idler [ˋaɪdlər] *s* haragán *m,* ocioso
idling [ˋaɪdlɪŋ] *s* ralentí m
idol [ˋaɪdəl] *s* ídolo
idola•try [aɪˋdɑlətri] *s* (*pl* **-tries**) idolatría
idolize [ˋaɪdəˌlaɪz] *tr* idolatrar
idyll [ˋaɪdəl] *s* idilio
idyllic [aɪˋdɪlɪk] *adj* idílico
if [ɪf] *conj* si; **as if** como si; **even if** aunque; **if so** si es así; **if true** si es cierto
ignis fatuus [ˋɪgnɪsˋfætʃʊ•əs] *s* (*pl* **ignes fatui** [ˋɪgnizˋfætʃʊˌaɪ]) fuego fatuo
ignite [ɪgˋnaɪt] *tr* encender ‖ *intr* encenderse
ignition [ɪgˋnɪʃən] *s* inflamación; (aut) encendido, ignición
ignition key *s* (auto) llave *f* de contacto o de incendio
ignition switch *s* (aut) interruptor *m* de encendido
ignoble [ɪgˋnobəl] *adj* innoble
ignominious [ˌɪgnəˋmɪnɪ•əs] *adj* ignominioso
ignoramus [ˌɪgnəˋreməs] *s* ignorante *mf*
ignorance [ˋɪgnərəns] *s* ignorancia
ignorant [ˋɪgnərənt] *adj* ignorante
ignore [ɪgˋnor] *tr* no hacer caso de, pasar por alto
ilk [ɪlk] *s* especie *f,* jaez *m*
ill. *abbr* **illustrated, illustration**
I'll *contr* **I will**
ill [ɪl] *adj* (*comp* **worse** [wʌrs]; *super* **worst** [wʌrst]) enfermo, malo ‖ *adv* mal; **to take ill** tomar a mal; caer enfermo
ill-advised [ˋɪlədˋvaɪzd] *adj* desaconsejado, malaconsejado, desavisado
ill at ease *adj* inquieto, incómodo
ill-bred [ˋɪlˋbrɛd] *adj* malcriado
ill-considered [ˋɪlkənˋsɪdərd] *adj* des considerado, mal considerado
ill-disposed [ˋɪldɪsˋpozd] *adj* malintencionado, maldispuesto
illegal [ɪˋligəl] *adj* ilegal
illegible [ɪˋlɛdʒɪbəl] *adj* ilegible
illegitimate [ˌɪlɪˋdʒɪtɪmɪt] *adj* ilegítimo
ill fame *s* mala fama, reputación de inmoral
ill-fated [ˋɪlˋfetɪd] *adj* aciago, funesto
ill-gotten [ˋɪlˋgɑtən] *adj* mal ganado
ill health *s* mala salud
ill-humored [ˋɪlˋhjumərd] *adj* malhumorado
illicit [ɪˋlɪsɪt] *adj* ilícito
illitera•cy [ɪˋlɪtərəsi] *s* (*pl* **-cies**) ignorancia analfabetismo
illiterate [ɪˋlɪtərɪt] *adj* (*uneducated*) iliterato; (*unable to read or write*) analfabeto ‖ *s* analfabeto
ill-mannered [ˋɪlˋmænərd] *adj* de malos modales
illness [ˋɪlnɪs] *s* enfermedad
illogical [ɪˋlɑdʒɪkəl] *adj* ilógico
ill-spent [ˋɪlˋspɛnt] *adj* malgastado
ill-starred [ˋɪlˋstɑrd] *adj* malhadado
ill-tempered [ˋɪlˋtɛmpərd] *adj* de mal genio
ill-timed [ˋɪlˋtaɪmd] *adj* inoportuno, intempestivo
ill'-treat' *tr* maltratar
ill'-treat'ment *s* malos tratos
illuminate [ɪˋlumɪˌnet] *tr* alumbrar, iluminar; miniar (*un manuscrito*)
illumination [ɪˌlumɪˋneʃən] *s* iluminación
illusion [ɪˋluʒən] *s* ilusión
illusive [ɪˋlusɪv] *adj* ilusivo
illusory [ɪˋlusəri] *adj* ilusorio
illustrate [ˋɪləsˌtret] o [ɪˋlʌstret] *tr* ilustrar
illustration [ˌɪləsˋtreʃən] *s* ilustración
illustrious [ɪˋlʌstrɪ•əs] *adj* ilustre
ill will *s* mala voluntad, rencor *m*
I'm *contr* **I am**
image [ˋɪmɪdʒ] *s* imagen *f;* **the very image of** la propia estampa de
image map *s* (compu) mapa de vínculos, mapa de imágenes

image•ry [ˈɪmɪdʒri] *s* (*pl* **-ries**) (*formation of mental images; product of the imagination*) fantasía; (*images collectively*) imágenes *fpl*
imaginary [ɪˈmædʒɪ,nɛri] *adj* imaginario
imagination [ɪ,mædʒɪˈneʃən] *s* imaginación
imagine [ɪˈmædʒɪn] *tr & intr* imaginar; (*to conjecture*) imaginarse
imbecile [ˈɪmbɪsɪl] *adj & s* imbécil *mf*
imbecili•ty [,ɪmbɪˈsɪlɪti] *s* (*pl* **-ties**) imbecilidad
imbibe [ɪmˈbaɪb] *tr* (*to drink*) beber; (*to absorb*) embeber; (*to become absorbed in*) embeberse de o en ‖ *intr* beber, empinar el codo
imbue [ɪmˈbju] *tr* imbuir
imitate [ˈɪmɪ,tet] *tr* imitar
imitation [,ɪmɪˈteʃən] *adj* (*e.g., jewelry*) imitado, imitación, de imitación ‖ *s* imitación; **in imitation of** a imitación de
immaculate [ɪˈmækjəlɪt] *adj* inmaculado
immaterial [,ɪməˈtɪrɪ•əl] *adj* inmaterial; poco importante
immature [,ɪməˈtjʊr] *adj* inmaturo
immeasurable [ɪˈmɛʒərəbəl] *adj* inmensurable
immediacy [ɪˈmidɪ•əsi] *s* inmediación
immediate [ɪˈmidɪ•ɪt] *adj* inmediato
immediately [ɪˈmidɪ•ɪtli] *adv* inmediatamente, en seguida
immemorial [,ɪmɪˈmorɪ•əl] *adj* inmemorial
immense [ɪˈmɛns] *adj* inmenso; (coll) excelente
immerge [ɪˈmʌrdʒ] *intr* sumergirse
immerse [ɪˈmʌrs] *tr* sumergir, inmergir
immersion [ɪˈmʌrʃən] o [ɪˈmʌrʒən] *s* sumersión, inmersión
immigrant [ˈɪmɪgrənt] *adj & s* inmigrante *mf*
immigrate [ˈɪmɪ,gret] *intr* inmigrar
immigration [,ɪmɪˈgreʃən] *s* inmigración
imminent [ˈɪmɪnənt] *adj* inminente
immobile [ɪˈmobɪl] *adj* inmoble, inmóvil
immobilize [ɪˈmobɪ,laɪz] *tr* inmovilizar
immoderate [ɪˈmɑdərɪt] *adj* inmoderado
immodest [ɪˈmɑdɪst] *adj* inmodesto
immoral [ɪˈmɔrəl] *adj* inmoral
immortal [ɪˈmɔrtəl] *adj & s* inmortal *mf*
immortalize [ɪˈmɔrtə,laɪz] *tr* inmortalizar
immune [ɪˈmjun] *adj* inmune
immunity [ɪˈmjunətɪ] *s* inmunidad
immunize [ˈɪmjə,naɪz] *tr* inmunizar
immunodeficiency [ˈɪmjənodɪˈfɪʃənsi] *s* inmunodeficiencia
imp [ɪmp] *s* diablillo; (*child*) niño travieso
impact [ˈɪmpækt] *s* impacto
impair [ɪmˈpɛr] *tr* empeorar, deteriorar
impan•el [ɪmˈpænəl] *v* (*pret & pp* **-eled** o **-elled;** *ger* **-eling** o **-elling**) *tr* inscribir en la lista de los jurados; elegir (*un jurado*)
impart [ɪmˈpɑrt] *tr* (*to make known*) dar a conocer, hacer saber; (*to transmit, communicate*) imprimir
impartial [ɪmˈpɑrʃəl] *adj* imparcial
impassable [ɪmˈpæsəbəl] *adj* intransitable, impracticable
impasse [ɪmˈpæs] o [ˈɪmpæs] *s* callejón *m* sin salida, impasse *m*
impassible [ɪmˈpæsɪbəl] *adj* impasible
impassioned [ɪmˈpæʃənd] *adj* ardiente, vehemente
impassive [ɪmˈpæsɪv] *adj* impasible
impatience [ɪmˈpeʃəns] *s* impaciencia
impatient [ɪmˈpeʃənt] *adj* impaciente
impeach [ɪmˈpɪtʃ] *tr* (*to accuse*) acusar, residenciar; (*to prosecute*) enjuiciar; (*to discredit*) poner on tela de juicio, impugnar
impeachment [ɪmˈpitʃmənt] *s* acusación, residencia; (*prosecution*) enjuiciamiento
impeccable [ɪmˈpɛkəbəl] *adj* impecable
impecunious [,ɪmpɪˈkjunɪ•əs] *adj* inope
impedance [ɪmˈpidəns] *s* impedancia
impede [ɪmˈpid] *tr* estorbar, dificultar
impediment [ɪmˈpɛdɪmənt] *s* impedimento; (*e.g., in speech*) defecto
im•pel [ɪmˈpɛl] *v* (*pret & pp* **-pelled;** *ger* **-pelling**) *tr* impeler, impulsar
impending [ɪmˈpɛndɪŋ] *adj* inminente
impenetrable [ɪmˈpɛnətrəbəl] *adj* impenetrable
impenitent [ɪmˈpɛnɪtənt] *adj & s* impenitente *mf*
imperative [ɪmˈpɛrɪtɪv] *adj* (*commanding*) imperativo; (*urgent, absolutely necessary*) imperioso ‖ *s* imperativo
imperceptible [,ɪmpərˈsɛptɪbəl] *adj* imperceptible, inapreciable
imperfect [ɪmˈpʌrfɪkt] *adj & s* imperfecto
imperfection [,ɪmpərˈfɛkʃən] *s* imperfección
imperial [ɪmˈpɪrɪ•əl] *adj* imperial; majestuoso ‖ *s* (*goatee*) perilla; (*top of coach*) imperial *f*
imperialist [ɪmˈpɪrɪ•əlɪst] *adj & s* imperialista *mf*
imper•il [ɪmˈpɛrɪl] *v* (*pret & pp* **-iled** o **-illed;** *ger* **-iling** o **-illing**) *tr* poner en peligro
imperious [ɪmˈpɪrɪ•əs] *adj* imperioso
imperishable [ɪmˈpɛrɪʃəbəl] *adj* imperecedero
impersonal [ɪmˈpʌrsənəl] *adj* impersonal
impersonate [ɪmˈpʌrsə,net] *tr* personificar; hacer el papel de
impertinence [ɪmˈpʌrtɪnəns] *s* impertinencia
impertinent [ɪmˈpʌrtɪnənt] *adj & s* impertinente *mf*
impetuous [ɪmˈpɛtʃʊ•əs] *adj* impetuoso
impetus [ˈɪmpɪtəs] *s* ímpetu *m*
impie•ty [ɪmˈpaɪ•əti] *s* (*pl* **-ties**) impiedad
impinge [ɪmˈpɪndʒ] *intr* — **to impinge on** o **upon** incidir eno sobre, herir; infringir, violar
impious [ˈɪmpɪ•əs] *adj* impío
impish [ˈɪmpɪʃ] *adj* endiablado, travieso
implant [ɪmˈplænt] *tr* implantar
implement [ˈɪmplɪmənt] *s* instrumento, utensilio, herramienta; **implements** implementos *mpl* ‖ [ˈimplɪ,mɛnt] *tr* poner por obra, llevar a cabo; (*to provide with implements*) pertrechar
implicate [ˈɪmplɪ,ket] *tr* implicar, comprometer, enredar
implicit [ɪmˈplɪsɪt] *adj* implícito; (*unquestioning*) absoluto, ciego
implied [ɪmˈplaɪd] *adj* implícito, sobrentendido
implore [ɪmˈplor] *tr* implorar, suplicar
im•ply [ɪmˈplaɪ] *v* (*pret & pp* **-plied**) *tr* dar a entender; implicar, incluir en esencia

impolite [ˌɪmpəˈlaɪt] *s* descortés; desacomodido (SAm)
import [ˈɪmport] *s* importación; artículo importado; importancia, significación ‖ *tr* importar; significar ‖ *intr* importar
importance [ɪmˈpɔrtəns] *s* importancia
important [ɪmˈpɔrtənt] *adj* importante
importation [ˌɪmporˈteʃən] *s* importación
importer [ɪmˈportər] *s* importador *m*
importunate [ɪmˈpɔrtʃənɪt] *adj* importuno
importune [ˌɪmpɔrˈtjun] *tr* importunar
impose [ɪmˈpoz] *tr* imponer ‖ *intr* — **to impose on** o **upon** abusar de
imposing [ɪmˈpozɪŋ] *adj* imponente
imposition [ˌɪmpəˈzɪʃən] *s* (*of someone's will*) imposición; abuso, engaño
impossible [ɪmˈpɑsɪbəl] *adj* imposible
impostor [ɪmˈpɑstər] *s* impostor *m*, embaucador *m*
imposture [ɪmˈpɑstʃər] *s* impostura
impotence [ˈɪmpətəns] *s* impotencia
impotent [ˈɪmpətənt] *adj* impotente
impound [ɪmˈpaʊnd] *tr* acorralar, encerrar; rebalsar (*agua*); (law) embargar, secuestrar
impoverish [ɪmˈpɑvərɪʃ] *tr* empobrecer
impracticable [ɪmˈpræktɪkəbəl] *adj* impracticable; (*intractable*) intratable
impractical [ɪmˈpræktkəl] *adj* impracticable; soñador, utópico
impregnable [ɪmˈprɛgnəbəl] *adj* inexpugnable
impregnate [ɪmˈprɛgnet] *tr* (*to make pregnant*) empreñar; (*to soak*) empapar; (*to fill the interstices of*) impregnar; (*to infuse, infect*) imbuir
impresari•o [ˌɪmprɪˈsɑrɪˌo] *s* (*pl* **-os**) empresario, empresario de teatro
impress [ɪmˈprɛs] *tr* (*to have an effect on the mind or emotions of*) impresionar; (*to mark by using pressure*) imprimir; (*on the memory*) grabar; (mil) enganchar
impression [ɪmˈprɛʃən] *s* impresión
impressionable [ɪmˈprɛʃənəbəl] *adj* impresionable
impressive [ɪmˈprɛsɪv] *adj* impresionante
imprint [ˈɪmprɪnt] *s* impresión; (typ) pie *m* de imprenta ‖ [ɪmˈprɪnt] *tr* imprimir
imprison [ɪmˈprɪzən] *tr* encarcelar
imprisonment [ɪmˈprɪzənmənt] *s* encarcelamiento; pena privativa de libertad
improbable [ɪmˈprɑbəbəl] *adj* improbable
impromptu [ɪmˈprɑmptju] o [ɪmˈprɑmptu] *adj* improvisado ‖ *adv* de improviso ‖ *s* improvisación; (mus) impromptu *m*
improper [ɪmˈprɑpər] *adj* impropio; (*contrary to good taste or decency*) indecoroso
improve [ɪmˈpruv] *tr* perfeccionar, mejorar; aprovechar (*la oportunidad*) ‖ *intr* perfeccionarse, mejorar; **to improve on** o **upon** mejorar
improvement [ɪmˈpruvmənt] *s* perfeccionamiento, mejoramiento; (*e.g., in health*) mejoría; (*useful employment, e.g., of time*) aprovechamiento
improvident [ɪmˈprɑvɪdənt] *adj* imprevisor
improvise [ˈɪmprəˌvaɪz] *tr* & *intr* improvisar
imprudent [ɪmˈprudənt] *adj* imprudente
impudence [ˈɪmpjədəns] *s* insolencia, descaro, impertinencia
impudent [ˈɪmpjədənt] *adj* insolente, descarado, impertinente
impugn [ɪmˈpjun] *tr* poner en tela de juicio
impulse [ˈɪmpʌls] *s* impulso
impulsive [ɪmˈpʌlsɪv] *adj* impulsivo
impunity [ɪmˈpjunɪti] *s* impunidad
impure [ɪmˈpjʊr] *adj* impuro
impuri•ty [ɪmˈpjʊrɪti] *s* (*pl* **-ties**) impureza, impuridad
impute [ɪmˈpjut] *tr* imputar
in [ɪn] *adj* interior ‖ *adv* dentro; en casa, en la oficina; **in here** aquí dentro; **in there** allí dentro; **to be in** estar en casa; **to be in for** estar expuesto a; **to be in with** gozar del favor de ‖ *prep* en; (*within*) dentro de; (*over, through*) por; (*a period of the day*) en o por; **dressed in . . .** vestido de . . . ; **in so far as** en tanto que; **in that** en que, por cuanto ‖ *s* — **ins and outs** recovecos, pormenores minuciosos
inability [ˌɪnəˈbɪlɪti] *s* inhabilidad, incapacidad
inaccessible [ˌɪnækˈsɛsɪbəl] *adj* inaccesible
inaccura•cy [ɪnˈækjərəsi] *s* (*pl* **-cies**) inexactitud, incorrección
inaccurate [ɪnˈækjərɪt] *adj* inexacto, incorrecto
inaction [ɪnˈækʃən] *s* inacción
inactive [ɪnˈæktɪv] *adj* inactivo
inactivity [ˌɪnækˈtɪvɪti] *s* inactividad
inadequate [ɪnˈædɪkwɪt] *adj* insuficiente, inadecuado
inadvertent [ˌɪnədˈvʌrtənt] *adj* inadvertido
inadvisable [ˌɪnədˈvaɪzəbəl] *adj* poco aconsejable, imprudente
inane [ɪnˈen] *adj* inane
inanimate [ɪnˈænɪmɪt] *adj* inanimado
inappreciable [ˌɪnəˈpriʃi•əbəl] *adj* inapreciable
inappropriate [ˌɪnəˈpropri•ɪt] *adj* no apropiado, no a propósito
inarticulate [ˌɪnɑrˈtɪkjəlɪt] *adj* (*sounds, words*) inarticulado; (*person*) incapaz de expresarse
inartistic [ˌɪnɑrˈtɪstɪk] *adj* antiartístico, inartístico
inasmuch as [ˌɪnəzˈmʌtʃˌæz] *conj* ya que, puesto que; en cuanto, hasta donde
inattentive [ˌɪnəˈtɛntɪv] *adj* desatento
inaugural [ɪnˈɔgjərəl] *adj* inaugural ‖ *s* discurso inaugural
inaugurate [ɪnˈɔgjəˌret] *tr* inaugurar
inauguration [ɪnˌɔgjəˈreʃən] *s* (*formal initiation or opening*) inauguración; (*investiture of a head of government*) toma de posesión
inborn [ˈɪnˈbɔrn] *adj* innato, ingénito
inbreeding [ˈɪnˌbridɪŋ] *s* intracruzamiento
inc. *abbr* **inclosure, included, including, incorporated, increase**
Inca [ˈɪŋkə] *adj* incaico ‖ *s* inca *mf*
incandescent [ˌɪnkənˈdɛsənt] *adj* incandescente
incapable [ɪnˈkepəbəl] *adj* incapaz
incapacitate [ˌɪnkəˈpæsɪˌtet] *tr* incapacitar, inhabilitar

incapaci•ty [,ɪnkə'pæsɪti] *s* (*pl* **-ties**) incapacidad
incarcerate [ɪn'kɑrsə,ret] *tr* encarcelar
incarnate [ɪn'kɑrnɪt] *adj* encarnado ‖ [ɪn'kɑrnet] *tr* encarnar
incarnation [,ɪnkɑr'neʃən] *s* encarnación
incendiarism [ɪn'sɛndɪ•ə,rɪzəm] *s* incendio intencionado; incitación al desorden
incendiar•y [ɪn'sɛndɪ,ɛri] *adj* incendiario ‖ *s* (*pl* **-ies**) incendiario
incense ['ɪnsɛns] *s* incienso ‖ *tr* (*to burn incense before*) incensar ‖ [ɪn'sɛns] *tr* exasperar, encolerizar
incense burner *s* incensario
incentive [ɪn'sɛntɪv] *adj & s* incentivo
inception [ɪn'sɛpʃən] *s* principio, comienzo
incertitude [ɪn'sʌrt,tjud] *s* incertidumbre
incessant [ɪn'sɛsənt] *adj* incesante
incest ['ɪnsɛst] *s* incesto
incestuous [ɪn'sɛstʃʊ•əs] *adj* incestuoso
inch [ɪntʃ] *s* (*2.54 centimeters*) pulgada; **to be within an inch of** estar a dos dedos de ‖ *intr* — **to inch ahead** avanzar poco a poco
incidence ['ɪnsɪdəns] *s* incidencia; (*range of occurrence*) extensión
incident ['ɪnsɪdənt] *adj & s* incidente *m*
incidental [,ɪnsɪ'dɛntəl] *adj* incidente; (*incurred in addition to the regular amount*) obvencional ‖ *s* elemento incidental; **incidentals** gastos menudos
incidentally [,ɪnsɪ'dɛntəli] *adv* incidentemente; a propósito
incipient [ɪn'sɪpɪ•ənt] *adj* incipiente
incision [ɪn'sɪʒən] *s* incisión
incisive [ɪn'saɪsɪv] *adj* incisivo
incite [ɪn'saɪt] *tr* incitar
incl. *abbr* **inclosure, inclusive**
inclemen•cy [ɪn'klɛmənsi] *s* (*pl* **-cies**) inclemencia
inclement [ɪn'klɛmənt] *adj* inclemente
inclination [,ɪnklɪ'neʃən] *s* inclinación
incline ['ɪnklaɪn] o [ɪn'klaɪn] *s* declive *m*, pendiente *f* ‖ [ɪn'klaɪn] *tr* inclinar ‖ *intr* inclinarse
inclined plane *s* plano inclinado
inclose [ɪn'kloz] *tr* encerrar; (*in a letter*) remitir adjunto, adjuntar, incluir
inclosed [ɪn'klozd] *adj* cerrado; (*in a letter*) adjunto; **please find inclosed** . . . se adjunta, se acompaña
inclosure [ɪn'kloʒər] *s* recinto; cosa inclusa, carta inclusa, documento anexo
include [ɪn'klud] *tr* incluir, comprender
including [ɪn'kludɪŋ] *prep* incluso, inclusive; imbíbito (Guat, Mex)
inclusive [ɪn'klusɪv] *adj* inclusivo; **inclusive of** comprensivo de ‖ *adv* inclusive
incogni•to [ɪn'kɑgnɪ,to] *adj* incógnito ‖ *adv* de incógnito ‖ *s* (*pl* **-tos**) incógnito
incoherent [,ɪnko'hɪrənt] *adj* incoherente
incombustible [,ɪnkəm'bʌstɪbəl] *adj* incombustible
income ['ɪnkʌm] *s* renta, ingreso, utilidad
income tax *s* impuesto sobre la renta, impuesto sobre los ingresos
in'come-tax' return *s* declaración de impuesto sobre la renta
in'com'ing *adj* de entrada, entrante; (*tide*) ascendente ‖ *s* entrada
incommunicado [,ɪnkə,mjunə'kɑdo] *adj* incomunicado
incomparable [ɪn'kɑmpərəbəl] *adj* incomparable; inigualable
incompatible [,ɪnkəm'pætɪbəl] *adj* incompatible; (compu, electron, med, pharm) incompatible
incompetent [ɪn'kɑmpɪtənt] *adj* incompetente
incomplete [,ɪnkəm'plit] *adj* incompleto
incomprehensible [,ɪnkɑmprɪ'hɛnsɪbəl] *adj* incomprehensible
incomprehension [ɪn,kɑmprɪ'hɛnʃən] *s* incomprensión
inconceivable [,ɪnkən'sivəbəl] *adj* inconcebible
inconclusive [,ɪnkən'klusɪv] *adj* inconcluyente
incongruous [ɪn'kɑŋgrʊ•əs] *adj* incongruo
inconsequential [ɪn,kɑnsɪ'kwɛnʃəl] *adj* (*lacking proper sequence of thought or speech*) inconsecuente; (*trivial*) de poca importancia
inconsiderate [,ɪnkən'sɪdərɪt] *adj* desconsiderado, inconsiderado
inconsisten•cy [,ɪnkən'sɪstənsi] *s* (*pl* **-cies**) (*lack of coherence*) inconsistencia; (*lack of logical connection or uniformity*) inconsecuencia
inconsistent [,ɪnkən'sɪstənt] *adj* (*lacking coherence of parts*) inconsistente; (*not agreeing with itself or oneself*) inconsecuente
inconsolable [,ɪnkən'soləbəl] *adj* inconsolable
inconspicuous [,ɪnkən'spɪkjʊ•əs] *adj* poco impresionante, poco aparente
inconstant [ɪn'kɑnstənt] *adj* inconstante
incontinent [ɪn'kɑntɪnənt] *adj* incontinente
incontrovertible [,ɪnkɑntrə'vʌrtɪbəl] *adj* incontrovertible
inconvenience [,ɪnkən'vinɪ•əns] *s* incomodidad, inconveniencia, molestia ‖ *tr* incomodar, molestar
inconvenient [,ɪnkən'vzinɪ•ənt] *adj* incómodo, inconveniente, molesto
incorporate [ɪn'kɔrpə,ret] *tr* incorporar; constituir en sociedad anónima ‖ *intr* incorporarse; constituirse en sociedad anónima
incorporation [ɪn'kɔrpə'reʃən] *s* incorporación; constitución en sociedad anónima
incorrect [,ɪnkə'rɛkt] *adj* incorrecto
increase ['ɪnkris] *s* aumento; ganancia, interés *m*; **to be on the increase** ir en aumento ‖ [ɪn'kris] *tr* aumentar; (*by propagation*) multiplicar ‖ *intr* aumentar; multiplicarse
increasingly [ɪn'krisɪŋli] *adv* cada vez más
incredible [ɪn'krɛdɪbəl] *adj* increíble
incredulous [ɪn'krɛdʒələs] *adj* incrédulo
increment ['ɪnkrɪmənt] *s* incremento
incriminate [ɪn'krɪmɪ,net] *tr* acriminar, incriminar
incrust [ɪn'krʌst] *tr* incrustar

incubate [ˈɪnkjə,bet] *tr & intr* incubar
incubator [ˈɪnkjə,betər] *s* incubadora
inculcate [ɪnˈkʌlket] o [ˈɪnkʌl,ket] *tr* inculcar
incumben•cy [ɪnˈkʌmbənsi] *s* (*pl* **-cies**) incumbencia
incumbent [ɪnˈkʌmbənt] *adj* — **to be incumbent on** incumbir a ‖ *s* titular *m*
incunabula [,ɪnkjʊˈnæbjələ] *spl* (*beginnings*) orígenes *mpl;* (*early printed books*) incunables *mpl*
in•cur [ɪnˈkʌr] *v* (*pret & pp* **-curred;** *ger* **-curring**) *tr* incurrir en; (*a debt*) contraer
incurable [ɪnˈkjʊrəbəl] *adj & s* incurable *mf*
incursion [ɪnˈkʌrʒən] *s* incursión, correría
ind. *abbr* **independent, industrial**
indebted [ɪnˈdɛtɪd] *adj* adeudado; obligado
indebtedness [ɪnˈdɛtɪdnɪs] *s* endeudamiento
indecen•cy [ɪnˈdisənsi] *s* (*pl* **-cies**) indecencia, deshonestidad
indecent [ɪnˈdisənt] *adj* indecente, deshonesto; lépero (CAm, Mex)
indecisive [,ɪndɪˈsaɪsɪv] *adj* indeciso
indeclinable [,ɪndɪˈklaɪnəbəl] *adj* (gram) indeclinable
indeed [ɪnˈdid] *adv* verdaderamente, claro ‖ *interj* ¡de veras!
indefatigable [,ɪndɪˈfætɪgəbəl] *adj* incansable, infatigable
indefensible [,ɪndɪˈfɛnsɪbəl] *adj* indefendible
indefinable [,ɪndɪˈfaɪnəbəl] *adj* indefinible
indefinite [ɪnˈdɛfɪnɪt] *adj* indefinido
indelible [ɪnˈdɛlɪbəl] *adj* indeleble
indelicate [ɪnˈdɛlɪkɪt] *adj* indelicado
indemnification [ɪn,dɛmnɪfɪˈkəʃən] *s* indemnización
indemni•fy [ɪnˈdɛmnɪ,faɪ] *v* (*pret & pp* **-fied**) *tr* indemnizar
indemni•ty [ɪnˈdɛmnɪti] *s* (*pl* **-ties**) (*security against loss*) indemnidad; (*compensation*) indemnización
indent [ɪnˈdɛnt] *tr* dentar, mellar; (typ) sangrar
indentation [,ɪndɛnˈteʃən] *s* mella, muesca; (typ) sangría
indenture [ɪnˈdɛntʃər] *s* escritura, contrato; contrato de aprendizaje ‖ *tr* obligar por contrato
independence [,ɪndɪˈpɛndəns] *s* independencia
independen•cy [,ɪndɪˈpɛndənsi] *s* (*pl* **-cies**) independencia; país *m* independiente
independent [,ɪndɪˈpɛndənt] *adj & s* independiente *mf*
indescribable [,ɪndɪˈskraɪbəbəl] *adj* indescriptible
indestructible [,ɪndɪˈstrʌktɪbəl] *adj* indestructible
indeterminate [,ɪndɪˈtʌrmɪnɪt] *adj* indeterminado
index [ˈɪndɛks] *s* (*pl* **indexes** o **indices** [ˈɪndɪ,siz] *s* índice *m;* (typ) manecilla ‖ *tr* poner índice a; poner en un índice; (econ) indexar, indiciar; **to index salaries to inflation** indexar o indiciar los salarios a la inflación ‖ **index** *s* (eccl) Índice *m*
index card *s* ficha catalográfica
index finger *s* dedo índice
index tab *s* pestaña
India [ˈɪndɪ•ə] *s* la India
India ink *s* tinta china
Indian [ˈɪndɪ•ən] *adj & s* indio
Indian club *s* maza de gimnasia
Indian corn *s* maíz *m,* panizo
Indian file *s* fila india ‖ *adv* en fila india
Indian Ocean *s* mar *m* de las Indias, Océano Índico
Indian summer *s* veranillo de San Martín
India paper *s* papel *m* de China
India rubber *s* caucho
indicate [ˈɪndɪ,ket] *tr* indicar
indication [,ɪndɪˈkeʃən] *s* indicación
indicative [ɪnˈdɪkətɪv] *adj & s* indicativo
indicator [ˈɪndɪ,ketər] *s* indicador *m*
indict [ɪnˈdaɪt] *tr* (law) acusar, procesar
indictment [ɪnˈdaɪtmənt] *s* acusación, procesamiento; auto de acusación formulado por el gran jurado
indifferent [ɪnˈdɪfərənt] *adj* indiferente; (*not particularly good*) pasadero, mediano
indigenous [ɪnˈdɪdʒɪnəs] *adj* indígena
indigent [ˈɪndɪdʒənt] *adj* indigente
indigestible [,ɪndɪˈdʒɛstɪbəl] *adj* indigestible
indigestion [,ɪndɪˈdʒɛstʃən] *s* indigestión
indignant [ɪnˈdɪgnənt] *adj* indignado
indignation [,ɪndɪgˈneʃən] *s* indignación
indigni•ty [ɪnˈdɪgnɪti] *s* (*pl* **-ties**) indignidad
indi•go [ˈɪndɪgo] *adj* azul de añil ‖ *s* (*pl* **-gos** o **-goes**) índigo
indirect [,ɪndɪˈrɛkt] *adj* indirecto
indirect discourse *s* estilo indirecto
indiscernible [,ɪndɪˈzʌrnɪbəl] o [,ɪndɪˈsʌrnɪbəl] *adj* indiscernible
indiscreet [,ɪndɪsˈkrit] *adj* indiscreto
indiscriminate [,ɪndɪsˈkrɪmənɪt] *adj* indiscriminado
indispensable [ˈɪndɪsˈpɛnsəbəl] *adj* indispensable, imprescindible
indispose [,ɪndsˈpoz] *tr* indisponer
indisposed [,ɪndɪsˈpozd] *adj* (*disinclined*) maldispuesto; (*somewhat ill*) indispuesto
indissoluble [,ɪndɪˈsɑljəbəl] *adj* indisoluble
indistinct [,ɪndɪˈstɪŋkt] *adj* indistinto
individual [,ɪndɪˈvɪdʒʊ•əl] *adj* individual ‖ *s* individuo; persona física o natural
individuali•ty [,ɪndɪ,vɪdʒʊˈælɪti] *s* (*pl* **-ties**) individualidad; (*person of distinctive character*) personaje *m*
Indochina [ˈɪndoˈtʃaɪnə] *s* la Indochina
Indo-Chi•nese [ˈɪndotʃaɪˈniz] *adj* indochino ‖ *s* (*pl* **-nese**) indochino
indoctrinate [ɪnˈdɑktrɪ,net] *tr* adoctrinar
Indo-European [ˈɪndo,jʊrəˈpi•ən] *adj & s* indoeuropeo
indolent [ˈɪndələnt] *adj* indolente
Indonesia [,ɪndoˈniʃə] o [,ɪndoˈniʒə] *s* la Indonesia
Indonesian [,ɪndoˈniʃən] o [,ɪndoˈniʒən] *adj & s* indonesio

indoor [ˈɪn,dor] *adj* interior, de puertas adentro; (*inclined to stay in the house*) casero
indoors [ˈɪnˈdorz] *adv* dentro, en casa, bajo techado, bajo cubierto
indorse [ɪnˈdɔrs] *tr* endosar; (fig) apoyar, aprobar
indorsee [,ɪndɔrˈsi] *s* endosatario
indorsement [ɪnˈdɔrsmənt] *s* endoso; (fig) apoyo, aprobación
indorser [ɪnˈdɔrsər] *s* endosante *mf*
induce [ɪnˈdjus] *tr* inducir; causar, ocasionar
inducement [ɪnˈdjusmənt] *s* aliciente *m, estímulo, incentivo*
induct [ɪnˈdʌkt] *tr* instalar; introducir, iniciar; (mil) quintar
induction [ɪnˈdʌkʃən] *s* instalación; introducción; (elec & log) inducción; (mil) quinta
indulge [ɪnˈdʌldʒ] *tr* gratificar (*p.ej., los deseos de uno*); mimar (*a un niño*) ‖ *intr* abandonar; **to indulge in** entregarse a, permitirse el placer de
indulgence [ɪnˈdʌldʒəns] *s* gusto, inclinación; intemperancia, desenfreno; (*leniency*) indulgencia
indulgent [ɪnˈdʌldʒənt] *adj* indulgente
industrial [ɪnˈdʌstrɪ•əl] *adj* industrial
industrialist [ɪnˈdʌstrɪ•əlɪst] *s* industrial *m*
industrialize [ɪnˈdʌstrɪ•ə,laɪz] *tr* industrializar
industrial park *s* zona industrial
industrious [ɪnˈdʌstrɪ•əs] *adj* industrioso, aplicado
indus•try [ˈɪndəstri] *s* (*pl* **-tries**) industria
inebriation [ɪn,ibrɪˈeʃən] *s* embriaguez *f*
inedible [ɪnˈɛdɪbəl] *adj* incomible
ineffable [ɪnˈɛfəbəl] *adj* inefable
ineffective [,ɪnɪˈfɛktɪv] *adj* ineficaz; (*person*) incapaz
ineffectual [,ɪnɪˈfɛktʃʊ•əl] *adj* ineficaz, fútil
inefficacy [ɪnˈɛfɪkəsi] *s* ineficacia
inefficient [,ɪnɪˈfɪʃənt] *adj* de mal rendimiento, ineficaz, ineficiente; (*worker*) incompetente, ineficiente, ineficaz
ineligible [ɪnˈɛlɪdʒɪbəl] *adj* inelegible, inhábil
inequali•ty [,ɪnɪˈkwɑlɪti] *s* (*pl* **-ties**) desigualdad
inequi•ty [ɪnˈɛkwɪti] *s* (*pl* **-ties**) inequidad
ineradicable [,ɪnɪˈrædɪkəbəl] *adj* inextirpable
inertia [ɪnˈʌrʃə] *s* inercia
inescapable [,ɪnɛsˈkepəbəl] *adj* ineludible
inevitable [ɪnˈɛvɪtəbəl] *adj* inevitable
inexact [,ɪnɛgˈzækt] *adj* inexacto
inexcusable [,ɪnɛksˈkjuzəbəl] *adj* indisculpable, inexcusable
inexhaustible [,ɪnɛgˈzɔstɪbəl] *adj* inagotable
inexorable [ɪnˈɛksərəbəl] *adj* inexorable
inexpedient [,ɪnɛkˈspidɪ•ənt] *adj* malaconsejado, inoportuno
inexpensive [,ɪnɛkˈspɛnsɪv] *adj* barato, poco costoso
inexperience [,ɪnɛkˈspɪrɪ•əns] *s* inexperiencia
inexplicable [ɪnˈɛksplɪkəbəl] *adj* inexplicable
inexpressible [,ɪnɛkˈsprɛsɪbəl] *adj* inexpresable
Inf. *abbr* **Infantry**
infallible [ɪnˈfælɪbəl] *adj* infalible
infamous [ˈɪnfəməs] *adj* infame
infa•my [ˈɪnfəmi] *s* (*pl* **-mies**) infamia
infan•cy [ˈɪnfənsi] *s* (*pl* **-cies**) infancia
infant [ˈinfənt] *adj* infantil; (*in the earliest stage*) (fig) naciente ‖ *s* criatura, nene *m*
infant care *s* puericultura
infantile [ˈɪnfən,taɪl] o [ˈɪnfəntɪl] *adj* infantil; (*childish*) aniñado, infantil
infan•try [ˈɪnfəntri] *s* (*pl* **-tries**) infantería
infantry•man [ˈɪnfəntrimən] *s* (*pl* **-men** [mən]) infante *m*, soldado de infantería
infarct [ɪnˈfɑrkt] *s* infarto
infatuated [ɪnˈfætʃʊ,etɪd] *adj* apasionado, locamente enamorado
infect [ɪnˈfɛkt] *tr* inficionar, infectar; influir sobre
infection [ɪnˈfɛkʃən] *s* infección
infectious [ɪnˈfɛkʃəs] *adj* infeccioso
in•fer [ɪnˈf,r] *v* (*pret & pp* **-ferred;** *ger* **-ferring**) *tr* inferir; (coll) conjeturar, suponer
inferior [ɪnˈfɪrɪ•ər] *adj & s* inferior *m*
inferiority [ɪn,fɪrɪˈɑrɪti] *s* inferioridad
inferiority complex *s* complejo de inferioridad
infernal [ɪnˈfʌrnəl] *adj* infernal
infest [ɪnˈfɛst] *tr* infestar
infidel [ˈɪnfɪdəl] *adj & s* infiel *mf*
infideli•ty [,ɪnfɪˈdɛlɪti] *s* (*pl* **-ties**) infidelidad
inˈfieldˈ *s* (baseball) cuadro interior
infiltrate [ˈɪnfɪl,tret] *tr* infiltrar; infiltrarse en ‖ *intr* infiltrarse
infinite [ˈɪnfɪnɪt] *adj & s* infinito
infinitive [ɪnˈfɪnɪtɪv] *adj & s* infinitivo
infini•ty [ɪnˈfɪnɪti] *s* (*pl* **-ties**) infinidad; (math) infinito
infirm [ɪnˈfʌrm] *adj* infirme, achacoso; (*unsteady*) inestable, inseguro; poco firme, poco sólido
infirma•ry [ɪnˈfʌrməri] *s* (*pl* **-ries**) enfermería
infirmi•ty [ɪnˈfʌrmɪti] *s* (*pl* **-ties**) achaque *m;* inestabilidad
inˈfix *s* (gram) infijo
inflame [ɪnˈflem] *tr* inflamar
inflammable [ɪnˈflæməbəl] *adj* inflamable
inflammation [,ɪnfləˈmeʃən] *s* inflamación
inflate [ɪnˈflet] *tr* inflar ‖ *intr* inflarse
inflation [ɪnˈfleʃən] *s* inflación; (*of a tire*) inflado
inflationary [ɪnˈfleʃən,ɛri] *adj* inflacionario
inflect [ɪnˈflɛkt] *tr* doblar, torcer; modular (*la voz*); (gram) modificar por inflexión
inflection [ɪnˈflɛkʃən] *s* inflexión
inflexible [ɪnˈflɛksɪbəl] *adj* inflexible
inflict [ɪnˈflɪkt] *tr* infligir
inˈflight *adj* de a bordo, en vuelo
influence [ˈɪnflu•əns] *s* influencia ‖ *tr* influir sobre, influenciar
influential [,ɪnfluˈɛnʃəl] *adj* influyente
influenza [,ɪnfluˈɛnzə] *s* influenza
inform [ɪnˈfɔrm] *tr* informar, avisar, enterar ‖ *intr* informar
informal [ɪnˈfɔrməl] *adj* (*not according to es-*

tablished rules) informal; (*unceremonious; colloquial*) familiar
information [,ɪnfər'meʃən] *s* información, informes *mpl;* (compu) información, datos
informational [,ɪnfər'meʃənəl] *adj* informativo
information highway *s* (compu) autopista de información
information processing *s* tratamiento de la información
information science *s* informática
information theory *s* teoría de la información
informed sources *spl* los entendidos
infraction [ɪn'frækʃən] *s* infracción
infrared [,ɪnfrə'rɛd] *adj & s* infrarrojo; (compu) infrarrojos
infrequent [ɪn'frikwənt] *adj* infrecuente
infringe [ɪn'frɪndʒ] *tr* infringir ‖ *intr*—**to infringe on** o **upon** invadir, abusar de
infringement [ɪn'frɪndʒmənt] *s* infración
infuriate [ɪn'fjʊrɪ,et] *tr* enfurecer
infuse [ɪn'fjuz] *tr* infundir
infusion [ɪn'fjuʒən] *s* infusión
ingenious [ɪn'dʒinjəs] *adj* ingenioso
ingenui•ty [,ɪndʒɪ'nju•ɪti] o [,ɪndʒɪ'nu•ɪti] *s* (*pl* **-ties**) ingeniosidad
ingenuous [ɪn'dʒɛnjʊ•əs] *adj* ingenuo
ingenuousness [ɪn'dʒɛnjʊ•əsnɪs] *s* ingenuidad
ingest [ɪn'dʒɛst] *tr* ingerir
in'go'ing *adj* entrante
ingot ['ɪngət] *s* lingote *m*
ingraft [ɪn'græft] *tr* (hort & surg) injertar; (fig) implantar
ingrained [ɪn'grend] *adj* arraigado; (*dirt*) incrustado
ingrate ['ɪngret] *s* ingrato
ingratiate [ɪn'greʃi,et] *tr*—**to ingratiate oneself with** congraciarse con
ingratiating [ɪn'greʃi,etɪŋ] *adj* atrayente, obsequioso
ingratitude [ɪn'grætɪ,tjud] *s* ingratitud, desagradecimiento
ingredient [ɪn'gridɪ•ənt] *s* ingrediente *m*
in'grow'ing nail *s* uñero
ingulf [ɪn'gʌlf] *tr* hundir, inundar
inhabit [ɪn'hæbɪt] *tr* habitar, poblar
inhabitant [ɪn'hæbɪtənt] *s* habitante *mf*
inhale [ɪn'hel] *tr* aspirar, inspirar, inhalar ‖ *intr* aspirar, inspirar; tragar el humo
inherent [ɪn'hɪrənt] *adj* inherente
inherit [ɪn'hɛrɪt] *tr & intr* heredar
inheritance [ɪn'hɛrɪtəns] *s* herencia; mortual *m* (CAm, Mex)
inheritance tax *s* impuesto sucesorio, impuesto sobre sucesiones, impuesto a la herencia
inheritor [ɪn'hɛrɪtər] *s* heredero
inhibit [ɪn'hɪbɪt] *tr* inhibir, prohibir
inhospitable [ɪn'hɑspɪtəbəl] o [,ɪnhɑs'pɪtəbəl] *adj* inhospitalario; (*affording no shelter or protection*) inhóspito
in'-house *adj & adv* en la empresa
inhuman [ɪn'hjumən] *adj* inhumano
inhumane [,ɪnhju'men] *adj* inhumano
inhumani•ty [,inhju'mænɪti] *s* (*pl* **-ties**) inhumanidad
inimical [ɪ'nɪmɪkəl] *adj* enemigo
iniqui•ty [ɪ'nɪkwɪti] *s* (*pl* **-ties**) iniquidad
ini•tial [ɪ'nɪʃəl] *adj & s* inicial *f* ‖ *v* (*pret* **-tialed** o **-tialled;** *ger* **-tialing** o **tialling**) *tr* firmar con sus iniciales; marcar (*p.ej., un pañuelo*)
initiate [ɪ'nɪʃi,et] *tr* iniciar
initiation [ɪ,nɪʃi'eʃən] *s* iniciación
initiative [ɪ'nɪʃi•ətɪv] o [ɪ'nɪʃətɪv] *s* iniciativa
inject [ɪn'dʒɛkt] *tr* inyectar; introducir (*una especie, una advertencia*)
injection [ɪn'dʒɛkʃən] *s* inyección
injudicious [,ɪndʒu'dɪʃəs] *adj* imprudente
injunction [ɪn'dʒʌŋkʃən] *s* admonición, mandato; (law) entredicho
injure ['ɪndʒər] *tr* (*to harm*) dañar, hacer daño a; (*to wound*) herir, lisiar, lastimar; (*to offend*) agraviar
injurious [ɪn'dʒʊrɪ•əs] *adj* dañoso, perjudicial; (*offensive*) agravioso
inju•ry ['ɪndʒəri] *s* (*pl* **-ries**) (*harm*) daño; (*wound*) herida, lesión; (*offense*) agravio
injustice [ɪn'dʒʌstɪs] *s* injusticia
ink [ɪŋk] *s* tinta ‖ *tr* entintar
ink'-jet print'er *s* (compu) impresora de chorro de tinta
inkling ['ɪŋklɪŋ] *s* sospecha, indicio, noción vaga, vislumbre *f*
ink'stand' *s* (*cuplike container*) tintero; (*stand for ink, pens, etc.*) portatintero
ink'well' *s* tintero
ink•y ['ɪŋki] *adj* (*comp* **-ier;** *super* **-iest**) entintado; negro
inlaid ['ɪn,led] o [,ɪn'led] *adj* embutido, taraceado
inland ['ɪnlənd] *adj & s* interior *m* ‖ *adv* tierra adentro
in'-law' *s* (coll) pariente político
in•lay ['ɪn,le] *s* embutido ‖ [ɪn'le] o ['ɪn,le] *v* (*pret & pp* **-laid**) *tr* embutir, taracear
in'let *s* ensenada, cala, caleta, brazo de mar
in'mate' *s* (*in a hospital or home*) asilado, recluso, acogido; (*in a jail*) presidiario, preso
inn [ɪn] *s* mesón *m,* posada
innate [ɪ'net] o ['ɪnet] *adj* ingénito, innato
inner ['ɪnər] *adj* interior; secreto
in'ner-cit'y o **in'ner-core'** *adj* de las zonas urbanas deprimidas
in'ner•spring' mattress *s* colchón *m* de muelles interiores
inner tube *s* cámara (de neumático)
inning ['ɪnɪŋ] *s* mano *f,* entrada, turno
inn'keep'er *s* mesonero, posadero
innocence ['ɪnəsəns] *s* inocencia
innocent ['ɪnəsənt] *adj & s* inocente *mf*
innovate ['ɪnə,vet] *tr* innovar
innovation [,ɪnə'veʃən] *s* innovación
innuen•do [,ɪnjʊ'ɛndo] *s* (*pl* **-does**) indirecta, insinuación
innumerable [ɪ'numərəbəl] *adj* innumerable, incontable
inoculate [ɪn'ɑkjə,let] *tr* inocular; (fig) imbuir

inoculation [ɪn,ɑkjəˈleʃən] *s* inoculación
inoffensive [,ɪnəˈfɛnsɪv] *adj* inofensivo
inoperative [ɪnˈɑpərətɪv] *adj* fuera de servicio
inopportune [ɪn,ɑpərˈtjun] *adj* inoportuno
inordinate [ɪnˈɔrdɪnɪt] *adj* excesivo; (*unrestrained*) desenfrenado
inorganic [,ɪnɔrˈgænɪk] *adj* inorgánico
in'put' *s* aportación, gasto, consumo; (*advice, comment, opinion*) consejos o comentarios; (compu, elec) entrada; (mech) potencia consumida
inquest [ˈɪnkwɛst] *s* encuesta; (*of coroner*) pesquisa judicial, levantamiento del cadáver
inquire [ɪnˈkwaɪr] *tr* averiguar, inquirir ‖ *intr* preguntar; **to inquire about, after** o **for** preguntar por; **to inquire into** averiguar, inquirir
inquir•y [ɪnˈkwaɪri] o [ˈɪnkwɪri] *s* (*pl* **-ies**) averiguación, encuesta; pregunta
inquisition [,ɪnkwɪˈzɪʃən] *s* inquisición
inquisitive [ɪnˈkwɪzɪtɪv] *adj* curioso, preguntón
in'road' *s* incursión
ins. *abbr* **insulated, insurance**
insane [ɪnˈsen] *adj* loco, insano, dementado ‖ *spl*—**the insane** los enfermos mentales
insani•ty [ɪnˈsænɪti] *s* (*pl* **-ties**) demencia, locura, insania, loquera
insatiable [ɪnˈseʃəbəl] *adj* insaciable
inscribe [ɪnˈskraɪb] *tr* inscribir; dedicar (*una obra literaria*)
inscription [ɪnˈskrɪpʃən] *s* inscripción; (*of a book*) dedicatoria
inscrutable [ɪnˈskrutəbəl] *adj* inescrutable
insect [ˈɪnsɛkt] *s* insecto
insect control *s* desinsectación
insecticide [ɪnˈsɛktɪ,saɪd] *adj & s* insecticida *m*
insecure [,ɪnsɪˈkjʊr] *adj* inseguro
insemination [ɪn,sɛməˈneʃən] *s* inseminación
insensitive [ɪnˈsɛnsɪtɪv] *adj* insensible
inseparable [ɪnˈsɛpərəbəl] *adj* inseparable
insert [ˈɪnsʌrt] *s* inserción; (typ) encarte *m*, encaje *m* ‖ [ɪnˈsʌrt] *tr* insertar; (*an object, a finger*) introducir; (compu) insertar
insertion [ɪnˈsʌrʃən] *s* inserción; (*strip of lace*) entredós *m*
in•set [ˈɪn,sɛt] *s* intercalación ‖ [ɪnˈsɛt] o [ˈɪn,sɛt] *v* (*pret & pp* **-set;** *ger* **-setting**) *tr* intercalar, encastrar
in'shore' *adj* cercano a la orilla ‖ *adv* cerca de la orilla; hacia la orilla
in'side' *adj* interior; interno; secreto ‖ *adv* dentro, adentro; **inside of** dentro de; **to turn inside out** volver al revés; volverse al revés ‖ *prep* dentro de ‖ *s* interior *m;* **insides** (coll) entrañas; **on the inside** (coll) en el secreto de las cosas
inside information *s* informes *mpl* confidenciales
insider [,ɪnˈsaɪdər] *s* persona enterada
insider trading *s* (econ) abuso de información privilegiada
insidious [ɪnˈsɪdɪ•əs] *adj* insidioso
in'sight' *s* penetración, perspicacia
insigni•a [ɪnˈsɪgnɪ•ə] *s* (*pl* **-a** o **-as**) insignia
insignificant [,ɪnsɪgˈnɪfɪkənt] *adj* insignificante
insincere [,ɪnsɪnˈsɪr] *adj* insincero; malo (Mex)
insinuate [ɪnˈsɪnjʊ,et] *tr* insinuar
insipid [ɪnˈsɪpɪd] *adj* insípido
insist [ɪnˈsɪst] *intr* insistir
insofar as [,ɪnsoˈfɑr,æz] *conj* en cuanto a, en la medida en que, en tanto que
insolence [ˈɪnsələns] *s* insolencia
insolent [ˈɪnsələnt] *adj* insolente
insoluble [ɪnˈsɑljəbəl] *adj* insoluble
insolven•cy [ɪnˈsɑlvənsi] *s* (*pl* **-cies**) insolvencia
insomnia [ɪnˈsɑmnɪ•ə] *s* insomnio
insomuch [,ɪnsoˈmʌtʃ] *adv* hasta tal punto; **insomuch as** ya que, puesto que; **insomuch that** hasta el punto que
inspect [ɪnˈspɛkt] *tr* inspeccionar
inspection [ɪnˈspɛkʃən] *s* inspección
inspector [ɪnˈspɛktər] *s* inspector m
inspiration [,ɪnspɪˈreʃən] *s* inspiración
inspire [ɪnˈspaɪr] *tr & intr* inspirar
inspiring [ɪnˈspaɪrɪŋ] *adj* inspirante
Inst. *abbr* **Institute, Institution**
install [ɪnˈstɔl] *tr* instalar
installer [ɪnˈstɔlər] *s* (compu) instalador *m*
installment [ɪnˈstɔlmənt] *s* instalación; entrega; **in installments** por entregas; a plazos
installment buying *s* compra a plazos
installment plan *s* pago a plazos; compra a plazos; venta a plazos; **on the installment plan** con facilidades de pago
instance [ˈɪnstəns] *s* caso, ejemplo; **for instance** por ejemplo
instant [ˈɪnstənt] *adj* instantáneo ‖ *s* instante *m*, momento; mes *m* corriente
instantaneous [,ɪnstənˈtenɪ•əs] *adj* instantáneo
instant coffee *s* café instantáneo, café soluble
instantly [ˈɪnstəntli] *adv* al instante
instant replay *s* (sport) repetición (de la jugada)
instead [ɪnˈstɛd] *adv* preferiblemente; en su lugar; **instead of** en vez de, en lugar de
in'step' *s* empeine *m*
instigate [ˈɪnstɪ,get] *tr* instigar
in•still' *tr* instilar
instinct [ˈɪnstɪŋkt] *s* instinto
instinctive [ɪnˈstɪŋktɪv] *adj* instintivo
institute [ˈɪnstɪ,tjut] *s* instituto ‖ *tr* instituir
institution [,ɪnstɪˈtjuʃən] *s* institución
instruct [ɪnˈstrʌkt] *tr* instruir
instruction [ɪnˈstrʌkʃən] *s* instrucción
instructions for use *spl* modo de empleo
instructive [ɪnˈstrʌktɪv] *adj* instructivo
instructor [ɪnˈstrʌktər] *s* instructor *m*
instrument [ˈɪnstrəmənt] *s* instrumento ‖ [ˈɪnstrə,mɛnt] *tr* instrumentar
instrumentalist [,ɪnstrəˈmɛntəlɪst] *s* instrumentista *mf*
instrumentali•ty [,ɪnstrəmənˈtælɪti] *s* (*pl* **-ties**) agencia, mediación
instrument panel *s* cuadro de mando; salpicadero
insubordinate [,ɪnsəˈbɔrdɪnɪt] *adj* insubordinado

insufferable [ɪn'sʌfərəbel] *adj* insufrible
insufficient [,insə'fɪʃənt] *adj* insuficiente
insular ['ɪnsələr] o ['ɪnsjʊlər] *adj* insular; (fig) de miras estrechas
insulate ['ɪnsə,let] *tr* aislar
insulation [,ɪnsə'leʃən] *s* aislación
insulator ['ɪnsə,lətər] *s* aislador *m*
insulin ['ɪnsəlɪn] *s* insulina
insult ['ɪnsʌlt] *s* insulto, insultada, escopetazo ‖ [ɪn'sʌlt] *tr* insultar
insurable [ɪn'ʃʊrəbəl] *adj* asegurable
insurance [ɪn'ʃʊrəns] *s* seguro
insurance policy *s* póliza de seguros; (fig) medida preventiva
insure [ɪn'ʃʊr] *tr* asegurar
insurer [ɪn'ʃʊrər] *s* asegurador *m*
insurgent [ɪn'sʌrdʒənt] *adj & s* insurgente *mf*
insurmountable [,ɪnsər'maʊntəbəl] *adj* insuperable
insurrection [,ɪnsə'rɛkʃən] *s* insurrección
insusceptible [,ɪnsə'sɛptɪbəl] *adj* insusceptible
int. *abbr* **interest, interior, internal, international**
intact [ɪn'tækt] *adj* intacto, ileso
intaglio [ɪn'tælyo] *s* grabado en hueco, talla dulce
in'take' *s* (*place of taking in*) entrada; (*act or amount*) toma; (mach) admisión
intake manifold *s* múltiple *m* de admisión, colector *m* de admisión
intake valve *s* válvula de admisión
intangible [ɪn'tændʒɪbəl] *adj* intangible; vago, indefinido
integer ['ɪntɪdʒər] *s* (arith) entero
integral ['ɪntɪgrəl] *adj* íntegro; **integral with** solidario de ‖ *s* conjunto
integrate ['ɪntəgret] *tr* integrar; (*to desegregate*) eliminar la segregación de
integrated ['ɪntəgretəd] *adj* integrado; no segregacionista, sin separación racial, integrado; (compu) integrado
integrated circuit *s* circuito integrado
integration [,ɪntɪ'greʃən] *s* integración
integrity [ɪŋ'tɛgrɪti] *s* integridad
intellect ['ɪntə,lɛkt] *s* intelecto; (*person*) intelectual *mf*
intellectual [,ɪntə'lɛktʃʊ•əl] *adj & s* intelectual *mf*
intellectuali•ty [,ɪntə,lɛktʃʊ'ælɪti] *s* (*pl* **-ties**) intelectualidad
intelligence [ɪn'tɛlɪdʒəns] *s* inteligencia; información
intelligence bureau *s* departamento de inteligencia
intelligence quotient *s* cociente *m* intelectual
intelligent [ɪn'tɛlɪdʒənt] *adj* inteligente; espabilado
intelligentsia [ɪn,tɛlɪ'dʒəntsɪ•ə] o [ɪn,tɛlɪ'gɛntsɪ•ə] *s* intelectualidad (*conjunto de los intelectuales de un país o región*)
intelligible [ɪn'tɛlɪdʒɪbəl] *adj* inteligible
intemperance [ɪn'tɛmpərəns] *s* intemperancia
intemperate [ɪn'tɛmpərɪt] *adj* intemperante; (*climate*) riguroso
intend [ɪn'tɛnd] *tr* pensar, proponerse, intentar; (*to mean for a particular purpose*) destinar; (*to signify*) querer decir
intendance [ɪn'tɛndəns] *s* intendencia
intendant [ɪn'tɛndənt] *s* intendente *m*
intended [ɪn'tɛndɪd] *adj & s* (coll) prometido, prometida
intense [ɪn'tɛns] *adj* intenso
intensi•fy [ɪn'tɛnsɪ,faɪ] *v* (*pret & pp* **-fied**) *tr* intensificar, intensar; (phot) reforzar ‖ *intr* intensificarse, intensarse
intensi•ty [ɪn'tɛnsɪti] *s* (*pl* **-ties**) intensidad
intensive [ɪn'tɛnsiv] *adj* intensivo
intensive course *s* (educ) curso acelerado o intensivo
intent [ɪn'tɛnt] *adj* atento; resuelto; intenso; **intent on** resuelto a ‖ *s* (*purpose*) intento; (*meaning*) acepción, sentido; **to all intents and purposes** en realidad de verdad
intention [ɪn'tɛnʃən] *s* intención
intentional [ɪn'tɛnʃənəl] *adj* intencional, deliberado
in•ter [ɪn'tʌr] *v* (*pret & pp* **-terred;** *ger* **-terring**) *tr* enterrar
interact ['ɪntər,ækt] *s* (theat) entreacto ‖ [,ɪntər'ækt] *intr* obrar recíprocamente
interaction [,ɪntər'ækʃən] *s* interacción
in'ter•ac'tive *adj* interactivo
inter-American [,ɪntərə'mɛrɪkən] *adj* interamericano
inter•breed [,ɪntər'brid] *v* (*pret & pp* **-bred** ['brɛd]) *tr* entrecruzar ‖ *intr* entrecruzarse
intercalate [ɪn'tʌrkə,let] *tr* intercalar
intercede [,ɪntər'sid] *intr* interceder
intercept [,ɪntər'sɛpt] *tr* interceptar
interceptor [,ɪntər'sɛptər] *s* interceptor *m*
interchange ['ɪntər,tʃendʒ] *s* intercambio; (*on a highway*) correspondencia ‖ [,ɪntər'tʃendʒ] *tr* intercambiar ‖ *intr* intercambiarse
in'ter•cit'y *adj* interurbano
intercollegiate [,ɪntərkə'lidʒɪ•ɪt] *adj* interescolar
intercom ['ɪntər,kɑm] *s* interfono, intercomunicador *m*
intercourse ['ɪntər,kors] *s* comunicación, trato; (*interchange of products, ideas, etc.*) intercambio; (*copulation*) cópula, comercio; **to have intercourse** juntarse
intercross [,ɪntər'krɔs] o [,ɪntər'krɑs] *tr* entrecruzar ‖ *intr* entrecruzarse
interest rate *s* tasa *or* tipo de interés
interdict ['ɪntər,dɪkt] *s* entredicho ‖ [,ɪntər'dɪkt] *tr* interdecir
interest ['ɪntərɪst] *s* interés *m;* **the interests** las grandes empresas, el grupo influyente; **to put out at interest** poner a interés ‖ *tr* interesar
interested ['ɪntə,rɛstɪd] *adj* interesado
interesting ['ɪntə,rɛstɪŋ] *adj* interesante
interface ['ɪntər,fes] *s* interfase *f;* (compu) interfaz *f* ‖ *tr* (compu) conectar ‖ *intr* (*to interact*) relacionarse, e.g., **to interface with someone**

relacionarse con alguno; **to interface with something** (compu) colaborar
interfere [,ɪntər'fɪr] *intr* inmiscuirse, injerirse, interferir; (sport) parar una jugada; **to interfere with** dificultar, impedir, interferir
interference [,ɪntər'fɪrəns] *s* injerencia, intromisión; (compu, phys, rad, sport, telv) interferencia
interferon ['ɪntər'fɪrɑn] *s* (pharm) interferón *m*
interim ['ɪntərɪm] *adj* interino || *s* intermedio, intervalo; **in the interim** entretanto
interior [ɪn'tɪrɪ•ər] *adj & s* interior *m*
interior decorator *s* interiorista *mf*
interject [,ɪntər'dʒɛkt] *tr* interponer || *intr* interponerse
interjection [,ɪntər'dʒekʃən] *s* interposición; exclamación; (gram) interjección
interlard [,ɪntər'lɑrd] *tr* interpolar; mechar (*la carne*)
interline [,ɪntər'laɪn] *tr* interlinear; entretelar (*una prenda de vestir*)
interlining ['ɪntər,laɪnɪŋ] *s* (*of a garment*) entretela
interlink [,ɪntər'lɪŋk] *tr* eslabonar
interlock [,ɪntər'lɑk] *tr* trabar || *intr* trabarse
interlope [,ɪntər'lop] *intr* entremeterse; traficar sin derecho
interloper [,ɪntər'lopər] *s* intruso
interlude ['ɪntər,lud] *s* intervalo; (mus) interludio; (theat) intermedio
intermarriage [,ɪntər'mærɪdʒ] *s* casamiento entre parientes; casamiento entre personas de distintas razas, castas, etc.
intermediar•y [,ɪntər'midɪ,ɛri] *adj* intermediario || *s* (*pl* **-ies**) intermediario
intermediate [,ɪntər'midɪ•ɪt] *adj* intermedio
in•ter•me'di•ate-range' missile *s* cohete *m* de alcance medio
interment [ɪn'tʌrmənt] *s* entierro
intermez•zo [,ɪntər'mɛtso] o [,ɪntərmɛdzo] *s* (*pl* **-zos** o **-zi** [tsi] o [dzi]) (mus) intermedio, intermezzo
intermingle [,ɪntər'mɪŋgəl] *tr* entremezclar || *intr* entremezclarse
intermittent [,ɪntər'mɪtənt] *adj* intermitente
intermix [,ɪntər'mɪks] *tr* entremezclar || *intr* entremezclarse
intern ['ɪntʌrn] *s* interno de hospital, residente *mf* || [ɪn'tʌrn] *tr* internar, recluir
internal [ɪn'tʌrnəl] *adj* interno
inter'nal-combus'tion engine *s* motor *m* de explosión
internal revenue *s* rentas internas
international [,ɪntər'næʃənəl] *adj* internacional
international date line *s* línea internacional de cambio de fecha
internationalize [,ɪntər'næʃənə,laɪz] *tr* internacionalizar
internecine [,ɪntər'nisɪn] *adj* sanguinario
internee [,ɪntʌr'ni] *s* (mil) internado
internet ['ɪntʌrnɛt] *adj* (compu) internáutico || *s* (compu) **Internet** internet *f*
internist [ɪn'tʌrnɪst] *s* internista *mf*
internment [ɪn'tʌrnmənt] *s* internamiento
internship ['ɪntʌrn,ʃɪp] *s* residencia de un médico en un hospital
interpellate [,ɪntər'pɛlet] o [ɪn'tʌrpɪ,let] *tr* interpelar
interplay ['ɪntər,ple] *s* interacción
interpolate [ɪn'tʌrpə,let] *tr* interpolar
interpose [,ɪntər'poz] *tr* interponer
interpret [ɪn'tʌrprɪt] *tr* interpretar
interpretation [ɪn,tʌrprɪ'teʃən] *s* interpretación
interpreter [ɪn'tʌrprɪtər] *s* intérprete *mf;* (fig) exponente *mf*
interracial ['ɪntər'reʃəl] *adj* interracial
interrogate [ɪn'tɛrə,get] *tr & intr* interrogar
interrogation [ɪn,tɛrə'geʃən] *s* interrogación
interrogation mark o **point** *s* signo de interrogación
interrupt [,ɪntə'rʌpt] *tr* interrumpir
interscholastic [,ɪntərskə'læstɪk] *adj* interescolar
intersection [,ɪntər'sɛkʃən] *s* (*of streets, roads, etc.*) cruce *m,* bocacalle *f;* cruza (SAm); (geom) intersección
intersperse [,ɪntər'spʌrs] *tr* entremezclar, esparcir
interstice [ɪn'tʌrstɪs] *s* intersticio
intertwine [,ɪntər'twaɪn] *tr* entrelazar || *intr* entrelazarse
interval ['ɪntərvəl] *s* intervalo; **at intervals** (*now and then*) de vez en cuando; (*here and there*) de trecho en trecho
intervene [,ɪntər'vin] *intr* intervenir
intervening [,ɪntər'vinɪŋ] *adj* intermedio
intervention [,ɪntər'vɛnʃən] *s* intervención
interview ['ɪntər,vju] *s* entrevista, interview *m* || *tr* entrevistarse con
inter•weave [,ɪntər'wiv] *v* (*pret* **-wove** ['wov] o **-weaved;** *pp* **-wove, woven** o **weaved**) *tr* entretejer
intestate [ɪn'tɛstet] *adj & s* intestado
intestine [ɪn'tɛstɪn] *s* intestino
inthrall [ɪn'θrɔl] *tr* cautivar, encantar; esclavizar, sojuzgar
inthrone [ɪn'θron] *tr* entronizar
intima•cy ['ɪntɪməsi] *s* (*pl* **-cies**) intimidad
intimate ['ɪntɪmɪt] *adj* íntimo || *s* amigo íntimo || ['ɪntɪ,met] *tr* insinuar, intimar
intimation [,ɪntɪ'meʃən] *s* insinuación
intimidate [ɪn'tɪmɪ,det] *tr* intimidar
intitle [ɪn'taɪtəl] *tr* dar derecho a; (*to give a name to; to honor with a title*) intitular
into ['ɪntu] o ['ɪntʊ] *prep* en; hacia; hacia el interior de
intolerant [ɪn'tɑlərənt] *adj & s* intolerante *mf*
intomb [ɪn'tum] *tr* sepultar
intombment [ɪn'tummənt] *s* sepultura
intonation [,ɪnto'neʃən] *s* entonación
intone [ɪn'ton] *tr* entonar
intoxicant [ɪn'tɑksɪkənt] *s* bebida alcohólica
intoxicate [ɪn'tɑksɪ,ket] *tr* embriagar, emborrachar; (*to exhilarate*) alegrar, excitar; (*to poison*) envenenar, intoxicar
intoxication [ɪn,tɑksɪ'keʃən] *s* embriaguez *f;*

alegría, excitación; (*poisoning*) envenenamiento, intoxicación
intractable [ɪnˈtræktəbəl] *adj* intratable
intranet [ˈɪntrəˈnɛt] *adj* intranáutico
intransigent [ɪnˈtrænsɪdʒənt] *adj & s* intransigente *mf*
intransitive [ɪnˈtrænsɪtɪv] *adj* intransitivo
intravenous [ˌɪntrəˈvinəs] *adj* intravenoso
intrench [ɪnˈtrɛntʃ] *tr* atrincherar ‖ *intr*—**to intrench on** o **upon** infringir, violar
intrepid [ɪnˈtrɛpɪd] *adj* intrépido
intrepidity [ˌɪntrɪˈpɪdɪti] *s* intrepidez *f*
intricate [ˈɪntrɪkɪt] *adj* intrincado
intrigue [ɪnˈtrig] *s* intriga; intriga amorosa, enredo amoroso ‖ *tr* (*to arouse the curiosity of*) intrigar ‖ *intr* intrigar; tener intrigas amorosas
intrinsic(al) [ɪnˈtrɪnsɪk(əl)] *adj* intrínseco
introd. *abbr* **introduction**
introduce [ˌɪntrəˈdjus] *tr* introducir; (*to make acquainted*) presentar
introduction [ˌɪntrəˈdʌkʃən] *s* introducción; (*of one person to another or others*) presentación
introductory offer [ˌɪntrəˈdʌktəri] *s* ofrecimiento de presentación, oferta preliminar
introit [ˈɪntro•ɪt] *s* (eccl) introito
introspective [ˌɪntrəˈspɛktɪv] *adj* introspectivo
introvert [ˈɪntrəˌvʌrt] *s* introvertido
intrude [ɪnˈtrud] *intr* injerirse, entremeterse
intruder [ɪnˈtrudər] *s* intruso, entremetido
intrusive [ɪnˈtrusɪv] *adj* intruso
intrust [ɪnˈtrʌst] *tr* confiar
intuition [ˌɪntjʊˈɪʃən] *s* intuición
inundate [ˈɪnənˌdet] *tr* inundar
inundation [ˌɪnənˈdeʃən] *s* inundación
inure [ɪnˈjʊr] *tr* acostumbrar, endurecer, aguerrir ‖ *intr* ponerse en efecto; **to inure to** redundar en
inv. *abbr* **inventor, invoice**
invade [ɪnˈved] *tr* invadir
invader [ɪnˈvedər] *s* invasor *m*
invalid [ɪnˈvælɪd] *adj* inválido (*nulo, de ningún valor*) ‖ [ˈɪnvəlɪd] *adj* inválido (*por viejo o por enfermo*) ‖ [ˈɪnvəlɪd] *s* inválido
invalidate [ɪnˈvælɪˌdet] *tr* invalidar
invalidity [ˌɪnvəˈlɪdɪti] *s* invalidez *f*
invaluable [ɪnˈvæljʊ•əbəl] *adj* inestimable, inapreciable
invariable [ɪnˈvɛrɪ•əbəl] *adj* invariable
invasion [ɪnˈveʒən] *s* invasión
invective [ɪnˈvɛktɪv] *s* invectiva
inveigh [ɪnˈve] *intr*—**to inveigh against** lanzar invectivas contra
inveigle [ɪnˈvegəl] o [ɪnˈvigəl] *tr* engatusar
invent [ɪnˈvɛnt] *tr* inventar
invention [ɪnˈvɛnʃən] *s* invención, invento
inventive [ɪnˈvɛntɪv] *adj* inventivo
inventiveness [ɪnˈvɛntivnɪs] *s* inventiva
inventor [ɪnˈvɛntər] *s* inventor *m*
invento•ry [ˈɪnvənˌtori] *s* (*pl* **-ries**) inventario; stock *m* ‖ *v* (*pret & pp* **-ried**) *tr* inventariar
inverse [ɪnˈvʌrs] *adj* inverso
inversion [ɪnˈvʌrʒən] o [ɪnˈvʌrʃən] *s* inversión
invert [ɪnˈvʌrt] *tr* invertir
invertebrate [ɪnˈvʌrtɪˌbret] o [ɪnˈvʌrtɪbrɪt] *adj & s* invertebrado
inverted exclamation point *s* principio de admiración
inverted question mark *s* principio de interrogación
invest [ɪnˈvɛst] *tr* (*to vest, to install*) investir; invertir (*dinero*); (*to besiege*) cercar, sitiar; (*to surround, envelop*) cubrir, envolver
investigate [ɪnˈvɛstɪˌget] *tr* investigar
investigation [ɪnˌvɛstɪ•geʃən] *s* investigación
investment [ɪnˈvɛstmənt] *s* (*of money*) inversión; (*with an office or dignity*) investidura; (*siege*) cerco, sitio
investment capital *s* capital *m* de inversión
investor [ɪnˈvɛstər] *s* inversionista *mf;* inversor *m*
inveterate [ɪnˈvɛtərɪt] *adj* inveterado, empedernido
invidious [ɪnˈvɪdɪ•əs] *adj* irritante, odioso, injusto
invigorate [ɪnˈvɪgəˌret] *tr* vigorizar
invigorating [ɪnˈvɪgəˌretɪŋ] *adj* vigorizador, vigorizante
invincible [ɪnˈvɪnsɪbəl] *adj* invencible
invisible [ɪnˈvɪzɪbəl] *adj* invisible
invisible ink *s* tinta simpática
invitation [ˌɪnvɪˈteʃən] *s* invitación, convite *m*
invite [ɪnˈvaɪt] *tr* invitar, convidar
inviting [ɪnˈvaɪtɪŋ] *adj* atractivo, seductor; (*e.g., food*) apetitoso
in vitro *adj invar*—**in vitro fertilization** fecundación in vitro ‖ *adv* en vitro
invoice [ˈɪnvɔɪs] *s* factura; **as per invoice** según factura ‖ *tr* facturar
invoke [ɪnˈvok] *tr* invocar; evocar, conjurar (*p.ej., los demonios*)
involuntary [ɪnˈvɑlənˌtɛri] *adj* involuntario
involution [ˌɪnvəˈluʃən] *s* (math) elevación a potencias, potenciación
involve [ɪnˈvɑlv] *tr* envolver, comprometer
invulnerable [ɪnˈvʌlnərəbəl] *adj* invulnerable
inward [ˈɪnwərd] *adj* interior ‖ *adv* interiormente, hacia dentro
iodide [ˈaɪ•əˌdaɪd] *s* yoduro
iodine [ˈaɪ•əˌdin] *s* yodo ‖ [ˈaɪ•əˌdaɪn] *s* tintura de yodo
ion [ˈaɪ•ən] o [ˈaɪ•ɑn] *s* ion *m*
ionize [ˈaɪ•əˌnaɪz] *tr* ionizar
ionosphere [aɪˈɑnəˌsfɪr] *s* ionosfera
IOU [ˈaɪˌoˈju] *s* (letterword) pagaré *m*
IPA [ˈaɪˈpiˈe] *s* (letterword) (**International Phonetic Alphabet**) AFI *m* (Alfabeto Fonético Internacional)
I.Q. [ˈaɪˈkju] *s* (letterword) (**Intelligence Quotient**) C.I. *m* (cociente intelectual, cociente de inteligencia)
IRA *abbr* **Irish Republican Army; Individual Retirement Account**
Iran [ɪˈrɑn] o [aɪˈræn] *s* el Irán
Iranian [ɪˈreni•ən] o [aɪˈrenɪ•ən] *adj & s* iranés *m* o iranio
Iraq [ɪˈrɑk] *s* el Irak

Ira•qi [ɪˈrɑki] *adj* iraqués o iraquiano ‖ *s* (*pl* -**qis**) iraqués *m* o iraquiano
irate [ˈaɪret] o [aɪˈret] *adj* airado
ire [aɪr] *s* ira, cólera
Ireland [ˈaɪrlənd] *s* Irlanda
iris [ˈaɪrɪs] *s* (*of the eye*) iris *m;* (*rainbow*) iris, arco iris; (bot) lirio
Irish [ˈaɪrɪʃ] *adj* irlandés ‖ *s* (*language*) irlandés *m;* whisky *m* de Irlanda; **the Irish** los irlandeses
Irish•man [ˈaɪrɪʃmən] *s* (*pl* **-men** [mən]) irlandés *m*
Irish stew *s* guisado de carne con patatas y cebollas
I'rish•wom'an *s* (*pl* **-wom'en**) irlandesa
irk [ʌrk] *tr* fastidiar, molestar
irksome [ˈʌrksəm] *adj* fastidioso, molesto
iron [ˈaɪ•ərn] *adj* férreo ‖ *s* hierro; (*implement used to press or smooth clothes*) plancha; **irons** (*fetters*) hierros, grilletes *mpl;* **strike while the iron is hot** a hierro caliente batir de repente ‖ *tr* planchar (*la ropa*); **to iron out** allanar (*una dificultad*)
i'ron-bound' *adj* zunchado con hierro; (*unyielding*) férreo, duro, inflexible; (*rockbound*) escabroso, rocoso
ironclad [ˈaɪ•ərnˈklæd] *adj* acorazado, blindado; inflexible, exigente
iron curtain *s* (fig) telón *m* de hierro, cortina de hierro
iron digestion *s* estómago de avestruz
ironhanded [ˈaɪ•ərn,hændɪd] *adj* severo; riguroso; de mano férrea
iron horse *s* (coll) locomotora
ironic(al) [aɪˈrɑnɪk(əl)] *adj* irónico
ironing [ˈaɪ•ərnɪŋ] *s* planchado; ropa planchada; ropa por planchar
ironing board *s* tabla de planchar
iron lung *s* pulmón *m* de acero o de hierro
i'ron•ware' *s* ferretería
iron will *s* voluntad de hierro
i'ron•work' *s* herraje *m;* **ironworks** ferrería, herrería
i'ron•work'er *s* herrero de grueso; (*metal-worker*) cerrajero
iro•ny [ˈaɪrəni] *s* (*pl* **-nies**) ironía
irradiate [ɪˈredɪ,et] *tr* irradiar; (med) someter a radiación ‖ *intr* irradiar
irrational [ˈɪræʃənəl] *adj* irracional
irrecoverable [,ɪrɪˈkʌvərəbəl] *adj* incobrable, irrecuperable
irredeemable [,ɪrɪˈdiməbəl] *adj* irredimible
irrefutable [,ɪrɪˈfjutəbəl] o [ɪˈrɛfjutəbəl] *adj* irrebatible
irregular [ɪˈrɛgələr] *adj* irregular ‖ *s* (mil) irregular *m*
irrelevance [ɪˈrɛləvəns] *s* impertinencia, inaplicabilidad
irrelevant [ɪˈrɛləvənt] *adj* impertinente, inaplicable; irrelevante
irreligious [,ɪrɪˈlɪdʒəs] *adj* irreligioso
irremediable [,ɪrɪˈmidɪ•əbəl] *adj* irremediable
irremovable [,ɪrɪˈmuvəbəl] *adj* inamovible
irreparable [ɪˈrɛpərəbəl] ıadj irreparable
irreplaceable [,ɪrɪˈplesəbəl] *adj* insubstituíble, irreemplazable
irrepressible [,ɪrɪˈprɛsɪbəl] *adj* irreprimible, incontenible
irreproachable [,ɪrɪˈprotʃəbəl] *adj* irreprochable
irresistible [,ɪrɪˈzɪstɪbəl] *adj* irresistible
irrespective [,ɪrɪˈspɛktɪv] *adj* — **irrespective of** sin hacer caso de, independiente de
irresponsible [,ɪrɪˈspɑnsɪbəl] *adj* irresponsable
irretrievable [,ɪrɪˈtrivəbəl] *adj* irrecuperable
irreverent [ɪˈrɛvərənt] *adj* irreverente
irreversible [ˈɪrəˈvʌrsəbəl] *adj* irreversible
irrevocable [ɪˈrɛvəkəbəl] *adj* irrevocable
irrigate [ˈɪrɪ,get] *tr* irrigar
irrigation [,ɪrɪˈgeʃən] *s* irrigación
irritant [ˈɪrɪtənt] *adj & s* irritante *m*
irritate [ˈɪrɪ,tet] *tr* irritar
irruption [ɪˈrʌpʃən] *s* irrupción
IRS |ˈaɪˈarˈɛs| *s* (letterword) (**Internal Revenue Service**) (*equivalente a la*) Hacienda
isinglass [ˈaɪzɪŋ,glæs] o [ˈaɪzɪŋ,glɑs] *s* (*form of gelatine*) cola de pescado, colapez *f;* mica
Islam [ˈɪsləm] o [ɪsˈlɑm] *s* el Islam
Islamic [ɪsˈlæmɪk], [ɪsˈlɑmɪk] *adj* islámico
Islamism [ɪsˈlæm,ɪzəm], [ɪsˈlɑm,ɪzəm], [ˈɪzləmɪzəm] *s* islamismo
island [ˈaɪlənd] *adj* isleño ‖ *s* isla
islander [ˈaɪləndər] *s* isleño
isle [aɪl] *s* islote *m*
ism [ˈɪsəm] *s* (pej) ismo (pej)
isn't *contr* **is not**
isolate [ˈaɪsə,let] aislar
isolated [ˈaɪsə,letɪd] *adj* aislado; insulado; alejado
isolation [,aɪsəˈleʃən] *s* aislamiento
isolationist [,aɪsəˈleʃənɪst] *s* aislacionista *mf*
isometric [,aɪsəˈmɛtrɪk] *adj* isométrico
isometrics *s* isométrica
isosceles [aɪˈsɑsə,liz] *adj* isosceles
isotope [ˈaɪsə,top] *s* isótopo
Israel [ˈɪzrɪ•əl] *s* Israel *m*
Israe•li [ɪzˈreli] *adj* israelí ‖ *s* (*pl* **-lis** [liz] israelí *mf*
Israelite [ˈɪzrɪ•ə,laɪt] *adj & s* israelita *mf*
issuance [ˈɪʃʊ•əns] *s* emisión, expedición
issue [ˈɪʃʊ] *s* (*outgoing; outlet*) salida; (*result*) consecuencia, resultado; (*offspring*) descendencia, sucesión; (*of a magazine*) edición, impresión, tirada, número; (*e.g., of a bond*) emisión; (*yield, profit*) beneficios, producto; punto en disputa; (*distribution*) repartida; (pathol) flujo; **at issue** en disputa; **to face the issue** afrontar la situación; **to force the issue** forzar la solución; **to take issue with** llevar la contraria a ‖ *tr* publicar, dar a luz (*un nuevo libro, una revista, etc.*); emitir, expedir (*títulos, obligaciones, etc.*); distribuir (*ropa, alimento*) ‖ *intr* salir; **to issue from** provenir de
isthmus [ˈɪsməs] *s* istmo
it [ɪt] *pron pers* (aplícase a cosas inanimadas, a niños de teta, a animales cuyo sexo no se conoce; y muchas veces no se traduce) él, ella;

lo, la; **it is I** soy yo; **it is snowing** nieva; **it is three o'clock** son las tres
ital. *abbr* **italics**
Ital. *abbr* **Italian, Italy**
Italian [ɪˈtæljən] *adj & s* italiano
italic [ɪˈtælɪk] *adj* (typ) itálico ‖ **italics** *s* (typ) itálica, bastardilla, cursiva ‖ **Italic** *adj* itálico
italicize [ɪˈtælɪˌsaɪz] *tr* imprimir en bastardilla; subrayar
italic script *s* letra itálica, bastardilla o cursiva
Italy [ˈɪtəli] *s* Italia
itch [ɪtʃ] *s* comezón *f;* (pathol) sarna; (*eagerness*) (fig) comezón, prurito ‖ *tr* dar comezón a ‖ *intr* picar; **to itch to** tener prurito por
itch•y [ˈɪtʃi] *adj* (*comp* **-ier;** *super* **-iest**) picante, hormigoso; (pathol) sarnoso
item [ˈaɪtəm] *s* artículo; noticia, suelto; (*in an account*) partida
itemization [ˌaɪtəmaɪˈzeʃən] *s* rubricación
itemize [ˈaɪtəˌmaɪz] *tr* particularizar, especificar, pormenorizar
itinerant [aɪˈtɪnərənt] o [ɪˈtɪnərənt] *adj* ambulante, errante ‖ *s* viandante *mf*
itinerar•y [aɪˈtɪnəˌrɛri] o [ɪˈtɪnəˌrɛri] *adj* itinerario ‖ *s* (*pl* **-ies**) itinerario
it'll *contr* **it will**
it's *contr* **it is; it has**
its [ɪts] *adj poss su* ‖ *pron poss* el suyo; suyo
itself [ɪtˈsɛlf] *pron pers* mismo; sí, sí mismo; se
IV [ˌaɪˈvi] *s* (letterword) (**intravenous**) inyección intravenosa
I've *contr* **I have**
ivied [ˈaɪvid] *adj* cubierto de hiedra
IV stand *s* aparato de IV
ivo•ry [ˈaɪvəri] *adj* marfileño ‖ *s* (*pl* **-ries**) marfil *m;* **ivories** (slang) teclas del piano; (slang) bolas de billar; (*dice*) (slang) dados; (slang) dientes *mpl*
ivory tower *s* (fig) torre *f* de marfil; (fig) inocencia
ivy [ˈaɪvi] *s* (*pl* **-ivies**) hiedra

J

J. j [dʒe] décima letra del alfabeto inglés
jab [dʒæb] *s* hurgonazo; (*prick*) pinchazo; (*with elbow*) codazo ‖ *v* (*pret & pp* **jabbed;** *ger* **jabbing**) *tr* hurgonear; dar un codazo a ‖ *intr* hurgonear
jabber [ˈdʒæbər] *s* parloteo ‖ *tr & intr* farfullar
jack [dʒæk] *s* (*for lifting heavy objects*) gato, cric *m;* (*fellow*) mozo, sujeto, (*jackass*) asno, burro; (*in card games*) sota, valet *m;* (*small ball for bowling*) boliche *m;* (*jackstone*) cantillo; (*device for turning a spit*) torno de asador; (*figure which strikes a clock bell*) jaquernar *m;* (*to remove a boot*) sacabotas *m;* marinero; (*flag at the bow*) (naut) yac *m;* (rad & telv) jack *m;* (elec) caja de enchufe; (slang) dinero; **every man Jack** cada hijo de vecino; **Jack** Juanito; **jacks** cantillos, juego de los cantillos ‖ *tr* — **to jack up** alzar con el gato; (coll) subir (*sueldos, precios, etc.*); (coll) recordar su obligación a
jackal [ˈdʒækɔl] *s* chacal *m*
jack'ass' *s* asno, burro
jacket [ˈdʒækɪt] *s* chaqueta; (*folded paper*) cubierta, envoltura; (*paper cover of a book*) sobrecubierta; (*metal casing*) camisa
jack'ham'mer *s* martillo perforador
jack'-in-the-box' *s* caja de sorpresa, jugete-sorpresa *m,* muñeco en una caja de resorte
jack'knife' *s* (*pl* **-knives'**) navaja de bolsillo; (*fancy dive*) salto de carpa
jack'-of-all-trades' *s* hombre que hace toda clase de oficios dije *m,* todoterreno
jack-o'-lantern [ˈdʒækəˌlæntərn] *s* fuego fatuo; linterna hecha con una calabaza cortado de modo que remede una cabeza humana
jackpot *s* grande *f,* pozo, premio gordo; **to hit the jackpot** sacarse el premio gordo, llevarse el pozo, sacarse la lotería; (fig) tener gran éxito
jack rabbit *s* liebre grande norteamericana
jack'screw' *s* cric *m* o gato de tornillo
jackstraws [ˈdʒækˌstrɔz] *s* juego de las pajitas
jade [dʒed] *adj* verdoso como el jade ‖ *s* (*ornamental stone*) jade *m;* verde *m* de jade; (*worn-out horse*) jamelgo; picarona, mujerzuela ‖ *tr* cansar, ahitar, saciar
jaded [ˈdʒedɪd] *adj* ahito, saciado, harto
jag [dʒæg] *s* punta saliente, púa
jagged [ˈdʒægɪd] *adj* dentado, mellado; rasgado en sietes
jaguar [ˈdʒægwɑr] *s* jaguar *m*
jail [dʒel] *s* cárcel *f;* **to break out of jail** escaparse de la cárcel ‖ *tr* encarcelar
jail'bird' *s* (coll) preso, encarcelado; (coll) infractor *m* habitual
jail'break' *s* escapatoria de la cárcel
jailer [ˈdʒelər] *s* carcelero
jalop•y [dʒəˈlɑpi] *s* (*pl* **-ies**) (coll) cacharro
jam [dʒæm] *s* apiñadura, apretura; (*e.g., in traffic*) embotellamiento, bloqueo; (*preserve*) compota, conserva; (*difficult situation*) (coll) aprieto, apuros ‖ *v* (*pret & pp* **jammed;** *ger* **jamming**) *tr* apiñar, apretujar; machucarse (*p.ej., un dedo*); (rad) perturbar, sabotear; **to jam on the brakes** frenar de golpe
Jamaican [dʒəˈmekən] *adj & s* jamaicano; jamaiquino (Am)
jamb [dʒæm] *s* jamba
jamboree [ˌdʒæmbəˈri] *s* (coll) francachela, holgorio; congreso de niños exploradores

James [dʒemz] *s* Jaime *m,* Diego; (*British kings*) Jacobo
jamming [ˈdʒæmɪŋ] *s* radioperturbación
jam nut *s* contratuerca
jam-packed [ˈdʒæmˈpækt] *adj* (coll) apiñado, apretujado, atestado
jam session *s* sesión de jazz improvisada
Jane [dʒen] *s* Juana
jangle [ˈdʒæŋgəl] *s* cencerreo; altercado, riña ‖ *tr* hacer sonar con ruido discordante ‖ *intr* cencerrear; reñir
janitor [ˈdʒænɪtər] *s* portero, conserje *m*
janitress [ˈdʒænɪtrɪs] *s* portera
January [ˈdʒænjʊ,ɛri] *s* enero
Ja•pan [dʒəˈpæn] *s* laca japonesa; obra japonesa laqueada; aceite *m* secante japonés ‖ *v* (*pret & pp* **-panned;** *ger* **-panning**) *tr* barnizar, charolar, laquear con laca japonesa ‖ **Japan** *s* el Japón
Japa•nese [,dʒæpəˈniz] *adj* japonés ‖ *s* (*pl* **-nese**) japonés *m*
Japanese beetle *s* escarabajo japonés
Japanese lantern *s* farolillo veneciano
jar [dʒɑr] *s* tarro; (*e.g., of olives*) frasco; (*of a storage battery*) recipiente *m;* (*jolt*) sacudida; ruido desapacible; sorpresa desagradable; **on the jar** (*said of a door*) entreabierto, entornado ‖ *v* (*pret & pp* **jarred;** *ger* **jarring**) *tr* sacudir; chocar; (*with a noise*) traquetear ‖ *intr* sacudirse; traquetear; disputar; **to jar on** irritar
jardiniere [,dʒɑrdɪˈnɪr] *s* (*stand*) jardinera; (*pot, bowl*) florero
jargon [ˈdʒɑrgən] *s* jerga, jerigonza
jasmine [ˈdʒæsmɪn] *s* jazmín *m*
jasper [ˈdʒæspər] *s* jaspe *m*
jaundice [ˈdʒɔndɪs] o [ˈdʒɑndɪs] *s* ictericia; (fig) envidia, celos, negro humor
jaundiced [ˈdʒɔndɪst] o [ˈdʒɑndɪst] *adj* ictericiado; (fig) avinagrado
jaunt [dʒɔnt] o [dʒɑnt] *s* caminata, excursión, paseo
jaun•ty [ˈdʒɔnti] o [ˈdʒɑnti] *adj* (*comp* **-tier;** *super* **-tiest**) airoso, gallardo, vivo; elegante, de buen gusto
Java•nese [,dʒævəˈniz] *adj* javanés ‖ *s* (*pl* **-nese**) javanés *m*
javelin [ˈdʒævlɪn] o [ˈdʒævəlɪn] *s* jabalina
jaw [dʒɔ] *s* mandíbula, quijada; **into the jaws of death** a las garras de la muerte; **jaws** boca, fauces *fpl* ‖ *tr* (slang) regañar ‖ *intr* (slang) regañar; (slang) chacharear, chismear
jawʹboneʹ *s* mandíbula, quijada
jawʹbreakʹer *s* (*word*) (coll) trabalenguas *m;* (*candy*) (coll) hinchabocas *m;* (mach) trituradora de quijadas
jay [dʒe] *s* (orn) arrendajo; (coll) tonto, necio
jayʹwalkʹ *intr* (coll) cruzar la calle descuidadamente
jayʹwalkʹer *s* (coll) peatón descuidado
jazz [dʒæz] *s* (mus) jazz *m;* (coll) animación, viveza ‖ *tr*—**to jazz up** (coll) animar, dar viveza a
jazz band *s* orquesta de jazz
J.C. *abbr* **Jesus Christ, Julius Caesar**
jct. *abbr* **junction**
jealous [ˈdʒɛləs] *adj* celoso; envidioso; (*watchful in keeping or guarding something*) solícito, vigilante
jealous•y [ˈdʒɛləsi] *s* (*pl* **-ies**) celosía, celos; envidia; solicitud, vigilancia
jeans [dʒinz] *spl* vaqueros, jeans *mpl,* tejanos (Esp)
Jeanne d'Arc [,ʒɑnˈdɑrk] *s* Juana de Arco
jeep [dʒip] *s* jip *m,* jeep *m* (*pequeño automóvil, todoterreno, que se maniobra con gran facilidad y en poco espacio*)
jeer [dʒɪr] *s* befa, mofa, vaya ‖ *tr* befar ‖ *intr* mofarse; **to jeer at** befar, mofarse de
Jehovah's Witness [dʒɪˈhovə] *s* testigo de Jehová
jell [dʒɛl] *s* jalea ‖ *intr* (*to become jellylike*) cuajarse; (*to take hold, catch on*) (fig) cuajar
jellaba [ˈdʒɛləbə] *s* (*gown*) chilaba
jel•ly [ˈdʒɛli] *s* (*pl* **-lies**) jalea ‖ *v* (*pret & pp*) *tr* convertir en jalea ‖ *intr* convertirse en jalea
jelʹlyʹbeanʹ *s* frutilla
jelʹly•fishʹ *s* aguamala, medusa; (*weak person*) (coll) calzonazos *m*
jelly roll *s* brazo gitano
jeopardize [ˈdʒɛpər,daɪz] *tr* arriesgar, exponer, poner en peligro
jeopardy [ˈdʒɛpərdi] *s* riesgo, peligro
jeremiad [,dʒɛrɪˈmaɪ•æd] *s* jeremiada
Jericho [ˈdʒɛrɪ,ko] *s* Jericó
jerk [dʒʌrk] *s* arranque *m,* estirón *m,* tirón *m;* tic *m,* espasmo muscular; (*person*) (pej) estúpido, pendejo, memo; **by jerks** a sacudidas ‖ *tr* mover de un tirón; arrojar de un tirón; atasajar (*carne*) ‖ *intr* avanzar a tirones
jerked beef *s* tasajo
jerkin [ˈdʒʌrkɪn] *s* jubón *m,* justillo
jerkʹwaʹter *adj* (coll) de mala muerte, insignificante
jerk•y [ˈdʒʌrki] *adj* (*comp* **-ier;** *super* **-iest**) (*road; style*) desigual; que va dando tumbos, que anda a tirones
jersey [ˈdʒʌrsi] *s* jersey *m,* chaqueta de punto
Jerusalem [dʒɪˈrusələm] *s* Jerusalén
jest [dʒɛst] *s* broma, chanza, chiste *m;* cosa de risa; **in jest** en broma ‖ *intr* bromear
jester [ˈdʒɛstər] *s* bromista *mf,* burlón *m;* (*professional fool of medieval rulers*) bufón *m*
Jesuit [ˈdʒɛʒʊ•ɪt] o [ˈdʒɛzj,•ɪt] *adj & s* jesuíta *m*
Jesus [ˈdʒizəs] *s* Jesús *m*
Jesus Christ *s* Jesucristo
jet [dʒɛt] *adj* de azabache; azabachado ‖ *s* (*of a fountain*) surtidor *m;* (*of gas*) mechero; (*stream shooting forth from nozzle, etc.*) chorro; avión *m* a reacción, avión de chorro; (*hard black mineral; lustrous black*) azabache *m* ‖ *v* (*pret & pp* **jetted;** *ger* **jetting**) *tr* arrojar en chorro ‖ *intr* chorrear, salir en chorro; volar en avión de chorro

jet age *s* era de los aviones de chorro
jet′-black′ *adj* azabachado
jet bomber *s* bombardero de reacción a chorro
jet coal *s* carbón *m* de bujía, carbón de llama larga
jet engine *s* motor *m* a chorro, motor de reacción, reactor *m*
jet fighter *s* caza *m* de reacción, cazarreactor *m*
jet lag *s* jet lag *m* (*cansancio causado por el desfase horario*)
jet′lin′er *s* avión *m* de travesía con propulsión a chorro
jet plane *s* avión *m* de chorro, reactor *m*
jet propulsion *s* propulsión a chorro, propulsión de escape
jetsam [ˈdʒɛtsəm] *s* (naut) echazón *f;* cosas desechadas
jet set *s* gente acomodada que viajan mucho por avión
jet stream *s* escape *m* de un motor cohete; (meteor) chorros de viento (*que soplan de oeste a este a la altura de 10 kilómetros*)
jettison [ˈdʒɛtɪsən] *s* (naut) echazón *f* ‖ *tr* (naut) echar al mar; desechar, rechazar
jet•ty [ˈdʒɛti] *s* (*pl* **-ties**) (*structure projecting into sea to protect harbor*) excollera, malecón *m;* (*wharf*) muelle *m,* desembarcadero
Jew [dʒu] *s* judío
jewel [ˈdʒu•əl] *s* piedra preciosa; (*valuable personal ornament*) alhaja, joya; (*of a watch*) rubí *m;* (*article of costume jewelry*) joya de imitación; (*highly prized person or thing*) alhaja, joya
jewel case *s* guardajoyas *m,* estuche *m,* joyero
jeweler o **jeweller** [ˈdʒu•ələr] *s* joyero; relojero
jewelry [ˈdʒu•əlri] *s* joyería, joyas
jewelry shop *s* joyería; relojería
Jewish [ˈdʒu•ɪʃ] *adj* judío
Jew•ry [ˈdʒu•ri] *s* (*pl* **-ries**) judería
jib [dʒɪb] *s* (*of a crane*) aguilón *m,* pescante *m;* (naut) foque *m*
jib boom *s* (naut) botalón *m* de foque
jibe [dʒaɪb] *s* remoque *m,* mofa ‖ *intr* mofarse; (coll) concordar (*dos cosas*); **to jibe at** mofarse de
jif•fy [ˈdʒɪfi] *s* (*pl* **-fies**)—**in a jiffy** (coll) en un santiamén
jig [dʒɪg] *s* (*dance and music*) giga; **the jig is up** (slang) ya se acabó todo, estamos perdidos
jigger [ˈdʒɪgər] *s* (*for fishing*) anzuelo de cuchara; (*for separating ore*) criba de vaivén; (*flea*) nigua; (*gadget*) cosilla, chisme *m,* dispositivo; vasito para medir el licor de un coctel (*onza y media*)
jiggle [ˈdʒɪgəl] *s* zangoloteo ‖ *tr* zangolotear ‖ *intr* zangolotearse
jig saw *s* sierra de vaivén
jig′saw′ puzzle *s* rompecabezas *m* (*figura que ha sido cortada caprichosamente en trozos menudos y que hay que recomponer*)
jihad [dʒɪˈhɑd] *s* (*holy war*) guerra sagrada (del Islam), guerra santa; (*crusade*) cruzada
jilt [dʒɪlt] *tr* dar calabazas a (*un novio*)
jim•my [ˈdʒɪmi] *s* (*pl* **-mies**) palanqueta ‖ *v* (*pret & pp* **-mied**) *tr* forzar con palanqueta; **to jimmy open** abrir con palanqueta
jingle [ˈdʒɪŋgəl] *s* (*small bell*) cascabel *m;* (*of tambourine*) sonaja; (*sound*) cascabeleo; rima infantil; (rad, telv) anuncio rimado y cantado, jingle *m* ‖ *tr* hacer sonar ‖ *intr* cascabelear
jin•go [ˈdʒɪŋgo] *adj* jingoista ‖ *s* (*pl* **-goes**) jingoísta *mf;* **by jingo!** (coll) ¡caramba!
jingoism [ˈdʒɪŋgo,ɪzəm] *s* jingoísmo
jinx [dʒɪŋks] *s* gafe *m* ‖ *tr* (coll) traer mala suerte a
jitters [ˈdʒɪtərz] *spl* (coll) inquietud, nerviosidad; **to give the jitters to** (coll) poner nervioso; **to have the jitters** (coll) ponerse nervioso
jittery [ˈdʒɪtəri] *adj* (coll) nervioso
Joan of Arc [ˈdʒon əv ˈɑrk] *s* Juana de Arco
job [dʒɑb] *s* (*piece of work*) trabajo; (*task, chore*) quehacer *m,* tarea; (*work done by contract*) destajo; (*employment*) empleo, oficio; (coll) robo; **by the job** a destajo; **on the job** en su puesto, de trabajo; (slang) vigilante, atento a sus obligaciones; **to be out of a job** estar desocupado, estar sin trabajo; **to lie down on the job** (coll) echarse en el surco, estirar la pierna
job analysis *s* análisis *m* ocupacional
jobber [ˈdʒɑbər] *s* comerciante medianero; (*pieceworker*) destajero
job′hold′er *s* empleado; (*in the government*) burócrata *mf*
jobless [ˈjɑblɪs] *adj* desocupado, sin empleo
job lot *s* saldo de mercancías, lote *m*
job market *s* oportunidades *fpl* de empleo
job security *s* garantía de empleo continuo
jock [dʒɑk] *s* (slang) atleta *mf*
jockey [ˈdʒɑki] *s* jockey *m* ‖ *tr* montar (*un caballo*) en la pista; maniobrar; embaucar
jockstrap [ˈdʒɑk,stræp] *s* suspensorio, suspensor *m* (*para sostener el escroto*)
jocose [dʒoˈkos] *adj* jocoso
jocular [ˈdʒɑkjələr] *adj* jocoso, festivo
jodhpurs [ˈdʒɑdpərz] *spl* pantalones *mpl* de equitación, pantalones de montar
Joe [dʒo] *m* Pepe
jog [dʒɑg] *s* golpecito; (*to the memory*) estímulo; trote corto ‖ *v* (*pret & pp* **jogged;** *ger* **jogging**) *tr* empujar levemente; estimular (*la memoria*) ‖ *intr* hacer footing, hacer jogging; **to jog along** avanzar al trote corto
jogger [ˈdʒɑgər] *s* persona que corre despacio para hacer ejercicio
jogging [ˈdʒɑgɪŋ] *s* jogging *m,* footing *m*
jog trot *s* trote *m* de perro; (fig) rutina
john [dʒɑn] *s* (coll) inodoro, retrete, baño; (*prostitute's client*) (slang) putero; **John** Juan *m*
John Bull *s* el inglés típico, el pueblo ingles
John Hancock [ˈhænkɑk] *s* (coll) la firma de uno
johnnycake [ˈdʒɑni,kek] *s* pan *m* de maíz
John′ny-come′-late′ly *s* recién llegado

John′ny-jump′-up′ *s* (*pansy*) pensamiento, trinitaria, violeta
John′ny-on-the-spot′ *s* (coll) el que está siempre presente y listo
John the Baptist *s* San Juan Bautista
join [dʒɔɪn] *tr* juntar, unir, ensamblar; asociarse a, unirse a; incorporarse a, ingresar en; abrazar (*un partido*); hacerse socio de (una asociación); alistarse en (*el ejército*); trabar (*batalla*); desaguar en (*el océano*) ‖ *intr* juntarse, unirse; confluir (*p.ej., dos ríos*)
joiner [ˈdʒɔɪnər] *s* carpintero; (coll) el que tiene la manía de incorporarse a muchas asociaciones
joint [dʒɔɪnt] *s* (*in a pipe*) empalme *m,* juntura, (*of bones*) articulación, juntura, coyuntura; (*backbone of book*) nervura; (*hinge of book*) cartivana; (*in woodwork*) emsambladura; (*of meat*) tajada; (*marijuana*) porro, puerro; (elec) empalme *m;* (*gambling den*) (slang) garito; (slang) restaurante *m* de mala muerte; **out of joint** desencajado, descoyuntado; (fig) en desorden, desbarajustado; **to throw out of joint** descoyuntarse (*p.ej., el brazo*)
joint account *s* cuenta en común, cuenta conjunta
Joint Chiefs of Staff *spl* (U.S.A) Estado mayor conjunto
joint committee *s* comisión mixta
jointly [ˈdʒɔɪntli] *adv* juntamente, en común
joint owner *s* condueño
joint session *s* sesión conjunta
joint′-stock′ company *s* sociedad anónima, compañía por acciones
jointure [ˈdʒɔɪntʃər] *s* bienes *mpl* parafernales
joist [dʒɔɪst] *s* viga
joke [dʒok] *s* broma, chiste *m;* (*trifling matter*) cosa de reír; (*person laughed at*) bufón *m,* hazmerreír *m;* **no joke** cosa seria; **to tell a joke** contar un chiste, **to play a joke on** gastar una broma a ‖ *tr*—**to joke one's way into** conseguir (*p.ej., un empleo*) burla burlando ‖ *intr* bromear, hablar en broma; **joking aside** o **no joking** burlas aparte
joke book *s* libro de chistes
joker [ˈdʒokər] *s* bromista *mf;* (*wise guy*) sábelotodo; (*playing card*) comodín *m;* (*hidden provision*) cláusula engañadora
jol•ly [ˈdʒɑli] *adj* (*comp* **-lier;** *super* **-liest**) alegre, festivo ‖ *adv* (coll) muy, harto ‖ *v* (*pret & pp* **-lied**) *tr* (coll) candonguear
Jolly Roger *s* bandera pirata
jolt [dʒolt] *s* sacudida ‖ *tr* sacudir ‖ *intr* dar tumbos
Jonah [ˈdʒonə] *s* Jonás *m;* (fig) ave *f* de mal agüero
jongleur [ˈdʒɑŋglər] *s* juglar *m,* trovador *m*
jonquil [ˈdʒɑŋkwɪl] *s* junquillo
Jordan [ˈdʒɔrdən] *s* (*country*) Jordania; (*river*) Jordán *m*
Jordan almond *s* almendra de Málaga
Jordanian [dʒɔrˈdenɪ•ən] *adj & s* jordano
Joseph [ˈdʒosəf] *s* José *m*
josh [dʒɑʃ] *tr* (coll) dar broma a ‖ *intr* dar broma
jostle [ˈdʒɑsəl] *s* empellón *m,* empujón *m* ‖ *tr* empellar, empujar ‖ *intr* chocar, encontrarse; avanzar a fuerza de empujones o codazos
jot [dʒɑt] *s* —**I don't care a jot for** no se me da un bledo de *s v* (*pret & pp* **jotted;** *ger* **jotting**) *tr*—**to jot down** apuntar, anotar
jounce [dʒaʊns] *s* sacudida ‖ *tr* sacudir ‖ *intr* dar tumbos
journal [ˈdʒʌrnəl] *s* (*newspaper*) periódico; (*magazine*) revista; (*daily record*) diario; (com) libro diario; (naut) cuaderno de bitácora; (mach) gorrón *m,* muñón *m*
journalese [ˌdʒʌrnəˈliz] *s* (pej) jerga periodística
journalism [ˈdʒʌrnəˌlɪzəm] *s* periodismo
journalist [ˈdʒʌrnəlɪst] *s* periodista *mf*
journalistic [ˌdʒʌrnəˈlɪstɪk] *adj* periodístico
journey [ˈdʒʌrni] *s* viaje *m* ‖ *intr* viajar
journey•man [ˈdʒʌrnimən] *s* (*pl* **-men** [mən]) oficial *m*
joust [dʒʌst] o [dʒust] o [dʒaʊst] *s* justa ‖ *intr* justar
jovial [ˈdʒovɪ•əl] *adj* jovial
joviality [ˌdʒovɪˈælɪti] *s* jovialidad
jowl [dʒaʊl] *s* (*cheek*) moflete *m;* (*jawbone*) quijada; (*of cattle*) papada; (*of fowl*) barba
joy [dʒɔɪ] *s* alegría, regocijo; **to leap with joy** saltar de gozo
joyful [ˈdʒɔɪfəl] *adj* alegre; **joyful over** gozoso con o de
joyless [ˈdʒɔɪlɪs] *adj* triste, sin alegría
joyous [ˈdʒɔɪ•əs] *adj* alegre
joyride *s* (coll) paseo de recreo en coche; (coll) paseo alocado en coche
joy′stick *s* (aer) palanca de mando; (compu, electron) mando, joystick *m*
Jr. *abbr* **junior**
jubilant [ˈdʒubɪlənt] *adj* jubiloso
jubilation [ˌdʒubɪˈleʃən] *s* júbilo, viva alegría
jubilee [ˈdʒubɪˌli] *s* (*jubilation*) júbilo; aniversario; quincuagésimo aniversario; (eccl) jubileo
Judaism [ˈdʒudeˌɪzəm] *s* judaísmo
Judeo-Christian [dʒuˈde•oˈkrɪstʃən] *adj* judeocristiano
judge [dʒʌdʒ] *s* juez *m;* **to be a good judge of** ser buen juez de o en ‖ *tr & intr* juzgar; **judging by** a juzgar por
judge advocate *s* (*in the army*) auditor *m* de guerra; (*in the navy*) auditor de marina
judgeship [ˈdʒʌdʒʃɪp] *s* judicatura
judgment [ˈdʒʌdʒmənt] *s* juicio; (*legal decision*) sentencia, fallo
Judgment Day *s* Día del Juicio Final
judicature [ˈdʒudɪkətʃər] *s* judicatura
judicial [dʒuˈdɪʃəl *adj* judicial; (*becoming a judge*) crítico, juicioso
judiciar•y [dʒuˈdɪʃiˌɛri] *adj* judicial ‖ *s* (*pl* **-ies**) (*judges of a city, country, etc.*) judicatura; (*branch of government that administers justice*) poder *m* judicial
judicious [dʒuˈdɪʃəs] *adj* juicioso

jug [dʒʌg] *s* botija, jarra, cántaro; (*jail*) (slang) chirona
juggle [ˈdʒʌgəl] *s* juego de manos; (*trick, deception*) trampa ‖ *tr* hacer suertes con (*p.ej., bolas*); alterar fraudulentamente, falsear (*cuentas, documentos, etc.*); **to juggle away** escamotear ‖ *intr* hacer suertes; hacer trampas
juggler [ˈdʒʌglər] *s* malabarista *mf;* impostor *m*
juggling [ˈdʒʌglɪŋ] *s* juegos malabares
jugular [ˈdʒʌgjələr] *adj & s* yugular *f*
juice [dʒus] *s* jugo, zumo; (*natural fluid of an animal body*) jugo; (slang) electricidad; (slang) gasolina; **to stew in one's own juice** (coll) freír en su aceite
juic•y [ˈdʒusi] *adj* (*comp* **-ier;** *super* **-iest**) jugoso, zumoso; (*interesting, spicy*) picante
jukebox [ˈdʒuk,bɑks] *s* tocadiscos *m* tragamonedas
julep [ˈdʒulɪp] *s* julepe *m*
julienne [,dʒulɪˈɛn] *s* sopa juliana
July [dʒuˈlaɪ] *s* julio
jumble [ˈdʒʌmbəl] *s* revoltijo, masa confusa ‖ *tr* emburujar, revolver
jum•bo [ˈdʒʌmbo] *adj* (coll) enorme, colosal ‖ *s* (*pl* **-bos**) (*large clumsy person*) (coll) elefante *m;* (coll) objeto enorme
jump [dʒʌmp] *s* salto; (*in a parachute*) lanzamiento; (*of prices*) alza repentina; (coll) (aut) uso de cables de arranque; **to be always on the jump** (coll) andar siempre de aquí para allí; **to get** o **to have the jump on** (slang) ganar la ventaja a ‖ *tr* saltar; hacer saltar (*a un caballo*); (*in checkers*) comer; salir (*un tren*) fuera de (*el carril*); (*a motor*) hacer arrancar ‖ *intr* saltar; (*in a parachute from an airplane*) lanzarse; pasar del tope (*el carro de la máquina de escribir*); **to jump at** apresurarse a aceptar (*un convite*); apresurarse a aprovechar (*la oportunidad*); **to jump on** saltar a (*un tren*); (slang) regañar, criticar; **to jump over** saltar por, pasar de un salto; saltar (*la página de un libro*); **to jump to a conclusion** sacar una conclusión precipitadamente
jumper [ˈdʒʌmpər] *s* saltador *m;* blusa de obrero; **jumpers** traje holgado de juego para niños
jumper cables *spl* cables *mpl* de arranque
jumping jack [ˈdʒʌmpɪŋ] *s* cohete borracho
jump'ing-off' place *s* fin *m* del camino
jump seat *s* estrapontín *m,* traspuntín *m*
jump spark *s* (elec) chispa de entrehierro
jump'-start *tr* (aut) hacer arrancar (*un motor conectándolo con un cable de empalme a la batería de otro motor*); (fig) (*an economy, enthusiasm, patriotism, donations*) estimular
jump suit *s* vestido unitario (*como de paracaidista*)
jump wire *s* (elec) alambre *m* de cierre
jump•y [ˈdʒʌmpi] *adj* (*comp* **-ier;** *super* **-iest**) saltón; asustadizo, nervioso
junction [ˈdʒʌŋkʃən] *s* juntura, unión; (*of pieces of wood*) ensambladura; (*of two rivers*) confluencia; (*rail connection*) empalme *m;* (rr) estación de empalme
juncture [ˈdʒʌŋktʃər] *s* juntura, unión; (*time, occasion*) coyuntura; **at this juncture** a esta sazón, a estas alturas
June [dʒun] *s* junio
jungle [ˈdʒʌŋgəl] *s* jungla, selva; revoltijo, maraña
jungle fever *s* (*malaria*) fiebre palúdica
junior [ˈdʒunjər] *adj* menor, de menor edad; joven; del penúltimo año; hijo, p.ej., **John Jones, Junior** Juan Jones, hijo ‖ *s* menor *m;* socio menor; alumno del penúltimo año
junior college *s* escuela de estudios universitarios de primero y segundo años
junior high school *s* escuela intermedia entre la primaria y la secundaria
juniper [ˈdʒunɪpər] *s* enebro; (*red cedar*) cedro de Virginia
juniper berry *s* enebrina
junk [dʒʌŋk] *s* chatarra, hierro viejo; ropa vieja; (*useless stuff*) (coll) trastos viejos, baratijas viejas; (*old cable*) jarcia trozada; (*Chinese ship*) junco; (naut) carne salada ‖ *tr* (slang) echar a la basura; reducir a hierro viejo
junk dealer *s* chatarrero, chapucero
junket [ˈdʒʌŋkɪt] *s* manjar *m* de leche, cuajo y azúcar; (*outing*) viaje *m* de recreo; (*trip paid out of public funds*) jira ‖ *intr* hacer un viaje de recreo; ir de jira
junk food *s* comida malsana, alimento chatarra (Mex), comida chatarra (Mex)
junkie [ˈdʒʌŋki] *s* (slang) toxicómano, narcotómano, yonquí *m*
junk mail *s* propaganda que se recibe por correo
junk•man [ˈdʒʌŋk,mæn] *s* (*pl* **-men** [,mɛn]) chatarrero, chapucero; ropavejero
junk room *s* leonera, trastera
junk shop o **junk store** *s* tienda de trastos viejos; baratío (CAm); barata (Col, Mex)
junk yard *s* chatarrería
juridical [dʒʊˈrɪdɪkəl] *adj* jurídico
juried [ˈdʒʊrid] *adj* (fa) evaluado por un tribunal de expertos
jurisdiction [,dʒʊrɪsˈdɪkʃən] *s* jurisdicción
jurisprudence [,dʒʊrɪsˈprudəns] *s* jurisprudencia
jurist [ˈdʒʊrɪst] *s* jurista *mf*
juror [ˈdʒʊrər] *s* (*individual*) jurado
ju•ry [ˈdʒʊri] *s* (*pl* **-ries**) (*group*) jurado
jury box *s* tribuna del jurado
jury•man [ˈdʒʊrimən] *s* (*pl* **-men** [mən]) (*individual*) jurado
jury-rig [ˈdʒʊri,rɪg] *v* (*pret & pp* **-rigged;** *ger* **-rigging**) *tr* (naut) aparejar temporariamente
just [dʒʌst] *adj* justo ‖ *adv* justamente, justo; hace poco, apenas; sólo, nomás; (coll) absolutamente; **just** + *pp* acabado de + *inf,* p.ej., **just received** acabado de recibir; recién + *pp,* p.ej., **just arrived** recién llegado; **just as** como; en el momento en que; tal como, lo mismo que; **just beyond** un poco más allá (de); **just now** hace poco; ahora mismo; **just**

out acabado de aparecer, recién publicado; **to have just** + *pp* acabar de + *inf,* p.ej., **I have just arrived** acabo de llegar; **I had just arrived** acababa de llegar
justice [ˈdʒʌstɪs] *s* justicia; (*judge*) juez *m;* (*just deserts*) premio merecido; **to bring to justice** aprehender y condenar por justicia; **to do justice to** hacer justicia a; apreciar debidamente
justice of the peace *s* juez *m* de paz
justifiable [ˈdʒʌstɪ,faɪ•əbəl] *adj* justificable
justi•fy [ˈdʒʌstɪ,faɪ] *v* (*pret & pp* **-fied**) *tr* justificar; (typ) justificar
justly [ˈdʒʌstli] *adj* justamente, debidamente
jut [dʒʌt] *v* (*pre & pp* **jutted;** *ger* **jutting**) *intr*—**to jut out** resaltar, proyectarse
jute [dʒut] *s* yute *m* ‖ **Jute** *m* juto
Jutland [ˈdʒʌtlənd] *s* Jutlandia
juvenile [ˈdʒuvənɪl] o [ˈdʒuvə,naɪl] *adj* juvenil; para jóvenes ‖ *s* joven *mf,* mocito; libro para niños; (theat) galán *m,* galancete *m*
juvenile court *s* tribunal *m* tutelar de menores
juvenile delinquency *s* delincuencia de menores
juvenile lead [lid] *s* (theat) papel *m* de galancete; (theat) galancete *m*
juvenilia [,dʒuvəˈnɪlɪ•ə] *spl* obras de juventud
juxtapose [,dʒʌkstəˈpoz] *tr* yuxtaponer

K

K, k [ke] undécima letra del alfabeto inglés
k. *abbr* **karat, kilogram**
K. *abbr* **King, Knight**
kale [kel] *s* col *f,* berza; (slang) dinero, pasta
kaleidoscope [keˈlaɪdə,skop] *s* calidoscopio
kangaroo [,kæŋgəˈru] *s* canguro
kapok [ˈkepɑk] *s* capoc *m,* lana de ceiba
kaput [kəˈpʊt] *adj* (slang) roto; gastado; inútil
karate [kəˈrɑti] *m* karate *m,* karaté *m*
karate expert *s* karateka *m*
katydid [ˈketidɪd] *s* saltamontes *m* cuyo macho emite un sonido chillón
kayak [ˈkaɪæk] *s* kayak *m*
kc. *abbr* **kilocycle**
kedge [kɛdʒ] *s* (naut) anclote *m*
keel [kil] *s* quilla ‖ *intr*—**to keel over** (naut) dar de quilla; volcarse; (coll) desmayarse
keelson [ˈkɛlsən] o [ˈkilsən] *s* (naut) sobrequilla
keen [kin] *adj* (*having a sharp edge*) agudo, afilado; (*sharp, cutting*) mordaz, penetrante; (*sharp-witted*) sutil, astuto, perspicaz; (*eager, much interested*) entusiasta; intenso, vivo; (slang) maravilloso; **to be keen on** ser muy aficionado a
keep [kip] *s* manutención, subsistencia; (*of medieval castle*) torre *f* del homenaje; **for keeps** (coll) de veras; (coll) para siempre; **to earn one's keep** (coll) ganarse la vida ‖ *v* (*pret & pp* **kept** [kɛpt] *tr* guardar, conservar; (*deciding to make a purchase*) quedarse con; cumplir, guardar (*su palabra, su promesa*); llevar (*cuentas*); apuntar (*los tantos*); tener (*criados, caballos, huéspedes*); cultivar (*una huerta*); dirigir (*un hotel, una escuela*); celebrar (*una fiesta*); hacer tardar (*a una persona*); **to keep away** tener alejado; **to keep back** retener; beberse (*las lágrimas*); reservar, no divulgar; **to keep down** reprimir; reducir (*los gastos*) al mínimo; **to keep** (*a person*) **from** + *ger* no dejarle (*a una persona*) + *inf;* **to keep in** no dejar salir; **to keep off** tener a distancia; no dejar penetrar (*p.ej., la lluvia*); evitar (*p.ej., el polvo*); **to keep out** no dejar entrar; no dejar penetrar; **to keep someone informed (about)** ponerle a uno al corriente (de); **to keep someone waiting** hacerle a uno esperar; **to keep up** mantener, conservar ‖ *intr* permanecer, quedarse; conservarse, no echarse a perder; **to keep** + *ger* seguir + *ger;* **to keep away** mantenerse a distancia; no dejarse ver; **to keep from** + *ger* abstenerse de + *inf;* **to keep informed (about)** ponerse al corriente (de); **to keep in with** (coll) congraciarse con, no perder el favor de; **to keep off** no acercarse a; no pisar (*el césped*); **to keep on** + *ger* seguir + *ger;* **to keep on with** continuar con; **to keep out** mantenerse fuera, no entrar; **to keep out of** no entrar en; no meterse en; evitar (*el peligro*); **to keep quiet** estarse quieto; **to keep to** seguir por, llevar (*la derecha, la izquierda*); **to keep to oneself** quedarse a solas; **to keep up** continuar; no rezagarse; **to keep up with** correr parejas con; llevar adelante, proseguir
keeper [ˈkipər] *s* guardián *m,* custodio; (*of a game preserve*) guardabosque *m;* (*of a magnet*) armadura, culata
keeping [ˈkipɪŋ] *s* custodia, cuidado; (*of a holiday*) celebración; **in keeping with** de acuerdo con, en armonía con; **in safe keeping** en lugar seguro, a buen recaudo; **out of keeping with** en desacuerdo con
keep′sake′ *s* recuerdo
keg [kɛg] *s* cuñete *m,* cubeto
ken [kɛn] *s* alcance *m* de la vista, alcance del saber; **beyond the ken of** fuera del alcance de
kennel [ˈkɛnəl] *s* perrera
kep•i [ˈkepi] o [ˈkɛpi] *s* (*pl* **-is**) quepis *m*
kept woman [kɛpt] *s* entretenida, manceba
kerchief [ˈkʌrtʃif] *s* pañuelo, mantón *m*
kerchoo [kərˈtʃu] *interj* ¡ah-chís!

kernel [ˈkʌrnəl] *s* (*inner part of a nut or fruit stone*) almendra núcleo; (*of wheat or corn*) grano; (fig) medula

kerosene [ˈkɛrə,sin] o [,kɛrəˈsin] *s* keroseno

kerosene lamp *s* lámpara de petróleo

kerplunk [kərˈplʌŋk] *interj* ¡cataplúm!

ketchup [ˈkɛtʃəp] *s* salsa de tomate condimentada

kettle [ˈkɛtəl] *s* caldera, marmita; (*teakettle*) tetera

ket'tle•drum' *s* timbal *m,* tímpano

key [ki] *adj* clave ‖ *s* (*of door, trunk, etc.*) llave *f;* (*of piano, typewriter, computer, etc.*) tecla; (*wedge or cotter used to lock parts together*) clavija, cuña, chaveta; (*reef or low island*) cayo; (bot) sámara; (*tone of voice*) tono; (mus) clave *f* o llave *f;* (telg) manipulador *m;* (*to a puzzle, secret, translation, code*) (fig) clave o llave; (*place giving control to a region*) (fig) llave *f;* (fig) persona principal; **off key** desafinado; desafinadamente ‖ *tr* acuñar, enchavetar; **to key up** alentar, excitar

key'board' *s* teclado ‖ *tr* (compu) teclear, entrar

key'boarder *s* (compu) operador *m,* grabador *m,* operador de consola

key fruit *s* sámara

key'hole' *s* ojo de la cerradura; (*of a clock*) agujero de cuerda

key money *s* pago ilícito al casero

key'note' *s* (mus) tónica, nota tónica; (fig) idea fundamental

keynote speech *s* discurso de apertura (*en que se expone el programa de un partido político*)

key'pad *m* (compu, electron, telv) teclado numérico

key'punch'er *s* perforista *mf*

key ring *s* llavero

key'stone' *s* clave *f,* espinazo; (fig) piedra angular

Key West *s* Cayo Hueso

key word *s* palabra clave

kg. *abbr* **kilogram**

kha•ki [ˈkɑki] o [ˈkæki] *adj* caqui ‖ *s* (*pl* **-kis**) caqui *m*

khedive [kəˈdiv] *s* jedive *m*

kibitz [ˈkɪbɪts] *intr* (coll) dar consejos molestos a los jugadores

kibitzer [ˈkɪbɪtsər] *s* (coll) mirón molesto (*de una partida de juego*); (coll) entremetido

kiblah [ˈkɪblɑ] *s* alquibla

kibosh [ˈkaɪbɑʃ] o [kɪˈbɑʃ] *s* (coll) música celestial; **to put the kibosh on** (coll) desbaratar, imposibilitar

kick [kɪk] *s* puntapié *m;* (*of an animal*) coz *f;* (*of a gun*) coz, culatazo; (*complaint*) (slang) queja, protesta; (*of liquor*) (slang) fuerza, estímulo; (*thrill*) gusto, placer intenso; **to get a kick out of** (slang) hallar mucho placer en ‖ *tr* acocear, dar de puntapiés a; sacudir (*los pies*); **to kick out** (coll) echar a puntapiés a la calle; (coll) echar, despedir; **to kick the bucket** (coll) morir; **to kick up a row** (slang) armar un bochinche ‖ *intr* cocear; dar culetazos (*un arma de fuego*); (coll) quejarse; **to kick about** (coll) quejarse de; **to kick against the pricks** dar coces contra el aguijón; **to kick off** (football) dar el golpe de salida

kick'back' *s* (coll) contragolpe *m;* (slang) devolución a un cómplice de una parte de lo robado

kick'off' *s* (football) golpe *m* de salida, puntapié *m* inicial, patata de inicio

kid [kɪd] *s* (*young goat*) cabrito; (*leather*) cabritilla; (coll) chiquillo, chico; **kids** guantes *mpl* o zapatos de cabritilla; (*offspring*) prole *f* ‖ *v* (*pret & pp* **kidded;** *ger* **kidding**) *tr* (coll) embromar, tomar el pelo a; **to kid oneself** (coll) forjarse ilusiones ‖ *intr* (coll) decirlo en broma

kidder [ˈkɪdər] *s* (slang) bromista *mf*

kid gloves *spl* guantes *mpl* de cabritilla; **to handle with kid gloves** tratar con suma discreción o cautela

kid'nap' *v* (*pret & pp* **-naped** o **-napped;** *ger* **naping** o **-napping**) *tr* secuestrar

kidnaper o **kidnapper** [ˈkɪd,næpər] *s* secuestrador *m,* raptor *m;* (*of children*) ladrón *m* de niños

kidney [ˈkɪdni] *s* riñon *m;* (coll) clase *f,* especie *f;* (coll) carácter *m*

kidney bean *s* judía, frijol colorado

kidney stone *s* cálculo renal

kill [kɪl] *s* matanza; (*of a wild beast, an army, a pack of hounds*) ataque *m* final; (*creek*) arroyo, riachuelo; **for the kill** para el golpe final ‖ *tr* matar; ahogar (*un proyecto de ley*); quitar (*el sabor*); producir una impresión irresistible en

killer [ˈkɪlər] *s* matador *m*

killer bee *s* abeja asesina

killer whale *s* orca

killing [ˈkɪlɪŋ] *adj* matador; (*exhausting*) abrumador; (coll) muy divertido, de lo más ridículo ‖ *s* matanza; (*game killed on a hunt*) cacería, piezas; (coll) gran ganancia; **to make a killing** (coll) enriquecerse de golpe

kill'-joy' *s* aguafiestas *mf*

kiln [kɪl] o [kɪln] *s* horno

kil•o [ˈkɪlo] o [ˈkilo] *s* (*pl* **-os**) kilo, kilogramo; kilómetro

kilocycle [ˈkɪlə,saɪkəl] *s* kilociclo

kilogram [ˈkɪlə,græm] *s* kilogramo

kilometer [ˈkɪlə,mitər] [kɪˈlɑmətər] *s* (*0.621 mile*) kilómetro

kilometric [,kɪləˈmɛtrɪk] *adj* kilométrico

kilowatt [ˈkɪlə,wɑt] *s* kilovatio

kilowatt-hour [ˈkɪlə,wɑtˈaʊr] *s* (*pl* **kilowatt-hours**) kilovatio-hora

kilt [kɪlt] *s* enagüillas, falda corta

kilter [ˈkɪltər] *s*—**to be out of kilter** (coll) estar descompuesto

kimo•no [kɪˈmonə] *s* (*pl* **-nos**) quimono

kin [kɪn] *s* (*family relationship*) parentesco; (*relatives*) deudos; **near of kin** muy allegado; **of kin** allegado; **the next of kin** el pariente más próximo, los parientes próximos

kind [kaɪnd] *adj* bueno, bondadoso; (*greeting*) afectuoso; **kind to** bueno para con ‖ *s* clase *f,* especie *f,* suerte *f,* género; **a kind of** uno a modo de; **all kinds of** (coll) gran cantidad de; **in kind** en especie; en la misma moneda; **kind of** (coll) algo, más bien; **of a kind** de una misma clase; (*poor, mediocre*) de poco valor, de mala muerte; **of the kind** por el estilo
kindergarten [ˈkɪndər,gɑrtən] *s* parvulario, escuela de párvulos, jardín *m* de la infancia
kindergartner [ˈkɪndər,gɑrtnər] *s* (*child*) párvulo; (*teacher*) parvulista *mf*
kind-hearted [ˈkaɪndˈhɑrtɪd] *adj* bondadoso, de buen corazón
kindle [ˈkɪndəl] *tr* encender ‖ *intr* encenderse
kindling [ˈkɪndlɪŋ] *s* encendajas
kindling wood *s* leña
kind•ly [ˈkaɪndli] *adj* (*comp* **-lier;** *super* **-liest**) (*kind-hearted*) bondadoso; apacible, benigno; favorable ‖ *adv* bondadosamente; cordialmente; con gusto; por favor; **to not take kindly to** no aceptar de buen grado
kindness [ˈkaɪndnɪs] *s* bondad; **have the kindness to** tenga Ud. la bondad de
kindred [ˈkɪndrɪd] *adj* emparentado; afín, semejante ‖ *s* parentela; semejanza, afinidad
kinetic [kɪˈnɛtɪk] *adj* cinético ‖ **kinetics** *s* cinética
kinetic energy *s* fuerza viva, energía cinética
kinfolk [ˈkin,fok] *s* (coll) pariente(s)
king [kɪŋ] *s* rey *m;* (cards, chess, & fig) rey; (checkers) dama
kingˈboltˈ *s* pivote *m* central
kingdom [ˈkɪŋdəm] *s* reino
kingˈfishˈer *s* martín *m* pescador
king•ly [ˈkɪŋli] *adj* (*comp* **-lier;** *super* **-liest**) real, regio; (*stately*) majestuoso ‖ *adv* regiamente
kingˈpinˈ*s* (bowling) bolo delantero; pivote *m* central; (aut) pivote de dirección; (coll) persona principal; (coll) jefe *m* de criminales
king post *s* pendolón *m*
king's evil *s* escrófula
kingship [ˈkɪŋʃip] *s* dignidad real
kingˈ-sizeˈ *adj* de tamaño largo
king-sized bed *s* cama de tamaño grande
king's ransom *s* riquezas de Creso
kink [kɪŋk] *s* (*twist, e.g., in a rope*) enroscadura, coca; (*e.g., in hair*) pasa; (*soreness in neck*) tortícolis *m;* (*flaw, difficulty*) estorbo, traba; (*mental twist*) chifladura, manía ‖ *tr* enroscar ‖ *intr* enroscarse
kink•y [ˈkɪŋki] *adj* (*comp* **-ier;** *super* **-iest**) encarrujado, ensortijado; (coll) perverso, raro
kinsfolk [ˈkɪnz,fok] *s* parentela, familia, deudos
kinship [ˈkɪnʃip] *s* parentesco; semejanza, afinidad
kins•man [ˈkɪnzmən] *s* (*pl* **-men** [mən]) pariente *m*
kins•woman [ˈkɪnz,wʊmən] *s* (*pl* **-women** [,wɪmɪn]) *s* parienta
kipper [ˈkɪpər] *s* arenque acecinado, salmón acecinado ‖ *tr* acecinar (*el arenque o el salmón*)
kiss [kɪs] *s* beso; (billiards) retruco; (*confection*) dulce *m,* merengue *m* ‖ *tr* besar; **to kiss away** borrar con besos (*las pensas de una persona*) ‖ *intr* besar; besarse; (billiards) retrucar
kisser [ˈkɪsər] *s* (*face or mouth*) (slang) jeta
kit [kɪt] *s* cartera *or* caja de herramientas; (*case and its contents for various purposes*) estuche *m;* (*of a soldier*) equipo, pertrechos; (*of a traveler*) equipaje *m;* (*pail, tub*) balde *m;* (*collection of items*) juego; (compu) kit *m;* (*parts for assembly*) kit
kitchen [ˈkɪtʃən] *s* cocina
kitchen cabinet *s* armario de cocina
kitchenette [,kɪtʃəˈnɛt] *s* cocinilla
kitchen garden *s* huerto
kitchˈen•maidˈ *s* ayudanta de cocina, pincha
kitchen police *s* (mil) trabajo de cocina; soldados que están de cocina
kitchen sink *s* fregadero; **everything but the kitchen sink** sin faltar apenas nada; completísimo
kitchen stove *s* cocina, cocina económica, estufa (Col, Mex)
kitchˈen-wareˈ *s* utensilios de cocina
kite [kaɪt] *s* cometa; (orn) milano; **to fly a kite** hacer volar una cometa
kith and kin [kɪθ] *spl* parientes *mpl;* parientes y amigos
kitten [ˈkɪtən] *s* gatito, minino
kittenish [ˈkɪtənɪʃ] *adj* juguetón, retozón; (*coy, flirtatious*) coquetón
kit•ty [ˈkɪti] *s* (*pl* **-ties**) gatito, minino; (*in card games*) polla, puesta ‖ *interj* ¡mi chiquito!
kleptomaniac [,klɛptəˈmenɪ,æk] *s* cleptómano
km. *abbr* **kilometer**
knack [næk] *s* tino, tranquillo, maña
knapsack [ˈnæp,sæk] *s* mochila
knave [nev] *s* bribón *m,* pícaro; (cards) sota
knaver•y [ˈnevəri] *s* (*pl* **-ies**) bribonería, picardía
knead [nid] *tr* amasar, sobar
knee [ni] *s* rodilla; (*of animal*) codillo; (*e.g., of trousers*) rodillera; (mach) ángulo, codo; **to bring** (*someone*) **to his knees** rendir, vencer; **to go down on one's knees** hincarse de rodillas, caer de rodillas; **to go down on one's knees to** implorar de rodillas
knee breeches [ˈbrɪtʃiz] *spl* pantalones cortos
kneeˈcapˈ *s* rótula; (*protective covering*) rodillera
kneeˈ-deepˈ *adj* metido hasta las rodillas
kneeˈhighˈ *adj* que llega hasta la rodilla
kneeˈ-holeˈ *s* (*abajo de un escritorio*) hueco para acomodar las rodillas
knee jerk *s* reflejo rotuliano
kneel [nil] *v* (*pret & pp* **knelt** [nɛlt] o **kneeled**) *intr* arrodillarse; estar de rodillas
kneeˈpadˈ *s* rodillera
kneeˈpanˈ *s* rótula
knee swell *s* (*of organ*) (mus) rodillera
knell [nɛl] *s* doble *m,* toque *m* de difuntos; mal agüero; **to toll the knell of** anunciar la muerte

de, anunciar el fin de || *intr* doblar, tocar a muerto; sonar tristemente

knickers [ˈnɪkərz] *spl* pantalones *mpl* de media pierna

knickknack [ˈnɪk,næk] *s* chuchería, bujería, baratija

knife [naɪf] *s* (*pl* **-knives** [naɪvz] cuchillo; (*of a paper cutter or other instrument*) cuchilla; **to go under the knife** (coll) hacerse operar || *tr* acuchillar; (slang) traicionar

knife sharpener *s* afilador *m,* afilón *m*

knife switch *s* (elec) interruptor *m* de cuchilla

knight [naɪt] *s* caballero; (chess) caballo || *tr* armar caballero

knight-errant [ˈnaɪtˈɛrənt] *s* (*pl* **knights-errant**) caballero andante

knighthood [ˈnaɪt•hʊd] *s* caballería

knightly [ˈnaɪtli] *adj* caballeroso, caballeresco

knit [nɪt] *v* (*pret & pp* **knitted** o **knit;** *ger* **knitting**) *tr* tejer a punto de aguja; enlazar, unir; fruncir (*las cejas*) arrugar (*la frente*) || *intr* hacer calceta, hacer malla; trabarse, unirse; soldarse (*un hueso*)

knit goods *spl* géneros de punto

knitting [ˈnɪtɪŋ] *s* punto de media, trabajo de punto

knitting machine *s* máquina de hacer tejidos de punto

knitting needle *s* aguja de calceta, aguja de punta, aguja de tejer

knit′wear′ *s* géneros de punto

knob [nɑb] *s* (*lump*) bulto, protuberancia; (*of a door*) botón *m,* tirador *m;* (*of a radio set*) botón, perilla; (*ornament on furniture*) manzana; colina o montaña redondeada

knock [nɑk] *s* golpe *m;* (*e.g., on a door*) toque *m,* llamada; (*with a door knocker*) aldabazo; (*of an internal-combustion engine*) pistoneo; (slang) censura, crítica || *tr* golpear; (*repeatedly*) golpetear; (slang) censurar, criticar; **to knock down** (*with a blow, punch, etc.*) derribar; (*to the highest bidder*) rematar; desarmar, desmontar (*un aparato o máquina*); **to knock off** hacer saltar con un golpe; suspender (*el trabajo*); poner fin a; (slang) matar; **to knock out** agotar; (box) poner fuera de combate || *intr* tocar, llamar; golpear, pistonear (*el motor de combustión interna*); (slang) censurar, criticar; **to knock about** andar vagando; **to knock against** dar contra, tropezar con; **to knock at** tocar a, llamar a (*la puerta*); **to knock off** dejar de trabajar

knocker [ˈnɑkər] *s* (*on a door*) aldaba; (coll) criticón *m*

knock-kneed [ˈnɑk,nid] *adj* patizambo, zambo

knock′out′ *s* (box) knock-out *m,* nocaut *m,* K.O. *m;* (coll) exitazo, maravilla; (*person*) (coll) super bien; **she's a knockout** (coll) es una chica estupenda, es una real moza

knockout drops *spl* (slang) gotas narcóticas

knockout punch *s* (box) golpe decisivo, puñetazo que derriba

knoll [nol] *s* loma, otero

knot [nɑt] *s* nudo; (*worn as ornament*) lazo; corrillo, grupo; (*difficult matter; bond or tie*) nudo; nudo o lazo de matrimonio; (*protuberance in a fabric*) envoltorio; (naut) nudo; **to tie the knot** (coll) casarse || *v* (*pret & pp* **knotted;** *ger* **knotting**) *tr* anudar; fruncir (*las cejas*) || *intr* anudarse

knot′hole′ *s* agujero en la madera (*que deja un nudo al desprenderse*)

knot•ty [ˈnɑti] *adj* (*comp* **-tier;** *super* **-tiest**) nudoso; (fig) espinoso, difícil

know [no] *s* **—to be in the know** estar enterado, tener informes secretos || *v* (*pret* **knew** [nju] o [nu]; *pp* **known**) *tr & intr* (*by reasoning or learning*) saber; (*by the senses or by perception; through acquaintance or recognition*) conocer; **as far as I know** que yo sepa; **to know about** saber de; **to know best** ser el mejor juez, saber lo que más conviene; **to know how to** + *inf* saber + *inf;* **to know it all** (coll) sabérselo todo; **to know what one is doing** obrar con conocimiento de causa; **to know what's what** (coll) saber cuántas son cinco; **you ought to know better** deberías tener vergüenza

knowable [ˈno•əbəl] *adj* conocible

know′-how′ *s* conocimiento, destreza, habilidad

knowingly [ˈno•ɪŋli] *adv* a sabiendas, coll conocimiento de causa; (*on purpose*) adrede

know′-it-all′ *adj & s* (coll) sabidillo, sabelotodo *mf*

knowledge [ˈnɑlɪdʒ] *s* (*faculty*) ciencia, conocimientos, el saber; (*awareness, acquaintance, familiarity*) conocimiento; **to have a thorough knowledge of** conocer a fondo; **to my knowledge** que yo sepa; **to the best of my knowledge** según mi leal saber y entender; **with full knowledge** con conocimiento de causa; **without my knowledge** sin saberlo yo

knowledgeable [ˈnɑlɪdʒəbəl] *adj* (coll) conocedor, inteligente

know′-noth′ing *s* ignorante *mf*

knuckle [ˈnʌkəl] *s* nudillo; (*of a quadruped*) jarrete *m;* (*mach*) junta de charnela; **knuckles** bóxer *m* || *intr***—to knuckle down** aplicarse con empeño al trabajo; **to knuckle under** someterse, darse por vencido

knurl [nʌrl] *s* moleteado || *tr* moletear, cerrillar (*p.ej., las piezas de moneda*)

KO *abbr* **knockout**

kook [kuk] *s* (coll) tipo raro; excéntrico

Koran [koˈrɑn] o [koˈræn] *s* Corán *m*

Korea [koˈri•ə] *s* Corea

Korean [koˈri•ən] *adj & s* coreano

kosher [ˈkoʃər] *adj* autorizado por la ley judía; (coll) genuino, auténtico

kowtow [ˈkaʊ,taʊ] o [ˈko,taʊ] *intr* arrodillarse y tocar el suelo con la frente; doblegarse servilmente, mostrarse servilmente obsequioso

kudos [ˈkjudɑs] o [ˈkudɑs] *s* (coll) gloria, renombre *m,* fama

kw. *abbr* **kilowatt**

K.W.H. *abbr* **kilowatt-hour**

L

L, l [ɛl] duodécima letra del alfabeto inglés
la•bel [ˈlebəl] *s* etiqueta, marbete *m,* rótulo; (*descriptive word*) calificación; (*in a dictionary*) calificativo; (compu) etiqueta, rótulo || *v* (*pret & pp* **-beled** o **-belled;** *ger* **-beling** o **-belling**) *tr* poner etiqueta o marbete a, rotular, etiquetar; calificar
labeling [ˈlebəlɪn] *s* etiquetado
labial [ˈlebɪ•əl] *adj & s* labial *f*
labor [ˈlebər] *adj* obrero || *s* trabajo, labor *f;* (*job, task*) tarea, faena; (*manual work involved in an undertaking; the wages for such work*) mano *f* de obra; (*wage-earning workers as contrasted with capital and management*) los obreros; (*childbirth*) parto; **labors** esfuerzos; **to be in labor** estar de parto || *intr* trabajar; (*to exert oneself*) forcejar; estar de parto; moverse penosamente; cabecear y balancear (*un buque*); **to labor under** ser víctima de
laborato•ry [ˈlæbərə,tori] *s* (*pl* **-ries**) laboratorio
Labor Day *s* Día *m* del Trabajo
labored [ˈlebərd] *adj* penoso, dificultoso; artificial, forzado; (*breathing*) fatigoso, farragoso
laborer [ˈlebərər] *s* trabajador *m,* obrero; (*unskilled worker*) bracero, jornalero, peón *m*
laborious [ləˈborɪ•əs] *adj* laborioso
laˈbor-manˈagement *adj* obrero-patronal
labor union *s* gremio obrero, sindicato
Labrador [ˈlæbrə,dɔr] *s* el Labrador
labyrinth [ˈlæbɪrɪnθ] *s* laberinto
lace [les] *s* encaje *m;* (*string to tie shoe, corset, etc.*) cordón *m,* lazo; (*braid*) galón *m* de oro o plata || *tr* adornar con encaje; (*one's shoes*) atar; (*thrash*) dar una paliza a: (*mix*) echar licor a; echar una ponzoña a; **to lace into** arremeter contra
lace trimming *s* randa
laceˈ-up shoe *s* zapato de cordón
laceˈworkˈ *s* encaje *m,* obra de encaje
lachrymose [ˈlækrɪ,mos] *adj* lacrimoso
lacing [ˈlesɪŋ] *s* cordón *m;* lazo; galón *m;* (*thrashing*) paliza; (*with liquor*) gota de licor
lack [læk] *s* carencia, falta; (*complete lack*) defecto || *tr* carecer de, necesitar || *intr* (*to be lacking*) faltar
lackadaisical [,lækəˈdezɪkəl] *adj* desaprovechado, indiferente
lackey [ˈlæki] *s* lacayo; secuaz *m* servil
lacking [ˈlækɪŋ] *prep* sin, carente de
lackˈlusˈter *adj* delustrado, deslucido
laconic [ləˈkɑnɪk] *adj* lacónico
lacquer [ˈlækər] *s* laca || *tr* laquear
lacquer ware *s* lacas, objetos de laca
lacu•na [ləˈkjunə] *s* (*pl* **-nas** o **-nae** [ni]) laguna
lac•y [ˈlesi] *adj* (*comp* **-ier;** *super* **-iest**) de encaje; (fig) diáfano
lad [læd] *s* muchacho, chico
ladder [ˈlædər] *s* escalera; (*stepladder*) escala, escalera de mano; (*two ladders fastened together at the top with hinges*) escalera de tijera; (*stepping stone*) (fig) escalón *m*
ladder truck *s* carro de escaleras de incendio
ladiesˈ man *s* perico entre ellas, donjuán *m*
ladiesˈ room *s* (*powder room*) cuarto tocador; **Ladies** (*rest room*) *SIGN* Señoras, Damas
ladle [ˈledəl] *s* cazo; (*for soup*) cucharón *m;* (*of tinsmith*) cucharilla || *tr* servir con cucharón; sacar con cucharón
la•dy [ˈledi] *s* (*pl* **-dies**) señora, dama
laˈdy-birdˈ o **laˈdy•bugˈ** *s* mariquita, vaca de San Antón
laˈdy•finˈger *s* plantilla, soletilla (Esp)
lady-in-waiting *s* camarera de la reina
laˈdy-kilˈler *s* ladrón *m* de corazones
laˈdy•likeˈ *adj* elegante; **to be ladylike** ser muy dama
laˈdy•loveˈ *s* amada, amiga querida
lady of the house *s* ama de casa
ladyship [ˈledi,ʃɪp] *s* señoría
lag [læg] *s* retraso || *v* (*pret & pp* **lagged;** *ger* **lagging**) *intr* retrasarse; **to lag behind** quedarse atrás, rezagarse
lager beer [ˈlɑgər] *s* cerveza reposada
laggard [ˈlægərd] *s* perezoso, rezagado
lagoon [ləˈgun] *s* laguna
laid paper [led] *s* papel vergueteado
laid up *adj* almacenado, ahorrado; (naut) inactivo; (coll) encamado por estar enfermo
lair [lɛr] *s* cubil *m*
laissez-faire o **laisser-faire** [ˈleseˈfɛr] *s* (econ, pol) doctrina de no intervención
lai•ty [ˈle•ɪti] *s* (*nonprofessionals*) profanos; (eccl) laicos
lake [lek] *adj* lacustre || *s* lago
lamb [læm] *s* cordero; carne *f* de cordero; piel *f* de cordero; (*meek person*) (fig) cordero
lambaste [læmˈbest] *tr* (*to thrash*) (coll) dar una paliza a; (*to reprimand harshly*) (coll) dar una jabonadura a
lamb chop *s* chuleta de cordero
lambkin [ˈlæmkɪn] *s* corderito; (fig) nenito
lambˈskinˈ *s* piel *f* de cordero, corderina; (*dressed with its wool*) corderillo
lame [lem] *adj* cojo; (*sore*) dolorido; (*e.g., excuse*) débil, pobre || *tr* encojar
lament [ləˈmɛnt] *s* lamento; (*dirge*) elegía || *tr* lamentar || *intr* lamentarse
lamentable [ˈlæməntəbəl] *adj* lamentable
lamentation [,læmənˈteʃən] *s* lamentación
laminate [ˈlæmɪ,net] *tr* laminar
laminated *adj* laminado, plastificado
laminated glass *s* cristal laminado
lamp [læmp] *s* lámpara
lampˈblackˈ *s* negro de humo
lamp chimney *s* tubo de lámpara
lampˈlightˈ *s* luz *f* de lámpara
lampˈlightˈer *s* farolero
lampoon [læmˈpun] *s* pasquín *m,* libelo || *tr* pasquinar
lampˈpostˈ *s* poste *m* de farol

lamp shade *s* pantalla de lámpara
lamp'wick' *s* mecha de lámpara, torcida
lance [læns] o [lɑns] *s* lanza; (surg) lanceta ‖ *tr* alancear; (surg) abrir con lanceta
lance rest *s* ristre *m*
lancet [ˈlænsɪt] *s* (surg) lanceta
land [lænd] *adj* terrestre; (*wind*) terral ‖ *s* tierra; **on land, on sea, and in the air** en tierra, mar y aire; **to make land** atracar a tierra; **to see how the land lies** medir el terreno, ver el cariz que van tomando las cosas ‖ *tr* desembarcar; conducir (*un avión*) a tierra; coger (*un pez*); (coll) conseguir ‖ *intr* desembarcar; (*to reach land*) arribar, aterrar; aterrizar (*un avión*); (*to arrive or come to rest*) ir a dar, ir a parar; **to land on one's feet** caer de pies; **to land on one's head** caer de cabeza
land breeze *s* terral *m*
landed [ˈlændɪd] *adj* (*owning land*) hacendado; (*real-estate*) inmobiliario; **landed property** bienes *mpl* raíces
land'fall' *s* (*sighting land*) aterrada; (*landing of ship or plane*) aterraje *m;* tierra vista desde el mar; (*landslide*) derrumbe *m*
land'fill' *s* tierra y escombros
land grant *s* donación de tierras
land'hold'er *s* terrateniente *mf,* hacendado
landing [ˈlændɪŋ] *s* (*of ship or plane*) aterraje *m;* (*of passengers*) desembarco; (*place where passengers and goods are landed*) desembarcadero; (*of stairway*) desembarco, descanso
landing beacon *s* (aer) radiofaro de aterrizaje
landing craft *s* (nav) lancha de desembarco
landing field *s* (aer) pista de aterrizaje
landing force *s* (nav) compañía de desembarco
landing gear *s* (aer) tren *m* de aterrizaje
landing stage *s* embarcadero flotante
landing strip *s* (aer) faja *or* pista de aterrizaje
land'la'dy *s* (*pl* **-dies**) (*e.g., of an apartment*) casera, dueña; (*of a lodging house*) ama, patrona; (*of an inn*) mesonera, posadera
landlocked [ˈlænd,lɑkt] *adj* rodeado de tierra
land'lord' *s* (*e.g., of an apartment*) casero, dueño; (*of a lodging house*) amo, patrón *m;* (*of an inn*) mesonero, posadero
land'lub'ber *s* (*person unacquainted with the sea*) marinero de agua dulce; (*awkward and unskilled seaman*) marinero matalote
land'mark' *s* (*boundary stone*) mojón *m;* (*feature of landscape that marks a location*) guía; suceso que hace época; (naut) marca de reconocimiento
land office *s* oficina del catastro
land'-of'fice business *s* (coll) negocio de mucho movimiento
land'own'er *s* terrateniente *mf,* hacendado
landscape [ˈlænd,skep] *s* paisaje *m* ‖ *tr* ajardinar
landscape architect *s* arquitecto paisajista
landscape gardener *s* jardinero adornista, jardinista *mf*
landscape painter *s* paisajista *mf*
landscapist [ˈlænd,skepɪst] *s* paisajista *mf*
land'slide' *s* derrumbe *m,* derrumbamiento de tierra, corrimiento; (fig) mayoría de votos abrumadora; (fig) victoria arrolladora
landward [ˈlændwərd] *adv* hacia tierra, hacia la costa
land wind *s* terral *m*
lane [len] *s* (*narrow street or passage*) callejuela; (*path*) carril *m;* (*of an automobile highway*) faja; (*of an air or ocean route*) derrotero, vía
langsyne [ˈlæŋˈsaɪn] *adv* (Scotch) hace mucho tiempo ‖ *s* (Scotch) tiempo de antaño
language [ˈlæŋgwɪdʒ] *s* idioma *m,* lengua; (*way of speaking or writing, style; figurative or poetic expression; communication of meaning said to be employed by flowers, birds, art, etc.*) lenguaje *m;* (*of a special group of people*) jerga
language laboratory *s* laboratorio de idiomas
languid [ˈlæŋgwɪd] *adj* lánguido
languish [ˈlæŋgwɪʃ] *intr* languidecer; afectar languidez
languor [ˈlæŋgər] *s* languidez *f*
languorous [ˈlæŋgərəs] *adj* lánguido; (*causing languor*) enervante
lank [læŋk] *adj* descarnado, larguirucho; (*hair*) lacio
lank•y [ˈlæŋki] *adj* (*comp* **-ier;** *super* **-iest**) descarnado, larguirucho
lantern [ˈlæntərn] *s* linterna
lanyard [ˈlænjərd] *s* (naut) acollador *m*
lap [læp] *s* (*of human body or clothing*) regazo; (*loose fold*) caída, doblez *f;* (*overlap of garment*) traslapo; (*with the tongue*) lametada; (*of the waves*) chapaleteo; (*in a race*) (sport) etapa, vuelta; **to live in the lap of luxury** llevar una vida regalada ‖ *v* (*pret & pp* **lapped;** *ger* **lapping**) *tr* beber con la lengua; lamer (*las olas la playa*); (*to overlap*) traslapar; juntar a traslapo; **to lap up** tragar a lengüetadas; (coll) aceptar con entusiasmo ‖ *intr* traslapar; traslaparse (*dos o más cosas*); **to lap against** lamer (*las olas la playa*); **to lap over** salir fuera, rebosar
lap'board' *s* tabla faldera
lap dog *s* perro de falda
lapel [ləˈpɛl] *s* solapa
Lap'land' *s* Laponia
Laplander [ˈlæp,lændər] *s* lapón *m* (*habitante*)
lap of honor *s* (sport) vuelta de honor; (taur) vuelta al ruedo
Lapp [læp] *s* lapón *m* (*habitante; idioma*)
lap robe *s* manta de coche
lapse [læps] *s* (*passing of time; slipping into guilt or error*) lapso; (*fall, decline*) caída, caída en desuso; (*e.g., of an insurance policy*) invalidación ‖ *intr* caer en culpa o error; decaer, pasar (*p.ej., el entusiasmo*); caducar (*p.ej., una póliza de seguro*)
lap'top' *adj & s* portátil *m,* laptop *m*
lap'top computer *s* ordenador *m* portátil, computadora portátil
lap'wing' *s* ave fría
larce•ny [ˈlɑrsəni] *s* (*pl* **-nies**) hurto, robo

larch [lɑrtʃ] *s* alerce *m,* lárice *m*
lard [lɑrd] *s* cochevira, manteca de puerco || *tr* (culin) mechar
larder [ˈlɑrdər] *s* despensa
large [ˈlɑrdʒ] *adj* grande; **at large** en libertad
large intestine *s* intestino grueso
largely [ˈlɑrdʒli] *adj* por la mayor parte
largeness [ˈlɑrdʒnɪs] *s* grandeza
large′-scale′ *adj* en grande escala, grande escala
lariat [ˈlærɪ•ət] *s* (*for catching animals*) lazo; (*for tying grazing animals*) cuerda, soga
lark [lɑrk] *s* alondra; (coll) parranda; **to go on a lark** (coll) andar de parranda, echar una cana al aire
lark′spur′ *s* (*rocket larkspur*) espuela de caballero; (*field larkspur*) consuelda real
lar•va [ˈlɑrvə] *s* (*pl* **-vae** [vi]) larva
laryngeal [ləˈrɪndʒɪ•əl] *adj* laríngeo
laryngitis [ˌlærɪnˈdʒaɪtɪs] *s* laringitis *f*
laryngoscope [ləˈrɪŋgəˌskop] *s* laringoscopio
larynx [ˈlærɪŋks] *s* (*pl* **larynxes** o **larynges** [ləˈrɪndʒiz]) laringe *f*
lascivious [ləˈsɪvɪ•əs] *adj* lascivo
lasciviousness [ləˈsɪvɪ•əsnɪs] *s* lascivia
laser [ˈlezər] *s* láser *m*
laser beam *s* rayo láser
lash [læʃ] *s* (*cord on end of whip*) tralla; (*blow with whip; scolding*) latigazo; (*e.g., of animal's tail*) coletazo; (*of waves*) embate *m;* (*eyelash*) pestaña || *tr* (*to beat, whip*) azotar; (*to bind, tie*) atar; (*to shake, to switch*) agitar, sacudir; (*to attack with words*) increpar, reñir || *intr* lanzarse, pasar rápidamente; **to lash out at** azotar; embestir; vituperar
lashing [ˈlæʃɪŋ] *s* atadura; paliza, zurra; (*severe scolding*) latigazo
lass [læs] *s* muchacha, chica; amada
las•so [ˈlæso] o [læˈsu] *s* (*pl* **-sos** o **-soes**) lazo || *tr* lazar
last [læst] o [lɑst] *adj* (*after all others; the only remaining; utmost, extreme*) último; (*most recent*) pasado; **before last** antepasado; **every last one** todos sin excepción; **last but one** penúltimo || *adv* después de todos; por último; por última vez || *s* última persona; última cosa; fin *m;* (*for holding shoe*) horma; **at last** por fin; **at long last** al fin y al cabo; **stick to your last!** ¡zapatero, a tus zapatos!; **the last of the month** a fines del mes; **to breathe one's last** dar el último suspiro; **to see the last of** no volver a ver; **to the last** hasta el fin || *intr* durar; resistir; dar buen resultado (*p.ej., una prenda de vestir*); seguir así
lasting [ˈlæstɪŋ] *adj* perdurable, duradero
lastly [ˈlæstli] *adv* finalmente, por último
last′-min′ute news *s* noticias de última hora
last name *s* apellido
last night *adv* anoche
last quarter *s* cuarto menguante
last rites *spl* (theol) extremaunción
last sleep *s* último sueño
last straw *s* acabóse *m,* colmo
Last Supper, the la Cena, la Última Cena
last will and testament *s* última voluntad y testamento
last wishes *spl* última voluntad
last word *s* última palabra; (*latest style*) (coll) última palabra
lat. *abbr* **latitude**
Lat. *abbr* **Latin**
latch [lætʃ] *s* picaporte *m* || *tr* cerrar con picaporte
latch′key′ *s* llavín *m*
latch′string′ *s* cordón *m* de aldaba; **the latchstring is out** ya sabe Ud. que ésta es su casa
late [let] *adj* (*happening after the usual time*) tardío; (*person*) atrasado; (*hour of the night*) avanzado; (*news*) de última hora; (*party, meeting, etc.*) que termina tarde; (*coming toward the end of a period of time*) de fines de; (*incumbent of an office*) anterior; (*deceased*) difunto, fallecido; **of late** recientemente, últimamente; (*Middle Ages*) bajo; **to be late** ser tarde; tardar (*p.ej., el tren*); **to be late in** + *ger* tardar en + *inf;* **to grow late** hacerse tarde || *adv* tarde; **late in** (*the week, the month, etc.*) a fines de, hacia fines de; **late in life** a una edad avanzada
latecomer [ˈletˌkʌmər] *s* recién llegado; (*one who arrives late*) rezagado
lateen sail [læˈtin] *s* vela latina
lateen yard *s* entena
lately [ˈletli] *adv* recientemente, últimamente
latent [ˈletənt] *adj* latente
lateral [ˈlætərəl] *adj* lateral
lath [læθ] o [lɑθ] *s* lata, listón; enlistonado || *tr* enlistonar
lathe [leð] *s* torno (*máquina que sirve para labrar madera, hierro, etc. con un movimiento circular*)
lather [ˈlæðər] *s* espuma de jabón; espuma de sudor || *tr* enjabonar; (coll) tundir, zurrar || *intr* espumar
lathery [ˈlæðəri] *adj* espumoso, jabonoso
lathing [ˈlæθɪŋ] *s* enlistonado
Latin [ˈlætɪn] o [ˈlætən] *adj* latino || *s* (*language*) latín *m;* (*person*) latino
Latin America *s* Latinoamérica, América Latina
Latin American *s* latinoamericano
Lat′in-Amer′ican *adj* latinoamericano
latitude [ˈlætɪˌtjud] *s* latitud
latrine [ləˈtrin] *s* letrina
latter [ˈlætər] *adj* (*more recent*) posterior; segundo (*de dos*); **the latter** éste; **the latter part of** fines *mpl* de (*p.ej., el siglo*)
lattice [ˈlætɪs] *s* enrejado || *tr* enrejar
lat′tice•work′ *s* celosía, enrejado
Latvia [ˈlætvɪ•ə] *s* Letonia, Latvia
laudable [ˈlɔdəbəl] *adj* laudable
laudanum [ˈlɔdənəm] o [ˈlɔdnəm] *s* láudano
laudatory [ˈlɔdəˌtori] *adj* laudatorio
laugh [læf] *s* risa || *tr*—**to laugh away** ahogar en risas; **to laugh off** tomar a risa || *intr* reír, reírse
laughable [ˈlæfəbəl] *adj* risible

laughing [ˈlæfɪŋ] *adj* reidor; **to be no laughing matter** no ser cosa de risa ‖ *s* risa, (el) reír
laughing gas *s* gas *m* hilarante
laugh'ing•stock' *s* hazmerreír *m*
laughter [ˈlæftər] *s* risa, risas
launch [lɔntʃ] *s* (*of a ship*) botadura; (*of a rocket*) lanzamiento; (*open motorboat*) lancha automóvil; (nav) lancha ‖ *tr* botar, lanzar (*un buque*); (*to throw; to start, set going, send forth*) lanzar ‖ *intr* lanzarse
launcher [ˈlɔntʃər] *s* lanzador *m;* (compu) lanzadera
launching [ˈlɔntʃɪŋ] *s* lanzamiento
launching pad *s* plataforma de lanzamiento
launching tower *s* torre *f* de lanzamiento
launch site *s* base *f* de lanzamiento
launder [ˈlɔndər] *tr* lavar y planchar; (*money*) blanquear ‖ *intr* resistir el lavado
launderer [ˈlɔndərər] *s* lavandero
laundress [ˈlɔndrɪs] *s* lavandera
laun•dry [ˈlɔndri] *s* (*pl* **-dries**) lavadero; lavado de la ropa; ropa lavada o para lavar
laundry•man [ˈlɔndrimən] *s* (*pl* **-men** [mən]) lavandero
laun'dry•wom'an *s* (*pl* **-wom'en**) lavandera
laureate [ˈlɔrɪ•ɪt] *adj* laureado ‖ *s* laureado; poeta laureado
lau•rel [ˈlɔrəl] *s* laurel *m;* **laurels** laurel (*de la victoria*); **to rest** o **sleep on one's laurels** dormirse sobre sus laureles ‖ *v* (*pret & pp* **-reled** o **-relled;** *ger* **-reling** o **-relling**) *tr* laurear, coronar de laurel
lava [ˈlɑvə] o [ˈlævə] *s* lava
lavato•ry [ˈlævə,tori] *s* (*pl* **-ries**) (*room equipped for washing hands and face*) lavabo; (*bowl with running water*) lavamanos *m;* (*toilet*) retrete *m,* inodoro, baño, servicio, excusado (Mex)
lavender [ˈlævəndər] *s* alhucema, espliego, lavanda
lavish [ˈlævɪʃ] *adj* pródigo ‖ *tr* prodigar
law [lɔ] *s* (*of man, of nature, of science*) ley *f;* (*branch of knowledge concerned with law; body of laws; study of law; profession of law*) derecho; **to enter the law** hacerse abogado; **to go to law** recurrir a la ley; **to lay down the law** dar órdenes terminantes; **to maintain law and order** mantener la paz; **to practice law** ejercer la profesión de abogado; **to read law** estudiar derecho
law-abiding [ˈlɔ•ə,baɪdɪŋ] *adj* observante de la ley
law'break'er *s* infractor *m* de la ley
law court *s* tribunal *m* de justicia
lawful [ˈlɔfəl] *adj* legal, legítimo
lawless [ˈlɔlɪs] *adj* ilegal; (*unbridled*) desenfrenado, licencioso
law'mak'er *s* legislador *m*
lawn [lɔn] *s* césped *m;* (*fabric*) linón *m*
lawn mower *s* cortacésped *m,* tundidora de césped, cortadora de césped
law office *s* bufete *m,* despacho de abogado
law of nations *s* derecho de gentes
law of supply and demand ley *f* de la oferta y la demanda
law of the jungle *s* ley *f* de la selva
law'suit' *s* pleito, proceso, litigio
lawyer [ˈlɔjər] *s* abogado
lax [læks] *adj* (*in morals, discipline, etc.*) laxo, relajado; vago, indeterminado; (*loose, not tense*) laxo, flojo, suelto
laxative [ˈlæksətɪv] *adj & s* laxante *m*
lay [le] *adj* (*not belonging to clergy*) lego, seglar, laico; (*not having special training*) lego, profano ‖ *s* situación, orientación ‖ *v* (*pret & pp* **laid** [led]) *tr* poner, colocar; dejar en el suelo; tender (*un cable*); echar (*los cimientos; la culpa*); situar (*la acción de un drama*); asentar (*el polvo*); poner (*huevos la gallina; la mesa una criada*); formar (*planes*); hacer (*una apuesta*); **to be laid in** ser (*la escena*) en; **to lay aside** echar a un lado; ahorrar; **to lay down** afirmar, declarar; dar (*la vida*); deponer (*las armas*); **to lay low** abatir, derribar; obligar a guardar cama; matar; **to lay off** despedir (*a obreros*); (*to mark off the boundaries of*) marcar, trazar; **to lay open** descubrir, revelar; (*to a risk or danger*) exponer; **to lay out** diseñar; (*to spread out*) disponer, arreglar; (*to prepare for burial*) amortajar; (coll) gastar; (compu) hacer la maquetación de, maquetar; **to lay up** obligar a guardar cama; ahorrar; (naut) desarmar ‖ *intr* poner (*las gallinas*); **to lay about** dar palos de ciego; **to lay for** acechar; **to lay off** (coll) dejar de trabajar; (coll) dejar de molestar; **to lay over** detenerse durante un viaje; **to lay to** (naut) capear
lay brother *s* donado, lego
lay day *s* (naut) día *m* de estadía
layer [ˈle•ər] *s* (*e.g., of paint*) capa; (*e.g., of bricks*) camada; (*e.g., of coal, rocks*) estrato, capa; (hort) codadura ‖ *tr* (hort) acodar
layer cake *s* bizcocho de varias camadas
layette [leˈɛt] *s* canastilla
lay figure *s* maniquí *m*
laying [ˈle•ɪŋ] *s* colocación; (*of eggs*) postura; (*of a cable*) tendido; **laying on of hands** imposición de manos
laying hen *s* gallina ponedora
lay•man [ˈlemən] *s* (*pl* **-men** [mən]) (*person who is not a clergyman*) lego, seglar *m,* laico; (*person who has no special training*) lego, profano
lay'off' *s* (*dismissal of workmen*) despido; (*period of unemployment*) paro forzoso
lay of the land *s* cariz *m* que van tomando las cosas
lay'out' *s* plan *m;* (*of tools*) equipo; disposición, organización; (*of house*) distribución; (*dummy*) maqueta; (compu) maquetación; (typ) diseño, maquetación
lay'o'ver *s* parada en un viaje
lay sister *s* donada
laziness [ˈlezɪnɪs] *s* pereza; lerdera; (coll) galbana

la•zy [ˈlezi] *adj* (*comp* **-zier;** *super* **-ziest**) perezoso; (coll) galbanoso
la'zy•bones' *s* (coll) perezoso
lb. *abbr* **pound**
l.c. *abbr* **lower case; loco citato** (Lat) **(in the place cited)** Loc. cit. (en el lugar citado)
lea [li] *s* prado
lead [lɛd] *adj* plomizo ‖ *s* plomo; (*of lead pencil*) mina; (*for sounding depth*) (naut) escandallo; (typ) interlínea, regleta ‖ [lɛd] *v* (*pret & pp* **leaded;** *ger* **leading**) *tr* emplomar; (typ) interlinear, regletear ‖ *s* [lid] *s* (*foremost place*) primacía; (*guidance*) conducta, guía, dirección; indicación; ejemplo; (cards) salida; (*leash*) traílla; (*of a newspaper article*) primer párrafo; (elec) conductor *m;* (elec & mach) avance *m;* (min) filón *m;* (rad) alambre *m* de entrada; (theat) papel *m* principal; (theat) galán *m;* (theat) dama; **to take the lead** tomar la delantera ‖ [lid] *v* (*pret & pp* **led** [lɛd]) *tr* conducir, llevar; liderar; (*to command*) acaudillar, mandar; estar a la cabeza de; dirigir (*p.ej., una orquesta*); llevar (*buena o mala vida*); salir con (*cierto naipe*); (elec & mach) avanzar; **to lead someone to** + *inf* llevar a alguien a + *inf* ‖ *intr* ir delante, enseñar el camino; ser el primero; tener el mando; (cards) salir, ser mano; (mus) llevar la batuta; **to lead up to** conducir a, llevar a; llevar la conversación a
leaded gasoline [ˈlɛdɪd] *s* gasolina con plomo
leaden [ˈlɛdən] *adj* (*of lead; like lead*) plomizo; (*heavy as lead*) plúmbeo; (*sluggish*) tardo, indolente; (*with sleep*) cargado; triste, lóbrego
leader [ˈlidər] *s* caudillo, jefe *m,* líder *m;* (*ringleader*) cabecilla *m;* (*of an orchestra*) director *m;* (*in a dance; among animals*) guión *m;* (*horse*) guía; (*in a newspaper*) artículo de fondo
leader dog *s* perro-lazarillo
leadership [ˈlidərʃip] *s* caudillaje *m,* jefatura; dotes *fpl* de mando
leading [ˈlidɪŋ] *adj* primero, principal; preeminente; delantero; líder
leading article *s* artículo de fondo
leading edge *s* (aer) borde *m* de ataque
leading lady *s* primera actriz, dama
leading man *s* primer actor *m,* primer galán *m*
leading question *s* pregunta tendenciosa
lead-in wire [ˈlid,ɪn] *s* (rad) bajada de antena, alambre *m* de entrada
lead pencil [lɛd] *s* lápiz *m*
leaf [lif] *s* (*pl* **leaves** [livz]) hoja; (*of vine*) pámpano; (*hinged leaf of table*) trampilla; **to shake like a leaf** temblar como un azogado; **to turn over a new leaf** hacer libro nuevo ‖ *intr* echar hojas; **to leaf through** hojear, trashojar
leafless [ˈliflɪs] *adj* deshojado
leaflet [ˈliflɪt] *s* hoja suelta, hoja volante; (*blade of compound leaf*) hojuela
leaf'stalk' *s* pecíolo
leaf•y [ˈlifi] *adj* (*comp* **-ier;** *super* **-iest**) hojoso, frondoso
league [lig] *s* (*unit of distance*) legua; (*association, alliance*) liga; (*sports*) división ‖ *tr* asociar ‖ *intr* asociarse, ligarse
League of Nations *s* (hist) Sociedad de las Naciones
leak [lik] *s* (*in a roof*) gotera; (*in a ship*) agua, vía de agua; (*of water, gas, electricity, steam*) escape *m,* fuga, salida; agujero, grieta, raja (*por donde se escapa el agua, etc.*); (*of money, news, etc.*) filtración; **to spring a leak** tener un escape; (naut) empezar a hacer agua ‖ *tr* dejar escapar, dejar salir (*el agua, gas, etc.*); dejar filtrar (*una noticia*) ‖ *intr* rezumarse (*un barril*); escaparse, salirse (*el agua, gas, etc.*); (naut) hacer agua; **to leak away** filtrarse (*el dinero*); **to leak out** rezumarse (*una especie*); trascender (*un hecho que estaba oculto*)
leakage [ˈlikɪdʒ] *s* escape *m,* fuga, salida; (com) merma
leak•y [ˈliki] *adj* (*comp* **-ier;** *super* **-iest**) agujereado, roto; (*roof*) llovedizo; (naut) que hace agua; (coll) indiscreto
lean [lin] *adj* magro, mollar; (*thin*) flaco; (*gasoline mixture*) pobre; **lean years** años de carestía ‖ *v* (*pret & pp* **leaned** o **leant** [lɛnt] *tr* inclinar, ladear, arrimar ‖ *intr* inclinarse, ladearse, arrimarse; (fig) inclinarse, tender; **to lean against** arrimarse a, estar arrimado a; **to lean back** retreparse, recostarse; **to lean on** apoyarse en; (*with the elbows*) acodarse sobre; **to lean out (of)** asomarse (a); **to lean over backwards** (coll) extremar la imparcialidad; **to lean toward** (fig) inclinarse a, ladearse a
leaning [ˈlinɪŋ] *adj* inclinado ‖ *s* inclinación; (fig) inclinación, tendencia
lean'-to' *s* (*pl* **-tos**) colgadizo
leap [lip] *s* salto; **by leaps and bounds** a pasos agigantados; **leap in the dark** salto a ciegas, salto en vago ‖ *v* (*pret & pp* **leaped** o **leapt** [lɛpt]) *tr* saltar *s* ‖ *intr* saltar; dar un salto (*el corazón de uno*)
leap day *s* día *m* intercalar
leap'frog' *s* fil derecho, juego del salto; **to play leapfrog** jugar a la una la mula
leap year *s* año bisiesto
learn [lʌrn] *v* (*pret & pp* **learned** o **learnt** [lʌrnt]) *tr* aprender; oír decir; saber (*una noticia*) ‖ *intr* aprender
learned [ˈlʌrnɪd] *adj* docto, erudito; (*e.g., word*) culto
learned journal *s* revista científica
learned society *s* sociedad de eruditos
learned world *s* mundo de la erudición
learner [ˈlʌrnər] *s* principiante *mf,* aprendiz *m,* estudiante *mf*
learning [ˈlʌrnɪŋ] *s* (*act and time devoted*) aprendizaje *m;* (*scholarship*) erudición
lease [lis] *s* arrendamiento, locación; contrato de alquiler; **to give a new lease on life to**

renovar completamente; volver a hacer feliz || *tr* arrendar || *intr* arrendarse
lease'hold' *adj* arrendado || *s* arrendamiento; bienes raíces arrendados
leash [liʃ] *s* traílla; **to strain at the leash** sufrir la sujeción con impaciencia || *tr* atraillar
least [list] *adj* (el) menor, mínimo, más pequeño || *adv* menos || *s* (el) menor; (lo) menos; **at least** o **at the least** al menos, a los menos, por lo menos; **not in the least** de ninguna manera
leather [ˈlɛðər] *s* cuero
leath'er•back' turtle *s* laúd *m*
leath'er•neck' *s* (U.S.A.) (slang) marine *m,* infante *m* de marina
leathery [ˈlɛðəri] *adj* correoso, coriáceo
leave [liv] *s* (*permission*) permiso; (*permission to be absent*) licencia; (*farewell*) despedida; **on leave** con licencia; **to give leave to** dar licencia a; **to take leave (of)** despedirse (de) || *v* (*pret & pp* **left** [lɛft]) *tr* (*to let stay; to stop, give up; to disregard*) dejar; (*to go away from*) salir de; (*to bequeath*) legar; **leave it to me!** ¡déjemelo a mí!; **to be left** quedar p.ej., **the letter was left unanswered** la carta quedó sin contestar; **to leave alone** dejar en paz, dejar tranquilo; **to leave no stone unturned** no dejar piedra por mover; **to leave off** dejar; no ponerse (*una prenda de vestir*); **to leave out** omitir; **to leave things as they are** dejarlo como está || *intr* irse, marcharse; eliminarse (Mex); salir (*un avión, un tren, un vapor*)
leaven [ˈlɛvən] *s* levadura; (fig) influencia || *tr* leudar; (fig) transformar
leavening [ˈlɛvənɪŋ] *s* levadura
leave of absence *s* licencia
leave'-tak'ing *s* despedida
leavings [ˈlivɪŋz] *spl* desperdicios, sobras
Leba•nese [ˌlɛbəˈniz] *adj* libanés || *s* (*pl* **-nese**) libanés *m*
Lebanon [ˈlɛbənən] *s* el Líbano
lecher [ˈlɛtʃər] *s* libertino, lujurioso
lecherous [ˈlɛtʃərəs] *adj* lascivo, lujurioso
lechery [ˈlɛtʃəri] *s* lascivia, lujuria
lectern [ˈlɛktərn] *s* atril *m*
lecture [ˈlɛktʃər] *s* conferencia; (*tedious reprimand*) sermoneo; (educ) clase *f* || *tr* instruir por medio de una conferencia; sermonear || *intr* dar una conferencia, dar conferencias
lecturer [ˈlɛktʃərər] *s* conferenciante *mf*
ledge [lɛdʒ] *s* (*projection in a wall*) retallo; cama de roca; arrecife *m*
ledger [ˈlɛdʒər] *s* (com) libro mayor
ledger line *s* (mus) línea suplementaria
lee [li] *s* (*shelter*) (naut) socaire *m;* (*quarter sheltered from the wind*) sotavento; **lees** heces *fpl*
leech [litʃ] *s* sanguijuela; **to stick like a leech** pegarse como ladilla
leek [lik] *s* puerro
leer [lɪr] *s* mirada de soslayo, mirada lujuriosa || *intr*—**to leer at** mirar de soslayo, mirar lujuriosamente
leery [ˈlɪri] *adj* (coll) receloso, suspicaz
leeward [ˈliwərd] o [ˈlu•ərd] *adj* (naut) de sotavento || *adv* (naut) a sotavento || *s* (naut) sotavento
Leeward Islands [ˈliwərd] *spl* islas de Sotavento
lee'way' *s* (aer & naut) deriva; (coll) tiempo de sobra, espacio de sobra, dinero de sobra; libertad de acción
left [lɛft] *adj* izquierdo || *adv* hacia la izquierda || *s* (*left hand*) izquierda; (box) zurdazo; (pol) izquierda; **from left to right** de izquierda a derecha; **on the left** a la izquierda
left field *s* (baseball) jardín izquierdo
left'-hand' drive *s* conducción o dirección a la izquierda
left-handed [ˈlɛftˈhændɪd] *adj* (*individual*) zurdo; (*clumsy*) desmañado, torpe; insincero; contrario a las agujas del reloj
leftish [ˈlɛftɪʃ] *adj* izquierdizante
leftist [ˈlɛftɪst] *adj & s* izquierdista *mf*
left'o'ver *adj & s* sobrante *m;* **leftovers** *spl* sobras
left'-wing' *adj* izquierdista
left-winger [ˈlɛftˈwɪŋər] *s* (coll) izquierdista *mf*
leg [lɛg] *s* (*of man or animal*) pierna; (*of animal, table, chair, etc.*) pata; (*of boot or stocking*) caña; (*of trousers*) pernera; (*of a cooked fowl*) muslo; (*of a journey*) etapa, trecho; **to be on one's last legs** estar sin recursos; estar en las últimas; **to not have a leg to stand on** (coll) no tener justificación alguna, no tener disculpa alguna; **to pull the leg of** (coll) tomar el pelo a; **to shake a leg** (coll) darse prisa; (*to dance*) (coll) bailar; **to stretch one's legs** estirar las piernas, dar un paseíto
lega•cy [ˈlɛgəsi] *s* (*pl* **-cies**) legado
legal [ˈligəl] *adj* legal
legal holiday *s* día festivo oficial
legali•ty [lɪˈgælɪti] *s* (*pl* **-ties**) legalidad
legalization [ˌligələˈzeʃən] *s* legalización despenalización
legalize [ˈligəˌlaɪz] *tr* legalizar; despenalizar
legal tender *s* moneda de curso legal
legate [ˈlɛgɪt] *s* legado
legatee [ˌlɛgəˈti] *s* legatario
legation [lɪˈgeʃən] *s* legación
legend [ˈlɛdʒənd] *s* leyenda
legendary [ˈlɛdʒənˌdɛri] *adj* legendario
legerdemain [ˌlɛdʒərdɪˈmen] *s* juego de manos, prestidigitación; (*cheating, trickery*) trapacería
legging [ˈlɛgɪŋ] *s* polaina
leg•gy [ˈlɛgi] *adj* (*comp* **-gier;** *super* **-giest**) zanquilargo; de piernas largas y elegantes
legible [ˈlɛdʒɪbəl] *adj* legible
legion [ˈlidʒən] *s* legión
Legionnaires' disease [ˌlidʒəˈnɛrz] *s* enfermedad del legionario
legislate [ˈlɛdʒɪsˌlet] *tr* imponer mediante legislación || *intr* legislar
legislation [ˈlɛdʒɪsˈleʃən] *s* legislación
legislative [ˈlɛdʒɪsˌletɪv] *adj* legislativo

legislator [ˈlɛdʒɪs,letər] *s* legislador *m*
legislature [ˈlɛdʒɪs,letʃər] *s* asamblea legislativa, cuerpo legislativo
legitimacy [lɪˈdʒɪtɪməsi] *s* legitimidad
legitimate [lɪˈdʒɪtɪmɪt] *adj* legítimo ‖ [lɪˈdʒɪtɪ,met] *tr* legitimar
legitimize [lɪˈdʒɪtɪ,maɪz] *tr* legitimar
leg′work′ *s* (coll) el mucho caminar
leisure [ˈliʒər] o [ˈlɛʒər] *s* desocupación, ocio; **at leisure** desocupado, libre; **at one's leisure** a la comodidad de uno, cuando uno pueda
leisure activities *spl* recreos pasatiempos
leisure class *s* gente acomodada
leisure hours *spl* horas de ocio, ratos perdidos
leisurely [ˈliʒərli] o [ˈlɛʒərli] *adj* lento, pausado ‖ *adv* lentamente, despacio, sin prisa
leisure wear *s* ropa de recreo, traje *m* informal
lemon [ˈlɛmən] *s* limón *m;* (slang) artículo de fábrica defectuosa
lemonade [,lɛməˈned] *s* limonada
lemon squeezer *s* exprimidera de limón
lemon verbena (bot) *s* luisa, cedrón *m*
lend [lɛnd] *s* (*pret & pp* **lent** [lɛnt]) *tr* prestar
lending library *s* biblioteca de préstamo
length [lɛŋθ] *s* largura, largo; (*of time*) extensión; (naut) eslora; **at length** por fin; largamente; **to go to any length** hacer cuanto esté de su parte; **to keep at arm's length** mantener a distancia; mantenerse a distancia
lengthen [ˈlɛŋθən] *tr* alargar ‖ *intr* alargarse
length′wise′ *adj* longitudinal ‖ *adv* longitudinalmente
length•y [ˈlɛŋθi] *adj* (*comp* **-ier;** *super* **-iest**) muy largo, prolongado
leniency [ˈlinɪ•ənsi] *s* clemencia, indulgencia, lenidad
lenient [ˈlinɪ•ənt] *adj* clemente, indulgente
lens [lɛnz] *s* lente *m & f;* (*of the eye*) cristalino
Lent [lɛnt] *s* cuaresma *f*
Lenten [ˈlɛntən] *adj* cuaresmal
lentil [ˈlɛntəl] *s* lenteja
Leo [ˈli•o] *s* (astr) Leo
leopard [ˈlɛpərd] *s* leopardo
leotard [ˈli•ə,tɑrd] *s* leotardo
leper [ˈlɛpər] *s* leproso
leper house *s* leprosería
leprosy [ˈlɛprəsi] *s* lepra
leprous [ˈlɛprəs] *adj* leproso; (*covered with scales*) escamoso
lesbian [ˈlɛzbɪ•ən] *adj* lesbiano, lésbico ‖ *f* lesbiana
lesbianism [ˈlɛzbɪ•ə,nɪzəm] *s* lesbianismo
lese majesty [ˈlizˈmædʒɪsti] *s* delito de lesa majestad
lesion [ˈliʒən] *s* lesión
less [lɛs] *adj* menor ‖ *adv* menos; **less and less** cada vez menos; **less than** menos que; (*followed by numeral*) menos de; (*followed by verb*) menos de lo que ‖ *s* menos *m*
lessee [lɛsˈi] *s* arrendatario
lessen [ˈlɛsən] *tr* disminuir, reducir a menos; quitar importancia a ‖ *intr* disminuirse, reducirse; amainar (*el viento*)
lesser [ˈlɛsər] *adj* menor, más pequeño
lesson [ˈlɛsən] *s* lección
lessor [ˈlɛsər] *s* arrendador *m*
lest [lɛst] *conj* no sea que, de miedo que
let [lɛt] *v* (*pret & pp* **let;** *ger* **letting**) *tr* dejar, permitir; alquilar, arrendar; **let** + *inf* que + *subj,* p.ej., **let him come in** que entre; **let alone** y mucho menos; **let good enough alone** bueno está lo bueno; **let us** + *inf* vamos a + *inf,* p.ej., **let us eat** vamos a comer, comamos; **to let** se alquila; **to let alone** dejar en paz, dejar tranquilo; **to let be** no tocar; dejar en paz; **to let by** dejar pasar; **to let down** dejar bajar; desilusionar, traicionar; dejar plantado; **to let fly** disparar; (fig) disparar, soltar (*palabras injuriosas*); **to let go** soltar, desasirse de; vender; **to let in** dejar entrar, dejar entrar en; **to let it go at that** no hacer o decir nada más; **to let know** hacer saber; **to let loose** soltar; **to let on** (coll) dar a entender; **to let out** dejar salir; revelar, publicar; dar, soltar (*p.ej., más cuerda*); dar (*un grito*); ensanchar (*un vestido que aprieta*); dar en arrendamiento; (coll) despedir; **to let through** dejar pasar, dejar pasar por; **to let up** dejar subir; dejar levantarse ‖ *intr* alquilarse, arrendarse; **to let down** (coll) ir más despacio; **to let go** desasirse; **to let go of** desasirse de; **to let on** (coll) fingir; **to let out** (coll) despedirse, cerrarse (*p.ej., la escuela*); **to let up** (coll) desistir; (coll) aflojar, amainar
let′down′ *s* disminución; aflojamiento; desilusión, decepción; humillación
lethal [ˈliθəl] *adj* letal
lethargic [lɪˈθɑrdʒɪk] *adj* (*affected with lethargy*) letárgico; (*producing lethargy*) letargoso
lethar•gy [ˈlɛθərdʒi] *s* (*pl* **-gies**) letargo
letter [ˈlɛtər] *s* (*written message*) carta; (*of the alphabet*) letra; (*literal meaning*) (fig) letra; **letters** (*literature*) letras; **to the letter** al pie de la letra ‖ *tr* estampar o marcar con letras
letter bomb *s* carta bomba
letter box *s* buzón *m* (*caja*)
letter carrier *s* cartero
letter drop *s* buzón *m* (*agujero*)
letter file *s* guardacartas *m*
let′ter•head′ *s* membrete *m;* (*paper with printed heading*) memorándum *m*
lettering [ˈlɛtərɪŋ] *s* inscripción; letras
letter of credit *s* carta de crédito
letter opener [ˈopənər] *s* abrecartas *m*
letter paper *s* papel *m* de cartas
let′ter-per′fect *adj* que tiene bien aprendido su papel; correcto, exacto
let′ter•press′ *s* impresión tipográfica
letter scales *spl* pesacartas *m*
lettuce [ˈlɛtɪs] *s* lechuga
let′up *s* (coll) calma, interrupción; **without letup** (coll) sin cesar
leucorrhea [,lukəˈri•ə] *s* leucorrea
leukemia [luˈkimɪ•ə] *s* leucemia

Levant [lɪˋvænt] *s* Levante *m* (*países de la parte oriental del Mediterráneo*)
levee [ˋlɛvi] *s* (*embankment to hold back water*) ribero; (*reception at court*) besamanos *m*
lev•el [ˋlɛvəl] *adj* raso, llano; nivelado; (coll) sensato, juicioso; **level with** al nivel de, a flor de, a ras de || *s* (*device for determining horizontal position; degree of elevation*) nivel *m;* (*flat and even area of land*) terreno llano, llanura; (*part of a canal between two locks*) tramo; **to be on the level** obrar sin engaño, decir la pura verdad; **to find one's level** hallar su propio nivel || *v* (*pret & pp* **-eled** o **-elled;** *ger* **-eling** o **-elling**) *tr* nivelar; (*to smooth, flatten out*) arrasar, allanar; (*to bring down*) derribar, echar por tierra; apuntar (*un arma de fuego*); (fig) allanar (*dificultades*) || *intr*—**to level off** (aer) enderezarse para aterrizar
level-headed [ˋlɛvəlˋhɛdɪd] *adj* sensato, juicioso
leveling rod *s* (surv) jalón *m* de mira
lever [ˋlivər] o [lɛvər] *s* palanca || *tr* apalancar
leverage [ˋlivərɪdʒ] o [ˋlɛvərɪdʒ] *s* palancada; poder *m* de una palanca; (fig) influencia, poder *m;* (econ, phys) apalancamiento
leveraged buyout *s* (econ) compra apalancada compra con financiación ajena
leviathan [lɪˋvaɪ•əθən] *s* (Bib & fig) leviatán *m;* buque *m* muy grande
levitation [ˌlɛvɪˋteʃən] *s* levitación
levi•ty [ˋlɛvɪti] *s* (*pl* **-ties**) frivolidad; (*fickleness*) ligereza
lev•y [ˋlɛvi] *s* (*pl* **-ies**) (*of taxes*) exación, recaudación; dinero recaudado; (mil) leva, enganche *m,* recluta || *v* (*pret & pp* **-ied**) *tr* exigir, recaudar (*impuestos*); (mil) enganchar, reclutar; hacer (*la guerra*)
lewd [lud] *adj* lascivo, lujurioso; obsceno
lewdness [ˋludnɪs] *s* lascivia, lujuria; obscenidad
lexical [ˋlɛksɪkəl] *adj* léxico
lexicographer [ˌlɛksɪˋkɑgrəfər] *s* lexicógrafo
lexicographic(al) [ˌlɛksɪkəˋgræfɪk(əl)] lexicográfico
lexicography [ˌlɛksɪˋkɑgrəfi] *s* lexicografía
lexicology [ˌlɛksɪˋkɑlədʒi] *s* lexicología
lexicon [ˋlɛksɪkən] *s* léxico, lexicón *m*
liabili•ty [ˌlaɪ•əˋbɪlɪti] *s* (*pl* **-ties**) (*e.g., to disease*) propensión; responsabilidad, obligación; desventaja; **liabilities** deudas; (*as detailed in balance sheet*) pasivo
liability insurance *s* seguro de responsabilidad civil
liable [ˋlaɪ•əbəl] *adj* (*e.g., to disease*) propenso, expuesto; responsable; **to be liable to** + *inf* (coll) amenazar + *inf*
liaison [ˋli•əˌzɑn] o [liˋezən] *s* enlace *m,* unión; (*illicit relationship between a man and woman*) amancebamiento, enredo, lío; (mil, nav & phonet) enlace *m*
liaison officer *s* (mil) oficial *m* de enlace
liar [ˋlaɪ•ər] *s* mentiroso
li•bel [ˋlaɪbəl] *s* calumnia, difamación; levante (CAm, P-R); (*defamatory writing*) libelo || *v* (*pret & pp* **-beled** o **-belled;** *ger* **-beling** o **-belling**) *tr* calumniar, difamar
libelous [ˋlaɪbələs] *adj* calumniador
liberal [ˋlɪbərəl] *adj* (*generous; done or given generously*) liberal; (*open-minded*) tolerante, de amplias miras; (*translation*) libre; (pol) liberal || *s* liberal *mf*
liberali•ty [ˌlɪbəˋrælɪti] *s* (*pl* **-ties**) liberalidad
liberal-minded [ˋlɪbərəlˋmaɪndɪd] *adj* tolerante, de amplias miras
liberate [ˋlɪbəˌret] *tr* libertar; (*to disengage from a combination*) (chem) desprender
liberation [ˌlɪbəˋreʃən] *s* liberación; (chem) desprendimiento
liberation theology *s* teología liberacionista
liberator [ˋlɪbəˌretər] *s* libertador *m*
libertine [ˋlɪbərˌtin] *adj & s* libertino
liber•ty [ˋlɪbərti] *s* (*pl* **-ties**) libertad; **to take the liberty to** tomarse la libertad de
libidinous [lɪˋbɪdɪnəs] *adj* libidinoso
libido [lɪˋbido] o [lɪˋbaɪdo] *s* libídine *f,* libido *f*
Libra [ˋlibrə] *s* (astr) Libra
librarian [laɪˋbrɛrɪ•ən] *s* bibliotecario
librar•y [ˋlaɪˌbrɛri] o [ˋlaɪbrəri] *s* (*pl* **-ies**) biblioteca
library number *s* signatura
library school *s* escuela de bibliotecarios
library science *s* bibliotecnia; biblioteconomía
libret•to [lɪˋbrɛto] *s* (*pl* **-tos**) (mus) libreto
license [ˋlaɪsəns] *s* licencia || *tr* licenciar
license number *s* número de matrícula
license plate o **tag** *s* chapa de circulación, placa de matrícula
license plate lights *spl* luces *fpl* de placa
licentious [laɪˋsɛnʃəs] *adj* licencioso, disoluto
lichen [ˋlaɪkən] *s* liquen *m*
lick [lɪk] *s* lamedura; (*place where animals go to lick*) lamedero; (*blow*) (coll) bofetón *m;* (*speed*) (coll) velocidad; (*beating*) (coll) zurra; (*quick cleaning*) (coll) limpión *m;* **to give a lick and a promise to** (coll) hacer rápida y superficialmente || *tr* lamer; lamerse (*p.ej., los dedos*); lamer (*las llamas un tejado*); (*to beat, thrash*) (coll) zurrar; (*to conquer*) (coll) vencer || *intr* lengüetear
licorice [ˋlɪkərɪs] *s* regaliz *m,* orozuz *m;* dulce *m* de regaliz
lid [lɪd] *s* (*of a box, trunk, chest, etc.*) tapa, tapadera; (*of a dish, pot, etc.*) cobertera; (*eyelid*) párpado; (*hat*) (slang) techo
lie [laɪ] *s* mentira; **to catch in a lie** coger en una mentira; **to give the lie to** dar un mentís a || *v* (*pret & pp* **lied;** *ger* **lying**) *tr*—**to lie oneself out of** o **to lie one's way out of** librarse de un aprieto mintiendo || *intr* mentir || *v* (*pret* **lay** [le]; *pp* **lain** [len]; *ger* **lying**) *intr* estar echado; hallarse, estar situado; (*e.g., in the grave*) yacer, estar enterrado; **to lie down** echarse, acostarse
lie detector *s* detector *m* de mentiras
lien [lin] o [ˋli•ən] *s* gravamen *m,* derecho de retención

lieu [lu] *s*—**in lieu of** en lugar de, en vez de
lieutenant [lu'tɛnənt] *s* lugarteniente *m;* (mil) teniente *m;* (nav) teniente de navío
lieutenant colonel *s* (mil) teniente coronel *m*
lieutenant commander *s* (nav) capitán *m* de corbeta
lieutenant governor *s* (U.S.A.) vicegobernador *m* (*de un Estado*)
lieutenant junior grade *s* (nav) alférez *m* de navío
life [laɪf] *adj* (*animate*) vital; (*lifelong*) perpetuo; (*annuity, income*) vitalicio; (*working from nature*) (fa) del natural ‖ *s* (*pl* **lives** [laɪvz]) vida; (*of an insurance policy*) vigencia; **for life** de por vida; **for the life of me** así me maten; **the life and soul of** (*e.g., a party*) la alegría de; **to come to life** volver a la vida; **to depart this life** partir de esta vida; **to run for one's life** salvarse por los pies
life annuity *s* renta vitalicia
life belt *s* cinturón *m* salvavidas
life'boat' *s* bote *m* de salvamento, bote salvavidas; (*for shore-based rescue services*) lancha de auxilio
life buoy *s* boya salvavidas, guindola
life expectancy *s* expectación de vida
life float *s* balsa salvavidas
life'guard' *s* salvavidas *m,* bañero (SAm)
life imprisonment *s* cadena perpetua
life insurance *s* seguro sobre la vida
life jacket *s* chaleco salvavidas
lifeless ['laɪflɪs] *adj* muerto, sin vida; (*in a faint*) desmayado, exánime; (*dull, colorless*) deslucido
life'like' *adj* natural, vivo
life line *s* cuerda salvavidas; cuerda de buzo
life'long' *adj* perpetuo, de toda la vida
life member *s* socio vitalicio
life of leisure *s* vida de ocio
life of Riley ['raɪli] *s* (slang) vida regalada
life of the party *s* (coll) alegría de la fiesta, alma de la fiesta
life preserver [prɪ'zʌrvər] *s* chaleco salvavidas
lifer ['laɪfər] *s* (slang) presidiario de por vida
life'sav'er *s* salvavidas *m,* bañero; (*something that saves a person from a predicament*) (coll) tabla de salvación
lifesaving ['laɪf,sevɪŋ] *adj* de salvamento ‖ *s* salvamento (*de vidas*)
life sciences *spl* ciencias biológicas
life sentence *s* condena a cadena perpetua
life'-size' *adj* de tamaño natural
life span *s* período de vida
life'style' *s* estilo, tren *m or* régimen *m* de vida
life'time' *adj* vitalicio ‖ *s* vida, curso de la vida, jornada
life'work' *s* obra principal de la vida de uno
lift [lɪft] *s* elevación, levantamiento; ayuda (*para levantar una carga*); (aer) sustentación; **to give a lift to** invitar (*a un peatón*) a subir a un coche; llevar en un coche; (fig) reanimar ‖ *tr* elevar, levantar; quitarse (*el sombrero*); (naut) izar (*velas, vergas, etc.*); (fig) reanimar, exaltar; (coll) robar; (coll) plagiar ‖ *intr* elevarse, levantarse; disiparse (*las nubes, las nieblas, la obscuridad, etc.*)
lift bridge *s* puente levadizo
lift'-off *s* despegue *m* vertical
lift truck *s* carretilla elevadora
ligament ['lɪgəmənt] *s* ligamento
ligature ['lɪgətʃər] *s* (mus & surg) ligadura; (mus & typ) ligado
light [laɪt] *adj* (*in weight*) ligero, leve, liviano; (*having illumination; whitish*) claro; (*hair*) blondo, rubio; (*complexion*) blanco; (*oil*) flúido; (*beer*) claro; (*reading*) poco serio; (*heart*) alegre, despreocupado; (*carrying a small cargo or none at all*) (naut) boyante; **light in the head** (*dizzy*) aturdido, mareado; (*simple, silly*) tonto, necio; **to make light of** no dar importancia a, no tomar en serio ‖ *adv* sin carga; sin equipaje ‖ *s* luz *f;* (*to light a cigarette*) lumbre *f,* fuego; (*to control traffic*) luz, señal *f;* (*window or other opening in a wall*) luz, claro, hueco; (*example, shining figure*) lumbrera; **according to one's lights** según Dios le da a uno a entender; **against the light** al trasluz; **in this light** desde este punto de vista; **lights** noticias; (*of sheep, etc.*) bofes *mpl;* **to come to light** salir a luz, descubrirse; **to shed** o **throw light on** echar luz sobre; **to strike a light** echar una yesca; encender un fósforo ‖ *v* (*pret & pp* **lighted** o **lit** [lɪt] *tr* (*to furnish with illumination*) alumbrar, iluminar; (*to set afire, ignite*) encender; **to light up** iluminar ‖ *intr* alumbrarse; encenderse; posar (*un ave*); (*from an auto*) bajar; **to light into** (*to attack*) (slang) arremeter contra; (*to scold, berate*) (slang) poner de oro y azul; **to light out** (slang) poner pies en polvorosa; **to light upon** tropezar con, hallar por casualidad
light bulb *s* (elec) bombilla, bujía (CAm), ampolleta (Chile), bombillo (SAm), foco (Mex), bombita (SAm)
light complexion *s* tez blanca
lighten ['laɪtən] *tr* (*to make lighter in weight*) aligerar; iluminar; (*to cheer up*) alegrar, regocijar ‖ *intr* (*to become less dark*) iluminarse; (*to give off flashes of lightning*) relampaguear; (fig) iluminarse (*los ojos, la cara de una persona*)
lighter ['laɪtər] *s* (*to light a cigarette*) encendedor *m;* (*flat-bottomed barge*) alijador *m*
light-fingered ['laɪt'fɪŋgərd] *adj* (coll) largo de uñas, listo de manos
light-footed ['laɪt'fʊtɪd] *adj* ligero de pies
light-headed ['laɪt'hɛdɪd] *adj* (*dizzy*) aturdido, mareado; (*simple, silly*) tonto, necio, ligero de cascos
light-hearted ['laɪt'hɑrtɪd] *adj* alegre, libre de cuidados, desenfadado
light heavyweight *s* peso semipesado
light'house' *s* faro
lighthouse keeper *s* farero
lighting ['laɪtɪŋ] *s* alumbrado, iluminación

lighting engineer *s* iluminador *m*
lighting fixtures *spl* artefactos de alumbrado
lightly [ˈlaɪtli] *adj* ligeramente
light meter *s* exposímetro
lightness [ˈlaɪtnɪs] *s* (*in weight*) ligereza; (*in illumination*) claridad
lightning [ˈlaɪtnɪŋ] *s* relámpagos, relampagueo ‖ *intr* relampaguear
lightning arrester [əˈrɛstər] *s* pararrayos *m*
lightning bug *s* luciérnaga
lightning rod *s* pararrayos *m*
light opera *s* opereta
light pen *s* (compu) lápiz luminoso, óptico o fotosensible
light'ship' *s* buque *m* fanal, buque faro
light•struck [ˈlaɪt,strʌk] *adj* velado
light'weight' *adj* ligero, liviano, poco pesado ‖ *s* persona de poco peso; (*in boxing, wrestling*) peso ligero; **lightweight champion** campeón *m* de peso ligero
light'-year' *s* año luz
lignite [ˈlɪgnaɪt] *s* lignito
lignum vitae [ˈlɪgnəmˈvaɪti] *s* guayaco, palo santo
likable [ˈlaɪkəbəl] *adj* simpático
like [laɪk] *adj* parecido, semejante; parecido a, semejante a, p.ej., **this hat is like mine** este sombrero es parecido al mío; (elec) del mismo nombre; **like father like son** de tal palo tal astilla; **to feel like** + *ger* tener ganas de + *inf;* **to look like** parecerse a; parecer que, p.ej., **it looks like rain** parece que va a llover ‖ *adv* como; **like enough** (coll) probablemente; **nothing like** ni con mucho ‖ *prep* a semejanza de ‖ *conj* (coll) del mismo modo que; (coll) que, p.ej., **it seems like he is right** parece que tiene razón ‖ *s* (*liking*) gusto, preferencia; (*fellow, fellow man*) prójimo, semejante *m;* **and the like** y cosas por el estilo; **to give like for like** pagar en la misma moneda ‖ *tr* gustar, p.ej., **I like music** me gusta la música; p.ej., **Mary likes peaches** a María le gustan los melocotones; **to like best** o **better** preferir; **to like it in** encontrarse a gusto en (*p.ej., el campo*); **to like to** + *inf* gustarle a uno + *inf,* p.ej., **I like to travel** me gusta viajar; gustarle a uno que + *subj,* p.ej., **I should like him to come to see me** me gustaría que él viniese a verme ‖ *intr* querer, p.ej., **as you like** como Ud. quiera; **if you like** si Ud. quiere
likelihood [ˈlaɪklɪ,hʊd] *s* probabilidad
like•ly [ˈlaɪkli] *adj* (*comp* **-lier;** *super* **-liest**) probable; a propósito; prometedor; **to be likely to** + *inf* ser probable que + *ind,* p.ej., **Mary is likely to come to see us tomorrow** es probable que María vendrá a vernos mañana ‖ *adv* probablemente
like-minded [ˈlaɪkˈmaɪndɪd] *adj* del mismo parecer; de natural semejante
liken [ˈlaɪkən] *tr* asemejar, comparar
likeness [ˈlaɪknɪs] *s* (*picture or image*) retrato; (*similarity*) semejanza, parecido; forma, aspecto, apariencia
like'wise' *adv* igualmente, asimismo; **to do likewise** hacer lo mismo
liking [ˈlaɪkɪŋ] *s* gusto, afición, simpatía; **to be to the liking of** ser del gusto de; **to have a liking for** aficionarse a
lilac [ˈlaɪlək] *adj* de color lila ‖ *s* lilac *m,* lila
Lilliputian [,lɪlɪˈpjuʃən] *adj & s* liliputiense *mf*
lilt [lɪlt] *s* paso airoso, movimiento airoso; canción cadenciosa, música alegre
lil•y [ˈlɪli] *s* (*pl* **-ies**) (*Lilium candidum*) azucena, lirio blanco; cala, lirio de agua; (*fleur-de-lis, the royal arms of France*) flor *f* de lis; **to gild the lily** ponerle colores al oro
lily-livered [ˈlɪliˈlɪvərd] *adj* pusilánime
lily of the valley *s* lirio de los valles, muguete *m*
lily pad *s* hoja de nenúfar
lima bean [ˈlaɪmə] *s* judía de la peladilla, frijol *m* de media luna
limb [lɪm] *s* (*arm or leg*) miembro; (*of a tree*) rama; (*of a cross; of the sea*) brazo; **to be out on a limb** (coll) estar en un aprieto
limber [ˈlɪmbər] *adj* ágil; flexible ‖ *intr*—**to limber up** agilitarse
lim•bo [ˈlɪmbo] *s* (*pl* **-bos**) lugar *m* de olvido; (theol) limbo
lime [laɪm] *s* (*calcium oxide*) cal *f;* (*Citrus aurantifolia*) limero agrio; (*its fruit*) lima agria; (*linden tree*) tila o tilo
lime'kiln' *s* calera, horno de cal
lime'light' *s* —**to be in the limelight** estar a la vista del público
limerick [ˈlɪmərɪk] *s* quintilla jocosa
lime'stone' *adj* calizo ‖ *s* caliza, piedra caliza *or* de cal
limit [ˈlɪmɪt] *s* límite *m;* **to be the limit** (slang) ser el colmo; **to go the limit** no dejar piedra por mover ‖ *tr* limitar
lim'ited-ac'cess high'way *s* carretera de vía libre
limited edition *s* edición limitada o numerada
limited monarchy *s* monarquía constitucional
limitless [ˈlɪmɪtlɪs] *adj* ilimitado
limousine [ˈlɪmə,zin] o [,lɪməˈzin] *s* (aut) limusina
limp [lɪmp] *adj* flojo, débil, flexible ‖ *s* cojera ‖ *intr* cojear
limpid [ˈlɪmpɪd] *adj* diáfano, cristalino
linage [ˈlaɪnɪdʒ] *s* (typ) número de líneas
linchpin [ˈlɪntʃ,pɪn] *s* (*vital factor*) eje *m;* (mach) pezonera
linden [ˈlɪndən] *s* tila, tilo
line [laɪn] *s* línea; (*of people, houses, etc.*) hilera; (*rope, string*) cuerda, cordel *m;* (*wrinkle*) arruga; (*for fishing*) sedal *m;* (*written or printed line; line of goods*) renglón *m;* manera (*de pensar*); (*of the spectrum*) (phys) raya; **all along the line** por todas partes; desde cualquier punto de vista; **in line** alineado; dispuesto, preparado; **in line with** de acuerdo con; **on line** (compu) en línea; **out of line**

desalineado; en desacuerdo; **to bring into line** poner de acuerdo; **to draw the line at** no ir más allá de; **to fall in line** conformarse; formar cola; alinearse; **to have a line on** (coll) estar enterado de; **to read between the lines** leer entre líneas; **to stand in line** hacer cola; **to toe the line** obrar como se debe; **to wait in line** hacer cola, esperar vez || *tr* alinear, rayar; arrugar (*p.ej., la cara*); formar hilera a lo largo de (*la acera, la calle*); forrar (*un vestido*); guarnecer (*un freno*) || *intr*—**to line up** ponerse en fila; hacer cola

lineage [ˈlɪnɪ•ɪdʒ] *s* linaje *m*

lineaments [ˈlɪnɪ•əmənts] *spl* lineamentos

linear [ˈlɪnɪ•ər] *adj* lineal

line•man [ˈlaɪnmən] *s* (*pl* **-men** [mən]) (elec) celador *m,* recorredor *m* de la línea; (rr) guardavía *m;* (surv) cadenero

linen [ˈlɪnən] *adj* de lino || *s* (*fabric*) lienzo, lino; (*yarn*) hilo de lino; ropa blanca, ropa de cama

linen closet *s* armario para la ropa blanca

line of battle *s* línea de batalla

line of fire *s* (mil) línea de tiro

line of least resistance *s* ley *f* del menor esfuerzo; **to follow the line of least resistance** seguir el camino más fácil, seguir la corriente, no oponer resistencia

line of scrimmage *s* zona de escaramuza

line of sight *s* visual *f;* (*of firearm*) línea de mira

liner [ˈlaɪnər] *s* vapor *m* de travesía; (baseball) pelota rasa, lineazo

line′-up′ *s* agrupación, formación; (*of suspects*) rueda de identificación, rueda de sospechosos; (sport) alineación, plantel *m*

linger [ˈlɪŋgər] *intr* estarse, quedarse; (*to be tardy*) demorar, tardar; tardar en marcharse; tardar en morirse; pasearse con paso lento; **to linger over** contemplar, reflexionar

lingerie [ˌlænʒəˈri] *s* ropa interior de mujer

lingering [ˈlɪŋgərɪŋ] *adj* prolongado

lingual [ˈlɪŋgwəl] *adj & s* lingual *f*

linguist [ˈlɪŋgwɪst] *s* (*person skilled in several languages*) poligloto; (*specialist in linguistics*) lingüista *mf*

linguistic [lɪŋˈgwɪstɪk] *adj* lingüístico || **linguistics** *s* lingüística

liniment [ˈlɪnɪmənt] *s* linimento

lining [ˈlaɪnɪŋ] *s* (*of a coat*) forro, forrado; (*of auto brake*) guarnición; (*of a furnace*) camisa; (*of a wall*) revestimiento

link [lɪŋk] *s* eslabón *m;* **links** campo de golf; (compu) links *mpl,* vínculos || *tr* eslabonar || *intr* eslabonarse; (compu) vincularse

linkage [ˈlɪŋkɪdʒ] *s* conexión; (*mechanism*) acoplamiento; (compu) enlace *m*

linkup [ˈliŋk,ʌp] *s* conexión; (*in space*) acoplamiento; (rad, telv) conexión, enlace *m*

linnet [ˈlɪnɪt] *s* pardillo

linoleum [lɪˈnolɪ•əm] *s* linóleo

Linotype[T] [ˈlaɪnə,taɪp] *adj* linotípico || *s* (*machine*) linotipia; (*matter produced by machine*) linotipo || *tr* componer con linotipia

linotype operator *s* linotipista *mf*

linseed [ˈlɪn,sid] *s* linaza

linseed oil *s* aceite *m* de linaza

lint [lɪnt] *s* borra, pelusa, hilaza; (*used to dress wounds*) hilas

lintel [ˈlɪntəl] *s* dintel *m,* umbral *m*

lion [ˈlaɪ•ən] *s* león *m;* (*man of strength and courage*) (fig) león; (fig) celebridad muy solicitada; **to beard the lion in his den** ir a desafiar la cólera de un jefe; **to put one's head in the lion's mouth** meterse en la boca del lobo

lioness [ˈlaɪ•ənɪs] *s* leona

lion-hearted [ˈlaɪ•ən,hɑrtɪd] *adj* valiente

lionize [ˈlaɪ•ə,naɪz] *tr* agasajar

lions′ den *s* (Bib) fosa de los leónes

lion's share *s* (la) parte *f* del león

lip [lɪp] *s* labio; (slang) lenguaje *m* insolente; **to hang on the words of** estar pendiente de las palabras de; **to smack one's lips** chuparse los labios

lip′-read′ *v* (*pret & pp* **-read** [ˌrɛd]) *tr & intr* leer (en) los labios

lip reading *s* labiolectura

lip service *s* homenaje *m* de boca, jarabe *m* de pico

lip′stick′ *s* lápiz *m* de labios, lápiz labial

lique•fy [ˈlɪkwɪ,faɪ] *v* (*pret & pp* **-fied**) *tr* liquidar || *intr* liquidarse

liqueur [lɪˈkʌr] *s* licor *m*

liquid [ˈlɪkwɪd] *adj* líquido || *s* líquido; (phonet) líquida

liquidate [ˈlɪkwɪ,det] *tr & intr* liquidar

liquidity [lɪˈkwɪdɪti] *s* liquidez *f*

liquid measure *s* medida para líquidos

liquor [ˈlɪkər] *s* licor *m*

Lisbon [ˈlɪzbən] *s* Lisboa

lisle [laɪl] *s* hilo fino de algodón, muy retorcido, sedalina, hilo de Escocia

lisp [lɪsp] *s* ceceo || *intr* cecear

lissome [ˈlɪsəm] *adj* flexible, elástico; ágil, ligero

list [lɪst] *s* lista; (*strip*) lista, tira; (*border*) orilla; (*selvage*) orillo; (naut) ladeo; **lists** liza; **to enter the lists** entrar en liza; **to have a list** (naut) irse a la banda || *tr* alistar, listar; registrar || *intr* (naut) irse a la banda

listen [ˈlɪsən] *intr* escuchar; obedecer; **to listen in** escuchar a hurtadillas; escuchar por radio; **to listen to** escuchar; obedecer; **to listen to reason** meterse en razón

listener [ˈlɪsənər] *s* oyente *mf;* radioescucha *mf,* radioyente *mf*

listening post [ˈlɪsənɪŋ] *s* puesto de escucha

listing [ˈlɪstɪŋ] *s* (*items*) rubricación

listless [ˈlɪstlɪs] *adj* distraído, desatento, indiferente

listlessness [ˈlɪstlɪsnɪs] *s* apatía; indiferencia

list price *s* precio de catálogo, precio de tarifa

lit. *abbr* **liter, literal, literature**

lita•ny [ˈlɪtəni] *s* (*pl* **-nies**) letanía; (*repeated series*) (fig) letanía

liter [ˈlitər] *s* litro

literacy [ˈlɪtərəsi] *s* capacidad de leer y escribir; instrucción

literal [ˈlɪtərəl] *adj* literal

literary [ˈlɪtə,rɛri] *adj* literario; (*individual*) literato

literate [ˈlɪtərɪt] *adj* que sabe leer y escribir; (*well-read*) literato, muy leído; (*educated*) instruído || *s* persona que sabe leer y escribir; literato, erudito

literati [,lɪtəˈrɑti] *spl* literatos

literature [ˈlɪtərətʃər] *s* literatura; impresos, escritos de publicidad

lithe [laiθ] *adj* flexible, cimbreño

lithia [ˈlɪθ•ə] *s* (chem) litina

lithium [ˈlɪθɪ•əm] *s* (chem) litio

lithograph [ˈlɪθə,græf] *s* litografía || *tr* litografiar

lithographer [lɪˈθɑgrəfər] *s* litógrafo

lithography [lɪˈθɑgrəfi] *s* litografía

litigant [ˈlɪtɪgənt] *adj & s* litigante *mf*

litigate [ˈlɪtɪ,get] *tr & intr* litigar

litigation [,lɪtɪˈgəʃən] *s* litigación; (*lawsuit*) litigio

litigious [lɪˈtɪdʒəs] *adj* litigioso

litmus [ˈlɪtməs] *s* tornasol *m*

litmus paper *s* papel *m* de tornasol

litmus test *s* (chem) prueba de acidez; (fig) prueba determinante *or* decisiva

litter [ˈlɪtər] *s* desorden *m;* (*scattered rubbish*) basura, papelería; (*young brought forth at one birth*) camada, ventregada; (*bedding for animals*) cama, paja; (*vehicle carried by men or animals*) litera; (*stretcher*) camilla, parihuela || *tr* esparcir papeles por; esparcir (*desechos, papeles, etc.*); cubrir (*el suelo*) con paja || *intr* parir

litˈter•bugˈ *s* persona que ensucia las calles tirando papeles rotos

littering [ˈlɪtərɪŋ] *s*—**no littering** se prohibe tirar papeles rotos

little [ˈlɪtəl] *adj* (*in size*) pequeño; (*in amount*) poco, p.ej., **little money** poco dinero; **a little** un poco de, p.ej., **a little money** un poco de dinero || *adv* poco; **little by little** poco a poco || *s* poco; **a little** un poco; (*somewhat*) algo; **to make little of** no dar importancia a, no tomar en serio; **to think little of** tener en poco; no vacilar en

Little Bear *s* Osa Menor

Little Dipper *s* Carro Menor

little finger *s* dedo auricular, dedo meñique; **to twist around one's little finger** manejar con suma facilidad

litˈtle•neckˈ *s* almeja redonda (*Venus mercenaria*)

little owl *s* mochuelo (*Athene noctua*)

little people *spl* hadas; gente menuda

Little Red Ridinghood [ˈraɪdɪŋ,hʊd] *s* Caperucita Roja

little slam *s* (bridge) semibola

liturgic(al) [lɪˈtʌrdʒɪk(əl)] *adj* litúrgico

litur•gy [ˈlɪtərdʒi] *s* (*pl* **-gies**) liturgia

livable [ˈlɪvəbəl] *adj* habitable, vividero; llevadero, tolerable

live [laɪv] *adj* (*living; full of life; intense*) vivo; (*coals; flame*) ardiente; de actualidad; (elec) cargado || [lɪv] *tr* llevar (*tal o cual vida*); vivir (*una experiencia, una aventura; un actor sus personajes*); **to live down** borrar (*una falta*); **to live out** vivir (*toda la vida*); salir con vida de (*un desastre, una guerra*) || *intr* vivir; **to live and learn** vivir para ver; **to live and let live** vivir y dejar vivir; **to live high** darse buena vida; **to live on** seguir viviendo; vivir de (*p.ej., carne*); vivir a expensas de; **to live up to** cumplir (*lo prometido*); gastar (*todas sus rentas*)

live ammunition *s* fuego real

live coal *s* ascua

liveˈ-in *adj* residente, con cama

live-in partner *s* conviviente *mf*

livelihood [ˈlaɪvlɪ,hʊd] *s* vida; **to earn one's livelihood** ganarse la vida

livelong [ˈlɪv,lɔŋ] o [ˈlɪv,lɑŋ] *adj*—**all the livelong day** todo el santo día

live•ly [ˈlaɪvli] *adj* (*comp* **-lier;** *super* **-liest**) animado, vivaz; alegre, festivo; (*active, keen*) vivo; (*resilient*) elástico

liven [ˈlaɪvən] *tr* animar, regocijar || *intr* animarse, regocijarse

liver [ˈlɪvər] *s* vividor *m;* habitante *mf;* (anat) hígado

liver•y [ˈlɪvəri] *s* (*pl* **-ies**) librea

livery•man [ˈlɪvərimən] *s* (*pl* **-men** [mən]) dueño de una cochera; mozo de cuadra

livery stable *s* cochera de carruajes de alquiler, caballeriza

liveˈstockˈ *adj* ganadero || *s* ganadería

live wire *s* (elec) alambre cargado; (coll) persona vivaz y activa

livid [ˈlɪvɪd] *adj* lívido, amoratado; encolerizado; pálido

living [ˈlɪvɪŋ] *adj* vivo, viviente || *s* vida; **to earn** o **to make a living** ganarse la vida

living quarters *spl* aposentos, habitaciones

living room *s* sala, sala de estar, salón *m*

living wage *s* jornal *m* suficiente para vivir

lizard [ˈlɪzərd] *s* lagarto; (slang) holgón *m*

load [lod] *s* carga; **loads** (coll) muchísimo; **loads of** (coll) gran cantidad de; **to get a load of** (slang) escuchar, oír; (slang) mirar; **to have a load on** (slang) estar borracho || *tr* cargar || *intr* cargar; cargarse

loaded [ˈlodɪd] *adj* cargado; (slang) muy borracho; (slang) muy rico

loaded dice *spl* dados cargados

loadˈstoneˈ *s* piedra imán; (fig) imán *m*

loaf [lof] *s* (*pl* **loaves** [lovz]) pan *m;* (*of sugar*) pilón *m* || *intr* haraganear

loafer [ˈlofər] *s* haragán *m,* holgazán *m*

loam [lom] *s* suelo franco; (*mixture used in making molds*) tierra de moldeo

loamy [ˈlomi] *adj* franco

loan [lon] *s* (*among individuals*) préstamo; (*between companies or governments*) emprés-

tito; **to hit for a loan** (coll) dar un sablazo a ‖ *tr* prestar
loan shark *s* (coll) usurero
loan word *s* préstamo lingüístico
loath [loθ] *adj* poco dispuesto; **nothing loath** de buena gana
loathe [loð] *tr* abominar, detestar
loathing [ˈloðɪŋ] *s* abominación, detestación
loathsome [ˈloðsəm] *adj* abominable, asqueroso
lob [lɑb] *v* (*pret & pp* **lobbed;** *ger* **lobbing**) *tr* (tennis) volear desde muy alto
lob•by [ˈlɑbi] *s* (*pl* **-bies**) salón *m* de entrada, vestíbulo; cabilderos, grupo de presión ‖ *v* (*pret & pp* **-bied**) *tr* ejercer presión sobre ‖ *intr* cabildear, ejercer presiones
lobbying [ˈlɑbɪ•ɪŋ] *s* cabildeo
lobbyist [ˈlɑbɪ•ɪst] *s* cabildero (*procurador de influencia legislativa*)
lobster [ˈlɑbstər] *s* (*spiny lobster*) langosta; (*Homarus*) bogavante *m*
lobster pot *s* langostera
local [ˈlokəl] *adj* local ‖ *s* tren suburbano; (*branch of a union*) junta local; noticia de interés local
local call *s* (telp) llamada urbana
locale [loˈkæl] *s* localidad
locali•ty [loˈkælɪti] *s* (*pl* **-ties**) localidad
localize [ˈlokə,laɪz] *tr* localizar
locate [loˈket] o [ˈloket] *tr* (*to discover the location of*) localizar, ubicar; (*to place, to settle*) colocar, establecer; (*to ascribe a particular location to*) situar ‖ *intr* establecerse
location [loˈkeʃən] *s* (*place, position*) localidad; (*act of placing*) colocación; (*act of finding*) localización; (compu) ubicación; **on location** (mov) en exteriores
loc. cit. *abbr* **loco citato** (Lat) (**in the place cited**) Loc. cit. (en el lugar citado)
lock [lɑk] *s* cerradura; (*of a canal*) esclusa; (*of hair*) bucle *m;* (*of a firearm*) llave *f;* **lock, stock, and barrel** (coll) del todo, por completo; **under lock and key** bajo llave ‖ *tr* echar la llave a, cerrar con llave; (*to key*) acuñar; hacer pasar (*un buque*) por la esclusa; abrazar, enlazar; **to lock in** encerrar, poner debajo de llave; **to lock out** cerrar la puerta a, dejar en la calle; dejar sin trabajo (*a los obreros*); **to lock up** encerrar poner debajo de llave; encarcelar
locker [ˈlɑkər] *s* armario cerrado con llave; (*in a station*) consigna automática
locker room *s* vestuario (*de un gimnasio, club*)
locket [ˈlɑkɪt] *s* guardapelo, medallón *m*
lock′jaw′ *s* trismo, oclusión forzosa de la boca
lock nut *s* contratuerca
lock′out′ *s* huelga patronal
lock′smith′ *s* cerrajero
lock step *s* marcha en fila apretada
lock stitch *s* punto encadenado
lock tender *s* esclusero
lock′up′ *s* cárcel *f*
lock washer *s* arandela de seguridad
loco [ˈloko] *adj* (slang) chiflado, loco
locomotive [,lokəˈmotɪv] *s* locomotora
lo•cus [ˈlokəs] *s* (*pl* **-ci** [saɪ]) sitio, lugar *m;* lugar (geométrico)
locust [ˈlokəst] *s* (ent) langosta (*Pachytylus*); (ent) cigarra (*Cicada*); (bot) acacia falsa
lode [lod] *s* filón *m,* venero, veta
lode′star′ *s* (astr) estrella polar; estrella de guía; (*guide, direction*) guía, norte *m*
lodge [lɑdʒ] *s* casa de guarda; casa de campo; (*e.g., of Masons*) logia ‖ *tr* alojar, hospedar; depositar, colocar; presentar (*una queja*) ‖ alojarse, hospedarse; quedar colgado, ir a parar
lodger [ˈlɑdʒər] *s* inquilino (*en parte de una casa*)
lodging [ˈlɑdʒɪŋ] *s* alojamiento, hospedaje *m;* (*without meals*) cobijo
loft [lɔft] *s* (*attic*) desván *m,* sobrado; (*hayloft*) henal *m,* pajar *m;* (*in theater or church*) galería; (*in a store or office building*) piso alto
loft•y [ˈlɔfti] *adj* (*comp* **-ier;** *super* **-iest**) (*towering; sublime*) encumbrado; (*haughty*) altivo, orgulloso
log [lɔg] *s* leño, tronco; (*log chip*) (naut) barquilla; (*chip and line*) (naut) corredera; (aer) diario de vuelo; **to sleep like a log** dormir como un leño ‖ *v* (*pret & pp* **logged;** *ger* **logging**) *tr* registrar; recorrer (*cierta distancia*) ‖ *intr*—**to log in** o **on** (compu) iniciar la sesión, acceder; **to log out** *o* **off** (compu) finalizar la sesión, cerrar el programa
logarithm [ˈlɔgə,rɪðəm] *s* logaritmo
log′book′ *s* (aer) libro de vuelo; (naut) cuaderno de bitácora, diario de navegación
log cabin *s* cabaña de troncos
log chip *s* (naut) barquilla
log driver *s* ganchero, maderero
log driving *s* flotaje *m*
logger [ˈlɔgər] o [ˈlɑgər] *s* leñador *m,* maderero; grúa de troncos; tractor *m*
log′ger•head′ *s* (zool) tortuga boba; **at loggerheads** reñidos, en desacuerdo
loggia [ˈlodʒə] *s* (archit) logia
logic [ˈlɑdʒɪk] *s* lógica
logical [ˈlɑdʒɪkəl] *adj* lógico
logic board *s* (compu) placa lógica
logician [loˈdʒɪʃən] *s* lógico
logistic(al) [loˈdʒɪstɪk(əl)] *adj* logístico
logistics [loˈdʒɪstɪks] *s* logística
log′jam′ *s* atasco de rollizos; (fig) estancación, atolladero
log line *s* (naut) corredera
logo [ˈlogo] *s* logo, logotipo
log′roll′ *intr* trocar favores políticos
log′wood′ *s* campeche *m*
loin [lɔɪn] *s* lomo; **to gird up one's loins** apercibirse para la acción
loin′cloth′ *s* taparrabo
loiter [ˈlɔɪtər] *tr*—**to loiter away** malgastar (*el tiempo*) ‖ *intr* holgazanear, rezagarse
loiterer [ˈlɔɪtərər] *s* holgazán *m,* rezagado

loll [lɑl] *intr* colgar flojamente; arrellanarse, repantigarse
lollipop [ˈlɑli,pɑp] *s* perulí *m,* chupetín *m*
London [ˈlʌndən] *adj* londinense ‖ *s* Londres *m*
Londoner [ˈlʌndənər] *s* londinense *mf*
lone [lon] *adj* solo, solitario; (*sole, single*) único
loneliness [ˈlonlinɪs] *s* soledad
lone•ly [ˈlonli] *adj* (*comp* **-lier;** *super* **-liest**) soledoso
lonesome [ˈlonsəm] *adj* soledoso; (*spot, atmosphere*) solitario
lone wolf *s* (fig) lobo solitario
long. *abbr* **longitude**
long [lɔŋ] o [lɑŋ] (*comp* **longer** [ˈlɔŋgər] o [ˈlɑŋgər]; *super* **longest** [ˈlɔŋgɪst] o [ˈlɑŋgɪst]) *adj* largo; de largo, p.ej., **two meters long** dos metros de largo ‖ *adv* mucho tiempo, largo tiempo; **as long as** mientras; (*provided*) con tal de que; (*inasmuch as*) puesto que; **before long** dentro de poco; **how long** cuánto tiempo; **long ago** hace mucho tiempo; **long before** mucho antes; **longer** más tiempo; **long since** desde hace mucho tiempo; **no longer** ya no; **so long!** (coll) ¡hasta luego!; **so long as** con tal de que ‖ *intr* anhelar, suspirar; **to long for** anhelar por, ansiar
longˈboatˈ *s* (naut) lancha
longˈ-disˈtance call *s* (telp) llamada de larga distancia, conferencia o llamada interurbana
long-distance flight *s* (aer) vuelo a distancia
longˈ-drawnˈ-outˈ *adj* prolongado, pesado
longevity [lɑnˈdʒɛvɪti] *s* longevidad
long face *s* (coll) cara triste
longˈhairˈ *adj & s* melómano; (pej) hippie *mf,* melenudo, bohemio
longˈhandˈ *s* escritura a mano
longing [ˈlɔŋɪŋ] *adj* anhelante ‖ *s* anhelo, ansia
longitude [ˈlɑndʒɪ,tjud] *s* longitud
long johns *spl* ropa interior que cubre brazos y piernas
long jump *s* (sport) salto de longitud
long-lived [ˈlɔŋˈlaɪvd] o (coll) [ˈlɔŋˈlɪvd] *adj* longevo, de larga vida
long-playing record [ˈlɔŋˈple•ɪŋ] *s* disco de larga duración; elepé *m*
long primer [ˈprɪmər] *s* (typ) entredós *m*
longˈ-rangeˈ *adj* de largo alcance
longshore•man [ˈlɔŋ,ʃormən] *s* (*pl* **-men** [mən]) *s* estibador *m,* portuario
long shot *s* (phot) plano largo
longˈ-standˈing *adj* que existe desde hace mucho tiempo
longˈ-sufˈfering *adj* longánimo, sufrido
long suit *s* (cards) palo fuerte; (fig) fuerte *m*
longˈ-termˈ *adj* a largo plazo
longˈwaveˈ *s* onda larga
longˈ-windˈed *adj* difuso, palabrero; discursisto
look [lʊk] *s* (*appearance*) aspecto, apariencia; (*glance*) mirada; (*search*) búsqueda; **looks** aspecto, apariencia; **to take a look at** echar una mirada a ‖ *tr* expresar con la mirada; representar (*la edad que uno tiene*); **to look daggers at** apuñalar con la mirada; **to look the part** vestir el cargo; **to look up** (*e.g., in a dictionary*) buscar; ir a visitar, venir a ver ‖ *intr* mirar; buscar; parecer; **look out!** ¡cuidado!, ¡ojo!; **to look after** mirar por; ocuparse en; **to look at** mirar; **to look back** mirar hacia atrás; (fig) mirar el pasado; **to look down on** mirar por encima del hombro; **to look for** buscar; creer, p.ej., **I look for rain** creo que va a llover; **to look forward to** esperar con placer anticipado; **to look ill** tener mala cara; **to look in on** pasar por la casa o la oficina de; **to look into** averiguar, estudiar; **to look like** parecerse a; amenazar, p.ej., **it looks like rain** amenaza lluvia, parece que va a llover; **to look oneself** parecer el mismo; tener buena cara; **to look out** tener cuidado; mirar por (*p.ej., la ventana*); **to look out for** mirar por, cuidar de; guardarse de; **to look out on** dar a; **to look through** mirar por; hojear (*un libro*); **to look toward** dar a; **to look up to** admirar, mirar con respeto; **to look well** tener buena cara
lookalike [ˈlʊkə,laɪk] *adj & s* doble; parecido
looker-on [,lʊkərˈɑn] *s* (*pl* **lookers-on**) mirón *m,* espectador *m*
lookˈoutˈ *s* vigilancia; (*tower*) atalaya; (*person keeping watch*) vigilante *mf;* (*man watching from lookout tower*) atalaya *m;* (*care, concern*) (coll) cuidado; **to be on the lookout for** estar a la mira de
loom [lum] *s* telar *m* ‖ *intr* (*to appear indistinctly*) vislumbrarse; amenazar, parecer inevitable
loon [lun] *s* tonto, bobo; (orn) zambullidor *m*
loon•y [ˈluni] *adj* (*comp* **-ier;** *super* **-iest**) (slang) loco ‖ *s* (*pl* **-ies**) (slang) loco
loop [lup] *s* lazo; (*in a cable or rope*) vuelta; (*of a river*) meandro; (*of a road*) recoveco; (*for fastening a button*) presilla; (aer) rizo; (elec) circuito cerrado; (*part of vibrating body between two nodes*) vientre *m;* **to loop the loop** (aer) rizar el rizo ‖ *tr* hacer lazos en; enlazar ‖ *intr* formar lazo; (aer) hacer el rizo
loopˈholeˈ *s* (*narrow opening in wall*) lucerna; (*means of evasion*) efugio, escapatoria
loose [lus] *adj* (*dress, tooth, screw, bowels*) flojo; (*fitting, thread, wire, rivet, tongue, bowels*) suelto; (*sleeve*) perdido; (*earth, soil*) desmenuzado; (*unpackaged*) a granel, sin envase; (*unbound papers*) sin encuadernar; (*pulley*) loco; (*translation*) libre; (*life, morals*) relajado; (*woman*) fácil, frágil; **to become loose** desatarse, aflojarse; **to break loose** ponerse en libertad; **to turn loose** soltar ‖ *s*—**to be on the loose** ser libre, estar sin trabas; estar de juerga ‖ *tr* soltar; desatar, desencadenar
loose end *s* cabo suelto; **at loose ends** desarreglado, indeciso
looseˈ-leafˈ notebook *s* cuaderno de hojas cambiables, cuaderno de hojas sueltas
loosen [ˈlusən] *tr* desatar, aflojar, desapretar;

aflojar, laxar (*el vientre*) || *intr* desatarse, aflojarse, desapretarse
looseness [ˈlusnɪs] *s* flojedad, soltura; (*in morals*) relajamiento
loose'strife' *s* lisimaquia; salicaria
loose-tongued [ˈlusˈtʌŋd] *adj* largo de lengua, ligero de lengua
loot [lut] *s* botín *m*, presa || *tr* saquear, pillar
lop [lɑp] *v* (*pret & pp* **lopped;** *ger* **lopping**) *tr* dejar caer (*p.ej., los brazos*); **to lop off** cortar; podar (*un árbol, una vid*) || *intr* colgar
lopsided [ˈlɑpˈsaɪdɪd] *adj* ladeado, sesgado; desproporcionado, asimétrico, patituerto
loquacious [loˈkweʃəs] *adj* locuaz
loran [ˈlɔræn] *s* (naut) lorán *m*
lord [lɔrd] *s* señor *m;* (Brit) lord *m;* (hum & poet) marido || *tr*—**to lord it over** dominar despóticamente, imponerse a
lord•ly [ˈlɔrdli] *adj* (*comp* **-lier;** *super* **-liest**) señoril; magnífico; despótico, imperioso; altivo, arrogante
Lord's Day, the el domingo
lordship [ˈlɔrdʃɪp] *s* señora, excelencia
Lord's Prayer *s* oración dominical, padrenuestro
Lord's Supper *s* sagrada comunión; Cena del Señor
lore [lor] *s* ciencia, saber *m;* ciencia popular, saber *m* popular
lorgnette [lɔrnˈjɛt] *s* (*eyeglasses*) impertinentes *mpl;* (*opera glasses*) gemelos de teatro con manija
lor•ry [ˈlɑri] o [ˈlɔri] *s* (*pl* **-ries**) (*truck*) (Brit) camión *m;* (rr) (Brit) vagoneta
lose [luz] *v* (*pret & pp* **lost** [lɔst] o [lɑst]) *tr* perder; no lograr salvar (*el médico al enfermo*); **to lose heart** desalentarse; **to lose oneself** perderse, errar el camino; ensimismarse || *intr* perder; quedar vencido; retrasarse (*el reloj*)
loser [ˈluzər] *s* perdedor *m*
losing [ˈluzɪŋ] *adj* perdedor || **losings** *spl* pérdidas, dinero perdido
loss [lɔs] o [lɑs] *s* pérdida; **to be at a loss** estar perplejo, no saber qué hacer; **to be at a loss to** + *inf* no saber como + *inf;* **to sell at a loss** vender con pérdida
loss leader *s* artículo vendido a gran descuento
loss of face *s* pérdida de prestigio, desprestigio
lost [lɔst] o [lɑst] *adj* perdido; (fig) desviado; **lost in thought** ensimismado, abismado; **lost to** perdido para; insensible a
lost'-and-found' department *s* oficina de objetos perdidos
lost sheep *s* oveja perdida
lot [lɑt] *s* (*for building*) solar *m*, parcela; (*fate, destiny*) suerte *f;* (*portion, parcel*) lote *m;* (*of people*) grupo; (coll) gran cantidad, gran número; (coll) sujeto, tipo; **a lot (of)** o **lots of** (coll) mucho, muchos; **to cast** o **to throw in one's lot with** compartir la suerte de; **to draw** o **to cast lots** echar suertes
lotion [ˈloʃən] *s* loción
lotter•y [ˈlɑtəri] *s* (*pl* **-ies**) lotería
lotto [ˈlɑto] *s* lotería
lotus [ˈlotəs] *s* loto
Lou [lu] *m familiar form of* **Louis**
loud [laʊd] *adj* alto; (*noisy*) ruidoso; (*voice*) fuerte; (*garish*) chillón, llamativo; (*conspicuously vulgar*) charro, cursi; (*foul-smelling*) apestoso, maloliente || *adv* alto, en voz alta; ruidosamente
loud'mouth' *s* bocaza, bocona, bocón *m*
loudmouthed [ˈlaʊd,maʊθt] o [ˈlaʊd,maʊðd] *adj* vocinglero
loud'speak'er *s* altavoz *m*, parlante *m*, pantalla acústica
Louis [ˈlu•ɪs] *m* Luis
Louise [luˈiz] *f* Luisa
lounge [laʊndʒ] *s* diván *m*, sofá *m* cama; salón *m* de descanso, salón social || *intr* repantigarse a su sabor, recostarse cómodamente; **to lounge around** estar arrimado a la pared, pasearse perezosamente
louse [laʊs] *s* (*pl* **lice** [laɪs]) piojo
lous•y [ˈlaʊzi] *adj* (*comp* **-ier;** *super* **-iest**) piojoso; (*mean*) (coll) vil, ruin; (*filthy*) (coll) asqueroso, sucio; (*bungling*) (coll) chapucero; **lousy with** (slang) colmado de (*p.ej., dinero*); (slang) plagado de (*p.ej., policías*)
lout [laʊt] *s* patán *m*
louver [ˈluvər] *s* (*opening to let in air and light*) lumbrera; tablilla de persiana; (aut) persiana del radiador
lovable [ˈlʌvəbəl] *adj* amable
love [lʌv] *s* amor *m;* (*tennis*) cero, nada; **not for love nor money** ni a tiros; **to be in love (with)** estar enamorado (de); **to fall in love (with)** enamorarse (de); **to make love to** cortejar, galantear || *tr* amar, querer; gustar de, tener afición a
love affair *s* amores *mpl*, amorío; (*enthusiasm*) pasión
love'bird' *s* (*lover*) (coll) tortolito; (orn) periquito; **lovebirds** tórtolos
love child *s* hijo del amor
love feast *s* ágape *m*
love'-hate' *s* odio-amor *m*
loveless [ˈlʌvlɪs] *adj* abandonado, sin amor; (*feeling no love*) desamado
love letter *s* carta de amor
love life *s* vida amorosa
lovelorn [ˈlʌv,lɔrn] *adj* abandonado por su amor, herido de amor
love•ly [ˈlʌvli] *adj* (*comp* **-lier;** *super* **-liest**) bello, hermoso; adorable, precioso; (coll) encantador, gracioso
love match *s* matrimonio de amor
love potion *s* filtro, filtro de amor
lover [ˈlʌvər] *s* amante *mf;* (*e.g., of hunting, sports*) aficionado; (*e.g., of work*) amigo
love seat *s* confidente *m*
love'sick' *adj* enfermo de amor
love'sick'ness *s* mal *m* de amor
love song *s* canción de amor
loving [ˈlʌvɪŋ] *adj* amoroso, afectuoso

lov′ing-kind′ness *s* bondad infinita, misericordia
low [lo] *adj* bajo; (*diet; visibility; opinion*) malo; (*dress, waist*) escotado; (*depressed*) abatido; gravemente enfermo; (*fire*) lento; **to lay low** dejar tendido, derribar; matar; **to lie low** no dejarse ver ‖ *adv* bajo ‖ *s* punto bajo; precio más bajo, precio mínimo; (*moo of cow*) mugido; (aut) primera marcha, primera velocidad; (meteor) depresión ‖ *intr* mugir (*la vaca*)
low′born′ *adj* de humilde cuna
low′boy′ *s* cómoda baja con patas cortas
low′brow′ *adj* (coll) poco intelectual, de poco cultura; (*writer, culture*) popular
low′-cost′ *adj* barato, de bajo costo; (compu) de bajo costo *or* coste
low′-cost′ housing *s* casas baratas
Low Countries, the los Países Bajos
low′-down′ *adj* (coll) bajo, vil, ruin ‖ **low′-down′** *s* (slang) informes *mf* confidenciales, hechos verdaderos
lower [ˈlo•ər] *adj* bajo, inferior ‖ *tr & intr* bajar ‖ [ˈlaʊ•ər] *intr* poner mala cara, fruncir el entrecejo; encapotarse (*el cielo*)
lower berth [ˈlo•ər] *s* litera baja, cama baja
Lower California [ˈlo•ər] *s* la Baja California
low′er•case′ *s* (typ) caja baja
lowercase letter *s* letra minúscula
lower middle class [ˈlo•ər] *s* pequeña burguesía
lowermost [ˈlo•ər,most] *adj* (el) más bajo
low′-fre′quency *adj* de baja frecuencia
low gear *s* primera marcha, primera velocidad
low′-key′ *adj* modesto; moderado
lowland [ˈlolənd] *s* tierra baja ‖ **Lowlands** *spl* Tierra Baja (*de Escocia*)
low′-lev′el *adj* a bajo nivel; de baja intensidad; (*nuclear waste*) de baja radioactividad; (aer) rasante, a baja altura; (compu) de gama baja
low-level language *s* (compu) lenguaje *m* de bajo nivel
low life *s* gentuza
low•ly [ˈloli] *adj* (*comp* **-lier;** *super* **-liest**) humilde; (*in growth or position*) bajo
Low Mass *s* misa rezada
low-minded [ˈloˈmaɪndɪd] *adj* vil, ruin
low neck *s* escote *m,* escotado
low-necked [ˈloˈnɛkt] *adj* escotado
low-pitched [ˈloˈpɪtʃt] *adj* (*sound*) grave; (*roof*) de poco declive
low′-pres′sure *adj* de baja presión
low-priced [ˈloˈpraɪst] *adj* barato, de precio bajo
low shoe *s* zapato inglés
low′-speed′ *adj* de baja velocidad
low-spirited [ˈloˈspɪrɪtɪd] *adj* abatido
low spirits *spl* abatimiento
low tide *s* bajamar *f,* marea baja; (fig) punto más bajo
low visibility *s* (aer) poca visibilidad
low water *s* (*of a river*) nivel mínimo; (*because of drought*) estiaje *m;* bajamar *f,* marea baja
loyal [ˈlɔɪ•əl] *adj* leal
loyalist [ˈlɔɪ•əlɪst] *s* leal *m*
loyal•ty [ˈlɔɪ•əlti] *s* (*pl* **-ties**) lealtad
lozenge [ˈlɑzɪndʒ] *s* losange *m;* (*candy cough drop*) pastilla, tableta
LP[T] [ˈɛlˈpi] *s* (letterword) **(long-playing record)** disco de larga duración; elepé *m*
Ltd. *abbr* **limited**
lubricant [ˈlubrɪkənt] *adj & s* lubricante *m*
lubricate [ˈlubrɪ,ket] *tr* lubricar
lubricous [ˈlubrɪkəs] *adj* (*slippery; lewd*) lúbrico (*resbaladizo; lascivo*); incierto, inconstante
lucerne [luˈsʌrn] *s* mielga
lucid [ˈlusɪd] *adj* claro, inteligible; (*rational, sane*) lúcido; (*bright, shining*) luciente; (*clear, transparent*) cristalino
Lucifer [ˈlusɪfər] *s* Lucifer *m*
luck [lʌk] *s* (*good or bad*) suerte *f;* (*good*) suerte, buena suerte; **down on one's luck** de mala suerte, de malas; **in luck** de buena suerte, de buenas; **out of luck** de mala suerte, de malas; **to bring luck** traer buena suerte; **to try one's luck** probar fortuna; **worse luck** desgraciadamente
luckily [ˈlʌkɪli] *adj* afortunadamente
luckless [ˈlʌklɪs] *adj* desgraciado
luck•y [ˈlʌki] *adj* (*comp* **-ier;** *super* **-iest**) afortunado; derecho (CAm); (*supposed to bring luck*) de buen agüero; **to be lucky** tener suerte; quedar bien parado
lucky hit *s* (coll) golpe *m* de fortuna
lucrative [ˈlukrətɪv] *adj* lucrativo
ludicrous [ˈludɪkrəs] *adj* absurdo, ridículo
lug [lʌg] *s* orejeta; (*pull, tug*) estirón *m,* esfuerzo ‖ *v* (*pret & pp* **lugged;** *ger* **lugging**) *tr* tirar con fuerza de; (*to bring up irrelevantly*) (coll) traer a colación
luggage [ˈlʌgɪdʒ] *s* equipaje *m*
lugubrious [lʊˈgubrɪ•əs] o [lʊˈgjubrɪ•əs] *adj* lúgubre
lukewarm [ˈluk,wɔrm] *adj* tibio, templado
lull [lʌl] *s* momento de calma, momento de silencio; (naut) recalmón *m* ‖ *tr* adormecer; calmar, aquietar; apaciguar
lulla•by [ˈlʌlə,baɪ] *s* (*pl* **-bies**) arrullo, canción de cuna
lulu [ˈlulu] *s* **—that's a lulu!** (coll) ¡qué bárbaro!
lumbago [lʌmˈbego] *s* lumbago
lumber [ˈlʌmbər] *s* madera aserrada, madera aserradiza, madera de sierra; trastos viejos ‖ *intr* andar pesadamente
lum′ber•jack′ *s* leñador *m,* hachero
lumber•man [ˈlʌmbərmən] *s* (*pl* **-men** [mən]) (*dealer*) maderero; (*man who cuts down lumber*) leñador *m,* hachero
lumber room *s* leonera, trastera
lum′ber•yard′ *s* maderería, depósito de maderas
luminar•y [ˈlumɪ,nɛri] *s* (*pl* **-ies**) luminar *m,* lumbrera
luminescent [,lumɪˈnɛsənt] *adj* luminiscente
luminous[ˈlumɪnəs] *adj* luminoso
lummox [ˈlʌməks] *s* (coll) jergón *m*
lump [lʌmp] *s* terrón *m;* (*swelling*) chichón *m,*

bulto, hinchazón *m;* (*stupid person*) (coll) bodoque *m;* **in the lump** en grueso, por junto; **to get a lump in one's throat** hacérsele a (*uno*) un nudo en la garganta || *tr* juntar, mezclar; (*to make into lumps*) aterronar; (coll) aguantar, tragar (cosa repulsiva)
lumpish [ˈlʌmpɪʃ] *adj* hobachón, torpe, pesado
lump sum *s* suma global, suma total
lump•y [ˈlʌmpi] *adj* (*comp* **-ier;** *super* **-iest**) aterronado, borujoso; torpe, pesado; (*sea*) agitado
luna•cy [ˈlunəsi] *s* (*pl* **-cies**) demencia, locura
lunar [ˈlunər] *adj* lunar
lunar lander o **lunar module** *s* módulo lunar
lunar landing *s* alunizaje *m*
lunar module *s* módulo lunar
lunatic [ˈlunətɪk] *adj & s* lunático, loco
lunatic fringe *s* minoría fanática
lunch [lʌnʃ] *s* (*regular midday meal*) almuerzo; (*light meal*) colación, merienda || *intr* almorzar; merendar, tomar una colación
lunch basket *s* fiambrera
lunch cloth *s* mantelito
luncheon [ˈlʌntʃən] *s* almuerzo; almuerzo de ceremonia
lunch'room' *s* cantina, merendero
lung [lʌŋ] *s* pulmón *m*
lung cancer *s* cáncer *m* pulmonar
lunge [lʌndʒ] *s* arremetida, embestida; (*with a sword*) estocada || *intr* arremeter, lanzarse; **to lunge at** arremeter contra
lurch [lʌrtʃ] *s* sacudida, tumbo; (naut) bandazo; **to leave in the lurch** dejar en la estacada, dejar colgado || *intr* dar una sacudida, dar un tumbo; (naut) dar un bandazo
lure [lʊr] *s* (*decoy*) cebo, señuelo; (fig) aliciente *m,* señuelo || *tr* atraer con cebo, atraer con señuelo; (fig) atraer, tentar, seducir; **to lure away** llevarse con señuelo; (*from one's obligations*) desviar
lurid [ˈlʊrɪd] *adj* sensacional; (*gruesome*) espeluznante; (*fiery*) ardiente, encendido
lurk [lʌrk] *intr* acechar, andar furtivamente
luscious [ˈlʌʃəs] *adj* delicioso; lujoso; voluptuoso
lush [lʌʃ] *adj* jugoso, lozano; lujuriante; lujoso
Lusitanian [ˌlusɪˈtenɪ•ən] *adj & s* lusitano
lust [lʌst] *s* deseo vehemente; (*greed*) codicia; (*strong sexual appetite*) lujuria; entusiasmo || *intr* lujuriar; **to lust after** o **for** codiciar; desear con lujuria
luster [ˈlʌstər] *s* (*gloss*) lustre *m;* (*of certain fabrics*) viso; (*fame, glory*) (fig) lustre
lus'ter•ware' *s* loza con visos metálicos
lustful [ˈlʌstfəl] *adj* lujurioso
lustrous [ˈlʌstrəs] *adj* lustroso
lust•y [ˈlʌsti] *adj* (*comp* **-ier;** *super* **-iest**) fuerte, robusto, lozano
lute [lut] *s* (mus) laúd *m;* (*substance used to close or seal a joint*) (chem) lodo
Lutheran [ˈluθərən] *adj & s* luterano
luxuriance [lʌgˈʒʊrɪ•əns] *s* lozanía
luxuriant [lʌgˈʒʊrɪ•ənt] *adj* lozano, lujuriante; (*overornamented*) recargado
luxuriate [lʌgˈʒʊrɪˌet] o [lʌkˈʃʊrɪˌet] *intr* crecer con lozanía; entregarse al lujo; (*to find keen pleasure*) lozanearse
luxurious [lʌgˈʒʊrɪ•əs] o [lʌkˈʃʊrɪ•əs] *adj* lujoso
luxu•ry [ˈlʌkʃəri] o [ˈlʌgʒəri] *s* (*pl* **-ries**) lujo
luxury tax *s* impuesto de lujo
lye [laɪ] *s* lejía
lying [ˈlaɪ•ɪŋ] *adj* mentiroso || *s* el mentir
ly'ing-in' hospital *s* casa de maternidad, clínica de parturientas
lymph [lɪmf] *s* linfa
lymphatic [lɪmˈfætɪk] *adj* linfático
lynch [lɪntʃ] *tr* linchar
lynching [ˈlɪntʃɪŋ] *s* linchamiento
lynch law *s* justicia de la soga
lynx [lɪŋks] *s* lince *m,* lobo cervario
lynx-eyed [ˈlɪŋksˌaɪd] *adj* de ojos linces
lyonnaise [ˌlaɪ•əˈnez] *adj* (culin) a la lionesa
lyre [laɪr] *s* (mus) lira
lyric [ˈlɪrɪk] *adj* lírico || *s* poema lírico; (*words of a song*) (coll) letra
lyrical [ˈlɪrɪkəl] *adj* lírico
lyricism [ˈlɪrɪˌsɪzəm] *s* lirismo
lyricist [ˈlɪrɪsɪst] *s* (*writer of words for songs*) letrista *mf;* (*poet*) poeta lírico

M

M, m [ɛm] decimotercera letra del alfabeto inglés
m. *abbr* **married, masculine, meter, midnight, mile, minute, month**
ma [mɑ] *s* (coll) mamá
ma'am [mæm] o [mɑm] *s* (coll) señora
mac o **Mac** [mæk] *s* (*form of address*) (coll) amigo
macadam [məˈkædəm] *s* macadán *m*
macadamize [məˈkædəˌmaɪz] *tr* macadamizar
macaro•ni [ˌmækəˈroni] *s* (*pl* **-nis** o **-nies**) macarrones *mpl*
macaroon [ˌmækəˈrun] *s* mostachón *m,* almendrado
macaw [məˈkɔ] *s* aracanga, guacamayo
mace [mes] *s* maza; (*spice*) macis *m*
mace'bear'er *s* macero
Machiavellian [ˈmæki•əˈvɛli•ən] *adj* maquiavélico
machination [ˌmækɪˈneʃən] *s* maquinación

machine [məˈʃin] *s* máquina; automóvil *m,* coche *m;* (*of a political party*) camarilla ‖ *tr* trabajar a máquina
machine gun *s* ametralladora
ma•chine′-gun′ *tr* ametrallar
ma•chine′-made′ *adj* hecho a máquina
machiner•y [məˈʃinəri] *s* (*pl* **-ies**) maquinaria
machine screw *s* tornillo para metales
machine shop *s* taller mecánico
machine stenography *s* estenotipia
machine tool *s* máquina-herramienta
machine translation *s* traducción automática
machinist [məˈʃinɪst] *s* (*person who makes machines*) maquinista *mf;* (person who operates machines) mecánico; (naut) segundo maquinista; (theat) maquinista *mf,* tramoyista *mf*
mackerel [ˈmækərəl] *s* caballa, escombro
mackerel sky *s* cielo aborregado
mackintosh [ˈmækɪn,tɑʃ] *s* impermeable *m*
macrobiotic [ˈmækrobaɪˈɑtɪk] *adj* macrobiótico
macroeconomics [ˈmækro,ɛkəˈnɑmɪks] *s* macroeconomía, macroeconómica
macrophotography [ˈmækrofəˈtɑgrəfi] *s* macrofotografía
mad [mæd] *adj* (*comp* **madder;** *super* **maddest**) (*angry*) enojado, furioso; (*crazy*) loco; (*foolish*) tonto, necio; (*rabid*) rabioso; **to be mad about** (coll) estar loco por; **to drive mad** volver loco; **to go mad** volverse loco; rabiar (*un perro*)
madam [ˈmædəm] *s* señora
mad cow disease *s* (vet) encefalopatía espongiforme bovina
madden [ˈmædən] *tr* (*to make angry*) enojar, enfurecer; (*to make insane*) enloquecer
made-to-order [ˈmedtəˈɔrdər] *adj* hecho de encargo; (*clothing*) hecho a la medida
made′-up′ *adj* inventado, ficticio; (*artificial*) postizo; (*face*) pintado
mad′house′ *s* loquero, manicomio
madman [ˈmæd,mæn] *s* (*pl* **-men** [,mɛn]) loco
madness [ˈmædnɪs] *s* furia, rabia; locura; (*of a dog*) rabia
Madonna and Child, the [məˈdɑnə] *s* (fa) la Virgen y el Niño
Madonna lily [məˈdɑnə] *s* azucena
maelstrom [ˈmelstrəm] *s* remolino
magazine [ˈmægə,zin] o [,mægəˈzin] *s* (*periodical*) revista, magazine *m;* (*warehouse*) almacén *m;* (*for cartridges*) cámara; (*for powder*) polvorín *m;* (naut) santabárbara; (phot) almacén *m*
Magellan [məˈdʒələn] *s* Magallanes *m*
maggot [ˈmægət] *s* cresa, gusano
Magi [ˈmedʒaɪ] *spl* magos de Oriente, Reyes Magos
magic [ˈmædʒɪk] *adj* mágico ‖ *s* magia; ilusionismo, prestidigitación; **as if by magic** como por encanto
magician [məˈdʒɪʃən] *s* (*entertainer with sleight of hand*) ilusionista *mf,* prestidigitador *m;* (*sorcerer*) mágico
magistrate [ˈmædʒɪs,tret] *s* magistrado
magnanimous [mægˈnænɪməs] *adj* magnánimo
magnesium [mægˈniʃi•əm] o [mægˈnɪʒɪ•əm] *s* magnesio
magnet [ˈmægnɪt] *s* imán *m*
magnetic [mægˈnɛtɪk] *adj* magnético; (fig) atrayente, cautivador
magnetic curves *spl* fantasma magnético
magnetic deviation *s* variación magnética
magnetic field *s* campo magnético
magnetic recording *s* grabación magnética
magnetic tape *s* (audio, compu, video) cinta magnética
magnetism [ˈmægnɪ,tɪzəm] *s* magnetismo
magnetize [ˈmægnɪ,taɪz] *tr* magnetizar, imanar
magne•to [mægˈnito] *s* (*pl* **-tos**) magneto *m & f*
magnificent [mægˈnɪfɪsənt] *adj* magnífico
magni•fy [ˈmægnɪ,faɪ] *v* (*pret & pp* **-fied**) *tr* magnificar; exagerar
magnifying glass *s* lupa, vidrio de aumento
magnitude [ˈmægnɪ,tjud] *s* magnitud
magpie [ˈmæg,paɪ] *s* picaza, urraca
Magyar [ˈmægjɑr] *adj & s* magiar *mf*
mahoga•ny [meˈhɑgəni] *s* (*pl* **-nies**) caoba
mahout [məˈhaʊt] *s* naire *m,* cornaca *m*
maid [med] *s* (*female servant*) criada, moza; (*young girl; housemaid*) doncella; gata (Mex); (*spinster*) soltera
maiden [ˈmedən] *s* doncella
maid′en•hair′ *s* (bot) cabello de Venus
maid′en•head′ *s* himen *m*
maidenhood [ˈmedən,hʊd] *s* doncellez *f*
maiden lady *s* soltera
maiden name *s* apellido de soltera
maiden voyage *s* primera travesía
maid′-in-wait′ing *s* (*pl* **maids-in-waiting**) dama
maid of honor *s* (*at a wedding*) primera madrina de boda; (*attendant on a princess*) doncella de honor; (*attendant on a queen*) dama de honor
maid′serv′ant *s* criada, doméstica
mail [mel] *s* correspondencia, correo; (*of armor*) malla; **by return mail** a vuelta de correo ‖ *tr* echar al correo
mail′bag′ *s* valija
mail′boat′ *s* vapor *m* correo
mail′box′ *s* buzón *m*
mail car *s* carro correo, coche-correo, ambulancia de correos
mail carrier *s* cartero
mailing list *s* lista de envío *or* direcciones
mailing permit *s* porte concertado
mail•man [ˈmel,mæn] *s* (*pl* **-men** [,mɛn]) cartero
mail order *s* pedido postal, venta por catálogo *or* correo
mail′-or′der house *s* casa de ventas por correo o catálogo
mail′plane′ *s* avión-correo
mail train *s* tren *m* correo

maim [mem] *tr* estropear, mutilar
main [men] *adj* principal, primero, maestro, mayor || *s* cañería maestra; **in the main** mayormente
main clause *s* proposición dominante
main course *s* plato principal, plato fuerte
main deck *s* cubierta principal
mainland [ˈmen,lænd] o [ˈmenlənd] *s* continente *m,* tierra firme
main'line *tr & intr* (slang) picar(se), chutar(se), inyectar(se)
main line *s* (rr) tronco, línea principal
mainly [ˈmenli] *adv* principalmente, en su mayor parte
mainmast [ˈmenməst], o [ˈmen,mæst] o [ˈmen,mɑst] *s* palo mayor
mainsail [ˈmensəl] o [ˈmen,sel] *s* vela mayor
main'spring' *s* (*of watch*) muelle *m* real; (fig) móvil *m,* origen *m*
main'stay' *s* (naut) estay *m* mayor; (fig) soporte *m* principal
main'stream' *adj* establecido, dominante || *s* vía principal, corriente *f* principal *or* dominante, línea central
main street *s* calle *f* mayor
maintain [menˈten] *tr* mantener; (*to support*) (law) manutener
maintenance [ˈmentɪnəns] *s* mantenimiento; (*upkeep*) conservación; gastos de conservación
maître d'hôtel [,metər doˈtɛl] *s* (*butler*) mayordomo; (*headwaiter*) jefe *m* de comedor
maize [mez] *s* maíz *m*
majestic [məˈdʒəstɪk] *adj* majestuoso
majes•ty [ˈmædʒɪsti] *s* (*pl* **-ties**) majestad
major [ˈmedʒər] *adj* (*greater*) mayor; (*elder*) mayor de edad; (mus) mayor || *s* (educ) especialización; (mil) comandante *m* || *intr* (educ) especializarse
Majorca [məˈdʒɔrkə] *s* Mallorca
Majorcan [məˈdʒɔrkən] *adj & s* mallorquín *m*
major•do•mo [,medʒərˈdomo] *s* (*pl* **-mos**) mayordomo
major general *s* general *m* de división
majori•ty [məˈdʒɔrɪti] *adj* mayoritario || *s* (*pl* **-ties**) (*being of full age; larger number or part*) mayoría; (*full age*) mayoridad; (mil) comandancia
make [mek] *s* (*brand*) marca; (*form, build*) hechura; carácter *m,* natural *m;* **on the make** (slang) buscando provecho || *v* (*pret & pp* **made** [med]) *tr* hacer; cometer (*un error*); efectuar (*un pago*); ganar (*dinero; una baza*); coger (*un tren*); dar (*dinero una empresa*); pronunciar (*un discurso*); cerrar (*un circuito*); poner (*a uno, p.ej., nervioso*); ser, p.ej., **she will make a good wife** será una buena esposa; **to make** + *inf* hacer + *inf,* p.ej., **she made him study** le hizo estudiar; **to make into** convertir en; **to make known** declarar; dar a conocer; **to make of** pensar de; **to make oneself known** darse a conocer; **to make out** distinguir, vislumbrar; descifrar; escribir (*una receta*); llenar (*un cheque*); **to make over** convertir; rehacer (*un traje*); (com) transferir; **to make up** preparar, confeccionar; inventar (*un cuento*); recobrar (*el tiempo perdido*); (theat) maquillar || *intr* estar (*p.ej., seguro*); **to make away with** llevarse; deshacerse de; matar; **to make believe** fingir, p.ej., **he made believe he knew me** fingió conocerme; **to make for** ir hacia; embestir contra; contribuir a (*p.ej., mejores relaciones*); **to make much of** (coll) hacer fiestas a, mostrar cariño a; **to make off** largarse; **to make off with** llevarse, hacerse con; **to make out** arreglárselas; **to make toward** encaminarse a; **to make up** maquillarse, pintarse; componerse, hacer las paces; **to make up for** suplir; compensar por (*una pérdida*); **to make up to** (coll) tratar de congraciarse con
make'-be•lieve' *adj* simulado || *s* pretexto, simulación, fantasía
maker [ˈmekər] *s* constructor *m,* fabricante *mf*
make'shift' *adj* de fortuna, provisional || *s* expediente *m;* (*person*) tapagujeros *m*
make'-up' *s* composición, constitución; afeite *m,* maquillaje *m;* (typ) imposición
make-up man *s* (theat) maquillador *m*
make'weight' *s* contrapeso; suplente *mf*
making [ˈmekɪŋ] *s* fabricación; material necesario; causa del éxito; **makings** elementos, materiales *mpl;* (*personal qualities necessary for some purpose*) madera
malachite [ˈmælə,kaɪt] *s* malaquita
maladjustment [,mæləˈdʒʌstmənt] *s* desadaptación, inadaptación; (mech) desajuste *m*
mala•dy [ˈmælədi] *s* (*pl* **-dies**) dolencia, enfermedad
malaise [mæˈlez] *s* indisposición, malestar *m*
malapropos [,mælæprəˈpo] *adj* impropio || *adv* fuera de propósito
malaria [məˈlɛrɪ•ə] *s* malaria, paludismo
Malay [ˈmele] o [məˈle] *adj & s* malayo
malcontent [ˈmælkən,tɛnt] *adj & s* malcontento
male [mel] *adj* (*sex*) masculino; (*animal, plant, piece of a device*) macho; (*human being*) varón, p.ej., **male child** hijo varón || *s* macho; varón *m*
male chauvinism *s* machismo
male chauvinist *s* machista *m*
malediction [,mælɪˈdɪkʃən] *s* maldición
malefactor [ˈmælɪ,fæktər] *s* malhechor *m*
male menopause *s* andropausia
male nurse *s* enfermero
malevolent [məˈlɛvələnt] *adj* malévolo
malfunction [,mælˈfʌŋkʃən] *s* malfuncionamiento || intr ir de través; estropearse
malice [ˈmælɪs] *s* malicia, malevolencia; **to bear malice** guardar rencor; **with malice prepense** [prɪˈpɛns] (law) con malicia y premeditación
malicious [məˈlɪʃəs] *adj* malicioso, malévolo
malign [məˈlaɪn] *adj* maligno || *tr* calumniar
malignant [məˈlɪgnənt] *adj* maligno
maligni•ty [məˈlɪgnɪti] *s* (*pl* **-ties**) malignidad

malinger [məˋlɪŋgər] *intr* hacer la zanguanga, fingirse enfermo
mall [mɔl] o [mæl] *s* alameda, paseo de árboles; centro comercial (*grupo de establecimientos minoristas, con aparcamiento*)
mallard [ˋmælərd] *s* pato *or* ánade *m* real
mallet [ˋmælɪt] *s* (*wooden hammer*) mazo; (*for croquet and polo*) mallete *m*
mallow [ˋmælo] *s* malva
malnutrition [,mælnjuˋtrɪʃən] *s* desnutrición
malodorous [mælˋodərəs] *adj* maloliente
malt [mɔlt] *s* malta *m;* (coll) cerveza
maltreat [mælˋtrit] *tr* maltratar
mama [ˋmɑmə] *s* mamá, mama
mamma [ˋmɑmə] o [məˋmɑ] *s* (*mammary gland*) mama; (*mother*) (coll) mama, mamá *f*
mammal [ˋmæməl] *s* mamífero
mammalian [mæˋmelɪ•ən] *adj & s* mamífero
mammogram [ˋmæməgræm] *o* **mammograph** [ˋmæməgræf] *s* mamografía
mammography [məˋmɑgrəfi] *s* mamografía
mammoth [ˋmæməθ] *adj* gigantesco, enorme ‖ *s* mamut *m*
man [mæn] *s* (*pl* **-men** [mɛən]) *s* hombre *m;* (*in chess*) pieza; (*in checkers*) pieza, peón *m;* **a man** uno, p.ej., **a man can't get work in this town** uno no puede obtener empleo en este pueblo; **as one man** unánimamente; **man alive!** ¡hombre!; **man and wife** marido y mujer; **to be one's own man** no depender de nadie ‖ *v* (*pret & pp* **manned;** *ger* **manning**) *tr* dotar, tripular (*un buque*); guarnecer (*una fortaleza*); servir (*los cañones*)
man about town *s* bulevardero, hombre *m* de mucho mundo
manacle [ˋmænəkəl] *s* manilla; **manacles** esposas ‖ *tr* poner esposas a
manage [ˋmænɪdʒ] *tr* manejar ‖ *intr* arreglárselas; **to manage to** ingeniarse a o para; **to manage to get along** ingeniarse para ir viviendo
manageable [ˋmænɪdʒəbəl] *adj* manejable
management [ˋmænɪdʒmənt] *s* manejo, dirección, gerencia; (*group who manage a business*) la empresa, la parte patronal, los patronos
manager [ˋmænədʒər] *s* director *m,* administrador *m,* gerente *mf;* empresario; (compu) gestor *m;* (sport) manager *m*
managerial [,mænəˋdʒɪrɪ•əl] *adj* empresarial
mandate [ˋmændet] *s* autorización; (*command*) mandato, orden *f;* (*territory*) territorio bajo mandato; (law, pol) mandato ‖ *tr* autorizar; (*make compulsory*) exigir, ordenar; (*a territory*) asignar por mandato
mandatory [ˋmændətɔri] *adj* obligatorio
mandolin [ˋmændəlɪn] *s* mandolina
mandrake [ˋmændrek] *s* mandrágora
mane [men] *s* (*of horse*) crines *fpl;* (*of lion, of person*) melena
maneuver [məˋnuvər] *s* maniobra ‖ *tr* hacer maniobrar ‖ *intr* maniobrar
manful [ˋmænfəl] *adj* varonil, resuelto
manganese [ˋmæŋgə,nis] o [ˋmæŋgə,niz] *s* manganeso
mange [mendʒ] *s* (vet) sarna
manger [ˋmendʒər] *s* pesebre *m*
mangle [ˋmæŋgəl] *tr* lacerar, aplastar
man•gy [ˋmendʒi] *adj* (*comp* **-gier;** *super* **-giest**) sarnoso; (*dirty, squalid*) roñoso
man'han'dle *tr* maltratar
man'hole' *s* caja de registro, pozo de inspección
manhood [ˋmænhʊd] *s* virilidad; hombres *mpl*
man hunt *s* caza al hombre
mania [ˋmenɪ•ə] *s* manía
maniac [ˋmenɪ,æk] *adj & s* maníaco
manic-depressive [ˋmænɪkdɪˋprɛsɪv] *adj & s* maníaco-depresivo
manicure [ˋmænɪ,kjʊr] *s* (*care of hands*) manicura; (*person*) manicuro, manicura ‖ *tr* hacer la manicura a (*una persona*); hacer (*las manos y las uñas*)
manicurist [ˋmænɪ,kjʊrɪst] *s* manicuro, manicura
manifest [ˋmænɪ,fɛst] *adj* manifiesto ‖ *s* (naut) manifiesto ‖ *tr* manifestar
manifes•to [,mænɪˋfɛsto] *s* (*pl* **-toes**) manifiesto
manifold [ˋmænɪ,fold] *adj* múltiple, vario; polivalente ‖ *s* copia, ejemplar *m;* (*pipe with outlets or inlets*) colector *m,* múltiple *m*
manikin [ˋmænɪkɪn] *s* maniquí *m;* (*dwarf*) enano
man in the moon *s* cara o cuerpo de hombre imaginarios en la luna llena
man in the street *s* hombre *m* de la calle
manioc [ˋmæniɑk] *s* cazabe *m,* casabe *m*
manipulate [məˋnɪpjə,let] *tr* manipular
manipulation [məˋnɪpjəˋleʃən] *s* manipulation
man'kind' *s* el género humano ‖ **man'kind'** *s* el sexo masculino, los hombres
manliness [ˋmænlɪnɪs] *s* masculinidad, virilidad
man•ly [ˋmænli] *adj* (*comp* **-lier;** *super* **-liest**) masculino, varonil
man'-made' *adj* (*fibers*) sintético; (*lake*) artificial
man'-made' harbor *s* puerto artificial
manned spaceship [mænd] *s* astronave tripulada
mannequin [ˋmænɪkɪn] *s* maniquí *m;* (*young woman employed to exhibit clothing*) maniquí *f*
manner [ˋmænər] *s* manera; **bad manners** malcriadez *f,* malacrianza; **by all manner of means** de todos modos; **in a manner of speaking** como si dijéramos; **in the manner of** a la manera de; **manners** modales *mpl,* crianza; **to the manner born** avezado desde la cuna
mannish [ˋmænɪʃ] *adj* hombruno
man of letters *s* hombre *m* de letras
man of means *s* hombre *m* de dinero
man of parts *s* hombre *m* de buenas prendas
man of straw *s* hombre *m* de suposición
man of the world *s* hombre *m* de mundo
man-of-war [,mænəvˋwɔr] *s* (*pl* **men-of-war** [,mɛnəvˋwɔr]) *s* buque *m* de guerra

manor [ˈmænər] *s* señorío
manor house *s* casa solariega
man overboard *interj* ¡hombre al agua!
man′pow′er *s* número de hombres; personal *m* competente; (mil) fuerzas nacionales
mansard [ˈmænsɑrd] *s* mansarda; piso de mansarda
mansion [ˈmænʃən] *s* hotel *m*, palacio; (*manor house*) casa solariega
man′slaugh′ter *s* (law) homicidio sin premeditación
mantel [ˈmæntəl] *s* manto (*de chimenea*); (*shelf above it*) mesilla, repisa de chimenea
man′tel•piece′ *s* mesilla, repisa de chimenea
mantle [ˈmæntəl] *s* capa, manto || *tr* vestir con manto; cubrir, tapar; ocultar || *intr* encenderse (*el rostro*)
mantra [ˈmæntrə] *s* mantra *m*
manual [ˈmænjʊ•əl] *adj* manual || *s* (*book*) manual *m;* (mil) ejercicio; (mus) teclado manual
manual training *s* enseñanza de los artes y oficios
manufacture [ˌmænjəˈfæktjər] *s* fabricación; obraje *m;* (*thing manufactured*) manufactura || *tr* fabricar, manufacturar
manufacturer [ˌmænjəˈfæktjərər] *s* fabricante *mf*
manure [məˈnjʊr] o [məˈnʊr] *s* estiércol *m* || *tr* estercolar
manuscript [ˈmænjəˌskrɪpt] *adj* & *s* manuscrito
many [ˈmɛni] *adj* & *pron* muchos; **a good many** o **a great many** un buen número; **as many as** tantos como; hasta, p.ej., **as many as twenty** hasta veinte; **how many** cuántos; **many a** muchos, p.ej., **many a person** muchas personas; **many another** muchos otros; **many more** muchos más; **so many** tantos; **too many** demasiados; **twice as many as** dos veces más que
many-sided [ˈmɛniˌsaɪdɪd] *adj* multilátero; (*having many interests or capabilities*) polifacético
map [mæp] *s* mapa *m;* (*of a city*) plano || *v* (*pret & pp* **mapped;** *ger* **mapping**) *tr* trazar el mapa de; indicar en el mapa; **to map out** trazar el plan de
maple [ˈmepəl] *s* arce *m*
mapping [ˈmæpɪŋ] *s* (compu) mapeado
maquette [mɑˈkɛt] *s* maqueta
Mar. *abbr* **March**
mar [mɑr] *v* (*pret & pp* **marred;** *ger* **marring**) *tr* desfigurar, estropear; frustrar
maraud [məˈrɔd] *tr* saquear || *intr* merodear
marauder [məˈrɔdər] *s* merodeador *m*
marble [ˈmɑrbəl] *adj* marmóreo || *s* mármol *m;* (*little ball of glass, etc.*) canica; **marbles** (*game*) canica || *tr* crispir, jaspear
march [mɑrtʃ] *s* marcha; (*frontier, territory*) marca; **to steal a march on someone** ganarle a uno por la mano || *tr* hacer marchar || *intr* marchar || **March** *s* marzo
marchioness [ˈmɑrʃənɪs] *s* marquesa
mare [mɛr] *s* (*female horse*) yegua; (*female donkey*) asna
margarine [ˈmɑrdʒərɪn] *s* margarina
Margaret [ˈmɑrgərɪt] *s* Margarita
margin [ˈmɑrdʒɪn] *s* margen *m* & *f;* (*collateral deposited with a broker*) doble *m*
marginal [ˈmɑrdʒɪnəl] *adj* marginal
margin release *s* tecla de escape
margin stop *s* fijamárgenes *m*, cierrarrenglón *m*, cortarrenglón *m*
marigold [ˈmærɪˌgold] *s* clavelón *m;* (*Calendula*) maravilla, flamenquilla
marihuana o **marijuana** [ˌmɑrɪˈhwɑnə] *s* marihuana, mariguana; grifa, grifo (Mex)
marina [məˈrinə] *s* dársena, puerto deportivo
marinate [ˈmærɪˌnet] *tr* escabechar, marinar
marine [məˈrin] *adj* marino, marítimo || *s* marina; soldado de infantería de marina; **marines** infantería de marina; **tell that to the marines** (coll) cuénteselo a su abuela, a otro perro con ese hueso
marine basin *s* fosa marina
mariner [ˈmærɪnər] *s* marino
marionette [ˌmærɪ•əˈnɛt] *s* marioneta, títere *m*
marital status [ˈmærɪtəl] *s* estado civil
maritime [ˈmærɪˌtaɪm] *adj* marítimo
marjoram [ˈmɑrdʒərəm] *s* orégano; mejorana
mark [mɑrk] *s* marca, señal *f;* (*label*) marbete *m;* (*of punctuation*) punto; (*in an examination*) calificación, nota; (*used instead of signature by an illiterate person*) cruz *f*, signo; (*spot, stain*) mancha; (*coin*) marco; (*starting point in a race*) raya; (*target to shoot at*) blanco; **to be beside the mark** no venir al caso; **to hit the mark** dar en el blanco; **to leave one's mark** dejar memoria de sí; **to make one's mark** llegar a ser célebre; **to miss the mark** errar el tiro; **to toe the mark** ponerse en la raya; obedecer rigurosamente || *tr* marcar, señalar; dar nota a (*un alumno*); calificar (*un examen*); advertir, notar; **to mark down** poner por escrito; rebajar el precio de
mark′down′ *s* reducción de precio
market [ˈmɑrkɪt] *s* mercado; **to bear the market** jugar a la baja; **to bull the market** jugar al alza; **to play the market** jugar a la bolsa; **to put on the market** lanzar al mercado || *tr* llevar al mercado; vender, comercializar
marketable [ˈmɑrkɪtəbəl] *adj* comerciable, vendible
market basket *s* cesta para compras
marketing [ˈmɑrkɪtɪŋ] *s* *s* mercología, mercadotecnia
marketplace *s* plaza del mercado, lonja
market price *s* precio corriente
market research *s* investigación mercológica
marking gauge [ˈmɑrkɪŋ] *s* gramil *m*
marks•man [ˈmɑrksmən] *s* (*pl* **-men** [mən]) tirador *m;* **a good marksman** un buen tiro
marksmanship [ˈmɑrksmənˌʃɪp] *s* puntería
mark′up′ *s* aumento de precio
marl [mɑrl] *s* marga || *tr* margar

marmalade [ˈmɑrmə,led] *s* mermelada
marmot [ˈmɑrmət] *s* marmota
maroon [məˈrun] *adj & s* granate *m,* rojo oscuro, burdeos *m* ‖ *tr* dejar abandonado (*en una isla desierta*)
marquee [mɑʃrˈki] *s* marquesina
marquess [ˈmɑrkwɪs] *s* marqués *m*
marque•try [ˈmɑrkətri] *s* (*pl* **-tries**) marquetería (*taracea*)
marquis [ˈmɑrkwɪs] *s* marqués *m*
marquise [mɑrˈkiz] *s* marquesa; (*over the entrance to a hotel*) marquesina
marriage [ˈmærɪdʒ] *s* casamiento, matrimonio; (*married life; intimate union*) maridaje *m*
marriageable [ˈmærɪdʒəbəl] *adj* casadero
marriage portion *s* dote *m & f*
marriage rate *s* nupcialidad
married life [ˈmærid] *s* vida conyugal
marrow [ˈmæro] *s* médula, tuétano
mar•ry [ˈmæri] *v* (*pret & pp* **-ried**) *tr* casar (*el sacerdote o el juez a un hombre y una mujer*); (*to take in marriage*) casar con, casarse con; (*to unite intimately*) maridar; **to get married to** casar con, casarse con ‖ *intr* casar, casarse; **to marry into** emparentar con (*p.ej., una familia rica*); **to marry the second time** casarse en segundas nupcias
Mars [mɑrz] *s* (astr, myth) Marte *m*
Marseille [mɑrˈsɛ:j] *s* Marsella
marsh [mɑrʃ] *s* ciénaga, pantano
mar•shal [ˈmɑrʃəl] *s* cursor *m* de procesiones, maestro de ceremonias; (mil) mariscal *m;* (U.S.A.) oficial *m* de justicia ‖ *v* (*pret & pp* **-shaled** o **-shalled;** *ger* **-shaling** o **-shalling**) *tr* conducir con ceremonia; ordenar, reunir (*los hechos de una argumentación*)
marsh mallow *s* (bot) malvavisco
marsh′mal′low *s* bombón *m* de merengue y gelatina; bombón de malvavisco
marsh•y [ˈmɑrʃi] *adj* (*comp* **-ier;** *super* **-iest**) pantanoso, palúdico
marten [ˈmɑrtən] *s* (*pine marten*) marta; (*beech marten*) garduña
martial [ˈmɑrʃəl] *adj* marcial
martial law *s* ley *f* marcial; **to be under martial law** estar en estado de guerra
Martian [ˈmɑrʃən] *adj & s* marciano
martin [ˈmɑrtɪn] *s* (orn) avión *m*
martinet [,mɑrtɪˈnɛt] o [ˈmɑrtɪ,nɛt] *s* ordenancista *mf*
martyr [ˈmɑrtər] *s* mártir *mf*
martyrdom [ˈmɑrtərdəm] *s* martirio
mar•vel [ˈmɑrvəl] *s* maravilla ‖ *v* (*pret & pp* **-veled** o **-velled;** *ger* **-veling** o **-velling**) *intr* maravillarse; **to marvel at** maravillarse con o de
mar′vel-of-Peru′ *s* (bot) dondiego
marvelous [ˈmɑrvələs] *adj* maravilloso
Marxist [ˈmɑrksɪst] *adj & s* marxista *mf*
Mary [ˈmærɪ], [ˈmɛrɪ] *s* María
masc. *abbr* **masculine**
mascara [mæsˈkærə] *s* tinte *m* para las pestañas; rímel *m*
mascot [ˈmæskɑt] *s* mascota
masculine [ˈmæskjəlɪn] *adj & s* masculino
mash [mæʃ] *s* (*crushed mass*) masa; (*to form wort*) masa de cebada ‖ *tr* machacar, majar
mashed potatoes [mæʃt] *spl* puré *m* de patatas
masher [ˈmæʃər] *s* (*device*) mano *f;* (slang) galanteador atrevido
mask [mæsk] o [mɑsk] *s* máscara; (*of beekeeper*) carilla; (*made from a corpse*) mascarilla; (*person*) máscara *mf;* (phot) desvanecedor *m* ‖ *tr* enmascarar; (phot) desvanecer ‖ *intr* enmascararse
masked ball [mæskt] *s* baile *m* de máscaras
masking [ˈmæskɪŋ] *s* (compu) enmascaramiento
masking tape *s* cinta de enmascarar
masochism [ˈmæsə,kɪzəm] *s* masoquismo
masochist [ˈmæsəkɪst] *s* masoquista *mf*
masochistic [,mæsəˈkɪstɪk] *adj* masoquista
mason [ˈmesən] *s* albañil *m* ‖ **Mason** *s* masón *m*
mason•ry [ˈmesənri] *s* (*pl* **-ries**) albañilería ‖ **Masonry** *s* masonería
masquerade [,mæskəˈred] o [,mɑskəˈred] *s* mascarada; (*costume, disguise*) máscara; (*false show*) farsa ‖ *intr* enmascararse; **to masquerade as** disfrazarse de
masquerade ball *s* baile *m* de máscaras
mass [mæs] *s* masa; gran cantidad; (*bulk, heap*) mole *f;* (*something glimpsed, e.g., in the fog*) bulto informe; (*big splotch in a painting*) gran mancha; (*celebration of the Eucharist*) misa; **the masses** las masas ‖ *tr* juntar, reunir; enmasar (*tropas*) ‖ *intr* juntarse, reunirse
massacre [ˈmæsəkər] *s* carnicería, matanza ‖ *tr* degollar, matar
massage [məˈsɑʒ] *s* masaje *m* ‖ *tr* masar, masajear
masseur [mæˈsœr] *s* masajista *m*
masseuse [mæˈsœz] *s* masajista *f*
massive [ˈmæsɪv] *adj* macizo; sólido, imponente
mass media *spl* medios *spl* de comunicación
mass meeting *s* mitin *m* popular
mass production *s* fabricación en serie
mast [mæst] o [mɑst] *s* (*for a flag*) palo; (*of a ship*) palo, mástil *m;* (*food for swine*) bellotas, hayucos; **before the mast** como simple marinero
master [ˈmæstər] o [ˈmɑstər] *s* (*employer*) dueño, patrón *m;* (*male head of household*) amo; (*man who possesses some special skill; teacher*) maestro; (*commander of merchant vessel*) capitán *m;* (*title of respect for a boy*) señorito ‖ *tr* dominar
master bedroom *s* alcoba de respeto, dormitorio principal
master blade *s* hoja maestra (*de una ballesta*)
master builder *s* maestro de obras
masterful [ˈmæstərfəl] o [ˈmɑstərfəl] *adj* hábil, experto; dominante, imperioso
master key *s* llave maestra

masterly [ˈmæstərli] o [ˈmɑstərli] *adj* magistral || *adv* magistralmente
master mechanic *s* maestro mecánico
mas'ter•mind' *s* mente directora || *tr* dirigir con gran acierto
master of ceremonies *s* maestro de ceremonias; (*in a night club, radio, etc.*) animador *m*
mas'ter•piece' *s* obra maestra
master stroke *s* golpe maestro
mas'ter•work' *s* obra maestra
master•y [ˈmæstəri] o [ˈmɑstəri] *s* (*pl* **-ies**) (*command, as of a subject*) dominio; ventaja, superioridad; (*skill*) maestría
mast'head' *s* (*of a newspaper*) cabecera editorial; (naut) tope *m*
masticate [ˈmæstɪ,ket] *tr* masticar
mastiff [ˈmæstɪf] o [ˈmɑstɪf] *s* mastín *m*
masturbate [ˈmæstər,bet] *tr* masturbar || *intr* masturbarse
masturbation [,mæstərˈbeʃən] *s* masturbación
mat [mæt] *s* (*for floor*) estera; (*for a cup, vase, etc.*) esterilla, ruedo; (*before a door*) felpudo; (*around a picture*) borde *m* de cartón || *v* (*pret & pp* **matted;** *ger* **matting**) *tr* (*to cover with matting*) esterar; enmarañar || *intr* enmarañarse
match [mætʃ] *s* fósforo; (*wick*) mecha; (*counterpart*) compañero; (*suitable partner in marriage*) partido; (*suitably associated pair*) pareja; (*game, contest*) match *m,* partido; **to be a match for** poder con, poder vencer; **to meet one's match** hallar la horma de su zapato || *tr* igualar; aparear, emparejar; hacer juego con; **to match someone for the drinks** jugarle a uno las bebidas || *intr* hacer juego, correr parejas; **to match** a juego, p.ej., **a chair to match** una silla a juego
match'box' *s* fosforera; (*of wax matches*) cerillera
matchless [ˈmætʃlɪs] *adj* incomparable, sin par
matchmaker [ˈmætʃ,mekər] *s* casamentero
match point *s* (sport) bola de partido
mate [met] *s* compañero; (*e.g., of a shoe*) compañero, hermano; (*husband or wife*) cónyuge *mf;* (*to a female*) macho; (*to a male*) hembra; (*in chess*) mate *m;* (*naut*) piloto || *tr* aparear, casar; (*in chess*) dar jaque mate a; **to be well mated** hacer una buena pareja || *intr* aparearse, casarse
material [məˈtɪrɪ•əl] *adj* material; importante || *s* material *m;* (*what a thing is made of*) materia; (*cloth, fabric*) tela, género
materialism [məˈtɪrɪ•ə,lɪzəm] *s* materialismo
materialist [məˈtɪrɪ•əlɪst] *s* materialista *mf*
materialize [məˈtɪrɪ•ə,laɪz] *intr* realizarse
matériel [mə,tɪrɪˈɛl] *s* material *m;* material de guerra
maternal [məˈtʌrnəl] *adj* materno; (*motherly*) maternal
maternity [məˈtʌrnɪti] *s* maternidad
maternity hospital *s* casa de maternidad
maternity leave *s* baja por maternidad
math. *abbr* **mathematics**
mathematical [,mæθɪˈmætɪkəl] *adj* matemático
mathematician [,mæθɪməˈtɪʃən] *s* matemático
mathematics [,mæθɪˈmætɪks] *s* matemática, matemáticas
matinée [,mætɪˈne] *s* matinée *f,* función de tarde
mating season *s* época de celo
matins [ˈmætɪnz] *spl* maitines *mpl*
matriarch [ˈmetrɪ•ɑrk] *s* matriarca
matricidal [,metrɪˈsaɪdəl] *adj* matricida
matricide [ˈmetrɪ,saɪd] *s* (*act*) matricidio; (*person*) matricida *mf*
matriculate [məˈtrɪkjə,let] *tr* matricular || *intr* matricularse
matrimo•ny [ˈmætrɪ,moni] *s* (*pl* **-nies**) matrimonio
matron [ˈmetrən] *s* matrona
matronly [ˈmetrənli] *adj* matronal
matron of honor *s* primera madrina de boda
matter [ˈmætər] *s* (*physical substance; pus*) materia; (*subject talked or written about*) asunto; (*reason, ground*) motivo; (*copy for printer*) material *m;* (*printed material*) impresos; **a matter of** cosa de, obra de; **for that matter** en cuanto a eso; **in the matter** al respecto; **no matter** no importa; **no matter when** cuando quiera; **no matter where** dondequiera; **what is the matter?** ¿qué hay?; **what is the matter with you?** ¿qué tiene Ud.? || *intr* importar
matter of course *s* cosa de cajón; **as a matter of course** por rutina
matter of fact *s*—**as a matter of fact** en realidad, en honor a la verdad
matter-of-fact [ˈmætərəv,fækt] *adj* prosaico, práctico, de poca imaginación
mattock [ˈmætək] *s* zapapico
mattress [ˈmætrɪs] *s* colchón *m*
mature [məˈtʃʊr] o [məˈtʊr] *adj* maduro; (*due*) pagadero, vencido || *tr* madurar || *intr* madurar; (*to become due*) (com) vencer
maturity [məˈtʃʊrɪti] o [məˈtʊrɪti] *s* madurez *f;* (com) vencimiento
maudlin [ˈmɔdlɪn] *adj* lacrimoso, sensiblero; chispo y lloroso
maul [mɔl] *tr* aporrear, maltratar
mausole•um [,mɔsəˈli•əm] *s* (*pl* **-ums** o **-a** [ə]) mausoleo, panteón *m*
maw [mɔ] *s* (*of fowl*) buche *m;* (*of fish*) vejiga de aire
mawkish [ˈmɔkɪʃ] *adj* (*sickening*) empalagoso; (*sentimental*) sensiblero
max. *abbr* **maximum**
maxim [ˈmæksɪm] *s* máxima
maximum [ˈmæksɪməm] *adj & s* máximo
may *v aux* **it may be** puede ser; **may I come in?** ¿puedo entrar? **may you be happy!** ¡que seas feliz! || **May** *s* mayo
maybe [ˈmebi] o [ˈmebɪ] *adv* acaso, quizá, tal vez
May Day *s* primero de mayo; fiesta del primero de mayo

Mayday [ˈme,de] *interj* (*ships, airplanes*) ¡socorro!
mayhem [ˈmehɛm] o [ˈme•əm] *s* (law) mutilación criminal
mayonnaise [,me•əˈnez] *s* mayonesa
mayor [ˈme•ər] o [mɛr] *s* alcalde *m*
mayoress [ˈme•ərɪs] o [ˈmɛrɪs] *s* alcaldesa
May′pole′ *s* mayo
Maypole dance *s* danza de cintas
May queen *s* maya
maze [mez] *s* laberinto
M.C. *abbr* **Master of Ceremonies, Member of Congress**
mdse. *abbr* **merchandise**
me [mi] *pron pers* me; mí; **to me** me; a mí; **with me** conmigo
meadow [ˈmɛdo] *s* prado, vega
mead′ow•land′ *s* pradera
mead′ow sweet *s* reina de los prados
meager [ˈmigər] *adj* escaso, pobre; flaco, magro
meal [mil] *s* (*regular repast*) comida; (*edible grain coarsely ground*) harina
meal′time′ *s* hora de comer
mean [min] *adj* (*intermediate*) medio; (*low in station or rank*) humilde, obscuro; (*shabby*) andrajoso, raído; (*stingy*) mezquino, tacaño; (*of poor quality*) inferior, pobre; (*small-minded*) vil, ruin, innoble; insignificante; (*vicious, as a horse*) arisco, mal intencionado; (coll) indisupuesto; (coll) avergonzado; (coll) de mal genio; **no mean** famoso, excelente || *s* promedio, término medio; **by all means** sí, por cierto, sin falta; **by means of** por medio de; **by no means** de ningún modo, en ningún caso; **means** bienes *mpl* de fortuna; (*agency*) medio, medios; **means to an end** paso para lograr un fin; **to live on one's means** vivir de sus rentas || *v* (*pret & pp* **meant** [mɛnt]) *tr* significar, querer decir; **to mean to** pensar || *intr*—**to mean well** tener buenas intenciones
meander [mɪˈændər] *s* meandro || *intr* serpentear; vagar
meaning [ˈminɪŋ] *s* sentido, significado
meaningful [ˈminɪŋfəl] *adj* significativo
meaningless [ˈminɪŋlɪs] *adj* sin sentido
meanness [ˈminnɪs] *s* bajeza, vileza, ruindad; (*stinginess*) mezquindad; (*lowliness*) humildad, pobreza
mean′time′ *adv* entretanto, mientras tanto || *s* medio tiempo; **in the meantime** entretanto, mientras tanto
mean′while′ *adv & s* var de **meantime**
measles [ˈmizəlz] *s* sarampión *m;* (*German measles*) rubéola
mea•sly [ˈmizli] *adj* (*comp* **-slier;** *super* **-sliest**) sarampioso; (slang) despreciable, mezquino
measurable [ˈmɛʒərəbəl] *adj* medible
measure [ˈmɛʒər] *s* medida; (*step, procedure*) paso, gestión; (*legislative bill*) proyecto de ley; (*of verse*) pie *m;* (mus) compás *m;* **beyond measure** con exceso; **in a measure** hasta cierto punto; **in great measure** en gran parte; (*suit*) **to measure** hecho a la medida; **to take measures** tomar las medidas necesarias; **to take someone's measure** tomarle a uno las medidas || *tr* medir; recorrer (*cierta distancia*); **to measure out** medir; distribuir || *intr* medir
measurement [ˈmɛʒərmənt] *s* (*act of measuring*) medición; (*measuring; dimension*) medida
measuring glass *s* vaso graduado
meat [mit] *s* carne *f;* (*food in general*) manjar *m,* vianda; (*substance, gist*) meollo
meat ball *s* albóndiga
meat grinder *s* picador *m*
meat′hook′ *s* garabato de carnicero
meat loaf *s* pan *m* de carne
meat market *s* carniceria
meat•y [ˈmiti] *adj* (*comp* **-ier;** *super* **-iest**) carnoso; (fig) jugoso, substancioso
Mecca [ˈmɛkə] *s* La Meca
mechanic [mɪˈkænɪk] *s* mecánico
mechanical [mɪˈkænɪkəl] *adj* mecánico, maquinal; (*machinelike*) (fig) maquinal
mechanical toy *s* juguete *m* de movimiento
mechanics [mɪˈkænɪks] *ssg* mecánica
mechanism [ˈmɛkə,nɪzəm] *s* mecanismo
mechanize [ˈmɛkə,naɪz] *tr* mecanizar
med. *abbr* **medicine, medieval**
medal [ˈmɛdəl] *s* medalla
medallion [mɪˈdæljən] *s* medallón *m*
meddle [ˈmɛdəl] *intr* meterse, entremeterse
meddler [ˈmɛdlər] *s* entremetido
meddlesome [ˈmɛdəlsəm] *adj* entremetido
media [ˈmidɪ•ə] *abbr* **mass media**
median [ˈmidɪ•ən] *adj* intermedio, medio || *s* punto medio, número medio
median strip *s* faja central o divisoria
mediate [ˈmidɪ,et] *tr* dirimir (*una controversia*); reconciliar || *intr* (*to be in the middle*) mediar; (*to intervene to settle a dispute*) intervenir
mediation [,midɪˈeʃən] *s* mediación
mediator [ˈmidɪ,etər] *s* mediador *m*
medical [ˈmɛdɪkəl] *adj* médico
medical corps *s* cuerpo médico
medical examination *s* reconocimiento médico, revisión médica (Esp)
medical examiner *s* (law) médico forense
medical history *s* historia clínica
medical intern *s* interno, practicante *mf*
medical records *spl* ficha médica
medical student *s* estudiante *mf* de medicina
medicine [ˈmɛdɪsɪn] *s* (*science and art*) medicina; (*remedy, treatment*) medicina, medicamento
medicine cabinet *s* armario botiquín
medicine kit *s* botiquín *m*
medicine man *s* curandero, hechicero (*entre los pieles rojas*)
medieval [,midɪˈivəl] o [,mɛdɪˈivəl] *adj* medieval
medievalist [,midɪˈivəlɪst] o [,mɛdɪˈivəlɪst] *s* medievalista *mf*
mediocre [ˈmidɪ,okər] o [,midɪˈokər] *adj* mediocre

mediocri•ty [ˌmidɪˈɑkrɪti] *s* (*pl* **-ties**) mediocridad
meditate [ˈmɛdɪˌtet] *tr & intr* meditar
Mediterranean [ˌmɛdɪtəˈrenɪ•ən] *adj & s* Mediterráneo
medi•um [ˈmidɪ•əm] *adj* intermedio; a medio asar ‖ *s* (*pl* **-ums** o **-a** [ə]) medio; (*in spiritualism*) medio, médium *m;* (*publication*) órgano; **through the medium of** por medio de
me'dium-range' *adj* de alcance medio
medlar [ˈmɛdlər] *s* (*tree and fruit*) níspero; (*fruit*) níspola
medley [ˈmɛdli] *s* mescolanza; (mus) popurrí *m*
medul•la [mɪˈdʌlə] *s* (*pl* **-lae** [li]) médula
meek [mik] *adj* dócil, manso
meekness [ˈmiknɪs] *s* docilidad, mansedumbre
meerschaum [ˈmɪrʃəm] *s* [ˈmɪrʃɔm] *s* espuma de mar; pipa de espuma de mar
meet [mit] *adj* conveniente, a propósito ‖ *s* concurso deportivo ‖ *v* (*pret & pp* **met** [mɛ]) *tr* encontrar, encontrarse con; (*to make the acquaintance of*) conocer; empalmar con (*otro tren o autobús*); ir a esperar; honrar, pagar (*una letra*); hacer frente a (*gastos*); cumplir (*sus obligaciones*); batirse con; hallar (*la muerte*); tener (*mala suerte*); aparecer a (*la vista*) ‖ *intr* encontrarse; reunirse; conocerse; **till we meet again** hasta la vista; **to meet with** encontrarse con; reunirse con; empalmar (*un tren*) con (*otro tren*); tener (*un accidente*)
meeting [ˈmitɪŋ] *s* junta, sesión; reunión; encuentro; (*of two rivers or roads*) confluencia; desafío, duelo
meeting of the minds *s* concierto de voluntades
meeting place *s* lugar *m* de reunión
megabucks [ˈmɛgəˌbʌks] *s* (slang) vastas cantidades de dinero
megacycle [ˈmɛgəˌsaɪkəl] *s* megaciclo
megahertz [ˈmɛgəhʌrts] *s* megahercio
megaphone [ˈmɛgəˌfon] *s* megáfono
megohm [ˈmɛgˌom] *s* megohmio
melancholia [ˌmɛlənˈkolɪ•ə] *s* melancolía
melanchol•y [ˈmɛlənˌkɑli] *adj* melancólico ‖ *s* (*pl* **-ies**) melancolía
melee [ˈmele] o [ˈmɛle] *s* refriega, reyerta
mellow [ˈmɛlo] *adj* maduro, jugoso; suave, meloso; melodioso ‖ *tr* suavizar ‖ *intr* suavizarse
melodious [mɪˈlodɪ•əs] *adj* melodioso
melodramatic [ˌmɛlədrəˈmætɪk] *adj* melodramático
melo•dy [ˈmɛlədi] *s* (*pl* **-dies**) melodía
melon [ˈmɛlən] *s* melón *m*
melt [mɛlt] *tr* derretir; fundir (*metales*); ablandar, aplacar; **to melt down** fundir ‖ *intr* derretirse; fundirse; ablandarse, aplacarse; **to melt away** desvanecerse; **to melt down** (*core of a nuclear reactor*) fundirse (*accidentalmente*); **to melt into** convertirse gradualmente en; deshacerse en (*lágrimas*)
melt'down' *s* fusión; (*atomic reactor*) fusión del combustible por fisión no controlada
melting pot *s* crisol *m;* (fig) caldero de razas
member [ˈmɛmbər] *s* miembro
membership [ˈmɛmbərˌʃɪp] *s* asociación; (*e.g., of a club*) personal *m;* número de miembros
membrane [ˈmɛmbren] *s* membrana
memen•to [mɪˈmɛnto] *s* (*pl* **-tos** o **-toes**) recordatorio, prenda de recuerdo
mem•o [ˈmɛmo] *s* (*pl* **-os**) (coll) apunte *m,* membrete *m*
memoir [ˈmɛmwɑr] *s* memoria; biografía; **memoirs** memorias
memoran•dum [ˌmɛməˈrændəm] *s* (*pl* **-dums** o **-da** [də]) apunte *m,* membrete *m*
memorial [mɪˈmorɪ•əl] *adj* conmemorativo ‖ *s* monumento conmemorativo; (*petition*) memorial *m*
memorial arch *s* arco triunfal
Memorial Day *s* día *m* de los caídos
memorialize [mɪˈmorɪ•əˌlaɪz] *tr* conmemorar
memorize [ˈmɛməˌraɪz] *tr* aprender de memoria
memo•ry [ˈmɛməri] *s* (*pl* **-ries**) memoria; (*recall*) retentiva; (*computer*) memoria, almacenaje *m* o almacenamiento (de datos); **to commit to memory** encomendar a la memoria
Men *s* (*men's room*) *SIGN* Caballeros
menace [ˈmɛnɪs] *s* amenaza ‖ *tr & intr* amenazar
ménage [meˈnaʒ] *s* casa, hogar *m;* economía doméstica
menagerie [məˈnæʒəri] o [məˈnædʒəri] *s* casa de fieras; colección de fieras
mend [mɛnd] *s* remiendo; **to be on the mend** ir mejorando ‖ *tr* (*to repair*) componer, reparar; (*to patch*) remendar; (*to improve*) reformar, mejorar ‖ *intr* mejorar
mendacious [mɛnˈdeʃəs] *adj* mendaz
mendicant [ˈmɛndɪkənt] *adj & s* mendicante *mf*
mending [ˈmɛndɪŋ] *s* remiendo, zurcido
menfolk [ˈmɛnˌfok] *spl* hombres *mpl*
menial [ˈminɪ•əl] *adj* bajo, servil ‖ *s* criado, doméstico
menopause [ˈmɛnəpɔz] *s* menopausia
menses [ˈmɛnsiz] *spl* menstruo
men's furnishings *spl* artículos para caballeros
men's room *s* baño *or* servicio de caballeros
menstruate [ˈmɛnstrʊˌet] *intr* menstruar
mental case [ˈmɛntəl] *s* (coll) paciente *mf* mental; estrafalario
mental cruelty *s* crueldad mental
mental giant *s* (coll) genio
mental handicap *s* minusvalía
mental hygiene *s* higiene *f* mental
mental illness *s* enfermedad mental
mental reservation *s* reserva mental
mental telepathy *s* telepatía
mental test *s* prueba de inteligencia
mention [ˈmɛnʃən] *s* mención ‖ *tr* mencionar; **don't mention it** no hay de qué; **not to mention** sin contar
menu [ˈmɛnju] o [ˈmenju] *s* menú *m,* lista de comidas; comida
menu bar *s* (compu) barra de menús
meow [mɪˈaʊ] *s* maullido ‖ *intr* maullar
mercantile [ˈmʌrkənˌtil] o [ˈmʌrkənˌtaɪl] *adj* mercantil

mercenar•y [ˈmʌrsə,nɛri] *adj* mercenario, interesado, materialista ‖ *s* (*pl* **-ies**) mercenario
merchandise [ˈmʌrtʃən,daɪz] *s* mercancías, mercaderías ‖ *tr* comercializar
merchant [ˈmʌrtʃənt] *adj* mercante ‖ *s* mercante *m*, mercader *m*
merchant•man [ˈmʌrtʃəntmən] *s* (*pl* **-men** [mən]) buque *m* mercante
merchant marine *s* marina mercante
merchant vessel *s* buque *m* mercante
merciful [ˈmʌrsɪfəl] *adj* misericordioso
merciless [ˈmʌrsɪlɪs] *adj* despiadado, cruel, implacable
mercu•ry [ˈmʌrkjəri] *s* (*pl* **-ries**) mercurio, azogue *m;* columna de mercurio ‖ **Mercury** (astr, myth) Mercurio
mer•cy [ˈmʌrsi] *s* (*pl* **-cies**) misericordia; (*discretionary power*) merced *f;* **at the mercy of** a merced de
mercy killing *s* eutanasia
mere [mir] *adj* mero, puro; nada más que
meretricious [,mɛrɪˈtrɪʃəs] *adj* postizo, de oropel; cursi, llamativo
merge [mʌrdʒ] *tr* enchufar, fusionar ‖ *intr* enchufarse, fusionarse; convergir (*p.ej., dos caminos*); **to merge into** convertirse gradualmente en
merger [ˈmʌrdʒər] *s* fusión de empresas
meridian [məˈrɪdɪ•ən] *adj* meridiano; (el) más elevado ‖ *s* meridiano; (fig) auge *m*, apogeo
meringue [məˈræŋ] *s* merengue *m*
meri•no [məˈrino] *adj* merino ‖ *s* (*pl* **-nos**) merino
merit [ˈmɛrɪt] *s* mérito ‖ *tr* merecer
merlon [ˈmʌrlən] *s* almena, merlón *m*
mermaid [ˈmʌr,med] *s* sirena
mer•man [ˈmʌr,mæn] *s* (*pl* **-men** [,mɛn]) tritón *m*
merriment [ˈmɛrɪmənt] *s* alegría, regocijo
mer•ry [ˈmɛri] *adj* (*comp* **-rier;** *super* **-riest**) alegre, regocijado; **to make merry** divertirse
Merry Christmas *interj* ¡Felices Pascuas!, ¡Felices Navidades!
mer′ry-go-round′ *s* tiovivo, caballito; serie ininterrumpida (de fiestas, tertulias, etc.)
mer′ry•mak′er *s* fiestero, jaranero
mesh [mɛʃ] *s* (*net, network*) red *f;* (*each open space of net*) malla; (*engagement of gears*) engrane *m;* **meshes** celada, red *f* ‖ *tr* enredar; (mach) engranar ‖ *intr* enredarse; (mach) engranar
mess [mɛs] *s* (*dirty condition*) cochinería; fregado, lío, embrollo; (*meal for a group of people; such a group*) rancho; (*refuse*) bazofia; **to get into a mess** meterse en un lío; **to make a mess of** ensuciar, echar a perder ‖ *tr* ensuciar; desarreglar; estropear, echar a perder ‖ *intr* comer; **to mess around** (coll) ocuparse en fruslerías
message [ˈmɛsɪdʒ] *s* mensaje *m;* recado
message board *s* (compu) tablón *m* de mensajes
messenger [ˈmɛsəndʒər] *s* mensajero; (*one who goes on errands*) mandadero; precursor *m*
mess hall *s* sala de rancho; comedor *m* de militares
Messiah [məˈsaɪ•ə] *s* Mesías *m*
mess kit *s* utensilios de rancho
mess′mate′ *s* comensal *mf*, compañero de rancho
mess of pottage [ˈpɑtɪdʒ] *s* (Bib) plato de lentejas; cosa de ningún valor
Messrs. [ˈmɛsərz] *pl* de **Mr.**
mess•y [ˈmɛsi] *adj* (*comp* **-ier;** *super* **-iest**) desaliñado, desarreglado; sucio
metal [ˈmɛtəl] *adj* metálico ‖ *s* metal *m;* (fig) brío, ánimo
metallic [mɪˈtælɪk] *adj* metálico
metallurgy [ˈmɛtə,lʌrdʒi] *s* metalurgia
metal polish *s* limpiametales *m*
met′al•work′ *s* metalistería
metamorpho•sis [,mɛtəˈmɔrfəsɪs] *s* (*pl* **-ses** [,siz]) metamorfosis *f*
metaphor [ˈmɛtə,fɔr] *s* metáfora
metaphorical [,mɛtəˈfɑrɪkəl] o [,mɛtəˈfɔrɪkəl] *adj* metafórico
metastasis [məˈtæstəsɪs] *s* metástasis *f*
metathe•sis [mɪˈtæθɪsɪs] *s* (*pl* **-ses** [,siz]) metátesis *f*
mete [mit] *tr*—**to mete out** repartir
meteor [ˈmitɪ•ər] *s* estrella fugaz; (*atmospheric phenomenon*) meteoro
meteorology [,mitɪ•əˈrɑlədʒi] *s* meteorología
meteor shower *s* lluvia de estrellas
meter [ˈmitər] *s* (*unit of measurement; verse*) metro; (*instrument for measuring gas, electricity, water*) contador *m;* (mus) compás *m*, tiempo ‖ *tr* medir (con contador)
metering [ˈmitərɪŋ] *s* medición
meter reader *s* lector *m* (del contador)
methane [ˈmɛθen] *s* metano
method [ˈmɛθəd] *s* método
methodic(al) [mɪˈθɑdɪk(əl)] *adj* metódico
Methodist [ˈmɛθədɪst] *adj & s* metodista *mf*
Methuselah [miˈθuzələ] *s* Matusalén *m*
meticulous [mɪˈtɪkjələs] *adj* meticuloso, minucioso
metric(al) [ˈmɛtrɪk(əl)] *adj* métrico
metronome [ˈmɛtrə,nom] *s* metrónomo
metropolis [mɪˈtrɑpəlɪs] *s* metrópoli *f*
metropolitan [,mɛtrəˈpɑlɪtən] *adj* metropolitano ‖ *s* (eccl) metropolitano
mettle [ˈmɛtəl] *s* ánimo, brío; **on one's mettle** dispuesto a hacer todo el esfuerzo possible
mettlesome [ˈmɛtəlsəm] *adj* animoso, brioso
mew [mju] *s* maullido; (orn) gaviota; **mews** (Brit) caballerizas alrededor de un corral
Mexican [ˈmɛksɪkən] *adj & s* mejicano, mexicano
Mexico [ˈmɛksɪ,ko] *s* Méjico, México, el país de México
Mexico City *s* México, la Ciudad de Méjico
mezzanine [ˈmɛzə,nin] *s* entresuelo
mi. *abbr* **mile**
mica [ˈmaɪkə] *s* mica
microbe [ˈmaɪkrob] *s* microbio

microbiologist [ˈmaɪkrobaɪˈɑlədʒəst] *s* microbiólogo
microbiology [ˌmaɪkrəbaɪˈɑlədʒi] *s* microbiología
microcard [ˈmaɪkrəˌkɑrd] *s* microficha
microchip [ˈmaɪkrotʃip] *s* microchip *m*
microcomputer [ˈmaɪkrəkəmˌpjutər] *adj* microinformático || *s* microordenador *m*
microeconomics [ˈmaɪkroˌɛkəˈnɑmɪks] *s* microeconómica
microfarad [ˌmaɪkrəˈfæræd] *s* microfaradio
microfilm [ˈmaɪkrəˌfɪlm] *s* microfilm *m,* micropelícula || *tr* microfilmar
microgroove [ˈmaɪkrəˌgruv] *adj* microsurco || *s* microsurco; disco microsurco
microphone [ˈmaɪkrəˌfon] *s* micrófono
microprocessor [ˈmaɪkrəˌprɑsɛsər] *s* microprocesador *m*
microscope [ˈmaɪkrəˌskop] *s* microscopio
microscopic [ˌmaɪkrəˈskɑpɪk] *adj* microscópico
microsurgery [ˈmaɪkroˈsʌrdʒəri] *s* microcirugía
microwave [ˈmaɪkrəˌwev] *s* microonda; (*oven*) microondas *m,* horno (de) microondas
mid [mɪd] *adj* medio, p.ej., **in mid course a** medio camino
midˈdayˈ *adj* del mediodía || *s* mediodía *m*
middle [ˈmɪdəl] *adj* medio || *s* centro, medio; (*of the human body*) cintura; **about the middle of** a mediados de; **in the middle of** en medio de
middle age *s* mediana edad || **Middle Ages** *spl* Edad Media
middle class *s* burguesía, clase media
Middle East *s* Oriente Medio
Middle English *s* el inglés medio
middle finger *s* dedo cordial, de en medio o del corazón
midˈdle•manˈ *s* (*pl* **-men** [ˌmɛn]) intermediario
midˈdle weightˈ *s* peso medio *or* mediano
middling [ˈmɪdlɪŋ] *adj* mediano, regular, pasadero || *adv* (coll) medianamente; (coll) así, así || *s* (*coarsely ground wheat*) cabezuela; **middlings** artículos de calidad o precio medianos
mid•dy [ˈmɪdi] *s* (*pl* **-dies**) (coll) aspirante *m* de marina; (*child's blouse*) marinera
midget [ˈmɪdʒɪt] *s* enano, liliputiense *mf*
midland [ˈmɪdlənd] *adj* de tierra adentro || *s* región central
midˈnightˈ *adj* de medianoche; **to burn the midnight oil** quemarse las cejas || *s* medianoche *f*
midˈ-rangeˈ *s* (compu) gama media
midriff [ˈmɪdrɪf] *s* (anat) diafragma *m;* talle *m*
midship•man [ˈmɪdˌʃɪpmən] *s* (*pl* **-men** [mən]) guardia marina *m,* aspirante *m* de marina
midst [mɪdst] *s* centro; **in the midst of** en medio de; en lo más recio de
midˈstreamˈ *s*—**in midstream** en pleno río
midˈsumˈmer *s* pleno verano
midˈwayˈ *adj* situado a mitad del camino || *adv* a mitad del camino || *s* mitad del camino; (*of a fair or exposition*) avenida central
midˈweekˈ *s* mediados de la semana
midˈwifeˈ *s* (*pl* **-wives**) partera, comadrona
midˈwinˈter *s* pleno invierno
midˈyearˈ *adj* de mediados del año || *s* mediados del año; **midyears** (coll) examen *m* de mediados del año escolar
mien [min] *s* aspecto, semblante *m,* porte *m*
miff [mɪf] *s* (coll) desavenencia || *tr* (coll) ofender
might [maɪt] *s* fuerza, poder *m;* **with might and main** con todas sus fuerzas, a más no poder || *v aux* se emplea para formar el modo potencial, p.ej., **she might not come** es posible que no venga; se emplea para hacer una sugerencia, p.ej., **you might at least study tonight** al menos podrías estudiar esta noche; **you might shut the door** podrías cerrar la puerta; **you might have told me!** ¡habérmelo dicho!
mightn't *contr* **might not**
might•y [ˈmaɪti] *adj* (*comp* **-ier;** *super* **-iest**) potente, poderoso; (*of great size*) grandísimo || *adv* (coll) muy
migraine [ˈmaɪˈgren] *s* (*headache*) jaqueca, migraña
migrant worker [ˈmaɪgrənt] *s* bracero migratorio
migrate [ˈmaɪgret] *intr* emigrar
migratory [ˈmaɪgrəˌtori] *adj* migratorio
mil *abbr* **military, militia**
milch [mɪltʃ] *adj* lechero
mild [maɪld] *adj* blando, suave; dócil, manso; leve, ligero; (*climate*) templado
mildew [ˈmɪlˌdju] *s* (*mold*) moho; (*plant disease*) mildeu *m*
mile [maɪl] *s* milla inglesa
mileage [ˈmaɪlɪdʒ] *s* recorrido en millas
mileage ticket *s* billete contado por millas, semejante al billete kilométrico
mileˈpostˈ *s* poste miliario
mileˈstoneˈ *s* piedra miliaria; **to be a milestone** hacer época
milieu [mɪlˈjʊ] *s* ambiente *m,* medio
militancy [ˈmɪlɪtənsi] *s* belicosidad
militant [ˈmɪlɪtənt] *adj* militante, belicoso
militarism [ˈmɪlɪtəˌrɪzəm] *s* militarismo
militarist [ˈmɪlɪtərɪst] *adj & s* militarista *mf*
militarize [ˈmɪlɪtəˌraɪz] *tr* militarizar
military [ˈmɪlɪˌtɛri] *adj* militar || *s* (los) militares
military academy *s* academia militar
Military Academy *s* (U.S.A.) Academia General Militar
military court *s* tribunal *m* militar
military police *s* policía militar
military school *s var* de **military academy**
militate [ˈmɪlɪˌtet] *intr* militar
militia [mɪˈlɪʃə] *s* milicia
militia•man [ˈmɪˈlɪʃəmən] *s* (*pl* **-men** [mən]) miliciano
milk [mɪlk] *adj* lechero, de leche || *s* leche *f* || *tr* ordeñar; chupar (*los bienes de uno*); abusar de, explotar || *intr* dar leche
milk can *s* lechera
milk diet *s* régimen lácteo

milking [ˈmɪlkɪŋ] *s* ordeño
milk'maid' *s* lechera
milk•man [ˈmɪlk,mæn] *s* (*pl* **-men** [,mɛn]) lechero
milk of human kindness *s* compasión, humanidad
milk of magnesia *s* leche *f* de magnesia
milk pail *s* ordeñadero
milk shake *s* batido de leche
milk'sop' *s* calzonazos *m,* marica *m*
milk tooth *s* diente *m* de leche
milk'weed' *s* algodoncillo, vencetósigo
milk•y [ˈmɪlki] *adj* (*comp* **-ier;** *super* **-iest**) lechoso, lácteo
Milky Way *s* Vía Láctea
mill [mɪl] *s* (*for grinding grain*) molino; (*for making fabrics*) hilandería; (*for cutting wood*) aserradero; (*for refining sugar*) ingenio; (*for producing steel*) fábrica; (*to grind coffee*) molinillo; (*part of a dollar*) milésima; **to put through the mill** (coll) poner a prueba, someter a un entrenamiento riguroso ‖ *tr* moler (*granos*); acordonar, cerrillar (*monedas*); laminar (*el acero*); triturar (*mena*); (*with a milling cutter*) fresar; batir (*chocolate*) ‖ *intr*—**to mill about** o **around** arremolinarse
millennial [mɪˈlɛnɪ•əl] *adj* milenario
millenni•um [mɪˈlɛnɪ•əm] *s* (*pl* **-ums** o **-a** [ə]) milenario, milenio
miller [ˈmɪlər] *s* molinero; (ent) polilla blanca
millet [ˈmɪlɪt] *s* mijo, millo
milliampere [,mɪlɪˈæmpɪr] *s* miliamperio
milligram [ˈmɪlɪ,græm] *s* miligramo
millimeter [ˈmɪlɪ,mitər] *s* milímetro
milliner [ˈmɪlɪnər] *s* modista *mf* de sombreros
millinery [ˈmɪlɪ,nɛri] o [ˈmɪlɪnəri] *s* sombreros de señora; sombrerería
milling [ˈmɪlɪŋ] *s* (*of grain*) molienda; (*of coins*) acordonamiento, cordoncillo; fresado
milling machine *s* fresadora
million [ˈmɪljən] *adj* millón de, millones de ‖ *s* millón *m*
millionaire [,mɪljənˈɛr] *s* millonario
millionth [ˈmɪljənθ] *adj & s* millonésimo
millivolt [ˈmɪlɪ,volt] *s* milivoltio
mill'pond' *s* represa de molino
mill'race' *s* caz *m*
mill'stone' *s* muela de molino; (fig) carga pesada
mill wheel *s* rueda de molino
mill'work' *s* carpintería de taller
mime [maɪm] *s* mimo ‖ *tr* remedar
Mimeograph[T] [ˈmɪm•ə,græf] o [ˈmɪmɪ•ə,grɑf] *s* mimeógrafo ‖ *tr* mimeografiar
mim•ic [ˈmɪmɪk] *s* imitador *m,* remedador *m* ‖ *v* (*pret & pp* **-icked;** *ger* **-icking**) *tr* imitar, remedar
mimic•ry [ˈmɪmɪkri] *s* (*pl* **-ries**) mímica, remedo
min. *abbr* **minimum, minute**
minaret [,mɪnəˈrɛt] o [ˈmɪnə,rɛt] *s* alminar *m,* minarete *m*
mince [mɪns] *tr* desmenuzar; picar (*carne*) ‖ *intr* andar remilgadamente; hablar remilgadamente
mince'meat' *s* cuajado, picadillo
mince pie *s* pastel *m* de picadillo de fruta
mind [maɪnd] *s* mente *f,* espíritu *m;* **to bear in mind** tener presente; **to be not in one's right mind** no estar en sus cabales; **to be of one mind** estar de acuerdo; **to be out of one's mind** estar fuera de juicio; **to change one's mind** mudar de parecer; **to go out of one's mind** volverse loco; **to have a mind to** tener ganas de; **to have in mind to** pensar en; **to have on one's mind** preocuparse con; **to lose one's mind** perder el juicio; **to make up one's mind** resolverse; **to my mind** a mi parecer; **to say whatever comes into one's mind** decir lo que se le viene a la boca; **to set one's mind on** resolverse a; **to slip one's mind** escaparse de la memoria; **to speak one's mind** decir su parecer; **with one mind** unánimamente ‖ *tr* (*to take care of*) cuidar, estar al cuidado de; obedecer; fijarse en; sentir molestia por; **do you mind the smoke?** ¿le molesta el humo?; **mind your own business** no se meta Ud. en lo que no le toca ‖ *intr* tener inconveniente; tener cuidado; **never mind** no se preocupe, no se moleste
mind'-bend'ing *adj* (coll) alucinante
mind'-blow'ing *adj* (coll) alucinante en exceso
mind'-bog'gling *adj* deslumbrante; abrumador
mindful [ˈmaɪndfəl] *adj* atento; **mindful of** atento a, cuidadoso de
mind reader *s* adivinador *m* del pensamiento ajeno, lector *m* mental
mind reading *s* adivinación del pensamiento ajeno, lectura de la mente
mine [maɪn] *pron poss* el mío; mío ‖ *s* mina; **to work a mine** beneficiar una mina ‖ *tr* minar; beneficiar (*un terreno*); extraer (*mineral, carbón, etc.*) ‖ *intr* minar; abrir minas
mine field *s* campo de minas
mine layer *s* buque *m* portaminas, lanzaminas *m*
miner [ˈmaɪnər] *s* minero; (mil, nav) minador *m*
mineral [ˈmɪnərəl] *adj & s* mineral *m*
mineralogy [,mɪnəˈrælədʒi] *s* mineralogía
mineral oil *s* aceite *m* de parafina
mineral resources *spl* riquezas del subsuelo
mineral wool *s* lana de escorias
mine sweeper *s* dragaminas *m*
mingle [ˈmɪŋgəl] *tr* mezclar, confundir ‖ *intr* mezclarse, confundirse; asociarse
miniature [ˈmɪnɪ•ətʃər] o [ˈmɪnɪtʃər] *s* miniatura; **to paint in miniature** miniar, pintar de miniatura
miniaturization [,mɪnɪ•ətʃərɪˈzeʃən] o [,mɪnɪtʃərɪˈzeʃən] *s* miniaturización
minicomputer [ˈmɪnɪkəm,pjutər] *s* miniordenador *m*
minimal [ˈmɪnɪməl] *adj* mínimo
minimize [ˈmɪnɪ,maɪz] *tr* empequeñecer
minimum [ˈmɪnɪməm] *adj & s* mínimo

minimum wage *s* jornal mínimo
mining [ˈmaɪnɪŋ] *adj* minero || *s* mineraje *m,* minería; (nav) minado
minion [ˈmɪnjən] *s* paniaguado
minion of the law *s* esbirro, polizonte *m*
miniskirt [ˈmɪnɪ,skʌrt] *s* minifalda
minister [ˈmɪnɪstər] *s* ministro; pastor *m* protestante || *tr & intr* ministrar
ministerial [ˈmɪnɪsˈtɪrɪ•əl] *adj* ministerial
minis•try [ˈmɪnɪstri] *s* (*pl* **-tries**) ministerio
mink [mɪŋk] *s* visón *m*
minnow [ˈmɪno] *s* pececillo; (ichth) foxino
minor [ˈmaɪnər] *adj* (*smaller*) menor; de menor importancia; (*younger*) menor de edad; (mus) menor || *s* menor *m* de edad; (educ) asignatura secundaria
Minorca [mɪˈnɔrkə] *s* Menorca
Minorcan [mɪˈnɔrkən] *adj & s* menorquín *m*
minori•ty [maɪˈnɔrɪti] *adj* minoritario || *s* (*pl* **-ties**) (*being under age; smaller number or part*) minoría; (*less than full age*) minoridad
minstrel [ˈmɪnstrəl] *s* (*retainer who sang and played for his lord*) ministril *m;* (*medieval musician and poet*) juglar *m,* trovador *m;* (U.S.A.) cantor cómico disfrazado de negro
minstrel•sy [ˈmɪnstrəlsi] *s* (*pl* **-sies**) juglaría; compañía de juglares; poesía trovadoresca
mint [mɪnt] *s* casa de moneda; (*plant*) menta, hierbabuena; montón *m* de dinero; fuente *f* inagotable || *tr* acuñar; (fig) inventar
minuet [,mɪnjʊˈɛt] *s* minué *m,* minuete *m*
minus [ˈmaɪnəs] *adj* menos || *prep* menos; falto de, sin || *s* menos *m*
minus sign *s* signo de menos
minute [maɪˈnjut] o [maɪˈnut] *adj* diminuto, menudo || [ˈmɪnɪt] *s* minuto; (*short space of time*) momento; **minutes** acta; **to write up the minutes** levantar acta; **up to the minute** al corriente; de última hora
minute hand [ˈmɪnɪt] *s* minutero
minutiae [mɪˈnjuʃɪ,i] o [mɪˈnuʃɪ,i] *spl* minucias
minx [mɪŋks] *s* moza descarada
miracle [ˈmɪrəkəl] *s* milagro
miracle play *s* auto
miraculous [mɪˈrækjələs] *adj* milagroso
mirage [mɪˈrɑʒ] *s* espejismo
mire [maɪr] *s* fango, lodo
mirror [ˈmɪrər] *s* espejo; (aut) retrovisor *m* || *tr* reflejar
mirth [mʌrθ] *s* alegría, regocijo
mir•y [ˈmaɪri] *adj* (*comp* **-ier;** *super* **-iest**) fangoso, lodoso; sucio
misadventure [,mɪsədˈvɛntʃər] *s* desgracia, contratiempo
misanthrope [ˈmɪsən,θrop] *s* misántropo
misanthropy [mɪsˈænθrəpi] *s* misantropía
misapprehension [,mɪsæprɪˈhɛnʃən] *s* malentendido
misappropriation [,mɪsə,proprɪˈeʃən] *s* malversación
misbehave [,mɪsbɪˈhev] *intr* conducirse mal, portarse mal
misbehavior [,mɪsbɪˈhevɪ•ər] *s* mala conducta, mal comportamiento
misc. *abbr* **miscellaneous, miscellany**
miscalculation [,mɪskælkjəˈleʃən] *s* mal cálculo
miscarriage [mɪsˈkærɪdʒ] *s* aborto, malparto, aborto espontáneo; fracaso, malogro; (*of a letter*) extravío
miscar•ry [mɪsˈkæri] *v* (*pret & pp* **-ried**) *intr* abortar, malparir; malograrse; extraviarse (*una carta*)
miscellaneous [,mɪsəˈlenɪ•əs] *adj* misceláneo
miscella•ny [ˈmɪsə,leni] *s* (*pl* **-nies**) miscelánea
mischief [ˈmɪstʃɪf] *s* (*harm*) daño, mal *m;* (*disposition to annoy*) malicia; (*prankishness*) travesura
misˈchief-makˈer *s* malsín *m,* cizañero
mischievous [ˈmɪstʃɪvəs] *adj* dañoso, malo; malicioso; travieso
misconception [,mɪskənˈsɛpʃən] *s* concepto erróneo, mala interpretación
misconduct [mɪsˈkɑndəkt] *s* mala conducta
misconstrue [,mɪskənˈstru] o [mɪsˈkɑnstru] *tr* interpretar mal
miscount [mɪsˈkaʊnt] *s* cuenta errónea || *tr & intr* contar mal
miscue [mɪsˈkju] *s* (*in billiards*) pifia; (*slip*) pifia || *intr* pifiar; (theat) equivocarse de apunte
misdate [mɪsˈdet] *tr* fechar erróneamente
mis•deal [ˈmɪs,dil] *s* repartición errónea || [mɪsˈdil] *v* (*pret & pp* **-dealt** [ˈdɛlt]) *tr & intr* repartir mal
misdeed [mɪsˈdid] o [ˈmɪs,did] *s* malhecho, fechoría
misdemeanor [,mɪsdɪˈminər] *s* mala conducta; (law) delito de menor cuantía
misdirect [,mɪsdɪˈrɛkt] o [,mɪsdaɪˈrɛkt] *tr* dirigir erradamente; hacer perder el camino
misdoing [mɪsˈdu•ɪŋ] *s* mala acción
miser [ˈmaɪzər] *s* avaro, verrugo, rata; codo (Guat, Mex)
miserable [ˈmɪzərəbəl] *adj* miserable; (coll) achacoso, indispuesto
miserly [ˈmaɪzərli] *adj* avariento, mezquino
miser•y [ˈmɪzəri] *s* (*pl* **-ies**) miseria; pelazón *f*
misfeasance [mɪsˈfizəns] *s* (law) fraude *m*
misfire [mɪsˈfaɪr] *s* falla de tiro; (*of internal-combustion engine*) falla de encendido || *intr* fallar (*un arma de fuego, el encendido de un motor*)
mis•fit [ˈmɪs,fɪt] *s* vestido mal cortado; cosa que no encaja bien; persona mal adaptada a su ambiente || [mɪsˈfɪt] *v* (*pret & pp* **-fitted;** *ger* **-fitting**) *tr & intr* encajar mal, sentar mal
misfortune [mɪsˈfɔrtʃən] *s* desgracia
misgiving [mɪsˈgɪvɪŋ] *s* mal presentimiento, rescoldo
misgovern [mɪsˈgʌvərn] *tr* desgobernar
misguidance [mɪsˈgaɪdəns] *s* error *m,* extravío
misguided [mɪsˈgaɪdɪd] *adj* descarriado, malaconsejado

mishap [ˋmɪshæp] o [mɪsˋhæp] *s* accidente *m,* percance *m*
mishmash [ˋmɪʃ,mæʃ] *s* baturillo; mezcolanza
misinform [,mɪsɪnˋfɔrm] *tr* dar informes erróneos a
misinterpret [,mɪsɪnˋtɛrprɪt] *tr* interpretar mal
misjudge [mɪsˋdʒʌdʒ] *tr & intr* juzgar mal
mis•lay [misˋle] *v* (*pret & pp* **-laid** [,led]) *tr* extraviar, perder; (*among one's papers*) traspapelar
mis•lead [mɪsˋlid] *v* (*pret & pp* **-led** [,lɛd]) *tr* (*to lead astray*) extraviar, descaminar; (*to lead into wrongdoing*) seducir, inducir al mal; (*to deceive*) engañar
misleading [mɪsˋlɪdɪŋ] *adj* engañoso
mismanagement [mɪsˋmænɪdʒmənt] *s* mala administración, desgobierno
misnomer [mɪsˋnomər] *s* nombre impropio, mal nombre
misplace [mɪsˋples] *tr* colocar fuera de su lugar; colocar mal; (*to mislay*) (coll) extraviar, perder
misprint [ˋmɪs,prɪnt] *s* errata de imprenta ‖ [mɪsˋprɪnt] *tr* imprimir con erratas
mispronounce [,mɪsprəˋnaʊns] *tr* pronunciar mal
mispronunciation [,mɪsprə,nʌnsɪˋeʃən] o [,mɪsprə,nʌnʃɪˋeʃən] *s* pronunciación incorrecta
misquote [mɪsˋkwot] *tr* citar equivocadamente
misrepresent [,mɪsrɛprɪˋzɛnt] *tr* tergiversar
miss [mɪs] *s* falta, error *m;* fracaso, malogro; tiro errado; jovencita, muchacha ‖ *tr* echar de menos; perder (*el tren, la función, la oportunidad*); errar (*el blanco; la vocación*); no entender, no comprender; omitir; no ver; no dar con, no encontrar; librarse de (*p.ej., la muerte*); escapársele a uno, p.ej., **I missed what you said** se me escapó lo que dijo Ud.; por poco, p.ej., **the car missed hitting me** el coche por poco me atropella ‖ *intr* fallar; errar el blanco; malograrse ‖ **Miss** *s* señorita
missal [ˋmɪsəl] *s* misal *m*
misshapen [mɪsˋʃepən] *adj* deforme, contrahecho
missile [ˋmɪsɪl] *adj* arrojadizo ‖ *s* arma arrojadiza; proyectil *m;* proyectil dirigido, misil *m*
missile launcher *s* lanzamisiles *m*
missil(e)ry [ˋmɪsəlri] *s* cohetería; ciencia de las armas proyectiles
missing [ˋmɪsɪŋ] *adj* extraviado, perdido; desaparecido; ausente; **to be missing** hacer falta; haber desaparecido
missing link *s* hombre *m* mono
missing persons *spl* desaparecidos
mission [ˋmɪʃən] *s* misión; casa de misión
missionar•y [ˋmɪʃən,ɛri] *adj* misional ‖ *s* (*pl* **-ies**) (*one sent to work to propagate his faith*) misionario, misionero; (*on a political or diplomatic mission*) misionario
mission control *s* centro de control
missive [ˋmɪsɪv] *adj* misivo ‖ *s* misiva
mis•spell [mɪsˋspɛl] *v* (*pret & pp* **-spelled** o **-spelt** [ˋspɛlt]) *tr & intr* deletrear mal, escribir mal
misspelling [mɪsˋspɛlɪŋ] *s* falta de ortografía
misspent [mɪsˋspɛnt] *adj* malgastado
misstatement [mɪsˋstetmənt] *s* relación equivocada, relación falsa
misstep [mɪsˋstɛp] *s* paso falso; (*slip in conduct*) resbalón *m*
miss•y [ˋmɪsi] *s* (*pl* **-ies**) (coll) señorita
mist [mɪst] *s* neblina; (*of tears*) velo; (*fine spray*) vapor *m*
mis•take [mɪsˋtek] *s* error *m,* equivocación; **and no mistake** sin duda alguna; **by mistake** por descuido; **to make a mistake** equivocarse ‖ *v* (*pret* **-took** [ˋtʊk]; *pp* **-taken**) *tr* tomar (*por otro; por lo que no es*); entender mal; **to be mistaken for** equivocarse con
mistaken [mɪsˋtekən] *adj* (*person*) equivocado; (*idea*) erróneo; (*act*) desacertado
mistakenly [mɪsˋtekənli] *adv* equivocadamente, por error
mistletoe [ˋmɪsəl,to] *s* (*Viscum album*) muérdago; (*Phoradendron flavescens, used in Christmas decorations in the U.S.A.*) cabellera
mistreat [mɪsˋtrit] *tr* maltratar
mistreatment [mɪsˋtritmənt] *s* maltratamiento
mistress [ˋmɪstrɪs] *s* (*of a household*) ama, dueña; (*lover*) moza, querida, manceba; (*teacher*) (Brit) maestra de escuela
mistrial [mɪsˋtraɪ•əl] *s* pleito viciado de nulidad
mistrust [mɪsˋtrʌst] *s* desconfianza ‖ *tr* desconfiar de ‖ *intr* desconfiar
mistrustful [mɪsˋtrʌstfəl] *adj* desconfiado
mist•y [ˋmɪsti] *adj* (*comp* **-ier;** *super* **-iest**) brumoso, neblinoso; indistinto
misunder•stand [,mɪsʌndərˋstænd] *v* (*pret & pp* **-stood** [ˋstʊd]) *tr* no comprender, entender mal
misunderstanding [,mɪsʌndərˋstændɪŋ] *s* malentendido; (*disagreement*) desavenencia
misuse [mɪsˋjus] *s* abuso, mal uso; (*of funds*) malversación ‖ [mɪsˋjuz] *tr* abusar de, emplear mal; malversar (*fondos*)
misword [mɪsˋwʌrd] *tr* redactar mal
mite [maɪt] *s* (*small contribution*) óbolo; (*small amount*) pizca; (ent) ácaro
miter [ˋmaɪtər] *s* mitra; (carp) inglete *m* ‖ *tr* cortar ingletes en; juntar con junta a inglete
miter box *s* caja de ingletes
mitigate [ˋmɪtɪ,get] *tr* mitigar, atenuar, paliar
mitten [ˋmɪtən] *s* confortante *m,* mitón *m*
mix [mɪks] *tr* mezclar; amasar (*una torta*); aderezar (*ensalada*); **to mix up** equivocar, confundir ‖ *intr* mezclarse; asociarse
mixed [mɪkst] *adj* mixto, mezclado; (*e.g., candy*) variados; (coll) confundido
mixed company *s* reunión de personas de ambos sexos
mixed drink *s* bebida mezclada
mixed feelings *s* concepto vacilante
mixer [ˋmɪksər] *s* (*of concrete*) mezcladora, hormigonera; **to be a good mixer** (coll) tener don de gentes

mixture [ˈmɪkstʃər] *s* mezcla, mixtura
mix′-up′ *s* confusión; enredo, lío; (*of people*) equivocación
mizzenmast [ˈmɪzən,mæst] *s* palo de mesana
mo. *abbr* **month**
moan [mon] *s* gemido ‖ *intr* gemir
moat [mot] *s* foso
mob [mɑb] *s* chusma, populacho; (*crowd bent on violence*) muchedumbre airada ‖ *v* (*pret & pp* **mobbed;** *ger* **mobbing**) *tr* asaltar, atropellar
mobile [ˈmobɪl] o [ˈmobil] *adj* móvil
mobile home *s* caravana fija, casa rodante
mobile telephone *s* teléfono portátil, móvil, o celular
mobility [moˈbɪlɪti] *s* movilidad
mobilization [,mobɪlɪˈzeʃən] *s* movilización
mobilize [ˈmobɪ,laɪz] *tr* movilizar ‖ *intr* movilizar, movilizarse
mob rule *s* gobierno del populacho
mobster [ˈmɑbstər] *s* (slang) gamberro, pandillero, gángster
mobsterism [ˈmɑbstə,rɪzəm] *s* gangsterismo; acciones de los gangsters
moccasin [ˈmɑkəsɪn] *s* mocasín *m*
Mocha coffee [ˈmokə] *s* moca *m,* café *m* de moca
mock [mɑk] *adj* simulado, fingido ‖ *s* burla, mofa ‖ *tr* burlarse de, mofarse de; despreciar; engañar ‖ *intr* mofarse; **to mock at** mofarse de
mocker•y [ˈmɑkəri] *s* (*pl* **-ies**) burla, mofa, escarnio; (*subject of derision*) hazmerreír *m;* (*poor imitation*) mal remedo; (*e.g., of justice*) negación
mock′ing•bird′ *s* burlón *m,* sinsonte *m*
mock orange *s* jeringuilla, celinda
mock privet *s* olivillo
mock turtle soup *s* sopa de cabeza de ternera
mock′-up′ *s* maqueta
mode [mod] *s* modo, manera; (*fashion*) moda; (gram) modo
mod•el [ˈmɑdəl] *adj* modelo, p.ej., **model city** ciudad modelo ‖ *s* modelo ‖ *v* (*pret & pp* **-eled** o **-elled;** *ger* **-eling** o **-elling**) *tr* (*to fashion in clay, wax, etc.*) modelar ‖ *intr* modelarse; servir de modelo
model airplane *s* aeromodelo
mod′el-air′plane builder *s* aeromodelista *mf*
model-airplane building *s* aeromodelismo
model apartment *s* (com) piso piloto (Esp)
model home *s* (com) casa modelo, casa piloto
modeling [ˈmɑdlɪŋ] *s* profesión de modelo; (*making models*) modelismo; (compu) modelado; (econ) modelización; (fa) modelado
model sailing *s* navegación de modelos a vela
modem [ˈmo,dɛm] *s* (compu) módem *m*
moderate [ˈmɑdərɪt] *adj* moderado; (*tiempo*) templado; (*precio*) módico ‖ [mɑdə,ret] *tr* moderar; presidir (*una asamblea*) ‖ *intr* moderarse
moderator [ˈmɑdə,retər] *s* (*over an assembly*) presidente *m;* (*mediator*) árbitro; (telv) presentador *m,* presentadora; (*for slowing down neutrons*) moderador *m*
modern [mɑdərn] *adj* moderno
modernize [ˈmɑdər,naɪz] *tr* modernizar
modest [ˈmɑdɪst] *adj* modesto
modes•ty [ˈmɑdɪsti] *s* (*pl* **-ties**) modestia
modicum [ˈmɑdɪkəm] *s* pequeña cantidad
modifier [ˈmɑdɪ,faɪ•ər] *s* (gram) modificante *m*
modi•fy [ˈmɑdɪ,faɪ] *v* (*pret & pp* **-fied**) *tr* modificar
modish [ˈmodɪʃ] *adj* de moda, elegante
modulate [ˈmɑdʒə,let] *tr & intr* modular
modulation [,mɑdʒəˈleʃən] *s* modulación
module [ˈmɑdʒul] *s* módulo; (aerosp, compu) módulo
mohair [ˈmo,hɛr] *s* mohair *m* (*pelo de cabra de Angora*)
moist [mɔɪst] *adj* húmedo, mojdo; (*weather*) lluvioso; (*eyes*) lagrimoso
moisten [ˈmɔɪsən] *tr* humedecer ‖ *intr* humedecerse
moisture [ˈmɔɪstʃər] *s* humedad
moisturize [ˈmɔɪstʃəraɪz] *tr* hidratar, humectar
moisturizing lotion *s* leche *f* hidratante *or* humectante
molar [ˈmolər] *s* diente *m* molar
molasses [məˈlæsɪz] *s* melaza
molasses candy *s* melcocha
mold [mold] *s* molde *m;* cosa moldeada; (*shape*) forma; (*fungus*) moho; (*humus*) mantillo; (fig) carácter *m,* índole *f* ‖ *tr* amoldar, moldear; (*to make moldy*) enmohecer ‖ *intr* enmohecerse
molder [ˈmoldər] *s* moldeador *m* ‖ *intr* convertirse en polvo, consumirse
molding [ˈmoldɪŋ] *s* moldeado; (*cornice, shaped strip of wood, etc.*) moldura
mold•y [ˈmoldi] *adj* (*comp* **-ier;** *super* **-iest**) (*overgrown with mold*) mohoso; (*stale*) rancio, pasado
mole [mol] *s* (*breakwater*) rompeolas *m;* (*inner harbor*) dársena; (*spot on skin*) lunar *m;* (*small mammal*) topo
molecular physics [məˈlɛkjələr] *s* física molecular
molecular weight *s* peso molecular
molecule [ˈmɑlɪ,kjul] *s* molécula
mole′hill′ *s* topinera
mole′skin′ *s* piel *f* de topo, molesquina
molest [məˈlɛst] *tr* molestar; faltar al respeto a (*una mujer*)
moll [mɑl] *s* (slang) mujer *f* del hampa; (slang) ramera
molli•fy [ˈmɑlɪ,faɪ] *v* (*pret & pp* **-fied**) *tr* apaciguar, aplacar
mollusk [ˈmɑləsk] *s* molusco
mollycoddle [ˈmɑlɪ,kɑdəl] *s* mantecón *m,* marica *m* ‖ *tr* consentir, mimar
molt [molt] *s* muda ‖ *intr* hacer la muda
molten [ˈmoltən] *adj* fundido, derretido; fundido, vaciado
molybdenum [məˈlɪbdɪnəm] o [,mɑlɪbˈdinəm] *s* molibdeno

mom [mɑm] *s* (coll) mamá
moment [ˈmomənt] *s* momento; **at any moment** de un momento a otro
momentary [ˈmomən,tɛri] *adj* momentáneo
momentous [moˈmɛntəs] *adj* importante, grave
momen•tum [moˈmɛntəm] *s* (*pl* **-tums** o **-ta** [tə]) ímpetu *m;* (mech) cantidad de movimiento
momma [ˈmɑmə] *s* (coll) mamá
mommy [ˈmɑmi] *s* (coll) mami, mamita
monarch [ˈmɑnərk] *s* monarca *m*
monarchic(al) [məˈnɑrkɪk(əl)] *adj* monárquico
monarchist [ˈmɑnərkɪst] *adj & s* monárquico, monarquista *mf*
monar•chy [ˈmɑnərki] *s* (*pl* **-chies**) monarquía
monaster•y [ˈmɑnəs,tɛri] *s* (*pl* **-ies**) monasterio
monastic [məˈnæstɪk] *adj* monástico
monasticism [məˈnæstɪ,sɪzəm] *s* monaquismo
Monday [ˈmʌndi] *s* lunes *m*
monetary [ˈmɑnɪ,tɛri] *adj* monetario; pecuniario
money [ˈmʌni] *s* dinero; **to make money** ganar dinero; dar dinero (*una empresa*)
mon′ey•bag′ *s* monedero, talega; **moneybags** (*wealth*) (coll) talegas; (*wealthy person*) (coll) ricacho
moneychanger [ˈmʌni,tʃendʒər] *s* cambista *mf*
moneyed [ˈmʌnid] *adj* adinerado
moneylender [ˈmʌni,lɛndər] *s* prestamista *mf*
mon′ey•mak′er *s* acaudalador *m;* (fig) manantial *m* de beneficios
money market *s* mercado de dinero, mercado monetario
money order *s* giro postal, orden *m* de pago
Mongol [ˈmɑŋgəl] *adj & s* mogol *mf*
Mongolian [mɑŋˈgolɪ•ən] *adj & s* mogol *mf*
mon•goose [ˈmɑŋgus] *s* (*pl* **-gooses**) mangosta
mongrel [ˈmʌŋgrəl] *adj & s* mestizo
monitor [ˈmɑnɪtər] *s* monitor *m* ‖ *tr* controlar (*la señal*); escuchar (*radio-transmisiones*); superentender
monk [mʌŋk] *s* monje *m*
monkey [ˈmʌŋki] *s* mono; simio; **to make a monkey of** tomar el pelo a ‖ *intr*—**to monkey around** haraganear; **to monkey with** ajar, manosear
monkey business *s* (coll) trapicheo, chanchullos; (*of children*) diabluras, travesuras; **to be up to some monkey business** (coll) estar haciendo alguna travesura
mon′key•shines′ *spl* (coll) monería, monada, payasada
monkey wrench *s* llave inglesa
monkhood [ˈmɑŋkhʊd] *s* monacato; los monjes
monkshood [ˈmɑŋks•hʊd] *s* cogulla de fraile
monocle [ˈmɑnəkəl] *s* monóculo
monogamy [məˈnɑgəmi] *s* monogamia
monogram [ˈmɑnə,græm] *s* monograma *m*
monograph [ˈmɑnə,græf] *s* monografía
monolithic [,mɑnəˈlɪθɪk] *adj* monolítico
monologue [ˈmɑnə,lɔg] *s* monólogo
monomania [,mɑnəˈmenɪ•ə] *s* monomanía
monomial [məˈnomɪ•əl] *s* monomio
monopolize [məˈnɑpə,laɪz] *tr* monopolizar; acaparar (*p.ej., la conversación*)
monopo•ly [məˈnɑpəli] *s* (*pl* **-lies**) monopolio
monorail [ˈmɑnə,rel] *s* monorriel *m*
monosyllable [ˈmɑnə,sɪləbəl] *s* monosílabo
monotheist [ˈmɑnə,θi•ɪst] *adj & s* monoteísta *mf*
monotonous [meˈnətənəs] *adj* monótono
monotony [meˈnətəni] *s* monotonía
monotype [ˈmɑnə,taɪp] *s* (*machine; method*) monotipia; (*machine*) monotipo
monotype operator *s* monotipista *mf*
monoxide [məˈnɑksaɪd] *s* monóxido
monseigneur [,mɑnsenˈjœr] *s* monseñor *m*
monsignor [mɑnˈsinjər] *s* (*pl* **monsignors** o **monsignori** [,mɔnsiˈnjori]) (eccl) monseñor *m*
monsoon [mɑnˈsun] *s* monsón *m*
monster [ˈmɑnstər] *adj* monstruoso ‖ *s* monstruo
monstrance [ˈmɑnstrəns] *s* (eccl) custodia, ostensorio
monstrosi•ty [mɑnˈstrɑsɪti] *s* (*pl* **-ties**) monstruosidad; esperpento
monstrous [ˈmɑnstrəs] *adj* monstruoso
month [mʌnθ] *s* mes *m*
month•ly [ˈmʌnθli] *adj* mensual ‖ *adv* mensualmente ‖ *s* (*pl* **-lies**) revista mensual; **monthlies** (coll) reglas
monument [ˈmɑnjəmənt] *s* monumento
moo [mu] *s* mugido ‖ *intr* mugir
mooch [mutʃ] *tr & intr* (coll) gorrear (Ecuad)
mood [mud] *s* humor *m,* genio; (gram) modo; **moods** accesos de mal humor
mood•y [ˈmudi] *adj* (*comp* **-ier;** *super* **-iest**) triste, hosco, melancólico; caprichoso, veleidoso
moon [mun] *s* luna
moon′beam′ *s* rayo lunar
moon′light′ *s* claror *m* de luna, luz *f* de la luna
moon′light′ing *s* multiempleo, pluriempleo
moon′sail′ *s* (naut) monterilla
moonscape [ˈmunskep] *s* paisaje *m* lunar
moon′shine′ *s* luz *f* de la luna; (*idle talk*) cháchara, música celestial; (coll) whisky destilado ilegalmente
moon shot *s* lanzamiento a la Luna
moor [mʊr] *s* brezal *m,* páramo ‖ *tr* (naut) amarrar ‖ *intr* (naut) echar las amarras ‖ **Moor** *s* moro
mooring [ˈmʊrɪŋ] *s* amarradero; **moorings** (*ropes*) amarras
Moorish [ˈmʊrɪʃ] *adj* moro
moor′land′ *s* brezal *m*
moose [mus] *s* (*pl* **moose**) alce *m* de América
moot [mut] *adj* discutible, dudoso
mop [mɑp] *s* aljofifa, fregasuelos *m,* estropajo; (*of hair*) espesura ‖ *v* (*pret & pp* **mopped;** *ger* **mopping**) *tr* aljofifar; enjugarse (*la frente con un pañuelo*); **to mop up** limpiar de enemigos
mope [mop] *intr* andar abatido, entregarse a la melancolía

moped [ˈmopɛd] *s* motoneta
mopish [ˈmopɪʃ] *adj* abatido, melancólico
moppet [ˈmapət] *s* (coll) angelito
moral [ˈmarəl] o [ˈmɔrəl] *adj* moral || *s* (*of a fable*) moraleja, moral *f;* **morals** (*ethics; conduct*) moral *f,* moralidad
morale [məˈræl] o [məˈral] *s* moral *f* (*estado de ánimo, confianza en sí mismo*)
moralistic [ˌmɔrəˈlɪstɪk] *adj* moralizador
morali•ty [məˈrælɪti] *s* (*pl* **-ties**) moralidad
morass [məˈræs] *s* pantano
moratori•um [ˌmɔrəˈtorɪ•əm] o [ˌmarəˈtorɪ•əm] *s* (*pl* **-ums** o **-a** [əl]) *s* moratoria
morbid [ˈmɔrbɪd] *adj* (*feelings, curiosity*) malsano; (*gruesome*) horripilante; (*pertaining to disease; pathologic*) morboso
mordacious [mɔrˈdeʃəs] *adj* mordaz
mordant [ˈmɔrdənt] *adj* mordaz || *s* mordiente *m*
more [mor] *adj & adv* más; **more and more** cada vez más; **more than** más que; (*followed by numeral*) más de; (*followed by verb*) más de lo que || *s* más *m*
more•o′ver *adv* además, por otra parte
Moresque [moˈrɛsk] *adj* moro; (archit) árabe || *s* estilo árabe
morgue [mɔrg] *s* depósito de cadáveres
moribund [ˈmɔriˌbʌnd] o [ˈmarɪˌbʌnd] *adj* moribundo
Moris•co [məˈrɪsko] *adj* morisco, moro || *s* (*pl* **-cos** o **-coes**) moro; moro de España
morning [ˈmɔrnɪŋ] *adj* matinal || *s* mañana; (*time between midnight and dawn*) madrugada; **in the morning** de mañana, por la mañana
morning coat *s* chaqué *m*
morn′ing•glo′ry *s* (*pl* **-ries**) dondiego de día
morning sickness *s* vómitos del embarazo
morning star *s* lucero del alba
Moroccan [məˈrakən] *adj & s* marroquí *mf* o marroquín *m*
morocco [məˈrako] *s* (*leather*) marroquí *m* o marroquín *m* || **Morocco** *s* Marruecos *m*
moron [ˈmoran] *s* (*person of arrested intelligence*) morón *m;* (coll) imbécil *mf*
morose [məˈros] *adj* adusto, hosco, malhumorado
morphine [ˈmɔrfin] *s* morfina
morphology [mɔrˈfalədʒi] *s* morfología
Morris chair [ˈmarɪs] o [ˈmɔrɪs] *s* poltrona extensible
morrow [ˈmaro] o [ˈmɔro] *s* (*future time*) mañana *m;* (*time following some event*) día *m* siguiente; **on the morrow** en el día de mañana; el día siguiente
Morse code *s* código Morse
morsel [ˈmɔrsəl] *s* bocadito; pedacito
mortal [ˈmɔrtəl] *adj & s* mortal *m*
mortality [mɔrˈtælɪti] *s* mortalidad; (*death or destruction on a large scale*) mortandad
mortality rate *s* tasa de mortalidad
mortar [ˈmɔrtər] *s* (*bowl used for crushing; mixture of lime, etc.*) mortero; (arti) mortero
mor′tar•board′ *s* esparavel *m;* gorro académico cuadrado
mortgage [ˈmɔrgɪdʒ] *s* hipoteca, crédito de vivienda, crédito hipotecario || *tr* hipotecar
mortgagee [ˌmɔrgɪˈdʒi] *s* acreedor hipotecario
mortgagor [ˈmɔrgɪdʒər] *s* deudor hipotecario
mortician [mɔrˈtɪʃən] *s* empresario de pompas fúnebres
morti•fy [ˈmɔrtɪˌfaɪ] *v* (*pret & pp* **-fied**) *tr* humillar; mortificar (*el cuerpo, las pasiones*); **to be mortified** avergonzarse
mortise [ˈmɔrtɪs] *s* mortaja, muesca || *tr* amortajar, enmuescar
mortise lock *s* cerradura embutida
mortuar•y [ˈmɔrtʃʊˌɛri] *adj* mortuorio || *s* (*pl* **-ies**) depósito de cadáveres; funeraria
mosaic [moˈze•ɪk] *m* mosaico
Moscow [ˈmaskaʊ] o [ˈmasko] *s* Moscú
Moses [ˈmozɪz] o [ˈmozɪs] *s* Moisés *m*
Mos•lem [ˈmazləm] o [ˈmasləm] *adj & s* var of **Muslim,** musulmán *m*
mosque [mask] *s* mezquita
mosqui•to [məsˈkito] *s* (*pl* **-toes** o **-tos**) mosquito
mosquito net *s* mosquitero
moss [mɔs] o [mas] *s* musgo
moss′back′ *s* (coll) reaccionario; (*old-fashioned person*) (coll) fósil *m*
moss•y [ˈmɔsi] o [ˈmasi] *adj* (*comp* **-ier;** *super* **-iest**) musgoso
most [most] *adj* más; la mayor parte de, los más de || *adv* más; muy, sumamente; (coll) casi || *s* la mayor parte, el mayor número, los más; **most of** la mayor parte de, el mayor número de; **to make the most of** sacar el mejor partido de
mostly [ˈmostli] *adv* por la mayor parte, mayormente; casi
moth [mɔθ] o [maθ] *s* mariposa nocturna; (*clothes moth*) polilla
moth ball *s* bola de alcanfor, bola de naftalina
moth′-ball′ fleet *s* (nav) flota en conserva
moth′-eat′en *adj* apolillado; (fig) anticuado
mother [ˈmʌðər] *adj* (*love*) maternal; (*tongue*) materno; (*country*) madre, mamá; (*church*) metropolitano || *s* madre *f;* (*an elderly woman*) (coll) tía || *tr* servir de madre a
moth′er•board′ *s* (compu) placa madre
mother country *s* madre patria
Mother Goose *s* supuesta autora o narradora de una colección de cuentos infantiles (in Spain: *Cuentos de Calleja*)
motherhood [ˈmʌðərˌhʊd] *s* maternidad
moth′er-in-law′ *s* (*pl* **mothers-in-law**) suegra
moth′er•land′ *s* patria
motherless [ˈmʌðərlɪs] *adj* huérfano de madre, sin madre
motherly [ˈmʌðərli] *adj* maternal
mother-of-pearl [ˈmʌðərəvˈpʌrl] *adj* nacarado || *s* nácar *m*
Mother's Day *s* día *m* de la madre
mother superior *s* superiora
mother tongue *s* (*language naturally acquired*

by reason of nationality) lengua materna; (*language from which another language is derived*) lengua madre, lengua matriz

mother wit *s* gracia natural, chispa

moth hole *s* apolilladura

moth•y [ˋmɔθi] o [ˋmɑθi] *adj* (*comp* **-ier;** *super* **-iest**) apolillado

motif [moˋtif] *s* motivo

motion [ˋmoʃən] *s* movimiento; (*signal, gesture*) seña, indicación; (*in a deliberating assembly*) moción; **to set in motion** poner en acción ‖ *intr* hacer señas con la mano o la cabeza

motionless [ˋmoʃənlɪs] *adj* inmoble, inmóvil

motion picture *s* película cinematográfica

mo'tion-pic'ture *adj* cinematográfico

motivate [ˋmotɪ,vet] *tr* animar, incitar, mover

motive [ˋmotɪv] *adj* (*promoting action*) motivo; (*producing motion*) motor ‖ *s* motivo

motive power *s* fuerza motriz, potencia motora o motriz; (rr) conjunto de locomotoras de un ferrocarril

motley [ˋmɑtli] *adj* abigarrado; mezclado, variado

motor [ˋmotər] *adj* motor ‖ *s* motor *m;* motor eléctrico; automóvil *m* ‖ *intr* viajar en automóvil

mo'tor•boat' *s* gasolinera, canoa automóvil

mo'tor•bus' *s* autobús *m*

motorcade [ˋmotər,ked] *s* caravana de automóviles

mo'tor•car' *s* automóvil *m*

mo'tor•cy'cle *s* motocicleta

motorcyclist [ˋmotərˋsaɪklɪst] *s* motociclista *mf*

motorist [ˋmotərɪst] *s* motorista *mf,* automovilista *mf*

motorize [ˋmotə,raɪz] *tr* motorizar

motor launch *s* lancha automóvil

motor•man [ˋmotərmən] *s* (*pl* **-men** [mən]) conductor *m* de tranvía, conductor de locomotora eléctrica

motor sailer [ˋselər] *s* motovelero

motor scooter *s* motoneta

motor ship *s* motonave *f*

motor truck *s* autocamión *m*

motor vehicle *s* vehículo motor, autovehículo

mottle [ˋmɑtəl] *tr* abigarrar, jaspear, motear

mot•to [ˋmɑto] *s* (*pl* **-toes** o **-tos**) lema *m,* divisa

mould [mold] *s, tr, & intr* var de **mold**

moulder [ˋmoldər] *s & intr* var de **molder**

moulding [ˋmoldɪŋ] *s* var de **molding**

mouldy [ˋmoldi] *adj* var de **moldy**

mound [maʊnd] *s* montón *m* de tierra; montecillo

mount [maʊnt] *s* (*hill, mountain*) monte *m;* (*horse for riding*) montura; (*setting for a jewel*) montadura; soporte *m;* cartón *m,* tela (*en que está pegada una fotografía*); (mach) montaje *m* ‖ *tr* subir (*una escalera, una cuesta*); subir a (*una plataforma*); escalar (*una muralla*); montar (*un servicio; una piedra preciosa*); poner a caballo; pegar (*vistas, pruebas*); (mil) montar (*la guardia*) ‖ *intr* montar, montarse; aumentar, subir (*los precios*)

mountain [ˋmaʊntən] *s* montaña; **to make a mountain out of a molehill** hacer de una pulga un camello

mountain climbing *s* alpinismo, montañismo

mountaineer [,maʊntəˋnɪr] *s* montañés *m*

mountainous [ˋmaʊntənəs] *adj* montañoso

mountain railroad *s* ferrocarril *m* de cremallera

mountain range *s* cordillera, sierra, cadena de montañas

mountain sickness *s* mal *m* de las montañas

mountebank [ˋmaʊntɪ,bæŋk] *s* saltabanco

mounting [ˋmaʊntɪŋ] *s* (*of a precious stone, of an astronomical instrument*) montura; papel *m* de soporte; papel o tela (*en que está pegada una fotografía*); (mach) montaje *m*

mourn [morn] *tr* llorar (*p.ej., la muerte de una persona*); lamentar (*una desgracia*) ‖ *intr* lamentarse; vestir de luto

mourner [ˋmornər] *s* doliente *mf;* (*person who makes a public profession of penitence*) penitente *mf;* (*person hired to attend a funeral*) plañidera; **mourners** duelo

mournful [ˋmornfəl] *adj* (*sorrowful*) doloroso; (*gloomy*) lúgubre

mourning [ˋmornɪŋ] *s* luto; **to be in mourning** estar de luto

mourning band *s* crespón *m* fúnebre, brazal *m* de luto

mouse [maʊs] *s* (*pl* **mice** [maɪs]) ratón *m,* laucha (Arg, Chile); (compu) ratón ‖ [maʊz] *intr* cazar ratones

mouse'hole' *s* ratonera

mouser [ˋmaʊzər] *s* cazador *m* de ratones

mouse'trap' *s* ratonera

moustache [məsˋtæʃ] o [məsˋtɑʃ] *s* bigote *m,* mostacho

mouth [maʊθ] *s* (*pl* **mouths** [maʊðz]) boca; (*of a river*) desembocadura, embocadura; **by mouth** por vía bucal; **to be born with a silver spoon in one's mouth** nacer de pie; **to make one's mouth water** hacérsele a uno la boca agua; **to not open one's mouth** no decir nunca esta boca es mía

mouthful [ˋmaʊθ,fʊl] *s* bocado

mouth organ *s* armónica de boca

mouth'piece' *s* (*of wind instrument*) boquilla; (*of bridle*) embocadura; (*spokesman*) portavoz *m*

mouth'wash' *s* enjuague *m,* enjuagadientes *m*

movable [ˋmuvəbəl] *adj* movible, móvil

move [muv] *s* movimiento; (*démarche*) acción, gestión, paso; (*from one house to another*) mudanza; **on the move** en marcha, en movimiento; **to get a move on** (slang) menearse, darse prisa; **to make a move** dar un paso; hacer una jugada ‖ *tr* mover; evacuar (*el vientre*); (*to stir, excite the feelings of*) conmover, enternecer; **to move up** adelantar (*una fecha*) ‖ *intr* moverse; desplazarse (*un viajante; un planeta*); mudarse, mudar de casa; (*e.g., to another store, to another city*) transladarse;

hacer una jugada; hacer una moción; venderse, tener salida (*una mercancía*); evacuarse, moverse (*el vientre*); **to move away** apartarse; marcharse; mudarse de casa; **to move in** instalarse; alternar con, frecuentar (*la buena sociedad*); **to move off** alejarse

movement [ˋmuvmənt] *s* movimiento; aparato de relojería; (*of the bowels*) evacuación; (*e.g., of a symphony*) tiempo

movie [ˋmuvi] *s* película, cinta

movie camera *s* filmadora, cámara cinematográfica

movie•goer [ˋmovi,go•ər] *s* aficionado al cine

movie star *s* cineasta *m*

moving [ˋmuvɪŋ] *adj* conmovedor, impresionante ‖ *s* movimiento; (*from one house to another*) mudanza

moving picture *s* película cinematográfica

moving spirit *s* alma (*de una empresa*)

moving van *s* camión *m* de mudanzas

mow [mo] *v* (*pret* **mowed;** *pp* **mowed** o **mown**) *tr* segar; **to mow down** matar (*soldados*) con fuego graneado ‖ *intr* segar

mower [ˋmo•ər] *s* segador *m;* segadora mecánica

mowing machine *s* segadora mecánica

Mozarab [moˋzærəb] *s* mozárabe *mf*

Mozarabic [moˋzærəbɪk] *adj* mozárabe

M.P. *abbr* **Member of Parliament, Military Police**

m.p.h. *abbr* **miles per hour**

Mr. [ˋmɪstər] *s* (*pl* **Messrs.** [ˋmɛsərz]) señor *m* (*tratamiento*)

Mrs. [ˋmɪsɪz] *s* señora (*tratamiento*)

MS. o **ms.** *abbr* **manuscript**

Mt. *abbr* **Mount**

much [mʌtʃ] *adj & pron* mucho; **too much** demasiado ‖ *adv* mucho; **however much** por mucho que; **how much** cuánto; **too much** demasiado; **very much** muchísimo

mucilage [ˋmjusɪlɪdʒ] *s* goma para pegar; (*gummy secretion in plants*) mucílago

muck [mʌk] *s* estiércol húmedo; suciedad, porquería; (min) zafra

muck′rake′ *intr* (coll) exponer ruindades

mucous [ˋmjukəs] *adj* mucoso

mucus [ˋmjukəs] *s* moco

mud [mʌd] *s* barro, o fango, lodo; **to sling mud at** llenar de fango

mud′bath *s* baño de lodo o fango

muddle [ˋmʌdəl] *s* confusión, embrollo ‖ *tr* confundir, embrollar; atontar, aturdir ‖ *intr* obrar torpemente; **to muddle through** salir del paso a pesar suyo

mud′dle•head′ *s* farraguista *mf,* cajón *m* de sastre

mud•dy [ˋmʌdi] *adj* (*comp* **-dier;** *super* **-diest**) barroso, fangoso, lodoso; (*obscure*) turbio ‖ *v* (*pret & pp* **-died**) *tr* embarrar, enturbiar

mud′guard′ *s* guardabarros *m*

mud′hole′ *s* atolladero, ciénaga

muezzin [mjuˋɛzɪn] *s* almuecín *m,* almuédano

muff [mʌf] *s* manguito ‖ *tr & intr* chapucear

muffin [ˋmʌfɪn] *s* mollete *m*

muffle [ˋmʌfəl] *tr* arropar; (*about the face*) embozar; amortiguar (*un ruido*); enfundar (*un tambor*)

muffler [ˋmʌflər] *s* bufanda, tapaboca; (aut) silenciador *m,* silencioso

mufti [ˋmʌfti] *s* traje *m* de paisano

mug [mʌg] *s* pichel *m;* (slang) jeta, hocico ‖ *v* (*pret & pp* **mugged;** *ger* **mugging**) *tr* (slang) fotografiar; (slang) atacar ‖ *intr* (slang) hacer muecas

mugger [ˋmʌgər] *s* ladron *m* asaltador

mugging [ˋmʌgɪŋ] *s* atraco

mug•gy [ˋmʌgi] *adj* (*comp* **-gier;** *super* **-giest**) bochornoso, sofocante

Muhammad [muˋhæməd] *s* Mahoma *m*

mulber•ry [ˋmʌl,bɛri] *s* (*pl* **-ries**) (*tree*) moral *m;* (*fruit*) mora

mulct [mʌlkt] *tr* defraudar

mule [mjul] *s* mulo, macho; (*slipper*) babucha

muleteer [,mjuləˋtɪr] *s* mulatero

mulish [ˋmjulɪʃ] *adj* terco, obstinado

mull [mʌl] *tr* calentar (*vino*) con especias ‖ *intr*—**to mull over** reflexionar sobre

mullion [ˋmʌljən] *s* parteluz *m*

multilateral [,mʌltɪˋlætərəl] *adj* (*having many sides*) multilátero; (*participated in by more than two nations*) multilateral

multimedia [ˋmʌltiˋmidi•ə] *adj* (compu) multimedia

multinational corporations *spl* multinacionales *mpl*

multiplatform [ˋmʌltiˋplætform] *s* (compu) multiplataforma

multiple [ˋmʌltɪpəl] *adj* múltiple, múltiplo ‖ *s* (math) múltiplo

mul′tiple-choice′ *adj* (*exam*) de opción múltiple

multiple sclerosis *s* esclerosis *f* múltiple

multiplex [ˋmʌltɪ,plɛks] *adj* múltiple

multiplici•ty [,mʌltɪˋplɪsɪti] *s* (*pl* **-ties**) multiplicidad

multi•ply [ˋmʌltɪ,plaɪ] *v* (*pret & pp* **-plied**) *tr* multiplicar ‖ *intr* multiplicar, multiplicarse

multipurpose [,mʌltɪˋpʌrpəs] *adj* múltiple de uso; versátil

multitasking [ˋmʌltiˋtæskɪŋ] *s* (compu) multitarea

multitude [ˋmʌltɪ,tjud] o [ˋmʌltɪ,tud] *s* multitud

multiuser [ˋmʌltiˋjuzər] *adj* multiusuario

mum [mʌm] *adj* callado; **mum's the word!** ¡punto en boca!; **to keep mum about** callar ‖ *interj* ¡chitón!

mumble [ˋmʌmbəl] *tr & intr* mascullar, mascujar

mumbo jumbo [ˋmʌmboˋdʒʌmbo] *s* (pej) jerga, jerigonza, galimatías *m*

mummer•y [ˋmʌməri] *s* (*pl* **-ies**) mojiganga

mum•my [ˋmʌmi] *s* (*pl* **-mies**) momia

mumps [mʌmps] *s* papera

munch [mʌntʃ] *tr* ronzar

mundane [ˈmʌnden] *adj* mundano
municipal [mjuˈnɪsɪpəl] *adj* municipal
municipali•ty [mju,nɪsɪˈpælɪti] *s* (*pl* **-ties**) municipio
munificent [mjuˈnɪfɪsənt] *adj* munífico
munition [mjuˈnɪʃən] *s* munición ‖ *tr* municionar
munition dump *s* depósito de municiones
mural [ˈmjʊrəl] *adj* mural ‖ *s* pintura mural; decoración mural
murder [ˈmʌrdər] *s* asesinato, homicidio ‖ *tr* asesinar; (*to spoil, mar*) (coll) estropear
murderer [ˈmʌrdərər] *s* asesino
murderess [ˈmʌrdərɪs] *s* asesina
murderous [ˈmʌrdərəs] *adj* asesino; cruel, sanguinario
murk•y [ˈmʌrki] *adj* (*comp* **-ier;** *super* **-iest**) (*hazy*) calinoso; (*gloomy*) lóbrego
murmur [ˈmʌrmər] *s* murmullo ‖ *tr & intr* murmurar
mus. *abbr* **museum, music**
muscle [ˈmʌsəl] *s* músculo; (fig) fuerza muscular
muscular [ˈmʌskjələr] *adj* musculoso
muse [mjuz] *s* musa; **the Muses** las Musas ‖ *intr* meditar, reflexionar; **to muse on** contemplar
museum [mjuˈzi•əm] *s* museo
mush [mʌʃ] *s* gachas; (coll) sentimentalismo exagerado, sensiblería
mush′room′ *s* hongo, seta ‖ *intr* aparecer de la noche a la mañana; **to mushroom into** convertirse rápidamente en
mushroom cloud *s* nube-hongo *f*
mush•y [ˈmʌʃi] *adj* (*comp* **-ier;** *super* **-iest**) mollar, pulposo; (coll) sensiblero, sobón; (*with women*) (coll) baboso; **to be mushy** (coll) hacerse unas gachas
music [ˈmjuzɪk] *s* música; **to face the music** (coll) afrontar las consecuencias; **to set to music** poner en música
musical [ˈmjuzɪkəl] *adj* musical; con dotes musicales ‖ *m* (*musical comedy*) comedia musical
musical chairs *spl* juego de las silletas vacías; (fig) un mero intercambio
musicale [,mjuzɪˈkæl] *s* velada musical, concierto casero
music box *s* caja de música
music cabinet *s* musiquero
music hall *s* salón *m* de conciertos; (Brit) teatro de variedades
musician [mjuˈzɪʃən] *s* músico
musicianship [mjuˈzɪʃən,ʃɪp] *s* musicalidad
musicologist [,mjuzɪˈkɑlədʒɪst] *s* musicólogo
musicology [,mjuzɪˈkɑlədʒi] *s* musicología
music rack o **music stand** *s* atril *m*
musk [mʌsk] *s* almizcle *m;* olor *m* de almizcle
musk deer *s* almizclero
musket [ˈmʌskɪt] *s* mosquete *m*
musketeer [,mʌskɪˈtɪr] *s* mosquetero
musk′mel′on *s* melón *m*
musk′rat′ *s* almizclera
Muslim [ˈmʌzləm] o [ˈmʌsləm] *adj & mf* musulmán, musulmana
Muslim calendar *s* calendario islámico
muslin [ˈmʌzlɪn] *s* muselina
muss [mʌs] *tr* (*the hair*) (coll) descabellar, desarreglar; (*clothing*) (coll) chafar, arrugar
muss•y [ˈmʌsi] *adj* (*comp* **-ier;** *super* **-iest**) desaliñado, desgreñado
must [mʌst] *s* mosto; (*mold*) moho; cosa que debe hacerse ‖ *v aux* **I must study my lesson** debo estudiar mi lección; **he must work tomorrow** tiene que trabajar mañana; **she must be ill** estará enferma
mustache [məsˈtæʃ], [məsˈtɑʃ], o [ˈmʌstæʃ] *s* bigote *m,* mostacho
mustard [ˈmʌstərd] *s* mostaza
mustard gas *s* gas *m* mostaza
mustard plaster *s* sinapismo, cataplasma *f*
muster [ˈmʌstər] *s* asamblea; matrícula de revista; **to pass muster** pasar revista; ser aceptable ‖ *tr* llamar a asamblea; reunir para pasar revista; reunir, acumular; **to muster in** alistar; **to muster out** dar de baja a; **to muster up courage** cobrar ánimo
muster roll *s* inventario; (mil) lista de revista; (naut) lista de dotación
mustn't *contr* **must not**
mus•ty [ˈmʌsti] *adj* (*comp* **-tier;** *super* **-tiest**) (*moldy*) mohoso; (*stale*) trasnochado; anticuado, pasado de moda
mutation [mjuˈteʃən] *s* mutación
mute [mjut] *adj & s* mudo ‖ *tr* poner sordina a
mute button *s* (telp, telv) tecla de silencio
mutilate [ˈmjutɪ,let] *tr* mutilar
mutilated *adj* mútilo, mutilado, mocho
mutineer [,mjutɪˈnɪr] *s* amotinado
mutinous [ˈmjutɪnəs] *adj* amotinado
muti•ny [ˈmjutɪni] *s* (*pl* **-nies**) motín *m* ‖ *v* (*pret & pp* **-nied**) *intr* amotinarse
mutt [mʌt] *s* (slang) perro cruzado; (slang) bobo, tonto
mutter [ˈmʌtər] *tr & intr* murmurar
mutton [ˈmʌtən] *s* carnero, carne *f* de carnero
mutton chop *s* chuleta de carnero
mutual [ˈmutʃʊ•əl] *adj* mutual, mutuo
mutual aid *s* apoyo mutuo
mutual benefit association *s* mutualidad
mutual fund *s* sociedad inversionista mutualista, fondo de inversión mobiliaria
mutual insurance company *s* mutua de seguros
mutual savings bank *s* mutua
muzzle [ˈmʌzəl] *s* (*projecting part of head of animal*) hocico; (*device to keep animal from biting*) bozal *m;* (*of firearm*) boca ‖ *tr* abozalar; (*to keep from speaking*) amordazar
my [maɪ] *adj poss* mi
myriad [ˈmɪrɪ•əd] *s* miríada
myrrh [mʌr] *s* mirra
myrtle [ˈmʌrtəl] *s* arrayán *m,* mirto
myself [maɪˈsɛlf] *pron pers* yo mismo; mí, mí mismo; me, p.ej., **I enjoyed myself** me divertí; **with myself** conmigo
mysterious [mɪsˈtɪrɪ•əs] *adj* misterioso

myster•y [ˈmɪstəri] *s* (*pl* **-ies**) misterio
mystic [ˈmɪstɪk] *adj & s* místico
mystical [ˈmɪstɪkəl] *adj* místico
mysticism [ˈmɪstɪˌsɪzəm] *s* misticismo
mystification [ˌmɪstɪfɪˈkeʃən] *s* confusión, mistificación
mysti•fy [ˈmɪstɪˌfaɪ] *v* (*pret & pp* **-fied**) *tr* rodear de misterio; (*to hoax*) confundir, mistificar
myth [mɪθ] *s* mito
mythical [ˈmɪθɪkəl] *adj* mítico
mythological [ˌmɪθəˈlɑdʒɪkəl] *adj* mitológico
mytholo•gy [mɪˈθɑlədʒi] *s* (*pl* **-gies**) mitología

N

N, n [ɛn] decimocuarta letra del alfabeto inglés
n. *abbr* **name, neuter, nominative, noon, north, northern, noun, number**
N. *abbr* **Nationalist, Navy, Noon, Norse, North, Northern, November**
NA *abbr* not applicable; not available
N.A. *abbr* **North America;** not applicable
NAACP *abbr* **National Association for the Advancement of Colored People**
nab [næb] *v* (*pret & pp* **nabbed;** *ger* **nabbing**) *tr* (slang) agarrar, coger; (slang) poner preso, prender
NAFTA [ˈnæftə] *s* (acronym) (**North American Free Trade Agreement**) NAFTA *m*
nag [næg] *s* caballejo, jaco; pequeño caballo de silla || *v* (*pret & pp* **nagged;** *ger* **nagging**) *tr* importunar regañando || *intr* regañar
nail [nel] *s* (*of finger*) uña; (*to fasten wood, etc.*) clavo; **to hit the nail on the head** dar en el clavo || *tr* clavar
nail brush *s* cepillo de uñas
nail clippers *spl* cortauñas *m*
nail file *s* lima para las uñas
nail polish *s* esmalte *m* para las uñas, laca de uñas
nailset [ˈnelˌsɛt] *s* contrapunzón *m*
naïve [nɑˈiv] *adj* cándido, ingenuo
naked [ˈnekɪd] *adj* desnudo; **to go naked** ir desnudo, andar a la cordobana; **to strip naked** desnudar; desnudarse; **with the naked eye** a simple vista
name [nem] *s* nombre *m;* (*first name*) nombre de pila; (*last name*) apellido; fama, reputación, renombre *m;* linaje, *m,* raza; **to call someone names** maltratar a uno de palabra; **to go by the name of** ser conocido por el nombre de; **to make a name for oneself** darse a conocer, hacerse un nombre; **what is your name?** ¿cómo se llama Ud.? || *tr* nombrar; fijar (*un precio*)
name day *s* santo
name dropping *s* costumbre de mencionar amigos o personas importantes para presumir
nameless [ˈnemlɪs] *adj* sin nombre, anónimo
namely [ˈnemli] *adv* a saber, es decir
namesake [ˈnemˌsek] *s* homónimo, tocayo
nanny goat [ˈnæni] *s* (coll) cabra
nap [næp] *s* lanilla, flojel *m;* sueñecillo; **to take a nap** descabezar un sueñecillo || *v* (*pret & pp* **napped;** *ger* **napping**) *intr* echar un sueñecillo; estar desprevenido; **to catch napping** coger desprevenido
napalm [ˈnepɑm] *s* (mil) gelatina incendiaria
nape [nep] *s* cogote *m,* nuca
naphtha [ˈnæfθə] *s* nafta
napkin [ˈnæpkɪn] *s* servilleta; (*of a baby*) (Brit) pañal *m*
napkin ring *s* servilletero
Napoleonic [nəˌpolɪˈɑnɪk] *adj* napoleónico
narc [nɑrk] *s* (slang) agente *m* de policía antidroga
narcissus [nɑrˈsɪsəs] *s* (bot) narciso || **Narcissus** *s* Narciso
narcotic [nɑrˈkɑtɪk] *adj & s* narcótico
narrate [næˈret] *tr* narrar
narration [næˈreʃən] *s* narración
narrative [ˈnærətɪv] *adj* narrativo || *s* (*story, tale; art of telling stories*) narrativa
narrator [næˈretər] *s* narrador *m*
narrow [ˈnæro] *adj* angosto, estrecho; intolerante; minucioso; (*sense of a word*) estricto || **narrows** *spl* angostura, paso estrecho || *tr* enangostar, estrechar; reducir, limitar || *intr* enangostarse, estrecharse; reducirse, limitarse
narrow escape *s* trance *m* difícil; **to have a narrow escape** escapar por un pelo, salvarse en una tabla
narrow gauge *s* trocha angosta, vía estrecha
narrow-minded [ˈnæroˈmaɪndɪd] *adj* intolerante, de miras estrechas, poco liberal
nasal [ˈnezəl] *adj & s* nasal *f*
nasalize [ˈnezəˌlaɪz] *tr* nasalizar || *intr* ganguear
nasturtium [nəˈstʌrʃəm] *s* capuchina, espuela de galán
nas•ty [ˈnæsti] *adj* (*comp* **-tier;** *super* **-tiest**) asqueroso, sucio; desagradable; horrible, feo; (*threatening*) amenazador; (*shameless*) desvergonzado; **to do the nasty** (slang) tener relaciones sexuales
nation [ˈneʃən] *s* nación
national [ˈnæʃənəl] *adj & s* nacional *mf*
national anthem *s* himno nacional
national hero *s* benemérito de la patria
national holiday *s* fiesta nacional
nationalism [ˈnæʃənəˌlɪzəm] *s* nacionalismo
nationalist [ˈnæˌʃənəlɪst] *adj & s* nacionalista *mf*

nationali•ty [ˈnæ,ʃən,ælɪti] *s* (*pl* **-ties**) nacionalidad, naturalidad
nationalize [ˈnæʃənə,laɪz] *tr* nacionalizar
na'tion-wide' *adj* de toda la nación
native [ˈnetɪv] *adj* nativo, natural; indígena; (*language*) materno; **to go native** vivir como los indígenas ‖ *s* natural *mf;* indígena *mf*
native land *s* patria
nativi•ty [nəˈtɪvɪti] *s* (*pl* **-ties**) nacimiento ‖ **Nativity** *s* (*day; festival; painting*) natividad
NATO [ˈneto] *s* (acronym) (**North Atlantic Treaty Organization**) la OTAN (Organización del Tratado del Atlántico Norte)
nat•ty [ˈnæti] *adj.* (*comp* **-tier;** *super* **-tier;** *super* **-tiest**) elegante, garboso
natural [ˈnætʃərəl] *adj* natural; (mus) natural ‖ *s* imbécil *mf;* (mus) tono natural, nota natural; (*sign*) (mus) becuadro; (mus) tecla blanca; (coll) cosa de éxito certero
naturalism [ˈnætʃərə,lɪzəm] *s* naturalismo
naturalist [ˈnætʃərəlɪst] *s* naturalista *mf*
naturalization [,nætʃərəlɪˈzəʃən] *s* naturalización
naturalization papers *spl* carta de naturaleza
naturalize [ˈnætʃərə,laɪz] *tr* naturalizar
naturally [ˈnætʃərəli] *adv* naturalmente; claro, desde luego, por supuesto
natural science *s* ciencias naturales
nature [ˈnetʃər] *s* naturaleza; **from nature** del natural
nature trail *s* ruta ecología (*circuito educativo en bosque*)
naught [nɔt] *s* nada; cero; **to bring to naught** anular, invalidar, destruir; **to come to naught** reducirse a nada, frustrarse
naugh•ty [ˈnɔti] *adj* (*comp* **-tier;** *super* **-tiest**) desobediente, pícaro; desvergonzado; (*story, tale*) verde
nausea [ˈnɔʃi•ə] o [ˈnɔsɪ•ə] *s* náusea
nauseate [ˈnɔʃi,et] o [ˈnɔsɪ,et] *tr* dar náuseas a ‖ *intr* nausear, marearse
nauseating [ˈnɔʃi,etɪŋ] o [ˈnɔsɪ,etɪŋ] *adj* nauseabundo, asqueroso
nauseous [ˈnɔʃi•əs] o [ˈnɔsɪ•əs] *adj* nauseabundo
nautical [ˈnɔtɪkəl] *adj* náutico, marino, naval
nav. *abbr* **naval, navigation**
naval [ˈnevəl] *adj* naval, naval militar
Naval Academy *s* (U.S.A.) Escuela Naval Militar
naval officer *s* official *m* de marina
naval station *s* apostadero
nave [nev] *s* (*of a church*) nave *f* central, nave principal; (*of a wheel*) cubo
navel [ˈnevəl] *s* ombligo; (*center point, middle*) (fig) ombligo
navel orange *s* navel *f,* naranja de ombligo
navigability [,nævɪgəˈbɪlɪti] *s* (*of a river*) navegabilidad; (*of a ship*) buen gobierno
navigable [ˈnævɪgəbəl] *adj* (*river, canal, etc.*) navegable; (*ship*) marinero, de buen gobierno
navigate [ˈnævɪ,get] *tr & intr* navegar
navigation [ˈnævɪ,geʃən] *s* navegacion
navigation lights *spl* faroles *mpl* de situación
navigator [ˈnævɪ,getər] *s* navegador *m,* navegante *mf;* (*he or she who is in charge of course of ship or plane*) oficial *m* de derrota; (aer) navegante; (compu) navegador
nav•vy [ˈnævi] *s* (*pl* **-vies**) (Brit) bracero, peón *m*
na•vy [ˈnevi] *adj* azul oscuro ‖ *s* (*pl* **-vies**) marina de guerra; (*personnel*) marina; azul oscuro
navy bean *s* frijol blanco común
navy blue *s* azul marino, azul oscuro
navy yard *s* arsenal *m* de puerto
Nazi [ˈnɑtsi] o [ˈnætsi] *adj & s* nazi *mf,* nacista *mf*
n.b. *abbr* **nota bene** (Lat) (**note well** nótese bien)
N-bomb [ˈɛn,bɑm] *s* bomba de neutrones
Neapolitan [,ni•əˈpɑlitən] *adj & s* napolitano
neap tide [nip] *s* marea muerta
near [nɪr] *adj* cercano, próximo; íntimo; imitado ‖ *adv* cerca; íntimamente ‖ *prep* cerca de; hacia, por ‖ *tr* acercarse a ‖ *intr* acercarse
nearby [ˈnɪr,baɪ] *adj* cercano, próximo ‖ *adv* cerca
Near East *s* Cercano Oriente, Próximo Oriente
nearly [ˈnɪrli] *adv* casi; de cerca; íntimamente; por poco, p.ej., **he nearly fell** por poco se cae
near miss *s* (aer, auto) casi una colisión
near-sighted [ˈnɪrˈsaɪtɪd] *adj* miope
near-sightedness *s* miopía
neat [nit] *adj* aseado, pulcro; pulido; diestro, primoroso; puro, sin mezcla, solo; (slang) fantástico ‖ *adv*—**I drink it neat** lo bebo solo
nebu•la [ˈnɛbjələ] *s* (*pl* **-lae** [,li] o **-las**) nebulosa
nebular [ˈnɛbjələr] *adj* nebular
nebulous [ˈnɛbjələs] *adj* nebuloso
necessary [ˈnɛsɪ,sɛri] *adj* necesario
necessitate [nɪˈsɛsɪ,tet] *tr* necesitar, exigir
necessitous [nɪˈsɛsɪtəs] *adj* necesitado
necessi•ty [nɪˈsɛsɪti] *s* (*pl* **-ties**) necesidad
neck [nɛk] *s* cuello; (*of a bottle*) gollete *m;* (*of violin or guitar*) mástil *m;* istmo, península; estrecho; **neck and neck** parejos; **to break one's neck** (coll) matarse trabajando; **to stick one's neck out** (coll) descubrir el cuerpo ‖ *intr* (coll) besuquearse, besucarse, acariciarse (*dos enamorados*)
neck and neck *adj* a la par, parejos ‖ *adv* a la par, parejo
neck'band' *s* tirilla de camisa
necklace [ˈnɛklɪs] *s* gargantilla, collar *m*
necktie [ˈnɛk,taɪ] *s* corbata
necktie pin *s* alfiler *m* de corbata
necrology [nɛˈkrɑlədʒi] *s* necrología
necromancy [ˈnɛkrə,mænsi] *s* necromancia, nigromancia
nectarine [,nɛktəˈrin] *s* griñón *m*
née o **nee** [ne] *adj* nacida o de soltera, p.ej., **Mary Wilson, née Miller** Maria Wilson, nacida Miller o María Wilson, de soltera Miller
need [nid] *s* necesidad; pobreza; **in need** necesitado ‖ *tr* necesitar ‖ *intr* estar necesitado; ser

necesario || *v aux*—**if need be** si fuere necesario; **to need** + *inf* deber, tener que + *inf*
needful [ˈnidfəl] *adj* necesario
needle [ˈnidəl] *s* aguja; **to look for a needle in a haystack** buscar una aguja en un pajar || *tr* coser con aguja; (coll) aguijonear, incitar; (coll) añadir alcohol a (*la cerveza o el vino*)
needle bath *s* ducha en alfileres
needle'case' *s* alfiletero
needle point *s* bordado al pasado; encaje *m* de mano
needless [ˈnidlɪs] *adj* innecesario, inútil
needle'work' *s* costura, labor *f*
needs [nidz] *adv* necesariamente, forzosamente
need•y [ˈnidi] *adj* (*comp* **-ier;** *super* **-iest**) necesitado, indigente || **the needy** los necesitados
ne'er-do-well [ˈnɛrdu,wɛl] *adj* & *s* holgazán, perdido
negation [nɪˈgeʃən] *s* negación
negative [ˈnɛgətɪv] *adj* negativo || *s* negativa; electricidad negativa, borne negativo; (gram) negación; (math) término negativo; (phot) prueba negativa; **to answer in the negative** contestar con una negativa
negative feedback *s* (electron, rad) realimentación negativa
neglect [nɪˈglɛkt] *s* negligencia, descuido || *tr* descuidar; **to neglect to** dejar de, olvidarse de
neglectful [nɪˈglɛktfəl] *adj* negligente, descuidado
négligée o **negligee** [,nɛglɪˈʒe] *s* bata de mujer, traje *m* de casa
negligence [ˈnɛglɪdʒəns] *s* negligencia, descuido
negligent [ˈnɛglɪdʒənt] *adj* negligente, descuidado
negligible [ˈnɛglɪdʒɪbəl] *adj* insignificante, imperceptible
negotiable [nɪˈgoʃi•əbəl] *adj* negociable; transitable
negotiate [nɪˈgoʃi,et] *tr* negociar; (coll) salvar, vencer || *intr* negociar
negotiation [nɪ,goʃiˈeʃən] *s* negociación; trámite *m;* **round of negotiations** ronda negociadora
Ne•gro [ˈnigro] *adj* (*usually offensive*) negro || *s* (*pl* **-groes**) (*usually offensive*) negro
neigh [ne] *s* relincho || *intr* relinchar
neighbor [ˈnebər] *adj* vecino || *s* vecino; (*fellow man*) prójimo || *tr* ser vecino de; ser amigo de || *intr* estar cercano; tener relaciones amistosas
neighborhood [ˈnebər,hʊd] *s* vecindad, vecindario, cercanías; **in the neighborhood of** en las inmediaciones de; (coll) cerca de, aproximadamente
neighboring [ˈnebərɪŋ] *adj* vecino, colindante
neighborly [ˈnebərli] *adj* buen vecino, amable, sociable
neither [ˈniðər] o [ˈnaɪðər] *adj indef* ninguno . . . (de los dos); **neither one** ninguno de los dos || *pron indef* ninguno (de los dos); ni uno ni otro, ni lo uno ni lo otro || *conj* ni; tampoco, ni . . . tampoco, p.ej., **neither do I** yo tampoco, ni yo tampoco; **neither . . . nor** ni . . . ni
neme•sis [ˈnɛmɪsɪs] *s* (*pl* **-ses** [,siz]) (*someone or something that punishes*) némesis *f* || **Nemesis** *s* Némesis *f*
neologism [niˈɑlə,dʒɪzəm] *s* neologismo
neomycin [,ni•əˈmaɪsɪn] *s* neomicina
neon [ˈni•ɑn] *s* neo, neón *m*
neon sign *s* letrero luminoso o de neón
neophyte [ˈni•ə,faɪt] *s* neófito
Nepal [nɪˈpɔl] *s* el Nepal
nephew [ˈnɛfju] o [ˈnɛvju] *s* sobrino
Neptune [ˈnɛptun] *s* (astr, myth) Neptuno
neptunium [nɛpˈtʃunɪ•əm] o [nɛpˈtjunɪ•əm] *s* neptunio
nerd [nʌrd] *s* (slang) tipo insípido; sujeto estúpido
Nero [ˈnɪro] *s* Nerón *m*
nerve [nʌrv] *adj* (*center; system; tonic; disease; prostration; breakdown*) nervioso || *s* nervio; ánimo, valor *m;* audacia; (coll) descaro; **nerves** excitabilidad nerviosa; **to get on one's nerves** irritar los nervios a uno; **to strain every nerve** esforzarse al máximo
nerve gas *s* gas *m* neurotóxico *or* nervioso
nerve-racking [ˈnʌrv,rækɪŋ] *adj* irritante, exasperante
nervous [ˈnʌrvəs] *adj* nervioso
nervous breakdown *s* colapso nervioso
nervousness [ˈnʌrvəsnɪs] *s* nerviosidad
nervous shudder *s* muerte chiquita
nerv•y [ˈnʌrvi] *adj* (*comp* **-ier;** *super* **-iest**) (*strong, vigorous*) nervioso; atrevido, audaz; (coll) descarado
nest [nɛst] *s* nido; (*where hen lays eggs*) nidal *m;* (*birds in a nest*) nidada; (*set of things fitting within each other*) juego; (*of, e.g., thieves*) nido; **to feather one's nest** hacer todo para enriquecerse || *tr* colocar en un nido || *intr* anidar
nest egg *s* (*eggs left in a nest to induce hen to lay more*) nidal *m;* (coll) ahorros, hucha
nestle [ˈnɛsəl] *tr* poner en un nido; arrimar afectuosamente || *intr* anidar; arrimarse cómodamente; **to nestle up to** arrimarse a
nest of tables *s* mesa nido
net [nɛt] *adj* neto, líquido || *s* red *f;* precio neto, peso neto, ganancia líquida || *v* (*pret & pp* **netted;** *super* **netting**) *tr* enredar, tejer; coger con red; producir (*cierta ganancia líquida*)
nether [ˈnɛðər] *adj* inferior, más bajo
Netherlander [ˈnɛðər,lændər] o [ˈnɛðərləndər] *s* neerlandés *m*
Netherlands, The [ˈnɛðərləndz] los Países Bajos (*Holanda*)
net income *s* ingresos netos
netting [ˈnɛtɪŋ] *s* red *f*
nettle [ˈnɛtəl] *s* ortiga || *tr* irritar, provocar
net'work' *s* red *f;* (rad & telv) cadena
neuralgia [njʊˈrældʒə] *s* neuralgia
neurology [njʊˈrɑlədʒi] *s* neurología
neuron [ˈnjʊrɑn] o [ˈnurɑn] *s* neurona

neuro•sis [njʊˋrosɪs] *s* (*pl* **-ses** [siz]) neurosis *f*
neurotic [njʊˋrɑtɪk] *adj & s* neurótico
neuter [ˋnjutər] *adj* neutro ‖ *s* género neutro; (aut) punto muerto ‖ *tr* castrar, capar
neutral [ˋnjutrəl] *adj* (*on neither side in a quarrel or war*) neutral; (*having little or no color*) neutro; (bot, chem, elec, phonet, zool) neutro ‖ *s* neutral *mf;* (aut) punto neutral, punto muerto
neutralist [ˋnjutrəlɪst] *adj & s* neutralista *mf*
neutrality [njuˋtrælɪti] *s* neutralidad
neutralize [ˋnjutrə,laɪz] *tr* neutralizar
neutron [ˋnjutrɑn] *s* neutrón *m*
neutron bomb *s* bomba de neutrones, bomba neutrónica
never [ˋnɛvər] *adv* nunca; en mi vida; de ningún modo; **never fear** no hay cuidado; **never mind** no importa
nev'er•more' *adv* nunca más
nevertheless [,nɛvərðəˋlɛs] *adv* no obstante, sin embargo
new [nju] o [nu] *adj* nuevo; **what's new?** ¿qué hay de nuevo?
new arrival *s* recién llegado; recién nacido
new'born' *adj* recién nacido; renacido
New Castile *s* Castilla la Nueva
New'cas'tle *s*—**to carry coals to Newcastle** echar agua al mar, llevar hierro a Vizcaya, llevar leña al monte
newcomer [ˋnju,kʌmər] *s* recién llegado, recién venido
New England *s* la Nueva Inglaterra
newfangled [ˋnju,fæŋgəld] *adj* de última moda, recién inventado
Newfoundland [ˋnjufənd,lænd] *s* (*island and province*) Terranova ‖ [njuˋfaʊndlənd] *s* (*dog*) Terranova *m*
newly [ˋnjuli] *adv* nuevamente; **newly** + *pp* recién + *pp*
new'ly•wed' *s* recién casado
New Mexican *adj & s* neomejicano, nuevomejicano
New Mexico *s* Nuevo Méjico
new moon *s* luna nueva, novilunio
news [njuz] o [nuz] *s* noticias; periódico; **a news item** una noticia; **a piece of news** una noticia
news agency *s* agencia de noticias
news beat *s* exclusiva, anticipación de una noticia por un periódico
news'boy' *s* vendedor *m* de periódicos
news bulletin *s* boletín informativo, boletín de noticias
news'cast' *s* noticiario, informativo
news'cast'er *s* presentador *m,* locutor *m*
news coverage *s* reportaje *m*
news'group' *s* (compu) tertulia
news'let'ter *s* circular *f* noticiera
news•man [ˋnjuzmən] *s* (*pl* **-men** [mən]) noticiero
news'pa'per *adj* periodístico ‖ *s* periódico
newspaper•man [ˋnjuz,pepər,mæn] *s* (*pl* **-men** [,mɛn]) periodista *m*
news'print' *s* papel-prensa *m,* papel *m* (de) periódico *or* prensa
news'reel' *s* noticiario cinematográfico
news'room' *s* sala de redacción
news'stand' *s* quiosco de periódicos, puesto de periódicos
news'week'ly *s* (*pl* **-lies**) semanario de noticias
news'wor'thy *adj* de gran actualidad, de interés periodístico
news•y [ˋnjuzi] *adj* (*comp* **-ier;** *super* **-iest**) (coll) informativo
new'-world' *adj* del Nuevo Mundo
New Year's card *s* tarjeta de felicitación de Año Nuevo
New Year's Day *s* el Día de Año Nuevo
New Year's Eve *s* la noche vieja, la víspera de año nuevo
New York [jɔrk] *adj* neoyorkino ‖ *s* Nueva York
New Yorker [ˋjɔrkər] *s* neoyorkino
New Zealand [ˋzilənd] *adj* neocelandés ‖ *s* Nueva Zelanda
New Zealander [ˋziləndər] *s* neocelandés *m*
next [nɛkst] *adj* próximo, siguiente; de al lado; venidero, que viene ‖ *adv* luego, después; la próxima vez; **next to** junto a; después de; **next to nothing** casi nada; **the next best** lo mejor después de eso; **to come next** venir después, ser el que sigue
next door *s* la casa de al lado; **next door to** en la casa siguiente de; (coll) casi
next'door' *adj* siguiente, de al lado
next of kin *s* (*pl* **next of kin**) pariente más cercano
niacin [ˋnaɪ•əsɪn] *s* niacina
Niagara Falls [naɪˋægərə] *spl* las Cataratas del Niágara
nibble [ˋnɪbəl] *s* mordisco ‖ *tr & intr* mordiscar; picar (*un pez*); **to nibble at** picar de o en
Nicaraguan [,nɪkəˋrɑgwən] *adj & s* nicaragüense, nicaragüeño
nice [naɪs] *adj* delicado, fino, sutil; primoroso, pulido, refinado; dengoso, melindroso; atento, cortés, culto; escrupuloso, esmerado; agradable, simpático; decoroso, conveniente; complaciente; preciso; satisfactorio; (*weather*) bueno; (*attractive*) bonito; **nice and . . .** (coll) muy, mucho; **not nice** (coll) feo
nice-looking [ˋnaɪsˋlʊkɪŋ] *adj* hermoso, guapo, bien parecido
nicely [ˋnaɪsli] *adv* con precisión; escrupulosamente; satisfactoriamente; (coll) muy bien
nice•ty [ˋnaɪsəti] *s* (*pl* **-ties**) precisión; sutileza; finura; **to a nicety** con la mayor precisión
niche [nɪtʃ] *s* hornacina, nicho; (ecol, econ) nicho; (fig) colocación, lugar *m*
Nicholas [ˋnɪkələs] *s* Nicolás *m*
nick [nɪk] *s* mella, muesca; **in the nick of time** en el momento crítico ‖ *tr* mellar, hacer muescas en; cortar
nickel [ˋnɪkəl] *s* níquel *m;* (U.S.A.) moneda de cinco centavos ‖ *tr* niquelar
nick'el-plate' *tr* niquelar
nicknack [ˋnɪk,næk] *s* chuchería, friolera
nick'name' *s* apodo, mote *m* ‖ *tr* apodar
nicotine [ˋnɪkə,tin] *s* nicotina

niece [nis] *s* sobrina
nif•ty [ˈnɪfti] *adj* (*comp* **-tier;** *super* **-tiest**) (coll) elegante; (coll) excelente
niggard [ˈnɪgərd] *adj & s* tacaño
night [naɪt] *adj* nocturno || *s* noche *f;* **at** o **by night** de noche or por la noche; **night before last** anteanoche; **to make a night of it** (coll) divertirse hasta muy entrada la noche
night'cap' *s* gorro de dormir; trago antes de acostarse, sosiega
nightclub *s* cabaret *m,* café *m* cantante, sala de fiestas
night driving *s* conducción de noche
night'fall' *s* anochecer *m,* caída de la noche
night'gown' *s* camisa de dormir
nightingale [ˈnaɪtən,gel] *s* ruiseñor *m*
night latch *s* cerradura de resorte
night letter *s* carta telegráfica nocturna
night'light' *s* lamparilla
night'long' *adj* de toda la noche || *adv* durante toda la noche
nightly [ˈnaɪtli] *adj* nocturno; de cada noche || *adv* de noche, por la noche; cada noche
night'mare' *s* pesadilla
nightmarish [ˈnaɪt,mɛrɪʃ] *adj* espeluznante, horroroso, pesadillesco
night owl *s* buho nocturno; (coll) anochecedor *m,* trasnochador *m,* sonámbulo
night school *s* escuela nocturna
night'shade' *s* (bot) solano
night'shirt' *s* camisa de dormir
night'time' *adj* nocturno || *s* noche *f*
night'walk'er *s* ladrón nocturno; ramera callejera nocturna
night watch *s* guardia de noche, ronda de noche; sereno; (mil) vigilia
night watchman *s* vigilante nocturno
nihilism [ˈnaɪ•ɪ,lɪzəm] *s* nihilismo
nihilist [ˈnaɪ•ɪlɪst] *s* nihilista *mf*
nil [nɪl] *s* nada
Nile [naɪl] *s* Nilo
nimble [ˈnɪmbəl] *adj* ágil, ligero; listo, vivo
nim•bus [ˈnɪmbəs] *s* (*pl* **-buses** o **-bi** [baɪ]) nimbo
Nimrod [ˈnɪmrɑd] *s* Nemrod *m*
nincompoop [ˈnɪnkəm,pup] *s* bobo, necio, tonto, papanatas *m,* papirote *m*
nine [naɪn] *adj & pron* nueve || *s* nueve *m;* equipo de béisbol; **nine o'clock** las nueve; **the Nine** las nueve musas
nine/eleven (9/11) o **9–11** o **Sept. 11** *s* (fecha de) la destrucción del Centro del Comercio Mundial de Nueva York por un ataque terrorista
nine hundred *adj & pron* novecientos || *s* novecientos *m*
nineteen [ˈnaɪnˈtin] *adj, pron & s* diecinueve *m,* diez y nueve *m*
nineteenth [ˈnaɪnˈtinθ] *adj & s* (*in a series*) decimonono; (*part*) diecinueveavo || *s* (*in dates*) diecinueve *m*
ninetieth [ˈnaɪntɪ•ɪθ] *adj & s* (*in a series*) nonagésimo; (*part*) noventavo
nine•ty [ˈnaɪnti] *adj & pron* noventa || *s* (*pl* **-ties**) noventa *m*
ninth [ˈnaɪnθ] *adj & s* nono, noveno || *s* (*in dates*) nueve *m*
nip [nɪp] *s* mordisco, pellizco; helada, escarcha; traguito; **nip and tuck** a quién ganará || *v* (*pret & pp* **nipped;** *ger* **nipping**) *tr* mordiscar, pellizcar; helar, escarchar; (slang) asir, coger; **to nip in the bud** atajar en el principio || *intr* beborrotear
nipple [ˈnɪpəl] *s* (*of female*) pezón *m;* (*of male; of nursing bottle*) tetilla; (mach) tubo roscado de unión, entrerrosca
Nippon [nɪˈpɑn] *s* el Japón
Nippon•ese [,nɪpəˈniz] *adj* nipón || *s* (*pl* **-ese**) nipón *m*
nip•py [ˈnɪpi] *adj* (*comp* **-pier;** *super* **-piest**) mordaz, picante; frío, helado; (Brit) ágil, ligero
nirvana [nɪrˈvɑnə] *s* el nirvana
nit [nɪt] *s* piojito; (*egg of insect*) liendre *f*
niter [ˈnaɪtər] *s* nitro; (agr) nitro de Chile
nit'pick' *intr* (coll) pararse en pequeñeces
nitrate [ˈnaɪtret] *s* nitrato; (agr) nitrato de potasio, nitrato de sodio
nitric acid [ˈnaɪtrɪk] *s* ácido nítrico
nitride [ˈnaɪtraɪd] *s* nitruro
nitrogen [ˈnaɪtrədʒən] *s* nitrógeno
nitroglycerin [,naɪtrəˈglɪsərɪn] *s* nitroglicerina
nitrous oxide [ˈnaɪtrəs] *s* óxido nitroso
nitwit [ˈnɪt,wɪt] *s* (slang) bobalicón *m*
no [no] *adj indef* ninguno; **no admittance** no se permite la entrada; **no matter** no importa; **no parking** se prohibe estacionarse; **no smoking** se prohibe fumar; **no thoroughfare** prohibido el paso; **no use** inútil; **with no** sin || *adv* no; **no good** de ningún valor; ruin, vil; **no longer** ya no; **no sooner** no bien || *interj* ¡no! || *s* (*pl* **noes** *o* **nos** [noz] no; voto en contra; **the noes have it** ha rechazado la moción
no., No., nº, o **Nº** *abbr* **number**
no admission *s* se prohíbe la entrada, prohibida la entrada o prohibido el paso
no admittance *s* se prohíbe la entrada, prohibido la entrada o el paso
Noah [ˈno•ə] *s* Noe *m*
nob•by [ˈnɑbi] *adj* (*comp* **-bier;** *super* **-biest**) (slang) elegante; (slang) excelente
nobili•ty [noˈbɪlɪti] *s* (*pl* **-ties**) nobleza; (*of sentiments, character, etc.*) nobleza, ennoblecimiento
noble [ˈnobəl] *adj & s* noble *m*
noble•man [ˈnobəlmən] *s* (*pl* **-men** [mən]) noble *m,* hidalgo
nobod•y [ˈno,bɑdi] o [ˈnobədi] *pron indef* nadie, ninguno; **nobody but** nadie más que; **nobody else** nadie más, ningún otro || *s* (*pl* **-ies**) nadie *m,* don nadie
no'-brain'er *s* (coll) asunto evidente y claro sin declaraciones
nocturnal [nɑkˈtʌrnəl] *adj* nocturno

nod [nɑd] *s* inclinación de cabeza; seña con la cabeza; (*of a person going to sleep*) cabezada ‖ *v* (*pret & pp* **nodded;** *ger* **nodding**) *tr* inclinar (*la cabeza*); indicar con una inclinación de cabeza ‖ *intr* inclinar la cabeza; (*in going to sleep*) cabecear

node [nod] *s* bulto, protuberancia; nudo, enredo; (astr, med & phys) nodo; (bot) nudo

no entry *s* se prohíbe la entrada, prohibida la entrada o prohibido el paso

no′-fault′ *adj* (*divorce, insurance*) libre de culpa

no′-go′ *adj* (slang) que no está listo

no′-good′ *adj* (coll) maldito, endemoniado

nohow [ˋno,haʊ] *adv* (coll) de ninguna manera, de ningún modo

noise [nɔɪz] *s* ruido ‖ *tr* divulgar

noiseless [ˋnɔɪzlɪs] *adj* silencioso, sin ruido

noise level *s* nivel sonoro

nois•y [ˋnɔɪzi] *adj* (*comp* **-ier;** *super* **-iest**) ruidoso; bullero; (*boisterous*) estrepitoso

no kidding? *s* (coll) ¿en serio?, ¿sin bromas?

nom. *abbr* **nominative**

nomad [ˋnomæ] *adj & s* nómada *mf*

nomadic [noˋmædɪk] *adj* nomádico

no man's land *s* terreno sin reclamar; (mil) la tierra de nadie

nominal [ˋnɑmɪnəl] *adj* nominal; (*price*) módico

nominate [ˋnɑmɪ,net] *tr* postular como candidato; (*to appoint*) nombrar, designar

nomination [,nɑmɪˋ neʃən] *s* postulación

nominative [ˋnɑmɪnətɪv] *adj & s* nominativo

nominee [,nɑmɪˋni] *s* propuesto, candidato

non′-aggres′sion pact *s* pacto de no agresión

nonaligned nations [,nɑnəˋlaɪnd] *spl* países no alineados; países no comprometidos; Tercer Mundo

nonbelligerent [,nɑnbəˋlɪdʒərənt] *adj & s* no beligerante *m*

nonbreakable [nɑnˋbrekəbəl] *adj* irrompible

nonchalance [ˋnɑnʃələns] *s* indiferencia, desenvoltura

nonchalant [ˋnɑnʃələnt] *adj* indiferente, desenvuelto

noncom [ˋnɑn,kɑm] *s* (coll) clase, suboficial *m*

noncombatant [nɑnˋkɑmbətənt] *adj & s* no combatiente *m*

noncommissioned officer [,nɑnkəˋmɪʃənd] *s* clase, suboficial *m*

noncommittal [,nɑnkəˋmɪtəl] *adj* evasivo, reticente

noncommitted [,nɑnkəˋmɪtɪd] *adj* no empeñado

non compos mentis [ˋnɑnˋkɑmpəsˋmɛntɪs] *adj* falto de juicio, loco

nonconformist [,nɑnkənˋfɔrmɪst] *s* disidente *mf;* inconformista *mf*

nonconformity [,nɑnkənˋfɔrmɪti] *s* inconformidad

nondelivery [,nɑndɪˋlɪvəri] *s* falta de entrega

nondescript [ˋnɑndɪ,skrɪpt] *adj* inclasificable, indefinido

none [nʌn] *pron indef* nadie, ninguno, ningunos; **none of** ninguno de; nada de; **none other** ningún otro ‖ *adv* nada, de ninguna manera; **none the less** sin embargo, no obstante

nonenti•ty [nɑnˋɛntɪti] *s* (*pl* **-ties**) cosa inexistente; (*person*) nulidad

nonessential [,nɑnɛˋsɛnʃəl] *adj* intrascendente

nonexistence [,nɑnɛgˋzɪstəns] *s* inexistencia

nonfiction [nɑnˋfɪkʃən] *s* literatura no novelesca

nonfulfillment [,nɑnfʊlˋfɪlmənt] *s* incumplimiento

nonintervention [,nɑnɪntərˋvɛnʃən] *s* no intervención

nonmetal [ˋnɑn,mɛtəl] *s* metaloide *m*

no′-no′ *s* algo prohibido, algo que no se hace

no′-non′ sense *adj* práctico, sensato: (*guidance*) firme y eficiente

nonpartisan [nɑnˋpɑrtɪzən] *adj* imparcial

nonpayment [nɑnˋpemənt] *s* falta de pago, impago

non•plus [ˋnɑnplʌs] o [nɑnˋplʌs] *s* estupefacción ‖ *v* (*pret & pp* **-plused** o **-plussed;** *ger* **-plusing** o **-plussing**) *tr* dejar estupefacto, dejar pegado a la pared

nonprofit [nɑnˋprɑfɪt] *adj* sin fin lucrativo

nonrefillable [,nɑnrɪˋfɪləbəl] *adj* irrellenable

nonresident [nɑnˋrɛzɪdənt] *s* transeúnte *mf*

nonresidential [nɑn,rɛzɪˋdɛnʃəl] *adj* comercial

nonscientific [nɑn,saɪ•ənˋtɪfɪk] *adj* anticientífico

nonsectarian [,nɑnsɛkˋtɛrɪ•ən] *adj* no sectario

nonsense [ˋnɑnsɛns] *s* disparate *m,* tontería; esperpento; **to talk nonsense** hablar en gringo ‖ *interj* ¡déjate de tonterías!

nonsensical [nɑnˋsɛnsɪkəl] *adj* disparatado, tonto

nonskid [ˋnɑnˋskɪd] *adj* antideslizante

nonstop [ˋnɑnˋstɑp] *adj & adv* sin parar, sin escala

nonsupport [,nɑnsəˋport] *s* falta de manutención

noodle [ˋnudəl] *s* tallarín *m,* fideo; (coll) coco, cabeza

noodle soup *s* sopa de pastas, sopa de fideos

nook [nʊk] *s* rinconcito

noon [nun] *s* mediodía *m;* **at high noon** en pleno mediodía

no one o **no-one** [ˋno,wʌn] *pron indef* nadie, ninguno; **no one else** nadie más, ningún otro

noontime [ˋnun,taɪm] *s* mediodía *m*

noose [nus] *s* lazo corredizo; (*to hang a criminal*) dogal *m;* trampa ‖ *tr* lazar; hacer un lazo corredizo en

no parking *s* prohibido estacionar

nor [nɔr] *conj* ni

Nordic [ˋnɔrdɪk] *adj & s* nórdico

norm [nɔrm] *s* norma

normal [ˋnɔrməl] *adj* normal

Norman [ˋnɔrmən] *adj & s* normando

Normandy [ˋnɔrməndi] *s* Normandía

Norse [nɔrs] *adj* nórdico; noruego ‖ *s* (*ancient*

Scandinavian language) nórdico; (*language of Norway*) noruego; **the Norse** los nórdicos; los noruegos

north [nɔrθ] *adj* septentrional, del norte ‖ *adv* al norte, hacia el norte ‖ *s* norte *m*

North America *s* Norteamérica, la América del Norte

North American *adj & s* norteamericano

north'east'er *s* (*wind*) nordestada, nordeste *m* (*viento*)

northern [ˈnɔrðərn] *adj* septentrional; (*Hemisphere*) boreal

Northern Ireland *s* Irlanda del Norte

North Korea *s* la Corea del Norte

North Korean *adj & s* norcoreano

North Star *s* (astr) estrella polar

northward [ˈnɔrθwərd] *adv* hacia el norte

north wind *s* norte *m,* aquilón *m*

Norway [ˈnɔrwe] *s* Noruega

Norwegian [nɔrˈwidʒən] *adj & s* noruego

nos. *abbr* **numbers**

nose [noz] *s* nariz *f;* (aer) proa; **to blow one's nose** sonarse las narices; **to count noses** averiguar cuántas personas hay; **to follow one's nose** seguir todo derecho; avanzar guiándose por el instinto; **to hold one's nose** tabicarse las narices; **to lead by the nose** llevar por la barba, tener agarrado por las narices; **to look down one's nose at** mirar por encima del hombro; **to pay through the nose** pagar un precio escandaloso; **to pick one's nose** hurgarse las narices; **to poke one's nose into** meter las narices en; **to speak through the nose** ganguear; **to thumb one's nose at** señalar (*a una persona*) poniendo el pulgar sobre la nariz en son de burla; tratar con sumo desprecio; **to turn up one's nose at** mirar con desprecio; **under the nose of** en las narices de, en las barbas de ‖ *tr* olfatear ‖ *intr* ventear; **to nose about** curiosear; **to nose over** capotar (*un avión*); **to nose up** encabritarse (*un buque, un avión*)

nose bag *s* cebadera, morral *m*

nose'band' *s* muserola, sobarba

nose'bleed' *s* hemorragia nasal

nose cone *s* cono de proa

nose dive *s* (aer) descenso de picado; **to take a nose dive;** (aer) descender en picada; (*prices*) caer en picada

nose'-dive' *intr* (aer) picar; (fig) descender precipidamente

nose drops *spl* gotas nasales

nosegay [ˈnoz,ge] *s* ramillete *m*

nose ring *s* nariguera

no'-show' *s* pasajero no presentado

no smoking *adj* (*section; room*) para no fumadores ‖ *s* prohibido fumar, se prohíbe fumar

nostalgia [nɑˈstældʒə] *s* nostalgia

nostril [ˈnɑstrɪl] *s* nariz *f,* ventana

no surrender *interj* ¡no nos rendimos!

nos•y [ˈnozi] *adj* (*comp* **-ier;** *super* **-iest**) (coll) curioso, husmeador

not [nɑt] *adv* no; **not at all** nada, de ningún modo; **not yet** todavía no; **to think not** creer que no; **why not?** ¿cómo no?

notable [ˈnotəbəl] *adj & s* notable *m*

notarize [ˈnotə,raɪz] *tr* abonar con fe notarial

nota•ry [ˈnotəri] *s* (*pl* **-ries**) notario

notch [nɑtʃ] *s* muesca, mella, corte *m;* (U.S.A.) desfiladero, paso; (coll) grado ‖ *tr* hacer muescas en, mellar

note [not] *s* nota; apunte *m;* esquela, cartita; marca, señal *f;* (com) pagaré *m,* vale *m;* canto, melodía; acento, voz *f;* (mus) nota ‖ *tr* notar, apuntar; marcar, señalar

note'book' *s* cuaderno, libro de apuntes

noted [ˈnotɪd] *adj* aramado, conocido

note paper *s* papel *m* de cartas

note'wor'thy *adj* notable, digno de notarse

not guilty *s* (*verdict*) declaración de no culpabilidad

nothing [ˈnʌθɪŋ] *pron indef* nada; **for nothing** inútilmente; de balde, gratis; **nothing doing** (slang) ni por pienso; **nothing else** nada más; **that's nothing to me** eso nada me importa; **to make nothing of** no hacer caso de; no aprovecharse de; no entender; despreciar; **to think nothing of** no hacer caso de; tener por fácil; despreciar ‖ *adv* nada, de ninguna manera; **nothing daunted** sin temor alguno ‖ *s* nada; nadería, friolera

notice [ˈnotɪs] *s* atención, reparo, advertencia; aviso, noticia; letrero; mención, reseña; llamada; notificación; **on short notice** con poco tiempo de aviso; **to escape one's notice** pasarle inadvertido a uno; **to serve notice** dar noticia, hacer saber ‖ *tr* notar, observar, reparar, reparar en; mencionar

noticeable [ˈnotɪsəbəl] *adj* sensible, perceptible; notable

noti•fy [ˈnotɪ,faɪ] *v* (*pret & pp* **-fied**) *tr* notificar, avisar, hacer saber

notion [ˈnoʃən] *s* noción; capricho; **notions** mercería, artículos menudos; **to have a notion to** + *inf* pensar + *inf,* tener ganas de + *inf*

notorie•ty [,notəˈraɪ•ɪti] *s* (*pl* **-ties**) mala reputación; (*condition of being well known*) notoriedad; (*person*) notable *mf*

notorious [noˈtorɪ•əs] *adj* reputado, mal reputado; bien conocido

no'-trump' *adj & s* sin triunfo; **a no-trump hand** un sin triunfo

notwithstanding [,nɑtwɪðˈstændɪŋ] o [,nɑtwɪθˈstændɪŋ] *adv* no obstante ‖ *prep* a pesar de ‖ *conj* a pesar de que

nougat [ˈnugət] *s* turrón *m*

noun [naʊn] *s* nombre, nombre sustantivo

nourish [ˈnʌrɪʃ] *tr* alimentar, nutrir; abrigar (*p.ej., esperanzas*)

nourishing [ˈnʌrɪʃɪŋ] *adj* alimenticio, nutritivo

nourishment [ˈnʌrɪʃmənt] *s* alimento, nutrimento

Nov. *abbr* **November**
Nova Scotia [ˈnovəˈskoʃə] *s* la Nueva Escocia
novel [ˈnɑvəl] *adj* nuevo; insólito, extraño, original ‖ *s* novela
novelist [ˈnɑvəlɪst] *s* novelista *mf*
novel•ty [ˈnɑvəlti] *s* (*pl* **-ties**) novedad, innovación; **novelties** bisutería, baratijas
November [noˈvɛmbər] *s* noviembre *m*
novice [ˈnɑvɪs] *s* novicio
novocaine [ˈnovəˌken] *s* novocaína
NOW *abbr* **National Organization for Women**
now [naʊ] *adv* ahora; ya; entonces; **from now on** de ahora en adelante; **how now?** ¿cómo?; **just now** hace un momento; **now and again** o **now and then** de vez en cuando; **now . . . now** ora . . . ora, ya . . . ya; **now that** ya que; **now then** ahora bien ‖ *interj* ¡vamos! ‖ *s* actualidad
nowadays [ˈnaʊ•əˌdez] *adv* hoy en día, hoy día
noʹwayʹ o **noʹwaysʹ** *adv* de ningún modo
noʹwhereʹ *adv* en ninguna parte, a ninguna parte; **nowhere else** en ninguna otra parte
noxious [ˈnɑkʃəs] *adj* nocivo
nozzle [ˈnɑzəl] *s* (*of hose*) lanza, boca; (*of oil can*) pico, pitorro; (*of sprinkling can*) rallo, roseta; (*of candlestick*) cubo; (*of blowtorch*) boquilla; (*of rocket or jet engine*) tobera; (slang) naríz *f*
nth [ɛnθ] *adj* n^{mo} (*enésimo*); **to the nth degree** elevado a la potencia *n;* a más no poder
nuance [njuˈɑns] o [ˈnju•ɑns] *s* matiz *m*
nub [nʌb] *s* protuberancia; pedazo; (coll) meollo
nuclear [ˈnuklɪ•ər] *adj* nuclear
nuclear energy *s* energía nuclear
nuclear fission *s* fisión nuclear
nuclear fusion *s* fusión nuclear
nuclear physics *s* física nuclear
nuclear power *s* energía nuclear
nuʹcle•ar-powʹered *adj* accionado por energía nuclear
nuclear power station *s* central *f* nuclear
nuclear reactor *s* reactor *m* nuclear
nuclear test ban *s* proscripción de las pruebas nucleares
nuclear war *s* guerra nuclear
nuclear waste *s* residuos *mpl* nucleares
nucle•us [ˈnuklɪ•əs] *s* (*pl* **-i** [ˌaɪ] o **-uses**) núcleo
nude [njud] o [nud] *adj* desnudo ‖ *s*— **in the nude** desnudo; **the nude** el desnudo
nudism [ˈnjudɪzəm] o [ˈnudɪzəm] *s* nudismo, desnudismo
nudge [nʌdʒ] *s* codazo suave ‖ *tr* dar un codazo suave a, empujar suavemente
nudist [ˈnjudɪst] *adj & s* nudista *mf,* desnudista *mf,* naturista *mf*
nudist colony *s* colonia nudista
nudity [ˈnjudəti] *s* desnudez *f,* desnudo
nugget [ˈnʌgɪt] *s* pedazo; (*of, e.g., gold*) pepita; preciosidad
nuisance [ˈnjusəns] o [ˈnusəns] *s* molestia, estorbo; majadería; persona o cosa fastidiosas; **to be a nuisance** ser un higado
nuke [njuk] o [nuk] *s* (coll) arma nuclear; (*power plant*) central *f* nuclear ‖ *tr* (coll) bombardear con armas nucleares
null [nʌl] *adj* nulo; **null and void** nulo, írrito, nulo y sin valor
nulli•fy [ˈnʌlifaɪ] *v* (*pret & pp* **-fied**) *tr* anular, invalidor
numb [nʌm] *adj* entumecido; **to get numb** envararse ‖ *tr* entumecer
number [ˈnʌmbər] *s* número; **a number of** varios ‖ *tr* numerar; ascender a (*cierto número*); **his days are numbered** tiene sus días contados o sus horas contadas; **to be numbered among** hallarse entre; **to number among** contar entre
numberless [ˈnʌmbərlɪs] *adj* innumerable
numeral [ˈnjumərəl] o [ˈnumərəl] *adj* numeral ‖ *s* número
numerical [njuˈmɛrɪkəl] o [nuˈmɛrɪkəl] *adj* numérico
numeric keypad *s* teclado numérico
numerous [ˈnjumərəs] o [ˈnumərəs] *adj* numeroso
numskull [ˈnʌmˌskʌl] *s* (coll) bodoque *m,* mentecato
nun [nʌn] *s* monja, religiosa
nuptial [ˈnʌpʃəl] *adj* nupcial ‖ **nuptials** *spl* nupcias, bodas
nurse [nʌrs] *s* enfermera, practicante *mf;* (*to suckle a child*) ama de cría, nodriza; (*to take care of a child*) niñera ‖ *tr* cuidar (*a una persona enferma*); amamantar; alimentar, criar; tratar de curarse de (*p.ej., un resfriado*); abrigar (*p.ej., odio*) ‖ *intr* ser enfermera
nurser•y [ˈnʌrsəri] *s* (*pl* **-ies**) cuarto de los niños; (*of plants*) criadero, plantel *m,* semillero; (fig) semillero
nursery•man [ˈnʌrsərɪmən] *s* (*pl* **-men** [mən]) cultivador *m* de semillero
nursery rhymes *spl* versos para niños
nursery school *s* pre-escolar *m,* parvulario, jardín *m* infantil
nursery tales *spl* cuentos para niños
nursing bottle *s* biberón *m*
nursing home *s* clínica de reposo; (*for the aged*) residencia de ancianos
nurture [ˈnʌrtʃər] *s* alimentación, nutrimento; crianza, educación ‖ *tr* alimentar, nutrir; criar, educar; acariciar (*p.ej., una esperanza*)
nut [nʌt] *s* fruto seco, e.g., nuez *f,* almendra, avellana; (*the walnut is sometimes used as a generic term for a nut or nuts*) nuez *f;* (*to screw on a bolt*) tuerca; (slang) estrafalario; **a hard nut to crack** (coll) hueso duro de roer
nutʹcrackʹer *s* cascanueces *m*
nutmeg [ˈnʌtˌmɛg] *s* nuez moscada; (*tree*) mirística
nutriment [ˈnjutrɪmənt] *s* nutrimento
nutrition [njuˈtrɪʃən] *s* nutrición
nutritious [njuˈtrɪʃəs] *adj* nutricioso, nutritivo

nuts *adj* (slang) loco; estrafalario; **nuts about** (slang) loco por || *interj* (slang) ¡no!, ¡niego!, ¡de ninguna manera!
nut'shell' *s* cáscara de nuez; **in a nutshell** en pocas palabras
nut•ty [ˈnʌti] *adj* (*comp* **-tier;** *super* **-tiest**) (*flavor*) a nueces, a almendras, a avellanas, etc.; (slang) chiflado, loco; **nutty about** (slang) loco por
nuzzle [ˈnʌzəl] *tr* hocicar, hozar || *intr* hocicar; arrimarse cómodamente; arroparse bien
nylon [ˈnaɪlɑn] *s* nilón *m;* **nylons** medias de nilón
nymph [nɪmf] *s* ninfa

O

O, o [o] decimoquinta letra del alfabeto inglés
O *interj* ¡oh!; ¡ay!, p.ej., **how pretty she is!** ¡Ay qué linda!; **O that. . . !** ¡Ojalá que. . . !
oaf [of] *s* zoquete *m,* zamacuco; niño contrahecho
oak [ok] *s* roble *m*
oaken [ˈokən] *adj* hecho de roble
oakum [ˈokəm] *s* estopa, estopa de calafatear
oar [or] *s* remo; **to lie** o **rest on one's oars** aguantar los remos; aflojar en el trabajo || *tr* conducir a remo || *intr* remar, bogar
oars•man [ˈorzmən] *s* (*pl* **-men** [mən]) remero
OAS [ˈoˈeˈɛs] *s* (letterword) (**Organization of American States**) OEA *f* (Organización de Estados Americanos)
oa•sis [oˈesɪs] *s* (*pl* **-ses** [siz]) oasis *m*
oat [ot] *s* avena; **oats** (*edible grain*) avena; **to feel one's oats** (slang) estar fogoso y brioso; (slang) estar muy pagado de sí mismo; **to sow one's wild oats** correrla, pasar las mocedades
oath [oθ] *s* juramento; **on oath** bajo juramento; **to take an oath** prestar juramento
oat'meal' *s* harina de avena; gachas de avena
ob. *abbr* **obiit** (Lat) **died**
obbligato [ˌɑblɪˈgɑto] *adj & s* obligado
obduracy [ˈɑbdjərəsi] *s* obduración
obdurate [ˈɑbdjərɪt] *adj* obstinado, terco; empedernido
obedience [oˈbidɪ•əns] *s* obediencia
obedient [oˈbidɪ•ənt] *adj* obediente
obeisance [oˈbesəns] u [oˈbisəns] *s* saludo respetuoso; homenaje *m,* respeto
obelisk [ˈɑbəlɪsk] *s* obelisco
obese [oˈbis] *adj* obeso
obesity [oˈbisɪti] *s* obesidad
obey [oˈbe] *tr & intr* obedecer
obfuscate [ɑbˈfʌsket] o [ˈɑbfəsˌket] *tr* ofuscar
obituar•y [oˈbɪtʃuˌɛri] *adj* necrológico || *s* (*pl* **-ies**) necrología, obituario
obj. *abbr* **object, objection, objective**
object [ˈɑbdʒɪkt] *s* objeto || [ɑbˈdʒɛkt] *tr* objetar || *intr* hacer objeciones
objection [ɑbˈdʒɛkʃən] *s* reparo, objeción; **to have no objections to make** no tener nada que objetar
objectionable [ɑbˈdʒɛkʃənəbəl] *adj* desagradable, reprensible; (*causing disapproval*) objetable
objective [ɑbˈdʒɛktɪv] *adj* objetivo || *s* objetivo; (*intention, aim, goal*) propósito
object lesson *s* perfecta demostración
obligate [ɑblɪˌget] *tr* obligar
obligation [ˌɑblɪˈgeʃən] *s* obligación; encargamiento; (com) compromiso
oblige [əˈblaɪdʒ] *tr* obligar; complacer; **much obliged** muchas gracias
obliging [əˈblaɪdʒɪŋ] *adj* complaciente, condescendiente, servicial
oblique [əˈblik] *adj* oblicuo; indirecto, evasivo
obliterate [əˈblɪtəˌret] *tr* borrar; arrasar, destruir
oblivion [əˈblɪvɪ•ən] *s* olvido
oblivious [əˈblɪvɪ•əs] *adj* olvidadizo
oblong [ˈɑblɔŋ] o [ˈɑblɑŋ] *adj* oblongo
obnoxious [əbˈnɑkʃəs] *adj* detestable, ofensivo
oboe [ˈobo] *s* oboe *m*
oboist [ˈobo•ɪst] *s* oboísta *mf*
obscene [ɑbˈsin] *adj* obsceno
obsceni•ty [ɑbˈsɛnɪti] o [ɑbˈsinɪti] *s* (*pl* **-ties**) obscenidad
obscure [əbˈskjʊr] *adj* obscuro
obscuri•ty [əbˈskjʊrɪti] *s* (*pl* **-ties**) obscuridad
obsequies [ˈɑbsɪkwiz] *spl* exequias
obsequious [əbˈsikwɪ•əs] *adj* obsequioso, servil, rastrero
observance [əbˈzʌrvəns] *s* observancia; ceremonia, rito
observant [əbˈzʌrvənt] *adj* observador
observation [ˌɑbzərˈveʃən] *s* observación; observancia
observation car *s* (rr) vagón mirador
observato•ry [əbˈzʌrvəˌtori] *s* (*pl* **-ries**) observatorio
observe [əbˈzʌrv] *tr* observar; (*a holiday; silence*) guardar
observer [əbˈzʌrvər] *s* observador *m*
obsess [əbˈsɛs] *tr* obsesionar
obsession [əbˈsɛʃən] *s* obsesión
obsolescent [ˌɑbsəˈlɛsənt] *adj* anticuado, cayendo en desuso
obsolete [ˈɑbsəˌlit] *adj* desusado, caído en desuso; obsoleto
obstacle [ˈɑbstəkəl] *s* obstáculo
obstetrical [ɑbˈstɛtrɪkəl] *adj* obstétrico
obstetrics [ɑbˈstɛtrɪks] *ssg* obstetricia
obstina•cy [ˈɑbstɪnəsi] *s* (*pl* **-cies**) obstinación
obstinate [ˈɑbstɪnɪt] *adj* obstinado

obstruct [ɑbˈstrʌkt] *tr* obstruir; obstruccionar
obstruction [əbˈstrʌkʃən] *s* obstrucción
obtain [əbˈten] *tr* obtener ‖ *intr* existir, prevalecer
obtrusive [əbˈtrusɪv] *adj* entremetido, intruso
obtuse [əbˈtjus] o [əbˈtus] *adj* obtuso
obviate [ˈɑbvɪˌet] *tr* obviar
obvious [ˈɑbvɪ•əs] *adj* obvio
occasion [əˈkeθən] *s* ocasión; **to improve the occasion** aprovechar la ocasión
occasional [əˈkeʒənəl] *adj* raro, poco frecuente; alguno que otro; de circunstancia
occasionally [əˈkeʒənəli] *adv* ocasionalmente, de vez en cuando
occident [ˈɑksɪdənt] *s* occidente *m*
occidental [ˌɑksɪˈdɛntəl] *adj* occidental
occlusive [əˈklusɪv] *adj* oclusivo ‖ *s* oclusiva
occult [əˈkʌlt] o [ˈɑkʌlt] *adj* oculto
occupancy [ˈɑkjepənsi] *s* ocupación
occupant [ˈɑkjepənt] *s* ocupante *mf;* inquilino
occupation [ˌɑkjəˈpeʃən] *s* ocupación
occupational therapy *s* terapia vocacional
occu•py [ˈɑkjəˌpaɪ] *v* (*pret & pp* **-pied**) *tr* ocupar; habitar
oc•cur [əˈkʌr] *v* (*pret & pp* **-curred;** *ger* **-curring**) *intr* ocurrir, acontecer, suceder; encontrarse; (*to come to mind*) ocurrir
occurrence [əˈkʌrəns] *s* acontecimiento; caso, aparición
ocean [ˈoʃən] *s* océano
o'cean-go'ing *adj* transoceánico
oceanic [ˌoʃɪˈænɪk] *adj* oceánico
ocean liner *s* buque transoceánico
oceanographer [ˌoʃəˈnɑgrəfər] *s* oceanógrafo
oceanography [ˌoʃəˈnɑgrəfi] *s* oceanografía
o'clock [əˈklɑk] *adv* por el reloj; **it is one o'clock** es la una; **it is two o'clock** son las dos; **what o'clock is it?** ¿qué hora es?
Oct. *abbr* **October**
octave [ˈɑktɪv] o [ˈɑktev] *s* octava
October [ɑkˈtobər] *s* octubre *m*
octo•pus [ˈɑktəpəs] *s* (*pl* **-puses** o **-pi** [ˌpaɪ]) pulpo
octoroon [ˌɑktəˈrun] *s* octavo
ocular [ˈɑkjələr] *adj & s* ocular *m*
oculist [ˈɑkjəlɪst] *s* oculista *mf*
odd [ɑd] *adj* suelto; (*number*) impar; (*that doesn't match*) dispar; libre, de ocio; sobrante; extraño, raro, singular; y pico, y tantos, p.ej., **two hundred odd** doscientos y pico ‖ **odds** *ssg* o *spl* (*in betting*) ventaja; apuesta desigual; puntos de ventaja; **at odds** de monos, riñendo; **by all odds** muy probablemente, sin duda alguna; **it makes no odds** lo mismo da; **the odds are** lo probable es; la ventaja es de; **to be at odds** estar de punta, estar encontrados; **to set at odds** enemistar, malquistar
odd'ball' *adj & s* excéntrico; disente
oddi•ty [ˈɑdɪti] *s* (*pl* **-ties**) rareza, cosa rara
odd jobs *spl* pequeñas tareas
odd lot *s* lote *m* inferior al centenar
odds and ends *spl* cajón *m* de sastre, retazos; cosas sueltas; (*junk*) cachivaches
ode [od] *s* oda
odious [ˈodɪ•əs] *adj* odioso, abominable
odometer [oˈdɑmətər] *s* (aut) odómetro
odor [ˈodər] *s* olor *m;* **to be in bad odor** tener mala fama
odorless [ˈodərlɪs] *adj* inodoro
odorous [ˈodərəs] *adj* oloroso
Odyssey [ˈɑdɪsi] *s* Odisea
Oedipus [ˈɛdɪpəs] o [ˈidɪpəs] *s* Edipo
of [ɑv] o [əv] *prep* de, p.ej., **the top of the mountain** la cima de la montaña; a: **to smell of** oler a; con: **to dream of** soñar con; en: **to think of** pensar en; menos: **a quarter of two** las dos menos un cuarto
off [ɔf] o [ɑf] *adj* malo, p.ej., **off day** día malo; (*account, sum*) errado; más distante; libre; sin trabajo; quitado; apagado; (*electric current*) cortado; de descuento, de rebaja; de la parte del mar; (*season*) muerto ‖ *adv* fuera, a distancia, lejos; allá; **off of** (coll) de; (coll) a expensas de; **to be off** ponerse en marcha ‖ *prep* de, desde, al lado de, a nivel de; fuera de; libre de; (naut) a la altura de ‖ *tr* (slang) matar, asesinar
offal [ˈɑfəl] u [ˈɔfəl] *s* (*of butchered meat*) carniza; basura, desperdicios
off and on *adv* unas veces sí y otras no
off'beat' *adj* (slang) insólito, chocante, original
off'-Broad'way *adj* fuera de Broadway
off'chance' *s* posibilidad poco probable
off'-col'or *adj* descolorido; indispuesto; (*indecent, risqué*) colorado, subido de color
offend [əˈfɛnd] *tr & intr* ofender
offender [əˈfɛndər] *s* ofensor *m*
offense [əˈfɛns] *s* ofensa; **to take offense (at)** ofenderse (de)
offensive [əˈfɛnsɪv] *adj* ofensivo ‖ *f* ofensiva
offer [ˈɔfər] o [ˈɑfər] *s* ofrecimiento, oferta ‖ *tr* ofrecer; rezar (*oraciones*); oponer (*resistencia*)
offering [ˈɔfərɪŋ] o [ˈɑfərɪŋ] *s* ofrecimiento; (*gift, present*) oferta; (*presentation in worship*) ofrenda
off'hand' *adj* hecho de improviso; brusco, desenvuelto ‖ *adv* de improviso, súbitamente; bruscamente
office [ˈɔfɪs] o [ˈɑfɪs] *s* oficina, despacho; función, oficio; cargo, ministerio; (*of a lawyer*) bufete *m;* (*of a doctor*) consultorio
office boy *s* mandadero
office desk *s* escritorio ministro
of'fice•hold'er *s* funcionario, burócrata *m*
office hours *spl* horas de oficina; (*of a doctor*) horas de consulta
officer [ˈɔfɪsər] o [ˈɑfɪsər] *s* jefe *m,* director *m;* (*of army, an order, a society, etc.*) oficial *m;* agente *m* de policía
office seeker [ˈsikər] *s* aspirante *m,* pretendiente *m*
office supplies *spl* suministros para oficinas
official [əˈfɪʃəl] *adj* oficial ‖ *s* jefe *m,* director *m;* (*of a society*) dignatario
officiate [əˈfɪʃɪˌet] *intr* oficiar

officious [əˈfɪʃəs] *adj* oficioso
off key *adj* desafinado, desentonado; **to go off key** desafinar
off limits *adj & adv* en zona prohibida
off′-line′ *adj* (*printer; storage*) (compu) autónomo
off′-peak′ *adj* (*hours, stop, etc.*) de valle; de menor tránsito
off-peak heater *s* (elec) termos *m* de acumulación
off-peak load *s* (elec) carga de las horas de valle
off′print′ *s* sobretiro
off season *s* temporada baja || *adv* durante la temporada baja
off,set′ *s* compensación; (typ) offset *m* || **off′set′** *v* (*pret & pp* **-set;** *ger* **-setting**) *tr* compensar; imprimir por offset
off′shoot′ *s* (*of plant*) retoño, renuevo; (*of a family or race*) descendiente *mf;* (*branch*) ramal *m;* consecuencia
off′shore′ *adj* (*wind*) terral; (*fishing*) de bajura; (*said of islands*) costero; **offshore drilling rig** barca perforador || *adv* a lo largo
off′side′ *adj* fuera de juego
off′spring′ *s* descendencia, sucesión; hijo, hijos
off′-stage′ *adj* de entre bastidores
off′-the-rec′ord *adj* extraoficial, confidencial
off′-the-wall′ *adj* (coll) estrambótico, estrafalario
often [ˈɔfən] o (ɑfən] *adv* a menudo, muchas veces; **how often?** ¿cuántas veces?; **not often** pocas veces
ogive [ˈodʒaɪv] u [oˈdʒaɪv] *s* ojiva
ogle [ˈogəl] *tr & intr* ojear; mirar amorosamente
ogre [ˈogər] *s* ogro
ohm [om] *s* ohmio
oho [oˈho] interj ¡ajá!
oil [ɔɪl] *adj* (*burner; field; well*) de petróleo; (*pump; stove*) de aceite; (*company, tanker*) petrolero; (*land*) petrolífero || *s* aceite *m;* (*consecrated oil; painting*) óleo; **to burn the midnight oil** quemarse las cejas; **to pour oil on troubled waters** mojar la pólvora; **to strike oil** encontrar una capa de petróleo; (fig) enriquecerse de súbito || *tr* aceitar; lubricar; lisonjear; (*to bribe*) untar || *intr* proveerse de petróleo (*un buque*)
oil′can′ *s* aceitera
oil′cloth′ *s* encerado, hule *m*
oil field *s* yacamiento de petróleo
oil gauge indicador *m* del nivel de aceite
oil pan *s* colector *m* de aceite
oil rig *s* plataforma petrolífera; torre *f* de perforación
oil shortage *s* carestía (o escasez *f*) de petróleo
oil slick *s* marea negra, mancha de petróleo
oil tanker *s* petrolero
oil•y [ˈɔɪli] *adj* (*comp* **-ier;** *super* **-iest**) aceitoso; liso, resbaladizo; zalamero
ointment [ˈɔɪntmənt] *s* ungüento
O.K. [ˈoˈke] *adj* (coll) aprobado, conforme || *adv* (coll) muy bien, está bien || *s* (coll) aprobación || *v* (*pret & pp* **O.K.'d;** *ger* **O.K.'ing**) *tr* (coll) aprobar
okra [ˈokrə] *s* quingombó *m*
old [old] *adj* viejo; antiguo; (*wine*) añejo; **how old is . . .?** ¿cuántos años tiene . . . ?; **of old** de antaño, antiguamente; **to be . . . years old** tener . . . años
old age *s* ancianidad, vejez *f;* **to die of old age** morir de viejo
old boy *s* viejo; graduado; **the Old Boy** (slang) el diablo
Old Castile *s* Castilla la Vieja
old-clothes•man [ˈoldˈkloðz,mæn] *s* (*pl* **-men** [mɛn]) ropavejero
old country *s* madre patria
old-fashioned [ˈoldˈfæʃənd] *adj* chapado a la antigua; anticuado, fuera de moda
old fo•gey u **old fo•gy** [ˈfogi] *s* (*pl* **-gies**) persona un poco ridícula por sus ideas o costumbres atrasadas
Old Glory *s* la bandera de los Estados Unidos
Old Guard *s* (U.S.A.) bando conservador del partido republicano
old hand *s* practicón *m,* veterano
old maid *s* solterona
old master *s* (paint) gran maestro; obra de un gran maestro
old moon *s* luna menguante
old salt *s* lobo de mar
old school *s* gente chapada a la antigua
old′-time′ *adj* del tiempo viejo
old-timer [ˈoldˈtaɪmər] *s* (coll) antiguo residente, veterano; (coll) persona chapada a la antigua
old wives' tale *s* cuento de viejas
old′-world′ *adj* del Viejo Mundo
oleander [,olɪˈændər] *s* adelfa
oligar•chy [ˈɑlɪ,gɑrki] *s* (*pl* **-chies**) oligarquía
olive [ˈɑlɪv] *adj* aceitunado || *s* aceituna
olive branch *s* ramo de olivo; (*peace*) oliva; hijo, vástago
olive grove *s* olivar *m*
olive oil *s* aceite *m,* aceite de oliva
olive tree *s* aceituno, olivo
Olympiad [oˈlɪmpɪ,æd] *s* Olimpíada
Olympian [oˈlɪmpɪ•ən] *adj* olímpico || *s* dios griego
Olympic [oˈlɪmpɪk] *adj* olímpico
omelet u **omelette** [ˈɑməlɪt] o [ˈɑmlɪt] *s* tortilla (de huevos)
omen [ˈomən] *s* agüero
ominous [ˈɑmɪnəs] *adj* ominoso
omission [oˈmɪʃən] *s* omisión
omit [oˈmɪt] *v* (*pret & pp* **omitted;** *ger* **omitting**) *tr* omitir
omnibus [ˈɑmnɪ,bʌs] o [ˈɑmnɪbəs] *adj* general; (*volume*) colecticio || *s* ómnibus *m*
omnipotent [ɑmˈnɪpətənt] *adj* omnipotente
omniscient [ɑmˈnɪʃənt] *adj* omnisciente
omnivorous [ɑmˈnɪvərəs] *adj* omnívoro
on [ɑn] u [ɔn] *adj* puesto, p.ej., **with his hat on** con el sombrero puesto; principiando; en funcionamiento; encendido; conectado; **the**

deal is on ya está concertado el trato; **the game is on** ya están jugando; **the race is on** allá van los corredores; **what is on at the theater this evening?** ¿qué representan esta noche? || *adv* adelante; encima; **and so on** y así sucesivamente; **come on!** ¡anda, anda!; **farther on** más allá, más adelante; **later on** más tarde, después; **to be on to a person** (coll) conocerle a uno el juego; **to have on** tener puesto; **to . . . on** sequir + *ger,* **he played on** siguió tocando || *prep* en, sobre, encima de; a, p.ej., **on foot** a pie; **on my arrival** a millegada; bajo, p.ej., **on my responsibility** bajo mi responsabilidad; contra, p.ej., **an attack on liberty** un ataque contra la libertad; de, p.ej., **on good authority** de buena tinta; **on a journey** de viaje; hacia, p.ej., **to march on the capital** marchar hacia la capital; por, p.ej., **on all sides** por todos lados; tras, p.ej., **defeat on defeat** derrota tras derrota; **on** + *ger* al + *inf,* p.ej., **on arriving** al llegar

on and on *adv* continuamente, sin cesar, sin parar

on′-board′ computer *s* ordenador *m* de viaje, computadora de viaje

once [wʌns] *adv* una vez; antes, p.ej., **once so happy** antes tan feliz; alguna vez, p.ej., **if this once becomes known** si esto llega a saberse alguna vez; **all at once** de súbito, de repente; **at once** en seguida; a la vez en el mismo momento; **for once** una vez por lo menos; **once and again** repetidas veces; **once in a blue moon** cada muerte de obispo; **once in a while** de vez en cuando; luego; **once more** otra vez; una vez más; **once upon a time there was** érase una vez, érase que se era || *conj* una vez que || *s* una vez; vez, p.ej., **this once** esta vez

once′-o′ver *s* (slang) examen rápido; **to give a thing the once-over** (coll) examinar una cosa superficialmente

oncology [ɑŋˋkɑlədʒi] *s* oncología

one [wʌn] *adj* un, uno; un tal, p.ej., **one Smith** un tal Smith; único, p.ej., **one price** precio único || *pron* uno, p.ej., **one does not know what to do here** uno no sabe qué hacer aquí; se, p.ej., **how does one go to the station?** ¿cómo se va a la estación?; **I for one** yo por lo menos; **it's all one and the same to me** me es igual; **my little one** mi chiquito; **of one another** el uno del otro, los unos de los otros, p.ej., **we took leave of one another** nos despedimos el uno del otro; **one and all** todos; **one another** se, p.ej., **they greeted one another** se saludaron; uno a otro, unos a otros, p.ej., **they looked at one another** se miraron uno a otro; **one by one** uno a uno; **one o'clock** la una; **one or two** unos pocos; **one's** su, el . . . de uno; **the blue book and the red one** el libro azul y el rojo; **the one and only** el único; **the one that** el que, la que; **this one** éste; **that one** ése, aquél; **to make one** unir; casar || *s* uno

one′-armed′ ban′dit *s* (*slot machine*) (coll) tragamonedas *m & f,* máquina sacaperras

one′-fam′i•ly house *s* vivienda unifamiliar

one′-horse′ *adj* de un solo caballo, tirado por un solo caballo; (coll) insignificante, de poca monta

one′-man′ band *s* hombre *m* orquesta

onerous [ˋɑnərəs] *adj* oneroso

one′self′ *pron* uno mismo; sí, sí mismo; se; **to be oneself** tener dominio de sí mismo; conducirse con naturalidad

one-sided [ˋwʌnˋsaɪdɪd] *adj* de un solo lado; injusto, parcial; desigual; unilateral

one′-track′ *adj* de carril único; (coll) con un solo interés

one′-way′ *adj* de una solo dirección, de dirección única; (*ticket*) sencillo, de ida

one-way street *s* calle de sentido único, calle de dirección única

one-way ticket *s* billete *m* sencillo, billete de ida

onion [ˋʌnjən] *s* cebolla

onion dome *s* (archit) cúpula de bulbo

on′ion•skin′ *s* papel *m* de seda, papel cebolla

on′line′ *adj* (compu) conectado, en línea

online *o* **on line** *adv* (compu) en línea; **to come on line** entrar en funcionamiento

on′look′er *s* mirón *m,* espectador *m*

only [ˋonlɪ] *adj* solo, único || *adv* solamente, sólo, únicamente; no . . . más que; **not only . . . but also** no sólo . . . sino también || *conj* sólo que, pero

only child *s* hijo único, hija única

onomatopoeic [ˌɑnəˌmætəˋpi•ɪk] *adj* onomatopéyico

on′set′ *s* arremetida, embestida; (*of an illness*) principio

on′side′ kick *s* (sport) patada corta

on′stage′ *adj* en escena

onward [ˋɑnwərd] u **onwards** [ˋɑnwərdz] *adv* adelante, hacia adelante

onyx [ˋɑnɪks] *s* ónice *m* u ónix *m*

oof [uf] *interj* ¡uf!

ooh [u] *interj* ¡uy!, ¡mmm!, ¡ah!; (*pain*) ¡ay!, ¡uy!

ooze [uz] *s* chorro suave; cieno; limo, lama || *tr* rezumar || *intr* rezumar, rezumarse; manar suavemente (*p.ej., la sangre de una herida*); agotarse poco a poco

op. *abbr* **opera, operation, opus, opposite**

opal [ˋopəl] *s* ópalo

opaque [oˋpek] *adj* opaco; (*writer's style*) obscuro; estúpido

open [ˋopən] *adj* abierto; descubierto, destapado; sin tejado; vacante; (*hour*) libre; discutible, pendiente; (*hand*) liberal; (*hunting season*) legal; **to break** o **to crack open** abrir con violencia, abrir por la fuerza; **to throw open** abrir de par en par || *s* abertura; (*in the woods*) claro; **in the open** al aire libre; a campo raso; en alta mar; abiertamente || *tr* abrir; desbullar (*una ostra*) || *intr* abrir; abrirse; estrenarse (*un drama*); **to open into**

desembocar en; **to open on** dar a; **to open up** descubrirse; descubrir el pecho
o'pen-air' *adj* al aire libre, a cielo abierto
open-air mass *s* (eccl) misa campal o de campaña
o'pen-ar'chitecture *s* (compu) arquitectura abierta
open-eyed [ˈopən,aɪd] *adj* alerta, vigilante; con ojos asombrados; hecho con los ojos abiertos
open-handed [ˈopənˈhændɪd] *adj* maniabierto, liberal
open-hearted (opənˈhɑrtɪd] *adj* franco, sincero
open house *s* coliche *m;* **to keep open house** recibir a todos, gustar de tener siempre convidados en casa
opening [ˈopənɪŋ] *s* abertura; (*of, e.g., school*) apertura; (*in the woods*) claro; (*vacancy*) hueco, vacante *f;* (*chance to say something*) ocasión
opening night *s* noche *f* de estreno
opening number *s* primer número
opening price *s* primer curso, precio de apertura
open-minded [ˈopənˈmaɪndɪd] *adj* receptivo, razonable, imparcial
open secret *s* secreto a voces
open shop *s* taller franco
open society *s* sociedad que permite los derechos civiles
open to the public *s* entrada libre
o'pen•work' *s* calado
opera [ˈɑpərə] *s* ópera
opera glasses *spl* gemelos de teatro
opera hat *s* clac *m,* sombrero de muelles
opera house *s* teatro de la ópera
operate [ˈɑpə,ret] *tr* hacer funcionar; dirigir, manejar; explotar || *intr* funcionar; operar; **to operate on** operar (*p.ej., una hernia; a un niño*)
operatic [,ɑpəˈrætɪk] *adj* operístico
operating expenses *spl* gastos de explotación
operating room *s* quirófano
operating table *s* mesa operatoria
operation [,ɑpə,retʃən] *s* operación; funcionamiento; (med) operación, intervención quirúrgica
operator [ˈɑpə,retər] *s* operador *m,* maquinista *m;* (com) empresario; (coll) corredor *m* de bolsa; (compu, electron, surg, telp) operador *m*
operetta [,ɑpəˈrɛtə] *s* opereta
opiate [ˈopɪ•ɪt] u [ˈop,et] *adj & s* opiato
opinion [əˈpɪnjən] *s* opinión; **in my opinion** a mi parecer; **to have a high opinion of** tener buen concepto de
opinionated [əˈpɪnjə,netɪd] *adj* porfiado en su parecer, dogmático
opinion poll *s* encuesta demoscópica
opium [ˈopɪ•əm] *s* opio
opium den *s* fumadero de opio
opossum [əˈpɑsəm] *s* zarigüeya
opponent [əˈponənt] *s* contrario
opportune [,ɑpərˈtjun] *adj* oportuno
opportunist [,ɑpərˈtjunɪst] *s* oportunista *mf;* maromero
opportuni•ty [,ɑpərˈtjunɪti] *s* (*pl* **-ties**) oportunidad, ocasión
oppose [əˈpoz] *tr* oponerse a
opposite [ˈɑpəsɪt] *adj* opuesto; de enfrente, p.ej., **the house opposite** la casa de enfrente || *prep* enfrente de || *s* contrario
opposite number *s* igual *mf,* doble *mf*
opposition [,ɑpəˈzɪʃən] *s* oposición
oppress [əˈprɛs] *tr* oprimir
oppression [əˈprɛʃən] *s* opresión
oppressive [əˈprɛsɪv] *adj* opresivo; sofocante, bochornoso
opprobrious [əˈprobrɪ•əs] *adj* oprobioso
opprobrium [əˈprobrɪ•əm] *s* oprobio
optic [ˈɑptɪk] *adj* óptico || *s* (coll) ojo; **optics** *ssg* óptica
optical [ˈɑptɪkəl] *adj* óptico
optical fiber *s* fibra óptica
optical scanner *s* lector óptico, lectura óptica
optician [ɑpˈtɪʃən] *s* óptico
optimism [ˈɑptɪ,mɪzəm] *s* optimismo
optimist [ˈɑptɪmɪst] *s* optimista *mf*
optimistic [,ɑptɪˈmɪstɪk] *adj* optimístico
optimize [ˈɑptə,maɪz] *tr* mejorar en todo lo posible
option [ˈɑpʃən] *s* opción
optional [ˈɑpʃənəl] *adj* facultativo, potestativo
optometrist [ɑp,tɑmɪtrɪst] *s* optometrista *mf*
opulent [ˈɑpjələnt] *adj* opulento
or [ɔr] *conj* o, u
oracle [ˈɑrəkəl] u [ˈɔrəkəl] *s* oráculo
oracular [oˈrækjələr] *adj* sentencioso; ambiguo, misterioso; fatídico; sabio
oral [ˈorəl] *adj* oral
orange [ˈɑrɪndʒ] u [ˈɔrɪndʒ] *adj* anaranjado || *s* naranja; (*color*) naranja *m*
orangeade [,ɑrɪndʒˈed] u [,ɔrɪndʒˈed] *s* naranjada
orange blossom *s* azahar *m*
orange grove *s* naranjal *m*
orange juice *s* zumo de naranja
orange peel *s* piel *f* de naranja
orange squeezer *s* exprimidera de naranjas
orange tree *s* naranjo
orangutan [əˈræŋə,tæŋ] *s* orangután *m*
oration [oˈreʃən] *s* oración, discurso
orator [ˈɑrətər] u [ˈɔrətər] *s* orador *m*
oratorical [,ɔrəˈtɔrɪkəl] *adj* oratorio
oratori•o [,ɔrəˈtorɪ,o] *s* (*pl* **-os**) oratorio
orato•ry [ˈɔrə,tori] *s* (*pl* **-ries**) (*art of public speaking*) oratoria; (*small chapel*) oratorio
orb [ɔrb] *s* orbe *m*
orbit [ˈɔrbɪt] *s* órbita; **to go into orbit** entrar en órbita || *tr* poner en órbita; moverse en órbita alrededor de || *intr* moverse enorbita
orbital space station [ˈɔrbɪtəl] *s* estación orbital
orbiter [ˈɔrbɪtər] *s* satélite *m* (artificial)
orchard [ˈɔrtʃərd] *s* huerto
orchestra [ˈɔkɪstrə] *s* orquesta; (*parquet*) platea, patio (Esp)
orchestrate [ˈɔrkɪs,tret] *tr* orquestar

orchid [ˈɔrkɪd] *s* orquídea
ordain [ɔrˈden] *tr* (eccl) ordenar; destinar; mandar
ordeal [ɔrˈdil] u [ɔrˈdi•əl] *s* prueba rigurosa o penosa; (hist) juicio de Dios
order [ˈɔrdər] *s* (*way one thing follows another; formal or methodical arrangement; peace, quiet; class, category*) orden *m;* (*command; honor society; monastic brotherhood; fraternal organization*) orden *f;* tarea, p.ej., **a big order** una tarea peliaguda; (com) pedido; (com) giro, libranza; (*formation*) (mil) orden *m;* (*command*) (mil) orden *f;* **in order that** para que, a fin de que; **in order to** + *inf* para + *inf,* a fin de + *inf;* **to get out of order** descomponerse; **to give an order** dar una orden; (com) hacer un pedido ‖ *tr* ordenar; mandar; encargar, pedir; mandar hacer; **to order around** ser muy mandón con; **to order someone away** mandar a uno que se marche
order blank *s* hoja de pedidos
order•ly [ˈɔrdərli] *adj* ordenado, gobernoso; tranquilo, obediente ‖ *s* (*pl* **-lies**) asistente *m* en un hospital; (mil) ordenanza *m*
ordinal [ˈɔrdɪnəl] *adj & s* ordinal *m*
ordinance [ˈɔrdɪnəns] *s* ordenanza
ordinary [ˈɔrdɪ,nɛri] *adj* ordinario
ordnance [ˈɔrdnəns] *s* artillería, cañones *mpl;* pertrechos de guerra
ore [or] *s* mena, mineral metalífero
organ [ˈɔrgən] *s* órgano
organ•dy [ˈɔrgəndi] *s* (*pl* **-dies**) organdí *m*
or′gan-grind′er *s* organillero
organic [ɔrˈgænɪk] *adj* orgánico
organic farming *s* agricultura biológica
organism [ˈɔrgə,nɪzəm] *s* organismo
organist [ˈɔrgənɪst] *s* organista *mf*
organize [ˈɔrgə,naɪz] *tr* organizar
organ loft *s* tribuna del órgano
orgasm [ˈɔrgæzəm] *s* orgasmo
orgiastic [,ɔrdʒiˈæstɪk] *adj* orgiástico
or•gy [ˈɔrdʒi] *s* (*pl* **-gies**) orgía
orient [ˈorɪ•ənt] *s* oriente *m* ‖ **Orient** *s* oriente ‖ **orient** [ˈorɪ,ɛnt] *tr* orientar
oriental [,orɪˈɛntəl] *adj* oriental
orientation [,ɔrɪ,ənˈteʃən] *s* orientación
orifice [ˈɔrɪfɪs] *s* orificio
origin [ˈɔrɪdʒɪn] *s* origen *m*
original [əˈrɪdʒɪnəl] *adj & s* original *m*
originate [əˈrɪdʒɪ,net] *tr* originar ‖ *intr* originarse
oriole [ˈorɪ,ol] *s* oropéndola
Orkney Islands [ˈɔrkni] *spl* Órcadas
ormolu [ˈɔrmə,lu] *s* (*gold powder used in gilding*) oro molido; (*alloy of zinc and copper*) similor m; bronce dorado
ornament [ˈɔrnəmənt] *s* ornamento ‖ [ˈɔrnə,mɛnt] *tr* ornamentar
ornate [ɔrˈnet] u [ˈɔrnet] *adj* muy ornado; (*style*) florido
orphan [ˈɔrfən] *adj & s* huérfano ‖ *tr* dejar huérfano
orphanage [ˈɔrfənɪdʒ] *s* (*institution*) orfanato; órfelinato (SAm); (*state, condition*) orfandad
orthodontic appliance [,ɔrθəˈdɑntɪk] *s* aparato de ortodoncia
orthodontics [,ɔrθəˈdɑntɪks] *s* ortodoncia
orthodox [ˈɔrθə,dɑks] *adj* ortodoxo
orthogra•phy [ɔrˈθɑgrəfɪ] *s* (*pl* **-phies**) ortografía
orthopedics [ˈɔrθəˈpidɪks] *s* ortopedia, traumatología
oscillate [ˈɑsɪ,let] *intr* oscilar
osier [ˈoʒər] *s* mimbre *m & f;* sauce mimbrero
ossi•fy [ˈɑsɪ,faɪ] *v* (*pret & pp* **-fied**) *tr* osificar ‖ *intr* osificarse
ostensible [ɑsˈtɛnsɪbəl] *adj* aparente, pretendido, supuesto
ostentatious [,ɑstɛnˈteʃəs] *adj* (*pretentious*) ostentativo; (*showy*) ostentoso
osteopath [ˈɑstɪ•ə,pæθ] *s* osteópata *mf*
osteopathy [,ɑstɪˈɑpəθi] *s* osteopatía
ostracism [ˈɑstrə,sɪzəm] *s* ostracismo
ostrich [ˈɑstrɪtʃ] *s* avestruz *m*
other [ˈʌðər] *adj & pron indef* otro ‖ *adv*—**other than** de otra manera que
otherwise [ˈʌðər,waɪz] *adv* otramente, de otra manera; en otras circunstancias; fuera de eso; si no, de otro modo
otherworldly [ˈʌðər,wʌrldli] *adj* extraterrestre
otter [ˈɑtər] *s* nutria, lobo acuático o de río
ottoman [ˈɑtəmən] *s* (*corded fabric*) otomán *m;* (*sofa*) otomana; escañuelo con cojín ‖ **Ottoman** *adj & s* otomano
ouch [aʊtʃ] *interj* ¡ay!
ought [ɔt] *s* alguna cosa; cero; **for ought I know** por lo que yo sepa ‖ *v aux* se emplea para formar el modo potencial, p.ej., **he ought to go at once** debiera salir en seguida
ounce [aʊns] *s* onza (*28,35 gramos*)
our [aʊr] *adj poss* nuestro
ours [aʊrz] *pron poss* el nuestro; nuestro
ourselves [aʊrˈsɛlvz] *pron pers* nosotros mismos; nos, p.ej., **we enjoyed ourselves** nos divertimos
oust [aʊst] *tr* echar fuera, desposeer; desahuciar (*al inquilino*)
out [aʊt] *adj* ausente; apagado; exterior; divulgado; publicado; (*size*) poco común ‖ *adv* afuera, fuera; al aire libre; hasta el fin; **out for** buscando; **out of** de; entre; de entre; fuera de; más allá de; (*kindness, fear, etc.*) por; (*money*) sin; (*a suit of cards*) fallo a; sobre, p.ej., **in nine out of ten cases** en nueve casos sobre diez; **out to** + *inf* esforzándose por + *inf* ‖ *prep* por; allá en ‖ *interj* ¡fuera de aquí! ‖ *s* cesante *mf;* **to be at outs** u **on the outs** estar de monos
out and away *adv* con mucho
out′-and-out′ *adj* perfecto, verdadero, rematado, a ultranza ‖ *adv* completamente
out′-and-out′er *s* intransigente *mf;* extremista *mf*
outbid′ *v* (*pret* **-bid;** *pp* **-bid** o **-bidden;** *ger*

-bidding) *tr* pujar más que (*otra persona*); (bridge) sobrepasar
out'board' motor *s* motor *m* fuera de borda, fuerabordo *m*
out'break' *s* tumulto, motín *m;* (*of anger*) arranque *m;* (*of war*) estallido; (*of an epidemic*) brote *m*
out'build'ing *s* dependencia, edificio accesorio
out'burst' *s* explosión, arranque *m;* **outburst of laughter** carcajada
out'cast' *s* proscripto, paria *mf;* vagabundo
out'come' *s* resultado
out'cry' *s* (*pl* **-cries**) grito; gritería, clamoreo
out•dat'ed *adj* fuera de moda, anticuado
out•do' *v* (**-did;** *pp* **-done**) *tr* exceder; **to outdo oneself** excederse a sí mismo
out'door' *adj* al aire libre
out'doors' *adv* al aire libre, fuera de casa || *s* aire *m* libre, campo raso
outer ear *s* pabellón *m* auricular
outer space ['autər] *s* espacio exterior
out'field' *s* (baseball) jardín *m*
out'field'er *s* (baseball) jardinero
out'fit *s* equipo; traje *m;* juego de herramientas; (*of soldiers*) cuerpo; (*of a bride*) ajuar *m;* (com) compañía || *v* (*pret & pp* **-fitted;** *ger* **-fitting**) *tr* equipar
out'go'ing *adj* de salida; cesante; (*tide*) descendente; (*nature, character*) exteriorista || *s* salida
out•grow' *v* (*pret* **-grew;** *pp* **-grown**) *tr* crecer más que; ser ya grande para; ser ya viejo para; ser ya más apto que; dejar (*las cosas de los niños; a los amigos de la niñez, etc.*) || *intr* extenderse
out'growth' *s* excrecencia, bulto; (*of leaves in springtime*) nacimiento; consecuencia, resultado
outing ['autɪŋ] *s* jira, gira, excursión al campo
outlandish [aut'lændɪʃ] *adj* estrafalario; de aspecto extranjero; de acento extranjero
out•last' *tr* durar más que; sobrevivir a
out'law' *s* forajido, bandido; prófugo, proscrito || *tr* proscribir; declarar ilegal
out'lay' *s* desembolso || **out•lay'** *v* (*pret & pp* **-laid**) *tr* desembolsar
out'let *s* salida; desaguadero; orificio de salida; (elec) caja de enchufe; (*tap*) (elec) toma de corriente *m*
out'line' *s* contorno; trazado; esquema *m;* esbozo, bosquejo; compendio || *tr* contornar; trazar; trazar el esquema de; esbozar, bosquejar; compendiar
out'lin'ing *s* (compu) silueteado
out•live' *tr* sobrevivir a; durar más que
out'look' *s* perspectiva; expectativa; concepto de la vida, punto de vista; atalaya
out'ly'ing *adj* remoto, circundante, de las afueras, periférico
out•mod'ed *adj* fuera de moda
out•num'ber *tr* exceder en número, ser más numeroso que
out'-of-date' *adj* fuera de moda, anticuado
out'-of-door' *adj* al aire libre
out'-of-doors' *adj* al aire libre || *adv* al aire libre, fuera de casa || *s* aire *m* libre, campo raso
out'-of-print' *adj* agotado
out'-of-the-way' *adj* apartado, remoto; poco usual, poco común
out of tune *adj* desafinado || *adv* desafinadamente
out of work *adj* desempleado, sin trabajo
out'pa'tient *s* paciente *mf* de consulta externa
out'post' *s* avanzada
out'put' *s* rendimiento; (compu, elec) salida; (mech) rendimiento de trabajo, efecto útil
out'rage *s* atrocidad; ultraje *m* || *tr* maltratar; ultrajar; escandalizar
outrageous [aut'redʒəs] *adj* (*grossly offensive*) ultrajoso; (*shocking, fierce*) atroz; (*extreme*) extravagante
out•rank' *tr* exceder en rango o grado
out'rid'er *s* carrerista *m;* (Brit) viajante *m* de comercio
out'right' *adj* cabal, completo; franco, sincero || *adv* enteramente; de una vez; sin rodeos; en seguida
out'run'ner *s* volante *m* (*criado*)
out'set' *s* principio
out'side' *adj* exterior; superficial; ajeno; (*price*) (el) máximo || *adv* fuera, afuera; **outside of** fuera de || *prep* fuera de; más allá de; (coll) a excepción de || *s* exterior *m;* superficie *f;* apariencia
outside broadcasting unit *s* equipo móvil, fuera de serie;
outsider [,aut'saɪdər] *s* forastero; intruso
out'skirts' *spl* afueras
out'spo'ken *adj* boquifresco, franco
out•stand'ing *adj* sobresaliente; prominente; sin pagar, sin cobrar
outward ['autwərd] *adj* exterior; superficial || *adv* exteriormente, hacia fuera
out•weigh' *tr* pesar más que; contrapesar, compensar
out•wit' *v* (*pret & pp* **-witted;** *ger* **-witting**) *tr* burlar, ser más listo que; despistar (*al perseguidor*)
oval ['ovəl] *adj* oval || *s* óvalo
ova•ry ['ovəri] *s* (*pl* **-ries**) ovario
ovation [o'veʃən] *s* ovación
oven ['ʌvən] *s* horno
o'ven•proof' *adj* de horno, refractario; **ovenproof dish** fuente de horno
over ['ovər] *adj* acabado, concluído; superior; adicional; excesivo || *adv* encima; al otro lado, a la otra orilla; hacia abajo; al revés; patas arriba; otra vez, de nuevo; de añadidura; (*at the bottom of a page*) a la vuelta; acá, p.ej., **hand over the money** déme acá el dinero; **over again** una vez más; **over against** enfrente de; a distinción de; en contraste con; **over and over** repetidas veces; **over here** acá; **over in** allá en; **over there** allá || *prep* sobre, encima de, por encima de; por; de un extremo a otro de; al otro lado de; más allá de; desde;

(*a certain number*) más de; acerca de; por causa de; durante; **over and above** además de, en exceso de

o'ver•all' *adj* cabal, completo; extremo, total || **overalls** *spl* pantalones *mf* de trabajo; overol *m,* mono

o'ver•bear'ing *adj* altanero, imperioso

o'ver•board' *adv* al agua; **man overboard!** ¡hombre al agua!; **to throw overboard** arrojar, echar o tirar por la borda

o'ver•cast' *adj* encapotado, nublado || *s* cielo encapotado || *v* (*pret & pp* **-cast**) *tr* nublar

o'ver•charge' *s* cargo excesivo; recargo de precio; sobrecarga; (elec) carga excesiva || **o'ver•charge'** *tr* hacer pagar más del valor, cobrar demasiado a; cargar (*p.ej., 50 pesetas*) de más; (elec) poner una carga excesiva a

o'ver•coat' *s* abrigo, gabán *m,* sobretodo

o'ver•come' *v* (*pret* **-came;** *pp* **-come**) *tr* vencer; rendir; superar (*dificultades*)

o'ver•crowd' *tr* atestar, apiñar; poblar con exceso

o'ver•do *v* (*pret* **-did;** *pp* **-done**) *tr* exagerar; agobiar; asurar, requemar || *intr* cansarse mucho, excederse en el trabajo

o'ver•dose' *s* sobredosis *f,* dosis excesiva || *intr* tomar una dosis excesiva

o'ver•draft *s* sobregiro, giro en descubierto

overdraft protection *s* crédito en cuenta corriente

o'ver•draw' *v* (*pret* **-drew;** *pp* **-drawn**) *tr & intr* sobregirar

o'ver•due' *adj* atrasado; vencido y no pagado

o'ver•eat' *v* (*pret* **-ate;** *pp* **-eaten**) *tr & intr* comer con exceso

o'ver•es'ti•mate *tr* sobreestimar

o'ver•exer'tion *s* esfuerzo excesivo

o'ver•ex'ploi•ta'tion *s* (*of resources*) explotación abusiva

o'ver•expose' *tr* sobreexponer

o'ver•expo'sure *s* sobreexposición

o'ver•flow' *s* desbordamiento, rebosamiento, derrame *m;* caño de reboso || **o'ver•flow** *intr* desbordar, rebosar

o'ver•fly' *v* (*pret* **-flew;** *pp* **-flown**) *tr* sobrevolar

o'ver•grown' *adj* demasiado grande para su edad; denso, frondoso

o'ver•hang' *v* (*pret & pp* **-hung**) *tr* sobresalir por encima de, estar pendiente o colgando sobre, salir fuera del nivel de; amenazar || *intr* estar pendiente, estar colgando

o'ver•haul' *tr* examinar, registrar, revisar; ir alcanzando, alcanzar; componer, rehabilitar, reacondicionar

o'ver•head' *adj* de arriba; aéreo, elevado; general, de conjunto || **o'ver•head'** *adv* por encima de la cabeza; arriba, en lo alto || **o'ver•head'** *s* gastos generales *or* fijos

o'ver•hear *v* (*pret & pp* **-heard**) *tr* oír por casualidad; acertar a oír, alcanzar a oír

o'ver•heat *tr* recalentar || *intr* recalentarse

overjoyed [,over'dʒɔɪd] *adj* lleno de alegría; **to be overjoyed** no caber de contento

o'ver•kill' *s* exceso de potencia; exceso de eficacia || *intr* exceder lo necesario

overland ['ovər,lænd] u ['ovərlənd] *adj & adv* por tierra, por vía terrestre

o'ver•lap' *v* (*pret & pp* **-lapped;** *ger* **-lapping**) *tr* solapar, traslapar || *intr* solapar, traslapar; traslaparse (*dos o más cosas*); suceder (*dos hechos*) en parte al mismo tiempo

o'ver•load' *s* sobrecarga || **o'ver•load'** *tr* sobrecargar

o'ver•look' *tr* dominar con la vista; pasar por alto, no hacer caso de; perdonar, tolerar; espiar, vigilar; cuidar de, dirigir; dar a, p.ej., **the window overlooks the garden** la ventana da al jardín

o'ver•lord' *s* jefe supremo || **o'ver•lord'** *tr* dominar despóticamente, imponerse a

overly ['ovərli] *adv* (coll) excesivamente, demasiado

o'ver•night' *adv* toda la noche; de la tarde a la mañana; **to stay overnight** pasar la noche

overnight bag *s* saco de noche

o'ver•pass' *s* viaducto, paso elevado

o'ver•pop'u•late' *tr* superpoblar

o'verpow'er *tr* dominar, supeditar, subyugar; colmar, dejar estupefacto

overpowering *adj* abrumador, arrollador, irresistible

o'ver•produc'tion *s* superproducción, sobreproducción

o'ver•rate' *tr* exagerar el valor de

o'ver•run' *v* (*pret* **-ran;** *pp* **-run;** *ger* **-running**) *tr* cubrir enteramente; infestar; exceder; **to overrun one's time** quedarse más de lo justo; hablar más de lo justo

o'ver•sea' u **o'ver•seas'** *adj* de ultramar || **o'ver•sea'** u **o'ver•seas'** *adv* allende los mares, en ultramar

o'ver•seer' *s* director *m,* superintendente *mf*

o'ver•shad'ow *tr* sombrear; (fig) eclipsar

o'ver•shoe' *s* chanclo, zapato de goma

o'ver•shoot' *v* (*pret & pp* **-shot**) *tr* tirar por encima de o más allá de; **to overshoot oneself** pasarse de listo, excederse

o'ver•sight' *s* inadvertencia, descuido

o'ver•sleep' *v* (*pret & pp* **-slept**) *intr* dormir demasiado tarde

o'ver•step' *v* (*pret & pp* **-stepped;** *ger* **-stepping**) *tr* exceder, traspasar

o'ver•stock' *tr* abarrotar

o'ver•sup•ply' *s* (*pl* **-plies**) provisión excesiva || **o'ver•sup•ply'** *v* (*pret* **-plied**) *tr* proveer en exceso

overt ['ovərt] u [o'vʌrt] *adj* abierto, manifiesto; premeditado

o'ver•take' *v* (*pret* **-took;** *pp* **-taken**) *tr* alcanzar; sobrepasar; sorprender; sobrevenir a

o'ver-the-count'er *adj* vendido directamente al comprador; vendido en tienda al por mayor

o'ver•throw' *s* derrocamiento; trastorno || **o'ver•throw'** *v* (*pret* **-threw;** *pp* **-thrown**) *tr* derrocar; trastornar

o'ver•time' *adj & adv* en exceso de las horas

regulares || *s* horas extraordinarias de trabajo, horas extra(s), tiempo suplementario; (sport) tiempo complementario

o'ver•trump *s* contrafallo ||

o'ver•trump' *tr & intr* contrafallar

overture ['ovərtʃər] *s* insinuación, proposición; (mus) obertura

o'ver•turn' *s* vuelco; movimiento de mercancías || **o'ver•turn'** *tr* volcar; trastornar; derrocar || *intr* volcar; trastornarse

overweening [,ovər'winɪŋ] *adj* arrogante, presuntuoso

o'ver•weight' *adj* excesivamente gordo o grueso || *s* sobrepeso; exceso de peso; peso de añadidura

overwhelm [,ovər'hwɛlm] *tr* abrumar; inundar; anonadar; (*with favors, gifts, etc.*) colmar

o'ver•work' *s* trabajo excesivo, exceso de trabajo; trabajo fuera de las horas regulares || **o'ver•work'** *tr* hacer trabajar demasiado; oprimir con el trabajo || *intr* trabajar demasiado

ovum ['ovəm] *s* óvulo

ow [aʊ] *interj* ¡ay!

owe [o] *tr* deber, adeudar || *intr* tener deudas

owing ['o•ɪŋ] *adj* adeudado; debido, pagadero; **owing to** debido a, por causa de

owl [aʊl] *s* buho, lechuza, mochuelo

own [on] *adj* propio, p.ej., **my own brother** mi propio hermano || *s* suyo, lo suyo; **on one's own** (coll) por su propia cuenta; (*without taking advice from anyone*) por su cabeza; (*without help from anyone*) de su cabeza; **to come into one's own** entrar en posesión de lo suyo; tener el éxito merecido, recibir el honor merecido; **to hold one's own** no aflojar, no cejar, mantenerse firme || *tr* poseer; reconocer || *intr* confesar; **to own up to** (coll) confesar de plano (*una culpa, un delito, etc.*)

owner ['onər] *s* amo, dueño, poseedor *m*, posesor *m*, proprietario

ownership ['onər,ʃɪp] *s* posesión, propiedad

owner's license *s* permiso de circulación, patente *f* de circulación

ox [ɑks] *s* (*pl* **oxen**) ['ɑksən] buey *m*

ox'cart' *s* carreta de bueyes

oxide ['ɑksaɪd] *s* óxido

oxidize ['ɑksɪ,daɪz] *tr* oxidar || *intr* oxidarse

oxygen ['ɑksɪdʒən] *s* oxígeno

oxygen tent *s* cámara o tienda de oxígeno

oxytone ['ɑksɪ,ton] *adj & s* oxítono

oyster ['ɔɪstər] *adj* ostrero || *s* ostra

oyster bed *s* ostrero

oyster cocktail *s* ostras en su concha

oyster fork *s* desbullador *m*

oys'ter•house' *s* ostrería

oys'ter•knife' *s* abreostras *m*

oyster•man ['ɔɪstərmən] *s* (*pl* **-men** [mən]) ostrero

oyster opener ['opənər] *s* desbullador *m*

oyster shell *s* desbulla, concha de ostra

oyster stew *s* sopa de ostras

oz. *abbr* **ounce, ounces**

ozone ['ozon] *s* ozono; (coll) aire fresco

ozone hole *s* agujero en la capa de ozono

ozone layer *s* capa de ozono

ozonosphere [o'zonə,sfɪr] *s* ozonosfera

P

P, p [pi] decimosexta letra del alfabeto inglés

p. *abbr* **page, participle**

P.A. *abbr* **Passenger Agent, power of attorney, Purchasing Agent**

pace [pes] *s* paso; **to keep pace with** ir, andar o avanzar al mismo paso que; **to put through one's paces** poner (*a uno*) a prueba; dar a (*uno*) ocasión de lucirse; **to set the pace** establecer el paso; dar el ejemplo || *tr* establecer el paso para; medir a pasos; recorrer a pasos; **to pace the floor** pasearse desesperadamente por la habitación || *intr* andar a pasos regulares

pace'mak'er *s* (med) marcapaso, marcapasos *m*

pacific [pə'sɪfɪk] *adj* pacífico || **Pacific** *adj & s* Pacífico; **Pacific Ocean** Océano Pacífico

pacifier ['pæsɪ,faɪ•ər] *s* pacificador *m*, chupon *m*; (*teething ring*) chupador *m*

pacifism ['pæsɪ,fɪzəm] *s* pacifismo

pacifist ['pæsɪfɪst] *adj & s* pacifista *mf*

paci•fy ['pæsɪ,faɪ] *v* (*pret & pp* **-fied**) *tr* pacificar

pack [pæk] *s* lío, fardo; paquete *m;* (*of hounds*) jauría; (*of cattle*) manada; (*of evildoers*) pandilla; (*of lies*) sarta, montón *m;* (*of playing cards*) baraja; (*of cigarettes*) cajetilla; (*of floating ice*) témpano; (med) compresa || *tr* empaquetar; embaular; encajonar; hacer (*el baúl, la maleta*); conservar en latas; apretar, atestar; cargar (*una acémila*); escoger de modo fraudulento (*un jurado*); **to be packed in** (coll) estar como sardinas en banasta || *intr* empaquetarse; hacer el baúl, hacer la maleta; consolidarse, formar masa compacta

package ['pækɪdʒ] *s* paquete *m* || *tr* empaquetar

package tour *s* viaje organizado

package store *s* tienda de bebidas alcohólicas

pack animal *s* acémila, animal *m* de carga

packer ['pækər] *s* (*company*) envasadora, frigorífico (SAm); (*in warehouse*) embalador *m*, envasador *m*

packing box o **case** *s* caja de embalaje

packing house *s* empresa de productos cárnicos, frigorífico (SAm)

packing slip *s* hoja de embalaje
pack rat *s* **—to be a pack rat** (coll) ser una urraca
pack′sad′dle *s* albarda
pack′thread′ *s* bramante *m*
pack train *s* recua
pact [pækt] *s* pacto
pad [pæd] *s* conjincillo, almohadilla; (*of writing paper*) bloc *m;* (*for inking*) tampón *m;* (*of an aquatic plant*) hoja; (*for launching a rocket*) plataforma *f;* (*sound of footsteps*) pisada; (*apartment*) (slang) bulín *m* (SAm); (*bed*) (slang) cama, catre *m* (SAm) ‖ *v* (*pret & pp* **padded;** *ger* **padding**) *tr* acolchar, rellenar; meter mucho ripio en (*un escrito*) ‖ *intr* andar, caminar; caminar despacio y pesadamente
paddle [ˋpædəl] *s* (*of a canoe*) canalete *m;* (*of a wheel*) pala, paleta; (*for spanking*) palo ‖ *tr* impulsar con canalete; (*to spank*) apalear ‖ *intr* remar con canalete; remar suavemente; (*to splash*) chapotear
paddle wheel *s* rueda de paletas
paddock [ˋpædək] *s* dehesa; (*at a racecourse*) paddock *m*
paddy wagon [ˋpædi] *s* (coll) camión *m* de policía
pad′lock′ *s* candado ‖ *tr* cerrar con candado; (*to lock up officially*) condenar (*una habitación, un teatro*)
pagan [ˋpegən] *adj & s* pagano
paganism [ˋpegə,nɪzəm] *s* paganismo
page [pedʒ] *s* (*of a book*) página; (*boy attendant*) paje *m;* (*in a hotel or club*) botones *m* ‖ *tr* paginar; buscar llamando
pageant [ˋpædʒənt] *s* espectáculo público
pageant•ry [ˋpædʒəntri] *s* (*pl* **-ries**) pompa, fausto; (*empty display*) bambolla
page setup *s* (compu, typ) compaginación
pail [pel] *s* balde *m,* cubo
pain [pen] *s* dolor *m;* **on pain of** so pena de; **pains** esmero, trabajo; dolores de parto; **to take pains** esmerarse ‖ *tr & intr* doler
painful [ˋpenfəl] *adj* doloroso; penoso
pain′kill′er *s* analgésico; calmante *m* del dolor
painless [ˋpenlɪs] *adj* sin dolor, indoloro; fácil, sin trabajo
pains′tak′ing *adj* esmerado
paint [pent] *s* pintura ‖ *tr* pintar ‖ *intr* pintar; pintarse, repintarse
paint′box′ *s* caja de colores
paint′brush′ *s* brocha, pincel *m*
painter [ˋpentər] *s* pintor *m*
painting [ˋpentɪŋ] *s* pintura
paint remover [rɪˋmuvər] *s* sacapintura *m,* quitapintura *m*
pair [pɛr] *s* par *m;* (*of people*) pareja; (*of cards*) parejas ‖ *tr* aparear ‖ *intr* aparearse
pair of scissors *s* tijeras
pair of trousers *s* pantalones *mpl*
pajamas [peˋdʒɑməz] o [peˋdʒæməz] *spl* pijama
Pakistan [,pɑkɪˋstɑn] *s* el Paquistán
Pakistani [,pɑkɪˋstɑni] *adj & s* paquistano, paquistaní *mf*
pal [pæl] *s* (coll) compañero; cumpa *m* (SAm) ‖ *v* (*pret & pp* **palled;** *ger* **palling**) *intr* (coll) ser compañeros
palace [ˋpælɪs] *s* palacio
palatable [ˋpælətəbəl] *adj* sabroso, apetitoso
palatal [ˋpælətəl] *adj & s* palatal *f*
palate [pælɪt] *s* paladar *m*
pale [pel] *adj* pálido; (*color*) claro ‖ *s* estaca; palizada; límite *m,* término ‖ *intr* palidecer
pale′face′ *s* carapálida, rostropálido (Esp)
palette [ˋpælɪt] *s* paleta
palfrey [ˋpɔlfri] *s* palafrén *m*
palimony [ˋpæləmoni] *s* pensión alimenticia que se paga a un antiguo o una antigua conviviente
palisade [,pælɪˋsed] *s* estaca; estacada; (*line of cliffs*) acantilado
pall [pɔl] *s* paño de ataúd, paño mortuorio; (eccl) palia ‖ *tr* hartar, saciar; quitar el sabor a ‖ *intr* perder el sabor
pall′bear′er *s* acompañante *m* de un cadáver; portador *m* del féretro
palliate [ˋpælɪ,et] *tr* paliar
pallid [ˋpælɪd] *adj* pálido
pallor [ˋpælər] *s* palidez *f,* palor *m*
palm [pɑm] *s* (*of the hand*) palma; (*measure*) palmo; (*tree and leaf*) palma; **to carry off the palm** llevarse la palma; **to grease the palm of** (slang) untar la mano a; **to yield the palm to** reconocer por vencedor ‖ *tr* esconder en la mano; escamotear (*una carta*); **to palm off something on someone** encajarle una cosa a uno
palmet•to [pælˋmɛto] *s* (*pl* **-tos** o **-toes**) palmito
palmist [ˋpɑmɪst] *s* quiromántico
palmistry [ˋpɑmɪstri] *s* quiromancia
palm leaf *s* palma, hoja de la palmera
palm oil *s* aceite *m* de palma; (slang) propina; (slang) soborno
Palm Sunday *s* domingo de ramos
palpable [ˋpælpəbəl] *adj* palpable
palpitate [ˋpælpɪ,tet] *intr* palpitar
pal•sy [ˋpɔlzi] *s* (*pl* **-sies**) perlesía, parálisis *f*
pal•try [ˋpɔltri] *adj* (*comp* **-trier;** *super* **-triest**) vil, ruin, mezquino
pamper [ˋpæmpər] *tr* mimar, consentir
pamphlet [ˋpæmflɪt] *s* folleto, panfleto
pan [pæn] *s* cacerola, cazuela, sartén *f;* caldera, perol *m* ‖ *v* (*pret & pp* **panned;** *ger* **panning**) *tr* cocer, freír; separar (*el oro*) en la gamella; (coll) criticar ásperamente ‖ *intr* separar el oro en la gamella; dar oro; **to pan out well** (coll) tener éxito, dar buen resultado ‖
Pan *s* Pan
panacea [,pænəˋsi•ə] *s* panacea
Panama Canal [ˋpænə,mɑ] *s* canal *m* de Panamá
Panama hat *s* panamá *m*
Panamanian [,pænəˋmenɪ•ən] *adj & s* panameño

Pan-American [,pænə'mɛrɪkən] *adj* panamericano

pan'cake' *s* (culin) panqueque *m,* crep *m,* tortada (de harina) a la plancha, hojuela ‖ *intr* (aer) desplomarse

pancake landing *s* aterrizaje aplastado, aterrizaje en desplome

pancreas ['pænkrɪ•əs] *s* páncreas *m*

panda ['pændə] *s* panda *mf*

pander ['pændər] *s* alcahuete *m* ‖ *intr* alcahuetear; **to pander to** gratificar

pane [pen] *s* cristal *m,* vidrio, hoja de vidrio

pan•el ['pænəl] *s* panel *m,* entrepaño, cuarterón *m;* grupo de personas en discusión cara al público, panel; (aut, elec) tablero, panel; (law) lista de personas que pueden servir como jurados ‖ *v* (pret & pp **peled** o **-elled;** *ger* **-elling** o **-elling**) *tr* adornar con cuarterones, labrar en cuarterones; artesonar (*un techo o bóveda*)

panel discussion *s* coloquio cara al público

panelist ['pænəlɪst] *s* miembro del panel; (*in a quiz show*) concursante *mf*

panel lights *spl* luces *fpl* del tablero

pang [pæŋ] *s* dolor agudo; (*of remorse*) punzada; (*of death*) agonía

pan'han'dle *s* mango de sartén ‖ *intr* (coll) mendigar, pedir limosna

pan•ic ['pænɪk] *adj & s* pánico ‖ *v* (*pret & pp* **-icked;** *ger* **-icking**) *tr* sobrecoger de pánico ‖ *intr* sobrecogerse de pánico

pan'ic-strick'en *adj* muerto de miedo, sobrecogido de terror

pano•ply ['pænəpli] *s* (*pl* **-plies**) panoplia, traje *m* ceremonial

panorama [,pænə'ræmə] o [,pænə'rɑmə] *s* panorama *m*

pan shot *s* (phot) plano general

pan•sy ['pænzi] *s* (*pl* **-sies**) pensamiento

pant [pænt] *s* jadeo; palpitación; **pants** pantalones *mpl;* **to wear the pants** (coll) calzarse los pantalones ‖ *intr* jadear; palpitar

pantheism ['pænθɪ,ɪzəm] *s* panteísmo

pantheon ['pænθɪ,ɑn] *s* panteón *m*

panther ['pænθər] *s* pantera; puma

panties ['pæntiz] *spl* pantaloncillos de mujer

pantomime ['pæntə,maɪm] *s* pantomima

pan•try ['pæntri] *s* (*pl* **-tries**) despensa

panty hose *s* pantimedias (Mex), panty *m* (Ven)

pap [pæp] *s* papilla, papas

papa•cy ['pepəsi] *s* (*pl* **-cies**) papado

paper ['pepər] *s* papel *m;* (*newspaper*) periódico; (*of needles*) paño ‖ *tr* empapelar

pa'per•back' *s* libro en rústica *or* de bolsillo

pa'per•boy' *s* vendedor *m* de periódicos

paper clip *s* clip *m,* sujetapapelas *m;* presilla; prensador (CAm); gancho de papel (Col)

paper cone *s* cucurucho

paper cutter *s* cortapapeles *m,* guillotina

paper doll *s* muñeca de papel

paper hanger *s* empapelador *m,* papelista *mf*

paper knife *s* cortapapeles *m*

paper mill *s* fábrica de papel, molino de papel

paper money *s* papel *m* moneda

paper profits *spl* ganancias no realizadas sobre valores no vendidos

paper tape *s* cinta perforada

pa'per•weight' *s* pisapapeles *m*

paper work *s* preparación o comprobación de escritos; papelerío

pap•py ['pæpi] *s* (*pl* **-pies**) (coll) papá, papi

paprika [pæ'prikə] o ['pæprɪkə] *s* pimentón *m*

Pap smear, Pap test *s* citología, frotis *m,* Papanicolau *m*

papy•rus [pe'paɪrəs] *s* (*pl* **-ri** [raɪ]) papiro

par. *abbr* **paragraph, parallel, parenthesis, parish**

par [pɑr] *adj* a la par; nominal; normal ‖ *s* paridad; valor *m* nominal; **above par** sobre la par; con beneficio; con premio; **below par** o **under par** bajo la par; con pérdida; (coll) indispuesto; **par value** valor *m* nominal; **to be on a par with** correr parejas con

parable ['pærəbəl] *s* parábola

parachute ['pærə,ʃut] *s* paracaídas *m* ‖ *intr* parachutar, lanzarse en paracaídas; **to parachute to safety** salvarse en paracaídas

parachute jump *s* salto en paracaídas

parachutist ['pærə,ʃutɪst] *s* paracaidista *mf*

parade [pə'red] *s* desfile *m;* paseo; ostentación ‖ *tr* ostentar, pasear ‖ *intr* desfilar, pasar por las calles; (mil) formar en parada

paradise ['pærə,daɪs] *s* paraíso

paradox ['pærə,dɑks] *s* paradoja; persona o cosa incomprensibles

paradoxical [,pærə'dɑksɪkəl] *adj* paradójico

paraffin ['pærəfɪn] *s* parafina

paragon ['pærə,gɑn] *s* dechado

paragraph ['pærə,græf] *s* párrafo

Paraguay *s* el Paraguay

Paraguayan [,pærə'gwaɪ•ən] *adj & s* paraguayano, paraguayo

parakeet ['pærə,kit] *s* perico, periquito

paral•lel ['pærə,lɛl] *adj* paralelo ‖ *s* (línea) paralela; (plano) paralelo; (geog) paralelo; **parallels** (typ) doble raya vertical ‖ *v* (*pret & pp* **-leled** o **-lelled;** *ger* **-leling** o **-lelling**) *tr* ser paralelo a; poner en dirección paralela; correr parejas con; (*to compare*) paralelizar

parallel bars *spl* paralelas, barras paralelas

paraly•sis [pə'rælɪsɪs] *s* (*pl* **-ses** [,siz]) parálisis *f*

paralytic [,pærə'lɪtɪk] *adj & s* paralítico

paralyze ['pærə,laɪz] *tr* paralizar

parameter [pə'ræmətər] *s* parámetro

paramount ['pærə,maʊnt] *adj* capital, supremo, principalísimo

paranoiac [,pærə'nɔɪ•æk] o **paranoid** [pærə,nɔɪd] *adj & s* paranoico

parapet [,pærə,pɛt] *s* parapeto

paraphernalia [,pærəfər'nelɪ•ə] *spl* trastos, atavíos

paraplegic [,pærə'plidʒɪk] *adj & s* parapléjico, parapléjica

parasite ['pærə,saɪt] *s* parásito

parasitic(al) [,pærə'sɪtɪk(el)] *adj* parasítico, parasitario

parasol [ˈpærə,sɔl] *s* quitasol *m,* parasol *m*
pa′ra•troop′er *s* paracaidista *m*
pa′ra•troops′ *spl* tropas paracaidistas
parboil [ˈpɑr,bɔɪl] *tr* sancochar; calentar con exceso
par•cel [pɑrsəl] *s* paquete *m,* atado, bulto ‖ *v* (*pret & pp* **-celed** o **-celled;** *ger* **-celing** o **-celling**) *tr* empaquetar; parcelar (*el terreno*); **to parcel out** repartir
parcel post *s* paquetes *mpl* postales
parch [pɑrtʃ] *tr* abrasar, tostar; **to be parched** tener mucha sed
parchment [ˈpɑrtʃmənt] *s* pergamino
pardon [ˈpɑrdən] *s* perdón *m;* (*remission of penalty by the state*) indulto; **I beg your pardon** dispense Ud.; **pardon me** perdóneme, perdón ‖ *tr* perdonar, dispensar; indultar
pardonable [ˈpɑrdənəbəl] *adj* perdonable
pardon board *s* junta de perdones
pare [pɛr] *tr* mondar (*fruta*); pelar (*patatas*); cortar (*callos, uñas*); despalmar (*la palma córnea de los animales*); adelgazar; reducir (*gastos*)
parent [ˈpɛrənt] *adj* madre, matriz, principal ‖ *s* padre o madre; autor *m,* fuente *f,* origen *m;* **parents** padres *mpl*
parentage [ˈpɛrəntɪdʒ] *s* paternidad o maternidad; abolengo, linaje *m*
parent company compañía matriz
parenthe•sis [pəˈrɛnθɪsɪs] *s* (*pl* **-ses** [,siz]) paréntesis *m*
parenthood [ˈpɛrənt,hʊd] *s* paternidad o maternidad
pariah [pəˈraɪ•ə] o [ˈpɑrɪ•ə] *s* paria *mf*
paring knife [ˈpɛrɪŋ] *s* cuchillo para mondar
Paris [ˈpærɪs] *s* París
parish [ˈpærɪʃ] *s* parroquia, feligresía
parishioner [pəˈrɪʃənər] *s* parroquiano, feligrés *m*
Parisian [pəˈrɪʒən] *adj & s* parisiense *mf*
parity [ˈpærɪti] *s* paridad
park [pɑrk] *s* parque *m* ‖ *tr* estacionar, parquear; (coll) colocar, dejar ‖ *intr* estacionar, parquear
parking [ˈpɑrkɪŋ] *s* aparcamiento, estacionamiento; (*space*) parking *m;* **no parking** se prohibe estacionarse; *SIGN* prohibido estacionar
parking lights *spl* (aut) faros de situación, luces *fpl* de ciudad
parking lot *s* parque *m* de estacionamiento, parking *m*
parking meter *s* reloj *m* de estacionamiento, parquímetro, parcómetro
parking ticket *s* aviso de multa
Parkinson's disease [ˈpɑrkənsənz] *s* enfermedad *f, or* mal *m* de Parkinson (*parálisis agitante o temblorosa*)
park′way *s* gran via adornado con árboles, avenida ajardinada; autopista
parley [ˈpɑrli] *s* parlamento ‖ *intr* parlamentar
parliament [ˈpɑrlɪmənt] *s* parlamento
parlor [ˈpɑrlər] *s* sala; parlatorio, locutorio
parlor car *s* coche-salón *m*
parlor politics *spl* política de café
parochial [pəˈrokɪ•əl] *adj* parroquial; estrecho, limitado
paro•dy [ˈpærədi] *s* (*pl* **-dies**) parodia ‖ *v* (*pret & pp* **-died**) *tr* parodiar
parole [pəˈrol] *s* palabra de honor; libertad bajo palabra, libertad provisional ‖ *tr* dejar libre bajo palabra
par•quet [pɑrˈke] *s* entarimado; (theat) platea ‖ *v* (*pret & pp* **-queted** [ˈked]); *ger* **-queting** [ˈke•ɪŋ] *tr* entarimar
parricide [ˈpærɪ,saɪd] *s* (*act*) parricidio; (*person*) parricida *mf*
parrot [ˈpærət] *s* papagayo, loro; (fig) papagayo ‖ *tr* repetir o imitar como loro
par•ry [ˈpæri] *s* (*pl* **-ries**) parada, quite *m* ‖ *v* (*pret & pp* **-ried**) *tr* parar; defenderse de
parse [pɑrs] *tr* analizar (*una oración*) gramaticalmente; describir (*una palabra*) gramaticalmente
parsley [ˈpɑrsli] *s* perejil *m*
parsnip [ˈpɑrsnɪp] *s* chirivía, pastinaca
parson [ˈpɑrsən] *s* cura *m,* párroco; clérigo; pastor *m* protestante
part [pɑrt] *s* parte *f;* (*of a machine*) pieza; (*of the hair*) raya; (theat) parte *f,* papel *m;* **part and parcel** parte esencial, parte inseparable, elemento esencial; **parts** partes *fpl;* prendas, dotes *fpl;* **to do one's part** cumplir con su obligación; **to look the part** vestir el cargo; **to take the part of** tomar el partido de, defender; desempeñar el papel de ‖ *tr* dividir, partir, separar; **to part the hair** hacerse la raya ‖ *intr* separarse; **to part with** deshacerse de, abandonar; despedirse de
par•take [pɑrˈtek] *v* (*pret* **-took** [ˈtʊk]; *pp* **-taken**) *tr* compartir; comer; beber ‖ *intr* participar
parthenogenesis [,pɑrθənoˈdʒɛnəsəs] *s* partenogénesis *f*
Parthenon [ˈpɑrθɪ,nɑn] *s* Partenón *m*
partial [ˈpɑrʃəl] *adj* parcial; aficionado
partiality [,pɑrʃiˈælətɪ] *s* (*bias*) parcialidad; (*fondness for*) afición a, debilidad por
participate [pɑrˈtɪsɪ,pet] *intr* participar
participation [pɑr,tɪsəˈpeʃən] *s* participación
participle [ˈpɑrtɪ,sɪpəl] *s* participio
particle [ˈpɑrtɪkəl] *s* partícula, corpúsculo
particle physics *s* física de las partículas
particular [pərˈtɪkjələr] *adj* particular; difícil, exigente, quisquilloso; esmerado; minucioso; **a particular . . .** cierto . . . ‖ *s* particular *m*
partisan [ˈpɑrtɪzən] *adj & s* partidario, partidista *mf;* (mil) partisano
partition [pɑrˈtɪʃən] *s* partición, distribución; división; proción; tabique *m* ‖ *tr* repartir; dividir en cuartos, aposentos; tabicar
partner [ˈpɑrtnər] *s* compañero; (*wife or husband*) cónyuge *mf;* (*in a dance*) pareja *f;* (*in business*) socio
partnership [ˈpɑrtnər,ʃip] *s* asociación; consorcio, vida en común; (com) sociedad, asociación comercial

part of speech *s* función gramatical
partridge [ˈpɑrtrɪdʒ] *s* perdiz *f*
part′-time′ *adj* por horas, parcial
par•ty [ˈpɑrti] *adj* de partido; de gala ‖ *s* (*pl* **-ties**) convite *m,* reunión, fiesta, tertulia, recepción; (*for fishing, hunting, etc.; of armed men*) partida; cómplice *mf,* interesado; (pol) partido; (coll) persona, individuo
party girl *s* chica de vida alegre
party-goer [ˈpɑrti,go•ər] *s* tertuliano; fiestero
party line *s* (*between two properties*) linde *m,* lindero; (pol) línea del partido; (telp) línea compartida o colectiva
party politics *s* política de partido
pass. *abbr* **passenger, passive**
pass [pæs] o [pɑs] *s* paso; (*permit; free ticket; movement of hands of mesmerist, of bullfighter*) pase *m;* (*in an examination*) aprobación; nota de aprobación ‖ *tr* pasar; pasar de largo (*una luz roja*); aprobar (*un proyecto de ley; un examen; a un alumno*); ser aprobado en (*un examen*); dejar atrás; cruzarse con; expresar (*una opinión*); pronunciar (*una sentencia*), dar (*la palabra*); dejar sin protestar, no pagar (*un dividendo*); **to pass off** colar, pasar, hacer aceptar (*una moneda falsa*); disimular (*p.ej., una ofensa con una risa*); **to pass over** omitir, pasar por alto; excusar; desdeñar; dejar sin protestar; postergar (*a un empleado*) ‖ *intr* pasar; pasarse (*introducirse*); aprobar; **to bring to pass** llevar a cabo; **to come to pass** suceder; **to pass as** pasar por; **to pass away** pasar, pasar a mejor vida; **to pass off** pasar (*una enfermedad, una tempestad, etc.*); tener lugar; **to pass out** salir; (slang) desmayarse; **to pass over** (*ignore, omit*) pasar por alto; **to pass over to** pasarse a (p.ej., el enemigo)
passable [ˈpæsəbəl] o [ˈpɑsəbəl] *adj* pasadero; (*law*) promulgable
passage [ˈpæsɪdʒ] *s* pasaje *m;* paso; pasillo; (*of time*) transcurso; (*of bowels*) evacuación
pass′book′ *s* cartilla, libreta de banco
passenger [ˈpæsəndʒer] *adj* de viajeros ‖ *s* pasajero, viajero
passer-by [ˈpæsərˈbaɪ] o [ˈpɑsərˈbaɪ] *s* (*pl* **passers-by**) transeúnte *mf*
passing [ˈpæsɪŋ] o [ˈpɑsɪŋ] *adj* pasajero; corriente; de aprobado ‖ *s* (*act of passing; death*) paso; (*in an examination*) aprobación
passion [ˈpæʃən] *s* pasión
passionate [ˈpæʃənɪt] *adj* apasionado
passive [ˈpæsɪv] *adj* pasivo ‖ *s* voz pasiva, verbo pasivo
pass′key′ *s* llave *f* de paso
Pass′o′ver *s* (eccl) Pascua
pass′port′ *s* pasaporte *m*
passport photo *s* foto de carnet o de pasaporte
pass′port-size′ *adj* de tamaño carné
pass′word′ *s* santo y seña; (compu) contraseña
past [pæst] o [pɑst] *adj* pasado; último; que fue, p.ej., **past president** presidente que fue; acabado, concluído ‖ *adv* más allá; por delante ‖ *prep* más allá de; más de; por delante de; fuera de; después de, p.ej., **past two o'clock** después de las dos; **past belief** increíble; **past cure** incurable; **past hope** sin esperanza ‖ *s* pasado
pasta [ˈpɑstə] *s* pasta
paste [pest] *s* (*dough; spaghetti, etc.*) pasta; (*for sticking things together*) engrudo ‖ *tr* engrudar, pegar con engrudo
paste′board′ *s* cartón *m*
pasteurize [ˈpæstə,raɪz] *tr* pasterizar
pastime [ˈpæs,taɪm] *s* pasatiempo
pastor [ˈpæstər] *s* pastor *m,* clérigo, cura *m*
pastoral [ˈpæstərəl] *adj & s* pastoral *f*
pas•try [ˈpestri] *s* (*pl* **-tries**) pastelería
pastry cook *s* pastelero, repostero
pastry shop *s* pastelería, repostería
pasture [ˈpæstər] *s* pasto, pastura, dehesa ‖ *tr* apacentar, pacer ‖ *intr* apacentarse, pacer
past•y [ˈpesti] *adj* (*comp* **-ier;** *super* **-iest**) pastoso; flojo, fofo, pálido
pat [pæt] *s* golpecito, palmadita; ruido de pasos ligeros; (*of butter*) pastelillo ‖ *v* (*pret & pp* **patted;** *ger* **patting**) *tr* dar golpecitos a, golpear ligeramente; palmotear, acariciar con la mano; **to pat on the back** elogiar, cumplimentar
patch [pætʃ] *s* remiendo, parche *m;* terreno, pedazo de terreno; mancha; lunar postizo ‖ *tr* remendar; **to patch up** componer (*una desavenencia*); componer lo mejor posible (*una cosa descompuesta*); hacer aprisa y mal
patch′work quilt *s* centón *m,* colcha de retazos
patent [ˈpetənt] *adj* patente; abierto ‖ [ˈpætənt] *adj* de patentes ‖ *s* patente *f,* patente de invención; propiedad industrial; **patent applied for** se ha solicitado patente ‖ *tr* patentar
patent leather [ˈpætənt] *s* charol *m*
patent medicine [ˈpætənt] *s* medicamento de patente
patent rights [ˈpætənt] *spl* derechos de patente, propiedad industrial
paternal [pəˈtʌrnəl] *adj* paterno; (*affection*) paternal
paternity [peˈtʌrnɪti] *s* paternidad
path [pæθ] *s* senda, sendero; trayectoria
pathetic [pəˈθɛtɪk] *adj* patético
path′find′er baquiano; explorador *m*
pathological [ˈpæθəˈlɑdʒɪkəl] *adj* patológico
patholo•gy [pəˈθɑlədʒi] *s* patología
pathos [ˈpeθɑs] *s* patetismo
path′way′ *s* senda, sendero
patience [ˈpeʃəns] *s* paciencia
patient [ˈpeʃənt] *adj* paciente ‖ *s* paciente *mf,* enfermo
patio [ˈpæti′o] *s* patio *m*
patriarch [ˈpetrɪ,ɑrk] *s* patriarca *m*
Patricia [pəˈtrɪʃə] *f* Patricia
patrician [pəˈtrɪʃən] *adj & s* patricio
patricide [ˈpætrɪ,saɪd] *s* (*act*) parricidio; (*person*) parricida *mf*
Patrick [ˈpætrɪk] *s* Patricio
patrimo•ny [ˈpætrɪ,moni] *s* (*pl* **-nies**) patrimonio

patriot [ˈpetrɪ•ət] *s* patriota *mf*
patriotic [ˌpetrɪˈɑtɪk] *adj* patriótico
patriotism [ˈpetrɪ•əˌtɪzəm] *s* patriotismo
pa•trol [pəˈtrol] *s* patrulla ‖ *v* (*pret & pp* **-troled** o **-trolled;** *ger* **-troling** o **-trolling**) *tr & intr* patrullar
patrol•man [pəˈtrolmən] *s* (*pl* **-men** [mən]) guardia *m* municipal, vigilante *m* de policía
patrol wagon *s* camion *m* de policía; carropatrulla *m* (SAm), camión *m* celular
patron [ˈpetrən] *adj* tutelar ‖ *s* parroquiano; patrocinador *m*
patronize [ˈpetrəˌnaɪz] *tr* ser parroquiano de (*un tendero*); comprar de costumbre en; patrocinar; tratar con aire protector
patron saint *s* patrón *m,* santo titular
patsy [ˈpætsi] *s* (*scapegoat*) (slang) cabeza *mf* de turco, chivo expiatorio; (*easy mark*) (slang) presa fácil, primo (Esp); **Patsy** apodo de Patricia; apodo de Patricio
patter [ˈpætər] *s* golpeteo; (*of rain*) chapaleteo; charla, parloteo ‖ *intr* golpetear; charlar, parlotear
pattern [ˈpætərn] *s* patrón *m;* modelo
P.A.U. *abbr* **Pan American Union**
paucity [ˈpɔsɪti] *s* corto número; falta, escasez *f, insuficiencia*
Paul [pɔl] *s* Pablo; (*name of popes*) Paulo
paunch [pɔntʃ] *s* panza
paunchy [ˈpɔntʃi] *adj* panzudo
pauper [ˈpɔpər] *s* pobre *mf,* indigente *mf*
pauper's grave *s* fosa común
pause [pɔz] *s* pausa; (mus) calderón *m;* **to give pause (to)** dar que pensar (a) ‖ *intr* hacer pausa, detenerse brevemente; vacilar
pave [pev] *tr* pavimentar; (*with flagstones*) enlosar; (*with bricks*) enladrillar; (*with pebbles*) enchinar; **to pave the way (for)** preparar el terreno (para), abrir el camino (a)
pavement [ˈpevmənt] *s* pavimento; (*of brick*) enladrillado; (*of flagstone*) enlosado; (*sidewalk*) acera
pavilion [pəˈvɪljən] *s* pabellón *m*
paw [pɔ] *s* pata; garra, zarpa; (coll) mano *f* ‖ *tr* dar zarpazos a, restregar con las uñas; golpear, patear (*el suelo los caballos*); (coll) manosear; (*to handle overfamiliarly*) (coll) sobar ‖ *intr* piafar (*el caballo*)
pawn [pɔn] *s* (*in chess*) peón *m;* (*security, pledge*) prenda; (*tool of another person*) instrumento; víctima ‖ *tr* empeñar, dar en prenda
pawn'bro'ker *s* prestamista *mf*
pawn'shop' *s* casa de empeños, monte *m* de piedad
pawn ticket *s* papeleta de empeño
pay [pe] *s* paga; recompensa; castigo merecido ‖ *v* (*pret & pp* **paid** [ped]) *tr* pagar; prestar o poner (*atención*); dar (*cumplidos*); dar (*dinero una actividad comercial*); dar dinero a, ser provechoso a; pagar en la misma moneda; pagar con creces; sufrir (*el castigo de una ofensa*); hacer (*una visita*); cubrir (*los gastos*); **to pay back** devolver; pagar en la misma moneda; **to pay off** pagar y despedir (*a un empleado*); pagar todo lo adeudado a; vengarse de; redimir (*una hipoteca*) ‖ *intr* pagar; ser provechoso, valer la pena; **pay as you enter** pague a la entrada; **pay as you go** pagar el impuesto de utilidades con descuentos anticipados; **pay as you leave** pague a la salida
payable [ˈpe•əbəl] *adj* pagadero
pay boost *s* aumento de salario
pay'check' *s* cheque *m* en pago del sueldo; sueldo
pay'day' *s* día *m* de pago
payee [peˈi] *s* portador *m* o tenedor *m* (*de un giro*)
pay envelope *s* sobre *m* con el jornal; jornal *m,* salario
payer [ˈpe•ər] *s* pagador *m*
pay load *s* carga útil
pay'mas'ter *s* pagador *m*
payment [ˈpemənt] *s* pago; castigo
pay roll *s* nómina, hoja de paga
pay station *s* teléfono público
PC *abbr* **personal computer**
pd. *abbr* **paid**
p.d. *abbr* **per diem, potential difference**
pea [pi] *s* guisante *m,* chícharo
peace [pis] *s* paz *f;* **to make peace with** hacer las paces con
peaceable [ˈpisəbəl] *adj* pacífico
Peace Corps *s* Cuerpo de Paz
peaceful [ˈpɪsfəl] *adj* tranquilo, pacífico, sosegado
peace'mak'er *s* iris *m* de paz, pacificador *m*
peace of mind *s* serenidad del espíritu
peace pipe *s* pipa ceremonial
peace'time' *s* época o tiempo de paz
peach [pitʃ] *s* melocotón *m;* (slang) persona o cosa admirables
peach tree *s* melocotonero
peach•y [ˈpitʃi] *adj* (*comp* **-ier;** *super* **-iest**) (slang) estupendo, magnífico
pea'cock' *s* pavo real, pavón *m;* (fig) pinturero
peak [pik] *s* pico, cima, cumbre *f;* punta, extremo; máximo; (*of a cap*) visera; (*of a curve*) cresta; (elec) pico
peak hour *s* hora punta
peak load *s* (elec) carga de punta; demanda máxima
peal [pil] *s* fragor *m;* estruendo; (*of bells*) repique *m;* juego de campanas ‖ *intr* repicar; resonar
peal of laughter *s* carcajada
peal of thunder *s* trueno
pea'nut' *s* cacahuete *m,* aráquida; **to work for peanuts** recibir poco sueldo
peanut butter *s* mantequilla de maní, mantequilla de cacahuete (Esp), mantequilla de cacahuate (Mex), manteca de maní (SAm)
peanut vendor *s* manicero
pear [pɛr] *s* pera
pearl [pʌrl] *s* margarita, perla; (*of running water*) murmullo ‖ *tr* alijofarar

pearl oyster *s* madreperla
pear tree *s* peral *m*
peasant [ˈpɛzənt] *adj & s* campesino, rústico
pea'shoot'er *s* cerbatana, bodoquera
pea soup *s* sopa de guisantes; (coll) neblina espesa y amarillenta
peat [pit] *s* turba
pebble [ˈpɛbəl] *s* china, guija ‖ *tr* agranelar (*el cuero*)
peck [pɛk] *s* medida de áridos (*nueve litros*); montón *m;* picotazo; beso dado de mala gana ‖ *tr* picotear ‖ *intr* picotear; (coll) comer melindrosamente; **to peck at** querer picar; regañar constantemente; (coll) comer melindrosamente
peculate [ˈpɛkjə,let] *tr & intr* malversar
peculiar [pɪˈkjuljər] *adj* peculiar; singular, raro; excéntrico
pedagogue [ˈpɛdə,gɑg] *s* pedagogo; dómine *m,* pedante *m*
pedagogy [ˈpɛdə,godʒi] o [ˈpɛdə,gɑdʒi] *s* pedagogía
ped•al [ˈpɛdəl] *s* pedal *m* ‖ *v* (*pret & pp* **-aled** o **-alled;** *ger* **-aling** o **-alling**) *tr* impulsar pedaleando ‖ *intr* pedalear
pedant [ˈpɛdənt] *s* pedante *mf*
pedantic [pɪˈdæntɪk] *adj* pedantesco
pedant•ry [ˈpɛdəntri] *s* (*pl* **-pries**) pedantería
peddle [ˈpɛdəl] *tr* ir vendiendo de puerta en puerta; traer y llevar (*chismes*); vender (*favores*) ‖ *intr* ser buhonero
peddler [ˈpɛdlər] *s* buhonero
pederasty [ˈpɛdə,ræsti] *s* pederastia
pedestal [ˈpɛdɪstəl] *s* pedestal *m*
pedestrian [pɪˈdɛstrɪ•ən] *adj* pedestre ‖ *s* peatón *m*
pediatrician [,pidɪ•əˈtrɪʃən] *s* pedíatra *mf*
pediatrics [,pidɪˈætrɪks] *ssg* pediatría
pedicure [ˈpɛdɪ,kjur] *s* pedicura
pedigree [ˈpɛdɪ,gri] *s* árbol genealógico; ascendencia; fuente *f,* origen *m*
pediment [ˈpɛdɪmənt] *s* frontón *m*
pee [pi] *s* (coll) pipí *m* ‖ *intr* (coll) hacer pipí
peek [pik] *s* mirada rápida y furtiva ‖ *intr* mirar a hurtadillas
peek'a boo' *interj* ¡cucú!
peel [pil] *s* cáscara, pellejo ‖ *tr* pelar ‖ *intr* pelarse
peep [pip] *s* mirada a hurtadillas; (*of chickens*) pío ‖ *intr* mirar a hurtadillas; piar (*los pollos*)
peep'hole' *s* atisbadero, ojo mágico; (*in a door*) mirilla, ventanillo
peep show *s* mundonuevo; (slang) vistas sicalípticas
peer [pir] *s* par *mf,* igual *mf;* (*contemporary*) coetáneo ‖ *intr* mirar fijando la vista de cerca; **to peer at** mirar con ojos de miope; **to peer into** mirar hacia lo interior de, escudriñar
peer group *s* grupo paritario (formal); compañeros
peerless [ˈpɪrlɪs] *adj* sin par, sin igual
peeve [piv] *s* (coll) cojijo ‖ *tr* (coll) enojar, irritar
peevish [ˈpivɪʃ] *adj* cojijoso, displicente
peg [pɛg] *s* clavija, claveta, estaquilla; **to take down a peg** (coll) bajar los humos a ‖ *v* (*pret & pp* **pegged;** *ger* **pegging**) *tr* enclavijar; señalar con clavijas; fijar (*precios*) ‖ *intr* trabajar con ahinco; **to peg away at** afanarse en
peg leg *s* pata de palo
peg top *s* peonza; **peg tops** pantalones anchos de caderas y perniles ajustados
Peking [ˈpiˈkɪŋ] *s* Pequín
Peking•ese [,pikɪˈniz] *adj* pequinés ‖ *s* (*pl* **-ese**) pequinés *m*
pelf [pɛlf] *s* dinero mal ganado
pell-mell [ˈpɛlˈmɛl] *adj* tumultuoso ‖ *adv* atropelladamente
pelota [pɛˈlotə] *s* pelota vasca
pelt [pɛlt] *s* pellejo; golpe violento; (*of a person*) (hum) pellejo ‖ *tr* golpear violentamente; apedrear ‖ *intr* golpear violentamente; caer con fuerza (*el granizo, la lluvia, etc.*); apresurarse
pen. *abbr* **peninsula**
pen [pɛn] *s* pluma; corral *m,* redil *m;* **the pen and the sword** las letras y las armas ‖ *v* (*pret & pp* **penned;** *ger* **penning**) *tr* escribir (*con pluma*); redactar ‖ *v* (*pret & pp* **penned** o **pent** [pɛnt]) *tr* acorralar, encerrar
penalize [ˈpinə,laɪz] *tr* penar; penalizar; (sport) sancionar
penal•ty [ˈpɛnəlti] *s* (*pl* **-ties**) pena; (*for late payment*) recargo; (sport) penalty *m,* penal *m,* pénal (Arg); **under penalty of** so pena de
penance [ˈpɛnəns] *s* penitencia; **to do penance** hacer penitencia
penchant [ˈpɛnʃənt] *s* afición, inclinación, tendencia
pen•cil [ˈpɛnsəl] *s* lápiz *m;* (*of light*) pincel *m,* haz *m* ‖ *v* (*pret & pp* **-ciled** o **-cilled;** *ger* **-ciling** o **-cilling**) *tr* marcar con lápiz; (med) pincelar
pencil sharpener *s* afilalápices *m,* cortalápices *m,* sacapuntas *m*
pendent [ˈpɛndənt] *adj* pendiente; sobresaliente ‖ *s* medallón *m;* (*earring*) pendiente *m*
pending [ˈpɛndɪŋ] *adj* pendiente ‖ *prep* hasta; durante
pendulum [ˈpɛndʒələm] *s* péndulo; (*of a clock*) péndola
pendulum bob *s* lenteja
penetrate [ˈpɛnɪ,tret] *tr & intr* penetrar
penguin [ˈpɛŋgwɪn] *s* pingüino, pájaro bobo
pen'hold'er *s* (*handle*) portaplumas *m;* (*box*) plumero
penicillin [,pɛnɪˈsɪlɪn] *s* penicilina
peninsula [pəˈnɪnsələ] *s* península
peninsular [pəˈnɪnsələr] *adj & s* peninsular *mf* ‖ **Peninsular** *adj & s* (*Iberian*) peninsular *mf*
penis [ˈpinəs] *s* pene *m;* (*phallus*) falo; (zool) verga
penitence [ˈpɛnɪtəns] *s* penitencia
penitent [ˈpɛnɪtənt] *adj & s* penitente *mf*
pen'knife' *s* (*pl* **-knives**) navaja, cortaplumas *m*
penmanship [ˈpɛnmən,ʃip] *s* caligrafía; (*hand of a person*) letra

pen name *s* seudónimo, nombre artístico
pennant [ˈpɛnənt] *s* gallardete *m*
penniless [ˈpɛnɪlɪs] *adj* pelón, sin dinero
pennon [ˈpɛnən] *s* pendón *m*
pen•ny [ˈpɛni] *s* (*pl* **-nies**) (U.S.A.) centavo ‖ *s* (*pl* **pence** [pɛns]) (Brit) penique *m*
pen′ny-an′te *adj* (coll) de poca monta, de pacotilla
pen′ny-pinch′ing *adj* cicatero, tacaño ‖ *s* cicatería, tacanaría
pen′ny•weight′ *s* peso de 24 granos
pen pal *s* (coll) amigo por correspondencia
pen point *s* punta de la pluma; puntilla de la pluma fuente
pension [ˈpɛnʃən] *s* pensión, jubilación ‖ *tr* pensionar, jubilar
pensioner [ˈpɛnʃənər] *s* pensionista *mf;* **pensioners** clases pasivas
pension fund *s* fondo de pensiones
pensive [ˈpɛnsɪv] *adj* pensativo; melancólico
Pentecost [ˈpɛntɪ,kɔst] *s* el Pentecostés
penthouse [ˈpɛnt,haʊs] *s* penthouse *m,* piso de lujo en la última planta de un hotel; (*luxurious top story of a building*) ático; (*shed*) alpende *m,* colgadizo
pent-up [ˈpɛnt,ʌp] *adj* contenido, reprimido
penult [ˈpinʌlt] *s* penúltima
penum•bra [pɪˈnʌmbrə] *s* (*pl* **-brae** [bri] o **-bras**) penumbra
penurious [pɪˈnʊrɪ•əs] *adj* (*stingy*) tacaño, mezquino; (*poor*) pobre, indigente
penury [ˈpɛnjəri] *s* tacañería, mezquindad; pobreza, miseria
pen′wip′er *s* limpiaplumas *m*
people [ˈpipəl] *spl* gente *f;* personas; gente del pueblo; se, p.ej., **people say** se dice ‖ *ssg* (*pl* **peoples**) pueblo, nación ‖ *tr* poblar
pep [pɛp] *s* (coll) ánimo, brío, vigor *m* ‖ *v* (*pret & pp* **pepped;** *ger* **pepping**) *tr*—**to pep up** (coll) animar, dar vigor a
pepper [ˈpɛpər] *s* (*spice*) *pimienta;* (*plant and fruit*) pimiento ‖ *tr* sazonar con pimienta; (*with bullets*) acribillar; salpicar
pep′per•box′ *s* pimentero
pep′per•mint′ *s* (*plant*) menta piperita; esencia de menta; pastilla de menta
pep talk *s* palabras alentadoras
per [pʌr] *prep* por; **as per** según
perambulator [pərˈæmbjə,letər] *s* cochecillo de niño
per capita [pər ˈkæpɪtə] por cabeza, por persona
perceive [pərˈsiv] *tr* percibir
per cent o **percent** [pərˈsɛnt] por ciento
percentage [pərˈsɛntɪdʒ] *s* porcentaje *m;* (slang) provecho, ventaja
perception [pərˈsɛpʃən] *s* percepción; comprensión, penetración
perch [pʌrtʃ] *s* percha, rama, varilla; sitio o posición elevada; (*fish*) perca ‖ *tr* colocar en un sitio algo elevado *intr* sentarse en un sitio algo elevado; posar (*un ave*)
percolator [ˈpʌrkə,letər] *s* cafetera filtradora
per diem [pərˈdaɪ•əm] por día
perdition [pərˈdɪʃən] *s* perdición
perennial [pəˈrɛnɪ•əl] *adj* perenne; (bot) vivaz ‖ *s* planta vivaz
perfect [ˈpʌrfɛkt] *adj & s* perfecto ‖ [pərˈfɛkt] *tr* perfeccionar
perfidious [pərˈfɪdɪ•əs] *adj* pérfido
perfi•dy [ˈpʌrfɪdi] *s* (*pl* **-dies**) perfidia
perforate [ˈpʌrfə,ret] *tr* perforar
perforce [pərˈfors] *adv* por fuerza, necesariamente
perform [pərˈfɔrm] *tr* ejecutar; (theat) representar ‖ *intr* ejecutar; funcionar
performance [pərˈfɔrməns] *s* ejecución; representación; funcionamiento; (compu) rendimiento; (theat) función
performer [pərˈfɔrmər] *s* ejecutante *mf;* actor *m;* acróbata *mf*
perfume [ˈpʌrfjum] *s* perfume *m* ‖ [pərˈfjum] *tr* perfumar
perfunctory [pərˈfʌŋktəri] *adj* hecho sin cuidado, hecho a la ligera; indiferente, negligente
perhaps [pərˈhæps] *adv* acaso, tal vez, quizá
per•il [ˈpɛrəl] *s* peligro ‖ *v* (*pret & pp* **-iled** o **-illed;** *ger* **-iling** o **-illing**) *tr* poner en peligro
perilous [ˈpɛrɪləs] *adj* peligroso
period [ˈpɪrɪ•əd] *s* período; (*in school*) hora; (gram) punto; (sport) division
period costume *s* traje *m* de época
periodic [,pɪrɪˈɑdɪk] *adj* periódico
periodical [,pɪrɪˈɑdɪkəl] *adj* periódico ‖ *s* periódico, revista periódica
peripheral [pəˈrɪfərəl] *adj* secundario, tangencial; (anat, compu, med) periférico
peripher•y [pəˈrɪfəri] *s* (*pl* **-ies**) periferia
periscope [ˈpɛrɪ,skop] *s* periscopio
perish [ˈpɛrɪʃ] *intr* perecer
perishable [ˈpɛrɪʃəbəl] *adj* perecedero; (*merchandise*) corruptible
periwig [ˈpɛrɪ,wɪg] *s* perico
perjure [ˈpʌrdʒər] *tr* hacer (*a una persona*) quebrantar el juramento; **to perjure oneself** perjurarse
perju•ry [ˈpʌrdʒəri] *s* (*pl* **-ries**) perjurio
perk [pʌrk] *s* (coll) beneficio extra, prebenda ‖ *tr* alzar (*la cabeza*); aguzar (*las orejas*) ‖ *intr* pavonearse; engalanarse; (*coffee*) hacerse, filtrarse; **to perk up** reanimarse, sentirse mejor
permanence [ˈpʌrmənəns] *s* permanencia
permanency [ˈpʌrmənənsi] *s* (*pl* **-cies**) permanencia; persona, cosa o posición peremanentes
permanent [ˈpʌrmənənt] *adj* permanente ‖ *s* permanente *f,* ondulación permanente
perm′anent-press′ *adj* inarrugable, de raya permanente
permeate [ˈpʌrmɪ,et] *tr & intr* penetrar
permission [pərˈmɪʃən] *s* permisión
permissive [pərˈmɪsɪv] *adj* permisivo, indulgente
per•mit [ˈpʌrmɪt] *s* permiso; cédula de aduana ‖ [pərˈmɪt] *v* (*pret & pp* **-mitted;** *ger* **-mitting**) *tr* permitir
permute [perˈmjut] *tr* permutar

pernicious [pərˈnɪʃəs] *adj* pernicioso
pernickety [perˈnɪkɪti] *adj* (coll) descontentadizo, quisquilloso
peroration [ˌpɛrəˈreʃən] *s* peroración
peroxide [pərˈɑksaɪd] *s* peróxido; peróxido de hidrógeno
peroxide blonde *s* rubia oxigenada
perpendicular [ˌpʌrpənˈdɪkjələr] *adj & s* perpendicular *f*
perpetrate [ˈpʌrpɪˌtret] *tr* perpetrar
perpetual [pərˈpɛtʃʊ•əl] *adj* perpetuo
perpetuate [pərˈpɛtʃʊˌet] *tr* perpetuar
perplex [pərˈplɛks] *tr* dejar perplejo
perplexed [pərˈplɛkst] *adj* perplejo
perplexi•ty [pərˈplɛksɪti] *s* (*pl* **-ties**) perplejidad; problema *m*
per se [per ˈsi] por sí mismo, en sí mismo, esencialmente
persecute [ˈpʌrsɪˌkjut] *tr* perseguir
persecution [ˌpʌrsɪˈkjuʃən] *s* persecución
persecution complex *s* mania persecutoria, mania de persecución
persevere [ˌpʌrsɪˈvɪr] *intr* perseverar
Persian [ˈpʌrʒən] *adj & s* persa *mf*
persimmon [pərˈsɪmən] *s* placaminero
persist [pərˈsɪst] o [pərˈzɪst] *intr* persistir; empecinarse
persistent [pərˈsɪstənt] o [pərˈzɪstənt] *adj* persistente; (*insistent*) porfiado; (*e.g., headache*) pertinaz
person [ˈpʌrsən] *s* persona; **no person** nadie
personage [ˈpʌrsənɪdʒ] *s* personaje *m;* persona
personal [ˈpʌrsənəl] *adj* personal; de uso personal ‖ *s* nota de sociedad; (*in a newspaper*) remitido
personal computer *s* ordenador *m* personal, computadora personal
personali•ty [ˌpʌrsəˈnælɪti] *s* (*pl* **-ties**) personalidad
personality cult *s* culto a la personalidad
personal property *s* bienes *mpl* muebles
personi•fy [pərˈsɑnɪˌfaɪ] *v* (*pret pp* **-fied**) *tr* personificar
personnel [ˌpʌrsəˈnɛl] *s* personal *m*
per′son-to-per′son *adv* (telp) particular a particular, persona a persona
perspective [pərˈspɛktɪv] *s* perspectiva
perspicacious [ˌpʌrspɪˈkeʃəs] *adj* perspicaz
perspire [pərˈspaɪr] *intr* sudar, transpirar
persuade [pərˈswed] *tr* persuadir
persuasion [pərˈsweʒən] *s* persuasión; creencia religiosa; creencia fuerte
pert [pʌrt] *adj* atrevido, descarado; (coll) animado, vivo
pertain [pərˈten] *intr* pertenecer; **pertaining to** perteneciente a
pertinacious [ˌpʌrtɪˈneʃəs] *adj* pertinaz
pertinent [ˈpʌrtɪnənt] *adj* pertinente
perturb [pərˈtʌrb] *tr* perturbar
Peru [pəˈru] *s* el Perú
perusal [pəˈruzəl] *s* lectura cuidadosa
peruse [pəˈruz] *tr* leer con atención
Peruvian [pəruvɪ•ən] *adj & s* peruano
pervade [pərˈved] *tr* penetrar, esparcirse por, extenderse por
perverse [pərˈvʌrs] *adj* perverso; avieso, díscolo; contumaz; malazo
perversion [pərˈvʌrʒən] *s* perversión
perversi•ty [pərˈvʌrsɪti] *s* (*pl* **-ties**) perversidad; indocilidad; contumacia
pervert [ˈpʌrvərt] *s* renegado, apóstata; pervertido ‖ [pərˈvʌrt] *tr* pervertir; emplear mal (*p.ej., los talentos que uno tiene*)
pes•ky [ˈpɛski] *adj* (*comp* **-kier;** *super* **-kiest**) (coll) cargante, molesto
pessimism [ˈpɛsɪˌmɪzəm] *s* pesimismo
pessimist [ˈpɛsɪmɪst] *s* pesimista *mf*
pessimistic [ˌpɛsɪˈmɪstɪk] *adj* pesimista
pest [pɛst] *s* peste *f;* insecto nocivo; (*misfortune*) plaga; (*annoying person, bore*) machaca *mf*
pester [ˈpɛstər] *tr* molestar, importunar
pesticide [ˈpɛstɪˌsaɪd] *s* pesticida *m*
pestiferous [pɛsˈtɪfərəs] *adj* pestifero; (coll) engorroso, molesto
pestilence [ˈpɛstɪləns] *s* pestilencia
pestle [ˈpɛsəl] *s* mano *f* de almirez
pet [pɛt] *s* animal mimado, animal casero; niño mimado; favorito; enojo pasajero ‖ *v* (*pret & pp* **petted;** *ger* **petting**) *tr* acariciar, mimar ‖ *intr* (slang) besuquearse
petal [pɛtəl] *s* pétalo
pet′cock′ *s* llave *f* de desagüe, llave de purga
Peter [ˈpitər] *s* Pedro; **to rob Peter to pay Paul** desnudar a un santo para vestir a otro
petit-bourgeois [pəˈtiˈbʊrʒwɑ] *adj* pequeñoburgués
petition [pɪˈtɪʃəŋ] *s* petición; (*formal request signed by a number of people*) memorial *m,* instancia, solicitud ‖ *tr* suplicar; dirigir una instancia a, solicitar
pet name *s* nombre *m* de cariño
petri•fy [ˈpɛtrɪˌfaɪ] *v* (*pret & pp* **-fied**) *tr* petrificar ‖ *intr* petrificarse
petrochemical [ˌpɛtroˈkɛmɪkəl] *adj* petroquímico
petroleum [pɪˈtrolɪ•əm] *s* petróleo
pet shop *s* pajarería
petticoat [ˈpɛtɪˌkot] *s* enaguas
pet•ty [ˈpɛti] *adj* (*comp* **-tier;** *super* **-tiest**) insignificante, pequeño; mezquino; intolerante
petty cash *s* caja de menores, efectivo para gastos menores
petty larceny *s* ratería, hurto
petty officer *s* (naut) suboficial *m*
petulant [ˈpɛtjələnt] *adj* malhumorado, enojadizo
pew [pju] *s* banco de iglesia
pewter [ˈpjutər] *s* peltre *m;* vajilla de peltre
phalanx [ˈfelæŋks] *s* falange *f*
phallic [ˈfælɪk] *adj* fálico
phallus [ˈfæləs] *s* falo
phantasm [ˈfæntæzəm] *s* fantasma *m*
phantom [ˈfæntəm] *s* fantasma *m*
Pharaoh [ˈfɛro] *s* Faraón *m*

pharisee [ˈfærɪ,si] *s* (pej) fariseo ‖ **Pharisee** *s* (Bib) fariseo
pharmaceutical [,fɑrməˈsutɪkəl] *adj* farmacéutico
pharmacist [ˈfɑrməsɪst] *s* farmacéutico
pharma•cy [ˈfɑrməsi] *s* (*pl* **-cies**) farmacia
pharynx [ˈfærɪŋks] *s* faringe *f*
phase [fez] *s* fase *f* ‖ *tr* poner en fase; llevar a cabo a etapas uniformes; (coll) inquietar, molestar; **to phase out** deshacer paulatinamente
pheasant [ˈfɛzənt] *s* faisán *m*
phenobarbital [,finoˈbɑrbɪ,tæl] *s* fenobarbital *m*
phenomenal [fɪˈnɑmɪ,nɑn] *s* (*pl* **-na** [nə]) fenómenal
phial [ˈfaɪ•əl] *s* frasco pequeño; inyectable *m*
philanderer [fɪˈlændərər] *s* galanteador *m,* tenorio
philanthropist [fɪˈlænθrəpɪst] *s* filántropo
philanthro•py [fɪˈlænθrəpi] *s* (*pl* **-pies**) filantropía
philatelist [fɪˈlætəlɪst] *s* filatelista *mf*
philately [fɪˈlætəli] *s* filatelia
Philip [ˈfɪlɪp] *s* Felipe *m*
Philippine [ˈfɪlɪ,pin] *adj* filipino ‖ **Philippines** *spl* Islas Filipinas
Philistine [ˈfɪlɪ,stin] o [ˈfɪlɪ,staɪn] *adj & s* (Bib) filisteo; **philistine** (pej) ignorante *mf,* inculto
philologist [fɪˈlɑlədʒɪst] *s* filólogo
philology [fɪˈlɑlədʒi] *s* filología
philosopher [fɪˈlɑsəfər] *s* filósofo
philosophic(al) [,fɪləsɑfɪk(əl)] *adj* filosófico
philoso•phy [fɪˈlɑsəfi] *s* (*pl* **-phies**) filosofía
philter [ˈfɪltər] *s* filtro
phlebitis [flɪˈbaɪtɪs] *s* flebitis *f*
phlegm [flɛm] *s* flema *f,* gargajo; **to cough up phlegm** gargajear
phlegmatic(al) [flɛgˈmætɪk(əl)] *adj* flemático; (coll) galbanoso
Phoebe [ˈfibi] *s* Febe *f*
Phoenicia [fɪˈnɪʃə] o [fɪˈniʃə] *s* Fenicia
Phoenician [fɪˈnɪʃən] o [fɪˈniʃən] *adj & s* fenicio
phoenix [ˈfɪnɪks] *s* fénix *m*
phone [fon] *s* (coll) teléfono; **to come** o **to go to the phone** acudir al teléfono, ponerse al aparato ‖ *tr & intr* (coll) telefonear
phone call *s* llamada telefónica
phone booth *s* cabina telefónica
phone′card′ *s* tarjeta telefónica
phone directory *s* guía telefónica
phoneme [ˈfonim] *s* fonema
phonetic [foˈnɛtɪk] *adj* fonético
phonics [ˈfɑnɪks] *s* fónica
phonograph [ˈfonə,græf] *s* fonógrafo
phonology [fəˈnɑlədʒi] *s* fonología
pho•ny [ˈfoni] *adj* (*comp* **-nier;** *super* **-niest**) falso, contrahecho ‖ *s* (*pl* **-nies**) (slang) farsa; (coll) farsante *mf*
phosphate [ˈfɑsfet] *s* fosfato
phosphorescent [,fɑsfəˈrɛsənt] *adj* fosforescente
phospho•rus [ˈfɑsfərəs] *s* (*pl* **-ri** [,raɪ]) fósforo
pho•to [ˈfoto] *s* (*pl* **-tos**) foto *f*
photo booth *s* fotomatón
photocopier [ˈfoto,kɑpɪ•ər] *s* fotocopiador *m;* fotóstato *m*
pho′to•cop′y *s* fotocopia ‖ *v* (*pret & pp* **-ied**) *tr* fotocopiar
pho′to elec′tric *adj* fotoeléctrico
photoelectric cell *s* fotocélula, célula fotoeléctrica
photoengraving [,foto•ɛnˈgrevɪŋ] *s* fotograbado
photo finish *s* (sport) fallo fotográfico
pho′to•fin′ish camera *s* fotofija *m*
photogenic [,fotoˈdʒɛnɪk] *adj* fotogénico
photograph [ˈfotə,græf] *s* fotografía ‖ *tr & intr* fotografiar
photographer [fəˈtɑgrəfər] *s* fotógrafo
photographic [,fotəˈgræfɪk] *adj* fotográfico
photography [fəˈtɑgrəfi] *s* fotografía
photojournalism [,fotəˈdʒʌrnə,lɪzəm] *s* fotoperiodismo
pho′to•play′ *s* fotodrama *m*
photostat [ˈfotə,stæt] *s* fotóstato ‖ *tr & intr* fotostatar
phototube [ˈfotə,tjub] fototubo
phrase [frez] *s* frase *f* ‖ *tr* frasear
phrenology [frɪˈnɑlədʒi] *s* frenología
phys. *abbr* **physical, physician, physics, physiology**
phys•ic [ˈfɪzɪk] *s* medicamento; purgante *m* ‖ *v* (*pret & pp* **-icked;** *ger* **-icking**) *tr* curar; purgar
physical [ˈfɪzɪkəl] *adj* físico
physical description *s* señas *fpl* personales
physical education *s* educación física
physical fitness *s* buena forma física
physical handicap *s* minusvalía
physical therapy *s* terapia física
physician [fɪˈzɪʃən] *s* médico
physicist [ˈfɪzɪsɪst] *s* físico
physics [ˈfɪzɪks] *s* física
physiognomy [,fɪzɪˈɑgnəmi] o [,fɪzɪˈɑnəmi] *s* fisonomía
physiological [,fɪzɪ•əˈlɑdʒɪkəl] *adj* fisiológico
physiology [,fɪzɪˈɑlədʒi] *s* fisiología
physique [fɪˈzik] *s* físico, talle *m,* exterior *m*
pi [paɪ] *s* (math) pi *f;* (typ) pastel *m* ‖ *v* (*pret & pp* **pied;** *ger* **piing**) *tr* (typ) empastelar
pian•o [pɪˈæno] *s* (*pl* **-os**) piano
picaresque [,pɪkəˈrɛsk] *adj* picaresco
picayune [,pɪkəˈjun] *adj* de poca monta, mezquino
picco•lo [ˈpɪkə,lo] *s* (*pl* **-los**) flautín *m*
pick [pɪk] *s* (*tool*) pico; (*choice*) selección; (*choicest*) flor *f* ‖ *tr* escoger; recoger (*p.ej., flores*); recolectar (*p.ej., algodón*); romper (*el hielo*) con un picahielos; escarbarse (*los dientes*); descañonar, desplumar (*un ave*); hurgarse (*la nariz*); rescarse (*una cicatriz, un grano*); roer (*un hueso*); mondar (*las frutas*); falsear, forzar (*una cerradura*); armar (*una pendencia*); herir (*las cuerdas de un instru-*

mento); buscar (*defectos*); hurtar de (*los bolsillos*); **to pick out** entresacar; **to pick someone to pieces** (coll) no dejarle a uno un hueso sano; **to pick up** recoger; recobrar (*ánimo; velocidad*); descolgar (*el receptor*); hallar por casualidad; aprender con la práctica; aprender de oidas; invitar a subir a un coche; entablar conservación con (*sin presentación previa*); captar (*una señal de radio*) ‖ *intr* comer melindrosamente; escoger esmeradamente; **to pick at** comer melindrosamente; tomarla con, regañar; **to pick on** escoger; (coll) regañar; (coll) molestar; **to pick over** ir revolviendo y examinando; **to pick up** (coll) ir mejor, sentirse mejor; recobrar velocidad

pick'ax' *s* zapapico

picket [ˈpɪkɪt] *s* (*stake, pale*) piquete *m;* (*of strikers; of soldiers*) piquete *m* ‖ *tr* poner un cordón de piquetes a ‖ *intr* servir de piquete

picket fence *s* cerca de estacas

picket line *s* línea de piquetes

pickle [ˈpɪkəl] *s* encurtido; escabeche *m,* salmuera; (coll) apuro, aprieto ‖ *tr* encurtir; escabechar

pick'pock'et *s* carterista *m,* ratero; bolsero (Mex)

pick'up' *s* recolección; (*of a motor*) recobro; (*of an automobile*) aceleración; (elec) pickup, fonocaptor *m*

pickup arm *s* (electron) brazo lector

pickup truck *s* camión *m* de reparto

pic•nic [ˈpɪknɪk] *s* jira, partida de campo ‖ *v* (*pret & pp* **-nicked;** *ger* **-nicking**) *intr* hacer una jira al campo, merendar en el campo

pictorial [pɪkˈtorɪ•əl] *adj* gráfico; ilustrado ‖ *s* revista ilustrada

picture [ˈpɪktʃər] *s* cuadro; retrato; imagen *f;* lámina, grabado; fotografía; película; pintura ‖ *tr* dibujar; pintar; describir; **to picture to oneself** representarse

picture book *s* libro en imágenes

picture gallery *s* galería de pinturas

picture postcard *s* postal ilustrada

picture show *s* exhibición de pinturas; cine *m*

picture signal *s* videoseñal *f*

picturesque [ˌpɪktjəˈrɛsk] *adj* pintoresco

picture tube *s* tubo de imagen

picture window *s* ventana panorámica

piddling [ˈpɪdlɪŋ] *adj* de poca monta, insignificante

pie [paɪ] *s* pastel *m;* (*bird*) picaza; (typ) pastel *m* ‖ *v* (*pret & pp* **pied;** *ger* **pieing**) *tr* (typ) empastelar

piece [pis] *s* (*fragment; section of cloth*) pedazo; (*part of a machine; drama; single composition of music; coin; figure or block used in checkers, chess, etc.*) pieza; (*of land*) lote *m,* parcela; **a piece of advice** un consejo; **a piece of baggage** un bulto; **a piece of furniture** un mueble; **to break to pieces** despedazar, hacer pedazos; despedazarse; **to fall to pieces** desbaratarse, caer en ruina; **to give someone a piece of one's mind** decirle a uno su parecer con toda franqueza; **to go to pieces** desvencijarse; darse a la desesperación; ir al desastre (*un negocio*); sufrir un ataque de nervios; perder por completo la salud; **to pick someone to pieces** (coll) no dejarle a uno un hueso sano ‖ *tr* formar juntando piezas; remendar ‖ *intr* (coll) comer a deshora

piece goods *spl* géneros de pieza

piece of evidence *s* pieza de convicción

piece'work' *s* destajo, trabajo a destajo

piece'work'er *s* destajero, destajista *mf*

pier [pɪr] *s* muelle *m;* (*of a bridge*) estribo, sostén *m;* (*of a harbor*) rompeolas *m;* (*wall between two openings*) (archit) entrepaño

pierce [pɪrs] *tr* agujerear, horadar, taladrar; atravesar, traspasar; picar; pinchar, punzar; (fig) traspasar (*de dolor*) ‖ *intr* penetrar, entrar a la fuerza

piercing [ˈpɪrsɪŋ] *adj* agudo, penetrante, desgarrador; (*pain*) lancinante

pier glass *s* espejo de cuerpo entero

pie•ty [ˈpaɪ•əti] *s* (*pl* **-ties**) piedad, devoción

piffle [ˈpɪfəl] *s* (coll) disparates *mpl,* música celestial

pig [pɪg] *s* cerdo; (*young hog*) lechón *m;* (*domestic hog*) puerco, cochino; carne *f* de puerco; (metal) lingote *m;* (*person who acts like a pig*) (coll) marrano, cochino

pigeon [ˈpidʒən] *s* paloma

pi'geon•hole' *s* hornilla, casilla de paloma; casilla ‖ *tr* encasillar

pigeon house *s* palomar *m*

piggish [ˈpɪgɪʃ] *adj* glotón, voraz

pig'gy•back' *adv* a cuestas, en hombros

pig'-head'ed *adj* terco, cabezudo

pig iron *s* arrabio, hierro en lingotes

pigment [ˈpɪgmənt] *s* pigmento ‖ *tr* pigmentar ‖ *intr* pigmentarse

pig'pen' *s* pocilga; (fig) pocilga, corral *m* de vacas

pig'skin' *s* piel *f* de cerdo; (coll) balón *m* (*con que se juega al fútbol*)

pig'sty' *s* (*pl* **-sties**) pocilga

pig'tail' *s* coleta, trenza; (*of tobacco*) andullo

pike [paɪk] *s* pica; (*of an arrow*) punta; carretera; camino de barrera; (*fish*) lucio

piker [ˈpaɪkər] *s* (slang) persona de poco fuste

Pilate [ˈpaɪlət] *s* Pilatos *m*

pile [paɪl] *s* pila, montón *m;* (*stake*) pilote *m;* lanilla, pelusa; pira; (elec, phys) pila; (coll) caudal *m;* **piles** almorranas ‖ *tr* apilar, amontonar ‖ *intr* apilarse, amontonarse; **to pile in** o **into** entrar atropelladamente en; entrar todos en; subir todos a (*p.ej., un coche*)

pile driver *s* martinete *m*

pileup [ˈpaɪlˌʌp] *s* (*collision*) choque en cadena

pilfer [ˈpɪlfər] *tr & intr* ratear

pilgrim [ˈpɪlgrɪm] *s* peregrino, romero

pilgrimage [ˈpɪlgrɪmɪdʒ] *s* peregrinación, romería

pill [pɪl] *s* píldora; mal trago, sinsabor *m;* (coll) persona molesta

pillage [ˈpɪlɪdʒ] *s* pillaje *m,* saqueo ‖ *tr & intr* pillar, saquear

pillar [ˈpɪlər] *s* pilar *m;* **from pillar to post** de acá para allá sin objeto determinado

pillo•ry [ˈpɪləri] *s* (*pl* **-ries**) picota ‖ *v* (*pret & pp* **-ried**) *tr* empicotar; (fig) motejar, poner en ridículo

pillow [ˈpɪlo] *s* almohada

pil′low•case′ o **pil′low•slip′** *s* funda de almohada

pillow fight *s* lucha de almohadas, guerra de almohadas (Arg, Chile)

pilot [ˈpaɪlət] *s* piloto; (*of a harbor*) práctico; (*of a gas range*) mechero encendedor; (rr) trompa, delantera ‖ *tr* pilotar; conducir

pilot light *s* llama piloto

pilot run o **pilot test** *s* experimento piloto

pimp [pɪmp] *s* alcahuete *m*

pimple [ˈpɪmpəl] *s* barro, grano

pim•ply [ˈpɪmpli] *adj* (*comp* **-plier;** *super* **-pliest**) granujoso

pin [pɪn] *s* alfiler *m;* (*brooch*) pin *m;* (*e.g., for a necktie*) prendedero; (*peg*) clavija; (*e.g., to hold scissors together*) clavillo, clavito; (bowling) bolo; (compu) pin; **to be on pins and needles** estar en espinas ‖ **PIN** *s* (acronym) (**personal identification number**) PIN *m* (número de identificación personal) ‖ *v* (*pret & pp* **pinned;** *ger* **pinning**) *tr* alfilerar; clavar, fijar, sujetar; **to pin something on someone** (coll) acusarle a uno de una cosa; **to pin up** recoger y apuntar con alfileres; fijar en la pred con alfileres

pinafore [ˈpɪnə,for] *s* delantal *m* de niño

pin′ball′ *s* billar romano, bagatela

pince-nez [ˈpæns,ne] *s* lentes *mpl* de nariz, lentes de pinzas

pincers [ˈpɪnsərz] *ssg* o *spl* pinzas

pinch [pɪntʃ] *s* pellizco; (*of hunger*) tormento; (slang) arresto; (slang) hurto, robo; **in a pinch** en un aprieto; en caso necesario ‖ *tr* pellizcar; cogerse (*los dedos, p.ej., en una puerta*); apretar (*p.ej., el zapato a una persona*); contraer (*el frío la cara de uno*); limitar los gastos de; (slang) arrestar, prender; (slang) hurtar, robar ‖ *intr* apretar; economizar, privarse de lo necesario

pinchers [ˈpɪntʃərz] *ssg* o *spl* var of **pincers**

pin′cush′ion *s* acerico

pine [paɪn] *s* pino ‖ *intr* languidecer; **to pine away** consumirse; **to pine for** penar por

pine′ap′ple *s* ananás *m,* piña

pine cone *s* piña

pine needle *s* pinocha

ping [pɪŋ] *s* silbido de bala ‖ *intr* silbar (*una bala*); silbar como una bala

pin′head′ *s* cabecilla de alfiler; cosa muy pequeña o insignificante; (coll) bobalicón *m*

pin′hole *s* agujerito; (compu) patilla

pink [pɪŋk] *adj* rosado, sonrosado ‖ *s* estado perfecto; comunistoide *mf;* (bot) clavel *m,* clavellina

pin money *s* alfileres *mpl*

pinnacle [ˈpɪnəkəl] *s* pináculo

pin′point′ *adj* exacto, preciso ‖ *s* punta de alfiler ‖ *tr & intr* señalar con precisión

pin′prick′ *s* alfilerazo

pinup girl [ˈpɪn,ʌp] *s* guapa

pin′wheel′ *s* rueda de fuego, rueda giratoria de fuegos artificiales; molinete *m* (Mex); (*child's toy*) rehilandera, ventolera

pioneer [,paɪ•əˈnɪr] *s* pionero; (mil) zapador *m* ‖ *intr* abrir nuevos caminos, explorar

pious [ˈpaɪ•əs] *adj* pío, piadoso; mojigato; respetuoso

pip [pɪp] *s* (*seed*) pepita; (*on a card, dice, etc.*) punto; (vet) pepita

pipe [paɪp] *s* caño, conducto, tubo; (*to smoke tobacco*) pipa; (mus) pipa, caramillo, zampoña; (*of an organ*) cañón *m* ‖ *tr* conducir por medio de tubos o cañerías; proveer de tuberías o cañerías ‖ *intr* tocar el caramillo; **to pipe down** (slang) callarse

pipe cleaner *s* limpiapipas *m*

piped music *s* música ambiental

pipe dream *s* esperanza imposible, castillo en el aire

pipe line *s* cañería; tubería; oleoducto; fuente *f* de informes confidenciales

pipe organ *s* (mus) órgano

piper [ˈpaɪpər] *s* flautista *m;* gaitero; **to pay the piper** pagar los vidrios rotos

pipe wrench *s* llave *f* para tubos

pippin [ˈpɪpɪn] *s* (*apple*) camuesa; (*tree*) camueso; (slang) real moza

piquancy [ˈpikənsi] *s* picante *m*

piquant [ˈpikənt] *adj* picante

pique [pik] *s* pique *m,* resentimiento ‖ *tr* picar, enojar; despertar, excitar

piracy [ˈpaɪrəsi] *s* piratería

pirate [ˈpaɪrɪt] *s* pirata *m* ‖ *tr* pillar, robar; publicar fraudulentamente ‖ *intr* piratear

pirouette [,pɪruˈɛt] *s* pirueta ‖ *intr* piruetear

Pisces [ˈpaɪsiz] *s* (astr) Piscis *m*

pistol [ˈpɪstəl] *s* pistola

piston [ˈpɪstən] *s* (mach) émbolo, pistón *m;* (mus) pistón *m*

piston displacement *s* cilindrada

piston ring *s* anillo de émbolo, aro de émbolo, segmento de émbolo

piston rod *s* vástago de émbolo

piston stroke *s* carrera de émbolo

pit [pɪt] *s* hoyo; (*in the skin*) cacaraña; (*of certain fruit*) hueso; (*for cockfights, etc.*) cancha, reñidero; (*of the stomach*) boca; abismo, infierno; (auto) fosa; (min) pozo; (theat) foso ‖ *v* (*pret & pp* **pitted;** *ger* **pitting**) *tr* marcar con hoyos; dejar hoyoso (*el rostro*); deshuesar (*p.ej., una ciruela*)

pitch [pɪtʃ] *s* (*black sticky substance*) pez *f;* echada, lanzamiento; cosa lanzada; pelota lanzada; (*of a boat*) arfada, cabezada; (*of a roof*) pendiente *f;* (*of, e.g., a screw*) paso; (*of a winding*) (elec) paso; (mus) tono, altura; (fig) grado, extremo; (coll) bombo, elogio ‖ *tr* echar, lanzar; elevar (*el heno*) con la horquilla; armar o plantar (*una tienda de cam-*

paña); embrear; (mus) graduar el tono de || *intr* caerse, caer de cabeza; bajar en declive, inclinarse; arfar, cabecear (*un buque*); **to pitch in** (coll) poner manos a la obra; (coll) comenzar a comer

pitch accent *s* acento de altura

pitcher [ˈpɪtʃər] *s* jarro; (*in baseball*) lanzador *m*

pitch′fork′ *s* horca, horquilla; **to rain pitchforks** (coll) llover a cántaros

pitch pipe *s* (mus) diapasón *m*

pit′fall′ *s* callejo, trampa; (*danger for the unwary*) escollo, atascadero

pith [pɪθ] *s* médula; (*essential part*) (fig) médula; (fig) fuerza, vigor *m*

pith•y [ˈpɪθi] *adj* (*comp* **-ier;** *super* **-iest**) medular; enérgico, expresivo

pitiful [ˈpɪtɪfəl] *adj* lastimoso; compasivo; despreciable

pitiless [ˈpɪtɪlɪs] *adj* despiadado, empedernido, incompasivo

pit•y [ˈpɪti] *s* (*pl* **-ies**) piedad, compasión, lástima; **for pity's sake!** ¡por piedad!; **to have** o **to take pity on** tener piedad de, apiadarse de; **what a pity!** ¡qué lástima!, !qué pena! || *v* (*pret & pp* **-ied**) *tr* apiadarse de, compadecer

pivot [ˈpɪvət] *s* pivote *m,* gorrón *m,* eje *m* de rotación; (fig) eje *m* || *intr* pivotar; **to pivot on** girar sobre; depender de

pixel [ˈpɪksɛl] *s* punto; (compu) píxel *m*

placard [ˈplækɑrd] *s* cartel *m* || *tr* fijar carteles en; fijar (*un anuncio*) en sitio público; publicar por medio de carteles

place [ples] *s* sitio, lugar *m;* (*of business*) local *m;* (*job*) puesto; grado, rango; **in no place** en ninguna parte; **in place of** en lugar de; **out of place** fuera de su lugar; fuera de propósito; **to be looking for a place to live** buscar piso; **to take place** tener lugar; situar || *tr* poner, colocar; acordarse bien de; dar empleo a; prestar (*dinero*) a interés || *intr* colocarse (*un caballo en las carreras*)

place•bo [pləˈsibo] *s* (*pl* **-bos** o **-boes**) placebo

place card *s* tarjetita con el nombre (*que indica la colocación de uno en la mesa*)

place kick *s* (sport) patada fija

placement [ˈplesmənt] *s* colocación

placement test *s* prueba de nivel

place name *s* nombre *m* de lugar, topónimo

placid [ˈplæsɪd] *adj* plácido, tranquilo

plagiarism [ˈpledʒəˌrɪzəm] *s* plagio

plagiarize [ˈpledʒəˌraɪz] *tr* plagiar

plague [pleg] *s* peste *f,* plaga; (*great public calamity*) plaga || *tr* apestar, plagar; atormentar, molestar

plaid [plæd] *s* (*cloth*) tartán *m;* cuadros a la escocesa

plain [plen] *adj* llano, claro, evidente; abierto, franco; ordinario; feo; humilde; solo, natural; **in plain English** sin rodeos; **in plain sight** o **view** en plena vista || *s* llano, llanura

plain clothes *spl* traje *m* de calle, traje de paisano

plainclothesman [ˈplenˈkloðzˌmæn] *s* (*pl* **-men** [ˌmɛn]) policía *m* que lleva traje de paisano

plain omelet *s* tortilla a la francesa

plains•man [ˈplenzmən] *s* (*pl* **-men** [mən]) llanero

plaintiff [ˈplentɪf] *s* (law) demandante *mf*

plaintive [ˈplentɪv] *adj* quejumbroso

plan [plæn] *s* plan *m,* intento, proyecto; (*drawing, diagram*) plan *m,* plano; **to change one's plans** cambiar de proyecto || *v* (*pret & pp* **planned;** *ger* **planning**) *tr* planear, planificar; **to plan to** proponerse || *intr* hacer proyectos

plane [plen] *adj* plano || *s* (*surface*) plano; aeroplano, avión *m;* (*of an airplane*) plano; (carp) cepillo; (*tree*) plátano; **by plane** (aer) en avión || *tr* cepillar || *intr* viajar en aeroplano

plane crash *s* accidente aéreo

plane sickness *s* mareo del aire, mal *m* de vuelo

planet [ˈplænɪt] *s* planeta *m*

plane tree *s* plátano

planing mill *s* [ˈplenɪŋ] *s* taller *m* de cepillado

plank [plæŋk] *s* tabla gruesa, tablón *m;* artículo de un programa político || *tr* entablar, entarimar

planning [ˈplænɪŋ] *s* planificación

plant [plænt] *s* fábrica, taller *m;* (*of an automobile*) grupo motor; (*educational establishment*) plantel *m;* (bot) planta || *tr* plantar; sembrar (*semillas*); inculcar (*doctrinas*); (slang) ocultar (*géneros robados*)

plantain [ˈplæntən] *s* (*fruit, tree*) plátano grande, plátano (Col, Ven), plátano macho (Mex)

plantation [plænˈteʃən] *s* plantación, campo de plantas; (*estate cultivated by workers living on it*) hacienda

planter [ˈplæntər] *s* plantador *m,* cultivador *m*

plaque [plæk] *s* (*tablet*) placa; (dent) sarro, placa (dental)

plasma [ˈplæzmə] *s* plasma *m*

plaster [ˈplæstər] *s* (*gypsum*) yeso; (*mixture of lime, sand, water, etc.*) argamasa; (*coating*) enlucido; (*poultice*) emplasto || *tr* enyesar; argamasar; enlucir; emplastar; embadurnar; pegar (*anuncios*)

plas′ter•board′ *s* cartón *m* de yeso y fieltro

plaster cast *s* (surg) vendaje enyesado; (sculp) yeso

plaster of Paris *s* estuco de París

plastic [ˈplæstɪk] *adj* plástico || *s* (*substance*) plástico; (*art of modeling*) plástica; (*credit card*) (coll) tarjeta de crédito

plastic explosive *s* goma dos

plastic surgery *s* cirugía plástica

plate [plet] *s* (*dish*) plato; (*sheet of metal, etc.*) chapa, placa; vajilla de oro, vajilla de plata; dentadura postiza, base *f* de la dentadura postiza; (baseball) puesto meta, puesto del batter; (anat, elec, electron, phot, zool) placa; (typ) clisé *m* || *tr* chapear, planchear; blindar; platear, dorar, niquelar (*por la galvanoplastia*); (typ) clisar

plateau [plæˈto] *s* meseta
plate glass *s* vidrio o cristal cilindrado
platelet [ˈpletlɛt] *s* plaqueta
platen [ˈplætən] *s* rodillo
platform [ˈplæt,fɔrm] *s* plataforma *f;* (*of passenger station*) andén *m;* (*of freight station*) cargadero; (*of a speaker*) tribuna; (*political program*) plataforma
platform car *s* plataforma *f*
platinum [ˈplætɪnəm] *s* platino
platinum blonde *s* rubia platino
platitude [ˈplætɪ,tjud] o [ˈplætɪ,tud] *s* perogrullada, trivialidad
Plato [ˈpleto] *s* Platón *m*
platonic [pləˈtɑnɪk] *adj* platónico
platoon [pləˈtun] *s* pelotón *m*
platter [ˈplætər] *s* fuente *f;* (slang) disco de fonógrafo
plausible [ˈplɔzɪbəl] *adj* aparente, especioso; bien hablado; (coll) creíble
play [ple] *s* juego; (*act or move in a game*) jugada; (*drama*) pieza; (*of water, colors, lights*) juego; (mach) huelgo, juego; **to give full play to** dar rienda suelta a ‖ *tr* jugar (*p.ej., un naipe, una partida de juego*); jugar a (*p.ej., los naipes*); jugar con (*un contrario*); dar (*un chasco*); gastar (*una broma*); hacer (*una mala jugada*); dirigir (*agua, una manguera*); desempeñar (*un papel*); desempeñar el papel de; representar (*una obra dramática, un film*); apostar por (*un caballo*); tocar (*un instrumento, una pieza, un disco de fonógrafo*) ‖ *intr* jugar; desempeñar un papel, representar; correr (*una fuente*); rielar (*la luz en la superficie del agua*); vagar (*p.ej., una sonrisa por los labios*); **to play out** rendirse; agotarse; acabarse; **to play safe** tomar sus precauciones; **to play sick** hacerse el enfermo; **to play up to** hacer la rueda a
play′back′ *s* lectura; aparato de lectura
playback head *s* célula fonorreceptora, cabeza de lectura, cabeza lectora
play′bill′ *s* (*poster*) cartel *m;* (*of a play*) programa *m*
player [ˈple•ər] *s* (compu) ejecutor *m;* (sport) jugador *m;* (theat) actor *m*
player piano [ˈple•ər] *s* autopiano, piano mecánico
playful [ˈplefəl] *adj* juguetón, retozón; dicho en broma
playgoer [ˈple,go•ər] *s* aficionado al teatro
play′ground′ *s* campo de juego; patio de recreo
play′house′ *s* casita de muñecas; teatro
playing card [ˈple•ɪŋ] *s* naipe *m*
playing field *s* campo de deportes
play′mate′ *s* compañero de juego
play′-off′ *s* partido de desempate
play′pen′ *s* parque *m,* corral *m* (*para bebés*)
play′thing′ *s* juguete *m*
play′time′ *s* hora de recreo, hora de juego
playwright [ˈple,raɪt] *s* dramaturgo, autor dramático; comediógrafo
play′writ′ing *s* dramaturgia, dramática

plea [pli] *s* ruego, súplica; disculpa, excusa; (law) contestación a la demanda
plead [plid] *v* (*pret & pp* **pleaded** o **pled** [plɛd]) *tr* defender (*una causa*) ‖ *intr* suplicar; abogar; **to plead guilty** confesarse culpable; **to plead not guilty** negar la acusación, declararse inocente
pleasant [ˈplɛzənt] *adj* agradable; simpático; sangriligero
pleasant•ry [ˈplɛzəntri] *s* (*pl* **-ries**) broma, chiste *m,* dicho gracioso
please [pliz] *tr & intr* gustar; **as you please** como Ud. quiera; **if you please** si me hace el favor; **please** + *inf* hágame Ud. el favor de + *inf;* **to be pleased to** alegrarse de, complacerse en; **to be pleased with** estar satisfecho de o con
pleasing [ˈplizɪŋ] *adj* agradable, grato
pleasure [ˈplɛʒər] *s* placer *m,* gusto; **what is your pleasure?** ¿en qué puedo servirle?, ¿qué es lo que Ud. desea?; **with pleasure** con mucho gusto
pleasure seeker [ˈsikər] *s* amigo de los placeres
pleasure trip *s* viaje *m* de placer
pleat [plit] *s* pliegue *m,* plisado ‖ *tr* plegar, plisar
plebeian [plɪˈbi•ən] *adj & s* plebeyo
pledge [plɛdʒ] *s* empeño, prenda; (*vow*) voto, promesa; (*toast*) brindis *m;* **as a pledge of** en prenda de; **to take the pledge** comprometerse a no tomar bebidas alcohólicas ‖ *tr* empeñar, prendar; dar (*la palabra*); brindar por
plentiful [ˈplɛntɪfəl] *adj* abundante, copioso
plenty [ˈplɛnti] *adv* (coll) completamente ‖ *s* abundancia, copia; suficiencia
pleurisy [ˈplʊrɪsi] *s* pleuresía
pliable [ˈplaɪ•əbəl] *adj* flexible, plegable, plástico; dócil
pliers [ˈplaɪ•ərz] *ssg* o *spl* alicates *mpl*
plight [plaɪt] *s* estado, situación; apuro, aprieto; compromiso solemne ‖ *tr* dar o empeñar (*su palabra*); **to plight one's troth** prometer fidelidad; dar palabra de casamiento
PLO [ˈpiˈɛlˈo] *s* (letterword) (**Palestine Liberation Organization**) OLP *f* (Organización para la Liberación de Palestina)
plod [plad] *v* (*pret & pp* **plodded;** *ger* **plodding**) *tr* recorrer (*un camino*) pausada y pesadamente ‖ *intr* caminar pausada y pesadamente; trabajar laboriosamente
plot [plat] *s* complot *m,* conspiración; (*of a play or novel*) argumento, trama, parcela, solar *m;* cuadro de flores; cuadro de hortalizas; plano, mapa *m* ‖ *v* (*pret & pp* **plotted;** *ger* **plotting**) *tr* fraguar, tramar, urdir, maquinar; dividir en parcelas o solares; trazar el plano de; trazar, tirar (*líneas*) ‖ *intr* conspirar
plough [plaʊ] *s, tr & intr* var de **plow**
plover [ˈplʌvər] o [ˈplovər] *s* chorlito
plow [plaʊ] *s* arado; quitanieve *m* ‖ *tr* arar; surcar; quitar o barrer (*la nieve*); **to plow back** reinvertir (*ganancias*) ‖ *intr* arar; avanzar como un arado

plow•man [ˈplaʊmən] *s* (*pl* **-men** [mən]) arador *m,* yuguero

plow'share' *s* reja de arado

pluck [plʌk] *s* ánimo, coraje *m,* valor *m;* tirón *m* ‖ *tr* arrancar; coger (*flores*); desplumar (*un ave*); puntear, pulsar (*p.ej., una guitarra*) ‖ *intr* dar un tirón; **to pluck up** recobrar ánimo

pluck•y [ˈplʌki] *adj* (*comp* **-ier;** *super* **-iest**) animoso, valiente

plug [plʌg] *s* taco, tarugo; boca de agua; tableta de tabaco; (*hat*) (slang) chistera; (elec) clavija, toma, ficha; (aut) bujía; (compu) toma; (coll) rocín; (coll) elogio incidental ‖ *v* (*pret & pp* **plugged;** *ger* **plugging**) *tr* atarugar; calar (*un melón*); **to plug in** (elec) enchufar ‖ *intr* (coll) trabajar con ahinco

plum [plʌm] *s* (*tree*) ciruelo; (*fruit*) ciruela; (slang) turrón *m,* pingüe destino

plumage [ˈplumɪdʒ] *s* plumaje *m*

plumb [plʌm] *adj* vertical; (coll) completo ‖ *adv* a plomo; (coll) verticalmente; (coll) directamente ‖ *tr* aplomar; sondear

plumb bob *s* plomada

plumber [ˈplʌmər] *s* fontanero; (*worker in lead*) plomero

plumbing [ˈplʌmɪŋ] *s* instalación sanitaria; conjunto de cañerías; (*working in lead*) plomería; sondeo

plumbing fixtures *spl* artefactos sanitarios

plumb line *s* cuerda de plomada

plume [plum] *s* (*of a bird*) pluma; (*tuft of feathers worn as ornament*) penacho ‖ *tr* emplumar; componerse (*las plumas*); **to plume oneself on** enorgulleclerse de

plummet [ˈplʌmɪt] *s* plomada ‖ *intr* caer a plomo, precipitarse

plump [plʌmp] *adj* rechoncho, regordete; brusco, franco ‖ *adv* de golpe; francamente ‖ *s* (coll) caída pesada; (coll) ruido sordo ‖ *intr* caer a plomo

plum tree *s* ciruelo

plunder [ˈplʌndər] *s* pillaje *m;* botín *m* ‖ *tr* pillar, saquear

plunge [plʌndʒ] *s* zambullida; caída a plomo; sacudida violenta; salto; baño de agua fría; (*of a boat*) cabeceo ‖ *tr* zambullir; sumergir; hundir (*p.ej., un puñal*) ‖ *intr* zambullirse; sumergirse; hundirse (*p.ej., en la tristeza*); caer a plomo; arrojarse, precipitarse; cabecear (*un buque*); (slang) entregarse al juego, entregarse a las especulaciones

plunger [ˈplʌndʒər] *s* zambullidor *m;* émbolo buzo; (*of a tire valve*) obús *m;* (slang) jugador o especulador desenfrenado

plunk [plʌŋk] *adv* (coll) con un golpe seco, con un ruido de golpe seco ‖ *tr* (coll) arrojar, empujar o dejar caer pesadamente ‖ *intr* sonar o caer con un ruido de golpe seco

plural [ˈplʊrəl] *adj & s* plural *m*

plus [plʌs] *adj* más; y pico; **to be plus** (coll) tener por añadidura ‖ *prep* más ‖ *s* (*sign*) más *m;* añadidura

plush [plʌʃ] *adj* afelpado; (coll) lujoso, suntuoso ‖ *s* felpa; peluche *m*

plus sign *s* signo de más

Pluto [ˈpluto] *s* (astr) Plutón *m;* (myth) Pluto

plutonium [pluˈtonɪ•əm] *s* plutonio

ply [plaɪ] *s* (*pl* **plies**) (*e.g., of a cloth*) capa, doblez *m;* (*of a cable*) cordón *m* ‖ *v* (*pret & pp* **plied**) *tr* manejar (*la aguja, etc.*); ejercer (*un oficio*); batir (*el agua con los remos*); importunar; navegar por (*p.ej., un río*) ‖ *intr* avanzar; **to ply between** hacer (*un barco*) el servicio entre

ply'wood' *s* chapeado, madera laminada

P.M. *abbr* **Postmaster, post meridiem** (Lat) **afternoon**

pneumatic [njuˈmætɪk] o [nuˈmætɪk] *adj* neumático

pneumatic drill *s* perforadora de aire comprimido

pneumonia [njuˈmonɪ•ə] o [nuˈmonɪ•ə] *s* neumonía o pulmonía

P.O. *abbr* **post office**

poach [potʃ] *tr* escalfar (*huevos*) ‖ *intr* cazar o pescar en vedado

poacher [ˈpotʃər] *s* cazador furtivo, pescador furtivo

pock [pɑk] *s* cacaraña, hoyuelo

pocket [ˈpɑkɪt] *s* bolsillo, faltriquera; (*in billiards*) tronera; (aer) bolsa de aire; (mil) bolsón *m* ‖ *tr* embolsar; entronerar (*una bola de billar*); tragarse (*injurias*)

pock'et•book' *s* portamonedas *m;* (*of a woman*) bolsa; (*paperback*) libro de bolsillo

pocket calculator *s* bolsicalculadora, calculadora de bolsillo

pocket handkerchief *s* pañuelo de bolsillo o de mano

pock'et•knife' *s* (*pl* **-knives**) navaja, cortaplumas *m*

pocket money *s* alfileres *mpl,* dinero de bolsillo

poc'ket-size' *adj* de tamaño bolsillo

pocket watch *s* reloj *m* de bolsillo

pock'mark' *s* cacaraña, hoyuelo

pod [pɑd] *s* vaina

podiatrist [pəˈdaɪ•ətrəst] *s* pedicuro, pediatra *mf*

podium [ˈpodi•əm] *s* podio

poem [ˈpo•ɪm] *s* poema *m,* poesía

poet [ˈpo•ɪt] *s* poeta *m*

poetess [ˈpo•ɪtɪs] *s* poetisa

poetic [poˈɛtɪk] *adj* poético ‖ **poetics** *ssg* poética

poetry [ˈpo•ɪtri] *s* poesía

pogrom [ˈpogrəm] *s* levantamiento contra los judíos

poignancy [ˈpɔɪnyənsi] *s* picante *m,* viveza, intensidad

poignant [ˈpɔɪnyənt] *adj* picante, vivo, intenso

poinsettia [pɔ•ɪnˈsɛtɪ•ə] *s* flor *f* de Pascua

point [pɔɪnt] *s* (*of a sword, pencil; of land*) punta; (*of pen*) pico; (*of fountain pen*) puntilla; (*mark of imperceptible dimensions*) punto; (*of a joke*) gracia; (elec) punta; (math, typ, sport, fig) punto; (coll) indirecta, insinuación; **beside the point** fuera de propósito; **on**

the point of a punto de; **to carry one's point** salirse con la suya; **to come to the point** venir al caso o al grano; **to get to the point** caer en la cuenta || *tr* aguzar, sacar punta a; apuntar (*p.ej., un arma de fuego*); resanar (*una pared*); **to point one's finger at** señalar con el dedo; **to point out** señalar, indicar, hacer notar || *intr* apuntar; pararse (*el perro de muestra*); **to point at** señalar con el dedo

point'blank' *adj & adv* a quemarropa

pointed [ˋpɔɪntɪd] *adj* puntiagudo; picante; acentuado, directo

pointer [ˋpɔɪntər] *s* puntero; indicador *m;* (*of a clock*) manecilla; perro de muestra; (mas) fijador *m;* (coll) indicación, dirección

pointing *adj* (compu) apuntador || *s* (*joints*) juntas; (*in a brick wall*) rejuntado

point of view *s* punto de vista

poise [pɔɪz] *s* aplomo, equilibrio || *tr* equilibrar; considerar || *intr* equilibrarse; estar suspendido

poison [ˋpɔɪzən] *s* veneno, ponzoña || *tr* envenenar

poison ivy *s* tosiguero

poisonous [ˋpɔɪzənəs] *adj* venenoso

poi'son-pen' letter *s* carta calumniosa

poke [pok] *s* (*push*) empuje *m,* empujón *m;* (*thrust*) hurgonazo; (*with elbow*) codazo; (*slow person*) tardón *m* || *tr* empujar; hacer (*un agujero*) a empujones; abrirse (*paso*) a empujones; atizar, hurgar (*el fuego*); **to poke fun at** burlarse de; **to poke one's nose into** entremeterse en || *intr* fisgar, husmear; andar perezosamente

poker [ˋpokər] *s* hurgón *m;* (*card game*) póker *m,* pócar *m*

poker face *s* cara de jugador de póker; **to keep a poker face** disfrazar la expresión del rostro, mantener una expresión imperturbable

pok•y [ˋpoki] *adj* (*comp* **-ier;** *super* **-iest**) (coll) tardo, roncero

Poland [ˋpolənd] *s* Polonia

polar bear [ˋpolər] *s* oso blanco

polar ice'cap *s* casquete *m* polar

polarize [ˋpolə,raɪz] *tr* polarizar

pole [pol] *s* (*long rod or staff*) pértiga; (*of a flag*) asta; (*upright support*) poste *m;* (*to push a boat*) botador *m;* (astr, biol, elec, geog, math) polo || *tr* impeler (*un barco*) con botador || **Pole** *s* polaco

pole'cat' *s* turón *m,* veso

pole'star' *s* estrella polar; (*guide*) norte *m;* (*center of interest*) miradero

pole vault *s* salto con garrocha o con pértiga

police [pəˋlis] *adj* policial || *s* policia || *tr* poner o mantener servicio de policía en; (mil) limpiar

police car *s* carro-patrulla *m*

police force *s* cuerpo de policía

police•man [pəˋlismən] *s* (*pl* **-men** [mən]) policía *m,* guardia urbano

police record *s* ficha policial

police state *s* estado-policía *m*

police station *s* cuartel *m* o estación de policía, casa cuartel, comisaría

police'wom'an *s* mujer *f* policía

poli•cy [ˋpɑlɪsi] *s* (*pl* **-cies**) política; (ins) póliza

pol'icy hold'er *s* asegurado

polio [ˋpolɪ•o] *s* (coll) polio *f*

polish [ˋpɑlɪʃ] *s* pulimento; cera de lustrar; (*for shoes*) bola, betún *m,* lustre *m;* (*diamond*) talla; elegancia; cultura, urbanidad || *tr* pulimentar, pulir; embolar, dar betún a (*los zapatos*); **to polish off** (coll) terminar de prisa; (slang) engullir (*la comida, un trago*) || **Polish** [ˋpolɪʃ] *adj & s* polaco

polisher [ˋpɑlɪʃər] *s* pulidor *m;* (*machine*) pulidora; (*for floors, tables, etc.*) enceradora

polite [pəˋlaɪt] *adj* cortés, fino, urbano; culto

politeness [pəˋlaɪtnɪs] *s* cortesía, fineza, urbanidad; cultura

politic [ˋpɑlɪtɪk] *adj* prudente, sagaz; astuto; juicioso

political [pəˋlɪtɪkəl] *adj* político

political asylum *s* asilo político

political correctness *s* corrección política (costumbre *f,* práctica o política de acuerdo con la ideología progresista)

politically correct *adj* de acuerdo con la ideología progresista

political science *s* ciencias políticas

politician [,pɑlɪˋtɪʃən] *s* político; (*politician seeking personal or partisan gain*) politiquero

politics [ˋpɑlɪtɪks] *ssg* o *spl* política

poll [pol] *s* (*questionnaire to determine opinion*) encuesta, sondeo; votación; lista electoral; cabeza; **polls** urnas electorales; **to go to the polls** acudir a las urnas; **to take a poll** hacer una encuesta || *tr* dar (*un voto*); recibir (*votos*)

pollen [ˋpɑlən] *s* polen *m*

pollinate [ˋpɑlɪ,net] *tr* polinizar

polling booth [ˋpolɪŋ] *s* cabina o caseta de votar

polliwog [ˋpɑlɪ,wɑg] *s* renacuajo; (slang) persona que atraviesa el ecuador en un barco por primera vez

pollster [ˋpolstʌr] *s* encuestador *m*

poll tax *s* capitación, impuesto por cabeza

pollutant [pəˋlutənt] *s* contaminante *m*

pollute [pəˋlut] *tr* contaminar, corromper, ensuciar

pollution [pəˋluʃən] *s* contaminación; (*of the environment*) polución; (fig) corrupción

polo [ˋpolo] *s* polo

polo player *s* polista *mf,* jugador *m* de polo

polo shirt *s* (Arg) chomba

polyester [ˋpɑlɪ,ɛstər] *s* poliéster

polygamist [pəˋlɪgəmɪst] *s* polígamo

polygamous [pəˋlɪgəməs] *adj* polígamo

polyglot [ˋpɑlɪ,glɑt] *adj & s* poligloto

polygon [ˋpɑlɪ,gɑn] *s* polígono

polynomial [,pɑlɪˋnomɪ•əl] *s* polinomio

polyp [ˋpɑlɪp] *s* pólipo

polytheist [ˋpɑlɪ,θi•ɪst] *s* politeísta *mf*

polytheistic [,pɑlɪθiˋɪstɪk] *adj* politeísta

polyvalent [,pɑli'velənt] *adj* (chem, bact) polivalente
pomade [pə'med] *s* pomada
pomegranate ['pɑm,grænɪt] *s* (*shrub*) granado; (*fruit*) granada
pom•mel ['pʌməl] o ['pɑməl] *s* (*on hilt of sword*) pomo; (*on saddle*) perilla || *v* (*pret & pp* **-meled** o **-melled;** *ger* **-meling** o **-melling**) *tr* apuñear, aporrear
pomp [pɑmp] *s* pompa, fausto
pompadour ['pɑmpə,dʊr] *s* copete *m*
pompous ['pɑmpəs] *adj* pomposo, faustoso
pon•cho ['pɑntʃo] *s* (*pl* **-chos**) capote *m* de monte, poncho
pond [pɑnd] *s* estanque *m,* charca
ponder ['pɑndər] *tr* ponderar || *intr* meditar; **to ponder over** ponderar, considerar con cuidado
ponderous ['pɑndərəs] *adj* pesado, inmanejable; tedioso, fastidioso
pond scum *s* lama, verdín *m*
poniard ['pɑnjərd] *s* puñal *m*
pontiff ['pɑntɪf] *s* pontífice *m*
pontoon [pɑn'tun] *s* pontón *m*
po•ny ['poni] *s* (*pl* **-nies**) jaca, caballito; (*for drinking liquor*) (coll) pequeño vaso; (*translation used dishonestly in school*) (coll) chuleta
poodle ['pudəl] *s* perro de lanas
pool [pul] *s* (*small puddle*) charco; (*for swimming*) piscina; (*game*) trucos; (*in certain games*) polla, puesta; combinación de intereses; caudales unidos para un fin || *tr* mancomunar
pool'room' *s* sala de trucos
pool table *s* mesa de trucos, mesa de billar
poop [pup] *s* popa; (*deck*) toldilla
poor [pʊr] *adj* (*having few possessions; arousing pity*) pobre; (*not good, inferior*) malo
poor box *s* cepillo, caja de limosnas
poor'house' *s* asilo de pobres, casa de caridad
poorly ['pʊrli] *adv* mal
pop. *abbr* **popular, population**
pop [pɑp] *s* estallido, taponazo; bebida gaseosa || *v* (*pret & pp* **popped;** *ger* **popping**) *tr* hacer estallar; **to pop the question** (coll) hacer una declaración de amor || *intr* estallar
pop'corn' *s* rosetas, palomitas (de maíz)
pope [pop] *s* papa *m*
popeyed ['pɑp,aɪd] *adj* de ojos saltones; (*with fear, surprise, etc.*) desorbitado
pop'gun' *s* tirabala
poplar ['pɑplər] *s* álamo, chopo
pop•py ['pɑpi] *s* (*pl* **-pies**) amapola
pop'py•cock' *s* (coll) necedad, tontería
popsicle ['pɑpsɪkəl] *s* polo
populace ['pɑpjəlɪs] *s* populacho; chamuchina
popular ['pɑpjələr] *adj* popular
popularize ['pɑpjələ,raɪz] *tr* popularizar, vulgarizar
populous ['pɑpjələs] *adj* populoso
pop'-up win'dow *s* (compu) ventana desplegable
porcelain ['pɔrsəlɪn] *s* porcelana
porch [portʃ] *s* porche *m,* pórtico
porcupine ['pɔrkjə,paɪn] *s* puerco espín
pore [por] *s* poro || *intr*—**to pore over** estudiar larga y detenidamente
pork [pork] *s* carne *f* de cerdo
pork chop *s* chuleta de cerdo
porn [pɔrn] *adj* (coll) porno || *s* (coll) pornografía
pornography [pɔr'nɑgræfi] *s* pornografía
pornographic [,pɔrnə'græfɪk] *adj* pornográfico
porno queen ['pɔrno] *s* (slang) actriz *f* de películas pornográficas
porous ['porəs] *adj* poroso
porphy•ry ['pɔrfɪri] *s* (*pl* **-ries**) pórfido
porpoise ['pɔrpəs] *s* marsopa, puerco de mar; (*dolphin*) delfín *m*
porridge ['pɔrɪdʒ] *s* gachas
port [port] *adj* portuario || *s* puerto; (*opening in ship's side*) portilla; (*left side of ship or airplane*) babor *m;* oporto, vino de Oporto; (mach) lumbrera
portable ['portəbəl] *adj* portátil
portal ['portəl] *s* portal *m*
portend [por'tɛnd] *tr* anunciar de antemano, presagiar
portent ['portent] *s* augurio, presagio
portentous [por'tɛntəs] *adj* portentoso, extraordinario; amenazante, ominoso
porter ['portər] *s* (*doorkeeper*) portero, conserje *m;* (*in hotels and trains*) mozo de servicio; pórter *m* (*cerveza de Inglaterra de color obscuro*)
portfoli•o [port'folɪ,o] *s* (*pl* **-os**) cartera
port'hole' *s* porta, portilla
porti•co ['portɪ,ko] *s* (*pl* **-coes** o **-cos**) pórtico
portion ['porʃən] *s* porción; (*dowry*) dote *m & f*
port•ly ['portli] *adj* (*comp* **-lier;** *super* **-liest**) corpulento; grave, majestuoso
port of call *s* escala
portrait ['portret] o ['portrɪt] *s* retrato; **to sit for a portrait** retratarse
portray [por'tre] *tr* retratar
portrayal [por'tre•əl] *s* representación gráfica; retrato, descripción acertada
Portugal ['portʃəgəl] *s* Portugal *m*
Portu•guese ['portʃə,giz] *adj* portugués || *s* (*pl* **-guese**) portugués *m*
port wine *s* vino de Oporto
pose [poz] *s* pose *f* || *tr* plantear (*una pregunta, cuestión, etc.*) || *intr* posar (*para retratarse; como modelo*); tomar una postura afectada; **to pose as** hacerse pasar por
posh [pɑʃ] *adj* (slang) elegante; (slang) lujoso, suntuoso
position [pə'zɪʃən] *s* posición; empleo, puesto; opinión; **to be in a position to** estar en condiciones de
positive ['pɑzɪtɪv] *adj* positivo || *s* positiva
possess [pə'zɛs] *tr* poseer
possession [pə'zɛʃən] *s* posesión
possible ['pɑsɪbəl] *adj* posible

possum [ˈpɑsəm] *s* zarigüeya; **to play possum** hacer la mortecina
post [post] *s* (*piece of wood, metal, etc., set upright*) poste *m;* (*position*) puesto; (*job*) puesto, cargo; casa de correos ‖ *tr* fijar (*carteles*); echar al correo; apostar, situar; tener al corriente; **post no bills** se prohibe fijar carteles; *SIGN* prohibido fijar carteles
postage [ˈpostɪdʒ] *s* porte *m,* franqueo; **postage will be paid by addressee** a franquear en destino
postage meter *s* franqueadora
postage stamp *s* sello de correo; estampilla, timbre *m* (Am)
postal [ˈpostəl] *adj* postal ‖ *s* postal *f*
postal card *s* tarjeta postal
postal permit *s* franqueo concertado
postal savings bank *s* caja postal de ahorros
postcard *s* tarjeta postal
post′date′ *s* posfecha ‖ **post′date′** *tr* posfechar
poster [ˈpostər] *s* cartel *m,* cartelón *m,* letrero; póster *m*
posterity [pɑsˈterɪti] *s* posteridad
postern [ˈpostərn] *s* postigo, portillo
post′grad′uate *adj* postgraduado
post′grad′uate course *s* postgrado
post′haste′ *adj* por la posta, a toda prisa
posthumous [ˈpɑstʃʊməs] *adj* póstumo
post•man [ˈpostmən] *s* (*pl* **-men** [mən]) cartero
post′mark′ *s* matasellos *m,* timbre *m* de correos ‖ *tr* matasellar, timbrar
post′mas′ter *s* administrador *m* de correos
post-mortem [ˌpostˈmɔrtəm] *adj* posterior a la muerte ‖ *s* examen *m* de un cadáver
post office *s* casa de correos
post′-of′fice box *s* apartado de correos, casilla postal
postpaid [ˈpostˌped] *adj* con porte pagado, franco de porte
postpone [post′pon] *tr* aplazar
postscript [ˈpostˌskrɪpt] *s* posdata
posttonic [postˈtɑnɪk] *adj* postónico
posture [ˈpɑstʃər] *s* postura ‖ *intr* adoptar una postura
post′war′ *adj* de la posguerra
post′war′ period *s* posguerra
po•sy [ˈpozi] *s* (*pl* **-sies**) flor *f,* ramillete *m*
pot [pɑt] *s* pote *m;* (*for flowers*) tiesto; (*for the kitchen*) caldera, olla, puchero; vaso de noche, orinal *m;* (*in gambling*) puesta; (coll) hierba (*marihuana*)
potash [ˈpɑtˌæʃ] *s* potasa
potassium [pəˈtæsɪ•əm] *s* potasio
pota•to [pəˈteto] *s* (*pl* **-toes**) patata, papa; (*sweet potato*) batata, buniato
potato chips *spl* papas fritas, patatas fritas (Esp), papas chip (Urug)
potato masher *s* pasapuré *m*
potato omelet *s* tortilla a la española
potato peeler *s* pelapapas *m,* pelapatatas *m*
potbellied [ˈpɑtˈbɛlid] *adj* barrigón, panzudo
poten•cy [ˈpotənsi] *s* (*pl* **-cies**) potencia
potent [ˈpotənt] *adj* potente
potentate [ˈpotənˌtet] *s* potentado
potential [pəˈtenʃəl] *adj & s* potencial *m*
pot′hang′er *s* llares *fpl*
pot′hook′ *s* garabato
potion [ˈpoʃən] *s* poción
pot′luck *s* lo que hay de comer; **to take potluck** hacer penitencia
potshot *s* tiro a corta distancia
potter [ˈpɑtər] *s* alfarero; ollero ‖ *intr* ocuparse en fruslerías
potter's clay *s* arcilla figulina
potter's field *s* cementerio de los pobres, hoyanca
potter's shop *s* ollería
potter's wheel *s* torno de alfarero
potter•y [ˈpɑtəri] *s* (*pl* **-ies**) alfarería; cacharros (de alfarería)
pouch [paʊtʃ] *s* bolsa, saquillo; (*of kangaroo*) bolsa; (*for tobacco*) petaca; valija
poulterer [ˈpoltərər] *s* pollero
poultice [ˈpoltɪs] *s* cataplasma *f*
poultry [ˈpoltri] *s* aves *fpl* de corral
pounce [paʊns] *intr*—**to pounce on** saltar sobre, precipitarse sobre
pound [paʊnd] *s* (*weight*) libra; (*for stray animals*) corral *m* de concejo ‖ *tr* golpear; machacar, moler; encerrar en el corral de concejo; bombardear incesantemente; (*to keep walking over*) desempedrar ‖ *intr* golpear
pound′cake′ *s* pastel *m* en que entra una libra de cada ingrediente; ponqué *m* (Am)
pound sterling *s* libra esterlina
pour [por] *tr* vaciar, verter, derramar; echar, servir (*p.ej., té*); escanciar (*vino*) ‖ *intr* fluir rápidamente; llover a torrentes; **to pour out of** salir a montones de (*p.ej., el teatro*)
pout [paʊt] *s* mala cara, puchero ‖ *intr* poner mala cara, hacer pucheros
poverty [ˈpɑvərti] *s* pobreza; pelazón *f*
POW [ˈpiˈoˈdʌbəlˌju] *s* (letterword) (**prisoner of war**) prisionero de guerra
powder [ˈpaʊdər] *s* polvo; (*for face*) polvos; (*explosive*) pólvora ‖ *tr* pulverizar; (*to sprinkle with powder*) empolvar, polvorear
powder keg *s* barril *m* de pólvora; (fig) polvorín *m*
powder puff *s* borla para empolvarse
powder room *s* tocador *m;* (*downstairs lavatory*) cuarto de aseo; *SIGN* Damas
powdery [ˈpaʊdəri] *adj* (*like powder*) polvoriento; (*sprinkled with powder*) empolvado; (*crumbly*) quebradizo
power [ˈpaʊ•ər] *s* (*ability to act or do something; possession*) poder *m;* (*control, influence; wealth*) poderío; (*influential nation; energy, force, strength*) potencia; **the powers that be** las autoridades, los que mandan ‖ *tr* accionar, impulsar
power brakes *spl* (auto) servofrenos, frenos asistidos
power dive *s* (aer) picado con motor
power failure *s* interrupción de fuerza; (compu) apagon *m*

powerful [ˈpaʊ•ərfəl] *adj* poderoso
pow′er•house′ *s* central eléctrica
powerless [ˈpaʊ•ərlɪs] *adj* impotente
power line *s* (elec) sector *m* de distribución
power lunch *s* cena de negocios
power mower *s* motosegadora
power of attorney *s* poder *m*
power plant *s* (aer) grupo motopropulsor; (aut) grupo motor; (elec) central eléctrica, estación generadora
power steering *s* (aut) servodirección, dirección asistida
power tool *s* herramienta motriz
pp. *abbr* **pages**
P.R. *abbr* **public relations**
practical [ˈpræktɪkəl] *adj* práctico
practically [ˈpræktɪkəli] *adv* poco más o menos
practice [ˈpræktɪs] *s* práctica; uso, costumbre; ensayo; (*of a profession*) ejercicio; (*of a doctor*) clientela ‖ *tr* practicar; ejercitar (*p.ej., la caridad*); ejercer (*una profesión*); estudiar (*p.ej., el piano*); tener por costumbre ‖ *intr* ejercitarse; practicar la medicina; ensayarse; entrenarse, adiestrarse; **to practice as** ejercer de (*p.ej., abogado*)
practitioner [prækˈtɪʃənər] *s* (*medical doctor*) práctico, practicante *mf*
Prague [prɑg] o [preg] *s* Praga
prairie [ˈprɛri] *s* pradera, llanura, pampa
prairie dog *s* ardilla ladradora
prairie wolf *s* coyote *m*
praise [prez] *s* alabanza, elogío ‖ *tr* alabar, elogiar
praise′wor′thy *adj* laudable, plausible
prance [præns] o [prɑns] *s* cabriola, trenzado ‖ *intr* cabriolar, trenzar
prank [præŋk] *s* travesura, broma
prate [pret] *intr* charlar, parlotear
prattle [ˈprætəl] *s* charla, parloteo ‖ *intr* charlar, parlotear, balbucear (*un niño*)
prawn [prɔn] *s* langostino, camarón *m*
pray [pre] *tr* implorar, rogar, suplicar; rezar (*una oración*) ‖ *intr* orar, rezar; **pray tell me** sírvase decirme
prayer [prɛr] *s* ruego, súplica; oración, rezo
prayer book *s* devocionario
preach [pritʃ] *tr* predicar; aconsejar (*p.ej., la paciencia*) ‖ *intr* predicar
preacher [ˈpritʃər] *s* predicador *m*
preamble [ˈpri,æmbəl] *s* preámbulo
prebend [ˈprɛbənd] *s* prebenda
precarious [priˈkɛrɪ•əs] *adj* precario
precaution [priˈkɔʃən] *s* precaución
precede [priˈsid] *tr & intr* preceder
precedent [ˈprɛsɪdənt] *s* precedente *m*
precept [ˈprisɛpt] *s* precepto
precinct [ˈprisɪŋkt] *s* barriada; distrito electoral
precious [ˈprɛʃəs] *adj* precioso; caro, amado; (coll) considerable ‖ *adv* (coll) muy, p.ej., **precious little** muy poco
precipice [ˈprɛsɪpɪs] *s* precipicio
precipitate [prɪˈsɪpɪ,tet] *adj & s* precipitado ‖ *tr* precipitar ‖ *intr* precipitarse
precipitous [prɪˈsɪpɪtəs] *adj* empinado, escarpado; (*hurried, reckless*) precipitoso
precise [prɪˈsaɪs] *adj* preciso; meticuloso
precision [prɪˈsɪʒən] *s* precisión
preclude [prɪˈklud] *tr* excluir, imposibilitar
precocious [prɪˈkoʃəs] *adj* precoz
predatory [ˈprɛdə,tori] *adj* predatorio; (zool) rapaz
predicament [prɪˈdɪkəmənt] *s* apuro, situación difícil
predict [prɪˈdɪkt] *tr* predecir
prediction [prɪˈdɪkʃən] *s* predicción
predispose [,pridɪsˈpoz] *tr* predisponer
predominant [prɪˈdɑmɪnənt] *adj* predominante
preeminent [prɪˈɛmɪnənt] *adj* preeminente
preempt [prɪˈɛmpt] *tr* apropiarse o apropiarse de; (*forestall*) adelantarse a; (rad, telv) reemplazar
preen [prin] *tr* arreglarse (*las plumas*) con el pico; **to preen oneself** componerse, vestirse cuidadosamente
pref. *abbr* **preface, preferred, prefix**
prefabricate [priˈfæbrɪ,ket] *tr* prefabricar
preface [ˈprɛfɪs] *s* prefacio, advertencia ‖ *tr* introducir, empezar
pre•fer [prɪˈfʌr] *v* (*pret & pp* **-ferred;** *ger* **-ferring**) *tr* preferir; presentar; promover
preferable [ˈprɛfərəbəl] *adj* preferible
preference [ˈprɛfərəns] *s* preferencia
prefix [ˈprifɪks] *s* prefijo ‖ *tr* prefijar
pregnan•cy [ˈprɛgnənsi] *s* (*pl* **-cies**) preñez *f*, embarazo
pregnant [ˈprɛgnənt] *adj* preñado; encinta; **to make pregnant** dejar encinta
prejudice [ˈprɛdʒədɪs] *s* prejuicio; (*detriment*) perjuicio; **to the prejudice of** con perjuicio de; **without prejudice** (law) sin detrimento de sus propios derechos ‖ *tr* predisponer, prevenir; (*to harm*) perjudicar
prejudicial [,prɛdʒəˈdɪʃəl] *adj* perjudicial
prelate [ˈprɛlɪt] *s* prelado
pre-Lenten [priˈlɛntən] *adj* carnavalesco
prelim [priˈlɪm] *s* (coll) examen *m* preliminar
preliminar•y [prɪˈlɪmɪ,nɛri] *adj* preliminar ‖ *s* (*pl* **-ies**) preliminar *m*
prelude [ˈprɛljud] o [ˈprilud] *s* preludio ‖ *tr* preludiar
premature [,priməˈtʊr] *adj* prematuro
premeditated [priˈmɛdɪ,tetəd] *adj* premeditado
premier [prɪˈmɪr] o [ˈpriˈmɪr] *s* primer ministro, presidente *m* del consejo
première [preˈmjɛr] o [ˈprimɪ•ər] *s* estreno; actriz *f* principal ‖ *intr* estrenarse
premise [ˈprɛmɪs] *s* premisa; **on the premises** en el local mismo; **premises** predio, local *m*
premium [ˈprimɪ•əm] *s* premio; (ins) prima
premonition [,priməˈnɪʃən] *s* presagio; presentimiento
preoccupancy [priˈɑkjəpənsi] *s* preocupación
preoccupation [priˈɑkjəˈpeʃən] *s* preocupación
preoccu•py [priˈɑkjə,paɪ] *v* (*pret & pp* **-pied**) *tr* preocupar

prepaid [pri`ped] *adj* pagado por adelantado; con porte pagado
preparation [,prɛpə`reʃən] *s* preparación; (*e.g., for a trip*) preparativo; (pharm) preparado
preparatory [prɪ`pærə,torɪ] *adj* preparativo, preparatorio
prepare [prɪ`pɛr] *tr* preparar ‖ *intr* prepararse
preparedness [prɪ`pɛrɪdnɪs] o [prɪ`pɛrdnɪs] *s* preparación; preparación militar
pre•pay [pri`pe] *v* (*pret & pp* **-paid**) *tr* pagar por adelantado
preponderant [prɪ`pɑndərənt] *adj* preponderante
preposition [,prɛpə`zɪʃən] *s* preposición
prepossessing [,pripə`zɛsɪŋ] *adj* atractivo, simpático
preposterous [prɪ`pɑstərəs] *adj* absurdo, ridículo
prep school [prɛp] *s* (coll) escuela preparatoria
prepuce [`pripjus] *s* prepucio
prerecorded [,prirɪ`kɔrdɪd] *adj* (rad & telv) grabado de antemano
prerequisite [,pri`rɛkwɪzɪt] *s* requisito previo
prerogative [prɪ`rɑgətɪv] *s* prerrogativa
Pres. *abbr* **Presbyterian, President**
presage [`prɛsɪdʒ] *s* presagio ‖ [prɪ`sedʒ] *tr* presagiar
Presbyterian [,prɛzbɪ`tɪrɪ•ən] *adj & s* presbiteriano
pre′school′ *adj* de edad preescolar; preescolar ‖ *s* preescolar *m*
prescribe [prɪ`skraɪb] *tr & intr* prescribir
prescription [prɪ`skrɪpʃən] *s* prescripción; (pharm) receta
prescription glasses *spl* gafas graduadas, lentes de aumento, de fórmula *or* ópticos
presence [`prɛzəns] *s* presencia
present [`prɛzənt] *adj* presente ‖ *s* presente *m,* regalo ‖ [prɪ`zənt] *tr* presentar, obsequiar
presentable [prɪ`zɛntəbəl] *adj* bien apersonado
presentation [,prɛzən`teʃən] o [,prizən`teʃən] *s* presentación
presentation copy *s* ejemplar *m* de cortesía con dedicatoria del autor
presentiment [prɪ`zɛntɪmənt] *s* presentimiento
presently [`prɛzəntli] *adv* luego, dentro de poco
preserve [prɪ`zʌrv] *s* conserva, compota; (*for game*) vedado ‖ *tr* conservar; preservar, proteger
preserved fruit *s* dulce *m* de almíbar
pre′shrunk′ *adj* preencogido
preside [prɪ`zaɪd] *intr* presidir; **to preside over** presidir
presiden•cy [`prɛzɪdənsi] *s* (*pl* **-cies**) presidencia
president [`prɛzɪdənt] *s* presidente *m,* presidenta; (*of a university*) rector *m*
pres′i•dent-e•lect′ *s* presidente *m* electo (*todavía sin gobierno*)
press [prɛs] *s* apretón *m,* empujón *m;* (*e.g., of business*) urgencia; muchedumbre; (*machine for printing, for making wine; newspapers and newspapermen*) prensa; (*printing*) imprenta; (*closet*) armario; **to go to press** entrar en prensa ‖ *tr* apretar (*p.ej., un botón*); (*in a press*) prensar; planchar (*la ropa*); imprimir (*discos de fonógrafo*); oprimir, pulsar (*una tecla*); apresurar; abrumar; apremiar, instar; insistir en
press agent *s* agente *m* de publicidad
press box *s* cabina de prensa
press conference *s* conferencia de prensa, rueda de prensa
pressing [`prɛsɪŋ] *adj* apremiante, urgente ‖ *s* planchado
press release *s* comunicado o nota de prensa
pressure [`prɛʃər] *s* presión; premura, urgencia
pressure cooker [`kʊkər] *s* olla de presión, cocina de presión
pressure group *s* grupo de interés o presión
pressurize [`prɛʃə,raɪz] *tr* (aer) sobrecargar
prestige [prɛs`tiʒ] o [`prɛstɪdʒ] *s* prestigio
presumably [prɪ`zuməbli] *adv* probablemente, verosímilmente
presume [prɪ`zjum] *tr* presumir; suponer; **to presume to** tomar la libertad de ‖ *intr* suponer; **to presume on** o **upon** abusar de
presumption [prɪ`zʌmpʃən] *s* presunción; pretensión
presumptuous [prɪ`zʌmptʃʊ•əs] *adj* confianzudo, desenvuelto
presuppose [,prisə`poz] *tr* presuponer
pretend [prɪ`tɛnd] *tr* aparentar, fingir ‖ *intr* fingir; **to pretend to** pretender (*p.ej., el trono*)
pretender [prɪ`tɛndər] *s* pretendiente *mf*
pretense [prɪ`tɛns] o [`pritɛns] *s* pretensión; fingimiento; **under false pretenses** con apariencias fingidas; **under pretense of** so pretexto de
pretentious [prɪ`tɛnʃəs] *adj* pretencioso, aparatoso; ambicioso, vasto
pre′trial′ prisoner *s* preso preventivo
pret•ty [`prɪti] *adj* (*comp* **-tier;** *super* **-tiest**) bonito, lindo; (coll) bastante, considerable ‖ *adv* algo; bastante; muy
prevail [prɪ`vel] *intr* prevalecer, reinar; **to prevail on** o **upon** persuadir
prevailing [prɪ`velɪŋ] *adj* prevaleciente, reinante; común, corriente
prevalent [`prɛvələnt] *adj* común, corriente, en boga
prevaricate [prɪ`værɪ,ket] *intr* mentir
prevent [prɪ`vɛnt] *tr* impedir ‖ *intr* obstar
prevention [prɪ`vɛnʃən] *s* (el) impedir; medidas de precaución
preventive [prɪ`vɛntɪv] *adj & s* preservativo
preventive detention *s* detención preventiva, arresto preventivo
preview [`pri,vju] *s* vista anticipada; (*private showing*) (mov) preestreno; (*showing of brief scenes for advertising*) (mov) avance *m;* (compu) previsualización
previous [`privɪ•əs] *adj* previo, anterior ‖ *adv* previamente; **previous to** con anterioridad a, antes de
prewar [`pri,wɔr] *adj* prebélico, de preguerra

prey [pre] *s* presa; víctima; **to be prey to** ser presa de || *intr* cazar; **to prey on** o **upon** apresar y devorar; pillar, robar; tener preocupado
price [praɪs] *s* precio || *tr* apreciar, estimar; fijar el precio de, poner precio a; pedir el precio de
price control *s* intervención de precios
price′-cut′ting *s* reducción de precios
price′-fix′ing *s* fijación de precios
price′-freez′ing *s* congelación de precios
priceless [ˈpraɪslɪs] *adj* inapreciable, sin precio; (coll) absurdo, divertido
price tag *s* etiqueta de precios; (fig) precio
price war *s* guerra de precios
prick [prɪk] *s* (*pointed weapon or instrument*) espiche *m;* (*sharp point*) púa; (*small hole made with sharp point*) agujerillo; (*spur*) aguijón *m;* (*jab; sharp pain*) pinchazo, punzada; **to kick against the pricks** dar coces contra el aguijón || *tr* pinchar; marcar con agujerillos; dar una punzada a; (*to sting*) punzar; **to prick up** aguzar (*las orejas*)
prick•ly [ˈprɪkli] *adj* (*comp* **-lier;** *super* **-liest**) espinoso, puado, punzante
prickly heat *s* salpullido causado por el calor
prickly pear *s* (*plant*) chumbera; (*fruit*) higo chumbo
pride [praɪd] *s* orgullo; arrogancia; **the pride of** la flor y nata de || *tr*—**to pride oneself on** o **upon** enorgullecerse de
priest [prist] *s* sacerdote *m*
priesthood [ˈprist•hʊd] *s* sacerdocio
priest•ly [ˈpristli] *adj* (*comp* **-lier;** *super* **-liest**) sacerdotal
prig [prɪg] *s* gazmoño, pedante *mf*
prim [prɪm] *adj* (*comp* **primmer;** *super* **primmest**) estirado, relamido
primary [ˈpraɪ,mɛri] o [ˈpraɪməri] *adj* primario || *s* (*pl* **-ries**) elección preliminar; (elec) primario
prime [praɪm] *adj* primero, principal; (*of the best quality*) primo || *s* flor *f,* juventud, primavera; alba, aurora; (la) flor y nata; (*of a degree*) (phys) minuto; (typ) virgulilla; **prime of life** edad viril, flor *f* de edad || *tr* informar de antemano; cebar (*un arma de fuego, una bomba, un carburador*); (*for painting*) imprimar; poner la primera capa o la primera mano a; poner virgulilla a
prime minister *s* primer ministro
primer [ˈprɪmər] *s* cartilla || [ˈpraɪmər] *s* (*for paint*) aprestado *m;* (mach) cebador *m*
primitive [ˈprɪmɪtɪv] *adj* primitivo
primp [prɪmp] *tr* acicalar, engalanar || *intr* acicalarse, engalanarse
prim′rose′ *s* primavera
primrose path *s* vida dada a los placeres de los sentidos
prin. *abbr* **principal**
prince [prɪns] *s* príncipe *m;* **to live like a prince** portarse como un príncipe
Prince Charming *s* el príncipe azul
prince consort *s* príncipe *m* consorte
Prince of Wales *s* príncipe *m* de Gales
princess [ˈprɪnsɪs] *s* princesa
principal [ˈprɪnsɪpəl] *adj* principal || *s* principal *m,* jefe *m;* (*of a school*) director *m;* criminal *mf;* (*main sum, not interest*) capital *m*
principle [ˈprɪnsɪpəl] *s* principio
print [prɪnt] *s* marca, impresión; (*printed cloth*) estampado; (*design in printed cloth*) diseño; grabado, lámina; letras de molde; (*act of printing*) impresión; edición; tirada; (phot) impresión; **in print** impreso, publicado; **out of print** agotado || *tr* imprimir; estampar; hacer imprimir; publicar; escribir en caracteres de imprenta; (phot) tirar, imprimir; (fig) imprimir o grabar (*en la memoria*)
printed circuit board *s* placa de circuitos impresos
printed matter *s* impresos
printer [ˈprɪntər] *s* impresor *m;* (compu) impresora
printer's devil *s* aprendiz *m* de imprenta
printer's error *s* error *m* de imprenta, error tipográfico
print′head′ *s* cabezal *m* de impresión
printer's ink *s* tinta de imprenta
printer's mark *s* pie *m* de imprenta
printing [ˈprɪntɪŋ] *s* impresión; caracteres impresos; edición; tirada; letras de mano imitación de las impresas; (phot) tiraje *m*
printing press *s* imprenta, prensa
printout [ˈprɪnt,aʊt] *s* (compu) salida impresa, listado
prior [ˈpraɪ•ər] *adj* anterior || *adv* anteriormente; **prior to** antes de
priori•ty [praɪˈɔrɪti] *s* (*pl* **-ties**) prioridad; **of the highest priority** de máxima prioridad
prism [ˈprɪzəm] *s* prisma *m*
prison [ˈprɪzən] *s* cárcel *f,* prisión || *tr* encarcelar
prisoner [ˈprɪzənər] o [ˈprɪznər] *s* preso; (mil) prisionero
prisoner of war *s* prisionero de guerra
prison van *s* coche *m* celular
pris•sy [ˈprɪsi] *adj* (*comp* **-sier;** *super* **-siest**) (coll) remilgado, melindroso
priva•cy [ˈpraɪvəsi] *s* (*pl* **-cies**) aislamiento, retiro; secreto, reserva
private [ˈpraɪvɪt] *adj* particular, privado; confidencial; || *s* soldado raso; **in private** privadamente; en secreto; **privates** partes pudendas
private first class *s* soldado de primera, aspirante *m* a cabo
private hospital *s* clínica, casa de salud
private lesson *s* clase *f* particular
private property *s* bienes *mpl* particulares
private school *s* colegio privado, centro de estudios
private view *s* día *m* de inauguración
privet [ˈprɪvɪt] *s* aligustre *m*
privilege [ˈprɪvɪlɪdʒ] *s* privilegio
priv•y [ˈprɪvi] *adj* privado; **privy to** enterado secretamente de || *s* (*pl* **-ies**) letrina

prize [praɪz] *s* premio; (*something captured*) presa || *tr* apreciar, estimar
prizefight *s* partido de boxeo profesional
prizefighter *s* boxeador *m* profesional
prize'win'ner *s* ganador *m* de un premio, premiado
pro [pro] *prep* en pro de || *s* (*pl* **pros**) voto afirmativo; (coll) deportista *mf* profesional; **the pros and the cons** el pro y el contra
probabili•ty [,prɑbə'bɪlɪti] *s* (*pl* **-ties**) probabilidad; acontecimiento probable; tiempo probable
probable ['prɑbəbəl] *adj* probable
probably ['prɑbəbli] *adv* probablemente, seguramente; presuntamente
probate ['probet] *s* (law) validación legal de un testamento || *tr* (*a will*) validar legalmente, autenticar
probation [pro'beʃən] *s* libertad vigilada; período de prueba
probe [prob] *s* encuesta, indagación; (*instrument*) sonda || *tr* indagar; sondar
problem ['prɑbləm] *s* problema *m*
procedure [pro'sidʒər] *s* procedimiento
proceed [pro'sid] *intr* proceder || **proceeds** ['prosidz] *spl* producto, ganancia
proceeding [pro'sidɪŋ] *s* procedimiento; **proceedings** actas; diligencias
process ['prɑsɛs] *s* procedimiento; proceso, progreso; **in the process of time** con el tiempo || *tr* elaborar; (*electronic data*) procesar
processed cheese *s* queso fundido
processing ['prɑsɛsɪŋ] *s* (*electronic data*) procesamiento
processor ['prɑ,sɛsər] *s* (compu) procesador *m*, unidad de proceso
process server ['sʌrvər] *s* entregador *m* de la citación
pro-choice ['pro'tʃoɪs] *adj* de pro-opción || *s* pro-opción
proclaim [pro'klem] *tr* proclamar
proclitic [pro'klɪtɪk] *adj & s* proclítico
procrastinate [pro'kræstɪ,net] *tr* diferir de un día para otro || *intr* tardar, no decidirse
procure [pro'kjʊr] *tr* conseguir, obtener || *intr* alcahuetear
prod [prɑd] *s* aguijada; empuje *m* || *v* (*pret & pp* **prodded;** *ger* **prodding**) *tr* aguijar, pinchar; aguijonear, estimular
prodigal ['prɑdɪgəl] *adj & s* pródigo
prodigal son *s* hijo pródigo
prodigious [pro'dɪdʒəs] *adj & s* prodigioso, maravilloso; enorme, inmenso
prodi•gy ['prɑdɪdʒi] *s* (*pl* **-gies**) prodigio
produce ['prodjus] o ['produs] *s* producto; productos agrícolas || [pro'djus] o [pro'dus] *tr* producir; presentar (*p.ej., un drama*) al público; (geom) prolongar
product ['prɑdəkt] *s* producto
production [pro'dʌkʃən] *s* producción
profane [pro'fen] *adj* profano; (*language*) injurioso, blasfemo || *s* profano || *tr* profanar
profani•ty [pro'fænɪti] *s* (*pl* **-ties**) blasfemia
profess [pro'fɛs] *tr & intr* profesar
profession [pro'fɛʃən] *s* profesión
professor [pro'fɛsər] *s* profesor *m*, catedrático; (coll) profesor, maestro
proffer ['prɑfər] *s* oferta, propuesta || *tr* ofrecer, proponer
proficient [pro'fɪʃənt] *adj* perito, diestro, hábil
profile ['profaɪl] *s* perfil *m* || *tr* perfilar
profit ['prɑfɪt] *s* provecho, beneficio, utilidad, ganancia; **at a profit** con ganancia || *tr* servir, ser de utilidad a || *intr* sacar provecho, ganar; adelantar, mejorar; **to profit by** aprovechar, sacar provecho de
profitable ['prɑfɪtəbəl] *adj* provechoso, rentable
profit and loss *s* ganancias y pérdidas
profiteer [,prɑfɪ'tɪr] *s* logrero, explotador *m* || *intr* logrear, explotar
profit margin *s* excedente *m* de ganancia
profit taking *s* realización de beneficios
profligate ['prɑflɪgɪt] *adj & s* libertino; pródigo
pro forma invoice [pro 'fɔrmə] *s* factura simulada
profound [pro'faʊnd] *adj* profundo
profuse [pro'fjus] *adj* (*extravagant*) pródigo; (*abundant*) profuso
proge•ny ['prɑdʒeni] *s* (*pl* **-nies**) prole *f*, progenie *f*
progno•sis [prɑg'nosɪs] *s* (*pl* **-ses** [siz]) pronóstico
prognostic [prɑg'nɑstɪk] *s* pronóstico
program ['prəgræm] *s* programa *m;* (*computer*) **program(me)** programa (para ordenador) || *tr* programar; (*computer*) **program(me)** programar
program(m)er ['prəgræmər] *s* (compu) programador *m*, programadora
program(m)ing ['prəgræmɪŋ] *s* (compu) programación (de ordenadores)
progress ['prɑgrɛs] *s* progreso; progresos; **to make progress** hacer progresos || [prə'grɛs] *intr* progresar
progressive [prə'grɛsɪv] *adj* progresivo; (pol) progresista || *s* (pol) progresista *mf*
prohibit [pro'hɪbɪt] *tr* prohibir
project ['prɑdʒɛkt] *s* proyecto || [prə'dʒɛkt] *tr* proyectar || *intr* proyectarse
projectile [prə'dʒɛktɪl] *s* proyectil *m*
projecting [prə'dʒɛtɪŋ] *adj* salido
projection [prə'dʒɛkʃən] *s* proyección
projectionist [prə'dʒɛkʃənɪst] *s* operador m, proyeccionista
projection room *s* cabina de proyección
projector [prə'dʒɛktər] *s* proyector *m*
proletarian [,prolɪ'tɛrɪ•ən] *adj & s* proletario
proletariat [,prolɪ'tɛrɪ•ət] *s* proletariado
proliferate [prə'lɪfə,ret] *intr* proliferar
prolific [prə'lɪfɪk] *adj* prolífico
prolix ['prolɪks] o [pro'lɪks] *adj* difuso, verboso
prologue ['prolɔg] *s* prólogo
prolong [pro'lɔŋ] *tr* prolongar

promenade [ˌprɑmɪˈned] *s* paseo; garbeo; baile *m* de gala ‖ *intr* pasear o pasearse
promenade deck *s* (naut) cubierta de paseo
prominent [ˈprɑmɪnənt] *adj* prominente
promise [ˈprɑmɪs] *s* promesa ‖ *tr & intr* prometer
promissory [ˈprɑmɪˌsori] *adj* promisorio
promissory note *s* pagaré *m*
promo [ˈpromo] *s* (coll) video promocional; (rad, telv) anuncio
promonto•ry [ˈprɑmənˌtori] *s* (*pl* **-ries**) promontorio
promote [prəˈmot] *tr* promover; fomentar
promoter [prəˈmotər] *s* (com) promotor *m;* (sport) empresario
promotion [prəˈmoʃən] *s* promoción; fomento
prompt [prɑmpt] *adj* pronto, puntual; listo, dispuesto ‖ *s* (*prompter*) apuntador *m;* (*reminder*) apunte *m;* (compu) mensaje *m* al operador, presto; (telp) mensaje informativo y automático para la persona que llama ‖ *tr* incitar, mover; inspirar, sugerir; (theat) apuntar
prompter [ˈprɑmptər] *s* (theat) apuntador *m*
prompter's box *s* (theat) concha
promulgate [ˈprɑməlˌget] o [proˈmʌlget] *tr* promulgar
prone [pron] *adj* postrado boca abajo; extendido sobre el suelo; dispuesto, propenso
prong [prɔŋ] o [prɑŋ] *s* punta (*de un tenedor, horquilla, etc.*)
pronoun [ˈpronaʊn] *s* pronombre *m*
pronounce [prəˈnaʊns] *tr* pronunciar
pronouncement [prəˈnaʊnsmənt] *s* declaración; decisión, opinión; (law) pronunciación
pronunciamen•to [prəˌnʌnsɪ•əˈmɛnto] *s* (*pl* **-tos**) pronunciamiento
pronunciation [prəˌnʌnsɪˈeʃən] o [prəˌnʌnʃɪˈeʃən] *s* pronunciación
proof [pruf] *adj* de prueba; **proof against** a prueba de ‖ *s* prueba
proof'read'er *s* corrector *m* de pruebas
prop [prɑp] *s* apoyo, puntal *m;* (*to hold up a plant*) rodrigón *m;* **props** (theat) accesorios ‖ *v* (*pret & pp* **propped;** *ger* **propping**) *tr* apoyar, apuntalar; poner un rodrigón a
propaganda [ˌprɑpəˈgændə] *s* propaganda
propagate [ˈprɑpəˌget] *tr* propagar
proparoxytone [ˌpropærˈɑksɪˌton] *adj & s* proparoxítono
pro•pel [prəˈpɛl] *v* (*pret & pp* **-pelled;** *ger* **-pelling**) *tr* propulsar, impeler
propeller [prəˈpɛlər] *s* hélice *f*
propensi•ty [prəˈpɛnsɪti] *s* (*pl* **-ties**) propensión
proper [ˈprɑpər] *adj* propio, conveniente; decente, decoroso; exacto, justo
proper name *s* nombre *m* propio
proper•ty [ˈprɑpərti] *s* (*pl* **-ties**) propiedad; **properties** (theat) accesorios
property developer *s* promotor inmobiliario
property owner *s* propietario de bienes raíces
prophe•cy [ˈprɑfɪsi] *s* (*pl* **-cies**) profecía
prophe•sy [ˈprɑfɪˌsaɪ] *v* (*pret & pp* **-sied**) *tr* profetizar
prophet [ˈprɑfɪt] *s* profeta *m*
prophetess [ˈprɑfɪtɪs] *s* profetisa
prophylactic [ˌprofɪˈlæktɪk] *adj & s* profiláctico
propitiate [prəˈpɪʃɪˌet] *tr* propiciar
propitious [prəˈpɪʃəs] *adj* propicio
prop'jet *s* turbohélice *m*
proportion [prəˈporʃən] *s* proporción; **in proportion as** a medida que; **out of proportion** desproporcionado ‖ *tr* proporcionar
proportionate [prəˈporʃənɪt] *adj* proporcionado
proposal [prəˈpozəl] *s* propuesta; proposición oferta de matrimonio
propose [prəˈpoz] *tr* proponer ‖ *intr* proponer matrimonio; **to propose to** pedir la mano a; proponerse a + *inf*
proposition [ˌprɑpəˈzɪʃən] *s* proposición, propuesta
propound [prəˈpaʊnd] *tr* proponer
proprietor [prəˈpraɪ•ətər] *s* propietario
proprietress [prəˈpraɪ•ətrɪs] *s* propietaria
proprie•ty [prəˈpraɪ•əti] *s* (*pl* **-ties**) corrección, conducta decorosa, conveniencia; **proprieties** cánones *mpl* sociales, convenciones
propulsion [prəˈpʌlʃən] *s* propulsión
prorate [proˈret] *tr* prorratear
prosaic [proˈze•ɪk] *adj* prosaico, pedestre
proscribe [proˈskraɪb] *tr* proscribir
prose [proz] *adj* prosaico ‖ *s* prosa
prosecute [ˈprɑsɪˌkjut] *tr* llevar a cabo; (law) procesar
prosecution [ˌprɑsɪˈkjuʃən] *s* prosecución; (law) procesamiento, enjuiciamiento; (*trial*) proceso, juicio
prosecutor [ˈprɑsɪˌkjutər] *s* acusador *m,* demandante *mf;* (*lawyer*) fiscal *m,* acusador (público)
proselyte [ˈprɑsɪˌlaɪt] *s* prosélito
prose writer *s* prosista *mf*
prosody [ˈprɑsədi] *s* métrica
prospect [ˈprɑspɛkt] *s* vista; esperanza; probabilidad de éxito; cliente *mf* o comprador *m* probable ‖ *tr & intr* prospectar; **to prospect for** buscar (*p.ej., oro, petróleo*)
prosper [ˈprɑspər] *tr & intr* prosperar
prosperi•ty [prɑsˈpɛrɪti] *s* (*pl* **-ties**) prosperidad
prosperous [ˈprɑspərəs] *adj* próspero
prostate [ˈprɑstet] *s* (anat) próstata
prostitute [ˈprɑstɪˌtjut] *s* prostituta; güila (Mex) ‖ *tr* prostituir
prostrate [ˈprɑstret] *adj* postrado, prosternado ‖ *tr* postrar
prostration [prɑsˈtreʃən] *s* postración
protagonist [proˈtægənɪst] *s* protagonista *mf*
protect [prəˈtɛkt] *tr* proteger
protection [prəˈtɛkʃən] *s* protección
protégé [ˈprotəˌʒe] *s* protegido
protégée [ˈprotəˌʒe] *s* protegida
protein [ˈproti•ɪn] o [ˈprotin] *s* proteína
pro-tempore [proˈtɛmpəri] *adj* interino

protest [ˈprotɛst] *s* protesta ‖ [proˈtɛst] *tr & intr* protestar
Protestant [ˈprɑtɪstənt] *adj & s* protestante *mf*
prothonotar•y [proˈθɑnə,tɛri] *s* (*pl* **-ies**) escribano principal (*de un tribunal*)
protocol [ˈprotə,kɑl] *s* protocolo
protoplasm [ˈprotə,plæzəm] *s* protoplasma *m*
prototype [ˈprotə,taɪp] *s* prototipo
protozoan [,protəˈzo•ɑn] *s* protozoo
protract [proˈtrækt] *tr* prolongar
protrude [proˈtrud] *intr* resaltar
proud [praʊd] *adj* orgulloso; soberbio; glorioso
proud flesh *s* carnosidad, bezo
prov. *abbr* **provincialism**
prove [pruv] *v* (*pret* **proved;** *pp* **proved** o **proven)** *tr* probar ‖ *intr* resultar; **to prove to be** venir a ser, resultar
proverb [ˈprɑvərb] *s* proverbio
provide [prəˈvaɪd] *tr* proporcionar, suministrar ‖ *intr*—**to provide for** proveer a; asegurarse (*el porvenir*)
provided [prəˈvaɪdɪd] *conj* a condición (de) que, con tal (de) que
providence [ˈprɑvɪdəns] *s* providencia
providential [,prɑvɪˈdɛnʃəl] *adj* providencial
provider [prəˈvaɪdər] *s* (*for a family*) sostén económico: (*of jobs*) fuente *f;* (compu) proveedor *m*
providing [prəˈvaɪdɪŋ] *conj* var de **provided**
province [ˈprɑvɪns] *s* provincia; (*sphere of activity or knowledge*) competencia
proving ground [ˈpruvɪŋ] *s* campo de ensayos
provision [prəˈvɪʒən] *s* provisión; condición, estipulación
provi•so [prəˈvaɪzo] *s* (*pl* **-sos** o **-soes**) condición, estipulación, salvedad
provoke [prəˈvok] *tr* provocar
provoking [prəˈvokɪŋ] *adj* provocador, irritante
provost [ˈprovost] *s* (educ) (U.S.A.) prevoste *mf* (*responsable del profesorado universitario*)
prow [praʊ] *s* proa
prowess [ˈpraʊ•ɪs] *s* proeza; destreza
prowl [praʊl] *intr* cazar al acecho, rodar, vagabundear
prowler [ˈpraʊlər] *s* rondador *m;* ladrón *m*
proximity [prɑkˈsɪmɪti] *s* proximidad
prox•y [ˈprɑksi] *s* (*pl* **-ies**) poder *m,* poderhabiente *mf*
prude [prud] *s* mojigato, gazmoño
prudence [ˈprudəns] *s* prudencia
prudent [ˈprudənt] *adj* prudente
pruder•y [ˈprudəri] *s* (*pl* **-ies**) mojigatería, gazmoñería
prudish [ˈprudɪʃ] *adj* mojigato, gazmoño
prune [prun] *s* ciruela pasa ‖ *tr* podar, escamondar
pry [praɪ] *v* (*pret & pp* **pried)** *tr*—**to pry open** forzar con la alzaprima o palanca; **to pry out of** arrancar (*p.ej., un secreto*) a (*una persona*) ‖ *intr* entremeterse; **to pry into** entremeterse en
P.S. *abbr* **postscript, Privy Seal**
psalm [sɑm] *s* salmo
Psalter [ˈsɔltər] *s* Salterio
pseudo [ˈsudo] o [ˈsjudo] *adj* supuesto, falso, fingido
pseudonym [ˈsudənɪm] o [ˈsjudənɪm] *s* seudónimo, anónimo
Psyche [ˈsaɪki] *s* Psique *f*
psychedelic [,saɪkəˈdɛlɪk] *adj* psicodélico
psychiatrist [saɪˈkaɪ•ətrɪst] *s* psiquiatra *mf*
psychiatry [saɪˈkaɪ•ətri] *s* psiquiatria
psychic [ˈsaɪkɪk] *adj* psíquico; mediúmnico ‖ *s* médium *mf*
psychoanalysis [,saɪko•əˈnælɪsɪs] *s* psicoanálisis *m*
psychoanalyze [,saɪkoˈænə,laɪz] *tr* psicoanalizar
psychologic(al) [,sɑɪkəˈlɑdʒɪk(əl)] *adj* psicológico
psychologist [saɪˈkɑlədʒɪst] *s* psicólogo
psychology [saɪˈkɑlədʒi] *s* psicología
psychopath [ˈsaɪkə,pæθ] *s* psicópata *mf*
psycho•sis [saɪˈkosɪs] *s* (*pl* **-ses** [siz]) psicosis *f;* estado mental
psychotherapy [,saɪkəˈθɛrəpi] *s* psicoterapia
psychotic [saɪˈkɑtɪk] *adj & s* psicótico
pt. *abbr* **part, pint, point**
pub [pʌb] *s* (Brit) taberna, bar *m*
puberty [ˈpjubərti] *s* pubertad
pubic [ˈpjubɪk] *adj* pubiano
public [ˈpʌblɪk] *adj & s* público
publication [,pʌblɪˈkeʃən] *s* publicación
public conveyance *s* vehículo de servicio público
public domain *s* dominio públic
public figure *s* figura pública
publicity [pʌbˈlɪsɪti] *s* publicidad
publicize [ˈpʌblɪ,saɪz] *tr* publicar
public library *s* biblioteca municipal
public relations *spl* relaciones publicas
public relations office *s* gabinete *m* de imagen
public safety *s* seguridad ciudadana
public school *s* (U.S.A.) escuela pública; (Brit) internado privado con dote
public speaking *s* elocución, oratoria
public spirit *s* celo patriótico del buen ciudadano
public toilet *s* baño público, servicios
public transportation *s* transporte colectivo
public utility *s* empresa de servicio público; **public utilities** acciones emitidas por empresas de servicio público
publish [ˈpʌblɪʃ] *tr* publicar
publisher [ˈpʌblɪʃər] *s* editor *m*
publishing house *s* casa editorial
pucker [ˈpʌkər] *s* (*small fold*) frunce *m;* pliego mal hecho ‖ *tr* fruncir (*una tela; la frente*); plegar mal ‖ *intr* plegarse mal
pudding [ˈpʊdɪŋ] *s* budín *m,* pudín *m*
puddle [ˈpʌdəl] *s* aguazal *m,* charco
pudg•y [ˈpʌdʒi] *adj* (*comp* **-ier;** *super* **-iest**) gordinflón, rechoncho
puerile [ˈpju•ərɪl] *adj* pueril
puerili•ty [,pju•əˈrɪlɪti] *s* (*pl* **-ties**) puerilidad

Puerto Rican [ˋpwɛrto ˋrikən] *adj & s* puertorriqueño
puff [pʌf] *s* soplo vivo; (*of smoke*) bocanada; (*in clothing*) bullón *m;* borla de polvos; pastelillo de crema o jalea; alabanza exagerada; ráfaga, ventolera ‖ *tr* soplar; hinchar; alabar exageradamente ‖ *intr* soplar; hincharse; enorgullecerse exageradamente
puff paste *s* hojaldre *m & f*
pugilism [ˋpjudʒɪ,lɪzəm] *s* pugilismo
pugilist [ˋpjudʒɪlɪst] *s* pugilista *m*
pug-nosed [ˋpʌg,nozd] *adj* braco
puke [pjuk] *s* (slang) vómito ‖ *tr & intr* (slang) vomitar
pull [pʊl] *s* estirón *m,* tirón *m;* (*on a cigar*) chupada; (*of a door*) tirador *m;* (*influence*) (coll) enchufe *m,* buenas aldabas, muñeca ‖ *tr* tirar de; torcer (*un ligamento*); (typ) sacar (*una impresión a prueba*); **to pull down** demoler, derribar; bajar (*p.ej., la cortinilla*); abatir, degradar; **to pull oneself together** componerse, recobrar la calma ‖ *intr* tirar; moverse despacio, moverse con esfuerzo; **to pull at** tirar de (*p.ej., la corbata*); chupar (*p.ej., un cigarro*); **to pull for** (slang) abogar por, ayudar; **to pull for oneself** tirar por su lado; **to pull in** llegar (*un tren*) a la estación; **to pull out** partir (*un tren*) de la estación; **to pull strings** usar enchufe; **to pull through** salir a flote; recobrar la salud
pull'-down menu *s* (compu) menú desplegable
pullet [ˋpʊlɪt] *s* polla
pulley [ˋpʊli] *s* polea
pulp [pʌlp] *s* pulpa; (*to make paper*) pasta; (*of tooth*) bulbo
pulpit [ˋpʊlpɪt] *s* púlpito
pulsate [ˋpʌlset] *intr* pulsar; vibrar
pulsation [pʌlˋseʃən] *s* pulsación; vibracion
pulse [pʌls] *s* pulso; **to feel** o **take the pulse of** tomar el pulso a
pulverize [ˋpʌlvə,raɪz] *tr* pulverizar
pumice stone [ˋpʌmɪs] *s* pómez *f,* piedra pómez
pum•mel [ˋpʌməl] *v* (*pret & pp* **-meled** o **-melled;** *ger* **-meling** o **-melling**) *tr* apuñear, aporrear
pump [pʌmp] *s* bomba; (*slipperlike shoe*) escarpín *m,* zapatilla, zapato de salón ‖ *tr* elevar o sacar (*agua*) por medio de una bomba; (coll) tirar de la lengua a (*una persona*); **to pump up** hinchar, inflar (*un neumático*)
pump handle *s* guimbalete *m*
pumpkin [ˋpʌmpkɪn] o [ˋpuŋkɪn] *s* calabaza común
pump-priming [ˋpʌmp,praɪmɪŋ] *s* inyección económica (*por parte del gobierno*)
pun [pʌn] *s* equívoco, retruécano ‖ *v* (*pret & pp* **punned;** *ger* **punning**) *intr* decir equívocos, jugar del vocablo
punch [pʌntʃ] *s* puñetazo; (*tool*) punzón *m;* (*for tickets*) sacabocado; (*drink*) ponche *m* ‖ *tr* dar un puñetazo a; taladrar, perforar (*un billete, una tarjeta*)
punch bowl *s* ponchera
punch card *s* tarjeta perforada, ficha perforada
punch clock *s* reloj *m* registrador de tarjetas
punch'-drunk' *adj* atontado (*p.ej., por una tunda de golpes*); completamente aturdido
punching bag *s* punching *m,* boxibalón *m*
punch line *s* broche *m* de oro, colofón *m* del artículo
punctilious [pʌŋkˋtɪlɪ•əs] *adj* puntilloso, pundonoroso
punctual [ˋpʌŋktʃʊ•əl] *adj* puntual
punctuate [ˋpʌŋktʃʊ,et] *tr* puntuar; acentuar, destacar; interrumpir ‖ *intr* puntuar
punctuation [,pʌŋktʃʊˋeʃən] *s* puntuación
punctuation mark *s* signo de puntuación
puncture [ˋpʌŋktʃər] *s* puntura; (*of a tire*) picadura, pinchazo ‖ *tr* pinchar, picar, perforar
punc'ture-proof' *adj* a prueba de pinchazos
pundit [ˋpʌndɪt] *s* erudito, sabio
pungent [ˋpʌndʒənt] *adj* picante; estimulante
punish [ˋpʌnɪʃ] *tr* castigar; penalizar; (coll) maltratar
punishable [ˋpʌnɪʃəbəl] *adj* delictivo
punishment [ˋpʌnɪʃmənt] *s* castigo; (coll) maltrato
punk [pʌŋk] *adj* (coll) malo, de mala calidad; (*hairstyle*) punk, punki ‖ *s* yesca, pebete *m;* (*decayed wood*) hupe *m;* (*rocker*) punk *mf,* punki *mf;* (mus) punk *m;* (coll) pillo, gamberro
punster [ˋpʌnstər] *s* equivoquista *mf,* vocablista *mf*
pu•ny [ˋpjuni] *adj* (*comp* **-nier;** *super* **-niest**) encanijado, débil; insignificante, mezquino
pup [pʌp] *s* cachorro
pupil [ˋpjupəl] *s* alumno; (*of the eye*) pupila
puppet [ˋpʌpɪt] *s* títere *m;* (*doll*) muñeca; (*person controlled by another*) maniquí *m;* (*stooge*) títere *m,* hombre *m* de paja
puppet government *s* gobierno de monigotes
puppet show *s* función de títeres
puppet theater *s* teatro de guiñol, marionetas o títeres
puppy love [ˋpʌpi] *s* (coll) primeros amores
purchase [ˋpʌrtʃəs] *s* compra; agarre *m* firme ‖ *tr* comprar
purchasing power *s* poder adquisitivo
pure [pjʊr] *adj* puro
purgative [ˋpʌrgətɪv] *adj & s* purgante *m*
purge [pʌrdʒ] *s* purga ‖ *tr* purgar
puri•fy [ˋpjʊrɪ,faɪ] *v* (*pret & pp* **-fied**) *tr* purificar
puritan [ˋpjʊrɪtən] *adj & s* puritano ‖ **Puritan** *adj & s* puritano
purity [ˋpjʊrɪti] *s* pureza
purloin [pərˋlɔɪn] *tr & intr* robar, hurtar
purple [ˋpʌrpəl] *adj* purpurado, rojo morado ‖ *m* púrpura, rojo morado
purport [ˋpʌrport] *s* significado, idea principal ‖ [pərˋport] *tr* significar, querer decir
purpose [ˋpʌrpəs] *s* intención, propósito; fin *m,* objeto; **for the purpose** al efecto; **for what purpose?** ¿con qué fin?; **on purpose** adrede,

de propósito; **to good purpose** con buenos resultados; **to no purpose** sin resultado; **to serve one's purpose** servir para el caso
purposely [ˈpʌrpəsli] *adv* adrede, de propósito
purr [pʌr] *s* ronroneo ‖ *intr* ronronear
purse [pʌrs] *s* bolsa; (*money collected for charity*) colecta ‖ *tr* fruncir
purser [ˈpʌrsər] *s* contador *m* de navío, comisario de a bordo
purse snatcher [ˈsnætʃər] *s* carterista *mf*
purse strings *spl* cordones *mpl* de la bolsa; **to hold the purse strings** tener las llaves de la caja
pursue [pərˈsu] o [pərˈsju] *tr* perseguir (*al que huye*); proseguir (*lo empezado*); seguir (*una carrera*); dedicarse a
pursuit [pərˈsut] o [pərˈsjut] *s* persecución; prosecución; (*e.g., of happiness*) busca o búsqueda; empleo
pursuit plane *s* caza *m,* avión *m* de caza
purvey [pərˈve] *tr* proveer, suministrar
pus [pʌs] *s* pus *m*
push [pʊʃ] *s* empuje *m,* empujón *m* ‖ *tr* empujar; pulsar (*un botón*); extender (*p.ej., conquistas*); **to push around** (coll) tratar a empujones; **to push aside** hacer a un lado; **to push through** forzar (*p.ej., una resolución*) ‖ *intr* empujar; **to push off** (coll) irse, salir; (naut) desatracarse
push button *s* botón *m* de llamada, botón interruptor
push′-but′ton *adj* de botones
push′cart′ *s* carretilla de mano
pusher [ˈpʊʃər] *s* (*drugs*) púcher *m*
pushing [ˈpʊʃɪŋ] *adj* emprendedor; entremetido, agresivo
pushy [ˈpʊʃi] *adj* (coll) agresivo; presumido
pusillanimous [ˌpjusɪˈlænɪməs] *adj* pusilánime
puss [pʊs] *interj* ¡miz! ‖ *s* micho; chica, muchacha; (slang) cara, boca
puss•y [ˈpʊsi] *s* (*pl* **-ies**) michito
puss′y foot′ing *adj* indeciso
pussy willow *s* sauce norteamericano de amentos muy sedosos
pustule [ˈpʌstʃʊl] *s* pústula
put [pʊt] *v* (*pret & pp* **put;** *ger* **putting**) *tr* poner, colocar; arrojar, echar, lanzar; hacer (*una pregunta*); **to put across** llevar a cabo; hacer aceptar; **to put aside** poner aparte; rechazar; ahorrar (*dinero*); **to put down** anotar, apuntar; sofocar (*una insurrección*); rebajar (*los precios*); **to put off** posponer; deshacerse de; **to put on** ponerse (*la ropa*); poner en escena; llevar (*p.ej., un drama a la pantalla*); accionar (*un freno*); cargar (*impuestos*); fingir; atribuir; **to put oneself out** incomodarse, molestarse; afanarse, desvivirse; **to put out** extender (*la mano*); apagar (*el fuego, la luz*); poner en la calle; dar a luz, publicar; decepcionar; (sport) sacar fuera de la partida; **to put over** o **through** (coll) llevar a cabo; **to put up** construir, edificar; abrir (*un paraguas*); conservar (*fruta, legumbres*); (coll) incitar ‖ *intr* dirigirse; **to put on** fingir; **to put up** parar, hospedarse; **to put up with** aguantar, tolerar
putative [ˈpjutətɪv] *adj* supuesto; (*father*) putativo
put option *s* opción de enajenación o de venta
put′-out′ *adj* contrariado, enojado
putrid [ˈpjutrɪd] *adj* pútrido; corrompido, perverso
putsch [pʊtʃ] *s* intentona de sublevación; sublevación; cuartelazo
putt [pʌt] *s* (golf) putt *m* ‖ *tr* golpear ‖ *intr* golpear la bola, potear
putter [ˈpʌtər] *s* (golf) putter *m* ‖ *intr* trabajar sin orden ni sistema; **to putter around** ocuparse en fruslerías, temporizar
put•ty [ˈpʌti] *s* (*pl* **-ties**) masilla ‖ *v* (*pret & pp* **-tied**) *tr* enmasillar
putty knife *s* cuchillo de vidriero, espátula
put′-up′ *adj* (coll) premeditado con malicia
puzzle [ˈpʌzəl] *s* enigma *m;* acertijo, rompecabezas *m* ‖ *tr* confundir, poner perplejo; **to puzzle out** descifrar ‖ *intr* estar perplejo; **to puzzle over** tratar de descifrar
puzzler [ˈpʌzlər] *s* quisicosa
PW *abbr* **prisoner of war**
pyg•my [ˈpɪgmi] *adj* pigmeo ‖ *s* (*pl* **-mies**) pigmeo
pylon [ˈpaɪlɑn] *s* pilón *m*
pyramid [ˈpɪrəmɪd] *s* pirámide *f* ‖ *tr* aumentar (*su dinero*) comprando o vendiendo al crédito y empleando las ganancias para comprar o vender más
pyre [paɪr] *s* pira
Pyrenean [ˌpɪrɪˈni•ən] *adj* pirineo
Pyrenees [ˈpɪrɪˌniz] *spl* Pirineos
pyrites [paɪˈraɪtiz] o [ˈpaɪraɪts] *s* pirita
pyrotechnical [ˌpaɪrəˈtɛknɪkəl] *adj* pirotécnico
pyrotechnics [ˌpaɪrəˈtɛknɪks] *spl* pirotecnia
python [ˈpaɪθən] *s* pitón *m*
pythoness [pɑɪθənɪs] *s* pitonisa
pyx [pɪks] *s* píxide *f,* copón *m*

Q

Q, q [kju] decimoséptima letra del alfabeto inglés
Q. *abbr* **quarto, queen, question, quire**
Q.M. *abbr* **quartermaster**
qr. *abbr* **quarter, quire**
qt. *abbr* **quantity, quart**

qu. *abbr* **quart, quarter, quarterly, queen, query, question**
quack [kwæk] *adj* falso || *s* graznido del pato; charlatán *m;* medicastro, curandero || *intr* parpar (*el pato*)
quacker•y [ˈkwækəri] *s* (*pl* **-ies**) charlatanismo
quadrangle [ˈkwɑd,ræŋgəl] *s* cuadrángulo; patio cuadrangular
quadrant [ˈkwɑdrənt] *s* cuadrante *m*
quadroon [kwɑdˈrun] *s* cuarterón *m*
quadruped [ˈkwɑdrʊ,pɛd] *adj & s* cuadrúpedo
quadruple [ˈkwɑdrʊpəl] o [kwɑdˈrupəl] *adj & s* cuádruple *m* || *tr* cuadruplicar || *intr* cuadruplicarse
quadruplet [ˈkwɑdrʊ,plɛt] o [kwɑdˈruplɛt] *s* cuatrillizo
quaff [kwɑf] o [kwæf] *s* trago grande || *tr & intr* beber en gran cantidad
quail [kwel] *s* codorniz *f* || *intr* acobardarse
quaint [kwent] *adj* curioso, raro; afectado, rebuscado; fantástico, singular
quake [kwek] *s* temblor *m,* terremoto || *intr* temblar
Quaker [ˈkwekər] *adj & s* cuáquero
Quaker meeting *s* reunión de cuáqueros; reunión en que hay poca conversación
qualification [,kwɑləfəˈkeʃən] *s* calificación; (*requirement*) requisito; **qualifications** capacidad, aptitude; (*credentials*) credenciales *fpl,* títulos; **without reservation** sin reserva
qualified [ˈkwɑlə,faɪd] *adj* calificado, capacitado; acreditado
quali•fy [ˈkwɑlɪ,faɪ] *v* (*pret & pp* **-fied**) *tr* calificar; capacitar, habilitar; (*to moderate*) atenuar || *intr* capacitarse, habilitarse; (sport) clasificarse
qualifying [ˈkwɑlə,faɪ•ɪŋ] *adj* calificativo; (*exam*) eliminatorio
quali•ty [ˈkwɑlɪti] *s* (*pl* **-ties**) (*characteristic; virtue*) calidad; (*property, attribute*) cualidad; (*of a sound*) timbre *m*
quality of life *s* calidad de vida
qualm [kwɑm] *s* escrúpulo de conciencia; duda, inquietud; (*nausea*) basca
quanda•ry [ˈkwɑndəri] *s* (*pl* **-ries**) incertidumbre, perplejidad
quanti•ty [ˈkwɑntɪti] *s* (*pl* **-ties**) cantidad
quan•tum [ˈkwɑntəm] *adj* cuántico || *s* (*pl* **-ta** [tə]) cuanto, quántum *m*
quantum physics *s* física cuántica
quantum theory *s* teoría cuántica
quarantine [ˈkwɑrən,tin] o [ˈkwɔrən,tin] *s* cuarentena; estación de cuarentena || *tr* poner en cuarentena
quar•rel [ˈkwɑrəl] o [ˈkwɔrəl] *s* disputa, riña, pelea; **to have no quarrel with** no estar en desacuerdo con; **to pick a quarrel with** tomarse con || v (*pret & pp* **-reled** o **-relled;** *ger* **-reling** o **-relling**) *intr* disputar, reñir, pelear
quarrelsome [ˈkwɑrəlsəm] o [ˈkwɔrəlsəm] *adj* pendenciero
quar•ry [ˈkwɑri] o [ˈkwɔri] *s* (*pl* **-ries**) cantera, pedrera; caza, presa || *v* (*pret & pp* **-ried**) *tr* sacar de una cantera; extraer, sacar
quart [kwɔrt] *s* cuarto de galón (*.94 litros*)
quarter [ˈkwɔrtər] *adj* cuarto || *s* cuarto, cuarta parte; (*three months*) trimestre *m;* moneda de 25 centavos; cuarto de luna; barrio; región, lugar *m;* (*clemency*) (mil) cuartel *m;* **quarters** morada, vivienda; local *m;* (mil) cuarteles *mpl;* **to take up quarters** alojarse || *tr* descuartizar
quar′ter•deck′ *s* alcázar *m*
quar′ter fi′nal *s* (sport) cuarto de final
quar′ter-hour′ *s* cuarto de hora; **on the quarter-hour** al cuarto en punto cada cuarto de hora
quarter•ly [ˈkwɔrtərli] *adj* trimestral || *adv* trimestralmente || *s* (*pl* **-lies**) publicación o revista trimestral
quar′ter•mas′ter *s* (mil) comisario; (nav) cabo de brigadas
quartet [kwɔrˈtɛt] *s* cuarteto
quartz [kwɔrts] *s* cuarzo
quartz watch *s* reloj de cuarzo
quasar [ˈkwesɑr] *s* (astr) quásar *m,* cuasar *m*
quash [kwɑʃ] *tr* sofocar, reprimir; anular, invalidar
quaver [ˈkwevər] *s* temblor *m,* estremecimiento; (mus) trémolo || *intr* temblar, estremecerse
quay [ki] *s* muelle *m,* desembarcadero
queen [kwin] *s* reina; (*in chess*) dama o reina; (*in cards*) dama (*que corresponde al caballo*); abeja reina
queen bee *s* abeja reina, abeja maestra; (slang) marimandona, la que lleva la voz cantante
queen dowager *s* reina viuda
queen•ly [ˈkwinli] *adj* (*comp* **-lier;** *super* **-liest**) de reina; como reina; regio
queen mother *s* reina madre
queen post *s* péndola
queen's English *s* inglés castizo
queer [kwɪr] *adj* curioso, raro; estrambótico, estrafalario; aturdido, indispuesto; (coll) sospechoso, misterioso || *s* (*gay*) (pej) maricón *m* || *tr* (slang) echar a perder; (slang) comprometer
quell [kwɛl] *tr* sofocar, reprimir; mitigar (*una pena o dolor*)
quench [kwɛntʃ] *tr* apagar (*el fuego; la sed*); sofocar, reprimir; (electron) amortiguar
que•ry [ˈkwɪri] *s* (*pl* **-ries**) pregunta; signo de interrogación; duda || *v* (*pret & pp* **-ried**) *tr* interrogar; marcar con signo de interrogación; dudar
quest [kwɛst] *s* búsqueda; (*of the Holy Grail*) demanda; **in quest of** en busca de
question [ˈkwɛstʃən] *s* pregunta; (*problem for discussion*) cuestión; asunto, proposición; **beside the question** que no viene al caso; **beyond question** fuera de duda; **out of the question** imposible, indiscutible; **to ask a question** hacer una pregunta; **to be a question of** tratarse de, ser cuestión de; **to call in question** poner en duda; **without question**

sin duda || *tr* interrogar; cuestionar (*poner en tela de juicio*)
questionable [ˈkwɛstʃənəbəl] *adj* cuestionable
question mark *s* punto interrogante, signo de interrogación
questionnaire [ˌkwɛstʃənˈɛr] *s* cuestionario
queue [kju] *s* (*of hair*) coleta; (*of people*) cola || *intr* hacer cola
quibble [kwɪbəl] *intr* sutilizar
quick [kwɪk] *adj* rápido, veloz; ágil, vivo; despierto, listo; **quick as a flash** como un rayo; **the quick and the dead** los vivos y los muertos; **to cut** o **to sting to the quick** herir en lo vivo, tocar en la herida
quick′-change′ artist *s* transformista *mf*
quick′-dry′ing *adj* de secado rápido
quicken [ˈkwɪkən] *tr* acelerar, avivar; animar || *intr* acelerarse; animarse
quickie [ˈkwɪki] *s*—**a quickie** (coll) un rápido, una rápida; (*drink*) una copita; (*question*) una preguntita
quick′lime′ *s* cal viva
quick lunch *s* servicio de la barra, servicio rápido
quick′sand′ *s* arena movediza
quick′sil′ver *s* azogue *m*
quick′-tem′pered *adj* irascible, de mucho genio
quick′wit′ted *adj* agudo, listo
quiet [ˈkwaɪ•et] *adj* (still) quieto; silencioso; (*market*) (com) encalmado; **to keep quiet** callarse || *s* quietud; silencio; **on the quiet** a las calladas || *tr* aquietar; acallar || *intr* aquietarse; callarse; **to quiet down** calmarse || *interj* ¡silencio!
quill [kwɪl] *s* pluma de ave; cañón *m* de pluma; (*of hedgehog, porcupine*) púa
quilt [kwɪlt] *s* edredón *m,* colcha || *tr* acolchar
quince [kwɪns] *s* membrillo
quinine [ˈkwaɪnaɪn] *s* quinina
quinsy [ˈkwɪnzi] *s* amigdalitis *f,* anginas *fpl*
quintessence [kwɪnˈtɛsəns] *s* quintaesencia
quintet [kwɪnˈtɛt] *s* quinteto
quintuplet [kwɪnˈtjuplɛt] o [kwɪnˈtuplɛt] *s* quintillizo
quip [kwɪp] *s* chufleta, pulla || *v* (*pret & pp* **quipped;** *ger* **quipping**) *tr* decir en son de burla || *intr* echar pullas
quire [kwaɪr] *s* mano *f* de papel; (bb) alzado
quirk [kwʌrk] *s* excentricidad, rareza; sutileza; vuelta repentina
quit [kwɪt] *adj* libre, descargado; **to be quits** estar desquitados; **to call it quits** no seguir; descontinuar; **to cry quits** pedir treguas || *v* (*pret & pp* **quit** o **quitted;** *ger* **quitting**) *tr* dejar || *intr* irse; (coll) dejar de trabajar
quit′claim′ *s* (law) renuncia || *tr* (law) renunciar
quite [kwaɪt] *adv* enteramente; verdaderamente; (coll) bastante, muy
quitter [ˈkwɪtər] *s* remolón *m;* (*of a cause*) desertor *m*
quiver [ˈkwɪvər] *s* temblor *m;* (*to hold arrows*) aljaba, carcaj *m* || *intr* temblar
quixotic [kwɪksˈɑtɪk] *adj* quijotesco
quiz [kwɪz] *s* (*pl* **quizzes**) examen *m;* interrogatorio || *v* (*pret & pp* **quizzed;** *ger* **quizzing**) *tr* examinar; interrogar
quiz game *s* torneo de preguntas y respuestas
quiz program *s* programa *m* de preguntas y respuestas, concurso de televisión
quiz section *s* grupo de práctica
quizzical [ˈkwɪzɪkəl] *adj* curioso; cómico; burlón
quoin [kɔɪn] o [kwɔɪn] *s* esquina; piedra angular; (*wedge*) cuña || *tr* (typ) acuñar
quoit [kwɔɪt] o [kɔɪt] *s* herrón *m,* tejo; **quoits** *ssg* hito
quondam [ˈkwɑndæm] *adj* antiguo, de otro tiempo
quorum [ˈkworəm] *s* quórum *m*
quota [ˈkwotə] *s* cuota
quotation [kwoˈteʃən] *s* (*from a book*) cita; (*of prices*) cotización
quotation marks *spl* comillas
quote [kwot] *s* (coll) cita; (coll) cotización; **close quote** fin de la cita; **quotes** (coll) comillas || *tr & intr* citar; cotizar; **quote** cito
quote unquote *adj* (coll) mal llamado
quotient [ˈkwoʃənt] *s* cociente *m*
Qur′an o **Quran** *var* de **Koran**
q.v. *abbr* **quod vide** (Lat) (**which see** véase)

R

R, r [ɑr] decimoctava letra del alfabeto inglés
r. *abbr* **railroad, railway, road, rod, ruble, rupee**
R. *abbr* **railroad, railway, Regina** (Lat) **Queen; Republican, response, Rex** (Lat) **King; River, Royal**
rabbet [ˈræbɪt] *s* barbilla, rebajo || *tr* embarbillar, rebajar
rab•bi [ˈræbaɪ] *s* (*pl* **-bis** o **-bies**) rabino
rabbit [ˈræbɪt] *s* conejo
rabbit ears *spl* (telv, rad) antena de conejo
rabble [ˈræbəl] *s* canalla, gentuza, palomilla, chamuchina
rabble-rouser [ˈraUzər] *s* populachero, alborotapueblos *mf,* demagogo
rabid [ˈræbɪd] *adj* virulento, feroz; (vet) rabioso
rabies [ˈrebiz] o [ˈrebɪˌiz] *s* rabia
raccoon [ræˈkun] *s* mapache *m,* oso lavador
race [res] *s* (*people of same stock*) raza; (*contest in speed, etc.*) carrera; (*channel to lead water*)

caz *m* || *tr* competir con, en una carrera; hacer correr de prisa; hacer funcionar (*un motor*) a velocidad excesiva || *intr* correr de prisa; correr en una carrera; competir en una carrera; embalarse (*un motor*); (naut) regatear
race'card *s* programa *m* de carreras
racehorse *s* caballo de carreras
race relations *spl* relaciones raciales
race riot *s* disturbio racista
racetrack *s* pista de carreras; hipódromo
racial [ˋreʃəl] *adj* racial
racing [ˋresɪn] *adj* de carreras || *s* carreras *mpl*
racing car *s* coche *m* de carreras
racism [ˋresizəm] *s* racismo
racist [ˋresist] *adj & s* racista
rack [ræk] *s* (*sort of shelf*) estante *m;* (*to hang clothes*) percha; (*for fodder for cattle*) pesebre *m;* (*for baggage*) red *f* de equipaje; (*for guns*) armero; (*bar made to gear with a pinion*) cremallera; **to go to rack and ruin** desvencijarse; ir al desastre || *tr* estirar, forzar; atormentar; despedazar; oprimir, agobiar; **to rack off** trasegar (*el vino*); **to rack one's brains** calentarse la cabeza, devanarse los sesos
racket [ˋrækɪt] *s* raqueta; (*noise*) baraúnda, alboroto; (slang) trapisonda, trapacería; **to raise a racket** armar un alboroto
racketeer [ˌrækɪˋtir] *s* trapisondista *mf,* trapacista *mf* || *intr* trapacear
rack railway *s* ferrocarril *m* de cremallera
rac•y [ˋresi] *adj* (*comp* **-ier;** *super* **-iest**) espiritoso, chispeante; perfumado; (*somewhat indecent*) picante
radar [ˋredɑr] *s* radar *m*
radar scanner *s* explorador *m* de radar
radiant [ˋredɪ•ənt] *adj* radiante, resplandeciente; (*cheerful, smiling*) radiante
radiate [ˋredɪˌet] *tr* radiar; difundir (*p.ej., felicidad*) || *intr* radiar, irradiar
radiation [ˌredɪˋeʃən] *s* radiación
radiation sickness *s* enfermedad de radiación, mal *m* de rayos
radiator [ˋredɪˌetər] *s* radiador *m*
radiator cap *s* tapón *m* de radiador
radical [ˋrædɪkəl] *adj & s* radical *m*
radi•o [ˋredɪˌo] *s* (*pl* **-os**) radio *f;* radiograma *m* || *tr* radiodifundir
radioactive [ˌredɪ•oˋæktɪv] *adj* radiactivo
radioactive waste *s* residuos radiactivos
radio amateur *s* radioaficionado
radio announcer *s* locutor *m* de radio
ra'dio•broad'cast'ing *s* radiodifusión
radio frequency *s* radiofrecuencia
radiogram [ˋredɪ•oˌgræm] *s* radiogram *m*
radio listener *s* radioescucha *mf,* radioyente *mf*
radiologist [ˋredɪˋɑlədʒəst] *s* radiólogo
radiology [ˌredɪˋɑlədʒi] *s* radiología
radio ministry *s* (eccl) ministerio radiofónico
radio network *s* red *f* de emisoras
radio newscaster *s* cronista *mf* de radio
radio receiver *s* radiorreceptor *m*
radio set *s* aparato de radio
radio station *s* radioemisora
ra'dio•(tel'e)phone' *s* radioteléfono
ra'di•o•ther'apy *s* radioterapia
radish [ˋrædɪ] *s* rábano
radium [redɪ•əm] *s* radio
radi•us [ˋredɪ•əs] *s* (*pl* **-i** [ˌɑɪ] o **-uses**) radio; (*range of operation*) radio; **within a radius of en** . . . a la redonda
raffle [ˋræfəl] *s* rifa, sorteo || *tr & intr* rifar, sortear; **to raffle off** rifar, sortear
raft [ræft] *s* armadía, balsa; (coll) gran número
rafter [ˋræftər] *s* cabrio, contrapar *m,* traviesa
rag [ræg] *s* trapo; **to chew the rag** (slang) dar la lengua; **in rags** hilachento
ragamuffin [ˋrægəˌmʌfɪn] *s* pelagatos *m;* golfo, chiquillo haraposo
rag baby o **rag doll** *s* muñeca de trapo
rage [redʒ] *s* rabia; **to be all the rage** estar en boga, hacer furor; **to fly into a rage** montar en cólera
ragged [ˋrægɪd] *adj* andrajoso; (*edge*) cortado en dientes
ragpicker [ˋrægˌpɪkər] *s* andrajero, trapero
rag'weed' *s* ambrosía
raid [red] *s* incursión, invasión; ataque de sorpresa; ataque aéreo || *tr* invadir; atacar inesperadamente; capturar (*p.ej., la policía un garito*)
raider [ˋredər] *s* asaltante *mf;* (econ) tiburón *m,* empresa tiburón
rail [rel] *s* carrill *m,* riel *m;* (*railing*) barandilla; (*of a bridge*) guardalado; (*at a bar*) apoyo para los pies; palo; **by rail** por ferocarril; **rails** títulos o valores de ferrocarril || *tr* poner barandilla a || *intr* quejarse amargamente; **to rail at** injuriar, ultrajar
rail fence *s* cerca hecha de palos horizontales
rail'head' *s* (rr) cabeza de línea
railing [ˋrelɪŋ] *s* barandilla, pasamano
rail'road' *adj* ferroviario || *s* ferrocarril *m* || *tr* (coll) llevar a cabo con demasiada precipitación; (slang) encarcelar falsamente || *intr* trabajar en el ferrocarril
railroad crossing *s* paso a nivel
railroad station *s* estación ferroviaria
rail'way' *adj* ferroviario || *s* ferrocarril *m*
rain [ren] *s* lluvia; **rain or shine** llueva o no, con buen o mal tiempo || *tr & intr* llover
rain'bow' *s* arco iris
rain'coat' *s* impermeable *m*
rain'fall' *s* lluvia repentina; precipitación acuosa
rain forest *s* selva tropical, bosque *m* ecuatorial, bosque pluvial
rain'water *s* aguas pluviales
rain•y [ˋreni] *adj* (*comp* **-ier;** *super* **-iest**) lluvioso
rainy day *s* día lluvioso; (*time of need*) tiempo futuro de posible necesidad
rainy season *s* temporada de lluvias
raise [rez] *s* aumento || *tr* levantar; aumentar; criar (*a niños, animales*); cultivar (*plantas*); reunir (*dinero*); suscitar (*una duda*); resucitar

(*a los muertos*); dejarse (*barba, bigote*); poner (*una objeción*); plantear (*una pregunta*); levantar (*tropas; un sitio*); (math) elevar; (*to come in sight of*) (naut) avistar

raisin [ˈrezən] *s* pasa, uva seca

rake [rek] *s* rastro, rastrillo; (*person*) calavera *m,* libertino || *tr* rastrillar; **to rake together** acumular (*dinero*)

rake′-off′ *s* descuento; comisión; (coll) tajada, pellizco (Esp)

rakish [ˈrekɪʃ] *adj* airoso, gallardo; listo, vivo; libertino

ral•ly [ˈræli] *s* (*pl* **-lies**) reunión popular, reunión política; recuperación, recobro || *v* (*pret & pp* **-lied**) *tr* reunir; reanimar; recobrar (*la fuerza, la salud, el ánimo*) || *intr* reunirse; recobrarse (*p.ej., los precios en la Bolsa*); recobrar la fuerza, la salud, el ánimo; **to rally to the side of** acudir a, ir en socorro de

RAM [ræm] *s* (acronym) (**random access memory**) (compu) RAM *f* (memoria de acceso aleatorio o directo)

ram [ræm] *s* (*male sheep*) morueco, carnero padre; (*device for battering, crushing, etc.*) pisón *m,* pisotón *m;* (*hydraulic*) martillo, ariete *m* || *v* (*pret & pp* **rammed;** *ger* **ramming**) *tr* dar contra, chocar en; atestar, rellenar || *intr* chocar; **to ram into** chocar en

Ramadan [ˈræmədɑn] *s* Ramadán *m*

ramble [ˈræmbəl] *s* paseo || *intr* pasear; serpentear (*p.ej., un río*); extenderse serpenteando (*las enredaderas*); (*to wander aimlessly; to talk in an aimless way*) divagar

rami•fy [ˈræmɪ,faɪ] *v* (*pret & pp* **-fied**) *tr* ramificar || *intr* ramificarse

ram′jet′ (engine) *s* motor *m* autorreactor; estatorreactor *m*

ramp [ræmp] *s* rampa; **off ramp** vía de salida; **on ramp** vía de acceso

rampage [ˈrɑmpedʒ] *s* alboroto; **to go on a rampage** alborotar, comportarse como un loco

rampart [ˈræmpɑrt] *s* muralla, terraplén *m;* amparo, defensa

ram′rod′ *s* atacador *m,* baqueta

ram′shack′le *adj* desvencijado, destartalado

ranch [ræntʃ] *s* granja, hacienda, rancho (Mex)

rancher [ˈræntʃər] *s* hacendado, ranchero (Mex), estanciero (SAm)

rancid [ˈrænsɪd] *adj* rancio

rancor [ˈræŋkər] *s* rencor *m*

random [ˈrændəm] *adj* casual, fortuito; **at random** al azar, a la ventura

random access memory *s* memoria de acceso aleatorio *or* directo

range [rendʒ] *s* (*row, line*) fila, hilera; (*scope, reach*) alcance *m;* (*of speeds, prices, etc.*) escala; campo de tiro; terreno de pasto; (*of a boat or airplane*) autonomía; (*of the voice*) extensión; (*of colors*) gama, serie *f;* (*stove*) cocina económica, cocina, estufa (Col, Mex); **within range of** al alcance de || *tr* alinear; recorrer (*un terreno*); ir a lo largo de (*la costa*); arreglar, ordenar || *intr* fluctuar, variar (*entre ciertos límites*); extenderse; divagar errar; **to range over** recorrer

range finder *s* telémetro

rank [ræŋk] *adj* exuberante, lozano; denso, espeso; grosero; maloliente; excesivo; incorregible, rematado; indecente, vulgar || *s* categoría, rango; condición, posición; distinción; (*line of soldiers standing abreast*) fila; (mil) empleo, grado || *tr* alinear; ordenar; tener grado o posición más alta que || *intr* ocupar el último grado; **to rank high** ocupar alta posición; ser tenido en alta estima; sobresalir; **to rank low** ocupar baja posición; **to rank with** estar al nivel de; tener el mismo grado que

rank and file *s* soldados de fila; pueblo, gente *f* común; (*of party or union*) bases *fpl*

rankle [ˈræŋkəl] *tr* enconar, irritar || *intr* enconarse

ransack [ˈrænsæk] *tr* registrar, escudriñar; robar, saquear

ransom [ˈrænsəm] *s* rescate *m* || *tr* rescatar

rant [rænt] *intr* desvariar, despotricar

rap [ræp] *s* golpe corto y seco; (*noise*) taque *m;* (coll) ardite *m,* bledo; (slang) crítica mordaz; **to beat the rap** (slang) escabullirse, quedar impune; **to take the rap** (slang) pagar la multa; sufrir las consecuencias || *v* (*pret & pp* **rapped;** *ger* **rapping**) *tr* golpear con golpe corto y seco; decir vivamente; (slang) criticar mordazmente || *intr* golpear con golpe corto y seco; (*to chat*) (coll) cotorrear **to rap at the door** tocar a la puerta

rapacious [rəˈpeʃəs] *adj* rapaz

rape [rep] *s* estupro, violación || *tr* estuprar, violar

rapid [ˈræpɪd] *adj* rápido || **rapids** *spl* (*of a river*) rápidos

rapid eye movement *s* movimientos oculares rápidos

rap′id-fire′ *adj* de tiro rápido; hecho vivamente

rapid transit *s* línea ferroviaria urbana

rapier [ˈrepɪ•ər] *s* estoque *m,* espadín *m*

rapist [ˈrepɪst] violador *m*

rapt [ræpt] *adj* arrebatado, extático, transportado; absorto

rapture [ˈræptʃər] *s* embeleso, éxtasis *f,* rapto

rare [rɛr] *adj* raro; (*word*) poco usado; (*meat*) poco asado; (*gem*) precioso

rare bird *s* mirlo blanco

rare•fy [ˈrɛrɪ,faɪ] *v* (*pret & pp* **-fied**) *tr* enrarecer || *intr* enrarecerse

rarely [ˈrɛrli] *adv* rara vez

rascal [ˈræskəl] *s* bellaco, bribón *m,* pícaro; pergenio

rash [ræʃ] *adj* temerario || *s* brote *m,* salpullido, erupción

rasp [ræsp] o [rɑsp] *s* escofina; (*sound of a rasp*) sonido áspero || *tr* escofinar; irritar, molestar; decir con voz ronca || *intr* hacer sonido áspero

raspber•ry [ˈræz,bɛri] o [ˈrɑz,bɛri] *s* (*pl* **-ries**) frambuesa, sangüesa
raspberry bush *s* frambueso, sangüeso
rat [ræt] *s* rata; (*false hair*) (coll) postizo; **to smell a rat** (coll) olerse una trama, sospechar una intriga
ratchet [ˈrætʃit] *s* trinquete *m*
rate [ret] *s* (*amount or degree measured in proportion to something else*) razón *f;* (*of interest*) tipo; velocidad; precio; **at any rate** de todos modos; **at the rate of** a razón de ‖ *tr* valuar; estimar, juzgar; clasificar ‖ *intr* ser considerado, ser tenido; estar clasificado
rate of exchange *s* tipo de cambio
rate table *s* baremo
rather [ˈræðər] o [ˈrɑðər] *adv* algo, un poco; bastante; antes, más bien; mejor dicho; por el contrario; muy, mucho; **rather than** antes que, más bien que ‖ *interj* ¡ya lo creo!
rati•fy [ˈrætɪ,faɪ] *v* (*pret & pp* **-fied**) *tr* ratificar
ratings [ˈretɪŋz] *spl* (telv) índice *m* de audencia
ra•tio [ˈreʃo] o [ˈreʃi,o] *s* (*pl* **-tios**) (math) razón *f;* (math) cociente *m*
ration [ˈreʃən] o [ˈræʃən] *s* ración ‖ *tr* racionar
rationing [ˈræʃənɪŋ] *s* racionamiento
rational [ˈræʃənəl] *adj* racional
rat poison *s* matarratas *m;* raticida
rat race *s* (coll) lucha diaria por ganarse el pan
rattle [ˈrætəl] *s* (*number of short, sharp sounds*) traqueteo; (*noise-making device*) carraca, matraca; (*child's toy*) sonajero; baraúnda; (*in the throat*) estertor *m* ‖ *tr* tabletear, traquetear; (*to confuse*) (coll) atortolar, desconcertar; **to rattle off** decir rápidamente ‖ *intr* tabletear, traquetear
ratˈtle•snakeˊ *s* serpiente *f* de cascabel
ratˈtrapˊ *s* ratonera; trance apurado, atolladero
raucous [ˈrɔkəs] *adj* ronco
ravage [ˈrævɪdʒ] *s* destrucción, estrago, ruina ‖ *tr* destruir, estragar, arruinar
rave [rev] *s* elogio muy entusiasta ‖ *intr* desvariar, delirar; bramar, enfurecerse; **to rave about** hacerse lenguas de, deshacerse en elogios de
raven [ˈrevən] *s* cuervo
ravenous [ˈrævənəs] *adj* famélico, hambriento, voraz; rapaz
ravine [rəˈvin] *s* cañón *m,* hondonada
ravish [ˈrævɪʃ] *tr* encantar, entusiasmar; raptar; violar (*a una mujer*)
ravishing [ˈrævɪʃɪŋ] *adj* encantador, deslumbrante
raw [rɔ] *adj* crudo; (*cotton, silk*) en rama; inexperto, principiante; ulceroso; (*weather, day*) crudo
raw deal *s* (slang) mala pasada
rawˈhideˊ *s* cuero en verde; látigo hecho de cuero en verde
raw material *s* primera materia, materia prima
ray [re] *s* (*of light*) rayo; (*fine line; fish*) raya
rayon [ˈre•ɑn] *s* rayón *m*
raze [rez] *tr* arrasar, asolar
razor [ˈrezər] *s* navaja de afeitar
razor blade *s* hoja u hojita de afeitar
razor strop *s* asentador *m,* suavizador *m*
razz [ræz] *s* (slang) irrisión ‖ *tr* (slang) mofarse de
R.C. *abbr* **Red Cross, Reserve Corps, Roman Catholic**
R.D. *abbr* **Rural Delivery**
reach [ritʃ] *s* alcance *m;* extensión; **out of reach (of)** fuera del alcance (de); **within reach of** al alcance de ‖ *tr* alcanzar; extender; entregar con la mano; llegar a; ponerse en contacto con; influenciar; cumplir (*cierto número de años*) ‖ *intr* alcanzar; extender la mano o el brazo; **to reach after** o **for** esforzarse por coger
react [rɪˈækt] *intr* reaccionar
reaction [rɪˈækʃən] *s* reacción
reactionar•y [rɪˈækʃən,ɛri] *adj* reaccionario; mocho (Mex) ‖ *s* (*pl* **-ies**) reaccionario
reactor [riˈæktər] *s* (*nuclear*) reactor *m;* (chem, phys) reactor
read [rid] *v* (*pret & pp* **read** [rɛd]) *tr* leer; recitar (*poesía*); estudiar (*derecho*); leer en, adivinar (*el pensamiento ajeno*); **to read over** recorrer, repasar ‖ *intr* leer; rezar, p.ej., **this page reads thus** esta página reza así; leerse, p.ej., **this book reads easily** este libro se lee con facilidad; **to read on** seguir leyendo
reader [ˈridər] *s* lector *m;* libro de lectura
readily [ˈrɛdɪli] *adv* de buena gana; fácilmente
reading [ˈridɪŋ] *s* lectura; recitación
reading desk *s* atril *m*
reading glass *s* lente *f* para leer, vidrio de aumento; **reading glasses** anteojos para la lectura, gafas de cerca *o* de leer
reading lamp *s* lámpara de sobremesa
reading room *s* gabinete *m* de lectura; sala de lectura
readˊ-onˈly memory *s* (compu) memoria de acceso aleatorio, memoria ROM
read•y [ˈrɛdi] *adj* (*comp* **-ier;** *super* **-iest**) listo, preparado, pronto; ágil, diestro; vivo; disponible; **to make ready** preparar; prepararse ‖ *v* (*pret & pp* **-ied**) *tr* preparar ‖ *intr* prepararse
ready cash *s* dinero a la mano, dinero contante y sonante
readˈy-madeˊ *adj* (culin) preparado, precocinado; (sew) de confección
readˈy-madeˊ clothing *s* ropa hecha
ready-made suit *s* el traje hecho
readˈy-mixˊ *adj* (*concrete*), ya mezclado; (culin) de sobre, de paquete
readˈy-to-wearˊ *s* ropa de confección
reagent [rɪˈedʒənt] *s* reactivo
real [ˈri•əl] *adj* real, verdadero
real estate *s* bienes *mpl* raíces, bienes inmuebles, propiedad inmobiliaria
reˈal-es•tateˊ *adj* inmobiliario
real-estate agency *s* agencia inmobiliaria
real-estate agent *s* agente *mf* inmobiliario, corredor *m* de propiedades
realism [ˈri•ə,lɪzəm] *s* realismo
realist [ˈri•əlɪst] *s* realista *mf*

reali•ty [rɪˈælɪti] *s* (*pl* **-ties**) realidad
realize [ˈri•ə,laɪz] *tr* darse cuenta de; realizar, llevar a cabo; adquirir (*ganancias*); reportar (*ganancias*) || *intr* (*to sell property for ready money*) realizar
realm [rɛlm] *s* reino
real time *s* (compu) tiempo real
Realtor [ˈri•əl,tɔr] o [ˈri•əltər] *s* corredor *m* de bienes raíces, agente *mf* inmobiliario
realty [ˈri•əlti] *s* bienes *mpl* raíces, bienes inmuebles
ream [rim] *s* resma; **reams** (coll) montones *mpl* || *tr* escariar
reap [rip] *tr & intr* (*to cut*) segar; (*to gather*), cosechar
reaper [ˈripər] *s* (*person*) segador *m;* máquina segadora
reappear [,ri•əˈpɪr] *intr* reaparecer
reapportionment [,ri•əˈporʃənmənt] *s* nuevo prorrateo
rear [rɪr] *adj* posterior, trasero; de atrás || *s* espalda; (*of a room*) fondo; (*of a row; of an automobile*) cola; retaguardia; (slang) culo, trasero || *tr* levantar; edificar; criar, educar || *intr* encabritarse (*un caballo*)
rear admiral *s* contraalmirante *m*
rear end *s* (*buttocks*) nalgas, pompis *m*
rearmament [riˈɑrməmənt] *s* rearme *m*
rearrange [,ri•əˈrendʒ] *tr* volver a arreglar; (*change order*) disponer de otro modo; (*furniture*) cambiar de lugar
rear′-view′ mirror *s* retrovisor *m,* espejo de retrovisión
rear′-wheel′ drive *s* tracción trasera
rear window *s* (aut) luneta, luneta posterior
reason [ˈrizən] *s* razón *f;* **by reason of** con motivo de, a causa de; **to listen to reason** meterse en razón; **to stand to reason** ser razonable || *tr & intr* razonar
reasonable [ˈrizənəbəl] *adj* razonable
reassessment [,ri•əˈsɛsmənt] *s* nuevo amillaramiento; nueva estimación
reassurance [,ri•əˈʃʊrəns] *s* (*promise*) promesa tranquilizadora; (*relief*) alivio, seguridades
reassure [,ri•əˈʃʊr] *tr* volver a asegurar; tranquilizar
reawaken [,ri•əˈwekən] *tr* volver a despertar || *intr* volver a despertarse
rebate [ˈribet] o [rɪˈbet] *s* rebaja || *tr* rebajar
rebel [ˈrɛbəl] *adj & s* rebelde *mf* || re•bel [rɪˈbɛl] *v* (*pret & pp* **-belled;** *ger* **-belling**) *intr* rebelarse
rebellion [rɪˈbɛljən] *s* rebelión
rebellious [rɪˈbɛljəs] *adj* rebelde
re•bind [riˈbaɪnd] *v* (*pret & pp* **-bound** [ˈbaund]) reatar; (*to edge, to border*) ribetear; (bb) reencuadernar
rebirth [ˈribʌrθ] o [riˈbʌrθ] *s* renacimiento
rebore [riˈbor] *tr* rectificar
rebound [ˈri,baʊnd] o [riˈbaʊnd] *s* rebote *m* || [riˈbaʊnd] *intr* rebotar
rebroad•cast [riˈbrɔd,kæst] *s* retransmisión || *v* (*pret & pp* **-cast** o **-casted**) *tr* retransmitir
rebuff [rɪˈbʌf] *s* desaire *m,* rechazo || *tr* desairar, rechazar
re•build [riˈbɪld] *v* (*pret & pp* **-built** [ˈbɪlt]) *tr* reconstruir, reedificar
rebuke [rɪˈbjuk] *s* reprensión || *tr* reprender
re•but [rɪˈbʌt] *v* (*pret & pp* **-butted;** *ger* **-butting**) *tr* rebatir, refutar
rebuttal [rɪˈbʌtəl] *s* rebatimiento, refutación
rec. *abbr* **receipt, recipe, record, recorder**
recall [rɪˈkɔl] o [ˈrikɔl] *s* llamada; (*memory*) recordación, retentiva; (*repeal*) revocación, revocatoria; (*of a diplomat*) retirada || [rɪˈkɔl] *tr* hacer volver, mandar volver; recordar; revocar; retirar (*a un diplomático*)
recant [rɪˈkænt] *tr* retractar || *intr* retractarse
re•cap [ˈri,kæp] o [riˈkæp] *s* (*summary*) (coll) resumen *m;* (auto) neumático recauchutado || *v* (*pret & pp* **-capped;** *ger* **-capping**) *tr* (*summarize*) (coll) resumir; (auto) recauchutar
recapitalization [ri,kæpɪtəlɪˈzeʃən] *s* recapitalización
recapitulation [,rikə,pɪtʃəˈleʃən] *s* recapitulación
re•cast [ˈri,kæst] *s* refundición; (*of a sentence*) reconstrucción || [riˈkæst] *v* (*pret & pp* **-cast**) *tr* refundir; reconstruir (*p.ej., una frase*)
recd. o **rec'd.** *abbr* **received**
recede [rɪˈsid] *intr* (*to move back*) retroceder; (*to move away*) alejarse, retirarse; deprimirse (*p.ej., la frente de una persona*)
receipt [rɪˈsit] *s* recepción; (*acknowledgment*) recibo; (*acknowledgment of payment*) recibí *m;* (*recipe*) receta; **receipt in full** finiquito; **receipts** entradas, ingresos || *tr* poner el recibí a
receive [rɪˈsiv] *tr* recibir; receptar (*cosas que son materia de delito*); **received payment** recibí || *intr* recibir
receiver [rɪˈsivər] *s* receptor *m;* (*in bankruptcy*) contador *m,* síndico; receptor telefónico
receivership [rɪˈsivər,ʃɪp] *s* (law) sindicatura
receiving set *s* aparato receptor
receiving teller *s* recibidor *m* (*de un banco*)
recent [ˈrisənt] *adj* reciente
recently [ˈrisəntli] *adv* recientemente; endenantes; recién, p.ej., **recently arrived** recién llegado
receptacle [rɪˈsɛptəkəl] *s* receptáculo; (*wall socket*) enchufe *m* (hembra); (elec) caja de enchufe
reception [rɪˈsɛpʃən] *s* recepción; recibida; (*welcome*) recibimiento; (rad, telv) sintonía
reception desk *s* recepción
receptionist [rɪˈsɛpʃənɪst] *s* recepcionista *f*
reception room *s* salón *m*
receptive [rɪˈsɛptɪv] *adj* receptivo
recess [rɪˈsɛs] o [ˈrisɛs] *s* intermisión; descanso; hora de recreo; (*in a surface*) depresión; (*in a wall*) hueco, nicho; escondrijo || [rɪˈsɛs] *tr* ahuecar; empotrar; deprimir || *intr* prorrogarse, suspenderse
recession [rɪˈsɛʃən] *s* retroceso, retirada; (*e.g.,*

in a wall) depresión; procesión de vuelta; (econ) recesión, contracción económica
rechargeable [rɪˋtʃɑrdʒəbəl] *adj* recargable
recipe [ˋrɛsɪ,pi] *s* receta (*de cocina*)
recipient [rɪˋsɪpɪ•ənt] *s* destinatario; (med) receptor *m*
reciprocal [rɪˋsɪprəkəl] *adj* recíproco
reciprocity [,rɛsɪˋprɑsɪti] *s* reciprocidad
recital [rɪˋsaɪtəl] *s* narración; (*of music or poetry*) recital *m*
recite [rɪˋsaɪt] *tr* narrar; (*formally*) recitar
reckless [ˋrɛklɪs] *adj* atolondrado, temerario
reckon [ˋrɛkən] *tr* calcular; considerar; (coll) calcular, conjeturar || *intr* calcular; **to reckon on** contar con; **to reckon with** tener en cuenta
reclaim [rɪˋklem] *tr* hacer utilizable; hacer labrantío (*un terreno*); ganar (*terreno*) a la mar; recuperar (*materiales usados*); conducir, guiar (*a los que hacen mala vida*)
reclamation [,rɪkləˋmeʃən] *s* (agr) roturación
recline [rɪˋklaɪn] *intr* reclinarse
recluse [rɪˋklus] o [ˋrɛklus] *s* solitario, ermitaño
recognize [ˋrɛkəg,naɪz] *tr* reconocer
recoil [rɪˋkɔɪl] *s* reculada; (*of a firearm*) reculada, culetazo || *intr* recular, apartarse; recular (*un arma de fuego*)
recollect [,rɛkəˋlɛkt] *tr & intr* recordar
recombinant [rɪˋkɑmbɪnənt] *adj* (*genetics*) recombinado
recommend [,rɛkəˋmɛnd] *tr* recomendar
recompense [ˋrɛkəm,pɛns] *s* recompensa || *tr* recompensar
reconcile [ˋrɛkən,saɪ] *tr* reconciliar; **to reconcile oneself** resignarse
reconnaissance [rɪˋkɑnɪsəns] *s* reconocimiento
reconnoiter [,rɛkəˋnɔɪtɛr] o [,rikɛˋnɔɪtɛr] *tr & intr* reconocer
reconquest [riˋkɑŋkwɛst] *s* reconquista
reconsider [,rikənˋsɪdər] *tr* reconsiderar
reconstruct [,rikənˋstrʌkt] *tr* reconstruir
reconversion [,rikənˋvʌrʒən] *s* reconversión
record [ˋrɛkərd] *s* anotación; ficha, historial *m*, historia personal; (*of a notary*) protocolo; (*of a phonograph*) disco; (educ) expediente académico; (sport) record *m*, plusmarca; **off the record** confidencialmente; **records** anales *mpl*, memorias; archivo; **to break a record** batir un record; **to have no (criminal) record** (coll) estar limpio; **to make a record** establecer un record; grabar un disco || [rɪˋkɔrd] *tr* asentar; registrar; inscribir; grabar (*un sonido, una canción, un disco fonográfico, etc.*)
record breaker *s* plusmarquista *mf*
record changer [ˋtʃendʒər] *s* cambiadiscos *m*, tocadiscos automático
recorder [rɪˋkɔrdər] *s* registrador *m;* (electron) grabadora; (mus) flauta dulce
recordholder s (sport) recordman *m*, plusmarquista *mf*
recording [rɪˋkɔrdɪŋ] *adj* registrador; (wire or tape) magnetofónico || *s* registro; (*of phonograph records*) grabación o grabado
recording head *s* (electron) cabeza de grabación
recording secretary *s* secretario escribiente, secretario de actas
record player *s* tocadiscos *m*, pícap *m*, fonógrafo, vitrola, radiola
record store *s* disquería
recount [ˋri,kaʊnt] *tr* (*to count again*) recontar || [rɪˋkaʊnt] *tr* (*to narrate*) recontar
recourse [rɪˋkors] o [ˋrikors] *s* recurso; (*helping hand*) paño de lágrimas; **to have recourse to** recurrir a
recover [rɪˋkʌvər] *tr* recobrar; rescatar; **to recover consciousness** recobrar el conocimiento, volver en sí || *intr* recobrarse; recobrar la salud; ganar un pleito
recover•y [rɪˋkʌvəri] *s* (*pl* **-ies**) recobro, recuperación; **past recovery** sin remedio
recreation [,rɛkrɪˋeʃən] *s* recreación
recruit [rɪˋkrut] *s* recluta *m* || *tr* reclutar || *intr* alistar reclutas; ganar reclutas; restablecerse, reponerse
recruitment [rɪˋkrutmənt] *s* reclutamiento
rect. *abbr* **receipt, rector, rectory**
rectangle [ˋrɛk,tæŋgəl] *s* rectángulo
recti•fy [ˋrɛktɪ,faɪ] *v* (*pret & pp* **-fied**) *tr* rectificar
rec•tum [ˋrɛktəm] *s* (*pl* **-ta** [tə]) recto
recumbent [rɪˋkʌmbənt] *adj* reclinado, recostado
recuperate [rɪˋkjupə,ret] *tr* recuperar; restablecer, reponer || *intr* recuperarse, recobrarse
re•cur [rɪˋkʌr] *v* (*pret & pp* **-curred;** *ger* **-curring**) *intr* volver a ocurrir; volver a presentarse (*a la memoria*); volver (*a un asunto*)
recurrent [rɪˋkʌrənt] *adj* repetido; periódico; (*illness*) recurrente
recyclable [rɪˋsaɪkləbəl] *adj* reciclable
recycling [rɪˋsaɪklɪŋ] *s* reciclado, reciclaje *m*
red [rɛd] *adj* (*comp* **redder;** *super* **reddest**) rojo, colorado; (*wine*) tinto; enrojecido, inflamado || *s* rojo; **in the red** (coll) endeudado; **to see red** (coll) enfurecerse || **Red** *adj & s* (*communist*) rojo
red′bird′ *s* cardenal *m;* piranga
red blood cell *s* glóbulo rojo, hematié *m*
red-blooded [ˋrɛd,blʌdɪd] *adj* fuerte, valiente, vigoroso
red′breast′ *s* (orn) petirrojo; (ichth) pez luna
red′bud′ *s* ciclamor *m* del Canadá
red′cap′ *s* (Brit) policía militar; (U.S.A.) mozo de estación
red cell *s* glóbulo rojo, hematíe *m*
red corpuscle *s* glóbulo rojo
Red Cross *s* Cruz Roja
redden [ˋrɛdən] *tr* enrojecer || *intr* enrojecerse
redeem [rɪˋdim] *tr* redimir; cumplir (*una promesa*)
redeemer [rɪˋdimər] *s* redentor *m*
redemption [rɪˋdɛmpʃən] *s* redención
red-haired [ˋrɛd,hɛrd] *adj* pelirrojo
red′head′ *s* pelirrojo

red herring *s* artificio para distraer la atención del asunto de que se trata
red′-hot′ *adj* candente, calentado al rojo; ardiente, entusiasta; fresco, nuevo
redial [`ri`daɪl] *s* rellamada, rediscado ‖ *tr & intr* volver a marcar, volver a discar
rediscount rate [rɪ`dɪskaʊnt] *s* tipo de redescuento
rediscover [,ridɪs`kʌvər] *tr* redescubrir
red′-let′ter day *s* día *m* memorable
red′-light′ district *s* barrio de los lupanares, barrio de mala vida
re•do [`ri`du] *v* (*pret* **-did** [`dɪd]; *pp* **-done** [`dʌn]) *tr* rehacer, repetir; refundir; reformar
redolent [`rɛdələnt] *adj* fragante, perfumado; **redolent of** que huele a
redoubt [rɪ`daʊt] *s* (fort) reducto
redound [rɪ`daʊnd] *intr* redundar; **to redound to** redundar en
red pepper *s* pimentón *m*
redress [rɪ`drɛs] o [`ridrɛs] *s* reparación; remedio ‖ [rɪ`drɛs] *tr* repara; remediar
Red Ridinghood [`raɪdɪŋ,hʊd] *s* Caperucita Roja
red tape *s* expedienteo, papeleo
reduce [rɪ`djus] o [rɪ`dus] *tr* reducir; (mil) degradar ‖ *intr* reducirse; reducir peso
reducing exercises *spl* ejercicios físicos para reducir peso
redundant [rɪ`dʌndənt] *adj* redundante
redux [`ridʌks] *adj* devuelto, renaciente ‖ *s* repetición
red′wood′ *s* secoya
reed [rid] *adj* (*organ, musical instrument*) de lengüeta ‖ *s* (*stalk*) caña; (*plant*) carrizo, caña; (mus) instrumento de lengüeta; (*of instrument*) lengüeta
re-edit [ri`ɛdɪt] *tr* refundir
reef [rif] *s* arrecife *m,* escollo; (min) filón *m,* veta ‖ *tr* (naut) arrizar
reefer [`rifər] *s* (slang) pitillo de mariguana
reek [rik] *intr* vahear, humear; estar bañado en sudor; estar mojado con sangre; **to reek of** o **with** oler a
reel [ril] *s* (*spool*) carrete *m;* (*of a shuttle*) broca; (*of motion pictures*) cinta; (*sway, staggering*) tambaleo; **off the reel** (coll) fácil y prestamente ‖ *tr* aspar, devanar; **to reel off** (coll) narrar fácil y prestamente ‖ *intr* tambalear; cejar (*p.ej., el enemigo*)
re-election [,ri•ɪ`lɛkʃən] *s* reelección
reenact [,ri•ɪn`ækt] *tr* recrear, representar; (*a crime*) reconstruir
reenlist [,ri•ɛn`lɪst] *tr* reenganchar ‖ *intr* reengancharse
reen•try [rɪ`ɛntri] *s* (*pl* **-tries**) reingreso, nueva entrada; (*return to earth's atmosphere*) reentrada
reexamination [,ri•ɛg,zæmɪ`neʃən] *s* reexaminación
ref. *abbr* **referee, reference, reformation**
re•fer [rɪ`fʌr] *v* (*pret & pp* **-ferred;** *ger* **-ferring**) *tr* referir ‖ *intr* referirse
referee [,rɛfə`ri] *s* árbitro ‖ *tr & intr* arbitrar
reference [`rɛfərəns] *adj* (*library, book, work*) de consulta ‖ *s* referencia
referen•dum [,rɛfə`rɛndəm] *s* (*pl* **-da** [də]) *s* referéndum *m,* referendo, plebiscito
refill [`rifɪl] *s* relleno ‖ [ri`fɪl] *tr* rellenar
refine [rɪ`faɪn] *tr* refinar
refinement [rɪ`faɪnmənt] *s* refinamiento; buena crianza, cultura
refiner•y [rɪ`faɪnəri] *s* (*pl* **-ies**) refinería
reflect [rɪ`flɛkt] *tr* reflejar; (*to meditate*) reflexionar; **to reflect on** o **upon** reflexionar en o sobre; perjudicar
reflecting telescope [rɪ`flɛktɪŋ] *s* reflector *m,* telescopio de espejo
reflection [rɪ`flɛkʃən] *s* (*thinking*) reflexión; (*reflected light; image*) reflejo
reflector [rɪ`flɛktər] *s* reflector *m*
reflex [`riflɛks] *s* reflejo
reflex action *s* acto reflejo
reforestation [,rifɑrɪs`teʃən] o [,rifarɪs`teʃən] *s* reforestación
reform [rɪ`fɔrm] *s* reforma ‖ *tr* reformar ‖ *intr* reformarse
reformation [,rɛfər`meʃən] *s* reformación ‖ **the Reformation** (eccl) la Reforma
reformato•ry [rɪ`fɔrmə,tori] *s* (*pl* **-ries**) reformatorio
reform school *s* casa de corrección
refraction [rɪ`frækʃən] *s* refracción
refrain [rɪ`fren] *s* estribillo ‖ *intr* abstenerse
refresh [rɪ`frɛʃ] *tr* refrescar ‖ *intr* refrescarse
refreshing [rɪ`frɛʃɪŋ] *adj* confortante, restaurante
refreshment [rɪ`frɛʃmənt] *s* refresco
refrigerator [rɪ`frɪdʒəretər] *s* heladera, nevera, refrigerador *m,* frigorífico (Esp)
refrigerator car *s* carro o vagón frigorífico
refuel [ri`fjul] *tr & intr* repostar
refuge [`rɛfjudʒ] *s* refugio; expediente *m,* subterfugio; **to take refuge (in)** refugiarse (en)
refugee [,rɛfju`dʒi] *s* refugiado
refugee camp *s* campo de refugiados
refund [`rifʌnd] *s* reembolso ‖ [rɪ`fʌnd] *tr* reembolsar ‖ [ri`fʌnd] *tr* consolidar
refurnish [ri`fʌrnɪʃ] *tr* amueblar de nuevo
refusal [rɪ`fjuzəl] *s* negativa
refuse [`rɛfjus] *s* basura, desecho, desperdicios ‖ [rɪ`fjuz] *tr* rehusar; rechazar, no querer aceptar; **to refuse to** negarse a
refute [rɪ`fjut] *tr* refutar
reg. *abbr* **register, registrar, registry, regular**
regain [rɪ`gen] *tr* recobrar, recuperar; volver a alcanzar; **to regain consciousness** recobrar el conocimiento, volver en sí
regal [`rigəl] *adj* regio
regale [rɪ`gel] *tr* regalar, agasajar
regalia [rɪ`gelɪ•ə] *spl* (*of an office or order*) distinctivos; galas, trajes *mpl* de lujo
regard [rɪ`gɑrd] *s* consideración, miramiento; (*esteem*) respeto; (*particular matter*) respecto; (*look*) mirada; **in regard to** respecto a o de; **regards** recuerdos; **without regard to**

sin hacer caso de; **with regard to** respecto a o de || *tr* considerar; mirar; tocar a, referirse a; **as regards** en cuanto a
regarding [rɪˋgɑrdɪŋ] *prep* tocante a, con respecto a o de, en cuanto a
regardless [rɪˋgɑrdlɪs] *adj* desatento, indiferente || *adj* (coll) pese a quien pese, cueste lo que cueste; **regardless of** sin hacer caso de; a pesar de
regenerate [rɪˋdʒɛnə,ret] *tr* regenerar || *intr* regenerarse
regeneration [rɪˋdʒɛnəˋreʃən] *s* renovación; (biol) regeneration
regent [,ridʒənt] *s* regente *mf*
regicide [ˋrɛdʒɪ,saɪd] *s* (*act*) regicidio; (*person*) regicida *mf*
regime o **régime** [reˋʒim] *s* régimen *m*
regiment [ˋrɛdʒɪmənt] *s* regimiento || [ˋrɛdʒɪ,mɛnt] *tr* regimentar
regimental [,rɛdʒɪ,mɛntəl] *adj* regimental || **regimentals** *spl* uniforme *m* militar
region [ˋridʒən] *s* región, comarca
regionalism [ˋridʒənə,lɪzəm] *s* regionalismo
register [ˋrɛdʒɪstər] *s* (*record; book for keeping such a record*) registro; reja regulable de calefacción; (*of the voice or an instrument*) extensión || *tr* (*to indicate by a record; to show, as on a scale*) registrar; empadronar (*los vecinos en el padrón*); manifestar, dar a conocer; certificar (*envíos por correo*); inscribir || *intr* registrarse; empadronarse; inscribirse
registered letter *s* carta certificada
registrar [ˋrɛdʒɪs,trɑr] *s* registrador *m*, archivero
registration fee [,rɛdʒɪsˋtreʃən] *s* derechos de matrícula
re•gret [rɪˋgrɛt] *s* pesar *m*, sentimiento; pesadumbre, remordimiento; **regrets** excusas || *v* (*pret & pp* **-gretted;** *ger* **-gretting**) *tr* sentir, lamentar; lamentar la pérdida de; arrepentirse de; **I regret** (*apology*) lo siento; me sabe mal; **to regret to** sentir
regrettable [rɪˋgrɛtəbəl] *adj* lamentable
regular [ˋrɛgjələr] *adj* regular; (coll) cabal, completo, verdadero || *s* obrero permanente; parroquiano regular; **regulars** tropas regulares
regulate [ˋrɛgjə,let] *tr* regular
regulation [,rɛgjəˋleʃən] *s* regulación; (*rule*) regla, norma
rehabilitate [,rihəˋbɪlɪ,tet] *tr* rehabilitar
rehabilitation [,rihə,bɪlɪˋteʃən] *s* rehabilitación; recuperación
rehearsal [rɪˋhʌrsəl] *s* ensayo
rehearse [rɪˋhʌrs] *tr* ensayar || *intr* ensayarse
reign [ren] *s* reinado || *intr* reinar
reimburse [,ri•ɪmˋbʌrs] *tr* reembolsar, rembolsar
rein [ren] *s* rienda; **to give free rein to** dar rienda suelta a || *tr* dirigir por medio de riendas; contener, refrenar, gobernar
reincarnation [,ri•ɪnkɑrˋneʃən] *s* reencarnación
reindeer [ˋren,dɪr] *s* reno
reinforce [,ri•ɪnˋfors] *tr* reforzar; armar (*el hormigón*)
reinforcement [,ri•ɪnˋforsmənt] *s* refuerzo
reinstate [,ri•ɪnˋstet] *tr* reinstalar
reiterate [riˋɪtə,ret] *tr* reiterar
reject [rɪˋdʒɛkt] *tr* rechazar
rejection [rɪˋdʒɛkʃən] *s* rechazamiento
rejoice [rɪˋdʒɔɪs] *intr* regocijarse
rejoinder [rɪˋdʒɔɪndər] *s* contestación; (law) contrarréplica
rejuvenation [rɪ,dʒuvɪˋneʃən] *s* rejuvenecimiento
rel. *abbr* **relating, relative, religion, religious**
relapse [rɪˋlæps] *s* recaída || *intr* recaer
relate [rɪˋlet] *tr* (*to establish relationship between*) relacionar; (*to narrate*) contar, relatar
relation [rɪˋleʃən] *s* (*connection; narration*) relación; (*narration*) relato; (*relative*) pariente *mf;* (*kinship*) parentesco; **in relation to** o **with** tocante a, respecto a o de
relationship [rɪˋleʃən,ʃɪp] *s* (*connection*) relación; (*kinship*) parentesco
relative [ˋrɛlətɪv] *adj* relativo || *s* deudo, pariente *mf*
relax [rɪˋlæks] *tr & intr* relajar
relaxation [,rilæksˋeʃən] *s* relajación; distracción; (*lessening*) disminución
relaxation of tension *s* disminución de tensión; disminución de la tirantez internacional
relaxing [rɪˋlæksɪŋ] *adj* relajador; despreocupante, tranquilizador
relay [ˋrile] o [rɪˋle] *s* (elec) relais *m*, relevador *m*, relevo; (mil & sport) relevo; (sport) carrera de relevos || *v* (*pret & pp* **-layed**) transmitir relevándose; transmitir con un relais; retransmitir (*una emisión*); reexpedir (*un radiotelegrama*) || [rɪˋle] *v* (*pret & pp* **-laid**) *tr* volver a colocar, volver a tender
relay race *s* canera de relevos
release [rɪˋlis] *s* liberación; (*from jail*) excarcelación; alivio; permiso de publicación, venta, etc.; obra o pieza lista para la publicación, venta, etc.; (aer) lanzamiento; (mach) escape *m*, disparador *m* || *tr* soltar; libertar; excarcelar (*a un preso*); permitir la publicación, venta, etc. de; (aer) lanzar (*una bomba*)
relent [rɪˋlɛnt] *intr* ablandarse, aplacarse
relentless [rɪˋlɛntlɪs] *adj* implacable
relevance [ˋrɛlɪvəns] *s* relevancia
relevant [ˋrɛlɪvənt] *adj* pertinente
reliable [rɪˋlaɪ•əbəl] *adj* confiable, fidedigno; (*source*) solvente
reliance [rɪˋlaɪ•əns] *s* confianza
relic [ˋrɛlɪk] *s* reliquia
relief [rɪˋlif] *s* alivio; caridad; (*projection of figures; elevation*) relieve *m;* (mil) relevo; **in relief** en relieve; **on relief** viviendo de socorro, recibiendo auxilio social
relieve [rɪˋliv] *tr* (*to release from a post*) relevar; aliviar; auxiliar (*a los necesitados*); (mil) relevar
religion [rɪˋlɪdʒən] *s* religión

religious [rɪˈlɪdʒəs] *adj* religioso
relinquish [rɪˈlɪŋkwɪʃ] *tr* abandonar, dejar, renunciar
relish [ˈrɛlɪʃ] *s* buen sabor, gusto; condimento, sazón *f;* entremés *m;* buen apetito ‖ *tr* gustar de; comer o beber con placer
relocate [riˈloket] *tr* trasladar, reubicar ‖ *intr* trasladarse
relocation [ˌriloˈkeʃən] *s* traslado, reubicación
reluctance [rɪˈlʌktəns] *s* renuencia, aversión
reluctant [rɪˈlʌktənt] *adj* renuente, maldispuesto
re•ly [rɪˈlaɪ] *v* (*pret & pp* **-lied**) *intr* depender, confiar; **to rely on** depender de, confiar en
REM [rɛm] *s* (acronym) (**rapid eye movement**) REM *m* (movimientos oculares rápidos)
remain [rɪˈmen] *intr* permanecer, quedarse ‖ **remains** *spl* desechos, restos; restos mortales; obra póstuma
remainder [rɪˈmendər] *s* resto, residuo; libro casi invendible ‖ *tr* saldar (*libros que ya no se venden*)
re•make [riˈmek] *v* (*pret & pp* **-made** [ˈmed]) *tr* rehacer
remark [rɪˈmɑrk] *s* observación ‖ *tr & intr* observar; **to remark on** aludir a, comentar
remarkable [rɪˈmɑrkəbəl] *adj* notable, extraordinario
remar•ry [riˈmæri] *v* (*pret & pp* **-ried**) *intr* volver a casarse
remedial [rɪˈmidɪ•əl] *adj* (educ) de recuperación; (med) de rehabilitación
reme•dy [ˈrɛmɪdi] *s* (*pl* **-dies**) remedio ‖ *v* (*pret & pp* **-died**) *tr* remediar
remember [rɪˈmɛmbər] *tr* acordarse de, recordar; dar recuerdos de parte de, p.ej., **remember me to your brother** déle Ud. a su hermano recuerdos de mi parte ‖ *intr* acordarse, recordar; **if I remember correctly** si mal no me acuerdo
remembrance [rɪˈmɛmbrəns] *s* recuerdo
remind [rɪˈmaɪnd] *tr* recordar
reminder [rɪˈmaɪndər] *s* recordatorio, recordativo
reminisce [ˌrɛmɪˈnɪs] *intr* entregarse a los recuerdos, contar sus recuerdos
remiss [rɪˈmɪs] *adj* descuidado, negligente
re•mit [rɪˈmɪt] *v* (*pret & pp* **-mitted;** *ger* **-mitting**) *tr* (*to send, to ship; to pardon*) remitir
remittance [rɪˈmɪtəns] *s* remesa
remnant [ˈrɛmnənt] *s* (*something left over*) remanente *m;* (*of cloth*) retal *m,* retazo; (*piece of cloth to be sold at reduced price*) saldo; vestigio
remod•el [riˈmɑdəl] *v* (*pret & pp* **-eled** o **-elled;** *ger* **-eling** o **-elling**) *tr* modelar de nuevo; rehacer, reconstruir; convertir, transformar; remodelar
remodeling [riˈmɑdəlɪŋ] *s* remodelación
remonstrate [rɪˈmɑnstret] *intr* protestar; **to remonstrate with** reconvenir
remorse [rɪˈmɔrs] *s* remordimiento
remorseful [rɪˈmɔrsfəl] *adj* compungido, arrepentido
remote [rɪˈmot] *adj* remoto
remote control *s* mando a distancia, telecontrol *m,* control remoto, telemando; **to operate by remote control** (co)mandar a distancia
remote′-controlled′ *adj* teledirigido
remote server *s* (compu) servidor remoto
removable [rɪˈmuvəbəl] *adj* (*partition, shelf; handle*) desmontable, amovible; (*part of clothing*) de quita y pon; (compu) extraíble, removible
removal [rɪˈmuvəl] *s* remoción; mudanza, traslado; (*dismissal*) deposición
remove [rɪˈmuv] *tr* remover; quitar de en medio, apartar matando ‖ *intr* removerse
remuneration [rɪˌmjunərˈeʃən] *s* remuneración
renaissance [ˌrɛnəˈsɑns] o [rɪˈnesəns] *s* renacimiento
rend [rɛnd] *v* (*pret & pp* **rent** [rɛnt]) *tr* (*to tear*) desgarrar; (*to split*) hender, rajar; estremecer (*un ruido el aire*)
render [ˈrɛndər] *tr* rendir (*gracias, obsequios, homenaje*); prestar, suministrar (*ayuda*); pagar (*tributo*); desempeñar (*un papel*); traducir (*sentimientos*); (*from one language to another*) verter; hacer (*justicia*); ejecutar (*una pieza de música*); derretir (*cera, manteca*); extraer la grasa o el sebo de; poner, volver
rendezvous [ˈrɑndəˌvu] *s* (*pl* **-vous** [ˌvuz]) cita; (*in space*) encuentro, reunión ‖ *v* (*pret & pp* **-voused** [ˌvud]; *ger* **-vousing** [ˌvu•ɪŋ]) *intr* reunirse en una cita
rendition [rɛnˈdɪʃən] *s* rendición; traducción; (mus) ejecución
renege [rɪˈnɪg] *s* renuncio ‖ *intr* renunciar; (coll) volverse atrás
renegotiation [ˌrinɪˌgoʃiˈeʃən] *s* renegociación
renew [rɪˈnju] o [rɪˈnu] *tr* renovar ‖ *intr* renovarse
renewable [rɪˈnju•əbəl] o [rɪˈnu•əbəl] *adj* renovable
renewal [rɪˈnju•əl] o [rɪˈnu•əl] *s* renovación
renounce [rɪˈnaʊns] *tr* renunciar; renunciar a (*p.ej., el mundo*) ‖ *intr* renunciar
renovate [ˈrɛnəˌvet] *tr* renovar; refaccionar; reformar (*p.ej., una tienda, una casa*)
renown [rɪˈnaʊn] *s* renombre *m*
renowned [rɪˈnaʊnd] *adj* renombrado
rent [rɛnt] *adj* desgarrado ‖ *s* alquiler *m,* arriendo; (*tear, slit*) desgarro ‖ *tr* alquilar, arrendar ‖ *intr* alquilarse, arrendarse
rental [ˈrɛntəl] *s* alquiler *m,* arriendo
rental agreement *s* contrato de alquiler
renunciation [rɪˌnʌnsɪˈeʃən] o [rɪˌnʌnʃɪˈeʃən] *s* renunciación
reopen [riˈopən] *tr* reabrir ‖ *intr* reabrirse
reorganize [riˈɔrgəˌnaɪz] *tr* reorganizar ‖ *intr* reorganizarse
reorientation [riˌɔrɪ•ənˈteʃən] *s* reorientación
rep [rɛp] *s* (com) representante *mf;* (sport) repetición; (slang) reputación

rep. *abbr* **report, reporter, representative, republic**
repair [rɪˋpɛr] *s* reparación; recompostura; **in repair** en buen estado ‖ *tr* reparar; refaccionar ‖ *intr* dirigirse; volver
repaper [riˋpepər] *tr* empapelar de nuevo
reparation [ˌrɛpəˋreʃən] *s* reparación
repartee [ˌrɛpɑrˋti] *s* respuesta viva; agudeza y gracia en responder
repast [rɪˋpæst] o [rɪˋpɑst] *s* comida, comilona
repatriate [riˋpetrɪˌet] *tr* repatriar
re•pay [rɪˋpe] *v* (*pret & pp* **-paid** [ˋped]) *tr* reembolsar, rembolsar; resarcir (*un daño, una injuria*); compensar
repayment [rɪˋpemənt] *s* reembolso; resarcimiento; compensación
repeal [rɪˋpil] *s* abrogación, revocación; revocatoria ‖ *tr* abrogar, revocar
repeat [rɪˋpit] *s* repetición ‖ *tr & intr* repetir
re•pel [rɪˋpɛl] *v* (*pret & pp* **-pelled;** *ger* **-pelling**) *tr* rechazar, repeler; repugnar
repent [rɪˋpɛnt] *tr* arrepentirse de ‖ *intr* arrepentirse
repentance [rɪˋpɛntəns] *s* arrepentimiento
repentant [rɪˋpɛntənt] *adj* arrepentido
repertory theater [ˋrɛpərˌtori] *s* teatro de repertorio
repetition [ˌrɛpɪˋtɪʃən] *s* repetición
repine [rɪˋpaɪn] *intr* afligirse, quejarse
replace [rɪˋples] *tr* (*to put back*) reponer; (*to take the place of*) reemplazar
replacement [rɪˋplesmənt] *s* reposición; reemplazo; pieza de repuesto; soldado reemplazante
replenish [rɪˋplɛnɪʃ] *tr* rellenar; reaprovisionar
replete [rɪˋplit] *adj* repleto
replica [ˋrɛplɪkə] *s* réplica
re•ply [rɪˋplaɪ] *s* (*pl* **-plies**) contestación, respuesta; contesto (Mex) ‖ *v* (*pret & pp* **-plied**) *tr & intr* contestar, responder
reply coupon *s* vale *m* respuesta
report [rɪˋport] *s* relato, informe *m;* (*summary*) reseña; voz *f,* rumor *m;* (*e.g., of a firearm*) detonación, tiro; denuncia ‖ *tr* relatar, informar acerca de; denunciar ‖ *intr* hacer un relato; redactar un informe; ser repórter; presentarse; **to report on** dar cuenta de, notificar
report card *s* certificado escolar, boletín *m* de calificaciones, boletín de notas
reportedly [rɪˋportɪdli] *adv* según se informa
reporter [rɪˋportər] *s* repórter *m,* reportero
reporting [rɪˋportɪŋ] *s* reportaje *m*
repose [rɪˋpoz] *s* descanso ‖ *tr* descansar; poner (*confianza*) ‖ *intr* descansar
reprehend [ˌrɛprɪˋhɛnd] *tr* reprender
represent [ˌrɛprɪˋzɛnt] *tr* representar
representative [ˌrɛprɪˋzɛntətɪv] *adj* representativo ‖ *s* representante *mf*
repress [rɪˋprɛs] *tr* reprimir
reprieve [rɪˋpriv] *s* suspensión temporal de un castigo, suspensión temporal de la pena de muerte; respiro, alivio temporal ‖ *tr* suspender temporalmente el castigo de o la pena de muerte de; aliviar temporalmente
reprimand [ˋrɛprɪˌmænd] *s* reprimenda ‖ *tr* reconvenir, reprender
reprint [ˋriˌprɪnt] *s* reimpresión; tirada aparte ‖ [riˋprɪnt] *tr* reimprimir
reprisal [rɪˋpraɪzəl] *s* represalia
reproach [rɪˋprotʃ] *s* reproche *m;* oprobio ‖ *tr* reprochar; oprobiar
reproduce [ˌriprəˋdjus] *tr* reproducir ‖ *intr* reproducirse
reproduction [ˌriprəˋdʌkʃən] *s* reproducción
reproof [rɪˋpruf] *s* reprobación
reprove [rɪˋpruv] *tr* reprobar
reptile [ˋrɛptɪl] *s* reptil *m*
republic [rɪˋpʌblɪk] *s* república
republican [rɪˋpʌblɪkən] *adj & s* republicano
repudiate [rɪˋpjudɪˌet] *tr* repudiar; no reconocer (*p.ej., una deuda*)
repugnant [rɪˋpʌgnənt] *adj* repugnante
repulse [rɪˋpʌls] *s* repulsión, rechazo ‖ *tr* repeler, rechazar
repulsive [rɪˋpʌlsɪv] *adj* repulsivo
reputation [ˌrɛpjəˋteʃən] *s* reputación; buena reputación
repute [rɪˋpjut] *s* reputación; buena reputación ‖ *tr* reputar
reputedly [rɪˋpjutɪdli] *adv* según la opinión común
request [rɪˋkwɛst] *s* petición, solicitud; **at the request of** a petición de ‖ *tr* pedir
Requiem mass [ˋrɛkwi•əm] *s* (eccl) misa de réquiem o difuntos
require [rɪˋkwaɪr] *tr* exigir, requerir
requirement [rɪˋkwaɪrmənt] *s* requisito; necesidad
requisite [ˋrɛkwɪzɪt] *adj & s* requisito
requital [rɪˋkwaɪtəl] *s* compensación, retorno
requite [rɪˋkwaɪt] *tr* corresponder a (*los beneficios, el amor, etc.*); corresponder con (*el bienhechor*)
re•read [riˋrid] *v* (*pret & pp* **-read** [ˋrɛd]) *tr* releer
rerun [ˋriˌrʌn] *s* (*film, play, etc.*) exhibición repetida, programa *m* repetido
resale [ˋriˌsel] o [riˋsel] *s* reventa
rescind [rɪˋsɪnd] *tr* rescindir
rescue [ˋrɛskju] *s* salvación, rescate *m,* liberación; **to go to the rescue of** acudir al socorro de ‖ *tr* salvar, rescatar, libertar
rescue party *s* pelotón *m* de salvamento
rescue team *s* brigada de salvamento
research [rɪˋsʌrtʃ] o [ˋrisʌrtʃ] *s* investigación ‖ *intr* investigar
research and development *s* investigación y desarrollo
re•sell [riˋsɛl] *v* (*pret & pp* **-sold** [ˋsold]) *tr* revender; rescatar (Mex)
resemblance [rɪˋzɛmbləns] *s* parecido, semejanza
resemble [rɪˋzɛmbəl] *tr* parecerse a, asemejarse a
resent [rɪ-zɛnt] *tr* resentirse de o por

resentful [rɪˈzɛntfəl] *adj* resentido
resentment [rɪˈzɛntmənt] *s* resentimiento
reservation [ˌrɛzərˈveʃən] *s* reserva
reserve [rɪˈzʌrv] *s* reserva ‖ *tr* reservar
reservoir [ˈrɛzərˌvwɑr] *s* depósito; (*where water is dammed back*) embalse *m,* pantano; (*of wisdom*) fondo
resettlement [riˈsɛtəlmənt] *s* (*of land*) repoblación, nueva colonización; (*of people*) reasentamiento
re•ship [riˈʃɪp] *v* (pret & pp **-shipped;** *ger* **-shipping**) *tr* reenviar, reexpedir; (*on a ship*) reembarcar ‖ *intr* reembarcarse
reshipment [riˈʃɪpmənt] *s* reenvío, reexpedición; (*of persons*) reembarco; (*of goods*) reembarque *m*
reshuffle [riˈʃʌfəl] *tr* reorganizar, redistribuir; (cards) volver a barajar
reside [rɪˈzaɪd] *intr* residir
residence [ˈrɛzɪdəns] *s* residencia
resident [ˈrɛzɪdənt] *adj & s* residente *mf,* vecino
residue [ˈrɛzɪˌdju] *s* residuo
resign [rɪˈzaɪn] *tr* dimitir, resignar, renunciar ‖ *intr* dimitir; (*to yield, submit*) resignarse; **to resign to** resignarse con (*p.ej., su suerte*)
resignation [ˌrɛzigˈneʃən] *s* (*from a job, etc.*) dimisión; (*state of being submissive*) resignación
resin [ˈrɛzɪn] *s* resina
resist [rɪˈzɪst] *tr* resistir (*la tentación*); resistir a (*la violencia; la risa*) ‖ *intr* resistirse
resistance [rɪˈzɪstəns] *s* resistencia; **without resistance** sin rechistar
resole [riˈsol] *tr* sobresolar
resolute [ˈrɛzəˌlut] *adj* resuelto
resolution [ˌrɛzəˈluʃən] *s* resolución; **good resolutions** buenos propósitos
resolve [rɪˈzɔlv] *s* resolución ‖ *tr* resolver ‖ *intr* resolverse
resort [rɪˈzɔrt] *s* lugar muy frecuentado; (*e.g., for vacations*) estación; (*for help or support*) recurso; **as a last resort** como último recurso ‖ *intr* recurrir
resound [rɪˈzaʊnd] *intr* resonar
resource [rɪˈsors] o [ˈrisors] *s* recurso
resourceful [rɪˈsorsfəl] *adj* ingenioso
respect [rɪˈspɛkt] *s* (*deference, esteem*) respeto; (*reference, relation; detail*) respecto; **respects** recuerdos, saludos; **to pay one's respects (to)** ofrecer sus respetos (a); **with respect to** respecto a o de ‖ *tr* respetar
respectable [rɪˈspɛktəbəl] *adj* respetable; decente, presentable
respectful [rɪˈspɛktfəl] *adj* respetuoso
respectfully [rɪˈspɛktfəli] *adj* respetuosamente; **respectfully yours** de Ud. atento y seguro servidor
respecting [rɪˈspɛktɪŋ] *prep* con respecto a, respecto de, en cuanto a
respective [rɪˈspɛktɪv] *adj* respectivo
respiration [ˌrɛspəˈreʃən] *s* respiración
respire [rɪˈspaɪr] *tr & intr* respirar
respite [ˈrɛspɪt] *s* (*temporary relief*) respiro; (*postponement, especially of death sentence*) suspensión; **without respite** sin respirar
resplendent [rɪˈsplɛndənt] *adj* resplandeciente
respond [rɪˈspɑnd] *intr* responder
response [rɪˈspɑns] *s* respuesta
responsibility [rɪˌspɑnsɪˈbɪlɪti] *s* responsabilidad, incumbencia; **to assume responsibility** responsabilizarse
responsible [rɪˈspɑnsɪbəl] *adj* responsable; (*job, position*) de confianza; **to hold responsible** responsabilizar; **responsible for** responsable de
rest [rɛst] *s* (*after exertion or work; sleep*) descanso; (*lack of motion*) reposo; (*of the dead*) paz *f;* (*what remains*) resto; (mus) pausa; **at rest** (*not moving*) en reposo; tranquilo; dormido; (*dead*) muerto; **the rest** lo demás; los demás; **to come to rest** venir a parar; **to lay to rest** enterrar ‖ *tr* descansar; parar; poner (*p.ej., confianza*) ‖ *intr* descansar; estar, hallarse; **to rest assured (that)** estar seguro, tener la seguridad (de que); **to rest on** descansar en o sobre, estribar en
restart [ˈriˈstart] *tr* (*a race*) volver a empezar; (*an engine*) volver a poner en marcha; (compu) reiniciar
restaurant [ˈrɛstərənt] *s* restaurante *m*
rest cure *s* cura de reposo
restful [ˈrɛstfəl] *adj* descansado, tranquilo, reposado
rest home *s* casa de reposo
resting place *s* lugar *m* de descanso; (*of a staircase*) descansadero; (*of the dead*) última morada
restitution [ˌrɛstɪˈtjuʃən] *s* restitución
restless [ˈrɛstlɪs] *adj* intranquilo, revuelta; (*sleepless*) insomne
restock [riˈstɑk] *tr* reaprovisionar; repoblar (*p.ej., un acuario*)
restore [rɪˈstor] *tr* restaurar; (*to give back*) devolver; (compu) recuperar
restrain [rɪˈstren] *tr* contener, refrenar; aprisionar
restraint [rɪˌˈstrent] *s* restricción; comedimiento, moderación
restrict [rɪˈstrɪkt] *tr* restringir
rest room *s* baño, servicio(s), retrete *m,* excusado (Mex)
result [rɪˈzʌlt] *s* resultado; **as a result of** de resultas de ‖ *intr* resultar; **to result in** dar por resultado, parar en
resume [rɪˈzum] o [rɪˈzjum] *tr* reasumir; reanudar (*el viaje, el vuelo, etc.*); volver a tomar (*su asiento*) ‖ *intr* continuar; recomenzar; reanudar el hilo del discurso
résumé [ˌrɛzʊˈme] *s* resumen *m*
resurface [riˈsʌrfɪs] *tr* dar nueva superficie a ‖ *intr* volver a emerger (*un submarino*)
resurrect [ˌrɛzəˈrɛkt] *tr & intr* resucitar
resurrection [ˌrɛzəˈrɛkʃən] *s* resurrección
resuscitate [rɪˈsʌsɪˌtet] *tr & intr* resucitar
retail [ˈritel] *adj & adv* al por menor ‖ *s* venta al por menor ‖ *tr* detallar, vendor al por menor

|| *intr* vender al por menor; venderse al por menor
retailer [ˈritelər] *s* detallista *mf,* minorista *m,* comerciante *mf* al por menor
retain [rɪˈten] *tr* retener; contratar (*a un abogado*)
retainer [rɪˈtenər] *s* (*fee*) anticipo, iguala
retaliate [rɪˈtælɪ,et] *intr* desquitarse, vengarse
retaliation [rɪ,tælɪˈeʃən] *s* desquite *m,* venganza
retard [ˈritɑrd] *s* (coll) retardo || [rɪˈtɑrd] *tr* retardar
retardation [,ritɑrˈdeʃən] *s* retardación
retarded [rɪˈtɑrdɪd] *adj* subnormal, atrasado, retrasado
retch [rɛtʃ] *tr* vomitar || *intr* arquear, esforzarse por vomitar
retching [ˈrɛtʃɪŋ] *s* arcadas
ret'd. *abbr* **returned**
reticence [ˈrɛtɪsəns] *s* reserva, circunspección, sigilo
reticent [ˈrɛtɪsənt] *adj* reservado, circunspecto
retina [ˈrɛtənə] *s* retina
retinue [ˈrɛtɪ,nju] *s* comitiva, séquito
retire [rɪˈtaɪr] *tr* retirar; jubilar (*a un empleado*) || *intr* retirarse; jubilarse; (*to go to bed*) recogerse; (mil) retirarse
retirement [rɪˈtaɪrmənt] *s* retiro; (*of an employee with pension*) jubilación; (mil) retirada
retirement age *s* tercera edad
retirement annuity *s* jubilación
retirement pension *s* pensión de jubilación
retir'ing *adj* (*shy*) retraído
retort [rɪˈtɔrt] *s* respuesta pronta y aguda, réplica; (chem) retorta || *intr* replicar
retouch [riˈtʌtʃ] *tr* retocar
retrace [rɪˈtres] *tr* repasar; **to retrace one's steps** volver sobre sus pasos
retract [rɪˈtrækt] *tr* retractarse de, desdecirse de (*lo que se ha dicho*) || *intr* retractarse, desdecirse
retractable [rɪˈtræktəbəl] *adj* retráctil
retraction [rɪˈtrækʃən] *s* retracción
re•tread [ˈri,trɛd] *s* neumático recauchutado; neumático ranurado || [riˈtrɛd] *v* (*pret & pp* **-treaded**) *tr* recauchutar; volver a ranurar || *v* (*pret* **-trod** [ˈtrɑd]; *pp* **-trod** o **-trodden**) *tr* desandar || *intr* volverse atrás
retreat [rɪˈtrit] *s* (*act of withdrawing; place of seclusion*) retiro; (eccl) retiro; (mil) retreta, retirada; (*signal*) (mil) retreta; **to beat a retreat** retirarse; (mil) batirse en retirada || *intr* retirarse
retrench [rɪˈtrɛntʃ] *tr* cercenar || *intr* recogerse
retrench'ment *s* reducción de gastos
retribution [,rɛtrɪˈbjuʃən] *s* justo castigo; (theol) juicio final
retrieve [rɪˈtriv] *tr* cobrar; reparar (*p.ej., un daño*); desquitarse de (*una pérdida, una derrota*); (hunt) cobrar, portar || *intr* (hunt) cobrar, portar
retriever [rɪˈtrivər] *s* perro cobrador, perro traedor
retroactive [,rɛtroˈæktɪv] *adj* retroactivo
retrofiring [,rɛtroˈfaɪrɪŋ] *s* retrodisparo
retrogress [ˈrɛtrə,grɛs] *intr* retroceder; empeorar
retrorocket [,rɛtroˈrɑkɪt] *s* retrocohete *m*
retrospect [ˈrɛtrə,spɛkt] *s* retrospección; **in retrospect** retrospectivamente
retrospective [,rɛtrə,spɛktɪv] *adj* retrospectivo
re'tro•vir'us *s* retrovirus *m*
re•try [riˈtraɪ] *v* (*pret & pp* **-tried**) *tr* reensayar; rever (*un caso legal*); procesar de nuevo (*a una persona*)
return [rɪˈtʌrn] *adj* repetido; de vuelta; **by return mail** a vuelta de correo || *s* vuelta; devolución; recompensa; respuesta; informe *m,* noticia; ganancia, beneficio, rédito; (*of an election*) resultado; (*of income tax*) declaración; **in return (for)** en cambio (de); **many happy returns of the day!** ¡que cumpla muchos más! || *tr* devolver; dar en cambio; corresponder a (*un favor*); dar (*una respuesta, las gracias*) || *intr* volver; responder
return address *s* dirección del remitente
return bout o **engagement** *s* (box) combate *m* revancha
return game *s* desquite *m*
return ticket *s* billete *m* de vuelta; billete de ida y vuelta
return trip *s* viaje *m* de vuelta
reunification [ri,junɪfɪˈkeʃən] *s* reunificación
reunion [riˈjunjən] *s* reunión
reunite [,rijʊˈnaɪt] *tr* reunir || *intr* reunirse
rev. *abbr* **revenue, reverse, review, revised, revision, revolution**
Rev. *abbr.* **Revelation, Reverend**
rev [rev] *s* revolución || *v* (*pret & pp* **revved;** *ger* **revving**) *tr* cambiar la velocidad de; **to rev up** acelerar || *intr* acelerarse
revaluate [riˈvæljʊ,et] *tr* revalorar, revalorizar, revaluar
revamp [riˈvæmp] *tr* componer, renovar, remendar
reveal [rɪˈvil] *tr* revelar
reveille [ˈrɛvəli] *s* diana, toque *m* de diana
rev•el [ˈrɛvəl] *s* jarana, regocijo tumultuoso || *v* (*pret & pp* **-eled** o **-elled;** *ger* **-eling** o **-elling**) *intr* jaranear; deleitarse
revelation [,rɛvəˈleʃən] *s* revelación
revel•ry [ˈrɛvəlri] *s* (*pl* **-ries**) jarana, diversión tumultuosa
revenge [rɪˈvɛndʒ] *s* venganza || *tr* vengar
revengeful [rɪˈvɛndʒfəl] *adj* vengativo
revenue [ˈrɛvə,nju] *s* renta, rédito; rentas públicas
revenue cutter *s* escampavía
revenue stamp *s* sello fiscal, timbre *m* del estado, timbre *m* fiscal
reverberate [rɪˈvʌrbə,ret] *intr* reverberar
revere [rɪˈvɪr] *tr* reverenciar, venerar
reverence [ˈrɛvərəns] *s* reverencia || *tr* reverenciar

Reverend [ˈrɛvərənd] *adj & s* reverendo
reverie [ˈrɛvəri] *s* ensueño
reversal [rɪˈvʌrsəl] *s* inversión (*e.g., of opinion*) cambio
reverse [rɪˈvʌrs] *adj* invertido; contrario; de marcha atrás ‖ *s* (*opposite or rear*) revés *m;* contrario; contramarcha, marcha atrás; (*check, defeat*) revés *m,* contratiempo ‖ *tr* invertir; dar vuelta a; poner en marcha atrás; **to reverse oneself** cambiar de opinión; **to reverse the charges** cobrar al destinatario; (telp) cobrar al número llamado ‖ *intr* invertirse
reverse lever *s* palanca de marcha atrás
reversible [rɪˈvʌrsəbəl] *adj* revocable; (*jacket*) reversible
revert [rɪˈvʌrt] *intr* revertir; saltar atrás; **to revert to one's old tricks** volver a las andadas
review [rɪˈvju] *s* (*reexamination; survey; magazine; musical show*) revista; (*of a book*) reseña, revista; (*of a lesson*) repaso; (mil) reseña, revista ‖ *tr* rever, revisar; reseñar (*un libro*); repasar (*una lección*); (mil) revistar
reviewer [rɪˈvju•ər] *s* (*critic*) reseñador *m*
revile [rɪˈvaɪl] *tr* ultrajar, vilipendiar
revise [rɪˈvaɪz] *s* revisión; refundición; (typ) segunda prueba ‖ *tr* rever, revisar; refundir (*un libro*); enmendar
revision [rɪˈvɪʒən] *s* revisión; revisada; (*of a book*) refundición; enmienda
revisionism [rɪˈvɪʒə,nɪzəm] *s* revisionismo
revisionist [rɪˈvɪʒənɪst] *adj & s* revisionista
revival [rɪˈvaɪvəl] *s* resucitación; reanimación; (*e.g., of learning*) renacimiento; (eccl) despertamiento religioso; (theat) reestreno, reposición
revive [rɪˈvaɪv] *tr* revivir; (theat) reestrenar, reponer ‖ *intr* revivir; volver en sí, recordar
revoke [rɪˈvok] *tr* revocar
revolt [rɪˈvolt] *s* rebelión, sublevación, revuelta ‖ *tr* dar asco a, repugnar ‖ *intr* rebelarse, sublevarse
revolting [rɪˈvoltiŋ] *adj* asqueroso, repugnante; rebelde
revolution [,rɛvəˈluʃən] *s* revolución
revolutionar•y [,rɛvəˈluʃə,nɛri] *adj* revolucionario ‖ *s* (*pl* **-ies**) revolucionario
revolve [rɪˈvɑlv] *tr* hacer girar; (*in one's mind*) revolver ‖ *intr* girar; revolverse (*un astro en su órbita*)
revolver [rɪˈvɑlvər] *s* revólver *m*
revolving bookcase *s* giratoria
revolving door *s* puerta giratoria
revolving fund *s* fondo rotativo
revue [rɪˈvju] *s* (theat) revista
revulsion [rɪˈvʌlʃən] *s* aversión, repugnancia; reacción fuerte
reward [rɪˈwɔrd] *s* premio, recompensa; (*money used to recapture or recover*) rescate *m;* hallazgo, p.ej., **five dollars reward** cinco dólares de hallazgo ‖ *tr* premiar, recompensar
rewarding [rɪˈwɔrdɪŋ] *adj* remunerador, provechoso, agradecido
re•wind [ˈri,waɪnd] *s* (mach, mov) retroceso ‖ [riˈwaɪnd] *v* (*pret & pp* **-wound** [waʊnd] *tr* (mach, mov) rebobinar
re•write [riˈraɪt] *v* (*pret* **-wrote** [ˈrot]; *pp* **-written** [ˈrɪtən]) *tr* escribir de nuevo; refundir (*un escrito*); redactar (*un escrito de otra persona*)
rezone [ˈriˈzon] *tr* rezonificar
R.F. *abbr* **radio frequency**
R.F.D. *abbr* **Rural Free Delivery**
R.H. *abbr* **Royal Highness**
rhapso•dy [ˈræpsədi] *s* (*pl* **-dies**) rapsodia
rheostat [ˈri•ə,stæt] *s* reóstato
rhesus [ˈrisəs] *s* (zool) macaco de la India
rhetoric [ˈrɛtərɪk] *s* retórica
rhetorical [rɪˈtɔrɪkəl] *adj* retórico
rheumatic [ruˈmætɪk] *adj & s* reumático
rheumatism [ˈrumə,tɪzəm] *s* reumatismo
Rhine [raɪn] *s* Rin *m*
Rhineland [ˈraɪn,lænd] *s* Renania
rhine'stone' *s* diamante de imitación hecho de vidrio
rhinoceros [raɪˈnɑsərəs] *s* rinoceronte *m*
Rhodes[rodz] *s* Rodas *f*
Rhone [ron] *s* Ródano
rhubarb [ˈrubɑrb] *s* ruibarbo
rhyme [raɪm] *s* rima; **without rhyme or reason** sin ton ni son ‖ *tr & intr* rimar
rhythm [ˈrɪðəm] *s* ritmo
rhythmic(al) [ˈrɪðmɪk(əl)] *adj* rítmico
rial•to [rɪˈælto] *s* (*pl* **-tos**) mercado ‖ **the Rialto** el puente del Rialto; el centro teatral de Nueva York
rib [rɪb] *s* costilla; (*of a fan or umbrella*) varilla; (*of a tire*) cuerda; (*in cloth*) canilla; (*of the wing of an insect*) nervio ‖ *v* (*pret & pp* **ribbed;** *ger* **ribbing**) *tr* proveer de costillas; hacer canillas en; (slang) tomar el pelo a
ribald [ˈrɪbəld] *adj* grosero y obsceno
ribbon [ˈrɪbən] *s* cinta
rice [raɪs] *s* arroz *m*
rice'field' *s* arrozal *m*
rich [rɪtʃ] *adj* rico; (coll) platudo; (*color*) vivo; (*voice*) sonoro; (*wine*) generoso; azucarado, condimentado; (coll) divertido; (coll) ridículo; **to strike it rich** descubrir un buen filón ‖ **riches** *spl* riquezas; **the rich** los ricos
Richard [ˈrɪtʃərd] *s* Ricardo
rickets [ˈrɪkɪts] *s* raquitis *f*
rickety [ˈrɪkɪti] *adj* (*object*) destartalado, desvencijado; (*person*) tambaleante, vacilante; (*suffering from rickets*) raquítico
ricochet [,rɪkəˈʃe] *s* (*pl* **-chets** [-ʃez]) rebote *m,* retacho (Mex) ‖ *v* (*pret & pp* **-cheted** [-ʃed]; *ger* **-cheting** [-ʃe•ɪŋ]) *intr* rebotar, retachar (Mex)
rid [rɪd] *v* (*pret & pp* **rid;** *ger* **ridding**) *tr* desembarazar; **to get rid of** desembarazarse de, deshacerse de; matar
riddance [ˈrɪdəns] *s* supresión, libramiento; **good riddance!** ¡adiós, gracias!, ¡de buena me he librado!

riddle [ˈrɪdəl] *s* acertijo, adivinanza; (*person or thing hard to understand*) enigma *m;* criba gruesa || *tr* acribillar; destruir (*un argumento; la reputación de una persona*); **to riddle with bullets** acribillar a balazos; **to riddle with questions** acribillar a preguntas

ride [raɪd] *s* paseo || *v* (*pret* **rode** [rod] *pp* **ridden** [ˈrɪdən]) *tr* montar (*un caballo*); montar sobre (*los hombros de una persona*); recorrer a caballo; flotar sobre (*las olas*); dominar, tiranizar; (coll) burlarse de; **to ride down** atropellar; vencer; **to ride out** luchar felizmente con (*una tempestad*); aguantar con buen éxito (*una desgracia*) || *intr* montar; pasear en coche o carruaje; **to let ride** (slang) dejar correr; **to take riding** llevar de paseo

rider [ˈraɪdər] *s* jinete *m;* pasajero

ridge [rɪdʒ] *s* (*of a roof; of earth between two furrows*) caballete *m;* (*of a fabric*) cordoncillo; (*of mountains*) cordillera; (*of two plane surfaces*) arista

ridge′pole′ *s* parhilera

ridicule [ˈrɪdɪˌkjul] *s* irrisión; **to expose to ridicule** poner en ridículo || *tr* ridiculizar

ridiculous [rɪˈdɪkjələs] *adj* ridículo

riding academy *s* escuela de equitación

riding boot *s* bota de montar

riding habit *s* amazona, traje *m* de montar

rife [raɪf] *adj* común, corriente, general; abundante, lleno; **rife with** abundante en, lleno de

riffraff [ˈrɪfˌræf] *s* bahorrina, canalla

rifle [ˈraɪfəl] *s* rifle *m,* fusil *m* || *tr* hurtar, robar; escudriñar y robar; desnudar, despojar

rifle range *s* tiro de rifle

rift [rɪft] *s* abertura, raja; desacuerdo, desavenencia

rig [rɪg] *s* equipaje *m;* carruaje *m* con caballo o caballos; traje extraño; (naut) aparejo || *v* (*pret & pp* **rigged;** *ger* **rigging**) *tr* equipar; aprestar, disponer; improvisar; vestir de una manera extraña; arreglar de una manera fraudulenta; (naut) aparejar

rigging [ˈrɪgɪŋ] *s* avíos, instrumentos, equipo; (naut) aparejo, cordaje *m*

right [raɪt] *adj* derecho; verdadero; exacto; conveniente; favorable; sano, normal; bien, correcto; señalado; correspondiente; que se busca, p.ej., **this is the right house** ésta es la casa que se busca; que se necesita, p.ej., **this is the right train** éste es el tren que se necesita; que debe, p.ej., **he is going the right way** sigue el camino que debe; **right or wrong** con razón o sin ella, bueno o malo; **to be all right** estar bien; estar bien de salud; **to be right** tener razón || *adv* derechamente; directamente; correctamente; exactamente; favorablemente; en orden, en buen estado; hacia la derecha; completamente; (coll) muy; mismo, p.ej., **right here** aquí mismo; **all right** muy bien || *interj* ¡bien! || *s* (*justice, reason*) derecho; (*right hand*) derecha; (box) derechazo; (com) derecho; (pol) derecha; **by right** según derecho; **on the right** a la derecha; **to be in the right** tener razón || *tr* enderezar; corregir, rectificar; hacer justicia a; deshacer (*un entuerto*) || *intr* enderezarse

righteous [ˈraɪtʃəs] *adj* recto, justo; virtuoso

right field *s* (baseball) jardín derecho

rightful [ˈraɪtfəl] *adj* justo; legítimo

right′-hand′ drive *s* conducción o dirección a la derecha

right-hand man *s* mano derecha, brazo derecho, persona *f* de confianza

rightist [ˈraɪtɪst] *adj & s* derechista *mf*

rightly [ˈraɪtli] *adv* derechamente; correctamente; con razón; convenientemente; **rightly or wrongly** con razón o sin ella; **rightly so** a justo título

right mind *s* entero juicio

right of asylum *s* derecho de asilo

right of way *s* derecho de tránsito o de paso, preferencia; (law) servidumbre de paso; (rr) servidumbre de vía; **to have the right of way** tener preferencia; **to yield the right of way** ceder el paso

rights of man *spl* derechos del hombre

right′-to-life′ *adj* derecho a la vida, antiabortista

right′-wing′ *adj* derechista || *s* derecha

right-winger [ˈraɪtˈwɪŋər] *s* (coll) derechista *mf*

rigid [ˈrɪdʒɪd] *adj* rígido

rigmarole [ˈrɪgməˌrol] *s* galimatías *m*

rigor [ˈrɪgər] *s* rigor *m*

rigor mortis [ˈrɪgərˈmɔrtəs] *s* rigidez cadavérica, rigor *m* mortis

rigorous [ˈrɪgərəs] *adj* riguroso

rile [raɪl] *tr* (coll) exasperar

rill [rɪl] *s* arroyuelo

rim [rɪm] *s* canto, borde *m;* (*of a wheel*) llanta; (*of a tire*) aro

rime [raɪm] *s* (*in verse*) rima; (*frost*) escarcha; **without rime or reason** sin ton ni son || *tr & intr* rimar

rind [raɪnd] *s* cáscara, corteza

ring [rɪŋ] *s* (*circular band, line, or mark*) anillo; (*for the finger*) sortija; (*for curtains; for gymnastics*) anilla; (*for nose of animal*) argolla; (*for fruit jars*) círculo de goma; (*for some sport or exhibition*) circo; (*for boxing*) cuadrilátero, ruedo; (*for bullfight*) redondel *m,* ruedo; boxeo; (*of a group of people*) corro; (*of evildoers*) pandilla; (*under the eyes*) ojera; (*of the anchor*) arganeo; (*sound of a bell, of a clock*) campanada; (*of a small bell; of the glass of glassware*) tintineo; (*to summon a person*) llamada; (*character, nature, spirit*) tono; **to be in the ring (for)** ser candidato (a); **to run rings around** dar cien vueltas a || *v* (*pret & pp* **ringed**) *tr* cercar, rodear; (*to put a ring on*) anillar || *intr* formar círculo o corro || *v* (*pret* **rang** [ræŋ]; *pp* **rung** [rʌŋ] *tr* tañer, tocar; (*to peal, ring out*) repicar; llamar al timbre; dar (*las horas la campana del reloj*); llamar por teléfono; **to ring up** llamar por teléfono; marcar (*una compra*) con el timbre || *intr* sonar (*una campana, un timbre, el teléfono*); tintinear (*el choque de copas, una campanilla*); resonar, retumbar; llamar; zumbar (*los oídos*); **to ring for** llamar, llamar al timbre; **to ring off** terminar una llamada por teléfono; **to ring up** llamar por teléfono

ring-around-a-rosy [ˈrɪŋə,raʊŋdəˈrozi] *s* juego del corro

ring finger *s* dedo anular

ringing [ˈrɪŋɪŋ] *adj* resonante, retumbante || *s* anillamiento; campaneo, repique *m;* (*of the glass of glassware*) tintineo; (*in the ears*) retintín *m,* silbido

ringʹleadʹer *s* cabecilla *m*

ringʹmasʹter *s* hombre encargado de los ejercicios ecuestres y acrobáticos de un circo

ringʹsideʹ *s* lugar junto al cuadrilátero; lugar desde el cual se puede ver de cerca

ringʹwormʹ *s* tiña

rink [rɪŋk] *s* patinadero

rinse [rɪns] *s* aclaración, enjuague *m* || *tr* aclarar, enjuagar

riot [ˈraɪ•ət] *s* alboroto, tumulto; regocijos ruidosos; (*of colors*) exhibición brillante; **to run riot** desenfrenarse; crecer lozanamente (*las plantas*) || *intr* alborotarse, amotinarse

rioter [ˈraɪ•ətər] *s* alborotador *m,* amotinado

riot squad *s* pelotón *m* de asalto

rip [rɪp] *s* rasgón *m,* siete *m;* (*open seam*) descosido || *v* (*pret & pp* **ripped;** *ger* **ripping**) *tr* desgarrar, rasgar; descoser (*lo que estaba cosido*) || *intr* desgarrarse, rasgarse; (coll) adelantar o moverse de prisa o con violencia; **to rip out with** (coll) decir con violencia

rip cord *s* cordón *m* de apertura

ripe [raɪp] *adj* maduro; acabado, hecho; dispuesto, preparado; (*boil, tumor*) madurado; (*olive*) negro

ripen [ˈraɪpən] *tr & intr* madurar

ripoff [ˈrɪp,ɔf] *s* (slang) estafa; timo

ripple [ˈrɪpəl] *s* temblor *m,* rizo; (*sound*) murmullo, susurro || *tr* rizar || *intr* rizarse; murmurar, susurrar

ripʹroarʹing *adj* (coll) animadísimo, bullicioso

rise [raɪz] *s* (*of temperature, prices, a road*) subida; (*of ground, of the voice*) elevación; (*of a heavenly body*) salida; (*of a step*) altura; (*in one's employment*) ascenso; (*of water*) crecida; (*of a source of water*) nacimiento; (*of a valve*) levantamiento; **to get a rise out of** (slang) sacar una réplica mordaz a; **to give rise to** dar origen a || *v* (*pret* **rose** [roz]; *pp* **risen** [ˈrɪzən]) *intr* subir; levantarse; salir (*un astro*); asomar (*un peligro*); brotar (*un manantial, una planta*); (*in someone's esteem*) ganar; resucitar; **to rise above** alzarse por encima de; mostrarse superior a; **to rise early** madrugar; **to rise to** ponerse a la altura de

riser [ˈraɪzər] *s* contraescalón *m,* contrahuella; **early riser** madrugador *m;* **late riser** dormilón *m*

risk [rɪsk] *s* riesgo; **to run** o **take a risk** correr riesgo, correr peligro || *tr* arriesgar; arriesgarse en (*una empresa dudosa*)

risk•y [ˈrɪski] *adj* (*comp* **-ier;** *super* **-iest**) arriesgado; riesgoso; escabroso

risqué [rɪsˈke] *adj* escabroso

rite [raɪt] *s* rito; **last rites** honras fúnebres

ritual [ˈrɪtʃʊ•əl] *adj & s* ritual *m*

riv. *abbr* **river**

ri•val [ˈraɪvəl] *s* rival *mf* || *v* (*pret & pp* **-valed** o **-valled;** *ger* **-valing** o **-valling**) *tr* rivalizar con

rival•ry [ˈraɪvəlri] *s* (*pl* **-ries**) rivalidad

river [ˈrɪvər] *s* río; **down the river** río abajo; **up the river** río arriba

rivʹer•bankʹ *s* ribera, margen *f*

river basin *s* cuenca de río

riverbed *s* cauce *m*

riverfront *s* orilla del río

rivʹer•sideʹ *adj* ribereño || *s* ribera

rivet [ˈrɪvɪt] *s* roblón *m,* remache *m;* (*e.g., to hold scissors together*) clavillo || *tr* remachar; clavar (*p.ej., los ojos en una persona*)

rm. *abbr* **ream, room**

R.N. *abbr* **registered nurse, Royal Navy**

roach [rotʃ] *s* cucaracha

road [rod] *adj* itinerario, caminero || *s* camino; (naut) rada; **to be in the road** estorbar el paso; incomodar; **to get out of the road** quitarse de en medio

roadʹbedʹ *s* (*of a highway*) firme *m;* (rr) infraestructura

roadʹblockʹ *s* (mil) barricada; (fig) obstáculo

road closed *s SIGN* carretera cerrada

road hog *s* (coll) loco del volante

roadʹhouseʹ *s* posada en el camino

road laborer *s* peón caminero

road map *s* mapa itinerario o de carreteras

road rage *s* (coll) furia de conductor, acto de enfurecimiento debido al tráfico

road service *s* auxilio en carretera

roadʹsideʹ *s* borde *m* del camino, borde de la carretera

roadside inn *s* posada en el camino

road sign *s* señal *f* de carretera, poste *m* indicador

roadʹsteadʹ *s* rada, fondeadero

roadʹwayʹ *s* camino, vía

road worker *s* peón caminero

roam [rom] *s* vagabundeo || *tr* vagar por, recorrer a la ventura || *intr* vagar, andar errante

roar [ror] *s* bramido, rugido || *intr* bramar, rugir; reírse a carcajadas

roast [rost] *s* asado; café tostado || *tr* asar; tostar (*café*); (coll) despellejar || *intr* asarse; tostarse

roast beef *s* rosbif *m,* rosbi *m & f*

roast pork *s* carne de cerdo asada

rob [rɑb] *v* (*pret & pp* **robbed;** *ger* **robbing**) *tr & intr* robar

robber [ˈrɑbər] *s* robador *m,* ladrón *m*

robber•y [ˈrɑbəri] *s* (*pl* **-ies**) robo, atraco

robe [rob] *s* manto; abrigo; (*of a woman*) traje *m,* vestido; (*of a professor, judge, etc.*) toga, túnica; (*of a priest*) traje *m* talar; (*dressing gown*) bata; (*for lap in a carriage*) manta || *tr* vestir || *intr* vestirse

Robert [ˈrabərt] *s* Roberto

robin [ˈrabɪn] *s* (*in Europe*) petirrojo; (*in North America*) primavera

robot [ˈrobat] *s* robot *m*

robotics [roˈbatɪks] *s* robótica

robust [roˈbʌst] *adj* robusto; vigoroso

rock [rak] *s* roca; (*sticking out of water*) escollo; (*one that is thrown*) piedra; (slang) diamante *m*, piedra preciosa; **on the rocks** arruinado, en pobreza extrema; (*said of hard liquor*) (coll) sobre hielo || *tr* acunar, mecer; (*to sleep*) arrullar; sacudir; **to rock to sleep** adormecer meciendo || *intr* mecerse; sacudirse || *abbr* **—rock-'n'-roll**

rock′-bot′tom *adj* (el) mínimo, (el) más bajo; **to hit** *o* **reach rockbottom** tocar fondo

rock candy *s* azúcar *m* cande

rock crystal *s* cristal *m* de roca

rocker [ˈrakər] *s* (*chair*) mecedora; (*curved piece at bottom of rocking chair or cradle*) arco; (mach) balancín *m;* (mach) eje *m* de balancín

rocket [ˈrakɪt] *s* cohete *m* || *intr* subir como un cohete

rocket bomb *s* bomba cohete

rocket launcher [lɔntʃər] *s* lanzacohetes *m*

rocket ship *s* aeronave *f* cohete

rock garden *s* jardín *m* entre rocas

rocking chair *s* mecedora, sillón *m* de hamaca

rocking horse*s* caballo mecedor

rock-′n′-roll [ˈrakənˈrol] *s* rock *m,* rocanrol *m,* rock and roll *m*

Rock of Gibraltar [dʒɪˈbrɔltər] *s* peñón *m* de Gibraltar

rock salt *s* sal *f* de compás, sal gema

rock singer *s* rockero, rockera

rock wool *s* lana mineral

rock•y [ˈraki] *adj* (*comp* **-ier;** *super* **-iest**) rocoso, roqueño; (slange) débil, poco firme

rod [rad] *s* vara; varilla; barra; (*authority*) vara alta; opresión, tiranía; (*of the retina*) bastoncillo; (*elongated microorganism*) bastoncito; (mach) vástago; (surv) jalón *m;* (Bib) linaje *m,* raza, vástago; (slang) revólver *m,* pistola; **to spare the rod** excusar la vara

rodent [ˈrodənt] *adj & s* roedor *m*

rod•man [ˈradmən] *s* (*pl* **-men** [mən]) jalonero, portamira *m*

roe [ro] *s* (*deer*) corzo; (*of fish*) hueva

Roger [ˈradʒər] *s* Rogelio || **roger** *interj* (*telecommunications*) ¡comprendido!, ¡roger!

rogue [rog] *s* bribón *m,* pícaro

rogues' gallery *s* colección de retratos de malhechores para uso de la policía

roguish [ˈrogɪʃ] *adj* bribón, pícaro; travieso, retozón

rôle o **role** [rol] *s* papel *m;* **to play a rôle** desempeñar un papel

roll [rol] *s* (*of cloth, film, paper, fat, etc.*) rollo; (*roller*) rodillo; (*cake of bread*) panecillo; (*of dice*) echada; (*of a boat*) balance *m;* (*of a drum*) redoble *m;* (*of thunder*) retumbo; bamboleo; ondulación; rol *m;* lista; (*of paper money*) fajo; **to call the roll** pasar lista || *tr* hacer rodar; empujar hacia adelante; cilindrar, laminar; (*to wrap up with rolling motion*) arrollar; alisar con rodillo; liar (*un cigarrillo*); mover de un lado a otro; poner (*los ojos*) en blanco; tocar redobles con (*el tambor*); vibrar (*la voz; la r*); **to roll back** (*wages; prices*) reducir, bajar; **to roll one's own** liárselos; **to roll up** arremangar (*p.ej., las mangas*); amontonar (*p.ej., una fortuna*) || *intr* rodar; bambolear; balancear (*un barco*); girar; retumbar (*el trueno*); redoblar (*un tambor*); **to roll around** revolcarse

roll call *s* lista, (el) pasar lista

roller [ˈrolər] *s* rodillo; (*of a piece of furniture*) ruedecilla; (*of a skate*) rueda; ola larga y creciente

roller bearing *s* cojinete *m* de rodillos

roller coaster *s* montaña rusa

roller skate *s* patín *m* de ruedas

roller towel *s* toalla sin fin

rolling blackout *s* apagon escalonado, parón cíclico

rolling mill [ˈrolɪŋ] *s* taller *m* de laminación; tren *m* de laminadores

rolling pin *s* rodillo, hataca, rulo

rolling stock *s* (rr) material *m* móvil, material rodante

rolling stone *s* piedra movediza

roll′-top′ desk *s* escritorio norteamericano, escritorio de cortina corrediza

roly-poly [ˈroliˈpoli] *adj* regordete, rechoncho

ROM [ram] *s* (acronym) (**read-only memory**) (compu) ROM *f* (memoria de acceso aleatorio)

Rom. *abbr* **Roman, Romance**

roman [ˈromən] *adj* (typ) redondo || *s* (typ) letra redonda || **Roman** *adj & s* romano

Roman candle *s* vela romana

Roman Catholic *adj & s* católico romano

romance [roˈmæns] o [ˈromæns] *s* (*tale of chivalry*) roman *m;* cuento de aventuras; cuento de amor; intriga amorosa; novela sentimental; (mus) romanza || [roˈmæns] *intr* contar o escribir romances, cuentos de aventuras o cuentos de amor; pensar o hablar de un modo romántico; exagerar, mentir || **Romance** [ˈromæns] o [roˈmæns] *adj* (*Neo-Latin*) romance o románico

romance languages *spl* lenguas romances o románicas

romance of chivalry *s* libro de caballerías

Roman Empire *s* Imperio romano

Romanesque [ˌromənˈɛsk] *adj & s* románico

Roman nose *s* nariz aguileña

Roman numeral *s* número romano

romantic [roˈmæntɪk] *adj* romántico; (*spot, place*) encantador

romanticism [roˋmæntɪ,sɪzəm] *s* romanticismo
romp [rɑmp] *intr* corretear, triscar
rompers [ˋrɑmpərz] *spl* (*for children and infants*) mameluco, pelele *m*
roof [ruf] o [rʊf] *s* (*top outer covering of a house*) tejado; (*of a car or bus*) imperial *f,* tejadillo; (*of the mouth*) paladar *m;* (*of heaven*) bóveda; (*home, dwelling*) (fig) techo; **to raise the roof** (slang) poner el grito en el cielo || *tr* techar
roofer [ˋrufər] o [ˋrʊfər] *s* techador *m,* pizarrero
roof garden *s* (*garden on the roof*) pérgola, azotea de baile y diversión
rook [rʊk] *s* (*bird*) grajo; (*in chess*) roque *m* || *tr* trampear
rookie [ˋrʊki] *s* (slang) bisoño, novato
room [rum] o [rʊm] *s* aposento, cuarto, habitación, pieza; espacio, sitio, lugar *m;* ocasión; **to make room** abrir paso, hacer lugar || *intr* alojarse
room and board *s* pensión completa
room clerk *s* empleado en la recepción, encargado de las reservas, recepcionista *mf*
roomer [ˋrumər] *s* inquilino
rooming house *s* casa donde se alquilan cuartos, pensión
room′mate′ *s* compañero de cuarto
room temperature *s* temperatura ambiente
room•y [ˋrumɪ] *adj* (*comp* **-ier;** *super* **-iest**) amplio, espacioso
roost [rust] *s* percha de gallinero; gallinero; lugar *m* de descanso; **to rule the roost** ser el amo del cotarro, tener el mando y el palo || *intr* descansar (*las aves*) en la percha; estar alojado; pasar la noche
rooster [ˋrustər] *s* gallo
root [rut] o [rʊt] *s* raíz *f;* **to get to the root of** profundizar; **to take root** echar raíces || *tr* hocicar, hozar || *intr* arraigar; **to root for** (slang) gritar alentando
rooter [ˋrutər] o [ˋrʊtər] *s* (slang) hincha *mf*
rope [rop] *s* cuerda; (*of a hangman*) dogal *m;* (*to catch an animal*) lazo; **to jump rope** saltar a la comba; **to know the ropes** (slang) saber todas las tretas; espabilarse || *tr* atar con una cuerda; coger con lazo; **to rope in** (slang) embaucar, engañar
rope ladder *s* escala de cuerda *or* de viento
rope′walk′er *s*l funámbulo, volatinero
rosa•ry [ˋrozəri] *s* (*pl* **-ries**) rosario
rose [roz] *adj* de color de rosa || *s* rosa
rose′bud′ *s* pimpollo, capullo de rosa
rose′bush′ *s* rosal *m*
rose′-col′ored *adj* rosado; **to see everything through rose-colored glasses** verlo todo de color de rosa
rose garden *s* rosaleda, rosalera
rose hip *s* (bot) cinarrodón *m;* eterio
rosemar•y [ˋroz,mɛri] *s* (*pl* **-ies**) romero
rose of Sharon [ˋʃɛrən] *s* granado blanco, rosa de Siria
rose window *s* rosetón *m*
rose′wood′ *s* palisandro
rosin [ˋrɑzɪn] *s* colofonia, brea seca
roster [ˋrɑstər] *s* catálogo, lista; horario escolar, horas de clase
rostrum [ˋrɑstrəm] *s* tribuna
ros•y [ˋrozi] *adj* (*comp* **-ier;** *super* **-iest**) rosado, sonrosado; alegre
rot [rɑt] *s* podredumbre; (slang) tontería || *v* (*pret & pp* **rotted;** *ger* **rotting**) *tr* pudrir || *intr* pudrirse
rotate [ˋrotet] o [roˋtet] *tr* hacer girar; alternar || *intr* girar; alternar
rotation [roˋteʃən] *s* rotación
rote [rot] *s* rutina, repetición maquinal; **by rote** de memoria, maquinalmente
rot′gut′ *s* (slang) matarratas *m*
rotten [ˋrɑtən] *adj* putrefacto, pútrido; corrompido
rotund [roˋtʌnd] *adj* redondo de cuerpo; (*language*) redondo
rouge [rʊʒ] *s* arrebol *m,* colorete *m* || *tr* arrebolar, pintar || *intr* arrebolarse, pintarse
rough [rʌf] *adj* áspero; (*sea*) agitado, picado, grueso; (*crude, unwrought*) tosco, grosero; aproximado; (meteor) revuelta || *tr*—**to rough it** vivir sin comodidades, hacer vida campestre
rough′cast′ *s* modelo tosco; mezcla gruesa || *v* (*pret & pp* **-cast**) *tr* (*to prepare in rough form*) bosquejar; dar a (*la pared*) una capa de mezcla gruesa
rough copy *s* borrador *m*
roughly [ˋrʌfli] *adv* asperamente; brutalmente; aproximadamente
roughshod [ˋrʌfˋʃɑd] *adv*—**to ride roughshod over** tratar sin miramientos
roulette [rʊˋlɛt] *s* ruleta
round [raʊnd] *adj* redondo, redondeado || *adv* redondamente; alrededor; de boca en boca; por todas partes || *prep* alrededor de; (*e.g., the corner*) a la vuelta de; cerca de; acá y allá en || *s* camino, circuito; (*of a policeman; of visits; of drinks or cigars*) ronda; (*of applause; discharge of guns*) salva; (*discharge of a single gun*) disparo, tiro; (*of people*) corro, círculo; (*of golf*) partido; rutina, serie *f,* sucesión; redondez *f;* revolución; (box) asalto; **to go the rounds** ir de boca en boca; ir de mano en mano || *tr* (*to make round*) redondear; cercar, rodear; doblar (*una esquina, un promontorio*); **to round off** u **out** redondear; acabar, completar, perfeccionar; **to round up** juntar, recoger; rodear (*el ganado*)
roundabout [ˋraʊndə,baʊt] *adj* indirecto, con rodeos || *s* curso indirecto; glorieta de tráfico
rounder [ˋraʊndər] *s* (coll) pródigo; (coll) catavinos *m,* borrachín habitual
round′house′ *s* cocherón *m,* casa de máquinas, depósito de locomotoras
round-shouldered [ˋraʊndʃoldərd] *adj* cargado de espaldas
Round Table *s* Tabla Redonda
round′-trip′ ticket *s* billete *m* de ida y vuelta

round′up′ *s* (*of cattle*) rodeo; (*of criminals*) redada; (*of old friends*) reunión
rouse [rauz] *tr* despertar; excitar, provocar; levantar (*la caza*) ‖ *intr* despertarse, despabilarse
rousing [ˈrauzɪŋ] *adj* (*stirring*) conmovedor m; (*applause*) caluroso, entusiasta
rout [raut] *s* derrota; fuga desordenada ‖ *tr* derrotar; poner en fuga desordenada; arrancar hozando ‖ *intr* hozar
route [rut] o [raut] *s* ruta; itinerario ‖ *tr* encaminar
routine [ruˈtin] *adj* rutinario ‖ *s* rutina
rove [rov] *intr* andar errante, vagar
row [rau] *s* (coll) camorra, pendencia, riña; (coll) alboroto, bullicio; (coll) balumba; **to raise a row** (coll) armar camorra ‖ [ro] *s* fila, hilera; (*of houses*) crujía; **in a row** seguidos, p.ej., **five hours in a row** cinco horas seguidas ‖ *intr* remar
rowboat [ˈro,bot] *s* bote *m,* bote de remos
row•dy [ˈraudi] *adj* (*comp* **-dier;** *super* **-diest**) gamberro ‖ *s* (*pl* **-dies**) gamberro
rower [ˈro•ər] *s* remero
royal [ˈrɔɪ•əl] *adj* real; (*magnificent, splendid*) regio
royal flush *s* escala o escalera real
royalist [ˈrɔɪ•əlɪst] *s* realista *mf*
royal•ty [ˈrɔɪ•əlti] *s* (*pl* **-ties**) realeza; personaje *m* real, personajes reales; derechos de autor; derechos de inventor
r.p.m. *abbr* **revolutions per minute**
R.R. *abbr* **railroad, Right Reverend**
rub [rʌb] *s* frotación, roce *m;* **there's the rub** ahí está el busilis ‖ *v* (*pret & pp* **rubbed;** *ger* **rubbing**) *tr* frotar; **to rub elbows with** rozarse mucho con; **to rub out** borrar; (slang) asesinar ‖ *intr* frotar; **to rub off** quitarse frotando; borrarse
rubber [ˈrʌbər] *s* caucho, goma; goma de borrar; chanclo, zapato de goma; (*in bridge*) robre *m;* (*condom*) (slang) globo, paracaídas *m,* forro (SAm), goma (Esp); **rubbers** (*low overshoe*) chanclos, galochas
rubber band *s* liga de goma
rubber bullet *s* bala de goma
rubber plant *s* árbol *m* del caucho
rubber plantation *s* cauchal *m*
rubber stamp *s* cajetín *m,* sello de goma; (*with a person's signature*) estampilla; (coll) persona que aprueba sin reflexionar
rub′ber-stamp′ *tr* estampar con un sello de goma; (*with a person's signature*) estampillar; (coll) aprobar sin reflexionar
rubbish [ˈrʌbɪʃ] *s* basura, desecho, desperdicios; (coll) disparate *m,* tontería
rubble [ˈrʌbəl] *s* escombros; (*broken stone*) ripio; (*masonry*) mampostería
rub′down′ *s* masaje *m,* fricción
rube [rub] *s* (slang) isidro, rústico
rubella [ruˈbɛlə] *s* rubéola, rubeola
ruble [ˈrubəl] *s* rublo
ru•by [ˈrubi] *s* (*pl* **-bies**) rubí *m*
rudder [ˈrʌdər] *s* timón *m,* gobernalle *m*
rud•dy [ˈrʌdi] *adj* (*comp* **-dier;** *super* **-diest**) coloradote, rubicundo
rude [rud] *adj* rudo; desacomodido (SAm)
rudiment [ˈrudɪmənt] *s* rudimento
rudeness [ˈrudnɪs] *s* malcriadez *f,* malacrianza
rue [ru] *tr* lamentar, arrepentirse de
rueful [ˈrufəl] *adj* lamentable; triste
ruffian [ˈrʌfɪ•ən] *s* hombre grosero y brutal
ruffle [ˈrʌfəl] *s* arruga; (*of drum*) redoble *m;* (sew) volante *m* ‖ *tr* arrugar; agitar, descomponer; enojar, molestar; confundir; redoblar (*el tambor*); (sew) fruncir un volante en, adornar o guarnecer con volante
rug [rʌg] *s* alfombra; alfombrilla; (*lap robe*) manta
rugged [ˈrʌgɪd] *adj* áspero, rugoso; recio, vigoroso; tempestuoso
ruin [ˈru•ɪn] *s* ruina ‖ *tr* arruinar; estropear; echar a perder
rule [rul] *s* regla; autoridad, mando; regla de imprenta; (*reign*) reinado; (*of a court of law*) decisión, fallo; **as a rule** por regla general; **to be the rule** ser lo que se hace ‖ *tr* gobernar, regir; dirigir, guiar; contener, reprimir; (*to mark with lines*) reglar; (law) decidir, determinar; **to rule out** excluir, rechazar ‖ *intr* gobernar, regir; prevalecer; **to rule over** gobernar, regir
rule of law *s* régimen *m* de justicia
ruler [ˈrulər] *s* gobernante *mf;* soberano; (*for ruling lines*) regla
ruling [ˈrulɪŋ] *adj* gobernante, dirigente, imperante ‖ *s* (*of a court or judge*) decisión, fallo; (*of paper*) rayado
rum [rʌm] *s* ron *m;* (*any alcoholic drink*) (U.S.A.) aguardiente *m*
Rumanian [ruˈmenɪ•ən] *adj & s* rumano
rumble [ˈrʌmbəl] *s* retumbo; (*of the intestines*) rugido; (slang) riña entre pandillas ‖ *intr* retumbar; avanzar retumbando
rumble strip *s* (aut) banda sonora
ruminate [ˈrumɪ,net] *tr & intr* rumiar
rummage [ˈrʌmɪdʒ] *tr & intr* buscar revolviéndolo todo
rummage sale *s* venta de prendas usadas
rumor [ˈrumər] *s* rumor *m;* (coll) díceres *mpl;* bolado (CAm) ‖ *tr* rumorear; **it is rumored that** se rumorea que
rump [rʌmp] *s* anca, nalga; (*cut of beef*) cuarto trasero
rumple [ˈrʌmpəl] *s* arruga ‖ *tr* arrugar, ajar, chafar ‖ *intr* arrugarse
rumpus [ˈrʌmpəs] *s* (coll) batahola, alboroto; **to raise a rumpus** (coll) armar la de San Quintín
run [rʌn] *s* carrera; clase *f,* tipo; arroyo; (*e.g., in a stocking*) carrera; (*on a bank by depositors*) asedio; (*of consecutive performances of a play*) serie *f;* (baseball & mus) carrera; **in the long run** a la larga; **on the run** a escape; en fuga desordenada; **the common run of people** el común de las gentes; **the general run of** la generalidad de; **to have a long run** per-

manecer en cartel durante mucho tiempo; **to have the run of** hallar el secreto de; tener libertad de ir y venir por || *v* (*pret* **ran** [ræn]; *pp* **run;** *ger* **running**) *tr* hacer funcionar; dirigir, manejar; trazar, tirar (*una línea*); exhibir (*un cine*); hacer (*mandados*); tener como candidato; burlar, violar (*un bloqueo*); tener (*calentura*); correr (*un caballo; un riesgo*); (compu) desplegar, correr, ejecutar; **to run down** cazar y matar; derribar; atropellar (*a un peatón*); (coll) denigrar, desacreditar; **to run in** rodar (*un nuevo coche*); **to run off** tocar (*una pieza de música*); tirar, imprimir; **to run up** (coll) aumentar (*gastos*) || *intr* correr; (*on wheels*) rodar; darse prisa; trepar (*la vid*); ir y venir (*un vapor*); supurar (*una llaga*); colar (*un líquido*); correrse (*un color o tinte*); presentar su candidatura; andar, funcionar, marchar; deshilarse (*las medias*); migrar (*los peces*); estar en fuerza; (*to be worded or written*) rezar; **to run across** dar con, tropezar con; **to run away** correr, huir; desbocarse (*un caballo*); **to run down** escurrir, gotear (*un líquido*); descargarse (*un acumulador*); distenderse (*el muelle de un reloj*); acabarse la cuerda, p.ej., **the watch ran down** se acabó la cuerda; **to run for** presentar su candidatura a; **to run in the family** venir de familia; **to run into** tropezar con; chocar con, topar con; **to run off the track** descarrilar (*un tren*); **to run out** salir; expirar, terminar; acabarse; agotarse; **to run out of** acabársele a uno, e.g., **I have run out of money** se me ha acabado el dinero; **to run over** atropellar (*a un peatón*); registrar a la ligera; pasar por encima; leer rápidamente; rebosar (*un líquido*); **to run through** disipar rápidamente (*una fortuna*); registrar a la ligera; estar difundido en

run'a•way' *adj* fugitivo; (*horse*) desbocado || *s* fugitivo; caballo desbocado; fuga

run'-down' *adj* desmedrado; desmantelado; inculto; (*clock spring*) sin cuerda, distendido; (*storage battery*) descargado

rung [rʌŋ] *s* (*of ladder or chair*) travesaño; (*of wheel*) radio, rayo

runner [ˈrʌnər] *s* corredor *m;* caballo de carreras; mensajero; (*of an ice skate*) cuchilla; (*of a sleigh*) patín *m;* (*long narrow rug*) pasacaminos *m;* (*strip of cloth for table top*) tapete *m;* (*in stockings*) carrera

run'ner-up' *s* (*pl* **runners-up**) subcampeón *m*

running [ˈrʌnɪŋ] *adj* corredor; (*expenses; water*) corriente; (*knot*) corredizo; (*sore*) supurante; (*writing*) cursivo; continuo; consecutivo; en marcha; (*start*) (*sport*) lanzado || *s* carrera, corrida; administración, dirección; marcha, funcionamiento; **to be in the running** tener esperanzas o posibilidades de ganar

running board *s* estribo

running head *s* titulillo

running start *s* (*sport*) salida lanzada

run'off e•lec'tion *s* votación de desempate

run-of-mine coal [ˈrʌnəvˈmaɪn] *s* carbón *m* tal como sale

run'-of-the-mill' *adj* (coll) ordinario; mediocre

run'proof' *adj* indesmallable

runt [rʌnt] *s* enano, hombrecillo; (*little child*) redrojo; animal achaparrado

run'time' *s* (compu) tiempo de ejecución

run'way' *s* (*of a stream*) cauce *m;* senda trillada; (aer) pista de aterrizaje

rupture [ˈrʌptʃər] *s* ruptura; (*pathol*) quebradura; (*break in relations*) ruptura || *tr* romper; causar una hernia en || *intr* romperse; padecer hernia

rural free delivery [ˈrʊrəl] *s* distribución gratuita del correo en el campo

rural police *s* guardia civil

rural policeman *s* guardia civil *m*

ruse [ruz] *s* astucia, artimaña

rush [rʌʃ] *adj* urgente || *s* prisa grande, precipitación; agolpamiento de gente; (bot) junco; **in a rush** de prisa || *tr* empujar con violencia o prisa; despachar con prontitud; (slang) cortejar insistentemente (*a una mujer*); **to rush through** ejecutar de prisa, despachar rápidamente; expediar || *intr* lanzarse, precipitarse; venir de prisa, ir de prisa; actuar con prontitud; **to rush through** lanzarse a través de, lanzarse por entre

rush-bottomed chair [ˈrʌʃbɑtəmd] *s* silla de junco

rush hour *s* hora de aglomeración, horas de punta, horas de afluencia

rush'light' *s* mariposa, lamparilla

rush order *s* pedido urgente

russet [ˈrʌsɪt] *adj* canelo

Russia [ˈrʌʃə] *s* Rusia

Russian [ˈrʌʃən] *adj & s* ruso

rust [rʌst] *s* orín *m,* moho, herrumbre; (agr) roña, roya; color rojizo o anaranjado || *tr* aherrumbrar || *intr* aherrumbrarse

rustic [ˈrʌstɪk] *adj* rústico; sencillo, sin artificio || *s* rústico

rustle [ˈrʌsəl] *s* susurro, crujido || *tr* hacer susurrar, hacer crujir; hurtar (*ganado*) || *intr* susurrar, crujir; (slang) trabajar con ahinco

rustler [ˈrʌslər] *s* ladrón *m* de ganado, cuatrero

rusty [ˈrʌsti] *adj* (*comp* **-ier;** *super* **-iest**) herrumbroso, mohoso; rojizo; (*out of practice*) empolvado, desusado, remoto

rut [rʌt] *s* (*track, groove in road*) rodada, bache *m;* hábito arraigado; (*sexual excitement in animals*) celo; (*period of this excitement*) brama

ruthless [ˈruθlɪs] *adj* despiadado, cruel

Ry. *abbr* **railway**

rye [raɪ] *s* centeno; whisky de centeno

S

S, s [ɛs] decimonona letra del alfabeto inglés
Sabbath [ˈsæbəθ] *s* dia de la oración del descanso; (*Saturday*) sábado; (*Sunday*) domingo; descanso dominical; (*Friday*) viernes *m*
sabbatical [səˈbætɪkəl] *adj* sabático ‖ *s* año *or* período sabático; **to go on sabbatical** tomarse un año sabático
saber [ˈsebər] *s* sable *m*
saber rattling *s* ruido de sables
sable [ˈsebəl] *adj* negro ‖ *s* marta cebellina; **sables** vestidos de luto
sabotage [ˈsæbə,tɑʒ] *s* sabotaje *m* ‖ *tr & intr* sabotear
saccharin [ˈsækərɪn] *s* sacarina
sachet [ˈsæʃe] o [sæˈʃe] *s* polvo oloroso; saquito de perfumes
sack [sæk] *s* saco; vino blanco generoso; (mil) saqueo, saco; (*of an employee*) (slang) despedida ‖ *tr* ensacar; saquear, pillar; (coll) despedir (*a un empleado*)
sack'cloth' *s* harpillera; (*worn for penitence*) cilicio
sacrament [ˈsækrəmənt] *s* sacramento
sacred [ˈsekrəd] *adj* sagrado
sacred cow *s* (fig) vaca sagrada
sacrifice [ˈsækrɪ,faɪs] *s* sacrificio; **at a sacrifice** con pérdida ‖ *tr* sacrificar; (*to sell at a loss*) malvender ‖ *intr* sacrificar; sacrificarse
Sacrifice of the Mass *s* sacrificio del altar
sacrilege [ˈsækrɪlɪdʒ] *s* sacrilegio
sacrilegious [,sækrɪˈlɪdʒəs] o [,sækrɪˈlidʒəs] *adj* sacrílego
sacristan [ˈsækrɪstən] *s* sacristán *m*
sacris•ty [ˈsækrɪsti] *s* (*pl* **-ties**) sacristía
sad [sæd] *adj* (*comp* **sadder;** *super* **saddest**) triste; (slang) malo
sadden [ˈsædən] *tr* entristecer ‖ *intr* entristecerse
saddle [ˈsædəl] *s* silla de montar; (*of a bicycle*) sillín *m* ‖ *tr* ensillar; **to saddle with** echar a cuestas a ‖ *intr* montar en la silla; **to saddle up** ensillar
sad'dle•bags' *spl* alforjas
sad'dle•bow' [,bo] *s* arzón delantero
sad'dle•tree' *s* arzón *m*
sadist [ˈsædɪst] *s* sádico
sadistic [ˈsæˈdɪstɪk] *adj* sádico
sadness [ˈsædnɪs] *s* tristeza
safe [sef] *adj* seguro, ileso, salvo; cierto, digno de confianza; sin peligro, a salvo; **safe and sound** sano y salvo; **safe from** a salvo de ‖ *s* caja fuerte, caja de caudales
safe'-con'duct *s* salvoconducto
safe'-crack'er *s* ladrón *m* de cajas de caudales
safe'-depos'it box *s* caja de seguridad
safe'guard' *s* salvaguardia, medida de seguridad ‖ *tr* salvaguardar
safe house *s* piso franco, (Arg, Urug) enterradero
safely [ˈsefli] *adv* sano y salvo, sin peligro, (*driving*) con cuidado; (*with certainty*) con toda seguridad
safe•ty [ˈsefti] *adj* de seguridad ‖ *s* (*pl* **-ties**) seguridad; **to parachute to safety** lanzarse en paracaídas; **to reach safety** ponerse a salvo, llegar a lugar seguro
safety belt *s* (aer, aut) correa de seguridad, cinturón *m* de seguridad; (naut) cinturón *m* salvavidas; **retractable safety belt** cinturón *m* retráctil
safety match *s* fósforo de seguridad
safety pin *s* imperdible *m*, alfiler *m* de seguridad, gacilla, gancho de nodriza (Col)
safety rail *s* guardarriel *m*
safety razor *s* maquinilla de seguridad
safety valve *s* válvula de seguridad
safety zone *s* (*for pedestrians*) isla de peatones o de seguridad
saffron [ˈsæfrən] *adj* azafranado ‖ *s* azafrán *m* ‖ *tr* azafranar
sag [sæg] *s* comba, combadura; (*e.g., of a cable*) flecha ‖ *v* (*pret & pp* **sagged;** *ger* **sagging**) *intr* combarse; (*to slacken, yield*) aflojar, ceder, doblegarse; bajar (*los precios*)
sagacious [səˈgeʃəs] *adj* sagaz
sage [ˈsedʒ] *adj* sabio, cuerdo ‖ *s* sabio; (bot) salvia; (bot) artemisa
sage'brush' *s* (bot) artemisa
Sagittarius [,sædʒəˈtɛri•əs] *s* (astr) Sagitario
sail [sel] *s* vela; barco de vela; paseo en barco de vela; **to set sail** hacerse a la vela; **under full sail** a vela llena ‖ *tr* gobernar (*un barco de vela*); navegar (*un mar, río, etc.*) ‖ *intr* navegar, navegar a la vela; salir, salir de viaje; deslizarse, flotar, volar; **to sail into** (slang) atacar, regañar, reñir
sail'boat' *s* barco de vela, buque *m* de vela, velero
sail'board' *s* plancha de vela
sail'cloth' *s* lona, paño
sailing [ˈselɪŋ] *adj* de salida ‖ *s* paseo en barco de vela; navegación a vela; salida
sailing vessel *s* buque velero
sailor [ˈselər] *s* (*one who makes a living sailing*) marinero; (*an enlisted man in the navy*) marino
saint [sent] *adj & s* santo ‖ *tr* (coll) canonizar
saintliness [ˈsentlɪnɪs] *s* santidad
Saint Vitus's dance [ˈvaɪtəsəs] *s* (pathol) baile *m* de San Vito
sake [sek] *s* respeto, bien, amor *m;* **for his sake** por su bien; **for the sake of** por, por motivo de, por amor a; **for your own sake** por su propio bien
salaam [səˈlɑm] *s* zalema ‖ *tr* saludar con zalemas, hacer zalemas a
salable [ˈseləbəl] *adj* vendible
salad [ˈsæləd] *s* ensalada
salad bowl *s* ensaladera
salad oil *s* aceite *m* de comer
salaried [ˈsælərid] *adj* a sueldo

sala•ry [ˈsæləri] *s* (*pl* **-ries**) sueldo
sale [sel] *s* venta; (*auction*) almoneda, subasta; **for sale** de venta; se vende(n)
sales'clerk' *s* dependiente *mf* de tienda, vendedor, vendedora
sales exhibit *s* exhibición-venta, exposición-venta
sales•man [ˈselzmən] *s* (*pl* **-men** [mən]) vendedor *m,* dependiente *m* de tienda
sales manager *s* gerente *m* o jefe *m* de ventas
sales'man•ship' *s* arte de vender
sales outlet *s* boca de expendio
sales representative vendedor, vendedora; promotor *m* comercial, promotor de ventas
sales'room' *s* salón *m* de ventas; salón de exhibición
sales talk *s* argumento para inducir a comprar
sales tax *s* impuesto sobre ventas
sales•woman [ˈselzwʊmən] *s* (*pl* **-women** [ˈwɪmɪn]) vendedora, dependiente *f* de tienda
saliva [səˈlaɪvə] *s* saliva
sallow [ˈsælo] *adj* cetrino
sal•ly [ˈsæli] *s* (*pl* **-lies**) paseo, viaje *m;* ímpetu *m,* arranque *m;* salida, ocurrencia; (mil) salida, surtida || *v,* (*pret & pp* **-lied**) *intr* salir, hacer una salida; ir de paseo; **to sally forth** salir, avanzar con denuedo
salmon [ˈsæmən] *s* salmón *m*
salon [sæˈlɑn] *s* salón *m*
saloon [səˈlun] *s* bar *m,* taberna; (*lounge*) salón *m,* sala
salt [sɔlt] *s* sal *f;* **to be not worth one's salt** no valer (*uno*) el pan que come || *tr* salar; (*to preserve with salt*) salpresar; marinar (*el pescado*); salgar (*al ganado*); **to salt away** (slang) ahorrar, guardar para uso futuro
salt'cel'lar *s* salero
salted peanuts *spl* saladillos
saltine [sɔlˈtin] *s* galletita salada
saltish [ˈsɔltɪʃ] *adj* salobre
salt lick *s* salero, lamedero
salt of the earth, the lo mejor del mundo
salt'pe'ter *s* (*potassium nitrate*) salitre *m;* (*sodium nitrate*) nitro de Chile
salt'sha'ker *s* salero
salt•y [ˈsɔlti] *adj* (*comp* **-ier;** *super* **-iest**) salado
salubrious [səˈlubrɪ•əs] *adj* salubre
salutation [ˌsæljəˈteʃən] *s* salutación
salute [səˈlut] *s* saludo || *tr* saludar
Salvadoran [ˌsælvəˈdorən] o **Salvadorian** [ˌsælvəˈdorɪ•ən] *adj & s* salvadoreño
salvage [ˈsælvɪdʒ] *s* salvamento || *tr* salvar; recobrar
Salvation Army [sælˈveʃən] *s* Ejército de Salvación
salve [sæv] o [sɑv] *s* ungüento || *tr* curar con ungüento; preservar; aliviar
sal•vo [ˈsælvo] *s* (*pl* **-vos** o **-voes**) salva
Samaritan [səˈmærɪtən] *adj & s* samaritano
same [sem] *adj & pron indef* mismo; **it's all the same to me** lo mismo me da; **just the same** lo mismo, sin embargo; **same . . . as** mismo . . . que
samite [ˈsæmaɪt] o [ˈsemaɪt] *s* jamete *m*
sample [ˈsæmpəl] *s* muestra || *tr* catar, probar
sample copy *s* ejemplar *m* muestra
sample home *s* casa modelo
sancti•fy [ˈsæŋktɪˌfaɪ] *v* (*pret & pp* **-fied**) *tr* santificar
sanctimonious [ˌsæŋktɪˈmonɪ•əs] *adj* santurrón
sanction [ˈsæŋkʃən] *s* sanción || *tr* sancionar
sanctuar•y [ˈsæŋktʃʊˌɛri] *s* (*pl* **-ies**) santuario; asilo, refugio; **to take sanctuary** acogerse a sagrado
sand [sænd] *s* arena || *tr* enarenar; lijar con papel de lija
sandal [ˈsændəl] *s* sandalia; cacle *m* (Mex)
san'dal•wood' *s* (bot) sándalo
sand'bag' *s* saco de arena, saco terreno || *tr* proteger con sacos de arena; (*bully*) (coll) forzar, obligar; (*deceive*) (slang) no estar jugando a tope, engañar, ocultar
sand'bank' *s* banco de arena
sand bar *s* barra de arena
sand'blast' *s* chorro de arena || *tr* limpiar con chorro de arena
sand'box' *s* (rr) arenero
sand dune *s* duna, médano
sand'glass' *s* reloj *m* de arena, ampolleta
sand'pa'per *s* papel *m* de lija || *tr* lijar
sand'stone' *s* piedra arenisca
sand'storm' *s* tempestad de arena
sandwich [ˈsændwɪtʃ] *s* emparedado, sandwich *m,* sándwich, sándwiche *m* || *tr* intercalar
sandwich man *s* hombre-anuncio
sand•y [ˈsændi] *adj* (*comp* **-ier;** *super* **-iest**) arenoso; (*hair*) rufo; cambiante, movible
sane [sen] *adj* cuerdo, sensato; (*principles*) sano
sanguinary [ˈsæŋgwɪnˌɛri] *adj* sanguinario
sanguine [ˈsæŋgwɪn] *adj* confiado, esperanzado; (*countenance*) coloradote
sanitary [ˈsænɪˌtɛri] *adj* sanitario
sanitary napkin *s* compresa, toalla o paño higiénico
sanitation [ˌsænɪˈteʃən] *s* (*sanitary measures*) sanidad; (*drainage*) saneamiento
sanity [ˈsænɪti] *s* cordura, sensatez *f*
Santa Claus [ˈsæntəˌklɔz] *s* el Papá Noel, San Nicolás
sap [sæp] *s* savia; (mil) zapa; (coll) necio, tonto || *v* (*pret & pp* **sapped;** *ger* **sapping**) *tr* agotar, debilitar; zapar, socavar
sap'head' *s* (coll) cabeza de chorlito
sapling [ˈsæplɪŋ] *s* árbol *m* muy joven, pimpollo; jovenzuelo, mozuelo
sapphire [ˈsæfaɪr] *s* zafiro
saraband [ˈsærəˌbænd] *s* zarabanda
Saracen [ˈsærəsən] *adj & s* sarraceno
Saragossa [ˌsærəˈgɑsə] *s* Zaragoza
Sarah [ˈsɛrɑ], [ˈsærɑ] *f* Sara
sarcasm [ˈsɑrkæzəm] *s* sarcasmo, sorna; escopetazo (SAm)
sarcastic [sɑrˈkæstɪk] *adj* sarcástico
sardine [sɑrˈdin] *s* sardina; **packed in like sardines** como sardinas en banasta o en lata
Sardinia [sɑrˈdɪnɪ•ə] *s* Cerdeña

Sardinian [sɑrˈdɪnɪ•ən] *adj & s* sardo
sarsaparilla [ˌsɑrsəpəˈrɪlə] *s* zarzaparrilla
sash [sæʃ] *s* banda, faja; (*of a window*) marco
sash window *s* ventana de guillotina
sas•sy [ˈsæsi] *adj* (*comp* **-sier;** *super* **-siest**) (coll) descarado, fresco; (*jazzy*) (coll) llamativo y atrevido
satchel [ˈsætʃəl] *s* maletín *m;* (*of a schoolboy*) cartapacio
sateen [sæˈtin] *s* satén *m*
satellite [ˈsætəˌlaɪt] *s* satélite *m*
satellite country *s* país *m* satélite
satellite dish *s* antena parabólica
satiate [ˈseʃiˌet] *adj* ahito, harto ‖ *tr* saciar
satin [ˈsætən] *s* raso
satinet [ˌsætɪˈnɛt] *s* rasete *m*
satiric(al) [səˈtɪrɪk(əl)] *adj* satírico
satirist [ˈsætɪrɪst] *s* satírico
satirize [ˈsætɪˌraɪz] *tr & intr* satirizar
satisfaction [ˌsætɪsˈfækʃən] *s* satisfacción
satisfactory [ˌsætɪsˈfæktəri] *adj* satisfactorio
satis•fy [ˈsætɪsˌfaɪ] *v* (*pret & pp* **-ified**) *tr & intr* satisfacer
saturate [ˈsætʃəˌret] *tr* saturar
Saturday [ˈsætərdi] *s* sábado
Saturn [ˈsætərn] *s* (astr, myth) Saturno
sauce [sɔs] *s* salsa; moje *f,* mojete *m;* (*of fruit*) compota; (*of chocolate*) crema; gracia, viveza; (coll) insolencia, lenguaje descomedido ‖ *tr* condimentar ‖ [sɔs] o [sæs] *tr* (coll) ser respondón con
sauce'pan' *s* cacerola
saucer [ˈsɔsər] *s* platillo
sau•cy [ˈsɔsi] *adj* (*comp* **-cier;** *super* **-ciest**) descarado, insolente; gracioso, vivo
sauerkraut [ˈsaʊrˌkraʊt] *s* chucruta
saunter [ˈsɔntər] *s* paseo tranquilo y alegre ‖ *intr* dar un paseo tranquilo y alegre; pasear tranquila y alegremente
sausage [ˈsɔsɪdʒ] *s* salchicha, embutido; moronga (Mex)
savage [ˈsævidʒ] *adj & s* salvaje, *mf*
savant [ˈsævənt] *s* sabio, erudito
save [sev] *prep* salvo, excepto, menos ‖ *tr* salvar (*p.ej., una vida, un alma*); ahorrar (*dinero*); conservar, guardar, horrar; proteger, amparar; **God save the Queen!** ¡Dios guarde a la Reina!; **to save face** salvar las apariencias
saving [ˈseviŋ] *prep,* salvo, excepto; con el debido respeto a ‖ *adj* económico ‖ **savings** *spl* ahorros, economías
savings account *s* cuenta de ahorros
savings and loan (institution) *s* sociedad de crédito hipotecario, sociedad de ahorro y préstamos
savings bank *s* banco de ahorros, caja de ahorros
savior [ˈsevjər] *s* salvador *m*
Saviour [ˈsevjər] *s* Salvador *m*
savor [ˈsevər] *s* sabor *m* ‖ *tr* saborear ‖ *intr* oler; **to savor of** oler a, saber a
savor•y [ˈsevəri] *adj* (*comp* **-ier;** *super* **-iest**) sabroso; picante; fragante ‖ *s* (*pl* **-ies**) (bot) ajedrea
saw [sɔ] *s* (*tool*) sierra; proverbio, refrán *m* ‖ *tr* aserrar, serrar
saw'buck' *s* cabrilla, caballete *m*
saw'dust' *s* aserrín *m,* serrín *m*
saw'horse' *s* cabrilla, caballete *m*
saw'mill' *s* aserradero, serrería; montero (Mex)
Saxon [ˈsæksən] *adj & s* sajón *m*
saxophone [ˈsæksəˌfon] *s* saxofón *m*
say [se] *s* decir *m;* **to have one's say** decir su parecer ‖ *v* (*pret & pp* **said** [sɛd] *tr* decir; **I should say so!** ¡ya lo creo!; **it is said** se dice; **no sooner said than done** dicho y hecho; **that is to say** es decir, esto es; **to go without saying** caerse de su peso
saying [ˈse•ɪŋ] *s* dicho; proverbio, refrán *m;* **sayings** (*rumor*) díceres *mpl*
sc. *abbr* **scene, science, scruple, scilicet** (Lat) **namely**
scab [skæb] *s* (*of wound*) costra, postilla; (*strikebreaker*) (pej) esquirol *m,* rompehuelgas *mf;* (*rascal*) (slang) bribón *m,* golfo
scabbard [ˈskæbərd] *s* funda, vaina
scab•by [ˈskæbi] *adj* (*comp* **-bier;** *super* **-biest**) costroso; (coll) ruin, vil
scabies [ˈskebiz] *s* sarna
scabrous [ˈskæbrəs] *adj* escabroso
scads [skædz] *spl* (slang) montones *mpl*
scaffold [ˈskæfəld] *s* andamio; (*to execute a criminal*) cadalso, patíbulo
scaffolding [ˈskæfəldɪŋ] *s* andamiaje *m*
scald [skɔld] *tr* escaldar
scale [skel] *s* escama; balanza; platillo de balanza; (*e.g., of a map*) escala; (mus) escala; **on a scale of** en escala de; **on a large scale** en grande escala; **scales** balanza ‖ *tr* escamer; descortezar, descostrar; escalar, subir, trepar; graduar ‖ *intr* descamarse; descortezarse, descostrarse; subir, trepar
scallop [ˈskɑləp] o [ˈskæləp] *s* concha de peregrino, vieira; (*shell or dish for serving fish*) concha, venera; (*thin slice of meat*) escalope *m;* (*on edge of cloth*) festón ‖ *tr* cocer (*p.ej., ostras*) en su concha; festonear
scalp [skælp] *s* cuero cabelludo ‖ *tr* escalpar; comprar y revender (*entradas*) a precios extraoficiales
scalpel [ˈskælpəl] *s* escalpelo
scal•y [ˈskeli] *adj* (*comp* **-ier;** *super* **-iest**) escamoso
scamp [skæmp] *s* bribón *m,* golfo
scamper [ˈskæmpər] *intr* escaparse precipitadamente; **to scamper away** escaparse precipitadamente
scan [skæn] *s* (astr, compu, mil) exploración; (med) escáner *m,* scanner *m,* escanograma *m;* (*ultrasound*) ecografía ‖ *v* (*pret & pp* **scanned;** *ger* **scanning**) *tr* escudriñar; escandir (*versos*); (astr, compu, mil, telv) explorar; (med) hacer un escáner (*or* un scanner o una ecografía) de; (compu) escanear; (coll) dar un vistazo a

scandal [ˈskændəl] *s* escándalo
scandalize [ˈskændəˌlaɪz] *tr* escandalizar
scandalous [ˈskændələs] *adj* escandaloso
Scandinavian [ˌskændɪˈnevɪ•ən] *adj & s* escandinavo
scanner [ˈskænər] *s* (compu) analizador *m* de léxico, explorador *m;* (med) escáner *m,* scanner *m,* escanógrafo; (*ultrasound*) ecógrafo
scanning [ˈskænɪŋ] *s* (telv) escansión, exploración
scansion [ˈskænʃən] *s* escansión
scant [skænt] *adj* escaso, insuficiente; solo, apenas suficiente ‖ *tr* escatimar
scant•y [ˈskænti] *adj* (*comp* **-ier;** *super* **-iest**) escaso, insuficiente, poco suficiente; (*clothing*) ligero
scape′goat′ *s* cabeza de turco, víctima propiciatoria, chivo expiatorio *or* emisario
scar [skɑr] *s* cicatriz *f,* señal *f,* lacra ‖ *v* (*pret & pp* **scarred;** *ger* **scarring**) *tr* señalar, marcar ‖ *intr* cicatrizarse
scarce [skɛrs] *adj* escaso, raro; **to make oneself scarce** (coll) no dejarse ver
scarcely [ˈskɛrsli] *adv* apenas; probablemente no; ciertamente no; **scarcely ever** raramente
scarci•ty [ˈskɛrsɪti] *s* (*pl* **-ties**) escasez *f,* carestía
scare [skɛr] *s* susto, alarma ‖ *tr* asustar, espantar; **to scare away** espantar, ahuyentar; **to scare up** (coll) juntar, recoger (*dinero*)
scare′crow′ *s* espantajo, espantapájaros *m*
scarf [skɑrf] *s* (*pl* **scarfs** o **scarves** [skɑrvz]) bufanda; pañuelo para el cuello; (*cover for a table, bureau, etc.*) tapete *m;* corbata
scarf′pin′ *s* alfiler *m* de corbata
scarlet [ˈskɑrlɪt] *adj* escarlata
scarlet fever *s* escarlata
scar•y [ˈskɛri] *adj* (*comp* **-ier;** *super* **-iest**) (*easily frightened*) (coll) asustadizo, espantadizo; (*causing fright*) (coll) espantoso
scathing [ˈskeðɪŋ] *adj* acerbo, duro
scatter [ˈskætər] *tr* esparcir, dispersar ‖ *intr* esparcirse, dispersarse
scatterbrain [ˈskætərˌbren] *s* (coll) farraquista *m*
scatterbrained *adj* (coll) alegre de cascos, casquivano
scattered showers *spl* lluvias aisladas
scavenge [ˈskævəndʒ] *intr* escarbar, hurgar
scenari•o [sɪˈnɛrɪˌo] o [sɪˈnɑrɪˌo] *s* (*pls* **-os**) guión *m,* escenario
scenarist [sɪˈnɛrɪst] o [sɪˈnɑrɪst] *s* guionista *mf,* escenarista *mf*
scene [sin] *s* (*view*) paisaje *m;* (*in literature, art, the theater, the movie*) escena; escándalo, demostración de pasión; **behind the scenes** entre bastidores; **to make a scene** causar escándalo
scener•y [ˈsinəri] *s* (*pl* **-ies**) paisaje *m;* (theat) decoraciones
scenic [ˈsinɪk] o [ˈsɛnɪk] *adj* pintoresco; (*representing an action graphically*) gráfico; (*pertaining to the stage*) escénico
scent [sɛnt] *s* olor *m;* perfume *m;* (*sense of smell*) olfato; (*trail*) rastro, pista ‖ *tr* oler; perfumar; olfatear, ventear; sospechar
scepter [ˈsɛptər] *s* cetro
sceptic [ˈskɛptɪk] *adj & s* escéptico
sceptical [ˈskɛptɪkəl] *adj* escéptico
schedule [ˈskɛdjʊl] *s* catálogo, cuadro, lista; plan *m,* programa *m;* (*of trains, planes, etc.*) horario ‖ *tr* catalogar; proyectar; fijar la hora de
scheduled flight *s* vuelo regular
scheme [skim] *s* esquema *m;* plan *m,* proyecto; (*trick*) ardid *m,* treta; (*plot*) intriga, trama ‖ *tr & intr* proyectar; tramar
schemer [ˈskimər] *s* proyectista *mf;* intrigante *mf*
scheming [ˈskimɪŋ] *adj* astuto, mañoso, intrigante ‖ *s* intriga
schism [ˈsɪzəm] *s* cisma *m;* facción cismática
schist [ʃist] *s* esquisto
schizophrenia [ˌskɪtzəˈfrini•ə] *s* esquizofrenia
scholar [ˈskɑlər] *s* (*pupil*) alumno; (*scholarship holder*) becario; (*learned person*) sabio, erudito
scholarly [ˈskɑkərli] *adj* sabio, erudito
scholarship [ˈskɑlərˌʃip] *s* erudición; (*grant to study*) beca
scholarship holder *s* bequista *mf* (CAm, Cuba)
school [skul] *s* escuela; (*of a university*) facultad; (*of fish*) banco, cardume *m;* **school of languages** academia de idiomas ‖ *tr* enseñar, instruir, disciplinar
school age *s* edad escolar
school attendance *s* escolaridad
school board *s* junta de instrucción pública, consejo escolar
school′boy′ *s* alumno de escuela
school day *s* día lectivo
school′girl′ *s* alumna de escuela
school′house′ *s* escuela
schooling [ˈskulɪŋ] *s* instrucción, enseñanza; experiencia
school′mate′ *s* compañero de escuela
school′room′ *s* aula, sala de clase
school′teach′er *s* maestro de escuela
school year *s* año lectivo
schooner [ˈskunər] *s* goleta
sci. *abbr* **science, scientific**
science [ˈsaɪ•əns] *s* ciencia
science fiction *s* ciencia-ficción; novela científica
scientific [ˌsaɪ•ənˈtɪfɪk] *adj* científico
scientist [ˈsaɪ•əntɪst] *s* científico, sabio, hombre *m* de ciencia
sci-fi [ˈsaɪˈfaɪ] *s* (slang) *abbr* **science fiction**
scil. *abbr* **scilicet** (Lat) **namely**
scimitar [ˈsɪmɪtər] *s* cimitarra
scintillate [ˈsɪntɪˌlet] *intr* chispear, centellear
scion [ˈsaɪ•ən] *s* vástago
scissors [ˈsɪzərz] *ssg* o *spl* tijeras
scoff [skɔf] o [skɑf] *s* burla, mofa ‖ *intr* burlarse, mofarse; **to scoff at** burlarse de, mofarse de
scold [skold] *s* regañón *m,* regañona ‖ *tr & intr* regañar

scoop [skup] *s* (*instrument like a spoon*) cuchara, cucharón *m;* (*tool like a shovel*) pala; (*kitchen utensil*) paleta; (*for water*) achicador *m;* cucharada, palada, paletada; (*hollow made by a scoop*) hueco; (*big haul*) (coll) buena ganancia || *tr* sacar con cuchara, pala, paleta; achicar (*agua*); **to scoop out** ahuecar, vaciar

scoot [skut] *s* (coll) carrera precipitada || *intr* (coll) correr precipitadamente

scooter [ˈskutər] *s* monopatín *m,* patinete *m*

scope [skop] *s* alcance *m,* extensión; campo, espacio; **to give free scope to** dar campo libre a

scorch [skɔrtʃ] *s* chamusco || *tr* chamuscar; (*to dry wither*) abrasar; criticar acerbamente || *intr* chamuscarse; abrasarse

scorching [ˈskɔrtʃɪŋ] *adj* abrasador; acerbo, duro, mordaz

score [skor] *s* (*in a game*) cuenta, tantos; (*in an examination*) nota; entalladura, muesca; línea, raya; (*twenty*) veintena; (mus) partitura; **on the score of** a título de; **to keep score** apuntar los tantos || *tr* anotar (*los tantos*); ganar, tantear (*tantos*); rayar, señalar; regañar acerbamente; (mus) instrumentar || *intr* ganar tantos; marcar los tantos

scoreboard *s* marcador *m,* cuadro indicador

scorn [skɔrn] *s* desdén *m,* desprecio || *tr & intr* desdeñar, despreciar; **to scorn to** no dignarse

scornful[ˈskɔrnfəl] *adj* desdeñoso

Scorpio [ˈskɔrpɪ•o] *s* (astr) Escorpión *m*

scorpion [ˈskɔrpɪ•ən] *s* alacrán *m,* escorpión *m*

Scot [skɑt] *s* escocés *m*

Scotch [skɑtʃ] *adj* escocés; (coll) frugal; (*stingy*) tacaño || *s* (*dialect*) escocés *m;* whiskey *m* escocés; **the Scotch** los escoceses

scotch [skɑtʃ] *tr* frustrar; (*rumors*) poner fin a

Scotch•man [ˈskɑtʃmən] *s* (*pl* **-men** [mən]) escocés *m*

Scotch tape[T] *s* cinta durex[T], huincha adhesiva

scot′-free′ *adj* sin pagar; impune, sin castigo; (*unhurt*) ileso

Scotland [ˈskɑtlənd] *s* Escocia

Scottish [ˈskɑtɪʃ] *adj* escocés || *s* (*dialect*) escocés *m;* **the Scottish** los escoceses

scoundrel [ˈskaʊndrəl] *s* bribón *m,* pícaro

scour [skaʊr] *tr* fregar, estregar; recorrer, explorar detenidamente

scourge [skʌrdʒ] *s* azote *m* || *tr* azotar

scout [skaʊt] *s* (mil) escucha, explorador *m;* niño explorador, niña exploradora; exploración, reconocimiento; (slang) individuo, sujeto, tipo || *tr* explorar, reconocer (*un territorio*); observar (*al enemigo*); negarse a creer

scout′mas′ter *s* jefe *m* de tropa de niños exploradores

scowl [skaʊl] *s* ceño, semblante ceñudo || *intr* mirar con ceño, poner mal gesto, poner mala cara

scramble [ˈskræmbəl] *s* arrebatiña || *tr* arrebatar; recoger de prisa; revolver; hacer un revoltillo de (*huevos*); trepar || *intr* luchar; trepar

scrambled eggs *spl* revoltillo, huevos revueltos

scrap [skræp] *s* fragmento, pedacito; desecho; chatarra; (slang) riña, contienda; **scraps** desperdicios, desechos; (*from the table*) sobras || *v* (*pret & pp* **scrapped;** *ger* **scrapping**) *tr* desechar, descartar, echar a la basura; reducir a hierro viejo || *intr* (slang) reñir, pelear

scrap′book′ *s* álbum *m* de recortes, libro de recuerdos

scrape [skrep] *s* raspadura; (*place scratched*) raspaza; aprieto, enredo; || *tr* raspar; (*to gather together with much difficulty*) arañar || *intr* raspar; **to scrape along** ir tirando; **to scrape through** aprobar justo

scrap heap *s* montón *m* de cachivaches

scrap iron *s* chatarra, desecho de hierro

scrap paper *s* papel *m* para apuntes; papel de desecho

scratch [skrætʃ] *s* arañazo, rasguño; marca, raya, garrapato; (billiards) chiripa; (sport) línea de partida; **to start from scratch** empezar desde el principio, empezar de cero; **up to scratch** en buena condición || *tr* arañar, rasguñar; borrar, rasgar (*lo escrito*); garrapatear; (sport) borrar (*a un corredor o caballo*) || *intr* arañar, rasguñar; garrapatear; raspear (*una pluma*)

scratch pad *s* cuadernillo de apuntes

scratch paper *s* papel *m* para apuntes

scratch′-re•sist′ant *adj* resistente al rayado

scrawl [skrɔl] *s* garrapatos || *tr & intr* garrapatear

scraw•ny [ˈskrɔni] *adj* (*comp* **-nier;** *super* **-niest**) huesudo, flaco

scream [skrim] *s* chillido, grito || *tr* vociferar || *intr* chillar, gritar; reírse a gritos

screech [skritʃ] *s* chillido || *intr* chillar

screech owl *s* buharro; (*barn owl*) lechuza

screed [skrid] *s* escrito largo y pesado; (pej) diatriba

screen [skrin] *s* mampara, biombo; (*in front of chimney*) pantalla; (*to keep flies out*) alambrera; (*to sift sand*) tamiz *m;* (compu, mov, phys, telv) pantalla; **to put on the screen** llevar a la pantalla, llevar al celuloide || *tr* defender, proteger; cubrir, ocultar; cinematografiar; rodar, proyectar (*una película*); adaptar para el cine; tamizar (*p.ej., arena*)

screen grid *s* (electron) rejilla blindada

screen′play′ *s* cinedrama *m*

screw [skru] *s* tornillo; (*internal or female screw*) rosca, tuerca; (*of a boat*) hélice *f;* **to have a screw loose** (slang) tener flojos los tornillos; **to put the screws on** apretar los tornillos a || *tr* atornillar; (*to twist, twist in*) enroscar; **to screw up** torcer (*el rostro*) || *intr* atornillarse

screw′ball′ *s* (slang) estrafalario, excéntrico

screw′driv′er *s* destornillador *m,* desatornillador *m*

screw eye *s* armella

screw jack *s* gato de tornillo

screw propeller *s* hélice *f*

screw top *s* tapa *or* tapón *m* de rosca

scribal error [ˈskraɪbəl] *s* error *m* de escribiente

scribble [ˈskrɪbəl] *s* garrapatos ‖ *tr & intr* garrapatear
scribe [skraɪb] *s* (*teacher of Jewish law*) escriba *m;* escribiente *mf;* copista *mf;* autor *m,* escritor *m* ‖ *tr* arañar, rayar; trazar con punzón
scrimmage [ˈskrɪmɪdʒ] *s* refriega; (sport) escaramuza
scrimp [skrɪmp] *tr & intr* escatimar
script [skrɪpt] *s* escritura, letra cursiva; manuscrito, texto; (*of a play, movie, etc.*) palabras; (com) divisa; (rad, telv) guión *m;* (typ) plumilla inglesa
scripture [ˈskrɪptʃər] *s* escrito sagrado ‖ **Scripture** *s* Escritura
script'writ'er *s* guionista *mf,* cinematurgo
scrofula [ˈskrɑfjələ] *s* escrófula
scroll [skrol] *s* rollo de papel, rollo de pergamino; (archit) voluta
scroll'work' *s* obra de volutas, adornos de voluta
scrub [skrʌb] *s* chaparral *m,* monte bajo; animal achaparrado; persona de poca monta; (*act of scrubbing*) fregado; (sport) jugador *m* no oficial ‖ *v* (*pret & pp* **scrubbed;** *ger* **scrubbing**) *tr* fregar, restregar
scrub oak *s* chaparro
scrub woman *s* fregona
scruff [skrʌf] *s* nuca; piel *f* que cubre la nuca; capa, superficie *f;* espuma
scruple [ˈskrupəl] *s* escrúpulo
scrupulous [ˈskrupjələs] *adj* escrupuloso
scrutinize [ˈskrutɪ,naɪz] *tr* escudriñar, escrutar
scruti•ny [ˈskrutɪni] *s* (*pl* **-nies**) escudriñamiento, escrutinio
scubadiver [ˈskubə,dɪvər] *s* submarinista *mf*
scuff [skʌf] *s* rascadura, desgaste *m* ‖ *tr* rascar, desgastar
scuffle [ˈskʌfəl] *s* lucha, sarracina ‖ *intr* forcejear, luchar
scull [skʌl] *s* espadilla‖ *tr* impulsar con espadilla ‖ *intr* remar con espadilla
sculler•y [ˈskʌləri] *s* (*pl* **-ies**) trascocina
scullery maid *s* fregona
scullion [ˈskʌljən] *s* pinche *m*
sculptor [ˈskʌlptər] *s* escultor *m*
sculptress [ˈskʌlptrɪs] *s* escultora
sculpture [ˈskʌlptʃər] *s* escultura ‖ *tr & intr* esculpir
scum [skʌm] *s* espuma, nata; (*on metals*) escoria; (fig) escoria, canalla, gente baja; palomilla ‖ *v* (*pret & pp* **scummed;** *ger* **scumming**) *tr & intr* espumar
scum•my [ˈskʌmi] *adj* (*comp* **-mier;** *super* **-miest**) espumoso; (fig) vil, ruin
scurf [skʌrf] *s* (*shed by the skin*) caspa; (*shed by any surface*) costra
scurrilous [ˈskʌrɪləs] *adj* chocarrero, grosero, insolente, difamatorio
scur•ry [ˈskʌri] *v* (*pret & pp* **-ried**) *intr* echar a correr, escabullirse; **to scurry around** menearse; **to scurry away** ir respailando
scur•vy [ˈskʌril] *adj* (*comp* **-vier;** *super* **-viest**) despreciable, ruin, vil ‖ *s* escorbuto
scuttle [ˈskʌtəl] *s* (*bucket for coal*) cubo, balde *m;* (*trap door*) escotillón *m;* fuga, paso acelerado; (naut) escotilla ‖ *tr* barrenar, dar barreno a ‖ *intr* echar a correr
scythe [saɪð] *s* dalle *m,* guadaña
sea [si] *s* mar *m & f;* **at sea** en el mar; confuso, perplejo; **by the sea** a la orilla del mar; **to follow the sea** correr los mares, ser marinero; **to put to sea** hacerse a la mar
sea'board' *adj* costanero, costero ‖ *s* costa del mar, litoral *m*
sea breeze *s* brisa de mar
sea'coast' *s* costa marítima, litoral *m*
sea dog *s* (*seal*) foca; (coll) marinero viejo, lobo de mar
seafarer [ˈsi,fɛrər] *s* marinero; viajero por mar
sea'food' *s* mariscos
seafood restaurant *s* marisquería
seagoing [ˈsi,go•ɪŋ] *adj* de alta mar
sea gull *s* gaviota
sea horse *s* caballito de mar
seal [sil] *s* (*raised design; stamp; mark*) sello; (*sea animal*) foca, lobo marino ‖ *tr* sellar; cerrar herméticamente; decidir irrevocablemente; (*with sealing wax*) lacrar
sea legs *spl* pie marino
sea level *s* nivel *m* del mar
sealing wax *s* lacre *m*
seal'skin' *s* piel *f* de foca
seam [sim] *s* costura; (*edges left after making a seam*) metido; (*mark, line*) arruga; (*scar*) costurón *m;* grieta, juntura; (min) filón *m,* veta
sea•man [ˈsimən] *s* (*pl* **-men** [mən]) marinero; (nav) marino
sea mile *s* milla náutica
seamless [ˈsimlɪs] *adj* inconsútil, sin costura
seamstress [ˈsimstrɪs] *s* costurera; (*dressmaker's helper*) modistilla
seam•y [ˈsimi] *adj* (*comp* **-ier;** *super* **-iest**) lleno de costuras; tosco, burdo; vil, soez; miserable
séance [ˈse•ɑns] *s* sesión de espiritistas
sea'plane' *s* hidroavión *m,* hidroplano
sea'port' *s* puerto de mar
sea power *s* potencia naval
sear [sɪr] *adj* seco, marchito; gastado, raído ‖ *s* chamusco, socarra ‖ *tr* chamuscar, socarrar; quemar; marchitar; cauterizar
search [sʌrtʃ] *s* busca; pesquisa, indagación; (*frisking a person*) cacheo; (*police, soldiers*) peinado; **in search of** en busca de ‖ *tr* averiguar, explorar; registrar ‖ *intr* buscar; (*police, soldiers*) peinar; **to search for** buscar; **to search into** indagar, investigar
search engine *s* (compu) motor *m* de búsqueda, buscador *m*
search'light' *s* reflector *m,* proyector *m*
search warrant *s* auto de registro domiciliario, orden *f* de allanamiento
sea'scape' *s* vista del mar; (*painting*) marina
sea shell *s* concha marina
sea'shore' *s* costa, playa, ribera del mar
sea'sick' *adj* mareado
sea'sick'ness *s* mareo

sea'side' *s* orilla del mar, ribera del mar, playa
season ['sizən] *s* (*one of four parts of year*) estación; (*period of the year; period marked by certain activities*) temporada; (*opportune time; time of maturity, of ripening*) sazón *f;* **in season** en sazón; **in season and out of season** en tiempo y a destiempo; **out of season** fuera de sazón || *tr* condimentar, sazonar; curar (*la madera*); moderar, templar
seasonal ['sizənəl] *adj* estacional
seasoning ['sizənɪŋ] *s* aderezo, aliño, condimento; (*of wood*) cura; (fig) sal *f,* chiste *m*
season ticket *s* billete *m* de abono
seat [sit] *s* asiento; (*of trousers*) fondillos; morada; sitio, lugar *m;* (*e.g., of government*) sede *f;* (*in parliament*) escaño; (*e.g., of a war*) teatro; (*e.g., of learning*) centro; (*of a saddle*) batalla; (*of human body*) nalgas; (theat) localidad; **reclining seat** (*as in car*) asiento abatible; || *tr* sentar; tener asientos para; poner asiento a (*una silla*); echar fondillos a (*pantalones*); arraigar, establecer; **to be seated** estar sentado; **to seat oneself** sentarse
seat belt *s* cinturón *m* de asiento
seat cover *s* funda de asiento, cubreasiento
SEATO ['sito] *s* (acronym) (**South-East Asia Treaty Organization**) la OTASE, la O.T.A.S.E. (Organización del Tratado del Sudeste Asiático)
sea wall *s* dique marítimo
sea'way' *s* ruta marítima; avance *m* de un buque por mar; vía de agua interior para buques de alta mar; mar gruesa
sea'weed' *s* alga marina; plantas marinas
sea wind *s* viento que sopla del mar
sea'wor'thy *adj* marinero, en condiciones de navegar
sec. *abbr* **secant, second, secondary, secretary, section, sector**
secede [sɪ'sid] *intr* separarse, retirarse
secession [sɪ'sɛʃən] *s* secesión
seclude [sɪ'klud] *tr* recluir
secluded [sɪ'kludɪd] *adj* aislado, apartado, solitario
seclusion [sɪ'kluʒən] *s* reclusión, soledad
second ['sɛkənd] *adj* segundo; **to be second to none** ser tan bueno como el que más, no tener segundo || *adv* en segundo lugar || *s* segundo; artículo de segunda calidad; (*in dates*) dos *m;* (*in a challenge*) padrino; (aut) segunda (velocidad); (mus) segunda || *tr* secundar; apoyar (*una moción*)
secondar•y ['sɛkən,dɛri] *adj* secundario || *s* (*pl* **-ies**) (elec) secundario
sec'ond-best' *adj* (el) mejor después del primero
sec'ond-class' *adj* de segunda clase
second floor *s* primer piso
second hand *s* segundero
sec'ond-hand' *adj* de segunda mano, de ocasión
second-hand bookshop *s* librería de viejo
second in command *s* segundo
second lieutenant *s* alférez *m,* subteniente *m*
sec'ond•rate' *adj* de segundo orden; de calidad inferior
second sight *s* doble vista
second wind *s* nuevo aliento
secre•cy ['sikrəsi] *s* (*pl* **-cies**) secreto; **in secrecy** en secreto
secret ['sikrɪt] *adj* & *s* secreto; **in secret** en secreto
secretar•y ['sɛkrɪ,tɛri] *s* (*pl* **-ies**) secretario; (*desk*) secreter *m,* escritorio
secrete [sɪ'krit] *tr* encubrir, esconder; (physiol) secretar
secretive [sɪ'kritɪv] *adj* callado, reservado
Secret Service *s* Servicio Secreto
sect [sɛkt] *s* secta, comunión
sectarian [sɛk'tɛrɪ•ən] *adj* & *s* sectario
section ['sɛkʃən] *s* sección; (*of a country*) región; (*of a city*) barrio; (*of a law*) artículo; (*department, bureau*) negociado; (rr) tramo
secular ['sɛkjələr] *adj* secular, seglar, laico || *s* clérigo secular
secularism ['sɛkjələ,rɪzəm] *s* laicismo
secure [sɪ'kjʊr] *adj* seguro || *tr* asegurar; conseguir, obtener
securi•ty [sɪ'kjʊrɪti] *s* (*pl* **-ties**) seguridad; (*person*) segurador *m;* **securities** valores *mpl,* obligaciones, títulos
security guard *s* guarda *mf,* guarda jurado
security risk *s* peligro para la seguridad
secy. o **sec'y.** *abbr* **secretary**
sedan [sɪ'dæn] *s* silla de manos; (aut) sedán *m*
sedate [sɪ'det] *adj* sentado, sosegado
sedative ['sɛdətɪv] *adj* & *s* sedativo
sedentary ['sɛdən,tɛri] *adj* sedentario
sedge [sɛdʒ] *s* juncia
sediment ['sɛdɪmənt] *s* sedimento
sedition [sɪ'dɪʃən] *s* sedición
seditious [sɪ'dɪʃəs] *adj* sedicioso
seduce [sɪ'djus] *tr* seducir
seducer [sɪ'djusər] *s* seductor *m*
seduction [sɪ'dʌkʃən] *s* seducción
seductive [sɪ'dʌktɪv] *adj* seductivo
sedulous ['sɛdjələs] *adj* cuidadoso, diligente
see [si] *s* (eccl) sede *f* || *v* (*pret* **saw** [sɔ; *pp* **seen** [sin] *tr* ver; **to see off** ir a despedir; **to see through** llevar a cabo; ayudar en un trance difícil || *intr* ver; **see here!** ¡mire Ud.!; **to see into** o **to see through** conocer el juego de
seed [sid] *s* semilla, simiente *f;* **to go to seed** dar semilla; echarse a perder || *tr* sembrar; (*to remove the seeds from*) despepitar || *intr* sembrar; dejar caer semillas
seed'bed' *s* semillero
seedling ['sidlɪŋ] *s* planta de semilla; árbol *m* de pie
seed•y ['sidi] *adj* (*comp* **-ier;** *super* **-iest**) lleno de granos; (coll) andrajoso, raído
seeing ['si•ɪŋ] *adj* vidente || *s* vista, visión || *conj* visto que
Seeing Eye dog *s* perro-lazarillo
seek [sik] *v* (*pret* & *pp* **sought** [sɔt] *tr* buscar; recorrer buscando; dirigirse a || *intr* buscar;

to seek after tratar de obtener; **to seek to** esforzarse por
seem [sim] *intr* parecer
seemingly [ˈsimɪŋli] *adv* aparentemente, al parecer
seem·ly [ˈsimli] *adj* (*comp* **-lier;** *super* **-liest**) decente, decoroso, correcto; bien parecido
seep [sip] *intr* escurrirse, rezumarse
seer [sɪr] *s* profeta *m,* vidente *m*
see′saw′ *s* balancín *m,* columpio de tabla; (*motion*) vaivén *m* ‖ *intr* columpiarse; alternar; vacilar
seethe [ˈsið] *intr* hervir
segment [ˈsɛgmənt] *s* segmento
segregate [ˈsɛgrɪ,get] *tr* segregar
segregation [ˈsɛgrɪˈgeʃən] *s* segregación
segregationist [,sɛgrɪˈgeʃənɪst] *adj & s* segregacionista *mf*
Seine [sen] *s* Sena *m*
seismograph [ˈsaɪzmə,græf] *s* sismógrafo
seismology [saɪzˈmɑlədʒi] *s* sismología
seize [siz] *tr* agarrar, asir, coger; atar, prender, sujetar; apoderarse de; comprender; (law) embargar, secuestrar; aprovecharse de (*una oportunidad*)
seizure [ˈsiʒər] *s* prendimiento, prisión; captura, toma; (*of an illness*) ataque *m;* (law) embargo, secuestro
seldom [ˈsɛldəm] *adv* raramente, rara vez
select [sɪˈlɛkt] *adj* escogido, selecto; (*elite*) exclusivo; (*fruit*) de primera calidad ‖ *tr* seleccionar
selectee [sɪ,lɛkˈti] *s* (mil) quinto
selection [sɪˈlɛkʃən] *s* selección; trozo escogido; (*of goods for sale*) surtido
selective [sɪˈlɛktɪv] *adj* selectivo
selective service *s* servicio militar obligatorio
self [sɛlf] *adj* mismo ‖ *pron* sí mismo ‖ *s* (*pl* **selves** [sɛlvz]) uno mismo; ser *m;* yo; **all by one's self** sin ayuda de nadie
self′-abuse′ *s* abuso de sí mismo; masturbación
self′-addressed′ envelope *s* sobre *m* con el nombre y dirección del remitente
self′-cen′tered *adj* egocéntrico
self′-con′scious *adj* cohibido, apocado, tímido
self′-con·trol′ *s* dominio de sí mismo; autodisciplina
self′-de·fense′ *s* autodefensa, defensa personal, defensa propria; **in self-defense** en defensa propia
self′-de·ni′al *s* abnegación
self′-de·ter′mi·na′tion *s* autodeterminación
self′-dis′cipline *s* autodisciplina
self′-ed′u·cat′ed *adj* autodidacto
self′-em·ployed′ worker *s* trabajador autónomo, independiente *or* por su cuenta propia
self′-ev′i·dent *adj* patente, manifiesto
self′-ex·plan′a·tor′y *adj* que se explica por sí mismo
self′-glor′i·fi·ca′tion *s* egolatría
self′-gov′ernment *s* autogobierno, autonomía; dominio sobre sí mismo
self′-im·por′tant *adj* altivo, arrogante
self′-in·dul′gence *s* intemperancia, desenfreno
self′-in′terest *s* egoísmo, interés *m* personal
selfish [ˈsɛlfɪʃ] *adj* egoísta
selfishness [ˈsɛlfɪʃnɪs] *s* egoísmo
selfless [ˈsɛlflɪs] *adj* desinteresado
self′-liq′ui·dat′ing *adj* autoamortizable
self′-love′ *s* amor propio, egoísmo
self′-made′ man *s* hijo de sus propias obras
self′-por′trait *s* autorretrato
self′-pos·sessed′ *adj* dueño de sí mismo
self′-pres′er·va′tion *s* propia conservación
self′-re·li′ant *adj* confiado en sí mismo
self′-re·spect′ing *adj* lleno de dignidad, decoroso
self′-right′eous *adj* santurrón
self′-sac′ri·fice′ *s* sacrificio de sí mismo
self′-same′ *adj* mismísimo
self′-sat′is·fied′ *adj* pagado de sí mismo
self′-seal′ing *adj* autopegado
self′-seek′ing *adj* egoísta ‖ *s* egoísmo
self′-ser′vice restaurant *s* restaurante *m* de libre servicio, restaurante de autoservicio
self′-start′er *s* arranque automático
self′-sup·port′ *s* mantenimiento económico propio
self′-taught′ *adj* autodidacto
self′-willed′ *adj* obstinado, terco
self′-wind′ing clock *s* reloj *m* de cuerda automática, reloj de autocuerda
self′-wor′ship *s* egolatría
sell [sɛl] *v* (*pret & pp* **sold** [sold] *tr* vender; **sold out** (*tickets*) agotadas las localidades; **to sell out** realizar, saldar; (*to betray*) vender ‖ *intr* venderse, estar de venta; **to sell for** venderse a o en (*p.ej., cien pesetas*); **to sell off** bajar (*el mercado de valores*); **to sell out** venderlo todo, realizar
seller [ˈsɛlər] *s* vendedor *m*
sell′out′ *s* (com) liquidación total; (sport, theat) éxito de taquilla; (*traitor*) traidor *m;* (*betrayal*) capitulación
Seltzer water [ˈsɛltsər] *s* agua de seltz
selvage [ˈsɛlvɪdʒ] *s* orillo, vendo
semantic [sɪˈmæntɪk] *adj* semántico ‖ **semantics** *s* semántica
semaphore [ˈsɛmə,for] *s* semáforo; (rr) disco de señales
semblance [ˈsɛmbləns] *s* apariencia, imagen *f,* simulacro
semen [ˈsimɛn] *s* semen *m*
semester [sɪˈmɛstər] *adj* semestral ‖ *s* semestre *m*
semester hour *s* hora semestral
sem′ico′lon *s* punto y coma
sem′iconduc′tor *s* semiconductor *m*
sem′icon′scious *adj* semiconsciente
sem′ifi′nal *adj & s* (sport) semifinal *f*
sem′ilearn′ed *adj* semiculto
sem′imonth′ly *adj* quincenal ‖ *s* (*pl* **-lies**) periódico quincenal
seminar [ˈsɛmɪ,nɑr] *s* seminario
seminar·y [ˈsɛmɪ,nɛri] *s* (*pl* **-ies**) seminario

sem'ipre'cious *adj* semiprecioso, fino
Semite ['sɛmaɪt] o ['simaɪt] *s* semita *mf*
Semitic [sɪ'mɪtɪk] *adj* semítico || *s* semita *mf;* (*language*) semita *m*
sem'itrail'er *s* semi-remolque *m,* camión articulado
sem'iweek'ly *adj* bisemanal || *s* (*pl* **-lies**) periódico bisemanal
sem'iyear'ly *adj* semestral
Sen. o **sen.** *abbr* **Senate, Senator, Senior**
senate ['sɛnɪt] *s* senado
senator ['sɛnətər] *s* senador *m*
senatorship ['sɛnətərʃɪp] *s* senaduría
send [sɛnd] *v* (*pret & pp* **sent** [sɛnt]) *tr* enviar, mandar; expedir, remitir; lanzar (*una bola, flecha, etc.*); **to send back** devolver, reenviar; **to send packing** despedir con cajas destempladas || *intr* (rad) transmitir; **to send for** enviar por, enviar a buscar
sender ['sɛndər] *s* remitente *mf;* (telg) transmisor *m*
send'-off' *s* (coll) despedida afectuosa
senile ['sinaɪl] o ['sinɪl] *adj* senil
senility [sɪ'nɪlɪti] *s* senilidad; (pathol) senilismo
senior ['sinjər] *adj* mayor, de mayor edad; viejo; del último año; padre, p.ej., **John Jones, Senior** Juan Jones, padre || *s* mayor *m;* socio más antiguo; alumno del último año
senior citizen *s* anciano, persona de la tercera edad; **senior citizens** gente *f* de edad
seniority [sin'jɔrɪti] *s* antigüedad; precedencia, prioridad
sensation [sɛn'seʃən] *s* sensación
sense [sɛns] *s* sentido; **to make sense out of** comprender, explicarse || *tr* intuir, sentir, sospechar; comprender
senseless ['sɛnslɪs] *adj* falto de sentido; desmayado; insensato, necio
sense of guilt *s* cargo de conciencia
sense of humor *s* sentido de humor
sense organ *s* órgano sensorio
sensibili•ty [,sɛnsɪ'bɪlɪti] *s* (*pl* **-ties**) sensibilidad; **sensibilities** sentimientos delicados
sensible ['sɛnsɪbəl] *adj* cuerdo, sensato; perceptible, sensible; equilibrado
sensitive ['sɛnsɪtɪv] *adj* sensible; (*of the senses*) sensorio, sensitivo
sensitize ['sɛnsɪ,taɪz] *tr* sensibilizar
sensory ['sɛnsəri] *adj* sensorio
sensual ['sɛnʃʊ•əl] *adj* sensual, voluptuoso
sensuous ['sɛnʃʊ•əs] *adj* sensual
sentence ['sɛntəns] *s* (gram) frase *f,* oración; (law) sentencia || *tr* sentenciar, condenar
sentiment ['sɛntɪmənt] *s* sentimiento
sentimentali•ty [,sɛntɪmən'tælɪti] *s* (*pl* **-ties**) sentimentalismo
sentinel ['sɛntɪnəl] *s* centinela *m* or *f;* **to stand sentinel** estar de centinela, hacer centinela
sen•try ['sɛntri] *s* (*pl* **-tries**) centinela *m* or *f*
sentry box *s* garita de centinela
separate ['sɛpərɪt] *adj* separado; suelto || ['sɛpə,ret] *tr* separar || *intr* separarse
separation [,sɛpə'reʃən] *s* separación
separation of powers *s* (pol) separación de poderes
Sephardic [sɪ'fɑrdɪk] *adj* sefardí, sefardita
Sephardim [sɪ'fɑrdɪm] *spl* sefardíes *mpl*
September [sɛp'tɛmbər] *s* septiembre *m*
septet [sɛp'tɛt] *s* septeto
septic ['sɛptɪk] *adj* séptico
septic tank *s* cámara séptica, pozo negro, séptico o ciego
sepulcher ['sɛpəlkər] *s* sepulcro
seq. *abbr* (Lat) (**the following**) lo siguiente
sequel ['sikwəl] *s* resultado, secuela; continuación
sequence ['sikwəns] *s* serie *f,* sucesión; (cards) secansa, escalera, runfla; (gram, mov & mus) secuencia
sequester [sɪ'kwɛstər] *tr* apartar, separar; (*jury*) aislar; (law) secuestrar
sequin ['sikwɪn] *s* lentejuela
ser•aph ['sɛrəf] *s* (*pl* **-aphs** o **-aphim** [əfɪm]) serafín *m*
Serb [sʌrb] *adj & s* servio
Serbia ['sʌrbɪ•ə] *s* Servia
Serbian ['sʌrbɪ•ən] *adj & s* servio
Serbo-Croatian [,sʌrbokro'eʃən] *adj & s* servocroata *mf*
sere [sɪr] *adj* seco, marchito
serenade [,sɛrə'ned] *s* serenata || *tr* dar serenata a || *intr* dar serenatas
serene [sɪ'rin] *adj* sereno
serenity [sɪ'rɛnɪti] *s* serenidad
serf [sʌrf] *s* siervo de la gleba
serfdom ['sʌrfdəm] *s* servidumbre de la gleba
serge [sʌrdʒ] *s* sarga
sergeant ['sɑrdʒənt] *s* sargento
ser'geant•at-arms' *s* (*pl* **sergeants-at-arms**) oficial *m* de orden
sergeant major *s* (*pl* **sergeant majors**) sargento mayor
serial ['sɪrɪ•əl] *adj* serial; publicado por entregas || *s* cuento o novela por entregas; (rad) serial *m,* serial radiado, emisión seriada
serially ['sɪrɪ•əli] *adv* en serie, por series; por entregas
serial number *s* número de serie
serial port *s* (compu) puerto serie
se•ries ['sɪriz] *s* (*pl* **-ries**) serie *f*
serious ['sɪrɪ•əs] *adj* (*e.g., person, face, matter*) serio; (*e.g., condition, illness*) grave
sermon ['sʌrmən] *s* sermón *m*
sermonize ['sʌrmə,naɪz] *tr & intr* sermonear
seropositive ['sɪrə'pɑzətɪv] *adj* seropositivo
serpent ['sʌrpənt] *s* serpiente *f*
serrated ['sɛr,etəd] *adj* serrado, dentado
se•rum ['sɪrəm] *s* (*pl* **-rums** o **-ra** [rə]) suero
servant ['sʌrvənt] *s* criado, sirviente *m*
servant girl *s* criada, sirvienta
serve [sʌrv] *s* (*in tennis*) saque *m,* servicio || *tr* servir; (*to supply*) abastecer, proporcionar; cumplir (*una condena*); (*in tennis*) servir; **it serves me right** bien me lo merezco || *intr* servir; **to serve as** servir de
server ['sʌrvər] *s* (compu) servidor *m,* ordena-

dor *m* patrón, computadora patrón; (culin) cubierto de servir; (sport) saque *m,* servidor

service [ˈsʌrvɪs] *s* servicio; **at your service** para servir a Ud.; **out of service** fuera de servicio; **the services** las fuerzas armadas ‖ *tr* instalar; mantener, reparar

serviceable [ˈsʌrvɪsəbəl] *adj* útil; duradero; cómodo

service charge *s* servicio; (*in banking*) comisión

serviceman [ˈsʌrvis,mæn] *s* (*pl* **-men** [,mən]) reparador *m,* mecánico; militar *m*

service record *s* hoja de servicios

service station *s* estación de servicio, taller *m* de reparaciones

service stripe *s* galón *m* de servicio

servile [ˈsʌrvɪl] *adj* servil

servitude [ˈsʌrvi,tjud] *s* servidumbre; trabajos forzados

sesame [ˈsɛsəmi] *s* sésamo; **open sesame** sésamo ábrete

session [ˈsɛʃən] *s* sesión; **to be in session** sesionar

set [sɛt] *adj* determinado, resuelto; inflexible, obstinado; fijo, firme; estudiado, meditado ‖ *s* (*of books, chairs, dishes, keys, etc.*) juego; (*of gears*) tren *m;* (*of horses*) pareja; (*of diamonds*) aderezo; (*of tennis*) partida; (*of dishes*) servicio; (*of kitchen utensils*) batería; clase *f,* grupo; equipo; porte *m,* postura; (*of a garment*) caída, ajuste *m;* (*of glue*) endurecimiento; (*of cement*) fraguado; (*of artificial teeth*) caja; (mov) plató *m;* (rad) aparato; (theat) decoración ‖ *v* (*pret & pp* **set;** *ger* **setting**) *tr* asentar; colocar, poner; establecer, instalar; arreglar, preparar; adornar; apostar; poner (*un reloj*) en hora; (*in bridge*) reenvidar; poner, meter, pegar (*fuego*); fijar (*el precio*); engastar, montar (*una piedra preciosa*); encasar (*un hueso dislocado*); disponer (*los tipos*); triscar (*una sierra*); armar, colocar (*una trampa*); fijar (*el peinado*); poner (*la mesa*); dar (*un ejemplo*); **to set back** parar; poner obstáculos a; hacer retroceder; atrasar, retrasar (*el reloj*); **to set forth** exponer, dar a conocer; **to set one's heart on** tener la esperanza puesta en; **to set store by** dar mucha importancia a; **to set up shop** poner tienda; **to set up the drinks** (coll) convidar a beber ‖ *intr* ponerse (*el Sol, la Luna, etc.*); cuajarse (*un líquido*); endurecerse (*la cola*); fraguar (*el cemento, el yeso*); empollar (*una gallina*); caer, sentar (*una prenda de vestir*); **to set about** ponerse a; **to set out** ponerse en camino; emprender un negocio, **to set out to** ponerse a; **to set to work** poner manos a la obra; **to set upon** acometer, atacar

set'back' *s* revés *m,* contrariedad

set'screw' *s* tornillo de presión

settee [sɛˈti] *s* sofá *m,* canapé *m*

setting [ˈsɛtɪŋ] *s* (*environment*) ambiente *m;* (*of a gem*) engaste *m,* montadura; (*of cement*) fraguado; (*e.g., of the sun*) puesta, ocaso; (theat) escena; (theat) puesta en escena, decoración

set'ting-up' exercises *spl* ejercicios sin aparatos, gimnasia sueca

settle [ˈsɛtəl] *tr* asentar, colocar; asegurar, fijar; componer, conciliar; calmar, moderar; matar (*el polvo*); casar; poblar, colonizar; ajustar, arreglar (*cuentas*); (*settle out of court*) transigir ‖ *intr* asentarse (*un líquido, un edificio*); establecerse; componerse; calmarse, moderarse; solidificarse; (law) transigir; **to settle down to work** ponerse seriamente a trabajar; **to settle on** escoger; fijar (*p.ej., una fecha*)

settlement [ˈsɛtəlmənt] *s* establecimiento; colonia, caserío; decisión; (*of accounts*) arreglo, ajuste *m;* traspaso; casa de beneficencia

settler [ˈsɛtlər] *s* fundador *m;* poblador *m;* colono; árbitro, conciliador *m*

set'up' *s* porte *m,* postura; (*e.g., of the parts of a machine*) disposición; (coll) organización; (slang) invitación a beber

seven [ˈsɛvən] *adj & pron* siete ‖ *s* siete *m;* **seven o'clock** las siete

seven hundred *adj & pron* setecientos ‖ *s* setecientos *m*

seventeen [ˈsɛvənˈtin] *adj, pron & s* diecisiete *m,* diez y siete

seventeenth [ˈsɛvənˈtinθ] *adj & s* (*in a series*) decimoséptimo; (*part*) diecisieteavo ‖ *s* (*in dates*) diecisiete *m*

seventh [ˈsɛvənθ] *adj & s* séptimo ‖ *s* (*in dates*) siete *m*

seventieth [ˈsɛvəntɪ•ɪθ] *adj & s* (*in a series*) septuagésimo; (*part*) setentavo

seven•ty [ˈsɛvənti] *adj & pron* setenta ‖ *s* (*pl* **-ties**) setenta *m*

sever [ˈsɛvər] *tr* desunir, separar; romper (*relaciones*) ‖ *intr* desunirse, separarse

several [ˈsɛvərəl] *adj* diversos, varios; distintos, respectivos ‖ *spl* varios; algunos

severance pay [ˈsɛvərəns] *s* indemnización por despido

severe [sɪˈvɪr] *adj* severo; (*weather*) riguroso; recio, violento; (*look*) adusto; (*pain*) agudo; (*illness*) grave

sew [so] *v* (*pret* **sewed;** *pp* **sewed** o **sewn**) *tr & intr* coser

sewage [ˈsu•ɪdʒ] o [ˈsju•ɪdʒ] *s* agua de albañal, aguas cloacales, aguas negras

sew'age-dis•pos'al plant *s* estación depuradora

sewer [ˈsu•ər] o [ˈsju•ər] *s* albañal *m,* cloaca, alcantarilla ‖ *tr* alcantarillar

sewerage [ˈsu•ərɪdʒ] o [ˈsju•ərɪdʒ] *s* desagüe *m;* (*system*) alcantarillado; aguas de albañal

sewer rat *s* rata de alcantarilla

sewing basket [ˈso•ɪŋ] *s* cesta de costura

sewing machine *s* máquina de coser

sex [sɛks] *s* sexo; **the opposite sex** el sexo opuesto; **to have sex with** tener relaciones sexuales con

sex appeal *s* sex-appeal *m* (*attracción sexual*)

sex change operation *s* operación de cambio de sexo

sex education *s* educación sexual
sexism [ˈsɛksɪzəm] *s* sexismo
sex offender *s* delicuente *mf* sexual
sexist [ˈsɛksɪst] *adj & s* sexista
sextant [ˈsɛkstənt] *s* sextante *m*
sextet [sɛksˈtɛt] *s* sexteto
sexton [ˈsɛkstən] *s* sacristán *m*
sexual [ˈsɛkʃʊ•əl] *adj* sexual
sexual abuse *s* abusos deshonestos
sexual harassment *s* acoso sexual, hostigamiento sexual
sexual intercourse *s* relaciones sexuales
sexually transmitted disease *s* enfermedad de transmisión sexual
sexual orientation *s* orientación sexual
sex•y [ˈsɛksi] *adj* (*comp* **-ier;** *super* **-iest**) (slang) sicalíptico, erótico
shab•by [ˈʃæbi] *adj* (*comp* **-bier;** *super* **-biest**) gastado, raído, usado; andrajoso, desaseado; ruin, vil
shack [ʃæk] *s* casucha, choza
shackle [ˈʃækəl] *s* grillete *m;* (*to tie an animal*) maniota; (*of a lock*) gancho; (fig) impedimento, traba; **shackles** cadenas, esposas, grillos ‖ *tr* poner grilletes a; poner esposas a; encadenar; (fig) trabar
shad [ʃæd] *s* sábalo, alosa
shade [ʃed] *s* sombra; (*of a lamp*) pantalla; (*of a window*) cortina, estor *m,* visillo, cortina de resorte; (*for the eyes*) visera; (*hue; slight difference*) matiz *m;* **shades** (slang) gafas *fpl* de sol; **the shades** las tinieblas; (*of the dead*) las sombras ‖ *tr* sombrear; obscurecer; rebajar ligeramente (*el precio*)
shadow [ˈʃædo] *s* sombra ‖ *tr* sombrear; simbolizar; acechar, espiar (*a una persona*); **to shadow forth** representar vagamente, representar de un modo profético
shadow cabinet *s* (pol) gabinete *m* fantasma, gabinete en la sombra
shadowy [ˈʃædo•i] *adj* sombroso; ligero, vago; imaginario; simbólico
shad•y [ˈʃedi] *adj* (*comp* **-ier;** *super* **-iest**) sombrío, umbroso; (coll) sospechoso; (coll) de mala fama; (*story*) (coll) verde; **to keep shady** (slang) no dejarse ver
shaft [ʃæft] *s* dardo, flecha, saeta; (*of an arrow; of a feather*) astil *m;* (*of light*) rayo; (*of a wagon*) vara alcándara, limonera; (*of a mine; of an elevator*) pozo; (*of a column*) fuste *m,* caña; (*of a flag*) asta; (*of a motor*) árbol *m;* (*to make fun of someone*) dardo
shag•gy [ˈʃægi] *adj* (*comp* **-gier;** *super* **-giest**) hirsuto, peludo, veludo; lanudo; áspero
shake [ʃek] *s* sacudida; (coll) apretón *m* de manos; (slang) instante *m,* momento ‖ *v* (*pret* **shook** [ʃʊk]; *pp* **shaken**) *tr* sacudir; agitar; apretar, estrechar (*la mano a uno*); inquietar, perturbar; (*to get rid of*) (slang) dar esquinazo a, zafarse de ‖ *intr* sacudirse; agitarse; temblar; inquietarse, perturbarse; (*from cold*) tiritar; **shake!** (coll) ¡choque Ud. esos cinco!, ¡vengan esos cinco!
shake′down′ *s* (*trial*) prueba; (*search*) registro; (*extortion*) (coll) timo, estafa, concusión
shakedown cruise *s* viaje *m* de pruebas
shake′-up′ *s* profunda conmoción; cambio de personal, reorganización completa
shak•y [ˈʃeki] *adj* (*comp* **-ier;** *super* **-iest**) trémulo, vacilante, movedizo; indigno de confianza
shall [ʃæl] *v* (*cond* **should** [ʃʊd]) *v aux* empléase para formar (1) el fut de ind, p.ej., **I shall do it** lo haré; (2) el fut perf de ind, p.ej., **I shall have done it** lo habré hecho; (3) el modo potencial, p.ej., **what shall I do?** ¿qué he de hacer?, ¿qué debo hacer?
shallow [ˈʃælo] *adj* bajo, poco profundo; (fig) frívolo, superficial
sham [ʃæm] *adj* falso, fingido; postizo ‖ *s* fingimiento, falsificación, engaño; (*person*) (coll) farsante *mf;* ‖ *v* (*pret & pp* **shammed;** *ger* **shamming**) *tr & intr* fingir
sham battle *s* simulacro de combate
shambles [ˈʃæmbəlz] *s* destrucción, ruina; (*confusion, mess*) lío, revoltijo
shame [ʃem] *s* vergüenza; deshonra; (*disgrace*) metedura; **shame on you!** ¡qué vergüenza!; **what a shame!** ¡qué lástima! ‖ *tr* avergonzar; deshonrar
shameful [ˈʃemfəl] *adj* vergonzoso
shameless [ˈʃemlɪs] *adj* descarado, desvergonzado
shampoo [ʃæmˈpu] *s* champú *m* ‖ *tr* lavar (*la cabeza*); lavar la cabeza a
shamrock [ˈʃæmrɑk] *s* trébol *m* irlandés
shanghai [ˈʃæŋhaɪ] o [ʃæŋˈhaɪ] *tr* embarcar emborrachando, embarcar narcotizando; llevarse con violencia, llevarse con engaño
shank [ʃæŋk] *s* (*of the leg*) caña, canilla; (*of an animal*) pierna; (*of a bird*) zanca; (*of an anchor*) caña; (*of the sole of a shoe*) enfranque *m;* astil *m,* caña, fuste *m;* extremidad, remate *m*
shan′t *contr* **shall not**
shan•ty [ˈʃænti] *s* (*pl* **-ties**) chabola, choza
shape [ʃep] *s* forma; **in bad shape** (coll) arruinado; (coll) muy enfermo; **out of shape** deformado; descompuesto; (*twisted*) sobornado ‖ *tr* formar, dar forma a; amoldar ‖ *intr* formarse; **to shape up** tomar forma; desarrollarse bien
shapeless [ˈʃeplɪs] *adj* informe
shape•ly [ˈʃepli] *adj* (*comp* **-lier:** *super* **-liest**) bien formado, esbelto
share [ʃɛr] *s* parte *f,* porción; (*of stock in a company*) acción; **to go shares** ir a la parte ‖ *tr* (*to enjoy jointly*) compartir; (*to apportion*) repartir ‖ *intr* participar, tener parte
share certificate *s* certificado de acciones
sharecropper [ˈʃɛr,krɑpər] *s* aparcero
share′hold′er *s* accionista *mf,* socio accionista
share′ware *s* (compu) shareware *m* (*herramientas para trabajar*)
shark [ʃɑrk] *s* tiburón *m;* (*swindler*) estafador *m;* (slang) experto, perito

sharp [ʃɑrp] *adj* afilado, agudo; anguloso; (*curve, slope, etc.*) fuerte, pronunciado; (*photograph*) nítido; (*hearing*) fino; (*step, gait*) rápido; atento, despierto; picante, mordaz; listo, vivo; (mus) sostenido; (slang) elegante; **sharp features** facciones bien marcadas ‖ *adv* agudamente; en punto, p.ej., **at four o'clock sharp** a las cuatro en punto ‖ *s* (mus) sostenido

sharpen [ˈʃɑrpən] *tr* aguzar; sacar punta a (*un lápiz*) ‖ *intr* afilarse

sharper [ˈʃɑrpər] *s* fullero, jugador *m* de ventaja

sharp'shoot'er *s* tirador certero; (mil) tirador distinguido

shatter [ˈfætər] *tr* hacer astillas, romper de un golpe; quebrantar (*la salud*); destruir, destrozar; agitar, perturbar ‖ *intr* hacerse pedazos, romperse

shat'ter•proof' *adj* inastillable

shave [ʃev] *s* afeitado; rebanada delgada; **to have a close shave** (coll) escapar en una tabla ‖ *tr* afeitar (*la cara*); raer, raspar; (*to graze; to cut close*) rozar; (*to slice thin*) rebanar; (carp) cepillar ‖ *intr* afeitarse

shaving [ˈʃevɪŋ] *adj* de afeitar, para afeitar, p.ej., **shaving soap** jabón *m* de o para afeitar ‖ *s* afeitado; **shavings** acepilladuras, virutas

shaving cream *s* crema de afeitar

shaving foam *s* espuma de afeitar

shaving lotion *s* loción facial

shawl [ʃɔl] *s* chal *m*, mantón *m*

she [ʃi] *pron pers* (*pl* **they**) ella ‖ *s* (*pl* **shes**) hembra

sheaf [ʃif] *s* (*pl* **sheaves** [ʃivz] gavilla; (*of paper*) atado

shear [ʃir] *s* hoja de la tijera; **shears** tijeras grandes); (*to cut metal*) cizallas ‖ *v* (*pret* **sheared;** *pp* **sheared** o **shorn** [ʃorn]) *tr* esquilar, trasquilar (*las ovejas*); cizallar; quitar cortando; tundir (*paño*)

sheath [ʃiθ] *s* (**sheaths** [ʃiðz]) envoltura, estuche *m*, funda; (*for a sword*) funda, vaina

sheathe [ʃið] *tr* enfundar, envainar

she'd *contr* **she would**

shed [fɛd] *s* cobertizo; (*line from which water flows in two directions*) vertiente *m & f* ‖ *v* (*pret & pp* **shed;** *ger* **shedding**) *tr* derramar, verter (*p.ej., sangre*); dar, echar, esparcir (*luz*); mudar (*la pluma, el pellejo*)

sheen [ʃin] *s* brillo, lustre *m;* (*of pressed cloth*) prensado

sheep [ʃip] *s* (*pl* **sheep**) carnero; (*female*) oveja; tonto; **to make sheep's eyes (at)** mirar con ojos de carnero degollado

sheep dog *s* perro ovejero, perro de pastor

sheep'fold' *s* aprisco, redil *m*

sheepish [ˈʃipɪʃ] *adj* avergonzado, corrido; tímido, tonto

sheep'skin' *s* (*undressed*) zalea; (*dressed*) badana; (coll) diploma *m*

sheer [ʃir] *adj* delgado, fino, ligero; casi transparente; escarpado; puro, sin mezcla; completo ‖ *intr* desviarse

sheet [ʃit] *s* (e.g., for the bed) sábana; (*of paper*) hoja; (*of metal*) hoja, lámina; (*of water*) extensión; hoja impresa; periódico; (naut) escota

sheet lightning *s* fucilazo

sheet metal *s* metal laminado

sheet music *s* música en hojas sueltas

sheik [ʃik] *s* jeque *m;* (*great lover*) (slang) sultán *m*

shelf [ʃɛlf] *s* (*pl* **shelves** [ʃɛlvz]) estante *m,* anaquel *m;* bajío, banco de arena; **on the shelf** arrinconado, desechado, olvidado

she'll *contr* **she will**

shell [ʃɛl] *s* (*of an egg, nut, etc.*) cáscara; (*of a crustacean*) caparazón *m,* concha; (*of a vegetable*) vaina; (*of a cartridge*) cápsula; (*of a boiler*) cuerpo; armazón *f,* esqueleto; bomba, proyectil *m;* (*long, narrow racing boat*) (sport) yola ‖ *tr* descascarar; desgranar, desvainar (*legumbres*); bombardear, cañonear; **to shell out** (coll) entregar (*dinero*)

shel•lac [ʃəˈlæk] *s* laca, goma laca ‖ *v* (*pret & pp* **-lacked;** *ger* **-lacking**) *tr* barnizar con goma laca; (slang) azotar, zurrar; (slang) derrotar

shell'fish' *s* marisco, mariscos

shell hole *s* (mil) embudo

shell shock *s* neurosis *f* de guerra

shelter [ˈʃɛltər] *s* abrigo, asilo, amparo, refugio; **to take shelter** abrigarse, refugiarse ‖ *tr* abrigar, amparar, proteger

shelve [ʃɛlv] *tr* poner sobre un estante; proveer de estantes; arrinconar, dejar a un lado; diferir indefinidamente

shepherd [ˈʃɛpərd] *s* pastor *m* ‖ *tr* pastorear (*a las ovejas o los fieles*)

shepherd dog *s* perro ovejero, perro de pastor

shepherdess [ˈʃɛpərdɪs] *s* pastora

sherbet [ˈʃʌrbət] *s* sorbete *m*

shereef [ʃɛˈrif] *s* jerife *m*

sheriff [ˈʃɛrɪf] *s* alguacil *m* mayor

sher•ry [ˈʃɛri] *s* (*pl* **-ries**) jerez *m,* vino de Jerez

she's [ʃiz], [ʃiz] *contr* **she is; she has**

Shia [ˈʃi•ə] *mfpl* shiíes

shibboleth [ˈʃibəlɛθ] *s* rasgo distintivo; dogma *m*

shield [ʃild] *s* escudo; (*for armpit*) sobaquera; (elec) blindaje *m* ‖ *tr* amparar, defender, escudar; (elec) blindar

shift [ʃift] *s* cambio; (*order of work or other activity*) turno; (*group of workmen*) tanda; maña, subterfugio ‖ *tr* cambiar; deshacerse de; echar (*la culpa*); (aut) cambiar de (*marcha*) ‖ *intr* cambiar, cambiar de puesto; mañear; (naut) correrse (*el lastre*); (rr) maniobrar; **to shift for oneself** ayudarse, ingeniarse

shift key *s* tecla de cambio, palanca de mayúsculas

shiftless [ˈʃiftlɪs] *adj* desidioso, perezoso

shiftlessness [ˈʃiftlɪsnɪs] *s* galbana

shift•y [ˈʃifti] *adj* (*comp* **-ier;** *super* **-iest**) ingenioso, mañoso; evasivo, tramoyista; (*glance*) huyente

Shiite [ˈʃi•aɪt] *adj & s* chiíta, shií
shill [ʃil] *s* (slang) cómplice *mf* (que sirve para engañar a un bobo)
shilling [ˈʃilɪŋ] *s* chelín *m*
shimmer [ˈʃimər] *s* luz trémula ‖ *intr* rielar
shin [ʃin] *s* espinilla ‖ *v* (*pret & pp* **shinned;** *ger* **shinning**) *tr & intr* trepar
shin'bone' *s* espinilla
shine [ʃaɪn] *s* brillo, luz *f;* bruñido, lustre *m;* buen tiempo; (*on shoes*) (coll) lustre *m;* **to take a shine to** (slang) tomar simpatía a ‖ *v* (*pret & pp* **shined**) *tr* pulir, lustrar; (coll) embolar, limpiar (*el calzado*) ‖ *v* (*pret & pp* **shone** [ʃon]) *intr* brillar, lucir, resplandecer; hacer sol, hacer buen tiempo; (*to be distinguished, to stand out*) (fig) brillar, lucir
shingle [ˈʃɪŋgəl] *s* ripia, teja de madera; tejamaní *m* (Am); pelo a la garçonne; (coll) letrero de oficina; **shingles** (pathol) zona; **to hang out one's shingle** (coll) abrir una oficina; (coll) abrir un consultorio médico ‖ *tr* cubrir con ripias; cortar (*el pelo*) a la garçonne
shining [ˈʃaɪnɪŋ] *adj* brillante, luciente
shin•y [ˈʃaɪni] *adj* (*comp* **-ier;** *super* **-iest**) brillante, lustroso; (*paper*) glaseado; (*from much wear*) brilloso
ship [ʃip] *s* nave *f,* buque *m,* barco, navío; (*steamer*) vapor *m;* aeronave *f* ‖ *v* (*pret & pp* **shipped;** *ger* **shipping**) *tr* embarcar; enviar, remitir, remesar; armar (*los remos*); embarcar (*agua*) ‖ *intr* embarcarse
ship'board' *s* bordo; **on shipboard** a bordo
ship'build'er *s* arquitecto naval, constructor *m* de buques
ship'build'ing *s* arquitectura naval, construcción de buques
ship'mate' *s* camarada *m* de a bordo
shipment [ˈʃipmənt] *s* embarque *m* (*por agua*); envío, expedición, remesa
shipper [ˈʃipər] *s* embarcador *m;* expedidor *m,* remitente *mf*
shipping memo [ˈʃipɪŋ] *s* nota de remisión
ship'shape' *adj & adv* en buen orden
ship'side' *adj & adv* al costado del buque ‖ *s* zona de embarque y desembarque; muelle *m*
ship's papers *spl* documentación del buque
ship's time *s* hora local del buque
ship'wreck' *s* naufragio; barco náufrago ‖ *tr* hacer naufragar ‖ *intr* naufragar
ship'yard' *s* astillero, varadero
shirk [ʃʌrk] *tr* evitar (*el trabajo*); faltar a (*un deber*) ‖ *intr* escurrir el hombro
shirred eggs [ʃʌrd] *spl* huevos al plato
shirt [ʃʌrt] *s* camisa; **to keep one's shirt on** (slang) quedarse sereno; **to lose one's shirt** (slang) perder hasta la camisa
shirt'band' *s* cuello de camisa
shirtfront *s* pechera de camisa, cami solín *m*
shirtsleeve *s* manga de camisa; **in shirt sleeves** en mangas de camisa
shirt'tail' *s* faldón *m,* pañal *m*
shirt'waist' *s* blusa (*de mujer*)
shiver [ˈʃivər] *s* estremecimiento, tiritón *m* ‖ *intr* estremecerse, tiritar
shoal [ʃol] *s* bajío, banco de arena
shock [ʃak] *s* (*sudden and violent blow or encounter*) choque *m;* (*sudden agitation of mind or emotions*) sobresalto; temblor *m* de tierra; (*of hair*) greña; (agr) tresnal *m;* (elec) sacudida; (med) choque *m;* (*profound depression*) (pathol) choque *m;* (coll) parálisis *f* ‖ *tr* chocar; sobresaltar; dar una sacudida eléctrica a; chocar, escandalizar
shock absorber [æbˈsɔrbər] *s* amortiguador *m*
shocker [ˈʃɑkər] *s* (slang) novelucha; película horripilante
shocking [ˈʃɑkɪŋ] *adj* chocante, escandalizador
shock troops *spl* tropas de asalto
shod•dy [ˈʃɑdi] *adj* (*comp* **-dier;** *super* **-diest**) falso, de imitación; fullero
shoe [ʃu] *s* (*which goes above the ankle*) bota, botina; (*which does not go above the ankle*) zapato; (*of a tire*) cubierta; **to put on one's shoes** calzarse ‖ *v* (*pret & pp* **shod** [ʃɑd]) *tr* calzar; herrar (*un caballo*)
shoe'black' *s* limpiabotas *m*
shoe'horn' *s* calzador *m*
shoe'lace' *s* cordón *m* de zapato, lazo de zapato
shoe'mak'er *s* zapatero; zapatero remendón
shoe polish *s* betún *m,* bola
shoe'shine' *s* brillo, lustre *m;* limpiabotas *m*
shoe store *s* zapatería
shoe'string' *s* cordón *m* de zapato, lazo de zapato; **on a shoestring** con muy poco dinero
shoe tree *s* horma
shoo [ʃu] *tr & intr* oxear
shoot [ʃut] *s* (*sprout, twig*) renuevo, vástago; conducto inclinado; (*for grain, sand, etc.*) tolva; tiro al blanco, cortamen *m* de tiradores; (*hunting party*) partida de caza ‖ *v* (*pret & pp* **shot** [ʃɑt]) *tr* tirar, disparar (*un arma*); herir o matar con arma; (*to execute with a discharge of rifles*) fusilar; fotografiar; (*to take a moving picture of*) rodar, filmar; echar (*los dados*); medir la altura de (*p.ej., el Sol*); **to shoot down** derribar (*un avión*); **to shoot up** (slang) destrozar echando balas a diestra y siniestra; (*drugs*) picarse, pincharse ‖ *intr* tirar; nacer, brotar; lanzarse, precipitarse, moverse rápidamente; punzar (*un dolor, una llaga*); **to shoot at** tirar a; (*to strive for*) (coll) poner el tiro en
shooting gallery *s* galería de tiro al blanco
shooting match *s* certamen *m* de tiro al blanco; (slang) conjunto, totalidad
shooting star *s* estrella fugaz, estrella filante
shoot'out' *s* balaceo, balacera (SAm)
shop [ʃɑp] *s* (*store*) tienda; (*workshop*) taller *m;* **to talk shop** hablar de su oficio, hablar del propio trabajo (*fuera de tiempo*) ‖ *v* (*pret & pp* **shopped;** *ger* **shopping**) *intr* ir de compras, ir de tiendas; **to go shopping** ir de compras, ir de tiendas; **to send shopping** mandar a la compra; **to shop around** ir de tienda en tienda buscando gangas

shop′keep′er *s* tendero, baratero
shoplifter [ˈʃɑpˌlɪftər] *s* mechera, ratero de tiendas
shopper [ˈʃɑpər] *s* comprador *m*
shopping bag *s* bolsa de la compra
shopping cart *s* carrito (de la compra)
shopping center *s* centro comercial (*grupo de establecimientos minoristas, con aparcamiento*)
shopping district *s* barrio comercial
shopping list *s* lista de la compra
shopping mall *s* galería comercial
shop steward *s* representante *mf* sindical, enlace *mf* sindical (Esp)
shop′talk′ *s* conversación sobre el trabajo
shop′win′dow *s* escaparate *m* (de tienda); aparador *m* (Mex)
shop′work′ *s* trabajo de taller
shop′worn′ *adj* desgastado con el trajín de la tienda
shore [ʃor] *s* orilla, ribera; costa, playa; **shores** (poet) clima *m,* región ‖ *tr* acodalar, apuntalar
shore dinner *s* comida de pescado y mariscos
shore leave *s* (nav) permiso para ir a tierra
shoreline *s* línea de la playa; línea de buques costeros
shore patrol *s* (nav) patrulla en tierra
short [ʃɔrt] *adj* (*in space, time, and quantity*) corto; (*in time*) breve; (*in stature*) bajo; (fig) corto, sucinto; (fig) brusco, seco; **in a short time** dentro de poco; **in short** en fin; **on short notice** con poco tiempo de aviso; **to be short of** estar escaso de; **short of breath** corto de resuello ‖ *adv* brevemente; bruscamente; (*without possessing the stock sold*) al descubierto, p.ej., **to sell short** vender al descubierto; **to run short of** acabársele a uno, p.ej., **I am running short of gasoline** se me acaba la gasolina; **to stop short** parar de repente ‖ *s* (elec) cortocircuito; (mov) cortometraje *m;* **shorts** calzones cortos, calzoncillos ‖ *tr* (elec) poner en cortocircuito ‖ *intr* (elec) ponerse en cortocircuito
shortage [ˈʃɔrtɪdʒ] *s* carestía, escasez *f,* falta; déficit *m;* (*from pilfering*) substracción
short′cake′ *s* torta de frutas; torta quebradiza
short′change′ *tr* (coll) no devolver la vuelta debida a
short circuit *s* (elec) cortocircuito
short′cir′cuit *tr* (elec) cortocircuitar ‖ *intr* (elec) cortocircuitarse
short′com′ing *s* falta, defecto, desperfecto
short cut *s* atajo; (*method*) remediavagos *m*
shorten [ˈʃɔrtən] *tr* acortar, abreviar ‖ *intr* acortarse, abreviarse
short′hand′ *adj* taquigráfico ‖ *s* taquigrafía; **to take shorthand** taquigrafiar
short-lived [ˈʃɔrtˈlaɪvd] o (coll) [ˈʃɔrtˈlɪvd] *adj* de breve vida, de breve duración
shortly [ˈʃɔrtli] *adv* en breve, luego; descortésmente; **shortly after** poco tiempo después (de)
short′-range′ *adj* de poco alcance
short sale *s* (coll) venta al descubierto
short-sighted [ˈʃɔrtˈsaɪtɪd] *adj* miope; (fig) falto de perspicacia
short′stop′ *s* (baseball) medio, paracorto (Col, Ven), paradas cortas (Mex); (*player*) torpedero, parador *m* en corto (Mex)
short story *s* cuento
short-tempered [ˈʃɔrtˈtɛmpərd] *adj* de mal genio
short′-term′ *adj* a corto plazo
short′wave′ *s* onda corta
shot [ʃɑt] *s* tiro, disparo; (*hit or wound made with a bullet*) balazo; (*distance*) alcance *m;* (*in certain games*) jugada, tirada, golpe *m;* (*of a rocket into space*) lanzamiento; conjetura, tentativa; fotografía, instantánea; (*small pellets of lead*) perdigones *mpl;* munición; (*marksman*) tiro; (*heavy metal ball*) (sport) pesa; (*hypodermic injection*) (slang) jeringazo; (*drink of liquor*) (slang) trago; (compu) disparo; **not by a long shot** ni con mucho, ni por pienso; **to start like a shot** salir disparado
shot′gun′ *s* escopeta
shot′-put′ *s* (sport) tiro de la pesa, lanzamiento de bala
should [ʃʊd] *v aux* empléase para formar (1) el pres de cond, *p.ej.,* **if I should wait for him, I should miss the train** si yo le esperase, perdería el tren; (2) el perf de cond, *p.ej.,* **if I had waited for him, I should have missed the train** si yo le hubiese esperado, habría, perdido el tren; y (3) el modo potencial, *p.ej.,* **he should go at once** debiera salir en seguida; **he should have gone at once** debiera haber salido en seguida
shoulder [ˈʃoldər] *s* hombro; (*of slaughtered animal*) brazuelo; (*of a garment*) hombrera; **across the shoulder** en bandolera; **to put one's shoulders to the wheel** arrimar el hombro, echar el pecho al agua; **to turn a cold shoulder to** volver las espaldas a ‖ *tr* cargar sobre las espaldas; tomar sobre sí, hacerse responsable de; empujar con el hombro para abrirse paso
shoulder blade *s* escápula, omóplato
shoulder strap *s* (*of underwear*) presilla; (*of garment*) tirante *m;* (*of bag*) correa; (mil) charretera
shouldn't *contr* **should not**
shout [ʃaʊt] *s* grito, voz *f* ‖ *tr* gritar, vocear; **to shout down** hacer callar a gritos ‖ *intr* gritar, dar voces
shove [ʃʌv] *s* empujón *m* ‖ *tr* empujar ‖ *intr* dar empujones, avanzar a empujones; **to shove off** alejarse de la costa; (slang) ponerse en marcha, salir
shov•el [ˈʃʌvəl] *s* pala ‖ *v* (*pret & pp* **-eled** o **-elled;** *ger* **-eling** o **-elling**) *tr* traspalar; espalar (*p.ej., la nieve*) ‖ *intr* trabajar con pala
show [ʃo] *s* exhibición, exposición, muestra; espectáculo; (*in the theater*) función; (*each performance of a play or movie*) sesión; demostración, prueba; indicación, señal *f,* signo;

apariencia; (*e.g., of confidence*) alarde *m;* (coll) ocasión, oportunidad; ostentación; espectáculo ridículo, hazmerreír *m;* **to make a show of** hacer gala de; **to steal the show from** robar la obra a (*otro actor*) || *tr* mostrar, enseñar; demostrar, probar; poner, proyectar (*un film*); (*e.g., to the door*) acompañar; **to show up** (coll) desenmascarar || *intr* mostrarse, aparecer, asomar; salir (*p.ej., las enaguas*); **to show off** fachendear; **to show through** clarearse, transparentarse; **to show up** (coll) presentarse, dejarse ver

show bill *s* cartel *m*

showbiz [ˋsobɪz] *s* (coll) el mundo del espectáculo

show'boat *s* barco donde se dan espectáculos

show business *s* comercio de los espectáculos, el mundo del espectáculo

show'case' *s* vitrina (de exposición), escaparate *m* || *tr* exhibir

show'down' *s* cartas boca arriba; (coll) revelación forzosa, arreglo terminante

shower [ˋʃaʊ•ər] *s* (*sudden fall of rain*) aguacero, chaparrón *m;* (*shower bath*) ducha; (*e.g., of bullets*) rociada; despedida de soltera || *tr* regar; **to shower with** colmar de || *intr* llover

shower bath *s* ducha, baño de ducha

shower curtain *s* cortina de ducha

showgirl *s* (theat) corista *f,* conjuntista *f*

show•man [ˋʃomən] *s* (*pl* **-men** [mən]) empresario de teatro, empresario de circo

show'-off' *s* (coll) fanfarrón *m,* presumido

show'piece' *s* objeto de arte sobresaliente

show'place' *s* sitio o edificio que se exhibe por su belleza o lujo

show'room' *s* sala de muestras, sala de exhibición

show window *s* escaparate *m* (de tienda); aparador *m* (Mex)

show•y [ˋʃo•i] *adj* (*comp* **-ier;** *super* **-iest**) aparatoso, cursi, ostentoso

shrapnel [ˋʃræpnəl] *s* granada de metralla

shred [ʃrɛd] *s* jirón *m,* tira, triza; fragmento, pizca; **to tear to shreds** hacer trizas || *v* (*pret & pp* **shredded** o **shred;** *ger* **shredding**) *tr* desmenuzar, hacer trizas; deshilar (*carne*); (*documents*) destruir, triturar

shredder [ˋʃrɛdər] *s* trituradora; (culin) cortadora

shrew [ʃru] *s* (*nagging woman*) arpía, fierecilla; (*animal*) musaraña

shrewd [ʃrud] *adj* astuto; despierto; listo

shriek [ʃrik] *s* chillido, grito agudo; risotada chillona || *intr* chillar

shrill [ʃrɪl] *adj* agudo, chillón

shrimp [ʃrɪmp] *s* camarón *m;* (*little insignificant person*) renacuajo

shrine [ʃraɪn] *s* relicario; sepulcro de santo; lugar sagrado

shrink [ʃrɪŋk] *v* (*pret* **shrank** [ʃræŋk] o **shrunk** [ʃrʌŋk]; *pp* **shrunk** o **shrunken**) *tr* contraer, encoger || *intr* contraerse, encogerse; moverse hacia atrás; rehuirse, retirarse

shrinkage [ˋʃrɪŋkɪdʒ] *s* contracción, encogimiento; disminución, reducción; merma, pérdida

shriv•el [ˋʃrɪvəl] *v* (*pret & pp* **-eled** o **-elled;** *ger* **-eling** o **-elling**) *tr* arrugar, marchitar, fruncir || *intr* arrugarse, marchitarse, fruncirse; **to shrivel up** avellanarse

shroud [ʃraʊd] *s* mortaja sudario; cubierta, velo || *tr* amortajar; cubrir, velar

Shrove Tuesday [ʃrov] *s* martes *m* de carnaval

shrub [ʃrʌb] *s* arbusto

shrubber•y [ˋʃrʌbəri] *s* (*pl* **-ies**) arbustos; plantío de arbustos

shrug [ʃrʌg] *s* encogimiento de hombros || *v* (*pret & pp* **shrugged;** *ger* **shrugging**) *tr* contraer; **to shrug one's shoulders** encogerse de hombros || *intr* encogerse de hombros

shudder [ˋʃʌdər] *s* estremecimiento || *intr* estremecerse

shuffle [ˋʃʌfəl] *s* (*of cards*) barajadura; turno de barajar; (*of feet*) arrastramiento; evasiva; recomposición || *tr* barajar (*naipes*); arrastrar (*los pies*); mezclar, revolver || *intr* barajar; caminar arrastrando los pies; bailar arrastrando los pies; moverse rápidamente de un lado a otro; **to shuffle along** ir arrastrando los pies; ir tirando; **to shuffle off** irse arrastrando los pies

shuf'fle•board' *s* juego de tejo

shun [ʃʌn] *v* (*pret & pp* **shunned;** *ger* **shunning**) *tr* esquivar, evitar, rehuir

shunt [ʃʌnt] *tr* apartar, desviar; (elec) poner en derivación; (rr) desviar

shut [ʃʌt] *adj* cerrado || *v* (*pret & pp* **shut;** *ger* **shutting**) *tr* cerrar; **to shut in** encerrar; **to shut off** cortar (*electricidad, gas, etc.*); **to shut up** cerrar bien; aprisionar; (coll) hacer callar || *intr* cerrarse; **to shut up** (coll) callarse la boca

shut'down' *s* cierre *m,* paro

shutter [ˋʃʌtər] *s* celosía, persiana; (*outside a window*) contraventana; (*outside a show window*) cierre metálico; (phot) obturador *m*

shutter speed *s* tiempo de exposición, velocidad de obturación

shuttle [ˋʃʌtəl] *s* (*used in sewing*) lanzadera || *intr* hacer viajes cortos de ida y vuelta

shuttle train *s* tren *m* lanzadera

shy [ʃaɪ] *adj* (*comp* **shyer** o **shier;** *super* **shyest** o **shiest**) arisco, recatado, tímido; (*fearful*) asustadizo; escaso, pobre; **I am shy a dollar** me falta un dólar || *v* (*pret & pp* **shied**) *intr* esquivarse, hacerse a un lado; espantarse, respingar; **to shy away** alejarse asustado

shyness [ˋʃaɪnəs] *s* timidez *f;* (*of animal*) lo asustadizo

shyster [ˋʃaɪstər] *s* (coll) abogado trampista

Sia•mese [,saɪ•əˋmiz] *adj* siamés || *s* (*pl* **-mese**) siamés *m*

Siamese twins *spl* hermanos siameses

Siberian [saɪˋbɪrɪ•ən] *adj & s* siberiano

sibilant [ˈsɪbɪlənt] *adj & s* sibilante *f*
sibling [ˈsɪblɪŋ] *s* hermano o hermana
sibyl [ˈsɪbɪl] *s* sibila
Sicilian [sɪˈsɪljən] *adj & s* siciliano
Sicily [ˈsɪsɪli] *s* Sicilia
sick [sɪk] *adj* enfermo, malo; nauseado; (coll) mórbido, perverso; **sick and tired of** (coll) harto y cansado de; **sick at heart** afligido de corazón; **to be sick at one's stomach** tener náuseas; **to take sick** caer enfermo || *tr* azuzar (*a un perro*)
sick'bed' *s* lecho de enfermo
sicken [ˈsɪkən] *tr & intr* enfermar
sickening [ˈsɪkənɪŋ] *adj* repelente, repugnante, nauseabundo
sick headache *s* jaqueca con náuseas
sickle [ˈsɪkəl] *s* hoz *f*
sick'le-cell' anemia *s* anemia drepanocítica, drepanocitosis *f*
sick leave *s* licencia por enfermedad
sick•ly [ˈsɪkli] *adj* (*comp* **-lier;** *super* **-liest**) enfermizo
sickness [ˈsɪknɪs] *s* enfermedad; náusea
side [saɪd] *adj* lateral || *s* lado; (*of a solid; of a phonograph record*) cara; (*of a hill*) falda; (*of human body, of a ship*) costado; facción, partido || *intr* tomar partido; **to side with** tomar el partido de
side arms *spl* armas de cinto
side'board' *s* aparador *m*
side'burns' *spl* patillas
side dish *s* plato servido con el plato principal
side door *s* puerta lateral; puerta excusada
side effect *s* efecto secundario perjudicial (*de ciertos medicamentos*)
side glance *s* mirada de soslayo
side issue *s* cuestión secundaria
side'kick' *s* (coll) compañero regular
side'light' *s* detalle *m* incidental, anécdota
side line *s* negocio accesorio; **on the side lines** sin tomar parte || *tr* (pol) marginar; (sport) dejar fuera del equipo, dejar al margen
sidereal [saɪˈdɪrɪ•əl] *adj* sidéreo
side'sad'dle *adv* a asentadillas, a mujeriegas
sideshow *s* función secundaria, espectáculo de atracciones
side'split'ting *adj* desternillante
side'step *v* (*pret & pp* **-stepped;** *ger* **-stepping**) *tr* esquivar, eludir
side'swipe *s* roce *m;* crítica hecha al pasar || *tr* rozar
side table *s* mesa auxiliar
side'track' *s* apartadero, desviadero, vía muerta || *tr* desviar (*un tren*); echar a un lado
side view *s* perfil *m,* vista de lado
side'walk' *s* acera; banqueta (Guat, Mex); vereda (Arg, Cuba, Peru)
sidewalk café *s* terraza, café *m* en la acera
sideward [ˈsaɪdwərd] *adj* oblicuo, sesgado || *adv* de lado, hacia un lado
side'ways' *adj* oblicuo, sesgado || *adv* de lado, hacia un lado; a través
side whiskers *spl* patillas
side'wise' *s* oblicuo, sesgado || *adv* de lado, hacia un lado; a través
siding [ˈsaɪdɪŋ] *s* (rr) apartadero, desviadero, vía muerta
sidle [ˈsaɪdəl] *intr* ir de lado; **to sidle up to** acercarse de lado a (*una persona*) para no ser visto
siege [sidʒ] *s* sitio, cerco; **to lay siege to** poner sitio o cerco a; (fig) asediar (*p.ej., el corazón de una mujer*)
siesta [sɪˈɛstə] *s* siesta; **to take a siesta** echarse una siesta
sieve [sɪv] *s* cedazo, tamiz *m* || *tr* cerner, tamizar
sift [sɪft] *tr* cerner, cribar; escudriñar, examinar; (*to screen, separate*) entresacar; (*to scatter with or as with a sieve*) empolvar
sifter [ˈsɪftər] *s* tamiz *m*
sigh [saɪ] *s* suspiro; **to breathe a sigh of relief** respirar || *tr* decir con suspiros || *intr* suspirar; **to sigh for** suspirar por
sight [saɪt] *s* vista; cosa digna de verse; (*of a firearm, telescope, etc.*) mira; (coll) gran cantidad, montón *m;* (coll) horror *m,* atrocidad; **at first sight** a primera vista; **at sight** a primera vista; (*translation*) a libro abierto; (com) a la vista; **out of sight** fuera del alcance de la vista; (*prices*) por las nubes; **to catch sight of** alcanzar a ver; **to know by sight** conocer de vista; **to not be able to stand the sight of** no poder ver ni en pintura; **to see the sights** visitar los puntos de interés || *tr* avistar, alcanzar con la vista || *intr* apuntar con una mira; (arti & surv) visar
sight draft *s* (com) giro a la vista, letra a la vista
sightless [ˈsaɪtlɪs] *adj* ciego
sight'-read' *v* (*pret & pp* **-read** [ˌrɛd]) *tr* leer a libro abierto; (mus) ejecutar a la primera lectura || *intr* leer a libro abierto; (mus) repentizar
sight reader *s* lector *m* a libro abierto; (mus) repentista *mf*
sight'see'ing *s* turismo, visita de puntos de interés; **to go sightseeing** ir a ver los puntos de interés
sightseer [ˈsaɪtˌsi•ər] *s* turista *mf,* excursionista *mf*
sign [saɪn] *s* signo; señal *f,* marca; huella, vestigio; letrero, muestra; **to show signs of** dar muestras de, tener trazas de; **to make the sign of the cross** hacerse la señal de la cruz || *tr* firmar; contratar; ceder, traspasar || *intr* firmar; usar el alfabeto de los sordomudos; **to sign off** (rad) terminar la transmisión; **to sign up** (coll) firmar el contrato
sig•nal [ˈsɪgnəl] *adj* señalado, notable || *s* señal *f* || *v* (*pret & pp* **-naled** o **-nalled;** *ger* **-naling** o **-nalling**) *tr* señalar || *intr* hacer señales
signal tower *s* (rr) garita de señales
signato•ry [ˈsɪgnɪˌtori] *s* (*pl* **-ries**) firmante *mf*
signature [ˈsɪgnətʃər] *s* firma; (mus & typ) signatura
sign'board' *s* cartelón *m,* letrero
signer [ˈsaɪnər] *s* firmante *mf*
signet ring [ˈsɪgnɪt] *s* anillo sigilar, sortija de sello

significance [sɪg'nɪfəkəns] *s* significación; relevancia, importancia
significant [sɪg'nɪfɪkənt] *adj* significativo; (*look, smile*) expresivo, elocuente; (*of consequence*) importante
significant other *s* (*lover*) novio, novia, amante *mf;* (*spouse*) esposo, esposa; (*parent*) padre *m,* madre *f*
signi•fy ['sɪgnɪ,faɪ] *v* (*pret & pp* **-fied**) *tr* significar
sign language *s* lenguaje *m* gestual, lenguaje de gestos; **to talk in sign language** hablar por señas
Sign of the Cross *s* (eccl) Señal *f* de la Cruz
sign'post' *s* hito, poste *m* de guía
Sikh [sik] *adj & s* sij
silage [saɪlɪdʒ] *s* ensilaje *m,* ensilado
silence ['saɪləns] *s* silencio ‖ *tr* acallar; (mil) apagar el fuego de; (mil) apagar (*el fuego del enemigo*)
silent ['saɪlənt] *adj* silencioso
silent movie *s* cine mudo, película muda
silent partner *s* socio capitalista
silhouette [,sɪlu'ɛt] *s* silueta ‖ *tr* siluetear
silicon chip *s* placa de silicio
silk [sɪlk] *adj* sedeño ‖ *s* seda; **to hit the silk** (slang) lanzarse en paracaídas
silken ['sɪlkən] *adj* sedeño
silk hat *s* sombrero de copa
silk screen *s* serigrafía
silk'-stock'ing *adj* aristocrático ‖ *s* aristócrata *mf*
silk'worm' *s* gusano de seda
silk•y ['sɪlki] *adj* (*comp* **-ier;** *super* **-iest**) sedoso, asedado
sill [sɪl] *s* travesaño; (*of a door*) umbral *m;* (*of a window*) antepecho
silliness ['sɪlinɪs] tontería, simpleza, pachotada
sil•ly ['sɪli] *adj* (*comp* **-lier;** *super* **-liest**) necio, tonto; (coll) pavo
si•lo ['saɪlo] *s* (*pl* **-los**) silo ‖ *tr* asilar
silt [sɪlt] *s* cieno, sedimento
silver ['sɪlvər] *ad* de plata; (*voice*) argentino; elocuente ‖ *s* plata ‖ *tr* platear; azogar (*un espejo*)
sil'ver•fish' *s* (ent) pez *m* de plata
silver foil *s* hoja de plata
silver lining *s* aspecto agradable de una condición desgraciada o triste
silver plate *s* vajilla de plata
silver screen *s* pantalla de plata
sil'ver•smith' *s* platero, orfebre *m*
silver spoon *s* riqueza heredada; **to be born with a silver spoon in one's mouth** nacer de pie
sil'ver-tongue' *s* (coll) pico de oro
sil'ver•ware' *s* plata, vajilla de plata; plata; cubertería
similar ['sɪmɪlər] *adj* similar, semejante, análogo
simile ['sɪmɪli] *s* (rhet) símil *m*
simmer ['sɪmər] *tr* cocer a fuego lento ‖ *intr* cocer a fuego lento; (coll) estar a punto de estallar; **to simmer down** (coll) tranquilizarse lentamente
simoon [sɪ'mun] *s* simún *m*
simper ['sɪmpər] *s* sonrisa boba ‖ *intr* sonreír bobamente
simple ['sɪmpəl] *adj* simple, sencillo ‖ *s* (*medicinal plant*) simple *m*
simple-minded ['sɪmpəl'maɪndɪd] *adj* candoroso, ingenuo; idiota, mentecato; estúpido, ignorante
simple substance *s* (chem) cuerpo simple
simpleton ['sɪmpəltən] *s* simple *mf,* bobo, mentecato
simplify ['sɪmplə,faɪ] *tr* simplificar
simulate ['sɪmjə,let] *tr* simular
simulator ['sɪmjə,letər] *s* (compu) simulador *m*
simultaneous [,saɪməl'tenɪ•əs] o [,sɪməl 'tenɪ•əs] *adj* simultáneo ‖ *adv*—**to do simultaneously** simultanear
sin [sɪn] *s* pecado ‖ *v* (*pret & pp* **sinned;** *ger* **sinning**) *intr* pecar
since [sɪns] *adv* desde entonces, después ‖ *prep* desde; después de ‖ *conj* desde que; después (de) que; ya que, puesto que
sincere [sɪn'sɪr] *adj* sincero
Sincerely yours [sɪn'sɪrlɪ] *adv* a usted atentamente, atentamente
sincerity [sɪn'sɛrɪti] *s* sinceridad
sinecure ['saɪnɪ,kjur] *s* sinecura
sinew ['sɪnju] *s* tendón *m;* (fig) fibra, nervio, vigor *m*
sinful ['sɪnfəl] *adj* (*person*) pecador; (*act, intention, etc.*) pecaminoso
sing [sɪŋ] *v* (*pret* **sang** [sæŋ] o **sung** [sʌŋ]; *pp* **sung**) *tr* cantar; **to sing to sleep** arrullar ‖ *intr* cantar
singe [sɪndʒ] *v* (*ger* **singeing**) *tr* chamuscar, socarrar
singer ['sɪŋər] *s* cantante *mf;* (*in a night club*) vocalista *mf*
single ['sɪŋgəl] *adj* solo, único; simple, sencillo; particular; (*e.g., room in a hotel*) individual; (*copy*) suelto; (*unmarried*) soltero; solteril, de soltero ‖ *s* (*record*) sencillo, single *m;* (*hotel room*) habitación individual; (*person*) soltero, soltera; (*in baseball*) sencillo ‖ *tr* escoger, elegir; **to single out** singularizar
single blessedness *s* el bendito celibato
single-breasted ['sɪŋgəl'brɛstɪd] *adj* sin cruzar, de un solo pecho
single entry *s* (com) partida simple
single file *s* fila india; **in single file** de reata
single-handed ['sɪŋgəl'hændɪd] *adj* solo, sin ayuda
single life *s* vida de soltero
single parent *s* madre *f* que cría a sus hijos sin pareja, padre *m* que cría a sus hijos sin pareja
sin'gle-par'ent family *s* familia monoparental
sin'gle-track' *adj* de vía única; (coll) de cortos alcances
sing'song' *adj* monótono ‖ *s* sonsonete *m*
singular ['sɪŋgjələr] *adj & s* singular *m*

sinister [ˈsɪnɪstər] *adj* amenazante, ominoso, funesto
sink [sɪŋk] *s* fregadero, pila ‖ *v* (*pret* **sank** [sæŋk] o **sunk** [sʌŋk]; *pp* **sunk**) *tr* hundir, sumergir; echar a pique; abrir, cavar (*un pozo*); hincar (*los dientes*); invertir (*mucho dinero*) perdiéndolo todo; (*basketball*) encestar ‖ *intr* hundirse; irse a pique; hundirse (*p.ej., el Sol en el horizonte*); descender, desaparecer; decaer (*un enfermo; una llama*); (*e.g., in a chair*) dejarse caer
sinking fund *s* fondo de amortización
sinless [ˈsɪnlɪs] *adj* impecable
sinner [ˈsɪnər] *s* pecador *m*
sinuous [ˈsɪnjʊ•əs] *adj* sinuoso
sinus [ˈsaɪnəs] *s* seno
sip [sɪp] *s* sorbo, trago ‖ *v* (*pret & pp* **sipped;** *ger* **sipping**) *tr* sorber, beber a tragos
siphon [ˈsaɪfən] *s* sifón *m* ‖ *tr* sacar con sifón, trasegar con sifón
siphon bottle *s* sifón *m*
sir [sʌr] *s* señor *m;* (*British title*) sir *m;* **Dear Sir**: Muy señor mío:, Estimado señor:
sire [saɪr] *s* padre *m,* semental *m;* caballo padre ‖ *tr* engendrar
siren [ˈsaɪrən] *s* sirena
Sirius [ˈsɪrɪ•əs] *s* (astr) Sirio
sirloin [ˈsʌrlɔɪn] *s* solomillo, lomo
sirup [ˈsɪrəp] o [ˈsʌrəp] *s* var de **syrup**
sis [sɪs] *s* (coll) hermanita
sissi•fy [ˈsɪsɪˌfaɪ] *v* (*pret & pp* **-fied**) *tr* (coll) afeminar
sis•sy [ˈsɪsi] *s* (*pl* **-sies**) (coll) persona tímida; (coll) afeminado, mariquita *mf* (pej); (coll) marica *m* (pej)
sister [ˈsɪstər] *adj* (*ship*) gemelo; (*language*) hermano ‖ *s* hermana
sis'ter-in-law' *s* (*pl* **sisters-in-law**) cuñada, hermana política; (*wife of one's husband's or wife's brother*) concuñada
sit [sɪt] *v* (*pret & pp* **sat** [sæt]; *ger* **sitting**) *intr* estar sentado; sentarse; echarse (*un ave sobre los huevos*); reunirse, celebrar junta; descansar; **to sit down** sentarse; **to sit still** estarse quieto; **to sit up** incorporarse (*el que estaba echado*)
sitcom [ˈsɪtˌkɑm] *s* (coll) telecomedia serial
sit'-down' strike *s* hulega de sentados, huelga de brazos caídos
site [saɪt] *s* sitio, paraje *m*; (compu) parcela
sit'-in' *s* sentada, sitin *m* (Mex) (manifestación pacífica a *modo de bloqueo*); (*strike*) encierro, ocupación o toma del lugar
sitting [ˈsɪtɪŋ] *s* (*period one remains seated*) sentada; (*before a painter*) estadía; (*of a court or legislature*) sesión; **at one sitting** de una sentada
sitting duck *s* pato sentado en el agua (*fácil de matar a tiro de escopeta*); (coll) blanco de fácil alcance
sitting room *s* sala de estar, salón *m*
situate [ˈsɪtʃʊˌet] *tr* situar
situation [ˌsɪtʃʊˈeʃən] *s* situación; colocación, puesto; medio ambiente
situation comedy *s* telecomedia serial
sitz bath [sɪts] *s* baño de asiento
six [sɪks] *adj & pron* seis ‖ *s* seis *m;* **at sixes and sevens** en confusión, en desacuerdo; **six o'clock** las seis
six hundred *adj & pron* seiscientos ‖ *s* seiscientos *m*
sixteen [ˈsɪksˈtin] *adj, pron & s* dieciséis *m,* diez y seis
sixteenth [ˈsɪksˈtinθ] *adj & s* (*in a series*) decimosexto; (*part*) dieciseisavo ‖ *s* (*in dates*) dieciséis *m*
sixth [sɪksθ] *adj & s* sexto ‖ *s* (*in dates*) seis *m*
sixtieth [ˈsɪkstɪ•ɪθ] *adj & s* (*in a series*) sexagésimo; (*part*) sesentavo
six•ty [ˈsɪksti] *adj & pron* sesenta ‖ *s* (*pl* **-ties**) sesenta *m*
sizable [ˈsaɪzəbəl] *adj* considerable, bastante grande
size [saɪz] *s* tamaño; (*of a person or garment*) talla; (*of a pipe, a wire*) diámetro; (*for gilding*) sisa, cola de retazo; (coll) verdadera situación ‖ *tr* clasificar según tamaño; sisar, encolar; **to size up** enfocar (*un problema*); medir con la vista
sizzle [ˈsɪzəl] *s* chispa ‖ *intr* chisporrotear, crepitar; (coll) echar chispas
skate [sket] *s* patín *m;* (slang) adefesio, tipo ‖ *intr* patinar; **to skate on thin ice** buscar el peligro
skate'board' *s* monopatín *m,* patineta (SAm)
skater [ˈsketər] *s* patinador
skating rink *s* patinadero, pista de patinar
skein [sken] *s* madeja; enredo, maraña
skeleton [ˈskɛlɪtən] *adj* esquelético ‖ *s* esqueleto
skeleton key *s* llave maestra
skeptic [ˈskɛptɪk] *adj & s* escéptico
skeptical [ˈskɛptɪkəl] *adj* escéptico
sketch [skɛtʃ] *s* boceto, dibujo; bosquejo, esbozo; drama corto, pieza corta ‖ *tr* dibujar; bosquejar, esbozar
sketch'book' *s* libro de bocetos; libro de esbozos literarios
skew [skju] *adj* torcido; sesgado ‖ *s* sesgo ‖ *tr* torcer; sesgar; **to be skewed** estar sesgado
skewer [ˈskju•ər] *s* broqueta ‖ *tr* espetar; traspasar con aguja
ski [ski] *s* (*pl* **skis** o **ski**) esquí *m intr* esquiar
ski boot *s* bota de esquiar, bota de esquí
skid [skɪd] *s* (*of an auto*) resbalón *m;* (*of a wheel*) patinaje *m,* patinazo; calzo ‖ *v* (*pret & pp* **skidded;** *ger* **skidding**) *tr* calzar ‖ *intr* resbalar (*un coche*); patinar (*una rueda*)
skid chain *s* cadena antirresbaladiza
skidding *s* (aut) patinada, derrapada, derrapaje *m*
skid row *s* barrio de mala vida
skier [ˈski•ər] *s* esquiador *m*
skiff [skɪf] *s* esquife *m*
skiing [ˈski•ɪŋ] *s* esquiismo
skiing goggles *spl* gafas de esquiar

ski jacket *s* plumífero
skijoring [ski'dʒorɪŋ] *s* esquí remolcado
ski jump *s* salto de esquí; cancha de esquiar; trampolín *m*
ski lift *s* telesquí *m*
skill [skɪl] *s* destreza, habilidad, pericia
skilled [skɪld] *adj* hábil, experimentado, experto
skillet ['skɪlɪt] *s* cacerola de mango largo; sartén *f*
skillful ['skɪlfəl] *adj* diestro, hábil
skim [skɪm] *v* (*pret & pp* **skimmed;** *ger* **skimming**) *tr* desnatar (*la leche*); espumar (*el caldo, el almíbar*); (*to graze*) rasar, rozar; examinar ligeramente || *intr* rozar; **to skim over** pasar rozando; examinar a la ligera
ski mask *s* pasamontaña *m*
skimmer ['skɪmər] *s* (*utensil*) espumadera; (*straw hat*) canotié *m*
skim milk *s* leche desnatada
skimp [skɪmp] *tr* escatimar; chapucear || *intr* economizar, apretarse; chapucear
skimp•y ['skɪmpi] *adj* (*comp* **-ier;** super **-iest**) escaso; tacaño, mezquino
skin [skɪn] *s* piel *f;* (*of an animal, of fruit*) pellejo; **to be nothing but skin and bones** estar hecho un costal de huesos, estar en los huesos; **to get soaked to the skin** calarse hasta los huesos; **to save one's skin** salvar el pellejo || *v* (*pret & pp* **skinned;** *ger* **skinning**) *tr* pelar, desollar; escoriarse (*p. ej., el codo*); (coll) timar; **to skin alive** (coll) desollar vivo; (coll) vencer completamente
skin'-deep' *adj* superficial
skin diver *s* submarinista *mf*
skin diving *s* submarinismo
skin'flint' *s* escasero, avaro
skin game *s* (slang) fullería
skin•ny ['skɪni] *adj* (*comp* **-nier;** *super* **-niest**) flaco, enjuto, magro, seco, delgaducho
skin'-tight' *adj* ajustado al cuerpo
skip [skɪp] *s* salto || *v* (*pret & pp* **skipped;** *ger* **skipping**) *tr* saltar || *intr* saltar; saltar espacios (*la máquina de escribir*); moverse saltando; irse precipitadamente
skip bombing *s* (aer) bombardeo de rebote
ski pole *s* bastón *m* de esquiar
skipper ['skɪpər] *s* caudillo, jefe *m;* (*of a boat*) patrón *m;* gusano del queso || *tr* patronear
ski resort *s* estación de esquí
skirmish ['skʌrmɪʃ] *s* escaramuza || *intr* escaramuzar
skirt [skʌrt] *s* falda; borde *m,* orilla; (*woman*) (slang) falda; **split skirt** falda pantalón; **straight skirt** falda de tubo || *tr* seguir el borde de; moverse a lo largo de
ski run *s* pista de esquí
ski stick *s* bastón *m* de esquiar
skit [skɪt] *s* boceto burlesco, paso cómico
skittish ['skɪtɪʃ] *adj* caprichoso; asustadizo; tímido; (*bull*) abanto
skulduggery [skʌl'dʌgəri] *s* (coll) trampa, embuste *m*
skull [skʌl] *s* cráneo, calavera
skull'cap' *s* casquete *m*
skunk [skʌŋk] *s* mofeta; (*person*) (coll) canalla *m*
sky [skaɪ] *s* (*pl* **skies**) cielo; **to praise to the skies** poner por las nubes, poner en el cielo
sky'box *s* (*in a stadium*) preferencia
sky'div'ing *s* paracaidismo con plomada suelta inicial
Skylab ['skaɪ,læb] *s* laboratorio espacial
sky'lark' *s* alondra || *intr* jaranear
sky'light' *s* tragaluz *m,* claraboya
sky'line' *s* línea del horizonte, línea de los edificios contra el cielo
sky'rock'et *s* cohete *m* || *intr* subir como un cohete
sky'scrap'er *s* rascacielos *m*
sky'writ'ing *s* escritura aérea
slab [slæb] *s* losa; plancha, tabla
slack [slæk] *adj* flojo; perezoso; negligente; inactivo || *s* flojedad; inactividad; estación muerta, temporada inactiva; **slacks** pantalones flojos; **to cut** (*someone*) **some slack** (slang) dar alguna libertad de acción a || *tr* aflojar; apagar (*la cal*) || *intr* atrasarse; descuidarse; **to slack up** aflojar el paso
slacker ['slækər] *s* perezoso; (mil) prófugo
slag [slæg] *s* escoria
slake [slek] *tr* aplacar, calmar; apagar (*la cal*)
slalom ['slɑləm] *s* eslálom *m*
slam [slæm] *s* golpe *m;* (*of a door*) portazo; (coll) crítica acerba || *v* (*pret & pp* **slammed;** *ger* **slamming**) *tr* cerrar de golpe; golpear o empujar estrepitosamente; (coll) criticar acerbamente || *intr* cerrarse de golpe
slam'-bang' *adv* (coll) de golpe y porrazo
slam dunk *s* clavado (*canasta marcada metiendo el balón con fuerza desde arriba*)
slammer ['slæmər] *s* (slang) cárcel *f,* chirona
slander ['slændər] *s* calumnia, difamación; levante (CAm, P-R) || *tr* calumniar, difamar
slanderous ['slændərəs] *adj* calumnioso, difamatorio
slang [slæŋ] *s* jerga
slant [slænt] *s* inclinación; parecer *m,* punto de vista || *tr* inclinar, sesgar; deformar, tergiversar (*un informe*) || *intr* inclinarse, sesgarse
slap [slæp] *s* manazo, palmada; (*in the face*) bofetada; (*in the back*) espaldarazo; desaire *m,* insulto || *v* (*pret & pp* **slapped;** *ger* **slapping**) *tr* dar una palmada a; abofetear
slash [slæʃ] *s* cuchillada || *tr* acuchillar; hacer fuerte rebaja de (*precios, sueldos, etc.*)
slat [slæt] *s* lámina, tablilla
slate [slet] *s* pizarra; candidatura, lista de candidatos || *tr* empizarrar; designar, destinar; poner en la lista de candidatos
slate pencil *s* pizarrín *m*
slate roof *s* empizarrado
slaughter ['slɔtər] *s* carnicería, matanza || *tr* matar
slaughter house *s* matadero
Slav [slɑv] o [slæv] *adj & s* eslavo

slave [slev] *adj & s* esclavo || *intr* trabajar como esclavo
slave driver *s* negrero; (fig) negrero
slave'hold'er *s* dueño de esclavos
slave labor *s* trabajo de esclavos
slavery [ˈslevəri] *s* esclavitud
slave trade *s* trata de esclavos
slave trader *s* negrero
Slavic [ˈslɑvɪk] o [ˈslævɪk] *adj & s* eslavo
slaw [slɔ] *s* ensalada de repollo
slay [sle] *v* (*pret* **slew** [slu]; *pp* **slain** [slen]) *tr* matar, asesinar
slayer [ˈsle•ər] *s* matador *m,* asesino
sled [slɛd] *s* luge *m* || *v* (*pret & pp* **sledded;** *ger* **sledding**) *intr* deslizarse en luge o trineo
sledge hammer [slɛdʒ] *s* acotillo
sleek [slik] *adj* liso y brillante || *tr* alisar y pulir; suavizar
sleep [slip] *s* sueño; **to be overcome with sleep** caerse de sueño; **to go to sleep** dormirse; dormirse, morirse (*un miembro*); **to put to sleep** adormecer; matar por anestesia || *v* (*pret & pp* **slept** [slɛpt]) *tr* pasar durmiendo; **to sleep it off** dormir la mona; **to sleep it over** consultar con la almohada; **to sleep off** dormir (*p.ej., una borrachera*) || *intr* dormir
sleeper [ˈslipər] *s* (*person*) durmiente *mf;* (*girder*) durmiente *m*
sleeping bag *s* saco de dormir, bolsa de dormir
Sleeping Beauty *s* la Bella Durmiente
sleeping car *s* coche-cama *m*
sleeping pill *s* píldora para dormir
sleeping sickness *s* enfermedad del sueño
sleepless [ˈsliplɪs] *adj* insomne, desvelado; pasado en vela
sleep'walk'er *s* sonámbulo; nochero
sleep•y [ˈslipi] *adj* (*comp* **-ier;** *super* **-iest**) soñoliento; **to be sleepy** tener sueño
sleep'y•head' *s* (coll) dormilón *m*
sleet [slit] *s* cellisca || *intr* cellisquear
sleeve [sliv] *s* manga; (mach) manguito; **to laugh in** o **up one's sleeve** reírse para sí
sleigh [sle] *s* trineo || *intr* pasearse en trineo
sleigh bell *s* cascabel *m*
sleigh ride *s* paseo en trineo
sleight of hand [slaɪt] *s* juego de manos, prestidigitación
slender [ˈslɛndər] *adj* esbelto, flaco, delgado; escaso, insuficiente
sleuth [sluθ] *s* sabueso
slew [slu] *s* (coll) montón *m*
slice [slaɪs] *s* rebanada, tajada; (*of an orange*) gajo || *tr* rebanar, tajar; dividir; cortar
slick [slɪk] *adj* liso y brillante; meloso, suave; (coll) astuto, mañoso || *s* lugar aceitoso y lustroso (*en el agua*)
slicker [ˈslɪkər] *s* impermeable *m* de hule; (coll) embaucador *m*
slide [slaɪd] *s* resbalón *m;* (*slippery place*) resbaladero; (*slippery surface*) desliz *m;* derrumbamiento de tierra; (*image for projection*) diapositiva, transparencia; (*of a microscope*) plaquilla de vidrio; (*piece of a device that slides*) cursor *m;* (*of a trombone*) corredera (tubular) || *v* (*pret & pp* **slid** [slɪd]) *tr* deslizar || *intr* deslizar, resbalar; **to let slide** dejar pasar, no hacer caso de
slide fastener *s* cierre *m* cremallera, cierre relámpago
slide rule *s* regla de cálculo
slide trombone *s* trombón *m* de varas
slide valve *s* corredera, válvula corrediza
sliding contact *s* cursor *m*
sliding door *s* puerta de corredera
sliding scale *s* regla de cálculo; (*of salaries*) escala móvil
slight [slaɪt] *adj* delgado; leve; pequeño; escaso; delgaducho || *s* desatención, descuido; desaire *m,* menosprecio || *tr* desatender, descuidar; desairar
slim [slɪm] *adj* (*comp* **slimmer;** *super* **slimmest**) delgado, esbelto; débil, leve, pequeño, escaso
slime [slaɪm] *s* légamo; (*of snakes, fish, etc.*) baba
slim•y [ˈslaɪmi] *adj* (*comp* **-ier;** *super* **-iest**) legamoso; baboso, viscoso; puerco, sucio
sling [slɪŋ] *s* (*to shoot stones*) honda; (*to hold up a broken arm*) cabestrillo || *v* (*pret & pp* **slung** [slʌŋ]) *tr* lanzar con una honda; lanzar, tirar; poner en cabestrillo; colgar flojamente
sling'shot' *s* honda
slink [slɪŋk] *v* (*pret & pp* **slunk** [slʌŋk]) *intr* andar furtivamente; **to slink away** esacabullirse, salir con el rabo entre piernas
slip [slɪp] *s* resbalón *m,* desliz *m;* falta, error *m,* desliz *m;* lapso; embarcadero; (*cover for a pillow, for furniture*) funda; (*piece of paper*) papeleta; (*cutting from a plant*) sarmiento; (*piece of underclothing*) combinación; (*of a dog*) traílla; huída, evasión; mozuelo, mozuela; **to give the slip to** burlar la vigilancia de || *v* (*pret & pp* **slipped;** *ger* **slipping**) *tr* poner rápidamente; quitar rápidamente; pasar por alto; eludir, evadir; **to slip off** (coll) quitarse de prisa; **to slip on** (coll) ponerse de prisa; **to slip one's mind** olvidársele a uno || *intr* deslizarse; patinar (*el embrague*); errar, equivocarse; (coll) declinar, deteriorarse; **to let slip** dejar pasar; decir inadvertidamente; **to slip away** escurrirse; **to slip by** pasar inadvertido; pasar rápidamente (*el tiempo*); **to slip out of one's hands** escurrirse de entre las manos; **to slip up** (coll) errar, equivocarse
slip cover *s* funda
slip of the pen *s* error *m* de pluma
slip of the tongue *s* error *m* de lengua
slipped disc [slɪpt] *s* hernia de disco
slipper [ˈslɪpər] *s* zapatilla, babucha
slippery [ˈslɪpəri] *adj* deslizadizo, resbaladizo; astuto, zorro, evasivo
slip'shod *adj* chapucero, descuidado
slip'-up' *s* (coll) error *m,* equivocación
slit [slɪt] *s* hendidura, raja; cortada, incisión || *v* (*pret & pp* **slit;** *ger* **slitting**) *tr* hender, rajar; cortar

sliver [ˈslɪvər] *s* astilla; (*of shrapnel or bone*) esquirla; (*thin slice*) tajada
slob [slɑb] *s* (slang) sujeto desaseado, puerco
slobber [ˈslɑbər] *s* baba; sensiblería || *intr* babear; hablar con sensiblería
sloe [slo] *s* (*shrub*) endrino; (*fruit*) endrina
slogan [ˈslogən] *s* lema *m,* mote *m;* grito de combate; (*striking phrase used in advertising*) eslogan *m*
sloop [slup] *s* balandra
slop [slɑp] *s* gacha, zupia, agua sucia || *v* (*pret & pp* **slopped;** *ger* **slopping**) *tr* salpicar, ensuciar || *intr* derramarse; chapotear
slope [slop] *s* cuesta, pendiente *f;* (*of a continent or a roof*) vertiente *m & f;* **slippery slope** camino, e.g. **the slippery slope to ruin** el camino de la perdición || *tr* inclinar || *intr* inclinarse
slop•py [ˈslɑpi] *adj* (*comp* **-pier;** *super* **-piest**) mojado y sucio; (*in one's dress*) desgalichado; (*in one's work*) chapucero
slot [slɑt] *s* ranura; (*for letters*) buzón *m;* (compu) ranura, zócalo
sloth [sloθ] o [slɔθ] *s* pereza; (zool) perezoso, perico ligero
slot machine *s* tragamonedas *m* máquina sacaperras, máquina de frutas
slot meter *s* contador automático
slouch [slaʊtʃ] *s* postura relajada; persona torpe de movimientos || *intr* agacharse, andar caído de hombros; **to slouch in a chair** repanchigarse
slouch hat *s* sombrero gacho
slough [slaʊ] *s* cenagal *m,* fangal *m;* estado de abandono moral || [slʌf] *s* (*of a snake*) camisa; (pathol) escara || *tr* mudar, echar de sí; **to slough off** librarse de, deshacerse de || *intr* caerse, desprenderse
Slovak [ˈslovæk] o [sloˈvæk] *adj & s* eslovaco
sloven•ly [ˈslʌvənli] *adj* (*comp* **-lier;** *super* **-liest**) desaseado, desaliñado
slow [slo] *adj* lento; (*sluggish*) cachazudo, despacioso; (*clock, watch*) atrasado; (*in understanding*) lerdo, tardo, torpe || *adv* despacio || *tr* retrasar; atrasar (*un reloj*) || *intr* retardarse, ir más despacio; atrasarse (*un reloj*)
slow′down′ *s* huelga de brazos caídos
slow motion *s* (*film*) ralentí *m;* **in slow motion** al ralentí, a cámara lenta
slow′-mo′tion *adj* a cámara lenta
slowness [ˈslonɪs] lentitud, lerdera
slow′poke′ *s* (coll) tardón *m*
slug [slʌg] *s* (*heavy piece of metal*) lingote *m;* (*metal disk used as a coin*) ficha; (zool) limaza, babosa; (coll) porrazo, puñetazo || *v* (*pret & pp* **slugged;** *ger* **slugging**) *tr* (coll) aporrear, apuñear
sluggard [ˈslʌgərd] *s* pachón *m,* perezoso
sluggish [ˈslʌgɪʃ] *adj* inactivo, indolente, tardo; pachorrudo, perezoso
sluice [slus] *s* canal *m;* (*floodgate*) compuerta; (*dam; flume*) presa
sluice gate *s* compuerta de presa
slum [slʌm] *s* barrio bajo || *v* (*pret & pp* **slummed;** *ger* **slumming**) *intr* visitar los barrios bajos
slumber [ˈslʌmbər] *s* sueño ligero, sueño tranquilo || *intr* dormir; dormitar
slump [slʌmp] *s* depresión, crisis económica; (*in prices, stocks, etc.*) baja repentina || *intr* hundirse, desplomarse; bajar repentinamente (*los precios, valores, etc.*)
slur [slʌr] *s* pronunciación indistinta; reparo crítico; (mus) ligado || *v* (*pret & pp* **slurred;** *ger* **slurring**) *tr* comerse (*sonidos, sílabas*); despreciar, insultar; (mus) ligar
slush [slʌʃ] *s* fango muy blando, aguanieve fangosa, nieve *f* a medio derretir; sentimentalismo tonto
slush fund *s* (coll) fondo de reptiles
slut [slʌt] *s* perra; (*slovenly woman*) pazpuerca; ramera, mala mujer
sly [slaɪ] *adj* (*comp* **slyer** o **slier;** *super* **slyest** o **sliest**) furtivo, secreto; astuto, socarrón; travieso; **on the sly** a hurtadillas
smack [smæk] *adv* (coll) de golpe, de sopetón || *s* dejo, gustillo; palmada, manotada; golpe *m;* beso sonado; (*of a whip*) chasquido || *tr* dar una manotada a; golpear; hacer chasquidos con (*un látigo*); besar sonoramente; **to smack one's lips** chuparse los labios || *intr*—**to smack of** saber a, oler a
small [smɔl] *adj* pequeño, chico; (*short in stature*) bajo; pobre, obscuro, humilde; (typ) minúsculo
small arms *spl* armas ligeras
small business *s* pequeña empresa
small capital *s* (typ) versalilla o versalita
small change *s* suelto, dinero menudo
small fry *s* gente menuda; gente de poca monta
small′-fry′ *adj* de niños, para niños; de poca monta
small intestine *s* intestino delgado
small-minded [ˈsmɔlˈmaɪndɪd] *adj* tacaño, mezquino; intolerante
smallpox [ˈsmɔlˌpɑks] *s* viruela
small print *s* tipo menudo, letra pequeña
small talk *s* palique *m,* charlas frívolas
small′-time′ *adj* de poca monta
small′-town′ *adj* lugareño, apegado a cosas lugareñas
smart [smɑrt] *adj* listo, vivo, inteligente; agudo, penetrante; astuto; elegante, majo; picante, punzante; (coll) grande, considerable || *s* escozor *m;* dolor vivo || *intr* escocer, picar; padecer, sufrir
smart aleck [ˈælɪk] *s* (coll) fatuo, sabihondo
smart bomb *s* (coll) bomba inteligente
smart card *s* tarjeta inteligente
smart money *s* (fig) inversionistas *mpl/fpl* astutos; gente *f* bien informada
smart set *s* gente *f* chic, gente de buen tono
smash [smæʃ] *s* rotura violenta; fracaso, ruina; quiebra, bancarrota; (coll) choque violento, tope violento || *tr* romper con fuerza; arruinar, destrozar; aplastar || *intr* romperse con fuerza;

arruinarse, destrozarse; aplastarse; **to smash into** chocar con, topar con

smash hit *s* (coll) éxito rotundo

smash'-up' *s* colisión violenta; ruina, desastre *m;* quiebra, bancarrota

smattering [ˈsmætərɪŋ] *s* barniz *m,* tintura, migaja

smear [smɪr] *s* embarradura; calumnia; (bact) frotis *m* || *tr* embarrar; calumniar || *intr* embarrarse

smear campaign *s* campaña de calumnias

smell [smɛl] *s* olor *m;* (*sense*) olfato; fragancia, perfume *m* || *v* (*pret & pp* **smelled** o **smelt** [smɛlt]) *tr* oler, olfatear || *intr* oler; heder, oler mal; **to smell of** oler a

smelling salts *spl* sales aromáticas

smell•y [ˈsmɛli] *adj* (*comp* **-ier;** *super* **-iest**) hediondo, maloliente

smelt [smɛlt] *s* (*fish*) eperlano, esperinque *m* || *tr & intr* fundir

smile [smaɪl] *s* sonrisa || *intr* sonreír, sonreírse

smiling [ˈsmaɪlɪŋ] *adj* risueño

smirk [smʌrk] *s* sonrisa fatua y afectada || *intr* sonreír fatua y afectadamente

smite [smaɪt] *v* (*pret* **smote** [smot]; *pp* **smitten** [ˈsmɪtən] o **smit** [smɪt]) *tr* (archaic) golpear o herir súbitamente y con fuerza; caer con fuerza sobre; apenar, afligir; castigar

smith [smɪθ] *s* forjador *m,* herrero

smith•y [ˈsmɪθi] *s* (*pl* **-ies**) herrería

smitten [ˈsmɪtən] *adj* afligido; muy enamorado

smock [smɑk] *s* bata

smock frock *s* blusa de obrero

smog [smɑg] *s* smog *m,* niebla tóxica

smoke [smok] *s* humo; **to go up in smoke** irse todo en humo || *tr* (*to cure or treat with smoke*) ahumar; fumar (*tabaco*); **to smoke out** ahuyentar con humo, dar humazo a; descubrir || *intr* humear; fumar; hacer humo (*una chimenea dentro de la habitación*)

smoke detector *s* detector *m* de incendios

smoked glasses *spl* gafas ahumadas

smoke evacuator *s* extractor de humos

smokeless powder [ˈsmoklɪs] *s* pólvora sin humo

smokeless tobacco *s* tabaco sin humo

smoker [ˈsmokər] *s* fumador *m;* (*room*) fumadero; (rr) coche-fumador *m;* reunión de fumadores

smoke rings *spl* anillos de humo; **to blow smoke rings** sacar humo formando anillos

smoke screen *s* cortina de humo

smoke signal *s* señal *f* de humo

smoke'stack' *s* chimenea

smoking [ˈsmokɪŋ] *s* el fumar; **no smoking** se prohibe fumar; *SIGN* prohibido fumar

smoking car *s* coche-fumador *m,* vagón *m* de fumar

smoking jacket *s* batín *m*

smoking room *s* fumadero, saloncito para fumadores

smok•y [ˈsmoki] *adj* (*comp* **-ier;** *super* **-iest**) humoso; (*emitting smoke*) humeante

smolder [ˈsmoldər] *s* fuego lento sin llama y con mucho humo || *intr* arder en rescoldo, arder sin llamas; (fig) estar latente; (*to burn within*) (fig) requemarse; (fig) expresar (*p.ej., los ojos*) una ira latente

smooch [smutʃ] *intr* besuquearse

smooth [smuð] *adj* liso, terso, suave; plano, llano; igual; acaramelado, afable, blando, meloso; (*water*) tranquilo; (*style*) fluido; **smooth as butter** como manteca || *tr* alisar, suavizar; allanar; facilitar; **to smooth away** quitar (*p.ej., obstáculos*) suavemente; **to smooth down** ablandar, calmar

smooth-faced [ˈsmuðˌfest] *adj* barbilampiño

smooth-spoken [ˈsmuθˌspokən] *adj* meloso, lisonjero, con mucha labia

smooth•y o **smooth•ie** [ˈsmuði] *s* (*pl* **-ies**) galante *m;* elegante *m;* adulador *m* con mucha labia

smother [ˈsmʌðər] *tr* ahogar, sofocar; suprimir; reprimir

smudge [smʌdʒ] *s* tiznón *m;* mancha || *tr* tiznar; manchar; ahumar, fumigar (*una huerta*)

smug [smʌg] *adj* (*comp* **smugger;** *super* **smuggest**) pagado de sí mismo; compuesto, pulcro; relamido

smuggle [ˈsmʌgəl] *tr* meter de contrabando || *intr* contrabandear

smuggler [ˈsmʌglər] *s* contrabandista *mf*

smuggling [ˈsmʌglɪŋ] *s* contrabando

smut [smʌt] *s* tiznón *m;* obscenidad; (agr) carbón *m,* tizón *m*

smut•ty [ˈsmʌti] *adj* (*comp* **-tier;** *super* **-tiest**) tiznado, manchado; obsceno; (agr) atizonado

snack [snæk] *s* parte *f,* porción; bocadillo, tentempié *m*

snack bar *s* lonchería

snag [snæg] *s* (*of a tree*) tocón *m;* (*of a tooth*) raigón *m;* obstáculo, tropiezo; **to strike** o **to hit a snag** tropezar con un obstáculo

snail [snel] *s* caracol *m;* (*slow person*) pachón *m;* **at a snail's pace** a paso de caracol, a paso de tortuga

snake [snek] *s* culebra, serpiente *f*

snake in the grass *s* traidor *m,* amigo pérfido

snap [snæp] *s* (*crackling sound*) chasquido, estallido; (*of the fingers*) castañetazo; (*bite*) mordisco; (*cracker*) galletita; (*of cold weather*) corto período; (*catch or fastener*) broche *m* de presión; (phot) instantánea; (coll) brío, vigor *m;* (slang) breva, cosa fácil || *v* (*pret & pp* **snapped;** *ger* **snapping**) *tr* asir, cerrar, etc. de golpe; castañetear (*los dedos*); chasquear (*el látigo*); fotografiar instantáneamente; tomar (*una instantánea*); **to snap one's fingers at** tratar con desprecio; **to snap up** aceptar con avidez, comprar con avidez; cortar la palabra a || *intr* chasquear, estallar; (*to crack*) saltar; (*from fatigue*) estallar; **to snap at** querer morder; asir (*una oportunidad*); **to snap out of it** (slang) cambiarse repentinamente; **to snap shut** cerrarse de golpe

snap'drag'on *s* (bot) boca de dragón

snap fastener *s* corchete *m* de presión
snap judgment *s* decisión atolondrada
snap•py [ˈsnæpi] *adj* (*comp* **-pier;** *super* **-piest**) mordaz; (coll) elegante, garboso; (coll) enérgico, vivo; (*food*) acre, picante
snap′shot′ *s* instantánea
snap switch *s* (elec) interruptor *m* de resorte
snare [snɛr] *s* lazo, trampa: (*of a drum*) bordón *m,* tirante *m*
snare drum *s* caja clara
snarl [snɑrl] *s* gruñido; regaño; maraña, enredo ‖ *tr* decir con un gruñido; enmarañar, enredar ‖ *intr* gruñir; regañar; enmarañarse, enredarse
snatch [snætʃ] *s* arrebatamiento; pedacito, trocito; ratito ‖ *tr & intr* arrebatar; **to snatch at** tratar de asir o agarrar; **to snatch from** arrebatar a
sneak [snik] *adj* furtivo ‖ *s* sujeto solapado ‖ *tr* mover a hurtadillas ‖ *intr* andar furtivamente, moverse a hurtadillas
sneaker [ˈsnikər] *s* sujeto solapado; (*shoe*) zapato de goma o lona, zapato blando; **sneakers** (*sport shoe*) zapatillas (de deporte) *fpl,* tenis *mpl,* playeras *fpl* (Esp), championes *mpl* (Arg; Urug)
sneak thief *s* ratero, descuidero
sneak•y [ˈsniki] *adj* (*comp* **-ier;** *super* **-iest**) solapado, furtivo
sneer [snɪr] *s* expresión de desprecio ‖ *intr* hablar con desprecio, echar una mirada de desprecio; **to sneer at** mofarse de
sneeze [sniz] *s* estornudo ‖ *intr* estornudar; **not to be sneezed at** (coll) no ser despreciable
snicker [ˈsnɪkər] *s* risa tonta ‖ *intr* reírse tontamente
snide [snaɪd] *adj* malicioso, insidioso
sniff [snɪf] *s* husmeo, venteo; sorbo por las narices ‖ *tr* husmear, ventear; sorber por las narices; (fig) husmear, averiguar; (fig) sospechar; (*heroin*) esnifar (*caballo*) ‖ *intr* ventear; **to sniff at** husmear; menospreciar
sniffle [ˈsnɪfəl] *s* resuello fuerte y repetido; **the sniffles** ataque *m* de resoplidos ‖ *intr* resollar fuerte y repetidamente
snip [snɪp] *s* tijeretada; recorte *m,* pedacito; (coll) persona pequeña e insignificante ‖ *v* (*pret & pp* **snipped;** *ger* **snipping**) *tr* tijeretear
snipe [snaɪp] *s* agachadiza, becacín *m* ‖ *intr* tirar desde un escondite; criticar; **to snipe at** disparar sobre
sniper [ˈsnaɪpər] *s* (*tirador emboscado*) francotirador *m*
snippet [ˈsnɪpɪt] *s* recorte *m,* fragmento, trozo
snip•py [ˈsnɪpi] *adj* (*comp* **-pier;** *super* **-piest**) (coll) arrogante, desdeñoso; (coll) acre, brusco
snitch [snɪtʃ] *s* (*thief*) ratero, ladrón *m;* (*informer*) chivato, soplón *m* ‖ *tr* birlar, robar ‖ *intr* chivarse, soplar; **to snitch on** acusar a, chivarse de (Esp)
sniv•el [ˈsnɪvəl] *s* gimoteo, lloriqueo; moqueo ‖ *v* (*pret & pp* **-eled** o **-elled;** *ger* **-eling** o **-elling**) *intr* gimotear, lloriquear; (*to have a runny nose*) moquear
snob [snɑb] *s* esnob *mf*
snobbery [ˈsnɑbəri] *s* esnobismo
snobbish [ˈsnɑbɪʃ] *adj* esnob, esnobista
snoop [snup] *s* buscavidas *mf,* curioso ‖ *intr* curiosear, ventear
snoopy [ˈsnupi] *adj* curioso, entremetido
snoot [snut] *s* (slang) cara, narices *fpl*
snoot•y [ˈsnuti] *adj* (*comp* **-ier;** *super* **-iest**) (slang) esnob
snooze [snuz] *s* (coll) sueñecito ‖ *intr* echar un sueñecito
snore [snor] *s* ronquido ‖ *intr* roncar
snort [snɔrt] *s* bufido ‖ *intr* bufar
snot [snɑt] *s* (slang) mocarro
snot•ty [ˈsnɑti] *adj* (*comp* **-tier;** *super* **-tiest**) mocoso; asqueroso, sucio; (slang) engreído
snout [snaut] *s* hocico; (*something shaped like the snout of an animal*) morro; (*of a person*) (coll) hocico
snow [sno] *s* nieve *f* ‖ *intr* nevar
snow′ball′ *s* bola de nieve ‖ *tr* lanzar bolas de nieve a ‖ *intr* aumentar rápidamente
snow′-blind′ *adj* cegado por reflejos de la nieve
snow-capped [ˈsno,kæpt] *adj* coronado de nieve
snow′drift′ *s* ventisquero, masa de nieve
snow′fall′ *s* nevada
snow fence *s* valla paranieves
snow′flake′ *s* copo de nieve, ampo
snow flurry *s* nevisca
snow job *s* (slang) decepción, cuento chino; engaño, embaucamiento
snow line o **limit** *s* límite *m* de las nieves perpetuas
snow man *s* figura o muñeco de nieve
snow′plow′ *s* expulsanieves *m,* quitanieves *m*
snow′shoe′ *s* raqueta de nieve
snow′storm′ *s* nevasca, fuerte nevada
snow tire *s* llanta de invierno
snow′-white′ *adj* blanco como la nieve
snow•y [ˈsno•i] *adj* (*comp* **-ier;** *super* **-iest**) nevoso
snowy owl *s* lechuza blanca
snub [snʌb] *s* desaire *m* ‖ *v* (*pret & pp* **snubbed;** *ger* **snubbing**) *tr* desairar
snub•by [ˈsnʌbi] *adj* (*comp* **-bier;** *super* **-biest**) (*nose*) respingona
snuff [snʌf] *s* rapé; (*of a candlewick*) moco; **up to snuff** (slang) en buena condición; (slang) difícil de engañar ‖ *tr* husmear, olfatear; sorber por la nariz; despabilar (*una candela*); **to snuff out** apagar, extinguir
snuff′box′ *s* tabaquera
snuffers [ˈsnʌfərz] *spl* despabiladeras
snug [snʌg] *adj* (*comp* **snugger;** *super* **snuggest**) cómodo; (*garment*) ajustado, ceñido; (*well-off*) acomodado; (*in hiding*) escondido
snuggle [ˈsnʌgəl] *intr* apretarse, arrimarse; dormir bien abrigado; **to snuggle up to** arrimarse a
so [so] *adv* así; tan + *adj* o *adv;* por tanto; también; **and so** así pues; también, lo mismo;

and so on y así sucesivamente; **or so** más o menos; **to think so** creer que sí; **so as to** + *inf* para + *inf;* **so far** hasta aquí; hasta ahora; **so long** hasta la vista; **so many** tantos; **so much** tanto; **so so** tal cual, así así; **so that** de modo que, de suerte que, así que; para que; con tal de que; **so to speak** por decirlo así || *conj* as que || *interj* ¡bien!; ¡verdad!

soak [sok] *s* mojada; (*toper*) (coll) potista *mf* || *tr* empapar, remojar; embeber; (slang) aporrear; (slang) hacer pagar un precio exorbitante; **to soak up** absorber, embeber; (fig) entender; **soaked to the skin** calado hasta los huesos || *intr* empaparse, remojarse

so′-and-so′ *s* (*pl* **-sos**) fulano, fulano de tal; tal cosa

soap [sop] *s* jabón *m* || *tr* jabonar

soap′box′ *s* caja de jabón; tribuna callejera

soapbox orator *s* orador *m* de plazuela

soap bubble *s* burbuja de jabón, pompa de jabón

soap dish *s* jabonera

soap flakes *spl* copos de jabón, jabón *m* en escamas

soap′mak′er *s* jabonero

soap opera *s* (coll) telenovela; serial lacrimógeno, dramón *m*

soap powder *s* jabón *m* en polvo, polvo de jabón

soap′stone′ *s* jaboncillo de sastre

soap′suds′ *spl* jabonaduras

soap•y [ˈsopi] *adj* (*comp* **-ier;** *super* **-iest**) jabonoso

soar [sor] *intr* encumbrarse, subir muy alto, volar a gran altura; aspirar, pretender; (aer) planear

sob [sɑb] *s* sollozo || *v* (*pret & pp* **sobbed;** *ger* **sobbing**) *tr* decir o expresar sollozando || *intr* sollozar

sobbing *s* llorera

sober [ˈsobər] *adj* sobrio; no embriagado; grave, serio; cuerdo, sensato; sereno, tranquilo; (*color*) apagado || *tr* poner sobrio; desemborrachar; **to sober up** desintoxicar || *intr* volverse sobrio; desemborracharse; **to sober down** calmarse, sosegarse; **to sober up** desemborracharse

sobriety [soˈbraɪ•əti] *s* sobriedad, moderación; gravedad, seriedad; cordura, sensatez; serenidad

sobriquet [ˈsobrɪˌke] *s* apodo

sob sister *s* (slang) periodista llorona

sob story *s* (coll) historia de lagrimitas

soc. o **Soc.** *abbr* **society**

so′-called′ *adj* llamado, así llamado; supuesto

soccer [ˈsɑkər] *s* fútbol *m* asociación

sociable [ˈsoʃəbəl] *adj* sociable

social [ˈsoʃəl] *adj* social || *s* reunión social

social climber [ˈklaɪmər] *s* ambicioso de figurar

socialism [ˈsoʃəˌlɪzəm] *s* socialismo

socialist [ˈsoʃəlɪst] *s* socialista *mf*

socialite [ˈsoʃəˌlaɪt] *s* (coll) personaje *m* de la buena sociedad

social register *s* guía *m* social, registro de la buena sociedad

social security *s* seguro social

social worker *s* asistente *mf* social

socie•ty [səˈsaɪ•əti] *s* (*pl* **-ties**) sociedad; (*companionship or company*) compañía; buena sociedad, mundo elegante

society editor *s* cronista *mf* de la vida social

sociology [ˌsosɪˈɑlədʒi] *s* sociología

sock [sɑk] *s* calcetín *m;* (slang) golpe *m* fuerte || *tr* (slang) golpear con fuerza

socket [ˈsɑkɪt] *s* (*of the eyes*) cuenca; (*of a tooth*) alvéolo; (*of a candlestick*) cañón *m;* (*of a socket wrench*) cubo; (*of a light bulb*) portalámparas *m,* casquillo; (*in a wall*) enchufe *m* (hembra)

socket wrench *s* llave *f* de caja, llave de cubo

Socratic [soˈkrætɪk] *adj* socrático

sod [sɑd] *s* césped *m;* terrón *m* de césped || *v* (*pret & pp* **sodded;** *ger* **sodding**) *tr* encespedar

soda [ˈsodə] *s* soda, sosa; (*drink*) soda

soda fountain *s* fuente *f* de sodas, heladería

soda jerk *s* (slang) dependiente *mf* de una heladería

soda water *s* agua gaseosa

sodium [ˈsodɪ•əm] *adj* sódico, de sodio || *s* sodio

sofa [ˈsofə] *s* sofá *m*

sofa bed *s* sofá *m* cama

soft [sɔft] o [sɑft] *adj* blando, muelle; (*skin*) suave; (*iron*) dulce; (*hat*) flexible; (*solder*) tierno; (coll) fácil

soft-boiled egg [ˈsɔftˈbɔɪld] *s* huevo pasado por agua

soft coal *s* hulla grasa

soft drink *s* bebida no alcohólica, refresco

soften [ˈsɔfən] o [ˈsɑfən] *tr* ablandar; **to soften up** (*by bombardment*) ablandar || *intr* ablandarse

soft′head′ed *adj* tonto, bobo

soft′heart′ed *adj* bondadoso, compasivo

soft′-ped′al *tr* (mus) disminuir la intensidad de, por medio del pedal suave; (slang) moderar

soft soap *tr* jabón blando o graso; (coll) adulación

soft′-soap′ *s* (coll) enjabonar, dar jabón a

soft′ware′ *s* (compu) software *m,* logicial *m* (*programa para ordenador*)

sog•gy [ˈsɑgi] *adj* (*comp* **-gier;** *super* **-giest**) remojado, ensopado

soil [sɔɪl] *s* suelo; país *m,* región; (*spot, stain*) mancha; (fig) mancha, deshonra || *tr* manchar, ensuciar; manchar, deshonrar; viciar, corromper || *intr* mancharse, ensuciarse

soil pipe *s* tubo de desagüe sanitario

soiree o **soirée** [swɑˈre] *s* sarao, velada

sojourn [ˈsodʒʌrn] *s* estancia, permanencia || [ˈsodʒʌrn] o [soˈdʒʌrn] *intr* estarse, permanecer

solace [ˈsɑlɪs] *s* solaz *m,* consuelo || *tr* solazar, consolar

solar [ˈsolər] *adj* solar

solar battery *s* fotopila

solar cell *s* célula fotovoltaica o solar, placa de energía solar

solder [ˈsɑdər] *s* soldadura ‖ *tr* soldar
soldering iron *s* cautín *m,* soldador *m*
soldier [ˈsoldʒər] *s* (*enlisted man as distinguished from an officer*) soldado; (*man in military service*) militar *m* ‖ *intr* servir como soldado
soldier of fortune *s* aventurero militar
soldier•y [ˈsoldʒəri] *s* (*pl* **-ies**) soldadesca
sold out [sold] *adj* agotado; **the theater is sold out** todas las localidades están vendidas; **we are sold out of those neckties** se nos han agotado esas corbatas
sole [sol] *adj* solo, único; exclusivo ‖ *s* (*of foot*) planta; (*of shoe*) suela; (*fish*) lenguado ‖ *tr* solar
solenoid [ˈsolənɔɪ] *s* solenoide *m*
solely [ˈsolli] *adv* solamente, únicamente
solemn [ˈsɑləm] *adj* solemne
solicit [səˈlɪsɪt] *tr* solicitar; intentar seducir
solicitor [səˈlɪsɪtər] *s* solicitador *m,* agente *m;* (law) procurador *m*
solicitous [səˈlɪsɪtəs] *adj* solícito
solicitude [səˈlɪsɪ,tjud] o [səˈlɪsɪ,tud] *s* solicitud
solid [ˈsɑlɪd] *adj* sólido; unánime; (*sound, good*) sólido, macizo; (*e.g., clouds*) denso; (*without pause or interruption*) entero; (*e.g., gold*) puro ‖ *s* sólido
solidarity [,sɑlɪˈderɪtɪ] *s* solidaridad; **to declare one's solidarity with** solidarizar con
solid geometry *s* geometría del espacio
solidity [səˈlɪdɪti] *s* (*pl* **-ties**) solidez *f*
solid majority *s* mayoría cómoda
sol'id-state' *adj* transistorizado
solid-state physics *s* física del estado sólido
solid tire *s* (aut) macizo
solilo•quy [səˈlɪləkwi] *s* (*pl* **-quies**) soliloquio
solitaire [ˈsɑlɪ,tɛr] *s* (*game and diamond*) solitario; sortija solitario
solitar•y [ˈsɑlɪ,tɛri] *adj* solitario; **in solitary confinement** incomunicado ‖ *s* (*pl* **-ies**) solitario
solitary confinement *s* incomunicación, aislamiento penal
solitude [ˈsɑlɪ,tjud] o [ˈsɑlɪ,tud] *s* soledad
so•lo [ˈsolo] *adj* (*instrument*) solista; a solas, hecho a solas ‖ *s* (*pl* **-los**) (mus) solo
soloist [ˈsolo•ɪst] *s* solista *mf*
so long *interj* (coll) hasta luego, hasta la vista
solstice [ˈsɑlstɪs] *s* solsticio
solution [səˈluʃən] *s* solución
solve [sɑlv] *tr* resolver, solucionar; adivinar (*un enigma*)
solvent [ˈsɑlvənt] *adj* & *s* solvente *m*
somber [ˈsɑmbər] *adj* sombrío
some [sʌm] *adj indef* algún; un poco de; unos; (coll) grande, bueno, famoso ‖ *pron indef pl* algunos, unos
some'bod'y *pron indef* alguien; **somebody else** algún otro, otra persona ‖ *s* (*pl* **-ies**) (coll) personaje *m*
some'day' *adv* algúna día
some'how' *adv* de algún modo, de alguna manera; **somehow or other** de un modo u otro
some'one' *pron indef* alguien; **someone else** algún otro, otra persona
somersault [ˈsʌmər,sɔlt] *s* salto mortal, vuelta de campana ‖ *intr* dar un salto mortal
something [ˈsʌmθɪŋ] *adv* algo, un poco; (coll) muy, excesivamente ‖ *pron inde,* alguna cosa, algo; **something else** otra cosa
some'time' *adj* antiguo, de otro tiempo ‖ *adv* alguna vez; antiguamente
some'times' *adv* a veces, algunas veces
some'way' *adv* de algún modo
some'what' *adv* algo, un poco ‖ *s* alguna cosa, algo
some'where' *adv* en alguna parte, a alguna parte; en algún tiempo; **somewhere else** en otra parte, a otra parte
somnambulist [sɑmˈnæmbjəlɪst] *s* sonámbulo
somnolent [ˈsɑmnələnt] *adj* soñoliento
son [sʌn] *s* hijo; **my son** hijo mío
song [sɔŋ] o [sɑŋ] *s* canción, canto; **for a song** muy barato; **to sing the same old song** volver a la misma canción
song and dance *s*—**to make a song and dance about** hacer muchos aspavientos por
song'bird' *s* ave canora
Song of Songs *s* Cantar *m* de los Cantares
song writer *s* cantautor *m*
sonic [ˈsɑnɪk] *adj* sónico
sonic boom *s* (aer) estampido sónico
son'-in-law' *s* (*pl* **sons-in-law**) yerno, hijo político
sonnet [ˈsɑnɪt] *s* soneto
sonneteer [,sɑnɪˈtɪr] *s* sonetista *mf;* poetastro ‖ *intr* sonetizar
son•ny [ˈsʌni] *s* (*pl* **-nies**) hijito
sonori•ty [səˈnɔrɪti] *s* (*pl* **-ties**) sonoridad
soon [sun] *adv* pronto, en breve; temprano; de buena gana; **as soon as** así que, en cuanto, luego que, tan pronto como; **as soon as possible** cuanto antes, lo más pronto posible; **had sooner** preferiría; **how soon?** ¿cuándo?; **soon after** poco después, poco después de; **sooner or later** tarde o temprano
soot [sʊt] o [sut] *s* hollín *m*
soothe [suð] *tr* aliviar, calmar, sosegar
soothsayer [ˈsuθ,se•ər] *s* adivino
soot•y [ˈsʊti] o [ˈsuti] *adv* (*comp* **-ier;** *super* **-iest**) holliniento, tiznado
sop [sɑp] *s* (*food soaked in milk, etc.*) sopa; regalo (*para acallar, apaciguar o sobornar*) ‖ *v* (*pret* & *pp* **sopped;** *ger* **sopping**) *tr* empapar, ensopar; **to sop up** absorber
sophisticated [səˈfɪstɪ,ketɪd] *adj* mundano, falto de simplicidad, corrido
sophomore [ˈsɑfə,mor] *s* estudiante *mf* de segundo año
sopping [ˈsɑpɪŋ] *adj* empapado; **sopping wet** hecho una sopa
sopran•o [səˈpræno] o [səˈprɑno] *adj* de soprano; para soprano ‖ *s* (*pl* **-os**) soprano *mf*
sorcerer [ˈsɔrsərər] *s* brujo, hechicero
sorceress [ˈsɔrsərɪs] *s* bruja, hechicera

sorcer•y [ˈsɔrsəri] *s* (*pl* **-ies**) brujería, hechicería, sortilegio
sordid [ˈsɔrdɪd] *adj* sórdido
sore [sor] *adj* enrojecido, inflamado; (coll) resentido, picado; **to be sore at** (coll) estar enojado con || *s* llaga, úlcera; pena, dolor *m,* aflicción; **to open an old sore** renovar la herida
sorely [ˈsorli] *adv* penosamente; con urgencia
sore throat *s* dolor *m* de garganta
sorori•ty [səˈrɔrɪti] *s* (*pl* **-ties**) hermandad de estudiantas
sorrel [ˈsɔrəl] *adj* alazán
sorrow [ˈsɔro] *s* dolor *m,* pena pesar *m;* arrepentimiento || *intr* dolerse, apenarse, sentir pena; arrepentirse; **to sorrow for** añorar
sorrowful [ˈsɔrəfəl] *adj* doloroso, pesaroso, acongojado
sor•ry [ˈsɑri] o [ˈsɔri] *adj* (*comp* **-rier;** *super* **-riest**) afligido, apenado, pesaroso; arrepentido; malo, pésimo; despreciable, ridículo; **to be** o **feel sorry** sentir; arrepentirse; **to be** o **feel sorry for** compadecer; arrepentirse de; **I am sorry** lo siento, me sabe mal
sort [sɔrt] *s* clase *f,* especie *f;* modo, manera; **a sort of** uno a modo de; **out of sorts** de mal humor; **sort of** (coll) algo, en cierta medida || *tr* clasificar, separar; escoger, entresacar
soʹ-soʹ *adj* mediano, regular, talcualillo || *adv* así así, tal cual
sot [sɑt] *s* borracho
sotto voce [ˈsɑto ˈvotʃə] *adv* a sovoz, en voz baja
soubrette [suˈbrɛt] *s* (theat) confidenta de comedia; (theat) doncella coquetona
soul [sol] *s* alma; **upon my soul!** ¡por vida mía!
soul food *s comida tradicional en el Sur de EE.UU.*
soul kiss *s* beso profundo
soulʹmateʹ *s* alma gemela
sound [saʊnd] *adj* sano: sólido, firme; solvente; sonoro; (*sleep*) profundo; prudente; legal, válido || *adv* profundamente || *s* sonido; ruido; (*passage of water*) estrecho, brazo de mar; (surg) sonda, tienta; **within sound of** al alcance de || *tr* sonar; tocar (*p.ej., campanas*); tantear, sondear; auscultar (*p.ej., los pulmones*); entonar (*p.ej., alabanzas*); **to sound out** sondar, sondear || *intr* sonar, resonar; sondar; parecer; **to sound like** sonar a, sonar como
soundʹ-ab•sorbʹent *adj* fonoabsorbente
sound barrier *s* muro del sonido, barrera de sonido, barrera sónica
soundʹ-deadʹen•ing *adj* fonoabsorbente
sound effects *spl* efectos sonoros
sounding [ˈsaʊndɪŋ] *s* (naut) sondeo
sounding board *s* (*for ideas*) caja de resonancia; (*above stage*) tornavoz *m;* (mus) tabla de armonía
soundly [ˈsaʊndli] *adv* sanamente; profundamente; a fondo, completamente
soundʹproofʹ *adj* antisonoro; insonorizado || *tr* insonorizar
soundproofing [ˈsaʊnd,prufɪŋ] *s* insonorización; aislamiento acústico
sound system *s* equipo de música o sonido
sound track *s* banda sonora
soup [sup] *s* sopa
soup kitchen *s* comedor *m* de beneficencia, dispensario de alimentos, olla común
soup spoon *s* cuchara de sopa
sour [saʊr] *adj* agrio || *tr* agriar || *intr* agriarse
source [sors] *s* fuente *f,* manantial *m*
source material *s* fuentes *fpl* originales
sour cherry *s* (*tree*) guindo; (*fruit*) guinda
sour grapes *interj* ¡están verdes las uvas!
south [saʊθ] *adj* meridional, del sur || *adv* al sur, hacia el sur || *s* sur *m,* mediodía *m*
South America *s* Sudamérica, la América del Sur
South American *adj & s* sudamericano
southern [ˈsʌðərn] *adj* meridional
Southern Cross *s* Cruz *f* del Sur
southerner [ˈsʌðərnər] *s* meridional *mf;* sureño (Am)
South Korea *s* la Corea del Sur
South Korean *adj & s* surcoreano
southʹpawʹ *adj & s* (slang in sport) zurdo
South Pole *s* polo sur, polo antártico
southward [ˈsaʊθwərd] *adv* hacia el sur
south wind *s* austro, noto
souvenir [,suvəˈnɪr] o [ˈsuvə,nɪr] *s* recuerdo, memoria
sovereign [ˈsɑvrɪn] o [ˈsʌvrɪn] *adj* soberano || *s* (*king; coin*) soberano; (*queen*) soberana
sovereign•ty [ˈsɑvrɪnti] o [ˈsʌvrɪnti] *s* (*pl* **-ties**) soberanía
soviet [ˈsovɪ,ɛt] o [,sovɪˈɛt] *adj* soviético || *s* soviet *m*
sow [saʊ] *s* puerca || [so] *v* (*pret* **sowed;** *pp* **sown** o **sowed**) *tr* sembrar; (*with mines*) plagar
soybean [ˈsɔɪ,bin] *s* soja; soya; semilla de soja
sp. *abbr* **special, species, specific, specimen, spelling**
spa [spɑ] *s* caldas, balneario
space [spes] *adj* espacial, del espacio || *s* espacio; **in the space of** por espacio de || *tr* espaciar
spaceʹ-age *adj* futurista, espacial || *s* era espacial
space bar *s* espaciador *m,* tecla de espacios
space center *s* centro espacial
spaceʹcraftʹ *s* astronave *f,* cosmonave *f*
space flight *s* vuelo espacial
space heater *s* calentador *m*
space key *s* llave *f* espacial
space•man [ˈspes,mæn] *s* (*pl* **-men** [,mɛn]) navegador *m* del espacio; astronauta *m;* visitante *m* a la Tierra del espacio exterior
space probe *s* cohete *m* sonda, sonda espacial
space race *s* carrera espacial
space rocket *s* cohete *m* espacial
spaceʹshipʹ *s* nave *f* del espacio
space shuttle *s* transbordador *m* espacial
space station *s* apostadero espacial
space suit *s* escafandra espacial
spaceʹ-timeʹ *s* espacio-tiempo

space travel *s* cosmonavegación, navegación espacial
space vehicle *s* vehículo espacial
spacious [ˈspeʃəs] *adj* espacioso
spade [sped] *s* laya; (cards) pica, pique *m* (*baraja francesa*); **spades** (cards) picas, piques *mpl;* un palo negro de naipes representandos picas estilizadas; equivalente al palo de espadas; **to call a spade a spade** llamar al pan pan y al vino vino
spade′work′ *s* trabajo preliminar
spaghetti [spəˈgɛti] *s* espagueti *m*
Spain [spen] *s* España
Spam[T] [spæm] *s* fiambre enlatado; **spam** (compu) (slang) mensajes inútiles enviados por correo electrónico
span [spæn] *s* palmo, cuarta, llave *f* de la mano; espacio, lapso, trecho; (*of horses*) pareja; (*of a bridge*) ojo; (aer) envergadura ‖ *v* (*pret & pp* **spanned;** *ger* **spanning**) *tr* medir a palmos; atravesar, extenderse sobre
spangle [ˈspæŋgəl] *s* lentejuela ‖ *tr* adornar con lentejuelas; (*to stud with bright objects*) estrellar ‖ *intr* brillar
Spanglish [ˈspænglɪʃ] *s* (hum) espanglés *m*
Spaniard [ˈspænjərd] *s* español *m*
spaniel [ˈspænjəl] *s* perro de aguas, spaniel
Spanish [ˈspænɪʃ] *adj & s* español *m;* **the Spanish** los españoles
Spanish America *s* la América Española, Hispanoamérica
Spanish broom *s* retama
Spanish fly *s* abadejo, cantárida
Spanish guitar *s* guitarra clásica
Spanish Main *s* Costa Firme, Tierra Firme; mar *m* Caribe
Spanish moss *s* barba española
Spanish omelet *s* tortilla de tomate
Span′ish-speak′ing *adj* de habla española, hispanohablante, hispanoparlante
spank [spæŋk] *tr* azotar, zurrar
spanking [ˈspæŋkɪŋ] *adj* rápido; fuerte; (coll) muy grande, muy hermoso, extraordinario ‖ *s* azote *m*
spar *s* (mineral) espato; (naut) mástil *m,* palo, verga ‖ *v* (*pret & pp* **sparred;** *ger* **sparring**) *intr* pelear, reñir; boxear
spare [spɛr] *adj* sobrante; libre, disponible; de repuesto; delgado, enjuto, flaco; parco, sobrio ‖ *tr* pasar sin; perdonar; guardar, salvar; ahorrar; **to have . . . to spare** tener de sobra; **to spare oneself** ahorrarse esfuerzos
spare bed *s* cama de sobra
spare parts *spl* piezas de repuesto o de recambio
spare room *s* cuarto de reserva
spare time *s* horas libres, tiempo libre
sparing [ˈspɛrɪŋ] *adj* económico; (*scanty*) escaso
spark [spɑrk] *s* chispa; (*e.g., of truth*) centellita ‖ *tr* (coll) cortejar, galantear (*a una mujer*) ‖ *intr* chispear
spark coil *s* bobina de chispas, bobina de encendido
spark gap *s* (*of induction coil*) entrehierro; (*of spark plug*) espacio de chispa
sparkle [ˈspɑrkəl] *s* chispita, destello; (*wit*) travesura; alegría, viveza ‖ *intr* chispear; ser alegre; espumar, ser efervescente
sparkling [ˈspɑrklɪŋ] *adj* centelleante, chispeante; (*wine*) espumante, espumoso; (*water*) gaseoso
spark plug *s* bujía (CAm), chispero (CAm)
sparrow [ˈspæro] *s* gorrión *m*
sparse [spɑrs] *adj* (*population*) poco denso; (*hair*) ralo
Spartan [ˈspɑrtən] *adj & s* espartano
spasm [ˈspæzəm] *s* espasmo; esfuerzo súbito y de breve duración
spasmodic [ˈspæzˈmɑdɪk] *adj* espasmódico; intermitente; caprichoso
spastic [ˈspæstɪk] *adj* espástico
spat [spæt] *s* disputa, riña; botín *m,* polaina corta
spatial [ˈspeʃəl] *adj* espacial
spatter [ˈspætər] *tr* salpicar, manchar ‖ *intr* chorrear, chapotear
spatula [ˈspætʃələ] *s* espátula
spavin [ˈspævɪn] *s* esparaván *m*
spawn [spɔn] *s* freza; prole *f;* producto, resultado ‖ *tr* engendrar ‖ *intr* desovar, frezar (*los peces*)
speak [spik] *v* (*pret* **spoke** [spok]; *pp* **spoken**) *tr* hablar (*un idioma*); decir (*la verdad*) ‖ *intr* hablar; **so to speak** por decirlo así; **speaking!** ¡al habla!; **to speak out** o **up** osar hablar, elevar la voz
speak′-eas′y *s* (*pl* **-ies**) (slang) taberna clandestina
speaker [ˈspikər] *s* hablante *mf;* orador *m;* (*of a legislative assembly*) presidente *m;* (rad) altavoz *m*
speaking [ˈspikɪŋ] *adj* hablante; **to be on speaking terms** hablarse ‖ *s* habla; elocuencia
speaking tube *s* tubo acústico
spear [spɪr] *s* lanza; (*for fishing*) arpón *m;* (*of grass*) hoja ‖ *tr* alancear, herir con lanza
spear′head′ *s* punta de lanza ‖ *tr* dirigir, conducir; encabezar; dar impulso a
spear′mint′ *s* menta verde, menta romana
special [ˈspɛʃəl] *adj* especial; **nothing special** (*no great thing*) nada del otro mundo ‖ *s* tren *m* especial
spe′cial•deliv′ery *adj* urgente, de urgencia
special education *s* educación especial
specialist [ˈspɛʃəlɪst] *s* especialista *mf*
speciali•ty [ˌspɛʃɪˈælɪti] *s* (*pl* **-ties**) especialidad
specialize [ˈspɛʃəˌlaɪz] *tr* especializar ‖ *intr* especializar o especializarse
special•ty [ˈspɛʃəltɪ] *s* (*pl* **-ties**) especialidad
spe•cies [ˈspisiz] *s* (*pl* **-cies**) especie *f*
specific [spɪˈsɪfɪk] *adj & s* específico
speci•fy [ˈspɛsɪˌfaɪ] *v* (*pret & pp* **-fied**) *tr* especificar
specimen [ˈspɛsɪmən] *s* espécimen *m;* (coll) tipo, sujeto
specious [ˈspiʃəs] *adj* especioso, engañoso

speck [spɛk] *s* mota, manchita || *tr* motear, manchar, salpicar de manchas
speckle [ˈspɛkəl] *s* mota, punto || *tr* motear, puntear
spectacle [ˈspɛktəkəl] *s* espectáculo; **spectacles** anteojos, gafas
spectator [ˈspɛktetər] *s* espectador *m*
specter [ˈspɛktər] *s* espectro
spec•trum [ˈspɛktrəm] *s* (*pl* **-tra** [trə] o **-trums**) espectro
speculate [ˈspɛkjə,let] *intr* especular
speech [spitʃ] *s* habla; (*of an actor*) parlamento; (*talk before an audience*) conferencia, discurso
speech clinic *s* clínica de la palabra
speech correction *s* foniatría, logopedía
speech defect *s* defecto del habla
speechless [ˈspitʃlɪs] *adj* sin habla; estupefacto
speed [spid] *s* velocidad; (aut) marcha, velocidad; (slang) anfetaminas tomadas como alucinantes || *v* (*pret & pp* **sped** [spɛd]) *tr* apresurar; despedir; ayudar || *intr* apresurarse; adelantar, progresar; ir con exceso de velocidad
speed bump *s* badén *m;* policía acostado (Col), guardia tumbado (Esp), tope *m* (Mex), lomo de burro (SAm)
speeding [ˈspidɪŋ] *s* exceso de velocidad
speed king *s* as *m* del volante
speed limit *s* velocidad permitida
speedometer [spiˈdɑmɪtər] *s* (*to indicate speed*) velocímetro, indicador *m* de velocidad; velocímetro y cuenta-kilómetros unidos
speed record *s* marca de velocidad
speed skating *s* patinaje *m* de velocidad
speed trap *s* control *m* de velocidad por radar
speed•y [ˈspidi] *adj* (*comp* **-ier;** *super* **-iest**) rápido, veloz
spell [spɛl] *s* encanto, hechizo; tanda, turno; rato, poco tiempo; (*e.g., of good weather*) temporada; **to cast a spell on** encantar, hechizar || *v* (*pret & pp* **spelled** o **spelt** [spɛlt]) *tr* deletrear; indicar, significar; **to spell out** (coll) explicar detalladamente || *intr* deletrear || *v* (*pret & pp* **spelled**) *tr* reemplazar, relevar
spell'bind'er *s* (coll) orador *m* fascinante, orador persuasivo
spell'bound *adj* embelesado, cautivado
spell checker *s* (compu) verificador ortográfico
spelling [ˈspɛlɪŋ] *adj* ortográfico || *s* (*act*) deletreo; (*subject or study*) ortografía; (*way a word is spelled*) grafía
spelunker [ˈspɪˈlʌŋkər] *s* espeleólogo de afición
spend [spɛnd] *v* (*pret & pp* **spent** [spɛnt]) *tr* gastar; pasar (*una hora, un día, etc.*)
spender [ˈspɛndər] *s* gastador *m*
spending money *s* dinero para gastos menudos
spend'thrift' *s* derrochador *m,* pródigo
sperm [spʌrm] *s* esperma; (coll) leche *f*
sperm bank *s* banco de esperma, banco de semen
sperm whale *s* cachalote *m*
spew [spju] *tr & intr* vomitar
sp. gr. *abbr* **specific gravity**
sphere [sfɪr] *s* esfera; astro, cuerpo celeste; (fig) esfera, ámbito, campo
spherical [ˈsfɛrɪkəl] *adj* esférico
sphinx [sfɪŋks] *s* (*pl* **sphinxes** o **sphinges** [ˈsfɪndʒiz]) esfinge *f*
spice [spaɪs] *s* especia; (*zest, piquancy*) sainete *m;* fragancia || *tr* especiar; dar gusto o picante a
spice box *s* especiero
spick-and-span [ˈspɪkəndˈspæn] *adj* flamante; limpio, pulcro
spic•y [ˈspaɪsi] *adj* (*comp* **-ier;** *super* **-iest**) especiado; picante; aromático; enchiloso (CAm, Mex); sicalíptico
spider [ˈspaɪdər] *s* araña
spider web *s* tela de araña, telaraña
spiff•y [ˈspɪfi] *adj* (*comp* **-ier;** *super* **-iest**) (coll) guapo, elegante
spigot [ˈspɪgət] *s* grifo; (*plug to stop a vent*) espiche *m*
spike [spaɪk] *s* (*long, heavy nail*) estaca, escarpia; (*sharp projection or part*) punta, pico, púa; (bot) espiga; (econ) aumento improvisto || *tr* empernar; acabar, poner fin a
spill [spɪl] *s* derrame *m;* líquido derramado; (coll) caída, vuelco || *v* (*pret & pp* **spilled** o **spilt** [spɪlt]) *tr* derramar, verter; (coll) hacer caer, volcar || *intr* derramarse, verterse; (coll) caer, volcarse
spillage [ˈspɪlɪdʒ] *s* derrame *m,* vertido
spill'way' *s* bocacaz *m,* canal *m* de desagüe
spin [spɪn] *s* vuelta, giro muy rápido; (coll) paseo en coche, etc.; (coll) operación de relaciones públicas; **to go into a spin** (aer) entrar en barrena || *v* (*pret & pp* **spun** [spʌn]; *ger* **spinning**) *tr* hacer girar; hilar (*p.ej., lino*); bailar (*un trompo*); **to spin off** (*derivative*) rendir; **to spin out** extender, prolongar; **to spin yarns** contar cuentos increíbles || *intr* dar vueltas, girar; hilar; bailar (*un trompo*); (aer) entrar en barrena
spinach [ˈspɪnɪtʃ] o [ˈspɪnɪdʒ] *s* espinaca; (*leaves used as food*) espinacas
spinal [ˈspaɪnəl] *adj* espinal
spinal column *s* espina dorsal, columna vertebral
spinal cord *s* médula espinal
spinal disk *s* disco vertebral
spindle [ˈspɪndəl] *s* (*rounded rod tapering toward each end*) huso; (*small shaft, axle*) eje *m;* (*turned ornament in a baluster*) mazorca
spin doctor *s* (coll) experto en relaciones públicas
spin drier *s* centrifugadora
spin'-dry' *v* (*pret & pp* **-dried;** *ger* **-drying**) *tr* centrifugar
spine [spaɪn] *s* espina, púa; (*rib, ridge*) cordoncillo; loma, cerro; (anat) espina; (bb) lomo; (fig) ánimo, valor *m*
spine'-chill'ing *adj* espeluznante, escalofriante

spineless [ˈspaɪnlɪs] *adj* sin espinas, sin espinazo; sin firmeza de carácter
spinet [ˈspɪnɪt] *s* espineta
spinner [ˈspɪnər] *s* hilandero; máquina de hilar
spinning [ˈspɪnɪŋ] *adj* hilador || *s* (*act*) hila; (*art*) hilandería
spinning wheel *s* torno de hilar
spin′-off′ *s* derivado; subproducto
spin rate *s* (compu) velocidad de giro
spinster [ˈspɪnstər] *s* (*obs, pej*) solterona
spi•ral [ˈspaɪrəl] *adj & s* espiral *f* || *v* (*pret & pp* **-raled** o **-ralled;** *ger* **-raling** o **-ralling**) *intr* dar vueltas como una espiral; (aer) volar en espiral
spi′ral-bound′ note′book *s* cuaderno de espiral
spiral staircase *s* escalera de caracol, escalera espiral
spire [spaɪr] *s* cima, ápice *m;* (*of a steeple*) aguja, chapitel *m;* (*e.g., of grass*) tallo
spirit [ˈspɪrɪt] *s* espíritu *m;* humor *m,* temple *m;* personaje *m;* licur *m* || *tr*—**to spirit away** llevarse misteriosamente
spirited [ˈspɪrɪtɪd] *adj* fogoso, espiritoso
spirit lamp *s* lámpara de alcohol
spiritless [ˈspɪrɪtlɪs] *adj* apocado tímido, sin ánimo
spirit level *s* nivel *m* de burbuja
spiritual [ˈspɪrɪtʃʊ•əl] *adj* espiritual
spiritualism [ˈspɪrɪtʃʊəˌlɪzəm] *s* espiritismo; (*belief that all reality is spiritual*) espiritualismo
spirituous liquors [ˈspɪrɪtʃʊ•əs] *spl* licores espirituosos
spit [spɪt] *s* esputo, saliva; (*for roasting*) asador *m,* espetón *m;* punta o lengua de tierra; **the spit and image of** la segunda edición de, el retrato de || *v* (*pret & pp* **spat** [spæt] o **spit;** *ger* **spitting**) *tr* escupir || *intr* escupir; lloviznar; neviscar; fufar (*el gato*)
spit′ball′ *s* bola de papel; (baseball) bola ensalivada
spite [spaɪt] *s* despecho, rencor *m,* inquina; **in spite of** a pesar de, a despecho de; **out of spite** por despecho || *tr* despechar, molestar, picar
spiteful [ˈspaɪtfəl] *adj* despechado, rencoroso
spit′fire′ *s* fierabrás *m;* mujer *f* de mal genio
spittoon [spɪˈtun] *s* escupidera
splash [splæʃ] *s* rociada, salpicadura; (*e.g., with the hands*) chapaleo, chapoteo; **to make a splash** (coll) hacer impresión, llamar la atención, causar furor || *tr & intr* salpicar; chapotear
splash′down′ *s* (aerosp) acuatizaje *m*
splatter [ˈsplætər] *tr* salpicar, manchar || *intr* chorrear, chapotear
spleen [splin] *s* mal humor *m;* (anat) bazo; **to vent one's spleen** descargar la bilis
splendid [ˈsplɛndɪd] *adj* espléndido; (coll) magnífico, maravilloso
splendor [ˈsplɛndər] *s* esplendor *m*
splice [splaɪs] *s* empalme *m,* junta || *tr* empalmar, juntar
splint [splɪnt] *s* (*splinter*) astilla, tablilla; (surg) tablilla || *tr* entablillar (*un hueso roto*)
splinter [ˈsplɪntər] *s* astilla; (*of shrapnel or bone*) esquirla || *tr* astillar || *intr* astillarse, hacerse astillas
splinter group *s* grupúsculo; grupo disidente
split [splɪt] *adj* hendido, partido; dividido || *s* división, fractura; (slang) porción || *v* (*pret & pp* **split;** *ger* **splitting**) *tr* dividir, partir; **to split one's sides with laughter** desternillarse de risa || *intr* dividirse a lo largo; (slang) abrirse, largarse; **to split away (from)** separarse (de)
split fee *s* dicotomía (*entre médicos*)
split′-lev′el *adj* en dos niveles
split personality *s* personalidad desdoblada
split screen *s* (compu, mov, telv) pantalla dividida
split second *s* fracción de segundo
splitting [ˈsplɪtɪŋ] *adj* partidor; fuerte, violento; (*headache*) enloquecedor
splotch [splɑtʃ] *s* borrón *m,* mancha grande || *tr* salpicar, manchar
splurge [splʌrdʒ] *s* (coll) fachenda, ostentación || *intr* (coll) fachendear
splutter [ˈsplʌtər] *s* chisporroteo; (*manner of speaking*) farfulla || *tr* farfullar || *intr* chisporrotear; farfullar
spoil [spɔɪl] *s* botín *m,* presa; **spoils** (*taken from an enemy*) botín, despojos; (*of political victory*) enchufes *mpl* || *v* (*pret & pp* **spoiled** o **spoilt** [spɔɪlt]) *tr* echar a perder, estropear; mimar (*a un niño*); amargar (*una tertulia*) || *intr* echarse a perder
spoiled [spɔɪld] *adj* (*child*) consentido, mimado; (*food*) pasado, podrido
spoils•man [ˈspɔɪlzmən] *s* (*pl* **-men** [mən]) enchufista *m*
spoils system *s* enchufismo
spoke [spok] *s* (*of a wheel*) radio, rayo; (*of a ladder*) escalón *m*
spokes•man [ˈspoksmən] *s* (*pl* **-men** [mən]) o **spokesperson** *s* portavoz *m,* vocero
sponge [spʌndʒ] *s* esponja; **to throw in** (o **up**) **the sponge** (coll) tirar la esponja || *tr* limpiar con esponja; borrar; absorber || *intr* ser absorbente; **to sponge on** (coll) vivir a costa de
sponge cake *s* bizcocho muy ligero
sponger [ˈspʌndʒər] *s* esponja (*gorrón, parásito*); bolsero (SAm)
sponge rubber *s* caucho esponjoso
spon•gy [ˈspʌndʒi] *adj* (*comp* **-gier;** *super* **-giest**) esponjoso
sponsor [ˈspɑnsər] *s* patrocinador *m;* (*godfather*) padrino; (*godmother*) madrina || *tr* patrocinar
sponsorship [ˈspɑnsərˌʃɪp] *s* patrocinio
spontaneous [spɑnˈtenɪ•əs] *adj* espontáneo
spoof [spuf] *s* (slang) mistificación, engaño; (slang) broma || *tr* (slang) mistificar, engañar || *intr* (slang) bromear, burlar; (slang) parodiar
spook [spuk] *s* aparecido, espectro

spook•y [ˈspuki] *adj* (*comp* **-ier;** *super* **-iest**) espectral, espeluznante; (*horse*) asustadizo
spool [spul] *s* carrete *m,* bobina
spoon [spun] *s* cuchara ‖ *tr* cucharear ‖ *intr* (slang) besuquearse (*los enamorados*)
spoonful [ˈspun,fʊl] *s* cucharada
spoon•y [ˈspuni] *adj* (*comp* **-ier;** *super* **-iest**) (coll) baboso, sobón
sporadic(al) [spəˈrædɪk(əl)] *adj* esporádico
spore [spor] *s* espora
sport [sport] *adj* deportivo, de deporte ‖ *s* deporte *m;* deportista *mf;* (*person or thing controlled by some power or passion*) juguete *m;* (*laughingstock*) hazmerreír *m;* (*gambler*) (coll) tahur *m,* jugador *m;* (*in gambling or playing games*) (coll) buen perdedor; (*flashy fellow*) (coll) guapo, majo; (biol) mutación; **to make sport of** burlarse de, reírse de ‖ *tr* (coll) lucir (*p.ej., un traje nuevo*) ‖ *intr* divertirse; estar de burla; juguetear
sport clothes *spl* trajes *mpl* de sport
sport fan *s* aficionado al deporte, deportista *mf*
sporting chance *s* riesgo de buen perdedor
sporting goods *spl* artículos de deporte
sporting house *s* casa de juego; casa de rameras
sports′cast′er *s* locutor deportivo
sports•man [ˈsportsmən] *s* (*pl* **-men** [mən]) deportista *m;* jugador honrado
sports news *s* noticiario deportivo
sports′wear′ *s* trajes deportivos
sports writer *s* cronista deportivo
sport•y [ˈsporti] *adj* (*comp* **-ier;** *super* **-iest**) elegante, guapo; alegre, brillante; magnánimo; disipado, libertino
spot [spɑt] *s* mancha; sitio, lugar *m;* (coll) poquito; **on the spot** allí mismo; al punto; (slang) en dificultad; (slang) en peligro de muerte; **to hit the spot** tener razón; dar completa satisfacción ‖ *v* (*pret & pp* **spotted;** *ger* **spotting**) *tr* manchar; descubrir, reconocer ‖ *intr* mancharse, tener manchas
spot cash *s* dinero contante
spot check *s* verificación a la ventura
spotless [ˈspɑtlɪs] *adj* inmaculado, sin manchas
spot′light′ *s* proyector *m* orientable, reflector *m;* luz concentrada; (aut) faro piloto, faro giratorio; (fig) atención del público
spot remover [rɪˈmuvər] *s* (*person*) quitamanchas *mf;* (*material*) quitamanchas *m*
spot welding *s* soldadura por puntos
spouse [spaʊz] o [spaʊs] *s* cónyuge *mf,* consorte *mf*
spout [spaʊt] *s* (*to carry off water from roof*) canalón *m;* (*of a jar, pitcher, etc.*) pico; (*of a sprinkling can*) rallo, roseta; (*jet*) chorro; **up the spout** (slang) acabado, arruinado ‖ *tr* echar en chorro; (coll) declamar ‖ *intr* chorrear; (coll) declamar
sprain [spren] *s* torcedura, esguince *m* ‖ *tr* torcer, torcerse
sprawl [sprɔl] *intr* arrellanarse
spray [spre] *s* rociada; (*of the sea*) espuma; (*device*) pulverizador *m;* (*twig*) ramita ‖ *tr & intr* rociar
sprayer [ˈspre•ər] *s* rociador *m,* pulverizador *m,* vaporizador *m*
spread [sprɛd] *s* extensión; amplitud, anchura; difusión; diferencia; cubrecama, sobrecama; mantel *m,* tapete *m;* (*of the wings of a bird; of the wings of an airplane*) envergadura; (coll) festín *m,* comilona ‖ *v* (*pret & pp* **spread**) *tr* extender; difundir, propagar; esparcir; escalonar; abrir, separar; poner (*la mesa*) ‖ *intr* extenderse; difundirse; esparcirse; abrirse, separarse
spread′sheet *s* hoja de cálculo
spree [spri] *s* juerga, parranda; borrachera; **to go on a spree** ir de juerga; pillar una mona
sprig [sprɪg] *s* ramita
spright•ly [ˈspraɪtli] *adj* (*comp* **-lier;** *super* **-liest**) alegre, animado, vivo
spring [sprɪŋ] *adj* primaveral; de manantial; de muelle, de resorte ‖ *s* (*season of the year*) primavera; (*issue of water from earth*) fuente *f,* manantial *m;* (*elastic device*) muelle *m,* resorte *m;* (*of an automobile or wagon*) ballesta; (*leap, jump*) brinco, salto; abertura, grieta; tensión, tirantez *f* ‖ *v* (*pret* **sprang** [spræŋ] o **sprung** [sprʌŋ]; *pp* **sprung**) *tr* soltar (*un muelle o resorte*); torcer, combar, encorvar; hacer saltar (*una trampa, una mina*) ‖ *intr* saltar; saltar de golpe; brotar, nacer, proceder; torcerse, combarse, encorvarse; **to spring at** abalanzarse sobre; **to spring forth** precipitarse; brotar; **to spring up** levantarse de un salto; brotar, nacer; presentarse a la vista
spring′board′ *s* trampolín *m*
spring chicken *s* polluelo; (*young person*) (coll) pollita
spring fever *s* (hum) ataque *m* primaveral, galbana
spring mattress *s* colchón *m* de muelles, somier *m*
spring′time′ *s* primavera
sprinkle [ˈsprɪŋkəl] *s* rociada; llovizna; pizca ‖ *tr* regar, rociar; salpicar, sembrar; espolvorear (*p.ej., azúcar*) ‖ *intr* rociar; lloviznar, gotear
sprinkling can *s* regadera, rociadera
sprint [sprɪnt] *s* (sport) embalaje *m* ‖ *intr* (sport) embalarse, lanzarse
sprite [spraɪt] *s* duende *m,* trasgo
sprocket [ˈsprɑkɪt] *s* diente *m* de rueda de cadena; rueda de cadena
sprout [spraʊt] *s* brote *m,* renuevo, retoño ‖ *intr* brotar, germinar, echar renuevos; crecer rápidamente
spruce [sprus] *adj* apuesto, elegante, garboso ‖ *s* abeto del Norte, abeto falso, pícea ‖ *tr* ataviar, componer ‖ *intr* ataviarse, componerse; **to spruce up** emperifollarse
spry [spraɪ] *adj* (*comp* **spryer** o **sprier;** *super* **spryest** o **spriest**) activo, ágil
spud [spʌd] *s* (*chisel*) escoplo; (agr) escoda; (coll) patata

spun glass [spʌn] *s* vidrio hilado, cristal hilado
spunk [spʌŋk] *s* (coll) ánimo, coraje *m,* corazón *m,* valor *m*
spun silk *s* seda cardada o hilada
spur [spʌr] *s* espuela; (*central point of an auger*) gusanillo; (*of a cock, mountain, warship*) espolón *m;* (rr) ramal corto; (*goad, stimulus*) (fig) espuela; **on the spur of the moment** impulsivamente, sin la reflexión debida || *v* (*pret & pp* **spurred;** *ger* **spurring**) *tr* espolear; espuelar (SAm); **to spur on** espolear, aguijonear
spurious [ˈspjʊrɪ•əs] *adj* espurio
spurn [spʌrn] desdén *m,* menosprecio || *tr* desdeñar, menospreciar; rechazar con desdén
spurt [spʌrt] *s* chorro repentino; esfuerzo repentino; arranque *m* || *intr* salir en chorro, salir a borbotones
sputnik [ˈspʌtnɪk] *s* sputnik *m;* satélite *m* artificial
sputter [ˈspʌtər] *s* (*manner of speaking*) farfulla; (*sizzling*) chisporroteo || *tr* farfullar || *intr* farfullar; chisporrotear
spy [spaɪ] *s* (*pl* **spies**) espía *mf* || *v* (*pret & pp* **spied**) *tr* columbrar, divisar || *intr* espiar; **to spy on** espiar
spy'glass' *s* catalejo, anteojo
spy satellite *s* satélite *m* espía
squabble [ˈskwɑbəl] *s* reyerta, riña || *intr* reñir, disputar
squad [skwɑd] *s* escuadra
squadron [ˈskwɑdrən] *s* (aer) escuadrilla; (*of cavalry*) (mil) escuadrón *m;* (nav) escuadra
squalid [ˈskwɑlɪd] *adj* escuálido
squall [skwɔl] *s* grupada, turbión *m;* (*quarrel*) (coll) riña; (*upset, commotion*) (coll) chubasco
squalor [ˈskwɑlər] *s* escualidez *f*
squander [ˈskwɑndər] *tr* despilfarrar, malgastar
square [skwɛr] *adj* cuadrado, p.ej., **eight square inches** ocho pulgadas cuadradas; en cuadro, de lado, p.ej., **eight inches square** ocho pulgadas en cuadro, ocho pulgadas de lado; rectangular; justo, recto; honrado, leal; saldado; fuerte, sólido; (coll) abundante, completo; **to get square with** (coll) hacérselas pagar a || *adv* en cuadro; en ángulo recto; honradamente, lealmente || *s* cuadrado; (*of checkerboard or chessboard*) casilla, escaque *m;* (*city block*) manzana; (*open area in town or city*) plaza; (*carpenter's tool*) escuadra; **to be on the square** (coll) obrar de buena fe || *tr* cuadrar; dividir en cuadros; ajustar, nivelar, conformar; saldar (*una cuenta*); (carp) escuadrar || *intr* cuadrarse; **to square off** (coll) colocarse en posición de defensa
square dance *s* danza de figuras
square deal *s* (coll) trato equitativo
square meal *s* (coll) comida abundante
square shooter [ˈʃutər] *s* (coll) persona leal y honrada
squash [skwɑʃ] *s* aplastamiento; (bot) calabaza; (sport) frontón *m* con raqueta; || *tr* aplastar, despachurrar; confutar (*un argumento*); acallar con un argumento, respuesta, etc. || *intr* aplastarse
squash•y [ˈskwɑʃi] *adj* (*comp* **-ier;** *super* **-iest**) mojado y blando; (*muddy*) lodoso; (*fruit*) modorro
squat [skwɑt] *adj* en cuclillas; rechoncho || *v* (*pret & pp* **squatted;** *ger* **squatting**) *intr* acuclillarse, agacharse; sentarse en el suelo; establecerse en terreno ajeno sin derecho; establecerse en terreno público para crear un derecho
squatter [ˈskwɑtər] *s* advenedizo, intruso, colono usurpador
squaw [skwɔ] *s* (pej) aborígen norteamericana
squawk [skwɔk] *s* graznido; (slang) queja chillona || *intr* graznar; (slang) quejarse chillando
squeak [skwik] *s* chillido; chirrido || *intr* dar chillidos; chirriar
squeal [skwil] *s* chillido || *intr* dar chillidos; (slang) delatar, soplar; **to squeal on** (slang) delatar, soplar (*a una persona*)
squealer [ˈskwilər] *s* (coll) soplón *m*
squeamish [ˈskwimɪʃ] *adj* escrupuloso, remilgado; excesivamente modesto; (*easily nauseated*) asqueroso
squeeze [skwiz] *s* apretón *m;* **to put the squeeze on someone** (coll) hacer a uno la forzosa, meter en prensa a uno || *tr* apretar; agobiar, oprimir; exprimir || *intr* apretar; **to squeeze through** abrirse paso a estrujones por entre; salir de un aprieto a duras penas
squeezer [ˈskwizər] *s* exprimidera
squelch [skwɛltʃ] *s* (coll) tapaboca || *tr* apabullar, despachurrar
squid [skwɪd] *s* calamar *m*
squint [skwɪnt] *s* mirada bizca; mirada furtiva; (*strabismus*) bizquera || *tr* achicar, entornar (*los ojos*) || *intr* bizquear; torcer la vista; tener los ojos medio cerrados
squint-eyed [ˈskwɪnt,aɪd] *adj* bisojo, bizco; malévolo, sospechoso
squire [skwaɪr] *s* acompañante *m* (*de una señora*); (Brit) terrateniente *m* de antigua heredad; (U.S.A.) juez *m* de paz, juez local || *tr* acompañar (*a una señora*)
squirm [skwʌrm] *s* retorcimiento || *intr* retorcerse; **to squirm out of** escaparse de (*p.ej., un aprieto*) haciendo mucho esfuerzo
squirrel [ˈskwʌrəl] *s* ardilla
squirt [skwʌrt] *s* chorro; jeringazo; (coll) mono, presuntuoso || *tr* arrojar a chorros || *intr* salir a chorros
Sr. *abbr* **senior, Sir**
St. *abbr* **Saint, Strait, Street**
stab [stæb] *s* puñalada; (coll) tentativa; **to make a stab at** (slang) esforzarse por hacer || *v* (*pret & pp* **stabbed;** *ger* **stabbing**) *tr* apuñalar; traspasar || *intr* apuñalar
stab in the back *s* puñalada trapera
stable [ˈstebəl] *adj* estable || *s* establo, cuadra, caballeriza
stack [stæk] *s* montón *m,* pila; (*of rifles*) pabe-

llón *m;* (*of books in a library*) estantería, depósito; (*of a chimney*) cañón *m;* (*of straw*) niara; (*of firewood*) hacina; (coll) montón *m,* gran número || *tr* amontonar, apilar; florear (*el naipe*); hacinar (*leña*)

stadi•um [ˈstedɪ•əm] *s* (*pl* **-ums** o **-a [ə]**) estadio

staff [stæf] *s* bastón *m,* apoyo, sostén *m;* personal *m,* plantel *m;* (mil) estado mayor; (mus) pentagrama *m* || *tr* dotar, proveer de personal, nombrar personal para

stag [stæg] *adj* exclusivo para hombres, de hombres solos || *s* (*male deer*) ciervo; varón *m;* varón solo (*no acompañado de mujeres*)

stage [stedʒ] *s* escena; etapa, jornada; (*coach*) diligencia; (*scene of an event*) teatro; (*of a microscope*) portaobjeto; (rad) etapa; **by easy stages** a pequeñas etapas; lentamente; **to go on the stage** hacerse actor || *tr* poner en escena, representar; preparar, organizar

stage′coach′ *s* diligencia

stage′craft′ *s* arte *f* teatral

stage door *s* (theat) entrada de los artistas, salida de artistas

stage fright *s* trac *m,* miedo al público

stage′hand′ *s* tramoyista *m,* metemuertos *m,* metesillas *m*

stage manager *s* director *m* de escena

stage name *s* nombre artístico

stage′-struck′ *adj* loco por el teatro

stage whisper *s* susurro en voz alta

stagger [ˈstægər] *tr* sorprender; asustar; escalonar (*las horas de trabajo*) || *intr* tambalear, hacer eses al andar

staggering *adj* tambaleante; sorprendente

staging area *s* (mil) zona de estacionamiento

stagnant [ˈstægnənt] *adj* estancado; (fig) estancado, inactivo, paralizado

staid [sted] *adj* grave, serio, formal

stain [sten] *s* mancha; tinte *m,* tintura; materia colorante || *tr* manchar; teñir; colorar || *intr* mancharse; hacer manchas

stained glass *s* vidrio de color

stained′glass′ window *s* vidriera de colores, vidriera pintada, vitral *m*

stainless [ˈstenlɪs] *adj* inmanchable; (*steel*) inoxidable; inmaculado

stainless steel *s* acero inoxidable

stair [stɛr] *s* escalera; (*step of a series*) escalón *m;* **stairs** escalera

stair′case′ *s* escalera

stair′way′ *s* escalera

stair well *s* hueco o caja de la escalera

stake [stek] *s* estaca; (*of a cart or truck*) telero; (*to hold up a plant*) rodrigón *m;* (*in gambling*) puesta; premio del vencedor; **at stake** en juego; en gran peligro; **to die at the stake** morir en la hoguera; **to pull up stakes** (coll) irse; (coll) mudarse de casa || *tr* estacar; atar a una estaca; rodrigar (*plantas*); apostar; arriesgar, aventurar; **to stake all** jugarse el todo por el todo; **to stake off** o **to stake out** estacar, señalar con estacas

stake′out *s* (slang) operación de vigilancia

stale [stel] *adj* añejo, rancio, viejo; (*air*) viciado; (*joke*) mohoso; anticuado

stale′mate′ *s* mate ahogado; **to reach a stalemate** llegar a un punto muerto || *tr* dar mate ahogado a; estancar, paralizar

stalk [stɔk] *s* tallo || *tr* cazar al acecho; acechar, espiar || *intr* cazar al acecho; andar con paso majestuoso; andar con paso altivo; **to stalk out** salir con paso airado

stall [stɔl] *s* cuadra, establo; pesebre *m;* (*booth in a market*) puesto; (*at a fair*) caseta; (Brit) butaca; (slang) pretexto || *tr* encerrar en un establo; poner trabas a; parar (*un motor*); **to stall off** (coll) eludir, evitar || *intr* atascarse, atollarse; pararse (*un motor*); (slang) eludir para engañar o demorar; **to stall for time** (slang) tardar para ganar tiempo

stallion [ˈstæljən] *s* caballo padre, caballo semental

stalwart [ˈstɔlwərt] *adj* fornido, forzudo; valiente; leal, constante || *s* persona fornida; partidario leal

stamen [ˈstemən] *s* estambre *m*

stamina [ˈstæmɪnə] *s* fuerza, nervio, vigor *m,* resistencia

stammer [ˈstæmər] *s* balbuceo, tartamudeo || *tr* balbucear (*p.ej., excusas*) || *intr* balbucear, tartamudear

stamp [stæmp] *s* (*device used for making an impression; mark made with it; piece of paper or mark used to show payment of postage*) sello; (*tool used for crushing or marking*) pisón *m;* (*tool for stamping coins and medals*) cuño, troquel *m;* marca, impresión; clase *f,* tipo || *tr* sellar; troquelar; estampar, imprimir; hollar, pisotear; indicar, señalar; poner el sello a; bocartear (*el mineral*); **to stamp out** apagar pateando; extinguir por la fuerza; suprimir; **to stamp the feet** dar patadas || *intr* patalear

stamp collector *s* coleccionista *mf* de sellos, filatelista

stampede [stæmˈpid] *s* fuga precipitada; estampida (Am) || *tr* hacer huir en desorden; provocar a pánico || *intr* huir en tropel; obrar por común impulso

stamping ground *s* sitio frecuentado por una persona

stamp pad *s* tampón *m*

stamp′-vend′ing machine *s* máquina expendedora de sellos

stance [stæns] *s* (sport) postura, planta

stanch [stɑntʃ] *adj* firme, fuerte; constante, leal; (*watertight*) estanco || *tr* estancar; retañar (*la sangre de una herida*)

stand [stænd] *s* parada; alto para defenderse; postura, posición; resistencia; estrado, tribuna; sostén *m* soporte *m,* pie *m;* puesto, quiosco || *v* (*pret & pp* **stood** [stʊd]) *tr* poner, colocar; poner derecho; soportar, tolerar, resistir; (coll) aguantar (*a una persona*); (coll) sufragar (*un gasto*); **to stand off** tener a raya; **to stand one's ground** mantenerse firme || *intr* estar, estar situado; estar parado; estacionarse; estar de pie, estar derecho; ponerse de pie, levantarse; resultar; persistir; mantenerse; **to stand aloof, apart** o **aside** mantenerse apartado; **to stand back of** respaldar; **to stand for** significar, representar; apoyar, defender; apadrinar; mantener (*p.ej., una opinión*); presentarse como candidato de; navegar hacia; (coll) tolerar; **to stand in line** hacer cola; **to stand out** sobresalir; destacarse, resaltar; **to stand up** ponerse de pie, levantarse; durar; **to stand up to** hacer; resueltamente frente a

stand'-alone' *adj* (compu) autoejecutable

standard ['stændərd] *adj* normal; (*typewriter keyboard*) universal; corriente, regular; legal; clásico || *s* patrón *m;* norma, regla establecida; bandera, estandarte *m;* emblema *m,* símbolo; soporte *m,* pilar *m;* (compu) estandar *m*

stan'dard-bear'er *s* portaestandarte *mf*

standardize ['stændər,daɪz] *tr* normalizar, estandardizar

standard of living *s* nivel *m* de vida, estandar *m* de vida

standard time *s* hora legal, hora oficial

stand'by *adj* de reserva, de emergencia; (aer) stand-by

standee [stæn'di] *s* (coll) espectador *m* que asiste de pie; (coll) pasajero de pie

stand'-in' *s* (theat & mov) doble *mf;* (coll) buenas aldabas

standing ['stændɪŋ] *adj* derecho, en pie; de pie; parado, inmóvil; (*water*) encharcado, estancado; (*army; committee*) permanente; vigente || *s* condición, posición; reputación; parada; **in good standing** en posición acreditada; **of long standing** de mucho tiempo, de antigua fecha

standing army *s* ejército permanente

standing committee *s* comisión permanente

standing count *s* cuenta de protección

standing room *s* sitio para estar de pie

stand'off *s* callejón sin salida, empate *m*

standoffishness [,stænd'ɔfɪʃnɪs] *s* desarrimo

stand'out *s* destacada

stand'point' *s* punto de vista

stand'still' *s* detención, parada; alto; descanso, inactividad; **to come to a standstill** cesar, pararse

stanza ['stænzə] *s* estancia, estrofa

staple ['stepəl] *adj* primero, principal; corriente, establecido || *s* (*to fasten papers*) grapa; artículo o producto de primera necesidad; materia prima; fibra textil || *tr* sujetar con grapas

stapler ['steplər] *s* (*for paper*) grapadora; (*for cardboard*) engrapadora

star [stɑr] *s* (*heavenly body*) astro; (*heavenly body except sun and moon; figure that represents a star*) estrella; (mov & theat) estrella; (*of football*) as *m;* (typ) estrella o asterisco; (*fate, destiny*) (fig) estrella; **to see stars** (coll) ver las estrellas; **to thank one's lucky stars** estar agradecido por su buena suerte || *v* (*pret & pp* **starred;** *ger* **starring**) *tr* estrellar, adornar o señalar con estrellas; marcar con asterisco; presentar como estrella (*a un actor*) || *intr* ser la estrella; lucirse; sobresalir

starboard ['stɑrbərd] o ['stɑr,bord] *adj* de estribor || *adv* a estribor || *s* estribor *m*

starch [stɑrʃ] *s* almidón *m,* fécula; arrogancia, entono; (slang) fuerza, vigor *m* || *tr* almidonar

stare [stɛr] *s* mirada fija || *intr* mirar fijamente; **to stare at** clavar la vista en mirar con fijeza

star'fish' *s* estrella de mar, estrellamar *m*

star'gaze' *intr* mirar las estrellas; ser distraído, soñar despierto

stark [stɑrk] *adj* cabal, completo, puro; rígido, tiesco; duro, severo || *adv* completamente, enteramente; rígidamente, severamente

stark'-na'ked *adj* en pelota, en cueros

star'light' *s* luz *f* de las estrellas

starling ['stɑrlɪŋ] *s* estornino

Stars and Stripes, the *s* la bandera de las barras y las estrellas

Star'-Span'gled Banner *s* bandera estrellada (*bandera de los EE.UU.*)

start [stɑrt] *s* comienzo, principio; salida, partida; lugar *m* de partida; (*scare*) sobresalto; (*sudden start*) arranque *m;* (*advantage*) ventaja || *tr* empezar, principiar; poner en marcha; hacer arrancar; dar la señal de partida a; entablar (*una conversación*); levantar (*la caza*) || *intr* empezar, principiar; ponerse en marcha; arrancar; (*to be startled*) sobresaltar; nacer, provenir; **starting from** o **with** a partir de; **to start after** salir en busca de

starter ['stɑrtər] *s* iniciador *m;* (*of a series*) primero; (aut) arranque *m,* motor *m* de arranque; (sport) juez *m* de salida

starting ['stɑrtɪŋ] *adj* de salida; de arranque || *s* puesta en marcha

starting crank *s* manivela de arranque

starting pistol *s* pistola de fogueo

starting point *s* punto de partida, arrancadero

startle ['stɑrtəl] *tr* asustar, sorprender, sobrecoger || *intr* asustarse, sorprenderse, sobrecogerse

startling ['stɑrtlɪŋ] *adj* alarmante, asombroso

start'-up *adj* inicial, de puesta en marcha || *s* (compu) arranque *m*

starvation [stɑr'veʃən] *s* hambre *f,* inanición

starvation diet *s* régimen *m* de hambre, cura de hambre

starvation wages *spl* salario de hambre

starve [stɑrv] *tr* hambrear; hacer morir de hambre; **to starve out** hacer rendirse por hambre || *intr* hambrear; morir de hambre; (coll) tener hambre

starving ['stɑrvɪŋ] *adj* hambriento, famélico

state [stet] *adj* de estado; del estado; estatal; público; de gala, de lujo || *s* estado; fausto, ceremonia, pompa; **to lie in state** estar expuesto en capilla ardiente, estar de cuerpo presente; **to live in state** gastar mucho lujo; **to ride in state** pasear en carruaje de lujo || *tr* afirmar, declarar; exponer, manifestar; plantear (*un problema*)

State Department *s* Ministerio de Relaciones Exteriores *or* de Asuntos Exteriores
state•ly [ˈstetli] *adj* (*comp* **-lier;** *super* **-liest**) imponente, majestuoso
statement [ˈstetmənt] *s* declaración; exposición, informe *m,* relación; (com) estado de cuentas
state of mind *s* estado de ánimo
state′-of-the-art′ *adj* de punta, de vanguardia; último modelo
state′room′ *s* camarote *m;* (rr) compartimiento particular
state′side′ *adv* (coll) en (*or* a) los Estados Unidos
states•man [ˈstetsmən] *s* (*pl* **-men** [mən]) estadista *m,* hombre *m* de estado
states′man•like *adj* propio de un estadista
states rights *spl derechos y atribuciones propias de cada estado de los EE.UU.*
static [ˈstætɪk] *adj* estático; (rad) atmosférico ‖ *s* (rad) parásitos atmosféricos
station [ˈsteʃən] *s* estación; condición, situación ‖ *tr* estacionar, apostar
stationary [ˈsteʃən,ɛri] *adj* estacionario
station break *s* (rad) descanso, intermedio
stationer [ˈsteʃənər] *s* papelero
stationery [ˈsteʃən,ɛri] *s* efectos de escritorio; papel *m* para cartas
stationery store *s* papelería
station house *s* cuartelillo de policía
station identification *s* (rad & telv) indicativo de la emisora
sta′tion•mas′ter *s* jefe *m* de estación
station wagon *s* vagoneta, rubia, coche *m* rural; camioneta (Arg, CAm, Col. Pan, Peru, S-D); esteishon wagon *m* (Chile, Col, Cuba, P-R); guagüita (Cuba, P-R); camionetilla (Guat); carmelita (Hond); ranchera (Ven)
statistical [stə,tɪstɪkəl] *adj* estadístico
statistician [,stætɪs,tɪʃən] *s* estadístico
statistics [stə,tɪstɪks] *ssg* (*science*) estadística; *spl* (*data*) estadística o estadísticas
statue [ˈstætʃu] *s* estatua
statuesque [,stætʃu,ɛsk] *adj* escultural
stature [,stætʃər] *s* estatura, talla; carácter *m,* habilidad
status [ˈstetəs] *s* condición, estado; situación social, legal o profesional; (*prestige or superior rank*) categoría
status quo [kwo] *s* statu quo *m*
status seeking *s* esfuerzo por adquirir categoría
status symbol *s* símbolo de categoría social
statute [ˈstætʃut] *s* estatuto, ley *f*
statutory [ˈstæʃu,tori] *adj* estatutario, legal
staunch [stɔntʃ] o [stɑntʃ] *adj & tr* var de **stanch**
stave [stev] *s* (*of a barrel*) duela; (*of a ladder*) peldaño; (mus) pentagrama *m* ‖ *v* (*pret & pp* **staved** o **stove** [stov]) *tr* romper, destrozar; (*to break a hole in*) desfondar; **to stave off** mantener a distancia; evitar, impedir, diferir
stay [ste] *s* morada, permanencia, estancia; suspensión; (*of a corset*) ballena, varilla; apoyo, sostén *m;* (law) espera; (naut) estay *m* ‖ *tr* aplazar, detener; poner freno a ‖ *intr* quedar, quedarse, permanecer; parar, hospedarse; habitar; **to stay up** no acostarse, velar
stay′-at-home′ *adj & s* hogareño
stead [stɛd] *s* lugar *m;* **in his stead** en su lugar, en lugar de él; **to stand in good stead** ser de provecho, ser ventajoso
stead′fast′ *adj* fijo; resuelto; constante
stead•y [ˈstɛdi] *adj* (*comp* **-ier;** *super* **-iest**) constante, fijo, firme, seguro; regular, uniforme; resuelto; asentado, serio ‖ *v* (*pret & pp* **-ied**) *tr* estabilizar, reforzar; calmar (*los nervios*) ‖ *intr* estabilizarse; calmarse
steak [stek] *s* (*beef*) bistec *m,* biftec *m,* bife *m* (Arg, Bol, Urug), churrasco (SAm); (*slice*) lonja, tajada, filete *m;* (*ground beef*) hamburguesa
steal [stil] *s* (coll) hurto, robo ‖ *v* (*pret* **stole** [stol]; *pp* **stolen**) *tr* hurtar, robar; atraer, cautivar; manotear (Arg, Mex) ‖ *intr* hurtar, robar; **to steal away** escabullirse; **to steal into** meterse a hurtadillas en; **to steal upon** aproximarse sin ruido a
stealth [stɛlθ] *s* cautela, recato; **by stealth** a hurtadillas
steam [stim] *adj* de vapor ‖ *s* vapor *m;* vaho, humo; **to get up steam** dar presión; **to let off steam** descargar vapor; (fig) desahogarse ‖ *tr* cocer al vapor; saturar de vapor; empañar (*p.ej., las ventanas*) ‖ *intr* echar vapor, emitir vapor; evaporarse; funcionar o marchar a vapor; **to steam ahead** avanzar por medio del vapor; (fig) hacer grandes progresos
steam′boat′ *s* buque *m* de vapor
steamer [ˈstimər] *s* vapor *m*
steamer trunk *s* baúl *m* de camarote
steam heat *s* calefacción por vapor
steam iron *s* plancha de vapor
steam roller *s* apisonadora movida a vapor; (coll) fuerza arrolladora
steam′ship′ *s* vapor *m,* buque *m* de vapor
steam shovel *s* pala mecánica de vapor
steam table *s* plancha caliente
steed [stid] *s* caballo; (*high-spirited horse*) corcel *m*
steel [stil] *adj* acerado; (*business, industry*) siderúrgico; (fig) duro, frío ‖ *s* acero; (*for striking fire from flint; for sharpening knives*) eslabón *m* ‖ *tr* acerar; **to steel oneself** acerarse
steel wool *s* virutillas de acero, estopa de acero
steelyard [ˈstil,jɑrd] *s* romana
steep [stip] *adj* escarpado, empinado; (*price*) alto, excesivo ‖ *tr* empapar, remojar; **steeped in** absorbido en
steeple [ˈstipəl] *s* aguja, campanario
stee′ple•chase′ *s* carrera de campanario, carrera de obstáculos
stee′ple•jack′ *s* escalatorres *m*
steer [stɪr] *s* buey *m* ‖ *tr* conducir, gobernar, guiar ‖ *intr* conducirse; **to steer clear of** (coll) evitar, eludir
steerage [ˈstɪrɪdʒ] *s* dirección; (naut) proa, entrepuente *m*

steering column *s* columna de dirección
steering committee *s* comité *m* paneador
steering wheel *s* (aut) volante *m;* (naut) rueda del timón
stem [stɛm] *s* (*of a goblet*) pie *m;* (*of a pipe, of a feather*) cañón *m;* (*of a column*) fuste *m;* (*of a watch*) botón *m;* (*of a key*) espiga, tija; (*of a word*) tema *m;* (bot) tallo, vástago; **from stem to stern** de proa a popa ‖ *v* (*pret & pp* **stemmed;** *ger* **stemming**) *tr* (*to remove the stem from*) desgranar; (*to check*) detener, refrenar; (*to plug*) estancar; hacer frente a; rendir (*la marea*) ‖ *intr* nacer, provenir; **to stem from** originarse en, provenir de
stem cell *s* célula madre; **stem cells** células madre
stench [stɛntʃ] *s* hedor *m,* hediondez *f*
sten•cil [ˈstɛnsəl] *s* cartón picado; (*work produced by it*) estarcido ‖ *v* (*pret & pp* **-ciled** o **-cilled;** *ger* **-ciling** o **-cilling**) *tr* estarcir
stenographer [stəˈnɑgrəfər] *s* estenógrafo
stenography [stəˈnɑgrəfi] *s* estenografía
step [stɛp] *s* paso; (*of staircase*) grada, peldaño; (*footprint*) huella, pisada; (*of carriage*) estribo; (*measure, démarche*) gestión, medida; (mus) intervalo; **step by step** paso a paso; **to watch one's step** proceder con cautela, andarse con tiento ‖ *v* (*pret & pp* **stepped;** *ger* **stepping**) *tr* escalonar; **to step off** medir a pasos ‖ *intr* dar un paso, dar pasos; caminar, ir; (coll) andar de prisa; **to step on it** (coll) acelerar la marcha, darse prisa; **to step on the starter** pisar el arranque
step'broth'er *s* medio hermano, hermanastro
step'child' *s* (*pl* **-children** [ˌtʃildrən]) hijastro
step'daugh'ter *s* hijastra
step'fa'ther *s* padrastro
step'lad'der *s* escala, escalera de tijera
step'moth'er *s* madrasta
steppe [stɛp] *s* estepa
stepping stone *s* estriberón *m,* pasadera; (fig) escalón *m,* escabel *m*
step'sis'ter *s* media hermana, hermanastra
step'son' *s* hijastro
stere•o [ˈstɛriˌo] o [ˈstɪrɪˌo] *adj* estereofónico, estereo; estereoscópico ‖ *s* (*pl* **-os**) música estereofónica, disco estereofónico, estereo; radiodifusión estereofónica; fotografía estereoscópica
stereophonic [ˈstɛrɪ•əˈfɑnɪk] *adj* estereofónico
stereo system *s* equipo de alta fidelidad, estereo, estereofonía
ster'e•o•type' *s* clisé *m,* estereotipo; concepción tradicional
stereotyped [ˈstɛrɪ•əˌtaɪpt] o [ˈstɪrɪ•əˌtaɪpt] *adj* estereotipado
sterile [ˈstɛrɪl] *adj* estéril
sterilization [ˌstɛrɪlɪˈzeʃən] *s* esterilización
sterilize [ˈstɛrɪˌlaɪz] *tr* esterilizar
sterling [ˈstʌrlɪŋ] *adj* fino, de ley; verdadero, genuino, puro, excelente ‖ *s* libras esterlinas; plata de ley; vajilla de plata
stern [stʌrn] *adj* austero, severo; decidido, firme ‖ *s* popa
stethoscope [ˈstɛθəˌskop] *s* estetoscopio
stevedore [ˈstivəˌdor] *s* estibador *m*
stew [stju] o [stu] *s* guisado, estofado ‖ *tr* guisar, estofar ‖ *intr* abrasarse; (coll) estar apurado
steward [ˈstu•ərd] *s* mayordomo; administrador *m;* (*of ship or plane*) camarero
stewardess [ˈstu•ərdɪs] *s* mayordoma; (*of ship or plane*) camarera; (*of plane*) azafata, aeromoza
stewed fruit *s* compota de frutas
stick [stɪk] *s* palo, palillo; bastón *m,* vara; (*of dynamite*) barra; (naut) mástil *m,* verga; (typ) componedor *m* ‖ *v* (*pret & pp* **stuck** [stʌk]) *tr* picar, punzar; apuñalar; clavar, hincar; pegar; (coll) confundir; **to stick out** asomar (*la cabeza*); sacar (*la lengua*); **to stick up** (*in order to rob*) (slang) asaltar, atracar ‖ *intr* estar prendido, estar hincado; pegarse; agarrarse (*la pintura*); encastillarse (*p.ej., una ventana*); resaltar, sobresalir; continuar, persistir; permanecer; atascarse; **to stick out** salir (*p.ej., el pañuelo del bolsillo*); sobresalir, proyectarse; velar (*un escollo*); resultar evidente; **to stick together** (coll) quedarse unidos, no abandonarse; **to stick up** destacarse; estar de punta (*el pelo*); **to stick up for** (coll) defender
sticker [ˈstɪkər] *s* etiqueta engomada, marbete engomado; pegatina; punta, espina; (coll) problema arduo
stick'pin' *s* alfiler *m* de corbata
stick'-up' *s* (slang) asalto, atraco
stick•y [ˈstɪki] *adj* (*comp* **-ier;** *super* **-iest**) pegajoso; (coll) húmedo, mojado; (*weather*) bochornoso
sticky menu *s* (compu) menú pegajoso
stiff [stɪf] *adj* tieso, duro, rigido; (*muscles*) anquilosado, entorpecido, entumecido; arduo, difícil; (*price*) (coll) excesivo; **to get stiff** envararse ‖ *s* (slang) cadáver *m* ‖ *tr* (slang) largarse sin pagar
stiff collar *s* cuello almidonado
stiffen [ˈstɪfən] *tr* atiesar; endurecer; espesar ‖ *intr* atiesarse; endurecerse; espesarse; obstinarse
stiff neck *s* torticolis *m;* obstinación
stiff-necked [ˈstɪfˌnɛkt] *adj* terco, obstinado
stiffness [ˈstɪfnɪs] *s* envaramiento, rigidez *f*
stifle [ˈstaɪfəl] *tr* ahogar, sofocar; apagar, suprimir
stig•ma [ˈstɪgmə] *s* (*pl* **-mas** o **-mata** [mətə]) estigma *m*
stigmatize [ˈstɪgməˌtaɪz] *tr* estigmatizar
stilet•to [stɪˈlɛto] *s* (*pl* **-tos**) estilete *m,* puñal *m*
still [stɪl] *adj* inmóvil, quieto, tranquilo; callado, silencioso; (*wine*) no espumoso ‖ *adv* tranquilamente; silenciosamente; aún, todavía ‖ *conj* con todo, sin embargo ‖ *s* alambique *m,* destiladera; destilería; fotografía de lo inmóvil; (poet) silencio ‖ *tr* acallar; amortiguar; calmar ‖ *intr* callar; calmarse
still'birth' *s* parto muerto

still'born' *adj* nacido muerto
still life *s* (*pl* **still lifes** o **still lives**) bodegón *m,* naturaleza muerta
stilt [stɪlt] *s* zanco; (*in the water*) pilote *m*
stilted [ˈstɪltɪd] *adj* elevado; hinchado, pomposo, tieso
stimulant [ˈstɪmjələnt] *adj & s* estimulante *m,* excitante *m*
stimulate [ˈstɪmjəˌlet] *tr* estimular
stimu•lus [ˈstɪmjələs] *s* (*pl* **-li** [ˌlaɪ]) estímulo
sting [stɪŋ] *s* picadura; aguijón *m;* lanceta ‖ *v* (*pret & pp* **stung** [stʌŋ]) *tr* picar; aguijonear ‖ *intr* picar
stin•gy [ˈstɪndʒi] *adj* (*comp* **-gier;** *super* **-giest**) mezquino, tacaño, rata
stink [stiŋk] *s* hedor *m,* mal olor *m* ‖ *v* (*pret* **stank** [stæŋk] o **stunk** [stʌŋk]; *pp* **stunk**) *tr* dar mal olor a ‖ *intr* heder, oler muy mal; **to stink of** heder a; (slang) poseer (*p.ej., dinero*) en un grado que da asco
stint [stɪnt] *s* faena, tarea ‖ *tr* limitar, restringir ‖ *intr* ser económico, ahorrar con mezquindad
stipend [ˈstaɪpənd] *s* estipendio
stipulate [ˈstɪpjəˌlet] *tr* estipular
stir [stʌr] *s* agitación, meneo; alboroto, tumulto; **to create a stir** meter ruido, causar furor ‖ *v* (*pret & pp* **stirred;** *ger* **stirring**) *tr* agitar, mover; revolver; conmover, excitar; atizar, avivar (*el fuego*); remover (*un líquido*); **to stir up** revolver; despertar; conmover; fomentar (*discordias*) ‖ *intr* bullirse, moverse; (*say a word*) rechistar
stirring [ˈstʌrɪŋ] *adj* conmovedor, emocionante
stirrup [ˈstʌrəp] o [ˈstɪrəp] *s* estribo
stitch [stɪtʃ] *s* puntada, punto; pedazo de tela; punzada, dolor *m* punzante; (coll) poquito; **to be in stitches** (coll) desternillarse de risa ‖ *tr* coser, bastear, hilvanar ‖ *intr* coser
stock [stɑk] *adj* común, regular; banal, vulgar; bursátil; ganadero, del ganado; (theat) de repertorio ‖ *s* surtido; capital *f* comercial; acciones, valores *mpl;* (*inventory*) stock *m;* (*of meat*) caldo; (*of a tree*) tronco; (*of an anvil*) cepo; (*of a rifle*) caja, culata; (*of a tree; of a family*) cepa; mango, manija; palo, madero; leño; (*livestock*) ganado; (theat) programa *m,* repertorio; **to have in stock** tener en stock; **in stock** en existencia; **out of stock** agotado; **to take stock** hacer el inventario; **to take stock in** (coll) dar importancia a, confiar en ‖ *tr* abastecer, surtir; tener existencias de; acopiar, acumular; poblar (*un estanque, una colmena, etc.*)
stockade [stɑˈked] *s* estacada, empalizada ‖ *tr* empalizar
stock'breed'er *s* criador *m* de ganado
stock'bro'ker *s* bolsista *mf,* corredor *m* de bolsa, agente *mf* de bolsa
stock car *s* (aut) coche *m* de serie; (rr) vagón *m* de ganado
stock certificate *s* título de acciones
stock company *s* (com) sociedad anónima; (theat) teatro de repertorio
stock dividend *s* acción liberada
stock exchange *s* bolsa
stock'hold'er *s* accionista *mf,* tenedor *m* de acciones
stockholder of record *s* accionista *mf* que como tal figura en el libro registro de la compañía
Stockholm [ˈstɑkhom] *s* Estocolmo
stocking [ˈstɑkɪŋ] *s* media
stock market *s* bolsa, mercado de valores; **to play the stock market** jugar a la bolsa
stock'pile' *s* reserva de materias primas ‖ *tr* acumular (*materias primas*) ‖ *intr* acumular materias primas
stock raising *s* ganadería
stock'room' *s* almacén *m;* sala de exposición
stock split *s* reparto de acciones gratis
stock•y [ˈstɑki] *s* adj (*comp* **-ier;** *super* **-iest**) bajo, grueso y fornido
stock'yard' *s* corral *m* de concentración de ganado
stodgy [ˈstɑdʒi] *adj* aburrido, pesado
stoic [ˈsto•ɪk] *adj & s* estoico
stoke [stok] *tr* atizar, avivar (*el fuego*); alimentar, cebar (*el horno*)
stoker [ˈstokər] *s* fogonero
stolid [ˈstɑlɪd] *adj* impasible, insensible
stomach [ˈstʌmək] *s* estómago; apetito; deseo, inclinación ‖ *tr* tragar; **to not be able to stomach** (coll) no poder tragar
stomach pump *s* bomba estomacal
stone [ston] *s* piedra; (*of fruit*) hueso; (pathol) mal *m* de piedra ‖ *tr* lapidar, apedrear; deshuesar (*la fruta*)
stone'-broke' *adj* arrancado, sin blanca
stone'-deaf' *adj* sordo como una tapia
stone'ma'son *s* albañil *m*
stone quarry *s* cantera, pedrera
stone's throw *s* tiro de piedra; **within a stone's throw** a tiro de piedra
stone'wall' *tr* bloquear. contestar con evasivas, negarse a cooperar con ‖ *intr* andarse con evasivas, utilizar tácticas obstruccionistas, ganar tiempo
ston•y [ˈstoni] *adj* (*comp* **-ier;** *super* **-iest**) pedregoso; duro, empedernido
stool [stul] *s* escabel *m,* taburete *m;* sillico, retrete *m;* (*bowel movement*) cámara, evacuación
stoop [stup] *s* encorvada, inclinación; escalinata de entrada ‖ *intr* doblarse, inclinarse, encorvarse; andar encorvado; humillarse, rebajarse
stoop•shouldered [ˈstupˈʃoldərd] *adj* cargado de espaldas
stop [stɑp] *s* parada, alto; parón; estada, estancia; cesación, fin *m,* suspensión; cerradura, tapadura; impedimento, obstáculo; freno; tope *m,* retén *m;* (*in writing; in telegrams*) punto; (*of a guitar*) llave *f,* traste *m;* **to put a stop to** poner fin a ‖ *v* (*pret & pp* **stopped;** *ger* **stopping**) *tr* parar, detener; acabar, terminar; estorbar, obstruir; interceptar; suspender; cerrar, tapar; rechazar (*un golpe*); retener (*un sueldo o parte de él*); **to stop up** cegar,

obstruir, tapar || *intr* parar, pararse, detenerse; quedarse, permanecer; alojarse, hospedarse; acabarse, terminarse; **to stop** + *ger* cesar de + *inf*, dejar de + *inf*

stop'cock' *s* llave *f* de cierre, llave de paso

stop'gap' *adj* provisional || *s* substituto provisional

stop light *s* luz *f* de parada

stop'o'ver *s* parada intermedia, escala; billete *m* de parada intermedia

stoppage [ˋstɑpɪdʒ] *s* parada, detención; (*of work*) paro; interrupción; suspensión; obstáculo; (*of wages*) retención; (pathol) obstrucción

stopper [ˋstɑpər] *s* tapón *m;* taco, tarugo

stop sign o **stop signal** *s* señal *f* de alto, señal de parada

stopwatch *s* reloj *m* de segundos muertos, cronómetro

storage [ˋstorɪdʒ] *s* depósito, almacenaje *m;* (*costs*) derechos de almacenaje; (compu) almacenamiento

storage battery *s* (elec) acumulador *m*

storage device *s* (compu) dispositivo de almacenamiento

storage tank *s* tanque *m* de almacenamiento

store [stor] *s* tienda, almacén *m;* **I know what is in store for you** sé lo que le espera; **to set store by** dar mucha importancia a || *tr* abastecer; tener guardado, almacenar; (compu) almacenar; **to store away** acumular

store'front' *s* frente *m* de una tienda

storefront church *s* iglesia en una antigua tienda que da a la calle

store'house' *s* almacén *m,* depósito; (*e.g., of wisdom*) (fig) mina

store'keep'er *s* tendero, almacenista *mf*

store'room' *s* cuarto de almacenar; (*for furniture*) guardamuebles *m;* (naut) despensa

store window *s* escaparate *m* (de tienda); aparador *m* (Mex)

stork [stɔrk] *s* cigüeña; **to have a visit from the stork** recibir a la cigüeña

storm [stɔrm] *s* borrasca, tempestad, tormenta; (mil) asalto; (naut) borrasca; (fig) tempestad, tumulto; **to take by storm** tomar por asalto || *tr* asaltar || *intr* tempestear; precipitarse

storm cloud *s* nubarrón *m*

storm door *s* contrapuerta, guardapuerta

storm sash *s* contravidriera

storm troops *spl* tropas de asalto

storm window *s* guardaventana, sobrevidriera

storm•y [ˋstɔrmi] *adj* (*comp* **-ier;** *super* **-iest**) borrascoso, tempestuoso; (*session, meeting, etc.*) tumultuoso

sto•ry [ˋstori] *s* (*pl* **-ries**) historia, cuento, anécdota; enredo, trama; (coll) mentira; piso, alto || *v* (*pret & pp* **-ried**) *tr* historiar

sto'ry•tel'ler *s* narrador *m;* (coll) mentiroso

stout [staʊt] *adj* corpulento, gordo, robusto; animoso; leal; terco || *s* cerveza obscura fuerte

stove [stov] *s* (*for heating a house or room*) estufa; (*for cooking*) hornillo, cocina de gas, cocina eléctrica

stove'pipe' *s* tubo de estufa, tubo de hornillo; (*hat*) (coll) chistera, chimenea

stow [sto] *tr* guardar, meter, esconder; (naut) arrumar, estibar || *intr*—**to stow away** embarcarse clandestinamente, esconderse en un barco o avión

stowage [ˋsto•ɪdʒ] *s* arrumaje *m,* estiba

stow'a•way' *s* llovido, polizón *m*

str. *abbr* **strait, steamer**

straddle [ˋstrædəl] *s* esparrancamiento || *tr* montar a horcajadas; (coll) tratar de favorecer a ambas partes en (*p.ej., un pleito*) || *intr* ponerse a horcajadas; (coll) tratar de favorecer a ambas partes

strafe [strɑf] o [stref] *s* bombardeo violento || *tr* bombardear violentamente

straggle [ˋstrægəl] *intr* errar, vagar; andar perdido, extraviarse; separarse; estar esparcido

straggly [strægli] *adj* desordenado, desgreñado, descuidado

straight [stret] *adj* derecho; recto; erguido; (*hair*) lacio; continuo, seguido; honrado, sincero; correcto; decidido, intransigente; (*e.g., whiskey*) solo; **to set a person straight** mostrar el camino a una persona; dar consejo a una persona; mostrar a una persona el modo de proceder || *adv* derecho; sin interrupción; sinceramente; exactamente; en seguida; **straight ahead** todo seguido, derecho; **to go straight** enmendarse

straighten [ˋstretən] *tr* enderezar; poner en orden || *intr* enderezarse

straight face *s* cara seria

straight'for'ward *adj* franco, sincero; honrado

straight off *adv* luego, en seguida

straight razor *s* navaja barbera

straight'way' *adv* luego, en seguida

strain [stren] *s* tensión, tirantez *f;* esfuerzo muy grande; fatiga excesiva, agotamiento; (*of a muscle*) torcedura; aire *m,* melodía; (*of a family or lineage*) cepa; linaje *m,* raza; rasgo racial; genio, vena; huella, rastro || *tr* estirar; torcer o torcerse (*p.ej., la muñeca*); forzar (*p.ej., los nervios, la vista*); apretar; deformar; colar, tamizar || *intr* esforzarse; deformarse; colarse, tamizarse; filtrarse; exprimirse (*un jugo*); resistirse; **to strain at** hacer grandes esfuerzos por

strained [strend] *adj* (*smile*) forzado; (*friendship*) tirante

strainer [ˋstrenər] *s* colador *m*

strait [stret] *s* estrecho; **straits** estrecho; **to be in dire straits** estar en el mayor apuro, hallarse en gran estrechez

strait jacket *s* camisa de fuerza

strait-laced [ˋstret,lest] *adj* gazmoño, mojigato, puritano

strand [strænd] *s* playa; filamento; (*of rope or cable*) torón *m,* ramal *m;* (*of pearls*) hilo; pelo || *tr* deshebrar; retorcer, trenzar (*cuerda, cable, etc.*); dejar extraviado; (naut) varar

stranded [ˋstrændɪd] *adj* desprovisto, desamparado; (*ship*) encallado; (*rope or cable*) trenzado, retorcido
strange [strendʒ] *adj* extraño, singular; nuevo, desconocido; novel, no acostumbrado
stranger [ˋstrendʒər] *s* forastero; visitador *m;* intruso; desconocido; principiante *mf*
strangle [ˋstræŋgəl] *tr* estrangular; reprimir, suprimir ‖ *intr* estrangularse
strap [stræp] *s* (*of leather*) correa; (*of cloth, metal, etc.*) banda, tira; (*to sharpen a razor*) asentador *m* ‖ *v* (*pret & pp* **strapped;** *ger* **strapping**) *tr* atar o liar con correa, banda o tira; azotar con una correa; fajar, vendar; asentar (*una navaja*)
strap'hang'er *s* (coll) pasajero colgado
stratagem [ˋstrætədʒəm] *s* estratagema *f*
strategic(al) [strəˋtidʒɪk(əl)] *adj* estratégico
strategist [ˋstrætɪdʒɪst] *s* estratega *m*
strate•gy [ˋstrætɪdʒi] *s* (*pl* **-gies**) estrategia
strati•fy [ˋstrætɪ,faɪ] *v* (*pret & pp* **-fied**) *tr* estratificar ‖ *intr* estratificarse
stratosphere [ˋstrætə,sfɪr] o [ˋstretə,sfɪr] *s* estratosfera
stra•tum [ˋstretəm] o [ˋstrætəm] *s* (*pl* **-ta** [tə] o **-tums**) estrato; (*e.g., of society*) clase *f*
straw [strɔ] *adj* pajizo; baladí, de poca importancia; falso; ficticio ‖ *s* paja; (*for drinking*) pajita; **I don't care a straw** no se me da un bledo; **to be the last straw** ser el colmo, no faltar más
straw'ber'ry *s* (*pl* **-ries**) fresa
straw hat *s* sombrero de paja; chupalla *m;* (*with low flat crown*) canotié *m*
straw man *s* figura de paja; (*figurehead*) testaferro, hombre *m* de paja; testigo falso
straw vote *s* voto informativo
stray [stre] *adj* extraviado, perdido; aislado, suelto ‖ *s* animal extraviado o perdido; (*dog*) perro callejero ‖ *intr* extraviarse, perderse
streak [strik] *s* lista, raya; vena, veta; rasgo, traza; (*of light*) rayo; (*of good luck*) racha; (coll) tiempo muy breve; **like a streak** (coll) como un rayo ‖ *tr* listar, rayar; abigarrar ‖ *intr* rayarse; (coll) andar o pasar como un rayo
streaker [ˋstrikər] *s* (coll) streaker *mf*
stream [strim] *s* (*current*) corriente *f;* arroyo, río; chorro, flujo; (*of people*) torrente *m;* (*e.g., of automobiles*) desfile *m* ‖ *intr* correr, manar (*un líquido*); chorrear; flotar, ondear; salir a torrentes
streamer [ˋstrimər] *s* flámula, banderola; cinta ondeante; rayo de luz
streamlined [ˋstrim,laɪnd] *adj* aerodinámico, perfilado, aerofluyente
stream'lin'er *s* tren aerodinámico de lujo
street [strit] *adj* callejero ‖ *s* calle *f*
street'car' *s* tranvía *m*
street cleaner *s* basurero; (*device*) barredera
street clothes *spl* traje *m* de calle
street door *s* puerta de (la) calle
street fighting *s* riñas callejeras
street floor *s* piso bajo
street lamp *s* farol *m* (de la calle)
street lighting *s* alumbrado público
street musician *s* músico callejero
street sprinkler [ˋsprɪŋklər] *s* carricuba, carro de riego, regadera
street'walk'er *s* prostituta
street'wise *adj* (coll) espabilado, avispado, taimado
strength [strɛŋθ] *s* fuerza; intensidad; (*of spirituous liquors*) graduación; (com) tendencia a la subida; (mil) número; **on the strength of** fundándose en, confiando en
strengthen [ˋstrɛŋθən] *tr* fortificar, reforzar; confirmar ‖ *intr* fortificarse, reforzarse
strenuous [ˋstrɛnjʊ•əs] *adj* estrenuo, enérgico, vigoroso; arduo, difícil
strep throat [strɛp] *s* (coll) inflamación estreptocócica de la garganta
streptomycin [ˋstrɛptoˋmaɪsən] *s* (pharm) estreptomicina
stress [strɛs] *s* tensión, fuerza; compulsión; acento; (mech) tensión; **to lay stress on** hacer hincapié en ‖ *tr* someter a esfuerzo; hacer hincapié en; acentuar
stress accent *s* acento prosódico
stretch [strɛtʃ] *s* estiramiento, estirón *m;* (*distance in time or space*) trecho; (*section of road*) tramo; extensión; (*of the imagination*) esfuerzo; (*confinement in jail*) (slang) condena; **at a stretch** de un tirón ‖ *tr* estirar; extender; tender; forzar, violentar; (fig) estirar (*el dinero*); **to stretch a point** hacer una concesión; **to stretch oneself** desperezarse ‖ *intr* estirarse; extenderse; tenderse; desperezarse; **to stretch out** (coll) echarse
stretcher [ˋstrɛtʃər] *s* (*for gloves*) ensanchador *m;* (*for a painting*) bastidor *m;* (*to carry sick or wounded*) camilla
stretch'er-bear'er *s* camillero
strew [stru] *v* (*pret* **strewed;** *pp* **strewed** o **strewn**) *tr* derramar, esparcir; sembrar, salpicar; polvorear
stricken [ˋstrɪkən] *adj* afligido; inhabilitado; herido; **stricken in years** debilitado por los años
strict [strɪkt] *adj* estricto, riguroso; (*exacting*) severo
stricture [ˋstrɪktʃər] *s* crítica severa; (pathol) estrictura
stride [straɪd] *s* zancada, tranco; **to hit one's stride** alcanzar la actividad o velocidad acostumbrada; **to make great** (o **rapid**) **strides** avanzar a grandes pasos; **to take in one's stride** hacer sin esfuerzo ‖ *v* (*pret* **strode** [strod]; *pp* **stridden** [ˋstrɪdən]) *tr* cruzar de un tranco; montar a horcajadas ‖ *intr* dar zancadas, caminar a paso largo, andar a trancos
strident [ˋstraɪdənt] *adj* estridente
strife [straɪf] *s* contienda; rivalidad
strike [straɪk] *s* (*blow*) golpe *m;* (*stopping of work*) huelga, paro; (*discovery of ore, oil, etc.*) descubrimiento repentino; golpe *m* de

fortuna; **to go on strike** ir a la huelga || *v* (*pret & pp* **struck** [strʌk]) *tr* golpear; pulsar (*una tecla*); herir, percutir; topar, dar con; acuñar (*monedas*); echar (*raíces*); frotar, rayar, encender (*un fóstoro*); descubrir repentinamente (*mineral, aceite, etc.*); cerrar (*un trato*); arriar (*las velas*); dar (*la hora*); asumir, tomar (*una postura*); borrar, cancelar; impresionar; atraer (*la atención*); **to strike it rich** descubrir un buen filón, tener un golpe de fortuna || *intr* dar, sonar (*una campana, un reloj*); declararse en huelga; (mil) dar el asalto; **to strike out** ponerse en marcha, echar camino adelante

strike'break'er *s* rompehuelgas *m,* esquirol *m*

strike pay *s* sueldo de huelguista

striker [ˈstraɪkər] *s* golpeador *m;* huelguista *mf*

striking [ˈstraɪkɪŋ] *adj* impresionante, llamativo, sorprendente; en huelga

striking power *s* potencia de choque

string [strɪŋ] *s* cuerdecilla; piola; pita; (*of pearls; of lies*) sarta; (*of beans*) hebra; (*of onions or garlic*) ristra; (row) hilera; (mus) cuerda; (*limitation, proviso*) (coll) condición; **strings** instrumentos de cuerda; **to pull strings** tocar resortes || *v* (*pret & pp* **strung** [strʌŋ]) *tr* enhebrar, ensartar; atar con cuerdas; proveer de cuerdas; colgar de una cuerda; tender (*un cable, un alambre*); encordar (*un violín, una raqueta*); colocar en fila; (slang) engañar, burlar; **to string along** (slang) traer al retortero; **to string up** (coll) ahorcar

string bean *s* habichuela verde, judía verde

stringed instrument [strɪŋd] *s* instrumento de cuerda

stringent [ˈstrɪndʒənt] *adj* riguroso, severo, estricto; convincente

string quartet *s* cuarteto de cuerdas

strip [strɪp] *s* tira; (*of metal*) lámina; (*of land*) faja || *v* (*pret & pp* **stripped;** *ger* **stripping**) *tr* desnudar; despojar; desforrar; deshacer (*la cama*); estropear (*el engranaje, un tornillo*); desvenar (*tabaco*); descortezar; **to strip of** despojar de || *intr* desnudarse; despojarse; descortezarse

stripe [straɪp] *s* banda, lista, raya; gaya; cinta, franja; (mil & nav) galón *m;* índole *f,* tipo; **to win one's stripes** ganar los entorchados || *tr* listar, rayar; gayar

strip mining *s* mineraje *m* a tajo abierto

stripper [ˈstrɪpər] *s* (*performer*) striptisero, striptisera; (*paint remover*) líquido quitapintura

strip'-search' *tr* hacer desnudar y registrar

strip'tease' *s* strip-tease *m* (*espectáculo de desnudamiento sensual*)

strive [straɪv] *v* (*pret* **strove** [strov]; *pp* **striven** [ˈstrɪvən]) *intr* esforzarse; luchar

strobe (light) [strob] *s* luz estroboscópica

stroke [strok] *s* golpe *m;* (*of bell or clock*) campanada; (*of pen*) plumada; (*of brush*) pincelada, brochada; (*of arms in swimming*) brazada; (*in a game*) jugada; (*caress with hand*) caricia; (*with a racket*) raquetazo; (*of a piston*) carrera, embolada; (*of a paddle*) palada; (*of an oar*) remada; (*of lightning*) rayo; (*line, mark*) raya; (*of good luck*) golpe *m;* (*of wit*) agudeza, chiste *m;* (*of genius*) rasgo; ataque *m* de parálisis; **at the stroke of** (*e.g., five*) al dar las (*p.ej., cinco*); **to not do a stroke of work** no dar golpe, no levantar paja del suelo || *tr* frotar suavemente, acariciar con la mano

stroll [strol] *s* paseo; **to take a stroll** dar un paseo || *intr* pasear, pasearse; callejear, errar, vagar

stroller [ˈstrolər] *s* paseante *mf;* cochecito para niños

strong [strɔŋ] o [strɑŋ] *adj* fuerte, resistente; recio, robusto; intenso; (*stock market*) firme; enérgico; marcado; picante; rancio

strong'-arm' man *s* (coll) gorila

strong'box' *s* cofre *m* fuerte, caja de caudales

strong drink *s* bebida alcohólica, bebida fuerte

strong'hold' *s* plaza fuerte

strong man *s* (*e.g., in a circus*) hércules *m;* (*leader, good planner*) alma, promotor *m;* (*dictator*) hombre *m* fuerte

strong-minded [ˈstrɔŋ,maɪndɪd] o [strɑŋˈmaɪndɪd] *adj* independiente; de inteligencia vigorosa; (*e.g., woman*) hombruna

strontium [ˈstrɑnʃi•əm] *s* estroncio

strop [strɑp] *s* suavizador *m* || *v* (*pret & pp* **stropped;** *ger* **stropping**) *tr* suavizar, afilar

strophe [ˈstrofi] *s* estrofa

structure [ˈstrʌktʃər] *s* estructura; edificio

struggle [ˈstrʌgəl] *s* lucha; esfuerzo, forcejeo || *intr* luchar; esforzarse, forcejear

strum [strʌm] *v* (*pret & pp* **strummed;** *ger* **strumming**) *tr* arañar (*un instrumento músico*) sin arte || *intr* cencerrear; **to strum on** rasguear

strumpet [ˈstrʌmpɪt] *s* ramera

strut [strʌt] *s* (*brace, prop*) riostra, tornapunta; contoneo, pavoneo || *v* (*pret & pp* **strutted;** *ger* **strutting**) *intr* contonearse, pavonearse

strychnine [ˈstrɪknaɪn] o [ˈstrɪknin] *s* estricnina

stub [stʌb] *s* fragmento, trozo; (*of a cigar*) colilla; (*of a tree*) tocón *m;* (*of a pencil*) cabo; (*of a check*) talón *m* || *v* (*pret & pp* **stubbed;** *ger* **stubbing**) *tr* —**to stub one's toe** dar un tropezón

stubble [ˈstʌbəl] *s* rastrojo; (*of beard*) cañon *m*

stubborn [ˈstʌbərn] *adj* terco, testarudo, obstinado; porfiado; intratable; **to be stubborn** ser obstinado, empecinarse

stubbornness [ˈstʌbərnɪs] obstinación, *s* empecinamiento

stuc•co [ˈstʌko] *s* (*pl* **-coes** o **-cos**) estuco || *tr* estucar

stuck'-up' *adj* (coll) estirado, orgulloso

stud [stʌd] *s* tachón *m;* botón *m* de camisa; montante *m,* pie derecho; clavo de adorno; (*bolt*) espárrago; caballeriza; (*group of animals*) cuadro; (*stallion*) semental *m;* (*man*) (coll) hombre *m* viril, semental *m;* **at**

stud de cría || *v* (*pret & pp* **studded;** *ger* **studding**) *tr* tachonar
stud bolt *s* espárrago
stud'book' *s* registro genealógico de caballos
student [ˈstjudənt] o [ˈstudənt] *adj* estudiantil || *s* estudiante *mf;* (*person who investigates*), estudioso
student body *s* estudiantado, alumnado
student center *s* (*building*) centro estudiantil (*en el campus*)
student representative *s* delegado de curso
student teacher *s* estudiante *mf* de profesorado, practicante *mf*
student union *s* asociación de estudiantes
stud'horse' *s* caballo padre, caballo semental
studied [ˈstʌdid] *adj* premeditado, hecho adrede; (*affected*) estudiado
studi•o [ˈstudɪ,o] *s* (*pl* **-os**) estudio, taller *m;* (mov & rad) estudio
studious [ˈstjudɪ•əs] o [ˈstudɪ•əs] *adj* estudioso; asiduo, solícito
stud•y [ˈstʌdi] *s* (*pl* **-ies**) estudio; solicitud; meditación profunda; (*e.g., of a professor*) gabinete *m,* estudio || *v* (*pret & pp* **-ied**) *tr & intr* estudiar
stuff [stʌf] *s* materia; género, paño, tela; muebles *mpl,* baratijas; medicina; fruslerías; cosa, cosas || *tr* rellenar; henchir, llenar; atascar, cerrar, tapar; embutir; (*with food*) atracar; meter sin orden, llenar sin orden; disecar (*un animal muerto*) || *intr* atracarse, hartarse
stuffed shirt *s* (slang) tragavirotes *m*
stuffing [ˈstʌfɪŋ] *s* relleno
stuff•y [ˈstʌfi] *adj* (*comp* **-ier;** *super* **-iest**) sofocante, mal ventilado; aburrido, sin interés; (*prim*) (coll) relamido
stumble [ˈstʌmbəl] *intr* tropezar, dar un traspié; moverse a tropezones; hablar a tropezones; **to stumble on** o **upon** tropezar con
stumbling block *s* escollo, tropezadero
stump [stʌmp] *s* (*of a tree, arm, etc.*) tocón *m;* (*of an arm*) muñon *m;* (*of a tooth*) raigón *m;* (*of a cigar*) colilla; (*of a tail*) rabo; paso pesado; fragmento, resto; tribuna pública; (*for shading drawings*) esfumino || *tr* recorrer (*el país*) pronunciando discursos políticos; (coll) confundir, dejar sin habla; esfumar
stump speaker *s* orador callejero
stump speech *s* arenga electoral
stun [stʌn] *v* (*pret & pp* **stunned;** *ger* **stunning**) *tr* atolondrar, aturdir
stunning [ˈstʌnɪŋ] *adj* (coll) pasmoso, estupendo, pistonudo, elegante
stunt [stʌnt] *s* atrofia; (*underdeveloped creature*) engendro; (coll) suerte acrobática; (coll) faena, hazaña, proeza || *tr* atrofiar || *intr* (coll) hacer suertes acrobáticas
stunt flying *s* vuelo acrobático
stunt man *s* (mov) doble *m* que hace suertes peligrosas
stupe•fy [ˈstjupɪ,faɪ] *v* (*pret & pp* **-fied**) *tr* dejar estupefacto, pasmar; causar estupor a
stupendous [stuˈpɛndəs] *adj* estupendo; enorme
stupid [ˈstupɪd] *adj* estúpido; (coll) sonso, pavo, gilí
stupor [ˈstjupər] o [ˈstupər] *s* estupor *m,* modorra
stur•dy [ˈstʌrdi] *adj* (*comp* **-dier;** *super* **-diest**) fuerte, robusto, fornido; firme, tenaz
sturgeon [ˈstʌrdʒən] *s* esturión *m*
stutter [ˈstʌtər] *s* tartamudeo || *tr* decir tartamudeando || *intr* tartamudear
sty [staɪ] *s* (*pl* **sties**) pocilga, zahurda; (pathol) orzuelo
style [staɪl] *s* estilo; moda; elegancia; (*type*) diseño, modelo; (compu) tipo; **to live in great style** vivir en gran lujo || *tr* intitular, nombrar; (*clothes*) diseñar; (*hair*) peinar a la moda
stylish [ˈstaɪlɪʃ] *adj* de moda, elegante
stylus [ˈstaɪləs] *s* (*on record player*) aguja, púa; (*for writing*) estilo
sty•mie [ˈstaɪmi] *v* (*pret & pp* **-mied;** *ger* **-mying**) *tr* obstaculizar, frustrar, bloquear
styptic pencil [ˈstɪptɪk] *s* lápiz estíptico
Styx [stɪks] *s* Estigia
suave [swɑv] o [swev] *adj* suave; afable, fino, zalamero, pulido
sub. *abbr* **subscription, substitute, suburban**
sub [sʌb] *s* (coll) substituto, suplente *mf;* (coll) submarino || *vi*—**to sub for** (coll) substituir a
subaltern [səbˈɔltərn] *adj & s* subalterno
subconscious [səbˈkɑnʃəs] *adj* subconsciente || *s* subconsciencia
subconsciousness [səbˈkɑnʃəsnɪs] *s* subconsciencia
subdeb [ˈsʌb,dɛb] *s* tobillera
subdivide [ˈsʌbdɪ,vaɪd] o [,sʌbdɪˈvaɪd] *tr* subdividir || *intr* subdividirse
sub'divi'sion *s* (*of land*) parcelación; (*plot*) parcela
subdue [səbˈdju] *tr* sojuzgar, subyugar; amansar, dominar; suavizar
subdued [səbˈdjud] *adj* sojuzgado; sumiso; (*e.g., light*) suave
subheading [ˈsʌb,hɛdɪŋ] *s* subtítulo
subject [ˈsʌbdʒɪkt] *adj* sujeto; súbdito || *s* asunto, materia, tema *m;* (*person in his relationship to a ruler or government*) súbdito; (gram, med, philos) sujeto || [səbˈdʒɛkt] *tr* sujetar, someter, sojuzgar
subject index *s* índice *m* de materias
subjection [səbˈdʒɛkʃən] *s* sumisión, sometimiento
subjective [səbˈdʒɛktɪv] *adj* subjetivo
subject matter *s* asunto, materia
subjugate [ˈsʌbdʒə,get] *tr* subyugar
subjunctive [səbˈdʒʌŋktɪv] *adj & s* subjunctivo
sub•let [sʌbˈlɛt] o [ˈsʌb,lɛt] *v* (*pret & pp* **-let;** *ger* **-letting**) *tr* realquilar, subarrendar
submachine gun [,sʌbməˈʃin] *s* subfusil *m* ametrallador
submarine [ˈsʌbmə,rin] *adj & s* submarino || *tr* (coll) atacar o hundir con un submarino

submarine chaser [ˈtʃesər] *s* cazasubmarinos *m*
submerge [səbˈmʌrdʒ] *tr* sumergir || *intr* sumergirse
submersion [səbˈmʌrʒən] o [səbˈmʌrʃən] *s* sumersión
submission [səbˈmɪʃən] *s* sumisión
submissive [səbˈmɪsɪv] *adj* sumiso
sub•mit [səbˈmɪt] *v* (*pret & pp* **-mitted;** *ger* **-mitting**) *tr* someter; proponer, permitirse decir || *intr* someterse
subˈnormˈal *adj* por debajo de lo normal
subordinate [səbˈɔrdɪnɪt] *adj & s* subordinado || [səbˈɔrdɪˌnet] *tr* subordinar
subornation of perjury [ˌsʌbɔrˈneʃən] *s* (law) soborno de testigo
subplot [ˈsʌbˌplɑt] *s* trama secundaria
subpoena o **subpena** [sʌbˈpinə] o [səˈpinə] *s* comparendo || *tr* mandar comparecer
sub rosa [sʌbˈrozə] *adv* en secreto, en confianza
subscribe [səbˈskraɪb] *tr* subscribir || *intr* subscribir; subscribirse, abonarse; **to subscribe to** subscribirse a, abonarse a (*una publicación periódica*); subscribir (*una opinión*)
subscriber [səbˈskraɪbər] *s* abonado
subsequent [ˈsʌbsɪkwənt] *adj* subsiguiente, posterior
subservient [səbˈsʌrvɪ•ənt] *adj* servil; subordinado; útil
subside [səbˈsaɪd] *intr* calmarse; acabarse, cesar; bajar (*el nivel del agua*); amainar (*el viento*)
subsidiary [səbˈsɪdɪˌɛri] *adj & s* subsidiario
subsidize [ˈsʌbsɪˌdaɪz] *tr* subsidiar, subvencionar; (*to bribe*) sobornar
subsi•dy [ˈsʌbsɪdi] *s* (*pl* **-dies**) subsidio, subvención
subsist [səbˈsɪst] *intr* subsistir
subsistence [səbˈsɪstəns] *s* subsistencia
subsonic [səbˈsɑnɪk] *adj* subsónico
substance [ˈsʌbstəns] *s* substancia
substandard [sʌbˈstændərd] *adj* inferior al nivel normal
substantial [səbˈstænʃəl] *adj* considerable, importante; fuerte, sólido; acomodado, rico; esencial; (*food*) substancial
substantiate [səbˈstænʃiˌet] *tr* comprobar, establecer, verificar
substantive [ˈsʌbstəntɪv] *adj & s* substantivo
substation [ˈsʌbˌsteʃən] *s* (elec) subcentral *f*
substitute [ˈsʌbstɪˌtjut] o [ˈsʌbstɪˌtut] *adj* substitutivo || *s* (*person*) substituto; (*thing, substance*) substitutivo; (mil) reemplazo || *tr* poner (*a una persona o cosa*) en lugar de otra || *intr* actuar de substituto; **to substitute for** substituir (with personal a)
substitute teacher *s* suplente *mf,* profesor *m* suplente
substitution [ˌsʌbstɪˈtjuʃən] *s* empleo o uso (*de una persona o cosa en lugar de otra*); (chem, law, math) substitución; imitación fraudulenta

subterranean [ˌsʌbtəˈrenɪ•ən] *adj & s* subterráneo
subtitle [ˈsʌbˌtaɪtəl] *s* substítulo || *tr* subtitular
subtle [ˈsʌtəl] *adj* sutil; astuto; insidioso
subtle•ty [ˈsʌtəlti] *s* (*pl* **-ties**) sutileza; agudeza; distinción sutil
subtract [səbˈtrækt] *tr* substraer; (math) substraer, restar
suburb [ˈsʌbʌrb] *s* suburbio, arrabal *m;* **the suburbs** las afueras, los barrios externos
suburban development [səˈbʌrbən] *s* ensanche *m*
subvention [səbˈvɛnʃən] *s* subvención || *tr* subvencionar
subversive [səbˈvʌrsɪv] *adj* subversivo || *s* subversor *m*
subvert [səbˈvʌrt] *tr* subvertir
subway [ˈsʌbˌwe] *s* galería subterránea; metro, ferrocarril subterráneo
subway entrance *s* boca de metro
succeed [səkˈsid] *tr* suceder (*a una persona o cosa*) || *intr* tener buen éxito
success [səkˈsɛs] *s* buen éxito
successful [səkˈsɛsfəl] *adj* feliz, próspero; acertado; logrado
succession [səkˈsɛʃən] *s* sucesión; **in succession** seguidos, uno tras otro
successive [səkˈsɛsɪv] *adj* sucesivo
succor [ˈsʌkər] *s* socorro || *tr* socorrer
succotash [ˈsʌkəˌtæʃ] *s* guiso de maíz tierno y habas
succumb [səˈkʌm] *intr* sucumbir
such [sʌtʃ] *adj & pron indef* tal, semejante; **such a** tal, semejante; **such a** + *adj* un tan + *adj;* **such as** quienes, los que
suck [sʌk] *s* chupada; mamada || *tr* chupar; mamar; aspirar (*el aire*)
sucker [ˈsʌkər] *s* chupador *m;* mamón *m;* (bot & mach) chupón *m;* (coll) bobo, primo
suckle [ˈsʌkəl] *tr* lactar; criar, educar
suckling pig [ˈsʌklɪŋ] *s* lechón *m,* cerdo de leche
suction [ˈsʌkʃən] *adj* aspirante || *s* succión
sudden [ˈsʌdən] *adj* súbito, repentino; **all of a sudden** de repente
sudden death *s* (football, tennis) muerte súbita
sudden infant death syndrome *s* muerte *f* de cuna
suds [sʌdz] *spl* jabonadura; (coll) espuma, cerveza
sue [su] *tr* demandar; pedir; (law) procesar || *intr* (law) poner pleito, entablar juicio; **to sue for damages** demandar por daños y perjuicios; **to sue for peace** pedir la paz
suede [swed] *s* gamuza, ante *m*
suet [ˈsu•ɪt] o [ˈsju•ɪt] *s* sebo
suffer [ˈsʌfər] *tr & intr* sufrir, padecer
sufferance [ˈsʌfərəns] *s* tolerancia; paciencia; **on sufferance** por tolerancia
suffering [ˈsʌfərɪŋ] *adj* doliente || *s* dolencia, sufrimiento
suffice [səˈfaɪs] *intr* bastar, ser suficiente
sufficient [səˈfɪʃənt] *adj* suficiente

suffix [ˋsʌfɪks] *s* sufijo
suffocate [ˋsʌfə,ket] *tr* sofocar ‖ *intr* sofocarse
suffrage [ˋsʌfrɪdʒ] *s* sufragio; aprobación, voto favorable
suffragette [,sʌfrəˋdʒɛt] *s* sufragista (*mujer*)
suffuse [səˋfjuz] *tr* saturar, bañar
sugar [ˋʃʊgər] *adj* azucarero ‖ *s* azúcar *m* ‖ *tr* azucarar
sugar beet *s* remolacha azucarera
sugar bowl *s* azucarero
sugar cane *s* caña de azúcar
sug′ar-coat′ *tr* azucarar; (fig) endulzar, dorar
suggest [səgˋdʒɛst] *tr* sugerir
suggestion [səgˋdʒɛstʃən] *s* sugestión, sugerencia; sombra, traza ligera
suggestive [səgˋdʒɛstɪv] *adj* sugestivo; evocador; insinuante, provocativo
suicidal [,su•ɪˋsaɪdəl] o [,sju•ɪˋsaɪdəl] *adj* suicida
suicide [ˋsu•ɪ,saɪd] *s* (*act*) suicidio; (*person*) suicida *mf;* **to commit suicide** suicidarse
suicide bomber *s* terrorista *mf* suicida
suicide bombing *s* atentado suicida, suicidio terrorista
suicide squad *s* comando suicida
suit [sut] o [sjut] *s* traje *m,* terno; (*of a lady*) traje *m* sastre; (*group forming a set*) juego; (*of cards*) palo; petición, súplica; cortejo, galanteo; (law) pleito, proceso; **to follow suit** servir del palo; seguir la corriente ‖ *tr* adaptar, ajustar; adaptarse a; sentar, ir o venir bien a; favorecer, satisfacer; **to be suited for** tener madera de; **to be suited to** ser apropiado para; **to suit oneself** hacer (*uno*) lo que le guste ‖ *intr* convenir, ser a propósito
suitable [ˋsutəbəl] *adj* apropiado, conveniente, adecuado
suit′case′ *s* maleta, valija
suite [swit] *s* comitiva, séquito; (*group forming a set*) juego; serie *f;* (*of rooms*) crujía; habitación salón; (mus) suite *f*
suiting [ˋsutɪŋ] *s* corte *m* de traje
suit of clothes *s* traje completo (*de hombre*)
suitor [ˋsutər] o [ˋsjutər] *s* pretendiente *m;* (law) demandante *mf*
sulfa drugs [ˋsʌlfə] *spl* medicamentos sulfas
sulfate [ˋsʌlfet] *s* sulfato
sulfide [ˋsʌlfaɪd] *s* sulfuro
sulfite [ˋsʌlfaɪt] *s* sulfito
sulfur [ˋsʌlfər] *s* (chem) azufre *m;* véase **sulphur**
sulfuric [sʌlˋfjʊrɪk] *adj* sulfúrico
sulfur mine *s* azufrera
sulfurous [ˋsʌlfərəs] *adj* sulfuroso ‖ *adj* (chem) sulfuroso
sulk [sʌlk] *s* murria ‖ *intr* amorrarse, enfurruñarse
sulk•y [ˋsʌlki] *adj* (*comp* **-ier;** *super* **-iest**) enfurruñado, murrio, resentido
sullen [ˋsʌlən] *adj* hosco, malhumorado, taciturno, triste
sul•ly [ˋsʌli] *v* (*pret & pp* **-lied**) *tr* empañar, manchar
sulphur [ˋsʌlfər] *adj* azufrado ‖ *s* azufre *m;* color de azufre ‖ *tr* azufrar
sultan [ˋsʌltən] *s* sultán *m*
sul•try [ˋsʌltri] *adj* (*comp* **-trier;** *super* **-triest**) bochornoso, sofocante
sum [sʌm] *s* suma; (coll) problema *m* de aritmética ‖ *v* (*pret & pp* **summed;** *ger* **summing**) *tr* sumar; **to sum up** sumar, resumir
sumac o **sumach** [ˋʃumæk] o [sumæk] *s* zumaque *m*
summarize [ˋsʌmə,raɪz] *tr* resumir
summa•ry [ˋsʌməri] *adj* sumario ‖ *s* (*pl* **-ries**) sumario, resumen *m,* reseña
summer [ˋsʌmər] *adj* estival, veraniego ‖ *s* verano, estío ‖ *intr* veranear
summer resort *s* lugar *m* de veraneo
summersault [ˋsʌmər,sɔlt] *s* salto mortal ‖ *intr* dar un salto mortal
summer school *s* escuela de verano
summery [ˋsʌməri] *adj* estival, veraniego
summit [ˋsʌmɪt] *s* cima, cumbre *f*
summit conference o **summit meeting** *s* conferencia en la cumbre
summon [ˋsʌmən] *tr* convocar, llamar; evocar; (law) citar, emplazar
summons [ˋsʌmənz] *s* orden *f,* señal *f;* (law) citación, emplazamiento ‖ *tr* (coll) citar, emplazar
sumptuous [ˋsʌmptʃʊ•əs] *adj* suntuoso
sun [sʌn] *s* sol *m;* **to have a place in the sun** ocupar su puesto en el mundo ‖ *v* (*pret & pp* **sunned;** *ger* **sunning**) *tr* asolear; **to sun oneself** tomar el sol ‖ *intr* asolearse
sun′-baked′ *adj* secado al sol
sun bath *s* baño de sol
sun′bathe *intr* tomar el sol, asolearse
sun′beam′ *s* rayo de sol
sun′bon′net *s* papalina
sun′burn′ *s* quemadura de sol ‖ *v* (*pret & pp* **-burned** o **burnt**) *tr* quemar al sol ‖ *intr* quemarse al sol
sundae [ˋsʌndi] *s* helado con frutas, jarabes o nueces, copa de helado, copa helado
Sunday [ˋsʌndi] *adj* dominical; (*used or worn on Sunday*) dominguero ‖ *s* domingo
Sunday school *s* escuela dominical, doctrina dominical
sunder [ˋsʌndər] *tr* separar; romper
sun′di′al *s* reloj *m* de sol, cuadrante *m* solar
sun′down′ *s* puesta del sol
sundries [ˋsʌndriz] *spl* articulos diversos
sundry [ˋsʌndri] *adj* diversos, varios
sun′flow′er *s* girasol *m,* tornasol *m*
sun′glass′es *spl* gafas de sol, gafas para el sol, lentes de sol
sung mass *s* (eccl) misa cantada
sunken [ˋsʌŋkən] *adj* hundido, sumido
sun lamp *s* lámpara de rayos ultravioletas
sun′light′ *s* luz *f* del sol
sun′lit′ *adj* iluminado por el sol
Sunni [ˋsʊni] *adj & s* suní *mf,* sunita *mf*
sun•ny [ˋsʌni] *adj* (*comp* **-nier;** *super* **-iest**) de

sol; asoleado; brillante, resplandeciente; alegre, risueño; **to be sunny** hacer sol
sunny side *s* sol *m;* (fig) lado bueno, lado favorable
sun porch *s* solana
sun'rise' *s* salida del sol; **from sunrise to sunset** de sol a sol
sun'roof' *s* techo corredizo
sun'set' *s* puesta del sol
sun'shade' *s* quitasol *m,* sombrilla; toldo; visera contra el sol
sun'shine' *s* claridad del sol; alegría; **in the sunshine** al sol
sun'spot' *s* mancha solar
sun'stroke' *s* (pathol) insolación
sun'tan' *s* bronceado
suntan lotion *s* bronceador *m,* aceite *m* solar
sup [sʌp] *v* (*pret & pp* **supped;** *ger* **supping**) *intr* cenar
super [ˈsupər] *adj* (coll) estupendo, formidable, genial; **super!** ¡fantástico! ‖ *s* (*building superintendent*) (coll) portero, conserje *m;* (theat) (coll) comparsa *mf,* figurante *mf,* extra *mf*
superannuated [ˌsupərˈænjuˌetɪd] *adj* jubilado, inhabilitado por ancianidad o enfermedad; fuera de moda
superb [səˈpʌrb] *adj* soberbio, estupendo, magnífico
supercar•go [ˈsupərˌkɑrgo] *s* (*pl* **-goes** o **-gos**) (naut) sobrecargo
supercharge [ˌsupərˈtʃɑrdʒ] *tr* sobrealimentar
supercilious [ˌsupərˈsɪlɪ•əs] *adj* arrogante, altanero, desdeñoso
superficial [ˌsupərˈfɪʃəl] *adj* superficial
superfluous [sʊˈpʌrflʊ•əs] *adj* superfluo
sup'er•high'way *s* autopista
superhuman [ˌsupərˈhjumən] *adj* sobrehumano
superimpose [ˌsupərɪmˈpoz] *tr* sobreponer
superintendent [ˌsupərɪnˈtɛndənt] *s* superintendente *mf*
superior [səˈpɪrɪ•ər] *adj* superior; indiferente, sereno; arrogante; (typ) volado ‖ *s* superior *m*
superiority [səˌpɪrɪˈɑrɪti] *s* superioridad; indiferencia, serenidad; arrogancia
superlative [səˈpʌrlətɪv] *adj & s* superlativo
super•man [ˈsupərˌmæn] *s* (*pl* **-men** [ˌmɛn]) sobrehombre *m,* superhombre *m*
supermarket [ˈsupərˌmɑrkɪt] *s* supermercado, autoservicio; (*large*) gran superficie *f*
supernatural [ˌsupərˈnætʃərəl] *adj* sobrenatural
superpose [ˌsupərˈpoz] *tr* sobreponer, superponer
supersede [ˌsupərˈsid] *tr* reemplazar; desalojar
supersonic [ˌsupərˈsɑnɪk] *adj* supersónico ‖ **supersonics** *ssg* supersónica
superstitious [ˌsupərˈstɪʃəs] *adj* supersticioso
supertanker [ˈsupərˌtæŋkər] *s* superpetrolero, supertanquero
supervene [ˌsupərˈvin] *intr* sobrevenir
supervise [ˈsupərˌvaɪz] *tr* superintender, supervisar, dirigir
supervisor [ˈsupərˌvaɪzər] *s* superintendente *mf,* supervisor *m,* dirigente *mf*
supper [ˈsʌpər] *s* cena
supplant [səˈplænt] *tr* reemplazar
supple [ˈsʌpəl] *adj* flexible, ágil; (*leather*) fino y flexible; dócil, adaptable
supplement [ˈsʌplɪmənt] *s* suplemento ‖ [ˈsʌplɪˌmɛnt] *tr* suplir, completar
suppliant [ˈsʌplɪ•ənt] *adj & s* suplicante *mf*
supplication [ˌsʌplɪˈkeʃən] *s* súplica
sup•ply [səˈplaɪ] *s* (*pl* **-plies**) suministro, provisión; surtido, repuesto; oferta, existencia; **supplies** pertrechos, provisiones, víveres *mf;* artículos, efectos ‖ *v* (*pret & pp* **-plied**) *tr* suministrar, aprovisionar; reemplazar
supply and demand *spl* oferta y demanda
supply'-side economics *s* economía de la oferta
support [səˈport] *s* apoyo, soporte *m,* sostén *m;* sustento; (compu) soporte *m* ‖ *tr* apoyar, soportar, sostener; sustentar; aguantar; (compu) soportar; admitir
supporter [səˈportər] *s* partidario; (*jockstrap*) suspensorio; faja abdominal, faja medical
suppose [səˈpoz] *tr* suponer; creer; **to be supposed to** deber; **to suppose so** creer que sí
supposed [səˈpozd] *adj* supuesto
supposition [ˌsʌpəˈzɪʃən] *s* suposición
supposito•ry [səˈpɑzɪˌtori] *s* (*pl* **-ries**) supositorio
suppress [səˈprɛs] *tr* suprimir
suppression [səˈprɛʃən] *s* supresión
suppurate [ˈsʌpjəˌret] *intr* supurar
supreme [səˈprim] o [suˈprim] *adj* supremo
Supreme Court, the *s* el Tribunal Supremo
supt. *abbr* **superintendent**
surcharge [ˈsʌrˌtʃɑrdʒ] *s* sobrecarga ‖ [ˌsʌrˈtʃɑrdʒ] o [ˈsʌrˌtʃɑrdʒ] *tr* sobrecargar
sure [ʃʊr] *adj* seguro; **to be sure** seguramente, sin duda ‖ *adv* (coll) seguramente, claro; **sure enough** efectivamente
surely [ˈʃʊrli] *adv* seguramente, ciertamente, sin duda ‖ *interj* ¡por supuesto!
sure thing *interj* ¡claro!, ¡por supuesto!, ¡seguro! ‖ *s* (coll) apuesta segura
sure•ty [ˈʃʊrti] o [ˈʃʊrɪti] *s* (*pl* **-ties**) seguridad, garantía, fianza
surf [sʌrf] *s* cachones *mpl,* olas que rompen en la playa, oleaje *m,* espuma ‖ *intr* hacer surf, hacer surfing
surface [ˈsʌrfɪs] *adj* superficial ‖ *s* superficie *f* ‖ *tr* alisar, allanar; recubrir ‖ *intr* emerger (*p.ej., un submarino*)
surface mail *s* correo por vía ordinaria
surf'board' *s* patín *m* de mar
surfeit [ˈsʌrfɪt] *s* exceso; hartura, hastío; empacho, indigestión ‖ *tr* atracar, hastiar; encebadar (*las bestias*) ‖ *intr* atracarse, hastiarse; encebadarse
surfer [ˈsʌrfər] *s* surfista *mf*
surfing [ˈsʌrfɪŋ] *s* surf *m,* surfing *m*
surf'-rid'ing *s* patinaje *m* sobre las olas
surge [sʌrdʒ] *s* oleada; (elec) sobretensión ‖ *intr* agitarse, ondular

surgeon [ˋsʌrdʒən] *s* cirujano
Surgeon General, the *s* La Dirección General de Salud Pública, Cirujano General
surger•y [ˋsʌrdʒəri] *s* (*pl* **-ies**) cirugía; sala de operaciones
surgical [ˋsʌrdʒɪkəl] *adj* quirúrgico
surgical gloves *s* guantes *mpl* de cirujano
sur•ly [ˋsʌrli] *adj* (*comp* **-lier;** *super* **-liest**) áspero, rudo, hosco, insolente
surmise [sərˋmaɪz] o [ˋsʌrmaɪz] *s* conjetura, suposición ‖ [sərˋmaɪz] *tr & intr* conjeturar, suponer
surmount [sərˋmaʊnt] *tr* levantarse sobre; aventajar, sobrepujar; superar; coronar
surname [ˋsʌr,nem] *s* apellido: (*added name*) sobrenombre *m* ‖ *tr* apellidar; sobrenombrar
surpass [sərˋpæs] o [sərˋpɑs] *tr* aventajar, sobrepasar
surplice [ˋsʌrplɪs] *s* sobrepelliz *f*
surplus [ˋsʌrplʌs] *adj* sobrante, excedente ‖ *s* sobrante *m,* exceso; (com) superávit *m*
surplus material *s* rezago
surprise [sərˋpraɪz] *adj* inesperado, improviso ‖ *s* sorpresa; **to take by surprise** coger por sorpresa ‖ *tr* sorprender
surprise package *s* sorpresa
surprise party *s* reunión improvisada para felicitar por sorpresa a una persona
surprising [sərˋpraɪzɪŋ] *adj* sorprendente, sorpresivo
surrealism [səˋri•ə,lɪzəm] *s* surrealismo
surrender [səˋrɛndər] *s* rendición ‖ *tr* rendir ‖ *intr* rendirse
surrender value *s* (ins) valor *m* de rescate
surreptitious [,sʌrɛpˋtɪʃəs] *adj* subrepticio
surrogate [ˋsʌrəgət] *adj* sucedáneo ‖ *s* substituto
surrogate mother *s* madre alquilada, de alquiler o suplente
surround [səˋraʊnd] *tr* cercar, rodear, circundar; (mil) sitiar
surrounding [səˋraʊndɪŋ] *adj* circundante, circunstante ‖ **surroundings** *spl* alrededores *mpl,* contornos; ambiente *m,* medio
surtax [ˋsʌr,tæks] *s* impuesto complementario
surveillance [sərˋveləns] o [sərˋveljəns] *s* vigilancia
survey [ˋsʌrve] *s* estudio, examen *m,* inspección, reconocimiento; agrimensura, medición, plano; levantamiento de planos; (*of opinion*) encuesta, sondeo; (*of literature*) bosquejo ‖ [sʌrˋve] o [ˋsʌrve] *tr* estudiar, examinar, inspeccionar, reconocer; medir; levantar el plano de ‖ *intr* levantar el plano
surveyor [sərˋve•ər] *s* inspector *m;* agrimensor *m*
survival [sərˋvaɪvəl] *s* supervivencia
survive [sərˋvaɪv] *tr* sobrevivir a (*otra persona; algún acontecimiento*) ‖ *intr* sobrevivir
surviving [sərˋvaɪvɪŋ] *adj* sobreviviente
survivor [sərˋvaɪvər] *s* sobreviviente *mf*
survivorship [sərˋvaɪvər,ʃɪp] *s* (law) sobrevivencia
susceptible [səˋsɛptɪbəl] *adj* susceptible; (*to love*) enamoradizo
suspect [ˋsʌspɛkt] *adj & s* sospechoso ‖ [səsˋpɛkt] *tr* sospechar
suspend [səsˋpɛnd] *tr* suspender ‖ *intr* dejar de obrar; suspender pagos
suspenders [səsˋpɛndərz] *spl* tirantes *mpl*
suspense [səsˋpɛns] *s* suspenso, suspensión; duda, incertidumbre; indecisión, irresolución; ansiedad
suspension bridge [səsˋpɛnʃən] *s* puente *m* colgante
suspension points *spl* puntos suspensivos
suspicion [səsˋpɪʃən] *s* sospecha, suspicacia; sombra, traza ligera
suspicious [səsˋpɪʃəs] *adj* (*inclined to suspect*) suspicaz; (*subject to suspicion*) sospechoso
sustain [səsˋten] *tr* sostener, sustentar; apoyar, defender; confirmar, probar; sufrir (*p.ej., un daño, una pérdida*)
sustenance [ˋsʌstɪnəns] *s* sustento, alimentos; sostenimiento
suture [ˋsutʃər] *s* (*thread*) (med) hilo de sutura, sedal *m;* (*stitch*) (med) sutura ‖ *tr* suturar
swab [swɑb] *s* escobón *m,* estropajo; (naut) lampazo; (surg) tapón *m* de algodón ‖ *v* (*pret & pp* **swabbed;** *ger* **swabbing**) *tr* fregar, limpiar; (naut) lampacear; (surg) limpiar con algodón
swaddle [ˋswɑdəl] *tr* empañar, fajar
swaddling clothes *spl* pañales *mpl*
swagger [ˋswægər] *adj* (coll) muy elegante ‖ *s* fanfarronada; contoneo, paso jactancioso ‖ *intr* fanfarronear; contonear
swain [swen] *s* (*lad*) (archaic o hum) mozo (archaic); (*suitor*) (archaic o hum) festejante *m* (archaic)
swallow [ˋswɑlo] *s* trago; (orn) golondrina ‖ *tr* tragar, deglutir; (fig) tragar, tragarse ‖ *intr* tragar, deglutir
swallow-tailed coat [ˋswɑlo,teld] *s* frac *m*
swal′low•wort′ *s* vencetósigo
swamp [swɑmp] *s* pantano, marisma ‖ *tr* encharcar, inundar; (*e.g., with work*) abrumar
swamp•y [ˋswɑmpi] *adj* (*comp* **-ier;** *super* **-iest**) pantanoso
swan [swɑn] *s* cisne *m*
swan dive *s* salto de ángel
swank [swæŋk] *adj* (slang) elegante, vistoso ‖ *s* (slang) elegancia vistosa
swan knight *s* caballero del cisne
swan's-down [ˋswɑnz,daʊn] *s* plumón *m* de cisne; moletón *m,* paño de vicuña
swan song *s* canto del cisne
swap [swɑp] *s* truque *m,* cambalache *m* trueque, cambalache, cambio ‖ *v* (*pret & pp* **swapped;** *ger* **swapping**) *tr & intr* trocar, cambalachear, intercambiar, cambiar
swarm [swɔrm] *s* enjambre *m* ‖ *intr* enjambrar; volar en enjambres; hormiguear (*una multitud de gente o animales*)
swarth•y [ˋswɔrði] o [ˋswɔrθi] *adj* (*comp* **-ier;** *super* **-iest**) atezado, carinegro, moreno

swashbuckler [ˈswɑʃ,bʌklər] *s* espada chín *m,* matasiete *m,* valentón *m*
swat [swɑt] *s* (coll) golpe violento || *v* (*pret & pp* **swatted;** *ger* **swatting**) *tr* (coll) golpear con fuerza; (coll) aporrear, aplastar (*una mosca*)
sway [swe] *s* oscilación, vaivén *m;* dominio, imperio || *tr* hacer oscilar; conmover; disuadir; gobernar, dominar || *intr* oscilar; desviarse; tambalear, flaquear
swear [swɛr] *v* (*pret* **swore** [swor]; *pp* **sworn** [sworn]) *tr* jurar; juramentar; prestar (*juramento*); **to swear in** tomar juramento a; **to swear off** jurar renunciar a; **to swear out** obtener mediante juramento || *intr* jurar; **to swear at** maldecir; **to swear by** jurar por; poner toda su confianza en; **to swear to** prestar juramento a; declarar bajo juramento; jurar + *inf*
swear′word′ *s* palabrota, taco
sweat [swɛt] *s* sudor *m* || *v* (*pret & pp* **sweat** o **sweated**) *tr* sudar (*agua por los poros; la ropa*); (slang) hacer sudar; **to sweat it out** (slang) aguantarlo hasta el fin || *intr* sudar
sweat′band *s* cinta, vincha; (*in hat*) faja interior
sweater [ˈswɛtər] *s* suéter *m,* pulóver *m,* jersey *m,* chomba (Chile), buzo (Urug), chompa (Peru)
sweat′shirt *s* sudadera, camiseta gruesa, buzo (Arg) polerón (Chile), camiseta de entrenamiento
sweat′shop′ *s* taller *m* de trabajo afanoso y de poco sueldo
sweat′suit *s* equipo de deportes, chandal *m,* pants *mpl* (Mex), buzo (Chile, Peru), sudadera (Col)
sweat•y [ˈswɛti] *adj* (*comp* **-ier;** *super* **-iest**) sudoroso, sudado, transpirado
Swede [swid] *s* sueco
Sweden [ˈswidən] *s* Suecia
Swedish [ˈswidɪʃ] *adj & s* sueco
sweep [swip] *s* barrido; alcance *m,* extensión; (*of wind*) soplo; (*of a well*) cigoñal *m;* (*by the police*) rastreo policial (*de una zona*) || *v* (*pret & pp* **swept** [swɛpt]) *tr* barrer; arrastrar; rozar, tocar; recorrer con la mirada, los dedos, etc. || *intr* barrer; pasar rápidamente; extenderse; precipitarse; andar con paso majestuoso
sweeper [ˈswipər] *s* (*person*) barrendero; (*machine for sweeping streets*) barredera; barredera de alfombra; (nav) dragaminas *m*
sweeping [ˈswipɪŋ] *adj* arrebatador; comprensivo, extenso, vasto || **sweepings** *spl* barreduras
sweep′sec′ond *s* segundero central
sweep′stakes′ *ssg* o *spl* lotería en la cual una persona gana todas las apuestas; carrera que decide todas las apuestas; premio en las carreras de caballos
sweet [swit] *adj* dulce; oloroso; melodioso, grato al oído; fresco; bonito, lindo; amable; querido; **to be sweet on** (coll) estar enamorado de || *adv* dulcemente; **to smell sweet** tener buen olor || **sweets** *spl* dulces *mpl,* golosinas
sweet′-and-sour′ *adj* agridulce
sweet′bread′ *s* lechecillas, mollejas
sweet′bri′er *s* eglantina
sweet corn *s* maíz tierno, elote *m* (Mex), choclo (SAm), jojoto (Ven)
sweeten [ˈswitən] *tr* azucarar, endulzar; suavizar; purificar || *intr* azucararse, endulzarse; suavizarse
sweetener [ˈswitənər] *s* eculcorante
sweet′heart′ *s* enamorado o enamorada; amiga querida; galán *m,* cortejo
sweetie [ˈswiti] *s* (coll) encanto: (*as form of address*) tesoro, mi vida
sweetish [ˈswitɪʃ] *adj* dulzoso
sweet marjoram *s* mejorana
sweet′meats′ *spl* dulces *mpl,* confites *mpl,* confitura
sweet pea *s* guisante *m* de olor
sweet potato *s* batata, camote *m,* papa dulce
sweet-scented [ˈswit,sɛntɪd] *adj* oloroso, perfumado
sweet′-talk′ *tr* (coll) engatusar, camelar (Esp)
sweet tooth *s* gusto por los dulces
sweet-toothed [ˈswit,tuθt] *adj* dulcero, goloso
sweet william *s* clavel *m* de ramillete, minutisa
swell [swɛl] *adj* (coll) muy elegante; (slang) de órdago, magnífico || *s* hinchazón *f;* bulto; marejada, mar de fondo; oleaje *m;* (*of a crowd of people*) oleada; (coll) petimetre *m,* pisaverde *m* || *v* (*pret* **swelled;** *pp* **swelled** o **swollen** [ˈswolən]) *tr* hinchar, inflar; abultar, aumentar; elevar, levantar; (fig) hinchar, engreír || *intr* hincharse; abultarse, aumentar, crecer; elevarse, levantarse; embravecerse (*el mar*); (fig) hincharse, engreírse
swelter [ˈswɛltər] *intr* sofocarse de sudor
sweltering [ˈswɛltərɪŋ] *adj* sofocante, bochornoso
swept′back′ wing *s* (aer) ala en flecha
swerve [swʌrv] *s* viraje *m,* desvío brusco || *tr* desviar || *intr* desviarse, torcer
swift [swɪft] *adj* rápido, veloz; pronto; repentino; correlón (SAm) || *adv* rápidamente, velozmente || *s* vencejo
swig [swɪg] *s* chisguete, tragantada || *v* (*pret & pp* **swigged;** *ger* **swigging**) *tr & intr* beber a grandes tragos
swill [swɪl] *s* basura, inmundicia; tragantada || *tr* beber a grandes tragos; emborrachar || *intr* beber a grandes tragos; emborracharse
swim [swɪm] *s* natación; **the swim** (*in affairs, society, etc.*) (coll) la corriente || *v* (*pret* **swam** [swæm]; *pp* **swum** [swʌm]; *ger* **swimming**) *tr* pasar a nado || *intr* nadar; deslizarse, escurrirse; padecer vahidos; dar vueltas (*la cabeza*); **to swim across** atravesar a nado
swimmer [ˈswɪmər] *s* nadador *m*
swimming pool *s* piscina
swimming trunks *spl* traje *m* de baño, bañador *m* de hombre (Esp)

swim'suit *s* traje *m de* baño, bañador *m,* malla de baño, vestido de baño (Col)
swindle [ˈswɪndəl] *s* estafa, timo; leva (CAm, Col); embelequería (Col, Mex, P-R) || *tr & intr* estafar, timar
swindler [ˈswɪndlər] *s* estafador *m,* estafadora; lana *m* (CAm)
swine [swaɪn] *s* cerdo, puerco; *spl* ganado porcino
swing [swɪŋ] *s* balance *m,* oscilación, vaivén *m;* (*device used for recreation*) columpio; hamaca; turno, período; fuerza, ímpetu *m;* (*trip*) jira; (box) golpe *m* de lado; (mus) ritmo constantemente repetido; **in full swing** en plena marcha || *v* (*pret & pp* **swung** [swʌŋ]) *tr* blandir (*p.ej., un arma*); menear (*los brazos*); hacer oscilar; columpiar; manejar con éxito || *intr* oscilar; balancearse; columpiar; estar colgado; dar una vuelta; **to swing open** abrirse de pronto (*una puerta*)
swinger [ˈswɪŋər] *s* (coll) desinhibido
swinging door [ˈswɪŋɪŋ] *s* batiente *m* oscilante, puerta de vaivén
swing shift *s* turno de tarde
swinish [ˈswaɪnɪʃ] *adj* porcuno; (fig) cochino, puerco
swipe [swaɪp] *s* (coll) golpe *m* fuerte || *tr* (com) pasar (*una tarjeta electrónica*) por la ranura de una máquina; (coll) dar un golpe fuerte a; (coll) hurtar, robar
swirl [swʌrl] *s* remolino, torbellino || *tr* hacer girar || *intr* arremolinarse, remolinar; girar
swish [swɪʃ] *s* (*e.g., of a whip*) chasquido; (*of a dress*) crujido || *tr* chasquear (*el látigo*) || *intr* chasquear; crujir (*un vestido*)
Swiss [swɪs] *adj & s* suizo
Swiss chard [tʃɑrd] *s* acelga
Swiss cheese *s* Gruyère *m,* queso suizo
Swiss Guards *spl* guardia suiza
switch [swɪtʃ] *s* bastoncillo, latiguillo; latigazo; coletazo; (*false hair*) trenza postiza, moño postizo; (elec) llave *f,* interruptor *m,* conmutador *m;* (rr) agujas || *tr* azotar, fustigar; (elec) conmutar; (rr) desviar; **to switch off** (elec) cortar, desconectar; **to switch on** (elec) cerrar (*el circuito*); (elec) encender, poner (*la luz, etc.*) || *intr* cambiarse, moverse; desviarse
switch'back' *s* vía en zigzag
switch'blade (knife) *s* navaja automática o de botón, navaja de resorte (Mex)
switch'board' *s* cuadro de distribución, centralita
switching engine *s* locomotora de maniobras
switch•man [ˈswɪtʃmən] *s* (*pl* **-men** [mən]) agujetero, guardagujas *m*
switch'yard' *s* patio de maniobras
Switzerland [ˈswɪtsərlənd] *s* Suiza
swiv•el [ˈswɪvəl] *s* eslabón giratorio || *v* (*pret & pp* **-eled** o **-elled;** *ger* **-eling** o **-elling**) *intr* girar sobre un eje
swivel chair *s* silla giratoria
swizzle stick [ˈswɪzəl] *s* agitador *m,* bastoncito *m* para cóctel
swoon [swun] *s* desmayo || *intr* desmayarse
swoop [swup] *s* descenso súbito; (*of a bird of prey*) calada || *intr* bajar rápidamente, precipitarse; abatirse (*p.ej., el ave de rapiña*)
sword [sord] *s* espada; **at swords' points** enemistados a sangre y fuego; **to put to the sword** pasar al filo de la espada, pasar a cuchillo
sword belt *s* cinturón *m*
sword'fish' *s* pez *m* espada
sword handler *s* (taur) mozo de estoques
sword rattling *s* fanfarronería
swords•man [ˈsordzmən] *s* (*pl* **-men** [mən]) espada *m;* esgrimidor *m*
sword swallower [ˈswɑlo•ər] *s* tragasable *m*
sword thrust *s* estocada, golpe *m* de espada
sworn [sworn] *adj* (*enemy*) jurado
sworn statement *s* declaración jurada
sycamore [ˈsɪkəmɔr] *s* (bot) plátano de sombra
sycophant [ˈsɪkəfənt] *s* adulador *m;* parásito
syllable [ˈsɪləbəl] *s* sílaba
sylla•bus [ˈsɪləbəs] *s* (*pl* **-buses**) plan *m* de estudios, programa *m*
syllogism [ˈsɪlə,dʒɪzəm] *s* silogismo
sylph [sɪlf] *s* sílfide *f*
sym. *abbr* **symbol, symmetrical, symphony**
symbiosis [,sɪmbaɪˈosɪs] o [,sɪmbiˈosɪs] *s* simbiosis
symbiotic [,sɪmbaɪˈɑtɪk] o [,sɪmbiˈɑtɪk] *adj* simbiótico
symbol [ˈsɪmbəl] *s* símbolo
symbolic(al) [sɪmˈbɑlɪk(əl)] *adj* simbólico
symbolize [ˈsɪmbə,laɪz] *tr* simbolizar
symmetric(al) [sɪˈmɛtrɪk(əl)] *adj* simétrico
symme•try [ˈsɪmɪtri] *s* (*pl* **-tries**) simetría
sympathetic [,sɪmpəˈθɛtɪk] *adj* compasivo, comprensivo; favorablemente dispuesto; (*nervous system*) simpático
sympathize [ˈsɪmpə,θaɪz] *intr* compadecerse; **to sympathize with** compadecerse de; comprender
sympathizer [ˈsɪmpə,θaɪzər] *s* (pol) simpatizante *mf,* partidario
sympa•thy [ˈsɪmpəθi] *s* (*pl* **-thies**) compasión, conmiseración; **sympathies** (pol) simpatías; **to be in sympathy with** estar de acuerdo con, ser partidario de; **to extend one's sympathy to** dar el pésame a, expresar las condolencias a
sympathy strike *s* huelga por solidaridad
symphonic [sɪmˈfɑnɪk] *adj* sinfónico
sympho•ny [ˈsɪmfəni] *s* (*pl* **-nies**) sinfonía
symposi•um [sɪmˈpozɪ•əm] *s* (*pl* **-a** [ə]) coloquio
symptom [ˈsɪmptəm] *s* síntoma *m*
syn. *abbr* **synonym, synonymous**
synagogue [ˈsɪnə,gɔg] *s* sinagoga
sync, synch [sɪŋk] *s* (coll) sincronización; **to be in sync with** estar sincronizado con; **to be out of sync with** no estar sincronizado con
synchronize [ˈsɪŋkrə,naɪz] *tr & intr* sincronizar
synchronous [ˈsɪŋkrənəs] *adj* sincrónico
syncopated [ˈsɪŋkə,petəd] *adj* sincopado

syncope [ˈsɪŋkə,pi] *s* (phonet) síncopa
syndicate [ˈsɪndɪkɪt] *s* sindicato ‖ [ˈsɪndɪ,ket] *tr* sindicar ‖ *intr* sindicarse
syndrome [ˈsɪndrom] *s* síndrome *m*
synonym [ˈsɪnənɪm] *s* sinónimo
synonym dictionary *s* diccionario de sinónimos
synonymous [sɪˈnɑnɪməs] *adj* sinónimo
synop•sis [sɪˈnɑpsɪs] *s* (*pl* **-ses** [siz]) sinopsis *f*
syntax [ˈsɪntæks] *s* sintaxis *f*
synthe•sis [ˈsɪnθɪsɪs] *s* (*pl* **-ses** [,siz]) síntesis *f*
synthesize [ˈsɪnθɪ,saɪz] *tr* sintetizar
synthesizer *s* sintetizador *m*
synthetic(al) [sɪnˈθɛtɪk(əl)] *adj* sintético
synthetic leather *s* piel sintética
syphillis [ˈsɪfɪlɪs] *s* sífilis *f*
Syria [ˈsɪrɪ•ə] *s* Siria
Syrian [ˈsɪrɪ•ən] *adj* & *s* sirio
syringe [sɪˈrɪndʒ] o [ˈsɪrɪndʒ] *s* jeringa; (*fountain syringe*) mangueta; (*syringe fitted with needle for hypodermic injections*) jeringuilla ‖ *tr* jeringar
syrup [ˈsɪrəp] *s* almíbar *m;* (*with fruit juices or medicinal substances*) jarabe *m*
system [ˈsɪstəm] *s* sistema *m*
systematic(al) [,sɪstəˈmætɪk(əl)] *adj* sistemático
systematize [ˈsɪstəmə,taɪz] *tr* sistematizar
systems analysis *s* análisis *m* & *f* de sistemas
systole [ˈsɪstəli] *s* sístole *f*

T

T, t [ti] vigésima letra del alfabeto inglés
t. *abbr* **teaspoon, temperature, tenor, tense, territory, town**
T. *abbr* **Territory, Testament**
tab [tæb] *s* apéndice *m,* proyección; marbete *m;* (compu) pestaña; **to keep tab on** (coll) tener a la vista; **to pick up the tab** (coll) pagar la cuenta
tab•by [ˈtæbi] *s* (*pl* **-bies**) gato atigrado; gata; solterona; chismosa
tabernacle [ˈtæbər,nækəl] *s* tabernáculo
table [ˈtebəl] *s* mesa; (*list, catalogue; index of a book*) tabla; **to set the table** poner la mesa; **to turn the tables** volver las tornas; **under the table** completamente emborrachado ‖ *tr* aplazar la discusión de
tab•leau [ˈtæblo] *s* (*pl* **-leaus** o **-leaux** [loz]) cuadro vivo
ta′ble•cloth′ *s* mantel *m;* **tablecloths** ropa de mesa
table d′hôte [ˈtɑbəlˈdot] *s* mesa redonda; comida a precio fijo
ta′ble•land′ *s* meseta
table linen *s* mantelería
table manners *spl* modales *mpl* que uno tiene en la mesa
table mat *s* posafuentes *m*
table of contents *s* índice *m* de materias, tabla de materias, índice temático
ta′ble•spoon′ *s* cuchara de servir
tablespoonful [ˈtebəl,spun,ful] *s* cucharada
tablet [ˈtæblɪt] *s* (*writing pad*) bloc *m;* (*slab*) lápida, placa; (*lozenge, pastille*) comprimido, tableta
table talk *s* conversación de sobremesa
table tennis *s* tenis de mesa
ta′ble•ware′ *s* servicio de mesa, artículos para la mesa
tabloid [ˈtæblɔɪd] *adj* de formato reducido; sensacionalista ‖ *s* tabloide *m,* periódico sensacional
taboo [təˈbu] *adj* prohibido ‖ *s* tabú *m* ‖ *tr* prohibir
tabulate [ˈtæbjə,let] *tr* tabular
tabulator [ˈtæbjə,letər] *s* tabulador *m*
tacit [ˈtæsɪt] *adj* tácito
taciturn [ˈtæsɪ,tʌrn] *adj* taciturno
tack [tæk] *s* tachuela; nuevo plan de acción; (naut) virada; (sew) hilván *m* ‖ *tr* clavar con tachuelas; añadir; unir; (naut) virar; (sew) hilvanar ‖ *intr* cambiar de plan; (naut) virar
tackle [ˈtækəl] *s* avíos, enseres *mpl;* (naut) poleame *m* ‖ *tr* atacar, embestir; emprender
tack•y [ˈtæki] *adj* (*comp* **-ier;** *super* **-iest**) pegajoso; (coll) desaliñado
tact [tækt] *s* tacto, juicio, tino
tactful [ˈtæktfəl] *adj* discreto, político
tactical [ˈtæktɪkəl] *adj* táctico
tactician [tækˈtɪʃən] *s* táctico
tactics [ˈtæktɪks] *ssg* (mil) táctica ‖ *spl* táctica
tactless [ˈtæklɪs] *adj* indiscreto
tad′pole′ *s* renacuajo
taffeta [ˈtæfɪtə] *s* tafetán *m*
taffy [ˈtæfi] *s* arropía, melcocha; (coll) lisonja, zalamería
tag [tæg] *s* etiqueta, marbete *m;* herrete *m;* pingajo; mechón *m;* vedija; (*curlicue in writing*) ringorrango; **to play tag** jugar al tócame tú ‖ *v* (*pret* & *pp* **tagged;** *ger* **tagging**) *tr* pegar un marbete a; marcar con marbete ‖ *intr* (coll) seguir de cerca
tag end *s* cabo flojo; (*remnant*) retal *m,* retazo
Tagus [ˈtegəs] *s* Tajo
tail [tel] *adj* de cola ‖ *s* cola; **tails** (*of a coin*) cruz *f;* (coll) frac *m;* **to turn tail** mostrar los talones ‖ *tr* atar, juntar ‖ *intr* formar cola; **to tail after** pisar los talones a
tail assembly *s* (aer) empenaje *m,* planos de cola
tail end *s* cola, extremo; conclusión; últimos minutos, última parte; **at the tail end** al final
tail′gate′ *tr* & *intr* (aut) seguir demasiado de cerca

tail'light' *s* faro trasero; (rr) disco de cola
tailor [ˈtelər] *s* sastre *m* || *tr* entallar (*un traje*) || *intr* ser sastre
tailoring [ˈtelərɪŋ] *s* sastrería, costura
tai'lor-made' suit *s* traje *m* de sastre, traje hecho a la medida
tailor's chalk *s* jabón *m* de sastre
tail'piece' *s* apéndice *m,* cabo; (*of stringed instrument*) (mus) cordal *m;* (typ) florón *m*
tail'race' *s* cauce *m* de salida; (min) canal *m* de desechos
tail spin *s* (aer) barrena picada
tail wind *s* (aer) viento de cola; (naut) viento en popa
taint [tent] *s* mancha; corrupción, infección || *tr* manchar; corromper, inficionar
Taiwan [ˈtaɪˈwɑn] *s* Taiwán *m*
take [tek] *s* toma; presa, redada; (mov) toma; (slang) entradas, ingresos || *v* (*pret* **took** [tʊk]; *pp* **taken**) *tr* tomar; (*to carry off with one*) llevarse; (*to remove*) quitar; quedarse con (*p.ej., una compra en una tienda*); comer (*una pieza, en el juego de ajedrez y en el de damas*); dar (*un paso, un salto, un paseo*); hacer (*un viaje; ejercicio*); seguir (*un consejo; una asignatura*); sacar (*una fotografía*); calzar, usar (*cierto tamaño de zapatos o guantes*); estudiar (*p.ej., historia, francés, matemáticas*); echar (*una siesta*); tomar (*un tren, autobús, tranvía*); aguantar, tolerar; soportar; **to take amiss** llevar a mal; **to take apart** descomponer, desarmar, desmontar; **to take down** bajar; descolgar; poner por escrito, tomar nota de; desmontar; (*to humble*) quitar los humos a; **to take for** tomar por, p.ej., **I took you for someone else** le tomé por otra persona; **to take from** quitar a; **to take in** acoger, admitir; (*to welcome into one's home, one's company*) recibir; (*to encompass*) abarcar, comprender; ganar (dinero); visitar (*los puntos de interés*); (*to win over by flattery or deceit*) cazar; meter (*p.ej., las costuras de una prenda de vestir*); **to take it that** suponer que; **to take off** quitarse (*p.ej., el sombrero*); descontar; (coll) imitar, parodiar; **to take on** tomar, contratar; empezar; cargar con, tomar sobre sí; desafiar; **to take out** sacar; pasear (*p.ej., a un niño, un caballo*); omitir; extraer, separar; **to take place** tener lugar; **to take up** subir; levantar; apretar; coger; recoger; emprender, comenzar; tomar posesión de (*un cargo, un puesto*); tomar, estudiar; ocupar, llenar (*un espacio*) || *intr* arraigar, prender; cuajar; actuar, obrar; salir, resultar; adherirse; pegar; (coll) tener éxito; **to take after** parecerse a; **to take off** levantarse; salir; (aer) despegar; **to take up with** (coll) estrechar amistad con; (coll) vivir con; **to take well** (coll) sacar buen retrato
take'-home' pay *s* salario neto
take'-off' *s* (aer) despegue *m;* (coll) imitación burlesca, parodia
take'-out' *adj* para llevar || *s* comida para llevar
take'-o'ver *s* toma del poder
takeover bid *s* (econ) oferta pública de adquisición, OPA *f*
talcum powder [ˈtælkəm] *s* polvos de talco; talco en polvo
tale [tel] *s* cuento, relato; embuste *m,* mentira
tale'bear'er *s* chismoso, cuentista *mf*
talent [ˈtælənt] *s* talento; gente *f* de talento
talented [ˈtæləntɪd] *adj* talentoso
talent scout *s* buscador *m* de nuevas figuras
talk [tɔk] *s* charla, plática; (*gossip*) fábula, comidilla; (*lecture*) conferencia; **to cause talk** dar que hablar || *tr* hablar; convencer hablando; **to talk up** ensalzar || *intr* hablar; parlar (*el loro*); **to talk on** discutir (*un asunto*); hablar sin para; continuar hablando; **to talk up** elevar la voz, osar hablar
talkative [ˈtɔkətɪv] *adj* hablador, locuaz, palabrudo
talker [ˈtɔkər] *s* hablador *m;* orador *m;* charlatán *m,* parlón *m;* discursista *mf*
talking doll [ˈtɔkɪŋ] *s* muñeca parlante
talk show *s* (telv, rad) programa *m* de conversación e interviú
tall [tɔl] *adj* alto; (coll) exagerado
tall-case clock [ˈtɔlkes] *s* reloj *m* de caja, reloj de pie
tallow [ˈtælo] *s* sebo
tal·ly [ˈtæli] *s* (*pl* **-lies**) cuenta || *v* (*pret & pp* **-lied**) *tr* echar la cuenta de || *intr* echar la cuenta; concordar, corresponder, conformarse
tally sheet *s* hoja en que se anota una cuenta
talon [ˈtælən] *s* garra
tambourine [ˌtæmbəˈrin] *s* pandereta
tame [tem] *adj* manso, domesticado; dócil, sumiso; insípido || *tr* amansar, domesticar; domar (*a un animal salvaje*); someter; captar (*una caída de agua*)
tamp [tæmp] *tr* atacar (*un barreno*); apisonar
tamper [ˈtæmpər] *s* (*person*) apisonador *m;* (*ram*) pisón *m* || *intr* entremeterse; **to tamper with** manosear, tocar ajando; tratar de forzar (*una cerradura*); falsificar (*un documento*); corromper (*p.ej., a un testigo*)
tampon [ˈtæmpɑn] *s* (surg) tapón *m* || *tr* (surg) taponar
tan [tæn] *adj* requemado, tostado; de color de canela; marrón; café (Am) || *v* (*pret & pp* **tanned;** *ger* **tanning**) *tr* adobar, curtir, zurrar; quemar, tostar; (coll) zurrar, dar una paliza a
tang [tæŋ] *s* sabor *m* u olor *m* fuerte y picante; dejo, gustillo; (*ringing sound*) tañido
tangent [ˈtændʒənt] *adj* tangente || *s* tangente *f;* **to fly off at a tangent** tomar subitamente nuevo rumbo, cambiar de repente
tangerine [ˌtændʒəˈrin] *s* mandarina
tangible [ˈtændʒɪbəl] *adj* palpable, tangible
Tangier [tænˈdʒɪr] *s* Tánger *f*
tangle [ˈtæŋgəl] *s* enredo, maraña, lío || *tr* enredar, enmarañar || *intr* enredarse, enmarañarse
tank [tæŋk] *s* tanque *m,* depósito; (mil) tanque,

carro de combate; (rr) ténder *m;* (*heavy drinker*) (slang) bodega
tank car *s* (rr) carro cuba, vagón *m* tanque
tanker [ˈtæŋkər] *s* barco tanque, buque *m* cisterna, barco cisternas; avión-nodriza *m*
tanker fleet *s* flota petrolera
tank farming *s* quimicultura, cultivo hidropónico
tank top o **tank** *s* (*shirt or blouse*) camiseta tanque, camiseta con tirantes, camiseta de espaldas desnudas
tank truck *s* camión *m* tanque
tanner [ˈtænər] *s* curtidor *m*
tanner•y [ˈtænəri] *s* (*pl* **-ies**) curtiduría, tenería
tantalize [ˈtæntəˌlaɪz] *tr* atormentar con falsas promesas
tantamount [ˈtæntəˌmaʊnt] *adj* equivalente
tantrum [ˈtæntrəm] *s* berrinche *m,* rabieta
tap [tæp] *s* golpecito, palmadita; canilla, espita; grifo; (elec) toma; (mach) macho de terraja; **on tap** sacado del barril, servido al grifo; listo, a mano; **taps** (*signal to put out lights*) (mil) silencio ‖ *v* (*pret & pp* **tapped;** *ger* **tapping**) *tr* dar golpecitos o un golpecito a o en; espitar, poner la espita a; sacar o tomar (*quitando la espita*); sangrar (*un árbol*); intervenir (*un teléfono*); derivar (*electricidad*); aterrajar (*tuercas*) ‖ *intr* dar golpecitos
tap dance *s* zapateo americano
tap′-dance′ *intr* zapatear, hacer zapateo americano
tap dancer *s* bailarín *m* de zapateo americano
tape [tep] *s* cinta ‖ *tr* proveer de cinta; medir con cinta; (coll) grabar en cinta magnetofónica
tape deck *s* platina, pletina
tape measure *s* cinta de medir
taper [ˈtepər] *s* cerilla, velita larga y delgada ‖ *tr* ahusar ‖ *intr* ahusarse; ir disminuyendo
tape′-re•cord′ *tr* grabar sobre cinta
tape recorder [rɪˈkɔrdər] *s* magnetófono, grabadora de cinta
tape recording *s* grabación sobre cinta
tapes•try [ˈtæpɪstri] *s* (*pl* **-tries**) tapiz *m* ‖ *v* (*pret & pp* **-tried**) *tr* tapizar
tape′worm′ *s* solitaria, lombriz solitaria
tappet [ˈtæpɪt] *s* (aut) alzaválvulas *m,* taqué *m*
tap′room′ *s* bodegón *m,* taberna
taps [tæps] *s* toque *m* de silencio; (slang) fin *m,* muerte *f*
tap water *s* agua de grifo
tap wrench *s* volvedor *m* de machos
tar [tɑr] *s* alquitrán *m;* (coll) marinero ‖ *v* (*pret & pp* **tarred;** *ger* **tarring**) *tr* alquitranar; **to tar and feather** embrear y emplumar
tar•dy [ˈtɑrdi] *adj* (*comp* **-dier;** *super* **-diest**) tardío
target [ˈtɑrgɪt] *s* blanco
target area *s* zona a batir
target practice *s* tiro al blanco
tariff [ˈtærɪf] *adj* arancelario ‖ (*duties*) arancel *m;* (*rates in general*) tarifa
tarnish [ˈtɑrnɪʃ] *s* deslustre *m* ‖ *tr* deslustrar ‖ *intr* deslustrarse
tar paper *s* papel alquitranado
tarpaulin [tɑrˈpɔlɪn] *s* alquitranado, encerado, empegado
tar•ry [ˈtɑri] *adj* alquitranado, embreado ‖ [ˈtæri] *v* (*pret & pp* **-ried**) *intr* detenerse, quedarse; tardar
tart [tɑrt] *adj* acre, agrio; (fig) áspero, mordaz ‖ *s* tarta; (coll) puta
task [tæsk] *s* tarea; **to bring** o **take to task** llamar a capítulo
task′mas′ter *s* amo, superintendente *mf;* ordenancista *mf,* tirano
tassel [ˈtæsəl] *s* borla; (bot) penacho
taste [test] *s* gusto, sabor *m;* sorbo, trago; muestra; gusto, buen gusto; **in bad taste** de mal gusto; **in good taste** de buen gusto; **to acquire a taste for** tomar gusto a ‖ *tr* gustar; (*to sample*) probar ‖ *intr* saber; **to taste of** saber a
taste bud *s* (physiol) papila gustativa
tasteless [ˈtestlɪs] *adj* desabrido, insípido; de mal gusto
tast•y [ˈtesti] *adj* (*comp* **-ier;** *super* **-iest**) sabroso; de buen gusto
tatter [ˈtætər] *s* andrajo, harapo, guiñapo ‖ *tr* hacer andrajos
tattered [ˈtætərd] *adj* andrajoso, haraposo, hilachento
tattle [ˈtætəl] *s* charla; habladuría ‖ *intr* charlar; chismear, murmurar
tat′tle•tale′ *adj* revelador ‖ *s* cuentista *mf,* chismoso
tatto [tæˈtu] *s* tatuaje *m;* (mil) retreta ‖ *tr* tatuar o tatuarse
taunt [tɔnt] o [tɑnt] *s* mofa, pulla ‖ *tr* provocar con insultos
Taurus [ˈtɔrəs] *s* (astr) Tauro
taut [tɔt] *adj* tieso, tirante
tavern [ˈtævərn] *s* taberna; mesón *m,* posada; bayun(c)a (CAm); borrachería (Mex)
taw•dry [ˈtɔdri] *adj* (*comp* **-drier;** *super* **-driest**) cursi, charro, vistoso
taw•ny [ˈtɔni] *adj* (*comp* **-nier;** *super* **-niest**) leonado
tax [tæks] *s* contribución, impuesto ‖ *tr* poner impuestos a (*una persona*); poner impuestos sobre (*la propiedad*); abrumar, cargar; agotar (*la paciencia de uno*)
taxable [ˈtæksəbəl] *adj* imponible
taxable income *s* renta gravable o imponible
taxation [tækˈseʃən] *s* imposición de contribuciones; contribuciones, impuestos
tax base *s* base *f* imponible
tax collector *s* recaudador *m* de impuestos
tax cut *s* reducción de impuestos
tax deduction *s* exclusión de contribución
tax evader [ɪˈvedər] *s* burlador *m* de impuestos
tax evasion *s* fraude *m* fiscal
tax′-ex•empt′ *adj* exento de impuesto
tax exemption *s* desgravación fiscal
tax haven *s* asilo de los impuestos
tax•i [ˈtæksi] *s* (*pl* **-is**) taxi *m* ‖ *v* (*pret & pp*

-ied; *ger* **-iing** o **-ying)** *tr* (aer) carretear || *intr* ir en taxi; (aer) carretear, taxear
tax'i•cab' *s* taxi *m*
taxi dancer *s* taxi *f*
taxi driver *s* taxista *mf*
tax'i•plane' *s* avioneta de alquiler
taxi stand *s* parada de taxis
tax loss *s* pérdida de reclamable
tax'pay'er *s* contribuyente *mf*
tax rate *s* tipo impositivo
tax refund *s* devolución de impuestos
tax relief *s* aligeramiento de impuestos, desgravación
tax return *s* declaración de renta
tax shelter *s* refugio fiscal, inversión que reduce el impuesto a pagar
t.b. *abbr* **tuberculosis**
tbs. o **tbsp.** *abbr* **tablespoon, tablespoons**
tea [ti] *s* té *m;* (*medicinal infusion*) tisana; caldo de carne
tea bag *s* bolsita de té
tea ball *s* huevo del té
tea'cart' *s* mesita de té (*con ruedas*)
teach [titʃ] *v* (*pret & pp* **taught** [tɔt]) *tr & intr* enseñar
teacher [ˈtitʃər] *s* maestro, instructor *m;* (*such as adversity*) (fig) maestra
teacher's pet *s* alumno mimado
teaching [ˈtitʃɪŋ] *adj* docente || *s* enseñanza; doctrina
teaching aids *spl* material *m* auxiliar de instrucción
teaching staff *s* personal *m* docente, profesorado
tea'cup' *s* taza para té
tea dance *s* té *m* bailable
teak [tik] *s* teca
tea'ket'tle *s* tetera
team [tim] *s* (*e.g., of horses*) tiro, tronco; (*of oxen*) yunta; (sport) equipo, plantel *m* || *tr* enganchar, uncir, enyugar || *intr*—**to team up** asociarse, unirse; formar un equipo
team'mate' *s* compañero de equipo, equipier *m*
teamster [ˈtimstər] *s* (*of horses*) tronquista *m;* (*of a truck*) camionista *m*
team'work' *s* espíritu de equipo; trabajo de equipo
tea'pot' *s* tetera
tear [tɪr] *s* lágrima; **to burst into tears** romper a llorar; **to fill with tears** arrasarse (*los ojos*) de o en lágrimas; **to hold back one's tears** beberse las lágrimas; **to laugh away one's tears** convertir las lágrimas en risas || [tɛr] *s* desgarro, rasgón *m* || [tɛr] *v* (*pret* **tore** [tor]; *pp* **torn** [torn]) *tr* desgarrar, rasgar; acongojar, afligir; mesarse (*los cabellos*); **to tear apart** romper en dos; **to tear down** derribar (*un edificio*); desarmar (*una máquina*); **to tear off** desgajar; **to tear up** romper (*p.ej., un papel*) || *intr* desgarrarse, rasgarse; **to tear along** correr a toda velocidad
tear bomb [tɪr] *s* bomba lacrimógena
tearful [ˈtɪrfəl] *adj* lacrimoso
tear gas [tɪr] *s* gas lacrimógeno
tear-jerker [ˈtɪr,dʒʌrkər] *s* (slang) drama *m* o cine *m* que arrancan lágrimas
tear-off [ˈtɛr,ɔf] *adj* exfoliador
tea'room' *s* salón *m* de té
tear sheet [tɛr] *s* hoja del anunciante
tease [tiz] *tr* embromar, azuzar
tea'spoon' *s* cucharilla, cucharita
teaspoonful [ˈti,spun,fʊl] *s* cucharadita
teat [tit] *s* teta, pezón *m*
tea time *s* hora del té
technical [ˈtɛknɪkəl] *adj* técnico
technical knockout *s* (box) K.O. técnico
technicali•ty [,tɛknɪˈkælɪti] *s* (*pl* **-ties**) detalle técnico
technician [tɛkˈnɪʃən] *s* técnico
technics [ˈtɛknɪks] *ssg* técnica
technique [tɛkˈnik] *s* técnica
technology [tɛkˈnɑlədʒi] *s* tecnología
teddy bear [ˈtɛdi] *s* oso de juguete, oso de trapo, osito de felpa o peluche
tedious [ˈtidɪ•əs] o [ˈtidʒəs] *adj* tedioso, enfadoso
teem [tim] *intr* hormiguear; llover a cántaros; **to teem with** hervir de
teeming [ˈtimɪŋ] *adj* hormigueante; (*rain*) torrencial
teenage [tin] *s* edad de 13 a 19 años
teen-ager [ˈtin,edʒər] *s* joven *mf* de 13 a 19 años de edad
teens [tinz] *spl* números ingleses que terminan en **-teen** (de 13 a 19); edad de 13 a 19 años; **to be in one's teens** tener de 13 a 19 años
tee•ny [ˈtini] *adj* (*comp* **-nier;** *super* **-niest**) (coll) diminuto, pequeñito
teeter [ˈtitər] *s* vaivén *m,* balanceo || *intr* balancear, oscilar
teethe [tið] *intr* endentecer
teething [ˈtiðɪŋ] *s* dentición
teething ring *s* chupador *m*
teetotaler [tiˈtotələr] *s* teetotalista *mf,* nefalista *mf,* abstemio
tel. *abbr* **telegram, telegraph, telephone**
tele•cast [ˈtɛlɪ,kæst] *s* teledifusión || *v* (*pret & pp* **-cast** o **-casted**) *tr & intr* teledifundir
telecommunications [ˈtɛlɪkəˈmjunəˈkeʃənz] *spl* telecomunicaciones
teleconference [ˈtɛlɪˈkɑnfərəns] *s* teleconferencia
telefax [ˈtɛləˈfæks] *s* telefax *m*
telegram [ˈtɛlɪ,græm] *s* telegrama *m*
telegraph [ˈtɛlɪ,græf] *s* telégrafo || *tr & intr* telegrafiar
telegrapher [tɪ,lɛgrəfər] *s* telegrafista *mf*
telegraph pole *s* poste *m* de telégrafo
Telemachus [tɪˈlɛməkəs] *s* Telémaco
telemarketing [,tɛləˈmɑrkətɪŋ] *s* telemarketing *m* (*uso de los medios de telecommunicación al servicio del marketing*)
telemeter [tɪˈlɛmɪtər] *s* telémetro || *tr* telemetrar
telemetry [tɪˈlɛmɪtri] *s* telemetría
telepathy [təˈlɛpəθɪ] *s* telepatía

telephone [ˈtɛlɪ,fon] *s* teléfono ‖ *tr & intr* telefonear
telephone booth *s* cabina telefónica
telephone call *s* llamada telefónica
telephone directory *s* guía telefónica
telephone exchange *s* estación telefónica, central *f* de teléfonos; conmutador *m* (SAm)
telephone number *s* número de teléfono
telephone operator *s* telefonista *mf,* centralista *mf*
telephone receiver *s* receptor telefónico
telephone table *s* mesita portateléfono
telephoto (lens) [ˈtɛlɪ,fotə] *s* teleobjectivo
teleprinter [ˈtɛlɪ,prɪntər] *s* teleimpresor *m,* teletipo
TelePrompTer[T] [ˈtɛlə,prɑmptər] *s* autocue *m,* teleprompter *m* (*dispositivo visual*)
telescope [ˈtɛlɪ,skop] *s* telescopio ‖ *tr* telescopar ‖ *intr* telescoparse
Teletype[T], **teletype** [ˈtɛlɪ,taɪp] *s* teletipo ‖ *tr & intr* transmitir por teletipo
teleview [ˈtɛlɪ,vju] *tr & intr* ver por televisión
televiewer [ˈtɛlɪ,vju•ər] *s* televidente *mf,* telespectador *m*
televise [ˈtɛlɪ,vaɪz] *tr* televisar
television [ˈtɛlɪ,vɪʃən] *adj* televisor ‖ *s* televisión
television audience *s* telespectadores
television ministry *s* (eccl) ministerio televisivo
television screen *s* pantalla televisora, pequeña pantalla
television set *s* televisor *m,* telerreceptor *m*
television viewer *s* telespectador *m,* televidente *mf*
telex [ˈtɛlɛks] *s* servicio comercial de teletipo
tell [tɛl] *v* (*pret & pp* **told** [told]) *tr* decir; (*to narrate; to count*) contar; determinar; conocer, distinguir; **I told you so!** ¡por algo te lo dije!; **to tell someone to** + *inf* decircle a uno que + *subj* ‖ *intr* hablar; surtir efecto; **to tell on** dejarse ver en (*p.ej., la salud de uno*); (coll) denunciar
teller [ˈtɛlər] *s* narrador *m;* (*of a bank*) cajero; (*of votes*) escrutador *m*
tell'tale' *adj* revelador
temper [ˈtɛmpər] *s* temple *m,* natural *m,* genio; cólera, mal genio; (*of steel, glass, etc.*) temple *m;* **to keep one's temper** dominar su mal genio; **to lose one's temper** encolerizarse, perder la paciencia ‖ *tr* templar *intr* templarse
temperament [ˈtɛmpərəmənt] *s* disposición; temperamento sensible o excitable
temperamental [,tɛmpərəˈmɛntəl] *adj* temperamental
temperance [ˈtɛmpərəns] *s* templanza; abstinencia de bebidas alcohólicas; antialcohólico
temperate [ˈtɛmpərɪt] *adj* templado
temperature [,tɛmpərətʃər] *s* temperatura
tempest [ˈtɛmpɪst] *s* tempestad
tempestuous [tɛmˈpɛstʃʊ•əs] *adj* tempestuoso
template [ˈtɛmplet] *s* plantilla, patrón *m*
temple [ˈtɛmpəl] *s* (*place of worship*) templo; (*side of forehead*) sien *f;* (*sidepiece of spectacles*) gafa
tem•po [ˈtɛmpo] *s* (*pl* **-pos** o **-pi** [pi]) (mus) tiempo; (fig) ritmo (*p.ej., de la vida*)
temporal [ˈtɛmpərəl] *adj* temporal
temporary [ˈtɛmpə,rɛri] *adj* temporáneo, temporario, provisional, interino
temporize [ˈtɛmpə,raɪz] *intr* contemporizar, temporizar
tempt [tɛmpt] *tr* tentar
temptation [tɛmptˈteʃən] *s* tentación
tempter [ˈtɛmptər] *s* tentador *m*
tempting [ˈtɛmptɪŋ] *adj* tentador
ten [tɛn] *adj & pron* diez ‖ *s* diez *m;* **ten o'clock** las diez
tenable [ˈtɛnəbəl] *adj* defendible
tenacious [tɪˈneʃəs] *adj* tenaz
tenacity [tɪˈnæsɪti] *s* tenacidad
tenant [ˈtɛnənt] *s* arrendatario, inquilino; morador *m,* residente *mf*
tend [tɛnd] *tr* cuidar, vigilar; servir ‖ *intr* tender, dirigirse; **to tend to** atender a; **to tend to** + *inf* tender a + *inf*
tenden•cy [ˈtɛndənsi] *s* (*pl* **-cies**) tendencia
tender [ˈtɛndər] *adj* tierno; (*painfully sensitive*) dolorido ‖ *n* oferta; (naut) alijador *m,* falúa; (rr) ténder *m* ‖ *tr* ofrecer, tender
tender-hearted [ˈtɛndər,hɑrtɪd] *adj* compasivo, tierno de corazón
ten'der•loin' *s* filete *m,* lomo ‖ **Tenderloin** *s* barrio de mala vida
tenderness [ˈtɛndərnɪs] *s* ternura, terneza; sensibilidad
tendon [ˈtɛndən] *s* tendón *m*
tendril [ˈtɛndrɪl] *s* zarcillo
tenement [ˈtɛnɪmənt] *s* habitación, vivienda; casa de vecindad, edificio de apartamentos
tenement house *s* (*in the slums*) conventillo
tenet [ˈtɛnɪt] *s* dogma *m,* credo, principio
tennis [ˈtɛnɪs] *s* tenis *m*
tennis court *s* campo de tenis
tennis player *s* tenista *mf*
tennis shoe *s* zapato de goma
tenor [ˈtɛnər] *s* tenor *m,* carácter *m,* curso, tendencia; (mus) tenor
tense [tɛns] *adj* tenso, tieso; (*person; situation*) (fig) tenso; (*relations*) tirante ‖ *s* (gram) tiempo
tension [ˈtɛnʃən] *s* tensión; ansia, congoja, esfuerzo mental; (*in personal or diplomatic relations*) tirantez *f*
tent [tɛnt] *s* tienda; tienda de campaña
tentacle [ˈtɛntəkəl] *s* tentáculo
tentative [ˈtɛntətɪv] *adj* tentativo
tenth [tɛnθ] *adj & s* décimo ‖ *s* (*in dates*) diez *m*
tenuous [ˈtɛnjʊ•əs] *adj* tenue; (*thin in consistency*) raro
tenure [ˈtɛnjər] *s* (*of property*) tenencia; (*of an office*) ejercicio; (*protection from dismissal*) inamovilidad
tepid [ˈtɛpɪd] *adj* tibio
tercet [ˈtʌrsɪt] *s* terceto

term [tʌrm] *s* término; (*of imprisonment*) condena; semestre *m,* período escolar; (*of the presidency of the U.S.A.*) mandato, período; **terms** condiciones || *tr* llamar, nombrar
termagant [ˈtʌrməgənt] *s* mujer regañona, mujer de mal genio
terminal [ˈtʌrmɪnəl] *adj* terminal || *s* término, fin *m;* (compu) videoterminal *m;* (elec) terminal *m;* (rr) estación de fin de línea
terminate [ˈtʌrmɪˌnet] *tr & intr* terminar
termination [ˌtʌrmɪˈneʃən] *s* terminación
terminus [ˈtʌrmɪnəs] *s* término; (rr) estación de cabeza, estación extrema
termite [ˈtʌrmaɪt] *s* termite *m,* comején *m*
terrace [ˈtɛrəs] *s* terraza; (*flat roof of a house*) azotea
terra firma [ˈtɛrə ˈfʌrmə] *s* tierra firme; **on terra firma** sobre suelo firme
terrain [tɛˈren] *s* terreno
terrapin [ˈtɛrəpən] *s* tortuga de agua dulce
terrestrial [təˈrɛstrɪ•əl] *adj* terrestre
terrible [ˈtɛrɪbəl] *adj* terrible; muy desagradable
terrific [təˈrɪfɪk] *adj* terrífico; (coll) enorme, intenso, brutal
terri•fy [ˈtɛriˌfaɪ] *v* (*pret & pp* **-fied**) *tr* aterrorizar, atemorizar
territorial waters [ˈtɛrəˈtɔri•əl] *s* mar *m & f* territorial, jurisdiccional o patrimonial
territo•ry [ˈtɛrɪˌtori] *s* (*pl* **-ries**) territorio
terror [ˈtɛrər] *s* terror *m*
terrorism [ˈtɛrərˌɪzəm] *s* terrorismo
terrorist [ˈtɛrərəst] *s* terrorista *mf*
terrorize [ˈtɛrəˌraɪz] *tr* aterrorizar; imponerse a, mediante el terror
terry cloth [ˈtɛri] *s* felpa, tela de toalla
terse [tʌrs] *adj* breve, sucinto
tertiary [ˈtʌrʃiˌɛri] o [ˈtʌrʃəri] *adj* terciario
test [tɛst] *s* prueba, ensayo; examen *m* || *tr* probar, poner a prueba; examinar; **to test out** probar, poner a prueba; (compu) testear
testament [ˈtɛstəmənt] *s* testamento
test drilling *s* sondeo
test drive *s* prueba de circulación en carretera
test flight *s* vuelo de ensayo
testicle [ˈtɛstɪkəl] *s* testículo
testi•fy [ˈtɛstɪˌfaɪ] *v* (*pret & pp* **-fied**) *tr & intr* testificar
testimonial [ˌtɛstɪˈmonɪ•əl] *s* recomendación, certificado; (*expression of esteem, gratitude, etc.*) homenaje *m*
testimo•ny [ˈtɛstɪˌmoni] *s* (*pl* **-nies**) testimonio
testing grounds [ˈtɛstɪŋ] *spl* campo de pruebas
test pilot *s* (aer) piloto de pruebas
test tube *s* probeta, tubo de ensayo
test′-tube′ baby *s* niño probeta
tether [ˈtɛðər] *s* atadura, traba; **at the end of one's tether** al límite de las posibilidades o la paciencia de uno || *tr* apersogar
tetter [ˈtɛtər] *s* empeine *m*
Texan [ˈtɛksən] *adj & s* tejano
Texas [ˈtɛksəs] *s* Tejas
text [tɛkst] *s* texto; tema *m,* lema *m*
text′book′ *s* libro de texto
text′flow′ *s* (compu) flujo de texto
textile [ˈtɛkstɪl] o [ˈtɛkstaɪl] *adj & s* textil *m*
texture [ˈtɛkstʃər] *s* textura
Thai [ˈtɑ•i] o [ˈtaɪ] *adj & s* tailandés *m*
Thailand [ˈtaɪlənd] *s* Tailandia
Thames [tɛmz] *s* Támesis *m*
than [ðæn] *conj* que, p.ej., **he is richer than I** es más rico que yo; (*before a numeral*) de, p.ej., **more than twenty** más de veinte; (*before a verb*) de lo que, p.ej., **the crop is larger than was expected** la cosecha es mayor de lo que se esperaba; (*before a verb with direct object understood*) del (de la, de los, de las) que, p.ej., **they sent us more coffee than we ordered** nos enviaron más café del que pedimos
thanatology [ˌθænəˈtɑlədʒi] *s* tanatología
thank [θæŋk] *tr* agradecer, dar las gracias a; **to thank someone for something** agradecerle a uno una cosa || **thanks** *spl* gracias, agradecimiento; **thanks to** gracias a, merced a || **thanks** *interj* ¡gracias!
thankful [ˈθæŋkfəl] *adj* agradecido
thankless [ˈθæŋklɪs] *adj* ingrato
thanksgiving [ˌθæŋksˈgɪvɪŋ] *s* acción de gracias
Thanksgiving Day *s* (U.S.A.) Día *m* de Acción de Gracias
that [ðæt] *adj dem* (*pl* **those**) ese; aquel; **that one** ése; aquél || *pron dem* (*pl* **those**) ése; aquél; eso; aquello || *pron rel* que, quien, el cual, el que || *adv* tan; **that far** tan lejos; hasta allí; **that many** tantos; **that much** tanto || *conj* que; para que
thatch [θætʃ] *s* barda, paja; techo de paja || *tr* cubrir de paja, techar con paja, bardar
thaw [θɔ] *s* deshielo, derretimiento; descongelación || *tr* deshelar, derretir || *intr* deshelarse, derretirse
the [ðə], [ðɪ], o [ði] *art def* el || *adv* cuanto, p.ej., **the more the merrier** cuanto más mejor; **the more . . . the more** cuanto más . . . tanto más
theater [ˈθi•ətər] *s* teatro
the′ater-go′er *s* teatrero
theater news *s* actualidad escénica
theater page *s* noticiario teatral
theatrical [θɪˈætrɪkəl] *adj* teatral
thee [ði] *pron pers* (archaic, poet, Bib) te; ti; **with thee** contigo
theft [θɛft] *s* hurto, robo
theft′-proof′ *adj* antirroba
their [ðɛr] *adj poss* su; el . . . de ellos
theirs [ðɛrz] *pron poss* el suyo, el de ellos
them [ðɛm] *pron pers* los; ellos; **to them** les; a ellos
theme [θim] *s* tema *m;* (mus) tema *m*
theme song *s* (mus) tema *m* central; (rad, telv) sintonía
them•selves′ *pron pers* ellos mismos; sí, sí mismos; se, p.ej., **they enjoyed themselves** se divirtieron; **with themselves** consigo
then [ðɛn] *adv* entonces; después, luego, en se-

guida; además, también; **by then** para entonces; **from then on** desde entonces, de allí en adelante; **then and there** ahí mismo
thence [ðɛns] *adv* desde allí; desde entonces; por eso
thence'forth' *adv* de allí en adelante; desde entonces
theocra•cy [θɪ'ɑkrəsɪ] *s* (*pl* **-cies**) teocracia
theolo•gy [θi'ɑlədʒi] *s* (*pl* **-gies**) teología
theorem ['θi•ərəm] *s* teorema *m*
theo•ry ['θi•əri] *s* (*pl* **-ries**) teoría
therapeutic [,θɛrə'pjutɪk] *adj* terapéutico || **therapeutics** *ssg* terapéutica
therapist ['θɛrəpəst] *s* terapeuta *mf*
thera•py ['θɛrəpi] *s* (*pl* **-pies**) terapia
there [ðɛr] *adv* allí, allá; **there is** o **there are** hay; aquí tiene Ud.
there'a-abouts' *adv* por allí; cerca, aproximadamente
there•af'ter *adv* de allí en adelante, después de eso
there•by' *adv* con eso; así, de tal modo; por allí cerca
there'd *contr* **there would**
therefore ['ðɛrfor] *adv* por lo tanto, por consiguiente
there•in' *adv* en esto, en eso; en ese respecto
there'll *contr* **there will**
there•of' *adv* de ello, de eso
there's *contr* **there is**
Theresa [tə'risə] o [tə'rɛsə] *s* Teresa
there'u•pon' *adv* sobre eso, encima de eso; por consiguiente; en seguida
thermistor [θər'mɪstər] *s* (elec) termistor *m*
thermocouple ['θʌrmo,kʌpəl] *s* (elec) termopar *m*
thermodynamic [,θʌrmodaɪ'næmɪk] *adj* termodinámico || **thermodynamics** *ssg* termodinámica
thermometer [θər'mɑmɪtər] *s* termómetro
thermonuclear [,θʌrmo'nuklɪ•ər] *adj* termonuclear
Thermopylae [θər'mɑpɪ,li] *s* las Termópilas
Thermos[T] o **thermos (bottle)** ['θʌrməs] *s* termos *m*, botella termos, bolsa isotérmica
thermostat ['θʌrmə,stæt] *s* termóstato
thesau•rus [θɪ'sɔrəs] *s* (*pl* **-ri** [raɪ]) tesauro, tesoro, diccionario de ideas afines, diccionario ideológico; diccionario de sinónimos
these [ðiz] *pl de* **this**
the•sis ['θisɪs] *s* (*pl* **-ses** [siz]) tesis *f*
Thespis ['θɛspɪs] *s* Tespis *m*
Thessaly ['θɛsəli] *s* la Tesalia
they [ðe] *pron pers* ellos, ellas
they'd *contr* **they would; they had**
they'd've ['ðedəv] *contr* **they would have**
they'll *contr* **they will**
they're *contr* **they are**
they've *contr* **they have**
thick [θɪk] *adj* espeso; grueso; denso; (coll) estúpido; (coll) íntimo || *s* espesor *m;* **the thick of** (*e.g., a crowd*) lo más denso de; (*e.g., a battle*) lo más reñido de; **through thick and thin** contra viento y marea
thicken ['θɪkən] *tr* espesar || *intr* espesarse; complicarse (*el enredo*)
thicket ['θɪkɪt] *s* espesura, matorral *m*, soto
thick-headed ['θɪk'hɛdɪd] *adj* (coll) torpe, estúpido
thickness ['θɪknəs] *s* grosor *m*, espesor *m;* (*layer*) capa; (*of sauce*) lo espeso
thick'-set' *adj* grueso, rechoncho
thick'-skinned' *adj* insensible
thief [θif] *s* (*pl* **thieves** [θivz]) ladrón *m*
thieve [θiv] *intr* hurtar, robar
thiever•y ['θivəri] *s* (*pl* **-ies**) latrocinio, hurto, robo
thigh [θaɪ] *s* muslo
thigh'bone' *s* hueso del muslo, fémur *m*
thimble ['θɪmbəl] *s* dedal *m*
thin [θɪn] *adj* (*comp* **thinner;** *super* **thinnest**) delgado, flaco, tenue; (*cloth, paper, sole of shoe, etc.*) fino; (*hair*) ralo; (*broth*) aguado; (*excuse*) débil; claro, ligero, escaso || *v* (*pret & pp* **thinned;** *ger* **thinning**) *tr* adelgazar, enflaquecer; enrarecer; aclarar; aguar; desleír (*los colores*) || *intr* adelgazarse, enflaquecerse; enrarecerse; **to thin out** ralear (*el pelo*)
thine [ðaɪn] *adj poss* (archaic & poet) tu || *pron poss* (*archaic & poet*) tuyo; el tuyo
thing [θɪŋ] *s* cosa; **of all things!** ¡qué sorpresa!; **to be the thing** ser la última moda; **to be the thing to do** ser lo que debe hacerse; **to see things** ver visiones, padecer alucinaciones
think [θɪŋk] *v* (*pret & pp* **thought** [θɔt]) *tr* pensar; **to think it over** pensarlo; **to think nothing of** tener en poco; creer fácil; no dar importancia a; **to think of** pensar de, p.ej., what do you think of this book? ¿qué piensa Ud. de este libro?; **to think up** imaginar; inventar (*p.ej., una excusa*) || *intr* pensar; **to think not** creer que no; **to think of** (*to turn one's thoughts to*) pensar en; pensar (*un número, un naipe, etc.*); **to think so** creer que sí; **to think well of** tener buena opinión de
thinker ['θɪŋkər] *s* pensador *m*
think tank *s* gabinete *m* estratégico, comité *m* asesor
third [θʌrd] *adj* tercero || *s* (*in a series*) tercero; (*one of three equal parts*) tercio; (*in dates*) tres *m*
third degree *s* (coll) interrogatorio bajo tortura
third rail *s* (rr) tercer carril *m*, carril de toma
third'-rate' *adj* de tercer orden; (fig) inferior
Third World *adj* tercermundista || *s* Tercer Mundo
Third World countries *spl* países no alineados
thirst [θʌrst] *s* sed *f* || *intr* tener sed; **to thirst for** tener sed de
thirst•y ['θʌrsti] *adj* (*comp* **-ier;** *super* **-iest**) sediento; **to be thirsty** tener sed
thirteen ['θʌr'tin] *adj, pron & s* trece *m*
thirteenth ['θʌrtinθ] *adj & s* (*in a series*) de-

cimotercero; (*part*) trezavo || *s* (*in dates*) trece *m*

thirtieth [ˈθʌrtɪ•ɪθ] *adj & s* (*in a series*) trigésimo; (*part*) treintavo || *s* (*in dates*) treinta *m*

thir•ty [ˈθʌrti] *adj & pron* treinta || *s* (*pl* **-ties**) treinta *m*

this [ðɪs] *adj dem* (*pl* **these**) este; **this one** éste || *pron dem* (*pl* **these**) éste; esto || *adv* tan

thistle [ˈθɪsəl] *s* cardo

thither [ˈθɪðər] o [ˈðɪðər] *adv* allá, hacia allá

Thomas [ˈtɑməs] *s* Tomás *m*

thong [θɔŋ] o [θɑŋ] *s* correa

tho•rax [ˈθoræks] *s* (*pl* **-roxes** o **-raxes** o **-races** [rə,siz]) tórax *m*

thorn [θɔrn] *s* espina

thorn•y [ˈθɔrni] *adj* (*comp* **-ier;** *super* **-iest**) espinoso; espinudo; (*difficult*) (fig) espinoso, espinudo

thorough [ˈθʌro] *adj* cabal, completo; concienzudo, cuidadoso

thor′ough•bred *adj* de pura sangre; bien nacido || *s* pura sangre *m;* persona bien nacida

thor′ough•fare′ *s* vía pública; **no thoroughfare** se prohibe el paso

thor′ough•go′ing *adj* cabal, completo, esmerado, perfecto

thoroughly [ˈθʌroli] *adv* a fondo

those [ðoz] *pl de* **that**

thou [ðaʊ] *pron pers* (archaic, poet & Bib) tú || *tr & intr* tutear

though [ðo] *adv* sin embargo || *conj* aunque, bien que; **as though** como sí

thought [θɔt] *s* pensamiento

thoughtful [ˈθɔtfəl] *adj* pensativo; atento, considerado

thoughtless [ˈθɔtlɪs] *adj* irreflexivo; descuidado; inconsiderado

thought transference *s* transmisión del pensamiento

thousand [ˈθaʊzənd] *adj & s* mil *m;* **a thousand** o **one thousand** mil *m*

thousandth [ˈθaʊzəndθ] *adj & s* milésimo

thralldom [ˈθrɔldəm] *s* esclavitud, servidumbre

thrash [θræʃ] *tr* (agr) trillar; azotar, zurrar; **to thrash out** decidir después de una discusión cabal || *intr* trillar; agitarse, menearse

thread [θrɛd] *s* hilo; (mach) filete *m,* rosca; (*of a speech, of life*) hilo; **to lose the thread of** perder el hilo de || *tr* enhebrar, enhilar; ensartar (*p.ej., cuentas*); (mach) aterrajar, filetear

thread′bare′ *adj* raído; gastado, desgastado, usado, viejo

threat [θrɛt] *s* amenaza

threaten [ˈθrɛtən] *tr & intr* amenazar

threatening [ˈθrɛtənɪŋ] *adj* amenazante

three [θri] *adj & pron* tres || *s* tres *m;* **three o'clock** las tres

three′-cor′nered *adj* triangular; (*hat*) de tres picos

three hundred *adj & pron* trescientos || *s* trescientos *m*

three′-ply′ *adj* de tres capas

three′-quar′ters *pron* las tres cuartes partes

three R's [ɑrz] *spl* lectura, escritura y aritmética (*primeras letras*)

three-ring circus *s* circo de tres pistas; (coll) jaleo *m,* caos *m*

three′score′ *adj* tres veintenas de

thresh [θrɛʃ] *tr* (agr) trillar; **to thresh out** decidir después de una discusión cabal || *intr* trillar; agitarse, menearse

threshing machine *s* máquina trilladora

threshold [ˈθrɛʃold] *s* umbral *m;* (physiol, psychol & fig) umbral, limen *m;* **to be on the threshold of** estar en los umbrales de; **to cross the threshold** atravesar o pisar los embrales

thrice [θraɪs] *adv* tres veces; repetidamente, sumamente

thrift [θrɪft] *s* economía, parquedad

thrift•y [ˈθrɪfti] *adj* (*comp* **-ier;** *super* **-iest**) económico, parco; próspero

thrill [θrɪl] *s* emoción viva || *tr* emocionar, conmover || *intr* emocionarse, conmoverse

thriller [ˈθrɪlər] *s* cuento o pieza de teatro espeluznante

thrilling [ˈθrɪlɪŋ] *adj* emocionante; espeluznante

thrive [θraɪv] *v* (*pret* **thrived** o **throve** [θrov]; *pp* **thrived** o **thriven** [ˈθrɪvən]) *intr* medrar, prosperar

throat [θrot] *s* garganta; **to clear one's throat** aclarar la voz

throb [θrɑb] *s* latido, palpitación, pulsación || *v* (*pret & pp* **throbbed;** *ger* **throbbing**) *intr* latir, palpitar, pulsar

throe [θro] *s* congoja, dolor *m;* **throes** angustia, agonía, esfuerzo penoso

thrombo•sis [θramˈbosəs] *s* (*pl* **-ses**) trombosis *f*

throne [θron] *s* trono

throng [θrɔŋ] *s* gentío, tropel *m,* muchedumbre || *intr* agolparse, apiñarse

throttle [ˈθrɑtəl] *s* válvula reguladora; (*of a locomotive*) regulador *m;* (*of an automobile*) acelerador *m* || *tr* ahogar, sofocar; impedir, suprimir; (mach) regular; **to throttle down** reducir la velocidad de

through [θru] *adj* directo, sin paradas; acabado, terminado; **to be through with** haber terminado; no querer ocuparse más de || *adv* a través, de un lado a otro; completamente || *prep* por, a través de; por medio de; a causa de; todo lo largo de

through•out′ *adv* por todas partes; en todos respectos; desde el principio hasta el fin || *prep* por todo . . .; durante todo . . .; a lo largo de

through′way′ o **thru′way′** *s* autopista, carretera directa

throw [θro] *s* echada, tirada, lance *m;* cobertor ligero || *v* (*pret* **threw** [θru]; *pp* **thrown**) *tr* arrojar, echar, lanzar; tirar (*los dados*); lanzar (*una mirada*); desarzonar (*a un jinete*); proyectar (*una sombra*); tender (*un puente*); perder con premeditación (*un juego, una carrera*); **to throw away** tirar; malgastar; perder, no aprovechar; **to throw in** añadir, dar de más; **to throw out** arrojar, botar, desechar; echar a la calle; chispar; **to throw over** abandonar, dejar || *intr* arrojar, echar, lanzar; **to throw up** vomitar

throw'back *s* retroceso

thrum [θrʌm] *v* (*pret & pp* **thrummed;** *ger* **thrumming**) *intr* teclear; zangarrear; **to thrum on** rasguear

thrush [θrʌʃ] *s* tordo

thrust [θrʌst] *s* empuje *m;* acometida; (*with horns*) cornada; (*with dagger*) puñalada; (*with sword*) estocada; (*with knife*) cuchillada || *v* (*pret & pp* **thrust**) *tr* empujar; acometer; clavar, hincar; atravesar, traspasar

thruway [ˋθruwe] *s* autopista, carretera directa

thud [θʌd] *s* baque *m,* ruido sordo || *v* (*pret & pp* **thudded;** *ger* **thudding**) *tr & intr* golpear con ruido sordo

thug [θʌg] *s* ladrón *m,* asesino; (coll) gorila

thumb [θʌm] *s* pulgar *m,* dedo gordo; **all thumbs** desmañado, chapucero, torpe; **to twiddle one's thumbs** menear ociosamente los pulgares; no hacer nada; **under the thumb of** bajo la férula de || *tr* manosear sin suidado; ensuciar con los dedos; hojear (*un libro*) con el pulgar; **to thumb a ride** pedir ser llevado en automóvil indicando la dirección con el pulgar; **to thumb one's nose at** señalar (*a una persona*) poniendo el pulgar sobre la nariz en son de burla; tratar con sumo desprecio

thumb index *s* escalerilla, índice *m* con pestañas, índice en el corte

thumb'print' *s* impresión del pulgar || *tr* marcar con impresión del pulgar

thumb'screw' *s* tornillo de mariposa, tornillo de orejas

thumb'tack' *s* chinche *m*

thump [θʌmp] *s* golpazo, porrazo || *tr* golpear, aporrear || *intr* caer con golpe pesado; andar con pasos pesados; latir (*el corazón*) con golpes pesados

thumping [ˋθʌmpɪŋ] *adj* (coll) enorme, pesado

thunder [ˋθʌndər] *s* trueno; (*of applause*) estruendo; amenaza || *tr* fulminar (*p.ej., censuras*) || *intr* tronar; **to thunder at** tronar contra

thun'der•bolt' *s* rayo

thun'der•clap' *s* tronido

thunderous [ˋθʌndərəs] *adj* atronador, tronitoso

thun'der•show'er *s* chubasco con truenos

thun'der•storm' *s* tronada

thun'der•struck' *adj* atónito, estupefacto, pasmado

Thursday [ˋθʌrsdi] *s* jueves *m*

thus [ðʌs] *adv* así; **thus far** hasta aquí, hasta ahora

thwack [θwæk] *s* golpe *m,* porrazo || *tr* golpear, pegar

thwart [θwɔrt] *adj* transversal, oblicuo || *adv* de través || *tr* desbaratar, impedir, frustrar

thy [ðaɪ] *adj poss* (archaic & poet) tu

thyme [taɪm] *s* tomillo

thyroid gland [ˋθaɪrɔɪd] *s* glándula tiroides

thyself [ðaɪˋsɛlf] *pron* (archaic & poet) tú mismo; ti mismo; te; ti

tiara [taɪˋɑrə] o [taɪˋɛrə] *s* (*papal miter*) tiara; (*female adornment*) diadema *f*

tic [tɪk] *s* (pathol) tic *m*

tick [tɪk] *s* tictac *m;* funda (*de almohada o colchón*) (coll) crédito; (ent) garrapata; **on tick** (coll) al fiado || *intr* hacer tictac; latir (*el corazón*)

ticker [ˋtɪkər] *s* teleimpresor *m* de cinta; (slang) reloj *m;* (slang) corazón *m*

ticker tape *s* cinta de teleimpresor

ticket [ˋtɪkɪt] *s* billete *m;* boleto (Am); (theat) entrada, localidad; (*for wrong parking*) (coll) aviso de multa; (*of a political party*) (U.S.A.) lista de candidatos; **that's the ticket** (coll) eso es, eso es lo que se necesita

ticket agent *s* taquillero

ticket collector *s* revisor *m*

ticket office *s* taquilla, despacho de billetes

ticket scalper [ˋskælpər] *s* revendedor *m* de entradas

ticket window *s* taquilla, ventanilla

ticking [ˋtɪkɪŋ] *s* cutí *m,* terliz *m*

tickle [ˋtɪkəl] *s* cosquillas || *tr* cosquillear; gustar, satisfacer; divertir || *intr* cosquillear

ticklish [ˋtɪklɪʃ] *adj* cosquilloso; difícil, delicado; inseguro

tick-tock [ˋtɪk,tɑk] *s* tictac m

tidal wave [ˋtaɪdəl] *s* aguaje *m,* ola de marea; (*e.g., of popular indignation*) ola

tidbit [ˋtɪd,bɪt] *s* buen bocado, bocadito

tiddlywinks [ˋtɪdli,wɪŋks] *s* juego de la pulga

tide [taɪd] *s* marea; temporada; **to go against the tide** ir contra la corriente; **to stem the tide** rendir la marea || *tr* llevar, hacer flotar; **to tide over** ayudar un poco; superar (*una dificultad*)

tide'wa'ter *adj* costanero || *s* agua de marea; orilla del mar

tidings [ˋtaɪdɪŋz] *spl* noticias, informes *mpl*

ti•dy [ˋtaɪdi] *adj* (*comp* **-dier;** *super* **-diest**) aseado, limpio, pulcro, ordenado || *s* (*pl* **-dies**) pañito bordado, cubierta de respaldar || *v* (*pret & pp* **-died**) *tr* asear, limpiar, arreglar, poner en orden || *intr* asearse

tie [taɪ] *s* atadura; lazo, nudo; (*worn on neck*) corbata; (*in games and elections*) empate *m;* (mus) ligado; (rr) traviesa || *v* (*pret & pp* **tied;** *ger* **tying**) *tr* atar, liar; enlazar; hacer (*la corbata*); confinar, limitar; empatar (*p.ej., una elección*); empatársela a (*una persona*); **to be tied up** estar ocupado; **to tie down** confinar, limitar; **to tie up** atar; envolver; obstruir (*el tráfico*) || *intr* atar; empatar o empatarse (*dos candidatos, dos equipos*)

tie'pin' *s* alfiler *m* de corbata

tier [tɪr] *s* fila, ringlera; (theat) fila de palcos

tiger [ˋtaɪgər] *s* tigre *m*

tiger lily *s* azucena atigrada

tight [taɪt] *adj* apretado, estrecho, ajustado; bien

cerrado, hermético; compacto, denso; fijo, firme, sólido; (com) escaso; (sport) casi igual; (coll) agarrado, tacaño; (slang) borracho || *adv* firmemente; **to hold tight** mantener fijo; agarrarse bien || **tights** *spl* traje *m* de malla

tighten [ˈtaɪtən] *tr* apretar; atiesar, estirar || *intr* apretarse; atiesarse, estirarse

tight-fisted [ˈtaɪtˈfɪstɪd] *adj* agarrado, tacaño

tight′-fit′ting *adj* ceñido, muy ajustado

tight′rope′ *s* cuerda tirante, cuerda floja

tight squeeze *s* (coll) brete *m,* aprieto

tightwad [ˈtaɪt,wɑd] *s* avaro, rata; codo (Guat, Mex)

tigress [ˈtaɪgrɪs] *s* tigresa

tile [taɪl] *s* azulejo; (*for floors*) baldosa; (*for roofs*) reja || *tr* azulejar; embaldosar; tejar

tile roof *s* tejado (de tejas)

till [tɪl] *prep* hasta || *conj* hasta que || *s* cajón *m* o gaveta del dinero || *tr* labrar, cultivar

tilt [tɪlt] *s* inclinación; justa, torneo; **full tilt** a toda velocidad || *tr* inclinar; asestar (*una lanza*) || *intr* inclinarse; justar, tornear; luchar; **to tilt at** luchar con, arremeter contra; protestar contra

timber [ˈtɪmbər] *s* madera de construcción; madero, viga; bosque *m,* árboles *mpl* de monte

tim′ber•land′ *s* bosque *m* maderable

timber line *s* límite *m* de la vegetación, límite del bosque maderable

timbre [ˈtɪmbər] *s* (phonet & phys) timbre *m*

time [taɪm] *s* tiempo; hora, p.ej., **time to eat** hora de comer; vez, p.ej., **five times** cinco veces; rato, p.ej., **a nice time** un buen rato; (*period for payment*) plazo; horas de trabajo; sueldo; tiempo de parir, término del embarazo; última hora; (phot) tiempo de exposición; **all the time** a cada momento; **for the time being** por ahora, por el momento; **on time** a tiempo, a la hora debida; (*in installments*) a plazos, **to bide one's time** esperar la hora propicia; **to do time** (coll) cumplir una condena; **to have a good time** darse buen tiempo; **to have no time for** no poder tolerar; **to lose time** atrasarse (*el reloj*); **to make time** avanzar con rapidez; **to pass the time of day** saludarse (*dos personas*); **to serve time** (*in prison*) tirarse; **to take one's time** no darse prisa, ir despacio; **what time is it?** ¿qué hora es? || *tr* calcular el tiempo de; medir el tiempo de; (sport) cronometrar

time bomb *s* bomba-reloj *f*

time capsule *s* cápsula del tiempo

time′card′ *s* hoja de presencia, tarjeta registradora

time clock *s* reloj *m* registrador

time delay lock *s* cerradura horaria de bloqueo

time exposure *s* exposición de tiempo

time fuse *s* espoleta de tiempos

time′keep′er *s* alistador *m* de tiempo; reloj *m;* (sport) cronometrador *m,* juez *m* de tiempo

time limit *s* plazo

time•ly [ˈtaɪmli] *adj* (*comp* **-lier;** *super* **-liest**) oportuno

time out *s* (sport) tiempo muerto; (*break*) descanso, pausa

time′piece′ *s* reloj *m*

timer [ˈtaɪmər] *s* (culin, electron) reloj automático

times [taɪmz] *prep* multiplicado por, por

time′-share′ *s* multipropiedad; (compu) tiempo compartido

time′-shar′ing *s* (compu) trabajo en tiempo compartido

time signal *s* señal horaria

time′ta′ble *s* horario, itinerario

time warp *s* salto en el tiempo, deformación espacio-temporal; **stuck in a time warp** detenido en el tiempo

time′work′ *s* trabajo ajornal

time′worn′ *adj* gastado por el tiempo

time zone *s* huso horario

timid [ˈtɪmɪd] *adj* tímido

timidity [təˈmɪdəti] *s* timidez *f*

timing gears [ˈtaɪmɪŋ] *spl* engranaje *m* de distribución, mando de las válvulas

timorous [ˈtɪmərəs] *adj* tímido, miedoso

tin [tɪn] *s* (*element*) estaño; (*tin plate*) hojalata; (*cup, box, etc.*) lata || *v* (*pret & pp* **tinned;** *ger* **tinning**) *tr* estañar; (*to pack in cans*) enlatar; recubrir de hojalata

tin can *s* lata, envase *m* de hojalata

tincture [ˈtɪŋktʃər] *s* tintura

tin cup *s* taza de hojalata

tinder [ˈtɪndər] *s* yesca

tin′der•box′ *s* lumbres *fpl,* yesquero; persona muy excitable; semillero de violencia

tinfoil *s* hojuela de estaño, papel *m* de estaño

ting-a-ling [ˈtɪŋə,lɪŋ] *s* tilín *m*

tinge [tɪndʒ] *s* matiz *m,* tinte *m;* dejo, gustillo || *v* (*ger* **tingeing** o **tinging**) *tr* matizar, teñir; dar gusto o sabor a

tingle [ˈtɪŋgəl] *s* comezón *f,* picazón *f* || *intr* sentir comezón; zumbar (*los oídos*); (*e.g., with enthusiasm*) estremecerse

tin hat *s* (coll) yelmo de acero

tinker [ˈtɪŋkər] *s* calderero remendón; chapucero || *intr* ocuparse vanamente

tinkle [ˈtɪŋkəl] *s* retintín *m* || *tr* hacer retiñir *m* || *tr* hacer retiñir || *intr* retiñir

tin plate *s* hojalata

tin roof *s* tejdo de hojalata

tinsel [ˈtɪnsəl] *s* oropel *m;* (*e.g., for a Christmas tree*) lentejuelas de hojas de estaño

tin′smith′ *s* hojalatero

tin soldier *s* soldadito de plomo

tint [tɪnt] *s* tinte *m,* matiz *m* || *tr* teñir, matizar, colorar ligeramente

tin′type′ *s* ferrotipo

tin′ware′ *s* objetos de hojalata

ti•ny [ˈtaɪni] *adj* (*comp* **-nier;** *super* **-niest**) diminuto, menudo, pequeñito

tip [tɪp] *s* extremo, extremidad; (*of shoestring*) herrete *m;* (*of arrow*) casquillo; (*of umbrella*) regatón *m;* (*of tongue*) punta; (*of shoe*) puntera; (*of cigarette*) embocadura; inclinación; golpecito; soplo, aviso confidencial; (*fee*) propina, feria || *v* (*pret & pp* **tipped;** *ger* **tipping**) *tr* herretear; inclinar, ladear; volcar; golpear ligeramente; dar propina a; informar por debajo de cuerda; tocarse (*el sombrero en señal de cortesía*); **to tip in** (typ) encañonar (*un pliego*) || *intr* dar una propina o propinas; inclinarse, ladearse; volcarse

tip'cart' *s* volquete *m*

tip'-off' *s* (coll) informe dado por debajo de cuerda

tipped'-in' *adj* (bb) fuera de texto

tipple ['tɪpəl] *intr* beborrotear

tip'staff' *s* vara de justicia; alguacil *m* de vara

tip•sy ['tɪpsi] *adj* (*comp* **-sier;** *super* **-siest**) achispado

tip'toe' *s* punta del pie; **on tiptoe** de puntillas; alerta; furtivamente || *v* (*pret & pp* **-toed;** *ger* **-toeing**) *intr* andar de puntillas

tirade ['taɪred] *s* diatriba, invectiva

tire [taɪr] *s* neumático, llanta de goma; (*of metal*) calce *m*, llanta || *tr* cansar; aburrir, fastidiar || *intr* (*to be tiresome*) cansar; (*to get tired*) cansarse; aburrirse, fastidiarse

tire chain *s* cadena llanta, cadena antirres-baladiza

tired [taɪrd] *adj* cansado, rendido, deshecho

tire gauge *s* indicador *m* de presión de inflado

tireless ['taɪrlɪs] *adj* incansable, infatigable

tire pressure *s* presión de inflado

tire pump *s* bomba para inflar neumáticos

tiresome ['taɪrsəm] *adj* cansado, fatigante, aburrido, pesado

tissue ['tɪʃʊ] *s* tejido fino; papel *m* de seda; (biol & fig) tejido

tissue paper *s* papel *m* de seda

tit [tɪt] *s* (slang) teta; (zool) paro

titanic [taɪ'tænɪk] *adj* titánico; (chem) de titanio

titanium [tai'tenɪ•əm] o [tɪ'tenɪ•əm] *s* titanio

tithe [taɪð] *s* décimo, décima parte; (*tax paid to church*) diezmo || *tr* dizmar

Titian ['tɪʃən] *adj* castaño rojizo || *s* el Ticiano

title ['taɪtəl] *s* título; (sport) campeonato || *tr* titular

title deed *s* título de propiedad

ti'tle•hold'er *s* titulado; (sport) campeón *m*

title page *s* portada, frontispicio

title role *s* (theat) papel *m* principal (*el que corresponde al título de la abra*)

titter ['tɪtər] *s* risita ahogada, risita disimulada || *intr* reír a medias, reír con disimulo

titular ['tɪtʃələr] *adj* titular; nominal

tn. *abbr* **ton**

to [tu] o [tʊ] o [tə] *adv* hacia adelante; **to and fro** de una parte a otra, de aquí para allá; **to come to** volver en sí || *prep* a, p.ej., **he is going to Madrid** va a Madrid; **they gave something to the beggar** dieron algo al pobre; **we are learning to dance** aprendemos a bailar; para, p.ej., **he is reading to himself** lee para sí; por, p.ej., **work to do** trabajo por hacer; hasta, p.ej., **to a certain extent** hasta cierto punto; en, p.ej., **from door to door** de puerta en puerta; con, p.ej., **kind to her** amable con ella; segun, p.ej., **to my way of thinking** según mi modo de pensar; menos, p.ej., **five minutes to ten** las diez menos cinco

toad [tod] *s* sapo

toad'stool' *s* agárico, seta; seta venenosa

to-and-fro ['tu•ənd'fro] *adj* alternativo, de vaivén

toast [tost] *s* tostadas; (*drink*) brindis *m;* **a piece of toast** una tostada || *tr* tostar; brindar a o por || *intr* tostarse; brindar

toaster ['tostər] *s* (*of bread*) tostador *m;* brindador *m*

toast'mas'ter *s* el que presenta a los oradores en un banquete, maestro de ceremonias

tobac•co [tə'bæko] *s* (*pl* **-cos**) tabaco

tobacco grower *s* tabacalero

tobacconist [tə'bækənəst] *s* tabaquero

tobacco pouch *s* petaca

tobacco shop *s* tabaquería

toboggan [tə'bɑgən] *s* tobogán *m* || *intr* deslizarse en tobogán

tocsin ['tɑksɪn] *s* campana de alarma; campanada de alarma

today [tʊ'de] *adv & s* hoy

toddle ['tɑdəl] *s* pasitos vacilantes || *intr* andar con pasitos vacilantes; hacer pinitos (*un niño o un enfermo*)

tod•dy ['tɑdi] *s* (*pl* **-dies**) ponche *m*

to-do [tə'du] *s* (coll) alharaca, alboroto

toe [to] *s* dedo del pie; (*of stocking*) punta || *v* (*pret & pp* **toed;** *ger* **toeing**) *tr*—**to toe the line** o **the mark** ponerse a la raya; obrar como se debe

toe'nail' *s* uña del dedo del pie

tofu ['tofu] *s* tofu *m,* queso de soja

tog [tɑg] *s* (coll) prenda de vestir

toga ['togə] *s* toga

together [tʊ'gɛðər] *adv* juntamente; juntos; al mismo tiempo; sin interrupción; de acuerdo; **to bring together** reunir; confrontar; reconciliar; **to call together** convocar; **to go together** ir juntos; ser novios; hacerjuego; **to stick together** (coll) quedarse unidos, no abandonarse

toggle ['tɑgəl] *s* (compu) flip-flop *m;* (naut) cazonete *m*

toggle switch *s* (compu) flip-flop *m* de conmutación

toil [tɔɪl] *s* afán *m,* fatiga; faena, obra laboriosa; **toils** red *f,* lazo || *intr* atrafagar; moverse con fatiga

toilet ['tɔɪlɪt] *s* (*dress or adornment*) tocado, atavio; (*dressing table*) tocador *m;* (*rest room*) retrete *m,* inodoro, baño, servicio, excusado (Mex), wáter *m* (Bol, Col, Chile, Peru, Urug), taza (Bol, Col, Guat, Mex), poseta (Ven); **to flush the toilet** tirar de la cadena; **to make one's toilet** asearse, acicalarse

toilet articles *spl* artículos de tocador

toilet paper *s* papel higiénico

toilet powder *s* polvos de tocador

toilet soap *s* jabón *m* de olor, jabón de tocador

toilet tank *s* cisterna
toilet water *s* colonia, agua de colonia
token [ˈtokən] *s* señal *f,* prueba; prenda, recuerdo; (*used as money*) ficha, tanto; **by the same token** por el mismo motivo; **in token of** en señal de
tolerance [ˈtɑlərəns] *s* tolerancia
tolerate [ˈtɑləˌret] *tr* tolerar, transigir con
toll [tol] *s* (*of bells*) doble *m;* (*to pass along a road or over a bridge*) peaje *m;* (*to use a canal*) derechos de paso; (*to use a telephone*) tarifa; (*number of victims*) baja, mortalidad ‖ *tr* tocar a muerto (*una campana*); llamar con toque de difuntos ‖ *intr* doblar
toll′booth′ *s* cabina de peaje
toll′bridge′ *s* puente *m* de peaje
toll call *s* (telp) llamada a larga distancia
toll′gate′ *s* barrera de peaje
toma•to [təˈmeto] o [təˈmɑto] *s* (*pl* **-toes**) (*plant*) tomatera o tomate *m;* (*fruit*) tomate
tomato paste *s* extracto de tomate
tomb [tum] *s* tumba, sepulcro
tomboy [ˈtɑmˌbɔɪ] *s* moza retozona, muchacha traviesa
tomb′stone′ *s* piedra o lápida sepulcral
tomcat [ˈtɑmˌkæt] *s* gato macho
tome [tom] *s* tomo; libro grueso
tomorrow [tʊˈmɔro] *adv* mañana ‖ *s* mañana *m;* **the day after tomorrow** pasado mañana
Tom Thumb *s* Pulgarcito
tom-tom [ˈtɑmˌtɑm] *s* tantán *m,* tom-tom *m*
ton [tʌn] *s* tonelada; **tons** (coll) montones *mpl*
tone [ton] *s* tono ‖ *tr* entonar ‖ *intr* armonizar; **to tone down** moderarse; **to tone up** reforzarse
tone poem *s* poema sinfónico
tongs [tɔŋz] o [tɑŋz] *spl* tenazas; (*e.g., for sugar*) tenacillas
tongue [tʌŋ] *s* (anat) lengua; (*of a wagon*) vara, lanza; (*of a belt buckle*) tarabilla; (*of shoe*) lengua, lengüeta; (*language*) lengua, idioma *m;* **to hold one's tongue** morderse la lengua
tongue′-lash′ing *s* (coll) bronca
tongue twister [ˈtwɪstər] *s* trabalenguas *m*
tonic [ˈtɑnɪk] *adj & s* tónico
tonic accent *s* acento prosódico
tonight [tʊˈnaɪt] *adv & s* esta noche
tonnage [ˈtʌnɪdʒ] *s* tonelaje *m*
tonsil [ˈtɑnsəl] *s* tonsila, amígdala
tonsillitis [ˌtɑnsɪˈlaɪtɪs] *s* tonsilitis *f,* amigdalitis *f*
ton•y [ˈtoni] *adj* (*comp* **-ier;** *super* **-iest**) (slang) elegante, aristocrático
too [tu] *adv* (*also*) también; (*more than enough*) demasiado; **too bad!** ¡qué lástima!; **too many** demasiados; **too much** demasiado
tool [tul] *s* herramienta; (*person used for one's own ends*) instrumento; **tools** implementos *mpl* ‖ *tr* trabajar con herramienta; (bb) filetear, estampar
tool bag *s* bolsa de herramientas
tool bar *s* (compu) barra de herramientas
toolmak′er *s* tallador *m* de herramientas, herrero de herramientas
toot [tut] *s* (*of horn*) toque *m;* (*of klaxon*) bocinazo; (*of locomotive*) pitazo; (coll) parranda ‖ *tr* sonar; **to toot one's own horn** cantar sus propias alabanzas ‖ *intr* sonar
tooth [tuθ] *s* (*pl* **teeth** [tiθ]) diente *m*
tooth′ache′ *s* dolor *m* de muelas
tooth′brush′ *s* cepillo de dientes
toothless [ˈtuθlɪs] *adj* desdentado
tooth′paste′ *s* pasta dentifrica, crema dental, crema dentífrica
tooth′pick′ *s* limpiadientes *m,* mondadientes *m,* palillo
tooth powder *s* polvo dentífrico
top [tɑp] *s* (*of a mountain, tree, etc.*) cima; (*of a mountain; high point*) cumbre *f;* (*of a tree*) copa; (*of a barrel, box, etc.*) tapa; (*of a page*) principio; (*of a table*) tablero; (*of a wall*) coronamiento; (*of a bathing suit*) camiseta; (*of a carriage or auto*) capota; (*toy*) peón *m,* peonza; (naut) cofa; **at the top of** en lo alto de; (*e.g., one's class*) a la cabeza de; **at the top of one's voice** a voz en grito; **from top to bottom** de arriba abajo; de alto a bajo; completamente; **on top of** en lo alto de; encima de; **the tops** (slang) la flor de la canela; **to sleep like a top** dormir como un leño ‖ *v* (*pret & pp* **topped;** ger **topping**) *tr* coronar, rematar; cubrir; aventajar, superar; descopar (*p.ej., un árbol*)
topaz [ˈtopæz] *s* topacio
top billing *s* cabecera de cartel
top′coat′ *s* sobretodo; abrigo de entretiempo
toper [ˈtopər] *s* borrachín *m*
top hat *s* chistera, sombrero de copa
top′-heav′y *adj* más pesado arriba que abajo
topic [ˈtɑpɪk] *s* asunto, materia, tema *m*
top′knot′ *s* moño
top′less *adj* topless (*con el busto desnudo*)
top′-lev′el *adj* alto, de alto nivel
top′mast′ *s* (naut) mastelero
top′most *adj* (el) más alto
top′notch′ *adj* de primera
topogra•phy [təˈpɑgrəfi] *s* (*pl* **-phies**) topografía
topple [ˈtɑpəl] *tr* derribar, volcar ‖ *intr* derribarse, volcarse; caerse, venirse abajo
top priority *s* máxima prioridad
top′-rank′ing′ *adj* de alto nivel, importante
topsail [ˈtɑpsəl] o [ˈtɑpˌsel] *s* (naut) gavia
top secret *adj* de mayor confidencia, ultrasecreto
top′soil′ *s* capa superficial del suelo
topsy-turvy [ˈtɑpsiˈtʌrvi] *adj* desbarajustado ‖ *adv* en cuadro, patas arriba ‖ *s* desbarajuste *m*
torch [tɔrtʃ] *s* antorcha; **to carry the torch for** (slang) amar desesperadamente
torch′bear′er *s* hachero; (fig) adicto, partidario
torch′light′ *s* luz *f* de antorcha
torch song *s* canción lenta y melancólica de amor no correspondido
torment [ˈtɔrmɛnt] *s* tormento; murga ‖ [tɔrˈmɛnt] *tr* atormentar

torna•do [tɔrˋnedo] *s* (*pl* **-does** o **-dos**) tornado, tromba terrestre
torpe•do [tɔrˋpido] *s* (*pl* **-does**) torpedo || *tr* torpedear
torque [tɔrk] *s* (mech, phys) momento *or* par *m* de torsión
torrent [ˋtɔrənt] *s* torrente *m*
torrid [ˋtɔrɪd] *adj* tórrido
tor•so [ˋtɔrso] *s* (*pl* **-sos**) torso
tort [tɔrt] *s* (law) agravio
tortoise [ˋtɔrtəs] *s* tortuga
tortoise shell *s* carey *m*
torture [ˋtɔrtʃər] *s* tortura || *tr* torturar, atormentar
toss [tɑs] *s* echada; alcance *m* de una echada || *tr* arrojar, echar; lanzar al aire; agitar, menear; levantar airosamente (*la cabeza*); lanzar (*p.ej., un comentario*); echar a cara o cruz; **to toss off** hacer muy rápidamente; tragar de un golpe || *intr* agitarse, menearse; **to toss and turn** (*in bed*) revolverse, dar vueltas
toss'-up' *s* cara o cruz; probabilidad igual
tot [tɑt] *s* párvulo, peque *m,* chiquitín *m*
to•tal [ˋtotəl] *adj* total; (*e.g., loss*) completo || *s* total *m* || *v* (*pret & pp* **-taled** o **-talled;** *ger* **-taling** o **-talling**) *tr* ascender a sumar
totalitarian [toˌtæləˋtɛrɪ•ən] *adj* totalitario
totem pole [ˋtotəm] *s* pilar totémico
totter [ˋtɑtər] *s* tambaleo || *intr* tambalear; estar para desplomarse
touch [tʌtʃ] *s* (*act*) toque *m;* (*sense*) tacto, tiento; (*of piano, pianist, typewriter, typist*) tacto; (*of an illness*) ramo, ataque ligero; pizca, poquito; **to get in touch with** ponerse en comunicación o contacto con; **to lose one's touch** perder el tiento || *tr* tocar; conmover, enternecer; probar (*vino, licor*); (*for a loan*) (slang) pedir prestado a, dar un sablazo a; **to touch up** retocar || *intr* tocar; **to touch at** tocar en (*un puerto*)
touching [ˋtʌtʃɪŋ] *adj* conmovedor, enternecedor || *prep* tocante a
touch typewriting *s* escritura al tacto
touch•y [ˋtʌtʃi] *adj* (*comp* **-ier;** *super* **-iest**) quisquilloso, enojadizo
tough [tʌf] *adj* correoso; tenaz; difícil; gamberro; (*e.g., luck*) malo || *s* gamberro, guapetón *m;* (coll) gorila
toughen [ˋtʌfən] *tr* hacer correoso; hacer tenaz; dificultar || *intr* ponerse correoso; hacerse tenaz; hacerse difícil
toupee [tuˋpe] *s* peluquín *m*
tour [tʊr] *s* jira, paseo, vuelta; viaje largo; **on tour** de jira, de viaje || *tr* viajar por, recorrer || *intr* viajar por distracción o diversión
touring car [ˋtʊrɪŋ] *s* coche *m* de turismo
tourist [ˋtʊrɪst] *adj* turístico || *s* turista *mf*
tourist guide *s* guía turística
tourist resort *s* complejo turístico
tournament [ˋtʊrnəmənt] o [ˋtʌrnəmənt] *s* torneo
tourney [ˋtʊrni] o [ˋtʌrni] *s* torneo || *intr* tornear
tourniquet [ˋtʊrnɪˌkɛt] *s* torniquete *m*
tousle [ˋtaʊzəl] *tr* despeinar, enmarañar
tow [to] *s* remolque *m;* (*e.g., of hemp*) estopa; **to take in tow** dar remolque a; (fig) encargarse de || *tr* remolcar
towage [ˋto•ɪdʒ] *s* remolque *m;* derechos de remolque
toward(s) [tord(z)] o [təˋwɔrd(z)] *prep* (*in the direction of*) hacia; (*with regard to*) para con; (*a certain hour*) cerca de, a eso de
tow'boat' *s* remolcador *m*
tow•el [ˋtaʊ•əl] *s* toalla || *v* (*pret & pp* **-eled** o **-elled;** *ger* **-eling** o **-elling**) *tr* secar con toalla
towelette [ˌtaʊˋlɛt] *s* toalla refrescante
towel rack *s* toallero
tower [ˋtaʊ•ər] *s* torre *f* || *intr* encumbrarse, empinarse
towering [ˋtaʊ•ərɪŋ] *adj* encumbrado; sobresaliente; excesivo
towing service [ˋto•ɪŋ] *s* servicio de grúa
tow'line' *s* cable *m* de remolque, sirga
town [taʊn] *s* problación, pueblo, villa; **in town** a la ciudad, en la ciudad
town clerk *s* escribano municipal
town council *s* concejo municipal
town crier *s* pregonero público
town hall *s* ayuntamiento, casa de ayuntamiento
town planning *s* planificación urbana
towns'folk' *spl* vecinos del pueblo
township [ˋtaʊnʃɪp] *s* sexmo; terreno público de seis millas en cuadro
towns•man [ˋtaʊnzmən] *s* (*pl* **-men** [mən]) ciudadano, vecino; conciudadano, paisano
towns'peo'ple *spl* vecinos del pueblo
town talk *s* comidilla o hablillas del pueblo
tow'path' *s* camino de sirga
tow plane *s* avión *m* de remolque
tow'rope' *s* cuerda de remolque
tow truck *s* grúa, camión *m* remolcador
toxic [ˋtɑksɪk] *adj & s* tóxico
toxic shock syndrome *s* síndrome *m* de choque tóxico
toy [tɔɪ] *adj* de juguete || *s* juguete *m;* (*trifle*) bagatela; (*trinket*) dije *m,* bujería || *intr* jugar; divertirse; **to toy with** jugar con (*los sentimientos de una persona*); acariciar (*una idea*)
toy bank *s* alcancía hucha
toy soldier *s* soldado de juguete
trace [tres] *s* huella, rastro; indicio, vestigio; (*of harness*) tirante *m;* pizca || *tr* rastrear; trazar (*p.ej., una curva; los rasgos de una persona o cosa*); averiguar el paradero de; remontar al origen de
trace element *s* elemento rastro
trache•a [ˋtrekɪ•ə] *s* (*pl* **-ae** [ˌi]) tráquea
track [træk] *s* (*of foot*) huella; (*of a wheel*) rodada, carril *m;* (*of a boat*) estela; (*of railroad*) vía; (*of an airplane, a hurricane*) trayectoria; (*of a tractor*) llanta de oruga; camino, senda; (*course followed by a boat*) derrota; (*of ideas, events, etc.*) sucesión; (compu, sport) pista; **to keep track of** no perder de vista; no olvidar; **to lose track of** perder de vista; olvidar;

to make tracks dejar pisadas; irse muy de prisa; **off the track** (*also* fig) desviado ‖ *tr* rastrear; seguir la huella o la pista de; dejar pisadas en, manchar pisando; **to track down** seguir y capturar; averiguar el origen de

track and field *s* (sport) competencia de atletismo

tracking [ˈtrækɪŋ] *s* (aerosp) seguimiento (*de vehículos espaciales*); (educ) agrupamiento de estudiantes según sus habilidades

tracing station *s* estación de seguimiento

trackless trolley [ˈtræklɪs] *s* filobús *m,* trolebús *m*

track meet *s* concurso de carreras y saltos

track record *s* historial *m,* antecedentes *mpl*

tract [trækt] *s* espacio, tracto; folleto; (anat) canal *m,* sistema *m*

traction [ˈtrækʃən] *s* tracción

traction company *s* empresa de tranvías

tractor [ˈtræktər] *s* tractor *m*

trade [tred] *s* comercio; negocio, trato; trueque *m,* canje *m;* (*calling, job*) oficio; clientela, parroquia; (*e.g., in slaves*) trata ‖ *tr* cambiar, trocar; **to trade in** dar como parte del pago; **to trade off** cambalachear; ‖ *intr* comerciar; comprar; **to trade in** comerciar en; **to trade on** aprovecharse de

trade fair *s* exposición comercial o industrial

tradeˈmarkˊ *s* marca de fábrica, marca registrada

trade name *s* nombre *m* comercial; razón *f* social, nombre de fábrica

trader [ˈtredər] *s* traficante *mf*

trade school *s* escuela de artes y oficios

trades•man [ˈtredzmən] *s* (*pl* **-men** [mən]) tendero; comerciante *m;* (Brit) artesano

trade union *s* sindicato, gremio de obreros

trade unionist *s* sindicalista *mf*

trade war *s* guerra comercial

trade winds *spl* vientos alisios

trading post [ˈtredɪŋ] *s* factoría; (*in stock exchange*) puesto de compraventa

trading stamp *s* sello de premio, sello de descuento

tradition [trəˈdɪʃən] *s* tradición

traduce [trəˈdjus] *tr* calumniar

traf•fic [ˈtræfɪk] *s* tráfico, comercio; tráfico, circulación; (*e.g., in slaves*) trata ‖ *v* (*pret & pp* **-ficked;** *ger* **-ficking**) *intr* traficar

traffic accident *s* accidente *m* de circulación, accidente de tráfico

traffic circle *s* glorieta de tráfico

traffic court *s* juzgado de tráfico

traffic jam *s* embotellamiento, tapón *m* de tráfico

traffic light *s* luz *f* de tráfico, semáforo

traffic sign o **signal** *s* señal *f* de tráfico, seña de tráfico

traffic ticket *s* aviso de multa

tragedian [trəˈdʒidɪ•ən] *s* trágico

trage•dy [ˈtrædʒɪdi] *s* (*pl* **-dies**) tragedia

tragic [ˈtrædʒɪk] *adj* trágico

trail [trel] *s* rastro, huella, pista; (*path through rough country*) trocha, senda, vereda; (*of a gown*) cola; (*of smoke, a rocket, etc.*) estela ‖ *tr* arrastrar; seguir la pista de; andar detrás de; llevar (*p.ej., barro*) con los pies ‖ *intr* arrastrar; rezagarse; arrastrarse, trepar (*una planta*); **to trail off** desaparecer poco a poco

trail bike *s* moto *f* de motocross

trailblazer [ˈtrel,blezər] *s* pionero

trailer [ˈtrelər] *s* remolque *m,* cochehabitación *m,* casa rodante; planta rastrera

trailer home *s* casa rodante, casa-remolque

trailing arbutus [ˈtrelɪŋ] *s* epigea rastrera

train [tren] *s* (*of railway cars; of waves*) tren *m;* (*of thought*) hilo ‖ *tr* adiestrar; guiar (*las plantas*); (sport) entrenar ‖ *intr* adiestrarse; (sport) entrenarse

train crash *s* accidente ferroviario

trained nurse *s* enfermera graduada

trainee [ˈtreˈni] *s* persona que se adiestra; (*apprentice*) aprendiz *mf*

trainer [ˈtrenər] *s* (sport) entrenador *m;* (*of animals*) amaestrador *m*

training [ˈtrenɪŋ] *s* adiestramiento; instrucción; (sport) entrenamiento

training school *s* escuela práctica; reformatorio

training ship *s* buque *m* escuela

trait [tret] *s* característica, rasgo

traitor [ˈtretər] *s* traidor *m*

traitress [ˈtretrɪs] *s* traidora

trajecto•ry [trəˈdʒɛktəri] *s* (*pl* **-ries**) trayectoria

tramp [træmp] *s* vagabundo; marcha pesada, ruido de pisadas ‖ *tr* pisar con fuerza; recorrer a pie ‖ *intr* andar a pie; vagabundear

trample [ˈtræmpəl] *tr* pisotear ‖ *intr*—**to trample on** o **upon** pisotear

trampoline [ˈtræmpə,lin] *s* cama elástica

tramp steamer *s* vapor volandero

trance [træns] o [trɑns] *s* arrobamiento, rapto; estado hipnótico

tranquil [ˈtræŋkwɪl] *adj* tranquilo

tranquilize [ˈtræŋkwɪ,laɪz] *tr & intr* tranquilizar

tranquilizer [ˈtræŋkwɪ,laɪzər] *s* tranquilizante *m*

tranquillity [træŋkwɪlɪti] *s* tranquilidad

transact [trænˈzækt] o [trænsˈækt] *tr* tramitar; llevar a cabo

transaction [trænˈzækʃən] o [trænsˈækʃən] *s* tramitación, transacción

transatlantic [,trænsətˈlæntɪk] *adj & s* transatlántico

transcend [trænˈsɛnd] *tr* exceder, superar ‖ *intr* sobresalir

transcribe [trænˈskraɪb] *tr* transcribir

transcript [ˈtrænskrɪpt] *s* trasunto, traslado; (educ) hoja de estudios, certificado de estudios

transcription [trænˈskrɪpʃən] *s* transcripción

transept [ˈtrænsɛpt] *s* crucero, transepto

trans•fer [ˈtrænsfər] *s* traslado; transbordo; contraseña o billete *m* de transferencia; (com) transferencia, transmisión ‖ [trænsˈfʌr] o [ˈtrænsfər] *s* (*pret & pp* **-ferred;** *ger* **-ferring**)

tr trasladar, transferir; transbordar || *intr* cambiar de tren, tranvía, etc.
transfix [træns'fɪks] *tr* espetar, traspasar; dejar atónito
transform [træns'fɔrm] *tr* transformar || *intr* transformarse
transformer [træns'fɔrmər] *s* transformador *m*
transfusion [træns'fjuʃən] *s* transfusión; (med) transfusión de la sangre
transgress [træns'grɛs] *tr* transgredir, violar; exceder, traspasar (*p.ej., los límites de la prudencia*) || *intr* pecar, prevaricar
transgression [træns'grɛʃən] *s* transgresión; pecado, prevaricación
transient ['trænʃənt] *adj* pasajero, transitorio; de tránsito || *s* transeúnte *mf*
transistor [træn'zɪstər] *s* transistor *m*
transistor radio *s* radio a transistores, radio de transistores
transistorize [træn'zɪstə,raɪz] *tr* transistorizar
transit ['trænsɪt] o ['trænzɪt] *s* tránsito
transitive ['trænsɪtɪv] *adj* transitivo || *s* verbo transitivo
transitory ['trænsɪ,tori] *adj* transitorio
translate [træns'let] o ['trænslet] *tr* (*from one language to another*) traducir; (*from one place to another*) trasladar; (compu) traducir; (eccl, math) trasladar || *intr* traducirse
translation [træns'leʃən] *s* traducción; traslación; (compu) traducción; (eccl) traslado; (math) traslación
translator [træns'letər] *s* traductor *m*
transliterate [træns'lɪtə,ret] *tr* transcribir
translucent [træns'lusənt] *adj* translúcido
transmission [træns'mɪʃən] *s* transmissión; (aut) cambio de marchas, cambio de velocidades
transmis'sion-gear' box *s* caja de cambio de marchas, caja de velocidades
trans•mit [træns'mɪt] *v* (*pret & pp* **-mitted;** *ger* **-mitting**) *tr & intr* transmitir
transmitter [træns'mɪtər] *s* transmisor *m;* (rad) radioemisora
transmitting set *s* aparato transmisor
transmitting station *s* estacion transmisora, emisora
transmute [træns'mjut] *tr & intr* transmutar
transom [trænsəm] *s* (*crosspiece*) travesaño; (*window over door*) montante *m;* (*of ship*) yugo de popa
transparen•cy [træns'pɛrənsi] *s* (*pl* **-cies**) transparencia
transparent [træns'pɛrənt] *adj* transparente
transpire [træns'paɪr] *intr* transpirar; (*to become known, leak out*) transpirar; (*to happen*) acontecer, tener lugar
transplant ['træns,plænt] *s* transplante; injerto || *tr* transplantar || *intr* transplantarse
transport ['trænsport] *s* transporte *m;* (aer & naut) transporte *m;* rapto, éxtasis *m,* transporte *m* || [træns'port] *tr* transportar
transportation [,trænspor'teʃən] *s* transporte *m;* (U.S.A.) pasaje *m,* billete *m* de viaje
transport worker *s* transportista *mf*
transpose [træns'poz] *tr* transponer; (mus) transportar
transsexual [,træns'sɛkʃʊ•əl] *adj & s* transexual *mf*
trans•ship [træns'ʃɪp] *v* (*pret & pp* **-shipped;** *ger* **-shipping**) *tr* transbordar
transshipment [træns'ʃɪpmənt] *s* transbordo
transvestism [træns'vɛstɪzəm] *s* travestismo
transvestite [træns'vɛstaɪt] *adj & s* travestí
trap [træp] *s* trampa; (*double-curved pipe*) sifón *m;* coche ligero de dos ruedas; (sport) lanzaplatos *m* || *v* (*pret & pp* **trapped;** *ger* **trapping**) *tr* entrampar; atrapar (*a un ladrón*)
trap door *s* escotillón *m,* trampa; (theat) escotillón *m,* pescante *m*
trapeze [trə'piz] *s* trapecio
trapezold ['træpɪ,zɔɪd] *s* trapecio
trapper ['træpər] *s* cazador *m* de alforja
trappings ['træpɪŋz] *spl* (*adornments*) adornos, altavíos; (*of a horse's harness*) jaeces *mpl*
trap'shoot'ing *s* tiro al vuelo *or* plato
trash [træʃ] *s* broza, basura, desecho; (*junk*) cachivaches *mpl;* (*nonsense*) disparates *mpl;* (*worthless people*) gentuza
trash can *s* basurero; (compu) papelera
trash pile *s* basural *m* (SAm)
traumatism ['traʊmə,tɪzəm] *s* traumatismo
travail ['trævel] o [trə'vel] *s* afán *m,* labor *f,* pena; dolores *mpl* del parto
trav•el ['trævəl] *s* viaje *m;* el viajar; (mach) recorrido || *v* (*pret & pp* **-eled** o **-elled;** *ger* **-eling** o **-elling**) *tr* viajar por; recorrer || *intr* vaijar; andar, recorrer
travel agency *s* agencia de viajes
travel agent *s* agente *mf* de viajes
travel bureau *s* oficina de turismo
travel expenses *spl* gastos de viaje
traveler ['trævələr] *s* viajero; (*salesman*) viajante *m*
traveler's check *s* cheque *m* de viajeros
traveling expenses *spl* gastos de viaje
traveling salesman *s* viajante *m,* agente viajero
travel trailer *s* casa rodante, casa-remolque *m*
traverse ['trævərs] o [trə'vʌrs] *tr* atravesar; recorrer, pasar por
traves•ty ['trævɪsti] *s* (*pl* **-ties**) parodia || *v* (*pret & pp* **-tied**) *tr* parodiar
trawl [trɔl] *s* red barredera, espinel *m,* palangre *m* || *tr & intr* pescar a la rastra
trawling *s* pesca de arrastre
tray [tre] *s* bandeja; (chem & phot) cubeta
treacherous ['trɛtʃərəs] *adj* traicionero, traidor; incierto, poco seguro
treacher•y ['trɛtʃəri] *s* (*pl* **-ies**) traición alevosía
tread [trɛd] *s* (*stepping*) pisada; (*of stairs*) grada, huella, peldaño; (*of stilts*) horquilla; (*of a tire*) banda de rodamiento; (*of shoe*) suela; (*of an egg*) meaje, galladura || *v* (*pret* **trod** [trɑd]; *pp* **trodden** ['trɑdən] o **trod**) *tr* pisar, pisotear; abrumar, agobiar || *intr* andar, caminar
treadle ['trɛdəl] *s* pedal *m*

treadless [ˈtrɛdlɪs] *adj* (*tire*) desgastado
tread′mill′ *s* rueda de andar; (*futile drudgery*) noria
treas. *abbr* **treasurer, treasury**
treason [ˈtrizən] *s* traición
treasonable [ˈtrizənəbəl] *adj* traicionero, traidor
treasure [ˈtrɛʒər] *s* tesoro ‖ *tr* atesorar
treasure hunt *s* caza al tesoro
treasurer [ˈtrɛʒərər] *s* tesorero
treasur•y [ˈtrɛʒəri] *s* (*pl* **-ies**) tesorería; tesoro
treat [trit] *s* convite *m;* (*to a drink*) convidada; (*something providing particular enjoyment*) regalo, deleite *m* ‖ *tr* tratar; convidar, regalar; curar (*a un enfermo*) ‖ *intr* tratar; convidar, regalar; **to treat of** tratar de
treatise [ˈtritɪs] *s* tratado
treatment [ˈtritmənt] *s* tratamiento
trea•ty [ˈtriti] *s* (*pl* **-ties**) tratado
treble [ˈtrɛbəl] *adj* (*threefold*) tresdoble, triple; sobreagudo; (mus) atiplado; (mus) de tiple ‖ *s* (*person*) tiple *mf;* (*voice*) tiple ‖ *tr* triplicar ‖ *intr* triplicarse
treble clef *s* clave *f* de sol
tree [tri] *s* árbol *m*
tree farm *s* monte *m* tallar
treeless [ˈtrilɪs] *adj* pelado, sin árboles
tree′top′ *s* copa, cima de árbol
trek [trɛk] *s* caminata
trellis [ˈtrɛlɪs] *s* enrejado, espaldera; emparrado
tremble [ˈtrɛmbəl] *s* temblor *m,* estremecimiento ‖ *intr* temblar, estremecerse
tremendous [trɪˈmɛndəs] *adj* tremendo
tremor [ˈtrɛmər] o [ˈtrimər] *s* temblor *m*
trench [trɛntʃ] *s* foso, zanja; (*for irrigation*) acequia; (mil) trinchera
trenchant [ˈtrɛntʃənt] *adj* mordaz, punzante; enérgico, bien definido
trench coat *s* trinchera
trench mortar *s* (mil) lanzabombas *m*
trench′-plow′ *tr* (agr) desfondar
trench warfare *s* guerra de trincheros
trend [trɛnd] *s* curso, dirección, tendencia ‖ *intr* dirigirse, tender
tren•dy [ˈtrɛndi] *adj* (*comp* **-dier;** *super* **-diest**) al día, de (última) moda
trespass [ˈtrɛspəs] *s* entrada sin derecho; infracción, violación; culpa, pecado ‖ *intr* entrar sin derecho; pecar; **no trespassing** prohibida la entrada; **to trespass against** pecar contra; **to trespass on** entrar sin derecho en; infringir, violar; abusar de (*p.ej., la paciencia de uno*)
tress [trɛs] *s* (*braid of hair*) trenza; (*curl*) bucle *m,* rizo
trestle [ˈtrɛsəl] *s* caballete *m;* puente *m* o viaducto de caballetes
trial [ˈtraɪ•əl] *s* ensayo, prueba; aflicción, desgracia; (law) juicio, proceso, vista; **on trial** a prueba; (law) en juicio; **to bring to trial** encausar
trial and error *s* método de tanteos
trial balance *s* balance de comprobación
trial balloon *s* globo sonda; **to send up a trial balloon** (fig) lanzar un globo sonda
trial by jury *s* juicio por jurado
trial jury *s* jurado procesal
trial order *s* (com) pedido de ensayo
trial run *s* experimento piloto
triangle [ˈtraɪˌæŋgəl] *s* triángulo
tribe [traɪb] *s* tribu *f*
tribunal [trɪˈbjunəl] o [traɪˈbjunəl] *s* tribunal *m*
tribune [ˈtrɪbjun] *s* tribuna
tributar•y [ˈtrɪbjəˌtɛri] *adj* tributario ‖ *s* (*pl* **-ies**) tributario
tribute [ˈtrɪbjut] *s* tributo
trice [traɪs] *s* momento, instante *m;* **in a trice** en un periquete
trick [trɪk] *s* ardid *m,* artimaña; leva (CAm, Col); (*knack*) maña; (*feat*) suerte *f;* (*prank*) travesura, burla, chasco; tanda, turno; ilusión; (*feat with cards*) truco; (*cards in one round*) baza; (coll) chiquita; **to be up to one's old tricks** hacer de las suyas; **to play a dirty trick on** hacer una mala jugada a ‖ *tr* trampear; burlar, engañar; ataviar
tricker•y [ˈtrɪkəri] *s* (*pl* **-ies**) trampería, malas mañas
trickle [ˈtrɪkəl] *s* chorro delgado, goteo ‖ *intr* escurrir, gotear; pasar gradual e irregularmente
trickster [ˈtrɪkstər] *s* tramposo, embustero, embaucador *m,* embaucadora
trick•y [ˈtrɪki] *adj* (*comp* **-ier;** *super* **-iest**) tramposo, engañoso, difícil; (*animal*) vicioso; (*ticklish to deal with*) delicado
tricorn [ˈtraɪkɔrn] *adj & s* tricornio
tried [traɪd] *adj* fiel, probado, seguro
trifle [ˈtraɪfəl] *s* bagatela, friolera, fruslería, basurita, chiquitura; (*trinket*) bagatela, baratija ‖ *tr*—**to trifle away** malgastar ‖ *intr* estar ocioso, holgar; **to trifle with** manosear; jugar con, burlarse de
trifling [ˈtraɪflɪŋ] *adj* frívolo, fútil, ligero; insignificante, trivial
trifocal [traɪˈfokəl] *adj* trifocal ‖ *s* lente *f* trifocal; **trifocals** anteojos trifocales
trigger [ˈtrɪgər] *s* (*e.g., of a gun*) disparador *m,* gatillo; (*of any device*) disparador ‖ *tr* poner en movimiento, provocar
trigonometry [ˌtrɪgəˈnɑmɪtri] *s* trigonometría
trill [trɪl] *s* trinado, trino; (*made with voice, esp. of birds*) gorjeo; (phonet) vibración ‖ *tr* decir o cantar gorjeando; pronunciar con vibración ‖ *intr* trinar; gorjear
trillion [ˈtrɪljən] *s* (U.S.A.) billón *m;* (Brit) trillón *m*
trilo•gy [ˈtrɪlədʒi] *s* (*pl* **-gies**) trilogía
trim [trɪm] *adj* (*comp* **trimmer;** *super* **trimmest**) acicalado, compuesto, elegante ‖ *s* condición, estado; buena condición; adorno, atavío; traje *m,* vestido; (*of sails*) orientación ‖ *v* (*pret & pp* **trimmed;** *ger* **trimming**) *tr* ajustar, adaptar; arreglar, componer; adornar, decorar; decorar, enguirnaldar (*el árbol de Navidad*); recortar; cortar ligeramente (*el

pelo); despabilar (*una lámpara o vela*); mondar, podar (*árboles, plantas*); acepillar, desbastar; (naut) orientar (*las velas*); (coll) derrotar, vencer; (coll) regañar

trimming [ˈtrɪmɪŋ] *s* adorno, guarnición; franja, orla; (coll) paliza, zurra; (coll) derrota; **trimmings** accesorios, arrequives *mpl;* recortes *mpl*

trini•ty [ˈtrɪnɪti] *s* (*pl* **-ties**) (*group of three*) trinca ‖ **Trinity** *s* Trinidad

trinket [ˈtrɪŋkɪt] *s* (*small ornament*) dije *m;* (*trivial object*) baratija, bujería, chuchería

tri•o [ˈtri•o] *s* (*pl* **-os**) (*group of three*) terna, trío; (mus) trío

trip [trɪp] *s* viaje *m;* jira, recorrido; (*stumble*) tropiezo; (*act of causing a person to stumble*) traspié *m,* zancadilla; (*blunder*) desliz *m;* (*drugs*) viaje ‖ *v* (*pret & pp* **tripped;** *ger* **tripping**) *tr* trompicar, echar la zancadilla a; detener, estorbar; inclinar; coger en falta; coger en una mentira ‖ *intr* ir conpaso rápido y ligero; brincar, saltar, correr; tropezar; **to trip over** tropezar con, contra o en

tripe [traɪp] *s* callos, mondongo; (coll) disparate *m,* barbaridad, paparruchas *fpl*

trip'ham'mer *s* martillo pilón

triphthong [ˈtrɪfθɔŋ] *s* triptongo

triple [ˈtrɪpəl] *adj & s* triple *m* ‖ *tr* triplicar ‖ *intr* triplicarse

triplet [ˈtrɪplɪt] *s* (*offspring*) trillizo; (*stanza of three lines*) terceto; (mus) terceto, tresillo

triplicate [ˈtrɪplɪkɪt] *adj & s* triplicado; **in triplicate** por triplicado ‖ [ˈtrɪplɪˌket] *tr* triplicar

tripod [ˈtraɪpɑd] *m* trípode *m*

triptych [ˈtrɪptɪk] *s* tríptico

trite [traɪt] *adj* gastado, trillado, trivial

triumph [ˈtraɪ•əmf] *s* triunfo ‖ *intr* triunfar; **to triumph over** triunfar de

triumphal arch [traɪˈʌmfəl] *s* arco triunfal

triumphant [traɪˈʌmfənt] *adj* triunfante

trivia [ˈtrɪvɪ•ə] *spl* bagatelas, trivialidades

trivial [ˈtrɪvɪ•əl] *adj* trivial, insignificante

triviali•ty [ˌtrɪvɪˈælɪti] *s* (*pl* **-ties**) trivialidad

Trojan [ˈtrodʒən] *adj & s* troyano

Trojan horse *s* caballo de Troya

troll [trol] *tr & intr* pescar a la cacea

trolley [ˈtrɑli] *s* polea o arco de trole; tranvía *m*

trolley bus *s* trolebús *m*

trolley car *s* coche *m* de tranvía

trolley pole *s* trole *m*

trolling [ˈtrolɪŋ] *s* cacea, pesca a la cacea

trollop [ˈtrɑləp] *s* (*slovenly woman*) cochina; mujer *f* de mala vida

trombone [ˈtrɑmbon] *s* trombón *m*

troop [trup] *s* tropa; (*of actors*) compañía; (*of cavalry*) escuadrón *m;* **troops** tropas; soldados ‖ *intr* agruparse; marcharse en tropel

troop carrier *s* transporte *m* de tropas

trooper [ˈtrupər] *s* soldado de caballería; corcel *m* de guerra; policía *m* de a caballo; (*ship*) transporte *m;* **to swear like a trooper** jurar como un carretero

tro•phy [ˈtrofi] *s* (*pl* **-phies**) trofeo; (*any memento*) recuerdo

tropic [ˈtrɑpɪk] *adj* tropical ‖ *s* trópico

tropical [ˈtrɑpɪkəl] *adj* tropical

tropics o **Tropics** [ˈtrɑpɪks] *spl* zona tropical

troposphere [ˈtrɑpəˌsfɪr] *s* troposfera

trot [trɑt] *s* trote *m* ‖ *v* (*pret & pp* **trotted;** *ger* **trotting**) *tr* hacer trotar; **to trot out** (slang) sacar para mostrar ‖ *intr* trotar

troth [trɔθ] o [troθ] *s* fe *f;* verdad; esponsales *mpl;* **in troth** en verdad; **to plight one's troth** prometer fidelidad; dar palabra de casamiento

troubadour [ˈtrubəˌdor] o [ˈtrubəˌdʊr] *adj* trovadoresco ‖ *s* trovador *m*

trouble [ˈtrʌbəl] *s* apuro, dificultad; confusión, estorbo; conflicto; inquietud, preocupación; pena, molestia; mal *m,* enfermedad; murga; (*of a mechanical nature*) avería, falla, pana; **not to be worth the trouble** no valer la pena; **to pour out one's troubles** jeremiquear; **that's the trouble** ahí está el busilis; **the trouble is that . . .** lo malo es que . . .; **to be in trouble** estar en un aprieto; **to be looking for trouble** buscar tres pies al gato; **to get into trouble** enredarse, meterse en líos; **to take the trouble to** tomarse la molestia de ‖ *tr* apurar; confundir, estorbar; inquietar, preocupar; apenar, afligir; incomodar, molestar; dar que hacer a; **to be troubled with** padecer de; **to trouble oneself** molestarse ‖ *intr* apurarse; inquietarse, preocuparse; molestarse, darse molestia; **to trouble to** molestarse en

trou'ble-free' *adj* sin problemas

trouble lamp *s* lámpara de socorro

trou'ble•mak'er *s* perturbador *m,* alborotador *m*

troubleshooter [ˈtrʌbəlˌʃutər] *s* localizador *m* de averías; (*in disputes*) componedor *m*

troubleshooting [ˈtrʌbəlˌʃutɪŋ] *s* localización de averías; solución de problemas; (*of disputes*) composición, arbitraje *m*

troublesome [ˈtrʌbəlsəm] *adj* molesto, pesado, gravoso; impertinente; perturbador

trouble spot *s* lugar *m* de conflicto

trough [trɔf] o [trɑf] *s* (*e.g., to knead bread*) artesa; (*for water for animals*) abrevadero; (*for feeding animals*) comedero; (*under eaves*) canal *f;* (*between two waves*) seno

troupe [trup] *s* (*in circus*) troupe *f;* (theat) compañía

trousers [ˈtraʊsərz] *spl* pantalones *mpl*

trous•seau [truˈso] o [ˈtruso] *s* (*pl* **-seaux** o **-seaus**) ajuar *m* de novia, equipo de novia

trout [traʊt] *s* trucha

trouvère [truˈvɛr] *s* trovero

trowel [ˈtraʊ•əl] *s* paleta, llana

Troy [trɔɪ] *s* Troya

troy (weight) *s* sistema *m* de pesos troy

truant [ˈtru•ənt] *s* novillero; **to play truant** hacer novillos

truce [trus] *s* tregua

truck [trʌk] *s* carro; vegoneta; camión *m;* autocamión *m;* (*to be moved by hand*) carretilla;

(*of locomotive or car*) carretón *m;* hortalizas para el mercado; (coll) desperdicios; (coll) negocio, relaciones ‖ *tr* acarrear

truck driver *s* camionista *mf;* materialista *m* (Mex)

truck farming *s* horticultura

truck garden *s* huerto de hortalizas (*para el mercado*)

truculent [ˈtrʌkjələnt] o [ˈtrukjələnt] *adj* truculento

trudge [trʌdʒ] *intr* caminar, ir a pie; **to trudge along** marchar con pena y trabajo

true [tru] *adj* verdadero; exacto; constante, uniforme; fiel, leal; alineado; a plomo, a nivel; **to come true** hacerse realidad; **true to life** conforme a la realidad

true copy *s* copia fiel

true-hearted [ˈtruˌhɑrtɪd] *adj* fiel, leal, sincero

true'love' *s* fiel amante *mf;* (bot) hierba de París

truelove knot *s* lazo de amor

truffle [ˈtrʌfəl] o [ˈtrufəl] *s* trufa

truism [ˈtru•ɪzəm] *s* perogrullada, verdad trillada

truly [ˈtruli] *adv* verdaderamente; efectivamente; fielmente; **truly yours** de Ud. atto. y S.S., su seguro servidor

trump [trʌmp] *s* triunfo; (coll) buen chico, buena chica; **no trump** sin triunfo ‖ *tr* matar con un triunfo; aventajar, sobrepujar; **to trump up** forjar, inventar (*para engañar*) ‖ *intr* triunfar

trumpet [ˈtrʌmpɪt] *s* trompeta; trompeta acústica; **to blow one's own trumpet** cantar sus propias alabanzas ‖ *tr* pregonar a son de trompeta ‖ *intr* trompetear

truncheon [ˈtrʌntʃən] *s* cachiporra; bastón *m* de mando

trundle bed [ˈtrʌndəl] *s* cama nido

trunk [trʌŋk] *s* (*of living body, tree, family, railroad*) tronco; (*chest for clothes, etc.*) baúl *m;* (*of an automobile*) portaequipaje *m;* (*of elephant*) trompa; **trunks** (*for swimming*) traje *m* de baño, bañador *m* de hombre (Esp); (*for sports*) shorts *mpl*

trunk hose *spl* trusas

trunk light (*aut*) luz *f* de maletero

truss [trʌs] *s* (*framework*) armadura; haz *m,* paquete *m,* lío; (*for holding back a hernia*) braguero ‖ *tr* armar; empaquetar; espetar; apretar (*barriles*)

trust [trʌst] *s* confianza; esperanza; cargo, custodia; depósito; crédito; obligación; (econ) trust *m,* cartel *m;* (law) fideicomiso; **in trust** en confianza; en depósito; **on trust** a crédito, al fiado ‖ *tr* confiar; confiar en; vender a crédito a ‖ *intr* confiar; fiar; **to trust in** fiarse a o de

trust company *s* banco fideicomisario, banco de depósitos

trust fund *s* fondo de fideicomiso, fondo fiduciario

trustee [trʌsˈti] *s* administrador *m,* comisario; regente (universitario); (*of an estate*) fideicomisario

trusteeship [trʌsˈtiʃɪp] *s* cargo de administrador, fideicomisario; (*of the UN*) fideicomiso

trustful [ˈtrʌstfəl] *adj* confiado

trust'wor'thy *adj* confiable fidedigno

trust•y [ˈtrʌsti] *adj* (comp **-ier;** *super* **-iest**) honrado, fidedigno ‖ *s* (*pl* **-ies**) presidiario fidedigno (*que se ha merecido ciertos privilegios*)

truth [truθ] *s* verdad; **in truth** a la verdad, en verdad

truthful [ˈtruθfəl] *adj* verídico, veraz

try [traɪ] *s* (*pl* **-tries**) ensayo, intento, prueba ‖ *v* (*pret & pp* **tried**) *tr* ensayar, intentar, probar; comprobar, verificar; cansar; exasperar, irritar; (law) procesar (*a una persona*); (law) ver (*un pleito*); **to try on** probarse (*una prenda de vestir*) ‖ *intr* ensayar, probar; esforzarse; **to try to** tratar de, intentar

trying [ˈtraɪ•ɪŋ] *adj* cansado, molesto, irritante; penoso

try'out' *s* prueba; audición

tryst [trɪst] o [traɪst] *s* cita; lugar *m* de cita

T-shirt [ˈtiʃʌrt] *s* camiseta

tsp. *abbr* **teaspoon, teaspoons**

T'-square *s* regla T

tub [tʌb] *s* cuba, tina; (coll) baño; (*clumsy boat*) (coll) carcamán *m,* trompo; (*fat person*) (coll) cuba

tube [tjub] o [tub] *s* tubo; túnel *m;* (*of a tire*) cámara; (coll) ferrocarril subterráneo

tube'less tire *s* cubierta sin cámara

tuber [ˈtjuber] o [ˈtubər] *s* tubérculo

tubercle [ˈtubərkəl] *s* tubérculo

tubercular [tuˈbʌrkjələr] *adj & s* tísico

tuberculosis [tuˌbʌrkjəˈlosɪs] *s* tuberculosis *f*

tuck [tʌk] *s* alforza ‖ *tr* alforzar; **to tuck away** encubrir, ocultar; **to tuck in** arropar, enmantar; remeter (*p.ej., la ropa de cama*); **to tuck up** arremangar (*un vestido*); guarnecer (*la cama*)

tucker [ˈtʌkər] *s* escote *m* ‖ *tr* **—to tucker out** (coll) agotar, cansar

Tuesday [ˈtjuzdi] *s* martes *m*

tuft [tʌft] *s* (*of feathers, hair, etc.*) penacho, copete *m;* manojo, racimo, ramillete *m;* borla ‖ *tr* empenachar ‖ *intr* crecer formando mechones

tug [tʌg] *s* estirón *m,* tirón *m;* (*boat*) remolcador *m* ‖ *v* (*pret & pp* **tugged;** *ger* **tugging**) *tr* arrastrar, tirar con fuerza de; remolcar (*un barco*) ‖ *intr* tirar con fuerza; esforzarse, luchar

tug'boat' *s* remolcador *m*

tug of war *s* lucha de la cuerda

tuition [tjuˈɪʃən] *s* enseñanza; precio de la enseñanza

tulip [ˈtulɪp] *s* tulipán *m*

tumble [ˈtʌmbəl] *s* caída, tumbo; (*somersault*) voltereta, tumba; confusión, desorden *m* ‖ *intr* caerse, rodar; voltear; derribarse, volcarse; brincar, dar saltos; (*into bed*) echarse; (*to* *catch on*) (slang) caer, comprender; **to tumble down** desplomarse, hundirse, venirse abajo

tum'ble-down' *adj* destartalado, desvencijado

tumble dry *tr* secar en secadora

tumbler [ˋtʌmblər] *s* (*for drinking*) vaso; (*person who performs bodily feats*) volatinero; (*self-righting toy*) dominguillo, tentemozo

tumor [ˋtjumər] o [ˋtumər] *s* tumor *m*

tumult [ˋtumʌlt] *s* tumulto

tun [tʌn] *s* barril *m,* tonel *m;* (*measure of capacity for wine*) tonelada

tuna [ˋtunə] *s* atún *m*

tune [tjun] o [tun] *s* tonada, aire *m;* (*manner of acting or speaking*) tono; **in tune** afinado; afinadamente; **in tune with** en sintonía con; **out of tune** desafinado; desafinadamente; **to change one's tune** mudar de tono || *tr* acordar, afinar; (rad) sintonizar; **to tune in** (rad) sintonizar; **to tune out** (rad) desintonizar; **to tune up** poner a punto; poner a tono (*un motor de automóvil*)

tungsten [ˋtʌŋstən] *s* tungsteno

tunic [ˋtjunɪk] o [ˋtunɪk] *s* túnica

tuning *s* (aut) puesto a punto; (rad, telv) sintonía

tuning coil *s* (rad) bobina de sintonía

tuning fork *s* diapasón *m*

Tunis [ˋtunɪs] *s* Túnez (*ciudad*)

Tunisia [tuˋniʒə] *s* Túnez (*país*)

Tunisian [tuˋniʒən] *adj & s* tunecino

tun•nel [ˋtʌnəl] *s* túnel *m;* (min) galería || *v* (*pret & pp* **-neled** o **-nelled;** *ger* **-neling** o **-nelling**) *tr* construir un túnel a través de o debajo de

tunnel vision *s* (opt) visión de túnel; (fig) estrechez *f* de miras

turban [ˋtʌrbən] *s* turbante *m*

turbid [ˋtʌrbɪd] *adj* turbio

turbine [ˋtʌrbɪn] o [ˋtʌrbaɪn] *s* turbina

turbocharger [ˋtʌrbo,tʃɑrdʒər] *s* turbocompresor *m*

turbofan [ˋtʌrbo,fæn] *s* turboventilador *m*

turbojet [ˋtʌrbo,dʒet] *s* turborreactor *m;* avión *m* de turborreacción

turboprop [ˋtʌrbo,prɑp] *s* turbopropulsor *m;* turbohelice *m* avión *m* de turbopropulsión

turbosupercharger [,tʌrboˋsupər,tʃɑrdʒər] *s* turbosupercargador *m*

turbulent [ˋtʌrbjələnt] *adj* turbulento

tureen [tʊˋrin] o [tjʊˋrin] *s* sopera

turf [tʌrf] *s* (*surface layer of grassland*) césped *m;* terrón *m* de césped; (*peat*) turba; **the turf** el hipódromo; las carreras de caballos

turf•man [ˋtʌrfmən] *s* (*pl* **-men** [mən]) turfista *m*

Turk [tʌrk] *s* turco

turkey [ˋtʌrki] *s* pavo; (slang) (theat) bodrio || **Turkey** *s* Turquía

turkey cock *s* pavo

turkey hen *s* pava

turkey vulture *s* aura

Turkish [ˋtʌrkɪʃ] *adj & s* turco

Turkish towel *s* toalla rusa

turmoil [ˋtʌrmɔɪl] *s* alboroto, disturbio, tumulto

turn [tʌrn] *s* vuelta; (*time of action*) turno; (*change of direction*) virada; (*bend*) recodo; (*walk*) paseo corto; (*of a spiral, roll of wire, etc.*) espira; (*complete turn*) vuelta en redondo; aspecto; inclinación; vahido, vértigo; giro, expresión; servicio; (coll) sacudida, susto; **at every turn** a cada paso; **in turn** por turno; **to be one's turn** tocarle a uno, p.ej., **it's your turn** le toca a Ud.; **to take turns** alternar, turnar; **to wait one's turn** aguardar turno, esperar vez || *tr* volver; dar vuelta a (*p.ej., una llave*); torcer (*p.ej., el tobillo*); doblar (*la esquina*); dirigir (*p.ej., los ojos*); (*to make sour*) agriar; (*on a lathe*) tornear; tener (*p.ej., veinte años cumplidos*); **to turn against** predisponer en contra de; **to turn around** volver; voltear; torcer (*las palabras de una persona*); **to turn aside** desviar; **to turn away** desviar; despedir; **to turn back** devolver; hacer retroceder; retrasar (*el reloj*); **to turn down** doblar hacia abajo; invertir; rechazar, rehusar; bajar (*p.ej., el gas*); **to turn in** doblar hacia adentro; entregar; **to turn off** apagar (*la luz, la radio*); cortar (*el agua, gas, etc.*); cerrar (*la llave del agua, gas, etc.; la radio, la televisión*); interrumpir (*la corriente eléctrica*); **to turn on** encender (*la luz*); poner (*la luz, la radio, etc.*); abrir (*la llave del agua, gas, etc.*); establecer (*la corriente eléctrica*); (slang) interesar; excitar; **to turn out** despedir echar al campo (*a los animales*); volver al revés; apagar (*la luz*); hacer, fabricar; **to turn up** doblar hacia arriba; levantar; arremangar (*p.ej., las mangas*); volver (*un naipe*); poner más alto o más fuerte (*la radio*); abrir la llave de (*p.ej., el gas*) || *intr* volver, p.ej., **the road turns to the right** el camino vuelve a la derecha; virar (*un automóvil, un avión, etc.*); (*to revolve*) girar; volverse (*p.ej., la conversación; la opinión; ciertos licores*); **to turn against** cobrar aversión a; rebelarse contra; **to turn around** dar vuelta; **to turn aside** o **away** desviarse; alejarse; **to turn back** volver, regresar; retroceder; **to turn down** doblarse hacia abajo; invertirse; **to turn in** doblarse hacia adentro; replegarse; recognerse, volver a casa; (coll) recogerse, acostarse; **to turn into** entrar en; convertirse en; **to turn on** volverse contra; depender de; versar sobre; ocuparse de; **to turn out badly** salir mal; **to turn out right** acabar bien; **to turn out to be** venir a ser; resultar, salir; **to turn over** volcar, derribarse (*un vehículo*); **to turn up** doblarse hacia arriba; levantarse; acontecer; aparecer

turn'around' *s* giro, cambio; (com) procesamiento

turnaround time *s* (compu) tiempo de devolución, tiempo de respuesta

turn'coat' *s* tránsfuga *mf,* apóstata *mf,* renegado; **to become a turncoat** volver la casaca, cambiarse la camisa

turn'down' *adj* (*collar*) caído || *s* rechazamiento

turning light *s* (aut) intermitente *m*
turning point *s* punto de transición, punto decisivo, revuelta
turnip [ˈtʌrnɪp] *s* nabo; (*cheap watch*) (slang) calentador *m;* (slang) tipo
turn'key' *s* carcelero, llavero de cárcel
turn of life *s* menopausia
turn of mind *s* natural *m,* inclinación
turn'out' *s* (*gathering of people*) con currencia; (*number attending a show, etc.*) entrada; (*side track or passage*) apartadero; (*amount produced*) producción; (*array, outfit*) equipaje *m;* carruaje *m* de lujo
turn'o'ver *s* (*spill, upset*) vuelco; cambio de personal; movimiento de mercancías, rotación; ciclo de compra y venta
turn'pike' *s* carretera o autopista de peaje
turnstile [ˈtʌrn,staɪl] *s* torniquete *m*
turn'ta'ble *s* (*of phonograph*) placa giratoria, plato giratorio; (rr) placa giratoria, plataforma giratoria
turpentine [ˈtʌrpən,taɪn] *s* trementina
turpitude [ˈtʌrpɪ,tjud] *s* torpeza, infamia, vileza
turquoise [ˈtʌrkɔɪz] o [ˈtʌrkwɔɪz] *s* turquesa
turret [ˈtʌrɪt] *s* torrecilla; (archit) torreón *m* (nav) torreta
turtle [ˈtʌrtəl] *s* tortuga; **to turn turtle** derribarse patas arriba
tur'tle•dove' *s* tórtola
tur'tle neck *s* cuello alto
Tuscan [ˈtʌskən] *adj & s* toscano
Tuscany [ˈtʌskəni] *s* la Toscana
tusk [tʌsk] *s* colmillo
tussle [ˈtʌsəl] *s* agarrada ‖ *intr* agarrarse, asirse, reñir
tutor [ˈtjutər] o [ˈtutər] *s* maestro particular; (*guardian*) tutor *m* ‖ *tr* dar enseñanza particular a ‖ *intr* dar enseñanza particular; (coll) tomar lecciones particulares
tuxe•do [tʌkˈsido] *s* (*pl* **-dos**) esmoquin *m,* smoking *m*
TV *abbr* **television**
twaddle [ˈtwɑdəl] *s* charla, tonterías, música celestial ‖ *intr* charlar, decir tonterías
twain [twen] *s* (archaic) dos *m*
twang [twæŋ] *s* (*of musical instrument*) tañido; (*of voice*) timbre *m* nasal ‖ *tr* tocar con un tañido; decir con timbre nasal ‖ *intr* hablar por la nariz
twang•y [twæŋi] *adj* (*comp* **-ier;** *super* **-iest**) (*device*) tañente; (*person, voice*) gangoso
'twas [twɑz], [twəz] *abbr* (poet) **it was** era, fue
tweed [twid] *s* mezcla de lana; traje *m* de mezcla de lana; **tweeds** ropa de mezcla de lana
tweet [twit] *s* pío ‖ *intr* piar
tweeter [ˈtwitər] *s* altavoz *m* para audiofrecuencias elevadas
tweezers [ˈtwizərz] *spl* bruselas, pinzas, tenacillas
twelfth [twɛlfθ] *adj & s* (*in a seris*) duodécimo; (*part*) dozavo ‖ *s* (*in dates*) doce *m*
twelve [twɛlv] *adj & pron* doce ‖ *s* doce *m;* **twelve o'clock** las doce
twentieth [ˈtwɛntɪ•ɪθ] *adj & s* (*in a series*) vigésimo; (*part*) veintavo ‖ *s* (*in dates*) veinte *m*
twen•ty [ˈtwɛnti] *adj & pron* veinte ‖ *s* (*pl* **-ties**) veinte *m*
twerp [twʌrp] *s* (coll) imbécil *mf,* papanatas *mf*
twice [twaɪs] *adv* dos veces
twice'-told' *adj* dicho dos veces; trillado, sabido
twiddle [ˈtwɪdəl] *tr* menear o revolver ociosamente
twig [twɪg] *s* ramito; **twigs** leña menuda
twilight [ˈtwaɪ,laɪt] *adj* crepuscular ‖ *s* crepúsculo
twill [twɪl] *s* tela cruzada; (*pattern of weave*) cruzado ‖ *tr* cruzar
twin [twɪn] *adj & s* gemelo
twin beds *spl* camas gemelas
twin brother *s* hermano gemelo
twin sister *s* hermana gemela
Twin Towers *spl* torres *fpl* gemelas
twine [twaɪn] *s* guita, cuerda, bramante *m* ‖ *tr* enroscar, retorcer ‖ *intr* enroscarse, retorcerse
twinge [twɪndʒ] *s* punzada, dolor agudo
twin'jet' plane *s* avión *m* birreactor
twinkle [ˈtwɪŋkəl] *s* centelleo; (*of eye*) pestañeo; instante *m* ‖ *intr* centellear; pestañear; moverse rápidamente
twin'-screw' *adj* (naut) de doble hélice
twirl [twʌrl] *s* vuelta, giro ‖ *tr* hacer girar; (baseball) lanzar (*la pelota*) ‖ *intr* dar vueltas, girar; piruetear
twist [twɪst] *s* torcedura; enroscadura; curva, recodo; giro, vuelta; propensión, prejuicio; (*of mind or disposition*) sesgo ‖ *tr* torcer; retorcer; enroscar; hacer girar; entrelazar; desviar; (*to give a different meaning to*) torcer ‖ *intr* torcerse; retorcerse; enroscarse; dar vueltas; entrelazarse; desviarse; serpentear; **to twist and turn** (*in bed*) dar vueltas
twisted [ˈtwɪstɪd] *adj* sobornado
twit [twɪt] *v* (*pret & pp* **twitted;** *ger* **twitting**) *tr* reprender (*a uno*) recordando algo desagradable o poniéndole en ridículo
twitch [twɪtʃ] *s* crispatura; ligero temblor ‖ *intr* crisparse; temblar (*p.ej., los párpados*)
twitter [ˈtwɪtər] *s* gorjeo; risita sofocada; inquietud ‖ *intr* gorjear; reír sofocadamente; temblar de inquietud
two [tu] *adj & pron* dos ‖ *s* dos *m;* **to put two and two together** atar cabos, sacar la conclusión evidente; **two o'clock** las dos
two'-cy'cle *adj* (mach) de dos tiempos
two'-cyl'inder *adj* (mach) de dos cilindros
two-edged [ˈtu,ɛdʒd] *adj* de dos filos
two'-faced' *adj* (coll) falso, doble
two'-fist'ed *adj* viril, vigoroso
two hundred *adj & pron* doscientos ‖ *s* doscientos *m*
twosome [ˈtusəm] *s* pareja; pareja de jugadores; juego de dos
two'-time' *tr* (coll) engañar en amor, ser infiel a (*un amante o una amante*)
two-way street *s* calle de doble sentido

tycoon [taɪˋkun] *s* (coll) magnate *m*
type [taɪp] *s* tipo; (*piece*) (typ) tipo, letra; (*pieces collectively*) (typ) letra; letras impresas, letras escritas a máquina ‖ *tr* escribir a máquina, tipiar; representar, simbolizar ‖ *intr* escribir a máquina
type′face′ *s* tipo de letra
type′script′ *s* material escrito a máquina
typesetter [ˋtaɪp,sɛtər] *s* (typ) cajista *mf;* (typ) máquina de componer
typesetting [ˋtaɪp,sɛtɪŋ] *s* composición de textos
type′write′ *v* (*pret* **-wrote** [,rot]; *pp* **-written** [,rɪtən]) *tr & intr* escribir a máquina, tipiar
type′writ′er *s* maq́uina de escribir
type′writ′ing *s* mecanografía; trabajo hecho con máquina de escribir
typhoid fever [ˋtaɪfɔɪd] *s* fiebre tifoidea
typhoon [taɪˋfun] *s* tifón *m*
typical [ˋtɪpɪkəl] *adj* típico
typi•fy [ˋtɪpɪ,faɪ] *v* (*pret & pp* **-fied**) *tr* simbolizar; ser ejemplo o modelo de
typist [ˋtaɪpɪst] *s* mecanógrafo, tipista *mf,* mecanógrafa
typographic(al) [,taɪpəˋgræfɪk(əl)] *adj* tipográfico
typographical error *s* error *m* de imprenta
typography [taɪˋpɑgrəfi] *s* tipografía
tyrannic(al) [tɪˋrænɪk(əl)] o [taɪˋrænɪk(əl)] *adj* tiránico
tyrannous [ˋtɪrənəs] *adj* tirano
tyran•ny [ˋtɪrəni] *s* (*pl* **-nies**) tiranía
tyrant [ˋtaɪrənt] *s* tirano
ty•ro [ˋtaɪro] *s* (*pl* **-ros**) tirón *m,* novicio

U

U, u [ju] vigésima primera letra del alfabeto inglés
U. *abbr* **University**
ubiquitous [juˋbɪkwɪtəs] *adj* ubicuo
udder [ˋʌdər] *s* ubre *f*
UFO [ˋuˋɛfˋo] *s* (letterword) (**Unidentified Flying Object**) OVNI, ovni *m* (objeto volante no identificado)
ugliness [ˋʌglɪnɪs] *s* fealdad; (coll) malhumor *m*
ug•ly [ˋʌgli] *adj* (*comp* **-lier;** *super* **-liest**) feo; (coll) malhumorado
ugly mug *s* (slang) carantamaula
Ukraine [ˋjukren] o [juˋkren] *s* Ucrania
Ukrainian [juˋkrenɪ•ən] *adj & s* ucraniano, ucranio
ulcer [ˋʌlsər] *s* llaga, úlcera; (*corrupting influence*) (fig) llaga
ulcerate [ˋʌlsə,ret] *tr* ulcerar ‖ *intr* ulcerarse
ulterior [ʌlˋtɪrɪ•ər] *adj* ulterior; (*concealed*) escondido, oculto
ultimate [ˋʌltɪmɪt] *adj* último
ultima•tum [,ʌltɪˋmetəm] *s* (*pl* **-tums** o **-ta** [tə]) ultimátum *m*
ultimo [ˋʌltɪ,mo] *adv* de o en el mes próximo pasado
ultrahigh [,ʌltrəˋhaɪ] *adj* (electron) ultraelevado
ultrasound [ˋʌltrə,saʊnd] *s* sonido silencioso, ultrasonido
ultraviolet [,ʌltrəˋvaɪ•əlɪt] *adj & s* ultravioleta, ultraviolado
umbilical cord [ʌmˋbɪlɪkəl] *s* cordón *m* umbilical
umbrage [ˋʌmbrɪdʒ] *s*—**to take umbrage at** resentirse de o por
umbrella [ʌmˋbrɛlə] *s* paraguas *m;* (mil) sombrilla protectora
umbrella stand *s* paragüero
umlaut [ˋʊmlaʊt] *s* inflexión vocálica, metafonía; (*mark*) diéresis *f* ‖ *tr* inflexionar; escribir con diéresis
umpire [ˋʌmpaɪr] *s* árbitro ‖ *tr & intr* arbitrar
umpteen [ˋʌmpˋtin] *adj* (coll) tropecientos
umpteenth [ˋʌmptinθ] *adj* (coll) enésimo
UN [ˋjuˋɛn] *s* (letterword) (**United Nations**) ONU *f* (Organización de las Naciones Unidas)
unable [ʌnˋebəl] *adj* incapaz, imposibilitado, inhábil; **to be unable to** no poder
unabridged [,ʌnəˋbrɪdʒd] *adj* sin abreviar, íntegro
unaccented [ʌnˋæksɛntɪd] o [,ʌnækˋsɛntɪd] *adj* inacentuado
unaccountable [,ʌnəˋkaʊntəbəl] *adj* inexplicable; irresponsable
unaccounted-for [,ʌnəˋkaʊntɪd,fɔr] *adj* inexplicado; no hallado
unaccustomed [,ʌnəˋkʌstəmd] *adj* (*unusual*) desacostumbrado; inhabituado
unafraid [,ʌnəˋfred] *adj* sin miedo
unaligned [,ʌnəˋlaɪnd] *adj* no empeñado
un′-Amer′ican *adj* antiamericano
unanimity [,junəˋnɪmɪti] *s* unanimidad
unanimous [jʊˋnænɪməs] *adj* unánime
unanswerable [ʌnˋænsərəbəl] *adj* incontestable; (*argument*) incontrastable
unappreciative [,ʌnəˋpriʃi,etɪv] *adj* ingrato, desagradecido
unapproachable [,ʌnəˋprotʃəbəl] *adj* inabordable; incomparable, único
unarmed [ʌnˋɑrmd] *adj* desarmado, inerme
unascertainable [ʌn,æsərˋtenəbəl] *adj* inaveriguable
unasked [ʌnˋæskt] *adj* no solicitado; no convidado

unassembled [,ʌnəˈsɛmbəld] *adj* desmontado, desarmado
unassuming [,ʌnəˈsumɪŋ] o [,ʌnəˈsjumɪŋ] *adj* modesto, sencillo
unattached [,ʌnəˈtætʃt] *adj* independiente; (*loose*) suelto; (*not engaged to be married*) no prometido; (law) no embargado; (mil & nav) de reemplazo
unattainable [,ʌnəˈtenəbəl] *adj* inasequible, inalcanzable
unattractive [,ʌnəˈtræktɪv] *adj* poco atrayente, desairado
unavailable [,ʌnəˈveləbəl] *adj* indisponible
unavailing [,ʌnəˈvelɪŋ] *adj* ineficaz, inútil, vano
unavoidable [,ʌnəˈvɔɪdəbəl] *adj* inevitable, ineluctable
unaware [,ʌnəˈwɛr] *adj*—**to be unaware of** no estar al corriente de ‖ *adv* de improviso; sin saberlo
unawares [,ʌnəˈwɛrz] *adv* (*unexpectedly*) de improviso; (*unknowingly*) sin saberlo
unbalanced [ʌnˈbælənst] *adj* desequilibrado
unbandage [ʌnˈbændɪdʒ] *tr* desvendar
un•bar [ʌnˈbɑr] *v* (*pret & pp* **-barred;** *ger* **-barring**) *tr* desatrancar
unbearable [ʌnˈbɛrəbəl] *adj* inaguantable
unbeatable [ʌnˈbitəbəl] *adj* imbatible
unbecoming [,ʌnbɪˈkʌmɪŋ] *adj* inconveniente, indecente; que sienta mal
unbelievable [,ʌnbɪˈlivəbəl] *adj* increíble
unbending [ʌnˈbɛndɪŋ] *adj* inflexible
unbiased o **unbiassed** [ʌnˈbaɪ•əst] *adj* imparcial
un•bind [ʌnˈbaɪnd] *v* (*pret & pp* **-bound** [ˈbaʊnd]) *tr* desatar
unbleached [ʌnˈblitʃt] *adj* sin blanquear
unbolt [ʌnˈbolt] *tr* desatrancar (*p.ej., una puerta*); (*to remove the bolts from*) desempernar
unborn [ʌnˈbɔrn] *adj* no nacido, por nacer, futuro
unbosom [ʌnˈbʊzəm] *tr* confesar, descubrir (*sus pensamientos, sus secretos*); **to unbosom oneself** abrir su pecho, desahogarse
unbound [ʌnˈbaʊnd] *adj* (*book*) sin encuadernar
unbreakable [ʌnˈbrekəbəl] *adj* irrompible
unbuckle [ʌnˈbʌkəl] *tr* deshebillar
unburden [ʌnˈbʌrdən] *tr* descargar; **to unburden oneself of** desahogarse de
unburied [ʌnˈbɛrid] *adj* insepulto
unbutton [ʌnˈbʌtən] *tr* desabotonar
uncalled-for [ʌnˈkɔld,fɔr] *adj* innecesario, no justificado; insolente
uncanny [ʌnˈkæni] *adj* espectral, misterioso; extraordinario, maravilloso
uncared-for [ʌnˈkɛrd,fɔr] *adj* desamparado, descuidado, abandonado
unceasing [ʌnˈsisɪŋ] *adj* incesante
unceremonious [,ʌnsɛriˈmonɪ•əs] *adj* inceremonioso
uncertain [ʌnˈsʌrtən] *adj* incierto
uncertain•ty [ʌnˈsʌrtənti] *s* (*pl* **-ties**) incertidumbre
unchain [ʌnˈtʃen] *tr* desencadenar
unchangeable [ʌnˈtʃendʒəbəl] *adj* incambiable, inmutable
uncharted [ʌnˈtʃɑrtɪd] *adj* inexplorado
unchecked [ʌnˈtʃɛkt] *adj* no verificado; no refrenado; desenfrenado
uncivilized [ʌnˈsɪvɪ,laɪzd] *adj* incivilizado
unclad [ʌnˈklæd] *adj* desvestido
unclaimed [ʌnˈklemd] *adj* sin reclamar; (*mail*) rechazado, sobrante
unclasp [ʌnˈklæsp] *tr* desabrochar
unclassified [ʌnˈklæsɪ,faɪd] *adj* no clasificado; no clasificado como secreto
uncle [ˈʌŋkəl] *s* tío
unclean [ʌnˈklin] *adj* desaseado, sucio; (*ritually prohibited*) impuro
Uncle Sam [sæm] *s* (coll) el Tío Sam
Uncle Tom *s* (pej) el Tío Tom
un•clog [ʌnˈklɑg] *v* (*pret & pp* **-clogged;** *ger* **-clogging**) *tr* desatrancar
unclouded [ʌnˈklaʊdɪd] *adj* despejado
uncollectible [,ʌnkəˈlɛktɪbəl] *adj* incobrable
uncomfortable [ʌnˈkʌmfərtəbəl] *adj* incomodo
uncommitted [,ʌnkəˈmɪtɪd] *adj* no empeñado, no comprometido
uncommon [ʌnˈkɑmən] *adj* raro, poco común
uncompromising [ʌnˈkɑmprə,maɪzɪŋ] *adj* intransigente
unconcerned [,ʌnkənˈsʌrnd] *adj* despreocupado, indiferente
unconditional [,ʌnkənˈdɪʃənəl] *adj* incondicional
uncongenial [,ʌnkənˈdʒinɪ•əl] *adj* antipático; incompatible; desagradable
unconquerable [ʌnˈkɑŋkərəbəl] *adj* inconquistable
unconquered [ʌnˈkɑŋkərd] *adj* invicto
unconscionable [ʌnˈkɑnʃənəbəl] *adj* inescrupuloso; desrazonable, excesivo
unconscious [ʌnˈkɑnʃəs] *adj* inconsciente; (*temporarily deprived of consciousness*) desmayado; (*unintentional*) involuntario
unconsciousness [ʌnˈkɑnʃəsnɪs] *s* inconsciencia; desmayo
unconstitutional [,ʌnkɑnstɪˈtjuʃənəl] *adj* inconstitucional
uncontrollable [,ʌnkənˈtroləbəl] *adj* ingobernable; incontrolable; (*laughter*) inextinguible
unconventional [,ʌnkənˈvɛnʃənəl] *adj* no convencional
uncork [ʌnˈkɔrk] *tr* destapar, descorchar
uncouth [ʌnˈkuθ] *adj* desgarbado, torpe, rústico
uncover [ʌnˈkʌvər] *tr* descubrir
unction [ˈʌŋkʃən] *s* (*anointing*) unción; suavidad hipócrita
unctuous [ˈʌŋktʃʊ•əs] *adj* untuoso; zalamero
uncultivated [ʌnˈkʌltɪ,vetɪd] *adj* inculto (*que no está cultivado; rústico, grosero*)
uncultured [ʌnˈkʌltʃərd] *adj* inculto, rústico, grosero

uncut [ʌnˋkʌt] *adj* sin cortar; (*book or magazine*) intonso
undamaged [ʌnˋdæmɪdʒd] *adj* indemne, ileso
undaunted [ʌnˋdɔntɪd] *adj* impávido, denodado
undecided [ˌʌndɪˋsaɪdɪd] *adj* indeciso
undefeated [ˌʌndɪˋfitɪd] *adj* invicto
undefended [ˌʌndɪˋfɛndɪd] *adj* indefenso
undefiled [ˌʌndɪˋfaɪld] *adj* inmaculado, impoluto
undeniable [ˌʌndɪˋnaɪ•əbəl] *adj* innegable
under [ˋʌndər] *adj* inferior; (*clothing*) interior || *adv* debajo; más abajo; **to go under** hundirse; (*to fail*) fracasar || *prep* bajo, debajo de; inferior a; **under full sail** a vela llena; **under lock and key** bajo llave; **under oath** bajo juramento; **under penalty of death** so pena de muerte; **under sail** a vela; **under separate cover** por separado, bajo cubierta separada; **under steam** bajo presión; **under the hand and seal of** firmado y sellado por; **under the nose of** en las barbas de; **under the weather** algo indispuesto; **under way** en camino
un′der•age′ *adj* menor de edad
un′der•bid′ *v* (*pret & pp* **-bid;** *ger* **-bidding**) *tr* ofrecer menos que
un′der•brush′ *s* maleza
un′der•car′riage *s* carro inferior; (aer) tren *m* de aterrizaje
un′der•clothes′ *s* ropa interior
un′der•con•sump′tion *s* infraconsumo
un′der•cov′er *adj* secreto
underdeveloped [ˌʌndərdɪˋvɛləpt] *adj* subdesarrollado
un′der•dog′ *s* víctima, perdidoso; **the underdogs** los de abajo
underdone [ˋʌndərˌdʌn] *adj* a medio asar, soasado
un′der•es′ti•mate′ *tr* subestimar
un′der•gar′ment *s* prenda de vestir interior
un′der•go′ *v* (*pret* **-went;** *pp* **-gone**) *tr* experimentar; sufrir, padecer
un′der•grad′uate *adj* no graduado; (*course*) para el bachillerato || *s* alumno no graduado de universidad
un′der•ground′ *adj* subterráneo; clandestino || *adv* bajo tierra; ocultamente || *s* ferrocarril subterráneo; movimiento de resistencia
un′der•growth′ *s* maleza
underhanded [ˋʌndərˋhændɪd] *adj* clandestino, taimado, disimulado
un′der•line′ o **un′der•line′** *tr* subrayar
underling [ˋʌndərlɪŋ] *s* subordinado, secuaz *m* servil
un′der•mine′ *tr* socavar, minar
underneath [ˌʌndərˋniθ] *adj* inferior, más bajo || *adv* debajo || *prep* debajo de || *s* parte baja, superficie *f* inferior
undernourished [ˌʌndərˋnʌrɪʃt] *adj* desnutrido
un′der•nour′ish•ment *s* desnutrición
un′der•pass′ *s* paso inferior, paso subterráneo
un′der•pay′ *s* pago insuficiente || *v* (*pret & pp* **-paid**) *tr & intr* pagar insuficientemente
un′der•pin′ *v* (*pret & pp* **-pinned;** *ger* **-pinning**) *tr* apuntalar, socalzar
underprivileged [ˌʌndərˋprɪvɪlɪdʒd] *adj* desheredado, desamparado, desfavorecido
un′der•rate′ *tr* menospreciar
un′der•score′ *tr* subrayar
un′der•sea′ *adj* submarino || **un′der•sea′** *adv* debajo de la superficie del mar
un′der•sec′re•tar′y *s* (*pl* **-ies**) subsecretario
un′der•sell′ *v* (*pret & pp* **-sold**) *tr* vender a menor precio que; (*for less than the actual value*) malbaratar
un′der•shirt′ *s* camiseta (interior)
undersigned [ˋʌndərˌsaɪnd] *adj* infrascrito, subscrito
un′der•skirt′ *s* enaguas, refajo
un′der•stand′ *v* (*pret & pp* **-stood**) *tr* entender, comprender; sobrentender, subentender (*una cosa que no está expresa*) || *intr* entender, comprender
understandable [ˌʌndərˋstændəbəl] *adj* comprensible
understanding [ˌʌndərˋstændɪŋ] *adj* entendedor; (*tolerant, sympathetic*) comprensivo || *s* comprensión; (*intellectual faculty, mind*) entendimiento; (*agreement*) acuerdo; **to come to an understanding** llegar a un acuerdo
un′der•stud′y *s* (*pl* **-ies**) sobresaliente *mf*
un′der•take′ *v* (*pret* **-took;** *pp* **-taken**) *tr* emprender; (*to agree to perform*) comprometerse a
undertaker [ˌʌndərˋtekər] o [ˋʌndərˌtekər] *s* empresario || (ˋʌndərˌtekər] *s* empresario de pompas fúnebres, director *m* de funeraria
undertaking [ˌʌndərˋtekɪŋ] *s* (*task*) empresa; (*pledge*) empeño || [ˋʌndərˌtekɪŋ] *s* (*business of funeral director*) funeraria
un′der•tak′ing establishment *s* funeraria, empresa de pompas fúnebres
un′der•tone′ *s* voz baja; (*background sound*) fondo; color apagado
un′der•tow′ *s* (*countercurrent below surface*) contracorriente *f;* (*on the beach*) resaca
un′derwa′ter fish′ing *s* caza submarina
un′der•wear′ *s* ropa interior, prendas interiores
un′der•world′ *s* (*criminal world*) inframundo, bajos fondos sociales; (*the earth*) mundo terrenal; (*pagan world of the dead*) averno, infierno; (*world under the water*) mundo submarino; (*opposite side of earth*) antípodas
un′der•write′ *v* (*pret* **-wrote;** *pp* **-written**) *tr* subscribir; (*to insure*) asegurar
un′der•writ′er *s* subscritor *m;* asegurador *m;* compañía aseguradora
undeserved [ˌʌndɪˋzʌrvd] *adj* inmerecido
undesirable [ˌʌndɪˋzaɪrəbəl] *adj & s* indeseable *mf*
undetachable [ˌʌndɪˋtætʃəbəl] *adj* inamovible
undignified [ʌnˋdɪgnɪˌfaɪd] *adj* poco digno, poco grave, indecoroso
undiscernible [ˌʌndɪˋzʌrnɪbəl] o [ˌʌndɪˋsʌrnəbəl] *adj* imperceptible, invisible

un•do′ *v* (*pret* **-did;** *pp* **-done**) *tr* deshacer; anular, borrar; arruinar
undoing [ʌnˈdu•ɪŋ] *s* destrucción, pérdida, ruina
undone [ʌnˈdʌn] *adj* sin hacer, por hacer; **to come undone** deshacerse, desatarse; **to leave nothing undone** no dejar nada por hacer
undoubtedly [ʌnˈdaʊtɪdli] *adv* indudablemente, sin duda
undramatic [ˌʌndrəˈmætɪk] *adj* poco dramático
undress [ˈʌnˌdrɛs] o [ʌnˈdrɛs] *s* traje *m* de casa; vestido de calle; (mil) traje de cuartel ‖ [ʌnˈdrɛs] *tr* desnudar; desvendar (*una herida*) ‖ desnudarse
undrinkable [ʌnˈdrɪŋkəbəl] *adj* impotable
undue [ʌnˈdju] *adj* indebido
undulate [ˈʌndjəˌlet] *intr* ondular
unduly [ʌnˈdjuli] *adv* indebidamente
undying [ʌnˈdaɪ•ɪŋ] *adj* imperecedero
unearned increment [ʌnˈʌrnd] *s* plusvalía
unearth [ʌnˈʌrθ] *tr* desenterrar
unearthly [ʌnˈʌrθli] *adj* sobrenatural; fantástico, espectral; extraordinario
uneasy [ʌnˈizi] *adj* (*worried*) inquieto; (*constrained*) encogido, embarazado
uneatable [ʌnˈitəbəl] *adj* incomible
uneconomic(al) [ˌʌnikəˈnɑmɪk(əl)] *adj* poco económico, antieconómico
uneducated [ʌnˈɛdjəˌketɪd] *adj* ineducado, sin instrucción; chontal
unemployed [ˌʌnɛmˈplɔɪd] *adj* desocupado, desempleado; improductivo
unemployment [ˌʌnɛmˈplɔɪmənt] *s* desocupación, desempleo
unemployment compensation *s* prestaciones por desempleo
unemployment insurance *s* seguro de desempleo o desocupación, seguro contra el paro obrero
unending [ʌnˈɛndɪŋ] *adj* interminable
unequal [ʌnˈikwəl] *adj* desigual; **to be unequal to** (*a task*) no estar a la altura de
unequaled o **unequalled** [ʌnˈikwəld] *adj* inigualado
unerring [ʌnˈʌrɪŋ] o [ʌnˈɛrɪŋ] *adj* infalible, seguro
unessential [ˌʌnɛsɛnʃəl] *adj* no esencial
uneven [ʌnˈivən] *adj* desigual; (*number*) impar
unexceptionable [ˌʌnɛkˈsɛpʃənəbəl] *adj* intachable, irreprensible
unexpected [ˌʌnɛkˈspɛktɪd] *adj* inesperado
unexplained [ˌʌnɛkˈsplend] *adj* inexplicado
unexplored [ˌʌnɛkˈsplord] *adj* inexplorado
unexposed [ˌʌnɛkˈspozd] *adj* (phot) inexpuesto
unfading [ʌnˈfedɪŋ] *adj* inmarcesible
unfailing [ʌnˈfelɪŋ] *adj* indefectible; (*inexhaustible*) inagotable
unfair [ʌnˈfɛr] *adj* injusto; desleal, doble, falso; (sport) sucio
unfaithful [ʌnˈfeθfəl] *adj* infiel
unfamiliar [ˌʌnfəˈmɪljər] *adj* poco familiar; poco familiarizado
unfasten [ʌnfˈæsən] *tr* desatacar, desatar, soltar
unfathomable [ʌnˈfæðəməbəl] *adj* insondable
unfavorable [ʌnˈfevərəbəl] *adj* desfavorable
unfeeling [ʌnˈfilɪŋ] *adj* insensible
unfetter [ʌnˈfɛtər] *tr* desencadenar
unfilled [ʌnˈfɪld] *adj* no lleno; por complir, pendiente
unfinished [ʌnˈfɪnɪʃt] *adj* sin acabar; imperfecto, mal acabado; (*business*) pendiente
unfit [ʌnˈfɪt] *adj* impropio, incapaz, inhábil; inservible, inútil
unfold [ʌnˈfold] *tr* desplegar ‖ *intr* desplegarse
unforeseeable [ˌʌnforˈsi•əbəl] *adj* imprevisible
unforeseen [ˌʌnforˈsin] *adj* imprevisto
unforgettable [ˌʌnfərˈgɛtəbəl] *adj* inolvidable
unforgivable [ˌʌnfərˈgɪvəbəl] *adj* imperdonable
unfortunate [ʌnˈfɔrtjənɪt] *adj & s* desgraciado
unfounded [ʌnˈfaʊndɪd] *adj* infundado
unfreeze [ʌnˈfriz] *tr* deshelar, descongelar; (*an account*) desbloquear; (*wages, prices*) descongelar
unfriendly [ʌnˈfrɛndli] *adj* inamistoso; desfavorable
unfruitful [ʌnˈfrutfəl] *adj* infructuoso
unfulfilled [ˌʌnfəlˈfɪld] *adj* incumplido
unfunded [ˈʌnˈfʌndəd] *adj* no dotado de fondos
unfurl [ʌnˈfʌrl] *tr* desplegar, extender
unfurnished [ʌnˈfʌrnɪʃt] *adj* desamueblado
ungainly [ʌnˈgenli] *adj* desgarbado, desmañado
ungentlemanly [ʌnˈdʒɛntəlmənli] *adj* poco caballeroso, descortés
ungird [ʌnˈgʌrd] *tr* desceñir
ungodly [ʌnˈgɑdli] *adj* impío, irreligioso; (*dreadful*) (coll) atroz
ungracious [ʌnˈgreʃəs] *adj* descortés; desagradable
ungrammatical [ˌʌngrəˈmætɪkəl] *adj* ingramatical
ungrateful [ʌnˈgretfəl] *adj* ingrato, desagradecido
ungrudgingly [ʌnˈgrʌdʒɪŋli] *adj* de buena gana, sin quejarse
unguarded [ʌnˈgɑrdɪd] *adj* indefenso; descuidado; (*moment*) de inadvertencia
unguent [ˈʌŋgwənt] *s* ungüento
unhandy [ʌnˈhændi] *adj* inmanejable; (*awkward*) desmañado
unhappiness [ʌnˈhæpɪnɪs] *s* infelicidad
unhap•py [ʌnˈhæpi] *adj* (*comp* **-pier;** *super* **-piest**) infeliz; (*unlucky*) desgraciado; (*fateful*) aciago
unharmed [ʌnˈhɑrmd] *adj* indemne
unharmonious [ˌʌnhɑrˈmonɪ•əs] *adj* inarmónico
unharness [ʌnˈhɑrnɪs] *tr* desenjaezar, desguarnecer; desenganchar
unhealthy [ʌnˈhɛlθi] *adj* malsano
unheard-of [ʌnˈhʌrdˌɑv] *adj* inaudito
unhinge [ʌnˈhɪndʒ] *tr* desgonzar; (fig) desequilibrar, trastornar
unhitch [ʌnˈhɪtʃ] *tr* desenganchar
unho•ly [ʌnˈholi] *adj* (*comp* **-lier;** *super* **-liest**) impío, malo, profano

unhook [ʌnˋhʊk] *tr* desabrochar; desenganchar; (*to take down from a hook*) descolgar
unhoped-for [ʌnˋhopt,fɔr] *adj* inesperado, no esperado
unhorse [ʌnˋhɔrs] *tr* desarzonar
unhurt [ʌnˋhʌrt] *adj* incólume, ileso
unicorn [ˋjunɪ,kɔrn] *s* unicornio
unidentified flying object (UFO) *s* objeto volante no identificado (ovni), OVNI *m*
unification [,junɪfɪˋkeʃən] *s* unificación
uniform [ˋjunɪ,fɔrm] *adj & s* uniforme *m* || *tr* uniformar
uniformi•ty [,junɪˋfɔrmɪti] *s* (*pl* **-ties**) uniformidad
uni•fy [ˋjunɪ,faɪ] *v* (*pret & pp* **-fied**) *tr* unificar
unilateral [,junɪˋlætərəl] *adj* unilateral
unimpeachable [,ʌnɪmˋpitʃəbəl] *adj* irrecusable, intachable
unimportant [,ʌnɪmˋpɔrtənt] *adj* poco importante; intrascendente
uninhabited [,ʌnɪnˋhæbɪtɪd] *adj* inhabitado
uninspired [,ʌnɪnˋspaɪrd] *adj* sin inspiración; aburrido, fastidioso
unintelligent [,ʌnɪnˋtɛlɪdʒənt] *adj* ininteligente
unintelligible [,ʌnɪnˋtɛlɪdʒɪbəl] *adj* ininteligible
uninterested [ʌnˋɪntrɪstɪd] o [ʌnˋɪntə,rɛstɪd] *adj* desinteresado
uninteresting [ʌnˋɪntə,rɛstɪŋ] *adj* poco interesante
uninterrupted [,ʌnɪntəˋrʌptɪd] *adj* ininterrumpido
union [ˋjunjən] *s* unión; (*organization of workmen*) gremio obrero, sindicato; unión matrimonial
unionize [ˋjunjə,naɪz] *tr* agremiar || *intr* agremiarse
union shop *s* taller *m* de obreros agremiados
union suit *s* traje *m* interior de una sola pieza
unique [jʊˋnik] *adj* único
unisex [ˋjunɪˋsɛks] *adj* unisex
unison [ˋjunisən] *s* unisonancia; **in unison (with)** al unísono (de)
unit [ˋjunɪt] *adj* unitario || *s* unidad; (mach & elec) grupo
unite [jʊˋnaɪt] *tr* unir || *intr* unirse
united [jʊˋnaɪtɪd] *adj* unido
United Kingdom *s* Reino Unido
United Nations *spl* Naciones Unidas
United States *adj* estadounidense || **the United States** *s* los Estados Unidos *mpl;* Estados Unidos *msg;* **the United States of America** los Estados Unidos de América
United States of Mexico, the los Estados Unidos Mexicanos
uni•ty [ˋjunɪti] *s* (*pl* **-ties**) unidad
univ. *abbr* **universal, university**
universal [,junɪˋvʌrsəl] *adj* universal
universal joint *s* cardán *m,* junta universal
universal product code (UPC) *s* código universal de producto
universe [ˋjunɪ,vʌrs] *s* universo
universi•ty [,junɪˋvʌrsɪti] *adj* universitario || *s* (*pl* **-ties**) universidad
university campus *s* ciudad universitaria
unjust [ʌnˋdʒʌst] *adj* injusto
unjustified [ʌnˋdʒʌstɪ,faɪd] *adj* injustificado
unkempt [ʌnˋkɛmpt] *adj* despeinado
unkind [ʌnˋkaɪnd] *adj* poco amable; duro, despiadado
unknowable [ʌnˋno•əbəl] *adj* inconocible insabible
unknowingly [ʌnˋno•ɪŋli] *adv* desconocidamente, sin saberlo
unknown [ʌnˋnon] *adj* desconocido, ignoto, incógnito || *s* desconocido; (math) incógnita
unknown quantity *s* (math & fig) incógnita
unknown soldier *s* soldado desconocido
unlace [ʌnˋles] *tr* desenlazar; desatar (*los cordones del zapato*)
unlatch [ʌnˋlætʃ] *tr* abrir levantando el picaporte
unlawful [ʌnˋlɔfəl] *adj* ilegal
unleaded [ʌnˋlɛdɪd] *adj* sin plomo
unleash [ʌnˋliʃ] *tr* destraillar; soltar, desencadenar
unleavened [ʌnˋlɛvənd] *adj* ázimo
unless [ʌnˋlɛs] *conj* a menos que, a no ser que
unlettered [ʌnˋlɛtərd] *adj* iletrado, indocto; sin rotular; (*illiterate*) analfabeto
unlike [ʌnˋlaɪk] *adj* desemejante; desemejante de; (*poles of a magnet*) (elec) de nombres contrarios; (elec) de signo contrario || *prep* a diferencia de
unlikely [ʌnˋlaɪkli] *adj* improbable
unlimber [ʌnˋlɪmbər] *tr* preparar para la acción || *intr* prepararse para la acción
unlined [ʌnˋlaɪnd] *adj* (*coat*) sin forro; (*paper*) sin rayar; (*face*) sin arrugas
unload [ʌnˋlod] *tr* descargar; (coll) deshacerse de || *intr* descargar
unloading [ʌnˋlodɪŋ] *s* descarga, descargue *m*
unlock [ʌnˋlɑk] *tr* abrir (*p.ej., una puerta*); (typ) desapretar
unloose [ʌnˋlus] *tr* aflojar, soltar, desatar
unloved [ʌnˋlʌvd] *adj* desamado
unlovely [ʌnˋlʌvli] *adj* desgraciado
unluck•y [ʌnˋlʌki] *adj* (*comp* **-ier;** *super* **-iest**) desgraciado, desdichado; aciago, nefasto; de mala suerte; **to be unlucky** quedar mal parado
un•make [ʌnˋmek] *v* (*pret & pp* **-made** [ˋmed]) *tr* deshacer; destruir
unmanageable [ʌnˋmænɪdʒəbəl] *adj* inmanejable
unmanly [ʌnˋmænli] *adj* afeminado, poco viril; bajo, cobarde
unmannerly [ʌnˋmænərli] *adj* descortés, malcriado
unmarketable [ʌnˋmɑrkɪtəbəl] *adj* incomerciable
unmarriageable [ʌnˋmærɪdʒəbəl] *adj* incasable
unmarried [ʌnˋmærid] *adj* soltero
unmarried mother *s* madre soltera

unmask [ʌn'mæsk] *tr* desenmascarar || *intr* desenmascararse
unmatchable [ʌn'mætʃəbəl] *adj* incomparable, sin igual; (*price*) incompetible
unmerciful [ʌn'mʌrsɪfəl] *adj* despiadado, inclemente
unmesh [ʌn'mɛʃ] *tr* desengranar || *intr* desengranarse
unmindful [ʌn'maɪndfəl] *adj* desatento, descuidado; **to be unmindful of** olvidar, no pensar en
unmistakable [,ʌnmɪs'tekəbəl] *adj* inequívoco, inconfundible
unmixed [ʌn'mɪkst] *adj* puro, sin mezcla
unmoor [ʌn'mʊr] *tr* desamarrar (*un buque*); desaferrar (*las áncoras*)
unmotivated [,ʌn'motɪ,vetɪd] *adj* inmotivado
unmoved [ʌn'muvd] *adj* fijo, inmoto; impasible
unmuzzle [,ʌn'mʌzəl] *tr* desbozalar
unnatural [ʌn'nætʃərəl] *adj* innatural; (*artificial, forced*) afectado; anormal; inhumano
unnecessary [ʌn'nɛsə,sɛri] *adj* innecessario
unnerve [ʌn'nʌrv] *tr* acobardar, trastornar
unnoticeable [ʌn'notɪsəbəl] *adj* imperceptible
unnoticed [ʌn'notɪst] *adj* inadvertido
unobliging [,ʌnə'blaɪdʒɪŋ] *adj* poco servicial, poco amable
unobserved [,ʌnəb'zʌrvd] *adj* inadvertido, sin ser visto
unobtainable [,ʌnəb'tenəbəl] *adj* inencontrable, inasequible
unobtrusive [,ʌnəb'trusɪv] *adj* discreto, reservado
unoccupied [ʌn'ɑkjə,paɪd] *adj* libre, vacante; (*not busy*) desocupado
unofficial [,ʌnə'fɪʃəl] *adj* extraoficial, oficioso
unopened [ʌn'opənd] *adj* sin abrir; (*book*) no cortado
unorthodox [ʌn'ɔrθə,dɑks] *adj* inortodoxo
unpack [ʌn'pæk] *tr* desembalar, desempaquetar
unpaid ['ʌn'ped] *adj* (*work*) no retribuido; (*debt*) impago, pendiente
unpalatable [ʌn'pælətəbəl] *adj* desabrido, ingustable
unparalleled [ʌn'pærə,lɛld] *adj* incomparable, sin par, sin igual
unpardonable [ʌn'pɑrdənəbəl] *adj* imperdonable
unpatriotic [,ʌnpetrɪ'ɑtɪk] o [,ʌnpætrɪ'ɑtɪk] *adj* antipatriótico
unperceived [,ʌnpər'sivd] *adj* inadvertido
unperturbable [,ʌnpər'tʌrbəbəl] *adj* infracto, imperturbable
unpleasant [ʌn'plɛzənt] *adj* antipático, desagradable; sangrigordo, sangripesado; bofe (CAm)
unpopular [ʌn'pɑpjələr] *adj* impopular
unpopularity [ʌn,pɑpjə'lærɪti] *s* impopularidad
unprecedented [ʌn'prɛsɪ,dɛntɪd] *adj* sin precedente, inaudito
unprejudiced [ʌn'prɛdʒədɪst] *adj* sin prejuicios, imparcial
unpremeditated [,ʌnprɪ'mɛdɪ,tetɪd] *adj* impremeditado
unprepared [,ʌnprɪ'pɛrd] *adj* desprevenido; falto de preparación
unprepossessing [,ʌnpripə'zɛsɪŋ] *adj* poco atrayente
unpresentable [,ʌnprɪ'zɛntəbəl] *adj* impresentable
unpretentious [,ʌnprɪ'tɛnʃəs] *adj* modesto, sencillo
unprincipled [ʌn'prɪnsɪpəld] *adj* sin principios, sin conciencia
unproductive [,ʌnprə'dʌktɪv] *adj* improductivo
unprofitable [ʌn'prɑfɪtəbəl] *adj* no provechoso, inútil
unpronounceable [,ʌnprə'naʊnsəbəl] *adj* impronunciable
unpropitious [,ʌnprə'pɪʃəs] *adj* impropicio
unpublished [ʌn'pʌblɪʃt] *adj* inédito
unpunished [ʌn'pʌnɪʃt] *adj* impune
unpurchasable [ʌn'pʌrtʃəsəbəl] *adj* incomprable
unqualified [ʌn'kwɑlə,faɪd] *adj* (*total*) incondicional, sin restricciones, absoluto; (*without qualifications*) sin titulación, no titulado, no calificado, inhábil
unquenchable [ʌn'kwɛntʃəbəl] *adj* inextinguible
unquestionable [ʌn'kwɛstʃənəbəl] *adj* incuestionable
unrav•el [ʌn'rævəl] *v* (*pret & pp* **-eled** o **-elled;** *ger* **-eling** o **-elling**) *tr* deshebrar; desenredar, desenmarañar || *intr* desenredarse, desenmarañarse
unreachable [ʌn'ritʃəbəl] *adj* inalcanzable
unreal [ʌn'ri•əl] *adj* irreal
unreali•ty [,ʌnrɪ,ælɪti] *s* (*pl* **-ties**) irrealidad
unreasonable [ʌn'rizənəbəl] *adj* irrazonable, desrazonable
unrecognizable [ʌn'rɛkəg,naɪzəbəl] *adj* irreconocible
unreel [ʌn'ril] *tr* desenrollar || *intr* desenrollarse
unrefined [,ʌnrɪ,faɪnd] *adj* no refinado, impuro; grosero, rudo, tosco
unrelenting [,ʌnrɪ'lɛntɪŋ] *adj* inexorable, inflexible, implacable
unreliable [,ʌnrɪ'laɪ•əbəl] *adj* indigno de confianza, informal
unremitting [,ʌnrɪ'mɪtɪŋ] *adj* constante, incesante; infatigable
unrenewable [,ʌnrɪ'nju•əbəl] o [,ʌnrɪ'nu•əbəl] *adj* irrenovable; (com) improrrogable
unrented [ʌn'rɛntɪd] *adj* desalquilado
unrepentant [,ʌnrɪ'pɛntənt] *adj* impenitente
unrequited love [,ʌnrɪ'kwaɪtɪd] *s* amor no correspondido
unresponsive [,ʌnrɪ'spɑnsɪv] *adj* insensible, frío, desinteresado
unrest [ʌn'rɛst] *s* intranquilidad, inquietud; alboroto, desorden *m*
un•rig [ʌn'rɪg] *v* (*pret & pp* **-rigged;** *ger* **-rigging**) *tr* (naut) desaparejar

unrighteous [ʌnˋraɪtʃəs] *adj* injusto, malvado, vicioso
unripe [ʌnˋraɪp] *adj* inmaturo, verde; prematuro, precoz
unrivaled o **unrivalled** [ʌnˋraɪvəld] *adj* sin rival, sin par
unroll [ʌnˋrol] *tr* desenrollar, desplegar
unromantic [ˌʌnroˋmæntɪk] *adj* poco romántico
unruffled [ʌnˋrʌfəld] *adj* tranquilo, sereno
unruly [ʌnˋruli] *adj* ingobernable, indómito, revoltoso
unsaddle [ʌnˋsædəl] *tr* desensillar (*un caballo*); desarzonar (*al jinete*)
unsafe [ʌnˋsef] *adj* inseguro, peligroso
unsaid [ʌnˋsɛd] *adj* callado, no dicho
unsalable [ʌnˋseləbəl] *adj* invendible
unsanitary [ʌnˋsænɪˌtɛri] *adj* antihigiénico, insalubre
unsatisfactory [ʌnˌsætɪsˋfæktəri] *adj* insatisfactorio, poco satisfactorio
unsatisfied [ʌnˋsætɪsˌfaɪd] *adj* insatisfecho
unsavory [ʌnˋsevəri] *adj* desabrido; (fig) infame, deshonroso
unscathed [ʌnˋskeðd] *adj* ileso, sano y salvo
unscientific [ˌʌnsaɪ•ənˋtɪfɪk] *adj* antiscientífico
unscrew [ʌnˋskru] *tr* destornillar ‖ *intr* destornillarse
unscrupulous [ʌnˋskrupjələs] *adj* inescrupuloso
unseal [ʌnˋsil] *tr* desellar; (fig) abrir
unseasonable [ʌnˋsizənəbəl] *adj* intempestivo, inoportuno
unseaworthy [ʌnˋsiˌwʌrði] *adj* innavegable
unseemly [ʌnˋsimli] *adj* impropio, indecoroso, indigno
unseen [ʌnˋsin] *adj* invisible, oculto
unselfish [ʌnˋsɛlfɪʃ] *adj* desinteresado, generoso, altruísta
unsettled [ʌnˋsɛtəld] *adj* inhabitado, despoblado; sin residencia fija; indeciso; descompuesto; (*bills*) por pagar
unshackle [ʌnˋʃækəl] *tr* desherrar, desencadenar
unshaken [ʌnˋʃekən] *adj* imperturbado
unshapely [ʌnˋʃepli] *adj* desproporcionado, mal formado
unshatterable [ʌnˋʃætərəbəl] *adj* inastillable
unshaven [ʌnˋʃevən] *adj* sin afeitar
unsheathe [ʌnˋʃið] *tr* desenvainar
unshod [ʌnˋʃɑd] *adj* descalzo; (*horse*) desherrado
unshrinkable [ʌnˋʃrɪŋkəbəl] *adj* inencogible
unsightly [ʌnˋsaɪtli] *adj* feo, de aspecto malo, repugnante
unsinkable [ʌnˋsɪŋkəbəl] *adj* insumergible
unskilled [ʌnˋskɪld] *adj* inexperto; (*worker*) no calificado; (*work*) no especializado
unskillful [ʌnˋskɪlfəl] *adj* desmañado
unsnarl [ʌnˋsnɑrl] *tr* desenredar
unsociable [ʌnˋsoʃəbəl] *adj* insociable, huraño
unsold [ʌnˋsold] *adj* invendido
unsolder [ʌnˋsɑdər] *tr* desoldar; (fig) desunir, separar
unsophisticated [ˌʌnsəˋfɪstɪˌketɪd] *adj* ingenuo, natural, sencillo
unsound [ʌnˋsaʊnd] *adj* poco firme; falso, erróneo; (*decayed*) podrido; (*sleep*) ligero
unsown [ʌnˋson] *adj* yermo, no sembrado
unspeakable [ʌnˋspikəbəl] *adj* indecible, inefable; (*atrocious, infamous*) incalificable
unsportsmanlike [ʌnˋsportsmənˌlaɪk] *adj* antideportivo, poco deportivo
unstable [ʌnˋstebəl] *adj* inestable
unsteady [ʌnˋstɛdi] *adj* inseguro, inestable; irresoluto, inconstante; poco juicioso
unstinted [ʌnˋstɪntɪd] *adj* no escatimado, generoso, liberal
unstitch [ʌnˋstɪtʃ] *tr* descoser
un•stop [ʌnˋstɑp] *v* (*pret & pp* **-stopped;** *ger* **-stopping**) *tr* destaponar
unstressed [ʌnˋstrɛst] *adj* sin énfasis; (*syllable*) inacentuado
unstrung [ʌnˋstrʌŋ] *adj* nervioso, trastornado
unsuccessful [ˌʌnsəkˋsɛsfəl] *adj* (*person*) desairado; (*undertaking*) impróspero; **to be unsuccessful** no tener éxito
unsuitable [ʌnˋsutəbəl] o [ʌnˋsjutəbəl] *adj* inadecuado, inconveniente
unsurpassable [ˌʌnsərˋpæsəbəl] *adj* insuperable
unsuspected [ˌʌnsəsˋpɛktɪd] *adj* insospechado
unswerving [ʌnˋswʌrvɪŋ] *adj* firme, inmutable, resoluto
unsymmetrical [ˌʌnsɪˋmɛtrɪkəl] *adj* asimétrico, disimétrico
unsympathetic [ˌʌnsɪmpəˋθɛtɪk] *adj* incompasivo, indiferente
unsystematic(al) [ˌʌnsɪstəˋmætɪk(əl)] *adj* poco sistemático, sin sistema
untactful [ʌnˋtæktfəl] *adj* indiscreto, falto de tacto
untamed [ʌnˋtemd] *adj* indomado, bravío
untangle [ʌnˋtæŋgəl] *tr* desenredar, desenmarañar
unteachable [ʌnˋtitʃəbəl] *adj* indócil
untenable [ʌnˋtɛnəbəl] *adj* insostenible
unthankful [ʌnˋθæŋkfəl] *adj* ingrato, desagradecido
unthinkable [ʌnˋθɪŋkəbəl] *adj* impensable; inconcebible, inimaginable
unthinking [ʌnˋθɪŋkɪŋ] *adj* irreflexivo, desatento; irracional, instintivo
untidy [ʌnˋtaɪdi] *adj* desaseado, desaliñado; descachalandrado
un•tie [ʌnˋtaɪ] *v* (*pret & pp* **-tied;** *ger* **-tying**) *tr* desatar; deshacer (*un nudo, una cuerda*); (*to free from restraint*) soltar; resolver ‖ *intr* desatarse
until [ʌnˋtɪl] *prep* hasta ‖ *conj* hasta que; **to wait until** aguardar a que, esperar a que
untillable [ʌnˋtɪləbəl] *adj* incultivable
untimely [ʌnˋtaɪmli] *adj* intempestivo
untiring [ʌnˋtaɪrɪŋ] *adj* incansable

untold [ʌn'told] *adj* nunca dicho; (*uncounted*) innumerable, incalculable
untouchable [ʌn'tʌtʃəbəl] *adj* intangible || *s* intocable *mf*
untouched [ʌn'tʌtʃt] *adj* intacto; íntegro; impasible; no mencionado
untoward [ʌn'tord] *adj* desfavorable; indecoroso
untrammeled o **untrammelled** [ʌn'træməld] *adj* libre, sin trabas
untried [ʌn'traɪd] *adj* no probado, no ensayado
untroubled [ʌn'trʌbləd] *adj* tranquilo, sosegado
untrue [ʌn'tru] *adj* falso; infiel
untrustworthy [ʌn'trʌst,wʌrði] *adj* indigno de confianza
untruth [ʌn'truθ] *s* falsedad, mentira
untruthful [ʌn'truθfəl] *adj* falso, mentiroso
untwist [ʌn'twɪst] *tr* destorcer || *intr* destorcerse
unused [ʌn'juzd] *adj* inutilizado, no usado; nuevo; **unused to** [ʌn'juzdtʊ] o [ʌn'justʊ] *adj* no acostumbrado a
unusual [ʌn'juʒʊ•əl] *adj* inusual, insólito
unutterable [ʌn'ʌtərəbəl] *adj* indecible, inexpresable
unvanquished [ʌn'væŋkwɪʃt] *adj* invicto
unvarnished [ʌn'vɑrnɪʃt] *adj* sin barnizar; (fig) sencillo, sin adornos
unveil [ʌn'vel] *tr* quitar el velo a; descubrir, develar, inaugurar, (*una estatua*) || *intr* quitarse el velo
unveiling [ʌn'velɪŋ] *s* develación, inauguración
unventilated [ʌn'vɛntɪ,letɪd] *adj* sin ventilar
unvoice [ʌn'vɔɪs] *tr* afonizar, ensordecer || *intr* afonizarse, ensordecerse
unwanted [ʌn'wɑntɪd] *adj* indeseado
unwarranted [ʌn'wɑrəntɪd] *adj* injustificado; no autorizado; sin garantía
unwary [ʌn'wɛri] *adj* incauto, imprudente
unwavering [ʌn'wevərɪŋ] *adj* firme, determinado, resuelto
unwelcome [ʌn'wɛlkəm] *adj* mal acogido; importuno, molesto
unwell [ʌn'wɛl] *adj* indispuesto, enfermo; (coll) menstruante
unwholesome [ʌn'holsəm] *adj* insalubre
unwieldy [ʌn'wildi] *adj* inmanejable, abultado, pesado
unwilling [ʌn'wɪlɪŋ] *adj* desinclinado, maldispuesto, renuente
unwillingly [ʌn'wɪlɪŋli] *adv* de mala gana
un•wind [ʌn'waɪnd] *v* (*pret & pp* **-wound** ['waʊnd]) *tr* desenvolver; (*rewind*) rebobinar || *intr* desenvolverse; distenderse (*el muelle del reloj*)
unwise [ʌn'waɪz] *adj* indiscreto, malaconsejado
unwished-for [ʌn'wɪʃt,fɔr] *adj* indeseado
unwitting [ʌn'wɪtɪŋ] *adj* inadvertido, inconsciente
unwonted [ʌn'wʌntɪd] *adj* poco común, raro, insólito
unworldly [ʌn'wʌrldi] *adj* no terrenal, no mundano, espiritual
unworthy [ʌn'wʌrði] *adj* indigno, desmerecedor
un•wrap [ʌn'ræp] *v* (*pret & pp* **-wrapped;** *ger* **wrapping**) *tr* desenvolver, desempapelar
unwrinkle [ʌn'rɪŋkəl] *tr* desarrugar || *intr* desarrugarse
unwritten [ʌn'rɪtən] *adj* no escrito; (*blank*) en blanco; oral
unyielding [ʌn'jildɪŋ] *adj* firme, inflexible; terco, reacio
unyoke [ʌn'jok] *tr* desuncir
up [ʌp] *adj* ascendente; alto, elevado; derecho, en pie; terminado; cumplido; levantado de la cama; **to be up and about** estar levantado (*el que estaba enfermo*) || *s* subida; **ups and downs** altibajos, vicisitudes || *adv* arriba; en el aire; hacia arriba; al norte; **to be up** estar levantado; vencer (*un plazo*); **to be up in arms** estar sobre las armas; protestar vehementemente; **to be up to a person** tocarle a una persona; **to get up** levantarse; **to go up** subir; **to keep up** mantener; continuar; mantenerse firme; **to keep up with** correr parejas con; **up above** allá arriba; **up against it** (slang) en apuros; **up to** hasta; (*capable of*) a la altura de; (*informed of*) al corriente de; (*scheming*) armando, tramando; **what is up?** ¿qué pasa? || *prep* subiendo; **up the river** río arriba; **up the street** calle arriba
up-and-coming ['ʌpən'kʌmɪŋ] *adj* (coll) prometedor
up-and-doing ['ʌpən'du•ɪŋ] *adj* (coll) emprendedor
up-and-up ['ʌpən'ʌp] *s*—**on the up-and-up** (coll) mejorándose; (coll) abiertamente, sin dolo
up•braid′ *tr* regañar, reprender
upbringing ['ʌp,brɪŋɪŋ] *s* educación, crianza
UPC *abbr* **universal product code**
up′coun′try *adv* (coll) hacia el interior, tierra adentro || *s* (coll) interior *m* del país
up′-date *s* últimas novedades, información actualizada; (*act*) actualización
up•date′ *tr* poner al día
up′grade *s* ascenso; aumento de categoría; mejora; (compu) actualización
up′grade′ *tr* elevar de categoría, ascendar; aumentar, mejorar; (compu) actualizar
upheaval [ʌp'hivəl] *s* trastorno, cataclismo
up′hill′ *adj* ascendente; arduo, difícil, penoso || **up′hill′** *adv* cuesta arriba
up•hold′ *v* (*pret & pp* **-held**) *tr* levantar; apoyar, sostener; defender
upholster [ʌp'holstər] *tr* tapizar
upholsterer [ʌp'holstərər] *s* tapicero
upholster•y [ʌp'holstəri] *s* (*pl* **-ies**) tapicería
up′keep′ *s* conservación, manutención; gastos de conservación, gastos de entretenimiento
upland ['ʌplənd] o ['ʌplænd] *adj* alto, elevado || *s* tierra alta, terreno elevado
up′lift′ *s* (*lifting*) elevación, levantamiento; mejora social; (*moral or spiritual improvement*)

edificación || **up•lift′** *tr* elevar, levantar; edificar
up′link *s* (aerosp) transmisión de datos de la tierra al satélite
upon [ə`pɑn] *prep* en, sobre, encima de; **upon** + *ger* al + *inf*, p.ej., **upon arriving** al llegar; **upon my word!** ¡por mi palabra!
upper [`ʌpər] *adj* alto, superior; (*country*) interior; (*clothing*) exterior || *s* (*of shoe*) pala; **on one's uppers** con las suelas gastadas; (coll) andrajoso, pobre, sin blanca
upper berth *s* litera alta, cama alta
up′percase′ *s* (typ) caja alta
uppercase letter *s* letra mayúscula
upper classes *spl* altas clases
upper hand *s* dominio, ventaia; **to have the upper hand** tener vara alta
upper middle class *s* alta burguesía
up′per•most′ *adj* (el) más alto; (el) principal || *adv* en lo más alto primero, en primer lugar
uppish [`ʌpɪʃ] o **uppity** [`ʌpətɪ] *adj* (coll) copetudo, arrogante
up•raise′ *tr* levantar
up′right′ *adj* derecho, vertical; probo, recto; (compu) de torre || *adv* verticalmente || *s* montante *m*
upright piano *s* piano vertical
uprising [ʌp`raɪzɪŋ] [ [`ʌp,raɪzɪŋ] *s* insurrección, levantamiento
up′roar′ *s* alboroto, conmoción, tumulto
uproarious [ʌp`rorɪ•əs] *adj* tumultuoso; (*noisy*) ruidoso; (*funny*) muy cómico
up•root′ *tr* desarraigar
up′scale *adj* acomodado; de primera calidad
up•set′ o **up′set′** *adj* (*overturned*) volcado; trastornado; indispuesto || **up′set′** *s* (*overturn*) vuelco; (*unexpected defeat*) contratiempo; (*disturbance*) trastorno; (*illness*) indisposición, enfermedad || **up•set′** *v* (*pret & pp* **-set;** *ger* **-setting**) *tr* volcar; trastornar; indisponer || *intr* volcar
upset price *s* precio mínimo fijado en una subasta
upsetting [ʌp`sɛtɪŋ] *adj* desconcertante
up′shot′ *s* conclusión, resultado; esencia, quid *m*
up′side′ *s* parte *f* superior, lado superior; **on the upside** (*said of prices*) subiendo
upside down *adv* alrevés, lo de arriba abajo, patas arriba; en confusión, revuelto; **to turn upside down** volcar; trastornar; volcarse; trastornarse
up′stage′ *adj* situado al fondo de la escena; (coll) altanero, arrogante || *adv* al fondo de la escena || **up′stage′** *tr* (coll) mirar por encima del hombro, desairar
up′stairs′ *adj* de arriba || *adv* arriba || *s* piso superior, pisos superiores
upstanding [ʌp`stændɪŋ] *adj* derecho; gallardo; probo, recto
up′start′ *adj & s* advenedizo
up′stream′ *adv* aguas arriba, río arriba
up′stroke′ *s* carrera ascendente
up′swing′ *s* movimiento hacia arriba; mejora notable; **on the upswing** mejorando notablemente
up′tight *adj* (coll) tenso, nervioso; (*annoyed*) enojado, enfadado; (*conventional*) inflexible, rígido; (*short of money*) apretado, necesitado; **don't get so uptight** no te pongas tan neura
up′-to-date′ *adj* corriente; reciente, moderno; de última hora, de última moda
up′-to-the-min′ute *adj* al día, de actualidad
up′town′ *adj* de la parte alta de la ciudad || *adv* en la parte alta de la ciudad
up train *s* tren *m* ascendente
up′trend′ *s* tendencia al alza
up′turn′ *s* alza, subida, mejora
upturned [ʌp`tʌrnd] *adj* revuelto; (*part of clothing*) arremangado; (*nose*) respingada
upward [`ʌpwərd] *adj* ascendente || *adv* hacia arriba; **upward of** más de
upward mobility *s* movilidad ascendente
Ural [`jʊrəl] *adj* ural || **Urals** *spl* Urales *mpl*
uranium [jʊ`renɪ•əm] *s* uranio
Uranus [`jʊrənəs], [jʊ`renəs] *s* (astr, myth) Urano
urban [`ʌrbən] *adj* urbano (*perteneciente a la ciudad*)
urbane [ʌr`ben] *adj* urbano (*atento, cortés*)
urban development *s* urbanística
urban guerrilla *s* guerrillero urbano
urbanite [`ʌrbə,naɪt] *s* ciudadano
urbanity [ʌr`bænɪti] *s* urbanidad
urbanize [`ʌrbə,naɪz] *tr* urbanizar
urchin [`ʌrtʃɪn] *s* pilluelo, galopín *m;* patojo (CAm)
ure•thra [jʊ`riθrə] *s* (*pl* **-thras** o **-thrae** [θri]) uretra
urge [ʌrdʒ] *s* impulso, estímulo || *tr* apremiar, impeler, estimular; pedir con insistencia; (*to try to persuade*) instar || *intr* instar
urgen•cy [`ʌrdʒənsi] *s* (*pl* **-cies**) urgencia; instancia, apremio
urgent [`ʌrdʒənt] *adj* urgente; apremiante
urinal [`jʊrɪnəl] *s* (*receptacle*) orinal *m;* (*place*) urinario
urinary [`jʊrɪ,nɛri] *adj* urinario
urinate [`jʊrɪ,net] *tr* orinar (*p.ej., sangre*) || *intr* orinar, orinarse; (coll) hacer pipí
urine [`jʊrɪn] *s* orina, orines *mpl;* (coll) pipí *m*
urn [ʌrn] *s* (*decorative vase*) jarrón *m;* cafetera o tetera con grifo; (*to hold ashes of the dead after cremation*) urna
urology [jʊ`rɑlədʒi] *s* urología
Uruguay [`jʊrə,gwaɪ] *s* el Uruguay
Uruguayan [,jʊrə`gwaɪ•ən] *adj & s* uruguayo
us [ʌs] *pron pers* nos; nosotros; **to us** nos; a nosotros
U.S.A. *abbr* **United States of America, United States Army, Union of South Africa**
usable [`juzəbəl] *adj* aprovechable, utilizable
usage [`jusɪdʒ] o [`juzɪdʒ] *s* usanza; (*e.g., of a language*) uso
usage dictionary *s* diccionario de uso
usage instructions *spl* modo de empleo

use [jus] *s* uso, empleo; utilidad; **in use** en uso; **out of use** desusado; **to be of no use** no servir para nada; **to have no use for** no necesitar; no servirse de; (coll) tener en poco; **to make use of** servirse de || [juz] *tr* usar, emplear, servirse de; **to use badly** maltratar; **to use up** agotar, consumir || *intr* (empléase sólo en el pretérito y se traduce al español con el pretérito imperfecto o el verbo **soler**), p.ej., **I used to go out for a walk every evening** salía de paseo todas las tardes o solía salir de paseo todas las tardes

used [juzd] *adj* (*customarily employed; worn, partly worn-out; accustomed*) usado; **used to** [ˈjuzdtʊ] o [ˈjustʊ] acostumbrado a

useful [ˈjusfəl] *adj* útil

usefulness [ˈjusfəlnɪs] *s* utilidad

useless [ˈjuslɪs] *adj* inservible, inútil

user [ˈjuzər] *s* usuario

usher [ˈʌʃər] *s* (*in a theater*) acomodador *m;* (*doorkeeper*) ujier *m,* portero || *tr* acomodar; **to usher in** anunciar, introducir

usual [ˈjuʒʊ•əl] *adj* usual, acostumbrado; **as usual** como de costumbre

usually [ˈjuʒʊ•əli] *adj* usualmente, de ordinario

usurp [jʊˈzʌrp] *tr* usurpar

usu•ry [ˈjuʒəri] *s* (*pl* **-ries**) usura

utensil [juˈtɛnsɪl] *s* utensilio; **utensils** corotos *mpl*

uter•us [ˈjutərəs] *s* (*pl* **-i** [,aɪ]); útero

utilitarian [,jutɪlɪˈtɛrɪ•ən] *adj* utilitario

utili•ty [juˈtɪlɪti] *s* (*pl* **-ties**) utilidad; empresa de servicio público; (compu) utilidad

utilize [ˈjutɪ,laɪz] *tr* utilizar

utmost [ˈʌt,most] *adj* sumo, extremo, último; más grande, mayor posible; más lejano || *s*—**the utmost** lo sumo, lo mayor, lo más; **to the utmost** a lo sumo, a más no poder; **to do one's utmost** hacer todo lo posible

utopia [juˈtopɪ•ə] *s* utopía

utopian [juˈtopɪ•ən] *adj* utópico, utopista || *s* utopista *mf*

utter [ˈʌtər] *adj* total, absoluto || *tr* proferir, pronunciar; dar (*un suspiro*)

utterance [ˈʌtərəns] *s* expresión, pronunciación; declaración

utterly [ˈʌtərli] *adj* completamente, totalmente, absolutamente

U′-turn′ *s* cambio de sentido, giro en U (CAm), vuelta en U (CAm)

uxoricide [ʌkˈsorɪ,saɪd] *s* (*husband*) uxoricida *m;* (*act*) uxoricidio

uxorious [ʌkˈsorɪ•əs] *adj* uxorio

V

V, v [vi] vigésima segunda letra del alfabeto inglés

v. *o* **vid.** *abbr* **vide** (Lat) (**see**) véase, vide

v. *abbr* **verb, verse, versus, voice, volt, volume**

VA [ˈviˈe] *s* (letterword) (**Veterans' Administration**) oficina encargada de los veteranos de las fuerzas armadas

vacan•cy [ˈvekənsi] *s* (*pl* **-cies**) (*emptiness; gap, opening*) vacío; (*unfilled position or job*) vacancia, vacante *f,* vacío; piso vacante; cargo vacante

vacant [ˈvekənt] *adj* (*empty*) vacío; (*having no occupant; untenanted*) vacante; (*expression, look*) vago; distraído

vacate [ˈveket] *tr* dejar vacante; anular, invalidar, revocar || *intr* (*to move out*) desalojar; (coll) irse, marcharse

vacation [veˈkeʃən] *s* vacaciones; **on vacation** de vacaciones || *intr* tomar vacaciones

vacation with pay *s* vacaciones retribuídas

vaccinate [ˈvæksɪ,net] *tr* vacunar

vaccination [,væksɪˈneʃən] *s* vacunación

vaccine[vækˈsin] *s* vacuna

vacillate [ˈvæsɪ,let] *intr* vacilar

vacillating [ˈvæsɪ,letɪŋ] *adj* vacilante

vacui•ty [væˈkjʊ•ɪti] *s* (*pl* **-ties**) vacuidad

vacu•um [ˈvækjʊ•əm] *s* (*pl* **-ums** o **-a** [ə]) vacío || *tr* (coll) limpiar

vacuum cleaner *s* aspiradora

vac′uum-packed′ *adj* envasado al vacío

vacuum tank *s* (aut) aspirador *m* de gasolina, nodriza

vacuum tube *s* tubo de vacío

vagabond [ˈvægə,bɑnd] *adj & s* vagabundo

vagar•y [vəˈgɛri] *s* (*pl* **-ies**) capricho

vagina [vəˈdʒaɪnə] *s* vagina

vagran•cy [ˈvegrənsi] *s* (*pl* **-cies**) vagancia

vagrant [ˈvegrənt] *adj & s* vagabundo

vague [veg] *adj* vago; impreciso

vain [ven] *adj* vano; (*conceited*) vanidoso; **in vain** en vano

vainglorious [venˈglorɪ•əs] *adj* vanaglorioso

valance [ˈvæləns] *s* (*across the top of a window*) guardamalleta; (*drapery*) doselera

vale [vel] *s* valle *m*

valedictorian [,vælɪdɪkˈtorɪ•ən] *s* alumno que pronuncia el discurso de despedida al fin del curso

valedicto•ry [,vælɪ dɪktəri] *adj* de despedida || *s* (*pl* **-ries**) discurso de despedida

valence [ˈveləns] *s* (chem) valencia

valentine [ˈvælən,taɪn] *s* tarjeta amorosa o jocosa del día de San Valentín

Valentine's Day *s* día *m* de los corazones, día de los enamorados (*14 de febrero*)

vale of tears *s* valle *m* de lágrimas

valet [ˈvælɪt] o [ˈvæle] *s* ayuda *m,* paje *m*

valiant [ˈvæljənt] *adj* valiente, valeroso
valid [ˈvælɪd] *adj* válido, valedero
validate [ˈvælɪˌdet] *tr* validar; (sport) homologar
validation [ˌvælɪˈdeʃən] *s* validación; (sport) homologación
validi•ty [vəˈlɪdɪti] *s* (*pl* **-ties**) validez *f*
valise [vəˈlis] *s* maleta
valley [ˈvæli] *s* valle *m;* (*of roof*) lima hoya
valor [ˈvælər] *s* valor *m,* ánimo
valorous [ˈvælərəs] *adj* valeroso
valuable [ˈvæljʊ•əbəl] o [ˈvæljəbəl] *adj* (*having monetary value*) valioso; (*highly thought of*) estimable ‖ **valuables** *spl* alhajas, objetos de valor
value [ˈvælju] *s* valor *m;* (*return for one's money in a purchase*) (coll) adquisición, inversión, p.ej., **an excellent value** una adquisición excelente ‖ *tr* (*to think highly of*) estimar; (*to set a price for*) valorar, valuar
valˈue-addˈed tax *s* impuesto sobre el valor añadido, impuesto al valor agregado
valueless [ˈvæljʊlɪs] *adj* sin valor
valve [vælv] *s* válvula; (*of mollusk*) valva; (mus) llava *f*
valve cap *s* capuchón *m*
valve gears *spl* distribución
valveˈ-in-headˈ engine *s* motor *m* con válvulas en cabeza
valve lifter [ˈlɪftər] *s* levantaválvulas *m*
valve seat *s* asiento de válvula
valve spring *s* muelle *m* de válvula
valve stem *s* vástago de válvula
vamp [væmp] *s* (*of shoe*) empella; (*patchwork*) remiendo; (*woman who preys on men*) (slang) mujer *f* fatal, vampiresa ‖ *tr* poner empella a (*un zapato*); remendar; (*to concoct*) componer, enmendar; (jazz) improvisar (*un acompañamiento*); (slang) seducir (*una mujer mundana a un hombre*)
vampire [ˈvæmpaɪr] *s* vampiro; (*woman who preys on men*) mujer *f* fatal, vampiresa
van [væn] *s* carro de carga, camión *m* de mudanzas; (mil & fig) vanguardia; (Brit) furgón *m* de equipajes
vanadium [vəˈnedɪ•əm] *s* vanadio
vandal [ˈvændəl] *adj & s* vándalo ‖ **Vandal** *adj & s* vándalo
vandalism [ˈvændəˌlɪzəm] *s* vandalismo
vane [ven] *s* (*weathervane*) veleta; (*of windmill*) aspa; (*of propeller or turbine*) paleta; (*of feather*) barba
vanguard [ˈvænˌgɑrd] *s* (mil & fig) vanguardia; **in the vanguard** a vanguardia
vanilla [vəˈnɪlə] *s* vainilla
vanish [ˈvænɪʃ] *intr* desvanecerse
vanishing cream [ˈvænɪʃɪŋ] *s* crema desvanecedora, crema evanescente
vani•ty [ˈvænɪti] *s* (*pl* **-ties**) vanidad; (*dressing table*) tocador *m;* (*vanity case*) estuche *m* de afeites
vanity case *s* estuche *m* de afeites, neceser *m* de belleza
vanquish [ˈvæŋkwɪʃ] *tr* vencer, rendir
vantage ground [ˈvæntɪdʒ] *s* posición ventajosa, posición estratégica
vapid [ˈvæpɪd] *adj* insípido
vapor [ˈvepər] *s* vapor *m* (*el visible; exhalación, vaho, niebla, etc.*)
vaporize [ˈvepəˌraɪz] *tr* vaporizar ‖ *intr* vaporizarse
vaporous [ˈvepərəs] *adj* vaporoso
vapor trail *s* (aer) estela de vapor, rastro de condensación
variable [ˈvɛrɪ•əbəl] *adj & s* variable *f*
variance [ˈvɛrɪ•əns] *s* diferencia, variación; **at variance with** en desacuerdo con
variant [ˈvɛrɪ•ənt] *adj & s* variante *f*
variation [ˌvɛrɪˈeʃən] *s* variación
varicose [ˈværɪˌkos] *adj* varicoso
varicose vein *s* (pathol) varice *f*
varied [ˈvɛrɪd] *adj* variado, vario
variegated [ˈvɛri•əˌgetɪd] o [ˈvɛrɪˌgetɪd] *adj* abigarrado, variado
varie•ty [vəˈraɪ•ɪti] *s* (*pl* **-ties**) variedad
variety show *s* variedades
variola [vəˈraɪ•ələ] *s* (pathol) viruela
various [ˈvɛrɪ•əs] *adj* (*several; of different kinds*) varios; (*many-sided; many-colored*) vario
varnish [ˈvɑrnɪʃ] *s* barniz *m;* (fig) capa, apariencia ‖ *tr* barnizar; (fig) dar apariencia falsa a
varsi•ty [ˈvɑrsɪti] *adj* (sport) universitario ‖ *s* (*pl* **-ties**) (sport) equipo principal de la universidad
var•y [ˈvɛri] *v* (*pret & pp* **-ied**) *tr & intr* variar
vase [ves] o [vez] *s* florero, jarrón *m*
Vaseline[T] [ˈvæsəˌlin] *s* vaselina
vassal [ˈvæsəl] *adj & s* vasallo
vast [væst] o [vɑst] *adj* vasto
vastly [ˈvæstli] *adv* enormemente
vastness [ˈvæstnɪs] *s* vastedad
vat [væt] *s* cuba, tina
vaudeville [ˈvodvɪl] o [ˈvɔdəvɪl] *s* variedades
vault [vɔlt] *s* (*underground chamber*) bodega; (*of a bank*) cámara acorazada; (*burial chamber*) sepultura, tumba; (*firmament*) bóveda celeste; (*leap*) salto; (archit) bóveda ‖ *tr* abovedar; saltar ‖ *intr* saltar
vaunt [vɔnt] *s* jactancia ‖ *tr* jactarse de ‖ *intr* jactarse
VCR [ˈviˈsiˈɑr] *s* (letterword) (**VideoCassette Recorder**) videograbadora
VDU [ˈviˈdiˈyu] *s* (letterword) (**Video Display Unit**) pantalla; (compu) videoterminal *f*
veal [vil] *s* ternera, carne *f* de ternera
veal chops *s* chuleta de ternera
vedette [vɪˈdɛt] *s* buque *m* escucha; centinela *m* de avanzada
veer [vɪr] *s* viraje *m* ‖ *tr* virar ‖ *intr* virar; (naut) llamar (*el viento*)
vegan [ˈvɛdʒən], [ˈvigən] *s* vegetariano estricto
vegetable [ˈvɛdʒɪtəbəl] *adj* vegetal ‖ *s* (*plant*) vegetal *m;* (*edible part of plant*) verdura, hortaliza legumbre *f*
vegetable garden *s* huerto de verduras

vegetable soup *s* sopa de verduras
vegetable stew *s* menestra, potaje *m*
vegetarian [,vɛdʒɪ'tɛrɪ•ən] *adj & s* vegetariano
vehemence ['vi•ɪməns] *s* vehemencia
vehement ['vi•ɪmənt] *adj* vehemente
vehicle ['vi•ɪkəl] *s* vehículo
veil [vel] *s* velo; **to take the veil** tomar el velo ‖ *tr* velar (*cubrir con un velo; cubrir, disimular*)
vein [ven] *s* vena; (*streak*) veta; (*distinctive quality*) rasgo ‖ *tr* vetear
velar ['vilər] *adj & s* velar *f*
vellum ['vɛləm] *s* vitela; papel *m* vitela
veloci•ty [vɪ'lɑsɪti] *s* (*pl* **-ties**) velocidad
velvet ['vɛlvɪt] *adj* de terciopelo ‖ *s* terciopelo; (slang) ganancia limpia
velveteen [,vɛlvɪ'tin] *s* velludillo
velvety ['vɛlvɪti] *adj* aterciopelado
Ven. *abbr* **Venerable**
vend [vɛnd] *tr* vender como buhonero
vending machine *s* distribuidor automático, máquina vendedora
vendor ['vɛndər] *s* vendedor *m,* buhonero
veneer [və'nɪr] *s* chapa, enchapado; (fig) apariencia, barniz *m* ‖ *tr* enchapar, chapar
venerable ['vɛnərəbəl] *adj* venerable
venerate ['vɛnə,ret] *tr* venerar
venereal [vɪ'nɪrɪ•əl] *adj* venéreo
venereal disease *s* enfermedad venérea
Venetia [vɪ'niʃi•ə] o [vɪ'niʃə] *s* Venecia (*provincia*)
Venetian [vɪ'niʃən] *adj & s* veneciano
Venetian blind *s* persiana veneciana
Venezuela [,vɛnɪ'zwilə] *s* Venezuela
Venezuelan [,vɛnɪzwilən] *adj & s* venezolano
vengeance ['vɛndʒəns] *s* venganza; **with a vengeance** con furia, con violencia; excesivamente, con creces
vengeful ['vɛndʒfəl] *adj* vengativo
Venice ['vɛnɪs] *s* Venecia (*ciudad*)
venire [vɪ'naɪri] *s* (law) auto de convocación del jurado
venison ['vɛnɪsən] o ['vɛnɪzən] *s* carne *f* de venado
venom ['vɛnəm] *s* veneno
venomous ['vɛnəməs] *adj* venenoso
vent [vɛnt] *s* agujero, orificio; (*outlet*) salida; **to give vent to** dar libre curso a ‖ *tr* proveer de abertura; desahogar, expresar; **to vent one's spleen** descargar la bilis
vent'hole' *s* respiradero
ventilate ['vɛntɪ,let] *tr* ventilar
ventilation ['vɛntɪ'leʃən] *s* ventilación
ventilation shaft *s* pozo o manga de ventilación
ventilator ['vɛntɪ,letər] *s* ventilador *m*
ventricle ['vɛntrɪkəl] *s* ventrículo
ventriloquism [vɛn'trɪlə,kwɪzəm] *s* ventriloquia
ventriloquist [vɛn'trɪləkwɪst] *s* ventrílocuo
venture ['vɛntʃər] *s* empresa arriesgada; **at a venture** a la buena ventura ‖ *tr* aventurar ‖ *intr* aventurarse; **to venture on** arriesgarse en
venture capital *s* capital aventurado
venturesome ['vɛntʃərsəm] *adj* (*bold, daring*) aventurero; (*hazardous*) aventurado
venturous ['vɛntʃərəs] *adj* (*bold, daring*) aventurero; (*hazardous*) aventurado, arriesgado
venue ['vɛnju] *s* lugar *m,* campo, sede *f;* (law) lugar *m* del crimen; (law) lugar donde se reúne el jurado, territorio jurisdiccional; **change of venue** cambio de lugar; (law) traslado de jurisdicción, cambio de tribunal
Venus ['vinəs] *s* (astr) Venus *m;* (myth) Venus *f;* (*very beautiful woman*) Venus *f*
veracious [vɪ'reʃəs] *adj* veraz
veraci•ty [vɪ'ræsɪti] *s* (*pl* **-ties**) veracidad
veranda o **verandah** [və'rændə] *s* terraza, veranda, galería
verb [vʌrb] *adj* verbal ‖ *s* verbo
verbatim [vər'betɪm] *adj* textual ‖ *adv* palabra por palabra, al pie de la letra
verbena [vər'binə] *s* (bot) verbena
verbiage ['vʌrbɪ•ɪdʒ] *s* palabrería, verbosidad
verbose [vər'bos] *adj* verboso
verdant ['vʌrdənt] *adj* verde; cándido, sencillo
verdict ['vʌrdɪkt] *s* (*of a jury*) veredicto; (*opinion*) opinión, juicio
verdigris ['vʌrdɪ,gris] *s* verdete *m*
verdure ['vʌrdʒər] *s* verdor *m*
verge [vʌrdʒ] *s* borde *m,* límite *m;* (*of a column*) fuste *m;* báculo; (eccl) cetro; **on the verge of** al borde de; a punto de; **within the verge of** al alcance de ‖ *intr*—**to verge on** o **upon** llegar casi hasta, rayar en
verification [,vɛrɪfɪ'keʃən] *s* verificatión
veri•fy ['vɛrɪ,faɪ] *v* (*pret & pp* **-fied**) *tr* verificar, comprobar; (law) afirmar bajo juramento
verily ['vɛrɪli] *adv* verdaderamente, en verdad
veritable ['vɛritəbəl] *adj* verdadero
vermicelli [,vʌrmɪ'sɛli] *s* fideos
vermilion [vər'mɪljən] *adj* bermejo ‖ *s* bermellón *m*
vermin ['vʌrmɪn] *ssg* (*objectionable person*) sabandija; bichería (SAm) ‖ *spl* (*objectionable animals or persons*) sabandijas
vermouth [vər'muθ] o ['vʌrmuθ] *s* vermú *m*
vernacular [vər'nækjələr] *adj* vernáculo ‖ *s* lenguaje vernáculo; idioma *m* corriente; (*language peculiar to a class or profession*) jerga
veronica [və'rɑnɪkə] *s* (bot & taur) verónica; lienzo de la Verónica
Versailles [vɛr'saɪ] *s* Versalles
versatile ['vʌrsətɪl] *adj* versátil; (*person*) de muchas habilidades; (*informed on many subjects*) polifacético, universal; (*device or tool*) útil para muchas cosas
verse [vʌrs] *s* verso; (*in the Bible*) versículo
versed [vʌrst] *adj* versado; **to become versed in** versarse en
versification [,vʌrsɪfɪ'keʃən] *s* versificación
versi•fy ['vʌrsɪ,faɪ] *v* (*pret & pp* **-fied**) *tr & intr* versificar
version ['vʌrʒən] *s* versión
ver•so ['vʌrso] *s* (*pl* **-sos**) (*e.g., of a coin*) reverso; (typ) verso

versus [ˈvʌrsəs] *prep* contra
verte•bra [ˈvʌrtɪbrə] *s* (*pl* **-brae** [ˌbri] o **-bras**) vértebra
vertebral disk [ˈvʌrtəˌbrəl] *s* disco vertebral
vertebrate [ˈvʌrtɪˌbret] *adj* & *s* vertebrado
ver•tex [ˈvʌrtɛks] *s* (*pl* **-texes** o **-tices** [tɪˌsiz]) (*top, summit*) ápice *m;* (geom) vértice *m*
vertical [ˈvʌrtɪkəl] *adj* & *s* vertical *f*
vertical rudder *s* (aer) timón *m* de dirección
vertical take-off *m* despegue *m* vertical
verti•go [ˈvʌrtɪˌgo] *s* (*pl* **-gos** o **-goes**) vértigo
verve [vʌrv] *s* brío, ánimo, vigor *m*
very [ˈvɛri] *adj* mismísimo; (*sheer, utter*) mero, puro; (*actual*) verdadero || *adv* muy; mucho, *p.ej.*, **to be very hungry** tener mucha hambre
vesicle [ˈvɛsɪkəl] *s* vesícula
vesper [ˈvɛspər] *s* tarde *f,* caída de la tarde; oración de la tarde; canción de la tarde; **vespers** (eccl) vísperas || **Vesper** *s* Véspero
vessel [ˈvɛsəl] *s* vasija, recipiente *m;* (*ship*) bajel *m,* embarcación, buque *m;* (anat) vaso
vest [vɛst] *s* (*of man's suit*) chaleco; (*jabot*) chorrera; (*undershirt*) (Brit) camiseta || *tr* vestir; **to vest in** conceder (*p.ej., poder*) a; **to vest with** investir de || *intr* vestirse; **to vest in** pasar a
vested interests *spl* intereses creados
vestibule [ˈvɛstɪˌbjul] *s* vestíbulo, zaguán *m*
vestige [ˈvɛstɪdʒ] *s* vestigio
vestment [ˈvɛstmənt] *s* vestidura
vest′-pock′et *adj* de bolsillo, en miniatura; diminuto
ves•try [ˈvɛstri] *s* (*pl* **-tries**) sacristía; junta parroquial
vestry•man [ˈvɛstrimən] *s* (*pl* **-men** [mən]) miembro de la junta parroquial
Vesuvius [vɪˈsuvɪ•əs] o [vɪˈsjuvɪ•əs] *s* el Vesubio
vet [vɛt] *s* (coll) veterinario; (coll) veterano || *v* (*pret* & *pp* **vetted;** *ger* **vetting**) *tr* someter a investigación, examinar, investigar; (*a manuscript*) revisar, corregir; (vet) examinar a un animal enfermo
vetch [vɛtʃ] *s* arveja, veza; (*grass pea*) almorta
veteran [ˈvɛtərən] *adj* & *s* veterano
Veterans Administration (VA) *s* oficina encargada de los veteranos de las fuerzas armadas
veterinarian [ˌvɛtərɪˈnɛrɪ•ən] *s* veterinario
veterinar•y [ˈvɛtərɪˌnɛri] *adj* veterinario || *s* (*pl* **-ies**) veterinario
veterinary medicine *s* veterinaria
ve•to [ˈvito] *s* (*pl* **-toes**) veto || *tr* vetar
vex [vɛks] *tr* vejar, molestar
vexation [vɛkˈseʃən] *s* vejación, molestia
v.g. *abbr* **verbi gratia** (Lat) **(for example)** p.ej., vg., e.g. (por ejemplo)
via [ˈvaɪ•ə] *prep* vía, p.ej., **via Lisbon** vía Lisboa; (*by means of*) por medio de, por
viaduct [ˈvaɪ•əˌdʌkt] *s* viaducto
vial [ˈvaɪ•əl] *s* redoma, frasco pequeño
viand [ˈvaɪ•ənd] *s* vianda, manjar *m*
vibrate [ˈvaɪbret] *tr* & *intr* vibrar
vibration [vaɪˈbreʃən] *s* vibración
vicar [ˈvɪkər] *s* vicario
vicarage [ˈvɪkərɪdʒ] *s* casa del vicario; (*duties of vicar*) vicaría
vicarious [vaɪˈkɛrɪ•əs] *adj* substituto; (*punishment*) sufrido por otro; (*power, authority*) delegado; (*enjoyment*) reflejado
vice [vaɪs] *s* vicio
vice′-ad′miral *s* vicealmirante *m*
vice′-pres′ident *s* vicepresidente *m*
viceroy [ˈvaɪsrɔɪ] *s* virrey *m*
vice versa [ˈvaɪsi ˈvʌrsə] o [ˈvaɪs ˈvʌrsə] *adv* viceversa
vicini•ty [vɪˈsɪnɪti] *s* (*pl* **-ties**) vecindad; (*area*) alrededores *mpl,* inmediaciones; **in the vicinity of** (*approximately*) aproximadamente, alrededor de
vicious [ˈvɪʃəs] *adj* vicioso; malazo; (*dog*) bravo; (*horse*) arisco
victim [ˈvɪktɪm] *s* víctima
victimize [ˈvɪktɪˌmaɪz] *tr* hacer víctima; engañar, estafar
victor [ˈvɪktər] *s* vencedor *m*
victorious [vɪkˈtorɪ•əs] *adj* victorioso
victo•ry [ˈvɪktəri] *s* (*pl* **-ries**) victoria
victuals [ˈvɪtəlz] *spl* vituallas, víveres *mpl*
vide [ˈvide] *tr* (*see*) véase, vide
video [ˈvɪdɪ•o] *s* (*pl* **videos**) video o vídeo (Esp); **on video** en video || *tr* (*3d pers pres* **videoes;** *pret* & *pp* **videoed;** *ger* **videoing**) grabar, videograbar
video arcade *s* sala recreativa con videojuegos
video camera *s* videocámara
videocassette *s* videocasete *m or* videocassette *m*
vid′eocassette′ recorder *s* magnetoscopio, video, videograbador *m,* videograbadora
vid′eocassette′ recording *s* grabación en video, videograbación
video clip *s* videoclip *m*
video club *s* videoclub *m*
videoconference *s* videoconferencia
videodisk *s* video disco, disco óptico
vid′eodisk′ player *s* videotocadiscos *m*
video display unit *s* pantalla; (compu) videoterminal *m*
video film *s* película de video, videofilm *m*
video game *s* videojuego
video library *s* videoteca
videophone *s* videófono, videoteléfono
video piracy *s* videopiratería
video projector *s* videoproyector *m*
videorecorder *s* aparato de video, reproductor *m* de video
videorecording *s* grabación en video
video signal *s* videoseñal *f*
videotape [ˈvɪdɪ•otep] *s* videocinta; (*recording*) video || *tr* grabar en video, videograbar
videotape recorder *s* video, videograbadora
videotape recording *s* video, videograma *m;* (*videotaping*) videograbación
videotaping [ˈvɪdɪ•o tepɪŋ] *s* videograbación
videotext [ˈvɪdɪ•oˌtɛkst] *s* videotexto

vie [vaɪ] *v* (*pret & pp* **vied; ger vying**) *intr* competir, emular, rivalizar
Vien•nese [,vi•əˋniz] *adj* vienés ‖ *s* (*pl* **-nese**) vienés *m*
Vietnam•ese [vɪ,ɛtnəˋmiz] *adj* vietnamés ‖ *s* (*pl* **-ese**) vietnamés *m*
view [vju] *s* vista; (*purpose*) intento, propósito, vista; **to be on view** estar expuesto (*p.ej., un cadáver*); **to keep in view** no perder de vista; no olvidar, tener presente; **to take a dim view of** no entusiasmarse por, mirar escépticamente; **with a view to** con vistas a ‖ *tr* ver, mirar; considerar, contemplar; examinar, inspeccionar; (compu) visualizar
viewer [ˋvju•ər] *s* espectador *m;* telespectador *m,* televidente *mf;* proyector *m* de transparencias; mirador *m* de transparencias; (compu) visualizador *m*
view finder *s* (phot) visor *m*
view′point′ *s* punto de vista
vigil [ˋvɪdʒɪl] *s* vigilia; **to keep vigil** velar
vigilance [ˋvɪdʒɪləns] *s* vigilancia
vigilant [ˋvɪdʒɪlənt] *adj* vigilante
vignette [vɪnˋjɛt] *s* viñeta
vigor [ˋvɪgər] *s* vigor *m*
vigorous [ˋvɪgərəs] *adj* vigoroso
vile [vaɪl] *adj* vil; (*disgusting*) asqueroso, repugnante; (*weather*) muy malo
vili•fy [ˋvɪlɪ,faɪ] *v* (*pret & pp* **-fied**) *tr* difamar, denigrar
villa [ˋvɪlə] *s* villa, quinta
village [ˋvɪlɪdʒ] *s* aldea
villager [ˋvɪlɪdʒər] *s* aldeano
villain [ˋvɪlən] *s* malvado; (*of a play*) malo, traidor *m*
villainous [ˋvɪlənəs] *adj* malvado
villain•y [ˋvɪləni] *s* (*pl* **-ies**) maldad, perfidia
vim [vɪm] *s* fuerza, brío, vigor *m*
vinaigrette sauce *s* (salsa) vinagreta
vindicate [ˋvɪndɪ,ket] *tr* vindicar, exculpar
vindictive [vɪnˋdɪktɪv] *adj* vengativo
vine [vaɪn] *s* (*creeping or climbing plant*) enredadera; (*grape plant*) vid *f,* parra
vine′dress′er *s* viñador *m,* viticultor *m*
vinegar [ˋvɪnɪgər] *s* vinagre *m*
vinegarish [ˋvɪnɪgərɪʃ] *adj* avinagrado
vinegary [ˋvɪnɪgəri] *adj* vinagroso
vineyard [ˋvɪnjərd] *s* viña, viñedo
vineyardist [ˋvɪnjərdɪst] *s* viñador *m,* viticultor *m*
vintage [ˋvɪntɪdʒ] *s* vendimia; vino de buena cosecha; (coll) categoría, clase *f*
vintager [ˋvɪntɪdʒər] *s* vendimiador *m*
vintage wine *s* vino de buena cosecha
vintage year *s* año de buen vino
vintner [ˋvɪntnər] *s* vinatero
vinyl [ˋvaɪnɪl] *s* vinilo
viola [viˋolə] *s* viola *f*
violate [ˋvaɪ•ə,let] *tr* violar
violation [ˋvaɪ•əˋleʃən] *s* violation; (*border; traffic*) infracción
violence [ˋvaɪ•ələns] *s* violencia
violent [ˋvaɪ•ələnt] *adj* violento
violet [ˋvaɪ•əlɪt] *adj* violado ‖ *s* (*color*) violeta *m,* violado; (*dye*) violeta *m;* (bot) violeta *f*
violin [,vaɪ•əˋlɪn] *s* violín *m*
violinist [,vaɪ•əˋlɪnɪst] *s* violinista *mf*
violoncel•lo [,vaɪ•ələnˋtʃɛlo] o [,viələnˋtʃɛlo] *s* (*pl* **-los**) violoncelo
viper [ˋvaɪpər] *s* víbora
VIP [ˈvi,aɪˈpi] *s* (letterword) (**Very Important Person**) VIP *mf;* **VIPs** VIPS, notables *mpl*
vira•go [vɪˋrego] *s* (*pl* **-goes** o **-gos**) mujer de mal genio
virgin [ˋvʌrdʒɪn] *adj & s* virgen *f*
virgin birth *s* parto virginal de María Santísima; (zool) partenogénesis *f*
Virginia creeper [vərˋdʒɪnɪ•ə] *s* (bot) guau *m*
Virgin Islands *mpl* Islas Vírgenes
virginity [vərˋdʒɪnɪti] *s* virginidad
Virgo [ˋvʌrgo] *s* (astr) Virgo
virility [vɪˋrɪlɪti] *s* virilidad
virology [vaɪˋrɑlədʒi] *s* virología
virtual [ˋvʌrtʃʊ•əl] *adj* virtual
virtual reality *s* realidad virtual
virtue [ˋvʌrtʃʊ] *s* virtud
virtuosi•ty [,vʌrtʃʊˋɑsɪti] *s* (*pl* **-ties**) virtuosismo
virtuo•so [,vʌrtʃʊˋoso] *s* (*pl* **-sos** o **-si** [si]) virtuoso
virtuous [ˋvʌrtʃʊ•əs] *adj* virtuoso
virulence [ˋvɪrjələns] *s* virulencia
virulent [ˋvɪrjələnt] *adj* virulento
virus [ˋvaɪrəs] *s* virus *m*
visa [ˋvɪzə] *s* visa ‖ *tr* visar
visage [ˋvɪzɪdʒ] *s* cara, semblante *m;* aspecto, apariencia
vis-à-vis [,vizəˋvi] *adj* enfrentados ‖ *adv* frente a frente ‖ *prep* enfrente de; respecto de
viscera [ˋvɪsərə] *spl* vísceras
viscount [ˋvaɪkaʊnt] *s* vizconde *m*
viscountess [ˋvaɪkaʊntɪs] *s* vizcondesa
viscous [ˋvɪskəs] *adj* viscoso
vise [vaɪs] *s* tornillo, torno
visé [ˋvize] o [viˋze] *s & tr* var de **visa**
visible [ˋvɪzɪbəl] *adj* visible
vision [ˋvɪʒən] *s* visión; (*sense of sight*) vista
visionar•y [ˋvɪʒə,nɛri] *adj* visionario ‖ *s* (*pl* **-ies**) visionario
visit [ˋvɪzɪt] *s* visita ‖ *tr* visitar; afligir, acometer; enviar (*p.ej., castigo, venganza*) ‖ *intr* hacer visitas; visitarse (*dos o más personas*)
visitation [,vɪzɪˋteʃən] *s* visitación; gracia del cielo, castigo del cielo; visita; **visitation rights** derechos de visita
visiting card *s* tarjeta de visita
visiting hours *spl* horas de visita
visiting nurse *s* enfermera ambulante
visiting team *s* equipo visitante, equipo de fuera
visitor [ˋvɪsɪtər] *s* visitante *mf*
visitors' book *s* libro de visitas
visor [ˋvaɪzər] *s* visera; (*disguise*) mascara
vista [ˋvɪstə] *s* vista, panorama *m*
visual [ˋvɪʒʊ•əl] *adj* visual
visual acuity *s* agudeza visual
visual display unit *s* (compu) visualizador *m*

visualize ['vɪʒʊ•ə,laɪz] *tr* representarse en la mente; hacer visible
vital ['vaɪtəl] *adj* vital; (*deadly*) mortal ‖ **vitals** *spl* partes *fpl* vitales, órganos vitales
vitality [vaɪ'tælɪti] *s* vitalidad
vitalize ['vaɪtə,laɪz] *tr* vitalizar
vitamin ['vaɪtəmɪn] *s* vitamina
vitiate ['vɪʃi,et] *tr* viciar
vitreous ['vɪtrɪ•əs] *adj* vítreo
vitriolic [,vɪtrɪ'ɑlɪk] *adj* (chem) vitriólico; (fig) cáustico, mordaz
vituperable [vaɪ'tupərəbəl] o [vaɪ'tjupərəbəl] *adj* vituperable
vituperate [vaɪ'tupə,ret] o [vaɪ'tjupə,ret] *tr* vituperar
viva ['vivə] *interj* ¡viva! ‖ *s* viva *m*
vivacious [vɪ'veʃəs] o [vaɪ'veʃəs] *adj* vivaz, vivaracho
vivaci•ty [vɪ'væsɪti] o [vaɪ'væsɪti] *s* (*pl* **-ties**) vivacidad, animación
viva voce ['vaɪvə 'vosi] *adv* de viva voz
vivid ['vɪvɪd] *adj* vivo (*intenso; brillante; expresivo*)
vivi•fy ['vɪvɪ,faɪ] *v* (*pret & pp* **-fied**) *tr* vivificar
vivisection [,vɪvɪ'sɛkʃən] *s* vivisección
vixen [vɪksən] *s* vulpeja; mujer regañona y colérica
viz. [vɪz] *adv* (letterword) (**videlicet**) (Lat) **namely, to wit**) a saber, es decir
vizier [vɪ'zɪr] o ['vɪzjər] *s* visir *m*
vocabular•y [vo'kæbjə,lɛri] *s* (*pl* **-ies**) vocabulario
vocal ['vokəl] *adj* vocal; (*inclined to express oneself freely*) expresivo
vocal chords *spl* cuerdas vocales
vocalist ['vokəlɪst] *s* vocalista *mf*
vocation [vo'keʃən] *s* vocación; empleo, ocupación
vocational guidance [vo'keʃənəl] *s* orientación profesional
vocative ['vɑkətɪv] *s* vocativo
vociferate [vo'sɪfə,ret] *intr* vociferar
vociferous [vo'sɪfərəs] *adj* clamoroso, vocinglero
vogue [vog] *s* boga, moda; **in vogue** en boga, de moda
voice [vɔɪs] *s* voz *f;* **in a loud voice** en alta voz; **in a low voice** en voz baja; **with one voice** a una voz ‖ *tr* expresar; sonorizar (*una consonante sorda*) ‖ *intr* sonorizarse
voiceless ['vɔɪslɪs] *adj* sin voz; mudo; silencioso; (phonet) sordo
voice menu *s* (compu) mensaje *m* al operador
voice'o'ver *s* voz superpuesta, voz en off
void [vɔɪd] *adj* (*empty*) vacío; (*useless*) vano; (law) inválido, nulo; **void of** desprovisto de ‖ *s* vacío; (*gap*) hueco ‖ *tr* vaciar; evacuar (*el vientre*); anular ‖ *intr* excretar
voile [vɔɪl] *s* espumilla
vol. *abbr* **volume**
volatile ['vɑlətɪl] *adj* volátil
volatilize ['vɑlətɪ,laɪz] *tr* volatilizar ‖ *intr* volatilizarse
volcanic [vɑl'kænɪk] *adj* volcánico
volca•no [vɑl'keno] *s* (*pl* **-noes** o **-nos**) volcán *m*
vole [vol] *s* ratón *m* de campo, campañol *m*
volition [və'lɪʃən] *s* voluntad; **of one's own volition** por su propia voluntad
volley ['vɑli] *s* (*of stones, bullets, etc.*) descarga, lluvia; (mil) descarga; (tennis) voleo ‖ *tr & intr* volear
vol'ley•ball' *s* balonvolea *m,* vóleibol o voleibol *m,* volibol *m* (Col, Mex, Ven)
volplane ['vɑl,plen] *s* vuelo planeado ‖ *intr* planear
volt [volt] *s* voltio
voltage ['voltɪdʒ] *s* voltaje *m*
voltage divider *s* (rad) divisor *m* de voltaje
voltaic [vɑl'te•ɪk] *adj* voltaico
volte-face [vɔlt'fɑs] *s* cambio de dirección; cambio de opinión
volt'me'ter *s* voltímetro
voluble ['vɑljəbəl] *adj* locuaz, hablador
volume ['vɑljəm] *s* (*book; bulk; mass, e.g., of water*) volumen *m;* (*each book in a set*) tomo; (*degree of loudness*) volumen sonoro; (geom) volumen *m;* **to speak volumes** ser muy significativo; ser muy expresivo
voluminous [və'lumɪnəs] *adj* voluminoso
voluntar•y ['vɑlən,tɛri] *adj* voluntario ‖ *s* (*pl* **-ties**) (eccl) solo de órgano
volunteer [,vɑlən'tɪr] *adj & s* voluntario ‖ *tr* ofrecer (*sus servicios*) ‖ *intr* ofrecerse; servir como voluntario; **to volunteer to** + *inf* ofrecerse a + *inf*
voluptuar•y [və'lʌptʃʊ,ɛri] *adj* voluptuoso ‖ *s* (*pl* **-ties**) voluptuoso, sibarita *mf*
voluptuous [və'lʌptʃʊ•əs] *adj* voluptuoso
volute [və'lut] *s* voluta
vomit ['vɑmɪt] *s* vómito; (*emetic*) vomitivo ‖ *tr & intr* vomitar
voodoo ['vudu] *adj* voduísta ‖ *s* (*practice*) vodú *m;* (*person*) voduísta *mf*
voracious [və'reʃəs] *adj* voraz
voracity [və'ræsɪti] *s* voracidad
vor•tex ['vɔrtɛks] *s* (*pl* **-texes** o **-tices** [tɪ,siz]) vórtice *m*
vota•ry ['votəri] *s* (*pl* **-ries**) persona ligada por votos solemnes; aficionado, partidario
vote [vot] *s* (*formal expression of choice; right to vote; person who votes*) voto; (*act of voting; votes considered together*) votación; **to put to the vote** poner a votación; **to tally the votes** regular los votos ‖ *tr* votar (*sí, no*); **to vote down** derrotar por votación; **to vote in** elegir por votación ‖ *intr* votar
vote getter ['gɛtər] *s* acaparador *m* de votos; (*slogan*) consigna que gana votos
voter ['votər] *s* votante *mf*
voting ['votɪŋ] *s* votación
voting machine ['votɪŋ] *s* máquina registradora de votos, máquina de votar
votive ['votɪv] *adj* votivo
votive offering *s* voto, exvoto
vouch [vaʊtʃ] *tr* garantizar ‖ *intr*—**to vouch fo**

responder de (*una cosa*); responder por (*una persona*)
voucher [ˈvaʊtʃər] *s* garante *mf;* (*certificate*) comprobante *m,* bono
vouch•safe′ *tr* conceder, otorgar; permitir ‖ *intr*— **to vouchsafe to** + *inf* dignarse + *inf*
vow [vaʊ] *s* voto; **to take vows** tomar el hábito religioso ‖ *tr* votar (*p.ej., un cirio a la Virgen*); jurar (*venganza*) ‖ *intr* votar; **to vow to** hacer votos de
vowel [ˈvaʊ•əl] *s* vocal *f*
voyage [ˈvɔɪ•ɪdʒ] *s* travesía, trayecto; (*any journey*) viaje *m* ‖ *tr* atravesar (*p.ej., el mar*) ‖ *intr* viajar
voyager [ˈvɔɪ•ɪdʒər] *s* pasajero, navegante *mf,* viajero
V.P. *abbr* **Vice-President**
vs. *abbr* **versus**
vulcanize [ˈvʌlkəˌnaɪz] *tr* vulcanizar
vulg. *abbr* **vulgar**
Vulg. *abbr* **Vulgate**
vulgar [ˈvʌlgər] *adj* grosero; (*popular, common; vernacular*) vulgar
vulgari•ty [vʌlˈgærɪti] *s* (*pl* **-ties**) grosería
Vulgar Latin *s* latín vulgar, latín rústico
Vulgate [ˈvʌlget] *s* Vulgata
vulnerable [ˈvʌlnərəbəl] *adj* vulnerable
vulture [ˈvʌltʃər] *s* buitre *m;* (*American vulture*) catartes *m,* aura (*buitre americano*)

W

W, w [ˈdʌbəlˌju] vigésima tercera letra del alfabeto inglés
W. *abbr* **Wednesday, west**
wad [wɑd] *s* (*of cotton*) bolita, tapón *m;* (*of papers*) fajo, lío; (*in a gun*) taco ‖ *v* (*pret & pp* **wadded;** *ger* **wadding**) *tr* emborrar, rellenar; atacar (*una escopeta*)
waddle [ˈwɑdəl] *s* anadeo ‖ *intr* anadear
wade [wed] *intr* andar sobre terreno cubierto de agua; andar descalzo por la orilla; chapotear (*los niños*) con los pies desnudos; **to wade into** (coll) embestir con violencia; (coll) meter el hombro a; **to wade through** (coll) avanzar con dificultad por; (coll) leer con dificultad
wading bird [ˈwedɪŋ] *s* ave zancuda
wafer [ˈwefər] *s* (*for sealing letters; pill*) oblea; (*thin, crisp cake*) hostia; (eccl) hostia
waffle [ˈwɑfəl] *s* barquillo
waffle iron *s* barquillero
waft [wæft] o [wɑft] *tr* llevar por el aire; llevar por encima del agua ‖ *intr* flotar
wag [wæg] *s* (*of head*) meneo; (*of tail*) coleada; (*jester*) bromista *mf* ‖ *v* (*pret & pp* **wagged;** *ger* **wagging**) *tr* menear (*la cabeza, la cola*) ‖ *intr* menearse
wage [wedʒ] *s* salario, sueldo, paga ‖ *tr* hacer (*la guerra*)
wage earner [ˈʌrnər] *s* asalariado
wager [ˈwedʒər] *s* apuesta; **to lay a wager** hacer una apuesta ‖ *tr & intr* apostar
wage′work′er *s* asalariado
waggish [ˈwægɪʃ] *adj* divertido, gracioso; (*person*) bromista
wagon [ˈwægən] *s* carro, furgón *m,* carretón *m;* **on the wagon** (slang) sin tomar bebidas alcohólicas; **to hitch one's wagon to a star** poner el tiro muy alto
wag′tail′ *s* aguanieves *m,* aguzanieves *m*
waif [wef] *s* (*foundling*) expósito; animal extraviado o abandonado; (*stray child*) granuja *m*
wail [wel] *s* gemido, lamento ‖ *intr* gemir, lamentar
wain•scot [ˈwenskət] o [ˈwenskɑt] *s* arrimadillo, friso de madera ‖ *v* (*pret & pp* **-scoted** o **-scotted;** *ger* **-scoting** o **-scotting**) *tr* poner arrimadillo o friso de madera a
waist [west] *s* (*of human body; corresponding part of garment*) talle *m,* cintura; (*garment*) corpiño, jubón *m,* blusa
waist′band′ *s* pretina
waist′cloth′ *s* taparrabo
waistcoat [ˈwestˌkot] o [ˈwɛskət] *s* chaleco
waist′line′ *s* cintura; (*of garment*) talle *m*
wait [wet] *s* espera; **to have a good wait** (coll) esperar sentado; **to lie in wait for** acechar emboscado ‖ *tr*—**to wait one's turn** esperar vez ‖ *intr* esperar, aguardar; **to wait for** esperar, aguardar; **to wait on** atender, despachar (*a los parroquianos en una tienda*); servir (*a una persona a la mesa*); **to wait until** esperar a que
waiter [ˈwetər] *s* camarero, mozo de restaurante; (*tray*) bandeja
waiting list *s* lista de espera
waiting room *s* (*of station*) sala de espera; (*of doctor's office*) antesala
waitress [ˈwetrɪs] *s* camarera, moza de restaurante
waive [wev] *tr* renunciar a (*un derecho*); diferir, poner a un lado
waiver [ˈwevər] *s* renuncia
wake [wek] *s* (*watch by the body of a dead person*) velatorio; (*of a boat or other moving object*) estela; **in the wake of** siguiendo inmediatamente; de resultas de ‖ *v* (*pret* **waked** o **woke** [wok]; *pp* **waked**) *tr* despertar ‖ *intr*— **to wake to** darse cuenta de; **to wake up** despertar

wakeful [ˈwekfəl] *adj* desvelado
wakefulness [ˈwekfəlnɪs] *s* desvelo
waken [ˈwekən] *tr & intr* despertar
wale [wel] *s* verdugón *m*
Wales [welz] *s* Gales, el país de Gales
walk [wɔk] *s* (*act*) paseo; (*distance*) caminata; (*way of walking, bearing*) andar *m*, paso; (*of a horse*) andadura; (*place to walk animals*) cercado; empleo, cargo, carrera; **at a walk** al paso de una persona; **to go for a walk** salir a pasear; **to take a walk** dar un paseo ‖ *tr* pasear (*a un niño, un caballo*); caminar (*recorrer caminando*); hacer ir al paso (*un caballo*); **to walk off** quitarse (*p.ej., un dolor de cabeza*) caminando; **to walk the dog on a leash** sacar al perro con correa ‖ *intr* andar, caminar, ir a pie; (*to stroll*) pasear; **to walk away from** alejarse caminando de; **to walk off with** cargar con, llevarse; **to walk out** salir repentinamente; declararse en huelga; **to walk out on** (coll) dejar airadamente
walkaway [ˈwɔkə,we] *s* (coll) triunfo fácil
walker [ˈwɔkər] *s* caminante *mf;* (*pedestrian*) peatón *m;* (*gocart*) andaderas
walkie-talkie [ˈwɔkiˈtɔki] *s* (rad) transmisor-receptor *m* portátil
walking papers *spl* (coll) nota de despedido, pasaporte *m*
walking stick *s* bastón *m*
walk'-on' *s* (theat) parte *f* de por medio
walk'out' *s* (coll) huelga
walk'o'ver *s* (coll) triunfo fácil
wall [wɔl] *s* muro; (*between rooms; of a pipe, boiler, etc.*) pared *f;* (*of a fortification*) muralla; **to drive to the wall** poner entre la espada y la pared; **to go to the wall** rendirse; fracasar ‖ *tr* murar, amurallar (*una ciudad, un castillo*); emparedar (*a un criminal*); **to wall up** cerrar con muro
wall'board' *s* cartón *m* tabla
wallet [ˈwɑlɪt] *s* cartera de bolsillo
wall'flow'er *s* alhelí *m;* **to be a wallflower** (coll) comer pavo, planchar el asiento
wallop [ˈwɑləp] *s* (coll) golpaza, puñetazo ‖ *tr* (coll) golpear fuertemente; (coll) vencer cabalmente
wallow [ˈwɑlo] *s* revuelco; (*place*) revolcadero ‖ *intr* revolcarse; (*e.g., in wealth*) nadar
wall'pa'per *s* papel *m* de empapelar, papel pintado ‖ *tr* empapelar
Wall Street *s* Wall Street *m* (*centro financiero de los EE.UU.*)
walnut [ˈwɔlnət] *s* (*tree and wood*) nogal *m;* nuez *f*
walrus [ˈwɔlrəs] o [ˈwɑlrəs] *s* morsa
Walter [ˈwɔltər] *s* Gualterio
waltz [wɔlts] *s* vals *m* ‖ *tr* hacer valsar; (coll) conducir directamente ‖ *intr* valsar
wan [wɑn] *adj* (*comp* **wanner;** *super* **wannest**) pálido, macilento; débil
wand [wɑnd] *s* vara; (*of deviner or magician*) varilla de virtudes
wander [ˈwɑndər] *tr* recorrer a la ventura ‖ *intr* errar, vagar; extraviarse, perderse; **to wander around** errar de una parte a otra
wanderer [ˈwɑndərər] *s* vagabundo; peregrino
wan'der•lust' *s* ansia de viajar
wane [wen] *s* decadencia, declinación; menguante *f* de la luna; **on the wane** decayendo, declinando; menguando (*la luna*) ‖ *intr* decaer, declinar; menguar (*la luna*)
wangle [ˈwɛŋgəl] *tr* (*to obtain by scheming*) (coll) mamar o mamarse; (coll) adulterar, falsear (*cuentas*); **to wangle one's way out of** (coll) salir con maña de ‖ *intr* (*to get along by scheming*) (coll) sacudirse
wannabe [ˈwɑnə,bi] *s* (coll) persona ambiciosa, solicitante *mf;* fingidor *m*
wannabe *abbr* **want to be**
want [wɑnt] o [wɔnt] *s* deseo; necesidad; carencia; **for want of** a falta de; **to be in want** pasar necesidad ‖ *tr* desear; necesitar; carecer de ‖ *intr* desear; **to want for** necesitar; carecer de
want ad *s* anuncio clasificado
wanton [ˈwɑntən] *adj* inconsiderado, desconsiderado; insensible, perverso; disoluto, licencioso; lascivo; cabezudo
war [wɔr] *s* guerra; **to go to war** declarar la guerra; (*as a soldier*) ir a la guerra; **to wage war** hacer la guerra ‖ *v* (*pret & pp* **warred;** *ger* **warring**) *intr* guerrear; **to war on** guerrear con, hacer la guerra a
warble [ˈwɔrbəl] *s* gorjeo, trino ‖ *intr* gorjear, trinar
warbler [ˈwɔrblər] *s* pájaro cantor; curruca de cabeza negra
war cloud *s* amenaza de guerra
ward [wɔrd] *s* (*person, usually a minor, under protection of another*) pupilo; (*guardianship*) custodia, tutela; (*of a city*) barrio, distrito; (*of a hospital*) cuadra, crujía; (*of a lock*) guarda ‖ *tr*— **to ward off** parar, desviar
warden [ˈwɔrdən] *s* guardián *m;* (*of a jail*) alcaide *m*, carcelero; (*of a church*) capiller *m;* (*in charge of fire prevention*) vigía *m*
ward heeler *s* muñidor *m*
ward'robe' *s* (*closet or cabinet for holding clothes*) guardarropa *m;* (*stock of clothing for a person*) vestuario; (theat) guardarropía
wardrobe trunk *s* baúl ropero
ward'room' *s* (nav) cámara de oficiales
ware [wɛr] *s* loza; **wares** efectos, artículos de comercio, mercancías
war game *s* juego de guerra; (mil) simulacro de combate
ware'house' *s* almacén *m;* (*for furniture*) guardamuebles *m*
warehouse•man [ˈwɛr,haʊsmən] *s* (*pl* **-men** [mən]) almacenista *m;* guardaalmacén *m*
war'fare' *s* guerra
war'head' *s* punta de combate
war'horse *s* veterano; ((*hackneyed work or idea*) caballo o caballito de batalla
warily [ˈwɛrɪli] *adv* cautelosamente
wariness [ˈwɛrɪnɪs] *s* cautela

war'like' *adj* guerrero
war lord *s* jefe *m* militar
warm [wɔrm] *adj* (*being moderately hot*) caliente; (*neither hot nor cold*) templado; (*clothing*) abrigador; (*climate, region*) caluroso; (*color*) cálido, (fig) caluroso, cordial; **to be warm** (*said of a person*) tener calor; (*said of the weather*) hacer calor || *tr* calentar, acalorar; (fig) animar, acalorar; **to warm up** recalentar (*p.ej., la comida*); hacer más amistoso || *intr* calentarse; **to warm up** templar (*el tiempo*); (*with work or exercise*) acalorarse; **to warm up to** cobrar afecto a
warm-blooded ['wɔrm'blʌdɪd] *adj* apasionado, ardiente; (*animals*) de sangre caliente
war memorial *s* monumento a los caídos
warmer ['wɔrmər] *s* calentador *m*
warm-hearted ['wɔrm'hɑrtɪd] *adj* afectuoso, de buen corazón; cariñoso; simpático
warming pan *s* mundillo
warmonger ['wɔr,mʌŋgər] *s* belicista *mf*
war mother *s* madrina de guerra
warmth [wɔrmθ] *s* calor *m;* ardor *m,* entusiasmo; cordialidad
warm'-up' *s* calentón *m*
warn [wɔrn] *tr* advertir, avisar; (*to exhort*) amonestar; (*to advise*) aconsejar
warning *adj* de aviso || *s* advertencia, aviso
war of attrition *s* guerra de desgaste
war of nerves *s* guerra de nervios
War of the Roses *s* guerra de las dos Rosas
warp [wɔrp] *s* (*of a fabric*) urdimbre *f;* (*of a board or record*) alabeo, deformación, pandeo; aberracion mental; (naut) espía || *tr* (*wood, metal, or plastic*) alabear, deformar, pandear; (*yarn, thread*) urdir; pervertir (*el juicio de una persona*); (naut) mover con espía || *intr* alabearse, pandearse; (naut) espiar con espía || *intr* combarse, alabearse; (naut) espiar
war'path' *s*—**to be on the warpath** prepararse para la guerra; estar buscando pendencia
warping [wɔrpɪŋ] *s* alabeo, deformación, pandeo
war'plane' *s* avión *m* de guerra
warp speed *s* (*in science fiction*) velocidad de la luz
warrant ['wɑrənt] o ['wɔrənt] *s* garantía, promesa; (*for arrest*) orden *f* de prisión; (*before a judge*) citación; cédula, certificado || *tr* garantizar, prometer; autorizar; justificar
warrantable ['wɑrəntəbəl] o ['wɔrəntəbəl] *adj* garantizable; justificable
warrant officer *s* suboficial *m* de las clases
warren ['wɑrən] o ['wɔrən] *s* (*where rabbits breed*) conejera, madriguera
warrior ['wɔrjər] *s* guerrero
Warsaw ['wɔrsɔ] *s* Varsovia
war'ship' *s* buque *m* de guerra
wart [wɔrt] *s* verruga
war'time' *s* tiempo de guerra
war'-torn' *adj* devastado por la guerra
war•y [wɛri] *adj* (*comp* **-ier;** *super* **-iest**) cauteloso
wash [wɑʃ] o [wɔʃ] *s* lavado; (*clothes washed or to be washed*) jabonado; (*dirty water*) lavazas; loción; (*place where surf breaks*) batiente *m;* (aer) estela turbulenta || *tr* lavar; fregar (*los platos*); bañar, mojar; **to wash away** quitar lavando; derrubiar (*las aguas corrientes la tierra de las riberas*) || *intr* lavarse; lavar la ropa; batir (*el agua*); derrubiarse
washable ['wɑʃəbəl] o ['wɔʃəbəl] *adj* lavable
wash and wear *adj* de lava y pon
wash'ba'sin *s* jofaina, palangana
wash'bas'ket *s* cesto de la colada
wash'board' *s* lavadero, tabla de lavar; (*baseboard*) rodapié *m*
washboard road *s* carretera llena de baches
wash'bowl' *s* jofaina, palangana
wash'cloth' *s* paño para lavarse; paño de cocina
wash'day' *s* día *m* de la colada
washed-out ['wɑʃt,aʊt] o ['wɔʃt,aʊt] *adj* desteñido; (coll) debilitado, rendido
washed-up ['wɑʃt,ʌp] o ['wɔʃt,ʌp] *adj* (coll) agotado, deslomado, acabado
washer ['wɑʃər] o [wɔʃər] *s* lavador *m;* (*machine*) lavadora; (*ring of metal placed under head of bolt*) arandela; (*ring of rubber, etc., to keep a spigot from leaking*) zapatilla; (phot) lavador
wash'er•wom'an *s* (*pl* **-wom'en**) lavandera
wash goods *spl* tejidos lavables
washing ['wɑʃɪŋ] o ['wɔʃɪŋ] *s* (*act of washing; washed clothes or clothes to be washed*) lavado; lavada; **washings** (*dirty water; abraded material*) lavadura
washing machine *s* lavadora, máquina de lavar
wash'out' *s* derrubio; derrumbe *m;* (coll) desilusión, fracaso
wash'rag' *s* paño para lavarse; paño de cocina
wash'room' *s* baño, servicio
wash'stand' *s* lavamanos *m,* lavabo
wash'tub' *s* cuba de colada, tina de lavar
wash water *s* lavazas
wasn't *contr* **was not**
wasp [wɑsp] *s* avispa
WASP [wɑsp] (acronym) (**White, Anglo-Saxon Protestant**) *persona de los EE.UU., blanca, anglo-sajona y protestante*
waste [west] *s* derroche *m,* desgaste *m;* (*garbage*) basura, despojo; (*wild region*) despoblado, yermo; (*of time*) pérdida; (*useless by-products*) desperdicios; excremento; (*for wiping machinery*) hilacha de algodón; **to lay waste** devastar, poner a fuego y sangre || *tr* malgastar, perder || *intr*—**to waste away** consumirse
waste'bas'ket *s* papelera
wasteful ['westfəl] *adj* derrochador, manirroto; devastador, destructivo
waste'-land' *s* peladero
waste paper *s* papeles usados, papel de desecho, papel viejo

waste pipe *s* tubo de desagüe
waste products *spl* desperdicios; materia excretada
wastrel [ˈwestrəl] *s* derrochador *m,* malgastador *m;* pródigo, perdido
watch [wɑtʃ] *s* reloj *m* (*de bolsillo o de pulsera*); (*lookout*) vigía *m;* (mil) vigilia; (naut) guardia; **to be on the watch for** estar a la mira de; **to keep watch over** velar ‖ *tr* (*to look at*) mirar; (*to oversee*) velar, vigilar; guardar; tener cuidado con ‖ *intr* mirar; (*to keep awake*) velar; **to watch for** acechar; **to watch out** tener cuidado; **to watch out for** estar a la mira de; tener cuidado con; guardarse de; **to watch over** velar, vigilar
watchʹcaseʹ *s* caja de reloj
watch charm *s* dije *m*
watch crystal *s* cristal *m* de reloj
watchʹdogʹ *s* perro de guarda, perro guardián; (fig) guardián *m* fiel
watchful [ˈwɑtʃfəl] *adj* desvelado, vigilante
watchfulness [ˈwɑtʃfəlnɪs] *s* desvelo, vigilancia
watchʹmakʹer *s* relojero
watch•man [ˈwɑtʃmən] *s* (*pl* **-men** [mən]) vigilante *m,* velador *m*
watch night *s* noche vieja; oficio de noche vieja
watch pocket *s* relojera
watch strap *s* pulsera
watchʹtowʹer *s* atalaya, vigía
watchʹwordʹ *s* santo y seña; (*slogan*) lema *m*
water [ˈwɔtər] o [ˈwɑtər] *s* agua; **of the first water** de lo mejor; **to back water** ciar; **to carry water on both shoulders** nadar entre dos aguas; **to fish in troubled waters** pescar en río revuelto; **to hold water** (coll) ser bien fundado; **to make water** (*to urinate*) hacer aguas; (naut) hacer agua; **to pour** o **throw cold water on** echar un jarro de agua (fría) a ‖ *tr* regar, rociar; abrevar (*el ganado*); aguar (*el vino*); proveer de agua ‖ *intr* abrevarse (*el ganado*); tomar agua (*una locomotora*); llorar (*los ojos*)
water bed *s* cama de agua
water blister *s* ampolla
water bottle *s* cantimplora
water carrier *s* aguador *m*
water color *s* acuarela
waʹter•courseʹ *s* corriente *f* de agua; lecho de corriente
water cress *s* berro
water cure *s* cura de aguas
waʹter•fallʹ *s* cascada, caída de agua
water front *s* terreno ribereño
water gap *s* garganta, hondonada
water hammer *s* golpe *m* de ariete
water heater *s* calentador *m* de agua
water ice *s* sorbete *m,* helado de agua
watering can *s* regadera
watering place *s* aguadero; balneario
watering pot *s* regadera
watering trough *s* abrevadero
water jacket *s* camisa de agua
water lily *s* ninfea, nenúfar *m*
water line *s* línea de agua, línea de flotación; nivel *m* de agua
waterlogged [ˈwɔtərˌlɔgd] *adj* anegado; empapado; impregnado de agua; (naut) pesado
water main *s* cañería de agua
waʹter•markʹ *s* (*in paper*) filigrana, timbre *m* de agua; marca de nivel de agua
waʹter•melʹon *s* sandía
water meter *s* contador *m* de agua
water pipe *s* cañería de agua
water polo *s* polo de agua
waterpower *s* hulla blanca, energía hidráulica
waʹter•proofʹ *adj & s* impermeable *m*
waʹter•shedʹ *s* divisoria de aguas; (*drainage area*) cuenca
water ski *s* esquí acuático
waʹter•spoutʹ *s* (*to carry water from roof*) canalón *m;* (*funnel of wet air extending from cloud to surface of water*) manga de agua, tromba marina
waʹter•sup•plyʹ system *s* fontanería
water table *s* nivel friático
waʹter•tightʹ *adj* estanco, hermético; (fig) seguro
water tower *s* arca de agua, tanque *m* de agua
water wagon *s* (mil) carro de agua; **on the water wagon** (slang) sin tomar bebidas alcohólicas
waʹter•wayʹ *s* vía de agua, vía fluvial; (naut) canalizo
waterwheel *s* rueda de agua; turbina de agua; (*of steamboat*) rueda de paletas
water wings *spl* nadaderas
waʹter•worksʹ *s* estación de bombas
watery [ˈwɔtəri] o [ˈwɑtəri] *adj* acuoso; (*said of the eyes*) lagrimoso, lloroso; insípido; húmedo, mojado
watt [wɑt] *s* vatio
wattage [ˈwɑtɪdʒ] *s* vatiaje *m*
wattʹ-hourʹ *s* (*pl* **watt-hours**) vatiohora
wattle [ˈwɑtəl] *s* (*of bird*) barba; (*of fish*) barbilla
wattʹmeʹter *s* vatímetro
wave [wev] *s* onda; (*of hair*) onda, ondulación; (*e.g., of heat or cold*) ola; (*greeting; signal*) señal hecha con la mano; (*surge, movement*) oleada ‖ *tr* (*e.g., a handkerchief*) agitar; (*the hair*) ondear, ondular; (*the hand*) hacer señal con; ondear, ondular (*el cabello*); hacer señal con (*la mano*); decir (*adiós*) con la mano; **to wave aside** rechazar ‖ *intr* ondear u ondearse; hacer señal con la mano
wave band *s* banda *or* gama de frecuencia
waver [ˈwevər] *intr* oscilar; (*to hesitate*) vacilar, titubear; (*to totter*) tambalear
waveʹlength *s* longitud de onda; **to be on the same wavelength** estar en la misma onda
wav•y [ˈwevi] *adj* (*comp* **-ier;** *super* **-iest**) undoso, ondoso; (*water*) ondulado; (*hair*) ondeado
wax [wæks] *s* cera; **to be wax in one's hands** ser como una cera ‖ *tr* encerar; cerotear (*el hilo*) ‖ *intr* hacerse, volverse; crecer (*la luna*)

wax paper *s* papel encerado, papel parafinado
wax taper *s* cerilla
wax'works' *s* museo de cera
way [we] *s* vía, camino; dirección, sentido; manera, modo; costumbre, hábito; **across the way** enfrente; **a good way** un buen trecho; **all the way** hasta el fin del camino; **any way** de cualquier modo; **by the way** a propósito; **in a way** hasta cierto punto; **in every way** en todos respectos; **in this way** de este modo; **on the way to** camino de, rumbo a; **on the way out** saliendo; desapareciendo; **out of the way** hecho, despachado; inconveniente, impropio; a un lado, apartado; fuera de lo común; **that way** por allí; de ese modo; **this way** por aquí; de este modo; **to be in the way** estorbar; **to feel one's way** tantear el camino; proceder con tiento; **to force one's way** abrirse paso por fuerza; **to get out of the way** quitarse de en medio; (*to finish*) quitarse de encima; **to give way** ceder, retroceder; romperse (*una cuerda*); fracasar; **to give way to** entregarse a; **to go out of one's way** dar un rodeo; dar un rodeo innecesario; darse molestia; **to have one's way** salirse con la suya; **to keep out of the way** no obstruir el paso; **to know one's way around** saber entendérselas; **to know one's way to** conocer el camino a, saber ir a; **to lead the way** enseñar el camino; ir o entrar primero; **to lose one's way** perder el camino, extraviarse; **to make one's way** avanzar; hacer carrera, acreditarse; **to make way for** dar paso a, hacer lugar para; **to mend one's ways** mudar de vida; **to not know which way to turn** no saber dónde meterse; **to put out of the way** alejar, apartar; quitar de en medio; **to see one's way to** ver el modo de; **to take one's way** irse, marcharse; **to wend one's way** seguir camino; **to wind one's way through** serpentear por; **to wing one's way** ir volando; **under way** en marcha, en camino; **way in** entrada; **way out** salida; **ways** maneras, modales *mpl;* (*for launching a ship*) anguilas; **which way?** ¿por dónde?; ¿cómo?
way'bill' *s* hoja de ruta
wayfarer [ˈweˌfɛrər] *s* caminante *mf*
way'lay' *v* (*pret & pp* **-laid'**) *tr* detener de improviso; (*to attack from ambush*) insidiar, asaltar
way of life *s* estilo de vida, tren *m* de vida
way'side' *s* borde *m* del camino; **to fall by the wayside** (*to disappear*) caer en el camino; fracasar
way station *s* apeadero
wayward [ˈwewərd] *adj* díscolo, voluntarioso; voltario, caprichoso
we [wi] *pron pers* nosotros
weak [wik] *adj* débil, flaco; caedizo; (*vowel; verb*) débil; (*coffee, tea*) flojo
weaken [ˈwikən] *tr* debilitar, enflaquecer ‖ *intr* debilitarse, enflaquecerse
weakling [ˈwiklɪŋ] *s* alfeñique *m,* canijo
weak-minded [ˈwikˈmaɪndɪd] *adj* irresoluto; simple, mentecato
weakness [ˈwiknɪs] *s* debilidad, flaqueza; caducidad; lado débil; afición, gusto
weal [wil] *s* verdugón *m*
wealth [wɛlθ] *s* riqueza
wealth•y [ˈwɛlθi] *adj* (*comp* **-ier;** *super* **-iest**) rico, adinerado
wean [win] *tr* destetar; **to wean away from** apartar gradualmente de
weanling [ˈwinlɪŋ] *adj & s* destetado
weapon [ˈwɛpən] *s* arma
weaponize [ˈwɛpənaɪz] *tr* convertir o transformar en un arma
wear [wɛr] *s* (*act of wearing*) uso; (*clothing*) ropa; estilo, moda; (*wasting away from use*) desgaste *m,* deterioro; (*lasting quality*) durabilidad; **for all kinds of wear** a todo llevar; **for everyday wear** para todo trote ‖ *v* (*pret* **wore** [wor]; *pp* **worn** [worn]) *tr* llevar, traer, llevar puesto; calzar (*cierto tamaño de zapato o guante*); (*to waste away by use*) desgastar, deteriorar; (*to tire*) agotar, cansar; **to wear out** consumir, gastar; agotar, cansar; abusar de (*la hospitalidad de una persona*) ‖ *intr* desgastarse, deteriorarse; **to wear off** pasar, desaparecer; **to wear out** gastarse, usarse; **to wear well** durar, ser duradero
wear and tear *s* uso y desgaste
weariness [ˈwɪrɪnɪs] *s* cansancio; aburrimiento
wearing apparel [ˈwɛrɪŋ] *s* ropaje *m,* prendas de vestir
wearisome [ˈwɪrɪsəm] *adj* aburrido, cansado, fastidioso
wea•ry [ˈwɪri] *adj* (*comp* **-rier;** *super* **-riest**) cansado ‖ *v* (*pret & pp* **-ried**) *tr* cansar ‖ *intr* cansarse
weasel [ˈwizəl] *s* comadreja
weaseler [ˈwizələr] *s* pancista *mf*
weasel words *spl* palabras ambiguas
weather [ˈwɛðər] *s* tiempo; mal tiempo; **to be under the weather** (coll) no estar muy católico; (coll) estar borracho ‖ *tr* aguantar (*el temporal, la adversidad*)
weather-beaten [ˈwɛðərˌbitən] *adj* curtido por la intemperie
weather bureau *s* meteo *f,* servicio meteorológico
weath'er•cock' *s* veleta
weather forecaster *s* metereologo, metereologa, meteorologista *mf*
weather forecasting *s* pronóstico del tiempo, previsión del tiempo
weather report *s* parte meteorológico
weather station *s* estación meteorológica
weather stripping [ˈstrɪpɪŋ] *s* burlete *m,* cierre hermético
weather vane *s* veleta
weave [wiv] *s* tejido ‖ *v* (*pret* **wove** [wov] o **weaved;** *pp* **wove** o **woven** [ˈwovən]) *tr* tejer; **to weave one's way** avanzar zigzagueando ‖ *intr* tejer; zigzaguear

weaver [ˈwivər] *s* tejedor *m*
web [wɛb] *s* tejido, tela; (*of spider*) tela; (*between toes of birds and other animals*) membrana; (*of an iron rail*) alma; (fig) tejido, tela, enredo; (compu) telaraña
web-footed [ˈwɛb,futɪd] *adj* palmípedo, de pie palmeado
Web page *s* (compu) página Web
Web site *s* (compu) sitio Web
we'd *contr* **we would**
wed [wɛd] *v* (*pret & pp* **wed** o **wedded;** *ger* **wedding**) *tr* (*to join in marriage*) casar; casarse con || *intr* casarse
wedding [ˈwɛdɪŋ] *adj* nupcial || *s* bodas, nupcias, matrimonio
wedding cake *s* tarta *or* pastel *m* de boda
wedding day *s* día *m* de bodas
wedding dress *s* vestido o traje *m* de novia
wedding march *s* marcha nupcial
wedding night *s* noche *f* de bodas
wedding present *s* regalo de boda o casamiento
wedding ring *s* anillo nupcial, anillo de boda, alianza
wedge [wɛdʒ] *s* cuña || *tr* acuñar, apretar con cuña
wed'lock' *s* matrimonio
Wednesday [ˈwɛnzdi] *s* miércoles *m*
wee [wi] *adj* pequeñito, diminuto
weed [wid] *s* mala hierba; (coll) tabaco; **weeds** ropa de luto (*especialmente, de una viuda*) || *tr* desherbar, escardar
weeding hoe *s* escardillo
weed killer *s* matamalezas *m,* herbicida *m*
week [wik] *s* semana; **week in week out** semana tras semana
week'day' *s* día *m* laborable, día de entresemana
week'days' *adv* entresemana (SAm)
week'end' *s* fin *m* de semana || *intr* pasar el fin de semana
week•ly [ˈwikli] *adj* semanal || *adv* cada semana || *s* (*pl* **-lies**) revista semanal, semanario
weep [wip] *v* (*pret & pp* **wept** [wɛpt]) *tr* llorar (*p.ej., la muerte de una persona*); derramar (*lágrimas*) || *intr* llorar
weeper [ˈwipər] *s* llorón *m;* (*hired mourner*) llorona, plañidera
weeping willow *s* sauce *m* llorón
weep•y [ˈwipi] *adj* (*comp* **-ier;** *super* **-iest**) (coll) lloroso
weevil [ˈwivəl] *s* gorgojo
weft [wɛft] *s* (*yarns running across warp*] trama; (*fabric*) tejido
weigh [we] *tr* pesar; (naut) levantar (*el ancla*) || *intr* pesar; **to weigh in** pesarse (*un jockey*)
weight [wet] *s* peso; (*of scales, clock, gymnasium, etc.*) pesa; **to lose weight** rebajar de peso; **to put on weight** ponerse gordo; **to throw one's weight around** (coll) hacer valer su poder || *tr* cargar, gravar; (*statistically*) ponderar
weightless [ˈwetlɪs] *adj* ingrávido
weightlessness [ˈwetlɪsnɪs] *s* ingravidez *f;* antigravedad
weight lifter *s* halterofilista *mf*
weight lifting *s* halterofilia
weight watcher *s* persona que cuida la línea
weight•y [ˈweti] *adj* (*comp* **-ier;** *super* **-iest**) (*heavy*) pesado; (*troublesome*) gravoso; importante, influyente
weir [wɪr] *s* presa, vertedero; (*for catching fish*) pescadera
weird [wɪrd] *adj* misterioso, sobrenatural, espectral; extraño, raro
welcome [ˈwɛlkəm] *adj* bienvenido; grato, agradable; **you are welcome** (*i.e., gladly received*) sea Ud. bienvenido; (*in answer to thanks*) no hay de qué; **you are welcome to it** está a la disposición de Ud.; **you are welcome to your opinion** piense Ud. lo que quiera || *interj* ¡bienvenido! || *s* bienvenida, buena acogida || *tr* dar la bienvenida a; acoger con gusto, recibir con amabilidad
weld [wɛld] *s* autógena; (bot) gualda || *tr* soldar con autógena; (fig) unir || *intr* soldarse
welder [ˈwɛldər] *s* soldador *m;* (*machine*) soldadora
welding [ˈwɛldɪŋ] *s* autógena, soldadura autógena
wel'fare' *s* bienestar *m;* (*de la seguridad social*) asistencia social; (*payment*) prestaciones sociales; **to be on welfare** recibir prestaciones sociales
welfare state *s* gobierno socializante, estado de beneficencia, estado de bienestar, estado asistencial *or* benefactor
we'll *contr* **we will, we shall**
well [wɛl] *adj* bien; bien de salud; **get well!** ¡que se mejore! || *adv* bien; pues; pues bien; **as well** también; **as well as** así como; además de || *interj* ¡vaya! || *s* pozo; (*natural source of water*) fuente *f,* manantial *m* || *intr*—**to well up** salir a borbotones
well'-adjust'ed *adj* (psychol) equilibrado
well-appointed [ˈwɛləˈpɔɪntɪd] *adj* bien amueblado, bien equipado
well-attended [ˈwɛləˈtɛndɪd] *adj* muy concurrido, con mucho público
well'-bal'anced *adj* equilibrado
well-behaved [ˈwɛlbɪˈhevd] *adj* de buena conducta
well'-be'ing *s* bienestar *m*
well'born' *adj* bien nacido
well-bred [ˈwɛlˈbrɛd] *adj* cortés, bien criado
well'-built' *adj* bien construido; (*person*) fornido
well'-dressed' *adj* bien vestido
well-disposed [ˈwɛldɪsˈpozd] *adj* bien dispuesto
well-done [ˈwɛlˈdʌn] *adj* bien hecho; (*meat*) bien asado
well'-ed'ucated *adj* culto, instruido
well-fixed [ˈwɛlˈfɪkst] *adj* (coll) acaudalado
well-formed [ˈwɛlˈfɔrmd] *adj* bien formado; (*nose*) perfilado
well-founded [ˈwɛlˈfaʊndɪd] *adj* bien fundado
well-groomed [ˈwɛlˈgrumd] *adj* de mucho aseo, atildado

well-heeled [ˈwɛlˈhild] *adj* (coll) acomodado; **to be well-heeled** (coll) tener bien cubierto el riñón
well-informed [ˈwɛlɪnˈfɔrmd] *adj* versado, bien enterado
well-intentioned [ˈwɛlɪnˈtɛnʃənd] *adj* bien intencionado
well-kept [ˈwɛlˈkɛpt] *adj* bien cuidado, bien atendido; (*secret*) bien guardado
well-known [ˈwɛlˈnon] *adj* bien conocido, sabido; familiar
well-meaning [ˈwɛlˈminɪŋ] *adj* bien intencionado
well-nigh [ˈwɛlˈnaɪ] *adv* casi
well′-off′ *adj* adinerado, acaudalado
well-preserved [ˈwɛlprɪˈzʌrvd] *adj* bien conservado
well-read [ˈwɛlˈrɛd] *adj* leído, muy leído
well-spent [ˈwɛlˈspɛnt] *adj* (*money, youth, life*) bien empleado
well-spoken [ˈwɛlˈspokən] *adj* (*person*) bienhablado; (*word*) bien dicho
well′spring′ *s* fuente *f,* manantial *m;* fuente inagotable
well-tempered [ˈwɛlˈtɛmpərd] *adj* bien templado
well-thought-of [ˈwɛlˈθɔt,ɑv] *adj* bien mirado
well-timed [ˈwɛlˈtaɪmd] *adj* oportuno
well-to-do [ˈwɛltəˈdu] *adj* adinerado, acaudalado; (coll) plateado
well-wisher [ˈwɛlˈwɪʃər] *s* amigo, favorecedor *m*
well-worn [ˈwɛlˈworn] *adj* trillado, vulgar
welsh [wɛlʃ] *intr* (slang) dejar de cumplir; **to welsh on** (slang) dejar de cumplir con ‖ **Welsh** *adj* galés ‖ *s* (*language*) galés *m;* **the Welsh** los galeses
Welsh•man [ˈwɛlʃmən] *s* (*pl* **-men** [mən]) galés *m*
Welsh rabbit o **rarebit** [ˈrɛrbɪt] *s* tostada cubierta de queso derretido en cerveza
welt [wɛlt] *s* (*finish along a seam*) ribete *m;* (*of a shoe*) vira; (*wale from a blow*) verdugón *m*
welter [ˈwɛltər] *s* confusión, conmoción; (*a tumbling about*) revuelco ‖ *intr* revolcar
wel′ter•weight′ *s* (box) peso mediano ligero
wen [wɛn] *s* lobanillo
wend [wɛnd] *tr*—**to wend one's way** dirigir sus pasos, seguir su camino
we′re *contr* **we are**
weren't *contr* **were not**
were′wolf *s* hombre lobo, lobizón *m*
west [wɛst] *adj* occidental, del oeste ‖ *adv* al oeste, hacia el oeste ‖ *s* oeste *m*
western [ˈwɛstərn] *adj* occidental ‖ *s* película del Oeste
West Indies [ˈɪndiz] *spl* Indias Occidentales
westward [ˈwɛstwərd] *adv* hacia el oeste
wet [wɛt] *adj* (*comp* **wetter;** *super* **wettest**) mojado; (*damp*) húmedo; (*paint*) fresco; (*weather*) lluvioso; (coll) antiprohibicionista ‖ *s* (coll) antiprohibicionista *mf* ‖ *v* (*pret & pp* **wet** o **wetted;** *ger* **wetting**) *tr* mojar ‖ *intr* mojarse
wet′back′ *s* (pej) espalda *mf* mojada, mojado
wet bar *s* bar *m* con agua corriente
wet blanket *s* aguafiestas *mf*
wet goods *spl* caldos
wet kiss *s* beso sonado
wet nurse *s* ama de cría o de leche
wet suit *s* traje *m* de neoprene o neopreno
we′ve *contr* **we have**
whack [hwæk] *s* (coll) golpe ruidoso; (coll) prueba, tentativa ‖ *tr* (coll) golpear ruidosamente
whale [hwel] *s* ballena; (*sperm whale*) cachalote *m;* **a whale at** (coll) un as de; **a whale for** (coll) un genio para; **a whale of a difference** (coll) una enorme diferencia; **a whale of a meal** (coll) una comida brutal ‖ *tr* (coll) azotar ‖ *intr* pescar ballenas
whale′bone′ *s* ballena
wham [hwæm] *tr* (coll) pegarle con fuerza a ‖ *interj* ¡pataplún!
wharf [hwɔrf] *s* (*pl* **wharves** [hwɔrvz] o **wharfs**) muelle *m,* embarcadero
what [hwɑt] *pron interr* qué; cuál; **what else?** ¿qué más?; **what if . . . ?** ¿y si . . . ?, ¿qué le parece si?; **what of it?** ¿qué importa? ‖ *pron rel* lo que; **what's what** lo que hay, toda la verdad ‖ *adj interr* qué ‖ *adj rel* el . . . que, la . . . que, etc. ‖ *interj* qué; **what a . . .!** qué . . . más o tan, p.ej., **what a beautiful day!** ¡qué día más (o tan) hermoso!
what•ev′er *pron* cualquiera; todo lo que ‖ *adj* cualquier; cualquier . . . que
what′not′ *s* juguetero
what's-his-name [ˈhwɑtsɪz,nem] *s* (coll) el señor fulano
wheal [hwil] *s* roncha
wheat [hwit] *s* trigo
wheedle [ˈhwidəl] *tr* engatusar; conseguir por medio de halagos
wheel [hwil] *s* rueda; (coll) bicicleta; **at the wheel** en el volante ‖ *tr* pasear (*a un niño*) en un cochecito; conducir (*a un enfermo*) en una silla de ruedas ‖ *intr* (coll) ir en bicicleta; **to wheel about** o **around** dar una vuelta; cambiar de opinión
wheelbarrow [ˈhwil,bæro] *s* carretilla
wheel base *s* batalla, paso, distancia entre ejes
wheel chair *s* silla de ruedas, cochecillo para inválidos
wheeler-dealer [ˈhwilərˈdilər] *s* (slang) negociante *m* de gran influencia e independencia
wheel horse *s* caballo de varas; (fig) esclavo (*el que trabaja mucho y cumple con sus obligaciones*)
wheelwright [ˈhwil,raɪt] *s* carpintero de carretas
wheeze [hwiz] *s* resuello ruidoso ‖ *intr* resollar produciendo un silbido
whelp [hwɛlp] *s* cachorro ‖ *intr* parir
when [hwɛn] *adv* cuándo ‖ *conj* cuando
whence [hwɛns] *adv* de dónde; por lo tanto ‖ *conj* de donde

when•ev′er *conj* siempre que, cada vez que
where [hwɛr] *adv* dónde; adónde || *conj* donde; adonde
whereabouts [ˈhwɛrə,bauts] *s* paradero
whereas [hwɛrˈæz] *conj* mientras que, al paso que; considerando || *s* considerando
where•by′ *adv* por medio del cual
wherefore [ˈhwɛrfor] *adv* por qué, para qué; por eso, por tanto || *conj* por lo cual || *s* motivo, razón *f*
where•from′ *adv* de donde
where•in′ *adv* donde, en qué || *conj* donde; en el que; en lo cual
where•of′ *adv* de qué || *conj* de que; de lo cual
where′up•on′ *adv* con lo cual, después de lo cual
wherever [hwɛrˈɛvər] *conj* dondequiera que
wherewithal [ˈhwɛrwɪð,ɔl] *s* cumquibus *m,* medios
whet [hwɛt] *v* (*pret & pp* **whetted;** *ger* **whetting**) *tr* afilar, aguzar; despertar, estimular; abrir (*el apetito*)
whether [ˈwɛðər] *conj* si; **whether or no** en todo caso, de todas maneras; **whether or not** si . . . o no, ya sea que . . . o no
whet′stone′ *s* piedra de afilar
whey [hwe] *s* suero de la leche
which [hwɪtʃ] *pron interr* cuál; **which is which** cuál es el uno y cuál el otro || *pron rel* que, el (la, etc.) que || *adj interr* qué; cuál, cuál de los (las) || *adj rel* el (la, etc.) . . . que
which•ev′er *pron rel* cualquiera || *adj rel* cualquier; **whichever ones** cualesquiera
whiff [hwɪf] *s* soplo; fumada; olorcillo; acceso, arranque *m;* **to get a whiff of** percibir un olor fugaz de || *intr* soplar (*el viento*); echar bocanadas (*el que fuma*)
while [hwaɪl] *conj* mientras, mientras que || *s* rato; **a long while** largo rato; **a while ago** hace un rato; **between whiles** de vez en cuando || *tr* **to while away** entretener (*el tiempo*); pasar (*p.ej., la tarde*) de un modo entretenido
whim [hwɪm] *s* capricho, antojo
whimper [ˈhwɪmpər] *s* lloriqueo || *tr* decir lloriqueando || *intr* lloriquear
whimsical [ˈhwɪmzɪkəl] *adj* caprichoso, extravagante, fantástico
whine [hwaɪn] *s* gimoteo, quejido || *intr* gimotear, quejarse
whin•ny [ˈhwɪni] *s* (*pl* **-nies**) relincho || *v* (*pret & pp* **-nied**) *intr* relinchar
whip [hwɪp] *s* látigo, zurriago; huevos batidos con nata || *v* (*pret & pp* **whipped** o **whipt;** *ger* **whipping**) *tr* azotar, zurriagar, fustigar; batir (*huevos y nata*); (coll) derrotar, vencer; **to whip off** (coll) escribir de prisa; **to whip out** sacar de repente; **to whip up** (coll) preparar de prisa; (coll) avivar, excitar
whip′cord′ *s* tralla; tejido fuerte con costurones diagonales
whip hand *s* mano *f* del látigo; (*upper hand*) vara alta
whip′lash′ *s* (*blow*) latigazo, trallazo; (*cord*) tralla
whiplash injury *s* traumatismo cervical
whipped cream *s* nata, crema batida
whipper-snapper [ˈhwɪpər,snæpər] *s* arrapiezo, mequetrefe *m*
whippet [ˈhwɪpɪt] *s* perro lebrel
whipping boy [ˈhwɪpɪŋ] *s* cabeza de turco, víctima inocente
whipping post *s* poste *m* de flagelación
whippoorwill [,hwɪpərˈwɪl] *s* chotacabras norteamericano (*Caprimulgus vociferus*)
whir [hwʌr] *s* zumbido || *v* (*pret & pp* **whirred;** *ger* **whirring**) *intr* girar zumbando
whirl [hwʌrl] *s* vuelta, giro; remolino; (*of events, parties, etc.*) serie *f* interminable || *tr & intr* remolinear; **my head whirls** siento vértigo
whirligig [ˈhwʌrlɪ,gɪg] *s* (ent) escribano del agua; tíovivo; (*pinwheel*) rehilandera, molinete *m;* peonza
whirl′pool′ *s* remolino, vorágine *f;* (*bath*) piscina de hidromasaje
whirl′wind′ *s* torbellino, manga de viento
whirlybird [ˈhwʌrli,bʌrd] *s* (coll) helicóptero
whish [hwɪʃ] *s* zumbido suave || *intr* zumbar suavemente
whisk [hwɪsk] *s* escobilla; toque ligero || *tr* barrer, cepillar; **to whisk out of sight** escamotear || *intr* moverse rápidamente
whisk broom *s* escobilla
whiskers [ˈhwɪskərz] *spl* barbas; (*on side of face*) patillas; (*of cat*) bigotes *mpl*
whiskey [ˈhwɪski] *adj* (*voice*) (coll) aguardentoso || *s* whisky *m*
whisper [ˈhwɪspər] *s* cuchicheo; (*of leaves*) susurro; **in a whisper** en voz baja || *tr* susurrar, decir al oído || *intr* cuchichear, hablar al oído; susurrar (*p.ej., las hojas*); (*to gossip*) susurrar, murmurar
whisperer [ˈhwɪspərər] *s* susurrón *m*
whispering [ˈhwɪspərɪŋ] *adj & s* (*gossiping*) susurrón *m*
whist [hwɪst] *s* whist *m* (*juego de naipes*)
whistle [ˈhwɪsəl] *s* (*sound*) silbido, silbo, pitido; (SAm) pitazo; (*device*) silbato, pito; **to wet one's whistle** (coll) remojar la palabra || *tr* silbar (*p.ej., una canción* || *intr* silbar; pitear; **to whistle for** llamar con un silbido; (coll) tener que componérselas sin
whistle stop *s* apeadero, pueblecito
whistle-stop tour *s* gira relámpago
whit [hwɪt] *s*—**not a whit** ni pizca; **to not care a whit** no importarle a (*uno*) un bledo
white [hwaɪt] *adj* blanco || *s* blanco; (*of an egg*) clara; **whites** (pathol) pérdidas blancas, flujo blanco
white blood cell *s* glóbulo blanco
white′caps′ *spl* cabrillas, palomas
white coal *s* hulla blanca
white′-col′lar *adj* oficinesco
white-collar crime *s* crímenes *mpl* de oficinistas

white corpuscle *s* glóbulo blanco
white feather *s*—**to show the white feather** mostrarse cobarde
white goods *spl* tejidos de algodón; ropa blanca; aparatos electrodomésticos
white-haired [ˋhwaɪt,hɛrd] *adj* de pelo blanco; (*gray-haired*) cano; (coll) favorito, predilecto
white heat *s* blanco, calor blanco; (fig) viva agitación
white lead [lɛd] *s* albayalde *m*
white lie *s* mentirilla, mentira inocente u oficiosa, mentira piadosa
white meat *s* pechuga, carne *f* de la pechuga del ave
whiten [ˋhwaɪtən] *tr* blanquear, emblanquecer ‖ *intr* blanquear, emblanquecerse; palidecer
whiteness [ˋhwaɪtnɪs] *s* blancura
white′out′ *s* líquido corrector
white plague *s* peste blanca (*tuberculosis*)
white noise *s* ruido blanco
white slavery *s* trata de blancas
white tie *s* corbatín blanco; traje *m* de etiqueta
white′wash′ *s* jalbegue *m,* lechada, blanqueadura; (*e.g., of a scandal*) encubrimiento ‖ *tr* jalbegar, enjalbegar, encalar; (*to exonerate falsely*) absolver sin justicia; (*to cover up*) encubrir (*un escándalo*)
whither [ˋhwɪðər] *adv* adónde ‖ *conj* adonde
whitish [ˋhwaɪtɪʃ] *adj* blanquecino, blancuzco
whitlow [ˋhwɪtlo] *s* (pathol) panadizo, uñero
Whitsuntide [ˋhwɪtsən,taɪd] *s* semana de Pentecostés
whittle [ˋhwɪtəl] *tr* sacar pedazos a (*un trozo de madera*); **to whittle away** o **down** reducir poco a poco
whiz o **whizz** [hwɪz] *s* silbido, zumbido; (slang) perito, fenómeno ‖ *v* (*pret & pp* **whizzed;** *ger* **whizzing**) *intr*—**to whiz by** rehilar, silbar; pasar como una flecha
who [hu] *pron interr* quién; **who else?** ¿quién más?; **who goes there?** (mil) ¿quién vive?; **who's who** quién es el uno y quién el otro; quiénes son gente de importancia ‖ *pron rel* que, quien; el (la, etc.) que
whoa [hwo] o [wo] *interj* ¡so!
who'd *contr* **who would**
who•ev′er *pron rel* quienquiera que, cualquiera que
whole [hol] *adj* todo, entero; (*intact*) ileso; (*not scattered or dispersed*) único, p.ej., **the whole interest for him was the child he was raising** el único interés para él era el niño que educaba; **made out of whole cloth** enteramente falso o imaginario ‖ *s* conjunto, todo; **as a whole** en conjunto; **on the whole** en general; por la mayor parte
wholehearted [ˋhol,hɑrtɪd] *adj* sincero, cordial
whole milk *s* leche entera
whole note *s* (mus) semibreve *f*
whole′sale′ *adj & adv* al por mayor ‖ *s* venta al por mayor ‖ *tr* vender al por mayor ‖ *intr* vender al por mayor; venderse al por mayor
wholesaler [ˋhol,selər] *s* comerciante *mf* al por mayor
wholesome [ˋholsəm] *adj* (*conducive to good health*) saludable; (*in good health*) fresco, rollizo
whole′-wheat bread *s* pan *m* integral
whole′-wheat flour *s* harina integral
wholly [ˋholi] *adv* enteramente, completamente
whole wheat *s* trigo entero
who'll *contr* **who will**
whom [hum] *pron interr* a quién ‖ *pron rel* que, a quien; al (a la, etc.) que
whom•ev′er *pron rel* a quienquiera que
whoop [hup] o [hwup] *s* ululato ‖ *tr*—**to whoop it up** (slang) armar una gritería ‖ *intr* ulular
whooping cough [ˋhupɪŋ] o [ˋhʊpɪŋ] *s* tos ferina, tos convulsiva
whopper [ˋhwɑpər] *s* (coll) enormidad; (coll) (*big lie*) mentirón *m*
whopping [ˋhwɑpɪŋ] *adj* (coll) enorme, grandísimo
whopping cough *s* (pathol) tos ferina o convulsa o convulsiva
whore o convulsiva [hor] *s* puta
whore′house′ *s* burdel *m;* congal *m* (Mex)
whortleber•ry [ˋhwʌrtəl,bɛri] *s* (*pl* **-ries**) arándano
who's *contr* **who is; who has**
whose [huz] *pron interr* de quién ‖ *pron rel* de quien, cuyo
why [hwaɪ] *adv* por qué; **why not?** ¿cómo no? ‖ *s* (*pl* **whys**) porqué *m* ‖ *interj* ¡toma!; **why, certainly!** ¡desde luego!, ¡por supuesto!; **why, yes!** ¡claro!, ¡pues sí!
wick [wɪk] *s* mecha, pabilo
wicked [ˋwɪkɪd] *adj* malo; malazo; (*mischievous*) travieso, revoltoso; (*vicious*) arisco; ofensivo
wicker [ˋwɪkər] *adj* mimbroso ‖ *s* mimbre *m&f*
wicket [ˋwɪkɪt] *s* (*small door in a larger one*) portillo, postigo; (*small opening in a door*) ventanillo; (*ticket window*) taquilla; (*gate to regulate flow of water*) compuerta; (cricket) meta; (croquet) aro
wide [waɪd] *adj* ancho; de ancho; (*sense of a word*) amplio, lato ‖ *adv* de par en par; enteramente; lejos; **wide of the mark** lejos del blanco; fuera de propósito
wide′-an′gle *adj* amplio; (phot, opt) gran angular, de ángulo ancho
wide-angle lens *s* (phot) gran angular *m,* objectivo gran angular
wide′-a•wake′ *adj* despabilado
widely [ˋwaɪdli] *adv* muy; mucho; extensamente
widen [ˋwaɪdən] *tr* ensanchar ‖ *intr* ensancharse
wide′-o′pen *adj* abierto de par en par; **to be wide-open** estar (*p.ej., una ciudad*) abierta a los jugadores
wide′-rang′ing *adj* amplio; variado; de gran alcance
wide screen *s* (mov) pantalla ancha
wide′spread′ *adj* (*arms, wings*) extendido; difundido, extenso

widow [ˈwɪdo] *s* viuda; (cards) baceta ‖ *tr* dejar viuda
widower [ˈwɪdo•ər] *s* viudo
widowhood [ˈwɪdo,hʊd] *s* viudez *f*
width [wɪdθ] *s* anchura
wield [wild] *tr* esgrimir, manejar (*la espada*); ejercer (*el poder*)
wife [waɪf] *s* (*pl* **wives** [waɪvz]) esposa, mujer *f*
wife′beat′er *s* esposo que maltrata a su esposa; (*undershirt*) (coll) camiseta sin mangas (*prenda interior para hombres*)
wig [wɪg] *s* peluca
wiggle [ˈwɪgəl] *s* meneo rápido ‖ *tr* menear rápidamente ‖ *intr* menearse rápidamente
wiggle room *s* (coll) un poco de espacio
wig′wag′ *s* comunicación con banderas ‖ *v* (*pret & pp* **-wagged;** *ger* **-wagging**) *tr* menear; mandar (*informes*) moviendo banderas ‖ *intr* menearse; señalar con banderas
wigwam [ˈwɪgwɑm] *s* wigwam *m*
wild [waɪld] *adj* (*not domesticated; growing without cultivation; uncivilized*) salvaje; (*unrestrained*) descabellado; (*frantic, mad*) frenético; (*riotous*) desenfrenado, revoltoso; extravagante; (*bullet, shot*) perdido; **wild about** loco por ‖ *adv* disparatadamente; **to run wild** crecer locamente; estar sin gobierno ‖ *s* desierto, yermo; **wilds** monte *m,* despoblado
wild boar *s* jabalí *m,* cerdo salvaje
wild card *s* comodín *m;* (fig) imponderable *m;* (compu) comodín
wild′cat′ *s* gato montés; lince *m;* empresa arriesgada
wildcat strike *s* huelga no autorizada por el sindicato, huelga salvaje (Esp)
wilderness [ˈwɪldərnɪs] *s* desierto, yermo
wild′fire′ *s* fuego fatuo; fucilazo; **to spread like wildfire** ser un reguero de pólvora, correr como pólvora en reguero
wild flower *s* flor *f* del campo
wild goose *s* ganso bravo
wild′-goose′ chase *s* caza de grillos
wild′life′ *s* animales *mf* salvajes
wild oats *spl* excesos de la juventud, mocedad; **to sow one's wild oats** llevar (*los mozos*) una vida de excesos
wild olive *s* acebuche *m*
wile [waɪl] *s* ardid *m* engaño; (*cunning*) astucia ‖ *tr* engatusar; **to wile away** entretener (*el tiempo*); pasar (*p.ej., la tarde*)
will [wɪl] *s* voluntad; (law) testamento; **at will** a voluntad ‖ *tr* querer; (*to bequeath*) legar ‖ *intr* querer; **do as you will** haga Ud. lo que quiera ‖ *v* (*pret & cond* **would**) *v aux* **he will arrive at six o'clock** llegará a las seis; **he will go for days without smoking** pasa días enteros sin fumar
willful [ˈwɪlfəl] *adj* voluntarioso
willfulness [ˈwɪlfəlnɪs] *s* voluntariedad
William [ˈwɪljəm] *s* Guillermo
willing [ˈwɪlɪŋ] *adj* dispuesto; gustoso, pronto; espontáneo; **willing or unwilling** que quiera, que no quiera
willingly [ˈwɪlɪŋli] *adv* de buena gana, de buena voluntad
willingness [ˈwɪlɪŋnɪs] *s* buena gana, buena voluntad
will-o'-the-wisp [ˈwɪləðəˈwɪsp] *s* fuego fatuo; ilusión, quimera
willow [ˈwɪlo] *s* sauce *m*
willowy [ˈwɪlo•i] *adj* (*pliant*) juncal, mimbreño; (*slender, graceful*) juncal, cimbreño, esbelto; lleno de sauces
will power *s* fuerza de voluntad
willy-nilly [ˈwɪliˈnɪli] *adv* de grado o por fuerza
wilt [wɪlt] *tr* marchitar ‖ *intr* marchitarse
wil•y [ˈwaɪli] *adj* (*comp* **-ier;** *super* **-iest**) artero, engañoso; astuto
wimp [wɪmp] *s* (coll) pelele *m,* mentecato, maricón *m* (pej)
wimple [ˈwɪmpəl] *s* griñón *m,* impla
win [wɪn] *s* (coll) éxito, triunfo ‖ *v* (*pret & pp* **won** [wʌn]; *ger* **winning**) *tr* ganar; **to win over** ganar, conquistar ‖ *intr* ganar; **to win out** ganar; (coll) tener éxito
wince [wɪns] *s* sobresalto ‖ *intr* sobresaltarse
winch [wɪntʃ] *s* maquinilla, torno; (*handle, crank*) manubrio
wind [wɪnd] *s* viento; (*gas in intestines*) (coll) viento; (*breath*) respiración, resuello; **to break wind** ventosear; **to get wind of** saber de, tener noticia de; **to sail close to the wind** (naut) ceñir el viento; **to take the wind out of one's sails** apagarle a uno los fuegos ‖ *tr* dejar sin aliento ‖ [waɪnd] *v* (*pret & pp* **wound** [waʊnd]) *tr* (*to coil; to wrap up*) arrollar, envolver, devanar (*alambre*); ovillar (*hilo*); torcer (*hebras*); hacer girar (*un manubrio*); dar cuerda a (*un reloj*); **to wind one's way through** serpentear por; **to wind up** arrollar, envolver; (coll) poner punto final a ‖ *intr* serpentear (*un camino*)
windbag [ˈwɪnd,bæg] *s* (*of bagpipe*) odre *m;* (coll) charlatán *m,* palabrero, discursista *mf*
windbreak [ˈwɪnd,brek] *s* guardavientos *m*
wind cone [wɪnd] *s* (aer) cono de viento
winded [ˈwɪndɪd] *adj* falto de respiración, sin resuello
windfall [ˈwɪnd,fɔl] *s* fruta caída del árbol; fortunón *m,* cosa llovida del cielo
wind farm *s* parque eólico
winding sheet [ˈwaɪndɪŋ] *s* sudario, mortaja
wind instrument [wɪnd] *s* (mus) instrumento de viento
windlass [ˈwɪndləs] *s* maquinilla, torno
windmill [ˈwɪnd,mɪl] *s* (*mill operated by wind*) molino de viento; (*modern wind-driven source of power*) aeromotor *m;* (*pinwheel*) molinete *m;* **to tilt at windmills** luchar con los molinos de viento
window [ˈwɪndo] *s* ventana; (*of ticket office; of envelope*) ventanilla; (*of coach, automobile*) ventanilla, portezuela; (compu) ventana, recuadro

window box *s* jardinera
window dresser *s* escaparatista *mf*
window dressing *s* adorno de escaparates
window frame *s* marco de ventana
win'dow•pane' *s* cristal *m* o vidrio de ventana
window screen *s* alambrera, sobrevidriera
window shade *s* visillo, transparente *m* de resorte
win'dow•shop' *v* (*pret & pp* **-shopped;** *ger* **-shopping**) *intr* curiosear en las tiendas, mirar vitrinas, vidrieras *or* escaparates
window shutter *s* contraventana
window sill *s* repisa de ventana
windpipe ['wɪnd,paɪp] *s* tráquea
wind power *s* energía eólica
wind shear *s* (aer) ráfaga violente
windshield ['wɪnd,ʃild] *s* parabrisa *m*
windshield washer *s* lavaparabrisas *m*
windshield wiper *s* limpiaparabrisas *m*
wind'shield-wip'er blade *s* escobilla de limpiaparabrisas
wind sock *s* (aer) cono o manga de viento
windstorm ['wɪnd,stɔrm] *s* ventarrón *m*
windsurfer ['wɪnd,sʌrfər] *s* (*person*) tablista *mf,* surfista *mf;* (*board*) tabla o plancha de windsurf
wind-up ['waɪnd,ʌp] *s* conclusión; (sport) final *f* de partido
windward ['wɪndwərd] *s* barlovento; **to turn to windward** barloventear
Windward Islands *spl* islas de Barlovento
Windward Passage *s* paso de los Vientos
wind•y ['wɪndi] *adj* (*comp* **-ier;** *super* **-iest**) ventoso; (*unsubstantial*) vacío; palabrero, ampuloso, discursisto; **it is windy** hace viento
wine [waɪn] *s* vino || *tr* obsequiar con vino || *intr* beber vino
wine cellar *s* bodega
wine'glass' *s* copa para vino
winegrower ['waɪn,gro•ər] *s* vinicultor *m*
winegrowing ['waɪn,gro•ɪŋ] *s* vinicultura
wine making *s* enotecnia
wine press *s* lagar *m*
winer•y ['waɪnəri] *s* (*pl* **-ies**) lagar *m*
wine'skin' *s* odre *m*
winetaster ['waɪn,testər] *s* catavinos *m*
wing [wɪŋ] *s* ala; facción; bando; (theat) bastidor *m;* **to take wing** alzar el vuelo || *tr* herir en el ala; **to wing one's way** avanzar volando
wing chair *s* sillón *m* de orejas
wing collar *s* cuello de pajarita
wing nut *s* tuerca mariposa o de aletas
wing'spread' *s* envergadura
wink [wɪŋk] *s* guiño; **to not sleep a wink** no pegar los ojos; **to take forty winks** (coll) descabezar el sueño || *tr* guiñar (*el ojo*) || *intr* guiñar; (*to blink*) parpadear, pestañear; **to wink at** guiñar el ojo a; fingir no ver
winner ['wɪnər] *s* ganador *m,* vencedor *m;* premiado
winning ['wɪnɪŋ] *adj* triunfante, victorioso; atrayente, simpático || **winnings** *spl* ganancias
winnow ['wɪno] *tr* aventar; entresacar || *intr* aletear
winsome ['wɪnsəm] *adj* atrayente, simpático, engañador; alegre
winter ['wɪntər] *adj* invernal || *s* invierno || *intr* invernar
win'ter•green' *s* gaulteria, té *m* del Canadá; esencia de gaulteria
win•try ['wɪntri] *adj* (*comp* **-trier;** *super* **-triest**) invernal, invernizo; helado, frío
wipe [waɪp] *tr* frotar para limpiar; enjugar (*la cara, el sudor, las manos*); **to wipe away** enjugar (*lágrimas*); **to wipe off** quitar frotando; **to wipe out** (coll) borrar, cancelar; (coll) aniquilar, destruir; (coll) enjugar (*deudas, un déficit*)
wiper ['waɪpər] *s* paño, trapo; (elec) contacto deslizante
wire [waɪr] *s* (*thread of metal*) alambre *m;* telégrafo; telegrama *m;* teléfono; **to pull wires** (coll) tocar resortes || *tr* alambrar; telegrafiar || *intr* telegrafiar
wire cutter *s* cortaalambres *m*
wire entanglement *s* (mil) alambrado
wire gauge *s* calibrador *m* de alambre
wire-haired ['waɪr,hɛrd] *adj* de pelo áspero
wireless ['waɪrlɪs] *adj* inalámbrico, sin hilos
wire nail *s* punta de París, clavo de alambre
wire pulling ['pʊlɪŋ] *s* (coll) empleo de resortes; enchufismo
wire recorder *s* grabadora de alambre
wire screen *s* alambrera, tela de alambre
wire service *s* servicio telegráfrico y telefónico
wire'tap' *s* escucha telefónica || *v* (*pret & pp* **-tapped;** *ger* **-tapping**) *tr* intervenir (*una conversación telefónica*)
wire tapping *s* escuchas telefónicas *fpl*
wiring ['waɪrɪŋ] *s* (elec) alambraje *m*
wir•y ['waɪri] *adj* (*comp* **-ier;** *super* **-iest**) alambrino; cimbreante; nervudo; vibrante
wisdom ['wɪzdəm] *s* sabiduría, cordura
wisdom tooth *s* muela cordal, muela del juicio
wise [waɪz] *adj* sabio, cuerdo; (*step, decision*) acertado, juicioso; **to be wise to** (slang) conocer el juego de; **to get wise** (coll) caer en el chiste || *s* modo, manera; **in no wise** de ningún modo
wiseacre ['waɪz,ekər] *s* sabihondo
wise'crack' *s* (slang) cuchufleta || *intr* (slang) cuchufletear
wise guy *s* (slang) sabelototodo
wish [wɪʃ] *s* deseo; **to make a wish** pensar algo que se desea || *tr* desear; dar (*los buenos días*) || *intr* desear; **to wish for** desear, anhelar
wish'bone' *s* espoleta, hueso de la suerte
wishful ['wɪʃfəl] *adj* deseoso
wishful thinking *s* optimismo a ultranza; **to indulge in wishful thinking** forjarse ilusiones
wishing well *s* fuente *f* de los deseos
wistful ['wɪstfəl] *adj* melancólico, tristón, pensativo
wit [wɪt] *s* agudeza; (*person*) chistoso; (*keen mental power*) juicio; **to be at one's wits'**

end no saber qué hacer; **to have the wit to** tener el tino de; **to live by one's wits** vivir del cuento
witch [wɪtʃ] *s* bruja, hechicera; (*old hag*) bruja
witch'craft' *s* brujería
witch'-hunt *s* caza de brujas
witches' Sabbath *s* aquelarre *m*
witch hazel *s* (*shrub*) nogal *m* de la brujería, planta del sortilegio; (*liquid*) hamamelina, hazelina
with [wɪð] o [wɪθ] *prep* con; de
with•draw' *v* (*pret* **-drew;** *pp* **-drawn**) *tr* retirar ‖ *intr* retirarse
withdrawal [wɪð'drɔ•əl] o [wɪθ'drɔ•əl] *s* retirada; suspensión
withdrawal symptom *s* síntoma *m* de abstinencia; (slang) mono
wither ['wɪðər] *tr* marchitar; (fig) aplastar, confundir ‖ *intr* marchitarse; confundirse
with•hold' *v* (*pret & pp* **-held**) *tr* retener; suspender (*pago*); negar (*un permiso*)
withholding tax *s* impuesto de retención, impuesto retenido
with•in' *adv* dentro ‖ *prep* dentro de; al alcance de; poco menos de; con un margen de
with•out' *adv* fuera ‖ *prep* fuera de; (*lacking, not with*) sin; **to do without** pasar sin; **without** + *ger* sin + *inf,* p.ej., **he left without saying goodbye** salió sin despedirse; sin que + *subj,* p.ej., **he came in without anyone seeing him** entró sin que nadie le viese
with•stand' *v* (*pret & pp* **-stood**) *tr* aguantar, resistir
witness ['wɪtnɪs] *s* testigo *mf;* (*for the defense*) testigo de descargo; (*for the prosecution*) testigo de cargo; **in witness whereof** en fe de lo cual; **to bear witness** dar testimonio ‖ *tr* (*to be present at*) presenciar; (*to attest*) atestiguar, testimoniar; firmar como testigo
witness stand *s* banquillo o estrado de los testigos
witticism ['wɪtɪ,sɪzəm] *s* agudeza, dicho agudo, ocurrencia
wittingly ['wɪtɪŋli] *adv* a sabiendas
wit•ty ['wɪti] *adj* (*comp* **-tier;** *super* **-tiest**) agudo, ingenioso; (*person*) ocurrente, chistoso
wizard ['wɪzərd] *s* brujo, hechicero; (coll) as *m,* experto
wizardry ['wɪzərdri] *s* hechicería, magia
wizened ['wɪzənd] *adj* acartonado, arrugado
woad [wod] *s* hierba pastel
wobble ['wɑbəl] *s* bamboleo, tambaleo ‖ *intr* bambolear, tambalear; bailar (*una silla*); (fig) vacilar, ser inconstante
wob•bly ['wɑbli] *adj* (*comp* **-blier;** *super* **-bliest**) bamboleante, inseguro; vacilante
woe [wo] *s* aflicción, miseria, infortunio ‖ *interj*—**woe is me!** ¡ay de mí!
woebegone ['wobɪ,gɔn] o ['wobɪ,gɑn] *adj* cariacontecido, triste
woeful ['wofəl] *adj* triste, miserable; (*of poor quality*) malo, pésimo
wolf [wʊlf] *s* (*pl* **wolves** [wʊlvz]) lobo; persona cruel, persona mañosa; (coll) tenorio; **to cry wolf** dar falsa alarma; **to keep the wolf from the door** ponerse a cubierto del hambre ‖ *tr & intr* comer vorazmente, engullir
wolf'hound' *s* galgo lobero
wolfram ['wʊlfrəm] *s* (*element*) volframio; (*mineral*) volframita
wolf's-bane o **wolfsbane** ['wʊlfs,ben] *s* matalobos *m*
woman ['wʊmən] *s* (*pl* **women** ['wɪmɪn]) mujer *f*
womanhood ['wʊmən,hʊd] *s* el sexo femenino; las mujeres
womanish ['wʊmənɪʃ] *adj* mujeril; (*effeminate*) afeminado
womanizer ['wumənaɪzər] *s* donjúan *m,* mujeriego
wom'an•kind' *s* las mujeres, la mujer
womanly ['wʊmənli] *adj* (*comp* **-lier;** *super* **-liest**) femenil, mujeriego
womb [wʊm] *s* útero; (fig) seno
Women *s* (*women's room*) *SIGN* Señoras, Damas
womenfolk ['wɪmɪn,fok] *spl* las mujeres
women's lib(eration movement) *s* movimiento feminista; feminismo
wonder ['wʌndər] *s* (*something strange or surprising*) maravilla; (*feeling of surprise*) admiración; (*something strange, miracle*) milagro; **for a wonder** cosa extraña; **no wonder that . . .** no es mucho que . . .; **to work wonders** hacer milagros ‖ *tr* preguntarse ‖ *intr* admirarse, maravillarse; **to wonder at** admirarse de, maravillarse con o de
wonder drugs *spl* drogas milagrosas
wonderful ['wʌndərfəl] *adj* maravilloso
won'der•land' *s* tierra de las maravillas; reino de las hadas
wonderment ['wʌndərmənt] *s* asombro, sorpresa
won't *contr* **will not**
wont [wʌnt] o [wɔnt] *adj* acostumbrado; **to be wont to** acostumbrar ‖ *s* costumbre, hábito
wonted ['wʌntɪd] o ['wɔntɪd] *adj* acostumbrado, habitual
woo [wu] *tr* cortejar (*a una mujer*); tratar de conquistar; tratar de persuadir
wood [wʊd] *s* madera; (*for making a fire*) leña; barril *m* de madera; **out of the woods** (coll) fuera de peligro; (coll) libre de dificultades; **to take to the woods** andar a monte; **woods** bosque *m*
woodbine ['wʊd,baɪn] *s* (*honeysuckle*) madreselva; (*Virginia creeper*) guau *m*
wood carving *s* labrado de madera
wood'chuck' *s* marmota de América
wood'cock' *s* becada, coalla, chocha
wood'cut' *s* (typ) grabado en madera
wood'cut'ter *s* leñador *m*
wooded ['wʊdɪd] *adj* arbolado, enselvado
wooden ['wʊdən] *adj* de madera, hecho de madera; torpe, estúpido; sin ánimo

wood engraving *s* (typ) grabado en madera
wooden-headed [ˈwʊdən,hɛdɪd] *adj* (coll) torpe, estúpido
wooden leg *s* pata de palo
wooden shoe *s* zueco
wood grouse *s* gallo de bosque
woodland [ˈwʊdlənd] *adj* selvático ‖ *s* bosque *m,* monte *m*
woodland scene *s* (paint) boscaje *m*
wood•man [ˈwʊdmən] *s* (*pl* **-men** [mən]) leñador *m;* silvicultor *m*
woodpecker [ˈwʊd,pɛkər] *s* carpintero, pájaro carpintero; (*green woodpecker*) picamaderos *m*
wood'pile' *s* montón *m* de leña
wood pulp *s* pasta de papel
wood screw *s* tirafondo
wood'shed' *s* leñero
woods•man [ˈwʊdzmən] *s* (*pl* **-men** [mən]) leñador *m;* silvicultor *m*
woodsy [ˈwʊdzi] *adj* selvático
wood'wind' *s* (mus) instrumento de viento de madera
wood'work' *s* (*working in wood*) ebanistería, obra de carpintería; (*things made of wood*) maderaje *m*
wood'work'er *s* ebanista *mf,* carpintero
wood'worm' *s* carcoma
wood•y [ˈwʊdi] *adj* (*comp* **-ier;** *super* **-iest**) arbolado, enselvado; (*like wood*) leñoso
wooer [ˈwʊ•ər] *s* pretendiente *m,* galán *m*
woof [wuf] *s* (*yarns running across warp*) trama; (*fabric*) tejido
woofer [ˈwʊfər] *s* altavoz *m* para audiofrecuencias bajas
wool [wʊl] *s* lana
woolen [ˈwʊlən] *adj* de lana, hecho de lana ‖ *s* tejido de lana; **woolens** lanerías
woolgrower [ˈwʊl ,gro•ər] *s* criador *m* de ganado lanar
wool•ly [ˈwʊli] *adj* (*comp* **-lier;** *super* **-liest**) lanoso, lanudo; borroso, confuso
Worcestershire sauce [ˈwʊstərʃər] *s* salsa inglesa
word [wʌrd] *s* palabra; **to be as good as one's word** cumplir lo prometido; **to have a word with** hablar cuatro palabras con; **to have word from** recibir noticias de; **to keep one's word** cumplir su palabra; **to leave word** dejar dicho; **to send word that** mandar decir que; **words** (*a quarrel*) palabras mayores; (*text of a song*) letra ‖ *tr* redactar, formular ‖ **Word** *s* (theol) Verbo
word count *s* recuento de vocabulario
word formation *s* (gram) formación de palabras
wording [ˈwʌrdɪŋ] *s* redacción, fraseología, estilo
word order *s* (gram) orden *m* de colocación
word processing *s* procesamiento de textos o palabras; tratamiento de textos
word processor *s* procesador *m* de textos o palabras
word'stock' *s* vocabulario, léxico
word•y [ˈwʌrdi] *adj* (*comp* **-ier;** *super* **-iest**) verboso, farragoso
work [wʌrk] *s* (*exertion; labor, toil*) trabajo; (*result of exertion; human output; engineering structure*) obra; (sew) labor *f;* **at work** trabajando; (*not at home*) en la oficina, en el taller, en la tienda; **out of work** sin trabajo, desempleado; **to shoot the works** (slang) echar el resto; **works** fábrica; mecanismo; (*of clock*) movimiento ‖ *tr* hacer trabajar; trabajar, obrar (*la madera, el hierro*); obrar (*un milagro*); explotar (*una mina*); **to work up** preparar; estimular, excitar ‖ *intr* trabajar; funcionar, marchar (*un aparato, un motor*); obrar (*p.ej., un remedio*); **to work loose** aflojarse; **to work out** resolverse
workable [ˈwʌrkəbəl] *adj* (*feasible*) practicable; (*that can be worked*) laborable
workaholic [,wʌrkəˈhɔlɪk] *s* (coll) trabajoadicto, fanático del trabajo
work'bench' *s* banco de trabajo, banco de taller
work'book' *s* (*manual of instructions*) libro de reglas; libro de ejercicios
work'box' *s* caja de herramientas; (*for needlework*) caja de labor
work'day' *adj* de cada día; ordinario, vulgar ‖ *s* día *m* de trabajo, día hábil, día laborable; (*number of hours of work*) jornada
work'days' *adv* entresemana (SAm)
worked-up [ˈwʌrktˈʌp] *adj* muy conmovido, sobreexcitado, exaltado
worker [ˈwʌrkər] *s* trabajador *m,* obrero
worker bee *s* abeja obrera
work force *s* mano *f* de obra, personal obrero
work'horse' *s* caballo de carga; (*tireless worker*) yunque *m*
work'house' *s* taller penitenciario; (Brit) asilo de pobres
working class *s* clase obrera
work'ing•girl' *s* trabajadora joven
working hours *spl* horas de trabajo
working hypothesis *s* hipótesis *f* de guía
working•man [ˈwʌrkɪŋ,mæn] *s* (*pl* **-men** [,mɛn]) *s* obrero, trabajador *m*
working•woman [ˈwʌrkɪŋ,wʊmən] *s* (*pl* **-women** [,wɪmɪn]) obrera, trabajadora
work•man [ˈwʌrkmən] *s* (*pl* **-men** [mən]) obrero, trabajador *m;* (*skilled worker*) artífice *m*
workmanship [ˈwʌrkmən,ʃip] *s* destreza en el trabajo; (*work executed*) hechura, obra, mano *f* de obra, trabajo
work of art *s* obra de arte
work'out' *s* ensayo, prueba; (*physical exercise*) sesión *f* de gimnasia
work'room' *s* (*for manual work*) obrador *m,* taller *m;* (*study*) gabinete *m* de trabajo
work'shop' *s* obrador *m,* taller *m*
work'sta'tion *s* (compu) estación o terminal *m* de trabajo
work stoppage *s* paro
work therapy *s* laborterapia
work'-to-rule' strike *s* huelga de celo (Esp)

world [wʌrld] *adj* mundial ‖ *s* mundo; **a world of** la mar de; **half the world** (*a lot of people*) medio mundo; **since the world began** desde que el mundo es mundo; **the other world** el otro mundo; **to be out of this world** ser increíble *or* fantástico, ser un sueño; **to bring into the world** echar al mundo; **to see the world** ver mundo; **to think the world of** tener un alto concepto de
world affairs *spl* asuntos internacionales
world'-class' *adj* sobresaliente
world history *s* historia universal
world•ly [ˈwʌrldli] *adj* (*comp* **-lier;** *super* **-liest**) mundano
world'ly-wise' *adj* que tiene mucho mundo
world's fair *s* exposición mundial
World Trade Center *s* World Trade Center *m* (*Centro del Comercio Mundial*)
World War *s* Guerra Mundial
world'-wide' *adj* global, mundial
World'-Wide' Web' *s* telaraña mundial
worm [wʌrm] *s* gusano; **worms** (pathol) lombrices *fpl* ‖ *tr* limpiar de lombrices; **to worm a secret out of a person** arrancar mañosamente un secreto a una persona; **to worm one's way into** insinuarse en
worm-eaten [ˈwʌrm,itən] *adj* carcomido; (fig) decaído, desgastado
worm gear *s* engranaje *m* de tornillo sin fin
worm'wood' *s* (*Artemisia*) ajenjo; (*Artemisia absinthium*) ajenjo del campo o ajenjo mayor; (*something bitter or grievous*) (fig) ajenjo
worm•y [ˈwʌrmi] *adj* (*comp* **-ier;** *super* **-iest**) gusaniento, gusanoso; (*worm-eaten*) carcomido; (*groveling*) rastrero, servil
worn [worn] *adj* roto, raído, gastado
worn'-out' *adj* muy gastado, inservible; (*by toil, illness*) consumido, rendido
worrisome [ˈwʌrisəm] *adj* inquietante; (*inclined to worry*) aprensivo, inquieto
wor•ry [ˈwʌri] *s* (*pl* **-ries**) inquietud, preocupación; (*cause of anxiety*) molestia ‖ *v* (*pret & pp* **-ried**) *tr* inquietar, preocupar; (*to harass, pester*) acosar, molestar; **to be worried** estar inquieto ‖ *intr* inquietarse, preocuparse; **don't worry** pierda Ud. cuidado
worse [wʌrs] *adj & adv comp* peor; **worse and worse** de mal en peor
worsen [ˈwʌrsən] *tr & intr* empeorar ‖ *ref* gravarse
wor•ship [ˈwʌrʃip] *s* adoración, culto; **your worship** vuestra merced ‖ *v* (*pret & pp* **-shiped** o **-shipped;** *ger* **-shiping** o **-shipping**) *tr & intr* adorar, venerar
worshiper o **worshipper** [ˈwʌrʃipər] *s* adorador *m,* devoto
worst [wʌrst] *adj & adv super* peor ‖ *s* (lo) peor; **at worst** en las peores circunstancias; **if worst comes to worst** si pasa lo peor; **to get the worst of** llevar la peor parte, salir perdiendo
worsted [ˈwʊstɪd] *adj* de estambre ‖ *s* estambre *m;* tela de estambre
wort [wʌrt] *s* (bot) hierba, planta; mosto de cerveza
worth [wʌrθ] *adj* del valor de; digno de; **to be worth** valer; tener una fortuna de; **to be worth** + *ger* valer la pena de + *inf;* **to be worth while** valer la pena; ser de mérito ‖ *s* valor *m;* mérito; **a dollar's worth of** un dólar de
worthless [ˈwʌrθlɪs] *adj* sin valor, inútil, inservible; (*person*) despreciable
worth'while' *adj* de mérito, digno de atención
wor•thy [ˈwʌrði] *adj* (*comp* **-thier;** *super* **-thiest**) digno; benemérito, meritorio ‖ *s* (*pl* **-thies**) benemérito; (*hum & iron*) personaje *m*
would [wʊd] *v aux* **she said she would do it** dijo que lo haría; **he would come if he could** vendría si pudiese; **he would go for days without smoking** pasaba días enteros sin fumar; **would that . . .!** ¡ojalá que . . .!
would'-be' *adj* llamado; supuesto ‖ *s* presumido
wouldn't *contr* **would not**
would've *contr* **would have**
wound [wund] *s* herida ‖ *tr* herir
wounded [ˈwundɪd] *adj* herido ‖ **the wounded** los heridos
wow [waʊ] *s* (*of phonograph record*) ululación; (slang) éxito rotundo ‖ *tr* (slang) entusiasmar ‖ *interj* ¡cielos!, ¡mecachis!
wrack [ræk] *s* naufragio; vestigio; (*fucaceous seaweed*) varec *m;* **to go to wrack and ruin** desvencijarse; ir al desastre
wraith [reθ] *s* fantasma *m,* espectro
wrangle [ˈræŋgəl] *s* pendencia, riña ‖ *intr* pelotear, reñir
wrap [ræp] *s* abrigo, manto ‖ *v* (*pret & pp* **wrapped;** *ger* **wrapping**) *tr* envolver; **to be wrapped up in** (fig) estar prendado de; **to wrap up** envolver; (*in clothing*) arropar; (coll) concluir ‖ *intr*—**to wrap up** arroparse
wrapper [ˈræpər] *s* bata, peinador *m;* (*of newspaper or magazine*) faja; (*of tobacco*) capa
wrapping paper [ˈræpɪŋ] *s* papel *m* de envolver, papel de embalar
wrath [ræθ] o [rɑθ] *s* cólera, ira; venganza
wrathful [ˈræθfəl] o [ˈrɑθfəl] *adj* colérico, iracundo
wreak [rik] *tr* descargar (*la cólera*); infligir (*venganza*)
wreath [riθ] *s* (*pl* **wreaths** [riðz]) guirnalda; corona funeraria; (*worn as a mark of honor or victory*) corona de laurel; (*of smoke*) espiral *f*
wreathe [rið] *tr* enguirnaldar; ceñir, envolver; tejer (*una guirnalda*) ‖ *intr* elevarse en espirales (*el humo*)
wreck [rɛk] *s* destrucción, ruina; naufragio; catástrofe *f,* desastre *m;* despojos, restos; (*of one's hopes*) naufragio; **to be a wreck** estar hecho un cascajo, estar hecho una ruina ‖ *tr* destruir, arruinar; hacer naufragar; hacer chocar, descarrilar (*un tren*)
wrecking ball *s* bola rompedora
wrecking car *s* (aut) camión *m* de auxilio; (rr) carro de grúa

wrecking crane *s* grúa de auxilio
wren [rɛn] *s* buscareta, coletero, rey *m* de zarza
wrench [rɛntʃ] *s* llave *f;* (*pull*) arranque *m,* tirón *m;* (*twist of a joint*) esguince *m* || *tr* torcerse (*p.ej., la muñeca*); (fig) torcer (*el sentido de una oración*)
wrest [rɛst] *tr* arrebatar, arrancar violentamente
wrestle [ˋrɛsəl] *s* lucha; partido de lucha || *tr* luchar contra || *intr* luchar
wrestler [ˋrɛslər] *s* luchador *m*
wrestling match [ˋrɛslɪŋ] *s* partido de lucha
wretch [rɛtʃ] *s* miserable *mf*
wretched [ˋrɛtʃid] *adj* miserable; (*poor, worthless*) malísimo, pésimo
wriggle [ˋrɪgəl] *s* culebreo, meneo serpentino || *tr* menear rápidamente || *intr* culebrear, ondular; **to wriggle out of** escabullirse de
wrig•gly [ˋrɪgli] *adj* (*comp* **-glier;** *super* **-gliest**) retorciéndose; (fig) evasivo, tramoyista
wring [rɪŋ] *v* (*pret & pp* **wrung** [rʌŋ]) *tr* torcer; retorcer (*las manos*); exprimir (*el zumo, la ropa, etc.*); sacar por fuerza (*la verdad*); arrancar (*dinero*); **to wring out** exprimir (*la ropa*)
wringer [ˋrɪŋər] *s* exprimidor *m*
wrinkle [ˋrɪŋkəl] *s* arruga; (*clever trick or idea*) (coll) ardid *m,* truco || *tr* arrugar || *intr* arrugarse
wrin•kly [ˋrɪŋkli] *adj* (*comp* **-klier;** *super* **-kliest**) arrugado
wrist [rɪst] *s* muñeca
wrist′band′ *s* bocamanga, puño, muñequera
wrist watch *s* reloj *m* de pulsera
writ [rɪt] *s* escrito, escritura; (law) mandato, orden *f*
write [raɪt] *v* (*pret* **wrote** [rot]; *pp* **written** [ˋrɪtən]) *tr* escribir; **to write down** poner por escrito; bajar el precio de; **to write off** cancelar (*una deuda*); dar por perdido; **to write up** describir extensamente por escrito; (*to ballyhoo*) dar bombo a || *intr* escribir; **to write back** contestar por carta
write′-off *s* (com) cancelación de una deuda (*que está incobrable*)
writer [ˋraɪtər] *s* escritor *m*
writer's cramp *s* grafospasmo
write′-up′ *s* (*favorable report*) bombo; (com) valoración excesiva
writhe [raɪð] *intr* contorcerse, retorcerse
writing [ˋraɪtɪŋ] *s* el escribir; (*something written*) escrito; profesión de escritor; **at this writing** al escribir ésta; **in one's own writing** de su puño y letra; **to put in writing** poner por escrito
writing desk *s* escritorio
writing materials *spl* recado de escribir
writing paper *s* papel *m* de escribir, papel de cartas
written accent [ˋrɪtən] *s* acento ortográfico
wrong [rɔŋ] *adj* injusto; malo; erróneo, equivocado; impropio; no . . . que se busca, p.ej., **this is the wrong house** ésta no es la casa que se busca; no . . . que se necesita, p.ej., **this is the wrong train** éste no es el tren que se necesita; no . . . que debe, p.ej., **he is going the wrong way** no sigue el camino que debe; **in the wrong place** mal colocado; **to be wrong** no tener razón; tener la culpa; **to be wrong with** pasar algo a, p.ej., **something is wrong with the motor** algo le pasa al motor || *adv* mal; sin razón; al revés; **to go wrong** ir por mal camino; darse a la mala vida || *s* daño, perjuicio; agravio, injusticia; error *m;* **to be in the wrong** no tener razón; tener la culpa; **to do wrong** obrar mal || *tr* agraviar, hacer daño a, ofender, ser injusto con
wrongdoer [ˋrɔŋ,du•ər] *s* malhechor *m*
wrongdoing [ˋrɔŋ,du•ɪŋ] *s* malhecho, maldad
wrong number *s* (telp) número equivocado
wrong side *s* contrahaz *f,* revés *m;* (*of the street*) lado contrario; **to get out of bed on the wrong side** levantarse del lado izquierdo; **wrong side out** al revés
wrought iron [rɔt] *s* hierro dulce
wrought′-up′ *adj* muy conmovido, sobreexcitado, exaltado
wry [raɪ] *adj* (*comp* **wrier;** *super* **wriest**) torcido; desviado, pervertido; irónico, burlón
wry′neck′ *s* (orn) torcecuello; (pathol) torticolis *m*
WTC *abbr* **World Trade Center**
www. *abbr* **World-Wide Web**

X

X, x [ɛks] vigésima cuarta letra del alfabeto inglés; **if you can't write, make an X** si no sabe escribir, ponga una cruz
Xanthippe [zænˋtɪpi] *s* Jantipa
Xavier [ˋzevɪ•ər] *s* Javier
xebec [ˋzibɛk] *s* (naut) jabeque *m*
xenia [ˋzinɪ•ə] *s* xenia
xenon [ˋzinɑn] o [ˋzɛnɑn] *s* xenón *m*
xenophobe [ˋzɛnə,fob] *s* xenófobo
xenophobia [,zɛnəˋfobɪ•ə] *s* xenofobia
Xenophon [ˋzɛnəfən] *s* Jenofonte *m*
xerography [zɪˋrɑgrəfɪ] *s* xerografía
xerox [ˋzɪrɑks], [ˋzirɑks] *tr* xerografiar, fotocopiar || *intr* hacer unas xerografías
Xeroxᵀ *s* Xeroxᵀ *m;* **to make a Xerox of** xerografiar, xerocopiar
Xerox copy *s* Xeroxᵀ *m,* xerografía, xerocopia, fotocopia

Xerox machine *s* fotocopiadora, Xerox[T] *f*
Xerxes [ˋzʌrksiz] *s* Jerjes *m*
Xmas [ˋkrɪsməs] *s* Navidad
X-rated [ˋɛks,retɪd] *adj* (*film, etc.*) sólo para adultos; pornográfico
X ray *s* rayo X; (*photograph*) radiografía
X-ray o **x-ray** [ˋɛks,re] *adj* radiográfico, de rayos X; **X-ray photograph** radiografía ‖ [ˋɛks're] *tr* hacer una radiografía de, radiografiar
xylem [ˋzaɪlɛm] *s* xilema *f*
xylograph [ˋzaɪlə,græt] *s* xilografía
xylography [zaɪˋlɑgrəfi] *s* xilografía
xylophone [ˋzaɪlə,fon] *s* (mus) xilófono

Y

Y, y [waɪ] vigésima quinta letra del alfabeto inglés
y. *abbr* **yard, year**
yacht [jɑt] *s* yate *m*
yacht club *s* club náutico
yak [jæk] *s* (zool) yac *m*
yam [jæm] *s* ñame *m;* (*sweet potato*) boniato, camote *m*
yank [jæŋk] *s* (coll) tirón *m* ‖ *tr* (coll) sacar de un tirón ‖ *intr* (coll) dar un tirón
Yankee [ˋjæŋki] *adj & s* yanqui *mf*
yap [jæp] *s* ladrido corto; (slang) charla necia y ruidosa ‖ *v* (*pret & pp* **yapped;** *ger* **yapping**) *intr* ladrar con ladrido corto; (slang) charlar necia y ruidosamente
yard [jɑrd] *s* cercado, patio; (*measure: 91.4 centimeters*) yarda; (naut) verga; (rr) patio
yard'arm' *s* (naut) penol *m*
yard goods *spl* géneros de pieza
yard'mas'ter *s* (rr) superintendente *m* de patio
yard'stick' *s* vara de medir una yarda; (fig) criterio, norma
yarn [jɑrn] *s* hilado, hilaza; (coll) cuento increíble, burlería
yarrow [ˋjæro] *s* milenrama
yaw [jɔ] *s* (naut) guiñada; **yaws** (pathol) frambesia ‖ *intr* (naut) guiñar
yawl [jɔl] *s* (naut) bote *m;* (naut) queche *m*
yawn [jɔn] *s* bostezo ‖ *intr* bostezar; abrirse desmesuradamente
yawning [ˋjɔnɪŋ] *adj* enorme; **a yawning chasm** un abismo ‖ *s* bostezo
yd. *abbr* **yard**
yea [je] *adv & s* sí *m*
yean [jin] *intr* parir (*la oveja, la cabra, etc.*)
year [jɪr] *s* año; **to be . . . years old** cumplir . . . años; **year in, year out** año tras año
year'book' *s* anuario
yearling [ˋjɪrlɪŋ] *adj & s* primal *m*
yearly [ˋjɪrli] *adj* anual ‖ *adv* anualmente
yearn [jʌrn] *intr* suspirar; **to yearn for** suspirar por, anhelar por
yearning [ˋjʌrnɪŋ] *s* anhelo, deseo ardiente
yeast [jist] *s* levadura
yell [jɛl] *s* grito, voz *f* ‖ *tr* decir a gritos ‖ *intr* gritar, dar voces
yellow [ˋjɛlo] *adj* amarillo; (*cowardly*) (coll) blanco; (*journalism*) sensacional ‖ *s* amarillo; yema de huevo ‖ *intr* amarillecer
yellowish [ˋjɛlo•ɪʃ] *adj* amarillento
yellow jacket *s* avispón *m*
yellowness [ˋjɛlonɪs] *s* amarillez *f*
yellow press *s* prensa amarilla
yellow streak *s* vena de cobarde
yelp [jɛlp] *s* gañido ‖ *intr* gañir
yeo•man [ˋjomən] *adj* sólido, de buena categoría ‖ *s* (*pl* **-men** [mən]) trabajador eficaz; (naut) pañolero; (naut) oficinista *m* de a bordo
yeoman of the guard *s* (Brit) alabardero de la Casa Real
yes [jɛs] *adv* sí ‖ *s* sí *m;* **to say yes** dar el sí ‖ *v* (*pret & pp* **yessed;** *ger* **yessing**) *tr* decir sí a ‖ *intr* decir sí
yes'-man *s* (coll) sacristán *m* de amén, idemista *mf*
yesterday [ˋjɛstərdi] o [ˋjɛstər,de] *adj & s* ayer *m*
yet [jɛt] *adv* todavía, aún; **as yet** hasta ahora; **not yet** todavía no ‖ *conj* sin embargo
yew tree [ju] *s* tejo
yield [jild] *s* producción, rendimiento; (*crop*) cosecha; (*income produced*) rédito ‖ *tr* producir, rendir, redituar ‖ *intr* entregarse, rendirse, someterse; acceder, ceder, consentir; producir
yippee [ˋjɪpi] *interj* ¡yupi!
yo [jo] *interj* (slang) ¡hola!
yodeling o **yodelling** [ˋjodəlɪŋ] *s* tirolesa
yoga [ˋjogə] *s* yoga
yogi [ˋjogi] *s* yogui *m*
yogurt [ˋjogərt] *s* yogurt *m*
yoke [jok] *s* (*pair of draft animals*) yunta; (*device to join a pair of draft animals*) yugo; (fig) yugo; (*of a shirt*) hombrillo; (elec) culata; **to throw off the yoke** sacudir el yugo ‖ *tr* uncir
yokel [ˋjokəl] *s* patán *m*
yolk [jok] *s* yema
yonder [ˋjɑndər] *adj* aquel, de más allá ‖ *adv* allá, más allá
yore [jor] *s*—**of yore** antaño, antiguamente
you [ju] *pron pers* usted, ustedes; le, la, les; **with you** consigo ‖ *pron indef se,* p.ej., **you go in this way** se entra por aquí
you'd *contr* **you had; you would**
you'll *contr* **you will**
young [jʌŋ] *adj* (*comp* **younger** [ˋjʌŋgər];

super **youngest** [ˈjʌŋgɪst]) joven ‖ **the young** los jóvenes, la gente joven
young people *spl* jóvenes *mpl,* gente *f* joven
youngster [ˈjʌŋstər] *s* jovencito; (*child*) chico, chiquillo
Young Turk *s* (fig) radical *mf*
your [jʊr] *adj poss* su, el (o su) de Ud. o de Uds.
you're *contr* **you are**
Yours [jʊrz] *pron poss* suyo; de Ud., de Uds.; el suyo; el de Ud., el de Uds.; **of yours** suyo; de Ud., de Uds.; **yours truly** su seguro servidor; (coll) este cura (*yo*)
your•self [jʊrˈsɛlf] *pron pers* (*pl* **-selves** [ˈsɛlvz]) usted mismo; sí, sí mismo; se, p.ej., **you enjoyed yourself** se divirtió Ud.
youth [juθ] *s* (*pl* **youths** [juθs] o [juðz]) juventud; (*person*) jovenzuelo; jovenzuelos, jóvenes *mpl*
youthful [ˈjuθfəl] *adj* juvenil, mocil
you've *contr* **you have**
yowl [jaʊl] *s* aullido, alarido ‖ *intr* aullar, dar alaridos
yr. *abbr* **year**
yuck [jʌk] [jək] *interj* (coll) ¡puaj!
Yugoslavˊ [ˈjugoˈslɑv] *adj & s* Yugoslavo
Yugoslavia [ˈjugoˈslɑvɪ•ə] *s* Yugoslavia
Yule [ˈjul] *s* la Navidad; la pascua de Navidad
Yule log *s* nochebueno, leño de nochebuena
Yuletide [ˈjul,taɪd] *s* la pascua de Navidad
yum•my [jʌmi] (*comp* **-mier;** *super* **-miest**) *adj* (coll) riquísimo ‖ *interj* (coll) ¡hmm!, ¡quérico
yum yum [ˈjʌmˈjʌm] *interj* (coll) ¡ñam ñam!
yuppie *o* **yuppy** [ˈjʌpi] *s* (*pl* **pies**) yuppy *mf;* (coll) yupi *mf*

Z

Z, z [zi] vigésima sexta letra del alfabeto inglés
za•ny [ˈzeni] *adj* (*comp* **-nier;** *super* **-niest**) cómico, gracioso, chiflado ‖ *s* (*pl* **-nies**) bufón *m,* payaso; mentecato
zap [zæp] *v* (*pret & pp* **zapped;** *ger* **zapping**) *tr* (coll) destruir, liquidar (coll); derrotar, vencer; sobresaltar; (compu) eliminar, borrar ‖ *intr* (coll) liquidarse, ir como una bala ‖ *interj* (coll) ¡zas!
zeal [zil] *s* celo, entusiasmo
zealot [ˈzɛlət] *s* fanático, entusiasta *mf*
zealotry [ˈzɛlətri] *s* fanatismo
zealous [ˈzɛləs] *adj* celoso, entusiasta
zebra [ˈzibrə] *s* cebra
zebu [ˈzibju] *s* cebú *m*
zenith [ˈzinɪθ] *s* cenit *m*
zephyr [ˈzɛfər] *s* céfiro
zeppelin [ˈzɛpəlɪn] *s* zepelín *m*
ze•ro [ˈzɪro] *s* (*pl* **-ros** o **-roes**) cero
zero gravity *s* gravedad nula
zero growth *s* crecimiento cero
zeˊro-growthˊ *adj* sin aumento; estable
zero option *s* opción cero, opción nula
zest [zɛst] *s* entusiasmo; (*agreeable and piquant flavor*) gusto, sabor *m*
Zeus [zus] *s* Zeus *m*
zig•zag [ˈzɪg,zæg] *adj & adv* en zigzag ‖ *s* zigzag *m,* ziszas *m* ‖ *v* (*pret & pp* **-zagged;** *ger* **-zagging**) *intr* zigzaguear
zinc [zɪŋk] *s* cinc *m*
zinc etching *s* cincograbado
zinnia [ˈzɪnɪ•ə] *s* rascamoño
Zionism [ˈzaɪ•ə,nɪzəm] *s* sionismo
zip [zɪp] *s* (coll) silbido, zumbido; (coll) energía, brío ‖ *v* (*pret & pp* **zipped;** *ger* **zipping**) *tr* cerrar con cierre relámpago, abrir con cierre relámpago; (coll) llevar con rapidez; **to zip up** dar gusto a ‖ *intr* silbar, zumbar; (coll) moverse con energía; **to zip by** (coll) pasar rápidamente
zip code *s* código postal
zipper [ˈzɪpər] *s* cierre *m* relámpago, cierre cremallera; chanclo con cierre relámpago; cíper (Mex)
zircon [ˈzʌrkɑn] *s* circón *m*
zirconium [zərˈkonɪ•əm] *s* circonio
zither [ˈzɪθər] *s* (mus) cítara
zodiac [ˈzodɪ,æk] *s* zodíaco
zone [zon] *s* zona; distrito postal ‖ *tr* dividir en zonas, zonificar
zoo [zu] *s* zoológico, jardín zoológico, zoo *m*
zoologic(al) [,zo•əˈlɑdʒɪk(əl)] *adj* zoológico
zoologist [zoˈɑlədʒɪst] *s* zoólogo
zoology [zoˈɑlədʒi] *s* zoología
zoom [zum] *s* zumbido; (aer) empinada; (phot) zoom *m* ‖ *tr* (aer) empinar ‖ *intr* zumbar; (aer) empinarse
zoom lens *s* zoom *m*
zoophyte [ˈzo•ə,faɪt] *s* zoófito
Zu•lu [ˈzulu] *adj* zulú ‖ *s* (*pl* **-lus**) zulú *mf*

Dictionaries in the Series

The New College French & English Dictionary
by Roger J. Steiner
The New College German & English Dictionary
by John C. Traupman
The New College Latin & English Dictionary
by John C. Traupman
The New College Spanish & English Dictionary
by Edwin B. Williams & Roger J. Steiner

AMSCO SCHOOL PUBLICATIONS, INC.